Mastering
Windows Server® 2008 R2

Mastering
Windows Server® 2008 R2

Mark Minasi

Darril Gibson

Aidan Finn

Wendy Henry

Byron Hynes

Acquisitions Editor: Agatha Kim
Development Editor: Thomas Cirtin
Technical Editors: John Mueller, Harold Wong
Production Editor: Elizabeth Ginns Britten
Copy Editor: Kim Wimpsett
Production Manager: Tim Tate
Vice President and Executive Group Publisher: Richard Swadley
Vice President and Publisher: Neil Edde
Book Designer: Maureen Forys, Happenstance Type-O-Rama; Judy Fung
Compositor: Craig Woods, Happenstance Type-O-Rama
Proofreader: Jen Larsen, Word One, New York
Indexer: Ted Laux
Project Coordinator, Cover: Lynsey Stanford
Cover Designer: Ryan Sneed
Cover Image: © Pete Gardner/Digital Vision/Getty Images

Copyright © 2010 by Wiley Publishing, Inc., Indianapolis, Indiana

Published by Wiley Publishing, Inc., Indianapolis, Indiana

Published simultaneously in Canada

ISBN: 978-0-470-53286-7

For general information on our other products and services or to obtain technical support, please contact our Customer Care Department within the U.S. at (877) 762-2974, outside the U.S. at (317) 572-3993 or fax (317) 572-4002.

Wiley also publishes its books in a variety of electronic formats. Some content that appears in print may not be available in electronic books.

Library of Congress Cataloging-in-Publication Data.

Minasi, Mark.
  Mastering Windows server 2008 R2 / Mark Minasi, Darril Gibson, Byron Hynes.
    p. cm.
  ISBN 978-0-470-53286-7 (pbk.)
  1. Microsoft Windows server. 2. Operating systems (Computers) I. Gibson, Darril. II. Hynes, Byron. III. Title.
  QA76.76.O63M57455 2010
  005.4'476—dc22
                    2009047999

10 9 8 7 6 5 4 3 2

Dear Reader,

Thank you for choosing *Mastering Windows Server 2008 R2*. This book is part of a family of premium-quality Sybex books, all of which are written by outstanding authors who combine practical experience with a gift for teaching.

Sybex was founded in 1976. More than 30 years later, we're still committed to producing consistently exceptional books. With each of our titles we're working hard to set a new standard for the industry. From the paper we print on to the authors we work with, our goal is to bring you the best books available.

I hope you see all that reflected in these pages. I'd be very interested to hear your comments and get your feedback on how we're doing. Feel free to let me know what you think about this or any other Sybex book by sending me an email at nedde@wiley.com, or if you think you've found a technical error in this book, please visit http://sybex.custhelp.com. Customer feedback is critical to our efforts at Sybex.

Best regards,

Neil Edde
Vice President and Publisher
Sybex, an Imprint of Wiley

To all those who've read my books, articles, or newsletters; joined my classes; or listened to my podcasts or web seminars. Thanks for the support, and now let's roll up our sleeves and get techie with this newest version of Server!

Acknowledgments

You're holding what is basically the 14th edition of a series of books about Windows Server, the 14th in a line that stretches back to 1994. Over time, the books have changed because the product that they explain—Microsoft Server operating systems from Windows NT Server 3.1 to Windows Server 2008 R2—have changed, and because the needs of those running networks have changed. (As you can guess, the section on Internet security in the NT Server 3.5 book was fairly short!) Another thing that's changed about the book over the years is the cast of hardworking folks who've made getting this done possible. This time I've called upon a variety of terrific writers.

Aidan Finn, one of the most active members on my online forum and a full-time cloud networking consultant, penned the chapter on upgrading your network to include Server 2008 systems (Chapter 2), the chapter on understanding the changes in TCP/IP that 2008 and R2 bring (Chapter 4), and the valuable chapters on managing users (Chapters 7 and 30). Willem Kasdorp, another forum member, put together the chapter on Hyper-V Server (Chapter 29). Derek Melber, an old friend from the consulting/speaking world, created the chapters on Group Policy and Active Directory delegation (Chapters 8 and 9). Alun Jones, one of the smartest guys I know on the subject of networking, offered the IP routing chapter (Chapter 19). Wendy Henry, another consultant/speaker friend, took time from her extremely hectic schedule to lead us through two big subjects with big chapters on Internet Information Server 7.x and Windows SharePoint Services (Chapters 16 and 28). Another old buddy, Kristin Griffin, helped out by updating the chapter that walks you through connecting Windows clients to servers (Chapter 15). Byron Hynes, who's worked with me on a previous book on Vista security, tackled the monster that is Windows' patching server, Windows Server Update Services (Chapter 27). Another veteran coauthor, Todd Phillips—we worked together on several editions of XP books—explains 2008's all-new backup tools, as well as how to get Macs hooked up with your Active Directory (Chapters 18 and 26). Chris Henley, a widely traveled speaker on technical Windows topics, provided the much-needed chapter on SYSVOL, Active Directory's essential file share, and how to upgrade it to 2008 compatibility (Chapter 12).

I also got to work with some new faces. Darril Gibson is a guy who professes to enjoy few things as much as he does teaching, and he's got six Windows-related books that can testify to that fact. He handled the AD-related chapters on building a simple AD, adding sites to it, and adding a read-only domain controller to an AD domain; the ones on sharing files, folders, and printers and monitoring servers, and on providing remote desktop services (both for remote administration and for delivering virtualized desktops); and the one on virtual private networks (Chapters 6, 10, 13–14, 17, 20–22, 25). Techie writer Stephen Sutton provided Active Directory–related chapters on DNS, multiple-domain ADs, and AD reshaping, as well as the chapter on Server Core (Chapters 3, 5, 23–24). Wallace McGhee wrote the DFS-N chapter (Chapter 11).

Once we writer types get our jobs done, it's time for a legion of editorial and production folks to fire up those word processors and convert our unprocessed words to nicely formatted, grammatically correct processed words. Agatha Kim and Pete Gaughan started things going, and then Tom Cirtin developed the material and provided the necessary pressure to keep things moving. Technical editor John Mueller checked facts, and copyeditor Kim Wimpsett kept participles from dangling, i's from going without dots, and the like, ensuring that you readers are supplied with sentences that make sense. Liz Britten kept all the production folks on track, Craig Woods made the pages pretty, Jen Larsen caught all those last-minute typos, and Ted Laux created the index for the monstrous book you now hold in your hands.

As always, thanks go to the people who created the Server product in the first place, the Microsoft folks. (Life would be pretty boring if the latest version we had to talk about was Windows NT Server 4.0, wouldn't it?) And finally, thank you to all of you, the readers; I hope you find this book useful.

—*Mark Minasi*

Contents at a Glance

Introduction . . . .*xxix*

Chapter 1 • What's New in Windows Server 2008 and 2008 R2 1

Chapter 2 • Installing and Upgrading to Windows Server 2008 R2 17

Chapter 3 • The New Server: Introduction to Server Core 111

Chapter 4 • Windows Server 2008 IPv4: What Has Changed? 165

Chapter 5 • DNS and Naming in Server 2008 and Active Directory 179

Chapter 6 • Creating the Simple AD: The One-Domain, One-Location AD 227

Chapter 7 • Creating and Managing User Accounts 279

Chapter 8 • Group Policy: AD's Gauntlet 359

Chapter 9 • Active Directory Delegation 419

Chapter 10 • Files, Folders, and Shares 431

Chapter 11 • Creating and Managing Shared Folders 471

Chapter 12 • SYSVOL: Old and New 517

Chapter 13 • Sharing Printers on Windows Server 2008 R2 Networks 539

Chapter 14 • Remote Server Administration 595

Chapter 15 • Connecting Windows Clients to the Server 627

Chapter 16 • Working the Web with IIS 7.0 and 7.5 683

Chapter 17 • Watching Your System 745

Chapter 18 • Windows Server 2008 R2 and Active Directory Backup
and Maintenance 793

Chapter 19 • Advanced IP: Routing with Windows 817

Chapter 20 • Getting from the Office to the Road: VPNs 853

Chapter 21 • Adding More Locations: Sites in Active Directory 909

Chapter 22 • The Third DC: Understanding Read-Only Domain Controllers 937

Chapter 23 • Creating Larger Active Directory Environments:
Beyond One Domain 967

Chapter 24 • Migrating, Merging, and Modifying Your Active Directory 1023

Chapter 25 • Installing, Using, and Administering Remote Desktop Services. . . . 1067

Chapter 26 • Connecting Mac OS X Clients 1117

Chapter 27 • Patch Management. 1127

Chapter 28 • File Shares Made Even Better: Windows SharePoint Services 3.0 . . . 1149

Chapter 29 • Server Virtualization with Hyper-V 1215

Chapter 30 • Advanced User Account Management and User Support. 1295

Appendix • The Bottom Line. 1363

Index. 1399

Contents

Introduction .... *xxix*

Chapter 1 • What's New in Windows Server 2008 and 2008 R2...............**1**
Server 2008 and R2 Goals 1
AD Changes 2
    Read-Only Domain Controllers 2
    New Windows Backup.. 2
    Fine-Grained Password Policies... 3
    PowerShell and AD Administrative Center 4
    DCPromo Improvements... 5
OS Changes Under the Hood... 5
    R2 Is 64-Bit Only 6
    Server Core.. 6
    Hyper-V 7
Networking Changes... 8
    TCP 8
    Network Access Protection (NAP)... 9
    Secure Socket Tunneling Protocol (SSTP) VPN 9
New Setup Technologies... 9
New Management Tools 10
    Server Manager... 10
    The New Remote Tools: WinRM and WinRS............................... 11
    Remote Desktop Services: Terminal Services with a New Name
      and New Features 11
    New Group Policies and Tools 12
    New Event Viewer 12
File and Print Sharing 13
    SMB 2.0.. 13
    More Reliable SYSVOL Replication 13
    Print Management Console and Printer Driver Isolation 13
Web-Based Services.. 14
    Web Server (IIS).. 14
    FTP Server 15
    Windows Server Update Services (WSUS).................................. 15

Chapter 2 • Installing and Upgrading to Windows Server 2008 R2..........**17**
What Has Changed Since 2000 and 2003?.. 17
    The Media 18
    Installation Requirements... 19
    64-bit Support 21

Installing the Operating System 22
   Performing a Clean Installation 23
   Performing an Upgrade Installation 33
   Initial Configuration Tasks Utility 46
Using Server Manager to Configure Your Servers 47
   Changes to Server Manager 49
   Common Configuration Tasks 50
   Adding and Removing Roles 58
   Troubleshooting Roles and Features 78
   Remote Management 80
   Wrapping Up Server Manager 82
Upgrading Active Directory. 82
   An Overview of Active Directory: New Functionality in
      Windows Server 2008 and 2008 R2 82
   New Active Directory Functionality in Windows Server 2008 R2 84
   Active Directory Upgrade Strategies 85
Unattended Installations. 88
   Installing Windows Automated Installation Kit (WAIK). 89
   Creating an Answer File 92
   Using an Answer File. 107
Installing a Sample Server Network for This Book's Examples 108
The Bottom Line. 109

Chapter 3 • The New Server: Introduction to Server Core **111**
What in the World Is Server Core? 111
Installing Server Core 113
Server Core Survival Guide 116
   Accessing the Task Manager. 116
   Closing the Command Prompt. 116
   Changing the Administrator's Password 117
   Accessing File Shares 118
   Finding Commands from A to Z 118
   Finding Command Syntax: The Question Mark 118
   Reading Text Files with Notepad 119
   Reverse Engineering 119
   Editing the Registry 120
   Rebooting and Shutting Down. 120
Initial Configurations for Server Core 120
   Step 1: Provide Computer Information 121
   Step 2: Update This Server 124
   Step 3: Customize This Server 127
Administering Server Core Remotely 130
Configuring Roles and Features 141
   Creating a Domain Controller and Managing DNS 142
   Configuring the DHCP Service 143
   Setting Up a File Server 146

Setting Up a Print Server... 151
Managing Licenses with Key Management Service......................... 155
Protecting Data with Windows Backup Server............................ 157
The Bottom Line.. 162

Chapter 4 • Windows Server 2008 IPv4: What Has Changed?.............165
TCP Then and Now... 165
Improving Transaction Time with Autoscaling............................ 167
Employing Policy-Based QoS.. 173
Sharing Files and Printers with SMB 2.0................................. 174
Alternatives for Network Performance.................................... 176
Wrapping Up the New and Improved TCP.................................... 177
DHCP and Network Access Protection.................................... 177
New to 2008 R2.. 177
The Bottom Line.. 178

Chapter 5 • DNS and Naming in Server 2008 and Active Directory.........179
Components of Microsoft's DNS.. 179
Understanding the DNS Server Role..................................... 179
Implementing Zones to Manage Namespaces.............................. 186
Understanding Record Types.. 194
Implementing the DNS Role on Server Core.............................. 198
Managing DNS Clients and Name Resolution.............................. 203
Understanding Active Directory's DNS.................................... 209
Configuring DNS Automatically... 210
Understanding SRV Records and Clients................................. 211
Windows Server 2008 R2's Additional Features.......................... 212
Supporting Internet-Based DNS Resolution................................ 216
Supporting External DNS Domains...................................... 216
Resolving External Namespaces... 218
Administration and Troubleshooting with DNS Tools....................... 219
Administering the DNS Server with the DNS Management Console
and DNSCmd.. 219
Leveraging Nslookup, DCDiag, and DNSLint............................. 221
The Bottom Line.. 225

Chapter 6 • Creating the Simple AD: The One-Domain, One-Location AD...227
An Introduction to Active Directory Basics............................... 227
A Single-Domain Forest.. 230
Benefits of a Single Domain... 231
Creating a Single-Domain Forest....................................... 231
Adding a Second DC.. 245
Before Running DCPromo... 245
Deployment Configuration for the Second DC........................... 246
DNS for the Second DC.. 246
Global Catalog for the Second DC..................................... 247
Running DCPromo for the Second DC.................................... 248

Creating Organizational Units, Accounts, and Groups. 250
    Creating Organizational Units. 250
    Creating Accounts 257
    Creating Groups 259
    Delegating Control 261
Domain Maintenance Tasks. 262
    Joining a Domain 262
    Decommissioning a DC. 263
    Troubleshooting ADI DNS 264
    Raising Domain and Forest Functional Levels 265
    Using NetDom. 268
    Managing the Domain Time. 269
Creating Fine-Grained Password Policies 271
    Requirements for Fine-Grained Password Policies. 272
    Creating a Password Settings Object. 272
The Bottom Line. 276

Chapter 7 • Creating and Managing User Accounts 279
User Accounts. 280
    Creating Local User Accounts 280
    Creating Domain User Accounts 284
    Setting Local User Account Properties 289
    Setting Domain-Based User Account Properties. 296
Group Management. 312
    Local Groups 312
    Active Directory Groups 321
Monday-Morning Admin Tasks 330
    Forgotten Passwords 330
    Locked-Out Users. 331
What's New in Windows Server 2008 R2 for User and Group Management. 333
    Active Directory Administrative Center. 333
    Active Directory Module for Windows PowerShell 343
The Bottom Line. 356

Chapter 8 • Group Policy: AD's Gauntlet 359
Group Policy Concepts 359
    Policies Are "All or Nothing" 360
    Policies Are Inherited and Cumulative. 361
    Group Policy Power! Refresh Intervals 361
Local Policies and Group Policy Objects 362
    Administrators or Non-Administrators LGPO 362
    User-Specific LGPO 363
Creating GPOs 365
Group Policy Basics 369
    Replication of Group Policy Is Built In 369
    GPOs Undo Themselves When Removed. 370
    You Needn't Log On to Apply GPO Settings 370

Modifying Group Policy Default Behavior 370
    Group Policy Policies 371
    Group Policy over Slow Links 373
Group Policy Application 374
    How Group Policy Is Applied............................... 375
    Filtering Group Policy with Access Control Lists 377
    Using WMI Filters with Group Policy........................... 378
    Enforcing and Blocking Inheritance 380
    Group Policy Example: Forcing Complex Passwords................... 381
Group Policy Setting Possibilities 382
    Decrypting User and Computer Configuration Settings...................... 383
    Using Group Policy to Set Password and Account Lockout Policy 399
    Group Policy Preferences.................................. 401
The New and Improved GPMC................................... 406
    Starter GPOs 407
    Backing Up and Restoring GPOs................................ 408
    Delegating Group Policy Administration........................... 410
Troubleshooting Group Policies.. 412
    The Resultant Set of Policy (RSOP) Tool 412
    Group Policy Results Using the GPMC............................. 412
    Group Policy Modeling Using the GPMC........................... 414
    gpresult... 414
    gpotool 415
    Using Event Viewer 416
    Troubleshooting 101: Keep It Simple 416
A Closing Thought or Two on Group Policy 416
The Bottom Line... 417

Chapter 9 • Active Directory Delegation **419**
AD Delegation vs. NT Domains 419
Delegating Control Using Organizational Units 421
    Creating a New Organizational Unit 422
    Moving User Accounts into an OU 422
    Creating a MktPswAdm Group 422
    Delegating the Marketing OU's Password Reset Control to MktPswAdm 423
Advanced Delegation: Manually Setting Permissions.......................... 424
Finding Out Which Delegations Have Been Set, or Undelegating. 428
The Bottom Line... 430

Chapter 10 • Files, Folders, and Shares **431**
Understanding the File Services Role.. 431
    Adding Role Services..................................... 432
    Adding the File Services Role 433
Creating Shares.. 435
    Creating Shares with Server Manager 435
    Creating Shares on Remote Computers Using Server Manager 437
    Publishing Shares in Active Directory 439

Managing Permissions 440

   NTFS Permissions. 441

   Share Permissions. 441

   Share and NTFS Permission Similarities 441

   Modifying Share and NTFS Permissions 444

   Combining Share and NTFS Permissions. 445

Connecting to Shares 446

   "A Set of Credentials Conflicts" 448

   Using net use on a WAN 448

   Common Shares 449

File Server Resource Manager 449

   Creating Quota Policies 450

   Creating File Screen Policies 454

   Generating Reports. 456

   File Server Resource Manager Options. 458

Understanding SMB 2.0 459

   Compatibility with SMB 1.0 459

   SMB 2.0 Security 460

Implementing BitLocker 461

   Hardware Requirements 461

   Enabling BitLocker 463

Using Offline Files/Client-Side Caching 465

   How Offline Files Works 465

   BranchCache 466

   Enabling Offline Files on the Server 467

The Bottom Line. 468

Chapter 11 • Creating and Managing Shared Folders **471**

Creating Shared Folders 471

   Creating Shares from Explorer. 473

   Remotely Creating Shares with the Computer Management Console. 474

Managing Permissions 476

   Creating Share Permissions 477

   Understanding File and Directory Permissions 480

Working with Hidden Shares. 494

Exploring the Distributed File System 496

   Understanding DFS Terminology 496

   Choosing Stand-Alone vs. Domain-Based DFS 498

   Creating a DFS Root 499

   Adding Links to a DFS Root 503

   Configuring DFS Replications 504

   Understanding DFS Replication. 506

   Managing DFS Replication 507

Exploring the Network File System. 510

The Bottom Line 515

Chapter 12 • SYSVOL: Old and New **517**
The Old: File Replication Service. 517
    File System Junctions 518
    Understanding File Replication Service 519
    How FRS Works with SYSVOL. 521
The New: Distributed File System Replication 524
    Understanding DFSR. 524
    Migrating to DFSR 525
The Bottom Line. 536

Chapter 13 • Sharing Printers on Windows Server 2008 R2 Networks **539**
Print Services Overview 539
    The Print Spooler 540
    The Printer Driver. 541
Installing the Print and Document Services Role. 544
    Adding the Print and Document Services Role. 544
    Working in the Print Management Console. 546
    Adding the Print Services Role to Server Core 556
Deploying Printers to the Masses 561
    Adding a Printer to a Client Manually 561
    Adding a Printer Using Active Directory Search 562
    Deploying Printers via GPO 565
    Viewing Deployed Printers. 568
Adjusting Print Server Settings. 569
    Server Properties 569
    Printer Migration 573
Managing Printer Properties 574
    Printer Properties Sharing Tab. 575
    Printer Properties Ports Tab 575
    Printer Properties Security Tab 576
    Printer Properties Advanced Tab. 581
Managing Print Jobs 587
Using Custom Filters 588
Troubleshooting Printer Problems 590
    Basic Troubleshooting: Identifying the Situation 590
    Restarting the Spooler Service 592
    Isolating Printer Drivers 592
The Bottom Line. 593

Chapter 14 • Remote Server Administration **595**
Remote Desktop for Administration. 595
    Configuring the Server for Remote Desktop 596
    Using Remote Desktop Connection. 597
    Remote Desktop Gateway 609
    Remote Desktops 614
    Configuring a Server for Remote Assistance 616

Windows Remote Management Service 618
   Enabling WinRM 619
   Using WinRS 620
Remote Server Administration Tools 622
   RSAT Compatibility Issues 622
   RSAT Tools 622
   Installing RSAT 624
The Bottom Line 625

Chapter 15 • Connecting Windows Clients to the Server 627
What to Know Before You Begin 627
   Understanding Client-Side Software Requirements 628
   Domain Accounts and Local Accounts 629
Verifying Your Network Configuration 630
   Verifying Local Area Connection Settings 630
   Test Network Connectivity with the ping Command 632
   Verifying and Setting Local Area Connection Information Using the GUI 634
Joining the Domain 642
   Joining a Domain from Windows 7 643
   Joining a Domain from Windows Vista 649
   Joining a Domain from Windows XP 651
   Joining a Domain from Windows 2000 Professional 652
Changing Domain User Passwords 653
   Changing Domain Passwords from Windows 7 and Windows Vista 655
   Changing Domain Passwords from Windows XP and Windows 2000
      Professional 656
Connecting to Network Resources 659
   Connecting to Network Resources from Windows 7 and Windows Vista 660
   Connecting to Network Resources from Windows XP 671
   Connecting to Network Resources from Windows 2000 679
The Bottom Line 680

Chapter 16 • Working the Web with IIS 7.0 and 7.5 683
Creating Simple Websites 683
   A Sum of Pages 684
   Lively Web Pages 685
What's So Different About IIS 7.0 and 7.5? 686
Introducing IIS 7 Modules 689
   What's Included? 689
   Feature Delegation 694
Installing IIS 7 695
   Adding the Web Server Role 695
   Installing IIS 7 via the Command Line 698
   Installing IIS 7 on Server Core 700
   Renovating IIS Construction 701

Website Provisioning. 707
   Understanding Global Settings 708
   Creating a Simple Website. 711
   Configuring Site Settings. 718
Hosting Multiple Websites 719
   Deploying Sites 720
   Site Uniqueness. 722
   Setting Up an Anonymous Account 722
   Delegating Administration. 723
Integrating SMTP into IIS 7 Web Pages 724
   Getting Started 725
   Adding the SMTP Server Feature 726
   Setting Up an SMTP Server. 728
   Adding the SMTP E-mail Feature to an IIS 7 Website 729
Integrating FTP into IIS 7 Web Pages 730
   The FTP7 File Transfer Publishing Service. 731
   Adding FTP to an IIS 7 Website 733
Advanced Administration 735
   Using Web Management Services 735
   Connecting, Securing, Auditing 737
   Windows System Resource Manager. 740
   Backing Up and Restoring Data. 741
The Bottom Line. 742

Chapter 17 • Watching Your System **745**
Monitoring Your System with Event Viewer. 745
   Viewing an Event 746
   Understanding Event Levels. 747
   Creating and Using Custom Views 748
   Modifying the Displayed Columns in the Event Viewer. 756
   Understanding Windows Logs. 757
   Understanding Applications and Services Logs 758
   Configuring Event Log Properties. 758
   Attaching Tasks to Events 760
   Viewing Events on Server Core 763
Subscribing to Event Logs. 766
   Understanding Subscription Types 766
   Selecting Events 770
   Setting Advanced Options 770
   Understanding Event Subscription Protocols 772
   Configuring Event Subscriptions. 772
Troubleshooting Event Forwarding 777
   Checking the Runtime Status. 777
   Using the Windows Event Collector Utility 778
Monitoring Performance. 780
   Using Monitoring Tools. 780
   Using Data Collector Sets 783
The Bottom Line. 791

**Chapter 18 • Windows Server 2008 R2 and Active Directory
Backup and Maintenance** **793**

Backing Up and Restoring Windows Server 793
   Backing Up and Restoring a Full Server 795
   Backing Up and Restoring Files and Folders 801
Stopping and Restarting Active Directory. 803
   Stopping and Starting AD DS. 804
   Defragmenting Active Directory Offline 804
   Checking the Integrity of an Active Directory Database 805
Capturing Active Directory Snapshots 807
   Creating an Active Directory Snapshot. 807
   Mounting an Active Directory Snapshot 808
   Working with Mounted Active Directory Snapshots 808
Backing Up and Restoring Active Directory 809
   Recovering Active Directory Objects 811
   Creating an Active Directory Backup 813
   Restoring an Active Directory Backup 813
   Performing an Authoritative Restore 814
The Bottom Line. 815

Chapter 19 • Advanced IP: Routing with Windows **817**

The Life of an IP Packet. 817
   First, the Simple Case: No Routing Required. 819
   Now the Hard Case: With Routing 822
From Classes to Classless 825
   In the Beginning Was the Class 825
   Unusable Host Addresses 826
   All Y'all. 827
   Broadcast Gets Narrower: The First Unroutable Addresses 827
   Routing the Unroutable Part I: Private Addresses 827
Sockets, Ports, and Winsock. 833
   Winsock: Why We Can All Use the Internet 835
   Routing the Unroutable Part II: NAPT and PAT 836
   Routing the Unroutable Part III: Application Layer Gateways 837
   Installing a NAT 838
Testing and Troubleshooting 846
   Using the Application Itself. 847
   Pinging a Remote Computer with ping 847
   Pinging a Remote Computer with traceroute. 848
   Checking Your Configuration with ipconfig 848
   Showing Routing and Neighbors. 849
   Using Network Monitor. 850
The Bottom Line. 851

Chapter 20 • Getting from the Office to the Road: VPNs **853**
Introducing VPNs 853
   The Many Names of VPN Servers 854
   Gateway-to-Gateway VPN 854
Understanding the Tunneling Protocols 855
   Layer 2 Tunneling Protocol 855
   Secure Socket Tunneling Protocol 855
   Internet Key Exchange Version 2 856
Using Network Policy and Access Services Role 856
   Routing and Remote Access 857
   Adding the Network Policy and Access Services Role 858
   Configuring Routing and Remote Access 858
   Configuring Policies 861
   Authenticating VPN Clients 882
   Configuring Accounting 884
   Exploring Routing and Remote Access 886
Protecting VPNs with IP Security (IPSec) 893
   Understanding IPSec: The Four Security Options 894
   Understanding IPSec Filters 895
   IPSec Rules = IPSec Actions + IPSec Filters 896
   Signing and Encrypting Need One More Piece: Authentication 896
   How IPSec Works in Windows 897
   Using IPSec to Protect Systems Through Packet Filtering 904
   A Few Final Thoughts About IPSec 908
The Bottom Line 908

Chapter 21 • Adding More Locations: Sites in Active Directory **909**
Mastering Site Concepts 909
   Sites and Replication 910
   Understanding Site Terminology 911
Exploring Sites 913
   How Sites Work 913
   Renaming Default-First-Site-Name 915
   Defining a Site 915
   Deciding on DCs in Remote Locations 916
   Defining a Subnet and Placing It in a Site 919
   Placing a Server in a Site 920
   Adding Site Links 920
Configuring Intersite Replication 924
   Bridgehead Servers 927
   Forcing Replication 928
Configuring Clients to Access the Next Closest Site 929
   Configuring Next Closest Site with Group Policy 930
   Configuring Next Closest Site Through the Registry 930
Using PowerShell 931
The Bottom Line 934

Chapter 22 • The Third DC: Understanding Read-Only Domain Controllers 937

Introducing RODCs 937
Making Changes on a Read-Only Domain Controller 938
RODC Contents 939
RODC Requirements 944
RODC and Server Applications 950
Installing the RODC 950
Installing RODC on Server Core 954
Viewing the RODC Properties 955
Modifying the Allowed List 957
Staged Installations 958
DNS on the RODC 963
The Bottom Line 964

Chapter 23 • Creating Larger Active Directory Environments: Beyond One Domain 967

The Foundations of Multiple-Domain Designs 967
Domains 967
Forests 970
Trees 971
You Must Build Trees and Forests Together 972
Planning Your Active Directory Environment 973
Satisfying Political Needs 973
Connectivity and Replication Issues 974
Multiple Domains: When They Make Sense 975
The Case for an Empty Root 976
Active Directory Design Pointers 978
Creating Multiple Domains 980
Naming Multidomain Structures 980
Preparing the DC for the Second Domain 981
Creating a Second Domain 982
Functional Levels 986
The Beginning of Functional Levels in Windows 2000 986
Domain Functional Levels 986
Forest Functional Levels 989
FSMOs and GCs 990
Multimaster vs. Single-Master Replication 991
But Not Everything Is Multimaster 991
Domain Naming: A FSMO Example 991
Why Administrators Must Know About FSMOs 992
Global Catalogs 992
FSMO Roles 994
Schema Master 994
Domain Naming Master FSMO 999
RID Pool FSMO 999
Infrastructure Master 1000

PDC Emulator FSMO 1001
Transferring FSMO Roles 1002
Time Sync. 1005
Trusts 1009
Defining the Domain: "Trust" 1009
Trust Relationships in More Detail 1009
Trusts Have Direction 1010
Some Trusts Are Transitive. 1011
Trusts Do Not Remove All Security. 1011
Trusts Involve Administrators from Both Sides 1011
Four Kinds of Trusts. 1012
Understanding Transitive Forest Trusts 1012
Manually Creating Trusts 1013
The Bottom Line. 1021

**Chapter 24 • Migrating, Merging, and Modifying Your
Active Directory. 1023**
Migration Strategies. 1023
Migrating with an In-Place Upgrade. 1024
Migrating with a Swing Migration 1027
Migrating with a Clean and Pristine Migration 1032
Using Microsoft's Free Migration Tool: ADMT. 1035
An Example Migration Setup 1037
Establishing the Trust 1038
Getting Both Sides ADMT-Friendly. 1039
Starting Up ADMT and Migrating 1042
Testing the Migrated Group's Access to Resources. 1050
Translating Local Profiles 1050
Migrating Computer Accounts. 1053
Rollback Considerations 1054
Renaming a Domain 1054
Understanding the Requirements 1055
Affecting Business Operations. 1055
Understanding the Business Risks. 1056
Performing the Domain Rename 1056
The Bottom Line. 1065

**Chapter 25 • Installing, Using, and Administering Remote
Desktop Services 1067**
Who Needs Remote Desktop Services? 1067
Centralized Deployment of Applications. 1068
Supporting Remote Users 1068
Supporting PC-Unfriendly Environments 1068
Reducing Hardware Refreshes. 1069
Simplifying the User Interface 1070
Providing Help-Desk Support 1070
Deploying RDS RemoteApp 1071

Understanding the Remote Desktop Services Processing Model 1071
    Son of Mainframe? 1071
    Anatomy of a Thin-Client Session 1072
Server and Client Requirements 1075
    Server Hardware. 1075
    Client Hardware 1079
Adding Remote Desktop Services. 1080
    Required Role Services 1081
    Easy Print. 1082
    Single Sign-On. 1082
    Network Level Authentication 1083
    Licensing Mode. 1083
    Remote Desktop Users Group. 1084
    Adding the Remote Desktop Services Role 1084
    Adding Applications 1087
    Connecting to an RDS Session 1087
    Adding an RDS RemoteApp Application. 1089
Monitoring Remote Desktop Services 1100
    Remote Desktop Services Manager 1100
    Remote Desktop Session Host Configuration 1103
    Remote Desktop Licensing Manager. 1113
The Bottom Line. 1115

Chapter 26 • Connecting Mac OS X Clients **1117**
Preparing Active Directory for Mac OS X Clients 1117
Connecting a Mac to the Domain 1120
Connecting to File Shares. 1122
Connecting to Printers 1122
Using Remote Desktop from a Mac Client. 1123
Troubleshooting 1124
The Bottom Line. 1125

Chapter 27 • Patch Management **1127**
The Four Phases of Patch Management 1127
    Phase 1: Assess 1127
    Phase 2: Identify 1128
    Phase 3: Evaluate and Plan 1130
    Phase 4: Deploy 1131
Dissecting a Security Update 1132
Digging into Windows Server Update Services 1132
    Features of WSUS 3.0 1132
    Software Requirements for WSUS Servers and Clients 1133
    Deployment Scenarios 1134
    Configuring Prerequisites for WSUS 3.0. 1135
    Installing and Configuring WSUS 3.0 1139
    Pointing Your Clients to the WSUS Server 1143
The Bottom Line. 1146

Chapter 28 • File Shares Made Even Better: Windows SharePoint Services 3.0 .... **1149**

Overview of Windows SharePoint Services 3.0. 1149
How Does WSS Work? 1151
Prerequisites 1151
Installing WSSv3 1152
Loading IIS 7.5 1153
Loading the .NET Framework 1155
Loading WSS 3.0 1156
Configuring Products and Technologies 1158
Introducing Central Administration 1159
SharePoint Website Provisioning. 1162
Creating a Web Application 1164
Creating a Site Collection 1167
Adding Sites to a Site Collection. 1168
Creating SharePoint Document Libraries 1170
Creating a Document Library. 1171
Populating a Document Library. 1172
Managing SharePoint Documents. 1174
Document Metadata. 1174
Document Library Settings. 1182
Workflows 1189
Accessing SharePoint Documents. 1194
Enforcing Security 1194
Creating Useful Navigation 1201
Updating Search Indexes. 1202
Using Alerts and RSS. 1203
Managing Information Rights 1205
Advanced WSS Administration. 1205
Authentication Providers. 1206
Managing Features. 1207
Limiting Content. 1208
Integrating Client Software 1210
Internet Explorer Integration 1211
Office 2007 Application Integration. 1211
The Bottom Line. 1213

Chapter 29 • Server Virtualization with Hyper-V **1215**

What Is Server Virtualization? 1215
What Use Is Server Virtualization? 1217
What Do You Need to Get Started with Hyper-V? 1218
The Hyper-V Feature Set 1220
Installing the Host with a Virtual Machine. 1222
Installing and Configuring Hyper-V. 1223
Configuring a Virtual Machine 1230
Installing a Virtual Machine. 1238

Understanding Hyper-V Architecture 1242
    The Hyper-V Parent Partition 1244
    Hyper-V Child Partitions 1248
    Security Design in Hyper-V 1249
Using Virtual Disks 1251
    Virtual Disks and Their Controllers 1251
    Virtual Disk Types and When to Use Them 1252
    Adding a Disk to an Existing VM 1253
    Disk Maintenance 1257
    Time Travel with Snapshots 1259
Using Virtual Networks 1263
    Understanding Virtual Switches 1264
    Connecting VMs to Virtual Switches 1266
Managing Virtual Machines 1269
    Licensing Hyper-V Hosts and Their VMs 1269
    Moving VMs Around: Export and Import 1270
    Backing Up and Restoring Virtual Machines 1274
    Server Core and the Hyper-V Server 1277
    Moving VMs: Quick Migration and Live Migration 1280
    Malware Protection and Patching 1287
    Scripting Hyper-V 1288
The Bottom Line 1293

Chapter 30 • Advanced User Account Management and User Support 1295
Experiencing the Flexible Desktop 1295
Configuring Home Directories 1297
    Setting Up the Lab 1298
    Creating the Home Directories 1299
    Creating Home Directories: The Easy Way 1304
    Creating Home Directories: The Hard Way 1307
    Home Directory vs. Local Storage 1309
Creating Roaming Profiles 1309
    Creating a Roaming Profiles Share: The Easy Way 1311
    Creating a Roaming Profiles Share: The Hard Way 1319
    Configuring Mandatory Profiles 1321
    Configuring Super Mandatory Profiles 1328
    Configuring a Default Network Profile 1329
Managing Roaming Profiles 1330
    Machine Settings 1331
    User Settings 1335
Redirecting Folders 1336
    Basic Folder Redirection 1338
    Advanced Folder Redirection 1345
    Managing Folder Redirection 1346
Managing the Desktop Using Group Policy 1347

Managing Users with Logon Scripts. 1352
    User Access Control and Logon Scripts 1357
    Multiple Logon Scripts. 1358
    Managing Logon Scripts with Group Policy 1359
    Managing Shutdown Tasks with Logoff Scripts 1360
The Bottom Line. 1361

Appendix • The Bottom Line **1363**
Chapter 2: Installing and Upgrading to Windows Server 2008 R2 1363
Chapter 3: The New Server: Introduction to Server Core 1364
Chapter 4: Windows Server 2008 IPv4: What Has Changed?. 1365
Chapter 5: DNS and Naming in Server 2008 and Active Directory. 1366
Chapter 6: Creating the Simple AD: The One-Domain, One-Location AD 1367
Chapter 7: Creating and Managing User Accounts 1368
Chapter 8: Group Policy: AD's Gauntlet. 1372
Chapter 9: Active Directory Delegation 1373
Chapter 10: Files, Folders, and Shares. 1374
Chapter 11: Creating and Managing Shared Folders 1375
Chapter 12: SYSVOL: Old and New 1376
Chapter 13: Sharing Printers on Windows Server 2008 R2 Networks. 1377
Chapter 14: Remote Server Administration. 1378
Chapter 15: Connecting Windows Clients to the Server 1379
Chapter 16: Working the Web with IIS 7.0 and 7.5 1380
Chapter 17: Watching Your System 1382
Chapter 18: Windows Server 2008 R2 and Active Directory Backup
    and Maintenance 1383
Chapter 19: Advanced IP: Routing with Windows. 1384
Chapter 20: Getting From the Office to the Road: VPNs. 1385
Chapter 21: Adding More Locations: Sites in Active Directory 1386
Chapter 22: The Third DC: Understanding Read-Only Domain Controllers 1387
Chapter 23: Creating Larger Active Directory Environments:
    Beyond One Domain 1388
Chapter 24: Migrating, Merging, and Modifying Your Active Directory 1390
Chapter 25: Installing, Using, and Administering Remote Desktop Services. 1391
Chapter 26: Connecting Mac OS X Clients 1392
Chapter 27: Patch Management 1393
Chapter 28: File Shares Made Even Better: Windows SharePoint Services 3.0 1394
Chapter 29: Server Virtualization with Hyper-V 1395
Chapter 30: Advanced User Account Management and User Support. 1397

Index. *1399*

Introduction

Welcome to *Mastering Windows Server 2008 R2*! I've got to tell you, I haven't been this excited about a new version of Server since Windows 2000, almost 10 years ago. Why? I guess because it feels...fun. Yeah, that's the word—*fun*. Here's what I mean.

R2's 10-year-old older brother, Windows Server 2000, was neat because it was such a game-changer, an OS lushly festooned with completely new concepts and tools to get to know. Now, I've seen big operating system upgrades before, like DOS 2.0 in 1982, OS 2.0 in 1992, or Windows 3.0 in 1990, and in every case things seemed to work out the same way: first we get the holy-moley-there's-so-much-new-stuff thrill of discovery and newness, then we sit down and start using the thing, and *then* we find ourselves shaking our heads saying, "OK, this [fill in the new feature] is cool, but why did they leave *this* part of it out," or "OK, this is cool, but it, um, doesn't exactly work as advertised."

In every one of those cases, the OS's vendor released the next version, better known as "version 1.1." Sure, they didn't all actually have a ".1" in their version numbers—DOS 2.0's "1.1" was DOS 3.0—but all of the 1.1s shared the same basic trait in that they were the *useful* upgrade of the game-changers. People ran those better-fitting 1.1s (MS-DOS 3.*x*, Windows 3.1, and OS/2 2.1 in the three examples I cited) and liked them so much that two of *their* successors—DOS 4.0 and OS/2 Warp 3—sold nary a copy. In fact, Windows 3.1's successor, Windows 95, sold well because Windows 95 itself was also a paradigm shifter. But even in the case of Windows 95, its popularity was far outpaced by *its* 1.1, Windows 98, and again, consider how *unwell* Windows Millennium Edition (Windows 98's putative replacement) sold.

Version 1.1s offer more, however, than bushels of much-needed bug fixes. They tend to sport a handful of completely new features as well, such as DOS 3.*x*'s support for larger drives, Windows 3.1's built-in multimedia capabilities (the birth of the Windows' "bonk!" error sounds, as well as Windows 98's USB support), and now Windows Server 2008 R2's AD Recycle Bin and a host of other things you'll read about in these pages.

Beyond fixes and features, however, it's always seemed to me that the best part of a 1.1 is its "broken-in" feel, a sort of "um, sorry; this was the version that we *meant* to ship" air to the follow-on OS versions, which brings me back to why I like Server 2008 R2. I'd argue that, in a sense, 2008 R2 is a "1.1" version not merely for Windows Server 2008, but indeed for Windows 2000 Server and Windows Server 2003. Why? Well, it seems like it's the first version of Server built since Windows NT 4.0 Server where the programmers actually got some time to look back at the previous version of Server and add a bit of that "broken-in" feel that I referred to earlier.

I know that sounds odd, but as far as I can see, it's true. Server 2003 didn't get to be a decent 1.1 because Bill Gates realized in January 2002 that Microsoft's software needed a top-to-bottom overhaul to make it more secure, making it a year and half late and causing it to lack quite a number of asked-for features. Heck, Microsoft couldn't even come up with a name for it until the last minute—its moniker was "Windows .NET Server 2003" in all of its betas and release candidates. 2008 was delayed when the embarrassing Blaster worm, which appeared about four months after Windows Server 2003's debut, sort of demonstrated that 2002's security cleanup job wasn't entirely effective, and led to a major reexamination of the kernel in Windows Vista and its companion product, Windows Server 2008. Server 2008's rushed nature is evident any number of places, but three jump to mind:

◆ Its arguably best new Active Directory feature, flexible password policies (which allow you to vary things like how often passwords have to be changed from person to person and from group to group within an AD domain) can't be accessed without donning AD "deep-diving" gear and working with the cryptic ADSI Edit tool.

◆ Its vastly improved new FTP server is indeed great, but it's not in the box in Server 2008; you've got to download it separately from a Microsoft site.

◆ Its enterprise-class server virtualization tool, Hyper-V Server, shipped with Server 2008 only as a beta and wasn't available in a finished version for another five months after 2008 released to the public.

WHAT ABOUT WINDOWS 2003 R2?

And before you ask, Windows Server 2003 R2 doesn't really count as a version of Server, much less a "1.1," because it was nothing more than Server 2003 SP1 with the new DFSR file replication service added.

So, how'd we get our first not-built-under-the-gun version of Server in nearly 10 years? Well, the main key to understanding this is in noticing that as of as of October 22, 2009, we got—for the first time in quite some time—*two* versions of Windows Server in less than two years. That hasn't been the case since the days of NT 3.*x* and NT 4, and we all know whom we can thank for this "bonus" version of Windows Server...Vista. Yup, in the end analysis, it was Vista's horrendous failure in the marketplace that made Microsoft decide to try to essentially "change the conversation" by taking advantage of the fact that two of the biggest objections voiced about Vista—"there are no drivers for Vista" and "Vista runs too slowly on my machine"—became largely insupportable with the passage of time, allowing them to make fairly small changes to Vista, rebrand it as "Windows 7," and release it. We Server folks can just be thankful that someone in Redmond decided, "Heck, as long as we're releasing a minor upgrade of the desktop OS, we may as well let the server guys do the same thing," which led to Windows Server 2008 *R2*. Without Vista, we might have been waiting until 2013 for new Server stuff to play with.

OH, AND BY THE WAY...

Let me clarify that I'm not casting aspersions about Windows 7, because I liked Vista from the very beginning for its largely overlooked under-the-hood security- and reliability-enhancing kernel changes. History may show that Windows 7 will turn out to be one of the most successful 1.1s in operating system history.

Who Is The Book For?

Like every other book in this 15-year-plus series, we've aimed this book at people who need to know how to install, configure, maintain, and troubleshoot a Windows network. Readers of previous editions, however, may recall that the books were getting a bit too large, so we split our Server 2008 and R2 coverage into two books: a "networking novice" volume, *Mastering Windows Server 2008 Networking Foundations*, and this book.

Now, if you *haven't* read *Networking Foundations*, must you go out and get a copy? Well, it depends on how much you already know about networking, and Windows networking in particular. Before tackling this book, I strongly recommend that you be comfortable with these topic areas (all of which are covered in *Networking Foundations*):

◆ What does a computer network do?

◆ How does Windows security work in general? What are authentication and authorization, and how do they differ? What is a file permission?

◆ How do you install a Windows operating system?

◆ Do you have a basic working level of comfort with the Windows GUI and Microsoft Management Consoles (MMCs) in particular? The command line? Can you use regedit.exe to do basic registry editing?

◆ Can you partition and format hard drives in Windows?

◆ Do you know how to configure IP addresses on a Windows system? Can you set up a Dynamic Host Configuration Protocol (DHCP) server on a Windows system to provide automatic IP addresses to clients on a network?

◆ How do you set up Windows name services with Windows Internet Name Services (WINS) and Domain Name Service (DNS)?

Please don't tackle this book until you're comfortable with these Windows networking basics—the last thing we'd want would for you to start reading and get immediately confused and frustrated. (After all, you could get confused and frustrated absolutely free of charge by reading most of the stuff on the Internet about Windows networking...why pay for it?)

What's Inside?

Chapter 1 starts out with an overview of Windows Server 2008 and Windows Server 2008 R2 (let's henceforth abbreviate that "Server 2008/R2"), as well as a high-level look at why you'd want to upgrade to either of them, and Chapter 2 shows you how to install them on your servers and how to begin to integrate them with your existing network, if you've got one. Chapter 2 is actually a great example of R2's "1.1-ness," because Server 2008's setup routine is a new platform named Panther that makes installation and deployment quite easy...and R2 installs with an updated Panther.

Veterans of Windows networking will expect Server 2008/R2 to look like other versions of Windows does, with a desktop, a Start menu, and a host of graphically based tools, but Server 2008 introduced a new option for Server installation called Server Core, a version of Server with no Start menu and a very limited GUI. Its great selling points are that it uses less CPU and RAM than the full versions of Server 2008/R2 and is easier to secure than them because there's less code to have to patch. (Not having to install Internet Explorer patches really thins out the "critical patch" list.) Chapter 3 gets you started on Server Core, and I recommend that you spend time learning it. Chapter 4 looks at how IPv4 networking changes with 2008/R2, and Chapter 5 does the same for DNS, answering the question, "How do I build a DNS infrastructure that is both secure and is also crafted to serve an Active Directory best?"

Speaking of AD, Chapter 6 is the first chapter to address that essential Windows Server technology, with an explanation of how to build the most common, and simplest, type of Active Directory: one that contains just one domain and just one location. Even if you're going to build huge, globe-spanning ADs, this first look provides a necessary foundation, so don't skip it. Then, once you've got your AD up, you'll need to create and manage user accounts, and Chapter 7 shows you how. Once you've got a working AD in place, then it's time to get some payback from all your design and setup work, and the tool for that is Group Policy. The good news is that Group Policy is a great way to control 10 or 10,000 machines and user accounts centrally; the bad news is that Group Policy can be a mite complex—but Chapter 8 helps on that score. The fourth AD-related chapter, Chapter 9, covers Active Directory delegation, a process that lets you create user accounts that are a bit more powerful than regular old users but not as all-powerful as a full-blown domain administrator, allowing you to fine-tune exactly how much power you give each user.

Chapter 10 starts out a three-part series on sharing files and folders in Windows Server. Chapter 10 covers the basics of sharing folders and files and using Windows' security to control who can get to particular files. Chapter 11 covers the Distributed File System or, as it's been renamed in the past few years, Distributed File System Namespaces (DFS-N), an overlay atop simple file sharing that combines multiple file shares into one unified, easy-to-understand unit for users and that lets you deploy multiple copies of those file shares around your company so that everyone can get local, high-speed access to those shares. Chapter 12 zooms in on the most important DFS/DFS-N-based file share of all, the SYSVOL share that every Active Directory domain controller can't live without; that chapter also covers how to accomplish an essential SYSVOL upgrade, which Server 2008 offers for the first time.

Many servers serve not only files but shared printers as well, and Chapter 13 shows you how to accomplish this with Server 2008/R2. Following that, Chapter 14 shows you how to maintain and control your servers remotely using a number of built-in technologies, including Remote Desktop, a Windows feature that got a lot of upgrades in Windows Server 2008 but that many folks don't know about, so don't miss that chapter. By now, you've got some working servers (which is nice) but no clients to use those services (which makes the whole thing sort of point-less), so Chapter 15 shows you how to hook up the various varieties of Windows created in the past decade to a Windows Server 2008/R2 network. What's that you say? You've got a Mac? OK, then skip ahead to Chapter 26, and you'll get the skinny on getting Our Team to talk with Their Team. (Note that the previous sentence was cleverly crafted so that you can project whatever OS you like onto "our team" and "their team." When I was a kid, I always heard that it's a bad idea to discuss politics and religion, but in the past 15 years or so it seems that both of those topics are far safer than the "PC or Mac?" question.)

Chapter 16 gets you up and running with one of Windows' most complex Server add-ons, Microsoft's Internet Information Services (IIS), better known as the web server. You'll learn how to get IIS running, how to set up a simple website, and how to find your way around the all-new IIS management tools built into Server 2008/R2. By now, you'll have a lot of time invested in getting your server up and running, so you'll be ready for Chapters 17 and 18—monitoring your system's performance and backing it up. If you've ever worked with a pre-2008 version of Windows Server, then get ready, because everything that you thought you knew is unfortunately wrong. (Fortunately, however, Chapter 18 will remedy that.)

Chapter 19 discusses how a Server 2008/R2 system can facilitate IP routing, which may sound like an odd topic until you consider that you need to understand a bit of IP-routing-on-a-Windows-Server before you can tackle Chapter 20, which shows you how to use your Server 2008/R2 system to set up a virtual private network. Hey, why spend money for a VPN appliance when you've already got a working server that can do it for you? (Well, there are several possible reasons, but we'll cover those in that chapter.)

Now it's time to return to Active Directory and take on some more advanced AD topics with four chapters. Chapter 21 shows you how to add multilocation awareness to your AD with a look at sites, site links, and subnets, AD-style. And if you've got multiple sites, then you may have some sites that you might be a bit uneasy about installing a domain controller into—which is why Server 2008 introduced the idea of read-only domain controllers (RODCs); learn about them in Chapter 22. After that, it's time to consider when you'd need to complicate your AD a bit by adding one, two, or a hundred more domains to it, in Chapter 23. Mergers, acquisitions, or just plain old reorganizations may require you to reshape your AD in a manner that's not all that easy, unless you learn about domain migrations, SID histories, and trust relationships—as you will in Chapter 24.

Back in Chapter 14, we considered how Windows Terminal Services let us easily control a server from hundreds of miles away, but Terminal Services—which R2 renames as Remote Desktop Services—can do a lot more than that. Chapter 25 delves more deeply into how Terminal Ser...oops, sorry, let's try it again...Remote Desktop Services lets you easily roll out applications across your network.

For our last few chapters, we cover several mildly advanced topics. Chapter 27 shows you how to set up and manage Windows Server Update Services (WSUS) on one of your services. WSUS handles one of those annoying but necessary jobs: keeping your systems patched. Chapter 28 helps you get started with a subsystem that was *supposed* to ship with Server 2008 but that instead makes you install it separately; I thought was important enough that the book needed a chapter on it: Windows SharePoint Services. Why learn SharePoint? Well, there are lots of reasons, but here's the unexpected one for many people: it's a web server that does many of the things that a file server does, and Microsoft has made very clear that it's the way it's going to go in the future when it comes to delivering file services.

You've already read that Hyper-V is a pretty big thing in Windows Server 2008 and R2, so we can't call the book complete without a chapter on that topic—and we've got a very comprehensive one on it for you, Chapter 29. Even if you don't do virtualization, give this a look, because it'll help you understand the technology and issues in server virtualization, which is a must-know field. Finally, in Chapter 30, we'll return to user management, expanding our earlier discussion of user management that we began in Chapter 7 into more advanced topics.

Stay Up-to-Date with My Free Newsletter

My coauthors and I have tried to cover as many of 2008 R2's good points and bad points, but we learn more as time goes on, and it'd be a shame for you to miss out on any of my additions to this volume. For the past decade, I've regularly put together a series of technical newsletters with tips I've recently learned, problems I've solved, and in-depth articles on things that somehow didn't make it into my books. I post these newsletters on my website at www.minasi.com, and the easiest way to learn about them is either to follow the RSS feed on my newsletters (it's at www.minasi.com/ rss.xml) or to sign up for my email notifications. The notifications are all short text notes with a sentence or two on what's in the new newsletter, the URL where you'll find that newsletter, and a line or two about any of my upcoming seminars. I never, never, never sell the list and in 10 years have used it only six times to send out a non-newsletter note, like the one I sent in September 2009 to inform my readers that I was doing a free webinar on managing Active Directory. Sign up at www.minasi.com/nwsreg.htm, or just browse the table of contents of the existing newsletters at www.minasi.com/nwstoc.htm.

For Help and Suggestions: Visit My Forum or Email Me

Very rarely have I picked up a technical book that answered my every question. Sometimes the book doesn't answer questions because the author arranged the material in a sequence that works in his or her brain but that doesn't match the way that your brain wants to hear it, and other times the question is just so specific to a particular environment ("I've got a Dell such-and-such server connected to our SAN with such-and-such iSCSI board running an Oracle database that's not working...") that the chances that the author has run into that particular situation is pretty small. So if you've got a question, what do you do?

Simple: just get in touch with me. I get a lot of the same questions all the time, so I try to cover them in my FAQ at www.minasi.com/gethelp. If the FAQ doesn't handle it, my email is in there. *But*, before you email me, visit my online forum at www.minasi.com/forum. There are lots of very smart folks there—some of whom made significant contributions to this book—who may well be better folks to ask. I've been running my online forum for seven years now and am blessed by a great crowd of members; it's so good a group that saying that I "run" it is probably overstating the case. From the forum's inception, I've tried to create a place on the Internet that's not only informative but is civil and polite. Too many forums consist of a few "regulars" hanging around the cracker barrel chattering with each other and giving short shrift to newbies' questions or, worse yet, flaming those newbies. I ask that folks use their real names as their handles and tell us what country they're from, and I think you'll find that it has worked out great—come join the forum crowd, and you'll find new friends from dozens of countries.

Again, that doesn't mean that you're not entirely welcome to email me, and I promise to get back to you as soon as I can, even if it's to say, "Heck, I don't know." As anyone knows who travels a lot, Internet access on the road can sometimes be ridiculously expensive or infuriatingly clumsy; therefore, I often am offline for a week or so, so please understand if I can't respond in four hours!

Thank you so much for picking up this copy of *Mastering Windows Server 2008 R2*. I hope it turns out to be the basis for getting your network questions answered and helps you have a little fun in the process. Happy reading and best of luck!

—*Mark Minasi*

Chapter 1

What's New in Windows Server 2008 and 2008 R2

As explained in the introduction, Microsoft had to delay Server 2008's appearance by years because of the change in the network security environment...a change for the worse. But once delivered, Server 2008 offered some very nice upgrades, and its "surprise" little sibling, Server 2008 R2, brought even more. Now, explaining all of those features would take much more than a chapter (which is, of course, why we wrote a book!), but let's use these first few pages to give you the lay of the land. Now, we realize that some reading this book are just getting started with Microsoft networking, and so for them, *everything* is new, but many others of you reading this already know tons about Windows networking, and would just like a summary of what's new in Server—this chapter summarizes that and where to find it in the book.

By now, I've sat through about a zillion Microsoft presentations on Windows Server 2008 and then R2, and they all start the same way, so apparently I'm required by law (or at least by custom) to present the following as the first heading when doing a 2008/R2 overview.

REMEMBER, WE DIDN'T COVER EVERYTHING HERE... SOME OF IT'S IN THE NETWORKING FOUNDATIONS BOOK!

In case you skipped the Introduction and are wondering, "where the heck are they going to explain TCP/IP basics, DHCP, DNS basics and the like," our total coverage of Server issues grew way beyond the size of any normal book, so we've broken out much of the sort of "network basics" stuff into a separate Wiley book named Mastering Windows Server 2008 Networking Fundamentals. If you've been doing Windows networking for the past five years or so, though, you may already know what Networking Fundamentals covers, so visit the Wiley site to give the book's table of contents a look before deciding you've got to buy another book.

Server 2008 and R2 Goals

Hmmm, I wonder what Microsoft's goals were in creating 2008 and R2. C'mon, this is an easy one. Microsoft basically has two goals in creating new versions of Server: to sell more Server licenses and to keep Windows Server a moving target so that Sun, Apple, Linux distros, and the other various Unix variants can't catch up. Fortunately, however, in order to accomplish those goals, Microsoft has to offer us some new tools, and really, Microsoft needs to offer us some new tools that will solve the most annoying problems that the version of Server we *currently* use can't solve.

Server 2008 and R2's new features basically fall into six categories:

◆ Active Directory

◆ New setup technologies

◆ Changes to the underlying operating system

◆ Networking changes

◆ File and print services

◆ Web-based services

And if you're wondering why I haven't included a bullet point with a name like "Changes to security," that's because better security was a major design goal in 2008 and, to a lesser extent, 2008 R2; therefore, you'll see that new and better security is "baked into" a large portion of these technologies, in addition to AD, the underlying OS, networking, file and print, and web-based features. The following sections offer a brief overview of what's new in this book and where to read more about those features.

AD Changes

As you may know, Active Directory (AD) is in many ways the keystone piece of Windows networking, in other words, the central database of user and machine authentication data. Server 2008 and 2008 R2's ADs include several useful new capabilities. Collectively, the new features simplify AD security and disaster recovery, offer new admin tools, and let us run our ADs more flexibly.

Read-Only Domain Controllers

As you may know (but if you don't, then don't worry—we'll cover this stuff later in the book), domain controllers (DCs) are the set of distributed servers that hold the information needed for users to authenticate to services, and as such they are pretty valuable things. If a bad guy can get close enough to steal a DC, then he could—with time, tools, and luck—retrieve usernames and passwords, enabling him to then attack your network with ease.

Now in a perfect world, we'd keep our DCs locked up, safe, and secure behind strong walls. But it ain't a perfect world, and sometimes we need to locate a DC in a branch office where there is no place to physically secure that DC—a fact that's kept many a Windows security professional up late at night since AD's inception in 2000. Windows Server 2008 offers a solution in the form of a new kind of DC called a *read-only domain controller* (RODC).

RODCs can act as DCs in that they can help users get authenticated to the file, print, and web servers that those users need to access. They are, however, different from traditional "read-write" DCs in that you can control exactly how much information they contain. (In a pre-2008 AD domain, every DC knows exactly the same amount as every other DC in that domain.) For instance, suppose you run an organization with 150 employees that has a branch office that houses only 10 of those employees. A standard read-write DC placed locally in that branch office would contain the usernames and passwords of all 150 employees. An RODC, in contrast, could be configured to hold only the passwords for the 10 employees who work in that office. Thus, if that RODC is stolen, then the most that the bad guys can extract from it are the 10 usernames and passwords, leaving the other 140 safe.

Read more about RODCs in Chapter 22.

New Windows Backup

There are many things that I like about Windows servers from NT Server 3.1 onward, but there's one thing that I have *never* liked about Windows servers: disaster recovery. Prior to Server 2008, the built-in backup software in Windows could back up all the files on a system, but if you'd lost the server altogether, then putting those files back together on a different piece of hardware so that you could bring the dead server back to life wasn't very easy. When it comes to functioning servers and backups, it's often the truth that the sum is *significantly* more than the sum of its parts. So, if you're looking at the smoking or waterlogged remains of a Server 2003 system after a fire or a flood, then having a complete set of backup tapes for that server is often cold comfort. For a long time, Windows just plain didn't have a very good disaster recovery solution.

Versions of Windows from Vista onward address this with a backup tool called Windows Server Backup, which can do a "bare-metal" backup, meaning that if you lose a server because of a hardware failure, then you can get a completely different piece of server hardware and restore the Windows Server Backup to that new hardware, and your new server hardware will behave just as your old server did. And the restore probably won't take more than an hour or so. Part of what "will behave just as your old server did" includes is DC functionality. Even if you have only one DC in your organization—something I strongly recommend against!—Windows Server Backup can turn what would have been a disaster in Server 2003 to just an annoying waste of time. Unfortunately, Windows Server Backup is a somewhat mixed blessing, because it cannot back up to tapes—it needs a network share or local hard drive to back up.

Read more about Windows Server Backup in Chapter 18.

Fine-Grained Password Policies

Active Directory does a lot of things besides just keep a list of user account names and passwords, but if we had to choose the most important of its tasks, I think it'd be reasonable to say that protecting and maintaining passwords would be that task.

That's why it's so odd that Windows authentication systems, both pre- and post-AD, lack some really obvious things. For example, using an English word as a password in a modern network is a painfully stupid thing to do, because about the only thing keeping the bad guys from guessing your password is the fact that Windows supports (theoretically, at least) around 300,000,000,000,000,000,000,000,000,000,000,000 different passwords, and even with today's computers, that's a *lot* of possibilities to brute-force. In contrast, there are only about 400,000 words in the English language, and brute-forcing that can be done in about 20 seconds by the average PC—simplicity itself, which is why anyone using an English word as a password might just as well choose a blank or the word *password*. So, why is there no feature in Windows that lets you scan user accounts for passwords that match English words? Unfortunately, Windows Server 2008 doesn't fix *that* problem, but it does address another long-term password annoyance.

In ADs based on Windows 2000 Server or Windows Server 2003, there's no way to tell Windows, "Let the nonadministrative users change their passwords every six months, and let them use eight-character passwords, but make the administrators change their passwords every 60 days, and require the passwords to be at least 12 characters." With Server 2008's ADs, in contrast, you can create as many different password policies as you like and attach them to groups and/or particular users. Called *fine-grained* password policies, they just may be the single coolest new thing in Windows Server 2008's AD.

Read more about fine-grained password policies in Chapter 6.

AD Snapshots and the AD Recycle Bin

Hey, we're all human. Once in a while, we drag the wrong icon or click OK when we meant to click "Oh, God, no, don't delete that user account!" It's in these times that we've got an unpleasant task ahead of us: rebuild or restore a user account or, if it's been a really bad day, rebuild or restore an entire organizational unit *and* the hapless users deleted with the OU. (OUs are essentially "sub-ADs" in that you can partition a piece of your organization and give someone god-like control of that piece of your organization while keeping him powerless to mess with the rest of the organization.) Windows Server 2008 and R2 each offer technologies intended to simplify undeleting AD objects.

Server 2008 introduced a notion that was a partial solution to the AD undelete problem, sort of an 8-foot ladder "solution" for scaling a 13-foot wall "problem." The idea is that you can, in a twinkling, take a complete backup of your Active Directory—a backup that is fast and lightweight but that you can't restore. I know, that sounds about as useful as a set of rectangular cement tires, but it can, with a bit of work, allow you to do something interesting: run a program named dsamain on a domain controller that lets you look at that backup as if it were a separate running Active Directory, almost like being able to fire up Active Directory Users and Computers (the program that most folks use to create and manage user accounts, often abbreviated ADUC), and tell it to go back in time three weeks, and voila! You see AD as it existed three weeks ago, not as it is now. You could then run various sorts of applications to retrieve information from that bygone AD to simplify rebuilding an accidentally deleted object. It's not the best answer, agreed, but it's potentially useful in being able to relatively quickly document what's changed in AD over time.

The better answer to the "How do I undelete a user account?" question comes with Server 2008 R2 and a thing called the AD Recycle Bin. Although its name makes you imagine some nice graphical user interface (GUI) tool like the Recycle Bin that has sat on Windows desktops for the past 15 years, R2's undeletion tool is actually a set of command-line tools that honestly ain't pretty, but they get the job done. You can see it in action in Figure 1.1.

FIGURE 1.1

Sample AD Recycle Bin run

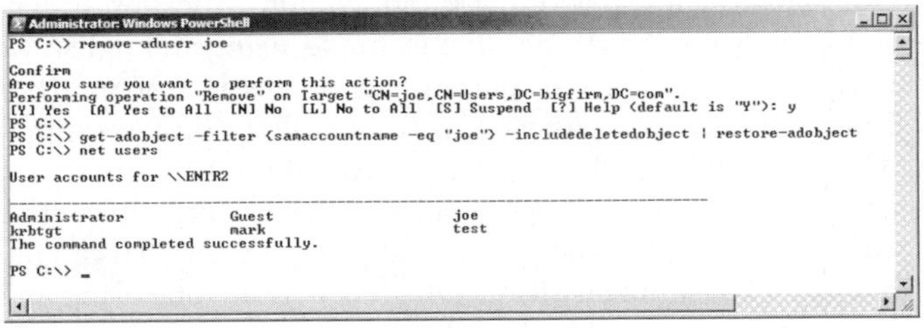

Learn more about AD snapshots and the AD Recycle Bin in Chapter 18.

PowerShell and AD Administrative Center

Ever since the advent of Windows, Microsoft has shipped operating systems whose administrative tools have, in the main, been graphically based tools; in fact, many Windows administrators can go weeks at a time without having to open a command line. That's good in that it means learning Windows administration is easier for new administrators than it would be for novices trying to learn Unix/Linux administration, because that latter group of operating systems is more heavily dependent on command-line administrative tools than GUI-based administrative tools.

What being command-line-centric does for the Unix/Linux world, however, is to make automating administrative tasks easier in Unix/Linux than it would be to automate many Windows administrative tasks. (You can put a command-line instruction into a batch file, which can then automate whatever task you're trying to accomplish. You can't, in contrast, put mouse clicks in a batch file.) So, Microsoft is trying to give Windows the "automate ability" that it lacks and that Unix and Linux have with a new command shell called PowerShell. It's designed to let you take boring, repetitive tasks and automate them easily (once you get over the initial learning curve, which is a mite steep), and so Microsoft intends to make PowerShell as important an administrative platform as is the host of GUI tools that exist today.

All of the good intentions in the world, however, are of no use if some of the Windows product groups choose not to build PowerShell cmdlets (PowerShell commands, pronounced "command-lets") to control their part of Windows. For example, 2008 R2 includes no PowerShell cmdlets to administer essential Windows networking tools like DHCP (the software that hands out Internet addresses to computers in your network) and DNS (the software that keeps track of which computer at what network address has what name). If you're rusty on DNS and DHCP, then you might consider picking up a copy of *Mastering Windows Server 2008 Networking Foundations*, our beginner's book on Windows networking. With Windows Server 2008 R2, however, the AD team has released more than 70 AD-related PowerShell cmdlets, one of which is `Restore-ADobject`, the heart of the AD Recycle Bin you just read about. You can see some more PowerShell in action in Figure 1.2.

FIGURE 1.2
Using PowerShell to install a server role

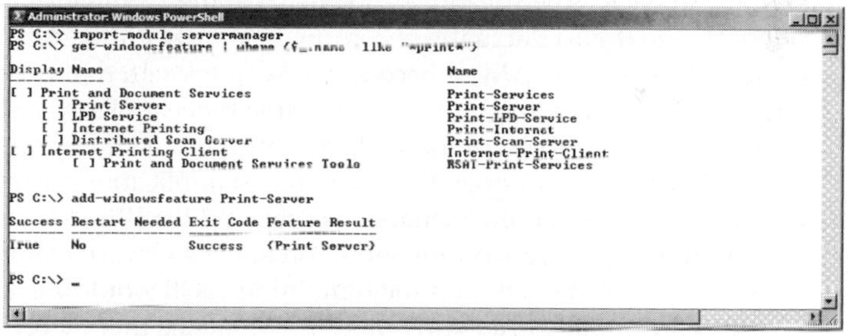

The version of PowerShell in Windows Server 2008 R2, version 2.0, even lets you create GUI tools, which is sort of interesting, and Windows Server 2008 R2 ships with an example PowerShell GUI AD administration tool called the Active Directory Administrative Center (ADAC), giving you two user management tools: ADUC and ADAC. You'll find it on the Start ➢ All Programs ➢ Administrative Tools menu on any Server 2008 R2 domain controller or any R2 or Windows 7 system where you've installed the Remote Server Administrative Tools (RSAT). We haven't covered it in any detail in the book because it is essentially no more than a differently organized subset of ADUC, but if you feel like a bit of variety, fire it up some time and see how you like it.

You can read about the various AD cmdlets throughout the book.

DCPromo Improvements

AD administrators have used the Active Directory installation wizard—or, as it's better known, DCPromo—to convert Windows servers to DCs (called *promotion*) or to convert DCs to simple member servers (called *demotion*) since Windows 2000. Server 2008 brought a number of changes to DCPromo in that you can now create the RODCs discussed earlier, *and* DCPromo will now actually write scripts for you, enabling you to automate DCPromo itself. Cool, eh? (*I* asked the Microsoft folks for that—well, me and about a million other people.)

You'll see DCPromo's new features in Chapters 6, 22, and 23.

OS Changes Under the Hood

Strictly speaking, a book on the Windows Server 2008 R2 operating system would say nothing about Active Directory or DNS or DHCP or file and print services because technically those are all nothing more than applications on the same level as Word or Excel...just stuff that sits atop the platform that is the core operating system. So, let's get purist for a moment and ask, "What's really new in Server 2008 and 2008 R2?" Server 2003's operating system platform was fairly solid, as anyone who's running a 2003 system right now can attest, but 2008 and R2 saw dozens of small changes, most of which work silently in the background and can be safely ignored; however, there are a few big OS changes that admins should know about.

R2 Is 64-Bit Only

It's been coming for quite some time, but starting with Server 2008 R2, it's official: you must have 64-bit hardware to run Server. This isn't a big surprise, particularly when Exchange Server 2007 (Microsoft's email server product) shipped in a 64-bit-only manner. But given that anything fast enough to run 2008 can run 2008 R2, it may frustrate a few admins who didn't know that R2 was coming so fast and so decided to save a couple of bucks and buy 32-bit hardware for their 2008 servers, only to see R2's new features and wish that they could just upgrade their 2008 boxes to R2 boxes.

As I write this, it's actually becoming a bit difficult to even *find* 32-bit server hardware, and computer memory (RAM) is becoming cheap enough that even a small outfit can afford servers with 16GB (that is, a bit more than 16 billion bytes) of RAM. (4GB RAM is the limit that most 32-bit *software* can access, and Windows imposes an additional limitation in that half of that 4GB is set aside for the operating system and applications—and remember that "applications" includes AD, SQL Server, Exchange Server, and the like—so even if you did buy a 16GB server and put most 32-bit versions of Server on it, the software would use just 2GB of RAM for the apps and 2GB for the OS, and the remaining 12GB would do nothing but heat the room.)

Why care about more RAM? More RAM means that there's enough room to hold entire databases in the system's RAM, which means much faster performance. What's that you say? You don't really *do* databases? Well, for example, AD is a database, Exchange Server is a database, and SharePoint is a database. In fact, "64-bitness" has been a major factor in deciding to go to Exchange Server 2007; my clients with large message stores tell me that Exchange Server just flies on a system with a ton of RAM.

GETTING THE MOST FROM 64 BITS

64 bits is pretty neat, but merely having a 64-bit OS may not be enough to offer the sort of better performance that I've promised here. For example, a Server 2008 R2 system running a 32-bit version of SQL Server 2008 (Microsoft's database server product) on a server containing 16GB of RAM could use most of that 16GB to store its AD but only 2GB to hold SQL Server databases because the SQL Server database engine only sees 32-bit-sized memory. So, remember, to get the most out of a 64-bit system, you need 64-bit apps as well.

There's not much more to know about Server's "64-bitness," because either an application is built to support 64 bits or it isn't, so there's really no other coverage in the book.

Server Core

Years ago, I wrote a book called *Linux for Windows Administrators* (Sybex, 2002) wherein I explained Linux in Windows terms—the idea was to create a sort of "fast path" to Linux for those already knowledgeable about Windows. As I did the research for that book, I couldn't help but notice a great strength of Linux over Windows: its ability to turn the GUI on or off at a whim without affecting the basic OS's server functionality.

On Unix/Linux systems, the GUI is nothing more than just another application, like Word or Solitaire on Windows. As you've already read, Unix/Linux systems boast a wide variety of command-line administration tools, and so it was quite easy to set up DHCP, DNS, or file servers without the need for a GUI, and that seemed pretty cool.

What's cool about it? Well, shutting off the GUI frees up RAM and CPU power, enabling a Unix/Linux server to be that—just a server. And when you think about it, how often are you really sitting at your server and administering it via its GUI? I'm sure the answer to that varies from system to system, but at least in my case, I don't think I'm actually logged onto our domain controllers either in person or via Remote Desktop Services (the new name for Terminal Services) more than about 1 percent of the time. If I could just turn the Windows GUI off when I was done doing some account management, think of how much faster our logins would be!

With Server 2008, Microsoft answered my prayers, kind of. You can choose to install a version of Server called Server Core that has, as you read in the introduction, no Start menu and a very, very limited GUI. There's no way to turn the full GUI back on temporarily in Server Core, but Server Core *is* a pretty powerful first step in that direction, and you'll learn how to set it up and get it going in Chapter 3. You'll also see how to administer a server from the command line pretty much throughout the rest of the book.

Hyper-V

Server virtualization—breaking one physical server up into a bunch of *virtual machines*—is one of the most significant changes in server management in the past 10 years. I wrote "server management" in lowercase because it's used not just in Windows Server but in various flavors of Linux, Unix, Sun Solaris, and so on. Being able to buy one big, powerful, reliable piece of hardware and fool it into believing that it's actually 10 or 20 smaller separate pieces of computer hardware and then installing separate server OSes on those bits of "virtual server hardware" has greatly simplified server management for operations big and small. Furthermore, it has solved a server management problem that has bedeviled server room planners for years: underutilized hardware. The tool that fools the computer into thinking that it is actually many separate computers is generically called a *virtual machine manager* (VMM).

You see, ever since the start of server computing, most organizations have preferred to put each server function—email, AD domain controller, file server, web server, database server—on its own separate physical server. Thus, if you needed a domain controller, a web server, and an email server for your domain, you would commonly buy three separate server computers, put a copy of Windows Server on each one, and make one a DC, one a web server (by enabling Internet Information Services, R2's built-in web server software, on the server), and one an Exchange server. You wouldn't do that because you *had* to for any technological reason but instead for a management reason: the web folks are probably different people from the Active Directory folks, who in turn are probably different people than the email folks. Rebuilding a three-in-one server, then, would require getting a lot of people together, and that seemed like a bad idea. The downside of this was that each of those servers would probably run at fairly low load levels: it wouldn't be surprising to learn that the DC ran about 5 percent of the CPU's maximum capacity, the web server a bit more, and the email server a bit more than that. Running a bunch of pieces of physical server hardware below their capacity meant wasting electricity, and that's just not green thinking, y'know? In contrast, buying one big physical server and using a VMM to chop it up into (for example) three virtual servers would probably lead to a physical server that's working near capacity, saving electricity and cooling needs.

In the past 10 years, then, VMMs have become important bits of operating system software, and since 2004, Microsoft has been trying to become a recognized leader in the VMM field with products such as Virtual PC and Virtual Server, neither of which have garnered much respect. But with Windows Server 2008, Microsoft shipped an all-new and quite powerful VMM called Hyper-V Server that's slowly finding its way into data centers everywhere. You can read about Hyper-V in Chapter 29.

Networking Changes

Servers are no good without the ability to talk to one another, but—of course—the downside of being able to communicate with other systems means that *infected* systems can try to spread their malware joy. ("Want to secure your server? Easy...disconnect the Ethernet cable!") Server 2008 and R2 offer some networking changes to make Windows networking a bit faster and a bit more secure.

TCP

Windows Server 2008 brought two changes to Transmission Control Protocol (TCP) and Internet Protocol (IP), the Internet's central pair of protocols. Windows' IP stack now includes IP version 6 (IPv6), the backbone of a slowly growing and newer Internet that will soon complement and eventually supplant the IP version 4 (IPv4)–based Internet that we've used for decades. We chose not to include much IPv6 coverage in this book because of space considerations and the fact that, at the moment, none of my clients unfortunately has the slightest interest in IPv6.

FOR MORE ON IPV6

IPv6 *is* covered in my Server 2008 audio course in some detail, if you need some background on this technology. That's also in part why I didn't cover Microsoft's VPN alternative DirectAccess, because DirectAccess requires that your network tunnel an IPv6 network over the IPv4 Internet— well, that and because the only clients that could take advantage of it were the top-priced Windows 7 Enterprise and Ultimate, because you need a certificate infrastructure, and because of a bunch of other stuff that's a bit exotic as I write this. In time, I'm sure that'll change, but not for a few years and certainly not before I get a chance to put another book together!

The TCP change, in contrast, cries out for coverage. Strange as it sounds, the Internet authorities decided way back in 1992 to enlarge the maximum size of TCP data blocks allowable on the Internet, but Windows essentially hasn't really supported those big blocks completely until Vista and Server 2008. Ordinarily, this would be a no-news bit of information, because you needn't do anything at all to get the benefit of larger TCP blocks and their attendant higher data transfer rates—it happens automatically. But many networks contain at least a small amount of creaky old network hardware that just plain can't handle big blocks, with the seemingly paradoxical result that

Vista, Windows 7, 2008, and 2008 R2's big blocks actually *slow things down*, sometimes significantly. Don't misunderstand, this is not a bug in Windows—it's just a Windows improvement that can trip over some long-unnoticed bugs in your hardware or your ISP's hardware. See how to smoke out and work around this problem in Chapter 4.

Network Access Protection (NAP)

Gone are the days when our company computers spent 99 percent of their lives inside the apparent safety of the organization's network firewalls, because we buy a lot more laptops than desktops nowadays, and it's getting pretty hard to find a cell phone that doesn't do email, which implies that the cell phone is a computer, has networking capabilities, and has an IP address.

As a result, you just never know what's going to happen when your users bring their Internet-enabled mobile devices back into your organization's network, and today's network administrator would be well justified to wonder each morning as the employees show up, "What fresh malware is this?" Many firewall and networking vendors, such as Cisco, have built so-called quarantine systems that refuse to give a system an IP address until it's been at least minimally patted down to assure that it's not infected, and Microsoft has a tool like that in Server 2008/R2 called Network Access Protection (NAP). It's still in its infancy (*very* early infancy!), so we didn't do extensive coverage of it, but you can get its basics in Chapter 20.

Secure Socket Tunneling Protocol (SSTP) VPN

Building some sort of quarantine system into our networks may exist only in the future for many of our networks, but virtual private networks (VPNs) are most assuredly *not* them—being able to punch through our firewalls from outside the office to get to company data and email is a "must-have" for almost every organization, and so you'll find VPNs on most networks today. Most folks choose to purchase a VPN appliance—there are many on the market and one for every budget—but Windows's Routing and Remote Access has always offered *some* kind of VPN. Unfortunately for Microsoft, however, encryption is the heart of any sort of virtual private networking system, and for a long time Microsoft insisted on creating its own home-brewed encryption system, and such systems are usually cracked, as was the case with Windows 2000 Server and Windows Server 2003's Point-to-Point Tunneling Protocol (PPTP) encryption technology. Windows Server 2008, however, offers a VPN technology built atop not a home-brewed encryption method but instead the well-known and well-trusted technologies used in SSL. Microsoft calls its SSL-based VPN a Secure Socket Tunneling Protocol (SSTP) connection. You'll get the scoop on implementing it (and other Microsoft VPN options) in Chapter 20.

New Setup Technologies

Rolling out more than four or five new servers soon gets a bit monotonous; we tire of clicking OK or Next as Setup runs on a soon-to-be-running system, and we long for a bit of automation. Microsoft has always included *some* sort of unattended installation abilities via various kinds of text setup files, but such automation tools have never appealed to many, because using them was considered to be only a hairsbreadth easier than just returning to clicking OK or Next.

The Setup programs for Windows Vista and newer, however, are far more flexible and far easier to automate than any you've ever seen from Microsoft; they incorporate a setup engine named Panther, and I can't recommend enough that you get to know Panther's new tools. Covering everything that Panther can do would constitute another book, so I'll point you to two places to find out more. First, I have some good information on working with Server 2008 and R2's Setup programs in Chapter 2. Second, documenting what Windows Setup can do has become something of a sideline job, and I have some fairly extensive articles on www.minasi.com, where you can find technical newsletters #59–62, 65, 71, and 72. (They're free.)

New Management Tools

Any good networking operating system should offer ways to simplify the job of keeping one server or one thousand servers up and running with the smallest amount of effort possible on the part of the humans doing the server administration. No one operating system has *the* answer for server administration, but Windows Server has gotten a bit better in 2008 and R2 with some useful new tools.

Server Manager

Prior to Windows Server 2008, the main "general management tool" was the Computer Management snap-in, compmgmt.msc. In 2008 and R2, however, right-clicking Computer and choosing Manage brings up a new GUI tool named Server Manager. It's the way to add capabilities to a server, such as when you want the server to offer DHCP or DNS services. You can see it displaying your server's installed roles in Figure 1.3.

FIGURE 1.3
Server Manager in action

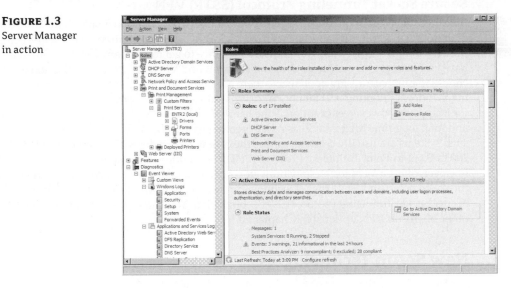

Server Manager's control of 2008's various capabilities—divided by 2008 into *roles* and *features*—extends as well to the command line, with tools named servermanagercmd.exe and ocsetup.exe.

With Server 2008 R2, Microsoft extended Server Manager's power by adding the ability to use Server Manager to control remote servers, or at least to control *some* things on remote servers, most notably adding and removing roles and features. It also scrapped both the servermanagercmd and ocsetup tools (or, rather, deprecated them), replacing them with the new dism.exe tool and a group of PowerShell cmdlets.

Where to read more on these tools? Well, Server Manager's use is so powerful and wide-ranging that it would have been ludicrous to put it all in one chapter, so you'll find it in at least part of a good number of chapters.

The New Remote Tools: WinRM and WinRS

It's the case all too often that new operating systems include some really important and useful features that go largely unnoticed. Windows Vista, Windows 7, Server 2008, and Server R2 contain one of those neat-but-largely-unknown features in a new network protocol called WinRM, short for "Windows Remote Management." To understand why WinRM is a great feature, let's consider what WinRM is intended to replace: a protocol known as the Remote Procedure Call (RPC).

Even if you've never heard of RPC, chances are that you've been using it for years. RPC's job is to allow one program to talk to another program, even if those programs are running on different computers. For example, if you've ever started up Outlook to read your email on an Exchange Server instance, then you've used RPC: it's how Outlook can tap Exchange on the shoulder and say, "Can I have my email, please?" Or if you've ever used an MMC snap-in like the DNS, DHCP, or Computer Management snap-in to remotely control those functions on a remote computer from your desktop, you've used RPC.

RPC is a protocol that has provided much service over the years, but it has one big problem: it's hard to secure. Microsoft invented RPC back in the days when there was no Internet, and the vast majority of LANs extended no farther than the distance from the first floor to the top floor in an office building, so security wasn't all that big a concern. Years later, when security became a big concern, Microsoft tried to retrofit security onto RPC with some optional changes wrought first by XP SP2, but by that point the horse was out of the barn, and requiring RPC security would just end up breaking hundreds or perhaps thousands of RPC-dependent applications.

Clearly, the time for a change in how Windows programs talk to each other had come, so Microsoft decided to adopt a protocol that did the same sort of thing that RPC did, with a few changes. First, it's not proprietary but is standards-based and platform-independent—there are similar implementations popping up on Linux and, I'm told, the Mac OS. Second, it's a modified form of HTTPS. Third, and not surprisingly, its communications are encrypted, and fourth, it requires authentication to use.

Components of Windows 2008 and R2 that use WinRM include event log collection; the ability to use the new Server Manager snap-in on remote servers; and my personal favorite, a secure remote command shell called Windows Remote Shell, or winrs. If you need a secure, low-bandwidth remote-control tool, look to winrs. (You can even retrofit it to XP and 2003 boxes with a hotfix referred to in Microsoft Knowledge Base article 936059.) Read more about WinRM in Chapter 14.

Remote Desktop Services: Terminal Services with a New Name and New Features

Ever since the latter days of NT 4, Windows has supported the notion of "terminal services," whereby a single powerful server creates, maintains, and presents a user's desktop across a network connection. This has the advantage of keeping the user's data, operating system, and user settings all on a server that's housed in a central location, making it simple to protect and back up all of that and allowing the user to view and interact with her desktop via a simple program running on just about any computer. Thus, she can start up Windows' terminal services client program, called the Remote Desktop Connection application, from anywhere and needn't worry if the computer she's sitting on crashes, because her session state and data are far away on that terminal services server.

As time has gone on, Terminal Services has grown to support the familiar Remote Desktop feature of XP and later versions of Windows. The XP/2003 version of Terminal Services was pretty good, but Terminal Services fans will be quite pleased with the new stuff that Server 2008 and R2 bring. The smallest and least change is a name change, because Windows 7 and Server 2008 R2 refer no longer to Terminal Services but instead to Remote Desktop Services (RDS). The other changes? Well, there's actually a whole bunch of them, but perhaps the most interesting is the ability to deliver not an entire desktop but optionally just one or two applications, enabling network administrators to deploy a single application simply via RDS with a new feature called *remote applications*.

Get all the details on Remote Desktop Services and what's new in them in Chapter 14 (which discusses remote administration) and Chapter 25 (which covers server-based RDS).

New Group Policies and Tools

Group Policy lets you set up a set of central rules about what users and computers can do and that configure parts of the computer's software, enabling you to simply make one change to those central rules and see that change quickly propagate to dozens, hundreds, or thousands of machines in an enterprise. Group Policy has been around since Windows 2000, but Windows Server 2008 and Vista introduced some big changes. (Windows 7 and R2 really produced very little in Group Policy changes, short of being able to create and manage Group Policy objects via PowerShell.)

What got better? Plenty. Managing Group Policy objects (GPOs) got easier with the now built-in Group Policy Management console. Want to control some registry entry, but Microsoft hasn't created a Group Policy setting for it? A new class of policies called *Group Policy preferences* lets you essentially build your own new policies from scratch, and not just registry entries—you can deploy printers, shortcuts, and the like. SYSVOL filling up from tons and tons of repetitious copies of administrative templates? No problem—just create a Central Store, and Group Policy trims more SYSVOL fat than a truckload of acai berries could.

In addition to better Group Policy management tools, Windows Vista and newer let you control a wider variety of things via Group Policy. For example, Vista and newer let you control power management settings via Group Policy, so for example you could create a domain-wide policy requiring all screens to dim after, say, five minutes of inactivity. Microsoft claims that being able to lock down power settings centrally saved the company $6 million in power bills, although I've never quite figured out how Microsoft "proved" that. Chapter 8 covers domain-based group policies and policy management tools in detail, and all throughout the book you'll see examples of the new Group Policy settings.

New Event Viewer

It seems hard to imagine that the Event Viewer application would be a featured "star of the show," but it is, believe it or not. The new Event Viewer is a complete from-the-ground-up rewrite that resolves some old problems—no more must you limit the size of your event logs or face blue screens from a lack of nonpaged pool memory—and adds some welcome new features. You can now tell a bunch of Windows computers, "Please centralize your event log entries by storing them on such-and-such computer." For the command-line junkies, there's even a new CLI version of the Event Viewer named `wevtutil.exe`. You'll learn more about the Event Viewer in Chapter 17.

File and Print Sharing

Back before we ran web or email services on our Windows servers, we only used Server to share just two things: big hard drives and expensive printers. File and print are the oldest services offered by Microsoft networks...but apparently they're not too old to learn a few new tricks.

SMB 2.0

Windows' file server service bears the official name of SMB, which stands unhelpfully for "Server Message Block." (Blame IBM, not Microsoft, because an IBM guy first designed it.) SMB has changed little over its roughly 25 years of life, with its biggest changes being support of somewhat bigger block sizes so as to be able to make use of networks faster than 100Mbps (appeared in 2000) and adding digital signatures so as to foil man-in-the-middle attacks (appeared in 2001). Windows Vista, Server 2008, and newer versions, however, sport a somewhat-reworked version of SMB that handles slow networks better, handles encryption more intelligently, and cranks up throughput on file transfers between Vista, Server 2008, Windows 7, and R2 systems. Chapter 4 covers this in more detail.

More Reliable SYSVOL Replication

File shares are all pretty much the same...except for SYSVOL. SYSVOL is a built-in file share created, maintained, and replicated on every domain controller in your Active Directory. On that share, AD stores Group Policy information and login scripts (among other things), so if SYSVOL fails, then AD can't get you started in the morning.

Now, in general, SYSVOL works fairly well, so long as you're careful to leave at least one gigabyte free on whatever drive SYSVOL resides upon and you don't have an excess of bad karma, but if, for some reason, SYSVOL starts to get out of whack, then your AD is done for. I'm not exaggerating; in 10 years of looking at ADs, I haven't seen one damaged by problems in Active Directory replication of user accounts, passwords, and the like. I *have*, however, seen a few ADs brought low by SYSVOL problems.

The major root cause of SYSVOL problems is the SYSVOL replication engine, a service called the File Replication Service (FRS). Fixing FRS is a bit of a pain because the more one gets to know FRS, the more that one is forced to conclude that FRS was designed and coded on a weekend. A weekend with tequila.

Windows Server 2008–based ADs can, however, rip out that wobbly FRS and replace it with a faster, less-bandwidth-intensive, more self-healing service called DFSR. Getting to DFSR on SYSVOL is a laudable goal, but consider this: do you *really* want to rip out *one* SYSVOL replication engine and replace it with another? On a production Active Directory?

The answer is, "You surely do, and as quickly as possible!" so long as you know how, and Chapter 12 shows you the way.

Print Management Console and Printer Driver Isolation

Windows Server 2003 R2 didn't offer us much in the way of all-new stuff, but it did have one desirable feature: a new tool called the Print Management console (PMC). The PMC offered one-stop-shopping for examining and controlling all of your print queues and would generate Group Policy objects allowing you to deploy printers via group policies—the answer to a perennial request. So if you skipped 2003 R2 and now run 2008 or 2008 R2, then give the PMC a look.

You probably know that in order to control a piece of hardware, such as a mouse, a display board, a network card, or a printer, Windows needs a program called a *device driver*, more commonly shortened to *driver*. Drivers have been a source of great pain over the years for Windows administrators because they're just about the only piece of "privileged" code running on your Windows system that didn't get the level of beta testing that the rest of the OS did, which is why when you get a blue screen, the chances are good that the culprit was a third-party device driver.

What most folks don't know, however, is that the print drivers are strange critters when compared to other device drivers because—and I'm simplifying here—print drivers end up running in the system not as separate pieces of code (as is the case for most types of drivers) but instead attach themselves to the print spooler service. A side effect of this is that when a print driver fails, it takes down the whole spooler service with it.

Windows Server 2008 R2 lets you change that by allowing you to enclose print drivers in their own processes, with the result that if the print driver fails, it doesn't crash the spooler service and all of the other print drivers!

Chapter 13 covers printing, including PMC and printer isolation.

Web-Based Services

Finally, there's the subset of the Internet that's become more important than all the rest of the 'Net put together: the Web and related services. They're important to Windows, and they've seen some big changes in 2008 and 2008 R2.

Web Server (IIS)

Windows' file services may not have changed much over the years, but that's not the case for Windows' *web* server. In the 90s, Windows Server's built-in web server software, Internet Information Services (IIS), changed rapidly to keep pace with the then-breakneck speed of Internet innovation. Then, in the first decade of the 21st century, IIS still had to run hard to keep up, but this time it was keeping up with the security needs facing *any* piece of software directly connected to an Internet that got scarier with the month. 2000's IIS 5.0 showcased a powerful web platform, but its vulnerabilities (which made possible the Code Red and Nimda worms) led 2003's IIS 6.0 to be a much harder-to-crack server.

One key to hardening any server product is to keep the amount of code exposed to the Internet to a bare minimum; if a web server can support (for example) something called FastCGI but your website doesn't *need* FastCGI, then why run FastCGI on an Internet-facing server and risk the possibility that someone discovers a way to use IIS's FastCGI to hack the server? Clearly you wouldn't, so it'd be nice to just strip your web server software of the things that you aren't going to need. (Security folks call this "minimizing the attack surface." Sometimes we think they play too much *Halo*.)

The perfect web server, then, would be composed of dozens of small modules, each of which could be removed or added as needed to allow the web administrator to build a web server that did exactly what she needed it to do...but no more. That was the guiding light for Windows Server 2008's IIS 7.0, a complete overhaul of IIS including some of the latest security technologies, including WinRM. (When you're doing remote administration of an IIS 7 box, you're using that protocol rather than RPC.)

No one has hacked IIS 7 yet to my knowledge, nor have they taken down IIS 7.5, which is the update shipped with Windows Server 2008 R2. Web admins will also like the cleaner, task-oriented interface of 7.*x*'s IIS Administration tools, which you can see in Figure 1.4. Even if you're not a web-slinger by trade, it's never a bad idea to understand the current Windows web server—so don't skip Chapter 16.

FIGURE 1.4
IIS's new management tool

FTP Server

Microsoft gets some things right and some things wrong. In a few cases, the company gets things terribly wrong, as was the case with the built-in File Transfer Protocol (FTP) server software that shipped with Windows for the past 15 years or so. It was so clunky, was so difficult to configure, offered such minimally useful logs and an inability to configure things that *should* have been childishly easy to configure (such as user home directories) that just about everyone that I know who needed a Windows FTP server ended up shelling out a few bucks for a third-party FTP server. (Many ended up buying WFTPD or WFTPD Pro from my friend Alun Jones, who wrote Chapter 19 of this book.)

With Windows Server 2008 and R2, however, things have changed considerably. As far as I can see, Microsoft tossed out all the FTP server code and rebuilt it from scratch, so if you need a Windows-based FTP server, flip over to the IIS chapter (Chapter 16) to learn about the new FTP server.

Windows Server Update Services (WSUS)

Having to download and deploy Windows patches on the second Tuesday of every month is a pain but necessary. For years, Microsoft has provided web-based services that simplify deploying and tracking patches in your domain. Windows Server 2008 Server is the first version of Server that includes the patch server, called Windows Server Update Services (WSUS). It's in the box now, so we cover it in Chapter 27.

Well, enough preliminaries—let's get on to the meat of the book!

Chapter 2

Installing and Upgrading to Windows Server 2008 R2

Experienced Windows Server administrators and consultants might feel the urge to skip this chapter. You might be thinking that you don't need to go through this material again. We urge you to think twice about that. We will be covering the fundamentals, but we will also be going through some details that you will probably not already know and that you will find useful.

Your first experience of Windows Server 2008 and Windows Server 2008 R2 is probably going to be a manual installation of the operating system on a lab or virtual machine. Depending on the complexity of your environment and your upgrade/migration plans, you may decide to continue with manual installations or even consider automated installations. No matter what you choose, you'll probably want to read this chapter to understand what the typical installation steps are.

In this chapter, we'll focus on Windows Server 2008 R2. It's pretty similar to Windows Server 2008, but we'll point out and explain the differences. We'll cover a clean manual installation and a manual upgrade of Windows Server 2003. From there we'll delve into installation and upgrade strategies for Active Directory. If you are performing many installations of Windows Server, then you will like this next piece. We will discuss how you can save some time and keyboard wear and tear by automating your installations of Windows Server 2008 R2 using an unattended installation answer file that you will create using Windows System Image Manager.

In this chapter, you'll learn to:

- ◆ Upgrade your old servers
- ◆ Configure your server
- ◆ Build a small server farm

What Has Changed Since 2000 and 2003?

We think you'll find installing Windows Server 2008 R2 much simpler than installing any previous version of Windows Server. If you have installed Windows Vista or Windows 7, then you have a good idea of what to expect from Windows Server 2008 R2 installations. The routine is much simpler, and it asks much fewer questions. Windows Server 2000 and 2003 ask for much more information and require much more "dialog box engineering." The installation routine really has been trimmed down to ask for just the basics to give you a secure installation that you can then customize.

Let's look at that last sentence. It's something we've heard before, but you might not have noticed much of a difference. You'll see it straightaway with Windows Server 2008 R2. The feature installation footprint of Windows Server 2008 or Windows Server 2008 R2 is much smaller than that of Windows Server 2003. What does that mean? There is much less functionality installed. Microsoft has not made any assumptions about what you will need this server to do. A clean, default installation of Windows Server 2008 or Windows Server 2008 R2 can't really do very much. It has no functionality installed. It's actually up to you to decide what this server will do on your network and what *functionality* should be installed. The result of this is that the server has a much smaller attack surface. What does that mean? The more functionality you install on a computer, the more targets you present to attackers. The goal should be to install only the functionality you require; in other words, to reduce the number of targets or minimize your attack surface. Furthermore, on the security side, the operating system is locked down by default. The first thing it does when it initially boots up is request a new administrator password. You'll also find that the Windows Firewall is on by default. This is an operating system that pretty much is isolating itself from the network until you configure it. Microsoft is putting you in total control of how this new server interacts with your network and/or the Internet.

Does this sound like it is going to be a lot of work to get a server up and running? Maybe, but actually Microsoft has made it pretty easy. If you are doing a few manual installations or upgrades, then you can quickly configure your servers using Group Policy and Server Manager. We'll talk about Server Manager later. If you're deploying many servers, then you'll want to look at automated solutions such as Windows Deployment Services or your favorite third-party solution. Again, you can use Group Policy to deploy policies and use the command-line version of Server Manager, `servermanagercmd.exe`, in a scripted manner to customize the roles and features of the server.

HOW ABOUT SERVER CORE?

You can learn a bit more about the Server Core installation of Windows Server in Chapter 3, "The New Server: Introduction to Server Core." The Server Core installation uses some different tools for configuring the functionality installed on a server.

How are you going to deploy Windows Server 2008 or Windows Server 2008 R2? There are some complications here. Windows Server 2008 is available as 32-bit and 64-bit architectures. Microsoft is shifting all of its server products to be 64-bit only. We've seen that with Exchange 2007. Windows Server 2008 R2 is available only as a 64-bit product. This means you cannot upgrade from 32-bit installations of Windows Server 2003 or Server 2008. You'll have to do a clean install on new hardware and move any services or data. If you have 64-bit server deployments, then you can do an in-place upgrade. This can be a time-saver, but it's not usually recommended. Microsoft pretty much urges you to do a clean install every time. However, if your server is running just Microsoft features, roles, and applications (all being 64-bit), then an in-place upgrade is possible. We've done this and had reliable servers afterward.

The Media

You may have seen Windows Server 2003 R2 media. It was two CDs. The first was a copy of Windows Server 2003. The second was the R2 upgrade. You could apply the second CD to a Windows Server 2003 installation to upgrade it to Windows Server 2003 R2. You could have viewed that as being like a service pack. Both versions were based on the same operating system.

Windows Server 2008 R2 is a different beast. It is a unique operating system, different from Windows Server 2008. Windows Server 2008 R2 comes on its own DVD and requires a complete upgrade from Windows Server 2008. Deploying Windows Server 2008 R2 on a Windows Server 2008 network is a complete operating system upgrade project.

Installation Requirements

As usual, we are given a set of minimum and recommended requirements with the operating system. Be aware that *minimum* means exactly that; the operating system will run, but it will not necessarily run very well. You should also take account of the applications that will be installed and the load that will be placed on your server.

This can vary wildly depending on applications and organizations, so there are no hard and fast rules on what your server specifications should be. The best thing to do to get accurate specifications is to develop a pilot environment and generate loads on your "proof-of-concept" servers while monitoring the performance and responsiveness of the servers and applications. However, if your server is going to have moderate loads in a small environment, then you're probably going to be OK with the recommended specifications.

Table 2.1 describes the requirements from Microsoft for Windows Server 2008.

TABLE 2.1: Windows Server 2008 Requirements

ITEM	MINIMUM	RECOMMENDED	MAXIMUM
CPU	1GHz for x86 1.4GHz for x64	2GHz	4 processors for Standard 8 processors for Enterprise 32 processors for Datacenter 32-bit 64 processor for Datacenter 64-bit
RAM	512MB	2GB or more	4GB for Standard x86 32GB for Standard x64 64GB for Enterprise x86 and Datacenter x86 2TB for Enterprise x64, Datacenter x64, and Itanium
Disk	10GB	40GB plus additional space for applications or data; note that servers with more than 16GB RAM require more disk space for paging	
DVD-ROM	Required to access the installation media; CD-ROM no longer supported		

TABLE 2.1: Windows Server 2008 Requirements *(CONTINUED)*

ITEM	MINIMUM	RECOMMENDED	MAXIMUM
Display	Super-VGA (800×600) or higher		
Input devices	Keyboard and compatible pointing device, such as a mouse		

Windows Server 2008 R2 shares pretty much the same requirements, as shown in Table 2.2, but you should read the next section before making plans for R2.

TABLE 2.2: Windows Server 2008 R2 Requirements

ITEM	MINIMUM	RECOMMENDED	MAXIMUM
CPU	1.4GHz	2GHz	4 processors for Standard 8 processors for Enterprise 64 processors
RAM	512MB	2GB or more	32GB for Standard 2TB for Enterprise, Datacenter, and Itanium
Disk	10GB	40GB plus additional space for applications or data; note that servers with more than 16GB RAM require more disk space for paging	
DVD-ROM	Required to access the installation media; CD-ROM no longer supported		
Display	Super-VGA (800×600) or higher		
Input Devices	Keyboard and compatible pointing device, such as a mouse		

AUDITING YOUR CURRENT INFRASTRUCTURE

It is critical that you accurately audit your existing infrastructure if planning a major change such as a server operating system deployment. Microsoft has provided a free suite of tools in the Microsoft Assessment and Planning Toolkit for Windows Server 2008 R2 (http://tinyurl.com/ycpuk3l). This easy to use toolkit can audit your servers as well as check hardware and driver compatibility. From this you can create reports to plan any changes.

64-bit Support

If you're working only with Windows Server 2008, then you might be relieved to hear that there are x86 and x64 builds of that release as there were with Windows Server 2003 and 2003 R2.

You've probably heard the rumblings or even heard or read the official statements before. Microsoft made it an official policy to end development of 32-bit server products several years ago. Microsoft Exchange 2007 is a 64-bit, or x64, product only. Yes, there was an x86 or 32-bit edition, but that was only for demonstration purposes. Windows Server 2008 R2 is available only as a 64-bit product. We'll reinforce that: *there are no x86 or 32-bit versions of Windows Server 2008 R2.*

Here are some notes on deploying x64 servers:

- *Your hardware support for x64 is probably not a huge issue*: The major vendors have been selling x64 processors for years for their mainstream products. You can do a quick audit of your server hardware and check for 64-bit support.

- *A lot of 32-bit applications should be able to run on the x64-only Windows Server 2008 R2*: This is thanks to 32-bit emulation provided by the Windows-on-Windows (WOW32) subsystem. Don't count just on this; please check with application vendors, and test in a lab before making firm plans to upgrade servers from Windows Server 2003 or Server 2008 to Windows Server 2008 R2.

- *You cannot do an upgrade from x86 to x64*: This precludes upgrading from an x86 installation of Windows Server 2003 or Windows Server 2008 to Windows Server 2008 R2. Getting your servers from x86 to x64 will require a migration plan from one physical server to another.

- *64-bit builds of Windows require digitally signed kernel mode drivers*: Sure, the operating system will allow you to install them with a warning, but those drivers will never actually load. Make sure your hardware vendor provides suitably signed x64 drivers for Windows Server 2008 or 2008 R2. Very often we see people complaining about Microsoft for driver issues, but this is really something that your hardware vendor is responsible for. Printer drivers do appear to be something in particular to watch out for!

As with any project, preparation is the key to success. Review the hardware requirements and check out application and service compatibility before moving forward with any deployment of Windows Server 2008 and Windows Server 2008 R2.

🌐 Real World Scenario

SO, WHAT ARE YOU GOING TO DEPLOY?

Many who deployed Windows Server 2008 knew that x86 support from Microsoft in the data center was ending. They deployed x64 builds wherever possible. They did the same for their customers. Key products like SQL Server 2008 have native x64 editions. When deploying Windows Server 2008, they were already doing an operating system deployment project, so they decided this was the best time to make that 64-bit jump. Sure, there have been times when they have been forced to go with x86 builds because of third-party application vendor support statements. That'll mean there will be a migration at some later point.

Our advice is simple. Go x64 now if you can. Check the hardware, drivers, application vendor support, and printers. Test it in a lab. If all is well, then deploy that server as either Windows Server 2008 x64 or Windows Server 2008 R2 depending on your licensing and your project aims. If not, deploy it as Windows Server 2008 x86, and make plans for a future migration to x64 on a different piece of hardware.

For a lab, you might want to look at Microsoft's virtualization solution, Hyper-V. Hyper-V is included as part of Windows Server 2008 and Windows Server 2008 R2. Watch out for Windows Server 2008 license SKUs that state "without Hyper-V." They will never allow you to turn on Hyper-V. Note that this isn't an issue with the Windows Server 2008 R2 licenses because those SKUs don't exist for that product. You can also use the free Microsoft product that is perfect for labs, Hyper-V Server 2008 or Hyper-V Server 2008 R2. All versions of Hyper-V only run on x64 builds; you run virtual machines with x64 or x86 operating systems, even Xen-enabled Linux. Hyper-V also requires CPU-assisted virtualization and Data Execution Prevention (DEP) to be turned on in the BIOS. We recommend taking advantage of this technology (or even one of the competitors if you prefer them) to test your deployment plans, whether they be x86 or x64. You can learn more about Hyper-V later in this book.

Installing the Operating System

Your first installations of Windows Server 2008 or 2008 R2 in your live or laboratory environment will probably be either a clean installation or an upgrade installation. There are some other, more advanced, ways to install Windows:

◆ An unattended installation. We'll talk about that a little later in this chapter.

◆ A cloned installation using ImageX from the Windows Automated Installation Kit.

◆ One of Microsoft's deployment solutions such as Windows Deployment Services (WDS). This is an advanced installation performed over the network using functionality that is included in Windows Server 2008 R2.

◆ Third-party solutions. Ghost is the classic example of a third-party cloning solution that works in conjunction with Microsoft's sysprep tool.

We're going to look at the clean installation and the upgrade installation processes now. We've already mentioned that the installation process is pretty simple.

The clean installation process is very simple in Windows Server 2008 and Windows Server 2008 R2. You're pretty much only being asked to do the following:

1. Enter a license key.

2. Choose an edition and build of Windows Server.

3. Choose between a manual and upgrade installation.

4. Configure the disk.

5. Set the default administrator password.

6. Log in.

There are some options during this flow:

◆ Read an installation guide.

◆ Repair an existing installation of the operating system on the computer.

◆ Create a password reset disk in case you lose or forget the existing administrator password.

In the next section, we'll cover completing this flow for a clean installation and an upgrade installation. Then we'll cover some of the options that are presented during the installation and follow that up with showing how to customize the installation of the operating system.

Performing a Clean Installation

A *clean* installation refers to installing the operating system onto a computer that does not have an installation present nor one that you want to keep. In our example, we are dealing with a computer that has no previous installations. We are assuming that you have not done any of this before, so we are going to get back to basics. More advanced readers might be tempted to skip ahead to another section, but we recommend that you at least skim this section to see what has changed.

Windows Server 2008 and Windows Server 2008 R2 each come on a DVD. It's a pretty large installation, so CDs no longer cut it. Ensure your server has a DVD-ROM drive, and then insert the DVD media. Alternatively, if you are using a virtual machine, you can redirect the virtual CD/DVD to the Windows Server DVD ISO image that you have downloaded from Microsoft or created from your original media.

WHAT, NO DVD DRIVE?

You may have a server that doesn't have a DVD drive. If so, you could look at one of the advanced network installation methods mentioned earlier. But you can also install Windows Server 2008 and 2008 R2 from a USB thumb drive. You can find a set of instructions on this blog post by a Microsoft employee: http://tinyurl.com/ktz5fq.

Once the media is loaded, you should power up your server and ensure that your server boots from the DVD drive. Normally, a computer with a blank hard disk will boot from the DVD drive by default. If the computer fails to boot from the DVD, then there may be one of a few things going on. There may be a valid operating system on the hard disk that is booting up by default. You might have a boot menu available in your computer that is briefly made available during or after the Power-On Self Test (POST). Alternatively, your server might not get the option to boot from DVD because of a boot configuration. You can alter this by entering the BIOS and making a change there. These two options will vary depending on your hardware, so you should consult your hardware vendor's documentation or contact their support desk. We have also seen situations where we have burned the DVD from an ISO file but we used a write speed that was too fast to ensure a good burn.

In the following examples, we'll cover how to install Windows Server 2008 R2. We will point out any differences that there may be if you are installing Windows Server 2008.

Figure 2.1 is the first screen you'll see. It allows you to customize the installation language and the regional and keyboard settings of the server. You'll need to change some settings here if the defaults do not match your language, region, and keyboard. For example, if you are in Ireland using an Irish-based keyboard, then these defaults won't suit you at all! The time zone won't work correctly, currency symbols will be wrong, and the keyboard layout will be totally wrong. For example, you will struggle to find the backslash (\), which is kind of important in the Windows world.

FIGURE 2.1
Setup environment to install Windows

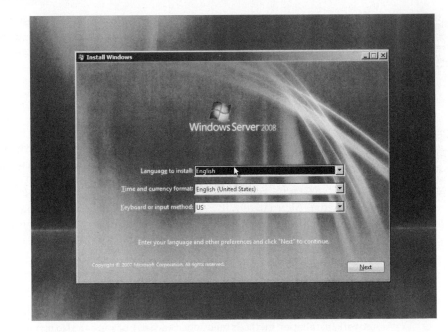

The "Language to install" option will vary depending on the languages supported by your DVD. Most people reading this book will probably deal with English-based media, even those in non-English nations. But you may be choosing Spanish, French, German, Chinese, and so on, depending on where you are and what your company standards are.

The "Time and currency format" setting affects how Windows presents and formats those regional-specific settings. You'll probably always want to ensure that this matches the location where your server is located.

The "Keyboard or input method" setting should match the keyboard that is physically attached to the keyboard. Keyboards can often vary from country to country, so make sure that this is correct. Don't worry; it won't affect your ability to manage a server using Remote Desktop. An RDP session will use the keyboard settings of the client computer that connects to the server.

The screen shown in Figure 2.2 allows you to do a few different things:

◆ You can kick off an installation.

◆ You can read about installation prerequisites and steps for upgrading Active Directory.

◆ You can repair an existing installation of Windows Server 2008 R2 or even Windows Vista if they can no longer boot up correctly.

FIGURE 2.2
Install
Windows now.

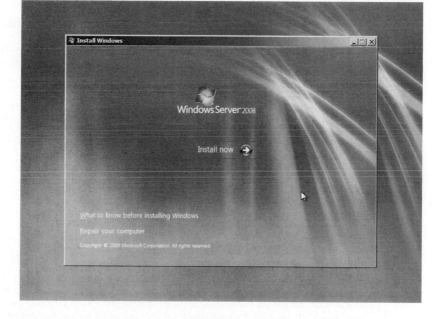

In this example, you'll install Windows Server 2008 R2, so click the Install Now button.

You may or may not see the screen shown in Figure 2.3 depending on your media. You will probably see it if you are using a retail or volume license media kit. This screen is where you start off with configuring your licensing configuration. We deliberately say "start off" because you can actually skip this step temporarily and then choose the version of the operating system that you are licensed to use. But you will have to activate Windows eventually, and that will require a product key.

FIGURE 2.3
Entering the
product key

FIGURE 2.3
Entering the
product key

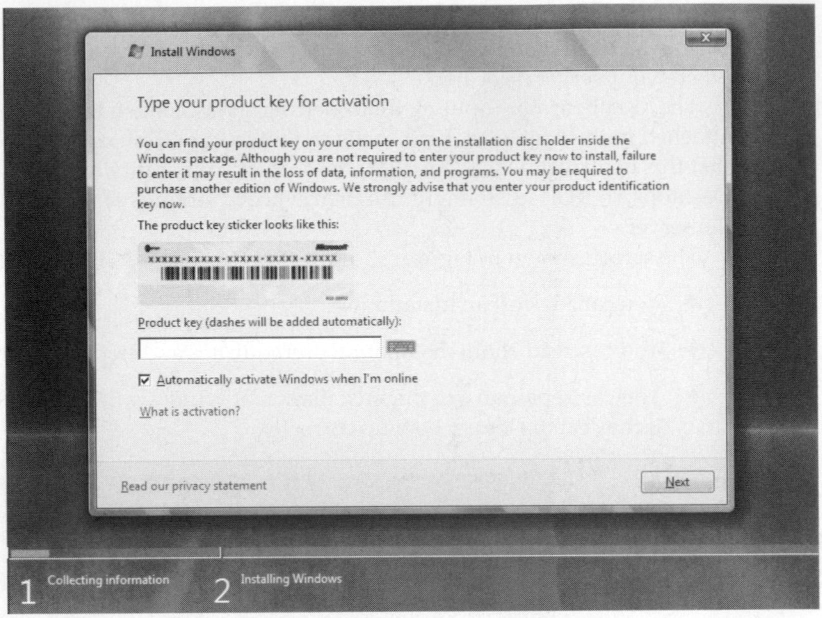

Let's assume you want to enter the product key now. If you are using an OEM license, then it will be on a sticker that is affixed to the case of your computer. That license and product key are tied to that computer and can be used only with that computer. If you purchased a retail or individual copy of the license, then the key will likely be in the DVD container. If you have volume licensing from Microsoft, then you will obtain your single reusable license key either from a Microsoft licensing website or from your channel supplier or large account reseller (LAR).

The check box shown in Figure 2.3 refers to activating this installation of Windows. Just like Windows Vista, all versions of licensing for Windows Server 2008 R2 require activation. It used to be that if you had volume licensing, there was an implicit trust that was backed up by product license usage reporting. This is no longer the case. Depending on your license agreement, you can activate each installation directly with Microsoft or via a locally hosted product activation service. Volume licensing and activation are pretty complex subjects, and they are subject to change over time. It's best to go directly to the latest materials that Microsoft has. Currently that's the Volume Activation 2.0 Technical Guidance, which you can find at http://tinyurl.com/yesoab.

You may find yourself in a situation where you need to legitimately install Windows Server 2008 R2 but you do not have access to the product key. If this was Windows Server 2003, you would be in trouble. But this is not the case with Windows Server 2008 R2. In this case, you can choose not enter your product key now, continue the installation, and then enter the product key later.

If you have your product key, then you should probably enter it here and select the activation check box. If you don't have it handy, click Next and then No when you are warned.

You have two ways to enter your product key after the install is complete. From the command line, you can use the slmgr.vbs script to set the product key, as in slmgr.vbs -ipk HFT6Y-IUTY3-P634B-PQYS8-365SV. In case you're wondering, that's a fake product key. Make sure you do not change that key after activating your installation. If you prefer the GUI, then you can go to the System Properties dialog box and use the hyperlink at the bottom to enter a new product key. That will also trigger an activation.

You can also use `slmgr.vbs` to activate your server from command line by running `slmgr.vbs -ato`.

This screen depicted in Figure 2.4 allows you to choose the particular edition and installation type of Windows Server 2008 R2 that you want to have, such as Web, Standard, Enterprise, or Datacenter. Each one requires an increasingly more expensive license with more features and scalability. Windows Server 2008 does not offer a choice of the Web edition in the normal media; there is specific media for Windows Server 2008 Web edition.

FIGURE 2.4
Choosing an edition and installation type

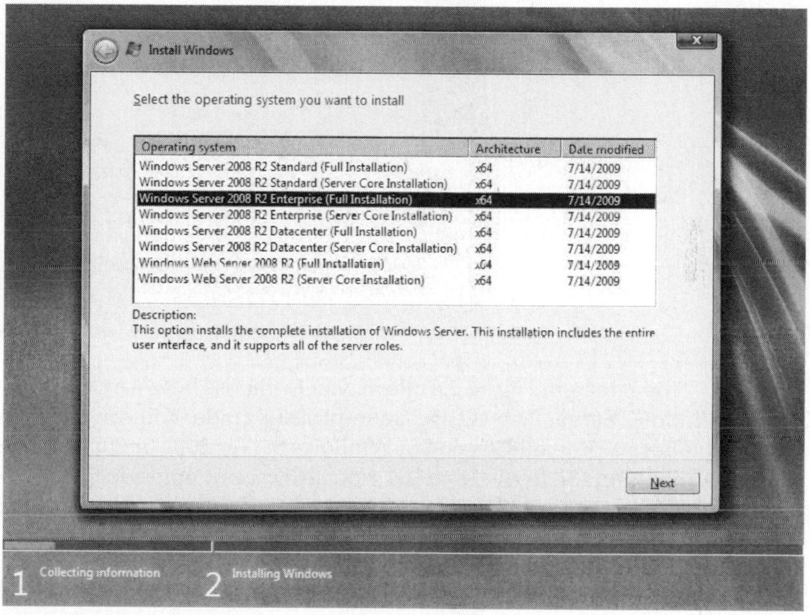

FULL INSTALLATION OR SERVER CORE

You'll also see that you have a choice of installation types. This was introduced with Windows Server 2008. The full installation has lots of Windows and graphical user interfaces. The Server Core installation strips that GUI away and assumes you're comfortable with command-line and remote administration techniques. Windows Server 2008 Server Core installation has less functionality than that included with Windows Server 2008 R2. It also doesn't have .NET support. That rules out a lot of installations. Windows Server 2008 R2 does include a version of .NET. You'll learn a lot more about the Server Core installation in Chapter 3, "The New Server: Introduction to Server Core."

In this example, we'll show how to set up a lab, so we want most of the functionality available in Windows Server 2008 R2. Select the Windows Server 2008 R2 Enterprise (Full Installation) option.

You now get the opportunity to read the legendary Microsoft end user license agreement (EULA), as shown in Figure 2.5. Most techies are going to just click "I accept the license terms" and click Next without ever reading it.

FIGURE 2.5
Agreeing to
the EULA

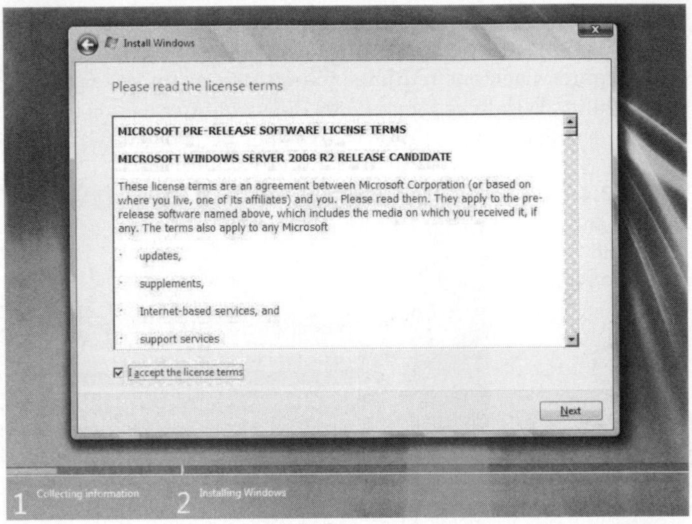

This screen in Figure 2.6 allows you to choose between a new or custom installation of Windows Server 2008 R2 and an in-place upgrade. You can choose to do an upgrade only when you have a previous version of Windows Server 2003 or 2008 to upgrade. Remember that you cannot upgrade from x86 to x64. You also cannot upgrade from a Server Core installation to a full installation, or vice versa. For this example, you're doing a clean or new installation, so choose Custom. Click Custom to continue.

FIGURE 2.6
Upgrade or clean
installation?

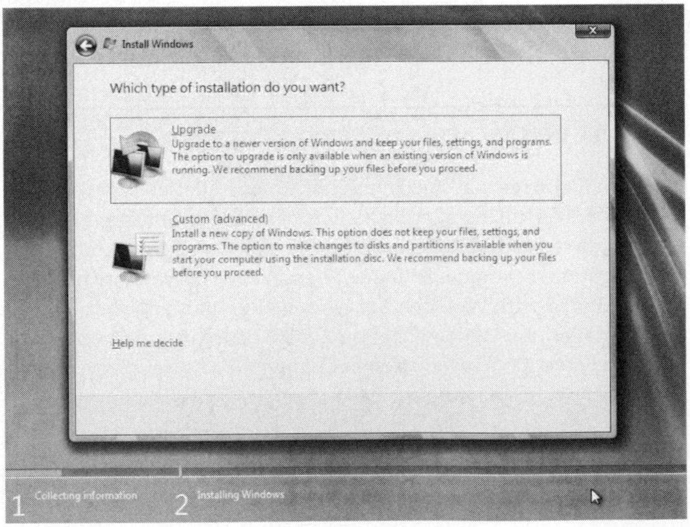

A few different things are going on in Figure 2.7. You'll probably click Next if you're dealing with a simple server where you want all the space in your first disk to be in your C drive. Clicking Next will cause Windows to create a volume called C that will consume the entire first disk in the server.

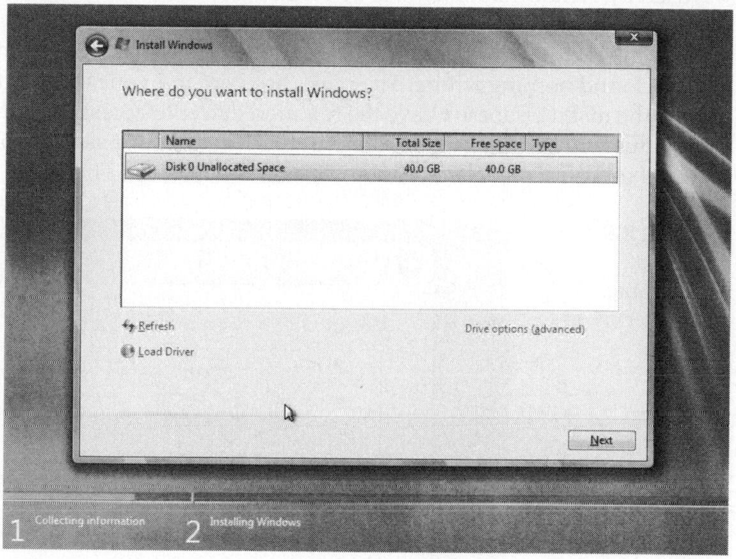

FIGURE 2.7
Where to install
Windows

However, what will you do if you want to partition that disk into different volumes? For example, you might want to create a volume to separate web content from the operating system for security reasons. To do this, you would click Drive Options. The screen shown in Figure 2.8 opens.

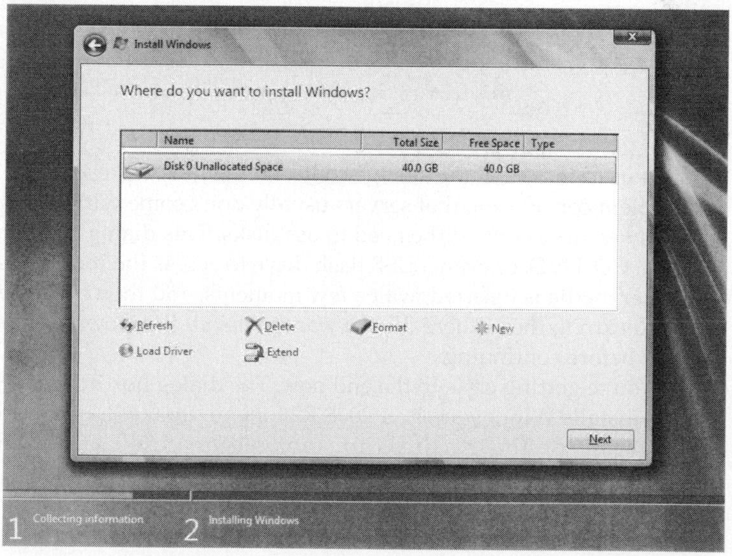

FIGURE 2.8
Drive options

On this screen, you can delete, create, and format volumes as you need them. You'll find yourself coming in here when you don't want to accept the default of using the entirety of your first disk (Disk 0) for the C drive. Make sure that you remember to format your volume with NT File System (NTFS) if you do create a custom volume to install Windows into. NTFS is the format used by Windows. NT used to be the name of the professional and server Windows products before Windows 2000; for example, Windows NT 4.0.

But what if your installer fails to find any disks at all? You've double-checked your hardware and found nothing wrong. The cables are fine, and your BIOS can see all of your disks. Well, odds are the installer doesn't have the required driver to access your storage controller. As time goes by, this will become more and more common as newer storage controllers are released into the market. You can add a driver by clicking Load Driver. The dialog box shown in Figure 2.9 opens.

FIGURE 2.9
Adding a
mass storage
controller driver

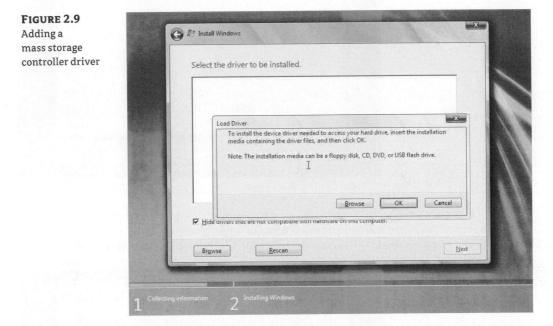

It used to be that the storage controller had to be present on a floppy drive. That would be a problem considering that servers usually don't come with a floppy drive anymore and Microsoft really wants to kill off the need to use disks. This dialog box allows you to navigate to a floppy disk, CD, DVD, or even a USB flash drive to access the required storage driver. Make sure your driver media is inserted, wait a few moments, and then navigate to find it.

Return to the "Where do you want to install Windows?" screen, and then configure your disk before continuing.

You're getting close to the end now. The dialog box in Figure 2.10 is where the installer actually installs Windows Server 2008 R2 for you. It takes a little while, depending on your install media and destination drive. You can probably get a coffee or answer some of those emails that never seem to stop arriving in your inbox.

FIGURE 2.10
Windows installation progress

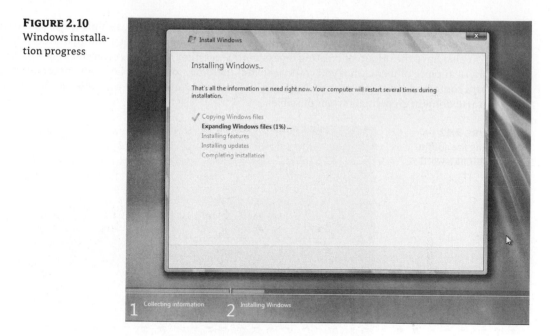

Figure 2.11 shows the first screen you'll see when you come back from your break. Before you can log in, Windows Server 2008 R2 wants you to set the password of the local administrator account. A complex password is required, comprised of eight or more characters with a mix of uppercase, lowercase, and numbers.

FIGURE 2.11
Installation is complete.

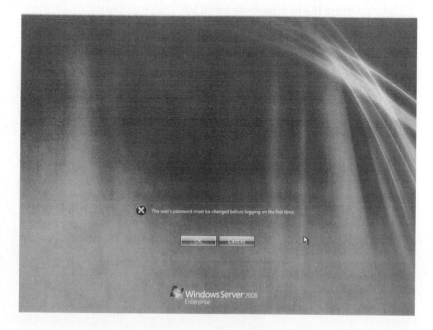

Set your password to something strong (see Figure 2.12). In fact, use a passphrase. We suggest you read "The Great Debates: Pass Phrases vs. Passwords" at http://tinyurl.com/3hrbg. You also have the option of creating a password reset disk. We don't recommend it. That's a physical piece of media that you could lose and therefore lose control of your server and the data contained on it. Instead, you can have alternative administrator accounts on the server or use domain credentials when possible.

FIGURE 2.12
Setting the administrator password

Setting the new password will log you on as the local administrator.

Be warned that your first time logging into Windows Server 2008 R2 might be a bit slower than expected (see Figure 2.13). It does seem to take just a few moments to prepare your profile.

FIGURE 2.13
Logging in for
the first time

You are eventually logged in (see Figure 2.14). The first thing you'll see is the Initial Configuration Tasks utility so that you can customize your server. You could use this, but we'll be looking at using Server Manager and the command-line alternative, `servermanagercmd.exe`, a little later in the chapter.

FIGURE 2.14
Logged in as administrator

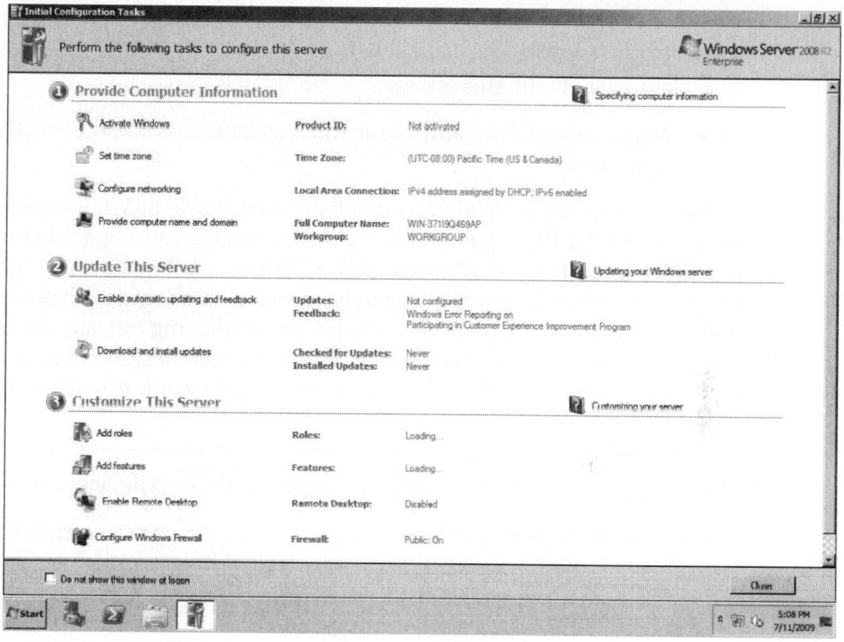

THE GUI: 2008 VS. 2008 R2

The Windows Server 2008 R2 user interface has a different look and feel from Windows Server 2008. Windows Server 2008 has a stripped-down version of the Vista interface. They're the same generation of operating system. Windows Server 2008 R2 has a newer Windows 7 interface, just toned down a little.

So, that's your first Windows Server 2008 R2 machine up and running. Congratulations! It doesn't do very much, but it is a minor victory. Grab a celebratory drink of something, and then we'll take a look at upgrading an existing installation of Windows Server to Windows Server 2008 R2.

Performing an Upgrade Installation

Most organizations will have existing servers in production, and they will want to know how they can deploy Windows Server 2008 R2 onto those networks without needlessly rebuilding their servers or migrating applications to new hardware.

Although Microsoft says that you should try to avoid in-place upgrades, there just seems to be certain scenarios where it just makes sense:

♦ A small organization that has recently invested in servers will not have the budget to buy a new server to do some sort of rolling upgrade. They will want to reuse existing installations.

♦ Large organizations will not consider a migration of all servers because of the huge costs associated with this process.

♦ Migrations of complex production environments could be costly in terms of effort and downtime.

We think it is realistic to expect that any move toward Windows Server 2008 or Windows Server 2008 R2 is likely going to include a mix of clean and upgrade installations. OK…the good news is that upgrade installations are supported, and they do work. It has been done before with production servers, but we believe in being selective about which servers to upgrade, wanting them to be without problems and completely supporting the new operating system. Tables 2.3 and 2.4 show the supported upgrade scenarios. Note that these are outline scenarios. Any upgrade that you are planning should be tested and cleared with vendors before you proceed.

TABLE 2.3:   Windows Server 2008 Supported Upgrade Scenarios

EXISTING OPERATING SYSTEM	SUPPORTED UPGRADE
Windows 2003 R2 Standard	Windows 2008 Standard
Windows 2003 Standard with Service Pack 1	Windows 2008 Enterprise
Windows 2003 Standard with Service Pack 2	
Windows 2003 R2 Enterprise	Windows 2008 Enterprise
Windows 2003 Enterprise with Service Pack 1	Windows 2008 Datacenter
Windows 2003 Enterprise with Service Pack 2	
Windows 2003 R2 Datacenter	Windows 2008 Datacenter
Windows 2003 Datacenter with Service Pack 1	
Windows 2003 Datacenter with Service Pack 2	

TABLE 2.4:   Windows Server 2008 R2 Supported Upgrade Scenarios

EXISTING OPERATING SYSTEM	SUPPORTED UPGRADE
Windows 2003 R2 Standard	Windows 2008 R2 Standard
Windows 2003 Standard with Service Pack 2	Windows 2008 R2 Enterprise
Windows 2008 Standard	

TABLE 2.4: Windows Server 2008 R2 Supported Upgrade Scenarios *(CONTINUED)*

EXISTING OPERATING SYSTEM	SUPPORTED UPGRADE
Windows 2003 R2 Standard	Windows 2008 R2 Standard
Windows 2003 Standard with Service Pack 2	Windows 2008 R2 Enterprise
Windows 2008 Standard	
Windows 2003 R2 Enterprise	Windows 2008 R2 Enterprise
Windows 2003 Enterprise with Service Pack 2	Windows 2008 R2 Datacenter
Windows 2008 Enterprise	
Windows 2003 R2 Datacenter	Windows 2008 R2 Datacenter
Windows 2003 Datacenter with Service Pack 2	
Windows 2008 Datacenter	

There are various upgrade scenarios to consider when you think about the combinations of x86, x64, Server Core, and full installations (see Figure 2.15).

FIGURE 2.15
Supported
upgrade paths

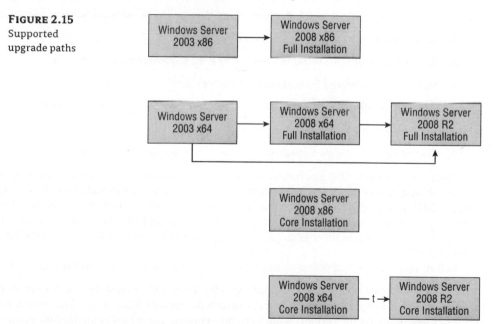

Here are some things to note:

◆ You cannot upgrade from x86 to x64, or vice versa.

◆ You cannot upgrade directly from Windows Server 2000. You will first have to upgrade to Windows Server 2003 before moving to Windows Server 2008.

◆ You cannot upgrade from Windows Server 2003 to Windows Server 2008 R2 Server Core editions.

◆ You cannot migrate from Windows Server 2008 R2 to Windows Server 2008 R2 Server Core editions.

◆ Although you can upgrade from one edition to a higher edition, such as Windows 2003 Standard to Windows 2008 Enterprise, you should ensure that you have a valid Windows license.

◆ You must have licensing for the upgrade operating system, such as Windows Server 2008 R2, before you can upgrade from Windows Server 2003. This will mean either having Software Assurance or purchasing the required Windows Server 2008 R2 license for each upgraded server and the required client access licenses (CALs) for end user access.

◆ You cannot upgrade from one language to another.

Getting from x86 servers to x64 servers is going to require some sort of migration. The likely process will involve introducing new hardware. This might be done as part of a scheduled recycling of all hardware that is no longer supported by the manufacturer. It could be part of a migration to a virtualized data center. Or it might be a rolling process, something we have seen done before because it minimizes hardware spending. For example:

1. Server A, server B, and so on, are running Windows 2003 x86 in the computer room.

2. Server X is purchased for the network upgrade.

3. Server X is built with Windows Server 2008 R2 to closely match server A.

4. Services are migrated from server A to server X.

5. Server A is rebuilt with Windows Server 2008 R2 to closely match server B.

6. Services are migrated from server B to server A.

7. The process continues with all remaining Windows Server 2003 machines.

Plenty of Windows 2000 machines are still knocking around. What are you going to do with them? To upgrade to Windows Server 2008, you will first have to upgrade them to Windows Server 2003. Realistically, that's probably not going to happen in most situations. Windows 2000 had no x64 release for Intel and AMD chipsets. There was an Itanium release, but that's not the same as x64. That means there is no in-place upgrade path from Windows 2000 to Windows Server 2008 R2.

Before you even look at doing an upgrade, you have a few chores to go through first:

◆ You will want to double-check that any software or drivers installed on the server that you are going to upgrade will support Windows Server 2008 R2. The products might work, but there is always the support issue from the vendors. There's a strong likelihood that third-party support will be a bit hit and miss in the early days, but that will improve over time.

◆ The most important driver to have is the mass storage controller driver. You've already seen in the clean installation process that you might need to provide this on removable media if Windows Server doesn't have a built-in driver for it.

◆ Check the health of your server hardware. Your vendor usually includes some free software for this. Microsoft recommends that you also use their memory diagnostics tool, which can be found at http://tinyurl.com/qoy4.

◆ If you are upgrading a production or an important server, then you should back it up before going any further. Test that backup if at all possible. If you're using a virtual machine, then this is a lot easier. You can take a snapshot and revert to that point in time if the upgrade fails. Check with your vendor for snapshot support in production environments first.

◆ You should either disable or uninstall your antivirus software on the server to be upgraded. Odds are, you will need to uninstall it because there is a good chance that it will interfere with the upgrade or even break the upgraded server. You should ensure that you have a version of your antivirus software ready to deploy for Windows Server 2008 R2 once the upgrade is completed.

◆ If you are running a monitoring solution such as System Center Operations Manager, you will want to either disable monitoring for a few hours or even remove the agent. Check with your vendor for supported scenarios.

◆ Finally, be prepared for the Windows Firewall. By default, it's turned on in Windows Server 2008 and Windows Server 2008 R2 and may block application traffic destined to your upgraded servers. Know what ports you will need to configure in advance. This may require checking with the application vendor or using a tool like the free Microsoft Network Monitor.

We cannot recommend enough that you try this upgrade process in a virtual lab first. You can do this pretty cheaply using TechNet or demonstration licenses and with one of a myriad of free virtualization solutions you can try. If you are testing Windows Server 2008 or Windows Server 2008 R2 then you can use:

◆ Microsoft's free Hyper-V Server 2008 R2.

◆ VMware Server, which will run on a Windows Server host.

◆ VMware ESXi, which is a hypervisor (it doesn't run on an operating system).

◆ Citrix XENServer, another hypervisor which that is a close relative of Microsoft's Hyper-V.

Note that you must use a virtualization technology, such as those just listed, that will support 64-bit virtual machines or guests when testing Windows Server 2008 R2.

USING HYPER-V

You're learning about Windows Server 2008 and Windows Server 2008 R2, so to us it seems logical to use Hyper-V. We strongly recommend reading Chapter 29, "Server Virtualization Using Hyper-V," to learn how you can deploy a virtualization environment for your test lab.

Those are all of the formalities out of the way, so now let's take a look at an upgrade in action. You cannot perform an in-place upgrade if you boot your server up from the DVD. This method allows only a clean installation. If you want to do an upgrade, then you will have to boot up your Windows server and insert the DVD or, in the case of a virtual machine, mount your Windows Server 2008 R2 media ISO image. This allows the upgrade program to download updates from Microsoft and to properly scan your server before any changes are made.

This is an existing Windows Server 2003 x64 machine that we are planning to upgrade to Windows Server 2008 R2 (see Figure 2.16). We ran winver.exe to check the version and build of the installed operating system. The presence of a C:\Program Files (x86) folder means that the installed operating system is a 64-bit one. The process is similar to upgrading from Windows Server 2003 x86 to Windows Server 2008 x86. To get moving, log into the server you want to upgrade, and insert or mount your Windows Server 2008 R2 media.

FIGURE 2.16
Windows 2003
is installed.

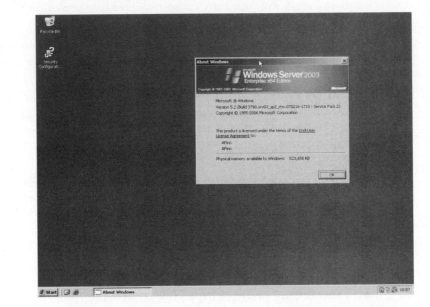

The dialog box in Figure 2.17 will appear automatically if you have autoplay enabled on your DVD drive. If it doesn't appear, then run setup.exe from the root of your Windows Server 2008 R2 media.

You'll notice that the upgrade process is almost identical to that of a clean install. It's pretty light on the keyboard and mouse work that you have to do.

You can see in this dialog box that you can read about what you should know before installing Windows Server 2008 R2. This is a good article to read, especially in the case of an upgrade. Click Install Now when you are ready to proceed with the upgrade.

The screen in Figure 2.18 allows you to download updates from Microsoft to improve the installation process. The process relies on the server and the currently logged in user having access to the Internet. Microsoft gives four reasons to go through an installation update:

◆ Updates for the installation process are downloaded. This can resolve issues that are discovered over time.

◆ Driver updates are available to improve the plug-and-play process during installation.

◆ Windows updates are included to patch the operating system.

◆ Updates for the Microsoft Windows Malicious Software Removal Tool are included to help protect your new server.

FIGURE 2.17
setup.exe
startup screen

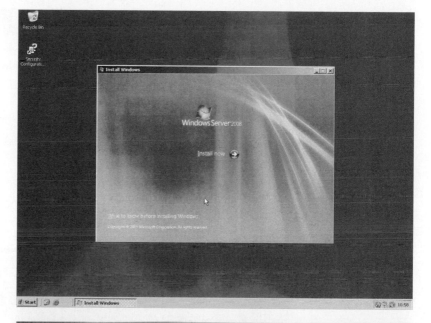

FIGURE 2.18
Getting updates
for the setup

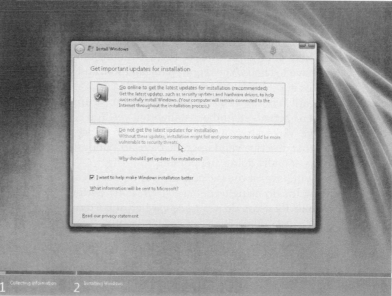

Our advice is that you should go through this process if your server is important to you. If you are just doing lab work, then you might not be concerned unless your installation fails and an update can resolve the issue.

As you can see in Figure 2.19, we've chosen to go through the update, so the installer connects to Microsoft to download any available updates.

FIGURE 2.19
Updates are downloaded.

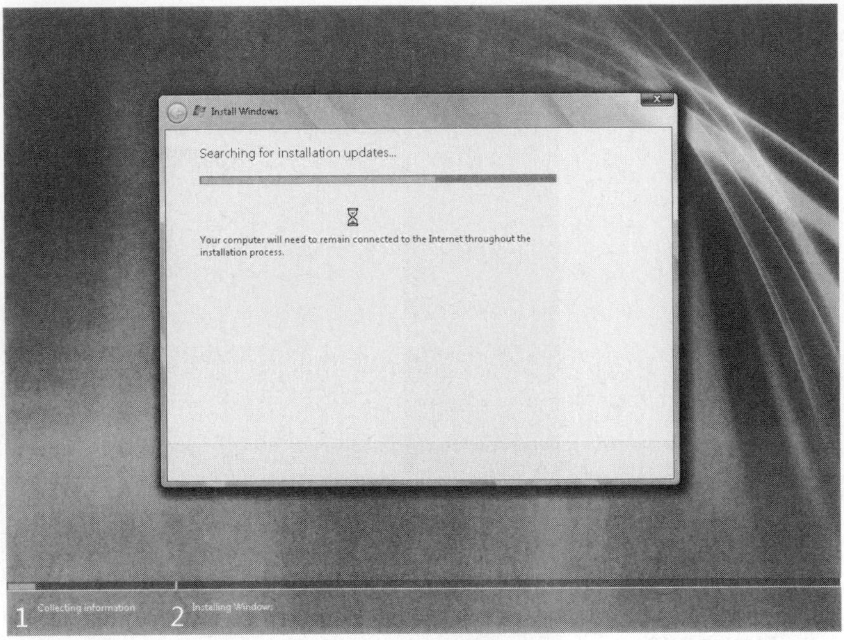

Depending on the media you are using, you come to a dialog box where you can enter your product key and choose to automatically update the installation. We've already discussed the options here; they're the same as in the clean installation process.

You have to choose the required installation, and you must also confirm that you have a license for it.

Hold on! Why are you seeing the screen in Figure 2.20? Aren't you doing an upgrade? Well, you haven't actually told the installer that yet. You could be installing a new operating system at this point. Make sure you pick a valid edition choice for your upgrade. Please refer to Tables 2.3 and 2.4 that describe valid upgrade paths to Windows Server 2008 and Windows Server 2008 R2 if you are actually doing an upgrade.

You will have, of course, poured over the EULA and have completely understood it before accepting the licensing terms (see Figure 2.21). Seriously, you will not be able to install Windows Server 2008 R2 if you do not agree to Microsoft's terms.

FIGURE 2.20
Choosing an
edition and
installation type

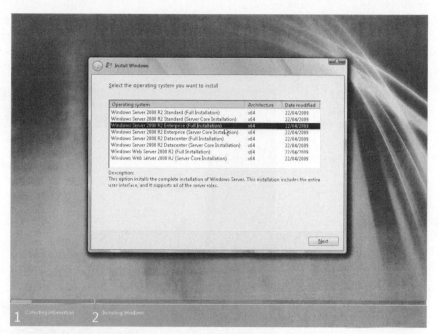

FIGURE 2.21
Accepting
the EULA

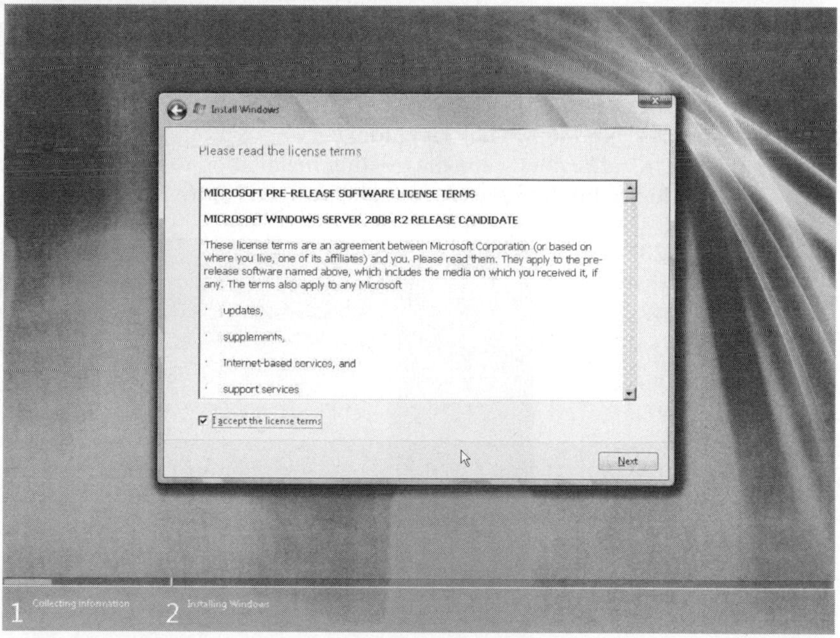

The dialog box shown in Figure 2.22 presents you with the option to either do an upgrade or a custom or clean installation of Windows Server 2008 R2. If you have followed the instructions correctly so far, then both options will be available to you. However, if you selected an invalid edition of Windows Server 2008 R2 to install, then you will not be able to upgrade.

FIGURE 2.22
Choosing to perform an upgrade

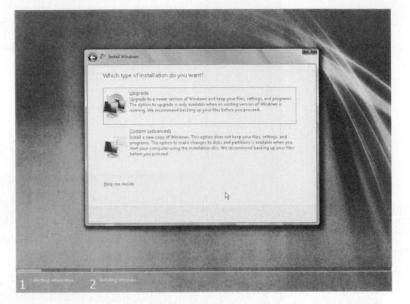

In this example, we are upgrading from Windows 2003 Enterprise edition to Windows 2008 Enterprise edition, so click Upgrade.

The installer now scans the existing installation to see whether there are any known incompatibilities with Windows Server 2008 R2 (see Figure 2.23).

FIGURE 2.23
Setup checks your compatibility.

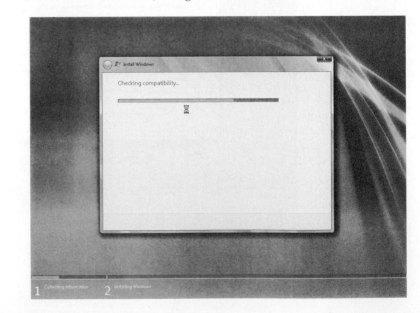

The installer will check to see whether the existing server is compatible. If it isn't, then you will get a reason why in a compatibility report, such as an unsupported upgrade path, as shown in Figure 2.24, and you will have to start the upgrade from the beginning after resolving any issues.

FIGURE 2.24
The compatibility report

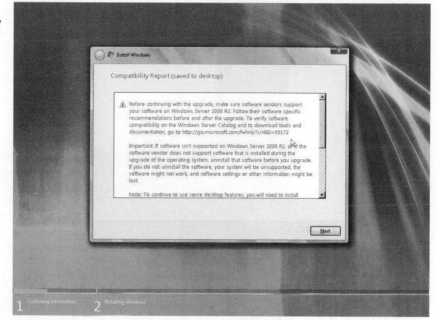

You have now arrived at the "last-chance gas station." You had better pull in here and fill up before proceeding. The installer is now giving you your last opportunity to confirm that all the hardware, software, and drivers on the existing server installation will work when you have completed the upgrade. After clicking Next, there is no going back! But seriously, any known incompatibilities with Windows Server 2008 R2 will be listed here.

If you get a warning that one of your drivers might not work after the upgrade, you can fix that after the upgrade is completed.

It is break time again (see Figure 2.25)! The installer now has enough information from you to proceed. It will perform the upgrade and reboot when required. Your next action will be to log into your shiny new Windows 2008 R2 server—assuming that all goes to plan. Don't stray too far because you will need to log in to make sure everything is working correctly and to make any required configuration modifications.

The server will reboot several times, and the screen in Figure 2.26 will appear while you're probably either taking a break or replying to emails. Eventually the screen in Figure 2.25 reappears, so it's nothing to worry about. This cycle will continue until the upgrade is complete.

FIGURE 2.25
Upgrade progress

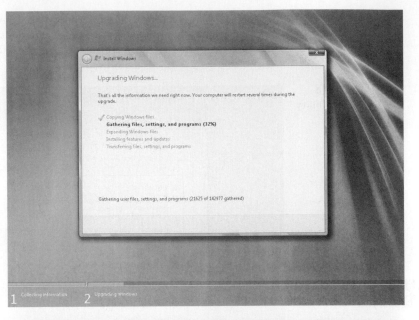

FIGURE 2.26
The server reboots
several times.

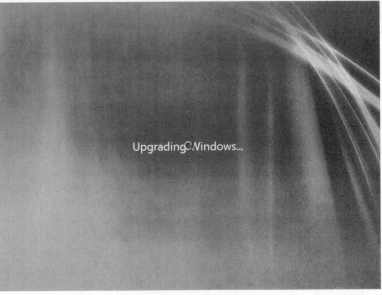

After a while, the server automatically will reboot into Windows Server 2008 R2 and wait for you to log in (see Figure 2.27). How long it takes to get here depends on your hardware. Your server might be quick or slow; for example, a computer with cheap and slow storage will obviously take longer to upgrade. That's why you are warned that the upgrade *may* take several hours.

FIGURE 2.27
The upgrade is
complete.

Go ahead and log in, and you will eventually see what your upgraded server looks like.
Instead of getting the Initial Configuration Tasks utility, you get to see Server Manager when
you log in (see Figure 2.28). For now, don't worry too much about Server Manager; you'll take a
much better look at it in a little while. That's the first difference you'll see between a clean installation and an upgrade. As you scroll through the details pane in the middle, you'll see that your
Windows Firewall status is inherited from the previous installation.

FIGURE 2.28
Server Manager

You can also see that some *roles* and *features* are installed. You may remember that we said that a Windows Server 2008 or Windows Server 2008 R2 installation has nothing installed by default. That's true. But in this example we just upgraded a server. The server that we just upgraded had no additional components installed. But Windows Server 2008 R2 sees it very differently. It saw important functionality that it believed should be retained in case it is being used. You'll later learn how to use Server Manager, `servermanagercmd.exe`, or PowerShell to add or remove roles and features.

You will probably want to ensure at this point that you complete the following:

◆ Check the logs in Event Viewer to see whether there are any problems that need to be resolved.

◆ Join a domain, if required, and make sure all applicable policies are applied.

◆ Install all available security updates.

◆ Install any security software such as antivirus software, and apply any required manual security configurations.

◆ You may have third-party software to install, configure, or diagnose.

That's an upgrade completed. It wasn't all that painful, was it? This would be an appropriate time for you to customize your server.

Initial Configuration Tasks Utility

The Initial Configuration Tasks utility has a pretty self-explanatory name (see Figure 2.29). When you do a clean installation of your server, this tool will allow you to quickly get some essential tasks done:

Activate Windows   Every copy of Windows Server 2008 and Windows Server 2008 R2 needs to be activated either via the Internet or via a telephone call with Microsoft. Failure to activate will render the server inoperable until you activate it.

Set time zone   Here you can set the time zone and the time.

Configure networking   This allows you to configure your server's connectivity to the network.

Provide Computer Name and Domain   Using this you can set the computer name and configure domain membership for the server.

Enable automatic updating and feedback   You really should do this either manually or via Group Policy. Automatic Updates will enable you to download important updates and security updates from Microsoft, usually on a monthly basis.

Download and install updates   You can manually force an update to protect your server immediately. We strongly recommend this.

Add roles   We'll talk more about *roles* and *features* in the next section.

Add features   Just like with the previous, this allows you to add functionality to the server.

Enable Remote Desktop   You probably will manage your server via Remote Desktop once it is on the network. This allows you to do that.

Configure Windows Firewall   Your server's Windows Firewall will be on by default. You can configure this automatically using Active Directory Group Policy, or you can do this manually. You need to configure the firewall to allow remote access to network services hosted on this server.

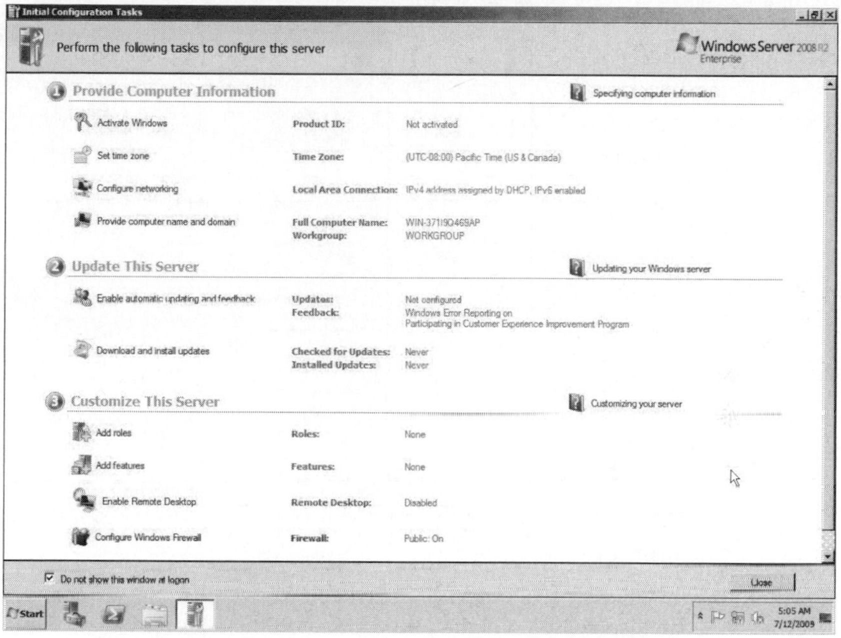

FIGURE 2.29
Initial Configuration Tasks window

We're not going into any detail in this section. We'll leave that until the next section when we talk about Server Manager.

By default, this tool will continue to appear whenever you log into the servers that you performed a clean installation on. You can disable that with the check box in the bottom-left corner.

Server Manager will now appear and will continue to do so whenever you log in. You'll now take a look at that tool and how you can manage your server with it.

Using Server Manager to Configure Your Servers

For many years, Microsoft has been trying to get people to use a single tool for managing the configuration of servers. In the past, when we logged into the newest version of Server, we were greeted by some tool that promised to do pretty much that. We looked at it briefly and saw a little check box that said something like "Do not display this again at logon," selected that, and then closed the tool so it would never again see the light of day. The only other time we heard of that tool was while studying for some sort of Microsoft certification exam. We just knew better…why use that tool when we could get exactly what we wanted from Control Panel's Add/Remove Programs in a much shorter time?

You probably noticed early on that Windows Server 2008 and Windows Server 2008 R2 are quite different from their predecessors. But Microsoft obviously wanted those of us who are familiar with Windows Server 2000 and 2003 to feel at home. Now you are greeted by the Initial Configuration Tasks utility every time you log in. Trust us; you will want to use Server Manager (see Figure 2.30) instead of this utility.

FIGURE 2.30
Server Manager

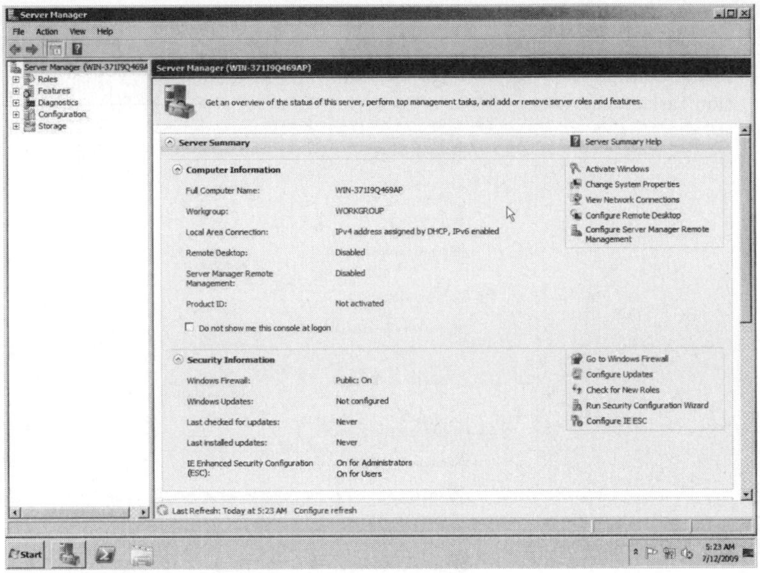

Now another tool pops up all by itself. Welcome to Server Manager. In Windows Server 2008 you can also get to it via the pinned area on the top of the Start menu. It's in the *superbar* (or the taskbar) in Windows Server 2008 R2. You will find additional ways to access Server Manager by starting it from Administrative Tools, by running `compmgmtlauncher.exe`, or by using Programs and Features in Control Panel.

SERVER MANAGER CAN BE ANNOYING

Server Manager has a habit of popping up every time you log in. That will get pretty old in a very short time. You can control this by editing the REG_DWORD value of DoNotOpenServerManagerAtLogon in HKEY_LOCAL_MACHINE\SOFTWARE\Microsoft\Server Manager. The default is 0, which causes Server Manager to appear every time you log in. Setting it to 1 will disable this. There's also a little check box in Server Manager called "Do not show me this console at logon." You will probably want to select this because waiting for Server Manager to open and closing it every time you log in could become tiresome pretty rapidly.

Server Manager is the tool that you will use to manage the configuration of your Windows Server 2008 and Windows Server 2008 R2 machines. Using it, you can add and remove native functionality, manage that functionality, and diagnose problems. You can also use a command-line alternative called `servermanagercmd.exe` to manage the native functionality that is installed on Windows Server 2008 and Windows Server 2008 R2.

Changes to Server Manager

There are some differences between Server Manager in Windows Server 2008 and Windows Server 2008 R2:

◆ Connect to Computer is different. Annoyingly, Server Manager in Windows Server 2008 could manage the local machine only. You can manage any Windows Server 2008 R2 machine using Server Manager from Windows Server 2008 R2.

◆ Some roles have been changed. We'll talk about what roles and features are soon.

  ◆ Terminal Services was expanded and renamed to Remote Desktop Services.

  ◆ Print Services is now called Print and Document Services.

  ◆ Windows Software Update Services (WSUS) is Microsoft's free centrally managed automatic updates solution, and it's included.

  ◆ Universal Description, Discovery, and Integration (UDDI) is not available in the new Server release.

◆ The following changes have been made to features:

  ◆ The Remote Server Administration Tools includes some new tools, including Active Directory Administrative Center, Remote Desktop Connection Broker, and the BitLocker Recovery Password Viewer.

  ◆ Windows Server Migration Tools are added to assist in migrating from older file servers.

  ◆ BranchCache is an advanced networking solution for caching file and web server content to help resolve WAN congestion issues in branch office networks.

  ◆ DirectAccess Management Console was added in Windows Server 2008 R2 to manage the new alternative for mobile worker remote access solutions.

  ◆ Windows Remote Management (WinRM) IIS Extension now allows clients to remotely manage servers using the WS-Management protocol.

  ◆ A new Windows Biometric Framework has been added to authenticate users.

  ◆ Windows 2000 support was removed from Message Queuing in the Windows Server 2008 R2 release.

  ◆ XPS Viewer is now a feature instead of being part of .NET Framework 3.0.

◆ A Best Practices Analyzer is available on Windows Server 2008 R2 to manage machines that are running:

  ◆ Active Directory Domain Services

  ◆ Active Directory Certificate Services

  ◆ Domain Names System (DNS)

  ◆ Remote Desktop Services

  ◆ Web Server (IIS)

◆ PowerShell cmdlets (pronounce "command-lets") have been added to managed roles and features:

◆ `Add-WindowsFeature`

◆ `Get-WindowsFeature`

◆ `Remove-WindowsFeature`

This sound like a lot of differences, but Server Manager is more alike than different on Windows Server 2008 and Windows Server 2008 R2.

Common Configuration Tasks

When you have installed a new server, you need to go through some common tasks to get the server onto the network. We'll now walk you through some samples using Server Manager.

CHANGING NETWORK PROPERTIES

One of the first things you will commonly do with a server is to give it a static IPv4 network configuration. This is required in an IPv4 network so that the server can see other network devices and services.

You can see a section called Computer Information in the details pane of Server Manager. On the left there is a link called View Network Connections. Clicking that will open the System applet from Control Panel (see Figure 2.31).

FIGURE 2.31
Network
Connections

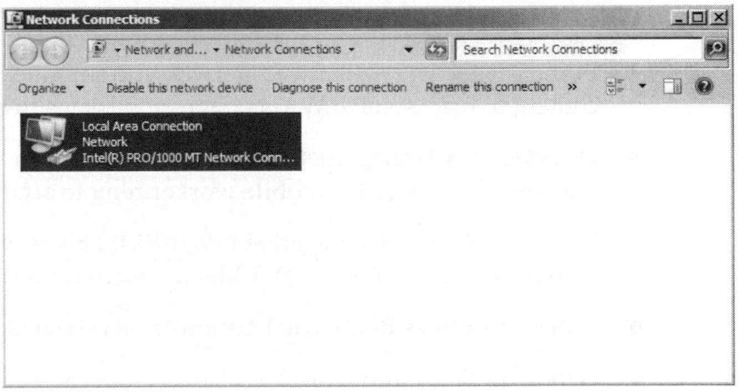

Here you can see each of the network interface cards (NICs) on your server. Our server is pretty simple. It only has one network interface for us to configure. Your server may have two. You might want to look into binding those two NICs into one fault-tolerant and/or load-balancing virtual interface. Your hardware vendor probably supplies software and instructions for doing that.

Here's a handy trick. You can run `ncpa.cpl` to quickly open the network connections properties sheet.

To configure your server's NIC, right-click it, and choose Properties. That opens the dialog box shown in Figure 2.32.

Next select Internet Protocol Version 4 (TCP/IPv4), and click Properties (see Figure 2.32). The dialog box shown in Figure 2.33 will open.

FIGURE 2.32

Local Area Connection properties

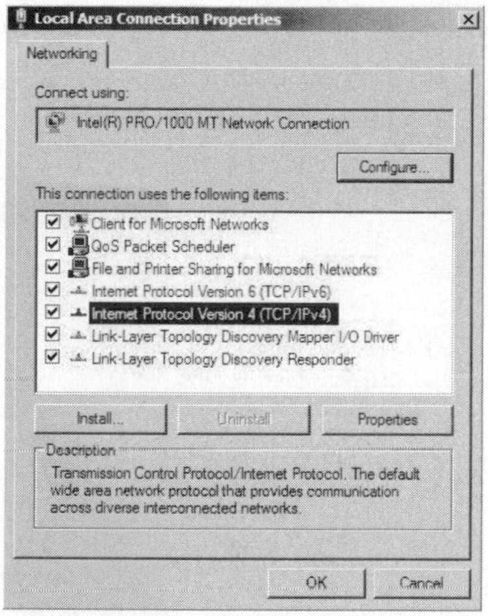

By default, a new Windows Server 2008 R2 server will not have a configured IP address. It will attempt to obtain a TCP/IPv4 configuration from a DHCP server. This is normally not desired for a production server, so you will want to change this to a static configuration (see Figure 2.34).

FIGURE 2.33

IPv4 properties

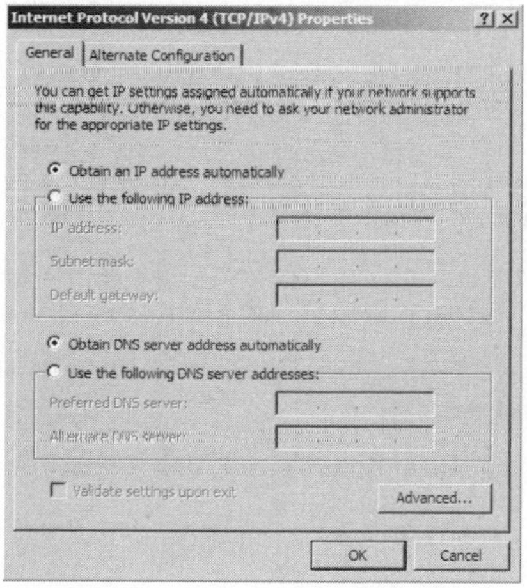

Obtain a configuration for the new server from your network administrators and then enter the details similar to how we have entered them in Figure 2.34. Click OK to save your settings, and close all the remaining dialog boxes.

There is a command-line way to do this too using the `netsh` command. You'll need to find the name of your network interface, and you can use the `ipconfig` command to get it:

```
C:\>netsh interface ip set address name="Local Area Connection" static 192.168.1
.51 255.255.255.0 192.168.1.1 1

C:\>
```

The syntax for the `netsh` command is as follows:

```
C:\>netsh interface ip set address name="<Name of the Network Interface" static
<Desired IP Address> <Desire Subnet Mask> <Desired Default Gateway>
```

FIGURE 2.34
Configured IPv4
properties

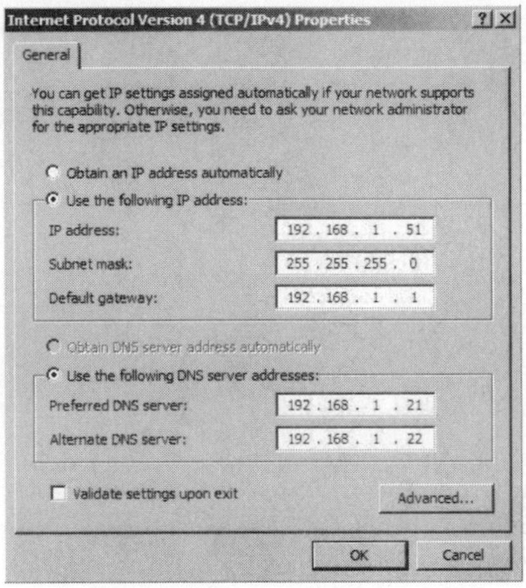

That saves the address configuration of the server. You'll also want to set the DNS server addresses. This first `netsh` command will set the primary DNS server:

```
C:\>netsh interface ip set dns "Local Area Connection" static 192.168.1.21

C:\>
```

The syntax is as follows:

```
netsh interface ip set dns "<Name of the Network Interface>" static <IP Address
of the Primary DNS Server>
```

If you have a secondary DNS server, then you should also configure it. The command is slightly different:

```
C:\>netsh interface ip add dns "Local Area Connection" 192.168.1.22

C:\>
```

Your new IPv4 configuration should be now applied. You might want to run the `ipconfig` command from command prompt to verify your work:

```
C:\>ipconfig
Windows IP Configuration

Ethernet adapter Local Area Connection:
    Connection-specific DNS Suffix  . :
    Link-local IPv6 Address . . . . . : fe80::5819:d35b:1b24:de7f%10
    IPv4 Address. . . . . . . . . . . : 192.168.1.51
```

```
       Subnet Mask . . . . . . . . . . : 255.255.255.0
       Default Gateway . . . . . . . . : 192.168.1.1

    Tunnel adapter Local Area Connection* 8:
       Media State . . . . . . . . . . : Media disconnected
       Connection-specific DNS Suffix  . :

    Tunnel adapter Local Area Connection* 9:
       Connection-specific DNS Suffix  . :
       IPv6 Address. . . . . . . . . . : 2001:0:4137:9e50:1817:3f21:3f57:fc97
       Link-local IPv6 Address . . . . : fe80::1817:3f21:3f57:fc97%12
       Default Gateway . . . . . . . . : ::

    C:\>
```

You can see that the adapter with the name Local Area Connection now has the new IPv4 configuration. Note that you can get lots more information by running ipconfig /all.

The next step is to test connectivity. You can do this from the command prompt by using the ping command to send a test packet to a network device or a server:

```
    C:\>ping 192.168.1.1

    Pinging 192.168.1.1 with 32 bytes of data:
    Reply from 192.168.1.1: bytes=32 time=13ms TTL=128
    Reply from 192.168.1.1: bytes=32 time<1ms TTL=128
    Reply from 192.168.1.1: bytes=32 time<1ms TTL=128
    Reply from 192.168.1.1: bytes=32 time<1ms TTL=128

    Ping statistics for 192.168.1.1:
        Packets: Sent = 4, Received = 4, Lost = 0 (0% loss),
    Approximate round trip times in milli-seconds:
        Minimum = 0ms, Maximum = 13ms, Average = 3ms

    C:\>
```

In our example, we tested using the default gateway that was defined in our IPv4 network configuration. That's normally a good first step. You can see that we got a response for every test packet that was sent. If you get no responses, then there is a problem with the hardware, drivers, network configuration, cables, or maybe even the network itself.

If you have devices beyond the local gateway, then you should try to ping one of them, assuming that your network administrators allow for such ICMP traffic. This test will confirm that your server can route to remote network nodes.

RENAMING THE SERVER

Every Windows computer should have a unique computer name to uniquely identify it on the network. Every organization has its own practice. Some have tightly structured names that describe the location and function, some use nondescriptive names with incremental numbers, and some use names of characters from their favorite TV show or players from a team that they support.

Click Change System Properties in the Computer Information section, which you can find in the details pane of Server Manager.

You can use the Computer Name tab, as shown in Figure 2.35, to control the name of this server and the domain or workgroup membership of this server. You should name this server according to the naming standards of the organization. You should click Change to do this in the dialog box shown in Figure 2.36.

FIGURE 2.35
System properties

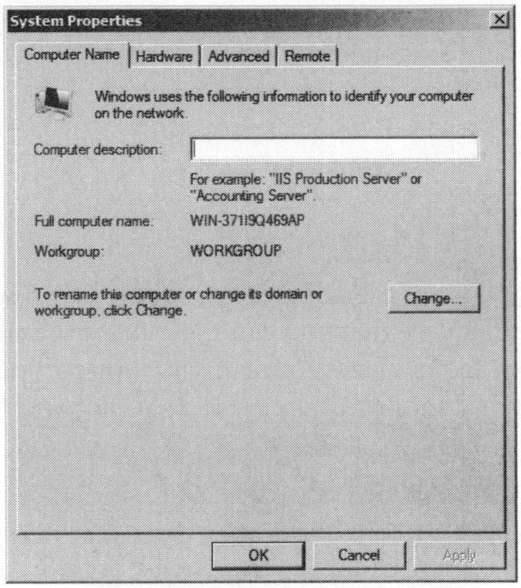

FIGURE 2.36
Computer name

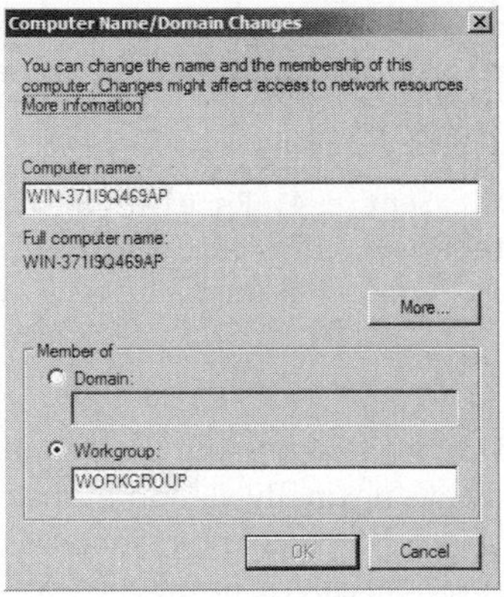

This was a clean installation of Windows. You may remember that the install routine didn't ask you for a computer name. Instead, the server was given a randomly generated name. Some security experts like this, but we like to be able to keep track of our servers, so we try to give them structured names.

To do this, you should change the name under "Computer name," and click OK (see Figure 2.37). Make sure that the name is unique on the network; otherwise, you will encounter problems.

You're now told that you need to reboot in order for this change to be applied (see Figure 2.38). Close down the remaining dialog boxes, and reboot the server when you are automatically prompted to do so. The server will assume the new computer name that you have assigned once the reboot is completed.

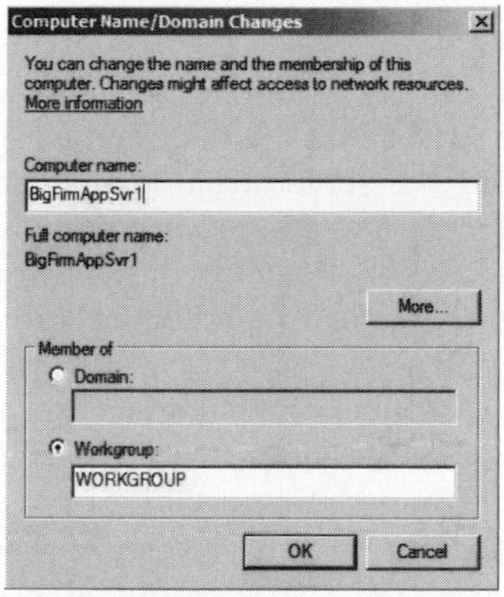

FIGURE 2.37
Configured computer name

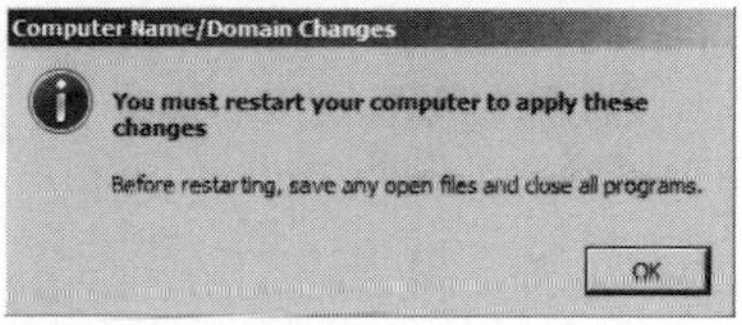

FIGURE 2.38
Restarting after
the computer
name change

You can alternatively accomplish the previous renaming procedure by running the `netdom` command from the command prompt:

```
C:\>netdom /renamecomputer WIN-DCL9MRNLVOH /newname:BIGFIRMAPPSVR1
This operation will rename the computer WIN-DCL9MRNLVOH
to BIGFIRMAPPSVR1.

Certain services, such as the Certificate Authority, rely on a fixed machine
name. If any services of this type are running on WIN-DCL9MRNLVOH,
then a computer name change would have an adverse impact.

Do you want to proceed (Y or N)?
y
The computer needs to be restarted in order to complete the operation.

The command completed successfully.
C:\>
```

The syntax for the command is as follows:

```
netdom /renamecomputer <Current Computer Name> /newname:<Desired Computer Name>
```

You will need to manually reboot the server after running this `netdom` command.

After the reboot, log in again, and fire up Server Manager. You'll see that your new computer name is present in Computer Information.

JOINING A DOMAIN

Odds are you will want to join the server to a domain so that it can use shared resources and be centrally managed. Return to the Computer Name tab in System Properties if this is the case.

We are joining this server to a domain that has the DNS name of bigfirm.com (see Figure 2.39). Once you've entered that name, click OK. You will then be asked to enter the username and password of a user that has permission to add this server to the domain. That might be bigfirm\administrator, or it might be bigfirm\jbloggs if the user jbloggs has been given those delegated rights in Active Directory. Close all the dialog boxes and reboot, and you'll soon have a server that is a member of the domain and able to take advantage of Group Policy, Active Directory user accounts and security groups, centralized administration, and so on.

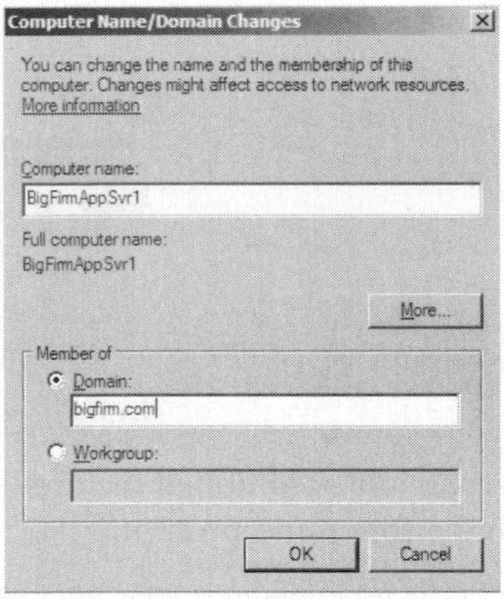

FIGURE 2.39
Domain member-
ship change

Alternatively, you can also do the previous procedure from command line:

```
C:\>netdom join bigfirmappsvr1 /Domain: bigfirm.com /UserD:bigfirm\administrator
/PasswordD:*
Type the password associated with the domain user:
```

The computer needs to be restarted in order to complete the operation:

```
The command completed successfully.
C:\>
```

The syntax for the command is as follows:

```
netdom join <name of computer joining domain> /Domain:<domain to be joined> /
UserD:<name of domain user with permission to join the domain> /PasswordD:*
```

After you run this command, you are prompted for the username of the user account. Once the join command is run, you are told that you need to reboot. You could initiate an automated reboot by adding the /REBoot flag, as shown here. You might prefer to control the timing of reboots as much as possible and instead initiate a manual reboot.

```
netdom join bigfirmappsvr1 /Domain: bigfirm.com /UserD:bigfirm\administrator /
PasswordD:* /REBoot
```

WHY THE COMMAND LINE?

You might be wonder why we are showing you these command-line alternatives. You will need to know these things if you are doing any of the following:

◆ Working with Windows Server 2008 Server Core where there is no alternative. Windows Server 2008 R2 includes a handy tool called `sconfig`.

◆ Being able to run these commands without reference can be quicker than navigating through a GUI.

◆ If you are building many servers by hand or using some third-party cloning solution, then you might want to script as much as possible.

ENABLING REMOTE ADMINISTRATION

Most Windows administrators want to be able to manage their servers from their desktops. Who really wants to go trotting off to the computer room every time you need to make some change on a server? You can do this by enabling Remote Desktop on your server. You can then use the Remote Desktop tool on your PC or laptop to connect to it over TCP 3389, in other words, the Remote Desktop Protocol (RDP). Your organization's security policies will define when this remote administration can be enabled, if at all.

If you want to enable RDP access, then you should click Configure Remote Desktop in the Computer Information section in Server Manager.

You can see in Figure 2.40 that RDP is disabled by default. There are two other options:

Allow connections from computers running any version of Remote Desktop (less secure)
This allows versions of the Remote Desktop tool prior to version 6 to connect to your new server. Version 6 includes new security functionality, so Microsoft would prefer you to use it. Note that Remote Desktop version 6 is included in Windows Vista and Windows Server 2008 R2. Older operating systems such as Windows XP and Windows Server 2003 require a free update that you can get from Windows Update or from the Microsoft website.

Allow connections only from computers running Remote Desktop with Network Level Authentication (more secure)   This is Microsoft's preference if you do enable RDP access. Note that you must have at least version 6 of Remote Desktop on all possible administrative computers to use this option.

By default, only those people who are members of the local Administrators group on your server will be able to access it via RDP. That suits most scenarios. However, you might want to delegate certain low-level functions to non-administrators. If so, you will need to click Select Users and add the user account names or, preferably, the security group names of those to whom you are granting RDP connectivity rights.

At this point, your server is on the network, you have added it to a domain, and you have enabled Remote Desktop so that you can work on it from your desktop. It's time to add some functionality to your Windows Server 2008 or Windows Server 2008 R2 machine.

FIGURE 2.40
Configuring
Remote Desktop

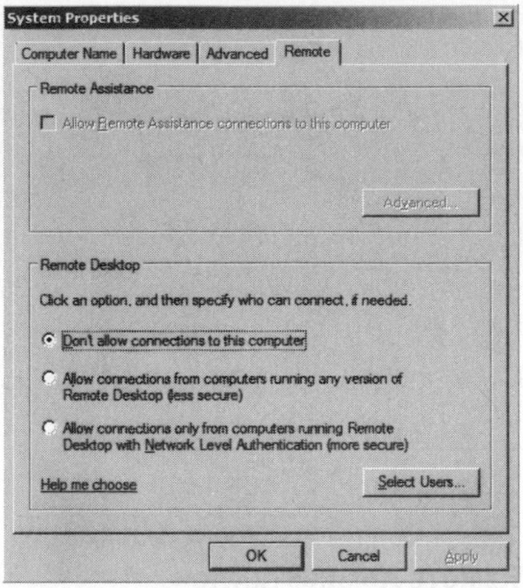

Adding and Removing Roles

So far, you have installed a new Windows Server 2008 machine, and you have configured it so that it is on the network and can be managed remotely. You're ideally sitting at your desk with a nice drink. You can complete the rest of the configuration in relative comfort. That sounds much better than standing in front of a tiny monitor in a noisy and cold server room.

Before you go forward with Server Manager, we'll define some terminology that you've seen several times in this chapter already:

Roles A role is a generic function that a server hosts. It could be something like a DNS server or a web server. Each role comes with a set of functionality that can be installed onto a server to allow that computer to perform those tasks. They're called *role services*.

Features A feature is a specific piece of software that adds a very granular piece of functionally to a server.

A set of roles and features are available in Windows Server 2008 and Windows Server 2008 R2. This set is extensible. This means that other roles and features can be made available by Microsoft as time goes by.

INHERITED ROLES AND FEATURES

A clean installation of Windows Server 2008 R2 or Windows Server 2008 will have no installed features or roles. Microsoft is not going to make any assumptions for you. This allows you to build customized servers with a minimized security risk. However, an upgraded server will include roles and features that Windows Server 2008 R2 can identify on the preexisting Windows 2003 server. For example, if your Windows 2003 server was a DNS server, then your upgraded server with Windows Server 2008 R2 will have a DNS Server role installed. You may actually decide that you want to remove some of these inherited roles or features because they are inappropriate for your Windows 2008 server.

ADDING A ROLE

A role can be described as a major function that a server can play in your network. When you install a role, you are installing a set of components to enable that functionality. There is a default set of components for each role that you can customize.

You'll now learn how you can add a role using Server Manager and `servermanagercmd.exe`. First, fire up Server Manager, and scroll down to Roles Summary (see Figure 2.41).

FIGURE 2.41
Roles Summary in
Server Manager

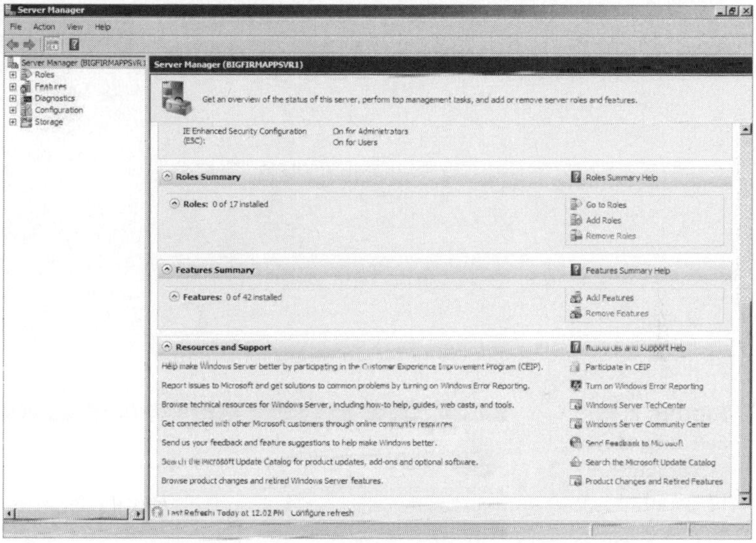

You can see in the summary that there are no roles installed. It's easy to see how to add a role; just click Add Roles. That will launch a wizard for you.

Lots of these new wizards have a welcome screen that describes the role of the wizard (see Figure 2.42). You can disable the welcome screen from popping up again by selecting the "Skip this page by default" box.

You can now see a listing of all the available roles that you can install (see Figure 2.43). Clicking each one gives you a brief description of that role. The new server is going to be a file server, so select File Services.

You can select many roles here if you want to install them all at once. Then click Next when you have selected all the required roles.

You now get an introduction to the role you've chosen to install, which is File Services in this example (see Figure 2.44). You can click each of the links available.

HMM...ROLES AND FEATURES DO MAKE SENSE

Note that you are told that you cannot install Windows Search Service and Indexing Service on the same computer. This is the first hint that there is some intelligence behind all of this roles and features functionality in Windows Server 2008 R2.

FIGURE 2.42
About adding roles

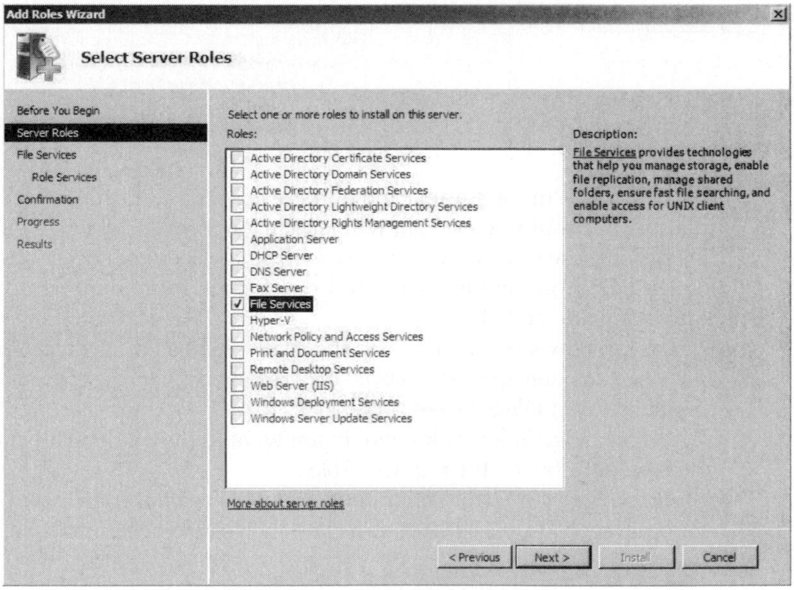

FIGURE 2.43
Selecting the
server roles
to install

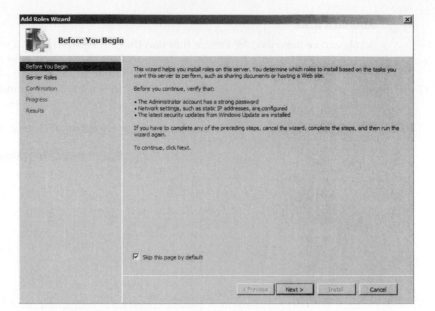

A role service is a subcomponent of a role. It is either the core component of the role or an optional component. Each role has one or a set of default role services. You can see that File Services has only the File Server role service on by default. You can also see a number of optional role services that you can install if you require them.

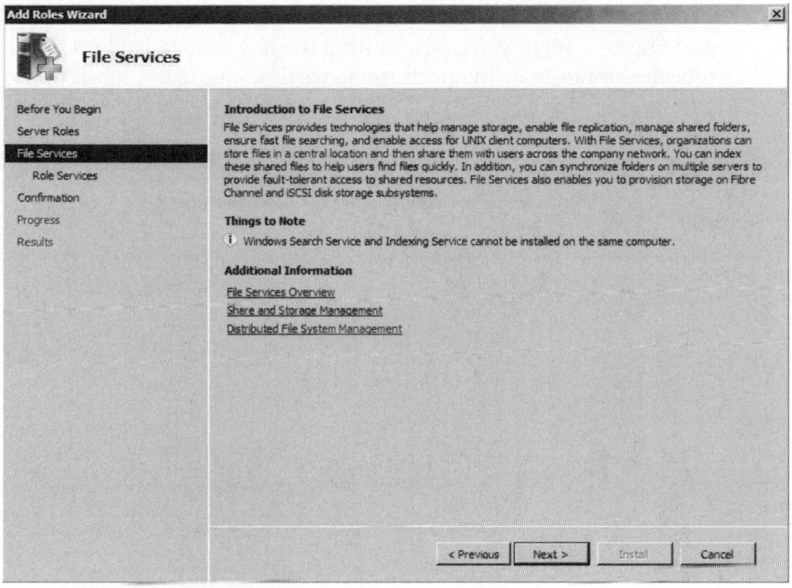

FIGURE 2.44
Introduction to the
role File Services

Microsoft has modeled all the available roles, role services, and features. It knows the relationships, the dependencies, and the conflicts. This is applied in Server Manager. For example, if a role requires a certain role service, then clearing that role service will result in clearing the role. It removes the guess work for administrators, which is a good thing.

In this example, you want to manage the storage utilization of your new file server, so select the File Server Resource Manager role service (see Figure 2.45).

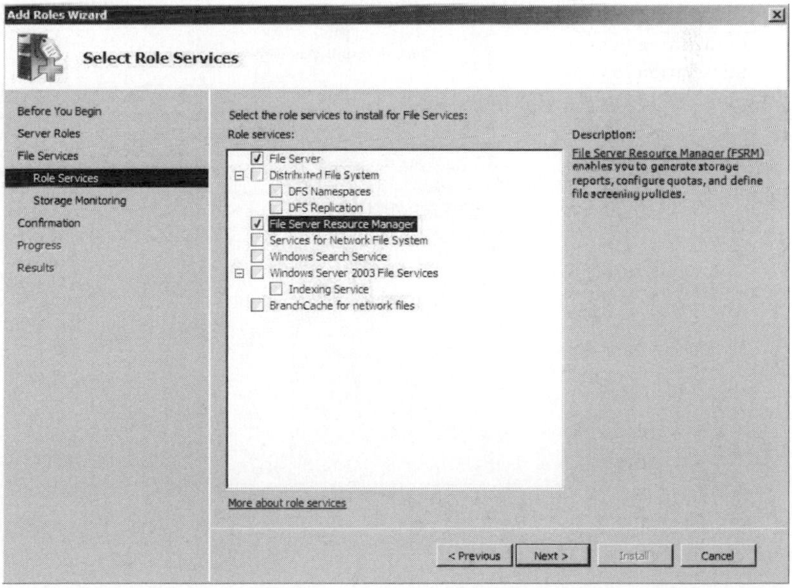

FIGURE 2.45
Selecting role
services

Some roles need to allow for some configuration before you install them. You can do this now (see Figure 2.46) or you can wait until the role is installed and use the associated administrative tools to configure it. In our example we're skipping the configuration so that the file server administrators can do the work.

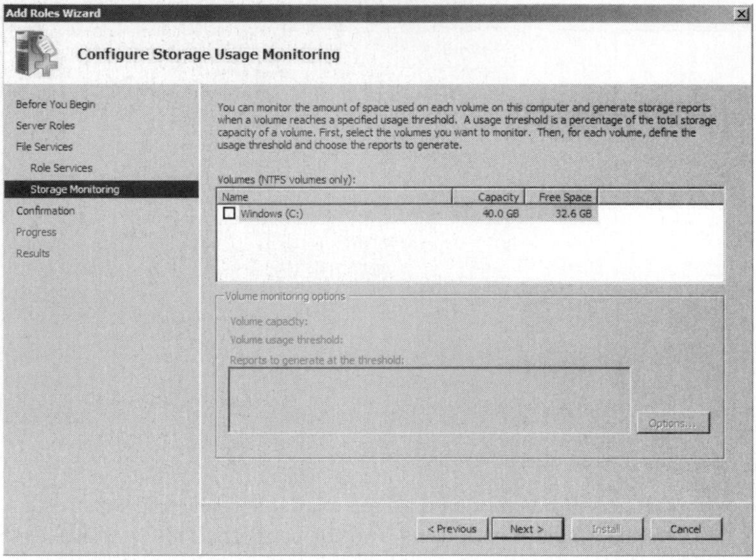

FIGURE 2.46
Configuring
the role

You get a summary screen where you can verify your new configuration before anything is installed (see Figure 2.47). Click Install to kick that off.

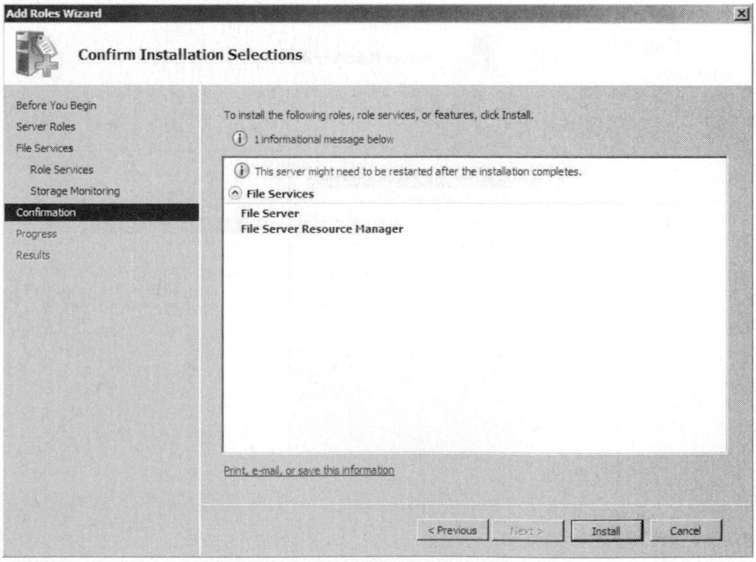

FIGURE 2.47
Confirming the
installation

Some roles and role services can take a little time to install (see Figure 2.48). You get a progress screen so you can track the progress.

FIGURE 2.48
Role installation progress

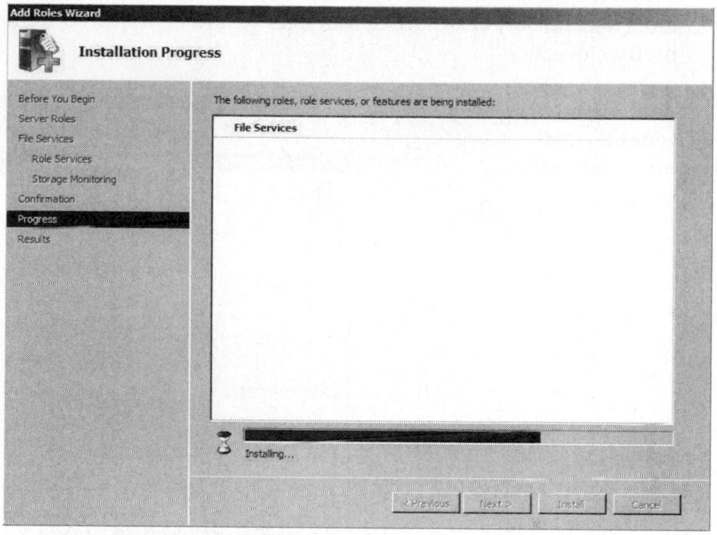

The installation will eventually finish (see Figure 2.49). We've deliberately shown you a warning that you can get while working with roles and features. You can see that our role installation succeeded with one warning. We have not configured automatic updating for patching this server yet. You'll probably see this while playing in a lab, so you can safely ignore it. It is a valid warning, though. You should configure your updates either manually or via Group Policy and then deploy them as soon as possible.

FIGURE 2.49
Role installation results

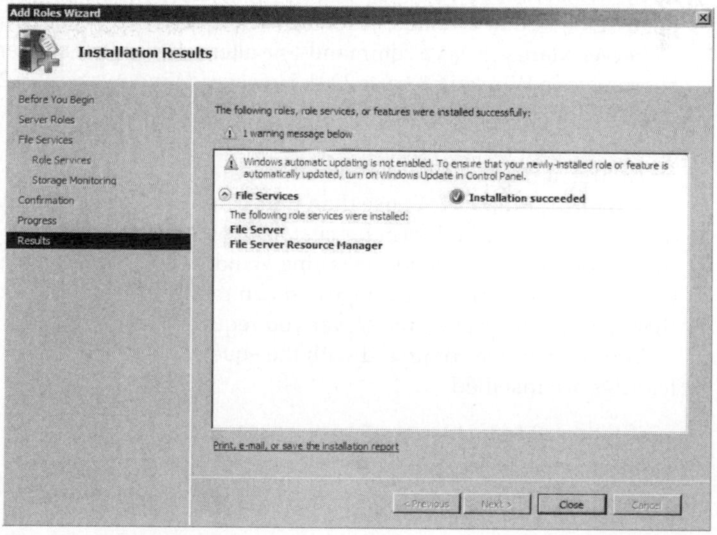

You can see that Roles Summary now lists the File Services role that you've just installed (see Figure 2.50). Have a look at Features Summary. You can see that File Server Resource Manager Tools was installed. The modeling that we mentioned earlier recognized that the management tools for File Server Resource Manager would be required to manage that role service. That's pretty clever!

FIGURE 2.50

Viewing the roles in Server Manager

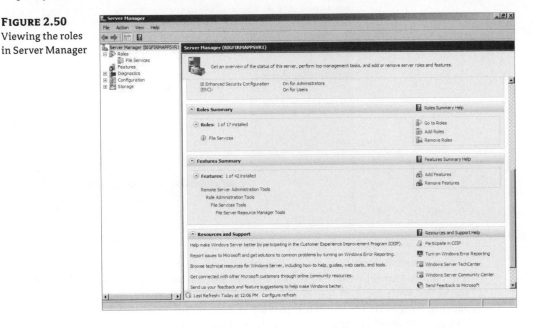

So, that's how you can add a role and role services by using the GUI. You can also do this using the command prompt. This is where a lot of Windows administrators start skipping pages. Don't do it! Trust us; you will want to know this stuff.

Server Manager has a command-line alternative called **servermanagercmd.exe**. It's the normal alternative in Windows Server 2008. However, Windows Server 2008 R2 warns you that it is deprecated and that you should use PowerShell instead. Still, we think that it is important to document the tool for Windows Server 2008 administrators.

At first, it might seem like something that's a bit clunky to use. But you will find that after a little while it is quicker to use than the GUI. Not only that, but you can also use it in a scripted or even an unattended form for customizing servers. That's very handy if you use a cloning or unattended mechanism for installing Windows or even if you are building loads of servers by hand. You just deploy one image and run the appropriate script or unattended file to customize that generic image to be the server you require.

You can run the command with the `-query` flag to report on what roles, role services, and features are installed:

```
C:\Users\Administrator>servermanagercmd.exe -query

----- Roles -----
```

```
[ ] Active Directory Certificate Services  [AD-Certificate]
    [ ] Certification Authority  [ADCS-Cert-Authority]
    [ ] Certification Authority Web Enrollment  [ADCS-Web-Enrollment]
    [ ] Online Responder  [ADCS-Online-Cert]
    [ ] Network Device Enrollment Service  [ADCS-Device-Enrollment]
  .
  .
  .

[ ] File Services
    [ ] File Server  [FS-FileServer]
    [ ] Distributed File System  [FS-DFS]
        [ ] DFS Namespaces  [FS-DFS-Namespace]
        [ ] DFS Replication  [FS-DFS-Replication]
    [ ] File Server Resource Manager  [FS-Resource-Manager]
    [ ] Services for Network File System  [FS-NFS-Services]
    [ ] Windows Search Service  [FS-Search-Service]
    [ ] Windows Server 2003 File Services  [FS-Win2003-Services]
        [ ] File Replication Service  [FS-Replication]
        [ ] Indexing Service  [FS-Indexing-Service]
  .
  .
  .


----- Features ----

[ ] .NET Framework 3.0 Features  [NET-Framework]
    [ ] .NET Framework 3.0  [NET-Framework-Core]
    [ ] XPS Viewer  [NET-XPS-Viewer]
    [ ] WCF Activation  [NET-Win-CFAC]
        [ ] HTTP Activation  [NET-HTTP-Activation]
        [ ] Non-HTTP Activation  [NET-Non-HTTP-Activ]
[ ] BitLocker Drive Encryption  [BitLocker]
[ ] BITS Server Extensions  [BITS]
  .
  .
  .


C:\Users\Administrator>
```

The generated report is pretty long, so you'll have to forgive us for not including the entire thing! We have rain forests to think about, so we've only included snippets of the query results.

None of the roles, role services, or features has an *X* next to them. That *X* designates that the role, role feature, or feature is installed. Hence, we are working with a blank server.

For this example, you want to install File Services and File Server Resource Manager just like you did with Server Manager. `servermanageercmd.exe` uses slightly different names that are command-prompt friendly. You can see them in the -`query` results. File Services is referred to as FS-`FileServer`, and File Server Resource Manager is referred to as FS-`Resource-Manager`. We'll use those designations in combination with the -`install` flag.

You can probably see that FS-FileServer is actually a role service and not a role. The File Server role appears to be the exception in servermanagercmd.exe because it does not have a reference for it to be installed as a role. Instead, we'll be installing the role service that we know is required.

```
C:\Users\Administrator>servermanagercmd.exe -install FS-FileServer FS-Resource-
Manager
..


Start Installation...
[Installation] Succeeded: [File Services] File Server.
[Installation] Succeeded: [File Services] File Server Resource Manager.
<100/100>

Success: Installation succeeded.

C:\Users\Administrator>
```

That was pretty simple, eh? And it was much faster than using the GUI wizard. We knew what we wanted, and we could run it as fast as we could type it, which, depending on your typing skills, may not have been all that fast! You could very easily add more complexity to that command and put it in a .bat file to be used as a script.

Some roles, role services, or features will require a reboot. You can have this be automatic by adding the -restart flag to the end of your command.

Let's verify the installation. Run servermanagercmd.exe with the -query flag again to check the results:

```
C:\Users\Administrator>servermanagercmd.exe -query
..


----- Roles -----

[ ] Active Directory Certificate Services  [AD-Certificate]
    [ ] Certification Authority  [ADCS-Cert-Authority]
    [ ] Certification Authority Web Enrollment  [ADCS-Web-Enrollment]
    [ ] Online Responder  [ADCS-Online-Cert]
    [ ] Network Device Enrollment Service  [ADCS-Device-Enrollment]
.
.

.
[X] File Services
    [X] File Server  [FS-FileServer]
    [ ] Distributed File System  [FS-DFS]
        [ ] DFS Namespaces  [FS-DFS-Namespace]
        [ ] DFS Replication  [FS-DFS-Replication]
    [X] File Server Resource Manager  [FS-Resource-Manager]
    [ ] Services for Network File System  [FS-NFS-Services]
    [ ] Windows Search Service  [FS-Search-Service]
    [ ] Windows Server 2003 File Services  [FS-Win2003-Services]
```

```
        [ ] File Replication Service  [FS-Replication]
        [ ] Indexing Service  [FS-Indexing-Service]
    .
    .
    .

----- Features -----

[ ] .NET Framework 3.0 Features  [NET-Framework]
    [ ] .NET Framework 3.0  [NET-Framework-Core]
    [ ] XPS Viewer  [NET-XPS-Viewer]
    [ ] WCF Activation  [NET-Win-CFAC]
        [ ] HTTP Activation  [NET-HTTP-Activation]
        [ ] Non-HTTP Activation  [NET-Non-HTTP-Activ]
    .
    .
    .

[X] Remote Server Administration Tools  [RSAT]
    [X] Role Administration Tools  [RSAT-Role-Tools]
        [ ] Active Directory Certificate Services Tools  [RSAT-ADCS]
            [ ] Certification Authority Tools  [RSAT-ADCS-Mgmt]
            [ ] Online Responder Tools  [RSAT-Online-Responder]
        [ ] Active Directory Domain Services Tools  [RSAT-ADDS]
            [ ] Active Directory Domain Controller Tools  [RSAT-ADDC]
            [ ] Server for NIS Tools  [RSAT-SNIS]
        [ ] Active Directory Lightweight Directory Services Tools  [RSAT-ADLDS]
        [ ] Active Directory Rights Management Services Tools  [RSAT-RMS]
        [ ] DHCP Server Tools  [RSAT-DHCP]
        [ ] DNS Server Tools  [RSAT-DNS-Server]
        [ ] Fax Server Tools  [RSAT-Fax]
        [X] File Services Tools  [RSAT-File-Services]
            [ ] Distributed File System Tools  [RSAT-DFS-Mgmt-Con]
            [X] File Server Resource Manager Tools  [RSAT-FSRM-Mgmt]
            [ ] Services for Network File System Tools  [RSAT-NFS-Admin]
        [ ] Network Policy and Access Services Tools  [RSAT-NPAS]
        [ ] Print Services Tools  [RSAT-Print-Services]
        [ ] Terminal Services Tools  [RSAT-TS]
            [ ] Terminal Server Tools  [RSAT-TS-RemoteApp]
            [ ] TS Gateway Tools  [RSAT-TS-Gateway]
            [ ] TS Licensing Tools  [RSAT-TS-Licensing]
        [ ] UDDI Services Tools  [RSAT-UDDI]
        [ ] Web Server (IIS) Tools  [RSAT-Web-Server]
        [ ] Windows Deployment Services Tools  [RSAT-WDS]
    [ ] Feature Administration Tools  [RSAT-Feature-Tools]
        [ ] BitLocker Drive Encryption Tools  [RSAT-BitLocker]
        [ ] BITS Server Extensions Tools  [RSAT-Bits-Server]
        [ ] Failover Clustering Tools  [RSAT-Clustering]
        [ ] Network Load Balancing Tools  [RSAT-NLB]
        [ ] SMTP Server Tools  [RSAT-SMTP]
```

```
    [ ] WINS Server Tools  [RSAT-WINS]
.
.
.


C:\Users\Administrator>
```

The roles and role services that you requested are designated with an *X*, which means that they are installed. You can also see that the required feature of File Server Resource Manager Tools is also installed. You can ensure that the results are identical to using the GUI by launching Server Manager.

Anyone who was a little scared of command-line administration might now be getting a little intrigued.

Let's look at using an unattended script with servermanagercmd.exe. You'll find it handy when you want to add many roles, role services, or features to a server. You can have a set of answer files available, one for every server configuration that you support. You can then use the appropriate answer file with a single execution of servermanagercmd.exe to customize your server. Here's an answer file for a web server:

```
<?xml version="1.0" encoding="utf-8" ?>
<ServerManagerConfiguration Action="Install" xmlns="http://schemas.microsoft.com/
sdm/Windows/ServerManager/Configuration/2007/1" xmlns:xs="http://www.w3.org/2001/
XMLSchema">
<Role Id="Application-Server" />
<RoleService Id="AS-Web-Support" />
<Role Id="Web-Server" />
</ServerManagerConfiguration>
```

It's an XML file. Don't be scared. You don't need to be a programmer to see how it works without too much difficulty. The ServerManagerConfiguration Action setting defines whether you are going to do an install or a remove. You can list a role ID for each role you want to manage. Just repeat that line, and add the name of the role as you see it in servermanagercmd.exe with the -query flag. The same applies to the role service ID, which lists each optional role service to configure. Save your XML file to a location where you'll be able to access it on your server.

Here is what we will be using in our FileServer.XML file:

```
<?xml version="1.0" encoding="utf-8" ?>
<ServerManagerConfiguration Action="Install"
xmlns="http://schemas.microsoft.com/sdm/Windows/ServerManager/
Configuration/2007/1" xmlns:xs="http://www.w3.org/2001/XMLSchema">
<RoleService Id="FS-FileServer" />
<RoleService Id="FS-Resource-Manager" />
</ServerManagerConfiguration>
```

Using an unattended answer file is considered a more complex task, so you will probably want to test the XML file before you use it. servermanagercmd.exe makes this possible thanks to the -whatif flag:

```
C:\Users\Administrator>servermanagercmd.exe -inputpath C:\FileServer.xml -whatif

..
```

```
Note: Running in 'WhatIf' Mode.
Specified for installation: [File Services] File Server Resource Manager
Specified for installation: [File Services] File Server

This server may need to be restarted after the installation completes.

C:\Users\Administrator>
```

Cool! The syntax has been confirmed to be OK. You can now execute the answer file:

```
C:\Users\Administrator>servermanagercmd.exe -inputpath C:\FileServer.xml
.

Start Installation...
[Installation] Succeeded: [File Services] File Server.
[Installation] Succeeded: [File Services] File Server Resource Manager.
<100/100>

Success: Installation succeeded.

C:\Users\Administrator>
```

You should, of course, follow this up with running servermanagercmd.exe -query to verify that everything is installed as expected.

If you are managing Windows Server 2008 R2, then you'll need to use PowerShell, Microsoft's scripting and command language. The subject of PowerShell is pretty huge. We'll just cover the relevant Server Manager–related cmdlets (pronounced "command-lets") here.

You can launch PowerShell from the superbar or by clicking Windows PowerShell Modules in Administrative Tools. Make sure you launch it with administrative rights; in other words, right-click the icon and select "Run as administrator." The PowerShell modules related to Server Manager are not loaded by default. Run this command to load them:

```
PS C:\Users\Administrator> import-module Servermanager
```

To display what roles and features you have installed, you run the confusingly named Get-WindowsFeature cmdlet:

```
PS C:\Users\Administrator> get-WindowsFeature

Display Name                                             Name
------------                                             ----
[ ] Active Directory Certificate Services               AD-Certificate
    [ ] Certification Authority                          ADCS-Cert-Authority
    [ ] Certification Authority Web Enrollment           ADCS-Web-Enrollment
    [ ] Online Responder                                 ADCS-Online-Cert
    [ ] Network Device Enrollment Service                ADCS-Device-Enrollment
    [ ] Certificate Enrollment Web Service               ADCS-Enroll-Web-Svc
    [ ] Certificate Enrollment Policy Web Service         ADCS-Enroll-Web-Pol
[ ] Active Directory Domain Services                     AD-Domain-Services
    [ ] Active Directory Domain Controller               ADDS-Domain-Controller
    [ ] Identity Management for UNIX                      ADDS-Identity-Mgmt
```

```
              [ ] Server for Network Information Services    ADDS-NIS
              [ ] Password Synchronization                   ADDS-Password-Sync
              [ ] Administration Tools                       ADDS-IDMU-Tools
          [ ] Active Directory Federation Services           AD-Federation-Services
              [ ] Federation Service                         ADFS-Federation
              [ ] Federation Service Proxy                   ADFS-Proxy
              [ ] AD FS Web Agents                            ADFS-Web-Agents
```

That takes a little while to execute. Any role, role service, or feature that is installed will be marked with an X. Take note of the Name column. You'll be using that for future commands. If you already know what role or feature you're interested in knowing about, then try running something like this:

```
PS C:\Users\Administrator> get-windowsfeature AD-Certificate

Display Name                                               Name
------------                                               ----
[ ] Active Directory Certificate Services                 AD-Certificate
```

If you want a text report on your server configuration, then you could run this next command. It will export the report to a file called c:\InstalledFeatures.txt.

```
PS C:\Users\Administrator> get-windowsfeature > C:\InstalledFeatures.txt
```

It's time to add a role. Say you want to set up a file server with the same configuration as you did earlier with Server Manager. You can use the Add-WindowsFeature cmdlet. The syntax is as follows:

```
Add-WindowsFeature Name
```

It's simple enough. Identify the role or feature name from the Get-WindowsFeature report, and specify it. A nice feature is that you can check out what would happen if you really ran the command. You can do that by adding the -whatif flag:

```
Add-WindowsFeature Name -whatif
```

You're going to add the File-Services role and the FS-Resource-Manager role service. Here's what would happen if you ran that command:

```
PS C:\Users\Administrator> add-windowsfeature File-Services,FS-Resource-Manager
-whatif
What if: Checking if running in 'WhatIf' Mode.
What if: Performing operation "Add-WindowsFeature" on Target "[File Services]
File Server Resource Manager".
What if: Performing operation "Add-WindowsFeature" on Target "[File Services]
File Server".
What if: This server may need to be restarted after the installation completes.

Success Restart Needed Exit Code Feature Result
------- -------------- --------- --------------
True    Maybe          Success   {}
```

Nothing has been changed on the server thanks to the -whatif flag. Notice that you might need to reboot? It is good to know that once this command executes, you'll need to do a reboot. This will allow you to plan for the reboot and warn users of any services hosted by this machine. You can automate the reboot by adding the -restart flag. It's handy for scripted or automated builds. We are going to stick with the manual reboot (if it is required) and run the command so that the role and role feature are actually installed:

```
PS C:\Users\Administrator> add-windowsfeature File-Services,FS-Resource-Manager
-concurrent

Success Restart Needed Exit Code Feature Result
------- -------------- --------- --------------
True    No             Success   {File Server, File Server Resource Manager}
```

That has installed the role and role service. What if you wanted to modify the configuration of many servers with minimum effort? You could create a PowerShell script to do the work for you:

```
PS C:\Users\Administrator> get-executionpolicy
Restricted
```

This command has shown you that scripts are disabled on your server. That's the default in PowerShell. To run the script, you'll have to run this command:

```
PS C:\Users\Administrator> set-executionpolicy unrestricted

Execution Policy Change
The execution policy helps protect you from scripts that you do not trust.
Changing the execution policy might expose
you to the security risks described in the about_Execution_Policies help topic.
Do you want to change the execution
policy?
[Y] Yes  [N] No  [S] Suspend  [?] Help (default is "Y"): Y
```

You can verify the change by rerunning the Get-ExecutionPolicy command:

```
PS C:\Users\Administrator> get-executionpolicy
Unrestricted
```

Now you can write a script and save it as C:\FileServer.PS1:

```
import-module Servermanager
add-windowsfeature File-Services,FS-Resource-Manager -restart
```

You can now browse to that file, right-click it, and choose Run with PowerShell. The components you want will be installed, and the server will reboot automatically if required.

You can also run the script from the command line. This would be handy if you were deploying it via some management or automation tool:

```
C:\>powershell.exe c:\fileserver.ps1
```

```
Success Restart Needed Exit Code Feature Result
------- -------------- --------- --------------
True    No             Success   {File Server, File Server Resource Manager}
```

Your third option is to run the command from within the PowerShell interface:

```
PS C:\> .\FileServer.PS1
```

Imagine that you were setting up many more roles, role services, and features. You could bundle everything into this one script and run it as required. With that command-line option, you could automatically reconfigure hundreds or thousands of servers using something like Microsoft System Center Configuration Manager. You should now understand the power of PowerShell. You could easily save hours of work on your server deployments or configuration projects.

REMOVING A ROLE

Removing a role is not all that different from adding one. Again, you'll do this in Server Manager and with the servermanagercmd.exe and PowerShell alternatives. In Server Manager, click Remove Roles (see Figure 2.51).

FIGURE 2.51
Removing
server roles

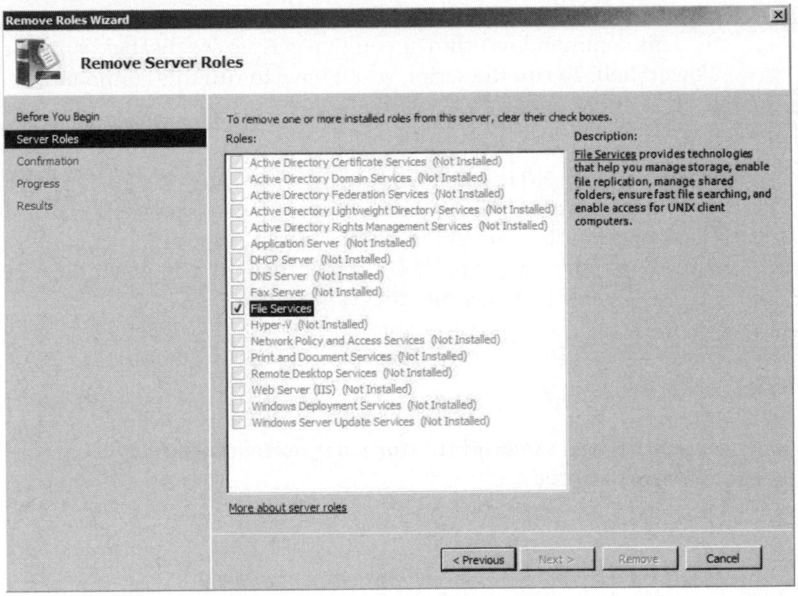

You can see all the installed roles. Any roles that are not installed will be grayed out. Deselect the roles that you want to uninstall, and click Next. You'll be brought to a summary screen. You can verify that you have selected the correct items before clicking Remove. You can click Cancel to terminate the process without affecting the server configuration.

A reboot might be required for the role you are removing. Reboot the server when prompted if this is the case, and then return to Server Manager to verify that the role has been removed (see Figure 2.52).

FIGURE 2.52
Role removal
results

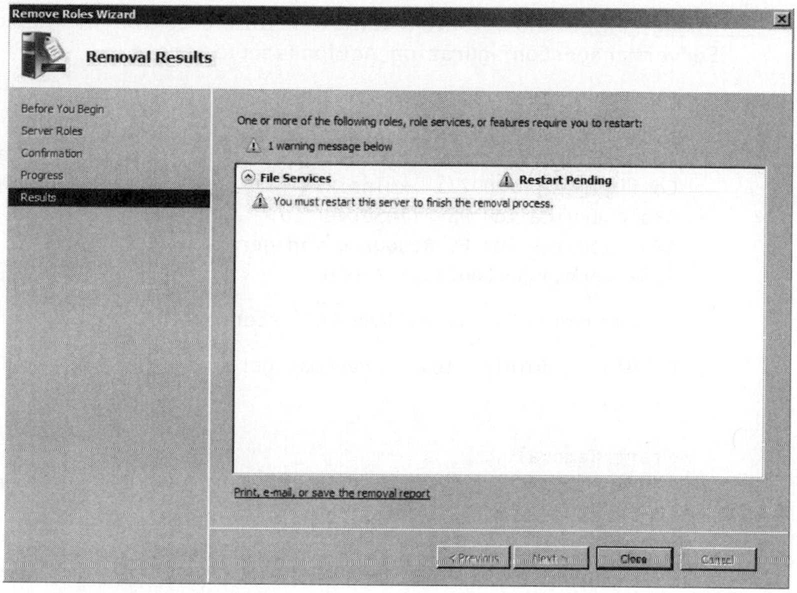

You can see that the example role was uninstalled as was the associated feature, thanks to Microsoft's modeling.

You can remove your role using servermanagercmd.exe as follows:

```
C:\Users\Administrator>servermanagercmd -remove FS-FileServer FS-Resource-Manager
.

Start Removal...
Warning: [Removal] Succeeded: [File Services] File Server Resource Manager. You
must restart this server to finish the removal process.

Warning: [Removal] Succeeded: [File Services] File Server. You must restart this
server to finish the removal process.

<100/100>

Success: A restart is required to complete the removal.

C:\Users\Administrator>
```

Reboot the server as prompted to complete the removal. Once you learn that removing a certain component requires a reboot, you might start using automated reboots as follows:

```
servermanagercmd -remove FS-FileServer FS-Resource-Manager -restart
```

It's probably unlikely that you will use an unattended answer file to remove components from a server, but here's a sample answer file for uninstalling the file server components in our configuration. Notice that the only difference from the previous answer file is that ServerManagerConfiguration Action is set to Remove.

```
<?xml version="1.0" encoding="utf-8" ?>
<ServerManagerConfiguration Action="Remove"
xmlns="http://schemas.microsoft.com/sdm/Windows/ServerManager/
Configuration/2007/1" xmlns:xs="http://www.w3.org/2001/XMLSchema">
<RoleService Id="FS-FileServer" />
<RoleService Id="FS-Resource-Manager" />
</ServerManagerConfiguration>
```

You can run this file called RemoveFileServer.xml, as shown here:

```
C:\Users\Administrator>servermanagercmd.exe -inputpath C:\RemoveFileServer.xml
..

Start Removal...
Warning: [Removal] Succeeded: [File Services] File Server Resource Manager. You
must restart this server to finish the removal process.

Warning: [Removal] Succeeded: [File Services] File Server. You must restart this
 server to finish the removal process.

<100/100>

Success: A restart is required to complete the removal.

C:\Users\Administrator>
```

Removing roles, role services, and features is just as easy with PowerShell as it was to install them. The Remove-WindowsFeature cmdlet is similar to the Add-WindowsFeature cmdlet:

```
Remove-WindowsFeature <Role>,<RoleService>,<Feature> -restart -whatif
```

Here's the syntax:

◆ Enter the role, role service, or feature that you want to remove. You can use commas to specify many of them.

◆ Use the -restart flag to initiate an automatic reboot if you need to do so.

◆ Use the -whatif flag to simulate the command.

This command will simulate removing everything you installed earlier:

```
PS C:\Users\Administrator> remove-windowsfeature File-Services, FS-Resource-
Manager -whatif
What if: Checking if running in 'WhatIf' Mode.
What if: Performing operation "Remove-WindowsFeature" on Target "[File Services]
File Server Resource Manager".
What if: Performing operation "Remove-WindowsFeature" on Target "[File Services]
File Server".
```

```
What if: This server may need to be restarted after the removal completes.

Success Restart Needed Exit Code Feature Result
------- -------------- --------- --------------
True    Maybe          Success   {}
```

Once you are happy that the command will run OK, you can remove the -whatif flag:

```
PS C:\Users\Administrator> remove-windowsfeature File-Services, FS-Resource-Manager
WARNING: [Removal] Succeeded: [File Services] File Server. You must restart this
server to finish the removal process.
WARNING: [Removal] Succeeded: [File Services] File Server Resource Manager. You
must restart this server to finish the
removal process.

Success Restart Needed Exit Code Feature Result
------- -------------- --------- --------------
True    Yes            Succes... {File Server, File Server Resource Manager}
```

You now need to manually reboot. You can automate the reboot with this:

```
PS C:\Users\Administrator> remove-windowsfeature File-Services,
FS-Resource-Manager -restart
```

That's role removal completed. We'll briefly cover feature installation and removal now.

INSTALLING AND REMOVING FEATURES

You'll now learn how to add a feature to your existing file server and then see how to remove that feature using Server Manager (see Figure 2.53), servermanagercmd.exe, and PowerShell. We won't go into great depth because it's not all that different from role management, as you'll see.

FIGURE 2.53
Add A Feature
Using Server
Manager

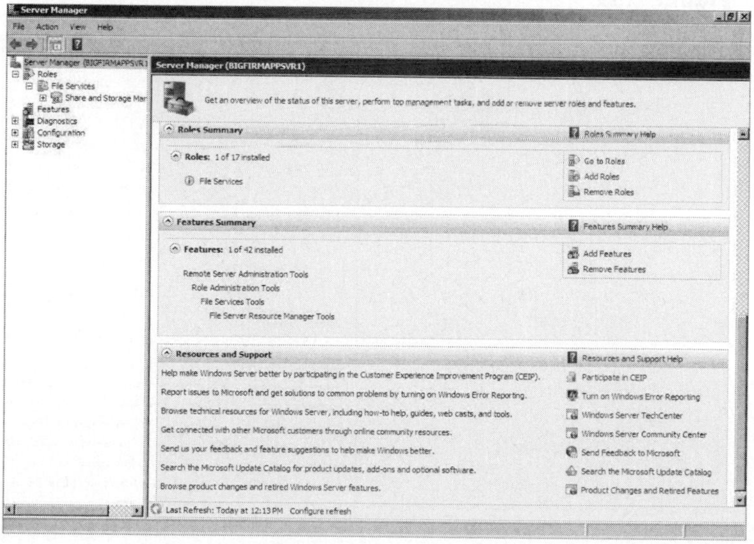

In Server Manager, click Add Features. That kicks off another wizard.

You'll install the Windows Server Migration Tools feature (see Figure 2.54), so select that, and then you'll progress through the wizard to install it.

FIGURE 2.54
Selecting features to install

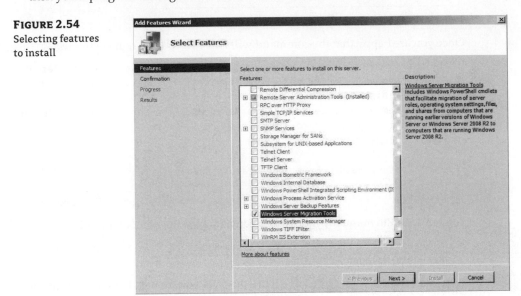

You can see that it is installed in Server Manager (see Figure 2.55). You could use the command prompt to install this feature using the following command:

```
servermanagercmd.exe -install Migration
```

FIGURE 2.55
Viewing the installed features

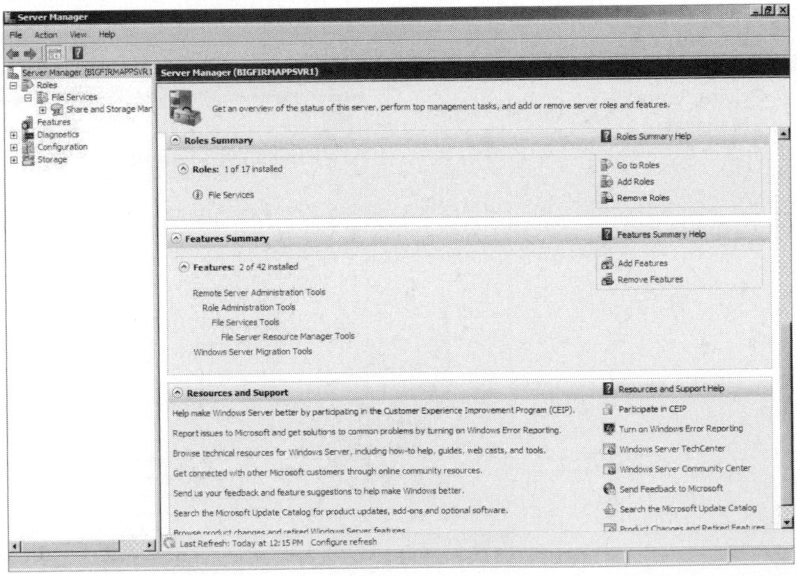

You could also use an unattended answer file named **InstallFeature.xml** to install the feature:

```
<?xml version="1.0" encoding="utf-8" ?>
<ServerManagerConfiguration Action="Install" xmlns="http://schemas.microsoft.com/
sdm/Windows/ServerManager/Configuration/2007/1" xmlns:xs="http://www.w3.org/2001/
XMLSchema">
<Feature Id="Migration" />
</ServerManagerConfiguration>
```

You would run this answer file as follows:

```
servermanagercmd.exe -inputpath C:\InstallFeature.xml
```

Here's the PowerShell cmdlet to do the same thing:

```
PS C:\Windows\system32> add-windowsfeature migration

Success Restart Needed Exit Code Feature Result
------- -------------- --------- --------------
True    No             Success   {Windows Server Migration Tools}
```

The removal process is pretty easy too. In Server Manager, you just click Remove Features. You can deselect the Removable Storage Manager feature, progress through the wizard, and then click the Remove button (see Figure 2.56).

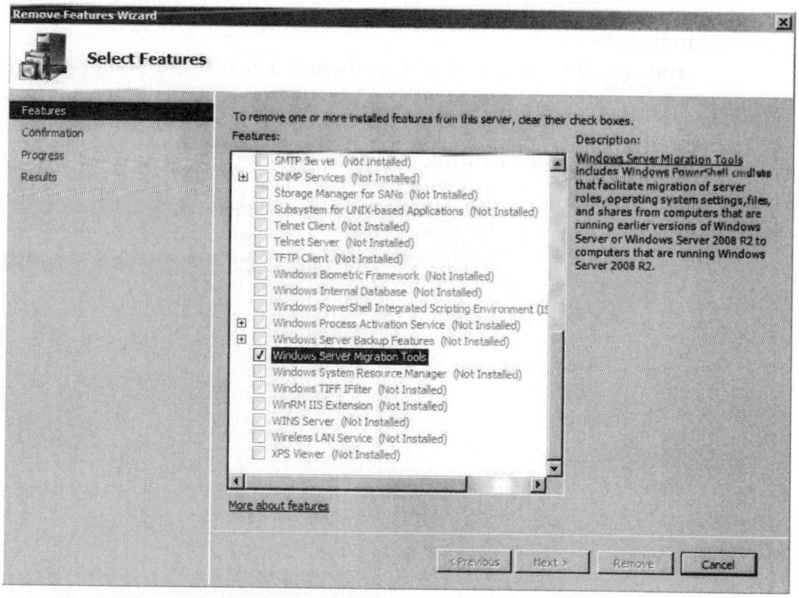

FIGURE 2.56
Selecting features to remove

The servermanagercmd.exe approach is similar to before:

```
servermanagercmd.exe -remove Migration
```

It's very unlikely that you would do this, but you could also use an answer file called RemoveFeature.xml to remove the feature:

```
<?xml version="1.0" encoding="utf-8" ?>
<ServerManagerConfiguration Action="Remove" xmlns="http://schemas.microsoft.com/
sdm/Windows/ServerManager/Configuration/2007/1" xmlns:xs="http://www.w3.org/2001/
XMLSchema">
<Feature Id="Migration" />
</ServerManagerConfiguration>
```

The command to remove the feature is as follows:

```
servermanagercmd.exe -inputpath C:\RemoveFeature.xml
```

The PowerShell method is as follows:

```
PS C:\Windows\system32> remove-windowsfeature migration

Success Restart Needed Exit Code Feature Result
------- -------------- --------- --------------
True    No             Success   {Windows Server Migration Tools}
```

Troubleshooting Roles and Features

By now you may have noticed that you can do a bit more with roles and features in Server Manager.

You can see in Figure 2.57 that there is a critical problem being reported with the File Services role on our example server. Something related to this role is not functioning and will affect the services that we are providing to the network. If this happens to you, you can start troubleshooting that problem by drilling into Roles and then clicking File Services.

FIGURE 2.57
Role error status

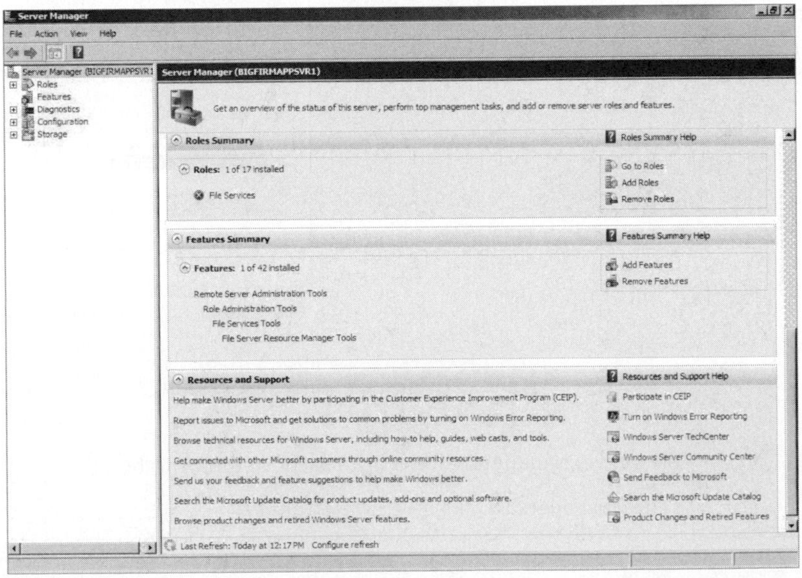

You are now presented with a summary of diagnostics information that is related to File Services. There is a filtered view of events from Windows Event Viewer (see Figure 2.58). You can also manage the services associated with your role.

FIGURE 2.58
Role events

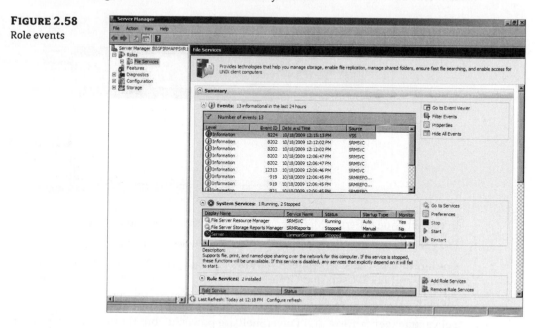

Further down the screen you can also see that there are some tips from Microsoft on how to keep a file server healthy (see Figure 2.59).

FIGURE 2.59
Resources and support

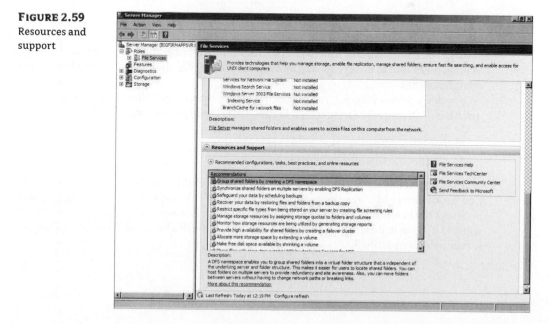

You can use Server Manager to manage the roles you have installed (see Figure 2.60). In this figure, we have drilled down into the File Services role. The relevant MMC consoles have been loaded. This allows you to do a lot of server management from a single console.

FIGURE 2.60
Role management
in Server Manager

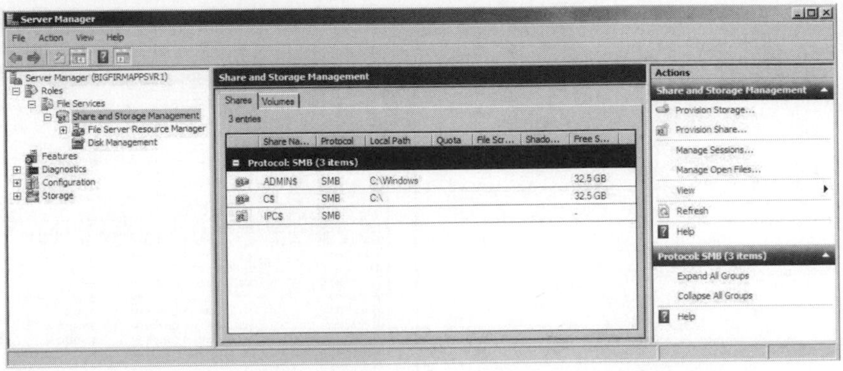

In the left pane of Server Manager, you can see other tools you can use:

Diagnostics   Event Viewer, Performance, and Device Manager.

Configuration   Task Scheduler, Windows Firewall with Advanced Security, Services, WMI Control, and Local Users and Groups.

Storage   Windows Server Backup and Disk Management.

`servermanagercmd.exe` and PowerShell are powerful, but they cannot replicate the management and diagnostics functionality that is in Server Manager. You'll want to keep that utility handy!

Remote Management

Windows Server 2008 Server Manager had one very annoying restriction. You could use it to manage only the local machine. We often found ourselves going back to the old Computer Management tool to do day-to-day management of servers because it allowed us to manage other machines.

Windows Server 2008 R2 introduces the ability to manage other Windows Server 2008 R2 machines with Server Manager (see Figure 2.61). There are two steps to the process:

1. Enable remote management on a server.

2. Connect to that server to manage it.

To enable remote management on a server, you should open Server Manager and click Configure Server Manager Remote Management. The dialog box shown in Figure 2.62 opens.

Select the box if you want to enable remote Server Manager management. Deselect it if you want to disable it. Be warned, though; disabling this will also disable remote management of the server using PowerShell.

FIGURE 2.61
Enable Remote
Management In
Server Manager

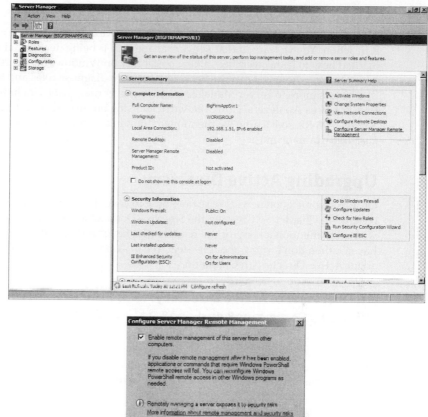

FIGURE 2.62
Enabling Server
Manager remote
management

You should be aware that enabling this feature enables remote management via PowerShell. The risk is that if someone steals administrator credentials, then they can remotely attack the services and data hosted on the server.

Now you can manage this machine from another machine running Windows Server 2008 R2 Server Manager. Right-click Server Manager in the top left, and then select Connect to Another Computer.

Enter the name of the computer you want to manage (see Figure 2.63), and you'll be connected to it, allowing you to manage that server.

FIGURE 2.63
Selecting a com-
puter to manage

Wrapping Up Server Manager

The command-line alternative, servermanagercmd.exe, can be very powerful, and you've seen it in action. You've learned that servermanagercmd is being deprecated by Microsoft, and you've learned how to use PowerShell, a new possibility on Windows Server 2008 R2, instead. And you have also seen how you can use Server Manager to diagnose roles and features.

There is more to Server Manager to aid in server diagnostics including some role-specific Best Practices Analyzers. However, we're focusing on installing and upgrading to Windows Server 2008 R2, so it's time we mentioned domain controllers and Active Directory—queue the *Jaws*-like dramatic music.

Upgrading Active Directory

OK folks, some good news. We're not going to cover this subject in detail yet. That will be covered in Chapter 6, "Creating the Simple AD: the One-Domain, One-Location AD," but we wanted to mention it here for the readers who have worked with an AD in the past. If you haven't, then don't worry about it—feel free to skip the next couple of pages, and you'll learn about Active Directory in Chapter 6.

An Overview of Active Directory: New Functionality in Windows Server 2008 and 2008 R2

As usual, a new version of Server comes along, and you get new functionality and design opportunities in Active Directory. A lot of this new functionality will be pretty exciting to people because it appears to be based on customer feedback. Some of these new options will definitely answer some of those questions we frequently see on Internet support forums.

FINE-GRAINED PASSWORD POLICIES

One of the most common questions since the initial release of Active Directory has been, "How can I have more than one password policy?" In fact, it makes for a nice trick question on the Windows 2000 and 2003 MCP exams! The official Microsoft answer was that you needed more than one domain to do this. Of course, this contradicts the basic design goal of trying to reduce the number of domains in networks. It also muddied the waters when it comes to no longer thinking of the domain as a security boundary—the domain is a policy boundary, and the forest is a security boundary.

The solution, without using third-party products that Microsoft might not support, was to create a domain for every password policy that you needed (which can create a lot of child domains) or to turn to a third-party solution that would allow you to have more than one password policy in a single domain.

With a Windows 2008 domain, you can create a password policy and associate this with a user or a group that resides in the same domain as the password policy. Note that you cannot associate it with an organizational unit (OU). You can probably bet that this will be the new trick password question on certification exams!

The objective of fine-grained password policies is that you should associate stronger policies with user accounts of greater significance, in other words, where they have greater access to systems or to valuable data.

READ-ONLY DOMAIN CONTROLLERS

Larger organizations with branch offices have had some conflicting directives to deal with in the past. Ideally, you should centralize your domain controllers as much as possible. The idea is to simplify your architecture. But you also want to minimize the risk of losing one of these servers. A domain controller contains sensitive information about the organization; in other words, the credentials of every user and system in the Active Directory forest. Branch offices often have poor physical security, and therefore placing a domain controller there is a bad risk. Unfortunately, the needs of the business usually prevail. The link to the branch office may have limited bandwidth or be unstable. This means that one domain controller, or maybe more, is placed in these risky offices. The business can now operate, but the risk of losing a domain controller is still there. What happens if you do lose a domain controller to an attacker? You've given the attacker a copy of your Active Directory, and they can use the information contained within to attack all your domain integrated services, such as SQL Server, SharePoint, Exchange, file servers, ISA, VPN, and so on. That's not good!

Windows Server 2008 and Windows Server 2008 R2 offers a solution in the form of a read-only domain controller (RODC). An RODC can be deployed to those branch offices where you need to offer network stability or a local domain presence for network performance reasons. The RODC contains copies of all data that you would expect to find on a normal domain controller with one notable exception; it does not store any passwords. This means that you can lose the server to a potential attacker and feel safe that your network credentials are protected.

ADMINISTRATOR ROLE SEPARATION

There is another annoying aspect of placing domain controllers in branch offices. Best practice is to minimize the numbers of domain administrators and the numbers of administrators who can log into branch offices. Often a branch office will have a local administrator with beginner skill levels. With Windows 2000 and Windows 2003, you could not grant that person the rights to log on locally because this would risk them being able to damage a corporate asset, namely, Active Directory. Also, in a single-domain architecture, an administrator with the rights to log onto one domain controller could log onto any domain controller in the domain. This might be contrary to company policies.

Windows Server 2008 and Windows Server 2008 R2 RODCs allow you to separate the role of domain controller server administrator from Active Directory administrator. Not only this, but you can delegate rights to a particular server and only that server.

RESTARTABLE ACTIVE DIRECTORY DOMAIN SERVICES

Maintenance such as some patching and offline defragmentation of the Active Directory database file requires a reboot of the domain controller in Windows Server 2000 and 2003. This means more downtime affecting service to users and unforgiving service-level agreements.

Windows Server 2008 and Windows Server 2008 R2 allows AD DS to be stopped and started as required so that maintenance does not require the domain controller to be rebooted quite as often as before. AD DS appears as a service called Domain Controller that an administrator can manage.

Auditing

By default, the global audit policy "Audit directory service access" is enabled in Windows Server 2008 and Windows Server 2008 R2. It is up to administrators to decide what objects should be audited. An entry is added into the Security log to note whenever an object is accessed. However, Windows Server 2008 and Windows Server 2008 R2 adds some new functionality. If an attribute of an object is changed, both the old value and the new value are recorded. This will allow administrators to track changes and allow them to undo them where appropriate.

Database Mounting Tool

A new tool called the Database Mounting Tool, `dsamain.exe`, allows administrators to mount old backups or snapshots of the AD DS database. This will allow the administrator to view old backups to decide which one should be recovered in a recovery scenario. It also allows an administrator to compare the current AD DS with historic copies in troubleshooting situations.

New Active Directory Functionality in Windows Server 2008 R2

The previous section contained information about the new features that were added to Active Directory in Windows Server 2008 and that are also present in Windows Server 2008 R2. This section will cover the new functionality of Active Directory in Windows Server 2008 R2. In other words, the following features are not present in Windows Server 2008 Active Directory.

Active Directory Recycle Bin

Do you hear that? That's the cheering of Active Directory administrators all around the world. Every domain administrator's worst nightmare has been the deletion of objects. It is now possible to recover them if they were recently deleted without going through nasty backup and recovery processes. The Active Directory Recycle Bin is a recycle bin to quickly recover accidentally deleted objects with a new simpler and supported process.

Active Directory Module for PowerShell

Microsoft didn't add cmdlets for Active Directory management when PowerShell was originally released. It was seen as something of an oversight. There were third-party offerings, but a native Microsoft solution was required. Now you can perform administrative, diagnostic, and engineering tasks in Active Directory using PowerShell.

Active Directory Administrative Center

This new tool is intended to replace the traditional MMC console approach for Active Directory management. It is task oriented, and it's based on PowerShell.

Active Directory Web Services

ADWS gives a web interface to Active Directory Domain Services and Active Directory Lightweight Directory Services.

AUTHENTICATION MECHANISM ASSURANCE

Administrators can map authentication methods to accounts to measure authentication reliability measurements for applications.

OFFLINE DOMAIN JOIN

Windows Server 2008 Active Directory administrators can allow remote workers with a new PC to join the domain by securely sending them a set of files. This speeds up the process by not requiring the remote worker to come into the office for a five-minute task.

MANAGED SERVICE ACCOUNTS

This requires less human effort and provides more security to set up and manage domain-based service accounts for applications and services.

Active Directory Upgrade Strategies

There are a few different scenarios for upgrading Active Directory. First we need to review some old territory. You cannot do a direct upgrade from Windows 2000 to Windows Server 2008. The only supported upgrade from Windows Server 2000 is to upgrade to Windows Server 2003 and then upgrade to Windows Server 2008. You cannot do any sort of in-place upgrade from Windows 2000 to Windows Server 2008 R2 because there was no x64 support for 2000. Also, Microsoft employees recommend not doing in-place upgrades to Windows Server 2008 or Windows Server 2008 R2.

Tables 2.5 and 2.6 show some Active Directory upgrade scenarios.

TABLE 2.5:   Windows Server 2008 Active Directory Upgrade Scenarios

EXISTING ACTIVE DIRECTORY	UPGRADE PATH
Windows 2000 (A) *When you want to decommission all old domain controllers*	1. Prepare forest. 2. Prepare domain. 3. Install new Windows 2008 member servers and promote to be domain controllers. 4. Update Group Policy permissions. 5. Decommission Windows 2000 domain controllers.
Windows 2000 (B) *When you want to retain all hardware*	1. Prepare forest. 2. Prepare domain. 3. Upgrade Windows 2000 domain controllers to Windows 2003. 4. Upgrade Windows 2003 domain controllers to Windows 2008.

TABLE 2.5: Windows Server 2008 Active Directory Upgrade Scenarios *(CONTINUED)*

EXISTING ACTIVE DIRECTORY	UPGRADE PATH
Windows 2003 (A) *When you want to decommission all old domain controllers*	1. Prepare forest 2. Prepare domain. 3. Install new Windows 2008 member servers and promote to be domain controllers. 4. Decommission Windows 2003 domain controllers.
Windows 2003 (B) *When you want to retain all hardware*	1. Prepare forest. 2. Prepare domain. 3. Upgrade Windows 2003 domain controllers to Windows 2008
Windows 2003 (C) *When you have a mix of old and new hardware and want to replace old*	1. Prepare forest. 2. Prepare domain. 3. Upgrade newer Windows 2003 domain controllers to Windows 2008 4. Install new Windows 2008 member servers and promote to be domain controllers. These will replace older Windows 2003 domain controllers. 5. Decommission remaining Windows 2003 domain controllers.

SAY GOODBYE TO X86

We strongly recommend that any newly installed domain controller be running a 64-bit operating system. This will simplify future upgrades and increase your upgrade plan options. There won't be any more x86 editions of Windows Server, so you should start switching to the new architecture at this point while you are deploying new servers. Many did this when they deployed Windows Server 2008 Active Directory, and it will pay off when they upgrade to Windows Server 2008 R2.

TABLE 2.6: Windows Server 2008 R2 Active Directory Upgrade Scenarios

EXISTING ACTIVE DIRECTORY	UPGRADE PATH
Windows 2000 (A) *No choice for Windows 2000 networks*	1. Prepare forest. 2. Prepare domain. 3. Install new Windows 2008 R2 member servers and promote to be domain controllers. 4. Update Group Policy permissions. 5. Decommission Windows 2000 domain controllers.

TABLE 2.6: Windows Server 2008 R2 Active Directory Upgrade Scenarios *(CONTINUED)*

EXISTING ACTIVE DIRECTORY	UPGRADE PATH
Windows 2003/2008 (A) *When you want to decommission all old domain controllers*	1. Prepare forest. 2. Prepare domain. 3. Install Windows 2008 R2 member servers and promote to be domain controllers. 5. Decommission old domain controllers.
Windows 2003/2008 (B) *When all old domain controllers are x64*	1. Prepare forest. 2. Prepare domain. 3. Upgrade x64 domain controllers to Windows 2008 R2.
Windows 2003/2008 (C) *When there is a mix of new and old hardware* *When there is a mix of x86 and x64 domain controllers*	1. Prepare forest. 2. Prepare domain. 3. Upgrade newer domain controllers to Windows 2008 R2. 4. Install new Windows 2008 R2 member servers to and promote to be domain controllers. These will replace older Windows domain controllers. 5. Decommission old domain controllers.

All of these strategies have a pair of steps in common. A tool called adprep is used to upgrade the forest schema; in other words, prepare the forest. This is done once by a user who is a member of Schema Admins, Enterprise Admins, and Domain Admins in the domain that contains the Schema Master forest-wide FSMO role. The same tool is also used to prepare any domain that will contain Windows 2008 domain controllers. This will be done by a user who is a domain administrator of that domain.

The side-by-side approach, shown as Windows 2000 (A) of upgrading from Windows 2000 Server to Windows Server 2008 or Windows Server 2008 R2, requires one more step. It is necessary to apply permissions to Group Policy objects so that they can be managed by the Group Policy Management console.

Your final way to get to Windows Server 2008 or Windows Server 2008 R2 is a drastic one. You may find that your network is not in a healthy or known state. Sometimes it's better to cut your losses and start again with a new Active Directory that is well planned, documented, controlled, and maintained. You can build a new forest/domain. You can then migrate users, data, and services to the new Active Directory. We've done that in the past when we joined a new company that was going through a spin-off closely followed by a series of mergers. It paid off with a much more stable and manageable working environment.

This all sounds very high level, and it is meant to be. It is just a taste of what you can expect in Chapter 6.

Unattended Installations

We bet you thought you were finally getting to the end of this chapter. Surely, there is no more we could discuss about installing Windows Server 2008 or Windows Server 2008 R2, right? Well, think again.

Smaller organizations will be happy with the manual approach for installing or upgrading Windows Server 2008 R2 that we discussed earlier in the chapter. However, you may want to invest some effort in alternative approaches. You could use a cloning solution such as Windows Deployment Services, as found in Windows Server since Service Pack 2 for Windows Server 2003 or the free Microsoft Deployment Toolkit 2010. Maybe you already use a third-party solution. There is another way that might be of interest for you that does not require a server to manage the process.

Unattended installations of Windows extend the installation media by customizing their installation. Part of the process is to answer those questions that you probably get sick of answering all the time. The idea is that you can start an installation and walk away knowing that you will not have to answer any questions. Your new server will install all by itself according to your predefined answers. The new installation routine for Windows Vista and Server 2008 is quite small, but if you are building lots of machines, you will soon get tired of entering product keys, selecting OS editions, and so on. The other, more powerful part is the ability to tweak the installation in ways that are not revealed in the manual installation process. How would you like to install some components of the operating system that are not revealed in the GUI? This could simplify your post-installation customization and streamline your deployments.

All of this is possible by using an answer file that you supply to the installation routine. This approach might be familiar to engineers who have deployed older versions of Windows. In the past you might have used a tool called Setup Manager to create a simple text-based answer file, which you probably then had to customize a fair bit in Notepad.

The release of Windows Vista changed all that. With Vista came the release of the Windows Automated Installation Kit (WAIK), which has seen some updates including support for Windows Server 2008, Windows 7, and Windows Server 2008 R2. WAIK is a very powerful set of tools that include the ability to create a boot DVD. This boots up using Windows PE, a trimmed-down version of Windows, that you can use for many tasks including OS deployment and troubleshooting. More important for this chapter, it includes Windows System Image Manager (WSIM). WSIM is the replacement for Setup Manager and is used to create answer files for Windows Vista, Windows Server 2008, Windows 7, and Windows Server 2008 R2.

The other big change you'll see is the format of the answer files that you are going to use. They used to be pretty simple to edit text files. Heck, Setup Manager actually did little other than set up the skeleton of the answer file. You generally had to do a lot more work on the answer file in Notepad. WSIM creates XML files. Uh-oh! There's that word: XML! Don't let it scare you. It scares many administrators at first because they are far from being a programmer. But the WSIM interface does pretty much everything you'll need. You can still go in and edit the file by hand in Notepad or whatever your favorite XML editor is. The only time you might really do that is to jump in and change a product key.

We'll now cover how to deploy Windows Server 2008 R2 in an unattended fashion. You'll see how to install WAIK, use WSIM to create an answer file, and then use that answer file to get a silent installation working.

Note that much, if not all, of what is covered in this section can also be used to deploy Windows Vista, Windows 7, and Windows Server 2008.

Installing Windows Automated Installation Kit (WAIK)

The exercise that you are now going to go through will demonstrate how to deploy an edition of Windows Server 2008 R2 with very little human intervention. You need to deploy several Windows Server 2008 R2 Enterprise edition servers. It makes sense to automate those builds. You do this by using an answer file to answer the questions that you encountered during the manual installation of Windows Server 2008 R2. We'll show how to create that answer file using Windows System Image Manager, and then we will go through the process of deploying Windows in an unattended fashion.

WAIK is a free set of tools that you can download from Microsoft. We are hesitant to include a URL for a download here because Microsoft has updated its deployment kits a few times since the initial release. Your best bet is to visit www.microsoft.com/downloads and search for *WAIK*. This will ensure that you get the latest version of WAIK. You'll be asked to download a rather large ISO file; it has reached about 1.6GB at the time of writing this chapter. Just in case you don't know, that ISO file is an image of a DVD that you can either mount or use to create a DVD. You may have previously downloaded WAIK before the release of Windows Server 2008 R2. However, Microsoft released a new version to coincide with the release of Windows Server 2008 R2 to support the new server operating systems and Windows 7, so you will need to download that.

You might need to burn the ISO file to a DVD if you want to use it. You can use the ISO burning feature that's included in Windows 7. For other operating systems, you'll need a special utility. Microsoft includes a tool in the Windows Server 2003 Resource Kit called DVDBURN that you can use. Or, ISO Recorder (http://tinyurl.com/yagdg5j) is a free tool for working with ISO images. If you are using Windows 7, you can use a free ISO mounting tool such as Virtual Clone Drive by Elaborate Bytes to mount the image and present it as a virtual drive to your PC. This saves you from using up blank disks for once-off jobs.

The next thing you are going to need is an administrative workstation. An administrative workstation is a PC that you will use to prepare future builds. This might just be your PC, but that might not be a good location because you're going to be messing around with WAIK and WSIM once you start getting to know them; you'll likely be making a mess of the administrative PC, so using your day-to-day machine might not be too sensible! Ensure you have lots of disk space to play with. You'll soon see why. Our preference is to have either a dedicated machine or, even better, a virtual machine. The latter offers the benefit of being economical and having the ability to save and restore states. With virtual machines, you can also mount ISO files, which is of great benefit because you won't waste time messing with utilities and blank disks. Speaking of virtual machines, you're going to need something to test your new answer files with. Virtual machines are great for testing for the same reasons that we like them as an administrative workstation.

You'll need to prepare your administrative workstation before you kick off the WAIK installation. You will have support if you are running Windows XP SP2 or later. The .NET Framework 2.0 and MSXML 6 SP1 or later are prerequisites.

Mount your newly downloaded WAIK media on your administrative PC, and then run `startcd.exe` from the root of the drive.

A splash screen will appear (see Figure 2.64). Users of Windows XP will note that they can install their prerequisites from here before installing WAIK. When you are ready, click Windows AIK Setup. Skip past the welcome screen shown in Figure 2.65.

Select I Agree if you agree to the licensing terms that are set out by Microsoft for WAIK (see Figure 2.66).

FIGURE 2.64
WAIK setup
splash screen

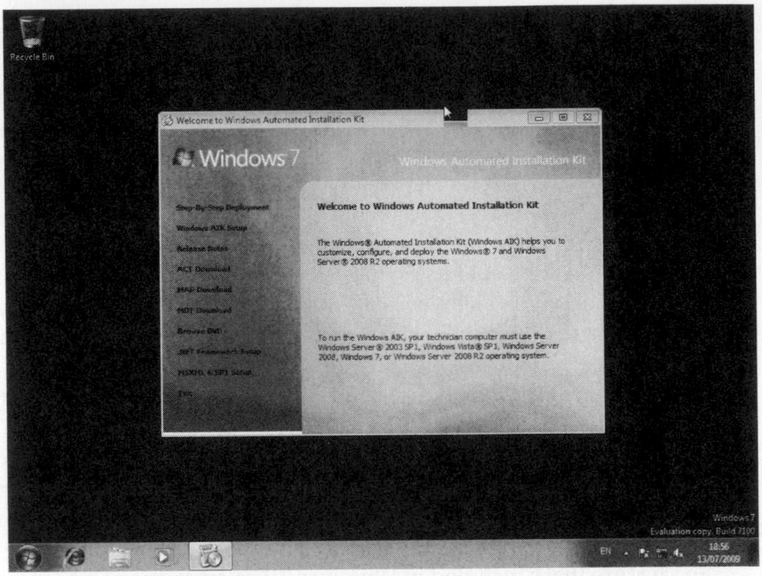

FIGURE 2.65
WAIK setup
welcome screen

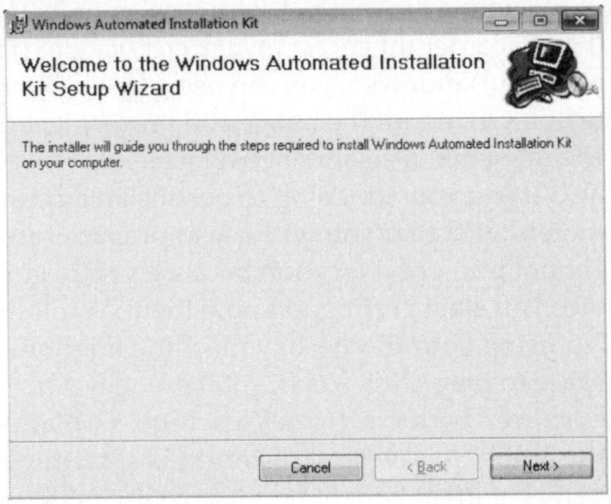

FIGURE 2.66
WAIK EULA

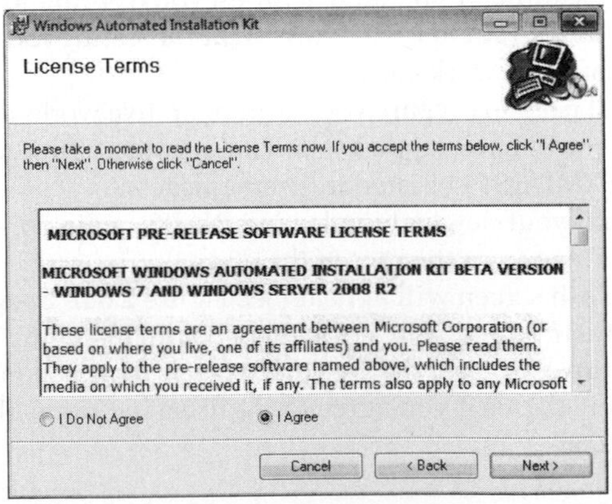

Real World Scenario

A BETTER DESTINATION

Rhonda Layfield, a colleague and a deployment guru, has a great tip for when you are installing WAIK. You're asked here to choose a location for installing WAIK. We usually choose the default of C:\Program Files. Once you start using WAIK a lot, however, you'll realize how much command-line stuff you might need to do. Burying your software in a deep path full of lots of long names isn't exactly command line friendly. Rhonda's tip is to simply install WAIK into C:\WAIK, as shown here. That will save a lot of keyboard wear and tear.

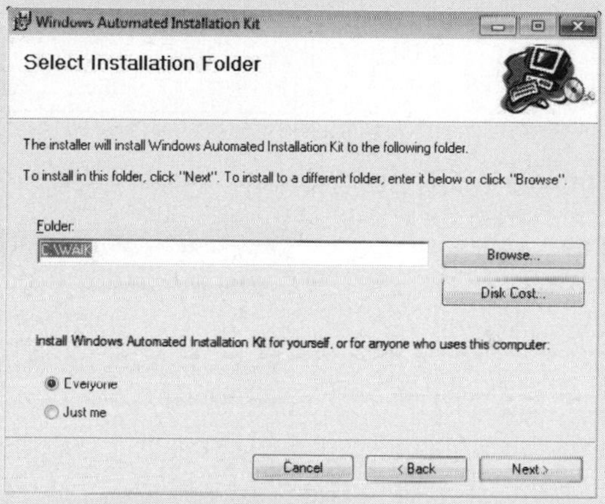

Click Next if you are ready to commit to the installation of WAIK (see Figure 2.67).

FIGURE 2.67
Confirming the
WAIK installation

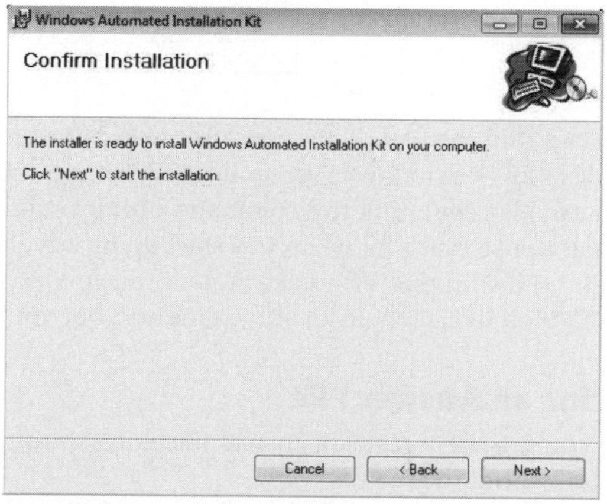

It can take several minutes for WAIK to install (see Figure 2.68). You now have yet another opportunity to respond to some emails.

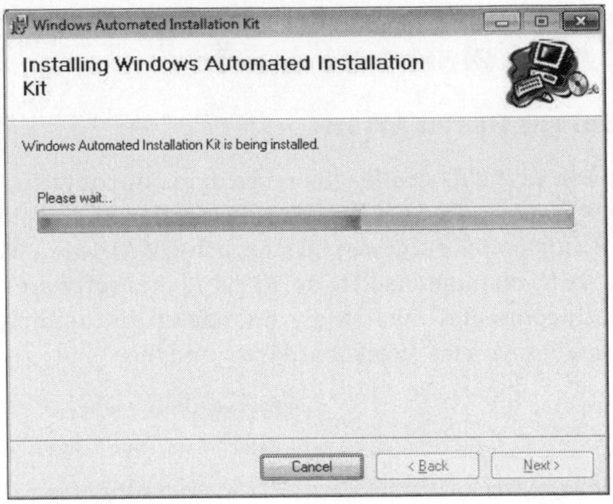

FIGURE 2.68
WAIK installation
progress

Eventually WAIK is installed (see Figure 2.69).

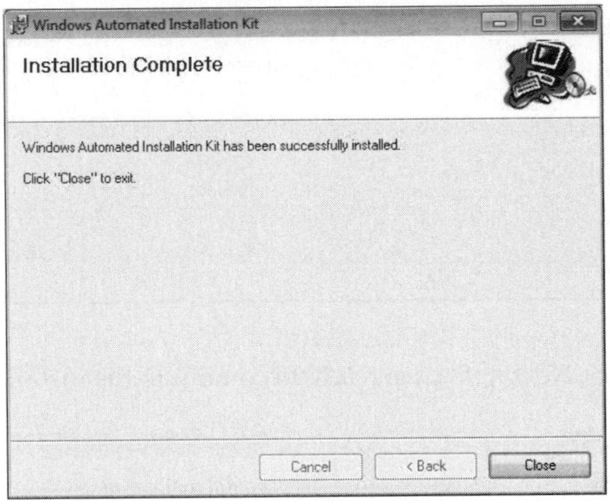

FIGURE 2.69
Completed WAIK
installation

You can find the tool that you're after in the Start menu under All Programs ➤ Microsoft Windows AIK ➤ Windows System Image Manager (see Figure 2.70).

You can also see a link to a command prompt called Windows PE Tools Command Prompt. You'll get to use that a lot when you start doing advanced operating system deployment tasks.

Clicking the link for Windows System Image Manager will launch that tool (see Figure 2.71). It doesn't look like a whole lot at the moment, but you'll change that in a few minutes.

Creating an Answer File

Before you actually create an answer file, you should get to understand a little bit of what is going on behind the scenes.

When Windows Vista, Windows 7, Server 2008, or Server 2008 R2 are installing, the installation routine goes through some or all of seven *configuration passes*, described in Table 2.7. Each of these passes is responsible for carrying out certain tasks. You can think of them as stages. Some tasks can be performed in more than one of the passes. Typically only three of those passes actually need to be executed for Windows to install.

FIGURE 2.70
WAIK on the
Start menu

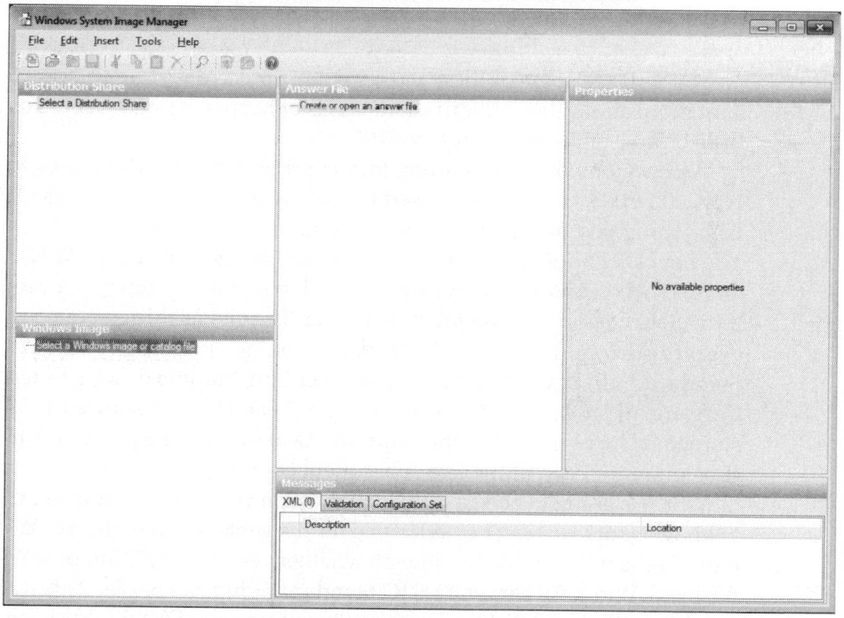

FIGURE 2.71
Windows System
Image Manager

TABLE 2.7: The Configuration Passes

PASS	DESCRIPTION
windowsPE	Boots up the WindowsPE installation environment, configures the product key, and configures the installation disk.
offlineServicing	Applies updates to the Windows image including packages, patches, and languages.
Specialize	Configures settings that might be unique to the system such as network configuration, regional, and domain.
Generalize	Removes system-specific information. It is executed only when you run sysprep /generalize.
auditSystem	Processes unattended setup steps before a user logs on. This pass runs only if you boot into audit mode.
auditUser	Processes unattended setup steps after a user logs on. It runs only if you boot into audit mode.
oobeSystem	Applies settings before the Windows welcome screen can start, in other words, before you log on.

You will see some of these passes when you create your answer file in WSIM. You can learn a lot more about the configuration passes at http://tinyurl.com/3dszvm. This will start to get a little clearer once you get into WSIM.

We have one other little thing to cover first. Anyone who has been working with Windows NT, 2000, 2003, or XP will be used to dealing with a folder such as i386 on the installation media. Everything you needed to configure Windows was in there. That changed with Windows Vista. The new DVD-only media used a file-based image called a *WIM file*. This WIM file, called install.wim, contains everything needed to install the new operating systems, and you can find it in \Sources on your installation media. The clever thing about this WIM file is that it contains everything required to install all editions of the operating system on the media. For example, Standard Full, Enterprise Full, Datacenter Full, Standard Core, Enterprise Core, and Datacenter Core are all on the Windows Server 2008 DVD. This is because the WIM file uses single-instance storage; instead of having the same identical file six times, it stores it once and creates a reference point for each of the five subsequent copies.

WSIM is going to need a copy of that file on your administrative PC. WSIM uses this *install image* to know what tasks can be performed for the version and edition of Windows that you are working with. These will vary depending on whether you're using Windows Vista Home, Windows Vista Business, Windows Server 2008 R2 Standard, Windows Server 2008 R2 Datacenter, and so on. Why put this on the hard disk and not use the one on your DVD? WSIM needs to create a catalog of the contents of the image file, and it uses the folder containing the image as a working folder. You cannot write to read-only media such as a DVD.

For this example, say you are working with the DVD for Windows Server 2008 R2. You have copied \sources\install.wim into C:\W2008R2\install.wim on our administrative PC.

Now launch WSIM and get this process rolling by selecting File ➢ Select Windows Image. Navigate to your install image (see Figure 2.72), which is C:\W2008R2\install.wim, and open it.

FIGURE 2.72
Adding a Windows image to WSIM

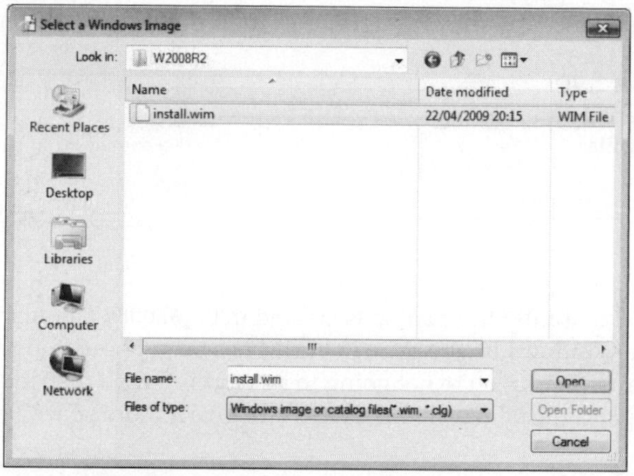

You can now see a little of the magic of the WIM file in action. The installation media has a number of different versions of Windows in it. The old architecture folder structure (such as i386) was not capable of this. Select the version of Windows that you want to install in an unattended fashion. We have selected the Enterprise edition of Windows Server 2008 R2 in Figure 2.73. Note that Microsoft has retained the preproduction code name of Longhorn in the Windows Server 2008 media.

FIGURE 2.73
Selecting the Windows image

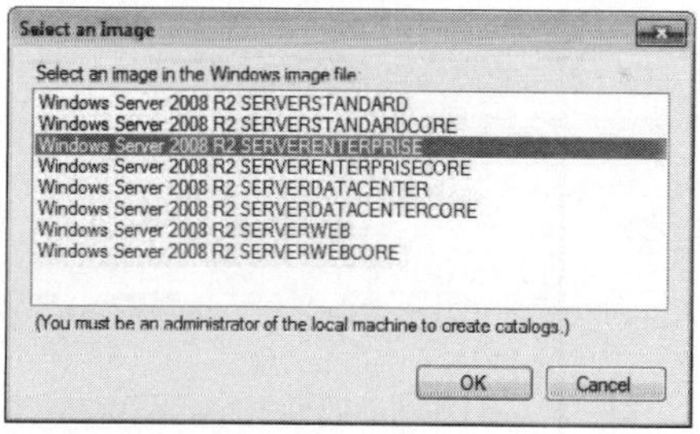

You are now warned that a catalog file of this image cannot be opened because it does not exist. You can either create a catalog file or cancel this process. Click Yes to create a catalog file in the dialog box shown in Figure 2.74. Note that you must be a local administrator on an administrative PC.

FIGURE 2.74
Building a catalog file

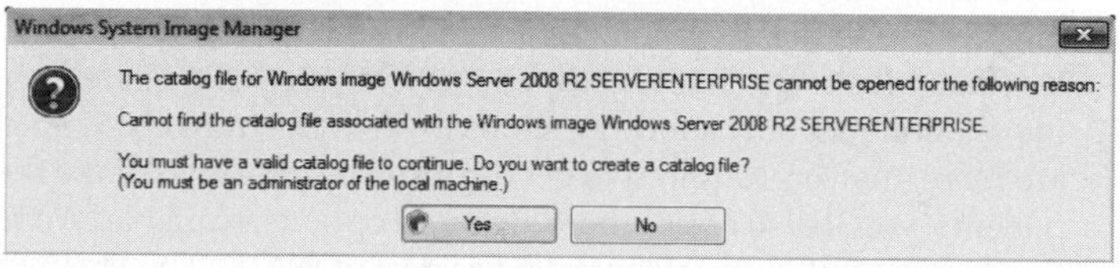

UAC might trigger a request before proceeding depending on the security configuration of your administrative workstation. It takes a little while for a catalog file to be created (see Figure 2.75). We really hope you have a lot of email to respond to or like to drink lots of coffee. Operating system deployment has been sometimes correctly referred to as "progress bar engineering"!

FIGURE 2.75
Generating the catalog file

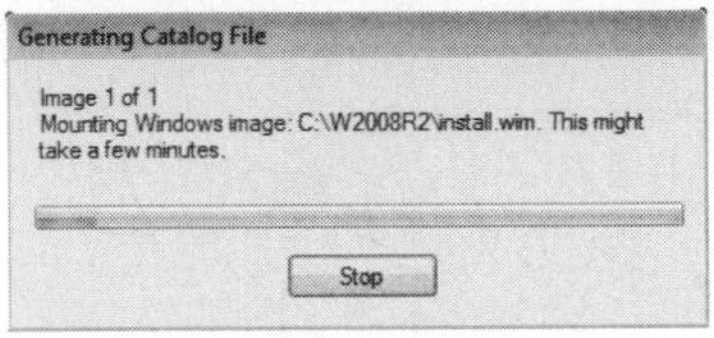

Eventually the catalog is created in C:\W2008R2 alongside the image file. You can see that the Windows Image pane in WSIM has been populated with Components and Packages (see Figure 2.76). You're not going to be working with distribution shares, so you might as well expand the Windows Image pane to give it more space.

FIGURE 2.76
Added Windows image

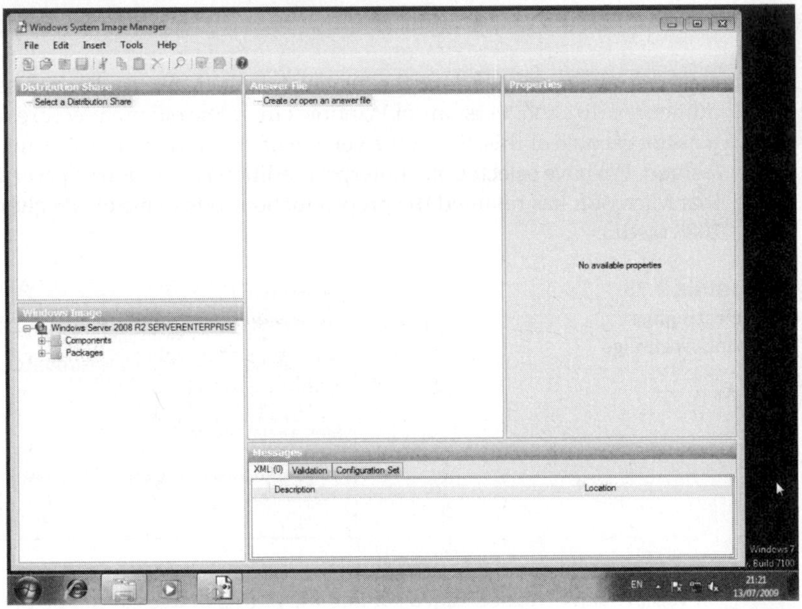

You're interested in working with Components here, so go ahead and expand that (see Figure 2.77). A *component* is a set of related settings that are used as building blocks for constructing an answer file. Each component answers a question or a set of questions during the installation. You can selectively choose components to create your desired unattended installation. The manual installation had only a few questions to answer; strangely, with an unattended installation, there are more answers required to get the same results. If you take the time to navigate around the components, you'll also notice there are more options available. We highly recommend that you read the documentation that is installed as part of WAIK. The Unattended Windows Setup Reference goes into great detail on what each of the components are responsible for.

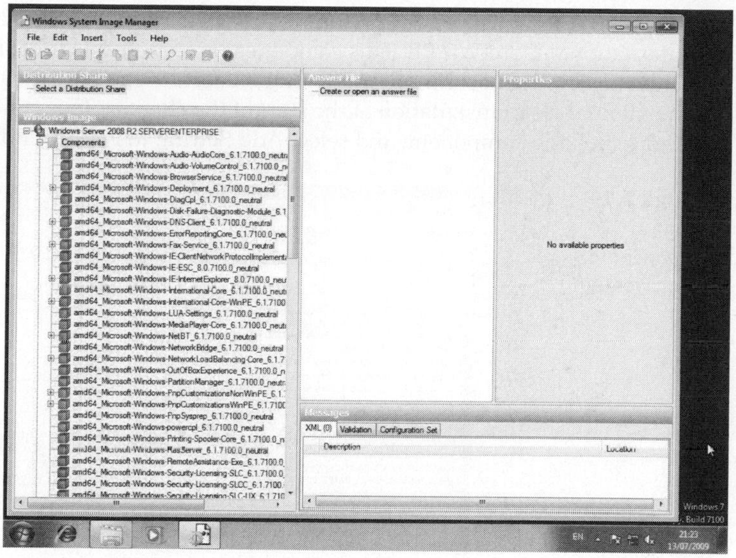

FIGURE 2.77
Browsing the
Windows image
components

The next step is to create a new answer file within WSIM. Open the File menu, and click New Answer File.

The Answer File pane is now populated (see Figure 2.78). Does what you see look familiar? It should. You can see each of the available configuration passes that are used for installing Windows underneath the Components object. You'll add components to the necessary passes to build up the answer file now.

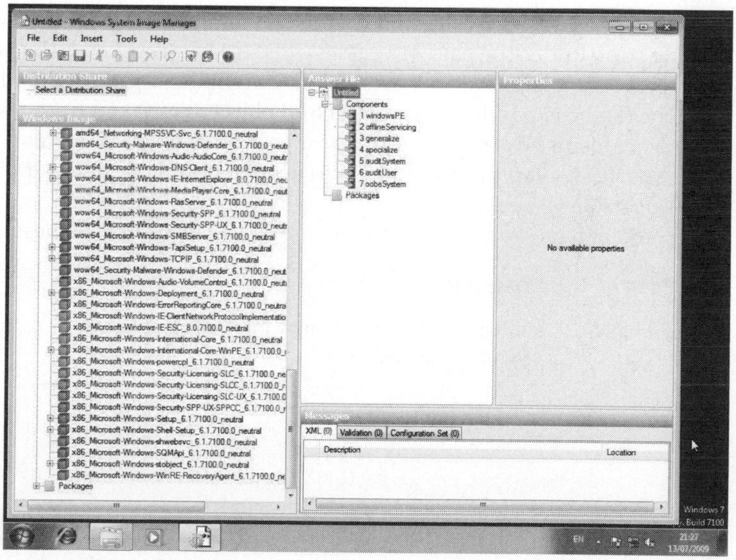

FIGURE 2.78
Starting a new
answer file

Under Components in the Windows Image pane, navigate to amd64_Microsoft-Windows-International-Core-WinPE. This component is responsible for configuring the Windows installation environment settings. You'll remember how you had to configure language settings in the manual clean installation at the start of the chapter. This component will automate that step. Right-click the component, and select Add Setting to Pass1 windowsPE (Figure 2.79).

FIGURE 2.79
Adding a component to the answer file

You can now see that this component has been added to the new answer file in the Answer File pane under the pass "1 windowsPE" (see Figure 2.80). You can also see that the properties of the component are now available to edit in the top-right details pane. Notice that this component can be expanded to reveal a child object. It also can have properties that can be edited. You select an edit box of a property value and press F1 on your keyboard to access the help on that property. As you progress, you will need to do that to find out what the property does and what its possible values are.

You can now edit the component. Add the following values:

PASS	COMPONENT	PROPERTY	VALUE
1	amd64_Microsoft-Windows-International-Core\ SetupUILanguage	InputLocale	en-us
		UserLocale	en-us
		UILanguage	en-us
		SystemLocale	en-us
		UILanguage	en-us

What you have done here is configured each of these settings to be US English (see Figure 2.81). Pressing F1 in any one of those properties will lead you to the help that gives the codes for alternative regional settings. Note that you have also edited the UILanguage property in the child component SetupUILanguage.

FIGURE 2.80
New component in the answer file

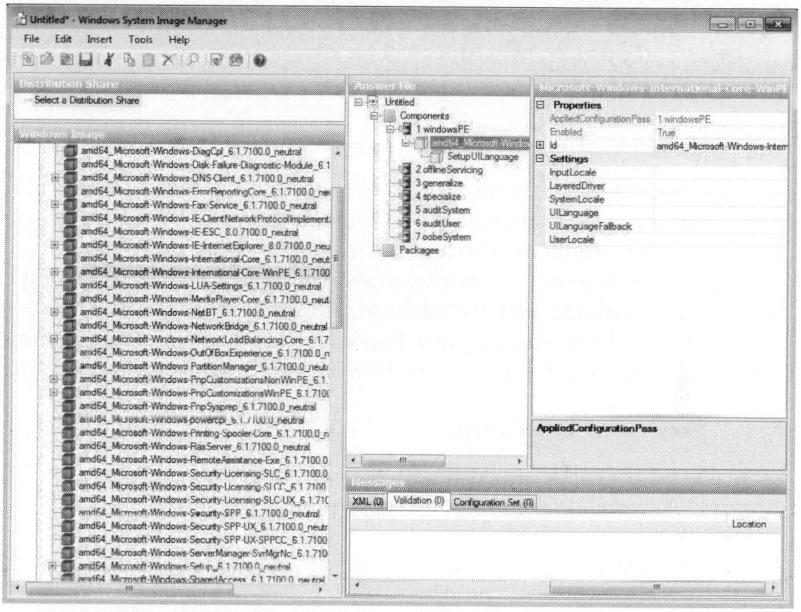

FIGURE 2.81
Configuring the answer file component

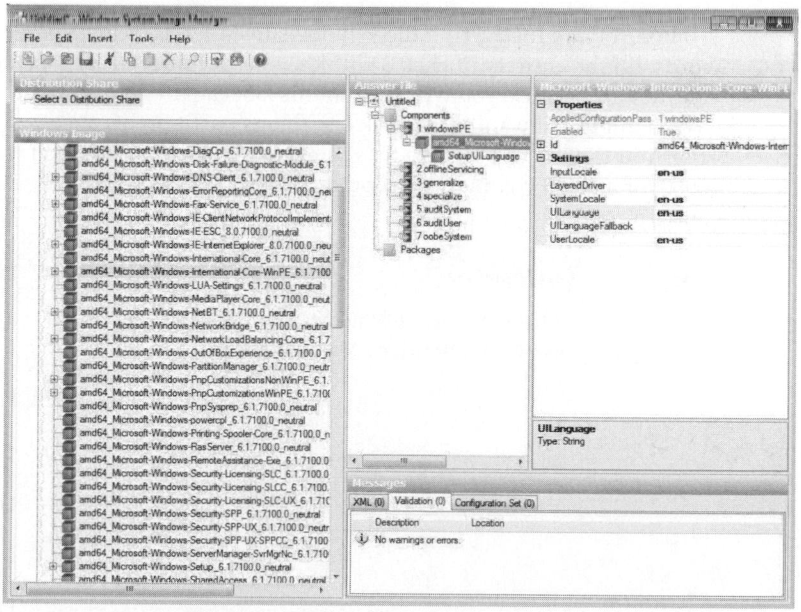

You'll now add some more components and edit their properties. (We will continue to use the previous table format; make sure you add the components to the pass mentioned in the first column of each table.)

PASS	COMPONENT	PROPERTY	VALUE
1	AMD64_Microsoft-Windows-Setup\ DiskConfiguration\Disk	DiskID	0
		WillWipeDisk	True

This Disk subcomponent that you are adding to the answer file in pass 1 tells the installer to manage Disk 0 in the server. Remember that in Microsoft-speak Disk 0 is the first disk in the computer. You have also told the installer to wipe this disk.

In the Answer File pane, you should expand the Disk subcomponent. You'll see two subcomponents called CreatePartitions and ModifyPartitions. Right-click each of those two subcomponents, and select Insert New. This will allow you to create a volume on your newly wiped Disk 0 and then format it using the following subcomponent property settings:

PASS	COMPONENT	PROPERTY	VALUE
1	AMD64_Microsoft-Windows-Setup\DiskConfiguration\ Disk\CreatePartitions\CreatePartition	Extend	True
		Order	1
		Type	Primary

Here you are instructing the Windows Installer to create a partition and extend it; in other words, fill the entirety of Disk 0 with the new volume. Order instructs the installer to label the volume as 1 because you will refer to this label again in a moment.

You might not want to fill Disk 0 with one partition because is signified by setting Extend = True. You can instead set Size to whatever size in megabytes you want partition 1 to be, such as 40960 for a 40GB volume. You should not set a value for size *and* set Extend = True because that causes a conflict.

PASS	COMPONENT	PROPERTY	VALUE
1	AMD64_Microsoft-Windows-Setup\DiskConfiguration\ Disk\CreatePartitions\ModifyPartition	Active	True
		Format	NTFS
		Label	Windows
		Letter	C
		Order	1
		PartitionsID	1

Here you can see where we refer to Order again. You're instructing the installer to format the previously created volume for you. It is set up as partition 1 using PartitionsID. In Microsoft-speak, partition 1 is the first partition; there is no partition 0. You set the volume as Active because you want to be able to boot from it. You format it with NTFS, label the volume as Windows, and give it the letter C.

The next bit is a bit tricky. We've found that using the help documentation that we have already referred to is useful. But you'll also see how you will need another tool from WAIK.

PASS	COMPONENT	PROPERTY	VALUE
1	AMD64_Microsoft-Windows-Setup\InstallImage\ OSImage\InstallFrom\Metadata	Key	/IMAGE/NAME
		Value	Windows Server 2008 R2 SERVERENTERPRISE

When we originally tried to install Windows Server 2008 R2 using an unattended approach, the install would always stop to ask us to choose between the available editions of Windows on the DVD. This was obviously not what we wanted; we wanted an unattended installation. A search through the help file in WAIK found that this subcomponent could help us select the correct edition. Unfortunately, it did not tell us what we should put in the property values. What it did tell us was that the values we needed were contained within our install image, install.wim.

So, we opened the Windows PE Tools Command Prompt, which is part of WAIK. We then ran the following command:

```
IMAGEX /info C:\W2008R2\INSTALL.WIM
```

The IMAGEX command is a WAIK utility that allows you to manage WIM files. The syntax for the previous is as follows:

```
IMAGEX.EXE /info <Path to Desired WIM File>
```

This produced a report on the contents of the Windows Server 2008 R2 x64 install image. Here's a snippet:

```
    .
    .

    <NAME>Windows Server 2008 R2 SERVERSTANDARD</NAME>
    <DESCRIPTION> Windows Server 2008 R2 SERVERSTANDARD</DESCRIPTION>
    <FLAGS>ServerStandard</FLAGS>
    <WINDOWS>

    .
    .

    <NAME>Windows Server 2008 R2 SERVERENTERPRISE</NAME>
    <DESCRIPTION> Server 2008 R2 SERVERENTERPRISE</DESCRIPTION>
    <FLAGS>ServerEnterprise</FLAGS>
    <WINDOWS>

    .
    .

    <NAME>Windows Server 2008 R2 SERVERDATACENTER</NAME>
```

```
<DESCRIPTION>Windows Server 2008 R2 SERVERDATACENTER</DESCRIPTION>
<FLAGS>ServerDatacenter</FLAGS>
<WINDOWS>
```

The Windows Server 2008 media that we have still uses the old product code name of Longhorn instead of Server 2008.

The Metadata subcomponent allows you to specify a key to search for in these results and then a value to match. In the previous snippet, you can see that there is a NAME key. It is under the path /IMAGE/PATH. The NAME key is used to uniquely identify each of the available editions of Windows contained within the install image. You can see the one you want for this example under IMAGE INDEX=1. That NAME key is set to Windows Server 2008 R2 SERVERENTERPRISE. Therefore, you set your Metadata component to search for and match a key called /IMAGE/NAME with a value of Windows Server 2008 R2 SERVERENTERPRISE. That image will be the one that the installer should install on the server. Phew! That's the hardest thing you'll do here; we promise.

The following tells the OS installer to install the selected image into the disk you previously selected and into the volume you have just created and formatted; in other words, the first partition on the first disk.

PASS	COMPONENT	PROPERTY	VALUE
1	AMD64_Microsoft-Windows-Setup\InstallImage\ OSImage\InstallTo	DiskID	0
		PartitionID	1

You use the UserData subcomponent to enter licensing information for this installation of Windows. You accept Microsoft's licensing terms by setting AcceptEula to True. Enter the name of the company for FullName and Organization, which is a common practice to signify ownership of the license. And our product key, which is shown only for illustrative purposes, is entered into Key in the subcomponent.

PASS	COMPONENT	PROPERTY	VALUE
1	AMD64_Microsoft-Windows-Setup\ UserData	AcceptEula	True
		FullName	Bigfirm
		Organization	Bigfirm
	AMD64_Microsoft-Windows-Setup\ UserData\ProductKey	Key	HFG76-34GFT-O6ID9-MNBW4-IYUSD

Add the following component into pass 4, "4 specialize." You use ComputerName, well, to set the name of the computer. That's not very mysterious. Set it to *. This tells the OS installer to generate a random name. You could type in something there if you wanted. Use TimeZone to configure the system clock. In this example, we've set it to the USA Eastern Time Zone. A list of available zones is available by pressing F1.

PASS	COMPONENT	PROPERTY	VALUE
4	AMD64_Microsoft-Windows-Shell-Setup	ComputerName	*
		TimeZone	Eastern Standard Time

Add the following subcomponent to pass 7, "7 oobeSystem." Configure the Windows Firewall using NetworkLocation. Setting it to Work configures the firewall to be enabled but loosened suitably for a typical corporate network. ProtectYourPC turns on automatic updates and configures it to install updates automatically.

This component shows you how you can add a little extra to your installation that is not otherwise available in a manual installation.

PASS	COMPONENT	PROPERTY	VALUE
7	AMD64_Microsoft-Windows-Shell-Setup\ OOBE	HideEULAPage	True
		NetworkLocation	Work
		ProtectYourPC	1

The last component you'll set up is a good one to keep in mind for laboratory environments where you might be using MSDN or TechNet licensing. Those subscriptions give you a limited number of activations for every license key. Your typical lab machine has a very short life, so it is pointless to use up your valuable activations.

This component may be called Wow64_Microsoft-Windows-Security-Licensing-SLC-UX in Windows Server 2008. It allows you to disable the default process of autoactivation of your installation.

PASS	COMPONENT	PROPERTY	VALUE
7	Wow64_Microsoft-Windows-Security-Licensing-SPP-UX	SkipAutoActivation	False

Those are all the components you want to add. What you're now going to do is validate the answer file. On the Tools menu, select Validate Answer File. This will go through the properties and the values that you have entered. Anything that is glaringly wrong will lead to an error in the Messages pane. Everything should be OK if you've entered the components and property values as illustrated so far (see Figure 2.82).

You can save your answer file now. Click the File menu, and select Save Answer File As.

Save it as `autounattend.xml` in a location of your choice, such as C:\Answer\autounattend.xml (see Figure 2.83).

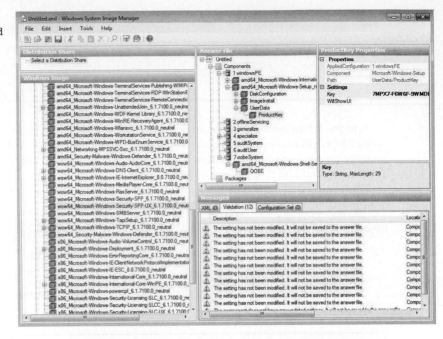

FIGURE 2.82
A fully configured answer file

FIGURE 2.83
Saving the answer file

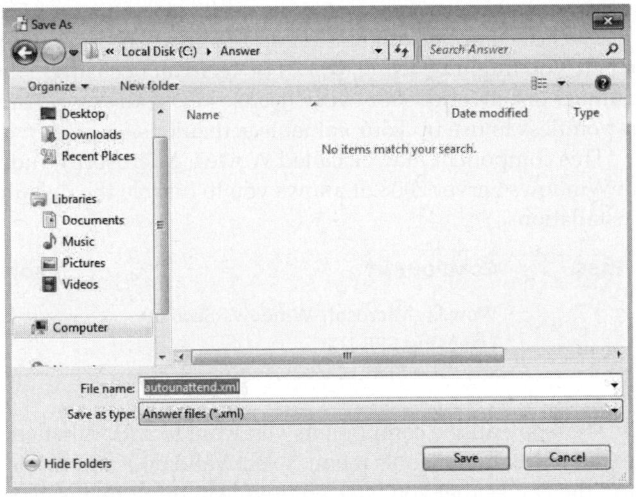

You might as well take a look at the XML file that you've created. Using Notepad, open your new answer file. You should have something like this:

```xml
<?xml version="1.0" encoding="utf-8"?>
<unattend xmlns="urn:schemas-microsoft-com:unattend">
    <settings pass="windowsPE">
```

```xml
        <component name="Microsoft-Windows-International-Core-WinPE"
processorArchitecture="amd64" publicKeyToken="31bf3856ad364e35"
language="neutral" versionScope="nonSxS" xmlns:wcm="http://schemas.microsoft.com/
WMIConfig/2002/State" xmlns:xsi="http://www.w3.org/2001/XMLSchema-instance">
        <SetupUILanguage>
            <UILanguage>en-us</UILanguage>
        </SetupUILanguage>
        <InputLocale>en-us</InputLocale>
        <UserLocale>en-us</UserLocale>
        <UILanguage>en-us</UILanguage>
        <SystemLocale>en-us</SystemLocale>
    </component>
    <component name="Microsoft-Windows-Setup" processorArchitecture="amd64" p
ublicKeyToken="31bf3856ad364e35" language="neutral" versionScope="nonSxS"
xmlns:wcm="http://schemas.microsoft.com/WMIConfig/2002/State" xmlns:xsi="http://
www.w3.org/2001/XMLSchema-instance">
        <DiskConfiguration>
            <Disk wcm:action="add">
                <CreatePartitions>
                    <CreatePartition wcm:action="add">
                        <Extend>true</Extend>
                        <Order>1</Order>
                        <Type>Primary</Type>
                    </CreatePartition>
                </CreatePartitions>
                <ModifyPartitions>
                    <ModifyPartition wcm:action="add">
                        <Active>true</Active>
                        <Format>NTFS</Format>
                        <Label>Windows</Label>
                        <Letter>C</Letter>
                        <Order>1</Order>
                        <PartitionID>1</PartitionID>
                    </ModifyPartition>
                </ModifyPartitions>
                <DiskID>0</DiskID>
                <WillWipeDisk>true</WillWipeDisk>
            </Disk>
        </DiskConfiguration>
        <ImageInstall>
            <OSImage>
                <InstallFrom>
                    <MetaData wcm:action="add">
                        <Key>/IMAGE/NAME</Key>
                        <Value>Windows Server 2008 R2 SERVERENTERPRISE</Value>
                    </MetaData>
                </InstallFrom>
```

```
                        <InstallTo>
                              <DiskID>0</DiskID>
                              <PartitionID>1</PartitionID>
                        </InstallTo>
                  </OSImage>
            </ImageInstall>
            <UserData>
                  <ProductKey>
                        <Key>7MPX7-F6W6F-9WMDB-9XFW8-VPH3M</Key>
                  </ProductKey>
                  <AcceptEula>true</AcceptEula>
                  <FullName>BigFirm</FullName>
                  <Organization>BigFirm</Organization>
            </UserData>
      </component>
  </settings>
  <settings pass="specialize">

<component name="Microsoft-Windows-Shell-Setup" processorArchitecture="amd64" pub
licKeyToken="31bf3856ad364e35" language="neutral" versionScope="nonSxS"
xmlns:wcm="http://schemas.microsoft.com/WMIConfig/2002/State" xmlns:xsi="http://
www.w3.org/2001/XMLSchema-instance">
            <ComputerName>*</ComputerName>
            <TimeZone>Eastern Standard Time</TimeZone>
      </component>
  </settings>
  <settings pass="oobeSystem">

<component name="Microsoft-Windows-Shell-Setup" processorArchitecture="amd64" pub
licKeyToken="31bf3856ad364e35" language="neutral" versionScope="nonSxS"
xmlns:wcm="http://schemas.microsoft.com/WMIConfig/2002/State" xmlns:xsi="http://
www.w3.org/2001/XMLSchema-instance">
            <OOBE>
                  <HideEULAPage>true</HideEULAPage>
                  <NetworkLocation>Work</NetworkLocation>
                  <ProtectYourPC>1</ProtectYourPC>
            </OOBE>
      </component>
  </settings>

<cpi:offlineImage cpi:source="wim:c:/w2008r2/install.wim#Windows Server 2008 R2
SERVERENTERPRISE" xmlns:cpi="urn:schemas-microsoft-com:cpi" />
</unattend>
```

You now have an answer file that is capable of answering all the questions that will be asked while installing Windows. All you need to do now is supply it to the OS installer.

Using an Answer File

This process is easy enough. You need to store the file `autounattend.xml` on the root of some form of removable storage. You will then boot up the new server using the correct Windows Server 2008 R2 media.

A WORD OF CAUTION

Don't go messing with this stuff on a machine that is valuable to you. Test it in a lab first. This is a destructive process; in other words, the hard disk on the computer you use for this will be wiped.

In our example, that will be the Windows Server 2008 R2 DVD. As soon as the server starts to boot from the DVD, you should also insert the removable storage that contains your answer file. The supported forms of removable storage are as follows:

CD/DVD   This requires your server to have two drives: a DVD drive to boot and install Windows Server 2008 R2 from and another drive to read the answer file CD or DVD.

Disk   How many servers have disk drives now? This will be OK for lab or older machines.

USB memory stick   This is the most likely of all the choices.

Pick your choice of media that is suitable for the server that you are going to build, and copy the answer file onto the root of that storage device.

If you are using a virtual machine, then here's a neat trick. Add a second virtual CD/DVD to the virtual machine where you intend to install Windows Server 2008 R2. Make sure your boot DVD has mounted the correct ISO for installing Windows. Create an ISO file that contains only your `autounattend.xml` file. Do not have a tool for that? That's OK, because there is one in WAIK. Try running the following from your Windows PE Tools command prompt:

```
oscdimg -n C:\Answer C:\answer.iso
```

This will create an ISO file on C:\ called `answer.iso` using the contents of the folder C:\ Answer. Please make sure you have not placed your `autounattend.xml` in C:\ and are trying to make an ISO file from your entire hard disk! It's an easy trap to fall into. The syntax for the previous is as follows:

```
oscdimg -n <Folder to Use as a Source> <Location and Name of the New ISO Image>
```

OK, let's get rocking! Insert your Windows Server 2008 R2 DVD into your boot DVD drive on your server.

You should insert your answer file media as soon as the server has started to boot from the DVD. The first few times you do this you should watch what goes on to make sure the process runs cleanly. What should happen is that Windows Server 2008 R2 silently kicks off an installation, reboots, and waits for you to set the administrator password so you can log in. If the answer file has a mistake, then something else will happen such as the following:

- A dialog box with a question will appear and wait for human input.

- An error dialog box will appear.

- A critical failure will occur and cause a reboot.

You will need to revisit your answer file in WSIM if any of these happens.

If you have gotten everything right, then you now have an answer file that will completely automate your manual installations of Windows Server 2008 R2. You've also gotten a peek into some of the steps required for automated installations.

Installing a Sample Server Network for This Book's Examples

You are going to need a laboratory or test network to practice what you learn in this book.

To follow along with the examples, build two servers using the clean installation or unattended installation method. Our recommendation is that you use both methods for your first attempt to build this lab network. You can then use the unattended installation method for all future builds to speed things along.

Customize each of the two servers using the following settings:

SERVER 1

ITEM	CONFIGURATION
Full Computer Name	bf1.bigfirm.com
IPv4 Configuration	Address: 192.168.1.51
	Subnet mask: 255.255.255.0
	Default gateway: 192.168.1.1
	DNS1: <blank>
	DNS2: <blank>

SERVER 2

ITEM	CONFIGURATION
Full Computer Name	bf2.bigfirm.com
IPv4 Configuration	Address: 192.168.1.52
	Subnet mask: 255.255.255.0
	Default gateway: 192.168.1.1
	DNS1: <blank>
	DNS2: <blank>

At this point, you will be the proud owner of your very first Windows Server 2008 R2 server network.

The Bottom Line

Upgrade your old servers   Microsoft has provided several upgrade options for Windows Server 2008 and Windows Server 2008 R2.

> **Master It**   You have a Windows 2000 file server. What will your upgrade path be to Windows Server 2008 R2?

Configure your server   Windows Server 2008 allows you to use Server Manager and `servermanagercmd.exe` to add or remove roles, role services, and features.

> **Master It**   You have started to deploy Windows Server 2008 R2. You are planning on automating as much of the build process as possible. What tool will you use to add or remove roles, role services, and features?

Build a small server farm   Installing Windows Server normally requires that you sit in front of the machine and answer a number of questions. This is time-consuming and distracts administrators from other engineering or project tasks that they could be working on. A number of alternative techniques can be employed.

> **Master It**   You have been instructed to build four new servers with Windows Server 2008 R2. This will be the first time your organization will deploy Windows Server 2008. Your department is short-staffed because a number of your colleagues are on vacation. You want to do this job quickly and efficiently. How will you do it?

Chapter 3

The New Server: Introduction to Server Core

Microsoft designs and develops the next version of its products based on what the market demands. In addition, it fends off the competition by integrating the strengths and features the others have to offer. Thus, with Server Core, Windows Server 2008 introduced a new approach to Windows operating systems to combat its competitors' edge and meet certain market demands of system administrators who want to work on the command line. Within this chapter, we'll explore this new operating system and how to manage it.

In this chapter, you will learn to:

- ◆ Explain the purposes for Server Core
- ◆ Install and configure Server Core
- ◆ Set up Server Core for a branch-office deployment
- ◆ Remotely manage the operating system

What in the World Is Server Core?

If you watch enough TV, you must endure the commercials of the shabbily dressed Mac slacker's cynical comments about the hard-working, productive PC guy. What productive thing does Mac have a corner on? Music and graphics. Yoo-hoo.

Well, there's another kid on the block that picks on PC. It's the ultra-geek who worships open source coding. He thinks that we can end world hunger and bring harmonic balance to the universe with the Linux operating system. Somehow, an OS that is free is better than one you pay for. Other than being "free," the ultra-geek's Linux system did have some serious advantages over Windows Server:

- ◆ With Linux, you don't have to install everything to run it. Windows Server 2003 and 2000 installation included the binaries for almost everything, and you couldn't trim out what you rarely run on a server such as Windows Audio and Internet Explorer.

- ◆ Since less is installed, less is taking up CPU cycles.

- ◆ Since less is installed, you have a reduced attack surface. Fewer services and less code within the server can be leveraged by the evil hacker to control the server.

- ◆ Since less is installed, less can break and needs to be patched. The stability of a system increases when you can strip away the extras.

Microsoft's answer to this is Server Core. It stripped Windows Server 2008 to the bare-minimum requirements to run an operating system. It removed the GUI, Windows Explorer, Internet Explorer, and other dependant components. Removing "extras" means we have to deal without much of the administration tools that we know and love, namely, snap-ins built on the Microsoft Management Console. This leaves the command prompt as our primary interface to the operating system.

Microsoft went on the marketing warpath with the following selling points:

Reduced maintenance   Less code has fewer updates to perform.

Reduced attack surface   Without the fluff, there is less to attack. Roles and features can be installed as needed and the limited number of services will reduce the areas for attack.

Reduced performance requirements   Server Core takes fewer CPU cycles and less hard disk space. So, the opportunity to repurpose hardware is increased with this option.

This brings us to the rub. You have a half dozen "pizza boxes" you want to turn around to do something else. (A *pizza box* is administrator slang for inexpensive 1U servers; these are thin rack mounted servers which could fit in a pizza box. They don't have much room for expansion.) You would like to add them to a web farm to support a newly released .NET web application that your company's developers cranked out in the past year. So, you take a look at Windows Server 2008 Server Core as a possible solution.

When Microsoft stripped the OS to the bare minimum, it had to leave out the .NET Framework too. The .NET Framework had specific dependencies to operating on Windows Server that were stripped from Server Core. This left a reduced list of available roles to work with. Basically, it was an infrastructure platform.

Here are the available roles for Windows Server 2008 Server Core:

◆ Active Directory Domain Services

◆ Active Directory Lightweight Directory Services (ADAM II)

◆ DHCP

◆ DNS

◆ File Services

◆ Print and Document Services

◆ Hyper-V

◆ Internet Information Services for static HTML and ASP pages

◆ Streaming Media

So, the "pizza boxes" have to be sidelined since .NET isn't available.

But Windows Server 2008 R2 improved on the first go by adding a compatible .NET Framework version. This means `.aspx` and `.asmx` web pages can be used. It also means PowerShell can run on it. Unfortunately, at the time of this writing, Windows Server 2008 R2 was not released as a 32-bit version. Because of hardware requirements, those "pizza boxes" may still be sidelined.

THE .NET ALTERNATIVE

In the world of competition, Novell produced a .NET Framework alternative that can run on the Windows Server 2008 Server Core installation. A major part of the .NET Framework is the runtime compilation of the .NET code. This allows the code to be transportable to other operating systems. However, somebody has to develop the engine or processes to translate the code into the host operating system for the transportability to work. Microsoft focused on Window systems only. Novell initiated the Mono project to support .NET code on Linux and Macs (http://mono-project.com). It also created a Windows version too, which can be installed on Server Core.

To get a feeling of how to implement this, you can visit the following site:

www.devsource.com/c/a/Architecture/Mixing-Server-Core-with-NET-Applications

This site gives an example of implementing a command-line .NET Framework application.

Here is the new list of roles available with Windows Server 2008 R2:

◆ Active Directory Certificate Services

◆ Active Directory Domain Services

◆ Active Directory Lightweight Directory Services (ADAM II)

◆ DHCP

◆ DNS

◆ File Services

◆ Print and Document Services

◆ Hyper-V

◆ Internet Information Services for static HTML and ASP pages and a subset of .NET pages

The infrastructure server will be a prevalent candidate for Server Core. With the inclusion of the read-only domain controller role and the Install from Media options for Active Directory, the operating system is a strong candidate for a branch-office deployment. This is the direction we'll take with Server Core in this chapter so you can repurpose those half dozen servers.

The infrastructure server is commonly deployed in every IT shop. It would provide basic file and print services and the big three Ds: domain controller, DNS, and DHCP. In the following example, we'll show how to set up a Server Core instance to provide these typical roles.

Installing Server Core

There is an important fact to keep in mind when planning to deploy Server Core. The operating system supports only a clean install. You cannot upgrade Server Core from a previous version of Windows. You cannot upgrade from a full Windows Server 2008 R2 installation. And you can't upgrade Server Core to a full Windows Server 2008 R2 installation.

The process for installing Windows Server 2008 R2 Server Core is as straightforward as other Windows Server 2008 R2 installations. You pop in the installation DVD and allow the server to boot from it. Then, you "follow the bouncing ball." An unattended installation .xml file can be used to configure the OS all the way down to the installed features. This can be generated with the Windows Automated Installation Kit, which will not be covered in this chapter.

The setup program offers the option of what operating system you would like to install, as shown in Figure 3.1. For Server Core, you can select the desired edition: Standard, Enterprise, or Datacenter.

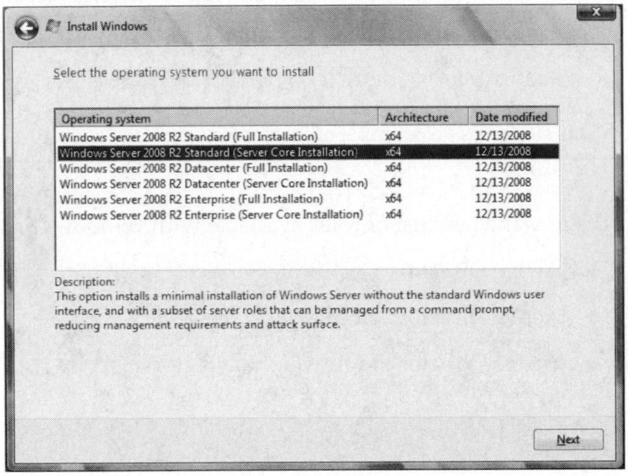

FIGURE 3.1
Selecting to install Server Core from the various editions of Windows Server 2008 R2

The next screen asks, "Where do you want to install Windows?" as shown in Figure 3.2. Assuming this is one of those "pizza boxes," they typically come with only two hard drives and an adequate SCSI controller to perform hardware-based mirroring. This would duplicate the contents on one drive to the other, providing a fault tolerance for one drive failure. So, the hardware would present only one drive to the OS and manage the mirroring in the background.

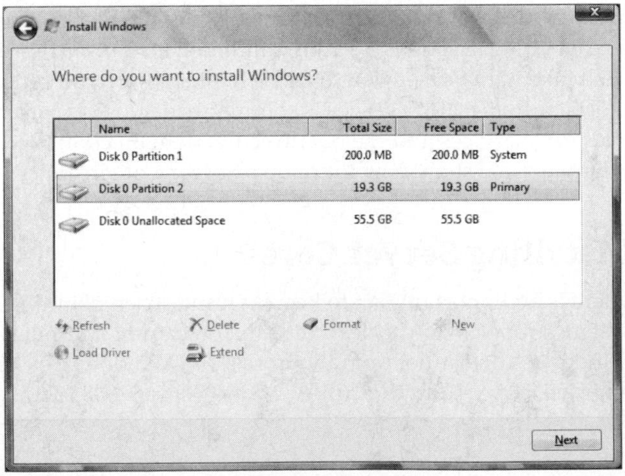

FIGURE 3.2
Choosing the installation partition

We prefer dividing the drive into two partitions: a small one such as 20GB for the operating system and the remainder for data or applications. This provides a smaller backup for the system drive. The tricky part of this is projecting the right size. Additional applications, service packs, security updates, and patches can drive up the overall size to the capacity of the small partition. This can cause system instability and potentially require a rebuild. The Server Core operating system does have a small footprint of 3GB, so 20GB will provide adequate headroom for growth.

Using the options on the bottom of the screen, we created the 20GB partition. The Windows setup also created the 200MB system partition. This holds the recovery console operating system. You can't delete this. Don't worry about this unavailable space; thumb drives come in bigger sizes now.

After an uneventful installation, you can select the Administrator account to log on as with a full installation. It doesn't have an assigned password, so you need to enter a new one. Once the installation has completed building the Administrator's profile, the desktop appears as shown in Figure 3.3, which looks very spartan. There's no Start menu, no taskbar, no system tray—no nuttin'. There's just an open command prompt.

Server Core lacks the dependencies, required code, that would support graphical user interfaces (GUIs). So, many current applications or services may not run on this installation as expected. Therefore, be certain to verify whether the application can run on it. An increasing number of server roles and applications will probably be modified to allow installation and administration on it in the next generation of releases.

FIGURE 3.3
The barren Server
Core user interface

For this book, the default settings for the command prompt have been changed for readability. The default is white letters on a black background. You can make these changes by right-clicking the upper-left corner and selecting Properties. Then you can modify the color of the fonts and backgrounds on the Colors tab, as shown in Figure 3.4.

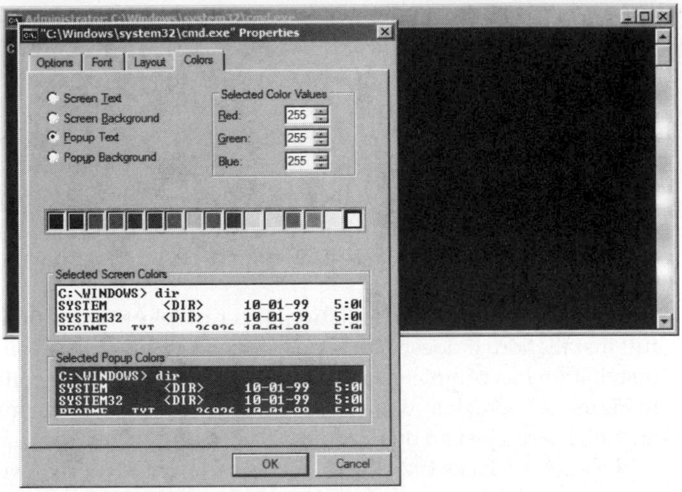

FIGURE 3.4
Modifying the
command prompt
window

Server Core Survival Guide

Before getting into the details of transforming this overgrown brick into a thriving infrastructure server, you need to learn a few survival tips on handling this operating system. The primary obstacle is getting used to the lack of GUI tools. We'll discuss accessing the Task Manager to control processes, start tasks, and view performance. Then we'll cover well-worn commands that we typically neglect when a flashy GUI is available. These will help you perform run-of-the-mill administration tasks and allow access to the network.

Accessing the Task Manager

Server Core provides a few graphical user interfaces. The most important is the Task Manager. It's the same one you have come to know and love with other Windows versions. There are two primary ways to open Task Manager.

Ctrl+Alt+Del   You can open the trustworthy Security dialog box by pressing the venerable Ctrl+Alt+Del key combination. On this page, you can opt to lock the workstation, log out, and even start Task Manager.

Ctrl+Shift+Esc   You can use the "MSCE secret handshake" method of the Ctrl+Shift+Esc key combination to start Task Manager. Now that you know this, you're part of an elite club. It was once one of those undocumented features.

Closing the Command Prompt

As a good system administrator, you close applications when you are done with them so as not to consume value resources such as memory and CPU cycles. Right? So, you will probably close the command prompt after completing a task while logged on to Server Core.

After the involuntary shriek or gasp of realizing you just closed your only interface to the OS, calmly perform the following steps:

1. Open the Task Manager, as discussed earlier.

2. Click File ➢ New Task (Run…). This is just like the Run prompt you find on the Start menu.

3. Enter **cmd**, and then click OK, as you can see in Figure 3.5.

Changing the Administrator's Password

After logging onto a Server Core installation for the first time, you might be thinking, "How am I going to change the Administrator password in the future?"

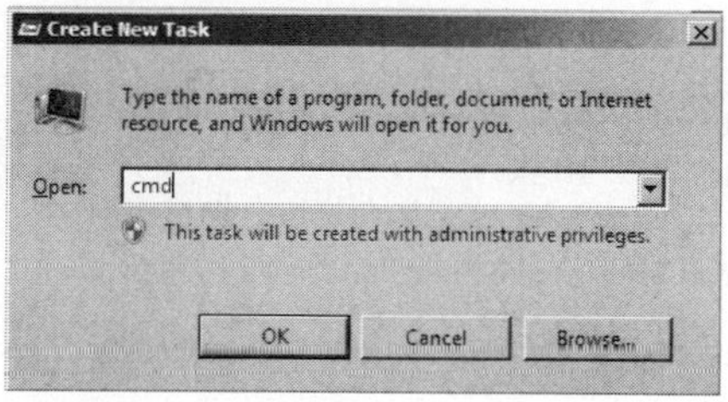

FIGURE 3.5
Create New
Task window

The answer is using the net user command. It is simply the following:

```
C:\Users\Administrator>net user administrator *
Type a password for the user:
Retype the password to confirm:
The command completed successfully.
```

The asterisk prompts for the new password.

Much of the commands used to administer Server Core have been available with previous versions. So, given your experience level with the command line on full installations of Windows, you may be able to get around Server Core with ease.

The net command is a really old one. It was old when NT was actually "new technology."

This command can perform a boatload of additional tasks that you would first think of doing using the Computer Management console. Here are just a few of the fun things you can do with it:

◆ Start and stop services

◆ Add local users

◆ Manage local groups

◆ Create share folders

Several of these will be covered later in the chapter. This command is also useful with another survival tip: accessing file shares.

Accessing File Shares

Given Windows Server is a network operating system, you will have to access shares on the network. If you're dependent on Windows Explorer, you may have never attempted to connect to a shared folder with the command prompt. First, to display the shares on a server, use the net view command:

```
C:\Users\Administrator>net view \\bf1
Shared resources at \\bf1

Share name  Type    Used as  Comment

-------------------------------------------------------------------------------
isos        Disk
netlogon    Disk
Public      Disk
SYSVOL      Disk
temp        Disk
The command completed successfully.
```

Then, to access a volume, use the net use command, which maps a share to a drive letter:

```
C:\Users\Administrator>net use Z: \\bf1\temp
The command completed successfully
```

Then within the command prompt, you can switch to that drive by entering the drive letter like **Z:**. Then use your MS-DOS commands to get around the folders.

To remove the mapped drive, use the following command:

```
C:\Users\Administrator>net use Z: /del
Z: was deleted successfully
```

Finding Commands from A to Z

Command-line references are very handy. There is one in Windows Server 2008 R2 for help on the full installation; however, it has Internet hyperlinks to the explanations for all of those commands. The best location for finding a listing of available commands is the *Command-Line Reference A-Z* (http://technet.microsoft.com/en-us/library/cc778084.aspx). To find a command that will do the job, this is the first place to go.

If a reference book is more your speed or you are in a seriously locked-down network where you can't even think of resourcing sites on the Internet, I recommend *Administering Windows Server 2008 Server Core* by John Paul Mueller (Sybex, 2008).

Finding Command Syntax: The Question Mark

When you need to know the syntax of a command with all of its parameters, just think about Batman's nemesis the Riddler. He had a big question mark on his chest. Type the command followed by a **?**, and you will most likely get a blur of lines. This is the embedded help documentation for the command. Even if you type the command parameters incorrectly, this will probably be the output. The computer is guessing you don't know what you are doing and need some help.

Oddly, ? doesn't always produce the best information. Sometimes you need -? or /? or even `help` for a more informed help explanation. But ? will get you on your way. Microsoft just didn't standardize this very well.

If you can't read very fast, that blur of lines is not very helpful. In fact, you may like to read it at your own leisure. A little trick is the port option >, which ports the output to a text file. For instance, if you need to know the parameters for the `ipconfig` command, you can port it to a file like this:

```
C:\Users\Administrator>ipconfig ? > documents\ipconfigCommand.txt
```

Another neat trick is the "double port" option >>, which appends the output to the end of the text file instead of overwriting it. Sweet!

Since the command prompt is open at the Administrator's profile location, the documents folder can be addressed without the full path. This dumps the file in the Administrator's My Documents folder.

Reading Text Files with Notepad

Now that you have produced a text file, you will need to read it. In a full installation, we use Notepad. It's also available in Server Core. This Notepad utility is "old school"; it was a rerelease of a very early version. It's not as old school as VI, but it has been resurrected from the days of NT. (If you get that comment, you *are* old.)

Incredibly, the designers of Server Core were actually thinking about dropping this handy tool until the marketing guys got feedback from users. This would have been a huge mistake. Notepad is an essential tool for Server Core.

To open the text file, use the following command:

```
C:\Users\Administrator>notepad documents\ipconfigCommand.txt
```

We like using Notepad to construct complex commands. At the bottom of a help text file like this one, you can cut, paste, and edit the examples to get what you need. Then you can cut and paste them into the command prompt. The output can be copied from the command window using the Mark command in the context menu, which you display by right-clicking the window. Then paste it back into Notepad for the record. Using the question mark and Notepad was the primary method of hashing out the commands throughout this chapter.

Reverse Engineering

Although this is not exactly reverse engineering, it reminds us of it.

All of the tasks performed on Server Core can be done on a standard installation using the graphical user interface such as the Microsoft Management Consoles. All of the commands that support Server Core are available on the standard installations also.

When encountering unfamiliar territory, one technique you might find useful is configuring a standard installation with the GUI as you would plan to a Server Core installation. With this step, you could reference what the essential parameters were and then run through the applicable commands to replicate the same settings. You could save the commands in a batch file and then run them on the Server Core without any issues.

Editing the Registry

SCRegedit.wsf is a script developed by the Server Core team to perform common tasks that involve editing the registry. You can use the parameter /cli to list common tasks on Server Core. It may not be all-inclusive for what you need to do, but it does list the "MSCE secret handshake" for opening the Task Manager.

Since scregedit.wsf is a VB script, you have to run it through an interpreter. It's located in the System32 folder, so you have to change the directory to it:

```
C:\Windows\System32>cscript scregedit.wsf /cli
```

Rebooting and Shutting Down

There's a command to reboot and shut down the server too. You can even enter the cause and comment for the reboot or shutdown. You can use the following for rebooting a server:

```
C:\Users\Administrator>shutdown /r /m \\bfscl /t 30
```

◆ /r is for reboot.

◆ /m is the machine using the UNC path. It can be used for shutting down remote machines too. This is fun to use in a classroom environment. (Ha-ha!) For work environments, it's not too funny. For some reason, people lose their sense of humor at work.

◆ /t is for seconds to delay the action.

TOO SEXY

A fellow admin, Chad, told us his experience with the shutdown command. At a large enterprise datacenter, he had the responsibility of applying security patches to hundreds of servers over one weekend. He generated a script that used this command to reboot the servers. Offhandedly, he added the comment "Chad is too sexy!" for the reason of the reboot.

When the script kicked off, it performed flawlessly. However, the company's network operation center was getting notifications of reboots along with the comment.

Monday morning, Chad was asked to explain to the IT manager why the servers were suffering spontaneous reboots when he walked through the datacenter.

Initial Configurations for Server Core

When you log onto a full installation, the Initial Configuration Tasks window, Figure 3.6, is displayed. As dutiful administrators, you follow the steps 1, 2, and 3, and you are good to go. You have transformed the brick into an infrastructure server. Unfortunately, this will never pop up in Server Core. So, we will walk you through these steps through the command prompt to get the server running.

FIGURE 3.6

Initial Configuration Tasks window on a standard Windows installation

Step 1: Provide Computer Information

In the Initial Configuration Tasks window, step 1 lists four essential tasks to get the ball rolling. All of these can be performed from the command line.

1. Add a product ID key and activate the server.

2. Set the time zone.

3. Configure networking.

4. Provide a computer name and domain.

ENTERING THE PRODUCT KEY AND ACTIVATING THE INSTALLATION

If you haven't noticed, the Windows Server 2008 R2 installation process doesn't require a product key. The operating system will require it eventually; for Windows Server 2008 R2, it's 60 days. On full installations when that happens, you will experience the reduced functionality mode (RFM). This will give you a black desktop and persistent notifications, and Windows Update will apply only critical security patches.

The slmgr.vbs script performs the operations of installing the product key and activation. The traditional process includes installing the key followed by online activation. Note in the following command example and later that rem is a remark that isn't processed by the command prompt or batch files.

```
rem Entering the product ID key
cscript c:\windows\system32\slmgr.vbs
-ipk q7y83-w4fvq-6mc6c-6qqtd-tpm88
Microsoft (R) Windows Script Host Version 5.8
```

```
Copyright (C) Microsoft Corporation. All rights reserved.

Installed product key q7y83-w4fvq-6mc6c-6qqtd-tpm88 successfully.
```

The online activation is also performed with the same script:

```
rem online activation
cscript  c:\windows\system32\slmgr.vbs -ato
```

In larger environments, volume licensing is the predominant method of obtaining Microsoft software. The volume activation process has changed significantly with the release of Windows Vista and Windows Server 2008. This new process can include the Key Management Service (KMS), which centralizes the activation to a server within the organization. Since this scenario is talking about a branch-office deployment, we'll discuss setting up the KMS on this server later in the section "Managing Licenses with Key Management Service."

SETTING THE TIME ZONE

Server Core isn't completely devoid of Control Panel graphic user interfaces: the Time and Date control panel is one that was left. The following command opens it:

```
control timedate.cpl
```

To validate the change, you can use this command:

```
C:\Users\Administrator>w32tm /tz
Time zone: Current:TIME_ZONE_ID_DAYLIGHT Bias: 300min (UTC=LocalTime+Bias)
  [Standard Name:"Eastern Standard Time" Bias:0min Date:(M:10 D:5 DoW:0)]
  [Daylight Name:"Eastern Daylight Time" Bias:-60min Date:(M:4 D:1 DoW:0)]
```

CONFIGURING THE NETWORK SETTINGS

The primary item that needs to change for the network is to assign a static IP address. To start off with, you need the name of the network connection. ipconfig /all will list the name of each network connection:

```
C:\Users\Administrator\Documents>ipconfig /all

Windows IP Configuration

        Host Name . . . . . . . . . . . : WIN-AG6PVO7DM2A
        Primary Dns Suffix  . . . . . . :
        Node Type . . . . . . . . . . . : Hybrid
        IP Routing Enabled. . . . . . . : No
        WINS Proxy Enabled. . . . . . . : No
        DNS Suffix Search List. . . . . : localdomain

Ethernet adapter Local Area Connection:

        Connection-specific DNS Suffix  . : localdomain
        Description . . . . . . . . . . : Intel(R) PRO/1000 MT Network Connection
```

```
Physical Address. . . . . . . . . : 00-0C-29-C9-F2-4B
DHCP Enabled. . . . . . . . . . . : Yes
Autoconfiguration Enabled . . . . : Yes
Link-local IPv6 Address . . . . . : fe80::b5a1:157f:7220:4f4c%3(Preferred)
IPv4 Address. . . . . . . . . . . : 192.168.1.136(Preferred)
Subnet Mask . . . . . . . . . . . : 255.255.255.0
Lease Obtained. . . . . . . . . . : Tuesday, May 19, 2009 1:42:26 PM
Lease Expires . . . . . . . . . . : Tuesday, May 19, 2009 2:12:25 PM
Default Gateway . . . . . . . . . :
DHCP Server . . . . . . . . . . . : 192.168.1.254
DHCPv6 IAID . . . . . . . . . . . : 50334761
DHCPv6 Client DUID. . . . . . . . : 00-01-00-01-11-A3-96-87-00-0C-29-C9-F2-4B

DNS Servers . . . . . . . . . . . : 192.168.1.254
NetBIOS over Tcpip. . . . . . . . : Enabled
```

By default, we have the aptly named Local Area Connection. This will be used in the `netsh interface` command:

```
netsh interface ipv4 set address name="Local Area Connection" source=static
address=192.168.1.11 mask=255.255.255.0 gateway=192.168.1.254
```

Since we don't like the default name, we want to change it to something like Internal. So, we did some pecking with the question mark and the `netsh` command. Eventually, we found this:

```
c:\Users\Administrator\Documents>netsh interface set interface /?

Usage set interface [name = ] IfName
            [ [admin = ] ENABLED|DISABLED
            [connect = ] CONNECTED|DISCONNECTED
            [newname = ] NewName ]

    Sets interface parameters.

    IfName  - the name of the interface
    admin   - whether the interface should be enabled
    connect - whether to connect the interface (non-LAN only).
    newname - new name for the interface (LAN only).

    Notes:
    - At least one option other than the name must be specified.
    - If connect = CONNECTED is specified, then the interface
      is automatically enabled even if the admin = DISABLED
      option is specified.

Examples:

    set interface name="Local Area Connection" admin=DISABLED
    set interface name="Local Area Connection" newname="Connection 1"
```

"Looky there, there's an example for changing the interface name." As we mentioned about Notepad, we copied the example and edited it. It ran effortlessly:

```
netsh interface set interface name="local area connection" newname="Internal"
```

We also changed the DNS server:

```
netsh interface ipv4 add dnsserver name="Internal" address=192.168.1.10 index=1
```

PROVIDING A COMPUTER NAME AND DOMAIN

The Windows setup program assigns a really imaginative computer name. You can find that using the hostname command:

```
c:\Users\Administrator\Documents>hostname
WIN-AG6PVO7DM2A
```

Since that isn't very user friendly, we'll change it to Bfsc1. (It's not a huge improvement, but at least we can type it without our fingers getting in a knot.) We will add it to the Bigfirm.com domain too. Both actions are performed with the netdom command. Now since we mentioned the netdom command, old-timers are starting to look for the support.msi file on the installation disk. This was where you once could find the command. Look no further because it is installed in the operating system by default.

The following command is to rename the computer:

```
netdom renamecomputer WIN-AG6PVO7DM2A /NewName:Bfsc1 /reboot:5
```

The /reboot parameter does just what you would think. Renames require reboots, so it can be added to the command to trigger it. Then the domain join can take place:

```
netdom join bfsc1 /domain:Bigfirm.com /userd:Administrator /passwordd:P@ssw0rd
/reboot:5
```

The netdom command is discussed in more detail in Chapter 23 because it is useful for creating trusts and assisting in the administration of computer accounts.

Step 2: Update This Server

Moving on to step 2, we'll perform the typical housekeeping chores to bring the server to the latest revisions and security patches. Step 2 consists of two substeps:

1. Enable automatic updating and feedback.

2. Download and install updates.

ENABLING AUTOMATIC UPDATING AND FEEDBACK

The scregedit.wsf script returns to action. The /au parameter enables or disables automatic updates with the values 4 and 0, respectively. Enabling is equivalent to Automatic in Windows Automatic Updates. If you are familiar with the Windows Automatic Updates options, there are two others: Notify and Download and Notify. These are not available with Server Core. So, if you have an environment that likes to test the security patches or control when they are applied, you will have to set up WSUS to manage this.

After the change is made, you need to restart the Automatic Updates service. This uses the net stop and net start commands. The tricky part of these commands is to get the right name of the service. Some of the time, you can use the display name such as Automatic Updates, but it should be contained in quotes and spelling counts. If the display name can't be located, the command doesn't perform the action. The actual service name works every time, and it is found in the registry under HKLM\System\CurrentControlSet\Services. However, the actual service name isn't as intuitive as the display name. You might guess that service for Automatic Updates starts with the letter *A*, but it does not. Its name is "wuauserv." (There is another command, sc, that you can use to perform restarts, which we'll discuss later in "Configuring the DHCP Service.") The following is the code to enable the Automatic Updates service:

```
rem navigate to the System32 folder
cd c:\windows\system32\
rem enable automatic updates
cscript scregedit /au 4

net stop wuauserv
net start wuauserv
```

To view the current settings for Automatic Updates, you can use the /v parameter:

```
c:\Windows\System32>cscript scregedit.wsf /au /v
Microsoft (R) Windows Script Host Version 5.8
Copyright (C) Microsoft Corporation. All rights reserved.

SOFTWARE\Microsoft\Windows\CurrentVersion\WindowsUpdate\Auto Update AUOptions
View registry setting.
4
```

If you play enough with this command, you may figure out how they got the name…probably "Server Core Regedit?" Hmmmm. It basically performs registry modifications, so you may be wondering if regedit is available.

Registry Editor is another GUI application available on Server Core, as shown in Figure 3.7.

FIGURE 3.7
The Registry Editor on Server Core

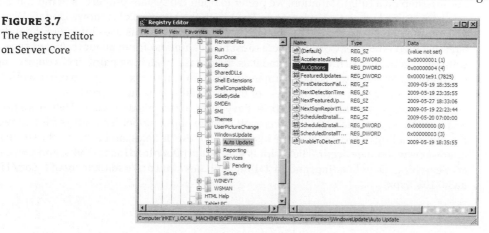

The highlighted value was modified to 4 to enable the Automatic Updates service. It's good to know this utility is available.

By default, error reporting/feedback is enabled on Windows Server 2008 R2 Server Core. To verify or disable it, you can use the serverweroptin.exe command. (You have to appreciate those developers who can come up with a name that you can't even pronounce.) The following is the output of the /query option:

```
C:\Users\administrator.BIGFIRM>serverweroptin /query

Current Windows Error Reporting Setting:
Automatically send detailed reports

Windows can send descriptions of problems
on this server to Microsoft. If you choose to
automatically send generic information about
a problem, Microsoft will use the information
to start working on a solution.

For more information on Windows Error Reporting,
refer to the privacy statement at
http://go.microsoft.com/fwlink/?linkid=50163
For Windows privacy information, please visit
http://go.microsoft.com/fwlink/?LinkID=104288
```

Just to make Server Core more confusing, the developers decided to change the method to modify error reporting from Windows Server 2008's release. With the previous version, you would use the SCRegedit.wsf /er command. This isn't the only instance where you need to know what version you are on when administering Server Core; we'll cover this later in "Adding Roles and Features."

DOWNLOADING AND INSTALLING UPDATES

For this step on a full installation, we prefer to open the system properties of the computer and navigate to the Automatic Updates tab. Then click the hyperlink Windows Update Web Site to kick off the download and installation of patches. However, this uses Internet Explorer, which isn't installed on Server Core. So, there must be a command for it: wuauclt /detectnow. This command generates as much excitement as the phrase "watching paint dry" conjures up. It just sits there. At least it returns the command prompt to you so you can get to other work, but it provides no indication of the progress of the application of security patches.

The developers of the MSDN website have recognized this deficiency. They have provided a sample VBS script that uses the Microsoft.Update object model. This VBS script allows for the downloading of the updates, the installation of the updates, and echoing the results of the operations when they occur. The script is WUA_SearchDownloadInstall.vbs, and you can find it at "Searching, Downloading, and Installing Updates" (http://msdn.microsoft.com/library/aa387102.aspx).

SAMPLE SCRIPT DISCLAIMER

Remember, scripts you might find on the Microsoft websites are samples, which means "You are on your own." Microsoft stands behind the object model that it develops, but scripting is different. You have the ability to modify it; thus, you have the opportunity to "destroy." You should understand that your scripts and samples may error out or have syntax errors. It's up to you to generate an error-free script to do what you want to do. Since this chapter is devoted to explaining Server Core, a description of VBS scripting and detailed discussions of any samples will be left for another time and place.

Step 3: Customize This Server

In this step, we get into applying the infrastructure roles and enabling for remote administration. The Initial Configuration Tasks window lists these substeps:

1. Add roles.
2. Add features.
3. Enable Remote Desktop.
4. Configure Windows Firewall.

ADDING ROLES AND FEATURES

The Server Manager console introduced in the full installation of Windows Server 2008 made the installation of roles and features straightforward. Basically, you select the box, and it's installed. If there are prerequisites that need to be installed in addition to the desired role, the Add Role Wizard will notify you. Then it will install them for you. In Server Core, it is similar. Typically, one command does the trick. The command results will notify you of any prerequisites but won't install them. So, you will have multiple commands to add prerequisites and the roles.

As mentioned in the "Enabling Automatic Updating and Feedback" discussion, the developers made changes to commands for Windows Server 2008 R2 Server Core from Windows Server 2008 Server Core. Here is another place to be on your toes about what version you are working with. Windows Server 2008 uses the `oclist` command to view available roles and the `ocsetup` command to install them. Windows Server 2008 R2 uses `dism`, which stands for the "Deployment Image Servicing and Management Tool." They work similarly, but no doubt you will be typing one of these commands on the wrong version eventually.

The roles we are going to add are a domain controller (Active Directory Domain Services), DNS, DHCP, and Print and Document Services. Basic file services are already installed and supported with the File Server role service. We'll add a couple features as well: Windows Server Backup to provide a backup capability and PowerShell.

The following statement lists the available roles and features together. Remember, with Windows Server 2008, you use OCList:

```
rem list available (enabled and disabled) roles
dism /online /get-features /format:table
```

Then you can use the same command to install each of the roles and features. For Windows Server 2008, you use the `ocsetup` command. Notice the `featurename` parameter is case sensitive.

```
rem add DHCP role
dism /online /enable-feature /featurename:DHCPServerCore

rem add printer role
dism /online /enable-feature /featurename:Printing-ServerCore-Role
rem this printer role is for 32 bit drivers
dism /online /enable-feature /featurename:Printing-ServerCore-Role-WOW64

rem a prerequisite for NetFx3-ServerCore
dism /online /enable-feature /featurename:NetFx2-ServerCore

rem add ad domain services and DNS server roles
dism /online /enable-feature /featurename:NetFx3-ServerCore
dism /online /enable-feature /featurename:DNS-Server-Core-Role
dism /online /enable-feature /featurename:DirectoryServices-DomainController-
ServerFoundation

rem add Windows Server Backup feature
dism /online /enable-feature /featurename:WindowsServerBackup

rem add powershell feature for the fun of it
dism /online /enable-feature /featurename:MicrosoftWindowsPowerShell
dism /online /enable-feature /featurename:ActiveDirectory-PowerShell
dism /online /enable-feature /featurename:WindowsServerBackupCommandlet
```

ENABLING REMOTE DESKTOP

Again, the SCRegedit.wsf script comes to our assistance. The command parameters are as follows:

- ◆ /ar: This means "Administration Remote Desktop" and is followed by a value of either 0 for enabled or 1 for disabled:

  ```
  c:\Windows\System32>cscript scregedit.wsf /ar 0
  ```

- ◆ Like the Automatic Updates option, the /v parameter allows you to view the current setting:

  ```
  rem view remote desktop settings
  c:\Windows\System32>cscript scregedit.wsf /ar /v
  Microsoft (R) Windows Script Host Version 5.8
  Copyright (C) Microsoft Corporation. All rights reserved.

  System\CurrentControlSet\Control\Terminal Server fDenyTSConnections
  View registry setting.
  0
  ```

♦ If you plan to connect to the installation with "legacy" workstations like XP, you will have to lower the security settings for RDP:

```
c:\windows\system32>cscript scregedit.wsf /cs 0
```

CONFIGURING THE FIREWALL

There are some firewall configurations to perform. The firewall needs to allow Remote Administration protocols through. This includes the ports to allow communication that the Microsoft Management Console snap-ins require. The following command enables protocols associated with the Remote Administration group:

```
netsh advfirewall firewall set rule group="Remote Administration" new enable=yes
```

This group includes all the MMC ports that can be accessed on the server. There are subsets of the protocols so you can have a finer-grained firewall policies to remotely manage specific MMC operations such as Event Viewer, Disk Management, File and Print Services, and Task Scheduler.

Surprisingly, this doesn't include Remote Desktop. This is part of its own group with the same name. It should be enabled with the following command, which by the way is the example in the embedded help of `netsh advfirewall firewall set rule`. No real wizardry was performed by generating this one. (The new parameter indicates adding a new setting to the rule.)

```
netsh advfirewall firewall set rule group="Remote Desktop" new enable=yes
```

If you want to administer the firewall from an MMC console, you will need to also run the following command:

```
netsh advfirewall set currentprofile settings remotemanagement enable
```

This is very helpful in administering the firewall because, as you may deduce from the command, `netsh advfirewall firewall set rule` tends to be bulky. Using a full Windows Server 2008 R2 installation, we created a new MMC console and added the Windows Firewall with Advanced Security snap-in while selecting to connect to the Server Core installation, as shown in Figure 3.8.

FIGURE 3.8
Windows Firewall snap-in

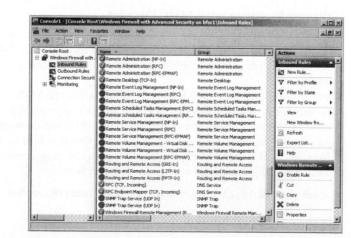

In Figure 3.8, the Remote Administration group and the Remote Desktop group are at the top of the center pane. When the Remote Administration group was enabled, it enabled three rules. The Remote Desktop group, which is also enabled, has only one rule. In addition, below these groups you will see four other "Remote…" groups. As we mentioned, these are the finer-tuned Remote Administration groups.

Administering Server Core Remotely

Before you get into configuring the roles you installed on the server, you need to be aware of the options for remote administration. We've touched on them briefly, and you will see them being used in the configurations of the roles in the following sections.

Remote Desktop is a very reliable and secure method of administering remote standard installations, and it is available on Server Core as well. The Microsoft Management Consoles or snap-ins are excellent for Server Core administration as long as the network supports it. A new option is Windows Remote Shell, which provides a command-line connection to the remote server.

MANAGING SERVERS WITH REMOTE DESKTOP

Terminal Services (Administration mode) was released with Windows 2000. It was the cat's meow because it provided a virtual desktop environment of that computer to which you connected. Windows Server 2003 improved it by making it a default installation. It is an essential method to perform remote work on servers. We have commonly installed and configured applications on Windows servers located on the opposite side of the North American continent using this method. So, this is a reliable option for Server Core.

With Windows Server 2008 R2 Server Core, you have to realize the desktop will still be just the command prompt and a few GUI tools. It will be the same as logged on locally. There are methods of publishing just the command prompt of Server Core to your desktop as a RemoteApp. However, we don't recommend using this. You will still need GUI tools such as Task Manager, Notepad, and the Registry Editor, which are part of your Server Core survival gear.

Remember, Remote Desktop and its firewall policy must be enabled to have it available. This was performed in the earlier "Initial Configurations for Server Core" section.

MANAGING REMOTELY WITH MMC SNAP-INS

Administrators have found the Microsoft Management Console to be a very versatile method of managing remote computers. Its strength lies in the use of the RPC protocol and the integrated Windows authentication. So, it is quick and efficient in managing domain-based computers within a LAN.

When computers are outside of these boundaries, the MMC snap-in loses its power. When the computer is behind a firewall, the RPC protocol is typically filtered out, so you lose connectivity with the tools. If the computer is part of a different domain or workgroup, authentication breaks down. So, you will have to consider whether this will be a viable option for your servers.

You can work around the authentication with alternate credentials. On the workstation, you run the following command to register these credentials:

```
cmdkey /add:bfsc1 /user:Administrator /pass:P@ssw0rd
```

You could opt to leave the /pass parameter off to be prompted for the password. After this is performed, you can connect to the server through the snap-in.

In previous versions of Windows Server, you needed to install the adminpak.msi package to have the snap-ins manage all the Windows services. Otherwise, you would have to install the service to make the snap-ins available. In Windows Server 2008 and R2, the adminpak.msi package is replaced by the Remote Server Administration Tools feature. This makes its installation easier and more fine-tuned. In Figure 3.9, you can see the DCHP Server Tools feature has been enabled through the Add Features Wizard.

FIGURE 3.9

Installing the
Remote Server
Administration
Tools feature

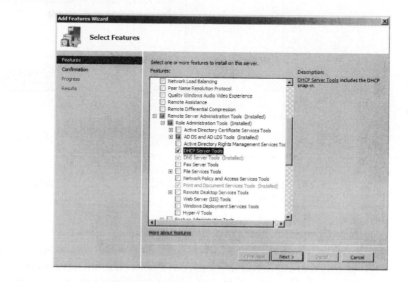

If you haven't tried before, you can connect to another computer when you add a snap-in to a new MMC. Some snap-ins allow multiple servers to be added into one tree for consolidated administration. The following steps create an MMC for managing the DHCP service on the Windows Server 2008 R2 Server Core installation. Please note that these steps can be performed only after the DHCP service is started and authorized. This is discussed in the "Configuring the DHCP Service" section.

1. After installing the DHCP Server Tools on a full installation, at the Run prompt enter **MMC**.

2. From the File drop-down menu, select Add/Remove Snap-in.

3. The Add/Remove Snap-in window is presented and lists the available snap-ins you can add to this MMC instance.

4. Select the DHCP snap-in, and click Add. And then click OK.

5. In the MMC, right-click the DHCP icon, and select Add Server.

6. In the Add Server window, the authorized DHCP servers are listed in the bottom area, as shown in Figure 3.10. Select the Server Core instance.

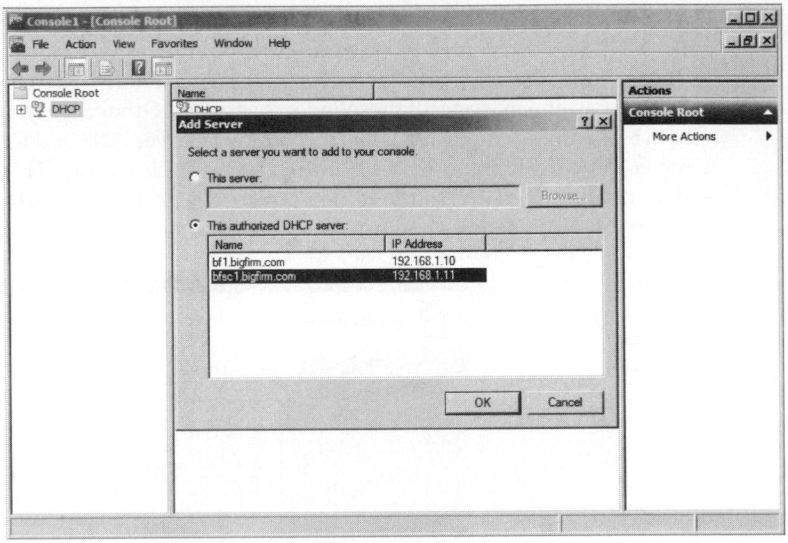

FIGURE 3.10
Adding a DHCP
server to an MMC

FIGURE 3.10
Adding a DHCP
server to an MMC

7. After clicking OK, the selected DHCP server is displayed and can be navigated through, as shown in Figure 3.11.

SENDING COMMANDS REMOTELY: WINDOWS REMOTE SHELL

Windows Remote Shell is relatively new; it allows commands to be sent to a server. Similar to Telnet, this will allow you to connect to a server and then run a command from a remote command prompt. However, it doesn't allow a continuous connection like Telnet provides. It sends the command, receives the results, and then closes the connection.

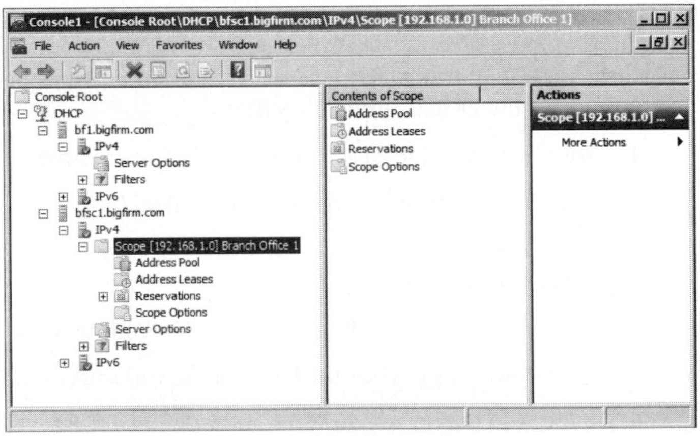

FIGURE 3.11
DHCP console
focused on the
Server Core
instance

This is a light client-server application based on the Simple Object Access Protocol (SOAP) technology. For this service, all you really need to understand about SOAP is that the client uses XML-formatted text to send the command to the server, and the output sent back to the client is in the same format using HTTP. Text-based communication can be easily read with text editors like Notepad, and HTTP is easy to sniff with a protocol analyzer. So, don't consider it a secure method of managing a server. You will have to lock it down.

Microsoft offers an option for test-driving Windows Remote Shell with the `winrm quickconfig` command. However, it sets it up with HTTP with the TCP port 5985. This, as they recommend, is not meant for production environments. To lock it down, you will want to ensure the communication is encrypted and the server is authenticated. IPsec provides this security. However, you may not have that available. You can set Windows Remote Shell for HTTPS (SSL) communication, which uses a server-based certificate to authenticate the server and encrypt the connection.

We will go through the basic steps to get this flying.

GETTING A CERTIFICATE

There are two options in getting a certificate: buy one from a repudiated certificate authority or set up your own certificate authority and request a certificate from it. The latter is much less expensive, especially using Windows Server.

Your own certificate authority is also not hard to set up; however, you should have a fully baked plan on how this will be accomplished for a production Active Directory environment. There are decisions to consider that will have lasting effects throughout the organization. And these effects will require manual administration to remove it. This section will not detail this. We're going to be "quick and dirty" on this as in a lab environment.

On the full installation Windows Server 2008 R2 domain controller, the Active Directory Certificate Services role is installed. A typical installation of this role would include the web enrollment component. This would require Internet Information Services (IIS). We don't want to go through the pain of getting that installed. We will only select the Certificate Authority service. This will allow the creation and administration of certificates. In addition, it will allow the computers of the domain to request certificates using the RPC protocol and Kerberos authentication. We will install a *trusted root enterprise certificate authority*. Root is selected because it is the first and only one in the organization. Enterprise is selected because it uses Active Directory to verify servers and users are trustworthy. Since it uses Active Directory, it automatically issues verified users and computers. Since Bfsc1 is a domain controller, it automatically requests a certificate. Quick and dirty.

On Server Core, we want to view the certificate. (We first tried using the MMC remotely, but for security reasons, this is not an option.) There are two methods of viewing certificates on the Server Core installation: the `certutil` command or PowerShell's `dir` command.

```
rem using certutil
C:\Users\Administrator.BIGFIRM\Documents>certutil -viewstore my
my
```

The my refers to the local machine store's own certificates. When this is run, a window is displayed listing the installed certificates, as shown in Figure 3.12.

FIGURE 3.12
Certificates
displayed by
`certutil`

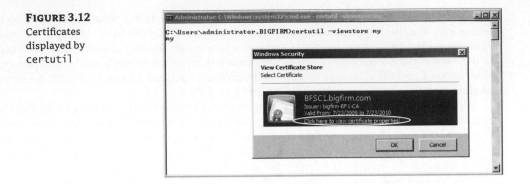

Notice there is a hyperlink underneath the only installed certificate, "Click here to view certificate properties." This will open the certificate information, as shown in Figure 3.13.

FIGURE 3.13
Certificate
properties

Thumbprint is highlighted because it will be used later in setting up the Windows Remote Shell HTTPS listener. You can copy and paste this value in Notepad.

PowerShell offers another route to get to the certificates through its providers. Generally, the provider is a group of objects that PowerShell navigates through. The file system is an example of a provider, so you can do operations on file and folder objects within it. Another provider is the certificate store. You can navigate through the certificate store to view and manage certificates.

The `dir` command is an alias created by the PowerShell developers for the `get-items` command. Thus, you can use your standard MS-DOS command to navigate through the file system. The following command lists the same location as the `certutil` command did earlier:

```
rem starting powershell
C:\Users\Administrator.BIGFIRM >powershell
```

```
Windows PowerShell V2
Copyright (C) 2008 Microsoft Corporation. All rights reserved.



PS C:\Users\administrator.BIGFIRM> dir cert:\localmachine\my | FL



Subject      : CN=BFSC1.bigfirm.com
Issuer       : CN-bigfirm-BF1-CA, DC=bigfirm, DC=com
Thumbprint   : 03ADB670C63E8D1CDB764CD7AA589C51D854307C
FriendlyName :
NotBefore    : 7/23/2009 6:55:41 PM
NotAfter     : 7/23/2010 6:55:41 PM
Extensions   : {System.Security.Cryptography.Oid, System.Security.Cryptography.
               Oid, System.Security.Cryptography.Oid, System.Security.Cryptogra
               phy.Oid...}
```

The | FL parameter is actually another command in shorthand. It formats the output of the dir command into a line-delimited list. We like using this format because the values are not truncated as the table format tends to do. In this specific case, the table format (not shown) doesn't truncate the most important value, the thumbprint.

CREATING A LISTENER

The listener tells the Windows Remote Shell service on what port and IP address to listen and respond to client requests. By default, the HTTP port is 5985, and the HTTPS port is 5986. You can view the default settings with the following command. In the following output, the attributes <cfg:HTTP> and <cfg:HTTPS> indicate the port settings. Despite what you may think about XML, the parameter of the command is format: pretty . The output appears redundant. However, the top half starting with <cfg:Client> is for the client settings which would send requests to other servers. The lower half starting with <cfg:Service> is for the service which receives the requests to run on this server.

```
C:\Users\administrator.BIGFIRM>winrm get winrm/config -format:pretty
<cfg:Config xml:lang="en-US" xmlns:cfg="http://schemas.microsoft.com/wbem/wsman/
1/config">
    <cfg:MaxEnvelopeSizekb>150</cfg:MaxEnvelopeSizekb>
    <cfg:MaxTimeoutms>60000</cfg:MaxTimeoutms>
    <cfg:MaxBatchItems>32000</cfg:MaxBatchItems>
    <cfg:MaxProviderRequests>4294967295</cfg:MaxProviderRequests>
    <cfg:Client>
        <cfg:NetworkDelayms>5000</cfg:NetworkDelayms>
        <cfg:URLPrefix>wsman</cfg:URLPrefix>
        <cfg:AllowUnencrypted>false</cfg:AllowUnencrypted>
        <cfg:Auth>
            <cfg:Basic>true</cfg:Basic>
            <cfg:Digest>true</cfg:Digest>
```

```
                    <cfg:Kerberos>true</cfg:Kerberos>
                    <cfg:Negotiate>true</cfg:Negotiate>
                    <cfg:Certificate>true</cfg:Certificate>
                    <cfg:CredSSP>false</cfg:CredSSP>
                </cfg:Auth>
                <cfg:DefaultPorts>
                    <cfg:HTTP>5985</cfg:HTTP>
                    <cfg:HTTPS>5986</cfg:HTTPS>
                </cfg:DefaultPorts>
                <cfg:TrustedHosts></cfg:TrustedHosts>
            </cfg:Client>
            <cfg:Service>
                <cfg:RootSDDL>O:NSG:BAD:P(A;;GA;;;BA)S:P(AU;FA;GA;;;WD)(AU;SA;GWGX;;;WD)
</cfg:RootSDDL>
                <cfg:MaxConcurrentOperations>4294967295</cfg:MaxConcurrentOperations>
                <cfg:MaxConcurrentOperationsPerUser>15</cfg:MaxConcurrentOperationsPerUs
er>
                <cfg:EnumerationTimeoutms>60000</cfg:EnumerationTimeoutms>
                <cfg:MaxConnections>25</cfg:MaxConnections>
                <cfg:MaxPacketRetrievalTimeSeconds>120</cfg:MaxPacketRetrievalTimeSecond
s>
                <cfg:AllowUnencrypted>false</cfg:AllowUnencrypted>
                <cfg:Auth>
                    <cfg:Basic>false</cfg:Basic>
                    <cfg:Kerberos>true</cfg:Kerberos>
                    <cfg:Negotiate>true</cfg:Negotiate>
                    <cfg:Certificate>false</cfg:Certificate>
                    <cfg:CredSSP>false</cfg:CredSSP>
                    <cfg:CbtHardeningLevel>Relaxed</cfg:CbtHardeningLevel>
                </cfg:Auth>
                <cfg:DefaultPorts>
                    <cfg:HTTP>5985</cfg:HTTP>
                    <cfg:HTTPS>5986</cfg:HTTPS>
                </cfg:DefaultPorts>
                <cfg:IPv4Filter>*</cfg:IPv4Filter>
                <cfg:IPv6Filter>*</cfg:IPv6Filter>
                <cfg:EnableCompatibilityHttpListener>false</cfg:EnableCompatibilityHttpL
istener>
                <cfg:EnableCompatibilityHttpsListener>false</cfg:EnableCompatibilityHttp
sListener>
                <cfg:CertificateThumbprint></cfg:CertificateThumbprint>
            </cfg:Service>
            <cfg:Winrs>
                <cfg:AllowRemoteShellAccess>true</cfg:AllowRemoteShellAccess>
                <cfg:IdleTimeout>180000</cfg:IdleTimeout>
                <cfg:MaxConcurrentUsers>5</cfg:MaxConcurrentUsers>
                <cfg:MaxShellRunTime>2147483647</cfg:MaxShellRunTime>
                <cfg:MaxProcessesPerShell>15</cfg:MaxProcessesPerShell>
```

```
        <cfg:MaxMemoryPerShellMB>150</cfg:MaxMemoryPerShellMB>
        <cfg:MaxShellsPerUser>5</cfg:MaxShellsPerUser>
    </cfg:Winrs>
</cfg:Config>
```

The listener also allows the mapping of a certificate to the port and IP address. So, using the trusty technique of copying the example from the embedded documentation from the `winrm /?` command, we crafted the following command to create a listener:

```
winrm create winrm/config/Listener?Address=*+Transport=HTTPS @{Hostname="bfscl.
bigfirm.com";CertificateThumbprint="03ADB670C63E8D1CDB764CD7AA589C51D854307C"}
```

Here's an explanation of the parameters:

Address=* The service will listen on all available IP addresses.

Transport=HTTPS There are only two options: HTTP and HTTPS. They use the default ports 5985 and 5986, respectively.

Hostname= This has to match the name of the host on the certificate.

CertificateThumbprint= As discussed, this is thumbprint obtained with the `certutil` command.

CREATING AN INBOUND FIREWALL RULE

The next requirement is to enable an inbound firewall rule to receive the client requests. There is one available for the unsecure HTTP protocol, which would be set up with the `/quickconfig` option, but we need to build one for the HTTPS port.

If you're a burly, leatherneck system admin type, you might be inclined to torture yourself learning the extensive parameters of the `netsh advfirewall firewall` command. The MMC console snap-in is for those French-vanilla-latte-sipping, pencil-neck-geek system admins. In this book, we appease both the leathernecks and the pencil necks.

So, we'll start with the latte-sipping style first. Primarily it helps us see what the essential parameters are in constructing a rule. Wizards like the New Inbound Rule Wizard are useful because they walk you through configurations without missing important ones. This will assist you in constructing a command line to create the same rule. Just as in the "Server Core Survival Guide" section's reverse engineering technique, we recommend creating the rules through a wizard first on a standard installation and then trying it with the command line.

Using the Windows Firewall with Advanced Security focused on the Server Core installation, we'll walk you through the New Inbound Rule Wizard.

The first page shown in Figure 3.14 allows you to select a port rule.

In the Protocols and Ports page, we select TCP port 5986 displayed in Figure 3.15.

The Action page provides three options, as shown in Figure 3.16:

◆ *Allow the connection*: This is what you want for this example.

◆ *Allow the connection if it is secure*: As the window explains, this requires IPsec communication to continue the connection. The Network Access Protection feature can be used to set the IPsec policies within a network for this.

◆ *Block the connection*: This blocks the connection.

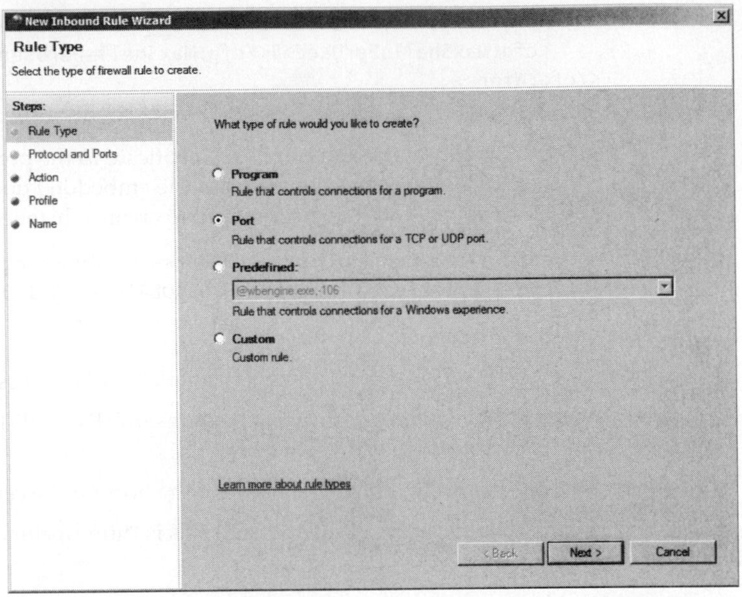

FIGURE 3.14
Selecting the type
of inbound rule

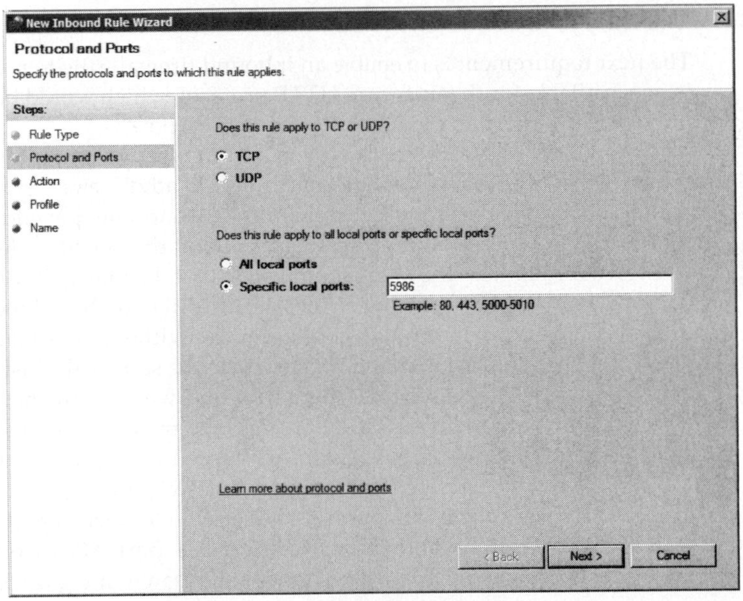

FIGURE 3.15
Entering the pro-
tocols and port for
the inbound rule

The Profile page applies the rule to the three profiles as in Figure 3.17. The public and private profiles are meant for computers that are mobile so you could work at home or at a wireless hotspot. Since this server is a domain controller, the concept of private and public don't really apply. We'll stick with just the domain profile just to be secure.

The final page allows you to enter the name and optional description for the new rule, as displayed in Figure 3.18.

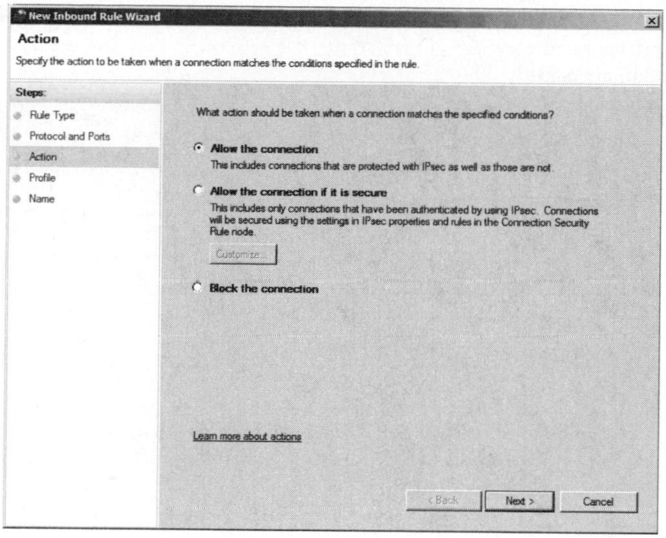

FIGURE 3.16
Selecting the
action for
the inbound rule

Now that you know the required parameters to create an inbound rule, you can take a look at the leatherneck's method. The embedded help information provides the following syntax for creating a firewall rule. Note that this was performed in the `netsh` interactive shell. It could be done as one command line as well:

```
netsh advfirewall firewall>add rule ?

Usage: add rule name=<string>
       dir=in|out
       action=allow|block|bypass
       [program=<program path>]
       [service=<service short name>|any]
       [description=<string>]
       [enable=yes|no (default=yes)]
       [profile=public|private|domain|any[,...]]
       [localip=any|<IPv4 address>|<IPv6 address>|<subnet>|<range>|<list>]
       [remoteip=any|localsubnet|dns|dhcp|wins|defaultgateway|
           <IPv4 address>|<IPv6 address>|<subnet>|<range>|<list>]
       [localport=0-65535|<port range>[,...]|RPC|RPC-EPMap|IPHTTPS|any
(default=any)]
       [remoteport=0-65535|<port range>[,...]|any (default=any)]
       [protocol=0-255|icmpv4|icmpv6|icmpv4:type,code|icmpv6:type,code|
           tcp|udp|any (default=any)]
       [interfacetype=wireless|lan|ras|any]
       [rmtcomputergrp=<SDDL string>]
       [rmtusrgrp=<SDDL string>]
       [edge=yes|deferapp|deferuser|no (default=no)]
       [security=authenticate|authenc|authdynenc|authnoencap|notrequired
           (default=notrequired)]
```

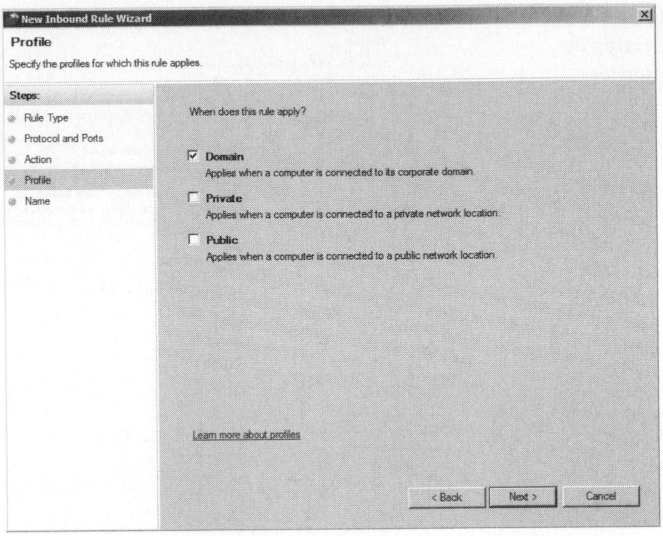

FIGURE 3.17
Limiting the rule
for domain com-
munication only

The list of parameters is long and intimidating. However, the "Server Core Survival Guide" section provided the tip of looking for examples at the end of the embedded help. Those can be edited in Notepad to create what we need. Notice the command line doesn't give us much fanfare for our accomplishment:

```
C:\Users\administrator.BIGFIRM> netsh advfirewall firewall add rule
name="Windows Remote Management HTTPS"
description="This is to open the 5986 port to allow remote management using
WinRM" protocol=TCP dir=in localport=5986 profile=domain action=allow
Ok
```

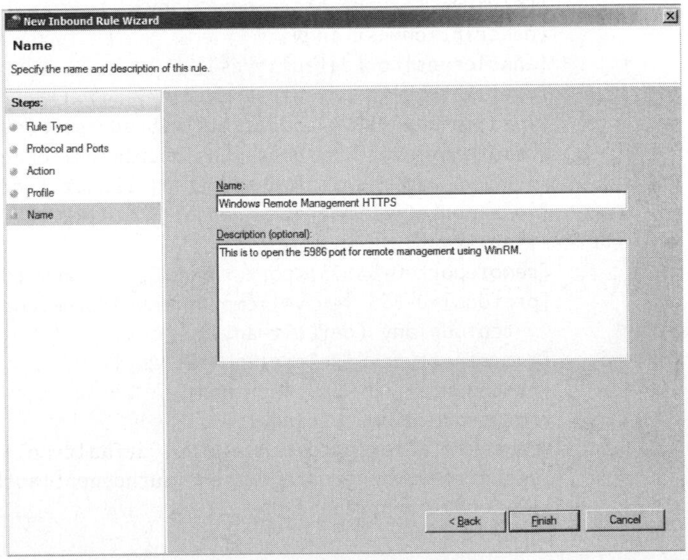

FIGURE 3.18
Providing a
descriptive name
for the rule

Here's an explanation of the parameters that translate to the earlier wizard pages:

Add rule   In the snap-in, we had to right-click the Inbound rules object and select New.

Name= & description=   This was the information added in the last page of the wizard, as shown in Figure 3.18.

Protocol= & localport=   This information was added in Figure 3.15.

Dir=   This indicates the inbound part of the rule. The direction was chosen by the selection of the New Inbound Rule Wizard.

Profile=   This was set in Figure 3.17. The options in the syntax gave the same values: [profile=public|private|domain|any[,...]].

Action=   This was set in Figure 3.16. The options are almost copied in the syntax: action=allow|block|bypass. However, bypass is the equivalent to "Allow if the connection is secure."

Note the option in Figure 3.14 that selecting the type of rule is implied with the selection of a local port. A rule that is based on a program or a service has its own structure that has examples listed in the embedded help text also.

Testing with WinRS

The current client available for Windows Remote Shell is winrs.exe. It is available on Windows Vista and Windows Server 2008 installations. So, the following command was hashed out using the winrs.exe help for the test of the service:

```
rem test winrs with fire wall enabled.
C:\Users\Administrator.BIGFIRM>winrs -r:https://bfsc1.bigfirm.com:5896 ipconfig

Windows IP Configuration


Ethernet adapter Internal:

   Connection-specific DNS Suffix  . :
   Link-local IPv6 Address . . . . . : fe80::b5a1:157f:7220:4f4c%3
   IPv4 Address. . . . . . . . . . . : 192.168.1.11
   Subnet Mask . . . . . . . . . . . : 255.255.255.0
   Default Gateway . . . . . . . . . : 192.168.1.254
```

Configuring Roles and Features

Now you are ready to get this lean, mean infrastructure machine into production. The plan for this Server Core instance was to provide a branch-office infrastructure server. This would provide authentication, file and print services, and other common network support for a small group of computers in a corporate network isolated by WAN links.

The roles that were installed on the computer during the initial tasks were Active Directory Domain Services, DNS, DHCP, and Print and Document Services. Each of these roles needs to be configured. We'll primarily cover the initial tasks for each service using both command-line and GUI tools.

Two additional services already installed are the File Server role service and the Key Management Service. We will configure the File Server role service to provide network access to local folders. The Key Management Service is to manage the activation of the volume-licensed operating systems within a network. As a branch-office server, it may prove to be the best platform to obtain the activation information from the Microsoft licensing servers for the branch.

Since the branch-office server is isolated from the corporate datacenter, it needs to perform backup operations of the data residing on the shared folders. Windows Server Backup feature was installed in the initial configurations as well, and we'll run through the commands to adequately back up its data.

Throughout the book, you will find additional details on configuring Server Core for a given feature.

Creating a Domain Controller and Managing DNS

To create a replica domain controller on a full installation, you run the Active Directory Domain Services Installation Wizard (DCpromo.exe) and walk through the wizard interface. However, with Server Core, the wizard interface isn't available. You have the unattend capability to input the specific configurations for this domain controller located in a text answer file. The following is the answer file we used:

```
[DCInstall]
ReplicaDomainDNSName=bigfirm.com
ReplicaOrNewDomain=ReadOnlyReplica
SiteName=Default-First-Site-Name
InstallDNS=yes
ConfirmGC=Yes
CreateDNSDelegation=No
UserDomain=bigfirm.com
UserName=bigfirm\Administrator
CriticalReplicationOnly=No
Password=P@ssw0rd
RebootOnCompletion=Yes
ReplicationSourceDC=bf1.bigfirm.com
SafeModeAdminPassword=P@ssw0rd
```

This server will be a read-only domain controller (RODC), which is indicated with the `ReplicaOrNewDomain=ReadOnlyReplica` option. Although this server will be an RODC, we will not be getting into the nifty extra features that come with it, such as password caching or delegating the RODC installation. We will be covering that in Chapter 22.

To get the network bulge to move, you can use the following command:

dcpromo /unattend:c:\temp\RODCanswerfile.txt

DCpromo also manages the configurations of the DNS services as well. It sets up the server as a name server for "read-only" queries. It attaches the domain's DNS zone and also reconfigures the primary DNS server in the IP properties.

The only thing we thought necessary was reconfiguring the IP properties. It listed the loop-back addresses for IPV4 and IPV6. We prefer listing the static IP address. This requires the `netsh interface` command:

```
rem remove all IPV4 entries
netsh interface ipv4 delete dnsserver name=Internal address=all
rem add the assigned IP address as the DNS server
netsh interface ipv4 add dnsserver name=Internal address=192.168.1.11 index=1
rem remove the IPV6 entry
netsh interface ipv6 delete dnsserver name=Internal address=::1
```

For the most part, that's all that is needed. The Active Directory database can be managed from full installations of Windows Server 2008. Any database maintenance can be performed locally with the `ntdsutil`, which is discussed in Chapter 18. The DNS Management console can remotely connect to the DNS service, and the `DNSCmd` utility can be used to administer the Server Core instance locally. See Chapter 5 concerning this command utility.

Configuring the DHCP Service

The first thing to do for the DHCP service is set it to autostart. The `sc` command is best at configuring the services. As we mentioned earlier, the tricky part is to get the right name of the service, which you can find in the registry. The DHCP service is named DHCPServer, not DHCP, which is for the DCHP client service. Once you figure that out, you are golden. The following are the example `sc` commands used to query, configure, and start the service:

```
rem verify the service is running or not
sc query dhcpserver

SERVICE_NAME: dhcpserver
        TYPE               : 20  WIN32_SHARE_PROCESS
        STATE              : 1   STOPPED
        WIN32_EXIT_CODE    : 1077  (0x435)
        SERVICE_EXIT_CODE  : 0  (0x0)
        CHECKPOINT         : 0x0
        WAIT_HINT          : 0x0

rem configure the service to auto-start
sc config dhcpserver start= auto
[SC] ChangeServiceConfig SUCCESS

rem start the service
sc start dhcpserver

SERVICE_NAME: dhcpserver
        TYPE               : 20  WIN32_SHARE_PROCESS
        STATE              : 2   START_PENDING
                                 (NOT_STOPPABLE, NOT_PAUSABLE, IGNORES_SHUTDOWN)
        WIN32_EXIT_CODE    : 0  (0x0)
        SERVICE_EXIT_CODE  : 0  (0x0)
```

```
           CHECKPOINT           : 0x0
           WAIT_HINT            : 0x7d0
           PID                  : 2564
           FLAGS                :

rem query the service again
sc query dhcpserver

SERVICE_NAME: dhcpserver
           TYPE                 : 20  WIN32_SHARE_PROCESS
           STATE                : 4   RUNNING
                                       (STOPPABLE, PAUSABLE, ACCEPTS_SHUTDOWN)
           WIN32_EXIT_CODE      : 0   (0x0)
           SERVICE_EXIT_CODE    : 0   (0x0)
           CHECKPOINT           : 0x0
           WAIT_HINT            : 0x0
```

When Windows Server 2003 came out, Microsoft was starting to kick up sand onto the ultra-geek's Linux system. It increased the available suite of commands to provide ultra-geek wanna-bes with the tools to configure as much as possible. That's when the netsh command came into fashion.

When considering how we could manage this service, this command came to mind. We looked up the command on the A–Z list and then printed out the documentation for netsh dhcp. After collating the 40 pages, we logged onto the Server Core instance to get busy. With netsh, you can construct one-line commands or use the interactive shell within the command prompt. In this instance, we will use the latter.

A branch office would require a basic DHCP implementation, including a single scope with standard scope options of a default gateway, DNS servers, and DNS domain name. But before that, we need to authorize it in Active Directory, which is performed by using the add server option. In the following code, the interactive mode is utilized to enter the commands:

```
netsh> dhcp
netsh dhcp>add server bfsc1.bigfirm.com 192.168.1.11

Adding server bfsc1.bigfirm.com, 192.168.1.11

Command completed successfully.
netsh dhcp>show server

1 Servers were found in the directory service:

        Server [bfsc1.bigfirm.com] Address [192.168.1.11] Ds location: c
n=bfsc1.bigfirm.com


Command completed successfully.
```

To add a scope, you need to switch to the `netsh dhcp server` prompt and use the `add scope` command. The required parameters are the subnet and subnet mask that the scope represents, the scope name, and any comments.

```
netsh dhcp>server
netsh dhcp server>add scope 192.168.1.0 255.255.255.0 "Branch Office 1"
 "Sample DHCP scope"


Command completed successfully.
netsh dhcp server>show scope

=============================================================================
 Scope Address  - Subnet Mask   - State   - Scope Name    - Comment

=============================================================================

 192.168.1.0   - 255.255.255.0  -Active    -Branch Office 1 -Sample DHCP scope

 Total No. of Scopes = 1
Command completed successfully.
```

The scope needs a range of IP addresses to serve to DHCP clients and the standard scope options. The scope options are identified with the option code, which is a three-digit identifier. You can see the code identifiers in the DHCP Management Console. The options have values in the format of byte, word, dword, string, or IP address. For our example, we have the following options, identifiers, and values:

- IP Range 192.168.1.50 - 100

- Default gateway, 003, 192.168.1.254

- DNS server, 006, 192.168.1.11

- DNS domain name, 015, bigfirm.com

```
netsh dhcp server>scope 192.168.1.0

Changed the current scope context to 192.168.1.0 scope.
netsh dhcp server scope>add iprange 192.168.1.50 192.168.1.100

Command completed successfully.
netsh dhcp server scope>set optionvalue 003 IPADDRESS 192.168.1.254

Command completed successfully.
netsh dhcp server scope>set optionvalue 006 IPADDRESS 192.168.1.11

Command completed successfully.
netsh dhcp server scope>set optionvalue 015 STRING bigfirm.com

Command completed successfully.
netsh dhcp server scope>show optionvalue
```

```
Options for Scope 192.168.1.0:

        DHCP Standard Options :
        General Option Values:
        OptionId : 51
        Option Value:
                Number of Option Elements = 1
                Option Element Type = DWORD
                Option Element Value = 691200
        OptionId : 3
        Option Value:
                Number of Option Elements = 1
                Option Element Type = IPADDRESS
                Option Element Value = 192.168.1.254
        OptionId : 6
        Option Value:
                Number of Option Elements = 1
                Option Element Type = IPADDRESS
                Option Element Value = 192.168.1.11
        OptionId : 15
        Option Value:
                Number of Option Elements = 1
                Option Element Type = STRING
                Option Element Value = bigfirm.com
Command completed successfully.
```

After running through these commands on Server Core, you can also connect to the service from a remote server and verify the configuration with a GUI, as shown earlier in Figure 3.10 and Figure 3.11.

Setting Up a File Server

The File Server role service provides basic file-sharing capabilities. We didn't have to install any specific role or feature to support this. Like much of the other roles, the procedures to share folders on full installations are typically handled by the MMC or other GUI-based applications such as Windows Explorer. We'll explore the command-line alternative for this.

CREATING A PRIMARY PARTITION

The first task to accomplish is to provide a data partition. Remember, in our pizza box example, the operating system's partition was carved from a 75GB hardware-based mirror array. It was sized at 20GB, so we have 55GB to create the data partition. In the following example, we decided to use 10GB of it.

The DiskPart command is the cat's meow for this operation. Again, this was part of the "sand kicking" when Windows Server 2003 was released. It manages all the functionality of the Disk Management Console in a command-line format or an interactive shell format. The following is in the interactive shell format. The first set of commands displays the disks and volumes on the computer. Notice the listed volumes will include volumes on other disks. Our data partition has not yet been allocated, so it is not listed in the volumes. To create the data partition, we have to select the disk, which is indicated by the value in the list disk output.

```
C:\Windows\system32>diskpart

Microsoft DiskPart version 6.1.7000
Copyright (C) 1999-2008 Microsoft Corporation.
On computer: BFSC1

DISKPART> list disk

  Disk ###  Status          Size     Free    Dyn  Gpt
  --------  -------------   -------  -------  ---  ---
  Disk 0    Online          75 GB    55 GB


DISKPART> list volume

  Volume ###  Ltr  Label        Fs     Type        Size     Status     Info
  ----------  ---  -----------  -----  ----------  -------  ---------  --------
  Volume 0    D    GB1SXFRE_EN  UDF    CD-ROM      2850 MB  Healthy
  Volume 1              NTFS    Partition          200 MB   Healthy    System
  Volume 2    C                NTFS   Partition    19 GB    Healthy    Boot
DISKPART> select disk 0

Disk 0 is now the selected disk.
```

Now, we will create the primary partition. The help information is displayed first. Noting that the size is listed in MB, we have some mental calculations to perform. *10GB = 10000 MB.* After the primary partition is created, it needs to be selected. This allows us to assign a drive letter to it.

```
DISKPART> help create partition primary
.....
Example:

    CREATE PARTITION PRIMARY SIZE=1000
rem size is in MB so 55 gb is 55000
DISKPART> create partition primary size=10000

DiskPart succeeded in creating the specified partition.

DISKPART> list partition

  Partition ###  Type             Size     Offset
  -------------  ---------------  -------  -------
    Partition 1  Primary          200 MB   1024 KB
    Partition 2  Primary          19 GB    201 MB
* Partition 3    Primary          10 GB    20 GB
```

```
DISKPART> select partition 3

Partition 3 is now the selected partition.

DISKPART> assign letter=e

DiskPart successfully assigned the drive letter or mount point.
```

With the partition created, we can view it as an available volume. We need to select it and then format it with the New Technology File System.

```
DISKPART> list volume
```

Volume ###	Ltr	Label	Fs	Type	Size	Status	Info
Volume 0	D	GB1SXFRE_EN	UDF	CD-ROM	2850 MB	Healthy	
Volume 1			NTFS	Partition	200 MB	Healthy	System
Volume 2	C		NTFS	Partition	19 GB	Healthy	Boot
* Volume 3	E		RAW	Partition	10 GB	Healthy	

```
DISKPART> select volume 3

Volume 3 is the selected volume.

DISKPART> format fs=ntfs label="Data volume" quick

    100 percent completed

DiskPart successfully formatted the volume.
```

CREATING THE FOLDERS AND EDITING PERMISSIONS

In our example, we'll create two folders:

◆ Users folder for their home folder location

◆ Sales folder as an example of a department accessible folder

To make our two folders, we'll use MS-DOS command md command, which stands for "make directory."

```
E:\>md sales
E:\>md users
```

We then have to trim the security for the folders. A group was created in Active Directory for the sales department. This will be assigned full control to their data folder.

The Users folder will be for home folders. When home folders are designated in user properties through Active Directory Users and Computers, the home folder is created automatically with the user having full control. Inherited permissions are applicable on this folder so the default Users group with read permissions are also assigned. We will need to remove the Users group's permissions from both the Sales and Users folders.

SPELLING COUNTS

You should use the %username% system variable to automatically apply usernames to the home folder path. Thus, in the Active Directory Users and Computers console, the home folder path found in the user's properties can look as follows: \\bfsc1.bigfirm.com\users\%username%. Remember, spelling counts. If this variable is spelled incorrectly, the literal string is applied as the user's folder name. Invariably we've seen some home folders named similarly to %usrename% or %usernam%.

What steps could you use to ensure you have the right spelling? The echo command! %username% is like other system variables in that it is effective within the command prompt as well. The echo command will repeat the variables value as follows:

```
rem spelled correctly
C:\>echo %username%
Administrator

rem not spelled correctly
C:\>echo %uesername%
%uesername%
```

Once confirming the correct spelling, you can cut and paste it for later use within Active Directory Users and Computers or within a script.

Again, referring to the A–Z command-line reference, you can find the cacls.exe utility. The following were the commands to modify the permissions on the sales folder. The work on the Users folder will be similar.

```
rem Display the permissions to the sales folder
cacls sales
E:\sales BUILTIN\Administrators:(OI)(CI)F
         NT AUTHORITY\SYSTEM:(OI)(CI)F
         BUILTIN\Administrators:F
         CREATOR OWNER:(OI)(CI)(IO)F
         BUILTIN\Users:(OI)(CI)R
         BUILTIN\Users:(CI)(special access:)
                        FILE_APPEND_DATA

         BUILTIN\Users:(CI)(special access:)
                        FILE_WRITE_DATA
    rem Remove the users group
```

```
cacls sales /E /R Users
processed dir: E:\sales
rem Add the Sales group with Full Control permissions
cacls sales /E /G bigfirm\sales:F
processed dir: E:\sales
rem View the Sales folder permissions
cacls sales
E:\sales BUILTIN\Administrators:(OI)(CI)F
        NT AUTHORITY\SYSTEM:(OI)(CI)F
        BUILTIN\Administrators:F
        CREATOR OWNER:(OI)(CI)(IO)F
        BIGFIRM\Sales:(OI)(CI)F
```

SHARING THE FOLDER

Sharing the folders is a piece of cake with the net share command. Yes, it's that venerable command introduced in the ancient days of LAN Manager. The following commands create both shares. The name of the share equals the path, followed by the permissions. The /Unlimited parameter is the number of connections allowed to this share.

```
rem create shares
E:\>net share SALES=e:\sales /grant:bigfirm\sales,FULL /Unlimited
Sales was shared successfully.

E:\>net share Users=e:\users /grant:"bigfirm\domain users",FULL /Unlimited
Users was shared successfully.
```

Of course, we need to validate the share. So, we went to a client and typed the UNC path in the Run prompt, and the results are displayed in Figure 3.19.

FIGURE 3.19
Verifying shares
on Server Core

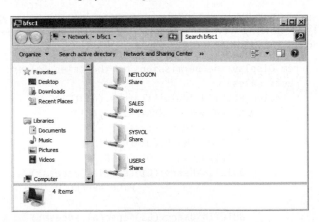

One more thing to test is the creation of the user's home folder. In Active Directory Users and Computers, we created a user and assigned \\bfsc1\users\%username% to the home folder field on the Profile tab. The home folder was created, and then we ran `calcs.exe` to verify the permissions on it.

```
rem verify permissions for the user
E:\users>cacls fbishop
E:\users\fbishop BIGFIRM\fbishop:F
                 BIGFIRM\fbishop:(OI)(CI)(IO)F
                 BUILTIN\Administrators:F
                 BUILTIN\Administrators:(OI)(CI)(IO)F
                 BUILTIN\Administrators:(OI)(CI)(ID)F
                 NT AUTHORITY\SYSTEM:(OI)(CI)(ID)F
                 CREATOR OWNER:(OI)(CI)(IO)(ID)F
```

Setting Up a Print Server

e-Print services require components of the Print and Document Services role to be installed. After that, like the other roles, you have to configure it. In previous versions of Windows, adding a printer was wizard driven, with all components rolled up into one routine. These components included the driver selection and port selection with possibly creating a TCP port and printer configurations. The functionality hasn't changed that much. Just the look has, so we won't be going into too much detail on this.

There may be commands to perform each of these procedures within the command prompt, but as in the Miller's tale, it would be "a pain in the arse." With Windows Server 2008, the printer configurations are managed in the Print Management Console, another MMC snap-in. We'll eagerly take that route first and then engage in our own Miller's tale.

An administrator responsible for printers will have to install the console by installing either the Print and Document Services role or just the Print and Document Services tool in Remote Server Administration Tools on a compatible workstation.

Once installed, the Print Management Console can be opened, and the Server Core instance can be added, as shown in Figure 3.20. Each component is separated into its own object category. So, now we have a wizard for each one of them.

FIGURE 3.20
The Print Management Console for configuring the print service

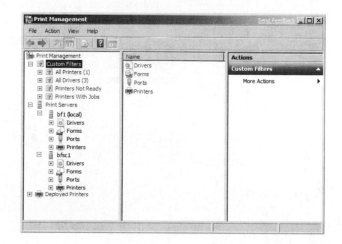

To add a driver, you need to right-click Drivers and then opt to add the driver. The wizard looks really familiar to previous Windows operating systems, as you can see in Figure 3.21.

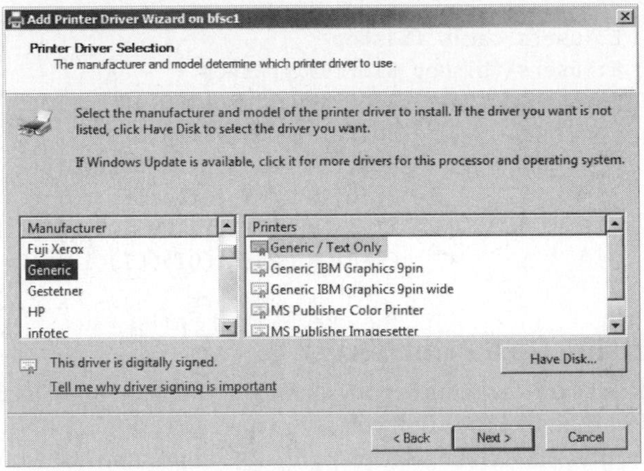

FIGURE 3.21
The Add Printer
Driver Wizard
looking familiar to
previous versions

Forms are pretty standard, so there's no need to mess with them; however, ports are very important. Typically, office printers are not locally attached to the server. They are connected to the network. So, we need to create a standard TCP port. Again, it looks eerily familiar, in Figure 3.22.

The printer can then be created with the specific driver, port, name, share name, permissions, and other configurations with the Network Printer Installation Wizard, as shown in Figure 3.23.

Now we will take it like the Nicholas the astrologer. We'll learn the Server Core commands for configuring the printer.

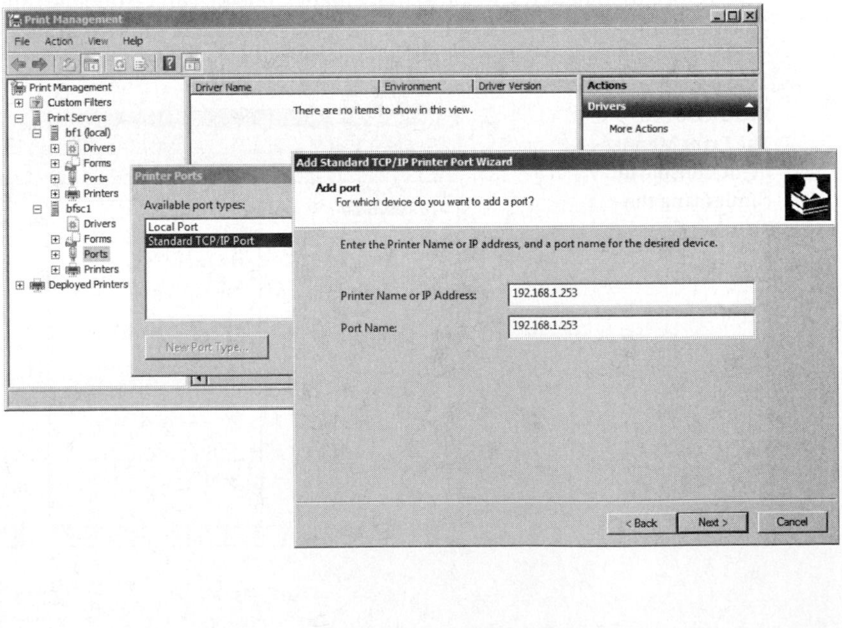

FIGURE 3.22
Adding a TCP port

FIGURE 3.23
Network Printer
Installation
Wizard

Actually, it isn't that painful. This is a great illustration of using the "Server Core Survival Guide" techniques to accomplish the tasks of administering a Server Core installation:

1. Consult the command-line reference sources. Using the A–Z command-line reference website, you start looking in the *P* section. "Printers start with P," you might think. And there within the P section, you find several commands that looked pertinent:

   ◆ Prncnfg.vbs configures the printer service.

   ◆ Prndrvr.vbs configures drivers for the printer service.

   ◆ Prnjobs.vbs manages print jobs.

   ◆ Prnmngr.vbs manages the printers supported by the service.

   Reviewing the wizards performed in the Printer Management Console, you would use the Prndrvr.vbs, prnmngr.vbs, and prncnfg.vbs scripts to get the job done. In the details found on the website of each of these commands, these scripts are located in the c:\windows\system32\ Printer_Admin_Scripts\en-us folder (assuming you are using the U.S. English version of Windows Server 2008 R2). The path differs according the language of the installation. You also have to run the script using the cscript.exe compiler.

2. Use the question mark. Entering a ? after the script produces the embedded help text, which also has useful examples to assist constructing the commands.

3. Port the output of the help text to Notepad to edit the command examples.

4. Reverse engineer the configurations made the GUI. This will help duplicate the settings using the commands.

In this example, a generic text-only printer will be configured on the TCP port 192.168.1.253. First, the printer driver is installed. In Figure 3.21, the "Generic / Text Only" driver was installed using the GUI. Reverse engineering produced this example on a standard installation. The –l parameter means list thus listing the installed drivers.

```
c:\Windows\System32\Printing_Admin_Scripts\en-US>cscript prndrvr.vbs -l
Microsoft (R) Windows Script Host Version 5.8
Copyright (C) Microsoft Corporation. All rights reserved.


Server name
Driver name Generic / Text Only,3,Windows x64
Version 3
Environment Windows x64
Monitor name
Driver path C:\Windows\system32\spool\DRIVERS\x64\3\UNIDRV.DLL
Data file C:\Windows\system32\spool\DRIVERS\x64\3\TTY.GPD
Config file C:\Windows\system32\spool\DRIVERS\x64\3\UNIDRVUI.DLL
Help file C:\Windows\system32\spool\DRIVERS\x64\3\UNIDRV.HLP
Dependent files
 C:\Windows\system32\spool\DRIVERS\x64\3\TTYRES.DLL
 C:\Windows\system32\spool\DRIVERS\x64\3\TTY.INI
 C:\Windows\system32\spool\DRIVERS\x64\3\TTY.DLL
 C:\Windows\system32\spool\DRIVERS\x64\3\TTYUI.DLL
 C:\Windows\system32\spool\DRIVERS\x64\3\TTYUI.HLP
 C:\Windows\system32\spool\DRIVERS\x64\3\UNIRES.DLL
 C:\Windows\system32\spool\DRIVERS\x64\3\STDNAMES.GPD
 C:\Windows\system32\spool\DRIVERS\x64\3\STDDTYPE.GDL
 C:\Windows\system32\spool\DRIVERS\x64\3\STDSCHEM.GDL
 C:\Windows\system32\spool\DRIVERS\x64\3\STDSCHMX.GDL
```

The previous listing displays the driver name or model, version, and environment, which are required in adding a driver. These are part of the prndrvr.vbs parameters:

```
c:\Windows\System32\Printing_Admin_Scripts\en-US>cscript prndrvr.vbs  -a
-m "Generic / Text Only" -v 3 -e "Windows x64"

Microsoft (R) Windows Script Host Version 5.8
Copyright (C) Microsoft Corporation. All rights reserved.

Added printer driver Generic / Text Only
```

Second, the TCP port is tackled:

```
c:\Windows\System32\Printing_Admin_Scripts\en-US>cscript prnport.vbs -a -s bf1
-r IP_192.168.1.253 -h 192.168.1.253 -o raw -n 9100

Microsoft (R) Windows Script Host Version 5.8
Copyright (C) Microsoft Corporation. All rights reserved.

Created/updated port IP_192.168.1.253
```

The previous command has two unfamiliar parameters in comparison to the Printer Port Wizard: -o raw and -n 9100. These values are displayed in the properties of a standard TCP port.

Third, the creation of the printer, which ties the driver with the port, is performed with the prnmngr.vbs script. Working through these scripts, you will see they share the same parameters. They are all text fields, so "spelling counts."

◆ -m: Model name of the printer

◆ -r: Name of the port

◆ -p: Name of the printer

```
c:\Windows\System32\Printing_Admin_Scripts\en-US>cscript prnmngr.vbs  -a
-p "GenericText" -m "Generic / Text Only" -r IP_192.168.1.253

Microsoft (R) Windows Script Host Version 5.8
Copyright (C) Microsoft Corporation. All rights reserved.

Added printer GenericText
```

5. The final operation is to configure the printer for sharing. The prncnfg.vbs script is used for this. Again, the examples found in the help text were copied and edited to enable it for sharing and add a location and a comment:

```
cscript prncnfg.vbs -t -p "GenericText" -h "GenericText" +shared
cscript prncnfg.vbs  -t -p "GenericText" -l "Building 1/Floor 100/Office 1"
-m "Comment Field"
```

Managing Licenses with Key Management Service

As we mentioned while discussing activation, Microsoft has introduced the Volume Activation 2.0 process with Windows Vista and Windows Server 2008. This differs from the familiar online activation. Volume-licensed installations connect to a central key management server within the LAN, which will register an activation "license" for the client with Microsoft over the Internet. This allows Microsoft to control the number of activations under the same volume product key.

By default, the Vista and Windows Server 2008 servers are configured to connect to the KMS server prior to attempting to connect online. If it can't find one but does activate online, it acts as a KMS server. So, you might want to control this process by getting ahead of it.

To consider deploying a KMS into a branch office, there are two key decision points. The first is secure TCP/IP connectivity. This process is seriously lightweight, so it isn't a tremendous drag on WAN connections; however, you still need connectivity that isn't the big white cloud to centralize activations to one site. The other is "25." A KMS doesn't start communicating with Microsoft until there are 25 qualified licenses to activate. This means 25 Vista installations. A Windows Server 2008 license counts as five Windows Vista installations. So, one Windows Server 2008 R2 and 20 Vista workstations would be enough to trigger communications.

Before the communication is triggered, the computers are running under a grace period and eventually will time out. This turns on the "reduced functionality mode."

In a branch office that has more than 25 licenses but not a secure TCP/IP connection to headquarters, setting up a KMS is a realistic option. If you don't meet the "25" threshold, Microsoft offers the Volume Multiple Activation Key (MAK), which works similarly to the online activation of product keys.

So, the following sections detail the steps to set up the KMS on a branch-office Server Core installation.

DETERMINING THE USE OF SRV PUBLISHING

SRV records are found in DNS and publish the existence of services within a network. This will be discussed in detail in Chapter 5. By default the KMS server publishes the service with an SRV record in the primary DNS domain. For our Windows Server 2008 R2 Server Core example, this is BigFirm.com.

In the BigFirm.com DNS domain, you would see an SRV record for `_VLMCS._TCP.Bigfirm.com`. It would have the properties as follows:

◆ Name: _vlmcs._TCP

◆ Type: SRV

◆ Priority: 0

◆ Weight: 0

◆ Port: 1688

◆ Hostname: Bfsc1.bigfirm.com

If you want this to happen, you would need to add permissions on the DNS zone to allow updates to the KMS servers. We recommend using a domain controller as the KMS server. The service is light, and the domain controller already has permissions to register SRV records in DNS.

However, with SRV records, there is no control on which KMS server the clients will go to if they are located in a branch office. They would query DNS and receive a response for a server located elsewhere. To keep the communication local, the KMS server must be registered on the client. In addition, DNS SRV publishing should also be disabled for the branch-office server. This is done by creating a `DisableDNSPublishing` dword value of 1 in the `HKEY_LOCAL_MACHINE\ SOFTWARE\Microsoft\Windows NT\CurrentVersion\SL` key.

ENABLING THE FIREWALL

There is already an inbound rule listed in the Windows Firewall configurations, and it's part of the Key Management Service rule group. You need to enable it. The command for this would be as follows:

```
netsh advfirewall firewall set rule group="Key Management Service" new enable=yes
```

ACTIVATING THE INSTALLATION

Just as we activated the Server Core instance, the branch-office KMS server needs to be activated with the `slmgr.vbs` `/ipk` and `/ato` options.

POINTING CLIENTS TO THE KMS

By default, Volume Activation 2.0 clients (Windows Vista and Windows Server 2008) attempt to connect to the KMS automatically using the SRV records. Since the process isn't site aware, it will go to any provided KMS server. You can manually assign the KMS host on each client of the branch location with the following command:

```
cscript c:\windows\system32\slmgr.vbs /skms bfsc1.bigfirm.com:1688
```

You could use a Group Policy object–assigned startup script to distribute this throughout the site.

Protecting Data with Windows Backup Server

This is the one of the features we added in the Server Core installation. It's a good idea to back up data. Now, your environment may pooh-pooh the use of native backup tools and prefer a third-party enterprise-class backup solution. We don't blame them. However, there's always a point in between installation and full production when the enterprise-class backup solution's client isn't installed or configured. We have found through experience that NTBackup Utility is excellent for CYA data backups.

Microsoft reengineered its native backup utility and named it Windows Backup Server. It takes advantage of the Volume Shadow Copy Service to freeze the state of the data for the backup. Originally, it was designed to provide only off-site backups on a set of portable hard drives. Tape backups were eliminated, so removable hard drives were the only backup options. Fortunately, Microsoft broadened the application to include UNC paths to shared folders and locally attached hard drives by time of the release.

EXCHANGE 2007 AND WINDOWS SERVER BACKUP

When it came to CYA backups, we truly relished the online backup capability available with NTBackup for Exchange Server. Occasionally, your third-party enterprise backup solution decides to not cooperate. Then the backup NTBackup becomes a lifesaver. Exchange Server relies on transaction logs to record changes to the database. Online backups provide a purge process of these transaction logs. If backups fail, transaction logs are not purged from the server. This can domino into stopping the Exchange services when the volume holding the transaction logs reaches capacity. So, NTBackup comes to the rescue by creating a secondary backup and clearing out the volume of unneeded files.

So, can you imagine the bally-hoo that erupted when administrators learned the news that Windows Backup Server doesn't support backing up Exchange 2007 datastores? Oh, the outrage! Oh, the angst! Oh, the inhumanity!

In actuality, it was Exchange that provided the capability. When it is installed, it adds the components to provide the online backup. Now with a brief examination of the names, Exchange 2007 and Windows Server 2008, you can see that this version of Exchange was released before the latest version of Windows. So, that explains why Exchange online backups weren't supported with Windows Server Backup.

The developers for Exchange and Windows Server Backup worked up a new compatible component. It will be released with Exchange 2007 SP2. It will support Volume Shadow Copy Service backups and purging of transaction logs rather than performing the original online backup as with NTBackup. Restores can overwrite the active location or go to an "out-of-place" location that can be attached to a recovery storage group.

What a relief!

In this discussion, we'll explore the wbadmin utility, which is the command-line tool for Windows Server Backup. For starters, the following is the initial help information:

```
c:\Windows\System32>wbadmin /?
wbadmin 1.0 - Backup command-line tool
(C) Copyright 2004 Microsoft Corp.


---- Commands Supported ----

ENABLE BACKUP              -- Creates or modifies a daily backup schedule.
DISABLE BACKUP             -- Disables the scheduled backups.
START BACKUP               -- Runs a one-time backup.
STOP JOB                   -- Stops the currently running backup or recovery
                              operation.
GET VERSIONS               -- List details of backups recoverable from a
                              specified location.
GET ITEMS                  -- Lists items contained in a backup.
START RECOVERY             -- Runs a recovery.
GET STATUS                 -- Reports the status of the currently running
                              operation.
GET DISKS                  -- Lists the disks that are currently online.
START SYSTEMSTATERECOVERY  -- Runs a system state recovery.
START SYSTEMSTATEBACKUP    -- Runs a system state backup.
DELETE SYSTEMSTATEBACKUP   -- Deletes one or more system state backups.
```

From the available command options, you can see it can back up and recover data and system state data, which will be beneficial for our Active Directory replica domain controller. We'll attach a removable USB hard drive (f:\) and walk through some of the commands to back up and restore some files.

Starting with a standard backup, we'll use the wbadmin start backup command. We'll back up the data drive (e:\), system drive (c:\), and the system state data. The c:\ drive is included in the -all critical parameter. The f:\ drive will be the target drive. The following is the command with the abbreviated output:

```
F:\WindowsImageBackup\BFSC1>wbadmin start backup -backupTarget:f:
-include:e: -allCritical -systemstate -quiet

wbadmin 1.0 - Backup command-line tool
(C) Copyright 2004 Microsoft Corp.


Retrieving volume information...
This will back up volume <Unlabeled Volume> (200.00 MB)(\\?\Volume{54a54ad2-43f9
-11de-9b46-806e6f6e6963}\),Local Disk(C:),Data volume(E:) to f:.
The backup operation to F: is starting.
Creating a shadow copy of the volumes specified for backup...
…
Creating a backup of volume <Unlabeled Volume> (200.00 MB)(\\?\Volume{54a54ad2-4
3f9-11de-9b46-806e6f6e6963}\), copied (38%).
```

```
The backup of volume <Unlabeled Volume> (200.00 MB)(\\?\Volume{54a54ad2-43f9-11d
e-9b46-806e6f6e6963}\) successfully completed.
Creating a backup of volume Local Disk(C:), copied (0%).
Creating a backup of volume Local Disk(C:), copied (1%).
...
Creating a backup of volume Local Disk(C:), copied (98%).
The backup of volume Local Disk(C:) successfully completed.
Creating a backup of volume Data volume(E:), copied (19%).
Creating a backup of volume Data volume(E:), copied (100%).
The backup operation successfully completed.
Summary of the backup operation:
------------------

The backup of volume <Unlabeled Volume> (200.00 MB)(\\?\Volume{54a54ad2-43f9-11d
e-9b46-806e6f6e6963}\) successfully completed.
The backup of volume Local Disk(C:) successfully completed.
The backup of volume Data volume(E:) successfully completed.
```

Since this is completed, we'll take a look at the results. On the f:\ drive, the utility created one folder called WindowsImageBackup. The contents of this folder are listed here:

```
F:\WindowsImageBackup\BFSC1>dir
 Volume in drive F is backup
 Volume Serial Number is 0AF2-4B31

 Directory of F:\WindowsImageBackup\BFSC1

05/24/2009  01:21 PM    <DIR>          .
05/24/2009  01:21 PM    <DIR>          ..
05/24/2009  01:21 PM    <DIR>          Backup 2009-05-24 171141
05/24/2009  01:21 PM    <DIR>          Catalog
05/24/2009  12:47 PM                16 MediaId
05/24/2009  01:21 PM    <DIR>          SPPMetadataCache
               1 File(s)             16 bytes
               5 Dir(s)  74,138,492,928 bytes free
```

Browsing through the Backup 2009-05-24 171141 folder, you will see several .xml files with very long names and a few .vhd files with similarly long names. Windows Server Backup uses the same Virtual Hard Disk technology as Virtual Server and Hyper-V to store data.

Now, we'll show a small restore. You have to first know what is in the backup. The wbadmin get items command lists the content of a backup, and the syntax of the command is shown next. The required parameter is the version. The version is the date timestamp found on the backup folder listed earlier. Note the time is in GMT.

```
wbadmin get items -version:05/24/2009-17:11
wbadmin 1.0 - Backup command-line tool
(C) Copyright 2004 Microsoft Corp.

Volume ID = {54a54ad2-43f9-11de-9b46-806e6f6e6963}
```

```
Volume '<Unlabeled Volume>', mounted at <not mounted> at the time the backup was
  created
Volume size = 200.00 MB
Can recover = Full volume

Volume ID = {54a54ad3-43f9-11de-9b46-806e6f6e6963}
Volume '<Unlabeled Volume>', mounted at C:
Volume size = 19.33 GB
Can recover = Full volume

Volume ID = {a8a658b4-454b-11de-9ff8-000c29c9f24b}
Volume 'Data volume', mounted at E:
Volume size = 9.76 GB
Can recover = Full volume

Application = FRS
Component = f95607bc-2b49-4b31-a0147ea3ee7f3545 (SYSVOL\f95607bc-2b49-4b31-a0147
ea3ee7f3545)

Application = AD
Component = ntds (C:_Windows_NTDS\ntds)

Application = Registry
Component = Registry (\Registry)
```

The contents include several components. The -allcritical parameter of the backup saved the 200MB system recovery partition and the c:\ drive. The e:\ drive was saved with the -include parameter. Then there are three application backups, FRS, Active Directory, and the registry, which are all part of the system state data.

Say you now want to recover a few files from c:\. We'll show how to restore the Administrator .BigFirm profile to a temporary location. Using the embedded help of the wbadmin start recovery command, we constructed a command from the examples to do the following:

◆ Use the 05/24/2009-17:11 backup.

◆ Perform a file restore.

◆ The files to restore are in c:\users\administrator.bigfirm.

◆ Restore the folder, files, subfolders, and their files too.

◆ Restore the files to c:\temp instead of the original location.

```
wbadmin start recovery -version:05/24/2009-17:11 -itemType:File
-items:c:\users\administrator.bigfirm
-recursive -recoveryTarget:c:\temp

wbadmin 1.0 - Backup command-line tool
(C) Copyright 2004 Microsoft Corp.

Retrieving volume information...
```

You have chosen to recover the file(s) c:\users\administrator.bigfirm from the backup created on 5/24/2009 1:11 PM to c:\temp.

Do you want to continue?
[Y] Yes [N] No y

Successfully recovered c:\users\administrator.bigfirm to c:\temp.
The recovery operation completed.
Summary of the recovery operation:

Recovery of c:\users\administrator.bigfirm to c:\temp successfully completed.
Total bytes recovered: 5.68 MB
Total files recovered: 116
Total files failed: 0

Log of files successfully recovered:
C:\Windows\Logs\WindowsServerBackup\FileRestore-24-05-2009_14-07-11.log

Drilling down through the restored folders, you can see the restore was successful:

```
c:\temp\administrator.bigfirm>dir
 Volume in drive C has no label.
 Volume Serial Number is E0B3-709F


 Directory of c:\temp\administrator.bigfirm

05/24/2009  02:07 PM    <DIR>          .
05/24/2009  02:07 PM    <DTR>          ..
05/19/2009  09:24 PM    <DIR>          Contacts
05/19/2009  09:24 PM    <DIR>          Desktop
05/24/2009  11:50 AM    <DIR>          Documents
05/19/2009  09:24 PM    <DIR>          Downloads
05/19/2009  09:24 PM    <DIR>          Favorites
05/19/2009  09:24 PM    <DIR>          Links
05/19/2009  09:24 PM    <DIR>          Music
05/19/2009  09:24 PM    <DIR>          Pictures
05/19/2009  09:24 PM    <DIR>          Saved Games
05/19/2009  09:24 PM    <DIR>          Searches
05/19/2009  09:24 PM    <DIR>          Videos
               0 File(s)              0 bytes
              13 Dir(s)  15,841,628,160 bytes free
```

The final command we'll cover is wbadmin enable backup. This has a similar syntax to the wbadmin start backup command, but its purpose is slightly different. It is meant to set up recurring scheduled backups.

The scheduled backup performs incremental backups of the data after the first full backup is performed. When the first backup is performed, the targeted location, specifically hard drives, is formatted, thus losing any previous data. Windows Server Backup manages disk space automatically by purging older backups versions. You also have the ability to add disks to the same schedule and allow for disk rotations to provide off-site backups. The following command will perform the same backup that we performed earlier but on a daily schedule at 9 p.m.

```
wbadmin enable backup -addtarget:F: -schedule:21:00 -include:e: -allCritical
-systemstate -vssFull -quiet
wbadmin 1.0 - Backup command-line tool
(C) Copyright 2004 Microsoft Corp.

Retrieving volume information...
The scheduled backup settings:

Bare metal recovery : Included
System state backup: Included
Volumes in backup: <Unlabeled Volume> (200.00 MB)(\\?\Volume{54a54ad2-43f9-11de-
9b46-806e6f6e6963}\),Local Disk(C:),Data volume(E:)
Advanced settings: VSS Backup Option (FULL)
Location to store backup: F:
Times of day to run backup: 21:00

The scheduled backup is enabled.
```

The Bottom Line

Explain the purposes for Server Core   The Windows Server 2008 R2 Server Core operating system is a trimmed-down version of its full installation. The removed code reduces the profile for security threats to leverage and also reduces performance demands. The primary administration interface is the command prompt. It can perform several but not all of the roles available with the full installation.

> **Master It**   The Windows Server 2008 R2 Server Core version differs from the original release in Windows Server 2008. What are those key differences, and how does that impact the roles the server can perform?

Install and configure Server Core   The installation of Server Core is the same as installing a full installation of Windows Server 2008 R2. The full installation provides a list of initial configuration tasks such as joining the domain, initiating automatic updates, and installing features. Each of these operations has a command associated with them.

> **Master It**   Server Core has a specific script to perform several common tasks that edit the registry. What is this script's name? What parameter can provide a list of additional commands to perform much of the common configuration tasks?

Set up Server Core for a branch-office deployment   The branch-office deployment was one possible purpose of the Server Core implementation. The infrastructure roles of Active Directory Domain Services, DNS server, DHCP, and File Services and Print and Document

Services would be installed and configured on a server, which would provide these basic services to the users within a small office environment. The configurations of these services could be performed remotely.

Master It To configure Active Directory Domain Services and DNS, the Active Directory Domain Services Installation Wizard (DCpromo) is run from the command line. What is needed to enter the parameters for the command?

Remotely manage the operating system Server Core can be remotely managed by three options. Remote Desktop administration is available, but only the command prompt and provided GUIs with Server Core can be used. The MMC console snap-ins can connect to the server's services to manage with the standard Windows tools. Finally, a new service, Windows Remote Shell, provides single-command connections to the server.

Master It The Windows Remote Shell offers a `quickconfig` option. What are the security concerns that system administrators should be aware of when using this option? What can be done to address these concerns?

Chapter 4

Windows Server 2008 IPv4: What Has Changed?

It's a safe bet that most people reading this book who wanted to get straight into the meat of Windows 2008 or Windows Server 2008 R2 would probably either quickly skim or skip through this chapter after reading its title. That would be a serious mistake, though, so don't be tempted to do that! Our author team started looking at, and working with, Windows Server 2008 long before the scheduled general general-release. Friends, colleagues, and customers often asked the same questions: "Why should we deploy Windows 2008? " "It's just a fancy upgraded version of Windows Server 2003, right?" Wrong. It's hard to put in one sentence how wrong that conclusion is. And that's even before we start thinking about Windows Server 2008 R2.

The first things to mention are the new networking features and how businesses, whether they be small, medium, or huge, will be able to take advantage of these features to resolve technical and, more critically, business issues that they face on a day-to-day basis. There are a bunch of new features, as you'll see by reading this book, but we always come back to networking and how optimized network performance and the new security solutions will resolve many of the issues that we have personally encountered in networks. We've been using the Internet Protocol for some time now. We've called it just IP, but the correct term would have been IPv4. We are going to spend this chapter briefly discussing what is new in IPv4 networking in Windows Server 2008 and Windows Server 2008 R2 and how it will resolve issues that you might just be fighting right now.

In this chapter, you will learn to:

- ◆ Understand the next-generation TCP stack
- ◆ Troubleshoot the improvements in the next-generation TCP stack
- ◆ Control bandwidth usage

TCP Then and Now

Let's go back in history a bit to explore the development of the Transmission Control Protocol (TCP). When combined with the Internet Protocol (IP), you get TCP/IP, which is the basis of all modern computer networking. Microsoft first developed its TCP stack in the 1990s. It evolved as Microsoft developed the various versions of its operating systems, but at its core it remained mostly unchanged right up to Windows Server 2003. That's right—you've been using 1990s technology at the heart of your state-of-the-art enterprise network. You can do only so much of that until you get to the point where the software cannot evolve anymore and becomes the bottleneck. Microsoft saw that there was a need for a new stack to be able to take advantage of new technologies and opportunities that its customers and partners were encountering. Microsoft started work on the new version of TCP while it was developing Windows 2000. In the meantime, it continued to evolve TCP for Windows 2000, Windows XP, and Windows Server 2003.

Our first glimpse of TCP for the new generation was in Windows Vista. The skeptical commentators did their usual flailing and panicking about this new TCP and how it would ruin us all. There really wasn't much need. Microsoft had spent years developing TCP, and Windows Vista had undergone one of the, if not the, biggest public beta testing programs ever. The same code is at the core of TCP in Windows Server 2008, and the public testing program for the new server product was quite impressive too. The release of Windows Server 2008 has come and gone, and now we're already looking at Windows 7, the successor to Windows Vista, and at Windows Server 2008 R2, the obvious successor to Windows Server 2008. Both Windows 7 and Windows Server 2008 R2 have the same "next-generation" TCP stack at the core of their networking.

You may get some network performance gains with Windows Server 2003 and Windows XP working in conjunction with Windows Server 2008 or Windows Server 2008 R2, but those legacy products will not be getting a new TCP stack. To get the very best networking performance, you need to pair up next-generation TCP stack operating systems:

◆ Windows Vista

◆ Windows 7

◆ Windows Server 2008

◆ Windows Server 2008 R2

Let's take a look at what we're talking about here. Figure 4.1 is a rather simplified view of the new TCP stack that is present in Windows Vista, Windows 7, Windows Server 2008, and Windows Server 2008 R2.

FIGURE 4.1
Windows 2008 TCP
stack simplified

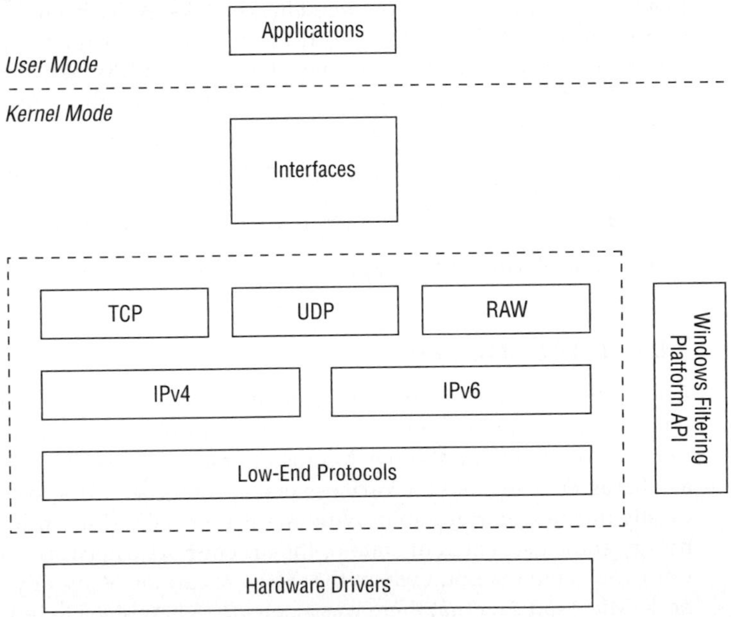

We've kept this diagram simple so you can get an idea of what's going on. Most administrators don't need to see a detailed view. That level of detail is normally reserved for programmers and people who like to talk about sockets. You should visit http://tinyurl.com/lp9q6e if you want to get more detail on the architecture of the stack.

At the top layer, you have the applications such as Windows Explorer. These applications generate and consume network traffic. They use an interface such as sockets to communicate with the lower levels of the stack that execute in kernel mode. The next layer in the architecture is where you find TCP and UDP, the transport protocols. They are responsible for managing connections between communicating network nodes. Beneath them you have the network protocols, IPv4 and IPv6. IPv6 is built by default into the new stack in Windows Server 2008 and Windows Vista and later, unlike previous versions of Windows. You then have lower-end protocols for handling things like IPsec (an IP-based protocol to secure network communications), WAN (wide area network—a network that spans wide geographic areas), and 802.1x (a way of securing access to a network by controlling access to ports on network equipment). They are responsible for dealing with your network card drivers. Another new feature is the Windows Filtering Platform API. This allows third-party solution providers to plug directly into the stack using documented APIs. This will be used by the likes of firewall and antivirus vendors.

OK, so what's the big fuss? Why are we even bothering to talk about TCP? Isn't that something boring for those network engineers? Maybe it is, and maybe it isn't. Keep reading, and you'll see what we mean.

Improving Transaction Time with Autoscaling

One of the biggest problems we've encountered working as consultants and administrators is how to provide optimal Windows networking across latent network links. We've been told that the most cost-effective solution for deploying servers is to centralize them into locations such as corporate or regional headquarters. The argument does make a lot of sense:

♦ You can reduce hardware costs by purchasing fewer servers.

♦ You can reduce infrastructure and operating costs by having fewer computer rooms to build, staff, power, and cool.

♦ You can locate servers where you have server administration and operational skills. Not all branch offices have adequate IT staff.

♦ You can increase data security by not locating sensitive data in nontrusted branch offices.

♦ You can simplify backups by having fewer backup infrastructure deployments and guarantee their management by using skilled operators. How many branch-office backups are run by the receptionist and have no offline storage? We've witnessed way too many of those in our time.

You can see the benefits of centralizing your servers, but are there any downsides? Unfortunately, there are. Users are used to accessing data at LAN speeds on local servers. You can't do that anymore because you've just moved the servers to remote locations across what are probably very expensive WAN links. Users will have a much slower experience, and that will generate a lot of help-desk calls.

The metric you have to focus on when you're looking at interactive services such as file sharing and application usage over the network is latency. *Latency* is the measure of how long packets take to get from the client to the server, and vice versa. It's a restriction of the laws of physics; in other words, how long it takes a packet to get from A to B across a cable, a satellite link, or even a wireless connection. Also, adding to the equation are network devices such as routers and switches and, of course, network congestion. If it takes longer for a message to get from A to B and to get a response, then the user will experience a slower service. We refer to a link as being latent if a message send takes a significant amount of time between transmission and receipt. Examples of latent links are leased lines, satellite links, and wireless WANs (see Figure 4.2). That's what we're going to look at here.

FIGURE 4.2
Latency explained

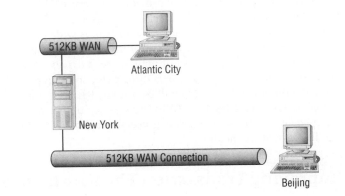

Let's take a look at a scenario to see what we mean. In this scenario, say we have a headquarters in New York and two branch offices, in Atlantic City and Beijing (see Figure 4.3). There is a dedicated 512KB connection from New York to each of the branch offices. Atlantic City is not so far from New York, so network latency is probably not so bad, maybe somewhere around 10 milliseconds. However, Beijing is on the other side of the world in China. Network latency will be pretty bad, probably well over 200 milliseconds. What does this mean for any network transaction?

A cross-network transaction is broken into a series of requests and acknowledgments that are transmitted in a sequential fashion. Each packet being sent across the WAN connection will take a certain amount of time to be transmitted across the network. It doesn't matter if the packet is large or small; the rules of physics dictate that the farther it has to travel, the longer it will take. If a transaction such as a file copy requires multiple packets to be transmitted, then the latency caused by distance will make things worse.

In this example, you can see that a user in each of our branch offices has downloaded a file from New York. The user in Atlantic City will notice that their performance is slower than using a local server, but they expected that. The performance isn't great, but the user can work with it. Beijing is a different matter! The same file is requested and is traveling over the same available bandwidth. However, those electrons traveling across the wire have a fixed speed determined by the laws of physics. The much longer distance and the introduction of more routers between the offices will slow things down to a trickle. You can see that the same transaction performed by both offices will take the Beijing user 20 times longer. That was just a simple transaction with only a few packets. Imagine how long downloading a 2MB Excel file would take. You can be sure that the users in Beijing won't be happy and that the directors will be rather upset that IT is ruining their business plans once again!

FIGURE 4.3
The impact
of latency

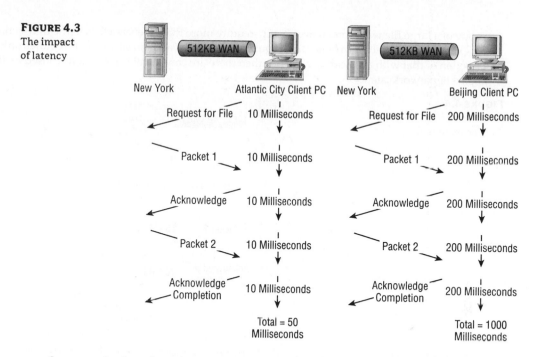

So, we get back to throwing more bandwidth at the problem. Think about the cause for a moment…our electrons have a fixed speed. It doesn't matter if we have a 512KB or 512MB pipe between New York and Beijing. The transaction time is still limited by the distance being covered by the link. Bear in mind that the link to Beijing might include hops between orbiting satellites and thus compound the latency problem for your colleagues in that office. Throwing more bandwidth at the problem only means that more people in Beijing can experience the same terrible performance at the same time. You need to look at how to make the best use of the available bandwidth.

Microsoft has introduced autoscaling in Windows Vista and Windows Server 2008 to resolve this problem (see Figure 4.4). Autoscaling includes two components:

The TCP receive window   This function is enabled by default in Windows Vista and Windows Server 2008. This determines how much data a computer can consume from the network in a single bite. The computer dynamically adjusts this setting based on the bandwidth delay product (a function of bandwidth and latency) and application retrieve rate (how fast the destination application can consume data).

Compound TCP   This allows a computer to send larger amounts of data to another computer with a large TCP receive window across latent connections, or in other words, slow turnaround times. This attempts to send as much data as possible in a single chunk. It is enabled by default on Windows Server 2008 but disabled by default on Windows Vista.

Working in conjunction, these two operations will increase the amount of data that is transmitted across the network between a client and a server in a single packet. This doesn't decrease the latency of the network, but it does reduce the impact of it.

You can see the impact of autoscaling in our simplified Beijing example of a file copy in Figure 4.4. The total operation took 600 milliseconds instead of 1,000. We did say it was simplified:

a copy of a large file will more than certainly require more than a few packets in the transaction. For example, if the network transaction requires 100 packets without scaling and requires only a fraction of that with autoscaling running, then there are considerable reductions caused by the impact of network latency.

FIGURE 4.4
Autoscaling trans-
fer time reduction

New York   Beijing Client PC

Request for File   200 Milliseconds

Packet 1   200 Milliseconds

Acknowledge
Completion   200 Milliseconds

Total = 600
Milliseconds

Some of you may have already dealt with receive window sizing in the previous generation of TCP found in Windows XP and Windows 2003. This allowed administrators to configure the maximum window on a per-machine basis by editing the registry. The value in question is a REG_DWORD called TcpWindowSize, which you can find in HKLM\SYSTEM\CurrentControlSet\ Services\Tcpip\Parameters. You can read a bit more about it at http://tinyurl.com/1slvbl. Windows Vista and Windows Server 2008 are different in the following ways:

◆ The tuning process is automated, so there is no need to deploy a registry edit, which is a time-consuming and potentially messy process.

◆ The tuning is done on a per-connection basis as opposed to a per-computer basis. You cannot assume that a receive window for one connection is correct for all connections. TCP will automatically determine the best connection for you.

◆ Autotuning is enabled by default on Windows Server 2008 and Windows Vista.

◆ The new TCP stack will normally advertise a much larger receive window size than one found in Windows XP or Windows Server 2003. This allows a Windows Vista or Windows Server 2008 computer to potentially allow their inbound connection to be more fully utilized and hence receive much more data per packet than those with legacy operating systems.

There is an assumption with autoscaling that you have bandwidth to spare in order to increase the receive window on the destination computer. In this chapter's scenario, the 512KB connection to the branch offices might be congested because of the number of clients simultaneously accessing the server in New York. With TCP autoscaling, they'll all want to use a larger receive window to optimize their usage of the pipe, but they can use only what is there. So, you still might have to add some bandwidth if you find utilization creeping higher. However, you will be safe in your job with the knowledge that Windows Vista and Windows Server 2008 will take advantage of the additional bandwidth by utilizing it more to reduce the impact of latency.

THINK BIG!

The example we've presented is a typical file-sharing scenario. It's easy fall into the trap of thinking about file sharing only. Think bigger, much bigger! The improvements in TCP affect *all* TCP applications that will run on your Windows Server 2008 servers. Think of your web servers, terminal servers, SharePoint, Oracle databases, Lotus Notes...all of these should perform much better across latent links such as WAN and Internet connections when working with other Windows Server 2008 and Windows Vista computers. That's pretty significant; it's possibly the biggest reason why Windows Server 2008 and Windows Server 2008 R2 are recommended to people who need to get the most from their WAN.

This performance gain isn't just limited to WAN links. Autoscaling will greatly improve cross-LAN traffic too. Network-intensive application and data-sharing servers running on Windows Server 2008 and Windows Server 2008 R2 that work with other next-generation TCP stack clients will perform much better, taking full advantage of the gigabit or greater networks that are provided to them. They'll be able to push more data down the network than they previously could.

If you want facts and figures on how Windows Vista and Windows Server 2008 autoscaling compares with Windows XP and Windows Server 2003, then you should read a report that was written by the Tolly Group (`http://tinyurl.com/la9jgq`). The Tolly Group was commissioned by Microsoft to analyze the performance of Windows Vista and Windows Server 2008 (aka Longhorn) networking. The group's white paper makes for very interesting reading. For example, the paper compares the time taken to open a 10MB Office document that is hosted on SharePoint. The pairing of Windows Server 2003 and Windows XP takes approximately twice as long as the pairing of Windows Vista and Windows Server 2008 to open the document. The important thing to note in the study, however, was that the group focused on WAN and LAN links with *high*-latency periods. The new TCP stack in Windows Server 2008 and Windows Vista doesn't improve matters all that much on low-latency networks such as your typical well-performing LAN.

TROUBLESHOOTING AUTOSCALING

As usual, all does not smell of roses, as some Windows Vista early adopters found out. There were many blog posts about people with Windows Vista laptops being unable to surf the Net while in airports or hotel rooms. TCP autoscaling can have some problems if you are using an outdated router, as Microsoft's KB article 932134 (`http://tinyurl.com/mkr59z`) will tell you. You may find that when your autoscaling-enabled computer tries to communicate over such a router, one of a few things may happen:

◆ You get download errors while surfing the Web.

◆ Network performance may actually be reduced.

◆ A router may actually stop working!

The cause of the problem lies in the router because it's not actually up-to-date. The receive window in Windows Vista, Windows 7, Windows Server 2008, and Windows Server 2008 R2 starts at 64KB by setting the window size of the TCP header to 256 and the scale factor to 8. That's calculated as $256*2^8=64\text{KB}$. This allows the window size to grow to 16,776,960 bytes, just a little shy of 16MB.

An older router can fail to inspect the scale factor and therefore sends data only in windows of 256 bytes. You can test your router using a Microsoft tool (http://tinyurl.com/3dc5g3) before deploying Windows Vista or Windows Server 2008. We recommend that you pay close attention to the potential of these scenarios given the amount of material in the blogosphere about people experiencing this problem. Test your network equipment, and educate "road warriors" whose laptops are loaded with Windows Vista or Windows 7. A little bit of work will help avoid a pink slip–generating event such as a new server crashing your network or your CEO not being able to send a critical email from his Vista laptop while on a hotel Wi-Fi network. Some network applications have also been found to ignore the scaling factor, so they will also appear to be quite slow at transferring data.

If you do find that autoscaling is causing you problems, then you can tune it until you get the desired result:

◆ You can reduce the scaling by running this command:

```
netsh interface tcp set global autotuning=restricted
```

That will allow the receive window to grow but restrict that growth. You can be more conservative with the scaling factor by running this command:

```
netsh interface tcp set global autotuning=highlyrestricted
```

◆ You can disable the receive window scaling by running the following from the command prompt:

```
netsh interface tcp set global autotuning=disabled
```

This restricts the receive window to 65,536 bytes, or 64KB. You might find that you don't need to completely turn off the scaling of the receive window:

◆ You can reenable the default settings for TCP autoscaling by running the following from the command prompt:

```
netsh interface tcp set global autotuninglevel=normal
```

And we're sure we're not the only people to wonder why the opposite of disabled is normal. It seems a bit...well...judgmental, don't you think?

◆ You can check the status of TCP autoscaling by running this from the command prompt:

```
netsh interface tcp show global
```

When you're troubleshooting networking issues that you believe are related to autoscaling, we recommend starting restricted and progress from there to highlyrestricted and disabled. If those don't fix the issue, then your issue probably isn't related to autoscaling, and you should switch autoscaling back to normal.

Autoscaling is all well and good, but you've just deployed an operating system that will try to consume bandwidth at any cost. Without any management, you can be sure that operations such as web browsing and downloads will be able to starve other interactive and critical applications such as VoIP of the bandwidth that they require. We'll cover how you can control your usage of bandwidth next.

Employing Policy-Based QoS

Quality of Service (QoS) allows administrators to deploy policies that predetermine which applications or services should be prioritized when it comes to allocating bandwidth. In other words, traffic for specific network applications will be transmitted before or after other applications. Alternatively, administrators can predetermine how much bandwidth is allocated to network applications by using *throttling*. Administrators can determine critical interactive services such as VoIP and line-of-business (LOB) applications that must have acceptable levels and bandwidth available to them whenever they seek it. Using Group Policy, you can determine an application's QoS by the following settings:

- The sending application and directory path
- The destination and source IP addresses and ports
- The protocol, either TCP or UDP
- Active Directory users or groups

Working together, these settings will determine the Differentiated Services Code Point (DSCP) value. TCP will use this to inject a value from 0 to 63 into the Type of Service (TOS) field in a TCP IPv4 packet. Note that it also injects the value into the Traffic Class field in an IPv6 packet. Routers on the network will then use the DSCP value to determine which packets to prioritize or throttle. The higher the DSCP value assigned by an administrator via Group Policy, the higher the routers will prioritize the associated packets.

Let's look at an example. An administrator needs to prioritize the LOB application when it is being used by sales staff and directors. We know it operates on TCP 3299 and that we have user groups in Active Directory for sales and for directors. We can build a group policy targeting TCP 3299 and the aforementioned user groups while placing a higher DSCP than normal of 60 on the application. This value will be injected into all packets on TCP 3299 that are associated with those users in the user groups. The network routers will then interrogate this value in the IPv4 or IPv6 packets and prioritize them as instructed.

The prerequisites for policy-based QoS are as follows:

- The managed computers must be running Windows Server 2008 or Windows Vista.
- They must be members of an Active Directory domain so that you can deploy your policies using Group Policy.
- The routers that reside between the clients and servers must be capable of being configured for DSCP (see RFC 2474 at http://tinyurl.com/nb852k).

Be sure to check off each of these prerequisites before you start your QoS deployment. You don't want to have deployed TCP autoscaling and think that you have control of everything using QoS only to find that QoS isn't actually doing anything all! The network routers are the one prerequisite that could cause the most pain. There could be significant cost and maybe even some difficulty if you've completely outsourced your WAN deployment. Deploying QoS will require a good deal of planning and research on your part. Every organization will have different needs, and you will have to work quite closely with management and the business to design your solution.

Microsoft has strongly recommended that policy-based QoS be deployed hand in hand with TCP autoscaling so as to prioritize the consumption of bandwidth. Failing to do this could have a serious impact on LOB and interactive services when autoscaling starts to increase its consumption of bandwidth.

Sharing Files and Printers with SMB 2.0

Server Message Block (SMB) is a protocol that dates back to the 1980s and the days of DOS.

THE DODO NAMED DOS

This might make some of us feel old. We used DOS, but it's recently been pointed out to us that there are people who have never even heard of it. DOS was the command-line-based Microsoft operating system that was the predecessor to Windows. You can learn more about it at http://tinyurl.com/nlz8la.

SMB is the protocol that is used by Windows for file and printer sharing. It had remained mostly unchanged at its core since the 1980s until the release of SMB 2.0 with Windows Vista (see Figure 4.5). Microsoft developed SMB 2.0 for a number of reasons:

◆ To reduce the size of the protocol and hence the attack surface in order to make it more secure

◆ To move on from the original, which had become hard to maintain and difficult to innovate

◆ To increase efficiency, particularly when dealing with latent networks

◆ To allow for future expansion, which was not possible with SMB 1.0

SMB 2.0 is included in both Windows Vista and Windows Server 2008 as well as in Windows 7 and Windows Server 2008 R2. There will not be a backport for legacy versions of Windows such as Windows Server 2003 or Windows XP. However, SMB 1.0 is still included in the newer operating systems and will be used when communicating with legacy machines.

The main point of interest for us with SMB 2.0 is the increase in efficiency. You'll remember when we discussed how latency was made worse by the fact that we have sequential transmission of packets. SMB 2.0 can build upon our autoscaling by reducing the amount of latency in this scenario by using data streaming. Let's revisit our friends in New York and Beijing to see what we mean.

There are two clients in Beijing, one using Windows XP with SMB 1.0 and the other using Windows Vista with SMB 2.0. Both of them request a file transfer from a Windows Server 2008 server in New York across our latent WAN connection. TCP autoscaling does quite a bit to minimize the impact of latency, but we still have a noticeable impact that users are complaining about when they use a file server in New York.

FIGURE 4.5
SMB 2.0, leveraging the next-generation TCP

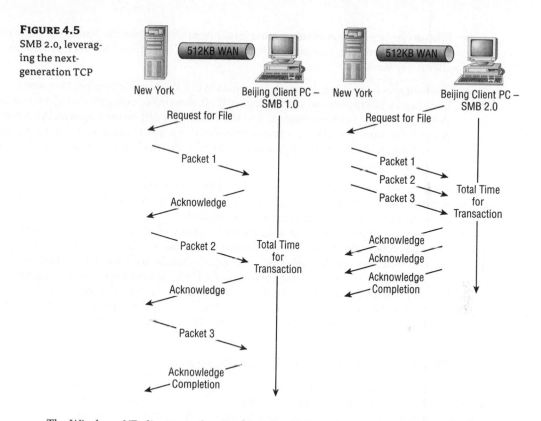

The Windows XP client transfers the file using SMB 1.0 in the now familiar form of a transmission followed by an acknowledgment. Each packet transmitted is subject to latency, and you already saw that there was a 200-millisecond delay on each packet. This process is repeated until the file download is completed. The time taken to do this for the Windows XP client is 200 milliseconds multiplied the number of packets transmitted by both parties in the transaction. That's a long time, even if you do minimize the number of packets being transmitted thanks to autoscaling.

The Windows Vista client can perform much faster because both it and the Windows Server 2008 file server are capable of using SMB 2.0. Instead of the sequential transmission of packets, SMB 2.0 uses data streaming, which sends out a compounded block of packets one after the other without waiting for the associated acknowledgments. Each packet still takes 200 milliseconds to transmit, but the server does not have to wait 400 milliseconds before sending the next packet. Instead, the server continues to send blocks of packets to the client. The client in turn sends a reply either acknowledging receipt of each packet or requesting a retransmission of a packet. The whole sequence is not sequential; instead, each party communicates as quickly as possible without waiting for the other. The result is that the impact of latency is lessened by the transmit/acknowledge sequence.

Latency isn't the only problem that impacts accessing a file share across a WAN connection. SMB 2.0 also offers us the following:

◆ Much larger buffer sizes to deal with the increase in traffic that we can expect because of measures deployed to deal with network latency. Remember that SMB is one of those applications that must be capable of consuming the larger amounts of data transmitted thanks to a larger autoscaling receive window.

◆ File servers are capable of supporting larger numbers of open file handles. This is necessary because you are now capable of running fewer centralized file servers with more clients per server.

◆ Brief outages in network coverage are common in a WAN environment. This would cause huge headaches to users who are using SMB 1.0. Imagine opening or saving a file and the WAN connection between your PC and the server goes offline for a second. What happens? Your transfer will fail and cause lots of dialog boxes to open, which in turn causes lots of help-desk calls. SMB 2.0 introduces durable file handles, which are capable of withstanding brief outages.

A new feature in Windows Vista Service Pack 1 builds on SMB 2.0 for file share improvements in latent environments. SP1 improves attribute and directory caching, reducing round-trips across the network when browsing remote file shares using Windows Explorer.

We will also see improvements in offline file caching that will allow client computers to work with an offline cache instead of directly accessing the file server. Background replication will take place and will improve the interactive experience that the user will have. There is the disadvantage that there will be a time lag between user 1 saving a document and it appearing in the offline cache of user 2, so this is one that administrators will need to think carefully about before enabling it. Remember, however, that you'll see only SMB 2.0–oriented performance improvement among Windows Vista and Windows 2008 and newer systems.

Alternatives for Network Performance

There are two schools of thought when it comes to accelerating network performance for centralized servers and remote branch offices. Both are caching or local transmission replay solutions that sit between the server and the client. The first is what we will call a *wide area file network*. It is a solution built to accelerate file server performance. That's pretty much all it can do. The second is sometimes called a *wide area data network* (WADN). The WADN attempts to accelerate all traffic based on TCP using cached data. The data is build by breaking up TCP transmission streams into smaller blocks that are uniquely identified using an algorithm. It is pretty successful, but it relies on seeing previously transmitted identical blocks of traffic.

The downside to both of these solutions is that there is a pretty significant capital investment required. They also can have certain restrictions such as being unable to accelerate certain types of signed or encrypted data because they can be viewed as "man-in-the-middle" hackers because of the way they operate. There is also the risk that these third-party hardware vendors don't keep up with the protocol advancements of the operating systems and applications and fail to accelerate those protocols or, worse, even break them. These hardware solutions will accelerate network performance for your legacy computers such as Windows Server 2003 and Windows XP.

Windows 7 paired with Windows Server 2008 R2 can provide an optimization similar to the wide area file network using BranchCache. By caching file data in the branch office, Windows 7 clients will be able to avoid the effects of latency with the file server or web application service—for example, SharePoint—based in the central office.

Wrapping Up the New and Improved TCP

So, we've covered the improvements you will see in TCP. They are pretty impressive, and you can probably see how they can impact your organization in a very positive way. In fact, you should be able to see how you can build a legitimate business case to deploy Windows Server 2008, Windows Server 2008 R2, Windows Vista, or Windows 7 to take advantage of the network performance improvements that are possible.

DHCP and Network Access Protection

Network Access Protection (NAP) is the new policy enforcement solution in Windows Server 2008 to restrict access to the Windows network to only those computers that meet certain pre-defined criteria. Those criteria used to determine access can include the presence of an antivirus product and up-to-date definition files, Windows patches, and the Windows Firewall status. By doing this, administrators are attempting to ensure that only "healthy" computers participate on the network. NAP can control access for computers running Windows Server 2008, Windows Vista, and Windows XP SP3.

DHCP is one of the four mechanisms that can be used by NAP to guarantee the health of a computer's connection to the network. DHCP integrates with NAP by allowing NAP policy enforcement on each DHCP scope. A DHCP client reports its health criteria with its DHCP request to the DHCP server. The DHCP server integrates with NAP to verify whether the client's health statement meets the required criteria. If it does, then the client is issued an IPv4 configuration from the requested DHCP scope by the DHCP server. If it fails to meet the criteria, it can be given an address for a restricted access network, thus allowing the client to rectify the problem that caused it to fail the health check. Upon rectifying the problem, the client can proceed to request an IPv4 configuration from the DHCP server once again.

DHCP NAP enforcement is actually considered quite weak because it relies on IPv4 address configuration. Any determined user with administrative rights on the failing computer can manually configure the IPv4 configuration to gain access to the network.

Note that Microsoft clearly states that NAP is not a security solution. NAP is intended to be a health and configuration policy enforcement solution. You should look at alternatives such as 802.1x or port-based network access control if you need a security solution to protect access to your network from malicious attackers.

New to 2008 R2

The big changes were introduced in Windows Vista and Server 2008. However, there is something that builds on the technologies developed in Windows Vista and Server 2008. It's seen as one of the business reasons to look at deploying Windows 7 and Server 2008 R2.

There's a new seamless remote connectivity solution called DirectAccess. This allows roaming Windows 7 clients to access a file share or HTTP/HTTPS site back in the office without asking the user to start up a VPN client. This is built on IPv6. Without any help, this could be very challenging. At this time, IPv6 is still not in widespread use. Microsoft facilitates this traffic by using a new communications protocol in Windows 7 and Server 2008 R2 called IP-HTTPS. This encapsulates the IPv6 traffic within an IPv4 (the IP protocol most of us know today) HTTPS session. Using HTTPS also simplifies and minimizes what has to be opened on the firewall.

The Bottom Line

Understand the next-generation TCP stack   The next-generation TCP stack includes technologies to optimize how data is sent across a network connection.

Master It   Can you name the technologies included in the next-generation TCP stack and what they do?

Troubleshoot the improvements in the next-generation TCP stack   You may encounter issues when you deploy the newer versions of Windows, such as Server 2008, Server 2008 R2, Vista, and Windows 7, on an older network or when roaming users are in airports or hotels.

Master It   What are the commands for configuring the TCP receive window when you encounter network appliance compatibility issues?

Control bandwidth usage   Windows Vista, Windows 7, Windows Server 2008, and Windows Server 2008 R2 all include functionality that allows you to fully utilize any bandwidth that you have.

Master It   Users in a branch office are complaining that access to network services that are hosted in your headquarters office are unbearably slow on a frequent basis. Network engineers report that the link between headquarters and the branch-office network has been fully utilized since you upgraded from Windows XP and Windows Server 2003. You need to resolve the issue.

Chapter 5

DNS and Naming in Server 2008 and Active Directory

Computers communicate with each other using IP addresses, whether IPv4 or IPv6. However, it is difficult for most people to remember the IP address for their favorite website or file server. They like using friendly text-based names. Thus, naming systems are implemented to resolve the friendly name of server with its assigned IP address. The Domain Name System (DNS) is the naming system that Windows Server 2008 R2 servers use. Not only does DNS help users, Active Directory requires DNS so that clients and servers can locate and communicate with domain controllers.

In this chapter, you will learn to:

◆ Explain the fundamental components and processes of DNS

◆ Configure DNS to support an Active Directory environment

◆ Manage and troubleshoot DNS resolution for both internal and external names

Components of Microsoft's DNS

DNS has been around for decades prior to Microsoft developing its edition of DNS in Microsoft NT 4.0. There are many varieties of DNS implementations that support the required features and processes that define DNS. We'll cover the components of Microsoft's Domain Name System and how it's applied in the Windows operating systems.

DNS is implemented with Windows Server 2008 R2 services to manage name resolution for Microsoft-based networks. Once installed, these services will need to communicate with other DNS name servers, which is accomplished with several different methods, such as forwarding, root hints, and delegation. The DNS service will also maintain databases, named *zones*, for the internal Active Directory domain or other namespaces. The domain computers will need to query this DNS service, so you must configure individual computers in order to provide efficient and rapid name resolution.

Understanding the DNS Server Role

Windows Server 2008 R2 and previous versions of Windows Servers offer a DNS server role. The Windows 2000 was the first version that could support the Active Directory requirements of DNS. So, you can integrate this version up to Windows Server 2008 R2 to meet your naming system requirement specifically for IPv4 addresses. Versions earlier than Windows Server 2008 do not support IPv6.

DNS FUNDAMENTAL CONCEPTS

Mastering Windows Server 2008 Networking Foundations (Sybex, 2008) covers DNS fundamentals. The following is a short summary of the DNS concepts referred to in this chapter. It is essential to have a complete understanding of the following terms and processes, so please refer to the *Networking Foundations* book for further details.

Hostname   This is the name of a computer. According to DNS standards, it can be up to 255 characters. It is equivalent to a computer's first name.

HOSTS file   This is a text file that lists hostnames to IP addresses. This is located in c:\windows\system32\drivers\etc for standard Windows Server 2008 R2 installations.

Namespace   This is the name of a domain, not specifically an Active Directory domain. This is a logical set of hosts signified by a name controlled by a set of name servers. This is equivalent to a computer's last name; they're all part of the same family. For example, Bigfirm.com is the namespace for hosts in the Bigfirm.com domain.

Fully qualified domain name (FQDN)   This is the hostname appended to the domain's namespace such as Bf1.Bigfirm.com.

Name server   This is a DNS server that will resolve FQDNs to IP addresses. Name servers also control namespaces for specified domains. They will resolve requests for that namespace from DNS clients throughout the network.

Hierarchical naming structure   The namespace is created so that the left part of a name is a subset of the right part of the name as shown in the FQDN. With this, the naming servers can start at the right side of the name, and the responses from the name servers will direct it to the correct naming server for a given namespace. For example, as shown in the following illustration, Ec1.Ecoast.Bigfirm.com is the FQDN for a server in the Ecoast.Bigfirm.com domain. This domain is actually a subset, or a *subdomain*, under the control of the Bigfirm.com domain. You can say the same thing about Bigfirm.com for the .com "top-level domain name." The strength is that you can ask the .com domain name server where the Bigfirm.com name server is. The same can be done for the Ecoast.Bigfirm.com server, and so on. The FQDN name directs the query to the right name server through a process named *recursion*.

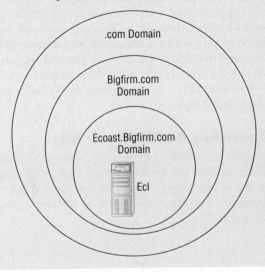

Recursion   This is a server-directed process to resolve an FQDN. If the server cannot resolve the FQDN with its own information, it will send the query to other name servers. The recursion process comprises root servers and domain name servers. Root servers are the top of the hierarchical naming structure. The root servers list the name servers that control the top-level domain names such as .com, .gov, and .edu. The top-level domain servers control the registry of subdomains beneath the top-level domain. For example, name servers for the Sybex.com subdomain are registered on the .com domain servers. When a query occurs, the following is performed (as shown in the following illustration):

1. The DNS client requests a name, like www.Sybex.com from its DNS server.
2. Through the recursive process, the DNS server queries the root servers for the .com domain name servers.
3. The root servers give a list of name servers for the .com domain.
4. Then the DNS server queries the .com name servers for Sybex.com.
5. It receives another list of name servers for the Sybex.com domain.
6. It queries the provided name servers for the www.Sybex.com FQDN.
7. The Sybex.com DNS server coughs up the IP address of the www server to the DNS server.
8. The DNS server passes the IP address to the client.
9. Armed with the IP address, the client connects with the web server www.Sybex.com.

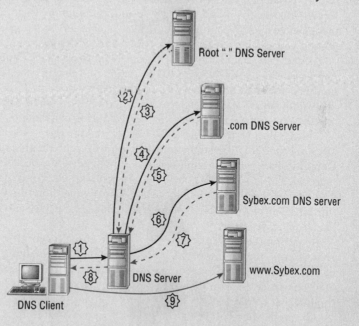

Delegation   This means allowing another name server to control a subdomain of a given namespace. For example, the Bigfirm.com name servers can delegate control to the Ecoast. Bigfirm.com namespace to another server.

Forwarding   This is an alternative to the recursion process. This is a lateral request to another name server within the network. The forwarding server obtains a response and relays it to the originating name server.

Iteration   This is a client-directed process to resolve an FQDN. If the client receives a negative request from a name server, it will query another name server.

NetBIOS naming system   This a legacy naming system used primarily within Microsoft NT 4.0 networks. Its processes are still part of the Windows operating systems.

Service resource records (SRVs)   This is a record within a DNS namespace to resolve a service to a hostname. This is an essential part of DNS supporting Active Directory.

Dynamic DNS (DDNS) update   This is a process that allows DNS clients to register their hostnames in an assigned namespace. This reduces the need of admins to manually enter records in the name server databases. This is another essential part of DNS supporting Active Directory.

Installing the DNS role is simple. First, you need to have a static IP address. Hitting a moving target is pretty tough for the DNS client. Remember, the Windows Server 2008 R2 setup configures a dynamically assigned IPv4 and IPv6 addresses by default. If you haven't implemented an IPv6 addressing scheme, the computer will receive IPv6's equivalent to the Automatic Private IP Addressing (APIPA) scheme (169.254.x.y) address in IPv4. So, it would be able to talk to computers within the subnet. You need to decide what you will do with the IPv6 configurations on the DNS server—disable them, assign a static IP address, or ignore them. The latter is fine for a test environment, but we don't recommend it for a production server. If you choose to ignore the IPv6 configurations, you will get a warning when installing DNS concerning the dynamically assigned address.

Second, you should add the primary DNS suffix, such as Bigfirm.com, in the computer's system properties. We use the word *should* because it isn't always necessary. The primary DNS suffix is modified automatically when the computer joins a domain. If the server is going to operate as part of a workgroup, you will need to add it so other DNS servers can locate it within the DNS structure and the DNS service is properly configured during installation.

Third, select to add the role. Within Server Manager's Add Role Wizard, you can select the DNS role, and it will install effortlessly. However, if you are going to install Active Directory Domain Services on the same server, you will get a kickback for attempting to select both roles together. The Add Role Wizard likes it when you select only Active Directory Domain Services in this instance. Although it doesn't specifically mention this as it does with the requirement for the .NET Framework, it will be installing the DNS service as a necessary component with the Domain Services role.

Installing the role creates a solitary DNS name server that is talking only with the Internet root servers. It can support a LAN environment for resolving Internet names, but that's about it. The Domain Name System leverages other naming servers to resolve names throughout the DNS structure. So, you'll have to configure the server to talk with other servers that exist in the internal network.

Although Microsoft leads you to believe it has the corner on any technology it touches, remember there are other DNS implementations. The Active Directory implementation of DNS is strong for internal requirements but rarely used on the Internet. In large environments, Unix or Linux-based DNS implementations may already be in place to support non-Microsoft servers.

Typically, these are referred to as BIND DNS servers. Integration between these servers is possible through forwarding. If database sharing is desired, the BIND DNS servers need to provide similar features of the Microsoft DNS role, and then you would rely on standard secondary zones to replicate the Microsoft DNS–based zones to the other servers, which are discussed in the following sections.

INTEGRATING WITH OTHER DNS SERVERS

In DNS Fundamental Concepts, we mentioned that there are different methods for resolving DNS names, such as forwarding, recursion, delegation, and iteration. These methods are related to the integration with other DNS servers. Before we get started, remember that iteration is basically client driven. If the DNS server doesn't have an answer, the client would go to another DNS server. The server or the client can be configured for iteration only, but it is not the default. It is rarely implemented. The other three, forwarding, recursion, and delegation, involve contacting other DNS servers by the queried DNS server.

Recursion is the primary process occurring on the Internet. The queried DNS server starts at the top and works its way down with the referrals it receives from each DNS server it contacts. In Windows DNS servers, the top servers are listed on the Root Hints tab of the DNS server properties, as shown in Figure 5.1. This can be displayed in the DNS Management snap-in by right-clicking the server icon and selecting Properties. By default, it is populated with "live" Internet DNS servers.

FIGURE 5.1
Root Hints tab

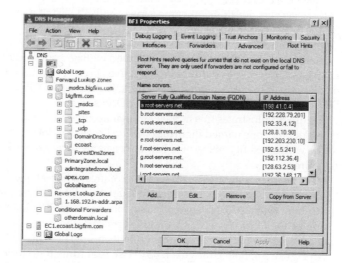

The list is located in a text file named Cache in the `c:\windows\system32\dns` folder displayed in Figure 5.2.

In a single Active Directory domain environment, you can leave this alone. DNS servers can use these references to resolve Internet-based namespaces such as Sybex.com when a client requests it. In larger environments, you can remove the root hint entries on other DNS servers and rely on one server to support DNS resolution throughout the external environment. This would be the "caching DNS server" of the internal structure.

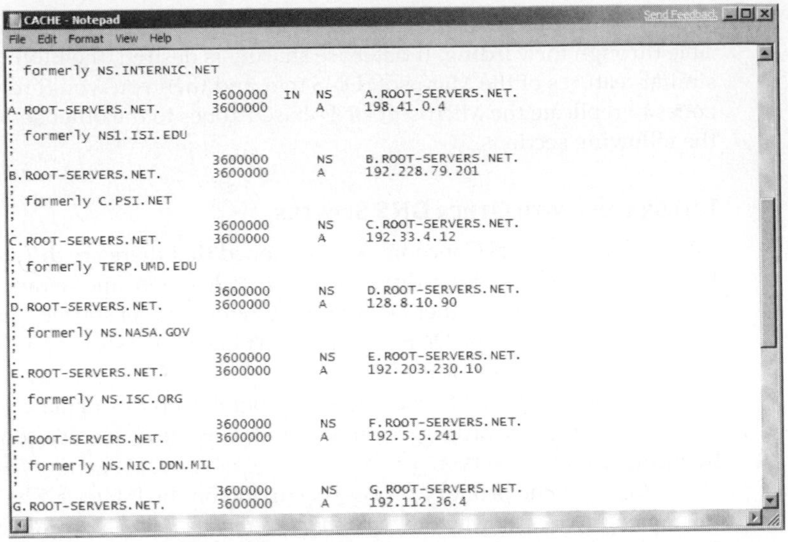

FIGURE 5.2

The Cache file listing root hints

While root hints manage the queries going up the DNS hierarchical structure, delegation manages queries going downward. In our example, the DNS servers that control the .com namespace delegate the control of registered subdomains like Sybex.com. The delegation is simply the listing of these servers. So, the .com name server sends the list of name servers to a DNS server looking for the Sybex.com namespace.

In a Windows environment, you can see delegation in play with multiple Active Directory domains. If you have an AD domain named Bigfirm.com, you have an associated Bigfirm.com DNS namespace. You could create an Active Directory domain named Ecoast.Bigfirm.com. Instead of keeping all the DNS namespaces on the Bigfirm.com DNS server, you can delegate the Ecoast.Bigfirm.com DNS namespace to another DNS server.

Figure 5.3 illustrates this in the DNS management console. The Bf1 DNS server supports a forward lookup zone named Bigfirm.com. The Ecoast subdomain, represented by an icon of a gray folder with a text file on top of it, lists only a name server record for Ec1.Ecoast.Bigfirm.com with its IP address.

A forwarder is another DNS server to request a lateral query. When a server cannot resolve the DNS name, it can forward the request to another DNS server rather than going through the root hints. In an internal DNS environment, forwarders can be used to resolve other namespaces. For example, the DNS server Ec1.Ecoast.Bigfirm.com needs to resolve Bigfirm.com servers and others namespaces, so a forwarder is entered in its properties shown in Figure 5.4.

In Figure 5.4, notice the check box "Use root hints if no forwarders are available." You can disable this in a larger environment if you want to centralize the Internet-based DNS queries. Also notice the text concerning conditional forwarders.

Conditional forwarders are a Windows Server 2003 feature in Windows DNS. However, the DNS management console for Windows Server 2008 R2 is different from that of Windows Server 2003. Instead of being located on the Forwarders tab, conditional forwarders have their own node in the left pane's tree. To manage resolution a specific namespace, the conditional forward can direct queries to a specific server. In Figure 5.5, a conditional forwarder was set up for the otherdomain.local namespace. Thus, any queries for this namespace will go to Od1.Otherdomain.local DNS server.

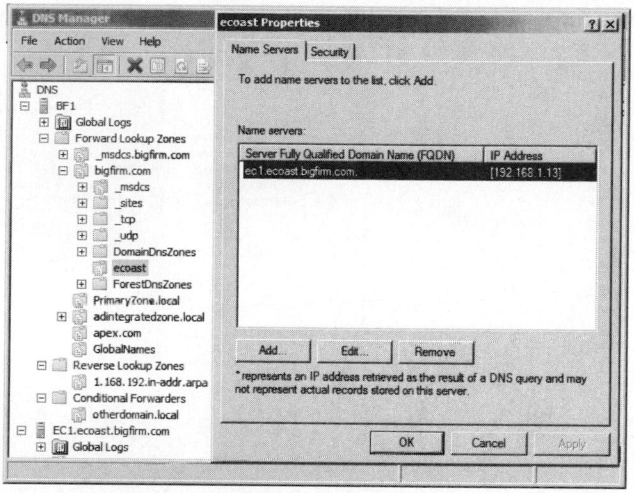

FIGURE 5.3

Delegated domain
for Ecoast
.Bigfirm.com

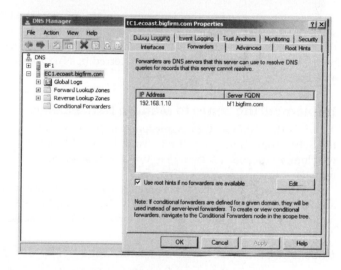

FIGURE 5.4

Forwarders tab

Conditional forwarders are created by right-clicking the Conditional Forwarder folder in the DNS management console and selecting New Conditional Forwarder. The New Conditional Forwarder dialog box provides an option to replicate the setting to other domain controllers in the domain or forest using Active Directory application partitions.

Forwarding also can be used to resolve Internet-based queries instead of using root hints. We prefer to use this in small environments that have an Internet service provider such as cable or DSL. These ISPs will have their own DNS servers that are found on the router configuration. So, these are entered as forwarders on the internal DNS servers. Although root hints can work in this environment, we find this technique more reliable. In addition, it limits the internal DNS server's communication to a specified external source.

FIGURE 5.5
Conditional
forwarder

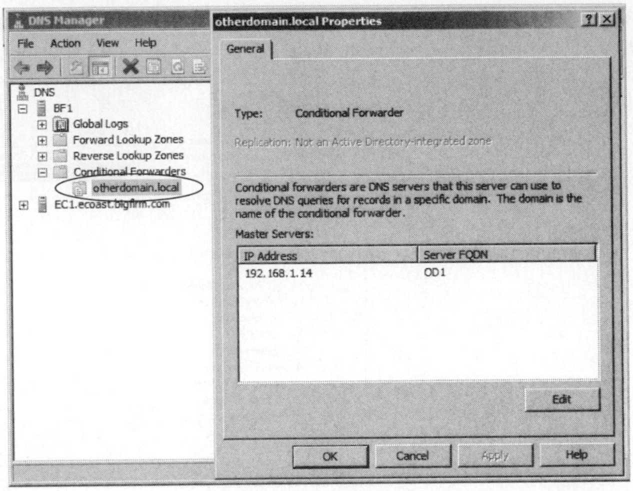

The integration with other DNS servers can complete the DNS role configurations. The DNS server could receive requests and then send these requests to other DNS servers. Once it receives the answer, it could cache the information for a period of time, which in Windows is set to one hour by default. This configuration is referred to as a *caching-only server*. If the server is to control a namespace, you have to add zones.

Implementing Zones to Manage Namespaces

A *zone* is the database for a namespace. In the Internet, there is a DNS server that controls the Sybex.com namespace. If you want the IP address for www.sybex.com , this DNS server will look in its zone (database) to find the answer. So, you can create zones on DNS servers to manage namespaces.

In Windows DNS servers, there are three types of zones: standard primary, standard secondary, and Active Directory integrated. Actually, there is another one, the stub zone, that doesn't manage a namespace. It's more like a conditional forwarder. We'll discuss that one as well.

UNDERSTANDING THE STANDARD PRIMARY ZONE

Name servers were designed to centralize name resolution for a network. Initially, DNS servers responded to requests based on its text-based HOSTS file. This is essentially what Microsoft named a *standard primary zone*. The standard primary zone is a text file in which the server maintains the records for a given namespace. That's what is *standard* about the Windows DNS implementation. *Primary* refers to replication.

As in the days of NT, there was one master domain controller named the *primary domain controller* (PDC), which controlled any writing to its database. The rest were *backup domain controllers* (BDCs), which had read-only copies. Primary zones mean there is only one master, and this server is it. Other DNS servers can have only read-only copies of this zone; these are secondary.

Creating a zone is easily accomplished with the New Zone Wizard, which you can initiate by right-clicking Forward Lookup Zones and selecting New Zone. The wizard prompts for the following information:

♦ The namespace or name of the domain such as Primaryzone.local.

♦ The name of the text file, which defaults to the .dns file extension.

♦ The Dynamic DNS Update option. We'll discuss this later in the "Updating DNS Dynamically" section.

After the zone creation, you can view the contents of the text file in the c:\windows\system32\dns folder displayed in Figure 5.6. Additional records, cname and hostrecord, were created for examples that are located at the bottom of the file.

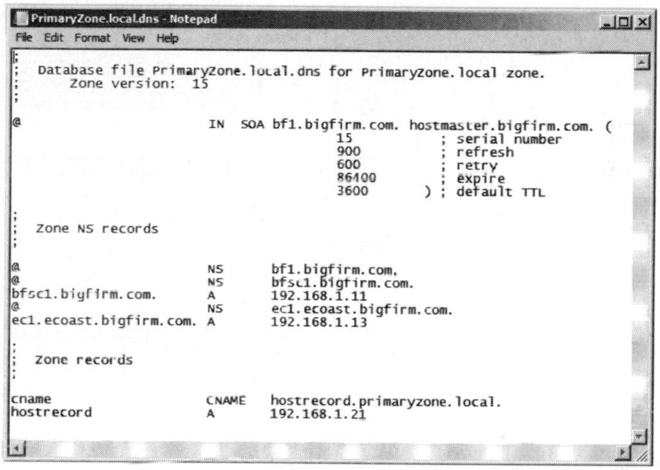

FIGURE 5.6
Standard primary
zone file

UNDERSTANDING THE STANDARD SECONDARY ZONE

The *standard secondary zone* is the read-only copy of the standard primary zone or an Active Directory integrated zone. Replication is performed through the zone transfer process, which is configured on the zone's properties. On Windows DNS servers, the default setting for zone transfers is to allow transfers to only the registered name servers of the zone, as shown in Figure 5.7.

So, you can add a name server such as Ec1.Ecoast.Bigfirm.com to the Name Servers tab, as in Figure 5.8, to permit replication to this server.

Once that is accomplished, you can run through the New Zone Wizard to create a standard secondary zone on Ec1. This will require the master server's IP address, which would be the server to request the zone transfer. It doesn't necessarily have to be the DNS server with the standard primary zone. The result is a successful transfer of the zone to Ec1, as shown in Figure 5.9.

FIGURE 5.7
Zone Transfers tab
for a primary zone

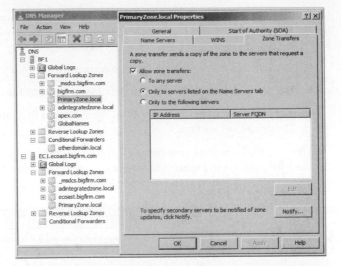

FIGURE 5.8
Name Servers tab
for a primary zone

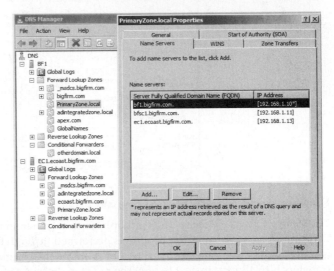

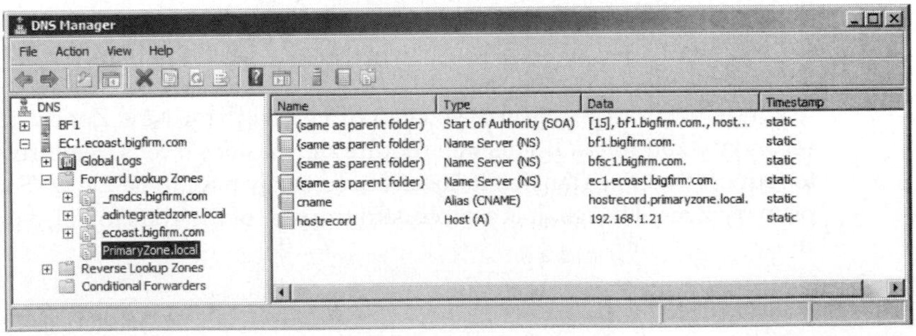

FIGURE 5.9
Standard
secondary zone

The zone transfer process is not complex. The server for the primary zone keeps track of the changes it has made and has a serial number for the change. When a secondary server contacts the primary server, it checks out the serial number in the Start of Authority record. If the serial number on the secondary server doesn't match, it's time to replicate the changes. This is simply a text-based blast of the database information. Earlier versions of DNS supported AXFR (all zone transfers) replication, which meant the entire zone was replicated to the secondary server. This could be too much traffic to throw onto the line. Windows DNS supports IXFR (which are incremental zone transfers), which just replicates the changes. Windows DNS also supports notification of secondary servers, which reduces the wait time to trigger replication.

UNDERSTANDING ACTIVE DIRECTORY INTEGRATED ZONES

The third zone, Active Directory Integrated, is the predominant implementation of Windows DNS servers. The name Active Directory says it all. First, the DNS records are stored in the Active Directory database rather than a text file. Second, the zones are replicated to all other Active Directory domain controllers in the domain rather than through the zone transfer process. Since Active Directory database uses multimaster replication, changes can be made to the DNS zone on any domain controller, and they would replicated to the other domain controllers. With the integration of DNS in Active Directory, the coupling of DNS and domain controller roles became the norm. For more information concerning the replication process, refer to Chapter 21.

Like the standard zones, an Active Directory integrated zone can be created with the New Zone Wizard. On the first page of the wizard, shown in Figure 5.10, you select the "Store the zone in Active Directory" check box.

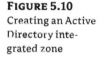

FIGURE 5.10

Creating an Active Directory integrated zone

Windows Server 2003 offered the capability to store the DNS zones in a separate application partition that is a division of the Active Directory database. This would allow the zones to be replicated to domain controllers in other parts of the forest and allowed admins to selectively choose which domain controller would support it.

In Figure 5.11, you have four options: forest wide, domain wide, domain wide (Windows 2000 compatible), and a specified custom application partition for storing the zone database. The first two options place the database in automatically created default application partitions: one for the forest and one for the domain that the domain controller is a member of The Windows 2000–compatible location is the domain partition of the Active Directory database so the zone database would be replicated to only domain controllers of that domain. You can create custom application partitions as well, such as those displayed in the figure.

FIGURE 5.11
Active Directory
zone replication
scope

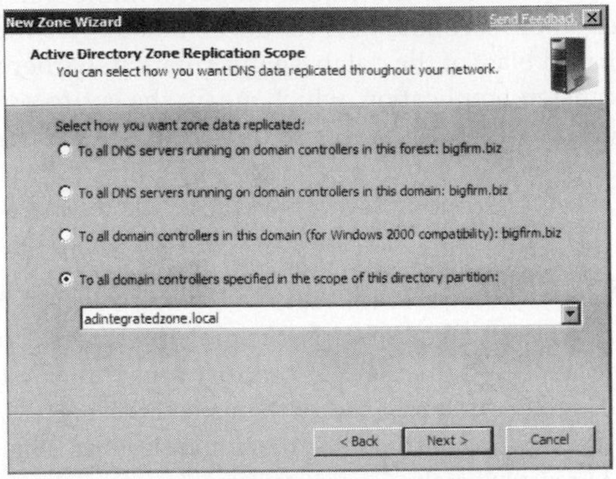

DNSCmd provides the ability to manage these partitions. The following creates a new application partition for the Active Directory integrated zone listed earlier. The name of the partition doesn't have to match the zone name. Using the same name makes it more understandable when viewing the configurations:

```
C:\Users\Administrator.BF1>dnscmd /createdirectoryPartition adintegratedzone.local

DNS Server . created directory partition: adintegratedzone.local
Command completed successfully.
```

Once it is created, then an Active Directory integrated zone can be assigned to it, as displayed in Figure 5.11.

Then the other domain controllers can be configured to support the zone using DNSCmd also. On Ec1, which is a domain controller for the Ecoast.Bigfirm.com domain, say you want to add two Active Directory zones.

◆ Adintegratedzone.local, which is placed in its own application partition

◆ The reverse lookup zone for 192.168.1.0 subnet, which is placed in the forest shared partition

First, add the server to the Name Servers tab in the properties of the desired zones similar to Figure 5.8.

Then, the following command lists the available partitions on Ec1:

```
C:\Users\administrator.BIGFIRM>dnscmd /enumdirectorypartitions
Enumerated directory partition list:

        Directory partition count = 4
    adintegratedzone.local                  Not-Enlisted
    DomainDnsZones.bigfirm.com              Not-Enlisted
```

```
DomainDnsZones.ecoast.Bigfirm.com          Enlisted Auto Domain
ForestDnsZones.bigfirm.com                 Enlisted Auto Forest
```

Command completed successfully.

From the output, you can see there are four application "directory" partitions. The first one is the custom one created earlier, which the server has not enlisted in sharing. The second is the domain application partition that is shared with all of the non-Windows 2000 domain controllers within the Bigfirm.com domain. The third is for the Ecoast.Bigfirm.com domain. The fourth is for all the domain controllers within the forest of domains. Ec1 is already enlisted for sharing these two partitions.

To start sharing the custom application partition, you use the /enlistdirectorypartition option:

```
C:\Users\administrator.BIGFIRM>dnscmd /enlistdirectorypartition adintegratedzone
.local

DNS Server . enlisted directory partition: adintegratedzone.local
Command completed successfully.
```

You should see the partition enlisted with the /enumdirectorypartitions option like you saw earlier. However, this seems to be affected by the "Microsoft Coffee Break Computation Process." Working with various Microsoft products, we've observed that some configurations do not take immediate effect as you would expect. Most times, you can quickly verify configurations after the changes have been made. Occasionally, the settings do not show a change, and they can't be verified. No matter what you do, including triggering Active Directory replication between the domain controllers as in this case, it doesn't help. Only after pulling your hair out in complete frustration, resolving to take a smoke or coffee break, and returning to the console do the verification of the settings work out and the server is performing as advertised. Therefore, the "Microsoft Coffee Break Computation Process" must have completed.

```
C:\Users\administrator.BIGFIRM>dnscmd /enumdirectorypartitions
Enumerated directory partition list:

        Directory partition count = 4
 adintegratedzone.local                 Enlisted
 DomainDnsZones.bigfirm.com             Not-Enlisted
 DomainDnsZones.ecoast.Bigfirm.com      Enlisted Auto Domain
 ForestDnsZones.bigfirm.com             Enlisted Auto Forest


Command completed successfully.
```

After the directory is displayed as enlisted and more "Microsoft Coffee Break Computation Process" completes, the zones should be listed on the server with the /enumzones option and be visible in the DNS management console. Notice in the following output, in the Storage column, the adintegratedzone.local zone is lists as AD-Custom, and the other two zones are AD-Forest.

These indicate the application partitions. The `Properties` column indicates the Dynamic DNS Update options, which will be discussed in the "Updating DNS Dynamically" section.

```
C:\Users\administrator.BIGFIRM>dnscmd /enumzones

Enumerated zone list:
      Zone count = 8

    Zone name                   Type        Storage        Properties

    .                           Cache       AD-Domain
    _msdcs.bigfirm.com          Primary     AD-Forest      Secure
    1.168.192.in-addr.arpa      Primary     AD-Forest      Update Rev
    adintegratedzone.local      Primary     AD-Custom      Secure
    ecoast.Bigfirm.com          Primary     AD-Domain      Secure
    PrimaryZone.local           Secondary   File
    TrustAnchors                Primary     AD-Forest
```

Using Stub Zones to Integrate with Other DNS Servers

The *stub zone* is another improvement that came with Windows 2003. It is actually another method to integrate with other DNS servers. The stub zone lists only the name server for a given namespace. It holds no control over the zone, so it indicates only what server could support name resolution for the namespace. Like conditional forwarders, it provides a lateral communication to the authoritative DNS server. These zones can also be replicated between domain controllers.

The New Zone Wizard sets up the stub zone with the following parameters:

◆ Type of zone: Stub

◆ Optionally stored in Active Directory with the desired application partition

◆ Namespace of the zone, such as Apex.com

◆ DNS server that supports this namespace

Once the stub zone is created, you can view the contents of it, as displayed in Figure 5.12. It lists the Start of Authority record for the namespace, the name server record for the namespace, and a host record for the name server.

FIGURE 5.12
Stub zone example

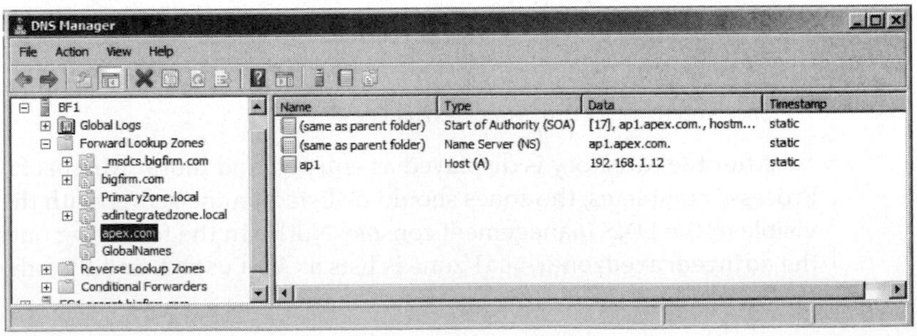

USING REVERSE LOOKUP ZONES TO INCREASE SECURITY

You may have noticed that the zones we created were found in the Forward Lookup Zones folder within the DNS management console. A *forward lookup* means the client provides a fully qualified domain name and the DNS server returns an IP address. A *reverse lookup* does the opposite: the client provides an IP address, and then the DNS server returns an FQDN.

You might be wondering to yourself, "Self, why would this be necessary?" Well, the primary reasons are security related. Consider an evil hacker who has set up a malicious service to listen for DNS queries for FQDNs starting with "www." on a network. When the rogue service gets a query, it automatically sends a bogus response to the client with the IP address of the evil hacker's web server. The website loads worms, viruses, Trojans, and other unsafe code before the user knows what's happening. Now, if the web browser could be configured to perform a reverse lookup on the provided IP address, it could compare the result with the queried name. If it didn't match, it wouldn't connect to the web server.

There are few Windows products that do this. The SMTP service on Windows and Exchange Server has an option to perform reverse lookups on connections to the server. The SMTP servers provide their domain names in the communication, and the TCP/IP address is provided in the connection. So, the reverse lookup can be performed to verify things match up. This option is not typically used, but it is available.

The nslookup command illustrates the use of the reverse lookup. In the following code, the command is started in the interactive mode to a server that doesn't have a pointer (PTR) record in a reverse lookup zone. Notice the default server is listed as UnKnown. DNS queries can be flaky when this is the case.

```
rem NsLookup without a proper ptr record
C:\Users\Administrator.BF1>nslookup
Default Server:  UnKnown
Address:  192.168.1.10
```

If the pointer record is created in the reverse lookup zone, the command output looks better. It lists the name of the server.

```
rem NsLookup with a proper ptr record
C:\Users\Administrator.BF1>nslookup
Default Server:  bf1.bigfirm.com
Address:  192.168.1.10
```

To correctly configure reverse lookup zones within your network, you need to understand how reverse resolution works. For IPv4, the IP address is in decimal dot notation with four octets, as in x.y.w.z. IPv6 is similar, but it uses hex numbers and a lot more. Either way, the process is the same. The DNS server that receives the query changes the order of the IP address. So, a query for the FQDN for the IP address of x.y.w.z becomes z.w.y.x, with .in-addr.arpa appended to the end of it. Then the DNS server attempts to resolve the FQDN of z.w.y.x.in-addr.arpa like a normal FQDN. It starts at the top-level domain of .arpa and works its way down to the in-addr. name servers. Each of the decimal values becomes a subdomain of the namespace to the right of it.

In small environments that include only one subnet, the subnet can be represented by a single zone. In our example, the 192.168.1.0 subnet is one zone, as shown in Figure 5.13. When the reverse lookup zone is created, the New Zone Wizard requests the name of the subnet to create the zone.

FIGURE 5.13
Reverse lookup
zone example

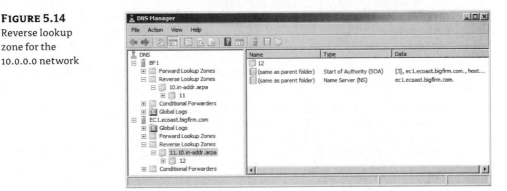

In larger environments where multiple subnets are in place, the zone for the higher-precedence octet needs to be created, and lower octets should be represented as subdomains or delegated subdomains. For example, if a large organization is using the 10.0.0.0 private IP addressing scheme, it would create a reverse lookup zone for the 10.in-addr.arpa domain name.

With dynamic updates occurring, subdomains would be automatically created for the next octet from 1 to 254, and pointer records would populate the subfolders of the structure. At some point, the subdomains could be delegated to another set of DNS servers such as domain controllers located in a site that contains these subnets. Then pointer records would be registered in the respective zone that represents the subnet.

In Figure 5.14, the 10.in-addr.arpa zone created was created on Bf1. If you wanted the 10.11.0.0 subnets controlled by another server, you would delegate the 11 subdomain. This was delegated to Ec1. Within it, the actual subnet of 10.11.12.0 is also represented as a delegated subdomain.

FIGURE 5.14
Reverse lookup
zone for the
10.0.0.0 network

Understanding Record Types

Now that the databases are set up for the clients to retrieve information, you need to add records to the databases. As mentioned previously, Dynamic DNS (DDNS) updates take care of this for the Windows computers within an environment. However, it will be necessary to add records manually and verify the correct records were created dynamically. More than 25 record types are available for a DNS zone. We will review the most common record types found in a Windows DNS implementation.

ROUND-ROBIN AND NETMASK ORDERING

On the Advanced tab in the properties of the DNS server, you will find three server options enabled:

◆ Enable round robin

◆ Enable netmask ordering

◆ Secure cache against pollution

Round-robin is a "poor man's" network load balancing technique. If you register multiple host records of the same name with different IP addresses, the DNS server responds randomly with a different IP address for each query. Although it doesn't spread the client load evenly or smartly to the available hosts, it still provides a balancing capability between servers.

Netmask ordering, like round-robin, uses multiple host records of the same name with a different IP address. Rather than picking randomly, the record that mathematically shows up as being closer is chosen. This is done through a comparison of the subnets. This is good if you have geographically separated hosts and your client needs to contact the one in its own network.

So, when using servers that are geographically separated, you need to decide which method is best. Netmask ordering will keep the response time minimized by nature of a shorter route. Round-robin will distribute the load more evenly if the clients are in a concentrated location.

However, a twist in these processes has come about with the release of Windows Server 2008 and Vista. The TCP/IP stack for IPv6 and IPv4 "when possible" will perform a similar process to netmask ordering named *default address selection*. Thus, it receives the IP addresses from the DNS server and decides on its own which is best.

Like most configurations, this can be overridden in the registry:

```
Hkey_Local_Machine\System\CurrentControlSet
\Services\Tcpip\Parameters\OverrideDefaultAddressSelection
```

A value of 1 will turn off default address selection and allow a random choice of the NLB round-robin servers.

You can see the effect on all this with the use of round-robin for geographically split servers. For example, an environment with a disaster recovery site would like to offer two servers located in different sites to perform the same servers. For example, two FTP servers could be available to download data. DNS is rigged to provide two IP addresses for the same name, ftp.Bigfirm.com. Round robin will distribute the names equally. If one server goes down such as in a disaster, the clients will still have connectivity to ftp.Bigfirm.com. (It will occasionally select the dead server's IP address, but reconnects are still available to keep the data flowing.)

However, if netmask ordering or default address selection is in place, the clients may never get the live FTP server. The DNS server would be making the choice or the client would be. So, this gotcha scenario tells you to apply the time-tried rule: "Test, test, test." Validate what servers are being used in a normal scenario, and validate what happens when a disaster scenario occurs.

HOST AND POINTER RECORDS

Host (A) and pointer (PTR) records are the most common records you will find in the forward lookup zones and the reverse lookup zones, respectively. The A records list the hostname of the computer and return the IP address. The PTR records list the IP address and return an FQDN.

You may have to create these for computers that do not have the DDNS update protocol available.

ALIAS RECORDS

Alias (CNAME) records are created to list a secondary name for a computer. This record will list the name and return the assigned computer's FQDN. These are useful in the event of replacing the server of a published name that the clients use to access applications or services. Without their reconfiguration, clients will still be able to access the alias after replacement.

MAIL EXCHANGER RECORDS

Mail exchanger (MX) records are for SMTP communication. Mail servers request MX records to contact the receiving SMTP server for that namespace. Typically, you will be setting these up in an external DNS zone. However, they may be required internally for specific applications. The MX record requires an FQDN of the SMTP server and a priority value.

The priority helps determine which MX record to contact first and next when more than one is available. The lower value wins out. Remember "number-one priority."

Say you have a primary SMTP server and a smart host SMTP server to support catching email when the primary server is unavailable. You would want to create MX records for both of them. The primary SMTP server needs a lower-priority value compared to the smart host such as 10 and 20, respectively. When the primary SMTP server is unavailable, the smart host is contacted.

SERVICE LOCATION RECORDS

Service location (SRV) records are the "big kahunas" for Windows DNS implementations. Without the SRV records, workstations and servers would not be able to find domain controllers. The SRV records by themselves involve only five values:

◆ *Service name*: This is a standard value typically preceded by an underscore such as "_gc." or "_ladp." This is equivalent to a hostname, and it would be tacked onto the FQDN of a service.

◆ *Server FQDN*: This is the server that provides the service.

◆ *Port*: This is the TCP or UDP port on which the service is available. The protocol is signified in the registered name such as _TCP.

◆ *Priority*: This works just like MX records—it has a "number-one priority."

◆ *Weight*: This is the tie-breaker for priority. Leave it at 0 if you not concerned with ties.

You will see a plethora of SRV records in a Windows DNS zone that supports Active Directory. They are found in subdomain folders because the service name is assigned different FQDNs. The required service is described by the FQDN like _gc._tcp.bigfirm.com. Figure 5.15 illustrates the SRV records.

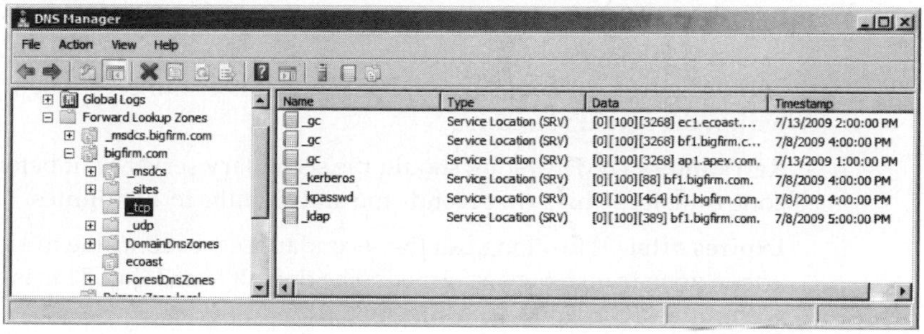

FIGURE 5.15
SRV record
example

START OF AUTHORITY RECORDS

A Start of Authority (SOA) record is a single record within each zone. It gives the information of what DNS server controls this zone and parameters on how to treat the resolved records. It contains several values that shouldn't be modified by editing the record. You should edit them on the Start of Authority (SOA) tab in the properties of the zone, as shown in Figure 5.16.

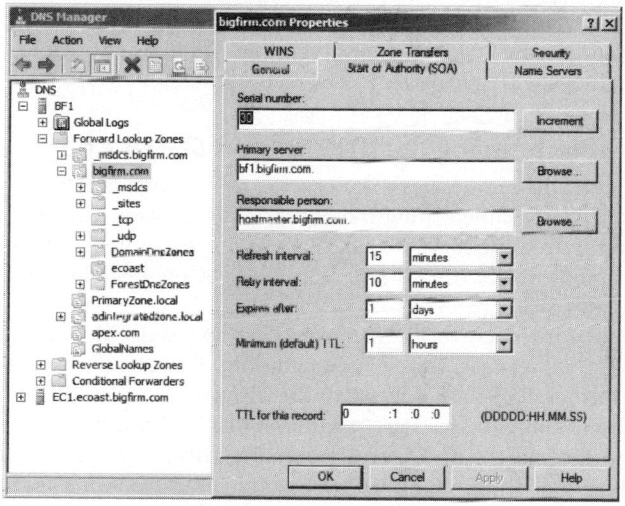

FIGURE 5.16
Start of Authority
(SOA) tab

The following are the fields on the tab:

Serial number   This is the revision number of the zone file. This really counts with standard primary zones because the Active Directory replication has its own serial number so to speak. Secondary zones can compare their number with it to see whether their information is up-to-date. If it isn't, it's time for a zone transfer.

Primary server   This is the server in which the zone was initially set up on.

Responsible person   This is supposed to be an email address of the person who administers the zone. Notice the @ is replaced by a dot (.). If you want to make someone really mad, you put their email address here.

Refresh interval   This is how much time the secondary server can wait before attempting to check changes on the primary server. At this point of time, it compares the serial number of the SOA record with its own. By default it is 15 minutes. The value is listed in seconds within the actual record.

Retry interval   How long should the secondary server wait before trying again after a failed zone transfer? This is in seconds too and defaults to 10 minutes.

Expires after   How long can the secondary server continue to answer requests on this zone after a zone transfer is performed? The default is one day. This is also in listed in seconds within the record, and the value is 86,400.

Minimum (default) TTL   How long should these records be cached? The default is an hour, or 3,600 seconds.

NAME SERVER RECORDS

Name server (NS) records list the servers that can respond to queries for this zone. There will be at least one of these records in the zone. Like the SOA record, this is modified in the properties of the zone on the Name Servers tab, as shown in Figure 5.8. The only value required in the NS record is the FQDN of the server. You'll notice a little note at the bottom of the Name Servers tab stating the IP address is a retrieved value.

Implementing the DNS Role on Server Core

One of the many roles that Server Core supports is DNS. As discussed in Chapter 3, the DNS role was installed using the Active Directory Domain Services role, and DCPromo automatically configured the service using Active Directory integrated zones. There may be opportunities to implement DNS on a stand-alone Server Core installation such as hosting an external domain namespace.

For instance, the Bigfirm.com IT shop has decided to control its own Internet-registered DNS namespace, which is Bigfirm.com. There are some pros and cons to hosting your own external DNS namespace that are discussed later in this chapter in the "Supporting External DNS Domains" section. In addition, the Bigfirm.com namespace is already used internally to support the Active Directory domain. This is sometimes referred as *split-brain DNS*. This is also discussed in the "Supporting External DNS Domains" section. For brevity, we'll say the IT shop has gone through the ropes and decided that Server Core would be the best option.

The steps would include installing the role, configuring the server, and adding zones as required. We discussed each of these procedures earlier but almost entirely used the DNS management console. Now you'll get your fingers dirty with DNSCmd, which provides the same functions as the snap-in and more.

INSTALLING THE DNS ROLE

You can install roles using the dism command. The following commands will list the available roles and features and then install the DNS role. Notice that the /featurename parameter is case sensitive. Since we haven't installed Active Directory Domain Services, this is a now stand-alone DNS server:

```
rem list roles available
dism /online /get-features /format:table
```

```
rem install DNS role
dism /online /enable-feature /featurename:DNS-Server-Core-Role
```

CONFIGURING THE DNS SERVER

As we discussed, the stand-alone DNS server needs to integrate with other DNS servers to leverage their information. This was performed with forwarding, root hints, delegation, stub zones, and conditional forwarders earlier in the chapter. In this example, we'll assume this DNS server is sitting in a DMZ or perimeter network so at most it will need to resolve external DNS names only. Root hints are available by default, but we will add a forwarder to an external DNS server.

The forwarders are entered as IP addresses after the /resetforwarders parameter. In addition, the /slave and /noslave parameters handle the functionality of the check box "Use root hints if no forwarders are available" on the Forwarders tab of the server properties (shown earlier in Figure 5.4). The default is /noslave, which is equivalent to selecting the check box and using root hints.

The following provides the syntax to add a forwarder:

```
rem add a forwarder
dnscmd /resetforwarders 123.45.67.89
```

To verify the forwarders, you can use the /info option. The following lists just the forwarder configurations of the output:

```
rem verify forwarders
dnscmd /info
  Forwarders:

        Ptr          = 0000000000143CD0
        MaxCount     = 1
        AddrCount    = 1
                Addr[0] => af=2, salen=16, [sub=0, flag=00000000] p=13568,
addr=123.45.67.89

        forward timeout  = 3
        slave            = 0
```

You can view the root hints in the cache.dns file using Notepad, as discussed earlier. The /recordadd and /recorddelete options discussed next are used to modify this file.

You can modify additional configurations using the /config option. You can find an example of this later in the chapter in the "Global Query Blocklist" section. The configuration options are so lengthy that we recommend using the question mark with the port option (>) to push the information to a text file. Then you can review what can be changed and how to do it. This is one of the "Server Core Survival Guide" techniques mentioned in Chapter 3.

```
Rem porting the help info to a text file
Dnscmd /config ? > "dnscmd_help.txt"
```

ADDING ZONES TO A DNS SERVER CORE INSTANCE

A stand-alone DNS server can support standard primary and standard secondary zones. In this scenario, this server will support a standard primary zone of Bigfirm.com and a standard secondary zone of PrimaryZone.local. For security reasons, the Bigfirm.com zone will be completely separate from the internal Bigfirm.com Active Directory integrated zone. This protects seriously critical data such as service resource records of the domain controllers from evil hackers on the Internet.

The PrimaryZone.local zone will be replicated from Bf1.Bigfirm.com. For this to work, a name server record is created on Bf1 for the Server Core instance, as shown in Figure 5.8.

The primary zone requires a filename that will hold the database:

```
rem create new zone for an external bigfirm.com
dnscmd /zoneadd bigfirm.com /primary /file bigfirm.com.dns
```

The secondary zone requires a filename and a master server's IP address:

```
rem create a secondary zone for PrimaryZone.local
dnscmd /zoneadd primaryzone.local /secondary 192.168.1.10 /file primaryzone.local.dns
```

To verify the creation of the zones, you can use the /enumzones parameter:

```
rem list zone
dnscmd /enumzones
Enumerated zone list:
      Zone count = 3

  Zone name                        Type      Storage      Properties

  .                                Cache     File
  bigfirm.com                      Primary   File
  primaryzone.local                Secondary File
```

For a Server Core installation with Active Directory Domain Services, you can add the zones using the /enlistdirectorypartition parameter discussed in "Understanding Active Directory Integrated Zones."

You can view the properties of a zone using the /zoneinfo parameter. The following is an example (the italics are added for clarification):

```
rem view properties of the zone
dnscmd /zoneinfo bigfirm.com

Zone query result:

Zone info:
        ptr                 = 0000000000352700
        zone name           = bigfirm.com
        zone type           = 1    (1 = primary, 2 = secondary, 3 = stub)
        shutdown            = 0
        paused              = 0
        update              = 0    (0 = none, 1 = non and secure updates,
2 = secure only.)
```

```
        DS integrated          = 0    (0 = non AD integrated, 1 = AD integrated.)
        read only zone         = 0
        data file              = bigfirm.com.dns
        using WINS             = 0
        using Nbstat           = 0
        aging                  = 0
          refresh interval     = 168
          no refresh           = 168
          scavenge available   = 0
        Zone Masters      NULL IP Array.
        Zone Secondaries       NULL IP Array.
        secure secs            = 1
Command completed successfully.
```

You can list the contents of the zone using the /zoneprint option. Since we haven't added any records in Bigfirm.com, this is not very exciting. PrimaryZone.local does have records indicating that the zone transfer worked from the master DNS server:

```
rem list zone contents
dnscmd /zoneprint bigfirm.com


;
;  Zone:    bigfirm.com
;  Server:  BFSC1.bigfirm.com
;  Time:    Mon Jul 13 15:50:53 2009 UTC
;
@ 3600 NS        bfsc1.bigfirm.com.
                 3600 SOA        bfsc1.bigfirm.com. hostmaster.bigfirm.com. 1 900
 600 86400 3600
bfsc1 3600 A     192.168.1.11


;
;  Finished zone: 2 nodes and 3 records in 0 seconds
;


dnscmd /zoneprint primaryzone.local


;
;  Zone:    primaryzone.local
;  Server:  BFSC1.bigfirm.com
;  Time:    Mon Jul 13 16:17:11 2009 UTC
;
@ 3600 NS        bf1.bigfirm.com.
                 3600 NS         192.168.1.11.
                 3600 NS         192.168.1.13.
                 3600 SOA        bf1.bigfirm.com. hostmaster.bigfirm.com. 9 900
 600 86400 3600
cname 3600 CNAME          hostrecord.primaryzone.local.
hostrecord 3600 A         192.168.1.21
```

```
;
;  Finished zone: 3 nodes and 5 records in 0 seconds
;
```

MANAGING RECORDS IN THE ZONE

External DNS namespaces are not typically complicated like the Active Directory integrated zones. They usually consist of a few standard records like A, MX, and CNAME. The /recordadd option adds these to a zone. Since more than 25 records are available, the help information is equally lengthy as the /config option, so porting the information to a text file assists in constructing the commands.

The following is the basic syntax for the option. The required values are the zone name, node name (computer name), resource record type (such as A, CNAME, or MX), and additional resource record data. The data is specific to the type of record.

```
rem add records to bigfirm.com zone
DnsCmd <ServerName> /RecordAdd <Zone> <NodeName> [/Aging] [/OpenAcl]
[/CreatePTR] [<Ttl>] <RRType> <RRData>
```

The following creates three host (A) records, a CNAME record, and an MX record for the Bigfirm.com domain:

```
dnscmd /recordadd bigfirm.com webserver A 192.168.1.15
dnscmd /recordadd bigfirm.com vpn A 192.168.1.16
dnscmd /recordadd bigfirm.com mailserver A 192.168.1.17
dnscmd /recordadd bigfirm.com www cname webserver.bigfirm.com
dnscmd /recordadd bigfirm.com bigfirm.com. MX 10 mailserver.bigfirm.com
```

In addition to these records, we will add a name server to provide high availability:

```
rem add a nameserver
dnscmd /recordadd bigfirm.com bfsc2 A 192.168.1.20
dnscmd /recordadd bigfirm.com bigfirm.com. NS bfsc2.bigfirm.com
```

When we run /zoneprint, the output is now more substantial:

```
dnscmd /zoneprint bigfirm.com


;
;  Zone:    bigfirm.com
;  Server:  BFSC1.bigfirm.com
;  Time:    Mon Jul 13 16:09:58 2009 UTC
;
@ 3600 NS       bfsc1.bigfirm.com.
                3600 NS     bfsc2.bigfirm.com.
                3600 SOA    bfsc1.bigfirm.com. hostmaster.bigfirm.com. 12 900
   600 86400 3600
                3600 MX     10 mailserver.bigfirm.com.
bfsc1 3600 A    192.168.1.11
bfsc2 3600 A    192.168.1.20
```

```
mailserver 3600 A        192.168.1.17
vpn 3600 A      192.168.1.16
webserver 3600 A         192.168.1.15
www 3600 CNAME  webserver.bigfirm.com.


;
;  Finished zone: 7 nodes and 10 records in 0 seconds
;
```

You can delete records using the /recorddelete option:

```
rem delete a record
dnscmd /recorddelete bigfirm.com vpn A 192.168.1.16
```

The key to implementing the DNS role on Server Core is the DNSCmd command-line utility. It will do all of the configurations that can be performed in the DNS management console. To get a handle on using this command, remember the "Server Core Survival Guide" technique of saving the help information to a text file. Then you can construct the desired commands and save them in the built-in text editor Notepad.

Managing DNS Clients and Name Resolution

You can deduce that every computer is a DNS client. The DNS service is a vital component of the network even if Active Directory is not part of it. In addition, it is the only method to getting to your favorite Internet websites like www.MarkMinasi.com.

On the Windows operating system, there are two areas concerning the clients of DNS: resolving hostnames and registering hostnames and IP addresses through Dynamic DNS updates.

HOSTNAME RESOLUTION

The Windows computer has two parts in the name resolution process. This process is so important that we'll call it the "circle of life." One, which is nearly dead, is NetBIOS, and the other is DNS. (You could call it the hostname process, but most admins call it DNS.) This circle consists of the steps a computer would take in resolving a given name, as illustrated in Figure 5.17.

The NetBIOS process involves the following steps:

1. Broadcast the name into the network and see whether someone answers.

2. Look the name up in WINS.

3. Look the name up in the LMHOSTS file. This is another text file similar to the HOSTS file located in the same place: c:\windows\system32\drivers\etc. It lists NetBIOS names instead of hostnames.

The order of the first two steps is configurable particularly through the DHCP server. The broadcast step can be skipped, or the WINS lookup can be skipped. The order can be changed too. The default on Windows Server 2008 R2 is resolve through WINS first and then resolve with a broadcast second. However, the LMHOSTS lookup is always last.

The DNS process involves a shorter list of steps:

1. Look the name up in HOSTS.

2. Look the name up in DNS.

FIGURE 5.17
The circle of life

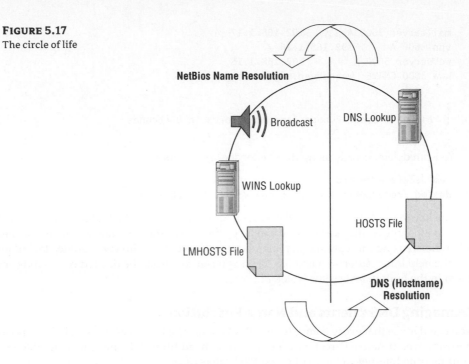

The order of the steps is not configurable, but you can modify the behavior of the DNS lookup. There are some good and bad points about the HOSTS file being first. If you are unable to access a DNS server or you need to redirect resolution of a name to another place, editing the HOSTS file works great. If the HOSTS file has stale or malicious entries, troubleshooting DNS can be difficult.

The name resolution process circles through both parts until it comes up with an IP address. It also has a choice of where to start in the circle, either NetBIOS or DNS. This is basically application dependent. Older Windows applications looked at a name and considered it NetBIOS. TCP/IP-based applications thought it was a hostname. This affects how the name is resolved, and it still is part of the Windows operating systems.

Examples of this include the `net view` command and the `ping` command.

The `net view` command is a command from the ancient days of LanManager, which relied entirely on NetBIOS. If you attempt to connect to a server using this command, you will see the NetBIOS name cache populated with the server name. This is displayed with the `nbtstat -c` command. The cache can be cleared with `nbtstat -R`.

```
rem view the NetBios cache
C:\Users\Administrator.BF1>nbtstat -c

Local Area Connection:
Node IpAddress: [192.168.1.10] Scope Id: []

    No names in cache

rem access the shares on bfsc1
```

```
C:\Users\Administrator.BF1>net view \\bfsc1
Shared resources at \\bfsc1



Share name  Type   Used as   Comment

---------------------------------------------------------------------------
NETLOGON    Disk             Logon server share
SALES       Disk
SYSVOL      Disk             Logon server share
Users       Disk
The command completed successfully.


rem view cache again
C:\Users\Administrator.BF1>nbtstat -c

Local Area Connection:
Node IpAddress: [192.168.1.10] Scope Id: []

                 NetBIOS Remote Cache Name Table

       Name            Type      Host Address    Life [sec]
       ------------------------------------------------------
       BFSC1   <00>  UNIQUE      192.168.1.11     600
```

When you ping a server, the DNS process is used because it was written as a TCP/IP utility. You can see that it resolved the server via DNS by displaying the DNS cache with the `ipconfig /displaydns` command. The cache is cleared with `ipconfig /flushdns`.

```
rem clear the DNS cache
C:\Users\Administrator.BF1>ipconfig /flushdns

Windows IP Configuration

Successfully flushed the DNS Resolver Cache.

C:\Users\Administrator.BF1>ping BFSC1

Pinging BFSC1.bigfirm.com [192.168.1.11] with 32 bytes of data:
Reply from 192.168. 1.11: bytes=32 time<1ms TTL=128
Reply from 192.168. 1.11: bytes=32 time<1ms TTL=128
Reply from 192.168. 1.11: bytes=32 time<1ms TTL=128
Reply from 192.168. 1.11: bytes=32 time<1ms TTL=128

Ping statistics for 192.168. 1.11:
    Packets: Sent = 4, Received = 4, Lost = 0 (0% loss),
Approximate round trip times in milli-seconds:
```

```
        Minimum = Oms, Maximum = Oms, Average = Oms

C:\Users\Administrator.BF1>ipconfig /displaydns

Windows IP Configuration

    BFSC1
    ----------------------------------------
    Record Name . . . . . : BFSC1.bigfirm.com
    Record Type . . . . . : 1
    Time To Live  . . . . : 1185
    Data Length . . . . . : 4
    Section . . . . . . . : Answer
    A (Host) Record . . . : 192.168. 1.11
```

Knowing this helps you decide how to support DNS client resolution process and effectively kill or support (as needed) NetBIOS names. The NetBIOS name process is chatty and takes up unnecessary CPU cycles. If the DNS server and client implementation are configured correctly, NetBIOS name resolution support can be eliminated or at least minimized.

CONFIGURING CLIENTS

You can find the DNS and NetBIOS configurations in the IP properties of the network connection. Both are in the advanced settings. You can find the NetBIOS configurations on the WINS tab. Figure 5.18 displays the WINS tab with the default configurations.

FIGURE 5.18
The WINS tab

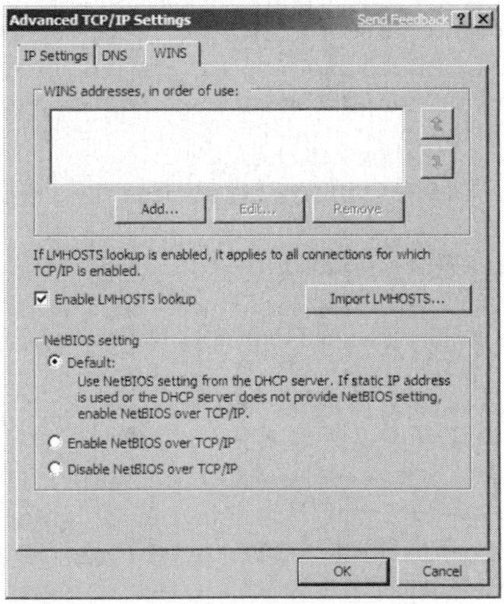

The settings enable LMHOSTS and default the NetBIOS configurations to the DHCP server settings. First, by default the LMHOSTS file is empty. It would be good to disable this because malicious viruses have entered data in this file in the past.

Next, the NetBIOS settings default to what's on the DHCP server. The DHCP server scopes have an option named NBT Node Type (046). This setting orders the first two steps in the NetBIOS process in the "circle of life." Four options are indicated by a decimal value:

◆ *Broadcast only*: "b-node," 1

◆ *Contact WINS only*: "p-node," 2

◆ *Broadcast first and then contact WINS*: "m-node," 4

◆ *Contact WINS and then broadcast*: "h-node," 8

"H-node" is best for a network relying on NetBIOS because it reduces the chatter in a WINS-supported environment. If no WINS server is available, the computer can at least get some answer in a subnet such as at home or in a workgroup. If DHCP is not configured with this value, the operating system's default configuration takes place. Windows Server 2008 R2 defaults to "h-node," or hybrid mode. This setting is displayed in `IPCONFIG /ALL`.

It would be best for Active Directory environments to disable NetBIOS because it reduces the extra chatter and processes. It also helps reduce security threats such as bots that search networks for computers to attack using this naming system. Before this is done, you need to ensure DNS name resolution is airtight.

You can find DNS client configurations on the DNS tab of the network properties, which is displayed in Figure 5.19. The obvious need is the DNS server's IP address. It should be connecting to the nearest server, typically a domain controller in its local site. A secondary DNS server is recommended.

FIGURE 5.19
DNS tab

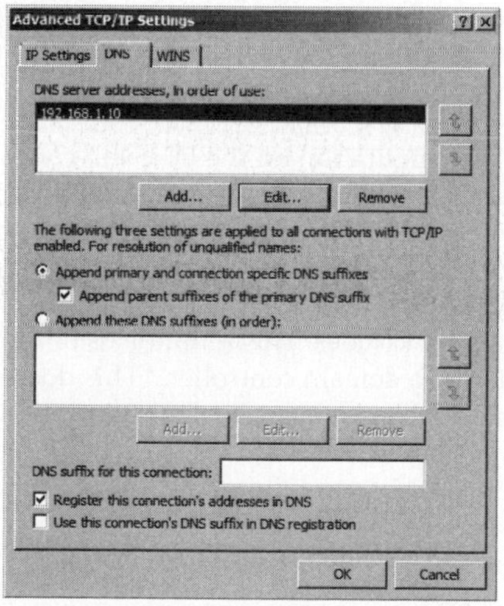

The middle portion of the tab deals with unqualified names. This is a hostname without its "last name," the DNS suffix (such as bfsc1 listed earlier in the ping example). The DNS server needs an FQDN, so the DNS client appends DNS suffixes, the "last name," before sending the request. The primary DNS suffix is listed in the System control panel (My Computer properties) under the Computer Name tab. This is managed automatically by the operating system when the computer joins the domain, so you shouldn't need to mess with it. Additional suffixes may be necessary in larger environments, but in single-domain environments, the default settings work. Only in rare occasions would you consider adding a connection DNS suffix.

All of this is moot if FQDNs are used regularly. When applications are configured, use FQDNs of servers. When configuring home folders or folder redirection, use FQDNs. When writing scripts that map network drives, use FQDNs. Get the point? On top of this, using FQDNs bypasses the NetBIOS process. Applications can tell the difference between NetBIOS names and FQDNs and will resort to DNS when they recognize an FQDN.

UPDATING DNS DYNAMICALLY

To make the DNS name resolution process airtight, you need to have all of the computers listed in DNS zones. In the past, DNS became a full-time job for system admins because they had to manually enter the ever-growing number of records for their network. To reduce the work for system admins, Microsoft sought a dynamic solution through WINS when developing NT and then switched to DNS when the Dynamic DNS (DDNS) update protocol was available.

The process is pretty simple:

1. The client queries the SOA record for its primary DNS suffix namespace. This will tell it what server can accept DDNS. It also does this for the reverse lookup zone that its IP address is associated with.

2. The client makes the DDNS request to that server.

On standard zones' Start of Authority records, the primary server is listed. On Active Directory integrated zones, the domain controller receiving the request modifies the SOA response with its name. Since it can change the Active Directory database, there's no need to hunt down a domain controller located elsewhere. If the update process fails, it can attempt to find other name servers to perform the update.

The only configuration on the DNS tab concerning DDNS you can make is to the two check boxes on the bottom, as shown in Figure 5.19. You can register the name with the primary DNS suffix or register the name with the connection suffix. The latter check box is deselected by default.

The silly part of this is that the DNS client service doesn't perform the DDNS process. The DHCP client service does. This reminds us of an eventful day that one of us disabled the DHCP client service on a domain controller. "This doesn't need the service running; it has a static IP address," he naively thought. As already mentioned, the DDNS process is used by the domain controllers to list the SRV records for Active Directory. Eventually, the clients couldn't find the domain controller because there were no SRV records for it. Oh, joy! Fortunately, this was in a lab environment.

There are two other locations that manage the DDNS process: the zone for a namespace and the DHCP server.

The DNS zone can be enabled for DDNS updates in the New Zone Wizard or can be modified in the properties of the zone. Figure 5.20 depicts the options for DDNS. The options are secure only, both secure and nonsecure, and disabled. Secure dynamic updates means the DNS client has authenticated with the domain controller prior to the update. Nonsecure means the update is accepted without authentication. Given the name, you can assume that evil hackers can exploit this option. Disabled prevents any DDNS updates from occurring.

FIGURE 5.20
Dynamic DNS
update options

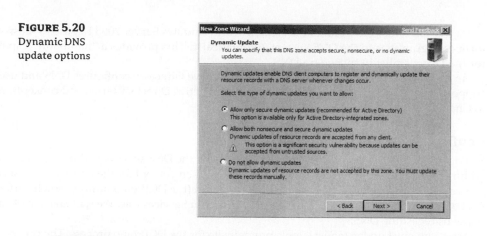

The DHCP server can also participate in the DDNS process. When Windows 2000 was released, there were plenty of Windows clients that didn't have DDNS capabilities. To resolve this, the DHCP server would identify these OSs and perform the updates for them. In addition, the DHCP server would perform the update upon request. Figure 5.21 shows the DNS tab of the IPv4 properties within the DHCP server.

FIGURE 5.21
DDNS options
on DHCP

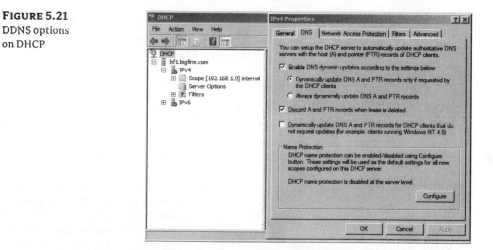

The default settings are displayed, and these settings will be rarely modified. Essentially, DHCP is not performing any updates because clients are doing it themselves. It does perform a cleanup when leases expire. Name protection, which is just a check box on the other side of the Configure button, basically prevents DHCP server from updating an existing DNS record.

Understanding Active Directory's DNS

We've discussed the components of the DNS system. Microsoft has integrated DNS and Active Directory so tightly together that it is difficult to discuss the two separately. When an Active Directory environment is created with Windows Server 2008 R2, the processes perform configurations to the DNS system automatically. This provides a "hands-off" capability for the IT generalist in setting up DNS.

In the following sections, we'll cover the way Active Directory configures DNS and uses it to support clients. For more detailed discussion of the Active Directory terms and concepts, refer to Chapter 6.

Configuring DNS Automatically

Windows Server 2008 R2 offers two ways of installing the DNS service: adding the DNS role or adding the Active Directory Domain Services role. When you opt for the latter, you must run the Active Directory Domain Services Installation Wizard (the DCPromo utility), which performs a host of configurations for the Active Directory Domain Services role. We will take a look at what happens regarding DNS.

First, you must understand a simple prerequisite for the DCPromo process. The prospective domain controller needs to have connectivity to the Active Directory DNS structure. Otherwise, it will not be able to connect to the domain controllers and obtain the necessary information. So, the IP configurations must list a DNS server within the Active Directory environment, preferably the forest root's DNS server or a DNS server in the parent domain. The only exception is when you create the very first domain controller in the Active Directory environment. At that point, there is no Active Directory DNS structure to point to.

When DCPromo is run, a new domain controller is configured. Depending on the options selected within a wizard, a new domain may be created. In either case, the DNS service and settings are configured automatically. The following changes are made.

CREATING APPLICATION PARTITIONS

Application partitions that are divisions within the Active Directory database are created for sharing DNS zones between different domains when a new domain or forest is created. The DomainDNSZones.domain.name partition is created for domain controllers within a domain. The ForestDNSZones.domain.name partition is created for sharing between domain controllers of an Active Directory forest.

If you look at Figure 5.3, you will notice the _msdcs.bigfirm.com subdomain is delegated just like Ecoast. It is delegated to the same domain controller, in this case, Bf1.Bigfirm.com. The _msdcs.Bigfirm.com zone is created in the ForestDNSZone.Bigfirm.com application partition. This allows this portion of the namespace to be replicated to all domain controllers in the forest.

When additional domain controllers are created, these domain controllers are automatically enlisted to these application partitions.

ADDING A FORWARDER

Within the DNS server's properties, a forwarder is added. This will be the IP address of the original DNS server that the server was using.

MODIFYING IP PROPERTIES

The new domain controller created by DCPromo is also a new DNS server. The primary DNS server's address in the IP properties is reconfigured to the loopback IP addresses, ::1 and 127.0.0.1.

DELEGATING THE SUBDOMAIN

A child domain has a name that is a subdomain within an existing domain namespace. For example, Ecoast.Bigfirm.com is a subdomain within the Bigfirm.com namespace. When DCPromo does its thing, the new domain's namespace will be supported on the new domain controller as a delegated subdomain.

On the parent domain, a subdomain like Ecoast.Bigfirm.com is delegated to the new domain controller. The delegation will link the parent to the child domain for name resolution. This was illustrated earlier in Figure 5.3.

ADDITIONAL RECOMMENDED CONFIGURATIONS

After a domain controller is created, we prefer to make the following configurations to the DNS system:

- Change the primary DNS server to the IP address of the primary network connection. When troubleshooting DNS with the NsLookup utility, the loopback address causes tests to be "unauthoritative." Although this may be merely cosmetic, I have found results to be squirrely using the loopback address.

- Create the reverse lookup zones in the ForestDNSZones.domain.name application partition. The reverse lookup zone for subnets may need to be shared between domain controllers of different domains.

- Create a stub zone for new domain trees on the root DNS server. A domain tree has a different name than the root DNS server. Since the original DNS server entry is listed as a forwarder like the other domain controller promotions, the DNS server can communicate with the rest of the Active Directory DNS structure. However, there are no automatic configurations on the rest of the Active Directory DNS structure to resolve names in the new namespace. We need to set up a conditional forwarder or a stub zone to point the DNS servers to the new domain controller for Apex.com, for example. In Figure 5.12, you can see a stub zone used to assist resolving Apex.com domain FQDNs.

Understanding SRV Records and Clients

Looking at a brand-spanking-new domain's DNS zone, you will notice it has a lot of new folders or subdomains. Drilling through these folders, you will find service location (SRV) records by the boatload, as shown earlier in Figure 5.15. As we mentioned, Microsoft needed SRV records and dynamic DNS update to make Active Directory work. This is the result of the two technologies working together.

The netlogon service performs DDNS requests to create the SRV records within the Active Directory DNS namespace. The sole reason is to ensure computers can find domain controllers in the domain.

Within the Windows operating system processes, the specific services are sought out with the use of the DNS. In Figure 5.15, you will notice a few different services:

- _gc, or global catalog: The LDAP service to look up data within the global catalog
- _kerberos: The authentication process

◆ _kpassword: Another part of the authentication process

◆ _ldap: The LDAP service to look up data within the domain

Each of these services is performed by domain controllers within the domain or forest. In Figure 5.15, you see Bf1.Bigfirm.com perform all of these roles and what TCP port it is listening on.

So, when a Windows computer needs a specific domain controller service such as LDAP, it would request an SRV answer for _ldap._tcp.Bigfirm.com. It would then have all it needed to get busy with an IP address and port.

If a Windows computer needs to find a domain controller in its own site, it can look for it within the _sites.Bigfirm.com subdomain. This subdomain will list all the created sites within the Active Directory Sites and Services console.

The idea that admins could possibly support this load of DNS entries is incredible. Microsoft stated that NT 4.0 SP4 could support an Active Directory environment since it could support SRV records. However, it would be without DDNS update. For one domain controller, you can expect at least 16 to 20 different SRV records to be registered. So, DDNS update is essential. Learning all of them is a daunting task as well. That's when tools like DCDiag and DNSLint come into play. See the section "Leveraging NsLookup, DCDiag, and DNSLint" later in this chapter for instructions for using these utilities.

Windows Server 2008 R2's Additional Features

With every release of Windows, the development teams of each technology are compelled to add something to their products. Windows DNS technology has been cooking with gas for the past 10 years. Any additional improvements are icing on the cake and may be bordering on job justification for the developers.

AN EXAMPLE OF JOB JUSTIFICATION

When Windows 2000 was released, the de-emphasis of WINS was very apparent. In the marketing and technical documents, WINS took a backseat to DNS. No one was talking about it.

In the Microsoft official curriculum for the MSCE upgrade to Windows 2000, Microsoft pushed the subject of WINS to the last day of the course. On the last day, the only person in a classroom interested in the course's information was the instructor, and he was watching the clock. WINS was mentioned in a few pages of a chapter dominated by the topic of DHCP.

The only change worth noting was that WINS clients could now add 12 WINS servers in the IP properties. Oh!

This is case of job justification. You can just picture the sole WINS product manager sadly tapping away on his keyboard in a dark basement cubicle in Redmond. His friends were transferred to the DNS product team, and he was left behind. He had to come up with something to earn his paycheck. (He must have been that guy who had change for Bill Gates in the Coke advertisement.)

In our discussion, we've been talking about the essentials for implementing DNS. This content would take you all the way there to handle a Windows network. The added features that come with Windows Server 2008 and Windows Server 2008 R2 are nice, but a very small percentage of IT shops may consider implementing these.

GLOBAL QUERY BLOCK LIST

There are a few common host records that can be registered in DNS by other services. Web Proxy Automatic Discovery Protocol (WPAD) is a very common one. This helps web browsers automatically download the proxy configurations from a server. Since the record doesn't belong to a specific computer, any computer including evil hacker computers could attempt to register the name. Another common host record is Intra-site Automatic Tunneling Addressing Protocol (ISATAP). This is to perform routing for IPv4 to IPv6 networks and is registered by the router performing this service.

The global query block list specifies the names blocked from DDNS registration. Thus, an evil hacker computer's attempt to register names such as WPAD or ISATAP is rejected.

The following commands illustrate how you can administer this list. You can see this list with DNSCmd. Notice it is populated with wpad and isatap by default. If you want to add a name to the list such as www, you can use the /config option listing all of the desired hostnames. (If you list just one, it will clear out the list and add just that one.) By default, the feature is enabled. You can disable or reenable it using the /config /enableglobalqueryblocklist option.

```
rem view current global query block list
C:\Users\Administrator.BF1>dnscmd bf1.bigfirm.com /info /globalqueryblocklist

Query result:
String:  wpad
String:  isatap

Command completed successfully.

rem adding www to the list
C:\Users\Administrator.BF1>dnscmd bf1.bigfirm.com /config
/globalqueryblocklist www wpad isatap



Registry property globalqueryblocklist successfully reset.
Command completed successfully.

rem view the modified list
C:\Users\Administrator.BF1>dnscmd bf1.bigfirm.com /info
/globalqueryblocklist

Query result:
String:  www
String:  wpad
String:  isatap

Command completed successfully.

rem enable the use of the global query block list
C:\Users\Administrator.BF1>dnscmd bf1.bigfirm.com /config
```

```
/enableglobalqueryblocklist 1
```

```
Registry property enableglobalqueryblocklist successfully reset.
Command completed successfully.
```

GLOBAL NAMES AND SINGLE NAME RESOLUTION

In this discussion, we've thrown WINS under the bus. However, there seems to be some require-ments in the marketplace to support some applications' use of the NetBIOS naming process. The GlobalNames feature is a special zone created to resolve a NetBIOS name (15 characters with no dots in it). The DNS client is supposed to perform the query to the GlobalName zone when the primary and alternate DNS suffix searches have failed.

The steps to configure this are not difficult given the earlier discussions:

1. Create a new zone with the name GlobalNames. An Active Directory integrated zone is recommended to provide replication to other domain controllers.

2. Enable GlobalNames support with the DNSCmd command:

```
C:\Users\Administrator.BF1>dnscmd bf1 /config /enableglobalnamessupport 1
```

```
Registry property enableglobalnamessupport successfully reset.
Command completed successfully.
```

3. Replicate the zone to other domain controllers. Remember to add these domain controllers to the name servers list of the zone.

4. Add CNAME records in the zone to redirect to specific hosts. In our example, www is redi-rected to hostrecord.PrimaryZone.local, as shown in Figure 5.22.

FIGURE 5.22
The GlobalNames
zone

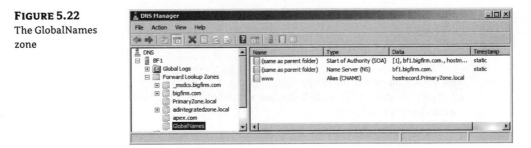

5. Add a service location record if you need other Active Directory forests to query this zone. This is illustrated in Figure 5.23.

You can use the NsLookup utility to test the resolution of the global name:

```
C:\Users\Administrator.BF1>nslookup
Default Server:  bf1.bigfirm.com
Address:  192.168.1.10
```

```
> www
```

```
Server:   bf1.bigfirm.com
Address:  192.168.1.10

Name:     hostrecord.primaryzone.local
Address:  192.168.1.21
Aliases:  www.bigfirm.com
```

FIGURE 5.23

The GlobalNames SRV record

In most environments that rely on Windows servers, the need for single names (NetBIOS) has been worked around, as we discussed earlier. It has also been minimized through the proper deployment of applications by using FQDNs.

BACKGROUND ZONE LOADING

Some environments have DNS zones so large that it takes the domain controllers more than an hour to restart the DNS service. If you have that problem, you're in luck with background zone loading! We expect a DNS zone must have more records than the Bible has verses to cause this issue.

While the DNS service is starting, it will start responding to zones it has loaded. Requests to zones that haven't loaded could be referred to other DNS servers.

DNSSEC AND TRUST ANCHORS

Like HTTP, DNS is an unencrypted and unauthenticated protocol. As we mentioned about reverse zones, hackers can spoof DNS responses. To counter this, DNSSec was developed, which allows a DNS server to digitally sign the resource records. Windows Server 2008 R2 provides the support to act as secondary zones for a DNSSec zone. It doesn't perform any validation of the digitally signed resource records. It only responds to queries for the record from a digitally signed zone. It will also provide the necessary resource records to authenticate the signature.

These records are the KEY, SIG, and NXT records. KEY is the public key of the signing DNS server. SIG is the digital signature of the resource record. NXT basically lists all the valid records in the namespace.

Trust anchors are the public certificates of DNSSec servers that the DNS server will trust for communications. The trust anchor certificates will be used to validate the digital signatures of the responses. These are added to the properties of the DNS server in the form of public keys.

Supporting Internet-Based DNS Resolution

Within an organization, there is the need to manage Internet namespaces as well. The users within a LAN will need to access websites and other Internet-based services. External users will need to access the organization's websites and mail servers at a minimum. So, you will have to be mindful of these requirements also.

To allow external users access to your websites, an external DNS domain needs to be in place. Thus, you need to consider whether deploying an external DNS server is necessary. The internal computers will resolve external names through the internal DNS servers. So, integration with the Internet DNS structure is required.

Supporting External DNS Domains

Most companies register a DNS namespace to support a website and email. Small and some medium-sized companies will allow an ISP to manage the namespace on their external DNS servers. The benefit is the availability of the servers and reduced headache of maintaining additional servers on a public Internet-facing subnet. These servers are managed through a web interface and allow only a few types of records such as host, cname, and MX.

Using a Windows Server 2008 R2 server for DNS operations is possible. The DNS role can be installed on a server that isn't a domain member, and then the registered DNS namespace's name server record can be modified to the public IP address of the server. Oh, sure, it can be done, but realistically there are some cons to the idea:

♦ Windows Server 2008 R2 is expensive. Maybe the Web edition would be OK to support this along with the websites, but it too has a high price tag.

♦ The Windows Server 2008 R2 server needs to be locked down and secure. So, now you are looking at Server Core and hardening that.

♦ It needs to be highly available, so you'll have to cluster the server or set up multiple DNS servers.

♦ If it hasn't already been taken care of, you'll need to have a highly available network connection to the Internet, too.

The cost of going in this direction is high, and many companies would rather spend the money elsewhere. This may be where a simple Linux implementation has an advantage. However, we recommend the approach most have taken—letting an ISP manage the namespace.

SPLIT BRAIN

Many companies have also implemented a "split-brain" scenario when it comes to DNS, although not intentionally. What this means is they have an internal namespace that is the same as the external namespace. For example, we have the registered namespace Bigfirm.com. The company has decided to build an Active Directory environment with the same name.

AVOID USING YOUR COMPANY'S EXTERNAL DNS NAMESPACE

This is one of those best practices to adhere to in Active Directory design: don't use your company's external DNS namespace. Use something different that may not be found on the Internet or a registered name you don't ever use.

When companies don't follow this rule, they soon realize that they have a conflict with resolving external resources that they own such as www.Bigfirm.com. The internal DNS server can't find the name, so it kicks back a big goose egg for a response. The admins try to fix this by adding the name manually with the external IP address, but adding the external IP address causes routing issues. In addition, the developers are whining that they can't upload new content with the external IP address. They need the internal IP address. This kind of additional administration hassle becomes the norm for dealing with "split-brain" issues.

The best practice is to name your Active Directory DNS namespace with an internal name or another registered domain name that you are not using. However, Active Directory has been around for nearly 10 years, and companies eagerly have adopted it through upgrades. You may not have the opportunity to apply this rule at this point of time.

Managing this scenario with one server would be ideal. A split-brain DNS implementation is a cool idea that is supposed to remedy this issue. You could have a single DNS server support an internal and external zone of the same namespace. The IP addresses for the external zone would be provided to external requests and internal IP addresses for the internal requests.

It's a nice idea that Windows Server 2008 R2 doesn't support. Primarily, Microsoft doesn't support your organization exposing the domain controller that hosts the internal DNS namespace to even the edge of the Internet. This is not a secure measure. The Active Directory database is too valuable to hang in a DMZ like a ripe peach. So, we have to come up with an alternative.

Our objective is to provide resolution of external requests with external IP addresses and internal requests with internal IP addresses. Using Microsoft DNS, you will have to administer two DNS servers. Here are the basic steps:

1. Implement an external DNS server to support Bigfirm.com. Typically, this is already in place with the registration of a domain name with the help of the ISP.

2. Implement the internal DNS structure. Using the Active Directory Domain Services Installation Wizard (DCPromo), this is handled quite readily.

3. Add any external records to the internal zone for Bigfirm.com. Remember, the DNS servers within the network will be authoritative for the Bigfirm.com domain. If it can't find www.Bigfirm.com, it doesn't exist. External records must be duplicated in the internal zone so a positive result can be returned. You will have to test routing to ensure that the IP address is accessible. If routing causes problems, you may have to use an internal address.

4. Configure resolving external namespaces using root hints or forwarders. This topic is covered in the following section.

Resolving External Namespaces

We discussed how to integrate a DNS server with others. The primary methods of resolving DNS names in the Internet are the root hints or the forwarders. The root hints were a list of DNS servers that were at the top of the Internet's DNS structure. The DNS server could communicate with these servers to perform recursive queries for external namespaces. Forwarders were lateral requests to another DNS server to see whether that server could come up with the name. We mentioned in small environments we prefer to use forwarders to an external DNS server that is supported by the ISP, but using root hints still work in this scenario too.

It is important to not mix the two. Don't list root hints servers as forwarders. A query to a root hint is a referral request that always returns the name server for a domain. So, it doesn't respond with host records, and it doesn't perform the recursive operation that a forwarder would. Forwarders also take precedence over root hints. In Figure 5.4 shown earlier in the chapter, the Forwarders tab includes the check box "Use root hints if no forwarders are available." You can infer that if a forwarder is listed and it comes up with a goose egg response, the query is over, and root hints won't be touched.

In extensive internal DNS environments, judicious use of the forwarders and root hints is necessary. The internal subdomain name servers need to resolve queries from the root DNS server. They also have to resolve Internet-based queries. Taking advantage of the caching capability of DNS, they can rely on a server to resolve and store common queries to reduce externally bound traffic. Microsoft recommends the caching server should not be the root server so the root server will not be overburdened with the additional workload. In addition, they warn internal DNS servers that host zones should not communicate directly with the Internet to reduce their exposure to Internet. So, Figure 5.24 depicts one solution that could work for our fictitious DNS structure.

FIGURE 5.24
Internal DNS structure

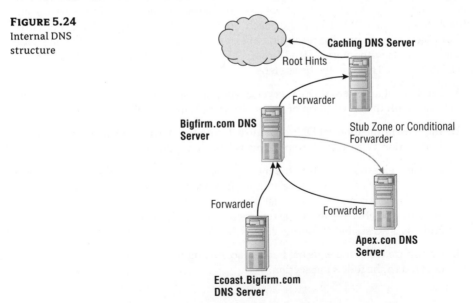

In this example, forwarders are used to send requests to the root DNS server in Bigfirm.com. Root hints could be used by removing the Internet root hints and listing Bf1.Bigfirm.com as the root hint server. The caching server is in place to remove the DNS servers hosting the Active Directory integrated zones from making queries into the Internet. It performs resolutions via the root hints. To handle queries in the Apex.com domain, a stub zone or a conditional forwarder is used.

Other solutions are possible and may have merit for different reasons. We prefer the simplicity of using the forwarders to manage the integration between the servers.

Administration and Troubleshooting with DNS Tools

In this section, we'll discuss the available tools and troubleshooting techniques for DNS name resolution. Given the importance of DNS, you need to be familiar with the tools that give valuable information to discern where problems lie with name resolution. The standard admin tools, the DNS management console, and the DNSCmd command-line utility provide additional information over and above configurations. The nslookup, DCDiag, and DNSLint utilities provide excellent initial indications of problems concerning DNS resolution.

Administering the DNS Server with the DNS Management Console and DNSCmd

To administer the DNS server, we have touched on two tools: the DNS management console, which is a MMC snap-in, and DNSCmd, which is a command-line tool. DNSCmd offers the capability of administering the entire server like the MMC console plus offers a little more functionality. For example, the DNS management console doesn't offer a method of modifying the global query block list or creating directory partitions.

Throughout the chapter, you have seen the DNS management console used to create zones and edit the properties of servers and zones, which are the run-of-the-mill types of tasks you do with it. You can also take advantage of some diagnostic configurations within the console. These are configured in the properties of the DNS server.

Event logging   A separate Event Viewer log is created for the DNS service. It is attached to the DNS management console. In addition, the server collects all events by default, which is set on the Event Logging tab.

Debugging log   A more detailed logging of the actual communication occurring on the DNS server can be gathered for inspection. Figure 5.25 displays the tab. This feature is valuable if the DNS server is not acting reliable. Although most DNS issues are resolved with proper IP connectivity, you will find this tool useful when IP connectivity is determined not to be the cause. On rare occasions, we have had to verify whether specific requests were hitting the server, and this tool provided the information.

Monitoring   This tab, displayed in Figure 5.26, is the equivalent to the million-dollar machine that goes "ping!" It's like a blinking light. It can test DNS queries from this server or to another server—not a specific server, mind you, just any indiscriminant server out there. Then you can perform the test at intervals. The output is just pass or fail. Basically, if the DNS server is having problems, it's a fail. This has not been a place we've found any comfort or valuable data in resolving DNS issues. Exhaust other troubleshooting techniques before you consider looking at the Monitoring tab. It won't tell you anything new.

FIGURE 5.25
Debug Logging tab

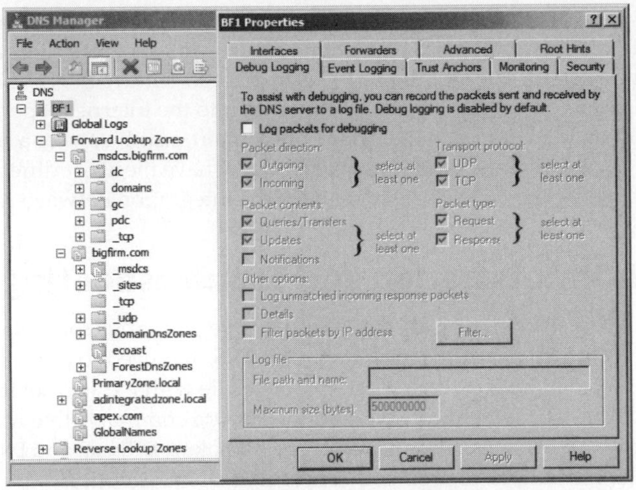

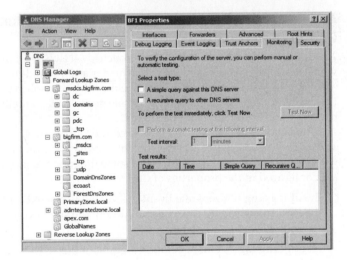

FIGURE 5.26
Monitoring tab

DNSCmd offers a few diagnostic features as well. These may be useful in collecting and examining data:

◆ DNSCmd /info provides configurations of the DNS server.

◆ DNSCmd /exportsettings generates a text file of the configurations and zone properties.

◆ DNSCmd /statistics is similar to the performance counters that are still available. This provides running tallies of specific operations on the server.

◆ DNSCmd /clearcache empties the cache. Occasionally, stale resolved records need to be removed after a problem has been resolved. This is also available in the DNS management console.

Each of these tools provides administration and monitoring features. We find they are useful for the deeper investigation where the frontline tools do not immediately indicate the problem. The frontline tools are Nslookup and DCDiag.

Leveraging Nslookup, DCDiag, and DNSLint

Nslookup, DCDiag, and DNSLint are the front-line tools. Nslookup provides immediate indications of what "doth stinketh in Denmark." DCDiag and DNSLint provide initial indications concerning Active Directory–related issues, such as DDNS registration and SRV records. If these tools do not reveal the problem, you can rely on the features of the DNS management console and DNSCmd.

NSLOOKUP

Nslookup is the first tool we go to when troubleshooting name resolution problems. It connects to the listed primary DNS server in the IP configurations and makes requests for DNS queries.

Notice that the utility doesn't perform the name resolution process, in other words, the "circle of life." It narrows down to one portion of the "circle of life." In our discussion on clients, the example of the ping and net view commands were provided to show the different parts of the process. The ping example showed the DNS process that included the first step of looking the name up in the HOSTS file. So, you will see a disconnect between ping and nslookup if the HOSTS file has records for the same hostname in it.

CONFICKER VIRUS

One example of malicious software is the conficker virus. This lovely bit of code prevents browsers from hitting important sites within specific DNS namespaces like Microsoft.com, Symantec.com, and Norton.com.

This has a crippling effect. The computer can't go to the Windows update site; It can't even look up possible solutions for the problem. Even after installing Norton AntiVirus onto the machine, it couldn't access the Symantec update site for the latest definition updates. The machine couldn't fix itself.

As mentioned, nslookup was our first tool of choice. The queries to Microsoft.com and Symantec.com were positive, but it wouldn't fly in Internet Explorer or Firefox instances on that computer. This difference helped narrow down where the issue lied. Therefore, the browsers were infected.

Of course, nslookup provides the IP addresses for the sites we need to hit. But—"Oh, no!"—the Microsoft websites don't play using just the IP address in the URL. So, trying that workaround doesn't work either.

We found the solution using the Microsoft Windows Malicious Software Removal Tool (MSRT). It had to be downloaded on a separate computer, and then using sneakernet, we transferred the MSRT package to the infected computer. It identified and removed the virus.

When an application cannot access a server, after checking TCP/IP connectivity, we start to poke around with the nslookup command. Here are some things we look for:

◆ *Is the DNS server responding?* The command will tell you right at the start if it can connect to the DNS server. If there is a delay or timeout, there's no need to continue. You have a connectivity issue.

◆ *Is the default server unknown?* This indicates the reverse lookup performed by nslookup failed. When it is in this state, we find the rest of nslookup tests get squirrely.

◆ *Can you resolve a local FQDN?* This bypasses a portion of the client's processing. The client will append primary DNS suffixes to search for hostnames.

◆ *Can you resolve a hostname without the DNS suffix?* This is what the client does so you can walk through the step.

◆ *Can you resolve external FQDNs?* This will validate that the default DNS server can get out to the Internet.

Nslookup has two methods: single-command queries and interactive mode. The interactive mode is much more powerful, so we opt to use that at the start. This mode offers the ability to perform queries on different types of resource records and allows you to switch to another server. The following are examples of queries we commonly perform (with remarks added for clarity):

```
C:\Users\Administrator.BF1>nslookup
Default Server:  bf1.bigfirm.com
Address:  192.168.1.10

rem  a host record query
> bf1.bigfirm.com
Server:  bf1.bigfirm.com
Address:  192.168.1.10

Name:    bf1.bigfirm.com
Address:  192.168.1.10

rem a reverse "ptr" record query
> set q=ptr
> 192.168.1.10
Server:  bf1.bigfirm.com
Address:  192.168.1.10

10.1.168.192.in-addr.arpa     name = bf1.bigfirm.com

rem a start of authority query
> set q=soa
> bigfirm.com
Server:  bf1.bigfirm.com
Address:  192.168.1.10

bigfirm.com
```

```
        primary name server = bf1.bigfirm.com
        responsible mail addr = hostmaster.bigfirm.com
        serial  = 124
        refresh = 900 (15 mins)
        retry   = 600 (10 mins)
        expire  = 86400 (1 day)
        default TTL = 3600 (1 hour)
bf1.bigfirm.com      internet address = 192.168.1.10


rem a name server query
> set q=ns
> bigfirm.com
Server:  bf1.bigfirm.com
Address:  192.168.1.10


bigfirm.com      nameserver = bf1.bigfirm.com
bf1.bigfirm.com      internet address = 192.168.1.10


rem a resource record query
> set q=srv
> _ldap._tcp.bigfirm.com
Server:  bf1.bigfirm.com
Address:  192.168.1.10


_ldap._tcp.bigfirm.com  SRV service location:
        priority    = 0
        weight      = 100
        port        = 389
        svr hostname = bf1.bigfirm.com
bf1.bigfirm.com      internet address = 192.168.1.10
```

DCDiag

DCDiag was part of the support tools from earlier versions and is included in the Windows Server 2008 R2 installation. It's our first choice to perform a quick health check on the DNS structure. Since it runs though a score of domain controller diagnostics, it must validate that DNS is working as needed. After running the standard battery of tests, you may see errors in attempting to connect to domain controllers. Then you could run additional DCDiag tests specifically for DNS. The following tests whether a domain controller can perform DDNS to register the SRV records:

```
dcdiag /test:RegisterInDNS /DnsDomain:bigfirm.com /f:documents\
dcdiagRegisterInDNS.txt
```

This produced the following text output:

```
Starting test: RegisterInDNS

    DNS configuration is sufficient to allow this domain controller to
```

```
     dynamically register the domain controller Locator records in DNS.

     The DNS configuration is sufficient to allow this computer to dynamically

     register the A record corresponding to its DNS name.

     ........................ bf1 passed test RegisterInDNS
```

DCDiag performs a boatload of domain controller–related tests including several DNS tests. We mentioned one, the `RegisterInDNS` test. These tests primarily focus on the integration between the DNS servers within an Active Directory environment. Tests can be performed on delegation, forwarders, dynamic update, and external DNS name resolution.

The following is a portion of the help information for the DCDiag utility. It lists the tests available for DNS. We rely on `NsLookup` to test external name resolution, so we never use /DnsForwarders and /DnsResolveExtName tests.

```
     DNS
             This test checks the health of DNS settings for the whole
             enterprise. Sub tests can be run individually using the switches
             below. By default, all tests except external name resolution are
             run)

/DnsBasic                      (basic tests, can't be skipped)
/DnsForwarders                 (forwarders and root hints tests)
/DnsDelegation                 (delegations tests)
/DnsDynamicUpdate              (dynamic update tests)
/DnsRecordRegistration         (records registration tests)
/DnsResolveExtName             (external name resolution test)
/DnsAll                        (includes all tests above)
/DnsInternetName:                <internet name> (for test /DnsResolveExtName)
(default is www.microsoft.com)
```

As discussed earlier with SRV records, the number of SRV records registered by a domain controller is so numerous that it is difficult to eyeball that it is working correctly. In addition to the /registerinDNS test, /DnsDynamicUpdate and /DnsRecordRegistration run through checks concerning SRV registration by the domain controllers. Opposed to /registerinDNS, these do not have to be run locally on the domain controller. The following command will verify the SRV records for a domain controller. The /v option is for "verbose." The output is lengthy because it lists all of the SRV records for the domain controller:

```
C:\Users\Administrator.BF1>dcdiag /s:bf1.bigfirm.com /test:dns /
dnsrecordregistration /v
```

The following will validate that DDNS update is operational on a zone. It will register a host and delete it from the DNS zone of the server. In this case, that is Ecoast.Bigfirm.com.

```
C:\Users\Administrator.BF1>dcdiag /s:ec1.Ecoast.Bigfirm.com /test:dns /
dnsdynamicupdate /v
```

DNSLint

Another useful utility introduced with the Windows Server 2003 support tools was DNSLint. This has to be run on other workstations and servers to validate DNS on a Windows Server 2008 R2 server.

DNSLint was not released with Windows Server 2008 R2, but it is available for download at the Microsoft support website, KB article 321045: http://support.microsoft.com/kb/321045.aspx.

DNSLINT ON R2?

As of this writing, DNSLint doesn't run on Windows Server 2008 R2. Our guess is that the Microsoft engineers prefer you to use DCDiag because it comes in the installation. DNSLint still can be run on legacy servers and connect to a Windows Server 2008 R2 DNS service.

DNSLint provides three types of tests:

Delegation   Proper configuration of subdomain delegation is critical in DNS integration, and this utility will attempt to validate that the configurations are correct. The following is an example command for this test:

```
dnslint /d ecoast.bigfirm.com
```

Active Directory replication   Primarily, DNSLint looks at the SRV of the domain controllers for replication processes. These records are located in the _msdsc.domain.com namespace. If DNSLint can't find the IP address of a domain controller to replicate to, other domain controllers will not find it either. The following is an example command for this test:

```
dnslint /ad 192.168.1.10 /s 192.168.1.10
```

An HTML-formatted output file will be generated with the name dnslint.htm.

Query list   You can create a list of records to query on the server. DNSLint will run through the list attempting to retrieve answers for them.

```
dnslint /ql c:\temp\querylist.txt
```

The Bottom Line

Explain the fundamental components and processes of DNS   DNS relies on integrated servers that manage a hierarchal naming structure. On the Internet, this structure starts with root servers and then top-level domain servers, which delegate subdomains to other DNS servers. Within a DNS server, the database of records is known as a *zone*, and it can be replicated between other DNS servers to provide distributed query resolution for a given namespace.

Master It   Several common DNS records were discussed in this chapter. The SRV and MX records both have a parameter named priority. If there were two SRV records for the same service with a priority parameter of 10 and 20, which SRV record would be selected first?

Configure DNS to support an Active Directory environment Active Directory requires a DNS namespace to be available to support the assigned name of the domain. Windows Server 2008 R2 provides an automatic capability to create the required DNS structure through the domain controller promotion process. The DNS zones can be stored in the Active Directory database, which provides multimaster replication of the DNS records. With the use of SRV records and DDNS update, the domain controllers can register their services in DNS for clients to access them.

> **Master It** The DNS service on DCs can create Active Directory integrated zones. In which locations within the Active Directory database can the zones be placed? What scope do these locations provide?

Manage and troubleshoot DNS resolution for both internal and external names Internal and external name resolution relies on the connectivity between DNS servers. Forwarding and root hints are the primary methods to provide DNS servers to send queries between them. Several tools are available to assist troubleshooting and monitoring DNS configurations and performance, including nslookup, DNSCmd, DCDiag, and DNSLint.

> **Master It** The SRV record registration for domain controllers is performed by the netlogon service. It is a very complex and demanding task to attempt to perform this manually. What tests can be performed to verify whether SRV records are correctly registered within a domain?

Chapter 6

Creating the Simple AD: The One-Domain, One-Location AD

Although a great deal has been written about the complex Active Directory structure in large organizations, the truth is that most organizations use just a simple one-domain structure. Indeed, unless your organization has more than 50,000 users or you have a specific reason to add more domains, a single domain structure is not only recommended, but it's also the simplest to implement.

A single domain is relatively easy to create once you have a server—just choose your domain name, run the domain controller promotion wizard (DCPromo), and you're in business. The primary tool you'll use to manage the domain is Active Directory Users and Computers. You can create user and computer objects (to represent the actual users and computers) in the domain and organize them in organizational units (OUs) using Active Directory Users and Computers. You can also create these Active Directory objects from the command line.

If you have special security requirements dictating that some users in your domain have different password policies, you can now implement fine-grained password policies. You no longer have to create a separate domain just to support a different password policy.

In this chapter, you will learn to:

♦ Create a single-domain forest

♦ Add a second DC to the domain

♦ Decide whether to add a global catalog

♦ Create accounts

♦ Create fine-grained password policies

An Introduction to Active Directory Basics

Before we get started covering Active Directory, we'll lay the foundation with some basics. These definitions aren't completely comprehensive but will give you the foundation you need to understand the topics in this chapter. Although there are a lot of terms to grasp, no term is that complex. We'll define them here with a short introduction and often expand on them later.

Workgroup   A workgroup is a group of users connected in a local area network (LAN) but with each computer having its own user accounts. A user who can log onto one computer will need a different user account to log onto a different computer, which can become a problem. A single user who needs to access several computers will have several different user accounts, often with different passwords.

Workgroups are often used in organizations with fewer than 10 computers. As more computers are added, a decentralized workgroup becomes harder to manage and administer, requiring it to be promoted to a domain.

Domain When an organization becomes too big for a workgroup, a domain is created by running the domain controller promotion wizard (DCPromo) on a server and promoting the server to a domain controller. A domain controller is a server that hosts a copy of Active Directory Domain Services.

Active Directory Domain Services Active Directory Domain Services (AD DS) is used to provide several services to an organization. At its core, it's a big database of objects (such as users, computers, and groups) and is used to centrally organize and manage all the objects within an organization. A single user would have a single user account in Active Directory and can use this single account to access multiple computers in the organization. This is often referred to as *single sign-on*.

Additional services include the ability to easily search AD DS so that objects can easily be located, as well as secure authentication using Kerberos.

Copies of Active Directory are kept on domain controllers. It's very common to have at least two domain controllers for redundancy purposes in case one goes down. Any changes to Active Directory are passed to each of the domain controllers using a process called *replication*.

Replication When any object (such as a user account) is added, deleted, or modified within Active Directory, the change is sent to all other domain controllers (DCs) in the domain. When a business is located in a single location, the changes are sent to all other DCs within a minute.

Modifications can be done on any DC. The initial change is sent from the DC where the change was created to other DCs (designated as replication partners) within 15 seconds. If there are more than four DCs in the organization, they are automatically organized in a logical circle, and the change is replicated through the replication circle until all the DCs have the change.

Objects Objects within AD are used to represent real-world items. Common objects are user objects and computer objects that represent people and their computers. The objects can be managed and administered using AD DS. For example, to represent a user named Sally, a user account object is created. Sally can then use this account to log onto the domain and access domain resources such as files, folders, printers, and email. Although we would often say that we give Sally permission to access the resources, we actually give Sally's user object permission to access the resources. Similarly, a computer account object is created to represent Sally's computer. All objects have properties that can be configured such as the user's first name, last name, display name, logon name, and password for a user object.

The types of objects and their properties are predefined. You won't find a kitchen-sink object in AD DS, and you won't find a favorite color property for users—at least not by default. All objects that can be added to AD DS and the properties used to define these objects are specified in the schema.

Schema The schema is the definition of all the object types that Active Directory can contain, and it includes a list of properties that can be used to describe the objects. You can think of the schema as a set of blueprints for each of the objects. Just as a blueprint for a house can be used to create a house, a schema definition for a user object can be used to create a user object.

Only objects that are defined by the schema can be added to Active Directory, and these objects can be described only by properties defined and identified by the schema. It's common for the schema to be modified a few times in the lifetime of an Active Directory enterprise. For example, to install Exchange Server 2007 (for mail), the schema must be modified to accept the different objects and properties required by Exchange. Modifying the schema is often referred to as *extending* the schema.

Organizational units   Organizational units are used to organize objects within Active Directory. You can think of an OU simply as a container for the objects. By placing the objects in different containers, they are easier to manage. For example, you can create a Sales OU and place all the objects representing users and computers in the sales department in the Sales OU.

OUs have two distinct benefits. You can delegate permissions to an OU, and you can link Group Policy to an OU. As an example, Maria may be responsible for administration for all users and computers in the sales department. If these objects were placed in the Sales OU, Maria could be delegated permission to administer the OU, and it would include all the objects in the OU. Similarly, you can use Group Policy to apply different settings and configurations to all the user and computer objects in an OU by applying a single Group Policy object to the OU.

Group Policy   Group Policy allows you to configure a setting once and have it apply to many user and/or computer objects. For example, if you want to ensure all the computers in the sales department have their firewall enabled, you could place the computers in an OU and call it Sales, configure a Group Policy object (GPO) that enables the firewall, and link the policy to the Sales OU. It doesn't matter if there are five computers in the OU or 5,000; a GPO will apply the setting to all the computers in the OU.

You can link GPOs to OUs, entire domains, or sites. When linked, a GPO applies to all the objects within the OU, domain, or site. For example, if you want all users in the entire domain to have firewalls enabled, instead of linking the GPO to the site, you'd link it to the domain. Two default GPOs are created when a domain is created: the default domain policy and the default domain controllers policy.

Default domain policy   The default domain policy is a preconfigured GPO that is added when a domain is created and linked at the domain level. Settings within the default domain policy apply to all user and computer objects within the domain. This policy starts with some basic security settings such as requirements for passwords but can be modified as desired.

Default domain controllers policy   The default domain controller policy is a preconfigured GPO that is added when a domain is created and linked at the Domain Controllers OU level. The Domain Controllers OU is created when a domain is created, and all domain controllers are automatically placed in this OU when they are promoted to a DC. Since the default domain controller policy is linked to the Domain Controllers OU, it applies to all domain controllers.

Site   A site is a group of well-connected computers and is sometimes referred to as a group of well-connected *subnets*. Small to medium-sized businesses often operate out of a single location, and all the computers in this location are connected via a single LAN. This is a site.

If a remote office is created and connected via a slower connection, it could be configured as a site. The remote office is well connected within the remote office but not well connected to the main office. Sites are explored in much more depth in Chapter 21.

Forest A forest is a group of one or more domains that share a common Active Directory. A single forest will have only one schema (only one definition of objects that can be created) and only one global catalog.

Global catalog The global catalog (GC) is a listing of all the objects in the entire forest. It is easily searchable and is often used by different applications to search AD DS for specific objects. The global catalog is hosted on domain controllers that are designated as GC servers. Since there is only one GC for a forest and a forest can include multiple domains, it can become quite large. To limit its size, objects in the GC have only a subset of properties included. For example, a user account may have 100 properties to describe it, but only about 10 are included in the GC.

Tree A tree is a group of domains with a common namespace. That simply means the two-part root domain name is common to other domains in the tree. The first domain in the forest may be called Bigfirm.com. A child domain could be created named sales.bigfirm.com. Notice the common name (Bigfirm.com). It is possible to create a separate tree within a forest. For example, another domain could be created named littlefirm.com. It's not the same namespace, but since it is in the same forest, it would share a common schema and global catalog.

A Single-Domain Forest

The majority of networks consist of just a single Active Directory domain. Any small business that has grown too big for a workgroup and any business that doesn't have a specific need to add domains will use a single domain.

It's generally recommended to move from a workgroup to a domain when the number of users reaches somewhere between 10 and 20. You're able to implement single sign-on capabilities, so users only need to remember one domain password instead of multiple workgroup passwords, and you can provide significantly better security with a domain than you can with a workgroup.

You can stick with a single domain unless you need a second domain. This may have you wondering, "When should I use more than one domain?" Generally, if none of the following situations applies to you, a single domain will meet your needs:

◆ You have more than 100,000 user and computer objects, and replication is slow.

◆ Replication performance is impacted by frequently changing attributes.

◆ You have multiple locations connected with slow WAN links, and replication performance is impacted.

◆ A legacy domain needs to be preserved.

Notice most of these are related to replication. If you have fewer than 100,000 user and computer objects (50,000 users with their own computers) all in a single well-connected network and replication works efficiently, then it's highly unlikely you'll need more than a single domain.

Technically, a single domain is also a forest (though it's a rather small forest). Every Active Directory implementation starts with a single forest. The first domain in the forest is the root domain, and a single-domain forest contains only the root domain.

In extremely large organizations, multiple forests may be used to enable multiple schemas, to manage resources differently, to segment administrator access, or even for geographic or political reasons. A multiple-domain forest requires consideration and management of trusts, but a single-domain forest implementation is comparatively simple.

Benefits of a Single Domain

This single domain includes all the Active Directory objects (users, computers, groups, and so on) used within the organization. A single domain provides several benefits:

Least expensive Every domain starts with a single domain controller and usually includes a second DC for redundancy. Each additional domain requires additional servers, incurring costs for hardware and software plus the added costs of the IT professionals like you needed to manage them.

Easier to manage A single domain is easier to manage than multiple domains. Each additional domain includes additional accounts, groups, group policies, and other details that must be managed.

Simpler disaster recovery You only need to plan for the recovery of a single domain. Backups only need to be done for a single domain, and the overall disaster recovery plan is simpler.

In the past, one of the biggest reasons why administrators were forced to create a separate domain was to enforce different password policies. However, Windows Server 2008 now allows fine-grained password policies, which means you can have multiple password policies in a single domain. Fine-grained policies are covered in more depth later in this chapter.

Creating a Single-Domain Forest

Once you have Windows Server 2008 R2 installed, it's pretty easy to create a domain—you simply run the domain controller promotion wizard (DCPromo) to promote the server to a domain controller.

DCPromo will install (and remove when necessary) Active Directory Domain Services on servers. You can run DCPromo on any Windows Server product to promote it to a DC. However, the operating system version you use will affect the capabilities of your domain. If you promote a Windows Server 2008 R2 server to a DC, you'll have significantly more capabilities than if you promote a Windows Server 2000 server.

Although DCPromo is a very well-written application guided by an intuitive wizard, you still have several decision points you need to understand:

- Server configuration
- Operating system compatibility
- Deployment configuration
- Domain name
- Forest functional level
- Domain functional level
- DNS
- File locations
- DSRM administrator password

These are explained in detail in the following sections.

BEFORE RUNNING DCPROMO (SERVER CONFIGURATION)

Before running DCPromo, you should ensure your server is properly configured. The two primary considerations are the name of the computer and the IP address:

Server name It's easiest to rename a domain controller before you promote it to a DC. Although it is possible to rename a domain controller using NetDom after you promote it, this frequently causes issues that are easier to just avoid. Many companies choose to name their DCs as DC1, DC2, and so on, but any intuitive name is acceptable.

IP addresses The domain controller should have a static IP address. Although Windows Server 2008 R2 supports both IPv4 and IPv6, many companies are still using only IPv4 internally and disabling or simply not actively using IPv6. Make sure you assign a static IP address for at least IPv4 to coincide with your network. If you assign a static IP address for IPv4 but leave IPv6 enabled and dynamically assigned, you'll receive an error similar to Figure 6.1 while running DCPromo.

FIGURE 6.1
DCPromo static
IP address error

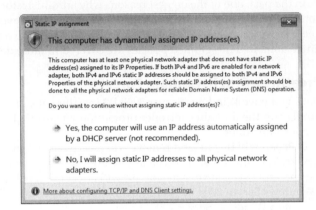

It is possible to complete DCPromo without statically assigning the address, but if you use DCPromo to also install DNS (a very common practice), you'll have some issues later. It's best to assign the address before running DCPromo.

In addition to statically assigning your IP address, you should also consider the IP address for DNS. If you're going to allow DCPromo to configure DNS for you (which is highly recommended), either leave the DNS address blank or use the same statically assigned address for the future DC.

OPERATING SYSTEM COMPATIBILITY

Every day we work with computers and computer systems, we hear or read something else about security. Systems are getting attacked daily. It used to be that attackers released viruses to damage systems just for the fun of it.

Times have changed. Viruses have become monetized. Attackers today want your data and your money and try every method possible to get into your systems without you knowing it. Administrators need to be proactive at plugging every security hole. One of the legacy security holes is related to how Windows NT 4.0 clients and non-Microsoft Server Message Block (SMB) clients try to authenticate with DCs.

USING PRIVATE IP ADDRESSES

When you statically assign IP addresses, you should use addresses in the private IP address ranges. In most networks, you'll see IPv4 addresses in use in one of the following ranges:

◆ 10.0.0.0/24 through 10.255.255.255

◆ 172.16.0.0 through 172.31.255.255

◆ 192.168.0.0 through 192.168.255.255

This is important because if you use an IP address that is also being used on the Internet (a public IP), you'll run into problems. As an example, Bing.com has an address of 64.4.8.147. If you assigned this address to an internal computer, users would never be able to reach Bing.com.

You can assign either IPv4 or IPv6 addresses. You should follow the standard used in your organization. If you're starting from scratch, use the version that you're most familiar with (either IPv4 or IPv6).

Several published papers identify acceptable addresses to use in private networks:

RFC 1918: Address Allocation for Private Internets   This paper outlines the use of IPv4 addresses in a private network. You can access it at http://www.faqs.org/rfcs/rfc1918.html.

RFC 4193: Unique Local IPv6 Unicast Addresses   If your internal network is using IPv6, you can look at this paper to identify IPv6 addresses to use internally: http://www.faqs.org/rfcs/rfc4193.html.

Early cryptography algorithms used with NT 4.0 clients are considered cracked today and shouldn't be used. To reinforce this, Microsoft has made the default installation of a domain in Windows Server 2008 and Windows Server 2008 R2 more secure. Specifically, the "Allow cryptography algorithms compatible with Windows NT 4.0" setting is configured to prevent these clients from connecting when using the weaker NT 4.0–style algorithms.

Of course, whenever you increase security, you sometimes impact usability. With this new setting, older NT 4.0 clients, some SAMBA SMB clients (such as Linux), and even some network attached storage (NAS) devices may have trouble connecting to the domain. Microsoft recommends upgrading the clients to resolve the issue without compromising security.

Although DCPromo doesn't give you a choice to modify these settings, it does give you a warning and an explanation on the Operating System Compatibility page, as shown in Figure 6.2.

If you find that you must support some older clients, check out the Knowledge Base article for the symptoms and workarounds at http://support.microsoft.com/kb/942564. The KB article includes information on the Group Policy settings that can be configured to enable the older clients to connect, along with some strong warnings that doing so will weaken security.

DEPLOYMENT CONFIGURATION

The deployment configuration choice allows you to identify whether you're creating a new domain in a new forest or adding it to an existing forest. If you're adding it to an existing forest, you can add another domain controller to an existing domain (which is covered later in this chapter) or create a new domain.

For the first DC, your choice is simple. You'll be creating a new domain in a new forest.

FIGURE 6.2
Operating System
Compatibility page

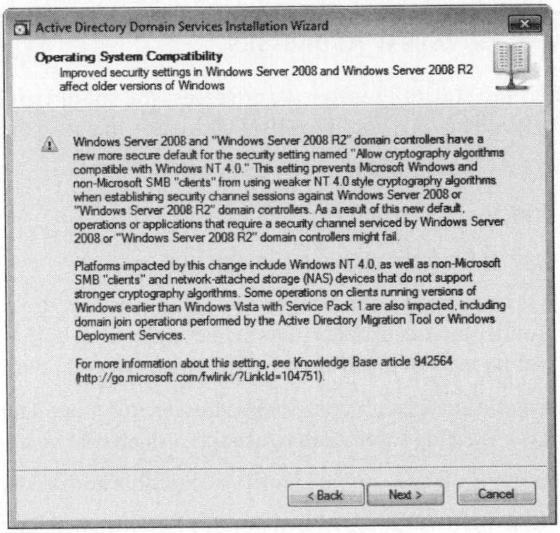

NAMING YOUR ROOT DOMAIN

The very first domain in the forest is referred to as the *forest root domain*. When creating the root domain, you need to use a fully qualified domain name (FQDN). This will have two elements, such as Bigfirm.com or Mydomain.net. The second part of the name (.com and .net in the examples) is referred to as the *top-level* domain name. Some other top-level domain names you've probably seen on the Internet are .biz, .mil, .gov, .tv, and many more.

Figure 6.3 shows the screen where you'll enter the name of your domain in DCPromo. In the figure, we've entered **bigfirm.com**.

FIGURE 6.3
Naming the forest
root domain

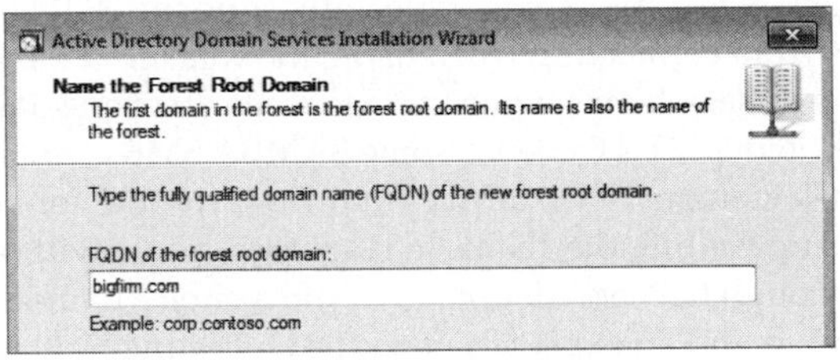

You must use a two-part name as your FQDN, but you don't have to use a valid top-level domain name that you may see on the Internet. If you want to use .hme, .home, .tst, .test, or any other name you can think of, go for it. Many administrators specifically try to avoid Internet top-level domains to avoid confusion for their internal networks.

ACTIVE DIRECTORY AND DNS

Chapter 5 covers the relationship between Active Directory and DNS in much greater depth, but in short you should know that DNS is a requirement for Active Directory. DNS SRV records are used to locate domain controllers running specific services.

CHANGING A DOMAIN NAME

Although it is possible to rename a domain, it's challenging, and some would say that it has never worked reliably. You'll be best served if you take your time to name the domain exactly what you want it to be when you create it. If you do need to change the domain name, you can use the Domain Rename tool (RenDom.exe). If you need to rename a domain, check out this TechNet article that outlines the process: http://technet.microsoft.com/library/cc786120.aspx.

We once provided some informal consultation to an organization that was faced with either renaming the domain or destroying it and starting over from scratch. The organization had about 100 users and just didn't want to flatten their domain unless they absolutely had to do so. In other words, they were willing to try the rename process and leave a complete domain rebuild as a last resort. The IT team took advantage of a long weekend (and were there all three days) and ended up with a successfully renamed domain.

Additionally, TechRepublic has an interesting article titled "Active Directory Domain Rename Not Difficult At All" that you can read at http://techrepublic.com.com/5208-6230-0.html? forumID=102&threadID=229757&start=0. Although the "Not Difficult At All" part of the title may be a little bit of a stretch, it does document one of many examples where a domain has been successfully renamed.

If you look around, though, you'll surely find some examples where it didn't succeed. The process is very tedious, and things can go wrong. If you can avoid the whole process completely, you're much better off.

DNS is so integral to Active Directory we've come to realize that if Active Directory has a problem, the first thing to check is DNS. It's often said that 70 percent of Active Directory problems are directly related to DNS. If DNS isn't working or configured properly, Active Directory won't be working.

Although DNS can be complex, DCPromo makes the initial installation and configuration of DNS quite simple. When you run DCPromo, it will recognize DNS isn't installed and will offer to configure it for you. If you let it, DCPromo does an excellent job.

DCPromo first tries to create a delegation for the DNS server, but if DNS isn't installed, this will fail and give an error message similar to Figure 6.4. This is normal.

FIGURE 6.4
DNS delegation
warning

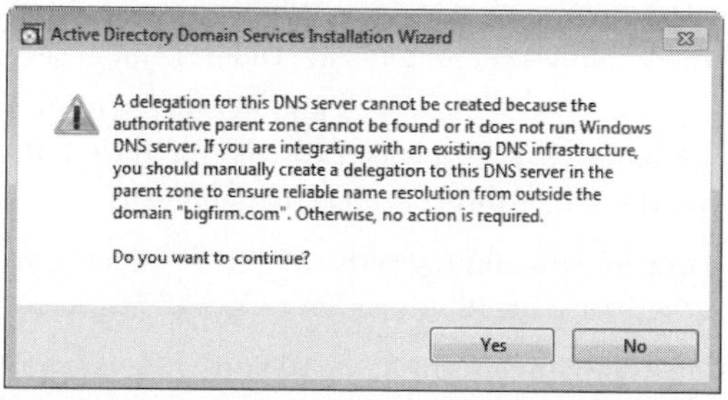

After receiving this warning, you simply click Yes to continue, and DCPromo will install and configure DNS for you. It will create the DNS zone as an Active Directory integrated zone.

DOMAIN FUNCTIONAL LEVELS

DCPromo will prompt you to set the domain functional level and the forest functional level. Your choice for the domain functional level will be based on the operating system that your domain controllers are using.

More specifically, you can only choose a domain functional level that matches the oldest operating system running on any of your DCs. The available domain functional levels are the following:

◆ Windows Server 2000 native

◆ Windows Server 2003

◆ Windows Server 2008

◆ Windows Server 2008 R2

If you're promoting a Windows Server 2008 R2 server to a domain controller, you can choose any of the domain functional levels up to and including Windows Server 2008 R2. However, if your server is running Windows Server 2003, the only choices will be Windows Server 2000 native and Windows Server 2003.

Your choice affects future DCs too. Imagine that you promoted a server running Windows Server 2008 R2 to a DC and chose the Windows Server 2008 R2 domain functional level. Later, you decide to add a second DC for redundancy. This second server must be running Windows Server 2008 R2. If you had another server running Windows Server 2003, you could not promote it to a DC in this domain.

Two important factors are worth considering:

◆ You can always raise the functional level to a higher level later.

◆ You can never lower the functional level.

This is like adding salt to soup, sauce, or gravy. You can always add more salt, but if you put too much in, you can't take it back out. It's best to be conservative—with salt and with functional levels. If you're unsure, choose a lower functional level such as Windows Server 2003 first.

FUNCTIONAL LEVEL APPLIES TO DCS, NOT MEMBER SERVERS

If the domain functional level is Windows Server 2008 R2, the domain will support only those DCs running Windows Server 2008 R2. Older member servers are OK, but not older DCs.

We've taught this concept to a lot of students in the classroom and have noticed an interesting phenomenon. Although we stress that the functional level directly relates to *DCs*, people often incorrectly change this to *servers* in their heads.

◆ Can a domain running at the Windows Server 2008 R2 domain functional level support *member* servers running Windows Server 2003? Yes. Absolutely!

◆ Can a domain running at the Windows Server 2008 R2 domain functional level support *domain controllers* running Windows Server 2003? No. DCPromo will not allow servers running older operating systems to be promoted.

Further, if your domain functional level is set to Windows Server 2003 and you have Windows Server 2003 domain controllers, you won't be able to raise the domain functional level any higher.

When you run DCPromo, you'll be prompted to select the domain functional level with a dialog box similar to Figure 6.5. If there's a possibility that you'll need to promote a server running an older operating system to a DC, choose the older domain functional level. You can always raise the domain functional level later. You'll see how to raise the functional levels later in this chapter.

FIGURE 6.5
Selecting the domain functional level

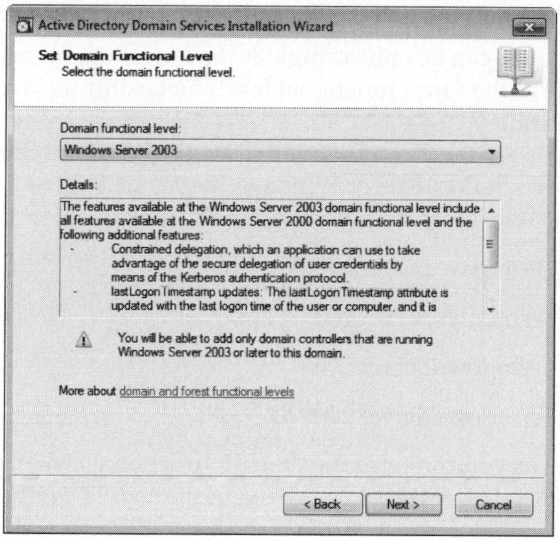

You'll enjoy different benefits depending on which domain functional level you choose.

Windows Server 2003   The Windows Server 2003 domain functional level includes several benefits:

♦ Can rename domain controllers using NetDom

♦ Delegation of user credentials using the Kerberos authentication protocol

♦ Use of the lastLogonTimestamp property

♦ Redirection of new user and computer objects to something other than the Users and Computers containers

Windows Server 2008   The Windows Server 2008 domain functional level includes several benefits:

♦ DFS support for SYSVOL

♦ AES 128 and AES 256 support for Kerberos

♦ More detailed last interactive logon information

♦ Fine-grained password policies

Fine-grained password policies are a significant feature related to single-domain forests and will be covered later in this chapter.

Windows Server 2008 R2 The Windows Server 2008 R2 domain functional level adds authentication assurance. This provides the ability to determine which logon method was used by a user; information is stored in the Kerberos token.

FOREST FUNCTIONAL LEVELS

The forest functional level identifies capabilities within the forest. Remember, the domain functional level can be only as high as the lowest operating system running on a DC in the domain. Similarly, the forest functional level can be only as high as the lowest domain functional level in the forest.

If you set the forest functional level to Windows Server 2008, you will only have the choice of Windows Server 2008 or Windows Server 2008 R2 for the domain functional level.

DCPromo offers the following forest functional level choices:

◆ Windows Server 2000

◆ Windows Server 2003

◆ Windows Server 2008

◆ Windows Server 2008 R2

Just as you can raise the domain functional level later, you can also raise the forest functional level after the DC has been promoted. The only thing to remember is that the domain functional level must be raised first, and then you can raise the forest functional level. If your network includes multiple domains, all the domains in the forest must be raised first.

When you run DCPromo, you'll be prompted with a page similar to Figure 6.6. For a single-domain forest, your choice is rather simple. You simply choose the same forest functional level as you plan to choose for the domain functional level. If your domain functional level is Server 2008 R2, your forest functional level should also be Windows Server 2008 R2.

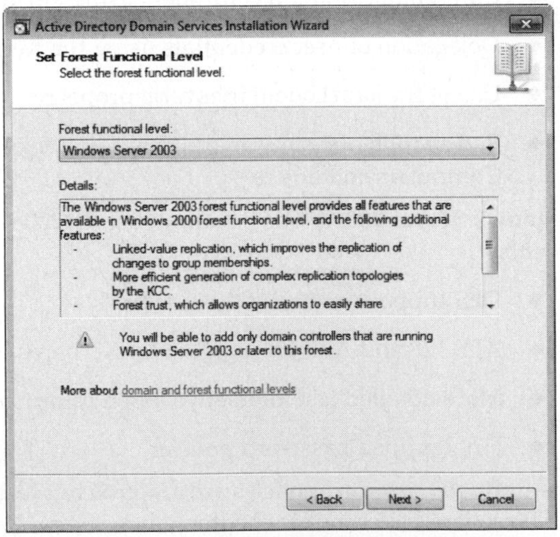

FIGURE 6.6
Selecting the forest functional level

Just as different domain functional levels provide different benefits, different forest functional levels also provide different benefits.

Windows Server 2003   The Windows Server 2003 forest functional level includes several benefits over the Windows Server 2000 forest functional level:

- Improved replication

- More efficient replication topologies automatically generated by KCC

- Ability to create forest trusts

- Ability to rename domains

- Can add a read-only domain controller (RODC)

Windows Server 2008   The Windows Server 2008 forest functional level doesn't provide any additional features. When the forest is raised to Windows Server 2008, all new domains in the forest will automatically be created using at least the Windows Server 2008 forest functional level.

Windows Server 2008 R2   The Windows Server 2008 R2 forest functional level adds the Active Directory Recycle Bin capability, which works similarly to the Windows Recycle Bin. The AD Recycle Bin allows you to easily restore Active Directory objects without entering Active Directory Restore Mode. The Active Directory Recycle Bin isn't enabled by default in Windows Server 2008 R2, but the capability is ready when you are.

The Active Directory Recycle Bin is a neat feature that should make you seriously consider using the forest functional level of Window Server 2008 R2. Although it is possible to restore accidentally deleted objects (such as users and computers) using NTDSUtil and authoritative restores, it is a time-consuming process. The Active Directory Recycle Bin makes things quite simpler.

FOREST FUNCTIONAL LEVEL CHOSEN FIRST

Although it's logical to think of the domain functional level first and then the forest functional level, DCPromo provides these choices as forest functional level first and then domain functional level. If you choose a forest functional level of Windows Server 2008 R2, the domain functional level must be Windows Server 2008 R2, and you won't even see the choice of a domain functional level.

LOCATIONS FOR FILES AND SYSVOL

DCPromo will prompt you for the location of different Active Directory files and the location of the SYSVOL shared folder. Figure 6.7 shows the screen that DCPromo presents.

The SYSVOL shared folder is used to share information such as scripts and elements of Group Policy objects between domain controllers. SYSVOL must be on an NTFS drive. The database and log files can be located on different drives for optimization.

At its core, Active Directory is a big database, and databases have a primary data file and a transaction log file. Changes to the database are first written to the transaction log file, and then periodically the transaction log file is checkpointed—that's just a fancy way of saying that changes in the transaction log are committed to the database.

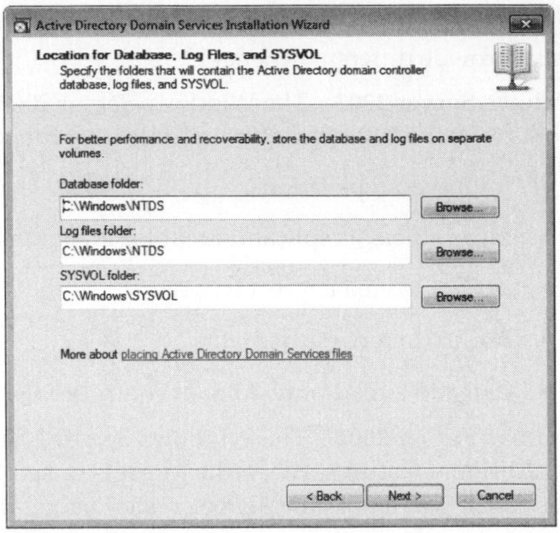

FIGURE 6.7
File locations and
SYSVOL location

The transaction log provides significant fault tolerance and recovery capabilities to the Active Directory database. If the server loses power in the middle of any change, Active Directory can use the log to ensure that the database is in a consistent state when the server is rebooted. Any changes recorded in the log are committed to the database, and any unfinished changes recorded in the log are ignored.

From a performance perspective, it's possible to increase the performance of your DC by moving the database and transaction log files to different drives. For optimal disk performance of Active Directory, you may use a configuration similar to this:

◆ C:\ drive: Operating system

◆ D:\ drive: Active Directory database file and SYSVOL

◆ E:\ drive: Transaction log file

In this configuration, each of the drives needs to be a separate spindle (a separate physical disk). A single drive with three partitions wouldn't provide any performance gain. Additionally, if your disk drives have different speeds, you should put the operating system on the fastest disk, the transaction log on the next fastest, and the Active Directory database file and SYSVOL on the slowest disk. The operating system and the transaction log file will receive the heaviest usage.

Let's add a moment of realism here, though. If your domain includes 100 users, you can store the database and log files on the C drive with the operating system and not notice any performance problems. On the other hand, if you're supporting 50,000 users, you may want to squeeze every ounce of performance gain out of the server, so you will locate the database and log files on different drives. If you're building a test system, there's nothing wrong with leaving everything on C.

MOVING THE DATABASE AND LOG FILES

If you later decide you want to move the database or log files onto different drives, you still can. The NTDSUtil command-line shell program includes the Files command that can be used to move these files. You must be in Directory Services Restore Mode to move files.

DIRECTORY SERVICES RESTORE MODE PASSWORD

If you ever need to perform maintenance or restoration of Active Directory, you need to do so using Directory Services Restore Mode (DSRM). You can access DSRM by pressing F8 to access the Advanced Options menu. You can also access the different Safe Mode options from this menu.

After selecting the Directory Services Restore Mode, you'll be prompted to log on. However, Active Directory will not be running, so you can't use an Active Directory account. Instead, you'll use a special administrator account with a different password.

DCPromo prompts you to set the password for the DSRM account, as shown in Figure 6.8.

FIGURE 6.8
Setting the DSRM password

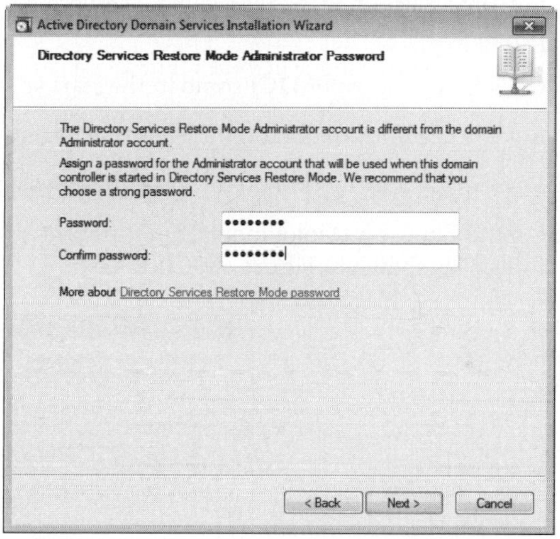

Make sure you document the password you set here. Many organizations document critical passwords by writing them down and storing them in a safe. You won't be able to access DSRM without it. The DSRM administrator account password is sometimes confused with the regular administrator password you set for the domain administrator account, but it's different.

CHANGING THE DSRM PASSWORD

If you later want to change the DSRM password (and it's a good practice to regularly do so), you can use the NTDSUtil command-line shell program to do so. NTDSUtil includes the Set DSRM Password command that can be used to change the DSRM password. For help at any of the NTDSUtil shell prompts, enter /?. Thankfully, you don't need to enter DSRM to change the password. You can change the password by launching NTDSUtil while the DC is running normally. This allows you to change the DSRM password even if you can't remember what the password was originally.

Check out this TechNet article on NTDSUtil to view the full command-line syntax for any NTDSUtil commands: http://technet.microsoft.com/library/cc753343.aspx.

RUNNING DCPROMO

Now that you know what you'll encounter when you run DCPromo, you can run it and create your single-domain forest. Although the Server Manager does give you the option of adding the Active Directory Domain Services role, it's not necessary to do so. Adding this role will add the binaries needed by DCPromo, but if the role hasn't been added, DCPromo will take care of all the details.

The following steps assume you have a clean installation of Windows Server 2008 R2 without any additional roles installed. If you have installed additional roles, you may see some minor differences.

1. Log onto a Windows Server 2008 R2 server using an account with local administrative privileges.

2. Click Start, and enter **DCPromo** in the start search box.

3. Review the information on the Welcome page, and click Next.

4. Review the information on the Operating System Compatibility page, and click Next.

5. On the Choose a Deployment Configuration page, select "Create a new domain in a new forest," as shown in Figure 6.9. Click Next.

FIGURE 6.9
Creating a new
domain in a
new forest

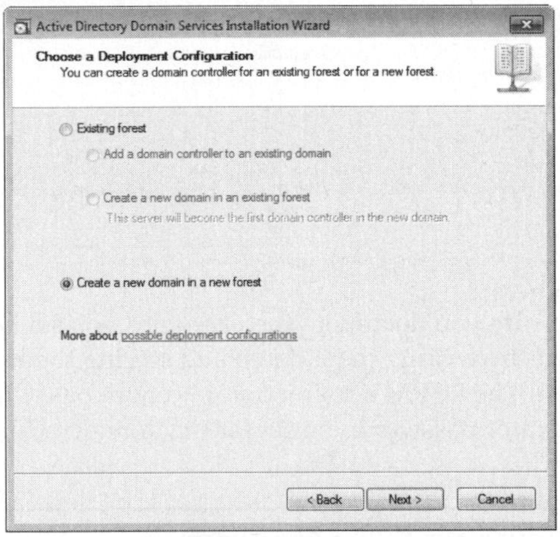

6. Enter the FQDN of your domain. In our domain, we entered **bigfirm.com**, but you can use any two-part FQDN you'd like. Click Next.

7. The Set Forest Functional Level page appears. Accept the default of Windows Server 2003, and click Next.

8. The Set Domain Functional Level page appears. Accept the default of Windows Server 2003, and click Next.

9. Ensure that DNS server is selected, as shown in Figure 6.10. DCPromo will install DNS as part of the process. Notice that global catalog is also selected but dimmed, preventing it from being changed. The first domain controller in the domain must be a global catalog server. Click Next.

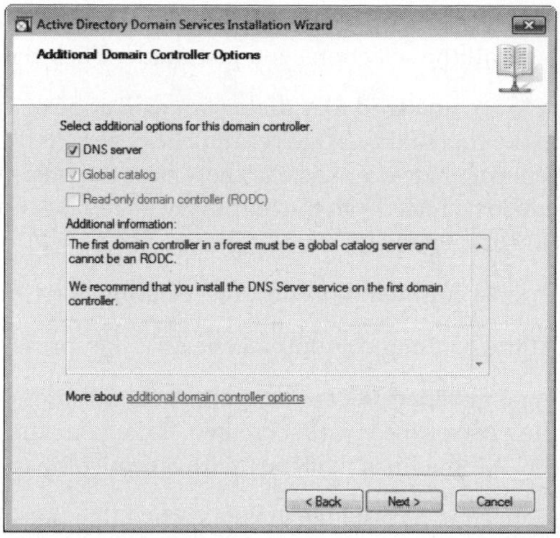

FIGURE 6.10
Adding DNS as
a domain control-
ler option

10. If either the IPv4 or IPv6 addresses are configured to receive their address from DHCP, you'll receive a warning. It's recommended that you assign a static IP address. If you have assigned a static IPv4 address but haven't disabled IPv6 or modified the IPv6 address, you can click Yes to continue the installation.

11. DCPromo will attempt to locate a DNS server. If you haven't prestaged a DNS server, you will now receive a warning letting you know the zone for your domain can't be created. This is normal. DCPromo will configure DNS. Click Yes to continue.

12. The Location for Database, Log Files, and SYSVOL page will appear. Click Next to accept the default locations.

13. On the Directory Services Restore Mode Administrator Password page, enter a password twice. In test beds, we often use **P@ssws0rd**. Click Next.

14. Review the information on the Summary page. It should look similar to Figure 6.11.

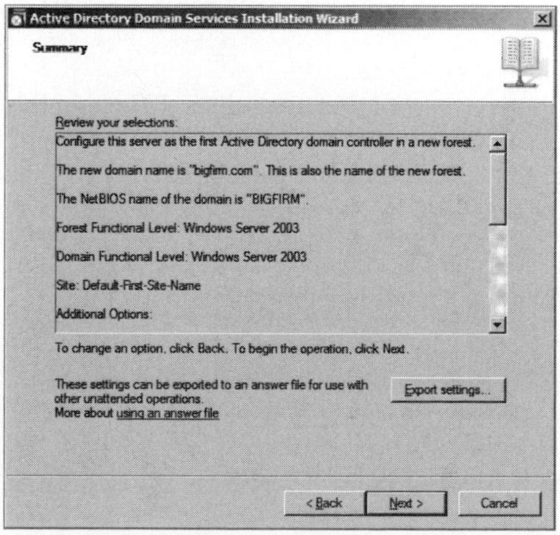

FIGURE 6.11
DCPromo
summary page

15. Notice there is a button named Export Settings. This will allow you to save an answer file with all the selections you just made. Click the Export Settings button.

16. A "Save unattend file" dialog box will appear. Type **DCPromoexport** in the text box. Browse to the root of the C:\ drive, and click Save. At this point, you could click Next, and DCPromo will run. However, instead these next few steps will show you how to run the DCPromo script you just created. On the Summary page, click Cancel, and click Yes to confirm you want to cancel DCPromo.

17. Open a command prompt by selecting Start ➢ Command Prompt.

18. At the command prompt, type **cd**, and press Return.

19. Type **notepad DCPromoexport.txt**, and press Return. Notepad should open showing you the answer file you just created. Take your time reviewing the information in this answer file. All the lines that start with a semicolon (;) are comment lines and will be ignored.

20. Notice the SafeModeAdminPassword line doesn't include a password. Type in a password after the equals sign (=) so that it looks something like this:

SafeModeAdminPassword=P@ssw0rd

As a security precaution, DCPromo scrubs out the password each time you run the script, so you'll either need to set the file to read-only or reenter the password before using the text file again. You can also remove the semicolon for RebootOnCompletion=Yes. You probably already guessed this will cause the server to reboot after DCPromo completes. Press Ctrl+S to save the file.

21. Return to the command prompt, and type in **DCPromo.exe /unattend:c:\DCPromoexport .txt.** Press Return. DCPromo will now run unattended using the answer file.

DCPROMO PARAMETERS

For a full listing of all the possible DCPromo parameters you can use when running DCPromo with an unattend file, check out http://technet.microsoft.com/library/cc732887.aspx.

Alternatively, you could have clicked Next on the Summary page back in step 14, and you'd get to the same result. About the only difference is that instead of the status messages coming out to the command line, you'd have a picture similar to Figure 6.12 showing the progress. Notice that you can select the check box "Reboot on completion."

22. If you want to take a break, now is a good time. Once DCPromo completes running and reboots, you will be prompted to log on.

23. Once the server reboots, press Ctrl+Alt+Delete to log on. The password for the domain administrator account is the same as the password was for the local administrator account before you ran DCPromo.

That's it. You've created a single-domain forest. Your next logical step is to create a second DC.

FIGURE 6.12
DCPromo on
autopilot

FIGURE 6.12
DCPromo on
autopilot

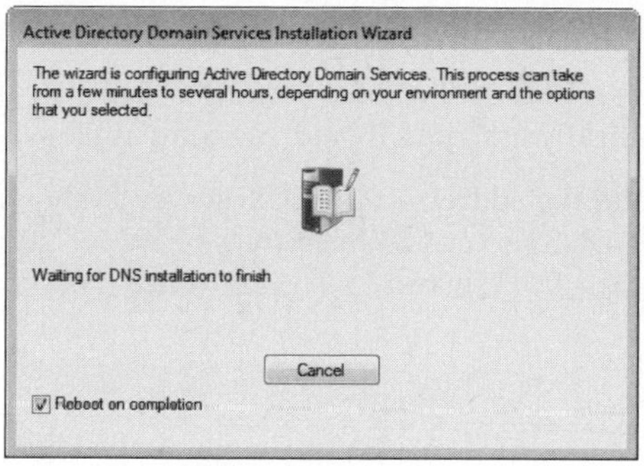

Adding a Second DC

Whenever possible, you should have a second DC. A second DC will make routine maintenance and disaster recovery planning much simpler. A single domain controller is a significant single point of failure risk. If it goes down, your entire network can go down, and you'll find yourself in crisis mode.

If you have a second DC and either the first or second DC fails, the network will continue to hum along. Users will still be able to log onto the domain, and they won't experience any interruption in their work, group policies will still be applied, and normal administration of the domain can still be done. You'll still have work to do, but it won't be a crisis. Additionally, restoring a failed DC is much simpler if a DC is still running in the domain. You can even create a new DC from scratch without a backup if it comes to that.

If your last DC in the domain has failed, you'll need a recent backup of Active Directory, and you'll have a significant amount of work to restore the domain. All the while, you'll also probably have several nervous managers hovering over your shoulder frequently asking things like "How much longer?"

Just as you ran DCPromo to create the first DC, you'll run DCPromo to create the second. An account with Domain Admins permissions is required to add a domain controller. You'll also need to consider the following choices:

◆ Deployment configuration

◆ DNS

◆ Global catalog

These are explained in detail in the following sections.

Before Running DCPromo

The computer you're promoting to a DC needs to have DNS configured so that it can locate the domain. And just as the first DC needs a static IP address, the second DC needs a statically assigned IP address.

You'll need to access the TCP/IP properties for the NIC. There are multiple ways to get there—here's one:

1. Click Start, right-click Network, and select Properties.

2. Click the Local Area Connection. Click the Properties button.

3. Select Internet Protocol Version 4 (TCP/IPv4), and select Properties. Ensure you have a statically assigned IP address compatible with your network.

4. Enter the address of the DNS server as shown in Figure 6.13. In this example network, the DNS server has an address of 192.168.20.10, so we've entered it as the IP address for the DNS server.

FIGURE 6.13
Configuring client
DNS settings

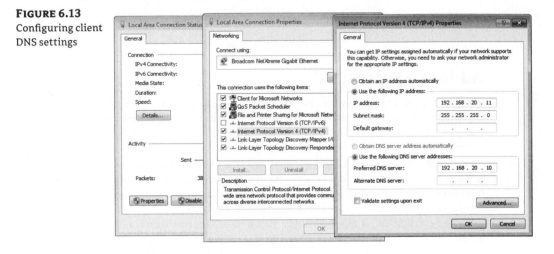

5. Close all the windows and dialog boxes.

It's not necessary for the computer to be a member of the domain prior to running DCPromo. If it's not a member of the domain, it will be joined as part of the promotion process.

Deployment Configuration for the Second DC

Since you already have a domain, you'll have a different choice to make with the deployment configuration. You want to add a second DC, so you'll select "Existing forest" and "Add a domain controller to an existing domain," as shown in Figure 6.14.

This would be the same selection you'd make for any subsequent domain controllers in the domain. If you wanted to create child domains in your forest, you'd instead select "Create a new domain in an existing forest."

DNS for the Second DC

Should you add DNS to the second DC? Here's the short answer—absolutely!

If your first DC is running DNS (a recommended configuration), then your second DC should also be running DNS. If you followed the steps promoting the first DC, than it's running an Active Directory integrated (ADI) zone. By adding DNS to the second DC, you'll add redundancy with very little overhead. You can also use the second DNS server for load balancing.

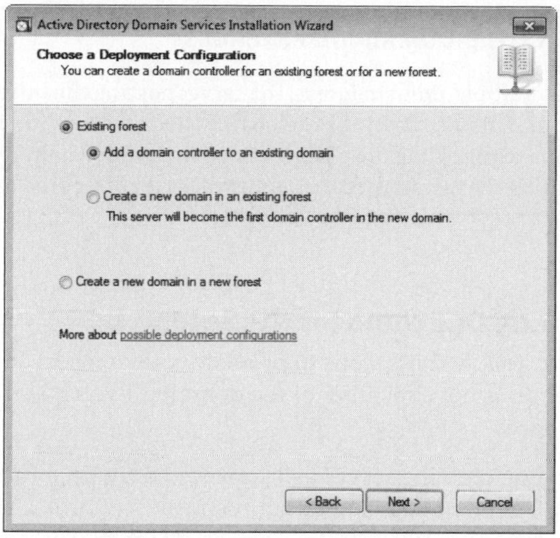

FIGURE 6.14
Choosing a deployment configuration

Remember, Active Directory is heavily dependent on DNS. Services use SRV records to locate the domain controller and to locate clients throughout the network. If you chose not to add DNS to the second DC and the first DC failed, your network would have no DNS available and would fall to its knees. A DC without DNS to locate it is about the same as no DC at all.

With two DNS servers, you can configure the clients to use both DNS servers. Clients should be configured with one preferred DNS server and can also be configured with one or more alternate DNS servers. Clients will only query the alternate DNS server if the preferred DNS server fails or doesn't respond to queries.

Imagine that you've configured two servers named BF1 and BF2 as domain controllers with ADI DNS. You could configure half the clients this way:

- Preferred DNS server: BF1

- Alternate DNS server: BF2

You would then configure the other half of the clients this way:

- Preferred DNS server: BF2

- Alternate DNS server: BF1

Global Catalog for the Second DC

Should the second DC be a global catalog server? Another short answer—yes!

In this chapter, you are creating a single-domain forest only. In a single-domain forest, you should always make all of your domain controllers global catalog servers. There is no additional cost involved, and it ensures that the DC provides full functionality if the other DC fails.

MULTIPLE-DOMAIN DIFFERENCES

In a multiple-domain forest, the server hosting the Infrastructure Master role won't function correctly if it's also hosting the global catalog server. With this in mind, you'll have different decisions to make regarding the global catalog server. Normally all of the domain controllers except the one hosting the Infrastructure Master role are configured as global catalog servers.

Running DCPromo for the Second DC

You can follow these steps to promote a second server to a domain controller. In these steps, the server is not a member of the domain. If you have joined the domain, you may see minor differences.

1. Log onto the server using an account with local administrative privileges. If you're logged in with a nonadministrative account, User Account Control will prompt you to enter administrator credentials when you run DCPromo.

2. Click Start, type in **DCPromo**, and press Enter.

3. Review the information on the wizard's Welcome page, and click Next.

4. Click Next on the Operating System Compatibility page.

5. On the Choose a Deployment Configuration page, select "Existing forest," and ensure "Add a domain controller to an existing domain" is selected. Click Next.

6. Enter the name of your existing domain on the Network Credentials page. We entered **bigfirm.com**.

7. If the account you logged onto the server with isn't a member of the Domain Admins group in the target domain, you'll also need to enter alternate credentials. Click Set, and enter the credentials for an account with Domain Admins permissions, as shown in Figure 6.15. Click OK, and then click Next.

FIGURE 6.15
Entering network credentials

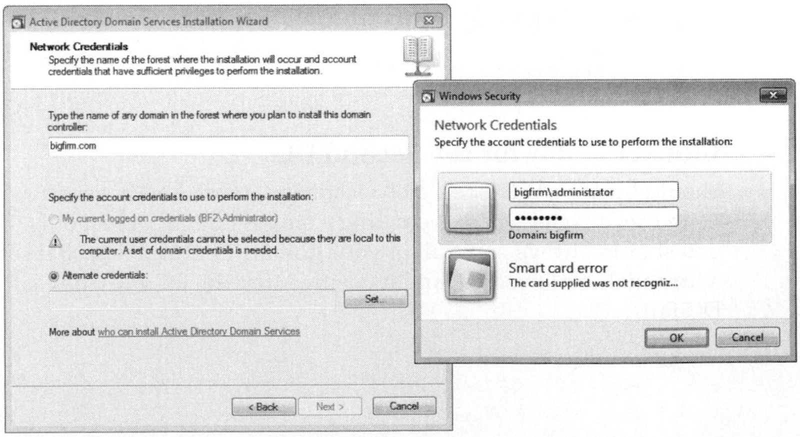

AD PROBLEMS? CHECK DNS!

If you receive an error indicating that a domain controller for the domain can't be contacted, double-check the spelling of the domain name and then check DNS. Ensure DNS is running on the DNS server, and ensure your system is configured to use this DNS server. A simple check is to ping the domain name. For example, if your domain name is Bigfirm.com, you would type in `ping bigfirm.com` and should receive four replies. If you don't see the four replies, it is a clear indication that you're either not reaching DNS (check TCP/IP) or DNS is not functioning correctly.

8. The Select a Domain page will appear. Ensure your domain is selected, and click Next.

9. On the Select a Site page, ensure the Default-First-Site-Name site is selected, and click Next. Chapter 21 covers multiple site environments in more depth, but if your network has multiple sites and they're configured correctly, the correct site for your DC should be selected automatically.

10. The Additional Domain Controller Options page will appear. You should select both DNS server and global catalog, as shown in Figure 6.16. (The read-only domain controller option is covered in Chapter 22 of this book.)

FIGURE 6.16
Selecting additional domain controller options

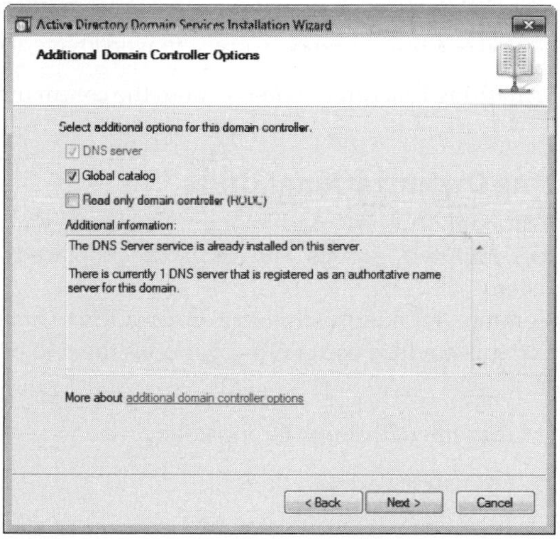

11. If a warning for DNS delegation appears, click Yes to continue.

12. On the Location for Database, Log Files, and SYSVOL page, click Next to accept the default locations.

13. Enter a DSRM password into the Password and Confirm Password text boxes. Click Next.

14. Review the information on the Summary page. If desired, you can click the Export Settings button to export the unattend file for DCPromo. (The installation for the first DC earlier in this chapter showed the procedure for an unattended DCPromo installation). Click Next.

UNATTENDED DCPROMO

The script file for a second DC can be very useful if you need to promote a server at a remote location. You can run through the steps just as you've done here, create the unattend file for DCPromo, and then send the file to the remote location. A technician at the other end doesn't need to know the intricacies of Active Directory to run the script.

---

15. Select the "Reboot on completion" check box.

16. Log on to the server after it reboots, and DCPromo will complete the process.

Creating Organizational Units, Accounts, and Groups

Once you've created your domain, you'll want to create your OUs, user accounts, computer accounts, groups, and so on. The primary tool you'll use is Active Directory Users and Computers (ADUC).

ADUC allows you to create everything with point-and-click ease. However, you can also do these tasks from the command line. Being able to create these objects from the command line is useful for two reasons:

◆ If you're running Server Core, you won't have access to ADUC locally.

◆ Anything that can be entered from the command line can be scripted.

Creating Organizational Units

Organizational units are used to organize objects within Active Directory. Any objects (such as users, computers, groups, and so on) can be placed within an OU to make them easier to administer.

It's common for administrators to create OUs to match each department in their organization. However, this obvious use of OUs overlooks the two primary technical reasons why you'll create an OU:

◆ Management through Group Policy

◆ Administrative delegation

MANAGEMENT THROUGH GROUP POLICY

Group Policy objects (GPOs) can be created and linked to sites, domains, and OUs. If you want some users to have a specific Group Policy assigned to them, you can create an OU, place the accounts within the OU, and link the GPO to the OUS.

However, if you haven't created any OUs, the only way GPOs can be assigned to regular accounts is through the default domain policy that is applied to all users and computers equally. Imagine that you wanted to deploy an application to all users in the sales department using Group Policy. If you linked your GPO to the domain, all users in the entire company would get the application, not just the users in the sales department.

Instead, you'd create an OU (let's call it Sales), move the sales department user and computer accounts into this OU, and then link the GPO to the Sales OU. If you had other groups of users that you wanted to apply specific Group Policy objects to, you'd create an OU for them and place their user and computer objects within that OU.

Administrative Delegation

The second technical reason to create an OU is related to delegation. Imagine Sally is the primary IT person providing IT support to personnel in the sales department. You want her to be able to create accounts for these users, reset passwords, and do basic troubleshooting. However, she should be able to do this only for users in the sales department.

If you've created an OU for the sales department and have placed all the user and computer accounts into that OU, you can use the Delegation of Control Wizard to grant appropriate privileges to Sally (or any other user or group you desire). You'll see how to use the Delegation of Control Wizard later in this chapter.

Creating OUs with ADUC

To create an OU using Active Directory Users and Computers, follow these steps:

1. Launch Active Directory Users and Computers by selecting Start ➤ Administrative Tools ➤ Active Directory Users and Computers.

2. Right-click the domain, and select New ➤ Organizational Unit.

3. Enter **Sales** as the name of the OU in the text box. Ensure the check box "Protect container from accidental deletion" is selected. Your display will look similar to Figure 6.17.

FIGURE 6.17
Creating an OU in ADUC

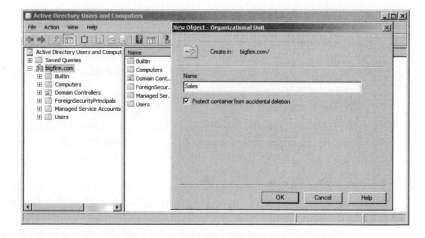

4. Click OK, and your OU is created.

5. It's also possible to create children OUs. Right-click the Sales OU you just created, and select New ➤ Organizational Unit.

6. Type in **Users** for the name, and click OK. Your display should look similar to Figure 6.18 with the Users OU as a child in the Sales OU.

PROTECT FROM DELETION

"Protect container from accidental deletion" is a neat feature that prevents anyone (even administrators) from accidentally deleting an object. Even though ADUC prompts you with the "Are you sure?" question, many of us quickly click right through these confirmation dialog boxes. However, when this option is set, the object cannot be deleted until the option is cleared.

If you really want to delete an object, you still can. Modify this setting by selecting View ➤ Advanced Features in ADUC, selecting the properties of the object, selecting the Object tab, and deselecting the "Protect object from accidental deletion" option.

FIGURE 6.18
Creating a child OU in ADUC

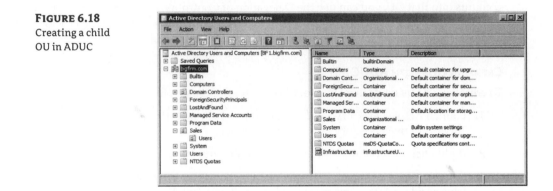

You may notice that you now have two Users objects within Active Directory. However, they are very different. The Users OU within the Sales OU is an OU and can have GPOs linked to it. The Users container under the domain is only a container (not an OU) and cannot have GPOs linked to it. OUs have a slightly different icon to identify them—it's not just a folder but instead a folder with an icon embedded on the front of the folder reminding you it's something more.

LDAP DISTINGUISHED NAMES

Active Directory uses the Lightweight Directory Access Protocol (LDAP) for communication. LDAP uses a distinguished name (DN) to uniquely identify each object within the directory. Before looking at how to create objects from the command line or scripts, you should understand the components of a DN.

The format of a DN uses objectType=objectName with several object types separated by commas. For example, a domain named Bigfirm.com has two domain components (`bigfirm` and `com`) that are identified this way: `dc=bigfirm,dc=com`.

Organizational units have an object type of OU and the Users and Computers containers are identified with `cn` (for "common name"). The Sales OU would have this DN:

    ou=Sales,dc=bigfirm,dc=com

The Users container would have this DN:

    cn=Users,dc=bigfirm,dc=com

An account with a name of Sally.Smith located in the Sales OU would have this DN:

`cn=Sally.Smith,ou=Sales,dc=bigfirm,dc=com`

An account with a name of Joe.Johnson located in the Users container would have this DN:

`cn=Joe.Johnson,cn=Users,dc=bigfirm,dc=com`

If OUs are nested, or have OUs within them, the lowest-level OU comes first in the DN name. For example, if the Sales OU had a child OU named Users and then had a user named Maria within it, the DN would be as follows:

`cn=Maria,ou=Users,ou=Sales,dc=bigfirm,dc=com`

Last, if the DN includes any spaces, it needs to be enclosed with quotes to ensure it is interpreted correctly. For example, this doesn't require quotes because there are no spaces:

`cn=Maria,ou=Users,ou=Sales,dc=bigfirm,dc=com`

However, the same DN with spaces must include quotes:

`"cn=Maria, ou=Users, ou=Sales, dc=bigfirm, dc=com"`

LDAP DNs are not case sensitive. The following two DNs will be interpreted as the same object:

`cn=Maria,ou=Users,ou=Sales,dc=bigfirm,dc=com`
`CN=maria,OU=users,OU=sales,DC=BigFirm,DC=Com`

CREATING OUs WITH DSADD

With a little bit of knowledge about DNs, you can now create some OUs using the command-line tool DSAdd. You can use DSAdd to create a variety of different objects:

- OUs
- Users
- Computers
- Groups
- Contacts
- Quotas

You need to execute the DSAdd command from the command line. Although it's easier to run the command from a domain controller, you can also run it from other locations by specifying the server and domain parameters. Once you launch the command line (click Start ➤ Command Prompt), you can enter DSAdd /? to view the help on DSAdd. If you want to see specific help on how to use DSAdd to create an OU, enter DSAdd ou /?. For more detailed help on DSAdd, check out the TechNet article at http://technet.microsoft.com/library/cc753708.aspx.

One of the things you'll notice is that a lot of help is available. A simple trick to capture the help information and store it in a text file is to use the redirection command (>) to redirect the help output to a text file. Instead of just entering DSAdd ou /?, enter it as DSAdd ou /? > DSAddhelp.txt.

To view the file, enter `notepad DSAddhelp.txt`.

The syntax of the DSAdd OU command is as follows:

```
Dsad ou DN
```

Although other optional parameters can be used, the only required parameter is the DN. Imagine you had a bunch of clowns in your organization that you wanted to manage using Group Policy. The following command can be entered from the command line to create an OU named Clowns in the Bigfirm.com domain. Notice the DN is ou=Clowns,dc=bigfirm,dc=com.

```
DSAdd ou "ou=Clowns,dc=bigfirm,dc=com"
```

If you launch Active Directory Users and Computers and refresh the view, you'll notice the Clowns OU has been added.

Remember, any of the commands you enter at the command line can also be saved as a batch file and easily run. For example, if you need to be able to re-create your live domain environment on a test-bed server, you could enter all the DSAdd commands into Notepad and then save the file with the .bat extension. Any file with the .bat extension is considered a batch file and can be executed from the command line. If you're going to enter the commands only once, it isn't much use to create the batch file. However, if there's a chance you'll need to enter the commands again, the batch file can save you a lot of time.

CREATING OUs WITH WINDOWS SCRIPTING HOST (WSH)

If you want to get a little fancier, you can create an OU with the Windows Scripting Host (WSH) program that is embedded in Windows. WSH could fill a book by itself (and it has filled many), so don't think these paragraphs will make you an expert—they won't. However, you will get a taste of what WSH can do.

> ### 🌐 Real World Scenario
>
> #### SCRIPTING ISN'T FOR EVERYONE
>
> We've taught scripting in the classroom and have come to realize that it isn't for everyone. It can sometimes be tedious and frustrating, and for some people it makes them want to pull their hair out. For others, it's tedious and frustrating but has an element of fun similar to solving a puzzle. Just remember, administrators don't need to be scripting experts. Usually, all you'll need to do is find a script that's close and slightly modify it to meet your needs. If you want to dig deeper into scripting, check out Microsoft's Scripting Center hosted by "The Scripting Guy" at http://technet.microsoft.com/en-us/scriptcenter/default.aspx.

You can enter the following script into a Notepad file saved with the .vbs extension (for example, CreateOU.vbs). You can then execute the script from the command line.

```
Set objDom = GetObject("LDAP://dc=bigfirm,dc=com")
Set objOU = objDom.Create("OrganizationalUnit","ou=SalesWSH")
objOU.SetInfo
Msgbox "Creating an OU", vbInformation, "Woo Hoo!"
```

The first line creates a variable named objDom (short for an "object of type domain"). The domain name is retrieved with the GetObject command and stored in this variable. This is one of the very few times when the Windows Scripting Host is case sensitive—LDAP must be capitalized. Additionally, you need to change the domain components (DC=xx) to match your domain. For example, if your domain name was testbed.hme, it would read as "LDAP:// dc=testbed,dc=hme".

The second line creates a variable named objOU (short for an "object of type OU"). It then uses the Create method of the objDom object to identify what you want to create. The variables are included in the parentheses—an "organizationalUnit" with the name of "SalesWSH" identified with a relative distinguished name of OU=SalesWSH.

SetInfo, in the third line, is the method that actually creates the object that was identified in the create method on the second line. At this point, you've completed the code needed to create the OU.

The fourth line launches a dialog-type message box that provides some feedback to you. The text within the first set of quotes identifies the message that will be displayed. VbInformation specifies that an information icon (white *i* within a blue circle) will be displayed. The text in the last set of quotes specifies a title for the message box.

CREATING OUs WITH POWERSHELL

You can also create OUs using PowerShell. PowerShell is installed by default in Server 2008 R2. You can launch it by selecting Start ➤ All Programs ➤ Accessories ➤ Windows PowerShell ➤ Windows PowerShell.

PowerShell will launch with a prompt of PS C:\Users\Administrator> (assuming you've logged in as an administrator). You can type the following lines of text to create an OU named PS_OU from the PowerShell prompt. You may need to modify the first line to match the name of your domain controller and your domain.

POWERSHELL IS SOMETIMES CASE SENSITIVE

Be careful when entering commands into PowerShell. Some commands are case sensitive. In particular, in the following code, LDAP must be capped as shown. It will accept other cases without an error on that line, but you won't succeed in creating the object.

```
$DCCon = "LDAP://BF1/DC=BigFirm,DC=Com"
$AD = [adsi] $DCCon
$OU = $AD.Create("OrganizationalUnit", "OU=PS_OU")
$OU.SetInfo()
```

If things don't work on the first try, verify that you don't have any typos, and verify that all the quotes and parentheses are in place. Just a single closing quote or parenthesis makes quite a bit of difference.

The first line identifies the instance of Active Directory on the domain controller named BF1 and stores it in the variable named $DCCon. Remember, LDAP must be all caps. The second line creates a variable named $AD and uses the Active Directory Services Interface (ADSI) to connect to the instance identified in the $DCCon variable.

Next, the $OU variable is created and uses the Create method of ADSI to indicate an OU named PS_OU wants to be created. The OU isn't created yet; instead, this line just indicates what you want to create. The last line uses the SetInfo() method to actually create the object.

We know what you're thinking. Isn't there a way to create this as a script?

Well, maybe a few of you are also thinking this is a pretty complex way to create an OU when all you have to do is point and click in Active Directory Users and Computers. The point is that you can automate processes with PowerShell. Say you want to re-create your live environment in a test bed by quickly creating a dozen OUs. This can be quick with a script.

You can create and execute a PowerShell script by following these steps:

1. Launch PowerShell if not already launched. It should be in the C:\Users\Administrator folder.

2. Type the following text, and press Enter to create a file and open it in Notepad.

   ```
   Notepad CreateOU.ps1
   ```

3. When prompted to create the file, click Yes.

4. Enter the following lines into the PowerShell script:

   ```
   $DCCon = "LDAP://BF1/DC=Bigfirm,DC=Com"
   $AD = [adsi] $DCCon
   $OU = $AD.Create("OrganizationalUnit", "OU=Script_OU1")
   $OU.SetInfo()
   $OU = $AD.Create("OrganizationalUnit", "OU=Script_OU2")
   $OU.SetInfo()
   ```

Notice that the first two lines ($DCCon and $AD) set up the environment, and then the next two lines create the OU. If you want to create multiple OUs, simply copy and paste the last two lines and modify the name of the OU.

5. Press Ctrl+S to save the file.

At this point, you have a PowerShell script you can run, but you probably won't be able to run it without modifying the environment.

6. Return to PowerShell. Type **Get-ex**, and press the Tab key. The command will become Get-ExecutionPolicy. Press Enter.

If you have a default installation, the result will show Restricted, and you can't run the script.

7. Type in the following command to change Execution Policy:

   ```
   Set-ExecutionPolicy RemoteSigned
   ```

When prompted to allow the change, press Y. This will allow you to execute local scripts.

8. You can now execute your script. If the script was in another directory, you would include the path. However, since it is in the current path, you'd use .\ to indicate the current path. Use the following command to execute the script:

   ```
   \CreateOU.ps1
   ```

If all goes well, you can launch Active Directory Users and Computers and view your new OUs. If there are errors, review the error and review the script. It's very common for errors to occur the first time you type the script, especially if there are several lines.

Creating Accounts

Once you've created some OUs, you'll want to create some accounts. Both users and computers need accounts in order to access the domain. Just as with OUs, you can use either Active Directory Users and Computers or DSAdd to create the accounts.

The creation of computer accounts is often automated. When a computer joins the domain, a computer account is automatically created. By default the account is created in the Computers container, but you can modify this using the `redircmp` command-line tool. The syntax is as follows:

```
Redircmp DN
```

For example, if a user joined a computer to a domain and you wanted the computer account to be created in the Sales OU, you'd enter the following command:

```
Redircmp "OU=Sales,DC=bigfirm,dc=com"
```

CREATING ACCOUNTS WITH ADUC

To create a user account using Active Directory Users and Computers, follow these steps:

1. Launch Active Directory Users and Computers by selecting Start ➤ Administrative Tools ➤ Active Directory Users and Computers.

2. Right-click the Sales OU you created earlier, and select New ➤ User.

3. Enter the first name, last name, and user logon name for the user. Your display will look similar to Figure 6.19.

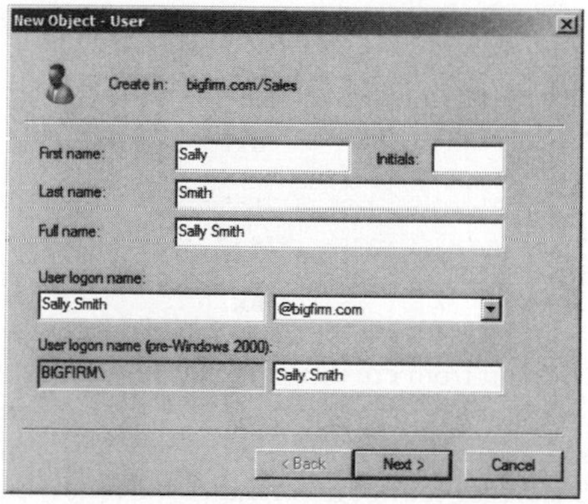

FIGURE 6.19
Creating a user
account in ADUC

4. Click Next. Enter a password for the user in the Password and Confirm Password text boxes. Ensure the check box is selected for "User must change password at next logon." This will ensure the user changes the password and no one else knows it, not even you. Your display will look similar to Figure 6.20.

USER LOGON NAME

Companies typically have an established standard of how logon names are created. Some common methods are first initial and last name, first name and last name, first name dot last name, and many more. If starting at a new company, you should learn what the standard is and ensure you follow this standard when creating accounts.

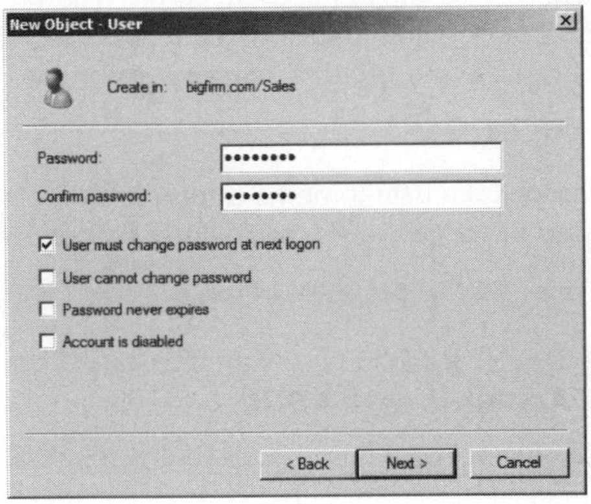

FIGURE 6.20
Setting the user
account password
settings

If the account is shared by multiple users (such as a temporary job filled by different workers each day), you may want to select "User cannot change password." If you're creating service accounts (user accounts used to start services), you may choose to select "Password never expires" to ensure an expired password doesn't lock out the account. Last, if the account isn't going to be used for a while, consider disabling it. Click Next.

5. Review the information on the Summary page, and click Finish.

CREATING ACCOUNTS AT THE COMMAND LINE

You can use the same DSAdd command-line tool to create user accounts. The basic syntax is as follows:

```
DSAdd user DN
```

Although all the other parameters are optional, you'll find that the default domain policy will prevent you from creating an enabled account with a blank password. Not only will it be disabled, but you won't be able to enable it until you set a password. Further, you'll probably want to add information such as first name, last name, and display name.

The DSAdd user command includes the following parameters that can be used for each of the following options:

- Pwd: Password
- Fn: First name
- Ln: Last name

- ◆ `Display`: Display name
- ◆ `Samid`: SAMID name
- ◆ `Upn`: User principal name

Figure 6.21 shows the dialog box you'd see if you created the account with ADUC. Although you probably guessed what first name and last name are, the others are a little cryptic.

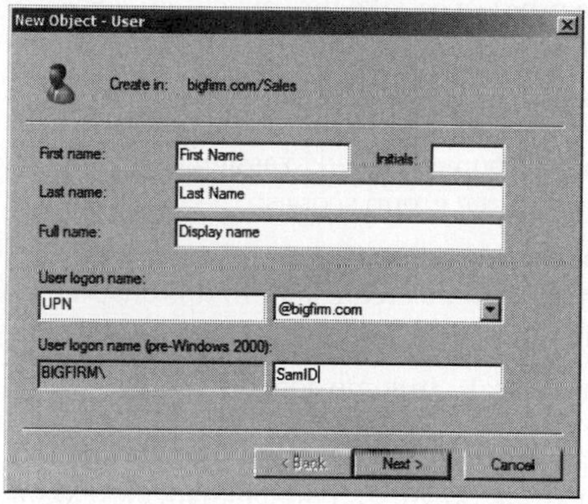

FIGURE 6.21
Mapping the
DSAdd parameters
for a user account

Notice that the full name in ADUC is the display name. When using ADUC, this is automatically created but needs to be specified with DSAdd or else it's left blank. The user logon name is developed from the UPN name, and the SAMID identifies the legacy logon name and is the same as the text in the user logon name text box.

One more thing: if you're creating the account with a password, you want to ensure the user changes the password as soon as they log on. The DSAdd command includes the `mustchpwd` parameter. When set to Yes, it will force the use to change their password.

So, to create a user named Maria.Smith in the Sales OU with a password of P@ssw0rd, you could use the following command. Even though this command spans multiple lines, it should be entered as a single command without any carriage returns.

```
DSAdd user "CN=Maria.Smith,OU=Sales,DC=Bigfirm,DC=Com" -pwd P@ssw0rd,
  -fn Maria, -ln Smith -display Maria Smith, -samid Maria.Smith,
  -upn Maria.Smith@bigfirm.com -mustchpwd Yes
```

That's a lot of code to enter on a single line. Don't be surprised if you have an error or two when you try to enter it. No problem. That's normal. Read the error message, and use the up arrow and back arrow. However, if you find yourself on a Server Core server and you need to create an account from the command line or if you need to create the accounts from a script, you know it's possible. Get back to the command line, and enter **DSAdd /?** to remind yourself how.

Creating Groups

You may also want to create some groups. The most common reason to create groups is to organize users. More specifically, global security groups are created to organize users and then assign permissions to the groups.

Whenever possible, you should assign permissions to groups rather than users. You may have heard the old saying "Users will come and go, but groups will stay forever." Well, maybe you haven't heard it before since we just made it up, but it makes sense, and it's a good way to remember that you should assign permissions to groups instead of users.

As an example, you could have several users in the sales department. Instead of assigning permissions to each individual in the sales department, you could create a single global security group named G_Sales. Place all the users in the sales department, and assign permissions to the G_Sales group. If a user leaves, take him out of the G_Sales group, and he'll no longer have the permissions of the group. If a user joins the Sales team, put her into the G_Sales group, and she'll have the permissions of everyone else in the group.

There are two types of groups: distribution and security. Distribution groups are used for email, and security groups are used to assign permissions. Security groups can also be used for email.

There are three group scopes:

Global   Global groups are used to organize users. This is the most commonly used group and the one you'll create later in this chapter. Users will be placed in the global group, and permission will be assigned to the global group.

Domain Local   In some domain implementations, domain local groups are used in an "A G DL P" group strategy, where the A indicates accounts, G indicates global groups, DL indicates domain local groups, and P indicates permissions. User accounts are placed in global groups. Global groups are placed into domain local groups, and permissions are assigned to the domain local groups. When used this way, the domain local groups are an added layer used to identify resources.

Universal   Universal groups are used only in multiple domain environments.

The most common way to create these groups is with Active Directory Users and Computers. You can use the following steps to create a global security group. These steps assume you have created a Sales OU in your domain.

1. Launch Active Directory Users and Computers by selecting Start ➤ Administrative Tools ➤ Active Directory Users and Computers.

2. Right-click the Sales OU, and select New ➤ Group. Enter **G_Sales** in the "Group name" box. Your display will look similar to Figure 6.22. Click OK.

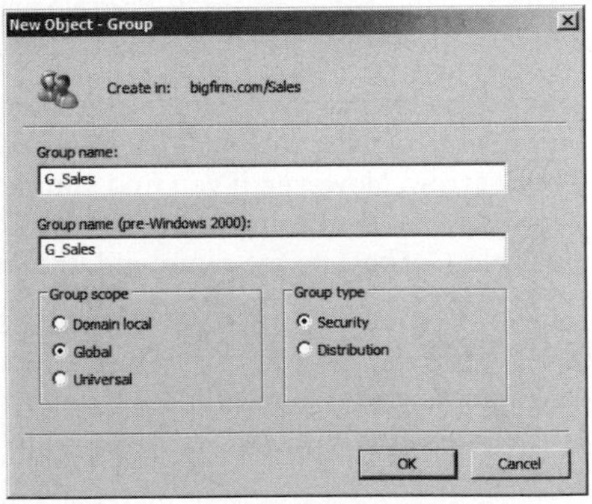

FIGURE 6.22
Creating a
global group

3. Right-click the Sales OU, and select New ➤ Group. Enter **G_SalesAdmins** in the "Group name" box. This group will be granted permissions needed to administer the Sales OU. Click OK.

Delegating Control

Earlier in the chapter, I mentioned that one of the reasons to create an OU was to delegate control. As an example, imagine that two users perform all the IT admin tasks for the sales department. You want these users to be able to do anything for any users in the sales department but not perform administrative tasks for other users in the domain.

As preparation, you should create a Sales OU and place all sales department users and computers into this OU. You should also create a global group (such as G_SalesAdmins) and place the sales IT administrator accounts into this group. You can now use the following steps to delegate permissions for this global group using the Delegation of Control Wizard:

1. Launch Active Directory Users and Computers by selecting Start ➤ Administrative Tools ➤ Active Directory Users and Computers.

2. Right-click the Sales OU, and select Delegate Control.

3. Review the information on the Welcome page, and click Next.

4. On the Users or Groups page, click Add.

5. Type in **G_SalesAdmins**, and click OK. Click Next.

6. Review the information on the Tasks to Delegate page. Notice you have several choices that you can select. For example, you could grant someone the ability to only reset passwords and nothing else. However, for our purposes, we want the group to be able to do anything. Select "Create a custom task to delegate." Your display will look similar to Figure 6.23. Click Next.

FIGURE 6.23
Selecting the tasks
to delegate

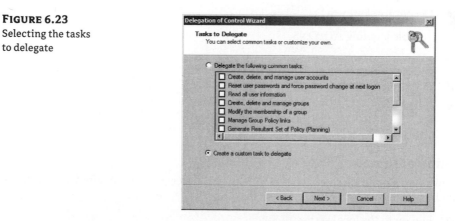

7. Review the selections on the Active Directory Object Type page. You have the ability to limit the actions to specific objects such as user objects, computer objects, or other types of Active Directory objects. Accept the default setting of "This folder, existing objects in this folder, and creation of new objects in this folder." Click Next.

8. Click Full Control on the Permission page. It will look similar to Figure 6.24. Click Next.

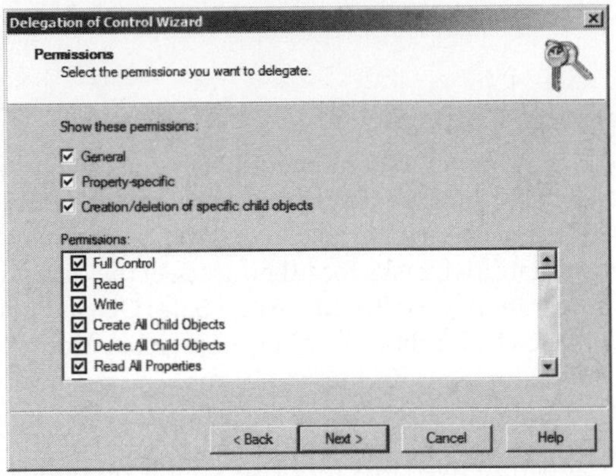

FIGURE 6.24
Granting Full Control permissions

9. Review the information on the completion page, and click Finish.

Remember, the Delegation of Control Wizard is a powerful tool that you can easily use to delegate permissions within Active Directory. A key point is that if you don't want to delegate domain-wide permissions, you must first create an OU and then launch the wizard from the OU.

Domain Maintenance Tasks

After you've established your domain, you'll need to do some domain maintenance. Although this section doesn't cover everything you'll need to do, it does cover some basic tasks:

♦ Joining a domain

♦ Decommissioning a DC

♦ Troubleshooting ADI DNS

♦ Raising the domain and forest functional levels

♦ Using NetDom

♦ Managing the domain time

These tasks are explained in detail in the following sections.

Joining a Domain

Follow these steps to join a Windows Server 2008 R2 server to a domain. Once the server is joined to a domain, it's referred to as a *member server*.

1. Log on to the local server.

2. Click Start, right-click Computer, and select Properties.

3. Click Advanced System Settings.

4. The System Properties dialog box will appear. Select the Computer Name tab, and click the Change button.

5. Select the Domain radio button, and enter the name of the domain you're joining. Your display will look similar to Figure 6.25. Click OK.

FIGURE 6.25
Joining a domain

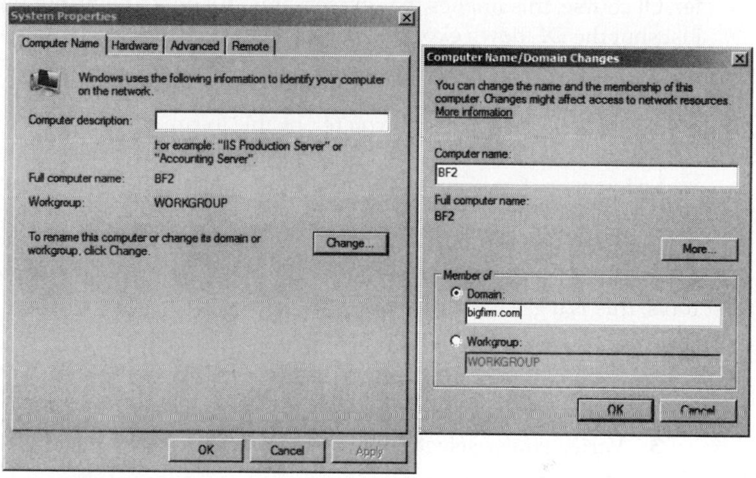

6. You'll be prompted to provide the credentials of an account that has permission on the domain. Enter the credentials, and click OK.

7. After a moment, you'll see a Welcome dialog box. Click OK. You will then be prompted to restart the computer. Click OK.

8. Click Close to close the System Properties dialog box. You'll receive another reminder saying the server must be restarted. Click Restart Now.

After the server has rebooted, it'll be a member of the domain—a member server.

OFFLINE DOMAIN JOIN

Windows Server 2008 R2 introduces a new feature that allows you to join a Windows 7 or Windows Server 2008 R2 system to a domain without contacting a domain controller. This can be useful if the computer doesn't have reliable connectivity to the corporate network. For more details about an offline domain join, check out the article on TechNet at http://technet.microsoft.com/library/dd392267.aspx.

Decommissioning a DC

If it's ever necessary to take one of the domain controllers out of service, it's imperative that you properly *decommission* it. When you decommission it, you remove all Active Directory components and return the domain controller to a member server role.

Properly decommissioning the DC is especially important if you need to take the first DC out of service. The first DC in the domain includes several Operations Master roles that are integral to the proper operation of the domain. If this server simply fails and you're never able to bring it back up, you're going to have some problems until you properly decommission it.

The easiest method of decommissioning a DC is to simply run DCPromo on the domain controller. Of course, this implies that the server is still operational, but the point is that you shouldn't just shut the DC down expecting things to work. If it's still operational, run DCPromo. DCPromo will transfer all the Operations Master roles, move the server object from the Domain Controllers OU to the Computers container, and take care of several other details.

If this server just fails and you're not able to run DCPromo, you'll need to remove it from Active Directory. In previous editions of Windows, this was a rather lengthy and tedious process. However, if you're using the Active Directory Users and Computers snap-in available with Windows Server 2008 or R2, you can simply delete the domain controller object in the Domain Controllers OU, and you're done.

For anyone who has gone through the lengthy metadata process using NTDSUtil and other tools, this is a great addition.

1. Launch Active Directory Users and Computers, and browse to the Domain Controllers OU.

2. Locate the DC you want to decommission. Right-click it, and select Delete.

3. Verify you've selected the correct DC, and click Yes in the confirmation dialog box.

4. A dialog box will appear warning that you're trying to delete a DC from AD without using DCPromo. It recommends you use DCPromo. Click the check box indicating "This Domain Controller is permanently offline and can no longer be demoted using the Active Directory Domain Services installation Wizard (DCPromo)," and click Delete.

5. If the DC is a global catalog server, you'll receive a warning asking you to continue. Click Yes.

6. If the server was holding any operations master roles, you'll be prompted to have the roles transferred to another domain controller. Click OK, and the role will be seized by this DC.

If the failed DC is later recovered, you won't be able to remove Active Directory using DCPromo normally. However, there's a workaround. Instead of just entering **dcpromo** alone, enter **dcpromo /forceremoval**. The /forceremoval switch will allow Active Directory to be removed without accessing another DC in the domain.

Troubleshooting ADI DNS

A common problem that occurs with DNS is that the SRV records aren't created when the server is rebooted. The netlogon service is responsible for creating these records, and sometimes it just seems to hiccup after rebooting the server.

As a reminder, the SRV records are used to locate domain controllers in a domain running specific services or holding specific roles within a domain. As a few examples, services within the domain often need to locate a global catalog server, a PDC emulator, a domain controller within a specific site, or simply a domain controller in the domain. Services query DNS for the appropriate SRV records, and as long as they exist, the server can be located.

However, occasionally these records aren't created after a reboot. Figure 6.26 shows the DNS console open to show that the records have been correctly created. Notice there are several folders starting with an underscore (_msdcs, _sites, _tcp, and _udp). Each of these folders includes the SRV records.

FIGURE 6.26
Viewing DNS
SRV records

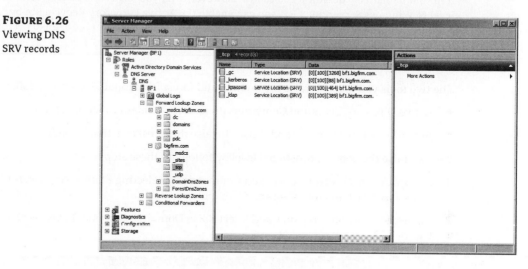

If you're experiencing connectivity problems and you notice that DNS is missing these records, there's a simple fix. Go to the command prompt, and issue the following two commands:

```
Net stop netlogon
Net start netlogon
```

The NetLogon service will re-create the records, and you'll be back in business.

Raising Domain and Forest Functional Levels

You may want to raise your domain and/or forest functional levels after you've initially created your forest. The primary reason why you'd want to do so is to take advantage of additional features available at the higher levels.

For example, Windows Server 2008 R2 introduced the Active Directory Recycle Bin. However, this isn't available until you raise the forest functional level to Windows Server 2008 R2. The big-picture steps you'd take are as follows:

1. First you must ensure all your domain controllers are running Windows Server 2008 R2.

2. Next, you'd raise the domain functional level to Windows Server 2008 R2.

3. Last, you'd raise the forest functional level to Windows Server 2008 R2.

It's important to remember that once you raise the level, there's no turning back. If your current domain functional level is Windows Server 2003 and you raise it to Windows Server 2008 R2, you'll no longer be able to promote anything less than a Windows Server 2008 R2 server to a domain controller. If that fits in with your plans, raise the levels.

ACTIVE DIRECTORY RECYCLE BIN

If the Active Directory Recycle Bin intrigues you as much as it intrigues me, you may want to enable it in your domain. By default it is disabled. However, after you have raised the forest functional level to Windows Server 2008 R2, you can enable the Active Directory Recycle Bin by following the procedures in this TechNet guide: http://technet.microsoft.com/en-us/library/dd392261(WS.10).aspx.

The two tools you'll use to raise the domain and forest functional levels are as follows:

◆ Active Directory Users and Computers (to raise the domain functional level)

◆ Active Directory Domains and Trusts (to raise the forest functional level)

You can raise the domain functional level by following these steps:

1. Launch Active Directory Users and Computers by selecting Start ➢ Administrative Tools ➢ Active Directory Users and Computers.

2. Right-click the domain name, and select Raise Domain Functional Level, as shown in Figure 6.27.

FIGURE 6.27
Raising the domain functional level

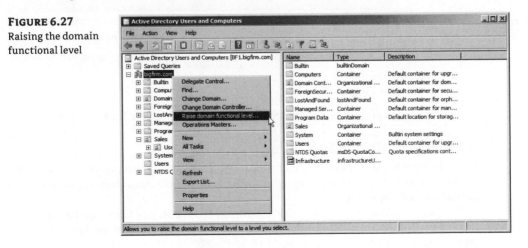

3. Review the information on the Raise Domain Functional Level page. Notice this page informs you what the current functional level is and gives you the option to raise it. Select Windows Server 2008 R2 from the drop-down box. Your display will look similar to Figure 6.28. Click Raise.

4. You'll receive another warning reminding you that this action isn't reversible. Click OK.

5. After a moment, a dialog box will indicate the level was raised successfully. Click OK.

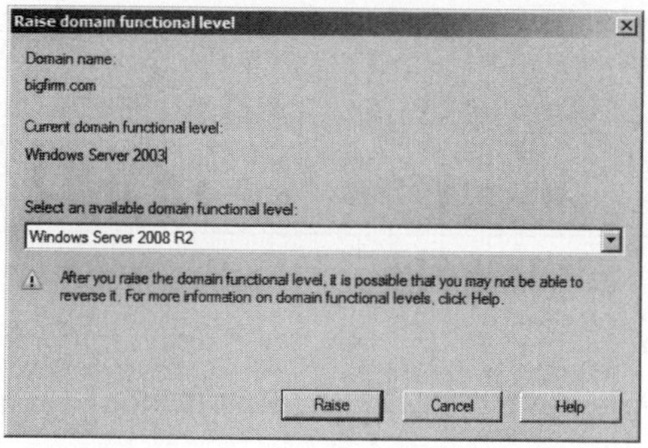

FIGURE 6.28
Selecting Windows
Server 2008 R2 as
the new domain
functional level

You can raise the forest functional level by following these steps:

1. Launch Active Directory Domains and Trusts by selecting Start ➤ Administrative Tools ➤ Active Directory Domains and Trusts.

2. Right-click Active Directory Domains and Trusts, and select Raise Forest Functional Level, as shown in Figure 6.29.

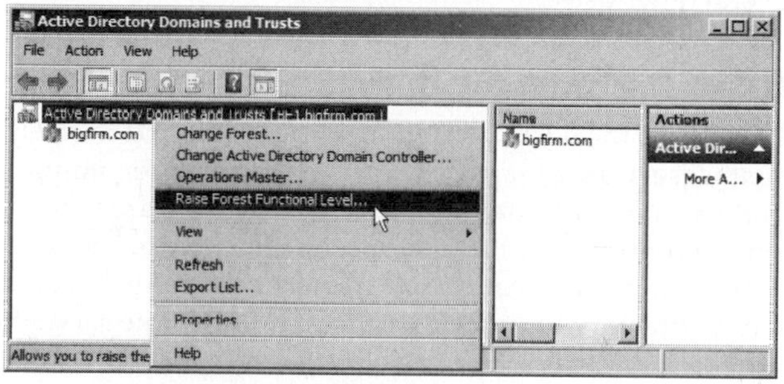

FIGURE 6.29
Raising the forest
functional level

3. Review the information on the Raise Forest Functional Level page. This page informs you what the current functional level is and gives you the option to raise it. Select Windows Server 2008 R2 from the drop-down box. Your display will look similar to Figure 6.30. Click Raise.

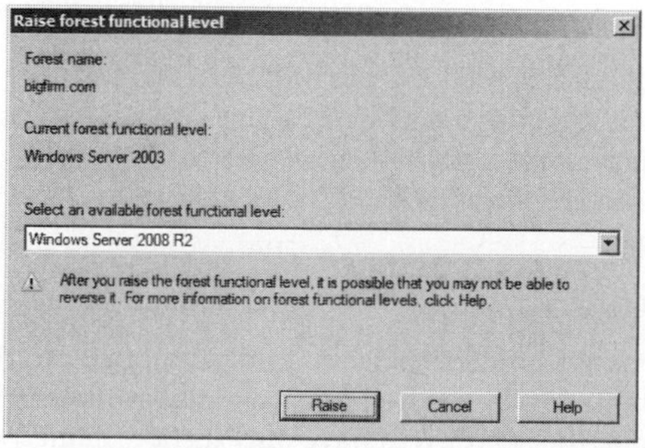

FIGURE 6.30
Selecting Windows
Server 2008 R2
as the new forest
functional level

> **SELECT AD DOMAINS AND TRUSTS TO RAISE FOREST FUNCTIONAL LEVEL**
>
> Notice that you don't right-click the domain name to raise the forest functional level. Instead, you click the line right above the domain name—Active Directory Domains and Trusts. It's common to ignore that first line in Microsoft Management Consoles (MMCs), but it is important here.

4. You'll receive a warning reminding you that this action isn't reversible. Click OK.

5. After a moment, a dialog box will indicate the level was raised successfully. Click OK.

Many of the additional features of the higher functional levels will be available automatically. Only a few (such as the Active Directory Recycle Bin) require additional steps to enable them.

Using NetDom

A valuable command-line tool is NetDom (short for "domain manager"). It's available at the command prompt on any server that's been promoted to a domain controller. Although NetDom is primarily used to manage trusts in environments with more than one domain, it also has several other uses.

RENAME COMPUTERS (INCLUDING DOMAIN CONTROLLERS)

You can use the netdom computername command to safely rename domain controllers and member servers. In early versions of Windows, renaming a domain controller wasn't possible unless you first demoted it with DCPromo. Be aware that even if you use NetDom to rename a domain controller, it may take a couple of reboots before everything settles—especially in DNS.

More important, you shouldn't rename servers that are certificate servers (those running Active Directory Certificate Services). A certificate server needs to keep the same name. The name embedded in a certificate identifies the server it's issued to and the server that issued the certificate. Certificates are validated by querying the original server, but if the name is changed, none of the certificates can be validated.

Renaming a DC involves giving it an alternate name and then changing the alternate name to the DC's primary name. For example, if you have a domain controller named Server9 in the domain Bigfirm.com but you want to rename it to BF2, you first give it an alternate name of BF2 with the following command:

```
Netdom computername Server9 /add:bf2.bigfirm.com
```

You'll need to reboot the server before issuing the second command. This ensures the alternate name is registered with DNS and on the system. At this point, the server has two names—its primary name and an alternate name.

After the reboot, you can rename the domain controller to the alternate name with this command:

```
Netdom computername Server9 /makeprimary:bf2.bigfirm.com
```

NetDom will indicate success and prompt you to reboot the server. In addition to making the alternate the primary name, it also removes the original primary name. In other words, after the reboot, the server will have only its new name.

JOIN A COMPUTER TO A DOMAIN

If you want to join a computer to a domain from the command prompt, or via a script, NetDom can be used. The simplest implementation is simply as follows:

```
Netdom join bf2 /d:bigfirm.com /reboot
```

The preceding command will join the computer named bf2 to the domain Bigfirm.com and then force a reboot. Normally, the computer account for a computer that just joined the domain is placed into the Computers container. As mentioned previously, you can use the redircmp command to have computer accounts created somewhere else.

It's also possible to get fancier with NetDom, but it tends to be more difficult than using the directory service command-line tools (such as DSMove). For example, if you want to move the computer account from the Computers container to the Sales OU, you could follow the NetDom Join command with the DSMove command as follows:

```
Dsmove "cn=bf3,cn=computers,dc=bigfirm,dc=com" -newparent
"ou=sales,dc=bigfirm,dc=com"
```

OTHER NETDOM COMMANDS

NetDom includes many other commands that can be used to manage your domain. Check out the full online reference for NetDom at http://technet.microsoft.com/library/cc772217.aspx. These are some other commands that may be of interest to you:

◆ NetDom Reset resets a machine's account. Sometimes you'll sit down at a system and be unable to log onto the domain because the machine has lost its domain account, or so it says. Sometimes just resetting it does the job.

◆ NetDom ResetPwd resets a machine's domain password. You must be sitting at the machine for this to run. If a machine has not connected to the domain for an extended period, it's possible for its account password to expire, and this command can resolve the problem.

◆ NetDom Remove removes a system from a domain.

Managing the Domain Time

The Kerberos authentication protocol used by Active Directory requires that all computers in the domain be synced with each other. If any computer becomes more than five minutes off from a domain controller, it will no longer be able to connect on the network.

Because of this, time synchronization is very important in a domain. Time synchronization is achieved through a hierarchy. It starts with the server holding the role of the PDC Operations Master (normally the first domain controller created in the domain) and extends to each system in a domain. You can check which server holds this role by following these steps:

1. Launch Active Users and Computers.

2. Right-click the domain, and select Operations Masters.

3. Select the PDC tab, as shown in Figure 6.31.

FIGURE 6.31

Identifying the
PDC Operations
Master

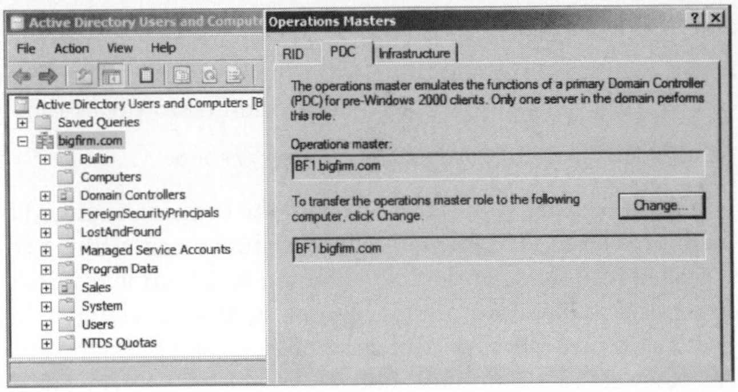

Ideally, the domain controller hosting the PDC role is configured to synchronize with a valid Network Time Protocol (NTP) source. The rest of the computers in the domain will get their time from this server.

- All domain controllers will synchronize their time with the time on the PDC.

- All computers and member servers will synchronize their time with the time on their authenticating domain controller.

- If a computer is specially configured so that it doesn't get its time from the authenticating DC, it should be synchronized with an NTP server just like the PDC Operations Master DC.

As long as the PDC has the correct time and users don't change the time on their systems, everything works well.

RESTRICT TIME CHANGES WITH GROUP POLICY

It's not uncommon for administrators to configure Group Policy to prevent users from changing the time and accidentally removing their systems from the domain. The Change the System Time Group Policy setting is located in the Computer Configuration ➤ Policies ➤ Windows Settings ➤ Security Settings ➤ Local Policies ➤ User Rights Assignment node.

You'll use the Windows Time Service (W32tm) to check and synchronize the time. W32tm is executed from the command line.

You can use the following command to check five samples of current time against Microsoft's time server (at time.windows.com) and verify how accurate it is. The output will indicate whether the time on your server is ahead (indicated with a +) or behind (indicated with a -).

```
W32tm /stripchart /computer:time.windows.com /samples:5 /dataonly
```

You can synchronize the time on the PDC Operations Master using an internal time source if you have one or an external time source. If you synchronize with an external NTP server using the W32 service, you'll need to ensure that UDP port 123 is open.

Use the following command to have your system synchronize its time with an external time server. Several time servers are available, but this example is using Microsoft's time server (time.windows.com) and the NIST time server (time.nist.gov):

```
W32tm /config "/manualpeerlist:time.nist.gov time.windows.com"
/syncfromflags:manual /reliable:yes /update
```

It's also a good idea to restart the time service using the following commands:

```
Net start w32time
Net stop w32time
```

The `syncfromflags` parameter specifies that the server will synchronize with one of the servers in the `manualpeerlist` group. You can add just a single time server (and omit the quotes) or add multiple time servers separated by a space as shown.

After you restart the service, you can use the earlier `W32tm` command to verify that the time is now accurate. If you change the time, it may take as long as long as five minutes before `W32tm` synchronizes again and resets the time to the proper time.

This section covered several maintenance tasks and techniques you'll likely find useful to keep your network running. It's certainly not an all-encompassing list but should help you master some of the basics. A neat new feature that can help you reduce the amount of maintenance you'll need to do is something called *fine-grained password policies*. This feature allows you to set multiple password or account lockout policies without creating a new domain.

Creating Fine-Grained Password Policies

Prior to Windows Server 2008, if you needed more than one password policy for your organization, you had to create a separate domain. This presented challenges for many organizations, but thankfully, you can now have a single domain with more than one password policy.

A common example is related to administrator accounts. Anyone with administrative privileges can do significantly more on a network than a regular user and the credentials for administrative accounts need to be more secure than regular user accounts. In some environments, administrators are told to make their passwords at least 15 characters long.

Although a 15 character password for an administrator account has some sound technical justification, it doesn't make sense for a regular user. In the past, the company needed to purchase a third-party password enforcement tool for the administrators or just ask them to use stronger passwords and hope they comply.

Today, you have fine-grained password policies. You can now assign specific password policies to individual users or groups to enforce any of the regular password policies including the following:

◆ Enforce password history

◆ Maximum password age

◆ Minimum password age

◆ Minimum password length

◆ Passwords must meet complexity requirements

◆ Store passwords using reversible encryption

They're referred to as *fine-grained* because you can assign them at the lowest level—similar to a grain of sand. If you have a single user who needs a special password policy, you can create a policy just for this user object. However, it's much more common to apply these policies to groups than to users.

PASSWORD AND ACCOUNT LOCKOUT POLICIES

Although all of the excitement centers on the ability to have multiple password policies, Windows Server 2008 also provides the ability to have multiple account lockout policies. This chapter focuses on fine-grained password policies, but you can use similar procedures to create fine-grained account lockout policies.

Password policies are implemented by the following:

◆ Creating a password settings object (PSO) and storing it in a password settings container (PSC)

◆ Applying the PSO to a user or global security group

Requirements for Fine-Grained Password Policies

Before you can implement fine-grained password policies, you need to ensure your environment meets the minimum requirements:

◆ If domain controllers have been upgraded from an earlier version of Windows, you must run adprep prior to upgrading to Windows Server 2008.

◆ The domain functional level must be at least Windows Server 2008.

Only members of the Domain Admins group can create PSOs.

Creating a Password Settings Object

You can create a PSO by using ADSI Edit. Once you create the PSO, you'll manipulate the different settings of the PSO. Some of the different PSO settings are as follows:

msDS-PSOAppliesTo   This value identifies to which objects that the PSO will apply. Entries use distinguished names of users or groups.

msDS-MinimumPasswordLength   This is the minimum password length for user accounts that use this PSO. Any number between 0 through 255 is valid.

msDS-MinimumPasswordAge   This is the minimum password age for user accounts. It identifies the soonest the password can be modified. Any number from 00:00:00:00 through the value of msDS-MaximumPasswordAge value can be used.

msDS-MaximumPasswordAge   This is the maximum password age for user accounts that identifies when the password must be changed. Any value between the msDS-MinimumPasswordAge value through Never is acceptable. For example, to ensure users change their passwords every 15 days, the following value could be used: 15:00:00:00. The msDS-MaximumPasswordAge value cannot be set to zero.

DURATION ENTRIES IN PSOs

Any duration entries are entered in the d:hh:mm:ss format to ensure that these time-related entries don't result in ADSI Edit errors. As an example, one day would be entered as 1:00:00:00, and one hour would be entered as 00:01:00:00. The values that require these four-part time entries are msDS-MaximumPasswordAge, msDS-MinimumPasswordAge, msDS-LockoutObservationWindow, and msDS-LockoutDuration.

msDS-PasswordHistoryLength This is the password history length for user accounts that identifies how many past passwords are remembered, or in other words, how many new passwords must be used before one is repeated. Any value between 0 through 1024 is valid.

msDS-PasswordComplexityEnabled This is the password complexity status for user accounts that ensures passwords meet minimum complexity requirements. The value can be False or True.

msDS-PasswordSettingsPrecedence The password settings precedence identifies which PSO will take precedence, if multiple PSO objects apply to a user. A lower value will have a higher precedence. For example, a PSO with a value of 10 would be used instead of a PSO with a value of 20. Any value greater than 0 is valid.

msDS-PasswordReversibleEncryptionEnabled The password reversible encryption status for user accounts specifies if reversible encryption is enabled or not. The value can be False or True.

msDS-LockoutThreshold This is the lockout threshold for lockout of user accounts. Identifies how many bad password attempts will be accepted before the account is locked out. Any value between 0 through 65535 is acceptable.

msDS-LockoutObservationWindow The observation window for lockout of user accounts identifies how long the invalid logon attempts are tracked. For example, imagine the lockout threshold is 3 and the LockoutObservationWindow is 0:00:30:00 (30 minutes). If a user enters an incorrect password twice, he would have only one more attempt before being locked out. However, he could take a coffee break for 30 minutes (the length of time set for the lockout observation window), and the counter would reset to 0. He could try his password three more times before being locked out. Valid values are anything between 00:00:00:01 through the msDS-LockoutDuration value.

msDS-LockoutDuration This is the lockout duration for locked-out user accounts. This identifies how long the user is locked out if the lockout threshold is exceeded. Valid values are the msDS-LockoutObservationWindow value through (Never).

CREATING PSOs WITH LDIFDE

It's also possible to create PSOs using the LDAP Data Interchange Format (LDIF) tool. This section only covers creating them using ADSI Edit. However, it doesn't matter how they are created. Once a PSO is created, it will work the same way no matter which method was used to create it.

With a little bit of knowledge of what the PSO settings are, you're now ready to create one. You can create and apply a PSO to the G_ITAdmins group with the following steps:

1. Launch ADUC, and create a global group named G_ITAdmins in the Users container.

2. Launch ADSI Edit by clicking Start, typing **ADSI**, and pressing Return.

3. Right-click ADSI Edit, and select Connect To.

4. Type in the fully qualified domain name of your domain in the Name text box, as shown in Figure 6.32. Click OK.

FIGURE 6.32
Entering the
domain name
in ADSI Edit

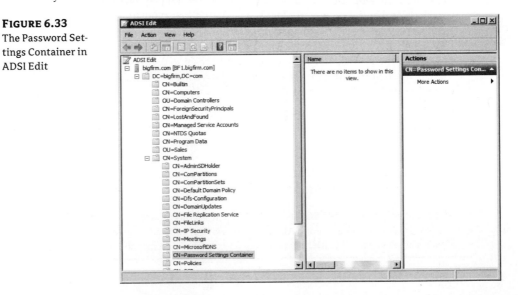

5. Expand the ADSI Edit console until you reach the CN=Password Settings Container within the CN=System node, as shown in Figure 6.33. This container starts empty, but you'll add a PSO here.

FIGURE 6.33
The Password Set-
tings Container in
ADSI Edit

6. Right-click CN=Password Settings Container, and select New ➢ Object.

7. The msDS-PasswordSettings class is selected as the only object. Click Next.

8. Enter **ITAdminsPSO** in the Value text box to name your PSO. Click Next.

9. For the msDS-PasswordSettingsPrecedence setting, enter **10**. Click Next.

10. For the msDS-PasswordReversibleEncryptionEnabled setting, enter **False.** Click Next.

11. For the msDS-PasswordHistoryLength setting, enter **24**. Click Next.

12. For the msDS-PasswordComplexityEnabled setting, enter **True**. Click Next.

13. For the msDS-MinimumPasswordLength setting, enter **15**. Click Next.

14. For the msDS-MinimumPasswordAge setting, enter **1:00:00:00** to set the value to one day. Click Next.

15. For the msDS-MaximumPasswordAge setting, enter **30:00:00:00** to set the value to 30 days. Click Next.

16. For the msDS-LockoutThreshold setting, enter **5**. Click Next.

17. For the msDS-LockoutObservationWindow, enter **0:00:30:00** to set the value to 30 minutes. Click Next.

18. For the msDS-LockoutDuration setting, enter **0:00:30:00** to set the value to 30 minutes. Click Next.

19. Instead of clicking Finish, click the More Attributes button.

20. Select the msDS-PSOAppliesTo property in the "Select a property to view" drop-down box.

21. Enter the distinguished name of the G_ITAdmins group you created earlier, and click Add. Your display will look similar to Figure 6.34. Click OK.

FIGURE 6.34
Applying the PSO
to a global group

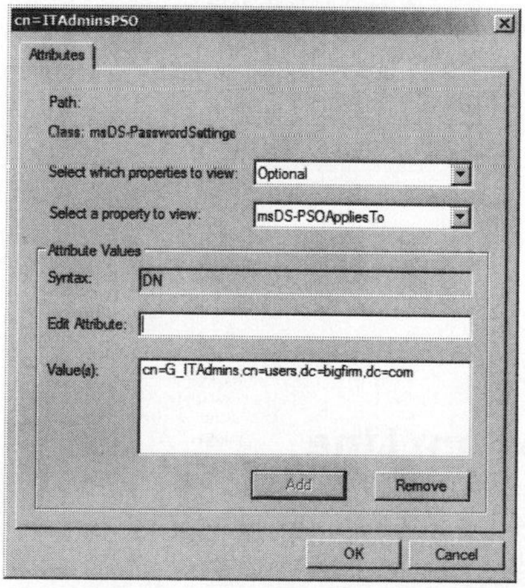

22. Click Finish. If you ever want to view or modify your settings, you can return to the CN=Password Settings Container in ADSI Edit and double-click the PSO to view the properties. Some settings can be modified, but other settings can be viewed only; when you select the setting, the button on the page will change to either Edit or View depending on whether it can be modified.

23. Close all the open windows.

Once the PSO exists, it's also possible to apply the PSO to other users or groups using Active Directory Users and Computers.

First ensure that advanced features are enabled by selecting View and that Advanced Features is selected. If it's not selected, select it.

Second, browse to the System ➤ Password Settings container in Active Directory Users and Computers. Right-click the PSO, and select Properties. Click the Attribute Editor, and your display will look similar to Figure 6.35.

FIGURE 6.35
Modifying the
PSO in ADUC

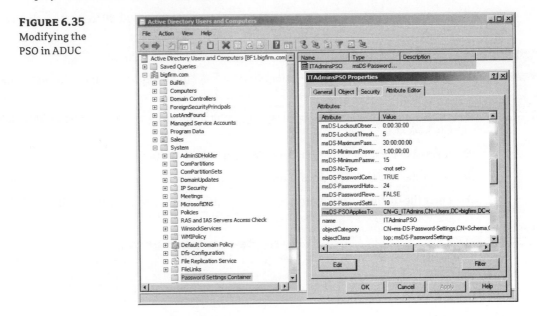

Notice that you can modify many of the properties here, but what we're most concerned with now is the msDS-PSOAppliesTo property. If you select it and click Edit, you can add users or groups.

The Bottom Line

Create a single-domain forest   Any Windows Server 2008 R2 server can be promoted to a domain controller to create a single-domain forest. A DC hosts an instance of Active Directory Domain Services.

Master It   You want to promote a server to a DC and create a single-domain forest. What should you do?

Add a second DC to the domain   A single DC represents a potential single point of failure. If it goes down, the domain goes down. Often administrators will add a second DC to the domain.

> **Master It**   You want to add a second DC to your domain. What should you do?

Decide whether to add a global catalog   A global catalog server hosts a copy of the global catalog. Any domain controller can become a GC, but only the first domain controller is a GC by default.

> **Master It**   You are promoting a second server to a domain controller in your single-domain forest. Should you make it a GC?

Create accounts   Any domain needs to host user and computer accounts representing users and computers that will access the domain. There are several ways to create user and computer accounts.

> **Master It**   What are two methods that can be used to create a user account? One is a GUI, and the other is a command-line tool.

Create fine-grained password policies   Windows Server 2008 introduced the ability to create multiple password policies within a domain by using fine-grained password policies. You can use a fine-grained password policy to assign a different password policy to a user or group within the domain.

> **Master It**   You want to create a fine-grained password policy for a group of administrators in your network. What should you create, and what tool should you use?

Chapter 7

Creating and Managing User Accounts

Probably one of the most common tasks an administrator will do, not only during deployment but also during the life of a network, is to create and manage user accounts. This sounds like a pretty simple task, but it is a very important one because of the time management and security implications. It's important for server administrators or consultants to understand the process. They might think they can ignore it because they don't create user accounts in normal operations. That may be true, but they are usually the people responsible for creating the first users in a new network, defining the processes, and handing over the operation to another team, department, or their customers. The same senior staff members also need to be able to be able to create and manage user accounts for services and applications on their servers by following best practices.

We'll cover the basics of creating and managing user accounts so that everyone has something to gain from this chapter. The Server Core installation option of Windows Server means that the old, reliable point-and-click solutions are not going to serve you in all scenarios. We'll cover how you can create and manage your user accounts from the command prompt. Don't let that scare you; you've already seen in previous chapters how the keyboard alternative can sometimes be a real time- and effort-saver; you'll see that this trend continues here.

We'll discuss some of the common properties and settings that you can configure for user accounts. We'll also discuss groups, why you would use them, how to add/remove users to/from groups, and best practices for group membership assignment. We'll cover all of these subjects in three environments: a stand-alone Windows Server machine, a Server Core installation, and Active Directory.

Everything we show will be identical in Windows Server 2008 and Windows Server 2008 R2. But Windows Server 2008 R2 has some new wrinkles, in the form of a new task-driven management tool called the Active Directory Administrative Center. And Microsoft has also added Active Directory modules for management via PowerShell, its shell and scripting language. So, we'll wrap up the chapter with a section covering those subjects. We that think you'll finish this chapter thinking that those tools will be a major time-saver.

In this chapter, you'll learn to:

◆ Manage local users and groups

◆ Manage users and groups in Active Directory

◆ Manage users and computers in Windows Server 2008 R2

◆ Delegate group management

◆ Deal with users leaving the organization

User Accounts

In this section, we'll cover how to create, manage, and delete local user accounts and domain-based user accounts. You'll learn how to do this using the GUI-based, command-line–based, and PowerShell-based administrative tools.

The working environment for this chapter contains a domain controller called bf1.bigfirm.com and a member server called bf2.bigfirm.com. This will allow us to demonstrate how to create and manage local and domain user accounts.

Creating Local User Accounts

We'll cover how to create local user accounts first. There are two MMC-based tools that you can use to manage user accounts. You can use Server Manager (which we discussed in Chapter 2), or you can use Computer Management. You can find both of these in the Start menu under Administrative Tools. Both tools will give you the same options when managing users and groups.

To follow along with this example, log into bf2.bigfirm.com as Administrator, open Computer Management, and navigate into \Local Users and Groups\Users (see Figure 7.1). You can see two existing user accounts:

Administrator This is the default administrative user account. We will talk a little more about this account in a few moments.

Guest The purpose of this account is to allow people who do not have an actual user account to log into the local computer. This might be something an administrator might want if they have lots of guest users coming and going. You'll notice that the Guest account has a little downward arrow on its icon. This is because best practices dictate this account should be disabled. Microsoft has done this by default for you. Having a Guest account is not a common requirement on a server, so you might never need to enable it.

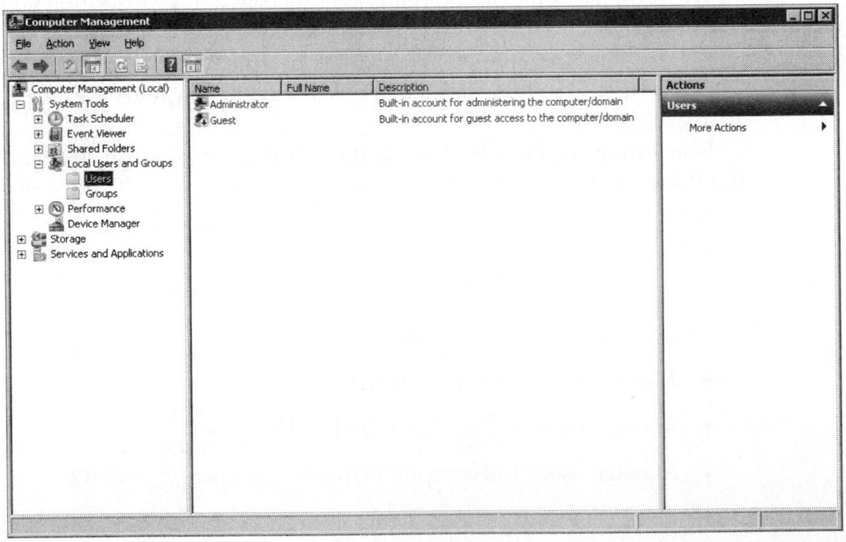

FIGURE 7.1
Local users
in Computer
Management

🌐 Real World Scenario

THE ADMINISTRATOR ACCOUNT

It is critical that you protect the Administrator account in a manner that is suitable for your organization. The local Administrator account has complete control over your server, and the domain Administrator account has complete control over your network! So, it makes sense to have a very strong password for this account.

Administrator is an anonymous account in larger organizations. Take a look at your security logs in the Event Viewer and ask yourself, "How do I know who did what using the Administrator account?" It is because of this that you should create a user account with suitable administrative or delegated rights for any administrator who needs them. Using the default Administrator account is often banned unless there is an emergency. This allows every member of IT to be accurately audited by the Security log. To do this sort of thing, you'll need to create Administrator user accounts for each administrator. You then need to ensure that each administrator has only the rights and permissions they need to do their job—and no more than necessary.

Some organizations choose to disable the Administrator account altogether. That's one solution that you might not be big on because this account is a great backdoor in the case of password lockouts. Administrator is the one user who cannot be locked out. Those organizations could take an alternative approach. You can think of it as the "nuclear" option. You've all seen those movies where two generals have to turn two different keys in order to start a nuclear missile launch. You can do the same thing with the Administrator password. It can be set by two different individuals or even departments, one typing the first half of the password and the other typing the second half. Organizations needing this sort of option probably have an IT security or internal audit department that is the holder of one half of the password while the server administration team retains the other half.

One final option is to rename the Administrator account. There's some debate about this option because the security identifier (SID; a code that Windows uses internally to uniquely identify an object) of the account can be predicted once you have access to the server or the domain. Some argue that renaming the account is pointless. However, most Internet-based attacks are actually rather robotic and unintelligent. They target typical names such as SA, root, or Administrator and try brute-force attacks to guess the password. It is still worthwhile to rename the Administrator account to defend against these forms of attack.

In the end, the same old security rules apply. Set a very strong password on your Administrator accounts, restrict knowledge of the passwords, restrict remote access where you can, and control physical access to your servers.

In this example, we'll show how to create a user account for a new member of staff called Joe Bloggs. Joe sure does get around, doesn't he? In \Local Users and Groups\Users, right-click in the middle pane and then select New User. The New User dialog box opens.

You now fill in some details about the user with the following fields (see Figure 7.2):

User name   This is the name that the user will enter whenever they log in. We strongly recommend implementing some sort of naming standard. A smaller organization might get away with JBloggs for Joe. What happens when John Bloggs joins the company, though? You might want to add a numeric scheme, such as JBloggs1, JBloggs01, or JBloggs10. Some organizations take things further. Some use the company employee ID as a username. Others use the person's initials (including the middle name) with a number, such as JRB10. These more anonymous systems might be appropriate where personal data is deemed sensitive.

Full name   The "Full name" field is just the name of the person who will use the account. You probably don't want to store those names on servers that will be facing the Internet.

Password   Next you need to set the password. You can see that we have set something rather long in Figure 7.2. Microsoft refers to this as a *passphrase*.

User must change password at next logon   We've left the "User must change password at next logon" option enabled for this example. That does exactly what it says on the tin. You can set an easy-to-communicate password such as "your new passphrase" and leave this box selected (it's on by default). The new user will be able to log on but *must* change their password to complete the logon process. This guarantees that no member of IT will know the user's password. You'll notice the next two check boxes are grayed out and unavailable to use. To change this, you should clear the "User must change password at next logon" check box. Logically, these boxes conflict with each other.

User cannot change password   You can decide to prevent the account user from being able to change their password. A scenario where you might use this is when you are creating a user account that will be used by an application or a service. Setting this option prevents the program or an attacker of the program from being able to change the password.

Password never expires   "Password never expires" overrides any password expiration policies that may be set elsewhere, such as on the local system or in a group policy. You'll likely use this option for service user accounts only. You don't want something like SQL Server shutting down because the service user account's password wasn't changed. Organizations with ultra-tight security might just have a 100 percent ban on this option.

Account is disabled   "Account is disabled" is pretty self-explanatory. The account will be created, but it cannot be used until this check box has been deselected. This is what was done with the Guest user account. You might do this if you are creating a large amount of users for the future and will enable them only when the users actually start. Remember that you may have set an easily communicated password for the user account only, and it's probably something that IT regularly or always uses. Using this option will protect the user account against unauthorized use until the employee starts and is forced to change their password using the aforementioned "User must change password at next logon" option.

FIGURE 7.2
Creating a new
local user

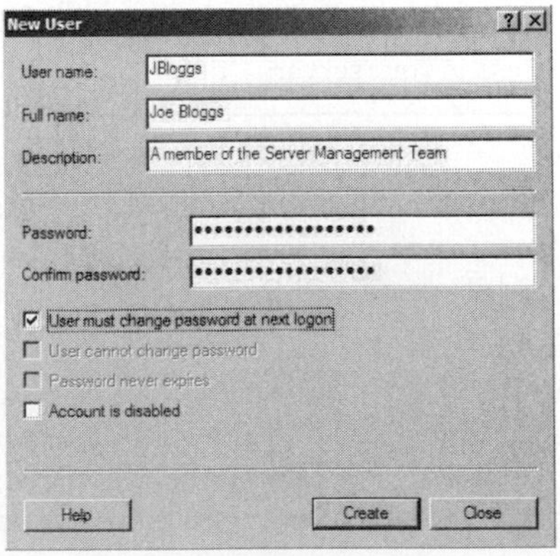

Clicking Create will create the JBloggs user for you and clear the fields in the New User dialog box. This allows you to quickly add new users without having to open more menus and click menu options. You can click Close to exit the dialog box once the user is created.

You can see the user is now created (see Figure 7.3), and you can either work on the account some more or allow it to be used.

FIGURE 7.3
The new user in Computer Management

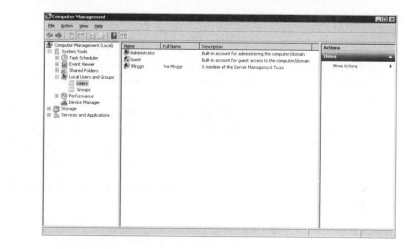

Real World Scenario

THE CASE FOR PASSPHRASES

Microsoft has been talking about passphrases for a few years now. There has always been some debate about what the best approach is with passwords. People have used seven or eight characters for their passwords. They've use complexity such as capital letters, numbers, or symbols to strengthen the password. However, that very same complexity makes that password harder to remember and harder to type. The end result is that the help desk has a fun time every Monday morning dealing with locked-out users and password reset requests. This is made worse when you force people to change their password every 30 days, which is done because you need the password to change before it could possibly be cracked by an attacker.

The alternative is to use longer passwords, such as 12 characters, with no enforced complexity. This lengthening makes the password mathematically stronger. You're already thinking—that will never fly with management or with the users. Hold on a moment.

The key to the solution is to advertise the concept of a passphrase. Up to now people enter things like "November1982-1" and increment it every month when their password expires. How about telling people to enter something that means something to them or is easy to remember? For example, a person with a yellow Italian sports car might have "my prancing pony is yellow." That's a long password, but it is easy for that person to remember, and it's easy to type. Here's the winner. The password is so strong that you could allow it to be used for six months. That would be popular! You could advertise the concept of passphrases using posters, emails, briefings, and so on, if you decided to introduce the policy. Thanks to fine-grained password policies, you could bring it in gradually with sympathetic pilot users who could spread the good word on your behalf.

You can also create users via the command line. This is helpful when using the Server Core installation of Windows Server 2008, but you may also find it's useful to learn for scripting as well. You can run the following command to create the local user JBloggs on your server:

```
C:\Users\administrator>net user JBloggs mydogisbrown /ADD
The command completed successfully.
```

The syntax of this command is as follows:

```
net user <user name to create> <password to set> /ADD
```

That command creates a user on the local computer. It does pretty much nothing else. None of the other options that we've just talked about are turned on or used. Note that if the password were more than 14 characters, then it would not be usable on computers running anything earlier than Windows 2000. You'll be prompted about this and asked to confirm that you want such a long password. You can add spaces into your password by surrounding the password with quotation marks. Here's an example:

```
net user JBloggs "My d0g is yellow" /ADD
```

You can add a few options to this command to completely re-create what you did in the Computer Management tool:

```
net user JBloggs Myd0giswhite /fullname:"Joe Bloggs" /comment:"A member of the
Server Management Team" /logonpasswordchg:yes /add
```

That's a long command. Here's what the options do:

/fullname This gives the user account a name for future reference.

/comment This completes the description field in the properties of the user account.

/logonpasswordchg:yes This forces the user to change their password when they first log into the server.

Here are some of the other options that we covered for Computer Management:

/passwordchg This is either set to yes or no to control whether a user can change their own password.

/expires This is either set to a date (in the format mm/dd/yy[yy]) or NEVER.

/active This either enables or disables the account.

You can get more information on other options by typing **net help user** at the command prompt. Don't fall into the trap of typing **net user /?**. There isn't exactly much information there.

Creating Domain User Accounts

Let's just quickly return to why you might prefer to use domain-based user accounts instead of local accounts. It turns out that your user, Joe Bloggs, will need to be able to log into many servers on the network, not just that stand-alone server. He's going to be using many services, and it has been determined that he needs a single sign-on experience. Administrators also want to set up only one user account and be able to grant rights to just one user account. Joe wants to have only one user account and one password. The solution is simple—use a domain and a domain user account.

To do this, log into your domain controller (in this example, it's bf1.bigfirm.com) to use a tool called Active Directory Users and Computers, which you can find in Administrative Tools on any domain controller. Using the free-to-download Remote Server Administration Tools, you can install this and other server management tools on your Vista or Windows 7 computer for remote management. You'll probably prefer to do this when managing a production environment on a day-to-day basis.

🌐 Real World Scenario

SEPARATION OF ADMINISTRATION

One of the things that Windows administrators have been slow to adopt is the concept of separating our roles as office employees and network administrators. Unix administrators have been doing it for decades by simply using the su command. In other words, they log into the network using an ordinary account with normal user rights and elevate their privileges to a higher account whenever they need to do any administrative work. Why would you want to do this? It's pretty simple. Imagine you are surfing the Internet or reading your email. A piece of malware manages to slip through your defense mechanisms and execute. What is it going to run as? That's right; it will run under your account. What is going to stop it from rampaging across your corporate network if you have logged in as a domain administrator or some other privileged account? Absolutely nothing! Windows does offer some protection with the User Account Control (UAC), but it's not a perfect defense. Just like physical security, sometimes the simplest solutions are the best ones.

The solution is quite simple and not quite as horrific as many Windows administrators try to make out when they hear it. Staff members with administrative rights should have two accounts. One account will be for their daily office work such as using Microsoft Word, surfing the Internet, or reading email. The second account will be for administrative work. This is where people throw their hands up in the air and start protesting. Let us finish—you'll soon see how easy this can be to use.

Let's say that you have set this scenario up for Joe Bloggs. Joe's normal daily account is JBloggs. That's what Joe logs into his computer with to do his non-administrative work. You've also set up another account that has rights to manage parts of Active Directory, some servers, and desktops in his office. This account is called JBloggs-Admin. You could have used a fine-grained password policy to enforce stricter requirements on the administrative account, but you've gone with passphrases for everyone. That's pretty secure.

How does Joe switch between different roles during the day? This is the normal argument against separation of administration: "I don't want to be constantly logging out and in again." There's a few ways to get around this.

You've been able to use the Run As feature since Windows 2000 to run programs under alternative user accounts. Some organizations have used this and even changed the shortcuts for the administrative MMC snap-ins in Administrative Tools to do this by default. Windows Vista and Windows 2008 allow you to quickly switch users without having to log out. Those are both OK but a little clumsy.

A commonly favored solution has been to go with the virtualization option. This allows you to separate the server administration account and the office/Internet account with no extra day-to-day effort. Microsoft's Virtual PC has been a free desktop-based virtualization solution for years. This allows you to run a virtual machine on your PC while you are logged in. You can set up the virtual machine with all your administrative tools. This accomplishes two things. First, you can be logged in twice at one time on one physical PC. Second, you have a portable "administrative toolkit" that can be easily cloned and deployed to IT staff. When you get a new PC, it can take a day and a half to get everything installed and configured the way you like it. Simply having a reproducible "machine" that is nothing more than a few files means that you can bring it from your old machine to your new machine with little or no customization. Combining this with sysprep allows you to copy the virtual machine whenever a new person joins the IT department so that they can use it too.

If you are using Windows 7, then take a look at the newest release of Virtual PC. It allows you install applications into your virtual machine and have shortcuts on the Start menu of your physical computer. You can start up those virtual applications, and they launch in seamless windows on the Windows 7 host. You never even see the virtual machine running.

There are other approaches to this solution. Some have used Citrix presentation virtualization products to provide an administrative environment in the past. Windows Server 2008 Terminal Services and Windows Server 2008 R2 Remote Desktop Services can easily duplicate this now by publishing either desktops or applications to people's computers. Or you could offer a variation on the virtual administrative PC solution by running that virtual PC on a server using Windows Server 2008 Hyper-V. The latter is a concept general referred to as *virtual desktop infrastructure* (VDI).

You should now understand the need to separate the two working lives of an administrator and can see that the solutions aren't all that hard to live with; in fact, they can be quite beneficial in saving time and effort.

Figure 7.4 shows Active Directory Users and Computers with the Users organizational unit (OU). Users contains a number of built-in users and groups that are important to the functions of Active Directory. Some of them are used now, and some of them will be used when you deploy other functionality on your network. One of our pet peeves is seeing people use this OU for user accounts that they create. This means that it becomes difficult to separate your ordinary user accounts from built-in ones. This makes applying policies to OUs and delegating administrative rights to OUs very difficult. We wish Microsoft had used a different name for this OU.

FIGURE 7.4
Active Directory
Users and
Computers

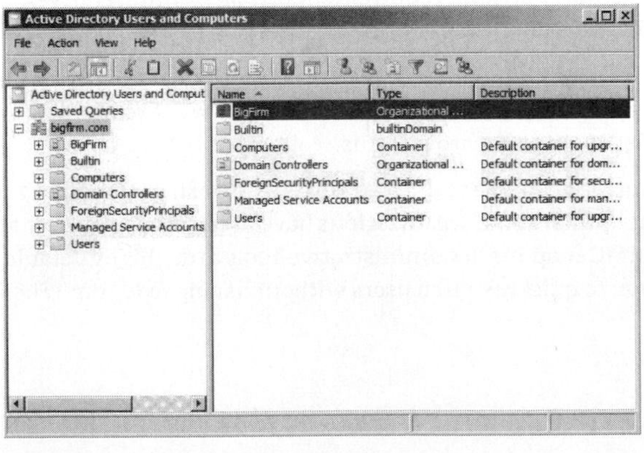

This solution is pretty simple. You create another OU, typically named after the domain or the organization, at the root of the domain. In this case, you'll create one called Bigfirm under bigfirm.com. Then you can create an OU architecture to suit the policy and administrative hierarchy of the organization within this domain. You have a single site organization, so create an OU for the users (Users), another for the computers (Computers), and one more for the security groups (Security Groups). You can see the solution in Figure 7.5. This allows you to give rights to each of these types of objects with granular control and to treat them differently. You'll be creating the users in the OU \BigFirm\Users within the domain bigfirm.com.

FIGURE 7.5
The Users OU

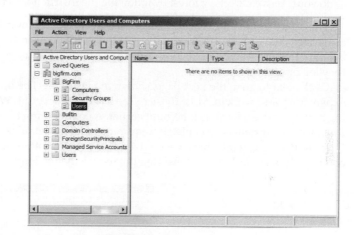

Navigate into the OU where you want to create you new user. Right-click in the OU, and select New ➢ User to create the user. This launches the New Object – User wizard.

You can see that things are pretty simple here. Enter the first name and last name of the user. This automatically completes the full name, which you can alter if you want. You can enter the logon name, such as **JBloggs**, as shown in Figure 7.6.

FIGURE 7.6
Creating a
new Active
Directory user

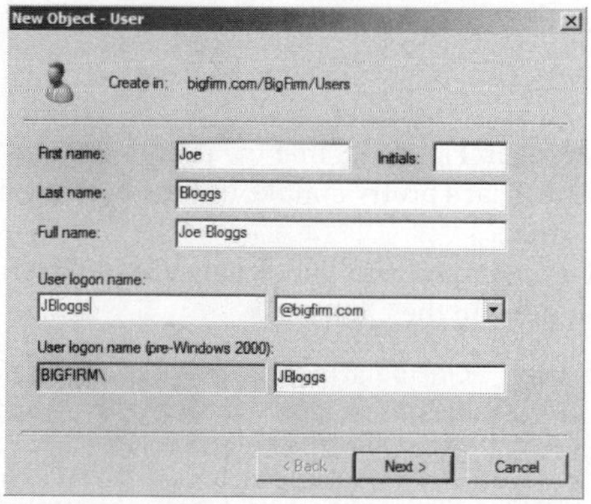

This is probably a good time to introduce some terminology for people new to Active Directory and user account management. Every user has two types of names with which they can access resources on the network:

User logon name   This is the name that you are probably most familiar with, such as JBloggs.

User principal name   Windows 2000 introduced the user principal name (UPN). This is a username that looks like an email address. You can see in Figure 7.6 that the UPN for Joe Bloggs is JBloggs@bigfirm.com. The UPN suffix (@bigfirm.com) is inherited from the name of the domain by default. This is bigfirm.com in our scenario. Note that you can add UPN suffixes to your Active Directory forest by following the instructions at http://tinyurl.com/3y4zdw.

The user logon name, which was retained by Microsoft for backward compatibility, is visible as JBloggs. You can also see that the pre–Windows 2000 username is Bigfirm\JBloggs. Funnily enough, this pre–Windows 2000 username is exactly what users will be prompted to enter when they log onto the domain!

Click Next to go to the next page, shown in Figure 7.7. The options here are pretty self-explanatory and work just like those in the local user account. We described them while showing how to create a local user account earlier. A common mistake here is to not enter a password that meets your defined complexity requirements. The default settings are defined in the Default Domain Policy. You may have customized these with another policy object. You won't be able to complete this wizard without meeting the requirements. Finish the wizard to create the user.

FIGURE 7.7
Setting the new AD
user password

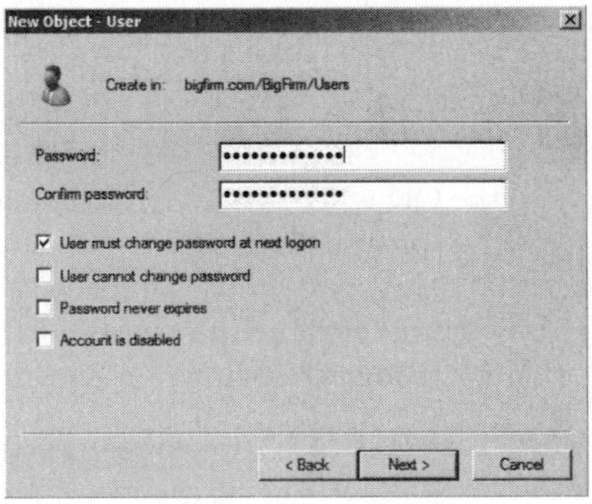

You can see in Figure 7.8 that the user is created and that it is located in the \BigFirm\Users OU. That's it. That's pretty simple, right? Let's take a look at how you can do the same thing from command line.

The first command you'll look at is dsadd. The following command will re-create what you've just done in the GUI:

```
dsadd user "CN=Joe Bloggs,OU=Users,OU=BigFirm,DC=bigfirm,DC=com" -samid JBloggs
-upn JBloggs@bigfirm.com -fn Joe -ln Bloggs -display "Joe Bloggs" -pwd
Mydogisblu3 -mustchpwd yes
```

Wow! That's quite a command. Here's the syntax:

```
dsadd user <Distinguished Name of the user> -samid <user logon name> -upn <user
principal name> -fn <firstname> -ln <surname> -display <full name> -pwd <password>
-mustchpwd <the user must change their password on first logon: yes or no>
```

FIGURE 7.8

The new user in
Active Directory

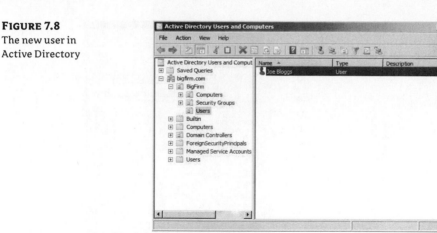

What's with this whole distinguished name (DN) thing? The DN describes where in Active Directory the user account object is created and how it is named. The DN in our case is CN=Joe Bloggs,OU=Users,OU=BigFirm,DC=bigfirm,DC=com. That breaks down as follows:

Component name (CN)   This is the name of an object. In this case, it is the name of the user account object.

Organization unit (OU)   You have a number of these to define your path of \BigFirm\Users. Have you noticed yet how the DN is working its way backward up through the path, as in CN=Joe Bloggs,OU=Users,OU=BigFirm?

Domain component (DC)   This describes the name of the domain, such as bigfirm.com. Notice that this is *not* backwards like the rest of the DN.

You can get more help on creating users using the dsadd command by typing **dsadd user /?**. There's a chance that you've probably seen that the net user command has a domain option. You are now thinking that it was a simpler command to use and wondering why we haven't chosen to use it here. The reason is that net user does not allow you to specify where in the domain that you should create the user account object. You want to create the user in \BigFirm\Users, and dsadd allows you to do this.

Let's now take a look at what you have created and how you can manage those user accounts.

Setting Local User Account Properties

Let's open the user account for Joe Bloggs that is created on the member server, bf2. You should right-click that user and click Properties. This opens the screen shown in Figure 7.9.

This dialog box will look pretty similar. These are the settings you defined for the user account when you created it. The grayed-out check box "Account is locked out" will be enabled and selected if the user is locked out. An account will be locked out if the password policy defines that it should be locked out after *x* number of failed password entry attempts within a specified time frame. By default, this is defined in the Default Domain Policy. Notice that you cannot select this box; that's because you cannot use this dialog box to lock out a user. The option becomes enabled only when the user is actually locked out.

We will go through the properties of the user object now and discuss the various attributes of a local user account.

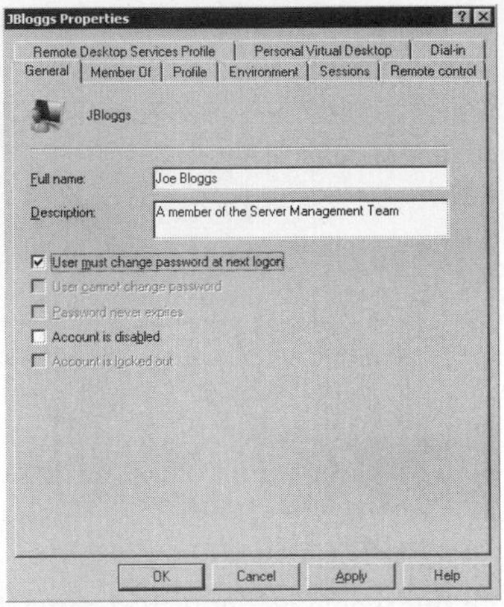

FIGURE 7.9
Local user general
properties

MEMBER OF TAB

The Member Of tab is used to control group membership of the user account (see Figure 7.10). We'll return to this tab when we cover groups later in this chapter.

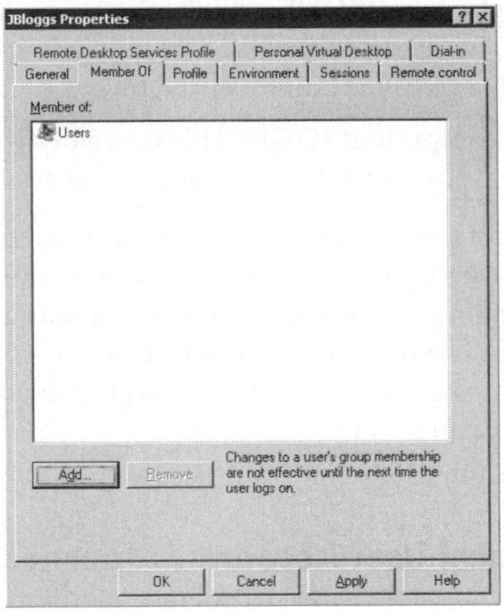

FIGURE 7.10
Local user group
membership

PROFILE TAB

Profile, which you can see in Figure 7.11, is used to control a number of settings:

Profile path   This setting is the location where the user profile is located. A *profile* is a folder structure that contains the settings that are unique to that user. It also contains things such as their My Documents and Favorites folders. We'll talk about profiles a little bit later in this chapter, but we'll go into much greater detail in Chapter 30.

Logon script   This setting allows you to define a script that will be stored on domain controllers and that will be run every time this user logs on. You might store this logon script locally for a local user account. This will be covered in Chapter 30 as well.

Home folder   This setting allows you to define a network drive that will be dedicated to this user and mapped as a particular drive letter when they log in. Guess what? You'll learn more about this in Chapter 30.

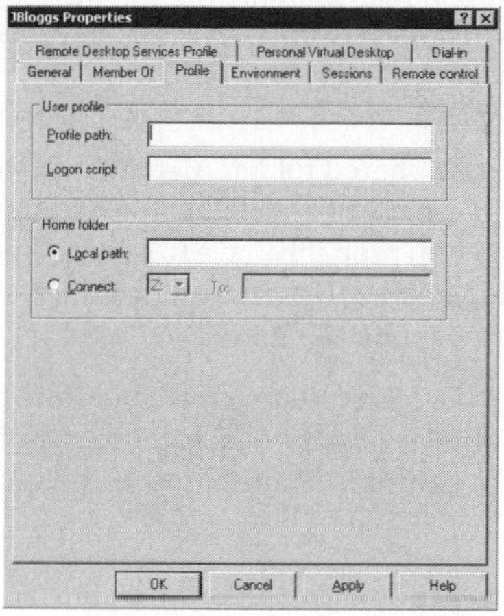

FIGURE 7.11
Local user profile settings

OBTAINING THE DN THE EASY WAY

Administrators can sometimes be pretty lazy, so you might hate typing this stuff. Our tip for obtaining the DN of the OU you are creating is to follow these steps:

1. Open Active Directory Users and Computers.

2. Select View ➢ Advanced Features.

3. Advanced Features should now be selected. This makes a lot of things visible to you in the Advanced Users and Computers MMC.

4. Navigate to the OU that you want the DN of, and open its properties.

5. Click the Attribute Editor tab, and scroll down to distinguishedName, as shown here. Double-click this and copy the DN for later reuse.

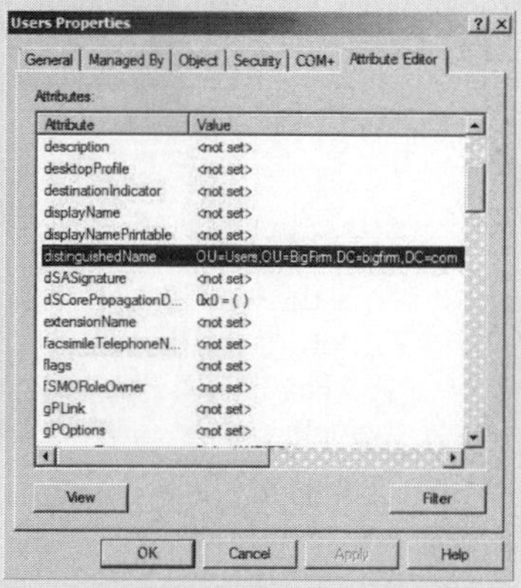

We mentioned profiles. Quite simply, an administrator will create a folder for the user to automatically store their personal data and settings and share the folder on a file server. It will have security permissions placed on it so that only the user in question (as well as local system and local administrators) can access the folder. This will allow the user's profile to be stored in this location when they log out and downloaded when they log in. An example of such a folder might be \\bf1\profiles\JBloggs. This is created as follows:

♦ bf1 is the file server.

♦ Profiles is a shared folder. All authenticated users can read and write to the share. The folder in the file system allows only authenticated users to read the contents. Local administrators will probably have full control permissions on the share and the folder. You might consider creating this share as a hidden share that is not visible when you browse the network by naming the share Profiles$.

♦ JBloggs is a folder that is created to store the profile of the user Joe Bloggs. Security on this folder allows only the user Joe Bloggs to read and write to this folder via the Modify permission. Administrators of the file server and System will have full control rights.

ENVIRONMENT TAB

The Environment tab in Figure 7.12 controls how the working environment is configured when the user logs into the server using Windows Server 2008 Terminal Services or Windows Server 2008 R2 Remote Desktop Services, such as by using the Remote Desktop Connection client.

You can configure a particular program to run every time a user logs in by selecting the "Start the following program at logon" option. You should enter the command to run that command and also enter a folder that will be the startup folder for that program.

The Remote Desktop Connection client allows a user to choose to map their local drives and local printers and choose to configure print jobs while using the server to always go to the client computer's default printer. Administrators can forcefully control these options using this tab.

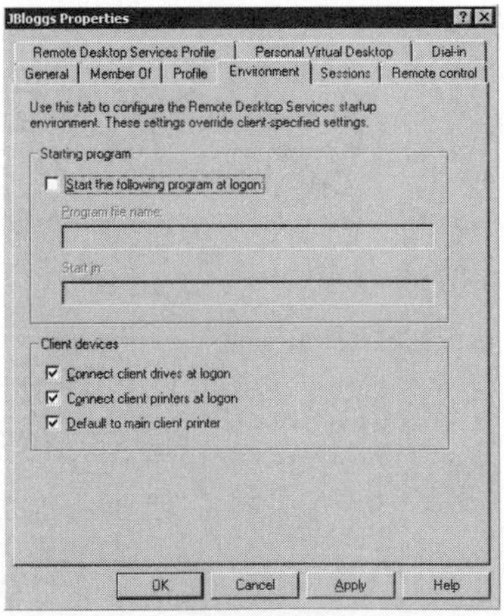

FIGURE 7.12
Local user environment settings

REMOTE DESKTOP SERVICES OR TERMINAL SERVICES

Windows Server 2008 R2 expanded the functionality in Terminal Services to include virtual desktop infrastructure. Microsoft rebranded Terminal Services as Remote Desktop Services. That can be a little confusing if you're reading this chapter and still working with Windows Server 2008. Just know that when we refer to Remote Desktop Services we are usually also talking about Terminal Services on Windows Server 2008.

SESSIONS TAB

You can see the Sessions tab in Figure 7.13. It also controls how Remote Desktop Services will work for this user. A user's session on a server will remain in a disconnected state on a server if they do not choose to log out. This means that they continue to use resources and that their programs continue to execute. More important, this means that one of the two freely available concurrent sessions that are used by administrators on servers will be consumed. Forgetful administrators can quickly consume both of those sessions, which will prevent other administrators from logging in normally by using the Remote Desktop Connection client. Note that administrators can terminate those sessions by using Remote Desktop Services Manager either locally or from a remote computer.

FIGURE 7.13
Local user
Sessions tab

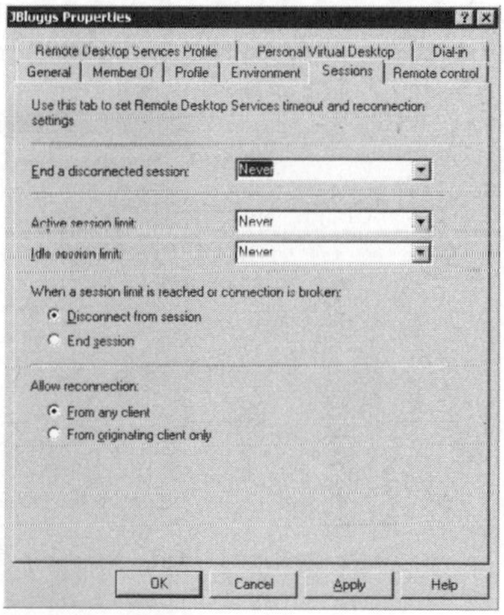

You can force disconnected sessions to terminate automatically after a defined time. Although it's more efficient to configure this centrally using Windows Server 2008 R2 Remote Desktop Services Configuration, you can do this on a per-user basis by using the "End a disconnected session" drop-down box on the Sessions tab.

Those valuable sessions can be made available by limiting how long an administrator's session can last. You can configure this maximum time by configuring the "Active session limit" drop-down box.

Idle sessions can be terminated automatically by choosing a time limit in the "Idle session limit" drop-down box.

The termination action for "Idle session limit" and "Active session limit" can be configured to be either disconnect the session (that is, the session still runs but is not interactive) or end the session completely.

A user can reconnect to a disconnected session to continue what they were previously doing. This is pretty useful:

◆ A session will be disconnected if there is a network outage between the client and server.

◆ A user or administrator may deliberately disconnect a session to leave some task running without any interaction.

It appears from the bottom of this tab that you can control how a user can reconnect to a disconnected session. You may choose to allow the user to reconnect from any client or only from the original client. This latter option might be used for security reasons, but it is a pretty restrictive idea. *Or so it would seem!* Windows help kindly informs you that the "From originating client" functionality is not currently enabled in Windows Remote Desktop Services. So, this means you actually cannot restrict reconnections using this control.

REMOTE CONTROL TAB

The Remote Control tab, shown in Figure 7.14, allows administrators to control how an administrator can interact with a user's Remote Desktop Services session. The concept is that an administrator can join the user's session to assist them with some task.

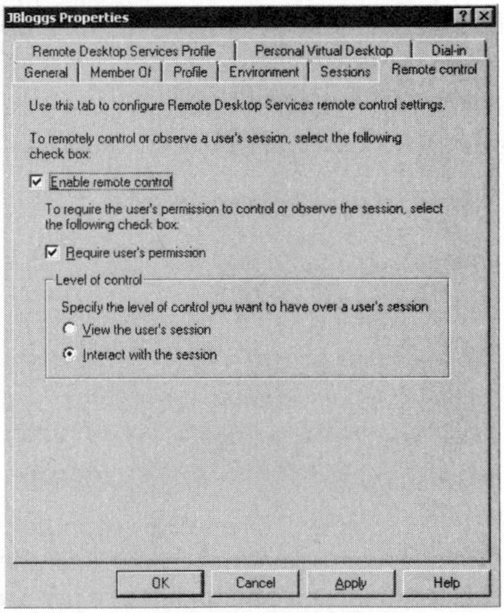

FIGURE 7.14
Local user Remote
Control tab

The default is that remote control is enabled. Maybe some user should never have remote control. You can disable remote control of that user's sessions by deselecting the "Enable remote control" check box.

This remote control thing might sound like it could be a little sneaky. The default is that a user will be prompted to either allow or disallow the remote control attempt by an administrator. You could deselect the "Require user's permission" check box to never involve the user in the process.

If you have allowed remote control, then you can configure the level of interaction that the administrator can have with the user's session. You can set it so that the administrator can only view; in other words, it is read-only with no control. The default is to allow an interactive session where an administrator can use the mouse and keyboard in the user's session.

REMOTE DESKTOP SERVICES PROFILE TAB

The Remote Desktop Services Profile tab, Figure 7.15, allows you to specify a custom profile for when this user logs into the server using Remote Desktop Services. This can allow administrators to provide a dedicated Remote Desktop Services profile or even a restricted profile for this user's session. We'll talk a bit about a relevant subject called *mandatory profiles* in Chapter 30. The path for your custom profile will logically be placed in the Profile Path field.

FIGURE 7.15

Local user Remote Desktop Services Profile tab

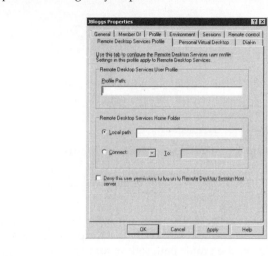

You can also offer this user a special home folder for storing personal information if they connect to the server by using Terminal Services.

At the bottom of the tab, you can see a check box to prevent the user from even being able to log into this server using Terminal Services. You might consider doing this with accounts such as those used for services. This means that even if the account's password should become compromised, you can still prevent it from being used by an attacker via Remote Desktop.

PERSONAL VIRTUAL DESKTOP TAB

We'll skip this for now but we will come back to it when talking about configuring the settings of domain-based user accounts in the next section.

DIAL-IN TAB

The Dial-in tab, as shown in Figure 7.16, allows an administrator to control if and how a user can remotely connect to this server, such as by initiating a VPN tunnel or using a modem to dial in.

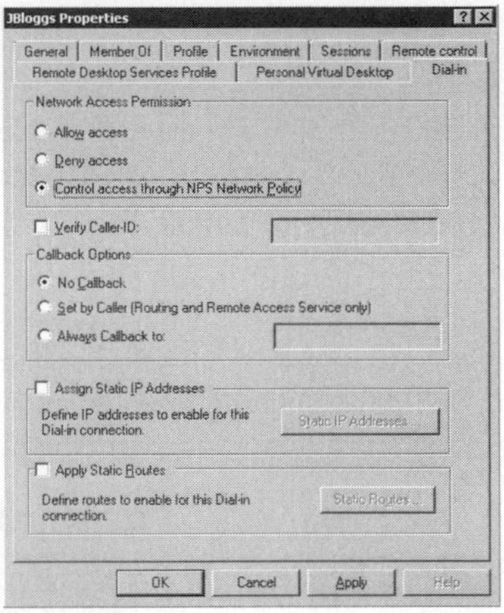

FIGURE 7.16

Local user
Dial-in tab

Changing any of the properties in this dialog box is pretty easy using Active Directory Users and Computers, as you've probably realized by now. You can control only *some* of these settings by using the `net user` command. Let's take a look at one or two. This command will change the full name of the local user account:

```
net user JBloggs /fullname:"Joeseph Bloggs"
```

This will set the home folder path to that of your choosing:

```
net user JBloggs /homedir:"D:\Home\JBloggs"
```

You should make sure that the path is valid before you run the command because the command does not check it. You should also verify that the permissions are OK for this user.

This configures the profile path setting for the user:

```
net user JBloggs /profilepath:"D:\Profiles\JBloggs"
```

Again, there is no error checking built into the command, so you should make sure that the path and permissions are valid first.

Setting Domain-Based User Account Properties

Let's compare what you've just looked at in a local user account with that of a domain-based user account. Log back into the domain controller, bf1.bigfirm.com, navigate to a user, select the user object, right-click, and select Properties. Note that you should have Advanced Features enabled in the View menu of Active Directory Users and Computers (ADUC). You can see the user's properties in Figure 7.17.

You should also disable the Advanced Features view in ADUC and see how it compares to the following sections. You'll notice the advanced view gives you much more power.

FIGURE 7.17

Active Directory
user account
properties

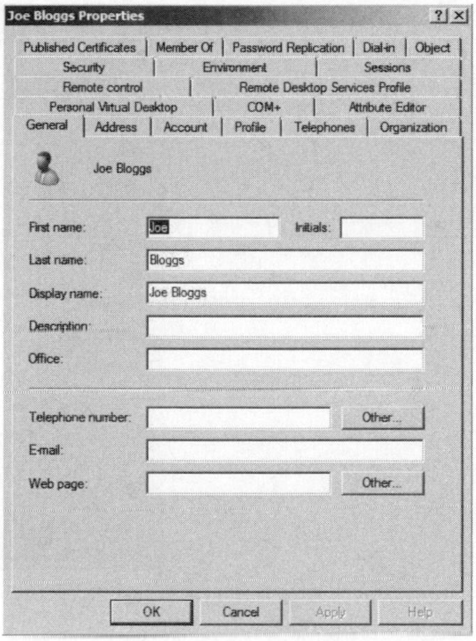

You can see two things here:

♦ There are a lot more tabs with many more settings available to you in a domain-based user account than there are in a local user account. This gives administrators much more control over their users. It also allows you to store more information with each user account. This information can be used by users or by applications.

♦ Both local user accounts and domain-based user accounts share a lot of common settings. We won't repeat ourselves when it comes to those settings in this section. We are assuming you've read the descriptions in the previous section on local user accounts.

Let's start by looking at the General tab.

GENERAL TAB

You can see, again in Figure 7.17, some descriptive information for your user. You'll see the usual first name and last name. You also have the ability to store some other information about the user in the user's account object in Active Directory such as their office, telephone number, email address, and web page. You'll find that you can make use of any defined email address or web page settings for this user by right-clicking the account object in Active Directory Users and Computers. This allows you to open the user's defined web page or send mail to their defined email address.

ADDRESS TAB

You can see the Address tab in Figure 7.18. This allows you to define a postal address for the user in question. Why would you want to do this? Active Directory can be used as a directory for users; in other words, it can be used by users to find out information about other users on the network, or it can be used by applications to store, retrieve, and share information about the users.

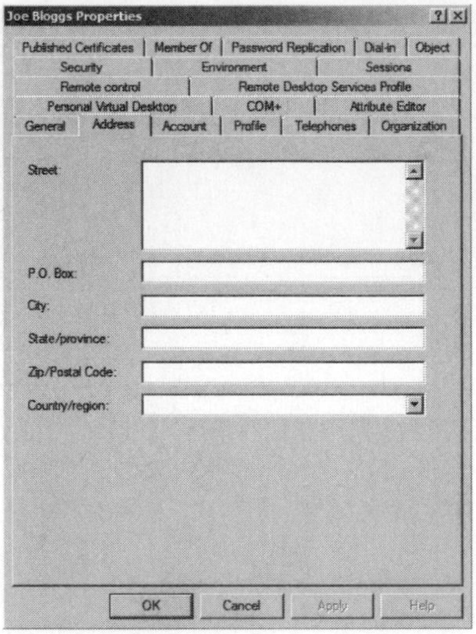

FIGURE 7.18
Active Directory
user Address tab

ACCOUNT TAB

You can see the user logon name, the UPN, and the pre–Windows 2000 user logon name that you defined while creating the user in Figure 7.19. You can use these controls to modify those usernames.

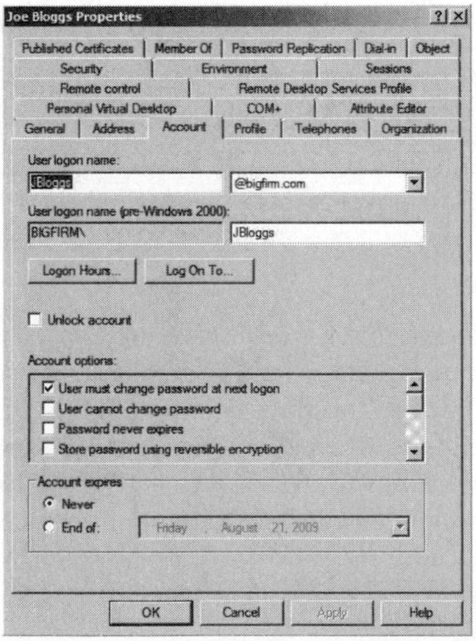

FIGURE 7.19
Active Directory
user Account tab

Clicking the Logon Hours button will open the dialog box in Figure 7.20. This allows you to control when a user can log on to the network to access resources. It does not forcibly log the user off. You might consider using this control where security is extremely strict. It's not a common requirement to configure this setting.

FIGURE 7.20

Active Directory user Logon Hours tab

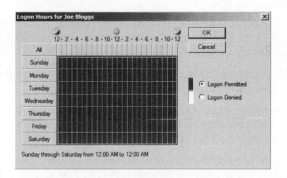

Back on the Account tab, you can see a button called Log On To. The dialog box in Figure 7.21 will open if you click it.

FIGURE 7.21

Active Directory user Logon Workstations dialog box

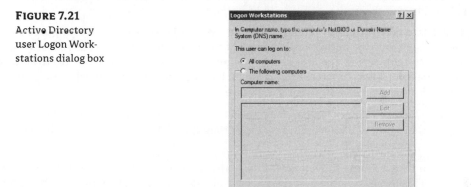

This dialog box allows you to control which computers this user can use to log in to Active Directory. You might consider doing this in a few scenarios:

◆ You need to control where some or all of your users log in. This isn't exactly a common configuration request, but we can imagine that some places that have CIA/NSA-like security might want to use this.

◆ You have a consultant or visiting engineer on-site, and you want to restrict the person to the computers they should be working on.

◆ You are creating a user account for an application or a service, and you need to ensure that it is used only on the designated servers. This will restrict any damage (temporarily!) that can be done if that user account is compromised.

You would imagine that both the Log On To and the Logon Hours settings would be used together to accomplish your domain-based user account logon restrictions.

Returning to Figure 7.19, have you noticed that you have many more options for controlling the account? It's not necessarily immediately obvious until you scroll that control in the middle of the dialog box:

User must change password at next logon   This is used by an administrator to force a user to change their password after an administrator has set or reset it. This means that the administrator should have no knowledge of what the user will use for their password.

User cannot change password   This would be used by an administrator for a service account to ensure that it cannot be changed.

Password never expires   This control overrides any password expiration policies that may be configured in Active Directory. Ideally it won't be used for ordinary user accounts, but it is typically used for service user accounts.

Store password using reversible encryption   Never enable this setting unless you absolutely know with 100 percent certainty that you need it. It is required when applications need to know a user's password for authentication purposes. Microsoft says that it is essentially the same as storing clear-text versions of the user's password.

Account is disabled   An administrator can disable a user account to prevent anyone from being able to authenticate or authorize by using the account.

Smart card is required for interactive logon   Active Directory can be configured to allow users to sign onto the network using a *smart card* device. It's referred to as *two-factor authentication*. In other words, the user uses something that they have (a unique token) and something that they know (a secret PIN) to log in. It is considered to be a much better solution for authentication than passwords or passphrases:

♦ The token cannot be shared or stolen easily. The device is unique, so it means that the owner will know if it is stolen, or they cannot log in themselves if they give it to someone else.

♦ It uses a simple-to-remember PIN. It also uses very strong encryption mechanisms. This means that the user doesn't have any passwords that change on a frequent basis—a common cause of headaches for IT on a Monday morning when users forget their long or complex passwords!

The added security might prompt administrators to deploy smart cards to either some or all users depending on security requirements. This check box will force users to log in using their assigned smart card and will not allow them to log in using the traditional username and password.

Account is sensitive and cannot be delegated   This configures whether the user can be impersonated by a service. This is done to allow the service to impersonate the user. You might possibly encounter this behavior in the middle tier of an n-tier architecture, such as a web front end, a middle-layer application server, and the back-end database architecture. The default is that this check box is cleared and allows impersonation of this user account.

Use Kerberos DES encryption types for this account   Some applications may require a service account that uses the DES encryption algorithm. You would enable this setting for those service user accounts. You may need to reset the password after changing this setting.

This account supports AES 128 bit encryption   The two AES encryption algorithm options are usable only when the domain functional level is set to either Windows Server 2003 or

Windows Server 2008. Again, some applications may require a service user account with AES 128-bit encryption. You would enable this setting for those accounts.

This account supports AES 256 bit encryption   See the previous item about AES 128-bit encryption.

Do not require Kerberos preauthentication   This setting can be used to enable users to be able to log in when the network contains mixed variety Kerberos realms, such as an Active Directory and Unix key distribution centers (KDCs). You can read more about Kerberos on the Microsoft TechNet site at `http://tinyurl.com/2ucaa7`.

Notice that there isn't a grayed-out check box to indicate that the user is locked out? This makes it very clear to you that you cannot just go to this dialog box to lock out a user. Instead, you only have a control to unlock a user account near the top middle of the tab.

The last control on this tab is for controlling the automated expiration of this account. You can define a date when the user account will no longer be able to be used. You might use this when creating a user account for visiting engineers/consultants or for temporary/contract staff. Since you would know how long they would be in the office for, you could preconfigure when the account would expire so that they could no longer log in. This protects the network nicely against user account misuse.

PROFILE TAB

We've discussed the reasons for having the Profile tab shown in Figure 7.22 in the local user account properties. We'll be covering this in more detail in Chapter 30 when we cover advanced user management.

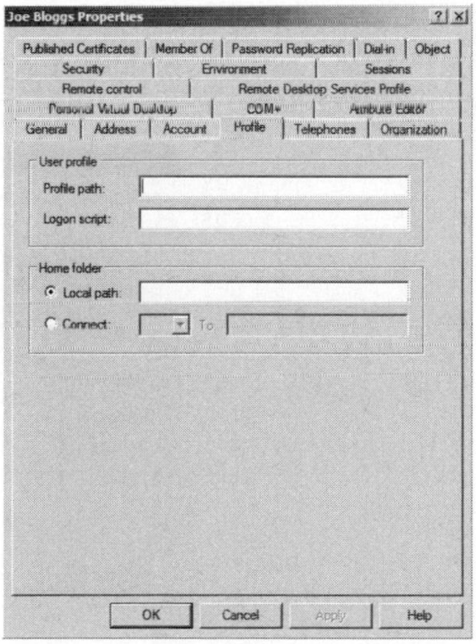

FIGURE 7.22
Active Directory
user Profile tab

TELEPHONES TAB

The Telephones tab is pretty self-explanatory (see Figure 7.23). You can store telecommunications contact information for the user in their user account object.

FIGURE 7.23
Active
Directory user
Telephones tab

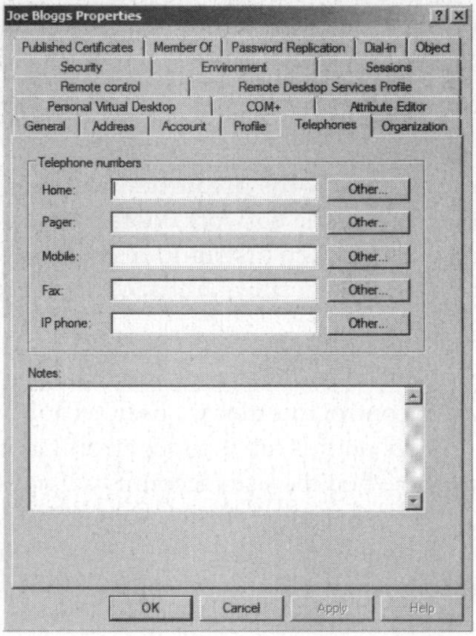

ORGANIZATION TAB

The Organization tab is another one of the information tabs (see Figure 7.24). We've mentioned several times that applications can use this sort of information. For example, the settings here could be used by a Windows SharePoint Services (WSS) implementation. This information is presented in a web interface when users look to find more about an owner of some documentation or a site within the WSS implementation. WSS loads this information from the user's Active Directory user account object. For example, if you browsed to view Joe Bloggs on a WSS server, then the properties of JBloggs would be read by WSS from Active Directory.

FIGURE 7.24
Active
Directory user
Organization tab

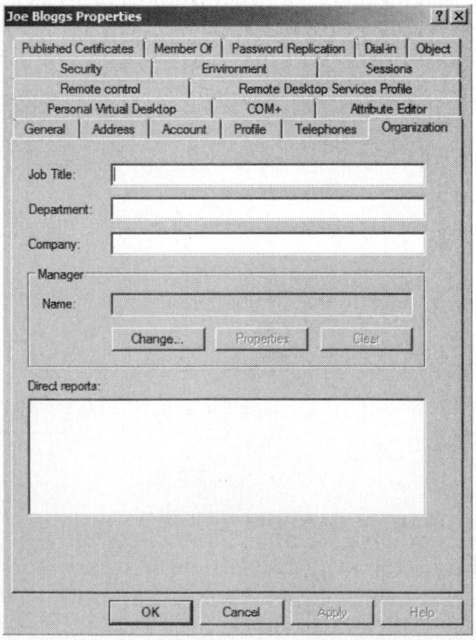

This tab allows you to describe the role of the user within the organization—it's more of a human resources thing and doesn't have anything to do with Active Directory delegation or administration. You can also select their line manager by browsing to another domain-based user account in Active Directory.

PERSONAL VIRTUAL DESKTOP TAB

This tab, which you can see in Figure 7.25, is a new one to Windows Server 2008 R2 and isn't available in previous editions of Windows Server. Personal virtual desktops are a form of VDI where a virtual machine with a copy of Windows Vista or Windows 7 runs on a server in the computer room. The user will log into it using Remote Desktop via a Remote Desktop Connection Broker. This broker is required to use the functionality in this tab.

COM+ TAB

You're delving into application programming country with the COM+ tab in Figure 7.26. A partition is an application configuration. An application can have many configurations. This means you can have many of these COM+ partitions within Active Directory. You can read more about application partitions on MSDN at `http://tinyurl.com/nm5tth`.

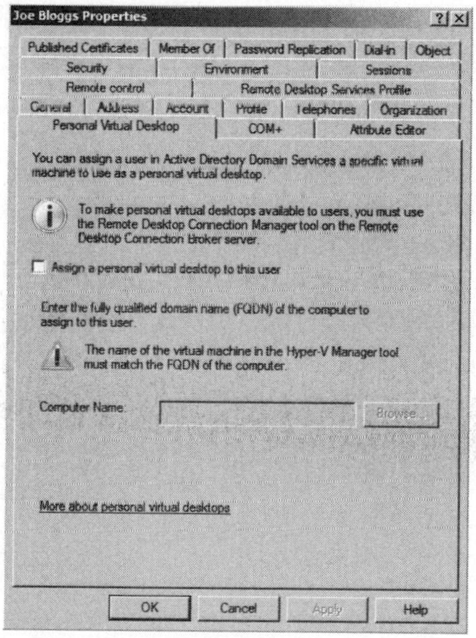

FIGURE 7.25
Active Directory user Personal Virtual Desktop tab

A partition set can contain many partitions. You can link users to partition sets and in turn to the contained partitions. Not only can you link a single user, but you can link all users in an OU by linking the OU to a partition set. You can read more about creating partition sets within Active Directory on MSDN at `http://tinyurl.com/2naoft`.

ATTRIBUTE EDITOR TAB

You've seen this tab before when you looked at the properties of an OU (see Figure 7.27). You can view or directly edit the properties of a user object here if you want.

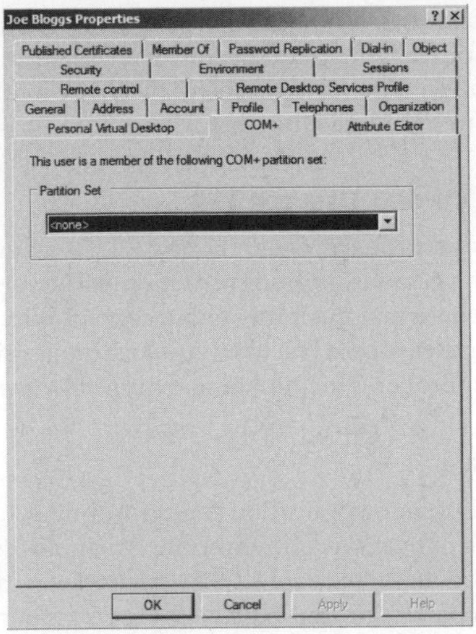

FIGURE 7.26
Active Directory
user COM+ tab

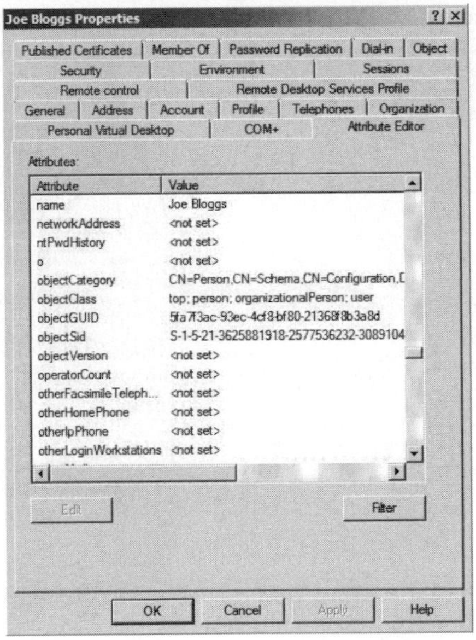

FIGURE 7.27
Active Directory
user Attribute
Editor tab

PUBLISHED CERTIFICATES TAB

Certificates give you an encryption-based security mechanism that is used to prove identity (see Figure 7.28).

Here you can view certificates that have been automatically assigned to the user through Active Directory using Certificate Services. You can actually manually assign certificates to a user from your own local certificate stores or from certificates that are stored on the file system.

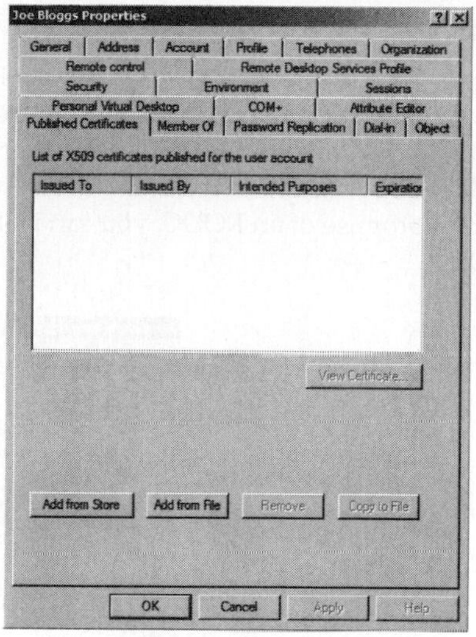

FIGURE 7.28

Active Directory
user Published
Certificates tab

MEMBER OF TAB

The Member Of tab allows you to control group membership of this user account (see Figure 7.29). We'll return to this later when we cover groups and group membership later in this chapter.

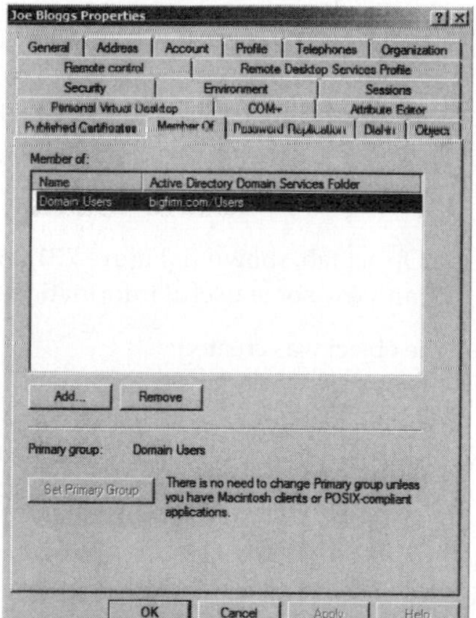

FIGURE 7.29

Active Directory
user group mem-
berships

You can see that you can also control the primary group of the user. This is required only in POSIX applications or Macintosh client computers. When one of these clients creates a file or folder on a Windows server, this primary group is assigned to the new object. The group must be in the user's own domain, and it must be either a global or universal security group.

PASSWORD REPLICATION TAB

The Password Replication tab is used to view which read-only domain controllers (RODCs) this user's password has been replicated to (see Figure 7.30). An RODC is an Active Directory architecture option that was added with Windows Server 2008. You can place an RODC in branch offices where the physical security of a normal domain controller cannot be guaranteed. In the event of the theft or compromise of an RODC, you can isolate user accounts that have their details stored on that RODC.

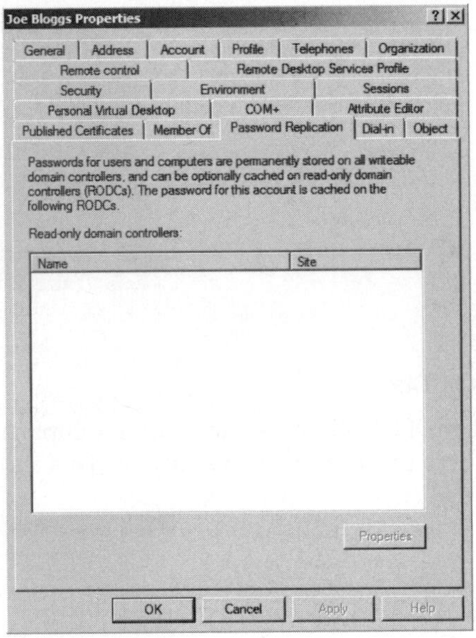

FIGURE 7.30

Active Directory
user Password
Replication tab

OBJECT TAB

You'll find the Object tab, shown in Figure 7.31, to be quite useful when doing some trouble-shooting. You can view some useful information such as the following:

- When the object was created

- When it was last modified

- USN information that is used to control Active Directory replication
   A nice new option on this tab is the ability to protect the user account against accidental deletion using the check box at the bottom. This would be pretty useful to ensure that no one unintentionally deletes the user account for a critical service account, such as the CEO or a senior government official.

SECURITY TAB

The Security tab, as shown in Figure 7.32, allows you to control who can do what to this user account object. This is known as *delegation*. We'll discuss this subject in great depth later in this book.

FIGURE 7.31
Active Directory
user Object
properties

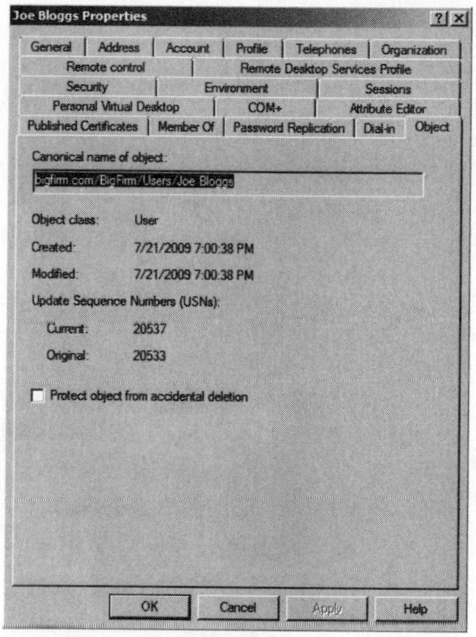

FIGURE 7.32
Active Directory
user Object
security

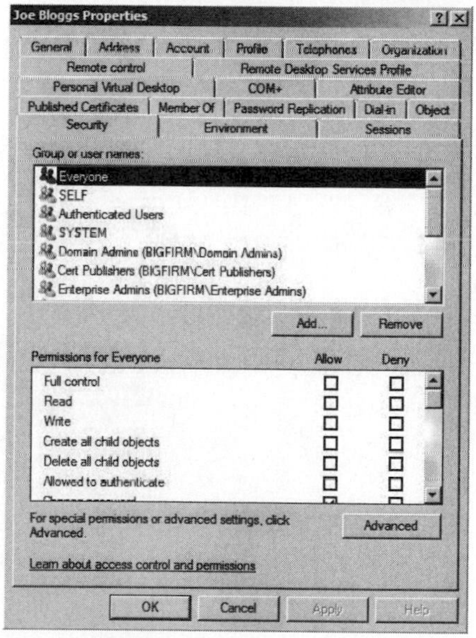

Take a look at the permissions assigned to SELF by clicking it. SELF is the user in question. That is, what can Joe Bloggs do to the JBloggs user account? If you scroll down in the Permissions for Self control, you will see that Joe can actually change a lot of settings in his own user account. This means that Joe can actually alter settings such as who his manager is, what his contact details are, and so on. In theory, you could present users with some web-like application that allows them to easily edit these settings. This approach would be much easier for them to understand than asking them to fire up Active Directory User and Computers and edit their accounts there!

EDITING MANY USER ACCOUNTS AT ONCE

It's pretty easy to change all of those settings for an individual account, as you've just seen. What if you want to modify more than one account at once? That's pretty easy too. For this example, create a couple of new users in the Users OU, as shown in Figure 7.33.

Say you want to modify settings for all the users in this OU. Select all the user accounts, right-click, and select Properties.

This opens up a properties dialog box, shown in Figure 7.34. It actually doesn't make sense to offer all the settings for more than one user, so you see only a subset of the options.

To modify a setting, select the check box associated with it. This makes the edit box available to you. You can now edit the setting for all the users who you previously selected, as shown in Figure 7.35.

FIGURE 7.33
Additional Active
Directory users

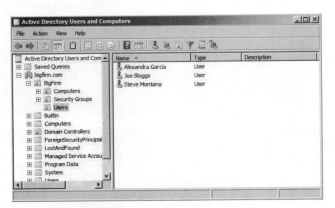

FIGURE 7.34
Properties of
multiple Active
Directory user
objects

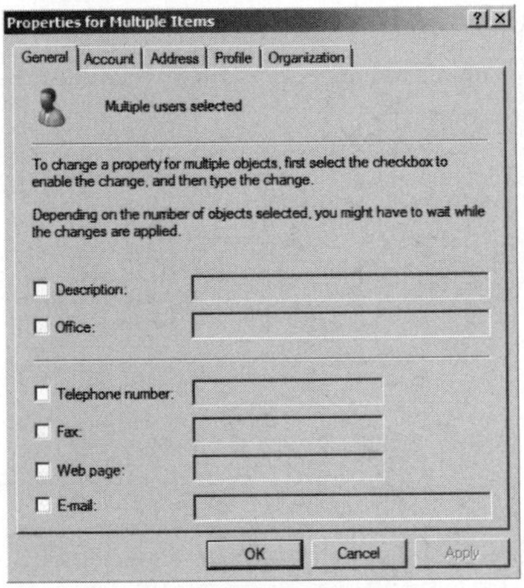

Managing domain-based user account objects is pretty easy when using Active Directory Users and Computers. You'll now take a look at how to do it when the command prompt is your only option.

FIGURE 7.35

Changing attributes of multiple Active Directory objects

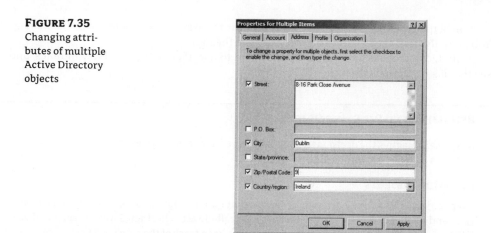

MANAGING DOMAIN-BASED USER PROPERTIES AT THE COMMAND LINE

Let's look at how you can do the same thing using the command prompt. You'll be using a command called dsmod with the user option. You can view the help for this by running the following:

```
dsmod user /?
```

Notice that you have to use the DN of the user that you want to modify. Check out the previous tip to get this from the distinguishedName property of the user account object on the Attribute Editor tab (see the "Obtaining the DN the Easy Way" sidebar). That's all well and good if you have a GUI available to you. What happens if you don't? If you know the UPN of the user, then you can run dsquery to get the DN:

```
dsquery user -upn jbloggs@bigfirm.com
"CN=Joe Bloggs,OU=Users,OU=BigFirm,DC=bigfirm,DC=com"
```

Alternatively, you can run the dsquery command using the SAM account name, which is the friendly name that you know as JBloggs:

```
C:\Users\Administrator>dsquery user -samid jbloggs
"CN=Joe Bloggs,OU=Users,OU=BigFirm,DC=bigfirm,DC=com"
```

dsquery is a really powerful command, so it's well worth getting to know it with dsquery /?.

Now you can proceed with dsmod. Let's see how you can configure a home drive and a drive letter to map it for Joe Bloggs:

```
dsmod user "CN=Joe Bloggs,OU=Users,OU=BigFirm,DC=bigfirm,DC=com" -hmdir \\bf1\
home$\JBloggs -hmdrv P
```

This will configure a home drive (a special network-based shared folder specific to this user) with the drive letter P mapped to \\bf1\home$\JBloggs whenever Joe Bloggs logs in.

You now want to configure the manager for Joe Bloggs. You've just learned that Alexandra Garcia has been promoted to be the department head. You can do this by running the following:

```
dsmod user "CN=Joe Bloggs,OU=Users,OU=BigFirm,DC=bigfirm,DC=com" -mgr "CN=
Alexandra Garcia,OU=Users,OU=BigFirm,DC=bigfirm,DC=com"
```

Notice that you didn't enter something like `bigfirm\agarcia` or `agarcia` as the manager? You actually used the DN for the account that is the manager.

At first, `dsmod` looks like a difficult command to use. Play with it for a few minutes, and you'll see that it's not actually that bad.

RENAMING AND DELETING OBJECTS

As you can imagine, the decision to rename or delete something should be considered very carefully. There's a very serious implication to this.

RENAMING OBJECTS

Every object in Windows has a name. You use that name for logins, scripts, application configuration, and so on. For example, if you create a user called SMurphy, then Sarah Murphy will use that label to log in. Windows does not use that name to keep track of the subject. That's because names change. Sarah might get married and change her surname to Sarah Kinsella. That will require changing her username to SKinsella. Windows needs to treat her exactly as it always did. Windows won't want to find every resource on the network where SMurphy was used to change the reference to SKinsella, such as group memberships, file share permissions, mailbox associations, and so on.

UNDERSTANDING HOW A SID COMES INTO PLAY

We humans need something we can remember and type easily, so a friendly label is used. Windows has a special code for each object called a *security identifier*. The SID is a globally unique identifier for every object in Active Directory. Every user object has a SID. Every computer object has a SID. Every group has a SID.

What happens when you rename a user or group, such as a *security principal*? Sure enough, the name you know changes. In the case of Sarah, she will need to remember her username. However, Windows tracks her user object only by the SID. Any resource permissions assigned to her user object or any group memberships associated with her user object won't change. Her user object name has changed, but her SID has not. Note that any third-party applications that use object names instead of SIDs will still require some administration to change the referenced object name. But anything that integrates tightly with Active Directory, such as SQL, SharePoint, or Exchange will be OK.

The thing to remember here is that when you change the name of an Active Directory object, such as a user or group, Windows still sees that as being the same object even if you don't. Permissions given to that object, attributes of that object, group memberships, and so on, will not have changed.

DELETING AN OBJECT

The other scenario you need to discuss is when you delete an object. If you assign permissions to SKinsella, then Windows is maintaining a list of permissions that are associated with her SID. The same happens if you assign permissions to a group of users. Windows will maintain the permissions associated with the SID of that group object, not with its name.

RESTORING A DELETED OBJECT

You have to be very careful about deleting that user or group object. If you accidentally delete them or you're told to restore them to their prior state, then you cannot just create a new object with an identical name. Remember that the SID is globally unique and is not tied to the name. A replacement SKinsella user object will have a different SID. The file share or mailbox that Sarah used to have access to won't recognize the new user object because it has a different SID than the old user object. The only way to restore access to a deleted group or user object is to restore the deleted object from a backup.

There's a few ways to do this, which Microsoft discusses at http://tinyurl.com/2wgo4g. Microsoft added a new Active Directory Recycle Bin in Windows Server 2008 R2, which will simplify the process of restoring recently deleted objects.

The point to remember is that the name of an object is not how Windows identifies the object. It uses a SID. You might re-create a copy of an object with the same name, but it will be a different object.

A BEST PRACTICE

For this reason, we strongly recommend that you disable users when you are asked to remove a user by your manager or the human resources department. That turns the user off and blocks them out from the network. There's always a chance that there has been a miscommunication or the person returns to work. Reenabling their access is easy: enable their account. After an agreed cooling-off period of 30 or 60 days, you can go ahead and delete that object.

For your Active Directory domain, you can use this command to find inactive and disabled accounts:

```
dsquery user -inactive <number of weeks> -disabled
```

For example, this command will find users that are disabled and have been inactive for eight weeks:

```
dsquery user -inactive 8 -disabled
```

To delete a user or a number of users, you simply select them, right-click, and select Delete. Deleting a user isn't much of a challenge from the command prompt. You can run the following to delete a local user account:

```
net user <username> /delete
```

This command will delete the JBloggs local user account:

```
net user JBloggs /delete
```

You'll use the dsrm command and the user object's DN to delete an Active Directory user account:

```
dsrm "CN=Joe Bloggs,OU=Users,OU=BigFirm,DC=bigfirm,DC=com"
```

You will be prompted to confirm the deletion. That's not necessarily a bad thing, but you won't want that to happen in a script. You can prevent a confirmation prompt by running this:

```
dsrm "CN=Joe Bloggs,OU=Users,OU=BigFirm,DC=bigfirm,DC=com" -noprompt
```

Group Management

Treating a collection of users as a single entity for one or a number of purposes eases a lot of administration tasks. For example, instead of performing 100 operations to assign permissions to each of 10 users to 10 resources, you can assign the users to a group (1 operation) and assign the group permissions to the resources (11 operations). The math makes it clear why you should use groups. Instead of dealing with individuals, you deal with the collective or the group.

In fact, best practice is that you always use groups for assigning permissions. Therefore, you need to know how to create groups, modify memberships, and remove groups.

You'll now learn about creating, controlling, and deleting local groups and domain-based groups. You'll see how to do this work using Active Directory Users and Computers and the command prompt.

Local Groups

Just like a local user, a local group exists within a member or stand-alone computer, be it a server, laptop, or desktop. It can contain local user accounts that exist on the server. It can also contain users or groups from the Active Directory that the server is a member of. You can manage groups using the same GUI tools that you use to manage local users.

Figure 7.36 shows where you manage local groups on a server. You can see that there are a number of them here by default. Windows will also add more groups if you add certain roles.

FIGURE 7.36
The default local groups

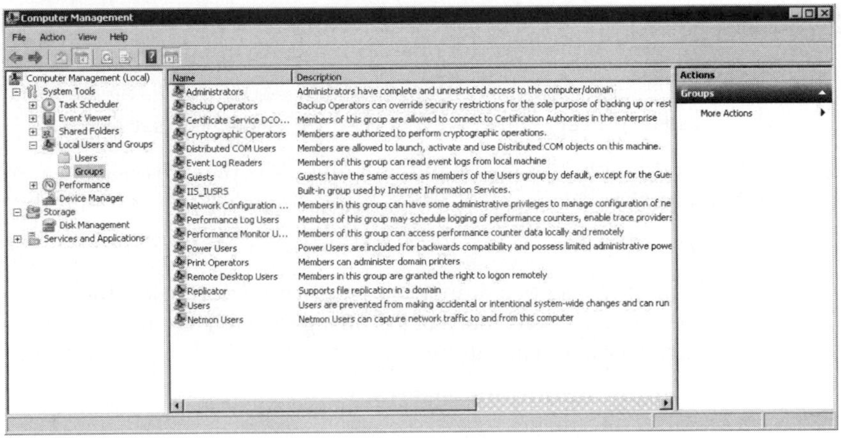

CREATING A GROUP

In this section, you'll create a new group called Fileshare. You can use it to assign permissions to a file share on this server to members of this group. You can either click the Action menu or right-click in the center pane and then select New Group.

The New Group dialog box will open. Enter the name of the group as **Fileshare**, as shown in Figure 7.37. We recommend that you enter a description for any groups you create. You might remember what this group is intended for now, but will you remember what it does in six months when you've been working on countless other projects and come back to fix an issue on this machine? Will your colleagues know what it does when you are out sick or away on vacation?

FIGURE 7.37
Creating a new
local group

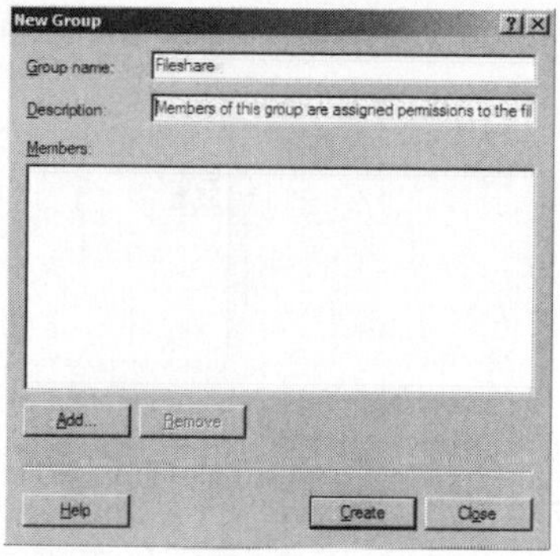

If you wanted, you could create this group now with no members. For this example, the local user for Joe Bloggs should be made a member of this group, so you'll do that now by clicking the Add button.

You can see in Figure 7.38 that the dialog box that opens allows you to search for and add the following to the group:

◆ Active Directory or local users

◆ Computer accounts from the Active Directory

◆ Active Directory Groups

FIGURE 7.38
Selecting group
members

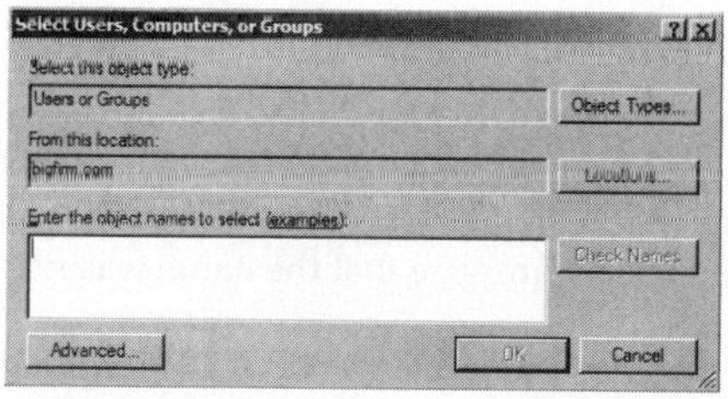

The Active Directory–based options are available only if this server is a member of a domain. The server that you are working with, BF2, is a member of bigfirm.com.

You can see that at the moment, the "Select this object type" setting allows you to add either users or groups to your group. You can modify this by clicking Object Types.

Now, in Figure 7.39, you can select or deselect computers, groups, or users. This will modify what you can add to/remove from your group during this membership edit.

Back in the Select Users, Computers, or Groups dialog box, you can see that "From this location" is set to the domain that the server is a member of. This is the default for a domain member computer. The location defines from where you can choose the objects that you have selected. A stand-alone server can have only itself as the location. In this example, you can choose either users or computers from the bigfirm.com domain. You want to change this, so you can select a local user account. You will click Locations to do this. Note that you could also select another trusted domain by clicking this button. Or you could even browse within the domain to a precise OU to reduce the size of the search for a domain-based user or computer.

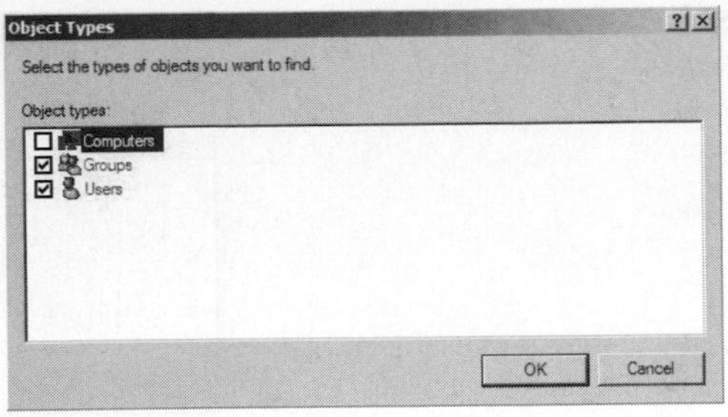

FIGURE 7.39
Potential group
member types

In Figure 7.40, we've expanded the domain to illustrate how you could browse through the OUs. However, you want to choose a local user account, so select the name of the local server, BF2. You could alternatively select the domain so you could add a group or user from the Active Directory domain to add into your local group.

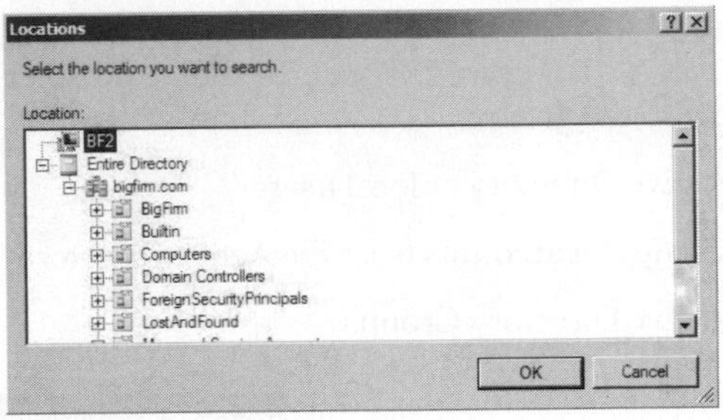

FIGURE 7.40
Selecting the
object source
location

If you believe that you know the username of the local user account to add, then you could simply type it in. If you type in **JBloggs** and then click Check Names, the dialog box searches the local account database and is able to confirm that JBloggs is actually BF2\JBloggs, as shown in Figure 7.41. Alternatively, if you are sure that the name was right, you could just type it and click OK.

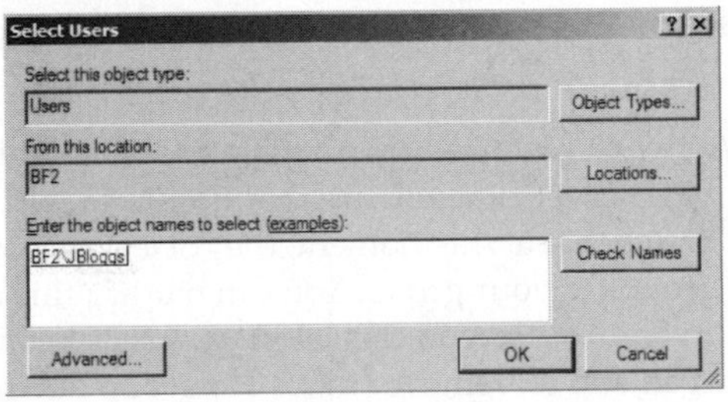

FIGURE 7.41
Adding a user to
the local group

If you don't know the precise name, then you can click Advanced to open the dialog box in Figure 7.42.

Lots of the search options here are grayed out because you have set the location to the local computer. These options work only when dealing with a domain location. However, you can click Find Now to list all the available accounts that you can add to the group based on the search criteria defined earlier.

FIGURE 7.42
Group
membership
advanced view

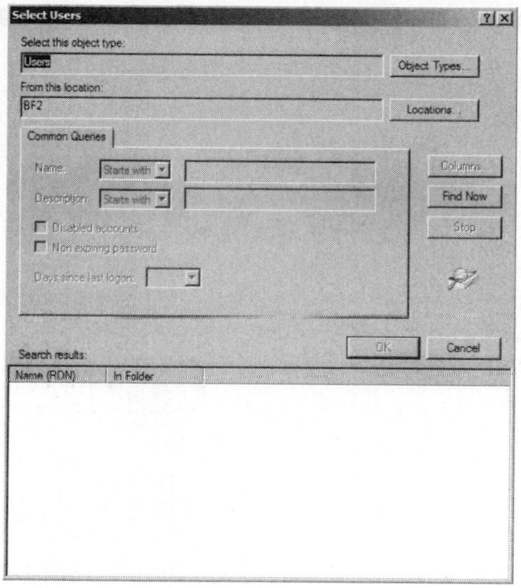

Figure 7.43 shows the results of this search. Here you can select the object or objects that you want to add to the group. Select JBloggs, and click OK.

FIGURE 7.43
Selecting a user
to add from the
advanced view

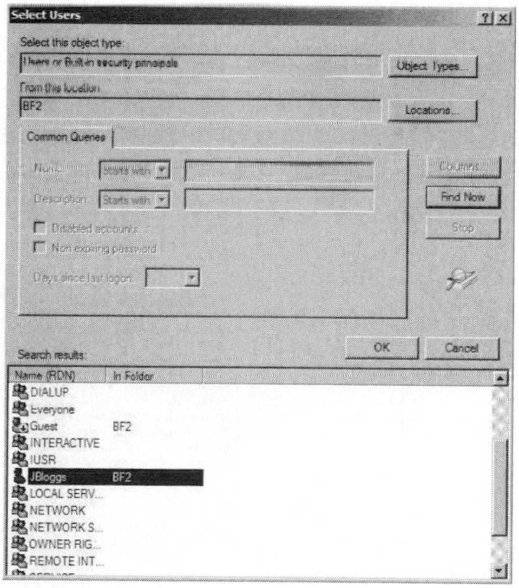

The selected objects are displayed in the Select Users dialog box, as shown in Figure 7.44. Click OK to save this membership.

You can see in Figure 7.45 that the group is ready to be created with its initial membership. You can complete the process by clicking Create.

FIGURE 7.44
Checked potential
group member

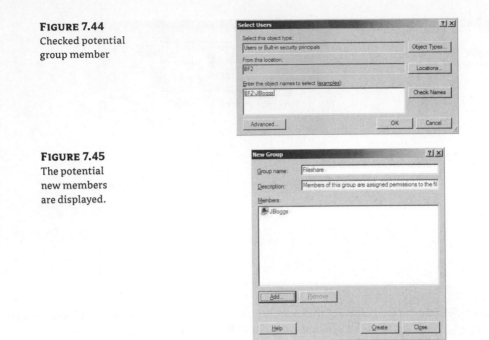

FIGURE 7.45
The potential
new members
are displayed.

You can see in Figure 7.46 that the new group is created and the user Joe Bloggs has been added to it.

FIGURE 7.46
The new group
is created.

LOGGING IN WITH A NEW GROUP MEMBERSHIP

Here's something important to note. It doesn't matter if you are working with Active Directory or local groups. A user can use its group membership only when it logs in *after* the group membership has been modified. Joe Bloggs would not be able to use his new group membership if he was currently logged in. You would have to advise him to log out and log back in again.

CREATING A GROUP AT THE COMMAND LINE

You can do the same thing with the command prompt by using the `net localgroup` command. You can get help by running the following:

```
net help localgroup
```

You can create the group by running this:

```
net localgroup Fileshare /add /comment:"Members assigned permission to the
fileshare on this server"
```

The syntax for this is as follows:

```
net localgroup <name of the new group> /add /comment:"<a description for the
group>"
```

Note that you cannot add a user to the group while creating it from the command prompt.

ADDING A USER TO GROUP

Let's add a new member to our group. You can do this via the MMC snap-in.

Open the properties of the group, which opens the window shown in Figure 7.47. Here you can see the existing membership of the group. Again, click Add to add a new member to the group.

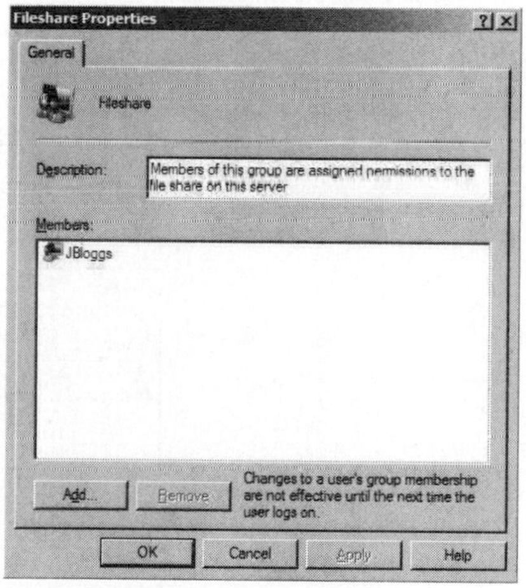

FIGURE 7.47
Group properties

Just like before, you can set the criteria for what will be added to the group and from where. You are going to add a domain-based group to the local group. You want everyone who is in the domain to be in the local group. You happen to know that a built-in domain-based group called Domain Users will do this for you.

Type in the name of the group, and click Check Name. You can see in Figure 7.48 that Domain Users will be added to the group.

A HANDY TECHNIQUE: ADDING A DOMAIN GROUP TO A LOCAL GROUP

The scenario of adding a domain group to a local group is a powerful one. It allows an administrator to reuse a collection of Active Directory objects in the form of an Active Directory group and give them rights to a resource that is shared on this server. You might consider doing this where an application owner has been granted local administrative access to a single server and nothing else. They can create local groups and populate them with domain groups and users. The application administrator can share their application with domain members without needing any domain administrative rights.

FIGURE 7.48
Adding a domain group to a local group

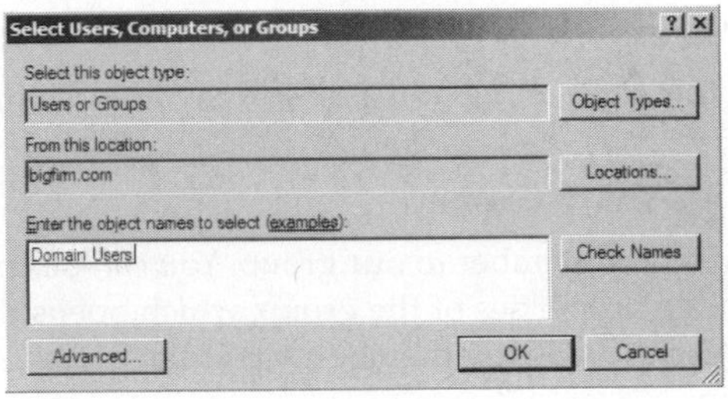

You can also see that BIGFIRM\Domain Users will join JBloggs as a member of the group once you click OK (see Figure 7.49).

FIGURE 7.49
The potential new membership of the group

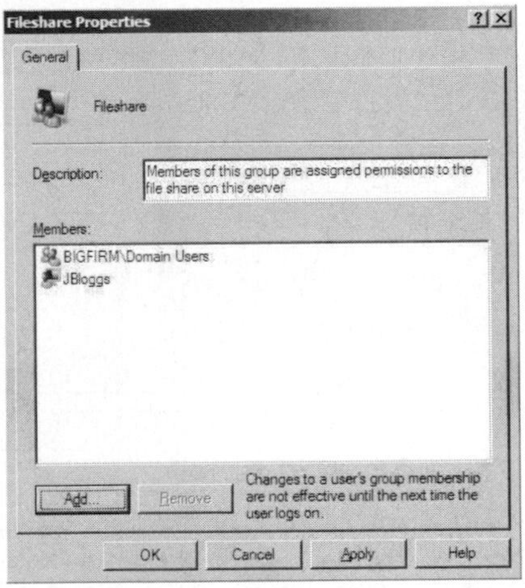

It's time for you to see how you can add members to a group using the command prompt. You'll be using net localgroup again:

```
net localgroup Fileshare jbloggs /add
```

That's a pretty simple command to add a user to a group. The syntax is pretty simple:

```
net localgroup Fileshare <name of object to add to the group> /add
```

The following quickly adds the Domain Users group from the BigFirm domain to your new local group:

```
net localgroup Fileshare "bigfirm\domain users" /add
```

Remember that Member Of tab in the local user account properties dialog box? Let's take a look at the user account object of JBloggs in Figure 7.50.

FIGURE 7.50

The user's group memberships

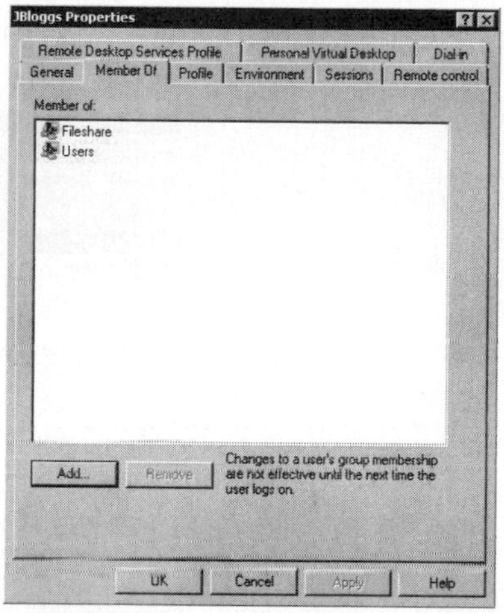

You can see that his group membership has been updated. You can just as easily add Joe to a group here. You have been asked to add Joe's local user account to the local Administrators group. This will make him an administrator of this server and only this server.

Click Add, and the dialog box in Figure 7.51 opens. You type in the name of the group that you want to add this user to. Then click Check Names to be sure that you have the group name correct. Note that you can only add local user accounts into local groups. You cannot add local users to domain groups.

FIGURE 7.51

Adding a user to a group via the user properties

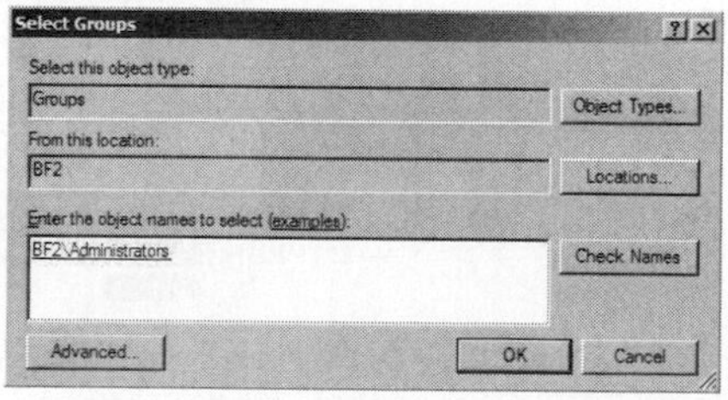

The listing of group memberships for the local user account has now been updated, as you can see in Figure 7.52. Click OK to save these changes.

The only way to replicate this using the command prompt is to manipulate the group itself instead of the user:

```
net localgroup administrators jbloggs /add
```

REMOVING A USER

Removing a user from a local group is easy too. You can do this in either of these ways:

◆ *Using the user account*: Use the user account if this is a one-off operation or if you're removing multiple rights from a user.

◆ *Using the group*: Use the group if you're removing identical rights from many users.

FIGURE 7.52
The user's group
memberships

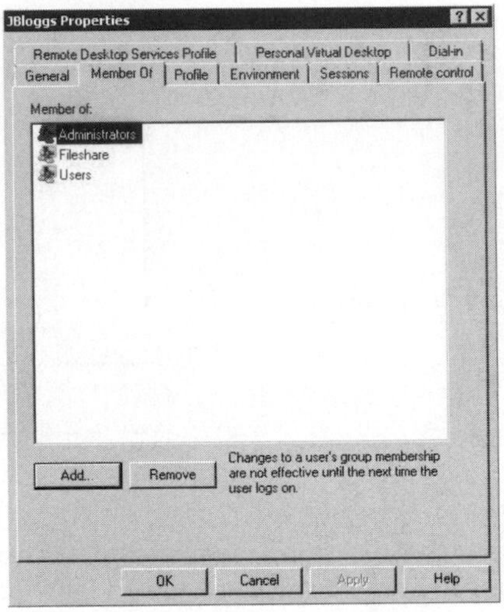

We'll now show how to modify the membership of Fileshare by removing Joe Bloggs. Open the properties of Fileshare, as shown in Figure 7.53.

FIGURE 7.53
Removing a user
from a local group

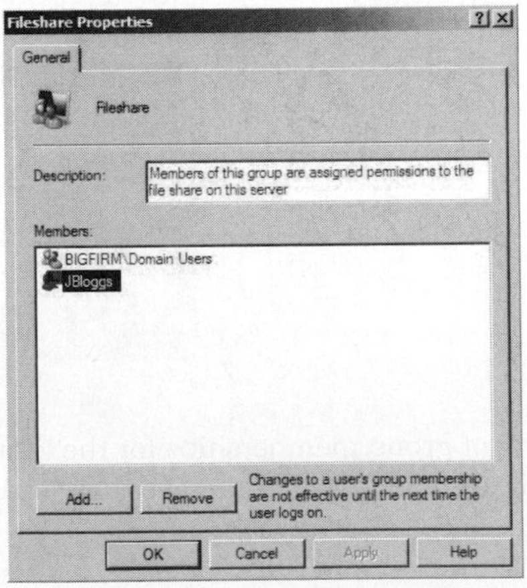

Select JBloggs. You can select more than one member to remove by using the Shift or Ctrl key. Click Remove once you have highlighted the members to remove. That's it; there's nothing more to removing a member from a group.

The following command will remove Joe Bloggs from the Fileshare group:

```
net localgroup fileshare jbloggs /delete
```

To delete a group using the MMC snap-in, you should browse to it and select it. You can then right-click the group and select Delete. Take note of the dialog box in Figure 7.54 that appears when you say you're going to delete a group. You are about to affect many users or computers who are members of this group.

FIGURE 7.54
Are you really sure
you want to delete
the group?

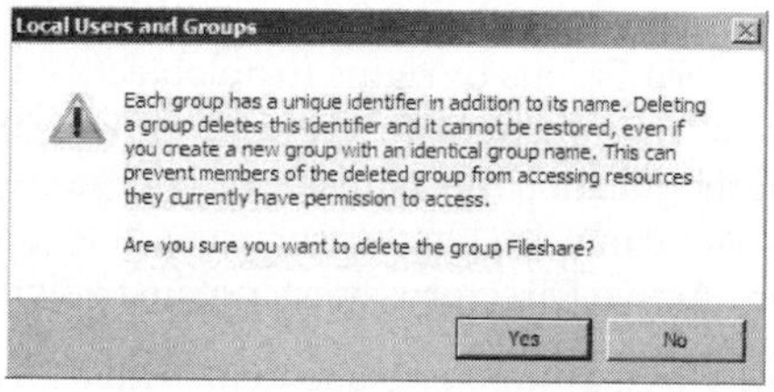

IT'S TIME TO PAY CLOSE ATTENTION AGAIN

This is important enough for us to repeat it: although you see users, computers, and groups as relatively friendly names such as JBloggs, BF2, or Fileshare, Windows does not. It uniquely identifies these *security principals* using a SID. A unique SID is created every time a new security principal is created. This means that if you create JBloggs, delete it, and re-create it, Windows will see the old and new objects as two different security principals. You see them as one, but they are not. The result is that permissions assigned to the old account are not retained by the new account. This is done deliberately to prevent administrators from trying to hijack an account.

The pop-up in Figure 7.54 warns you of this. You must be sure that the organization is 100 percent sure that it no longer needs a security principal before it deletes it. Here, you need to know that once you delete a group, its assigned permissions, as well as the group membership, are lost. Any user who was granted access to a resource, such as a file share, via membership of this group will lose access to that resource.

The following net localgroup command will delete the Fileshare group without any warnings or requests for confirmation:

```
net localgroup fileshare /delete
```

Active Directory Groups

The basic concept of Active Directory or domain-based groups does not differ from that of local groups. You use them to collectively treat a number of objects in an identical manner. However, you can do a lot more with Active Directory groups. This is made possible because this type of group is stored in Active Directory on domain controllers and a subset of domain controllers that are configured to be global catalogs. This enables a single group to contain many domain-based security principals, such as users and computers, and to be used across all computers within the domain that the group resides. In fact, you can use groups outside of their native domain, and there is even a category that can contain members from any domain in a forest.

For the purpose of this section, you should assume that when we say *group*, we mean Active Directory group. These are the two basic group types:

Distribution group   A distribution group is used to group a number of objects together that will be addressed collectively. A mail server, such as Microsoft Exchange, can present the distribution group to users as a destination address. The user can choose to send a mail to the distribution group, and the mail server will attempt to send the mail to all members of the group, assuming that they have email addresses configured.

Security group   A security group can also perform the mail distribution function. But its primary purpose of this type is given away by the name: security. You can use a security group to assign permissions or rights to an object or a set of objects, such as an organizational unit, a folder, or a component of an application. This allows Active Directory to become not only your single authentication mechanism for your network but also your authorization mechanism. An end user can use a single user account to gain authorization to secured resources across the entire Active Directory forest, not just a domain or a single computer.

There are three group scopes to deal with as well:

Domain local group   A domain local group is intended to be used only within the domain that it was created in. It can contain user/computer accounts, global groups, and universal groups from any domain in the forest and domain local groups from the same domain.

Global group   This is the default scope when you create a group in Active Directory. A global group can be used by computers within the domain that it is a member of and by members of other domains in the Active Directory forest. It can contain user/computer accounts from the domain that the global group is created in.

Universal group   One thing makes a universal group very different from both of the other group types. Both of the others are stored and replicated to all domain controllers within the domain that they were created in. A universal group is stored on domain controllers that are configured as global catalogs. This implies that the universal group is replicated to domains across the entire forest. That allows a universal group not only to able to be used by all computers in the forest but also to contain members from any domain within the forest.

Great care must be taken when designing a universal group in larger environments because you are adding to replication loads when you create or modify them. Active Directory will only replicate the changes to universal groups, but just be careful of large-scale changes. You also need to be sure that global catalog–enabled domain controllers are close to services that rely heavily on them. Single-domain networks do not really need to worry too much about universal groups because there isn't much use for them. Universal groups can contain user/computer accounts, global groups, and other universal groups from any domain in the forest.

You probably just noticed something there. Groups can contain other groups. This is commonly referred to as *group nesting*. Why would you consider doing this? Here are two things to consider:

◆   Say you have groups called Accounts Management and Sales Management. You want to be able to deal with both of them at once, maybe having one email address for them all that you will treat as a contact list. You can create a group called Management and add each of the three accounts as members. You can then configure an email address for the Management group.

♦ Another scenario, shown in Figure 7.55, is where you have created organizational units for different departments; for example, say you have \BigFirm, which contains \BigFirm \Accounts and \BigFirm\Sales. There are two levels of IT. BigFirm has an IT department that runs Active Directory and corporate IT functions. You work in this department. Both Accounts and Sales have small IT teams that can only manage objects in their OUs. This is called *delegation*. You want to be able to have a group called Management that will contain managers for all departments. You do not want to manage these members, and you want departmental IT staff to manage the process instead. You can create the group Accounts Management in \BigFirm\Accounts and Sales Management in \BigFirm\Sales. This allows departmental IT to manage those two groups. Create the group Management in \BigFirm. Now you can add the departmental groups as members of Management.

FIGURE 7.55
Nested groups

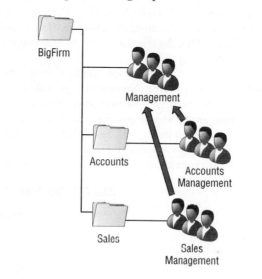

As you can see, there's a little more to Active Directory groups than there is to local groups. It is important to understand why you are creating a group and how that group will be used before you create the group. You can change group scopes and group types, but you must understand what the impact will be, such as that changing from a global group to a universal group will alter Active Directory replication from being between domain controllers within a domain to being between global catalog servers across an entire forest. The extra little bit of planning is well worth the effort as you will find as you progress through the rest of this book. As time goes by, you will find yourself using groups for all sorts of things:

♦ Assigning permissions to file shares

♦ Creating email distribution groups containing members across an entire corporate forest

♦ Assigning rights for deploying operating systems

◆ Controlling what computers will receive an automated deployment of Microsoft Visio

◆ Controlling who will be targeted by a Group Policy object

◆ Delegating administrative rights to parts of Active Directory

You may be thinking that the concept of group nesting sounds pretty complex and nasty. When you combine this with a descriptive naming standard for your groups, you can create a group mechanism that is very easy to deploy and manage and that allows for granular delegated administration.

CREATING ACTIVE DIRECTORY GROUPS

It's time for you to create some Active Directory groups. Say you want to create a group that will be used only within your domain. It will be used to assign rights to anyone who is a manager in the organization. This description tells you that you need a domain local group scope and that you need a security group type.

Earlier you created an OU called \BigFirm\Security Groups within the bigfirm.com domain. Navigate there using Active Directory Users and Groups. Right-click, and select New ➢ Group. This opens the New Object – Group dialog box.

Enter **Management** as the group name. This automatically fills in the pre–Windows 2000 group name, as shown in Figure 7.56, which is maintained to maintain backward compatibility with legacy operating systems. You selected the desired group scope of Domain Local and kept the default group type of Security. You can click the OK button to create the group.

FIGURE 7.56
Creating a
new Active
Directory group

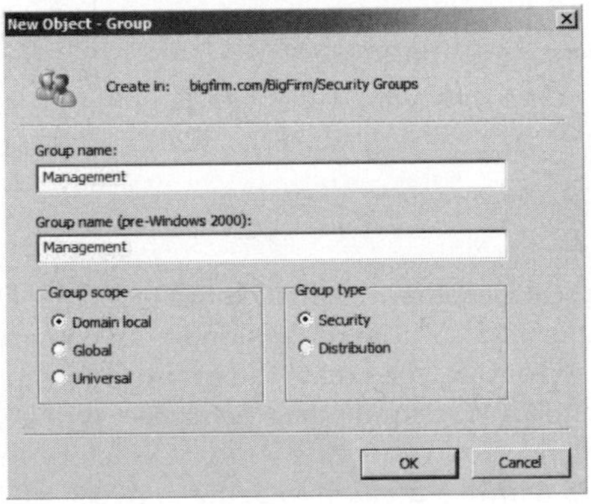

You've probably noticed that you didn't have the option to edit the properties of the group while you created it. You'll probably want to add a description and add members to the group. You can do this by right-clicking the group and selecting Properties to open the Management Properties dialog box shown in Figure 7.57.

We've already typed in the description for the group. This form of documentation makes it immediately clear to administrators what the purpose of the group is. We discussed the need to do this when we covered local groups. It's infinitely more important to document in this way when dealing with medium to large-sized Active Directory setups where there may be teams of administrators working with the servers.

DMANAGING USERACCOUNTS

FIGURE 7.57
Adding a group
description

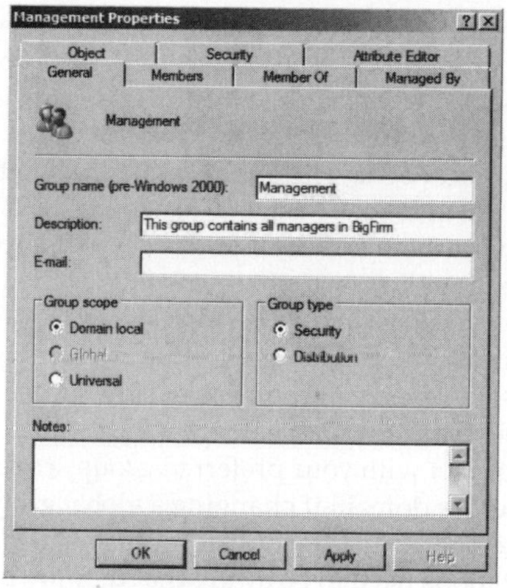

GROUP NAMING STANDARDS

It is important to adopt a naming standard for groups if your domain will grow to be large or it will be part of a forest. Remember that groups can be used anywhere within a domain or even an Active Directory forest. Even with just two domain controllers, you can support a large user base and a complex organization. How meaningful do you think the name Management would be in an organization containing hundreds or thousands of users? What about a corporate or government forest with many domains and tens of thousands of employees? Management is possibly suitable for a small/medium organization with a single site and a small IT team.

If you had an organization with many departments or many sites, you might consider having Milan—Accounts Management and Milan—IT Management. It immediately visible that each of these group names are associated with an office in the city of Milan and that the members of the groups are members of management for a department. If you had many domains in a forest, you could consider something like BigFirm—Milan—Senior Management. Any administrator in any domain in the forest knows that the group is from the BigFirm domain, the members are from the Milan office, and all members are from the senior management team in that office.

The bottom of the General tab shows you the type and scope of the group. You may notice that you can change these. However, there are some things to consider before making changes here.

Changing a group from being a security group to a distribution group means that it cannot be used for assigning permissions anymore. You are warned that any permission assigned using this group may fail to function anymore. This is especially important if you are denying access to critical resources using this group.

We've tested this with file shares to see how it worked. We shared a folder using a security group and added some members. We also applied permissions to the folder on the file system. We verified that the members had access to the share and everything looked good. We changed the group type to a distribution group. We checked the share and folder permissions, and the distribution group still had rights. Testing user access showed that the user still had rights to the folder. So far, so good. We then logged the user out and back in again. Uh-oh; the user lost rights. The group that is now a distribution group still has rights but is no longer effective. We then reversed the group back to being a security group. A logout and login was required to give the test user access to the share again.

This is typical behavior for groups. Anything that will affect members typically requires the user to log out and back in again. That's the third time we've stated this in this chapter; it has definitely been the solution to almost every group membership and rights assignment question we have dealt with at work. Remember this when you grant a user rights to a resource by adding them to a group.

You cannot directly change a group from being a domain local group to a global group, or vice versa. However, you can change either scope to being a universal group. From there, you can change it back to either a domain local or a global group. Make sure that the member list does not conflict with your preferred group scope. You need to be sure that your group is not used in another domain if changing a global group to a domain local group. This would cause loss of access to secured resources for members of the group. Administrators in larger forest implementations need to be aware that they are potentially adding new traffic to global catalog replication when converting an existing group into a universal group.

The member functionality for domain-based groups works just like that of local groups. Open the properties of a group in Figure 7.58. You can add and remove members using the Add and Remove buttons.

FIGURE 7.58

Adding new members to the Active Directory group

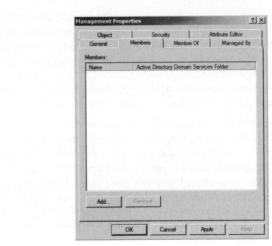

As you can see in Figure 7.59, domain-based groups are capable of containing more types of objects than local groups can, such as the following:

Other objects   This flexible solution allows you to add members that are created by applications, that is, not the usual users, computers, or groups.

Contacts   These objects are created in Active Directory to store contact information about people or organizations. This could be used for distribution groups.

Service accounts   This is a new feature of Windows Server 2008 R2 where you can set up dedicated service accounts instead of creating user accounts and assigning them to services.

FIGURE 7.59
Selecting
potential member
object types

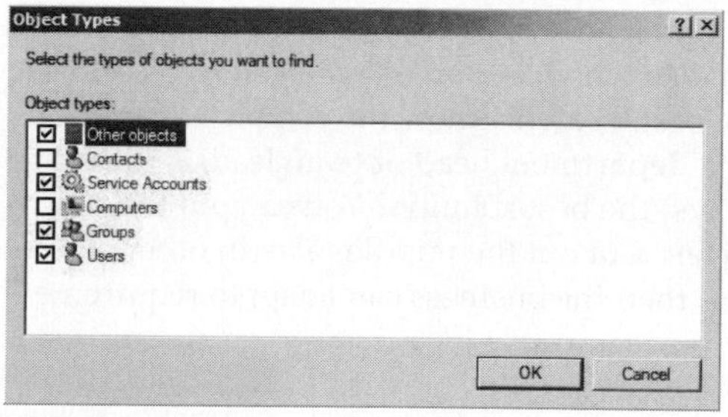

Seeing as you're dealing with the member list of a domain-based group, you cannot add security principals that are local machine based, that is, local users or local groups. These security principals exist only on their computer, so it makes no sense to add them to a domain-wide or forest-wide group. For this reason, the Locations dialog box in Figure 7.60 presents only domains that exist in your forest.

FIGURE 7.60
Choosing new
member object
location

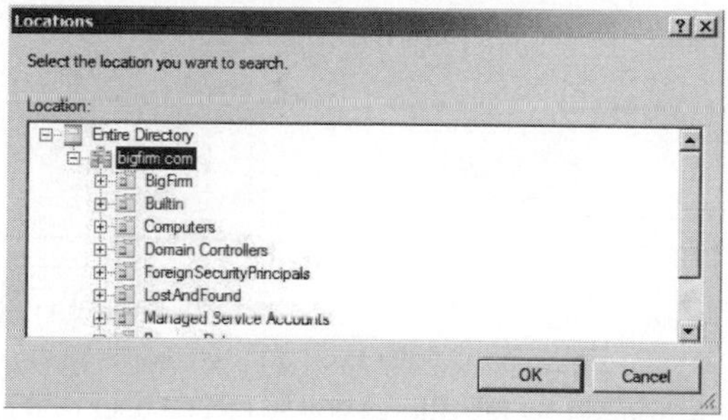

Domain-based groups can be nested; that is, a group can be a member of another group. The Member Of tab in the group's properties, shown in Figure 7.61, allows you to manage what groups this group is a member of.

FIGURE 7.61
What groups
is this group a
member of?

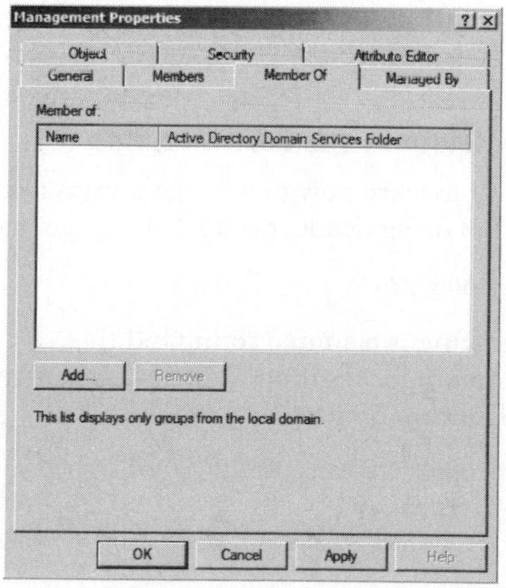

The Managed By tab in Figure 7.62 is a nice little feature. As an administrator, you probably have no idea who has a business reason to access secured data. You have enough to do to run the network, let alone know the complete operations of the business. The owner of the data, usually a department head or team lead, is the best person to decide this. What is often (but not always) the best solution? You can put the power of access control into the hands of the data owner. Cut out the middle man, in other words, IT. If the owner can mange access to the resource, then the business can adapt to requirements as needs arise.

FIGURE 7.62
Active Directory
group Managed
By tab

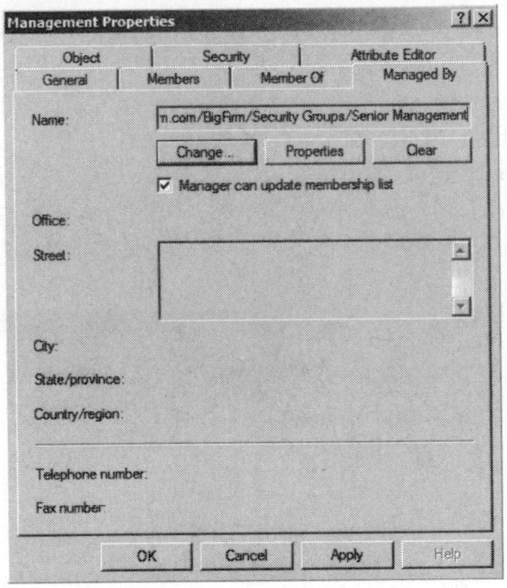

The Managed By tab allows you to elect a user or a group that can be the owner of this group. This group can be assigned rights to resources. We've saved the best bit for last. The selected owner can be given rights to manage the membership of the group by selecting the "Manager can update membership list" box. Superb! You don't have to give the manager rights to the mange the security rights of a shared folder. Can you imagine the disasters that could arise from that? The simple solution is to let them manage the membership of groups that have the right to use the shared folder. All you have to do is give them a mechanism for editing the group membership, such as the Active Directory Users and Computers snap-in, a script, or maybe a web applet.

CREATING A GROUP AT THE COMMAND LINE

It's important to learn how to manage groups from the command line. You'll first look at how to create a group using dsadd group. You can get more help by typing the following:

```
dsadd group /?
```

The following is a simple command that re-creates what you can do in the GUI. It creates a domain local group called Management in the \Bigfirm\Security Groups OU in the bigfirm.com domain.

```
dsadd group "CN=Management, OU=Security Groups,OU=BigFirm,DC=bigfirm,
DC=com" -scope 1
```

Here's the syntax:

```
dsadd group <distinguished name of the new group> -scope <Domain Local
= l | Global = g | Universal = u>
```

By default, this creates a security group. You can actually leave out the `-scope` option if a global group is what you want. You can make a global distribution group instead by running this:

```
dsadd group "CN=Management, OU=Security Groups,OU=BigFirm,DC=bigfirm,
DC=com" -secgrp no -scope g
```

The change in the syntax is as follows:

```
-secgrp <security group = yes | distribution group = no>
```

The default is to create a security group. You don't need to use this option in your command if a security group is what you need to create.

Remember that the GUI for creating domain-based groups didn't offer you anything other than the ability to create the group? You had to go back into the properties of the group to set the properties or add members? Well, you can use this command:

```
dsadd group "CN=Senior Management, OU=Security Groups,OU=BigFirm,
DC=bigfirm,DC=com" -scope g -desc "This group contains senior managers"
 -memberof "CN=Management,OU=Security Groups,OU=BigFirm,DC=bigfirm,DC=com"
 -members "CN=Joe Bloggs,OU=Users,OU=BigFirm,DC=bigfirm,DC=com"
 "CN=Alexandra Garcia,OU=Users,OU=BigFirm,DC=bigfirm,DC=com"
```

This command has done quite a bit. You've created a global security group called Senior Management in the Security Groups OU. You've set the group description to "This group contains senior managers." The Senior Management group was added as a member of the Managers group. And finally, you have added two users to the new Senior Managers group.

You can use the `dsmod group` command to modify an existing group. Here's the command to get some help:

```
dsmod group /?
```

This command will add Joe Bloggs and Alexandra Garcia to the Management group:

```
dsmod group "CN=Management, OU=Security Groups,OU=BigFirm,DC=bigfirm,DC=com"
 -addmbr "CN=Joe Bloggs,OU=Users,OU=BigFirm,DC=bigfirm,DC=com" "CN=Alexandra
 Garcia,OU=Users,OU=BigFirm,DC=bigfirm,DC=com"
```

The syntax is as follows:

```
dsmod group <DN of the group to manage> -addmbr
<DN's of the users to add to the group>
```

Next you want to remove Joe Bloggs from the group:

```
dsmod group "CN=Management, OU=Security Groups,OU=BigFirm,DC=bigfirm,DC=com"
 -rmmbr "CN=Joe Bloggs,OU=Users,OU=BigFirm,DC=bigfirm,DC=com"
```

You can erase the existing member list of a group and add a replacement member list by running this:

```
dsmod group "CN=Management, OU=Security Groups,OU=BigFirm,DC=bigfirm,DC=com"
 -chmbr "CN=Joe Bloggs,OU=Users,OU=BigFirm,DC=bigfirm,DC=com"
```

You can change the group scope to universal by running this:

```
dsmod group "CN=Management, OU=Security Groups,OU=BigFirm,DC=bigfirm,DC=com"
 -scope u
```

The syntax for the -scope option is as follows:

```
-scope <Domain Local = l | Global = g | Universal = u>
```

One disappointment here is that you cannot set the manager properties for a group using dsmod group.

How about deleting a group? That's pretty easy:

```
dsrm "CN=Management, OU=Security Groups,OU=BigFirm,DC=big firm,DC=com"
```

This command will delete the Management group. You'll get prompted to confirm the deletion. You can skip that by running this:

```
dsrm "CN=Management, OU=Security Groups,OU=BigFirm,DC=big firm,DC=com" -noprompt
```

Monday-Morning Admin Tasks

We'll now cover some common operational tasks that you may find yourself doing regularly. Our experience is that anyone in a help-desk role will find their Monday mornings consumed by these tasks if they don't carefully consider how to design their authentication mechanisms. Check out the discussions on passphrases and smart cards earlier in this chapter to see what we mean. We'll cover domain-based security principals because this is what you will find yourself working with the vast majority of the time.

Forgotten Passwords

The first challenge is dealing with a person who can't remember their password. This is usually the number-one call to the help desk after the weekend. Let's see how you can reset that password for your user. After all, the user is your customer, and you need to provide quality and timely service. If you are using the GUI, then you need to navigate to the user account in question in Active Directory Users and Computers. Then right-click the user and select Reset Password to open the Reset Password dialog box.

You can now enter in a new password for the user, as shown in Figure 7.63. This new password must comply with the password policies that apply to the user. Odds are that you are going to be communicating this password to the user over the phone. Our experience is that you should use a password that is easy to communicate. Be wary that you may be dealing with people whose first language is not the same as yours. Something like Password123456789 is easy to communicate over the phone and complies with the default password requirements. See that the check box to force the user to change their password after logon is selected? This is the default. This is very convenient because, as you can see, the password that you gave to this user is probably the same one that you will use for every user. Forcing the user to change their password will secure their user account, and this means that no one in IT will know their password.

FIGURE 7.63
Resetting the
user password

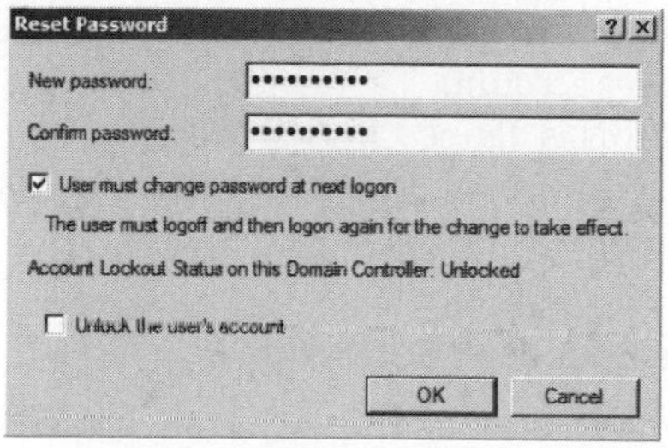

At the bottom is the check box to unlock the account. You can select this just in case the user has been locked out of their account. Users who aren't IT savvy might not be able to understand or communicate the messages on their desktop that explain why they can't log in. Changing the user's password without unlocking the account won't help them log in. It won't do any harm to select this check box if you're dealing with an unsure-sounding user or a repeat offender.

Here's how you can change a user's password using the dsmod user command:

```
C:\Users\Administrator>dsmod user "CN=Joe Bloggs,OU=Users,OU=BigFirm,
DC=bigfirm, DC=com" -pwd *
Enter User Password:

Confirm user password:

dsmod succeeded:CN=Joe Bloggs,OU=Users,OU=BigFirm,DC=bigfirm,DC=com
```

The -pwd * option instructs the command that you will enter the new password and confirm it. Alternatively, you can reset the password in the command:

```
dsmod user "CN=Joe Bloggs,OU=Users,OU=BigFirm,DC=bigfirm,DC=com"
 -pwd Password12345678
```

You can use an additional option with either of these commands to force the user to change their password when they log on:

```
dsmod user "CN=Joe Bloggs,OU=Users,OU=BigFirm,DC=bigfirm,DC=com"
 -pwd Password12345678 -mustchpwd yes
```

Locked-Out Users

Account lockout policies...oh, boy! Pretty much most of the "security experts" you will encounter on the Internet or in person love their "3 failed logons in 30 minutes should cause a lockout" policy. You know what? That's a great recipe for facilitating a denial-of-service attack. Get access to a desktop computer in your forest with an ordinary user account for a couple of minutes, and you can run a script that will fail five logons for every user on your Active Directory in no time at all. Every single user except for the default domain administrator accounts will be locked out. That'll shut down your business. It's for this reason that real security experts have been telling us to really think hard about using the lockout option for passwords. (Check out the earlier "The Case for Passphrases" sidebar to see an alternative.) It's for this reason that lockouts are disabled by default in the Default Domain Policy. Our opinion is that this is a very good thing. Nevertheless, some organizations will enable this policy. They may have a valid reason for it. For this reason, it's important to know how to unlock a user account.

Note that this is defined in Active Directory in the Default Domain Group Policy object (GPO). The default setting in Windows Server 2008 R2 is 0, that is, to not lock out user accounts after failed login attempts.

Two Simple Lock-Out Scenarios

The first scenario is when the user has reported that their computer is informing them that they are locked out. They know their password, so you don't need to reset it. You can navigate to the user account in Active Directory Users and Computers and open the properties of the account.

You can see in the Account tab, shown in Figure 7.64, that there is a message to inform you that the account is locked out. The solution is simple. You can unlock the account. Of course, the user may have forgotten their password, so you may need to reset that as well.

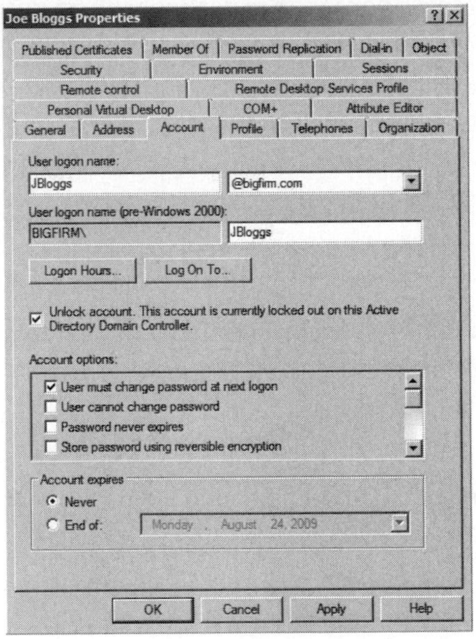

FIGURE 7.64
Active Directory
user locked out

The second scenario is the user whose only knowledge of their problem is that they cannot log in. There could be two problems here (to start with). The user could have forgotten their password, or they could have a locked account. You should just kill two birds with one stone and deal with both possibilities. You can open the dialog box to rest the user's password, shown in Figure 7.65.

Unfortunately, it appears that there is no command-line option for unlocking user accounts.

With that, we've covered all the options for basic user and group management that are common to both Windows Server 2008 and Windows Server 2008 R2. We'll now move on to cover what is new in Windows Server 2008 R2.

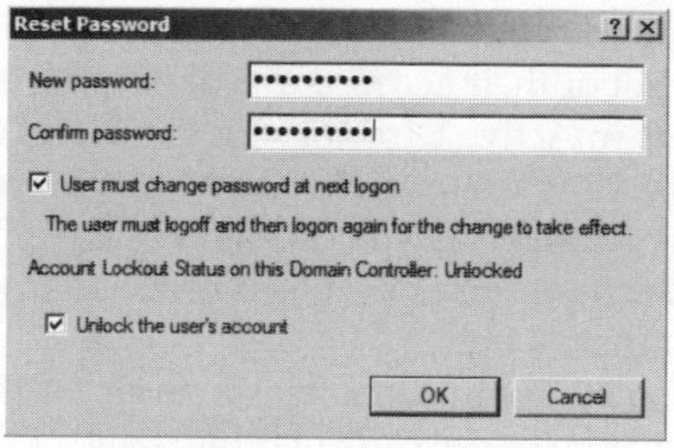

FIGURE 7.65
Unlocking user
account and
resetting password

What's New in Windows Server 2008 R2 for User and Group Management

Everything we have discussed in this chapter applies to both Windows Server 2008 and Windows Server 2008 R2. Windows Server 2008 R2 has two significant changes that are relevant to basic user and group management:

◆ Microsoft has added a new task-oriented GUI utility called the Active Directory Administrative Center (ADAC).

◆ Microsoft has added native PowerShell support for managing users and groups. This means you have a new command-line interface and a new scripting solution for doing the work discussed in this chapter.

Windows Server 2008 didn't have a native PowerShell method for managing Active Directory. However, you can download Quest's Free PowerShell Commands for Active Directory from http://tinyurl.com/5otmff. We'll be covering the native Windows Server 2008 R2 PowerShell cmdlets.

Active Directory Administrative Center

Microsoft added this new administrative tool to give you a more task-oriented command interface. Active Directory Users and Computers, a general administrative tool, has been with us since Windows 2000. Microsoft wanted to provide something to make it quick and easy to do frequent, repetitive tasks, such as dealing with those user lockouts on Monday mornings. You'll find Active Directory Administrative Center (ADAC) in Administrative Tools on a Windows Server 2008 R2 domain controller. You can also use it on Windows 7 if you install the Remote Server Administration Tools for Windows 7 (http://tinyurl.com/yers2eq). It takes a little longer than Active Directory Users and Computers to load, so you might fire this up in the morning and leave it running.

ADAC ESSENTIALS

You can see what we mean by "task-oriented" when ADAC opens, as shown in Figure 7.66. Right there in front of you in the center pane is an interface dedicated to resetting passwords and unlocking user accounts. Those are the most common Active Directory tasks for IT, so it makes sense that the tool is right there.

What happens without ADAC when a user calls the corporate help desk asking to have their password reset or their account unlocked? The help-desk engineer needs to search the organizational units in Active Directory for the user. Then they have to right-click the user and perform the task. This assumes the help-desk engineer knows how to search Active Directory. It's also time-consuming. As you can see in Figure 7.66, with ADAC the help-desk engineer simply enters the username and new password. The Unlock Account option is grayed out because the account isn't locked out.

ADAC also makes finding objects easier for that help-desk engineer. You can see in Figure 7.67 that he or she can enter the name of the object to search for.

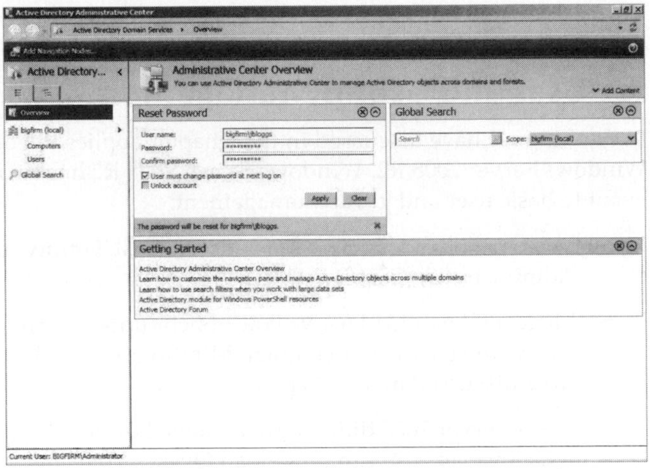

FIGURE 7.66
Resetting a user
password in ADAC

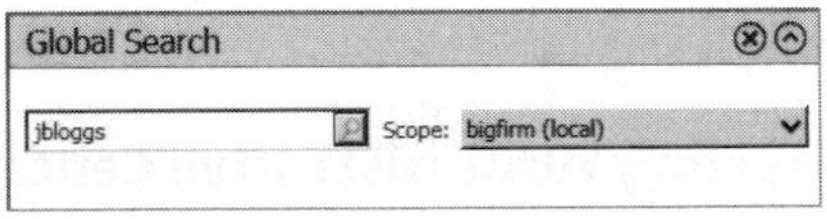

FIGURE 7.67
Searching for
an Active
Directory object

Figure 7.68 shows the results of that search. You can see how easy it was to search for JBloggs. The engineer can easily right-click this user object to perform administrative tasks on it. The search tool is pretty clever because it searches attributes of the object, that is, the object properties. The engineer could have searched for *J*, *Joe*, or *Joe Bloggs* and still found the JBloggs user object. This isn't limited to user objects either! You can search for any type of object in the domain, such as groups and computers.

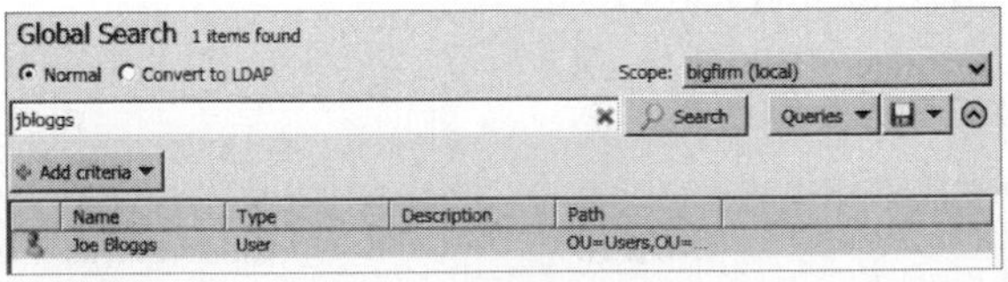

FIGURE 7.68
Finding the
user object

You can reach the Global Search tool by clicking Global Search in the navigation pane on the left. This allows you to jump right in and access some more powerful search options.

Clicking Add Criteria gives you some really powerful options to qualify the search, as shown in Figure 7.69. Look at those built-in criteria and imagine how useful they could be. Every morning you could kick off the day by searching for locked-out accounts and dealing with them before people get in. In the user section of this chapter, we recommended that you disable accounts instead of immediately deleting them. To use one of these criteria, select the associated box, and then click the Add button.

FIGURE 7.69

Potential search criteria

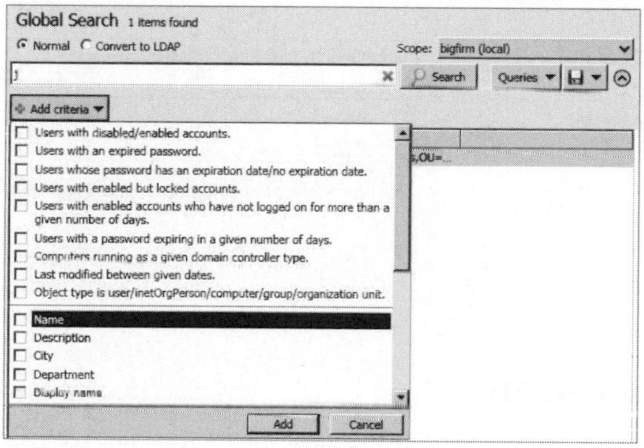

In the figure, we've selected the option "Users with enabled accounts who have not logged on for more than this number of days." You can see on the right of Figure 7.70 where you can select a number of days from a predefined range of options. This is very useful. Ideally, the human resources department should communicate with IT whenever an employee leaves the company. However, we are human, and we make mistakes. Using this query, you can identify "stale" user accounts and disable them. You can remove a search criterion by clicking the red X on the right.

FIGURE 7.70

Finding all users who have not logged in for 15 days

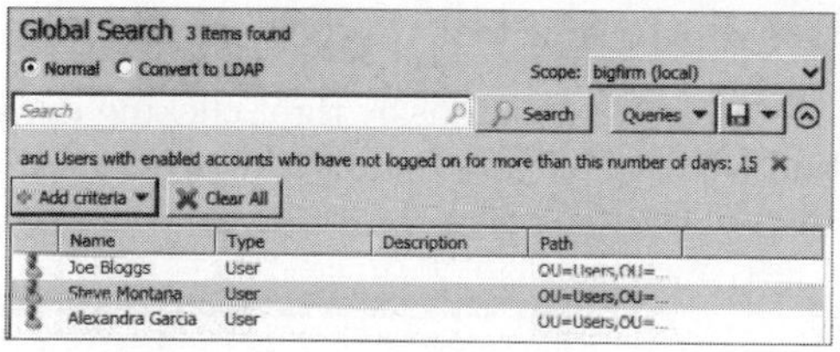

Figure 7.71 shows a more complex query. The object type is Computer, and the object name starts with *B*. This means you won't get search results that are polluted with other object types such as groups, users, and OUs.

FIGURE 7.71

Adding many search criteria

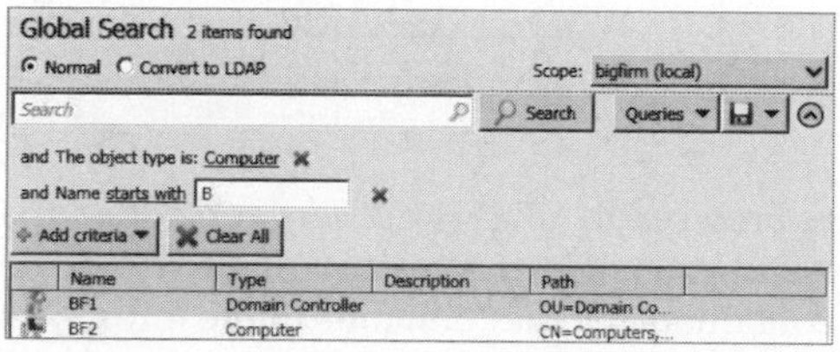

You can use that little disk icon on the right to save your query for later reuse. You give the query a name (use something descriptive), and you can access the query again by clicking the Queries drop-down box. That will load and execute the query for you.

Once you have found an object, you will want to do something with it. When you select an object, the Tasks pane on the right will display context-sensitive actions. There are examples of these context-sensitive tasks in Figure 7.72. You can click one of those tasks to manage the selected object.

FIGURE 7.72
Context-
sensitive tasks

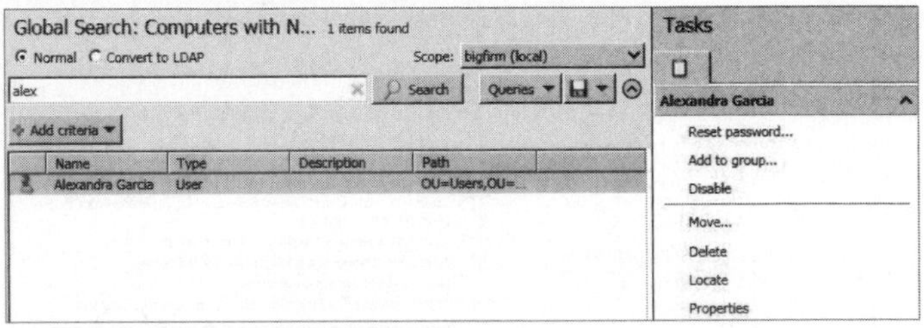

NAVIGATING ADAC

Now that we've covered the basics, let's start navigating ADAC. The navigation pane has a list view (the default) and a tree view. The list view contains a preselected set of locations. This includes the following:

◆ The Administrative Center Overview where you started out and where you can quickly deal with basic user requests and simple searches.

◆ The domain from which you can jump into any OU or container

◆ The Users and Computers containers where you're ideally not adding anything

◆ The Global Search tool, which we've already covered

You can add other locations by right-clicking in the navigation pane and selecting Add Navigation Nodes. That opens a window where you can navigate your Active Directory structure, shown in Figure 7.73.

FIGURE 7.73
Adding a naviga-
tion node

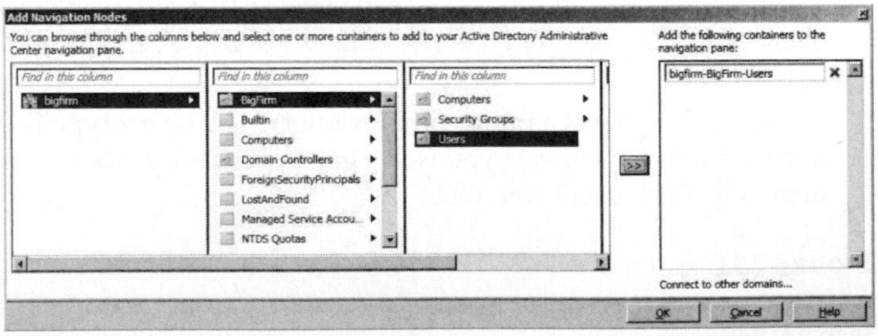

You've browsed to \BigFirm\Users and added that OU to the control in the right side of the window. Did you notice that you can use the "Connect to other domains..." control to navigate to OUs or containers in other domains in the forest? You can use this to manage many domains in many forests at once with ADAC.

In Figure 7.74, you can see that we have clicked OK to add the \BigFirm\Users OU to the list view in ADAC. Now you can quickly get to the OU where you are managing user accounts, another time-saver for day-to-day administration. You can see that the Tasks pane now contains new actions, allowing you to perform administration within the OU.

FIGURE 7.74
Using a
navigation node

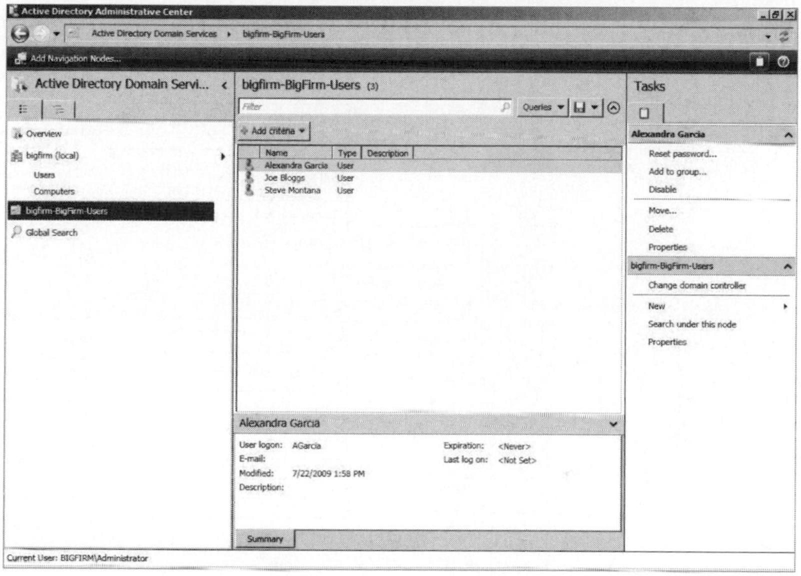

Note that any navigation nodes you create will appear in both the tree and list views.

The tree view in the navigation pane in Figure 7.75 gives you the more traditional navigation method you're used to having in ADUC.

FIGURE 7.75
The tree view
in ADAC

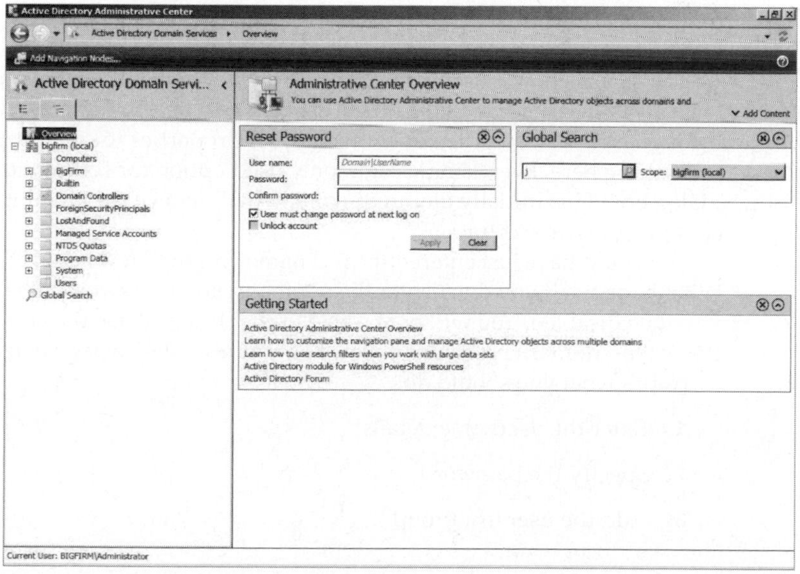

Let's do some work. In this example, you'll create a user. Navigate to \BigFirm\Users using the new navigation node that you just created in the list view, and click New ➢ User in the Tasks pane. That opens up the dialog box shown in Figure 7.76.

FIGURE 7.76
Creating a new
user in ADAC

FIGURE 7.76
Creating a new
user in ADAC

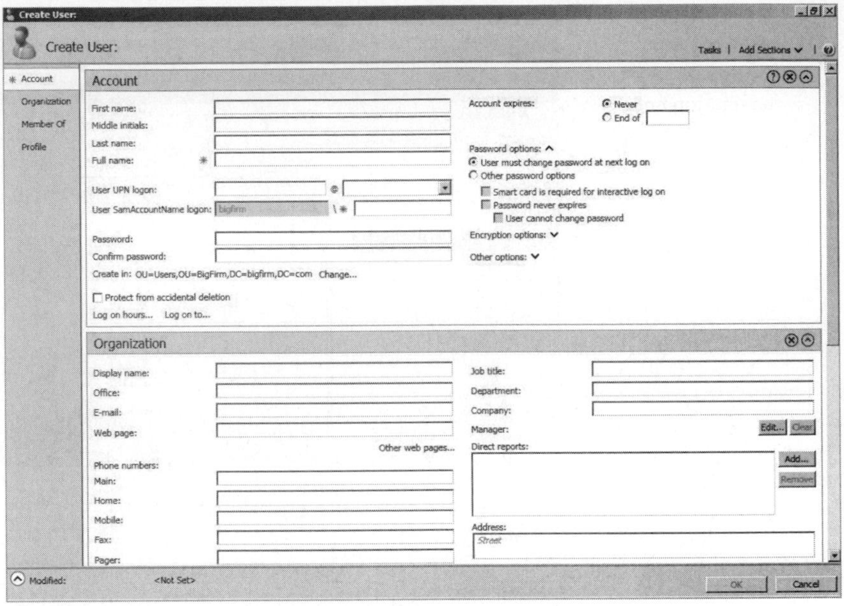

Wow! That's a hefty dialog box, and it might be a bit daunting at first. Let's take a look around before you do anything. First, let's simplify things. You only need to complete the fields with a red * beside them to be allowed to create a user. The left navigation pane tips you off that this window is broken up into sections. You can use the Add Sections button on the top right to hide or reveal those sections. This allows you to hide any section that you never use. ADAC will remember what sections are hidden or revealed.

You can see how we've removed the Organization and Profile sections in Figure 7.77. We have also filled out the dialog box to create a new user called Joe Elway. Instead of navigating through a wizard and then opening the user properties to complete the operation, you can do everything here. Every single commonly used option for setting up the user is available in this dialog box. This initially daunting window will reduce the amount of time it takes to create and configure a user account.

You could have just entered the full name and the SAM account name to create this user. What happens if you don't enter the nonmandatory password? The account will be created, but it will be disabled. You will not be able to enable it because the lack of a password contravenes the default domain password policy. You can reset the password and then enable the account.

Here's what you should do:

1. Enter the username details.

2. Specify the password.

3. Add the user to a group.

FIGURE 7.77
Removed dialog
box sections
in ADAC

You can see in Figure 7.78 that when you click OK, the user is created and added to the OU that you were in.

FIGURE 7.78
The new user
appears in the
navigation node.

You probably noticed that not every single attribute or property for user objects was available. The common ones were, but lots of others weren't. In Active Directory, you will probably configure those properties via policies instead. However, you can still access them.

Figure 7.79 shows the properties of the user account in ADAC. A new section appears in the window called Extensions. This allows you to view and configure those advanced features of the object.

FIGURE 7.79
Viewing the user
properties in ADAC

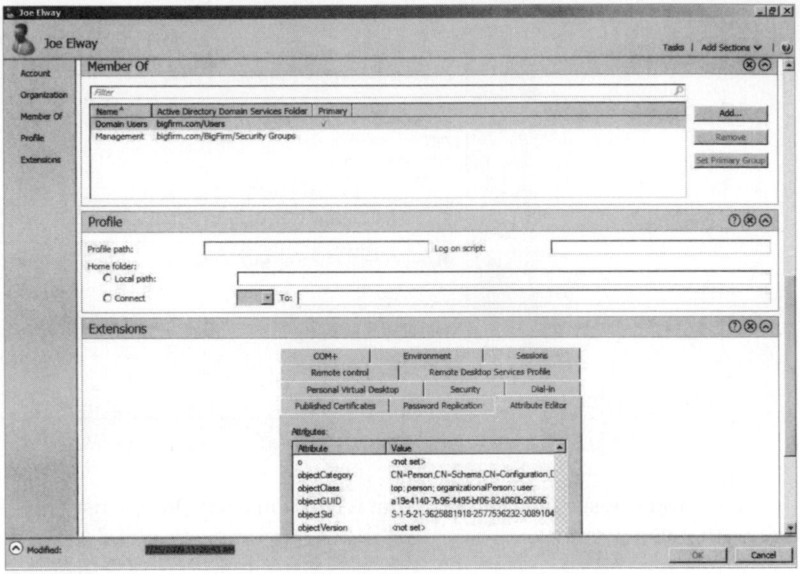

As shown in Figure 7.80, we have returned to the list view and created an additional navigation node for the \BigFirm\Security Groups OU. It's time to manage groups in ADAC. Click New and then Group in the Tasks pane.

FIGURE 7.80
An additional navi-
gation node for
security groups

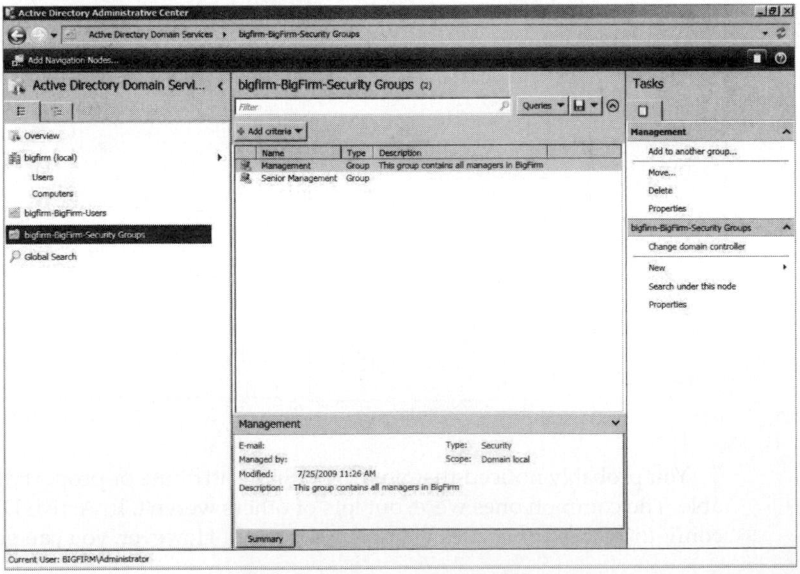

As you can see in Figure 7.81, like with the dialog box for creating a user, you can mask or hide some of the sections. You are going to do that now.

FIGURE 7.81

Creating a new group in ADAC

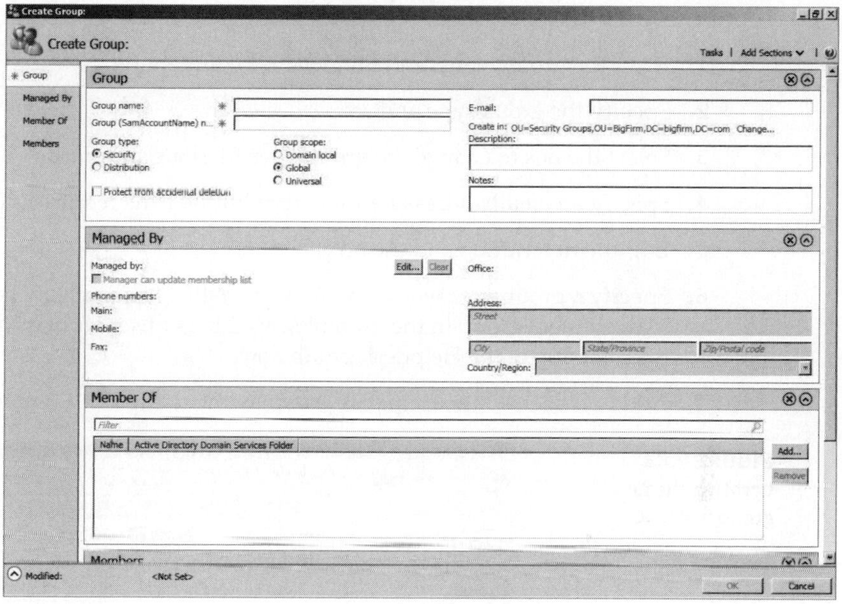

Figure 7.82 shows the simplified view; you can create this look by clicking the Add Sections button to remove the Member Of section.

FIGURE 7.82

A trimmed-down Create Group dialog box

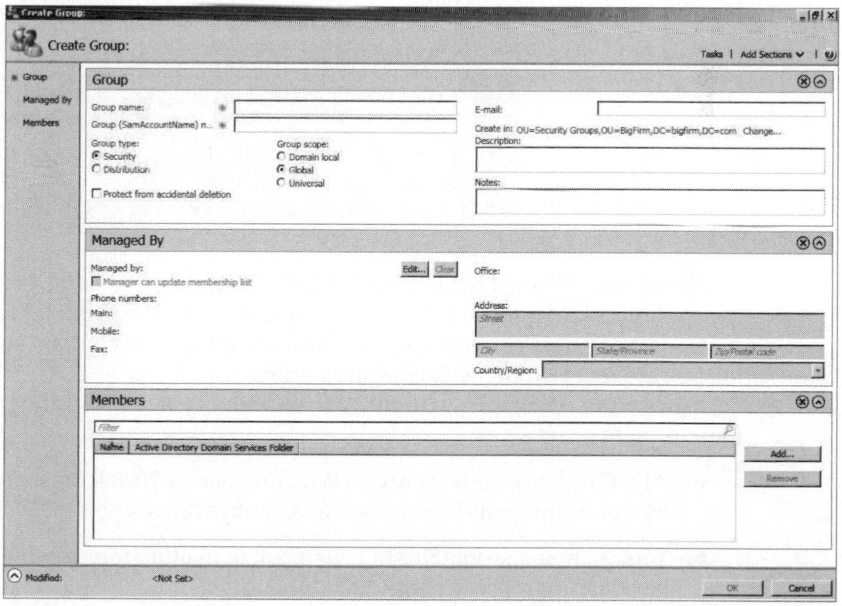

Let's create a group called Helpdesk. Figure 7.83 shows the completed dialog box to create the new Helpdesk group. Again, you can see that you can enter a lot of information into a single dialog box, saving you from going through a wizard and then editing the group object properties afterward. Do the following:

1. Enter the group name, and fill in SamAccountName.

2. Specify the group type and scope.

3. Select the box to change the group's permissions so you can't delete it accidentally.

4. Specify an email address for mail distribution (this requires a compatible mail service).

5. Edit the description and the notes.

6. Specify a group manager who can manage the group membership (we used the Senior Management group in the example). Members of senior management can alter the group membership of the Helpdesk group now.

7. Add two users to the Helpdesk group membership.

FIGURE 7.83
Creating the new
group in ADAC

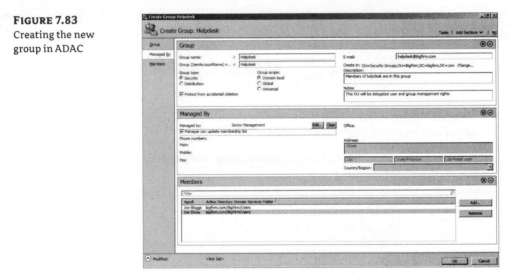

The group is created when you click OK. You can return to the group object properties to edit the configuration or the membership of the group, as shown in Figure 7.84.

As with the user object properties, those attributes you couldn't see in the object creation dialog box are revealed in the Extensions section.

As we wrap up dealing with the Active Directory Administrative Center, here are a few remaining tips:

◆ ADAC can be installed only on Windows Server 2008 R2 machines and Windows 7 computers running the Remote Server Administrative Tools (RSAT).

◆ You can manage domains in your forest or in other forests where a trust exists and you have the appropriate permissions.

◆ In the navigation pane, you can right-click the domain name to connect to different domain controllers. You might do this to work on a domain controller in another site, such as to do some work for local users and get immediate results without waiting for intersite replication.

◆ Active Directory Web Services (ADWS) must be installed on at least one domain controller in the domain to use ADAC to manage that domain. ADWS provides a web service interface for managing Active Directory using tools such as ADAC and PowerShell.

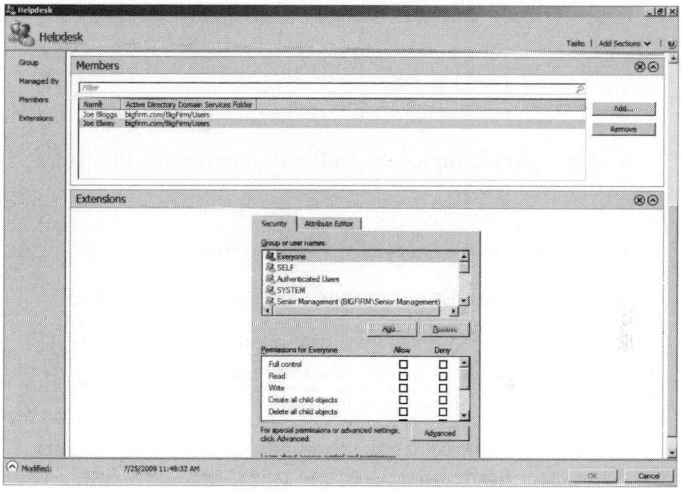

FIGURE 7.84
Viewing the group properties in ADAC

In the ADAC's Getting Started content in the Administrative Center Overview section (shown in Figure 7.85), you will find hyperlinks to online content for ADAC and the new PowerShell modules for Active Directory management using PowerShell.

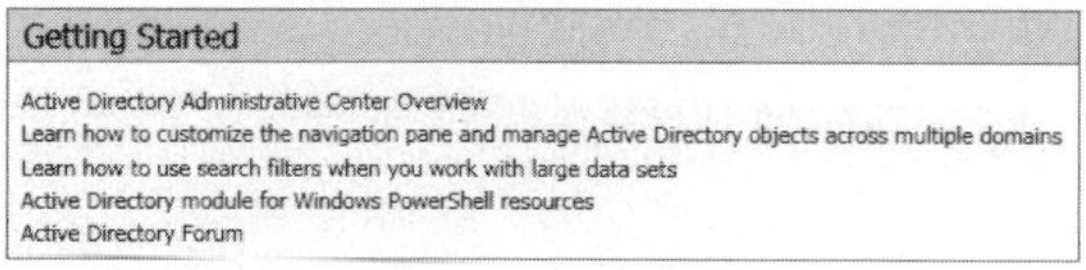

FIGURE 7.85
Getting started with Windows Server 2008 R2 AD

Active Directory Module for Windows PowerShell

The Active Directory module for Windows PowerShell allows you to perform command-line and scripted operations using Microsoft's new shell language. Like ADAC, it is available only for Windows Server 2008 R2 and Windows 7 (using the Remote Server Administration Tools). Also like ADAC, it requires the Directory Web Services role to be installed on at least one domain controller in the domain that you wish to manage. You can also install the Directory Web Services Gateway (http://tinyurl.com/yblxwey) on Windows Server 2003 or Windows Server 2008 domain controllers in your site for optimum performance. We'll now cover how to manage users and groups using this new PowerShell module. We'll cover the more common scenarios, but we strongly recommend that you check out the Microsoft site at http://tinyurl .com/m4ctao to read more about this subject.

You won't be using the normal PowerShell window. Instead, launch the Active Directory module for Windows PowerShell from Administrative Tools either on your Windows Server 2008 R2 domain controller or on a Windows 7 machine with RSAT installed.

CREATING USERS

You'll start with some user administration operations. It makes sense to create a user first. The PowerShell cmdlet for that is New-ADuser:

```
PS C:\Users\Administrator> new-aduser "Boomer Moon"
```

PowerShell contains help and examples. If you want help on New-ADuser, then you can run this:

```
PS C:\Users\Administrator> help new-aduser
```

You can get examples of cmdlet usage by running this:

```
PS C:\Users\Administrator> get-help new-aduser -examples
```

Finally, you can get in-depth information about the cmdlet by running this:

```
PS C:\Users\Administrator> get-help new-aduser -detailed
```

These help commands are consistent with all the cmdlets supplied by Microsoft's modules in PowerShell. There are a few other useful things to note. You can add a -whatif flag to a cmdlet to see what will happen if you run it:

```
PS C:\Users\Administrator> new-aduser BMoon -whatif
What if: Performing operation "New" on Target "CN=BMoon,CN=Users,
DC=bigfirm,DC=com".
```

Nothing is actually done; this just simulates the command and tells you what the result would be if you remove the -whatif flag. You can also tell PowerShell to seek a confirmation before executing the command. That's useful so you can double-check what you have typed before running the command:

```
PS C:\Users\Administrator> new-aduser BMoon -confirm

Confirm
Are you sure you want to perform this action?
Performing operation "New" on Target "CN=BMoon,CN=Users,DC=bigfirm,DC=com".
[Y] Yes  [A] Yes to All  [N] No  [L] No to All  [S] Suspend  [?] Help
(default is "Y"):
```

You can use -whatif and -confirm on all the following cmdlet examples so you can be sure that what you are doing is correct.

The previous new-aduser command creates the new user, BMoon, in the default location for new users, usually the Users container. As we stated earlier, that's not the best place for storing user accounts. It contains a number of special users and groups, so you should treat it as special. You've got a location in \BigFirm\Users for your user accounts. Say you want to specify a number of configurations for the user. So, this is what you can run:

```
PS C:\Users\Administrator> new-ADUser "Boomer Moon" -SamAccountName
  "BMoon" -GivenName "Boomer" -Surname "Moon" -DisplayName "Boomer Moon"
```

```
-Path 'OU=Users,OU=BigFirm,DC=bigfirm,DC=com' -UserPrincipalName
"BMoon@bigfirm.com"
```

Let's look at the flags in this:

-SamAccountName   This is the user logon name (pre–Windows 2000) property in the user object properties. For example, you entered **BMoon**, so the user will be able to log in using the domain name BigFirm\BMoon.

-GivenName   This refers to the first name of the user.

-Surname   This is the last name of the user.

-DisplayName   This will be the display property of the user object.

-Path   This refers to the distinguished name of the OU where you want to create the new user object. In this case, it will be in the \BigFirm\Users OU in the bigfirm.com domain.

-UserPrincipalName   The UPN is the user logon name property in the user object, that is, the one that takes an email-like form.

If you run this command, you'll find your new user is created in the OU that you have specified. You'll also find that the user is disabled. Why? PowerShell wants you to specify that the user should be enabled.

Why would you want to create a user this way? You may want to run a bulk job to create a lot of user accounts. You won't enable the user accounts until the associated people are ready to use them. At that point, you can set a password unique to the user and then enable the account. PowerShell is being flexible.

SETTING PASSWORDS

Speaking of passwords, you didn't set one, did you? You're not forced to do so. However, if you want to, you can specify a password using the -AccountPassword flag. There's a catch here. -AccountPassword requires a "secure string" to be entered, so you can't just add My Passw0rd. You have to create a secure string first before creating the user. There's a number of ways to do this; PowerShell is very open in how you can deal with things.

Let's assume you're creating 10 user objects and you want to set them all with the same password and enable the users. You also want to force the user to change their password when they log in for the first time. You can do something like this:

```
PS C:\Users\Administrator> $pw = read-host "Please Enter The Password"
 -AsSecureString

Please Enter The Password: ******************

PS C:\Users\Administrator> new-ADUser "Boomer Moon" -SamAccountName
 "BMoon" -GivenName "Boomer" -Surname "Moon" -DisplayName "Boomer Moon"
 -Path 'OU=Users,OU=BigFirm,DC=bigfirm,DC=com' -UserPrincipalName
 "BMoon@bigfirm.com" -AccountPassword $pw -Enabled 1 -ChangePasswordAtLogon 1
```

The first line prompts the administrator to enter a password. The text will be entered and converted into a secure string. It will then be stored in the $pw variable. The $ indicates to PowerShell that pw is a variable or a container where you want to store a value. The Read-Host cmdlet will prompt you for a value. ASSECURESTRING will convert the value you enter in response to the prompt into a secure string. $pw will be stored in memory by this PowerShell session until you either overwrite the value or close the PowerShell window.

When you run the command, you're prompted to enter the password. Respond with an easy-to-communicate string that meets the password complexity and length requirements.

The second command will create your user. You can add a few flags to meet your requirements:

AccountPassword Use the $pw password from the previous command. This passes your desired password for the new user object in a secure string format.

Enable This takes either a 1 (user object to be enabled) or 0 (user object to be disabled) value.

ChangePasswordAtLogon This takes either a 1 (force a password change) or 0 (do not force a password change) value.

The result of this combination is that the user object is created with your desired password and is enabled, and the user will be forced to change their password when they log in for the first time.

It seems wasteful to run two commands, doesn't it? It would be for just one user. But with this approach, you can repeat that second command for the other nine users you want to created. Each one would have the same password.

If you wanted to create just one user, then you can do everything in one command. This approach will take advantage of PowerShell's...power. You'll be nesting the Read-Host cmdlet:

```
PS C:\Users\Administrator> new-ADUser "Boomer Moon" -SamAccountName
 "BMoon" -GivenName "Boomer" -Surname "Moon" -DisplayName "Boomer Moon"
 -Path 'OU=Users,OU=BigFirm,DC=bigfirm,DC=com' -UserPrincipalName
 "BMoon@bigfirm.com" -AccountPassword (read-host "Please Enter The Password"
 -AsSecureString) -Enabled 1 -ChangePasswordAtLogon 1


Please Enter The Password: **********
```

What you've done here is substitute the Read-Host cmdlet for the $pw variable as shown in the previous approach. This will cause the Read-Host cmdlet to run before the New-ADuser cmdlet can complete and then enter the required secure string as a value for the –AccountPassword flag. When you run the command, you are prompted for a password, and then the user object is created.

CREATING MANY USERS AT ONCE

Imagine that you work in a university as an Active Directory administrator. You probably have a forest for students. Every summer you delete all the student user accounts. You then create new user accounts for each student attending the first semester of the year. You're looking at a task where you might be creating tens of thousands of user objects. Are you really going to use ADUC, ADAC, or one of the previous PowerShell examples to do that? We really hope you aren't planning on one of those approaches.

You can use a powerful one-line PowerShell command to do this work for you with very little effort. What you are going to do is create a comma-separated value (CSV) file in Excel or some other spreadsheet-editing tool. A more advanced network may have a personnel management system that can create this via some export process. The CSV file is a text file that contains a header row dictating value descriptions and is followed by one row for each user. Each row will contain the values that describe the user. Here are the contents of a file called users.csv that you can use to create three users:

Name	SamAccountName	GivenName	Surname
Rachel Kelly	RKelly	Rachel	Kelly
Ulrika Gerhardt	UGerhardt	Ulrika	Gerhardt
Tomasz Kozlowski	TKozlowski	Tomasz	Kozlowski

DisplayName	Path	UserPrincipalName	AccountPassword
Rachel Kelly	OU=Users, OU=BigFirm, DC=bigfirm, DC=com	RKelly@bigfirm.com	NewPassw0rd
Ulrika Gerhardt	OU=Users, OU=BigFirm, DC=bigfirm, DC=com	UGerhardt@bigfirm.com	NewPassw0rd
Tomasz Kozlowski	OU=Users, OU=BigFirm, DC=bigfirm, DC=com	TKozlowski@bigfirm.com	NewPassw0rd

If you open that CSV file, `users.csv`, in Notepad, it will look like this:

```
Name,SamAccountName,GivenName,Surname,DisplayName,Path,UserPrincipalName,
AccountPassword
Rachel Kelly,RKelly,Rachel,Kelly,Rachel Kelly,"OU=Users,OU=BigFirm,DC=bigfirm,DC=
com",RKelly@bigfirm.com,NewPassw0rd
Ulrika Gerhardt,UGerhardt,Ulrika,Gerhardt,Ulrika Gerhardt,"OU=Users,OU=BigFirm,
DC=bigfirm,DC=com",UGerhardt@bigfirm.com,NewPassw0rd
Tomasz Kozlowski, TKozlowski,Tomasz,Kozlowski,Tomaz Kozlowski,"OU=Users,OU=BigFir
m,DC=bigfirm,DC=com",TKozlowski@bigfirm
.com,NewPassw0rd
```

NOTICE THE HEADER ROW

The header row is the same as the variables you used earlier with the New-ADuser cmdlet. The rows below the header row in the CSV file contain the values for creating each user.

Now you want to run a command that will read each row from the CSV file that you've saved as C:\users.csv. The command will then execute the `New-ADuser` cmdlet using the values from the file. Here's the command:

```
PS C:\Users\Administrator> Import-CSV c:\users.csv | foreach
  {New-ADUser -Name $_.Name -SamAccountName $_.SamAccountName -GivenName
  $_.GivenName -Surname $_.Surname -DisplayName $_.DisplayName -Path $_.Path
```

```
-UserPrincipalName $_.UserPrincipalName -AccountPassword (ConvertTo-SecureString
-AsPlainText $_.AccountPassword -Force) -Enabled $true -ChangePasswordAtLogon 1}
```

Don't let the size of this command scare or confuse you. We promise it is simple to understand once you break it down into its components:

IMPORT-CSV   This PowerShell cmdlet will read the CSV file you created and saved as C:\users.csv.

| This is a pipe. It's the vertical bar on your keyboard. Part of the power that PowerShell gives you is the ability to feed the results of one cmdlet in as a parameter to another cmdlet. Here you're reading the CSV file and feeding it in to the next part of the command.

FOREACH   This cmdlet takes the CSV file, which is read as three items, that is, three rows of data (excluding the header row). The FOREACH cmdlet will now run a task using each of the rows as a parameter.

NEW-ADUSER   You know that this command will create a user. But how does it get its values?

$_   Each flag in the New-User cmdlet requires a value. You know that you have assigned a header to the CSV values. Each of the $_ entries in the command refers to one of those headers. For example, the $_.Name refers to the Name header in the CSV. So, New-ADuser will take the value Rachel Kelly from the first row and substitute it for $_.Name.

AccountPasword   You're again converting the password value to a secure string to meet the requirements of the flag.

This command will read each of the three data rows from the CSV file. It will load in the values and create three user objects based on these values, such as in the OU you specified in the CSV file. The users will have their passwords set, be enabled, and then be forced to change their password when they log in.

Nothing is stopping you from adding columns to this CSV and matching additional flags in the command to further populate the attributes of the user object, such as roaming profile, home directory, and so on.

Using this approach, you could manually or automatically (using some developed export tool from a personnel system) create this CSV file and then run this *one* command to create many user accounts. That's exactly what PowerShell is all about: making work easier by automation.

Unlocking a User Account

You can also use PowerShell to do the more mundane work. If you want to unlock a user account, you can run the following:

```
PS C:\Users\Administrator> Unlock-ADAccount -identity JBloggs
```

The -identity flag takes the name of the user object to unlock. In this example we've used the friendly user logon name. You might want to use the DN to identify the user object:

```
PS C:\Users\Administrator> Unlock-ADAccount -identity "CN=Joe Bloggs,OU=Users,OU=
BigFirm,DC=bigfirm,DC=com"
```

You can reset a user's password using this command:

```
PS C:\Users\Administrator> set-adaccountpassword -identity jbloggs -reset
 -newpassword (read-host "Please Enter The New Password" -AsSecureString)


Please Enter The New Password: **********
```

The Set-Adaccountpassword cmdlet also uses the -identity flag to specify a user object to manage. The -reset flag lets PowerShell know that you aren't doing a normal password change that requires knowing the old password. Instead, you want to change a password for a user object because the user has forgotten their password. You're again using the Read-Host cmdlet to read in a password and convert it to a secure string for the -newpassword flag.

The Get-ADuser cmdlet will retrieve a user object's properties:

```
PS C:\Users\Administrator> get-aduser jbloggs


DistinguishedName: CN=Joe Bloggs,OU=Users,OU=BigFirm,DC=bigfirm,DC=com
Enabled          : True
GivenName        : Joe
Name             : Joe Bloggs
ObjectClass      : user
ObjectGUID       : 5fa7f3ac-93ec-4cf8-bf80-21368f8b3a8d
SamAccountName   : JBloggs
SID              : S-1-5-21-3625881918-2577536232-3089104624-1108
Surname          : Bloggs
UserPrincipalName: JBloggs@bigfirm.com
```

By default it retrieves only a small set of the available attributes. If you want to see everything that's available in a user object, then run the Get-ADuser command and ask for all properties using a * wildcard:

```
PS C:\Users\Administrator> get-aduser jbloggs -properties * | more
```

Here you're piping the results into a More cmdlet so that the results pause and require you to press a key to continue. Otherwise, the results just scroll past faster than you can read. There's probably too many results included, so you can modify the previous results by specifying the properties you do want to see. You'll need to know what properties to ask for, so the wildcard approach is useful after all.

```
PS C:\Users\Administrator> get-aduser jbloggs -properties HomeDirectory


DistinguishedName: CN=Joe Bloggs,OU=Users,OU=BigFirm,DC=bigfirm,DC=com
Enabled          : True
GivenName        : Joe
HomeDirectory    : \\bf1\home$\JBloggs
Name             : Joe Bloggs
ObjectClass      : user
```

```
ObjectGUID       : 5fa7f3ac-93ec-4cf8-bf80-21368f8b3a8d
SamAccountName   : JBloggs
SID              : S-1-5-21-3625881918-2577536232-3089104624-1108
Surname          : Bloggs
UserPrincipalName: JBloggs@bigfirm.com
```

This example has requested that the default response to `Get-ADuser` is modified to also include the `HomeDirectory` attribute.

You can return the properties of a number of users at once by specifying some search criteria:

```
PS C:\Users\Administrator> Get-ADUser -Filter 'Name -like "*"' -SearchBase
"OU=Users,OU=BigFirm,DC=bigfirm,DC=com"
```

There are two flags here:

-Filter   Here you are specifying any object with a name similar to the wildcard *****, in other words, all user objects.

-SearchBase   You've further qualified the search by specifying the \BigFirm\Users OU in the domain.

That command will return the default properties of all user objects in the \BigFirm\ Users OU.

If you want to modify the property of a user object, then you will need to run the `Set-ADuser` cmdlet:

```
PS C:\Users\Administrator> Set-ADUser AGarcia -Description "IT Manager"
```

That command specifies the user, AGarcia, and that you want to modify the `-Description` attribute. This example will change this user object's description to IT Manager, giving Alexandra a promotion. You can get a list of the attributes to modify by running this:

```
PS C:\Users\Administrator> Help Set-ADUser
```

It's possible to change a property of a large number of objects at once. In this example, you'll modify every object in \BigFirm\Users. You'll use the `Get-ADuser` cmdlet that we just discussed to find the users in that OU and then feed the results into `Set-ADuser` using a pipe:

```
PS C:\Users\Administrator> Get-ADUser -Filter 'Name -like "*"' -SearchBase "OU=Us
ers,OU=BigFirm,DC=bigfirm,DC=com" | Set-ADUser -Description "Member of IT"
```

This uses the same example for finding users as we covered just a moment ago. Once you have the objects, you can feed them in as parameters via the pipe into `Set-ADuser`. You're changing the property of all the found users to Member of IT.

ENABLING AN ACCOUNT

Earlier we said that you might want to create a user object and enable it only when the human user was ready to use it. Here's how to enable a user object for Joe Bloggs:

```
PS C:\Users\Administrator> Enable-ADAccount -Identity BMoon
```

DISABLING AN ACCOUNT

We discussed why you might want to disable accounts for a certain amount of time before deleting them. Here's how to disable an account:

```
PS C:\Users\Administrator> Disable-ADAccount -Identity BMoon
```

Finally, you get to the point where you want to delete a user account:

```
PS C:\Users\Administrator> remove-aduser -Identity BMoon -confirm

Confirm
Are you sure you want to perform this action?
Performing operation "Remove" on Target "CN=BMoon,CN=Users,DC=bigfirm,DC=com".
[Y] Yes  [A] Yes to All  [N] No  [L] No to All  [S] Suspend  [?] Help
(default is "Y"):
```

We've been very careful by throwing on the -confirm flag at the end of the Remove-ADuser cmdlet. That will force you to read what the result will be and gives you a chance to decide whether you want to continue with this action. Doing things from the command line is very quick, so a deletion is something you need to be careful about. If this will be a script, then you will probably not want to use the -confirm flag because you might not want the script to pause halfway through the execution to ask you to interact with it.

That wraps up our coverage of user management using PowerShell. We'll now move on to group management. To get going, create a group by using the New-ADgroup cmdlet. Have you noticed how similar all these cmdlets are? That's a feature of PowerShell. There's a verb like Get, Set, or New and then something descriptive to indicate what the cmdlet does.

```
PS C:\Users\Administrator> New-ADGroup -Name "IT Administrators" -SamAccountName
"IT Administrators" -GroupCategory Security -GroupScope DomainLocal -DisplayName
"IT Administrators" -Path "OU=Security Groups,OU=BigFirm,DC=bigfirm,DC=com"
-Description "Members of this group are in IT"
```

That command will create a domain local security group called IT Administrators in the \BigFirm\Security Groups OU using these flags:

-Name   This is the name of the group!

-SamAccountName   This is the name associated with the pre–Windows 2000 group object attribute.

-GroupCategory   This will be either Security (or 1) or Distribution (or 0).

-GroupScope   This will be either DomainLocal (or 0), Global (or 1), or Universal (or 2).

-DisplayName   This is the name shown for the group.

-Path   This is the distinguished name of the OU where the group will be located.

-Description   This will fill the description field of the object for future reference.

Once you have a group, you'll want to start adding members to it. You'll be using the Add-ADGroupMember cmdlet to add members. You have lots of ways to do this. You'll start with the simplest one:

```
PS C:\Users\Administrator> Add-ADGroupMember "IT Administrators" -Member JBloggs
```

You can use the -Identify flag to tell PowerShell which group you want to edit. You then can specify a user to add using the -Member flag. The previous example adds the JBloggs user object to the IT Administrators security group. Odds are you'll want to add more than one user at once. If you're doing this from the PowerShell command prompt, then you could use this approach:

```
PS C:\Users\Administrator> add-adgroupmember "IT Administrators"

cmdlet Add-ADGroupMember at command pipeline position 1
Supply values for the following parameters:
Members[0]:AGarcia
Members[1]:JElway
Members[2]:
```

Using this method, you specify the group to be managed, but you do not list the new members in the command. PowerShell knows that something is missing, so it prompts for a member. You've entered **AGarcia** as member 0, entered **JElway** as member 1, and pressed Return on the prompt for another member to end the command. The users you entered will then be added to the group. Alternatively, you can use this approach:

```
PS C:\Users\Administrator> Add-ADGroupMember "IT Administrators" -Member
 JBloggs,AGarcia
```

You've used a comma delimiter to separate the name of each user account object that you want to add to the IT Administrators group.

You might want to add a very large number of users into a group. You can use a search result generated by using the Get-ADuser cmdlet to do this:

```
PS C:\Users\Administrator> Add-ADGroupMember "IT Administrators" -Member (Get-
ADUser -Filter 'Name -like "*"' -SearchBase "OU=Users,OU=BigFirm,DC=bigfirm,DC=
com")
```

This command nests the Get-ADuser query that you used earlier when you were dealing with user management via PowerShell. You've nested the Get-ADuser cmdlet as a value for the -Member flag of the Add-ADGroupMember cmdlet. Get-ADuser is searching for all users in the \BigFirm\Users OU. The resulting users are added as members to IT Administrators.

There's a catch to this approach. If one of the user objects specified in the Get-ADuser query is already in the group, then the entire Add-ADGroupMember operation will fail. No one will be added to the group. This means you have to build up the query carefully.

Remember that you're not limited to adding just users to a group in Active Directory. You can also add groups to create nested groups:

```
PS C:\Users\Administrator> add-adgroupmember "IT Administrators" "Helpdesk"
```

The previous command will add the Helpdesk group to the IT Administrators group.

When you have a group, you'll want to see who's a member. This is a simple command using the Get-ADGroupMember cmdlet to list all the members of the IT Administrators group:

```
PS C:\Users\Administrator> Get-ADGroupMember "IT Administrators"

distinguishedName: CN=Helpdesk,OU=Security Groups,OU=BigFirm,DC=bigfirm,DC=com
name             : Helpdesk
```

```
objectClass       : group
objectGUID        : 93e9b21b-023a-4e46-88b5-3c4cbf71f218
SamAccountName    : Helpdesk
SID               : S-1-5-21-3625881918-2577536232-3089104624-1115

distinguishedName: CN=Joe Bloggs,OU=Users,OU=BigFirm,DC=bigfirm,DC=com
name              : Joe Bloggs
objectClass       : user
objectGUID        : 5fa7f3ac-93ec-4cf8-bf80-21368f8b3a8d
SamAccountName    : JBloggs
SID               : S-1-5-21-3625881918-2577536232-3089104624-1108
```

That will return all direct members of the group, not the nested members. The returned list might not be very useful for something like a report. PowerShell allows you to specify which attributes of the returned objects should be presented.

```
PS C:\Users\Administrator> Get-ADGroupMember "IT Administrators" |
  FT ObjectClass,Name

ObjectClass                           Name
-----------                           ----
group                                 Helpdesk
user                                  Joe Bloggs
```

Here you've piped the results from Get-ADGroupMember into the FT cmdlet. That allows you to specify properties or attributes that you would like listed. In the previous example, you've asked for ObjectClass and Name. That gives you useful reports on what objects are direct members of the IT Administrators group.

However, if a group contains other groups as a member, then you might need a complete recursive list of members:

```
PS C:\Users\Administrator> Get-ADGroupMember "IT Administrators" -recursive |
  FT DistinguishedName

DistinguishedName
-----------------
CN=Joe Bloggs,OU=Users,OU=BigFirm,DC=bigfirm,DC=com
CN=Rachel Kelly,OU=Users,OU=BigFirm,DC=bigfirm,DC=com
CN=Joe Elway,OU=Users,OU=BigFirm,DC=bigfirm,DC=com
```

Here you've added the -Recursive flag to the cmdlet and piped the results into FT to get the distinguished names of all objects that can claim membership of the IT Administrators group.

The next operation you'll want to be able to do with groups is remove members. You'll use the Remove-ADGroupMember cmdlet for that:

```
PS C:\Users\Administrator> Remove-ADGroupMember "IT Administrators" -Member
  JBloggs

Confirm
```

```
Are you sure you want to perform this action?
Performing operation "Set" on Target "CN=IT Administrators,OU=Security
Groups,OU=BigFirm,DC=bigfirm,DC=com".
[Y] Yes  [A] Yes to All  [N] No  [L] No to All  [S] Suspend  [?] Help
(default is "Y"):
```

Here you've requested to remove the user JBloggs from the IT Administrators group. The Remove-ADGroupMember cmdlet always asks for confirmation. You can enter one of a number of options in response to the confirmation request:

Yes   Go ahead and remove the indicated user from the group.

Yes to All   Use this option if you have requested to remove multiple members from the group and you're sure you want to remove them all.

No   Do not remove the indicated user group the group.

L   Abandon all removal operations requested in the command.

S   Suspend the operation. This will return you to the command prompt. You can resume the command to this point by typing in Exit.

You can run this command for multiple users by using a comma delimiter:

```
PS C:\Users\Administrator> Remove-ADGroupMember -Identity "IT Administrators"
-Member AGarcia,JBloggs


Confirm
Are you sure you want to perform this action?
Performing operation "Set" on Target "CN=IT Administrators,OU=Security
Groups,OU=BigFirm,DC=bigfirm,DC=com".
[Y] Yes  [A] Yes to All  [N] No  [L] No to All  [S] Suspend  [?] Help
(default is "Y"):
```

Here you have separated AGarcia and JBloggs with a comma. You can add many users or even groups to the command this way.

You might want to remove many users or groups using some sort of search. In the following example, you're using the Get-ADuser cmdlet to search for all users in the \BigFirm\Users OU and then remove them from the IT Administrators group:

```
PS C:\Users\Administrator> Remove-ADGroupMember "IT Administrators" -Member
 (Get-ADUser -Filter 'Name -like "*"' -SearchBase "OU=Users,OU=BigFirm,DC=bigfirm,
DC=com")


Confirm
Are you sure you want to perform this action?
Performing operation "Set" on Target "CN=IT Administrators,OU=Security
Groups,OU=BigFirm,DC=bigfirm,DC=com".
[Y] Yes  [A] Yes to All  [N] No  [L] No to All  [S] Suspend  [?] Help
(default is "Y"):
```

You can see that you haven't specified a value for the -Member flag. Instead, you have nested the Get-ADuser cmdlet. That will find all the users you want to remove, and the result is passed to the Remove-ADGroupMember cmdlet. If you confirm this, every user object in the \BigFirm\Users OU will be removed from the IT Administrators group.

This has a similar catch to when you used the same query approach to add users to the group. The entire Remove-ADGroupMember operation will fail if any of the resulting objects from the Get-ADuser nested query are not members of the indicated group. So, if you query for all users in \BigFirm\OU and one of them is *not* already in the IT Administrators group, then the removal operation will fail.

Maybe you want to remove all members from a group. You can do that by querying for the members of the group and nesting that command in a command to remove members from the group

```
PS C:\Users\Administrator> Remove-ADGroupMember "IT Administrators" -Member
(Get-ADGroupMember "IT Administrators")

Confirm
Are you sure you want to perform this action?
Performing operation "Set" on Target "CN=IT Administrators,OU=Security
Groups,OU=BigFirm,DC=bigfirm,DC=com".
[Y] Yes  [A] Yes to All  [N] No  [L] No to All  [S] Suspend  [?] Help
(default is "Y"):
```

Here you are retrieving all the members of IT Administrators by running the Get-ADGroupMember cmdlet. That's nested in the Remove-ADGroupMember command and will return the answer as a value for the -Member flag of the command.

That gives you many ways to create a group using PowerShell, add members, query the membership, and remove members. All that remains is to delete that group.

REMOVING A GROUP

Removing a group is a pretty simple task. Just use the, you guessed it, Remove-ADGroup cmdlet and specify the name of the group:

```
PS C:\Users\Administrator> Remove-ADGroup "IT Administrators"

Confirm
Are you sure you want to perform this action?
Performing operation "Remove" on Target "CN=IT Administrators,OU=Security
Groups,OU=BigFirm,DC=bigfirm,DC=com".
[Y] Yes  [A] Yes to All  [N] No  [L] No to All  [S] Suspend  [?] Help
(default is "Y"):
```

Here you are deleting the IT Administrators group. It doesn't matter if the group has members or not; it will be removed. Be sure that you don't need the group anymore. Remember that you cannot just re-create the group to restore all the assigned permissions because the SID assigned to the group is globally unique.

Finally, you've reached the end of the section that deals with the Active Directory module for Windows PowerShell. At first it looks like something that will be very difficult to use. Sure, in a smaller environment there might not be any advantage to using PowerShell, but it's something you should learn. In medium-sized environments, you'll find it can be used to rapidly get results. In large environments, you'll find it's something you'll be able to use to get complex operations done very quickly and with minimum effort.

The Bottom Line

Manage local users and groups Local users and groups are stored on a computer and cannot be used to log in to or access resources on other computers.

> **Master It** You have 25 PCs with 25 users on a workgroup network; in other words, a network with no Active Directory or Windows domain. You are installing two file servers. You want to provide authorized-only access to shared resources on the file servers. How will you do this?

Manage users and groups in Active Directory Users and groups can be stored in Active Directory. That means administrators can create a single copy of each user and group that is stored in a replicated database and can be used by member computers across the entire Active Directory forest. You can use Active Directory Users and Computers and the command prompt to manage users and groups on Windows Server 2008 and Windows Server 2008 R2. Windows Server 2008 R2 adds a new task-oriented console called the Active Directory Administrative Center and an Active Directory module for PowerShell.

> **Master It** List the different types of Active Directory group types and scopes. Why would you use each of them?

Manage users and computers in Windows Server 2008 R2 Windows Server 2008 R2 adds two new ways to manage users and computers in an Active Directory. Once Active Directory Web Services is installed on one domain controller in the domain, you can manage its users and computers using either PowerShell or the new Active Directory Administrative Center (ADAC). ADAC makes it quicker and easier for administrators to perform day-to-day operations such as resetting passwords, unlocking user accounts, and finding objects in the forest that they want to manage. The Active Directory module for Windows PowerShell offers a new command-line interface and way to script Active Directory management tasks. You can use this to automate repetitive tasks using scripts or to perform complex and large operations that would consume too much time using an administrative console.

> **Master It** You are managing the Windows Server 2008 R2 Active Directory forest for an international corporation. The directors have announced that a new call center with 5,000 employees is to be opened soon. The human resources department will be able to produce a file from its database with the names of the new employees thanks to some in-house developers. You want to create the user objects as quickly as possible with minimum human effort. How will you do this?

Delegate group management Part of the power of Active Directory is the ability to delegate administrative rights. You can grant permissions to users or groups to manage any organizational unit or object in the domain. You can limit those rights so people only have permissions to do what they need to do for their role in the organization.

Master It You are a domain administrator in a large organization. Your network contains several file servers. File shares are secured using domain-based security groups. You have delegated rights to help-desk staff to manage these groups. The organization is relying on the help desk to know who should have read, read/write, and no access to the file shares. Mistakes are being made and changes are taking too long, causing employees to be unable to access critical information. You've considered a paper-based procedure where the business owners of the file shares document who should have access. This has proven to be unpopular because it slows down the business. You have been asked to implement a solution that ensures the business is not delayed and where only authorized people have access to sensitive information.

Deal with users leaving the organization It is important to understand that Windows tracks users, groups, and computers by their security identifier and not by their visible friendly name. When you delete and re-create an object, the new object is actually a different object and does not keep the old object's rights and permissions.

Master It The personnel department has informed you that an employee, BKavanagh, is leaving the organization immediately under bad circumstances. The security officer informs you that there is a security risk. You have been asked to deal with this risk without any delay. What do you do? Two hours later you are told that the personnel department gave you the wrong name. The correct name was BCavanagh. BKavanagh has called the help desk to say that she cannot do any work. What do you do to rectify the situation?

Chapter 8

Group Policy: AD's Gauntlet

When you talk about Active Directory, you must also talk about Group Policy. Group Policy is not a new technology for Active Directory, but it has grown and improved with every iteration of the operating system and service pack since it was first introduced in Windows 2000. The Group Policy technology and features that are delivered with Windows Server 2008 make such drastic improvements over the previous version that it can almost seem like new technology. Changes and enhancements have come for managing Group Policy (the Group Policy Management console and the Group Policy Management Editor), managing available settings (with now more than 5,000 settings), controlling targeting objects, and troubleshooting your Group Policy infrastructure. If you are a veteran of Group Policy, you will certainly want to focus on the Group Policy preferences, GPMC, and troubleshooting sections in this chapter.

In this chapter, you will learn to:

- ◆ Understand local policies and Group Policy objects

- ◆ Create GPOs

- ◆ Troubleshoot group policies

Group Policy Concepts

Let's start with some important concepts, terms, and rules you need to know to master Group Policy. In the process of explaining the functionality of Group Policy, we will mention several settings without actually showing you how to turn them on in the Group Policy snap-in. Just focus on the concepts for now. Later in this section, we'll take you on a full tour of the GPMC; we will cover Group Policy application (including settings such as Enforce and Block Inheritance) and the expanded settings.

Administrators configure and deploy Group Policy by building *Group Policy objects* (GPOs). GPOs are containers for groups of settings (*policy settings*) that can be applied to user and computer accounts throughout an Active Directory network. Policy objects are created using the Group Policy Management Editor (GPME), which is invoked by editing a GPO from within the GPMC. The same GPO could specify a set of applications to be installed on all users' desktops, implement a fascist policy of disk quotas and restrictions on the Explorer shell, and define domain-wide password and account lockout policies. It is possible to create one all-encompassing GPO or several different GPOs, one for each type of function.

There are two major nodes in the GPME: Computer Configuration and User Configuration. The computer configuration policies manage machine-specific settings such as disk quotas, security auditing, and Event Log management. User configuration policies apply user-specific settings such as application configuration, Start menu management, and folder redirection. However, there is a good bit of overlap between the two, especially now that Group Policy preferences have been introduced (more on Group Policy preferences later in this chapter). It's not unusual to find the same policy available in both the User Configuration and Computer Configuration nodes. Be prepared for a certain amount of head scratching as you search for the policy you want to activate and decide whether to employ the user-based policy or the computer policy. Keep in mind that you can create a policy that uses both types of settings, or you can create separate GPOs to control the User Configuration and Computer Configuration settings.

Contrary to the name, Group Policy objects aren't group oriented at all. Maybe they are called GPOs because a bunch of different configuration management settings are *grouped* together in one location. Regardless, you cannot apply them directly to groups, but only to sites, domains, and OUs (Microsoft abbreviates these collectively with SDOU) within a given forest. This act of assigning GPOs to a site, domain, or OU is called *linking*. GPOs also exist on each computer running Windows 2000, XP, Vista, Server 2003, and Server 2008, as you'll see in a moment. The GPO-to-SDOU relationship can be many-to-one (many GPOs linked to one OU, for example) or one-to-many (one GPO linked to several different OUs). Once linked to an SDOU, user policies affect user accounts within the OU (and sub-OUs), and computer policies affect computer accounts within the OU (and sub-OUs). Both types of policy settings apply at a periodic refresh rate, which is approximately every 90 minutes, for the most part.

When we said GPOs were stored in the AD, that wasn't exactly accurate. GPOs are stored in two parts—a Group Policy container (GPC) and a Group Policy template (GPT), which is a folder structure in the SYSVOL. The container part is stored in Active Directory and contains property information, version information, status, and a list of components. The folder structure path is `Windows\SYSVOL\sysvol\<Domainname>\Policies\`*GUID*`\` where *GUID* is the globally unique identifier for the GPO. This folder contains administrative templates (ADM files for your Windows 2000 and 2003 domains), security settings, information on available applications, registry settings, scripts, and much more.

GPOs are rooted in a domain's Active Directory. You can't directly copy them to other domains or forests, but you can link them across domain boundaries (although it's not recommended). Windows Server 2003 and 2008 support some cross-forest functionality. For example, a user in forest A can log on to a computer in forest B and still have the group policies apply from forest A. Also, Group Policy settings can contain references to servers in other forests now.

BEYOND THE REGISTRY

Group policies aren't just registry changes. All policy settings are applied with client-side extension (CSE) DLLs, which give them a broad and deep reach into the operating system. Examples include controlling disk quotas, folder redirection, and software installation. In fact, there is a CSE DLL that processes the registry changes, `Userenv.dll`.

Policies Are "All or Nothing"

Each GPO contains many possible settings for many functions; usually you'll configure only a handful of them in each GPO. The others will be left "inactive," sort of like putting REM (for a remark) in front of a command in a script or using a semicolon at the beginning of a line in an INF file. Once you've configured policy settings and told AD that "this GPO is linked to the Bigfirm.

com domain," for example, the individual settings or types of settings cannot be selectively applied. All User Configuration settings will be applied to all user accounts logged onto Windows 2000, XP, Vista, 2003, and 2008 systems in the linked domain. All Computer Configuration settings will be applied to all Windows 2000, XP, Vista, 2003, and 2008 machines in the domain. (Remember that neither will be applied to NT 4 or 9x clients.)

Now, let's say you've created a GPO that deploys a set of standard desktop applications such as Word, Excel, and Outlook and you threw in a bunch of shell restrictions to prevent users from changing their configurations. If you don't want your IT support group users to be subject to those ridiculously stringent shell restrictions (although those users may need them most of all!), you can do a couple of things. You can create a separate GPO for those policy settings and link the GPO to an OU that contains all the regular users. But that OU will be the only one that gets the Office applications. You can alternately set permissions on the GPO that prevent the policy from being applied to the IT support group (this is called *filtering*). However, if you use filtering to solve this problem, none of the settings in the GPO will apply to the IT support group at all.

Group Policy application is all or nothing, so sometimes you really need separate policies for separate functions. The best way to approach this might be to create a GPO for standard software deployment and a GPO for shell restrictions. Both could be applied at the domain level, but shell restrictions can be filtered for the IT support group. The point is, it's not possible to create one monolithic policy and then specify who gets what settings, and you wouldn't want to do that anyway. At least, you wouldn't want to troubleshoot it.

The only exceptions to this "all or nothing" concept are the new Group Policy preferences that are delivered with Windows Server 2008 and Vista SP1. All the Group Policy preferences come with item-level targeting, which is at the policy setting level. We'll cover more about these settings and their configurations later in this chapter.

Policies Are Inherited and Cumulative

Group Policy settings are cumulative and inherited from parent Active Directory containers. For example, the Bigfirm.com domain has several different GPOs. There is a GPO linked to the domain that sets password restrictions, account lockout, and standard security settings. Each OU in the domain also has a GPO linked to it that deploys and maintains standard applications, as well as folder redirection settings and desktop restrictions. User accounts and computer accounts that are located in the OUs receive settings from both the GPO linked to the domain and the GPO linked to the specific OU. So, some blanket policy settings can be applied to the entire domain, while others can target accounts according to OUs upon which they are linked.

Group Policy Power! Refresh Intervals

Policies apply in the background every 90 minutes, with up to a 30-minute "randomization" to keep the domain controller from getting hit by hundreds or even thousands of computers at once. DCs refresh group policies every five minutes. There is, however, a policy to configure all of this, as you'll see later in this chapter. Exceptions to the refresh interval include folder redirection, software installation, script application, Group Policy preference printers, and Group Policy preference drive maps. These are applied only at logon (for user accounts) or system startup (for computer accounts); otherwise, you might end up uninstalling an application while someone is trying to use it. Or a user might be working in a folder as it is being redirected to a new network location. In essence, for data integrity these policy settings apply only in the "foreground" refresh of Group Policy.

Local Policies and Group Policy Objects

When you open the Group Policy tool (`gpedit.msc`), it automatically focuses on the local machine GPO, as shown in Figure 8.1. Administrators can use the tool to configure account settings (such as the minimum password length and number of bad logon attempts before locking the account), to set up auditing, and to specify other miscellaneous settings. However, the domain-based policy editor, the Group Policy Management Editor, includes a number of settings (including software installation and folder redirection) that are not available for local policies.

GP FOLDER STRUCTURE

The local Group Policy folder structure is similar to that of other domain-based GPOs and is found in `\Windows\system32\GroupPolicy`.

FIGURE 8.1
The Local Group Policy Editor—local machine

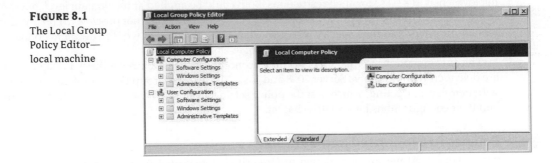

If you happen to be working on a Windows Server 2008 or Vista computer, you have more than the local GPO (LGPO) that you can configure. On these computers, you also have GPOs that can target groups of local users (Administrators or Non-Administrators LGPO) and individual users (User Specific LGPO).

Administrators or Non-Administrators LGPO

As their names represent, the settings in the Administrators and Non-Administrators LGPOs will target either the users in the Administrators group or the users in all other groups. The idea is that when a user has membership in the local Administrators group, that user should have more privileges than a user who is not in this group.

Note that the LGPOs that control these settings modify user-based settings only. There are no settings under these LGPOs that control computer-based settings, which are located under the Computer Configuration node.

Since there are two "types" of groups, there are two LGPOs that control them. For you to control both of these types of users, you will need to configure both LGPOs. To access these LGPOs, you must use the MMC. The steps are similar to those previously, with a slight alteration in the scoping of the Group Policy object that is loaded in the MMC. Instead of choosing Local Computer from the Group Policy Objects list, use the Browse button to look for the Administrators or Non-Administrators group listed on the Users tab, as shown in Figure 8.2.

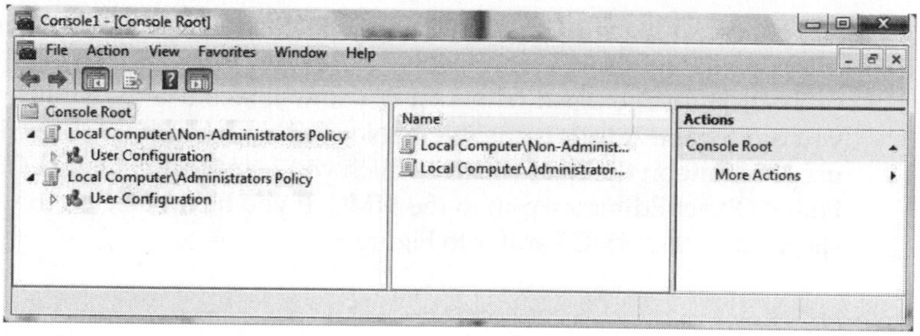

FIGURE 8.2
You can view
the Administrators
and Non-
Administrators
LGPOs using
the MMC.

To access both of these local GPOs for editing, follow these steps:

1. Select Start ➢ Run.

2. Type **MMC** in the Open text field.

PERMISSIONS REQUIRED

This is an administrative task; therefore, if you have UAC enabled, you will have to agree to the permissions that opening the Group Policy Management Editor MMC snap-in requires.

---

3. From within the MMC console, select the File menu from the toolbar.

4. Select Add/Remove Snap-in from the drop-down menu.

5. Select Group Policy Object Editor from the list of snap-ins.

6. Leave Local Computer as the entry under Group Policy Object.

7. Click the Browse button.

8. Select the Users tab in the Browse for a Group Policy Object dialog box.

9. Select Administrators from the list, and then click the OK button.

10. Select Finish in the Select Group Policy Object dialog box.

11. Click OK in the Add or Remove Snap-ins dialog box.

12. Expand the Local Computer\Administrators Policy node in the console window.

Repeat steps 4–12 for the Non-Administrators local GPO, replacing Non-Administrators for Administrators in the appropriate steps.

User-Specific LGPO

Finally, you can configure a very granular LGPO on every Windows Server 2008 and Vista computer. This policy is geared to target individual user accounts. There are only user-based policy settings in the LGPO, and the settings target only a single user.

The caveat to using this LGPO is that the user must have an account in the local SAM of the computer that you are configuring.

To view and configure this LGPO, you will also use the MMC and follow the same steps as you did for the Administrators and Non-Administrators LGPOs; however, you will select the user account on the Users tab for which you want to create the LGPO when adding the Group Policy Object Editor snap-in to the MMC. If you have selected the Administrator account, it will show up in the MMC similar to Figure 8.3.

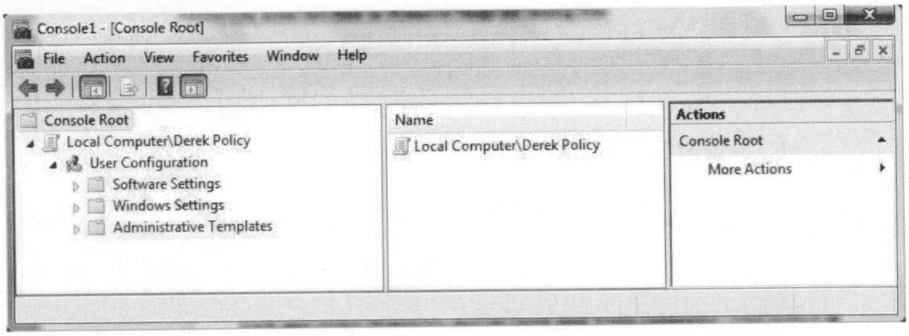

FIGURE 8.3
Once a user is selected for management of the LGPO, it will show up in the MMC with all the User Configuration settings exposed.

Here are the steps to follow to access the local user-specific GPOs:

1. Select Start ➢ Run.

2. Type **MMC** in the Open text field.

PERMISSIONS REQUIRED

This is an administrative task; therefore, if you have UAC enabled, you will have to agree to the permissions that opening the Group Policy Management Editor MMC snap-in requires.

---

3. From within the MMC console, select the File menu from the toolbar.

4. Select Add/Remove Snap-in from the drop-down menu.

5. Select Group Policy Object Editor from the list of snap-ins.

6. Leave Local Computer as the entry under Group Policy Object.

7. Click the Browse button.

8. Select the Users tab in the Browse for a Group Policy Object dialog box.

9. Select the desired user account from the list, and then click the OK button.

10. Click Finish in the Select Group Policy Object dialog box.

11. Click OK in the Add or Remove Snap-ins dialog box.

12. Expand the Local Computer\<username> Policy node in the console window.

Creating GPOs

Now that you understand the major concepts involved with Group Policy and know the difference between local GPOs and domain-based GPOs, let's go through the steps of creating and editing a domain-based GPO. In this section, we'll show you all the settings we discussed in the preceding "theory" section.

DOMAIN-BASED GPOS

From this point forward, we will be focusing on only domain-based GPOs, because they are the preferred, logical, and secure way to deploy the settings that exist in a GPO.

You will be using the GPMC to manage all domain-based GPOs. With Windows Server 2008, you will need to install the GPMC using the Server Manager, as you saw in Chapter 2.

After the GPMC is installed, it shows up under the Start ➤ Administrative Tools menu. Once it's selected from this list, the GPMC tool opens and displays the domain in which your management computer has membership, as shown in Figure 8.4.

FIGURE 8.4
GPMC is the preferred GPO management tool.

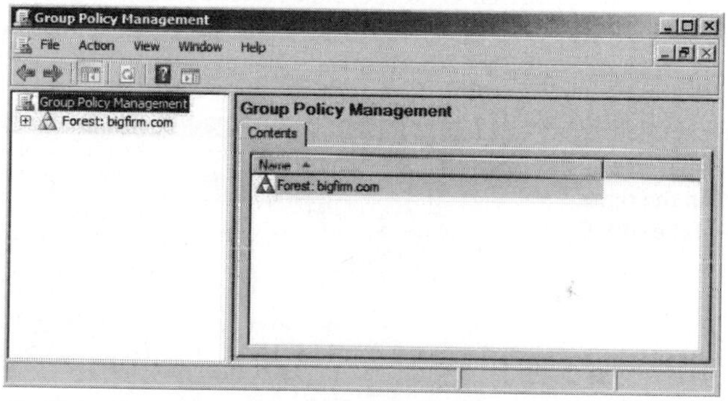

To create a new GPO in the domain, you will need to expand the GPMC structure such that you can see all the nodes that exist under the domain, as shown in Figure 8.5.

FIGURE 8.5
GPMC expands to display all the nodes under the domain.

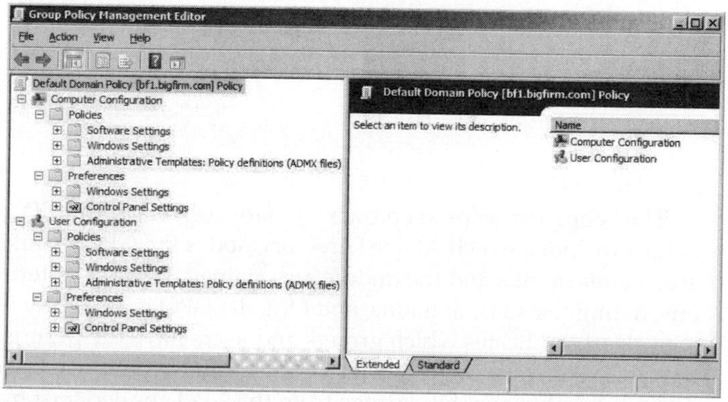

To create a GPO in the domain, follow these steps:

1. Right-click the Group Policy Objects node, and select New.

2. In the New GPO dialog box, type the name for the GPO (in this case **Desktop Security**), and then click the OK button.

This will create a GPO called Desktop Security, which is not linked to any container in the domain yet. At this point, you will want to configure the GPO settings and then link it to the site, the domain, or an OU. To link a GPO to a node in Active Directory, follow these steps:

1. Right-click the desired node, in this case Desktops OU.

2. Select the Link an Existing GPO menu option.

3. In the Select GPO dialog box, select the Desktop Security GPO, and then click the OK button.

Notice that the Desktops OU now has a linked GPO associated with it. If you want to create and link a GPO to an OU, you can do this in just a single step. By right-clicking the OU (or domain or site, for that matter), you can select the option called "Create a GPO in this domain, and link it here." This will perform both steps in just a single action.

Now, click your GPO, in this case Desktop Security. Notice that the GPO has some tabs and properties associated with it in the right pane of the GPMC. Four tabs are associated with each GPO: Scope, Details, Settings, and Delegation (see Figure 8.6).

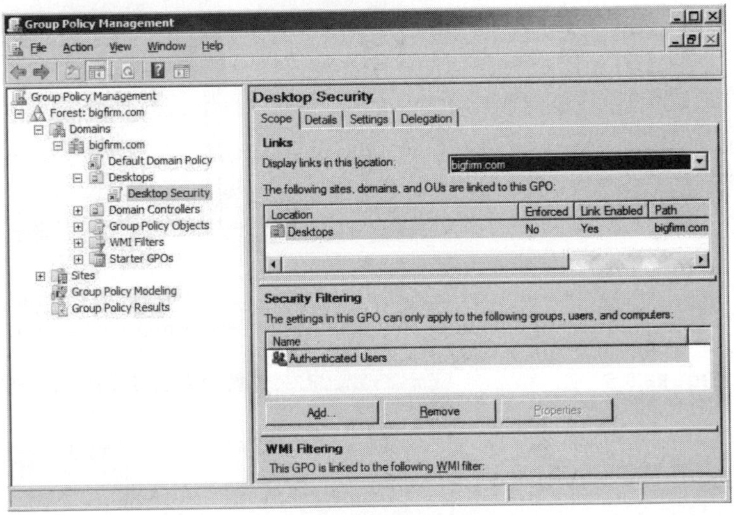

FIGURE 8.6
GPO tabs and properties in the right pane of the GPMC

The Scope tab helps keep track of many aspects of the GPO. The most important of these details includes which Active Directory nodes the GPO is linked to, indicated by the uppermost area named Links and the middle area named Security Filtering. The Links area is rather obvious, listing the sites, domains, and OUs the GPO is currently linked to. The Security Filtering area clearly indicates which groups and users have the permission to apply the settings in the GPO. This filtering was referenced earlier, when it was used to control which users in the domain would have the settings from the GPO applied, just by adding or removing them from this tab. The final area of the tab, WMI Filtering, lists the WMI filter that the GPO has a link to, if any. WMI filters allow the targeting of GPOs to computer accounts dependent on the state of the computer at the time the WMI query is run.

The Details tab, as shown in Figure 8.7, helps keep track of the GPO information that is associated with the creation and state of the GPO. Here you will be able to track down the GUID, creation date, version, and so on, related to the GPO. You can also configure whether all or part (computer and/or user) of the GPO is enabled or disabled.

FIGURE 8.7
The Details tab of the GPO provides key information about the GPO.

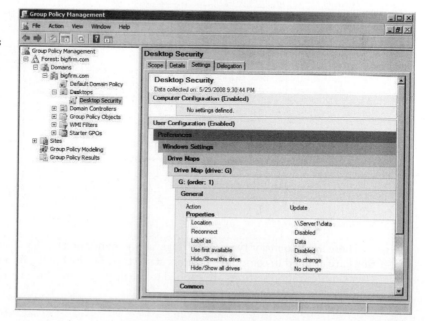

The Settings tab contains dynamic data related to the settings that are configured in the GPO. The tab displays an HTML version of the settings report, as shown in Figure 8.8.

FIGURE 8.8
The Settings tab of the GPO displays the current settings in the GPO.

Finally, the Delegation tab shows the current security controlling the administration of the GPO. There are three different levels of administration of the GPO on this tab, as shown in Figure 8.9. Two include editing the GPO, where one is just reading the settings of the GPO.

FIGURE 8.9

The Delegation tab of the GPO displays the level of administration permissions per group and user.

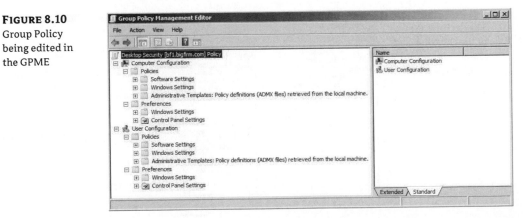

Now let's view and modify the new GPO. Back under the Group Policy Objects node in the GPMC, right-click the GPO, and click Edit. This will open the GPME in a separate window, and you'll see the policy object name at the root of the namespace, in this case Desktop Security [bf1.bigfirm.com] Policy. This indicates what policy is being viewed and edited. Figure 8.10 shows the policy expanded in the console tree to show the major nodes of the GPO. Remember that bf1 is the domain controller for the Bigfirm.com domain.

FIGURE 8.10

Group Policy being edited in the GPME

There are two major types of settings, as we mentioned earlier. Computer Configuration settings are applied to computer accounts at startup and during the background refresh interval. User Configuration settings are applied to the user accounts logon and during the background refresh interval.

We'll explore the various policies according to subject matter later, but prepare yourself for the fact that policies are not all configured in a uniform way as far as the interface is concerned. You'll need a few examples to see what we mean:

1. To specify software packages under Policies\Software Settings\Software Installation, open the folder and choose New ➢ Package from the Action menu. An Open dialog box asks for the location of the package. Once you've located and selected it, you configure the package properties.

2. To set the interval that users can wait before changing passwords, go to Policies\Computer Configuration\Windows Settings\Security Settings\Account Policies\Password Policy. Double-click Minimum Password Length in the details pane on the right, enable the setting by clicking the Define This Policy Setting check box, and supply a number of characters.

3. To set a policy that restricts group memberships, go to Restricted Groups under Security Settings in Policies\Computer Configuration\Windows Settings, and choose Add Group from the Action menu. A dialog box asks you to enter a group or browse for it. Once the group is added to the list in the details pane on the right, double-click the group name to open a dialog box, and supply the names of the users or domain groups who must have membership in the group. You can also define group memberships for the group itself.

4. To set up folder redirection, go to Policies\User Configuration\Windows Settings\Folder Redirection, and choose a folder (for example, Start Menu). The details pane on the right will be blank. Right-click whitespace in the details pane (or select the Action menu), and choose Properties. The properties sheet appears, and you can now specify a location for the Start menu and configure redirection settings.

The point of this wild ride through the array of GPO settings is not to disorient you but rather to illustrate the fact that the GPME has several nodes to accomplish various tasks, and the procedures to specify settings will vary with the node and the task. There is no one way to configure a setting, although many do follow the pattern of step 2. So, when in doubt, right-click or look at the Action menu. It's a strategy to live by.

Once you've configured your Group Policy settings, simply close the GPME window. There is no Save or Save Changes option. Changes are written to the GPO when you click OK or Apply on a particular setting, although the user or computer will not actually see the change until the policy is refreshed.

Group Policy Basics

To better understand how Group Policy technology works in your Active Directory environment, it is best to understand how some of the Group Policy technology works "under the hood." If you are just becoming familiar with Group Policy, you will quickly see that many of the features that Group Policy possesses are benefits over older technologies, such as system policies.

Replication of Group Policy Is Built In

GPOs live partially in the Active Directory and partly in SYSVOL, the Window 2000 and later replacement for netlogon. Both Active Directory and SYSVOL replicate themselves automatically, with no work required on your part. Active Directory is replicated using AD Replication (controlled by the Knowledge Consistency Checker and the Intersite Topology Generator), and SYSVOL is controlled by the File Replication Service or Distributed File Replication Service.

GPOs Undo Themselves When Removed

All the administrative template GPO settings write their information to certain parts of the registry and clean up after themselves when the policy setting is removed or the GPO is deleted.

This fixes the dreaded "tattooing" issue that has plagued "policy management" since it was first introduced. For example, suppose you had created an NT 4–type system policy that set everyone's background color to some nauseating hue and also set up a policy that kept them from changing the color. Those changes got written into the system's registry. If you then deleted the policy, the entries in the registry would not be removed, and therefore the ugly background would remain intact on the system. You'd actually have to write a *second* policy to undo the registry effects. With GPOs, that's not necessary. Just removing the policy will undo its effects.

You Needn't Log On to Apply GPO Settings

The true glory of Group Policy is related to the "background refresh." Since all domain-based computers check in to see whether there are any changes every 90 minutes or so, policy settings are constantly being applied. This means that a setting that you make at 6 a.m. on a Monday morning to control some security setting on each desktop won't require that the computers be up and running. Rather, the background refresh will apply to the computer before the user arrives at 8 a.m.

On Windows 2000 and later with Active Directory, machines get their policy settings from the domain they have membership within when they power up (recall that machines log on also), and users get policies from *their* domain when they log on.

GROUP POLICIES WORK ONLY ON WINDOWS 2000 AND LATER MACHINES

Group Policy was created as part of Windows 2000 and won't work on earlier operating systems. Also, to take advantage of domain-based GPOs, you must be running Active Directory, although it is possible to apply a more limited set of "local policies" without AD.

Windows 9x and Windows NT Workstation 4 use the same old tools as before—Windows 9x profiles, Windows NT 4 profiles, and system policies. Because there aren't many "ancient" OSs still in use, it's unlikely that you'll have to worry about one set of policies and profiles for the Windows 9x machines, another for the NT 4 machines, and a third set of GPOs for the 2000, XP, and Vista machines. If you're unlucky enough to be working in such an environment, you can store *all* of these things on Windows Server 2008—you don't have to keep an old NT 4 server around to hold the 9x/NT profiles. That's something of a consolation.

Modifying Group Policy Default Behavior

Group Policy is fantastic all by itself, but there are some behaviors that you might want to tweak or control. It might seem cyclical, but there are GPO settings to control the behavior of Group Policy and some of its settings. You will find that many of these settings don't need to be configured, but in the instances where you need to make some minor adjustments, they will come in handy.

Group Policy Policies

You can find the GPO settings to control Group Policy under Administrative Templates of both the User Configuration and Computer Configuration nodes (`Policies\Administrative Templates\System\Group Policy`). The Computer Configuration node contains most of the policies we'll be discussing. Figure 8.11 and Figure 8.12 show the User Configuration and Computer Configuration options for Group Policy. The following paragraphs summarize the most important configuration options.

FIGURE 8.11

User Configuration settings for Group Policy

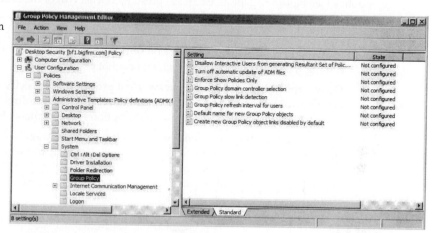

FIGURE 8.12

Computer Configuration settings for Group Policy

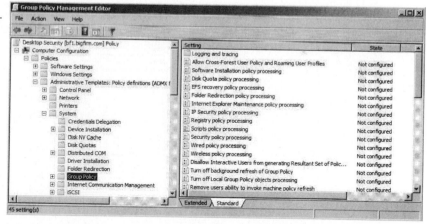

Group Policy refresh intervals for users/computers/domain controllers   These separate policies determine how often GPOs are refreshed in the background while users and computers are working. These parameters permit changes to the default background refresh intervals and tweaking of the offset time.

Turn off background refresh of Group Policy If you enable this setting, policies will be refreshed only at system startup and user logon. This might be useful for performance reasons in your branch offices, since having 1,500 computers refreshing policies every 90 minutes could cause congestion over the WAN.

Policy processing options These policies, with names such as Registry Policy Processing and Folder Redirection Policy Processing, are available to customize the behavior of the different GPO components. These policy settings exist under the Computer Configuration node. Each policy (see Figure 8.13 for an example) presents at least two of the following three options:

Allow processing across a slow network connection For slow connections, some policies can be turned off to enhance performance (you can define what a "slow link" is by using the Group Policy Slow Link Detection setting). Security settings and registry policy processing will always apply, however, and cannot be turned off.

Do not apply during periodic background processing Specify which components will be refreshed periodically. Software installation and folder redirection policies will never be refreshed while a user is logged in, so the option is not available for them.

Process even if the Group Policy objects have not changed To conserve network and system resources, GPOs are, by default, not refreshed if there have been no changes. To increase security, however, and guard against a user changing a policy setting, enable the policy to ensure that all settings are reapplied at each refresh interval. Please note that enabling this policy may cause noticeable performance degradation.

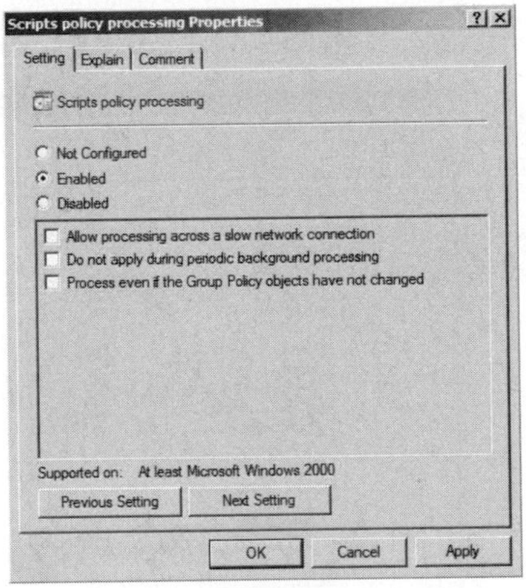

FIGURE 8.13
Scripts policy
processing options

Loopback processing mode: when you want a particular *machine* to have specific user settings By default, user policy settings are processed after Computer Configuration policies. Also by default, users receive their policy settings regardless of the machine they use to log in. Sometimes this is not appropriate and policy settings need to be applied according to the computer's policy objects instead (*loopback processing*). For example, if you log in to a server to do administration, it's not appropriate for your office productivity applications to start installing themselves. Another example of when you would want computer policies to override user policies is if you want to apply more stringent policies for machines that are exposed to the anonymous public (machines in libraries, university computer labs, or kiosks in shopping malls and tourist attractions, for instance). Two modes are used to control this behavior (see Figure 8.14):

Merge mode   Processes user policies first and then the "user configuration portion" of the computer GPO. All settings "merge" unless there is a conflict, upon which the user settings from the computer GPO will rule.

Replace mode   Disregards user policies and processes only the "user configuration portion" of the computer GPO.

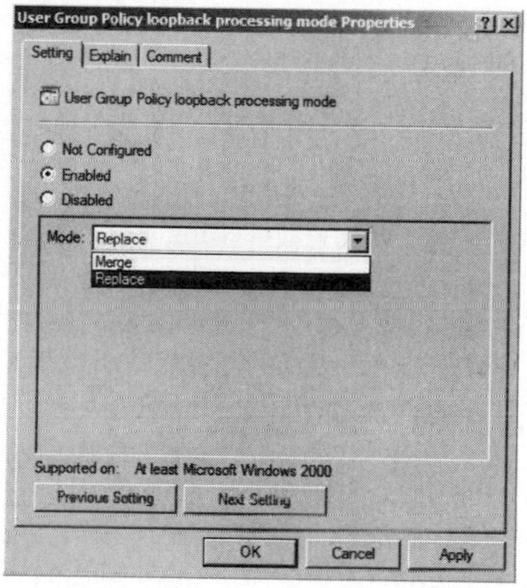

FIGURE 8.14

User Group Policy loopback processing mode policy

Group Policy over Slow Links

Group Policy still works over slow links such as dial-up connections. Even better, it's applied whether users log in using Dial-Up Networking or whether they log in with cached credentials and then initiate a connection. However, application of Group Policy over slow links can pose performance issues, so there are also policy settings to define a slow link and to define how policies are applied over a detected slow link.

Windows Server 2008 and Vista have moved to using Network Location Awareness (NLA) to determine the link speed, whereas in previous versions of Windows ping was used. The default definition of a slow link, as far as group policies are concerned, is anything slower than 500 kilobits per second. You can change the definition of a slow link, however. This policy setting, called Group Policy Slow Link Detection, is available in both User Configuration and Computer Configuration, under Policies\Administrative Templates\System\Group Policy (see Figure 8.15 for the properties sheet of the policy). To change the default parameter, enter a number in kilobits per second or enter 0 to disable slow-link detection altogether. If you disable slow-link detection, all policies will be applied regardless of the connection speed.

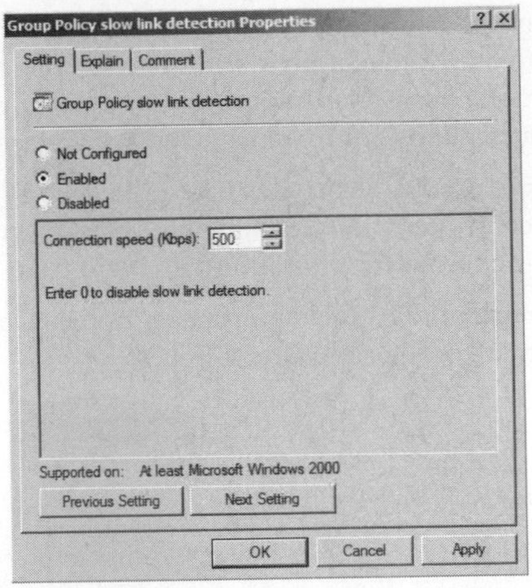

FIGURE 8.15
Group Policy's
slow-link detection
properties

As we mentioned in the preceding section, policy processing settings for individual policy components (these have names such as Folder Redirection Policy Processing and are found in the same path as the slow-link detection setting, under Computer Configuration\Administrative Templates\System\Group Policy) allow you to specify whether a portion of the policy object will be processed over a slow-link connection. Again, this is not an option for registry-based policies or for security settings; these will always be processed, even over slow links. The other modules will not be applied over slow links by default.

To have logon scripts run over slow links, for example, open the policy called Scripts Policy Processing. Enable the policy and select the "Allow processing across a slow network connection" box (shown earlier in Figure 8.13). Click OK, and the policy is set. Repeat as necessary for the other policy-processing entries.

Group Policy Application

Like most technologies, Group Policy has logic associated with it to ensure that it applies in a reliable manner. For the most part, the application of Group Policy will be straightforward. It is only when you start to have conflicting settings in multiple GPOs and you start to modify the default behavior that the logic becomes more complex. Regardless, when you sit down to design and implement your policy settings, you will need to fully grasp what the end result will be for all of your computers and users.

In this section, we will cover the default Group Policy application, which will resolve all your questions regarding GPO setting conflicts. You know, questions like "What if I have a GPO at the domain that removes the Run command from the Start menu, but a different GPO linked to the Desktops OU that adds the Run command to the Start menu?"

We will also delve into areas that will help you "target" your GPO settings for when too many users and computers (or not enough users and computers) are receiving the policy settings. With WMI filters, enforcement, blocking inheritance, and more, you will certainly not be without options.

How Group Policy Is Applied

Now that you have a GPO or two running, you'll soon find the troublesome part of Group Policy: figuring out what the end result is for each computer and user. Imagine, for example, that a user calls up and asks, "Why is my background purple?" You then realize that there are a *lot* of places that your system gets policies from, and they might disagree on things such as, for example, background color. So, which one *wins*?

POLICIES EXECUTE FROM THE BOTTOM UP IN THE GUI

Let's start by considering a simple situation: just policies in a domain. Suppose you look at the domain node using the GPMC and see that it has many GPOs linked to it, as shown in Figure 8.16.

FIGURE 8.16
Domain node and linked GPOs

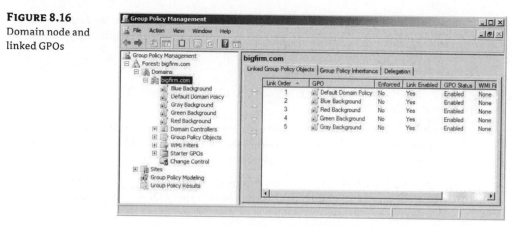

In this (admittedly fanciful) situation, the domain has five group policies, four of which attempt to set a workstation's background color to gray, green, red, or blue. (The other is the Default Domain Policy, which has nothing to say on the issue.) To see the order in which the GPOs have preference, you can click the domain node and view the Linked Group Policy Objects tab in the right pane. So, based on Figure 8.16, who wins? Gray, red, green, or blue?

The answer lies in two basic conflict resolution rules for GPOs:

Rule 1 Listen to the last policy that you heard from.

Rule 2 Execute policies from the bottom up, as they appear in the GUI.

Reading from the bottom of the dialog box up, you see that the system will first see the policy that sets the background gray, then the one that sets it green, then the one that sets it red, and finally the one that sets it blue. Because blue is the last one heard from, it wins, and the effects of the previous three are obviated.

You can also click the Group Policy Inheritance tab, which will display the order in which the GPOs apply from all locations within Active Directory. As you can see in Figure 8.17, the blue background policy wins out over the others.

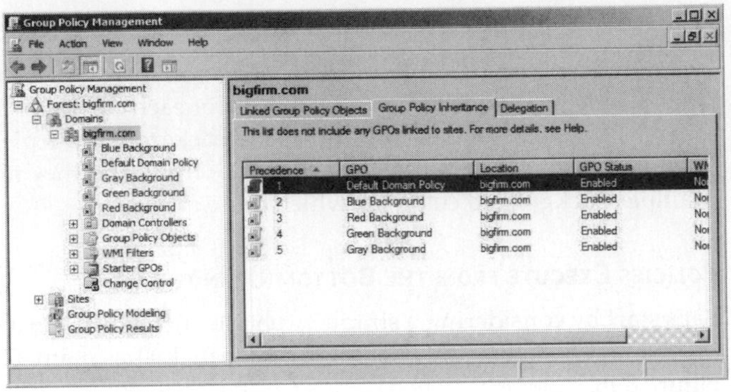

FIGURE 8.17
GPO inheritance
for the
domain node

But what if you *want* the red background policy to win? Notice the up and down arrows to the left of the Linked Group Policy Objects tab? You can shuffle them around to your heart's content.

GROUP POLICY APPLICATION ORDER

The previous example only considered GPOs that were linked to the domain. But you can apply policies to different AD nodes:

- Sites can have linked GPOs, and no matter what domain's machines and users are in that site, those policy settings within the GPO will apply. (That's why you have to be an Enterprise Administrator to create site policies.)

- OUs can have linked GPOs. Don't forget OUs can contain OUs, and OUs can contain OUs that contain OUs, and so on. Therefore, any of these OUs in the chain can have a GPO linked to it.

- There are also *local* policies, don't forget.

So, again, the question is, "Who wins?" Policies are applied in the following order:

1. Local policy
2. Sites
3. Domains
4. Organizational units
5. Child OUs

If the domain policy says, "You must be logged in before you can shut down the machine" and the OU policy says, "Allow shutdown before logon," the OU policy takes precedence because it is applied last. If one policy says, "Lock it down" and the next one says, "Not configured," the setting remains locked down. If one policy says, "Not configured" and the next one says, "Lock it down," then it's locked down in this case, as well. If one policy says, "Leave it on" and the next one says, "Turn it off," it's turned off. If one policy says, "Turn it off," then another, closer one says, "Turn it on," and then a third one says, "Turn it off," guess what? It ends up turned off. However, for the preservation of your sanity, it is desirable to avoid these little disagreements between GPOs and the settings.

Filtering Group Policy with Access Control Lists

But we're not *nearly* finished here. It *could* be that although it looks as if many policies apply to your system, in fact, only a small number do. The reason: GPOs have ACLs.

Click any GPO in the GPMC (in our example, the Desktop Security GPO), and view the Scope tab in the right pane. Here, in the Security Filtering section, you see the ACL for the GPO, as shown in Figure 8.18.

FIGURE 8.18

ACL for a GPO in the GPMC

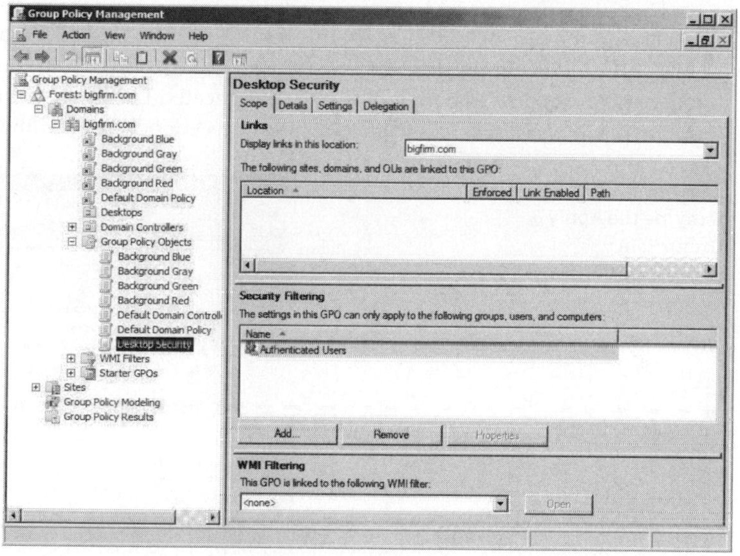

As we pointed out before, Domain Admins and Enterprise Admins have Read and Modify permissions, and Authenticated Users have Read and Apply Group Policy. However, notice that you only see Authenticated Users listed in the list. Why is that? Well, this is a list of only the users, computers, and groups that have the permission to apply the GPO settings. To view the full ACL, you must first select the Delegation tab and then click the Advanced button. The good ole Security Settings dialog box will display, as shown in Figure 8.19.

FIGURE 8.19

Security Settings dialog box for a GPO

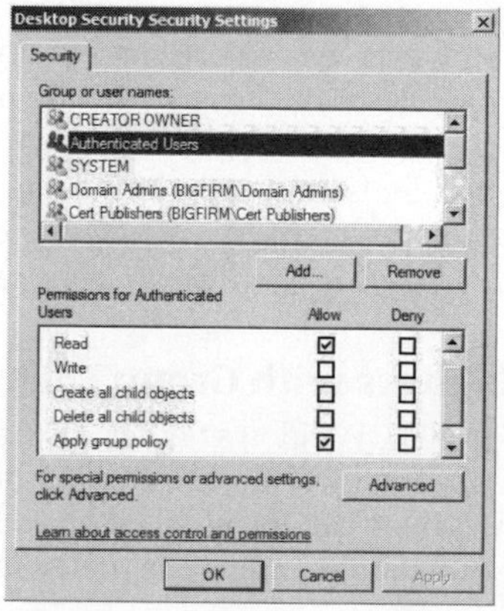

It may happen that you create a GPO to restrict desktops and you don't want to apply it to a certain group of people. The group Authenticated Users includes everyone (user and computer accounts) but guests, so by default the GPO will apply to everyone but guests; that means even Domain Admins and Enterprise Admins will receive the policy settings. To prevent Domain Admins and Enterprise Admins from receiving this policy, you must select the Deny box next to Apply Group Policy (Figure 8.20). A member of both groups will only need the Deny setting for one of the two groups, but you'll need to select the Deny box for both groups if the members of Domain Admins and Enterprise Admins are not the same people. To "excuse" others from receiving the policy, put them all in a security group and add that group to the list. It is not enough to deselect the granted box for Read and Apply Group Policy; the users in your special security group are also members of Authenticated Users, so you actually need to choose the Deny option for them as well. Deny takes precedence over Allow.

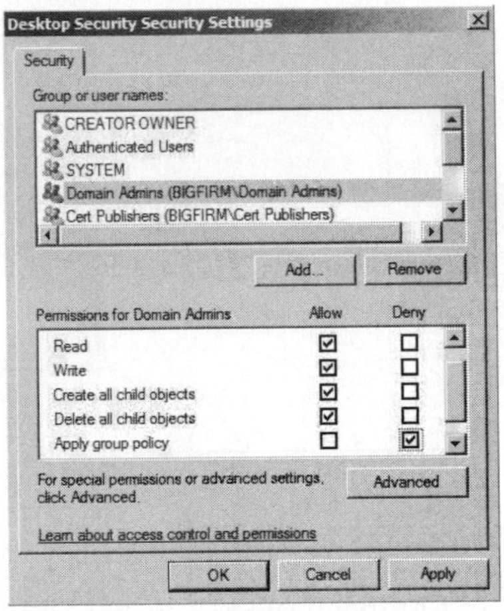

FIGURE 8.20

Denying the Apply Group Policy permission

As an alternative to all that ACLing, you can also remove the Authenticated Users group from the Security Filtering part of the Scope tab, add all the users who need to have the settings to a security group, and then add the security group to the Security Filtering part of the Scope tab. This is shown in Figure 8.21.

By the way, there is nothing to prevent you from adding individual users to the permissions list for a GPO. However, it is a horrible security and management practice to do so, because it is impossible to track individual users who are placed on ACLs throughout the enterprise! We'll stress, then, that policy filtering is incredibly powerful—you might say that it's the tool that lets you oppress individuals or groups. In the real world, however, adding ACLs to a policy can be a nightmare for the poor fool trying to figure out two years later why a policy is attached to a domain but *isn't bloody applying to most of the people in the domain!*

Using WMI Filters with Group Policy

Windows Server 2003, Windows Server 2008, and Windows Server 2008 R2 offer a WMI filtering option for GPOs, which was not offered in Windows 2000. WMI filters run queries created in WMI Query Language (WQL) to determine whether to apply all the settings in the entire GPO. You can't pick and choose among the policy settings. To use WMI filtering, select the GPO, select the Scope tab in the right pane, and look in the WMI Filtering section, as shown in Figure 8.22. Use the drop-down list to select which WMI filter you want to link the GPO to.

FIGURE 8.21
Group Policy security filtering without Authenticated Users

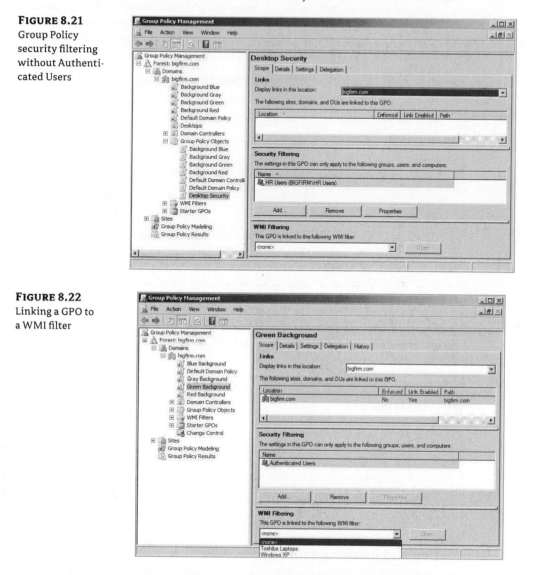

FIGURE 8.22
Linking a GPO to a WMI filter

You can choose from thousands of WMI-based variables. For instance, you might want to have policy settings apply only to laptops. First you'd need to determine the make and model of laptops used, and then you could create a query that looks something like this:

```
Root\CimV2; Select * from Win32_ComputerSystem where manufacturer =
  "Toshiba" and   Model = "Portege 2000" OR Model = "Portege 4010"
```

Other WMI criteria you could use to filter policies are disk space thresholds, version of the operating system, absence or presence of an existing software package, or even network information. To create your own WMI filter, you need to right-click the WMI Filters node and select New. In the New WMI Filter dialog box, type a name for your filter and then click the Add button to input your WMI query. Figure 8.23 shows a WMI filter for systems with an operating system name of Windows XP.

FIGURE 8.23
Managing WMI
filters for Group
Policy objects

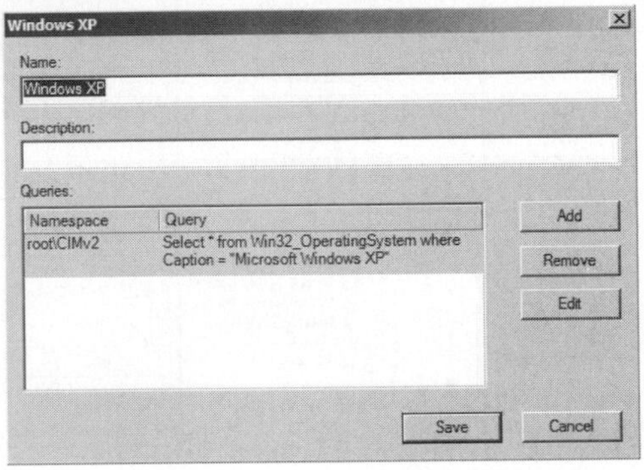

This WMI filter thing sounds great, right? Well, here's the downside: you can have only one WMI filter per GPO. If you use WMI filters, you'll probably end up creating more GPOs than you normally would. First you would create one or more "generic" GPOs, the ones that apply to the entire site, domain, or OU without any of the hardware or software-dependent settings. Then you would create a bunch of "mini-GPOs" that each use a WMI filter to determine whether to deploy.

WMI SCRIPTING

Another disadvantage of using WMI filters is that you have to learn the WMI scripting variables. Or you can cheat and download the unsupported Scriptomatic tool from www.microsoft.com/downloads/details.aspx?FamilyID=09dfc342-648b-4119-b7eb-783b0f7d1178&DisplayLang=en. This little hypertext application reveals all the WMI classes, properties, and methods you need to use the WMI filtering capability.

Enforcing and Blocking Inheritance

Just as security filtering can be used to counter the blanket application of policy application, the Block Inheritance setting is a special setting on an AD node (domain or OU) to prevent higher-level GPOs from trickling down. When the Block Inheritance setting is enabled, the settings of higher policies will not be applied to lower containers at all. For example, if you create a GPO for a specific OU, say Brunswick, and set up all the necessary settings for the Brunswick OU and then you want to prevent the Bigfirm domain GPOs from affecting the Brunswick OU, you'd enable the Block Inheritance setting on the Brunswick OU. The only GPOs applied will be those linked to the Brunswick OU.

There is also a counter to the block inheritance configuration. (Isn't this becoming like a *Batman* episode? "Robin, they've blocked our transmission. It's time for the block-anti-block Bat-transmitter!") When Enforce is turned on for a GPO, the Block Inheritance setting is neutralized for the enforced GPO. Also, the settings in subsequent GPOs are prevented from reversing the ones in the Enforce-enabled GPO. For example, if domain admins have a set of highly disputed settings turned on at the domain level and those renegade Brunswick admins set up their own OU with its own policy settings and select the Block Inheritance setting, the Brunswick OU effectively escapes the disputed settings, but only until the domain admins get wise and select the Enforce setting. Then the domain admins win, and the Brunswick OU people have to live with the same restrictions as everyone else. Enforce beats Block Inheritance (just like paper covers rock).

Like all secret weapons, the Enforce and Block Inheritance settings are best used sparingly. Otherwise, in a troubleshooting situation it becomes rather complicated to determine what GPOs are applied where. This could be detrimental to the mental health (and potentially the job security) of a network administrator.

Whew! Here's a summary of the factors that can decide which Group Policy object wins:

♦ Examine policies in this order: local GPOs, then site GPOs, then domain GPOs, then OU GPOs, then child OU GPOs, and so on.

♦ Within any AD node—site, domain, or OU—examine the policies as they appear in the GUI, from the bottom up.

♦ If policy settings conflict, pay attention only to the setting in the last GPO that you examined, *unless* you already saw a policy that said Enforce. This means that no matter what conflicting policy setting comes afterward, you should ignore these because of the Enforce-enabled GPO.

♦ Before you actually apply a GPO, check its ACL. If the target user or computer does not have the Read and Apply Group Policy permissions (usually through group membership), then the GPO doesn't apply.

Group Policy Example: Forcing Complex Passwords

Before leaving this topic, let's look at a conflict resolution example that will also offer an example of a useful situation for GPOs. Assume that you want to create a highly secure password policy for users in the domain. You decide to create a GPO that has the following criteria:

♦ Complex passwords

♦ Minimum of 12 characters in the password

To implement your solution, follow these steps:

1. Open GPMC.

2. Right-click the domain node, such as Bigfirm.

3. Create a GPO in this domain, and Link it here. Select the New menu option, and then type in **New Password Policy** for the name of the GPO. Then click the OK button.

4. Right-click the New Password Policy GPO, and select Edit.

5. In the GPME, maneuver down through the Computer Configuration\Policies\Windows Settings\Security Settings\Account Policies\Password Policy node.

6. Enable the "Password must meet complexity requirements" option, and then configure the minimum password length for 12 characters.

7. Exit the GPME.

But you're not done yet—don't expect this to take effect immediately. Domain controllers reapply policies every 15 seconds, but they can only apply a policy that they know about, so you also have to wait for the policy information to replicate to other domain controllers. (Obviously, if you have only one DC, then replication isn't a problem.)

Now, create a user account and try to give it a short seven-character password; you probably expect to get an error message. But you don't get one; the system accepts the short password despite the New Password Policy GPO. You can even open a command line and typed **gpupdate**, hoping that will push the system into seeing the policy. But it still won't work.

Why is that? Every AD domain automatically gets a GPO called Default Domain Policy. When you created the new GPO, New Password Policy, the system placed it below the Default Domain Policy, as it does by default—reading top to bottom, you can see the order in which policies were created or linked to the domain. The Default Domain Policy object has only a seven-character minimum password length!

So, there's a conflict in policies here. Your password length is set to 12 characters, and the Default Domain Policy says to only enforce a 7-character password. Who wins? Well, by default, a system pays attention to the *last* command that it heard, and the system executes GPOs from the one at the bottom of the list in the user interface to the top. (It's true, believe it or not.) So, the system first got the command to enforce a 12-character password, and then as it worked its way up the GPO hierarchy and it came across the Default Domain Policy, which said only force a seven-character password.

The answer? You could have set New Password Policy to Enforce, but this seems like overkill in this situation. Instead, you can just move it above Default Domain Policy in the UI. The result: 12-character passwords.

And one more note, embarrassing as it may be: we were originally going to have you just try this longer password policy on an organizational unit, but the policy didn't work. Then we remembered—duh—that account policies for domain user accounts don't work when linked to OUs; you have to make account policies on domains, or they'll be ignored.

Group Policy Setting Possibilities

You can do basically anything with Group Policy settings that you can do to the local system registry and most configurations. Here are a few examples:

Deploy software   You can gather all the files necessary to install a piece of software into a *package*, put that package on a server somewhere, and then use group policies to point a user's desktop at that package. The user sees that the application is available, and again, you accomplish all that from a central location rather than having to visit every desktop. The first time the user tries to start the application, it installs without any intervention from the user.

Set user rights   You may know that NT had the notion of "rights," or the ability to do a particular function. Examples include the ability to log on locally, back up files, and log on using Terminal Services. Under NT 4, you had to visit a machine to modify user rights; now it's controllable via a GPO, meaning again that you needn't wear out any shoe leather to change a distant machine's rights.

Restrict the applications that users can run You can control a user's desktop to the point where that user can run only a few applications—perhaps Outlook, Word, and Internet Explorer, for example.

Control system settings The easiest way to control disk space quotas is with GPOs. Many Windows systems are most easily controlled with policy settings; with some systems, policies are the *only* method to enable and control those systems.

Set logon, logoff, startup, and shutdown scripts GPOs allow any or all of these four events to trigger a script, and you use GPOs to control which scripts run.

Simplify and restrict programs You can use GPOs to remove many of the features from Internet Explorer, Windows Explorer, and other programs.

General desktop restriction You can remove most or all of the items on a user's Start button, keep her from adding printers, or disallow her from logging out or modifying her desktop configuration at all. With all the policy settings turned on, you can really lock down a user's desktop. (Too much locking down may lead to creating one unproductive employee, however, so be careful.)

There's lots more to work with in policies, but that was a basic introduction to get you started.

Decrypting User and Computer Configuration Settings

Windows Server 2008, Server 2008 R2, and Vista SP1 and later come with a completely new look and feel for the User and Computer Configuration settings in the GPME. The reason for this is that Microsoft has done us all a huge favor! The favor is that it has introduced nearly 3,000 more GPO settings. To give you a better grip on the volume of settings, Microsoft has also adjusted how the settings are presented in the GPME.

As you see in Figure 8.24, there are two main nodes to the GPME interface: User Configuration and Computer Configuration. Both nodes have the following subnodes: Policies and Preferences. The Policies subnode is further broken down into the following subnodes: Software Settings, Windows Settings, and Administrative Templates. The Preferences subnode is broken down into these subnodes: Control Panel and Windows Settings.

FIGURE 8.24
Group Policy nodes
and subnodes

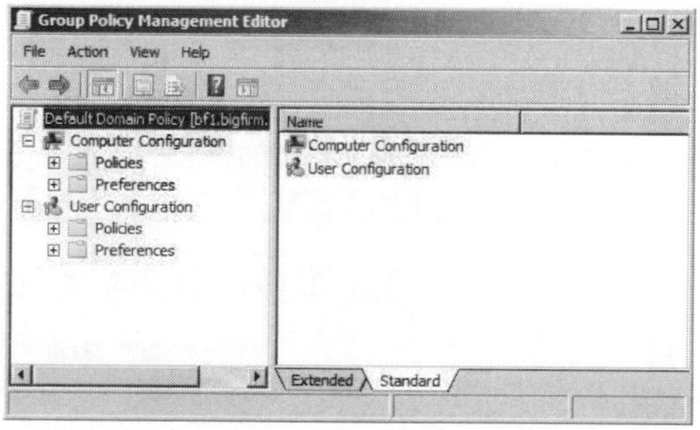

The difference between the two level of nodes is this: settings for User Configuration apply to user accounts, and settings for Computer Configuration apply to computer accounts. For example, if registry settings are involved, as is the case with administrative templates, the changes will be written to HKEY_CURRENT_USER (HKCU) for User Configuration stuff and to HKEY_LOCAL_MACHINE (HKLM) for Computer Configuration settings. You may want to create separate GPOs for machines and users to keep things straight. If a value set in the computer settings is also specified in the user policy settings, the Computer Configuration settings usually take precedence by default. To ensure the behavior, check out the Explain tab within the GPO setting, or, the best solution would be to test!

With more than 5,000 settings in a Windows Server 2008 GPO, it's impossible to go over every setting. However, to help you through the settings, you should check out the Excel spreadsheet that Microsoft has provided at http://www.microsoft.com/downloads/details.aspx?displaylang=en& FamilyID=18c90c80-8b0a-4906-a4f5-ff24cc2030fb.

We will go over some of the more useful policy settings and policy categories in the following sections.

SPECIFY SCRIPTS WITH GROUP POLICY

You can specify logon and logoff scripts, as well as scripts to run at system startup and shutdown, using Windows Settings in either the User Configuration node or the Computer Configuration node. Expand Policies\Windows Settings to reveal Scripts, and then select the script type (Startup, Shutdown, Logon, or Logoff) in the details pane on the right; Figure 8.25 shows the scripts available in User Configuration. From here, double-click the script type (such as Logon), or highlight it and choose Action ➤ Properties. Add Scripts to the list using the Add button (see Figure 8.26), and supply a script name and parameters when prompted. To edit the script name and parameters (not the script itself), choose Edit. If more than one script is specified, use the up and down buttons to indicate the order in which the scripts should run.

FIGURE 8.25
Group Policy
logon scripts

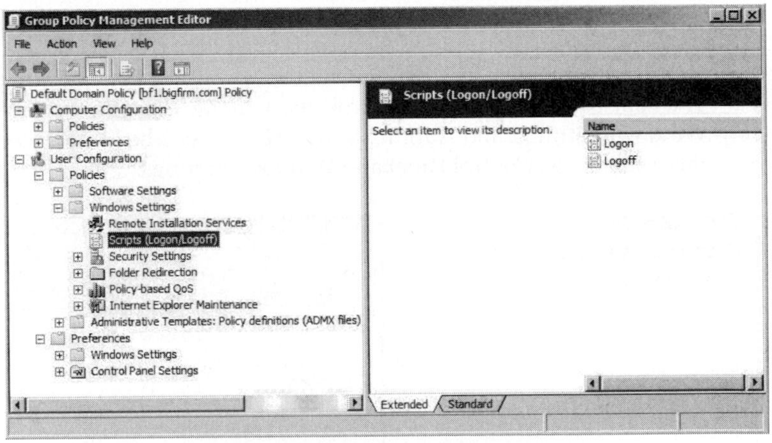

FIGURE 8.26
Adding a script to
Group Policy

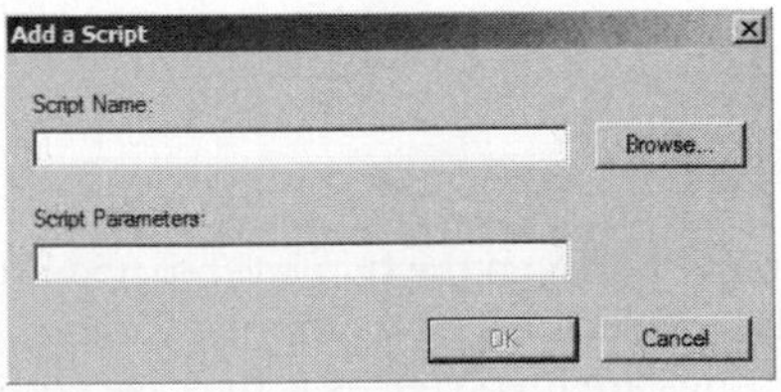

The scripts you create and assign should be copied to the following path in the SYSVOL directory: \Windows\SYSVOL\SysVol\domainname\Policies\{GUID}\Machine\Scripts\Startup (or Shutdown). (Or they can be copied to User\Scripts\Logon or User\Scripts\Logoff, depending on whether you are assigning scripts to the Computer Configuration node or to the User Configuration node.) The GUID for the Group Policy object is a long string that looks like {FA08AF41-38AB-11D3-BD1FC9B6902FA00B}. If you want to see the scripts stored in the GPO and possibly open them for editing, use the Show Files button at the bottom of the properties sheet. This will open the folder in Explorer.

As you may know, you can also specify a logon script in the properties sheet of the user account in dsa.msc. Microsoft calls these *legacy logon scripts* and encourages you to assign scripts with Group Policy for Windows AD–aware clients. Of course, Windows 9x/NT clients don't use GPOs, so you'll still assign their logon scripts in the account properties of the user account. Other than that, the only real advantage to using the Group Policy scripts is that they run asynchronously in a hidden window. So, if several scripts are assigned or if the scripts are complex, the user doesn't have to wait for them to end. Legacy logon scripts run in a window on the desktop. On the other hand, you might not want the scripts to run hidden (some scripts stop and supply information or wait for user input). In that case, several policy settings are available to help you define the behavior of Group Policy scripts. These settings are located in the System\Scripts\Administrative Templates node. There you'll find settings to specify whether to run a script synchronously or asynchronously and whether it should be visible or invisible. Legacy logon scripts can be run hidden, like Group Policy scripts, by using the setting shown in Figure 8.27. The Computer Configuration settings also include a maximum wait time for Group Policy scripts, which is 600 seconds by default. This changes the timeout period, which is the maximum allotted time allowed for the script to complete.

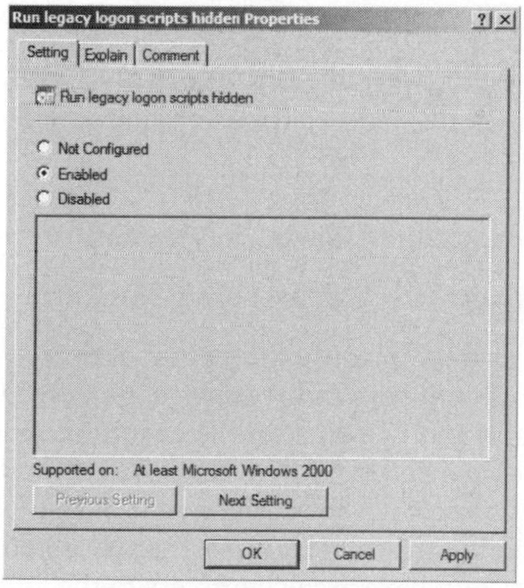

FIGURE 8.27
Policy to run legacy scripts hidden

FOLDER REDIRECTION

One of the more useful things you can do with User Configuration settings in Group Policy is to arrange for a user's AppData, Desktop, Start Menu, Documents, Favorites, and Links folders to follow the user around from computer to computer. These folders are important elements in a user's working environment. AppData stores application-specific user information (Internet Explorer uses it, for example), and Desktop may contain important folders and shortcuts that need to be just one click away for the user. The Start Menu folder contains program groups and shortcuts to programs, and My Documents is the default place to save and retrieve files, sort of like a local home directory.

There are several good reasons to use folder redirection. For one thing, it's convenient for users who log in from several different machines. Also, if you specify a network location for some or all of these folders, they can be backed up regularly and protected by the IT department. If roaming profiles are still in use, setting up folder redirection speeds up the synchronization of the server profile with the local profile at logon and logoff, since the redirected folders need not be updated. Redirecting the Desktop and Start Menu folders to a centralized, shared location facilitates standardization of users' working environments and helps with remote support issues, because help-desk personnel will know that all machines are configured in the same way. Best of all, you can mix and match. It's possible to specify a shared location for the Desktop and Start Menu folders while allowing each user to have their own Documents and AppData folders. Let's take a look.

To set a network location for the Documents folder in Group Policy, go to User Configuration\Policies\Windows Settings\Folder Redirection\Documents, right-click the highlighted Documents folder, and choose Properties from the context menu. The properties sheet reveals that this setting is not configured by default. Choose Basic from the drop-down list to specify a single location for the Documents folder, to be shared by all the users, or choose Advanced to set locations based on security group membership. If you want a single location for a shared Documents folder, just fill in the target location with a network path or browse for it. To designate different locations, first choose a security group and then specify a network path. Figure 8.28 demonstrates redirecting the My Documents folder for all members of Domain Engineering to the CentralEng share on the server Zooropa. Whether you choose the Basic or Advanced redirection option, the policy permits you to choose from four options:

◆ Redirect the folder to the user's home directory

◆ Create a folder for each user under the root path

◆ Redirect to the following location (which you specify)

◆ Redirect to the local user profile location

For this example, choose the second option; everyone in Engineering will use the same root path, but they will have individual Documents folders. When you use this option, the system creates a subfolder named after the user in the path you specify.

Now click the Settings tab to configure the redirection settings. For the sake of completeness, the redirection settings for Documents are shown in Figure 8.29.

The options you see in Figure 8.29 show default selections for the Documents folder. Notice that the user will have exclusive access to the folder by default. The contents of the corresponding folder will be moved to the new location by default. Even after the policy is removed, the folder will remain redirected unless you say to "unredirect" it.

SECURITY SETTINGS

Security settings, along with administrative templates, make up a significant part of Group Policy. The default security settings are purposely open to minimize administrative headaches and to ensure that users and applications work as intended. As security increases, users and applications have more restrictions, and support time goes up. In other words, security is inversely proportionate to convenience. As you start locking down systems, something is bound to stop working. Hey, regular users can't even install applications on a Windows Vista system by default. When you start enforcing passwords that are eight characters or more, contain both letters and numbers, can't use any part of a user's name, and cannot be reused until 15 other passwords have been used, things get complicated for the everyday Joe. For organizations that want to increase security, there are tools and guidelines.

FIGURE 8.28
Policy to redirect the user's Documents folder

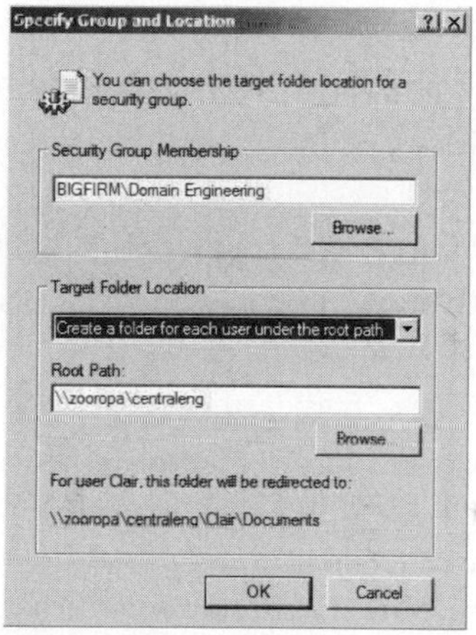

FIGURE 8.29
Additional settings in Policy to redirect the user's Documents folder

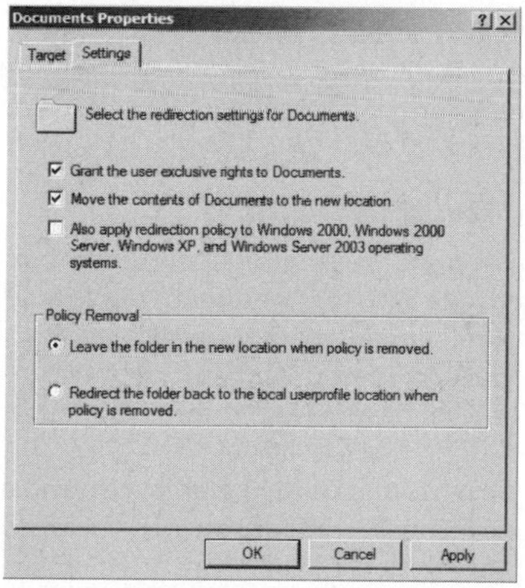

For example, if you have ever "hardened" a Windows server according to established military or other high-security guidelines, you know that you have to set particular permissions on particular folders, change the default permissions on certain registry keys, and change or create other registry entries as well. All in all, it takes a few hours of work on a single server, even for an efficient admin. What if you have 50 servers and 500 workstations? Some things can be scripted, but others can't. There is no Microsoft or third-party tool that does everything automatically for all machines.

Here's where Group Policy comes to the rescue. Assuming you are going to standardize throughout a grouping of servers or workstations, or even a portion of the organization, you have to change those sticky registry permissions and settings only once using Group Policy. You only have to set the NTFS permissions once. The permissions can even be set up in one policy and copied to another. Whether you need a lot of security or just a little more than the default, chances are you'll want to make at least some standardized changes, and the Security Settings node will certainly make your life easier. The bulk of security settings are found under Computer Configuration\Policies\Windows Settings\Security Settings, although public key policies and software restriction policies are also found in the User Configuration node in the same path. The following are the major categories of settings under Security Settings:

Account Policies   Specifies password restrictions, lockout policies, and Kerberos policy.

Local Policies   Configures auditing and assigns user rights and miscellaneous security settings.

Event Log   Centralizes configuration options for the event log.

Restricted Groups   Enforces and controls group memberships for certain groups, such as the Administrators group.

System Services   Standardizes services configurations and protects against changes.

Registry   Creates security templates for registry key permissions to control who can change what keys and to control read access to parts of the registry.

File System   Creates security templates for permissions on files and folders to ensure that files and directories have and keep the permissions you want them to have.

Public Key Policies   Manages settings for organizations using a public key infrastructure.

Software Restrictions Policies   Places restrictions on what software runs on a system. This new feature is designed to prevent viruses and untrusted software from running on a system. It works only on Windows XP or Server machines, though.

Leveraging Security Templates

To accomplish your "mass" security rollout from the previous example, you will need some way to get the settings "entered" and then "deployed." The deployment is rather easy, since we have AD and Group Policy. The question then becomes how do you "enter" the security information so it can be tracked, reused, and quickly modified? The answer is security templates. We suggest that if you've been overlooking them, then you *have* to start using them. In this section, you'll see why.

Worms, viruses, disgruntled employees, and our ever-growing reliance on computers all add up to one thing: a need for security. Clearly there are more and more reasons to secure our computers, and, for most of us, there are more and more computers around to secure! But who wants to make security a full-time job? Not us. That's why you should know about a set of tools that can simplify your job of locking down 2000 (and later) boxes.

Let's say that you've decided you want to ensure that the Power Users groups on your workstations should be empty—you don't want anyone in those groups. You also are awfully tired of stomping out the latest Web server worm on all of those computers that installed IIS, so you're going around and disabling Web Publishing Service on all servers that don't need it.

But, man, that's a lot of work. So, you adopt Plan B: the security requirements document. In this document, you outline exactly what must be done for any workstations or servers approved at Acme Corporation. You distribute the document. And no one has time to read it. Nor is there any easy way to check up on systems to see whether they meet the requirements. Or so it seems.

Wouldn't it be great to just click a button and make those changes on every system? You can, with a few tools: `secedit.exe`, which is an MMC snap-in named Security Configuration and Analysis, and security templates.

What Templates Can Do

Basically, a *security template* is an ASCII file that you feed into a program named `secedit.exe`. That template is a set of instructions—basically a script—that tells `secedit` to make various kinds of changes in your system.

Templates don't let you modify anything that you couldn't modify otherwise; they just provide a nice, scripted, reproducible way to make modifications and then easily audit systems to ensure that they meet the template's requirements. You could make any of these changes by hand with the GUI, but it'd be time-consuming. With templates, you can change the following:

NTFS permissions If you want the directory C:\STUFF to have NTFS permissions of System/Full Control and Administrators/Full Control and to deny access to everyone else, then a template can make that happen. And because you can apply templates not only to one machine but also to many (provided you're using group policies), you could enforce that set of NTFS permissions on the whole domain.

Local group membership Perhaps you have a policy that workstations are set up so that the only accounts in the local Administrators group should be the local Administrator account and the Domain Admins group from the domain. But now and then, some support person "temporarily" elevates a user account to the Administrators group, with the innocent intention of undoing the action "as soon as the need is over." And, because that support person is as busy as all support folks are, that undoing never gets done. By applying a security template that says that "only Administrator and Domain Admins can be in the local Administrators," reapplying the template kicks everybody out who's not supposed to be there.

ENFORCING SECURITY SETTINGS

Templates automate the process of setting some security information, just as if you had sat down and done it from the GUI. There's no magic guardian angel that constantly monitors a system to ensure that your desired template settings are always enforced. The only way to ensure that your settings remain in force is to either reapply the template on some regular basis or create a GPO to apply the template, because security settings in a GPO are updated, regardless of any changes, every 16 hours.

Disable IIS and control who can start and stop services Want to shut off IIS on all machines but a few? That can be a pain, because Windows 2000 (unlike Windows Server 2003, 2008 and 2008 R2) installs IIS on every server by default. With a security template, you can turn off or even disable services. Templates also let you control who has the permissions to *change* that—you can restrict who can turn a service on or off, or you can grant that power to some user who you want to be able to do that, but who you don't want to make into an administrator.

Registry key permissions The registry contains a lot of information that users can read but can't change. For example, you may have noticed that there are a number of desktop applications that worked fine under NT 4 and that allowed someone with just user privileges to run them, but those same applications won't let a user run them under Windows 2000, XP, or Vista—only an administrator can run them. What's the difference? There are a few keys in the registry that users could both read and write under NT 4 but that they can only read under Windows 2000/XP/Vista. Thus, if you have one of those applications—AutoCAD is one example—and you want users to be able to run those apps on their Windows 2000/XP/Vista desktops, then you can either make all of your users local administrators (which may not sound like a great idea) or just loosen up the permissions on the registry keys to dial them back to their NT 4 settings. You could do that painstakingly from `regedt32.exe`, but it's so much easier to just apply a template to accomplish the same thing.

Local security policy settings Every machine has dozens of local security settings, things like, "Should I show the name of the last person who logged in?" and "How often should passwords on locally stored accounts be changed?" and "Who should be allowed to change the time on this system?" to name a few.

Working with Templates

It's easiest to show you how to work with templates with an example, so let's build a template to do three things:

◆ We'll ensure that no one is in the local Power Users group.

◆ We'll set NTFS permissions so that the directory C:\SECRET will be accessible only to the local Administrators group.

◆ Finally, we'll shut down Internet Information Services, that pesky web server that seems to install itself on every operating system that Microsoft makes.

First, you'll need some tools. Let's build an all-in-one tool using the MMC. Also, you'll need two snap-ins: Security Templates and Security Configuration and Analysis. Set it up like so:

1. Click Start, type **mmc /a** in the Start Search field, and then press Enter to bring up the empty MMC.

2. In the empty MMC, choose Add/Remove Snap-in from the File menu.

3. In the Add or Remove Snap-ins dialog box, click Security Configuration and Analysis and then the Add button. Then click Security Templates and Add again.

4. Click OK.

5. Save your new custom tool for future use.

Your tool should look like the one in Figure 8.30.

Expand the Security Templates node, and add a new template search path. The path you want to add will be C:\Windows\Security\Templates. Expand that, and you'll see a DC security.inf prebuilt template.

EXPANDING THE SECURITY TEMPLATES

Expand the DC security.inf security template, and you'll see, in the right pane, folders corresponding to everything that you can control:

Account Policies   Sets password, account lockout, and Kerberos policies

Local Policies   Controls audit settings, user rights, and security options

Event Log settings   Controls parameters of how events are stored

Restricted Groups   Controls what goes into and stays out of various local groups

System Services   Turns services on and off and controls who has the rights to change any of that

Registry security   Sets permissions to change or view any given registry key (and which keys will have changes audited)

File System   Controls NTFS permissions on folders and files

But you're interested in building a new template from scratch. To do that, right-click the template path, and choose New Template from the context menu. Type in a name for the template and a description if you want. The new template will appear as a folder in the left pane, along with the prebuilt template. We've named ours Simple. First, let's clean out the Power Users group:

1. Open Simple.

2. Inside Simple, you'll see a folder named Restricted Groups. Click it so that it appears in the left pane.

3. Right-click Restricted Groups, and choose Add Group. Type in **Power Users** in the Add Group dialog box, or use the Browse function to select the Power Users group. Note that if you are working from a domain controller, then you won't, of course, have a Power Users group.

By default, including a group in a security template tells the template to remove everyone from the group, so you're done. If you wanted to use the security template to put someone in the group, then just right-click the group and choose Properties, which lets you specify members of the group.

Next, let's set up the security template so that any system with a folder named C:\SECRET will be accessible only to the local administrators.

1. Back in the left pane, right-click File System, and choose Add File.

2. In the dialog box that appears, you can either browse to a particular directory or simply type in the directory name. Yes, the menu item was Add File, but you can choose directories as well. Type **C:\SECRET**, and click OK.

3. Now you'll see the standard Windows NTFS permissions dialog box. Delete permissions for all users and groups except for Administrators. Grant Full Control Permission to Administrators.

4. The program will ask whether you want these permissions to apply only to this folder or to all child folders. Set it as you like, and click OK.

Finally, let's shut down IIS:

1. Click System Services.

2. In the right pane, right-click World Wide Web Publishing Services, and choose Properties.

3. Select the Define This Policy Setting in the Template check box, and click the Disabled radio button.

4. Click OK.

Now save the template—right-click Simple or whatever you called the template, and click Save. Unless you set up a separate folder for your templates as we described earlier, you now have a file named `simple.inf` in your `\Windows\Security\Templates` folder.

Creating a Security Database

To see how this template will modify a system or to apply the template setting using the MMC snap-in, you must create a security database. To do this, you have to essentially compile it from its simple ASCII form to a binary form called a *database*. You do that from the other snap-in, Security Configuration and Analysis.

1. Right-click Security Configuration and Analysis and choose Open Database to open the Open Database dialog box, which asks what database you want to load.

2. Within the Open Database dialog box, you want to create a new database, but there's no option for that; instead, just type the name of the new database. Using this example, type **Simple**, and press Enter. Typing in a name of a new database causes the snap-in to realize that you want to *create* a new database, so it then asks which template to build it out of. (Yup, it's nonintuitive.) By default, a dialog box shows you the files with `.inf` extensions in the `Windows\Security\Templates` folder.

3. If you're following this example, choose `simple.inf`. Before you click, though, notice the Clear This Database Before Importing check box. Select that option. Otherwise, when you're experimenting with a template, the snap-in makes your changes cumulative (which might well be your intention, but it's not usually ours) rather than wiping the slate clean and starting from scratch.

4. Choose the template, and click Open. Nothing obvious has happened, but the snap-in has now "compiled" (which is our word, not Microsoft's, but it seems a good shorthand for the process of converting your ASCII template into a binary security database) the template into a security template named `simple.sdb` in `My Documents\Security\Database`. In the details pane, you'll see the Configure and Analyze options.

5. Right-click Security Configuration and Analysis, and you'll see two options: Analyze Computer Now and Configure Computer Now. Analyze doesn't change the computer. Instead, it compares the computer's state to the one that you want to create with the template. It then shows you—and saves a log file that explains—how your system varies from what the template instructs. The log file is written to `\Documents\Security\Logs`.

6. To see how your computer measures up to the settings in the database, select the Analyze Computer Now option, and you can see what the current settings are compared to what you "want them to be." If you want to jump in headfirst and apply the settings, instead of choosing Analyze Computer Now, select Configure Computer Now to modify the system's settings to fall into line with the template.

That's all very nice, you may be thinking, but how do I apply it to dozens of computers? Do I have to visit each one? Well, you do if you want to use this tool! If you want to use other options, one would be to use a command-line tool for that. A command-line program called `secedit.exe` will both convert templates into databases and apply databases. To read a template, apply, and then create a database in the process, use the following syntax:

```
Secedit /configure /cfg templatefilename /db databasefilename/overwrite
/log logfilename
```

To apply an existing database without first reading the template, just leave off the `/cfg` switch and argument. To apply the template to your workstations, you could include the `secedit` command in a logon script (be sure to specify full path names for the template, database, and log files) that will reapply it with every logon. You could also use the Task Scheduler service to run a batch file and reapply the template at specific intervals. Or you could enable the Telnet server on your Windows server machines and just apply the template whenever you like.

Automation and scripting are nice, but what if you want to take advantage of the "automatic" background refreshes that Group Policy provides, as well as the 16-hour forced security settings update? That is right, you use Group Policy! You'll learn about this in the next section.

Using Domain-Based Group Policies to Apply Templates

`secedit` is nice, but it has to be invoked manually or from a batch file, which means a lot of messy editing of logon batch files or fiddling with the Scheduled Tasks on all your systems. If you use a login script, the security template gets applied at logon time only. How do you enforce security settings more often? With a GPO.

Domain-based GPOs have a few benefits. First, it's easy to control whom they apply to, which is much easier than having to figure out which batch files go where. Second, they reapply themselves not only at logon time but also throughout the day—the workstation seeks them out every 60 to 120 minutes. Third, security settings are "reapplied" every 16 hours, just in case a security setting was modified by the user, an application, and so on.

Importing Security Templates

You already have your security template, `simple.inf`, which you created in the previous section. Now, you want to leverage the deployment of the security settings in the template by using a GPO.

The steps to import the template are very simple. Follow these steps to import the `simple.inf` template into a GPO:

1. Launch the GPMC.

2. Go to an OU that contains the computers that you want to apply the security settings to; for example, the `simple.inf` template could apply to all the desktops in your organization.

3. Right-click the OU, and select the "Create a GPO in this domain, and Link it here" menu option.

4. Type in a name for your new GPO; ours is named Desktop Enforcement Policy.

5. Right-click Desktop Enforcement Policy, and select the Edit menu option.

6. From within the GPME, drill down and select the Security Settings node, which is found under Computer Configuration\Policies\Windows Settings.

7. Right-click the Security Settings node, and click the Import Policy menu option.

8. Click the `simple.inf` security template (you can browse for this template if you have it on a network share or a USB thumb drive), and select Open.

9. Verify that the settings were imported by going down one level below the Security Settings node to the Restricted Groups node.

10. Click the Restricted Groups node, and ensure your Power Users policy is there.

The big question is, what do you do now? Well, if you can just wait 90 minutes, you don't have to do anything! Just allow the standard background policy refresh to take over and—bam!—all your settings will apply to all computers in the Desktops OU.

LEGACY ADMINISTRATIVE TEMPLATES (ADMs)

Administrative templates are the part of Group Policy that is most like system policies in NT. Windows 2000, Sever 2003, Windows Server 2008 R2 and Windows XP all use ADM templates. The settings available here are based on template files (ADM files, like those used in NT and Windows 9x system policies). These settings specify registry entry changes to adjust various aspects of a user's environment or a machine configuration, including those famous options to restrict a user's desktop to the point where they can run only a limited set of programs and nothing else.

The user changes specified in administrative templates that are driven by ADM templates are written to HKEY_ CURRENT_USER\Software\Policies, and computer changes are written to HKEY_LOCAL_ MACHINE\Software\Policies. Like the NT 4 System Policy Editor, Group Policy Administrative Templates loads ADM files to disclose collections of configurable settings. These ADM files are in \Windows\inf. Capabilities of administrative templates can also be extended with custom ADM files. Custom ADM templates can be added to a GPO by right-clicking the Administrative Templates node and choosing Add/Remove Templates (shown in Figure 8.31). When you load an administrative template into a GPO, the ADM files are copied to \SYSVOL\<Domainname>\Policies\<GUID of GPO>\Adm.

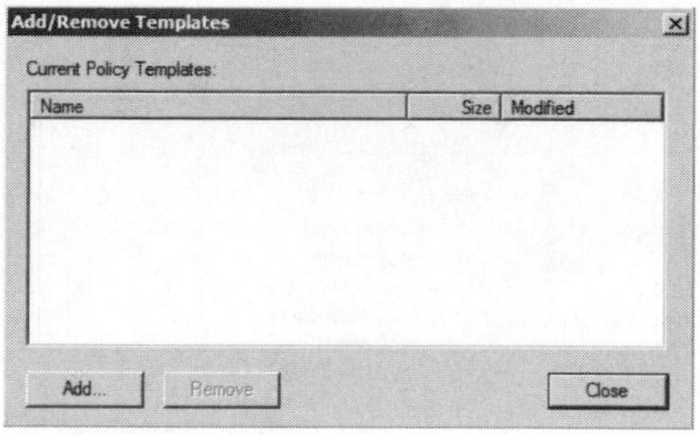

FIGURE 8.31
ADM files loaded
in Administrative
Templates node

New Administrative Templates (ADMX/ADML)

The old-style administrative templates were OK, but they had issues. In fact, these ADM templates were plagued with size issues, scripting complexity, and language barriers. To solve all these issues, Microsoft developed a new type of file that replaces the ADM template, which originated with Windows Server 2008. The new templates are XML based and come in pairs. The new file extensions are ADMX and ADML.

The ADMX and ADML files are now stored in C:\Windows\PolicyDefinitions. When you crack open this folder location, you will see more than 100 ADMX files, along with a default folder for English, which is named en-US. The en-US folder contains all the language-specific information for displaying the settings in the GPME.

The new ADMX/ADML files have a few benefits. First, these files are not stored in the SYSVOL folder structure of the GPO. Second, the files can be ported to nearly any language, as long as a new ADML file and folder structure is established for the new language. Third, there is a central store option that allows for centralized administration of the ADMX/ADML files.

Creating a central store for the storage and administration of these files is as easy as a copy of the folder structure! That is right—all that needs to be done to centralize the management of these files is to copy the folder structure to the domain controllers. In short, follow these steps to create the central store:

1. Open your Windows Vista or Sever 2008 computer to view the C:\Windows\PolicyDefinitions folder.

2. Right-click the PolicyDefinitions folder, and select Copy.

3. Open the C:\Windows\Sysvol\sysvol\<domainname>\Policies folder on any of the domain controllers for your domain.

4. Right-click the Policies folder, and select Paste.

The end result will be that you have now duplicated the ADMX/ADML folder structure and files on the domain controller, as shown in Figure 8.32. Since the folder exists in the SYSVOL of the domain controller, it will automatically be replicated to all the other domain controllers in the domain.

To verify that you are now consuming the ADMX files from the central store, just edit a GPO and view the text after the Administrative Templates node from within the GPME, as shown in Figure 8.33.

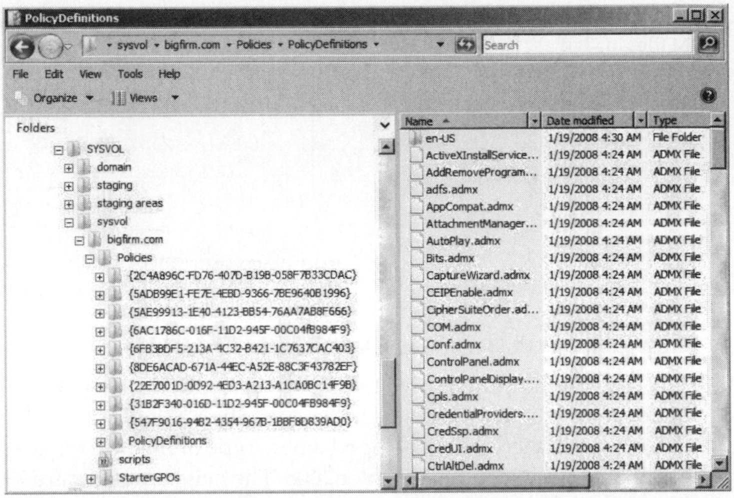

FIGURE 8.32
Central Store for
ADMX/ADML files

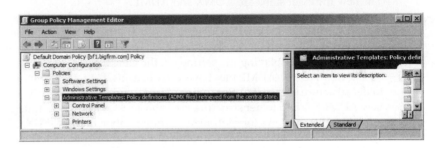

FIGURE 8.33
GPME interface
indicating which
ADMX files are
being used

If you have a custom ADMX/ADML file combo after creating the central store, all you need to do is copy the ADMX file to the PolicyDefinitions folder and the ADML file to the en-US folder. The new settings will show up in the GPME!

USING ADM TEMPLATES

You can still use your ADM templates in Windows Server 2008 and Vista. They are handled the same way, in that they are copied to the SYSVOL under the ADM folder per GPO. They will show up in the GPME interface under the Classic Administrative Templates (ADM) node, as shown in Figure 8.34.

Restricting Internet Explorer

For every setting in Internet Explorer, there seems to be policy to disable it. Considering that a good deal of time at work is spent surfing the Web, it's a particularly cruel and clever thing to impose such control over IE settings (unfortunately, many companies use Firefox instead of Internet Explorer). Here are a couple of settings that we find useful: if you want to prevent users from messing with the security zones you set up or if you want Internet Explorer to use the same security zones and proxy settings for all users on the computer, then enable the Security Zones and proxy settings under Computer Configuration/Policies/Administrative Templates/ Windows Components/Internet Explorer. To prevent users from downloading offline content to their workstations, enable the policy named Disable Adding Schedules for Offline Pages under User Configuration/Policies/Administrative Templates/Windows Components/Internet Explorer/Offline Pages. To prevent users from making any changes to IE's Security, Connections, or Advanced Properties pages, disable access to these and other IE Control Panel pages in the User Configuration node under Internet Explorer/Internet Control Panel. If you want to keep users from downloading any software from the Web, however, that's a little more difficult. There is a policy under User Configuration/.../Internet Explorer/Browser Menus that disables the Save This Program to Disk option. However, this won't prevent users from installing the software without saving it, and there are probably a couple of other ways around the restriction for a determined power user.

FIGURE 8.34

Legacy ADM templates imported into a GPO will show up under Classic Administrative Templates (ADM) node in GPME

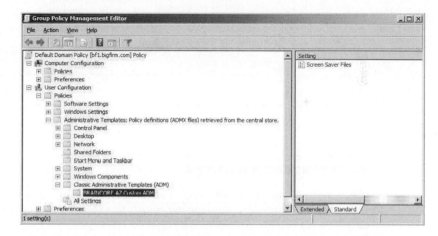

Prevent Users from Installing or Running Unauthorized Software

While we're on the subject of preventing users from installing software, enable the policy named Prevent Removable Media Source for Any Install found under User Configuration/.../ Windows Components/Windows Installer to keep users from running installations from a CD-ROM or a floppy drive (remember those?). And if you are going to do that, you should also enable the policy to hide the "Add a Program from CD-ROM or floppy disk" option in User Configuration/.../Control Panel/Add or Remove Programs. The Control Panel node includes several options to disable or remove all or part of the Add/Remove Programs applet. Disabling Add/Remove Programs will not prevent users from running setup routines in other ways, however. Anyone who can use a command line can circumvent these restrictions, so you'd need to open the System node of the User Configuration policies and enable the policy to Prevent Access to the Command Prompt. If you are looking for that infamous policy called Run Only Allowed Windows Applications, it's found in the System node of the User Configuration templates (shown in Figure 8.35). Be careful with this one, though; you have to make a list of all applications that can be launched from Windows Explorer. There is also a setting in the same location called Don't Run Specified Windows Applications. For this one, you'd need to make a list of disallowed programs.

FIGURE 8.35
Policy to run
only allowed
applications

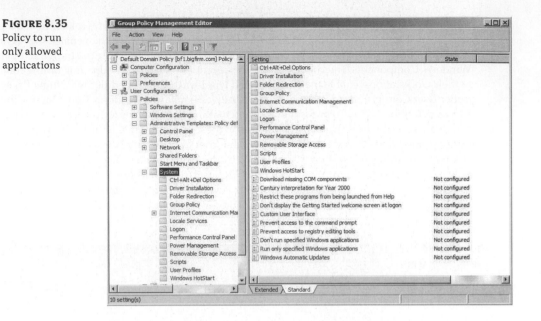

PREVENTING REGISTRY EDITING

Figure 8.35 also shows the location of a policy to prevent access to registry editing tools. Enabling this policy prevents users from running regedt32.exe and regedt.exe, although regular users only have Read access to the vast majority of the registry anyway.

The same principle applies to the Start menu and taskbar option called Run from the Start menu. Experienced users will not be prevented from running non-approved programs just because Run is removed from the Start menu, so you have to seek out all the other ways of launching programs and disable them as well (users can also launch programs from the Task Manager unless you disable it in the Ctrl+Alt+Delete options).

CREATING A CONSISTENT DESKTOP AND START MENU

If you want to achieve a simplified and consistent desktop and Start menu for your organization or department, you'll probably need to combine folder redirection with the restrictions that are available in the administrative templates.

Configure Time Servers and Clients Using Administrative Templates

Synchronizing time across a big network can be a bit of a headache. Admins often use login scripts to execute the net time command or install a third-party service on NT or 2000 systems. For Windows XP/2003 and greater, you can use the Computer Configuration administrative templates to enable and configure NTP clients and servers and to specify global parameters for time sources. You can find these settings in the System node under Windows Time Service.

Using Group Policy to Set Password and Account Lockout Policy

One of the most misunderstood and complex aspects of Windows AD is how and where password policies are configured and managed. In this section you will get the skinny on how it works to remove all doubt moving forward. Here is a list of truths and myths about Account Policy settings that should answer all of your FAQs.

TRUTHS

◆ The only way to modify the Account Policy settings for domain user accounts is in a GPO linked to the domain. (Note that this is applicable for Windows 2000 and Windows Server 2003 domains.)

◆ Fine-grained password policies can be set up to have users in the same domain have different Account Policy settings. In other words, IT users can have a 20-character password, and executives can have a three-character password. (Note that this is only for Windows Server 2008 domains.)

◆ A GPO linked to an OU will modify the local SAM Account Policy settings for the local users in the SAM of all computer accounts in that OU.

MYTHS

◆ A GPO can be linked to the Domain Controllers OU to modify the Account Policy settings for domain user accounts.

◆ A GPO can be linked to an OU to modify the Account Policy settings for the user accounts contained within the OU.

◆ The ACL for the Default Domain Policy can be modified to only include certain security groups, thus allowing different password policies in the same domain.

By default in a Windows Server 2008 domain, the Default Domain Policy is used to establish the Account Policy settings for all user accounts in the domain. (This includes both domain user accounts and all local SAM user accounts for computers joined to the domain.) Password and account lockout policy settings are located under Computer Configuration/Policies/Windows Settings/Security Settings. The password policy includes the following options:

Enforce password history   Enable this option to specify the required number of consecutive unique passwords before a given password can be used again.

Maximum password age This option sets the amount of time for which a password can be used before the system requires the user to pick a new one. Organizations usually set this interval somewhere between 30 and 90 days.

Minimum password age The value set here is the amount of time for which a password must be used before the user is allowed to change it again.

Minimum password length This option defines the smallest number of characters that a user's password can contain. Seven or eight characters is a good minimum length for passwords. Setting this policy also disallows blank passwords.

Passwords must meet complexity requirements In case you are wondering "What requirements?" this setting used to be called Passwords Must Meet Complexity Requirements of Installed Password Filter. A password filter DLL was available as an option for NT 4, but it's built in to Windows 2000 and later. Password filters define requirements such as the number of characters allowed, whether letters and numbers must be used, whether any part of the username is permitted, and so forth. If you enable this policy, all new passwords and changed passwords must meet the following requirements:

◆ They must be at least six characters long.

◆ They cannot contain the username or part of the username.

◆ They must use three of the four following types of characters: uppercase letters (A–Z), lowercase letters (a–z), numbers (0–9), and special characters (for example, @, %, &, #).

Store passwords using reversible encryption Yes, this policy is definitely a security downgrade, telling the domain controller that it's OK to store passwords in a reversible encryption. This is one step away from clear text; passwords are normally stored in a one-way hash encryption. If you need this for only individual user accounts (like Mac users), enable the option in the user account properties instead. Reversible encryption is required, however, if you are using CHAP authentication with remote access or Internet Authentication Services.

Account Lockout Policy, once enabled, prevents anyone from logging in to the account after a certain number of failed attempts. The options are as follows:

Account lockout duration This setting determines the interval for which the account will be locked out. After this time period expires, the user account will no longer be locked out and the user can try to log in again. If you enable the option but leave the minutes field blank, the account will stay locked out until an administrator unlocks it.

Account lockout threshold This value defines how many times the user can unsuccessfully attempt to log in before the account will be locked out. If you define this setting, be sure to specify the number of permitted attempts, or the account will never lock out.

Reset account lockout counter after This setting defines the time interval after which the count of bad logon attempts will start over. For example, suppose you have a reset count of two minutes and three logon attempts. If you mistype twice, you can wait two minutes after the second attempt, and you'll have three tries again.

Group Policy Preferences

One of the most impressive aspects of Windows Server 2008 (not just Group Policy related, but of the entire new OS) is Group Policy preferences (GPP). Group Policy preferences are extensions to Group Policy, which in normal speak is "new settings in a GPO." These new settings add more than 3,000 policy settings to a GPO, and some of them are just amazing! For example, now you can modify the local Administrator password on every desktop in your environment, within about 90 minutes. You can also control the membership of the local Administrators group on all desktops and servers, without removing the key service accounts and other domain groups that are unique to each computer.

GPP Settings

The GPP settings are a bit different from the other Group Policy settings, primarily because they exist in almost duplication under both the computer and user areas of a GPO. This gives you great flexibility and power over which setting you want to unleash on the desktops and users in the environment.

For the GPP settings, you will see the list of options displayed in Table 8.1.

TABLE 8.1:   Group Policy Preference Settings

Group Policy Preferences Setting	Available Under Computer Configuration?	Available Under User Configuration?
Applications	No	Yes
Drive Maps	No	Yes
Environment	Yes	Yes
Files	Yes	Yes
Folders	Yes	Yes
Ini Files	Yes	Yes
Network Shares	Yes	No
Registry	Yes	Yes
Shortcuts	Yes	Yes
Data Sources	Yes	Yes
Devices	Yes	Yes
Folder Options	Yes	Yes
Internet Settings	No	Yes

TABLE 8.1: Group Policy Preference Settings *(CONTINUED)*

GROUP POLICY PREFERENCES SETTING	AVAILABLE UNDER COMPUTER CONFIGURATION?	AVAILABLE UNDER USER CONFIGURATION?
Local Users and Groups	Yes	Yes
Network Options	Yes	Yes
Power Options	Yes	Yes
Printers	Yes	Yes
Regional Options	No	Yes
Scheduled Tasks	Yes	Yes
Services	Yes	No
Start Menu	No	Yes

Most of the settings in Table 8.1 are self-explanatory. However, we'll give you a jump start on how some of these settings might be used. For example, security is always on the top of the IT staff members' minds when it comes to securing desktops, but there is never enough time, right? Take the issue of resetting the local Administrator password on every desktop in your company. We know, we know…that is just crazy talk! However, when was the last time that this task was accomplished for your desktops? At installation? Two years ago? We have heard all of the possible answers, but now with GPP, you can change it as often as you like. To make this setting occur, modify a GPO that is targeting all of your desktops (the best bet here is to link a GPO to the OU that contains the desktop computers). When you have launched the GPME for the GPO, head to the Computer Configuration\Preferences\Control Panel\Local Users and Groups node. Right-click the node, and select New ➢ Local User, which will open the New Local User Properties dialog box, as shown in Figure 8.36.

FIGURE 8.36
Group Policy Preferences New Local User dialog box

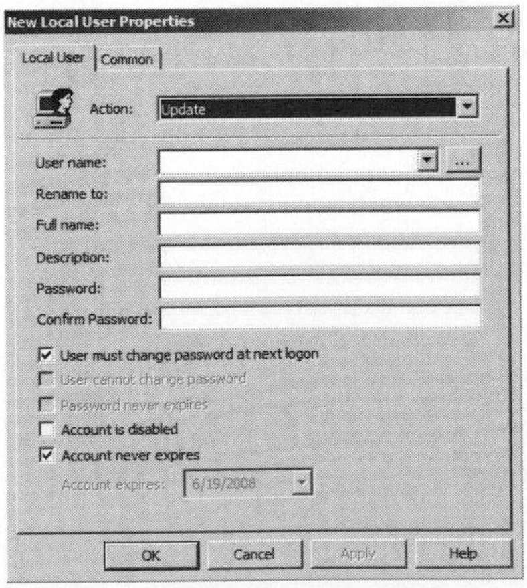

UNDERSTANDING NEW USER POLICY

You are not actually creating a new user when you select the New ➤ User option for GPP. Instead, think about it as creating a new user policy! You can create a new user, but there are many more options than just creating a new user. Use this "New XYZ policy" mentality when you create any new GPP setting, and it will help you figure out what you want to do with the setting.

From here, just type in the name of the user you want to control, which is **Administrator**. Then, type in the password that you want to use, retyping it as the dialog box clearly indicates. *Voila*! This will reset the password for the local Administrator account on every desktop that falls under the SOM to receive the GPO. After about two hours, all of the desktops that are connected to the domain and network will have the setting updated.

Now, wasn't that easy? The rest of the settings are just as easy, and the power that you now have at your fingertips is quite impressive. To give you an idea of what we have seen and what others have already done with GPP, here is a list of ideas per policy setting to get you started:

◆ Applications

  ◆ Enable the spell checker for Microsoft Word.

  ◆ Configure the Outlook autoarchive capability.

  ◆ Configure a "company-approved and consistent" signature for Outlook e-mail.

◆ Drive maps

  ◆ Replace all drive mappings in the logon script with a Group Policy preferences setting.

  ◆ Map drives for Terminal Services sessions only.

◆ Environment

  ◆ Create a laptop environment variable that is used with other Group Policy preferences settings.

  ◆ Establish environment variables for first name, last name, address, and so on, which can then be used in the Outlook signature.

◆ Files

  ◆ Transfer virus definitions from server to desktop.

  ◆ Deploy application configuration files to desktops.

◆ Folders

  ◆ Clean up the Temporary Internet Files folder.

  ◆ Create an application folder for desktops that run secured applications.

◆ Network shares

  ◆ Control network shares on a server only during business operating hours.

  ◆ Enable access-based enumeration for server.

◆ Registry

   ◆ Uh, you name it—it can and might have been done!

◆ Data sources

   ◆ Create a centralized data source configuration for salespeople.

   ◆ Create a custom data source configuration for help-desk employees.

◆ Folder options

   ◆ Allow all IT staff users to see hidden and super-hidden files at every desktop they administer.

   ◆ Configure all IT staff users to see file extensions in Windows Explorer on all desktops they touch.

◆ Internet settings

   ◆ Configure the Internet Explorer proxy setting for all users in branch office 1.

   ◆ Configure custom Internet Explorer settings that standard Group Policy settings can't handle, such as all the settings on the Advanced tab of the Internet Explorer settings configuration dialog box.

◆ Local users and groups

   ◆ Reset the local Administrator password on every desktop.

   ◆ Manage local Administrators group members on every desktop and server (by the way, without first deleting the members!).

◆ Power options

   ◆ Create 24-hour power options scheme where users never see a power option scheme during working hours, but after employees leave, their computer is put into Standby mode after five minutes of no activity. (This has been proven to save about $50 per PC per year.)

◆ Printers

   ◆ Eliminate printers from logon scripts.

   ◆ Configure printers for laptop users who go from remote office to remote office, only giving them the printers they need based on their location.

◆ Scheduled tasks

   ◆ Waking the computer up during the middle of the night to allow maintenance to occur (an excellent combo with Power Options!).

◆ Services

   ◆ Configure a different service account to increase overall security.

   ◆ Configure the service account password.

   ◆ Configure service behavior if it fails to start gracefully.

ITEM-LEVEL TARGETING

One of the most impressive aspects of GPP is the item-level targeting capabilities. You can now target and apply any GPP setting by first querying different aspects of the computer environment, only applying the setting if the environment is what you want it to be. For example, let's say you have the HR department running an application that exists in a Terminal Services environment. When they launch this application, they need to have a mapped drive for the application. The solution that most companies must use today is to map the drive for the user account, so they have a "bogus" drive mapping even when they are working on their desktop. GPP item-level targeting allows you to provide the drive mapping *only* when they are in the Terminal Services environment. Figure 8.37 illustrates what a filter might look like to provide this solution. Notice that in the configuration we have configured *only* the HR group and the fact that the user must be in a Terminal Services session access to apply the setting, which will map a drive for the HR application.

FIGURE 8.37
Item-level targeting allows you to precisely apply GPP settings.

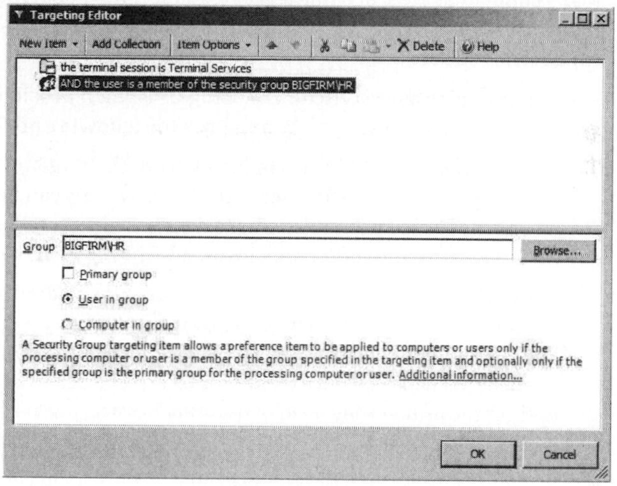

You can obtain this type of control by leveraging one of many different item-level targeting options. The full list of item-level targeting options is as follows:

Battery Present	IP Address Range
Computer Name	Language
CPU Speed	LDAP Query
Date Match	MAC Address Range
Dial-Up Connection	MSI Query
Disk Space	Operating System
Domain	Organizational Unit
Environment Variable	PCMCIA Present
File Match	Portable Computer

Processing Mode	Terminal Session
RAM	Time Range
Registry Match	User
Security Group	WMI Query
Site	

🌐 Real World Scenario

ELIMINATING LOGON SCRIPTS USING GROUP POLICY PREFERENCES

Many companies are still using legacy logon scripts to apply settings to desktops such as drive mappings and printer mappings. Using logon scripts is archaic in comparison to the new and improved capabilities of GPP.

Many companies have switched to using GPP when possible to eliminate some, if not all, of the settings in their logon scripts. You can use the following preferences in lieu of logon scripts:

Drive mappings Drive mappings can now be targeted to create "just-in-time" mappings that make more sense for users. Item-level targets can be used in conjunction with drive mappings to only provide access to data based on the user having the correct application installed, with the right patch installed, and only when in a Terminal Services session.

Printers Printers are often hard to manage for medium and large organizations that have mobile users. When a user goes to a company branch office, it can be difficult for the user to find and configure the correct printer. The GPP for printers can be used to map all printers in the company. When used with an item-level target (such as an IP address range or AD site), users will get the printer they need in the branch office, just because they are in the branch office.

Registry With the new registry preference, any registry entry can now be placed in a GPO without any custom ADM template or ADMX file. This includes binary and multistring values, which were not possible in ADM templates.

The New and Improved GPMC

The GPMC has been around for quite a while now. The first generation of the GPMC was revolutionary and made administration of GPOs much easier. This generation of the GPMC continues to make the administration of GPOs easy, efficient, and stable. No more are the days when you needed to launch the Active Directory Users and Computers to see, create, link, and manage GPOs. That was archaic to say the least. Now, the new GPMC can run on Windows Server 2008 and Vista SP1.

You will need to install the GPMC, because it is not installed by default. For your Windows Server 2008 computers, you can install the GPMC from the Server Manager. Launch the Server Manager, and select the Features menu option. From here, you just need to click the Add Features option, which will give you a full list of tools you can install, as shown in Figure 8.38.

FIGURE 8.38
The GPMC is
installed via the
Server Manager.

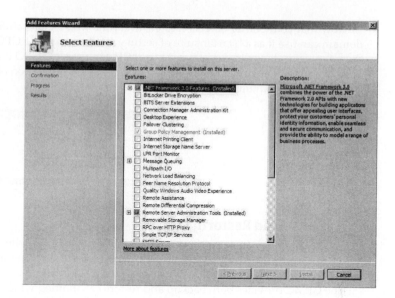

Select the Group Policy Management option, which will take you through some gyrations to get the tool installed. After a restart, you will now have the GPMC installed.

For your Windows Vista desktops, installing the GPMC is not nearly as straightforward. You will need to follow these steps to get the GPMC installed:

1. Install Windows Vista SP1.

2. Install the Remote Server Administrative Tools.

3. Open the Control Panel from the Start menu.

4. Click the Programs and Features applet.

5. Select the "Turn Windows features on or off" menu option.

Starter GPOs

Microsoft is making strides to make GPO management easier and more efficient. The first attempt at this is Starter GPOs. You can use Starter GPO to precreate a suite of GPO settings, only to use the Starter GPO again and again and again. Say, for example, that you are in charge of ensuring that Internet Explorer is configured properly for your organization. You could create a Starter GPO that includes all of the required Internet Explorer settings and save the Starter GPO. Then, when any new GPO is created, it uses the IE Starter GPO you created to ensure the Internet Explorer settings are included.

To create a new Starter GPO, select the Starter GPO node in the GPMC. Then, follow these steps:

1. Right-click the Starter GPO node, and select the New menu option.

2. Type in the name of your Starter GPO; we're using **IE Starter GPO**.

3. To configure your IE settings, you now only need to edit the GPO, just like you would any other GPO by right-clicking it in the GPMC and selecting Edit.

Now that your Starter GPO is created, everyone who has the ability to create a GPO in the domain can use it as a "starter suite of settings." When any new GPO is created in the GPMC, there is a drop-down list for Source Starter GPO in the New GPO dialog box, as shown in Figure 8.39. Keep in mind, however, that one significant limitation of Starter GPOs is that they only include the administrative template settings of the GPO.

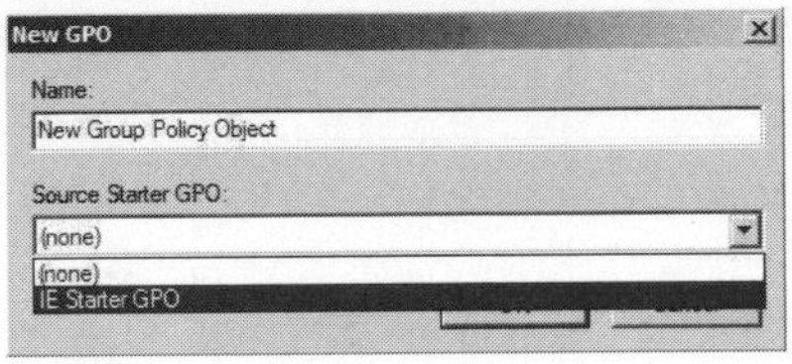

FIGURE 8.39
New GPOs can use a Source Starter GPO during creation.

Backing Up and Restoring GPOs

The GPMC is a one-stop shop for all GPO management. One of the most important aspects of protecting your GPO assets is to back them up. (It is like anything in a computer world, you are only as protected as the last time you backed up your data!)

The GPMC provides both backup and restore capabilities, which allows you to archive every version of the GPO that you create and implement. It is very convenient that the GPMC provides these capabilities directly in the interface, because there is no need to launch another application or tool to get this job done.

Backing up a GPO is simple; you just right-click the GPO that you want to back up and then select the "Back up" menu option. The Back Up Group Policy Object dialog box appears, where you will input the location to store your backups. This can be a predetermined location, or you can create a folder during this process. Type in the location or click the Browse button, whichever option suits you best. Now that you have a GPO archive folder selected, simply click the "Back up" button. You will see the progress of the backup process in the Backup dialog box, and then when the GPO has successfully been backed up, you can click out of that box.

BEFORE-AND-AFTER BACKUPS

Like data and other operating system changes, backups should be performed directly before a change is made, as well as after the change is made to ensure that both states of the GPO are captured.

There will be a time when you want to view the list of GPOs that you have backed up. To see this list, you will right-click the Group Policy Objects node within the GPMC and select the Manage Backups menu option. This will launch the Manage Backups interface, shown in Figure 8.40.

From here, you can restore, delete, and view the settings of a backed-up GPO. The Restore feature will allow you to restore the "archived GPO" over the "production GPO." You can imagine how important this might be! Imagine that you have a junior administrator who was working away in the production GPO, doing a bit of research on how to lock down Internet Explorer. Unfortunately, you granted edit capabilities to the GPO for the research, so the junior administrator accidentally modified the proxy settings for the entire stock trader GPO, which stopped them from being able to trade! The phone rings, and you track down the errant configuration. Since the change occurred on all 250 traders' computers, you need a solution fast! You dive into the GPMC and restore the last GPO version, and the problem is fixed without any need for an AD restore. Whew!

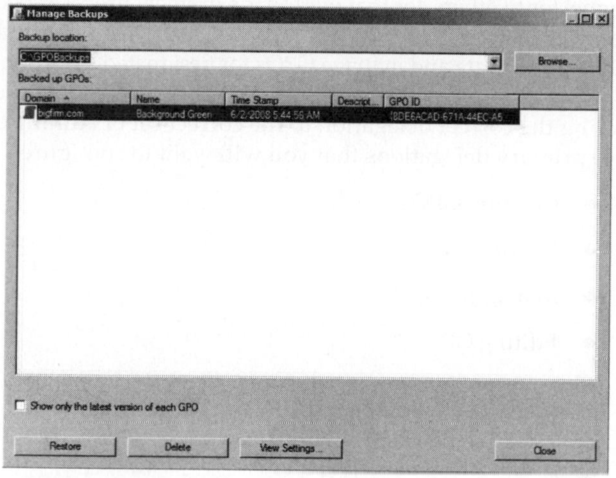

FIGURE 8.40
GPMC allows you to manage the GPOs that you have backed up.

The Delete option allows you to clean house of the archived GPOs, especially those that are of no use anymore or those that are *really* old. There's no reason to clog up your servers with information you will not need in the future.

The View option allows you to view the contents of the GPO, as well as all the other key information such as delegation, security, links, and so on. Figure 8.41 illustrates the HTML page that is displayed from selecting the View option.

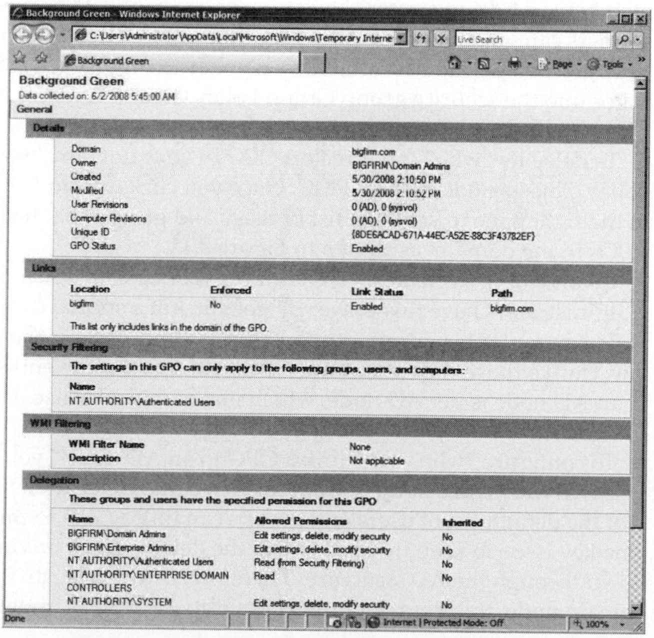

FIGURE 8.41
The View option in the backup tool allows you to see all the GPO information.

Delegating Group Policy Administration

The ability to delegate creation and configuration of GPOs and their settings to administrative personnel (or to others, for that matter) is extremely useful, especially in a large organization. In this section, we'll explain how to allow persons who are not members of Domain Admins or Enterprise Admins to create and manage GPOs for designated sites, domains, or organizational units.

The GPMC provides a simple, yet distributed, array of options to ensure that you are providing the correct delegation to the correct set of administrators. You will find that there are five primary delegations that you will want to configure:

◆ Creating GPOs

◆ Linking GPOs

◆ Managing GPOs

◆ Editing GPOs

◆ Reading GPOs

All of these are configured in the GPMC. The major confusion about establishing delegation in the GPMC for GPO management is scoping. This means that you need to know where to go to set up the delegation; then once you are there, you need to know how far the delegation will extend. For example, suppose that you are the HR OU administrator. This means that you control "everything for HR," including user accounts, group accounts, and even which GPOs are linked to your OU. How do you ensure that you are the only administrator who can link a GPO to your HR OU? Well, this is one of the delegated tasks that the GPMC can control. Let's take a look at each delegation and the scope.

GPOs, by default, can be created by a member of the Administrators group for the domain or by members of the global group called Group Policy Creator Owners. However, although members of Administrators have full control of all GPOs, members of Group Policy Creator Owners can only modify policies they themselves have created, unless they have been specifically granted permission to modify a policy. So, if you put a designated Group Policy administrator into the security group Group Policy Creator Owners (that's almost as awkward as Active Directory Users and Computers), that person can create new policy objects and modify them.

To delegate "who" can "create a GPO in your domain," you will head down to the Group Policy Objects node in the GPMC. Once you click this node, you will select the Delegation tab in the right pane to view the list of users and groups that have been granted the ability to create GPOs in the domain, as shown in Figure 8.42.

It's one thing to create a GPO; linking that GPO to a site, domain, or OU is another matter. Administrators have this power by default, but a special delegation can be configured, per AD node, to grant other administrators this capability. Here, the scoping is very important to follow. Unlike the ability to create a GPO, which is per the entire domain, the ability to link a GPO to an AD node is per AD node, which makes logical sense. How about the configuration of this delegation?

To configure "who" can "link a GPO to an AD node," you need to select the target AD node in the GPMC. Then, in the right pane, select the Delegation tab. Each AD node has one. Notice that the default list of users and groups can link a GPO to this node, as shown in Figure 8.43. One key issue to keep in mind is that the delegation of linking to an AD node does not inherit down through the AD structure. Therefore, if you delegate the ability to link a GPO to the domain node, this does not grant the ability to all OUs in the domain.

FIGURE 8.42
Delegation of the
creation of GPOs
using GPMC

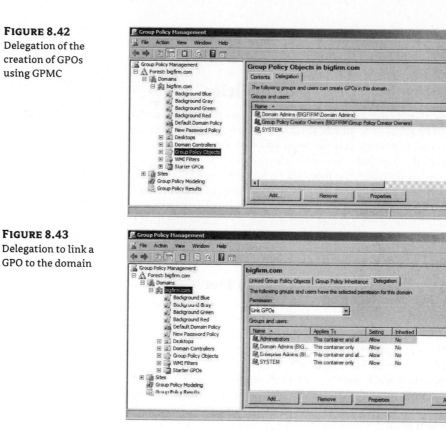

FIGURE 8.43
Delegation to link a
GPO to the domain

The final three delegations have the same scope, which is per GPO. Again, this makes logical sense, but sometimes logic does not always make it to the keyboard for some people. If this is logical, you should be able to select a GPO in the GPMC; then, in the right pane, you can select the Delegation tab to see the delegations per GPO. Well, this is exactly the case, and you can see the three levels of delegation per GPO in Figure 8.44. Here, you need to right-click the GPO to see the full list of delegations.

FIGURE 8.44
Delegations to
manage, edit, and
read a GPO

The interface does not say "Manage GPO." Instead, it says "Edit settings, delete, modify security" for the GPO.

Troubleshooting Group Policies

In case it's not clear by now, group policies are powerful…and also complex. And they can be kind of opaque—sometimes you create a bunch of policy settings for a domain controller that you intend to control some desktop and then restart the desktop, log in, and wait to see the effects of the new policies…but nothing happens.

A few troubleshooting tools are included to assist you in troubleshooting Group Policy issues. The Resultant Set of Policy (RSOP) snap-in and console tool provides a graphical interface, and `gpresult.exe` performs equivalent functions from the command line. `gpotool.exe` is a Windows Resource Kit tool, and it looks for inconsistencies between GPOs that are stored on domain controllers. This little utility can help you identify replication issues are causing a problem with Group Policy application.

The Resultant Set of Policy (RSOP) Tool

Troubleshooting group policies has been, for administrators, a major obstacle to complete control and domination of the network environment. The problem was the inability to view the cumulative policy settings that were in effect for a user or computer. This little capability to display actual policy settings, the Resultant Set of Policy tool, is built into Windows Server and XP/Vista systems. Although RSOP is not supported on Windows 2000 systems, even if you can't see the actual RSOP data, you can run a "what if" scenario using RSOP on a server and make an educated guess about the problem. Without RSOP, you have to look at the properties of each site, domain, and OU to see which policies and containers are linked. Then you must view the ACLs and WMI information to see whether there's any filtering and also check out the Disabled, Block Inheritance, and Enforce options. Don't forget the new item-level targeting, which can get very granular, thus confusing to try to evaluate by hand. Finally, you need to view the settings of the policies in question before you can get to the bottom of things. You'll need to take notes. Personally, we prefer the RSOP tool.

The RSOP tool is easily launched by typing **rsop.msc** at the command prompt. When it is launched, you will see it "working away" determining the resultant set of policy that has been applied based on the computer you are running it on and the user account that is logged in at the time the tool is run.

The result is a window that's similar to that shown in the GPME, as shown in Figure 8.45. Here are a few things to note about using the `rsop.msc` tool:

◆ The tool provides only the applied GPOs and the settings from those GPOs.

◆ The tool provides a view of which GPO each setting came from.

Group Policy Results Using the GPMC

Inside the GPMC is a tool that is similar to that of the localized version of the RSOP, but it allows you to query any computer and user on the network to get the RSOP. Imagine that a user calls to indicate that they can't access a website that is required for their job. You could visit their desk, but that would only take time, when you are sure that they are getting their Internet Explorer proxy settings from a GPO. So, instead, you launch the Group Policy Results Wizard in the GPMC, select the user and the desktop they are logged into, and browse to the IE proxy setting. You notice that the wrong GPO is applying to the computer, since someone set up an enforcement of the GPO linked to the OU above, which is negating your proxy setting. Problem found, so now, you only need to fix the Enforce issue on the GPO, and you are set!

FIGURE 8.45

rsop.msc generates a real time view of the policy settings that have been applied.

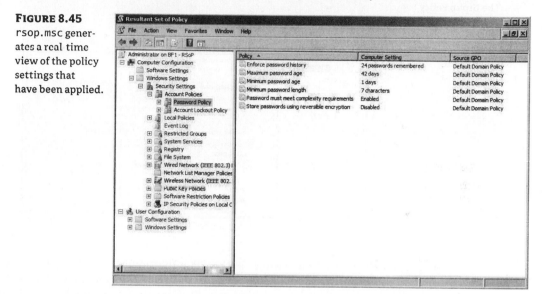

You can find the Group Policy Results Wizard toward the bottom of the GPMC. When you launch the wizard, you will just need to provide the computer and user you want to find results for, and the wizard takes care of the rest, as shown in Figure 8.46.

FIGURE 8.46

Group Policy Results Wizard in the GPMC

The results from the wizard will display in three different tabs on the right pane: Summary, Settings, and Policy Events. The Summary tab, shown in Figure 8.47, summarizes all the settings, including the GPOs that applied, those that failed, the security groups that were considered, WMI filters, and more.

FIGURE 8.47
The Group Policy Results Wizard displays information on three tabs in the GPMC.

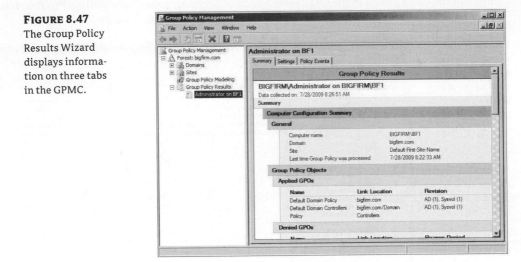

The Settings tab displays all the settings for the GPOs that applied, breaking them down into Computer and User sections. It also indicates the "winning GPO," so you know exactly where to go if you need to make a change to a setting, as well as any issues that might be occurring, if you thought the setting should be from a different GPO.

The Policy Events tab is very unique, in that it displays the settings from the Event Viewer that relate to Group Policy–related events and categories. If you can see that there is an issue with a setting applying, you can use the contents on all three tabs to track down the issue.

Group Policy Modeling Using the GPMC

The Group Policy Results Wizard in the GPMC is powerful, allowing you to view the "existing state" of the GPOs and their settings on any computer and user on the network. However, what if you have a scenario where you want to move a computer to a different OU or move a user to a different OU because they are being promoted? You would not want to just "move the account" and hope that the settings were correct based on the new location in AD.

gpresult

`gpresult.exe` is a Group Policy troubleshooting and reporting tool that complements the RSOP snap-in by adding command-line and batch file capabilities to the RSOP arsenal. When run without arguments or options, `gpresult` will generate the following RSOP information for the current user at the local machine:

◆ The DC that the workstation got the policies from

◆ When the policies applied

- Which policies applied

- Which policies were not applied because of filtering

- Group memberships

- User rights information (if used in verbose mode)

To generate RSOP information for a remote user on a remote machine, use the /S *systemname* and /USER *username* arguments. For instance, to get RSOP information on the remote workstation VISTACLIENT1 for the user dmelber, type **gpresult /S VISTACLIENT1 /USER dmelber**. The targeted remote system must be running Windows XP, Vista, Server 2003, and Server 2008, though. gpresult doesn't work remotely on Windows 2000 systems.

You can get more detailed information with options:

- /V says to give more verbose information: gpresult /V.

- /Z says to give even *more* information; it is the "Zuper-verbose" option: gpresult /Z.

- If you know that you're zeroing in on just a machine policy, add /SCOPE MACHINE; if you're interested only in user policies, add /SCOPE USER. So, for example, to get the maximum information about the user policies applied to this system, add gpresult /Z /SCOPE USER. It's also a simple matter to generate a report by redirecting the output of the command to a text file:

```
gpresult /S VISTACLIENT1 /USER dmelber /Z > c:\gpinfo.txt
```

gpotool

gpotool.exe checks all your group policies to ensure that they are "whole." Group policies exist in two parts: first, there is a text file in SYSVOL for each policy, which is called the Group Policy template (GPT), and second, each policy shows up as a record in the Active Directory called the Group Policy container (GPC). If one replicates and the other one does not, then the policy won't work.

gpotool checks each policy and ensures that it has replicated both in the GPC and in the GPT. But gpotool has one annoying feature. In fact, it's a feature shared by many GP tools: it doesn't refer to policies by their English name or "friendly name," as Microsoft calls it. Instead, it reports on policies by their GUID, a scary-looking hexadecimal string. You can look up a GUID's friendly name just by viewing the Details tab for the GPOs in the GPMC.

You can also grab the friendly name by using the techniques outlined in Knowledge Base article Q216359 or with a script like this one:

```
set RootDSE = GetObject("LDAP://RootDSE")
Domain = RootDSE.get("DefaultNamingContext")
wscript.echo "The domain name is: " & domain & vbCrLf
Set GPCContainer = GetObject("LDAP://cn=Policies,cn=System," & domain)
For Each object in GPCContainer
    wscript.echo "Friendly name: " & object.displayname
    wscript.echo "Container GUID: " & object.guid
    wscript.echo vbCrLf
Next
```

You can download the gpotool from this Microsoft link: http://technet.microsoft.com/en-us/library/cc759170(WS.10).aspx.

Using Event Viewer

You can stop chuckling now! We're serious! There are times that you need to really pat Microsoft on the back, and this is one of those times. The Event Viewer has been completely overhauled, and now, to the shock of many, there is an entire node dedicated to Group Policy!

The Group Policy Operation log is a replacement to the Userenv.log file that was generated by Group Policy in the past. Now, you don't need to set up any verbose or auditing settings; it just happens. To view the Group Policy log files in the new Event Viewer (Windows Server 2008 and Vista only, sorry!), just launch the Event Viewer. Once in the Event Viewer is open, expand the Applications and Services Logs\Microsoft\Windows\GroupPolicy node. Here, you will find the Operational log for Group Policy. After clicking the Operational log, you will see the list of events on the right pane.

Here are a few tips and features of the new environment:

◆ The Operational log replaces the Userenv.log from previous version of Windows Group Policy.

◆ There are General and Details tabs, each providing excellent information for troubleshooting issues.

◆ Double-clicking the event will launch the event in its own window, allowing a single view of the information.

◆ Clicking the System + sign on the Details tab will expose more information about the event.

Troubleshooting 101: Keep It Simple

We predict that, even with the RSOP tool, working with group policies will not be a walk in the park for most. Here are a few suggestions to help minimize troubleshooting time:

◆ Keep your policy strategy simple. Locate users and computers together in OUs if possible, and apply policies at the highest level possible.

◆ Avoid having multiple GPOs with conflicting policies that apply to the same recipients.

◆ Minimize the use of the Enforce and Block Inheritance settings.

◆ Document your Group Policy strategy. You may want to visually depict your policy structure and put it on the wall, like your network topology diagrams. That way, when a problem arises, you can consult the diagram to see what's going on before you go fishing.

◆ Test those GPO settings before deployment! This is absolutely essential to conserve your help-desk resources and ensure that applications and system services continue to run properly.

A Closing Thought or Two on Group Policy

In this chapter, we have discussed the concepts of Group Policy, focusing on domain-based GPOs. You have created a sample GPO and seen how to turn on the various settings, such as Enforce and Block Inheritance. You have looked at filtering policies for security groups and delegating policy administration to others. You have explored many of the actual policy settings, including administrative templates for desktop control, security settings, folder redirection, Group Policy preferences, and even Group Policy policies. But before you close this chapter and begin to configure group policies on your network, you want to be very aware that group policies affect network and system performance.

The more GPOs there are to apply, the longer the logon time. Each time a user logs in (or a computer is restarted), each of the GPOs associated with the user's or computer's containers (SDOUs) is read and applied. This can slow down logons considerably, and users may start calling the help desk to ask, "What's wrong with the network?" Therefore, you should keep the number of GPOs and the settings to a minimum. Another thing that can bog down a machine or a network is the background refresh rate. Most environments can get by with the default 90 minutes, but if you do decide to test a refresh rate that is more often, be careful not to overburden your network with too many refreshes. Another way to streamline GPO processing is to avoid assigning GPOs from different domains. Just because you can do it doesn't mean it's a good idea. A final note on performance is that permissions (for files, folders, and the registry) can destroy logon performance. If you must use Group Policy to set permissions, use it sparingly.

The Bottom Line

Understand local policies and Group Policy objects   Every Windows computer from Windows 2000 Professional and up has a local Group Policy. Windows Vista has many local group policies, which can accommodate for various situations where the computer might be located. There are Group Policy objects stored in Active Directory too, which allow for central administration of computers and users who are associated with the domain.

Master It   Which of the following is not a local Group Policy:

A.   Local Computer Policy

B.   Administrator

C.   Non-Administrator

D.   All Users

Create GPOs   Group Policy Objects can, and should be, created within your Active Directory domain. These additional GPOs will allow you to control settings, software, and security on the different users and computers that you have within the domain. GPOs are typically linked to OUs but can be linked to the domain node and to AD sites as well. GPOs are created within AD by using the Group Policy Management console.

Master It   Create a new GPO and link it to the HRUsers OU.

Troubleshoot group policies   There are times when a GPO setting or Group Policy itself fails to apply. There can be many reasons for this, because there are many tools to help you investigate the issue. There are some tools, such as the rsop.msc tool, which are presented in a resulting window, and other tools, such as gpresult, which is a command-line tool. Regardless of your tool that you use, troubleshooting Group Policy is sometimes required.

Master It   Which tool would you use to ensure that all settings in all GPOs linked to Active Directory have applied, even if there have not been any changes to a GPO or a setting in a GPO?

Chapter 9

Active Directory Delegation

Active Directory delegation is a powerful solution to the old-world style of Windows NT domains, where you had to create multiple domains to create separate control over users, groups, and computers. By implementing delegation within a single Active Directory domain, you don't need multiple domains, you can save money by reducing the number of domain controllers, managing the enterprise is easier with a single domain, and so on.

This feature of Active Directory is so compelling that many companies and enterprises have moved to Active Directory to take full advantage of the benefits that Active Directory delegation provides. One of the most compelling benefits of using delegation is the ability to grant one or more groups the privilege to reset passwords for user accounts. This is not your typical solution like the old NT domains had with account operators, no! This means you can allow a group of users to reset passwords for just a subset of the users in a domain. For example, the HR manager can reset passwords for all the employees in the HR department. No more privilege, no less privilege.

In this chapter, you will learn to:

◆ Delegate control using organizational units

◆ Use advanced delegation to manually set individual permissions

◆ Find out which delegations have been set

AD Delegation vs. NT Domains

To see how you can leverage delegation, let's consider an example scenario. Say some fictitious part of the U.S. Navy is spread across naval facilities across the world, but perhaps (to keep the example simple) its biggest offices are in San Diego, California, and Norfolk, Virginia. There are servers in San Diego and Norfolk, all tended by different groups. For all of the usual reasons, the officers in charge of the Norfolk facility don't want administrators from San Diego messing with the Norfolk servers, and the San Diego folks don't want the Norfolk guys anywhere near *their* servers, with the result that the Navy technology brass wants to be able to say, "Here's a group of servers we'll call Norfolk and a group of users we'll call Norfolk Admins. We want to be able to say that only the users in Norfolk Admins can control the servers in Norfolk." They want to the same thing for San Diego. How do you do this?

Under the old-world solution of Windows NT 4, they could do it only by creating two separate security entities called *domains*. Creating two different domains would solve the problem because separate domains in Windows NT 4 are like separate *universes*—they're not aware of each other (without additional coordination and configurations on both domains). With a Norfolk domain and a San Diego domain, they could separate their admins into two groups that wouldn't be able to meddle with one another. It's a perfectly acceptable answer, and indeed many organizations around the world still use NT 4 in that manner. However, it's a solution with a few problems—all solved by Active Directory delegation, we might add.

The first issue is that enterprises usually want *some* level of communication between domains, and to accomplish that, the enterprises must put in place connections between domains. We've briefly discussed these connections between domains before; they're called *trust relationships*. Without a trust relationship, it's difficult for a user in one domain to access something—a printer, a file share, a mail server, or the like—in another domain. The simple process of having a user in one domain access a resource in another requires a logon; the domain that contains the resource (printer, file share, mail, and so on) must recognize and log in the user.

Specifically, here's how the Navy would solve its problem with NT 4 domains:

1. First, the Navy would create two different NT 4 domains. NT 4 domains had names of up to 15 characters, so they might call the two domains NORFOLK and SANDIEGO.

When created, every NT 4 domain automatically creates a user group called Domain Admins. Anyone in that group has complete and total control over the domain. So, they'd just put the people they wanted to be Norfolk administrators into the Domain Admins group of the NORFOLK domain, and they'd put the people they wanted to be San Diego admins into the Domain Admins group in the SANDIEGO domain.

2. Once those domains were created, they'd next create a user account for each person at the Norfolk facility in the NORFOLK domain and create a user account for each person at the San Diego facility in the SANDIEGO domain. Similarly, any member servers and workstations in Norfolk would join the NORFOLK domain, and member servers and workstations at San Diego would join the SANDIEGO domain.

3. Finally, they'd create a trust relationship between NORFOLK and SANDIEGO; actually, they'd create *two* trusts, because NT 4–style trusts are one-way only. Two domains can trust one another only if the domain administrators on both sides agree, so both the NORFOLK and SANDIEGO Domain Admins groups would have to cooperate to create the "NORFOLK trusts SANDIEGO" trust and the "SANDIEGO trusts NORFOLK" trust.

This would work, but it might not be the most convenient thing to keep running. For one thing, we've already explained that NT 4 trust relationships can be quirky and unreliable, and this model relies upon two of those trusts. With AD domains, in contrast, the Navy needs to create only *one* domain and then divide it up using a notion that first appeared in the Microsoft world with Active Directory—a concept called *organizational units* (OUs).

More specifically, the Navy would solve their problem using Active Directory this way:

1. They'd create one domain named (for example) navy.mil. (Recall that AD domains have DNS-like names.)

2. Inside navy.mil, they'd create an organizational unit named Norfolk and another called San Diego. They would set up their servers and then place each server into the proper OU.

3. Also inside navy.mil, they'd create a user group named Norfolk Admins and another named San Diego Admins. They'd create accounts for their users and place any administrators into their proper group, depending on whether they were based in San Diego or Norfolk.

4. Finally, they'd give the San Diego Admins group complete control over the San Diego OU, and they'd give the Norfolk Admins group complete control over the Norfolk OU.

We'll clarify two things at this point. First, understand that the San Diego Admins didn't have any power until someone explicitly gave them control of the San Diego OU. There's no magic in Active Directory that says, "Well, there's an OU named San Diego and a group named San Diego Admins—I guess that must mean I should let these admin guys have total control over the servers in the San Diego OU." You have to create that link by *delegating control* of the San Diego OU to the user group San Diego Admins. (There's a wizard that assists in doing this, as you'll see when we walk you through a delegation example later in this chapter.) You'll see that OUs are a useful tool for organizing large domains into efficient "buckets."

Second, the facts that AD domains have DNS-like names and OUs are subunits of domains leads people to think that OUs also get DNS-like names. For example, many people presume that the Norfolk OU of navy.mil would be named norfolk.navy.mil or something like that. But that's not true—although you name *domains* using DNS, you name just about everything else in Active Directory using Lightweight Directory Access Protocol (LDAP) naming conventions. You can safely avoid a lot of LDAP by using the built-in administrative tools, but just for completeness sake, here's the LDAP path that you would use for the Norfolk OU in the navy.mil domain: ou=Norfolk,dc=navy,dc=mil. You'll meet more LDAP later.

Delegating Control Using Organizational Units

Certainly one of AD's strengths is that it can let you grant partial or complete administrative powers to a group of users, meaning that it would be possible for a one-domain network to subdivide itself into, say, Uptown and Downtown, Marketing and Engineering and Management, or whatever. Let's look at a simple example of how to do that.

Let's suppose that there are five people in marketing: Adam, Betty, Chip, Debbie, and Elaine. They want to designate one of their own, Elaine, to be able to reset passwords. They need this because "I forgot my password—can you reset it for me?" is probably the number-one thing that marketing calls the central IS support folks for. The central IS folks are happy to have someone local to marketing take the problem off their hands, freeing them up to fight other fires.

Here's the process:

1. Create an OU called Marketing. (You can call it anything that you like, of course, but Marketing is easier to remember later.)

2. Move Adam's, Betty's, Chip's, Debbie's, and Elaine's already-existing user accounts into the Marketing OU.

3. Create a group called MktPswAdm, which will be the people who can reset passwords for people in the Marketing OU. (Again, you can actually give it any name you want.)

4. Make Elaine a member of the MktPswAdm group.

5. Delegate password reset control for the Marketing OU to the MktPswAdm group.

If you want to follow this along as an exercise, get ready by creating accounts for Adam, Betty, Chip, Debbie, and Elaine, except don't make them administrators. Or do it from the command line; type **net user *username* /add**, and you'll get a basic user account built in the Users folder. For example, create Adam like so:

```
net user Adam Pa$$word /add
```

You've got to be sitting at the domain to do this. You can create domain users from any other system at the command line, but you must then add the option /domain, as follows:

```
net user adam /add /domain
```

Creating a New Organizational Unit

Creating a new OU is simple. Just open Active Directory Users and Computers (ADUC), right-click the domain's icon in the left pane, and choose New ➤ Organizational Unit. A dialog box will prompt you for a name of the new organizational unit. Enter **Marketing**, and click OK. You're done.

Moving User Accounts into an OU

Next, to move Adam, Betty, Chip, Debbie, and Elaine to the Marketing OU, open ADUC, open your domain (ours is Bigfirm.com; yours might have another name), and then open the Users folder. (If you created the five accounts somewhere other than Users, then look there.)

You can move all five users by clicking Adam and Ctrl+clicking the other four accounts. Then right-click one of the five accounts, and you'll get a context menu that includes a Move option; select Move, and you'll get a dialog box asking you where to move the "object." It'll originally show you your domain name with a plus sign next to it; just click the plus sign, and the domain will open to show the OUs in your domain. Choose Marketing, and click OK; all five accounts will move to the Marketing OU. In ADUC, you can open the Marketing OU, and you will see that all five accounts are now in that OU.

Or...you can use the drag-and-drop capability. In ADUC, click the Users folder in the left pane. You will be able to see the contents of Users in the right pane. In the left pane, you'll not only be able to see Users, but you should be able to see the Marketing OU as well. Select the users, and then drag them from the right pane to the Marketing OU. Instant OU movement! (What's that you say? You're not impressed? Well, believe us, when you do a lot of user management, you'll find this to be a lifesaver. Trust us on this.)

Creating a MktPswAdm Group

Next, you'll create a group for the folks who can reset Marketing passwords. Again, work in ADUC. First click the Marketing OU to highlight it, and then select Action ➤ New ➤ Group. (You can also right-click the Marketing OU and select New ➤ Group.) You'll see a dialog box like Figure 9.1.

FIGURE 9.1
Creating a
new group

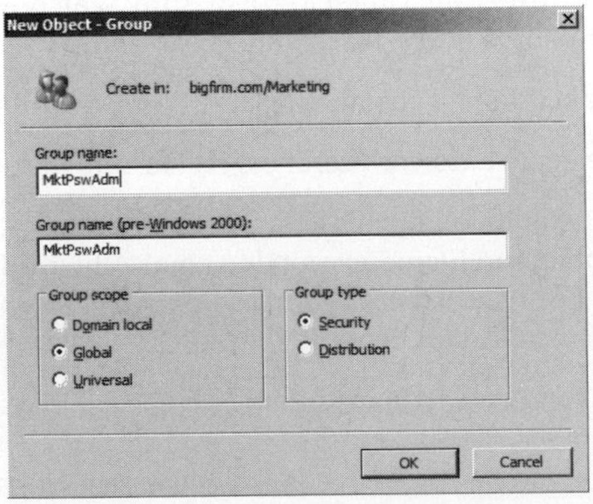

You see that the dialog box gives you the option of creating any one of the three types of groups in Active Directory. A global group will serve our purposes well, although in this particular case—the case of a group in a given domain getting control of an OU in that same domain—either a domain local, global, or universal group would suffice. We've called the group MktPswAdm. Click OK, and it's done.

Next, put Elaine in the MktPswAdm group. Right-click the icon for MktPswAdm, and choose Properties. Click the Members tab, then the Add button, then Elaine's account, then Add, and then OK. You'll see that Elaine is now a member of MktPswAdm. Click OK to clear the dialog box.

Delegating the Marketing OU's Password Reset Control to MktPswAdm

Now let's put them together. In ADUC again, right-click the Marketing OU. Choose Delegate Control, and the first screen of the Delegation of Control Wizard will appear.

The wizard is a simplified way to delegate, and it'll work fine for this first example. Click Next, and you'll see Figure 9.2.

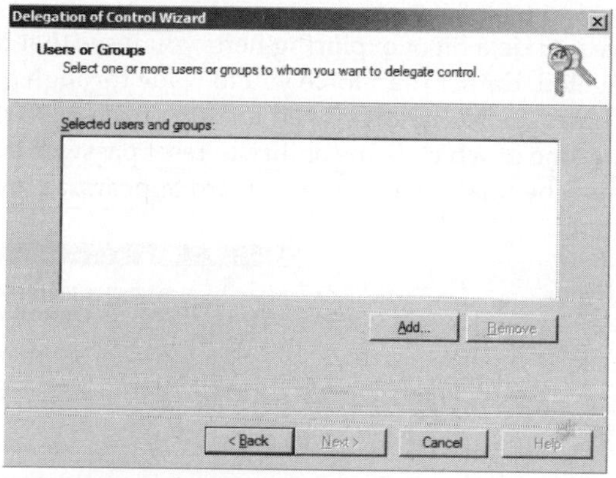

FIGURE 9.2
Before selecting
a group

Next, you have to tell it that you're about to delegate some power to a particular group, so you have to identify the group. Click Add, and choose the MktPswAdm group. After choosing MktPswAdm and clicking OK to dismiss the Add dialog box, the screen looks like Figure 9.3.

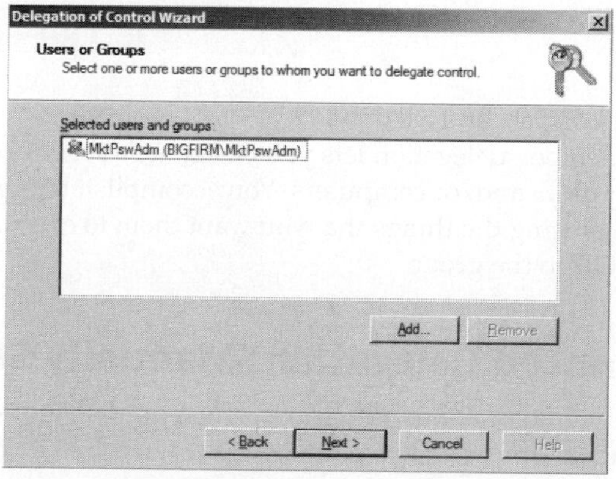

FIGURE 9.3
MktPswAdm
selected

Now click Next, and you'll get a menu of possible tasks to delegate, as you see in Figure 9.4.

FIGURE 9.4
Options for
delegation

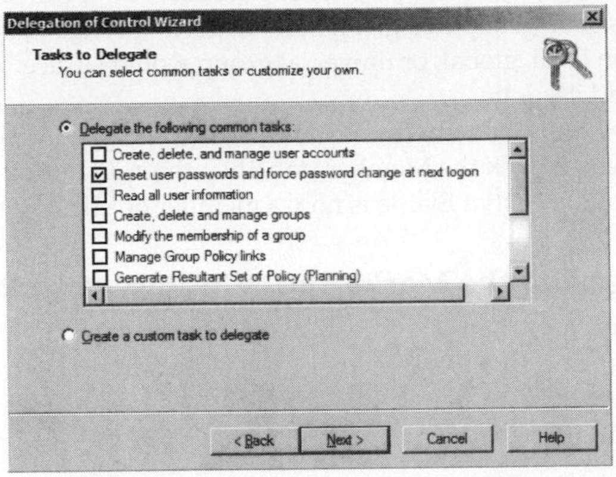

Once you do a bit of exploring here, you'll see that there are many, many functions that can be delegated. Rather than force you to wade through a long list of things that you'll never care about, however, Microsoft picked the top dozen or so things that you'd be most likely to want to delegate, one of which is the ability to reset passwords. We've selected that in the figure; click Next, and the final screen in the wizard appears, as you see in Figure 9.5.

FIGURE 9.5
Confirming your
choices

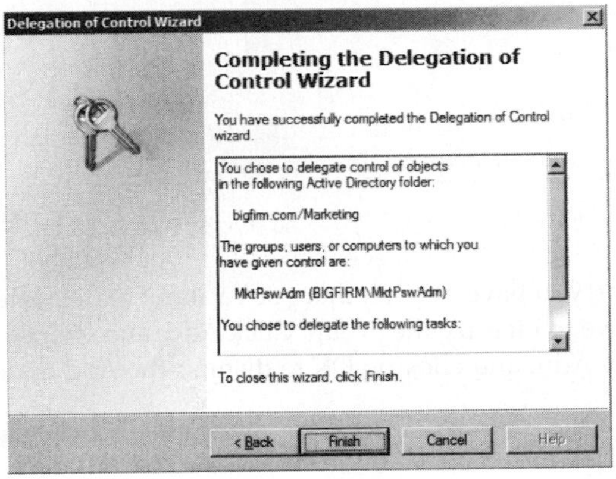

Click Finish, and it's done.

Remember, delegation lets you designate a set of users who have some kind of control over a set of users and/or computers. You accomplish that by putting the controlling users into a group, putting the things that you want them to control into an OU, and then delegating control of the OU to the group.

Advanced Delegation: Manually Setting Permissions

Although the previous scenario is a nice—and useful—example, it only hints at the power of delegation. You actually needn't use the wizard to delegate; it just makes things simpler for a range of common tasks.

BEST PRACTICES FOR DELEGATION

Delegation is a powerful tool for administering your network. If it is used carefully, it will prove quite helpful. So far in this section we have mentioned a few good practices to use when delegating; now we'll expand on these and explore more examples:

◆ *Create groups and OUs that will have delegation applied to them*: This facilitates security as well as administration.

◆ *Avoid assigning permissions directly to a user*: Create a group (see the earlier discussion), and place the user in that group. Creating a group to house one user is not as burdensome as it might seem initially; in fact, it will make your administrative life much easier than trying to track down why this one individual can still perform actions that she or he shouldn't.

◆ *Assign the least amount of permissions to users and groups.* This will help make your network *most* secure. Users might think they are entitled to full control for everything, but they rarely, if ever, require it.

◆ *Use full control sparingly*: Full control can backfire on you when users or groups start taking advantage of your largesse. Full control gives the user an opportunity to work with an object's permissions. That means the users could give themselves greater permissions than the administrator intended. In addition, if someone gains control of this account, then that person could cause more mayhem than they would otherwise.

◆ *To further enforce security and enhance good administration techniques, delegate object creation and object management to different groups*: This is known as *two-person integrity* (TPI). If you split the responsibility between two individuals or groups, there is less likelihood of mismanagement by either. Think of this as splitting the create-backup and restore permissions between two groups. For example, you could give one group of administrators the ability to create groups in an OU, where you give a different group of administrators the ability to control the group's members.

◆ *Create Taskpad views*: Taskpad views are great when you want to delegate tasks to help-desk personnel or other groups that require some permissions but don't want them to have access to the full console. This technique can help train new administrators before you give them the keys to the domain.

◆ *You can delegate at levels higher than an OU, but avoid doing this as a rule*: If you delegate permissions at the domain level, that user or group could have a potentially far greater impact on your network than you anticipated.

STICK AROUND

Even if you're not terribly interested in delegation, stay with this example. It shows how to navigate the three levels of progressive complexity in Windows Server 2008 security dialog boxes, which is something you'll be doing a lot of as an administrator in a Windows 2000, XP, 2003, Vista, and 2008 world.

Here's how you can directly manipulate delegation:

1. First, open ADUC, and select View ➤ Advanced Features. New items will appear on the screen, as in Figure 9.6.

FIGURE 9.6
ADUC with
View Advanced
Features enabled

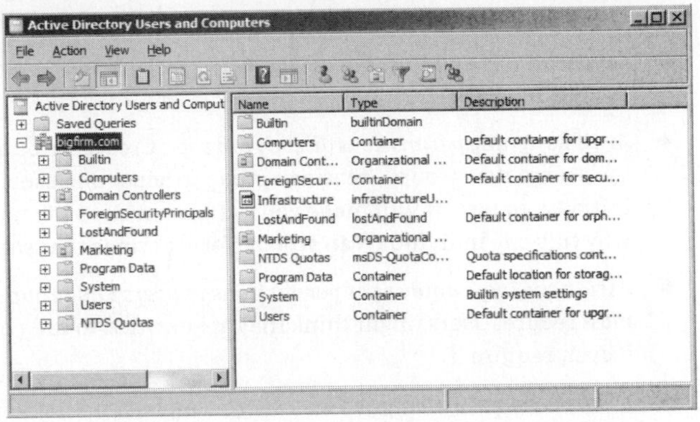

2. Right-click the Marketing OU, and choose Properties. You'll get a properties sheet with a Security tab. (By the way, without Advanced Features enabled, you will not have the Security tab available.) Click it, and you'll see something like Figure 9.7.

FIGURE 9.7
Security tab on
Marketing OU

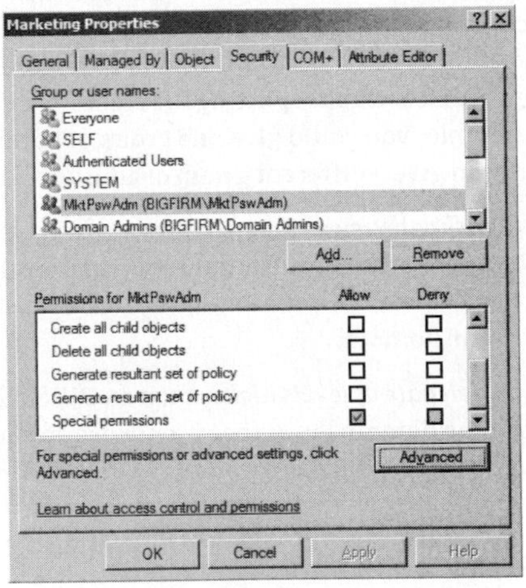

Here, I've scrolled down a bit to show what the dialog box tells you about the MktPswAdm group. It appears that the group has powers that can only be described as "special," which isn't all that helpful. This is the top level of a Windows 2008 security dialog box. Think of it as the overview level of security information. We quite frankly find this top-level view pretty limited. About all it really tells us is that there are many entries in this dialog box—you can't see that because they don't all fit in here—and you may recall that each of these entries are called *access control entries* (ACEs). The list in total is called the *access control list* (ACL), pronounced "ackull," rhyming with "shackle."

3. In theory, you should be able to click any of the ACEs in the top part of the dialog box, and in the bottom part you see what powers that ACE gives the thing named in the ACE. For example, you see in Figure 9.7 that MktPswAdm has "special" powers. That's one reason we don't like this dialog box all that much, because "special" doesn't say much. The other reason is that this dialog box only shows a really simplified list of possible powers, so what you see will be sometimes misleading. That's why it's nice that you can zoom in one level by clicking the Advanced button. Do that in ADUC, and you'll see a screen like Figure 9.8.

FIGURE 9.8
Advanced security
settings for
Marketing OU

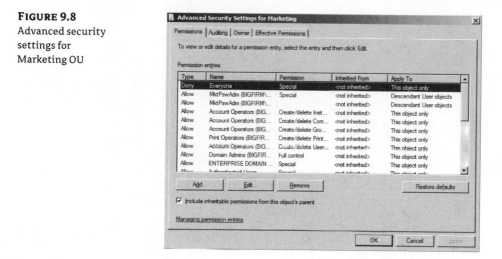

4. Scroll down to highlight MktPswAdm, and you see two entries for it. One lists the "special" permission, while the other does not list anything for the permissions, which is not very helpful at all. Click it and choose Edit when you have one of the entries highlighted, and you'll see something like Figure 9.9.

FIGURE 9.9
Specific
MktPswAdm
abilities

5. Here you see that we've given MktPswAdm the ability to read and write "Descendant User objects" properties, but *only* the pwdLastSet property—AD lingo for being able to select the check box that indicates "User must change password at next logon," which is available in the Reset Password dialog box. Now, go back and look at the other record for MktwPswAdm and edit it, and you'll see Figure 9.10.

FIGURE 9.10
Giving the power
to reset passwords

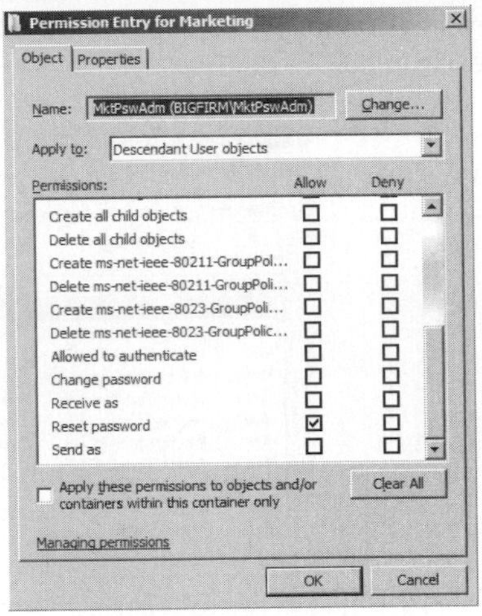

As you can see from the figure, there are a *lot* of powers that you can grant to a particular group in controlling a particular OU! Believe it or not, you can set more than 10,000 individual permissions for just one OU. And that's counting only the Allow permissions—it's double that for both Allow and Deny.

Where might you make use of this? Well, you gave MktPswAdm the ability to change passwords, but you didn't take it away from the groups that originally had it—the Domain Admins members, the Enterprise Admins members, and the like can still reset passwords. That's not a bad idea, but if you really ever *do* come across a "feuding departments" scenario, wherein marketing wants to be sure that they're the *only* people who can administer accounts, then you'd first delegate the Marketing OU to some group and then go in with the Security tab and rip out all of the other administrators.

Finding Out Which Delegations Have Been Set, or Undelegating

It's time for some not-so-good news and some bad news.

Suppose you're not the administrator who set up Active Directory. Suppose, instead, you're the *second* administrator—the person hired to clean up the mess that the *first* administrator made. You know these kinds of administrators; they're the "mad scientist" variety—the guys who just click things in the administrative tools until they solve the problem…they think. And *document*? Heck, real administrators don't document; there is never time to document. After all, this network was hard to design; it should be hard to understand!

So, you're wondering what this guy did. How did he change the company's AD from the default AD that you get when you run DCPromo? That's a hard question to answer. First, of course, the OUs that he created are obvious—just look in Active Directory Users and Computers, and you'll see the new folders. But what delegations did he do?

Here's the not-so-good news. Sad to say, but there is no program you can run that will compare the standard AD structure and delegations to the current AD structure and delegations and spit out a "this is what has changed" report. Considering this limitation, we'll offer a really heartfelt piece of advice: always document delegations. *Always*. Try to control who can do delegations, and make clear that delegations are authorized only sparingly. So, why is this news about comparisons *not-so-good* news, instead of *bad* news? The reason is a small tool called dsacls.exe. This tool, part of the core Windows Server 2008 command-line utilities, provides you with detailed listings of the directory service (the ds portion of the tool name) ACLs (the acls portion of the tool name).

To use the tool, you must get to a command prompt, so just select Start ➤ Run. From there, type **cmd**, and a command prompt window will open up. From here, you can type **dsacls** to get the full list of help that accompanies the tool. As the help will indicate, the tool requires that you input the path to the OU that you want to view in the official LDAP syntax. This will be something like ou=marketing,dc=bigfirm,dc=com for our example.

You can just type **dsacls ou=marketing,dc=bigfirm,dc=com**. This will pump the output to the command prompt window, which is not all that friendly or useful to analyze. So, instead of this option, you can pipe the output to a file, using the following syntax: **dsacls ou=marketing,dc=bigfirm,dc=com > c:\marketing_OU_delegation.txt**. When you open the marketing_OU_delegation.txt file, you will see a result similar to that in Figure 9.11.

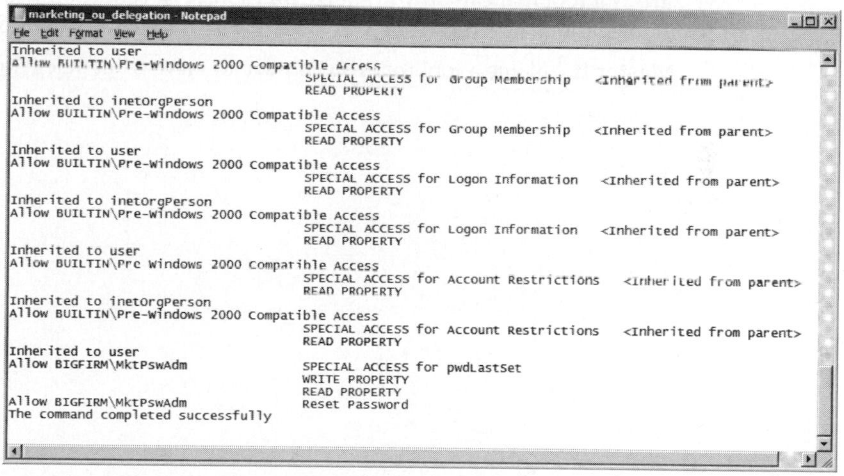

FIGURE 9.11

Giving the power to reset passwords

Now, here's the really bad news. The Delegation of Control Wizard is a nice little tool, but it's only a *delegation* wizard, not an *un*delegation wizard. If you want to remove MktPswAdm's ability to change marketing passwords, you have to go into the Security tab, find the references to MktPswAdm, and rip them out. We warn you, if there are some delegations you want to keep and others you want to remove, you will have to manually determine which ones correspond to the delegated task you configured.

The Bottom Line

Delegate control using organizational units Delegation is a powerful feature in Active Directory that allows domain administrators to "delegate" tasks to junior administrators. The idea is that the delegation granted is narrow in scope, providing only limited capabilities within Active Directory and the objects contained within.

Master It Establish delegation on the HRUsers organizational unit such that the HRHelpDesk can reset the passwords for all users in the HRUsers OU.

Use advanced delegation to manually set individual permissions There are thousands of individual permissions for any given AD object. Advanced delegation provides the ability to set any of these permissions to give a user or security group access to the object for the specified permission. The Delegation of Control Wizard is a useful tool to grant common tasks, but when the wizard does not provide the level of detail required, you must grant delegation manually.

Master It *Delegation* is another term for which of the following:

A. Replicating AD database

B. Read-only domain controller

C. Setting permissions on AD objects

D. Using Group Policy to set security

Find out which delegations have been set It is unfortunate, but the Delegation of Control Wizard is a tool that can only grant permissions, not report on what has been set. To find out what delegations have been set, you have to resort to using other tools.

Master It Name a tool that you can use to view what delegations have been set.

Chapter 10

Files, Folders, and Shares

One of the core functions of any server is to serve resources such as files and folders. In Windows Server 2008 R2, File Services is one of the key roles you can add. The File Services role includes additional role services such as the File Server Resource Manager (FSRM), services for Network File System (to support Unix clients), the Windows Search service, and BranchCache for remote offices.

If you plan on sharing files and folders, it's important that you understand not only how to share the data but also how to protect it with permissions including both New Technology File System (NTFS) and share permissions. Although both sets of permissions work independently, they also interact with each other. You should be able to quickly determine what the ultimate permissions are for a user who accesses a share over the network. And, if you want to protect entire hard drives, you can now use BitLocker Drive Encryption to encrypt them.

The underlying protocol that handles file transfers is Server Message Block (SMB), which has been upgraded to version 2.0. Although SMB 2.0 doesn't require any additional configuration, it does provide some significant benefits for file transfers over the network—as long as you're connecting to the right kinds of clients. SMB 1.0, with all of its inherent challenges, will still be used when connecting to legacy clients.

In this chapter, you will learn to:

◆ Install the File Services role on a server

◆ Combine share and NTFS permissions

◆ Implement BitLocker Drive Encryption

Understanding the File Services Role

The core component of any server is its ability to share files. In fact, the Server service in the entire Windows Server family (including Server 2008 R2) handles the server's basic file and print sharing capabilities. But what exactly does that mean, and why is it so important? By default, just because you have a server running doesn't mean it has anything available for your users. Before they can actually get to resources on the server, you must share your resources. Let's say you have a folder on your local F drive named Apps with three subfolders, as shown in Figure 10.1.

When you share this folder to the network under the name Apps, you allow your clients to map a new drive letter on their machines to your F:\Apps folder. By mapping a drive, you are placing a virtual pointer directly to the remote drive. If you map your client's M drive to the Apps share of the server, the M drive will look identical to the server's F:\Apps folder, as shown in Figure 10.2.

FIGURE 10.1

Subfolders in the
F:\Apps folder

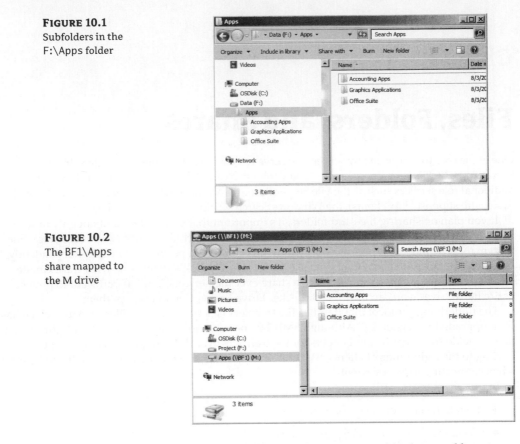

FIGURE 10.2

The BF1\Apps
share mapped to
the M drive

Don't worry, we'll slow down and explain how to create this share and how to connect to it later in this chapter. That's really all there is to it. Sharing resources means that you allow your users to access those resources from the network. No real processing goes into it as far as the server is concerned; it just hands out files and folders as they are.

Adding Role Services

Server Manager includes several consoles that can be used to manage the different server roles including the File Services role. File Services in Windows Server 2008 R2 helps you do much more than just share folders. The File Services role includes several additional role services:

File Server This is the primary role service required to support the File Services role. It is automatically added when a folder is shared.

Distributed File System (DFS) DFS includes both DFS Replication and DFS Namespaces and is covered in more depth in Chapter 11.

File Server Resource Manager (FSRM) The FSRM provides a rich set of additional tools that can be used to manage the storage of data on the server including configuring quotas, defining file screening policies, and generating storage reports. A full section on the FSRM is included later in this chapter in the "File Server Resource Manager" section.

Services for Network File System (NFS) This service enables you to grant access to files from Unix client computers.

Windows Search Service The Windows Search Service uses indexing to perform quicker file searches. It's intended for small file server scenarios and can impact performance on large enterprise file servers.

Windows Server 2003 File Services This includes the Indexing Service for backward compatibility with Windows Server 2003 File Services.

BranchCache for Network Files BranchCache can be used in a multiple-site environment to allow computers in branch offices to cache commonly downloaded files. BranchCache needs to be enabled on the shared folder. You'll see how to do this in the "Using Offline Files/Client-Side Caching" section later in this chapter.

FILE SERVICES ROLE ADDED WHEN A FOLDER IS SHARED

If you just use Windows Explorer to share a folder, the File Services role is added automatically. You don't have to add the role using Server Manager. However, when you use Server Manager to add the File Services role, it gives you the option to add the additional services in support of the role.

Adding the File Services Role

You can add the File Services role by following these steps:

1. Launch Server Manager by selecting Start ➢ Administrative Tools ➢ Server Manager.

2. Select Roles, and click the Add Roles link.

3. Review the information on the Before You Begin page, and click Next.

4. Select the File Services role, and click Next.

5. Review the information on the Introduction to File Services page, and click Next.

6. On the Select Role Services page, select the following role services, as shown in Figure 10.3: File Server, File Server Resource Manager, and BranchCache for network files. Click Next.

7. The Configure Storage Usage Monitoring page is used to identify which volumes you want to monitor. In this example, we have the operating system on C and will share data on the F volume. Select the volume that you plan on using to share data. You display will look similar to Figure 10.4. The File Server Resource Manager can monitor and generate storage reports on any volumes you choose to monitor. Click Next.

8. The Set Report Options page allows you to specify a location for storage reports. You can either accept the default location or browse to another location. You can also configure the reports to be emailed if you have an SMTP server available to send the reports. For now, accept the default location, and click Next.

9. Review the information on the Confirmation page, and click Install. After a moment, the file services will be installed. Click Close.

FIGURE 10.3
Selecting File
Services role
services

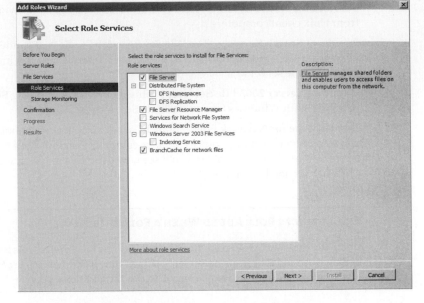

FIGURE 10.3
Selecting File
Services role
services

FIGURE 10.4
Identifying the vol-
ume to monitor

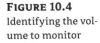

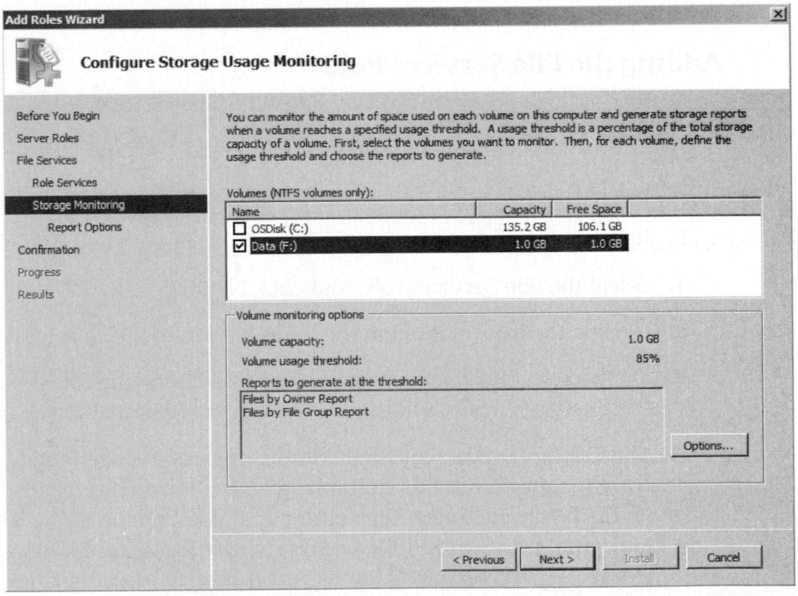

At this point, Server Manager includes the File Services role. If you open it, you'll see that it includes the Share and Storage Management node and several selections under the File Server Resource Manager, as shown in Figure 10.5.

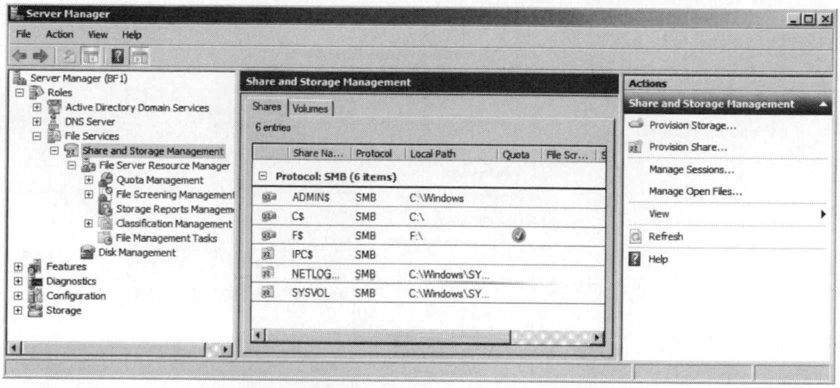

FIGURE 10.5
File Services, Share and Storage Management, and File Server Resource Manager tools

Creating Shares

◆ Chapter 11 will show a couple of methods of creating shares using Windows Explorer and the Computer Management console. This chapter will present the creation of shares with Server Manager. No matter which method you use, you'll need either Administrator or Power User rights on the computer where you're creating the shares.

Once a share is created, it can be published to Active Directory to make it easy for users to locate the share. You'll learn how to create shares using Server Manager and publish the shares to Active Directory in this section.

Creating Shares with Server Manager

It's relatively easy to add shares using Server Manager. The Share and Storage Management node includes a Provision a Shared Folder Wizard that you can use by following these steps:

1. If not started, launch Server Manager by selecting Start ➤ Administrative Tools ➤ Server Manager.

2. Browse to the Roles ➤ File Services ➤ Share and Storage Management node, right-click Share and Storage Management, and select Provision Share.

3. On the Shared Folder Location page, click Browse. Browse to a folder you want to share. For example, we've selected the Apps folder on the F drive in Figure 10.6. Click OK after browsing to and selecting a folder. Click Next.

4. The NTFS Permissions page gives you an opportunity to change the NTFS permissions if desired. We'll cover NTFS permissions later in the chapter, but for now click Next to accept the NTFS permissions.

5. On the Share Protocols page, you identify the protocols used to access the share and can also give the share a different share name. SMB is the primary protocol used by Windows clients to connect, and when this is selected, it allows both SMB version 1 and SMB version 2 depending on the client's capabilities. If you added NFS support for Unix clients, you could select NFS here. For this example, accept the default of SMB, and click Next.

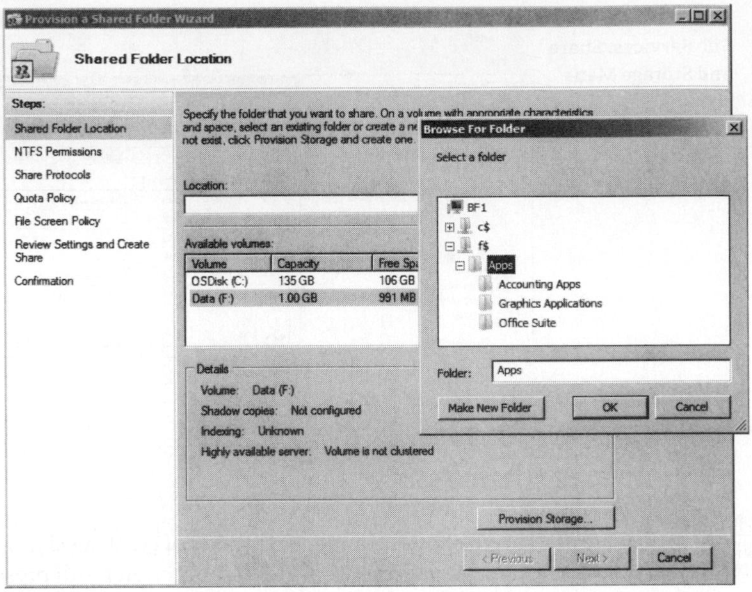

FIGURE 10.6
Selecting a folder
to share using the
Provision a Shared
Folder Wizard

NFS FOR UNIX CLIENTS

The NFS option will be grayed out if Services for Network File System (NFS) is not added. However, if you later decide you want to add support for Unix clients, you can add the service, and the NFS selection will be available.

6. The SMB Settings page allows you to manipulate some of the advanced settings by clicking the Advanced button. The User Limit option is set to Maximum Allowed by default, but you can limit it to a specific number of connections if desired. The Access-based Enumeration setting is related to DFS and is disabled if the DFS role service isn't added. Offline Settings affects Offline Folders and will be covered later in this chapter. Click Next.

7. On the SMB Permissions page, you'll have the opportunity to change the default share permissions. By default, the Everyone group is granted Read access to the share. You can accept this or choose one of the options shown in Figure 10.7 by selecting "Users and groups have custom share permissions" and clicking the Permissions button.

Granting the Administrators group Full Control ensures they can do anything with the share. Granting users Change permission grants them Read and Write access to the share. You can also configure custom permissions by selecting the last radio button and clicking the Permissions button. Accept the default permission, and click Next.

8. The Quota Policy page allows you to apply quotas to the share that are enforced with FSRM. As an example, if you wanted to ensure users were limited to no more than 100MB of storage space, you could create a quota policy to enforce the limit. Quota policies will be discussed in greater depth later in this chapter. Click Next.

FIGURE 10.7
Selecting custom share permissions

9. The File Screen Policy page allows you to apply a file screen that can be used to monitor or block specific types of files from being saved on the share. For example, if you wanted to ensure that users didn't store any audio and video files on the server, you could select the Block Audio and Video Files file screen. File screens will be discussed in greater depth later in this chapter. Click Next.

10. If you're using DFS, you can publish an SMB share to a DFS namespace. DFS is covered in the next chapter. Click Next.

11. Review the settings you've selected, and click Create.

12. After a moment, the wizard will complete the creation of the share and indicate success. Click Close.

Creating Shares on Remote Computers Using Server Manager

It's also possible to perform the previous procedure to create shares on remote computers using Server Manager. You first need to ensure the remote computer is configured correctly, which can be done by entering three commands:

1. Enter the following command at the command prompt on the computer that you want to administer remotely. This command will enable the WinRM listener.

```
winrm qc
```

When prompted, type **Y** and press Enter.

2. Ensure the Virtual Disk service is running on the remote computer. You can do this from the command line with the following command:

```
sc config vds start= auto
net start vds
```

Real World Scenario

SETTING USER LIMITS

You can configure how many users can connect to a share simultaneously on the User Limits tab of the SMB Settings screen's advanced settings, as shown here.

As an example, if an application under your share is licensed for 100 concurrent users, you can configure your server share to maintain that limit, even though you may have 200 users on your network. Just select the Allow This Number of Users radio button, and fill in the appropriate number (it defaults to 10). As users connect to the share, they build up to the user limit. As users log off or disconnect from the share, the number drops. This type of licensing enforcement can be handy in reducing your licensing costs.

Be careful with your licensing, however. Not all applications have a concurrent license mode, although they might have a client license mode. With client license mode, the manufacturer doesn't care how many users are accessing the application at any given time; they just care about how many people have installed the application altogether. This user limit option will not protect you in these cases.

Another thing to keep in mind is that this user connection concurrency limit is based on the entire share. It cannot be defined for each folder within a share. For example, you could have two applications in a single share. Application 1 has a concurrency limit of 100, and application 2 has no limits. You might inadvertently limit access to application 2 when the share limits the connections to 100. The easy solution is to use different shares if different limits are needed.

Finally, you need to consider how your users connect to the share to use these applications before you limit them based on concurrency. If your users all connect to the share upon logging in (such as with a mapped drive) but don't disconnect until logging off, your concurrency limit may be used up based on who shows up for work first, and you'll have 100 people using up your concurrency limit even if only a small percentage of them are actually using the application. If connections are made only when actually using the application, the user limit will work quite nicely.

If you need to modify the user limit after the share has been provisioned, you can return to Share and Storage Management, right-click the share, and select Properties.

WATCH THE SPACES WITH SC

The server config (sc) command is very particular about spaces. The following command has a space after the = symbol and will work:

```
sc config vds start= auto
```

On the other hand, this next command will fail since the space is missing:

```
sc config vds start=auto
```

---

3. Create a firewall exception for the remote volume management with the following command. Even though this spans two lines in the book, the entire command should be entered on a single line.

```
netsh advfirewall firewall
    set rule group="Remote Volume Management" new enable=yes
```

Although the command shown here spans two lines, you should enter it all on a single line. When the command is entered correctly, the output indicates that that it has "Updated 3 rules."

Once the remote computer is configured, you can launch Server Manager and your local computer, right-click Server Manager (the top line in the tree), and select Connect to Another Computer. Enter the name of the remote computer, and click OK. After a moment, Server Manager will be connected to the remote computer, and the same wizard can be launched to create a share (though you'll find it's a tad slower).

Publishing Shares in Active Directory

One of the great things about Active Directory is that it can unify all resources in an enterprise into a single directory, whether it's printers, groups, users, organizational units, or just about anything you can dream up—or more appropriately, serve up. This counts for shares too. The primary reason to publish a share to Active Directory is to allow users to easily find it.

To publish a share, you need to be in the Active Directory Users and Computers Management Console. Right-click the organizational unit of choice, and select New ➤ Shared Folder. From there, you'll be asked to provide a name for this publication of the share and, of course, the share name. That's all there is to it—your share is now published in Active Directory.

Once the share is published, you can also add keywords to help users easily find the published share. Right-click the shared folder object in Active Directory Users and Computers, select Properties, and click the Keywords button; then add any keywords you like that users might use to help them find this share. Figure 10.8 shows keywords being added to the Apps published share.

Users can then use the Active Directory Search tool to search based on the keyword. Figure 10.9 shows the Active Directory Search tool with Shared Folders selected in the Find drop-down box. We've added the keyword *apps* and clicked Find Now, and the share was located. At this point, we could just double-click the share to access it.

FIGURE 10.8
Adding
keywords to a
published share

FIGURE 10.9
Using Active Direc-
tory Search to
locate a published
share

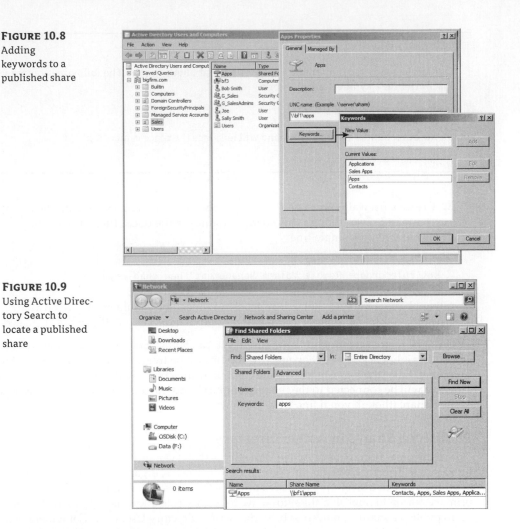

Managing Permissions

One of the great strengths of both NTFS formatted drives and shares is the ability to assign
permissions and control who can access different files and folders. While Chapter 11 will
cover the inner workings of these permissions in much greater detail, this chapter gives a
basic introduction to both NTFS and share permissions.

There are many similarities between NTFS and share permissions which you'll learn about in
this section. This includes how each permission can be assigned Allow or Deny, how permissions
are cumulative, how deny takes precedence, and how the principle of implicit deny is used.

When a user accesses a share that has both NTFS and Share permissions applied, the resulting
permission is commonly called the least restrictive permission. Since you may be asked to resolve
the problem of why a user can't access a file or folder, you should know how to calculate the resulting permission, which you'll learn in this section.

NTFS Permissions

NTFS permissions apply to any file or folder on a disk that has been formatted with NTFS.

Read   When a user is assigned Read permission, the user is allowed to view the contents, permissions, and attributes associated with a file or folder.

Read and Execute   The Read and Execute permission is used to grant permission for a user to execute files. Any executable files (such as .exe, .bat, and .com) are files that can be executed or launched. If a user has only Read permission, and not Read and Execute, the files can't be executed.

List Folder Contents   The List Folder Contents permission allows a user to view the contents of a folder. It will allow a user to see that files exist in a folder, but will not apply Read permissions to those files.

Write   If a user is assigned Write permission to a file or folder, the user can modify the file or folder. This includes adding new files or folders to a folder or making changes to existing files or folders. However, it does not include deleting files from a folder.

Modify   Modify includes all of the permissions from Read, Read & Execute, and Change, and adds the ability to delete files and folders.

Full Control   Full Control is a combination of all the available permissions. It adds the ability to change permissions and take ownership of files or folders.

Share Permissions

Share permissions only apply to shares when they are accessed over the network. There are only three share permissions. They are:

Read   Users granted Read permission can read files and folders within the share.

Change   Users granted Change permission can read, execute, modify, and delete files and folders within the share.

Full Control   Users granted Full Control permission have all the permissions from Change, and can also modify permissions on the share.

Share and NTFS Permission Similarities

Now that you have a basic understanding of the overall NTFS and share permissions, it's easier to explore the similarities, and there are many. These include:

- Both can be assigned either Allow or Deny
- Both are cumulative
- Deny takes precedence with both
- Both support implicit deny

ASSIGNING ALLOW OR DENY

As you start working with permissions, you'll notice that they have both Allow and Deny check boxes for each of the listed permissions. Here's an overview of how they work:

◆ If the permission is set to Allow for a user or group, the user or group has this permission.

◆ If the permission is set to Deny for a user or group, the user or group will not have the permission.

◆ Permissions are cumulative. If a user has multiple Allow permissions assigned (such as allow Read and Allow Change), the user has a combination of the assigned permissions.

◆ If both Allow and Deny permissions are assigned for a user, deny takes precedence.

If there aren't any permissions assigned to a user, then the user does not have access to the object. This is referred to as an *implicit deny*. Both share permissions and NTFS permissions use the discretionary access control (DAC) model to control access. Each object has a discretionary access control list (DACL; pronounced as "dackel"). The DACL is a list of access control entries (ACEs).

Each ACE identifies a user or a group with their associated security identifier (SID) and Allow or Deny permission. Any object can have multiple ACEs in the DACL; said another way, any object can have multiple permissions assigned.

SECURITY IDENTIFIERS (SIDS)

Every user and every group is uniquely identified with a SID. When the user logs on, a token is created that includes the user's SID and the SIDs of any groups where the user is a member. This token is used by the operating system to determine whether a user should have access. The SIDs in the token are compared to the SIDs in the access control entries of the DACL to determine access.

When a user accesses a file, folder, or share, the operating system compares the DACL with the user's account and group memberships. If there's a match, the user is granted the appropriate permission.

CUMULATIVE PERMISSIONS

Objects can have multiple permissions assigned. As an example, imagine a share named ProjectData. Administrators could be granted Full Control, another group could be granted Change, and another group could be granted Read permission. When multiple permissions are assigned, permissions are cumulative. In other words, if multiple permissions apply to a user, the user has the combination of all the permissions.

Imagine that Sally is a member of both the G_Sales group and the G_SalesAdmins group, and these groups are granted the following permissions to the Sales Share:

G_Sales	Allow Change permission
G_SalesAdmins	Allow Full Control permission

Since Sally is a member of both groups, she is granted both Change and Full Control; said another way, she is granted the combination of both the Change and Full Control permissions.

DENY TAKES PRECEDENCE

If both Allow and Deny for any permission are assigned to a user, Deny takes precedence. As an example, imagine you have granted the G_Sales group Full Control to a share that includes proprietary information. For some reason, Billy-Joe-Bob (who is a member of the G_Sales group) has fallen out of grace with the company. You're asked to leave him in the G_Sales group so he can access other shares but prevent him from accessing the proprietary share.

Figure 10.10 shows what you can do. The share permissions started with personnel in the G_Sales group having Full Control permissions on the share. To prevent Billy-Joe-Bob from accessing the data at all, his account was added and assigned Deny Full Control. Said another way, his account is explicitly denied.

FIGURE 10.10
Selecting custom share permissions

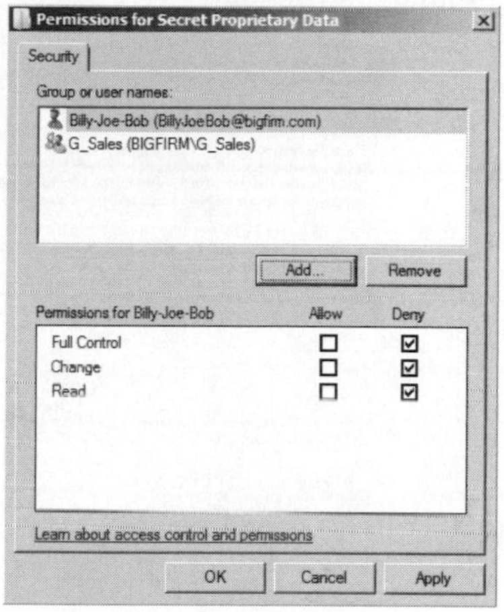

Notice the conflict. The user is granted access as a member of the G_Sales group and denied access for his specific account. The conflict is resolved in favor of the deny permission. This makes sense if you think about it. When you take the extra steps needed to deny access, you don't want anything overriding it. Deny takes precedence.

IMPLICIT DENY

There's also something known as *implicit deny*. If permissions aren't explicitly granted, they are implicitly denied.

Imagine a share named ProjectData where the only group granted access to the share is the G_Sales group. Maria is in the G_HR group and is not a member of the G_Sales group, so she does not have any access to the share. She hasn't been explicitly granted access, so she is implicitly denied access.

This is similar to your home. If you never give the keys to anyone for your house, they shouldn't be able to get in. Of course, you still need to worry about bandits and hackers, but from the basic perspective, giving no permissions results in no access.

Modifying Share and NTFS Permissions

You can modify both the share and NTFS permissions using Server Manager, Computer Management, or Windows Explorer. The steps are a little different for each method, but ultimately you'll get to the same permissions pages. For this discussion, we're limiting the procedure to using Server Manager.

Imagine that you've created a share and granted the Everyone group Read permission. However, now you want to change the permissions so that users in the G_Sales group have Change permission. You can follow these steps to make the changes:

1. Launch Server Manager, and browse to Roles ➢ File Services ➢ Share and Storage Management.

2. Right-click the share, and select Properties.

3. Click the Permissions tab, and then click the Share Permissions button. Your display will look similar to Figure 10.11.

FIGURE 10.11
Viewing the share permissions

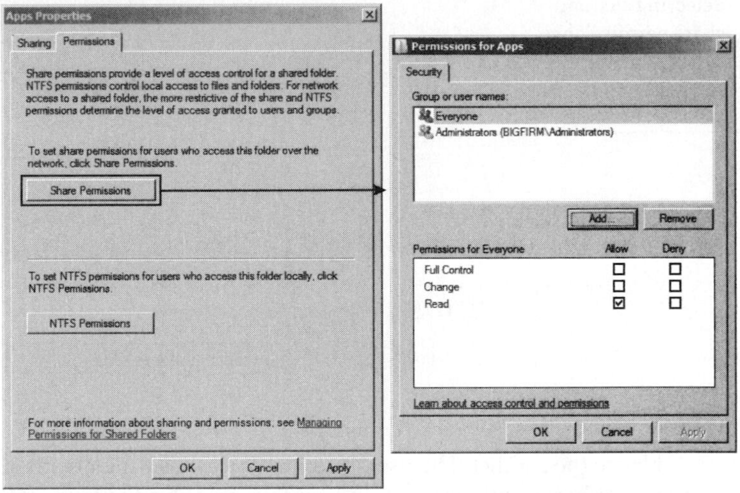

4. Click Add. Enter the name of the group you want to add (for example **G_Sales**), and click OK.

5. Select the Allow Change permission for the group you added.

6. Select the Everyone group, and click Remove. Click OK.

7. Click the NTFS Permissions button. Notice that you can also modify the NTFS permissions here.

8. Click Add, and enter the name of a group you want to add (such as **G_Sales**). Click OK after you've added the group.

9. By default any user or group you add is automatically granted Read, Read & Execute, and List Folder Contents permissions. Select the Allow Write permission for the group you've added to ensure they can also make changes to the files.

10. If you want to prevent other users from even reading the files, you can select the Everyone group and click Remove. Your display will look similar to Figure 10.12.

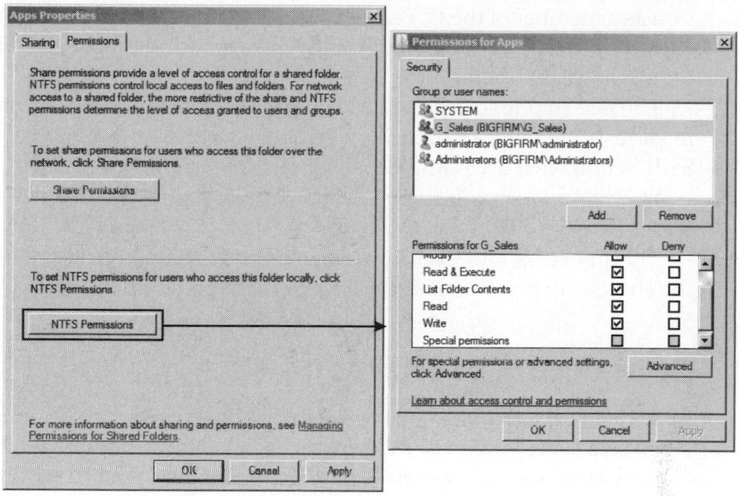

FIGURE 10.12
Viewing the NTFS permissions

11. Click OK to accept the changes. Click OK on the Apps properties sheet.

Combining Share and NTFS Permissions

People sometimes find it challenging to identify the permissions a user will have when they access a file or folder via a share. We like to keep it simple with these three steps:

1. Determine the cumulative NTFS permissions.

2. Determine the cumulative share permissions.

3. Determine which of the two provides the least access (commonly called the *most restrictive permission*).

Imagine that Sally is a member of the G_Sales and G_ITAdmins groups. The assigned permissions for the SalesData folder (shared as the SalesData share) are shown in Table 10.1.

TABLE 10.1: Combining NTFS and Share Permissions

GROUP	NTFS PERMISSIONS	SHARE PERMISSIONS
G_Sales	Read, Read & Execute, List Folder Contents	Read
G_ITSalesAdmins	Full Control	Change

In step 1, you need to determine the cumulative NTFS permissions. Sally has the Read, Read & Execute, and List Folder Contents permissions as a member of the G_Sales group. Additionally, she has Full Control permission as a member of the G_IT SalesAdmins group. Since Full Control includes all the other permissions, her cumulative NTFS permissions are Full Control.

In step 2, you need to determine the cumulative share permissions. Sally has the Read permission as a member of the G_Sales group. Additionally, she has the Change permission as a member of the G_IT SalesAdmins group. Since Change includes both Read and Write, her cumulative share permissions are Change.

The last step involves a simple question. Which permission provides the least access or is the most restrictive: Full Control or Change? The answer is Change. Change is the permission that Sally will have if accessing the share over the network.

How about a trick question? What is Sally's permission when she accesses the SalesData folder locally?

The answer is Full Control. Remember that share permissions apply only when a user accesses the share over a network. If the folder is accessed locally, only NTFS permissions apply.

Connecting to Shares

Now that you have these shares, how do people use them? Assuming that you have a share called Apps on a server called BF1, how would someone attached to the network access that share?

Primarily, you connect to a share using the universal naming convention (UNC) of \\ServerName\ShareName. As a simple example, you can click Start and in the search box enter **\\ServerName** (using the server name of any server on your network) followed by a backslash, as shown in Figure 10.13. In the figure, we've used **\\BF1** to connect to the server named BF1.

FIGURE 10.13
Searching for shares available on a network server

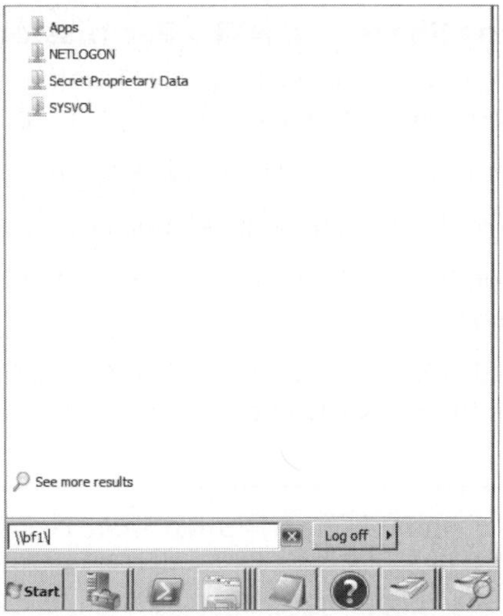

START SEARCH OR RUN

You can use the Start and Search menu on Windows Vista, Windows 7, Server 2008, and Server 2008 R2. In previous editions (such as Windows XP and Server 2003), you could achieve the same results by clicking Start, selecting Run, and entering the UNC path in the Run window.

Once the operating system connects, it retrieves a list of shares available. On this server there are currently four shares, well, four shares that aren't hidden. Chapter 11 will show you how additional hidden shares are available. You could type in **Apps** to the end of \\BF1\and complete the entry as **\\BF1\Apps,** or simply click the Apps share from the menu shown in Figure 10.13 to connect the Apps share.

Besides using the search menu, you can connect to the share in the following ways:

Mapping a drive You can map a drive letter to a share on your network. For example, users may need access to a share each time they boot. You can right-click either Computer or Network from the Start menu and select Map Network Drive. Figure 10.14 shows the Map Network Drive dialog box. With "Reconnect at logon" selected, the user will always have the Z drive mapped to the share when they boot.

FIGURE 10.14
Mapping a share to a drive letter

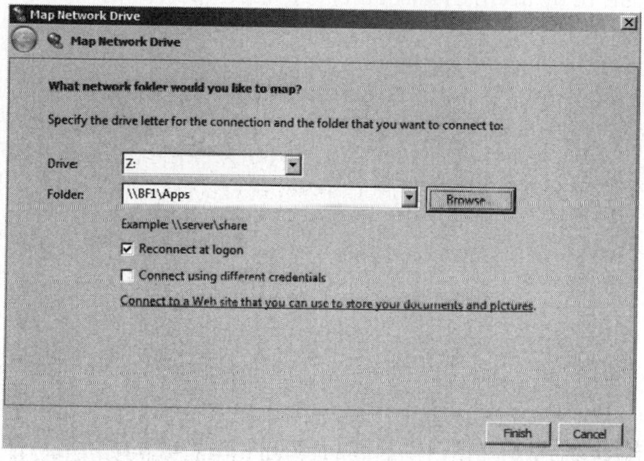

Searching Active Directory If a client is a member of a domain, the Search Active Directory command appears on the Network console. You can launch Network by selecting Start ➢ Network on Windows Server 2008 R2.

Using net use You can use the net use command at the command line. The basic syntax is as follows:

```
net use driveletter \\servername\sharename
```

For example, to attach to the share Apps on the server named BF1 and then to be able to refer to that share as drive Z, you could use this command:

```
net use Z: \\BF1\apps
```

If you later want to remove the mapping, you can use this command:

```
net use Z: /delete
```

"A Set of Credentials Conflicts"

Sometimes when you're trying to attach to a share, you'll get an error message that says something like "A set of credentials conflicts with an existing set of credentials on that share."

Here's what's happening. You've already tried to access this share and failed for some reason—perhaps you mistyped a password. The server that the share is on has constructed some security information about you that says you're a deadbeat, and it doesn't want to hear anything else about you. You need to get the server to forget about you so that you can start all over. You can do that with the /d option.

Suppose you've already tried to access the \\BF1\Apps share and apparently failed. It might be that you *are* actually connected to the share, but with no permissions. (We know it doesn't make sense, but it happens.) You can find out what shares you're connected to by typing just net use all by itself. Chances are, you'll see that \\BF1\Apps is on the list. You have to disconnect from that BF1 server so that you can start over. To do that, type this:

```
net use \\BF1\apps /d
```

Then do another net use to make sure that you have all of those connections cleaned up; you may find that you have *multiple* attachments to a particular server. Or…in a few cases, you may have to disconnect *all* of your file shares with this command:

```
net use * /d
```

With all the connections closed, you can try net use again, and it will work.

Using net use on a WAN

Now you are into one of the most difficult networking areas: connecting to your resources across long distances and great unknowns. If you've ever had to rely on long-distance remote computing, you know not to rely on it. But you have a new little function set in your net use arsenal that takes a lot of the "unknown" out of the picture.

Instead of relying on getting to the appropriate name resolution server, getting through to that server, and getting accurate reliable resolution over an inaccurate and unreliable network link, you can now just map a drive straight to your server via its IP address. Granted, you now need to know that IP address, but it is a good fail-safe. In our case, we work from several different locations connected with frame-relay WAN links. The network isn't always so good about being able to convert server names into IP addresses, so net use \\BF1 usually tells us that our machine couldn't *find* \\BF1. Even if it *does* work, *name resolution*—converting a name such as BF1 to a network address—takes time.

If you know the IP address of the server you're trying to contact, then you can use the IP address in lieu of the server's name. If you know that BF1's IP address is 134.81.12.4, you can simply type this:

```
net use \\134.81.12.4\apps
```

And, because you're probably connecting from a different network, you might have to add the /user: information. And it's never a bad idea to add /persistent:no so that your system doesn't spend five minutes trying to reconnect to it the next time that you start up. So, for example, if BF1 is a member of a domain named BigFirm.com and you have an account on BigFirm.com named boss, you could ensure that BF1 will know who you are and log you on like so:

```
net use \\134.81.12.4\apps /user:bigfirm.com\boss /persistent:no
```

Although there are many conventional methods of connecting to shares using different GUIs, don't overlook the net use command. You'll find it useful.

Common Shares

In Windows Server, several common shares have already been created for you. Most of these shares are hidden. If you know of these shares, you can connect to any of them using the UNC path.

C\$, D\$, and so on   All drives, including CD-ROM drives, are given a hidden share to the root of the drive. This share is what is called an *administrative share*. You cannot change the permissions or properties of these shares, other than to configure them for Offline Files (we'll talk about Offline Files at the end of this chapter). Only the Administrators and Backup Operators groups can connect to administrative shares, and you can't stop sharing these administrative shares without modifying the registry or by stopping the Server service (which stops all sharing). These shares come in handy for server administrators who do a lot of remote management. Mapping a drive to the C\$ share is the equivalent of being at C:\ on the server.

ADMIN\$ The ADMIN\$ share is another administrative share and it maps to the location of the operating system. If you installed the operating system at D:\Windows, the ADMIN\$ share would map to D:\Windows.

PRINT\$ Whenever you create a shared printer, the system places the drivers in this share. This allows the drivers to be easily downloaded when clients connect to the shared printer.

IPC\$ The IPC\$ share is probably one of the most widely used shares in interserver communications though you will rarely interact with it directly. When you try to access shared resources on other computers (to read event logs, for example), the system uses *named pipes*. A named pipe is a piece of memory that handles a communication channel between two processes, whether local or remote, and the IPC\$ is used by the named pipes.

NETLOGON   The NETLOGON share is used in conjunction with processing logon requests from users. Once users successfully log in, they are given any profile and script information that they are required to run. This script is often a batch file. For example, we have a common batch file that we want all of our users to run every time they log in. This allows us to have all clients run a standard set of commands, like copying updated network information, mapping standard network drives, and so on. These batch files, scripts, and profiles go in the NETLOGON share. The NETLOGON share is required on all domain controllers.

SYSVOL   The SYSVOL share is used to house Group Policy information and scripts that are accessed by clients on the network. You will always see SYSVOL shares on domain controllers, but they can be replicated to member servers.

File Server Resource Manager

The File Server Resource Manager is an important addition that's included with the File Services role. It includes several additional capabilities that make it easier to manage a file server:

◆   Creating and managing quota policies

◆   Creating and managing file screen policies

◆   Viewing reports

These techniques are covered in the following sections.

Creating Quota Policies

NTFS has long included quota management capabilities, but they have been significantly improved with FSRM. In short, quotas allow you to monitor and limit the space users can consume on a volume or folder.

STORAGE USAGE MONITORING VS. QUOTA POLICIES

You may remember configuring storage usage monitoring when you added the File Services role. You can refer to Figure 10.4 to jog your memory. Although storage usage monitoring uses the same technology as quota policies available with NTFS, it has a subtle difference from the quota policies. Storage monitoring monitors the entire volume and is configured by default to let you know when the drive reaches 85 percent of capacity. Quota policies can be configured on individual folders, which allows you to fine-tune what you monitor.

When creating quotas, you have the ability to set warning limits, set enforcement limits, provide notification of reached limits via email or event log entries, and even execute commands in response to any limit. Quotas can be set for any share on a server or any specific path.

Quotas can be very useful for monitoring storage on file servers. For example, you may have a file server with 2TB of storage. You may think this is more than enough space, but if some users are creating and editing audio and video files, 2TB of free space could disappear quickly. A quota policy can help you limit users to a specific amount. However, these audio and video files may be integral to your business, and you may not want to limit the storage space but instead just ensure you're informed when the storage space reaches a certain threshold. Instead of actually limiting the storage, you can use the quota policy to just monitor the usage.

On the surface, quota policies can be very simple to understand and implement. However, you can get pretty sophisticated with them if you need to do so.

QUOTA TEMPLATES

Microsoft has included several quota templates in FSRM that you can easily be applied as is, or you can modify them to fit your needs. You can even create your own templates. Figure 10.15 shows the Quota Templates screen with the default templates.

FIGURE 10.15
Viewing the available quota templates

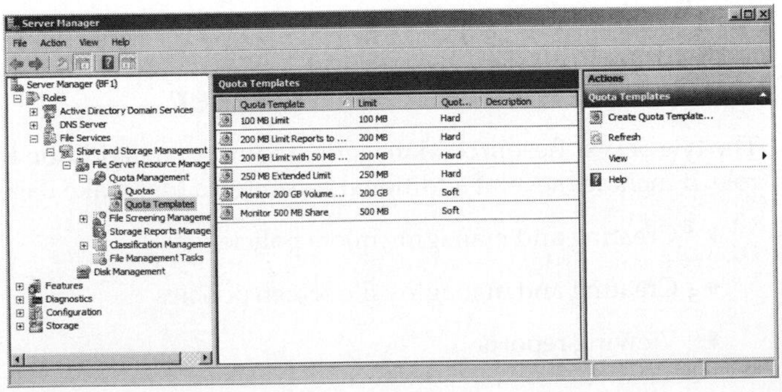

Once you have an idea of how the quotas work, the information on this page gives you the basic information you need to understand what the quota will do. A significant piece of information is the quota type: hard or soft. A *hard* quota limit will enforce the limit and prevent users from exceeding the limit. A *soft* quota limit is just used for monitoring; it will provide notification but does not enforce the limit.

The 200 MB Limit with 50 MB extension template provides an excellent example of responding to a quota limit being reached. You can view or edit the template properties of any template by right-clicking the template and selecting Edit Template Properties.

Figure 10.16 shows the template being edited. On the left you can see the basic template. Notice on the bottom that there are three notification thresholds that have been configured: 85 percent, 95 percent, and 100 percent. The 85 percent warning only sends an email, the 95 percent warning sends an email and logs an event, and the 100 percent warning also executes a command.

FIGURE 10.16
Viewing a quota template

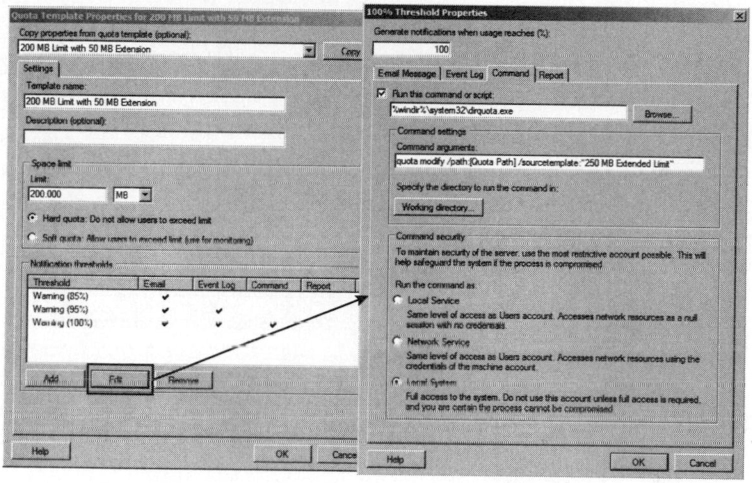

The page on the right of the figure was reached by selecting the Warning (100%) notification threshold and selecting Edit. It is using the `dirquota.exe` command-line tool to modify the quota. Specifically, it is changing the quota from a limit of 200MB to 250MB. The commands you put here are limited only by your imagination. If necessary, you also set the security context of the command depending on what permissions the command needs to execute.

In addition to executing a command, the other threshold responses are sending an email, logging an event, and creating a report.

E-mail Message Tab

The E-mail Message tab allows you to configure an email response if the threshold is reached. If you want an email sent to an administrator, simply add the administrator's email address (or an administrator's distribution group) on this page in the format of account@domain, such as ITAdmins@bigfirm.com. You can also configure it to send an email to the user who exceeded the threshold simply by selecting a box. FSRM uses Active Directory to look up the user's email address.

The templates include a preconfigured subject line and message body, and both can include variables. In Figure 10.17 the message body includes several variables: Source I/O Owner, Quota Path, Server, and more. If you click within either the subject line or the message body, the variable drop-down box will be enabled. You can select any of these variables to see a short explanation of what it is. We know when we first saw [Source lo Owner], we couldn't figure out what "lo" was, but after selecting it from the drop-down box, we saw it meant I/O as input/output.

FIGURE 10.17
Viewing the E-mail
Message tab

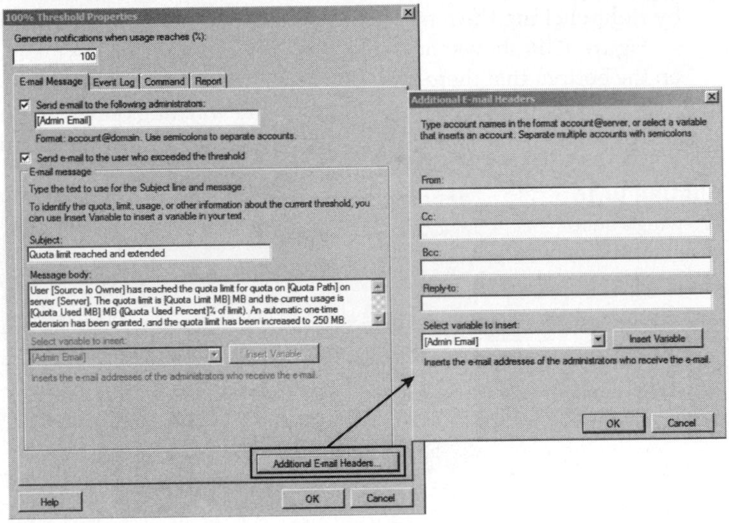

On the right side of the figure, you can see the additional headers you can add to your email messages by clicking the Additional E-mail Headers button. It also includes variables that you can add by selecting the variable in the drop-down box and clicking Insert Variable.

SMTP SERVER MUST BE CONFIGURED

For FSRM to send email messages, it must be configured with the server name or IP address of an SMTP server that will accept the email messages. This is done on the File Server Resource Manager Options page, covered later in this chapter.

Event Log Tab

You can configure the events to be logged in the Application log if desired. It's as simple as selecting the Event Log tab and selecting the box to send the warning to the event log, as shown in Figure 10.18. Any events sent from here are logged into the Application log.

Just as you can add variables to email messages, you can also add variables to log entries. In Figure 10.28, we've selected the variable drop-down box to show some of the variables that can be added. A lot of variables can be selected, but not all of them are showing in the figure.

FIGURE 10.18
Viewing the Event
Log tab

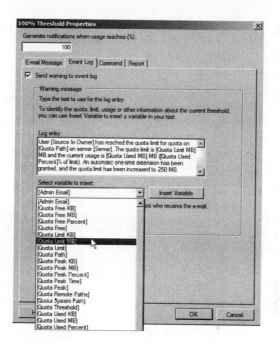

Report Tab

The fourth tab that can be manipulated for notification thresholds is the Report tab. You can configure reports to be generated in response to a threshold and automatically be sent via email to administrators and/or the user. Reports can also be created on demand, as you'll see later in this chapter.

CREATING A QUOTA

Once you understand the basics, it's pretty simple to create and apply a quota. Imagine you want to monitor the amount of data that is being stored in a folder named Graphics on your system. Specifically, you want to know whether the amount of storage used is getting close to 500MB. If the limit is reached, you want to send a report to the user letting her know which files are duplicates, which files are the largest, and which files haven't been used recently.

You can use the following steps to create this quota:

1. Launch Server Manager, and browse to the Roles ➤ File Services ➤ Share and Storage Management ➤ Quota Templates node.

2. Right-click the 200 MB Limit Reports to User quota template, and select Create Quota from Template.

3. Enter the path to the folder you want to monitor in the Quota Path text box. For example, you could enter **F:\Graphics**. Alternately, you could click Browse and browse to the path. Click Create.

4. Select Quotas (right above Quota Templates in the Server Manager navigation tree).

5. Right-click your new quota, and select Edit Quota Properties.

6. Change the Space Limit from 200MB to 500MB.

7. Select the Warning (100%) notification threshold, and select Edit.

8. Review the information on the E-mail Message, Event Log, and Command tabs. If a warning appears indicating that an SMTP server is not configured, review the information, and click Yes to continue; you can configure the SMTP server later. Notice that you can modify the data on any of these tabs.

9. Click the Report tab. Your display will look similar to Figure 10.19.

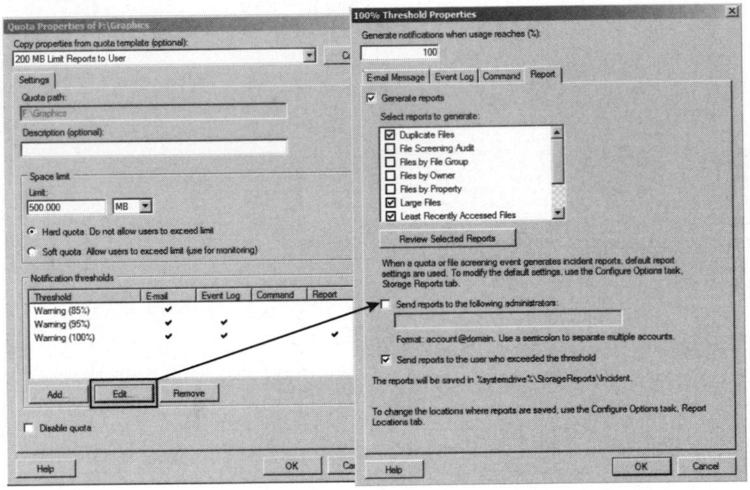

FIGURE 10.19

Viewing the Report tab of a new quota

10. Notice that the reports are already configured. The Generate Reports check box is checked, and three reports are configured to be generated: Duplicate Files, Large Files, and Least Recently Accessed Files. Additionally, it's configured to send the report to the user exceeding the threshold. Click OK to close the 100% Threshold Properties page.

11. Click OK to close the Quota Properties page.

Creating File Screen Policies

File screens are used to filter or screen files to ensure certain types of files aren't stored on a server. Imagine that after implementing a quota policy and reviewing some of the reports you realize that your F drive is almost full because one of the users has stored several gigabytes of backup MP3 files on the server.

Although it's admirable that the user is backing up his files, you may not want him using your server to back up his MP3 files. Additionally, you may not want anyone storing MP3 files or any other type of audio or video files on your server.

You can create a file screen that will block users from saving specific types of files and generate notifications when anyone attempts to save these blocked files on the server. File screens can be created on entire volumes or specific folders, and just as quotas have templates, file screens also have templates. Figure 10.20 shows Server Manager open to the file screen templates.

FIGURE 10.20
Viewing the file screen templates

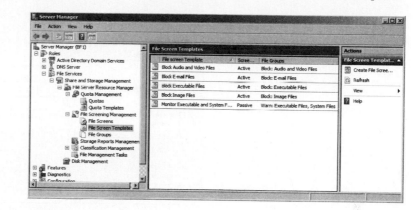

Notice that several well-known file group types are identified in the templates such as audio and video files and image files. The specific extensions of these file types are identified in the File Groups node. For example, audio and video files include .mp1, .mp2, .mp3, .mp4, and .mpeg—and that's not even all of the m's.

When you create a file screen, you can simply select one of the file groups. This will meet your needs most of the time, but if you want to add file types or exclude specific file types from the screen, you can modify the contents to meet your needs.

Imagine that your company has recently learned that many users are storing Outlook .pst files on a server that are more than 1GB in size and eating up the storage space. The company states that users cannot store email files on a file server. You can use the following steps to enforce the rule:

1. Launch Server Manager, and browse to the File Screen Templates node.

2. Right-click the Block E-mail Files template, and select Create File Screen from Template.

3. Enter the volume name that you want to screen (such as **F:**) in the File Screen Path text box. Click Create.

4. Select File Screens (right above File Screen Templates). Right-click the new file screen you just created, and select Edit File Screen Properties. Your display will look similar to Figure 10.21.

Notice that you can select either Active Screening or Passive Screening. Since you want to specifically block users from storing the files on the server, leave it as Active Screening.

5. Click through the Email Message, Event Log, Command, and Report tabs. If a warning appears indicating that an SMTP server is not configured, review the information, and click Yes to continue. You'll see that these are very similar to the tabs used with quotes. Only the notification content is changed.

6. Click OK once you've reviewed the tabs.

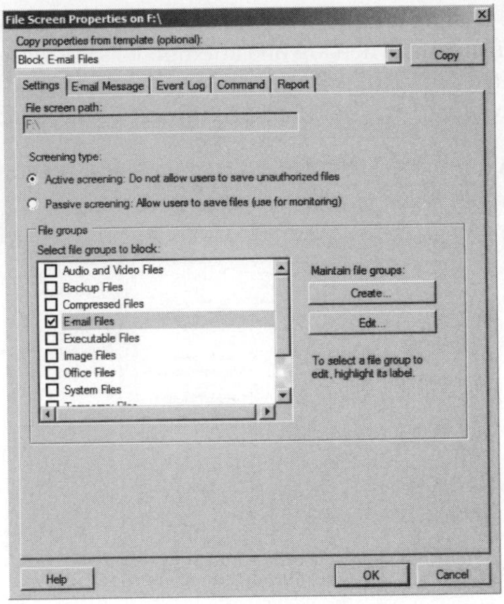

FIGURE 10.21
Viewing the
properties of a
file screen

FIGURE 10.21
Viewing the
properties of a
file screen

Generating Reports

Several different reports are available. You can generate reports as part of any quota policy or file screen policy. You can also configure reports to be generated on a schedule or generate them on demand.

Thankfully, the reports are well named, and it's easy to determine the primary content just by the name. The different reports available are Duplicate Files, File Screening Audit, Files by File Group, Files by Owner, Files by Property, Large Files, Least Recently Accessed Files, Most Recently Accessed Files, and Quota Usage.

Additionally, you can save the reports in several different formats such as DHTML, HTML, XML, CSV, and text. You can access the reports with the following steps:

1. Launch Server Manager. Right-click the Storage Reports Management node within the File Server Resource Manager, and select Generate Reports Now.

2. Click the Add button. Browse to a drive or a folder, and click OK. You can add multiple drives and folders.

3. You can select as many reports as you'd like to view, but if you select them all, be patient; they take some time to generate. Some of the reports have additional parameters that you can modify. For example, if you select the Quota Usage report, you can click the Edit Parameters button and modify the minimum quota usage that will be included in the report.

4. Select the check boxes next to the report formats that you'd like to view. Your display will look similar to Figure 10.22.

5. Click the Delivery tab. Notice you can add an email address and send the reports via email. Click OK.

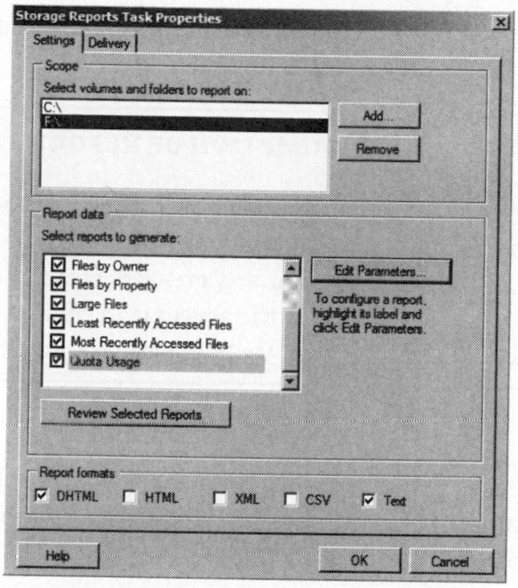

FIGURE 10.22
Selecting report
types and formats

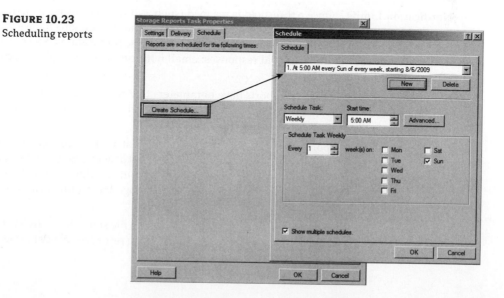

6. In the Generate Storage Reports dialog box, select Generate Reports in the Background, and click OK. This will create a report task that will be deleted after it completes.

Depending on the amount of data in the reports, this could take several minutes to complete.

7. While the report task is running, right-click Storage Reports Management, and select Schedule a New Report Task.

8. Click the Add button, and select any volumes or folders you want included in the report. Select the reports and the report formats desired.

9. Select the Schedule tab, and click the Create Schedule button. Click the New button.

10. Change the schedule task from Daily to Weekly. Select Sunday at 5 a.m. Your display will look similar to Figure 10.23.

FIGURE 10.23
Scheduling reports

11. Click OK to accept the schedule. Click OK again to close the Storage Reports Task page.

MONITOR DISK CONSUMPTION OF REPORTS

If you create a report schedule that will create report files on your system, you'll want to monitor the amount of space taken up by the reports. The worst-case scenario is that a report schedule is created and reports are regularly created, steadily consuming the disk space. One way to avoid this impacting the operation of the server is to change the default location of the reports by modifying the Report Locations tab of the File Server Resource Manager Options.

---

12. The report task you created earlier should be done at this point. By default, reports are located in the %systemdrive%\StorageReports\Interactive folder. Use Windows Explorer to browse to this folder.

13. Double-click some of the HTML files to view the available information. Double-click any of the text files to see how the information is displayed.

As you can see, FSRM provides rich reporting capabilities.

File Server Resource Manager Options

You can modify several FSRM options. One of them, Email Notifications, must be configured before you can use any of the email capabilities of the server. You can access the options page by right-clicking File Server Resource Manager within Server Manager and selecting Configure Options. A properties sheet appears with six tabs:

Email Notifications   If you want to use email notifications, you must enter the name or IP address of an SMTP server that will accept email from your server. You can also enter the default email address for administrator recipients and a default From address on this page.

Notification Limits   Once a threshold is reached (such as 85 percent usage on a disk), the threshold remains until action is taken. Instead of having the notifications harass the user every 30 seconds, you can set time limits in minutes for these notifications. The default is 60 minutes for each of the threshold responses: email notification, event log entry, command execution, and report generation.

Storage Reports   Many of the reports have parameters that can be modified. Each parameter that can be modified starts with a default. You can use this page to modify the default parameters.

Report Locations   Reports have default locations on the system drive (which is normally c:\). Three folders are created within the %systemdrive%\StorageReports folder. They are Incident (created from notifications), Scheduled (created from scheduled report tasks), and Interactive (created from on-demand reports). You can change the default locations for any of the reports from this page.

File Screen Audit   This page has only one option: "Record file screening activity in an auditing database." If selected, the screening activity will be recorded in a database, which can be reviewed by running a file screen auditing report.

Automatic Classification   It's possible to manage files based on classification properties and rules you create, instead of where files are located within a directory tree. If you use classification management (not many people do), you can use this tab to schedule the execution of classification rules and generate reports. If you'd like to learn more about file classification, check out this TechNet article: `http://technet.microsoft.com/library/dd758765.aspx`.

Although NTFS is a great file system and has included extras such as NTFS quotas, you can get a lot more capabilities by adding the File Server Resource Manager. If you're managing a file server, these extras are worth digging into.

Understanding SMB 2.0

After 15 years of running Server Message Block 1.0 on Windows systems, it has been upgraded to SMB 2.0 in Windows Server 2008. That's a long time in computer years for a protocol to be used without being upgraded; that it lasted that long says a lot about the developers.

However, SMB 1.0 had a few problems that Microsoft wanted to overcome with SMB 2.0:

Chattiness   SMB is noisy. It's not uncommon for common tasks to require several round-trips from the client to the server before the data is exchanged. This worked well in many environments, but not in slower WAN or high latency networks.

Speed   When SMB came out, the fastest networks operated at 10MB per second, but today it's not uncommon to see 1GB per second networks. SMB 1.0 just doesn't perform well on the faster networks, but SMB 2.0 excels.

Efficiency   Several data requests can be combined in one data packet with SMB 2.0, where SMB 1.0 required individual packets for each data request. More than 100 SMB 1.0 commands were reduced to only 19 commands in SMB 2.0. Additionally, data pipelining is possible in SMB 2.0. A data pipeline allows the client to send several requests one after another without having to wait for the response to one request before sending another request.

Security   Message signing is improved with SMB 2.0. It uses a 32-byte hash using HMAC SHA-256 of the entire message. In contrast, SMB 1.0 uses the 128-bit MD5.

SMB 2.0 PROTOCOL SPECIFICATION

Although we've highlighted some of the important features of SMB 2.0, we certainly haven't covered everything in depth. If you'd like to look at the full protocol specification, you can check it out at `http://msdn.microsoft.com/library/cc212614.aspx`.

Compatibility with SMB 1.0

To maintain backward compatibility, newer operating systems support both SMB 1.0 and SMB 2.0. The following clients support SMB 2.0 and can use either SMB 1.0 or SMB 2.0 depending on the client on the other side of the conversation:

◆   Windows Vista

◆   Windows 7

◆ Windows Server 2008

◆ Windows Server 2008 R2

SMB 2.0 is used whenever possible by the clients that support it. However, since it's not supported by other operating systems (such as Windows XP or Windows Server 2003 Server), newer clients can use SMB 1.0 to talk to legacy clients. The good news is that all of this is automatic. You don't need to do any special configuration to take advantage of SMB 2.0 or to switch back to SMB 1.0 for legacy clients. Here's what automatically occurs with SMB:

◆ If both clients support SMB 2.0, SMB 2.0 will automatically be used.

◆ If one of the clients does not support SMB 2.0 (Windows XP, for example), then SMB 1.0 will be used for the session.

You've probably heard some of Microsoft's "Better Together" marketing campaigns. That's not just marketing for marketing's sake. SMB is one example where you'll truly enjoy better performance when you match up new technologies with each other. A network running Windows Server 2008 and 2008 R2 servers but still running Windows XP desktops won't be using SMB 2.0. If it's a busy network, the difference is noticeable.

SMB 2.0 Security

SMB 2.0 uses Hashing Message Authentication Code (HMAC) Secure Hashing Algorithm-256 (SHA with 256 bits). This is much more secure than the 128-bit Message Digest version 5 (MD5) used in SMB 1.0.

HMAC SHA-256 provides data integrity—assurances that the data hasn't been modified. Although SMB 1.0 also provides data integrity, the security is better with HMAC SHA-256.

A *hash* is simply a number created by performing a hashing algorithm on a packet, message, or file. As long as the packet is the same (not modified), the hashing algorithm will always provide the same hash (the same number). Generically, a hash provides data integrity to packets, messages, or files by following these steps:

1. The packet is created.

2. The hash is calculated on the packet.

3. The packet and hash are sent to their destination.

4. The destination calculates hash on the received packet and compares it to received hash:

   ◆ If both hashes are the same, data integrity is maintained.

   ◆ If the hashes are different, data integrity has been lost. This could be because an attacker modified the data or simply because bits were lost in transit.

However, if an attacker could modify the data in transit, why not modify the hash in transit too? To prevent this, the hash is encrypted with a session key known only to the client and the server. This is called *digitally signing* the packet in SMB 1.0 and 2.0. The process is as follows:

1. Create the packet.

2. Calculate the hash on the packet.

3. Encrypt the hash with a session key (or shared key).

4. Send the packet with the encrypted hash.

5. The receiver decrypts the encrypted hash.

6. The receiver calculates the hash on the received packet.

7. The receiver compares the two hashes to determine whether integrity is lost.

Enabling digital signing for SMB 1.0 packets could decrease performance by as much as 10 to 15 percent. Although you'll still see a performance hit with SMB 2.0, it won't be as great. One of the primary reasons is that SMB 2.0 is streamlined, resulting in fewer packets being sent and fewer packets needing to be signed.

Implementing BitLocker

BitLocker Drive Encryption is a technology designed to provide protection for entire disk drives. BitLocker To Go is a newer technology that came out with Windows 7 and is designed to allow you to encrypt USB flash drives. Our focus here will simply be using BitLocker Drive Encryption to secure drives on Server 2008 R2.

The primary vision of BitLocker is to encrypt data on hard drives so that if the hard drive is stolen or lost, the data can't be accessed. This has significant application with laptops and servers located where physical security is weak. Laptops are easy to pilfer—people leave them in a conference room for lunch or forget them on a chair, and quickly they're gone.

Similarly, servers located in remote office locations often have weak physical security, or at least weaker physical security than the main business location. You probably have very strong physical security in your primary server room, but your server in a remote office may be hidden behind a closet door that can be jimmied with a crowbar or even a credit card.

BITLOCKER ENHANCES PHYSICAL SECURITY

BitLocker enhances physical security but can't protect against all possible attacks. Malware such as rootkits can introduce weaknesses that might allow access to data if the computer is later stolen.

Additionally, if disk drives on a decommissioned server are not cleaned, it may include data you wouldn't want shared. BitLocker will protect this data from being used inappropriately.

On the surface, it may look like the data on these drives are protected through permissions. However, an attacker could set up a domain and place his account in Enterprise Admins. If he had physical access to your server, he could then remove the drive from your server, place it into his server, and easily take ownership of all the files. At that point, he owns all your data. However, if the files are encrypted, it will be much more difficult to access the data—we hesitate to say impossible, but it will be difficult enough to deter the vast majority of attackers.

Hardware Requirements

To provide the best protection, your hardware should include Trusted Platform Module (TPM) version 1.2. TPM 1.2 is a hardware component built into the computer, typically on the motherboard.

If the system has TPM 1.2 and BitLocker has been enabled, the system will do an integrity check when it boots up. If it senses changes in the hardware that indicate the hard drive is in a different computer, the drive will lock. It will stay locked until it is manually unlocked using a recovery key.

However, many computers don't have TPM 1.2. There are alternatives that can be used to encrypt drives with BitLocker:

Password BitLocker can encrypt the drive, and a password can be used to unlock it.

Smart Card BitLocker can encrypt the drive, and a smart card with a PIN can be used to unlock the drive.

You select TPM, a password, or a smart card when enabling BitLocker on a specific drive. In Figure 10.24, the system does not have a TPM, so only the password and smart card options are shown.

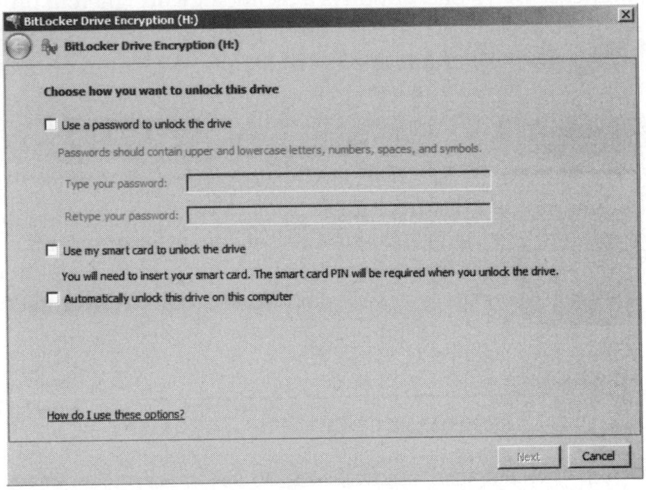

FIGURE 10.24
Choosing how to unlock a BitLocker-protected drive

It's also possible to select the option to have the drive automatically unlock when accessed on the same computer. This requires that the drive hosting Windows is also protected by BitLocker. When used this way, the encryption will be apparent only when the drive is moved to another computer (or enough hardware is changed in the current computer to make BitLocker think the drive has been moved).

BitLocker can be implemented on partitions without encrypting the entire drive. For example, if your system has a single physical hard drive divided into two partitions (C and D), you can lock the D drive with BitLocker without locking the C drive.

RECOVERY KEY

The BitLocker recovery key can be used if TPM detects that the drive has been moved onto a different computer. Once TPM detects that it has been moved (or the hardware has been changed), it will lock the drive until the recovery key is used to unlock it.

BitLocker includes a recovery mechanism in case the password is forgotten or the smart card is lost. Microsoft recommends that you save the recovery key to Active Directory Domain Services, a file, print it, or store it in safe place. The BitLocker wizard gives you three options:

◆ Save the recovery key to a USB flash drive

◆ Save the recovery to a file

◆ Print the recovery key

This key should be protected at a level comparable to the data stored on the drive. In other words, if you have secret proprietary data on the drive, protect the key like it's secret proprietary data.

Enabling BitLocker

BitLocker is not enabled by default. Before you can enable BitLocker, you must first add the BitLocker Drive Encryption feature. The following steps lead you through the process of adding the BitLocker Drive Encryption feature and enabling it. These steps assume that TPM 1.2 is not available on your system. If it is installed and available, the procedures will be slightly different.

1. Launch Server Manager. Select Features, and click Add Features.

2. Select the BitLocker Drive Encryption check box, as shown in Figure 10.25. Click Next.

FIGURE 10.25
Adding the
BitLocker Drive
Encryption feature

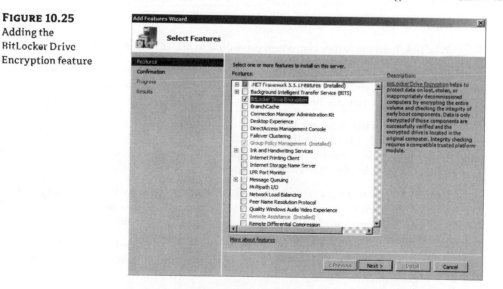

3. Click Install. When prompted, restart your computer to complete the installation.

4. After the reboot, log on. When the installation completes, click Close.

5. Launch the Control Panel, and click System and Security. At this point, you'll see the BitLocker Drive Encryption feature in the System and Security Center. If you looked here before adding the feature, it didn't appear.

SEARCHING CONTROL PANEL

Control Panel has a neat feature that is quite valuable but easily overlooked. In the upper-right corner is a search box. You can type in any search term (such as **BitLocker** or **User**), and it'll list only the relevant applets. This is also available in Windows Vista, Windows 7, and Windows Server 2008. Now if they could only make this feature available for Group Policy....

6. Click BitLocker Driver Encryption. You'll see a display similar to Figure 10.26.

FIGURE 10.26
Turning on BitLocker Drive Encryption for a drive

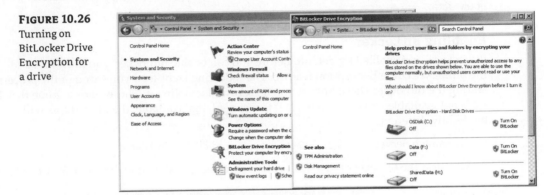

7. Click Turn On BitLocker. When prompted to start the BitLocker setup, click Yes.

8. Select Use a Password to Unlock the Drive, and enter your password twice. If you have a smart card and the system supports smart card usage, you could also choose to protect it with a smart card. Click Next.

9. Select Save the Recovery Key to a File. Browse to a location on your computer, and click Save. Ideally, you'd save this file on a separate drive (such as on a USB flash drive). If you attempt to save the file on the same physical drive, you'll be prompted to save it somewhere else, but you can click Yes to override the prompt. Click Next.

10. Click the Start Encrypting button. This can take quite a while depending on the size of the drive. We've seen 1GB take about 30 seconds, so if you have a 500 GB drive, this might be a good time for a break. Click Close when it is complete.

11. If you reboot your system, the drive is listed as encrypted and is not accessible. You can unlock it by right-clicking the drive and selecting Unlock Drive, as shown in Figure 10.27.

12. Once the drive is unlocked, you can access the data normally. Right-click the drive, and select Manage BitLocker. This menu gives you the ability to change the password and manipulate other options for the drive.

FIGURE 10.27
Unlocking an
encrypted drive

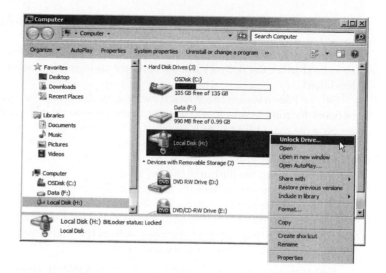

BITLOCKER TO GO

BitLocker To Go is a great capability that's easy to use once you've added the feature to the server. Access BitLocker Drive Encryption via the Control Panel, insert your USB flash drive, and click Turn On BitLocker. Enter a password, save your recovery key, and click Start Encrypting. If the drive is placed into another computer, it is not readable.

However, you can insert the drive into another computer and enter the password when prompted, and you'll have access to all your data. Although it works best on Windows 7 or Windows Server 2008 R2, you can also access your data on other systems such as Windows Vista by launching the BitLockerToGo.exe file to decrypt and copy the data.

Many organizations are taking extra steps to protect "data at rest," and BitLocker To Go looks like it will meet those needs. We fully expect it to be widely used in the near future.

Using Offline Files/Client-Side Caching

If you have laptop users in your network environment, you'll love the Offline Files, or Client-Side Caching (Microsoft uses both names interchangeably), feature. In fact, it will appeal to almost anyone who uses a network. Offline Files provides three main advantages: it makes the network appear faster to its users, smoothes out network "hiccups," and simplifies the task of keeping laptop files and server files in sync.

How Offline Files Works

Offline Files is enabled on shares hosted on a server. When enabled, it automatically caches accessed files, storing the cached copies in a folder on a local hard drive (a folder not surprisingly called Offline Files). It then uses those cached copies to speed up network access (or apparent network access), because subsequent accessing of a file can be handled out of the local hard disk's cached copy rather than over the network.

This is great for users on the road. Offline Files can use the cached copies of the files to act as a stand-in for the network if it isn't present (as it isn't for mobile users) or even if the network has failed.

Offline Files uses a write-through caching mechanism; when you write a file out, it goes to the network location to save it, and it is also cached to your local hard disk. And when you want to access a file that Offline Files has cached, Offline Files would *prefer* to give you the cached (and faster) copy, but first Offline Files checks that the file hasn't changed at the server by examining the file date, time, and size both on the server and in the cache. If they're the same, then Offline Files can give you the file out of the cache without any worries; otherwise, Offline Files fetches the network copy so you have the most up-to-date copy.

Offline Files increases the chances that it has the most up-to-date copies of your cached files by doing background synchronizations in several user-definable ways. This synchronization is largely invisible to the user, who simply utilizes the share over the network.

You'll like Offline Files for several reasons:

Faster access   Because these oft-used cached files will reside on the local hard disk in the Offline Files folder, you'll immediately see what seems to be an increase in network response speed. Opening a file that appears to be on the network but that is really in a local disk folder will yield apparently stunning improvements in response time, because little or no actual network activity is required.

Reduces network traffic   Since cached files don't need to be retransmitted over the LAN, network traffic is reduced. Having frequently used files in a local cache folder also solves the problem of "What do I do when the network's down and I need a file from a server?" If you try to access a file on a server that's not responding (or if you're not physically connected to the network), Offline Files shifts to "offline" mode. When in offline mode, Offline Files looks in your local Offline Files network cache and, if it finds a copy of that file in the cache, it delivers the file to you just as if the server were up, running, and attached to the user's workstation.

Automatic synchronization   Anyone who's ever had to get ready for a business trip knows two of the worst things about traveling with a laptop: the agony of getting on the plane only to realize that you've forgotten one or two essential files and the irritation of having to remember when you return to make sure that whatever files you changed while traveling get copied back to the network servers. Offline Files greatly reduces the chance of the first of those problems because, again, often-used files can be configured to automatically end up in the local network cache folder. It greatly reduces the work of the second task by automating the laptop-to-server file synchronization process.

BranchCache

BranchCache is designed to optimize the availability of data in branch offices that are connected with slower WAN links. When enabled, BranchCache allows data to be cached on computers in the remote office for use by other computers in the remote office.

Imagine your headquarters is located in Virginia Beach and a branch office is located in Atlanta via a slower link. If users in Atlanta needed to access data shared from a server in Virginia Beach, they'd have to connect over the WAN link, even if they just accessed and closed the file a moment previously.

With BranchCache, files can be cached on a computer in the remote office after they are accessed the first time. Users who need to access the file later can access the locally cached copy. BranchCache still checks to ensure the file is the most recent version, but a quick round-trip check of the timestamp is much quicker than downloading the entire file again.

BranchCache supports two modes:

Hosted Cache Data is hosted on a server in the remote office running Windows Server 2008 R2.

Distributed Cache Data is hosted on PCs in the branch office. A server is not needed, but data can only be cached on Windows 7 computers.

BranchCache is supported only on Windows Server 2008 R2 servers and Windows Vista and Windows 7 clients. You can't enable BranchCache on server versions before Windows Server 2008 R2. When using Distributed Cache mode, data will be cached only on Windows 7 computers, but both Windows Vista and Windows 7 computers can access data cached using BranchCache. Before it can be enabled, it must be added as a role service under the File Services role.

Group Policy includes several settings that you can use to enable and manage BranchCache. These settings are located in the Computer Configuration\Policies\Administrative Templates \Network\BranchCache node of Group Policy.

Enabling Offline Files on the Server

Offline Files is relatively easy to enable on the server. It's actually enabled by default when you create a share. If you launch Server Manager and browse to the File Services\Share and Storage Management console, you'll see all the shares that are currently shared.

Right-click any of the shares, and then select Properties. Click the Advanced button, and then select the Caching tab. Your display will look similar to Figure 10.28. This shows the default Offline Files setting.

FIGURE 10.28
Viewing Offline Files settings

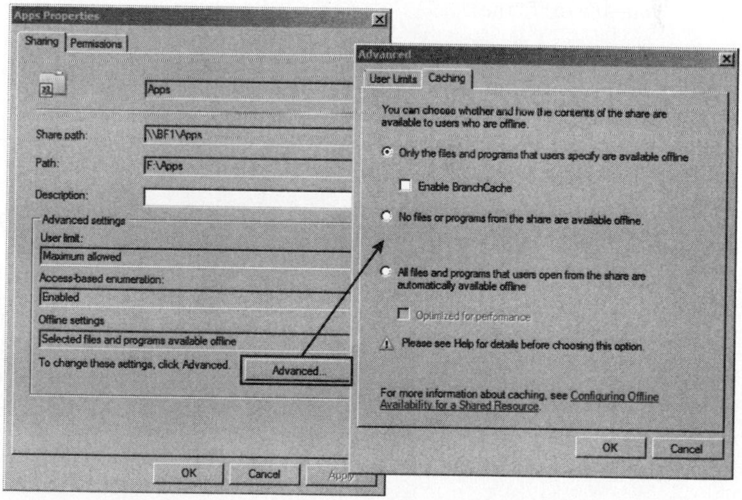

The different options for Offline Files are as follows:

Only the files and programs that users specify are available offline This is the default setting. Files aren't cached on the user's system unless they right-click the file and select Make Available Offline. BranchCache can be enabled with this setting.

No files or programs from the share are available offline This setting will disable Offline Files for the share.

All files and programs that users open from the share are automatically available offline Any file that a user opens is cached. Users do not have to right-click the file and select Make Available Offline. Instead, when the user expresses an interest in the file by opening it, the file will automatically be cached on the user's system.

Optimized for performance If the previous setting (All files and programs that users open from the share are automatically available offline) is enabled, you can also select Optimized for Performance. In short, this is one-way caching. In other words, when the user opens the file, it will be cached to their system. However, if the user modifies the file, the modifications are not uploaded to the server. This setting is useful for applications or other files (such as an employee manual) that users should not be modifying anyway.

While this section explained Offline Files and showed you how to configure it on the server, it also needs to be configured on the client. Different clients (Windows XP, Windows Vista, and Windows 7) approach this differently. You can check out these web links for different clients:

♦ Windows XP:

http://support.microsoft.com/kb/307853

♦ Windows Vista:

http://windows.microsoft.com/en-us/windows-vista/Working-with-network-files-when-you-are-offline

♦ Windows 7:

http://www.windows7update.com/Windows7-Offline-Files.html

The Bottom Line

Install the File Services role on a server The File Services role includes services designed to optimize serving files from the server. A significant addition is the File Server Resource Manager, which can be used to manage quotas, to add file screens, and to produce comprehensive reports.

    Master It How do you add FSRM to the server?

Combine share and NTFS permissions   When a folder is shared from an NTFS drive, it includes both share permissions and NTFS permissions. It's important to understand how these permissions interact so that users can be granted appropriate permission.

> **Master It**   Maria is in the G_HR and G_HRManagers groups. A folder named Policies is shared as Policies on a server with the following permissions:
>
> > NTFS: G_HR Read, G_HR_Managers Full Control
> >
> > Share: G_HR Read, G_HR Change
>
> What is Maria's permission when accessing the share? What is her permission when accessing the folder directly on the server?

Implement BitLocker Drive Encryption   BitLocker Drive Encryption allows you to encrypt an entire drive. If someone obtains the drive that shouldn't have access to the data, the encryption will prevent them from accessing the data.

> **Master It**   What are the hardware requirements for BitLocker Drive Encryption, and what needs to be done to the operating system to use BitLocker?

Chapter 11

Creating and Managing Shared Folders

Maybe you can still remember putting data on floppy disks that you wanted to share with peers. Sharing files and folders is one of the very reasons why server technologies were developed. Microsoft Windows Server 2008 has developed new ways to share files with services such as Network File System (NFS), which provides a file-sharing solution for enterprises that may be running a mix of operating systems. With NFS, you can now share files with not only other Windows servers but also Unix, Linux, and Mac OS clients if they exist in your organization.

Windows Server 2008 also has revamped its Distributed File System (DFS) technologies by offering WAN-friendly replication to simplify access to geographically dispersed files and folders. You can now share files and folders across the network, based on your groupings of them. This function streamlines a complex process that was both tedious and time-consuming.

In this chapter, we'll help you dig into DFS and then NFS with step-by-step guides on how to use these exciting functions. You'll find out what they are, how they work, and how to make them work for you.

In this chapter, you will learn to:

◆ Add a File Services role to your server

◆ Add a shared folder using NFS

◆ Add a DFS root

Creating Shared Folders

Before you can create a shared folder, you must have the appropriate rights to do so. This requires that you are either an Administrator or a Power User. You can create shares in a few ways: you can use the Windows Explorer interface when sitting at the server, or you can use the Share and Storage Management window to create shares either at the server or remotely.

SOME BASICS OF FILE SHARING

One of the core components of any server is its ability to share files. In fact, the Server service in each member of the Windows NT family, including Server 2008, handles the server's ability to share file and print resources. But what exactly does that mean, and why is it so important? By default, just because you have a server running doesn't mean it has anything available for your users. Before they can actually get to resources on the server, you must share your resources. Let's say you have a folder on your local I drive named APPS with three applications in subfolders, as shown here:

When you share this folder to the network under the name of APPS, you allow your clients to map a new drive letter on their machines to your I:\APPS folder. By mapping a drive, you are placing a virtual pointer directly to where you connected. If you map your client's M drive to the APPS share of the server, their M: drive will look identical to the server's I:\APPS, as shown here:

Creating Shares from Explorer

If you're sitting at the server, the Explorer interface provides a simple and direct means for creating and managing all properties of a share. Let's go back to the I:\APPS folder that you want to make available to the network under the name of APPS.

In Explorer, right-click the APPS folder, and select the Sharing and Security menu option. This will bring up the properties sheet for the folder APPS, already set to the Sharing tab. To share the folder, click the Share button, as shown in Figure 11.1.

FIGURE 11.1
Properties for the
APPS share

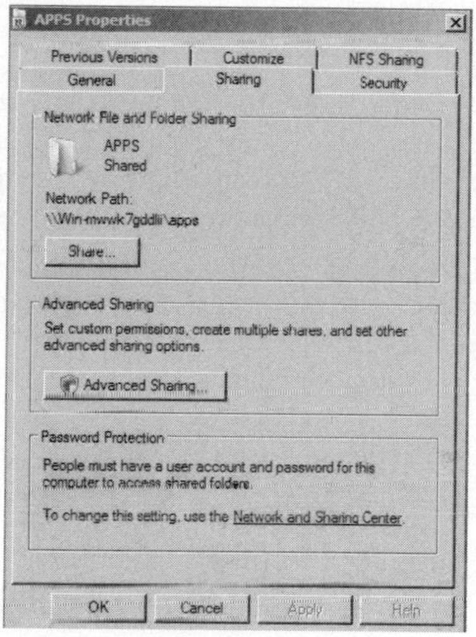

The Share Name option on this page is the most critical entry. This is how your users will reference this share. For our purposes, share this folder as APPS. The Comments field is used to provide more descriptive information about this share. Notice the description fields on the APPS folder and the APPS2 folder in Figure 11.2. The APPS folder shows the user that this folder is for the payroll application. Click OK, and your share is enabled and ready for immediate use by your users.

FIGURE 11.2
Browsing
network shares

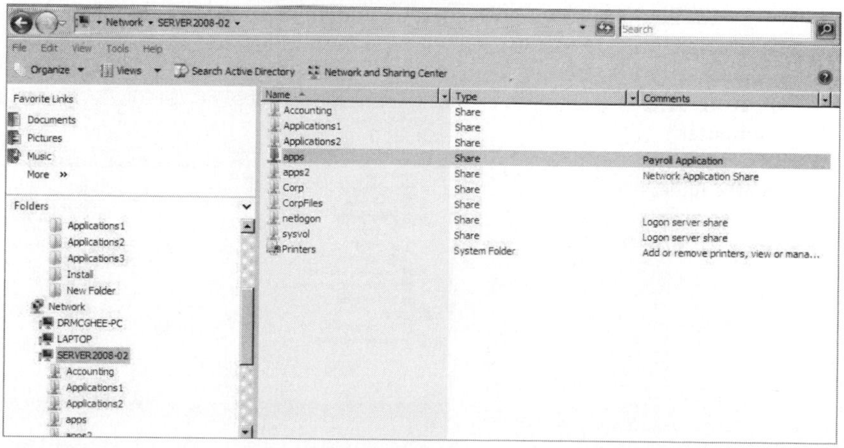

SETTING USER LIMITS

You can configure how many users can connect to a share simultaneously in the User Limit area of the Sharing properties sheet. If the applications under your share are each licensed for 100 concurrent users, you can configure your server share to maintain that limit, even though you may have 200 users on your network. As users connect to the share, they build up to the user limit. As users log off or disconnect from the share, the number drops. This type of licensing enforcement can be handy in reducing your licensing costs.

Be careful with your licensing, however. Not all applications have a concurrent license mode, although they might have a client license mode. (Unfortunately, as Microsoft has abandoned concurrent licensing, more and more other firms have stopped offering this useful licensing option.) With client license mode, the manufacturer doesn't care how many users are accessing the application at any given time; they just care about how many people have installed the application altogether. This user-limit option will not protect you in these cases.

Finally, you need to consider how your users connect to the share to use these applications before you limit them based on concurrency. If your users all connect to the share upon logging in but don't disconnect until logging off, your concurrency limit may be used up based on who shows up for work first, and you'll have 100 people using up your concurrency limit even if only a small percentage of them are actually using the application. If connections are made only when actually using the application, the user limit will work quite nicely.

Remotely Creating Shares with the Computer Management Console

Within your Administrative Tools program group is the Computer Management console. With this tool, you can, among other things, create and manage shares locally or remotely. In contrast, within the Explorer interface, if you right-click a folder that is not local to your machine, you won't see the Sharing menu option. If you are going to create a share using the Computer Management console from your local machine, you're set. If you want to manage a share on a remote server, you have to first connect to that server. Right-click the Computer Management (Local) icon, and select Connect to Another Computer. From there, you can type in the name of the server you want to manage, or you can browse the network for the computer you want.

To begin with the share management, you need to select Computer Management\System Tools\Shared Folders\Shares, as shown in Figure 11.3.

FIGURE 11.3
Computer
Management
shared folders

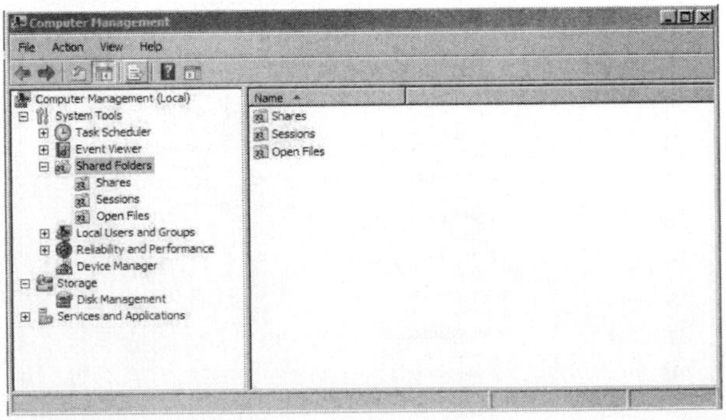

You can now either select the Action menu or right-click in the Shares window and select New Share. Click Next in the initial screen of the Create a Shared a Folder Wizard, and you will see the screen shown in Figure 11.4. Make sure that the "Computer name" field is correct so that you are creating the share on the right computer. To create the share, you can browse through the given drives and folders, or you can create a new folder on the fly by simply typing the full drive and folder name in the "Folder path" box. For this example, share the I:\APPS folder. Once you have completed the path, click Next.

FIGURE 11.4
Specifying a folder location in the Create A Shared Folder Wizard

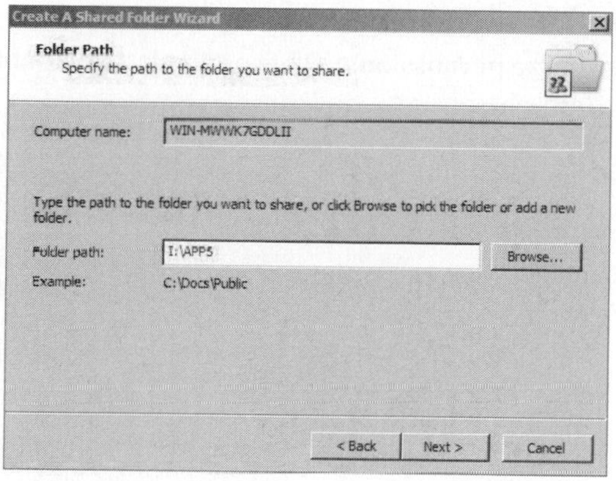

You'll then see the screen shown in Figure 11.5. Here you enter the name you want this share to be given, along with a brief description; click Next to continue through the wizard.

FIGURE 11.5
Assigning a share name and description

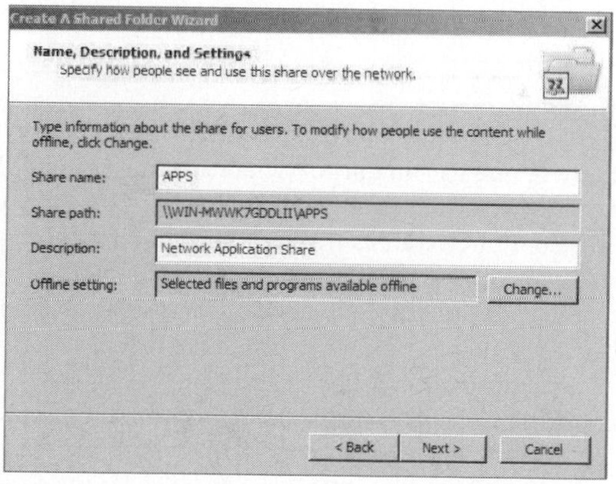

From there, you jump straight to defining your share permissions. On the next screen (Figure 11.6), you are given four options for defining permissions:

All users have read-only access   This option allows the Everyone group (which, in Server 2008, no longer contains Anonymous User) to have read-only access to the contents of the folder. This is the default setting in Server 2008 and is a great new feature that illustrates the extra focus Microsoft has given to security in the past year. Until now, the default, Everyone having Full Control, included anonymous users coming in across the network! Now when creating a share, you don't have to start with a wide-open door. You start with a closed door and open it per your specifications, at your leisure.

Administrators have full access; other users have read-only access This option ensures that your users can view data and run programs but can't modify or delete anything within the share. This still gives administrators the appropriate rights to manage the data.

Administrators have full access; other users have no access This option allows the users to do anything they want except delete files or folders, change permissions, or take ownership of the files.

Customize permissions This option lets you define permissions based on specific users or groups.

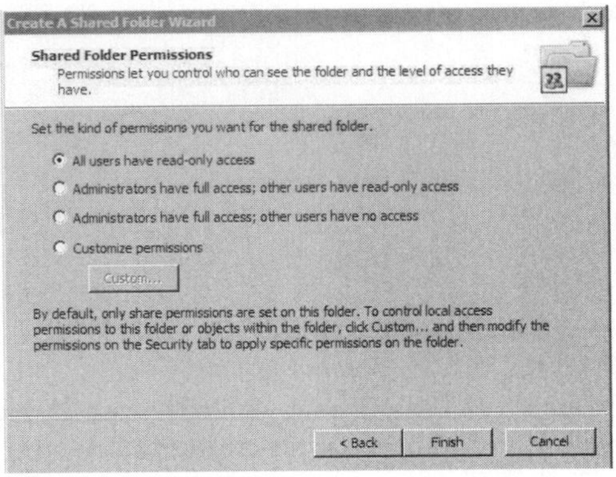

FIGURE 11.6
Controlling computer access in the Create a Shared Folder Wizard

---

OLDER SERVER OPTIONS

Windows 2000 had an option where administrators had Full Control rights and other users had no access. This was a handy option to choose when you knew that you wanted to customize the permissions but weren't sure how you wanted to set them up. You could choose this option and feel secure about the share until you opened it at your leisure. That option doesn't exist in Windows 2008, but there are still two ways to get almost the same thing. Either use the "Administrators have full access; other users have read and write access" option, which still allows users read access, or customize the share by choosing the fourth option. Then add the Administrator account with full control, and remove the Read attribute from the Everyone group.

Once you set up the permissions on your share, click Next to see the final screen of the Create a Shared a Folder Wizard, which lists the results and gives you the option to run the wizard again, as shown in Figure 11.7.

Managing Permissions

Share permissions are applied when a user accesses a file or folder across the network, but they are not taken into consideration when a user accesses those resources locally, like they would be when sitting directly at the computer or when using resources on a terminal server. NTFS permissions, in contrast, are applied no matter how a user accesses those same resources, whether they are connecting remotely or logging in at the console. So, when accessing files locally, only NTFS permissions are applied. When accessing those same files remotely, the sum of both share and NTFS permissions are applied by calculating the most restrictive permissions of the two types.

FIGURE 11.7
The final screen shows a summary of the share you created.

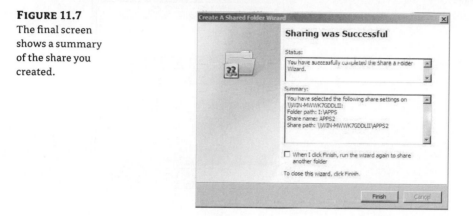

NTFS is the most common and the most secure file system used for Windows Server. For more information about NTFS, see Chapter 10.

Creating Share Permissions

Share permissions are possibly the easiest forms of access control you will deal with in Windows Server. Remember that share permissions take effect only whenever you try to access a computer over the network. Consider share permissions to be a kind of access pass to a secure building. When you walk up to the front door and show your identification, the guard looks up your name and gives you a pass that shows your access level for everything else on the inside. If your pass says "level 1 access," then your pass will get you into every door on level 1—and nowhere else. Once inside, try to get into a room with level 2 access requirements; it won't work. By defining share permissions, you can safely control the access level for each person at the front door.

Keep in mind, though, that this front door—or share-level permission—isn't the entire picture. The share-level permission represents only the *maximum* level of access you will get on the inside. If you get read permissions at the share, the best you can do once you've connected remotely to the share is read. Likewise, change permissions will grant change at best. If you want full control to *anything* inside the share, you need full control *at* the share. But understand that when we say the share permission is the *maximum* level of access you will get inside the share, it is entirely possible to restrict access more once you're inside by using file-level (or NTFS) permissions. You can have full control at the share, but an object inside can still have NTFS permissions that say you can only read it.

DEFINING SHARE PERMISSIONS

To define share permissions, we will walk you through the Computer Management console. Select the share you want to secure by right-clicking the share name, selecting Properties, and then selecting the Share Permissions tab. You can get to the same place from Explorer by right-clicking the locally shared folder, selecting Sharing and Security, and then clicking the Permissions button. Both methods will bring you to the dialog box shown in Figure 11.8.

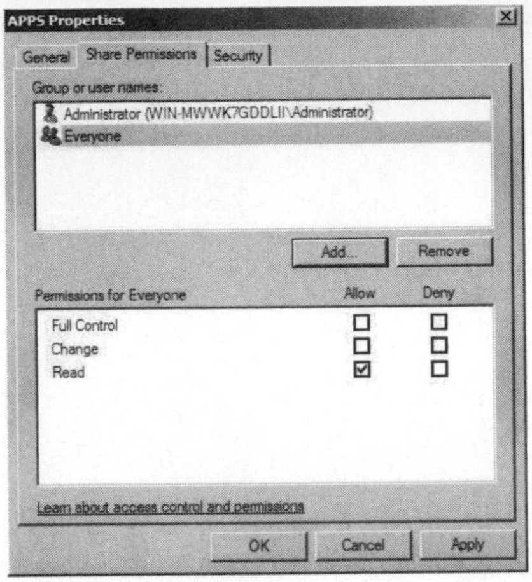

FIGURE 11.8
The Share Permissions tab

NO MORE EVERYONE

Note that the Everyone group, by default, has Read access permissions, which is a great step forward in the Windows world in terms of security. Until Server 2003, the Everyone group was given Full Control access by default. Another new feature in Server 2008 is that the Everyone group is no longer added to a folder when shared.

In this dialog box, you are shown a "Group or user names" box that lists users and groups assigned to the share; when a user or group is selected, the permissions for that user or group to access the share are revealed. You can assign different levels of permission for different users and groups. At the share level, you have the types of permission, shown in Table 11.1.

TABLE 11.1:   Types of Permissions

PERMISSION	LEVEL OF ACCESS
Full Control	The assigned group can perform any and all functions on all files and folders through the share.
Change	The assigned group can read and execute, as well as change and delete, files and folders through the share.
Read	The assigned group can read and execute files and folders but has no ability to modify or delete anything through the share.

The example in Figure 11.8 shows Read access for Everyone. Although you won't see the Administrator account listed with any specific rights, note that local administrators always have Full Control access of the shares on the computer. If you want to change share permissions to give all your network administrators Full Control, you will need to add the group and assign them rights. Click the Add button to see the dialog box shown in Figure 11.9.

FIGURE 11.9

Select Users or Groups dialog box

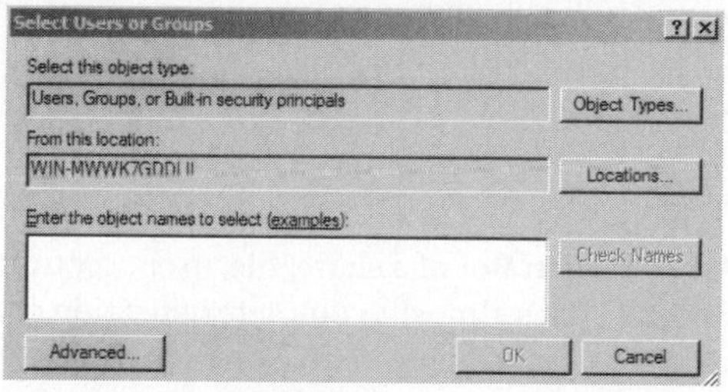

You can either type in the name of the account or group that you want to add or click the Advanced button, which will bring you to the second Select Users or Groups dialog box, shown in Figure 11.10. This dialog box enables you to search the directory.

FIGURE 11.10

Enumerate users and groups by clicking the Find Now button in this dialog box.

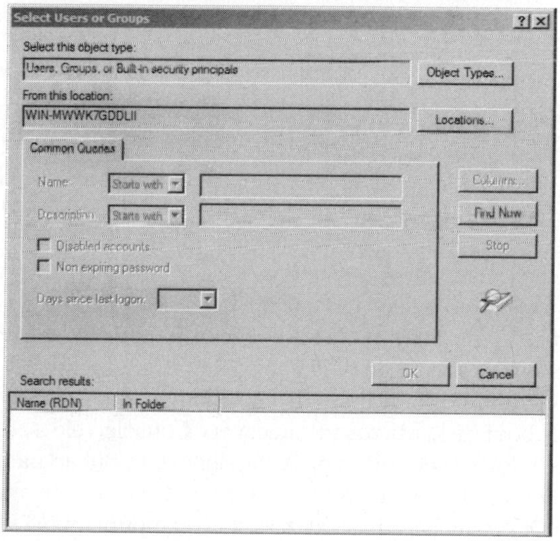

You can either use the Active Directory search functions on the Common Queries tab to narrow down your choices or click the Find Now button, which will enumerate all the users in the directory. From here you locate the group that you want to add—the Domain Administrators group in the example—and click OK and then OK again. This brings you back to the Share Permissions tab with the Domain Administrators group added to the display and highlighted. Select the Full Control check box.

Again, keep in mind that share-level permissions are just your first filter for users accessing files over the network. Whatever level of permissions you get at the share level will be the highest level of permissions you can get for files and directories (the most restrictive apply, remember?). If you get Read rights to the share but Full Control rights to the file, the share will not let you do anything other than read.

UNDERSTANDING ALLOW AND DENY

You probably noticed when you selected the Allow check box on the Full Control permission for the Domain Administrators group in the previous example that there also exists a Deny check box for each permission listed. Share permissions are just about the simplest set of permissions that you'll deal with, so they're a great place to explain this Allow and Deny notion. Here's how they work:

◆ An administrator of a share, file, user account, or whatever can change permissions on that object. (That's almost a complete definition of an administrator, actually.) There are several kinds of permissions—Full Control, Change, or Read in the case of shares. Anyone can be allowed or denied by the administrator, or the administrator can choose to clear *both* Allow and Deny, leaving a user with neither Allow nor Deny on that permission.

◆ If the user has no permissions—in other words, no Allow or Deny—then the user does not have access to the object.

◆ If the Allow permission is selected, the user can exercise the permission; if Deny is selected, the user can't. We know that's obvious, but let's see how it affects more complex situations.

Understanding File and Directory Permissions

The old days of Microsoft networking (before the arrival of the NTFS file system) utilized share-level permissions only. Once connected to a share with a given set of permissions, you had those permissions for everything under the share. If you had 1,000 users who all wanted private access to their data, you would have to create 1,000 shares with specific permissions on each share. Then, with the introduction of Windows NT to the Microsoft networking platform, you could create one share for all users and customize access via file and directory permissions—permissions that could be assigned directly to the files and folders. With this new feature came an unending ability to customize the security of your data.

Someone *did* come up with a utility that allows you to gain access to NTFS partitions via a simple boot disk. Microsoft's Recovery Console, released with Windows 2000, lets you boot from the Windows 2000 Server or Professional CD. But actually, there was a similar package that existed long before Microsoft gave it to us. Mark Russinovich and Bryce Cogswell wrote a utility called NTFSDOS way back in 1996 that lets you mount an NTFS volume from a boot disk. Mark is the same smart guy who discovered that the only difference between NT Workstation and NT Server code was just *one* registry entry. You can still find this tool—and many others—through Mark and Bryce's freeware company, Sysinternals, or its sister company, Wininternals. What all this means is that, to be secure, go back to square one: lock up your server so no one can sit at its keyboard.

PERMISSION TYPES

Before you assign permissions to your files and folders, you need to have a good understanding of what those permissions mean and how they work. There are two different levels of permissions.

To see the higher level, go to any NTFS folder, right-click it, choose Properties, and then select the Security tab. You'll see a permissions dialog box like the one in Figure 11.11.

FIGURE 11.11
Top-level NTFS permissions dialog box

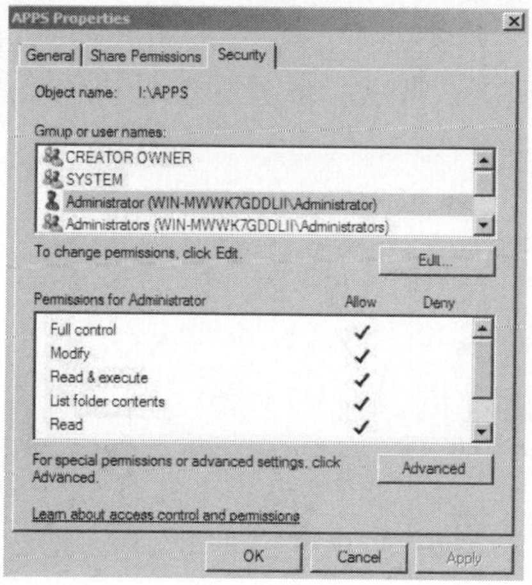

The permissions you see in Figure 11.11 are actually built up from the lower-level permissions. For example, the high-level permission List Folder Contents comprises five lower-level permissions—Traverse Folder/Execute File, List Folder/Read Data, Read Attributes, Read Extended Attributes, and Read Permissions. You may want to think of them as "molecular" and "atomic" permissions. There are 13 atomic permissions for NTFS. (Other sorts of Active Directory objects, such as organizational units, *can* have child objects because you can create users and other OUs inside OUs.) All AD object types share the same set of atomic permissions, even the ones that are irrelevant—go ahead and grant someone the ability to create child objects for a Group Policy object; it'll be about as useful as granting someone at a brick factory the ability to set the sex of the bricks.

Look at Table 11.2 to see how groups of atomic permissions in the left column make up molecular permissions.

TABLE 11.2: Atomic and Molecular Permissions

ATOMIC	WRITE	READ	LIST FOLDER CONTENTS	READ & EXECUTE	MODIFY	FULL CONTROL
Traverse Folder/ Execute File			X	X	X	X
List Folder/Read Data	X	X	X	X	X	X
Read Attributes	X	X	X	X	X	X
Read Extended Attributes	X	X	X	X	X	X

TABLE 11.2: Atomic and Molecular Permissions *(CONTINUED)*

ATOMIC	WRITE	READ	LIST FOLDER CONTENTS	READ & EXECUTE	MODIFY	FULL CONTROL
Create Files/ Write Data	X				X	X
Create Folders/ Append Data	X				X	X
Write Attributes	X				X	X
Write Extended Attributes	X				X	X
Delete Subfolders and Files						X
Delete					X	X
Read Permissions	X	X	X	X	X	X
Change Permissions						X
Take Ownership						X

ATOMIC PERMISSIONS

We'll start at the atomic level. These permissions are the building blocks of the permissions that we normally speak of, such as Read, Modify, and Full Control. You will probably never see these permissions, much less refer to them on their own.

Traverse Folder/Execute File The Traverse Folder permission lets you bypass all the locks on the upper levels and essentially "beam yourself" right into level 4. Like Execute File, it's a useful permission, but it has nothing to do with files. What's happening is this: when NTFS is examining a permission, it pulls up the 13 bits. When looking at the first one, it asks itself the question, "Is this a file or a folder?" If it's a file, then it interprets that first bit as the Execute File permission. If a folder, then it's the Traverse Folder permission. You'll see this in a somewhat less extreme manner on some of the other permissions as well.

List Folder/Read Data List Folder permissions allow you to view file and folder names within a folder. Read Data permissions allow you to view the contents of a file. This atomic right is the core component of Read.

Think of the separation between these two atomic permissions. Is there really much of a difference? Yes, but probably not for long. Remember the days when we called everything files and directories? Now the file and *folder* terminology has become mainstream. Just when we start really getting used to it, another term is coming into play: *objects*. Everything on your machine is an object—both files and folders. This atomic permission could almost be rephrased to *read object*. Regardless of whether this permission applies to a file or folder, this right lets you examine the contents of an object.

Read Attributes   Basic attributes are file properties such as Read-Only, Hidden, System, and Archive. This atomic-level permission allows you to see these attributes.

Read Extended Attributes   Certain programs include other attributes for their file types. For example, if you have Microsoft Word installed on your system and you view the file attributes of a DOC file, all sorts of attributes will show up, such as Author, Subject, Title, and so on. These are called *extended attributes*, and they vary from program to program. This atomic permission lets you view these attributes.

Create Files/Write Data   The Create Files atomic permission allows you to put new files within a folder. Write Data allows you to overwrite existing data within a file. This atomic permission will not allow you to add data to an existing file.

Create Folders/Append Data   Create Folders allows you to create folders within folders. Append Data allows you to add data to the end of an existing file but not change data within the file.

Write Attributes   This permission allows you to change the basic attributes of a file.

Write Extended Attributes   This permission allows you to change the extended attributes of a file.

Delete Subfolders and Files   This atomic permission is strange. Listen to this: with this permission, you can delete subfolders and files, even if *you don't have Delete permissions on that subfolder or file*. Now how could this possibly be? If you were to read ahead to the next atomic permission—Delete—you would see that that permission lets you delete a file or folder. What's the difference? Think of it this way: if you are sitting at a file or folder, Delete lets you delete it. But let's say you're sitting at a folder and want to delete its *contents*. This atomic permission gives you that right. There is a very vague difference between the two. One lets you delete a specific object; the other lets you delete the *contents* of an object. If you are given the right to delete the contents of a folder, you don't want to lose that right just because one object within that folder does not want to give you permissions. Hey, it's your folder—you can do with it what you want.

Delete   Plain and simple this time, Delete lets you delete an object. Or is it plain and simple? If you have only the atomic permission to delete a folder but not its big-brother atomic permission to delete subfolders and files and if one file within that folder has no access, can you delete the folder? No. You can't delete the folder until it is empty, which means that you need to delete that file. You can't delete that file without having either Delete rights to that file or having Delete Subfolders and Files rights to the file's parent folder.

Read Permissions   The Read Permissions atomic permission lets you view all NTFS permissions associated with a file or folder, but you can't change anything.

Change Permissions   This atomic permission lets you change the permissions assigned to a file or folder.

Take Ownership   We'll talk about what ownership is and what it does in more detail later in the chapter, but this atomic permission allows you to take ownership of a file. Once you are the owner, you have an inherent right to change permissions. By default, administrators can always take ownership of a file or folder.

MOLECULAR PERMISSIONS

A full understanding of what atomic permissions do, as well as an understanding of the atomic makeup of molecular permissions (shown in Table 11.2), provides exceptional insight into what these molecular permissions are and how they work. This section will try to put the atomic makeup of permissions in better perspective, but you should flip back and forth to Table 11.2 while you read about these permissions. This information will form a solid foundation to help you manage permissions later.

Read   Read permissions are your most basic rights. They allow you to view the contents, permissions, and attributes associated with an object. If that object is a file, you can view the file, which happens to include the ability to launch the file, should it be an executable program file. If the object in question is a folder, Read permissions let you view the contents of the folder.

Now, here is a tricky part of folder read. Let's say that you have a folder to which you have been assigned Read permissions. That folder contains a subfolder, to which you have been denied all access, including read access. Logic would say that you could not even see that subfolder at all. Well, the subfolder, before you even get into its own attributes, is *part of* the original folder. Because you can read the contents of the first folder, you can see that the subfolder exists. If you try to change to that subfolder, then—and only then—will you get an Access Denied message.

Write   Write permissions, as simple as they sound, have a catch. For starters, Write permissions on a folder let you create a new file or subfolder within that folder. What about Write permissions on a file? Does this mean you can change a file? Think about what happens when you *change* a file. To change a file, you must usually be able to open the file or read the file. To change a file, Read permissions must normally accompany your Write permissions. There is a loophole, though: if you can simply append data to a file, without needing to open the file, Write permissions will work.

However, if a programmer were to write an application that opens a file in a write-only mode, the file could then truncate it without reading it and then write to the file, all without reading the file; thus, the file would be changed without the reading process taking place.

Read & Execute   Read & Execute permissions are identical to Read but give you the added atomic privilege of traversing a folder.

Modify   Simply put, Modify permissions are the combination of Read & Execute and Write, but they give you the added luxury of Delete. Even when you could change a file, you never really could delete the file. You'll notice that, when you select permissions for files and folders, if you select Modify only, then Read, Read & Execute, and Write are automatically selected for you.

Full Control   Full Control is a combination of all the previously mentioned permissions, with the abilities to change permissions and take ownership of objects thrown in. Full Control also allows you to delete subfolders and files, even when the subfolders and files don't specifically allow you to delete them.

List Folder Contents   List Folder Contents permissions apply similar permissions as Read & Execute, but they apply only to folders. List Folder Contents allows you to view the contents of folders. More important, List Folder Contents is only *inherited* by folders, and it is shown only when looking into the security properties of a folder. The permission allows you to see that files exist in a folder—similar to Read—but will not apply Read & Execute permissions to those files. In comparison, if you applied Read & Execute permissions to a folder, you would be given the same capabilities to view folders and their contents but would also propagate Read & Execute rights to files within those folders.

Special Permissions   Special Permissions is simply a customized grouping of atomic rights you can create when one of the standard molecular permissions just covered isn't suited to your specific situation. Although it might appear that the Special Permissions feature was new in Server 2003, it did, in fact, exist in Windows 2000. It just wasn't visible as a molecular permission. In fact, in Windows 2000, there wasn't any way to tell whether a folder had customized atomic permissions unless you looked in the Advanced tab of the Securities properties sheet. In Server 2008, you can tell just by looking at the Allow/Deny check boxes used for Special Permissions whether the ACEs have been modified. If the check boxes appear shaded, then, by clicking the Advanced tab, you can view and edit those modifications.

INHERITED PERMISSIONS

A tool that has been around since Windows 2000 is the *inherited permissions* feature. By now, you are probably already accustomed to using this great feature, but for those of you who might not know about it yet or who are upgrading from NT4, we'll explain. In Windows NT, if you wanted to set permissions for all files and directories for an entire directory tree, you had to select a box to apply permissions down from the root. When that happened, the server went through every single file and set the permissions as defined—what a tedious process! Now, there is inheritance. If a file or folder is set to inherit permissions, it really has no permissions of its own; it just uses its parent folder's permissions. If the parent is also inheriting permissions, you simply keep moving up the chain of directories until you get one that actually has some cold, hard permissions assigned. That being said, the root directory cannot inherit permissions.

For example, say you have a folder named APPS, with three subfolders and files. All the subfolders and files allow inheritable permissions. If you set permissions on APPS to allow Read & Execute permissions for Users, all subfolders and files automatically mirror those new permissions. What if you want to customize the permissions on application 1 so that users can also write? You right-click application 1, select Properties, and then click the Security tab to view the permissions on the folder. If the check boxes for anything other than Special Permissions are grayed out, you can tell that the folder is inheriting permissions from its parent. From here, you need to select the Advanced tab in order to see the "Allow inheritable permissions from parent to propagate to this object and all child objects" option (now there's a mouthful). This option shows whether the object is inheriting permissions and lets you choose whether to allow inheritance.

ASSIGNING FILE AND DIRECTORY PERMISSIONS

Once you understand what the different permissions mean, assigning them to files and folders is a piece of cake. Start off in Explorer. Find the file or folder you want to assign rights to, right-click it, select Properties, and then select the Security tab. Take a look at Figure 11.12.

The top window shows the different groups or users to whom permissions are assigned, and the bottom window shows the permissions assigned to the selected user or group. You're starting off in an APPS folder for this example. Ideally, because this is for applications, you want all users to have Read & Execute permissions and not have the ability to change, add, or delete anything. You also want to keep administrators in full control so they can still maintain the data, and there is a group of database managers that you want to give Modify rights. Since the Users and Administrators groups already have an entry by default, you'll start by adding the Database Managers group and giving that group Modify rights. Click the Add button, and the Select Users or Groups dialog box appears, as shown earlier in Figure 11.9.

FIGURE 11.12
The Security properties tab

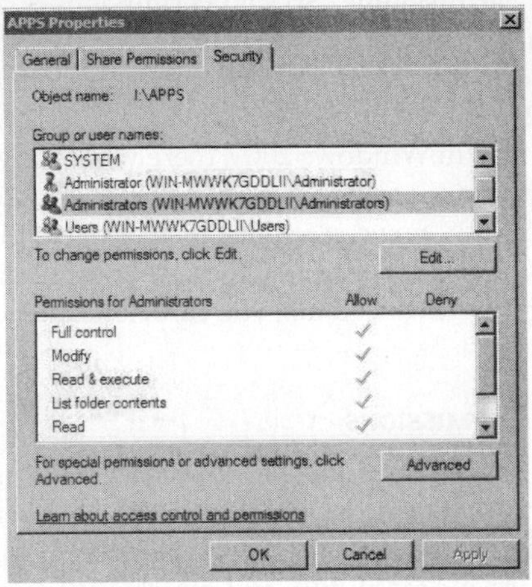

You can type in the name of the user or group, click the Advanced button, and click the Find Now button, or you can set up your query manually to enumerate a list of domain accounts. Since you know the name of the group you want to add in this example (Database Managers), you can just type it in the Select Users or Groups dialog box and then click the Check Names button. This will cross-check the manually typed entry with the list of names to find a match. Once the name appears with an underscore, click OK to return to the Security tab of the properties page of APPS. Now that you have added the Database Managers group, the dialog box should look like the one shown in Figure 11.13.

FIGURE 11.13
The Database Managers group is added.

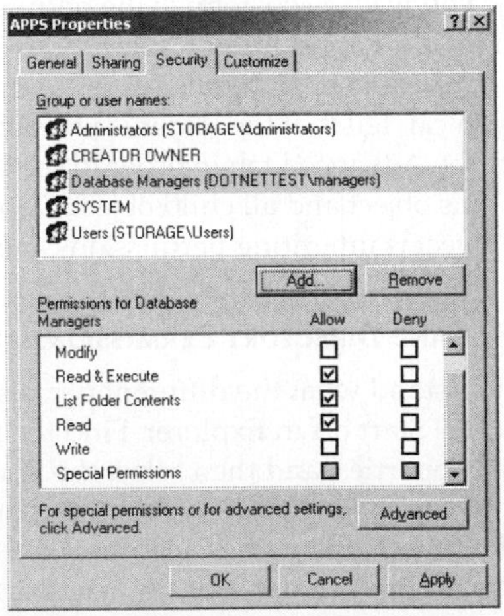

FASTER ADDITIONS OF USERS AND GROUPS

You can add multiple users and groups at one time using either interface in the previous example. When you type the names in manually, just type the first name, click the Check Names button, and start typing the next name. If you don't type a complete name before clicking Check Names, it will give you the closest match to your typed entry. If you choose to use the Active Directory search interface, you can select multiple accounts by clicking the first entry and then holding the Ctrl key down while you click additional entries.

Now that you have added the Database Managers group, all you have to do is assign the correct permissions, which are Modify rights. Highlight the Database Managers group, and select the Modify box in the Allow column. The Security tab should now look like Figure 11.13. Since the Users and Administrators groups were added by default when you created the share, let's look at the default permissions that were applied and see whether you need to make any adjustments. Click the User's Groups, and you will see the dialog box in Figure 11.14.

FIGURE 11.14
New permissions

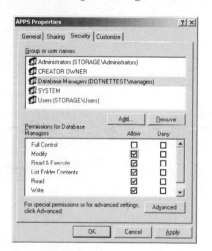

PERMISSION LEVEL CAUTION

You need to be careful when selecting some permission levels. Selecting Read & Execute includes all of the rights of Read, so Read is automatically selected. If, on the other hand, you want to clear Read & Execute, deselecting the Read & Execute box won't automatically deselect Read.

You can see, in Figure 11.15, that the Users group already has some default permissions, including Read & Execute, List Folder Contents, and Read. You can also tell that these are inherited because of the gray shading in the Allow boxes. However, as you may remember, the shading in the Special Permissions box doesn't mean that these permissions are inherited (although they might be). The shading here just represents that there are more permission entries than you can see in this particular dialog box; click the Advanced tab to find out more. If you look at Figure 11.16, you will see a much more complex version of the permission entries you saw in Figure 11.15. We're not quite sure why the good folks at Microsoft provide a sort of table of contents for the permissions story, when they could simply provide the whole story all at once.

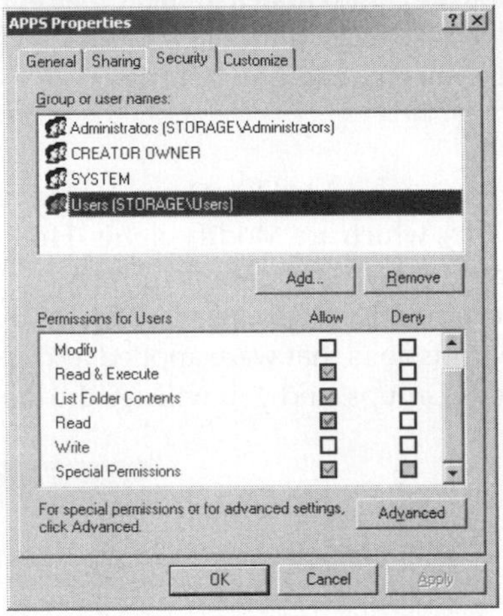

FIGURE 11.15
Default permissions for the Users group

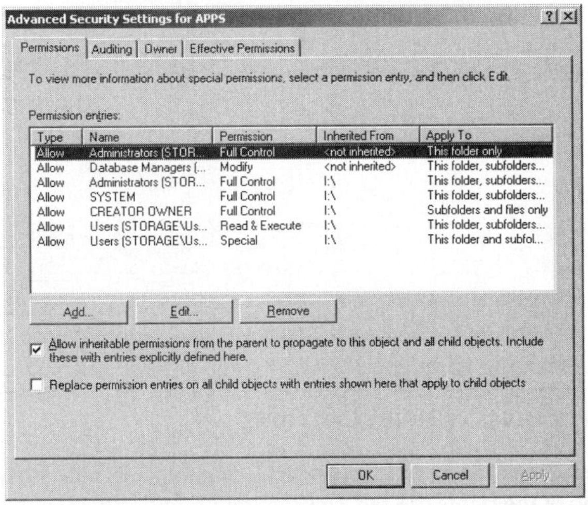

FIGURE 11.16
Advanced Security Settings for APPS dialog box

The "Permission entries" box shows your selected groups and users, with a description of their rights. The "Allow inheritable permissions from parent to propagate to this object" check box is the same, and you can still add and remove entries from this box. So, what is different here? In this window, you get to see a few more details. First, you can see that what might have been one entry (ACE) in the previous screen can become two or more detailed entries, allowing you to see exactly which rights are inherited and from where, or whether the entries were specifically created for this resource by hand. For example, notice that the Users group has two entries, both of which are inherited by the volume. You can also see exactly where the permissions flow downward by look-ing at the Apply To column. Of course, having all these details is great for troubleshooting because you finally have all the information in one place (well, almost).

You have the ability to tailor your extended permissions to the atomic level by choosing an entry and clicking the Edit button. Be careful, though. With so many permissions coming from so many different places (and we aren't even considering share permissions here!), this process can easily become messy to troubleshoot. Try to simplify your resources and users as much as possible, by volume, by group, or by machine, and your life will be a lot simpler when dealing with permissions.

To see what rights the Users group has so you can make sure it has the correct access to the APPS folder, select the Users entry with Read & Execute permissions, and then click the Edit button. You'll get the options shown in Figure 11.17.

FIGURE 11.17
Viewing and edit-ing the atomic permissions gives you the most information.

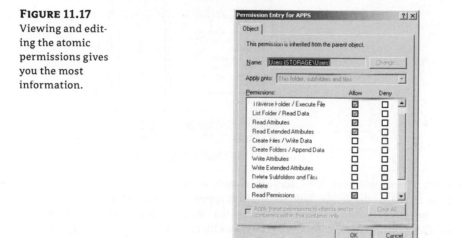

These permissions are Read & Execute by the book. No more, no less; these five atomic per-missions make up Read & Execute. Consider it law.

PERMISSION INHERITANCE

You might have noticed that the Apply Onto drop-down list is also unavailable for the Users group entry. Remember, you couldn't remove it because of inheritance, and this is yet another result of inheritance. You can consider inheritance as an order from on high. These permissions *will* be applied to this folder, subfolders, and files unless and until you remove the inheritance check box and create your own custom permissions. Or you could go straight to the source, since, as the administrator, you are the ruler when it comes to inheritance. If you open up the properties for the volume and edit the entries for the Users group, you can remove or modify the permissions; you can then specify exactly where you want them applied throughout the volume by using the Apply Onto button from there.

Notice there were two entries for the Users group. Server 2008's default permissions are more secure than those given to us in Windows 2003. Remember, in Windows 2000, Everyone had Full Control on *everything*!) Let's examine the atomic permissions for the other Users group entry. If you are still looking at the dialog box in Figure 11.17, click Cancel—you don't need to modify the Read & Execute entry because that is exactly what you want for the APPS directory. Back in the Advanced Security Settings for APPS window, click the other entry for the User group and then click Edit. You'll see the dialog box in Figure 11.18.

FIGURE 11.18
Editing the special permissions for the Users group

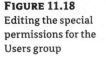

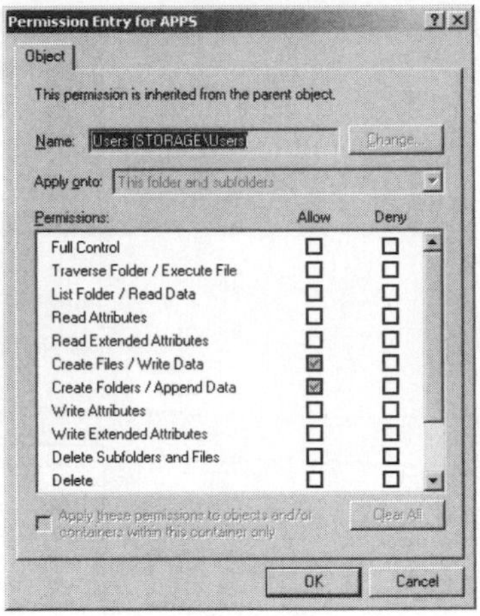

The default permissions for the Users group include the ability to create files and folders on the volume as well as the ability to write data and append data to the files contained within that volume—unless, of course, you specifically deny that ability to any particular resources on the volume. So, what you have here is a set of permissions that is in between two of the molecular groups discussed previously. The first set of atomic permissions you saw for the Users group made up the Read & Execute molecular permission. If you add these two atomic permissions, the molecular set falls somewhere between Read & Execute and Modify. In full, the Modify permission also includes the Write Attributes, Write Extended Attributes, and Delete Files and Folders rights.

For a couple of reasons, the easier of the two solutions is to use the Deny function. First, you don't have to worry about the rest of your inherited permissions from the volume, some of which you will need to keep. When you remove inheritance, you are given the right to copy the existing inherited permissions and can edit them as you like. Second, by removing inheritance, you take away your ability to push out permissions from the volume on a global scale, which is a pretty handy feature. As we said before, if you can simplify the permissions by doing things on a global scale, you can save yourself a lot of time and energy. To disable the ability for the Users group to create files or folders or to write or append data with the APPS folder, simply select the Deny check box (see Figure 11.19) for both of the atomic permission entries, and click OK.

Removing a Group or User

To remove a group or user entry, just click the Remove button from either of the two properties sheets you just saw. If a user or group is there because of inheritance, the Remove option will be unavailable, and you will have to disable inheritance by selecting the "Allow inheritable permissions from parent to propagate to this object and all child objects" option.

Using the Detailed Interface to Get the Whole Story

Look at Figure 11.19. Remember this dialog box? We'll remind you of something we said before about the interfaces used for managing NTFS permissions: this window just doesn't give enough information, and it's kludgey. If you decided to disable inheritance to get rid of the Users group's Write permissions and clicked the Remove button in this dialog box to accomplish that, you'd remove *both* of the Users entries that you saw in Figure 11.16. Also, if you used this window to add a user or group account, you'd only be able to select the molecular permissions boxes you see here— you wouldn't be able to specify exactly where you wanted those permissions applied using inheritance. You'd have to drill down to the dialog box in Figure 11.16 to do that. It's best to just bypass this unnecessary dialog box and go straight to the detailed view. That way, you have the full story to start with.

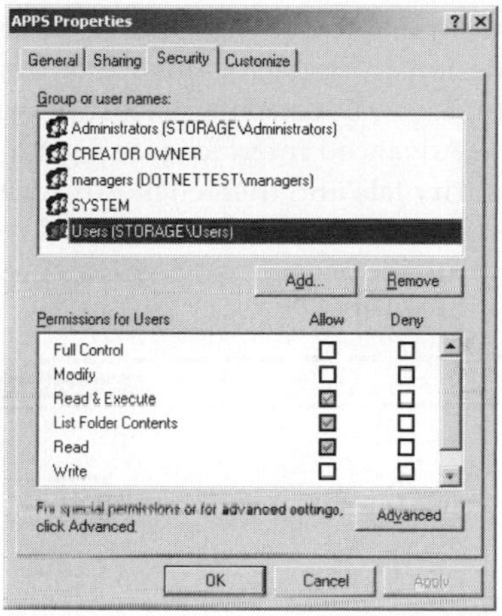

FIGURE 11.19

There isn't enough information to determine the *whole* permissions story from the initial properties sheet.

CONFLICTING PERMISSIONS

You can assign permissions to files, and you can assign permissions to directories. Just as share permissions can conflict with file and directory permissions, file permissions can conflict with directory permissions. In share-level conflicts, the share wins; in file and directory permission conflicts, the file wins. If you assign read-only rights to a directory but you assign change rights to a file within that directory, you will still be able to change the file.

MULTIPLE PERMISSIONS

Now for another problem. You have given your Administrators group full control over the APPS folder, and everyone else has Read & Execute permissions only. Here is where permissions once again come into conflict. Everyone is a user, right? Even administrators are users. Hmmm. How does this work? Well, in the case of multiple permissions, the *least restrictive* permissions will prevail, as long as share permissions aren't involved. Let's say you have an administrator named Bob. Bob is part of the Users group, which has read-only rights on a file. Bob is also part of the Administrators group, which has full control. In this case, Bob will get full control because it is least restrictive.

DENY PERMISSIONS

We talked about Deny permissions with respect to shares earlier and then briefly talked about the effects of inheriting permissions as it relates to Allow and Deny. The same thing applies in file and directory permissions, but in a way that's just a tad bit more complex because of the increased number of security options. Think of a corporate bonus-award spreadsheet file that you are trying to protect. You want everyone to see the file, but you only want the managers to be able to actually change the file. It makes sense: grant Employees the right to read and Managers full control. Imagine that, somewhere along the line, some low-level supervisor falls into both groups. They need to be part of Managers for some things but are more like Employees in others. If you leave the permissions just described, this supervisor is going to get the best of both worlds with this spreadsheet—full control. For this reason, you decide that you explicitly don't want anyone in Employees to have full control. Now what?

Easy enough: simply deny those excess permissions. What you need to do is find out which permissions you specifically do *not* want Employees to have and select them in the Deny column; this way you can make sure that Employees are given Read rights only. To do this, from the Advanced interface (see Figure 11.20), right-click the file, choose Properties, go to the Security tab, and then click Advanced. Remember this interface from Figure 11.16? From here, highlight the entry for the Employees group and click Edit, which will allow you to modify the atomic permissions for the spreadsheet. Check the Deny column for the entries that you see in Figure 11.20.

FIGURE 11.20
Deny permissions

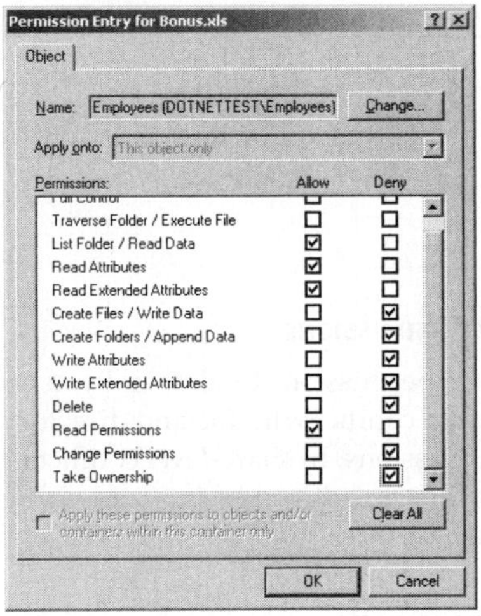

You'll need to individually select the Deny boxes for each attribute. If you check the Deny box for Full Control, however, everything else below that will automatically be selected in the Deny column because Full Control *includes* all permissions.

For this example, you want to allow Read and deny Write. When you click OK to have these new permissions take effect, you'll get a warning that tells you that Deny permissions override Allow permissions. Now, in the case of the multiple-permissions scenario, the Deny takes precedence, and even if the supervisor in question has both Managers and Employees memberships, he'll get cut off with the Deny.

EFFECTIVE PERMISSIONS

What is the end result of all of these permissions if some are inherited, some are not, some apply to users, and some apply to groups? Who will get to do what and with which files? How can you tell what the result of all these permissions will be for any group, user, or object? Well, Microsoft has included a tool in Server 2008 that allows you to calculate the effective permissions for any particular user or group on a particular object. Take a look at the dialog box in Figure 11.21. Once again, it's the advanced properties sheet for your APPS folder that, by now, you should know well. Remember that Administrators have Full Control, Database Managers have Modify, and Users have Read & Execute permissions?

FIGURE 11.21
Advanced permissions for the APPS folder

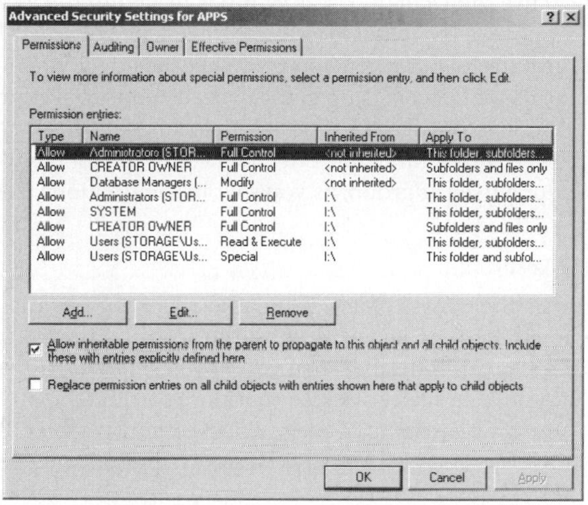

To see how exactly all these permissions work, click the Effective Permissions tab, and you will see the dialog box shown in Figure 11.22. It's simple. Just select a user or group name to view the permissions based on global and local group permissions, local permissions, and local privileges.

FIGURE 11.22
Effective Permissions tab

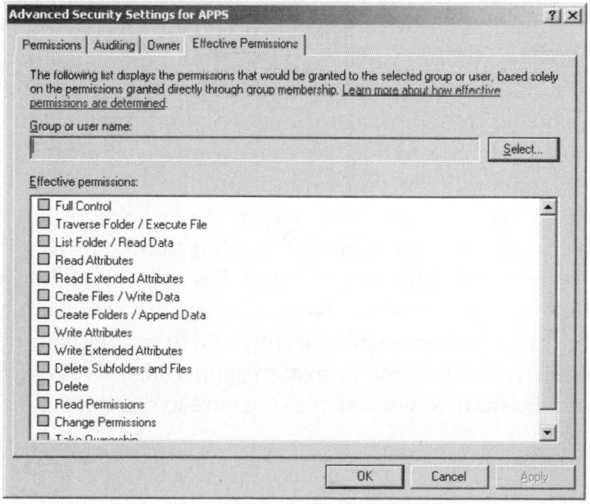

Of course, you need to have the appropriate rights to view the permissions on whatever resource you are checking, and there *are* some limitations in terms of the factors that are used to determine the effective permissions. For instance, you may not be able to view permissions for every user or group. Consider the local users group on the server called Storage, where your APPS share is located. Because this server is a member of an Active Directory domain, the global group called Domain Users is automatically nested within the local Users group. You can view the effective permissions on the local users group by selecting the local location called Storage (instead of the directory) after clicking the Select button from the screen in Figure 11.22. The results were obtained by calculating the permissions for the two entries that exist for the Users group in Figure 11.21.

Because the Domain Users group is nested in the local users group, domain users have the same rights to the folder, barring the existence of any other set of permissions that would conflict with these. But when you try to get the effective permissions for the Domain Users group using this tool, it comes up empty because this tool cannot calculate the effective permissions for domain groups that are nested in local groups.

This certainly limits the effectiveness of the tool, but you can still use it to calculate multiple ACEs for a user or group, as you saw in the previous example.

Ownership

Through the course of assigning and revoking permissions, you are bound to run into the problem where no one, including the administrators, can access a file. And you can't change the file's permissions because you need certain permissions in order to assign permissions. This could be a really sticky situation. Fortunately, ownership can help you.

There is an attribute of every object called an *owner*. The owner is completely separate from permissions. There will always be *some* owner for *every* object. But how does that help you? Well, the owner of an object has a special privilege—the ability to assign permissions.

Working with Hidden Shares

Once you share a folder to the network, it becomes visible to the user community. But what if you don't necessarily want everyone to see the share? For example, we have created an installation source share on a server so that whenever we go to a user's workstation, we can install whatever applications we need to without having to bring CDs. It's really just a convenience, but at the same time, we don't want the users clicking through the shares, installing every program they can get their hands on. Sure, we could limit the share to allow permissions only to us, but that is kind of a pain, too. We don't want to log off the user and log in as ourselves every time we do an install, especially if user profiles are being used. This is where creating hidden shares can help. We want the share to be there and available, but just not as easily visible. Although not a completely secure solution, it is a deterrent to browse-happy users.

To create a hidden share, proceed as normal in sharing a folder, but place a dollar sign at the end of the name. That's it. Now, whenever the server registers its information to the browse list with its available resources, it simply will not register that hidden share.

We'll now show how to create a share called INSTALL$, which will be shared from `D:\Install`. Create the share as normal, making sure to call it INSTALL$ instead of INSTALL (see Figure 11.23).

FIGURE 11.23
Creating a
hidden share

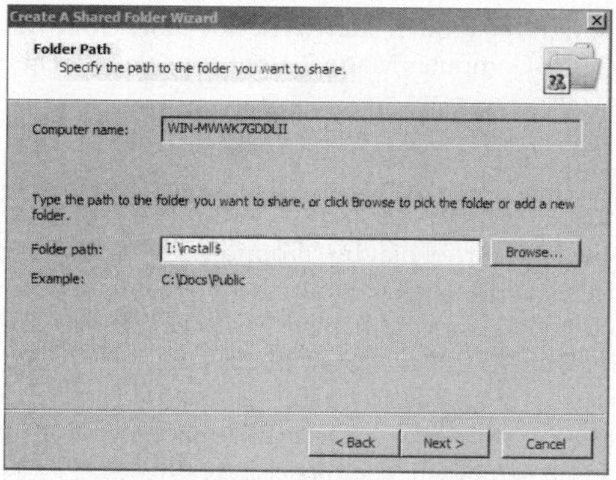

Select the permissions to allow access to *only* Administrators (see Figure 11.24).

FIGURE 11.24
Setting
Administrators
permissions on
a hidden share

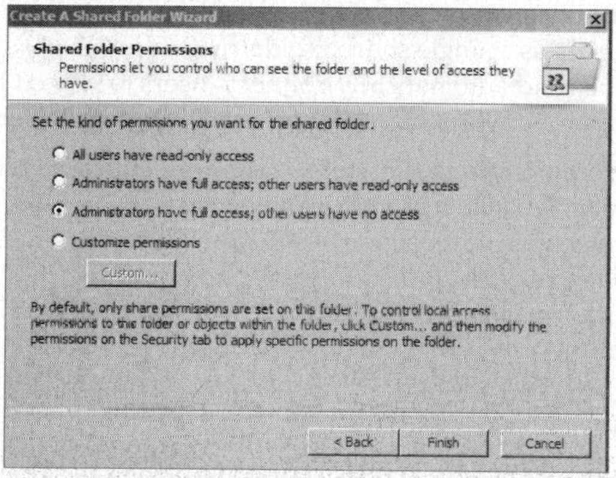

Now, from your client workstations, you will not see the INSTALL$ share listed in the browse list, but you can still map a drive to the INSTALL$ drive connection if you manually type the share name, as shown in Figure 11.25.

FIGURE 11.25
Mapping to a
hidden share

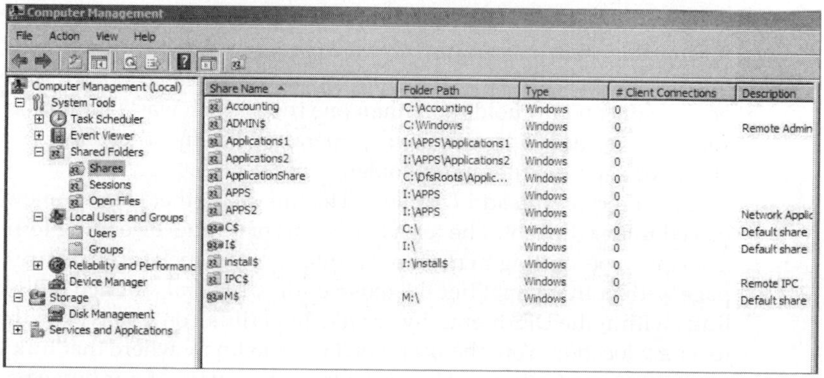

Although the hidden share will not show from your Explorer browser list, the share is visible through the Computer Management console. This helps keep you from forgetting which hidden shares you have created.

Exploring the Distributed File System

If you haven't started playing around with DFS, you should. Although Windows NT4 with SP3 can host a stand-alone DFS root, the tool really became useful with the release of Windows 2000 and Active Directory. And in Server 2008, there are even more enhancements that we will explore in more detail in this section. What is DFS? Well, with DFS, you can create a single share that encompasses every file share–based resource on your network. Think of it as a home for all the file shares on your network with a "links" page that points the clients to the particular server or servers that actually house those shares.

Server 2008 uses two new technologies:

DFS namespaces DFS namespaces enable you to group shared folders that are located on different servers into one or more logically structured namespaces. Each namespace appears to users as a single shared folder with a series of subfolders. This structure increases availability and automatically connects users to shared folders in the same Active Directory Domain Services site, when available, instead of routing them over WAN connections.

DFS replication DFS replication is an efficient, multiple-master replication engine that you can use to keep folders synchronized between servers across limited bandwidth network connections. It replaces the File Replication Service (FRS) as the replication engine for DFS namespaces, as well as for replicating the AD DS SYSVOL folder in domains that use the Windows Server 2008 domain functional level. In other words, you create shared folders by creating and using a namespace, and then you can keep them synchronized in an efficient manner by using the DFS replication feature.

Before you can use these features, you must first add a role to your server. The role you will add is the File Services role. Use the Select Server Roles screen to add the File Services role, as shown in Figure 11.26.

Understanding DFS Terminology

Before we go much further, you need to understand the terminology of DFS. Just like learning to understand Active Directory, a whole new set of concepts and terms comes into play.

You start with a *root*. This translates roughly into the share that will be visible to the network. In the example, APPS was the root. You can have many roots in your site, and with Server 2008 one server can now hold more than one root, which was a limitation in Windows 2003. A root is shared to the network and actually operates like any other share. You can have additional files and folders within the shared folder.

Under a root, you add *DFS links*. The link is another share somewhere on the network that is placed under the root. The term *link* is part of our never-ending terminology shift. In this case, it seems to be shifting to more of an Internet nomenclature. Picture the DFS root as a web home page with nothing on it but the name of the page and a bunch of links to other web pages. The links within the DFS hierarchy are like hyperlinks on a web page that automatically direct you to a new location. You, the user, don't need to know where that link will take you, as long as you get the web page you were looking for. Once you find your home page (the DFS root), you will be directed by those hyperlinks (your DFS links) to any other website you want (your shares).

FIGURE 11.26
Adding the File
Services role

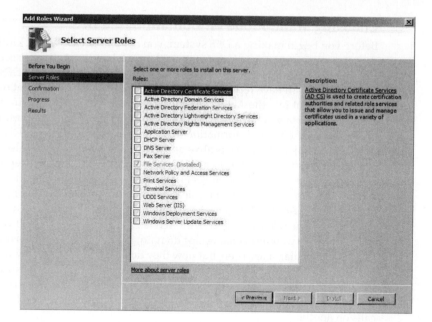

A *target or replica* can refer to either a root or a link. If you have two identical shares on the network, usually on separate servers, you can group them together within the same link, as *DFS targets*. You can also replicate an entire root—you know, the table of contents—as a *root replica member*. Once the targets are configured for replication, the File Replication Service keeps the contents of roots in sync.

🌐 Real World Scenario

DFS AND YOU

We started this chapter with a suggestion that you should look into or start playing around with DFS. Well let us tell you a short story about the day a server died. Now we know you are thinking about a song with a similar name; just read on and find out why using DFS can save critical files and reduce the time required to restore files and or folders.

One day a few years ago one of the authors of this book was looking at his servers and examining the event logs before he left for the day. Everything seemed OK, so he went home, some 45 miles away. Home for about 15 minutes, he got a page from the afternoon support person that the main server at one location was down and he could not log in or see it using the ping command. He drove back fearing the worst, only to arrive and see that production was ongoing and nothing needed to be done. Those critical files needed for that night's production were in use from another server.

The server was restored the next day (a problem with the motherboard), and the company never missed a beat. The time that would have been required to restore from backup would have doubled the mean time to restore (MTTR) and caused millions of dollars in lost production. Those costs included the people who could not work in the plants because of the missing data. If you want to keep the data in play, get comfortable using the DFS function.

Choosing Stand-Alone vs. Domain-Based DFS

Before you begin making a DFS system, you need to decide which kind of DFS you want. This decision will be primarily based on whether you have an Active Directory. The big difference is going to be on the root of the DFS. In an Active Directory–based DFS or domain-based DFS, the root itself can have replicas. In other words, that one single point of failure—the root—has been spread out into the Active Directory. Using root replicas, if you have 27 servers housing the Active Directory, you have 27 places where the DFS information lives. Well, it's not all DFS information; it's just enough information to point clients to one of the DFS root replicas. With that, as long as the Active Directory is alive and available, the DFS is too. Also, when integrated into the Active Directory, link replicas can be configured to use automatic replication. With automatic replication, the File Replication Service takes over the synchronization of the contents of replicated folders to ensure that all replicas contain the same information. It might be safe to say that if you have an Active Directory–based domain, you should choose domain-based DFS.

But here's the really cool part of an Active Directory–based DFS. If you host your DFS in the Active Directory of the dotnettest.loc domain, not only do your users not need to know which server a particular share is on, but now they don't even need to know which server the DFS itself is on. Instead of having to map a drive to \\servername\DFSname, your users could map a drive to \\dotnettest .loc\DFSname. Now, using the same logic a client uses to find an available domain controller for Active Directory, the client can search for a host of the DFS. If one fails, the client just calls on another.

A domain-based DFS automatically publishes its topology in Active Directory. What this means is that the actual DFS hierarchy—the roots, links, and targets—is published into Active Directory so that all domain controllers will know where the DFS lives, what it looks like, and how to get to it. It *doesn't* mean that every domain controller is a DFS root replica server.

If you've gotten this far, you probably don't have an Active Directory to publish to. What about the non-AD-based networks? Some companies have migrated to Active Directory (and most others are at least in the planning stages, since support for NT4 is ending). Some have at least put up a few member servers here and there. For those who have not gone through the process of migration, the DFS provides an enhancement to the basic file server that lets an enterprise step out of its physically bound shackles into a more user-friendly and manageable state. A stand-alone DFS is a solid step forward into the world of file sharing from previous Windows Server Versions, without requiring a major Active Directory initiative. With a stand-alone DFS, you don't get the nice fault tolerance of the root itself, you don't get the automatic replication, and you don't get the DFS published in the Active Directory. But you still get all the other goodies, such as combining all your network shares into a single namespace and finally killing the dependency on physical server names and locations when it comes to getting your users to their resources. In just a little bit, we'll talk about how these benefits brought to you by the DFS can be put to use in a practical environment—with or without an Active Directory—but first, let's jump into learning how to actually build these things.

Let's say you have the following set of shared resources across the network:

UNC Path	Users' Mapping	Resource Description
\\DC1\APPS	G:	All generic applications
\\RESOURCE1\APPS	G:	The same applications as \\DC1\APPS
\\STORAGE\SALES	S:	The corporate sales data

UNC Path	Users' Mapping	Resource Description
\\STORAGE2\USERS	H:	All user directories
\\STORAGE\FINANCE	Q:	The corporate financing data
\\RESOURCE2\APP2	P:	Miscellaneous applications

This could become a real pain for users (not to mention administrators!), who have to remember where to go to connect to their various resources. Here, there are five different servers housing resources. This also means that if a client needed to access APPS, SALES, USERS, and FINANCE all at the same time, they would be required to make three different connections. Well, three doesn't sound too bad, but we have been in large networks where there were no more available drive letters left on clients to map another share; every single letter from A to Z was mapped to something. You also have to remember which clients connect to \\DC1\APPS and which connect to \\RESOURCE1\APPS, which are identical shares housed on two different servers. Again, it's not a big deal in this particular example, but if you had 50 servers containing the same set of APPS, this could become a nightmare to keep track of.

BENEFITS OF DFS

As you can probably see, DFS is most beneficial in large enterprises and probably not worth the effort in small-office networks.

Now, let's put this same scenario into DFS instead. You would have one DFS root—we'll call it CORPfiles—with all your corporate shares listed within.

Creating a DFS Root

Your choices for the DFS root type are domain root and stand-alone root. A domain root will publish itself in Active Directory, while a stand-alone root will not. This fundamental difference is the deciding factor on how much functionality you will receive. Keep in mind that a domain DFS root must be hosted on a domain controller so that there is an Active Directory to post to. One of the most important benefits of being published in Active Directory is that domain roots can have replica roots. Again, a root replica lets you have any domain controller host the root, which greatly improves fault tolerance. Because the roots require Active Directory to be replicas at this level, stand-alone roots cannot be and cannot have replicas. Because our test server, Server2008-02, is a stand-alone server, we will choose that one when we get to that step.

You will then fire up the DFS Management screen, as shown in Figure 11.27, to begin using the DFS features, which we will describe in a bit.

You can see that you could either use the step-by-step guide or use the Action tab menus on the right side of the window to create DFS namespaces and DFS replication for your files. In this example, we will use the wizard method to create the first DFS namespace and DFS replications just to get used to these features. You can determine which method you prefer to use; maybe you may want to use the step-by-step method the first time.

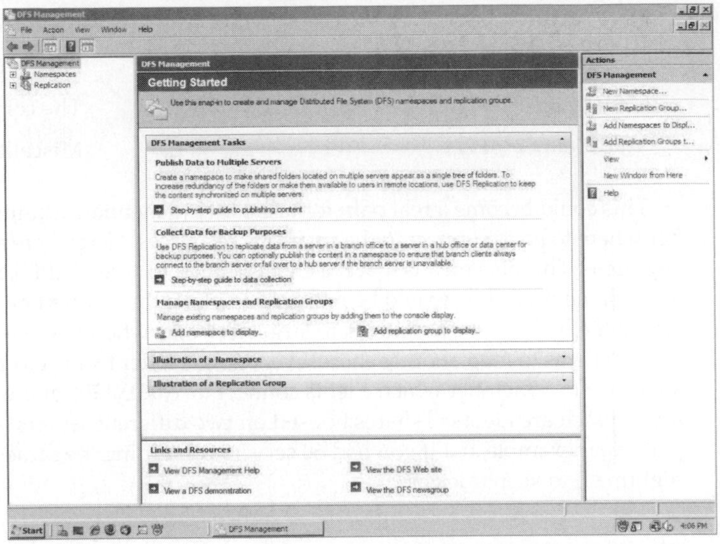

FIGURE 11.27
DFS Management screen

On the upper-right side of the DFS Management screen, click New Namespace. You will then see the Namespace Server Wizard. If you want, browse to find the correct server name to use. See Figure 11.28 with the server name displayed.

USING THE WIZARDS

We recommend using wizards until you are comfortable with the process; this recommendation is true for all of Server 2008.

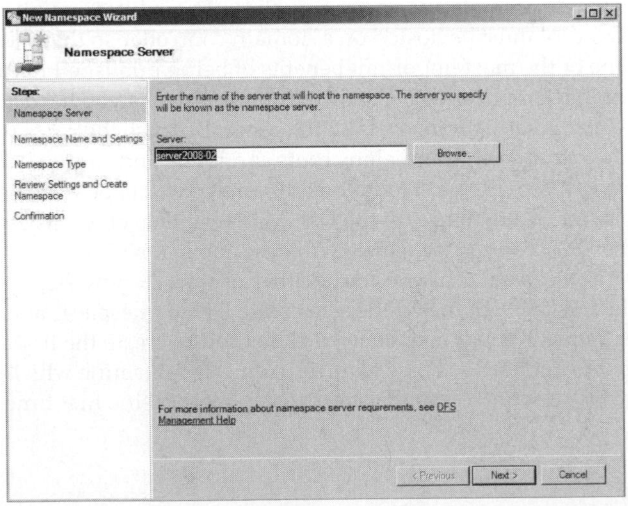

FIGURE 11.28
New namespace server

Next you will assign a name for the namespace, as shown in Figure 11.29. This name will appear after the server name and is used as the name for the collection of files and folders added to the namespace.

FIGURE 11.29

Namespace name

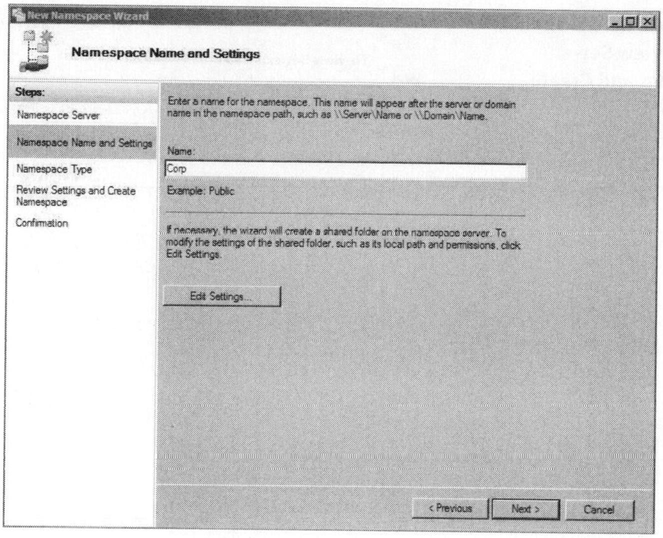

Now you will need to assign the types of namespace to create. Your choice is either a domain-based namespace or a stand-alone namespace. The domain-based namespace allows you to store the namespace on one or more namespace servers. The stand-alone namespace allows you to place the namespace on a single namespace server. We will use the stand-alone namespace for this example, as shown in Figure 11.30. This will allow you to add files and folders to the namespace later.

FIGURE 11.30

Namespace Type screen

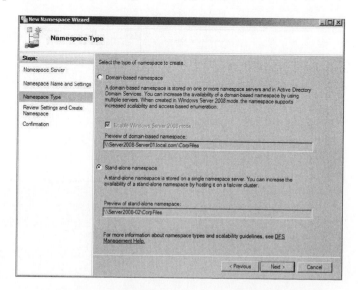

The final screen shows all the settings before the namespace is confirmed and created, as shown in Figure 11.31. If you are OK with these settings, click the Create button to create the namespace, as shown in Figure 11.32.

FIGURE 11.31
Review Settings and Create Namespace screen

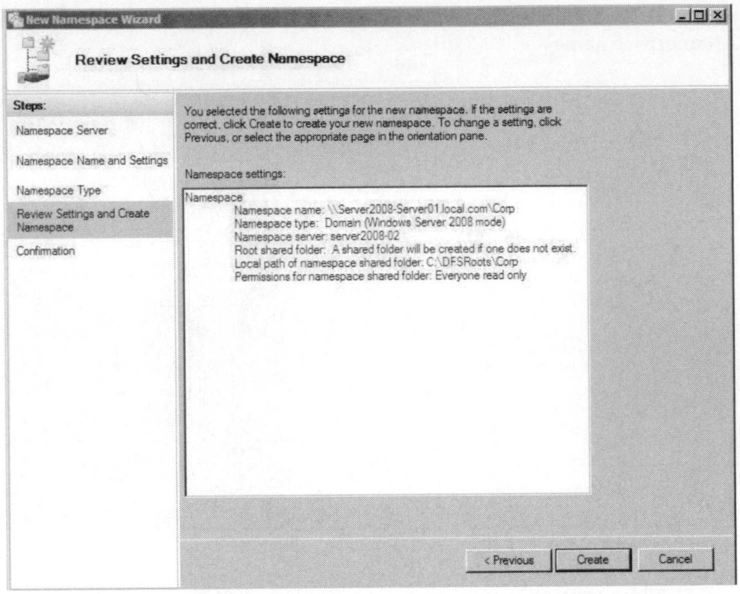

FIGURE 11.32
Confirmation screen

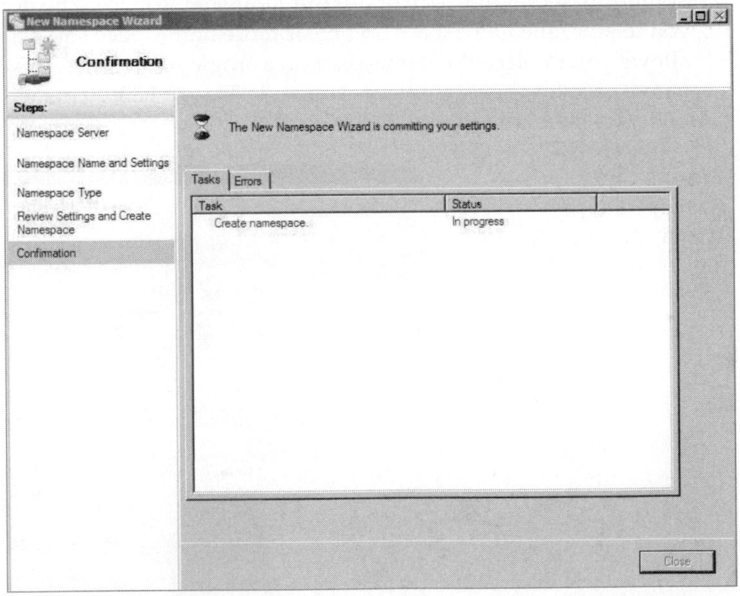

This process may take some time; however, when completed, you will be well on your way to having files and folders shared in one logical location from across the server environment with one name for easy access. In the Share and Storage Management window, you can then see the CORPfiles folder created with a local path of `c:\DFSroots\Corp`, as shown in Figure 11.33. Notice that the default space is 39GB.

FIGURE 11.33
DFS root path

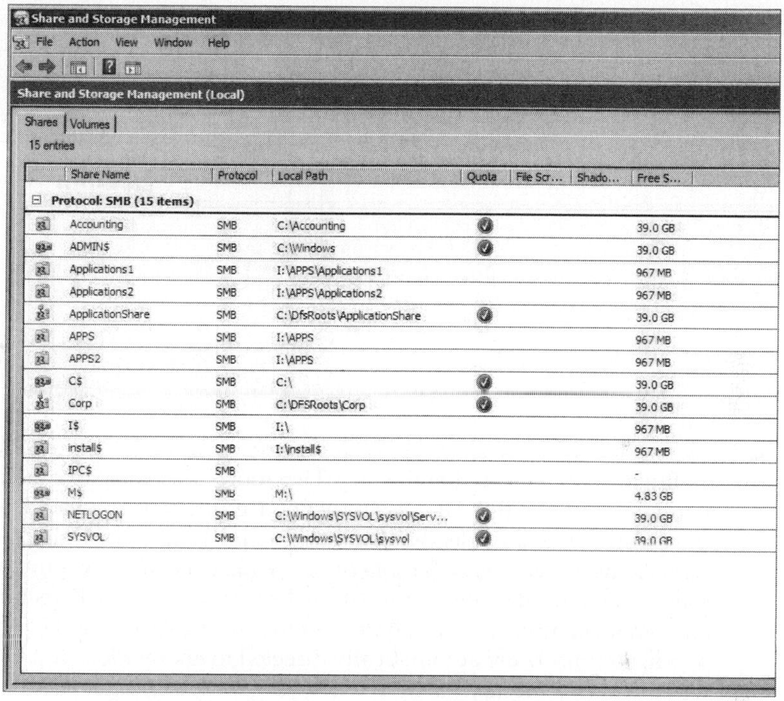

Adding Links to a DFS Root

Under this one root share, you can now add links or files and folders. To do this, all you need to do now is to click the Add Folder target and add any and all files and folders you want. So, let's create a new folder and add those target files and folders.

You will then need to create a new folder within the CORP namespace. To do this, click New Folder in the DFS Management window under Action on the right, click to add a name to it, and then browse for the folders. We used accounting files and the Accounting folder. Then just browse to add folder targets, as shown in Figure 11.34. Click OK. If you are using different servers, their names would change after the \\; however, in this example, we are only using one server, because we are in stand-alone mode. If we were using a domain-based mode, we would use only one target folder. Click OK, and if you have not created a replication for the new folder (and who would if you did not know what you were going to name it?), you can then create that now.

Understand, though, that DFS isn't a new kind of file server. In a sense, it's not a file server at all—it is, instead, a way of putting a kind of "table of contents" on a bunch of existing file shares and pointing the clients to that source of information when they need to connect to a share that is referenced in that table. DFS does *not* create file shares; you must create all the file shares on the various servers first and *then* use DFS to impose some order. To emphasize that point, here's another fact about DFS: the file shares needn't be NT, 2000, or Server 2003 file shares. If you had Unix NFS, Banyan VINES, and Novell NetWare client software on your computer, then you could actually create a DFS "share" that points only to NFS, VINES, and NetWare volumes! We will cover NFS next, but first let's finish with DFS.

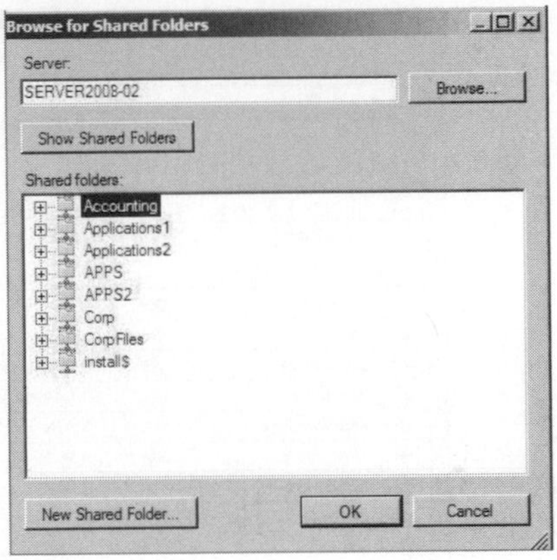

FIGURE 11.34

The Browse for Shared Folders dialog box

But does that mean that this new DFS root—this "table of contents"—constitutes a new single point of failure? If that one server that houses the root—the place where all your users go to find their resources—goes dead in the water, so do your users, right? Not necessarily. Combined with Active Directory, DFS roots can be made to be fault tolerant. Instead of the actual, physical root being housed on one server, it can be stored in Active Directory, which is maintained across all domain controllers. Now, if one of those servers housing the root—in Active Directory—goes down, your users are automatically directed to another location to retrieve root information without even a hiccup.

Again, we'll stress the function of DFS. "Fault-tolerant DFS" doesn't mean that you're backing up the data in the file shares. It only means that the "table of contents" that is a DFS root gets backed up so that if the computer hosting the DFS root goes down—and sorry to be stressing this point, but again there's a good chance that the machine hosting the DFS root *does not contain one single byte of shared files*, just the pointers to the servers that contain those files—then there's another computer standing by to assume the role of "table of contents server," or, in Server 2008 language, the DFS root.

Configuring DFS Replications

Can you somehow protect those file shares and their data with some kind of fault tolerance? Yes, you can by using replication. To do this, go to the DFS Management window, and click the Replication link under the Namespaces link, as shown in Figure 11.35.

Under the Action section, click New Replication Group. One of the new features of Server 2008 R2 that we have not pointed out is the use of wizards and how they look different. Notice once you open a wizard that all the steps are clearly listed on the left column. This helps you plan things because you know what to expect next—no more clicking OK or Next and finding something you were not expecting. Also, notice that these steps are explained better than previous Server technologies. Anyway, let's get back to work—on the first replication screen in the wizard, you have two choices. One is for a multipurpose replication group, and the other is for a replication group for data collection. If you are using the domain-based namespace or stand-alone namespace, then you would choose the default, which is Multipurpose. If you wanted to replicate data to back it up and "collect" data on, say, a hub server, then choose the second option. We will use the default.

FIGURE 11.35
DFS Replication
screen

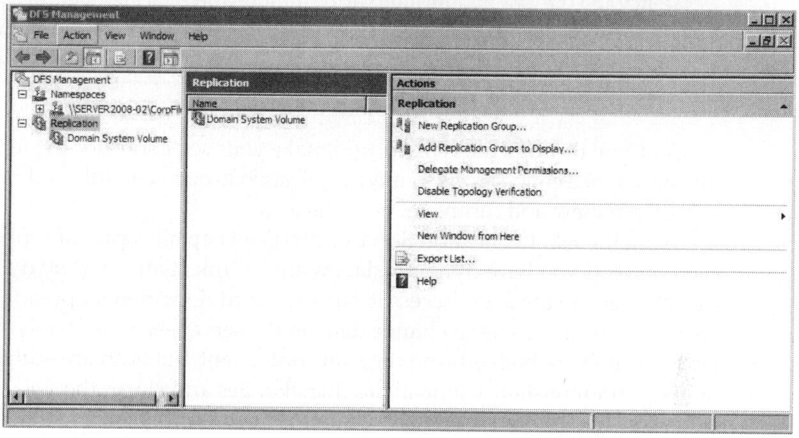

Next, you will need to give the replication group a name. We'll name it CorpRep, as shown in Figure 11.36.

FIGURE 11.36
New Replication
Group Wizard's
Name and Domain
screen

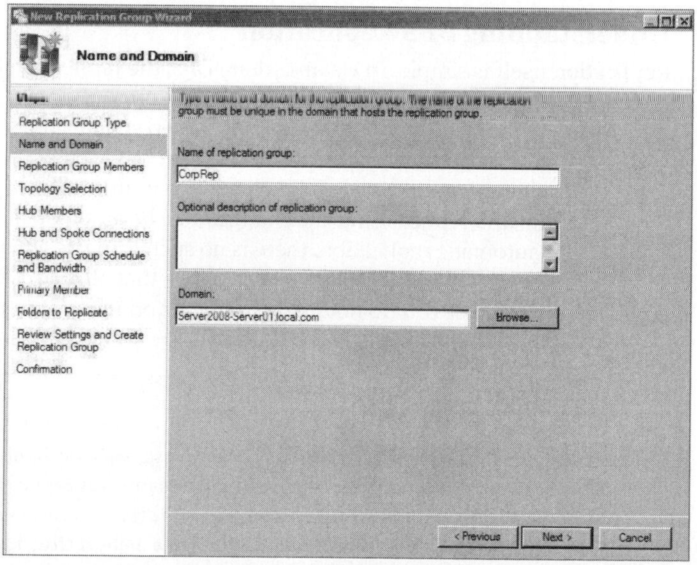

Next you will need to add the servers that will be part of the replication group. You should choose this with some thought, because you will add to the amount of data that will flow into and out of the servers selected.

WAITING FOR REPLICATION

Configuration changes are not applied immediately to all members. The new configuration must be replicated to all domain controllers, and each member in the replication group must poll its closest domain controller to obtain the changes. The amount of time this takes depends on AD DS replication latency and the long polling interval (60 minutes) on each member. To poll immediately for configuration changes, open a command prompt window, and then type the following command once for each member of the replication group: `dfsrdiag.exe PollAD /Member:DOMAIN\Server1`.

Continue through the wizard, and make your selections for the topology, hub members (if any), hub and spoke connections (if any), replication group schedule and bandwidth, and primary member; then review and complete the wizard.

Using the File Replication Service, DFS can keep all copies of replicated targets in sync with each other. If you have dynamic data within a link at all—and by dynamic we mean anything that changes as the users access it, such as Word documents, spreadsheets, databases, or anything else that requires users to change data on the server—you probably shouldn't replicate it. Let's say Jane and Bob are both editing the same document, but both are editing different replicated copies on two different shares. Jane makes her changes and closes the document, and then Bob makes different changes and saves his version. Who wins? Bob will win because he saved it last. Once saved, the document is replicated to the other share, overwriting Jane's changes. So, remember, if a user is editing a document and accessing it on a link that is a replica, their changes will get overwritten the next time the replication occurs. Use caution when using link replicas and replication.

Understanding DFS Replication

Replication itself is simple. In a stand-alone DFS, the replication is manual, and one link replica is the master. In other words, changes from that particular master server propagate to all other replica servers. If the physical share you want to keep synchronized resides on an NTFS volume on a Windows 2008 Server machine, replication is automatic based on the Active Directory replication schedule and uses multimaster replication. With multimaster replication, you can modify files on any one of the link replicas, and the changes will be automatically copied to the other members. Really, with automatic replication, there is no such thing as a master after the initial replication. The first replication will need a master to ensure that all shares have the same starting point. It is advised, though, that you do not mix automatic and manual replication within a single replica set.

THE MISSING LINK

Now that we have covered the replication process, we should note that both Active Directory and DFS replicate at the same time. They are not the same but replicate that way. Once we had problems replicating and found that if we corrected the Active Directory replication process, the FRS or in this case DFS would reestablish and replicate as well. If this does not correct replication on your DFS, then you will need to do a more detailed troubleshooting and correction process.

Managing DFS Replication

After you have configured your DFS, there are a few steps you must go through to properly manage the roots, links, and clients that are connected to them. Once you have set up your replication groups, there will come a time when you will need to make changes.

EDITING REPLICATION SCHEDULES AND BANDWIDTH

Perform the following tasks to make changes to the replication or bandwidth for your replication groups.

To edit the schedule and bandwidth for a replication group, follow these steps:

1. In the console tree under the Replication node, right-click the replication group with the schedule that you want to edit, and then click Edit Replication Group Schedule.

2. Use the Edit Schedule dialog box to control when replication occurs, as well as the maximum amount of bandwidth that replication can consume.

To edit the schedule and bandwidth for a specific connection, follow these steps:

1. In the console tree under the Replication node, select the appropriate replication group.

2. Click the Connections tab, right-click the connection that you want to edit, and then click Properties.

3. Click the Schedule tab, select "Custom connection schedule," and then click Edit Schedule.

4. Use the Edit Schedule dialog box to control when replication occurs, as well as the maximum amount of bandwidth that replication can consume.

ENABLING OR DISABLING REPLICATION

From time to time you will also need to enable or disable your replication groups.

TO REPLICATE OR NOT TO REPLICATE

If you are updating your network and need to control your bandwidth, you may want to disable replication. We always disable replication and change the time to replicate Active Directory whenever we upgrade servers or networking devices. You would not want to cause problems for yourself if you were adding equipment and the servers want to replicate and then fail. This will not only fill up error logs but start causing problems fast. The best thing here is to disable replication whenever you are making changes to the network's architecture.

To enable or disable replication for a specific connection, perform the following steps:

1. Select Start ➤ Administrative Tools ➤ DFS Management.

2. In the console tree, under the Replication node, click the replication group that contains the connection you want to edit.

3. In the details pane, click the Connections tab.

4. Do one of the following:

   ◆ To disable a connection, right-click the connection, and then click Disable.

   ◆ To enable a connection, right-click the connection, and then click Enable.

CONNECTION SUPPORT

Microsoft does not support one-way connections for DFS replication. Creating a one-way replication connection can cause numerous issues including health check topology errors, staging issues, and issues with the DFS replication database. To create a one-way connection, instead make the replicated folder on the appropriate member read-only.

ENABLING OR DISABLING REPLICATION ON A SPECIFIC MEMBER

Sometimes you may also need to enable or disable replication with specific members of a replication group. Caution should be the order of the day. After a disabled member is enabled, the member must complete an initial replication of the replicated folder. Initial replication will cause about 1KB of data to be transferred for each file or folder in the replicated folder, and any updated or new files present on the member will be moved to the DfsrPrivate\PreExisting folder on the member, and it will be replaced with authoritative files from another member. If all members are disabled, then the first member enabled becomes the primary member, which may not be want you want to do.

TO SHARE OR TO PUBLISH

Membership changes are not applied immediately. The membership changes must be replicated to all domain controllers, and the member must poll its closest domain controller to obtain the changes. The amount of time this takes depends on AD DS replication latency and the short polling interval (five minutes) on the member.

SHARING OR PUBLISHING A REPLICATED FOLDER

Once you have completed the replication wizard, you may want to share or publish the replicated folder. To do this, you must add the folder to an existing or new namespace.

To share a replicated folder without publishing the folder to a DFS namespace, perform the following steps:

1. Select Start ➤ Administrative Tools ➤ DFS Management.

2. In the console tree, under the Replication node, click the replication group that contains the replicated folder you want to share.

3. In the details pane, on the Replicated Folders tab, right-click the replicated folder that you want to share, and then click Share and Publish in Namespace.

4. In the Share and Publish Replicated Folder Wizard, click "Share the replicated folder," and then follow the steps in the wizard.

To share a replicated folder and publish it to a DFS namespace, perform the following steps:

1. Select Start ➤ Administrative Tools ➤ DFS Management.

2. In the console tree, under the Replication node, click the replication group that contains the replicated folder you want to share.

3. In the details pane, on the Replicated Folders tab, right-click the replicated folder that you want to share, and then click Share and Publish in Namespace.

4. In the Share and Publish Replicated Folder Wizard, click "Share and publish the replicated folder in a namespace," and then follow the steps in the wizard.

CHECK THE SECURITY REQUIREMENTS

To perform this procedure, you must meet the security requirements for managing DFS replication and namespaces. If folders will be shared as part of the Share and Publish Replicated Folder Wizard, you must also be a member of the local Administrators group on the servers where each folder is shared.

PRACTICAL USES

Before you start setting up your root, throwing in some links, and reorganizing the way your users access their resources, let's take a quick look at some good ways that DFS can actually add value to your network. Remember, it's not about playing with cool new features; it's about making life easier. When you reduce your time on the boxes, you become more efficient and thus more productive.

Consolidated Enterprise Resources

The example DFS we've worked through in this chapter would be a good way to consolidate enterprise resources. You can take all your shared resources across the network and put them under one logical share. Then, instead of having to know which logical drive a resource resides on, you only need to know the subdirectory. The neat thing is that actually configuring the DFS has absolutely no impact on the configuration of your network. You can build and experiment with DFS configurations all day long in a production environment without anyone even knowing that it exists. All of the old shares on your network remain in place, data is untouched, and users don't see anything different. Once you're ready with your new DFS, the hard part comes in—changing your users' drive mappings from one drive per \\server\share to one drive for all shares. Don't underestimate this task. It's more than just mapping a new drive letter to the DFS root. All applications need to know that they will no longer be on drive X but, rather, on drive Y.

Life-Cycle Management

The good news is that with DFS, this is the last time you'll ever deal with changing drive mappings. If you need to move data from one server to another for purposes of cycling a new server in and an old one out, you don't need to play the game of backing up data, wiping the server, rebuilding it new with the same name, and restoring data to make it look like it is the same physical machine. With DFS, you can set up a new server and configure it as an offline link replica for the share you want "moved." After you verify that all data has been ported over successfully, bring it online and take the old one off. The users don't know that they are hitting a new server. The DFS handles it all in stride.

Exploring the Network File System

We have covered DFS, so you now know how great it can be to point to one logical location to find files and folders. Now you get to talk to the animals—or share files with all those other knockoff operating systems. Just kidding, we want to be able to share files across the whole organization, and if we are using another OS, Server 2008 offers us a tool to do just that. We will be getting a bit technical in this section, and we want you to know that you may not need to do this; however, if you do, you will want these steps. You must select NFS when adding the File Services role to your server. You had to do this for the DFS section just completed. If you did not select NFS, simply go back into your File Services role and add NFS by selecting the appropriate box. So, we'll begin by discussing what NFS is and what Server 2008 can provide you. You will also need to add the File Services role as well, but you can wait for those directions later in this section.

Network File System provides a file-sharing solution for organizations that have a mixed Windows and Unix/Linux environment. NFS gives you the ability to share files across these different platforms when you are running Server 2008. NFS Services include the following improvements in Server 2008:

Active Directory lookup You have the ability to use Windows Active Directory to access files. The Identity Management for Unix Active Directory schema extension includes Unix user identifier (UID) and group identifier (GID) fields. This enables Server for NFS and Client for NFS to look up Windows-to-Unix user account mappings directly from Active Directory Domain Services. Identity Management for Unix simplifies Windows-to-Unix user account mapping management in Active Directory Domain Services.

Enhanced server performance Services for NFS include a file filter driver, which significantly reduces common server file access latencies.

Unix special device support Services for NFS support Unix special devices (mknod).

Enhanced Unix support Services for NFS support the following versions of Unix: Sun Microsystems Solaris version 9, Red Hat Linux version 9, IBM AIX version 5L 5.2, and Hewlett Packard HP-UX version 11i. However, newer versions will undoubtedly be supported in the future.

You can use command-line tools, but in Server 2008 you can use also the Services for Network File system console, as shown in Figure 11.37. The command-line tools and their use are listed in Figure 11.38 later in the chapter.

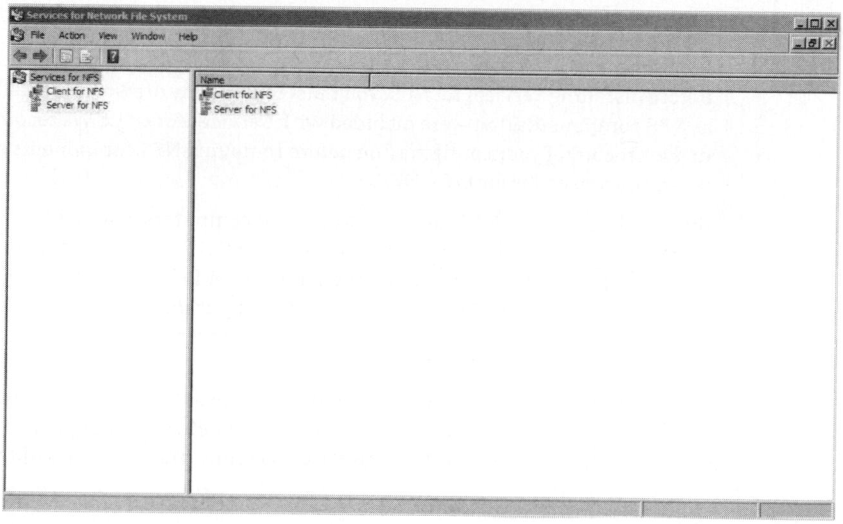

FIGURE 11.37
Services for Net-
work File System
console

One of the more common scenarios that would create the need to use NFS would be for users in a Windows environment using an ERP that is Unix based. While in the ERP system, users can create reports and or export accounting data into Microsoft Excel for further analysis. NFS allows you to access these files while still in Windows, which cuts down on both the technical skills and the time required to export the files using a Unix script and then import them into a Windows-based application. Another scenario may be that you have a Unix system used to store files in some storage area network (SAN). Having NFS running on Server 2008 allows users in the organization to access the files stored there without all the overhead of scripting on the Unix side.

NFS SERVICE COMPONENTS

There are two service components that help run NFS:

Server for NFS   Normally, a Unix-based computer cannot access files on a Windows-based computer. A computer running Windows Server 2008 and Server for NFS, however, can act as a file server for both Windows-based and Unix-based computers.

Client for NFS   Normally, a Windows-based computer cannot access files on a Unix-based computer. A computer running Windows Server 2008 and Client for NFS, however, can access files stored on a Unix-based NFS server.

NFS in Server 2008 also has administrator tools that you can use to manage NFS; you can find these administration functions in the Microsoft Management Console (MMC) snap-in discussed throughout this book.

Before using NFS, there are some prerequisites and assumptions that must be made. You will need to have a basic understanding of both Windows and Unix environments, have some file security knowledge, and know how to administrate Server 2008. A good understanding of what the users need is also a requirement.

NFS PRECAUTIONS

Before installing Services for NFS, you must remove any previously installed NFS components, such as NFS components that were included with Services for Unix. We recommend that you back up or make a record of your configuration before removing NFS components so that you can restore the configuration on Services for NFS.

By default, Server for NFS supports Unix client computers using NFS version 2 or version 3. You can override this, however, and configure Server for NFS to allow access only to clients running NFS version 2. For instructions, see "Configuring Server for NFS" in the Services for NFS help. Client for NFS supports both versions, and this is not configurable.

You will need to gather the list of users, groups, and computers that will be used. Begin with a test ID on both the Windows and Unix servers before you deploy and announce your genius. Start by creating user accounts on the both servers, and then install the File Services role by following these steps:

1. Select Start ➤ Administrative Tools ➤ Server Manager.

2. In the left pane, click Manage Roles.

3. Click Add Roles. The Add Roles Wizard appears.

4. Click Next. The Select Server Roles options appear.

5. Select the File Server check box, and click Next.

6. The File Server screen appears. Click Next to view the Role Services options.

7. Select the Services for Network File System (NFS) check box, and click Next.

8. Confirm your selection, and click Install.

9. When the installation completes, the installation results will appear. Click Close.

You now need to configure NFS authentication and create an NFS shared folder. Make sure you use Server 2008 for this and keep those security updates current. Follow these steps to create an NFS shared folder:

1. On the computer running Server for NFS, create a folder to use as the NFS shared folder.

2. Right-click the folder you created, and click NFS Sharing.

3. Select "Share this folder."

4. If you want to allow anonymous access, select "Allow anonymous access."

5. Click Permissions, click Add, and then do either of the following:

   ◆ In the Names list, click the clients and groups you want to add, and click Add.

   ◆ In the Add Names box, type the names of clients or groups you want to add, separating names in the list with a semicolon (;).

6. In the Type of Access list, click the type of access you want to give the selected clients and groups.

7. Select Allow Root Access if you want a user identified as root to have access other than as an anonymous user. By default, the user identifier (UID) root user is coerced to the anonymous UID.

8. In the Encoding list, click the type of directory name and filename encoding to be used for the selected clients and groups. Stay consistent here!

9. Click OK twice, and then click Apply.

SETTING DEFAULT PERMISSIONS

You will now apply some default permissions for the files and folders you will be creating and then make some minor changes to your firewall on the server you are using for NFS. Remember that the server you use should be behind the organization's main firewalls and be protected. You will need to open all the ports shown here to run NFS:

Services for NFS Component	Port to Open	Protocol	Port
User Name Mapping and Server for NFS	Portmapper	TCP, UDP	111
Server for NFS	Network Status Manager	TCP, UDP	1039
Server for NFS	Network Lock Manager	TCP, UDP	1047
Server for NFS	NFS Mount	TCP, UDP	1048
Server for NFS	Network File System	TCP, UDP	2049

PORT REQUIREMENTS

Depending on your requirements, you may need to open Transmission Control Protocol (TCP) ports, User Datagram Protocol (UDP) ports, or both TCP ports and UDP ports. For testing purposes, we recommend that you open both TCP and UDP transports for all protocols.

To open the firewall ports, follow these steps as necessary:

1. On a computer running the User Name Mapping service or Server above for NFS, select Start ➢ Run, type **firewall.cpl**, and then click OK.

2. Click the Exceptions tab, and then click Add Port.

3. In Name, type the name of a port to open, as listed in the "Setting Default Permissions" sidebar.

4. In "Port number," type the corresponding port number.

5. Select TCP or UDP, and click OK.

6. Repeat steps 2 through 5 for each port to open, and then click OK when finished.

You will then need to add `Mapsvc.exe` to the exception list in the firewall.

FIREWALL PRECAUTIONS

Before you make the firewall changes, be sure that the file server that is being used for NFS is well protected and behind the main enterprise firewalls. These directions assume you would never make these changes on a border server within the DMZ.

---

1. On the computer running the User Name Mapping service, select Start ➤ Run, type `firewall.cpl`, and then click OK.

2. Click the Exceptions tab, and then click Add Program.

3. Click Browse, click `mapsvc.exe`, and then click Open. By default, this file is located in `%windir%\System32`.

4. For testing purposes, click "Change scope," select "Any computer," and then click OK.

5. Click OK two times.

You are almost done with this process. Now you will need to enable file and print sharing on the computer running the NFS service. You probably know how to do this if you have been reading along to this point, but we want to be complete, so here are the steps:

1. On a computer running Services for NFS, select Start ➤ Run, type `firewall.cpl`, and then click OK.

2. Click the Exceptions tab, select the File and Printer Sharing check box, and then click OK.

3. Repeat these steps on each computer running Services for NFS.

You will want to test this to verify that all the functionality is there before you release it to the masses. The following Microsoft TechNet article will give you four tests you can run: `http://technet.microsoft.com/en-us/library/cc753302.aspx`.

You can use the `netsh` command-line tool to configure the firewall as well. See Figure 11.38 for an explanation and listing of available commands.

FIGURE 11.38
netsh command-
line utility

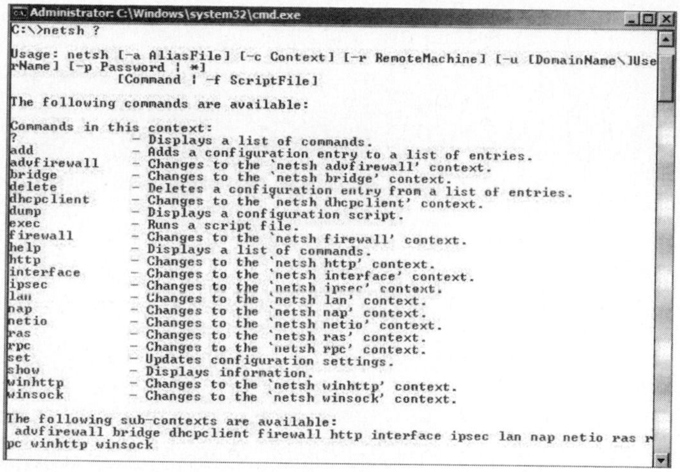

```
Administrator: C:\Windows\system32\cmd.exe                          _ | □ | x |
C:\>netsh ?

Usage: netsh [-a AliasFile] [-c Context] [-r RemoteMachine] [-u [DomainName\]Use
rName] [-p Password | *]
            [Command | -f ScriptFile]

The following commands are available:

Commands in this context:
?              - Displays a list of commands.
add            - Adds a configuration entry to a list of entries.
advfirewall    - Changes to the `netsh advfirewall' context.
bridge         - Changes to the `netsh bridge' context.
delete         - Deletes a configuration entry from a list of entries.
dhcpclient     - Changes to the `netsh dhcpclient' context.
dump           - Displays a configuration script.
exec           - Runs a script file.
firewall       - Changes to the `netsh firewall' context.
help           - Displays a list of commands.
http           - Changes to the `netsh http' context.
interface      - Changes to the `netsh interface' context.
ipsec          - Changes to the `netsh ipsec' context.
lan            - Changes to the `netsh lan' context.
nap            - Changes to the `netsh nap' context.
netio          - Changes to the `netsh netio' context.
ras            - Changes to the `netsh ras' context.
rpc            - Changes to the `netsh rpc' context.
set            - Updates configuration settings.
show           - Displays information.
winhttp        - Changes to the `netsh winhttp' context.
winsock        - Changes to the `netsh winsock' context.

The following sub-contexts are available:
 advfirewall bridge dhcpclient firewall http interface ipsec lan nap netio ras r
pc winhttp winsock
```

The Bottom Line

Add a File Services role to your server   Before you can create and use DFS, NFS, share files and folders, or any other file-related function across the domain in Server 2008, you will need to install the File Services role.

Master It   Go into the server master, and add the server role File Services.

Add a shared folder using NFS   Once the File Services role has been added, you can then share folders, such as a folder called APPS.

Master It   Create a shared folder called APPS on your Server 2008 server; when done, the wizard should show a successful share.

Add a DFS root   If your organization ends up with a lot of file servers created over time, you may have users who do not know where all the files are located. You can streamline these operations by creating a DFS root and consolidate the existing file servers into common namespaces.

Master It   Create a new namespace called MYFIRSTNS on your Windows Server 2008 server; when done, the wizard should show a new namespace called MYFIRSTNS.

Chapter 12

SYSVOL: Old and New

Microsoft's first version of Active Directory (if you don't count the testing done with Exchange 5.5) was released with Windows 2000 Server. This version of Active Directory was really exceptional. It had the capability to house objects in a secure, hierarchical, distributed database called NTDS.dit. It also had the ability to build both logical and physical constructs into functioning directory services, and the tools that were used to manage this version of Active Directory were well designed and pretty easy to use.

The really cool thing about Active Directory back in the year 2000, and still cool today, is that Active Directory is a distributed database. It can have more than one domain controller that houses a writable copy of the directory database, thus eliminating the need for primary (writable) and secondary (nonwritable) servers. Inside each Active Directory domain controller were a couple of folders, which were public-facing shares, used to provide access and replication capabilities for the various domain controllers throughout the domain. The directory that stored and made these shares available was titled SYSVOL, the principal topic of this chapter. It contains netlogon shares (logon scripts and Group Policy objects for client computers in the domain), user logon scripts, Windows Group Policy, File Replication Service staging folders and files for synchronization, and file system junctions.

In this chapter, you will learn to:

+ Understand the File Replication Service

◆ Migrate to Distributed File System Replication

◆ Discover the current migration state of a domain controller using the dfsrmig command-line utility

The Old: File Replication Service

Often when we consider something in the world of technology as *old*, there is a negative connotation associated with it. In this case, the old stuff simply makes reference to the way that something has been done in the past. In this particular case, the changes made to SYSVOL in Windows Server 2008 R2 are encompassed in a new methodology for conducting replication of SYSVOL materials between replication partners throughout the domain.

The new way of using Distributed File System Replication (DFSR) has some significant improvements over the old File Replication Service (FRS) method, but that doesn't necessarily mean the old way is bad. In fact, all versions of Active Directory with the exception of Windows Server 2008 R2 use the "old" method. It is worth exploring and gaining an understanding of FRS because it is so prevalent on the networks to which you will add Windows Server 2008 R2.

Before you start using the cool new features of DFS Replication, it is important that you understand FRS and its functionality so that you can easily migrate from FRS to DFSR. FRS replication uses something called *file system junctions* to maintain the integrity of the SYSVOL folder. You will want to understand the operation of FRS and some of the options associated with FRS replication. Each domain controller that runs FRS contains the following shares and components of SYSVOL:

◆ `netlogon` shares

◆ User logon scripts

◆ Windows Group Policy

◆ FRS staging folders and files

◆ File system junctions

File System Junctions

File system junctions are used extensively throughout the SYSVOL structure. They are a feature of the NTFS version 3.0 file system. That's the same file system that was released with Windows 2000 Server. Junction points work to eliminate data loss or corruption that can occur when you modify the SYSVOL structure.

SYSVOL uses junction points to manage a single instance store. Junction points are also referred to as *reparse points*. A junction point is a physical location on a hard disk that points to a piece of data that is located somewhere else on your hard drive or on some other physical storage device. In a single-instance store, the physical files exist only one time on the file system; however, in SYSVOL, the files exist in SYSVOL\staging\domain or in SYSVOL\enterprise and SYSVOL\staging\enterprise. These additional directory structures are the reparse points that redirect file input and or output to the original locations.

This configuration of junction points/reparse points maintains the data consistency by making sure that a single instance of the data exists. This configuration also permits more than one access point for a given piece of data. The idea is that you get data redundancy without data duplication.

Junction points do something called *grafting* of the namespace of the destination file system to the local NTFS volume. An underlying reparse point permits NTFS to transparently remap an operation to the destination object. The result is that if you modify the data in the SYSVOL structure, the changes will occur directly on these physical files. If you were to perform a cut-and-paste operation, for example, in the SYSVOL structure that contains the junction points, then the operation would occur in the junction point.

CUTTING (OR COPYING) AND PASTING OPERATIONS

Microsoft recommends that you avoid cut-and-paste operations or copy-and-paste operations on the SYSVOL structure. Imagine if you copy and paste a portion of the SYSVOL structure that includes a junction point. The data would not be copied; just the junction point would be, and you would now be dealing with a copy of a junction point that was really a pointer to the actual data files. Here's the crazy part. If you make a change to your copy of the junction point, the original files would be modified in their original location. Not only does Microsoft recommend that you do not cut copy and paste the SYSVOL structure, but it also recommends that you just plain don't modify the SYSVOL structure. Leave it alone.

There were some changes to file system junctions when Microsoft moved from Windows 2000 Server to Windows Server 2003. Specifically, if you copied systemroot\SYSVOL in a Windows Server 2003 environment, you would not copy the junction point too. Outside of this little tidbit, the concepts and recommendations around SYSVOL and junction points remained the same in both Windows 2000 Server and Windows Server 2003.

Understanding File Replication Service

FRS was released with Windows 2000 Server to replicate DFS folders and the SYSVOL folder. It replicates files and folders stored in SYSVOL on domain controllers and DFS shared folders. When FRS sees that a change has been made to a file or folder within a replicated share, then FRS will automatically replicate the updated folder to the other servers. FRS is a multimaster replication service, meaning any of the servers that participate in the replication can trigger updates and subsequent replications and can also resolve conflicts among both files and folders to maintain data consistency among the servers participating as replication partners.

FRS keeps data synchronized across multiple servers and enables networks to increase the availability of data to their clients. If a single server becomes unavailable, the files and folders are still available because they exist on another server. FRS is good at replication in geographically dispersed wide area network (WAN) environments because data can be synchronized to each physical location, which can eliminate the need for clients to use the WAN for access to information from SYSVOL or DFS.

FRS is probably most commonly known for its role in replicating SYSVOL data between domain controllers in a domain. Each domain controller has a SYSVOL folder structure containing files and folders that must be available and synchronized between domain controllers in a domain. The netlogon share, system policies, and Group Policy settings all are part of the SYSVOL structure and need to be replicated to each of the domain controllers for the domain.

BENEFITS OF REPLICATING WITH FRS

When you make additions, modifications, or deletions to SYSVOL, the FRS will take over and replicate those changes to the other domain controllers in the domain. FRS has some benefits that it implements when replicating data between servers, including the following:

Encrypted RPC   FRS uses Kerberos authentication for authenticating remote procedure calls (RPCs) to encrypt the data that is sent between members of a replication partnership.

Compression   FRS compresses files in the staging folder using NTFS compression. Files that are being sent across the network between replication members are sent in their compressed form to save network bandwidth.

Conflict resolution   FRS resolves conflicts with files and folders to make the data consistent among replica members. If two identically named files are created or modified, the FRS uses a simple rule to resolve the conflict. The rule is called "last writer wins." FRS will simply take the most recent update and use that as the authoritative file and will then replicate this version of the file to the other members of the replication partnership. Now if two identically named folders are created on separate servers, FRS will identify the conflict and use a different methodology to resolve the conflict. In this case, FRS will rename the folder that was most recently created and replicate both folders to the replication members. Using this strategy, an administrator is then able to manually resolve the conflict without potential data loss.

Continuous replication FRS provides continuous replication between members of replication groups. FRS changes are replicated within three seconds of the change being made.

Fault-tolerant replication path FRS does not use broadcasts to replicate. It can provide multiple paths for connection between servers. If a replica member is unavailable, then FRS will send the data on a different path. FRS prevents identical files from being sent more than once to any replica member.

Replication Scheduling One of the cool things about FRS is that you can schedule replication to occur at specified times and intervals. This really comes in handy when it is necessary to replicate data across WAN Links. You can schedule the replication to occur during off-peak hours on your WAN line.

Replication Integrity FRS maintains replication integrity using update sequence numbers to log changes to files on a replica member. FRS is able to manage replication even if one of the replica members is shut down without notice. When the member comes back online, FRS will replicate changes that happened in the members' absence as well as updates made to local files on the member before the shutdown.

In pre-Windows 2008 environments, FRS is used primarily in two network situations, DFS and SYSVOL replication. FRS can be used to keep data in DFS hierarchies synchronized among replica members in the replication topology. FRS and DFS are independent technologies, and DFS does not require FRS. You could use other replication methods to ensure the DFS members were kept up-to-date.

FRS REQUIREMENTS AND DEPENDENCIES

SYSVOL replication is handled by FRS. FRS replicates SYSVOL using the topology generated by the *Knowledge Consistency Checker* (KCC) and also has its own Active Directory objects that are replicated using Active Directory replication.

WHAT ABOUT AD?

It is important to remember that although FRS is used to replicate SYSVOL, it is not used as the mechanism for replicating Active Directory.

FRS does have some requirements and dependencies in order to operate:

Active Directory replication FRS requires Active Directory replication to be functioning properly so that the FRS objects in Active Directory reside on all domain controllers in the domain.

DFS If you are going to use FRS to keep data synchronized in folders on separate physical servers, you must first build a DFS namespace. (This does not apply to replicating SYSVOL.)

DNS FRS requires an operational DNS infrastructure. FRS uses DNS for name resolution services for the replica members.

Kerberos authentication FRS requires a functioning Kerberos environment.

NTFS FRS uses the USN journal in NTFS volumes to identify changes or updates to files.

Remote procedure calls FRS requires both traditional IP connections and RPC to communicate with replication members and domain controllers in the domain.

How FRS Works with SYSVOL

FRS is tied to NTFS volumes in its functions and to Active Directory for its replication members and objects. FRS works through a series of processes that will occur on domain controllers as they are added to, updated, and removed from the domain.

When you install Active Directory, you use a tool called DCPROMO.exe. This tool will effectively promote the server to the status of domain controller and add the necessary components for Active Directory. This promotion follows a step-by-step process and results in the creation of a SYSVOL folder hierarchy and the ability of FRS to replicate that hierarchy. The process works like this:

1. DCPROMO sends notification to FRS to prepare for promotion. It FRS is already running on the server that is being promoted, then DCPROMO will stop FRS.

2. DCPROMO deletes any information from previous promotions or demotions from the associated registry keys.

3. The netlogon service stops sharing the SYSVOL shared folder, and the SYSVOLReady registry key is set to 0, meaning false.

4. DCPROMO creates the SYSVOL folder and the subfolders and junction points.

5. FRS is started.

6. DCPROMO makes a call to FRS to start a promotion thread that sets the necessary registry keys.

7. DCPROMO reboots the server.

8. After the server is restarted, FRS detects that the server is now a domain controller and then checks for the registry value SYSVOLInformationIsCommited entry. The entry is set to 0, meaning false. FRS will create the necessary Active Directory objects and then populate those objects with information from the registry.

9. FRS starts to source the SYSVOL content from the server that is identified in the ReplicaSet Parent registry entry. This is a temporary entry and will be removed after successful replication occurs.

10. When SYSVOL is finished replicating, FRS changes the SYSVOLReady registry entry to 1, meaning true, and the netlogon service shares the SYSVOL folder and publishes the computer as a domain controller.

Many of you are familiar with the process of building domain controllers using DCPROMO and have used the prestaging process to prevent the necessary action of the initial replication of Active Directory or SYSVOL information across the network. The question is whether this can be done with FRS. If so, what are the steps in the process?

PRESTAGING DOMAIN CONTROLLERS WITH FRS

First it is important to note that in order to prestage a domain controller, you will be required to restore a system state backup (which includes the SYSVOL information) to be used as a source for data when you promote a server to domain controller status on Windows Server 2003 or Windows Server 2008.

When it comes right down to it, the process of prestaging domain controllers is really based on using a piece of media to store a backup copy of system state data to be used as the source to create additional domain controllers. FRS is going to follow essentially the same process as in a traditional DCPROMO, with a few exceptions:

◆ FRS must have a constructed MD5 checksum data for the files in the SYSVOL tree. This MD5 checksum data is constructed after one of two events occurs: first after there are two or more domain controllers in the domain, and second if all data is moved to a nonreplicated folder outside SYSVOL and then moved back into SYSVOL after there are two or more domain controllers in the domain.

◆ The system state backup must contain all the files in SYSVOL. If any files in the system state backup are out-of-date, those files are replicated across the network to the new member, which really defeats the purpose of prestaging in the first place.

◆ The outbound log on the upstream replication partner must be cleared if SYSVOL is less than seven days old. The join process will attempt to optimize the connections and will not look for prestaged content. To work around this, you clear the outbound log on the upstream partners. It is important to note here that you will not want to clear the outbound log on bridgehead servers. This would significantly impact a bridgehead server's performance as it generates new connections for each pending transfer.

So, you have seen what happens when you promote a server to a domain controller. Let's review what the process looks like if you were to demote a domain controller. DCPROMO will perform the following steps:

1. DCPROMO stops FRS.

2. Old demotion state entries are removed from the registry (if there are any).

3. DCPROMO starts FRS.

4. DCPROMO binds to Active Directory using a different domain controller in the domain. This happens because demotion will invalidate the local domain controller, and so Active Directory relocation will not take place after the system restarts.

5. The Replica Set command registry entry is set to Delete.

6. DCPROMO instructs FRS to tombstone the SYSVOL replica set.

7. DCPROMO commits the demotion by stopping FRS and setting the service to Manual.

8. The SYSVOLReady registry entry is set to 0.

9. The NTFRS Subscription object and the NTFRS replica object are deleted for SYSVOL.

How Files and Folders Are Replicated

Files are the basic unit of replication. FRS uses NTFS volumes' USN journal to determine when a change has occurred to a file and triggers replication. Replication can occur immediately upon a change being recognized or can be initiated based on replication schedule. All changes with the exception of changes made to a file or folder's last access time, its archive bit, changes to encrypted files, or changes related to reparse points will trigger replication.

FRS monitors the USN journal for changes. When FRS detects a close record for a file, FRS gathers information about the recently closed file, including the file's attributes and its MD5 checksum.

FRS computes an MD5 checksum for the recently closed file. This checksum is calculated based on the file's data and security descriptors. If there is a change in the MD5 checksum value, then FRS will initiate the process of replication. There are some changes that can be made to files that will not affect the MD5 checksum such as saving an identical copy of a file over the top of an existing copy.

When it is determined that files or folders will be replicated, FRS follows this process:

1. When a file in a replica set is changed and closed, NTFS makes a journal entry in the USN journal.

2. FRS monitors the USN journals for changes. There is a three-second delay called the *aging cache* that is used to prevent replication if a file is undergoing rapid updates.

3. FRS creates entries in the inbound log and file ID table so that recovery can occur if the server should fail. The inbound log contains the change orders from all inbound partners. They are listed in the order in which they are received.

4. FRS creates the staging file in the staging folder.

5. FRS creates the entry in the outbound log, which is eventually sent to all of the outbound replication partners.

6. FRS sends change notifications.

7. FRS members record and acknowledge the change notification.

8. FRS replicates the staging file from the source server to the replication member.

9. The replication member uses restore APIs to restore the file from the preinstall folder and then renames the file or folder in the replica tree.

SCHEDULING REPLICATION

It is possible to set the schedule for SYSVOL replication. Before setting SYSVOL schedules in FRS, it is important to understand that the domain controllers that are members of the same site have a persistent or always-on connection between them, so there is no need to configure a replication schedule. SYSVOL schedules are configured only for connections between sites.

If you are configuring a SYSVOL schedule between sites, the schedule will be defined between two members in different sites and will occur at the beginning of 15-minute intervals. The connection is treated as a trigger schedule. The upstream partner ignores the schedule and responds to any request by the downstream partner. When the schedule closes, the upstream partner unjoins the connection only after the current contents of the outbound log, at the time of join, have been sent and acknowledged by the replica member.

The replication schedule can be configured to take place four, two, one, or zero times per hour:

◆ If the schedule is set to four times per hour, then replication will start at 0:00, 15, 30, and 45. This schedule is essentially the same as having continuous replication.

◆ If the schedule is set to two times per hour, then replication will start at 15 and 45.

◆ If the schedule is set to one time per hour, then replication will start at 0:00 and end at 15 assuming that all changes are replicated at that time.

CHANGING THE SYSVOL SCHEDULE

It is possible to change the SYSVOL schedule, but this should be done only after careful consideration of the potential effects on network bandwidth and synchronization. It is also important to note that a change to an NTDS connection object will become a manual connection that cannot be managed by KCC.

The New: Distributed File System Replication

As you learned earlier in this chapter, FRS has been used since the inception of Active Directory on Windows 2000 Server for SYSVOL replication to domain controllers throughout the Active Directory domain. Windows Server 2008 R2 introduces a new option for replicating SYSVOL throughout the domain. This new option is called Distributed File System Replication. DFSR is a state-based, multimaster replication engine that supports replication scheduling and bandwidth throttling.

DFSR uses a compression algorithm known as *Remote Differential Compression* (RDC). RDC is a "difference over the wire" protocol used to update clients and servers over the network. RDC detects insertions, removals, and modifications of data files and replicates only the changes to its replication partners, instead of the entire files. RDC can provide significant improvements to the replication of SYSVOL between domain controllers in your domain.

Understanding DFSR

Many of you are familiar with a technology called the Distributed File System (DFS). DFS is used to provide a single transparent namespace in which users can access shared resources located in diverse target locations throughout the network. This DFS namespace can be hosted in multiple locations. As its title suggests, it is truly a distributed file system. DFS is not new to Windows Server 2008 R2; it has been around for years. In fact, the DFS namespace is one of the two scenarios (along with SYSVOL replication) under which you will find FRS. When Windows Server 2008 R2 was released, Microsoft updated the way in which DFS replicated files and folders. Instead of using FRS, it included a new feature with DFS called DFSR. DFSR replaces FRS in DFS, as well as in SYSVOL replication in Active Directory domains where the domain functional level is at least Windows Server 2008.

RDC, described in the previous section, is great because as it detects changes in files and folders, instead of replicating the entire file or folder (which is what FRS did), it will replicate only the changes made to the file or folder. RDC can save a tremendous amount of network bandwidth during replication.

DFSR uses something called *replication groups* to replicate files and folders. A replication group is really just a set of servers where each of the servers is called a *member* of the group. Each member participates in the replication of one or more replicated folders. A replicated folder is a folder that stays synchronized on each member of the replication group. The topology, schedule, and bandwidth throttling for the replication group are applied to each replicated folder. Each replicated folder has unique settings, such as the file and folder filters, so that you can filter out files and subfolders for each replicated folder.

DFSR can be managed by using the DFS management tool or from the command line using DFSRADMIN, DFSRDIAG, DFSUTIL, DFSCMD, and DFSDIAG.

The gotcha with DFSR is that your domain controllers need to be at Windows Server 2008 or Windows Server 2008 R2. If you are still running Window Server 2003, or heaven forbid Windows 2000, you will be stuck with FRS until you can arrange to migrate to the newer-version domain controllers and migrate to DFSR.

Migrating to DFSR

So, the requirement for using DFSR is that your domain functional level is at least Windows Server 2008. This means a little more than getting all your domain controllers (DCs) to Windows Server 2008. You would think you could just upgrade your Windows Server 2003 DCs to Windows Server 2008 and you would be good to go. It just doesn't quite work that way. The migration process from FRS to DFSR actually works through a number of "states," during which SYSVOL replication transitions from FRS replication to DFSR. The steps and states are each clearly defined in the following section.

MIGRATION STATES

The migration process involves setting migration rules on the domain controller that is the primary domain controller emulator (PDC emulator) and waiting for other domain controllers to act on those rules. Migration states can be defined as local to the DC or global to the DCs in the domain.

The global migration state is set with the dfsrmig command-line utility, which is used for setting one of the phases of the migration process. This setting is made in Active Directory and then is replicated to all domain controllers.

Each domain controller has its own local migration state. DFSR on each DC polls Active Directory to determine the global migration state to which the DC should migrate. If the global migration state is different from the local migration state, then DFSR will attempt to move the local state to match the global state. The local migration state can be any one of the stable states or the transition states.

The SYSVOL migration proceeds through four primary states (usually called *stable states*) and six temporary states (usually called *transition states*). The transition states lead a DC to the stable states.

Stable States

There are four stable states, or phases, to SYSVOL migration from FRS to DFSR. The states are called *start*, *prepared*, *redirected*, and *eliminated*. They are also referenced by ordinal numbers from 0 to 3, respectively:

Start (state 0) Before the SYSVOL migration begins, FRS replicates the shared SYSVOL folder.

Prepared (state 1) FRS still replicates the shared SYSVOL folder that the domain uses, while DFSR replicates a copy of the shared SYSVOL folder. This copy of SYSVOL is not used to service requests from other DCs.

Redirected (state 2) The DFSR copy of SYSVOL becomes responsible for servicing requests from other DCs. FRS continues to replicate the original SYSVOL folder, but DFSR now replicates the production SYSVOL folder that the DCs in the redirected state use.

Eliminated (state 3) DFSR continues to handle all the SYSVOL replication. Windows deletes the original SYSVOL folder, and FRS no longer replicates SYSVOL data.

You will use the dfsrmig command during the migration to step through the four stable states. There are some visible changes that occur during the process:

1. The migration process creates a copy of the SYSVOL folder. FRS replicates the original SYSVOL folder located at c:\windows\SYSVOL. DFSR replicates the copy of the SYSVOL folder located at c:\windows\SYSVOL_dfsr.

2. The mapping of the SYSVOL shared folder changes from FRS to DFSR. Originally the SYSVOL shared folder mapping, c:\windows\SYSVOL is used for the information that is actively replicated by FRS. Later in the migration process, the SYSVOL shared folder location will be mapped to c:\windows\SYSVOL_dfsr, and the information actively used by Active Directory will be replicated by DFSR.

3. The migration process will delete the original copy of the SYSVOL folder.

Transition States

Each domain controller will also cycle through a series of transition states as they are moving from one stable state to another. There are five transition states, and the states are numbered from 4 through 9. The states each have names that explain exactly what is occurring during the transition:

- Preparing (state 4)
- Waiting for initial synchronization (state 5)
- Redirecting (state 6)
- Eliminating (state 7)
- Undo redirecting (state 8)
- Undo preparing (state 9)

Figure 12.1 shows the process of migration through the four stable states and the transition states involved between each stable state.

FIGURE 12.1
The boxes show the stable states, and the numbered circles illustrate the transition states.

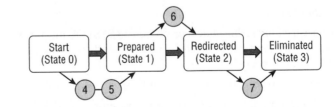

HOW DOES STATE MIGRATION WORK?

You are probably wondering exactly how DFSR migrates between states. Remember that the DFSR service on each DC polls Active Directory for the current global migration state. If the global state is different from the local state on the DC, then DFSR takes steps (transitional states) to match the state of the global state.

When you are ready to migrate the domain controllers in your domain to DFSR, all the domain controllers will begin at the start state. You will open a command prompt and use the `dfsrmig` tool to move your domain controllers from the start state to the eliminated state. The cool thing about this migration process is that not only can you move forward through the migration process, but you can also go backward if need be, as long as you have not completed step 3, the elimination.

For example, maybe you are working along and your DC is at the prepared state and you decide you need to move back to the start state, for whatever reason. You can use the `dfsrmig` tool and change the state back to start.

It is important to know that once you have moved to state 3, there is no going back. The migration will be complete at that point. The original SYSVOL will be deleted. There is no going back from eliminated.

You will want to methodically move from state to state as you migrate from FRS to DFSR.

MIGRATING TO THE PREPARED STATE

Before you actually get to the process of migrating anything, you will need to meet some requirements. Remember that in order to use DFSR, your domain will need to be raised to the functional level of Windows Server 2008. This means that each of your domain controllers will need to be Windows Server 2008 or Windows Server 2008 R2. If you are still using domain controllers from the 2000 or 2003 families, you are not quite ready for DFSR.

Verifying Active Directory

Before you raise the domain functional level to Windows 2008, you should check the health of Active Directory and verify that the existing SYSVOL is replicating correctly. If Active Directory replication is not working the way it should, then you need to take care of that problem before you try to migrate. A failure on a single domain controller could be perpetuated to the rest of the domain. This is your chance to address any existing issues with AD. Do the following:

1. Microsoft recommends that you use the `net share` command to verify that the SYSVOL folder is shared by each domain controller and that this share folder still maps to the SYSVOL folder that FRS is replicating. When you type the **net share** command, the output will display the share names for the `netlogon` share and the SYSVOL share along with their respective current directory locations.

2. You will want to make certain that you have sufficient disk space to make a copy of your SYSVOL folder structure.

3. Use the Ultrasound tool to monitor FRS and verify its functionality. It can be downloaded free of charge at http://go.microsoft.com/fwlink/?linkid=121859.

4. On one of the domain controllers of the domain, open a command prompt, and type **repadmin /replsum**. This command will verify that Active Directory replication is working properly. The output should not indicate any errors. If it does, take the opportunity to correct them before you continue.

5. Using the registry editor on each domain controller in the domain, navigate to HKEY_LOCAL_MACHINE\System\CurrentControlSet\Services\Netlogon\Parameters, and verify

the value of the SYSVOL Registry entry is drive:|\windows_folder\SYSVOL\SYSVOL and that the value of the SYSVOLReady registry entry is set to 1.

6. On each domain controller, go to the Services tool, and verify that the DFS Replication service is started and that the startup type is set to Automatic.

Raising the Domain Functional Level

Now that you have taken the steps to ensure the functionality of Active Directory, FRS, and SYSVOL, and you have checked the registry for the right entries and settings, you are now ready to raise the domain functional level to Windows Server 2008 (see Figure 12.2).

To raise the domain functional level to Windows Server 2008, perform the following steps:

1. Open Active Directory Domains and Trusts.

2. Right-click the domain, and click Raise Domain Functional Level.

3. In the domain functional level box, select Windows Server 2008.

4. Click Raise.

5. In the warning message box, click OK.

6. In the confirmation box, click OK.

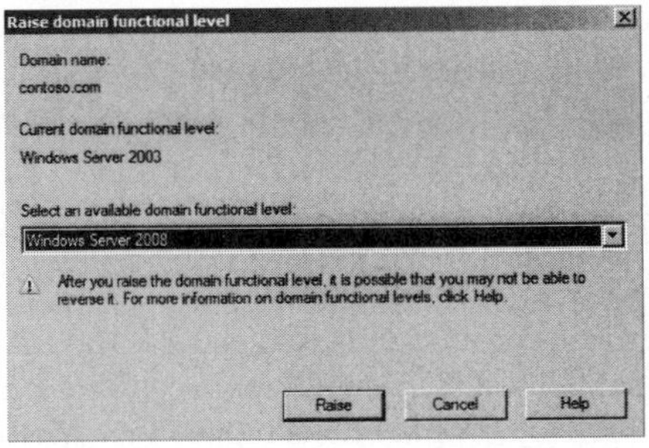

FIGURE 12.2
Raising the domain
functional level

Each time you move from one state to the next, you will do a series of verification activities. Once these activities are complete, then you make the move to the next state. In this case, you have verified Active Directory and SYSVOL for functionality. You have checked the registry and raised the domain functional level. There is one detail left before you make the migration to the prepared state, and that's a backup. At this point, it is time to make certain that you have a good current backup of your system state data. If things go really, really wrong, you want to be able to get back to this point. So, take a few minutes to make, and verify, a system state backup. You are now ready to migrate to the prepared state.

Performing the Migration

The process of migrating from the starting state to the prepared state is a short one. You will need to open a command prompt and type the following command:

```
dfsrmig /setglobalstate 1
```

That's it. See Figure 12.3 for the output.

FIGURE 12.3
Command-line
output from
setting the
global state

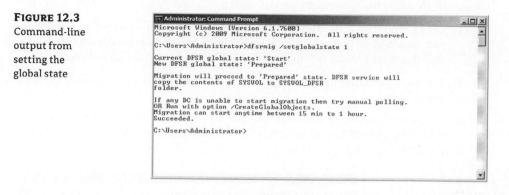

At this point, you will need to verify that the global migration state has been updated. To do this, you will again use the command prompt and type the following command:

```
dfsrmig /getglobalstate
```

This command will return the current global state with a message indicating success (see Figure 12.4).

FIGURE 12.4
Output of
getglobalstate
command

There is one last command to verify that all the domain controllers in the domain have moved to the prepared state:

```
dfsrmig /getmigrationstate
```

Remember that this command can take some time before it comes back with the message that all domain controllers in the domain have migrated to the prepared state (see Figure 12.5). Active Directory takes time to replicate, so be patient.

Now that you have set the process in motion for moving to the prepared state, you will want to verify that the domain has properly migrated to this state before you move to the next phase of the migration process. There are very simple steps you can perform to make certain you have successfully made the move to the prepared state:

1. On each domain controller in the domain, you can open a command prompt and type **net share** to verify that SYSVOL is shared by each domain controller in the domain and that the shared folder still maps to the SYSVOL folder that FRS is replicating.

2. Use the Ultrasound tool to verify that FRS on the original shared folder remains operational.

3. Check the file system, and verify the creation of the new SYSVOL_DFSR in the c:\windows\SYSVOL_dfsr and that the contents of the original SYSVOL have been copied there (see Figure 12.6).

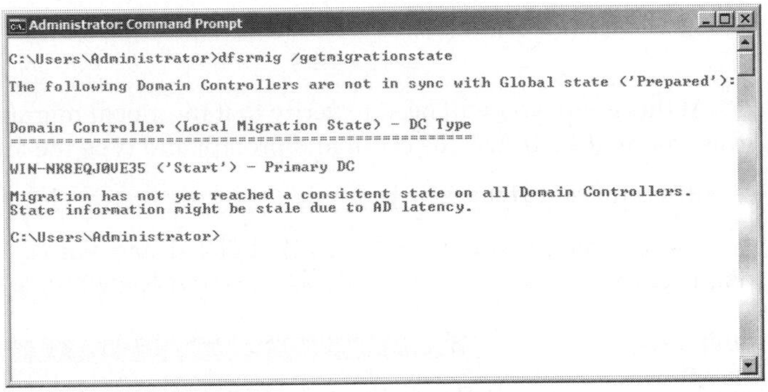

FIGURE 12.5
Output from getmigrationstaate command

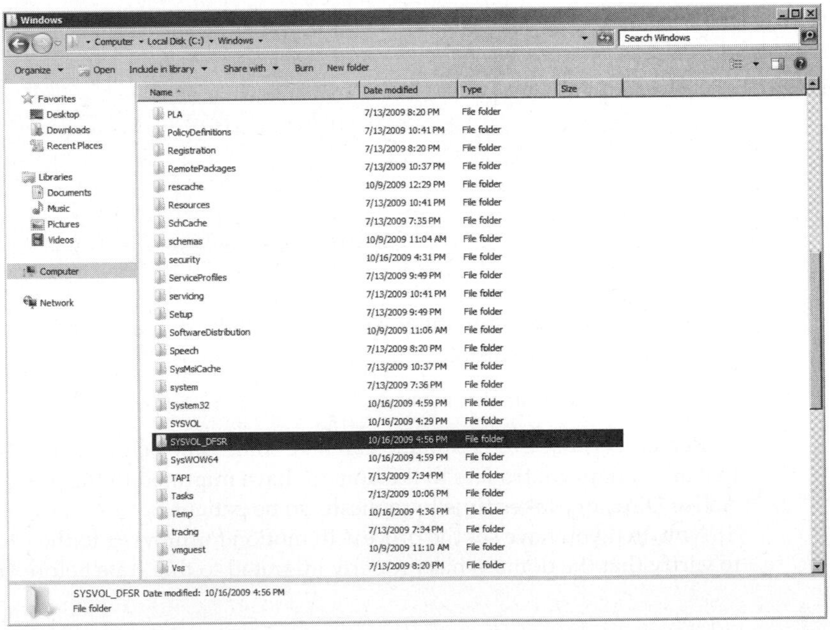

FIGURE 12.6
The new SYSVOL_DFSR folder

4. Use the DFS management tool to generate a diagnostic report. If you do not already have the DFS management tool installed, you can add it as a feature under Remote Server Administration Tools and File Services in Server Manager.

When you use the DFS Manager snap-in, it is possible to run two types of diagnostic reports called the *general health report* and the *propagation report*. You should really run both of the reports and review them to check for problems (see Figure 12.7).

To generate the reports, use the following steps:

1. Open the DFS Manager.

2. In the console tree under the Replication node, click Domain System Volume.

3. Click the Membership tab.

4. Click Membership Status.

5. Verify that the Enabled box is selected for a local path of `c:\windows\SYSVOL_dfsr\ yourdomain`.

6. Right-click System Volume.

7. Click Create Diagnostic Report.

FIGURE 12.7
Creating DFS
Manager reports

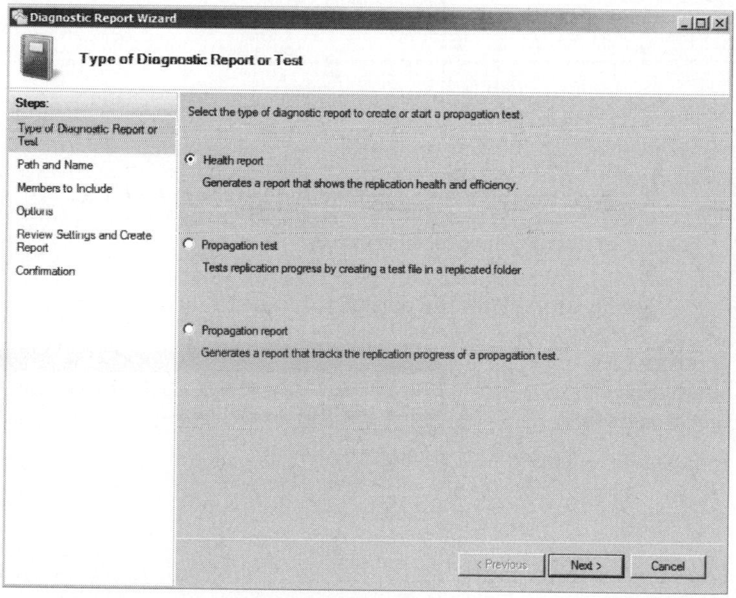

When you have verified the successful move of your DCs to the prepared state, you are ready to move on to the redirected state.

MIGRATING TO THE REDIRECTED STATE

After verifying that your DCs are successfully working in the prepared state, you are ready to move them to the redirected state. In the redirected state, DFSR will take on the responsibility of replicating the SYSVOL folder for the domain. There are two parts to this piece of the migration process. First you will migrate to the redirected state, and then you will verify that the domain has successfully migrated to the redirected state.

To migrate the domain to the redirected state, you will perform the following tasks:

1. Type the following command at the command line:

   ```
   dfsrmig /setglobalstate 2
   ```

   See Figure 12.8 for the output.

FIGURE 12.8
Output of the
setglobalstate
2 command

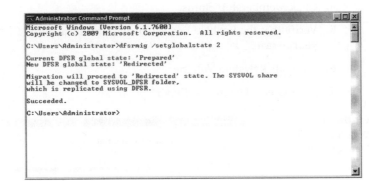

2. Type the following command at the command line:

   ```
   dfsrmig /getglobalstate
   ```

   See Figure 12.9 for the output.

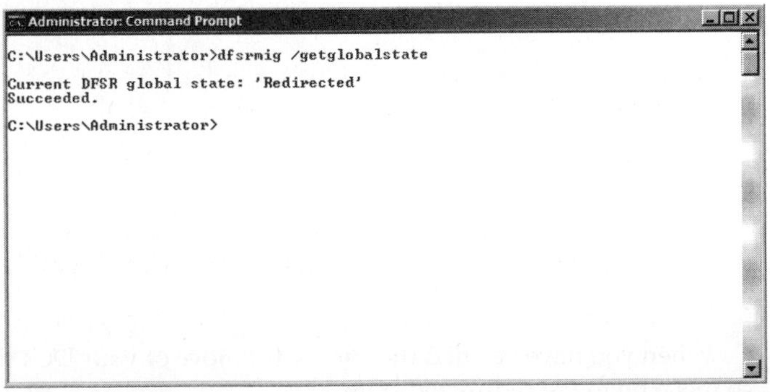

FIGURE 12.9
Output of
getglobalstate

3. Type **dfsrmig /getmigrationstate** to confirm that all DCs in the domain have reached the redirected state (see Figure 12.10).

FIGURE 12.10

Output of the
getmigrationstate
command

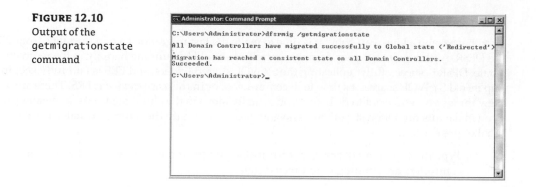

At this point, you have successfully completed the steps necessary to migrate the domain to the redirected state; however, before you move ahead to the eliminated state, you will want to verify that the domain has successfully moved to the redirected state. To verify successful migration into this state, you should do the following:

1. Open a command prompt, and type **netshare**. The output of this command will show you the new SYSVOL_DFSR share in its authoritative state, as shown in Figure 12.11.

FIGURE 12.11

New SYSVOL
folder location

2. Use the DFS management tool to create another set of diagnostic reports just like you did in the verification of the prepared state.

3. Use the Ultrasound tool to verify that the FRS replication of the original SYSVOL folder is healthy. You will recall that DFSR is actually responsible for the domain replication of the new SYSVOL folder share; however, it is important to verify the functionality of the FRS replication process should you want to go back to the prepared state.

When you have verified that the domain controllers in your domain have successfully made the migration to the redirected state, you can then make the final move to the eliminated state.

MIGRATING TO THE ELIMINATED STATE

You have come a long way, baby! It is time to make the last migration step in the move from FRS to DFSR. At this point, all your domain controllers should be running happily in the redirected state. DFSR is successfully replicating the SYSVOL shared folders, and FRS is faithfully keeping up its old SYSVOL shares. It's time to decommission, or in this case *eliminate*, FRS. There are a few things you will want to do before you actually move to the eliminated state. Remember, once you make this migration step, there is no going back. So, verify the redirected state once more to make sure everything is working:

1. Type the command **dfsrmig /getmigrationstate**, and make certain all your domain controllers are running in redirected state.

2. Type the command **repadmin /replsum** to verify that Active Directory replication is working properly. Make sure there are no errors.

3. Save the state of the Active Directory just in case you should need to recover from backup.

If you are satisfied that your domain is functioning as desired in the redirected state, then it is time to migrate to the eliminated state. Perform the following steps on the domain controller:

1. Type the command **dfsrmig /setglobalstate 3** (see Figure 12.12).

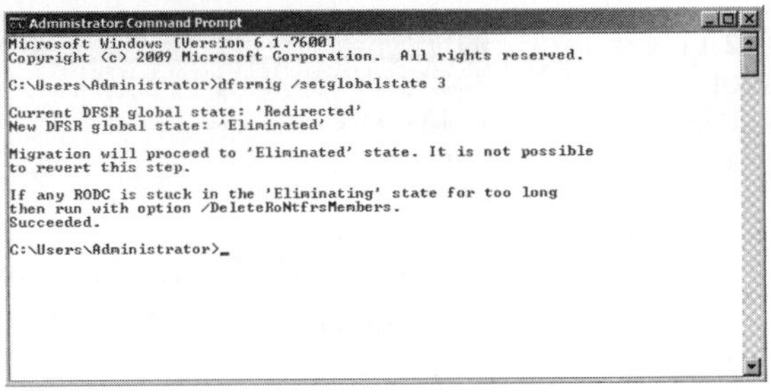

FIGURE 12.12
Output of setglobalstate command

2. Type **dfsrmig /getglobalstate** to verify that the global state is eliminated (see Figure 12.13).

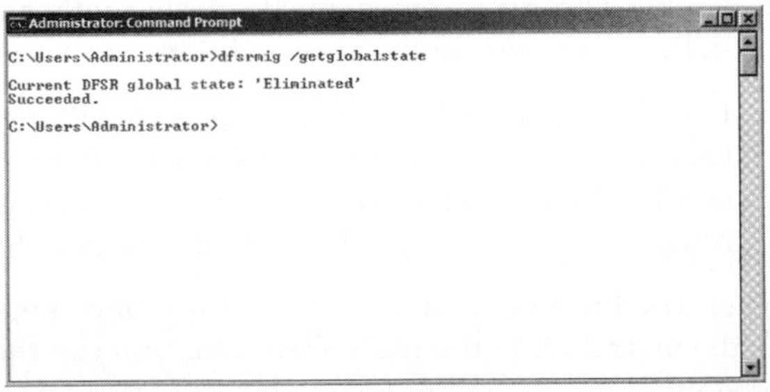

FIGURE 12.13
Output of getglobalstate

3. Type **dfsrmig /getmigrationstate** to confirm that all domain controllers in the domain have successfully migrated (see Figure 12.14).

FIGURE 12.14
Output of
getmigrationstate

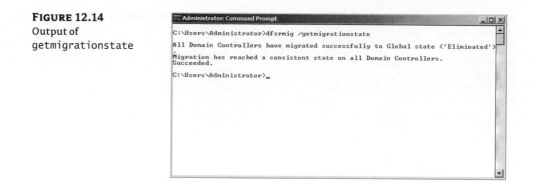

4. On each domain controller you will need to open a command prompt and type **net share** to verify the SYSVOL shared folder location (see Figure 12.15).

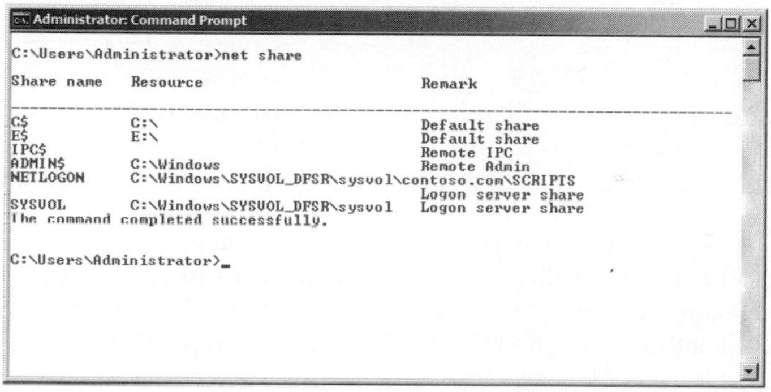

FIGURE 12.15
Final output of
the net share
command

5. Use the DFS Manager to generate the same general diagnostic and propagation reports you created in the prepared and redirected state verifications.

6. On each domain controller, you will need to open Windows Explorer and verify that the c:\windows\SYSVOL shared folder has been removed. It is OK if some of the folders stay resident; however, you will want to ensure that they are empty of any contents. The idea is to have only the new SYSVOL_DFSR structure, as shown in Figure 12.16.

Last but not least, if you are not using FRS for anything else, you can remove it from your system. To remove FRS, you can do the following:

1. Open Server Manager.

2. Select and expand Roles.

3. Right-click File Services, and select Remove.

4. Clear the File Replication Service check box, and click Next.

5. Click Remove.

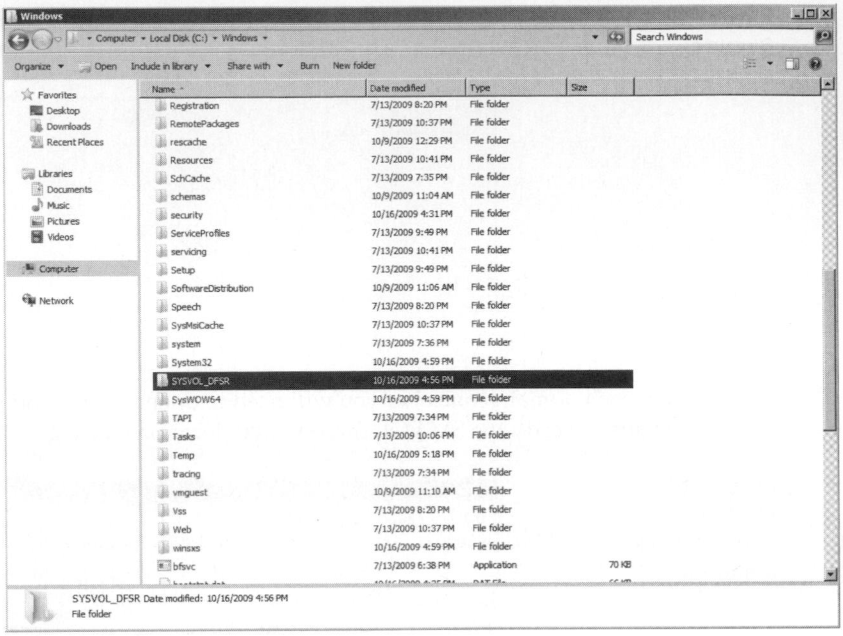

FIGURE 12.16
Eliminated state
file system with
no old SYSVOL
directory

With that stroke, you have successfully migrated your SYSVOL replication infrastructure from FRS to DFSR and garnered all the benefits of remote differential compression. You have taken something that is truly old in the SYSVOL folder and FRS replication and migrated it to something new in SYSVOL_DFSR and DFS replication.

The Bottom Line

Understand the File Replication Service   In the old world of SYSVOL (everything up until Windows Server 2008 R2), the duties of replicating the shared SYSVOL folder were handled by the File Replication Service. Any domain that has a domain functional level of Windows 2008, or later, can be migrated to DFSR.

> **Master It**   You have decided to adjust the replication schedule for FRS in your network. You are interested in setting the replication to occur continuously. Which replication setting would you choose?

Migrate to Distribute File System Replication   If you desire the benefits of remote differential compression displayed in DFSR, you can migrate your domain replication method from FRS to DFSR. This migration will occur in a series of four standard states: start, prepared, redirected, and eliminated.

> **Master It**   Use the Active Directory Domains and Trusts tool to move your domain to the Windows Server 2008 functional level.

Discover the current migration state of a domain controller using the dfsrmig **command-line utility** The process of migrating from the start state to the eliminated state is handled only by using the dfsrmig command-line utility. This utility is used to set the global state and to get the global migration state. This utility is used to move the process of migration forward and backward through its stages.

Master It Use dfsrmig to discover the current migration state of a domain controller.

🌐 Real World Scenario

MAKING THE TRANSITION: MIGRATING FROM FRS REPLICATION TO DFS REPLICATION

Henley Outdoor Products is a (hypothetical) medium-sized business with several domain controllers located in several geographical locations throughout the United States. Henley has domain controllers running the Windows Server 2003 and Windows Server 2008 operating systems. The domain functional level is set at 2003. Henley is currently using FRS to replicate SYSVOL information to the various domain controllers throughout the domain. The FRS replication schedule is set to continuous. The company uses several group policies and makes regular updates to these policies. LAN replication works without incident, although the IT staff would like to decrease the amount of traffic generated at each replication. The replication across WAN links has become an increasing issue as the company looks to maximize bandwidth and minimize its expenditures.

The Henley Outdoor Products IT team upgrades its Windows Server 2003 DCs to Windows Server 2008 R2 and moves the domain functional level to Windows Server 2008. After some discussion of the benefits of DFSR Replication and RDC, Henley decides to migrate from FRS replication to DFS Replication. They are particularly excited about the potential bandwidth savings that they will incur from the RDC.

The IT team coordinates a concerted migration strategy to migrate from the starting state (state 0) to the eliminated state (state 3). Using the dfsrmig command-line tool, they work through the migration process. At each phase of the migration, the team validates the operation of both FRS and DFSR, until they arrive at a completed eliminated state. The IT team removes FRS from their domain controllers. DFSR remains as the replication service responsible for replicating the SYSVOL folder throughout the domain.

DFSR using RDC produces significant reductions in replication traffic on both the WAN and LAN networks. Henley Outdoor Products continues to monitor replication traffic and look for ways to maximize network utilization while minimizing replication traffic.

Chapter 13

Sharing Printers on Windows Server 2008 R2 Networks

If your company has unlimited funds, it can afford to purchase a print device for every user. Can you imagine that? A print device on every desk? Neither can we. Even in the best of times, profitable companies wouldn't be so wasteful.

Instead, a company will often identify a ratio of print devices to people such as one printer for every five, ten, or twenty people. Not only do they save on the cost of the print devices, but they save on electricity and maintenance.

And, for better efficiency managing these printers, they are often hosted on print servers. A single print server can host hundreds of printers.

With Windows Server 2008 R2, you can add the Print and Document Services role, which comes with the Print Management console. Not only does this optimize the server to serve print jobs for end users, but the Print Management console allows you to manage multiple print servers from a central location.

In this chapter, you will learn to:

◆ Add the Print and Document Services role

◆ Manage printers using the Print Management console

◆ Manage print server properties

◆ Manage printer properties

Print Services Overview

Most of your users believe that a *printer* is the putty-colored box sitting within walking distance of their cubicles that they put paper into and create printed documents. But we all know that in the arcane world of systems administration, a printer is a logical software component that's an intermediary between user applications and the *print device*. All configuration settings apply to printers, not to print devices.

The ratio of printers to print devices is not necessarily one to one. You can have one printer and one print device, two printers for a single print device, or one printer and several print devices. We'll talk about *why* you might want to do any of these in the course of this chapter.

When you send documents to a printer, they become part of the printer's *queue*, the group of documents waiting to be printed. Documents wait in the queue until the print device is available to accept the print job.

Most people on your network won't have their own print device on their desk. Instead, users typically print to a network-accessible printer. This printer can be accessible directly on the network or available via a print server (the focus of this chapter).

Take a look at Figure 13.1 to see the different ways print devices can be configured on a network. Print device 1 is connected directly to a USB port on Sally's computer. This isn't considered a network printer unless Sally shares it. However, even if she shares it, the print device wouldn't be shared by the print server but instead by Sally's computer. In this context, Sally's computer is acting as a print server, even if she's just running Windows 7.

FIGURE 13.1

Print devices on a network

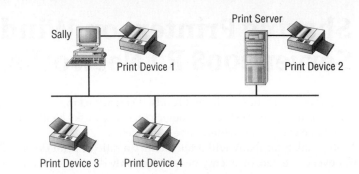

Print Device 1
Print Server
Print Device 2
Print Device 3
Print Device 4
Sally

Print device 2 is directly connected to the print server and would be shared by the print server, so it considered a network printer. Since print devices 3 and 4 are connected directly to the network, they are also considered network printers. Print devices 3 and 4 both must have NICs that can be assigned IP addresses to be accessible on the network.

What's not clear in Figure 13.1 is whether print devices 3 and 4 are being served by the print server. One could be, and the other could be a stand-alone network printer. Let's say that the print server is configured to serve print jobs for print device 3. All users would send their print jobs to the print server, and the print server would manage the queue for print device 3.

On the other hand, let's say that the print server is not configured to serve print jobs for print device 4. Users would instead need to configure the print device individually on each of their systems, and jobs would be sent directly to the print device instead of to the server. Print device 4 wouldn't have any of the benefits of the print server such as automatically downloading print jobs, controlling access to printers with permissions or schedules, or managing queues, unless this functionality is built into the device's software.

This chapter is focused on using a Windows Server 2008 R2 server as a print server. If the print devices are just connected to the network and not served by a printer, they are on their own.

The process of printing with Windows Server 2008 R2 is a bit more complex than it looks from the outside. The printing model uses several components to render application data for graphical output, get the data to a printer, and then help the printer manage multiple print jobs. Some of the following information on *how* printing works is background, but it's also helpful when it comes to troubleshooting.

The Print Spooler

Computers are much quicker than print devices. No surprise there. However, years ago, when print jobs were sent to print devices, the computer slowed to the speed of the print device until the entire print job was completed. During this time, the user wasn't able to do anything else with the computer.

🌐 Real World Scenario

WORKING WITHOUT A PRINT SERVER

We have spent a lot of time working in organizations that do not use print servers. Instead, print devices are placed directly on the network with an IP address, and each computer then needs to be configured to use the print device.

One of the significant drawbacks to this method is that users often have problems connecting to the print device and installing the correct driver. They'd have to learn the printer's IP address to connect, and even then, the wrong driver can be selected, resulting in useless printouts. The help desk is called, and unless the help-desk professional knows exactly what driver is needed, she often has to go on a driver hunt.

When a print server is used, users just need to use the universal naming convention (UNC) path of the printer (\\serverName\shareName) when adding it. The server will then automatically download the correct driver. As an example, a printer could be shared as Laser1 on a server named BF1, and users would only need to connect to \\BF1\Laser1 to automatically download the correct driver for their operating system. Additionally, if the print device is moved to a different subnet, only the server needs to be reconfigured, not every client.

The trade-off is the cost of the print server and associated maintenance. However, since servers can easily share roles, file servers often act as print servers too.

You can bet this irritated many users, so the *print spooler* was developed. Now, when print jobs are sent by the user, the print spooler service accepts the print job and stores it in memory or on the hard drive until the print device can accept it. If you print a document, you can almost immediately begin working on something else, even if it takes 10 minutes for your document to print.

When users print documents to a printer served by a print server, two spoolers are actually involved. The spooler service on the user's computer spools the document (usually only to memory) and then sends the spooled job to the print server. When the print server receives the print job, it also spools it. Since the print server may be working on other jobs, it will usually spool print jobs to the hard drive.

The default folder for spooled documents is C:\Windows\System322\Spool\Printers. You'll see how you can change this later in this chapter.

The Printer Driver

Printer drivers are the software that enables the operating system to communicate with a printer and ultimately send the print job to the print device. Print drivers have been unified in recent years, making them a little easier to work with. You'll come across three primary print drivers:

Itanium	Type 3 – User Mode
x64	Type 3 – User Mode
x86	Type 3 – User Mode

Notice that each of these is referred to as Type 3 – User Mode drivers. Drivers before Windows 2000 were referred to as version 2 Kernel mode drivers. They would interact with the kernel of the operating system and had the potential of crashing the system if something went wrong.

Type 3 drivers work only in user mode and are isolated from the operating system. Itanium is a special 64-bit architecture used in high-end servers. x64 indicates a 64-bit architecture, and x86 indicates a 32-bit architecture. The good news about this is that you can install an x86 Type 3—User Mode driver, and it will work with any 32-bit operating system—at least it should. You may run into problems if you're still running something like Windows 98.

Thankfully, you can load all three print drivers onto a Windows Server 2008 R2 server, and when different systems connect, the correct driver will automatically be downloaded. However, you'll still need to ensure the correct drivers are loaded on the server. In other words, if you're supporting 32-bit Windows XP and 64-bit Windows 7 clients, you'll need to ensure you have both x86 and x64 drivers.

PRINTER DRIVER HUNTS

Finding the correct print drivers (especially for new operating systems) is often very challenging. In a perfect world, as soon as a new operating system is released, every company would automatically have the correct driver so their hardware will work. However, a lot of things work against this scenario. Companies may create a print driver that works with the release candidate of an OS only to see that last-minute changes to the operating system result in their driver no longer working.

Of course, when a company realizes its driver no longer works, it tweaks and reengineers. And then it posts the new driver on its website as quickly as possible. However, the driver needs to be tested and validated before it's included with the operating system or available through Windows Update.

Meanwhile, users who have upgraded to a new OS realize that they can no longer print. They try Windows Update (which includes only those drivers that have gone through the lengthy submission and testing process) with no joy. Educated users (and administrators) know the best source in this situation is to go to the manufacturer's website.

They go to the manufacturer website, which may or may not have the correct driver listed, and often a lengthy game of trial and error is started until the user (or administrator) either finds something that will work or gives up. This was very apparent when Windows Vista came out and resulted in a lot of complaints from users.

As a last resort, if you find the manufacturer hasn't posted a new 64-bit driver, check out Microsoft's paper on using substitute drivers at www.microsoft.com/windowsserver2003/ techinfo/overview/x64printdriver.mspx. Even though the article was targeted for Windows 2003, it still applies to Windows Server 2008.

XML PAPER SPECIFICATION (XPS)

The XML Paper Specification (XPS) emerged with Windows Vista and Windows Server 2008. Updates have since been released for Windows XP and Server 2003 to make XPS backward compatible with these older operating systems.

XPS ON THE INTERNET

Microsoft has embraced XPS and has published a lot of material detailing how it is used in Microsoft products. The XPS home page is at www.microsoft.com/whdc/xps/default.mspx. Additionally, ECMA International is the driving force for standardizing XPS across multiple platforms. You can access details from meetings and available documents at www.ecma-international.org/memento/TC46-M.htm.

XPS is based on Extensible Markup Language (XML), an industry standard that has been steadily creeping into many current technologies including databases, web services, and now printing. HTML (used for web pages) is based on XML. XML data is contained in a simple text document that can be read with simple applications such as Notepad, and it can be used to hold a significant amount of data and metadata.

Metadata is used to describe the data. For example, metadata within a print document might be used to identify all the data on page 1, page 2, and so on. It could also be used to describe how the data should be displayed such as the font style or size.

Microsoft has embraced the XPS document format based on the Open XML Markup Compatibility specifications and Open Packaging Conventions (OPC). The vision is for much better efficiency, compatibility with more applications, and higher document quality when XPSDrv printer drivers are used.

XPS is similar in concept to the Portable Document Format (PDF) created by Adobe Systems for document exchange. We're betting that you've opened a few PDF documents during your travels since PDF documents are so widely used today. The cool thing about a PDF document is that the person who creates the document can control what it looks like when it prints. Compare this to a simple Word document that may print one way on one printer but another way on another printer.

You can create XPS documents from within Microsoft Office 2007, and these documents can be shared just as PDF files. Select Save As ➤ XPS Document to save your document in this format. Users who have an XPS view can view the documents, just as users can view PDF files if they have a matching version of Adobe Reader. In addition to saving files in the XPS format, documents can be translated to the XPS format so that they can be used by XPSDrv printer drivers.

XPSDRV: THE NEW PRINTER DRIVER MODEL

Print drivers created to take advantage of the new XPS format are referred to as XPSDrv printer drivers. These drivers provide greater flexibility than the older Graphics Device Interface (GDI) graphics processing functions that were used before XPSDrv printer drivers.

XPSDrv printer drivers use the XPS document format to provide a better what-you-see-is-what-you-get (WYSIWYG) output from printers. A greater range of colors can be used, and other graphic outputs such as transparent areas and gradients are possible.

Since the XPSDrv printer drivers use the XPS format and the XPS format produces smaller spooled files than the GDI format, the overall size of spooled printer files is reduced.

THE GRAPHICS DEVICE INTERFACE

GDI is the portion of the operating system that begins the process of producing visual output, whether that output is to the screen or to the printer. GDI has historically been used to produce WYSIWYG output to both the screen and the printed page. To produce screen output, the GDI calls the video driver; to produce printed output, the GDI calls the printer driver providing information about the print device needed and the type of data used.

Although GDI-based printer drivers are being replaced with XPSDrv-based printer drivers, you may still come across the older GDI-based printer drivers for a while.

Now that you have a little bit of an overview on print services, let's jump into the Print and Document Services role.

Installing the Print and Document Services Role

The Print and Document Services role is added to your server when you want it to become a print server. When you add this role, you'll have the option of adding several different services depending on what you want the print server to do:

Print Server The Print Server service includes the Print Management console that you'll use for the majority of management tasks on the print server. You can manage multiple printers and even multiple print servers through this snap-in. This is the primary service of a print server and is the focus of this chapter.

LPD Service If your organization includes Unix-based computers that will need to print to print devices served by your print server, you can add the Line Printer Daemon (LPD) service. The LPD service will allow any clients using the Line Printer Remote (LPR) service to print to printers shared on the print server.

Internet Printing The Internet Printing Protocol (IPP) can be used to allow clients that have the Internet Printing client installed to use a web browser to connect and print to printers shared on your server. Adding this service will also create a website where users can manage print jobs on the server instead of using the print console.

Distributed Scan Server This service allows the server to receive scanned documents from scanners on the network and route them to the correct destinations. When you add this service, it will also include the Scan Management snap-in.

Adding the Print and Document Services Role

The Print and Document Services role is fairly simple to install using Server Manager. The only choices you need to make are what services to add, and this will be decided based on what the clients are doing. You can use the following steps to add the Print and Document Services role to a Windows Server 2008 R2 server:

1. Launch Server Manager by selecting Start ➤ Administrative Tools ➤ Server Manager.

2. Select Roles, and click the Add Roles link.

3. Review the information on the Before You Begin page, and click Next.

4. On the Select Server Roles page, select Print and Document Services. Your display will look similar to Figure 13.2. Click Next.

FIGURE 13.2
Adding the Print
and Document
Services role

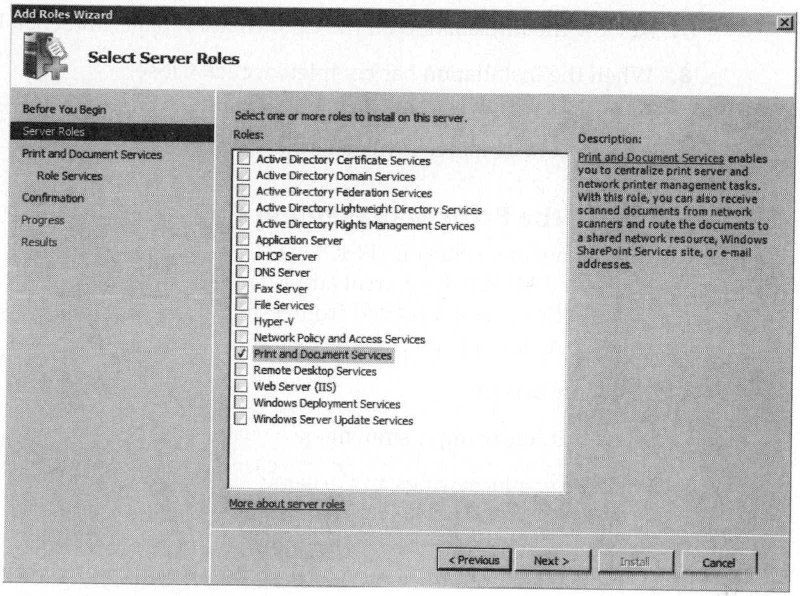

5. Review the information on the Introduction to Print and Document Services page, and click Next.

6. On the Select Role Services page, ensure the Print Server service is selected. Your display will similar to Figure 13.3. Click Next.

FIGURE 13.3
Adding the Print
Server service

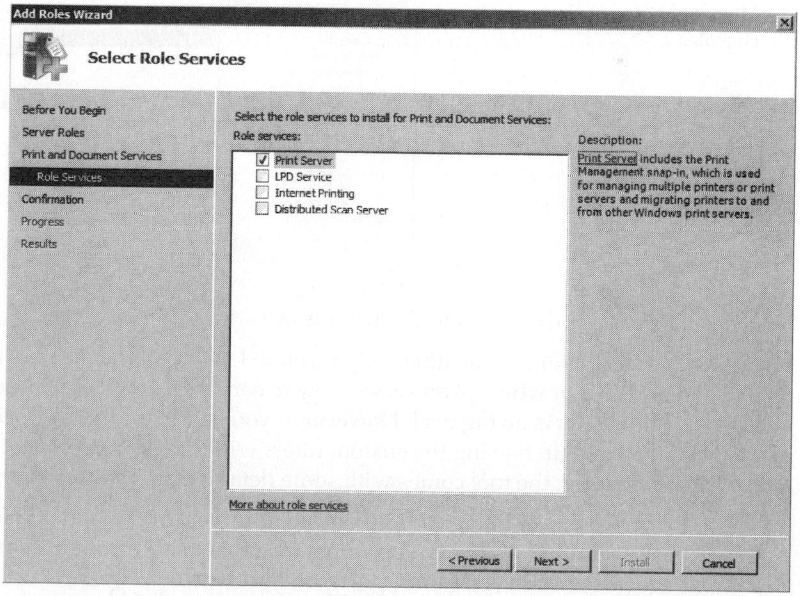

7. Review the information on the Confirmation page, and click Install.

8. When the installation has completed, click Close.

Once you've added the Print and Document Services role, you can access the Print Management console—your central source to manage all printing tasks.

Working in the Print Management Console

The Print Management console (PMC) was introduced in Windows Server 2003 R2 (that's not a typo—Server 2003 R2). It's a great addition to the operating system interface, finally allowing you to do *everything* printer related from a single console. It allows you to do just about anything with printers and other print servers, including the following:

◆ Add new drivers

◆ View printers using custom filters

◆ Manage printer settings and drivers

◆ Monitor printer status and configure alerts

◆ Connect to remote print servers so you can do all this for your entire enterprise

With the Print and Document Services role added to your server, you can launch the PMC by selecting Start ➢ Administrative Tools ➢ Print Management. It will look similar to Figure 13.4. It's also possible to view the PMC via Server Manager in the Roles node.

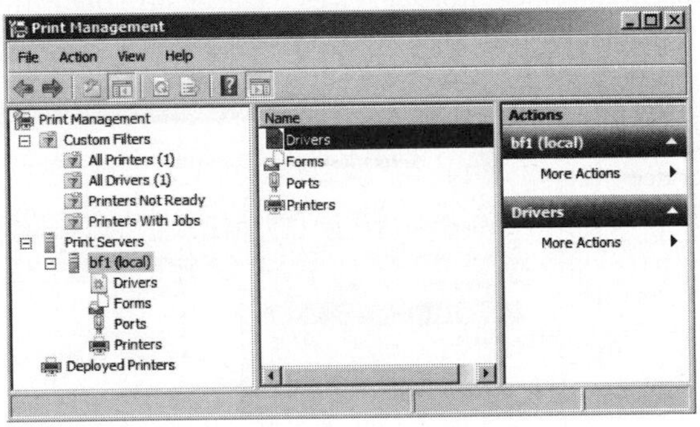

FIGURE 13.4
Viewing the Print
Management
console

The PMC is divided into three main sections:

Custom Filters   The filters allow you to look at all the printers managed from this console, regardless of which print server they're connected to. If a print server hosts just five print devices, this is no big deal. However, if you have hundreds of print devices connected, the ability to search using the custom filters will make your job a lot easier. As you'll see later in this chapter, the tool comes with some default filters, but you can also create your own.

Print Servers   In Figure 13.4, one print server (bf1) is added. However, if your organization has several print servers, you can manage them all through a single PMC. Each server would have its own drivers, forms, ports, and printers.

Deployed Printers Printers that have been deployed using Group Policy are listed here. You'll see how to deploy printers with Group Policy later in this chapter.

Additionally, within each print server, you have four primary nodes. These nodes are used to manage the different print devices and printers served by the print server.

Drivers You can add drivers that are needed for your printers here. Drivers have been simplified into three types: Itanium for high-end servers, x64 for 64-bit operating systems, and x86 for 32-bit operating systems.

Forms The forms on a server show the various print layouts the installed printers can support. They define the paper size and the printer area margins. The majority of time most people use letter-size paper (8.5×11), and the letter form defines letter-size paper. However, there are many other forms that can be selected, and you can make your own. The forms are shown on a per-server basis, not a per-printer basis.

Ports Ports are used to connect to print devices. The legacy ports are the serial ports (COM1 through COM4), parallel ports (LPT1 through LPT3), and FILE. If you plug in a USB printer, a USB port will be automatically added. A new port is XPSPort and is used to create Microsoft XPS documents. You can also create standard TCP/IP ports to connect to any network printer using an IP address.

Printers When you add a printer, it will be listed here. Remember, the printer is the software interface that you can manipulate on the print server, and it will send print jobs to the print device. You can have multiple printers for any print device, depending on your needs.

ADDING NEW PRINTERS

You use the PMC to add new printers, and one piece of good news is that you can use it to automatically detect printers on the same subnet as the print server. If you right-click Printers and select Add Printer, your display will look similar to Figure 13.5. Notice you have four choices.

FIGURE 13.5
Adding a new printer using the Network Printer Installation Wizard

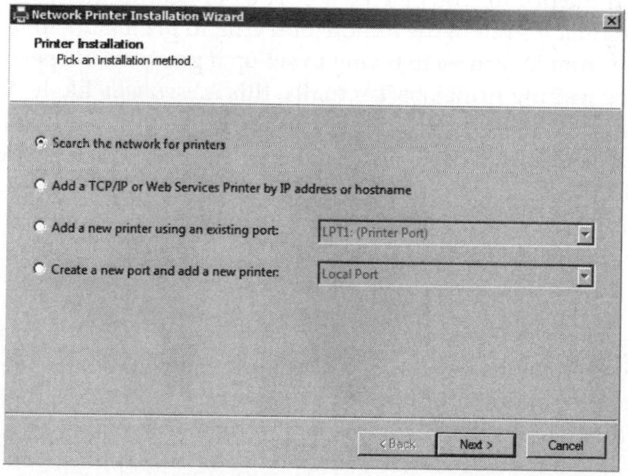

Search the network for printers   This method allows PMC to automatically detect printers. It will work only with network printers on the local subnet, but if your printers are on the same subnet, it can save you a step.

Add a TCP/IP or Web Services Printer by IP address or hostname   If the printer is on a separate subnet or configured as a web services printer (available from a web server), use this choice to manually add the IP address or hostname of the printer. If you use the hostname, you need to ensure that the name can be resolved by DNS or another name resolution method.

Add a new printer using an existing port   If a port already exists, you can use this method to add a printer to an existing port. A single printer would have one port configured for each print device. When printer pooling is enabled (you'll see how to enable printer pooling later), you can have multiple ports configured for a single printer; each port will be connected to a print device. You may also choose to add more printers for a single print device so that you can manipulate different properties such as printer permissions or schedules, as you'll see later in the chapter.

Create a new port and add a new printer   This method allows you to create new ports and add printers to them. The wizard doesn't give as many choices, and you can achieve what you want using other methods, so you may never use this method.

Printers connected to the USB port of the server don't need any additional steps. Simply plug the printer into the USB port; it will be automatically sensed, and the driver will be added. It won't be shared by default, but you can access the printer properties sheet (covered later in the chapter) and share it from the Sharing tab.

DELETING A PRINTER

Sometimes you'll need to delete a printer from a print server. Most of the time this process is extremely simple: you open the Printers node of the Print Management console, right-click the printer about to be sent to that big network in the sky, and choose Delete from the context menu. The printer should disappear immediately.

If the printer you deleted *doesn't* disappear immediately, you may receive an error. Make sure that it's not in the middle of trying to print a document. Even if a printer never worked— for example, you were trying to set up a printer and specified the wrong port name—it can still have waiting print jobs. (Actually, this is *especially* likely if the printer never worked but you insisted on setting it up, damn the errors and full speed ahead.)

Check the print queue of the printer you're trying to delete. If it has waiting print jobs, selecting Printer ➤ Cancel All Documents, and then try to delete the printer. Rebooting the print server will not clear the list of spooled print jobs—you must explicitly cancel them.

AUTOMATICALLY DETECTING NETWORK PRINTERS

The "Search the network for printers" method of finding a printer is pretty cool but a little misleading. It will search the local subnet where the print server is located, but if your network includes multiple subnets, it won't search the entire LAN. In other words, it can't search for any printers that are accessible only through a router.

If you have a network printer on your local subnet, you can use the following steps to install it:

1. Launch the Print Management console, and select your print server.

2. Right-click the Printers node, and select Add Printers.

NETWORK MUST BE CONFIGURED AS PRIVATE

If your network is configured as a Public network in the Network and Sharing Center, you won't be able to automatically detect network printers. You'll need to change the configuration to Private, indicating this is a home or work network.

3. Select "Search the network for printers," and click Next. This will begin a broadcast search on the subnet. If you have any printers on the subnet, you'll see them appear, as shown in Figure 13.6.

FIGURE 13.6
Searching the network for a printer (and finding one!)

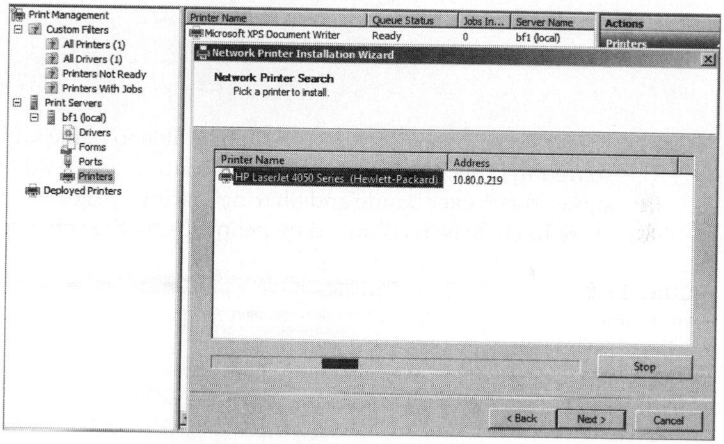

4. Once your printer has been located, select it, and click Next. Although it's not apparent here, this automatically creates a standard TCP/IP port with the IP address of your printer. You don't have to create the port as a separate step.

5. Windows will attempt to locate a driver for the printer. If successful, the printer driver will be selected on the Printer Driver page. If it can't find a driver, you'll need to install a new driver by selecting "Install a new driver" and clicking Next.

6. If the driver wasn't found automatically, there are three choices for finding the driver at this point. All three are available from the screen shown in Figure 13.7.

   A. Select the manufacturer and printer model from the screen. However, since Windows didn't find the driver, it's unlikely this will be successful.

   B. If the server has access to the Internet, you can click Windows Update and search for a driver there.

   C. You can click Have Disk. Since 64-bit drivers aren't that common yet, you may need to go to the manufacturer's website, download the 64-bit version, and unzip it onto your system. After clicking Have Disk, you can browse to where you've unzipped the files, select the driver, and click OK.

   D. Once you've selected the driver, click Next.

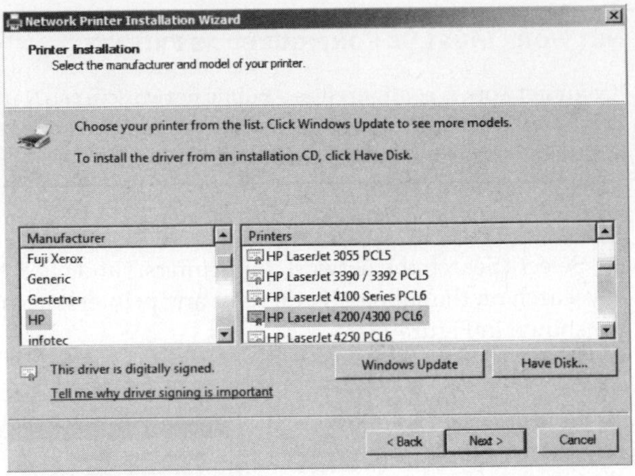

FIGURE 13.7
Adding the printer
driver manually

7. After you've loaded the driver, you'll be able to name and share it. The printer must be shared in order for users to be able to connect and send their print jobs to it. Figure 13.8 shows the Printer Name and Sharing Settings page. Feel free to give it a name that is more likely to be recognized by people using the printer.

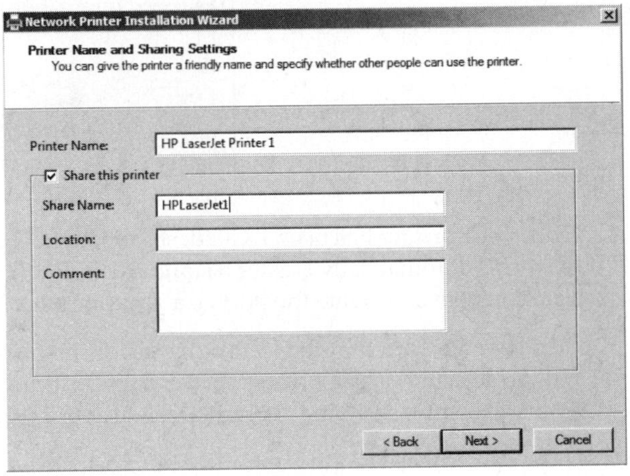

FIGURE 13.8
Naming and
sharing the printer

8. The Printer Found page will show the details you've selected. Click Next.

9. On the wizard completion page, the system will attempt to install the driver and then install the printer. If an incompatibility between the driver and the printer is discovered, it will show an error. Otherwise, you'll see the printer successfully added, as shown in Figure 13.9.

10. Select the "Print test page" box, and click Finish. This provides a final check to ensure things are working properly.

USING (OR NOT USING) PRINTER LOCATIONS

Although you can enter printer locations to allow users to search directly on this term, Printer Locations is also an advanced feature. However, it is usually not used because of its complexity.

When fully implemented, Printer Locations allows users to search for printers and returns a printer that is located close to them. For example, if a user searches for a printer that prints double-sided and there are 25 printers in the organization, only those printers that are close to them are used.

"Close to them" in this context means it's on the same subnet.

This requires subnets to be organized and implemented physically close together. For example, if an organization has multiple buildings, the buildings have multiple floors, and the floors have multiple wings, each wing of each floor of each building would need a separate subnet. If a single subnet spanned all floors of the east wing of a building, it wouldn't work because a user on the first floor could be referred to a printer on the third floor, which many users would not consider "close."

The Location property then needs to be accurately entered. First, it needs to be entered using Active Directory Sites and Services to add the location for each subnet. Second, it needs to be entered as the property for each printer. Spelling counts here. If the location for the subnet was entered as "Bldg 1, Floor 3, West wing" but the location for the printer was entered as "Bldg1, Floor 3, West wing" with no spaces between Bldg and 1, the location wouldn't match, and the printer wouldn't be found.

Although the idea of printer locations sounds good, we just don't see it being used. However, it still is possible to enter the location, and if users know what location to search, they can find it.

FIGURE 13.9
Printer successfully added

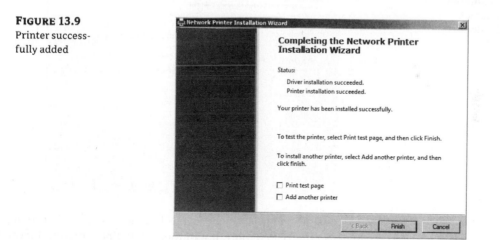

MANUALLY INSTALLING NEW PRINTERS

If you need to install a printer that isn't on your subnet, you can use the following procedure:

1. Right-click the Printers node within the PMC, and select Add Printers.

2. Select "Add a TCP/IP or Web Service Printer by IP address or hostname," and click Next.

3. Select TCP/IP Device as the type of device. Type the IP address of the printer, or if DNS has been configured to resolve the printer's name, you can enter the printer's name. Ensure that "Auto detect the printer driver to use" is selected. Your display will look similar to Figure 13.10. Click Next.

FIREWALL MUST BE ENABLED

Interestingly, if the Windows Firewall is not running, you'll receive an error indicating the operation couldn't be completed with an error code of 0x000006d9 similar to the following illustration. This can be a real head-banger problem since the error code doesn't give you any indication that it's related to the firewall. However, all you need to do is start the Windows Firewall service and try again.

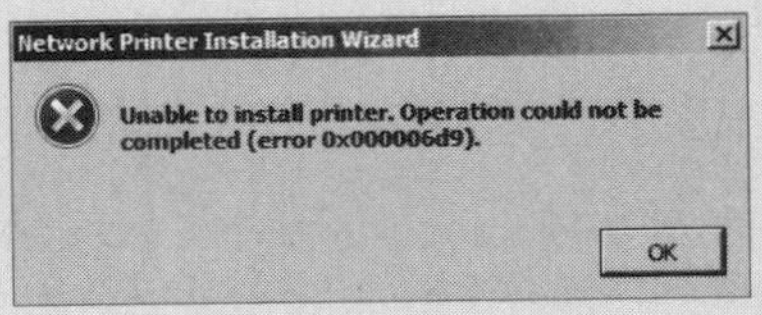

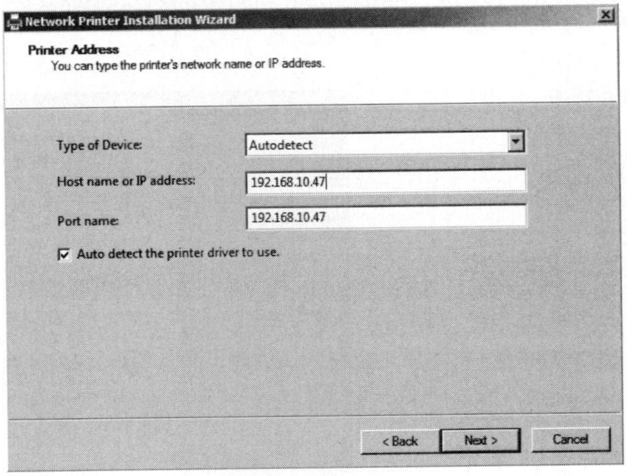

FIGURE 13.10
Adding the printer's IP address

4. At this point, the wizard will complete just as it did in the automatic detection process. It will first try to detect the TCP/IP port. It will then try to find a driver. If it can't find a driver, you'll need to select "Install a new driver," click Next, and browse to the correct driver. Click Next.

5. After you've installed the driver, give the printer a name, share it, and give it a share name. Click Next to review the details of your selections, and click Next again to install the driver and printer.

Notice that the only real difference here is that you're manually entering the IP address instead of allowing it to be found through a network search. As a reminder, you'll have to add it manually if the printer is on a different subnet.

CONFIGURING AND VIEWING SETTINGS AND RESOURCES

Installing a printer is the first step, but just installing the printer does not guarantee that it'll have the right drivers or the right forms available to users. In this section, we'll show you how the PMC organizes these settings to help you review and configure print server settings for drivers, ports, and available forms.

Managing Printer Drivers

If you want to add a printer to Windows Server 2008 R2 that users can print to, you'll need 64-bit drivers for it that are compatible with the print server. For end users to use the shared printers, the system needs drivers for their computers.

For example, if you are supporting clients running 32-bit operating systems, you'll need to add drivers to the print server for them. You can view a listing of all the drivers that are currently installed on your server by selecting the Drivers node in the PMC, as shown in Figure 13.11.

FIGURE 13.11
Viewing installed drivers

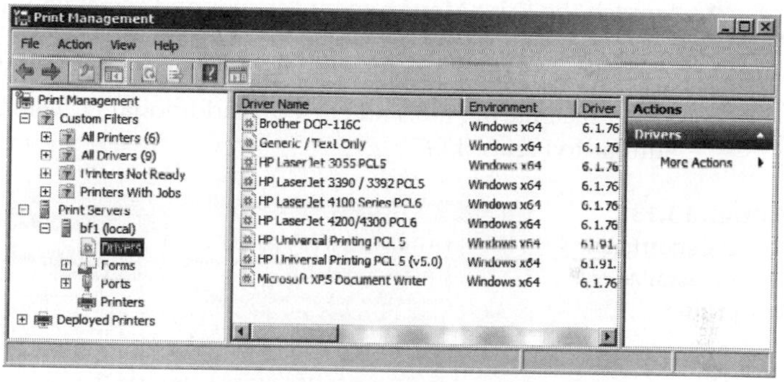

Notice in the figure that all the drivers are x64 based. They won't be useful to any x86 (or 32-bit) clients.

Changing Printer Driver Views

The printer driver view shows a lot of information on drivers, but you may be interested in more information. You can change the view to show additional information or remove information as desired. As an example, you can add the URL for the manufacturer to identify the source for an update.

Figure 13.12 shows the Add/Remove Columns selection for the driver view. With the Drivers node selected, select View ➤ Add/Remove Columns to access this page.

You can add any item in the "Available columns" list to the "Displayed columns" list by selecting it and clicking Add. Similarly, you can remove columns by selecting them from the "Displayed columns" list and clicking Remove. In the figure, we've added the URL for the driver to the view.

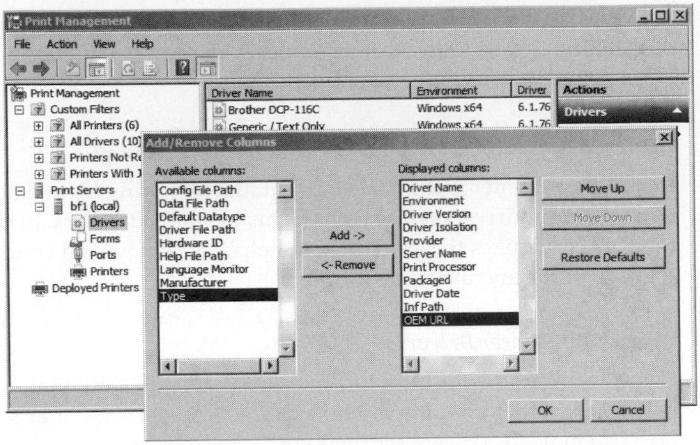

FIGURE 13.12
Modifying
the view for
installed drivers

Installing New Printer Drivers

You can install additional printer drivers by using the Drivers node or by adding the driver to a specific printer. Use the following steps to add the driver to a printer:

1. Launch the Print Management console, and select your print server.

2. Browse to the Printers container. Right-click any printer, and select Properties.

3. Select the Sharing tab, and click the Additional Drivers button. Your display will look similar to Figure 13.13.

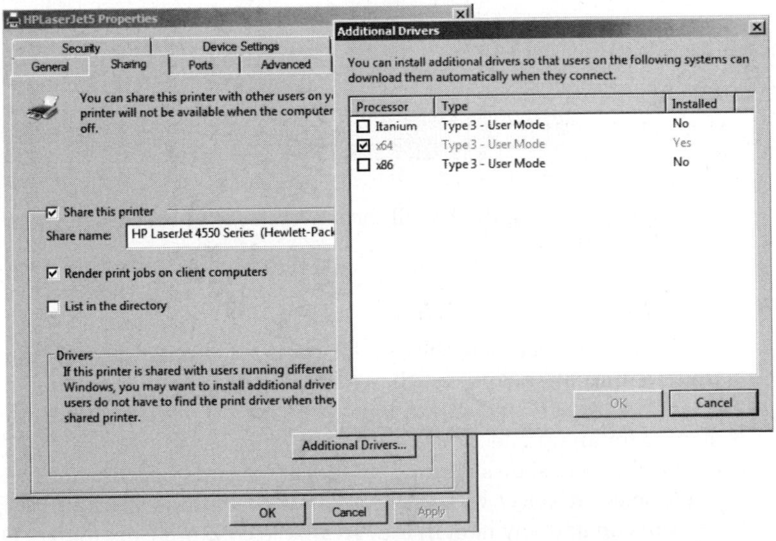

FIGURE 13.13
Viewing additional
drivers installed
for a printer

4. Select the x86 Type 3 – User Mode check box, and click OK. The server will search its internal driver store for a compatible driver. If it has a compatible driver, it will add it. If not, you'll be prompted to browse to the location of the driver. If the driver is not in the store, the best bet is to access the manufacturer website to locate the driver and download and unzip it to a location you can browse to. Browse the location, and click OK.

THE DRIVER STORE

All device drivers (including printer drivers in Windows Server 2008 R2) are installed in a secure folder referred to as the *driver store*. You can think of this as a regular store or mart where items can be purchased (except, of course, that the operating system doesn't charge you). When a driver is needed, the store is searched. If the driver is in the store, it's automatically installed. If the driver is not in the store, Windows can search additional locations (such as Windows Update) and may prompt the user for a path to the driver. Only signed drivers are stored in the driver store, making them a more secure option.

---

5. You can click the Additional Drivers button to verify the driver has been added. Instead of saying No for Installed, it will have changed to Yes.

Viewing and Editing Port Settings

Each printer server's ports are listed in its Ports folder. You can use this screen to identify which printers are connected to which port or which ports have printers attached.

Additionally, you can view or modify the properties of any port simply by right-clicking it and selecting Configure Port. Figure 13.14 shows port configuration page.

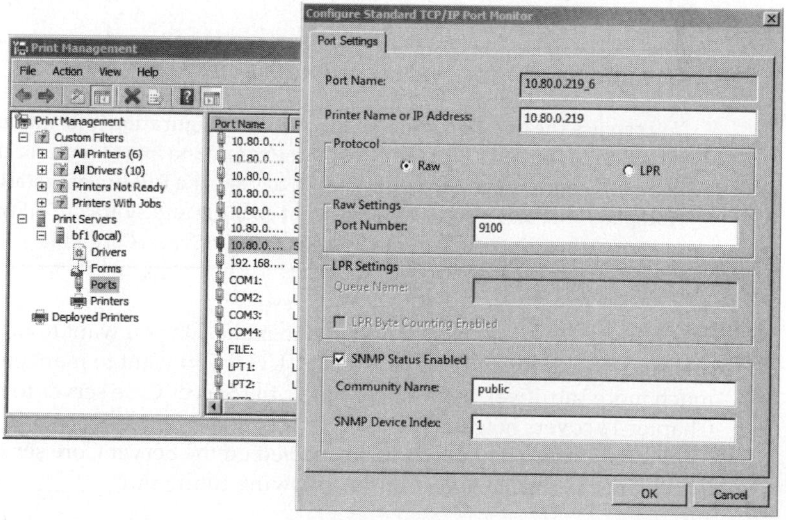

FIGURE 13.14
Viewing available ports on a server

If necessary, you can change the IP address of the port number that the printer is using. Changing the IP address would be necessary if the printer was moved to a different subnet or assigned a different IP address for some other reason.

The Simple Network Management Protocol (SNMP) is often used for managing network devices, and although the default community name is Public, this will be changed in a production environment. If you want your ports to be able to communicate with an SNMP management system, you'll need to change the community name to match your environment.

Viewing Forms

The forms on a server show the various print layouts that the installed printers can support. The forms are shown on a per-server basis. In other words, all the forms on the server are available to all the printers.

If you right-click the Forms folder and choose Manage Forms, you'll open the printer server properties to the Forms tab. You can also access this tab via the server properties sheet. If there is a special need for a custom form with specific margins or sizes, you can create a custom form from this page.

Adding the Print Services Role to Server Core

Windows Server 2008 R2 supports the Print and Document Services role on Server Core. Server Core does not have a GUI but instead requires you to manage it from the command line—at least the initial management must be done from the command line.

If you're running Server Core on a server and want to add the Print and Document Services role, use the following command from the Server Core command line:

```
Ocsetup Printing-ServerCore-Role
```

After a moment, you'll be prompted to restart the server. Click Yes to restart it, and when it restarts, log on.

USE OCLIST TO VIEW INSTALLED ROLES

You can use the `oclist` command to provide configuration information on your Server Core installation. Enter `oclist > oclist.txt` at the command line to redirect the output to a text file. When complete, enter **notepad oclist.txt** to view the full list of installed roles and services within Notepad. This also gives you the correct spelling and syntax of all the roles you want to add. For example, the printer role is identified as Printer-ServerCore-Role.

At this point, you'll have a decision to make. Do you want to manage the Print Services role from the command line or from a GUI? If you want to manage it from a GUI (which is much more intuitive), you can configure the Server Core server to be remotely administered. Chapter 14 covers how to do this.

Network Discovery needs to be enabled on the Server Core server for print server management. You can enable this with the following command:

```
netsh firewall set service fileandprint enable
```

You'll also need to enable the server to be managed by an MMC on a remote server with the following command. Even though it appears on two lines in the book, enter it as a single command.

```
netsh advfirewall firewall set rule group = "Remote Administration"
  new enable = yes
```

Once the Server Core server is configured for remote administration, you can then remotely administer it from a server that has the full operating system installed. For example, you may have 10 file and print servers all running Server Core but one central server with the full operating system installed that you'll use to remotely administer all the servers.

To add a print server to the PMC, right-click Print Servers, and select Add/Remove Servers. On the Add/Remove Servers page, enter the name of the remote server. You can also click Browse. If Network Discovery is turned off, you'll be prompted to turn it on so that other computers can be located. Select your server, and click the Select Server button.

If you need to do any tasks from the Server Core command line, several tools can help.

THE PRINTER USER INTERFACE COMMAND: PRINTUI

You can use the printer user interface command to perform several advanced tasks such as adding and removing printers, adding and removing drivers, and much more. Entering **printui** from the command line will launch a window showing the help file for this tool.

You can execute PrintUI via the rundll32 process using the following syntax:

```
start rundll32 PrintUI.dll, options
```

The options you provide can be quite complex depending on what task you're trying to accomplish. Some of the common tasks you may use this for are shown in the following sections.

One reason you may need the PrintUI command is if you try to install unsigned drivers remotely and receive an error of 0x00000572. This indicates that Server Core is not willing to install the unsigned driver using PMC.

You can resolve this by installing the driver from the Server Core prompt. First, copy the driver file to a folder on the Server Core system. Next run the following command. Notice that the options start after start rundll32 PrintUI.dll.

```
start rundll32 PrintUI.dll,PrintUIEntry /ia /K /v 3 /m
  "name of driver" /h "x64" /f "path\name to driver inf file"
```

The /ia switch indicates you're installing a print driver. The /K and /v 3 switches work together to indicate the driver is a Type 3 driver. (Note that the /K must be uppercase; the lowercase /k is used to print a test page.) The /m switch is used to provide the name of the driver, which you can get by opening the driver's information .inf file.

Use the /h switch to indicate the architecture as Windows NT x86 (32-bit), x64, or IA64 (Itanium). When the /K switch is used, /h can be indicated as 2, 3, or 4 to represent x86, x64, or IA64. Last, the /f switch includes the path and name of the .inf file.

With the driver added, you can then add the printer using the GUI from another server.

SERVER CORE PRINTER SCRIPTS

Server Core includes several scripts directly related to the print role on a Server Core installation. All of these scripts are located in the C:\Windows\System32\Printer_Admin_Scripts\en-US directory by default (for installations in the United States). If you're in a different country, check to see what folders exist in the C:\Windows\System32\Printer_Admin_Scripts\ folder. You'll either need to change to this directory or include the directory in the path when you launch the script. To change to the directory and view all the available scripts, enter these commands.

```
Cd\Windows\System32\Printer_Admin_Scripts\en-US
Dir
```

PRINT SCRIPTS ADDED WHEN SERVER ROLE ADDED

If you try to access these scripts without adding the Print Server role, you'll find that the Printer_Admin_Scripts folder doesn't exist. It is added only when the Print Server role is added.

The following examples assume the path has been changed to the Printer_Admin_Scripts folder using the cd command. Additionally, each of these scripts must be launched with the cscript command. In other words, to get help on the prncnfg.vbs command, you'd enter **cscript prncnfg.vbs help** after changing to the correct path.

Using the Printer Manager Script (prnmngr.vbs)

You can list, add, and delete printer connections with this command: prnmngr.vbs. You can also set or display the default printer.

You can list all the installed printers using the following command. Note that the –l is the letter *l*, not the number 1.

```
cscript prnmngr.vbs –l
```

If you want to delete a printer, use the -p switch to identify the name of the printer and the -d switch to delete, as shown in this command:

```
cscript prnmngr.vbs -d –p "printerName"
```

You can use the following command to add a printer shared on a server named BF1 with a share name of LaserPrinter. Note that this uses the standard UNC path of \\ServerName\ ShareName.

```
cscript prnmngr.vbs -ac –p \\BF1\LaserPrinter
```

The default printer can be identified with this command. Only the -g switch is needed.

```
cscript prnmngr.vbs -g
```

Using the Printer Configuration Script (prncnfg.vbs)

You can use the prncnfg.vbs script to configure a printer or display configuration about a printer.

You can use the following command to get configuration information about a printer. The -g switch is used to get the information, and the -p switch identifies the printer.

```
cscript prncnfg.vbs -g -p "printer name"
```

If you want to set any properties, you use the -t switch and specify the individual configuration property you want to change. As any example, you can use this command to change the printer's name. The -z switch gives the new name.

```
cscript prncnfg.vbs -t -p "printer name" -z "new name"
```

Similarly, you could change the priority of the printer to 50 using the -t and -o switches like this:

```
cscript prncnfg.vbs -t -p "printer name" -o 50
```

Using the Printer Jobs Script (prnjobs.vbs)

Use prnjobs.vbs to list, pause, resume, and cancel print jobs. As an example, you can use this command to list jobs on all printers. Note that the -l is the letter *l*, not the number 1.

```
cscript prncnfg.vbs -l
```

Or, use this command to list jobs on a specific printer:

```
cscript prncnfg.vbs -l -p "printer name"
```

Jobs are listed with a Job ID. You can use the -z switch to pause a job, the -x switch to cancel a job, or the -m switch to resume a paused job. You need to include both the printer name and the job ID to pause, cancel, or resume jobs. The syntax of each command is as follows:

```
cscript prncnfg.vbs -z -p "printer name" -j JobID
cscript prncnfg.vbs -x -p "printer name" -j JobID
cscript prncnfg.vbs -m -p "printer name" -j JobID
```

Using the Printer Driver Script (prndrvr.vbs)

Use prndrvr.vbs to add, delete, and list printer drivers. As an example, you can use this command to list all the print drivers. Note that the -l is the letter *l*, not the number 1.

```
cscript prndrvr.vbs -l
```

You may need to add a driver. First you'll download and unzip the file to a location. When you unzip a driver, it'll include several files including the information file with an .inf extension. Once you have unzipped the file, you can add a print driver by using the -m, -v, -e, -i, and -h switches like this:

```
cscript prndrvr.vbs -a -m "driver name" -v 3 -e "Windows xx"
 -I "path to inf file" -h "path to driver"
```

The -m switch specifies the driver model name (get this from the driver's .inf file). The -v switch specifies the type or version. All new drivers today are Type 3, so this should be a 3 all the time. The -e switch is used to identify the architecture and will be Windows NT x86 for 32-bit systems, Windows x64 for 64-bit systems, and Windows IA64 for Itanium systems. Last, you need to include the path and name of the .inf file and the path to the driver.

Using the Printer Ports Script (prnport.vbs)

You can list, create, and delete TCP/IP printer ports with the prnport.vbs script. To view a listing of the ports, use this command. As before, the –l is the letter *l*, not the number 1.

```
cscript prnport.vbs -l
```

You can add an IP port with the -a switch. You'll need to specify the IP name with the -r switch; the name is normally IP_ followed by the IP address. The IP address is specified with the -h switch. The following command shows how it'll work for a printer with an assigned IP address of 192.168.20.222.

```
cscript prnport.vbs -a -r IP_192.168.20.222 -h 192.168.20.222
```

The command does try to reach out and connect to the printer when this command is executed. If it can't reach a device using that IP, the command will fail.

Using the Printer Queue Script (prnqctl.vbs)

You can use the printer queue script, prnqctl.vbs, to print a test page, pause or resume a printer, and completely clear a printer queue. Print a test page with the -e switch using the -p switch to identify the name of the printer:

```
cscript prnqctl.vbs -e -p "HP Laser Jet 3055 PCL5"
```

Pause the printer and all print jobs with the -z switch:

```
cscript prnqctl.vbs -z -p "HP Laser Jet 3055 PCL5"
```

Cancel all print jobs (clear the queue) with the -x switch:

```
cscript prnqctl.vbs -x -p "HP Laser Jet 3055 PCL5"
```

Using the Publish Printers Script (pubprn.vbs)

Use pubprn.vbs to publish a printer to Active Directory. You'll need to identify your domain using a Lightweight Directory Access Protocol (LDAP) distinguished name to specify the location where the printer should be published. Distinguished names were explained in greater depth in Chapter 6, "Creating the Simple AD: The One-Domain, One-Location AD," but in short you'll start with LDAP:// and then use OU= to identify the organizational unit and DC to identify the domain name.

As an example, if you wanted to specify the Sales OU in the domain of BigFirm.com, you'd use the following. Note that LDAP must be all uppercase.

```
"LDAP://OU=Sales,DC=BigFirm,DC=Com"
```

Now, if you wanted to publish a printer shared on BF1 with a share name of LaserPrinter, you could use the UNC path name of \\BF1\LaserPrinter to identify the printer. To publish it to the Sales OU in the BigFirm.com domain, you could use this command:

```
Cscript pubprn.vbs \\BF1\LaserPrinter "LDAP://OU=Sales,DC=BigFirm,DC=Com"
```

Deploying Printers to the Masses

Once you've added printers to the server, you'll want them to be available for the clients. You can accomplish this in three ways:

◆ Manually

◆ Through the Active Directory Search tool

◆ Through Group Policy

If your computers are in an Active Directory domain, you'll probably use the second or third choice to provide some automation. In the following sections, you'll learn how to deploy printers using each of the three methods.

Adding a Printer to a Client Manually

When you've added printers to a print server, it's relatively easy to add printers to the client (and have the proper drivers automatically install). The following steps show how you can add a printer to a Windows Vista client:

1. With Windows Vista started, select Start ➤ Printers.

2. Click "Add a printer."

3. Select "Add a network, wireless, or Bluetooth printer."

4. The system will search for available printers on the network. Select "The printer that I want isn't listed."

5. Click "Select a shared printer by name," and enter **ServerName**\ to view a list of shared printers (but enter the actual server name). Figure 13.15 shows how we're connecting to a server named BF1.

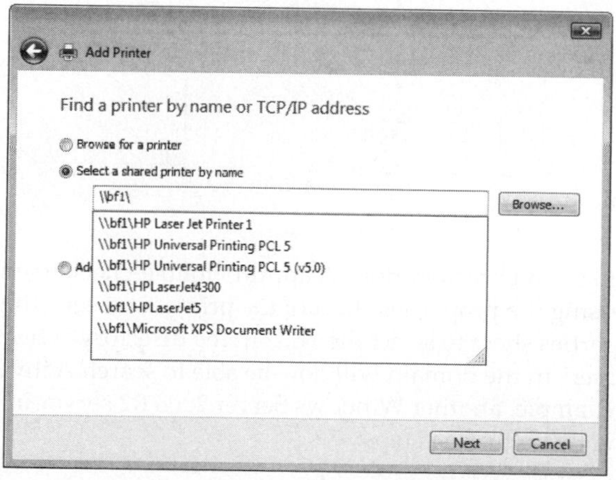

FIGURE 13.15
Connecting to a shared printer from Windows Vista

6. Select the desired shared printer, and click Next.

7. The driver that was installed on the server is automatically downloaded and installed on the client. The name of the printer will be the same as that given on the client. Click Next, and click Finish. That's it.

Of course, you may not want to do this for 500 clients in your organization. If not, you can configure the printer to be deployed automatically using Group Policy as shown in the Deploying Printers via GPO section later in this chapter.

Adding a Printer Using Active Directory Search

Active Directory is a huge database of objects that can be searched by both end users and administrators. Many objects are automatically published in Active Directory (such as users, computers, groups, and shares), allowing users to easily search for what they want. However, printers are not published in Active Directory by default. It's not hard to do so, and once they are listed in Active Directory, users can easily find them with a quick search.

Any printer that has been shared can also be listed in Active Directory as long as it is hosted on a server that is a member of the domain. In other words, network printers that aren't managed by a print server cannot be listed.

Open the Print Management console, browse to the Printers container, right-click the printer, and select List in Directory, as shown in Figure 13.16. That's it. The system will do the rest.

FIGURE 13.16
Listing a printer in Active Directory

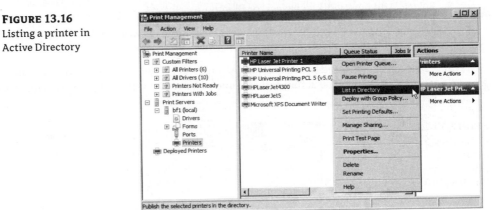

If List in Directory doesn't appear, double-check to ensure the printer is being shared by accessing the properties sheet of the printer and selecting the Sharing tab. You can also use this properties sheet to select the "List in the directory" check box.

Users in the domain will now be able to search Active Directory for the printer they want. For example, another Windows Server 2008 R2 server in the domain could locate this printer using the following steps:

1. Select Start ➢ Network.

2. Select Search Active Directory. The Search Active Directory choice is present only when the computer (including Vista and Windows 7 computers) is a member of a domain. Interestingly, it doesn't appear on Network page for a domain controller, but it can be accessed through Active Directory Users and Computers on domain controllers.

3. In the Active Directory search box, select Printers in the Find box. Type **HP** in the Model text box, and click Find Now. Figure 13.17 shows the result.

FIGURE 13.17
Searching for a printer listed in Active Directory

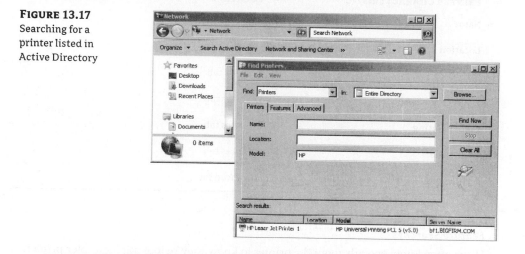

STRING SEARCHES

Notice that the full name of the model doesn't need to be entered. This is valuable since printer model names often have a length reminiscent of the names of minor royalty. Instead, the Active Directory Search tool looks for string matches, so any model starting with *HP* will be found. Although this example search worked, if all your models were HP, it wouldn't be as valuable.

Once the printer is located, a user could just double-click the printer to install it as an additional printer on their system. As long as the correct driver has been added to the print server, it will automatically be downloaded to the client, and the client doesn't need to take any additional steps to use the printer.

You can search for a printer based on just about any characteristic—or combination of characteristics—that you like. Searching for a printer by name doesn't seem very likely, since if you knew that much you'd probably know its domain and its server as well. However, you might know the printer's location. If the printer's location is entered when the printer is added, it can be used as a search term.

Since people may be using a printer's location to search Active Directory for that printer, keep printer locations short and consistent (such as Lab or Reception). As mentioned earlier, if you're using the full implementation of Printer Locations, you need to ensure that the printer location is entered exactly how it's entered in the Sites and Services subnet object.

Table 13.1 shows many of the common search criteria that can be used for finding printers in Active Directory.

TABLE 13.1: Common Search Criteria for Finding Printers in Active Directory

PRINTER CHARACTERISTIC	LOCATION
Name	Printers tab
Location	Printers tab
Model	Printers tab
Double-sided printing	Features tab
Color printing	Features tab
Can staple	Features tab
Search on specific property	Advanced tab

Feature Searches

Users often know enough about the printer to know they're looking for a color printer, one that can staple, or one that has some other features. Figure 13.18 shows the Features search tab. If a user is looking for a specific feature, they can select the desired feature and click Find Now.

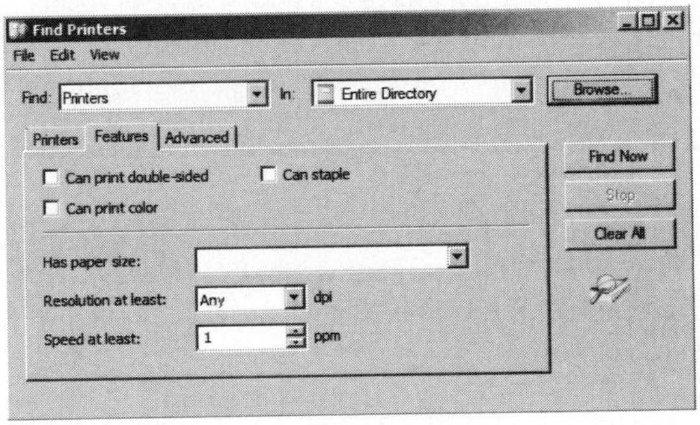

FIGURE 13.18
Searching for printers based on supported features

Advanced Searches

The contents of the Advanced tab will be most suited to people who *really* know their printers, since the search criteria there is more granular than most people will need. Whereas the first two tabs allow you to describe a printer in terms of where it is, what it's called, and what you want it to be able to do, the Advanced tab allows you to describe the printer exactly.

Figure 13.19 shows the Field drop-down menu with the Paper Available property highlighted. Notice there are many different properties you can search on. If a printer property exists, you can select it.

FIGURE 13.19
Searching for
printers using the
Advanced tab

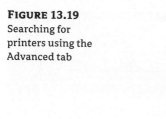

Once you select the property, you choose a condition such as "Starts with" and "Ends with" and then enter text in the Value field to match the property and condition. As an example, you could choose Server Name, select "Starts with," and enter **BF** in the value. After clicking Find Now, all printers hosted by any server that starts with BF will be shown.

Deploying Printers via GPO

You can also deploy printers using a Group Policy object. If you need to support Windows 7 clients and Windows Server 2008 R2 servers, there are a couple of warnings:

♦ Active Directory must be using a Windows Server 2008 R2 schema version. If you installed the first domain controller (DC) with Windows Server 2008 R2, you have the updated schema. If not, you'll need to run adprep to update the schema. You can find details on adprep at http://technet.microsoft.com/library/cc731728.aspx.

♦ Clients that are *not* running Windows 7 or Windows Server 2008 R2 must use the PushPrinterConnections.exe tool in a startup script or a logon script.

If your domain is completely Windows Server 2008 R2 or the schema has been updated with adprep, you can then follow these steps to deploy printers via GPOs:

1. Launch PMC and browse to the Printers node for the server. Right-click the printer, and select Deploy with Group Policy. This selection is right under List in Directory, discussed in the previous section.

2. On the Deploy with Group Policy page, click Browse.

3. Click the Create a New Group Policy Object icon, and name it **Deploy Printers**. (If you hover over the icons, a tooltip will appear; you want the middle icon.) Your display will look similar to Figure 13.20.

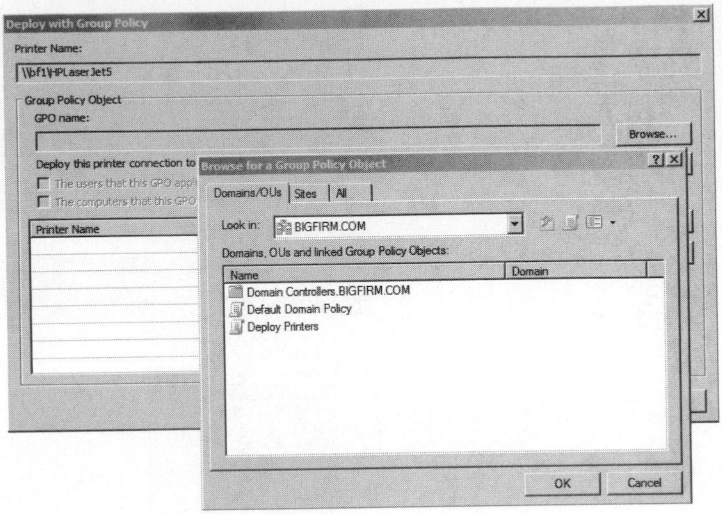

FIGURE 13.20
Creating a Group
Policy object

4. Select your Deploy Printers GPO, and click OK.

5. Select the "The computers that this GPO applies to (per machine)" check box. You could also select the "The users that this GPO applies to (per user)" check box if you wanted the GPO to apply to users without regard to who logged onto the computer or to the user no matter where they logged on.

6. Click Add. The settings you selected will be designated for the GPO. Click OK to apply the settings. After a moment, a dialog box will indicate the printer deployment GPO has been successfully added, as shown in Figure 13.21. Click OK to dismiss the dialog box, and click OK again to dismiss the Deploy GPO screen.

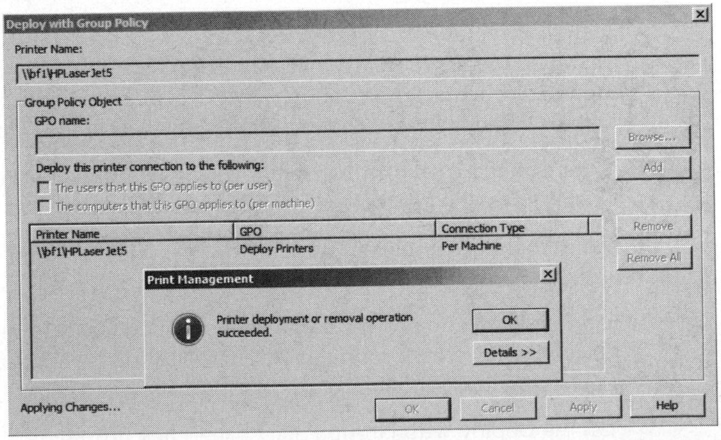

FIGURE 13.21
Adding the set-
tings to the GPO

The previous step added the printer as a deployed printer in the Computer Configuration\Policies\Windows Settings\Deployed Printers node of the Deploy Printers GPO you created.

7. You can now go to any Windows 7 or Windows 2008 R2 computer in the domain, type **gpupdate /force** at the command line to refresh Group Policy, and the printer will automatically appear with other devices and printers, with the correct driver.

If all your clients are running Windows 7 or Windows 2008 R2, you'd be done. However, if you have other clients such as Windows Vista and Windows XP, you'll need to configure the PushPrinterConnection.exe utility to run on each of them to have the printer deployed. This utility is not on the default installation of Windows Server 2008 R2 or Windows 7 since they don't need it, but it is in the Windows\System32 folder of Windows Server 2008 and Windows Vista.

You can configure this utility to run on clients that need it with the following steps:

1. Launch the Group Policy Management console (GPMC) by selecting Start ➤ Administrative Tools ➤ Group Policy Management.

2. Browse to the Deploy Printers GPO in the domain, and click Edit, as shown in Figure 13.22.

FIGURE 13.22
Selecting a
GPO to edit

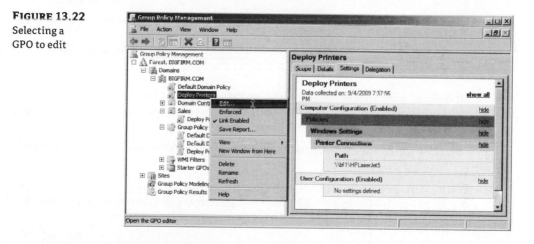

DEPLOYING VIA GPO DIRECTLY

You can also deploy printers from the Group Policy snap-in. Go to the Policies\Windows Settings\Deployed Printers section, and right-click its folder. From the context menu, choose **Deploy Printer**, and browse to the desired printer.

3. Browse to the Computer Configuration\Policies\Windows Settings\Scripts (Startup/Shutdown) node.

4. Double-click Startup, and click Show Files. Notice this is empty now. You need to copy the PushPrinterConnection.exe utility to this folder. Once the file is added, close Windows Explorer.

5. Click Add. Click Browse, and select PushPrinterConnections. Click Open. Your display will look similar to Figure 13.23.

FIGURE 13.23
Adding PushPrinter-
Connections to the
startup script

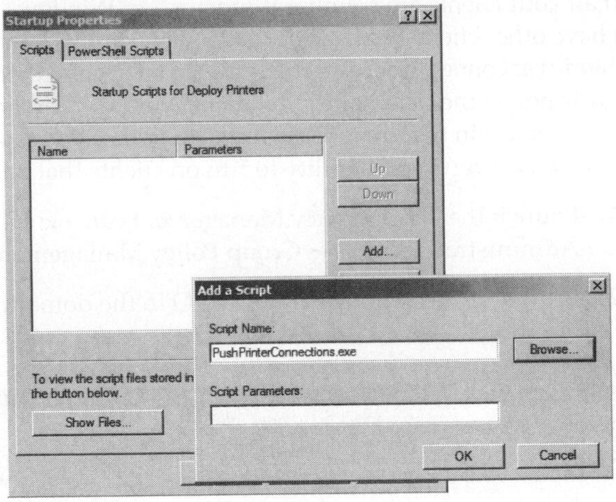

If desired, you can add –log to the Script Parameters text box to enable logging on computers where it runs. The log is located in the %Windir%\temp\ppcMachine.log file for computers or in the %temp%\ppcUser.log file for user connections.

6. Click OK to close the Add a Script dialog box. Click OK to close the Startup Properties dialog box.

That's it. A cool feature of the PushPrinterConnections utility is that if it attempts to start on a Windows 7 or Windows 2008 R2 computer, it automatically detects the environment and exits. You don't have to worry about deploying this in a mixed environment.

BEING SELECTIVE WITH GPOS

Although these steps will deploy the GPO to all users in the domain, you could be more selective. For example, if you wanted this printer deployed only to users in the Sales OU, you could launch the Group Policy Management console, delete the link at the domain for the Deploy Printers GPO, and link the GPO to the Sales OU. As soon as domain clients refresh Group Policy (or it's forced with gpupdate /force), the printer will be removed for all clients that aren't in the Sales OU.

Viewing Deployed Printers

You can easily view all deployed printers from within the Print Management console by select-ing the Deployed Printers container in the Print Management console. This will query Active Directory and show all the printers that are deployed via GPO.

Although you can't deploy additional printers from this view, you can remove the deployment option for printers using this view. Simply select any deployed printer, select Deploy with Group Policy, and remove the deployment option.

Adjusting Print Server Settings

Several settings apply at the server level and can be configured once to apply to all resources (drivers, forms, ports, and printers) managed by that server. You can also export and import printers to and from files and set notifications.

To edit server-wide printer settings, launch the Print Management console, browse to the Print Servers container, and right-click your server to view the context menu and access these choices.

Server Properties

If you select Server Properties from the context menu, you'll see that you can access five tabs. Figure 13.24 shows the print server properties sheet with the Forms tab selected. You can also reach this page by selecting Forms under the server and selecting Manage Forms.

FIGURE 13.24
Viewing the Forms tab of system properties

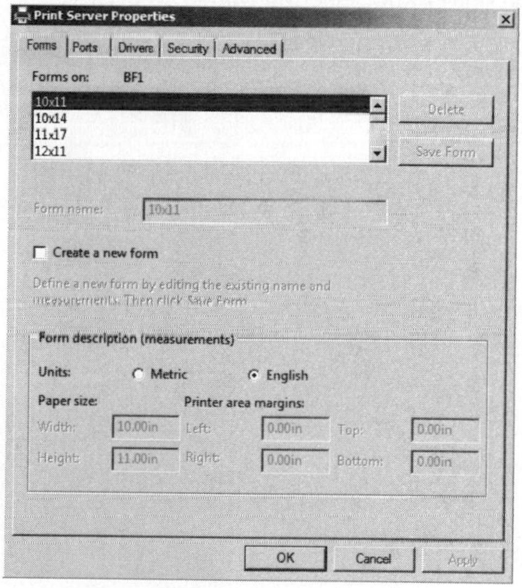

As you can see, several tabs allow you to configure server properties:

◆ Forms

◆ Ports

◆ Drivers

◆ Security

◆ Advanced

CHOOSING FORM SETTINGS

Print jobs are arranged on the paper based on forms, which define a template for where text should appear. Print servers come with a long list of predefined forms you can choose from, but they also allow you to define your own form settings for customized needs such as printing to company letterhead.

Print servers are set up to print on blank 8.5×11 paper (the standard size). To choose a new form, find it in the list.

If you want to create a new form, select the "Create a new form" check box, edit the form description as desired, and click OK. Any forms that you've created can be modified by selecting it, making your modifications, and then clicking Save Form.

You can't delete the preexisting forms, but you can delete any forms you've created.

CONFIGURING SERVER PORT SETTINGS

You can select the Ports tab to view all the ports available on the server. Figure 13.25 shows the Ports tab. Notice that you can add ports, delete ports, and configure ports here, though most ports have very little configuration needed. You can also reach this page by selecting Ports under the server and selecting Manage Ports.

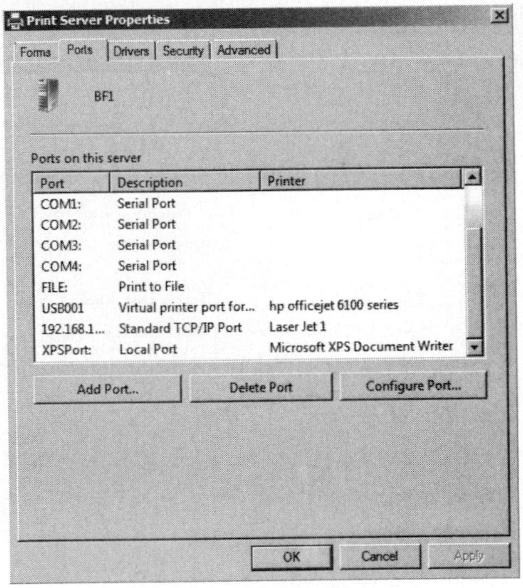

FIGURE 13.25
Viewing the Ports tab of system properties

You normally won't need to create a port by itself. Normally, when you add a network printer, you'll be adding the port as you saw earlier in the chapter. When you add a USB printer, the port will be added automatically. It's very rare to use LPT (parallel) or COM (serial) ports today, but if you do use them, several are already preconfigured.

If you're no longer using a port, you can simply select it and click Delete Port to delete it.

USB ports don't have any configurable options, and we covered the configuration of TCP/IP ports earlier in the chapter.

ADDING OR UPDATING THE PRINTER DRIVER ON A PRINT SERVER

Earlier, you saw how to add a printer driver to a printer. This is commonly done to support different clients. If you access the Drivers tab of the server properties, you can add printer drivers using a similar process.

Although most driver management will be done from within the printer, there may be times when you need to manage the drivers when the printer isn't installed on the server. For example, you may want to add drivers before adding the printer or remove unused drivers after the printer has been removed.

MANAGING PRINT SECURITY

You can manage permissions that apply to security for the entire server through the Security tab. There are differences in permissions that can apply to a server and permissions that apply to a printer.

Figure 13.26 shows the server permissions on the left and the printer permissions on the right.

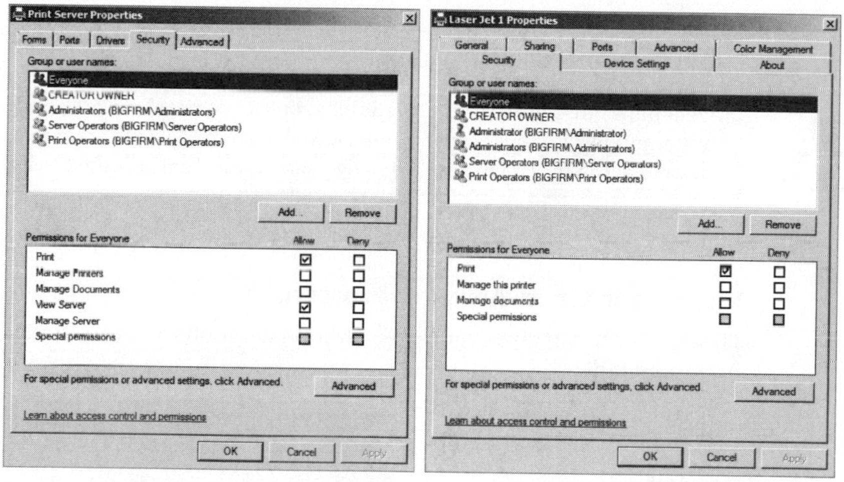

FIGURE 13.26
Viewing the security tabs; server security is on the left, and individual printer security is on the right.

Just as NTFS and share permissions (covered in Chapter 10) can be set to Allow or Deny for any individual user or group of users, permissions on the print server or individual printers can be set to Allow or Deny.

For any of the permissions that are the same on the server and printer, setting them at the server level will cause all new printer installations to receive the same permissions. Existing permissions are not modified; only permissions for new installations are.

The print server permissions are as follows:

Print   Users can send print jobs to the printer. The Everyone group is granted this permission by default.

Manage Printers   Users can change printer properties and permissions. This is granted to Administrators, Server Operators, and Print Operators groups by default.

Manage Documents   User can control document-specific settings and pause, resume, restart, and delete spooled print jobs. This is granted to the Creator Owner, Administrators, Server Operators, and Print Operators groups by default. When a user creates a print job, they become a member of the Creator Owner group for that job, allowing them to manage their own documents.

View Server   Users can view the server properties and settings. This does not give them permission to change the properties. The View Server permission is granted to the Everyone, Administrators, Server Operators, and Print Operators groups by default.

Manage Server   The Manage Server permission allows users to modify any of the server properties and settings. It is granted to the Administrators, Server Operators, and Print Operators groups by default.

Special Permissions   Individual permissions can be assigned at the granular level by clicking Advanced. If any granular permissions are assigned, the Special Permissions check box will be grayed out.

DELEGATION OF PERMISSIONS

Default permissions on Windows Server 2008 R2 do not allow nonadministrative users to perform any administrative print operations. However, it is possible to grant any specific printer permission desired at the server without granting users full system administrative rights.

VIEWING THE SERVER ADVANCED PROPERTIES

The Advanced tab gives you a few additional options you can configure. Figure 13.27 shows the Advanced tab.

FIGURE 13.27
Viewing the
Advanced tab

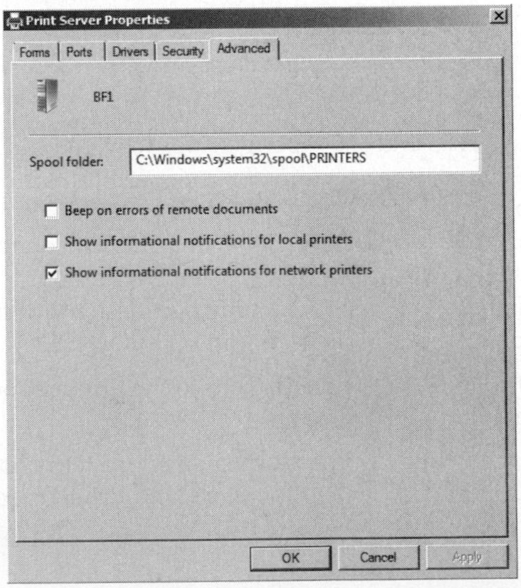

The most common reason to access this tab is to change the location of the spool folder. As a reminder, any documents that can't be sent to the printer right away are spooled to the hard drive and then sent as the printer becomes available. On a dedicated print server, it's common to move the spool folder to another dedicated drive.

There are two reasons to move the spool folder:

To give it more disk space   Since some print jobs can become quite large, they can consume the space available on the hard drive. Although a spooled job will be deleted after it's printed, if multiple jobs are spooled at the same time, you could run out of disk space.

To get better performance   The default location will compete with the operating system for disk access. If performance is an issue, you can move the spool folder to a dedicated hard drive separate from the operating system.

Moving the spool folder is as simple as entering the path to the new location. If the path doesn't exist, it will be created. Beware, though. The change will occur immediately, and any documents that have been spooled will not print. You should wait until there are no active documents waiting to print before moving the spooler.

The other settings are minor. You can enable the system beep on errors from remote documents and show informational notifications for both local and network printers. Although it's not configurable here, a cool new feature is the ability to send notifications via email, which you'll see a little later in this chapter.

Printer Migration

Printer migration from one server to another is relatively easy. Imagine that you've been running a server as a print server for a period of time, and it is hosting 20 or more printers. You need to decommission this server, but before you do so, you want to have a new server host the printers. Manually re-creating all the printers on the new server could take a substantial amount of time.

You can export the printers to a file on the original server and then import the printers from that same file onto the new server. At this point, both servers will act as print servers for the same print devices. You'll then need to configure the clients to use the new print server before taking the old one down. If you've deployed them with Group Policy, you can just change the Group Policy settings to point to the new server, and you're done.

To export the printers, simply right-click the server, and select Export Printers to a File, browse to a location, and save the file. You should then copy the file to a location accessible by the new server.

On the new server, right-click the server, select Import Printers from a File, and browse to the location of the exported file. The migration wizard gives you some import options, as shown in Figure 13.28.

You can choose to keep existing printers or completely overwrite existing printers. You can also choose how the printers will be listed in Active Directory by choosing to list only the printers that were previously listed, list them all, or don't list any.

You can also use this method to restore your printer configurations to a previous time. If you have exported the printers to a file and they become corrupt, modified, or deleted, you can simply import the file to restore the configuration.

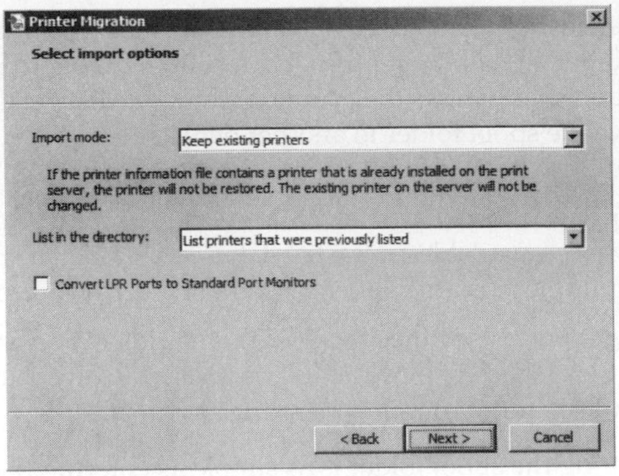

FIGURE 13.28
Importing
printers to a
new print server

Managing Printer Properties

Just as the print server has several properties that can be managed, viewed, and manipulated,
you can also manipulate properties for individual printers. Earlier in the chapter, you learned
how to add printers. If you later need to modify any of the printers, simply right-click the
printer, and select Properties.

Figure 13.29 shows the properties of a printer with the General tab selected. The General tab
shows basic information on the printer such as the name, location, comments (if added), model,
and features supported by the printer. This page will often include a preferences button that can
be used to modify specific user preferences for the printer. It also includes a button to print a
test page that can be very useful to verify connectivity with the printer.

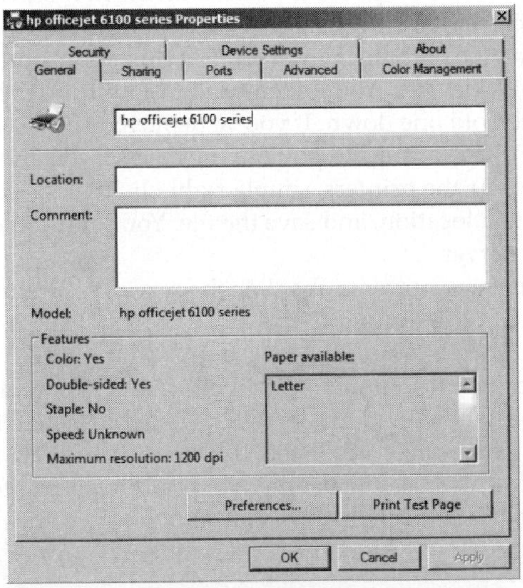

FIGURE 13.29
Viewing the
General tab of
printer properties

The properties sheet shows several tabs. Some printers will include more tabs depending on
the capabilities of the printer. These additional tabs are added from the print driver package.

Printer Properties Sharing Tab

The Sharing tab was shown earlier in this chapter in Figure 13.14 when describing how to add printer drivers to the printer. You can also use it to share (or stop sharing) a printer by simply selecting the check box. This page includes the "List in the directory" check box that can be modified here or by right-clicking the printer and selecting List in Directory.

Printer Properties Ports Tab

The Ports tab allows you to add, delete, and configure ports used by the printer. Most printers can receive data to print and also send data to the server to report on conditions such as low toner, low paper, and paper jam conditions. This page includes the "Enable bidirectional support" check box, which is selected by default to enable the printer to send and receive.

The most common reason to access this tab is to enable printer pooling. Printer pooling allows you add multiple print devices to a single printer.

As we mentioned earlier in this chapter, the ratio of printers to print devices isn't always one to one. You'll see later how to create multiple printers for a single print device, but here you'll see how to have single printer support multiple print devices.

Why would you want to do this? It's mostly a matter of efficiency. Even with the fast print devices available today, busy offices may have more print jobs coming through than one print device can handle. To keep things running smoother and reduce delays, you can distribute print jobs among multiple print devices. Print clients will all send their print jobs to the same printer, but the jobs will go to the printer that's least busy at any given time. This is called *printer pooling*. Figure 13.30 shows the Ports tab with print pooling enabled.

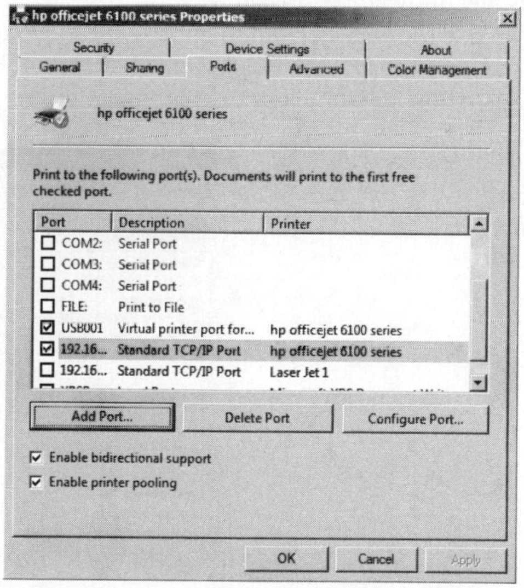

FIGURE 13.30

Enabling print pooling from the Ports tab

Notice in the figure that two ports are enabled. This is possible only when the "Enable printer pooling" check box is selected. You can add as many ports as you have print devices and your needs require.

There are a couple of catches to printer pooling. First, the print devices in the pool must use the same driver. Since many print devices use the same or similar internal parts, it's possible to have different print devices that use the same driver. However, if the devices require different drivers, they won't work in the same printer pool.

Second, we highly recommend putting the pooled print devices in the same physical location. Since users don't know which printer their job will print at, you don't want to have to wander from place to place looking for their print jobs.

SEPARATOR PAGES

Consider using separator pages with usernames in printer pools since users will not necessarily know which printer their job went to. Separator pages are explained in greater depth later in this chapter.

Printer Properties Security Tab

Those familiar with any current Windows-based operating system know that you secure the network by defining user rights for what people can *do* on the network and setting permissions for the resources that people can *use*. Printer security is controlled with permissions on a per-group or per-user basis. Permissions generally stack—that is, the most permissive set of permissions available to you applies—unless you're talking about denied access. Denied access overrides any allowed permissions.

You can use the Security tab to modify the permissions for the printer. You can assign four basic permissions to any user or group, as shown in Figure 13.31. Print permissions can be assigned as Allow or Deny just as other permissions in Windows.

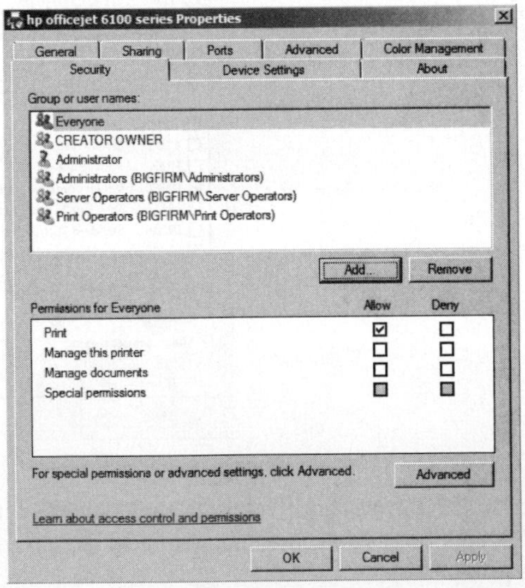

FIGURE 13.31
Printer permissions shown on the Security tab

Although three basic permissions are showing, there are actually a total of six granular permissions available.

You may remember from Chapter 10 that NTFS has basic permissions such as Read that map to granular permissions; the basic Read permission maps to the four granular permissions of Read Data, Read Permissions, Read Attributes, and Read Extended Attributes. By assigning the NTFS Read permission, you actually assign the four underlying permissions.

Print permissions work similarly, though they aren't as complex. There are three basic permissions and three additional granular permissions. The basic permissions are as follows:

Print   The user can send jobs to the printer. Print includes "Read permissions." The Everyone group is granted "Print permission" by default.

Manage this printer   The user can change printer properties and permissions on the printer. "Manage this printer" includes the following: Print, Read permissions, Change permissions, and Take ownership. The Administrators, Server Operators, and Print Operators groups are all assigned the "Manage this printer" permission by default.

Manage documents   User can control document-specific settings and pause, resume, restart, and delete spooled print jobs. This permission includes the following: "Read permissions," "Change permissions," and "Take ownership." The Creator Owner, Administrators, Server Operators, and Print Operators groups are all assigned the "Manage documents" permission by default.

When users send print jobs to the printer, they become a member of the Creator Owner group for that print job and manage that document.

PERMISSIONS ARE CUMULATIVE

If a user is granted multiple permissions because they are members of multiple groups, they will be granted the cumulative value of all the permissions. For example, if a user is a member of the Everyone group and is granted Print permission and is also a member of another group and is granted "Manage this printer" permission, they have a combination of all the permissions.

The only exception is if Deny is used. If a user is a member of group granted Print permission and a member of another group that is assigned Deny permission, Deny will always win. Just as Deny takes precedence in NTFS and share permissions, Deny takes precedence with printer permissions.

You can use the basic permissions to accomplish most, if not all, of your requirements. However, if you click the Advanced button on the Security tab and then click the Edit button, you'll see the advanced permissions, as shown in Figure 13.32.

The advanced permissions include the basic permissions and these three additional permissions:

Read permissions   The user can view the permissions assigned to any users and groups for the printer. The Everyone group is granted "Read permissions" by default.

Change permissions   The user can change the permissions all users and groups have for that printer. The Administrators, Server Operators, and Print Operators groups are all assigned "Change permission" by default.

Take ownership   The user can take ownership of the printer. As the owner, the user can grant themselves any of the permissions.

The Administrators, Server Operators, and Print Operators groups are all assigned the "Take ownership" permission by default.

FIGURE 13.32
Editing
advanced printer
permissions

To set or edit the permissions assigned to a printer, log in with an account that is granted "Change permissions," open the printer's properties sheets, and access the Security tab. If you want to add any user or group, click the Add button, and add the user or group just as you'd add a user or group for NTFS permissions (it's the same dialog box and procedure). With the user or group added, select Allow or Deny for the desired permission.

Now that you have a basic understanding of how print permissions work, we'll cover some common scenarios of how the permissions can be used.

USING PRINTER PERMISSIONS TO RESTRICT ACCESS

When a printer is created, the Everyone group is granted the Print permission. Although this often works just fine, there are some exceptions.

We once remember working in an organization where we had a very elaborate color printer used to produce some beautiful documents. It used special paper and special toner, and the cost to print each page was expensive. One day, the boss found several color pages printed out from a website using this printer and…well, let's just say he wasn't happy.

He wanted to change the permission so only a select group of users could print to this printer and so it wasn't available to everyone. We simply used the Security tab, removed the Everyone group, added a group that included the special users, and granted this group Allow for the Print permission.

If a user doesn't have the Print permission (and when the Everyone group is removed, most users will no longer have the Print permission), they are not able to send print jobs to the print device.

DON'T DENY EVERYONE

If you deny the Print permission to the Everyone group, instead of removing the Everyone group, no one will be able to print. Remember, Deny takes precedence. Since everyone is in the Everyone group, everyone will be denied. It doesn't matter who is granted Allow; Deny takes precedence.

USING PRINTER PERMISSIONS FOR DELEGATION

It's common to delegate permission to someone located close to the printer to manage documents on the printer. This person can then administer the common problems associated with the printer without needing an administrator.

As an example, a printer could be located in an office with six people. Let's say that Joe sends a lengthy print job to the printer and then heads off to a meeting. Unfortunately, his job hangs up. Not only is his job not printing, but the other jobs behind his are held in a queue, waiting for his job to finish. Everyone is on hold until Joe comes back and cancels his job. Since the job is owned by Joe, only he can cancel it (or someone else with the "Manage documents" permission).

A common solution is to assign someone responsible in the office the "Manage documents" permission. If anyone's job gets hung up, this person can then pause, resume, restart, and delete spooled print jobs. Users in the office don't need to wait until Joe comes back or ask a busy administrator for help.

AUDITING PRINTER ACCESS

Curious to know who's doing what to the printers under your care? You can turn to the Auditing tab (accessible by clicking the Advanced button in the Security section of a printer's properties) to set up auditing. All auditable events will be recorded in the Security log.

It's relatively easy to enable auditing. The following steps will enable auditing of any successful printing to a printer:

1. Access the properties of the printer you want to audit, and select the Security tab.

2. Click Advanced, and select the Auditing tab.

3. Click Add, and enter the name of the group you want to audit. If you want to audit all users, enter **Everyone**. Select Check Names to ensure the group is recognized. Your display will look similar to Figure 13.33. Click OK.

4. The permissions page will appear. Select the Successful check box next to Print, as shown in Figure 13.34. Notice that it also selects "Read permissions" automatically. Click OK. Click OK to close the advanced settings.

You're not quite done yet. Even though auditing has been enabled on the printer object, you still need to ensure that auditing is possible in the environment. This is typically done via Group Policy. You can use the Local Security Policy snap-in for a stand-alone server. If you're in a domain, you can create a new Group Policy object (GPO) or use an existing GPO such as the Default Domain Policy.

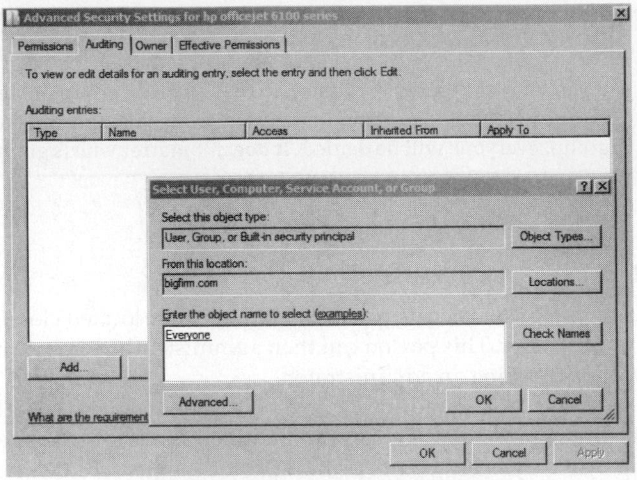

FIGURE 13.33
Enabling auditing
for Everyone

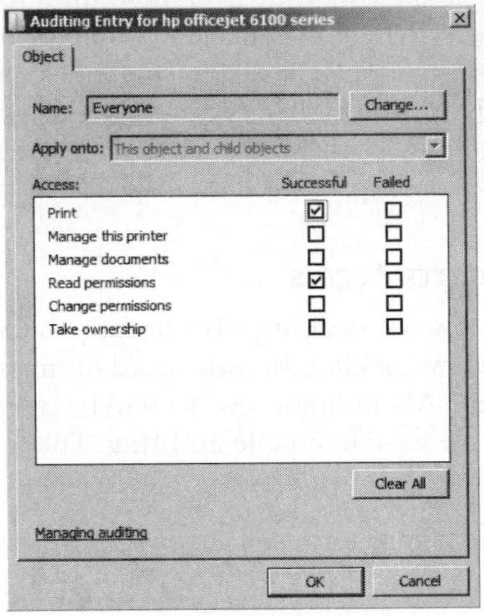

FIGURE 13.34
Auditing successful
printing attempts

Follow these steps to enable auditing of object access in the Default Domain Policy:

1. Launch the GPMC by selecting Start ➢ Administrative Tools ➢ Group Policy Management.

2. Browse to your domain, and select the Default Domain Policy. Right-click the Default Domain Policy, and select Edit, as shown in Figure 13.35.

3. The Group Policy Management Editor will launch. Browse to the Computer Configuration \Policies\Windows Settings\Security Settings\Local Policies\Audit Policy node.

4. Double-click the "Audit object access" property.

5. Select the "Define these policy settings" check box, and select the Success check box. Your display will look similar to Figure 13.36. Click OK.

FIGURE 13.35

Modifying the
Default Domain
Policy using
the GPMC

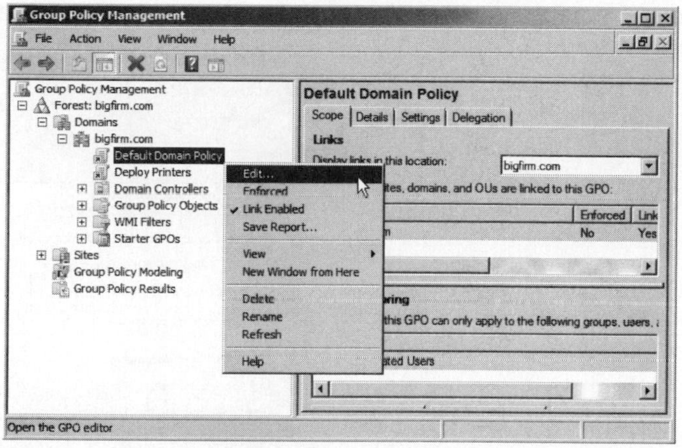

ENABLING OBJECT ACCESS AUDITING

Enabling object access auditing must be done before auditing on any individual objects will occur. In this context, objects are resources such as printers, files, and folders. Once object access auditing is enabled via Group Policy, then auditing can be enabled on any individual objects. However, if auditing is enabled on the object but object access auditing is not enabled, then auditing doesn't occur at all. Both steps must be done.

FIGURE 13.36

Enabling object
access auditing
in the Group Policy
Management
Editor

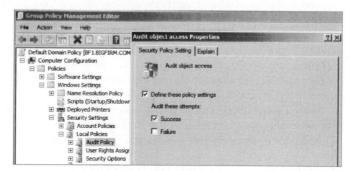

6. Close all the windows, and you're done.

Printer Properties Advanced Tab

The Advanced tab gives you the ability to set and configure a lot of different capabilities including adding a schedule for the printer, adding priorities for the printer, updating the driver, and doing some miscellaneous document management features and tasks.

Figure 13.37 shows the Advanced tab. Refer to this figure as we discuss the different capabilities.

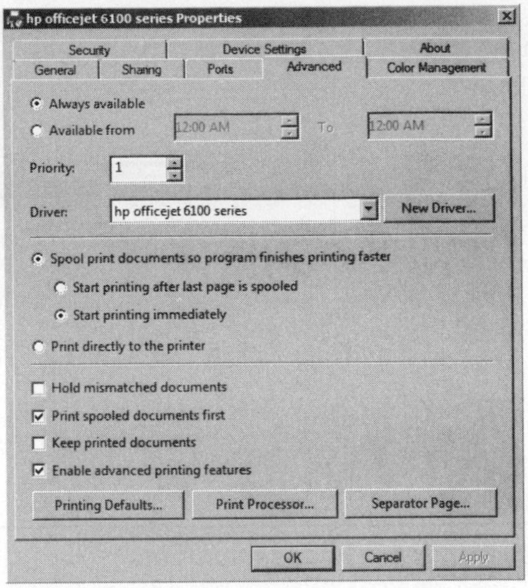

FIGURE 13.37
Printer properties
Advanced tab

SETTING AVAILABLE HOURS

You can make printers available all the time to everybody (which is the default), or you can pick and choose the times the printer will be available.

A printer will always accept print jobs, but you can manipulate the time when a printer will send jobs to the print device. If a print job is sent to a printer outside of these hours, the job will be queued and printed when the scheduled time arrives. Jobs queued in this manner won't prevent other jobs from printing.

As a simple example, suppose that Sally occasionally needs to print lengthy documents needed for the following day. Without a printer schedule, she'd print with everyone else. As her print jobs are printing, everyone else's print jobs will have to wait.

However, if you alter the printer schedule for Sally, her jobs could be set to print between the hours of 8 p.m. and 5 a.m.—when everyone else is gone.

There's an important point to grasp here, though. If you create a printer named LaserJet1 that everyone uses to print and then you alter the schedule for LaserJet1, you've just altered the schedule for everyone. What you must do is create a new printer.

Creating a Second Printer for a Single Print Device

You'd create new printer using the procedures covered earlier in this chapter. Remember, the printer is the software component, and the print device is the physical device that creates the printed output. When creating the new printer, make sure you do two things:

- ◆ Give the new printer a different name and share name.

- ◆ Choose the same settings (port, printer manufacturer and model, and so on) you chose for the first printer.

Sending documents to the new printer will cause them to print on the same print device. The only difference will lie in the configuration options you set for the new printer.

In this example, you could name your printer AfterHoursLaser. All the settings would be the same, except you'd edit the printer's hours of availability.

Modifying the New Printer

Once you've created the second printer, you simply access the Advanced tab, select Available From, and select the desired time. You'd need to provide some training to the user to ensure the user understood that any jobs sent to this printer would not print until the scheduled time.

You can also modify the security settings so only Sally could print to this printer. And, if desired, you can modify the share settings so other users can't find the share. If you place a $ symbol at the beginning of the share, it will be hidden. Users who know the printer name can still reach it, but it won't be visible.

SETTING PRINTER PRIORITIES

The default priority of a printer is 1, but you can choose different priorities between 1 and 99, where 99 is the highest priority. If several print jobs are waiting to be sent to a print device, they are queued. Print jobs with higher priorities (such as 99) will be placed in the queue ahead of print jobs with lower priorities (such as 1).

Print jobs that have a higher priority don't stop active print jobs. In other words, if a job with a priority of 1 is printing and a job with a priority of 99 is received, the priority 1 job will complete before the priority 99 job starts.

Let's state the obvious here, though. If everyone is using a printer named LaserJet1 and you change the priority of LaserJet1 to 50, you've just modified the priority for everyone. It doesn't matter what the priority is if it's the same for everyone.

Just as you need to create a new printer to assign a different schedule, you need to create a new printer to assign a different priority. It's also a good idea to modify the permissions so that only the person needing the higher priority printer can use it; include the $ symbol at the beginning of the share name to hide it.

CONFIGURING SPOOLER SETTINGS

The different settings in the middle of the Advanced tab of the properties sheet affect how the spooler works. Spooling documents means the application you're printing from is tied up only for the time it takes to create the spool file, not to print the entire document. This is called *printing in the background*.

Normally, they will be set with the following settings:

◆ Spool print documents so program finishes printing faster

◆ Start printing documents immediately

You can configure it so that printing starts only after the last page is spooled. This could be used if the printer is quicker than your computer (not likely today).

If you can't use print spooling for some reason—perhaps if the print server's hard disk is so full that it can't create the spool file—then you can send documents directly to the printer port, without creating a spool file or using print server resources. Select "Print directly to the printer" on the Advanced tab.

Disabling spooling is not something you'll often want to do. Spool files allow you to print large and complex documents without running out of printer memory. They also allow users to regain control of their applications quicker. Disable print spooling only if you can't print otherwise—it's something to mess around with if images aren't coming out properly.

MISCELLANEOUS SPOOLING SETTINGS

There are four additional miscellaneous settings close to the bottom of the Advanced tab of the printer properties:

Hold mismatched documents A mismatched document is a print job sent to the print device that needs a different form or tray. Instead of printing it incorrectly or deleting the job, the spooler holds the print jobs until the printer is reconfigured.

Print spooled documents first This is selected by default. It causes jobs that have completed spooling to print before jobs that are in the process of spooling—even if the job being spooled has a higher priority.

Keep printed documents Normally documents are deleted from the queue after they're printed, but it is possible to keep a copy of the documents by selecting this option. This option allows you to easily reprint documents. Make sure your hard drive has enough space to store these documents if this is selected.

Enable advanced printing features Many printers have advanced printing features. By selecting this option, the advanced features will be available. If they're causing problems, you can simply disable the advanced features by deselecting the box.

USING SEPARATOR PAGES

When a lot of people are using the same printer, keeping print jobs organized can get complicated. To help you minimize the number of people who wander off with each other's print jobs, the operating system supports separator pages. These extra pages are printed at the beginning of documents to identify the person doing the printing, the time, the job number, or whatever other information is defined in the page. (We'll explain how you can tell what information a page will print and how you can create your own custom separator pages in a minute.)

SEPARATOR PAGES ARE ASSIGNED TO PRINTERS

Like other printer options, separator pages are assigned to printers, not to print devices, so you can use a different separator page for each printer.

CHOOSING A SEPARATOR PAGE

Printers don't use separator pages by default. However, several separator pages are included in Windows Server 2008 R2 and can be added to your printer.

With the printer properties open to the Advanced tab, click the Separator Page button, and click Browse. It will open to the `Windows\System32` directory, and you can choose one of the four provided separator pages. Figure 13.38 shows the `sysprint.sep` separator page being added.

FIGURE 13.38

Adding a separator page

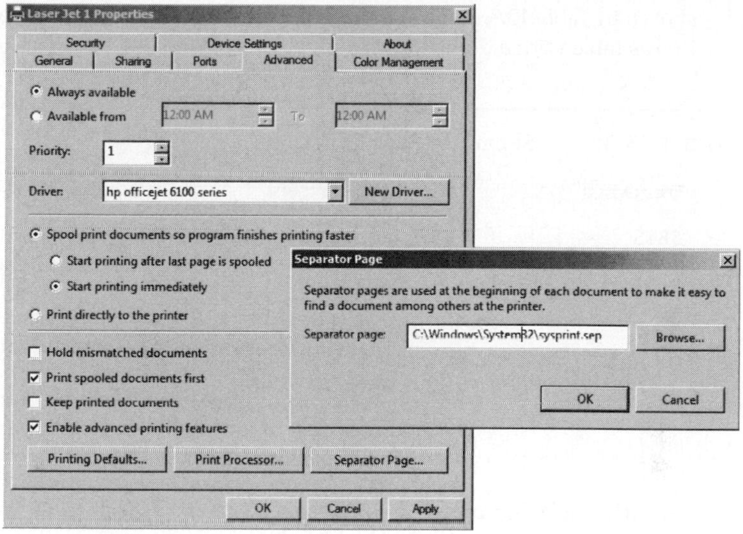

Table 13.2 describes the four built-in separator pages.

TABLE 13.2: Default Separator Pages

PAGE NAME	DESCRIPTION	COMPATIBILITY
sysprint.sep	Prints a separator page before print jobs	PostScript
pcl.sep	Switches a dual-language printer to PCL mode	PCL
pscript.sep	Switches a dual-language printer to PostScript mode	PostScript
sysprtj.sep	This is the same as the sysprint.sep page but with support for Japanese characters	PostScript

CREATING A NEW SEPARATOR PAGE

Given that the built-in separator pages are mostly necessary in specific instances, you'll probably want to create your own separator pages if you use them at all. Separator page files are just text files, so you can create the file in Notepad. You can also copy the original files and modify them to fit your needs.

On the first line of the new file, type a single character—any character will do—and press Enter. This character will now be the *escape character* that alerts the print server that you're performing a function, not entering text, so make it one that you won't need for anything else. Dollar signs ($) and pound signs (#) are both good escape characters, but the only rule is that you can't use the character as text.

Once you've picked an escape code, customize the separator page with any of the variables shown in Table 13.3. Be sure to include the escape character before each function, as we've shown in this table with a dollar sign.

TABLE 13.3:   Separator Page Functions

VARIABLE	FUNCTIONS
BS	Prints text in block characters created with pound signs (#) until you insert a $U. Be warned—printing text like this takes up a lot of room.
$D	Prints the date the job was printed, using the format defined on the Date tab of the Regional Options applet in the Control Panel.
$E	Equivalent to a page break in Word; all further functions will be executed on a new page. If you get an extra blank separator page when you print, remove this function from the SEP file.
$Fpathname\filename	Prints the contents of the specified file to the separator page, starting on a blank line. Because separator pages are strictly text only, only the text will be printed—no formatting.
$Hnn	Sets a printer-specific control sequence, where nn is a hex ASCII code that goes directly to the printer. Look in your printer manual for any codes that you might set this way and for instructions on how and when to use them.
$I	Prints the job number. Each print job has a job number associated with it.
$Lxxx	Prints all the characters following (represented here with xxx) until it comes to another escape code. Use this function to print any customized text you like.
$N	Prints the login name of the person who submitted the print job.
$n	Skips n lines (where n is a number from 0 to 9). Skipping 0 lines just moves printing to the next line, so you could use that function to define where line breaks should occur.
$T	Prints the time the job was printed, using the format defined on the Time tab of the Regional Options applet in the Control Panel.
$U	Turns off block character printing.
$Wnn	Sets the line width, where nn is a number of characters. Any characters in excess of this line width are truncated. The default (which you don't have to define) is 80 characters.

For example, you could use the following text in the SEP file:

```
$
$N
$n
$0
$D
$L This is a separator page. Only use these pages to organize
$L print jobs because they're otherwise a waste of paper.
```

It will produce this output:

```
Darril
10/31/09 This is a separator page. Only use these pages to organize
print jobs because they're otherwise a waste of paper.
```

Notice that there are line breaks only if you specifically include them. Without the $n codes, all output will be on a single line.

When you're done, save the separator page file with an .sep extension to the %*systemroot*%\ system32 folder if you want to store it with other separator pages. Otherwise, you can store the page anywhere on the print server. To use the new page, just load it as you would one of the defaults.

Managing Print Jobs

Managing print jobs is pretty straightforward. You can use the Print Management console and select Printers for the print server. You can then right-click the printer you're interested in and select Open Printer Queue.

Figure 13.39 shows the print queue open for a printer named Laser Jet 1. Notice in the figure that the Printers node also shows the queue status and the number of jobs in queue. We paused the printer so that the print jobs could build up as we sent several print jobs to the printer.

FIGURE 13.39
Viewing the print queue for a printer

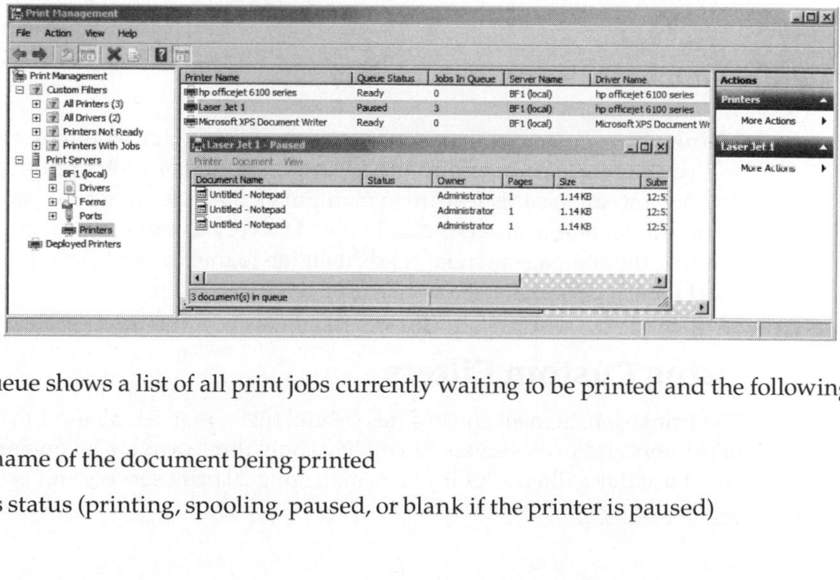

The print queue shows a list of all print jobs currently waiting to be printed and the following information:

◆ The filename of the document being printed

◆ The job's status (printing, spooling, paused, or blank if the printer is paused)

◆ Who sent the job to the printer

◆ How many pages are in the job and how many remain to be printed

◆ The file size of the print job

◆ The time and date the user submitted the job

When you select a job in the list, you can use the tools in the Document menu to pause a job, resume a paused job, restart a print job from the beginning, or cancel a print job. The only catch is that you have to do all this while the job is still spooling to the print device. You can't control the parts of the job that have already been sent to the print device.

If you pause a print job before it actually starts printing, you can edit its priority or printing times in the middle of printing. From the Document menu, choose Properties to open the dialog box in Figure 13.40.

FIGURE 13.40
Viewing the properties of a print job

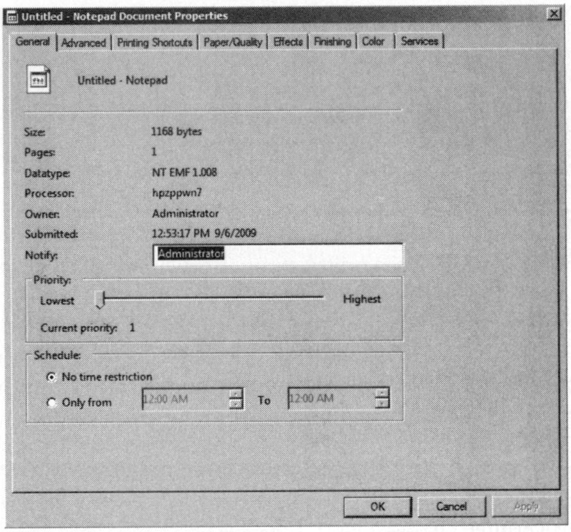

From here, you can view many properties inherited from the printer and passed to the job, and you can raise or lower the job's priority. The higher a job's priority, the higher its place in line, so you can use this feature to manipulate the order in which jobs print even if one job got to the printer before another did. This can be very useful on those occasions when the person printing the 200-page manual sends their job to the printer before the person creating a cover sheet for a FedEx package that has to be ready by 3:30 p.m.

Using Custom Filters

The Print Management console has several filters that can be used to assist with management of printers and print servers. If you have only three printers on one print server, you probably won't use these filters. But if you're managing 20 print servers and each print server has as many as 100 printers, these filters can be quite valuable.

The built-in filters are fairly straightforward:

All Printers   This shows all printers from all servers managed by the PMC. If the PMC is managing only a single server, this view will the same as the Printers node within the Servers node.

All Drivers   This shows all drivers from all servers managed by the PMC. If the PMC is managing only a single server, this view will the same as the Drivers node within the Servers node.

Printers Not Ready   If any printers are not reporting to the server because they are not ready (because of being offline, paused, out of paper, or any other reason), they will be listed here. Printers that aren't powered up or otherwise not reachable from the print server will not be listed here.

Printers with Jobs   If any printers have jobs that are either printing or in queue, they will be listed here.

You can also create custom filters to meet any specific needs. You can launch the wizard by right-clicking Custom Filters and selecting Add New Printer Filter or Add New Driver Filter. Give your filter a name and description, and then you can add your filter criteria. Figure 13.41 shows the filter criteria you can choose.

FIGURE 13.41
Defining a
custom filter

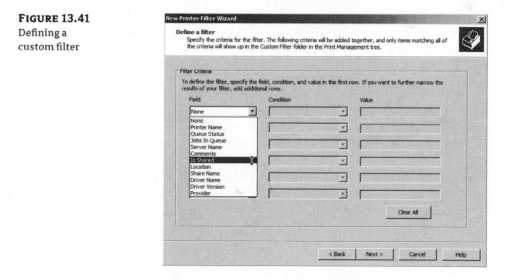

Depending on which field you select, you'll have different conditions that can be selected (such as "is exactly" or "is not exactly"), and you can then enter a value (such as **true** or **false**). It's possible to configure multiple conditions for any single filter. If all conditions are met, the filter will detect the printer or printers.

You also have the ability to configure notifications with your filter. Notifications can be configured to send an email or run a script. Figure 13.42 shows the notification page.

You wouldn't to do this for all your filters, or you'd start getting spammed by your print server. However, you could have a high-priority printer that needs to be fixed as soon as a problem is detected. You could create a filter with one condition to identify this printer and a second condition with a field of Queue Status, a condition of "is exactly," and a value of Error. Now whenever this filter detects this printer in error, it would send a notification. Or, if the solution was to run a script, you could configure the filter to automatically run the script.

FIGURE 13.42
Configuring the
notifications

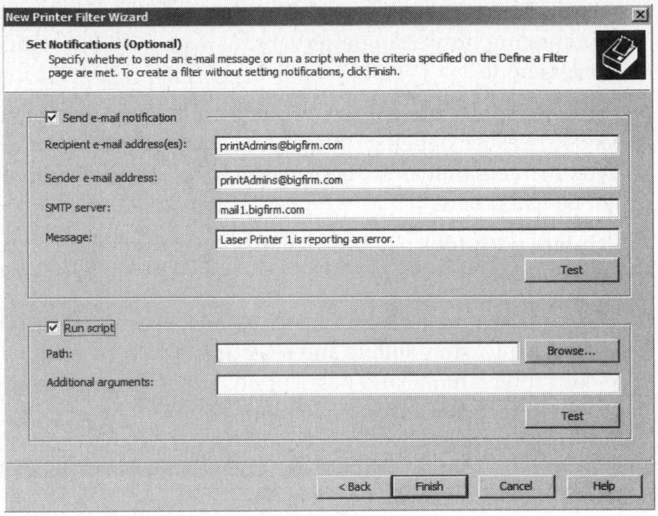

Troubleshooting Printer Problems

Printing under Server 2008 R2 is usually pretty trouble-free—in the software, at any rate—but every once in a while you may run into problems. The remainder of this chapter describes some of the more common printing problems and tells you how to solve them.

Basic Troubleshooting: Identifying the Situation

First, try to figure out *where* the problem lies. Is it the printer? The application? The network? If you can tell where the problem lies, you'll simplify the troubleshooting process.

PAPER JAMS

The printing problem that frustrates us most is paper jams. Getting that last shred of jammed paper out of the printer can drive you to madness. To minimize paper jams, store paper somewhere with low humidity (curled paper jams easier), don't overfill the paper tray, and keep paper neat before it goes in the tray. Further, some paper is designed to be printed to a specific side; it is packaged with an arrow on the ream and should be loaded with the arrow pointing up.

There are also a lot of differences between paper types. As one of many examples, copy paper and printer paper have many different properties, and using paper designed for copying machines may impact the quality in addition to increasing the risks of paper jams.

Printer troubles can happen because of any combination of three different causes:

◆ Hardware errors

◆ Software errors

◆ User errors

No One Can Print

If no one can print, check the print device and network connection. Check the easy stuff first. Is the printer on and online? Does the cartridge have ink? Is the printer server up and running? Did the printer *ever* work, or is this its maiden voyage? If it never worked, make sure you have the right driver installed, or try downloading a newer one from the manufacturer's website.

From the console, check the port settings. Is the printer sending data to the port the print device is connected to? Make sure to set up the TCP/IP port for a network-connected printer properly.

Also, see whether you can print from the print server's console. There could be a network problem preventing people from reaching the print server.

Make sure there's enough space on the print server's hard disk to store spool files. If the print server can't create spool files, it can't print from a spool.

Make sure the printer is set up to use the proper print processor.

If using Internet Printing, make sure that this service is enabled.

Some People Can't Print

What do those people have in common? Are they all in a single subnet? In the same user group? Using the same application? Printing to the same printer? Find the element they have in common, and that's probably the element that's causing the printing problem. For example, if everyone who's printing from one subnet can print but users from another subnet cannot print, the problem is with the network, not the printer.

One Person Can't Print

If only one person can't print, try to narrow down the source of the problem. Can the person print from another application? Can the person print from another computer? If this person can't print at all, see whether someone else can print from their computer. If so, check the permissions attached to the person who can't print. They may be denied access to the printer altogether.

REBOOTING SOLVES MANY ILLS

If only one person is having printing problems, try rebooting the computer and retrying the print job. You can resolve many issues by rebooting the user's computer. You won't always know what the exact problem was, but it'll be solved, and both you and the user will be off doing more important things.

Restarting the Spooler Service

A common problem that occurs with print servers is that the print spooler service occasionally hangs. When this occurs, print jobs don't print and can't be canceled. The solution is to stop and restart the Print Spooler service.

You can restart a service from the Services applet (available in Administrative Tools). Find the Print Spooler service, right-click it, and select Restart. Sometimes you'll need to select Stop and, then after it stops, select Start.

Of course, you can also do the same thing from the command line with the following commands:

```
Net stop spooler
Net start spooler
```

Isolating Printer Drivers

A new feature available with Windows Server 2008 R2 is the ability to isolate print drivers from the operating system. If you find that a print driver is not playing well with others but still allows users to print, you can simply isolate it. Figure 13.43 shows a driver that has been configured in driver isolation mode.

FIGURE 13.43
Setting print driver isolation

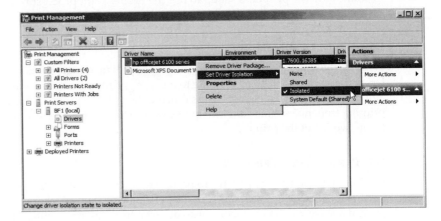

By isolating a printer driver, you can prevent a faulty driver from stopping all the print operations on a server. These are the three available choices:

None   Driver isolation isn't attempted.

Shared   Drivers operate in a shared process.

Isolated   The driver is isolated. This does take additional resources so should be used only when necessary and can be useful for testing new drivers.

System Default (Shared)   This is used by default for all new drivers added to the server.

The Bottom Line

Add the Print and Document Services role   Windows Server 2008 R2 servers can be configured to perform as print servers. One of the first steps you must take is to add the Print and Document Services role. There are different steps needed if you're adding the role to a full installation of Windows Server 2008 R2 vs. a Server Core installation.

> **Master It**   What tool would you use to add the Print and Document Services role on a full installation of Windows Server 2008 R2? What tool would you use to add the Print and Document Services role on a Server Core installation of Windows Server 2008 R2?

Manage printers using the Print Management console   After adding the Print and Documents Services role to the server, you can use the Print Management console to manage other print servers, printers, and print drivers.

> **Master It**   Your company has purchased a new print device, and you want it to be hosted on a server that is configured as a print server. How would you add the printer to the print server?

Manage print server properties   The spool folder can sometimes take a significant amount of space on the C drive, resulting in space problems and contention issues with the operating system. Because of these issues, the spool folder is often moved to another physical drive.

> **Master It**   You want to move the spool folder to another location. How can you do this?

Manage printer properties   Printers can be added to Active Directory so that they can be easily located by searching Active Directory. Printers must be shared first, but they aren't published to Active Directory by default when they are shared.

> **Master It**   You want users to be able to easily locate a shared printer. What can you do to ensure the shared printer can be located by searching Active Directory?

Chapter 14

Remote Server Administration

The day-to-day administration of any server rarely occurs at the server. Instead, administrators commonly connect to servers remotely.

The servers are humming along smoothly in a cool (and sometimes downright cold) server room protected with physical security. Administrators are often in a comfortable office running a desktop system like Windows XP, Windows Vista, or Windows 7. When administration is necessary, they connect to the servers remotely.

With this in mind, you need to know how to configure the servers for remote administration and connect to the servers from your desktop. Either that, or you will spend your time in the server room bundled up in a parka in the middle of the summer.

In this chapter, you will learn to:

- ◆ Configure Windows Server 2008 R2 servers for remote administration

- ◆ Remotely connect to Windows Server 2008 R2 servers using Remote Desktop Connection

- ◆ Remotely connect to Windows Server 2008 R2 servers using a Remote Desktop Protocol file

- ◆ Configure a server for Remote Assistance

- ◆ Install the Remote Server Administration Tools

Remote Desktop for Administration

Remote Desktop for Administration is the default implementation of Remote Desktop Services (RDS) on a Windows Server 2008 R2 server. In this mode, as many as two administrators can be remotely logged onto a server at the same time performing remote administration.

It's also possible to configure a server as a Remote Desktop Session Host server so that it can run desktops or desktop applications for remote users. However, configuring the server as a Remote Desktop Session Host server requires additional licenses and a licensing server. When using the server in the Remote Desktop for Administration mode, no additional licensing is required.

TERMINAL SERVICES RENAMED

If you've been working with previous versions of Windows, you're probably familiar with some of the RDS features, but by a different name. In past versions, Remote Desktop Services was known as Terminal Services. It was renamed to RDS in Windows Server 2008 R2.

Remote Desktop for Administration allows you to connect to a server and do just about anything remotely that you could if you were physically at the server. You can access the Start menu, launch tools, install applications, install updates, and do much more when connected remotely. The two primary tools you'll use are Remote Desktop Connection and Remote Desktop.

The primary limitation you have is if the remote system needs a reboot or restart. Although it is possible to reboot the system remotely, when you do so, you will be disconnected. If something prevents the system from rebooting, you won't know what the problem is or be able to resolve it.

Configuring the Server for Remote Desktop

You can enable Remote Desktop on the server in several ways. You can access the advanced properties page of the server by one of the following methods:

◆ Click Enable Remote Desktop in the Initial Configuration Tasks window that appears when the system first boots.

◆ Click Start, right-click Computer, and select Properties. Click Remote settings to access the Remote tab of the System Properties dialog box.

Figure 14.1 shows the configuration choices you have on the Remote tab.

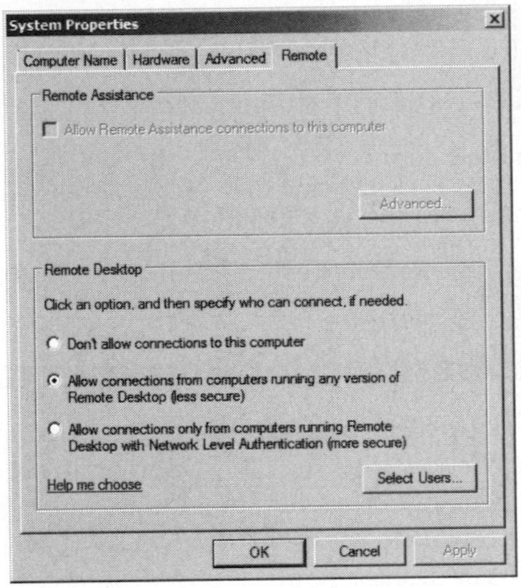

FIGURE 14.1
Configuring
Remote Desktop
from the Remote
tab of the System
Properties
dialog box

You can see that Windows Server 2008 R2 provides three choices for configuring the server for remote administration:

Don't allow connections to this computer   Remote Desktop is disabled.

Allow connections from computers running any version of Remote Desktop (less secure)
This will allow remote connections from clients that are using a version of RDC older than RDC 6.0, which provides less security. This setting supports users connecting with Windows XP running the older RDC.

Allow connections only from computers running Remote Desktop with Network Level Authentication (more secure)   This supports connections from clients using RDC 6.0 or newer. RDC 6.0 and newer is available on Windows Vista and Windows 7. RDC 6.1 can be installed on Windows XP systems with at least SP2 installed.

When you enable Remote Desktop Connection, an exception is automatically created in the firewall on the local system. It's not necessary to add other exceptions on the local firewall. However, if you connect through a network firewall, port 3389 needs to be opened to allow the remote connections through. If opening port 3389 on your network firewall is not feasible in your network, you can create a Remote Desktop Gateway server as described later in this chapter.

Network Level Authentication (NLA) is a security feature available in Remote Desktop Services when the more secure setting is selected. NLA provides added security by completing the user authentication before the remote connection is established. If NLA is not used, the server is vulnerable to a denial-of-service attack.

NLA should be used whenever possible. The following are the requirements to support NLA:

- The client computer must be running at least RDC 6.0. RDC 6.0 is natively supported in Windows Vista clients.

- The client computer must support the Credential Security Support Provider (CredSSP) protocol.

- The server must be running Windows Server 2008 R2.

RDC 6.1 FOR WINDOWS XP

The original version of RDC used in Windows XP doesn't support NLA. However, Microsoft later created RDC 6.1 for clients running Windows XP SP2 or SP3 that provides support for many of the features available in Windows Server 2008 R2 connections.

RDC 6.1 is available as a free download and is documented in KB article 952155 (`http://support` `.microsoft.com/kb/952155/`). RDC 6.0 is supported in Windows XP SP3.

Additionally, the CredSSP protocol can be enabled via a registry modification on Windows XP, as described in KB article 951608 (`http://support.microsoft.com/kb/951608/`).

Using Remote Desktop Connection

Remote Desktop Connection (RDC) is used to connect to a remote server. The version that works best with Windows Server 2008 R2 is RDC 6.0 or greater. Earlier versions don't support all of the features available, such as NLA.

You can launch RDC in Windows Vista, Windows 7, and Windows Server 2008 R2 by selecting Start ➢ All Programs ➢ Accessories ➢ Remote Desktop Connection. Once RDC is launched, you can click the Options button to view all the options available, as shown in Figure 14.2.

RDC includes six tabs that can be manipulated to provide different features, as detailed in the following sections.

RDC GENERAL TAB

The General tab is used to identify the remote computer you want to connect with and the user account you'll use to connect. Additionally, you can save your settings in a Remote Desktop Protocol (RDP) file from this page.

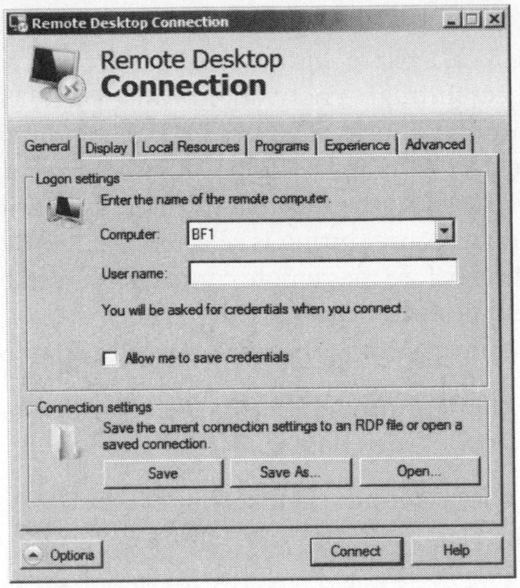

FIGURE 14.2
Remote Desktop
Connection with
Options expanded

By saving your settings in an RDP file, you can simply double-click the file to start the session. Follow these steps to save and use your RDP file.

REMOTE SESSIONS ARE POSSIBLE ON LOCAL COMPUTERS

If you have only one computer, you can still follow these steps. It's possible to log onto the remote session of a computer while logged on locally. You should use a different account with administrative permissions for the remote session. Although this wouldn't be very useful on the job, it does allow you to see the process in a test system.

---

1. Launch RDC by selecting Start ➤ All Programs ➤ Accessories ➤ Remote Desktop Connection.

2. Click the Options button to expand the options.

3. Enter the remote computer's computer name in the Computer text box.

4. Enter a username that has permission to use RDC on the remote computer. If you want this username to be saved, select the "Allow me to save credentials" check box. You will be prompted for the password later.

5. Click Save As, and browse to the desktop. Rename the file name to RDC.rdp, and click Save.

6. Close the Remote Desktop Connection application.

7. Access your computer's desktop, and double-click the RDC.rdp file to launch it. Review the warnings on this dialog box, as shown in Figure 14.3. Click Details in the dialog box.

This dialog box allows you to pick some local resources that you can bring to your remote session. You can also manipulate local resource settings on the Local Resources tab when the Remote Desktop Connection tool opens.

FIGURE 14.3
Remote Desktop Connection unknown publisher warning

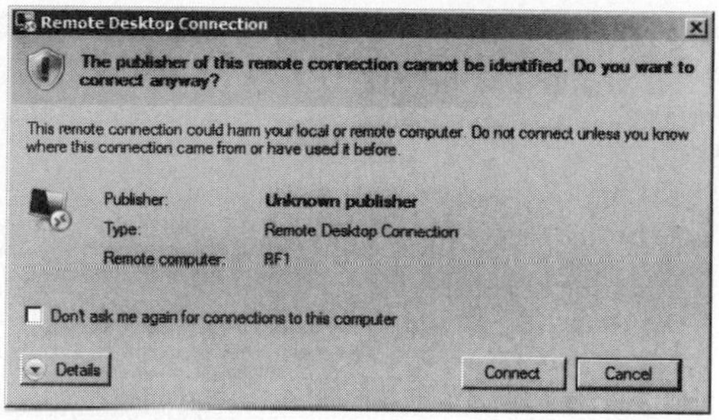

8. Since you created the RDP file, you can trust it and ignore the warnings. Click Connect.

9. A dialog box appears allowing you to enter the password for your account or use another account. Enter the password for an account with administrative privileges, and click OK.

10. After a moment, another warning will appear similar to Figure 14.4.

11. Click Yes to connect despite the warning. Your system will then connect to the remote session. Take your time looking around in the remote session.

12. If you used the defaults in RDC, the connection bar will display across the top of the screen with the name of the server. If you click the X to close the screen, you will disconnect the session, but you won't close it. The session will remain open consuming resources either until you reconnect or log off or until another administrator closes your session.

13. Click Start, and select Log Off to log off and close the session.

UNKNOWN PUBLISHER WARNINGS

When using an unsigned RDP file, you'll see two warnings indicating that the publisher of the remote connection cannot be identified and asking you whether you want to connect anyway. The first warning is shown at the top of the dialog box in Figure 14.3, and the second warning is shown in Figure 14.4.

RDP files can be signed using certificates for security. A signed RPP file has a signature within it indicating the identity of the client of the certificate authority (CA) that verified the identity. If you trust the CA, you'll trust this RDP file. When distributing RDP files to many clients, this added security feature can be quite valuable.

However, RDP files don't have to be signed. Since you are creating this RDP file, you can simply ignore the warnings.

If you'd like to learn more about signing the files or how to eliminate the errors, check out the following two Microsoft TechNet blog posts:

- http://blogs.technet.com/askperf/archive/2008/09/23/unknown-publisher-where-did-this-dialog-box-come-from.aspx

- http://blogs.technet.com/askperf/archive/2008/10/31/unknown-publisher-part-two.aspx

FIGURE 14.4
Remote Desktop Connection unknown certifying authority warning

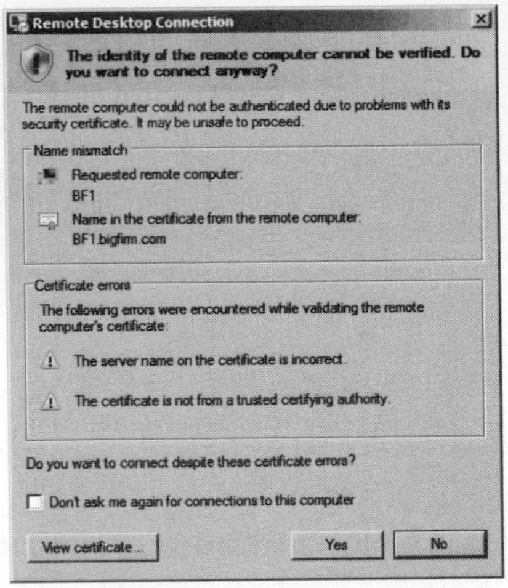

The RDP file is associated with the Remote Desktop Connection application, so by double-clicking it, you will launch RDC. However, this RDP file is simply a text file. If you want to look at the contents, you can launch Notepad and browse to the file to open the contents.

RDC DISPLAY TAB

The Display tab allows you to configure the display for the remote desktop. You can configure the size of the desktop and the colors from this page. Figure 14.5 shows the Display tab.

FIGURE 14.5
Remote Desktop Connection Display tab

If you drag the slider all the way to the right, the remote desktop will display in full-screen mode. By default, a connection bar will be displayed across the top when in full-screen mode.

INCREASED PERFORMANCE OVER A WAN LINK

If you're accessing the remote server over a slow WAN connection, you can get increased performance by using a smaller screen or reducing the number of colors displayed. This isn't a problem in a well-connected network with a maximum of two remote sessions, but with a slow link, every bit helps.

The connection bar includes the name of the remote server, which can be useful if have more than one instance of RDC running at a time. For example, if you're troubleshooting a problem and remote into three different servers using three different instances of RDC, you can quickly glance at the connection bar at the top of the window to remind yourself which server you're accessing.

When you remote into a server using RDC in full-screen mode, this connection bar is the only apparent difference you'll see. Everything else will look as if you're standing in front of the server.

At the left of the connection bar is a pushpin icon. It is selected by default and pins the connection bar to the top of the screen. You can deselect it to enable autohiding of the connection bar.

RDC LOCAL RESOURCES TAB

The Local Resources tab allows you to identify what resources you can bring to your remote session. For example, if you have a printer attached to your system and you want to print a log from the remote server, you can enable the local printer.

Microsoft introduced Easy Print in Windows Server 2008 that makes printer redirection easier with Remote Desktop Services and ensures that the client printers are installed in remote sessions. You don't have to install the print drivers on the server in order to print from an RDS session.

You can click the More button to enable additional resources during the remote session. Figure 14.6 shows the Local Resources tab and the additional resources that can be enabled after clicking the More button.

FIGURE 14.6
The Remote Desktop Connection Local Resources tab, with additional options

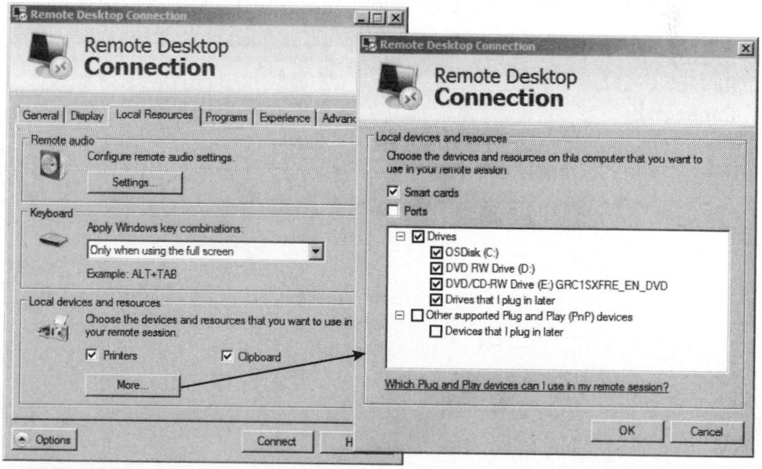

The primary reason why you'll access this tab is to enable or disable local devices and resources. Local printers and the local clipboard are enabled by default. The local clipboard allows you to copy text from your system (such as a script) and paste it into an application in the remote session.

Local drives are not enabled by default, but if you want to copy data from a local drive to the remote system, you can easily select the box. This does represent a security risk, though. If either the remote system or your local system is infected with malware, connecting the drives makes them accessible by the malware and susceptible to infection.

You can also configure the audio and keyboard settings. Audio settings include the following:

◆ Play on this computer (your local computer)

◆ Do not play

◆ Play on remote computer

If you're a fan of keyboard shortcuts, you may want to change the keyboard settings. The choices are as follows:

◆ On this computer

◆ On the remote computer

◆ Only when using the full screen

RDC PROGRAMS TAB

The Programs tab allows you to identify a program that will start when the remote connection is established. For example, you may always launch Server Manager when you start a specific server and want it to start automatically.

Figure 14.7 shows the RDC Programs tab. ServerManager.msc is entered in the text box, which will cause Server Manager to start when the connection is created.

FIGURE 14.7
Remote Desktop
Connection
Programs tab

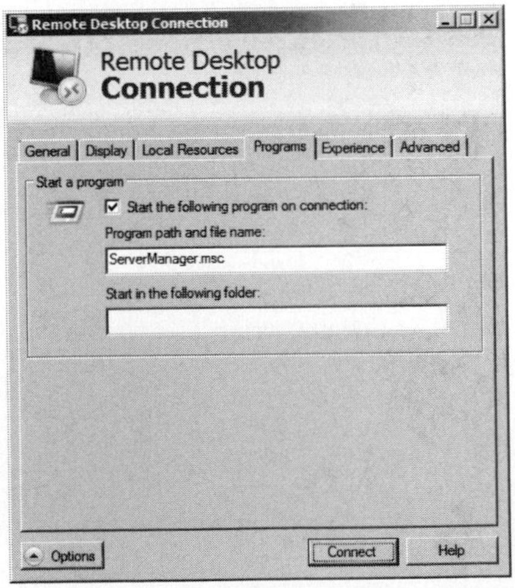

Since the path of Server Manager is already known by the system to be `%systemroot%\`
`System32`, the path doesn't need to be included. However, if you wanted to launch a different
program or script from an unknown path, you would need to include the full path.

SYSTEM PATH VARIABLE

You can identify what the known path of the system is by accessing the command line, typing
Path, and pressing Enter. Any applications in this path can be entered by just entering the name
of the application.

You can modify this path by clicking Start, right-clicking Computer, selecting Properties, and
then selecting Advanced system settings. Select the Advanced tab of System Properties, and click
the Environment Variables button. You can then select the Path system variable, and click Edit to
modify it. You shouldn't delete any paths, but you can add paths by entering a semicolon and the
additional path.

RDC EXPERIENCE TAB

You can add or remove different features from the RDC Experience tab. Different features such
as the desktop background, menu and window animations, and visual styles are available to
enhance the remote connection's display or experience.

Figure 14.8 shows the RDC Experience tab with the connection speed set to "LAN (10 Mbps
or higher)." These features take additional bandwidth, so default features are selected based on
the connection speed selected on this page.

FIGURE 14.8
Remote Desktop
Connection Expe-
rience tab

If you're connected in a local LAN, you have high-speed connectivity, so all of the features are
available. If you see a decrease in performance, you can deselect some of the features. Additionally,
if you connect using a modem over a 56Kbps connection, you could select the "Modem (56 Kbps)"
setting, and only persistent bitmap caching will be enabled by default.

The speed selection isn't automatically determined. When it is selected, default features are selected, but you can easily add or remove these features by selecting or deselecting the check box.

This page also includes the setting "Reconnect if the connection is dropped." This is useful on unreliable links. If the network connection is dropped, RDC will automatically try to reconnect.

RDC ADVANCED TAB

The RDC Advanced tab includes two sections: "Server authentication" and "Connect from anywhere."

Server authentication is a new security feature available when connecting to Windows Server 2008 servers. It provides verification that you are connecting to the computer that you intended to connect to, and it helps prevent the unintentional disclosure of confidential information.

You have three choices with server authentication:

Connect and don't warn me   You can use this if you are consistently connecting to pre–Windows Server 2008 servers that don't support server authentication. Since these servers don't support server authentication, they will always be giving warnings.

Warn me   This is the default. It would be used in a mixed environment of Windows Server 2008 servers and Windows 2003 (or older) servers.

Do not connect   If your environment is all Windows Server 2008 servers or newer, this setting will ensure that connections aren't created if the server can't authenticate.

Figure 14.9 shows the Remote Connection Advanced tab with the RD Gateway settings expanded.

FIGURE 14.9
Remote Desktop Connection Advanced tab and Remote Desktop Gateway settings

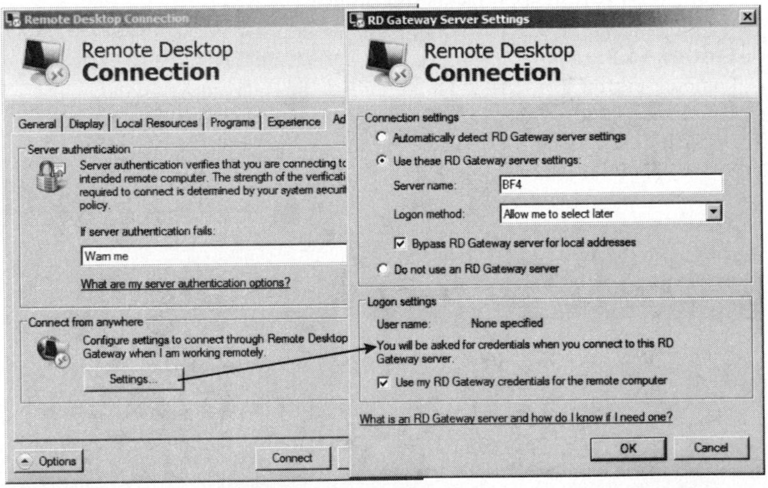

If you are connecting to a remote server through a Remote Desktop Gateway (RD Gateway) server, you would configure the connection settings here. RD Gateway will be covered in more detail later in this chapter.

The important thing to realize is that the server name you enter here is the gateway server. RDC will connect to this RDC server first and then to the remote server identified on the General tab.

You will need to authenticate with both the RD Gateway server and the remote computer. If you'll use the same credentials for both, you can leave the "Use my RD Gateway credentials for the remote computer" check box selected. With this check box selected, you will be challenged only once. If you deselect it, you will be challenged at both servers, and you can enter different credentials for each.

Although knowing what each of the tabs within the Remote Desktop Connection can do for you is useful, you'll want to know some other details. For example, you can launch it from the command line, and with any command-line command, there are useful switches to master. Additionally, you can control several different limitations on remote connections.

MSTSC

You can launch the Remote Desktop Connection from the Run line or the command line using the `mstsc.exe` command. The name `mstsc` is derived from Microsoft Terminal Services Connection. Even though Terminal Services has been renamed to Remote Desktop Services, the `mstsc` command is still the same.

You can access the help screen for `mstsc` by entering **mstsc /?** at the command line. The following items show some of the common usage for `mstsc`:

Default usage   Use the following command to launch Remote Desktop Connection (RDC):

```
mstsc
```

Identify a server   Connect to a server named Srv1 using the /v switch:

```
mstsc /v:Srv1
```

Use an RDP file   Launch RDC using an RDP file located in the path `c:\data\srv1.rdp`:

```
mstsc c:\data\Srv1.rdp
```

Connect in full-screen mode   Use the /f switch to launch RDC in full-screen mode after the connection is established:

```
mstsc /f
```

Use multiple monitors   If you want RDC to be able to span multiple monitors available on your local system, use the /span switch. This will cause the remote system to use the same width and height of your local desktop.

```
mstsc /span
```

Connect for administrative purposes   The /admin switch is used to connect to a Windows Server 2008 server for administrative purposes. This is meaningful only if the server has the Remote Desktop Services installed. In other words, when the server is being used for Remote Desktop for Administration mode only, all connections are for administrative purposes, and this switch isn't needed. However, if the server is configured as a Remote Desktop Session Host server, you can use this switch to connect to one of the two administrator sessions.

You can also use the /admin switch to launch RDC in legacy console mode when connecting to Windows Server 2003 servers. Windows Server 2003 servers support a console session that isn't supported in Windows Server 2008 R2. The /admin switch will connect to the console session in Windows Server 2003.

```
mstsc /admin
```

NO MORE /CONSOLE

Previous versions of mstsc had a console switch (mstsc /console) that allowed you to connect to the console session of the server. The console session was the same session you would connect to if you were standing in front of the server; it was also known as session 0.

However, in Windows Server 2008 R2, session 0 is a noninteractive session that is reserved for services. When you log onto the server while standing in front of it, the Remote Desktop Services Manager identifies the session as the console session, but it is not session 0.

When you were able to use Remote Desktop Connection to access the console session, you could access a total of three sessions. Since session 0 is no longer available, you are now limited to only two sessions.

For more information on the console session and why session 0 is no longer needed, check out KB article 947723 at http://support.microsoft.com/kb/947723.

CONNECTION LIMITATIONS

Only two connections are allowed to the server when it is used for normal administrative connections. In other words, only two administrators can be logged onto a single server at a time.

If the server is used to host desktops or applications for end users, then you can have as many connections as you need. Remote Desktop Services requires licenses for connections when used in Remote Desktop session host server mode. However, licenses are not required for the two administrator connections.

The two connections include either remote sessions or the session at the computer. Previous operating systems allowed you to connect to two remote sessions and the session at the computer. The session at the computer was referred to as the *console session* and you were even able to connect to this console session remotely but the console session is no longer available.

Figure 14.10 shows the result if a third user tries to connect when two sessions are already active.

In the figure, a user named Darril is physically located at the server and logged on. Sally is connected via a remote session. Joe tries to log on, but since his session will be the third session, it is blocked. Notice that the dialog box also indicates whether these sessions are active or idle. In the figure, Sally's session has been idle for 11 minutes, and Darril's session is active.

If Joe selects the check box next to "Force disconnect of this user" and selects one of the users, that user will be immediately disconnected with a message saying this:

"Your Remote Desktop session has ended. Another user connected to the remote computer so your connection was lost. Try connecting again, or contact your network administrator or technical support group."

FIGURE 14.10
Blocking the third
remote session

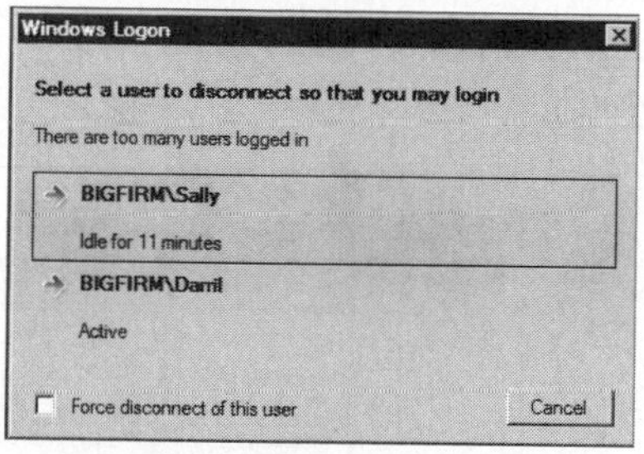

If Joe doesn't select the check box but instead just selects one of the users to disconnect the session, the user will get a notification. Figure 14.11 shows what appears on Darril's session when Joe tries to disconnect it without the check box selected. If Darril is working at the computer, he can see this connection attempt and click Cancel to block it. Otherwise, the request will automatically disconnect Darril's session after 30 seconds and allow Joe's session.

FIGURE 14.11
Disconnect request

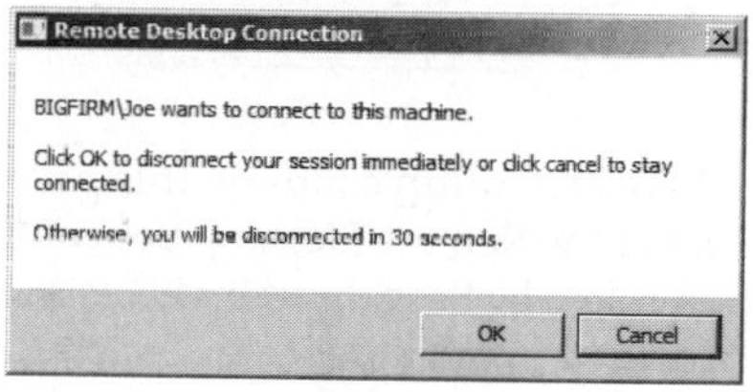

If Darril was active and clicked Cancel, Joe would receive a notification indicating that the logged-on user denied the disconnect request.

ACTIVE CONNECTIONS FOR INACTIVE SESSIONS

This method of closing an inactive administrator session provides a real-world solution to a common problem. We've worked in some large environments where administrators connect remotely to a server, but instead of logging off, they simply disconnect by closing the RDC application.

When this happens, the inactive session is left open on the server. If the server has reached the maximum number of sessions, other administrators can't log into a remote session. These inactive sessions would stay open until they timed out (if timeout settings were configured), the user logged back in and closed the session, or the session was closed in Remote Desktop Services Manager.

With the features now available in RDC, you can easily see who's connected, whether the session is active or idle, and even choose to disconnect the session.

CONFIGURING SESSION PROPERTIES

You can configure session properties for remote sessions in the Remote Desktop Session Host Configuration tool. You can access this tool by selecting Start ➤ Administrative Tools ➤ Remote Desktop Services ➤ Remote Desktop Session Host Configuration.

The primary configuration you'll use here when using Remote Desktop for Administration is the RDP-Tcp connection properties. Figure 14.12 shows the properties available on the session's tab.

FIGURE 14.12

Modifying the RDP-Tcp properties from the Remote Desktop Session Host Configuration tool

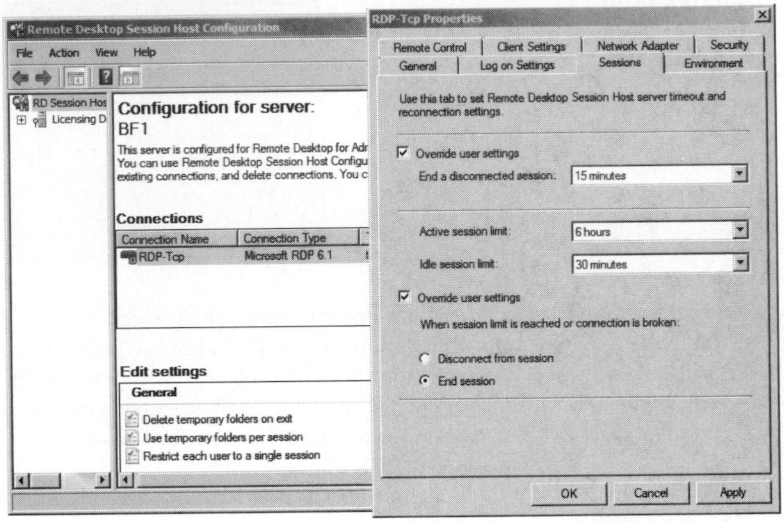

Although there are multiple tabs on this properties sheet, most of them will be manipulated when you're using the Remote Desktop Session Host server role, not the Remote Desktop for Administration role. The Sessions tab affects both roles. The Remote Desktop Session Host server role is covered in more depth in Chapter 25.

Override user settings   User's settings can be configured in Active Directory Users and Computers. Each user account has a Session tab where similar settings can be configured on a per-user basis. By selecting the "Override user settings" box, you can control the behavior of all users who connect to the server and override the settings of the Active Directory account.

End a disconnected session   You can set a time limit for users to reconnect to a disconnected session. When the time limit is exceeded, the session will end. This will free up the resources on the server and ensure the session is available for another administrator.

In a LAN setting, sessions would rarely become disconnected accidentally. Instead, sessions become disconnected when the user closes the RDC tool instead of logging off.

However, if a user connects with a 56Kbps modem, the session may be disconnected because of connectivity issues. By setting a time limit of 15 minutes or so, you allow the user to reconnect and access the original session before it is closed.

Active session limit   You can use the "Active session limit" setting to limit how long someone can stay connected.

Idle session limit   The idle session can limit how long a session can stay active even if the user is not using it. Be careful with this setting; an idle session is identified by a lack of keyboard or mouse inputs. It would not measure activity by applications. In other words, if an administrator is running an application such as a backup program that might take an hour or so, she would not be active on the computer, and this setting might end a session that is running the program.

Disconnect from session   If disconnected, the session will stay active on the server, and the user can reconnect.

End session   If set to end, the session will be closed and no longer available.

USING GROUP POLICY TO CONTROL SESSION TIME LIMITS

It's also possible to control session time limits using Group Policy. Several Group Policy settings are available in the following Group Policy node:

- Computer Configuration ➤ Policies ➤ Administrative Templates ➤ Windows Components ➤ Remote Desktop Services ➤ Remote Desktop Session Host ➤ Session Time Limits

- User Configuration ➤ Policies ➤ Administrative Templates ➤ Windows Components ➤ Remote Desktop Services ➤ Remote Desktop Session Host ➤ Session Time Limits

Each of these nodes includes several Group Policy settings that can be used to keep sessions under control and prevent an administrator from remoting into a server when necessary. The available Group Policy settings in these nodes are as follows:

- Set time limit for disconnected sessions

- Set time limit for active but idle Remote Desktop Services sessions

- Set time limit for active Remote Desktop Services sessions

- Terminate session when time limits are reached

- Set time limit for logoff of RemoteApp sessions

Although the Remote Desktop Connection is an extremely valuable tool to remotely administer servers within a controlled LAN, sometimes it won't meet your needs. For example, you may want to remotely connect to a server over the Internet, but the firewall administrators simply refuse to open the ports. Remote Desktop Gateway may be exactly what you need.

Remote Desktop Gateway

RD Gateway is used to allow connections to an internal network via the Internet. When RD Gateway is enabled, users can connect to resources on an internal network from any Internet-connected device. RD Gateway works the same way whether it's used to allow an administrator to access an internal resource, or to allow a regular user to access a Session Host server as covered in Chapter 25.

RD Gateway uses the Remote Desktop Protocol (RDP) over HTTPS to establish a secure, encrypted connection between the remote users and the internal resource.

Figure 14.13 shows how RD Gateway could be configured. A Windows Server 2008 R2 server named BF4 is placed in the DMZ with the Remote Desktop Gateway role service installed. The client can connect to BF4 over the Internet using RDP over HTTPS.

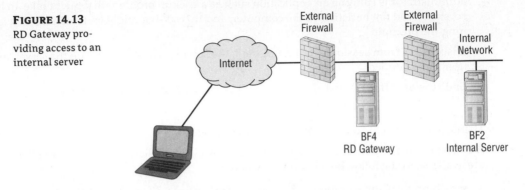

FIGURE 14.13
RD Gateway providing access to an internal server

HTTPS uses Secure Sockets Layer (SSL) to encrypt the session and uses port 443. The external firewall needs port 443 open to support the HTTPS traffic.

BF4 will authenticate the client and act as the gateway to internal resources. RD Gateway can be configured with a resource authorization policy to restrict access to a single server (such as BF2 in the figure) or any resources in the network.

Connection Authorization Policies (RD CAP) are used to restrict who can connect to the RD Gateway server. Resource Authorization Policies (RD RAP) are used to restrict what servers can be accessed once a user connects.

TS GATEWAY RENAMED TO RD GATEWAY

RD Gateway was previously known as Terminal Services Gateway (TS Gateway). Since Terminal Services has been renamed to Remote Desktop Services, it has affected other names, including the RD Gateway.

In past versions of Windows, it was possible to remotely administer servers from the Internet. However, you had to open port 3389 on the firewall (or convince the firewall administrator to open the port). However, every additional port opened on a firewall represents an additional vulnerability that needs to be managed.

From a security standpoint, it's much easier to simply leave the port closed. Even though remote administration through port 3389 was a useful feature, it was often blocked at the network firewall to mitigate the associated security risks.

Since RD Gateway uses RDP over HTTPS through port 443, the external firewall needs only port 443 open. Port 443 is commonly open to allow other HTTPS traffic through. If port 443 is open for other HTTPS traffic, you don't need to open additional ports to use RDP over HTTPS.

As an example, if a company was hosting a web server using HTTP and HTTPS, ports 80 and 443 would be open to support the web server. You can then implement RD Gateway on a server in the DMZ without modifying the firewall.

Even if port 443 isn't already open, the security of HTTPS is well understood by most administrators. It's easier for an administrator to weigh the risks of HTTPS and make a decision to open this port than it is for an administrator to consider opening port 3389 for remote administration traffic.

REMOTE DESKTOP CONNECTION CLIENT

RD Gateway supports connections from Remote Desktop Connection (RDC) 6.0 or greater. However, to support all the features available in RD Gateway in Windows Server 2008 R2, Remote Desktop Protocol 7.0 is recommended. This is natively provided in the RDC client supplied with Windows 7 and Windows 2008 R2, but not with the RDC client supported with Windows Vista and Windows Server 2008. Updates for pre-Windows 7 clients are scheduled for the end of 2009.

Although these features are most useful when using Remote Desktop Services to host desktops and remote applications, administrators may find them useful too. These are some of the additional features that are available:

Configurable idle and session timeouts   These features can be used to automatically close sessions and reclaim resources when the timeout has been reached.

Service and consent messages   This feature allows messages issued at the RD Gateway server to be viewed at the remote connection.

Secure device redirection   Secure device redirection helps prevent malicious code on remote clients from overriding security policies.

RD GATEWAY—REQUIRED SERVICES AND FEATURES

RD Gateway requires the following additional role services and features on the Windows Server 2008 R2 server where it is hosted:

◆ Web Server (IIS) role

  ◆ Management Tools (to manage IIS) feature

  ◆ Web Server (support for HTML websites and ASP.NET) services

◆ Network Policy and Access Services role

  ◆ Network Policy Server services

◆ RPC over HTTP Proxy feature

◆ Remote Server Administration Tools feature

When you add the RD Gateway role service, the wizard will prompt to automatically install all the required roles, services, and features. You won't need to install them individually. However, if they are already installed, the wizard recognizes they are active.

RD Gateway–Required Policies

Before users can connect through RD Gateway, you must have at least two policies:

RD Connection Authorization Policy (RD CAP) RD CAP specifies the users who can connect to the RD Gateway server. For example, you may choose to give anyone in the Administrators group of the RD Gateway server permission to connect, or you could create a global security group (such as G RD Gateway Users) specifically for this purpose. You would then place any users you want to grant connection access for into this new global group.

RD Resource Allocation Policy (RD RAP) RD RAP specifies the resources that users can access once they connect. For example, you may be creating this policy so that administrators can remotely administer a specific server. You would identify the server in RD RAP. Administrators could connect to this server, but not to any other servers via the RD Gateway server.

It's also possible to configure RD RAP so that users can connect to any computer on the network without any restrictions.

Enabling Remote Desktop Gateway

Follow these steps to enable the Remote Desktop Gateway role service on a Windows Server 2008 R2 server. These steps will also lead you through adding the required roles, services, and features, as well as RD CAP and RD RAP.

1. Launch Server Manager by selecting Start ➤ Administrative Tools ➤ Server Manager.

2. Select Roles, and click Add Roles.

3. Review the information on the Before You Begin page, and click Next.

4. Select Remote Desktop Services on the Select Server Roles page. Click Next.

5. Review the information on the Remote Desktop Services page, and click Next.

6. Select the Remote Desktop Gateway check box. When you select the check box, the Add Roles Wizard will appear showing the additional role services and features that need to be added to support RD Gateway, as shown in Figure 14.14.

7. Click the Add Required Role Services button. Click Next.

8. The Choose a Server Authentication Certificate for SSL Encryption page will appear. You can install an existing certificate, create a self-signed certificate, or choose a certificate later.

You can purchase a certificate from an external CA or obtain one from an internal CA. For these steps, choose the option "Create a self-signed certificate for SSL encryption." Click Next.

OBTAINING A CERTIFICATE FROM A CA

Self-signed certificates are useful for testing, but it is not recommended you use a self-signed certificate in a production environment. Instead, you should obtain a certificate from a certificate authority (CA). Since a certificate used by RD Gateway for administration will be used only by administrators, you can use an internal CA to create a certificate instead of purchasing a CA from an external CA.

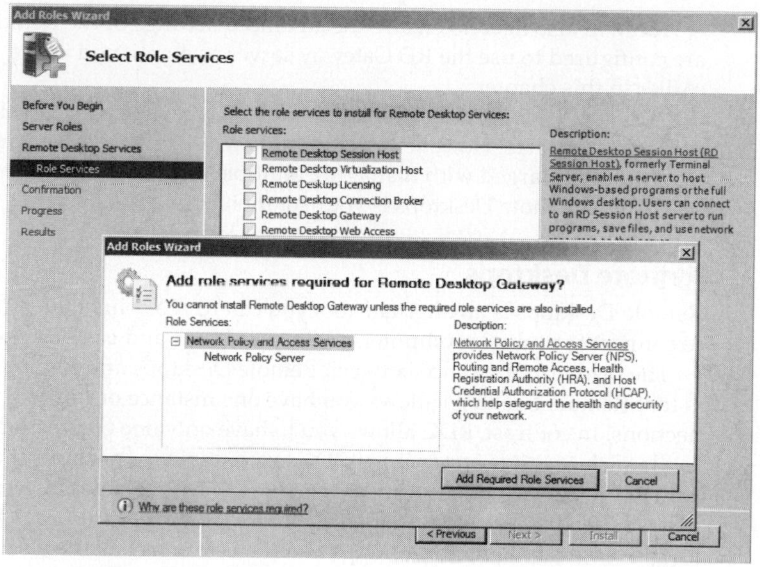

FIGURE 14.14
Adding the Remote
Desktop Gateway
services

9. Review the information on the Create Authorization Policies for RD Gateway page. Ensure that Now is selected, and click Next.

10. The Administrators group is added by default. You can remove this group and add other groups. For this example, leave the Administrators group alone, and click Next.

11. Change the name of RD CAP to RD_Administrators. Ensure that Password is selected. If your infrastructure supports it, you can also support smart cards. Click Next.

12. Change the name for RD RAP to RD_All. Select Allow Users to Connect to Any Computer On the Network. Click Next.

13. Review the information on the Network Policy and Access Services page, and click Next.

14. Verify the network policy server is selected, and click Next.

15. Review the information on the Web Server (IIS) page, and click Next.

16. Review the role services being added to support the Web Server role, and click Next.

17. Review your selections on the Confirmation page, and click Install. The installation of these roles, services, and features may take several minutes.

18. When the installation completes, click Close.

19. Select Start ➢ Administrative Tools ➢ Remote Desktop Services. You'll see that an additional program has been added in this node: Remote Desktop Gateway Manager. Select Remote Desktop Gateway Manager to launch it. The Remote Desktop Gateway Manager allows you to view the connections by selecting the server. If any connections are active, you can click Monitoring.

20. Close the Remote Desktop Gateway Manager.

You will also need to ensure the advanced settings of the Remote Desktop Connection client are configured to use the RD Gateway server as mentioned in the "RDC Advanced Tab" section earlier in this chapter.

Remote Desktop Connection and Remote Gateway are both valuable tools used to remotely administer servers. However, each of these will launch as single instances. There may be times when you're charged with managing multiple servers and you want to manage them through a single tool. Remote Desktops is your solution.

Remote Desktops

Remote Desktops is an alternate tool you can use to connect to remote computers. It allows you to connect to multiple computers at the same time and easily switch between connections.

The primary difference between Remote Desktops and Remote Desktop Connection (RDC) is that Remote Desktops allows you have one instance of the program running for multiple connections. In contrast, RDC allows you to have only one connection for every instance, but you can launch multiple instances of RDC for multiple connections if desired.

Remote Desktops is useful if you manage several related servers. For example, you may be a database administrator and manage several servers running SQL Server 2008. You could add all the servers to Remote Desktops and then simply click the name of the server to connect and remotely manage any of the servers.

Figure 14.15 shows Remote Desktops configured to manage several SQL Server 2008 servers. In the figure, we have logged onto a server named SQL6 and have accessed Server Manager on this remote server.

FIGURE 14.15
Remote Desktops

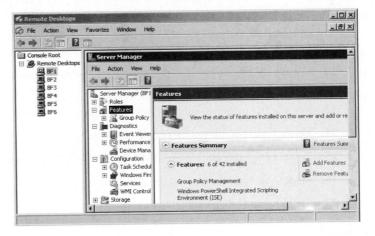

If connections are established between multiple remote computers, you can switch between the servers by selecting them in the left pane. The central pane allows interaction with the selected server.

You can add as many connections as desired to Remote Desktops. Each Windows Server 2008 R2 server will still support only two connections, but you can add as many servers to the Remote Desktops tool as desired.

Use the following steps to create a Remote Desktops console that you can use to easily administer multiple servers. These steps are run from a Windows Server 2008 R2 server but could be reproduced on a desktop system such as Windows Vista or Windows 7:

1. Launch Remote Desktops by selecting Start ➤ Administrative Tools ➤ Remote Desktop Services ➤ Remote Desktops.

2. Right-click Remote Desktops, and select "Add new connection."

3. Enter the computer name or IP address of a remote computer. Notice the same name appears in the "Connection name" text box. You can change the connection name to a name more familiar to you if desired.

4. Ensure the check box "Connect with /admin option" is selected. This ensures that you will connect for administrative purposes even if Remote Desktop Services for host applications is installed and running on the remote server. As a reminder, if Remote Desktop Services for host applications is not running on the remote server, the /admin option is meaningless; you will still connect to one of the two administrator sessions.

5. Enter the name of a user account used to connect to the server in the format of domain\username or computername\username. Notice that the Add New Connection dialog box doesn't include any other options. Click OK and then right-click the connection and select Properties. Your display will look similar to Figure 14.16 with the additional tabs available.

FIGURE 14.16
Configuring a remote connection

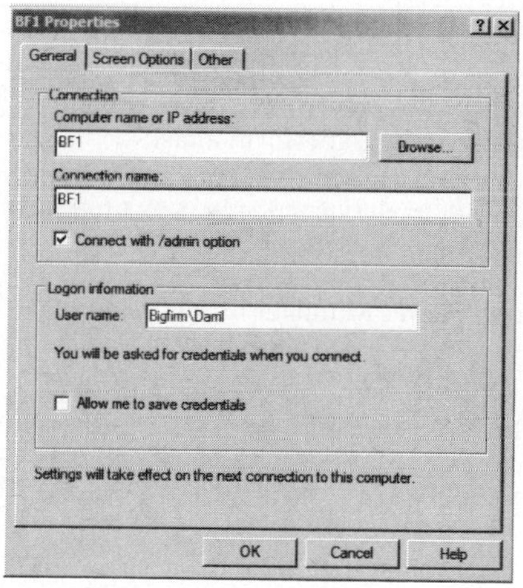

6. Click the Screen Options tab. Notice you can configure the screen size here. You can have the screen fill the entire result pane of the console, set a desktop size using standard resolutions such as 800×600, or select a custom desktop size.

7. Click the Other tab. The Other tab includes three settings:

   A. You can enter the name of a program to start when you connect. For example, if this were a SQL Server, you could configure it to launch SQL Server Management Studio each time you connect.

> **B.** The Security section allows you to configure whether you want to connect even if the server isn't able to authenticate to the client. This would normally be set to "Do Not Connect if Authentication Fails" but can be modified if connecting to older servers that don't support server authentication.
>
> **C.** If you want local drives available in your remote session, enable the "Redirect local drives when logged on to the remote computer" check box.

8. Click OK to close the connection properties of this connection. Repeat the steps starting at step 2 to add connections if desired.

9. Select File ➢ Save As. Browse to a location on your computer to save the file, type in a file-name, and click Save. You can launch this console by double-clicking the saved file.

Once you've created a Remote Desktops console, you can use it whenever you need to quickly connect to any server you manage with simple point-and-click functionality. Of course, any servers you want to connect to must be configured for remote connections.

Configuring a Server for Remote Assistance

Remote Assistance is primarily a feature used on desktop systems and is not enabled by default on Windows Server 2008 R2. However, if you have a large organization with junior administrators in remote locations, it can be very useful to you.

For example, imagine you work at the main location of your company and your company has a remote office with only 20 people. One of these employees occasionally performs routine tasks on the server located in the remote office but may need some help. With Remote Assistance enabled, he can send you a request for assistance. You can then access the remote server's desktop and demonstrate how to perform a task.

The Remote Assistance check box in System Properties is grayed out and can't be enabled until the Remote Assistance feature is added to Windows Server 2008 R2. The following steps show how to enable Remote Assistance:

1. Launch Server Manager by selecting Start ➢ Administrative Tools ➢ Server Manager.

2. Select Features.

3. Click Add Features.

4. Select the Remote Assistance check box, and click Next.

5. Click Install on the Confirmation page.

6. When the wizard completes, click Close.

With the Remote Assistance feature added, Remote Assistance should now be enabled on the server. You can verify it with these steps:

1. Click Start, right-click Computer, and select Properties.

2. Click Remote Settings.

3. Verify the "Allow Remote Assistance connections to this computer" check box is selected.

4. Click the Advanced button. Verify the "Allow this computer to be controlled remotely" check box is selected. The default lifetime of invitations is six hours, but it can be changed. After the time limit has passed, the invitation can no longer be used to connect.

This server is now configured for Remote Assistance. To start a Remote Assistance session, the user needs to send a Remote Assistance request.

SENDING A REMOTE ASSISTANCE REQUEST

The user who needs assistance should follow these steps to create a Remote Assistance request and begin the process:

1. Click Start, type **msra** in the Run box, and press Enter. The Windows Remote Assistance dialog box will appear.

2. Click "Invite someone you trust to help you."

3. Click "Save this invitation as a file."

4. Browse to a location on your hard drive. The invitation file is named `Invitation .msrcIncident` by default but can be changed if desired. Click Save.

5. A password is automatically created and can't be changed. You'll need to tell the helper this password.

6. Send the invitation to a helper as an email attachment, or place it on a share accessible to the helper.

At this point, the person needing help needs to wait for the response from the helper.

RESPONDING TO A REMOTE ASSISTANCE REQUEST

The helper can follow these steps with the person requesting assistance to begin a Remote Assistance session:

1. Double-click the invitation received from the person requesting help. This invitation could have been received via email or available on a share. It will take a moment for this invitation to open.

2. Enter the password in the Windows Remote Assistance dialog box. Click OK. (If you enter the incorrect password, you will be notified immediately.)

The user requesting help will see a dialog box appear asking whether they want to allow the connection. The user should click Yes.

3. At this point, you will be able to see everything on the user's desktop, but you won't be able to interact with the desktop. Click the Request Control button at the top of the Windows Remote Assistance window.

The user will see a dialog box appear asking whether he wants to allow the helper to share control of the desktop. The user should click Yes. Note that the user has complete control and can deny the request. However, since the user requested assistance and gave the password, they would click Yes.

4. The helper can now control the mouse on the remote computer. Figure 14.17 shows the Remote Assistance window viewed by the person being helped.

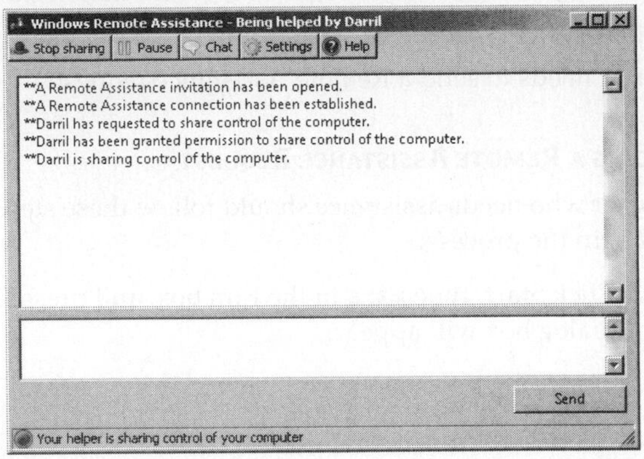

FIGURE 14.17
Remote Assistance session on a remote server

At this point, the helper can manipulate the mouse and keyboard of the remote desktop to demonstrate any tasks. This is shared control. In other words, both the helper and the user have control over the desktop.

It's useful if the helper and user are able to talk over the phone during this process, but it's not necessary. The Windows Remote Assistance boxes include a chat feature that allow each of the users to type questions and comments.

The helper could demonstrate a task and then simply type **now you try it** while observing the desktop. The helper can stop using the mouse, and the user could perform the same steps on his computer. Additionally, the user being helped can end the session whenever they want to by clicking Stop Sharing or Pause.

Windows Remote Management Service

The Windows Remote Management Service (WinRM) will allow you to issue any command-line command from one computer against a remote computer.

For example, you may be working on a Windows Vista or Windows 7 computer, but you want to query some information from a remote server. If the server has been configured with WinRM, you can execute a WinRS command-line command from the desktop system and get the results just as if you were at the computer or connected with RDC.

One of the benefits of this is that you don't need to consume one of the two remote sessions for a server, or even launch RDC. You can simply enter the command at your command prompt.

The following are the two commands used by the Windows Remote Management Service:

WinRM   The WinRM tool is executed on the remote server and enables the server to listen and respond to WinRS requests.

WinRS   The WinRS tool is executed from the command line on a desktop or other server accessed by an administrator. It allows the administrator to execute any command-line commands against the remote server.

Enabling WinRM

WinRM is not enabled by default on Windows Server 2008 R2. You can use the following steps to enable WinRM on the server.

RD GATEWAY ENABLES WINRM

WinRM is not enabled to allow remote access for management by default. However, if you followed the steps to enable RD Gateway earlier in this chapter, you'll find that WinRM has been enabled on the same server. RD Gateway uses the Windows Remote Management Service and enables it when the role service is installed. If you follow these steps, it will inform you that WinRM is already configured.

---

1. Select Start ➤ All Programs ➤ Accessories ➤ Command Prompt.

2. Type the following command, and press Enter.

   ```
   WinRM quickconfig
   ```

WinRM includes many shortcuts. Instead of the full command, you could shorten `quickconfig` to just `qc` and enter it as follows:

   ```
   WinRM qc
   ```

3. You will be promoted to allow the following changes to be made on your system:

   ◆ Create a WinRM listener on HTTP://* to access WS-Man requests to any IP on this machine.

   ◆ Enable the WinRM firewall exception.

   ◆ Configure LocalAccountTokenFilterPolicy to grant administrative rights remotely to local users.

4. Type **Y**, and press Enter to accept the changes. You will see a status message indicating the changes have been completed.

5. Type **WinRM** **/?** to see the help available for the Windows Remote Management command-line tool. `WinRM` includes a rich set of commands, and the help file can help you dig deeper if desired.

6. Type in the following command to enumerate (list) the properties for WinRM. Notice that there is a space between `WinRM` and `enumerate`, and there is a second space between `enumerate` and `WinRM`, but no other spaces are used.

   ```
   WinRM enumerate WinRM/config/listener
   ```

This command will give you some of the details on how the service is configured and verification that it is enabled to listen on the HTTP transport using all the available IP addresses on your system. Notice that you can also type in the command with just the first letter of *enumerate* (e) as follows:

```
WinRM e WinRM /config/listener
```

7. You can change the format of the output by modifying the -format switch. By default, the output in shown in text format, but you can output it as simple XML (using the - format:#XML switch) or formatted XML (using the -format:#pretty switch). Try the following commands:

```
WinRM e WinRM /config/listener -format:#text
WinRM e WinRM /config/listener -format:#xml
WinRM e WinRM /config/listener -format:#pretty
```

Although there is more you can do with WinRM on the server, its primary purpose for remote administration is to enable the listener with the quickconfig command. Once this is done, you'll probably turn your attention to the client where you'll do the actual administration.

Using WinRS

The Windows Remote Shell (WinRS) is used to execute commands against a remote server that has been configured with WinRM. For example, you could use WinRS from a Windows Vista or Windows 7 system to execute commands against a remote server.

WinRS commands are primarily formatted as follows:

```
WinRS -r:servername command
```

The -r switch is used to identify the name of the remote server. Although other switches are available, the -r switch is the switch used the most.

ISSUING WMIC COMMANDS WITH WINRS

WinRS commands can be any command that you would issue from the command line. As an example, you can use the Windows Management Instrumentation command (WMIC) to document the services running on computers.

Before using WinRS, you can use this command to show how WMIC can be used to document information on services running on any system. Launch a command line, and enter this command.

```
Wmic /output:services.htm /node:localhost service list brief /format:htable
```

This creates an HTML-formatted file named services.htm. You can view it by entering services.htm at the command prompt, which will launch Internet Explorer displaying the document. This lists all of the services on the system, as well as the start mode, the state, the status, and some additional details.

Now, use the same command to document the services of a remote computer that has been configured with WinRS. Substitute Srv08R2 for the name of the server you have configured with WinRS, and change the name of the HTML file:

```
WinRS -r:Srv08R2 Wmic /output:Srv08R2services.htm /node:Srv08R2 service list
brief /format:htable
```

You can view this file by entering the name of the file at the command prompt. In this example, it is Srv08R2services.htm.

If you want more details on the services, change `list brief` to `list full`. This simple tool can easily give you some important documentation on multiple servers that you can easily print or save.

ISSUING POWERSHELL COMMANDS WITH WINRS

Although WMIC is certainly feature-rich, it's not the only command you can use. Any command that you can enter at the server you can also enter remotely using WinRS. This includes PowerShell commands.

INSTALLING POWERSHELL

Windows PowerShell is included and installed by default on Windows Server 2008 R2. It isn't installed by default on Windows Server 2008 systems, but can be added by adding the feature using Server Manager. It's not included on older operating systems such as Windows Server 2003, but you can obtain Windows PowerShell (and a lot of great information on how to use it) from www.microsoft.com/windowsserver2003/technologies/management/powershell/default.mspx.

PowerShell commands follow a verb-noun format. The verb specifies an action, and the noun identifies the object on which the action will take place.

The most popular verb is `get`, and if you enter `get-` at the PowerShell command prompt, you can tab through all the nouns associated with the `get` verb.

Other verbs include `set`, `copy`, `move`, and many more. You can do the same thing with any of the verbs; enter the verb with a hyphen (-), and tab through all the possible nouns associated with the verb. For a full list of the verbs, check out this MSDN page: `http://msdn.microsoft.com/en-us/library/ms714428(VS.85).aspx`.

For example, you can enter the following PowerShell command from the PowerShell prompt to check the status of services on a system.

```
Get-Service
```

You don't even need to type in the entire command. You can just type **Get-S** and press the Tab key.

This command will list all the services on the system with the status (running or stopped), name, and display name. Using this with WinRS, you can execute the same command remotely:

```
WinRS -r:SRV08R2 PowerShell Get-Service
```

If you want to redirect this to a file, you can add the > redirect character as follows:

```
WinRS -r:SRV08R2 PowerShell Get-Service > services.txt
```

The output will be stored in a file named `services.txt`. You can then open the file with Notepad from the command line with this:

```
Notepad services.txt
```

Remote Server Administration Tools

The Remote Server Administration Tools (RSAT) are tools you need to manage roles and features on a Windows Server 2008 and Windows Server 2008 R2 server from your desktop operating system.

Although Remote Desktop Connection and Remote Desktops allow you to connect to the desktop of a server, sometimes you simply need to do a single task such as resetting a password on a user account or verifying that DNS is configured correctly.

RSAT includes tools like Active Directory Users and Computers (ADUC) and the DNS console. After installing RSAT on a desktop, you can launch ADUC to manipulate user accounts, or you can launch the DNS console to verify DNS configuration.

Users still need the appropriate permissions to run the installed tools. For example, a junior administrator who installs the tools on his desktop system won't be added to the Enterprise Admins role and suddenly be able to perform anything in the forest.

The tools available in RSAT can be used to do the following:

◆ Manage Windows Server 2008 and Windows Server 2008 R2 roles and features

◆ Manage Windows Server 2003 servers

RSAT REPLACES ADMIN PACK

If you've been working with previous editions of Windows, you're probably already familiar with RSAT, but by a different name. In previous editions, the Administration Tools Pack (commonly called the Admin Pack) was installed on Windows XP and prior desktop systems to remotely administer servers. RSAT is used on Windows Vista and Windows 7 to provide similar functionality.

RSAT Compatibility Issues

RSAT is not compatible with the Administration Tools Pack used to remotely administer Windows Server 2000 and Windows Server 2003 servers. If you have these tools installed on your system, you must first uninstall them before installing RSAT.

Additionally, RSAT won't allow you to remotely manage a server with the Streaming Media Services role. There is a separate Remote Server Administration Tools for the Streaming Media Services role you can download and install to manage a Windows Server 2008 and Windows Server 2008 R2 server hosting the Streaming Media Services role.

For more information on issues with a Streaming Media Services role server, check out the Microsoft KB article at http://support.microsoft.com/kb/934518. The RSAT information is contained near the end of the article.

RSAT Tools

After installing RSAT on a desktop system, you'll have access to a full suite of tools that you'd find on a Windows Server 2008 and Windows Server 2008 R2 server with all of the roles and features installed. As long as the remote server has the appropriate role or feature installed, you can use the client-side RSAT tool to administer it.

In other words, if a server is running the DHCP role, you can use the DHCP console to remotely administer it. However, if the server isn't a DHCP server, you can't use the RSAT-installed DHCP console to make it a DHCP server.

The following lists some of the more commonly used tools available with RSAT. This isn't meant to be an exhaustive list but instead a summary of some of the commonly used tools. For a complete listing, check out the Microsoft KB article at http://support.microsoft.com/kb/941314.

Active Directory Domain Services (AD DS) Tools   These tools include Active Directory Users and Computers, Active Directory Domains and Trusts, Active Directory Sites and Services, and other snap-ins and command-line tools for remotely managing Active Directory Domain Services.

Active Directory Certificate Services Tools   These tools include the Active Directory Certification Authority Tools used for enterprise certificate authorities and certificate authority tools used for stand-alone certificate authorities.

Dynamic Host Configuration Protocol (DHCP) Server Tools   The DHCP snap-in tool is included.

Domain Name System (DNS) Server Tools   DNS tools include the DNS Manager snap-in and the Dnscmd.exe command-line tool.

File Services Tools   These tools include the Share and Storage Management snap-in, Distributed File System Tools, and the File Server Resource Manager Tools.

Network Policy and Access Services Tools   The Routing and Remote Access snap-in is included for network policy and network access.

Remote Desktop Services Tools   Remote Desktops and Remote Desktop Services Manager snap-ins are included.

BitLocker Drive Encryption Tools   The Manage-bde.wsf script is included for BitLocker Drive Encryption.

Failover Clustering Tools   These tools include the Failover Cluster Manager snap-in and the Cluster.exe command-line tool.

Group Policy Management Tools   The Group Policy Management Console, Group Policy Management Editor, and Group Policy Starter GPO Editor are all included.

Network Load Balancing Tools   The Network Load Balancing Manager utility and the Nlb.exe and Wlbs.exe command-line tools are included.

SMTP Server Tools   The SMTP snap-in is available.

Storage Manager for SANs Tools   The Storage Manager for SANs snap-in and the ProvisionStorage.exe command-line tool are both included.

Windows System Resource Manager Tools   The Windows System Resource Manager snap-in and the Wsrmc.exe command-line tool are included.

All of the traditional tools needed to remotely administer Windows Server 2003 servers are also available in RSAT. These include the following:

◆ Active Directory Domain Services (AD DS) Tools

◆ Active Directory Certification Authority Tools

- ◆ DHCP Server Tools
- ◆ DNS Server Tools
- ◆ Terminal Services tools
- ◆ Group Policy Management Tools
- ◆ Network Load Balancing Tools

Installing RSAT

RSAT is available as a free download from Microsoft. You can download RSAT by going to the Microsoft download site at www.Microsoft.com/downloads and typing **RSAT**.

32-BIT AND 64-BIT VERSIONS OF RSAT

Both 32-bit and 64-bit versions of RSAT are available. These need to match the platform where you're installing RSAT. In other words, if you're running 32-bit Windows Vista on your desktop, you need the 32-bit version of RSAT to remotely manage a 64-bit Windows Server 2008 R2 server.

Once you've downloaded RSAT, you can follow these steps to install and enable RSAT. These steps were written for a Windows Vista system and may need to be modified slightly to work on Windows 7.

1. Use Windows Explorer to browse to where you saved the download. Double-click the installation package, and follow the wizard to complete the installation.

2. When the installation completes, click Close.

Normally you'd expect the installation to be complete at this point, but you need to take extra steps to enable RSAT on your system.

3. Select Start ➢ Control Panel to launch the Control Panel.

4. Select Programs and then click "Turn Windows features on or off." If prompted by User Account Control, click Continue.

5. Select the Remote Server Administration Tools check box. Your display will look similar to Figure 14.18.

You can pick and choose individual feature and role administration tools if desired, or you can simply add them all by selecting the Remote Server Administration Tools check box.

6. Click OK. The tools will be configured to work on your system.

If Administrative Tools are not showing on your Start menu, you can add them by following these steps:

1. Right-click the Start menu, and select Properties.

2. Ensure the Start Menu tab is selected, and click Customize.

3. Scroll to the "System administrative tools" section close to the bottom of the customization window. Select "Display on the All Programs menu and the Start menu."

4. Click OK twice.

Once RSAT is installed on a system, you can use the tools in the same way you would use them on a server.

FIGURE 14.18
Adding the Remote Server Administration Tools feature

The Bottom Line

Configure Windows Server 2008 R2 servers for remote administration   Servers must be configured to allow remote administration before administrators can connect remotely.

> **Master It**   Configure a server to allow remote connections by clients running RDC version 6.0 or greater.

Remotely connect to Windows Server 2008 R2 servers using Remote Desktop Connection
You can remotely connect to servers to do almost any administrative work. Servers are often located in a secure server room that is kept cool to protect the electronics. They can be in a different room, a different building, or even a separate geographical location, but they can still be remotely administered using either RDC or Remote Desktops.

> **Master It**   Connect to a server using RDC. Ensure your local drives are accessible when connected to the remote server.

Remotely connect to Windows Server 2008 R2 servers using a Remote Desktop Protocol file
If you regularly connect to a remote server using RDC, you can configure an RDP file that can be preconfigured based on your needs for this server. This RDP file will store all the settings you configure for this connection.

> **Master It**   Create an RDP file that you can use to connect with a server named Server1. Configure the file to automatically launch Server Manager when connected.

Configure a server for Remote Assistance When your environment includes remote locations where junior administrators may occasionally need assistance, you can use Remote Assistance to access their session and demonstrate procedures.

Master It Configure a server for Remote Assistance.

Install the Remote Server Administration Tools The Remote Assistance Server Administration Tools (RSAT) include the snap-ins and command-line tools needed to manage Server 2003 and Server 2008 and Server 2008 R2 servers from Windows Vista and Windows 7.

Master It Obtain and install RSAT on a Windows Vista or Windows 7 system.

Chapter 15

Connecting Windows Clients to the Server

You've built your server, created users, and shared network resources. Now you need to configure your client systems to connect to the network and use those resources. In this chapter, we'll show you how to set up various client systems with networking components, how to log on to the network, how to find and connect to shared resources, how to manage your passwords, and, when applicable, how to find and connect to Active Directory.

Although most of this book is geared toward the network administrator, this chapter is more for the end users since they'll often be the ones connecting to network resources (and ideally the ones giving themselves new passwords). This chapter, then, is less for the administrator's daily use than for teaching the user base how to perform key tasks.

In this chapter, you'll learn to:

- ◆ Verify your network configuration

- ◆ Join a client computer to a domain

- ◆ Change user passwords

- ◆ Connect to network resources

What to Know Before You Begin

Before you connect workstations to the domain, you should know a few things about client computers and the network environment. If you are new to Microsoft networks, you may want to review some other chapters before attempting to configure clients:

- ◆ Chapter 2, "Installing and Upgrading Your Network to Server 2008," covers the basics of networking software and security.

- ◆ Chapters 4, "Windows Server 2008 IPv4: The New Stuff," and Chapter 19, "Advanced IP: Routing with Windows," deal with TCP/IP protocol and infrastructure. Microsoft networks almost universally use TCP/IP.

- ◆ Chapter 7, "Creating and Managing User Accounts," shows you how to set up user accounts and computer accounts.

- ◆ Chapter 25, "Installing, Using, and Administering Remote Desktop Services," covers connecting clients to domain resources using Remote Desktop Services (previously known as Terminal Services).

If you've read these chapters or are generally familiar with the concepts, then read on to learn more about the client networking stack and about the kinds of accounts you'll need.

Throughout this chapter, we'll connect to the same server, on the same domain, and with the same user account:

◆ The username is mminasi (if acting as a regular user) or bigadmin (if acting as a domain administrator).

◆ The domain name is bigfirm.com.

◆ There is a Windows 2008 R2 domain controller on the network called bf1.bigfirm.com.

◆ There are several client machines on the network, representing the client operating systems we will deal with in this chapter. Their names are:

  ◆ WIN7CLIENT

  ◆ VISTACLIENT

  ◆ XPCLIENT

  ◆ 2KCLIENT

Understanding Client-Side Software Requirements

For each client you configure, you'll be loading three basic software components: a *driver* for the network interface card (NIC), a *network protocol*, and a *network client*. The good news is that on modern Windows operating systems, most—and sometimes all—of what you need is built into the OS.

The NIC driver allows the operating system to communicate with the NIC. Before loading any network protocol or client software, the operating system must recognize the network card and load the appropriate driver. Fortunately, because of the advancement of Universal Plug and Play (UPnP), most of the client systems in this chapter can automatically detect the NIC and load a driver included with the OS. If the driver is not included with the OS or if your client system fails to detect the network card, you must use the driver and installation instructions for your operating system that are provided by the manufacturer. If possible, use the most recent driver, which is likely the vendor-supplied driver rather than the one supplied with the OS. The network card's original equipment manufacturer (OEM) disk or CD usually includes release notes, installation instructions, and any available diagnostic software. The drivers on an OEM CD are usually not the most up-to-date versions, so if you have Internet access, the manufacturer's website is an even better source for support, because documentation and the latest drivers should be available there.

If feasible, use the same type of network card throughout your network. Consistency in your hardware will allow you to become familiar with its idiosyncrasies, and you can use the same installation procedures, drivers, and diagnostic software on all of your workstations.

The network protocol, built into the operating system, allows nodes on the same network to communicate with each other. To communicate, the nodes must all use the same protocol. TCP/IP is the de facto standard for Microsoft networks today. Since most networks use IPv4, we'll use that version throughout this chapter.

> **WINDOWS SERVER 2008 ADDS SUPPORT FOR IPV6**
>
> In Windows 2008, IPV6 is installed and enabled by default. For more information on this protocol and configuring it for your environment, refer to Chapter 19, "Advanced IP: Routing with Windows."

The clients in the examples throughout this chapter will obtain a unique IP address and other necessary protocol configuration information from a Dynamic Host Configuration Protocol (DHCP) server on the network. Most servers in production will have a static IP address. Workstations, however, most often have dynamically assigned IP addresses. Not only does a DHCP server assign IP addresses to client workstations, but it can also supply all of the other values required in your particular TCP/IP environment (including a subnet mask, DNS servers to use, the default gateway to route through, and the domain suffix to apply to the connection). DHCP also keeps track of IP assignments and updates clients dynamically when you want to make IP configuration changes. (There will be cases where you won't use a DHCP server to assign address information to the client. This chapter will also cover how to set this information manually for each client operating system.)

The network client locates network resources and connects to them. For any given flavor of file-mounting, printer-sharing software that runs on a server, there is a client connection counterpart.

Domain Accounts and Local Accounts

Two kinds of accounts are key to using a client workstation and getting to network resources: domain accounts and local accounts. In general, domain accounts are used to authenticate access to shared domain resources, and local accounts are used to authenticate access to use or manage the local computer.

A *domain* is a logical grouping of computers and user accounts and related network resources, all with a common security database called Active Directory. Domains provide centralized security, along with the resource grouping function of workgroups. Domain user accounts permit people to use a single login name to log on to any workstation and access resources on any server that belongs to the domain (provided that the user has permission to access the resources). Although Microsoft used to make some operating systems that could not join a domain, all the current ones can. (The Home editions of Windows XP, Vista, and Windows 7 are the exception, but you're unlikely to find Home editions in an office.) A user account that is not a member of the domain or a member of a trusted domain cannot access network resources protected by domain security. For more information about domains, see Chapter 6, "Creating the Simple AD: The One-Domain, One-Location AD."

A *workgroup* is a logical grouping of computers with no central security database but organized under a single name. Although today's operating systems can join workgroups, this isn't very common in production environments unless they're very small. Workgroup resources are much harder to manage access to and lack the discoverability that Active Directory provides.

Although domain membership is key to accessing centralized resources, local accounts also have their purposes: you need them for the local management of the workstation. All current Microsoft operating systems maintain local security databases. The configuration changes you are about to perform require administrative privileges, so you must log on using the local Administrator account (or an account in the local Administrators group) to make the changes.

GIVING USERS RIGHTS TO ADMINISTER A CLIENT COMPUTER

After joining computers to the domain, add the Domain User account for the person who typically uses that computer to the local Administrators group, if you want them to be able to administer the computer. This will save them from being prompted for user credentials when doing administrative tasks, while still allowing you to control who has this access (but also be aware that this gives the user full capabilities to the local machine).

Verifying Your Network Configuration

The first step in joining a domain is to connect to the domain IP network so the client computer can communicate with the domain controller. The steps for connecting to a network and are basically the same for each of the client operating systems we discuss in this chapter:

1. Install a working network interface card (NIC) and driver on the client computer.

2. Configure the NIC with the appropriate settings in order to communicate on the network.

We will address any UI (or other) differences between client operating systems as we go, but for now let's get ready to join a domain.

Log on to the system using a local Administrator account. Before trying to join the domain, it's good to verify that the NIC and its associated driver were installed correctly, and you'll need to have administrative rights to check everything.

Devices that your computer detects show up in Device Manager. To get there, open the Start menu, right-click Computer (for Vista and Windows 7) or My Computer (for Windows XP and Windows 2000), and click Manage. The Computer Management console will open. In the left pane, select Device Manager. In the right pane, expand the Network Adapters folder, and your NIC should be there.

If you have problems with the NIC, such as a driver issue, you will know it clearly because the network adapter will be missing or could be "banged out" (the device will be there but will have a yellow exclamation point next to it). The NIC could also be banged out and located under the Other Devices folder. Refer to the NIC manufacturer's documentation and the operating system's Help and Support to help you resolve hardware problems.

Verifying Local Area Connection Settings

If you accept the typical network settings during the installation, Setup will install and create a software representation of the NIC, called a Local Area Connection. The installation will also install the following Local Area Connection components:

◆ TCP/IP Protocol, which allows the computer to communicate with other network nodes and devices

◆ Client for Microsoft Networks, which allows a computer to access resources on a Microsoft network

By default the Local Area Connection will be configured to obtain the following configuration settings from a DHCP server:

IP address The address of the computer as relates to the network it is joining. Every node on the network must have a unique IP address.

Subnet mask A number that logically segments a larger network into separate subnetworks (the communication between these smaller subnetworks must be passed by a router).

Default gateway The IP address of the router that will route communications between nodes located in different subnetworks or other networks.

Domain Name System (DNS) server The IP address of a DNS server on the network.

DNS Suffix (optional) The Active Directory domain name to which the computer is or will be joined (in this chapter it is bigfirm.com).

The fastest way to tell whether your NIC obtained the appropriate settings automatically is to open a command prompt and type the following:

```
ipconfig /all
```

You should get results similar to Figure 15.1.

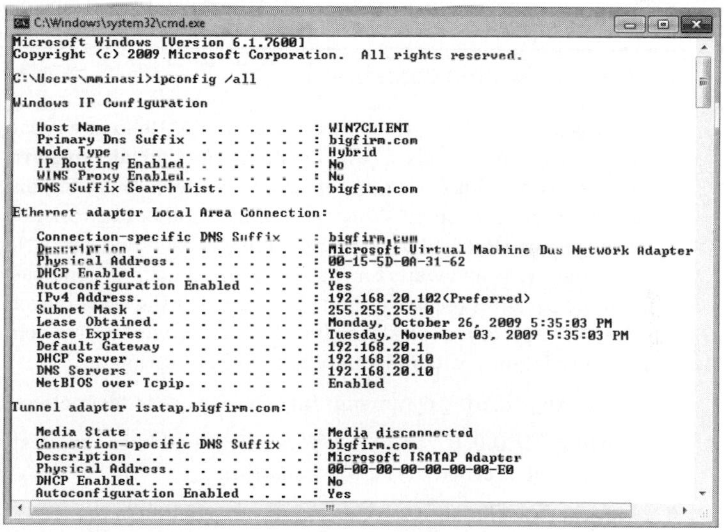

FIGURE 15.1
ipconfig
command results

```
C:\Windows\system32\cmd.exe

Microsoft Windows [Version 6.1.7600]
Copyright (c) 2009 Microsoft Corporation.  All rights reserved.

C:\Users\mminasi>ipconfig /all

Windows IP Configuration

   Host Name . . . . . . . . . . . . : WIN7CLIENT
   Primary Dns Suffix  . . . . . . . : bigfirm.com
   Node Type . . . . . . . . . . . . : Hybrid
   IP Routing Enabled. . . . . . . . : No
   WINS Proxy Enabled. . . . . . . . : No
   DNS Suffix Search List. . . . . . : bigfirm.com

Ethernet adapter Local Area Connection:

   Connection-specific DNS Suffix  . : bigfirm.com
   Description . . . . . . . . . . . : Microsoft Virtual Machine Bus Network Adapter
   Physical Address. . . . . . . . . : 00-15-5D-0A-31-62
   DHCP Enabled. . . . . . . . . . . : Yes
   Autoconfiguration Enabled . . . . : Yes
   IPv4 Address. . . . . . . . . . . : 192.168.20.102(Preferred)
   Subnet Mask . . . . . . . . . . . : 255.255.255.0
   Lease Obtained. . . . . . . . . . : Monday, October 26, 2009 5:35:03 PM
   Lease Expires . . . . . . . . . . : Tuesday, November 03, 2009 5:35:03 PM
   Default Gateway . . . . . . . . . : 192.168.20.1
   DHCP Server . . . . . . . . . . . : 192.168.20.10
   DNS Servers . . . . . . . . . . . : 192.168.20.10
   NetBIOS over Tcpip. . . . . . . . : Enabled

Tunnel adapter isatap.bigfirm.com:

   Media State . . . . . . . . . . . : Media disconnected
   Connection-specific DNS Suffix  . : bigfirm.com
   Description . . . . . . . . . . . : Microsoft ISATAP Adapter
   Physical Address. . . . . . . . . : 00-00-00-00-00-00-00-E0
   DHCP Enabled. . . . . . . . . . . : No
   Autoconfiguration Enabled . . . . : Yes
```

The lines from these results that will tell you that your NIC is configured properly are located in the Ethernet Adapter Local Area Connection section:

DHCP Enabled If this is set to Yes, then the NIC is set to obtain IP address information from a DHCP server. If it is set to No, then you will need to manually configure an IP address for your Local Area Connection.

Autoconfiguration Enabled This is set to Yes and is present only if the NIC is set to obtain IP addresses automatically from the DHCP server.

IPv4 Address This is the unique IP address assigned to the Local Area Connection.

Subnet Mask This is the subnetwork to which the node belongs.

Default Gateway This is the router that will route traffic between your assigned subnet and other subnets and networks.

DNS Servers DNS servers resolve IP addresses to computer names. You need to have a DNS server assigned, or you will not be able to join a domain. In most cases, the DNS server address is supplied by the DHCP server.

If the `ipconfig` results come up empty, then you may not have a DHCP server to allocate IP addresses, in which case you will need to configure your Local Area Connection settings manually. To do this, you will need to open the Local Area Connection associated with the NIC and enter the information by hand. For now, assume that the `ipconfig` results show that the NIC has the address information assigned.

Test Network Connectivity with the ping Command

To be absolutely certain that your network card and TCP/IP are working properly and the IP information assigned to the NIC is correct, open a command prompt, and use the `ping` command to test basic network connectivity.

WHAT IS THE PING COMMAND?

Imaging knocking on a friend's door and saying "Hello, is anybody home?" If your friend is home, then he/she would reply, "Yes, I am home" (and ideally open the door and let you in). The `ping` command does this for computers and other devices (nodes) on a network. The name stands for "Packet Internet Groper." When you "ping" another network node, your computer sends a packet (called an Echo Request packet) to the address (an IP address, a NetBIOS address, or a DNS address) of another node and waits for that destination node to send back a reply (an Echo Reply packet). If a reply packet is received, then you know that the node is accessible. The time required for the response to get to you can also tell you how much *latency*—the delay—this communication is facing. Too much latency can hinder network communication.

Here are typical `ping` commands that you can use to test network connectivity:

`ping 127.0.0.1` This pings yourself (this address always specifies the node you are pinging from and is called the *loopback address*).

`ping localhost -4` This pings yourself. It tells you that the Local Area Connection is able to send and receive information. Use the -4 option to receive results in IPv4 format.

`ping x.x.x.x` This pings another node (replace x.x.x.x with an IP address).

`ping DNSNAME.DOMAIN.SUFFIX` This pings a node using its fully qualified domain name (the name stored in DNS that is mapped to an IP address). An example is `ping bf1.bigfirm.com`.

`ping yahoo.com` This pings an address on the Internet to test connectivity with the Internet. (Not all domains accept pings, because they are protecting themselves from DoS attacks and have denied ICMP packets to their servers, but yahoo.com is pingable.)

Ping your IP address, the IP of the router, and the IP of the domain controller or another node on your network. While you are at it, ping a couple of systems by name to test your DNS resolution, and ping a node on the Internet (for example, yahoo.com) to test connectivity to the Internet and proper DNS resolution. Figure 15.2 shows the output of the computer WIN7CLIENT issuing `ping` commands and receiving replies.

FIGURE 15.2

ping command
successful results

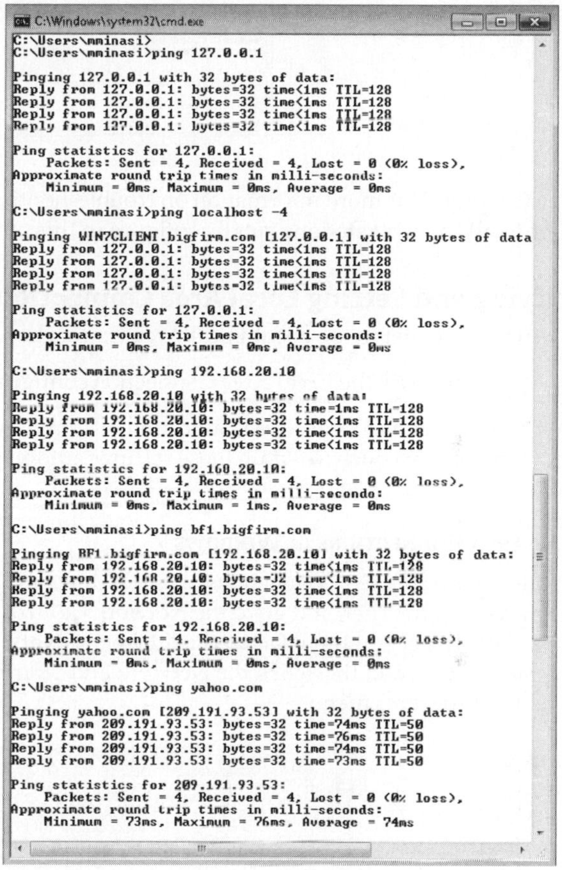

"Request timed out" or "Destination host unreachable" messages (both shown in Figure 15.3) mean that you were unable to communicate with the node specified. Again, this could signify network issues or could signify that the destination address doesn't accept ping requests (for example, microsoft.com does not accept ping requests). For known servers on your network, it's a good indication that the resource is unreachable. If you can ping only by IP address, double-check your DNS configuration, and check the DNS server to make sure it is operating correctly. Another possibility is that the computer you are pinging has its firewall turned on and is blocking ICMP.

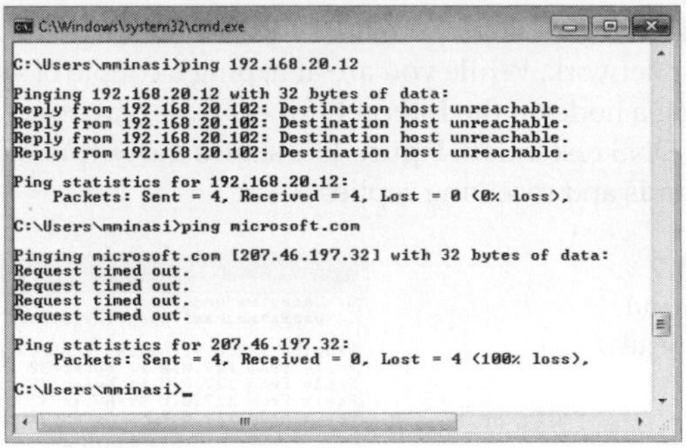

FIGURE 15.3
ping command
unsuccessful
results

See Chapter 4 for more information on troubleshooting network problems with TCP/IP. This applies to all the workstations you'll configure in this chapter.

Verifying and Setting Local Area Connection Information Using the GUI

Knowing how to get to the client Local Area Connection is important for these reasons:

◆ You can verify the Local Area Connection configuration using the GUI.

◆ You can set the Local Area Connection information manually if you do not have a DHCP server from which to obtain these settings automatically.

LOCAL AREA CONNECTIONS IN WINDOWS 7

To locate the Local Area Connections on a Windows 7 client, select Start ➢ Control Panel ➢ Network and Internet, and go to the Network Control and Sharing Center (shown in Figure 15.4). To get you there faster, type the word **Network** in the search area at the bottom of the Start menu, and then click the Network and Sharing Center that appears in the top portion on the Programs menu.

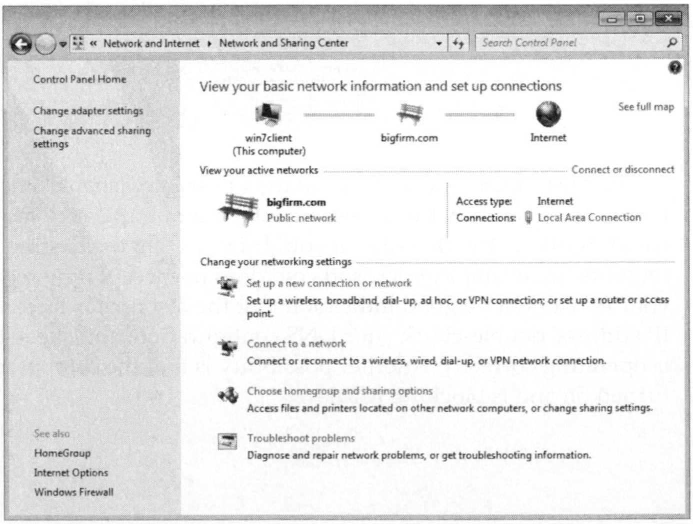

FIGURE 15.4
Windows 7:
The Local Area
Connection icon in
the Network and
Sharing Center

If you do not see a Local Area Connection icon, your NIC may not have been properly detected. Use Device Manager to isolate the problem, or try to add the network adapter manually using the Add Hardware Wizard in the Control Panel.

Click the Local Area Connection link to open the Local Area Connection Status window, as shown in Figure 15.5.

FIGURE 15.5
Windows 7:
The Local Area
Connection
Status window

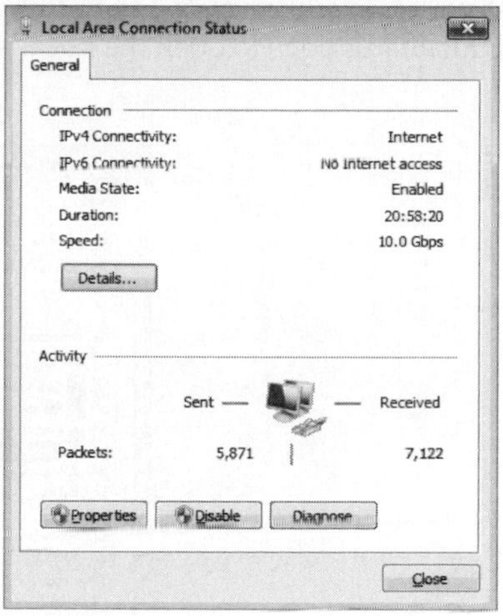

Here you can see that the connection is enabled (Media State is set to Enabled). Click the Details button to open the Network Connection Details window, as shown in Figure 15.6. The data found here is a subset of the data retrieved from using the ipconfig command.

FIGURE 15.6
Windows 7:
The Network
Connection
Details window

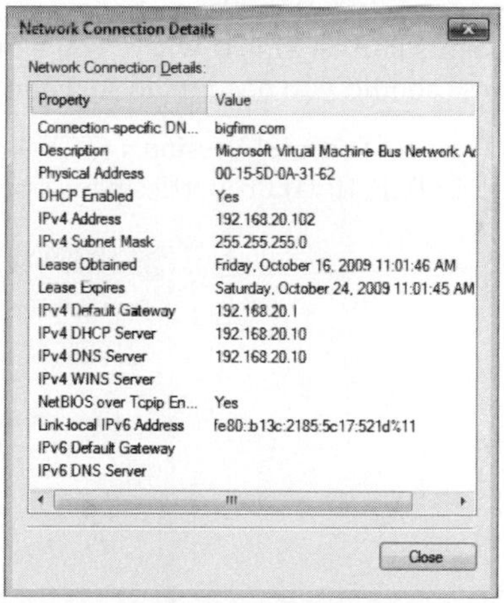

The network connection details results show that the Local Area Connection is DHCP enabled, so you know it is getting its configuration from a DHCP server. The connection is configured with the DNS suffix bigfirm.com, the IP address 192.168.20.102, the subnet mask

255.255.255.0, the default gateway address 192.168.20.1, and DNS server address 192.168.20.10. You can also see when the DHCP information was given out (by the date in the Lease Obtained value) and when it will expire (the date in the Lease Expires value).

MANUALLY CONFIGURING LOCAL AREA CONNECTION SETTINGS IN WINDOWS 7

Close the Network Connection Details window and click the Properties button on the Local Area Connection Status page to open the Local Area Connection Properties page shown in Figure 15.7.

FIGURE 15.7
Windows 7:
The Local Area
Connection
Properties page

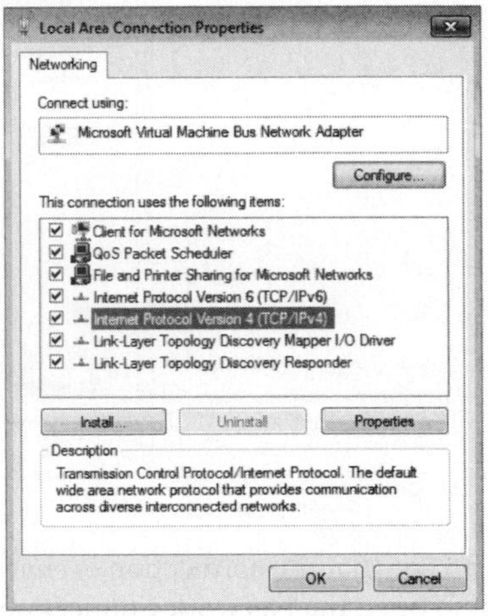

The Local Area Connection Properties page shows which NIC it's associated with, as well as the components it uses. This is where you would manually give the Local Area Connection a static IP address should you need to do so. Follow these steps:

1. Select Internet Protocol Version 4 (TCP/IPv4), and click Properties. The Internet Protocol Version 4 (TCP/IPv4) Properties page opens, as shown in Figure 15.8.

FIGURE 15.8
Windows 7:
The Internet
Protocol Version 4
(TCP/IPv4)
Properties page

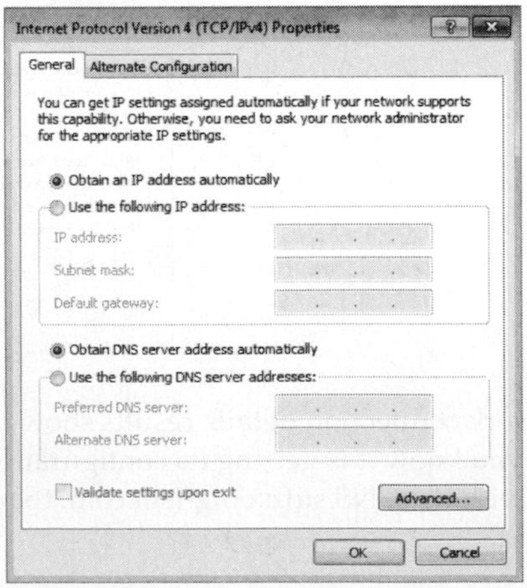

2. Select "Use the following IP address."

3. Enter the IP address, subnet mask, and default gateway address.

4. Click "Use the following DNS server addresses," and enter the preferred and alternate DNS server addresses.

5. Click the Advanced tab, click the DNS tab, and enter the DNS suffix you want appended to the name of this computer (to create the FQDN).

6. Select the "Validate settings upon exit" setting to run the Network Diagnostics applet. The applet will run when you exit the Local Area Connection Properties page and will validate your IP settings. If there is a problem, you will be notified and given information to help you solve the issue.

7. Click OK and OK again, and then close the remaining windows.

LOCAL AREA CONNECTIONS IN WINDOWS VISTA

In Windows Vista, locate the Local Area Connection by clicking Start ➢ Network and selecting the Network and Sharing Center, shown in Figure 15.9. Or type **Network** in the search area at the bottom of the Start menu and then choose Network and Sharing Center in the Programs menu. The interface is very much like the one in Windows 7.

FIGURE 15.9
Vista: The Local Area Connection Icon in the Network and Sharing Center

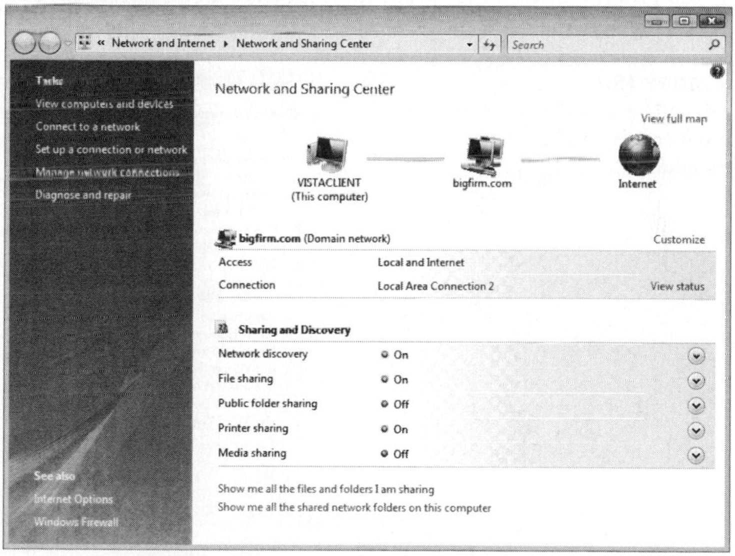

Again, if you don't see the Local Area Connection icon listed here, then you have a hardware or driver issue. Use Device Manager to isolate the problem, or try to add the network adapter manually using the Add Hardware Wizard in the Control Panel.

Click the "View status" link to open the Local Area Connection Status window, as shown in Figure 15.10.

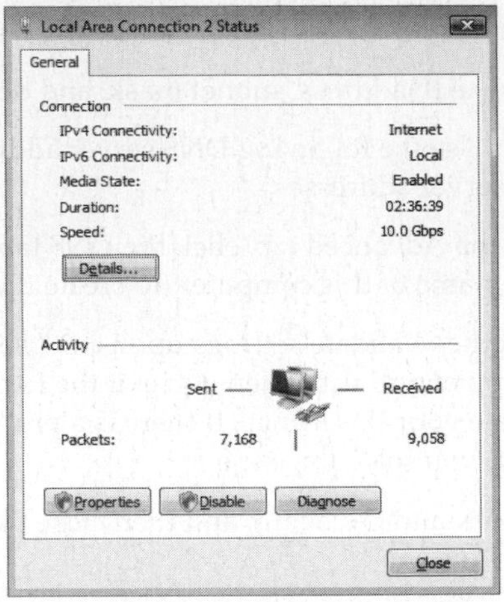

FIGURE 15.10
Vista: The Local
Area Connection
Status window

The Connection Media State value is set to Enabled, so you know the Local Area Connection is live. Click the Details button to open the Network Connection Details window, shown in Figure 15.11. The window is identical to the corresponding window in Windows 7. The data found here is a subset of the data retrieved from using the `ipconfig` command and verifies that the Local Area Connection has been configured, either manually or by DHCP.

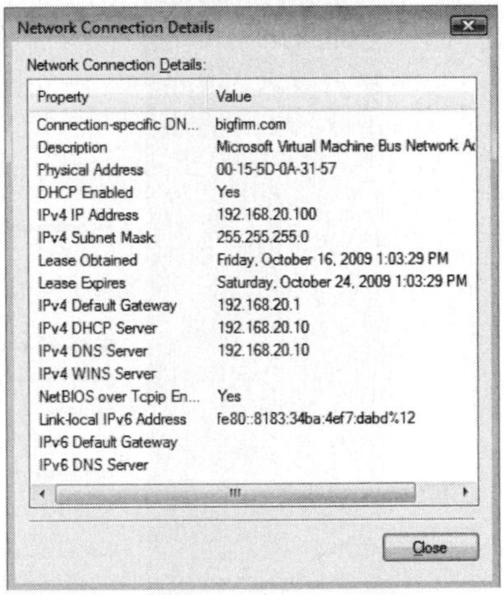

FIGURE 15.11
Vista: The Network
Connection Details
window

MANUALLY CONFIGURING LOCAL AREA CONNECTION SETTINGS IN WINDOWS VISTA

Close the Details window, and click the Properties button to open the Local Area Connection Properties page shown in Figure 15.12.

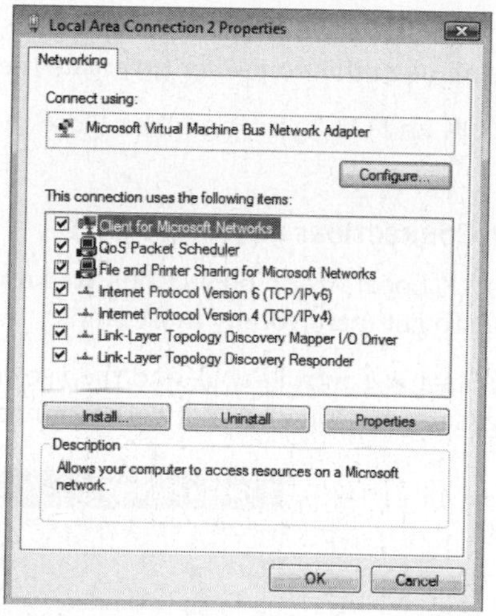

FIGURE 15.12
Vista: The Local
Area Connection
Properties page

The Local Area Connection Properties page in Vista is identical to the one in Windows 7. It shows which NIC it's associated with, as well as the components it uses. To configure static settings (instead of getting them from DHCP), follow these steps:

1. Select Internet Protocol Version 4 (TCP/IPv4), and click Properties. The Properties page opens, as shown in Figure 15.13.

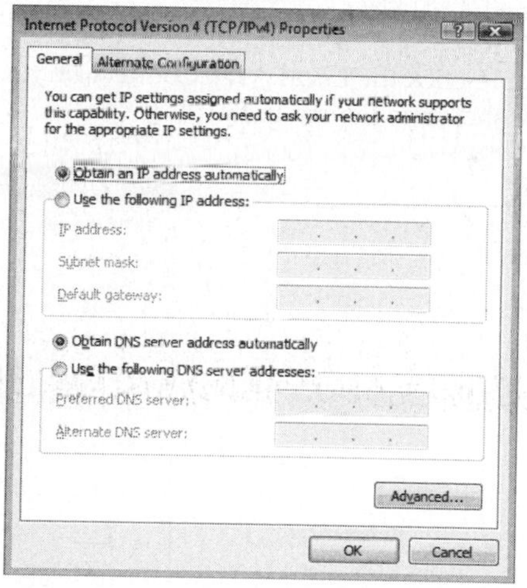

FIGURE 15.13
Vista: The Internet
Protocol Version 4
(TCP/IPv4)
Properties page

2. Select "Use the following IP address."

3. Enter the IP address, subnet mask, and default gateway.

4. Click "Use the following DNS server addresses," and enter the preferred and alternate DNS server addresses.

5. Click the Advanced tab, click the DNS tab, and enter the DNS suffix you want appended to the name of this computer (to create the FQDN).

6. Click OK and OK again, and then close the remaining windows.

LOCAL AREA CONNECTIONS IN WINDOWS XP

In Windows XP, Local Area Connections are kept in the Network Connections section (shown in Figure 15.14). To get there, follow these steps:

1. Click Start ➢ Control Panel, and then select Network and Internet Connections (if you are using Category View) or Network Connections (if you are using Classic View).

FIGURE 15.14
XP: The Network
Connections
window

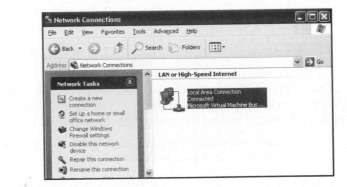

2. Double-click the Local Area Connection to open the Local Area Connection Status window shown in Figure 15.15.

FIGURE 15.15
XP: The Local
Area Connection
Status window

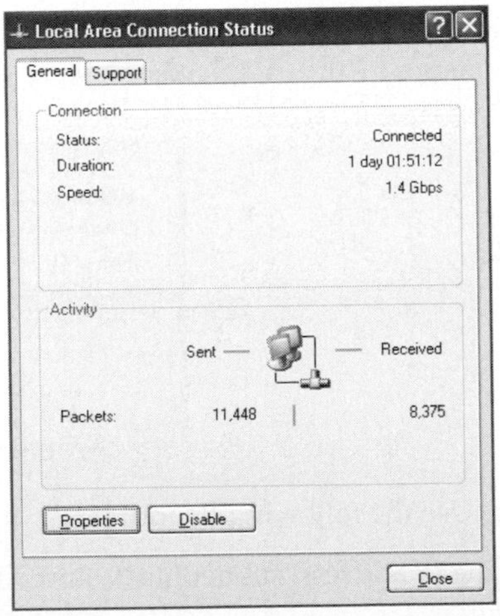

3. The Local Area Connection details are available by clicking the Support tab and then clicking the Details button, as shown in Figure 15.16.

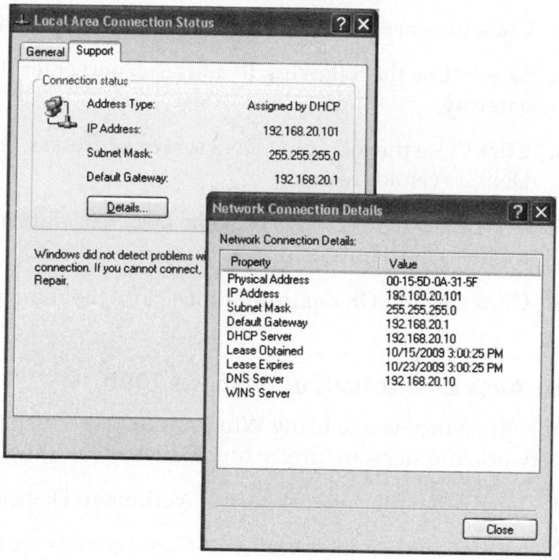

FIGURE 15.16

XP: The Network
Connection Details
window

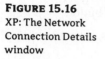

The Network Connection Details window in Windows XP does not give as many details as in Windows Vista or Windows 7, but you will see the details of the main settings you need to connect to a network.

MANUALLY CONFIGURING LOCAL AREA CONNECTION SETTINGS IN WINDOWS XP

To manually enter IP settings for the Local Area Connection, follow these steps:

1. Close the Details window, and click the Properties on the General tab of the Local Area Connection Status window. The Local Area Connection Properties window opens, as shown in Figure 15.17.

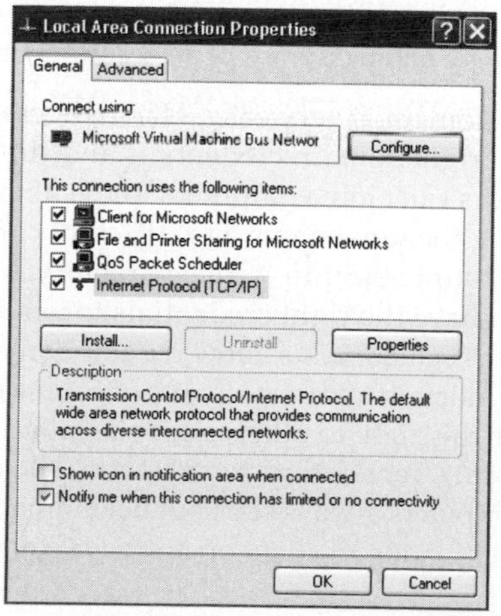

FIGURE 15.17

XP: Local Area
Connection Prop-
erties window

2. Click Internet Protocol (TCP/IP), and then click the Properties button.

3. Select "Use the following IP address," and enter the IP address, subnet mask, and default gateway.

4. Click "Use the following DNS server addresses," and enter the preferred and alternate DNS server addresses.

5. Click the Advanced tab, click the DNS tab, and enter the DNS suffix you want appended to the name of this computer (to create the FQDN).

6. Click OK and OK again, and then close the remaining windows.

LOCAL AREA CONNECTIONS IN WINDOWS 2000

On the off-chance you're using Windows 2000 Professional clients on your Windows Server 2008 R2 network, the steps are pretty much the same as they are for later operating systems:

1. Verify that the network card is working in Device Manager.

2. Verify that that the Local Area Connection is found in the Network and Dialup Connections applet in the Control Panel.

3. Make sure the Local Area Connection has an IP address, subnet mask, default gateway, and DNS server, as well as a DNS suffix assigned to it (by using the GUI or the `ipconfig` command).

If you need to manually assign this information to the Local Area Connection, follow the instructions for Windows XP.

Joining the Domain

To join a domain from any Windows operating system, you'll need the following information:

◆ The fully qualified domain name or NetBIOS name of the domain

◆ The name and password of an account with permission to join the domain

Joining a domain is very easy. The main places you're likely to run into trouble are not knowing the right domain credentials and supplying the wrong computer name. Local administrators can't join computers to the domain, and you shouldn't join a computer to the domain using the same name as a different computer that previously joined and that has a computer account object in Active Directory. Make sure that the computer name is unique and that you have the right credentials to join the domain.

By default, 2008 domains allow regular domain users to join up to 10 computers to a domain. Beyond that, domain admin accounts of course can add computers to a domain, and you can also delegate this right to other users via Group Policy. For information on how to delegate this right, see `http://technet.microsoft.com/library/dd392267(WS.10).aspx`.

Client computers always start out belonging to a workgroup called WORKGROUP. That's the beginning setting for all client operating systems discussed in this chapter.

ADDING DOMAIN ACCOUNTS TO LOCAL COMPUTER GROUPS

To log on and use a computer using a domain account, domain user accounts have to be added to a local group on the computer. This is true for all Windows 7, Vista, XP, and 2000 client computers that join a domain.

When a computer is joined to a domain, the Domain Admins group gets added to the local Administrators group on the computer. Domain Admins are now administrators of the local computer and can fully manage the machine (can add or remove hardware, install software, and so on). Likewise, the Domain Users group gets added to the Local Users group on the computer. Domain users are now afforded the normal local user rights on the computer (nonmanagement tasks, such as using software, accessing network resources, and so on).

Joining a Domain from Windows 7

Typically, you'll join the domain from a computer connected to it, but Windows 7 supports both online joins and offline joins.

JOINING THE DOMAIN WHILE ONLINE

To join a domain from Windows 7 when connected to the network, follow these steps:

1. Open the System applet. The fastest way to open it is by right-clicking the Computer icon in the Start menu and choosing Properties. You can also reach it from the Control Panel (select Start ➢ Control Panel ➢ System and Security, and select System). You should see a dialog box like the one in Figure 15.18.

FIGURE 15.18
System information for the Windows 7 client

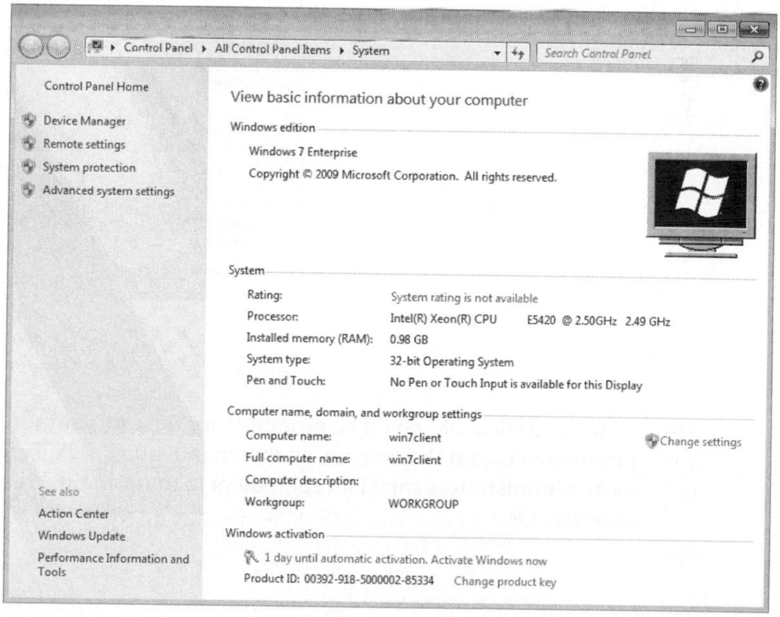

2. In this example, the computer hasn't yet joined the domain, so it's in the default work-group (called WORKGROUP) that all Windows computers start in. Click the "Change settings" link to open the System Properties dialog box, as shown in Figure 15.19.

FIGURE 15.19

System Properties
dialog box

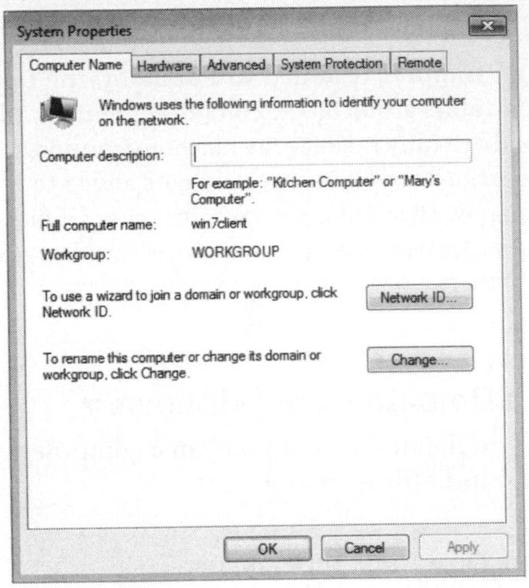

3. The simplest way to join a domain is to click the Change button to open the dialog box in Figure 15.20. Type the name of the domain (either the NetBIOS name or the FQDN), and click OK.

FIGURE 15.20

Type the domain
name to join the
domain.

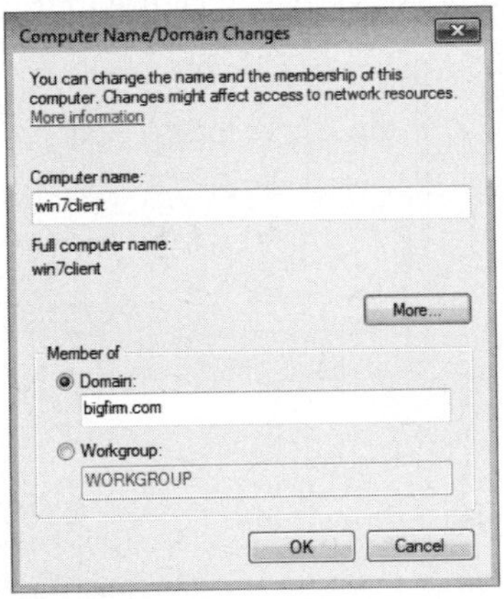

4. When you click OK, you'll be prompted for the username and password of an account with permission to join the domain, as shown in Figure 15.21. Type the credentials. Remember, local administrators can't join computers to the domain. You must supply a domain account and click OK.

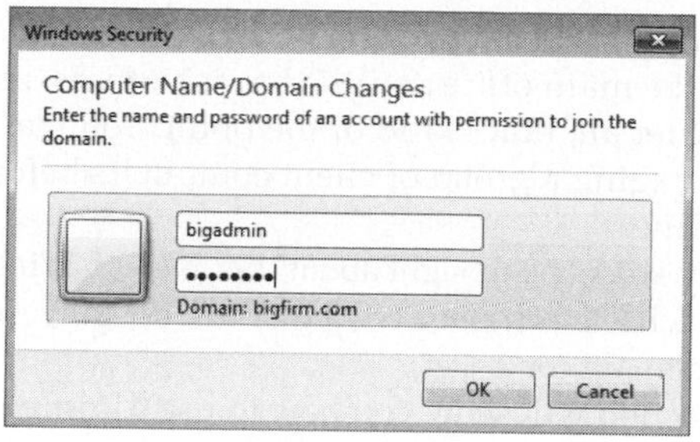

FIGURE 15.21
Provide credentials to join the domain.

5. You should see a dialog box welcoming you to the bigfirm domain. Click OK, and you'll see first a warning that you'll need to reboot (click OK again). Then you will be prompted to reboot the computer. (You'll need to reboot to complete the join.)

If you don't join successfully, check the credentials you used.

WHAT ABOUT THE NETWORK ID WIZARD?

Clicking the Network ID button shown in Figure 15.19 (this is also available in Windows Vista and XP, as well as Windows 2000 clients) starts the Join a Domain or Workgroup Wizard. It walks you through the steps in joining a domain (or workgroup) and adding domain accounts to local groups. It asks you questions about the kind of network you will be joining (whether it's part of a business network or it's a home computer) and configures the domain or workgroup name accordingly.

If you choose the "home" option, then the computer will be set to be part of a workgroup.

If you choose the "business network" option, then you are further prompted to tell whether the company uses a network with or without a domain. If you select "My company uses a network without a domain option," then next you are asked to give a workgroup name, and the computer will be configured to be part of that workgroup.

To join a domain using this wizard, select the "This computer is part of a business network" option. Click Next, and then choose "My computer uses a network with a domain." Click Next (twice), and then enter the username, password, and domain name for a domain account that has the rights to join a domain (an account that is a member of the Domain Admins group or other account that has been delegated this right).

The wizard then gives you the chance to add a domain user account to either the local Administrators group (giving a domain user full rights on the local machine) or the Local Users group.

JOINING THE DOMAIN WHILE OFFLINE WITH DJOIN.EXE

Domain joining has one problem: what if you can't get to the domain controller to create the computer account or you can't write to it? Windows Server 2008 introduced the concept of a *read-only domain controller* (RODC) for branch offices to cut down on the network traffic between the main office and the branch offices, but you can't write to Active Directory on an RODC. After all, that's kind of the point. You may also not be able to contact a domain controller if staging a group of client computers before deploying them or installing a client OS while offline.

Luckily, someone thought about this. New to Windows 7 and Windows 2008 R2 is the djoin.exe utility, which lets you join a computer to a domain even when the client computer can't communicate with the domain controller.

This section will show you how to use djoin.exe to join a new Windows 7 client computer (WIN7CLIENT2) to the domain bigfirm.com when the client is offline.

In a nutshell, djoin.exe provisions a computer account in AD and then exports the data (called a *blob*, which is needed for the computer with that computer name to join the domain) to a text file. The offline computer then imports the blob and joins the domain. The blob can also be added to an unattended setup answer file in order to join a computer to a domain (offline) as part of the OS installation.

One thing about the blob: if you provision the computer account in AD using djoin.exe and then open the resulting text file expecting to read it, you will be disappointed because it's not human-readable. However, it contains sensitive data, such as the machine account password and other important domain information.

These are the steps to join an offline computer to the domain:

1. Run djoin on a Windows 7 or Windows 2008 R2 machine that *can* communicate with the DC. This will create a computer account in AD for the computer name specified and create a text file used in step 3.

2. Move that file to the offline client computer (securely).

3. Run djoin on the offline machine, and import the text file.

djoin Requirements

You can run djoin only on Windows 7 and Windows 2008 R2 computers. It's possible to use djoin to join a Windows 7 or 2008 R2 computer to a "down-level" DC (via the /downlevel parameter), but the example in this chapter will join a Windows 7 client to a Windows 2008 R2 domain.

There are a few other general requirements as well. First, the user who runs djoin on the "provisioning machine" must have the right to add computers to the domain. Again, domain users have this permission although they can only add up to 10 computers to the domain by default.

You should also be familiar with the djoin parameters to understand the commands issued in the following example. Table 15.1 describes these parameters.

TABLE 15.1: djoin Parameters

PARAMETER	DESCRIPTION
/provision	Creates the computer account in Active Directory

TABLE 15.1:   djoin Parameters *(CONTINUED)*

PARAMETER	DESCRIPTION
/domain	Specifies the domain the computer will be joining
/machine	Specifies the name of the computer that will be added to ADDS and that you want to join the domain
/savefile <filepath>	Specifies the location and file to save the provisioning metadata
/dcname (optional)	Specifies the name of a specific DC you want to use to create the computer account
/reuse (optional)	Reuses an existing machine account (the machine account password will be reset)
/downlevel (optional)	Provides support for using DC that runs Windows 2008 or older
/printblob (optional)	Creates a blob correctly encoded for use in an unattended answer file
/defpwd (optional)	Uses default machine account password—not recommended
/requestodj	Requests an offline domain join (ODJ) on reboot
/loadfile <filepath>	Specifies the file (created with the /savefile parameter) to be imported to the offline computer
/windowspath	Specifies the path of the Windows directory in an offline image, typically %systemroot% or %windir%
/localos	Specifies a local OS as opposed to an offline image (requires a reboot)

Adding the Computer to the Domain While Offline

To use djoin to join a computer to the domain, you will need to execute djoin commands on two different machines. In this example, they are as follows:

win7client.bigfirm.com   This machine is already joined to the domain and can communicate with the DC. This machine will be used to provision the new computer account in AD (we refer to it as the *provisioning machine*).

win7client2   This is a newly created Windows 7 client that is in a workgroup and cannot communicate with a DC.

RUNNING DJOIN.EXE USING A REGULAR USER ACCOUNT

To avoid confusion, it's best to use an account that is a member of the Domain Admins group to run the djoin.exe command or to use an account that has been delegated the right to add computers to the domain. Regular users can run the djoin.exe command and create computer accounts, but only up to 10 times (because by default regular users are limited to joining no more than 10 computers to the domain). After that, the user will be denied, as shown in the following code:

```
Djoin djoin /provision /domain bigfirm.com /machine win7client11
/savefile c:\join.txt


Provisioning the computer account...

Failed to provision [win7client11] in the domain [bigfirm.com]: 0x216d.


Computer account provisioning failed: 0x216d.
Your computer could not be joined to the domain. You have exceeded
the maximum number of computer accounts you are allowed to create
in this domain. Contact your system administrator to have this
limit reset or increased.
```

From then on you will need to use a domain admin account or delegate this right to others (via Group Policy).

First, log onto the client computer win7client.bigfirm.com with a domain administrator account, and start an elevated command prompt. Then run the following command to create a computer account in Active Directory and also to create the provisioning text file:

```
C:\Users\bigadmin>djoin /provision /domain bigfirm.com
/machine win7client2 /savefile c:\join.txt
```

The results of this command are as follows:

```
Provisioning the computer account...

Successfully provisioned [win7client2] in the domain [bigfirm.com].
Provisioning data was saved successfully to [c:\join.txt].

Computer account provisioning completed successfully.
The operation completed successfully.
```

Active Directory Users and Computers on the DC (bf1) will now contain the computer account WIN7CLIENT2 stored in the default Computers folder, as shown in Figure 15.22.

Next, move the resulting text file join.txt from the provisioning computer (WIN7CLIENT) to the computer you want to join (WIN7CLIENT2). In this example, the file is placed in the root of the C drive. Then on the client computer (WIN7CLIENT2), open a command prompt with elevated permissions, and type the following:

```
Djoin /requestODJ /loadfile c:\join.txt /windowspath %systemroot% /localos
```

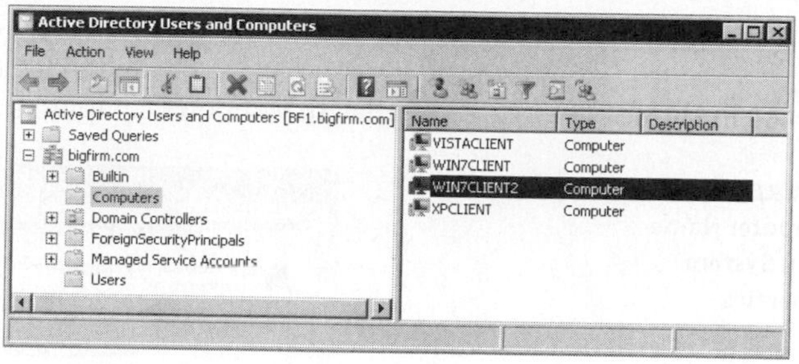

FIGURE 15.22
Running djoin
adds a computer
account to ADDS.

Reboot the computer, and when it comes back up, it will be joined to the domain.

For more information on using djoin with unattended setups and delegating the right to join computers to the domain, refer to http://technet.microsoft.com/library/dd392267(WS.10).aspx.

Joining a Domain from Windows Vista

To join a domain from Windows Vista, follow these steps:

1. Open the System applet. The fastest way to open it is by right-clicking the Computer icon in the Start menu and choosing Properties. You can also reach it from the Control Panel (select Start ➤ Control Panel ➤ System and Security, and select System). You should see a dialog box like the one in Figure 15.23.

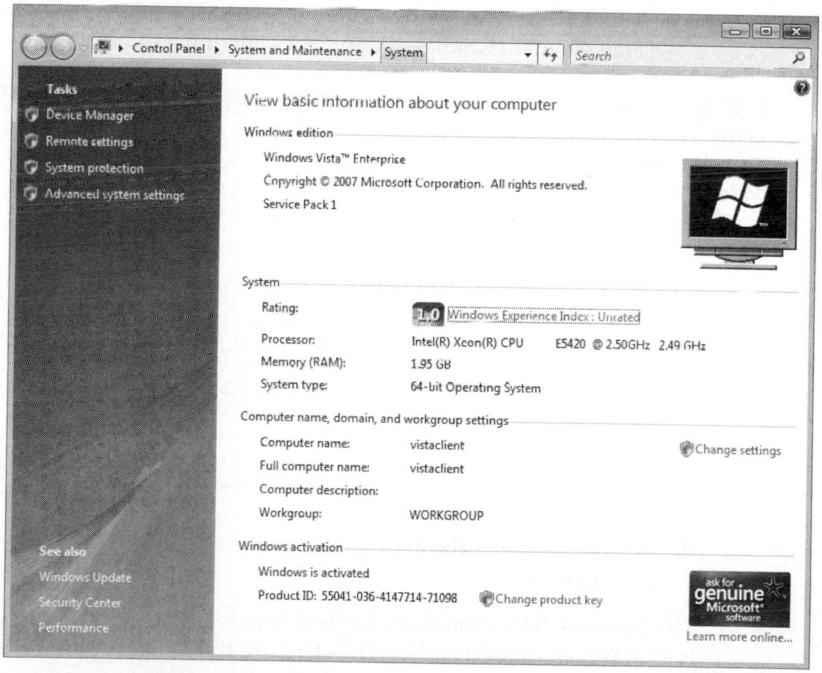

FIGURE 15.23
The System applet

2. Click the "Change settings" link, and the System Properties window opens (Figure 15.24). In this example, the computer hasn't yet joined the domain, so it's in the default workgroup (WORKGROUP) that all Windows computers start in.

FIGURE 15.24
Computer Name
tab in System
Properties

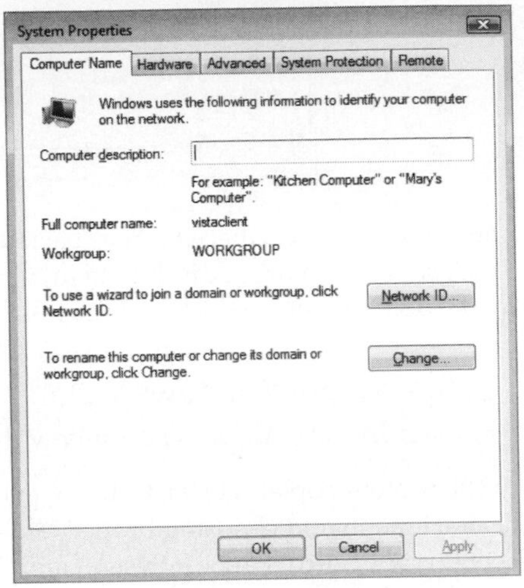

3. The simplest way to join a domain is to click the Change button to open the Computer Name/Domain Changes dialog box shown in Figure 15.25.

FIGURE 15.25
Computer Name/
Domain Changes
dialog box

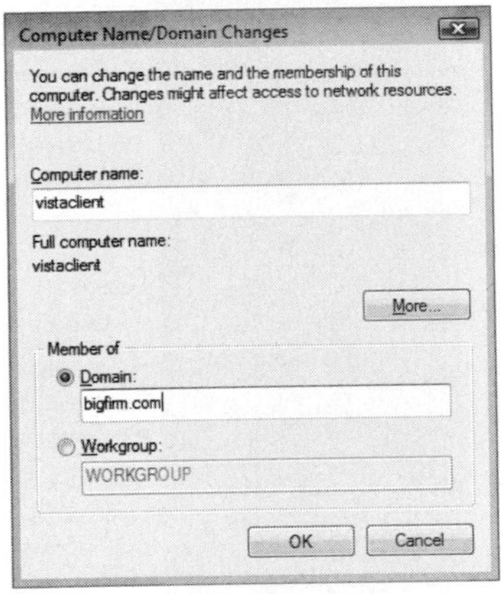

4. Type the name of the domain (either the NetBIOS name of the domain or the FQDN), and click OK.

The Network ID button will also help you do this; it just does it with a pretty wizard. This button was discussed earlier. The steps are the same for Windows Vista, so refer to the "What About the Network ID Wizard?" sidebar for more information on how to use this button to join a domain.

5. When you click OK, you'll be prompted for the username and password of an account with permission to join the domain, as shown in Figure 15.26.

6. Type the credentials—remember, you must provide domain credentials in order to join a domain. Then click OK.

FIGURE 15.26
Providing credentials to join the domain

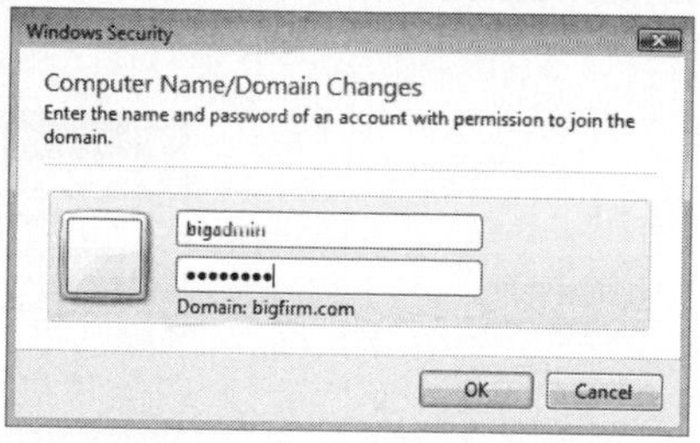

7. You should see a dialog box welcoming you to the bigfirm domain. Click OK, and you'll see first a warning that you'll need to reboot (click OK again) and then a prompt to reboot the computer. (You'll need to reboot to complete the join.)

If you don't join successfully, check the credentials you used.

Joining a Domain from Windows XP

To join a domain from Windows XP, follow these steps:

1. Open the System applet. The fastest way to open it is by right-clicking the My Computer icon in the Start menu and choosing Properties. You can also reach it from the Control Panel (select Start ➤ Control Panel, switch to Classic View, and click System). Navigate to the Computer Name tab (see Figure 15.27).

FIGURE 15.27
Computer Name tab in System Properties

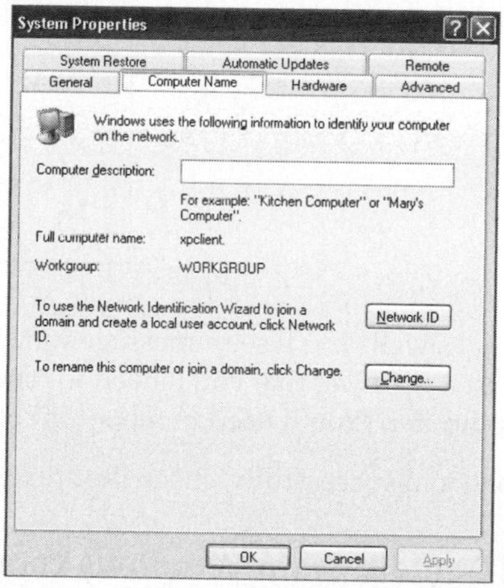

In this example, the computer hasn't yet joined the domain, so it's in the default WORKGROUP domain all Windows computers start in.

2. The simplest way to join a domain is to click the Change button to open the Computer Name Changes dialog box shown in Figure 15.28.

The Network ID button will also help you do this; it just does it with a pretty wizard. This button was discussed earlier. The steps are the same for Windows XP, so refer to the "What About the Network ID Wizard?" sidebar for more information on how to use this button to join a domain.

FIGURE 15.28
The Computer Name Changes dialog box

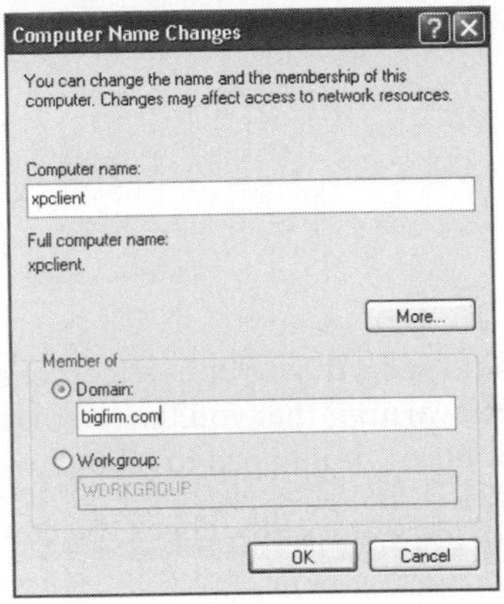

3. Type in the domain name (use either the NetBIOS or the FQDN name), and click OK. You will then be prompted to supply a domain username and password with permission to join the domain (see Figure 15.29).

FIGURE 15.29
Supplying a user-name and pass-word to join the domain

4. If all goes well, you'll see a message welcoming you to the domain. Click OK, and you'll see first a warning that you'll need to reboot (click OK again) and then a prompt to reboot the computer. (You'll need to reboot to complete the join.)

If you don't join successfully, check the credentials you used.

Joining a Domain from Windows 2000 Professional

In the unlikely event that you're using Windows 2000 Professional clients to connect to a Windows Server 2008 R2 domain, the basics are very much like those of connecting from the other operating systems: from the System applet in the Control Panel, change from the default WORKGROUP membership to the full domain name, supply the appropriate credentials, and reboot when required.

Changing Domain User Passwords

Good security practice demands that passwords be changed regularly and known only to the user. Therefore, the operating systems users will employ to connect to a Windows server 2008 domain will require some user intervention to change the passwords.

Although most of this book is geared toward the administrator, this section has information that the administrator will need to convey to the user population so they can do it themselves. The good news is that changing passwords is extremely simple, and the UI gives all the guidance the user needs:

- If policy requires a user to change their password when they first use an account, they'll be prompted to do this.

- If policy demands a user change a password because the password will soon expire, they'll be prompted to do so, told how to do it, and told how long they have until the password expires.

- If the password they type does not meet the security standards defined in Group Policy, they'll be told what those standards are so they can follow them.

If a user *forgets* their old password, they will not be able to change it themselves, and if you've followed best security practices, the administrator won't know it either. The administrator will need to update the password on their domain user account and then set the password to be changed at first logon.

Real World Scenario

P@SSW0RD POLICIES PROVIDE SECURITY AND ACCOUNTABILITY

Why do we have this section? Wouldn't it be easier to just edit Group Policy so that users never need to change their passwords and they just use the ones the administrator gave them when creating their user account?

That might be easier (although changing a password is hardly arduous), but it's a lot less secure. If users never change their passwords, then that increases the risk that the wrong person will learn or figure out the password—if nothing else, the bad guys will have an unlimited period to try to do so. And if the administrator chooses the password, then the user doesn't own the security of that account.

One of the authors of this book used to consult for a company that did not enforce regular password changes. The managers had determined that this was just too annoying to their employees. This lax security position hurt them. An employee was let go, and not long after that, work stored on the network started disappearing. After convincing the management that a companywide password change had to happen, the mysterious phenomenon of missing files stopped. Later we determined that the fired employee had been connecting to the network using a co-worker's username and password and deleting files. After that incident, the company management decided that regular password changes were a good idea.

The Windows 2008 default domain group policy enforces regular password changes and password complexity rules. The Group Policy setting is located at Computer Configuration\Policies\Windows Settings\Security Settings\Account Policies\Password Policy.

The default password policy settings are as follows:

Enforce password history This requires users to use a certain number of unique passwords before an old password can be reused. The default number is 24 passwords.

Maximum password age This is the number of days a password can be used before the user must change it. The default is 42 days.

Minimum password age This is the minimum number of days a password must be used before the user can change it. The default is one day.

Minimum password length This is the minimum number of characters a password must contain. The default is 7.

Password must meet complexity requirements Enabled by default, this enforces several rules about how a password must be created. For example, a password must not contain more than two consecutive characters that are part of the user's full name.

It's an even better idea to encourage users to use passphrases instead of mere passwords. A *passphrase* is a combination of words that together, in the exact right order, is the password. A passphrase as a whole still has to meet password policy complexity requirements but is generally longer and can contains spaces, so the passphrase can be much harder to figure out for the bad guys. Combined with vowel substitution (substituting some letters, namely vowels, for numbers), users can create very complex passphrases. For instance, a good passphrase could be My g00d d0g c4tch3s fr1sb33s! This is easy to remember but is long (29 characters long), complex (because of the use of multiple words, spaces, and vowel substitution), and would be difficult to crack.

See Chapter 8, "Group Policies in AD," for an example of creating a complex password GPO.

Windows Server 2008 also provides the ability (via GPO) to enforce different password policies for different groups of users. So, for users who work with more sensitive data, you can create a fine-grained password policy to have them change their password more often than other user groups.

Similarly, two people should not use the same account. Even if those two people never use the account at the same time (if they do, then doubling up on account usage will cause you all kinds of grief from lost profile changes), it's a bad idea. If more than one person uses an account, then you will never know who is using what on the network—or attempting to use resources that they're not authorized to touch. Security auditing requires a model of one account and one password for each user.

Incidentally, this advice about unique passwords for each user doesn't apply just to ordinary users. To enable security auditing, all Windows server administrators should have their own user account (instead of all administrators using the Administrator account) with Group Policy set to require regular password changes. Although this model requires more account management, it allows you to track which server administrator did what and allows you to easily disable administrative access when someone leaves the company, without having to change the administrative passwords for everybody. Password policies are domain-wide, so it makes sense to follow best practices for everyone in the domain.

Changing Domain Passwords from Windows 7 and Windows Vista

Most often, users will change passwords under two circumstances: when the administrator has just reset their domain account password and requires that it be changed, or when Group Policy is forcing the password to expire. Windows 7 and Windows Vista follow the same process and have the same GUI for this, so we'll combine the information about changing domain passwords for these two operating systems in the following sections.

CHANGING PASSWORDS AT FIRST LOGON

When the administrator forces a password reset (for security reasons or on a new account), the user will be prompted for the new password when they attempt to log on for the first time, as shown in Figure 15.30. The default password applied by the administrator is simply to prevent a user account from being unprotected before it's used.

FIGURE 15.30
Changing the password before logging on for the first time

When the user clicks OK, they'll be prompted for the new password, as shown in Figure 15.31.

FIGURE 15.31
Changing to the new password

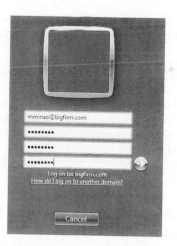

The old password is filled in, and the user types a new password. According to the Default Domain Policy, the password cannot be the same password and must meet length and complexity requirements, or else the user will be nagged for a password that meets the security guidelines and told how to meet them. When the user has successfully changed the password, they'll see a message telling them that the password has been changed. When they click OK, they'll be able to log on with the new password. That's it. After the password is changed, the user can log on normally.

CHANGING PASSWORDS ON DEMAND

When a password is about to expire, users will start seeing nag messages a few days ahead of time telling them that their passwords are about to expire and telling them how to change them. A user might also want to change their password on demand. The simplest way to change a password is to press Ctrl+Alt+Del to open the Windows Security GUI and choose the "Change a password..." option, as shown in Figure 15.32. You can also get to this screen from the Windows Security button located in the Start menu.

FIGURE 15.32
Changing a password from the Security GUI

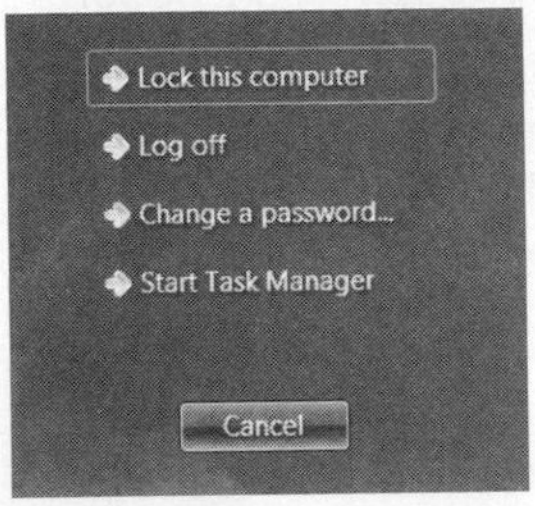

When the user chooses to change a password, they'll see the same dialog box as shown in Figure 15.31, prompting them to type the old password and the new one. Again, if the new password does not meet the security requirements, then they'll see an error message advising them of the password policies. Once the user enters their old and new password (twice), the user clicks the arrow button, and the password is changed.

AVOID REPEAT PASSWORD PROMPTS AFTER A PASSWORD CHANGE

If a user has more than one computer and is logged into both (for example, if they have both a laptop and a desktop computer), then they should log out and log back in on both computers after changing the password. The session will still work, but because their domain password will have changed, this can lead to repeated password prompts for network resources such as Exchange Servers, SharePoint sites, and other applications requiring authentication. They can keep typing in their passwords when prompted, but it's simplest just to log in with the new password to avoid the prompts.

Changing Domain Passwords from Windows XP and Windows 2000 Professional

Most often, users will change passwords under two circumstances: when the administrator has just reset their domain account password and requires that it be changed, or when Group Policy is forcing the password to expire. The steps for changing the password for Windows XP and Windows 2000 Professional are the same.

CHANGING PASSWORDS AT FIRST LOGON

When the administrator forces a password reset (for security reasons or on a new account), the user will be prompted for the new password when they attempt to log on for the first time, as shown in Figure 15.33. The default password applied by the administrator is simply to prevent a user account from being unprotected before it's used.

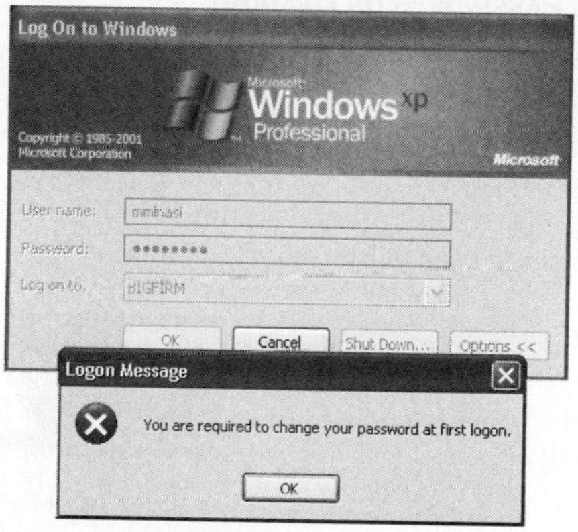

FIGURE 15.33
Prompting for a
new password

When the user clicks OK, they'll be prompted for the new password, as shown in Figure 15.34.

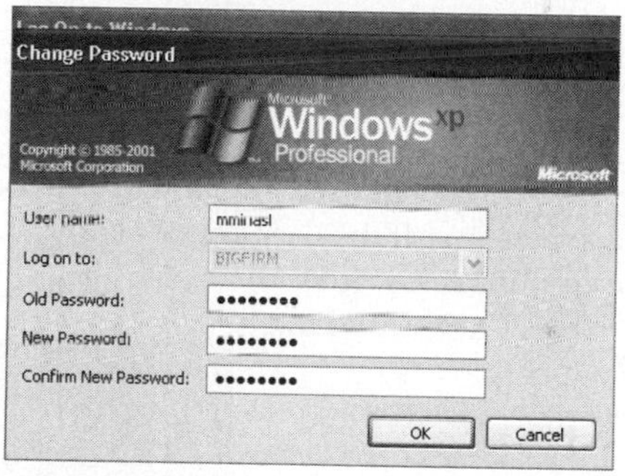

FIGURE 15.34
Typing the new
password

When the user has typed a password meeting the security requirements for the domain, they'll see a confirmation, as shown in Figure 15.35.

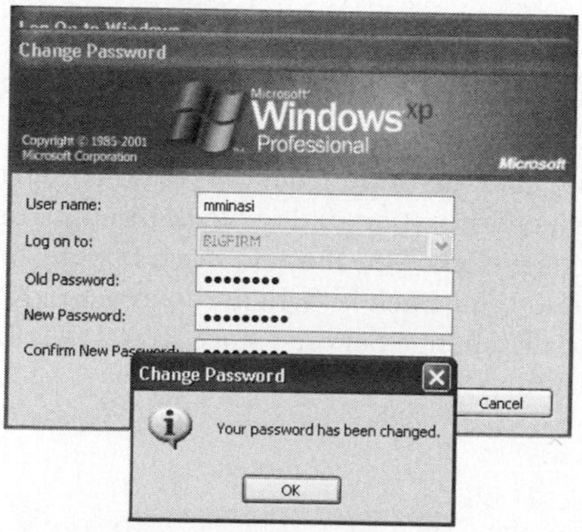

FIGURE 15.35
The password has
been changed.

The user can now log on normally using the new password.

CHANGING PASSWORDS ON DEMAND

When a password is about to expire, users will start seeing nag messages a few days ahead of time telling them that their passwords are about to expire and telling them how to change them. A user might also want to change their password on demand. The simplest way to change a password is to press Ctrl+Alt+Del to bring up the Windows Security dialog box and choose the Change Password option, as shown in Figure 15.36. You can also get to this screen from the Windows Security option in the Start menu.

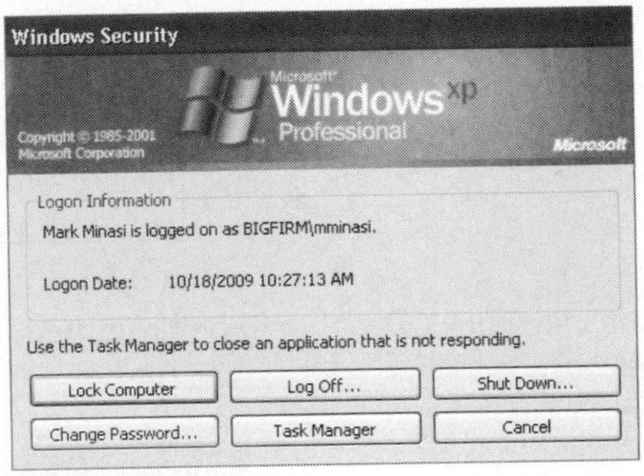

FIGURE 15.36

Changing passwords from the Windows Security dialog box

When they click Change Password, the user will see a dialog box like the one in Figure 15.37 prompting them to type the old and new passwords. The user must supply the old password to change to the new one. If the user doesn't know the old password, the administrator will need to reset the account password.

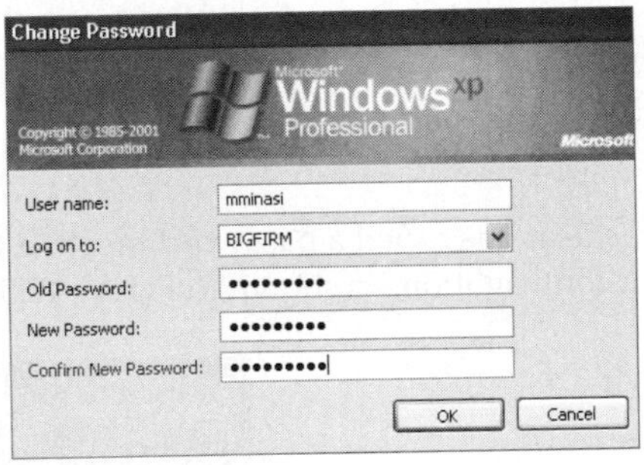

FIGURE 15.37

Changing to the new password

Once the user has supplied a password conforming to domain security policy requirements, they'll see a confirmation dialog box telling the user that the password has been changed. When the user clicks OK, they'll return to the Windows Security dialog box. From there, they can log out and log back in (which can avoid weird problems when connecting to network resources or Exchange Servers, since the user's domain password will be different) or click Cancel to return to their session.

NOTE   The same caveats apply here as in the earlier "Avoid Repeat Password Prompts After a Password Change" sidebar.

Connecting to Network Resources

One of the biggest reasons to join a domain is to access resources on the domain, such as the printer down the hall or some documents that you need to work on. You could access company photos, slide shows, and other media needed to make a marketing campaign. Whatever your need, the point is that you don't need to have these items and devices hooked or stored directly on your client machine. In fact, having them stored on the network is ideal because they are more secure there (access is centrally controlled, and ideally the files would be backed up regularly). Examples of network resources include the following:

- Printers
- Shared folders and files
- Wireless devices (such as wireless printers)
- Services (such as Certificate Services)
- Other computers

Connecting to shared resources is easy for users thanks to Network Discovery and Active Directory. Network Discovery is a setting that allows your computer to find resources on the network easily. It also means other computers (and users) will be able to see your client computer in their Network folder and be able to find shared resources located on your computer easily. Users can also search Active Directory for published resources. This means that the user doesn't need to know where the device is installed or contained. The user might not even know the exact name of a shared folder or printer or the server where it's stored. As long as the resource is published to Active Directory, with a little searching the user will most likely be able to find and utilize the resource.

There are several ways to access shared resources. Here are the more common ways that this section will expand upon for each of the client operating systems addressed in this chapter:

- You can search for and access resources that are published in Active Directory.
- You can attach to shared network resources (for example, shared folders and printers) from the command line.
- You can create a mapped drive to network folder shares.
- You can connect to uniform naming convention (UNC) paths from Windows Explorer that describe the path to a network location in the form of \\computername\sharename.
- You can add network folders to your desktop.

The following examples will access resources located on bigfirm.com domain. Table 15.2 lists those resources and their locations on the network.

TABLE 15.2: Network Resources Used in This Section's Examples

NETWORK RESOURCE TYPE	NETWORK RESOURCE PATH	NETWORK RESOURCE MACHINE LOCATION
Finance file share	\\bf1\BF_Finance	bf1.bigfirm.com
Marketing file share	\\bf1\BF_Marketing	bf1.bigfirm.com
HR file share	\\bf1\BF_HR	bf1.bigfirm.com
Black-and-white printer	\\bf1\BF_Main_Printer	bf1.bigfirm.com
Color printer	\\vistaclient\HP_LJ_2800	vistaclient.bigfirm.com

ADDING THE NETWORK ICON TO THE DESKTOP IN WINDOWS 7 AND VISTA

Capitalizing on the search feature to locate parts of the OS in Windows 7 and Windows Vista is great. But there multiple ways to get to places in these operating systems. The Network button is hidden in Windows 7 and Vista by default, but you can put this item on the desktop for easy access. This will come in handy when you go there frequently in this section. Follow these steps:

1. Right-click anywhere on the desktop, and select Personalize.
2. In the upper-left quadrant, click the Change Desktop Icons link.
3. Select the Network check box, and click OK.

You can also add the Network icon to the Start menu:

1. Right-click the Start menu.
2. Select Properties.
3. Choose the Start Menu tab.
4. Click Customize.
5. Select the Network check box.

Connecting to Network Resources from Windows 7 and Windows Vista

In Windows 7, Network Discovery is turned off by default. This doesn't mean you can't still access resources, providing you know where to look; it means you can't just "discover" them automatically using the Network and Sharing Center. It also means that other users cannot just see your computer and its shared resources.

To turn on Network Discovery, follow these steps:

1. Open the Network and Sharing Center by selecting Start ➢ Control Panel, Network and Internet, and Network and Sharing Center. Or type **Network** in the search box on the Start

menu, then clicking Network and Sharing Center in the list above. If you followed the earlier instructions and added the Network icon to the desktop, then just double-click the network icon on the desktop, and click Network and Sharing Center.

2. Click Change Advanced Sharing Settings in the upper-left quadrant of the Network and Sharing Center.

3. Because the computer is part of a domain, the Advanced Sharing Settings will open to the Domain profile. Under Network Discovery, select the "Turn on network discovery" option.

ADDING THE NETWORK ICON TO THE START MENU OF WINDOWS XP

If you are using Windows XP, you can add the My Network Places to the Start menu, making it simpler to get to network resources, such as network folders you've linked to. Follow these steps:

1. Right-click the Start menu, and select Properties.

2. Choose Customize Start Menu.

3. Select the Advanced tab.

4. Select the My Network Places box, as shown here:

Usually, domain administrators keep company files in centralized, secure, and fault-tolerant locations that can be backed up easily (that is, not stored on individual computers). There are circumstances where being able to share files stored on your local machine with others on the network could come in handy. For instance, maybe you and another user don't have access to the same network shares, but you need to collaborate on a project. By default File and Printer sharing is also turned on, meaning that you can share files and printers that are located/installed on this computer with other users on the network. If you don't want to share these items, you can turn this option off here.

A few more options in the Advanced Sharing settings will help you share files and folders located on the local machine with other users/computers in the domain. This chapter will concentrate on accessing network shares and files located on other computers (not the client computer sharing resources to others), but here are brief descriptions of these options:

Public Folder Sharing   Allows others to access items in your Public Folders folder. Users in the domain will be able to read and write to this directory, and all user accounts on the computer share this common folder. This permission is off by default.

Media Streaming   Allows users to access media files that are shared on the network through Windows Media Server (turned off by default).

Click Save Changes. Network Discovery might not occur immediately. You may have to log out and back into the computer to actually see anything. In a few cases, you may need to reboot the computer.

SEARCHING ACTIVE DIRECTORY

Now that Network Discovery is turned on, accessing network resources becomes much easier because the Windows 7 client will search for them on the network. One of the fastest ways to see what resources are available to you as a user is to search Active Directory for resources that have been published there. To do this in Windows 7, follow these steps:

1. Open the Network applet by typing **Network** into the search bar in the Start menu and then choosing Network from the resulting list.

2. When the Network applet opens, click Search Active Directory in the upper-left quadrant of the window, as shown in Figure 15.38.

FIGURE 15.38
Choosing Search
Active Directory
from the
Network applet

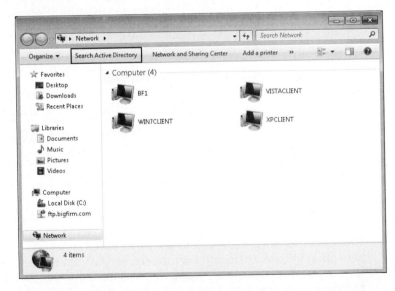

The Find Users, Groups, and Contacts dialog box appears. This dialog box gives you access to a searchable directory of computers, shared folders, and printers, as well as users, groups, and contacts. This is potentially a gold mine of information at the user's fingertips. For example, if a co-worker's telephone number is listed in their domain user account properties, a user can find it by searching for the co-worker's name. A user could find groups to join or what floor a particular printer is located. For the following examples, this section will focus on finding printers and network shares in Active Directory.

ADDING A NETWORK PRINTER

You can add a network printer by searching Active Directory from the GUI, using the command-line tools, or with the Network applet.

Finding a Printer in Active Directory

In the Find drop-down list, choose Printers. If there are multiple domains on the network, you can make the search more specific by choosing your domain name from the In drop-down list (located to the right of the Find drop-down list). If the list of printers is likely to be long, you can search by name or keyword or use the Advanced tab to search by other properties. Once you've set your search criteria, click Find Now. All printers published to Active Directory that meet your search criteria will appear in the Results window.

On the bigfirm.com network, there are two printers published to Active Directory, as shown in Figure 15.39.

FIGURE 15.39
Printers found by searching Active Directory

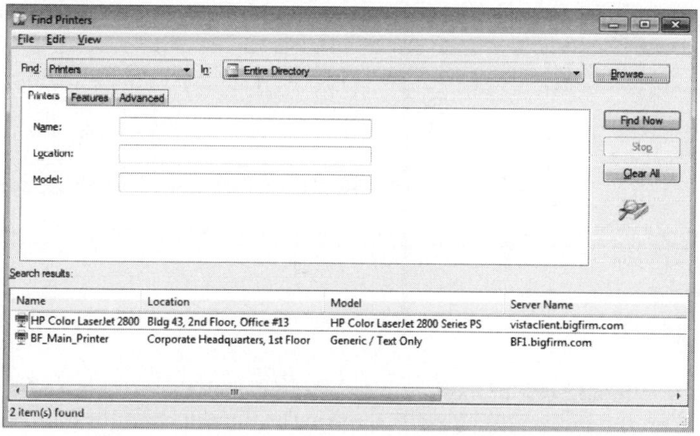

To add a found printer to your computer, right-click the printer, and choose Connect. The printer will install, and you will see it in your Printers folder.

Adding a Network Printer from the Command Line

If you know the name of the printer you want and the print server it's attached to, you can add it from the command line with the `start` command. For instance, to add the printer called bf_main_printer located on server bf1 to a Windows 7 or Windows Vista client, open a command prompt and type the following:

```
start \\bf1\bf_main_printer
```

When the printer installs, the print queue for that printer will open, and the printer will be listed for use in the Devices and Printers applet.

Adding a Network Printer Using the Network Applet

To add a network printer to a Windows 7 or Windows Vista client machine, open the Network applet, and click the Add a Printer link on the toolbar of the Network Folder dialog box. Clicking the link will initiate the Add Printer Wizard. This is the same wizard you get when you add a printer from the Devices and Printers button (located on the Start menu in Windows 7) and the Printers applet (located in the Control Panel in Windows Vista). Remember, you can get to operating system features in many ways.

Like all previous versions of the Add Printer Wizard, this version allows you to add local printers, Bluetooth printers, and printers that are located on the network. This section will concentrate on network resources, which are comprised of cabled or wireless network printers. To add a network printer, click "Add a network, wireless or Bluetooth printer," and click Next. As soon as you click this option, the wizard will search for printers on the network and return any it finds, as shown in Figure 15.40.

FIGURE 15.40
The Add Printer dialog box searches for and returns found network printers.

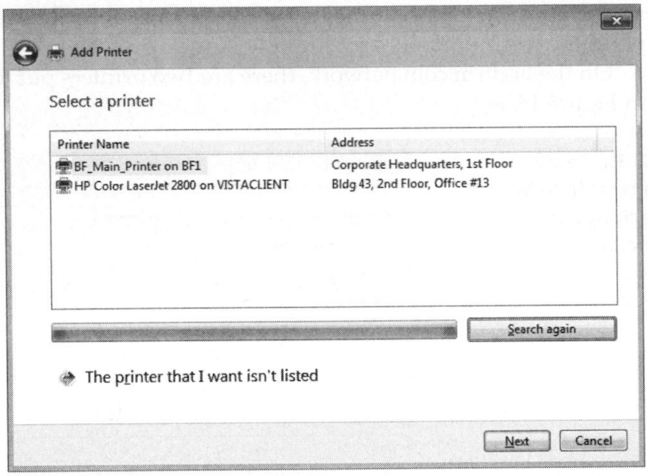

To add one of these printers, simply click the printer, and click Next; then click Next again on the proceeding Results screen. The default configuration is to make this printer the default printer, but you can change this by deselecting the "Set as default printer" box. Click the "Print a test page" button to send a test page to the printer, and click Finish.

If the printer you want to add is not located, click "The printer that I want isn't listed." The next screen offers three more ways to locate the printer you want (shown in Figure 15.41).

The options are to do the following:

◆ Search Active Directory for published network printers

◆ Enter a printer location and name (in the form of \\servername\printername)

◆ Specify a printer using its hostname or its TCP/IP address (often called a *TCP/IP printer*)

The option "Find a printer in the directory, based on location and feature" opens the Find Printers window. You search Active Directory for printers by specifying certain printer criteria (such as a name or a printer model) or a printing feature (such as the ability to print double-sided).

Click the Find Now button, and the wizard returns printers that match the specified criteria, as shown in Figure 15.42. You can also enter no criteria, and the search will return all printers in Active Directory.

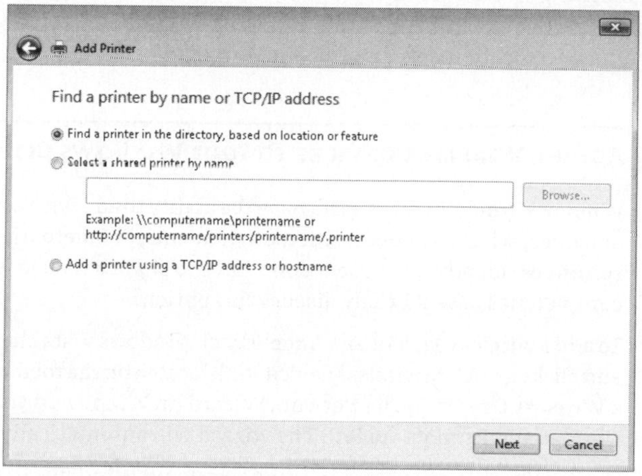

FIGURE 15.41
Add Printer dialog box for finding a printer manually

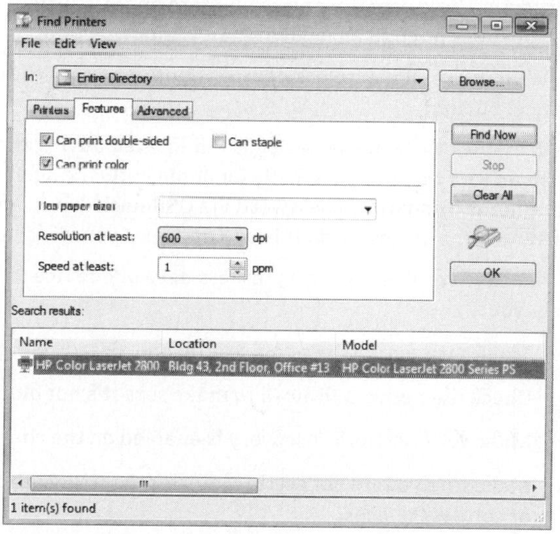

FIGURE 15.42
The Find Printers dialog box searches Active Directory for printers matching specified criteria.

Figure 15.42 shows that the printer search criteria specified included the ability to print double-sided and the ability to print in color. The wizard returned one result. Once you find the printer, select it, click OK, and the wizard will add the printer. Click Next on the following Results screen. Click "Print a test page" to test printing to the printer, and then click Finish.

Instead of searching Active Directory for a printer, you can also add a shared printer by name. Select the option "Select a shared printer by name" and then either enter the network path and name of the printer in the form \\servername\printername or click the Browse button to locate a printer on a specific computer on the network. Once the printer name is added, click Next, click Next again on the information screen, and then click Finish.

Lastly, choose the option "Add a printer using a TCP/IP address or hostname" to add a TCP/IP printer. Enter the IP address of the printer in the "Hostname or IP address" input box. The port name will automatically mimic the IP address (you can change this if you want to something more descriptive). The Device type defaults to AutoDetect. You should leave this setting alone unless you know the device type to specify. Click Next, and the wizard will attempt to locate the printer and install it.

ADDING WIRELESS DEVICES TO YOUR WINDOWS CLIENT COMPUTER

Windows 7 and Windows Vista have the ability to add wireless devices, such as Bluetooth keyboards and mice, wireless phones, Bluetooth modems, or Bluetooth printers. These aren't exactly network resources (ideally, your users don't have to share a mouse with someone else), but for the sake of completeness, we'll briefly discuss this option.

To add a wireless device to a Windows 7 or Windows Vista client computer, open the Network applet, and click the "Add a wireless device" link located on the toolbar. Clicking the link will initiate the Add a Wireless Device To The Network Wizard (in Windows 7 you can also invoke this wizard from the Devices and Printers applet). The wizard will automatically search for wireless devices for you.

One noticeable difference in Windows 7 and Windows Vista's Add Wireless Device GUI is that Windows Vista actually gives you more opportunity to add a wireless device that the operating system does not find on its own than Windows 7 does.

In Windows 7, if a wireless device is not detected, the system just searches until you click the Cancel button.

In Windows Vista, if the device is not located during the search, you can add one by using a USB flash drive. This feature is really for home networking. It allows you to network wireless devices in your home by sharing a password via USB flash drive. You can also add wireless devices manually (instructions on how to do this will appear if you click "Add the device or computer manually").

If you have trouble adding a wireless network device to your client system, here are a few tips to help you:

◆ Make sure the wireless device is on and already connected to the wireless network.

◆ Check the network firewall to make sure it's not blocking the discovery process.

◆ Make sure Network Discovery is enabled on the client computer.

◆ Make sure you are not getting interference from other wireless appliances such as microwaves or cordless phones.

◆ Make sure the device is in wireless range of the computer (6 feet for Bluetooth devices, 100 feet for Wi-Fi devices).

MAPPING A DRIVE TO A SHARED FOLDER

Sometimes it's easier to use a drive letter than a UNC path to connect to a network share, especially if you're browsing from the command line. Some applications demand it; they won't save to or execute from UNC paths. Therefore, you can add network shares to drive letters—at least until you run out of letters. In Windows 7 and Windows Vista, you can do this from the GUI, from the command line, or by creating network location shortcuts.

To map a drive to a shared network folder, follow these steps:

1. Open the Network applet, and click Search Active Directory.

2. In the Search Active Directory window, select Shared Folders in the Find drop-down menu.

3. Click Find Now, and shared folders that are published to Active Directory will appear in the Results window.

4. To connect to these shared folders, right-click the folder, and choose Map Network Drive, as shown in Figure 15.43.

FIGURE 15.43
Mapping a drive to shared folders found in Active Directory

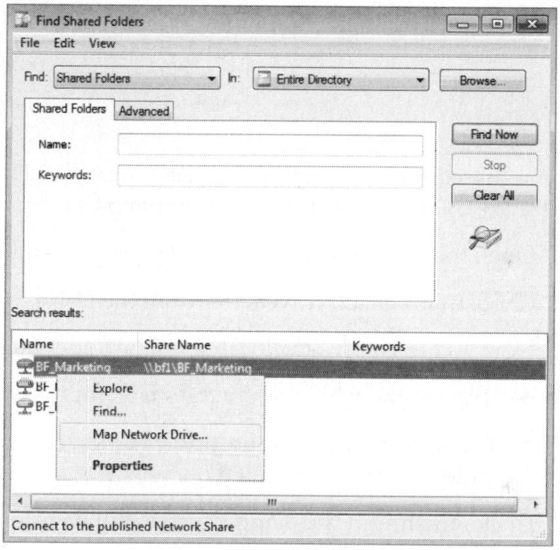

5. Every mapped drive needs to have a unique drive letter. The resulting Map Network Drive dialog box (shown in Figure 15.44) is already populated with an unused drive letter and automatically fills in the folder location. Mapped drives will be persistent unless you deselect the "Reconnect at logon" check box. By default, the current username and password will be used; click a different username link to specify a different account to use for the connection.

(The link "Connect to a Web site that you can use to store your documents and pictures" opens the Add Network Location Wizard, which is discussed later in the "Adding Network Location Shortcuts" section.)

6. Click Finish.

To access the mapped drive, select Start ➢ Computer, and double-click the mapped drive listed under the Network Location section of the main window. You can also click and drag a shortcut to the mapped drive and drop it on your desktop for fast access later. To disconnect from a mapped drive, simply right-click the drive and choose Disconnect.

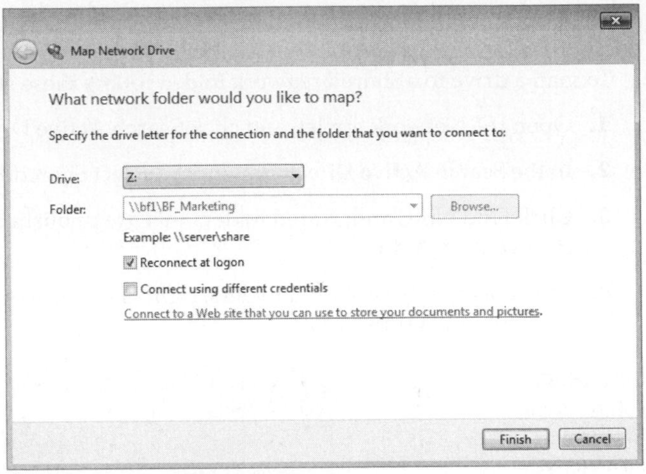

FIGURE 15.44
Map Network
Drive dialog box

Some shared folders might not be listed in Active Directory. To map a drive to an unpublished share on the network, follow these steps:

1. Open the Start menu, right-click Computer, and choose Map Network Drive.

2. Choose an unused drive letter from the Drive drop-down box.

3. Now you must give the location to the folder using one of these methods:

   ◆ Type in the UNC path to the share; for instance, type **\\BF1\BF_Marketing**.

   ◆ Click the Browse button, and visually locate shared folders by expanding the computer the share is located on, selecting the share, and clicking OK.

4. Click Finish, and the mapped drive will be listed in the Computer window under the Network Location section.

It's also possible to map drives from the command line with the `net use` command if you know the path to the share. In fact, administrators often create login scripts to automatically map drives for users when they log on to their computers. For instance, to map a drive to the bf_marketing share on server bf1, you would issue the following command:

```
net use M: \\bf1\bf_marketing /PERSISTENT:YES
```

Here's a breakdown of the parameters used in this example:

M: This represents the drive letter to which the drive will be mapped.

\\bf1\bf_marketing   This is the UNC path to the share.

/PERSISTENT:YES   This makes the mapped drive reconnect automatically each time the user logs on to this computer

To get a full list of parameters for the `net use` command, open command prompt and type **net use /?**.

But what if you don't know what's out there to connect to via CLI? No problem. You can use the `net view` command to get a list of shared resources on the network. Run it once, and you'll get a list of computers that are visible on the network. Now digging further, you can issue the `net view` command against a computer on the network to get a list of its shared resources. Figure 15.45 shows an example of using net view to first find computers on the network and then to find shared network resources on server BF1.

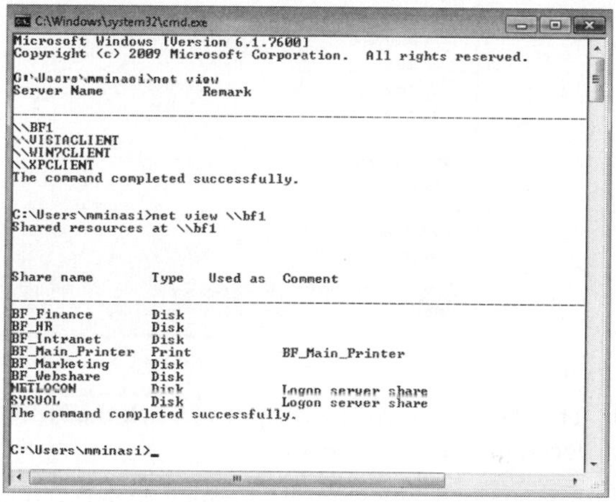

FIGURE 15.45
Using the net view command to find shared network resources

To delete a mapped drive from the command line, type **net use X: /delete**, where X is the drive letter of the mapped drive you want to delete.

CREATING A NETWORK FOLDER

You've learned how to map a drive in Windows 7 and Vista in ways very similar to older operating systems. But there is another way to access shared folders (and other network locations): by creating a *network folder* (basically a shortcut) to the shared location from within your Computer window. Why would you do this as opposed to just mapping a drive? There are both positive and negative differences between mapped drives and network location shortcuts. On one hand, a mapped drive acts like a local drive on the computer. So, applications that need to access items from drives will treat the network location as a local drive. However, you can't map a drive letter to other kinds of locations such as FTP sites and web shares. So, there are reasons to utilize both access techniques.

A network location includes shared folders, web shares, FTP sites, and UNC paths. You can add links to these network places in your Computer window by using the Add Network Location Wizard. The Add Network Location Wizard is a menu option in XP's My Network Places. My Network Places has since been morphed into the Network and Sharing Center in Vista and Windows 7—and the location of the Network Location Wizard in no longer a feature of that applet.

To open the Add Network Location Wizard in Windows Vista and Windows 7, follow these steps:

1. Select Start ➤ Computer.

2. Right-click in the resulting window, and choose Add Network Location, as shown in Figure 15.46.

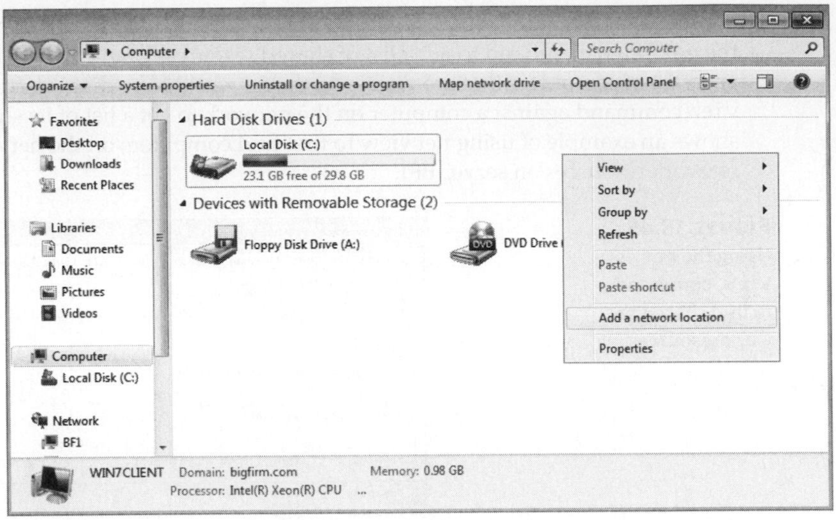

FIGURE 15.46
Starting the Add
Network Location
Wizard from the
Computer window

3. The Welcome screen will appear. Click the Next button, select "Choose a custom network location," and click Next.

4. Now you can either enter a location path if you know it (the UNC path to a network share, the FTP address of an FTP site, the URL of a web share), or you can click the Browse button to help you locate a folder share. (The Browse button will only allow you to search the network for folder shares, not other kinds of locations.)

5. Click Next. Figure 15.47 shows entering the URL for the bigfirm.com company FTP site: **ftp://ftp.bigfirm.com**.

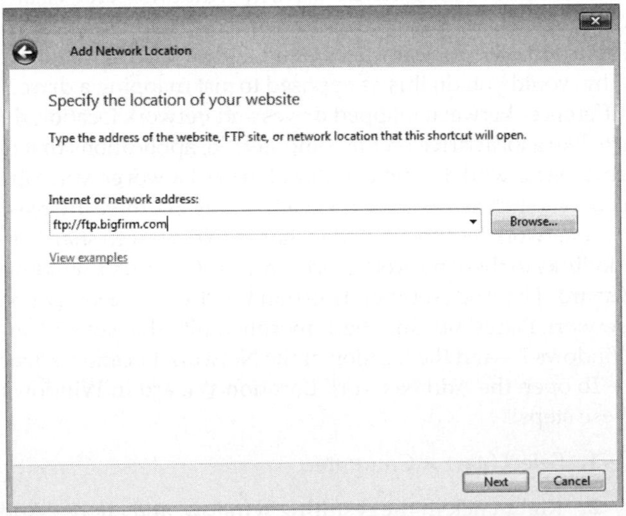

FIGURE 15.47
Enter the path to
the network loca-
tion or browse the
network to locate
a network location.

By default, the wizard allows for anonymous access to the FTP site. If you want to change this, follow these steps:

1. Deselect "Log on anonymously," and then type in a username you want to use to log on.

2. Click the Next button, and name the location (for example **ftp.bigfirm.com**).

3. Click the Next button, and then click Finish.

The network location will open, and the network location will be listed in the Network Location section of the Computer window, as shown in Figure 15.48.

FIGURE 15.48
The network location is added to the Computer window.

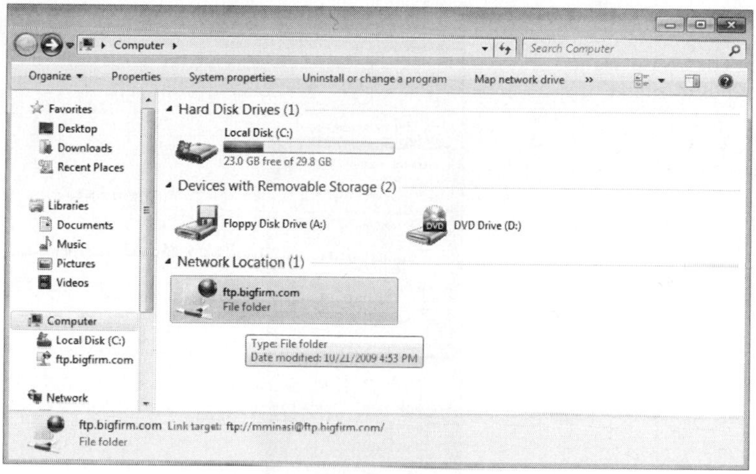

To disconnect a network location, simply right-click the network location, and select Delete.

Connecting to Network Resources from Windows XP

As previously stated, there are multiple ways to attach to network resources in Windows 7 and Windows Vista, and this is also true in Windows XP. This section of the chapter will concentrate on showing you how to find and attach to network printers, shared folders, and other network locations using the Windows XP My Network Places applet, the command line, and the My Computer applet.

One way to access network resources is through the My Network Places applet. In Windows XP, the My Network Places applet is kind of the hub of finding and accessing network resources. Remember, My Network Places is not located on the Start menu by default, so to make it easy to get to this place, add this applet to the Start menu:

1. Right-click the Start button, and choose Properties.

Make sure Start Menu is selected, and click the Customize button to its right.

2. Choose the Advanced tab, and in the "Start Menu items" scrollable box, scroll down and select My Network Places.

3. Now open the Start menu, and choose My Network Places.

As you can see in Figure 15.49, My Network Places offers three different options for finding and connecting to network resources:

◆ Use the Add Network Place Wizard to create a shortcut to a network resource. The wizard can locate the resource using a UNC name (\\servername\sharename), which you provide, or you can open a browse list from within the wizard.

◆ Use Search Active Directory for shared folders or printers that have been published in Active Directory.

◆ Browse the network by choosing Entire Network from Other Places.

FIGURE 15.49
The My Network Places applet

SEARCHING ACTIVE DIRECTORY

Click the Search Active Directory link. The corresponding dialog box opens, as shown in Figure 15.50.

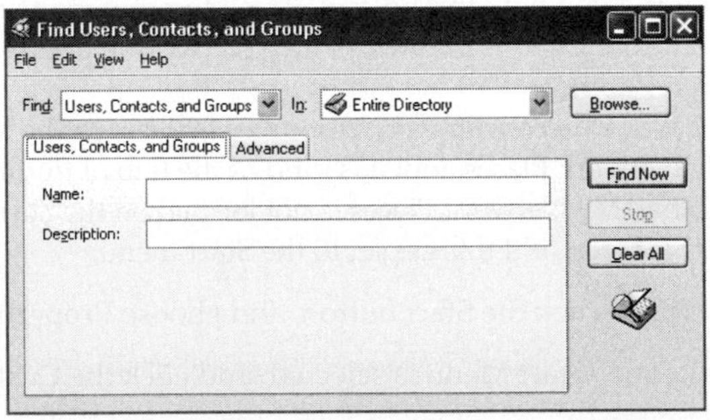

FIGURE 15.50
The Find Users, Contacts, and Groups dialog box

This dialog box gives you access to a searchable directory of computers, shared folders, and printers, as well as users, groups, and contacts. As in Windows 7 and Windows Vista, this dialog box can connect you to a gold mine of information, such as a co-worker's telephone number if it's stored in their user account properties or what floor a printer is located on.

In the Find drop-down menu, you can choose the types of resources you want to find in Active Directory such as users, computers, groups, printers, shared folders, and organizational units, or you can do a custom search for resources. You can also narrow your search to a particular domain by selecting the domain in the In drop-down menu (it defaults to searching the entire Active Directory).

On the Advanced tab, you can further narrow your search by specifying different criteria based on fields that are tied to the type of resource you are searching for.

You can narrow your search, but you don't have to do so. Select the type of resource you are looking for in the Find drop-down menu, and click the Find Now button. All resources of that type that are published to Active Directory will appear in the results.

ADDING A NETWORK PRINTER

You can add a network printer by searching Active Directory using the GUI, using the command-line tools, or using the Printers and Faxes applet.

Finding a Printer in Active Directory

In the Find Users, Contacts, and Groups dialog box, choose Printers in the Find drop-down menu. The dialog box name changes to Find Printers. Now you can narrow your search for printers, or you can just search AD for all printers. The Features tab (unique to the Find Printers dialog box), shown in Figure 15.51, allows you to add common search criteria to your search that is specific to printers.

FIGURE 15.51
The Features tab of the Find Printers dialog box

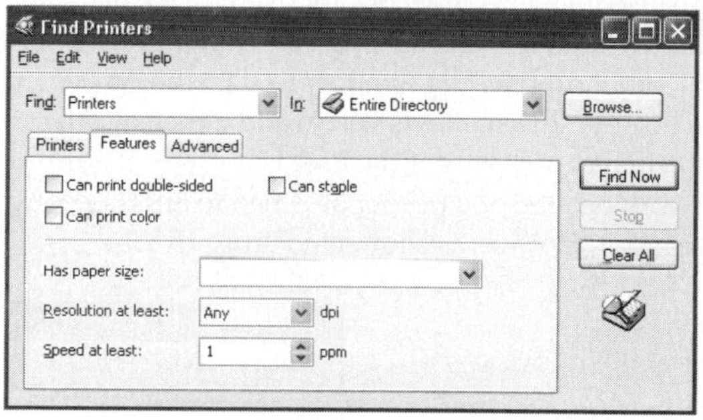

Select your search criteria, and click Find Now. The results of your search will appear in the results window. For example, to search the bigfirm.com domain for printers whose names begin with "HP," click the Advanced tab, click the Field drop-down menu, and select Name. Open the Condition drop-down menu, and select "Starts with." In the Value box, type **HP**. Figure 15.52 shows the results of this search: one printer located in building 43.

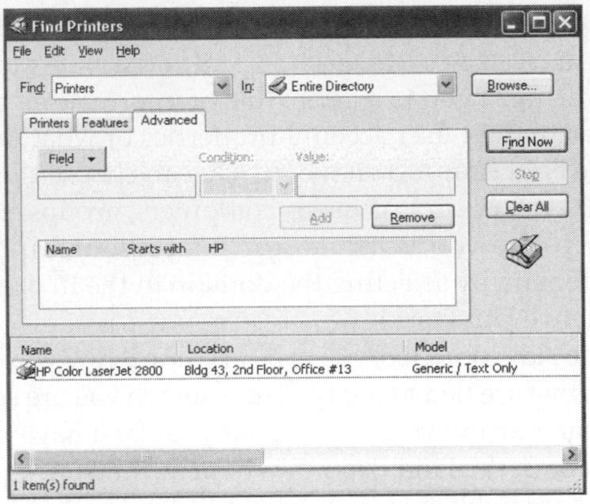

FIGURE 15.52

Active Directory
search results for
printers that meet
specific search
criteria

Adding a Network Printer from the Command Line

Add a network printer to the client computer from the command line by issuing the start command followed by the UNC path to the printer. For instance, to add the printer called bf_main_printer located on server bf1, open a command prompt, and type the following:

```
start \\bf1\bf_main_printer
```

When the printer installs, the print queue for that printer will open, and the printer will be listed for use in the Printers and Faxes applet accessible from the Start menu.

Adding a Network Printer Using the Printers and Faxes Applets

You can also add a network printer from the Printers and Faxes applet. Open the applet by clicking the Start menu and then clicking the Printers and Faxes button. Click the Add a Printer button in the upper-left quadrant of the window to start the Add Printer Wizard. On the Welcome screen, click Next. The next screen allows you to add either a local printer or a network printer (the local printer option will be grayed out if the user is not a local administrator on the computer). Select the option "A network printer, or a printer attached to another computer," and click Next. This brings up the Specify a Printer page, as shown in Figure 15.53.

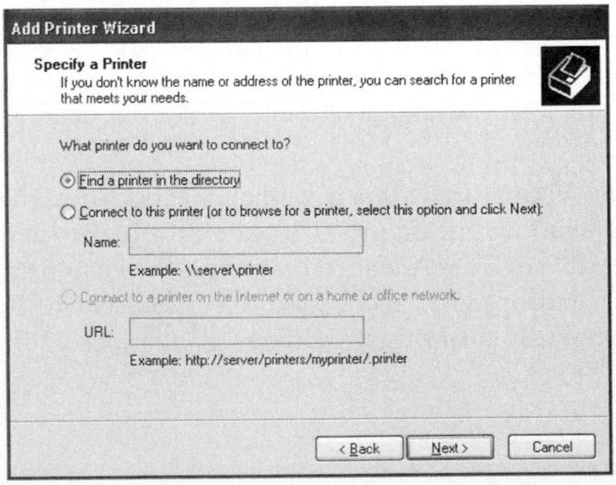

FIGURE 15.53

Specifying a
printer in the
Add Printer Wizard

To search Active Directory for the printer, leave the default selection, "Find a printer in the directory," selected, and click Next. This will start the familiar Search Active Directory dialog box.

Select "Connect to this printer" to add a network by entering its network path and name in the form of \\servername\printername. If you do not know its name, you can leave this field blank and click Next. This will bring up the Browse for Printer page, as shown in Figure 15.54.

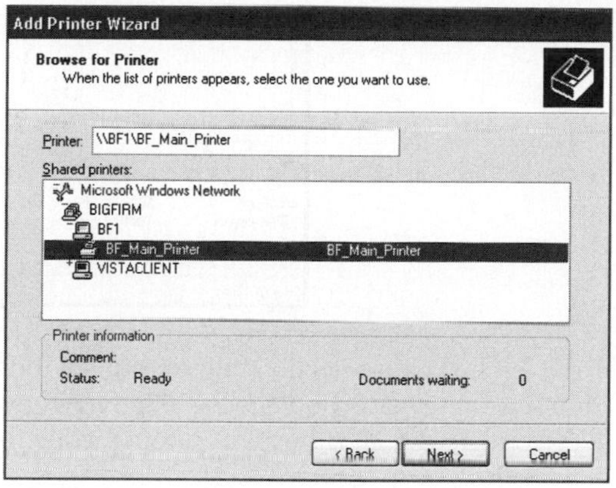

FIGURE 15.54
Browsing the network for a printer in the Add Printer Wizard

Browsing for a printer really means finding a printer located on a specific machine. Double-click a computer to reveal any printers shared from that computer. Figure 15.54 shows the server BF1 has one printer shared called BF_Main_Printer. Click the printer you want to install, and click Next. Click the Finish button on the next screen, and the printer will be added to the Printers and Faxes applet.

MAPPING A DRIVE TO A SHARED FOLDER

Sometimes it's easier to use a drive letter than a UNC path to connect to a network share. Some applications demand it; they won't save to or execute from UNC paths. Therefore, you can add network shares to drive letters—at least until you run out of letters. In Windows XP, you can do this from the GUI, from the command line, or by creating network location shortcuts.

To connect to a shared folder found by the Active Directory search engine, follow these steps:

1. Open My Network Places, and click the Search Active Directory link.

2. Choose Shared Folders in the Find drop-down link. You can narrow your search to a specific domain by picking it in the In drop-down menu.

3. Add a name or keywords on the Shared Folders tab to further narrow your search, or add other fields to search by on the Advanced tab.

Again, adding search criteria is optional. You can just specify Shared Folders in the Find drop-down menu and click Find Now to return all shared folders published in Active Directory.

The results of your search will appear in the results pane below the search criteria in the same window. For example, Figure 15.55 shows the results of searching the bigfirm.com Active Directory for all shared folders (no extra criteria specified).

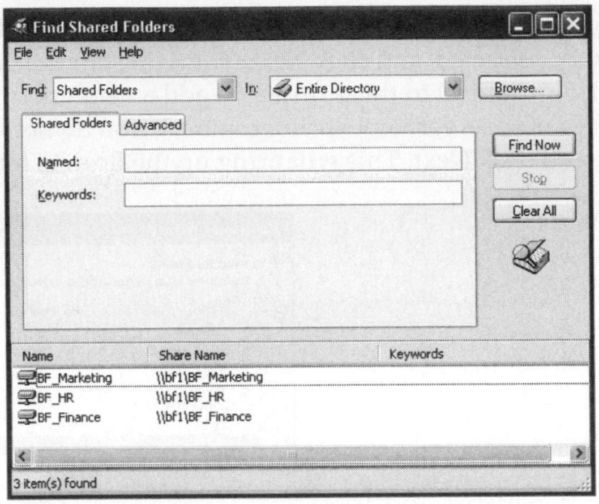

FIGURE 15.55

Searching Active Directory for shared folders

4. Double-click your selection in the results window to open the folder in Explorer, or right-click the folder and choose Map Network Drive. As shown in Figure 15.56, the Map Network Drive dialog box will automatically fill in the server and share information.

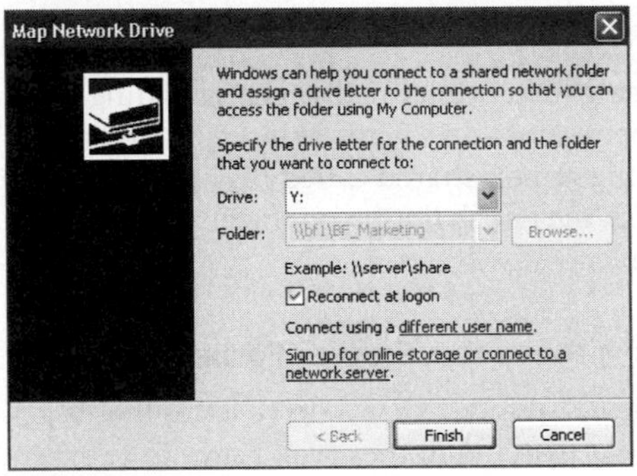

FIGURE 15.56

Mapping a network drive to a shared resource

5. Mapped drives will be persistent unless you deselect the "Reconnect at logon" check box. By default, the current username and password will be used; click "different user name" to specify a different account to use for the connection.

Clicking the "Sign up for online storage or connect to a network server" link starts the Add Network Place Wizard, which is discussed later in this chapter in the section "Adding Network Location Shortcuts in Windows XP."

6. Click Finish, and the mapped drive will be added to the Network Drives section of the My Computer window, accessible from the Start menu. To disconnect a mapped drive, open My Computer, right-click the network drive, and choose Disconnect.

Mapping a drive in XP is done the same way in Windows Vista and Windows 7, by using `net view` to find resources and `net use` to connect to them.

To find shared folders on the network from the command line, open a command prompt and type the following:

```
net view
```

This will return a list of computers on the network. To find shared folders located on a particular computer, use the `net view` command and add the computer name like this:

```
Net view \\computername
```

For example, Figure 15.57 shows the shared folders located on the server BF1. (It also shows other shared resources such as shared printers).

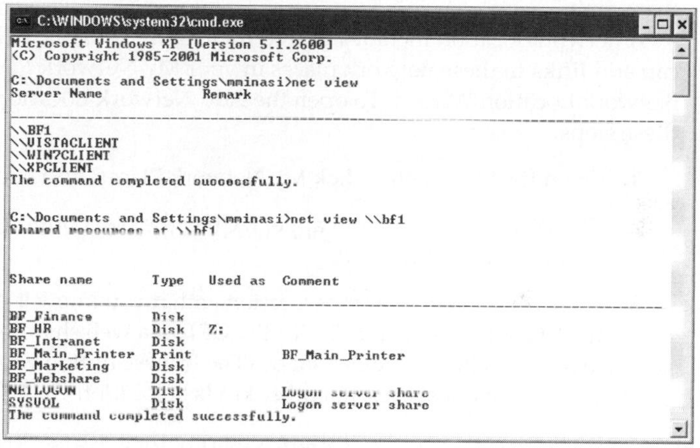

FIGURE 15.57

Using the net view command to find shared resources on the network

Now that you know what resources are available, you can add a mapped drive using `net use`. The basic syntax of the command is as follows:

```
Net use X: \\computername\sharename /PERSISTENT:YES
```

The breakdown of the command syntax shown is as follows:

X   This represents an unused drive letter (remember, all drives, local and mapped, must have a unique drive letter).

\\computername\sharename   This is the computer on which the share is located, followed by the name of the shared folder.

/PERSISTENT:YES   This reconnects the drive every time the user logs onto the computer.

Figure 15.58 shows the results of using the `net use` command to map a drive to the BF_Finance share located on server BF1.

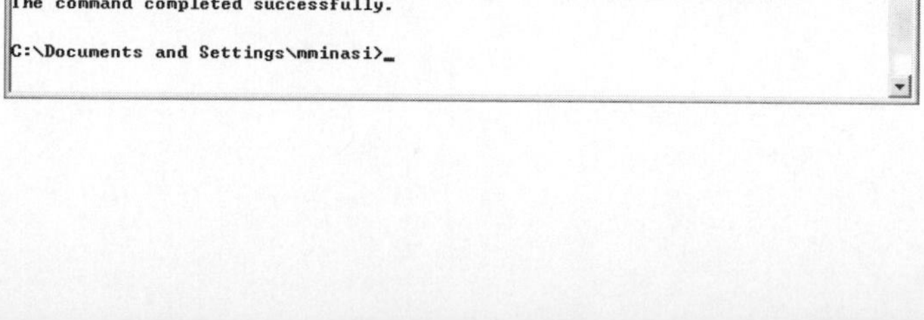

FIGURE 15.58

Using the net use command to map a drive to shared folder

For more information on net view or net use syntax and additional parameters, open a command prompt and type the following:

```
net view /? or net use /?
```

ADDING NETWORK LOCATION SHORTCUTS

You've learned how to map a drive in Windows XP. But there is another way to access shared folders (and other network locations): by creating a network folder (basically a shortcut) to the shared location from My Network Places. Just as in Windows 7 and Windows Vista, you'd do this because not all online resources can accept drive letters; FTP sites and web shares are two that won't.

A network location includes shared folders, web shares, FTP sites, and UNC paths. You can add links to these network places in your My Network Places window by using the Add Network Location Wizard. To open the Add Network Location Wizard in Windows XP, follow these steps:

1. Open the Start menu, click My Network Places, and click the "Add a network place" link.

2. The Welcome screen will appear. Click the Next button, select "Choose another network location," and click Next.

3. Now you can either enter a location path if you know it (the UNC path to a network share, the FTP address of an FTP site, the URL of a web share), or you can click the Browse button to help you locate a folder share. (The Browse button will only allow you to search the network for folder shares, not other kinds of locations.)

4. Click Next. Figure 15.59 shows entering the URL for the bigfirm company FTP site: **ftp://ftp.bigfirm.com**.

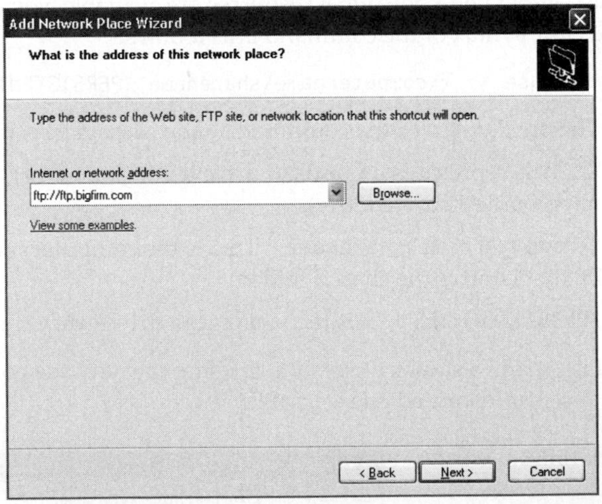

FIGURE 15.59
The Add Network Place Wizard in Windows XP

By default, the wizard allows for anonymous access to the FTP site. If you want to change this, follow these steps:

1. Deselect "Log on anonymously," and then type in a username you want to use to log on.

2. Click the Next button, and name the location (for example **ftp.bigfirm.com**).

3. Click the Next button, and then click Finish.

The network location will open, and the network location shortcut will be listed in My Network Places, as shown in Figure 15.60.

FIGURE 15.60
The network location is added to My Network Places.

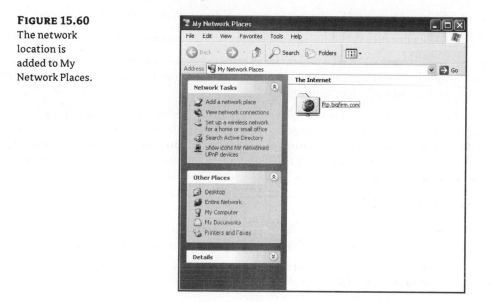

To disconnect a network location, simply right-click the network location and select Delete. Don't want to have to open My Network Places every time you want to access network short-cuts? Drag the shortcut from My Network Places (while holding down the Ctrl key on your key-board), and drop it onto your desktop.

Connecting to Network Resources from Windows 2000

To connect to network resources from a Windows 2000 Professional workstation, follow these steps:

1. Open My Network Places on the desktop, and you'll see two choices: Add Network Place and Entire Network.

2. Choose Add Network to open the Add Network Place Wizard.

3. Type the name of the resource, or select a share from a list using the Browse button. Click OK.

4. Provide a user-friendly name for the connection in the next window, and click Finish.

The wizard will automatically open the folder for viewing, and a shortcut will appear in the list of My Network Places. This shortcut can be moved or copied to a different location, such as the user's desktop.

To access resources using a browse list or by searching Active Directory, follow these steps:

1. Choose the Entire Network option in My Network Places. You'll see a list of links to search for different types of objects and a link to view the entire contents of the network.

2. Click the link to view the entire contents of the network, and you'll have two more choices (Microsoft Windows Network and Directory).

3. Choose Microsoft Windows Network. A list of domains and workgroups appears.

4. Click your domain name, and select a server from the list to see its shared folders.

5. Double-click a listed shared folder to open the shared folder, or right-click to see a list of options. These options include Map Network Drive or Create Shortcut. The latter choice will create a shortcut on your Desktop.

You cannot search for a list of shared folders using the Search for Files and Folders link in My Network Places/Entire Network, but you can search for computers. Once a list of computers is found, double-clicking a computer on the list will present a list of shares. However, this process is not as intuitive as the Active Directory search function you saw in Windows XP.

The Bottom Line

Verify your network configuration   DHCP provides centralized IP address configurations, and all Windows clients understand DHCP without any additional installations required.

> **Master It**   You need to verify that a client machine has received the correct IP address configuration via DHCP for the network you are working on. Which of the following commands would return these results?
>
> ```
> ipconfig /all
> ipconfig /refresh
> msconfig /show
> msconfig
> ```

Join a client computer to a domain   Joining an Active Directory domain is key for workstations, because this provides centralized management from the Domain Admins within the domain. Group Policy is centralized, security can be established, and even software can be controlled centrally.

> **Master It**   Is the following statement true or false? "When joining a computer to an Active Directory domain, the only way this can occur is if the user joining the computer to the domain is a Domain Admin."

Change user passwords   By default Windows AD provides a 42-day maximum password age limit. This limit is preceded by a 14-day reminder that you need to change your password. The 42-day maximum is designed to maintain a certain level of security for the enterprise, not allowing passwords to become stale.

> **Master It**   A user has become paranoid and wants to change his user account password right away. He does not know how to do this and calls the help desk. The computer he is using is running the Windows 7 operating system. What do you tell him?

Connect to network resources   A user wants to connect to a printer on the domain that does double-sided printing and also stapling. But the user does not know where the company keeps these printers. The user calls the help desk.

> **Master It**   Which of the following is the most efficient way for the user to find printers matching this description?
>
> **A.**   Tell the user to walk around the office complex and check each printer to see whether it has these features.
>
> **B.**   Tell the user to use the net view command to check for shared printers on a per-computer basis.
>
> **C.**   Tell the user to start the Add Printer Wizard and then select the Search Active Directory option.

Chapter 16

Working the Web with IIS 7.0 and 7.5

It is official: the Internet is here to stay. More than a passing fad for streaming video, comedy, and up-to-the-minute news, the Internet has also become a primary data distribution medium for the world. Whether you shop online, use the Internet for research, or even just use an application on your job that is supported by a web server, you have undoubtedly been touched by the technology that Microsoft's Internet Information Services is all about. According to the ISC's Internet Domain Survey, the number of hosted domains on the Internet currently exceeds 433 million. Meanwhile, www.internetworldstats.com reports that as of June 30, 2009 more than 1.2 billion folks are using the Internet in some capacity.

Although it is true that Microsoft has suffered less-than-stellar PR since its 1996 inception of IIS as an add-on to Windows NT Server 3.51 (thanks in part to stability issues and popularity among malicious coders), Microsoft has continued to bundle the web server product in its leading enterprise-class network operating system, Windows Server. Microsoft's efforts to capitalize on the Web are paying off because IIS enjoys second place among web server products according to www.netcraft.com. Slow and sure wins the race, and IIS has been steadily gaining on the leader to effectively reduce Apache's lead from 62 percent in 2003 to only 51 percent of the market share in 2008.

Given the growing popularity of IIS and Microsoft's recent trend toward all things web delivery, any smart network administrator will realize the benefits of IIS 7.5 sooner rather than later.

In this chapter, you'll learn to:

◆ Understand IIS 7 architecture and capabilities

◆ Plan for and install IIS 7.5

◆ Manage IIS 7's modularity and delegated administration

◆ Create and secure websites in IIS 7

◆ Manage IIS 7 with advanced administration techniques

Creating Simple Websites

As with most things in life, one must learn to walk before they can run, and IIS is no exception. For those of you who are experienced webmasters eager to push on to more advanced discussions of IIS 7, I assure you, this chapter will not disappoint. But before we can dissect IIS, a few fundamentals are in order. Many of us visit websites every day for work or to shop or just for entertainment, but do we really understand why the pages of the websites we visit look the way they do? For example, information on a web page can be either static or dynamic, but what does that really mean?

A Sum of Pages

A website is basically a collection of web pages that are managed as a whole, so before site visitors actually see anything interesting, there must be at least one web page. Writing a simple web page file is like writing a text file in Notepad, except the actual text is more than regular words and sentences. In addition to the text or pictures you want displayed on your web page, the web page file must also contain controls, or *tags*, that specify things like what color the text appears in, which lines start new paragraphs, and what picture to display. The specific tag nomenclature and layout is dictated by the markup language in which you choose to write the file. One of the oldest and simplest web markup languages for authoring static web pages is HyperText Markup Language (HTML). But there is also Dynamic HTML (DHTML), eXtensible Markup Language (XML), and others that can be used to write more complex web pages.

WRITING A SIMPLE WEB PAGE

Since this chapter is about IIS and not a walk down programming lane, let's just stick to HTML and write a very basic static web page using Notepad. A static web page's contents are delivered from the web server without any input from the client or user. In other words, the text and graphics are dictated by the web page author and cannot be customized by user preferences or actions. Dynamic web pages, on the other hand, change in response to either client programs or user authentication, preferences, or actions. Using the following syntax, you can create a simple static web page consisting of a title, text, and a picture of a bird:

```
<html>
  <head>
    <title>It's a Bird!!</title>
  </head>
  <body>
    <p>
      Below is a picture of a bird:
    </p>
<imgsrc=http://www.minasi.com/photos/flbrd0508/
  content/bin/images/large/flbirds0508_2644.jpg>
  </body>
</html>
```

The indentation isn't mandatory, but it helps to visually separate the different tags while illustrating the compartmentalized layout of HTML (that is, header vs. body). The text to be displayed was written directly in the web page file itself, but the picture required a pointer to the actual `.jpg` image file. If the path you specify in the `<imgsrc>` tag cannot be reached or does not contain the actual image, the web page will merely display a graphic placeholder icon instead of the picture. So, be careful, because using drive letter paths instead of UNC or hyperlink paths to image files can result in pictures missing from your website if you move your web page file to another server later!

SAVING A SIMPLE WEB PAGE

Now that you have the HTML written in Notepad, it's time to save the web page file with an `.htm` extension. First you should choose a name and location for the file dependent upon its purpose. To simply test the syntax from the previous section, you could name the file `test.htm` and save it to your personal folder. Simply double-clicking the `test.htm` file would automatically launch the application your OS has associated with `.htm` filename extensions (probably your web browser application), and *voila*! You should see something like Figure 16.1.

FIGURE 16.1
Simple web page

DELIVERING A SIMPLE WEB PAGE

Now that you've tested your simple static `test.htm` web page file, it's time to unveil it to the world. But it would be impractical to ask each user who wants to see the file to log into the server, navigate to your personal folder, and double-click the web page file from a directory browser application! A better method of delivering the page would be to incorporate it into an IIS website. Each IIS website can be associated with one or more virtual directories that map to local or remote file system folders. For instance, the default website automatically generated when IIS is installed uses a default virtual directory path of `%systemdrive%\inetpub\wwwroot`, so any `.htm` files saved into the wwwroot folder can be delivered by the default website.

Your name choice for the web page file can be either descriptive or indicate its purpose within the site. For example, if you rename your new web page file from `test.htm` to `default.htm`, you are indicating it will be the default page delivered to site users. Since most users arrive at websites by entering the URL without specifying a particular page, you can make your `default.htm` web page the first thing they see. Unfortunately, IIS 7 is not loaded by default during a Windows Server 2008 OS installation. Don't worry, there is a whole section coming up in this chapter that regales strategies and methods of IIS installation, so stay tuned!

Lively Web Pages

One of the drawbacks to static web pages is stale content. To liven the website up a bit, IIS programmers (you know who you are) can take advantage of several methods for creating dynamic web pages full of content that reacts to the user or client application. For example, have you ever logged into a website and the web page greets you personally by your logon or first name? Or perhaps you have used a shopping cart page while purchasing items from an online storefront. Internet search engines can even remember your past searches and help you find those resources again! How does that happen?

WEB APPLICATIONS

In essence, dynamic web pages get their pizzazz from embedded computer programs. When the user requests a typical URL via the common HyperText Transfer Protocol (HTTP), the web page delivered by the web server actually contains programming code instead of just simple text and pictures. Technologies have grown over the past decade to allow programmers to create sophisticated programs (or *web applications*) that produce and deliver dynamic content via web servers. Some of these technologies include Microsoft Active Server Pages (ASP and ASP.NET), Java, Common Gateway Interface (CGI), PHP, and more. Further discussion of these technologies falls outside the scope of this IIS chapter, so if you're interested in learning one of these programming languages, you'll need additional references.

DYNAMIC CONCERNS

Because dynamic web pages include programs that are vulnerable to security holes, bugs in the code, and possible viral infections, IIS administrators are often concerned for the safety of the IIS server. For instance, if a single IIS installation hosts multiple dynamic websites and one of those website's programs goes haywire, will it take down the other healthy sites as well? Or if a malicious user attacks one of the sites, is there a way to make sure that user cannot also jump to a second site and seize control of it? Keeping multiple sites safe from one another and keeping the Windows Server operating system safe from web applications that have run amok are some of the concerns that IIS administrators face and is why IIS 7.0 and 7.5 are gaining popularity among webmasters. So, keep reading for more information on what makes IIS 7 different from its predecessor!

What's So Different About IIS 7.0 and 7.5?

As you have just seen, the act of creating a simple static web page and dropping it into the wwwroot file system directory structure to be displayed on the default website has changed little since IIS 4. Where IIS 7.0 and 7.5 separate from the pack is more in the dynamic content arena. Monikers such as "overhauled" and "revamped" fail to convey the vast changes that have been made to the web service that ships with Windows Server 2008 and 2008 R2 to better support and secure web applications. You may be wondering why you should care. Over the years many Windows services have become web based, and as of Windows Server 2008, IIS is now a dependency service for several other Windows services (see Table 16.1).

TABLE 16.1:   Services That Depend On IIS 7.5

AD FS Web Agents	.NET Framework 3.0 Features
AD Rights Management Services	Network Device Enrollment Service

TABLE 16.1:   Services That Depend On IIS 7.5   *(CONTINUED)*

AD Rights Management Services Server	Online Responder
BITS Server Extensions	Remote Server Administration Tools
Certification Authority Web Enrollment	Remote Server Administration Tools Role Admin Tools
Claims-Aware Agent	RPC over HTTP Proxy
Feature Administration Tool	SMTP Server
Federation Service	TS Gateway
Federation Service Proxy	TS Web Access
Health Registration Authority	UDDI Services
Host Credential Authorization Protocol	UDDI Services Web Application
HTTP Activation	Web Server (IIS) Support
HTTP Support	WCF Activation Components
Identity Federation Support	Windows Process Activation Service Support
Internet Printing	Windows Token-Based Agent

Historically web server management in large IT departments has often been divided into two camps: the engineers who administrate the server and the programmers who develop the site content. Settings altered by the administrators could adversely affect dynamic programs written by the developers, while unsecure code written by the developers could wreak havoc for the administrators, so managing the IIS servers required communication and compromise between these two groups. In IIS 7.0, Microsoft introduces a new architecture that allows more granular control over site management and application oversight so that developers and administrators alike can be empowered or restricted while being held accountable for their work. The traditional role of webmaster will be redefined in this new environment.

Like the previous version 6.0, IIS 7 does not install as part of a default operating system installation. Instead, you have to deliberately add the Web Server role to Windows Server 2008 and 2008 R2. Also, only static content is supported upon default installation, much like IIS 6.0. However, unlike version 6.0, dynamic technologies such as ASP, CGI, and ASP.NET are completely absent until you add them. Security and a smaller, less vulnerable footprint are only two of the new priorities. With such deep revision to the conceptual and practical web server, one would anticipate IIS 7 could fill a whole book. And it has! But for the purpose of this chapter, we will focus on the cool new architecture, configuration, and management tools. These are some of the biggest changes to the 7.0 and 7.5 versions of IIS:

A simpler, but extensible, product   IIS 7.0 has been stripped down to be essentially nothing more than a very sophisticated web server engine. The true functionality of the product lies within the prepackaged feature sets called *modules* that can be added or removed from IIS at will. In fact, IIS 7.5 is even more extensible than 7.0 because it allows third-party features to be integrated directly into IIS so they appear as part of the application. As a web server administrator, you should be aware of the modules available, know which ones will best support your websites, and load only the modules you need in an effort to reduce the server's attack surface.

Integration of ASP.NET and IIS   IIS 7.0 introduces a new request-processing model made up of both native (Windows executable) and managed (.NET) code that integrates ASP.NET with IIS. We'll discuss native vs. managed in more detail later in this chapter. For now, just know that duplicate functionalities between ASP and ASP.NET have been trimmed out, and both feature sets are managed in the same, single location. Best of all, now all web files can take advantage of both native and managed features. What does this mean to you? Well, unlike IIS 6.0 (in which ASP.NET support was an add-on and incompatible with existing static or ASP sites), you can now have static, ASP, and ASP.NET web pages all in the same website on a leaner, more efficient server!

Distributed configuration model   Configuring IIS 7 can now be accomplished with a bit of XML knowledge and a text editor. The binary metabase has been gone since IIS 6.0 replaced it with the `metabase.xml` file. Now that single configuration file has further been replaced by several XML files that work together to provide the distributed configuration model for IIS 7. The `applicationhost.config` file (located in the `%windir%\system32\inetsrv\config` directory by default) dictates global settings, the `machine.config` file (located in the `%windir%\Microsoft.NET\Framework\{framework version}\config` directory by default) defines properties for all .NET Framework features, and the root `web.config` file (same default directory as `machine.config`) provides all default ASP.NET web application settings. Also, each site relies on a unique `web.config` file that stores any configuration settings for the specific site that have been changed from the inherited parent setting. This hierarchical architecture gives you control at different levels (at the server level, at the web application platform level, or at the site level). Plus, all these files can be managed without stopping the web services and can even be quickly copied to other servers for scaling.

New management tools   The IIS Manager console (GUI) has a whole new look and feel. No more flat, dreary Properties dialog boxes with tab after tab after tab. Now the management console is laid out in a hierarchical fashion with layers of drill-down management and more useful panes within the window. Also, a new command-line interface (CLI) application, `appcmd.exe`, provides flexible, scriptable administration of server and sites, while the new WinRM-based remote management feature allows access from anywhere through commonly exposed TCP ports without the dangerous security vulnerabilities that RPC used in previous IIS versions.

New administrative and troubleshooting tools   Newly packaged support in IIS 7.5 such as the Best Practice Analyzer, IIS Module for Windows PowerShell, configuration logging, and FastCGI failed request tracing make administering and troubleshooting IIS 7.5 a breeze!

New processing modes   For those of you responsible for web server security and performance, you may recall that IIS 6.0 addressed concerns about multiple dynamic websites endangering one another (or the OS) by introducing worker process isolation mode at the server level. Think of a dynamic website's spawned program processes being inked as belonging to a certain club (application pool) so that they can affect only other processes belonging to that same club. Unfortunately, ASP.NET sites in IIS 6.0 could not belong to the same club as non-ASP.NET sites; in fact, ASP.NET processes had to be executed outside of IIS. The following are the two new processing modes in IIS 7:

♦ *Integrated application pool mode*, which integrates IIS and ASP.NET pipelines for seamless processing within the same pool

♦ *Classic application pool mode*, which mimics IIS 6.0 worker process isolation mode (attention programmers: in classic application pool mode, the request is routed outside IIS to `Aspnet_isapi.dll` in order to handle ASP.NET instructions)

Also, now you can assign your chosen processing mode at the application pool level, so it is possible to support both processing modes on the same web server. IIS 7.5 introduces even more application pool control than IIS 7.0, such as thread warm-up to alleviate initial processing delays and less-privileged identity per pool via application pool identity accounts.

SSL support   For those of you responsible for transport protocol and network management of your web server, IIS 7 continues to use HTTP.sys, which was introduced in IIS 6.0 as its default protocol listener but now includes SSL support in this listener as well. And IIS 7 now takes advantage of the Windows Communication Foundation (WCF) listeners to support web applications that use protocols other than HTTP or HTTPS, giving your web programmers more options for developing managed-code websites. Also, the World Wide Web service (also known as WWW or W3SVC) is no longer the big shot in town. W3SVC is still employed as the listener adapter for HTTP.sys, but it is not the service responsible for managing the application pool configurations or worker processes. That distinct honor now belongs to the new Windows Process Activation Service (WAS) in Windows Server 2008.

Introducing IIS 7 Modules

Microsoft still endorses separating IIS onto its own dedicated server unless another network application needs it to run (such as the new Active Directory Rights Management Services). And to satisfy various workload or security arguments, you may agree. However, since the IIS 7 architecture is so modular (thanks to a new public web server extensibility API), you needn't worry about overburdening network application servers with a cumbersome IIS installation. IIS 7 can be as lean or as pudgy as you want; it's all in the modules you choose to install. So go ahead, install IIS 7 on any server you like.

What's Included?

In addition to the new modular design, things have changed under the hood. For example, the old ISAPI model and IIS metabase are gone, making IIS 7 one of the most secure versions of Microsoft web services ever produced. Although IIS 7 can still support backward compatibility for legacy ISAPI and metabase-dependent applications with the right modules installed, you can now avoid installing unnecessary processes that make a server vulnerable to attacks and exploitation.

For example, experienced web server installers may already be familiar with the enhancing protocols and services that have routinely shipped with previous versions of IIS such as SMTP for email-enabling your website and NNTP for supporting online discussion forums. We'll talk more about SMTP in a bit, but you should know that it can still be employed on your IIS 7 websites via the IIS 6.0 Metabase Compatibility native module for IIS 7 (attention programmers: this module intercepts API calls made to the legacy AdminBaseObject [ABO] and maps them instead to the new `applicationhost.config` system in IIS 7). Alas, this is not so for NNTP, which has been deprecated in Windows Server 2008. Another example would be FrontPage Server Extensions 2002 (FPSE2002), which was retired by Microsoft in 2006 but had been very popular for developing dynamic content up to that point and could still be employed by some older websites on an upgraded IIS server. FPSE2002 is supported in IIS 7 by downloading separate extension modules available at www.iis.net/downloads. Although these modules give you the ability to run your legacy sites, the security and performance benefits of ASP.NET should be motivation to update your sites.

One of the obstacles to understanding how IIS 7 is constructed may very well be the vocabulary that Microsoft publishes. The terms *module* and *feature* seem to be used almost interchangeably, such as in the Windows Server 2008 R2 GUI or help library. IIS *modules* represent compartmentalized processes that are now available in plug-in fashion to build the custom web server of your dreams. However, since the OS term for similar components of optional functionality in the OS itself is *feature*, the term *features* could apply to IIS modules as well. And just to confuse the matter even further, during a GUI installation of IIS 7, the phrase *role services* is used! Role services are software programs that provide functionality associated with a particular server role, whereas features may or may not be directly related to a particular server role. Features are more freelance in nature and simply enhance another program.

Confusing nomenclature aside, the idea during IIS 7 installation is to add only the modules necessary to support your planned web content. Table 16.2 lists some of the role services available while selecting the Web Server role in the OS along with their corresponding IIS feature names used by the CLI administration tools. By installing no more than absolutely necessary, you can build a lean web server with a smaller resource footprint and reduced attack surface. Following this strategy will give you a more secure, better-performing web server.

TABLE 16.2:   OS Role Services for IIS 7.5 (in the Same Order as in the Server Manager Wizard)

SERVICE NAME (GUI)	*Server Manager* .cmd FEATURE NAME	PACKAGE MANAGER/ OPTIONAL COMPONENT SETUP FEATURE NAME	DESCRIPTION	DEFAULT
Internet Information Services	Web-WebServer	IIS-WebServer	Publishes websites, web services and web applications	Yes
Static Content	Web-Static-Content	IIS-StaticContent	Publishes static web file formats	Yes
Default Document	Web-Default-Doc	IIS-DefaultDocument	Configures a default file for websites to deliver when page call is not specified in URL	Yes
Directory Browsing	Web-Dir-Browsing	IIS-DirectoryBrowsing	Autogenerates list of all directories/files for websites to deliver when page call is not specified in URL and default document is disabled or not configured	Yes

TABLE 16.2: OS Role Services for IIS 7.5 (in the Same Order as in the Server Manager Wizard) *(CONTINUED)*

SERVICE NAME (GUI)	*Server Manager* .cmd FEATURE NAME	PACKAGE MANAGER/ OPTIONAL COMPONENT SETUP FEATURE NAME	DESCRIPTION	DEFAULT
HTTP Errors	Web-Http-Errors	IIS-HttpErrors	Customizes error messages	Yes
HTTP Redirection	Web-Http-Redirect	IIS-HttpRedirect	Redirects one URL to another URL	No
WebDAV Publishing		IIS-WebDAV	Publishes files to/from a web server via HTTP	No
ASP.NET	Web-Asp-Net	IIS-ASPNET	Provides server-side object model for managed applications based on the .NET Framework	No
.NET Extensibility	Web-Net-Ext	IIS-NetFxExtensibility	Extends web server functionality in the request, configuration, or UI	No
ASP	Web-ASP	IIS-ASP	Provides Active Server Page server-side scripting (both VBScript and JScript)	No
CGI	Web-CGI	IIS-CGI	Provides CGI support for CGI scripting to external programs	No
ISAPI Extensions	Web-ISAPI-Ext	IIS-ISAPIExtensions	Supports dynamic web content via ISAPI extensions engaged upon request	No
ISAPI Filters	Web-ISAPI-Filter	IIS-ISAPIFilter	Supports files that filter requests to the web server in order to extend or change specific functionalities	No
Server-Side Includes (SSI)	Web-Includes	IIS-ServerSideIncludes	Provides script generation of dynamic HTML pages	No
HTTP Logging	Web-Http-Logging	IIS-HttpLogging	Provides logging of website activity	Yes
Logging Tools	Web-Log-Libraries	IIS-LoggingLibraries	Provides web server log management and automation infrastructure	No
Logging Tools	Web-Log-Libraries	IIS-LoggingLibraries	Provides web server log management and automation infrastructure	No

TABLE 16.2: OS Role Services for IIS 7.5 (in the Same Order as in the Server Manager Wizard) *(CONTINUED)*

SERVICE NAME (GUI)	*Server Manager* *.cmd* FEATURE NAME	PACKAGE MANAGER/ OPTIONAL COMPONENT SETUP FEATURE NAME	DESCRIPTION	DEFAULT
Request Monitor	Web-Request-Monitor	IIS-RequestMonitor	Provides infrastructure to capture IIS worker process information including HTTP request details	Yes
Tracing	Web-Http-Tracing	IIS-HttpTracing	Provides infrastructure to capture defined events	No
Custom Logging	Web-Custom-Logging	IIS-CustomLogging	Creates custom log modules	No
ODBC Logging	Web-ODBC-Logging	IIS-ODBCLogging	Provides infrastructure to log web server activity to an ODBC-compliant database and retrieve it for web display	No
Basic Authentication	Web-Basic-Auth	IIS-BasicAuthentication	Supports Basic authentication	No
Windows Authentication	Web-Windows-Auth	IIS-WindowsAuthentication	Supports Windows account authentication	No
Digest Authentication	Web-Digest-Auth	IIS-DigestAuthentication	Supports password hashing authentication	No
Client Certificate Mapping Authentication	Web-Client-Auth	IIS-ClientCertificateMapping Authentication	Supports client certificate authentication using Active Directory (one-to-one mappings across multiple web servers)	No
IIS Client Certificate Mapping Authentication	Web-Cert-Auth	IIS-IISCertificateMapping Authentication	Supports client certificate authentication using IIS (one-to-one or many-to-one mappings)	No
URL Authorization	Web-Url-Auth	IIS-URLAuthorization	Supports rules-based content restrictions associated with users, groups, or HTTP header verbs	No
Request Filtering	Web-Filtering	IIS-RequestFiltering	Filters incoming requests based on administrator-defined rules	Yes
IP and Domain Restrictions	Web-IP-Security	IIS-IPSecurity	Delivers content by originating requestor's IP address or domain name	No
Static Content Compression	Web-Stat-Compression	IIS-HttpCompressionStatic	Provides infrastructure to compress static content for caching	Yes

TABLE 16.2: OS Role Services for IIS 7.5 (in the Same Order as in the Server Manager Wizard) *(CONTINUED)*

SERVICE NAME (GUI)	*Server Manager* .*cmd* FEATURE NAME	PACKAGE MANAGER/ OPTIONAL COMPONENT SETUP FEATURE NAME	DESCRIPTION	DEFAULT
Dynamic Content Compression	Web-Dyn-Compression	IIS-HttpCompressionDynamic	Provides infrastructure to compress dynamic content	No
IIS Management Console	Web-Mgmt-Console	IIS-WebServerManagementTools	Provides GUI management of IIS 7.5 web services (not FTP or SMTP)	Yes
IIS Management Scripts and Tools	Web-Scripting-Tools	IIS-ManagementScriptingTools	Provides CLI and scripted management of IIS valuable for automating administration	No
Management Service	Web-Mgmt-Service	IIS-ManagementService	Provides infrastructure for remote GUI management of IIS	No
IIS 6 Management Compatibility	Web-Mgmt-Compat	IIS-IIS6ManagementCompatibility	Provides ABO and ADSI support for existing IIS 6.0 management scripts	No
IIS 6 Metabase Compatibility	Web-Metabase	IIS-Metabase	Provides IIS 6.0 metabase query and configuration support for ABO and ADSI applications	No
IIS 6 WMI Compatibility	Web-WMI	IIS-WMICompatibility	Provides WMI scripting interface for management and automation tasks using WMI CIM Studio, WMI Event Registration, WMI Event Viewer, and WMI Object Browser	No
IIS 6 Scripting Tools	Web-Lgcy-Scripting	IIS-LegacyScripts	Provides infrastructure to run IIS 6 scripts on IIS 7.5 including ADO and ADSI (requires WAS)	No
IIS 6 Management console	Web-Lgcy-Mgmt-Console	IIS-LegacySnapIn	Provides infrastructure for administration of remote IIS 6 web servers and for administration of FTP and SMTP	No
FTP Server	Web-Ftp-Server	IIS-FTPServer	Provides infrastructure to build FTP sites that use FTP for uploading and downloading	No
FTP Service		IIS-FTPSvc	Enables FTP publishing	

TABLE 16.2: OS Role Services for IIS 7.5 (in the Same Order as in the Server Manager Wizard) *(CONTINUED)*

SERVICE NAME (GUI)	*Server Manager* .cmd FEATURE NAME	PACKAGE MANAGER/ OPTIONAL COMPONENT SETUP FEATURE NAME	DESCRIPTION	DEFAULT
FTP Extensibility		IIS-FTPExtensibility	Supports FTP extensibility features such as custom providers, ASP.NET users, or IIS Manager users	No
IIS Hostable Web Core		IIS-ApplicationDevelopment	Enables applications outside of IIS to serve HTP requests using their own .config files	No

There are two classes of IIS modules: native and managed. *Native modules* are classic Windows executables (including ASP) that are available on all web servers as part of a full installation. Native modules execute their code under the identity of the IIS services' process threads according the website's application pool. *Managed modules*, however, integrate the use of managed code (programs) into IIS. Managed code can be any .NET program, including ASP.NET, written by a VB .NET or C# .NET programmer. Although managed modules extend IIS by allowing creative programmers to add custom code to any website, the modules may or may not execute their code under the identity of the IIS services' process threads (it depends on your processing mode choice: integrated or classic).

The use of managed code can be dictated by IIS-dependent applications or may be mandated to add custom behavior to a native website. Before you can add any managed modules, you must employ the native ManagedEngine module (`Microsoft.NET\Framework\v2.0.50727\webengine.dll`). This module gets loaded into those application pools that have been set to run in integrated mode thanks to a condition found in the `applicationhost.config` file. You can support websites that include managed modules by simply assigning the sites to an application pool that has been set to integrated mode.

Feature Delegation

Feature delegation is being touted as the best solution for distributing administration of IIS 7 between the administrators and other users. Essentially, feature delegation is the practice of unlocking certain server-level configuration settings in the `applicationhost.config` file so that other users such as developers and site administrators can override that setting's values on specific sites. However, planning efficient delegation can be like walking a tightrope—one false step and your IIS implementation could fall to the ground. When it comes to configuring the delegation setting on each feature, consider carefully whom you trust enough to make resource utilization and security decisions for your web server. If you delegate a feature to an inexperienced site administrator, they may unwittingly expose the entire server to malicious code or content and compromise all the websites on your server. Governing and planning feature delegation should rank high on your priority list.

In essence, the effect of delegating a feature involves unlocking specific sections of one or more sites' `web.config` files. Remember, these are the new XML files that dictate the site and ASP.NET configurations for a given website. By allowing certain configuration settings to be read-write for a named finite group of users, you are allowing those users to make configuration changes to one or more websites without needing to contact you, the server administrator, but only so far as to configure the unlocked feature. For example, say you delegate the Digest Authentication feature but not the ASP feature. The users will be able to make configuration changes to the site that affect digest authentication, but they will not be able to alter any settings that affect ASP behavior. Feature delegation can be performed either at the server level to identify site defaults or at the site level to disallow inheritance of the server default and configure unique delegation site by site. In other words, if there is a conflict as to which features are delegated to whom, then the site-level delegation setting wins the conflict.

But wait, there's more. Which sites your chosen users can make configuration changes to also depends on the ACLs of the web.config files. Just because a feature has been delegated doesn't mean that your chosen users have anything beyond Read permission to a site's web.config file. You now must grant your chosen users the Write permission to their sites' web.config files to allow them to alter whatever feature configuration settings have been unlocked. Feature delegation and NTFS ACLs must be maintained in unison to achieve the most effective security for website configuration.

Now that you are sold on using feature delegation to secure your web server, we will cover delegation in greater detail later in this chapter. The anticipation is building!

Installing IIS 7

Before we inadvertently put the proverbial cart before the horse, we should take a deeper look at installing IIS. Windows Server 2008 comes in several editions (R2 in 64-bit flavor only) and has new methods of employing different services, or *roles*, for the server. Without getting into detailed analysis of those editions in this chapter, keep in mind that IIS 7.0 is available on all full Windows Server 2008 editions including Server Core, and IIS 7.5 is available on all full Windows Server 2008 R2 editions (including Server Core) as well as Windows 7.

Although some IIS 7 servers may be internally deployed as intranet servers or to support a web-based network application, others will be relegated to the perimeter TCP/IP network address space, sometimes called the *demilitarized zone* (DMZ), as public front-end web servers. For security reasons, many enterprise administrators are reluctant to join DMZ hosts to the internal logical ADS structure (for good reason). Despite the IIS 7 server's intended purpose, the installation program will be the same—but unlike anything you've done before. You know, the same but different.

Adding the Web Server Role

Windows Server 2008 and R2 introduce a new concept of installing functionality into the OS by employing specific roles on the server. Assigning a role not only installs the corresponding services but also mandates dependency services and implies suggestions for hardening. To install IIS 7, you should employ the Web Server role on the server.

Every Microsoft product offers several methods to accomplish the same result, and adding roles to a Windows Server 2008 or 2008 R2 operating system is no exception. Table 16.3 outlines some of the tools that you can use to add roles to a server.

TABLE 16.3:   Tools for Adding Roles to a Server

UTILITY	COMMAND	PURPOSE
ICT (GUI)	OOBE.exe	This finishes the initial setup of the operating system (including assigning roles).
Server Manager (GUI)	compmgmtlauncher.exe	This configures the OS at any time (including roles, features, scheduled tasks, disk management, diagnostics, and so on).
Control Panel (GUI)	compmgmtlauncher.exe	The Programs and Features applet in Control Panel offers a "Turn Windows Features on or off" hyperlink that launches Server Manager.
Server Manager (CLI)	servermanagercmd.exe	This installs, uninstalls, and lists roles and features on the OS from the command line.
Package Manager (CLI)	pkgmgr.exe	This installs, uninstalls, and updates features on the OS from the command line.
Optional Component Setup (CLI)	ocsetup.exe	This installs and uninstalls features on the OS from the command line.

The Initial Configuration Tasks (ICT) utility offers easy-to-follow walk-through wizards meant to be used during the initial setup of the server (Figure 16.2). Once the initial setup is deemed complete, you can prevent the ICT utility from launching by simply selecting the "Do not show this window at logon" check box. Upon closing the ICT, Server Manager will automatically launch.

FIGURE 16.2
The Initial
Configuration
Tasks utility

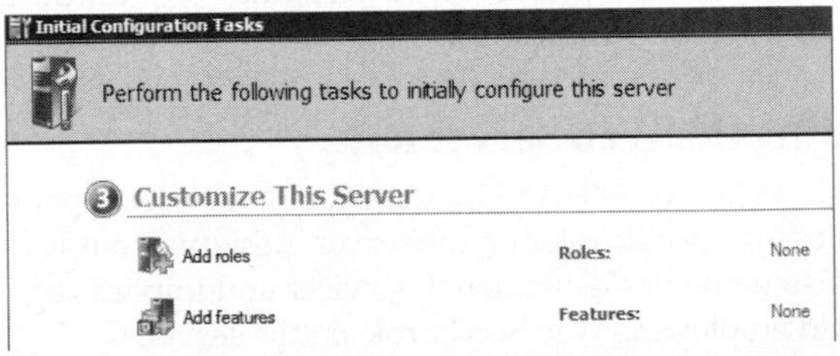

If the ICT (or Server Manager, for that matter) has been inactivated from launching upon logon, you can edit the Windows OS registry to resume logon invocation (see the "Reinitializing Server Management Utilities" sidebar). But reinitializing these utilities may be unnecessary (unless you are a hardware manufacturer preparing a server to be shipped to a customer) since the Server Manager GUI utility is always available from the Start menu's Administrative Tools program group and can be used to configure roles, services, and features at any time.

REINITIALIZING SERVER MANAGEMENT UTILITIES

To reinitialize ICT for automatic launch upon logon, change the HKEY_LOCAL_MACHINE\ SOFTWARE\MICROSOFT\SERVER MANAGER\OOBE registry subkey by resetting the DoNotOpenInitialConfigurationTasksAtLogon value to 0.

To reinitialize Server Manager for automatic launch upon logon, change the HKEY_LOCAL_ MACHINE\SOFTWARE\MICROSOFT\SERVER MANAGER registry subkey by resetting the DoNotOpenServerManagerAtLogon value to 0.

🌐 Real World Scenario

A WEB SERVER FOR BIGFIRM

Since IIS 7 installation might not have been your initial plan for the server back when you used the ICT utility to set up your server, we'll show how to use Server Manager to set up IIS for Bigfirm. Let's say you want to put up a couple of public websites proving to the world that although oranges may enjoy the media limelight as one of Earth's most delicious and nutritious fruits, the humble apple is just as beneficial and a much heartier fruit. And to stay true to our network, we'll use Microsoft IIS 7.5 on Windows Server 2008 R2 to host our new public sites.

To begin, launch Server Manager from the Administrative Tools program group or icon in the Quick Launch Toolbar on the taskbar, and visit the Roles node in the left tree pane to add the Web Server role to the server. Clicking the Add Roles hyperlink in Server Manager's Roles node, as shown here, launches the same wizard to add the Web Server role to the server that you would have seen if you had used the ICT utility. Alternatively, you could use the command line to install IIS 7.5 and even write scripts for automatic or remote installation (more on command line later).

To install IIS 7.5 via the Server Manager's Add Role Wizard, follow these steps:

1. Select Web Server (IIS) on the Select Server Roles page, and then click Next.

2. In the resulting pop-up, click Add Required Features to also employ the dependency OS features on which IIS 7.5 depends, and then click Next.

- ◆ Windows Process Activation Service (WAS) removes HTTP dependency by introducing .NET Framework Windows Communication Foundation (WCF) services that allow non-HTTP protocol support, and it provides message-based activation over HTTP.

- ◆ Process Model hosts Web and WCF services.

- ◆ Configuration APIs allows .NET Framework applications to configure WAS (not available on Server Core).

3. The Web Server (IIS) page simply educates you about the Web Server role and provides hyperlinks to various help articles about IIS 7.5. Do not get hasty here and click the Next button too quickly; there is some very good information in these articles (like the IIS checklists!) Each hyperlink opens a new window to the article, so the installation wizard remains uninterrupted while you read (now that's intuitive).

4. In the Available Role Services selection list, you can choose which IIS 7.5 modules to employ (see Table 16.1 for an explanation of each). To really get an idea of the power in IIS 7, select all the role services, and click Next to continue.

5. Having selected the IIS modules, the Confirm page merely reminds you of your choices thus far in the wizard. If you're certain enough, you can click Install and wait through the progress to reach the Installation Results page (which gives you an opportunity to save the installation report!) before closing the wizard by clicking Close. And don't go get coffee. IIS is so lean that it won't take very long (less than 10 minutes on a minimum spec virtual server).

Installing IIS 7 via the Command Line

Server Manager had a command-line cousin in Windows Server 2008, `ServerManagerCMD.exe`, that can also be used to install IIS. Alas, the `ServerManagerCMD.exe` utility is deprecated in R2 in favor of Windows PowerShell. Although the following commands can still be executed on R2, a warning will appear cautioning that future releases of the OS may no longer support the `ServerManagerCMD.exe` commands. Alternatively, Package Manager or Optional Component Setup can be scripted to install IIS 7 from the command line, but they are considered older utilities and do not have the inherent error control of `ServerManagerCMD.exe` or PowerShell. In addition, they are a bit more convoluted if you want to install all features at once because there is no AllFeatures parameter; each feature must be listed individually. The following are syntax examples of `ServerManagerCMD.exe` and Package Manager for comparison:

Here's the Server Manager command-line syntax for a full IIS 7.5 installation:

```
ServerManagerCMD.exe –install Web-Server –allsubfeatures
```

The following is the Package Manager command-line syntax for a full IIS 7.5 installation:

```
start /w pkgmgr /iu:IIS-WebServerRole;IIS-WebServer;IIS-CommonHttpFeatures;
IIS-StaticContent;IIS-DefaultDocument;IIS-DirectoryBrowsing;IIS-HttpErrors;
IIS-HttpRedirect;IIS-ApplicationDevelopment;IIS-ASPNET;IIS-NetFxExtensibility;
```

```
IIS-ASP;IIS-CGI;IIS-ISAPIExtensions;IIS-ISAPIFilter;IIS-ServerSideIncludes;
IIS-HealthAndDiagnostics;IIS-HttpLogging;IIS-LoggingLibraries;IIS-RequestMonitor;
IIS-HttpTracing;IIS-CustomLogging;IIS-ODBCLogging;IIS-Security;
IIS-BasicAuthentication;IIS-WindowsAuthentication;IIS-DigestAuthentication;
IIS-ClientCertificateMappingAuthentication;IIS-IISCertificateMappingAuthentication;
IIS-URLAuthorization;IIS-RequestFiltering;IIS-IPSecurity;IIS-Performance;
IIS-HttpCompressionStatic;IIS-HttpCompressionDynamic;IIS-WebServerManagementTools;
IIS-WebServerManagementTools;IIS-ManagementScriptingTools;IIS-ManagementService;
IIS-IIS6ManagementCompatibility;IIS-Metabase;IIS-WMICompatibility;
IIS-LegacyScripts;IIS-LegacySnapIn;IIS-FTPServer;IIS-FTPSrvc;IIS-FTPExtensibility;
IIS-WebDAV;WAS-WindowsActivationService;WAS-ProcessModel;WAS-NetFxEnvironment;
WAS-ConfigurationAPI
```

The start /w command in front of pkgmgr launches a second command prompt window to run the installation and monitor its progress, releasing the current command prompt window for subsequent unrelated work. Using start /w is not mandatory, but it sure is handy. Also, you can add setting configurations to each feature during installation by using the -setting switch to set *setting name = setting value*. Although ServerManagerCMD.exe certainly makes a full installation much simpler to invoke, you can also use the command to install granular feature selection in case you need to trim down the web server, such as supporting only static content with a default page, as follows:

```
ServerManagerCMD.exe -install Web-Server
ServerManagerCMD.exe -install Web-Static-Content
ServerManagerCMD.exe -install Web-Default-Doc
```

The most difficult part of a granular ServerManagerCMD.exe installation may be translating the role services as shown in the GUI into the command values understood by ServerManagerCMD.exe. Reviewing Table 16.2 in the previous section of this chapter may help you with this task. The entire list of OS features, and their ServerManagerCMD.exe setting names, is available in the "Role, Role Services, and Feature Command Identifiers" article in the Windows Server 2008 R2 help files. To configure multiple setting identifiers in one ServerManagerCMD.exe command, use spaces as the delimiter.

A WORD ABOUT WINDOWS POWERSHELL

Windows PowerShell includes an extensive library of cmdlets (single-operation commands) that can be used to manipulate almost every nuance of the Windows Server 2008 R2 OS. An education on using these cmdlets could fill entire books and is beyond the scope of this IIS chapter. However, there are three cmdlets that lend well to installing the Web Server role onto Windows Server 2008 R2:

Import-Module servermanager   Loads the module that contains the next two cmdlets

Get-WindowsFeature   Lists modules available for OS, both installed and uninstalled

Add-WindowsFeature {feature name}   Installs a module by name, in this case Web-Server

Installing IIS 7 on Server Core

Now that you are well versed in IIS 7 installation on any of the full Windows Server 2008 editions, let's embark on one remaining frontier yet unexplored: Windows Server 2008 Server Core. Similar to digital cameras and mobile telephones in recent years, Microsoft's server operating system has been slimmed down and offers a variation of the OS with a smaller footprint and more efficient performance that is ripe for virtualization. But with every peach comes a pit, so you need to be careful here.

Before we begin, note that the following discussion specifies Windows Server 2008 R2 Server Core. Windows Server 2008 Server Core was rather limited in its IIS 7 support; for example, it did not support the .NET Framework. So, what do you get, and what don't you get? Table 16.4 outlines the limitations (we mean "boundaries") of employing Windows Server 2008 R2 Server Core as an IIS 7.5 web server.

TABLE 16.4:   Limitations of Server Core

FUNCTIONALITY	AVAILABILITY
IIS 7.5 support	Available on all Server Core editions except Itanium (at the time of this writing).
Windows Explorer shell	Not included in any Server Core editions (no GUI installation options).
.NET Framework	Not installed by default. Must be added before adding Web Server role.
Server Manager (CLI)	Not included in any Server Core editions.
IIS 7.5 features	Unavailable in Server Core: IIS-WebServerManagementTools (IIS 7 Manager console) and IIS-LegacySnapIn (IIS 6 Manager console).

With these idiosyncrasies, Server Core may not immediately capture your heart as the desirable operating system for your new web server. But keep in mind that if your objective is a lean, safe, low-maintenance IIS 7.5 implementation, then installing only select IIS 7.5 features onto Server Core becomes a pretty attractive option.

Unfortunately, ServerManagerCMD.exe is not available on both Server Core versions (Windows Server 2008 and R2). So, you are left with either Package Manager or Optional Component Setup to install IIS 7.0 onto Windows Server 2008 Server Core and potentially Windows PowerShell to install IIS 7.5 onto Windows Server 2008 R2 Server Core. The following is an example of using the Optional Component Setup syntax to add a default installation of IIS 7 to Server Core:

```
ocsetup IIS-WebServerRole
```

You can also use the following switches to manipulate the ocsetup utility:

```
/passive  (unattended mode, progress only)
/quiet  (quiet mode, no user interaction)
/norestart  (will not restart)
/log:<file> (specify a non-default log location)
/x:<parameters>  (supply expected parameter values to installer)
```

By specifying the entire Web Server role, Optional Component Setup will install IIS-CommonHttpFeatures, IIS-HealthandMonitoring, IIS-Performance, IIS-Security, and IIS-WebServerManagementTools, as well as automatically create firewall exceptions for HTTP traffic. Keep in mind that Optional Component Setup does not configure features for you; it just installs or removes them. All the features are installed with default settings. You may want to confirm that IIS 7 has not yet been installed prior to installing it with Optional Component Setup. To display a list of uninstalled OS features, Server Core includes a command called Optional Component List that will display a result set of all features (by name) that are not installed on the OS, as shown in Figure 16.3. This `oclist` command is similar in nature to running the full Windows Server 2008 R2 ServerManagerCMD.exe -query switch. But get ready—the list of all features not installed can be quite long!

FIGURE 16.3

Typical abbreviated `oclist` result

```
============================================
Microsoft-Windows-ServerCore-Package
Not Installed:BitLocker
Not Installed:BitLocker-RemoteAdminTool
```

However, unlike ServerManagerCMD.exe, the Optional Component Setup utility will *not* automatically install necessary dependency services! You must manually install any services on which IIS depends prior to installing IIS via `ocsetup.exe` (namely, WAS and WAS-ProcessModel) as well as any optional features:

```
ocsetup.exe WAS-WindowsActivationService
ocsetup.exe WAS-ProcessModel
ocsetup.exe WAS-NetFxEnvironment        *to support .NET functionality
ocsetup.exe MicrosoftWindowsPowershell *for remote IIS Manager administration
```

Although the installation procedures may differ, once installed on any Windows Server 2008 or R2 edition, the new IIS 7 will give you the flexibility and power to support your most robust web-based applications. Well, that's what the marketing materials claim anyway. After initial installation, you may find it occasionally necessary to extend the list of components available on your web server. To employ modules beyond the default installation, you will need to master adding and removing OS role services and IIS modules, which we will discuss next. However, be aware that if IIS 7 doesn't live up to your expectations and you want to remove it, the product's uninstallation behavior leaves a lot to be desired. From the Server Manager GUI, the uninstall seems so simple; just remove the Web Server role from the server. But you will see that although IIS can check out any time it likes, it never really leaves.

Removing the Web Server role from the OS leaves data behind in the registry and on the file system. All site virtual directories will remain along with the `%windir%\system32\inetsrv` directory. To truly clean off a soon-to-be-ex-IIS server, you should delete the sites first (including their directory structures) and then remove the role. Even then the `applicationhost.config` file will remain, and if you reinstall IIS, the new installation will use the previous installation's `applicationhost.config` file, which may present issues until you clean it up.

Renovating IIS Construction

Altering the construction of IIS is as easy as unplugging the A/C adapter of your laptop computer in favor of plugging in your mobile phone charger instead! Feel free to add or remove modules for exploration, testing, or actual production use. The addition of a feature to IIS is not a permanent decision. You can always remove the feature later down the road by simply deselecting the check box.

If you did not perform a *full* installation of all Web Server role services in the OS when you initially installed IIS, then you will need to add the appropriate role service before that role service's associated native modules will be available to add to an IIS website. The "Adding Role Services to the Web Server Role for Bigfirm" case study will show how to register a native module using the OS, allowing Windows Server 2008 to trust the code and give it unrestricted access to all resources. As with any escalated code, be careful to only register native IIS modules from trusted sources because they will have very privileged access to the system.

🌐 Real World Scenario

ADDING ROLE SERVICES TO THE WEB SERVER ROLE FOR BIGFIRM

During the campaign to prove apples are good for you, you'll need ASP page support on the oranges site until you rewrite some of the content, and then you will use HTTP redirection to port visitors to the new content once we get it written. You can add role services to an already applied server role in the Server Manager GUI or with the ServerManagerCMD.exe CLI utility. For example, to add the ASP role service to an existing Web Server role on the BF1 server at Bigfirm via the Server Manager GUI, follow these steps:

1. Launch Server Manager (click Continue at the User Account Control to confirm administrative privilege).

2. Expand the Roles node in the left tree pane, and highlight the Web Server role.

3. Scroll down the right details pane to reach the Role Services section for a summary of the Web Server role's available role services and the installation status of each:

4. Use the Add Role Services hyperlink on the right to install any of the Not Installed role services. The resulting dialog box, as shown here, will only install role services. If you want to remove a role service, you should use the Remove Role Services hyperlink instead.

5. In the Add Role Service dialog box that pops up, simply highlight any of the available role services for the Web Server role to see a description of it on the right. Select the check box if, in fact, you want to add the role service to the Web Server role. Notice that already installed role services appear in gray and cannot be removed from this dialog box. If you want to remove a role service, cancel this dialog box (confirm the cancellation), and use the Remove Role Services hyperlink in the details pane of Server Manager instead.

6. Because the newly added ASP role service requires the dependency role service entitled ISAPI Extensions, which is not yet installed, an Add Role Services dialog box appears informing you of the requirement and giving you the chance to also install the dependency role service on the fly, as shown here. Click the Add Required Role Services button to allow the installation of the dependencies.

7. After you click Next, the Confirmation dialog box will simply summarize your choices, and you can just click Install to finalize the installation, returning you to Server Manager.

Notice that you do not get prompted for the Windows Server 2008 installation media. You no longer need to frantically search every software-supply closet prior to administrating your IIS server!

If you prefer to use the CLI to add role services to the Web Server role in the OS, ServerManagerCMD or the Optional Component Setup utility will get the job done. Recall that Microsoft strongly encourages ServerManagerCMD over ocsetup because of the limitations of the ocsetup command discussed earlier. However, also recall that ServerManagerCMD is not available on Windows Server 2008 Server Core, so you will have to use the Optional Component Setup utility instead. To illustrate the difference between the two utilities, the following is the syntax for each.

Here's the Server Manager command-line syntax for adding the HTTP Redirection role service:

```
ServerManagerCMD.exe —install Web-Http-Redirect
```

The following is the Optional Component Setup command-line syntax for adding the HTTP Redirection role service:

```
ocsetup.exe IIS-HttpRedirect
```

If you employed ServerManagerCMD to add the new role service, a progression percentage count ascends to 100/100 (100 percent of a potential 100 percent), after which the command prompt window should contain the lines in Figure 16.4.

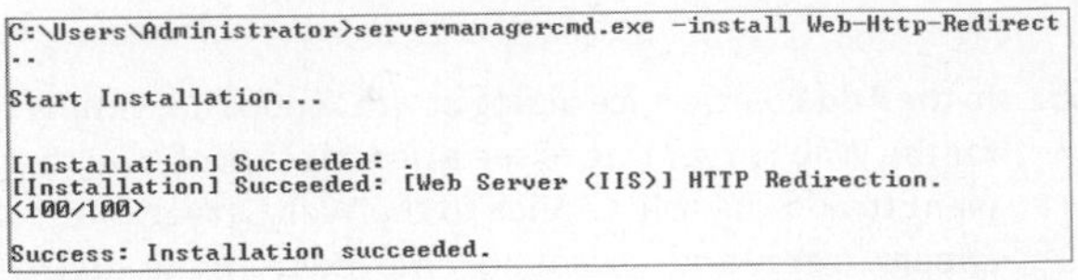

FIGURE 16.4
Completed role service
installation via
ServerManagerCMD

```
C:\Users\Administrator>servermanagercmd.exe -install Web-Http-Redirect
..
Start Installation...

[Installation] Succeeded: .
[Installation] Succeeded: [Web Server (IIS)] HTTP Redirection.
<100/100>
Success: Installation succeeded.
```

FIGURE 16.4
Completed role service
installation via
ServerManagerCMD

REGISTERING NATIVE MODULES USING IIS MANAGER

When it comes to native modules, you could register a native module using the IIS Manager GUI. This is not as intuitive as using Server Manager, but if you are the kind of administrator who prefers to spend your whole day in one utility and IIS Manager is your preference, you can accomplish this very important task in IIS Manager as well. To register a native module on the fly, follow these steps:

1. Launch IIS Manager, and connect to or highlight a specific IIS server that you want to examine using the Connections pane on the left.

2. The center page of IIS Manager reflects the categories of management tools by default. Within the IIS category, click the Modules icon to see a list of modules installed at the server level.

3. Click the Configure Native Modules hyperlink from the modules-specific Actions pane on the right. This produces a dialog box listing the native modules currently installed (see Figure 16.5).

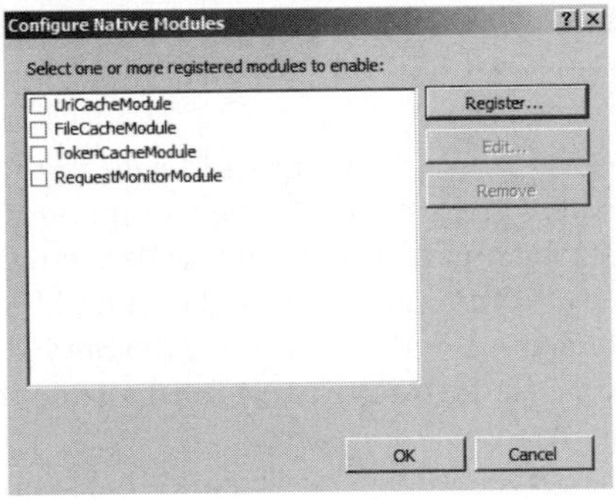

FIGURE 16.5
Configure Native
Modules dialog box

4. Click the Register button in the dialog box to manually register a native module on the fly (see Figure 16.6). This, of course, requires that you know the actual filename of the native module. Upon adding the native module to the list, you can then select it to enable it at the server level.

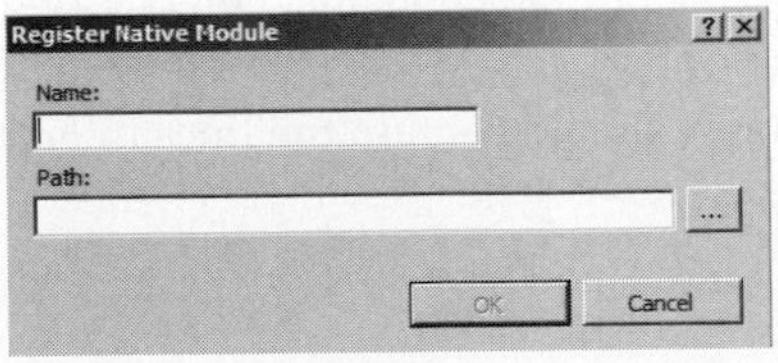

FIGURE 16.6
Register Native
Module dialog box

DETERMINING IIS MODULE FILENAMES

There is a wonderful article entitled "Feature to Configuration Reference" available at Microsoft's IIS 7.5 Product website (http://learn.iis.net/page.aspx/153/feature-to-configuration-reference/). This article lists all the system-supplied features and their corresponding consumers by .dll filename. Be aware, this article is geared toward programmers, not engineers.

Adding role services to an already installed server role makes the associated native modules available within IIS to be enabled or disabled on individual websites. Remember that IIS 7 uses various XML files in a hierarchical fashion to store configuration information, and because the applicationhost.config file is the server-level configuration file, any role services added to it will be inherited by all sites on the IIS server by default. The server-level applicationhost.config configuration file will be modified to include the newly added role services. For instance, the ISAPI Extensions role service that was added to the Web Server role earlier is now recorded as an installed native module in the following sections of the applicationhost.config file (IIS calls them sections, but XML lingo refers to the hierarchical pieces of an XML file as *elements*):

```
<globalModules>
    <add name="IsapiModule" image="%windir%\system32\inetsrv\isapi.dll" />

<modules>
    <add name="IsapiModule" lockItem="true" />
```

The <globalModules> section lists all native modules available at the server level along with the physical path to each module's compiled code file. The beauty here is that if you pro-grammatically customize a native module, you can simply redirect the module's image value in applicationhost.config to point to the custom .dll file you wrote. Of course, Microsoft does not support altering the native modules, but you have to admit that pointing IIS to new code doesn't get any easier than that!

The <modules> section merely lists all the native and managed modules and their current lock status regarding whether administration of the module can be delegated at a lower level. For instance, the ISAPI Extensions module listed earlier is currently locked at the server level, so it cannot be removed from IIS by a lower-level administrator. We will discuss more about securing IIS configuration in the Advanced Administration section.

🌐 Real World Scenario

LISTING THE ASP ROLE SERVICE

But what about the ASP role service we added? Why isn't it explicitly listed in either the <globalModules> or <modules> section? The ASP role service is a web application that sup-ports classic ASP web applications through the dependency ISAPI Extensions role service, so it is not explicitly listed under <modules> in applicationhost.config. However, it does get its own <system.webserver> section identifying it as a web application on the server. We will dive deeper into the applicationhost.config and web.config sections later in this chapter.

To retrieve a list of the installed global modules from applicationhost.config, you do not have to open the file with Notepad (although this is entirely possible to do if you are an OS administrator). Instead, you can use the new IIS CLI management command %windir%\system32\inetsrv\ appcmd.exe to expose particular sections of applicationhost.config. For example, to view the globalModules section, use a command prompt window to execute the following:

```
Appcmd list config "{web server process URL}" -section:globalModules
```

Whether you expose the list of global modules in a command prompt for read-only purposes or gain full edit access to the applicationhost.config file with a text editor, you can quickly identify which IIS modules will be automatically enabled on your websites.

MODULE MANAGEMENT VIA THE COMMAND LINE INTERFACE (CLI)

Now that you've tried it, you may find managing the modules available at either the server level or site level more convenient via the CLI. If you prefer to use appcmd.exe to install native modules at the server level so they can be automatically installed at every site, the following commands will prove useful.

◆ To install a module, use this:

```
Appcmd.exe install module /name:{module name} /image:{module path}
```

◆ To uninstall a module, use this:

```
Appcmd.exe uninstall module {module name}
```

◆ To enable a module, use this:

```
Appcmd.exe add module /name:{module name} /type:{MGD type}
```

◆ To disable a module, use this:

```
Appcmd.exe delete module /name:{module name} /app.name:{application name}
```

CONFIGURING MODULES AT THE SITE LEVEL

Once you have installed the necessary role services, the associated modules are available in IIS to process client requests properly. In fact, the native modules are automatically enabled on all websites that are inheriting their configuration from the parent applicationhost.config file. IIS modules can be configured or disabled at the site level by directly modifying the site's web.config file in a text editor, by using the appcmd.exe CLI utility, or by navigating the IIS Manager GUI. For example, beginning with the friendly GUI interface, follow these steps:

1. Launch IIS Manager, and connect to or highlight a specific IIS server that you want to examine using the Connections pane on the left.

2. The center page of IIS Manager reflects the categories of management tools by default. Within the IIS category, click the Modules icon to see a list of modules installed at the server level that are available to be managed at the site level. Note that any website set to inherit its feature structure from its parent will be inheriting these modules from the server level.

3. Navigate to Default Web Site under Sites in the Connections pane on the left, and highlight it. Notice the Home icons available, particularly the ASP and HTTP Redirect icons, which are available now only because we installed the necessary role services at the server level (they did not appear here before).

4. Double-click the Modules icon, and peruse the list of installed modules, both native and managed, that are available for use on Default Web Site. Notice that ASP does not appear separately listed but rather is hidden within the IsapiModule.

5. To disable one of the inherited native modules here at the site level on Default Web Site, such as IsapiModule, simply highlight the module, and click the Remove link in the Actions pane on the right. Of course, the OS will prompt you to confirm the removal, so be ready to be sure. Notice that the module disappears from the list.

6. To enable an already installed native module (one that is registered in `applicationhost .config`) at the site level isn't as obvious. If you want to reenable the IsapiModule on Default Web Site, click the Configure Native Modules hyperlink in the modules-specific Actions pane on the right. This produces a dialog box such as Figure 16.7 that allows you enable IsapiModule by simply selecting its check box.

FIGURE 16.7
Configure Native
Modules dialog box

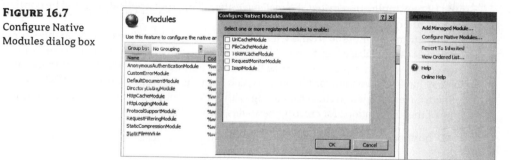

Remember, modules registered in the server-level `applicationhost.config` configuration file are automatically enabled on all sites that inherit their module structure from the server. There is no reason to enable the modules at every site in your IIS instance. And although there is much ado being made about the new site-specific `web.config` files, the reality is that a site doesn't even get a `web.config` file created for itself until you make a configuration change to the site that disallows inheritance from the parent level. Once you make such a change, only the newly unique configuration setting is written into the site-specific `web.config` file, and the write happens immediately. So, by employing native modules by registering them at the server level, you have not yet caused any site-specific `web.config` file to be generated. You'll take a look at customizing websites in the next section.

Website Provisioning

Provisioning is the art of allocating resources and creating the structure for a new website. Several client access protocols are supported these days (HTTP, FTP, SOAP, and so on), so an accurate discourse on the subject of creating a website should clarify which type of traffic you expect the website to support. Vocabulary may again provide challenges when researching the best method of creating sites. Remember that a *site* in IIS is a logical entity that merely defines protocol handling and endpoint listening behavior in order to receive client requests and respond to them. For example, to create an HTTP site, you would configure the IP address, port number, and host header information that the server will recognize on an inbound request from a client in order to respond to it. Any client request bearing a destination IP address, destination port, or requested host header in the URL that matches your new site's configuration will immediately be directed to your new site as opposed to any other site existing on that same IIS server. These address, port, and header assignments are referred to in IIS 7 as *bindings*.

Because each HTTP site's binding values must be unique in order to correctly route processing, IIS 7 will throw an error if you attempt to create identical site protocol bindings on more than one site. However, there are many possible combinations of IP address, port, and host header that would allow you to build multiple sites on the same instance of IIS 7 without conflict. We'll discuss hosting multiple sites in more detail in a bit.

Within a site, a smaller logical unit that represents part or all of the site's functionality is called an *application*. Multiple applications may exist within a single site and can be configured separately for performance and security reasons. Each application's URL namespace is mapped to a physical drive via a *virtual directory* configuration parameter. A site must contain a minimum of one application called the *root application*. This root application must be configured with a minimum of one virtual directory.

Before jumping into site creation, it is important to conceptualize the new architecture in IIS 7. Recall that the metabase has been banished in favor of a distributed XML file configuration system. The server-level settings are now being held in the new `applicationhost.config` file, and each site may have its own `web.config` file in which both site configuration and ASP.NET settings are defined. Given the new architecture along with the continued binding uniqueness requirements, some of the justifications for creating new sites include the following:

- Supporting different domain names
- Supporting different authentication protocols
- Hosting multiple sites on a single instance of IIS
- Hosting separate ASP.NET applications on a single instance of IIS
- Maximizing performance by isolating applications into separate app pools
- Maximizing disk space utilization with separate virtual directories
- Delegating site administration

Understanding Global Settings

Before creating a new website, you should understand which global settings defined at the server level in `applicationhost.config` will be enforced for your new site. New to IIS 7, this file is securely settled within the `%windir%\system32\inetsrv\config` directory, which is a folder with very limited NTFS ACL access by default (see Table 16.5).

🌐 Real World Scenario

PLANNING BIGFIRM'S APPLES AND ORANGES WEBSITES

One of the most popular protocols is still HTTP for delivery of static content, so let's concentrate on creating simple static HTTP websites for our "apples trump oranges" campaign. First you will create an apples virtual directory within the Default Web Site, and then you will create a separate oranges website using different protocol bindings. Since the oranges site is going to need to support ASP pages, you should probably run it in a separate application pool. And given that both of your sites need to have different bindings and URLs, you should create the oranges pages as a new, separate website. However, the apples pages will use the same settings and application pool as the Default Web Site, so you can simply add the apples content as a new virtual directory into the Default Web Site.

When deciding between adding apples as a virtual directory to the existing Default Web Site root application vs. creating a second application within the Default Web Site to support the apples content, the ultimate factor is code support. Recall that applications are designed to provide both content and code and thus give you the opportunity to assign a unique application pool to them. Since the apples pages are simply delivering static .htm content, creating a whole new application for these pages would be overkill for this illustration. However, when planning your own IIS implementation, plan for growth, scale, and development. If you think a set of pages will eventually need to include code, go ahead and build them an application at the beginning and grow into it down the road.

IIS 7 still offers a Default Web Site that listens on TCP port 80 across all network interfaces and is not configured for any particular host header. If these dimensions are acceptable for your new website, feel free to direct the Default Web Site to your content directories instead of creating an additional site. This will work fine for the apples site.

TABLE 16.5: NTFS Permissions on applicationhost.config

ACCESS CONTROL ENTRY	ALLOWED PERMISSION
Administrators	Full Control
SYSTEM	Full Control
TrustedInstaller	Full Control
WMSvc	Read

To make server-level configuration changes, you can either edit the applicationhost.config file directly or use the IIS Manager GUI or the appcmd.exe CLI utility. If you decide to alter the applicationhost.config file directly, pay close attention to the %windir%\system32\inetsrv\config\schema\IIS_schema.xml file that dictates the allowable structure you can write into applicationhost.config. You may also decide to back up the applicationhost.config file prior to making any changes…just in case. If you are going to frequently edit the application-host.config file directly, it would be prudent to invest in a true XML-editing application such as Microsoft's XML Notepad 2007. At the time of this writing, XML Notepad 2007 is available for free download at www.microsoft.com/downloads/details.aspx?FamilyID=72d6aa49-787d-4118-ba5f-4f30fe913628&displaylang=en.

IMPORTANT SECTIONS OF APPLICATIONHOST.CONFIG

There are so many elements in an applicationhost.config XML file that at first glance it may be difficult to figure out which section of the file has what type of configuration settings in it! To help you navigate this critical server-level configuration file, here are some descriptions of important sections indented to indicate their hierarchy level in the applicationhost.config XML schema:

<configuration>: Root element

    <configSections>: Registrations of non-nested sections organized into groups

        <Section>: Building blocks of deployable, lockable, searchable settings

    <configProtectedData>: Registrations of cryptography providers (algorithms)

    <system.applicationHost>: Site, web app, virtual directory, and app pool configurations

        <applicationPools>: Registrations of application pools of isolated execution

        <customMetadata>: ABO compatibility data (*do not modify this!*)

        <listenerAdapters>: WAS bindings

        <log>: Binary and W3C log definitions

        <sites>: Site definitions

    <system.webServer>: Global web defaults not found in system.applicationHost

    <globalModules>: Registrations of native modules

    <http…>: HTTP compression, custom errors, custom headers, redirect, and tracing

    <security>: Server-level security settings

    <modules>: Module locking status for distributed management

---

There are many settings you may want to control from the server level. Registration and security of the modules come immediately to mind. And many of these settings are more easily managed in the IIS Manager GUI or appcmd.exe CLI. We will cover more administration topics later, but suffice it to say that it would be a good idea to identify which settings from the server level you will be customizing on your new site and plan for disallowing inheritance once your new site is created.

Creating a Simple Website

You can use either the GUI administration tools or the `appcmd.exe` CLI utility to create new websites in IIS 7, depending on your comfort level and scripting needs. The new `appcmd.exe` utility will be covered in more depth later, so for now we will concentrate on the GUI. Before you can begin actually creating the site, planning is required to determine the appropriate settings for the new site:

◆ What IP address should be associated with the site?

◆ What TCP/IP port number should be associated with the site?

◆ Will the site use a custom host header in the URL?

◆ What application pools will the site's applications use?

◆ Where will the virtual directory point to locate content for the site?

To begin, you must become familiar with the new IIS Manager interface.

SITE SETUP VIA IIS MANAGER

Upon launching the new Internet Information Services (IIS) Manager, you undoubtedly recognized that the snap-in has undergone an extreme makeover. Rest assured that this is still a preconfigured console file and that you can build the IIS Manager snap-in into any custom management console. The start page (see Figure 16.8) is mostly links to news and resources, although the "Recent connections" and "Connection tasks" panes can prove helpful when troubleshooting multiple IIS servers from a single management console.

FIGURE 16.8
Internet Information Services (IIS) Manager

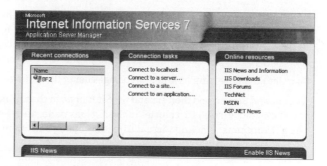

Once connected to a web server, the Connections pane on the left is easily navigated vertically to expose the application pools and sites of various IIS servers the management console is currently connected to. This pane remains visible when using the console. The path across the top of the console is reminiscent of an Internet Explorer 7 ribbon with Forward, Back, Refresh, and Help buttons. However, a big difference is the breadcrumb navigation appearing automatically in the position field as you navigate the Connections pane vertically (instead of manually entering website URLs).

Once you highlight a connected server in the Connections pane, the start page disappears and is replaced with the server's Home page in Features view and grouped by area as the default. An Actions pane will also appear on the right, and the tasks hyperlinked in this pane will change relative to the Connections pane node being focused on (see Figure 16.9 for an example of the console pane's layout).

FIGURE 16.9

IIS Manager:
server focus

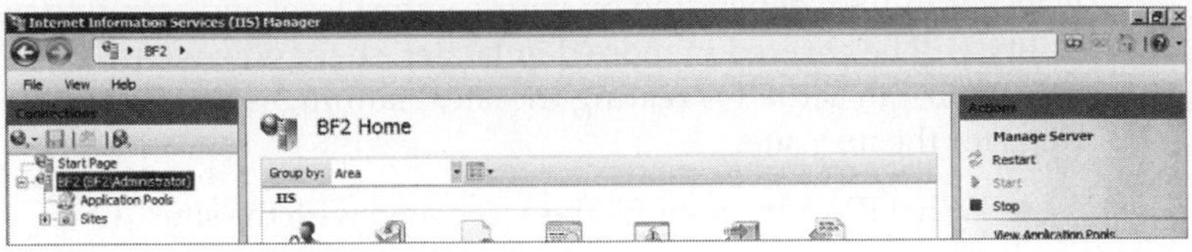

Performing administration via IIS Manager will be covered in greater detail throughout this chapter. For now, we will focus on creating a new website. Make note of the features listed at the server level, because you will be limited to only these functionalities for your new site. If there is a trick your new site must perform that is missing from the server, it is best to add the necessary feature to the server prior to creating your new site. You may also notice that the Actions pane on the right offers many of the same configuration capabilities as the right-click menu would if you were to right-click the Connections node. Imagine that—more than one way to accomplish the same task in a Microsoft product! Regardless, you may want to take this opportunity to acquaint yourself with using the Actions pane instead of using right-click menus.

Real World Scenario

CONSTRUCTING BIGFIRM'S WEBSITES

For illustrative purposes, assume the new "Apples Rule!!" pages will be part of the bigfirm.com domain and will serve static .htm content across all server network interfaces through TCP port 80. Also, assume that the text and image content for these new pages are already stored in an apples directory you created under the default IIS 7 content directory of %systemdrive%\inetpub.

To create the new "Apples Rule!" web pages using IIS Manager, do the following:

1. Expand Server, and then expand the Sites node in the Connections pane. Click Default Web Site, click View Virtual Directories in the Actions pane, and then click Add Virtual Directory in the Actions pane. The Add Virtual Directory dialog box opens.

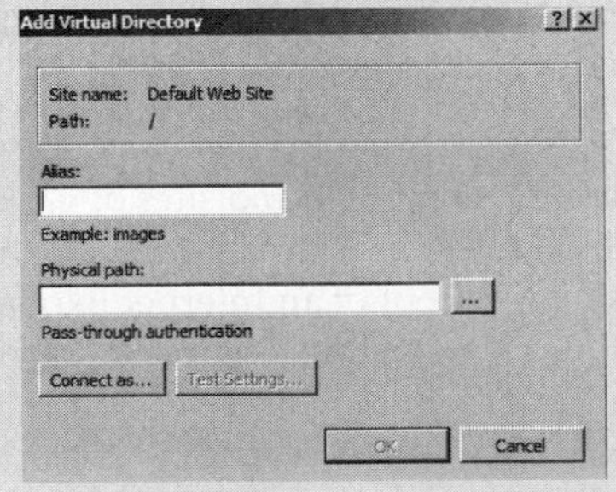

2. For the alias, enter a URL-friendly name that is descriptive but concise. In this case, the new name is **apples**.

3. For the physical path, enter the UNC or local path to the content for this virtual directory, such as the `\inetpub\apples` content folder. If the content is stored in a local folder on the IIS server that happens to also be shared, use the local path instead of the UNC path for maximum performance. As is always true when using UNC paths to remote folders, for performance or confidence reasons, you can always replace the hostname of the path with an IP address. Just beware of DHCP environments or networks that frequently change server IP addresses!

4. Clicking "Connect as" produces a subsequent dialog box in which to provide a specific user account and password that IIS should always use to access the content directory instead of passing through the application user credentials. For the apples pages, use pass-through. Remember that if you set a credential here, you will need to update it if the credential password changes in Windows.

Once you click OK in the Add Virtual Directory dialog box, the new virtual directory should appear in the Virtual Directories list in the details pane of IIS Manager. From there you can manage the new virtual directory's properties and permissions. And be careful if you add a new virtual directory folder in Explorer or Computer (Windows Server 2008's and 2008 R2's new Windows Explorer and My Computer type of utilities) by adding or moving a folder beneath `%systemdrive%\inetpub\wwwroot`. IIS Manager will show the new folder structure beneath the Default Web Site, but the virtual directory will not be registered in the Virtual Directories list for the root application. Management of the folder will need to be performed directly via `web.config` and Explorer. Adding virtual directories using the appropriate IIS management tools is the preferred method.

Now that you have created a virtual directory that points to the "Apples Rule!!" content, you should test the new environment by browsing to the "Apples Rule!!" page. Without leaving IIS Manager, you can do either of the following:

◆ Right-click the new virtual directory in the Connections pane, choose Manage Virtual Directory, and click Browse.

◆ Click the new virtual directory in Virtual Directories list, and click the Browse *.80 (http) link in the Actions pane.

No matter which method you employ, a new instance of Internet Explorer will launch and navigate directly to the new "Apples Rule!!" page (as shown here). Just a side note, Windows Server 2008 R2 includes IE 8 with enhanced security engaged by default. If your new page will not display, consider either adding the URL to Trusted Sites or disengaging the IE Enhanced Security Configuration setting.

Now that the "Apples Rule!!" content is up, it is time to build the "Oranges" site. Remember, you plan to employ additional modules and some code on this site, so you need it to be completely separate from the Default Web Site and run in a separate application pool.

To create the new "Oranges" website using IIS Manager, follow these steps:

1. Expand Server in Connections pane, click the Sites node in Connections pane, and click Add Web Site in the Actions pane. The Add Web Site dialog box opens.

2. Enter a site name that is descriptive but concise (the maximum is 64 characters). In this case, the new site name is Oranges. The value entered in this field will automatically generate a new .NET integrated-mode application pool by default and assign it to the new site unless you specify an already existing application pool with the Select button. The new application pool will be created with the parameter settings defined using the Set Application Pool Defaults link available in the Actions pane when focused on the Application Pools node in Connections. Also, by default a new system-generated identity account will be automatically created of the same name as the pool for security purposes.

3. Enter the full UNC or local drive letter path to the directory on the physical drive in which the site content is stored. If the directory is a local drive that happens to also be shared, use the volume letter instead of the share UNC to avoid potential performance degradation. The virtual directory will be located at \inetpub\oranges (assuming you have already created the oranges directory under the default IIS content directory of %systemdrive%\inetpub).

4. Choose between static or pass-through credentials that will gain IIS services access to the physical path defined earlier. You may even want to confirm that the credential has sufficient permissions to the directory by using the Test Connection button. For the example's purposes, pass-through authentication keeps access to only valid Windows accounts that have ACL privilege to the oranges directory.

5. Decide whether to assign HTTP or HTTPS as the initial protocol being bound to the new site. FTP may also appear as a third choice if you have the IIS 6.0 Metabase Compatibility and FTP Server modules installed. You can always add bindings to the site after creation by using the Bindings link on the site's Actions pane. Since the new "Oranges" site will host nonconfidential static content, we'll use HTTP.

6. Use the All Unassigned value for "IP address" to bind the new "Oranges" site to any and all IP addresses configured on all server network interfaces but that are not already assigned to other websites in IIS. Alternatively, you can enter a specific IP address or select a specific IP address from the drop-down menu, which is populated by the network connections of the OS. Regardless of how you populate this field, notice that it is a single-value field, preventing you from binding a single website to more than one specific IP address (but not all of them) simultaneously. You will need to invoke teaming services to employ some but not all of your network interfaces for a single website. Use caution when manually entering an IPv6 address into the "IP address" field. At the time of this writing, the % character (such as at the end of a link-local IPv6 address) can be misunderstood by WAS and may prevent a new site from starting. Simply leave off the % section of an IPv6 address when entering it into the Binding information if this becomes a problem.

7. For the Port setting, specify the port number on which IIS will listen for inbound client requests. Note that customizing this value requires the clients to provide the chosen custom port number upon each request. For our illustration, we will leave the new site on the default TCP port of 80.

8. For the Host name setting, enter a custom host header for the new site as a method of differentiating it from other sites that share the same port number or IP addresses. Note that this field becomes ineligible if HTTPS is the binding type. This is because HTTPS uses SSL, which requires a certificate. The certificate will include the domain name, so adding a custom host header may cause SSL to fail because the certificate will not match the site. The new oranges site needs a custom host header of "oranges" to differentiate it from the apples pages within the Default Web Site.

9. The "SSL certificate" field appears only after selecting HTTPS for the binding type. The certificate that was enrolled for by the server for the specific purpose of SSL identification must be present on the machine before it can be chosen in this drop-down field. You can add certificates to IIS by managing the Server Certificates feature at the server level in IIS Manager. Since you won't be invoking encryption or authentication on either of the new sites, you won't need SSL.

To easily force all new sites created going forward to have specific settings, consider altering the Application Pool Defaults and Web Site Defaults settings to affect future site creations. Links to these dialog boxes appear in the Actions pane of IIS Manager when highlighting the Application Pools node or Sites node, respectively, in the Connections pane.

Now that the new "Oranges" site has been created, you can employ either of the two IIS Managers' navigation methods you learned earlier to test the new site by browsing to it (as shown here). Remember to disengage the IE Enhanced Security Configuration setting or add the http://oranges URL to your list of trusted sites if necessary.

CREATING A SITE AT THE COMMAND LINE

Alternatively, you can use the CLI to create a site on your web server. The beauty of command-line methods is that you can script them for later use. In fact, the scripts could even be parameterized to allow the insertion of the site name and other values at runtime. Scripted creation helps you deploy a like site structure and content across a network load balanced web server farm as well as disaster recovery and documentation for change control.

The CLI utility `appcmd.exe` is the most common tool for command-line site creation. Here's the `appcmd.exe` syntax that would create a site called "Oranges" on TCP port 80 pointing to the assumed directory path ending in `\inetpub\oranges` and using a custom host header of `oranges`:

```
appcmd.exe add site /name:Oranges
 /bindings:http/*:80:oranges /physicalPath:{path}\inetpub\oranges
```

When creating a new site with `appcmd.exe`, if you omit the `/id` parameter (as shown here), it causes IIS to simply assign the next available ID number to the new site. Also, if you had failed to provide the `/physicalPath` parameter, then no applications or virtual directory would have been created for the new site, and you would have to manually add those settings to the new site once it was created. Lastly, because no authentication credential was included in the `appcmd.exe` `add site` command, the default pass-through authentication would be used on the new site.

If instead you prefer to script with WMI, the following is an example of commands that would create the same "Oranges" site:

```
Set oService = GetObject("winmgmts:root\WebAdministration")
Set oBinding = oService.Get("BindingElement").SpawnInstance_
  oBinding.BindingInformation="*:80:oranges"
oBinding.Protocol = "http"
oService.Get("Site").Create "NewSite", array(oBinding), "{path}\inetpub\oranges"
```

WMI is usually reserved for disaster recovery or to create custom scripts for distributed site creation because the scripts can be built to accept input parameter values. The `appcmd.exe` CLI utility is a much simpler tool that can also be included in automated batch files for execution. The `appcmd.exe` utility is efficient enough to be used to create hundreds of sites but may need monitoring so as not to overload the server. The `appcmd.exe` utility can also display existing sites for inventory or troubleshooting purposes:

```
Appcmd list sites
```

This is the result:

```
SITE "Default Web Site" (id:1,bindings:HTTP/*80,status:started)
SITE "Oranges" (id:2,bindings:HTTP/*80:oranges,status:stopped)
```

Configuring Site Settings

Once a site has been created, you may need to refine the site's configuration prior to unleashing visitors upon it. For example, the "Oranges" site needs to support ASP and HTTP redirection, but the apples pages do not. By default, a new website will immediately begin inheriting configuration settings from the `applicationhost.config` file. Right now both our apples and oranges pages are enabling all settings in the server-level file that have the `enabled` attribute set equal to `true`. Additionally, all modules listed in the `<globalModules>` section of `applicationhost.config` are also initiated on the Default Web Site that governs the apples pages as well as on the "Oranges" site.

Before you make any changes to the default build of a new site, you should know that it does not possess a `web.config` file. If, however, you were to alter a site, a new `web.config` file would appear in the site's root virtual directory. The new `web.config` file would contain only the changed parameter, and all else would continue to be inherited from the `applicationhost.config` file. However, it depends on the nature of the customization as to whether it warrants a `web.config` entry. For example, disengaging native modules does not generate a `web.config` entry. To disengage HTTP redirection and ASP (the ISAPI module) on the Default Web Site, follow these steps:

1. Launch IIS Manager, and expand the IIS server in the Connections pane on the left.

2. Expand the Sites folder, and highlight Default Web Site. The center pane becomes the home page of the site in Features view by default.

3. Double-click the Modules icon to see a list of the enlisted native modules. Note that HttpRedirectionModule and IsapiModule are both listed.

4. Highlight both the HttpRedirectionModule and IsapiModule, and click the Remove hyperlink in the Actions pane on the right.

5. Confirm the removal by clicking Yes to the prompt.

But what if the customization was not based on module employment but rather was simply the altering of a site setting? For instance, what if on a page currently being supported by the Default Web Site you decide to engage directory browsing? This change will construct a new `web.config` file in the \inetpub\wwwroot subfolder that contains the new directory browsing behavior. To enable directory browsing on the Default Web Site, follow these steps:

1. Launch IIS Manager, and expand the IIS server in the Connections pane on the left.

2. Expand the Sites folder, and highlight Default Web Site. The center pane becomes the home page of the site in Features view by default.

3. Double-click the Directory Browsing icon.

4. Click the Enable hyperlink in the Actions pane on the right.

By enabling the directory browsing setting, you have caused a new entry to be added to the `web.config` file for the Default Web Site:

```
<?xml version="1.0" encoding="UTF-8"?>
<configuration>
    <system.webServer>
        <directoryBrowse enabled="true" />
    </system.webServer>
</configuration>
```

What is nice about the `web.config` file is that now, regardless of what a server-level administrator might decide about directory browsing, the Default Web Site pages will allow browsing thanks to the custom `web.config` file. Now, this is possible only because the `applicationhost.config` file is generously "allowing" the `overrideMode` on the `directoryBrowse` configuration. If the server-level administrator really wanted to control your site's behavior, they could modify the `applicationhost.config` file so that the site level administrator could not change the `directoryBrowse` setting (by changing `overrideModule="Deny"`). There will be more about administration in a bit.

Hosting Multiple Websites

There are many reasons to host multiple sites on a single IIS 7 server. Sometimes it is simply a matter of making the most of your hardware potential. Another strategy may be to host the same site on multiple servers in order to establish a workload-balanced web server farm. And then do the same for a second site, a third site, and on and on. When it comes to hosting multiple sites, several decisions must be made to assure smooth administration and delivery of the content. First, delegating administration allows distribution of duties so that administrators do not become overwhelmed with the responsibilities associated with multiple sites. Distributed management may even be a political *requirement* of the environment. Second, if a site is going to be deployed to multiple servers (such as in a web server farm design), then settling on a preferred deployment method can streamline the process and enforce consistency. Uniqueness of site bindings, application pool account assignment, and authentication processes round out some of the other points that should be settled before embarking on multiple-site hosting.

Deploying Sites

One of the benefits of the new configuration design in IIS 7 is that site configuration as well as content can all be located in the same directory. The site-specific `web.config` file now contains both website configuration as well as ASP.NET configuration, so all necessary site settings are self-contained. The point here is that you can now port entire websites and their configurations between servers easily and efficiently!

Another improvement in IIS 7 is the replacement of the old IIS_WPG local group with the IIS_IUSRS group. The new IIS_IUSRS built-in group receives each process as a member at runtime, and it is through this membership that the process receives access to the website's configuration files and content. Since the IIS_IUSRS built-in group uses the same SID on all Windows Server 2008 operating systems, deploying sites to new servers no longer requires extensive redefining of directory permissions!

To disable automatic insertion of process identities as members into the IIS_IUSRS built-in group at runtime, enable `manualGroupMembership` by changing the following:

```
<applicationPools>
    <add name="DefaultAppPool">
        <processModel manualGroupMembership="true" />
    </add>
</applicationPools>
```

This is one of those defaults that need to be edited directly in the `applicationhost.config` file, because it is not exposed in the IIS Manager GUI.

If you are a big fan of raw file copy, then the CLI utility `xcopy.exe` may be your choice for porting IIS 7 websites between servers. But there may be a better way. The new Microsoft Web Deployment Tool (`msdeploy.exe`) is available in 32-bit or 64-bit versions and fully supports both IIS 6 and 7 for upgrading, synchronizing, or moving entire websites. In fact, the Deployment Tool can be custom configured to migrate IIS supporting structure such as registry keys and ACLs as well. To investigate the Web Deployment Tool beyond this book, see the following Internet sites:

- ◆ For a full dissertation on the Microsoft Web Deployment Tool: `www.iis.net/extensions/WebDeploymentTool`

- ◆ To download the Microsoft Web Deployment Tool: `www.microsoft.com/downloads/details.aspx?displaylang=en&FamilyID=32a781a2-4961-49fc-b34d-170bfa78414f`

In addition to migrating or porting websites, the new Web Deployment Tool also has the capability of producing a *snapshot*, or archive, of a website. Although this snapshot is no substitute for a dependable backup strategy, it can provide a quick copy of a website for troubleshooting, for recovery, or to be deployed onto another machine. The new Deployment Tool can be installed in remote service mode or offline mode. Offline mode is nothing more than using `msdeploy.exe` to create a snapshot of a website and manually copying that snapshot to another server. Remote service mode allows `msdeploy.exe` to be executed from a destination server and request data from the source server running the dependency *remote service* (which has a startup type of Manual and status of Not Started by default). The remote service listens on `http://+:80/MSDEPLOY/` by default, but a custom URL can be specified during installation.

Before using `msdeploy.exe` to port a website, you may need to identify a list of any dependency components that would need to be in place on the target destination server in order for the site to function properly in its new habitat. The CLI syntax to view a list of dependencies is as follows:

```
Msdeploy -verb:getDependencies -source:apphostconfig="{site name}"
```

Once you have assured that all dependency objects have been successfully set up on the destination server, you can now use `msdeploy.exe` to synchronize the site from one IIS 7.5 instance to another:

1. Take an archive of the existing site on the destination (*if* any copying has been done in the past):

```
Msdeploy -verb:sync -source:apphostconfig="{site name}"
-dest:archivedir={path}
```

2. Run a mock synchronization to validate activity prior to actually copying data:

```
Msdeploy -verb:sync -source:archivedire={path}
-dest:apphostconfig="site name" -whatif > {filename}.log
```

3. Once the log file has been approved, synchronize the source site to the destination:

```
Msdeploy -verb:sync -source:archivedire={path} -dest:apphostconfig="site name"
```

The aforementioned method will synchronize from an `msdeploy.exe`-generated archive or snapshot to an IIS 7 instance destination—well, so long as the source and destination servers are full editions of Windows Server 2008, full editions of Windows Server 2008 R2, or Server Core editions of Windows Server 2008 R2. The `msdeploy.exe` utility requires .NET Framework 2.0 SP1+, which is unsupported on Windows Server 2008 Server Core (non-R2), so you will need to stick with `xcopy` as the method of copying websites. Consider employing the following switches to be sure `xcopy` transfers all the pertinent file information:

- The /E switch to include all subdirectories

- The /S switch if you want to ignore empty directories for improved performance

- The /O switch to copy file ownership and ACL information in such an environment

Site Uniqueness

Earlier in this chapter we discussed defining multiple sites within a single instance of IIS by employing unique site bindings, namely, selecting a particular IP address configured on one or more NIC interfaces or specifying a custom "non-80" TCP port number or by adding a custom host header to the new site. Although they assist in correctly routing requests, TCP/IP bindings are not the only way to differentiate a site from other sites on the same server.

Recall that by default the creation of a new website automatically creates a new application pool for the new site and spells the application pool name the same as the site's name. Keeping in mind that new application pools are created according to the application pool defaults mentioned earlier in this chapter, you can affect the identity of all new application pools by editing the Identity property in the Application Pool Defaults settings (Figure 16.10). The default Identity value in IIS 7 is the new Application Pool Identity Account (autogenerated during pool creation), but this can be altered to LocalService, LocalSystem, NetworkService, or a named account of your choice.

FIGURE 16.10
Application Pool
Defaults dialog box

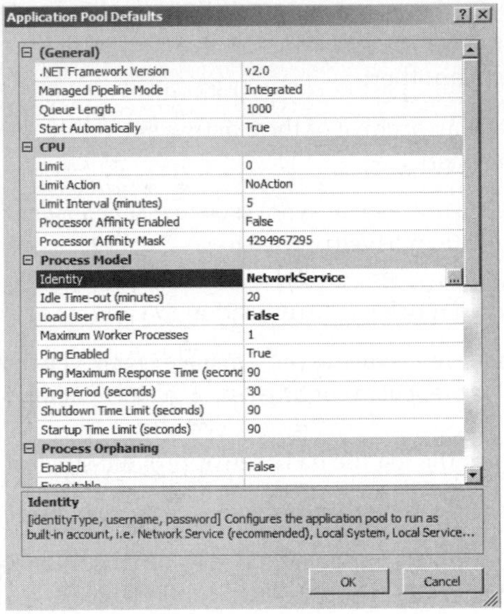

Setting Up an Anonymous Account

Now that we have discussed how you can apply a specific user account to an application pool either during creation (uniquely or via the application pool defaults), wouldn't it be nice to employ that same user account for more than simply application pool identity? By the old IIS 6.0 definition, you would expect to see an IUSR_*machinename* account in Windows that is automatically assigned to all anonymous activity. However, IUSR_*machinename* has now been replaced with the IUSR account to avoid deployment issues in a multiweb server farm. You can still create an IUSR_*machinename* account for backward compatibility if you must, but beware that you will be limiting that account's capabilities in nontrusted domains.

> ### 🌐 Real World Scenario
>
> #### Managing Multiple Sites for Bigfirm
>
> Remember that the "Oranges" site needed the HTTP redirection module because you plan to establish a new oranges site and eventually roll onto it. You cannot build the new oranges site with the same IP address, TCP port, and host header as the current "Oranges" site. That would just be wrong on so many levels!
>
> Imagine you are auditing the "Oranges" site for I/O access and process initialization. Because the "Oranges" site can be configured to use a unique application pool and because each application pool can be configured to identify itself by a unique account credential, narrowing a long log file down to the exact website issuing the error can be simplified by using application pool identities.

It may prove advantageous for developing ASP.NET applications on your new site or for differentiating between applications running in the same site to set the anonymous account to something other than IUSR. This can be accomplished by assigning the user account of your choice to the authentication properties of the site:

1. Launch IIS Manager, and expand the IIS server in the Connections pane on the left.

2. Expand the Sites folder, and highlight Oranges. The center pane becomes the home page of the site in Features view by default.

3. Double-click the Authentication icon, and highlight Anonymous Authentication in the list of providers.

4. Click the Edit hyperlink in the Actions pane on the right.

5. Set the anonymous credential either to a specific user or to the application pool identity (see Figure 16.11).

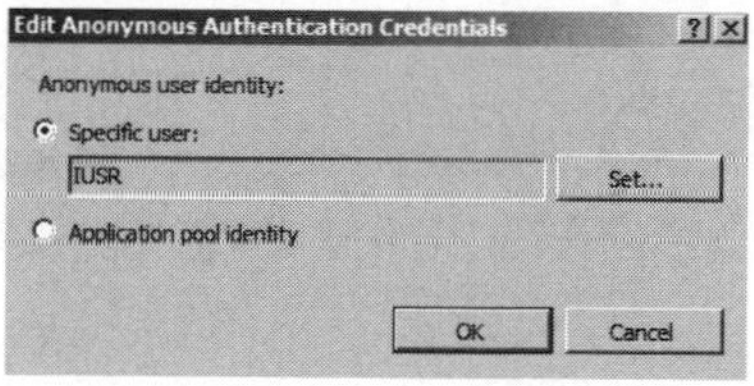

FIGURE 16.11
Edit Anonymous
Authentication
Credentials
dialog box

The "Application pool identity" choice for the anonymous credential might come in handy on a website that supports multiple applications, each of which uses a unique application pool that is configured with a unique service account. Now your audit reports would show exactly which application within a site may be suffering abuse by anonymous visitors.

Delegating Administration

In a large IIS environment supported by a legion of IT administrators, it stands to reason that different personnel may be held responsible for managing different sites. On a single instance of IIS, delegating administrative responsibilities at the site level requires that the server-level administrator unlock specific aspects of the lower site levels. Remember the brief conversation regarding feature delegation earlier in this chapter? Well, now is the time to unlock your sites.

In the server-level `applicationhost.config` file, the preferred method of unlocking specific configurable sections of lower website definitions so that they can be managed by website administrators is to add a `<location>` tag. For example, if you want to manage HTTP logging at the website by website level, you can alter the `applicationhost.config` file as follows:

```
<location path="Default Web Site" overrideMode="Allow">
        <system.webServer>
            <httpLogging />
        </system.webServer>
    </location>
```

Of course, allowing override of server-level default settings at the lower website level does not guarantee that the lower website level administrator will actually take up the challenge and manage his own logs. The successful delegation of duties requires strong training and accountability management. But at least now the `applicationhost.config` file does not prevent editing of site settings via IIS Manager.

Integrating SMTP into IIS 7 Web Pages

Before you deem the following paragraphs as mere insomnia medication for anyone other than a messaging engineer, stop to consider the breadth of network communication handled by Simple Mail Transfer Protocol (SMTP) services on your web servers to provide messaging on behalf of human users. Think of every web page you have ever visited that includes a Contact Us button graphic. There must be some service running on the web servers hosting such pages that is equipped to forward your information to interested parties (see Figure 16.12). Or when you purchase a travel reservation online, certainly it isn't just mist and magic that produces a thank-you or confirmation email in your inbox, is it?

FIGURE 16.12
Typical SMTP use on web server

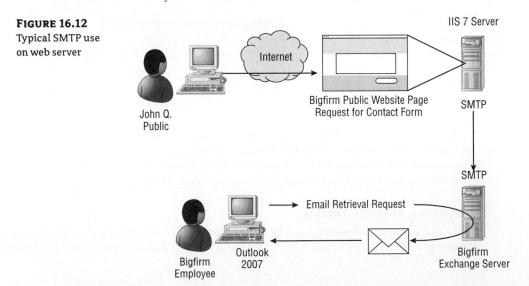

From a security standpoint, you would not want to enlist SMTP services on any web server that does not need to push messages to another SMTP host or receive messages from another SMTP host. Enabling SMTP unnecessarily would leave the server vulnerable to attacks, not to mention potentially being blacklisted on the Internet, if in fact the server were improperly exposed and registered in DNS. SMTP services are appropriate for those web servers that will handle inbound user information submitted to a website that must be forwarded to another SMTP-capable system for processing. But for those websites that need SMTP protocol support, we will cover a bit about installing the feature and enabling the necessary components on your website. However, please understand, gentle reader, that a detailed discussion about managing SMTP on Windows Server 2008 falls beyond the scope of this IIS chapter.

SMTP Is Under New Management

Although SMTP services are available in Windows Server 2008 and R2 as a server feature, actual support of the SMTP services is no longer under the umbrella of Microsoft's Internet Information Services team as in versions past. Perhaps it's because SMTP has been taken out of IIS as a subservice and been made a server feature in the OS in its own right. However, at the time of this writing, the new Windows Server 2008 OS SMTP server feature is really just the old IIS 6.0 SMTP protocol stack in a shiny new wrapper, as evidenced by its dependency on the Web Server role's IIS 6.0 Compatibility role services.

Currently, it appears the newly freed SMTP server feature has temporarily fallen through the support cracks at Microsoft. The Microsoft IIS 7 website (http://www.iis.net) and even TechNet (see http://technet.microsoft.com/en-us/library/cc772058(WS.10).aspx) offer some information for employing SMTP on an IIS 7 website, but they fall short of assisting with diagnostics, failures, or the SMTP server feature. Meanwhile, it appears that the Exchange team is now going to support SMTP on Windows Server 2008 (not the IIS or OS teams); however, this has yet to materialize in any support media from the Exchange folks unless the server in question is, in fact, an Exchange server (which most web servers are not).

So, what does this mean to you? Independent forums or external resources such as Microsoft Valued Professionals (MVPs) may be your best avenue until the question of supporting SMTP in Windows Server 2008 and R2 gets resolved at Microsoft.

Getting Started

The SMTP server feature depends on the prior successful installation of the Internet Information Services (IIS) 6.0 Manager console *and* the IIS 6 Metabase modules from the IIS 6 Management Compatibility role service of IIS 7 (among others, more about installation in a bit) in order to load. These IIS 6.0 modules use an IIS 7 configuration file named metabase.xml (%systemroot%\ System32\inetsrv), which gains several new entries upon SMTP installation. Some of the most noteworthy are as follows:

- ◆ `<IISConfigObject Location="/LM.../DisplayName">`: Sets the SMTP server feature's display name to SMTP Server

- ◆ `<IISConfigObject Location="/LM.../BindingManagerMoniker">`: Sets the event binding for the SMTP server to smtpsvc1

◆ `<IISConfigObject Location="/LM.../Sources.../DisplayName">`: Sets the bound service's OS object display name to smtpsvc1

◆ `<IISSmtpService Location="/LM/SmtpSvc"`: Contains all the settings for the SMTP services (such as timeouts, max connections, NTAuthenticationProviders, and options)

◆ `<IISSmtpServer Location="/LM/SmtpSvc/1"...>`: Contains mail settings for the SMTP services (such as directories, TCP port, and route settings)

Managing the SMTP Server service could be performed by directly editing the `metabase. xml` file, but there is an easier way: the Internet Information Services (IIS) 6.0 Manager console (see Figure 16.13). This is basically the same console used by past administrators to configure the SMTP services that shipped with IIS 6.0. To expose the SMTP node, simply expand the server node of the SMTP hosting machine you want to configure in the tree pane on the left of the console.

FIGURE 16.13
Internet Information Services (IIS) 6.0 Manager console

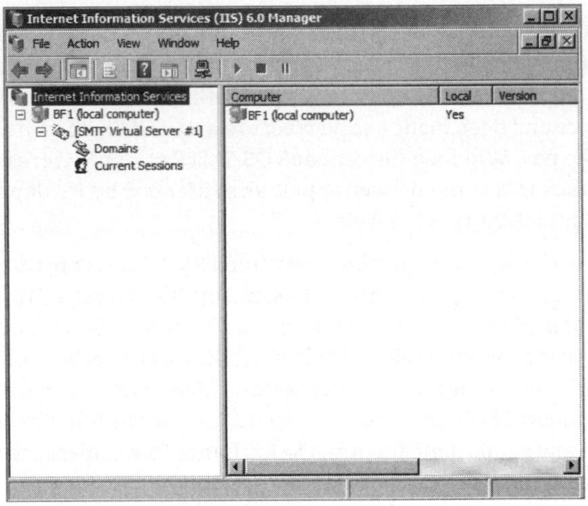

The first thing you will notice is that the SMTP service installs in a Manual startup configuration and is most likely initially stopped, as indicated by a red *x* graphic on the node icon, if you performed less than a full IIS 7 installation. To configure the startup parameters, you should configure the service itself using the Services console from the Administrative Tools program group (see Figure 16.14).

If you install more than the prerequisite IIS 7 role services, the SMTP service startup behavior differs upon installation. Specifically, if you install all IIS 7 Web Server role services, then SMTP services will start immediately upon adding the SMTP feature, even though the service configuration has a startup setting of Manual. And although this may be helpful initially, the first time the web server gets rebooted, you'll be wondering why your SMTP services did not restart on their own as well. So, consider changing the startup setting of the service from Manual to Automatic.

Adding the SMTP Server Feature

In addition to IIS 7's role services of IIS 6 Metabase Compatibility and the Internet Information Services (IIS) 6.0 Manager console, the SMTP feature also requires the SMTP Server Tools feature. Server Manager utilities, both GUI and CLI, are kind enough to install these dependencies during SMTP installation. However, if you choose to use one of the CLI utilities that do not, such as `ocsetup.exe`, you must be sure to install all necessary role services and features in order to successfully enable SMTP services. The SMTP Server Tools feature provides the snap-in to the Internet Information Services (IIS) 6.0 Manager console needed to administer SMTP services. To install this required SMTP Server Tools feature using the GUI, select SMTP Server Tools from the Feature Administration Tools group under the Remote Server Administration Tools group when running the Add Features Wizard. Could Microsoft have hidden it any deeper?

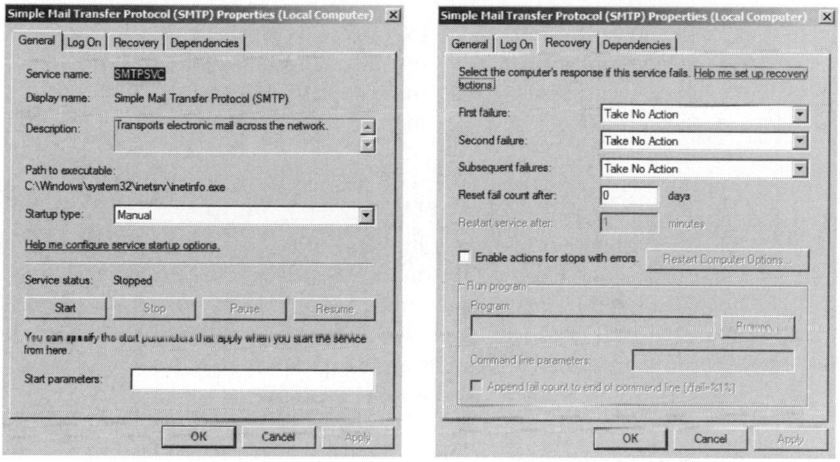

FIGURE 16.14
Simple Mail Transfer Protocol (SMTP) service properties

A WORD ABOUT OS SERVICE CONFIGURATION

The default OS name for the SMTP service is SMTPSVC with a display name of Simple Mail Transfer Protocol (SMTP), and it has a dependency on the IIS Admin service. By default it authenticates as the Local System account, is enabled for all hardware profiles, and has no recovery options configured. To protect SMTP services availability on your websites, consider configuring restart recovery options as you would any mission-critical service.

WHEN MINIMUM REQUIREMENTS AREN'T *REALLY* ENOUGH

The minimal installation of only the IIS 6.0 Metabase Compatibility and the Internet Information Services (IIS) 6.0 Manager console role services for IIS 7 will not be enough to employ the IIS 7 feature named SMTP E-mail on your websites. In fact, not even a default installation of the Web Server role will provide enough role services to facilitate configuring SMTP support on your sites! Microsoft's answer is a complete installation of all IIS 7 role services in order to incorporate SMTP into a website. Talk about a security concern! Thankfully, you can disable needless site features in the `applicationhost.config`, root `web.config`, or site-specific `web.config` files to harden the server.

To install the SMTP Server feature via the Server Manager GUI, simply right-click the Features node and choose Add Features, or click the Add Features link in the details pane to launch the Add Features Wizard. Should you instead decide to install the SMTP Server feature via CLI, be sure to right-click the Command Prompt shortcut and choose Run As Administrator launch the CLI with elevated privileges if you are not logged in as the built-in Administrator account. Otherwise, your endeavor will be a very short trip. The following are syntax examples of using ServerManagerCMD to install both the prerequisite Web Server role services and the SMTP features:

```
ServerManagerCMD.exe –install Web-Metabase
ServerManagerCMD.exe –install Web-Lgcy-Mgmt-Console
ServerManagerCMD.exe –install RSAT-SMTP
ServerManagerCMD.exe –install SMTP-Server
```

Setting Up an SMTP Server

Once installed, you can customize the SMTP Server configuration and build additional domain support via the Internet Information Services (6.0) Manager console. Though the service itself is maintained in this console, embedding SMTP services onto an IIS 7 website takes place elsewhere (you'll look deeper into that in a moment). Navigating the Internet Information Services (6.0) Manager console is a nostalgic trip down memory lane because the interface is the same console from IIS 6.0 in Windows Server 2003.

VIRTUAL SERVERS AND DOMAINS

The SMTP Server feature offers mail transfer capability per the configuration settings of a SMTP virtual server. By default, only one SMTP virtual server is created during SMTP installation, but you can create additional virtual servers if you will be hosting mail for different domain names and need them all to be configured separately. Within each SMTP virtual server, one or more domains must exist to associate the related file system directory for mail delivery to a particular fully qualified domain name (FQDN). By default, the initially created SMTP virtual server will house only one domain—that of the resident machine's FQDN.

Differing security and delivery limit requirements of additional domains may dictate that they be serviced by separate SMTP virtual servers. Before deciding which domains should be governed by which SMTP virtual server, you should know what the virtual server settings are that will affect the domains. Each new virtual server will store its configuration settings in the IIS 6.0–compatible metabase.xml file under a separate IIsSmtpServer element with a Location attribute of /LM/SmtpSvc/{number} where {number} is a sequential integer assigned to new virtual servers in creation order. Feel free to create as many virtual servers as can be assigned to unique combinations of IP addresses and TCP port numbers supported by the server.

If instead you find that all email conforms to the same restrictions and limitations and can be serviced by a single virtual server, then using the default SMTP Virtual Server #1 constructed during feature installation is the easiest way to go. Simply add as many domains as must be supported for message routing to the Domains folder underneath the default virtual server. You can create a new domain into the folder by right-clicking the Domains folder and choosing to create a new domain via the New SMTP Domain Wizard. The wizard will identify the following:

Domain Type Remote or alias

Domain Name x400-compliant fully qualified address space of mail to be delivered by the new domain (be sure DNS is configured to resolve)

Upon completing the wizard, enter the new domain's properties to specify whether it must adhere to drop directory quota limits set forth in its resident virtual server's configuration settings. Each new domain will garner its own IIsSmtpDomain element in the `metabase.xml` configuration file.

SOME CHANGES REQUIRE SERVICE RESTART

Adding SMTP virtual servers and/or domains to Windows Server 2008 will not take effect until the SMTP services are stopped and restarted. The Internet Information Services (IIS) 6.0 Manager console offers a quick method of restarting all IIS services by right-clicking the computer name at the top of the tree pane, choosing All Tasks, and then selecting Restart IIS.

AUTHENTICATION

SMTP services can be configured to demand authentication from other SMTP hosts attempting to transfer messages to it for security. By default, only anonymous access is permitted, allowing any and all SMTP servers that want to push email messages for supported domain namespaces to flood the drop directory with items. In a secure environment and for auditing purposes, you may need to enforce an authentication method so that other SMTP hosts are required to identify themselves before being allowed to forward messages to your SMTP service.

Adding the SMTP E-mail Feature to an IIS 7 Website

Once both the SMTP feature and the entire Web Server role set of role services have been installed, the SMTP E-mail feature will appear in the Internet Information Services (IIS) Manager console for IIS 7 websites. Despite the SMTP virtual servers' state(s), the SMTP E-mail feature can be enabled or disabled for the entire IIS server or for only a few chosen sites or web applications. Global settings for SMTP defined at the server-level `applicationhost.config` file can be inherited by one or more websites.

The SMTP E-mail feature is listed at the server level under the area entitled ASP.NET (see Figure 16.15). From the Features view, the Actions menu for the SMTP E-mail feature, like any other feature, offers quick links to open the feature's settings page, restart/start/stop the feature, view application pools that are configured to service the feature, view sites that have been configured to use the feature, or get help about SMTP email.

Upon opening the SMTP E-mail feature's settings page (see Figure 16.16), you can set the configuration parameters shown in Table 16.6.

FIGURE 16.15
Server-level
features for BF1
IIS 7.0 server

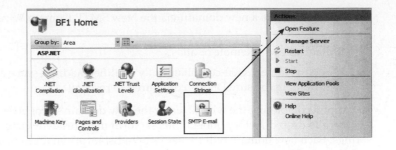

TABLE 16.6: SMTP E-mail Feature Settings

SETTING	POSSIBLE VALUES	PURPOSE
E-mail address	A valid email box address from the sending domain	Declare the "sent from" email address that will be used when IIS 7.0 sends email from a web application.
Deliver e-mail to SMTP server: SMTP Server	A functioning SMTP server Note: Select the "Use localhost" check box to use the SMTP services on this same server.	Declare an SMTP server handling the domain declared on the "E-mail address" setting.
Port	Any available TCP port number Default = 25	Declare the TCP port on which the SMTP server will be listening for SMTP traffic.
Authentication Settings	Not Required Windows Specify credentials	Declare the authentication method supported by the SMTP server. Enter a username and password for "Specify credentials."
Store e-mail in pickup directory	Valid file system directory	An alternative to delivering email to the SMTP server. Holds email instead in a file system directory for later pickup by a mail retrieval application.

Once configured at the server level, individual websites and web applications can be modified to send email to alternate SMTP servers or support different domain namespaces in their email addresses. Simply click the SMTP E-mail feature icon at any website or web application to alter the mail behavior for that entity. In fact, you might even consider scheduling appcmd.exe commands to automate modifications to SMTP E-mail feature settings.

Integrating FTP into IIS 7 Web Pages

With the popularity of glossy graphics and endless streaming on today's Internet, you might think that the good old FTP protocol has become a thing of the past. But the tried-and-true act of a simple file transfer still holds a sentimental, if not functional, place in our hearts. And although it is true that many web applications developed in today's market make use of complex ASP.NET programming code to hide the actual movement of data between the server and client systems, sometimes the old adage "less is more" rings true when it comes to managing file transfers in a heterogeneous network. Microsoft has made FTP 7 more versatile than its predecessor version and given you new security tools that will help protect data access and transport while keeping the user experience streamlined and easy. For example, FTP 7 now supports IPv6 for improved packet construction and UTF-8 for improved response, as well as Windows Server 2008 disk quota integration for improved storage management. A deeper dive into the FTP services falls beyond the scope of this IIS chapter, so let's just take a quick look at incorporating FTP features into IIS 7 websites.

FIGURE 16.16
SMTP E-mail
feature's
settings page

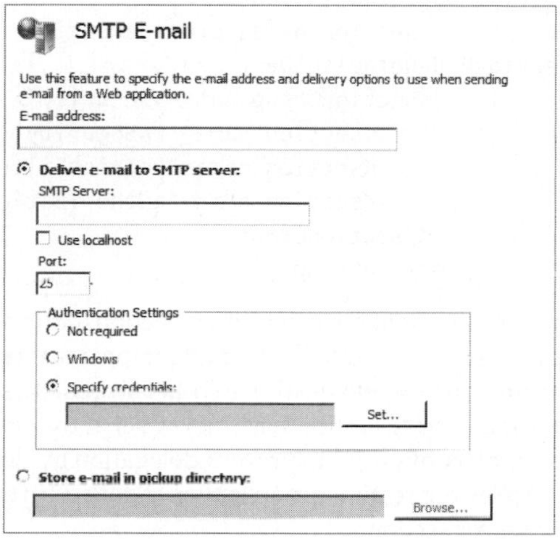

The FTP7 File Transfer Publishing Service

In Windows Server 2008, FTP 7 is a separate download available at www.iis.net that requires installation (whereas in Windows Server 2008 R2, FTP 7 is included in IIS 7.5 out of the box). Assuming you execute the downloaded .msi on Windows Server 2008 and accept all default settings, there will be little indication in Server Manager that anything important has happened to the server. The new FTP 7 application is not listed as a role or feature. In fact, burrowing into the Web Server (IIS) role and taking a look at the role services listed doesn't reflect the recent FTP 7 installation either. The only FTP role services listed are those for the old FTP module based on IIS 6 (and they show as uninstalled because you cannot run both versions simultaneously). But a quick look at the Application log in Event Viewer or the applicationhost.config file will prove that FTP 7 is, indeed, installed.

In Windows Server 2008 R2, FTP 7 has been incorporated into IIS 7.5, so you need only add the FTP role service to the Web Server role in order to take advantage of simple file transfers via your websites. Since we covered adding role services to IIS 7 earlier in this chapter, let's not digress. But as with all features, roles, and role services, do not add FTP to your web server unless you truly need to employ it on a website; otherwise, you could be introducing a security vulnerability. The FTP role service can be added to Windows Server 2008 R2 Server Core as well.

Once FTP 7 has been installed or the role service added (R2), the server-level `applicationhost.config` file will contain two new sections, the first of which outlines the structure of the second:

```
Section Group Definition

<sectionGroup name="system.ftpServer">
        <section name="log" allowDefinition="AppHostOnly"
  overrideModeDefault="Deny" />
        <section name="firewallSupport" allowDefinition="AppHostOnly"
  overrideModeDefault="Deny" />
        <section name="caching" allowDefinition="AppHostOnly"
  overrideModeDefault="Deny" />
        <section name="providerDefinitions" allowDefinition="AppHostOnly"
  overrideModeDefault="Deny" />
            <sectionGroup name="security">
                <section name="ipSecurity" overrideModeDefault="Deny" />
                <section name="requestFiltering" overrideModeDefault="Deny" />
                <section name="authorization" overrideModeDefault="Deny" />
            </sectionGroup>
        </sectionGroup>
</sectionGroup>
```

In the first `sectionGroup` definition section, notice that all the configuration sections are only allowed to be defined in `applicationhost.config` as a global IIS setting (allowDefinition=AppHostOnly). In other words, these configuration settings cannot be inherited from `machine.config` (entire machine) or set at the site level in `web.config`. Notice also that these sections are all configured to prevent delegation by default (overrideModeDefault=Deny). The new `system.ftpServer` section group is then detailed further down in the `applicationhost.config` file's FTP server section:

```
FTP Server Section

<system.ftpServer>
        <providerDefinitions>
            <add name="IisManagerAuth" type="Microsoft.Web.FtpServer.Security.
  IisManagerAuthenticationProvider,
  Microsoft.Web.FtpServer,version=7.0.0.0,Culture=neutral,
  PublicKeyToken=31bf3856ad364e35" />
            <add name="AspNetAuth" type="Microsoft.Web.FtpServer.Security.
  AspNetFtpMembershipProvider,
  Microsoft.Web.FtpServer,version=7.0.0.0,Culture=neutral,
  PublicKeyToken=31bf3856ad364e35" />
        </providerDefinitions>
        <security>
            <requestFiltering>
                <hiddenSegments>
                    <add segment="_vti_bin" />
                </hiddenSegments>
            </requestFiltering>
        </security>
    </system.ftpServer>
```

In the second section, the only default authentication providers are IisManagerAuth (new to IIS 7, you can manage non-AD user accounts in IIS Manager for your FTP users) and AspNetAuth (for forms-based authentication in ASP.NET applications). Furthermore, a default `requestFiltering` of `_vti_bin` prevents clients from accessing this segment of a URL. Additionally, the `administration.config` file found in the `%systemdrive%\windows\system32\inetsrv\config` directory will have several new FTP moduleProvider listings added to it. These new listings coincide with the management icons shown in the FTP area of the IIS Manager console (see Figure 16.17) and specify the libraries available for module management.

FIGURE 16.17

IIS Manager:
FTP area

Adding FTP to an IIS 7 Website

One of the advantages of the new FTP 7 Publishing service is that you can now add FTP functionality to an existing website in IIS 7 right alongside HTTP! From the Actions pane in the IIS Manager console, you need simply click the Add FTP Publishing link to kick off FTP configuration for the HTTP site. Before you add file transfer, however, you need to make some preliminary decisions.

First, because FTP will be a separate protocol, you must identify a unique set of bindings for the services. Namely, the IP address, port number, and virtual host must be planned. Yes, we said virtual host. New to FTP 7, the FTP services can operate under a custom header name much like HTTP sites, making it easier for users to correctly connect to friendly-named sites. Also, you must decide whether the FTP site starts automatically and whether to engage SSL. Notice in Figure 16.18 that SSL is not an all-or-nothing proposition. You can select either the Require SSL (thus alienating clients who are unable to participate in SSL) or soften the security by choosing Allow SSL (which offers unsecure file transfer for those clients who cannot participate in SSL).

FIGURE 16.18

Add FTP Site
Publishing
dialog box

Second, you must plan whether to allow the embedded FTP 7 Publishing service to accept anonymous connections and support basic clear-text authentication strings. You can also limit access to anonymous users only or specific users/groups (see Figure 16.19). Additionally, you must decide whether allowed users may contribute or only read.

FIGURE 16.19
FTP site authentication and authorization

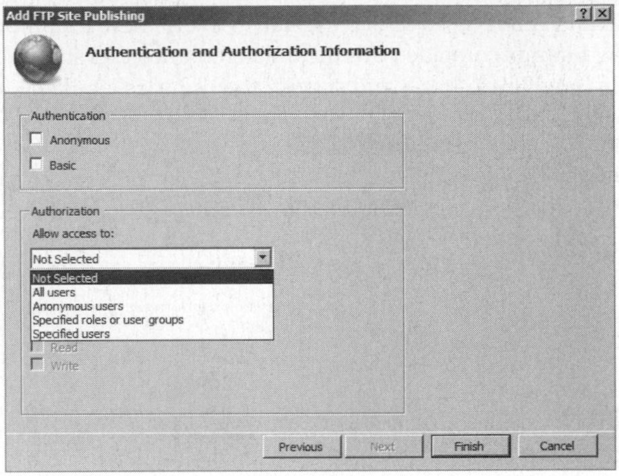

To prove that FTP 7 Publishing services have been successfully embedded into the R&D website, in the Connections pane you need expand the application to which FTP was added. A new group of icons for FTP management now appear in the Features view. FTP authorization rules allows you to configure more rules that will either allow or deny a specific group of users a particular permission-level of access to the FTP services on this site. FTP IPv4 address and domain restrictions allow you to restrict FTP services to only a particular IP address or subnet range.

As an alternative method of creating a new FTP 7 Publishing service site, you could use the CLI utility appcmd.exe. Some benefits of using the command line as the creation method include scripting, automation, and remote management. For example, to create a new FTP site named FTPTest with default parameters and using a custom port number of 2121 with an explicit physical directory of c:\FTPTest, the syntax would look something like this:

```
appcmd.exe add site /name:FTPTest /bindings:ftp/*:2121 /physicalPath:C:\FTPTest
```

Keep in mind the new FTP site will be created with the next available ID number since this syntax did not specify one. Also, the default authentication protocols and authorization entities will be configured. Another method of automating creation of FTP 7 sites is by using WMI scripts. The same site example as earlier would be as follows:

```
Set oService = GetObject("winmgmts:root\WebAdministration")
Set oBinding = oService.Get("BindingElement").SpawnInstance_
  oBinding.BindingInformation="*:2121:accounting"
oBinding.Protocol = "ftp"
oService.Get("Site").Create "FTPTest", array(oBinding), "c:\FTPTest"
```

Remember, FTP 7 is a powerful role service in its own right, and there is much to consider when employing it on your web server. Entire chapters and short books have been written on the FTP 7 product! Though a deeper dive into administration and security of FTP 7 falls outside the scope of this IIS chapter, you would be wise to brush up on the protocol before you unwittingly open your websites up to potential vulnerabilities.

Advanced Administration

So far, we have covered a great deal of information about installing and configuring IIS 7 as well as site creation and management. But there are still a few loose ends we need to tie up. The beauty of IIS 7 administration is the bevy of tools Microsoft offers to accommodate a multitude of engineering tastes. For GUI aficionados, there is the very powerful IIS Manager. For engineers more comfortable in the CLI, you have appcmd.exe and WMI. For Server Core managers, there are the Optional Component List and Optional Component Setup utilities. And for developers savvy in XML, there is always direct editing of the *.config files. The list doesn't seem to end.

And although it may be a comforting thought to believe that any time you need to manage IIS 7, the server will be readily accessible and you can perform all of your maintenance from its keyboard, the reality is most administrators prefer the convenience of remote management over the reliability of local administration on the server itself. The new Web Management Service (WMSVC) in IIS 7 allows a remote connection into a Windows Server 2008 or Windows 7 installation of IIS (not Vista) by using the IIS Manager GUI console. Of course, the traditional Remote Administration and VPN approaches of remotely connecting to the operating system are still a possibility, but why introduce the extra bandwidth utilization if you don't have to? Considering that WMSVC uses a static TCP port assignment, punching the firewall for remote access from the beach seems easier than maintaining a VPN or RDP connection.

But if your heart is set on full OS access while remotely managing your IIS installation, Microsoft offers a robust remote management platform called Windows Remote Management (WinRM) that provides SOAP-based access to the Windows Server 2008 R2 OS across commonly allowed firewall port calls. WinRM became available on Windows Server 2003 R2 but had to be added to the OS in Control Panel. Windows Remote Management uses WMI calls to remotely manage hardware via baseboard management controllers (BMCs). Windows Remote Management falls out of the scope of this chapter, but it is very cool. For more information on using WinRM, see http://msdn.microsoft.com/library/aa384426.aspx.

Using Web Management Services

Before you can sit at your desk in your comfy leather chair and launch an IIS Manager console that will connect to your IIS Server down the hall, you must do some prep work. The days of IIS 6.0 are gone, and the new versions do not automatically allow remote administration. The basic tasks you need to perform to set up remote management services are the following:

1. Install WMSVC.

2. Enable remote connectivity.

3. Configure optional settings.

4. Start WMSVC.

Although the last task may seem to go without saying, the order of its execution is paramount. Try not to get overzealous and start the newly installed WMSVC service before configuring it. The service cannot be altered while it is running.

To install WMSVC onto the IIS server, add the Management Service role service to the Web Server role in the OS. We covered different methods of adding role services earlier in this chapter. Recall that the Management Service role service is not available on Windows Server 2008 R2 Server Core. To enable remote connectivity on full editions of Windows Server 2008 and 2008 R2, follow these steps:

1. Launch IIS Manager, and click the IIS server to be remotely managed in the Connections pane on the left. The center pane becomes the home page of the server in Features view by default (see Figure 16.20).

2. Double-click the Management Service icon under the Management area.

3. Select the Enable Remote Connections check box (see Figure 16.21).

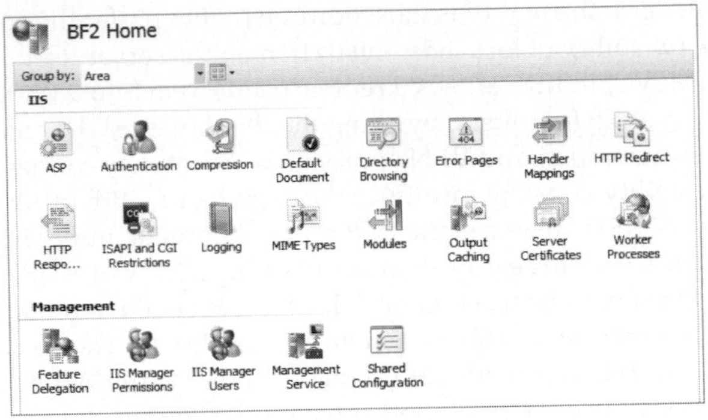

FIGURE 16.20
Server home in
IIS Manager

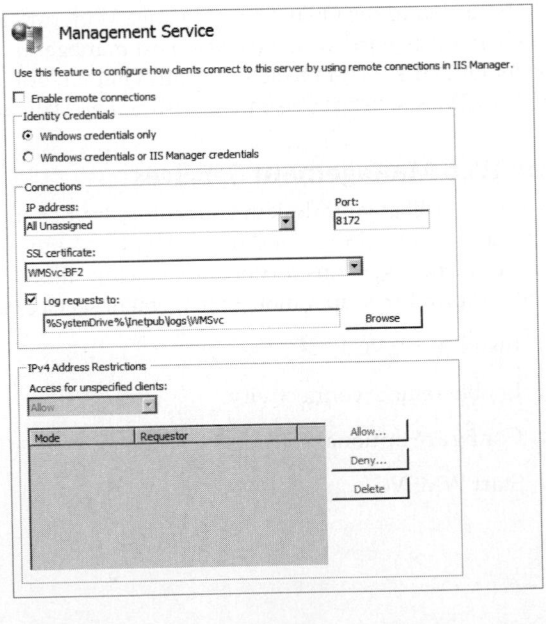

FIGURE 16.21
Management
Service

You can also enable remote connectivity by setting the EnableRemoteManagement dword data value to 00000001in the following registry key:

```
HKEY_LOCAL_MACHINE\Software\Microsoft\WebManagement\{server}
```

Optional WMSVC settings you may want to configure include binding the service to a custom IP address or TCP port structure. By default, WMSVC listens on TCP port 8172 across all IP addresses on the server. Or you may want to explicitly list the IPv4 addresses allowed to connect as well as whether WMSVC will accept both Windows credentials and IIS Manager credentials. To configure optional settings, follow these steps:

1. Launch IIS Manager, and click the IIS server to be remotely managed in the Connections pane on the left. The center pane becomes the home page of the server in Features view by default.

2. Double-click the Management Service icon under the Management area.

Once all configuration settings are complete, start WMSVC as you would any other service. For your convenience, there is a Start hyperlink in the Actions pane when IIS Manager is focused on Management Service. And just for the record, `net start` commands still work in Windows Server 2008 R2!

Once WMSVC is running on the IIS server, even a Windows Server 2008 R2 Server Core server, you can connect any IIS Manager console GUI to the IIS server by following these steps:

1. Launch IIS Manager on the remote computer.

2. On the Welcome home page of IIS Manager, click the "Connect to a server" hyperlink under the "Connection tasks" section.

3. Provide the IIS server's name to which you want to connect.

4. Provide credentials for the connection.

BEWARE OF MULTIPLE CONNECTIONS

Allowing too many concurrent connections into WMSVC is a recipe for conflicting administration. Consider limiting WMSVC to receive connections only from specific administrators' machines, and train those administrators!

Connecting, Securing, Auditing

In the grand scheme of securing a website, many factors play an important role in keeping the site content safe from harm. First, and most obvious, are visitor permissions while on the site. Additionally, there are encryption settings that protect data during transport, and services that will help you keep the IIS server from overloading and crashing. Lastly, there is the small matter of backing up the site configuration and content to recover in the wake of a disaster.

IIS 7.5 introduces some new authentication parameters and failed request tracing to assist administrators in becoming proactive toward user access needs. Windows Server 2008 R2 can now take advantage of the Windows System Resource Manager (WSRM) to manage resource utilization being usurped by IIS. Feature delegation restricts elevated privilege to site configurations, while user permissions dictate access to the content.

AUTHENTICATION

Several possible authentication mechanisms are available on an IIS 7 website. Table 16.7 outlines the differences between authentication methods.

TABLE 16.7:   Authentication Methods

FEATURE METHOD	PURPOSE
AD Client Certificate	This maps AD users to client certificates.
Anonymous	The visitor doesn't need to supply credentials.
ASP.NET Impersonate	This runs ASP.NET applications under an alternative security context (instead of the default ASP.NET account).
Basic	The visitor must provide the username and password (transported in plain clear text).
Digest	The visitor must provide AD username and password (HTTP 1.1 browser required); the password does not traverse medium.
Forms	The client-side redirection transparently forwards user to HTML form into which they enter credentials before transparently transferring back to the page requested.
Windows	NTLM or Kerberos authenticates Windows username and password.

Choose the authentication method wisely for your site. If you select an authentication method that is less secure, unwanted visitors may get in. If you select an authentication method that is too strict, you may inadvertently alienate valid visitors.

PERMISSIONS

You can use the IIS Manager Permissions page in IIS Manager to grant IIS Manager user objects, Windows user accounts, or Windows group objects the permission to connect to a site or application for the purpose of managing it. Keep in mind that only features that have been delegated ("unlocked") at the server level will be available to the permission holders for site-level administration (see Figure 16.22).

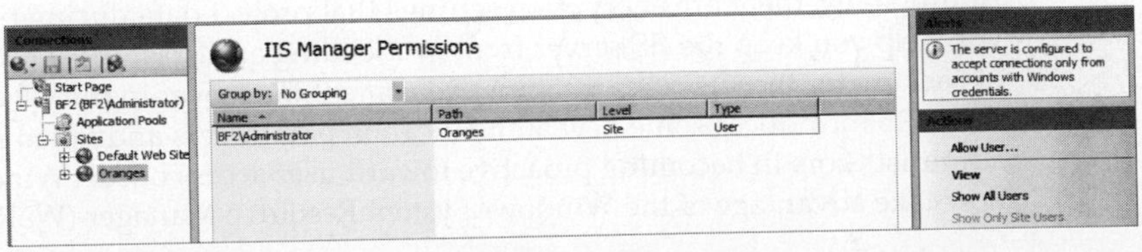

FIGURE 16.22
IIS Manager Permissions page

Permission to access a site for browsing or uploading purposes revolves around the virtual directories of the site's applications. You can manage an individual virtual directory's permission structure by following these steps:

1. Launch IIS Manager, and expand the IIS server in the Connections pane on the left.

2. Expand the Sites folder, and highlight the particular site. The center pane becomes the home page of the site in Features view by default.

3. Click the View Virtual Directories link in the Actions pane on the right.

4. Highlight (single-click) the virtual directory of choice and click the Edit Permissions hyperlink in the Actions pane on the right.

5. Set the permissions on the Security tab of the virtual directory's Properties dialog box.

You can use either the appcmd.exe command-line utility or the IIS Manager GUI to specify which features are delegated and to what degree. To delegate a feature using IIS Manager, follow these steps:

1. Launch IIS Manager, and highlight the IIS server in the Connections pane on the left. The center pane becomes the home page of the site in Features view by default.

2. Click the Feature Delegation icon in the Management area.

3. Click the feature to be delegated, and click the hyperlink in the Actions pane on the right that denotes your intended level of delegation (Read Only, Read/Write, Reset to Inherited).

Keep in mind that delegating a feature at the server level makes it possible for that feature's configuration parameters to be altered on any and all websites throughout the server that are employing the delegated feature (depending on the individual site's web.config permissions, of course). This could endanger some sites so use server-wide delegation cautiously. The appcmd command to delegate a feature is simply as follows:

```
appcmd.exe unlock config -section:{section name}  ← server-wide
```

CODE ACCESS SECURITY

You can configure the .NET trust levels to dictate a specific level of access that the .NET applications on a site will have to underlying content. You can edit the .NET trust levels in IIS Manager by clicking the .NET Trust Level icon or by editing the web.config file directly. Editing the .NET code's authority level will generate an entry into the site's web.config file. Table 16.8 outlines the possible settings for .NET trust levels and what they give away.

TABLE 16.8:   .NET Trust Levels

TRUST LEVEL	PURPOSE
Full (internal)	Access to all resources pursuant to OS security.
High (web_hightrust.config)	Cannot call code or services, write to event log, or access MSMQ, ODBC, OleDb.

TABLE 16.8:   .NET Trust Levels   *(CONTINUED)*

TRUST LEVEL	PURPOSE
Medium (web_mediumtrust.config)	High restrictions, plus cannot access files outside the application directory hierarchy, access the registry, or make network/web service calls.
Low (web_lowtrust.config)	High and medium restrictions, plus cannot write to file system and cannot call the Assert method.
Minimal (web_minimaltrust.config)	Execute permissions only by default.

INVOKING SSL

Secure Sockets Layer (SSL) protection has been around for many generations of the IIS product. By now, you likely realize that SSL is used to protect data that is passed to and from an IIS server. To invoke SSL on an IIS 7 website, you must first create an HTTPS binding on the site. To add bindings to a site, follow these steps:

1. Launch IIS Manager, and expand the IIS server in the Connections pane on the left.

2. Expand the Sites folder, and highlight the site requiring SSL.

3. In the Actions pane on the right, click Bindings.

4. Click the Add button in the Site Bindings dialog box.

5. Change the binding type from HTTP to HTTPS, and specify the certificate to be used.

Now that SSL has been bound to the website, you can fine-tune its behavior by double-clicking the SSL Settings icon on the home page of the site. Choose the bit level and whether client-side certificates will be required or even honored.

Windows System Resource Manager

Windows System Resource Manager is a tool that allows you to monitor the resource utilization of various processes occurring on a Windows Server 2008 R2 OS. For IIS 7, this means process worker threads and how badly they may be overwhelming the CPU of the server. Thankfully, WSRM is not only a passive monitoring tool, but it can also be configured to automatically allocate resources to IIS. Unfortunately, WSRM doesn't kick in until the processor load exceeds 70 percent. As long as combined efforts by multiple visitors do not cause excessive simultaneous processes, the WSRM may never invoke one of its management policies.

Use WSRM to perform the following resource management objectives, among others:

◆ Preconfigure policies to allocate CPU and RAM resources by process, user, or application pool.

◆ Define calendar rules to schedule policy enforcement with no manual reconfiguration.

♦ Invoke resource throttling policies in response to server events.

♦ Report usage data to a SQL database.

Windows System Resource Manager was originally offered in Windows Server 2003 and now has become an integral part of Windows Server 2008 Enterprise edition. The WSRM feature in the OS is not installed by default but rather must be added via Server Manager. Once installed, it can monitor processor and memory utilization by many applications, not just IIS. Windows System Resource Manager is beyond the scope of this chapter. For more information on using WSRM, see `http://technet.microsoft.com/ library/cc755056.aspx`.

Backing Up and Restoring Data

No discussion of IIS 7 would be complete without at least mentioning disaster recovery. After all, no one ever anticipates corruption or system failures, but it's best to have a plan in place for the inevitable. Luckily, the new architecture of IIS 7 makes it a rather simple network application to back up. We have already discussed taking snapshots of sites for porting; those same snapshots could be used to restore a site to a previous version. Also, the new XML configuration files reside on the NTFS file system and as such need only be backed up as part of the regular I/O backup strategy to be available in the event a recovery is necessary.

So, if it's all just a matter of backing up the configuration and content files, is there anything unique to IIS about backing up? Just one thing—the `appcmd.exe` commands that can be used to create, restore, delete, and list backups.

♦ To generate a backup, use this:

```
appcmd.exe add backup {backup name}
```

♦ To restore a backup, use this:

```
appcmd.exe restore backup {backup name}
```

♦ To delete a backup (clean up), use this:

```
appcmd.exe delete backup {backup name}
```

♦ To list backups, use this:

```
appcmd.exe list backup
```

These `appcmd.exe` commands can be written into a batch file and scheduled with the OS. But what if something goes wrong with the OS, and unbeknownst to the IIS administrator there has been no good backup created of the `applicationhost.config` file in weeks? Not to worry, IIS 7 maintains a configuration history of `applicationhost.config` according to the default schedule found in the `%windir%\system32\inetsrv\config\schema\iis_schema.xml` file. These automatic backups, for that is what they are, will appear in the results of an `appcmd.exe` list backup command along with manually generated backup files and can be restored with the `appcmd.exe` restore backup command.

By default, IIS 7 stores the automatically generated historical versions of `applicationhost.config` in the history subdirectory under `%systemdrive%\inetpub`.

This may not be the most secure location for these all important files. To redirect future history backups of `applicationhost.config` to be placed in another location, for instance `c:\myhistfiles`, execute the following command:

```
appcmd.exe set config -section:configHistory -path:"c:\myhistfiles"
```

The Bottom Line

Understand IIS 7 architecture and capabilities   IIS 7 redefined the structure of Microsoft's web server by compartmentalizing functionality and vertically managing behavior in a hierarchy. The new features of IIS 7.5 enhance application pools and include native modules for application protocols such as FTP that were absent from the previous revision. A dependency for many other services, IIS has become an integral part of the OS.

> **Master It**   Which of the following does *not* require IIS?
>
> Remote Server Administration Tools
>
> AD Rights Management Services
>
> Windows SharePoint Services 3.0
>
> Windows Management Service
>
> Federation Service

Plan for and install IIS 7.5   Relatively lean by default, IIS 7.5 must be carefully and painstakingly planned so as not to install more modular functionality than you need. More than a resource concern, leaving unnecessary role services off the server is also a method of securing your websites. As always with Microsoft, there are multiple ways to install IIS 7.5, from interactive GUI to CLI utility scripting to Windows PowerShell.

> **Master It**   You are planning a Windows Server 2008 R2 web server and need to make sure the requisite features are already installed in the OS. What three role services should you verify are installed?

Manage IIS 7's modularity and delegated administration   IIS 7.5 modules are only one piece of evidence of the product's compartmentalization. Web applications and individual configuration settings per site can be independently managed as well. A hierarchical ladder of global, web, application, and page settings allow granular administration by multiple engineers.

> **Master It**   What is feature delegation?

Create and secure websites in IIS 7   Designing and generating new websites in IIS 7.5 can be accomplished via the GUI or CLI, allowing you to automate routine site creation. Permission structure can be copied from one site to another or managed from the upper layers of the settings hierarchy to simplify permission granting. IIS 7.5 eases site generation by packaging your website.

> **Master It**   You need to create a new website that has all the characteristics of the Default Web Site but must also support ASP.NET pages. You do not want to add ASP.NET support to the Default Web Site for fear of adding vulnerability to existing web content. How would you implement this?

Manage IIS 7 with advanced administration techniques   Day-to-day site maintenance and content posting may be the bulk of your IIS 7.5 administration. But additional higher-level management is what assures consistent and uninterrupted service of your web pages. Important configuring tasks including recovering from disasters, monitoring performance, setting access or code security, and defining encryption can be accomplished either locally or remotely.

Master It   Because of limited storage space, you are revising your disaster recovery plan. You are considering delaying backups of the IIS `applicationhost.config` file to monthly. However, you are concerned that minor global configuration changes made throughout the month may get lost if a failure occurs before the monthly backup. How would you recover a mid-month edit?

Chapter 17

Watching Your System

The best time to know about a problem is before it happens. This is as true in the IT world as much as anywhere else. If you want to know about potential problems with servers before they morph into a full-blown crisis, you have to watch the servers or, said another way, *monitor* them.

With just a little bit of proactive monitoring, you can identify minor errors and negative trends before they bloom into hardcore problems.

Two monitoring tools you'll find very effective when watching your servers are Event Viewer and Performance Monitor. Event Viewer includes a sophisticated feature called *event forwarding* that you can use to monitor events from multiple servers. Performance Monitor includes powerful data collector sets that can be used for sophisticated system monitoring and reporting.

In this chapter, you will learn to:

♦ View administrative events on your system

♦ Attach a task to an event

♦ View the System Performance data collector set report

Monitoring Your System with Event Viewer

The Event Viewer in Windows Server 2008 R2 is one of the primary tools used to watch your system. Often, it's one of the first places you'll look once you realize your server has a problem, but it can also be used to proactively monitor servers. Event Viewer can often help you to quickly identify the source of a problem, or at least gain enough knowledge to know where to look next.

You can launch the Event Viewer by selecting Start ➤ Administrative Tools ➤ Event Viewer or via Server Manager in the Diagnostics node.

Figure 17.1 shows the Event Viewer with several nodes open. You can see that you have quite a selection of logs available in the Event Viewer. As the saying goes, this ain't your daddy's Event Viewer. It's significantly different from the Event Viewer available in Windows Server 2003.

The left pane shows all the selectable logs. The center pane shows the events from the selected log, and it shows information from the selected event at the bottom. The right pane shows all the available actions for the selected log or event.

Note that all the logs aren't necessarily used or may be used only for a specific purpose. As a simple example, the Setup log is used to log events only during installation. If this log is cleared, you won't ever see events here again. If you dig into some of these lesser used logs, you may indeed see they are empty, but that doesn't indicate a problem exists.

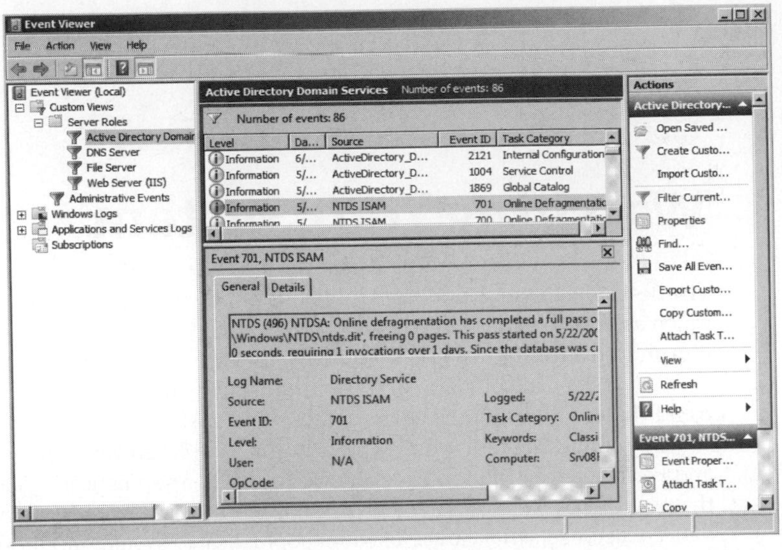

DIFFERENT LOGS AVAILABLE

Logs are dynamically added as different roles and features are added. A clean installation without any added roles or features won't have any logs in the Custom Views ➢ Server Roles node. As different roles and features are added, additional logs are added in the Applications and Services Logs node, and custom views are added in the Server Roles node.

Viewing an Event

You can double-click any event in the center pane, and a dialog box will appear providing all the details on the event. Details in many of the events are robust and much better than the generic "Contact your administrator" so many of us have seen in the past. Figure 17.2 shows an example error event.

FIGURE 17.2
Event Viewer error
providing helpful
information

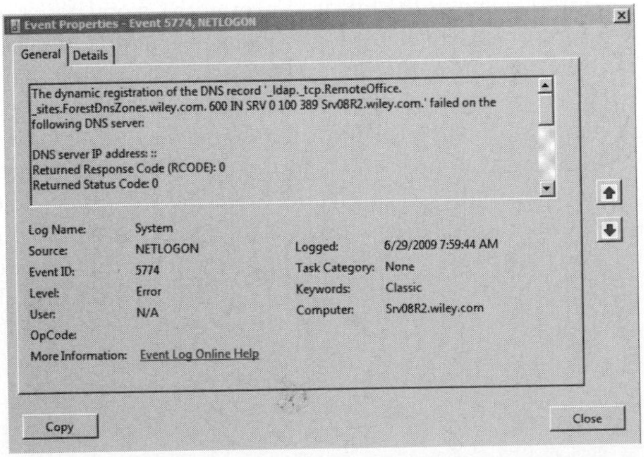

Even though this event is logged in the System log, the details point to a problem with a DNS record. It's clear that dynamic registration of the gc._msdcs.bigfirm.com record has a problem. If you know a little about Active Directory, you realize that *gc* is short for the *global catalog* and DNS records beginning with an underscore (_msdcs) are SRV (short for service) records. In other words, the SRV record used to locate the global catalog server has a problem, which can indeed be serious.

If you scroll down on the details of events, you'll see a USER ACTION section. For this event, it gives instructions to run DCDiag to identify the source of the problem and a suggestion to run nltest.exe /dsregdns or restart the netlogon service to resolve the problem.

You can also click the Event Log Online Help icon. If the server has access to the Internet, it will transmit information on the error and bring up a Microsoft TechNet page related to the error. For some of the common errors, the online check can be useful.

A neat extra feature is the ability to click the Copy button to copy all the details to the clipboard. You can then paste it into a document to easily review it or even paste it into a troubleshooting log or database.

Understanding Event Levels

Events are categorized by their level. These levels have both names and numbers associated with them. You'll see the level identified by the name and icon when looking at events, but if you're configuring custom views, you may use the level numbers in the XML file.

Information events: level 0 and level 4   These entries are used to indicate a change has occurred or to describe the successful completion of an operation. The icon used to represent Information events is an *i* in a circle.

Critical events: level 1   A critical event is one that an application or component cannot automatically recover from. Critical events are the most serious. The icon used to represent Critical events is a white *x* in a red circle.

Error events: level 2   Error events indicate a problem occurred external to the application or component that might impact the functionality of the application or component. The icon used to represent error events is a white exclamation point in a red circle. Errors aren't always as significant as they appear. As an example, if the system has a problem reading a scratched CD, an error will indicate reading a block of data from the CD, but there is nothing wrong with the CD reader.

Warning events: level 3   Warning events indicate events that may lead to a problem in the future. The event isn't necessarily significant. Sometimes you can trace back from critical or error events to identify a preceding warning. The icon used to represent Warning events is a black exclamation point in a yellow triangle.

Verbose: Level 5   Verbose logging provides more details in the log entry. If the log entry supports verbose logging, these additional details will be recorded in the log when this check box is checked.

The event levels are shown by default in all logs except the Security log. The Security log is focused more on audit success and audit failure so lists these audit keywords instead of the levels.

Creating and Using Custom Views

Custom views are a useful new feature in Windows Server 2008 and Server 2008 R2. Often when you're looking at the logs, you're looking for specific events, or at least events related to a specific issue or problem. The custom views provide predefined focused views of the events and allow you to create your own views.

This concept isn't new. You could always create a filter in the Event Viewer. However, in the past, the filtered view was gone once you created another filter. In Windows Server 2008 and Server 2008 R2, you can save the filter as a custom view, and you don't have to re-create the view each time you want to look at these events.

Some custom views are automatically created:

Server roles   Each time you add a server role, an associated custom view is automatically created. For example, if you promote a server to a domain controller, a custom view named Active Directory Domain Services will be added to show system events for Active Directory Domain Services.

Administrative Events   The Administrative Events custom view shows critical, error, and warning events from all the administrative logs. In other words, it shows everything except for the informational events. This view includes the basic administrative logs (Application, Security, and System) found on any system. It also includes logs in the Applications and Services Logs node and some of the logs in the Applications and Services logs ➤ Microsoft ➤ Windows node.

When the server is configured with a new role or feature and additional logs are added, the custom view is modified to include these additional logs.

You can view the properties for any custom view, but a few steps are involved. Although you can't modify these predefined custom views, you can create your own custom views and modify them. The next two sections show you how to view the properties of a custom view and create your own modifiable custom views.

VIEWING THE PROPERTIES OF A CUSTOM VIEW

Use the following steps to view the properties of a custom view:

1. Launch the Event Viewer by selecting Start ➤ Administrative Tools ➤ Event Viewer.

Open the Custom Views node, and select Administrative Events. Right-click Administrative Events, and select Properties.

The Administrative Events Properties page appears. It will look similar to Figure 17.3. The description is too long to fit in the viewable area of the text box. However, you can click in the Description text box and use your right arrow key to scroll to the right to view the full description.

FIGURE 17.3
Administrative
Events properties

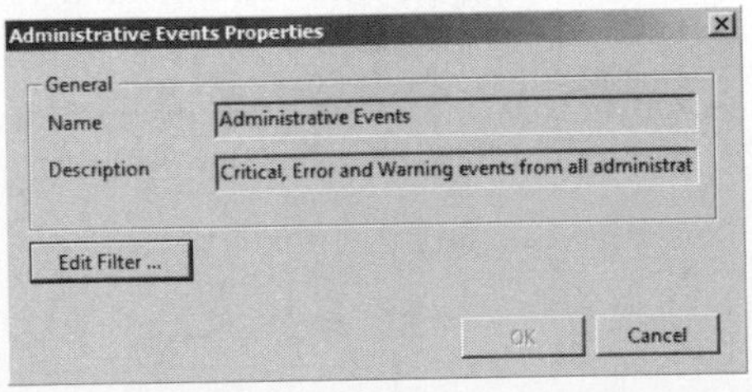

Click the Edit Filter button. The Custom View Properties page will appear and will look similar to Figure 17.4.

FIGURE 17.4
Custom View Properties page

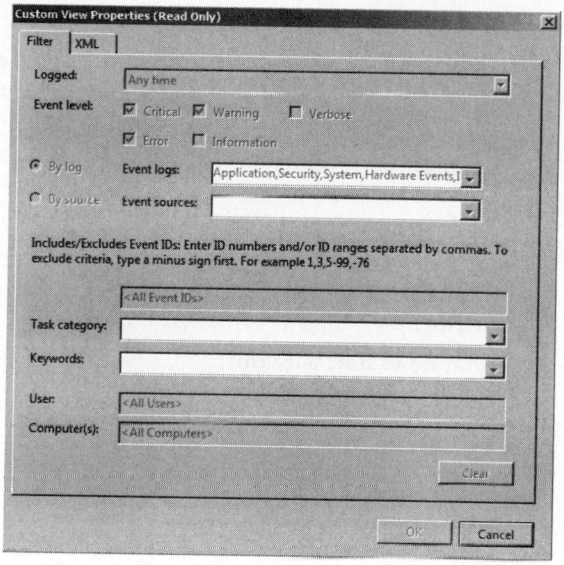

All the properties on this page are dimmed because they are read-only, but you can see what is selected. Notice that the Critical, Warning, and Error check boxes are selected. The Event Logs drop-down box includes a listing of the event logs included. However, you can't select the drop-down box, so you can't identify all the logs that are selected in this view.

Click the XML tab.

The XML tab shows the XML version of the selections in the GUI. Each statement that starts with `<Select Path ="Logname"` identifies the name of the log. The levels identify what event levels (critical, warning, error, or information) are selected.

Click Cancel twice to close the properties sheet.

Perform the following steps if you've added a role to your server:

A. Open the Custom Views ➢ Server Roles folder.

B. Right-click any custom view, and select Properties.

C. Click the Edit Filter button. Notice this puts you into the XML view of the custom view. You can view the XML data to identify what has been selected.

D. Click the Filter tab. An error appears indicating that you can't switch to the Filter tab because the query is configured for manual editing. The only way you can view the properties of the view is via the XML tab.

E. Click Cancel twice to close the Properties sheet.

⊕ Real World Scenario

XML AND XPATH

The Extensible Markup Language (XML) is simple on the surface but can be incredibly complex in the details. If you have a programmer's mind-set, you may enjoy manipulating the XML in the custom views, but if not, you may find it incredibly frustrating.

There isn't much documentation on the use of XML and XPath within the Event Viewer to create custom views. Much of the manual manipulation will be trial and error. However, there are some basic rules for working with XML and XPath with custom view properties:

All tags must be well formed.   In other words, every tag that is opened must have a matching closing tag. For example, <QueryList> starts the document, and </QueryList> is the closing tag.

Custom views start with this:

```
<QueryList>
  <Query ID="0" Path="Application">
and end with this:
  </Query>
<QueryList>
```

XML tags must be properly nested.   In other words, each element must be completely contained within another element. In the preceding example, <Query></Query> is completely contained within <QueryList></QueryList>. The following code would be incorrect since it is not properly nested:

```
<QueryList>
    <Query ID="0" Path="Application">
<QueryList>
  </Query>
```

XML tags are case sensitive.   A query opened with <QueryList> and closed with <queryList> will fail since the Q is uppercase in the opening tag and lowercase in the closing tag. Logs are selected with a Select statement using the following format:

```
<Select Path="logName">*</Select>
```

Parameters can be added after the * to filter the selected log (but before the closing </Select> tag). You can specify the event levels, event sources, event IDs, task categories, keywords, users, or computers. Each selected log will have a separate Select Path statement, and each of these statements can have multiple parameters.

The best way learn this is to manipulate a single log with these steps:

1. Create a custom view. Select a single log, and view the XML query.

2. Modify the logged time by selecting Last 24 Hours, and view the XML query. Note: 86400000 is the number of milliseconds in 24 hours (24 * 60 * 60 * 100).

3. Modify the event level by selecting Critical, and view the XML query. Notice the levels are represented with numbers, not names, and critical events are identified with level 1.

4. Modify the event sources by selecting ActionQueue, and view the XML query. Note: Task category selections are available only if an event source is selected. Also, the task category is coded with a Task=1000 statement.

5. Enter an event ID of **7000 -7004**, and view the XML query.

6. Select a task category of Process Action Queue, and view the XML query. Note that task.

7. Select a keyword of Response Time, and view the XML query. Note that the keywords entry has a complex code of (band(Keywords,281474976710656)).

8. Enter **Administrator** in the User text box, and view the XML query. Note that the user is identified by the SID, not the username.

9. If you view the XML, it will look similar to the following (though we have added a few line breaks for readability):

```
<Select Path="Application">
  *[System[Provider[@Name='Microsoft-Windows-ActionQueue']
  and (Computer='localhost')
  and (Level=1 )
  and Task = 1000
  and (band(Keywords,281474976710656))
  and ( (EventID &gt;= 7000 and EventID &lt;= 7004) )
  and Security[@UserID='S 1-5-21-213145904-2160082392-954785620-500']
  and TimeCreated[timediff(@SystemTime) &lt;= 86400000]]]
</Select>
```

Although it's highly unlikely you'll type this full statement from scratch, you can use this process to identify how to modify a specific parameter within the XPath statement.

CREATING A COPY OF A CUSTOM VIEW

You may like one of the predefined custom views but want to make a slight modification. Instead of starting from scratch, you can create a copy of the custom view.

PREDEFINED CUSTOM VIEWS CAN'T BE FILTERED

Neither the Administrative Events custom view nor any of the server role custom views can be filtered. If you want to filter these logs, you need to create a copy of the custom view first.

As an example, you may want to use the Administrative Events log as a template but add information events and filter it so only the last 24 hours are viewable. The following steps will show you how to create this log:

1. Launch the Event Viewer by selecting Start ➤ Administrative Tools ➤ Event Viewer.

2. Right-click the Administrative Events custom view, and select Copy Custom View.

3. Change the name to **Today's Core Log Events**.

4. Click New Folder. Type **My Custom Views** in the Name text box, and click OK.

5. Click OK to create the copy of the Administrative Events custom view in the My Custom Views folder.

6. Right-click the Today's Core Log Events log, and select Properties. Click the Edit Filter button. Notice that the properties are the same as the original Administrative Events custom view, but you can edit them.

7. Select the drop-down box for Logged, and select Last 24 Hours.

8. Select the Event Level check box for Information. The check boxes for Critical, Warning, and Error should already be checked.

9. Select the Event Logs drop-down box. The Application and Services Logs has the check box dimmed indicating that some of the logs are selected. Select it once to select all the logs. Click it again to deselect it, and all of the logs will be deselected. Your display will look similar to Figure 17.5. In the figure, we have clicked the plus sign to show all the available logs, but only three of the Windows logs are actually selected.

FIGURE 17.5
Modifying a custom view

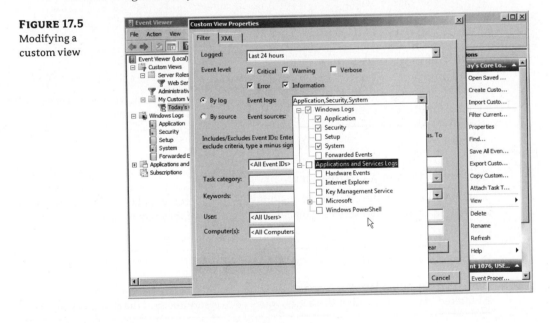

10. Click OK twice to save your new custom view.

CREATING A CUSTOM VIEW

You can also create custom views from scratch. This is useful if you're troubleshooting specific issues. For example, you may need to monitor the starting and stopping of services.

You can use the following steps to create a custom view that allows you to quickly view all the events related to a service starting or stopping.

1. Launch the Event Viewer by selecting Start ➢ Administrative Tools ➢ Event Viewer.

2. Right-click Custom Views, and select Create Custom View.

3. Select the Critical, Warning, Error, and Information check boxes.

4. Select the By Source radio button.

5. Select the Event Sources drop-down box, scroll down, and click the check box next to Service Control Manager and Service Control Manager Performance Diagnostic Provider. Notice that two logs are automatically selected: the System log and the Microsoft-Windows-Services/Diagnostic log.

6. Click OK. Enter **Monitor Services** as the name of the custom view. Click OK. This custom view will show only those events related to the Service Control Manager.

FILTERING A CUSTOM VIEW

Custom views can be filtered just as any regular event log can be filtered. A log could contain hundreds or thousands of events. If you're looking for a specific event, it may take you hours to comb through the events one by one, but you can use a filter to quickly narrow your search.

FILTERING LOGS

Although this section covers how to filter a custom view, you can follow the same steps to filter any log within the Event Viewer.

The following steps show how to filter a log. Although these steps use a log created earlier in this chapter (named Today's Core Log Events), you can use these steps as a guideline to filter any log.

1. Launch the Event Viewer by selecting Start ➢ Administrative Tools ➢ Event Viewer.

2. Open the Custom Views node.

3. Select a custom view that you've created such as the Today's Core Log Events created in the preceding section.

4. Create a filter to show different event levels:

   A. Right-click the log, and select Filter Current Custom View.

   B. Deselect the Event Level check boxes for Warning, Error, and Information. This will leave only the Critical level selected.

   C. Click OK. Your log will now show only Critical events.

   D. Right-click the log, and select Clear Filter.

5. Create a filter to show specific event sources:

   A. Right-click the log, and select Filter Current Custom View.

   B. Select the Event Sources drop-down box, and select the check box next to Service Control Manager. You can select as many event sources as desired. Your display will look similar to Figure 17.6.

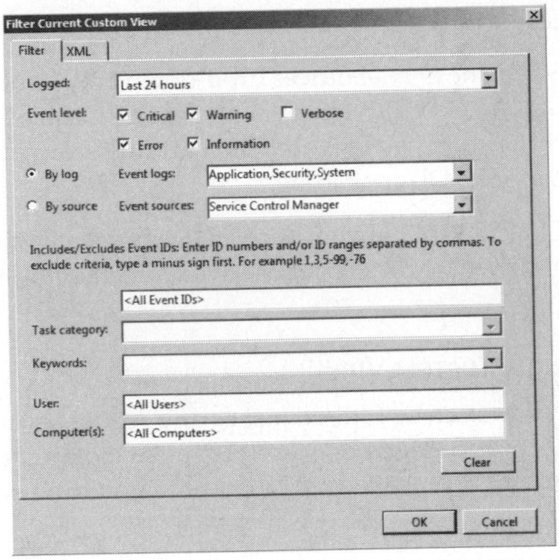

FIGURE 17.6
Filtering event sources

SELECTING BY LOG OR BY SOURCE

The By Log and By Source radio buttons are a little misleading. Radio buttons are usually used to choose only one option, so these buttons imply that you can filter only by log or by source, but you can actually choose both.

When the By Log radio button is chosen, you can select the event logs and then narrow the search by selecting specific event sources in the Event Sources drop-down box.

If you select the By Source radio button and select an event source in the Event Sources drop-down box, the available logs in the Event Logs drop-down box change, showing only the logs that include this event source.

   C. Click OK. Your log will now show events related to services.

   D. Right-click the log, and select Clear Filter.

6. Create a filter to show only specific event IDs:

   A. Right-click the log, and select Filter Current Custom View.

   B. Click in the text box that shows <All Event IDs>.

   C. Enter **7000-7999, 8224** to select Event ID 8224 and all events between 7000–7999.

SELECTING EVENT IDS

You can select ranges of event IDs by using a hyphen (as in **7000-7999**). You can add multiple ranges by separating each range with a comma (as in **7000-7999, 8050-8059**). You can filter for any specific event IDs by separating each one with a comma (as in **7036, 7042**). You can also combine any of these methods (as in **7000-7999, 8050-8059, 8042, 636**).

 D. Click OK to view the filtered log.

 E. Right-click the log, and select Clear Filter.

These steps lead you through modifying the filter for specific reasons, but you can filter based on other criteria depending on your needs.

EXPORTING AND IMPORTING CUSTOM VIEWS

Custom views created on one server can be exported and then imported onto another server. Although it's certainly possible to manually create the custom view on another system, it may be difficult, or at least time-consuming, to reproduce the filter without any errors. However, the export and import process will be reproduced quickly and exactly.

XML-BASED LOGS

All event logs since Windows Vista share a common XML-based infrastructure. A great strength of XML is that it's a common format stored in a simple text file. Custom views are exported as an XML file and can then be copied just as you'd copy any file.

Use the following steps to export a custom view. These steps export the predefined Administrative Events custom view, but you could just as easily use the same steps for any custom view you have created.

1. Launch the Event Viewer by selecting Start ➤ Administrative Tools ➤ Event Viewer.

2. Open the Custom Views node.

3. Right-click the Administrative Events custom view, and select Export Custom View.

4. Browse to a location on your computer where you want to save the file. Type in the name of the file such as **ExportedCustomView**, and click Save.

The XML file can be copied to another server or a share that is accessible by another server. It can even be imported on the same server if the original file has become corrupt. Use the following steps to import the XML file:

1. If the Event Viewer is not open, launch it by selecting Start ➤ Administrative Tools ➤ Event Viewer.

2. Right-click the Custom Views node, and select Import Custom View.

3. Browse to the location of the exported XML file. Select the XML file, and click Open. Enter a different name for the imported view. Your display will look similar to Figure 17.7.

FIGURE 17.7
Importing a
custom view

FIGURE 17.7
Importing a
custom view

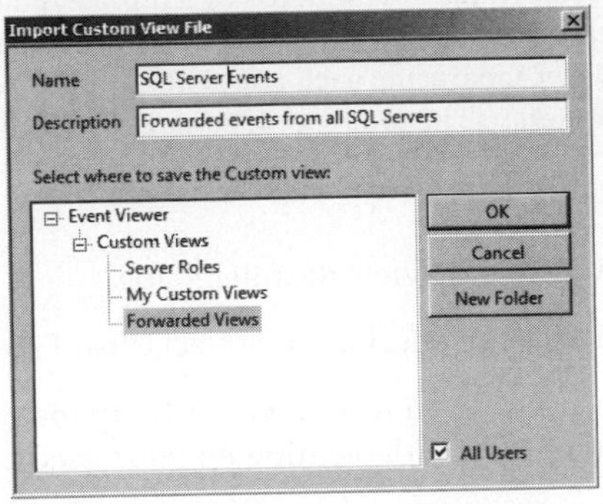

4. You can give the file a new description if desired. You can also organize your custom views by creating folders.

Once you have imported a custom view, you can manipulate the filter just as you can manipulate any other custom views. The original XML file used to import the custom view won't be affected if the custom view is modified.

Modifying the Displayed Columns in the Event Viewer

Although the Event Viewer display pane does show most of the key information, you may want to modify what is displayed. For example, when viewing the Administrative Events custom views log, you may want to know at a glance which log is generating the event.

You can add or remove columns from the Event Viewer display pane with the following steps:

1. Launch the Event Viewer by selecting Start ➤ Administrative Tools ➤ Event Viewer.

2. Open the Custom Views node, and select Administrative Events. (You can perform these same steps with any log, but for demonstration purposes, the Administrative Events log is used.)

3. With the Administrative Events log selected, click the View drop-down menu of the Event Viewer MMC and select Add/Remove Columns.

4. Select Log from the Available Columns display, and click Add. You'll see the Log column move to the Displayed Columns side. You can add as many of the available columns to the display as you like. You can also reorder the columns. For example, if you want the log displayed in the first column, you can select it and click the Move Up button to reposition it.

5. Click OK. Your display will look similar to Figure 17.8.

You may notice that the Log column was placed first in the Add/Remove Columns display, but the Level column is first. The event level will always show first except for Security logs, where the Keywords column (Audit Success or Audit Failure) will always be the first column.

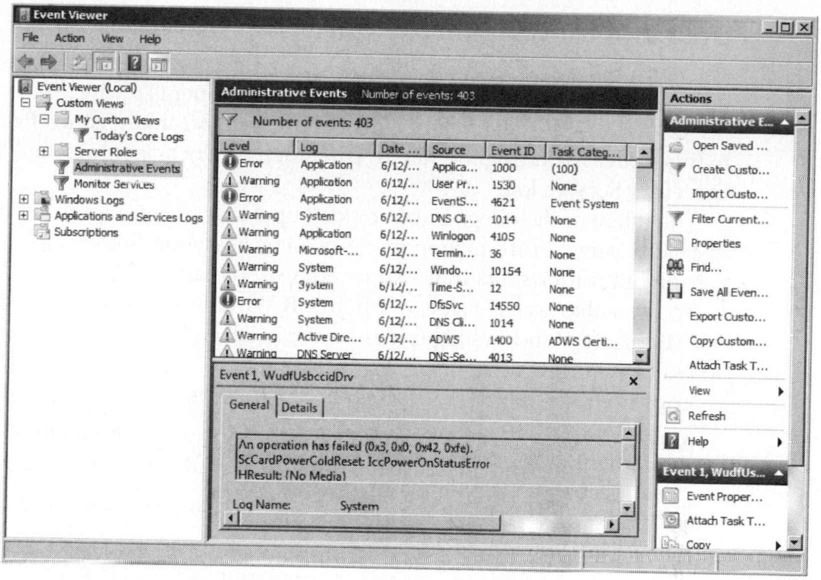

FIGURE 17.8
Adding a column to
the Event Viewer

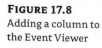

Understanding Windows Logs

The Windows logs are the traditional logs that have been available in past versions of Windows, plus the Setup and Forwarded Events logs:

Application   The Application log is used to log events from applications. The application developer can choose to log events in this log or create an additional application log specifically for the application. As an example, SQL Server will log applications into this log, but the Windows PowerShell application will log events into the Windows PowerShell log in the Applications and Services Logs section. Additionally, Internet Explorer, which didn't have its own log before, now has a dedicated log in the Applications and Services Logs section.

Security   The Security log will show all audited events. Audited events include logons, files, and other object usage, as well as any other auditing events the administrator has enabled. Audited events can be specified to include both success and failure events. Windows Server 2008 R2 does enable auditing of specific events by default, so these logs will have events even if the administrator hasn't modified auditing.

Setup   The Setup log includes events related to the setup of the operating system or installed applications. These logs include the addition or removal of any roles or features.

System   The System log records events related to the operating system. It includes information related to system drivers and system services.

Forwarded Events   If subscriptions are enabled, the Forwarded Events log will show all events forwarded to this computer. Event subscriptions must be configured before events show in this log.

Understanding Applications and Services Logs

The Applications and Services Logs folder is new in Windows Server 2008 and Server 2008 R2. It includes logs for specific applications or components.

As an example, when a server is promoted to a domain controller, additional logs are added to this folder including the Active Directory Web Services log, the DFS Replication log, and the Directory Service log.

The intent of these logs is to provide important relevant information to targeted personnel, instead of generic information that is used by everyone. Some of the extra logs existed in previous version of Windows, but they're now organized in this folder.

You can also access a slew of Microsoft Windows logs from this folder. Many of the logs in the Microsoft\Windows log folder also existed in previous editions of Windows but weren't accessible via the Event Viewer.

Logs in this folder fall into one of four categories:

Admin   Admin logs are targeted at administrators and support personnel. The goal is to identify issues and include a solution that an administrator can take to resolve a problem.

Operational   Operational logs are intended to be used to analyze or diagnose a problem or occurrence of an event.

Analytic   Analytic logs are used to log and describe the details of operation of a program or component. An analytic log will typically have a large number of events that log each step.

Debug   Debug logs are intended to be used by application developers with troubleshooting programs during the development phase.

Configuring Event Log Properties

Every event log has a properties page that identifies details on the log. You can configure where the log is located, the maximum size of the log, and what to do when the maximum size is reached from this page.

Figure 17.9 shows the properties page of the System log. You can access this page by right-clicking the log file and selecting Properties.

FIGURE 17.9
System log
properties page

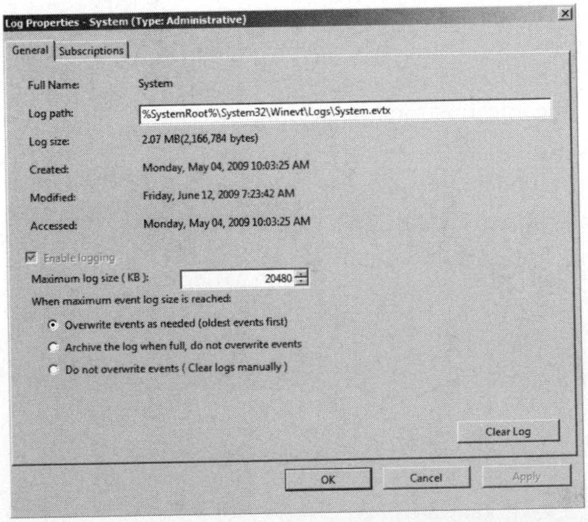

CUSTOM VIEW LOG SIZES CAN'T BE CONFIGURED

You can't configure the maximum log size on a custom view. This is because a custom view isn't actually a file. Instead, it's simply a filtered view of one or more existing files. Each time you select a custom view, it retrieves the data from the original log files.

The log path shows the location of the log file. Moving the location of the log file is as simple as typing in a new path.

Interestingly, when you move the log file, the existing events are retained in the original location. All new events are logged in the new location. However, Event Viewer remembers where the original events are and displays events from both locations. You can click the Clear Log button after moving it, and you will be prompted to save the contents of the log file.

You can set the maximum log size from this page. Different log files have different default sizes. For example, the System log defaults to 20MB, and the Security log defaults to about 130MB. Set the maximum log size to a size that won't consume too much of the hard drive space but that also will allow you to view the events.

Last, you can determine what to do when the maximum log size is reached. The choices are as follows.

- ◆ Overwrite events as needed (oldest events first)

- ◆ Archive the log when full, do not overwrite events

- ◆ Do not overwrite events (clear logs manually)

SAVING A LOG FILE

Many organizations have policies in place that require log files to be archived. Once archived, the original file is saved and can be viewed later, and new events won't overwrite archived events.

If you right-click a log file in the Event Viewer and select Clear Log, you will be prompted to save the contents of the log file. Click the Save and Clear buttons. You can then give it a name and browse to a location where you want to save the file.

You can also right-click the log file and select Save All Events As. Again, you'll be able to give the file a name and browse to a location where you want to save it. The difference is that if you click Save As instead of Clear Log, the saved events will remain in the log.

You may also be prompted to save display information. If you work in a bilingual environment, this ensures the data can be displayed properly on other computers with a different default language.

DISPLAYING A SAVED LOG FILE

You can open any saved log from Event Viewer. Right-click any node in the Event Viewer, and select Open Saved Log. You can then browse to the location of the saved log, select it, and click Open.

Figure 17.10 shows the Open Saved Log dialog box. The default location is a new folder named Saved Logs. You can use this as the location to display the saved log, or you can create a new folder to display the new logs.

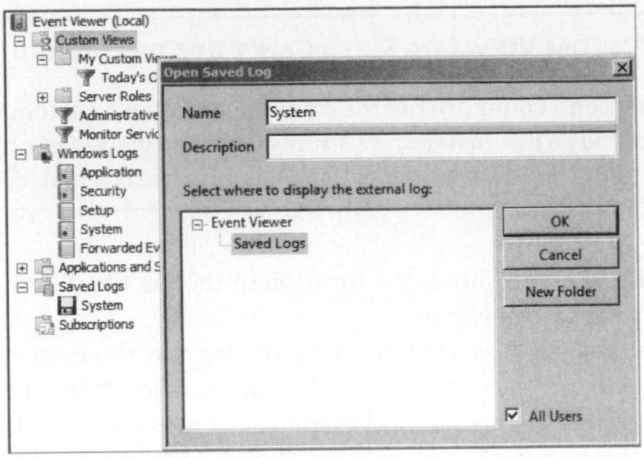

FIGURE 17.10
Opening a
saved log

If you use the default location, a new folder named Saved Logs will appear. You can go back and forth between the live log and the saved log just by pointing and clicking.

Attaching Tasks to Events

A significant new feature available with the Event Viewer is the ability to attach tasks to events. You can do this for any event that can be logged in any of the logs.

It's not uncommon for serious problems to be preceded by information events or warnings. By attaching a task to an event, you can take preemptive steps to prevent the minor problems from becoming serious.

As an example, a backup application may log the success or failure of a backup when it completes. You could have an intermittent problem that occasionally results in a backup failure. When this occurs, you want to ensure you're notified. By attaching a task to the failure event, you can automate a response to the failure.

The response to an event can be one of three possible actions:

Send an email   If you have an SMTP server, you can send an email to a user or distribution group in response to an event.

Display a message   A dialog box will display on the desktop. A drawback to this choice is that a user must be logged onto the system to view the event.

Start a program   The program can be any executable including a batch file or a script. Since you can launch a script in response to the event, your possible responses are endless. For example, you could write a script to run a different program, send an email, and display a message.

Use the following steps to attach a task to an event:

1. Launch the Event Viewer by selecting Start ➤ Administrative Tools ➤ Event Viewer.

2. Select the System log. Right-click any event, and select Attach Task To This Event. This will launch the Create a Basic Task Wizard.

3. You can give the task a new name or accept the default. Click Next.

4. Review the information on the When a Specific Event Is Logged page. Click Next.

5. On the Action page, accept the default of a program. Your display will look similar to Figure 17.11. Click Next.

FIGURE 17.11
Choosing an action
for an event task

FIGURE 17.11
Choosing an action
for an event task

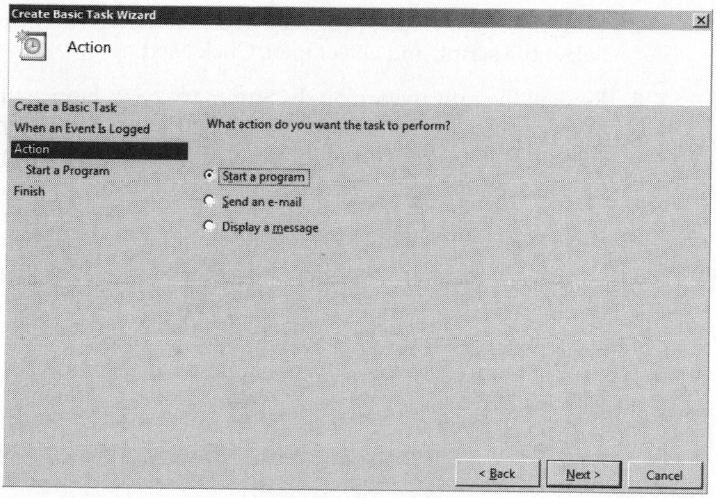

6. On the Start a Program page, you can enter the name of any program or script you may want to run. Create a simple script file with the following steps:

   A. Select Start. Type **Notepad** in the Search box, and press Enter. Notepad will launch.

   B. Enter the following text in a single line in Notepad:

   ```
   msgbox "An error occurred", vbExclamation, "Event Task Action"
   ```

   This script is simplistic, but you can do just about anything you can imagine with scripting. To test the script, you can use Windows Explorer to browse to it and simply double-click the file to execute the script.

WRITING TO A FILE WITH A SCRIPT

You may want to do a little more than just create a pop-up (especially on a server where the pop-up won't be seen right away). Here's a simple script you can use to write something to a text file that you or someone else may periodically review. If you dig into scripting, you'll find that you can do just about anything.

```
Set objFSO = CreateObject("Scripting.FileSystemObject")
Set Report = objFSO.OpenTextFile ("c:\scripts\LogEvent.txt", 8, True)
Report.Write "Date: " & date & ". Time: " & time & ". "
Report.Writeline "Something Happened."
```

   C. Select File Save. Type **EventScript.vbs** as the name of the file. Create a folder named scripts, browse to it, and click Save.

7. With the script created, click Browse, and browse to the location where you saved it. Select the script, and click Open. Click Next.

8. Review the information on the Summary page. Notice that you have access only to the basic settings for the task. If you need to access the advanced properties for the task, select the "Open the Properties dialog for this task when I click Finish" check box. For now, leave this box unchecked, and click Finish.

9. Review the information in the dialog box, and click OK.

After tasks are created, you can modify them via Task Scheduler. You can launch the Task Scheduler by selecting Start ➤ Administrative Tools ➤ Task Scheduler.

Figure 17.12 shows the Task Scheduler with Event Viewer Tasks selected. Each task you attach to an event or to an event log will appear here. You can also access the advanced properties of the tasks from here.

FIGURE 17.12
Task Scheduler

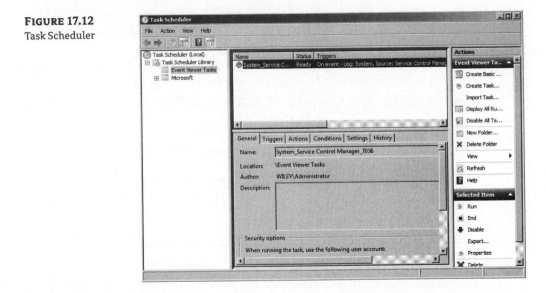

The advanced properties include six tabs:

General   The General tab provides general information such as the name and author of the task. You can also change the security context of the task. By default it will run only when the author is logged on, but it's common to change it to run under the context of a service account.

Triggers   The trigger is the event ID of the event that you selected. However, if you edit the trigger, you'll see that you have a lot of additional advanced settings that can be manipulated. For example, you can delay execution of the task for a certain time period, cause the task to repeat, set a time period for it to be active, and set it to be enabled or not.

Actions   When creating the task, you could only choose to start a program, send an email, or display a message. However, using the Actions tab, you can select multiple actions and pick and choose the order of the actions.

Conditions   The Conditions tab allows you to specify certain conditions when the task will execute or not execute. For example, you can set it to execute only if the computer is idle, only if it is on AC power, or only if a network connection is available.

Settings   The Settings tab allows you to modify the behavior of the task. By default any task can be executed by right-clicking it and selecting Run. You can prevent the task from running on demand by deselecting the check box to "Allow task to be run on demand." This tab also has choices for other miscellaneous task behaviors.

History   The History tab logs all the details of the task, including when it was created, when it was triggered, which task was executed, and when it completed. This can be valuable when troubleshooting the task.

Viewing Events on Server Core

If you're running Server Core, you may want to view different events on the server. Although the Event Viewer isn't available locally, you can still view events using the Windows Event utility (wevtutil).

This is the basic syntax of the command:

```
wevtutil command /options
```

Notice that instead of using options, or switches, you must first use a command. Then, the individual commands may have available switches or additional options that need to be used. The following sections show some common uses of the available commands.

VIEWING SERVER CORE EVENTS REMOTELY WITH EVENT VIEWER

Although it is possible to use wevtutil from the command line to view and access events on a Server Core installation, there is an easier way. You can view the events remotely.

If you execute the following command at a Server Core command prompt, you can then view events using the Event Viewer from another computer:

```
Netsh advfirewall firewall set rule group = "Remote Administration" new enable = yes
```

After executing the command, log onto another Windows Server 2008 R2 server, launch the Event Viewer, and select "Connect to computer." Type in the name of the Server Core server (or browse to it). You will then be able to view all the events on the Server Core server.

LIST LOGS

The el (enum logs) command will *enumerate*, or list, all the logs stored on the server. The syntax of the command is very simple:

```
wevtutil el
```

You may be a little surprised by how many logs scroll past on the screen. This output shows the basic logs (such as System, Application, and Security) and also all the Microsoft Windows logs.

SEND THE OUTPUT TO NOTEPAD

Remember, an easy way to send any command output to a text file is by using the > symbol to redirect it. For example, `wevtutil el > loglist.txt` will create a text file of all the logs on the server. You can then open the file on Server Core in Notepad by using Notepad `loglist.txt`.

GET LOG INFORMATION

You may be interested in knowing details about a log's configuration such as where it's stored and the maximum size. The `gl` (get logs) command will show you these settings. You need to include the name of the log in which you're interested.

The following command will show the configuration information for the System log:

```
wevtutil gl system
```

Some of this information is straightforward such as `Enabled: True` or `Enabled: False`. However, some of it is not so easy to figure out. You may be interested in what is done when the event log maximum size is reached. These choices are configured from the retention and autobackup properties. The following three choices are available from the GUI:

Overwrite events as needed (oldest events first)   Retention is set to False, and autobackup is set to False.

Archive the log when full, do not overwrite events   Retention is set to True, and autobackup is set to True.

Do not overwrite events (Clear logs manually)   Retention is set to True, and autobackup is set to False.

SET LOG INFORMATION

You can use the `sl` (set log) command to change the configuration. The command changes slightly depending on what you're trying to change.

The following command will change the maximum log size to 30MB for the System log:

```
wevtutil sl system /ms: 30720000
```

You can set the retention (/rt) and autobackup (/ab) settings with the following command. Both switches will accept either a `True` or `False`.

```
wevtutil sl system /rt:False /ab: False
```

It's not possible to set retention as `True` and autobackup as `False` since there is no associated setting. It will give a syntax error.

QUERY EVENTS

The qe (query events) command allows you to perform complex queries of the logs. For example, you may want to see only the warning events from the System log. You'll see that the qe command provides a rich set of capabilities to query specific events. The simplest command will query all the events from a specific log such as the System log in the following command:

```
wevtutil qe system
```

Events are returned in XML format. However, since this isn't very easy to read, you can add the /f:text switch to display the data in text format. Additionally, data is presented with oldest events first. You can use the /rd switch to provide the data in the reverse direction or the oldest events last if desired. The command would then look like this:

```
wevtutil qe system /f:text /rd:true
```

If you want to limit the number of events that are output (such as only the first 10 events), you can use /c (count) to identify how many events to display. For example, this command would show only the 10 most recent events:

```
wevtutil qe system /c: 10 /f:text /rd:true
```

If you want to get a little fancier, you can use the /q switch (query) and embed some XML phrases using XPath into the request to really narrow your results. You learned a little about XPath earlier in this chapter.

As an example, you may want to retrieve warning events only. Warning events are defined with a level of 3 (information is 4, error is 3, and critical is 1). The following command will retrieve all the warning events from the System log in a text format:

```
wevtutil qe system "/q:*[System [(Level=2)]]" /f:text /rd:true
```

Be careful with this. XML is much pickier than most command-line apps, and you must enter the case exactly: xml is not the same as XML. If you just change the case of System to system, the command wouldn't retrieve any data (and also doesn't give an error).

If you still don't see any events after double-checking the syntax and case and you're not getting any error messages, change the level to 4 to view the information events. It could be your system just doesn't have any warnings.

Also, note that the first instance of system indicates the System log, while the second instance of system within the query indicates the type of query. If you wanted to query the application log, you'd use this query:

```
wevtutil qe application "/q:*[System [(Level=2)]]" /f:text /rd:true
```

EXPORT LOG

The epl (export log) command can be used to export the log to a file in the Event Viewer format (.evtx). This file can then be copied to another system and opened using the Event Viewer. You need to identify the log to be copied, as well as the target path and filename.

You can use the following command to export the System log to a file named System.evtx in the C:\Logs folder:

```
wevtutil epl system c:\Logs\System.evtx
```

The folder must exist, and the folder cannot contain a file with the same name. Otherwise, the command will fail.

CLEAR LOG

You can use the cl (clear log) command to clear all the events from the log. It includes the ability to back up all the cleared events to a file using the /bu switch. If you use the /bu switch, the path to the folder must exist and can't contain a file with the same name.

The following command will clear the System log and create a backup in the Logs folder.

```
wevtutil cl system c:\Logs\Bacuups\System.evtx
```

Subscribing to Event Logs

Event log subscriptions allow you to configure a single server to collect copies of events from multiple systems. The single server collecting the events is called the *collector computer*, and events are forwarded to the collector computer from source computers.

Figure 17.13 shows how the source and collector computers work together with event subscriptions. In the figure, the collector computer is collecting copies of event log events from several source computers.

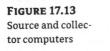

FIGURE 17.13
Source and collector computers

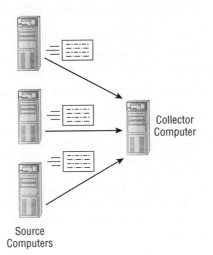

Collector
Computer

Source
Computers

Having a central server monitor events can make it a lot easier to maintain and administer several servers. As an example, you may administer multiple Microsoft SQL Server instances. You can create subscriptions to forward events from each of the SQL Server instances to a central monitoring server.

Once the events are captured on the collector computer, you can manipulate and filter them just like any other events on the computer. You can also create custom views for forwarded events.

Understanding Subscription Types

Subscriptions can be either collector initiated or source computer initiated. A collector-initiated subscription identifies all the computers that the collector will receive events from and will normally pull events from these computers. In a source computer–initiated subscription, source computers push events to the collector.

🌐 Real World Scenario

USING EVENT SUBSCRIPTIONS TO MANAGE SERVERS

In one large organization that shall remain nameless, event subscriptions were used to manage and reduce specific problems with Microsoft Exchange Server. Microsoft Exchange Server is used for email in many organizations, and since email is so important today, any outage is quickly felt throughout the organization.

The problem started because backups were occasionally failing on some servers. A side effect when a backup fails is that the Exchange database transaction logs aren't truncated. From a recovery perspective, this is important because you can still recover if a failure occurs. However, if the transaction logs aren't truncated, they continue to grow until they consume the entire drive. Once the drive fills up, Exchange will stop sending and receiving email.

The obvious solution was to improve the backup process, but the size and hierarchy of the organization resulted in some communication problems. Administrators responsible for Exchange backups and the tier 4 administrators charged with troubleshooting a failed Exchange server worked in different areas of the company with different supervisors and managers.

By the time the tier 4 administrators received the problem, it was a crisis. However, they realized it could be resolved earlier if the Exchange administrators were aware of the problem when the backups failed.

The tier 4 administrators set up event subscriptions for all the Exchange servers. Using the event subscriptions, they created a task associated with specific backup failure events and configured the task to send an email notifying them of the problem.

Now when a backup fails, the tier 4 administrators send a courtesy notification to the Exchange administrators of the problem. After a while, the Exchange administrators got tired of being informed of problems with their servers by the tier 4 administrators and became more proactive in monitoring backups themselves. They even improved the overall backup process.

COLLECTOR-INITIATED SUBSCRIPTIONS

Collector-initiated subscriptions list all the computers that will forward events (event sources). This is the most common type of subscription used by server administrators.

Figure 17.14 shows the configuration page for a collector-initiated subscription named CollectSQLEvents.

When configuring a collector-initiated subscription, you need to add the source computers by clicking the Add Computers button. If the source computers stay the same, the collector-initiated subscription is the best choice. You identify the list of computers once, and it only needs to be reconfigured if you want to add or remove a computer to/from the subscription.

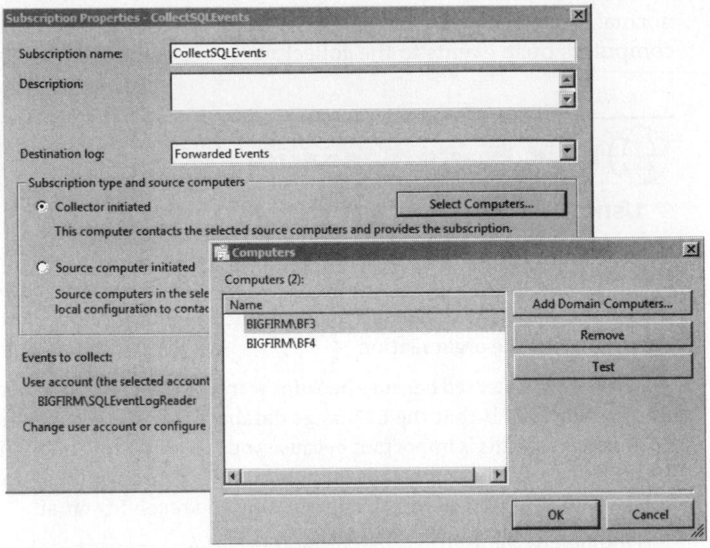

FIGURE 17.14
Creating a
collector-initiated
subscription

Collector-initiated subscriptions also need to be configured with the credentials of an account that has read permissions on the source logs. Since subscriptions will include events from multiple computers, you should use a domain account that can easily be granted Read permission on multiple computers.

In the figure, you can see that a domain account named SQLEventLogReader was created. This account was added to the Event Log Readers group.

EVENT LOG READERS GROUP

The easiest way to grant Read permission on the source logs is to add a user account to the Event Log Readers group. You can add an account to this group on each computer, or you can add a user account to the domain Event Log Readers group located in the Builtin container.

SOURCE COMPUTER–INITIATED SUBSCRIPTIONS

In a source computer–initiated subscription, the source computers push the subscriptions to the collector computer. The source computers can be identified individually or by using a global group within Active Directory.

Source computer–initiated subscriptions work best when the list of source computers changes frequently. The subscription can be created once using a global group, and then the groups can be added and removed from this global group in Active Directory.

Figure 17.15 shows the configuration page for a source computer–initiated subscription. In the figure, a global group named G Event Monitored Computers from the Bigfirm domain is added to the subscription. This global group includes a list of computers that will act as source computers in the subscription.

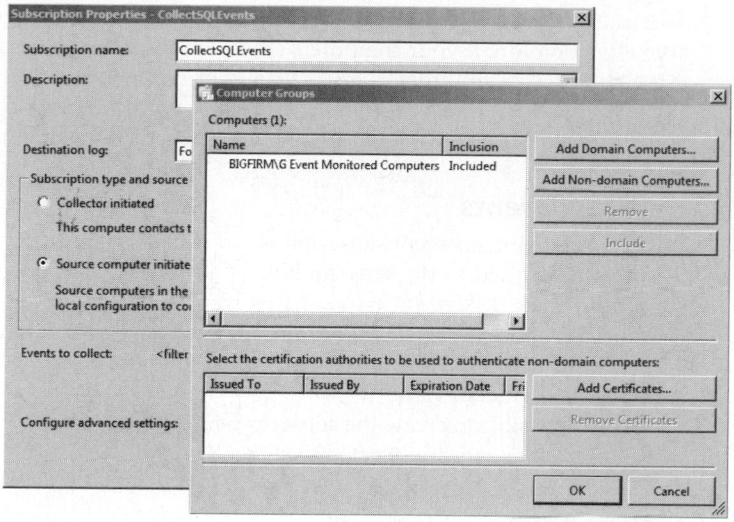

FIGURE 17.15
Creating a source computer–initiated subscription

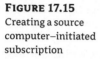

Additional configuration of the source computers is done through Group Policy. Specifically, you would configure the Computer Configuration ➤ Policies ➤ Administrative Templates ➤ Windows Components ➤ Event Forwarding node.

The setting to configure is Configure the Server Address, Refresh Interval and Issuer Certificate Authority of a Target Subscription Manager.

You must add the fully qualified domain name of the collector computer as the subscription manager. Once you enable the setting, you can click Show and then add the name of the server on the Subscription Managers page.

As an example, a server named BF5 in the Bigfirm.com domain would be identified with a value of Server="BF5.Bigfirm.Com", as shown in Figure 17.16.

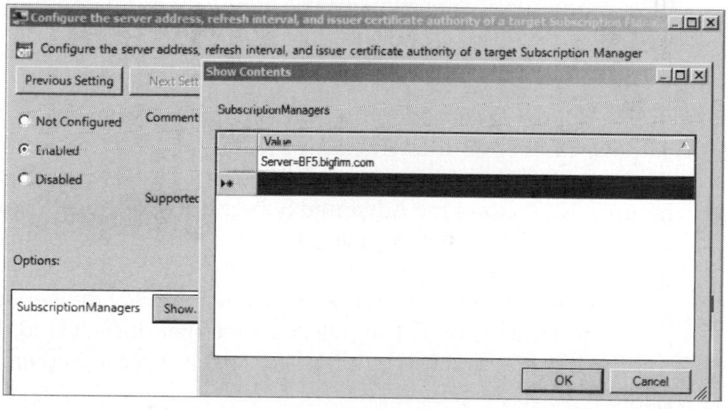

FIGURE 17.16
Configuring Group Policy for a source-initiated subscription

As a reminder, Group Policy objects (GPOs) can be linked to sites, domains, and organizational units (OUs). For this scenario, it makes sense to place all the servers you want to manage in an OU and then link the GPO to the OU.

It's also possible to configure this setting on each of the source computers manually if they aren't in a domain. If your computers are in a workgroup instead of a domain, you also need to use certificates issued from a certificate authority for authentication.

Given the additional requirements for source-initiated subscriptions within a workgroup, you'll probably stick with collector-initiated subscriptions in nondomain environments.

Selecting Events

When configuring an event subscription, you need to identify which events will be forwarded. Selecting events works the same for both collector-initiated or source computer–initiated subscriptions.

You can choose to forward all events for specific logs or forward only specific events. When you click the Select Events button, you will see the same page you use to filter any Event Viewer log or create a custom view.

It's also possible to create the subscription from the command line. When using the command line, the events are selected using an XML query.

Setting Advanced Options

Advanced options include the user account, the event delivery optimization settings, and the protocol and port. The user account is configurable only in a collector-initiated subscription. The other advanced options are available in both types of subscriptions.

Configuring User Accounts

The collector-initiated subscription will actually read the logs on the source computers and need to have at least Read permission on the logs. You have to configure the account on the subscription and ensure the account has appropriate permission on each of the source computers.

The easiest way to meet the requirements within a domain is to create a domain account and add this account to the Event Log Readers built-in domain local group.

User accounts are not configurable on source computer–initiated subscriptions.

Optimizing Event Delivery

When configuring subscriptions, you can optimize them for environments with different bandwidth capabilities or different latency requirements. These settings can be configured for both collector-initiated and source computer–initiated subscriptions.

Figure 17.17 shows the Advanced Subscription Settings dialog box for a collector-initiated subscription. Notice that there are three Event Delivery Optimization options: Normal, Minimize Bandwidth, and Minimize Latency.

A source-initiated subscription has the same event delivery optimization choices but omits the user account settings. The collector computer doesn't read the logs on the source computer in a source-initiated subscription but instead just receives them, so an account with appropriate permissions isn't required.

Normally, the servers will all be in a well-connected environment within the same LAN and use the Normal mode. Events are forwarded within 15 minutes and don't require excessive bandwidth. However, if your servers are separated by WAN links or you need the events sent to the collector quicker, you can optimize delivery of the events.

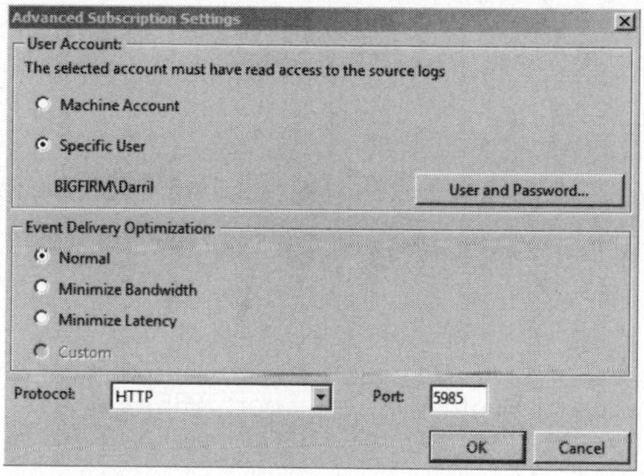

FIGURE 17.17
Advanced Subscription Settings dialog box

The different delivery modes use batches and batch timeouts. Before understanding the delivery modes, you need to understand the basics of batches and batch timeouts.

Batches   Events can be sent one at a time, but they are usually sent in batches. A batch is simply several events grouped together for transmission. Different optimization modes have thresholds of how many events are included in a batch. For example, the Normal mode waits until five events are received and sends them as a batch of five items.

Batch timeout   A batch timeout specifies the maximum amount of time a system will wait before sending the events, even if the batch threshold isn't reached. For example, the Normal mode has a batch timeout of 15 minutes. If the subscription specifies five items per batch but only three items are received in 15 minutes, these three items will be sent as a batch after 15 minutes.

Each of the three event delivery optimization options uses batches and batch timeouts a little differently. The event delivery optimization options are as follows:

Normal   The Normal mode is used in a typical well-connected LAN. It doesn't attempt to conserve bandwidth and sends events often. The default threshold for batches is five events, and the default batch timeout is 15 minutes.

Minimize Bandwidth   The Minimize Bandwidth option significantly limits how often events are sent no matter how many events are collected. It doesn't use a batch threshold, and the default batch timeout is six hours. In other words, it will send all the collected events only every six hours.

Use this option if the source computers are connected to the collector computer via a WAN link.

The trade-off with this option is that messages on the collector computer have a high degree of latency. Events occurring on the source computer may take as long as six hours to appear on the collector.

Minimize Latency   This option sends events to the collector computer every 30 seconds by default using the push delivery mode. It doesn't monitor the batch threshold but instead uses the batch timeout of 30 seconds.

Understanding Event Subscription Protocols

Subscriptions use HTTP for unencrypted transmissions and HTTPS for encrypted transmissions. Although HTTP and HTTPS use the default ports of 80 and 443 on the Internet, event subscriptions use different ports for these protocols.

The default ports used by event subscriptions are as follows:

◆ *HTTP:* 5985

◆ *HTTPS:* 5986

The only reason to change the default ports is if there is a conflict with another application on your network. In other words, if port 5985 or 5986 is already in use on your network, you could use other ports.

If you do change the ports in the subscription configuration, the servers involved in the subscription will need to be reconfigured using the WinRM command. This is the format of the WinRM command:

```
Winrm set winrm/config/listener?Address=*+Transport=HTTP @{Port="8888"}
```

Since event subscriptions use different ports than is typically used with HTTP and HTTPS, event subscriptions won't conflict with an installed IIS server.

Configuring Event Subscriptions

These are the overall requirements to configure event subscriptions:

◆ Ensure the required services are enabled on source and collector computers.

◆ Configure the source and collector computers.

◆ Configure the subscription.

ENABLING REQUIRED SERVICES

Two services are needed to support event log subscriptions. Both of these services must be running on both the source and collector computers:

Windows Event Collector (Wecutil) service Wecutil is the primary service used to manage subscriptions. It should be set to Automatic or Automatic (Delayed Start). Wecutil supports the WS-Management protocol that is implemented in Windows with the WinRM service.

Windows Remote Management (WinRM) service WinRM uses web services over HTTP and HTTPS to implement remote software and hardware management. It should be set to Automatic or Automatic (Delayed Start). WinRM doesn't depend on the Web Services (IIS) role and can coexist if this role is installed on the same server.

CONFIGURING THE COMPUTERS

Before event subscriptions can be created, you must configure both the source and collector computers. Use the following steps to configure the source computer to receive events.

These steps will configure the Windows Remote Management (WinRM) on the source server.

1. Launch a command prompt with administrative permissions. Select Start, right-click Command Prompt, and select Run As Administrator.

2. Enter the following command:

```
Winrm quickconfig
```

WINDOWS EVENT COLLECTOR SERVICE

The first time you select the Subscriptions node of Event Viewer or the Subscription tab of any log, a dialog box will appear stating that the Windows Event Collector Service must be running and configured. It then asks whether you want to start and configure the service. If you click Yes, it starts the service and changes the startup type from Manual to Automatic (Delayed Start), causing it to start each time Windows starts.

If WinRM hasn't been configured yet, you will be prompted to do the following:

♦ Create a WinRM listener on HTTTP://* to accept WS-Man requests to any IP on this machine.

♦ Enable the WinRM firewall exception.

3. Type **Y** and press Enter to make these changes. The system will respond indicating that WinRM was updated for remote management.

Use the following steps to configure the collector computer to receive events. These steps will configure the Windows Event Collector (Wecutil) service on the collector server.

1. Launch a command prompt with administrative permissions. Select Start, right-click Command Prompt, and select Run As Administrator.

2. Enter the following command:

```
Wecutil qc
```

It will reply with a message indicating the service startup mode will be changed to Delay-Start and prompt you to type Y or N.

3. Type **Y** and press Enter to make these changes. The system will respond indicating that the Windows Event Collector service was configured successfully.

CREATING A COLLECTOR-INITIATED SUBSCRIPTION

Use the following steps to create a collector-initiated subscription within a domain environment:

1. Launch the Event Viewer by selecting Start ➤ Administrative Tools ➤ Event Viewer.

2. Right-click Subscriptions, and select Create Subscription.

3. Enter **Collector Initiated** as the Subscription Name. Notice that Forwarded Events is selected as the destination log.

4. Ensure that Collector Initiated is selected, and click Select Computers.

5. Click Add Domain Computers. Enter **LocalHost** as the computer name, and click OK. LocalHost will be resolved to your actual computer name.

In a live environment, there would be no need to create a subscription for your own computer. However, this does allow you to follow the steps to create a subscription. Add other computers if desired.

6. Click the Test button. This verifies that you have connectivity to the server. Your display will look similar to Figure 17.18 with different computer names.

FIGURE 17.18
Testing
connectivity in
a subscription

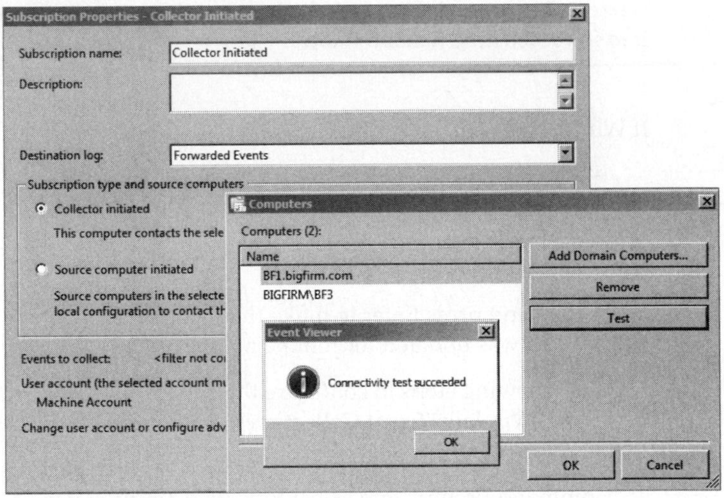

FQDN OR LOGON NAME

When you add the server, the system attempts to reach it, and if it can, it displays the fully qualified domain name (FQDN) of the server (as in BF1.Bigfirm.com). If it can't reach it, it will display the name in the logon format of domain\account (as in Bigfirm\BF3). If the server doesn't exist in Active Directory, it can't be added.

---

7. Click OK to dismiss the Connectivity Test Succeeded dialog box. Click OK in the Computers dialog box.

8. Click the Select Events button. Click the check boxes for Critical, Warning, Error, and Information. You can choose different event levels to meet your needs.

9. Select the drop-down box next to Event Logs. Select the plus (+) sign next Windows Logs, and select the Application and System logs. You can also choose any logs in the Application and Services Logs node.

SELECT FEWER THAN 10 LOGS

Any time you select more than 10 logs, a warning appears indicating this isn't a wise action. Selecting too many logs can consume a large amount of server resources and affect system performance. Avoid the temptation to monitor everything, and instead identify exactly what you want to monitor.

---

10. Click OK to close the Query Filter selection.

11. Click the Advanced button. Notice that the machine Account is selected by default. It will not have read access to the source logs on any remote server.

12. Use the following steps to create a domain account, and grant it read access to the source logs on remote systems:

   A. Launch Active Directory Users and Computers by selecting Start ➢ Administrative Tools ➢ Active Directory Users and Computers.

   B. Right-click in the Users node, and select New ➢ User.

   C. Type **EventLogReader** in the First Name and User Logon Name text boxes. Click Next.

   D. Enter a password that meets the complexity requirements of your domain in the Password and Confirm Password text boxes. Deselect the User Mush Change Password at Next Logon check box. Select the User Cannot Change Password and Password Never Expires check boxes. Your display will look similar to Figure 17.19.

FIGURE 17.19
Creating a user account to read the logs

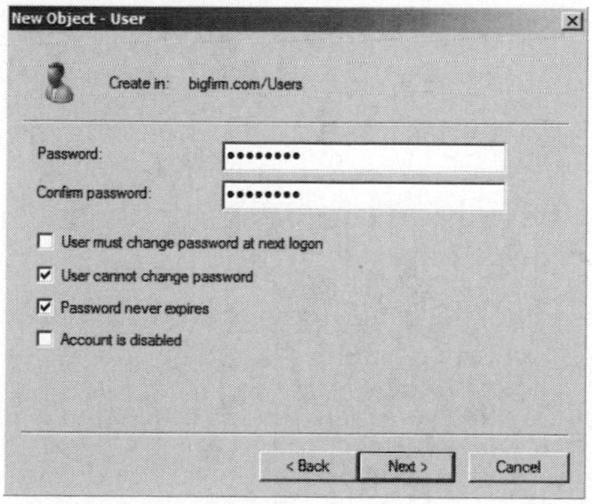

EVENT LOG READER ACCOUNT

You should treat the event log reader account as a service account. Service accounts are often configured so that the password does not expire. However, service accounts (and the event log reader account) should still be managed. In other words, you should have a process in place to periodically change the passwords of these accounts, or better yet, use the new Managed Service Accounts feature available with Windows Server 2008 R2.

E. Click Next, and then click Finish to create the account.

F. Double-click the EventLogReader account to access the properties.

G. Click the Member Of tab, and click Add.

H. Type **Event Log Readers**, and click OK to add the account to the Event Log Readers group. Your display will look similar to Figure 17.20. Click OK.

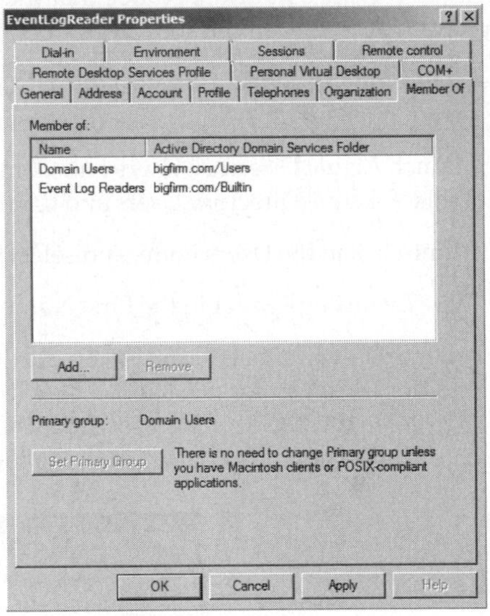

FIGURE 17.20
Adding the user account to the Event Log Readers global group

13. Return to the Advanced Subscription Settings page, and select Specific User. Click the User and Password button.

14. Enter the username and password of the account you just created in the Credentials dialog box. The username should be entered in the format of domain\username. Click OK.

15. Review the Event Delivery Optimization choices, and ensure the Normal option is selected.

16. Review the protocols and ports. The default port for HTTP is 5985, and the default port for HTTPS is 5986. You can view the port for HTTPS by selecting HTTPS in the Protocol drop-down dialog box. Your display should look similar to Figure 17.21.

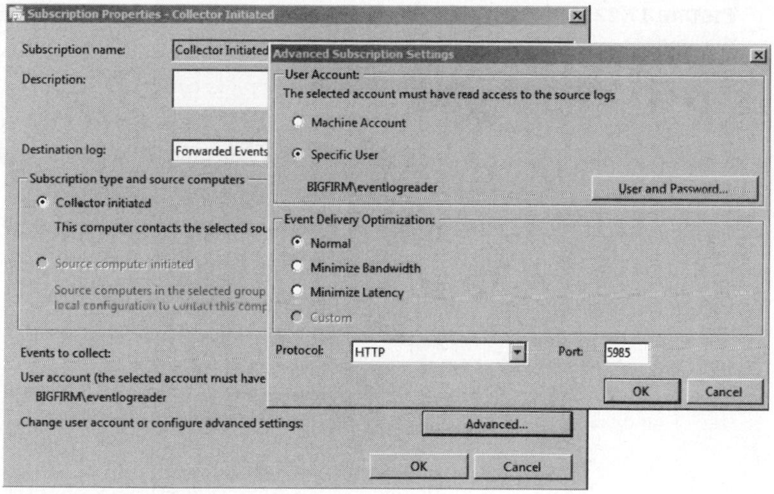

FIGURE 17.21
Verifying the advanced subscription settings

17. Click OK to accept your changes.

18. Click OK to complete the creation of your subscription.

ERRORS WHEN CREATING SUBSCRIPTION

If you receive any errors when creating the subscription, verify the computers that you've added to the subscription are operational and reachable by your server. You can easily verify this by clicking the Select Computers button, selecting each of the computers, and clicking Test.

After a subscription is created, you can right-click it and select Properties to reconfigure most of the properties of the subscription. You can't change the subscription type (collector initiated or source computer initiated) or the subscription name, but you can modify any of the other properties.

Troubleshooting Event Forwarding

The most common problems associated with event forwarding errors are that the servers involved in the subscription aren't accessible in the network, the subscription is configured incorrectly, or the user account doesn't have the right permissions.

Checking the Runtime Status

A useful check is the runtime status of the event subscription. You can access it by right-clicking the subscription and selecting Runtime Status.

Figure 17.22 shows the runtime status of a subscription created with an account problem. When the error is selected, the details of the error are displayed in the bottom pane.

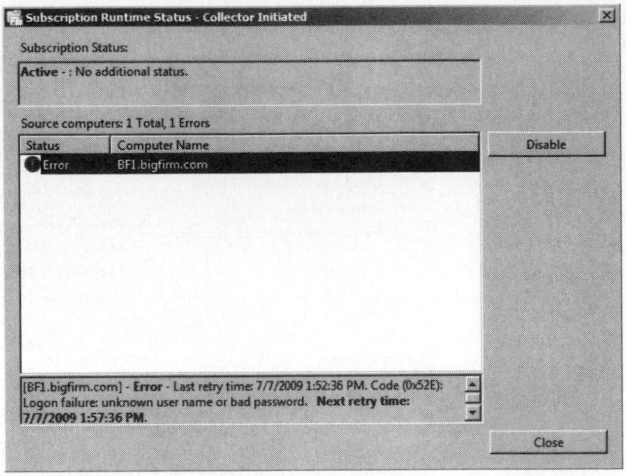

FIGURE 17.22
Viewing the
runtime status

In this case, the error message is "Access is denied." The account used for the subscription doesn't have permission to read the logs on the remote computer. This can be resolved by adding the user account to the Event Log Readers group.

Using the Windows Event Collector Utility

You can also run the Windows Event Collector Utility at the command line to configure and troubleshoot event forwarding.

COMMAND LINE OR GUI

You can accomplish most of the same tasks using either the Event Viewer GUI or the `wecutil` commands. So, you may be asking why you'd really need the `wecutil` commands. Two reasons:

◆ The first and most important reason is that `wecutil` commands can be executed remotely using the WinRS command. Chapter 14 covered the WinRS command in more detail, but if it is configured, any of the `wecutil` commands can be executed from the command line of a remote computer.

◆ The second reason is that the `wecutil` commands can be scripted. Any commands you can enter at the command line can be put into a batch file and easily executed. For example, if you created a subscription using a batch file, you could easily re-create it by simply rerunning the batch file. Table 17.1 shows the various switches available with `wecutil`.

The most common way to use these commands for troubleshooting event subscriptions is to first list the subscriptions with this command:

```
Wecutil es
```

This will list the event subscriptions with their name. For example, if you did the earlier steps to create a collector-initiated subscription named Collector Initiated, the output would be `Collector Initiated`.

With the name of the subscription known, you can now retrieve the runtime status of the subscription with the following command:

```
Wecutil gr "Collector Initiated"
```

Note that the name of the subscription has a space in it so it must be enclosed in quotes. If the subscription doesn't have a space, you can omit the quotes.

TABLE 17.1: `wecutil` **COMMANDS**

wecutil COMMAND	COMMENTS
Wecutil /?	Help. Shows the basic commands.
	You can ask for additional help on any command by using the /? switch after the command, as in `wecutil es /?`.
Wecutil es	Enumerate subscription. You can list all the subscriptions on your system. Use this command to get the subscription ID to use with other commands.
Wecutil gs <subscription id>	Get subscription. The gs command will list all the parameters and options for a created subscription.
Wecutil gr <subscription id>	Get subscription runtime status. This command is useful when troubleshooting subscriptions. If the subscription isn't working, it will include details of the last error message.
	You can also access this information by right-clicking the subscription in the Event Viewer and selecting Runtime Status.
Wecutil ss	Set subscription. You can use this command to set the parameters of a subscription. There is a lot of additional help on this command. Use the following command to pipe it into a text file named sshelp.txt:
	Wecutil ss /? > sshelp.txt.
	Open the help file with this: Notepad sshelp.txt
Wecutil cs	Create subscription. You can use this command to create a subscription. There is a lot of additional help on this command by using the /? switch.
Wecutil ds <subscription id>	Delete subscription.

TABLE 17.1: wecutil **COMMANDS** *(CONTINUED)*

wecutil COMMAND	COMMENTS
Wecutil rs <subscription id>	Retry subscription. This command will attempt to establish a connection and send a remote subscription request. You can follow it with a gr command to get the current status after the retry attempt.
Wecutil qc	The quick configure switch is used to configure the Windows Event Collector service.

Monitoring Performance

Performance Monitor has been around in the Windows operating systems for several versions, but it enjoys some significant improvements today. It can be used to watch your system in real time or create log files that you can use to identify changes in performance.

Figure 17.23 shows the Performance Monitor. The left pane shows all the tools available to you from this snap-in. In the center pane is the system summary that appears by default. The four core resources (memory, network interface, physical disk, and processor) are monitored in real time with counters showing you details of their performance.

FIGURE 17.23
Performance
Monitor

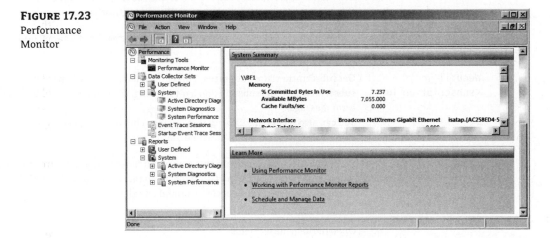

The most significant improvements with the Performance Monitor are with the data collector sets. Data collector sets allow you to collect and view key performance data on your system.

Using Monitoring Tools

This section includes the legacy Performance Monitor, the Resource Monitor, and a system reliability report.

The Performance Monitor shows by default, but if you right-click the Monitoring Tools node, you'll also see Resource Monitor and "View system reliability," as shown in Figure 17.24.

PERFORMANCE OR PERFORMANCE MONITOR

In different versions of Windows, this tool has been called both Performance and Performance Monitor. In Windows Server 2008 R2, it's called both. When you launch it, you launch Performance Monitor (Start ➤ Administrative Tools ➤ Performance Monitor). You can also launch it by entering **perfmon** from the Run line or the command line.

Once it's launched, the title bar names it Performance Monitor.

However, the top node is Performance. Within the Monitoring Tools node, you'll see the familiar Performance Monitor you may have used in previous editions of Windows. In this chapter we refer to the full suite of tools as Performance Monitor and the older Performance Monitor (in the Monitoring Tools node) as the legacy Performance Monitor.

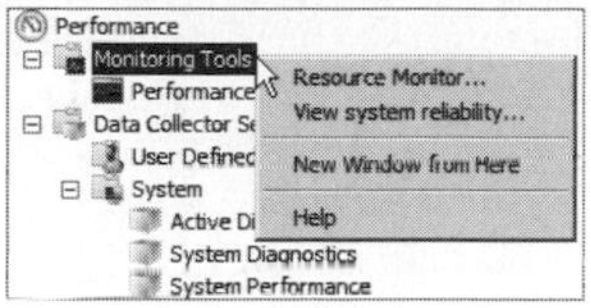

FIGURE 17.24
Accessing the additional monitoring tools

PERFORMANCE MONITOR

If you've worked with previous versions of Windows, you've probably worked with Performance Monitor. The functionality is the same in Windows Server 2008 R2. Performance Monitor uses objects and counters.

Objects   Performance Monitor objects are specific resources that can be measured. Some commonly measured objects are Processor, Memory, Network Interface, and Physical Disk.

Counters   Counters are the individual metrics within an object. For example, the Processor object includes counters such as the % Processor Time, % User Time, and Interrupts/Sec counters.

Counters monitored in this Performance Monitor are used throughout the entire suite of Performance Monitor tools including the data collector sets.

RESOURCE MONITOR

The Resource Monitor is constantly running and capturing counters on the core four resources of your system. You can access it by right-clicking Monitoring Tools and selecting Resource Monitor. You can also access via Task Manager. Select the Performance tab, and click the Resource Monitor button.

Figure 17.25 shows the Resource Monitor with the Overview tab selected. The left pane shows details on each of the resources, and the right pane shows a graphic of each of the resources.

You can select the tab for any of the four resources to drill into additional details on the performance of the processor, memory, disk subsystem, or network interface.

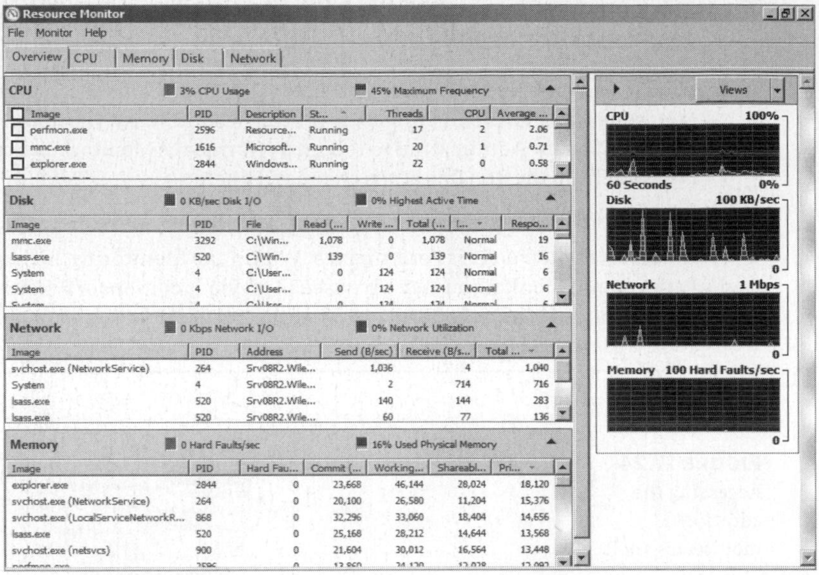

FIGURE 17.25
Accessing the additional monitoring tools

One of the primary benefits of the Resource Monitor is the ability to filter the results according to specific processes or services. For example, if you want to identify the load a specific application is placing on your system, you can select only that application's processes.

You can also use the Resource Monitor to help you identify what process may be locking a file or DLL. As an example, malware will often prevent files from being deleted by locking it. If you try to delete the malware file, the system balks because it claims the file is locked. However, you can use Resource Monitor to get some more details on what's happening.

Select the CPU tab, and open the Associated Handles section. You can type in the name of the file in the text box and click the Search button. Details on the handle will be displayed. You can right-click the result and select End Process, and you should be able to delete the file now.

BE CAREFUL WITH ENDING PROCESSES

Ending processes may result in system instability. You should end a process only as a last resort. It's sometimes a good solution but not a good first solution. Additionally, some processes are resilient, and if stopped, they'll automatically be restarted. This happens with some system resources and some malware.

Sometimes you may need to dig a little deeper. Identify the process ID (in the PID column), click the Overview tab, and look at the CPU section. The second column is labeled PID, and if you click it, you can sort the processes in ascending or descending order to easily find the process. When you click it once, an up arrow will indicate ascending order, and when you click it again, a down arrow will display.

Once you've found the process, you can right-click it and end it here or gather more information. If you select Analyze Wait Chain, it will show all the processes using or waiting to use the same resource.

VIEWING SYSTEM RELIABILITY

System reliability is tracked by the Reliability Monitor. It uses a stability index to assess the system's stability on a scale of 1 to 10, with 10 indicating perfect reliability.

The Reliability Monitor monitors hardware failures, application failures, Windows failures, and other miscellaneous failures and warnings. When a failure occurs, the stability index is reduced depending on the severity of the problem. The longer the system runs without any failures, the higher the stability index.

Information is displayed on a graph and shows icons for information, warnings, and failures. You can select any of the icons to view details on the failure.

The Reliability Monitor can be useful in identifying trends of systems. Most of your servers should have similar stability indexes. However, if you identify a server that has a significantly lower index, it could be because of problems with incompatible hardware or buggy applications.

Using Data Collector Sets

Data collector sets are an exciting feature available within Performance Monitor that appeared in Windows Server 2008. Each data collector set is a predefined set of performance counters, event trace data, and configuration information used to monitor key elements within a system.

Performance Monitor includes prebuilt system data collector sets you can use to monitor your system. You can also use these system data collector sets as templates to create your own data collector sets.

Membership in the Administrators group is required on the local system to run or access data collector sets. Although the Performance Log Users group exists in Windows Server 2008 R2, these users will have only minimal access to tools within the Performance Monitor.

SYSTEM DATA COLLECTOR SETS

The two prebuilt data collector sets are System Diagnostics and System Performance. If you promote a server to a domain controller, the Active Directory Diagnostics data collector set is also added.

Unlike the Resource Monitor, which is constantly running, the data collector sets are not configured to automatically run. You can start them by right-clicking any data collector set and selecting Start.

Data collected from these data collector sets is stored in the c:\Perflogs folder.

System Diagnostics The System Diagnostics data collector set provides details on local hardware resources, system response times, and processes on the local computer. It includes system information and configuration data. The resulting report includes suggestions to maximize performance and streamline the system's operation. It will run for 10 minutes after being started.

System Performance The System Performance data collector set can be used to identify possible causes of performance issues. It includes information on local hardware resources, system response times, and processes. It will run for one minute after being started.

Active Directory Diagnostics The Active Directory Diagnostics data collector set collects Active Directory–related data including performance counters, trace events, and registry keys that can be used to troubleshoot Active Directory performance issues. It will run for five minutes after being started.

The configuration details and properties of each of the prebuilt data collector sets can be viewed, but they can't be modified.

Use the following steps to run the System Performance and System Diagnostics data collector sets and view their results:

1. Launch Performance Monitor by selecting Start ➢ Administrative Tools ➢ Performance Monitor.

2. Browse to the Data Collector Sets ➢ System node to access the prebuilt data collector sets.

3. Right-click the System Performance data collector set, and select Start. The Data Collector Set will run for one minute. When it completes, you can view the report. When it's running, it has a green icon similar to the Play button for a CD or DVD player.

4. After the data collector set completes, right-click the System Diagnostics data collector set, and select Start. This will run while you're viewing the System Performance data collector set report.

5. Browse to the Reports ➢ System ➢ System Performance node within Performance Monitor. Select the report. Your display will similar to Figure 17.26.

FIGURE 17.26
Data collector set report

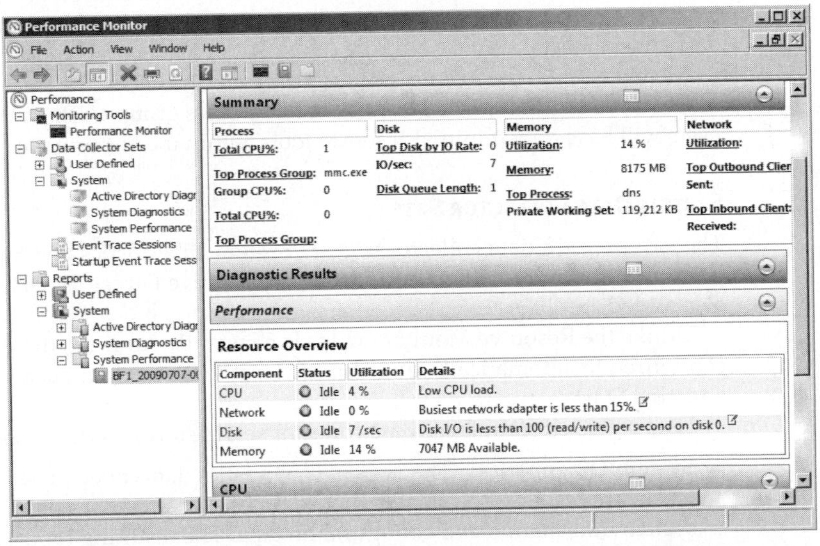

6. Browse through the details of the report. It includes details on the overall performance of your system and the CPU, network, disk, and memory resources. At the end of the report are overall report statistics.

7. Right-click the report, and select View ➢ Performance Monitor. Your display will look similar to Figure 17.27

FIGURE 17.27
Data collector set
report viewed in
graph mode

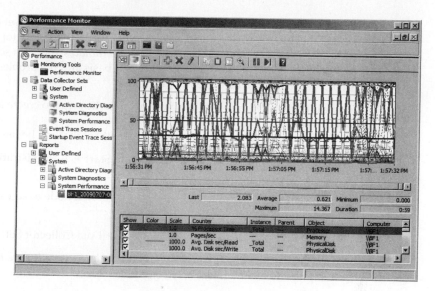

This shows the same report data within the legacy Performance Monitor, but it's quite a bit messier. Although a picture is worth a thousand words, a thousand data points on the legacy Performance Monitor graph doesn't easily tell you a story. Microsoft has done a great job in cleaning this data up and displaying it in the report format.

8. Right-click the report, and select View ➢ Folder. This shows you the actual Windows Explorer view of the files used to create the report. System Performance data collector sets are stored in the c:\Perflogs\System\Performance folder by default. Each report will be contained within a separate folder.

9. When the System Diagnostics data collector set finishes, right-click the System Diagnostics data collector set, and select Latest Report. Browse through this report. Notice that the Warnings section includes the symptoms, cause, details, and a suggested resolution for each error. Additionally, it often includes a link to a website in the Related section where you can look for information related to the error.

USER-DEFINED DATA COLLECTOR SETS

You can create your own data collector sets to meet specific needs. Unlike the prebuilt data collector sets, you can modify any of the properties of a user-defined data collector set. This includes the length of time it runs and the schedule used to launch it.

When creating a user-defined data collector set, you typically start with a template, and each of the prebuilt system data collector sets can be used as a template. You can also create a data collector set from scratch, though it's a little like re-creating the wheel. The templates provide you with a good starting point.

These are the two most common reasons to create a user-defined data collector set:

To create a baseline   A baseline will document the system operation at a point in time. If the performance degrades later, you can easily identify which resource or which application is causing the problem.

To schedule a data collector set   A user-defined data collector set can be scheduled to run on a regular basis. For example, you could create two data collector sets from the System Diagnostics and System Performance built-in templates and then schedule them to run once a day. You can review the reports on a regular basis and if a problem appears on your server, you'll have a history you can easily reference.

The next two procedures will lead you through the steps to create a baseline and to schedule a data collector set to run on a regular basis.

Use the following steps to create a data collector set that can be used as a baseline:

1. Launch Performance Monitor by selecting Start ➢ Administrative Tools ➢ Performance Monitor.

2. Browse to the Data Collector Sets ➢ User Defined node to access the prebuilt data collector sets.

3. Right-click User Defined, and select New ➢ Data Collector Set.

4. Enter **Baseline** as the name for your data collector set. Ensure that Create From a Template (Recommended) is selected. Click Next.

5. Select the System Performance template, and click Next.

6. Accept the default location for the data to be stored by clicking Next. On a production server, you may want to change this path to a different partition that won't compete with the operating system.

7. On the Create the Data Collector Set page, you can designate another account to run the data collector set. The default user account is the built-in System account and will work for the local system. Click Finish.

8. Right-click the Baseline data collector set, and select Start. It will run for a minute and then complete. An icon similar to a Play button appears while it is running. When the schedule completes, the icon will disappear.

9. Browse to the Reports ➢ User Defined ➢ Baseline node. Select the report from your baseline, and view it. At this point, there's no difference between your user-defined data collector set and the System Performance data collector set.

10. Right-click your Baseline data collector set, and select Properties.

11. Click the Stop Condition tab. Change the Overall Duration Units from Minutes to Weeks. Your display will look similar to Figure 17.28.

12. Click the Directory tab. Notice that you can modify where the report is stored and the format of the report's name. By default, the reports are named with the following convention: ServerName_dateyyyymmdd-sequential number. As you modify the settings on this page, the example directory is shown at the bottom of the page.

13. Select each of the tabs in the properties of your data collector set. Notice that you can configure many properties, but the sample interval isn't available on any of the property pages. Click OK to save your changes.

FIGURE 17.28
Modifying data
collector set
properties

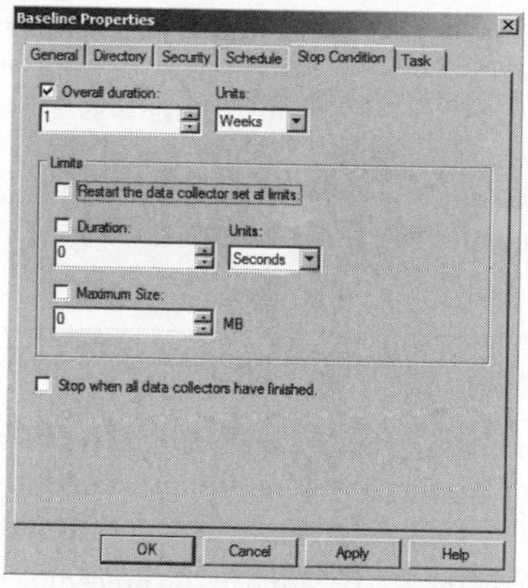

MODIFY THE DEFAULT SAMPLE INTERVAL

The default sample interval is set to one second, meaning that the data collector set will capture all the metrics every second. When capturing the data for 60 seconds, sampling every second is useful. However, if you're capturing data for a full week as part of a baseline, you only need to capture the samples every 30 to 45 minutes to get an accurate picture of the system's performance.

---

14. With the baseline data collector set selected, right-click the Performance Counter element, and select Properties.

15. You can add or remove performance counters from this page. For example, if you were monitoring a server hosting SQL Server, you may want to add some of the SQL Server performance counters in addition to the core resource counters.

16. Change Sample Interval from 1 to 45, and change Units from Seconds to Minutes. Your display will look similar to Figure 17.29. Click OK.

FIGURE 17.29
Modifying Perfor-
mance Counter
properties

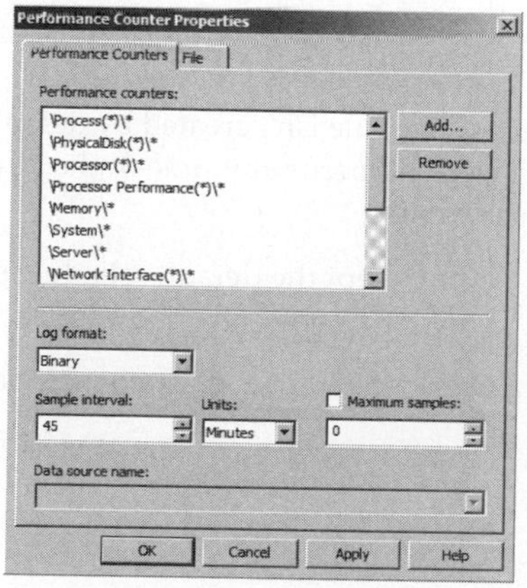

At this point, you have a data collector set that will run for a week and will capture samples every 45 minutes. It can be manually started, or you could modify the properties to add a schedule to start it on a specific date. Either way, it will run for seven days and create a baseline report of your system.

You can also manually stop any data collector set. Right-click the data collector set that is running, and select Stop.

ONLY ONE DATA COLLECTOR SET AT A TIME

Data collector sets require exclusive access to some system resources. Because of this, you can run only one data collector set at a time. If one is running and you try to start another, you will receive an error. Once the first data collector set finishes, another can be started, but they aren't queued.

If you've created the baseline in the preceding exercise and started it, you'll need to stop it before you can run the data collector set created in the following exercise.

Use the following steps to create a system diagnostics data collector set and schedule it to run once a day:

1. Launch Performance Monitor by selecting Start ➢ Administrative Tools ➢ Performance Monitor.

2. Browse to the Data Collector Sets ➢ User Defined node to access the prebuilt data collector sets.

3. Right-click User Defined, and select New ➢ Data Collector Set.

4. Enter **Routine Diagnostics** as the name for your data collector set. Ensure that Create From a Template (Recommended) is selected. Click Next.

5. Select the System Diagnostics template, and click Next.

6. Accept the default location for the data to be stored by clicking Next.

7. Select Open Properties for this Data Collector Set, and click Finish.

8. Click the Schedule tab, and click Add to add a schedule. Your display will look similar to Figure 17.30.

Notice that a schedule isn't created by default. However, you can add schedules to occur any day of the week, to occur any time of the day, to start on any date on the calendar, and to expire on any date.

9. Click OK to accept the default schedule starting at midnight for each day of the week.

10. Click OK to complete the creation of the routine diagnostics data collector set. You now have a user-defined data collector set that will run daily.

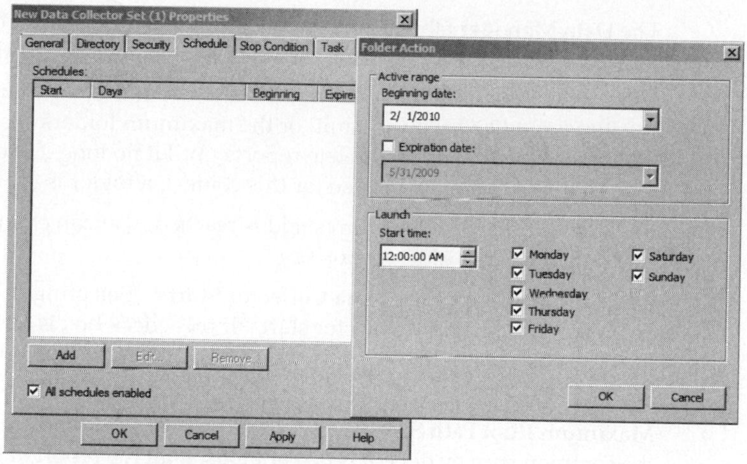

FIGURE 17.30
Scheduling routing
diagnostics

REPORT MAINTENANCE

After creating reports to run on a regular basis, the only other thing you need to consider is the data retention policies. The worst-case scenario is that the reports consume the disk space and the system shuts down. Thankfully, there are built-in protections that will prevent this from happening. However, these protections can delete reports you may want to keep.

Reports are grouped together for each data collector set and managed by individual data retention policies. Each time you run a data collector set, another report is created in the same node or folder, and other reports are examined to determine whether they should be deleted or archived.

The data retention policy is managed using the Data Manager tab and the Actions tab of the report properties sheet.

Figure 17.31 shows the Data Manager tab for a user-defined data collector set named Routine Diagnostics. You can access this page by right-clicking the report group and selecting Properties. The report group will have the same name as the data collector set. In this example, you can locate the report group at Reports ➢ User Defined ➢ Routine Diagnostics.

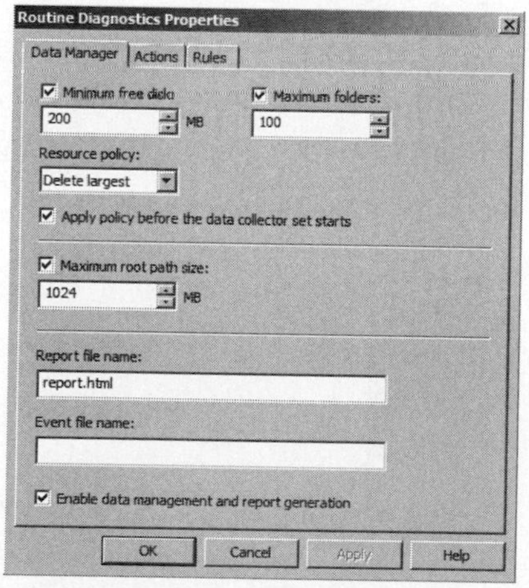

FIGURE 17.31
Managing reports

The Data Manager tab provides details on when reports will be deleted based on disk usage. These settings are used to prevent the reports from consuming the entire disk.

Minimum Free Disk and Maximum Folders   If the minimum free disk space drops below the threshold (200MB by default) or the maximum folders exceed the threshold (100 reports by default), the policy will delete reports until it no longer exceeds the threshold. Each report is contained within a folder, so for this context, a folder is the same as a report.

Resource Policy   When a threshold is reached, you can choose to delete the largest reports (the default) or the oldest reports.

Apply Policy Before the Data Collector Starts   Selecting this box will cause data to be deleted before the data collector starts. If this check box is deselected, the data manager limits will be ignored. Data retention will be managed exclusively by the rules defined on the Actions tab.

Maximum Root Path Size   This refers to all the report data in this common path. For example, the common path by default is c:\Perflogs. If all the report data exceeds 1GB, then this policy will cause files to be deleted or archived. This setting will override the Minimum Free Disk and Maximum Folders settings.

PERFLOGS FOLDER

You can access the reports using Windows Explorer. If you browse to the c:\Perflogs folder, you'll see two folders: Admin and System. The Admin folder holds report data from all the user-defined data collector sets. The System folder holds report data from all the system data collector sets. It's also possible to choose a different path including a different partition for any user-defined data collector sets.

The Actions tab provides details on how reports are archived and deleted even if the disk usage doesn't exceed the defined thresholds. Figure 17.32 shows the Actions tab and the Folder Action page used to create any scheduled action. The Folder Action page is accessed by clicking Edit to edit an existing action or by clicking New to create a new action.

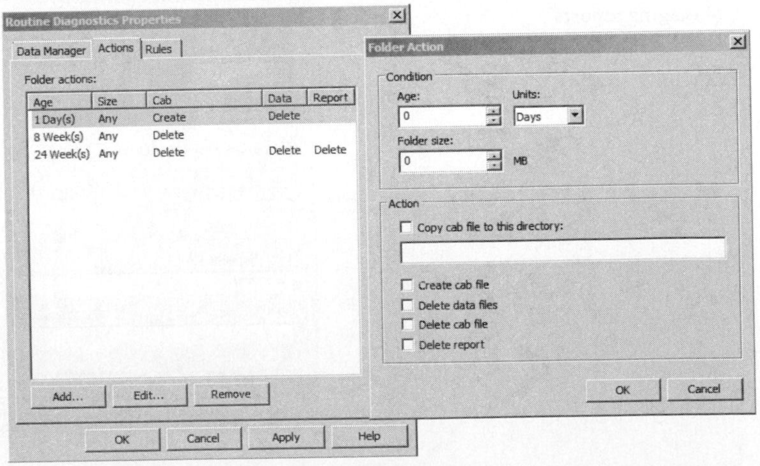

FIGURE 17.32
Defining data
retention actions

Reports created from templates have three default folder actions:

1 day   After a day, a cabinet file will be created, and the source data will be deleted. A cabinet file is an archive format that can be used by a user to retrieve the original data. Data must first be extracted from the cabinet file before it can be viewed in a report. Data archived into a cabinet file will disappear from the Reports view in Performance Monitor. However, you can extract the data into a different folder and double-click the `report.html` file to view the report.

8 weeks   The cabinet file will be deleted. A `report.xml` file will remain that holds the raw data from the report.

24 weeks   The report will be deleted. This rule will also check for the original data and the cabinet file. If either of these exists, it will also be deleted.

> ### SAVE YOUR REPORT
>
> If you want to save any report and ensure it's not deleted as part of the data retention policies, you should copy the entire folder and save it in a different location using Windows Explorer. Any time you want to view the report, open the folder and double-click the `report.html` document. The entire report is viewable in Internet Explorer. You can also modify the data retention policy so that it doesn't automatically remove it.

The Bottom Line

View administrative events on your system   The Event Viewer includes many logs showing events on your system. It includes a built-in custom view that can be used to view all administrative events from multiple logs.

> **Master It**   Access the Administrative Events custom view log.

Attach a task to an event   You can create a response to any event by attaching a task. The response can be a notification with a dialog box, an email, or the execution of a program.

> **Master It**   Create a task to display a dialog box if the Print Spooler service stops.

View the System Performance data collector set report   Data collector sets can be used to measure and monitor the performance of a server. The Performance Monitor includes built-in data collector sets that can be run on demand, and you can also create your own user-defined data collector set.

> **Master It**   Run the System Performance data collector set, and view the resulting report.

Chapter 18

Windows Server 2008 R2 and Active Directory Backup and Maintenance

Backup and recovery are familiar tasks to most server administrators. Protecting data and applications is important enough, but recovering your Active Directory can be even more vital to continued operations.

In this chapter, we cover the various types of backup and recovery available in Windows Server 2008 R2 as well as describe how they apply to Active Directory. You will also learn about an exciting new feature in Active Directory that will help you recover deleted objects without relying on backups, the Active Directory Recycle Bin.

In addition, we'll describe Active Directory maintenance, such as the ability to stop and restart Active Directory without having to restart the server computer. The ability to stop Active Directory lets you perform offline maintenance of the Active Directory database, such as defragmentation and integrity checks.

In this chapter, you will learn to:

- Use Windows Server Backup to back up and restore a Windows Server 2008 R2 computer

- Defragment AD DS offline

- Install the Active Directory Recycle Bin

- Create and recover a system state backup for Active Directory

Backing Up and Restoring Windows Server

Backup has long been part of Windows Server, and in Windows Server 2008 R2 the backup tasks are performed by Windows Server Backup. Although Windows Server Backup may not provide every feature you might want in an enterprise environment, it does a good job of backing up and restoring a Windows Server 2008 R2 server. Windows Server Backup can be used to back up remote computers, but it most suited to backing up the local server.

The Windows Server Backup tool included with Windows Server 2008 R2 has some improvements over the version in Windows Server 2008. Perhaps the most notable addition is the ability to back up single files and folders, where the previous version required you to back up entire volumes. Some of the new and updated features include the following:

- System state backups and recoveries can now be performed using the Windows Server Backup snap-in in Server Manager. You can also select a system state backup and add other data to that backup. A system state backup contains all the data necessary to restore the operating system to the state it was in when the backup was made. This includes the operating system files and registry but does not include user data that is stored on the computer.

◆ The Windows Server Backup tool includes full functionality from both the command line and Windows PowerShell utilities. You can do everything from the command line or through scripting that you can do from the Windows Server Backup snap-in.

◆ Remote storage options for backups include remote shared folders and volumes (such as iSCSI or Fibre Channel volumes) and virtual disks.

◆ You can perform automatic management of stored backups. Windows Server Backup will automatically delete old backups to make room for current backups.

LIMITATIONS OF WINDOWS SERVER BACKUP

Windows Server Backup has a few limitations of which you should be aware, particularly if you are coming from an earlier version of Windows Server in which you used NTbackup.exe:

◆ Unlike earlier versions of Windows Server, Windows Server 2008 R2 only supports backing up to internal or external disks or to optical media such as CD or DVD. Tape backups are no longer supported, and tape drivers are no longer supplied.

◆ There is a data size limit of 2TB (2048GB) per volume that can be backed up using Windows Server Backup. This means that if you have files and folders on a single volume that exceed that 2TB limit, you must split the operation into two or more backups. The real concern with this limit is when performing a full server backup where the server has more than 2TB on a single volume. In this case, the full server backup would truncate to 2TB, and data beyond that limit would not be backed up.

◆ Windows Server Backup only works with volumes that are formatted with NTFS. To back up FAT volumes, you would need to convert them to NTFS before performing the backup operation.

◆ Windows Server Backup cannot read backups made with NTbackup.exe. Thus, restoring data from backups made in a previous version of Windows Server, such as Windows Server 2000, cannot be restored using Windows Server Backup. Microsoft does make a read-capable version of NTbackup.exe available in its Download Center. Using this version of NTbackup.exe, you could mount those older backups and restore data to your Windows Server 2008 R2 computer.

◆ Windows Server Backup is available in all editions of Windows Server 2008 R2 with the exception of the Server Core installation. However, you can back up a Server Core installation by using the command-line and Windows PowerShell utilities or by backing up the volumes remotely from another server running a full installation of Windows Server 2008 R2. You can find more information on using Windows Server Backup from the command line at http://technet .microsoft.com/en-us/library/cc771583(WS.10).aspx.

Windows Server Backup is installed as a feature within the File Services role in Windows Server 2008 R2 and comprises three distinct parts:

◆ Microsoft Management Console (MMC) snap-in

◆ Command-line tools (Wbadmin.exe)

◆ Windows PowerShell cmdlets

Windows Server Backup is not installed by default in Windows Server 2008 R2. To install all components, do the following:

1. In Server Manager, click Features in the left tree pane, and then in the right Actions pane click Add Features.

2. On the Select Features page of the Add Features Wizard, select Windows Server Backup Features. To also add the command-line tools, expand Windows Server Backup Features, and select Command-line Tools.

3. Click Next. Review your installation choices, and then click Install.

Windows Server Backup lets you back up to local disks (disks that are physically attached to the server computer) or to remote shared folders and volumes. If you choose to back up to a remote location, be sure that your network connection to that remote location has enough bandwidth to ensure that the backup can complete in the time you have allocated for backup. Since most backup operations are scheduled for off-hours when few users will be accessing the server, you would want the backup to complete before the users come into the office in the morning.

The biggest difference between storing backups in a network shared folder vs. using a local disk is that Windows Server Backup will store multiple versions of backups on a local disk but will store only the most recent version of a backup in a remote location. Having multiple backups for a specific server computer means that you can recover from changes made on those dates as well as recover from a complete data loss. This is most useful when restoring files that may have been changed or deleted prior to the most recent backup.

When backing up to disks, consider using some type of removable disk, such as an external USB or eSATA hard disk. A better implementation would include multiple removable disks that could then be rotated to off-site storage to provide a higher level of disaster recovery protection. Windows Server Backup can identify disks to be used for backup and automatically use whichever disk is present, deleting the oldest backup on the disk to make room for the current backup operation.

Backing Up and Restoring a Full Server

Performing a full server backup is one of the easiest types of backup to perform and is also one of the best types in terms of recovery. A full server backup includes the following parts:

◆ All local volumes (virtual disks hosted on local volumes will not be backed up if they are online)

◆ Critical volumes

◆ System state

With a full server backup, you can recover individual files and folders and entire volumes in case of disk failure. You can also perform a "bare-metal" recovery in which you have replaced the entire server computer (or at least the hard disks containing the operating system and system state) and there is no operating system installed. The drawbacks to a full server backup are the size of the backup and the time required to perform the backup.

PERFORMING A FULL SERVER BACKUP

These steps assume that you will be performing a full server backup to a local disk and defining a schedule for the backup operation to be automatically repeated:

1. Open Windows Server Backup. In Server Manager, expand Storage in the left tree pane, and then click Windows Server Backup.

2. In the right Actions pane, click Backup Schedule. Click Next.

3. Select "Full server" for the backup type, as shown in Figure 18.1. Click Next.

FIGURE 18.1
Selecting the backup type

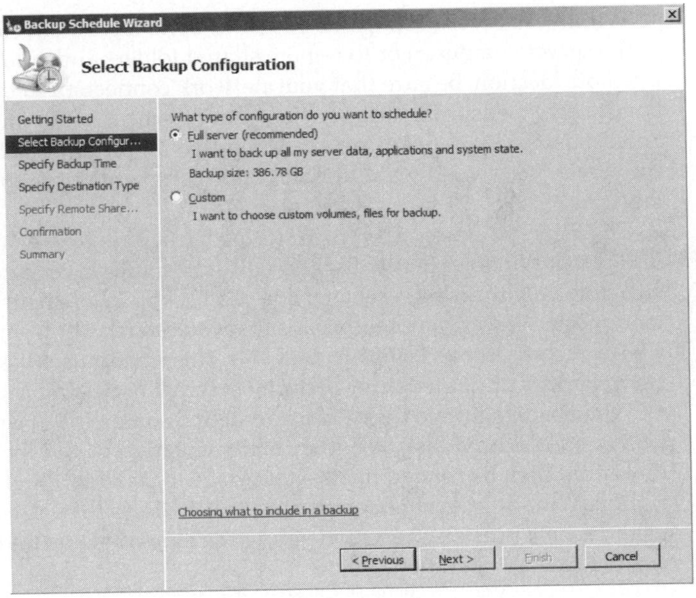

4. Set the time of day to start the backup, as shown in Figure 18.2. Your options include "Once a day," for which you select the time of day to start the backup, and "More than once a day," where you select an available time and click Add to move it to the "Scheduled time" list. Using the "More than once a day" option lets you schedule as many backups as you want, with the caveat that you want to leave enough time between backup operations that they are able to complete before the next is triggered. Click Next.

Remember that performing a backup requires heavy disk activity and processor cycles. Because of this, backups should be performed only when user activity on the server is low, such as overnight during off-hours. If you perform backups during peak usage times, your users may complain of slow access, and their activities on the server may delay the backup.

5. Select the option "Back up to a hard disk that is dedicated for backups," as shown in Figure 18.3. To use this option, you must have at least one disk attached to the server computer that has no existing volume. The disk should be raw, with no partition or file system. Click Next.

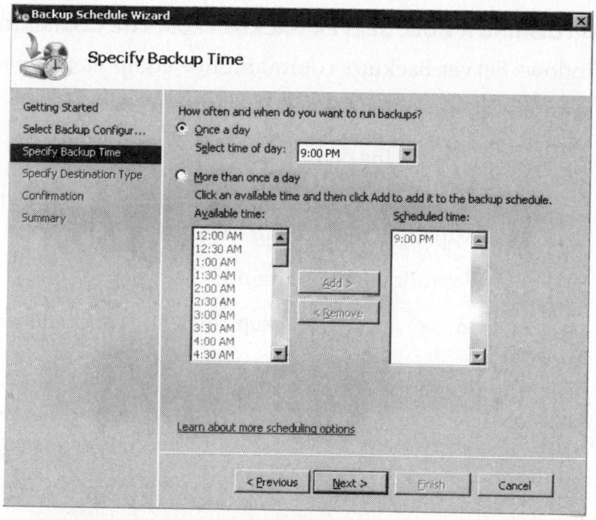

FIGURE 18.2
Selecting the
time of day

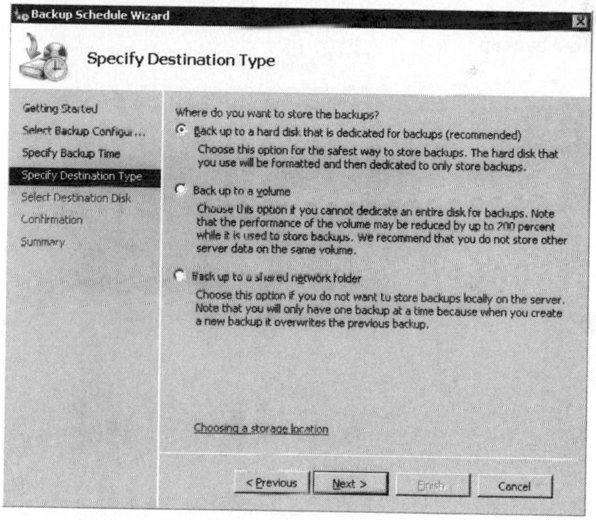

FIGURE 18.3
Selecting the
type of disk

6. Select the disk to use for the backup volume. To use off-site disk rotation, specify multiple disks on this page. Click Next. You will be warned that finishing this wizard will cause the selected disks to be formatted, losing any existing data on the disks. If you are certain you want to use the selected disks, click Yes to proceed.

7. Review your selected options for the scheduled full server backup. If you are satisfied with the options, click Finish to format the disks and schedule the backup.

PERFORMING A FULL SERVER BACKUP FROM THE COMMAND LINE

Windows Server Backup's command-line component, Wbadmin.exe, should be used in cases where you want to script backup operations or when you prefer to use the command line to maintain a server computer. These steps assume that you will be creating a scheduled full server backup using the command line:

1. Open an elevated command prompt. You must be a member of either the Administrators or Backup Operators group to perform these steps.

2. Enter the following command:

   Wbadmin.exe enable backup -vssFull -schedule:02:00 -addtarget:E: -include:C:\

   The -vssFull switch indicates a full server backup, and -addtarget defines the destination path to store the backup as the E drive. -include:C:\ indicates that the C drive should be included. Whenever you use a drive letter with -include, you must include the final backslash. Figure 18.4 shows the result of this command.

FIGURE 18.4
Creating a new
scheduled backup

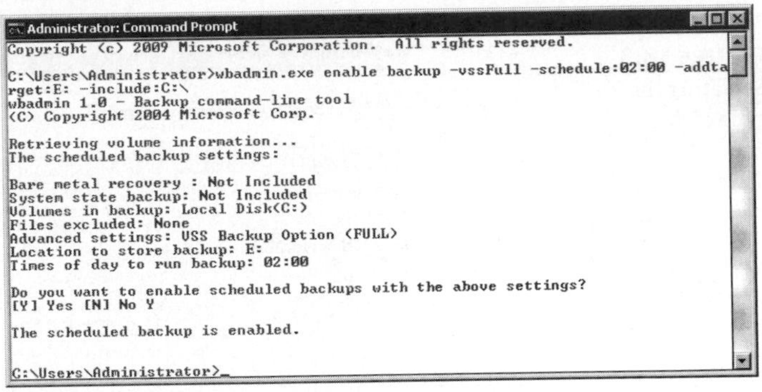

3. Enter the following command to start the backup you just created:

   Wbadmin.exe start backup

PERFORMING A FULL SERVER RESTORE

You can recover your server using different methods depending on the amount of data that must be recovered and the time you want to spend on the recovery. Consider the worst-case scenario of complete data loss on the server, either from hardware failure or from data corruption. In this case, you could choose to reinstall the Windows Server 2008 R2 operating system and then perform a full server restore using Windows Server Backup. Or you could choose to perform a bare-metal restore using the Windows Server 2008 R2 installation DVD and the full server backup.

The following steps assume that your server computer has suffered total data loss and that you have resolved the hardware issues, replacing the failed hard disks. Make sure that the new hard disks are at least equal in capacity to the disks being replaced. Be sure to attach the drive containing the backup that will be restored so that Windows Setup will be able to locate it. Alternatively, you can access a backup located in a shared folder on the network.

1. Boot the computer with your Windows Server 2008 R2 DVD.

2. In Install Windows, select the correct language options, and click Next.

3. Click "Repair your computer."

4. Windows Setup will attempt to identify any existing Windows installations on the hard disks and, if found, offer to repair them. If you are restoring onto a fresh hard disk, the list should be empty. Click Next.

5. In System Recovery Options, click System Image Recovery.

6. In "Re-image your computer," select either "Use the latest available system image" or "Restore a different backup." If you select "Restore a different backup," you will be prompted to select from available backups or to provide a network path to the backup.

7. In "Choose additional restore options," select the appropriate options:

   ◆ Select the "Format and repartition disks" box to repartition and format the disks you are recovering to. When you select this option, the option "Exclude disks" becomes available, and you can choose to exclude some disks from the formatting. This is particularly important when you are only recovering the disk containing the operating system and do not want to affect data stored on other volumes.

   ◆ If you want to only restore the operating system, click "Only restore system drives."

   ◆ If you do not see all the disks installed in the computer, you may need to install drivers. Click "Install drivers."

   ◆ In the Advanced options, specify whether the computer will automatically be restarted and whether to check for disk errors upon restart.

8. Review your selected options, and then click Finish to begin the recovery.

If you are restoring from a network location, be aware that your server is not functioning as a domain computer while being recovered. The server containing the backups must be available to nondomain computers in order to be accessible during the recovery. For this reason, it is often easier to perform a recovery from a locally attached external drive.

A full server restore is most useful on a server computer that requires a complete restore of the operating system and all data on each disk. If you are restoring only the operating system or everything on the critical drives (such as operating system and registry files), restoring from Windows Setup works well provided you are careful to exclude disks where the data is not being recovered.

RECOVERING THE SYSTEM STATE

You can also recover the server by reinstalling the operating system and then using Windows Server Backup to restore the system state. This might be the preferred method if the backup is stored on a domain computer that cannot be accessed through Windows Setup.

WHEN THINGS GO WRONG

As a server administrator, you take steps to protect your data just in case something goes wrong. As a case in point, we recently heard from a client who had done everything right in preparing for data recovery. The domain controller for this small office housed not only Active Directory for the domain but also several important applications and user data. The operating system, applications, and user data were all stored on a RAID 5 set comprising four physical disks. Backups were scheduled to run every night, and they ran full manual backups at least once a month to be stored off-site.

RAID 5 sets are resilient enough to lose a single hard disk without downtime. You can add a new disk to replace the failed disk and tell the RAID 5 set to rebuild, all on the fly. The client's domain controller, however, suffered the loss of two physical disks in the set on the same night. It was a freak occurrence, but it was something they weren't able to recover from.

After discovering the problem the next morning, the administrator was able to recover the domain controller by replacing the failed disks, establishing a new RAID 5 set, and then performing a full server restore. The process included booting the computer with the installation DVD with the backup drive attached and then using the backup to perform a bare-metal restore. The server was up and running in a few short hours.

CAUTION REQUIRED

Once you start a system state recovery, you must not stop it or restart the computer until it has completed. If the system state recovery is interrupted, the server computer may be left in an unbootable state.

To use Windows Server Backup to recover the system state of your server, follow these steps:

1. Open Windows Server Backup. Either select Start ➤ Administrative Tools ➤ Windows Server Backup or in Server Manager expand Storage and then click Windows Server Backup.

2. In the Actions pane, click Recover.

3. On the Getting Started page, select the server to recover:

   ◆ "This server:" The local server will be recovered.

   ◆ "Another server": You will be restoring data to a remote server. If you select the option, you will be prompted to select the location of the backup files to use, either on the local computer or on a network shared folder.

4. On the Select Backup Date page, use the calendar control to select the date of the backup to restore, and select the time if there was more than one backup made on that date.

5. On the Select Recovery Type page, select System State.

6. Select the location to restore to, either "Original location" or "Select another location." If you choose to restore to another location, either type the path to the restore location or use the Browse button to specify the location.

7. Review your settings, and then click Recover to begin the restore.

In Windows Server 2008 R2, you can also restore the system state from the command line using the Wbadmin.exe tool:

```
Wbadmin.exe start systemstate recovery -version -backupTarget
-machine -recoveryTarget -authsysvol -autoreboot
```

-version   Defines the date and time of the backup. For example, to specify the backup made on June 10, 2009, at 11 p.m., use -version:06/10/2009-23:00.

-backupTarget   Defines the computer where the backup file is stored. For example: -backupTarget:\\server1\share.

-machine   Defines the name of the computer being recovered; use this switch with -backupTarget if there are backups for multiple computers stored in that location. For example: -machine:Server1.

-recoveryTarget   Defines the destination of the backup if not being restored to the original location.

-authsysvol   Indicates that the restore should perform an authoritative restore of the system volume shared folder (SYSVOL).

-autoreboot   Tells the recovery to automatically restart the computer once the system state restore has completed.

Backing Up and Restoring Files and Folders

In addition to full server and system state backups, Windows Server Backup lets you back up and restore individual files, folders, and volumes. This is the method to use when you are more concerned about recovering data than the operating system itself or when performing interim backups of important data that changes frequently. Backing up data folders can be useful for recovery scenarios where the operating system can be restored through imaging and then the data is restored through backup.

PERFORMING A MANUAL BACKUP OF FILES AND FOLDERS

Data backups (of files and folders) either can be scheduled or can be manual operations in Windows Server Backup. One common backup configuration for a server that houses important data would be for a full server backup each night with an additional file and folder backup of data during the day.

These steps assume that Windows Server Backup is installed and that you have folders containing data to be backed up:

1. Open Windows Server Backup. Either select Start ➢ Administrative Tools ➢ Windows Server Backup or in Server Manager expand Storage and then click Windows Server Backup.

2. In the right Actions pane, click Backup Once. Click Next.

3. On the Select Backup Configuration page, select Custom, as shown in Figure 18.5. Click Next.

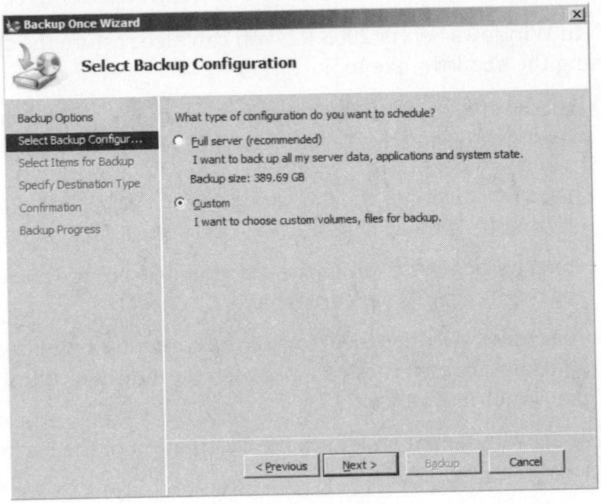

FIGURE 18.5
Selecting Custom to perform a backup of specific files and folders

4. Click Add Items to select the files and folders to back up. Repeat the process until you have added all the folders and files you want to back up.

5. Click Advanced Settings. On the Exclusions tab, you can add file exclusions to omit certain files from the backup such as if you have temporary files in the folders you will be backing up. On the VSS Settings tab, you can modify the behavior of Windows Server Backup regarding backup history flags. Select VSS Full Backup if Windows Server Backup is the only backup software you will use with these files and folders. Otherwise, if you use additional backup software and want the backup flags to remain unchanged after this manual backup, select VSS Copy Backup. Click OK, and then click Next.

6. Specify the backup destination type, either a local disk or a network location. Click Next.

7. Specify the location for the backup. This page will vary depending on the type of destination you selected previously. If you selected a network location, you can also determine whether the created backup file will inherit the permissions of the shared folder destination or maintain specific permissions. If you select "Do not inherit," you will be prompted to provide user credentials to assign permissions to the file. Click Next.

8. Review the settings for the backup, and then click Backup to begin the operation. The Backup Progress page shows the progress of the backup including any errors encountered and the completion.

RECOVERING A FOLDER FROM A BACKUP

Recovering individual files and folders is a rather common task for many administrators. Consider how many times a user has said that they accidentally deleted a presentation or spreadsheet that they need to have for an important meeting. This can be accomplished easily using a custom recovery in Windows Server Backup, provided the backup files are accessible:

1. Open Windows Server Backup. Either select Start ➢ Administrative Tools ➢ Windows Server Backup or in Server Manager expand Storage and then click Windows Server Backup.

2. In the right Actions pane, click Recover.

3. Select the location of the backup file that you will use for this recovery. If you select a remote location, you must provide the type of location and the location path in subsequent steps. Click Next.

4. Select the backup date and time that you want to use. If there is only one backup present, the date and time will default to that backup. If there are multiple backups, it will default to the most recent. Click Next.

5. On the Select Recovery Type page, click Files and Folders. Click Next.

6. Use the tree view under "Available items" to locate the folder you want to recover. If you are trying to restore individual files, select the files in the "Items to recover" pane. Click Next.

7. On the Specify Recovery Options page, select the recovery location, permissions for the recovered files and folders, and what to do if there are existing copies of the files in the location you are restoring to. Click Next.

8. Review the settings for accuracy, and then click Recover.

You can also recover a single folder from the command line. The following example recovers the C:\Library folder:

```
Wbadmin.exe START RECOVERY -version:07/20/2009-18:39
-items:C:\Library -itemtype:File -backupTarget:C: -recursive
```

START RECOVERY   This switch tells **Wbadmin.exe** to begin a restore operation.

-version   The **-version** switch defines the backup version to use for the restore. It is specified in a MM/DD/YYYY-HH:MM format. You can use the Wbadmin.exe GET VERSIONS command to list all available backup versions.

-items   This switch provides a comma-delimited list of items to restore.

-itemtype   This option specifies the type of objects in the **-items** list and can include FILE, APP, and VOLUME. Use separate switches to specify more than one type in a restore operation.

-backupTarget   This specifies the location of the backup file you want to use for the restore operation.

Stopping and Restarting Active Directory

Restartable Active Directory Domain Services (AD DS), introduced in Windows Server 2008, lets you stop AD DS to perform maintenance on the server without requiring you to restart the server in Active Directory Recovery Mode (ADRM). The benefits of being able to stop and restart AD DS include offline defragmentation and the application of server updates without requiring a restart of the computer. However, performing a system state recovery is not supported without restarting the server computer in ADRM.

Once you stop AD DS on the server, users can continue to log on to the domain if other domain controllers are available. In addition, you will be able to log on to the server using your domain administrator account to perform tasks on the server if there is another domain controller available to process your logon. Otherwise, if you have stopped AD DS on the only domain controller, you must log on to the server using the ADRM administrator credentials. To enable this option, you must modify the DSRMAdminLogonBehavior registry value to either 1 (the Directory Services Restore Mode administrator account can log on when AD DS is stopped on the server) or 2 (the Directory Services Restore administrator account can always log on to the server). The option to allow the Directory Services Restore (DSRM) administrator account to always log on to the server, whether AD DS is stopped or not, is not a good idea since the credentials are not checked against any password policies. The registry value is located here:

```
HKLM\System\CurrentControlSet\Control\Lsa\DSRMAdminLogonBehavior
```

Stopping and Starting AD DS

Stopping AD DS is done exactly like stopping any service in Windows, by using the Services snap-in in Server Manager or Computer Management.

You must be a member of the Domain Administrators group to perform these steps:

1. Open Server Manager. Select Start ➢ Administrative Tools ➢ Server Manager, or click the Server Manager button on the taskbar.

2. Expand Services and Applications, and then click Services. In Server Manager, expand Configuration, and then click Services.

3. Right-click Active Directory Domain Services in the details pane. Click Stop on the context menu. You will be prompted to approve a list of other services upon which AD DS depends. Accept the list, and those services will also be stopped. They will be restarted when you start AD DS again.

4. To start AD DS, right-click Active Directory Domain Services, and then click Start.

Defragmenting Active Directory Offline

In Windows Server 2008, you had to restart a domain controller in DSRM to perform an offline defragmentation and integrity check of the AD DS database. Windows Server 2008 R2 gives you the ability to perform these tasks without having to restart the computer and enter DSRM. Instead, you can stop AD DS and then use Ntdsutil.exe from an elevated command prompt to perform the offline defragmentation and integrity check.

Before performing an offline defragmentation, it would be wise to back up the system state and critical drives of the domain controller to be sure you can recover from any serious errors that might occur. You should verify that there is ample free space on the volume that contains the AD DS database (Ntds.dit) for temporary space. Microsoft recommends free space equal to at least 15 percent of the Ntds.dit file size for temporary space needs.

Active Directory automatically performs online defragmentation to optimize the storage of data within the Ntds.dit file part of the daily garbage collection process. This does help optimize the database, but it does nothing to reduce the size of the database file. Offline defragmentation is the only effective way to reduce the size of the database.

PERFORMING OFFLINE DEFRAGMENTATION OF NTDS.DIT

These steps assume that you will be compacting the `Ntds.dit` file to a local folder. If you plan to defragment and compact the database to a remote shared folder, map a drive letter to that shared folder before you begin these steps, and use that drive letter in the path where appropriate.

1. Open an elevated command prompt. Click Start, and then right-click Command Prompt. Click Run as Administrator.

2. Type **ntdsutil**, and then press Enter.

3. Type **Activate instance NTDS**, and press Enter.

4. At the resulting `ntdsutil` prompt, type **Files** (case sensitive), and then press Enter.

5. At the `file maintenance` prompt, type **compact to** followed by the path to the destination folder for the defragmentation, and then press Enter. If there are spaces in your path to the destination folder, enclose the entire path in double quotation marks (such as **"c:\temp folder\"**). Ntdsutil.exe will display a progress indicator. Upon completion, it instructs you to perform an immediate backup of the original and the compacted files.

6. Copy the new `Ntds.dit` file to your `%systemroot%\NTDS\` (for example c:\Windows\NTDS\ Ntds.dit).

7. Delete all the log files in the NTDS folder (for example, type **del C:\Windows\NTDS*.log**).

8. Type **quit** and press Enter to exit file maintenance mode, and then type **quit** and press Enter again to exit `Ntdsutil.exe`.

9. After you complete all these steps, restart AD DS.

It may be interesting to note that you will not be able to access files and folders on the server computer after stopping AD DS without providing the DSRM administrator credentials.

Checking the Integrity of an Active Directory Database

Active Directory uses the same indexed sequential access manager (ISAM) database engine that is used in Exchange Server and various Windows Server internal databases such as Windows Internet Naming Service (WINS). The version used in Windows Server 2008 R2 is called the *extensible storage engine* (ESENT), which is essentially a newer version of the JET database engine used by Microsoft for many years.

You can check the integrity of the `Ntds.dit` file in two ways; the first uses the `Files` subcommand of `Ntdsutil.exe`, and the second uses the `Semantic database analysis` subcommand of `Ntdsutil.exe`. Microsoft warns that `Semantic database analysis` subcommand should not be used as part of normal database management because improper use can result in severe data loss for Active Directory; instead, it is used only as part of troubleshooting when working with Microsoft product support. Even though Microsoft warns against using `Semantic database analysis`, each time you use the integrity and recover subcommands under `Files`, it will prompt you to also run `Semantic database analysis`.

PERFORMING AN INTEGRITY CHECK OF NTDS.DIT

Using the Files subcommand in Ntdsutil.exe lets you verify the integrity of the database file and repair any corruption that is found. You should always use the recover command before performing an integrity check. The recover command flushes all transactions to the database file, ensuring that the file has the most up-to-date information. recover uses the Esentutl.exe program to perform a soft recovery of the Ntds.dit database and commits all outstanding transactions.

Perform these steps after stopping the AD DS service:

1. Open an elevated command prompt. Click Start, right-click Command Prompt, and select Run as Administrator.

2. Type **ntdsutil**, and press Enter.

3. Type **Activate instance NTDS**, and press Enter.

4. At the resulting ntdsutil prompt, type **Files** (case sensitive), and then press Enter.

5. At the file maintenance prompt, type **recover**, and press Enter.

6. Type **integrity**, and then press Enter.

7. Type **quit** and press Enter to exit file maintenance mode, and then type **quit** and press Enter again to exit Ntdsutil.exe.

8. After you have completed these steps, restart AD DS.

USING SEMANTIC DATABASE ANALYSIS

While using the Files subcommand of Ntdsutil.exe checks the Ntds.dit file for normal file corruption, using the Semantic database analysis subcommand checks the internal structure of Ntds.dit to ensure it complies with the normal semantics of Active Directory and outputs a report of the number of records currently in the database, including deleted and phantom records. The report is named dsdit.dmp.x, where x is a number that is incremented each time you run the report.

Perform these steps after stopping the AD DS service:

1. Open an elevated command prompt. Click Start, right-click Command Prompt, and select Run as Administrator.

2. Type **ntdsutil**, and press Enter.

3. Type **Activate instance NTDS**, and press Enter.

4. Type **Semantic database analysis** (case sensitive), and then press Enter.

5. At the semantic checker prompt, type **Go** to start the analysis. Use **Go Fixup** to run the analysis and repair semantic errors in the file.

6. Type **quit** and press Enter to exit semantic checker mode, and then type **quit** and press Enter again to exit Ntdsutil.exe.

7. After you have completed these steps, restart AD DS.

The report file generated by the Semantic database analysis subcommand is in the current folder from which you ran Ntdsutil.exe, typically c:\Users%username%. The system variable %username% will be automatically replaced with the name of the currently logged on user.

Capturing Active Directory Snapshots

In Windows Server 2008 R2 you can use the Volume Shadow Copy Service (VSS) to create a snapshot of the AD DS database. You can then use this snapshot as an offline copy to view data, or it can be processed to be used as an Lightweight Directory Access Protocol (LDAP) directory database. Snapshots can be used to view current objects in AD DS without risking the current state of the database. An easier method for recovering deleted objects in AD DS in Windows Server 2008 R2 is the Active Directory Recycle Bin, which is described in the "Recovering Active Directory Objects" section later in this chapter.

Creating an Active Directory Snapshot

You can create AD DS snapshots with the Ntdsutil.exe tool from an elevated command prompt. Because you do not have to stop AD DS before creating a snapshot, they are ideal for viewing objects from a domain controller without taking it offline.

1. Open an elevated command prompt. Click Start, right-click Command Prompt, and select Run as Administrator.

2. Type **ntdsutil**, and press Enter.

3. Type **Snapshot**, and then press Enter.

4. At the snapshot prompt, type **Activate instance NTDS**, and then press Enter.

5. Type **Create**, and then press Enter. The snapshot will be created, and the GUID of the snapshot will be displayed, as shown in Figure 18.6.

FIGURE 18.6
Creating an Active Directory snapshot

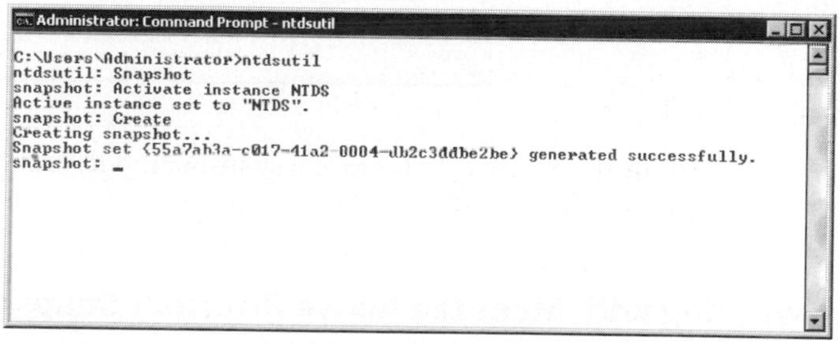

6. Type **quit** and press Enter to exit snapshot mode, and then type **quit** and press Enter again to exit Ntdsutil.exe.

Mounting an Active Directory Snapshot

You won't be able to work with an AD DS snapshot until you have mounted it. Mounting takes the snapshot and makes it available as a local path on the server computer. Once mounted, you can access the AD DS files in the NTDS folder under Windows.

1. Open an elevated command prompt. Click Start, right-click Command Prompt, and select Run as Administrator.

2. Type **ntdsutil**, and press Enter.

3. Type **Snapshot**, and then press Enter.

4. At the snapshot prompt, type **Activate instance NTDS**, and then press Enter.

5. Type **List All**, and then press Enter. This will display all the snapshots currently on the server computer. Each entry will have an index number and then display the GUID of the snapshot.

6. Type **mount x**, where x is either the index number or the GUID of the snapshot you want to mount, and then press Enter. If the command completes successfully, it will return the local mount path of the snapshot, typically a folder off the C drive root. The result should be similar to Figure 18.7.

FIGURE 18.7
Mounting an Active Directory snapshot

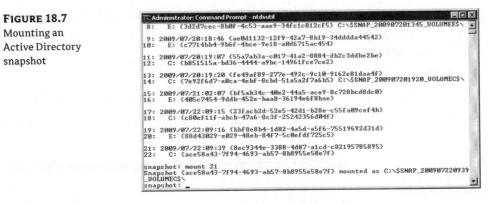

7. Type **quit** and press Enter to exit snapshot mode, and then type **quit** and press Enter again to exit Ntdsutil.exe.

Working with Mounted Active Directory Snapshots

After you have created and mounted an Active Directory snapshot, you need to make it available by using the Dsamain.exe command. Dsamain.exe is installed on Windows Server 2008 R2 with the AD DS role or the Active Directory Lightweight Directory Services (AD LDS) role, and it requires that you be a member of the Domain Administrators or Enterprise Administrators group to use it.

USING DSAMAIN.EXE

Dsamain.exe makes a copy of the AD DS database available through the LDAP from the server computer. Using LDAP, you can access this version of AD DS using a variety of tools such as Ldp.exe or any of the Active Directory snap-ins in Windows Server 2008 R2.

These steps assume that you have created and mounted a snapshot using the previous procedures:

1. Use Windows Explorer to browse to the Ntds.dit file in the mounted snapshot. The path will be similar to c:\$SNAP_200906191422_VOLUMEC$\Windows\NTDS\Ntds.dit.

2. Hold down the Shift key, and right-click Ntds.dit. Click "Copy as path."

3. Open an elevated command prompt. Click Start, right-click Command Prompt, and select Run as Administrator.

4. Type **dsamain /dbpath <path> /ldapPort 10389**. For the <path> value, right-click the command prompt, and select Paste to paste in the copied path. The result should be similar to this:

```
Dsamain /dbpath "C:\$SNAP_200906191422_VOLUMEC$\Windows\NTDS\Ntds.dit"
/ldapPort 10389
```

5. If the command completes successfully, leave the command prompt open while you work with the mounted snapshot. Once you close the command prompt, you will close the Dsamain.exe session. To quit Dsamain.exe, you can press Ctrl+C.

Now that you have the snapshot mounted and have made it available as an LDAP instance, you can view it with any tool that can connect to LDAP, such as adsiedit.

1. From an elevated command prompt, type **adsiedit**, and then press Enter.

2. On the Action menu, click "Connect to."

3. Click Advanced.

4. In Port, type the port number you assigned previously in the Dsamain.exe command line. Click OK.

5. Click OK to connect to the LDAP instance.

You can use adsiedit to view the contents of the snapshot such as when verifying that objects have been created.

Backing Up and Restoring Active Directory

Active Directory is backed up as part of the system state on a domain controller whenever you perform a backup using Windows Server Backup or Wbadmin.exe. As described earlier in this chapter, Windows Server Backup must be installed through features in Server Manager before you can use it to back up or recover your server computer.

The type of backup you select for your domain controllers will depend on the frequency of changes to Active Directory and the data or applications that might be installed on the domain controller. The bare minimum you need to back up to protect AD DS on a domain controller is the system state. The system state includes the following plus additional items depending on the roles that are installed:

◆ Active Directory database (`Ntds.dit`)

◆ Registry

◆ COM+ registration database

◆ Active Directory Certificate Services database

◆ Boot files

◆ SYSVOL folder

◆ Cluster service information

◆ Any system files that are protected by Windows Resource protection

◆ Microsoft Internet Information Services metadirectory

The next level of backup protection is provided by a critical volumes backup, which includes the following:

◆ Volume containing the boot files, including the Bootmgr and Boot Configuration Data (BCD) store

◆ Volume that contains the Windows operating system and registry

◆ Volume containing the SYSVOL folder structure

◆ Volume containing the AD DS database (`Ntds.dit`) and log files

These backup types can be run manually on demand, or they can be scheduled either using Windows Server Backup or using `Wbadmin.exe` and Scheduled Tasks.

LIMITATIONS OF ACTIVE DIRECTORY BACKUPS

You can use either Windows Server backup or `Wbadmin.exe` to perform a system state backup of a domain controller to back up Active Directory. Microsoft recommends using either a dedicated internal disk or an external removable disk such as a USB hard disk to perform the backups. External disks have the advantage of being easily rotated for off-site storage as part of your normal disaster recovery planning.

You must have administrative credentials to schedule a system state backup or restore; backup operators do not have privileges required to schedule backups. System state backups will back up Active Directory integrated DNS zones but will not back up file-based DNS zones. File-based DNS zones must be backed up as part of a volume-level backup such as a critical volumes backup or full server backup.

Recovering Active Directory Objects

Active Directory has allowed you to recover objects that have been deleted for a short period. You had to recover the object before garbage collection occurred and permanently removed any item marked as deleted. Windows Server 2008 R2 introduces the Active Directory Recycle Bin to provide a longer protection for deleted objects.

In Windows Server 2008 R2 without the Active Directory Recycle Bin and in earlier versions of Windows Server when you deleted an object, it was flagged for deletion (*tombstoned*) rather than being immediately deleted. Tombstoned object are permanently deleted when the garbage collection process runs.

With the Active Directory Recycle Bin installed on Windows Server 2008 R2, the process changes. Now when an object is deleted, it is flagged as a deleted object for the span of time determined by the `msDS-DeletedObjectLifetime` property in AD DS, which defaults to null. Once the deleted object lifetime expires, the object is flagged as a recycled object and is stripped of most of its attributes. It still resides in the Deleted Objects container and can be recovered for the duration of its lifetime, which is defined by the `tombstoneLifetime` attribute in AD DS.

WHAT ABOUT OLD TOMBSTONED OBJECTS?

When you install the Active Directory Recycle Bin, any preexisting tombstoned objects automatically become recycled objects, but they cannot be recovered like any other recycled objects from that point on. To prevent this situation, you should check that you have recovered any tombstoned objects you might want to save prior to installing the Active Directory Recycle Bin.

You may have completed these preparatory steps when you installed your first Windows Server 2008 R2 domain controllers. If so, then you can safely move on to enabling Active Directory Recycle Bin. If you have not prepared your forest, then before installing the Active Directory Recycle Bin, be sure to complete the following preparatory steps:

1. If you have upgraded an existing domain to Windows Server 2008 R2, make sure all domain controllers are upgraded before proceeding.

2. Run `Adprep.exe` to prepare the schema of AD DS:

   A. Run `adprep /forestprep` on the domain controller that holds the schema master role.

   B. Run `adprep /domainprep /gpprep` on the domain controller that holds the infrastructure master role.

   C. If you have a read-only domain controller in your network environment, use the `adprep /rodcprep` command on that server.

3. Raise the functional level of the domain to Windows Server 2008 R2, as follows:

   A. Open Active Directory Domains and Trusts. Select Start ➤ Administrative Tools ➤ Active Directory Domains and Trusts.

B. Right-click the domain root in the left tree pane, and select "Raise domain functional level." If you have installed a fresh domain using only Windows Server 2008 R2, these steps are unnecessary.

C. Select Windows Server 2008 R2, and click OK.

You can enable Active Directory Recycle Bin using either Ldp.exe or Windows PowerShell. Once the domain functional level is raised successfully, you can enable the Active Directory Recycle Bin. If your domain is part of a forest, you must raise the entire forest to Windows Server 2008 R2 mode.

ENABLING THE ACTIVE DIRECTORY RECYCLE BIN USING WINDOWS POWERSHELL

You can use Windows PowerShell to modify the AD DS schema in your forest to activate the Active Directory Recycle Bin. This is the method that Microsoft recommends:

1. Open the Windows PowerShell modules. Click Start ➤ Administrative Tools ➤ Windows PowerShell Modules. This will open Windows PowerShell and automatically load the required modules.

2. At the prompt, type the following: **Enable-ADOptionalFeature -Identity <ADOptionalFeature> -Scope <ADOptionalFeatureScope> -Target <ADEntity>**.

The result should look similar to Figure 18.8.

FIGURE 18.8
Installing the Active Directory Recycle Bin

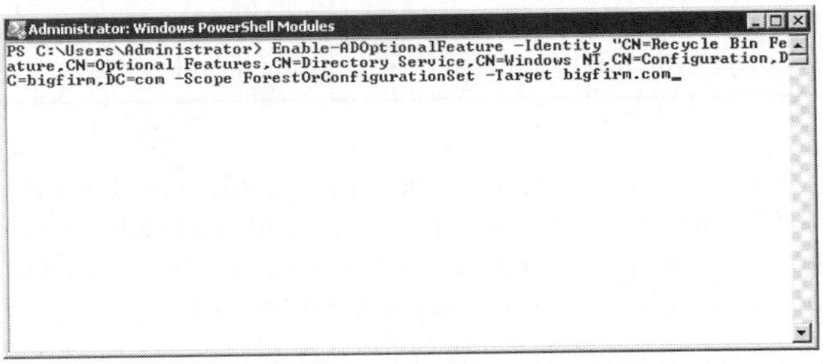

◆ <ADOptionalFeature> must be replaced with the distinguished name for the Active Directory Recycle Bin, which is CN=Recycle Bin Feature,CN=Optional Features,CN=Directory Service,CN=Windows NT,CN=Services,CN=Configuration ,DC=<your root domain>,DC=<com>, where <yourdomain> and <com> represent the name of your root domain in Active Directory such as DC=testdomain,DC=com for the Bigfirm.com domain.

◆ The possible values for -Scope are Unknown, ForestOrConfigurationSet, and Domain.

◆ The value for -Target is your root domain name, such as testdomain.local.

ENABLING THE ACTIVE DIRECTORY RECYCLE BIN USING LDP.EXE

As an alternative to using Windows PowerShell to install the Active Directory Recycle Bin, you can use Ldp.exe to modify the AD DS schema in your forest to activate the Recycle Bin:

1. Open Ldp.exe. Select Start ➤ Run, type in **Ldp.exe**, and then click OK.

2. To connect and bind to the server that hosts the root domain of your organization, click Connection, click Connect, type the name of the server, and then click OK.

3. Click Connection, and then click Bind. To bind using your current credentials, click OK. Otherwise, click "Bind with credentials," provide the credentials to use, and then click Next.

4. Click View, click Tree, and then in BaseDN select the configuration directory partition. Then click OK.

5. In the tree view, expand **CN=Configuration**, right-click CN=Partitions, and select Modify.

6. In the Modify dialog box, in Edit Entry Attribute, type **enableOptionalFeature**.

7. In Values, type CN=Partitions,CN=Configuration,DC=<yourdomain>,DC=<com>:766d dcd8-acd0-445e-f3b9-a7f9b6744f2a, where <yourdomain> and <com> represent your domain name. For example, you'd type DC=testdomain,DC=local. 766ddcd8-acd0-445e-f3b9-a7f9b6744f2a is the GUID for Active Directory Recycle Bin.

8. Under Operation, click Add ➢ Enter ➢ Run.

Creating an Active Directory Backup

To create a system backup from a command line, use the command Wbadmin.exe start systemstatebackup -target <volumename> from an elevated command prompt, where <volumename> is the drive letter of a local disk.

1. Open Windows Server Backup. In Server Manager, expand Storage, and then click Windows Server Backup.

2. Click Backup Once. Click Next.

3. Click Custom, and then click Next.

4. Click Add Items. Select System State, and then click OK. Click Next.

5. Select the type of storage for the backup location, either local drives or remote shared folder. Click Next.

6. Depending on the backup destination type, provide either the local path for the destination or the network location. Click Next.

7. Review your selected options, and then click Backup.

Be careful to maintain appropriate security for your Active Directory backups because they contain complete copies of your domain's security objects and credentials.

Restoring an Active Directory Backup

There are two types of restore operations for Active Directory: authoritative and nonauthoritative. Authoritative restore will be covered in the next section. Both methods are performed in DSRM, which require restarting the server computer and using the F8 option menu to select DSRM. If the server is not able to boot to this mode using the installed operating system such as after recovering from failed hard drives, you can boot from the Windows Server 2008 R2 DVD and enter DSRM by selecting "Repair your computer" at the Setup screen.

1. Power on the server computer, and after POST, press the F8 key to bring up the Windows Server 2008 R2 boot options screen.

2. Select "Launch startup recovery," and then press Enter.

3. On System Recovery Options, select the language (if there is more than one language pack installed) and the keyboard input method. Click Next.

4. Provide the DSRM administrator credentials, and then click OK.

5. Click Command Prompt.

6. At the prompt, type **wbadmin get versions -backuptarget:<drive>:- machine:<computername>**, where <drive> is the drive letter of the drive where the backup is located, and <computername> is the name of the computer being restored. The -machine switch is required only if there are backups from multiple computers on the backup disk. Press Enter.

7. Note the version that you want to restore as the version ID must be entered exactly to work. At the prompt, type **wbadmin start systemstaterecovery -version:<MM:DD:YYYY-HH:MM> -backuptarget:<drive>: -machine:<computername> -quiet**. The -quiet parameter suppresses prompts to verify that you want to start the restore and that SYSVOL has not changed. The command should look similar to Figure 18.9.

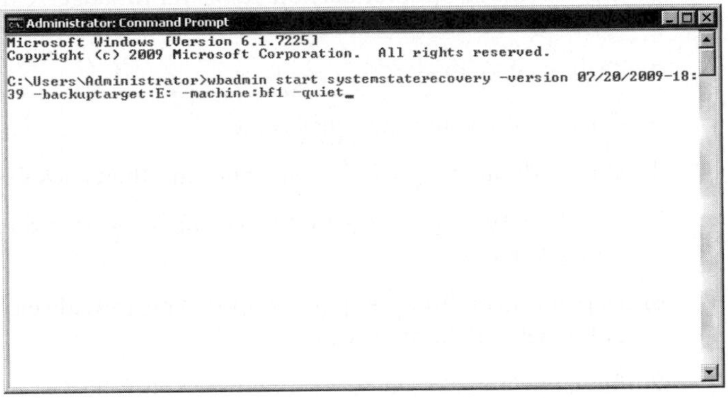

FIGURE 18.9
Restoring the system state

```
Administrator: Command Prompt                                           _ □ X
Microsoft Windows [Version 6.1.7225]
Copyright (c) 2009 Microsoft Corporation.  All rights reserved.

C:\Users\Administrator>wbadmin start systemstaterecovery -version 07/20/2009-18:
39 -backuptarget:E: -machine:bf1 -quiet_
```

If you will be performing an authoritative restore after the nonauthoritative restore completes, do not restart the server. Once you restart the domain controller, AD DS and Active Directory Certificate Services detect that a restore has occurred, and they run automatic integrity checks of their databases.

Performing an Authoritative Restore

An authoritative restore is performed after a nonauthoritative restore in most cases. The purpose is to recover deleted AD DS objects by marking the restored objects as authoritative or by marking the new copy that should be replicated to the other domain controllers. Every time a change is made to AD DS, the version number of the database is incremented. Making an authoritative restore of deleted objects involves setting the version number higher than the currently replicated version of the AD DS database.

Wherever possible, authoritative restores should be made on the global catalog server so that group information can be fully recovered. If you can isolate the global catalog server before it receives replication of the deletion you are trying to recover, you can restore the objects without first performing a nonauthoritative restore. In other words, if you are quick enough, you can unplug the network cable from the global catalog server and avoid having to recover from a backup.

To perform an authoritative restore before the change has replicated, do the following:

1. Isolate the server either by disconnecting the network cables or by typing the **repadmin /options <servername> +DISABLE_INBOUND_REPL** command.

2. Stop AD DS either by using Services in Server Manager, as described earlier in this chapter, or by typing the **net stop ntds** command at an elevated command prompt.

3. At an elevated command prompt, type **ntdsutil**, and press Enter.

4. At the ntdsutil prompt, type **authoritative restore**, and press Enter.

5. Type the appropriate command for the type of object being restored:

   ◆ To restore a subtree such as an entire OU, type **restore subtree <DN>**, where <DN> is the full distinguished name of the object being restored. For example, to restore the HR OU in Bigfirm.com, type **restore object "OU=HR,DC=bigfirm,DC=com"**.

   ◆ To restore a single object, such as a user account, type **restore object <DN>**, where <DN> is the full distinguished name of the object.

6. Make a note of any .txt or .ldif files that are generated because they can be used to re-create any back links for the objects being restored. Back links contain the information for group memberships. The .txt files can be used to re-create group memberships in other domains for the restored user accounts using the create ldif file from command in Ntdsutil in the other domains. The .ldif files can be used to restore group memberships in the local domain using the Ldifde.exe utility.

7. Type **quit** to exit authoritative restore mode, and then type **quit** again to exit Ntdsutil. Restart the server normally.

Performing an authoritative restore where the changes have already replicated will require a nonauthoritative restore from backup first and then the same steps to perform authoritative restores of the deleted objects.

The Bottom Line

Use Windows Server Backup to back up and restore a Windows Server 2008 R2 computer Windows Server Backup is installed as a feature in Windows Server 2008 R2 and can be used to create various types of backups to protect your server computer. Full server backups contain the operating system, critical volumes, and all data on the server, while critical volume backups protect all volumes the operating system depends on but not necessarily the additional data stored on the server.

Master It   Your server contains two hard disks; the first contains the operating system, and the second contains user data. How can you use Windows Server Backup to protect the operating system and the user data?

Defragment AD DS offline   In Windows Server 2008, you had to restart a domain controller in DSRM to perform an offline defragmentation and integrity check of the AD DS database. Windows Server 2008 R2 gives you the ability to perform these tasks without having to restart the computer and enter DSRM. Instead, you can stop AD DS and then use Ntdsutil.exe from an elevated command prompt to perform the offline defragmentation and integrity check.

Master it   You want to defragment your AD DS database but do not want to shut down the server and restart it in DSRM. How do you do that?

Install the Active Directory Recycle Bin   In previous versions of Windows Server, recovering deleted objects in Active Directory required recovering from a backup. Windows Server 2008 R2 introduces the Active Directory Recycle Bin, which enables you to recover objects from Active Directory as if you were restoring a file that had been sent to the Windows Recycle Bin.

Master it   You want to provide additional protection against accidental deletion of objects in Active Directory. How can you provide an extra 180 days of recovery for deleted objects?

Create and recover a system state backup for Active Directory   Because domain controllers contain all the database information for Active Directory, recovering a failed domain controller server is critically important. When using Windows Server Backup or the command-line utility Wbadmin.exe, perform backups containing the system state at a minimum to preserve Active Directory.

Master it   You want to protect your Active Directory data from the possibility of complete hardware failure of the server computer. Which type of backups will provide this protection?

Chapter 19

Advanced IP: Routing with Windows

Why route from Windows? The short answer is, because you can and because it's very informative.

A decade or more ago, routers were expensive, and it was common for network-savvy companies to use cast-off PCs as cheap routers. For example, by putting a couple of network cards in the PC and installing a copy of KA9Q NOS (a network operating system that could be configured to do nothing but route), a network engineer saved the company a lot of money on buying a huge chunk of iron from a major network vendor.

Today, as ever, routing is a vital part of maintaining a network infrastructure, so it is important to understand how routing works in order to correctly manage your network and the hosts on it. Knowing a little about routing will also help you troubleshoot connection issues on your own hosts.

In this chapter, we will take you through the life of an IP packet as it finds itself being routed across your network, and we will explore the difference between class-based and classless routing. We will explain how network address translator (NAT) devices allow you to route TCP traffic and how the arrival of Winsock shaped the Internet boom.

We will walk you through the processes of installing the Routing and Remote Access Server (RRAS) role and installing a NAT. (We will revisit the RRAS role more in the next chapter, when we discuss VPNs.) We will cover how to configure a Windows Server 2008 R2 computer to route IP traffic, and we will discuss tunneling. Finally, you will learn how you can use the knowledge in this chapter, and a few common tools, to troubleshoot network communication difficulties.

In this chapter, you will learn to:

◆ Document the life of an IP packet routed through your network

◆ Explain the class-based and classless views of IP routing

◆ Use NAT devices to route TCP traffic

The Life of an IP Packet

The designers of the original Internet Protocol achieved something that goes beyond being merely clever: they made something that is just about as simple as it can be to achieve its purpose. As a result, you will notice that we are not going to tell you how to route UDP or TCP, because those protocols each can assume that IP takes care of all that fussiness for them. We are also not going to tell you how to route Ethernet, because Ethernet doesn't route; it only communicates on a single subnet.

But this does mean that if you are to understand routing in TCP/IP, you have to know what makes an IP packet move through the system. To this end, we will describe the life cycle of a typical IP packet using a sample network that should be familiar to you if you've read other books by Mark Minasi.

FIRST, A RECAP

Before we get into the nuts and bolts of routing with Windows, we'll start with a quick recap of what we expect you to know about TCP/IP for this chapter.

◆ *IP addresses identify individual interfaces*: Each active interface on a TCP/IP host (whether it's a PC or a device such as a router or firewall) owns one or more IP addresses; these IP addresses are 32-bit numbers for IPv4 and 128-bit numbers for IPv6. IPv4 addresses are commonly written as "dotted quads"—four numbers from 0 to 255, separated by dots, such as 198.162.1.234. IPv6 addresses are written grouped as hex digits, representing 16 bits at a time, with colons to separate groups, such as 2001:db8::12af:d4f2:1cab:1002. (The double colon represents a string of zeros that has been removed for brevity, in this case, 32 bits worth, or the equivalent of 0:0.)

◆ *IP is an inherently unreliable protocol*: It makes no effort to guarantee delivery or to report on a failure of data to reach its destination.

◆ *UDP is an unreliable protocol built on top of IP*: To IP, it adds the concept of ports—one each for destination and source.

◆ *TCP is a reliable protocol built on top of IP*: Apart from the size of addresses, there is no difference between TCP over IPv6 and TCP over IPv4. To IP, TCP adds the concepts of *ports* for the destination and source, a *connection* lasting from initial greeting to end of life, a *handshake* protocol for opening and gracefully closing the connection, sequencing to maintain the order of each byte in the connection stream, and a way to abort a connection when either end has detected an error condition.

In the example IP packet lifetimes in this section, we will be using Mark's old, but still applicable, network diagram, as reinterpreted in Figure 19.1. Rumor has it that there is a version of this diagram with Roman numerals for IP addresses.

FIGURE 19.1
The Carthage/
Rome network

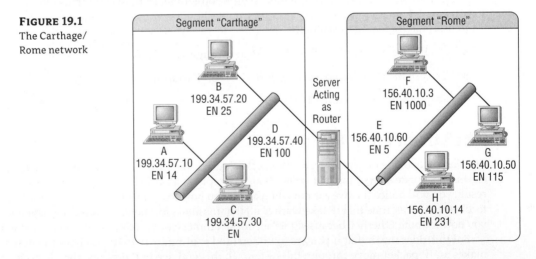

First, the Simple Case: No Routing Required

The simplest case is one where the two computers that want to talk are on the same Ethernet segment. Let's choose a communication from computer A (IP address 199.34.57.10, MAC address 14) to computer C (IP 199.34.57.30, MAC 30). The procedure is as follows:

1. A's application, or its network layer, sends an IP packet to the IP layer.

2. A's IP layer examines the header for the destination IP address.

3. A's IP layer finds B's MAC address using ARP (IPv4) or ND (IPv6).

4. A's IP layer creates an Ethernet packet and sends it.

5. C's Ethernet card recognizes the address, reads the packet, and forwards it to the IP layer.

6. C's IP layer examines the header and passes the payload to the protocol's handler.

That list of steps is something you'll refer to later when troubleshooting connectivity problems, but for now it needs some explanation.

If an IP packet had *parents*, they would be the source and destination IP addresses. Every IP packet has to know where it's starting and where it's going. In IPv4, it also needs a name, just in case it gets split into parts by an intermediate router. That way, the receiver will know which parts to plug together. Finally, it needs a piece of information that tells the receiver how to treat its payload, whether it is to be handed to the TCP or UDP stack, or perhaps a different protocol, with abbreviations such as ICMP, IGMP, GRE, and so on. To IP, they are protocols 1, 2, 47, and so on.

When a packet is created, all this information—and perhaps some optional parts—is placed into the *IP header*, and the header and payload are sent to the IP layer of the network stack for forwarding.

The IP layer at any computer or router reads the source and destination addresses and uses them to determine where to send the packet. In this "simple" case, the source and destination addresses are clearly both on the same subnet, or local link. In that case, no routing is required for the packet.

The IP layer on the source computer has to tell the network layer (in most cases, this would be the Ethernet driver) to put the packet onto the right network card, with the right network destination and source address, and to do that it must know the Ethernet address (the MAC address) corresponding to each IP address.

From Figure 19.1, it's clear that the MAC address for the source should be 14 and that the MAC address for the destination should be 30, but the source computer doesn't have this diagram, and since it's never spoken to C before, it has no idea that it's at MAC address 30. All it knows is that the IP address 199.34.57.30 is where this packet needs to go.

MAC ADDRESS EXAMPLES

Note that the examples we have chosen are unlikely to be seen in real life. The Media Access Control (MAC) address is a globally unique identifier, expressed as a long string of hexadecimal digits, usually separated into pairs by dashes.

IPv4: Address Resolution Protocol

This is where the Address Resolution Protocol (ARP) comes into the picture. ARP is an Ethernet broadcast. Technically, all Ethernet packets are broadcast across the whole subnet, but most of them carry a destination MAC address and are discarded by other Ethernet cards when they are received. An Ethernet broadcast packet is meant to be picked up by any Ethernet card.

The ARP packet contains the source MAC address of the requester and the IP address that is being searched for. Every Ethernet card on this segment will receive this request and has to forward it to its IP layer. The IP layer will check to see whether it owns the IP address being requested. The interface that does own this IP address will then respond affirmatively to the ARP request, with a unicast response that identifies itself as the owner of the requested address.

The requester receives this response and adds an association to its *ARP table* between the IP address and the Ethernet address. You can view this ARP table at any time in Windows using a number of different methods. The easiest to remember is probably the command arp -a, which shows the addresses that have been assigned to network cards, as you will see in Figure 19.2.

FIGURE 19.2
Displaying the ARP table

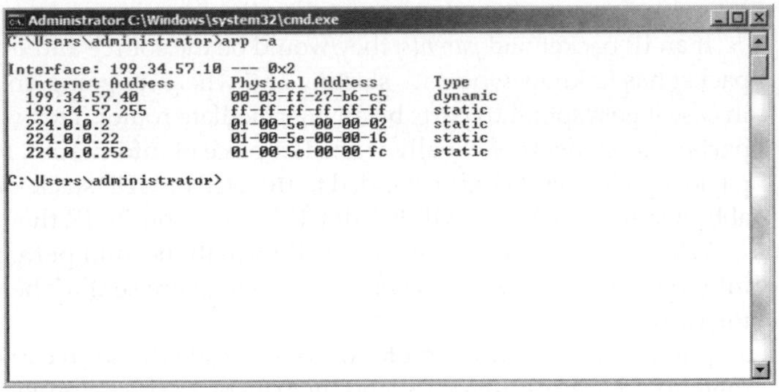

As with most network facilities, you can also see this table using a netsh command, netsh interface ipv4 show neighbors, as shown in Figure 19.3.

FIGURE 19.3
Using netsh to show the neighbors table

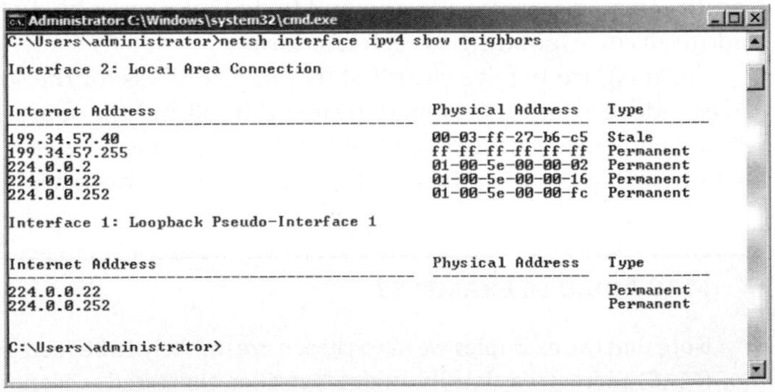

In this example, the IP layer at computer A will create a packet that says, "I am an ARP request packet from the machine at IP 199.34.57.10 (EN 14), and I want to know the MAC address for the interface with IP 199.34.57.30." Computer A will then "shout" that message to the whole of Carthage, most of whom will stop what they're doing, check their IP addresses to see whether they are 199.34.57.30, and only one (C) will send a response back to A, saying, "I am an ARP response packet from the machine at IP 199.34.57.30, and my MAC address is 30."

IPv6: Neighbor Discovery

In IPv4, the IP layer of every computer on a subnet needs to pause what it's doing to inspect incoming ARP requests. If you can imagine how annoying it would be for everyone to stop their work every time someone called *anyone* in the company, that's roughly what it is like for IPv4 hosts.

IPv6 discards the concept of broadcast-based protocols—they become multicast-based protocols—and the same is true of Neighbor Discovery (ND), which (among other things) takes over the resolution process from ARP, which is not supported on IPv6.

Rather cleverly, the IPv6 layer will take the last 24 bits of the IP address being queried for and will build a multicast address known as the *solicited node multicast address* by putting those 24 bits into the placeholder X bits of the destination address FF02:0:0:0:1:FFXX:XXXX. It is this address that the Neighbor Solicitation message is sent to. Because there are more than 16 million possibilities for those last 24 bits, it's almost certain that this multicast message will only interrupt the Ethernet card and interface that owns this IP address.

The Neighbor Advertisement message that comes back tells the requester what MAC address corresponds to the IP address requested—as with ARP, this is kept in a table that is always checked when sending an IP packet, so as to save repeatedly requesting the same Neighbor Solicitation.

To show the neighbors table for IPv6, can you use the ARP command? No, because ARP is strictly for IPv4 only. The way to get the neighbor discovery table that is in use for your IPv6 layer is to run the `netsh` command, specifically, `netsh interface ipv6 show neighbors`, as shown in Figure 19.4.

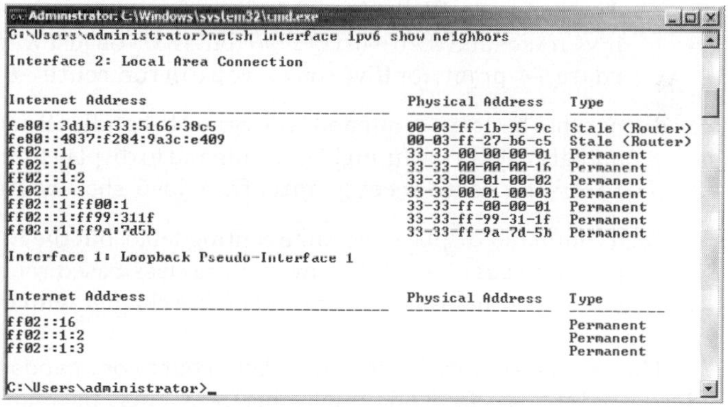

FIGURE 19.4
Showing the IPv6 Neighbors Table

Finally, You Can Send the Packet!

Now that you know who you are trying to talk to, the computer at interface A can finally send the data by building an Ethernet packet, whose payload is the IP packet (IP header and IP payload) and whose header contains the source and destination address, length, and type of protocol (to say that this is IP, as opposed to SPX or DEC/LAT or some other protocol that nobody really much uses anymore).

This packet is then handed down to the Ethernet card, which sends it on.

ETHERNET TRIVIA

Did you know that although IP is an unreliable, "best-effort" protocol, which is free to lose packets of data for pretty much any reason (much like the postal service), Ethernet itself is a reliable protocol? It's true: Ethernet uses electrical properties of the wire on which it runs to monitor whether a packet that it tried to send might have been confused with any other packet that was on the cable at the same time—if it finds this, it pauses a random length of time and tries again.

Now the Hard Case: With Routing

This really isn't all that hard, actually, but we thought it best to approach you with as few confusing issues as possible, which is why we have separated the two parts of packet routing into different sections of this chapter.

EVERY HOST IS A LITTLE BIT ROUTER

Every computer with an IP address is part host, part router. It may not forward packets received from other hosts, like routers normally do, but it most certainly needs to keep a table of routes out from its own interfaces to the rest of the world, exactly as a router would do.

Just as with the ARP table, although you don't generally want to mess with the table's contents, you can always view them. Again, as with the ARP table, you can use several commands:

◆ route print: This command is the old standby for routing, and with no parameters other than print, it will display a list of interfaces and their MAC addresses, followed by a list of IPv4 routes and then a list of IPv6 routes. If you just want the IPv4 routes, you can run route -4 print; for IPv6 routes, you can run route -6 print.

◆ netsh: The netsh command is designed to handle all network-related configuration settings and displays in the future. The command to display the routing table is netsh interface ipv4 show route or netsh interface ipv6 show route.

Each command displays the same routing table, but the information and presentation vary. The command route print displays a more class-based routing table and is familiar to many. You should feel comfortable by the end of this chapter with outputs such as that shown in Figure 19.5.

The two netsh interface *ipvX* show route commands are a little more compact—if you don't need the interface index table, this format may be more what you need.

In both of the netsh outputs, the network destinations are in the newer Classless Inter-Domain Routing (CIDR) format, which we will describe in more detail shortly. Figure 19.6 shows the IPv4 routing table, and Figure 19.7 shows the IPv6 routing table. There is little difference between them except for the format and size of the prefix.

As you can see, that's a lot of confusing data to understand.

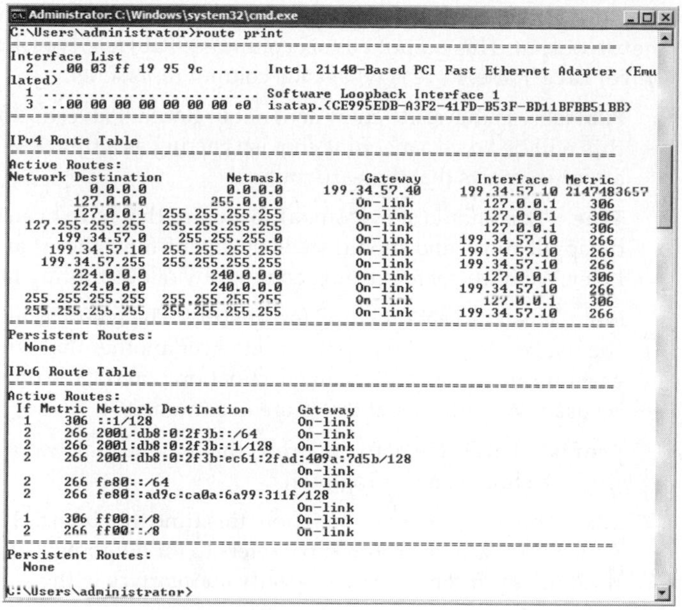

FIGURE 19.5
Showing the IPv4 and IPv6 routing tables with route print

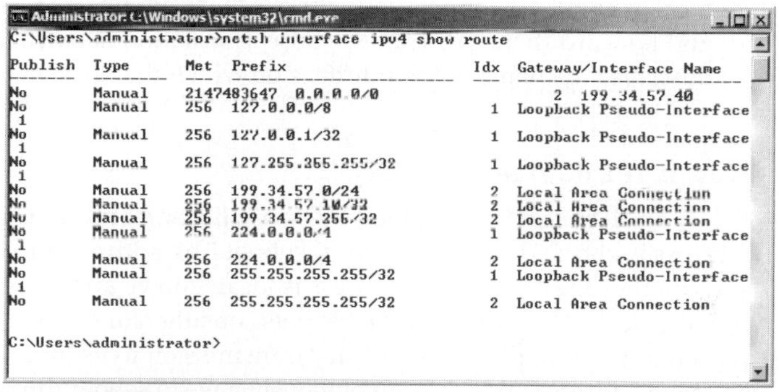

FIGURE 19.6
Using netsh to view the IPv4 routing table

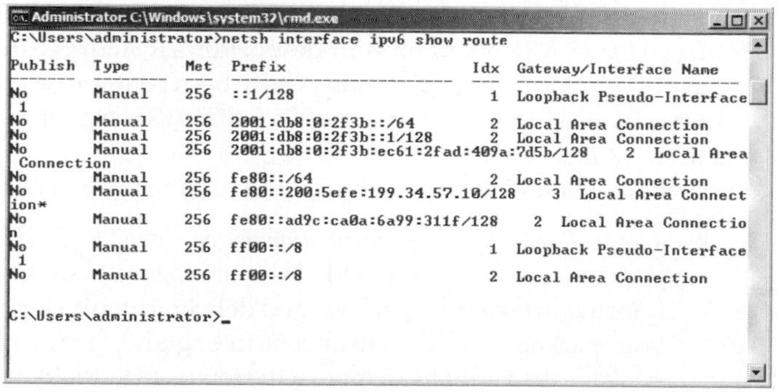

FIGURE 19.7
Using netsh to view the IPv6 routing table

Let's pick one of those outputs and analyze it. Because it's new to everyone, let's go with the netsh output. This output has six columns—Publish, Type, Met, Prefix, Idx, and Gateway/ Interface Name. Here is what each column represents:

Publish Is this route entry sent out in Router Advertisements to other computers? Usually this will be No on a machine that isn't acting as a router—only routers should be providing advertisements that they are routers!

Type This should show Manual for routes that have been statically added either by hand or by applications and should show Autoconf for routes that are added automatically by the IP layer. We have yet to see Autoconf in any of our routing tables.

Met This is an abbreviation for "metric." The metric is an arbitrary number that indicates the relative "cost" of using this route over another that will get to the same destination. When several routes match the same destination criteria, the one with the lowest metric will always be used. We will look at this more in a moment.

Prefix This is the network prefix that will be matched against the destination address to find the shortest matching prefix.

Idx This is another abbreviation, this time for "interface index." This is a number indicating which interface this route entry refers to for outgoing traffic. The interface index can often be used in netsh commands to specify an interface without remembering its name.

Gateway/Interface Name For routes containing destination network prefixes outside the local subnet, this column contains the local subnet address of a router that can take packets and forward them. For routes whose destination network is on the local subnet, this column describes the name of the interface on which that local subnet lies.

How Is the Routing Table Used?

When an IP packet is assembled by an application and sent to the IP layer, its destination address is checked against the local subnet link address and mask of every network interface to see whether the destination address is local. You've already seen what happens if the address is indeed local—the ARP or ND table gets consulted and, if necessary, refreshed, and the packet is placed onto the appropriate NIC for transmission to its target.

If the address isn't local, you obviously have to send it through a router. You will find a router to send the packet to, and you will act as if the router's MAC address is actually the MAC address returned by an ARP query on your destination's IP address. In fact, in some very strange environments, this is exactly what the routers have been configured to do—respond to every ARP as if the router is indeed the host being searched for. That's a sign of a dysfunctional network, though, so we'll say no more about that.

How do you find the right route in the routing table? There are three simple criteria:

◆ *The routing table entry's destination network must be the closest match to the destination address of your packet*: In the real world, this is analogous to saying that if you had two mail carriers offering to take your package and deliver it, you'd skip over the one who says, "I can get your package delivered to anyone in England," in favor of one who says, "I can get your package delivered to anyone in the town of Hadfield in England"—the latter will get your package there much faster, because he's already local.

◆ *If there are two possible routing entries, the one with the lowest metric is chosen*: Metrics are rather arbitrary numbers, and their only purpose is to act as tiebreakers in this step of finding a matching route in the routing table. All that is necessary is to ensure that routes to the same destination can be sorted by metric to indicate the network designer's preference as to which router should be tried first.

◆ *If there is still more than one matching entry, the first one in the list is chosen*: Note that "the first one in the list" is rather difficult to control accurately. As a result, you should be careful to choose metrics appropriately so that you can always predict which route gets chosen.

Once the IP layer has chosen a routing entry, as we mentioned earlier, it will send the IP packet to the router listed as the gateway in that entry. Of course, that means that the IP layer must use ARP to determine what MAC address corresponds to the IP address of the router. Note that the destination IP address in the IP packet that is eventually sent to the router is the original destination IP address, not that of the router.

Let's use Carthage host A as an example, revisiting the routing table in Figure 19.8.

FIGURE 19.8

Looking at the Carthage host A routing table again

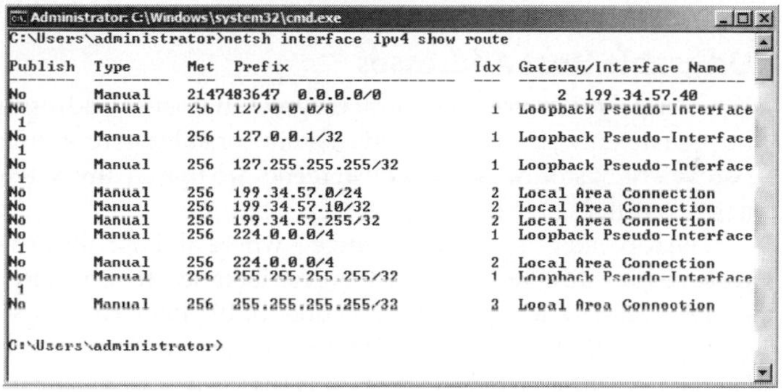

How do you figure out from that where to send a packet from Carthage A, destined for machine H on subnet Rome? To answer that, first you need to know about network masks.

From Classes to Classless

We have deliberately chosen the `netsh` version of the router table, because it uses the more recent CIDR format, as opposed to the older `netmask` format that appears in the `route print` output in Figure 19.5.

Wherever you work with networks, you will encounter some people who were taught the new format and some who learned the old format; therefore, it's best to learn both, so you can be the interpreter between these two groups. The following description may not be entirely historically accurate, but it is logically accurate and will help you understand why the Internet is the way it is today.

In the Beginning Was the Class

When the Internet was young and there were huge swaths of wide-open address space available to be assigned, addresses were, well, not quite handed out like candy but were certainly assigned less strictly than they are today. Internet users were categorized into different classes, and along with them came different classes of address ranges to suit them.

The classes were named A through C, and they were each distinguished by the number of bits devoted to the network address and the number of bits devoted to the host address. With only 32 bits of IP address, a class A assignment would use 8 bits to signify the network address and the remaining 24 to signify the host address, a class B assignment would use 16 bits for network address and 16 for host address, and a class C assignment would use the first 24 bits for network address and 8 bits for host address.

Classes are identified by reading the binary form to see how many of the "most significant bits" are set to 1, before reaching the first zero. Class A addresses start with a zero, so the first octet is in the range 0000 0000 to 0111 1111 (or in decimal, 0 to 127). A class B address has a single 1 before the first zero, as in 1000 0000 to 1011 1111 (in decimal, 128 to 191). Class C addresses start with two 1s and then their first 0, so their range is 1100 0000 to 1101 1111 (or 192 to 223).

This all seemed very equitable, with class A users getting the ability to have nearly 2 to the power of 24 (16,777,216) hosts. Class B users received nearly 2 to the power of 16 (65,536) hosts, and class C users got nearly 256 hosts each.

Unusable Host Addresses

Why "nearly"? In every network range, a number of addresses are not available to be assigned to hosts. The only absolute, carved-in-stone (or at least, written in the RFCs, which are the Internet's equivalent of stone tablets) requirements are that in any network the top and bottom end of the address ranges are reserved.

The top end of the address range—where all host bits are set to 1 (the *all 1s address*)—is reserved for directed broadcast. So, for instance, if your network was a class B assignment and had addresses starting with the sequence 192.168.*something.something*, the directed broadcast address would be 192.168.255.255, where the two 255 octets represent a binary sequence of 1111 1111. All 1s, see?

A packet sent to this address would reach every computer on the 192.168.*something.something* network. Every computer would pass that message up to its own IP layer, where something might be listening for that broadcasted traffic. (You will see this 192.168.*something.something* network appear in lots of documentation, and we will explain why in a few paragraphs.)

The bottom end of the address range—where all host bits are set to 0 (the *all 0s address*)—is technically reserved for broadcasting.

Wait, we already said that the all 1s address was reserved for broadcasting, didn't we? Well, yes, that's true—and you won't find a system today that uses all 0s for broadcasting. But back in the Internet's equivalent of the Bronze Age, Internet developments were being made by several different groups at once. Apparently the broadcast was invented by more than one company. Sun chose to broadcast at all 0s, and everyone else chose to broadcast at all 1s. Much to Sun's surprise (because at the time, it was a major force in Internet development), everyone else won out.

But the all 0s address hasn't become available for use because it also represents another concept, that of the "network address." In router tables, as well as in network diagrams and other documentation, it refers to the network as a whole, so, instead of talking about the 192.168.*something.something* network, you could now talk about the 192.168.0.0 network.

All Y'all

As an Englishman living in Texas, the first few years in this country for this chapter's author proved to be educational as to the way in which the language he had previously considered "his" could be contorted and yet still vaguely recognizable as English. The most interesting example was that not only was there now a second-person plural, "y'all" (an abbreviation of "you all"), but there was a plural of the second-person plural, "all y'all."

Internet addressing in IPv4 has a similar concept—the all-all-1s and all-all-0s addresses, 255.255.255.255 and 0.0.0.0.

Given that the all 0s address 192.168.0.0 now represents the network of machines from 192.168.0.1 to 192.168.255.254, what would 0.0.0.0 represent? It generally represents a network of one computer—"this" computer.

By extension, 255.255.255.255 represents "broadcast to every computer out there." That's the "all y'all" address, if you like.

Broadcast Gets Narrower: The First Unroutable Addresses

When the Internet was small, these broadcast addresses were great. If you wanted to know what computers a company had connected to the Internet, all you had to do was find that their network address was 192.168.0.0, and that meant you could enumerate their network by pinging 192.168.255.255. You would get a response from every machine they had. Then you could try to connect to random machines and see which ones were interesting.

Similarly, if you wanted to enumerate the entire Internet, that was no problem either—you simply used `ping 255.255.255.255`, and you got in return a response from every machine that currently existed (and a stern warning from the university network administrators not to ever, ever do that again!).

Because each of these actions had their own risks—the first, a risk of disclosure, and the second a risk of flooding your own network (or someone else's, if you could direct the responses to their directed broadcast address!) pretty soon routers were being configured to disallow packets with these destinations from crossing them.

As a result, 192.168.255.255 could now be used only from inside the 192.168.0.0 network, so it became a directed broadcast that you could only direct at yourself; and 255.255.255 became a global broadcast that would only reach machines on your side of the router. Essentially, this meant that both broadcasts reached the same place—your local subnet—and since the 192.168.255.255 directed broadcast address required calculation but the 255.255.255.255 address could be hard-coded, pretty much nobody uses the directed broadcast form anymore. Unfortunately, this doesn't mean you can get that address back and use it for a host.

Routing the Unroutable Part 1: Private Addresses

The document that defines the all 0s and all 1s addresses (RFC 1122, "Requirements for Internet Hosts—Communication Layers") also defines a specific class A address as being reserved for the purpose of *loopback* communication. This is the network 127.0.0.0, but out of that 16 million address range, almost nobody ever uses anything other than the single address 127.0.0.1, which is usually given the alias *localhost*.

A useful convention that has grown over the years is to use the first address in a network as the location for the default router. Note that this is only a convention, and nothing forces you to do this (in our Rome/Carthage example, for instance, the router does not follow this convention).

However, following this convention may make it simpler for the person who follows you to find the router. An example would be in the 192.168.0.0 network, you'd use 192.168.0.1 as the address of the default router.

There's that network again—192.168.0.0. Why do we keep using that network? Quite simply, it's because we know we won't get sued by the owners for accidentally directing traffic their way. How do we know this? This address is not owned by any one individual. Another RFC document (RFC 1918, "Address Allocation for Private Internets") lays out a series of network ranges that are reserved for private use. By default, these addresses are not routed—a router will not forward an IP packet whose destination is in these ranges:

10.0.0.0–10.255.255.255

172.16.0.0–172.31.255.255

192.168.0.0–192.168.255.255

Those of you who can do binary math in your heads, or have memorized the class ranges, will have realized that the range 172.16.0.0–172.31.255.255 is not a network range that matches a class. It is, in fact, a supernetwork, or *supernet*, of 16 class B address ranges between 172.16.0.0–172.16.255.255 and 172.31.0.0–172.31.255.255. The 192.168.*.* range is also a supernet of 256 class C networks.

Of course, if you're in one of these networks, you'll realize that your packets do make it outside the router—what you may not realize is that they do so by virtue of a NAT, which alters the source address to something that the router will be willing to pass.

Originally, NATs would assume that only a certain number of internal users would be accessing the Internet at any one time so that number of external addresses were assigned to the NAT, and each time a user's traffic needed forwarding to the Internet, that user's internal address was mapped to a free external address. For some organizations, this is still the way in which internal systems become accessible to the outside Internet.

SUBNETTING AND SUPERNETTING

Something that was realized early on in the design of the IP class system was that even a huge multinational corporation that might want a class A address would not actually have one physical Ethernet wire to which 16 million devices were attached. So, a scheme was developed whereby a larger network could be divided into several subnetworks, or *subnets*.

The way to do this was to say that class distinctions were no longer so important; every host would have its own notion of how many of its address bits defined "the network" and how many of its address bits defined "me on the network." Because this divided the binary address into two portions, not on an 8-bit octet boundary, they used a term borrowed from graphics processing—and called it a *mask*. Specifically, this would be a *netmask*. You can imagine it as a sheet of paper with holes cut in it (just like a mask you might make for your kids at Halloween). The holes allow the network part of your address to show through and hide the host part, replacing those bits with 0s.

In Figure 19.9, we are looking at the effect of the netmask 255.252.0.0 on the address 192.168.143.8. The netmask is equivalent to the binary string 1111 1111 1111 1100 0000 0000 0000 0000—that's 14 bits set to 1 and 18 bits set to 0.

FIGURE 19.9
Demonstrating
how a netmask
works

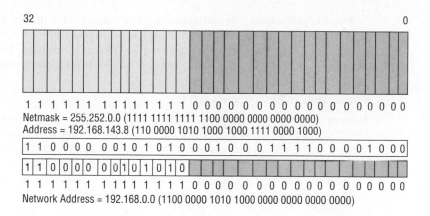

Network Address = 192.168.0.0 (1100 0000 1010 1000 0000 0000 0000 0000)

The address 192.168.143.8 is equivalent to the bits 1100 0000 1010 1000 1000 1111 0000 1000, and when you line this up underneath the netmask, you can see which bits to ignore when calculating the network address and which bits to count:

1111 1111 1111 1100 0000 0000 0000 0000: Netmask

1100 0000 1010 1000 1000 1111 0000 1000: Host address

1100 0000 1010 1000 0000 0000 0000 0000: Network address

In binary mathematics, this is equivalent to defining the mask as a number that's the same width as your address, with a 1 in every bit in the network portion, with a 0 in every bit in the host portion, and using the binary AND operation with your network address. The binary AND compares bits in the two inputs one position at a time—where the two bits are set to 1, the result will have a 1 bit; if any or both are set to 0, the result will have a 0 bit. Check our binary math, and make sure that we got it right!

As you've guessed from this section's heading, there were also organizations that bought a class C and then realized that they needed to use more than 254 addresses within their organization. They could buy another class C, of course, but if they could buy a class C that was next door to their existing one, they could "supernet" the two to create a network of 2^9–2 addresses—510 in all. The savings in number of addresses were not the main point, however—the savings that were important in supernetting were in the sizes of the routing tables on the way to this network.

You will see these network masks in the output from `route -4 print`, but they are a pain to calculate and to understand what number of bits each represents. The key to remember is that there are only eight values that can appear in any octet of a netmask: 255, 254, 252, 248, 240, 224, 192, 128, 0—that's 8, 7, 6, 5, 4, 3, 2, 1 and 0 bits, respectively. Add up the number of bits in each octet to come up with the total number of bits in a network mask to see how many bits of your host address are tied to the network.

Because a network might be subnetted at several different places, the netmask for an address depends on where you are in the network. The address 10.1.2.3, for instance, might be the third host in the network 10.1.2.0–10.1.2.255, or it might be the 66,051st host in the network 10.0.0.0–10.255.255.255.

Another casualty of subnetting and supernetting was the directed broadcast—even if the router allowed a directed broadcast to pass, how do you know how many bits to direct your broadcast at? This was yet another nail in the coffin of the directed broadcast, which now only truly exists as an annoying reason not to use the all 1s address in your network.

SUBNETTING BY RFC OR BY REALITY

Many of you may have already encountered a subnet range chosen from RFC 1918 (www.ietf.org/rfc/rfc1918.txt) values. Every time the author of this chapter connects to the wireless in a local coffee shop, he gets an address in the 10.0.0.0 class A range that is reserved for private networking. But his netmask isn't 255.0.0.0. It's generally 255.255.255.0—allowing for only a maximum of 253 devices (the router takes up one address!) using wireless inside the coffee store. This being Seattle, the home of many Microsoft employees, it's a little optimistic to think that this limit won't be reached!

This 10.* range is also used frequently in home networks set up by cable installers or those that follow the instructions for the default configuration of several brands of routers. If you use 10.0.0.0–10.0.0.255 with a netmask of 255.255.255.0 in your home, technically you're in violation of RFC 950, which says that you shouldn't use a subnet of all 0s or all 1s. However, we doubt the Internet police would come knocking on your door.

If you're trying to take an exam based on this RFC and RFC 1122, you will want to trim off two subnets from your calculations—the all 0s subnet and the all 1s subnet.

CLASSLESS INTER-DOMAIN ROUTING (CIDR): THE INTERNET LOSES ITS CLASS

As you can see from our assertion that the use of an all 1s or all 0s subnet address is no big deal, as well as from the widespread use of supernetting (which has no subnet part or perhaps a negative-length subnet part!), it was pretty clear that the Internet's scheme of segregating network addresses by classes was becoming completely irrelevant.

Added to this was the sheer tedium of having to calculate the network masks. Network masks were always a string of some number of bits set to 1, followed by a number of bits set to 0, with the total number of bits being 32, which is the size of an IPv4 address. To save having to write network addresses as "10.0.0.0–10.0.255.255" or "10.0.0.0 with netmask 255.255.0.0," network administrators used a shorthand notation, writing a slash after the network number and then writing just the number of bits set to one. So "10.0.0.0–10.0.255.255" would become "10.0.0.0/16." The default allocation of the 10.0.0.0 address as a class A network with netmask of 255.0.0.0 would be noted by describing it as "10.0.0.0/8."

The Internet is ruled by RFCs, as we think we've already mentioned, and this new shorthand notation was no exception. RFC 1519 defined the original solution as Classless Inter-Domain Routing, and the name has held up.

In fact, the CIDR shortcut has been carried over into IPv6; you will see that IPv6 network prefixes throughout Windows Server 2008 R2 are specified in exactly this manner.

ROUTING TCP: NAPT AND PAT

Remember that we told you early on in this chapter that IP is the only layer that is routed—that Ethernet is a broadcast system and TCP doesn't need routing? That's a bit of a fib, we're afraid.

DECIPHERING THE ROUTER TABLE

Do you have enough information to read that router table in Figure 19.8? Let's look at the Carthage A router table again.

Reading from top to bottom and ignoring the `Publish`, `Metric`, and `Idx` fields, you have the following routes:

CARTHAGE A'S ROUTING ENTRIES

PREFIX	GATEWAY/INTERFACE	COMMENTS
0.0.0.0/0	199.34.57.40	The default route—this means "if you don't find a better match below, send the packet to 199.34.57.40, or Carthage D." 0.0.0.0/0 is a special value and should not be thought of as anything other than a placeholder meaning "default."
127.0.0.0/8 127.0.0.1/32 127.255.255.255/32	Loopback	Even the loopback address has to be routed! The first entry indicates that the entire loopback network can be reached through the loopback interface; the second entry indicates that the specific address 127.0.0.1 is on that interface, and the third entry indicates that directed broadcasts for this network can be sent there. Strictly speaking, the first entry should cover the others.
199.34.57.0/24 199.34.57.10/32 199.34.57.255/32	Local Area Connection	This indicates that any address on Carthage, even the router Mediterranean, can be reached through the Local Area Connection interface.
224.0.0.0/4	Loopback Local Area Connection	These entries indicate that multicast traffic can be sent on either of the available interfaces.
255.255.255.255/32	Loopback Local Area Connection	Again, these entries indicate that broadcasts can be sent on either interface.

As you can see, the table is displayed in order from least-specific route to most-specific route. You can think of the router inside this computer comparing the destination in the Prefix column against the destination of an IP packet:

"Hmm, I have a packet here for 199.34.57.20—where do I send it? Well, 0.0.0.0/0 matches anything, so if I don't find anything else, that entry will win out. What about the next few? They all start with 127, and the prefix hasn't masked that out. My destination address doesn't start with 127, so that won't work. 199.34.57.0/24 matches, because my destination address is 199.34.57.20, and if I zero everything past the first 24 bits (like the prefix says I should), I get 199.34.57.0, which is the same as the network address of the prefix for this entry. That's a match that I will choose instead of the less-specific match I have. No others match, so I am left with sending my packet through the local area connection."

As long as the routing table is complete and correct, the computer will always follow this procedure of checking the prefix against the destination address, masking the destination address with the number of bits in the prefix first, and always discarding a less-specific match when a more-specific match is found. The metric is used only as a "tiebreaker" in case two entries have the same prefixes that are the closest match—the one with the lowest metric is chosen.

COMPLETING THE TABLE

How do you correct an incomplete router table? More to the point, how do you tell if a router table is incomplete?

You've already seen that the router table is consulted for every IP packet. So, a correct and complete router table must be able to tell you the right place to send every packet.

It must have at least one default route, with a prefix of 0.0.0.0/0 (or ::/0 for IPv6 routes); otherwise, there will be some packets it has no idea what to do with. Don't forget that the routing table may have more than one default route; in the case, there are several routers that volunteer for the task. Remember that the one with the lowest metric value will win.

Other than that, it must know exactly how to route to every destination address that does not go to the default router. In most home environments, this is not a problem. The default router is usually the one that connects to the DSL or cable router, and everything can be sent there.

In an enterprise environment, however, there are often several routers in your immediate subnet. Each leads to a different portion of your network. If you list the routers and the networks to which they lead, you should have a list that matches all the entries in your routing table.

If you find that you need to add a route to your routing table, that can be done very easily from the command line. There are two basic commands to use—the old route add and our good friend netsh. Suppose you wanted to add a route to the prefix 192.168.0.0/16 with a metric of 100 that leads to the router at 10.0.0.1. The commands to do this could be any of the following:

```
route add 192.168.0.0 mask 255.255.0.0 10.0.0.1 metric 100
route add 192.168.0.0/16 10.0.0.1 metric 100
netsh interface ipv4 add route 192.168.0.0/16 "Local Area Connection" 10.0.0.1
```

The netsh command is a little more typing than the route command, even if you abbreviate it to

```
netsh int ipv4 add ro 192.168.0.0/16 "Local" 10.0.0.1
```

Similarly, you can delete a route—though if it is one that is automatically added because of a router advertisement, it will come back as follows:

```
route del 192.168.0.0
netsh interface ipv4 delete route 129.0.0.0/8 "Local Area Connection"
```

It is certainly the original design that IP should be the only point that requires routing, and it was an original goal of IP. What was the original design for TCP that it didn't require routing, and how did that change over time?

Why TCP: What Doesn't IP Have?

So, just what is wrong with IP that TCP needed inventing?

IP doesn't have any concept of a connection—if we had to describe it as analogous to an existing system we're comfortable with, it would be the postal service. Every IP packet is like a postcard that goes through the system. Much like the postal service, some IP packets get lost in transit, and if you send two IP packets one soon after the other, they may arrive in the opposite order. Unlike the postal service, some IP packets get delivered twice!

An IP packet, just like a postcard, cannot contain as simple a message as "please ignore the previous message" because it is impossible to be certain that the sender and recipient will agree on what the previous message is. With occasional packet duplication, a recipient could even believe that he is to ignore the message that told him to ignore the previous message.

So, for some kind of communications, these restrictions needed to be overcome—and a system of connected communications needed to be developed to allow for something more akin to a telephone conversation, with a start, an ordered exchange of information, and an end. This is what TCP provides.

Strictly speaking, TCP adds to IP the following attributes:

Handshaking   An exchange like "How do you do?"; "Fine, thanks. How are you?"; "Oh, fine too" in TCP is known as the *three-way handshake* and consists of very short messages, known as SYN, SYN/ACK, and ACK. SYN is short for synchronize, and ACK is short for acknowledgment.

Sequencing   A counter of bytes sent/received is used to ensure that no two bytes are presented twice to the application and that bytes received out of sequence can be reordered. These sequences (one on each side of the connection) are set by the initial SYN and acknowledged with every ACK.

Flow control   A clever system called *sliding windows* keeps traffic flowing without having to wait and without taking up too much memory in the sender or receiver.

Error indication   An application that closes unexpectedly (akin to a hang up on a phone conversation) can be signaled to its communicating partner with a reset (RST) packet.

Ports   This is a little like having a switchboard that allows you to call a company at one number and be directed to any of thousands of extensions so that your conversation can be separated from other conversations with employees at that company.

Sockets, Ports, and Winsock

Almost no one actually writes applications that talk directly in IP. Fewer still write applications that directly control TCP, particularly on Windows, because various security measures prevent any application other than the network stack from creating TCP packets.

Instead, applications communicate to the TCP layer by using something known as a *socket*. Sockets are not unique to Windows; they have been around since some of the earliest days of the Internet.

A socket, in Internet terms, consists of five things—a source address, a destination address, a source port, a destination port, and a protocol (in this case, the protocol is TCP). A pair of matching sockets (where the source address and port of one socket is the destination address and port of the other, and vice versa) constitute a TCP connection. A socket is *unconnected* if its destination port and address are zero, and it is *unbound* if its source port and address are zero. An unbound socket is also unconnected.

Although you know what an address is, we have not yet told you what a port is. Quite simply, it's a number from 1 to 65535, chosen to make sure that sockets can be distinguished from one another. The ports below 1024 are considered reserved, in that they are assigned to a particular protocol. For instance, ports 21 and 20 are assigned to the FTP protocol.

The life cycle of a connection starts in one of two states, depending on whether it is a server-side socket or a client-side socket. A server-side socket will start off in the LISTENING state, which requires a socket to be bound to a source address and port. The client-side socket, meanwhile, will start in the SYN-SENT state, when it starts its handshake with the server socket. This requires that the socket be bound and associated with a destination address and port. The server responds with its SYN-ACK, creating a new socket with the same source address and port as the listening socket, which it puts into the SYN-RECEIVED state. Ending the handshake, the client sends its ACK and puts its socket into the ESTABLISHED state. On the server side, when the initial ACK is received, the server too will put its socket into the ESTABLISHED state.

ONE PORT PER END MEANS TWO PORTS

It is not true to say that a connection to a listening socket creates a connection on a different port. This is an erroneous statement made by many who do not understand that there are two ports in play—one at each side. An example is a connection to a web server—say a client at 192.168.1.2 wants to connect to the web server at 10.20.30.40, and this is the client's first connection since it started.

Let's use some shorthand to describe the sockets. Each socket will be described as {source address, source port, protocol, destination address, destination port}. The web server is LISTENING at port 80, meaning it has a socket bound to source address 10.20.30.40, source port 80, protocol TCP, destination address 0.0.0.0, destination port 0—{10.20.30.40, 80, TCP, 0.0.0.0, 0}. The client creates a socket {192.168.1.2, 1025, TCP, 10.20.30.40, 80}. Huh? Where did 1025 come from? It's the first number above 1024, so it's the first port from the unreserved range and will be used as the source port for the first connection. The next connection will be from port 1026, and so on.

The client sends a SYN on its socket to start the handshake. When the LISTENING socket receives the SYN, the TCP layer creates a copy of the LISTENING socket and sets the destination address and port to match the incoming connection request, so it now has two sockets: {10.20.30.40, 80, TCP, 0.0.0.0, 0} in the LISTENING state and {10.20.30.40, 80, TCP, 192.168.1.2, 1025} in the SYN-RECEIVED state after the SYN-ACK is sent. This socket is paired with the client socket of {192.168.1.2, 1025, TCP, 10.20.30.40, 80} to form the connection. When the client receives the SYN-ACK and sends its ACK in response, both sockets can go to the ESTABLISHED state. A new socket, but not a new port, has been created at the server.

From now on, it is meaningless to call one socket the server and one socket the client; they are both on an equal footing. Each can send and receive data at any time. Although many protocols insist on strict synchronization between command and response, TCP is an asynchronous communications protocol, meaning that any side can send at any time.

To terminate the connection gracefully, one side of the communication (we'll call it the *closer*) will send a FIN and set its socket into the FIN-WAIT-1 state to indicate that it is waiting for an acknowledgment of its FIN, as well as for the other end (we'll call it the *closee*) to close the socket with a FIN. The closee can carry on sending data but will not receive more data from the closer after the FIN that it received.

At some point, usually pretty quickly after receiving the FIN, the closee will send an ACK that acknowledges the FIN. This will cause the closee to enter the CLOSE-WAIT state, indicating that it knows that it won't receive anything more but that it's still waiting for the application to finish sending and close. When the closer receives this ACK, it will enter the FIN-WAIT-2 state.

The closee will eventually finish sending data and will send a FIN to indicate that the application on its end is finished, too. After sending the FIN, the closee enters the LAST-ACK state (it's waiting for an ACK—the last ACK—from the closer), and when the closer receives the FIN, it will enter the TIME_WAIT state and send an ACK to the closee.

The closee will close its socket on receiving this ACK, at which point it is free to forget all about that connection. Technically, the socket is in the CLOSED state. The poor closer, on the other hand, has to keep its socket in the TIME_WAIT state for about four minutes, before it too can move the socket to the CLOSED state and forget about it. (This is to prevent packets that are still bouncing around in the network from being responded to with RST messages.)

Winsock: Why We Can All Use the Internet

Fortunately, even application developers don't need to handle this all for themselves. Wherever there is a network stack, there is an interface used for programming it. Back in the Iron Age of the Internet, there were as many different interfaces—or application programming interfaces (APIs)—as there were network stacks.

There were about a dozen network stacks.

For us poor network programmers, that meant either we had to write a dozen different versions of our software or we had to pick one or two network stacks and hope we had backed the right horse. The "right horse" could change midstream, if you don't mind us mixing a metaphor, whenever the next "killer app" came along and its authors chose a different network stack than the one you had chosen.

Then in 1992 or 1993, the network stack vendors realized that this was constricting their market, because no one was producing applications for Windows networking. They banded together in what they called a spirit of "coopetition" and developed, over the course of several months, a common API that they would all stand behind. They called this Windows Sockets, because it was very similar to the BSD Sockets API on Unix systems. Everyone else quickly called it Winsock, because that's the name of the library with which you linked your network program.

It's some coincidence (but not much) that at this time the National Center for Supercomputing Applications released a hugely popular web browser called NCSA Mosaic that was available for Windows among other platforms.

IMPORTANCE OF WINSOCK

This chapter's author, too, took this opportunity to release his own networking programs, most notably WFTPD, an FTP server that is still selling strong today at http://www.wftpd.com/. He could not have done this without Winsock, and it is his belief that Winsock was a key component of the rise of the Internet around the world.

The graphical web browser from NCSA played a huge part in popularizing the Internet (fans of the musical *Avenue Q* will realize immediately why), as did the arrival of America Online (AOL), and its subsequent adoption of Winsock as the chief method of connecting applications to its dial-up stack.

Of course, these days, there are no "dozen network stacks" for Windows. For most of us, there is just one, and it comes from Microsoft. But it still supports Winsock, and developers can still write networking programs that they can feel reasonably certain will run on any Windows system.

Thanks, Winsock!

Routing the Unroutable Part II: NAPT and PAT

So, now that you know all about sockets and ports, we can explain the next big leap in technology for routing private networks to the Internet. With a plain NAT, we have shown that you could only have as many externally connected clients as you had external IP addresses—and this during a time when the number of available IP addresses is drying up.

The next bright idea, then, was to make possible the use of one external IP address for several internal IP addresses. This kind of NAT router would have to look beyond the IP layer into the TCP (or UDP) layer and use the IP address and port to map connections, rather than entire IP addresses, to external connections.

Such a router is called a *network address/port translator* (NAPT). Some people may also call it a *port/address translator* (PAT). We prefer NAPT, partly because this is what the RFCs refer to, but mostly because the "network" part of the job hasn't been lost, so the initial doesn't need to be tossed.

Because NAPT routers are so useful compared to NAT routers and because NAPT is a little harder to say, for the most part what you hear referred to as a NAT router is actually a NAPT router. Some enterprises will still use a NAT router as an IP-level NAT router with no port translation, but that is somewhat of an oddity these days.

When a NAPT router sees a SYN crossing its bows from an internal address, it will assign an external IP address and a port (usually the same number as the internal port, but in case of conflicts, this can be assigned essentially at random) to that connection attempt. Then, whenever it sees the internal IP and port in a TCP-bearing IP packet coming from its inside edge, it will edit that packet and insert the external IP and port before forwarding the packet to the Internet. Likewise, when it sees an incoming TCP-bearing IP packet on its outside edge, it will find the matching internal IP address and port to replace that with, before forwarding the edited packet to its internal target.

NAPT's Unintended Consequences Part I: An Accidental Firewall

For most applications, this works really well.

Indeed, it has an unexpected benefit to those of us who beg for security devices to "fail closed" and to be "deny by default." Every NAPT device acts as a firewall, because by default a NAPT will not know where to send any incoming packet. Rather than guessing, the NAPT will either drop the packet or respond with a failure indication such as a RST response.

Most NAPTs will allow you to configure port mappings, for instance to tell the NAPT that "we have a web server running at 192.168.230.21, port 80," in which case it will assign a static mapping from its external IP address, which is port 80, to its internal address 192.168.230.21, which is port 80.

You can also configure most NAPT devices to forward any unknown traffic to a particular IP address, sometimes known as the *DMZ host*. Try to resist the temptation to do this, because this will result in that host being bombarded with every network attack known to man. The Internet is a little hostile to those without a firewall.

NAPT's Unintended Consequences Part II: App Killer

For some applications, however, NAPT devices have practically killed the protocols on which they rely. There are several protocols, such as FTP (file transfer), SIP (session initiation—for phone-like communication), and H.323 (again, for voice and video phones), that send information about IP addresses and ports in their communication with their connection partners. Even IPsec, the secured protocol for IP that allows for authentication and encryption of IP traffic, will sometimes need to quote its IP address.

For instance, an FTP client will tell the FTP server "connect back to me at my address 192.168.230.21 on port 1025," with a command such as PORT 192,168,230,21,4,1. The server can't connect to that address and port because it's a nonroutable address. This usually results in a timeout when the upcoming file transfer is attempted and makes FTP very hard to use from behind a firewall.

Routing the Unroutable Part III: Application Layer Gateways

The developers of the NAPT specification (again, it's in an RFC—this time RFC 3022, "Traditional IP Network Address Translator") were aware of this kind of problem and suggested that Application Layer Gateways (ALGs) could be added to any NAPT router.

Such an ALG would inspect the contents of the TCP payloads for recognized protocols and commands, editing the TCP stream itself to change IP addresses and port numbers quoted there and opening up mappings to allow incoming connections as requested.

This works acceptably well except in the case where a protocol is unrecognized by the NAPT as belonging to a particular ALG. The cause of this can be as simple as the use of a different port or as complex as the use of encryption (IPsec, for instance, or FTP over SSL/TLS). In the former case, the NAPT doesn't know that you're sending FTP traffic because the server is not at port 21; in the latter case, the NAPT sees only encrypted data, which it can neither read nor modify.

NAPTs Will Someday Become Irrelevant

IPv6 offers a new reality. There are so many addresses in IPv6 that we will never have the exhaustion problem that afflicted IPv4.

Yes, we know, we said that with IPv4, but this time we mean it. Really. Even if you gave an IPv6 address to every blade of grass in your lawn, you'd still have plenty of space in your own IPv6 address assignment to accommodate an address for each item in your refrigerator, every device you own, and every square inch of your house. Then there would still be room to spare between those addresses.

As a result of this huge address space, there will be no NATs or NAPTs for IPv6. If you need the "accidental firewall" feature of NAPTs, you will need to get a more "deliberate" firewall, one that operates only as a firewall.

Installing a NAT

Possibly the most likely use you will have for making a Windows Server 2008 R2 machine into a router is if you want to create a NAT over which you have finer control than you would get from a normal NAT device.

Installing NAT in Windows Server 2008 R2 is relatively simple, although it has many steps.

The first of these steps is to install the Routing and Remote Access Service (RRAS; pronounced "r-razz"). This is part of the Network Policy and Access Services role, so the first part of the process is to open Server Manager and click Add Roles. The familiar Add Roles Wizard appears, as shown in Figure 19.10.

FIGURE 19.10
Adding the server role that contains RRAS

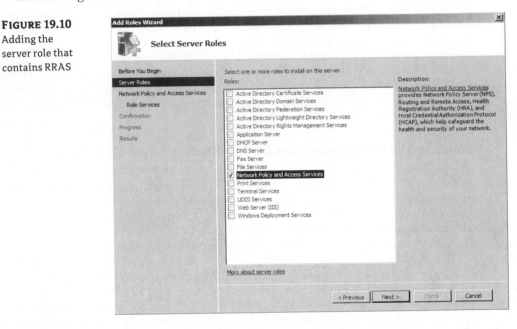

Check Network Policy and Access Services, because that is where the Routing and Remote Access Service resides. Click Next to accept. As usual, the first thing you are presented with is a brief note about the role you are about to add, as shown in Figure 19.11.

Click Next to view the services for this role, which should appear as in Figure 19.12. Note that the Routing and Remote Access Service is listed prominently as one of the services provided in this role.

Select to install Routing and Remote Access Services. You will need both the Remote Access Service and the Routing component.

Now click Next again to go to the Confirmation page for your installation selections, as in Figure 19.13.

Confirm that you are ready to install this role by clicking the Install button, and wait for the role to install (see Figure 19.14). You should not need to reboot.

FIGURE 19.11
Reading the
preamble for
the role install

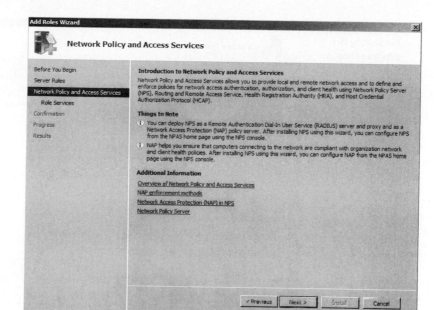

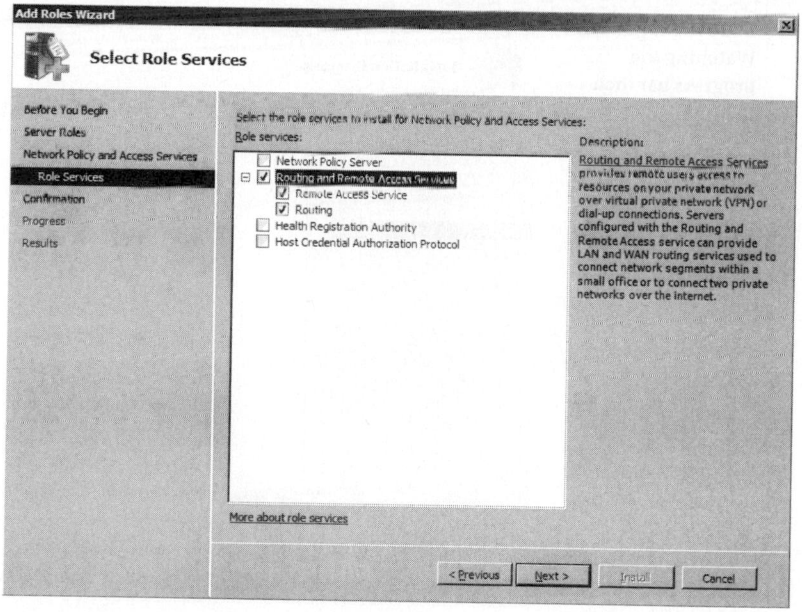

FIGURE 19.12
Selecting the Rout-
ing and Remote
Access Service

FIGURE 19.13
Reviewing the
services chosen
to install

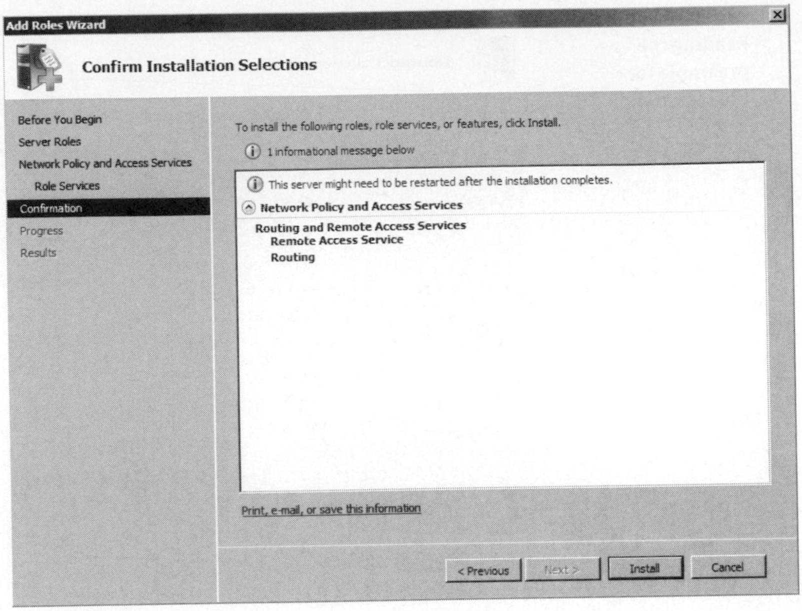

FIGURE 19.14
Watching the
progress bar inch
its way across

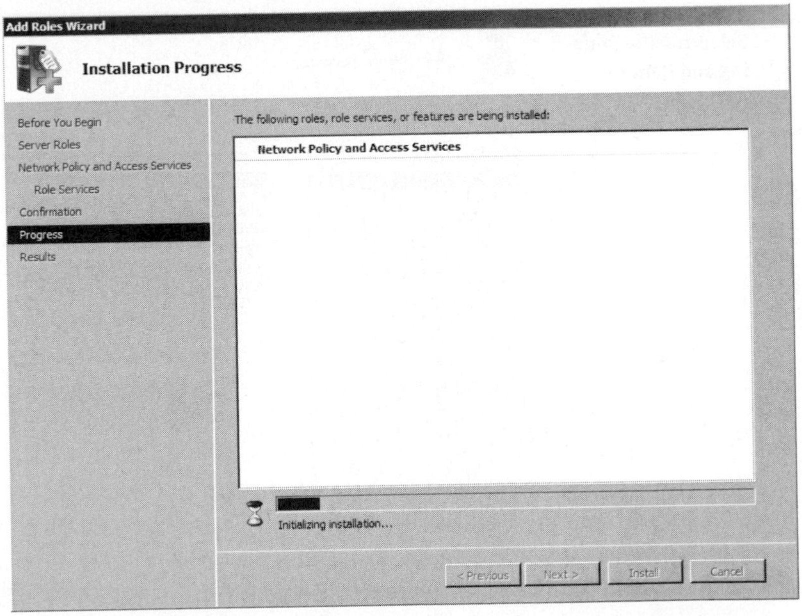

You should see the success prompt as in Figure 19.15.

Click Close to end the Add Roles Wizard. Now, open the Routing and Remote Access tool by selecting Start ➤ Administrative Tools ➤ Routing and Remote Access, as shown in Figure 19.16.

FIGURE 19.15
Installation suc-
cessful—you did
get this, yes?

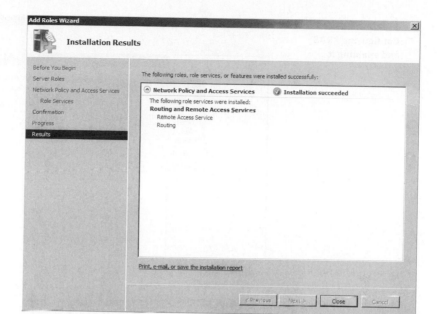

FIGURE 19.16
Finding the Rout-
ing and Remote
Access tool

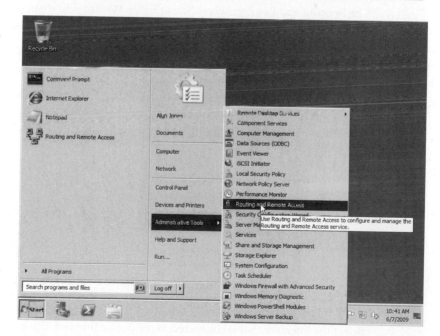

You can now configure and enable routing and remote access for this server, which is available from the Action menu or by right-clicking the name of this server and then selecting Configure and Enable Routing and Remote Access, as in Figure 19.17.

FIGURE 19.17
Configuring RRAS
and enabling it

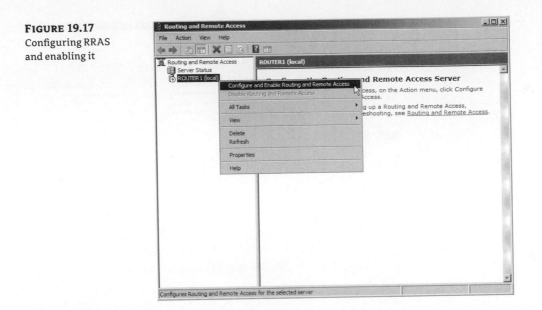

The Routing and Remote Access Server Setup Wizard will display, as you will see in Figure 19.18.

FIGURE 19.18
The RRAS
Setup Wizard

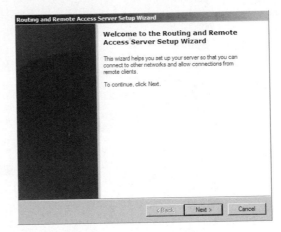

Click Next, and select that you want to configure a NAT, as we have done in Figure 19.19.

Click Next, and you will be prompted to select the "public" side of this NAT router, as shown in Figure 19.20.

Select the interface that is connected to the public Internet. Click Next to open the Name and Address Translation Services page shown in Figure 19.21.

FIGURE 19.19
Selecting to configure RRAS for NAT

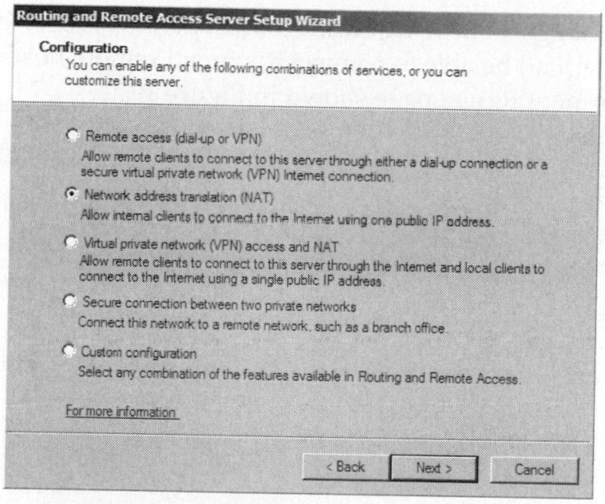

FIGURE 19.20
Choosing which interface will provide network sharing

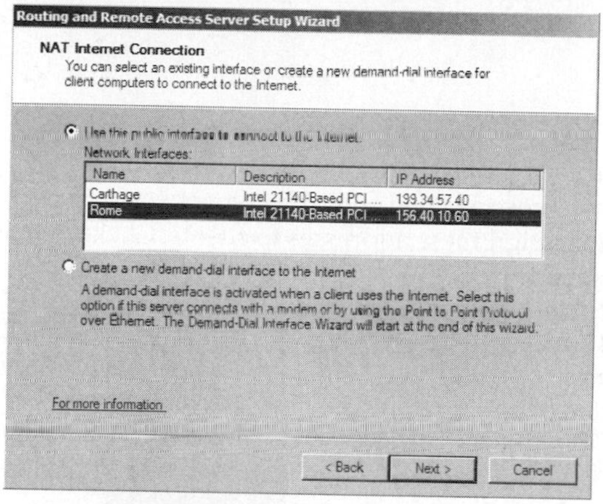

FIGURE 19.21
Letting the NAT provide DHCP and DNS service

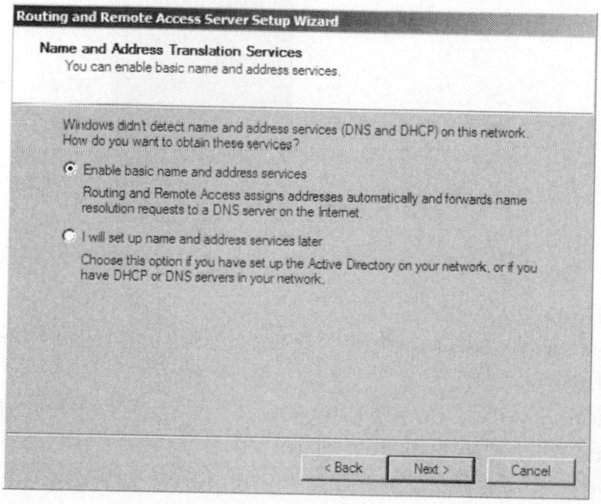

We suggest allowing basic name and address services to be enabled so that your internal hosts will all be able to connect to named remote hosts. Now click Next again to see the Address Assignment Range page shown in Figure 19.22.

FIGURE 19.22
Checking the
NAT address
assignment

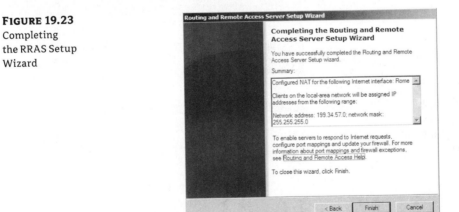

The address picked for this NAT is the address assigned to the network interface that you did not choose as your public-facing network connection. The NAT will act as a DHCP server in order to assign these addresses to clients. Click Next again for the summary page, which should look something like Figure 19.23.

FIGURE 19.23
Completing
the RRAS Setup
Wizard

Assuming you agree with everything processed so far and displayed on the summary page, click Finish.

There—you're done! Now, any DHCP-client system connecting to the interface you've defined as internal (in our example, this was the Carthage subnet) will be given an IP address and be configured to connect to the public Internet.

You've probably guessed that, like so many other NATs, the NAT in Windows Server 2008 R2 RRAS is really a NAPT, in that it will translate and map ports as necessary. There are also some built-in ALGs to support the use of FTP and PPTP.

CREATING A ROUTER

What is a router?

A *router* is a multihomed machine (that is, one with more than one network interface) that has been set up to forward packets received from one network to another network.

The computer that sits between the Carthage and Rome networks, which we shall call the Mediterranean computer, is well placed to be a router—it is multihomed, and each interface is on a different network. But is it a router yet?

Not until it has been configured to forward.

By default, Windows Server 2008 R2 computers are not configured to forward. To cause a Windows Server 2008 R2 computer to forward IPv4 packets, you need to edit a registry setting. The setting is HKEY_LOCAL_MACHINE\SYSTEM\CurrentControlSet\Services\Tcp\Parameters\ IPEnableRouter; it should already exist as a dword value set to 0, so set it to 1 in order to enable IP routing, and then restart the computer.

That's all you need to do to create a router between two local subnets. This computer will now automatically forward packets received on one interface to the interface corresponding with the network containing the destination address of the packets.

Again, you can use the route add (or netsh, if you like typing) command to add any routes that are not already present in the router.

TUNNELING: NEARLY ROUTING

Network tunneling is a form of routing in which network traffic is encapsulated or transformed in some way by a tunnel endpoint so that it can reach another tunnel endpoint, at which point it is either deencapsulated or transformed back.

In a way, NAT is a form of tunneling, in which the transformation is to change the source and/ or destination IP address and port along its travels. As with other tunneling methods, several NATs may be between the start of the packet's travel and its end.

CHEAT TUNNELING WITH PORTPROXY

The last netsh tunnel you'll visit is a very useful one, called portproxy. You can use it to cheat port restrictions by forwarding a "safe" port such as 80 (for the Web, using HTTP) to an "unsafe" port such as 119 (Network News Transfer Protocol—often blocked by enterprises to limit employees' access to this information source).

At the other end, forwarding port 119 to port 80, you begin by encapsulating the NNTP traffic from your newsreader into a connection that seems to the firewall to be a connection to a web server.

Assuming that your home computer is at address 10.20.30.40 and the news server you want to reach but can't is msnews.microsoft.com, these are the commands to use:

```
[At the work computer] netsh interface portproxy add v4tov4 119 10.20.30.40 80
[At the home computer] netsh interface portproxy add v4tov4 80 msnews.microsoft.
com 119
```

Connecting to systems at home using this method is probably going to get you into trouble, but there may be some work uses you can put this method to. Note that portproxy does not offer any kind of authentication, and it does not provide any encryption to protect your data in transit. You may find that a virtual private network (VPN) offers you more what you need in this direction. Read the next chapter to find out how to configure Windows Server 2008 R2 as your VPN endpoint.

IPv6 TUNNEL COMMANDS

In the absence of native IPv6 support from your ISP, you may be testing IPv6 Internet access through the use of an IPv6 tunneling service, such as that provided by Hurricane Electric. We do this, and we set up our tunnel—IPv6 tunneling through IPv4—as follows:

```
netsh interface ipv6 add v6v4tunnel IP6Tunnel myIPv4Address 72.52.104.74
netsh interface ipv6 add address IP6Tunnel 2001:db8:1234:567:2
netsh interface ipv6 add route ::/0 IP6Tunnel 2001:db8:1234:567:1 publish=yes
netsh interface ipv6 set interface IP6Tunnel forwarding=enable
netsh interface ipv6 add route 2001:db8:fedc:ba98::/64 "Local Area Connection"
publish=yes
netsh interface ipv6 set interface "Local Area Connection" forwarding=enable
advertising=enable
```

The first command creates the tunnel itself from this server to the machine at 72.52.104.74, and the server on which you run this command is now capable of communicating in IPv6 through this tunnel. The second command creates an address and assigns it to the tunnel interface, while the third command creates a route that forwards traffic to the IPv6 tunnel if it has nowhere else more specific defined—::/0 is the IPv6 placeholder for a default destination in a routing entry.

The fourth command enables forwarding on the IPv6 tunnel so that any traffic coming through the tunnel for other machines on our network will be forwarded to them. The fifth command adds a route from this machine to other machines in our local network, and the sixth command enables forwarding and advertising for traffic on the local network so that we are able to forward packets received on that network and so that the computers on that network will know that we are willing to forward their traffic.

Another use for `portproxy` is to "IPv6-enable" an application that is able to use IPv4 traffic only. Again, picking on NNTP as the protocol in question, if you have an IPv4-only newsreader and an IPv6-only news server, you can connect the two with a `portproxy` command like this:

```
netsh interface portproxy add v4tov6 119 news6server.example.com 119
```

Then simply set your newsreader to point to localhost:119, and it will connect through the proxy to the IPv6 news server!

Testing and Troubleshooting

You will never need this section, because the information we have given you in this chapter should teach you how to understand routing in the context of a Windows Server 2008 R2 server. Oh, maybe that's a bit of an exaggeration—some basic troubleshooting will allow you to determine which machine beyond your control is administered by someone without your knowledge and is causing the problem you are experiencing.

Using the Application Itself

You can use many tools to debug the state of a network. Which you use, and when, will depend on what the problem is that you are trying to fix. The first tool, as ever, is the one you actually plan to use. Let's say you're trying to make an FTP connection—first, read the errors that the FTP client is giving you.

If the FTP client says "Connection refused," then the client has received a TCP RST ostensibly from the IP address you tried to reach. This could be a sign of a firewall between you and the server, or the server application itself might not be running.

If the FTP client says "Timed out," then the client has received nothing in response to multiple requests to connect. This means either a "stealth" firewall is in between client and server or the server computer isn't reachable right now, either because there is no network route to it or because the computer is not currently running.

Avoid Stealth Firewalls

Although some security proponents suggest using stealth firewalls, we do not. Stealth firewalls do not respond to unexpected incoming requests, preferring instead to remain silent. The appropriate TCP expression for "go away and don't talk to me" is a TCP RST; silence traditionally means "try again in a little while." Not only is a RST going to restrict accidental connections from retrying, but it will also prevent someone from using IP spoofing to pretend to be the server. If an IP spoofing session is underway, the genuine server will still receive a SYN, and the RST it sends in response will cause the client to abort its connection. In the absence of a RST, the client will continue to trust the spoofed server, which is a security risk.

Pinging a Remote Computer with ping

ping is the classic tool that many of us have used for decades. Its design has varied a little, but the basic principle is to send a packet to a remote machine that the remote machine is supposed to reply to and then wait for the reply and indicate whether it is successful. Windows Server 2008 R2 still uses the "classic" ping method of sending an ICMP Echo Request to the remote machine (with extra data consisting of "abcdefghijklmnopqrstuvwabcdefghi") and waiting for the ICMP Echo Reply to come back.

As such, it is important to remember that ping tests only ICMP Echo connectivity; it does not test the TCP connection to a server port. Only a TCP connection to the server port will do that (which is why we suggested earlier that your first debugging tool is the application you're trying to debug!).

Many firewalls block the ICMP echo service, so, as you can demonstrate by first pinging and then connecting with a web browser to www.microsoft.com, a failed ping does not necessarily mean a failed connection will result.

A successful ping, however, indicates that a machine somewhere is responding to your echo requests. You can also use the output from the ping command to ensure that you are resolving the name to the right IP address. Where the NsLookup tool allows you to query a DNS server, that makes it only a good tool for debugging the DNS server—to find out what the DNS client is going to do with a name, ping is as good as any other tool.

ping has a bewildering array of arguments. The most useful are the following:

◆ -t: This pings the host until stopped. It's useful for detecting when a downed server comes back up.

◆ -4 and -6: This is used to choose between either IPv4 or IPv6, respectively. Note that this will affect the choice of DNS name resolution as well as the route to send the ping packets.

For most troubleshooting, however, all the default parameters will generally be sufficient, and you can use ping server.example.com to give a rough-and-ready estimation of whether the server is resolvable and reachable.

Pinging a Remote Computer with traceroute

tracert, as Microsoft chose to abbreviate it (does anyone still remember the days when eight-dot-three filenames were all we had?), is a tool whose purpose is to detail the route to a destination.

As with ping, tracert is not necessarily an absolute indication that a TCP connection to a remote host will or will not work. But it's generally going to give you information that you can use.

tracert acts in a very similar way to ping, in that it sends an ICMP echo request and waits for an ICMP echo reply. How it differs is that tracert sets the TTL (hop count) on outgoing echo requests. The first three packets are sent with a hop count of 1, the next three are sent with a hop count of 2, and so on, up to a number you can specify (but that defaults to 30).

Since routers decrease the hop count on packets as they pass through, the first three packets will encounter an error at the first router on the way to the destination computer. Fortunately for tracert, this router reports that it discarded the packet, and the tracert program uses this information to display the address of the first router. Similarly, the second three packets will show where the second router is, and so on.

Some routers are not configured to respond with this information or are so busy that they don't have time to do so. These routers will be seen as a "timeout" in the tracert output. This may happen at one or two hops along a route. When you see several timeouts in a row, it usually indicates that the last router before the string of timeouts is unable to forward packets toward your destination or that your destination is not responding.

As you can see from the tracert output in Figure 19.24, the host for www.microsoft.com in this part of the world is lb1.www.ms.akadns.net. This may be different if you reproduce this test. We know already, from trying to ping this host, that it does not answer to ICMP echo requests, and for that reason, packets with hop counts of 14 or more are not replied to, either with echo replies or with errors.

However, this tracert output does give you a fairly good idea of the route toward Microsoft's website. We're not sure that the bouncing around from Everett (north of Seattle) to Burien (so far south of Seattle that it's nearly closer to Tacoma) and then back up to Seattle is all that efficient.

Again, tracert has the parameters -4 and -6, which you can use to force the trace to go over IPv4 or IPv6, respectively.

Checking Your Configuration with ipconfig

ipconfig will show information about the configuration of some or all of your network cards. ipconfig /all shows very detailed information, and ipconfig on its own shows a limited subset of that information. The best use of `ipconfig` is to ensure that your configuration matches what it is supposed to be, at least according to the network diagrams you're trying to match reality to.

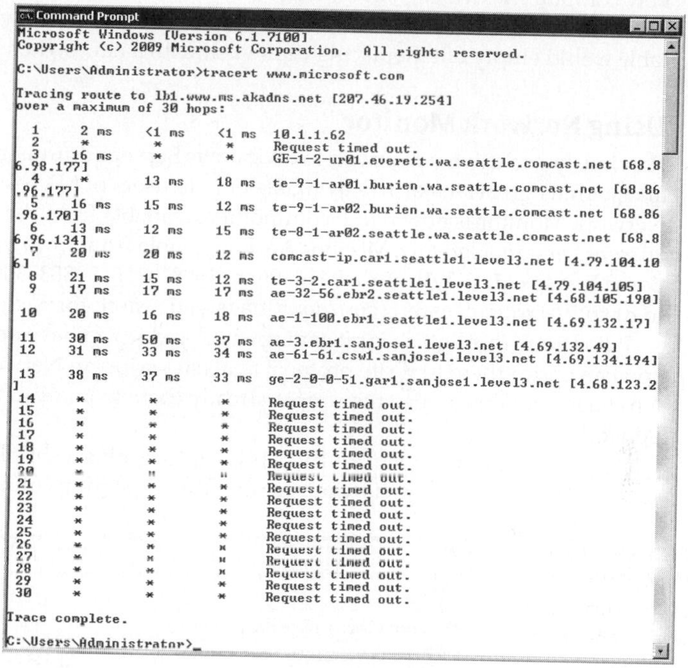

FIGURE 19.24

Tracing the route to Microsoft's website

```
Command Prompt                                                          _ □ ×
Microsoft Windows [Version 6.1.7100]
Copyright (c) 2009 Microsoft Corporation.  All rights reserved.

C:\Users\Administrator>tracert www.microsoft.com

Tracing route to lb1.www.ms.akadns.net [207.46.19.254]
over a maximum of 30 hops:

  1     2 ms    <1 ms    <1 ms  10.1.1.62
  2     *        *        *     Request timed out.
  3    16 ms     *        *     GE-1-2-ur01.everett.wa.seattle.comcast.net [68.8
6.98.177]
  4     *       13 ms    18 ms  te-9-1-ar01.burien.wa.seattle.comcast.net [68.86
.96.177]
  5    16 ms    15 ms    12 ms  te-9-1-ar02.burien.wa.seattle.comcast.net [68.86
.96.170]
  6    13 ms    12 ms    15 ms  te-8-1-ar02.seattle.wa.seattle.comcast.net [68.8
6.96.134]
  7    20 ms    20 ms    12 ms  comcast-ip.car1.seattle1.level3.net [4.79.104.10
6]
  8    21 ms    15 ms    12 ms  te-3-2.car1.seattle1.level3.net [4.79.104.105]
  9    17 ms    17 ms    17 ms  ae-32-56.ebr2.seattle1.level3.net [4.68.105.190]
 10    20 ms    16 ms    18 ms  ae-1-100.ebr1.seattle1.level3.net [4.69.132.17]
 11    30 ms    50 ms    37 ms  ae-3.ebr1.sanjose1.level3.net [4.69.132.49]
 12    31 ms    33 ms    34 ms  ae-61-61.csw1.sanjose1.level3.net [4.69.134.194]
 13    38 ms    37 ms    33 ms  ge-2-0-0-51.gar1.sanjose1.level3.net [4.68.123.2
]
 14     *        *        *     Request timed out.
 15     *        *        *     Request timed out.
 16     *        *        *     Request timed out.
 17     *        *        *     Request timed out.
 18     *        *        *     Request timed out.
 19     *        *        *     Request timed out.
 20     *        !!        !!    Request timed out.
 21     *        *        *     Request timed out.
 22     *        *        *     Request timed out.
 23     *        *        *     Request timed out.
 24     *        *        *     Request timed out.
 25     *        *        *     Request timed out.
 26     *        *        *     Request timed out.
 27     *        *        *     Request timed out.
 28     *        *        *     Request timed out.
 29     *        *        *     Request timed out.
 30     *        *        *     Request timed out.

Trace complete.

C:\Users\Administrator>_
```

Note that a number of virtual interfaces will show up in this listing. For instance, if you have enabled a VPN server or RRAS as a dial-up access point, an interface will be assigned for those connections to use.

For network interfaces that assign addresses through DHCP, it can be useful to run `ipconfig /renew` or `ipconfig /release` followed by `ipconfig /renew`. It may be just as quick, and require fewer privileges, to simply unplug and replug the associated network cable—that, too, causes a release and renew against the DHCP server.

Showing Routing and Neighbors

We have talked about the routing table in Windows Server 2008 R2 in this chapter, and you should find that analyzing the routing table as if you were the router can be constructive in tracing where a fault lies. If your routing table is very large and is not easily understood, that can be a fault in itself, in that no one thoroughly understands even a small section of the network enough to say that it is working as designed.

In addition to the routing table, using `arp -a` or `netsh interface ipv6 show neighbors` will let you know who this computer has recently been talking to on the local area link. If there are no entries in the table, except for those used by multicast addresses and loopback adapters, this indicates that the computer is probably not able to reach any of its neighbors on the local network link. This is often a sign of a faulty cable or switch port, and swapping out the cable or plugging it into a different port at the switch is a good option to try.

A lack of neighbors may also indicate an inability to negotiate network speeds with the switch. A recent case we worked on involved an old but generally serviceable 10/100Mbps switch and a new computer with a Gigabit Ethernet card. The Ethernet card always negotiated down to 10Mbps, and when we forced it to 100Mbps, it would not see any other systems on the network—its ARP table would empty out. Replacing the switch with a new switch fixed that issue.

Using Network Monitor

Previously exclusively reserved for Windows Server administrators who knew where it was, and with its greatest features available only to users of Microsoft's System Management Server, Network Monitor is now a free commodity, available from the Microsoft download site. The current version, Network Monitor 3.3, is available from `http://www.microsoft.com/downloads/details.aspx?FamilyID=983b941d-06cb-4658-b7f6-3088333d062f`. Or you can simply connect to `http://www.microsoft.com/downloads` and search for *Network Monitor*.

It has gone through a significant rewrite, and if you have any developers in your enterprise, you can entice them to write protocol analysis scripts in Network Monitor's own C/JScript-like language. Or you can use the scripts already there to analyze what traffic is present on your network.

As you can see from Figure 19.25, this capture, plus a simple filter `protocol.ICMP`, allows us to see all the traffic generated by our earlier use of the `ping` command.

FIGURE 19.25
Viewing a ping capture using Network Monitor 3.1

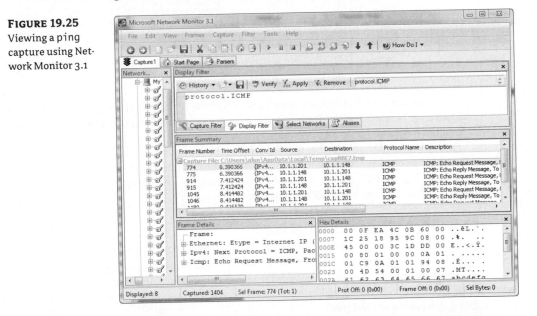

WHICH CARD DO YOU MONITOR?

If you want to capture data from only one card using Network Monitor, how do you decide which one to use? In most situations, this is relatively obvious because there is only one network card in most systems, and therefore there is no choice to make. However, one wrinkle comes out of the changes made between IPv4 and IPv6, and that is the topic of weak sends and weak receives:

♦ A *weak send* is one where the source IP address of the packet does not match an IP address belonging to the network interface to which it is sent.

♦ A *weak receive*, by analogy then, is one where the destination IP address of the packet does not match an IP address belonging to the network interface on which it is received.

IPv4 for decades has confused network administrators with its behavior. Weak sends are enabled by default in IPv4 interfaces, which means that the interface that is chosen for sending an IP packet depends on the destination IP address, not the source IP address. The interface that is chosen is the one that is closest to the "next-hop" address in the route toward the destination.

That's *not* the case in Windows Server 2008 R2, however. In Windows Vista and Windows Server 2008, Microsoft took the bold step of requiring that IP packets go out on the interface that matches their source address and, similarly, that IP packets will be discarded if their destination address does not match that of the interface on which they were received.

IPv6 by comparison does not enable weak sends by default, so the packet will always be sent to the interface whose IP address matches the source IP address of the outgoing packet. No change there in Windows Server 2008.

The change, however, is that you can change this behavior.

As with all new network configuration commands, you can achieve this through `netsh`:

```
netsh interface ipv4 set interface <NameOrIndex> weakhostsend=enabled
netsh interface ipv4 set interface <NameOrIndex> weakhostreceive=enabled
netsh interface ipv6 set interface <NameOrIndex> weakhostsend=enabled
netsh interface ipv6 set interface <NameOrIndex> weakhostreceive=enabled
```

Of course, you can set any of these values back to `disabled`, as the default, if you prefer that behavior.

Disabling weak host receives is a security feature for a multihomed computer, in that packets will be discarded if they are not received on the anticipated interface, but this may discard valid traffic that really should reach your computer, if the routing and the cabling sends it to the wrong interface. If that is the case, then your network design needs revisiting. A local link, or subnet, should not find itself split across two network cards in a single computer.

In this chapter, we have given you a flavor of some of the routing capabilities of Windows Server 2008 R2. You will shortly encounter a big routing ability in Chapter 20's description of virtual private networks.

The Bottom Line

Document the life of an IP packet routed through your network   Understanding how the routing components work inside your hosts and routers will allow you to predict where network traffic will travel throughout your network. With this understanding comes the ability to troubleshoot network issues that appear perplexing.

Master It   In the Carthage/Rome network from Figure 19.1, use your understanding of the route taken by an IP packet from host A to host G to determine which addresses you should ping in order to discover routing issues that are preventing packets from traveling between A and G.

Explain the class-based and classless views of IP routing When discussing routing with networking professionals, it is important to understand the old class-based terminology to allow for conversations and documentation that may still linger on these terms. Understanding how classless IP routing works is key to avoiding inefficiencies brought on by too strict an adherence to class boundaries in network addressing.

> **Master It** The address 172.24.255.255 lies inside class B, whose default netmask is 255.255.0.0. It also lies in the 172.16/20 RFC 1918 private network range, whose default netmask is 255.255.240.5. Given this information, is the address 172.24.255.255 a host address or a subnet broadcast address?

Use NAT devices to route TCP traffic Until we all switch to using IPv6, we will need to use NAT devices to route TCP traffic from our many networked hosts to the outside world, while using only a few of the increasingly rare public IP addresses. Understanding how NAT devices change the source and destination addresses of IP packets will allow you to read network packet traces and interpret which systems are intended as recipients of data.

> **Master It** A user complains that when he tries to connect to an FTP site, the connection initially succeeds, but the first time that a file listing is attempted, his connection is severed, and the server states that it cannot connect to 192.168.0.10. What are likely causes of this problem, and how could this be addressed?

Chapter 20

Getting from the Office to the Road: VPNs

Users often need access to data in the office even when they're away from the office. Traveling salespeople, telecommuters, and others need to be able to connect, and virtual private networks (VPNs) are often used to meet this need.

A VPN is a private connection that is created over a public network such as the Internet. If the users can access the Internet (and this is becoming much easier and much more common, even for mobile workers), they can access the office over the VPN. Once connected, users can access any office resources just as if they were there—this includes email, shared folders, and more.

To configure a VPN server, you'll need to add the Network Policy and Access Services role, configure the VPN server, and create or manipulate remote access policies.

Internet Protocol Security is an encryption protocol commonly used with Layer 2 Tunneling Protocol. You can also use IPSec by itself within a network to encrypt or digitally sign traffic on the wire. When IPSec is configured to encrypt the data, it thwarts attackers from intercepting data and therefore provides an extra layer of confidentiality. Or, you can configure IPSec to just use digital signatures to provide assurances that data has not been modified.

In this chapter, you will learn to:

◆ Add the Network Policy and Access Services role

◆ Configure a VPN server

◆ Create a remote access policy to allow VPN connections

◆ Use IPSec to encrypt traffic

Introducing VPNs

A VPN is used to provide access to a private network over a public network. The public network is often the Internet, but it could also be leased lines that are shared by different companies. Figure 20.1 shows a common example of a how a VPN server is configured.

The VPN server has at least two network interface cards (NICs). One NIC has a public IP address and can be reached by any user who has access to the Internet. The other NIC has a private address connected to the internal network.

VPN servers are often hosted in a *demilitarized zone* (DMZ) as shown in the figure. A DMZ would have two firewalls. One firewall provides a layer of protection to hosts in the DMZ from potential Internet attackers, and the second internal firewall provides an extra layer of protection for internal clients. Although the figure is simplified to show the VPN server, a DMZ can be configured with more than just a VPN server.

FIGURE 20.1
VPN used
for mobile
connectivity

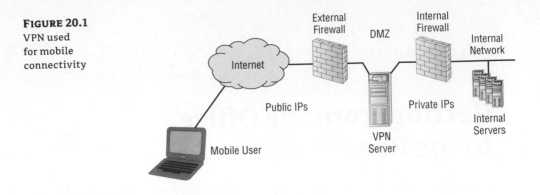

The mobile user can use the VPN connection to connect to the internal network by first connecting to the VPN server. Once connected, the user is able to access internal resources just as if they were physically located in the internal network. One drawback is that the connection is often slower.

First, the mobile user would gain access to the Internet. This could be via a broadband connection, a dial-up connection, or even via a wireless connection. How the user connects to the Internet isn't important, only that the user is connected. The VPN server then routes traffic between the mobile user and the internal network.

The Many Names of VPN Servers

A VPN server is often known by different names. Besides being called a VPN server, it could be called a *network access services (NAS) server* or a *remote access services (RAS) server*. The concept is the same—the server provides access to an internal network from a remote location.

The biggest difference with the names is that a VPN server is more specific about the connection. A VPN server uses a virtual private connection over a public network—the user connects to the Internet first and then connects to the public IP of the VPN server over the Internet.

However, a NAS server and a RAS server can support both VPN and direct dial-up connections. In a dial-up connection, a client could have a modem and a phone line and connect to the server that also has a modem and a phone line. A VPN server never uses direct-dial connections.

The specific role that supports VPNs in Windows Server 2008 R2 is the Network Policy and Access Services role. The Routing and Remote Access service within this role can be used for both VPNs and direct-dial connections.

Gateway-to-Gateway VPN

Although this chapter is focused on allowing mobile users to connect, it's also possible to configure VPNs to allow two different offices to connect. This is referred to as a *gateway-to-gateway VPN* and is shown in Figure 20.2.

In a gateway-to-gateway VPN, two VPN servers are connected over the public network. It's common for the public network in this situation to be semiprivate leased lines, but the Internet can also be used. This allows users in the branch office to easily connect to resources at the main office via the VPN. Users may notice that connectivity is slower, but otherwise the connection appears just as if the server were located in the remote office.

FIGURE 20.2
Gateway-to-gate-
way VPN

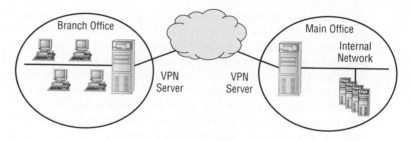

Understanding the Tunneling Protocols

When configuring a VPN, security is always a consideration. Data can't be sent across the Internet in clear text without the risk of someone using a sniffer to capture it. To combat this risk, VPNs use tunneling protocols.

Currently there are three primary tunneling protocols in use for Windows VPNs: Layer 2 Tunneling Protocol (L2TP), Secure Socket Tunneling Protocol (SSTP), and Internet Key Exchange version 2 (IKEv2). The Point-to-Point Tunneling Protocol (PPTP) has been used in the past but has known vulnerabilities and is used less and less as administrators become even more concerned about security.

Both the VPN server and the VPN client must be configured to use the same tunneling protocol.

Layer 2 Tunneling Protocol

Layer 2 Tunneling Protocol is a popular tunneling protocol used with VPNs. It commonly encrypts traffic with IPSec (which is explained in depth later in this chapter), and you'll often see it expressed as L2TP/IPSec.

When used with IPSec, L2TP encrypts the data, providing confidentiality, and signs the data, providing integrity. However, IPSec has a weakness that prevents it from being used all the time—IPSec can't travel through a Network Address Translation (NAT) server.

NAT is commonly used to translate private IP addresses to public IP addresses and public back to private. However, because of the way that IPSec packets are put together, NAT effectively breaks IPSec packets. If you need to go through a NAT server, you simply can't use L2TP/IPSec.

In the past, if you had to go through a NAT server to connect to a Microsoft VPN server, you'd need to use Point-to-Point Tunneling Protocol. PPTP has security concerns, so you'll rarely see it being used today. However, if you need to go through a NAT server, you have another choice today—Secure Socket Tunneling Protocol.

Secure Socket Tunneling Protocol

Secure Socket Tunneling Protocol is a newer tunneling protocol that was introduced with Windows Server 2008. It uses Secure Sockets Layer (SSL) over port 443 to secure VPN traffic.

This is actually a big deal. SSL is a well-respected, heavily used, and well-understood security protocol. Because of this, IT administrators and security professionals are willing to trust it much easier than something new. That might not seem like much, but if you've ever tried to get a firewall administrator to open a port on an enterprise firewall, you'll know what we mean. Firewall administrators notoriously (and rightfully) want to ensure that only the necessary ports are open. And even if they're convinced a port must be open to perform a specific task, they need to be thoroughly convinced that it's safe to open the port.

However, since SSTP uses SSL over port 443, a firewall administrator is more willing to open the port (if it's not open already). They know SSL is secure, so as long as SSTP is being implemented for the business model, it's acceptable to the firewall administrator. Additionally, if the enterprise is already hosting a web server that uses HTTPS, port 443 is already open, and you won't need to beg or bribe the firewall administrator to open the port.

An SSTP session works by first creating an HTTPS session. This HTTPS session is encrypted with SSL, ensuring the session is secure before any data or authentication credentials are sent over the network. After the HTTPS session is established, the SSTP session sends authentication credentials and data over the encrypted channel.

A certificate must be installed on the VPN server from a trusted certificate authority to support SSL. When VPN clients connect, the certificate is sent to the client and used to create a secure session.

Internet Key Exchange Version 2

Internet Key Exchange version 2 was added in Windows Server 2008 R2 as a new VPN type. The biggest advantage of IKEv2 is its ability to support VPN Reconnect.

VPN Reconnect allows VPN clients to survive short interruptions in network connectivity without losing the entire connection. After the temporary loss of network connectivity, the VPN client is able to continue without starting the connection over from the start.

IKEv2 is useful in environments where clients may move from one wireless client to another or even move from a wireless to a wired connection. IKEv2 requires a certificate from a trusted certificate authority, but it can use the same certificate that is used by SSTP.

Using Network Policy and Access Services Role

The Network Policy and Access Services role includes much more than just the ability to create a VPN server, though that will be the focus in this chapter. The individual services within this role include the following:

Routing and Remote Access   This service is used to host either a VPN server or a dial-up server and will be the focus in this chapter. The server must have at least two NICs to be used as a VPN server.

Network Policy Server (NPS)   NPS is Microsoft's implementation of a Remote Authentication Dial-in User Service (RADIUS) server and includes network access policies, accounting, Network Access Protection (NAP), and more. NAP can be used to ensure the "health" of clients before they are allowed access to network resources. Health is determined by examining the clients to ensure they meet certain conditions predefined by the administrator and can include items such as being current with updates, having a firewall enabled, and having antivirus software running. These health policies can be applied to any clients— those within a wired network, those in a wireless network, or those connecting remotely.

Figure 20.3 shows the NPS console when launched directly from the Administrative Tools menu. When accessed this way, all the features and capabilities are shown that can easily fill another chapter. However, the focus within this chapter is on the Network Policies and Accounting nodes used with Routing and Remote Access Services (RRAS).

You can create a VPN server without adding the NPS role service, but when you do, the Network Policy Server console will still be available. However, if you access it using the RRAS console (as you'll do in this chapter), you'll see only what applies to RRAS.

FIGURE 20.3
Network Policy Server console when accessed from Administrative Tools

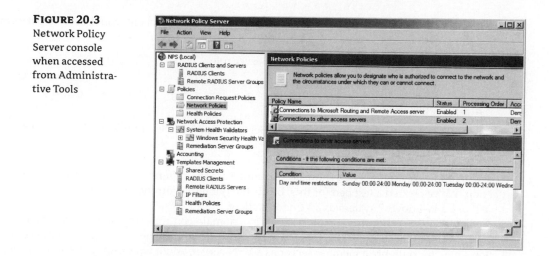

Health Registration Authority (HRA)   HRA is part of NAP and is used to issue health certificates for the NAP IPSec enforcement. If the client passes the health policy verification performed by NPS, the HRA will issue a clean bill of health in the form of a health certificate.

Host Credential Authorization Protocol (HCAP)   HCAP is used to integrate Microsoft's NAP solution with Cisco's Network Access Control Server.

Routing and Remote Access

Routing and Remote Access Services (RRAS) is the core component that provides remote access, or network access, to internal networks by external clients. This service provides two capabilities:

Remote access   Remote Access is used to configure your system as a VPN server or as a dial-up remote access server. This is the primary reason why Routing and Remote Access will be added to a server.

Routing   It's also possible to configure a Windows Server 2008 R2 server as a dedicated router with this service. The router is a software router. Although RRAS will perform routing as part of its role as a VPN server, it'll be rare to use RRAS as only a dedicated router in a production environment. It can be done, but most production environments require the better performance gained by using a hardware router.

WINDOWS SERVER 2008 R2 SERVER AS A ROUTER?

Yes, it's possible to configure a Windows Server 2008 R2 server as a router, but don't expect to see this very often. There are a lot of dedicated routers in the IT world (you may have heard of a little company called Cisco) that will perform as a router much more efficiently and cheaper than the cost of a server hosting Windows Server 2008 R2. However, there may be a time when you need a temporary router and you have a server with two NICs. You could use the server while waiting for the hardware router to arrive.

To configure your server as a VPN server and connect with a client, you'll need to perform the following:

1. Add the Network Policy and Access Server role.

2. Configure Routing and Remote Access.

3. Add policies to allow connections.

4. Add the Active Directory Certificate Services and Web Server roles to the VPN server.

5. Configure the VPN client, and connect.

The following sections will show how to configure the different pieces to see a VPN server in action. We've created a test bed for this. BF1 is the domain controller, BF2 is the VPN server, and we'll use a Windows 7 system as a Windows client.

Chapter 6 shows how to promote a server to a domain controller in a single-forest domain. You can refer to that chapter if necessary to configure your DC. The meat of the following section shows how to configure a member server as a VPN server, and it wraps up with showing you how to configure the client and connect to the server.

Adding the Network Policy and Access Services Role

The Network Policy and Access Services role includes several different functions and capabilities. The focus of this section is to create a VPN server by adding the Network Access Services portion of the role. A network access server could be a dial-in server or a VPN server, but we'll focus on a VPN server.

You can follow these steps to add the Network Policy and Access Services role:

1. Launch Server Manager. Select Roles, and click Add Roles.

2. If the Before You Begin page appears, click Next.

3. On the Select Server Roles page, select the Network Policy and Access Services role, and click Next.

4. Review the information on the Network Policy and Access Services page, and click Next.

5. Select the Remote Access Services role services. Your display will look similar to Figure 20.4. Although you aren't adding the Network Policy Server role service, the Network Policy Server console will be added with enough capabilities to support Remote Access Services as a VPN server. Click Next.

6. Review the information on the confirmation page, and click Install.

7. After the installation completes, click Close.

Although this adds the service, you'll need to configure it and either add or modify policies before it can be used as a VPN server.

Configuring Routing and Remote Access

The following steps will lead you through the process of configuring the Routing and Remote Access Service as a VPN server. You can access this service via Server Manager or directly via

Administrative Tools. You should be logged on to an account with domain administrator permissions, not just local administrator permissions.

1. Launch Routing and Remote Access by selecting Start ➢ Administrative Tools ➢ Routing and Remote Access. You can also access Routing and Remote Access within Server Manager.

2. Right-click the server, and select Configure and Enable Routing and Remote Access. This will launch the setup wizard.

3. Click Next on the wizard introduction page.

FIGURE 20.4
Adding the Remote Access Service role services

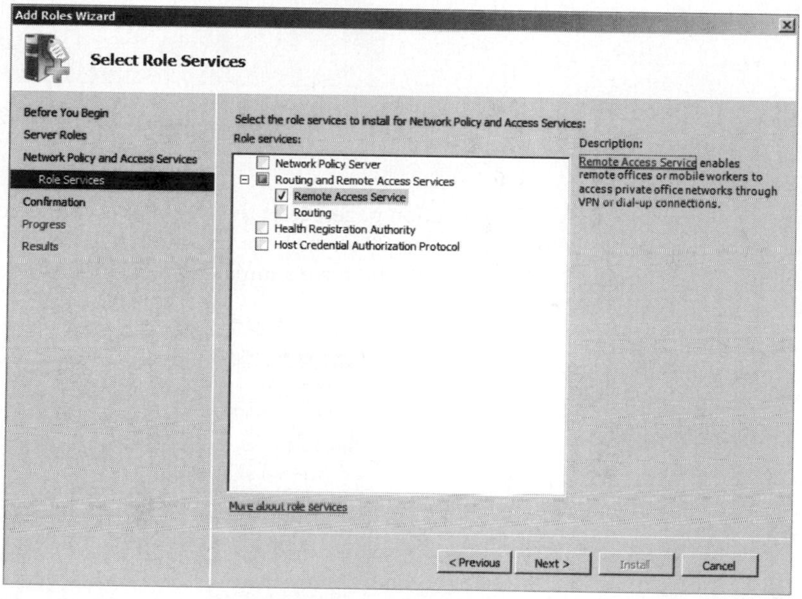

TWO NICS REQUIRED FOR VPN

As a reminder, two NICs are required to fully configure RRAS as a VPN server. However, if you have only one NIC, you can still configure RRAS so that you can explore both RRAS and NPS. Instead of choosing "Virtual private network (VPN) access and NAT" on the Configuration page, choose Custom configuration, and select VPN access and NAT on the Custom Configuration page. Once complete, you'll also need to access the properties page of the server and add a static address pool from the IPv4 tab.

4. On the Configuration page, select "Virtual private network (VPN) access and NAT," as shown in Figure 20.5. Click Next.

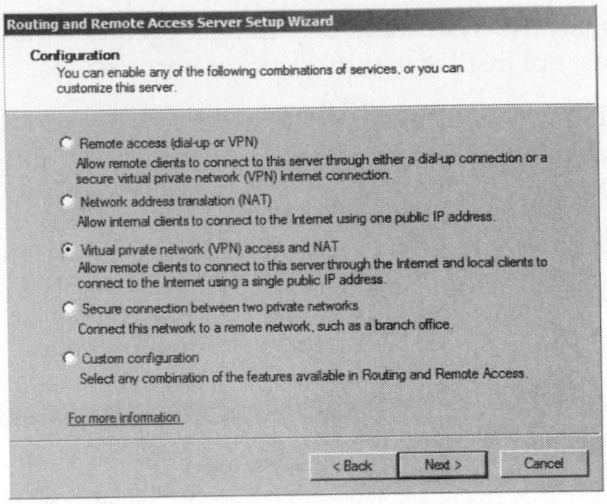

FIGURE 20.5

Configuring RRAS for remote access

5. On the VPN Connection page, select the NIC that is connected to the Internet. On this example system (Figure 20.6), we have renamed the NIC connected to the NIC Internet Facing NIC, selected it, and have simulated an public IP address by assigning it 74.1.2.3. Click Next.

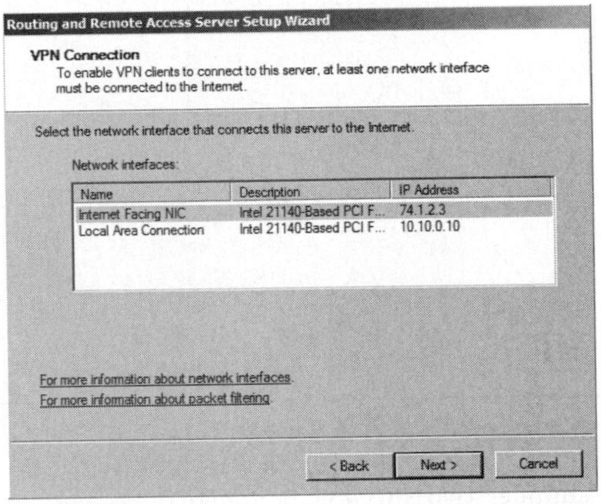

FIGURE 20.6

Identifying the NIC connected to the Internet

6. On the IP Address Assignment page, select "From a specified range of addresses," and click Next.

7. Click New. Enter a starting IP address and an ending IP address. These will be assigned to VPN clients and should be chosen to allow access to the network. In Figure 20.7, we've chosen the range of 192.168.20.200 through 192.168.20.250 to be used. Click OK, and then click Next.

8. On the Managing Multiple Remote Access Servers page, accept the default of "No, use Routing and Remote Access to authenticate connection requests," and click Next. Click Finish.

FIGURE 20.7

Specifying the
IP address range

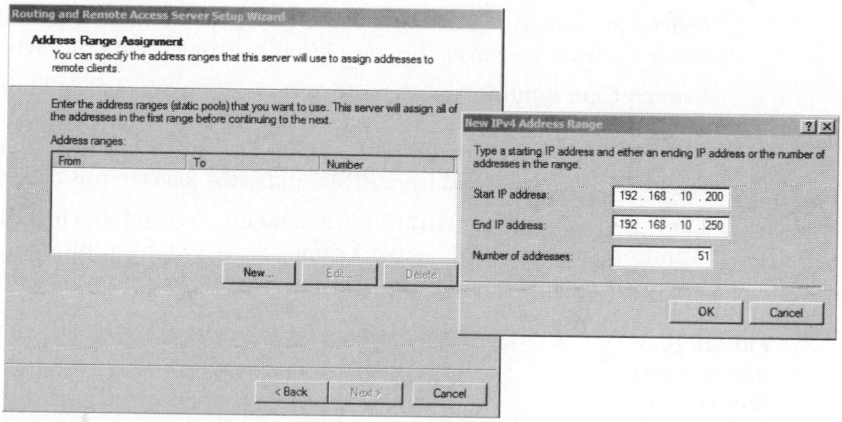

You may receive a message indicating that Windows was unable to add this computer to the list of valid remote access servers; however, it will still be added. Review the message, and click OK.

9. A dialog box will appear indicating that the DHCP relay agent must be added if DHCP is being used to give out IP addresses. This is not relevant with a static IP range as used in these steps. Review the information, and click OK to dismiss the dialog box.

10. You will then be prompted to start the Routing and Remote Access service. Click Start Service.

At this point, you have a VPN server joined to a domain with Routing and Remote Access Services installed and configured. However, clients will not be able to connect until a network access policy is configured.

Configuring Policies

Network access policies are an integral component required for VPN access. If a client doesn't meet the conditions of any policy, the client will not be able to connect. If the VPN server doesn't have any policies, clients can't meet the conditions of a policy, and they can't connect.

NETWORK ACCESS POLICIES PREVIOUSLY KNOWN AS REMOTE ACCESS POLICIES

Network access policies were previously known as *remote access policies* and were accessed from within the RRAS console. However, since Windows Server 2008, the NPS console is used to configure and manage policies, and they are now referred to as *network access policies*.

This reflects the broader application of NPS. NPS can be used to create and enforce network access policies throughout an organization. Although this chapter focuses only on VPNs, NPS can be used to create advanced policies to check any computers, including those in an internal network. Computers that don't meet the predefined conditions set by the administrator can be quarantined, and network access can be denied.

Policies are configured within the NPS console, and the NPS console can be accessed from two different methods. However, the console has different capabilities when accessed differently:

Launch from Routing and Remote Access With Routing and Remote Access launched, you can right-click Remote Access Logging & Policies and select Launch NPS. When launched this way, NPS will show only the options that are directly related with RRAS. The top console in Figure 20.8 was launched from RRAS and is the focus in this chapter.

Launch via the Administrative Tools menu When launched by selecting Start ➢ Administrative Tools ➢ Network Policy Server, many additional tools are available. The bottom console shown in Figure 20.8 was launched from the Administrative Tools menu.

FIGURE 20.8
Network Policy Server consoles when launched from RRAS (top) and when launched from Administrative Tools (bottom).

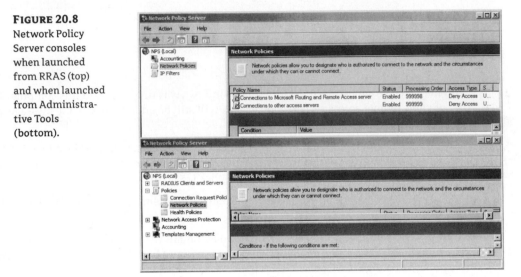

NPS includes two default policies in the Network Policies node. Each of these policies is set to Deny Access when created but can be changed if desired. The two policies are as follows:

Connections to Microsoft Routing and Remote Access Service Policy This includes a single condition that specifies that the RADIUS client must be a Microsoft client (specified as MS-RAS Vendor ^311$). This applies only to RADIUS clients.

Connections to Other Access Servers This includes a single condition of any time of the day and any day of the week. If no other conditions are met by previous policies, this policy will be used. Notice the processing order of this starts with a default of 999999, which is the highest possible number that can be assigned. Although you can't assign the processing order directly, you can modify the order such as which policy is processed first, second, and so on.

Policies have four important elements: conditions, permissions, constraints, and settings. For a big picture perspective, here's an overview. In the following pages, we'll cover each of these elements in much more depth.

Conditions Each policy must have one or more conditions that must be met for the client to use the policy. If the condition is not met, the policy will not be used. Many conditions can be specified, such as being a member of a Windows group or connecting at a certain time of day or day of week.

If a user meets the condition of a policy, the policy will be used even if the policy prevents a user from accessing the VPN server. No other policies will be used. For example, consider a VPN server that has five policies. If a user meets the condition of the first policy and access is denied from this policy, the other four policies will not be checked.

Permissions Permissions help determine whether a user is granted access once it's determined that they will use this policy (by meeting the conditions of the policy). On the surface, permissions sound simple since they can be set to Grant Access or Deny Access. However, individual user account settings can override the permission of the policy, and the policy can be set to override the user account setting. As you dig in, you realize it isn't as simple as just Grant Access or Deny Access.

Constraints Constraints can be used to ensure that clients follow some specific rules for the connection. Constraints include authentication methods, timeouts for the session or idle time, and more. If a user meets the condition and is allowed permission but doesn't meet one of the constraints, the connection will be refused.

Settings Settings are applied if the policy meets the conditions and constraints of a policy. Settings include encryption choices, IP settings, and IP filters.

POLICY CONDITIONS AND POLICY ORDER

The conditions are very important to set and understand for policies. Consider these basic rules that govern policies:

- A user must meet all the conditions of a policy to use a policy.

- A user will use only the first policy where all the conditions are met.

- If a user is denied access from a policy where conditions are met, additional policies are not evaluated.

- If a user doesn't meet the conditions of any policy, access cannot be granted.

- If there are no policies, conditions cannot be met, and access cannot be granted.

As a simple example, you may want to configure a policy for users in the Sales group. You can create a condition for the policy that includes the Sales group (assuming you have a Sales group in your domain). Any user who is a member of the Sales group will meet this condition, and this policy will be used.

Understanding Policy Order

Policies are evaluated in a specific order, and when creating policies, it's important to consider the logic of each to determine which policy will be used. Imagine that after you've created the policy for the Sales group, you now have three administrative-created policies with the conditions and permissions shown in Table 20.1.

TABLE 20.1: Evaluating Policy Conditions

POLICY NAME	CONDITIONS	PERMISSION
Domain Users	Member of Domain Users group	Deny Access
IT Admins	Member of IT Admins group in domain	Grant Access
Sales	Member of Sales group in domain	Grant Access

Figure 20.9 shows these policies. Notice in the figure that each of the policies includes a processing order. The Domain Users policy is at the top with a processing order of 1, the IT Admins policy has a processing order of 2, and so on. This identifies the order that the policies will be evaluated and helps show a serious flaw with the current design.

FIGURE 20.9
Network access policies

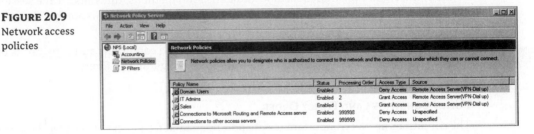

In this example, only the first policy (Domain Users) would ever be used. Anyone in either the IT Admins group or the Sales group is a member of the domain and would also be a member of the Domain Users group. Since these users are members of the Domain Users group, they would meet the conditions of the first policy and would use this policy. As shown, the IT Admins and Sales policies would never be used, and since the Domain Users policy is set to Deny Access, no one would ever be allowed access.

However, the problem is easy to fix. By right-clicking any of the policies, you can click Move Up or Move Down to change the processing order. Table 20.2 shows a more appropriate processing order. In general, policies should be ordered from most specific to least specific, but you also need to think through the logic.

TABLE 20.2: Modifying Policy Order

POLICY NAME	CONDITIONS	PERMISSION	POLICY ORDER
IT Admins	Member of IT Admins group in domain	Grant Access	1
Sales	Member of Sales group in domain	Grant Access	2
Domain Users	Member of Domain Users group	Deny Access	3

It's possible to add more than one condition to a policy. If a policy includes more than one condition, all the conditions must be met in order to use the policy. The categories of the different conditions that can be used are Groups, Host Credential Authorization Protocol (HCAP), Day and Time Restrictions, Connection Properties, RADIUS Client Properties, and Gateway.

Employing the Groups Condition

You can use the Groups condition to restrict access to specific users or computers. Any valid group that is supported within a domain or any local group supported on individual systems can be added. Groups can include Windows groups, machine groups, and user groups.

Using groups can be an effective way to identify the user who is trying to access the VPN server. For example, if you want users in the IT Admins group to be able to dial in any time but users in the Sales group to be able to dial in only at certain times, you can create two policies with one condition for each group. The constraints can then be configured to restrict access to a specific time.

The Host Credential Authorization Protocol

The HCAP can be used for communication between NPS and third-party network access servers. If all VPN servers are Microsoft, HCAP would not be used. However, HCAP allows you to support a hybrid environment with different types of VPN servers.

Day and Time Restrictions

Figure 20.10 shows the screen for Day and Time Restrictions. Imagine that you have reserved the hours of midnight to 4 a.m. for maintenance tasks on the server and want to ensure the server doesn't accept any connections during this time. You could configure the settings as shown.

FIGURE 20.10
Restricting access using Day and Time Restrictions

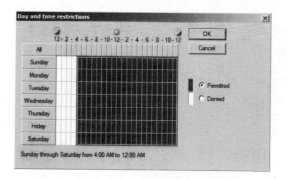

The Day and Time Restrictions condition is one of the most often used to control access to the VPN server. You'll see later that you can also use Day and Time Restrictions as a constraint.

Connection Properties

The Connection Properties category includes several different protocols and specifics about the protocol that can be required by the client. The choices are as follows:

Access Client IPv4 and IPv6 Addresses You can specify a specific IP address or IP subnet for the client. This can be useful in gateway-to-gateway VPNs where a remote office is connected to the main office via a VPN. If the remote office has a specific IP address that doesn't change, the condition can specify this IP address.

Authentication Type Authentication protocols are used to allow the client to prove their identity. Many different authentication types can be used, and they can be identified in the condition or in the constraints section.

Allowed EAP Types Extensible Authentication Protocol (EAP) is used to allow advanced authentication protocols. This allows the use of smart cards and other more secure methods of authentication.

Framed Protocol Framed protocols include Point-to-Point Protocol (PPP) and Serial Line Interface Protocol (SLIP). The most common type is PPP and is used by the client for their initial connection to the Internet. For example, a client could dial into the Internet and then use a tunneling protocol to access the VPN server over the Internet. Several other less used framed protocols are also supported.

Service Type You can specify which service type a client is using such as Callback Framed or Framed protocol.

Tunnel Type The Tunnel Type setting can be used to specify the tunneling protocol used by the client. Tunnel types supported include L2TP, PPTP, and SSTP.

RADIUS Client Properties

RADIUS client properties can be used to identify specifics about RADIUS clients. Several conditions can be configured including the calling station ID, the RADIUS client's friendly name, the IPv4 or IPv6 address, and even the vendor of the client. These settings are used to configure a policy for a RADIUS server but not a VPN server.

Configuring a Gateway

If your VPN server has multiple points of access, you can configure a gateway to ensure that clients are accessing it in a specific way. The different gateway conditions include the phone number called, the name of the server, the IPv4 or IPv6 address, and the port type.

Imagine your VPN server has two NICs with different public IP addresses. One NIC may have a lot of bandwidth available, but another does not. You can restrict access to the higher-bandwidth NIC to a select group by combining a gateway condition with a Windows group condition.

SETTING POLICY PERMISSIONS

Policy permissions can be affected by several different elements. Figure 20.11 shows the Overview tab of a policy. The access permissions are identified in the center of the page.

The "Grant access" and "Deny access" permissions mean access will be granted or denied if the condition of the policy is met, but only if the user account is configured to use the permissions of the policy and the "Ignore user account dial-in properties" check box is not selected. The user account properties are set on the user's Active Directory account.

🌐 Real World Scenario

RADIUS CLIENT VS. VPN CLIENT

The term *RADIUS client* is sometimes misunderstood. When RADIUS is used, the end user is not the RADIUS client, but instead the VPN server is the RADIUS client.

Imagine that you have several VPN servers. You could install NPS on another server to act as a RADIUS server and as a central point of authentication for all the VPN servers. Now, instead of each of these VPN servers authenticating the client, they could instead pass the authentication requests on to a RADIUS server.

Take a look at the illustration shown here. The end user is a VPN client and is accessing VPN Server 2. In this role, VPN Server 2 is acting as a server to the client. However, the VPN server then passes the authentication credentials on to the RADIUS server, and in this role, Server 2 is also RADIUS client.

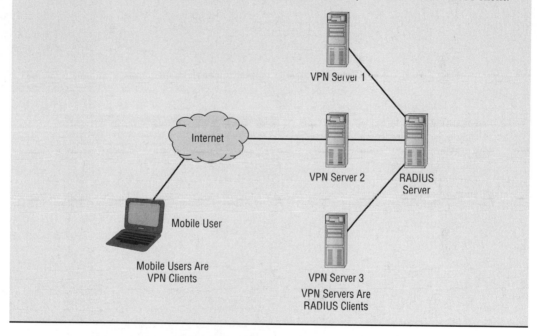

Figure 20.12 shows the properties of a user account with the Dial-in tab selected. The Network Access Permission area includes three settings: "Allow access," "Deny access," and "Control access through NPS Network Policy." As shown, the permissions of the policy will be used. However, if the permissions here are set to "Allow access" or "Deny access," the permissions of the policy will not take precedence unless you take an additional step.

Alarm bells may be going off in your head. Wait a minute. You have to set the network access permission for every user in you network? If you have five users, that's no big deal, but if you have 5,000 users, this might take some time. There's an easier way.

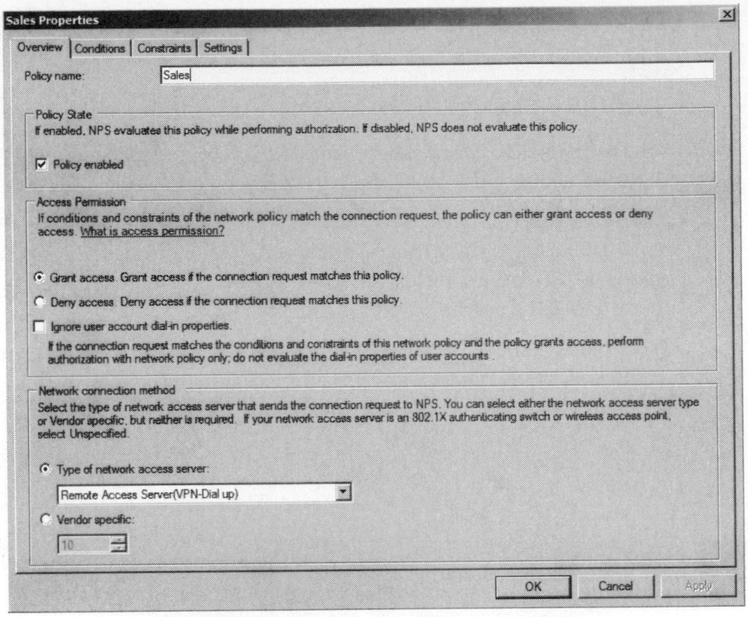

FIGURE 20.11
Viewing access
permissions in an
access policy

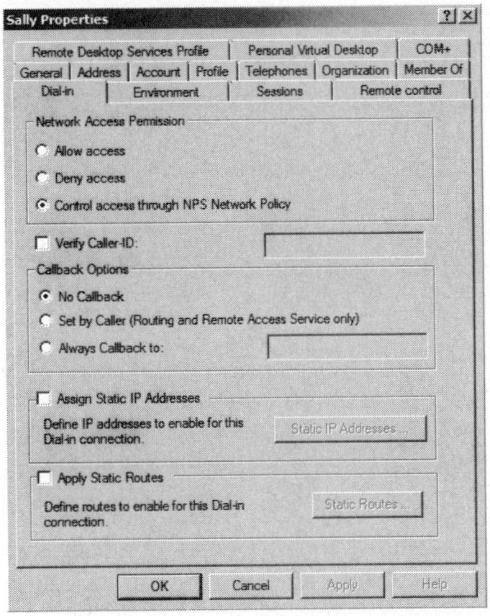

FIGURE 20.12
Viewing user Net-
work Access Per-
missions in Active
Directory Users
and Computers

If you look back at Figure 20.11, you can see a third choice in the Access Permission section: "Ignore user account dial-in properties" check box. You can select it in addition to either "Grant access" and "Deny access," and when selected, the user setting for the user account shown in Figure 20.12 will be overridden.

CONFIGURING POLICY CONSTRAINTS

Policy constraints are additional elements you can configure to control the connections. Constraints can then be used to deny access or disconnect users based on other qualifiers.

Figure 20.13 shows the constraints page for a network access policy. You may notice some crossover with the conditions and the constraints. Four elements can be configured as either conditions or constraints: Authentication Methods, Called Station ID, Day and Time Restrictions, and NAS Port Type.

FIGURE 20.13
Configuring constraints for a network access policy

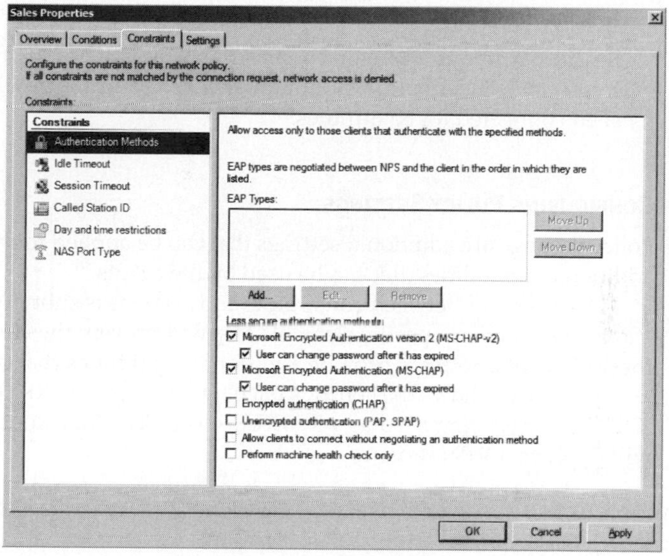

A logical question is, "Should I use the element as a condition or a constraint?" The answer lies in the purpose of the condition—a condition is used to identify the policy to be used. Remember, all conditions of a policy must be met for the policy to be used, and then you set permissions, constraints, and settings to further restrict or control the connection.

As an example, you may want to allow Sales users to be able to connect any time of any day, but Domain Users to only connect between 7 a.m. and 5 p.m. Monday through Friday. The following two policies could be created:

POLICY 1

- ◆ Condition: Sales group, Allow access

- ◆ Constraints: None

POLICY 2

- ◆ Condition: Domain Users group, Allow access

- ◆ Constraints: Day and Time Restrictions (7 a.m. to 5 p.m. Monday through Friday)

If users in the Sales group access the server, they will use Policy 1 based on the Sales group condition and the constraints won't restrict their access. If any domain user that's not in the Sales group accesses the server, they will use Policy 2 based on the Domain Users group condition. If they access the server between 7 a.m. and 5 p.m. Monday through Friday, the connection will complete. However, if they access it at any other time, they'll still use Policy 2, but the constraint will prevent the connection.

The two extra constraints are as follows:

Idle Timeout   You can configure this to close the connection if the session is idle for a period of time, just as a screen saver can be configured to start if a system is idle.

Session Timeout   The total connection time can be configured to control how long a user connects. For example, enabling this and setting it to 60 will disconnect users after they've been connected for 60 minutes.

CONFIGURING POLICY SETTINGS

Policy settings are additional settings that can be applied to the connection. The settings provide additional capabilities that can be used by the clients.

The difference between constraints and settings is subtle. Constraints are used to ensure a VPN client is using specific elements and will prevent the connection if the client does not use these elements. Settings provide additional capabilities that clients are free to use.

Figure 20.14 shows the settings page for a policy. The RADIUS Attributes section applies only if the server is being used as a RADIUS server. The four Routing and Remote Access settings will apply to a VPN server.

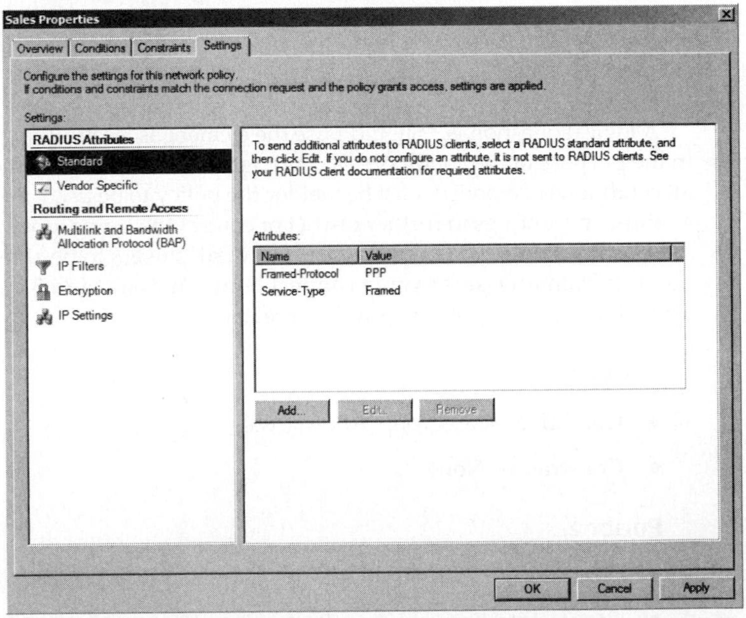

FIGURE 20.14
Configuring settings for a network access policy

Multilink and Bandwidth Allocation Protocol

Multilink allows clients to use multiple lines for a connection. Although this isn't commonly used for a VPN, it can be valuable for dial-up connections. If a user connects via a single phone line, they are limited to a 56Kbps modem, and even the modem is limited to slower speeds than 56Kbps over a phone line.

However, if the client has two phone lines and two modems and the server also has at least two phone lines and two modems, the client is able to make a single shared connection over both phone lines and modems.

When multilink is used, the Bandwidth Allocation Protocol (BAP) can also be used. It can be used to dynamically disconnect unused multilink connections. In other words, if a user connected with two multilink connections but was using only a small fraction of the bandwidth, BAP can disconnect the unused line so that it is available for another user.

Figure 20.15 shows the settings page for Multilink and BAP with the default selections.

FIGURE 20.15
Configuring multilink settings for a network access policy

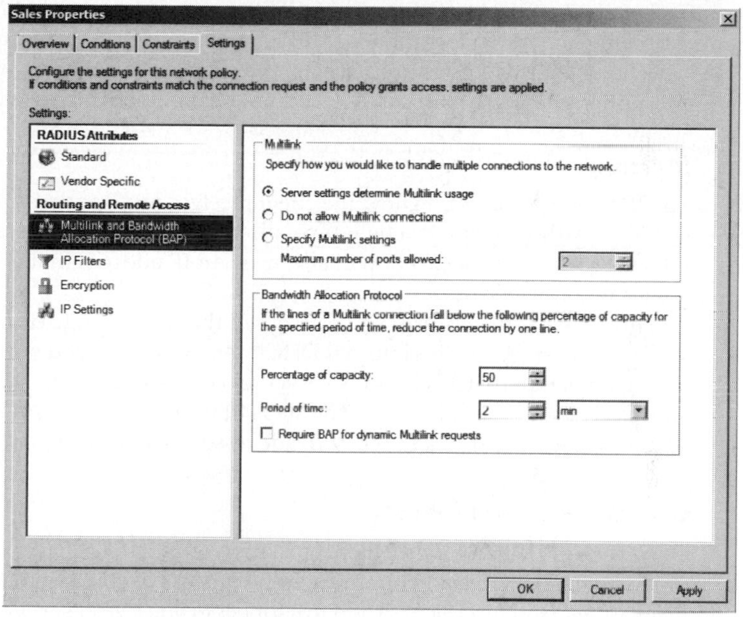

IP Filters

IPv4 and IPv6 input and output filters can be used to control traffic going across the connection. The settings that can be configured are the same type of settings that can be configured on a basic packet filtering router.

Packets can be filtered based on IP addresses, subnets, protocols, and ports. For example, if the VPN clients are supposed to have access only to a single subnet in the network, a filter could be created to grant access to this subnet and no others. Similarly, a filter could be granted to block access to a specific subnet while granting access to all others.

Encryption Settings

Encryption settings help determine what encryption will be used for the connection. Encryption will cipher the data so that it is not easily readable if intercepted. This page gives four encryption choices:

◆ Basic Encryption (MPPE 40-bit)

◆ Strong Encryption (MPPE 56-bit)

◆ Strongest Encryption (MPPE (128-bit)

◆ No Encryption

The actual encryption used is determined by other protocols. For example, if you're using PPTP, it will use Microsoft Point to Point Encryption (MPPE) with the bit lengths shown. However, if you're using L2TP, it uses IPSec instead of MPPE, and if you're using Secure Sockets Layer Tunneling Protocol (SSTP), it uses SSL instead of MPPE. Additionally, each of the different encryption techniques (MPPE, IPSec, and SSL) has different strengths of encryption.

When all four settings are selected, the client and the server will negotiate the strongest encryption that they both can use. It is not recommended to use the No Encryption setting.

IP Settings

The IP settings determine how the client receives an IP address that is used for internal connections. Although a VPN client typically has a public IP address used to tunnel through the Internet to the VPN server, it will also need an IP address that is local to the internal network after it is connected.

This internal IP address can be assigned through a range of addresses assigned by the VPN server, requested from an internal DHCP server, or assigned statically. For a gateway-to-gateway VPN connection (where the VPN server accepts only a single connection), a statically assigned address is used. If you followed the steps in the chapter to configure Routing and Remote Access, you configured a range of IP addresses that are assigned to VPN clients.

CREATING A NETWORK POLICY

Once you understand the elements of a network access policy, you can create your own. The following steps will lead you through the process of creating a network access policy to allow users in the Domain Users group to connect to your VPN server. These steps assume your VPN server is a member server in the domain so that the Domain Users group can be used.

1. Launch the Routing and Remote Access Server (RRAS) console by selecting Start ➢ Administrative Tools ➢ Routing and Remote Access.

2. Launch the Network Policy Server console by right-clicking Remote Access Logging and Policies and selecting Launch NPS.

3. Select Network Policies in the Network Policy Server console. Right-click Network Policies, and select New.

4. Type **Domain Users** as the policy name. Select Remote Access Server (VPN-Dial up) from the drop-down box as the type of network access server. Your display will look similar to Figure 20.16. Click Next.

5. On the Specify Conditions page, click Add. Select Windows Groups, click Add, and then click the Add Groups button.

6. Enter **Domain Users** as the object name, and click Check Names. If prompted, enter credentials for the domain. Your display will look similar to Figure 20.17. Click OK to accept the group on the Select Group page. Click OK on the Windows Groups page, and click Next on the Specify Conditions page.

You can add as many conditions as you like on the Specify Conditions page. However, if more than one condition is added, all conditions must be met to use the policy.

7. The Specify Access Permission page allows you to grant or deny access and override the user's dial-in properties. Ensure "Access granted" is selected. Select the "Access is determined by User Dial-in properties (which override NPS policy)" box to ensure that dial-in user properties cannot override this policy. Click Next.

8. On the Configure Authentication Methods page, you can identify what authentication methods the server and clients will use. Click Add to view the extensible authentication protocols that can be added. Your display will look similar to Figure 20.18.

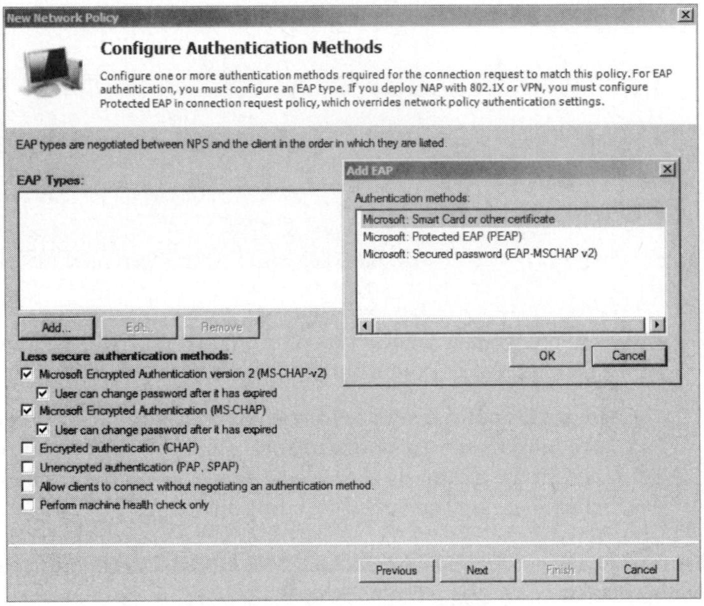

FIGURE 20.18
Choosing from the different authentication methods

You can add the additional EAP methods, but for now just leave the defaults. Click Cancel to dismiss the Add EAP dialog box. You'll explore the different authentication methods in greater depth in the next section. Click Next.

9. On the Configure Constraints page, ensure Idle Timeout is selected, and select the "Disconnect after the maximum idle time" box. Change the 1 to 15 to indicate 15 minutes. Feel free to click through the other constraints to view them. Click Next.

10. The Configure Settings page will appear. Select Encryption, and deselect "No encryption." Only "Basic encryption," "Strong encryption," or "Strongest encryption" should be selected. This will ensure that any connections will use some type of encryption. Click Next.

11. Review the information on the Completing New Network Policy page, and click Finish. At this point, you have created a VPN policy that can be used to grant access to any user who has a domain account.

At this point, you have a domain controller (named BF1 in our example test bed) and a member server (named BF2 in our lab). The Routing and Remote Access Services role has been added and configured on the server, and a network access policy has been created.

The next step is to configure a client to connect to the VPN server.

CONFIGURING AND CONNECTING WITH A VPN CLIENT

With your domain controller and VPN server created and configured, it's time to configure your client and connect. Although a VPN server would actually have one NIC connected to the Internet, a test bed will look more like Figure 20.19.

FIGURE 20.19
Connecting to a
VPN server

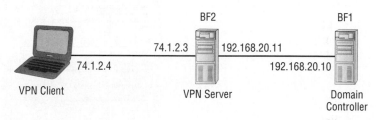

Notice that the VPN server has two NICs. The back-end NIC is connected to the network with an IP of 192.168.20.11/24, which is on the same subnet as the DC with 192.168.20.10/24.

The Internet-facing NIC has a public IP with a manually assigned IP of 74.1.2.3/8. The client will obtain any public IP from the Internet service provider (ISP), but for our lab we're manually assigning the NIC with an IP of 74.1.2.4/8, which is on the same subnet as the public IP.

One of the biggest challenges is getting a certificate to work with both the server and the client, so for initial testing, we'll do this without a certificate. Afterward, we'll show how to add a certificate and configure the server to use L2TP/IPSec.

Configure the RRAS server to use SSTP without SSL by following these steps:

1. Launch the Routing and Remote Access console.

2. Right-click the server, and select Properties.

3. Select the Security tab, and select the Use HTTP check box. This bypasses the need for a certificate. Your display will look similar to Figure 20.20.

Now all that's left is to configure the Windows 7 client and connect with a domain account. You can do so with the following steps:

1. Assign your Windows 7 client the IP address of 74.1.2.4/8 to simulate the public IP address that will reach the VPN server with these steps:

   A. Click Start, right-click Network, and select Properties to launch the Network and Sharing Center.

   B. Select Change Adapter Settings. Right-click the Local Area Connection, and select Properties.

   C. Select Internet Protocol Version 4 (TCP/IPv4), and select Properties.

D. Enter the IP address of 74.1.2.4 with a subnet mask of 255.0.0.0. Click OK to dismiss IPv4 Properties. Click Close to close the Local Area Connection Properties. At this point, you should be able to access the command prompt and ping the IP address of the VPN server at 74.1.2.3. If you can't ping the server, you won't be able to connect with a VPN connection.

FIGURE 20.20
Modifying
VPN security

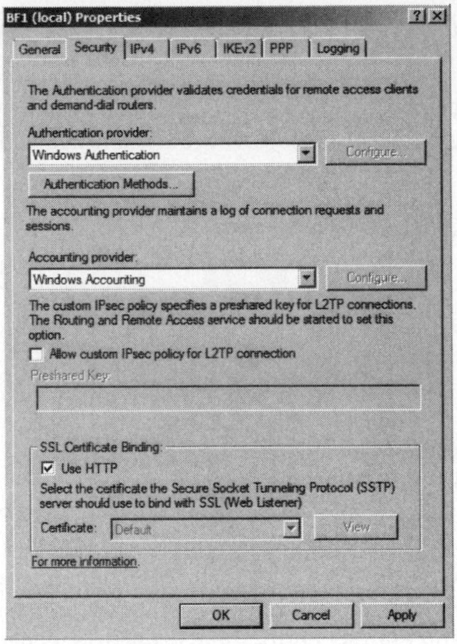

2. Click Back in the Explorer window to return to the Network and Sharing Center.

3. Create a VPN connection with these steps:

A. Click "Set up a new connection or network."

B. On the "Choose a connection option" page, select "Connect to a workplace." Click Next.

C. You'll be prompted to use an existing connection or create one. Select "No, create a new connection." Click Next.

D. On the "How do you want to connect?" page, select "Use my Internet connection (VPN)."

E. You'll be prompted to identify how you want to connect to the Internet. For this lab, Select "Let me decide later." Click Next.

F. Enter **74.1.2.3** as the Internet address. This is the IP address of the public-facing NIC on the VPN server. Click Next.

G. Enter **administrator** as the username and the domain name in the Domain (optional) text box. It's not necessary to enter the password at this point. Click Create.

H. Although a message indicates you must create an Internet connection, this isn't needed for the test bed. It would be needed for a client connecting over the Internet. Click Close.

4. Connect to the VPN server with the following steps:

   A. In the Network and Sharing Center, click Connect to a Network.

   B. Select the VPN connection you just created, and click Connect.

   C. Enter the password of the domain account you entered when creating the connection. You can also enter a new username and password if desired. Your display will look similar to Figure 20.21. Click Connect.

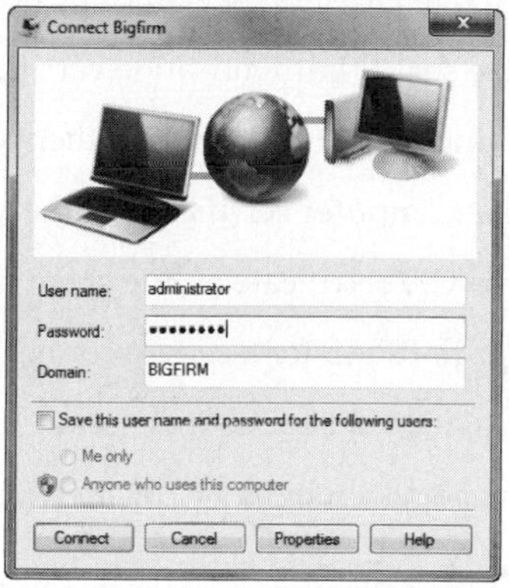

FIGURE 20.21
Launching the
VPN connection
in Windows 7

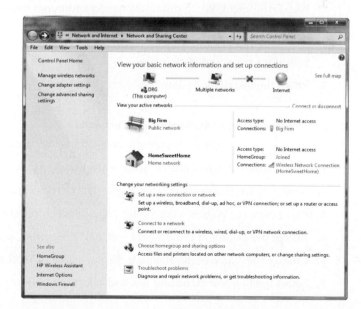

The connection will try to connect to the server. It tries the SSTP connection first and then others if it's not successful.

Since SSTP is enabled without SSL, it will connect. The Network and Sharing Center will look similar to Figure 20.22. Notice that both the Bigfirm VPN connection and the home network are shown as connected.

FIGURE 20.22
Windows 7
client connected
to Bigfirm VPN
connection and
home wireless
connection

ADDING A CERTIFICATE

Now that you know the pieces are working, you can add a certificate to the server to secure the connection. There are several ways to obtain a certificate. You can purchase a certificate from a trusted root authority or add Active Directory Certificate Services and issue and install certificates for free.

We're taking the free route even though it does require the completion of several tasks. You'll need to do the following:

1. Install Active Directory Certificate Services.

2. Create the server authentication certificate.

3. Request and install the server authentication certificate.

4. Install the computer certificate on the VPN server.

5. Install the CA certificate on the client.

6. Reconfigure RRAS for a secure connection.

7. Connect with a secure connection.

The next few pages include the detailed steps needed to accomplish these tasks.

Step 1: Install Active Directory Certificate Services

Perform the following steps to install Active Directory Certificates Services onto your VPN server:

1. Log onto your VPN server, and launch Server Manager. Select Add Roles.

2. Select Active Directory Certificate Services, and click Next twice.

3. On the Select Roles Services page, select Certification Authority and Certificate Authority Web Enrollment. When prompted to add additional role services, click the Add Required Role Services button. Click Next.

4. Accept all the defaults of the wizard. Review the information on the Confirm Installation Selections page, and click Install.

5. When the installation completes, click Close.

Step 2: Create the Server Authentication Certificate

Perform these steps on the VPN server to create the server authentication certificate:

1. Select Start ➤ Administrative Tools ➤ Certificate Authority.

2. Browse to Certificate Templates. Right-click Certificate Templates, and click Manage.

3. Right-click the Web Server template, and select Duplicate Template.

4. Accept the default of Windows Server 2003 Enterprise, and click OK.

5. Change the Name of the Template display name to **VPN IPSec**.

6. Select the Request Handling tab, and select the "Allow private key to be exported" check box.

7. Select the Subject Name tab. Review the information in the warning dialog box, and click OK. Select "Supply in the request."

8. Select the Extensions tab. Select Application Policies, and click Edit. Click Add. Select Server Authentication, and click OK. Your display will look similar to Figure 20.23. Click OK again to return to the Extensions tab.

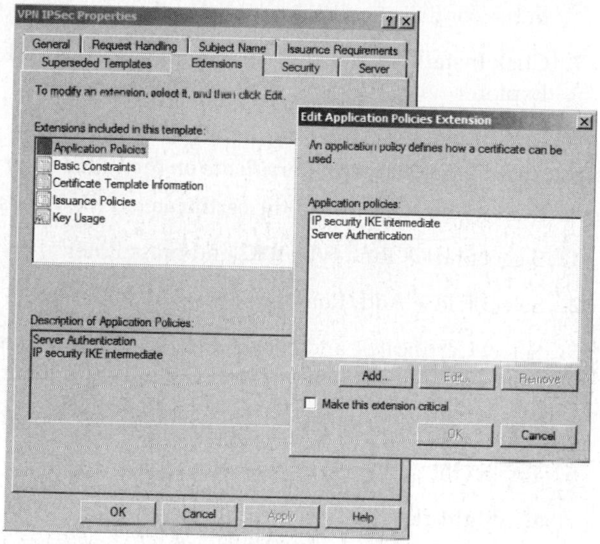

FIGURE 20.23

Adding the Server Authentication application policy extension for the certificate

9. Click OK to save the template.

10. Return to the Certificate Authority console.

11. Right-click Certificate Templates, and select New ➤ Certificate Template to Issue.

12. Select VPN IPSec, and click OK.

Step 3: Request and Install the Server Authentication Certificate

Perform these steps on the VPN server to install the server authentication certificate:

1. Use the following steps to configure Internet Explorer security so that you can use it to add the certificate:

   A. Launch Internet Explorer with administrative privileges (using Run As Administrator).

   B. Select Tools ➤ Internet Options, and select the Security tab.

   C. Select the Local intranet zone, and change the slider from Medium-low to Low. Click OK.

2. Enter **http://localhost/certsrv** in the address bar of Internet Explorer to connect to Certificate Services.

3. Click Request a Certificate. Then click Advanced Certificate Request.

4. Select Create, and submit a request to this CA. When prompted to allow an ActiveX control, click Yes. Review the confirmation message, and click Yes again.

5. Select VPN IPSec as the certificate template. Enter the name of your server and the domain in the Name box. For the example lab, this is BF2.Bigfirm.com.

6. Click Submit. When prompted to allow the ActiveX control, click Yes, and click Yes again in the confirmation dialog box. At this point, the certificate has been created.

7. Click Install This Certificate, though you will need to take additional steps. Close Internet Explorer.

Step 4: Install the Computer Certificate on the VPN Server

Use the following steps to add the certificate on the VPN server's to the certificate store:

1. Select Start ➤ Run, type **MMC**, and press Enter.

2. Select File ➤ Add/Remove Snap-in.

3. Select Certificates, and click Add. Click Finish to add the "My user account certificate" snap-in. Click Add again, select Computer Account, and click Next. Click Finish. Click OK.

4. Browse to the Certificates – Current User\Personal\Certificates container.

5. Export the server certificate with these steps:

   A. Right-click the server certificate, and select All Tasks ➤ Export.

   B. Click Next on the Welcome page. Select "Yes, export the private key," and click Next. Accept the default file format, and click Next.

   C. Enter a password in the Password and Confirm password text boxes on the Password page, and click Next.

   D. Click Browse, and browse to the C:\Certs folder (create it if needed). Name the file **VPNIPsec**, and click Save. Click Next, click Finish, and click OK.

6. Back in the MMC, import the certificate using these steps:

   A. Browse to the Certificates (Local Computer)\ Personal\Certificates container.

   B. Right-click Certificates, and select All Tasks ➤ Import.

   C. Click Next on the Welcome page. Click Browse, and browse to C:\Certs. Change the extension to All Files (*.*) so that the file you exported appears. Select your certificate, and click Open.

   D. Click Next on the File to Import page. Enter the password you used to protect the certificate, and click Next. Click Next to accept the default location of the certificate store, and click Next. Click OK.

7. Use the following steps to generate a trusted root certificate on the VPN server:

   A. Launch Internet Explorer using Run As Administrator.

B. Enter **http://localhost/certsrv** in the address bar.

C. Click "Download a CA certificate, certificate chain, or CRL." When the ActiveX warning appears, click Yes. Click Yes again on the confirmation dialog pop-up.

D. Select Download CA certificate. Click Save. Notice that the name is certnew. Browse to the C:\Certs folder, click Save, and then click Close.

You will install this root certificate on the client.

Step 5: Install the CA Certificate on the Client

When the client connects to the VPN server, the VPN server will pass the certificate to use to establish the session. However, the client won't trust this certificate as valid by default. Instead, the root CA certificate needs to be installed on the client so that the server's certificate is trusted. The following steps will install the root certificate on the client:

1. Copy the certnew certificate created in the previous steps from the server to the client in a folder named C:\Certs.

2. On the Windows 7 client, select Start ➤ Run, type **MMC**, and press Enter. If a User Account Control dialog box appears, click Yes to allow the action.

3. Select File ➤ Add/Remove Snap-in.

4. Select Certificates, and click Add. Select Computer Account, and click Next. Accept Local Computer, and click Finish. Click OK.

5. Browse to Certificates (Local Computers)\ Trusted Root Certification Authorities\ Certificates. Right-click Certificates, and select All Tasks ➤ Import.

6. Click Next on the Welcome page.

7. Browse to the C:\Certs folder, and select the certnew.cer certification file. Click Open. Click Next.

8. On the Certificate Store page, click Next to accept the default location. Click Finish. Click OK.

Step 6: Reconfigure RRAS for Secure Connection

You can now configure the RRAS server to use the certificate with the following steps:

1. If it's not open, launch the Routing and Remote Access console.

2. Right-click the server, and select Properties.

3. Select the Security tab.

4. Deselect Use HTTP in the SSL Certificate Binding area. Select the certificate you created earlier.

Step 7: Connect with a Secure Connection

At this point, you can connect using the same Windows 7 connection you created earlier. No changes are needed for Windows 7. It will automatically connect.

Connect to the VPN server with the following steps:

1. Access the Network and Sharing Center on Windows 7.

2. Click Connect to a Network.

3. Select the VPN Connection you created earlier, and click Connect.

4. Enter the password of the domain account you entered when creating the connection. Click Connect, and you'll be connected with a secure connection.

In the previous steps, you accepted the defaults for authentication. However, you may choose to use different types of authentication methods. The following topic includes more details on the available authentication choices.

Authenticating VPN Clients

Authentication allows a client to prove who they are. Once that's been established, the network access policy is able to determine whether the client should be granted access. Obviously, authentication is very important. You wouldn't want just anyone to connect to your VPN server and have access to your network.

If an attacker can obtain another user's credentials, it's possible for the attacker to impersonate the legitimate user and gain access to the server. Because of this, authentication becomes a significant security concern, and there are many different ways to authenticate individuals.

As attackers have gotten better at attacks, IT pros have had to improve security to thwart the attacks. Then the attackers improve, and the IT pros improve…it's never-ending. In the next page or so, you'll see many different authentication methods that show the progression and improvements with authentication.

The oldest authentication method of Password Authentication Protocol sent passwords across in clear text and was easily beatable with just a sniffer to capture the relevant packets. Today, the more secure authentication methods are referred to as Extensible Authentication Protocol methods. They are extensions of the core authentication methods.

When more than one authentication method is chosen, the client and the server negotiate the most secure authentication method available to both of them. It's not uncommon for a VPN server to need to support multiple types of clients, so a VPN server will commonly support multiple authentication methods. You'll need to ensure your VPN server supports the authentication mechanisms for all the clients you choose to support.

On the other hand, you can choose to use only the most secure authentication mechanism. Clients will then need to ensure they can use this method, or they won't be able to connect.

The Domain Users policy created earlier in this chapter was created using the default authentication methods. Authentication can be strengthened by adding the "Microsoft: Secured password (EAP-MS-MSCHAP v2)" authentication method to this policy by clicking Add and selecting the authentication method, as shown in Figure 20.24. This method does require adding a certificate from a certificate authority. If your users are issued smart cards, you can add the "Microsoft: Smart Card or other certificate" choice for the most secure authentication.

All the available authentication methods are listed here from the least secure to the most secure:

Perform Machine Health Check Only   If a network policy server is configured, this can be used to validate the health of the client. It isn't actually authentication since it validates only health but is listed in the authentication page.

FIGURE 20.24
Modifying authentication methods for a policy

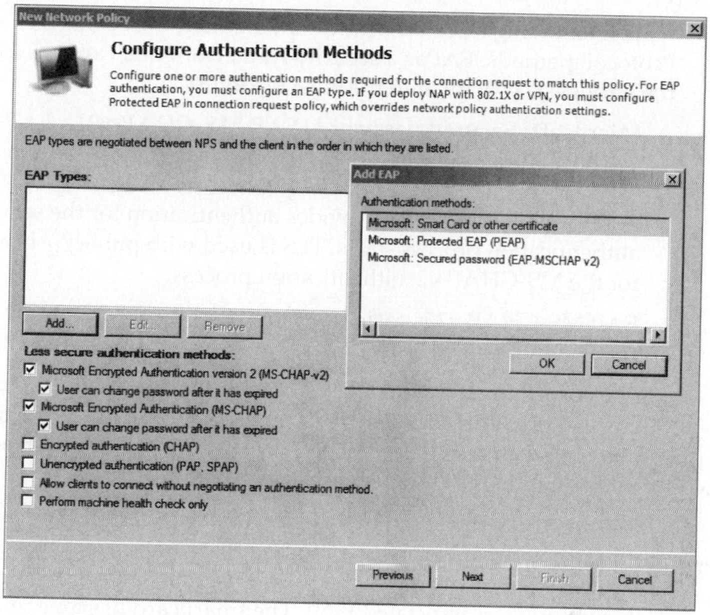

Allow Clients to Connect without Negotiating an Authentication Method   No authentication is used. Any clients can connect without any proof of identity.

Unencrypted Authentication (PAP, SPAP)   Authentication is passed across the transmission lines in clear text. A protocol analyzer (commonly called a *sniffer*) can capture the packets and read the credentials. This includes the generic Password Authentication Protocol (PAP) and the proprietary Shiva Password Authentication Protocol (SPAP). We'd be surprised to see this being used in any production environment today.

Encrypted Authentication (CHAP)   Challenge Handshake Authentication Protocol was the first widely used encrypted authentication protocol. When a client connected, the client was challenged with a nonce (a number used once) that was combined with credential information, hashed, encrypted, and returned to the server. The server periodically sent a new nonce to the client and forced another challenge handshake during the session. CHAP has historically been used on Microsoft RRAS servers to support non-Microsoft clients, but the more secure EAP methods are recommended today instead of CHAP.

Microsoft Encrypted Authentication (MS-CHAP)   This was Microsoft's first improvement over CHAP. It worked only on Microsoft clients and has been replaced with MS-CHAP-v2. MS-CHAP also encrypts the authentication to thwart sniffing attempts.

Microsoft Encrypted Authentication version 2 (MS-CHAP-v2)   MS-CHAP-v2 was created as an enhancement over MS-CHAP. It provided several improvements over MS-CHAP including mutual authentication. With mutual authentication, the server authenticates to the client before the client sends user credentials.

The following three authentication methods are referred to as Extensible Authentication Protocol methods. EAP is a security framework that can be used by any vendor and provides the strongest security with the most flexibility.

Microsoft: Secured password (EAP-MS-CHAP-v2)   EAP-MS-CHAP-v2 uses certificates on the VPN server to provide better security. The certificate is issued by a CA that is trusted by the VPN client and is provided when the VPN client contacts the VPN server. Since the CA is trusted, the certificate provides authentication for the server to the client before the client authentication process starts. TLS is used with public/private keys to create a secure channel for the MS-CHAP-v2 authentication process.

EAP-MS-CHAP-v2 is easier to deploy than EAP-TLS (smart card authentication) but still provides significant security enhancements over MS-CHAP-v2.

Microsoft: Protected EAP (PEAP)   PEAP doesn't specify an authentication method but instead provides additional security for whatever authentication method is used. PEAP provides a protected channel that helps prevent an attacker from injecting packets between the client and the VPN server.

Microsoft: Smart Card or other certificate   Certificate-based authentication is considered the strongest authentication method that can be used by a VPN server. Smart cards provide multifactor authentication because a user must have something (the smart card) and know something (an associated PIN). The smart card has an embedded digital certificate obtained from a trusted certificate authority (CA).

Smart cards can add significant expense. They require a CA to issue certificates, the hardware to create the smart cards with the embedded certificates, and the hardware to read the smart cards.

This method uses Transport Layer Security (TLS) and is sometimes referred to as EAP-TLS.

Configuring Accounting

Accounting is used in a VPN server to log details of who accesses the server and daily operations of the server. All the accounting is configured via the NPS console for a VPN server on Windows Server 2008 R2.

NPS includes a wizard that can be used to configure accounting and gives you four choices of how to store the accounting data:

◆ SQL Server database

◆ Text file

◆ SQL Server database and a local text file

◆ SQL Server database with text file logging for failover

If your network includes a SQL Server and someone is familiar with how to configure SQL Server to provide the data, it is the best choice. However, if you don't have SQL Server running on your network, logging the data to a text file should be selected.

Logging allows you to log several different types of data:

◆ Accounting requests

◆ Authentication requests

♦ Periodic accounting status

♦ Periodic authentication status

The authentication request and status information records all authentication events. This includes both failed and successful authentication attempts. Although it's obvious that authentication occurs when a user first connects, it's not so obvious that the server periodically challenges the client. This is transparent to the user but ensures that the client's session isn't hijacked by a malicious attacker. A hijack attempt will disconnect the original user and allow the attacker access to data within the session.

Accounting requests and status comments record information that is often used for billing purposes such as when a user connected, how long they stay connected, and activity during the connection.

You can use the following steps to configure accounting on a VPN server:

1. Launch the Routing and Remote Access Services console by selecting Start ➢ Administrative Tools ➢ Routing and Remote Access.

2. Launch the NPS console by right-clicking Remote Access Logging and Policies and selecting Launch NPS.

3. In the NPS console, select Accounting. Click the Configure Accounting link in the middle pane.

4. Review the information on the Introduction page, and click Next.

5. On the Select Accounting Options page, select Log to a Text File on the Local Computer, and click Next.

6. The Configure Local File Logging page allows you to pick and choose what type of information you want logged. Figure 20.25 shows the default selections. If you want to select a different location, you can simply click Browse and browse to the new location.

FIGURE 20.25
Modifying authentication methods for a policy

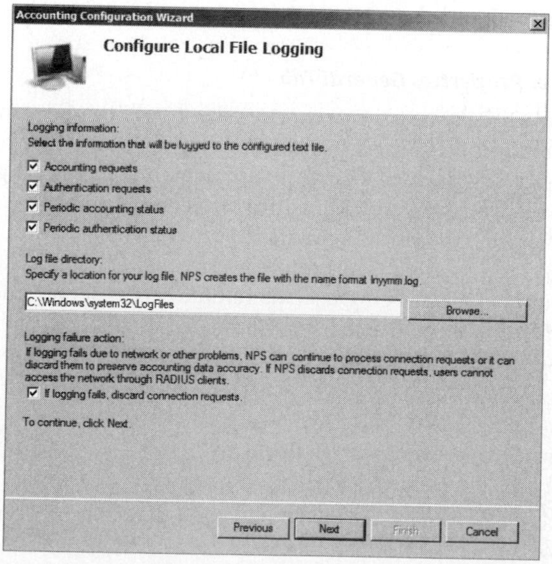

An important selection is at the bottom of the screen: "If logging fails, disconnect connection requests." You need to know what's most important to you and your organization—the logging of accounting data, or access to the VPN server. If it's most important for all access to be logged, select the box, and if logging fails, the VPN server won't allow any connections. If access to the VPN server is most important, deselect the box. If logging fails, users can still connect, but you won't have a record of the connections.

Accept the defaults, and click Next.

7. Review the information on the Summary page, and click Next. Click Close.

At this point, you've added the Routing and Remote Access Server, configured it to act as a VPN server, added a network access policy, and configured accounting. One thing we haven't done is explore the Routing and Remote Access console; we'll do so in the next section.

Exploring Routing and Remote Access

Once Routing and Remote Access has been added and configured using Server Manager, you can use the Routing and Remote Access console to modify the settings and view information on clients that have connected.

There are three primary areas where you'll want to explore:

◆ Server properties

◆ Ports

◆ Remote access clients

CONFIGURING SERVER PROPERTIES

You can view the server properties by right-clicking the server within the Routing and Remote Access console and selecting Properties. This properties sheet includes several tabs that can all be viewed and changed for the server.

Server Properties General Tab

Figure 20.26 shows the properties sheet with the General tab selected. Since the server was configured as a VPN server, it includes both the Router and the Remote Access Server settings.

The IPv4 Router and "LAN and demand-dial routing" settings allow the VPN server to route packets from the public IP address (received from the VPN clients) the internal LAN. At this point, both IPv4 and IPv6 are supported as the Internet is migrating to IPv6, so either IPv4 or IPv6 could be used. The bottom section has the "IPv4 Remote access server" check box selected to indicate this is being used as remote access server and the internal network is using IPv4 addresses. From this page, you really can't tell whether it's being used as a VPN server or a dial-up server, but when you look at the ports available (shown later in this chapter), it becomes clear this is being used as a VPN server.

Server Properties Security Tab

If you click the Security tab, you'll see a tab similar to Figure 20.27. In the figure, the Authentication Methods button was clicked to show the available authentication methods for the server.

FIGURE 20.26
General tab for
RRAS server

FIGURE 20.27
Security tab for
RRAS server

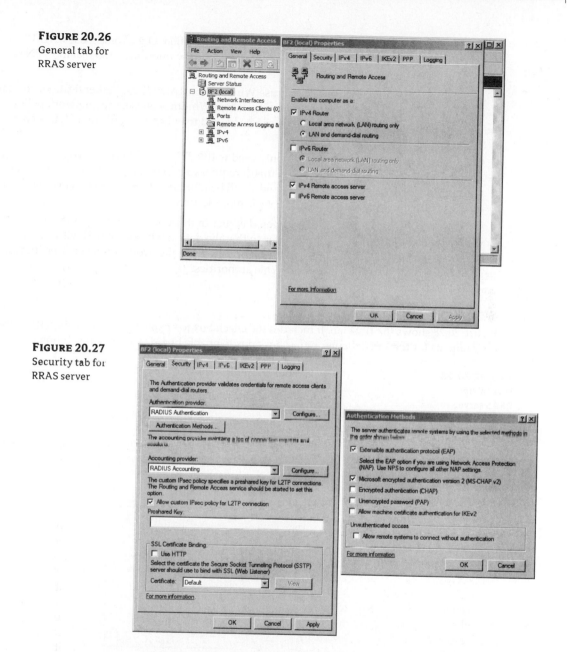

This tab has four main settings including authentication:

Authentication provider   If you have a single VPN server, this would be set to Windows
Authentication, meaning that the VPN server will authenticate the client using typical Windows
credentials. However, if your organization has multiple VPN servers, you very likely have

a RADIUS server, and you can choose RADIUS Authentication. Once you choose RADIUS Authentication, you'll need to click Configure to provide the information so that the VPN server can connect to the RADIUS server.

Accounting provider   Just as you can use Windows or RADIUS for authentication, you can choose Windows or RADIUS for accounting. When Windows is used, the network policy server is used for the logging, and data can be logged to either a text file or a SQL Server as discussed previously in this chapter.

Custom IPSec policy   IPSec is commonly used with L2TP. If L2TP is used, you can configure a custom IPSec policy. When you select this, it requires a preshared key. IPSec is covered in much more depth later in this chapter, and you'll be reminded that although a preshared key can be used, either Kerberos or a certificate is more secure.

SSL certificate binding   SSTP was covered earlier in this chapter. If you plan on using this, you need to add a certificate to the server so that the data can be encrypted with SSL. Once the certificate is added, you can select the certificate from the drop-down box. Certificates should be obtained from trusted certificate authorities.

Server Properties IPv4 Tab

Figure 20.28 shows the IPv4 tab. It includes the check box to enable IPv4 forwarding, IP address assignments for the VPN clients, and a check box to enable broadcast name resolution.

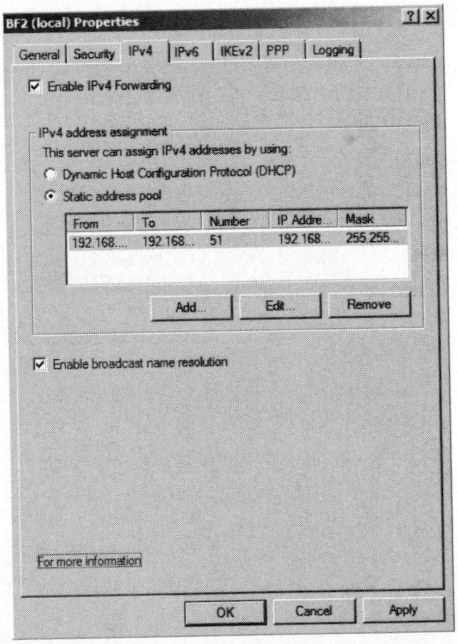

FIGURE 20.28
IPv4 tab for
RRAS server

If you added the Routing and Remote Access server role and configured it using the steps in this chapter, you'll have a static address pool of 51 IP addresses (192.168.10.200 through 192.168.10.250) that can be assigned to VPN clients. It's also possible to use an existing DHCP server to assign the IP addresses.

The DHCP server doesn't need to be on the same server or even the same subnet as the VPN server. It can be any DHCP server that is reachable by the VPN server. However, since the VPN server must relay the DHCP requests from the VPN clients to the DHCP server, you must add the DHCP Relay Agent as an additional Routing and Remote Access service.

If "Enable broadcast name resolution" is selected (the default), clients are able to resolve names on the internal LAN using broadcasts. However, it's important to remember that broadcasts can't pass a router. In other words, broadcasts will only resolve names on the same internal subnet that the client's assigned IP address is on.

For example, if a client receives an IP address from the VPN server of 192.168.10.101 with a subnet mask of 255.255.255.0, broadcasts will only resolve IP addresses for clients on the 192.168.10.0 subnet. Clients on other subnets will need to be resolved using other means such as DNS.

Server Properties IPv6 Tab

You can use the IPv6 tab if you're using IPv6 on your internal network. Although IPv6 is becoming much more common on the Internet, its usage hasn't been widely embraced on internal networks, so you may not need to touch this. This tab has three settings.

Select Enable IPv6 Forwarding if you want the VPN server to act as a router for IPv6 packets. Selecting Default Route Advertisement specifies whether a default route is advertised on the server. If the server is enabled to route IPv6 packets, this should be selected.

Last, you can specify an IPv6 prefix assignment to be compatible with IPv6 addresses on your internal network.

Server Properties IKEv2 Tab

Internet Protocol Security (IPSec) uses security associations to establish secure channels between the client and server. IKEv2 is used on Windows Server 2008 R2 to establish these security associations. Additionally, IKEv2 is used to establish a secure channel when using EAP-MS-CHAPv2 for authentication.

Figure 20.29 shows the IKEv2 tab for the RRAS server with the default settings. The different settings can be modified to meet different needs or environments.

FIGURE 20.29
IKEv2 tab for
RRAS server

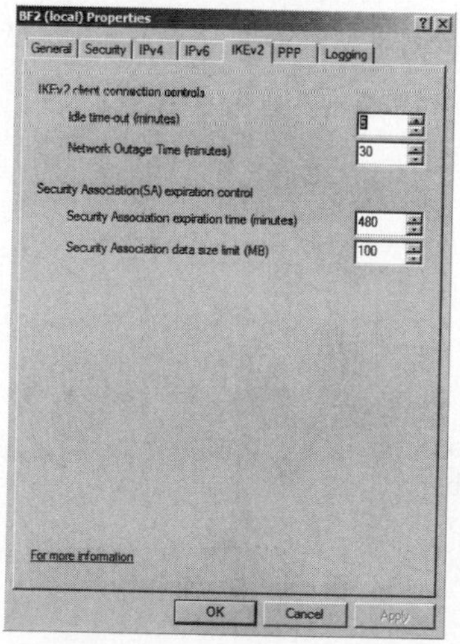

The settings are as follows:

Idle time-out   This identifies how long (in minutes) the connection can be idle before IKEv2 will terminate the connection. The default value is 5 minutes.

Network Outage Time   This setting specifies how many minutes that IKEv2 packets can be retransmitted without receiving a response. This is useful if the network experiences network outages by allowing the persistent connections. The default value is 30 minutes.

Security Association expiration time   When the expiration time has been reached, a new security association (SA) is negotiated and created before additional data can be transmitted. The default value is 8 hours (480 minutes).

Security Association data size limit   When the data size limit has been reached, a new security association (SA) is negotiated and created before additional data can be transmitted. The default value is 100MB.

Server Properties PPP Tab

The Point-to-Point Protocol is used for dial-up connections, and dial-up connections can be enhanced with various techniques such as using multilink connections. Figure 20.30 shows the settings available on the PPP tab.

FIGURE 20.30
PPP tab for
RRAS server

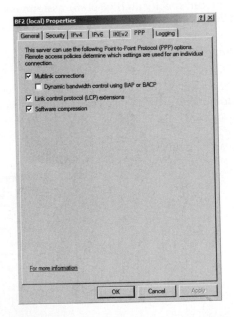

Settings configured on this tab won't necessarily apply to all users. Instead, these settings define what is possible on the server, and individual network access policy settings define what can be used for the policy. As an example, you could configure these settings to allow multilink connections on the server. A policy defined for IT Admins could be configured to allow multilink, while another policy defined for regular users could be defined so that multilink connections are not allowed. The available settings are as follows:

Multilink connections   When enabled, remote access clients can combine multiple connections to increase the overall bandwidth available. This can also be used in demand-dial router connections used in gateway-to-gateway VPNS connecting a remote office with main office. Two 56Kbps lines could be connected to achieve throughput of 112Kbps.

Dynamic bandwidth control using BAP or BACP   BAP and BACP allow lines to be dynamically added or deleted based on usage. For example, if a single user was using two lines but only using 10 percent of the bandwidth, the user's second line could be automatically dropped to make it available for other users.

Link control protocol (LCP) extensions   LCP extensions are used to send additional traffic related to time remaining and identification used in accounting and logs. If this data is not needed, this box can be deselected to eliminate this extra traffic on the line.

Software compression   With this box selected, the Microsoft Point-to-Point Compression Protocol (MPPC) is used to compress data.

Server Properties Logging Tab

The Logging tab is used to control what events are logged and where they are logged. Figure 20.31 shows the details in the Logging tab. Although it's not apparent, these setting are actually for different logs.

FIGURE 20.31
Logging tab for
RRAS server

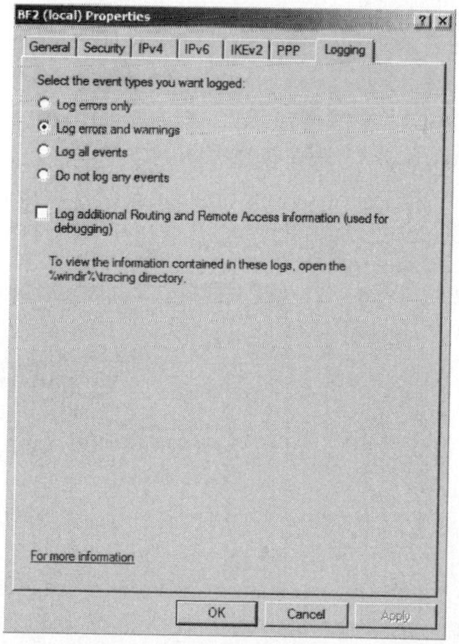

Events specified by the radio buttons are logged into the event log and can be viewed by the Event Viewer. The choices are errors only, errors and warnings, all events, or no logging. For more information on how to view the event logs, check out Chapter 17.

The "Log additional Routing and Remote Access information (used for debugging)" check box is completely separate from the event log. This check box is used only when you're troubleshooting specific problems but can be quite valuable to help you find the source of problems.

Any time you come across trace or debug logs, you should keep an important consideration in mind—they should be enabled only long enough to troubleshoot a problem and then should be immediately turned off. Trace and debug logs have the potential to consume a significant amount of resources, including processing power, memory, and disk space. Yes, they are useful when troubleshooting, but they may impact normal operation if left on.

Trace logs are stored in the %windir%\tracing directory. By default, this directory is empty, but when you select it, several dozen files will be created in this directory.

%WINDIR% OFTEN = C:\WINDOWS

%windir% is an environment variable that points to where Windows is installed on a system. You don't have to install Windows on the C drive, and in older operating systems, the Windows folder could be called something else. However, the operating system always needs to be able to locate this directory so when it boots, it populates the variable %windir% with the actual path to the Windows directory.

You can verify the value by going to the command line and typing **%windir%**. The command line will interpret the variable as C:\Windows (or wherever Windows is located). C:\Windows isn't a valid command, so it will give an error, but the first part of the error will tell you how %windir% is being interpreted. You can do this same procedure for any variables such as %systemroot% or %programfiles%.

MONITORING REMOTE ACCESS CLIENTS

Once your VPN server starts hosting VPN clients, you'll occasionally need to view the activity. Figure 20.32 shows the Remote Access Clients node with a remote client connected.

FIGURE 20.32
Viewing active clients

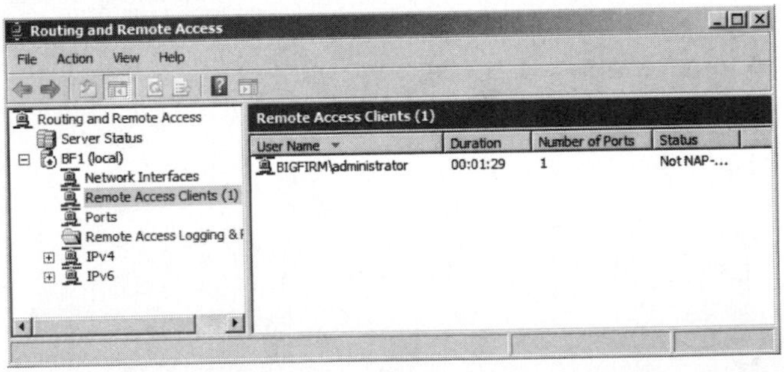

This view shows who is currently connected, how long they've been connected (duration), the number of ports they're using (if the connection is using multilink), and their current status (active or idle). You can disconnect any user by right-clicking the connection and selecting Disconnect.

CONFIGURING PORTS

When you create a VPN server, many ports are automatically created. These include 128 PPTP ports, 128 SSTP ports, 128 IKE-v2 ports, and 128 L2TP ports. Figure 20.33 shows the ports that are created. Typically, you'll use only one type of port. In other words, if you're using SSTP for VPN connections, you would not be using PPTP and probably wouldn't be using L2TP or IKEv2.

FIGURE 20.33
Viewing port properties on the RAS server

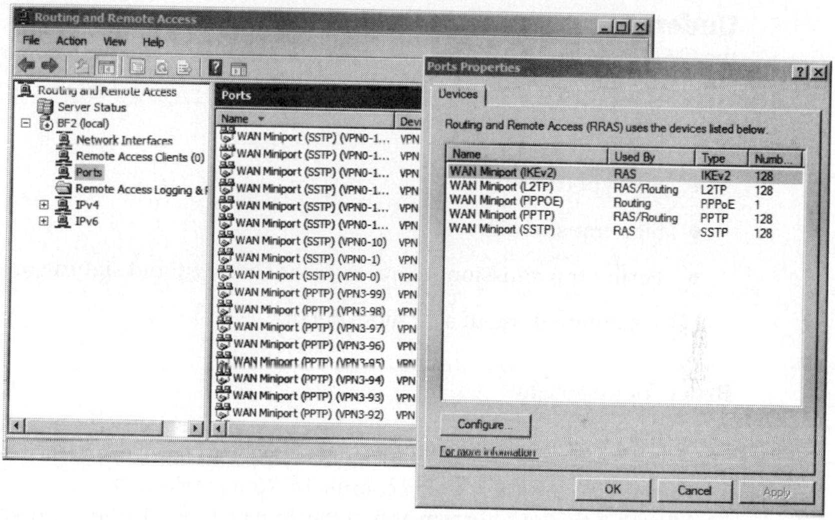

The number of ports that can be used is relative to how much bandwidth each user needs and the total amount of bandwidth for the server's connection. If the NIC is connected with a T3 connection with 44.7Mbps (lucky you!), you can support a lot more than 128 connections for your chosen protocol, as follows:

1. Select the port.

2. Click Configure.

3. Change the number to allow more connections.

On the other hand, if your bandwidth is only about 256Kbps, the performance will be dismal if all 128 connections are used simultaneously. In this situation, you'll likely reduce the number of possible connections.

Up to this point in the chapter, you've learned how to add the Network Policy and Access Services role and configure your server as a VPN server. One of the protocols that is heavily used with L2TP to encrypt traffic is IPSec. However, you can also use IPSec by itself to encrypt traffic.

Protecting VPNs with IP Security (IPSec)

Basic garden-variety IP lacks security, and that's fine in most cases—if you're just accessing files on a file server within your network, then you don't expect someone to be snooping. However, it is possible for someone between your computer and the server to intercept the data with a *protocol analyzer* (often called a *sniffer*). There's even the possibility for malicious users to modify the data in transit.

IPSec provides a generic solution for securing IP-based networks. IPSec operates at the same layer as IP and is a necessary part of using the VPN protocol L2TP—you can't run L2TP without IPSec. IPSec is supported by both IPv4 and IPv6.

Understanding IPSec: The Four Security Options

IPSec lets you choose how secure a communication between two computers will be. Basically, it offers four levels of security:

◆ Block transmissions

◆ Encrypt transmissions

◆ Sign transmissions

◆ Permit transmissions to travel unchanged, without signing or encrypting them

Let's examine those in a bit more detail.

BLOCK TRANSMISSION

This does just what it sounds like: it blocks transmissions or stops them from connecting. When you tell IPSec to "block" traffic from machine X to machine Y, then the IPSec code on machine Y just simply discards any traffic coming in from machine X.

Although this might seem at first blush to be kind of useless, if you think about it from a security perspective, then you'll see that it can be quite useful. In some senses, blocking traffic is the most extreme option for security, right? For example, a firm might have a competitor whose systems run on subnet 200.200.100.0, and you don't want them to be able to send you mail, visit your website, or communicate with your network in any way. (These could be mortal-enemy types of competitors.) You could set up IPSec on you systems to block that subnet, just discarding any packets that arrive.

ENCRYPT TRANSMISSION

Here, you *want* to allow traffic to pass from machine X to machine Y, but you're worried that someone will eavesdrop on the network connection between X and Y. So, you tell IPSec to use a protocol called the Encapsulating Security Payload—and we'll bet you don't need to be precognitive to guess that its acronym is ESP—to encrypt the traffic before putting it on the network. Snoopers will only see an unreadable, random-looking stream of bytes.

Notice how convenient it is that IPSec works way down at the network protocol layer—it can encrypt *anything*. Do you like the convenience of Telnet but hate that it sends its information in clear text? Just tell IPSec that whenever machine X and machine Y are using Telnet to communicate that IPSec should use ESP to encrypt the communication. No modification required at all to the Telnet server or client.

When would encryption be useful? Perhaps you have a few machines inside your intranet that handle very sensitive information—payroll information or perhaps customer credit cards. The data might be kept on a machine named SQL1, and it might be entered and edited only from workstations WS1, WS2, and WS3. You might fear that an insider might set up a sniffer on the network to capture this traffic as it goes by, collecting privileged information. You can keep people from accessing SQL1's database in the first place with permissions, as you probably already know. Additionally, you can keep people from listening on the wire by creating IPSec policies on SQL1 that force it to encrypt any communications to and from WS1, WS2, or WS3, and you can create similar policies on those workstations.

Or, in another instance, suppose you had a server in Chicago and offices all around the country, containing workstations that need to access data on that server. Suppose also that the only way that the offices connect to Chicago is over the public Internet, and you're (rightly) concerned that running company data over the public Internet might not be the best idea, security-wise. You could create an IPSec policy on the Chicago server so that it will accept encrypted traffic only—it would never accept clear-text communications. You would then create IPSec policies on the workstations so that they communicate with the Chicago server only via ESP.

SIGN TRANSMISSION

In certain kinds of network attacks, the bad guys fool your computer into thinking that transmissions from them are transmissions from someone you trust. Or other attacks involve grabbing transmission packets somewhere between you and the trusted person, modifying the packets, and sending them along to you—a so-called man-in-the-middle attack. IPSec lets you guard against this with a protocol called Authentication Header (AH). AH is a method for digitally *signing* communications.

If your computer and mine are performing signed communications, then you're *not* encrypting your data—anyone listening on the wire could overhear your communications. Instead, digital signing adds a bit of data to your network packets that you can use to verify that the data wasn't changed in transit. Another way of saying this is that digital signing provides data integrity, or an assurance that the data hasn't been modified.

IPSEC AND FIREWALLS

"What if a company had firewalls at every location? Would IPSec work through the firewalls?" The answer is yes. However, you must open UDP port 500 and permit protocol numbers 50 and 51. Protocol number 50 identifies the traffic as ESP, and protocol number 51 identifies the traffic as AH.

PERMIT TRANSMISSION

Permit is IPSec's phrase for "no security at all." It just tells IPSec to let the traffic pass without any changes to it and does not check on its integrity. This is basically what happens in a TCP/IP-based network that doesn't include any IPSec. Why, then, have a "permit" action at all? It's so that you can create rules that restrict some things but not others, such as a rule (which you'll see later in this chapter) that says, "Block all incoming traffic *except* for traffic on ports 80 and 443—permit that traffic."

Understanding IPSec Filters

Now that you know what IPSec can do, let's examine an important flexibility about IPSec—its filters. In the examples so far, we've said that you can direct IPSec to encrypt traffic between two particular systems. In another example, we said that not only can you tell IPSec to encrypt transmissions between two particular systems but that you could further refine IPSec's mission by saying that it should encrypt transmissions between those two systems *only when running Telnet*. In the section on blocking traffic altogether, we suggested you might want to tell your web server to block any traffic from subnet 200.200.100.0.

More specifically, you can use filters to restrict IPSec to securing communications:

◆ By the source computer's IP address, IP subnet, or DNS name

◆ By the destination computer's IP address, IP subnet, or DNS name

◆ By the port and port type (TCP, UDP, ICMP, and so on)

All of this makes for a very nice amount of flexibility with IPSec.

IPSec Rules = IPSec Actions + IPSec Filters

Blocking, encrypting, signing, or permitting traffic is said to be an IPSec *action*. You've just met IPSec filters. But to use IPSec, you combine a filter and an action to produce a *rule*. For example, suppose you want to tell the IPSec system on a given computer, "Encrypt all Telnet traffic from the computer at 10.10.11.3." *That's* a rule. It has a filter part and an action part:

◆ The *filter* part says, "Activate this rule only if there is traffic that is (1) from IP address 10.10.11.3 and (2) uses TCP port 23." (In case you didn't know, Telnet uses port 23.)

◆ The *action* part says, "Encrypt the traffic."

We'll show how to build some IPSec rules, filters, and actions in a bit, once we've gotten a few more concepts out of the way.

Signing and Encrypting Need One More Piece: Authentication

To make either digital signatures or encryption work, you need a set of agreed-upon *keys*—passwords, basically. So whenever you create an IPSec rule, then you'll have to tell IPSec how to authenticate.

Microsoft's IPSec supports three methods of authenticating: Kerberos, certificates, or an agreed-upon key. The Kerberos option only works between computers that are either in an Active Directory domain or in AD domains that trust one another. Simply having two computers that have Kerberos clients won't be sufficient, and, insofar as we can see, even two Windows systems that are members of the same Unix-based Kerberos version 5 realm (the Kerberos version of what we call a *domain* in the Microsoft world) can't use IPSec to communicate while authenticating with Kerberos. Perhaps Microsoft should have called this option "Active Directory" rather than "Kerberos."

The *certificates* option allows you to use Public Key Infrastructure (PKI) certificates to identify a machine. The *preshared key* option lets you use a regular clear-text string as the key.

We love the preshared key option, because it's great for experimentation. There's no need to set up a certificate or an AD domain—just tell both machines to use a preshared key and then type in some text, like **this is a secret**, on both machines. We wouldn't use it in a production environment, but for teaching and testing purposes, it's great.

AUTHENTICATION REQUIRED IN MICROSOFT'S IPSEC

Microsoft's IPSec implementation of authentication has a sort of annoying habit: it demands an authentication method whether IPSec needs it or not. You see, simply permitting traffic through without changing it, or blocking it altogether, does not require any agreed-upon keys, so in theory any rule that only includes permitting and blocking should not require choosing an authentication method. It'd be like the Department of Motor Vehicles asking you whether you put regular or high-test gas in your electric car when you registered it. But, again, Microsoft's IPSec asks you for an authentication method anyway, even though it'll never use it. So if you're building an IPSec rule that only permits and/or blocks, then go ahead and choose any authentication method; it doesn't matter.

How IPSec Works in Windows

That was the theory. Let's see how to actually use IPSec. There isn't really an "IPSec manager" program built into Windows; instead, Microsoft set things up so that you do IPSec entirely through policies, whether local policies or domain-based policies.

LOCAL POLICES VS. DOMAIN-BASED POLICIES

Within a domain, Active Directory includes three default IPSec policies, though none of the policies are applied by default:

◆ Client (Respond Only)

◆ Secure Server (Require Security)

◆ Server (Request Security)

Local security policies on previous editions of Windows also included these three default IPSec policies, but Windows Server 2008 R2 does not. You can still apply IPSec, but for member servers and stand-alone servers you'll need to create these policies from scratch.

To make IPSec do your bidding, you'll first open the Local Security Policy snap-in: select Start ➤ Programs ➤ Administrative Tools ➤ Local Security Policy; alternatively, select Start ➤ Run, type **secpol.msc**, and press Enter. It's a standard MMC snap-in, and in the left "command" pane, you'll see icons for several security policies including Account Policies, Local Policies, Public Key Policies, and one called IP Security Policies on Local Machine.

You can see a similar console within Group Policy:

1. Launch the Group Policy Management Console (GPMC) by selecting Start ➤ Administrative Tools ➤ Group Policy Management.

2. Right-click the Group Policy Objects node, and select New.

3. Type **IPSec** as the name of the new GPO, and click OK.

4. Right-click the IPSec GPO, and click Edit.

5. Browse to the Computer Configuration\Policies\Windows Settings\Security Settings\ IP Security Policies on Active Directory node, and select it. You'll see a screen like Figure 20.34.

FIGURE 20.34

Initial IPSec policies

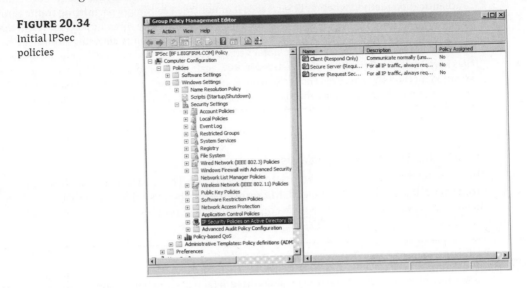

The big difference between the IPSec policies on the local machine and in the domain is that the domain includes three default policies in the right pane—Client (Respond Only), Secure Server (Require Security), and Server (Request Security). Those are three prebuilt policies that Microsoft adds to the domain. In the extreme right column, you see No next to each one; that means none of them are activated, or *assigned* in Windows lingo. You can activate any policy by right-clicking it and choosing Assign. But you can have only one policy assigned at a time. That's important—if you want to add some functionality to a current IPSec policy, then you can't just create a new policy and assign it, because that will *un*assign whatever policy is currently in force.

So, for example, suppose you were configuring IPSec on a server and you wanted to instruct that server to always encrypt communications when talking to server SRV1 and to always digitally sign communications when talking to server SRV2. You could create a policy that forces your system to encrypt when talking to SRV1 and a second policy that forces your system to sign when talking to SRV2. But if you did, then you'd see that you can have only one policy in force at a time. The *correct* way to deal with this requirement is to create *one* policy that contains *two* rules—one for SRV1 and one for SRV2. And note that you do not need to have *any* IPSec policies assigned at a given time; in fact, by default no policies are assigned.

Let's review what you've learned so far about IPSec:

- You control and enable IPSec on Microsoft operating systems through policies. You can have only one IPSec policy active on any given machine.

- Policies contain rules, which tell IPSec what to do, and authentication methods, which tell IPSec how the receiver (or receivers) and the transmitter (or transmitters) will exchange a password. They will then use that password in order to sign or encrypt the traffic. Even though permit and block rules don't use authentication, Windows requires that you specify an authentication method.

♦ IPSec lets you authenticate via Active Directory, PKI certificates, or a preshared key.

♦ Rules contain a filter or filters that tell the rule when to kick in, and rules contain actions that tell the rule what to do.

♦ There are four possible actions: block, encrypt, sign, and permit.

If that sounds like perhaps more work than you bargained for just to get a bit of secure traffic, then wait, don't run away—Microsoft has prebuilt those three nice, generic policies that might just fill the bill for you. As long as you're working in a domain, you may not have to write any policies at all—just find the one that works for your needs and turn it on.

DEFAULT IPSEC POLICIES

The three policies that come with IPSec in a domain are called Client (Respond Only), Server (Request Security), and Secure Server (Require Security). These three policies were previously included with the operating system installation. However, you won't see them on Windows Vista, Windows 7, or Windows Server 2008 or Windows Server 2008 R2 installations. The policies can still be applied through Group Policy in a domain, though.

The Client (Respond Only) policy tells a computer not to use IPSec unless requested. So, for example, suppose you set this policy to apply to all the systems in your domain. Then, one of the users tries to access a server that doesn't require IPSec. In that case, the server won't try to initiate IPSec with the computer, and the computer won't insist on using IPSec for the transaction, so all is well. But if your computer tries to connect to a server that *does* use IPSec, then the server will say to your workstation, "Let's do IPSec," and your workstation will be able to oblige.

The Server (Request Security) policy will cause the computer to attempt to initiate IPSec whenever possible. But if the other computer either can't or won't use IPSec, then both computers will still be able to communicate without IPSec.

As you'd expect, the Secure Server (Require Security) policy is designed to disallow any communications that don't use IPSec.

CREATING A CUSTOM IPSEC POLICY

Let's walk through a simple example of creating and configuring an IPSec policy that will ensure an encrypted connection between two machines. Suppose you work at home and have a persistent connection to the Internet—DSL, cable modem, or the like—with a static IP address of 199.10.10.3. Your job involves updating a database on a machine across the Internet with an IP address of 206.20.20.10. You want that connection to be encrypted, and, just for simplicity's sake, you'll use a preshared key. In this simple example, assume that the only system that 199.10.10.3 wants to use IPSec with is the 206.20.20.10 machine, and vice versa.

You'll need two policies—one for the 199.10.10.3 machine and one for the 206.20.20.10 machine. Each has two rules in addition to the default rule. The first rule for 199.10.10.3 will consist of the following:

Filter   Trigger the rule whenever there is traffic to 206.20.20.10, over any port.

Action   Encrypt the data.

The second rule is the reverse—trigger the rule whenever there is traffic *from* 206.20.20.10; the rest of the rule is the same as the first.

When building these rules, a preshared key with "this is a secret" as the key will be used for authentication.

The easiest way to create a rule is to first define filters and actions and *then* create the rule out of the new filter and action.

Define a Filter

You can create a filter in Local Security Policy by following these steps:

1. Launch Local Security Policy, and browse to IP Security Policies on the Local Computer node.

2. Right-click the object labeled IP Security Policies on Local Machine, and choose Manage IP Filter Lists and Filter Actions.

LOCAL POLICY AND DOMAIN GPO POLICY DIFFERENCES

In a domain GPO, two filters will already be added—All ICMP Traffic and All IP Traffic. These are needed to define the three prebuilt policies, but since the three prebuilt policies aren't included in the Local Security Policy, they aren't present.

---

3. Click the Add button to start the creation of the "traffic to 206.20.20.10." This dialog box doesn't actually let you create a new filter; it's sort of a staging area for new filters. (Don't ask us why it was built this way.)

4. Name the filter **Comms with 206.20.20.10**. To define the filter, deselect the Use Add Wizard check box, and click Add to open the IP Filter Properties dialog box. Your display will look similar to Figure 20.35. The "Destination address" drop-down is selected to show the different choices available.

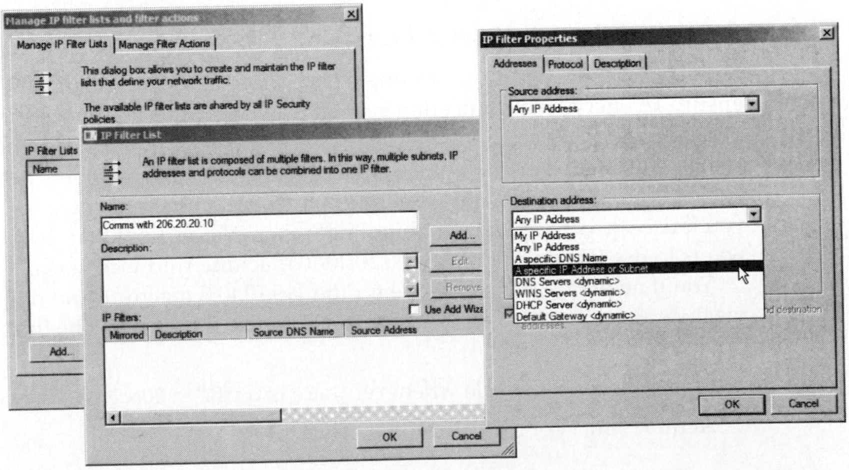

FIGURE 20.35
IP Filter Properties dialog box

5. Leave the source address as Any IP Address. Click the "Destination address" drop-down, and you'll see the options shown in Figure 20.30. Choose "A specific IP Address or Subnet," and punch in **206.20.20.10**.

6. If you like, click the Description tab, and describe the filter. If you were going to specify only traffic on a particular port, then you'd click the Protocol tab—it lets you specify the protocol type (UDP, TCP, ICMP, and others) and a port number.

7. One more thing before you click OK—leave the Mirrored check box selected. *Mirror* means to use the rule in both directions. Don't just activate it from "my address" to 206.20.20.10; also activate it from 206.20.20.10 to "my address." This saves you the trouble of creating that second rule, which is quite convenient. Now you're ready to click OK until you're back to the Manage IP Filter Lists and Filter Actions dialog box.

Define an Action

Next, follow these steps to define an action. These steps assume you've just created the filter and the Manage IP Filter Lists and the Filter Actions dialog box is still open.

1. Click the Manage Filter Actions tab.

2. As before, skip the wizard. Deselect Use Add Wizard, and click Add to show a dialog box like Figure 20.36.

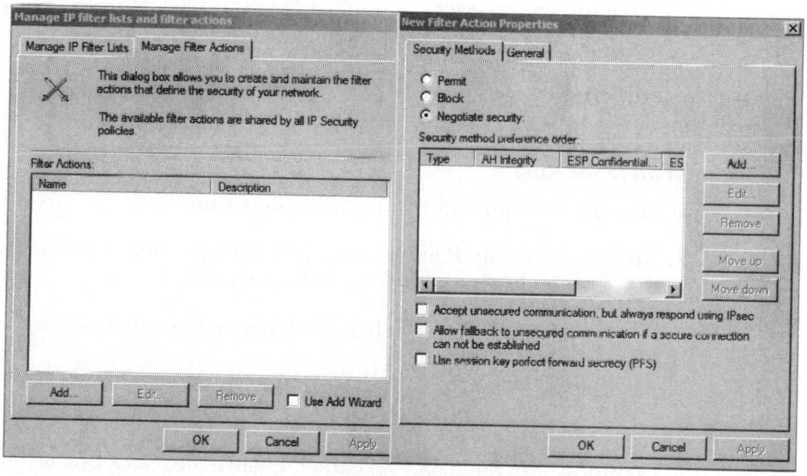

FIGURE 20.36
Creating a new filter action

Thus far, we've said that IPSec offers four possible actions, but you see only three here—Permit, Block, and Negotiate security. That's because "Negotiate security" can include both signing and encryption. You can see the check box that tells your system to accept nonsecured information, but leave it deselected. You want to be sure that this communication is secured, or you don't want to do it at all.

3. To specify the encryption, ensure that the radio button "Negotiate security" is chosen, and then click Add to see a dialog box like the one in Figure 20.37. Notice that "Integrity and encryption" is selected.

FIGURE 20.37
Defining the
filter action

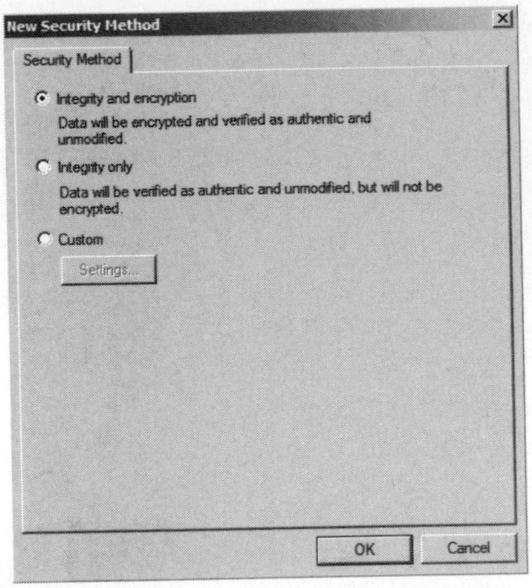

As you can see, you could choose "Integrity only." This will ensure that the packets are digitally signed to ensure that any loss of integrity is immediately noticed.

4. Click OK to accept the default of "Integrity and encryption," and return to New Filter Action Properties.

5. Click the General tab and give the filter a name, such as **Require Encryption**.

6. Click OK to return to the Manage IP Filter Lists and Filter Actions dialog box, and then click Close to close that dialog box.

Build an IPSec Rule

Now let's assemble the filter and action into a rule:

1. In Local Security Policy, again right-click the object labeled IP Security Policies on Local Machine, and choose Create IP Security Policy.

2. After the wizard starts, click Next. Name the rule **Secure comms to 206.20.20.10**, and click Next.

3. Next, the IPSec Policy Wizard will give you the option to activate the default response rule. The default response rule is supported only in operating systems running Windows XP, Windows Server 2003, and earlier. Ensure the check box is not selected, and click Next.

4. Leave the Edit Properties box selected, and click Finish on the Completion page.

5. Make sure that the Use Add Wizard check box is deselected, and click Add to show a dialog box like you see in Figure 20.38.

6. You've done most of the hard work; now just stitch a filter to an action, choose an authentication method, name the rule, and you'll be done:

   A. Choose the filter by clicking its radio button—Comms with 206.20.20.10.

B. Click the Filter Action tab to reveal the possible actions. Click the radio button next to your desired action—Require Encryption.

C. Click the tab labeled Authentication Methods. Click Add, select "Use this string (pre-shared key)," and type **this is a secret**. Your display will be similar to Figure 20.39.

FIGURE 20.38
Defining the IPSec policy rule

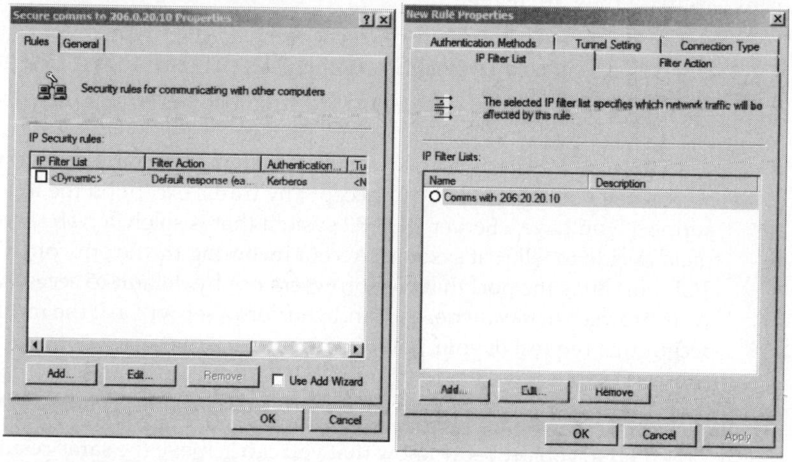

FIGURE 20.39
Choosing an authentication method

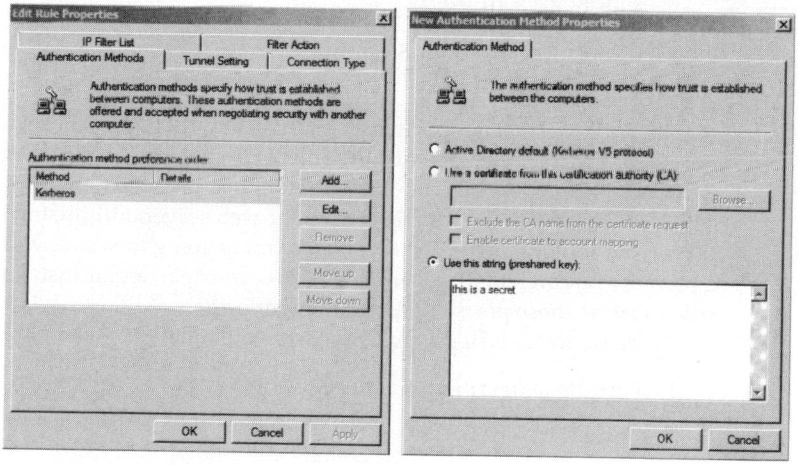

Here you can see the three options for authentication—Kerberos, certificate, or a preshared key. If both machines were in the same Active Directory domain, then the easiest thing to do would be use the default, which is Kerberos (and which we've suggested should be labeled "Active Directory" instead). But for simplicity's sake, we're using a preshared key—the extremely hard to guess "this is a secret."

7. Click OK three times, and you'll be back in Local Security Settings.

8. In the right pane, you'll see the newly created IPSec policies. To assign the policy, right-click the policy, and choose Assign.

Now you're done on the 199.10.10.3 side. Next, you'd go to the 206.20.20.10 machine and create an identical policy, *except* that you'd replace the references to 206.20.20.10 with 199.10.10.3.

But how could you check that you actually have encryption working between the two systems? With a program called Ipsecmon—just select Start ➤ Run, type **ipsecmon**, and click OK. Ipsecmon isn't very pretty, but it *will* identify systems that are using IPSec and the level of security they are using.

Using IPSec to Protect Systems Through Packet Filtering

Here's another neat thing you can do with IPSec—filter packets. It's not a common use of IPSec, but it works pretty well.

One way to at least partially secure a system is to shut down unused ports—or, in other words, tell your system, "Don't accept any traffic except on the following ports." For example, suppose you have a Server 2008 R2 system that is solely a web server; that's all that it does. You *could* decide to tell that system, "Accept incoming traffic only on TCP ports 80 and 443," because TCP port 80 is the port that web browsers use by default to access a website using HTTP. Point your browser to www.acme.com, and your browser will ask the machine at www.acme.com, "Please accept this request at your port 80." Your web server uses port 443 for *secured* communications using HTTPS or HTTP with SSL. In this section, we'll show you how to use IPSec to disable every port on your system except ports 80 and 443. But before we do, two notes on this process:

◆ First, you probably know that you can achieve the same result by configuring the system's built-in firewall.

◆ Second, filtering ports 80 and 443 on a web server is a very simple approach to security and is probably *too* simple.

The built-in SMTP server that can run on any IIS box wouldn't work, because SMTP needs port 25 open to send and receive email. And, worse, any remote access tool, such as Telnet or Remote Desktop Services, wouldn't work either, because they employ ports other than 80 and 443. You would then have to do all of your web server administration by sitting down at the web server and logging in locally. If you were *really* going to secure your system, you'd want to do a bit more research to discover which ports your particular installation uses and configure the rule to allow those ports but block all other ports.

These are the two steps you'd take to create the IPSec filters:

1. Formulate the rules by stating the objectives.

2. Build the rules within an IP filter.

FORMULATING THE RULES

In this example, you'll create the policy and add the rules to it. Each rule will be composed of a filter and a filter action. (We'll spare you the dialog box screenshots; the process is the same as in the earlier example. We'll just focus on what you'll need to know to make this work.) This time, you'll need more than one rule—four, actually. If they don't make sense upon an initial reading, don't worry. We're about to explain them. In IPSec-ese, you'd state the objective "Block all traffic except the traffic coming in on TCP ports 80 and 443" with four rules:

Rule 1 If network traffic of any kind or any port *enters* this computer from any other computer, block it.

Rule 2   If network traffic of any kind or any port *originates* at this computer and is addressed to go to any computer on the Internet, let it pass.

Rule 3   If TCP traffic on port 80 enters this computer from any other computer, let it pass.

Rule 4   If TCP traffic on port 443 enters this computer from any other computer, let it pass.

Upon first reading those four points, you're likely to say, "Wait…the first rule says to block *all* traffic of any kind, and the third one says to allow TCP port 80 traffic. Doesn't that conflict?" It looks that way, but it's the only way that you can give IPSec an even mildly complicated filtering rule.

What happens when two IPSec rules conflict with each other in the same policy? The simple guideline is that the specific rule beats the more generic rule. When IPSec comes across a conflict in rules, the more specific of the conflicting rules applies.

So, for example, suppose traffic comes in on TCP port 80. Rule 1 says, "It's incoming data; ignore it." Rule 2 says, "It's incoming data *on port 80*; keep it." Rule 2 is more specific, so it wins.

BUILDING THE RULES

Let's see how to build the policy's four rules. First you'd create a new IPSec policy by right-clicking IP Security Policy on Local Computer and selecting Create IP Security Policy. After naming the policy something like Block Non-Web Traffic, you would edit the properties and add each of the four rules.

Building Rule 1

Rule 1 says block all incoming traffic and could be named All Incoming Traffic. Let's break that down into its filter and its action. As you've seen, you create a filter by specifying the following parameters.

Create an IP filter list named All Incoming Traffic with the following values:

- All Incoming Traffic
- Source address: Any IP address
- Destination address: Your IP address
- Port and protocol: Any
- Mirroring: No

Notice that in this situation you do *not* want mirroring. That's because you want to block all incoming traffic and permit all outgoing traffic. If you wanted to block all incoming and outgoing traffic, then you'd mirror the rule. Because all four rules are *asymmetric*, you won't mirror any of them. To create rule 1, perform the following steps:

1. Set the action for this rule to Block by selecting the Manage Filter Actions tab and clicking Add.

2. Select Block, and click the General tab.

3. Name the filter action **Block**, and click OK.

Don't forget about authentication. You can leave the default of Kerberos or pick another.

DEFAULTING TO KERBEROS

If you pick Kerberos on a system that is not a member of an Active Directory domain, then the GUI will offer a dire-sounding dialog box that basically says, "Are you sure?" For the purposes of the exercise, just tell it that yes, you're sure.

Building Rule 2

The second rule permits all outgoing traffic and could be named All Outgoing Traffic. The filter is very much like the last one, although source and destination are reversed:

◆ Source: Your IP address

◆ Destination: Any IP address

◆ Ports and protocols: Any

◆ Mirroring: No

To create rule 2, follow these steps:

1. Set the action for this rule to Permit by selecting the Manage Filter Actions tab and clicking Add.

2. Select Permit, and click the General tab.

3. Name the filter action Permit, and click OK.

4. For authentication, you can leave the default of Kerberos or choose another.

At this point, your policy will have two rules added and will look similar to Figure 20.40.

FIGURE 20.40
Two rules added and selected for the Web Traffic IPSec policy

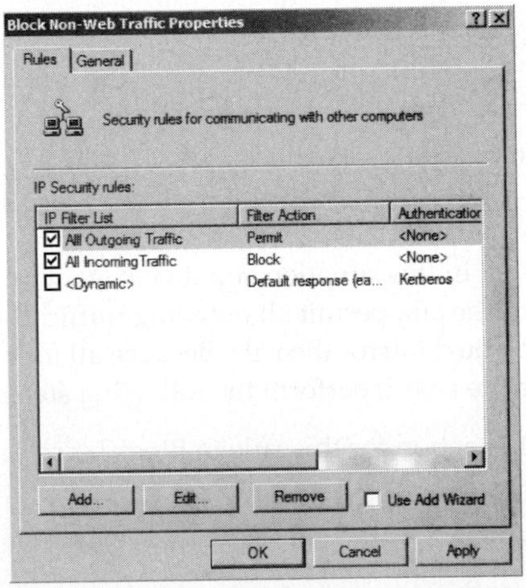

Building Rules 3 and 4

Next, you'll build the rules that pass traffic on ports 80 and 443, and you'll name them as TCP Port 80 and TCP Port 443. The filters are a trifle more complicated because you need to add port and protocol information, as follows:

1. As before, click Add to add the rule.

2. On the New Rule Properties page, click Add to add the filter, and name it **TCP Port 80**.

3. Enter the following parameters for the port 80 filter:

    ◆ Source address: Any IP address

    ◆ Destination address: Your IP address

    ◆ Ports and protocol: To port 80 on TCP

    ◆ Mirrored: No

4. Modify the ports and protocol on the Protocol tab of the IP Filter properties, as shown in Figure 20.41.

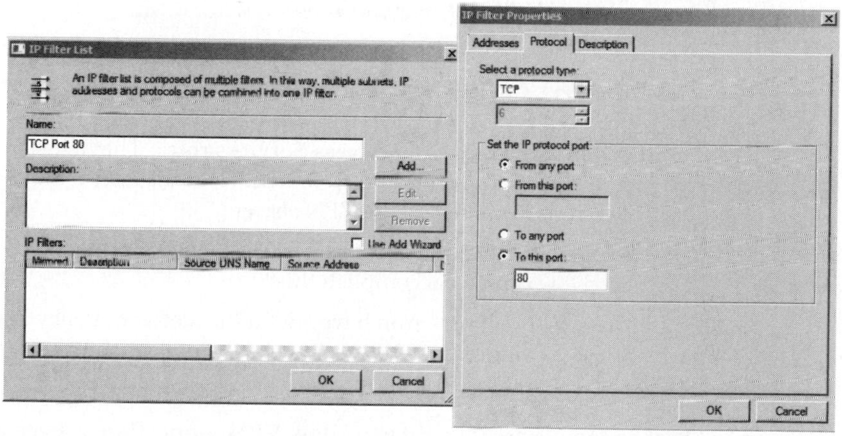

FIGURE 20.41
Specifying the protocol in the IP Filter

5. Choose the Permit action that was created in rule 2, and select the desired authentication

6. Repeat these steps to create the fourth rule with a filter named **TCP Port 443** by specifying TCP port 443 instead of TCP port 80. Again, choose the Permit action and the desired authentication.

This policy could then be assigned to a web server. Remember, though, it will block all incoming traffic that isn't using either TCP port 80 or TCP port 443. This includes SMTP traffic, FTP traffic, or even a simple ping to check connectivity. But you *will* be able to access its web pages, both secured on port 443 and unsecured on port 80.

A Few Final Thoughts About IPSec

We haven't covered all of IPSec here, because IPSec could probably fill a book. We've just tried to hit the high points. But we don't want to leave without mentioning a few things.

First, IPSec will *not* work in conjunction with NAT. A solution was attempted with something called IPSEC NAT traversal, but because of security concerns, it's not used very often. In general, if you need to go through a NAT, you'll need to consider something other than IPSec.

Second, we've been talking about IPSec as a one-to-one way for systems to communicate. But IPSec also has a feature called *tunneling* whereby most of your systems needn't be IPSec aware at all. Instead, they'd tunnel all their communications through a single IPSec-aware computer that is prepared to "relay" their communications to another IPSec-aware computer on a remote site. Thus, if you had 100 machines at one location and 100 machines at another location, you wanted machines at each location to be able to talk to all the machines on the other location, but you wanted security while the data traveled from one location to another, then you could just designate one machine at each location as a sort of "firewall" box. Those boxes would tunnel IP traffic from one site to another.

Third, IPSec is a standard, not just a Microsoft functionality. So in theory, you should be able to use Microsoft's IPSec to communicate with other vendors' tools. But test that before you start to rely upon it—we've heard that many non-Microsoft implementations can run into trouble trying to talk with IPSec-enabled Windows boxes.

The Bottom Line

Add the Network Policy and Access Services role   The first step to create a VPN server is to add the Network Policy and Access Services role. Once the role is added, you can take additional steps to configure the VPN server.

> **Master It**   You need to add the Network Policy and Access Services role to create a VPN server. How can you accomplish this?

Configure a VPN server   You have added the Network Policy and Access Services role and now want to configure your VPN server to accept connections from clients.

> **Master It**   What should you do to configure your VPN server?

Create a remote access policy to allow VPN connections   Even after the VPN role has been added and the Routing and Remote Access service has been configured, the VPN server will not accept any connections until the default remote access policies are modified or new ones are created.

> **Master It**   You want to allow users that have domain accounts to be able to access the VPN server remotely. What should you do to create a remote access policy?

Use IPSec to encrypt traffic   IPSec can be used to encrypt normal IP traffic between two computers to protect it against sniffing attacks. Policies can be created with Group Policy or via a local policy.

> **Master It**   You want to ensure that traffic between two DNS servers is encrypted. What should you do?

Chapter 21

Adding More Locations: Sites in Active Directory

If all your domain controllers are located in a single physical location, you can skip this chapter. However, if you have some domain controllers that aren't in the same location, you'll need to teach Active Directory about the wide area network (WAN) links connecting the different locations.

Active Directory uses sites to identify different locations. However, Active Directory knows about only one site by default. This default first site is named Default-First-Site-Name. If your organization is in a single location, everything will work as expected without problems.

However, if you have more than one site, you will need to create additional sites, subnets, and site links. The sites represent the locations, the subnet objects represent the actual subnets that exist in the locations, and the site links represent the WAN links that connect the different locations.

This chapter covers creating sites and subnets, configuring intersite replication with site links, optimizing intersite replication by modifying site link properties, and configuring the next nearest site for clients.

In this chapter, you will learn to:

◆ Create a site

◆ Add subnets to sites

◆ Configure a site link to replicate only during certain times

◆ Configure Group Policy for the next nearest site

Mastering Site Concepts

Many organizations have more than one physical location. Production, sales, and other activities are often spread across a city, a country, or even the world. These organizations have to take extra steps to ensure that the day-to-day operations of Active Directory are optimized.

Consider Figure 21.1. It represents an organization named Bigfirm.com that has three physical locations: the headquarters (HQ), a crosstown office, and a remote office.

Each physical location is well connected. In other words, all the routers, switches, NICs, and cabling at HQ are capable of transmitting data at 1Gbps, and all the components at the other two sites support 100Mbps transfer rates. This is actually the basic definition of a *site*—a group of well-connected hosts or subnets.

Between the sites, the connection is something less than the well-connected sites. In the figure, a T1 (1.544Mbps) WAN link connects the HQ location with the crosstown office. The remote office is connected to HQ with a slower 256Kbps connection, and a backup 56Kbps connection connects the crosstown and remote offices.

FIGURE 21.1
A multiple-
location company

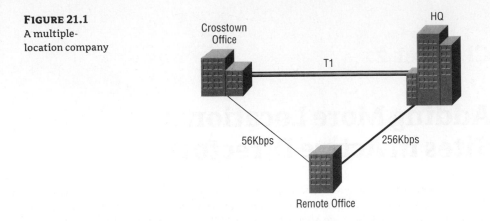

Assume that each location has at least one domain controller, and consider these questions:

◆ When users log on in the remote office, what domain controller (DC) should authenticate them?

◆ If a domain controller in the remote office replicates Active Directory data with a domain controller at HQ, what path should it take?

◆ If the T1 line went down, how should a domain controller in HQ replicate with a domain controller in the crosstown office?

The answers are obvious when you look at Figure 21.1 shown previously:

◆ Remote office users should log onto a DC in the remote office.

◆ Replication between HQ and the remote office should occur using the 256Kbps link.

◆ If the T1 link goes down, the replication path from HQ to the crosstown office should be through the 256Kbps and then the 56Kbps connections.

However, the answers aren't obvious to Active Directory. You have to teach Active Directory by configuring objects in Active Directory Sites and Services.

Remember, Active Directory is a huge database of objects such as users, computers, and groups that refer to real-world entities. When you create a user object in Active Directory, you aren't creating a person; instead, you're creating an object representing the user.

Similarly, when you create a site in Active Directory Sites and Services, you aren't creating a physical location. Instead, you're creating an object that refers to the physical location or physical site.

Sites and Replication

As a reminder, Active Directory replication is the replication of all the additions, deletions, and modifications to Active Directory. When a user account is added or a user changes their password, this change needs to be replicated to Active Directory.

Within a site, this replication occurs very quickly and uses a notification process. For example, consider a site with four domain controllers named BF1, BF2, BF3, and BF4, as shown in Figure 21.2.

FIGURE 21.2
Intra-site replication
topology

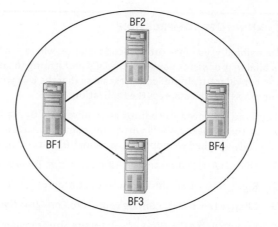

If a user account is added to BF1, BF1 would notify BF2 and BF3 of the change. BF2 and BF3 don't have this change, so they request it, and all three are up-to-date.

Both BF2 and BF3 will send a notification to BF4 of the change. BF4 will request the change from the first notification it receives, but not from both DCs.

Imagine that BF2's notification was received first. BF4 will request the change from BF2, but when it receives the notification from BF3, it will recognize that it already has the change, and the notification will be ignored. This notification process is called *propagation dampening*, and it prevents changes from endlessly being replicated to each other.

Replication *between* sites is optimized by omitting this notification mechanism and by compressing the replicated data.

No notification between sites   Replication between sites is sent based on the schedule. All replicated data that has been collected since the last replication is sent without using a notification process.

Replication compressed between sites   Replicated data is compressed before being replicated. In a well-connected site, compression isn't needed. However, since WAN links have less bandwidth, this compression is quite valuable.

Understanding Site Terminology

You should understand several terms and concepts regarding sites before digging into the details. These are some of the key concepts related to sites:

Sites   A site is a group of well-connected hosts or well-connected subnets located together in a physical location.

The phrase *well-connected* is relative. One site may include all the network infrastructure components to run at 10Mbps, and another site may be running at 1Gbps. However, within each site, all the components are functioning in a well-connected LAN and referred to as a site even though there is such a disparity in their speeds.

Physical locations   A physical location refers to the location of the LAN. A physical location could be a single remote office with 25 users or an entire building with thousands of users. If a physical location includes a domain controller, a site object should be configured in Active Directory representing the physical location.

TURNING OFF COMPRESSION

Occasionally, you may run across a situation where you have more bandwidth between sites than available processing power on the DCs performing the intersite replication. In this situation, you can consider turning off compression so that the DCs won't spend the processing time required to compress and decompress the replication.

This is an advanced procedure and requires modifying Active Directory settings using ADSI Edit, which should be done only when you're sure you have a good backup of Active Directory. If you've carefully weighed your options, you can turn off compression by following these steps:

1. Launch ADSI Edit from the Administrative Tools menu.

2. Right-click ADSI Edit, and select Connect to.

3. Change the default naming context to Configuration.

4. Browse to the CN=Sites, CN=Intersite Site Transport, CN=IP container.

5. Double-click the site link you want to modify to access the properties.

6. Double-click the "options" property.

7. If this has a value of <not set>, change it to 4, and click OK. You'll see that the value is now 0x4 = (DISABLE_COMPRESSION).

   If the "options" property has a value, you'll need to add 4 to it. For example, if it is set to 2, add 4 + 2 for a value of 6. You'd then enter 6.

Subnets   Every LAN will have one or more subnets. These subnets already exist at each physical location. Site objects are added to Active Directory to represent physical locations, and subnet objects are added to the site objects to represent the actual subnets at these locations.

Site links   Sites connect to other sites through slower WAN connections. For example, one site may connect to another through a fast T1 WAN link. Two other sites may connect using slower 128Kbps WAN links. Site link objects are used to teach Active Directory about these WAN links, and site link properties are configured to provide details on the links such as which site link to use and when to use it.

Site link bridges   Site link bridges are automatically created within Active Directory, allowing replication between all sites. Even if a site doesn't have a direct path to another site, Active Directory *bridges* the sites together and provides connectivity through one or more other site links. Site link bridging can be disabled to exclude the use of specific site links.

ISTG   The Inter-site Topology Generator (ISTG) manages advanced replication management tasks. The ISTG designates the bridgehead server within the site and monitors it to ensure it is operational. If the bridgehead server fails, the ISTG will designate another domain controller as the bridgehead server.

Bridgehead servers   A bridgehead server is the designated domain controller within a site that replicates Active Directory data to domain controllers in other sites. Each site has one bridgehead server designated by the ISTG. It's also possible to override the ISTG by identifying preferred bridgehead servers.

Preferred bridgehead servers Preferred bridgehead servers can be manually identified to prevent domain controllers with inadequate resources from being picked to act as a bridgehead server. Once one preferred bridgehead server is configured, any DCs that aren't configured as a preferred bridgehead server will not be designated as a bridgehead server.

Exploring Sites

Once you've built your TCP/IP infrastructure, you need to tell Active Directory about it. After Active Directory has the key information about your infrastructure, it can make intelligent decisions on how the bandwidth is used.

When replicating from one domain controller to another domain controller, each domain controller needs to know whether it's communicating via a high-speed link within a well-connected site, or communicating with another domain controller over a 56Kbps link and needs to take the time to compress the data.

But the domain controller can't know what kind of link it is unless you help it. A DC knows that it can communicate at high speed with another DC if they're both in the same *site*. But it doesn't know that DCs are not in the same site unless you tell it.

How Sites Work

The obvious question is, "How can you tell AD that the DCs are in different sites?" The answer is by using the Active Directory Sites and Services snap-in.

DCs are located in the Servers container of one of the Sites containers of Active Directory. There is a separate container for each *site*. Remember, a site is defined as one or more subnets that communicate with each other at relatively high data rates. You define sites and then place domain controllers in sites.

Workstations and servers aren't added to AD Sites and Services. However, they still use the information here to identify DCs that are close to them when they log on. A process called the DC Locator service identifies which site a workstation is in based on the host's subnet. It then identifies a domain controller in the same site.

"But," you might wonder, "how did Active Directory figure out what sites it had, what subnets it had, and which subnets go into what sites?" *That's* the part that requires a little administrative elbow grease, so let's see how to apply that elbow grease using Active Directory Sites and Services.

You can launch it by selecting Start ➤ Administrative Tools ➤ Active Directory Sites and Services. Figure 21.3 shows the Active Directory Sites and Services snap-in.

FIGURE 21.3
Active Directory
Sites and Services

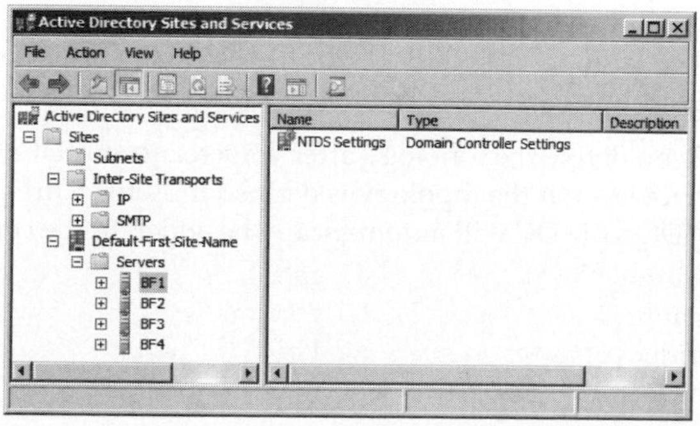

Notice that there's only one site, with the highly creative name Default-First-Site-Name. This example domain has four domain controllers (named BF1, BF2, BF3, and BF4), and they are all located in this default site.

When you create an Active Directory forest, AD creates this default site and assumes that everything is in it. If you have a single site, you can open Default-First-Site-Name, and you'll see that your domain controllers are in there.

DCPROMO AUTOMATICALLY ADDS SERVERS TO THE CORRECT SITE

DCPromo is used to promote a server to a domain controller. One of the actions DCPromo takes is to place the server object into a site. It will be placed in the Default-First-Site-Name site by default. However, if another site exists with subnets defined and the server you're promoting has an IP address in a defined subnet, the server object will be placed into the appropriate site.

The following are the steps and requirements to set up AD's site topology:

1. Define each site.

A *site* refers to a well-connected location. The terms *site* and *location* are often used interchangeably. Within Active Directory, a site is an Active Directory object that refers to a well-connected location.

2. Define each subnet.

For each subnet that has been created in your physical environment, a subnet object needs to be created in Active Directory.

3. Assign each subnet to a site.

Each subnet is linked to the actual location by linking the subnet object with the site object.

4. Create site links to connect the sites.

Physical locations are connected with WAN links. These WAN links are represented by site link objects. Each site link object includes two or more sites.

5. Configure the site link properties.

Site links include three key properties that must be configured: cost, replicate every, and schedule. The "cost" property helps Active Directory decide whether the site link should be used using a lowest-cost algorithm, the "replicate every" property identifies how often to replicate, and the "schedule" property identifies when to replicate.

If you define the topology after you create your DCs, you'll need to move DCs to the correct site. However, if the topology is defined in Active Directory Sites and Services before promoting your DCs, the DC will automatically be added to the correct site.

Renaming Default-First-Site-Name

You can rename your first site from that goofy Default-First-Site-Name to something simple like HQ:

1. Open Active Directory Sites and Services.

2. Open the Sites folder to reveal the folder labeled Default-First-Site-Name.

3. Right-click the Default-First-Site-Name folder, and select Rename.

4. The name Default-First-Site-Name will be highlighted. Just overtype it with **HQ**, and click anywhere else on the screen.

This works best if you do it *early* in your AD creation. In fact, it's really best to rename Default-First-Site-Name when you create your first DC. You may have to reboot your DCs to make this take effect, although restarting the `netlogon` service on them may do the trick.

Defining a Site

Suppose you set up another site across town from the first site. Active Directory needs to know about that site. Right-click the Sites folder, and choose New Site; you'll see a screen like Figure 21.4.

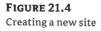

FIGURE 21.4

Creating a new site

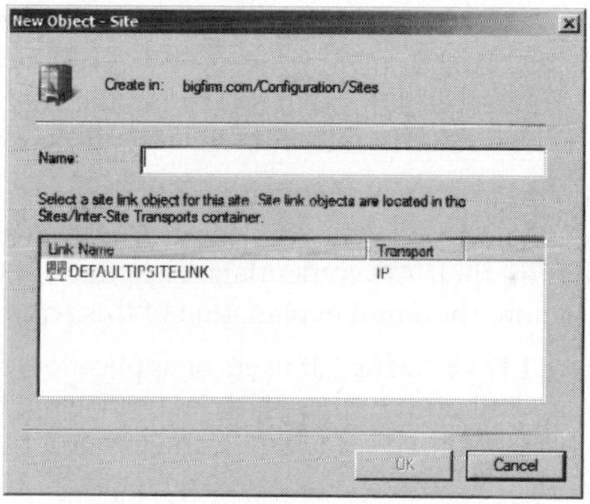

Next, fill in a name for the new site (such as **Crosstown**), click the DEFAULTIPSITELINK object, and click OK. When you do, you get a message box like Figure 21.5.

FIGURE 21.5

Checklist for hooking up the new site

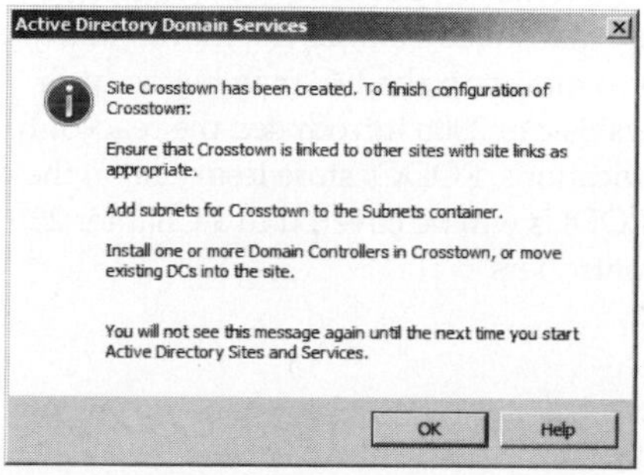

You don't need to create a site for every location. In fact, the only reason you will create a site is if you plan on putting a domain controller into the location. If the location won't host a domain controller, don't create a site.

Deciding on DCs in Remote Locations

OK, if you should create a site only if the location will host a DC, you may be wondering when you should add a DC to a location. Good question.

Domain controllers are expensive—in both hardware and maintenance costs. Just because you have a separate location doesn't necessarily mean it needs a domain controller. For example, if a location has only five users connected via a WAN link, you probably won't add the expense of a domain controller at this location. The users can log on via the WAN link.

You should consider placing a DC into a location if one of the following situations exists:

100 or more users   In general, if there are more than 100 users at a location, you should place a DC there. It's possible to place a DC in a site with fewer users, but beyond 100 users, you should a have DC there. The decision is easy.

WAN link unacceptably slow   If it's taking users too long to log on, a DC in the site will significantly reduce the logon time. Of course, *too long* is relative. In one environment, 10 minutes may be considered unacceptable, while another environment may consider it unacceptable when the logon time takes 2 minutes.

WAN link is unreliable for logon when needed   If users can't reliably log on when they need to, consider placing a DC at the location. For example, if users need to log on between 8 a.m. and 5 p.m., Monday through Friday, but the WAN link is 100 percent utilized during this time, users won't be able to authenticate with the domain.

You should also consider whether remote users are accessing resources such as a file server in the remote site. If users can't authenticate with a DC, they won't be able to access resources that require their AD credentials. The "Cached Credentials" section later in this chapter provides a more thorough explanation of this scenario.

Frequent LDAP traffic   If users or applications will frequently query Active Directory, a DC in the site will prevent these queries from using the WAN links. Lightweight Directory Access Protocol (LDAP) is used to query and/or modify data within Active Directory, and applications frequently query the global catalog. Frequent LDAP traffic often requires making the DC a global catalog (GC) server.

One reason you should *avoid* placing a DC into a remote site is if inadequate physical security exists or inadequate expertise is available for regular maintenance. If a domain controller is stolen, the contents of your entire forest could be compromised. If no one at the remote location can do basic maintenance (and the maintenance can't be done remotely), the cost of travel for a technician to maintain the DC may be too high.

Windows Server 2008 introduced the read-only domain controller (RODC) that can be deployed in smaller locations. RODCs store less data on the domain controller and can be used in remote locations. RODCs will be covered in a Chapter 22, "The Third DC: Understanding Read-Only Domain Controllers."

DC AND DNS

If you place a DC in a site, you should seriously consider making it a DNS server. When a user logs on, the `netlogon` service will query DNS to locate a domain controller in the user's site. If a DNS server isn't in the site, the WAN link will have to be used to query DNS.

Active Directory integrated (ADI) DNS is commonly used. ADI DNS is updated through regular Active Directory replication and doesn't require as much administration for the zones and zone transfer.

CACHED CREDENTIALS

You may remember that if a user has logged on to a system once before, then they can log on to the same system with the same domain credentials even if a domain controller is not available. Cached credentials are used.

Consider a user with a mobile computer. She plugs her laptop into a docking station at work and logs onto the domain. Later while waiting for a plane at the airport, she wants to use the same laptop computer to work on a report. She can use the same account to log onto her computer. However, the company's DC isn't available at the airport. Instead, she logs on using credentials that were cached on her laptop.

From the user's perspective, there is nothing different in the process. The user enters the same username and password, and the desktop appears.

This works the same way for users in remote locations without a DC and without reliable WAN links. If a user has logged onto his computer at the remote location over the WAN link before, he can log on again using the same credentials.

However, if a user is logged in with cached credentials, he is not able to access any resources requiring the credentials. For example, consider a remote site with a file server configured to restrict access to shares using domain accounts. Users logged on with cached credentials haven't been authenticated in this session and access is denied.

While a user is logged on using cached credentials, the system will periodically try to access a domain controller. If the WAN link becomes available, the system will log on, and they will be able to access resources normally.

CACHED CREDENTIALS AND THE GC

Cached credentials work a little differently if a DC is available but a DC hosting the global catalog is not available. The global catalog is the only location where universal group membership is held, and universal group membership must be identified for a successful logon.

When a user logs on, a token is built that includes the SIDs of any groups the user is a member of and the user's SID. However, if the GC isn't available, universal group membership can't be identified.

The reason is that access can be explicitly denied to members of a universal group. However, if universal group membership can't be identified and logon was allowed, it's possible that members of a universal group gain access to resources that should be denied.

Consider Figure 21.6. A user is logging on in the remote office. The WAN link is currently unavailable, but he can access BF2 in the remote office. Notice that BF1 is a global catalog server, but BF2 is not a global catalog server.

FIGURE 21.6
Logging on with-
out access to a GC

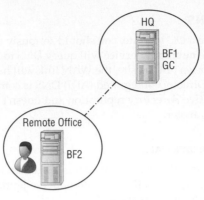

The `netlogon` service is able to validate his credentials on BF2, but since a GC can't be reached and universal group membership can't be identified, the logon is denied. The user isn't even logged on with cached credentials.

To avoid this problem, you should either make the DC at the remote site a global catalog server or enable universal group membership caching.

GC OR UNIVERSAL GROUP MEMBERSHIP CACHING

Once you've decided to place a domain controller into a site, you also need to decide whether you want to make the DC a global catalog server. A global catalog server will host the global catalog.

If you don't make the DC a GC, you should enable universal group membership caching on the site. When this is enabled, the domain controller will cache the user's universal group membership data the first time the user logs on and use it to create the user's token for subsequent logons.

Universal group membership for any users who have logged onto the DC is refreshed every eight hours. The DC can hold universal group membership cached data for as many as 500 users.

The primary reason why you wouldn't want to make a DC a GC in a remote site is that the replication of the global catalog will consume too much bandwidth. For example, if bandwidth utilization is already at 80 percent, making the DC a GC could cause utilization to peak at 100 percent.

You can make any DC a GC by modifying the NTDS Settings properties sheet of the server. Figure 21.7 shows this sheet with the Global Catalog check box selected.

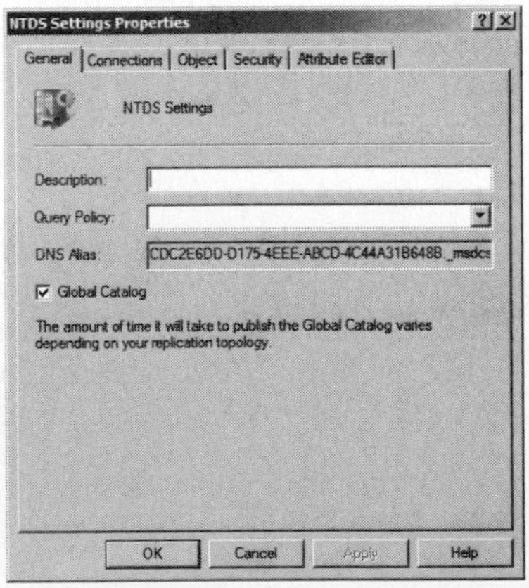

FIGURE 21.7
Making a domain
controller a global
catalog server

To access the server's NTDS Settings properties sheet, locate the server object within the site in Active Directory Sites and Services. Right-click NTDS Settings, and select Properties.

You can enable universal group membership caching on a site by modifying the NTDS Settings properties sheet of the site. Figure 21.8 shows this sheet with universal group membership caching enabled.

FIGURE 21.8

Enabling universal group membership caching

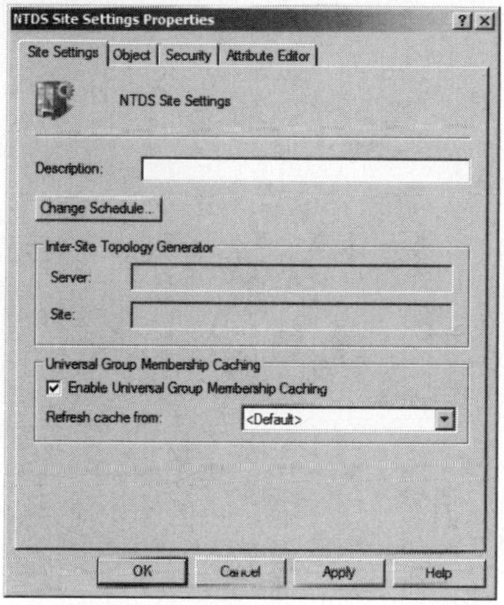

To access the site's NTDS Settings properties sheet, locate the site object within the Sites container in Active Directory Sites and Services. Right-click NTDS Settings for the site, and select Properties.

Defining a Subnet and Placing It in a Site

Next, you need to describe the subnets in your enterprise. Suppose the original site has a single subnet of 192.168.20.0/24 and the Crosstown site has a subnet of 192.168.1.0/24. You need to tell Active Directory about these subnets:

1. Right-click the Subnets folder, and choose New Subnet.

2. Enter **192.168.20.0/24** to identify the subnet.

3. Select the HQ site to associate this subnet with HQ.

Your display will look similar to Figure 21.9.

IPV4 OR IPV6

You can add both IPv4 and IPv6 subnets to Active Directory Sites and Services, but only one at a time. When adding the subnets, you need to identify the subnet mask using Classless Inter-Domain Routing (CIDR) notation. In CIDR notation, you identify how many bits a 1 is in the subnet mask. The /24 indicates the first 24 bits in the subnet mask are 1s; in other words, the subnet mask is 255.255.255.0.

FIGURE 21.9
Creating a
new subnet

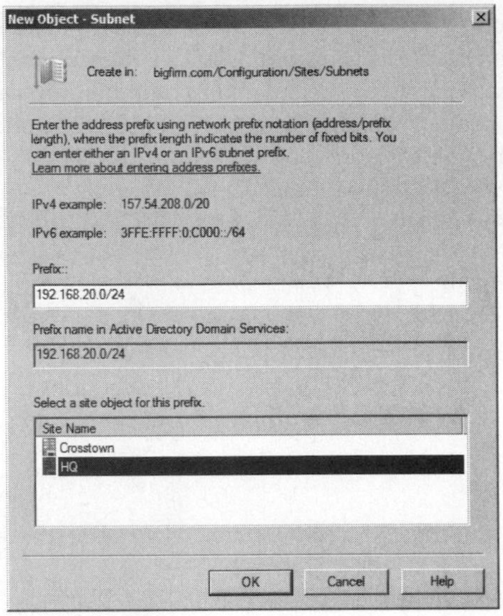

Add the 192.168.1.0/24 subnet, and associate it with the Crosstown site. Your display will now look like Figure 21.10.

FIGURE 21.10
Sites and Services
after adding
subnets

Placing a Server in a Site

Right now all four of the enterprise's DCs are in HQ. Suppose BF3 belongs in Crosstown. You could tell AD that BF3 is physically located in the Crosstown site by moving it there. Navigate to Sites ➤ HQ ➤ Servers, right-click BF3, and choose Move to see a dialog box like Figure 21.11.

It's a little bit of work, but arranging your servers in Active Directory Sites and Services pays off if your enterprise includes multiple locations over WAN links.

Adding Site Links

Site links are used to identify the actual WAN links. Active Directory Sites and Services starts with a default site link with another highly creative name: DefaultIPSiteLink. Just as you can rename the default site and add sites, you can rename the default site link and create other site links.

FIGURE 21.11

Moving a server

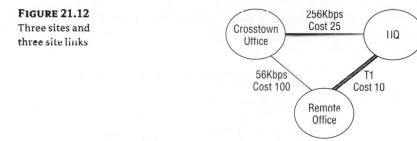

Consider Figure 21.12. It shows three sites within an enterprise: HQ, a crosstown office, and a remote office. This site diagram shows the three sites connected with three WAN links and different WAN link speeds. Later in this section, we'll show how to create site links to match these WAN links.

FIGURE 21.12

Three sites and
three site links

Consider Figure 21.12. It shows three sites within an enterprise: HQ, a crosstown office, and a remote office. This site diagram shows the three sites connected with three WAN links and different WAN link speeds. Later in this section, we'll show how to create site links to match these WAN links.

When creating site links, you have two choices: IP site links and SMTP site links. You will almost always use IP site links.

IP SITE LINK

IP site links use a remote procedure call (RPC) over IP transport connection. You will use IP site links almost all the time. One of the core requirements is that you have an IP connection available between the sites. If you can ping between the sites, you have an IP connection and should use an IP site link.

SMTP SITE LINK

If a direct IP connection isn't available and you aren't replicating domain data, you can configure an SMTP site link. On the surface, SMTP *sounds* like a great answer: it doesn't need to be running all the time, the link needn't be up that often, and—heck—you might even be able to send replication updates via Hotmail!

Unfortunately, it's not that useful. First, you can only replicate the forest-wide schema and configuration naming contexts, so you couldn't use SMTP to replicate updates between domain controllers in the same domain. In other words, simple tasks such as adding or modifying users, computers, or groups within a domain can't be replicated with SMTP.

Additionally, you can't use just any old mail server. You need a certificate issued from an enterprise certification authority to ensure secure mail delivery before security-conscious AD will let you use it to replicate.

CREATING SITE LINKS

You can configure Active Directory Sites and Services to mimic the configuration shown previously in Figure 21.12 by following these steps:

1. Launch Active Directory Sites and Services.

2. Add a site named RemoteOffice using the procedure provided earlier in this chapter.

3. Add a 192.168.30.0/24 subnet to the RemoteOffice site using the procedure provided earlier in this chapter.

4. Browse to the Sites ➤ Inter-Site Transports ➤ IP folder. Right-click DEFAULTIPSITELINK, and select Rename. Enter **CrossHQ** as the name. Crosstown, HQ, and RemoteOffice are added to this site link. You'll remove RemoteOffice in a moment.

5. Right-click IP, and select New Site Link. Name the new site link **CrossRemote**. Select the Crosstown and RemoteOffice sites, and click Add. Your display will look similar to Figure 21.13. Click OK.

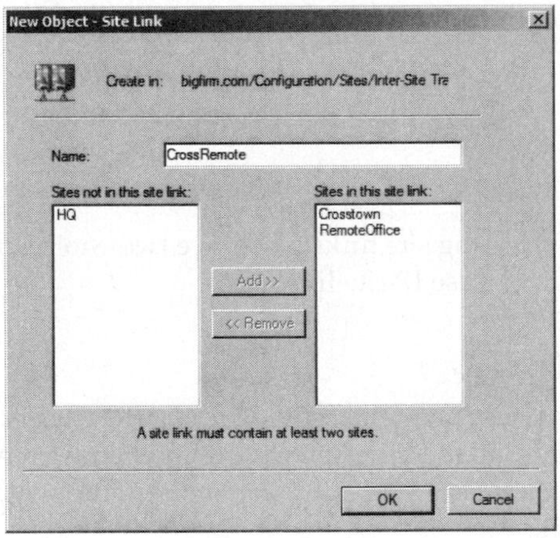

FIGURE 21.13
Adding a site link

6. Right-click IP, and select New Site Link again. Name the new site link **HQRemote**. Select the HQ and RemoteOffice sites, and click Add. Click OK.

7. When you created the RemoteOffice site, the only site link available was the DEFAULTIPSITELINK that you then renamed to CrossHQ. Right-click CrossHQ, and select Properties. Select RemoteOffice, and click Remove. Your display will look similar to Figure 21.14. Click OK.

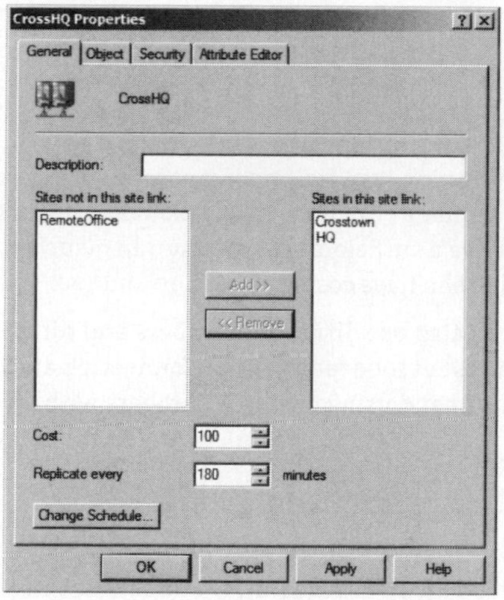

FIGURE 21.14
Removing a site
from a site link

SITE LINK PROPERTIES

Site links include three important properties that are used by Active Directory to identify when the site link will be used. These three properties are the cost, how often replication will occur, and the replication schedule.

Cost Active Directory uses the cost to determine the lowest cost path to get from one site to another. If one path has a cost of 10 and another path has a cost of 100, the path with the least cost (10) will be used. When multiple site links are used to get to a site, each of the site link costs will be added together to determine the least cost. When you create a site link, the default cost is 100, but this can be changed to any value between 1 and 99,999.

Replicate every This identifies how often replication occurs between sites. Initial replication within a site occurs every 15 seconds between domain controllers. However, replicating every 15 seconds over a WAN link is just too often. By default, replication over WAN links occurs every 180 minutes. You can change this value to anything between 15 and 10,080 minutes.

Schedule The schedule identifies when the link will be used. The default schedule is 24/7— 24 hours a day every day of the week. However, you can limit when the link will be used for replication by modifying the schedule. For example, if the link has limited usage between midnight and 6 a.m. but is close to maximum use during normal hours, you can configure replication between sites to occur only between midnight and 6 a.m.

CALCULATING THE COST

You have a wide range of numbers (1 to 99,999) you can assign to the cost of your IP site links. Remember, these numbers will be used by Active Directory to determine which link to use to reach another site.

🌐 **Real World Scenario**

COST IS RELATIVE

When assigning cost, it's important to ensure the costs accurately reflect the speed. For example, if one T1 line has a cost of 10, all T1s should have a cost of 10. Similarly, if a T1 has a cost of 10, a 56Kbps should have a sufficiently higher number (such as 100); speeds between 56Kbps and a 1.544Mbps T1 would then have costs between 10 and 100.

You could also use different numbers and different ranges of numbers. For example, you could assign a cost of 1000 for a 56Kbps connection and a cost of 100 for a T1 connection. However, we do not recommend using only low numbers with a very narrow range, such as a cost of 1 for a T1 and 10 for a 56K. If you added a T3 line in the future, you couldn't assign a cost lower than 1, so you'd need to redesign and reassign all the costs.

Consider Figure 21.15. It shows our three sites, with the site links and the speeds of the WAN links. Additionally, costs have been assigned to each link.

FIGURE 21.15
Three sites connected with three site links

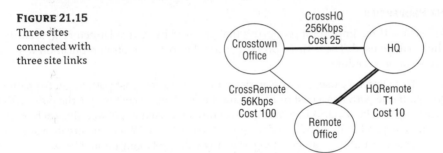

Since the HQRemote link is connected with the fastest link (a T1 line), I have assigned it a cost of 10—the lowest cost of each of the links. The CrossRemote link is the slowest at 56Kbps, and I have assigned it the highest cost of 100. CrossHQ has a 256Kbps WAN link, and I have assigned it a cost of 25.

When HQ wants to replicate with the remote office, it sees that the direct path using HQRemote has the lowest cost of 10 as compared to a cost of 125 (100 + 25) if it went through the crosstown office.

However, when the remote office wants to replicate with the crosstown office, the least cost path is via HQ with a cost of 35 (10 + 25). The direct path using the CrossRemote link has a cost of 100, so it would be used only if one of the paths failed.

Configuring Intersite Replication

Now that you've seen how to create subnets, sites, and site links, you'll learn how to configure them to match your network infrastructure.

You already know that within a site AD replicates by building a replication topology between domain controllers. But the same topology across WAN links would be inefficient, so AD instead creates a minimal spanning tree, meaning that it creates a set of site-to-site replication paths that minimizes the load on your WAN bandwidth.

Take a look at the AD Sites and Services snap-in shown in Figure 21.16 with the overlaid sites diagram. It shows three sites with three IP site links.

FIGURE 21.16
Active Directory
Sites and Services
with three sites
and three site links

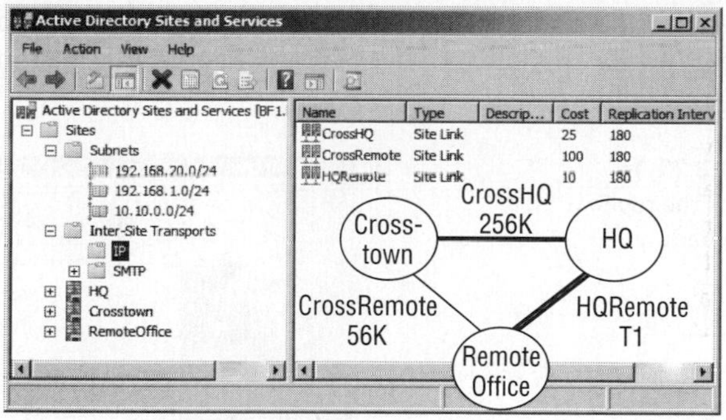

Notice that the cost of each of the site links has been modified within Active Directory Sites and Services. You'll see how to do this in a moment.

This is a simple enterprise, but it'll serve fine to understand the issues in a multisite environment. You see, once you set up your sites, DCs figure out how to replicate all by themselves *within the site*. But across sites, they need a little help.

You tell AD about connections between sites by creating site links. You help AD identify which path to use for replication, when to perform replication, and how often to perform replication by configuring the site link properties.

If you double-click any site link object, you'll see a dialog box similar to Figure 21.17.

FIGURE 21.17
Site link
properties page

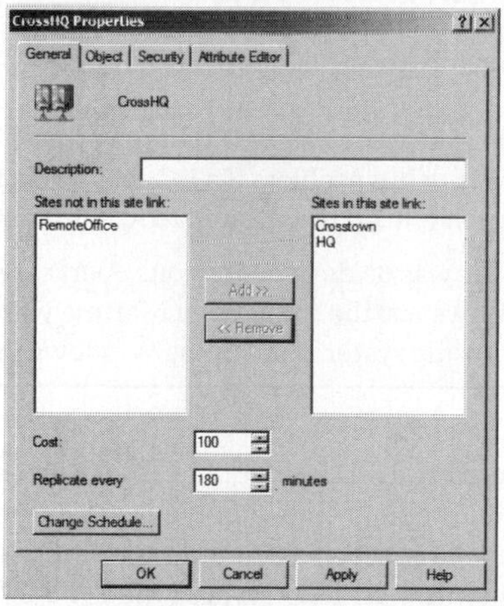

This dialog box is *very* important for three reasons:

◆ The Cost spinner box is used to help AD identify which link to use. AD will choose lower-cost paths over higher-cost paths. It is set to a cost of 100 by default.

◆ The Replicate Every *xx* Minutes spinner box is used to control how often AD tries to replicate over this link. It is set to 180 minutes by default.

◆ Last, the Change Schedule button allows you to modify when replication occurs based on a schedule.

Click the Change Schedule button, and you'll see a dialog box similar to Figure 21.18. The schedule for this site link has been changed to allow replication only during the nonpeak hours of midnight to 6 a.m.

FIGURE 21.18
Setting the replication schedule

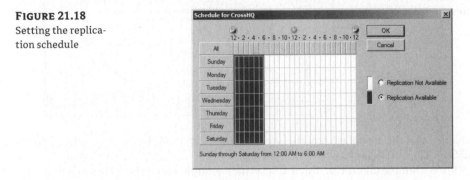

It could be that the HQ-to-Crosstown link is heavily used during the daytime hours, and you want replication to occur only during nonbusiness hours. Setting the schedule tells AD not to bother trying to replicate before 6 p.m. daily.

REPLICATE AT LEAST EVERY 180 DAYS

AD sites must replicate at least once every 180 days or less. AD throws away objects that have been inactive for 180 days, so if one site and another didn't talk for a few months, then they'd start deleting objects from their copies of AD that they weren't using but that other DCs in other sites were still using. This is only a problem if a DC goes down for a long period of time. Do not reconnect a DC to the network if it hasn't replicated to AD for more than 180 days.

This number was 60 days in previous operating system versions, based on the default tombstone lifetime. However, the tombstone lifetime was changed to 180 days in Server 2003 with SP1 and newer operating systems including Windows Server 2008 R2.

Once you tell AD all these things about sites, a souped-up version of the Knowledge Consistency Checker called the Inter-Site Topology Generator (ISTG) identifies what links to use and when to use them. One DC at each site is automatically designated as the ISTG.

You can identify which server is the ISTP by viewing the Site NTDS Site Settings properties sheet. Select the site, and double-click NTDS Site Settings to access this page. However, the ISTG needs very little oversight.

An important function of the ISTG is to assign bridgehead servers. Additionally, you can override the ISTG by assigning preferred bridgehead servers.

Bridgehead Servers

A *bridgehead server* is a DC within a site that will replicate to DCs in other sites. Every site will have only one active bridgehead server at any time.

The ISTG designates a DC as a bridgehead server and periodically checks this DC to ensure it's still operational. If this DC crashes or is taken offline, the ISTG will automatically designate another server as the bridgehead server.

At least this is the way it works normally assuming you haven't overridden the ISTG by assigning a preferred bridgehead server.

PREFERRED BRIDGEHEAD SERVERS

Occasionally, you may want to exclude a DC from becoming a bridgehead server. For example, a DC may be close to full capacity with the processing power hovering close to 80 percent and the paging file usage excessively high. When the ISTG designates this as the bridgehead server, the processing power could peak at 100 percent, significantly impacting the performance of other functions on the server.

> ### USE PREFERRED BRIDGEHEAD SERVERS FOR EXCLUSION MANAGEMENT
>
> Notice the subtlety here. You aren't picking a DC as a preferred bridgehead server because you want it to be the bridgehead server as much as you don't want *another* DC to be a bridgehead server. In other words, you select preferred bridgehead servers to exclude one or more DCs from the selection process. Once you designate any DC as a preferred bridgehead server, the ISTG will only pick preferred bridgehead servers to fill this role.

You can't directly exclude a DC as a preferred bridgehead server. However, you can designate other DCs as preferred bridgehead servers. For example, if you have four DCs and you don't want BF4 to be a bridgehead server, you'd designate BF1, BF2, and BF3 as preferred bridgehead servers.

This brings up a special consideration. If you ever designate a single DC as a preferred bridgehead server, you should also designate at least one more DC as a preferred bridgehead server. If only one is designated and it fails, the ISTG will not automatically switch the role to other DCs.

You can designate a server as a preferred bridgehead server by following these steps:

1. Launch AD Sites and Services.

2. Browse to the Servers container within the site you want to manipulate.

3. Right-click the server you want to add, and select Properties.

4. Select IP, and click Add. Your display will look similar to Figure 21.19.

5. Click OK to close the properties sheet. Repeat these steps for each server you want to designate as a preferred bridgehead server.

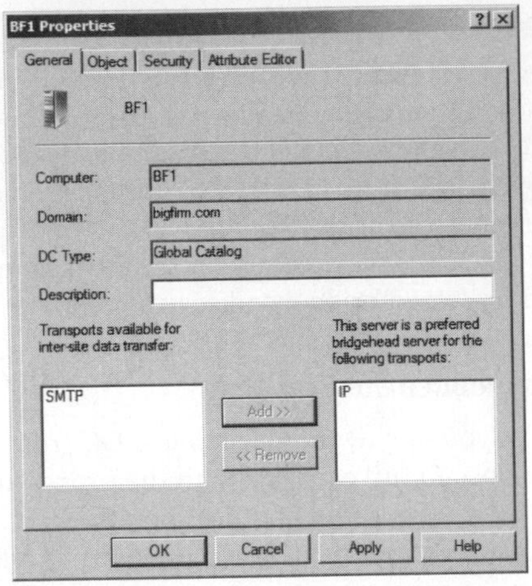

FIGURE 21.19
Designating
a server as a
preferred bridge-
head server

Forcing Replication

The repadmin command-line tool includes a neat feature that you can use to replicate data between two domain controllers even if it's outside the schedule. This can be useful when troubleshooting replication problems between sites. The repadmin switch is /replsingleobj.

REPLSINGLEOBJECT REPLACED WITH REPLSINGLEOBJ

In previous editions of Windows, the replsingleobject switch was used to replicate objects between DCs even if there wasn't a connection. However, this has been shortened to just replsingleobj (*obj* instead of *object*) in Windows Server 2008 R2. This shorter version was also available in Windows Server 2003 with the longer version, but in 2008 R2, only the shorter version is available. We can tell you from experience that no matter how many times you try it without shortening object to obj, it simply won't work.

This is the basic syntax for the repadmin tool:

```
repadmin <command> <arguments>
```

When using the replsingleobj command or switch, the syntax is as follows:

```
repadmin /replsingleobjc sourceDC destinationDC ObjectDN
```

Both the source and destination domain controllers can be identified with their name (such as BF1) or with their fully qualified domain name (such as BF1.Bigfirm.com).

The object distinguished name (DN) follows the LDAP DN rules. For example, a computer named TestCPU created in the Sales OU of the Bigfirm.com domain would have the following DN: CN=TestCPU,OU=Sales,DC=bigfirm,DC=com.

If the DN has any spaces in it, it must be enclosed in quotes.

To replicate the `TestCPU` object from BF1 to BF1, you can use the following command. Notice that the command wraps to multiple lines in the book, but it should be entered on a single line.

```
repadmin /replsingleobj BF1.bigfirm.com BF2.bigfirm.com
  CN=TestCPU,OU=Sales,DC=bigfirm.DC=com
```

Configuring Clients to Access the Next Closest Site

A new capability available with Windows Server 2008 is the ability to teach clients what site to access if the domain controller in their site is down. Consider the Bigfirm.com enterprise shown in Figure 21.20.

FIGURE 21.20

Next closest site

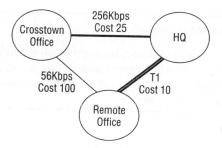

Each site has at least one domain controller, and normally users will log onto a domain controller in their own site. However, what if the domain controller in the remote office site goes down?

You probably wouldn't want the users to use the 56Kbps connection and log onto DCs in the crosstown office site. However, this is exactly what might happen if the next closest site setting isn't enabled. The DC Locator service first tries to locate a DC in the same site as the client. If unsuccessful, it then looks for any DC regardless of the location unless the next closest site setting is enabled.

The term *closest site* is somewhat of a misnomer. Active Directory doesn't have any concept of distance, but it does understand the cost configured in the site link properties. Although it's likely that the closest sites will have the fastest WAN links and would be configured with the lowest cost, an organization could be configured differently.

As an example, the remote office could be 1 mile away from the crosstown office but 5 miles away from the headquarters location. The link between the remote office and HQ has a cost of 10, and the link between the crosstown office and the remote office is 100. If distance was used, the crosstown office would be considered closest, but since cost is considered, HQ would be identified as the next closest site since the cost is lowest.

NEXT CLOSEST SITE NOT AVAILABLE ON PRE–WINDOWS VISTA CLIENTS

The next closest site feature will work on only Windows Vista, Windows 7, and Windows Server 2008 or greater clients. This feature will not affect how Windows XP, Windows Server 2003, or previous clients behave.

You can configure Windows Vista, Windows 7, and Windows Server 2008 servers to use the cost to locate the next closest site. These are the two methods that can be used to configure this feature:

◆ Group Policy

◆ Registry modification

Configuring Next Closest Site with Group Policy

If you want to configure multiple clients to use the cost to determine which sites are the closest, you can modify Group Policy to do so. You can use the following steps to configure all clients in the domain.

> **SITE, DOMAIN, OR OU**
>
> The following procedure takes you through the steps to configure all the clients in the domain by modifying the default domain policy. However, you could slightly modify these steps to create or alter any GPO and link it to a site, domain, or organizational unit (OU) depending on which computers you want to affect.

1. Launch the Group Policy Management console by selecting Start ➢ Administrative Tools ➢ Group Policy Management.

2. Browse to the Default Domain Policy object within the Forest ➢ Domains ➢ *Domain Name* folder.

3. Right-click Default Domain Policy, and click Edit.

4. Browse to the Computer Configuration ➢ Policies ➢ Administrative Templates ➢ System ➢ Net Logon ➢ DC Locator DNS Records Group Policy folder.

5. Double-click the Try Next Closest Site setting, and click Enabled. Your display will look similar to Figure 21.21. Click OK.

6. Close the Group Policy Management Editor and the Group Policy Management console.

You can wait until Group Policy is applied through the normal refresh cycle or use the gpupdate /force command from the command line to update any individual clients.

Configuring Next Closest Site Through the Registry

Group Policy allows you to configure a setting once and affect multiple clients. However, if you want only a single client to use the next closest site capability, you can modify the registry.

> **BE CAREFUL WITH THE REGISTRY**
>
> You should be cautious any time you modify the registry. Incorrectly editing the registry may severely damage your system. It's recommended that you back up valuable data on your computer before modifying the registry.

FIGURE 21.21
Configuring
Try Next Closest
Site through
Group Policy

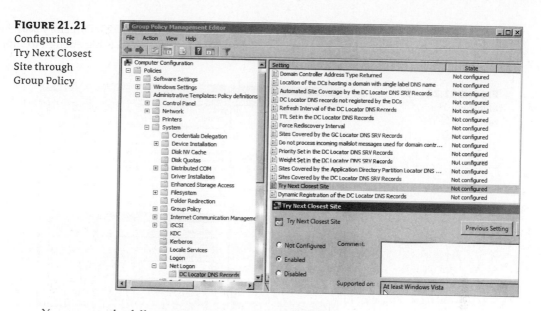

You can use the following steps to enable the Try Next Closest Site setting for a single Windows Vista, Windows 7, or Windows Server 2008 client.

1. Launch the Registry Editor by clicking Start, typing **regedit** or **regedit32** in the Start Search box, and pressing Enter. Both commands launch the same Registry Editor.

2. Select the HKEY_LOCAL_MACHINE (HKLM) hive.

3. Browse to the System\CurrentControlSet\Services\Netlogon\Parameters folder.

4. Look for a registry key named Try Next Closest Site. If it doesn't exist, follow these steps to create it:

   A. Right-click Parameters, and select New ➢ DWORD (32-bit) Value.

   B. Rename the new key as **Try Next Closest Site** using spaces between each word.

5. Double-click the Try Next Closest Site key. Change the value to **1**. Your display will look similar to Figure 21.22.

6. Click OK. Close the Registry Editor.

As a reminder, this setting is referenced only if a domain controller can't be contacted in the same site as the client.

If the value is 1 for this key, the DC Locator process will use the cost value of the site links to find a domain controller in the next closest site. If the value is 0, the DC Locator won't use the cost value and could contact any domain controller regardless of the location.

Using PowerShell

PowerShell cmdlets are covered in many chapters throughout this book, so you've probably already seen many. This section highlights a few cmdlets you can use and combine to retrieve information from Active Directory. It includes some basics on the Active Directory searcher tool built in to PowerShell, which can be very useful if your organization is big enough to support multiple sites.

FIGURE 21.22
Modifying the registry

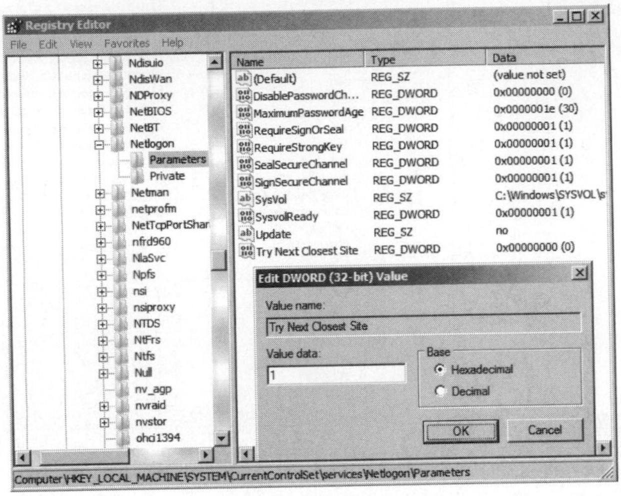

USING DISTINGUISHED NAMES

These steps talk about distinguished names (DNs), which were covered in much greater depth in Chapter 6 and mentioned earlier in this chapter. It will take a little bit of practice before you can create a DN on the fly, but you'll find the ability to create and identify the DN useful, especially when scripting or digging into Active Directory details.

---

1. Launch an instance of Windows PowerShell.

2. Get some information about your environment by first creating a variable to represent the domain with the following cmdlet. It populates the variable $dom with the DN of the domain. Note that LDAP must be all caps:

   ```
   $dom=[adsi]"LDAP://RootDSE"
   ```

3. You can now query information about the domain using the $dom variable with these commands:

   A. View the naming context of the root domain:

   ```
   Write-Host $obj.RootDomainNamingContext
   ```

   Our result: DC=bigfirm,DC=com

B. View the naming context of all domains in the forest:

```
Write-Host $obj.NamingContexts
```

Our result: DC=bigfirm,DC=com

C. View the default naming context (or the partial DN of your domain):

```
Write-Host $obj.DefaultNamingContext
```

Our result: DC=bigfirm,DC=com

D. Identify the number of the highest update sequence number (USN) used for replication:

```
Write-Host $obj.HighestCommittedUSN
```

Our result: 86051

4. There are times when you don't know the distinguished name of a user because you don't know what OU they're in. If you know some details about the account (such as the display name), you can retrieve the distinguished name using the built-in Active Directory searcher. This example assumes accounts use a display name of first name, period, last name (as in John.Smith). All you need to know are the user's first and last names to search.

A. First create a variable for the filter (your search item) with this line:

```
$filter = "(&(ObjectCategory=User)(DisplayName=John.Smith*))"
```

The wildcard * is used to find all instances (such as John.Smith.2 and John.Smith.3).

B. Next, create an instance of the searcher using the filter with this line.

```
$Searcher = New-Object System.DirectoryServices.DirectorySearcher($Filter)
```

C. Last, find all instances with this command:

```
Searcher.Findall()
```

The DNs of all accounts matching this display name will be displayed.

5. You can even make the previous code into a script designed to accept a parameter (such as the username).

A. Type the following lines into any text editor (such as Notepad), and save it in the C:\Scripts folder as FindUser.ps1. The first identifies the parameter that will be accepted, and the second line uses this parameter in the filter. The rest is the same.

```
Param($filterName)
$filter = "(&(ObjectCategory=User)(DisplayName=$filterName))"
    $Searcher = New-Object System.DirectoryServices.DirectorySearcher($Filter)
Searcher.Findall()
```

B. Execute the script with this line in PowerShell:

```
C:\Scripts\FindUser.ps1 John.Smith*
```

6. You may want to retrieve a list of group memberships for a user. If you know the DN, you can use these steps to do so:

A. First, create a variable for a user object in your domain using the DN. In this code, we're using the Administrator account, but you can use any account (including computer accounts):

```
$user=[adsi]"LDAP://CN=Administrator,CN=Users,Dc=bigfirm,DC=com"
```

B. Retrieve the group membership for the user with this command:

```
Write-Host $user.memberof -separator " >>> "
```

This will show a list of groups in DN format. The separator switch makes it a little easier to see where one group stops and another starts.

The Bottom Line

Create a site   Site objects are added to Active Directory to represent well-connected physical locations that will host domain controllers. Once a decision has been made to place a DC in a physical location, you need to add a site.

> **Master It**   Create a site to represent a new business location in Virginia Beach.

Add subnets to sites   Active Directory uses clients' subnets to determine which site they are in. For this to work, subnet objects need to be created and associated with sites.

> **Master It**   Create a subnet object to represent the 10.15.0.0/16 subnet that exists in the Virginia Beach location. Associate the subnet object with the VB site.

Configure a site link to replicate only during certain times   It's often desirable to restrict when replication occurs between sites. If the defaults are used, replication will occur every 180 minutes. If the WAN link is heavily used during certain periods, you can configure the schedule so that it replicates only during certain times.

> **Master It**   Configure the Default-First-Site-Name site (or another site) to replicate only between midnight and 5 a.m.

Configure Group Policy for the next nearest site   If a domain controller can't be reached in a client's site, the client will look for any domain controller without regard to how close it is. This can negatively impact logons for enterprises with several locations connected with different speed WAN links. You can configure Windows Vista (and newer) clients to locate and log on to a DC in the next nearest site if a DC can't be located in their site. This can be done using Group Policy or the Registry Editor.

Master It   Which of the following Group Policy settings can be manipulated to enable the next nearest site setting?

1. Computer Configuration ➢ Policies ➢ Administrative Templates ➢ System ➢ Logon ➢ DC Locator DNS Records

2. Computer Configuration ➢ Policies ➢ Administrative Templates ➢ System ➢ Net Logon ➢ DC Locator DNS Records

3. User Configuration ➢ Policies ➢ Administrative Templates ➢ System ➢ Logon ➢ DC Locator DNS Records

4. User Configuration ➢ Policies ➢ Administrative Templates ➢ System ➢ Net Logon ➢ DC Locator DNS Records

Chapter 22

The Third DC: Understanding Read-Only Domain Controllers

Most domain controllers (DCs) hold a full copy of Active Directory, including all of the administrative accounts and their passwords. Also, most domain controllers enjoy a safe lifetime locked behind doors to a server room or server closet. As long as a DC is well protected with physical security, this arrangement works perfectly.

However, domain controllers sometimes need to be deployed to other locations to support users working in branch offices or remote locations. Ideally, these branch offices enjoy the same physical security as the main location, but in reality this just isn't true.

In the past, administrators have had to weigh the risk of a DC being stolen or attacked after it's been placed in a remote location against the benefit of providing better performance for users in the remote office. Today, administrators have another choice.

With the introduction of read-only domain controllers (RODCs) in Windows Server 2008, administrators can now have it both ways. They can place their RODCs in a remote location to support the users, and they significantly reduce the risks if the RODC is stolen or attacked.

In this chapter, you will learn to

- ◆ Prepare a forest and a domain for RODCs
- ◆ Prepare the domain
- ◆ Allow passwords on any RODC
- ◆ Allow passwords on a single RODC

Introducing RODCs

A read-only domain controller is a new type of a domain controller that was introduced in Windows Server 2008. It's specifically designed to be used in remote office locations where physical security cannot be guaranteed.

THE THIRD DC

Any domain starts with a single writable domain controller. Companies often add a second DC for routine fault tolerance in case the first DC fails. Although you're not required to have two DCs before creating an RODC, this is what most companies will do. An RODC cannot be used for fault tolerance. If there's only one writable DC and it fails, the RODC can't be used to seize FSMO roles and won't hold the majority of passwords.

In Chapter 21, "Adding More Locations: Sites in Active Directory," you learned about adding sites in Active Directory for different geographical locations of your enterprise. As an example, imagine your company has a primary location and a remote office connected via a slow link, as shown in Figure 22.1.

FIGURE 22.1
Company with
a remote site

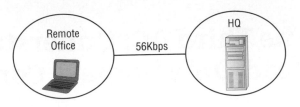

Any users in the remote office would have to use the slow 56Kbps WAN link to log on to their computers. You could improve their logon times by adding a domain controller to the remote office and configuring a site within Active Directory.

Moving the DC to the remote office will certainly improve the logon times for users there. However, it presents a significant security risk if the DC in the remote office is stolen or compromised.

A social engineer would probably not succeed if he came to your headquarters location and told people he was there to pick up the DC for its annual cleaning. However, employees at a remote office may be convinced by a cunning attacker that a DC does need to be taken away to be "cleaned."

If an attacker were able to gain unrestricted physical access to the DC, he could gain access to passwords of key accounts, including administrator accounts. However, if an RODC is placed at the remote location instead of a regular DC, the attacker will not be able to access all the passwords in the domain because the RODC holds only a limited amount of data that can be exploited.

Making Changes on a Read-Only Domain Controller

What does *read-only* really mean on a read-only domain controller? It doesn't mean that changes never occur on the RODC; instead, it means that changes cannot originate on the read-only domain controller. Changes can originate on a writable domain controller and replicate to the RODC.

A writable DC is any normal DC where additions, deletions, and modifications to Active Directory can be recorded. Normally when changes occur in Active Directory such as adding an account or changing a password, they can occur on any DC in the domain. Changes are then replicated to other DCs.

RODCs are not writable DCs. This means that any changes that a user attempts while connected to an RODC are not made on the RODC. Instead, a writable DC is contacted, and the change is made on the writable DC after the credentials are checked. If appropriate, the change is then replicated back down to the RODC.

This prevents an attacker from taking over an RODC at a remote location, making changes to Active Directory, and having those changes replicate back to the writable DCs.

Even though an RODC will receive replicated data from a writable DC, it will not store all the same contents as a writable DC.

🌐 Real World Scenario

STOLEN DOMAIN CONTROLLER

One company we know of had a remote office with about 15 users. They were separated from their main office by railroad tracks, and the railroad company would not allow cables to be run beneath the tracks. Users connected using a 56Kbps dial-up modem that created a VPN between the main office and the remote office.

Not surprisingly, the users often complained that the logon times were taking too long. Eventually, domain administrators created a domain controller and placed it in the remote office. Unfortunately, the remote office had very poor physical security.

About a month after they placed the DC in the remote office, it disappeared. Users weren't even sure exactly when it disappeared, though administrators were able to narrow down the time frame using logs. A lot of circumstantial evidence pointed to an employee who had access to the office after-hours, but nothing was ever proven.

Since the DC had a full copy of Active Directory including all the administrative accounts and their passwords, the IT department was soon in panic mode. They spent a great deal of time changing passwords and renaming accounts. They even seriously considered deleting their one-domain forest and starting over.

Management spent a lot of time evaluating the risk of not rebuilding the forest and weighing it against the business impact of deleting the forest and rebuilding it from scratch. Eventually they accepted the risk. It paid off. They never saw any evidence that anything was compromised from this theft.

If the DC were an RODC instead, the company would have lost the cost of the server, but the added risks that caused so much administrative and managerial headaches could have been avoided.

RODC Contents

An RODC holds all the Active Directory accounts and *most* of the attributes that can be found on a writable DC. A significant difference between an RODC and a writable DC is that an RODC holds very few passwords.

More specifically, the RODC will typically only hold the passwords of nonadministrator users who log on in the remote office. Other passwords are specifically blocked from being stored on the RODC.

Figure 22.2 shows the process if an RODC is placed in a remote office. Imagine Sally is logging onto the RODC for the first time. Her system will contact the RODC. The RODC doesn't have her account cached, so it will query the DC at the headquarters location.

FIGURE 22.2
RODC logon process

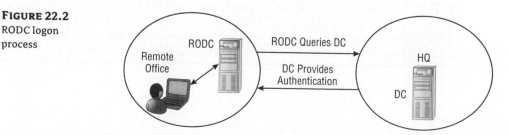

The DC at HQ will authenticate Sally's credentials, and it will also check the password replication policy to determine whether her credentials can be cached on the RODC. By default, no passwords will be cached on the RODC. However, it's common to allow credentials for nonadministrator users working at the remote office location to be cached. Any passwords that aren't specifically allowed will not be cached on the RODC.

The next time Sally logs on at the remote site, her credentials are verified with the cached credentials on the RODC. The term *cached credentials* means that they are stored in a temporary location on the server's hard drive.

CACHED ON THE RODC HARD DRIVE

If you're a hardware guy or gal, you may be thinking of *cache* because it refers to memory used to improve performance. For example, L1 and L2 cache is additional memory to improve the performance of the processor. Memory is volatile, and its contents will be lost when the system is shut down or rebooted. However, credentials cached on an RODC are stored on the hard drive of the RODC. These credentials will be maintained even if the RODC loses power or is rebooted.

Most notably, passwords for users in the domain who have not logged on at the remote location are not stored or replicated to the RODC.

What if an administrator logs onto the RODC using an administrative account? The purpose of the RODC is to protect against a physical attack by not including administrator passwords on the server. But if an administrator logs on and the administrator password is cached, it defeats the purpose.

To specifically address this issue, a password replication policy is configured to ensure administrator accounts are not cached on the RODC. You can modify the password replication policy, and you can also identify specific groups that can have password replication allowed or denied.

PASSWORD REPLICATION POLICY

The password replication policy was added in Windows Server 2008 to support RODCs. It identifies which passwords will be cached on the RODC. By default, no passwords are cached on the RODC, so you will need to understand how this works so you can make some modifications.

Figure 22.3 shows the properties of an RODC named BFRODC2 with the Password Replication Policy tab selected. Each RODC has its own password replication policy.

REPLICATION OR CACHING

You may notice the terms *replication* and *caching* are both used. Once a password is cached on an RODC, it will be replicated back to the RODC when changes occur through normal replication. Additionally, it's possible to designate specific user passwords to be replicated to an RODC even before a user logs on. Once the password is replicated to the RODC, it is considered cached on the RODC.

FIGURE 22.3
Password Replication Policy tab

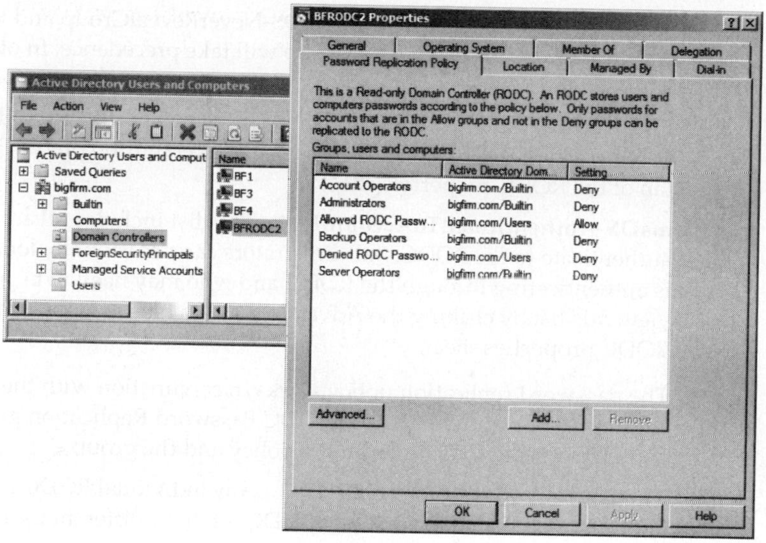

Notice that the following groups have a setting of Deny:

◆ Account Operators

◆ Administrators

◆ Backup Operators

◆ Denied RODC Password Replication

◆ Server Operators

Users with membership in any of these groups can log onto the RODC, but their credentials will not be cached on the RODC. The only group that has a setting of Allow by default is the Allowed RODC Password Replication group. Users in this group can have their passwords cached.

Windows Server 2008 modifies the Active Directory schema to include several new Active Directory attributes to support the password replication policy. These attributes are as follows:

msDS-Reveal-OnDemandGroup This is also known as the *allowed list*. It identifies which accounts can have passwords cached on an RODC. It includes only one value by default: the Allowed RODC Password Replication group. In other words, only users in the Allowed RODC Password Replication group (which is a domain local group) can have passwords cached on the RODC. The Allowed RODC Password Replication group starts empty, so by default no passwords will be cached on the RODC.

msDS-NeverRevealGroup This is also known as the *denied list*. It identifies which accounts cannot be cached on the RODC and includes the Account Operators, Server Operators, Backup Operators, and Administrators groups in addition to the members of the Denied RODC Password Replication group.

If an account is a member of the msDS-NeverRevealGroup and the msDS-Reveal-OnDemand-Group, the msDS-NeverRevealGroup will take precedence. In other words, if an account is both denied and allowed, Deny takes precedence.

msDS-RevealedList This is the list of accounts that have credentials cached on the RODC. You can view this list by clicking the Advanced button on the Password Replication Policy tab of the RODC properties sheet.

msDS-AuthenticatedToAccountList This list includes all accounts that have attempted to authenticate to the RODC. Administrators can occasionally look at this list to determine who is authenticating through the RODC and who may need to be added to the allow list. You can view this list by clicking the Advanced button on the Password Replication Policy tab of the RODC properties sheet.

The password replication policy works in conjunction with the Allowed RODC Password Replication group and the Denied RODC Password Replication group. The following are two important points to consider with the policy and the groups:

The policy is specific to each RODC Any individual RODC can have specific users or groups allowed or denied, while another RODC can have different users or groups specifically allowed or denied.

Groups apply to all RODCs universally The Allowed RODC Password Replication and Denied RODC Password Replication groups apply to all RODCs. For example, if a user is added to the Denied RODC Password Replication group, her credentials will not be cached on any RODC in the domain.

DENIED RODC PASSWORD REPLICATION GROUP

The Denied RODC Password Replication group is automatically added to Active Directory. Any users added to this group, or anyone who is a member of a group added to this group, will not have their passwords cached on any RODC in the domain.

For example, if Joe's account is added this group, his account can't be cached on any RODC. If Sally is a member of the IT Admins group and the IT Admins group is added to the Denied RODC Password Replication group, Sally's account can't be cached on any RODC in the domain.

Figure 22.4 shows the group with the Members tab selected.

This group is a domain local security group and includes the following members by default:

◆ Cert Publishers

◆ Domain Admins

◆ Domain Controllers

◆ Enterprise Admins

◆ Group Policy Creator Owners

◆ krbtgt

◆ Read-only Domain Controllers

◆ Schema Admins

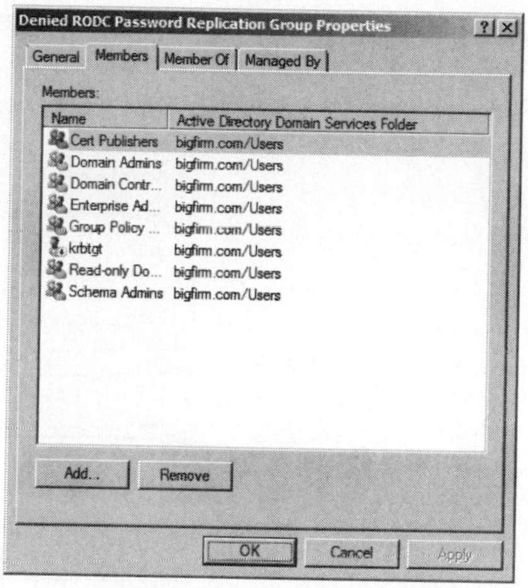

FIGURE 22.4
Denied RODC Pass-
word Replication
group members

FIGURE 22.4
Denied RODC Pass-
word Replication
group members

> ## KRBTGT AND KRBTGT123
>
> Writable DCs use the krbtgt account with Kerberos. You can think of it as the Kerberos ticket-granting ticket account, and its password is known by all writable DCs. When tickets need to be created for authentication, they are encrypted with a symmetric key that is derived from the password. Since all DCs use the same password for this account, all DCs can decrypt tickets granted by other DCs.
>
> The Kerberos ticket-granting ticket account works differently on RODCs. First, it has a different name such as krbtgt123 (or another semirandom string of numbers after krbtgt). Second, it has a different password. Writable DCs know the password of the RODC; however, the RODCs don't know the password of the krbtgt account used by writable DCs.

Users with accounts in any of these groups can still log onto the RODC. The only difference is that their credentials won't be cached, preventing the security risk if the RODC is stolen.

ALLOWED RODC PASSWORD REPLICATION GROUP

The Allowed RODC Password Replication group is also a domain local security group located in the Users container. Figure 22.5 shows the Allowed RODC Password Replication group.

Unlike the Denied RODC Password Replication group, which includes several members by default, the Allowed RODC Password Replication group does not include any members. Members added to this group can have their passwords replicated or cached to any RODC in the domain.

If a user is a member of both this group and the Denied RODC Password Replication group, the Denied RODC Password Replication group will take precedence.

DELEGATING ADMINISTRATION FOR AN RODC

When you promote a server to an RODC, you will be prompted to identify a specific user or group that will administer the RODC or that may finish the promotion of the RODC. If a user at the remote office will be performing administration, this is the best way to delegate appropriate permissions to the user.

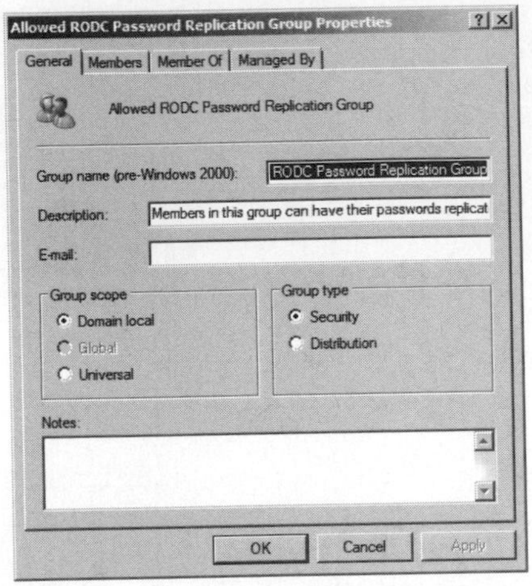

FIGURE 22.5
Allowed RODC
Password Replica-
tion group

Whenever possible, it's recommended to use groups instead of users to designate permissions or privileges, and this is no exception. You should create a group and add the user (or users) to the group that will administer the RODC.

Users in this group will be able to complete the RODC installation at the remote site if needed and will also have specific permissions granted for administration of the RODC. They do not have any type of administrative permissions in the domain from this group.

Even though the group is granted specific permissions to the RODC, it is not added to the Allowed RODC Replication group by default. However, you probably will want to add this account to the allowed group so that the user's credentials will be cached on the DC and the user can perform local administrative tasks even if the WAN link is down.

RODC Requirements

Before an RODC can be deployed, Active Directory must meet some basic requirements:

At least one DC must be running Windows Server 2008   The RODC needs to replicate with a Windows Server 2008 or Windows Server 2008 R2 rewritable domain controller. If none of the domain controllers in the domain is running at least Windows Server 2008, you won't be able to install an RODC. If you are promoting the first Windows Server 2008 server to a domain controller in a preexisting domain (running Windows Server 2003, for example), you'll first need to prepare the domain and forest with adprep /forestprep and adprep /domain prep. If the forest was built on Windows Server 2008 servers, it is not necessary to run adprep /forestprep and adprep /domain prep.

The domain functional level must be at least Windows Server 2003   Windows Server 2003 domain functional level provides Kerberos-constrained delegation. This provides the necessary security for the RODC.

The forest functional level must be at least Windows Server 2003   The RODC requires linked value replication, which is available when the forest functional level has been raised to Windows Server 2003.

The forest must be prepared by running adprep You must run adprep **/rodcprep** before installing the first RODC.

DOMAIN FUNCTIONAL LEVEL

Different domain functional levels provide different capabilities. When all the domain controllers in a domain are upgraded to newer operating systems, you can upgrade the domain functional level to take advantage of the new capabilities.

FUNCTIONAL LEVELS CANNOT BE REVERSED

Although it's possible to raise a functional level from a lower level to a higher level, once you raise it, there's no turning back. This applies to both a domain functional level and a forest functional level. Since the higher functional levels provide extra capabilities, a logical question is, "Why not always choose the highest level?" The answer is that the domain functional level dictates the minimum operating system that must be running on domain controllers.

As an example, if you have an existing domain with Windows Server 2003 DCs, you can add a Windows Server 2008 DC, but you won't be able to raise the level higher than 2003. Similarly, if you build a domain by promoting a Windows Server 2008 R2 server to a DC and select Windows Server 2008 R2 as both the domain and forest functional levels, you will never be able to promote anything less than a Windows Server 2008 R2 server to a DC.

The different domain functional levels are as follows:

Windows Server 2000 mixed Provides backward compatibility support for NT 4.0 domain controllers.

Windows Server 2000 native Used when all domain controllers are running at least Windows Server 2000.

Windows Server 2003 Used when all domain controllers are running at least Windows Server 2003. As a reminder, this is the minimum domain functional level that will support RODCs.

Windows Server 2008 Used when all domain controllers are running at least Windows Server 2008.

Windows Server 2008 R2 Used when all domain controllers are running at least Windows Server 2008 R2.

You can verify (and upgrade if needed) the domain functional level that your domain is currently using with the following steps:

1. Log onto a domain controller.

2. Launch Active Directory Users and Computers by selecting Start ➤ Administrator Tools ➤ Active Directory Users and Computers.

3. Right-click the domain name, and select Raise Domain Functional Level. Your display will look similar to Figure 22.6.

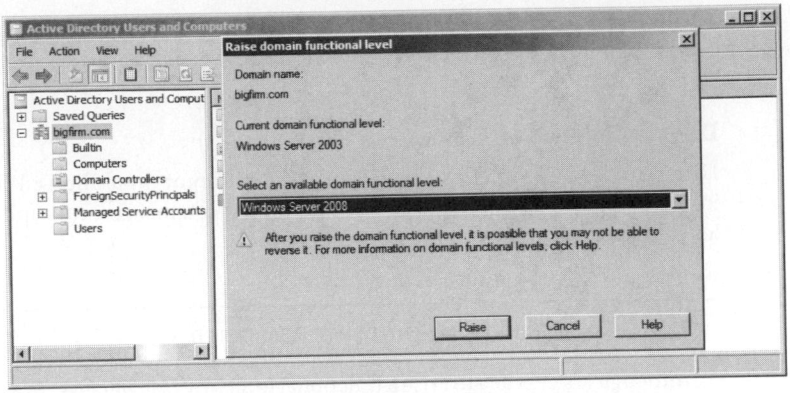

FIGURE 22.6
Verifying
the domain func-
tional level

In the figure, the current domain functional level is Windows Server 2003 and can be raised to either Windows Server 2008 or Windows Server 2008 R2.

4. If the domain functional level is not at least Windows Server 2003, raise it to Windows Server 2003 by selecting Windows Server 2003 and clicking Raise.

You need to raise the domain functional level on only one domain controller in the domain. It will replicate to all domain controllers within a short period of time.

If all domain controllers aren't running at least Windows Server 2003, you won't be able to raise the domain functional level to Windows Server 2003. After you click the Raise button, you will receive an error. Domain controllers running older operating systems will need to be removed from the domain or upgraded.

FOREST FUNCTIONAL LEVELS

Just as domain functional levels provide different capabilities, different forest functional levels provide different capabilities. The different forest functional levels are as follows:

Windows Server 2000 Native   Used when all domains are running at least Windows Server 2000 native domain functional level.

Windows Server 2003   Used when all domains are running at least Windows Server 2003 domain functional level. As a reminder, this is the minimum forest functional level required to support RODCs.

Windows Server 2008   Used when all domains are running at least Windows Server 2008 domain functional level.

Windows Server 2008 R2   Used when all domains are running at least Windows Server 2008 R2 domain functional level.

You can't raise the forest functional level higher than the lowest domain functional level. You must first upgrade all domain controllers in the domain so that you can upgrade the domain functional level. You can then upgrade the forest functional level.

To verify (and upgrade if needed) the forest functional level that your forest is currently using, follow these steps:

1. Log onto a domain controller.

2. Launch Active Directory Domains and Trusts by selecting Start ➢ Administrator Tools ➢ Active Directory Domains and Trusts.

3. Right-click Active Directory Domains and Trusts, and select Raise Forest Functional Level. Your display will look similar to Figure 22.7. In the figure, the current forest functional level is Windows Server 2003 and can be raised to either Windows Server 2008 or Windows Server 2008 R2.

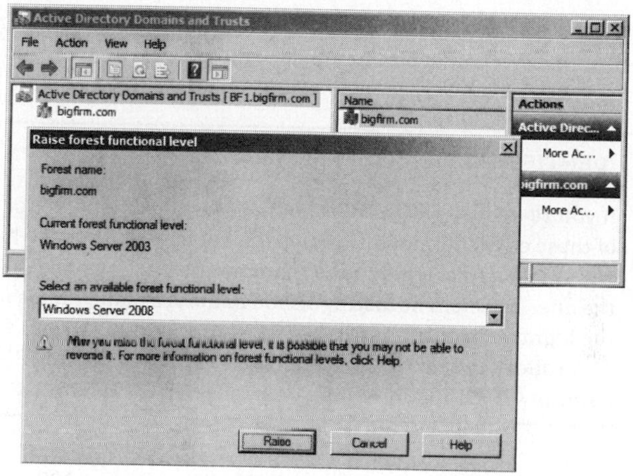

FIGURE 22.7
Verifying the forest functional level

4. If the forest functional level is not at least Windows Server 2003, raise it to Windows Server 2003 by selecting Windows Server 2003 and clicking Raise.

If any of the domains are not raised to the selected forest level, it will fail. In other words, if any of the domains in your forest are currently set to Window Server 2000 native domain functional level and you try to raise the forest functional to Windows Server 2003, it will fail.

Once both the domain functional level and the forest functional level have been raised to at least Windows Server 2003, you can then run adprep to prepare your environment for read-only domain controllers.

RUNNING ADPREP

You can use the command-line tool adprep to prepare Active Directory for different environments. It modifies the Active Directory schema and update permissions to prepare the forest and domain for different capabilities.

Remember, to support an RODC, you must have at least one Windows Server 2008 domain controller, but other domain controllers could be running Windows Server 2003. Since the domain functional level must be at least Windows Server 2003, all domain controllers must be running at least Windows Server 2003.

If the forest started with domain controllers running pre–Windows Server 2008 operating systems (such as Windows Server 2003), you need to run both adprep /forestprep and adprep /domainprep. However, if the forest started with Windows Server 2008 domain controllers, these two commands are not needed. However, the adprep /rodcprep command is still required.

For best performance, you should run `adprep` on computers holding specific roles.

◆ `adprep /forestPrep` should be run on the domain controller holding the schema master role. You must be a member of both the Schema Admins and Enterprise Admins groups to run this command.

◆ `adprep /domainPrep` should be run on the domain controller holding the infrastructure master role. You must be a member of the Domain Admins group to run this command.

◆ `adprep /rodcPrep` should be run on the domain controller holding the infrastructure master role. You must be a member of the Enterprise Admins group to run this command.

IDENTIFYING THE SCHEMA MASTER

If you're unsure which DC is holding the schema master or infrastructure roles, you can use one of these easy command-line queries: `dsquery server -hasfsmo schema` or `dsquery server -hasfsmo infr`. The `dsquery` command will return the distinguished name of the server holding the queried role. The distinguished name is a name that is used to uniquely identify objects using the Lightweight Directory Access Protocol (LDAP). For example, a DC named BF1 in the Domain Controller's organizational unit (OU) in a domain named Bigfirm.com would have a distinguished name of CN=BF1,OU=Domain Controllers, DC=Bigfirm,DC=Com.

`adprep` is available on both the Windows Server 2008 and Windows Server 2008 R2 installation DVDs in the following locations:

Windows Server 2008   `adprep` is located in the `x:\Sources\Adprep` folder of the Windows Server 2008 installation DVD.

Windows Server 2008 R2   `adprep` is located in the `x:\Support\Adprep` folder of the Windows Server 2008 R2 installation DVD. This folder includes both a 64-bit version (named `adprep.exe`) and a 32-bit version (named `adprep32.exe`).

Since you will be modifying the schema of the forest, you'll need to log on with an account that is in the Schema Admins and Enterprise Admins groups when running the `adprep /forestprep` command. For the `adprep /domainprep` command, you will need to be logged on with an account in the Domain Admins group. The `adprep /rodcprep` command requires membership in the Enterprise Admins group.

You can prepare your forest to install an RODC by following these steps:

1. Log onto the domain controller that is also the schema master with an administrative account in the Enterprise Admins group.

2. Insert the Windows Server 2008 R2 DVD.

3. Click Start, right-click Command Prompt, and select "Run as administrator."

4. Enter the drive letter of the DVD, enter a colon (:), and press Enter. For example, if the DVD is in the D drive, enter **D:**, and press Enter.

5. Change the path to the `x:\support\adprep` directory, where x is the actual name of your CD drive, by entering **cd \support\adprep** and pressing Enter.

6. Prepare the forest by following these steps:

    A. Type **adprep /forestprep**, and press Enter. If you are running `adprep` on a 32-bit version of Windows Server, you would substitute `adprep32` for `adprep`.

    B. An ADPREP Warning dialog box will appear asking you to confirm that all Windows Server 2000 domain controllers have been upgraded to at least Windows 2000 SP4. Since the requirement to add an RODC is that all DCs must be running at least Windows Server 2003, this shouldn't be an issue. Type **C**, and press Enter to continue.

FOREST ALREADY UPDATED ON WINDOWS SERVER 2008

If the first domain controller in your forest was Windows Server 2008, the forest-wide information is up-to-date when the server is promoted to a domain controller. There is no harm in running it again and verifying it is up-to-date. If it is, adprep will notify you that the forest-wide information has already been updated.

    C. `adprep` will complete several import commands and output the progress onto the screen. This will take a few minutes to complete. When `adprep` is completed, you will see a message indicating that "Adprep successfully updated the forest-wide information" and be returned to the drive prompt.

7. Prepare the domain with `adprep` by following these steps:

    A. Type **adprep /domainprep**, and press Enter. If you are running `adprep` on a 32-bit version of Windows Server, you would substitute `adprep32` for `adprep`.

DOMAIN ALREADY UPDATED ON WINDOWS SERVER 2008

If your domain and forest started with Windows Server 2008 domain controllers, the domain will already be updated. There is no harm in running it again and verifying it is up-to-date. If it is, adprep will notify you that the domain-wide information has already been updated.

    B. `adprep` will update the domain and output a message indicating "Adprep successfully updated the domain-wide information."

8. Prepare the domain to create RODCs by following these steps:

    A. Type **adprep /rodcprep**, and press Enter. If you are running `adprep` on a 32-bit version of Windows Server, you would substitute `adprep32` for `adprep`.

    B. `adprep` will update the ForestDnsZones partition, the DomainDnsZones partition, and the domain partition. You should see a message indicating that "Adprep completed without errors."

It will take time for the changes to replicate through the forest. Once the changes have replicated, you can then successfully promote a domain controller to an RODC.

RODC and Server Applications

Although some server applications will work normally on an RODC just as they would on a regular DC, you'll run into problems with applications that need to do much interaction with Active Directory. Considering that an RODC would be deployed to a remote office that doesn't have much IT support, it's possible that there aren't any other applications out there.

However, if you do have server applications that are deployed in the remote office or you want to install on the RODC, you'll need to do a little research.

Microsoft has posted an article titled "Applications that are known to work with RODCs" that you can view at `http://technet.microsoft.com/library/cc732790.aspx`. The meat of the article covers what you need to do to make these applications work. Several server applications will work without any problems or with only minor preparation:

- Microsoft Internet Security and Acceleration (ISA) Server
- Microsoft Office Live Communications Server
- Microsoft Systems Management Server (SMS)
- Microsoft Operations Manager (MOM)
- Windows SharePoint Services
- Microsoft SQL Server 2005

A big gotcha is when Exchange Server tries to interact with the global catalog (GC) on an RODC. An RODC can act as a GC, but not enough of a GC to service a local Exchange Server instance.

The big message here is if you're trying to deploy an RODC to a remote office and the remote office is using other applications, you need to do some testing. Some will work with no problems, others require some minor tweaking, and others simply won't play with your RODC at all.

Installing the RODC

You can promote a Windows Server 2008 R2 server to a read-only domain controller by following these steps:

1. To start, ensure all of the following:
   - The server has joined the domain.
   - The domain is running at least Server 2003 domain functional level.
   - The forest is running at least Server 2003 forest functional level.
   - The forest and domain has been prepared with the following commands, if needed:
     - `adprep /forestprep`
     - `adprep /domainprep`
     - `adprep /rodcprep`
   - The changes from `adprep` have replicated through the forest.

WHEN IS ADPREP NEEDED?

In some situations adprep isn't needed. If your domain was built using Windows Server 2008 R2 servers, the schema is already up-to-date, and adprep isn't needed.

However, if you're running a Windows Server 2003 domain, you'll need to run adprep /domainprep and adprep /forestprep before promoting the first Windows Server 2008 R2 server (which is required before creating an RODC). You'll then need to run adprep /rodcprep before creating the RODC.

2. Create a site for your RODC in an existing domain by following these steps:

   A. Log onto a domain controller, and launch Active Directory Sites and Services by selecting Start ➤ Administrative Tools ➤ Active Directory Sites and Services.

   B. Right-click Sites, and select New Site.

   C. Name the site **RemoteOffice**, and select DefaultIPSiteLink. Your display will look similar to Figure 22.8. Click OK.

   D. Review the information displayed in the dialog box, and click OK. Check out Chapter 21 in this book for a review of how to completely configure a site.

   E. Close Active Directory Sites and Services.

3. Create a group that will be used to administer RODCs by following these steps:

   A. Launch Active Directory Users and Computers by selecting Start ➤ Administrative Tools ➤ Active Directory Users and Computers.

   B. Right-click the Users container, and select New ➤ Group.

   C. In the New Object – Group dialog box, enter **Remote Office Admins** as the name of the group. Ensure Group Scope is set to Global and Group Type is set to Security. Your display should look similar to Figure 22.9. Click OK.

FIGURE 22.8
Adding a site to
Active Directory
Sites and Services

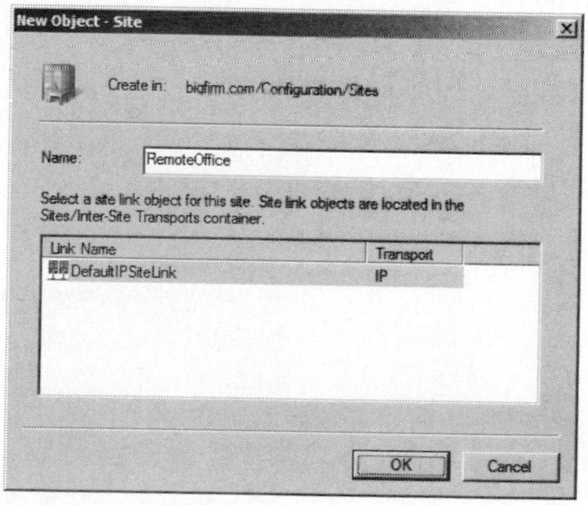

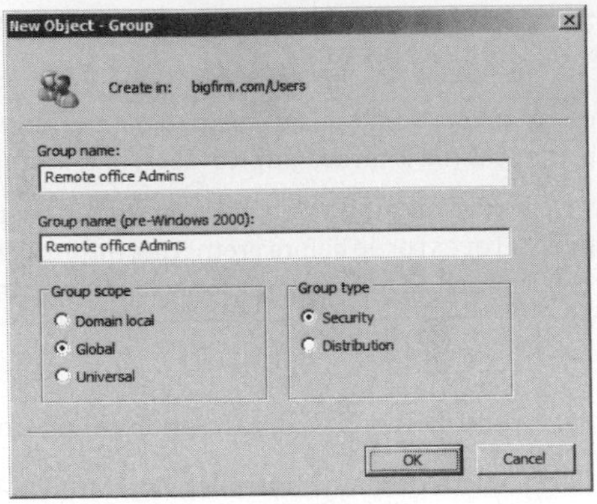

FIGURE 22.9
Adding a group
for RODC
administration

4. Log onto the Windows Server 2008 R2 server that you want to promote to an RODC. This
   is a different server than you just used to create a site named RemoteOffice.

5. Click Start, type **DCPromo** in the search text box, and press Enter.

6. Review the information on the Welcome page, and click Next.

7 Review the information on the Operating System Compatibility page, and click Next.

8. On the Choose a Deployment Configuration page, select "Existing forest," and ensure
   that "Add a domain controller to an existing domain" is selected. Your display should
   look similar to Figure 22.10. Click Next.

9. The Network Credentials page will appear. The name of the domain you have joined
   will already be entered. Click the Set button next "Alternate credentials," and enter the
   credentials of an account that has permission to promote a server to a domain controller
   within your domain. Your display will look similar to Figure 22.11. Click Next.

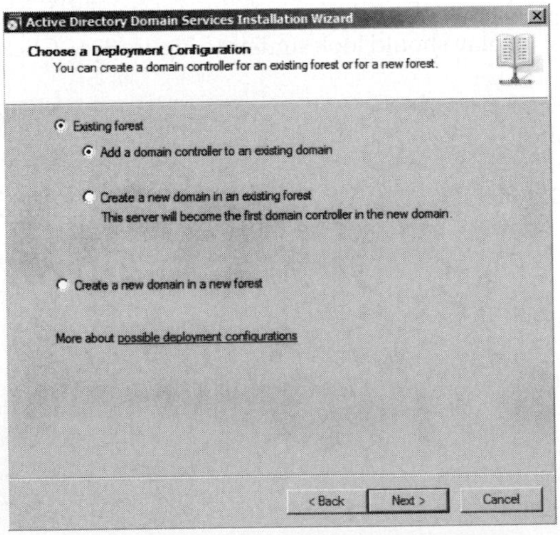

FIGURE 22.10
Choosing a deploy-
ment configuration

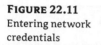

FIGURE 22.11
Entering network
credentials

10. The Select a Domain page will appear. Select the domain where you want to create your RODC, and click Next.

11. Select the RemoteOffice site you created earlier in this exercise. If subnets have been configured in your sites, you may need to deselect the "Use the site that corresponds to the IP address of the computer" box. Click Next.

12. The Additional Domain Controller Options page will appear. Select the "DNS server" and "Read-only domain controller (RODC)" boxes. Deselect the "Global catalog" check box. Your display will look similar to Figure 22.12. Click Next.

FIGURE 22.12
Adding domain
controller options

GLOBAL CATALOG OR UNIVERSAL GROUP MEMBERSHIP CACHING

When configuring an RODC in a site, you will need to consider whether to make it a global catalog server or enable universal group membership caching. Chapter 21 includes details that can help you decide what to use in a production site, but for a test lab, you can get away without either.

13. The Delegation of RODC Installation and Administration page will appear. Enter the name of your domain, a backslash (\), and **Remote Office Admins** to identify the group that will be delegated permission for administration on the RODCs. This is the same group you created earlier in this exercise. You can also use the Set button to browse to the group. Your display will look similar to Figure 22.13. Click Next.

FIGURE 22.13
Delegating installation and administration privileges to a group

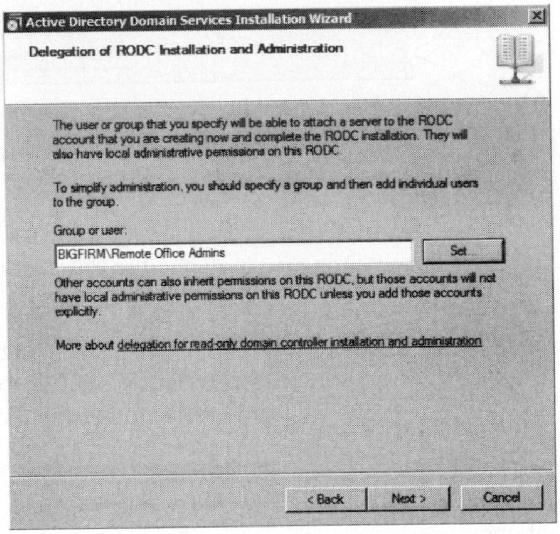

14. Accept the default locations for the database, log files, and SYSVOL. Click Next.

15. Enter a password in the Password and Confirm Password text boxes that will meet your domain's password complexity requirements. For a test bed environment, you can use **P@ssw0rd**. Click Next.

16. Review the information on the Summary page, and click Next to begin the installation. DCPromo takes several minutes and requires a reboot upon completion.

Installing RODC on Server Core

Server Core will support the installation of an RODC. As a reminder, Server Core gives you a command prompt only, so you'll need to run DCPromo with an unattend file.

You can create the unattend file in two ways:

- Run DCPromo on another member server with a full installation of Windows Server 2008. When you get to the summary page, click the Export Settings button, and follow the wizard to save the file. (Chapter 6, "Creating the Simple AD: The One-Domain, One-Location AD," showed this process, including how to run DCPromo with the unattend file.)

- Create the text file using Notepad. Here's a sample file:

```
[DCInstall]
InstallDNS=Yes
ConfirmGc=Yes
CriticalReplicationOnly=No
DisableCancelForDnsInstall=No
Password=P@ssw0rd
RebootOnCompletion=Yes
ReplicaDomainDNSName= DomainDNSName
ReplicaOrNewDomain=ReadOnlyReplica
ReplicationSourceDC=bf1.bigfirm.com
SafeModeAdminPassword=P@ssw0rd
SiteName=RemoteOffice
UserDomain=bigfirm.com
UserName=Administrator
```

Once you have the unattend file, you can execute DCPromo at the Server Core prompt with the following:

```
dcpromo /unattend:<unattendfileName>)
```

Viewing the RODC Properties

After you have promoted a server to an RODC, you can view and modify the properties of the server using Active Directory Users and Computers. You can do this on the RODC itself or on any other DC in the domain.

The following steps will show you how to view the different properties of the RODC:

1. Log on to a domain controller with administrative privileges.

2. Launch Active Directory Users and Computers by selecting Start ➤ Administrative Tools ➤ Active Directory Users and Computers.

3. Browse to the Domain Controllers container in the domain, and select it. Locate the RODC you created. Right-click it, and select Properties.

4. Select the Password Replication Policy tab. Notice that the Allowed RODC Password Replication group has been granted Allow access, but all other groups are denied.

5. Click the Add button. Select the "Allow passwords for the account to replicate to this RODC" radio button. Your display will look similar to Figure 22.14. Click OK.

6. Enter **Remote Office Admins** in the text box. This is the name of a group created earlier in this chapter. If desired, you can also click the Advanced button, browse to locate a

group, and add it here. Once you've added a group, click OK. You'll see that your group has been added with the Allow setting.

FIGURE 22.14
Viewing the RODC properties

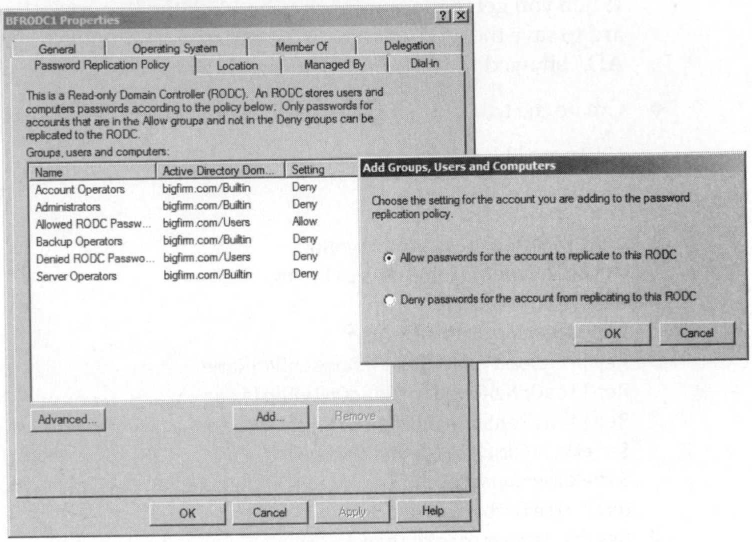

Notice that you can add or remove any groups using this page. However, the setting of Allow or Deny can be configured only when you add the group. It's not possible to modify the setting directly. If you want to change the setting, you'll need to remove the group and then add it again using the different setting.

7. You should be back on the Password Replication Policy tab of the RODC properties sheet. Click the Advanced button. Your display should look similar to Figure 22.15.

This page has two selections. You can view the any accounts that have been cached onto the RODC, and you can view any accounts that have been used to log onto the RODC.

FIGURE 22.15
Viewing the Policy Usage tab

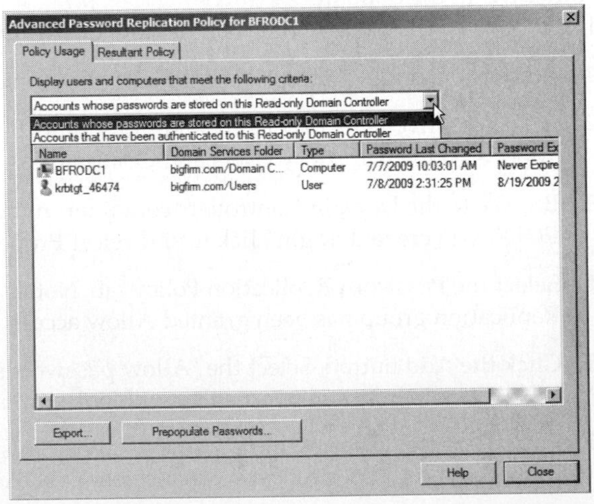

You can use this page to identify any regular users who are logging onto the RODC that may need their accounts added to the password replication policy or the Allowed RODC Password Replication group.

8. Click the Prepopulate Passwords button. Notice that this takes you to the Active Directory search tool. You can identify any user or computer accounts whose passwords you want to replicate to the RODC before the user actually logs on. This can be useful if the remote office has an unreliable WAN link and you want to ensure a user's account is cached on the RODC before they log on for the first time.

9. Click Cancel to close the Active Directory search page. Click Close to close the Advanced Password Replication Policy page. Click OK to close the RODC's properties sheet.

Users or groups added to this page will be able to have their passwords replicated or cached onto this RODC. However, if you want a user or group to be able to have their passwords replicated or cached onto any RODC, you need to modify the Allowed RODC Password Replication group.

Modifying the Allowed List

If you want to allow users to be able to have their passwords replicated or cached onto any RODC instead of just a specific RODC, you can modify the properties of the Allowed RODC Password Replication group by following these steps:

1. Launch Active Directory Users and Computers.

2. Browse to the Users container.

3. Right-click the Allowed RODC Password Replication group, and select Properties.

4. Select the Members tab.

5. Click the Add button.

6. Enter **Remote Office Admins** in the text box. This is the name of a group created earlier in this chapter. If desired, you can also click the Advanced button and browse to locate a user or group. Your display will look similar to Figure 22.16. Notice that you can add or remove groups from this page.

7. Click OK to close the properties page.

You can follow a similar process to modify the members of the Denied RODC Password Replication group. The Denied RODC Password Replication group includes several groups by default. You can add or remove groups using this page.

SECURITY WARNING

Although it is possible to remove members from the Denied RODC Password Replication group, Microsoft recommends you don't modify any of the prepopulated groups. These groups help ensure that passwords for accounts with elevated permissions are not cached on the server. If a group is removed and a member of the group logs onto the RODC, it is possible their account credentials will be stored on the RODC and subject to compromise if the RODC is stolen or attacked.

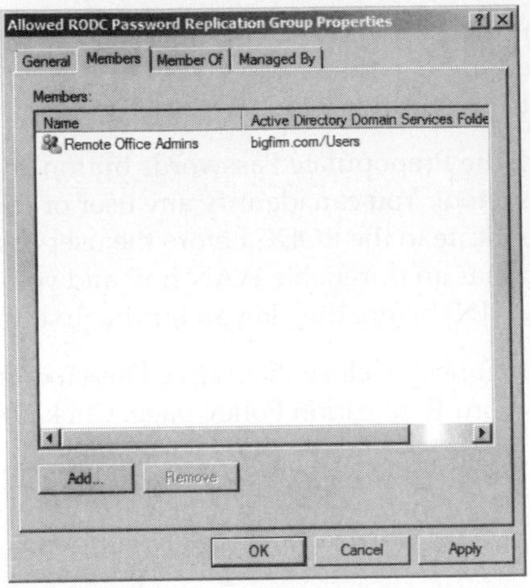

FIGURE 22.16
Adding a group to
the Allowed RODC
Password Replica-
tion group

Staged Installations

Normally, you need to be at least a member of the Domain Admins group to be able to run
DCPromo on a server. However, it's highly unlikely that a member of the Domain Admins group
will be assigned to work at a remote office.

This may not be a problem in many scenarios, but situations may arise when it is difficult for
a member of the Domain Admins group to travel to the remote office. With this in mind, you
have several options:

Build the RODC at the main office and ship it to the remote site   This could be expensive
and time-consuming. If the server is a new purchase, it would be cheaper to ship it directly to
the remote office and build it there.

Have a domain admin travel to the remote site to perform the installation   If the office is
across the street, this would be an ideal solution. However, if the office is across the country,
the cost of travel isn't justified.

Promote the server remotely   Chapter 14, "Remote Server Administration," covers a lot of
the remote administration technologies you can use to remotely administer a server. However,
since DCPromo requires a reboot, conventional wisdom dictates that someone should be physically present.

Perform a staged installation   A staged installation is performed in two steps. A domain
administrator prestages the account (which you'll see how to do in the "Prestaging the RODC
Account" section in this chapter), and an administrator with limited privileges at the remote
location can then promote the server.

USING INSTALLATION MEDIA

Active Directory can be very large, and if the WAN link doesn't have a lot of available bandwidth, promoting a server to a domain controller can take a long time and may prevent other
users from performing normal work with this link.

One way to avoid the problem is to create installation media that includes Active Directory. It can be stored on a CD and then shipped to the remote site.

To create the installation media, you need to run `ntdsutil` from the command line of a writable domain controller with the `ifm` command, which is short for "installing from media." The following steps will lead you through the process of creating the media:

1. Log onto a domain controller in the same domain where the RODC will be installed.

2. Launch a command prompt with administrative permissions by selecting Start, right-clicking Command Prompt, and selecting "Run as administrator."

3. Create an empty directory with the following command:

   `md c:\ifm`

You can name your directory anything you desire and can also store it on a different drive if desired.

4. Type **ntdsutil** at the command prompt, and press Enter. The `ntdsutil` prompt will appear.

5. Type **Activate instance ntds**, and press Return. `ntdsutil` will connect to the instance of Active Directory on the domain controller and will output "Active instance set to ntds."

6. Type **ifm**, and press Return. The `ifm` prompt will appear.

7. Type **Create rodc c:\ifm**, and press Return.

A folder named Active Directory will be created in the ifm folder with a single file named `ntds.dit`. You can copy this file to installation media such as a CD and ship it to the remote office.

After the installation media is created, you can install it on the remote server using `DCPromo` with the `/adv` switch.

PRESTAGING THE **RODC** ACCOUNT

Prestaging an RODC account is just a fancy way of saying you create an account for the RODC before it is promoted. You must be a member of the Domain Admins group to prestage an RODC account.

Follow these steps to prestage an RODC account:

1. Launch Active Directory Users and Computers by selecting Start ➢ Administrative Tools ➢ Active Directory Users and Computers.

2. Browse to the Domain Controllers OU. Right-click the Domain Controllers OU, and then select Pre-create Read-only Domain Controller account, as shown in Figure 22.17.

3. Review the information on the Welcome page, and click Next.

4. Review the Operating System Compatibility page, and click Next.

5. On the Network Credentials page, click Alternate Credentials, and enter the credentials of an account in the Domain Admins group. Click OK, and click Next.

6. On the Specify the Computer Name page, enter the name of the RODC. Your display will look similar to Figure 22.18. Click Next.

FIGURE 22.17
Precreating an
RODC account
from Active Direc-
tory Users and
Computers

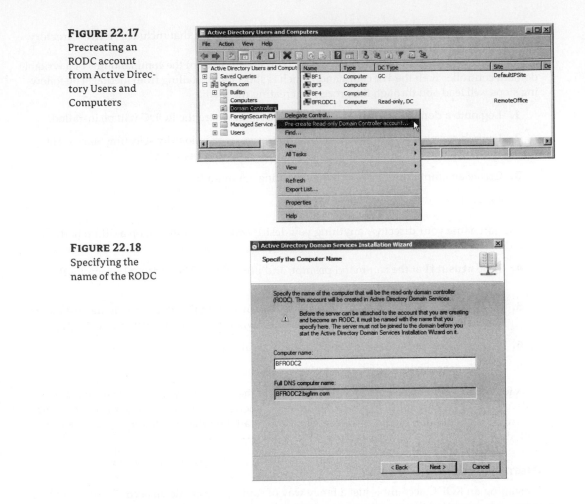

FIGURE 22.18
Specifying the
name of the RODC

7. On the Select a Site page, select the site where the RODC will be placed. Click Next.

8. The Additional Domain Controller Options page will appear with the DNS Server, Global Catalog, and Read-only Domain Controller (RODC) choices selected. You can deselect the DNS server or global catalog if desired, but the RODC selection is dimmed. Click Next.

9. The Delegation of RODC Installation and Administration page will appear. Enter the name of a group or user who will run DCPromo at the remote site. The account that you specify will have local administrative permissions on the RODC. Click Next.

10. Review the information on the Summary page, and click next.

11. DCPromo will create the account for the RODC, assign appropriate permissions and settings, and report success. Click Finish.

12. Active Directory Users and Computers will show the RODC account in Domain Controllers, as shown in Figure 22.19.

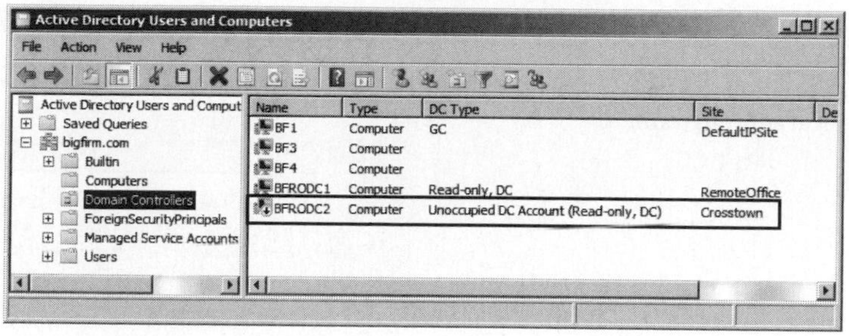

FIGURE 22.19

A prestaged RODC account

Notice that the RODC2 account has a down arrow indicating that it is not enabled. It will be enabled when DCPromo is run to promote it to an RODC. You can also see that the DC type is listed as Unoccupied DC Account (Read-only Domain Controller), which indicates it is a prestaged account.

With the account prestaged, the local administrator at the remote site can now run DCPromo to promote it.

THE SECOND STAGE OF INSTALLING A PRESTAGED RODC

The local administrator can use the following steps to complete the installation of a prestaged RODC. The name of the computer where DCPromo is run must be the same name as the prestaged account.

DON'T JOIN THE DOMAIN

The prestaged account creates an actual computer account in the Domain Controllers OU. Since any computer can have only one account, the prestaged RODC cannot be a member of the domain before it is promoted. Instead, it starts as a member of a workgroup and is added to the domain as part of the DCPromo process.

---

1. Log onto the server using the local administrator account.

2. Click Start, type **DCPromo** in the Start Search text box, and press Enter.

3. Review the information on the Welcome page, and click Next.

4. Review the information on the Operating System Compatibility page, and click Next.

5. On the Choose a Deployment Configuration page, select "Existing forest" and "Add a domain controller to an existing domain." Click Next.

6. On the Network Credentials page, enter the name of the domain. Click Set to enter alternate credentials. Enter the username and password of a user who is in the group that has been delegated permissions to complete the installation. Your display will look similar to Figure 22.20. Click Next.

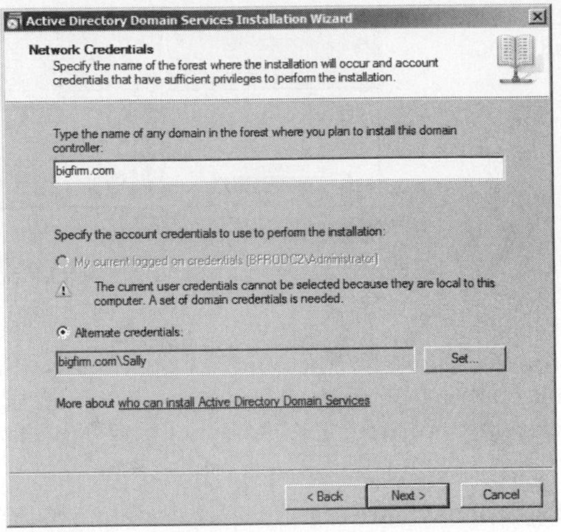

FIGURE 22.20
Entering the credentials of the local administrator

7. The Select a Domain page will appear. Select the domain where the RODC should be located, and click Next.

8. An error message will appear, as shown in Figure 22.21.

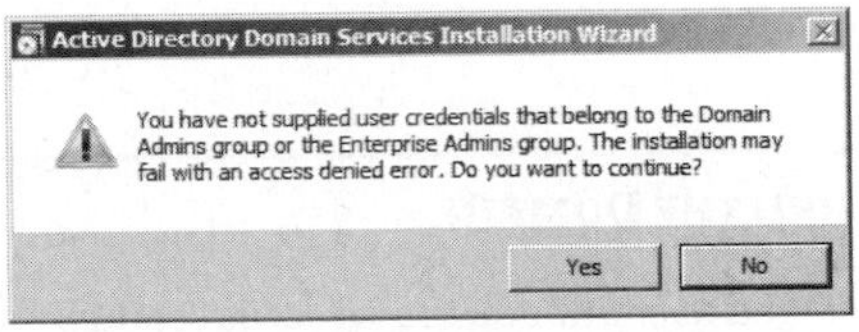

FIGURE 22.21
DCPromo error message

DCPromo has detected that the user account is not a member of either the Domain Admins group or the Enterprise Admins group, and it may fail. This is normal and expected. As long as this user is a member of the group that was delegated appropriate permissions when the RODC account was prestaged, DCPromo will succeed. Review the message, and click Yes.

9. DCPromo will detect that the RODC account is prestaged and display the message shown in Figure 22.22.

Review the message, and click OK.

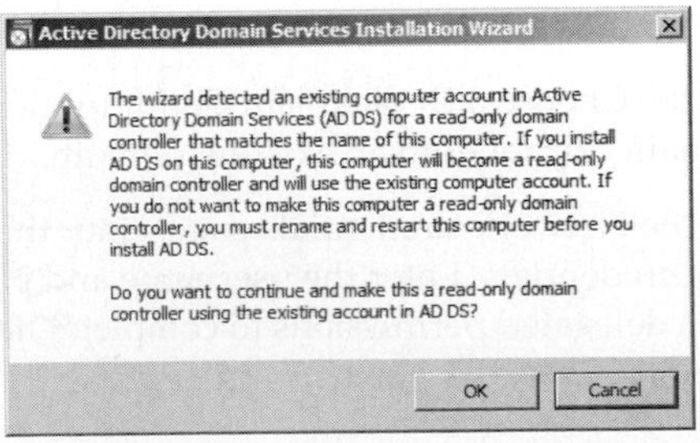

FIGURE 22.22
DCPromo detected the prestaged RODC.

10. Accept the default location for the database, log files, and SYSVOL by clicking Next.

11. On the Directory Services Restore Mode Administrator Password page, enter a password in the Password and Confirm password text boxes. Click Next.

12. Review the information on the Summary page, and click Next.

13. DCPromo will begin as shown in Figure 22.23.

FIGURE 22.23

DCPromo completes the promotion of the server to an RODC.

> **Active Directory Domain Services Installation Wizard**
>
> The wizard is configuring Active Directory Domain Services. This process can take from a few minutes to several hours, depending on your environment and the options that you selected.
>
> Configuring the local computer to host Active Directory Domain Services
>
> Cancel
>
> ☐ Reboot on completion

DCPromo takes several minutes to run and requires a reboot upon completion. You can select the "Reboot on completion" check box to allow it to reboot automatically.

After DCPromo completes, the server will be fully configured as an RODC.

DNS on the RODC

It's strongly recommended that you install the DNS service on the RODC. In the steps used in this chapter, DNS was selected each time. It has very little overhead and provides significant gains.

If a DNS server isn't located in the branch office but a DC is located there, the users will still have to traverse the WAN link to query DNS to locate the DC. Additionally, normal DNS name resolution will still be required at the remote office.

Take a look at Figure 22.24 as you review the process of a normal logon.

When a user logs on, the following actions are taken:

1. The user enters their credentials and the netlogon service takes over.

2. The netlogon process queries DNS to locate the name and IP address of a domain controller located in the same site as the user. Both the SRV and host record of the server needs to be retrieved.

FIGURE 22.24

DNS and the logon process

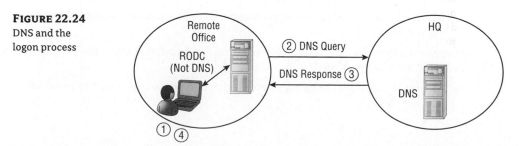

3. DNS responds.

4. The `netlogon` service passes the user's credentials to the RODC located in the site.

By configuring DNS on the RODC, the DNS queries over the WAN link will be avoided. The `netlogon` service queries the DNS service on the RODC and then passes the credentials to the RODC.

ACTIVE DIRECTORY INTEGRATED DNS

If other DNS servers are configured as Active Directory integrated (ADI), then the RODC will also be set as an Active Directory integrated zone. ADI DNS takes advantage of Active Directory replication to replicate zone data and is strongly recommended in Windows domains.

When the sites are configured, Active Directory replication is significantly optimized.

◆ All replication traffic is compressed to about 10–15 percent of its original size.

◆ It can be scheduled to occur after-hours or during nonpeak hours.

READ-ONLY DNS

When DNS is added to the RODC, it will be a read-only DNS server. This is actually a new type of zone introduced in Windows Server 2008 known as a *primary read-only zone.*

Normally, the Start of Authority (SOA) record for an ADI DNS server will list itself as the primary server. In other words, updates can occur on the server. However, an ADI DNS server on an RODC will hold a copy of an SOA record from a writable DNS server.

Traditional DNS works with a single DNS server hosting the primary zone data. You can then add multiple DNS servers hosting secondary zones. The secondary DNS servers are read-only and receive their updates from the primary DNS Server.

A read-only ADI DNS server on an RODC works similarly to a primary/secondary DNS configuration. Updates can't occur on the RODC just as they can't occur on the secondary DNS server. However, the biggest difference is that you don't need to manage the DNS zone transfers as you would with traditional DNS servers. Zone transfers are managed through Active Directory replication.

The Bottom Line

Prepare a forest and a domain for RODCs   RODCs are new to Windows Server 2008 and can't be added until the forest and domain are prepared. The preparation will modify the schema and permissions.

> **Master It**   Identify the command that needs to be executed to prepare the forest to support RODCs.

Prepare the domain   In addition to preparing the forest, you must also prepare the domain before RODCs can be added.

> **Master It**   Identify the two commands that need to be executed to prepare the domain to support RODCs.

Allow passwords on any RODC The RODC can cache passwords for users based on how it's configured. When a user's password is cached on the RODC, the authentication process doesn't have to traverse the WAN link and is quicker. However, a cached password is susceptible to an attack, so privileged accounts should not be cached on the server.

> **Master It** What should you modify to allow users to have their passwords cached on any RODC in the domain?
>
> ◆ The Allowed RODC Password Replication group
>
> ◆ The Denied RODC Password Replication group
>
> ◆ The password replication policy

Allow passwords on a single RODC It's possible to configure the environment so members of a group can have their passwords replicated and cached to any RODC in the domain. It's also possible to configure the environment so that the passwords will be replicated or cached only to a single RODC.

> **Master It** What should you modify to allow users to have their passwords cached on a specific RODC in the domain?
>
> ◆ The Allowed RODC Password Replication group
>
> ◆ The Denied RODC Password Replication group
>
> ◆ The password replication policy

Chapter 23

Creating Larger Active Directory Environments: Beyond One Domain

Throughout this book, we've been dealing with the plain vanilla Active Directory (AD) implementation of one domain. Although Active Directory can support large enterprises with a single domain, IT shops are faced with administrating multiple domains for various reasons. Sometimes it is part of the plan, yet on occasion it is forced upon them by their company restructuring or acquiring other businesses.

Administrators need to understand the impact of multiple domains in an organization. They need to know the decision points that direct an organization to consider multiple domains.

In this chapter, you will learn to:

◆ Explain the fundamental concepts of Active Directory with clarity

◆ Choose between using domains, multiple domains, or multiple forests with an Active Directory design

◆ Add domains to an Active Directory environment

◆ Manage function levels, trusts, FSMO roles, and the global catalog

The Foundations of Multiple-Domain Designs

Before you consider adding multiple domains to an Active Directory environment, you need to understand the essential concepts. Specifically, you need to understand the logical and physical components of Active Directory to help you plan the Active Directory design. Knowing the benefits and differences between a single domain, multiple domains in the single forest, and multiple forests will assist you in deciding on the proper implementation to meet the needs of your organization.

"Under-the-hood" processes—such as multimaster replication, the Kerberos authentication protocol, and programmed limitations of Active Directory—further define the structure of the Active Directory implementation. Each has pros and cons to consider.

Domains

The typical way to explain an AD domain is to say that it is a security boundary for users and computers in sharing resources and that it uses multimaster replication to distribute the information of these users and computers. That's true, but it's not very illuminating, so let's see what it means.

THE SECURITY BOUNDARY

Every network with any kind of security at all needs to keep a list of information about users—the names, passwords, and other information about people authorized to use the system. You also know that once you have more than one machine, you run into a problem—how do you share that list with all the machines in your company? Recall that you do that by setting up a small number of servers called *domain controllers* with a database of your users, called NTDS.DIT. This essential database file was named after "new technology directory services," and the file extension stands for "directory information tree," which is an industry-standardized format.

The member servers and workstations still have their lists of *local* user accounts, a list maintained in a security account management (SAM) database, but in most cases you won't make much use of these local accounts. Rather, you configure your workstations and member servers to *trust* the list of users on the domain controllers. When someone tries to sit down at a workstation and claims to be a member of your domain, then the workstation takes the name and password offered by the user and hands it to the domain controller (DC), saying, "Is this a valid username and password on your domain database?" And, again, if the DC says that the name/password combination is OK, then the workstation *trusts* that the DC is telling the truth.

The domain defines a security boundary. The domain provides a boundary to administer accounts and resource access. Members of the Domain Admins group are assigned full control over the domain's objects. The domain also controls application of GPOs to its users and computers.

In previous versions of Windows Server, the domain was also a boundary for password policies and account lockout options. A new feature of Windows Server 2008 is fine-grained password policies. These allow different password policies to be applied throughout a domain. Although Windows Server 2008 R2 provides this feature, existing Active Directory implementations may have included multiple domains to provide differing password policies.

If you have one domain, access to resources is managed through the domain's groups and accounts. If there are multiple domains, a trust relationship is required that allows another domain's users and groups to be recognized by the domain's computers. The trust is similar to a gate in a fence that allows users in or out.

You must fully understand the security boundaries of the domain, forest, and physical domain controllers in order to design a secure Active Directory implementation.

MULTIMASTER REPLICATION

The second part of the domain's definition, *replication*, refers to the process that ensures that every copy of the domain database matches every other one. In other words, if you're sitting in the Topeka office and you create a user account, then that new record—the user account—exists only on the Active Directory domain controller in Topeka at that moment. Part of the job of AD's database engine is to get that new information to the other DCs as quickly as is reasonably possible—that's replication. The *multimaster* part comes from the fact that you can insert a change into the AD database from any DC. That's a change from many replicated database approaches, including the one for NT 4. With NT 4, you could have lots of DCs, but only one of them accepted database changes. Whether creating a new user account, changing a password, or joining a machine to a domain, the resulting modification to the domain's SAM had to happen on the one machine with the ability to change the SAM database—the machine called the *primary domain controller* (PDC). AD mainly does away with the idea of a PDC, and all DCs are basically equal. (We say "basically" because of something called *operations masters* that we'll cover in the section "FSMOs and GCs.")

NOT THE ONLY SECURITY BOUNDARY

Now, the domain provides a security boundary for access and control to resources. Yet it is not the *only* security boundary. The domain is not an impenetrable wall where information is protected. There is information about the domain shared between other domain controllers within the Active Directory forest, and a group of domains have a built-in relationship with each other. So, another security boundary is the forest that protects information shared between domain controllers.

User and group information of the domain can be found in global catalog servers, which can be located in other domains. The domain controllers of the forest replicate additional information such as Active Directory configuration data.

The physical security boundary of Active Directory is the domain controllers. A domain controller contains the database on its physical disks and replicates changes to other domain controllers.

If any of these security boundaries are compromised, the Active Directory environment is compromised and subject to the whims of an evil hacker, who is commonly depicted as a black silhouette with a wool cap and trench coat.

When Microsoft became security conscientious, it discovered how damaging to an Active Directory environment the evil hacker can be. He could change configurations with administrative privileges in another domain, and the changes would be replicated to the rest of the domain controllers. With a physical domain controller, he could decrypt passwords for access. This was the primary impetus for Windows Server 2008 features of read-only domain controllers and password replication policies for caching passwords. If an evil hacker could get his hands on a domain controller in an unsecured area, at least the domain controller could not replicate changes to other domain controllers, and it would have a limited number of passwords to decrypt.

WHY TALK ABOUT NT 4?

Since Active Directory was introduced 10 years ago, NT 4 is an operating system that has gone into history along with the Altair. It is very surprising finding a computer running this version of Windows in any production IT environment. So, why use it as a comparison with Active Directory? Windows Server 2008 R2 is still built on NT technology. There are portions of the operating system that are throwbacks to its origins. Windows Server 2008 R2 member servers still have a SAM. The operating system still uses security tokens created by domain controllers and the member server to permit access to user accounts. Users' logons can still be controlled with the same technology that came with NT. Although young system administrators reading this book may have never installed NT and have no reference point to it, they should know how good they have it.

When you created your first domain by running DCPromo on the first domain controller, the Active Directory database was created, which would be replicated using the multimaster replication process. The database is structured with three basic parts, or partitions:

Domain partition This contains the information of users, groups, and computers that are associated with accessing resources.

Configuration partition   This contains replication parameters and other nifty configurations to the Active Directory environment like Exchange Server information.

Schema partition   This contains the definition of objects. It tells Active Directory how to build a user account or a group, and it tells what data can be assigned to a user.

The domain partition is the largest portion of the database and is replicated to only domain controllers within the same domain. It will also be the growing portion of the database because organizations will create far more users, computers, and other domain-based objects than adding data to the configuration or schema partitions.

If you want to limit the amount of replication across wide area network (WAN) links, you would consider segregating users and groups in one location from other locations by defining separate domains for each location.

That's basically how domains are structured. It is a security boundary administering access to resources and authenticating users. It is also a replication unit in that its information is shared with domain controllers in the same domain. Now let's look at options to expand Active Directory with more domains.

Forests

When considering additional domains in Active Directory, we get back to nature using familiar terms such as *forests* and *trees*. Although you can't start a forest without a tree, we'll begin with the concept of a forest.

After creating the first domain with DCPromo, you can create replica domain controllers for the same domain or create domain controllers for new domains in relation to this first domain. When additional domains are created in relation to this first domain, as you will do later in the "Creating Multiple Domains" section, not all the Active Directory database information is replicated to those domain controllers. The domain partition is not replicated to new domains' domain controllers. Configuration and schema partitions will be replicated to every domain controller in the forest. The phrase *in the forest* means a group of domains that replicate the configuration and schema partitions.

In addition, being *in the forest* means that the domains are built in relation to each other. The relation is the trust built between the domains with DCPromo. A nonconfigurable "two-way transitive" trust is built automatically between the new domain and another one in the forest. This means users and groups of one domain can access resources such as files and printers in the other domain, and vice versa. In fact, users in any domain could access resources in any other domain in the forest.

Getting back to nature, when you created the first domain on the first domain controller, you created a one-domain, one-tree forest. It is important to understand that building a domain from scratch, as you did in Chapter 6, "Creating the Simple AD: The One-Domain, One-Location AD," will create a stand-alone pristine forest that stands by itself and doesn't interact with anything else. It's just like you find in nature. A forest is a collection of trees. It is a security boundary for all the furry woodland creatures to remain hidden and safe. They can peacefully forage for food under the shade of the trees whose branches and roots are interconnected. The furry woodland creatures don't go prancing around to other forests. ("Don't go out into the meadow, Bambi. It's not safe.") So, separate forests don't share information, and users don't venture into the other forests on their own. In addition, you can only add more trees to a forest. Roots of trees don't extend to the other forests. You can't transplant forests next to each other and expect them to be unified. The back to nature analogy works.

This security boundary for the furry woodland creatures is important because evil hackers dressed as lions, tigers, or bears can cause havoc if they are permitted in the forest. To avoid security breaches, the Active Directory design might include a separate forest for the carnivores. In other words, if you want to ensure one portion of your network is locked down, you may consider a separate forest to prevent sharing resources with others.

Trees

When creating a new domain in an Active Directory forest, you have to name it. Primarily, a *tree* is a group of domains in the forest with the same last name, or namespace.

THE ROOT OF A FOREST

You would think we were done with this "back to nature" analogy. However, we have to modify it. The root of a tree is the new namespace for a group of domains such as the Bigfirm.com namespace. The root domain of a forest of Active Directory domains is the first domain that you installed in the forest. Occasionally, it will be referred as the *forest root*. It is commonly depicted at the top of the tree.

For example, the first domain or forest root domain was named Bigfirm.com. You can assign a name to the next domain as Ecoast.Bigfirm.com. Thus, it shares the same namespace Bigfirm.com, and it is part of the same tree. If you create another domain named Consolidated. com, it doesn't have the same namespace. Ecoast is considered a child domain to Bigfirm.com. Consolidated.com is a new tree within the forest. Consolidated.com is also a tree root even though it has no child domains.

In an Active Directory forest with just a couple domains, this doesn't make much difference, specifically when it comes to accessing resources through the trust relationships. Things are pretty much equal. With several domains, the effect of how the domains are named impacts the trust relationships. This is because of how the Kerberos authentication protocol works.

KERBEROS AND TRUSTS

Kerberos authentication is similar to dating in high school. Savvy guys learned getting a date can't be done by simple pick-up lines or cute smiles; they learned to network. They have to get someone to vouch for them.

Say you see a cute potential date in the halls of school, but you don't know her. You can't talk to her directly, and there's that security device named Mother who gets hot and bothered when you try to call her house. But your security device, Mom, knows the other security device; they're friends. So, you ask your mom to talk to her mother to initiate conversations between the user (you) and the resource (cute potential date).

When your mom isn't friends with the other security device, she knows of another friend who does. This friend is the forest root of the neighborhood; she's a friend with everyone. Now, your mom talks with her friend, who talks to the mother of the cute date. Ba-da-bing, you're there!

Logically, the trust relations between the domains are either parent-child or forest root–tree root. As we mentioned, Ecoast.Bigfirm.com is a child domain to Bigfirm.com, so it has a parent-to-child relation. Consolidated.com has a forest root–tree root relation. Figure 23.1 illustrates the trust relationship of the forest.

FIGURE 23.1
Active Directory
forest example

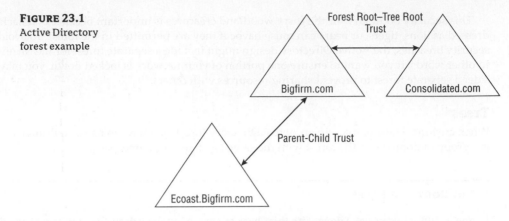

Active Directory Forest Trusts

Kerberos works in this fashion across the domains' trust relations. A user account starts with its domain controller for a voucher (a *ticket*). If the resource is in another domain, it has to travel across the trust relations to the resource domain. It needs to go up the parent-child trust, across the forest root–tree root trust, and if needed down the other tree's parent-child trust path. If the user is in Ecoast.Bigfirm.com, this means the user must contact the Ecoast.Bigfirm.com domain controller. If the resource is in Consolidated.com, the Ecoast.Bigfirm.com domain controller contacts one in Bigfirm.com. Then the Bigfirm.com domain controller needs to contact a domain controller in Consolidated.com. It takes three jumps to get to the resource because that is the path the automatic trusts provide. Having taller trees means more jumps, more traffic, and more delay.

You Must Build Trees and Forests Together

Multiple domains sound great, and they of course have been a terrific improvement over NT 4. But hidden in this potentially rich notion of many domains joined into a tree and many trees joined into a forest is a dirty little secret. You cannot join already-existing domains into a tree. Remember, in nature, you can't transplant a forest next to another one. Nor can you join already-existing trees into a forest; transplanting trees is tough too. Just like the mighty oak comes from an acorn, the only way to build a forest is from scratch. You start with one domain, the forest root. Then you can add a domain to an existing tree (a child domain) or add a tree to an existing forest (a tree root). Other domains will remain outside your forest forever.

Hard to believe? Well, it's true. Once you place domains in a forest, you cannot move them to another forest. You also can't delete them if they have any child domains. AD's forest structure is painfully inflexible, and that's true even if you're completely upgraded to Server 2008.

You Can't Graft nor Prune

So, suppose you were to create an AD domain named Bigfirm.com on one network. Then, on a completely separate network totally unconnected to Bigfirm.com's network, you create an AD domain named Eastcoast.Bigfirm.com. You cannot then attach the two networks and create a tearful reunion of parent and child domain. Nor could you build Consolidated.com and Bigfirm.com AD trees in isolation and then connect them, after the fact, to create a forest.

Attaching existing domains to existing trees or forests is called *grafting*, and it can't be done, at least not with the tools supplied by Microsoft. Thus, for example, if Exxon buys Mobil and Exxon already has a domain named Exxon.com and Mobil has a domain named Mobil.com, it's not possible to join them together in a tree with the supplied Microsoft Active Directory tools.

And don't get anxious if you aren't finding any third-party grating tools. Microsoft just doesn't support it. The biggest deterrent from creating a solution that grafts a domain to a forest is the schema. The schema that defines objects within Active Directory can also be modified, which we'll discuss in the "FSMOs and GCs" section. If two companies modify their schemas in different manners, it would be impossible to develop a method to merge the differences.

Pruning can't be done either. If Consolidated.com is part of the forest and its company is spun off from Bigfirm, the domain can't run independently from the rest of the domains. There's no little check box to make this happen.

You Must Be an Enterprise Admin

Another factor to remember is you can't be just an average domain administrator to build another domain or two into your forest. You may have thought you could rule supremely with your domain admin credentials but you are mistaken. You need to be a member of the Enterprise Admins group.

If you create an AD domain named Bigfirm.com and want to create a child domain in its tree named Ecoast.Bigfirm.com, then you sit down at the machine that you want to be the first DC in Ecoast.Bigfirm.com and create the Ecoast.Bigfirm.com domain, explaining to the domain controller promotion wizard that you want it to be part of an existing tree, Bigfirm.com. Before the wizard will go any further, it demands the name and password of an all-powerful enterprise admin for the Bigfirm.com domain. DCPromo will refuse to create a child domain unless it can contact the parent domain right at that moment and get permission. In the same way, if you want to create a second tree in a forest, then the wizard will require that you tell it the name and password of an enterprise admin account for the first tree. (What about the third tree or fourth tree—what account do *they* need to provide? From the second to the millionth tree in a forest, you have to provide an enterprise admin account from the first tree in the forest.)

Planning Your Active Directory Environment

Before you run DCPromo on the first domain controller, you need to consider the overall vision of the Active Directory network. In addition to the organizational unit structure, DNS namespace, domain controller placement, and replication, which are all part of a single-domain plan, you need to consider the need for multiple domains. Several factors lead to the correct decision. The following is a broad discussion of these factors.

Satisfying Political Needs

"That's *my* data, so I want it on *my* servers!" Because information has become the most important asset of many firms, occasionally parts of management have been reluctant to yield control of that information to a central IT group. And that isn't that irrational: if you were in charge of maintaining a five-million-person mailing list and if that list generated one half of your firm's sales leads, then you might well want to see that data housed on machines run by people who report directly to you.

Of course, on the other side of the story, there is the IT director who wants total control of all the servers in the building, and her reasoning is just as valid. You see, if a badly run server goes down and that failure affects the rest of the network, it's *her* head on the chopping block.

So, the department head or VP wants to control the iron and silicon that happens to be where his data lives, but the IT director who's concerned with making sure that all data is safe and that everything on the network plays well with others wants to control said data and network pieces. Who wins? It depends—and that's the "politics" part.

What does Active Directory do to ameliorate the political problems? Well, not as much as would be preferred—there is no "make the vice presidents get along well" wizard—but AD's variety of options for domain design gives the network designers the flexibility to build whatever kind of network structure they want. Got a relatively small organization that would fit nicely into a single domain but one VP with server ownership lust? No problem, give her an OU of her own within the domain. Got a firm with two moderately large offices with independent IT shops? Two domains and a trust relationship may be the answer. Because Windows Server 2008 R2 AD domain controllers are extremely parsimonious with WAN bandwidth in comparison with earlier versions, you might find that a single domain makes sense because it's easier to administer than two domains, but it's not impossible from a network bandwidth point of view. And bandwidth utilization is our next consideration.

Connectivity and Replication Issues

More and more companies don't just live in one place. They've purchased another firm across the country, and what once were two separate *local* area networks are now one firm with a WAN need. The design of Active Directory is affected by the available bandwidth across the WAN. The decision point on a single domain or multiple domains is determined by how fast the WAN link is. *Fast* is a relative term. Some designs can tolerate links of 1.5Mbps bandwidth, while others can't. This is primarily dependent on the size of the domain partition and how often it is modified.

If the WAN bandwidth can handle it, then hook the two offices up and create only one domain. A single-domain design is beneficial because it will be easier to administer. Each site will contain at least one domain controller that manages all the users and computers. If the WAN link is lost, the domain controller in each office can manage logins.

But those domain controllers must communicate with each other whenever something changes, such as when a user's password changes or when an administrator creates a new user account. This replication would occur across the WAN link.

If the link was not capable of supporting the replication traffic, you should consider multiple domains. Thus, the domain partition, the largest part of an Active Directory database, would be limited to the office location in which it resides. The configuration and schema partitions would be replicated across the WAN link, but it would not change frequently. This would greatly reduce the amount of replication traffic.

Active Directory allows you to tell it how it should replicate its information, but all parts of its database are subjected to be replicated. So, organizations with multiple locations need to consider whether the available bandwidth can support the replication traffic.

While on the subject, the global catalog (GC), which contains objects from every domain, is receiving changes from domains across the forest. The GC is essential for the user login process and Exchange Server, so it must be located near the users. Thus, every domain will replicate information to GCs across the WAN links to other sites as well. The available bandwidth may not support this traffic; therefore, separate forests may be the ticket.

Multiple Domains: When They Make Sense

When, then, should you use one domain divided into OUs, and when should you have different domains or even different forests? Well, in general, a rule of thumb is, "Don't use multiple domains unless you must." So, the real question is, "When do multiple domains make sense?" They make sense in a few cases:

Replication problems due to poor bandwidth This is probably the best reason. All domain controllers in a domain really need to be online and available to each other all the time. Replication between domain controllers must be consistent, otherwise the domain controllers fail. If the WAN link can't support the replication traffic, it's better to implement multiple domains. Think of it this way: suppose you had one office in Chicago and another in Sydney (Australia) with an expensive link between the two. Suppose also that you had 20,000 people in the Chicago office and 150 in the Sydney office. Every time the Chicago people changed their passwords, you'd have to replicate all that traffic over the costly WAN link to the domain controllers in Sydney. That's not a great use of WAN links. It'd be better to just build two domains.

Legal requirements There may be legal consideration that would require separate domains and possibly separate forests. Although you don't initially think that multiple forests are part of Active Directory design, there are situations where it is necessary.

Since you can't prune a tree from a forest, you have to consider what the organization is thinking on the topic of restructuring. A spin-off would need to be a separate forest to ensure a clean separation from the main Active Directory forest.

Some national laws may prevent sharing of information across national boundaries. The global catalog role lists private information for everyone in the forest. It also includes contacts with their information. Some countries may have a problem with that. Thus, separate forests may be required.

Organizations may have similar regulations for users. Control of specific user accounts must be contained within four walls of a certain building, or resources must be segregated with tighter security control. Given the legal mandates, a separate domain or forest may be needed. With the potential security intrusions within a forest, separate forests may be required here as well.

Politics We talked about this in the section "Satisfying Political Needs."

We just found it this way, honest! Your firm buys another firm, and you have to blend the two organizations. Third-party tools can help assimilate the new domain into your existing domain, but that'll be a big undertaking. You probably don't have the time to do that just at the moment. In that case, you're living in a multidomain world for a while. Multi*forest*, most likely. If you can, however, consider merging the two domains with a tool like Active Directory Migration Tool, which we'll cover in Chapter 24, "Migrating, Merging, and Modifying Your AD."

We know we've said it already, but we'll weigh in again with our opinion about multiple domains—or rather, why we'd avoid them. First, NT 4 multiple-domain enterprises were a major pain, because trusts tended to break. Supposedly this won't happen under Active Directory, and thus far we haven't seen it, but in general, the fewer "moving parts" in your enterprise, the better. Additionally, NT has had its growing pains over the years about security. What if the next NT security hole appears in AD trusts?

Some requirements for multiple domains have been alleviated by improvements in Windows Server 2008. Password policies can now be set for different users within a domain. In the past, if you wanted that, you were making separate domains. Branch offices dictated separate domains. The security boundaries were threatened because the domain controller was sitting underneath someone's desk. The entire domain could be comprised if the domain controller was stolen. A separate domain would limit the amount of compromised information. The read-only domain controller and password caching policies address this security threat.

The Case for an Empty Root

Refer again to Figure 23.1. In that figure, you see an extra tree root domain, Consolidated.com, in addition to Bigfirm.com, as well as Bigfirm.com's child domain Ecoast.Bigfirm.com. We did that to make the diagram "look" right— but we're used to seeing hierarchies end up at a single point.

In a tree, it's simple to see which domain is the root or top-level domain—Consolidated. com is the top of the Consolidated.com tree, and Bigfirm.com is the top of the Bigfirm.com tree. But when you build two trees (Consolidated.com and Bigfirm.com) into one forest, then which domain is the top, or root, domain? Perhaps there isn't a root and all trees are equal?

In an Active Directory forest built of several trees, there *is* a single-forest domain root. It's just not obvious which one it is.

So, suppose you came across an AD forest that contained just three domains—Bigfirm.com, Apex.com, and Consolidated.com. Which domain is the forest root? The answer isn't obvious because the three domains seem to sit at the same level. We don't know of a quick way to find out which domain is the forest root, but here's a slightly slower one. Remember that only the forest root domain contains a group named Enterprise Admins; that's how you'll find the root.

Start Active Directory Users and Computers (Start ➢ Programs ➢ Administrative Tools ➢ Active Directory Users and Computers). In the left pane of the MMC snap-in, you'll see an icon representing a domain; it looks like three tower PCs clustered together. Right-click that icon, and choose Find. In the resulting dialog box, there's a drop-down list box labeled In, which lets you tell the program which domain to search in; click it, and you'll see that you have the ability to search any one of your forest's domains. Choose one of your top-level domains. Then notice the field labeled Name; enter **enterprise***, and press Enter. If the search finds a group called Enterprise Admins, then you've found the root. If not, open the In list box, and try another domain until you locate the one with Enterprise Admins.

Suppose Bigfirm.com turned out to be the root domain in our Bigfirm/Ecoast/Consolidated example. There are probably three domains because there are, or were at some time, three different business entities that for some reason are one firm now. Who *cares* if the Bigfirm guys happen to be the forest root?

Well, the Consolidated and Ecoast guys, that's who—whether they know it or not. You see, members of the Enterprise Admins group, which happens to live in the Bigfirm domain, have powers in *every domain in the forest*. They're not members of the Domain Admins group in those domains, but they might as well be, because Enterprise Admins have Domain Admins–like powers everywhere.

That means that although in *theory* Bigfirm, Ecoast, and Consolidated have separate domains, with those nice, convenient security boundaries, in *practice* the Ecoast and Consolidated folks have to hope that the Bigfirm guys don't get the lust for power one day and decide to do something scary in the Ecoast or Consolidated domains. The answer? Don't create three domains; create four. The first domain—the root domain—should be some domain that you're never going to use—e-gobbledygook.com or something like that. Create one administrative account in that domain, including Enterprise Admins in it. Let the CIO create it and then have her write down that account name and password, stuff the paper on which she's written them into her safe, and use the *Sopranos* personnel-termination procedure on anyone who knows the password besides you and her. (Just kidding. But this *is* a powerful account, and you don't want any nonessential people getting access to it.) At the same time, create the other three domains. You'll need the CIO for a while. She'll have to type in the username and password for that enterprise admin account in order to create those three domains. Then you can put away the enterprise admin account, and you'll need it only now and then.

This idea of creating a first domain, populating it with only an account or two, and then doing nothing else with it, is called an *empty root* AD design.

Some firms create an empty root domain even if it's just a one-domain enterprise in case it acquires other companies at some time in the future. It's not a bad bit of bet-hedging, and we recommend it to some. Of course, the downside of it is that you need to have a DC or, better yet, two DCs, sitting around running, doing nothing to support the root domain, and each of them will need a copy of Server 2003 or Windows Server 2008 depending on the forest level you want. But, again, it may not be a bad investment——an empty root is one case where we'd break our single-domain-preferred preference.

🌐 Real World Scenario

THE CASE FOR TWO DOMAIN CONTROLLERS

It's a good practice in any environment to address availability and disaster recovery for services and systems. The multimaster replication model provided with Active Directory makes these concerns a piece of cake. All you need to do is install another replica domain controller in a site for availability or in another site for disaster recovery.

It's a *best practice* to add at least two domain controllers into an empty forest root domain. Although it may not have any users or resources in it, it still is an irreplaceable (literally) part of your Active Directory environment. It needs to be highly available and able to withstand a disaster. If it is supported by only one domain controller, that domain controller is going to do a lot of work. If you lose it and can't restore it, you probably will be calling Microsoft premier support and then polishing your resume.

Consider the impact of the solitary empty root domain controller:

◆ All Kerberos authentication traffic goes through the forest root domain. Remember, it is "friends with everyone," specifically, the root of each tree.

◆ Time synchronization is centralized on the PDC emulator of the forest root, which happens to be the first domain controller by default.

◆ Two FSMO roles, domain naming master and schema master, reside in this domain and on that sole DC.

So, if that solitary empty root domain controller goes down, the rest of the forest will see the effect. You can't make a replica domain controller without one from which to replicate, so you will be stuck performing a cold-iron restore. And you can't build a replacement domain controller from scratch using DCPromo. You may have to rebuild the Active Directory environment from scratch and migrate users and computers to it if a restore is not available.

Active Directory Design Pointers

The idea of this chapter is to give you an overall idea of how AD's pieces work. Earlier we discussed the primary decision areas for an Active Directory design. We strongly suggest that you peruse the rest of this book before starting to build your AD structure, because the AD *permeates* Windows-based networks. But the following sections provide a few hints on how to get started designing your AD structure.

Examine Your WAN Topology

Domain controllers in a domain must replicate among themselves in order to keep domain information consistent across the domain. DCs need not be connected exactly 24/7—you *could* just dial connections between branch offices and the home office every day or so and then try to force replication to occur, although that's not simple and may lead to problems down the road—but on the whole you'll find that domains work best if they have a constant end-to-end connection. If you have an area that's poorly or sporadically served by your WAN connections, perhaps it's best to make it a separate domain or a separate forest.

Lay Out Your Sites

Once you know where the WAN connections are, list the sites that you'll have, name them, and figure out which machines go in what sites. Also, document the nature of their connections— speed and cost—to assist Active Directory in using the intersite bandwidth wisely.

Figure Out Which Existing Domains to Merge and Merge Them

You'll probably want to reduce the number of domains in your enterprise. One way to do that would be to merge resource domains into a master domain. The idea here would be that you first upgrade the master domain to Server 2008 and then merge other domains into that master domain as organizational units using the Active Directory Migration Tool (ADMT) or whatever other migration tools you might buy. Merging domains and using the ADMT are topics discussed in detail in Chapter 24.

What Needs an OU, and What Needs a Domain?

As you read earlier, you can divide up enterprises by breaking them into multiple domains. In addition, you can create a single domain and use organizational units to parcel out administrative control, or you can do any combination of those.

This is partially a political question, but you can get a head start by looking at the perceived needs of the organization. Is administration centralized or decentralized? Who manages user accounts? Who manages the resources such as file servers? Do the company's divisions work together closely, or is there not very much collaboration?

The choice of OUs or multiple domains is to divide the network to the controlling forces so they can administrate it. OUs provide particular admins to control the computer, user or group accounts that they are responsible for. So if admins have just this need, organizational units is the way to go. The multiple domain choice is dependent on who will manage the domain controllers. If there is a separate group of admins who will control the domain controllers apart from the forest root domain, the additional domain would be justified.

From a technical point of view, there are really only a few reasons to use more than one domain, as you've read. The biggest reason is replication traffic. If you have two large domains connected only by a slow WAN link, then you may find that it makes sense to keep them as separate domains. But think carefully about it—Active Directory is very efficient at using WAN links for domain replication traffic.

DEVELOP NAMES FOR YOUR DOMAINS/TREES

Active Directory allows a wider variety of domain names, but sometimes you can have too much of a good thing with too *many* options. If you're going multidomain, how will the domains fit together? Do you divide geographically, by division, or by function? Where are the lines of control in the organization now?

It's important to understand that the names of domains are primarily political. With the exception of the parent-child trust relation, there is hardly any other technical impact concerning the name. The name will occasionally be reflected to the user through technology such as domain-based Distributed File Systems (DFSs) and depending on how they log on to computers. So, because the name will be seen by users, management might care what the domain is named.

GET THE DNS INFRASTRUCTURE READY

Once you know the names of your domains, you need to map out the DNS infrastructure. Know which servers will support it. Plan how clients will be able to resolve internal names and external names. Remember the following:

◆ Plan a DNS zone whose name matches your AD domain's, and don't be afraid to use an imaginary top-level domain.

◆ It's recommended you don't use your externally registered DNS names.

◆ Although Windows Server 2008 R2 sets up the DNS infrastructure automatically, it will be rare that you will be starting from scratch. If the DNS namespaces are already in place, ensure the DNS server supports dynamic DNS updates and service resource records. You needn't use a Microsoft DNS server, but it's not a bad idea, particularly with Active Directory integrated zones.

◆ If you have to use your company's registered DNS names, split-brain DNS is the *right* idea to protect your zones from external prying eyes for 99 percent of the AD.

OVERALL AD DESIGN ADVICE

There's a lot to consider in building your AD, and only you know what your organization needs and wants—we can't pass along a standard one-size-fits-all design for AD. But overall, remember the following:

◆ Use sites to control bandwidth and replication.

◆ Use organizational units to create islands of users and/or computers, which you can then delegate administrative control over.

◆ Use domains to solve replication problems, security, legal and possible political problems.

Use forests to create completely separate network systems. If, for example, your enterprise had a subsidiary that wasn't completely trusted (in the human sense, not the AD sense) and you were worried that the automatic trust relationships (in the AD sense) created by common membership in a forest might lead to unwanted security links, then make them separate forests. The value of separate forests is that there is no security relationship at all between two forests unless you explicitly create the relationship using a trust relationship.

Creating Multiple Domains

After the hard thinking is accomplished and the boss buys the idea of how you want to implement Active Directory, it is high time to put your ideas on the street. If not in production, you can at least deploy your desired Active Directory structure in a lab. So you need to know the straightforward steps for building multiple domains.

The process of creating a new domain is similar to creating the first domain. Beforehand, the domain name must be determined. Since changing a domain name is a hugely intrusive process, it needs to be locked down as in "There's no changing it." Like the initial domain, the new domain controller needs to be prepared to support Active Directory. It must also be able to resolve the forest root domain names through DNS. Then you'll run DCPromo to create the new domain.

Naming Multidomain Structures

Real-world experience has shown that in large enterprises a hierarchy of domains works best. In Active Directory, we call this a *tree structure* despite that computer trees tend to have their roots up top in the air and their "leaves" at bottom. (We know, some of the "back to nature" analogy isn't consistent.) Microsoft designed AD to use DNS as a naming system, and DNS is hierarchical in nature anyway, so Active Directory exploits this happy coincidence and encourages you to build multidomain enterprises as hierarchies.

The multiple-domain namespaces must be supported by DNS. The preferred method is letting DCPromo handle this. Child domains, since they have the same last name as an existing parent domain, have a DNS namespace. However, the Active Directory Wizard will automatically configure the new domain controllers to support the child domain's namespace. A new tree's namespace doesn't need to be created either because the domain controller promotion will automatically configure DNS to support it. However, the prospective domain controller needs to resolve names of the forest root domain to execute the new tree creation without error.

If the DNS environment is established beforehand, it will need to support service resource records and dynamic DNS updates.

YOU CAN'T ALWAYS GET WHAT YOU WANT

Although the domain's NetBIOS name's importance is diminished, you will still see this name throughout the network. Prior to running through DCPromo, double check the NetBIOS name is available. The utility will do that too. If it isn't available, the utility will generate something else. If you are not aware of the name's availability, you could be stuck with a misnamed domain.

We have seen test domains assigned with the desired NetBIOS name. Thus when the real domain is built, the conflicting names becomes readily apparent and stops the process in its tracks.

Preparing the DC for the Second Domain

For our Bigfirm example, you'll now set up the first DC in another domain—Ecoast.Bigfirm.com. As we mentioned earlier, a big change from Windows Server 2003 to Windows Server 2008 R2 is the requirement to set up DNS for a domain. In earlier Windows versions, you would need to get DNS ready prior to building the domain. The DCPromo process will identify the need to build DNS and run through the steps for you.

After the creation of the child domain, you will see the following:

◆ An Active Directory integrated zone on the new domain controller for the child domain name, such as Ecoast.Bigfirm.com

◆ A forwarder DNS server listing on this domain controller for the Bigfirm.com DNS servers

◆ A delegated DNS subdomain on Bigfirm.com to the new domain controller

First, set up a machine that will be the domain controller for Ecoast.Bigfirm.com. Call it Ec1. Ecoast.Bigfirm.com. It will need to be able to support Active Directory for the given number of users and computers in your organization. In a production environment, you should plan to build at least two domain controllers for the domain. The second domain controller will be a replica of the first one and provide fault tolerance of the domain database.

When you log on as an administrator, the Initial Configuration Tasks window pops up. This lists the typical steps for getting a server up and running. Step 1 lists the Configure Networking link. This opens the Network control panel where you can change the IP configurations. In most networks, IPv4 will be used. So, assign it an appropriate static IP address, and assign its DNS server as one for Bigfirm.com. It will need this to resolve the Bigfirm.com domain controller's IP addresses. Windows Server 2008 R2 also installs IPv6 by default with a dynamically assigned address. Although it doesn't "hurt" anything in lab environments, network admins need to decide to keep it installed or to assign a static IP address to the configurations. Otherwise, DCPromo will kick up the warning shown in Figure 23.2.

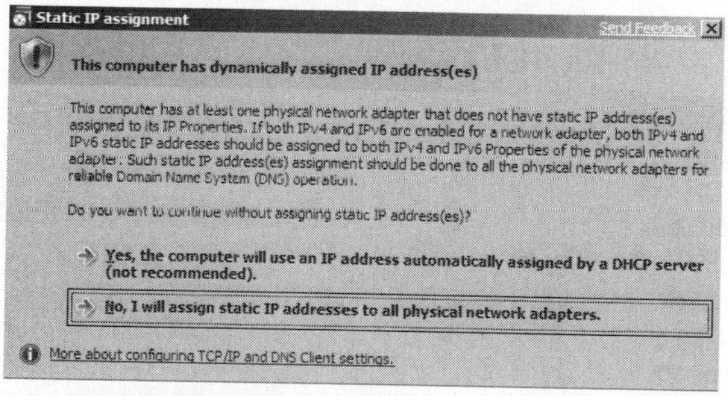

FIGURE 23.2
DCPromo
warning because
of a dynamic
IPv6 address

Step 3 of the Initial Configuration Tasks window leads you to add Roles and Features. For Active Directory, you need to install the Active Directory Domain Services role. Just as you did with the first domain controller for Bigfirm.com, the Add Role Wizard allows this role to be selected but not with the DNS role at the same time. It will install all the binaries required to set up a domain controller including the .NET Framework and the DNS service. It will not run DCPromo. This must be performed separately.

Prior to running DCPromo, ensure you have the logon credentials for an account in the Enterprise Admins group.

Creating a Second Domain

After the role is installed, you can push on with installing the new domain. Logged on as an administrator on Ec1.Ecoast.Bigfirm.com, run DCPromo.

DCPromo starts out as before. It first allows you to opt for the Advanced mode installation. It gives more details and choices for the process.

The wizard notifies you of the tightened security policy concerning cryptography algorithms. The take-away of this is "research, plan, and test." Production workstations and NAS servers may be impacted when part of this domain. Be certain you know what your systems will do within a Windows Server 2008 R2 domain.

On the next page, as shown in Figure 23.3, you tell the wizard that you want to create a new domain in an existing forest but not to create a new tree. The check box "Create a new domain tree root instead of a new child domain" must remain deselected.

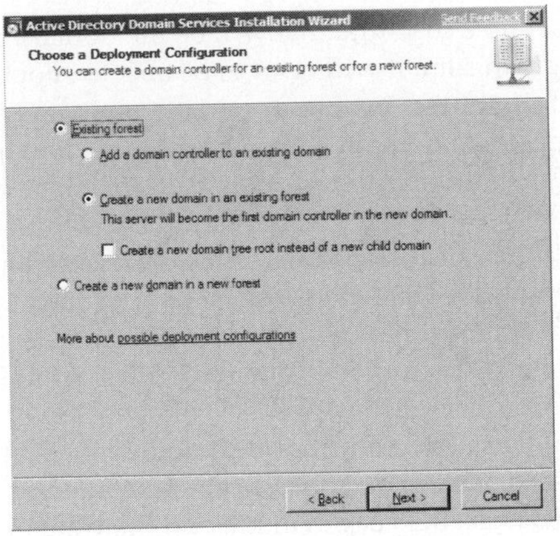

FIGURE 23.3
Choosing a deployment configuration for a new domain in an existing forest

Before you go any further, DCPromo asks you to log in. This requires listing the forest domain and credentials for an account in the Enterprise Admins group, as shown in Figure 23.4. Here, we've filled in the administrator's login information; by default this is a member of the Enterprise Admin group. DCPromo pauses a bit to authenticate the account.

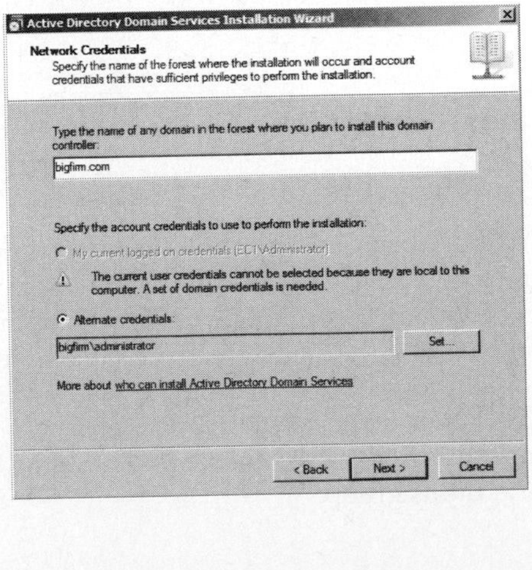

FIGURE 23.4
Establishing credentials for creating a child domain

Once you've filled that in, click Next, and the screen in Figure 23.5 appears. You set the names of the parent and child domains here. DCPromo now needs to know which domain to add a child to and what to call the child. You can fill in that the parent's name is Bigfirm.com, or you can click the Browse button and choose from the domains in the forest. The child domain will be named Ecoast.Bigfirm.com, but DCPromo just wants you to type in **Ecoast** for the child name, and it then assembles it and the parent domain into the complete Ecoast.Bigfirm.com for the child domain.

FIGURE 23.5

Naming the child domain

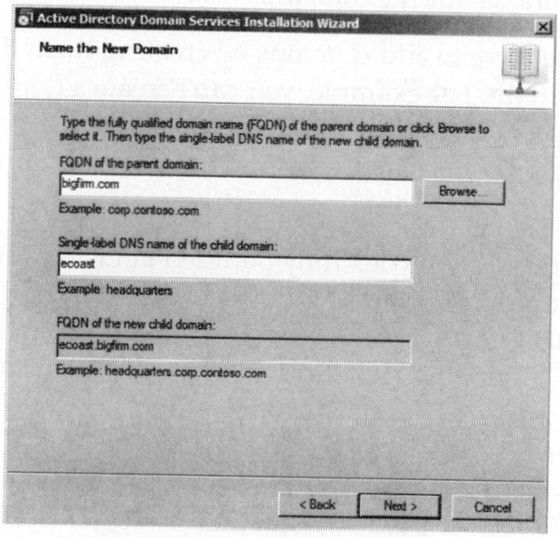

The Bigfirm.com domain got the down-level name (or NT 4 or NetBIOS name, take your pick; they all mean the same thing) of Bigfirm. But how do you name the child domains with the more complex names? Just take out the periods and take the leftmost 15 characters? Do some kind of truncated name with tildes on the end, in the same way that long filenames get converted to 8.3 names? Well, you can actually give your domains any down-level name that you like, but the default ones are just the leftmost portion of the domain name, as you see in Figure 23.6. Because Ecoast is the leftmost portion of the domain name, the domain gets the down-level name Ecoast by default.

From this point on, you'll just answer DCPromo's questions as you did for the first domain, so we'll spare you the rest of the wizard pages.

FIGURE 23.6

NetBIOS name for child domain

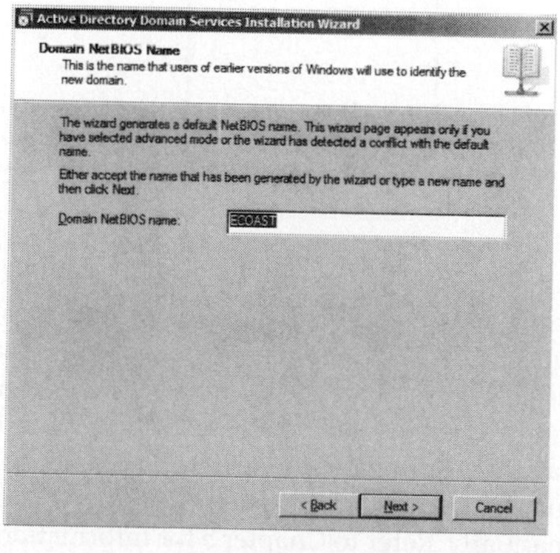

Before leaving this topic, we'll make a few points about using DCPromo to build domains. DCPromo is kind of rigid about the order in which you create domains:

1. The first domain that you create in a forest is the forest root domain, and there's no changing that.

2. You should create replica domain controllers for the new domain. This provides fault tolerance for the domain.

3. You have to add domains by creating them through DCPromo in relation to the existing domain. For example, you can't create a domain Green.com and another Yellow.com separately and then decide later to merge them into a forest. Instead, you must first create Green.com as the first domain in a forest and then create Yellow.com as the first domain in a new tree but in an existing forest.

After the reboot, your fully outfitted Ec1.Ecoast.Bigfirm.com should be examined. Check its IP configurations with **ipconfig /all**, and verify it is listing itself as the DNS server (::1 for IPv6 and 127.0.0.1 for IPv4). Open the DNS management console on the new domain controller, as shown in Figure 23.7. Look for the Ecoast.Bigfirm.com zone listing the domain controller Ec1 as the name server. The Ecoast.Bigfirm.com zone should include the DC's A record and the domain's SRV records registered in it.

FIGURE 23.7
The DNS zone for
the new domain

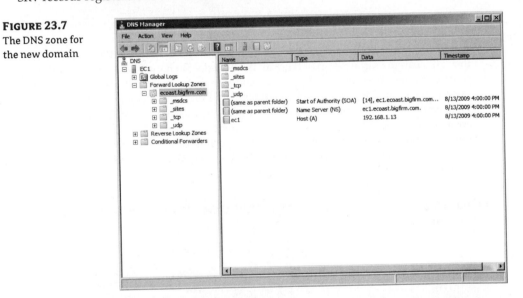

Check the properties of the DNS server; you'll see there is at least one forwarder listing for Bf1.Bigfirm.com or the domain controllers of the parent domain, as shown in Figure 23.8.

Also check Bf1's DNS management console to make sure that delegation of the Ecoast sub-domain is added, as shown in Figure 23.9. Additional checks include the same for building any domain controller such as the creation of database files, the SYSVOL folder, and services.

Once again, Windows Server 2008 R2 automatically configures the DNS infrastructure to support the new domains. If things aren't flying as expected, you may have to configure the DNS integration manually. Refer to Chapter 5 for information about doing this and other DNS issues.

FIGURE 23.8
DNS forwarders on new domain controller

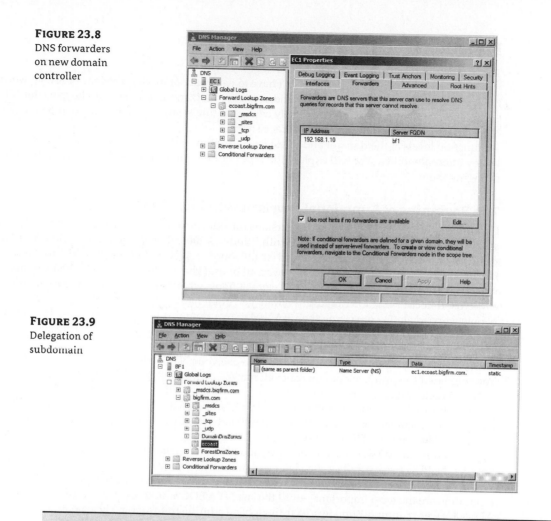

FIGURE 23.9
Delegation of subdomain

MISSPELLED DOMAINS

Misspelling a domain during this procedure is possible. In writing this book, we have created the Bigifrm.com domain and the Bigfrim.com domain in our virtual lab environment. Since we weren't paying attention, the wizard accepted the typing and got the "pencil" flying. So, when building a new domain in a production environment, have at least two sets of eyes on the monitor, and double-check what was typed in the summary screen.

If the name is still misspelled after the creation of the first DC, you can run through DCPromo again on the same server. In this case, it will identify that the server is a domain controller. It will assume you want to remove Active Directory from it. The only option it will provide is whether this is the last domain controller in the domain. For this case, it is. The eraser end of the pencil gets busy and cleanly removes the instance of Active Directory from this server and the environment.

Any other solution would be intrusive to Active Directory such as the domain rename process or destructive such as shutting down and removing the operating system.

Functional Levels

Too bad previous versions of NT weren't a flop.

If they *had* been flops, then we wouldn't have to worry about mixing versions of NT. However, NT worked pretty good, and Microsoft understood organizations with skin in the game for NT weren't going to jump ship for a completely new operating system. So, it had to build on top of the NT technology to support upgrades and coexistence.

Function levels at the domain and forest levels are the configuration options to manage legacy interoperability. We will explore the types of function levels and the considerations in changing them.

The Beginning of Functional Levels in Windows 2000

Combining different Active Directory versions introduces some problems as to what ADs can and can't do. When Microsoft came out with Windows 2000, then it might have said, "You can't use 2000-based AD domains until you `fdisk` all your NT 4 DCs," but that would have been a marketing disaster and would have annoyed all of us. (That's what we meant when we said that it was too bad that earlier versions of NT weren't flops; when NT came out, in theory it followed a Microsoft networking OS called LAN Manager, but it had a tiny market share, so very few people worried about converting their LAN Manager domains to NT 3.1 domains. That's not the story for Windows Server 2008 R2, however, because previous Microsoft operating systems were hugely successful.)

So, Microsoft said that you could continue to use your NT 4–based BDCs in Active Directory. You upgraded the primary domain controller to Windows 2000 and that 2000 box created an Active Directory domain, but it also continued to work with the old NT 4–based BDCs. Clearly, the NT 4 boxes don't understand (for example) OUs, and so the NT 4–based BDCs couldn't really be full members of the DC family if the 2000-based DCs exercised a lot of their new-to-Windows-2000 powers. The result was mixed mode.

A mixed-mode AD was one that had a Windows 2000 system acting as a domain controller and holding the PDC role (or, rather, the PDC emulator role) and any number of BDCs running NT 4. Windows 2000–based ADs would not exercise a few powers—universal groups and multimaster replication are the most important—until the last NT 4 BDC was shut off. Once all of a 2000-based AD's DCs were running Windows 2000, though, an administrator could click a button in Active Directory Users and Computers that would shift the domain into native mode, and at that point a 2000-based AD could strut its stuff.

We'll stress that all you have to upgrade to go to native mode are the DCs. All other systems could be NT 4 systems for all that a 2000-based AD cares. Native vs. mixed mode is only a matter of the OSs on the DCs. As you'll see, that's the case with 2003 and 2008's "modes" as well.

Domain Functional Levels

In Windows 2000–based ADs, there were only two possible conditions: either a population of DCs that were all 2000-based or a population of DCs that included both 2000 and NT 4—that's why there were only two modes. But ADs that include Server 2003 or 2008 can have several possible combinations of DCs, each with their own mode. (Server 2003's preferred term is *functional level*; we sometimes write it as *domain functional level* to distinguish it from *forest* functional levels that you'll meet soon.)

You change a domain's functional level by opening Active Directory Users and Computers and right-clicking the icon representing the domain. Choose Raise Domain Functional Level, and you'll see a dialog box like Figure 23.10.

FIGURE 23.10
Viewing a domain's
functional level

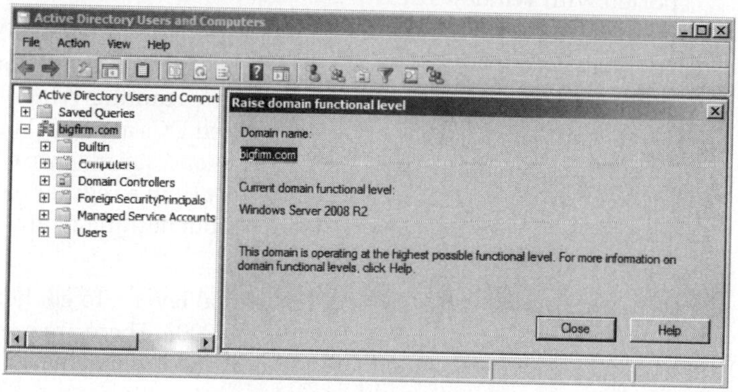

In this case, the domain is at something called Windows Server 2008 R2 domain functional level, which is described as the highest domain functional level available. Also, the dialog box doesn't provide the option of changing it. Functional levels can be changed upward and not downward. In this case, it's as far as we can go with this domain.

Changing the domain functional level should be performed with caution and consideration. Since it is a one-way operation, you need to ensure all domain controllers within the domain can meet that functional level. Otherwise, a legacy domain controller can be left out of the loop, per se. It will not get the proper replication and end up with stale or incompatible data within its database.

Here's what you get from each functional level:

Windows 2000 mixed domain functional level This is a domain that can have some DCs running Windows Server 2003, others Windows 2000 Server, and still others NT 4 Server. This still works if you're running only 2003 and 2000 or just 2003, but in those cases you'll want to raise the functional level to enable your AD to use as many features as possible. This is basically just Windows 2000's mixed mode but with 2003 servers added. Newly built AD domains, domains upgraded from 2000-based mixed mode ADs, and domains directly upgraded from NT 4 domains start in this functional level. Even if your network consists of a forest composed of one domain, which in turn contains just one DC and that DC is running Server 2003, it'll be in Windows 2000 mixed domain functional level. Like 2000's mixed mode domains, these domains lack multimaster replication and universal groups. They also cannot use something called *SID histories*, which we'll cover in Chapter 24, and they cannot convert distribution groups (email lists) to security groups (that is, regular old groups), and vice versa. Notice that Windows Server 2008 R2 does not list this as a supported function level.

Windows 2000 native domain functional level This is a domain with only 2000-based or newer DCs. When you upgrade a 2000-based AD, then you get this functional level, or you get it if you raise the functional level yourself. You can't use 2000 native functional level if you have any NT 4–based DCs. Systems in 2000 native domain functional level can use universal groups, group nesting, multimaster replication, and SID histories, and they can convert between distribution and security groups. They really only miss out on one thing: they cannot rename domains, or at least they can't use the new-to-2003 simplified domain renaming feature. This functional level has the most impact on administration. The use of universal groups and group nesting are very valuable features for administering groups. This is supported with Windows Server 2008 R2.

Windows Server 2003 interim domain functional level   We honestly don't know much about this because we haven't found much of a use for it. You can raise your domain to this level only if none of your domain's DCs are running Windows 2000. NT 4 BDCs are OK, and of course Windows Server 2003–based DCs are fine. You can only get to this functional level with a separate tool from Microsoft, and as far as we can see, you get nothing out of an interim functional level that you don't get from a regular old 2000 mixed domain functional level. (Well, there are a few small things but nothing of any significance.) Again, this is not supported by Windows Server 2008.

Windows Server 2003 domain functional level   To get here, you need to have all your DCs in the domain running Windows Server 2003. There are several exotic features here. These changes don't change your job significantly. You may never see them working for you:

◆ Domain rename. See Chapter 24.

◆ User and computer containers can be redirected.

◆ Constrained delegation.

◆ Selective authorization. This is related to trusts.

◆ Logon timestamp update.

Windows Server 2008 domain functional level   Again, you need to have all your domain controllers at this version. However, there is a caveat in the Windows Server 2008 R2 help. Specifically, if you plan to add earlier versions as domain controllers such as Windows Server 2008 or 2003, you could set the domain function level to this value. Here are some features of this level:

◆ DFS replication support. In Chapter 11, "File Shares Made Better: DFS and DFS-N," you read about the improved DDFS replication. These improvements can be applied to the SYSVOL folder as well.

◆ Advanced Encryption Services (AES 128 and 256).

◆ Track last interactive logon information for users on workstations.

◆ Password policies.

Windows Server 2008 R2 domain function level   Yes, even this version has its own domain function level. Its sole feature is authentication mechanism assurance. This modifies the security token for users passed to member servers for access to resources. Basically, it notifies that the user was authenticated with a certificate instead of username/password credentials. Applications and resources then can be configured to grant permission based on this information.

There's another important reason to get to 2003 functional level or above. You see, you can't upgrade your *forest* functional level until all the domains in the forest are at 2003 domain functional level.

Forest Functional Levels

Windows 2000 only had different kinds of domains because that's all that NT 4 had—domains. But both Windows 2000–based ADs and 2003-based ADs have forests, leading inevitably to different functional levels for forests.

When you upgrade DCs or domains in an existing forest or if you create a new forest, then 2003 assumes for safety's sake that not all DCs and domains are entirely 2003-based, and so it will not stretch its wings to use all the new capabilities that 2003 offers. To get all those abilities, you must shift the forest from its default level, which is called Windows 2000 forest functional level, to the all-2003 setting, which is Windows Server 2003 forest functional level.

You raise a forest's functional level with Active Directory Domains and Trusts (Start ➢ Administrative Tools ➢ Active Directory Domains and Trusts). Right-click the icon in the left pane labeled Active Directory Domains and Trusts, and you'll see Figure 23.11. Notice you don't right-click the domain icon. You'll get Raise Domain Function Level when right-clicking the domain icon.

FIGURE 23.11
Raising a forest's functional level

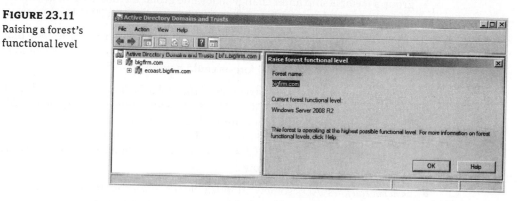

In Figure 23.11, in this example, the forest functional level is as high as it can go just as with the domain functional level. In addition, you can't switch downward on the functional level.

You can't go to Windows Server 2003 forest functional level unless every single DC in every single domain in the forest is running Windows 2003 or higher. But think about that: doesn't that mean that all your domains must be in 2003 domain functional level before Domains and Trusts lets you raise the forest functional level? No, it doesn't, as it turns out:

1. When you open the dialog box in Figure 23.11, then you'll get the screen that you see in that figure, or you'll get a message that says, "You can't go to 2003 level," and tells you (or, rather, offers to generate a text file telling you) exactly which DCs must be upgraded before you can go to 2003 forest functional level.

2. When you right-click AD Domains and Trusts, the forest does a quick census of its list of DCs:

   ◆ If they're all 2003-based DCs, then you get the option to raise the forest functional level.

   ◆ If not, you get the option to see which ones must be upgraded.

3. That leads to what seemed, to us anyway, an odd thing: you can raise your forest's functional level even *if* the domains are all set at Windows 2000 native domain functional level—they needn't be at Windows Server 2003 domain functional level.

As it turns out, this is something of a convenience. Provided that all your DCs are running 2003 or 2008 and you raise your forest's functional level, then AD Domains and Trusts also automatically raises the functional level of all your domains to 2003 domain functional level.

So, what do you get from this improved functional level? You get several items that we've discussed elsewhere but that we'll summarize here:

Windows Server 2003 forest function level   This contains the following:

♦ *Transitive forest trusts*: One trust makes every domain in each of two forests trust each other...but only if both forests are at 2003 forest functional level.

♦ *More flexible group membership replication*: 2000's old problem about "if you change a group's membership and I change that same group membership at about the same time, then one of our changes will be lost" goes away in a 2003-level forest.

♦ *Better intersite routing*: 2003 saw a completely massive rewrite of the code that handles site-to-site replication, with the result that where 2000-based forests would fall apart at about 200 sites, 2003-based forests could handle up to 5,000 sites.

♦ *GC fixes*: Any change to the structure of the global catalog, such as the type that usually happens when you install an AD-aware application, causes GCs on a 2000-level forest to completely panic; they dump their entire databases and rebuild them from scratch, causing massive replication loads over the network. 2003-level forests are much smarter, because their GCs focus only on the changes to the database, rather than restarting from square one.

♦ *Schema redefines*: AD's somewhat inflexible schema structure loosens up a bit on a 2003-level forest. You still can't delete or undo schema changes, but the schema manages itself to ensure that you'll never have one AD-aware app accidentally step on another AD-aware app's schema changes.

Windows Server 2008 forest function level   There's actually nothing special about this level. So, there is no impetus to switch to this.

Windows Server 2008 R2 forest function level: Active Directory DS Recycle Bin   This offers the sweet ability to restore Active Directory objects while Active Directory DS is running. "It's about time!"

As anyone who lived through an initial AD rollout under 2000 knows, the road to native mode was sometimes long, and we're sure that'll be the case when moving a forest to Windows Server 2008 R2 forest functional level. But once there, it's worth it. As we've observed elsewhere, you *paid* for this stuff...you may as well get what you paid for.

FSMOs and GCs

Thus far, you've seen how to set up AD multiple domains but there's more to AD planning than that. Making an AD run also requires knowing about the following:

Operations masters and global catalogs   These are particular functions that some DCs must assume. Placement of these roles need to considered to ensure proper Active Directory functioning.

Time synchronization   Believe it or not, AD simply will not run unless all the AD members and DCs all agree on what time it is to within five minutes. This is controlled by one of the operations masters, namely, the PDC emulator of the forest root domain.

In the next few sections, we'll take on this kind of intermediate-level AD planning and operation. First, we'll talk about operations masters.

Multimaster vs. Single-Master Replication

As we've mentioned, one of the things that differentiates AD domains and DCs from NT 4 and earlier domains is *multimaster* replication rather than *single-master* replication. Under multimaster, *any* DC can accept changes to the user account, so a local Tulsa admin could start up an administration tool such as Active Directory Users and Computers and make a change to a user's account on an available domain controller. Because any DC can accept changes, any DC is then a "master," which is why it's called *multimaster*.

But Not Everything Is Multimaster

In general, the Active Directory tries to carry this notion of decentralized control throughout its structure. In general, all DCs are equal, but, to paraphrase George Orwell, some DCs are more equal than others. Those DCs are the ones that serve in any of five roles called either *operations master* or *flexible single master of operations* roles. By the way, no one says *flexible single master of operations*; it gets made into an acronym to FSMO and is pronounced "fizz-moe." Strictly speaking, FSMO was the phrase that Microsoft used through most of Windows 2000's development process, but it renamed FSMOs to *operations masters* late in the beta process. As a result, you'll hear some people say *operations master*, but the FSMO name has stuck with many, even now in the days of Windows Server 2008 R2, probably because it's quicker to say "fizz-moe" (and more fun). So, for example, the phrases *domain-naming operations master* and *domain-naming FSMO* refer to the same thing.

Certain jobs in the AD just need to be centralized, and so we end up with FSMOs. For example, take the job of creating new domains. Suppose you have a domain Bigfirm.com and someone decides to set up a new domain controller and thereby create a child domain, Ecoast.Bigfirm.com. Creating a domain causes AD to build a lot of data structures—a domain for Ecoast.Bigfirm.com, more work for the global catalog, changes to the overall forest AD database, and so on. Now imagine that two people both try to create a new domain named Ecoast.Bigfirm.com at roughly the same time. That could be a nightmare—the parent domain would be receiving conflicting requests to modify the AD database, there might be potential security issues, and it might keep the whole forest from functioning.

Domain Naming: A FSMO Example

To avoid the situation of duplicate names and to oversee the forest structure, Microsoft developed one DC to act as a sort of central clearinghouse for new domain creation, and whenever you attempt to create a new child domain or new domain tree, DCPromo stops and locates the one DC in the entire forest that is the "keeper of the domain names." That DC is said to be the *domain-naming*

FSMO or *domain-naming operations master*. If DCPromo on the new would-be DC cannot establish contact with the domain-naming FSMO, then it flatly refuses to go any further.

Remember, even if you have a worldwide enterprise with dozens of domains, hundreds of offices all around the world, thousands of domain controllers, and hundreds of thousands of workstations, there is one and only one computer that serves as the domain-naming FSMO. If it were, for example, in the Okinawa office and you were in the New York office sitting at a server trying to create a new domain in the forest, then your computer would be unable to proceed until it contacted the Okinawa computer and got its OK on building the new domain.

Why Administrators Must Know About FSMOs

In general, you won't think about the DCs that act as FSMOs in your forest much at all. However, you *do* need to do a little planning about which DCs will be FSMOs, and you need to know how to assign a particular FSMO role to a particular DC.

That reminds us, you *do* have to manage the FSMO roles by hand. The AD automatically picks a particular DC to act in each FSMO role—the first DC that you install—but it's not bright enough to move those roles around. So, for example, consider this scenario. Your company decides to play around with AD and sets up its first DC on a "junk" machine in a test lab—say, the old 750MHz system with 254MB of RAM. They see that AD works pretty well, so you start buying some "big guns" to be the production DCs. They roll out these big DCs, and things seem to work pretty well.

They work well until one Monday, folks come to work, and the AD apparently still thinks it's the weekend because AD is not working. Administrators find that they can't create new user accounts or join machines to a domain. Someone has tried to install Exchange Server, but it complains about not having the authorization to change something called the *schema*. The Cleveland office was scheduled to create a new child domain, but that's refused, too. The remaining NT 4 domain controllers—perhaps the firm has decided to run in mixed mode for a while—complain that they can't find the PDC, and account changes like password resets are clearly not getting to those NT 4 backup domain controllers.

What happened? Well, someone was playing around in the lab that weekend and needed an extra machine with which to do some experimenting. The 750MHz system was just sitting there, still running Server 2003 and acting as an AD domain controller. But it wasn't really relevant anymore, the weekend noodler reasoned, because the firm now has several dozen big DCs running. So, the experimenter wiped the hard disk on the 750MHz system and put Linux on it.

You see, by default, AD assigns the FSMO roles to the first DC that you install. In this little story, that 750MHz system quietly served a very important role. But now it can't. And AD isn't smart enough to figure that out and then to nominate a new computer in that role. You might say that our "sparkling" forest has lost its "fizz-moe." It's now your job to transfer the FSMO roles to other DCs.

That's why you care about FSMOs.

Global Catalogs

We've mentioned global catalog servers throughout the chapter. So, you might expect that with their hype they would fall into this FSMO category. Well, they don't really, since they are not "single." Although you start out with one, you can enable other domain controllers to assume the role. However, like the FSMO roles, it is important to know which domain controllers have the role and where they are located.

Real World Scenario

DECOMMISSIONING WITH DCPROMO

This little story about the 750MHz domain controller is not unrealistic. We've encountered situations where an uninformed admin wiped away the hard drives of a failed domain controller since they already had a couple replica domain controllers keeping the domain going. "It was old anyway." It just happened to be the first DC of the domain.

There *is* one case where AD automatically moves the FSMO role—when you use DCPromo to demote a domain controller that holds one or more FSMO roles into a member server. DCPromo finds another appropriate domain controller and moves the FSMO roles to that DC. In that case, decommissioning the Pentium 750 would have resulted in no problems. So, perhaps the best advice here is, "When you want to get rid of a domain controller, always use DCPromo to decommission it before fdisking it."

If you run into a disaster and can't recover the system, there are methods, discussed next, to move the FSMOs from that failed domain controller.

For starters, the first one is the first domain controller you build. Since all the necessary roles are required from the get-go, the FSMOs and the global catalog role are slammed onto that first server. So, with the previous example, the ghost of the 750MHz workstation will rear its ugly head when the global catalog is needed in the logon process. Errors in the other domain controllers and workstation event logs will probably give you a subtle hint of this condition.

The global catalog has a "little bit of everything." It has a subset of the properties or attributes for every object in the forest. Remember, an object includes users, contacts, groups, computers, and other entities described in Active Directory. So, all domain controllers that are GCs will have personal information for every user in the forest even if the global catalog isn't in the same domain as the user.

How many GCs are necessary? Typically it is dictated by how many sites you have. There are many uses for GCs. The most prominent is assisting in the logon process. If all users are assigned user principal names (UPNs) such as bdavis@bigfirm.com within a multiple domain forest, the domain controllers need to resolve to which domain they actually belong. The global catalog provides this information. So, it would be nice if a global catalog were in a site where the users are logging on to the domain.

Since a global catalog has all of this information, Active Directory–aware applications like Exchange Server love global catalogs. Exchange Server uses the GC to find all recipients and distribution group members in the organization. It would be nice if the Exchange Server instances had a GC in the same site.

You'll have to weigh this against the potential replication traffic that the servers will receive from the other domains. All domains will replicate its domain information to each Global Catalog. Typically, the importance of global catalogs for logon and Exchange Server significantly outweighs this consideration.

Once you have decided how many GCs are needed, you need to log on as an enterprise admin and enable domain controllers within the forest. This is done in the Active Directory Sites and Services console. Drilling down through Sites, to a specific site, and to the Servers object, you'll see that the properties of the NTDS settings has a Global Catalog check box with a lot of punch, as shown in Figure 23.12.

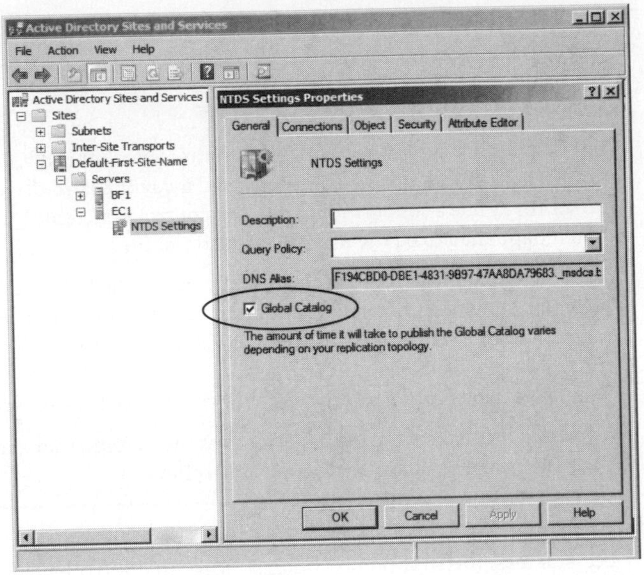

FIGURE 23.12
Enabling a
global catalog

FSMO Roles

AD has five FSMO roles:

- Schema master

- Domain naming master

- Relative identifier (RID) master

- PDC emulator

- Infrastructure master

There is only one schema master FSMO in the entire forest and similarly only one domain naming master FSMO. Each domain in the forest, however, has its own RID, PDC, and infrastructure operation masters.

We look at each role's function and consider any requirements relating to its assignment on domain controllers.

Schema Master

Schema is the word for the structure of the AD database—the fields. It's the definition of things in the database, such as the usernames, passwords, and so on. In some senses, it's the directory to your Active Directory.

EXAMINING THE SCHEMA WITH THE SCHEMA SNAP-IN

You can look at the schema with the Active Directory Schema snap-in. It's not sitting in Administrative Tools, however; follow these steps to run it.

1. Open a command prompt, and type **regsvr32 schmmgmt.dll**. You should get a message box that says "DllRegisterServer in schmmgmt.dll succeeded." Click OK to clear it.

2. Select Start ➤ Run, enter **mmc** **/a**, then press Enter to start the Microsoft Management Console in Author mode.

3. Click Console and then Add/Remove Snap-in.

4. In the resulting dialog box, click the Add button, which will open yet another dialog box, called Add Standalone Snap-in.

5. In the Add Standalone Snap-in dialog box, click the Active Directory Schema object, and then click the Add and Close buttons.

6. Back in the Add/Remove Snap-in dialog box, click OK to close.

You'll then see a screen like Figure 23.13.

FIGURE 23.13
Schema Manager
snap-in

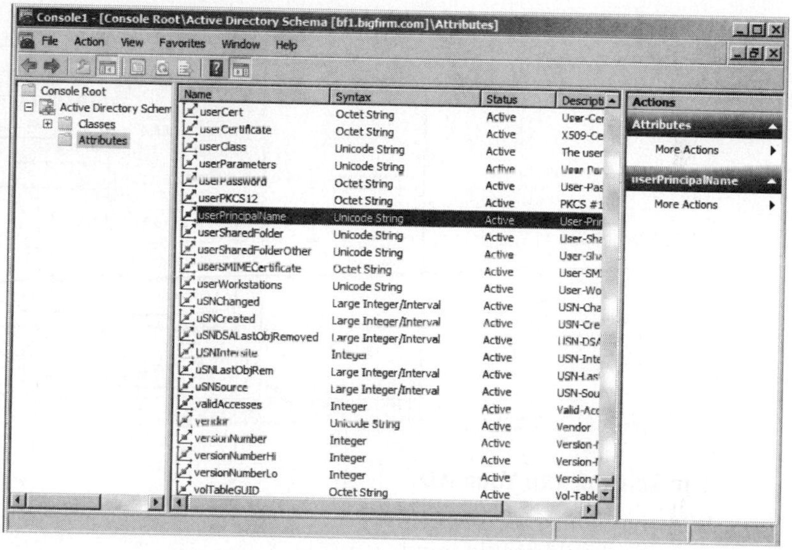

Here, we've highlighted the part of the schema that tells you that there's an attribute called userPrincipalName, which is one of the login names available to the user. Double-click it, and you'll see a dialog box describing its properties, but they'll probably be grayed out, even if you're a member of the Enterprise Admin group. Recall that even Enterprise Admins can't modify the schema—you must be a member of the Schema Admins group to do that. But if you're a schema admin, then you'll see the properties page with everything enabled, as in Figure 23.14.

Like the enterprise admin, a schema admin is a user account which is a member of a group within the forest root domain. The group is named Schema Admins. By default, the Administrator account of this domain populates this group.

Notice the "Replicate this attribute to the Global Catalog" check box. You can, using this check box, control which attributes can replicate in the GC.

UNREGISTERING A DLL

To remove the Active Directory Schema snap-in from your server for security reasons, perform the following command:

```
REGSVR32 /u C:\Windows\System32\schmmgmt.dll
```

FIGURE 23.14
Properties page
for UPN

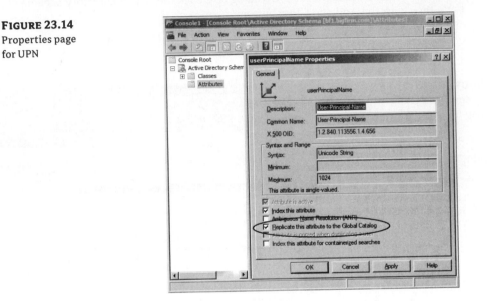

THE SCHEMA AND YOUR AD

Will you change the schema very much or very often? Probably not. But there are few things that you should bear in mind.

First, remember that there is only one schema for the entire forest; it's not meaningful to talk of changing the schema for a particular domain, because any changes to the schema are changes to the schema of an entire forest. So, a bit of innocent schema-dabbling will affect every domain controller in every domain in the forest, because all of those DCs will have to be notified of the changes and thus will have to make room for the new schema items in their copy of the schema, which burns up some CPU and disk time.

Second, when will you change the schema? Usually the only thing that you'll do that will cause the schema to change will be adding new server-based applications such as Exchange Server 2007 or other server-based apps that were designed with Active Directory in mind. In Chapter 24, you will read about adprep for preparing earlier domains for Windows Server 2008 R2. This will modify the schema as well.

KEEPING SCHEMA CHANGES ORDERLY

Inasmuch as schema changes affect the whole forest, it's reasonable to say that the schema *does* change. You want it to change in an orderly fashion, and it'd be really bad if two people both modified the schema at the same time.

For that reason and because there's only one schema for the entire forest, there's only one computer that can approve schema changes in the entire forest. That computer is said to have the *schema FSMO* role. By default, the AD places the schema FSMO role on the first domain controller that you install in the first domain of the forest. So, the first DC that you set up should be a well-protected one!

You can see which computer is the schema FSMO computer like so:

1. Right-click the Active Directory Schema object, and choose Change Domain Controller.

2. Right-click the Active Directory Schema object, and choose Operations Master to see a dialog box like Figure 23.15.

You must be a schema admin to move the schema FSMO role.

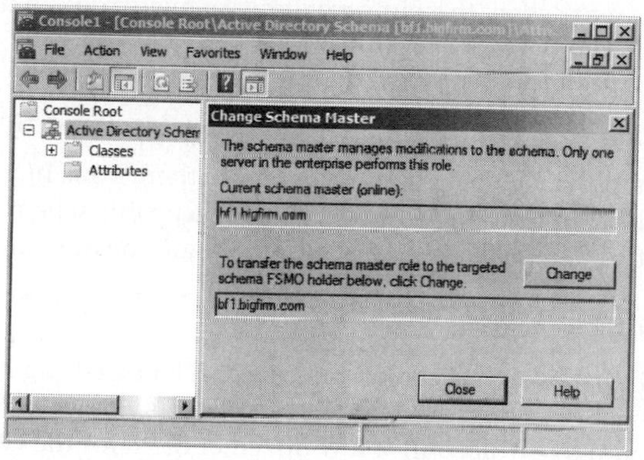

FIGURE 23.15
Viewing the schema FSMO

PLANNING FOR SCHEMA CHANGES...AND CONFLICTS

Before leaving the subject of the schema, we'll offer a thought about how it will affect your organization. There are truthfully very few AD-aware applications. But now let's consider what happens if conflicts arise within the schema. Let's imagine that you work at a big university with a lot of independent departments. The university's forest has many domains—Chemistry, English, Microbiology, Astronomy, Music, Geology, and others—that all live in a single forest and therefore have only one schema. Now imagine that Astronomy just got a cool new application that will aid its professors in researching something, and so they put it in AD. It adds a few dozen things to the schema, including a Magnitude field, which stores a star's brightness. Then suppose Geology buys some neat new application that will help them in seismology research, which also adds a few things to the schema—such as a Magnitude field, where they'd store information on earthquake power. What happens when Geology tries to install an application that wants to create a schema field whose name already exists? Well, to make a long story short, it depends...and not all possible outcomes are good.

Our point is this: Geology should have *known* when it first installed its app that the app would conflict with an existing one. But how could Geology have known? Well—and here's the part you won't like—every forest should consider keeping a testing lab up and running all the time, with a DC or two that run a working but independent version of your forest. Prior to rolling out any server-based apps, you should test them on the test lab to see whether they create schema changes that will make AD bellyache.

What's that you say? Astronomy and Geology are used to running things independently, not having to ask each other's permission to run applications? Yes, we can believe that—research and educational institutions have that tradition. But once you make the decision to stitch your organization together into a single forest, then your organizational components must communicate a bit more to keep things working. And *somebody* is going to have to keep that test lab up and running all the time, which means staffing it and finding space, machines, and software for it. Golly, that argument about how Windows lowers total cost of ownership (TCO) doesn't seem quite as compelling now. At least Windows Server 2008 offers Hyper-V. This test lab gives you a reason to buy it and play around with it.

In case it's not clear, this is a bit of a weakness in Active Directory. Basically, in this case, the AD is just another piece of software that says, "If you want to use me, you'll have to modify the way that you do business," and that seems awfully backward—sort of like a mouse manufacturer saying, "Gosh, we're sorry that our revolutionary mouse design doesn't fit your hand…have you perhaps considered surgery?"

GLOBAL CATALOG REPLICATION AND CHANGES IN THE SCHEMA

Although we're discussing the schema, there's one more side effect of schema changes that you ought to know about: what happens when your schema change impacts the global catalog's structure. This is dependent on the version the domain controller is running.

Windows 2000

Recall that every schema item has a check box telling AD whether to include it in the global catalog. Select the box, and you tell the GCs, "Listen, there's about 1,000 items in the AD, but I need you to extract only a few dozen of them for the GC. I just added a new item." That leads to a nonintuitive result.

Suppose the GC used to keep track of, say, 25 items in Active Directory. You select a box, so now the GC must build a slightly larger GC. How does it do it? Now, you might guess that it would just say to itself, "Well, I have 25 of the 26 already…so I'll just contact my DC partners in the other domains and go get that 26th item."

But it doesn't.

Instead, it says, "Hmm…things have changed. The only way to be absolutely sure that I'm not missing something important is to just *dump the whole global catalog and start over.*" Yikes! This means that any change to the list of items in the GC kicks off a message to every global catalog server in the forest to just flush its copy of the GC and to start contacting other DCs to rebuild the GC from scratch. In other words, get ready for some network activity and a set of global catalog servers that will be fairly unresponsive for a while.

What can you do about this? Two things: install the server-based apps early on, when there are only a small number of global catalog servers, or wait a bit and make sure that all your domain controllers are running a version of Windows Server that is later than Windows 2000.

In the first approach, you start out creating your Active Directory by creating your first DC, and you immediately install the server-based applications to that DC. Then, any future DCs will have your augmented schema and global catalog structure from the very beginning, and you'll never see the global catalog servers decide to quit working and have a midday party just because someone installed an application on a server. Some apps make that easier to do; for example, Exchange Server 2007's Setup program has an option that allows you to modify only the schema.

It doesn't install any files; it just makes room for Exchange's schema needs, should you ever decide to install Exchange Server later. If you're even thinking about running Exchange Server, we suppose it's not a bad idea to pump up the schema in anticipation of a possible Exchange Server future. (However, we should point out that installing Exchange on a virgin AD roughly triples the number of fields in the schema.)

Windows Server 2003 and later

The second approach just says something like, "Don't modify the schema until all Windows 2000 domain controllers are upgraded." Windows Server 2003 to Windows Server 2008 R2 helps out by changing the global catalog's behavior. Under a forest populated by post–Windows 2000 global catalog servers, changes to the GC only cause the global catalog servers to contact other DCs for just the changes—adding a 26th item to the GC would only cause GC servers to get the 26th item and add it to the GC, rather than dumping the whole thing and starting over. The neat thing about this is that it works in *any* functional level. Thus, if you have some GCs built on 2000 and some on 2003, a change in the GC will still cause panic amongst the 2000-based GCs but not the 2003 or later based GCs.

Domain Naming Master FSMO

You've already met this one—we used this FSMO as the example earlier of why you'd need an operations master in the first place. There is only one of these for the entire forest. As with the schema operations master, the AD places the domain naming operations master role on the first domain controller in the first domain.

> **DOMAIN NAMING MASTER PLACEMENT**
>
> The domain naming FSMO role should be placed *only* on a DC that is also a global catalog server. Apparently the AD developers got a little lazy and decided that, inasmuch as the global catalog knows about things from all over the forest, the domain naming FSMO could exploit the GC's knowledge.

RID Pool FSMO

One of the things that any native-mode AD domain controller can do is to create new accounts (user and machine) without having to go find some "central" or "primary" DC. In the NT/2000 world, everything has a unique identifier, called its *security ID* (SID). SIDs look like this:

S-1-5-21-*D1-D2-D3-RID*

The 1-5-21 applies to all SIDs. What we've called D1, D2, and D3 are actually three randomly generated 32-bit numbers. When AD first creates a domain, it generates these three unique 32-bit numbers, and they remain constant for any SID generated in that domain. And it's not just a matter of a separate D1/D2/D3 for a domain—the local SAM on a workstation or member server also has its own set of three unique 32-bit numbers.

So, for example, if you created a domain named Bigfirm.com and it happened to come up with D1=55, D2=1044, and D3=7, then every SID in Bigfirm.com would look like S-1-5-21-55-1044-7-*something*, where *something* is a 32-bit number. In other words, all SIDs in a domain are identical, save for the last 32 bits. That last 32 bits are the only *relative* difference between SIDs; these bits are therefore called the *relative identifier* (RID). Some RIDs are fixed, such as the SID for the default Administrator account on a computer.

Anyway, if a DC needs to generate a new SID, then it *knows* what the first part of the SID will be. It just needs a unique RID. So, there's one DC in every domain that hands out pools of 500 RIDs at a clip. Each DC can, then, create up to 500 accounts before it has to go back to this one central DC, which then doles out 500 more RIDs. (Actually, DCs don't wait until they're "on empty." They refill their pool once they've used 100 or 250 of them—100 if they're Windows 2000 Servers running SP3 or 250 if running 2000 and SP4 or Server 2003.) The computer that hands out the 500-RID bunches is called the *RID operations master*, or the RID FSMO. By default, it is the first DC installed *in a domain*. Note that there is a RID FSMO for each domain, not just one per forest.

You can view the RID FSMO assignment in the Active Directory Users and Computers snap-in. In the snap-in, right-click the domain object, and choose Operations Master in the context menu. The dialog box displayed in Figure 23.16 shows the RID master assignment as Bf1.Bigfirm.com. The other tabs, PDC and Infrastructure, show the assignments of the PDC emulator and infrastructure master roles for the domain.

FIGURE 23.16

Viewing the RID, PDC, and infrastructure operations masters

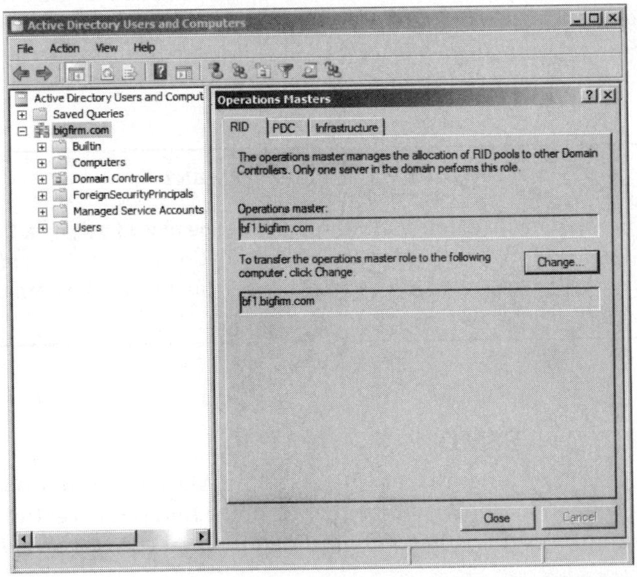

Infrastructure Master

In a multidomain network, it is, according to the Microsoft folks, difficult to quickly reflect changes to group and user accounts across domains. So, you might rename a user or put a user in a group in the domain that you administer, but that change might not show up in other domains for a while. This period of time is based on the replication between domain controllers. With a single site with a couple domain controllers, it may be only five minutes. Within a single site with a large number of domain controllers, this period could be as long as fifteen minutes. If the replication goes between sites, it is subject to the replication configurations of site links such as its interval and schedule. Something called the *infrastructure operations master* speeds this process up. You change its role in the same way that you'd change the RID FSMO. There is one infrastructure FSMO per domain.

INFRASTRUCTURE MASTER PLACEMENT

There's one oddity about the infrastructure operations master role: don't make a DC that is a global catalog server into an infrastructure FSMO, unless you have a single-domain forest. The very first DC that you set up assumes all five operations master roles, which means that initially your infrastructure master is on a global catalog server. That's OK so long as you have one domain, and of course that's true if you have only *one* DC. If you have a single-domain forest, the global catalog will have the same information as the single domain, so it's one and the same. When multiple domains become a reality, it's time to consider reassigning the role to another domain controller.

PDC Emulator FSMO

Finally, there's the PDC emulator FSMO. It's a very important one.

◆ In many cases, computers running a pre–Windows 2000 operating system need to find the PDC of the domain that they're a member of. Some of those cases will be obvious. For example, clearly an NT 4 BDC will look for its PDC when the BDC needs to update the information in its SAM.

Arbitrarily dubbing one of an AD domain's DCs as the "primary" DC, then, makes sense. And although an AD domain is in mixed mode, the PDC emulator FSMO is more than just an emulator; it's the only DC that can accept account changes.

But does that mean that a PDC emulator becomes irrelevant once you're in native mode and have no pre-2000 boxes around? Not at all. The PDC emulator still serves in two extremely important functions. Since we cover replication earlier in the book, you probably know that replicating AD changes can take time—sometimes a significant amount of time. So, suppose the following happens: you're working in St. Louis and need your password changed. You call the company help desk, which is, unknown to you, in Ottawa. The help-desk person changes your password, and it seems that all will be well.

But what DC did the help-desk person change your password on? Well, she probably did it on a DC that was physically close to her, in other words, a DC in Ottawa. So, an Ottawa DC knows your new password. But how long will it be before your local St. Louis DCs know your new password? Well, it could be hours. Does that mean that you'll have to just twiddle your thumbs for a few hours waiting for your new password to find its way to Missouri? Well, if you were talking about any other attribute besides a password, then the answer would be yes—but passwords are special.

When an admin changes a password on some DC somewhere, that DC immediately contacts the system acting as the PDC emulator FSMO for that domain. So, the PDC FSMO almost always knows the most up-to-date passwords. When you try to log in to the domain, it is a local DC that tries to log you in. As you tell that DC your new password, the local DC is inclined at first to decline your logon, because the password that you offer doesn't match what the DC has. But before declining your logon, the DC connects to the PDC emulator FSMO for its domain and double-checks, and if the password that you gave your local DC matches the new one that the PDC has, then you're logged in.

This "high-priority replication" also occurs for one other user attribute—account unlocks. Thus, when a user forgets his password and retries to log on with the wrong password over and over, then not only does he need a new password but he probably also locks himself out of his account. So, when the administrator resets the user's password, the admin probably also has to unlock the account. Immediately replicating the new password without replicating the account unlock wouldn't be very helpful.

That's one important job for the PDC FSMO. What's the other one? We'll cover that in an upcoming section, "Time Sync."

Transferring FSMO Roles

If you want to move a FSMO assignment to another domain controller, you are going to transfer the role. This process is pretty simple. As you saw earlier, you can view the FSMO assignment in three different MMC snap-ins:

◆ The Active Directory Domains and Trusts snap-in manages the domain naming master role.

◆ The Active Directory Schema snap-in manages the schema master role.

◆ The Active Directory Users and Computers snap-in manages the PDC emulator, RID master, and infrastructure master.

So, to transfer the role, you can perform the following procedure:

1. Open the specific snap-in for the desired role.

2. Change the focus of the snap-in to your target domain controller, which will receive the role assignment. Just open respective snap-in, right-click the top object in that MMC snap-in, and then choose Connect to Domain Controller. The dialog box displayed in Figure 23.17 is produced. Then the target domain controller can be selected.

FIGURE 23.17
Changing the focus DC

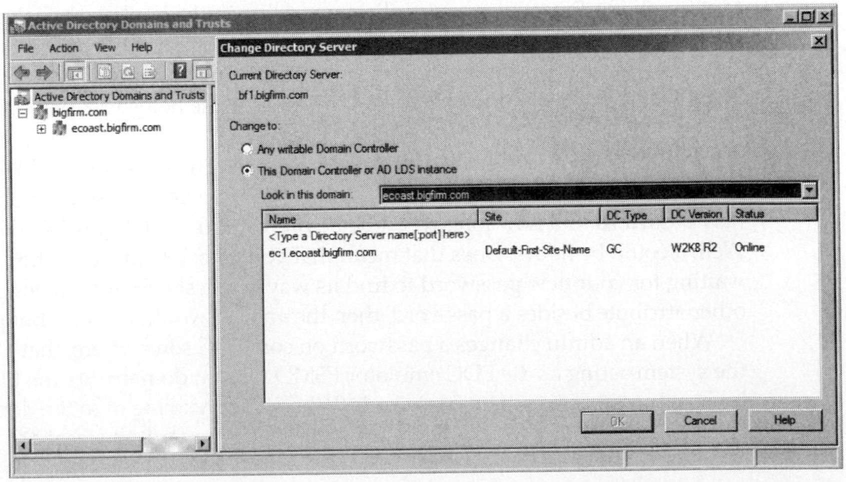

3. View the role by right-clicking the top object of the tree in the left panel and selecting Operation Masters. The new dialog box displays the current FSMO assignment. The earlier Figure 23.16 shows tabs for the domain-related roles (RID, PDC, and infrastructure). Figure 23.15 shows the schema role.

4. In each of these dialog boxes, the bottom field displays the target domain controller. To transfer the role to the target domain controller, click the Change button.

You must be a Domain Admin for a given domain to transfer the RID, PDC, or infrastructure role for that domain. You must be an enterprise admin for transferring the domain naming master role and a schema admin to transfer to schema master role.

Transferring FSMO roles is very simple via the GUI, as you've seen. But there's a catch: you can use the GUI to transfer a FSMO role *if the current FSMO is up and running*. If you fdisked the computer that was acting as your domain naming master, then there's no one around to "approve" transferring the role to another computer. In that case, you don't just *transfer* the operations master role—you must, using your best pirate accent, "Seize the master! Argh."

If your PDC emulator or infrastructure master goes offline, then it's perfectly safe to transfer those FSMO/operations master roles to another computer, and you can actually do it through the GUI. It'll tell you that the operations master is offline and that you can't transfer the role, but ignore it and click Change anyway.

But to seize the RID, domain naming, or schema FSMO, you'll need to use a command-line tool, ntdsutil. You can also transfer the FSMO roles with ntdsutil, but the GUI is so much easier. You could use this to administer Server Core installations. You start it from the command line by typing **ntdsutil**. Then do this:

1. Type **roles**; ntdsutil will respond by changing the prompt to fsmo maintenance:.

2. Type **connections** to point to the computer that you are going to transfer the FSMO role to. ntdsutil will respond by changing the prompt to server connections:.

3. Type **connect to server *servername***, where *servername* is the target domain controller that you want to transfer the FSMO role to.

4. Type **quit** to return to FSMO maintenance.

5. You can use the question mark to list the possible commands. This will give you the correct spelling of the roles.

```
fsmo maintenance: ?

?                              - Show this help information
Connections                    - Connect to a specific AD DC/LDS instance
Help                           - Show this help information
Quit                           - Return to the prior menu
Seize infrastructure master    - Overwrite infrastructure role on connected
server
Seize naming master            - Overwrite Naming Master role on connected
server
Seize PDC                      - Overwrite PDC role on connected server
Seize RID master               - Overwrite RID role on connected server
```

```
Seize schema master            - Overwrite schema role on connected server
Select operation target        - Select sites, servers, domains, roles and
                                   naming contexts
Transfer infrastructure master - Make connected server the infrastructure
master
Transfer naming master         - Make connected server the naming master
Transfer PDC                   - Make connected server the PDC
Transfer RID master            - Make connected server the RID master
Transfer schema master         - Make connected server the schema master
```

6. Type **transfer** *fsmotype* **master**. You'll get a dialog box request for confirmation if ntd-sutil finds that it cannot contact the current FSMO to get its approval. Confirm that you want to force a transfer.

7. If that works—if there are no error messages—then you're done. But if the transfer fails, then type **seize** *fsmotype* **master**. That's a bit more drastic, but it always works.

8. Type **quit** twice, and you should be done.

For example, here is a session where we seized the RID master role from a computer called Bf2.Bigfirm.com to a computer named Bf1.Bigfirm.com (what we typed is in bold; the computer's responses are not bold):

```
C:\>ntdsutil
ntdsutil: roles
fsmo maintenance: connections
server connections: connect to server bf1.bigfirm.com
Binding to bf1.bigfirm.com ...
Connected to bf1.bigfirm.com using credentials of locally logged on user.
server connections: quitfsmo maintenance: transfer rid master
ldap_modify_sW error 0x34(52 (Unavailable).
Ldap extended error message is 000020AF: SvcErr: DSID-03210CB1, problem 5002
(UNAVAILABLE), data 1722

Win32 error returned is 0x20af(The requested FSMO operation failed.
The current FSMO holder could not be contacted.)
)
Depending on the error code this may indicate a connection,
ldap, or role transfer error.
Server "bf1.bigfirm.com" knows about 5 roles
Schema - CN=NTDS Settings,CN=BF1,CN=Servers,CN=Default-First-Site-Name,CN=Sites,
CN=Configuration,DC=bigfirm,DC=com
Naming Master - CN=NTDS Settings,CN=BF1,CN=Servers,CN=Default-First-Site-Name,
CN=Sites,CN=Configuration,DC=bigfirm,DC=comPDC - CN=NTDS Settings,CN=BF1,
CN=Servers,CN=Default-First-Site-Name,CN=Sites,
CN=Configuration,DC=bigfirm,DC=com
RID - CN=NTDS Settings,CN=BF2,CN=Servers,CN=Default-First-Site-Name,CN=Sites,
CN=Configuration,DC=bigfirm,DC=com
```

```
Infrastructure - CN=NTDS Settings,CN=BF1,CN=Servers,CN=Default-First-Site-Name,
CN=Sites,CN=Configuration,DC=bigfirm,DC=com

fsmo maintenance:
```

Hmmm, the transfer didn't work. Let's seize:

```
fsmo maintenance: seize rid master
Attempting safe transfer of RID FSMO before seizure.
ldap_modify_sW error 0x34(52 (Unavailable).
Ldap extended error message is 000020AF: SvcErr: DSID-03210CB1, problem 5002
(UNAVAILABLE), data 1722

Win32 error returned is 0x20af(The requested FSMO operation failed.
The current FSMO holder could not be contacted.)
)
Depending on the error code this may indicate a connection,
ldap, or role transfer error.
Transfer of RID FSMO failed, proceeding with seizure ...
Searching for highest rid pool in domain
Server "bf1.bigfirm.com" knows about 5 roles
Schema - CN=NTDS Settings,CN=BF1,CN=Servers,CN=Default-First-Site-Name,CN=Sites,
CN=Configuration,DC=bigfirm,DC=com
Naming Master - CN=NTDS Settings,CN=BF1,CN=Servers,CN=Default-First-Site-Name,
CN=Sites,CN=Configuration,DC=bigfirm,DC=com
PDC - CN=NTDS Settings,CN=BF1,CN=Servers,CN=Default-First-Site-Name,CN=Sites,
CN=Configuration,DC=bigfirm,DC=com
RID - CN=NTDS Settings,CN=BF1,CN=Servers,CN=Default-First-Site-Name,CN=Sites,
CN=Configuration,DC=bigfirm,DC=com
Infrastructure - CN=NTDS Settings,CN=BF1,CN=Servers,CN=Default-First-Site-Name,
CN=Sites,CN=Configuration,DC=bigfirm,DC=comfsmo maintenance:
```

SEIZE AND SLICK

If you seize an RID, domain naming, or schema master, make sure that the old master never comes online again, or AD havoc will result! If this domain controller comes up again, it will think it still has the FSMO role. So, contention between the old one and the new one will occur.

It is highly recommended that you remove the network cable and erase the hard drive. We recommend grabbing the installation CD and booting it up to delete the system partition for a clean installation.

Time Sync

When it comes to replication and trusts, the AD needs all of its domain controllers to pretty much agree about the current time and date. They don't have to be *exactly* the same, but they need to be close—Kerberos fails if a domain controller and the system trying to use that DC to authenticate disagree about what time it is by more than five minutes. Under NT 4 and earlier, establishing time synchronization across a domain was difficult. But Windows Servers include a service called the Windows Time service that keeps all your Windows 2000 and later workstations and servers in good time sync.

Machines in AD stay in sync this way. The PDC emulator FSMO of the forest root—the first created domain's first domain controller—is the "Master Time Server Dude." All other servers automatically create a hierarchy, sort of like a "telephone tree," to distribute time synchronization information. Everyone below that top dog automatically gets time synced from someone above it in the hierarchy. Specifically:

◆ Member servers and workstations synchronize to the DC that logged them in.

◆ DCs in a domain all look to the DC in their domain that holds the PDC emulator operations master role.

◆ If there is more than one domain in the forest, then there will be more than one PDC emulator, because each domain has a PDC emulator. The PDC emulators must agree on the time, so they choose one of their number to be "the source"—the PDC emulator for the *first* domain in the forest, the forest root. So, again, it's the PDC emulator FSMO for the forest root domain that is the ultimate time authority.

But who syncs that top dog, the forest root domain's PDC FSMO?

First, odd as this sounds, you don't need to sync the FSMO. All that matters in AD is that all the servers think it's the same time. Sure, it'd be nice if it was the *actual* time, but that's not necessary. If your whole enterprise were ten minutes early, that would constitute no problem for AD, as long as *all the* servers are ten minutes early.

🌐 Real World Scenario

TIME ZONES AND TIME SYNC

But it's *very important* that you set the time zones correctly on all your systems! AD stores and syncs time in "universal time," so in its heart of hearts AD is always working on Greenwich, England, time. Windows operating systems use the time zones to understand the system clock's time and to display time that you'll understand. So, if you were to leave everyone's time zone to Pacific and then just set the system clocks to whatever the local time was, each of those systems would think that the time in universal time was hours different…and synchronization would fail. Such a situation will drive you crazy, because you'll be looking at a DC and a workstation whose time *looks* identical—but unknown to you, their time zones are set differently—so, it's a mystery why they won't talk to one another. It wouldn't be if you could see their beliefs about what the *universal* time was! You can quickly check a system's time zone by opening a command prompt and typing *w32tm /tz*.

But as long as we've got this hierarchy, let's do it right and sync that root domain PDC somewhere reliable. You could purchase an Network Time Protocol appliance that syncs its time with the Global Positioning System (GPS). Or you could save a buck or two and just let the Internet set your time.

The suite of Internet standards includes a way of sharing time information called the Simple Network Time Protocol (SNTP); see RFC 1769 at www.faqs.org/rfcs/rfc1769.html. Many, many machines on the Internet serve as NTP servers and will provide up-to-date time information to any machine running an NTP client. Fortunately, Windows 2000 and later systems include an NTP client—in fact, it is *the* protocol that AD uses to synchronize its member systems. You can tell a Windows Server 2008 R2 machine to synchronize its clock from a given Internet time server with the w32tm command:

```
w32tm /config /computer:bf1 /update /manualpeerlist:time.windows.com
/syncfromflags:manual /reliable:yes
```

Let's parse out some of the strange parameters:

◆ /computer: The name of the computer. In this case, we would use the name of the forest root PDC emulator.

◆ /Reliable: Yes, it is reliable time source for other computers.

◆ /manualpeerlist: This is the list of specific time servers you want to sync with.

◆ /syncfromflags: This is manual because you want to sync with only the servers in the manual peer list.

You can specify multiple time servers by separating them with spaces and surrounding them with double quotes, like so:

```
w32tm /config /computer:bf1 /update
/manualpeerlist:"time.windows.com AnotherTimeServer.com StillAnotherOne.com"
/syncfromflags:manual /reliable:yes
```

If you forget what server you told the clock to sync with, you can find out by typing this:

```
w32tm /query /computer:bf1 /source
```

By default, the forest root's PDC FSMO will try to synchronize with its time source once every six minutes until it successfully connects with the time source. Then it does it again in six minutes and again six minutes later. It keeps resynchronizing every six minutes until it has successfully synchronized three times in a row. Then it reduces its frequency to once every 100 minutes. You can change this with a registry entry, although we're not sure why you'd need to do so. (All Time service parameters are in HKLM\System\CurrentControlSet\Services\W32Time\Config.) Alternatively, you can run the following command to view the configurations:

```
C:\Users\Administrator.BF1>w32tm /query /computer:bf1 /configuration
[Configuration]

EventLogFlags: 2 (Local)
AnnounceFlags: 10 (Local)
TimeJumpAuditOffset: 28800 (Local)
MinPollInterval: 6 (Local)
MaxPollInterval: 10 (Local)
MaxNegPhaseCorrection: 172800 (Local)
```

```
MaxPosPhaseCorrection: 172800 (Local)
MaxAllowedPhaseOffset: 300 (Local)

FrequencyCorrectRate: 4 (Local)
PollAdjustFactor: 5 (Local)
LargePhaseOffset: 50000000 (Local)
SpikeWatchPeriod: 900 (Local)
LocalClockDispersion: 10 (Local)
HoldPeriod: 5 (Local)
PhaseCorrectRate: 7 (Local)
UpdateInterval: 100 (Local)
```

But where do you find an SNTP server? Oddly enough, there are many around. Most ISPs' big DNS servers seem to act as SNTP servers. You can find out whether a particular machine is an SNTP server with a neat little free tool called ntpquery.exe from www.bytefusion.com/products/fs/fs.htm. You just point it at a DNS name or IP address, and if that machine is a time server, you get a screen full of incomprehensible long numbers.

There doesn't seem to be a way to enable success/failure logging to the event log. But there is a diagnostic program that you can use to figure out whether you're connected to a useful time server. Shipped on all Windows machines, the program is called w32tm. Although it's not as pretty as ntpquery.exe, it's free and integrates with the Time service.

To find out whether a system's time server is working, open a command prompt, and type **w32tm /resync**. It'd look like this:

```
c:\>w32tm /resync
Sending resync command to local computer...
The command completed successfully.
```

Or, if it *didn't* work, you'll see this:

```
The computer did not resync because no time data was available.
```

This service requires that port 123 be open to the outside world, so set your firewalls appropriately.

TIME SYNC FOR ALL

You can even use this if you *don't* have an Active Directory running. If, for example, your home machine were a Windows XP or later operating system, then you could use the w32tm /config command to give your workstation the name of a time server, and the workstation would periodically resynchronize with that server. But only do this if you're connected to the Internet via cable modem or DSL...it might be quite unsettling to have your workstation dial up EarthLink at 3:30 in the morning just to get the time! You can set the time server from the GUI—just double-click the time in the system notification area (most of us call it the *system tray*), and you'll see the Internet Time tab where you can set a server. You won't see it on an AD member system, because AD selects time servers in Active Directory.

Trusts

As discussed earlier in the chapter, computers within a domain allow users authenticated by the domain controllers to access to their resources. The computers trusted the domain controllers. For users outside the domain, an explicit trust was created between the domain controllers to authorize the users to access the computers' resources. This section will go into more detail on concepts behind these explicit trusts and how to administer them.

The trusts have characteristics that can be configured when they are created. They can have one direction or two. They can be transitive or nontransitive. Each of these characteristics is considered in the type of trust that will be created.

You can create and administer the trust using the Active Directory Domains and Trusts snap-in. In addition, the `netdom` utility can perform the same operations.

Defining the Domain: "Trust"

So, now you have a server that can authenticate a user, a DC. But for whom will it do this authenticating? Not just any system. A PC (whether workstation or server) can only use a domain's DCs to authenticate if that PC "joins" a domain to become a "domain member." Systems that are not members of any domain can authenticate using the user accounts in their local SAM database; systems that are domain members can either authenticate a user with those local SAM accounts or ask one of their domain's DCs to authenticate the user. In the world of Microsoft networking, we say that systems not in any domain *trust* only their local SAM but that systems in a domain *trust* their SAM and their domain's DCs. Joining a domain creates a *trust relationship* between the PC and the DCs. Before a workstation will trust a domain controller to provide it with logon services and before a domain controller will trust a workstation enough to *provide* those logon services, Microsoft software requires the agreement both of a domain-level administrator and of a workstation-level administrator.

When you join a machine to a domain, you are typically logged in using an account that workstation recognizes as a local administrator, but when you try to join the machine to a domain, you'll see that the domain then comes back and says, "Now I need to see an administrative account that the *domain* recognizes." Just as a treaty between two countries requires signatures from leaders of *both* countries, so also does trust between machines and domains require authorization from both local and domain-level admins.

But trusts can go further than that. As we discussed earlier, trusts occur between domains in the forest. You can also create trust relationships between forest domains and other domains. Thus, if your PC is a member of the Bigfirm.com domain and if the Bigfirm.com domain trusts the Apex.com domain, then your local DCs can authenticate information about not only user accounts in Bigfirm.com but also user accounts in Apex.com.

Trust Relationships in More Detail

If you want to connect an old domain and a new domain to do a clean and pristine migration, if you want domains in one forest to trust domains in another forest due to a corporate merger, or if you're even just sharing data between domains, then you must create a trust relationship. When a domain trusts another domain, then the first domain is saying that it once was only willing to accept authentications from its own DCs, but now it'll accept authentications from the second domain's DCs as well.

But how do you build one of those trusts? In the case of domain-to-domain trusts, you can use the GUI or a command-line tool named `netdom`.

Trusts Have Direction

To understand trusts in depth, the first thing to grasp is that trusts have direction. That shows up particularly clearly in trusts with NT 4 domains, because NT 4 trusts are all one-way only. Now, we know NT 4 is as old as dirt in the relative age of Windows operating systems. However, the NT 4 trust still lives on in the form of external trusts. Other AD trusts are two-way, and of course you can simulate a two-way trust with NT 4 by building two trusts—one in each direction. But let's take a moment to discuss trust directions.

The language to describe the NT 4 trust relationship seems to muddle the concepts. Refer to Figure 23.18 to get this concept down and use it to remind yourself of the terminology to get the trust creation correct.

FIGURE 23.18
Trusts

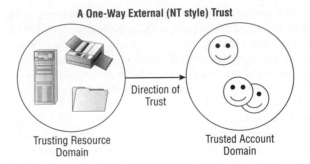

A One-Way External (NT style) Trust

Direction of Trust

Trusting Resource Domain

Trusted Account Domain

Any trust between two domains has a trusting domain and a trusted domain. The *trusting* domain is willing to accept login information and authentications from the *trusted* domain. For example, suppose you have two domains—a domain named Factory.com and another domain named Workers.com. Suppose also that Factory.com is a domain that contains very few user accounts; instead, it contains the machine accounts for several hundred servers. People with user accounts in Workers.com need to get access to data in Factory.com's servers.

Or, in other words, you need the Factory.com domain to *trust* the Workers.com domain. "Resources" trust "accounts."

If you haven't messed around with trust relationships in the past, then read that again so you're clear on it. The primary goal is to give Worker.com people access to Factory.com's data. But Factory.com's servers will not, of course, let any users get to that data unless they can authenticate those users. But Factory.com can't authenticate the users; only their home domain's DCs can. Therefore, Factory.com must begin accepting authentication from Workers.com. That's the definition of "to trust" here: to accept authentications of another domain's DCs. So, Worker.com folks get to use Factory.com's data because Workers.com is *trusted*, and Factory.com lets them because it is *trusting*.

This notion of one-way trusts is largely irrelevant in Active Directory networks that have no NT 4 DCs, but not entirely. The automatically created trusts between domains within a forest are two-way in direction. Each domain trusts each other. Manually created trusts may have no need to allow the trust in both directions, so the option to create one-way trusts is still available.

Some Trusts Are Transitive

A neat thing about a forest is that all of its domains trust each other because of transitive trusts—even if domain A doesn't trust domain B directly, it might be that A trusts D, D trusts C, and C trusts B.

We illustrated how the trust relationships worked with the cute potential date earlier in the chapter in the "Kerberos and Trusts" section. If the cute potential date had an equally geeky brother as yourself and he considers your sister hot stuff, the trust relationship between Mother and Mom works in the opposite direction. It would work if there was a forest root of the neighborhood or even more motherly security devices to network through. As these trusts "flow through," there's a kind of "six degrees of Kevin Bacon" in that everyone trusts everyone.

This is the transitive nature of some trusts. The automatically built parent-child trusts and the forest root–tree root trusts are transitive. Shortcut trusts and forest trusts are transitive, but they are created manually. The transitive nature reduces the number of trusts needed to be created.

Trusts Do Not Remove All Security

People sometimes fear creating trusts between two domains, thinking that if domain A and domain B trust one another, then anyone with a user account in A can make mischief in B, and vice versa. That's not true at all. Establishing trusts between two domains just means that a system in the A domain can recognize a user in B, and B in A. To see why this isn't the end of the world, consider this question: can a user in domain A do anything that he wants on any system in domain A? Of course not—group policies, user rights, and permissions control all of those things.

People get that idea because they're used to working in networks running older versions of NT that have been configured with default permissions and rights. Because earlier versions of NT's permissions were something like "Everyone in the world is welcome here," hooking up domain A and domain B meant that yes, anyone from A could do anything to any machine in B (and the other way around as well). But modern networks are tighter for two reasons. First, the default permissions and rights that a user has in a network running Windows XP Professional and later Windows operating systems and Windows Server 2003/2008–based domains are a lot more restrictive than the ones for a network running NT 4 or Windows 2000 workstations and domain controllers. Second, administrators are just plain more aware of security and so more likely to take a close look at how they secure their servers. Once a server in domain A is well protected from the users in domain A, then it'll be pretty much automatically protected from users in any other trusting domain.

Trusts Involve Administrators from Both Sides

The decision to let domain A accept authentications from domain B (to use a one-way trust example) isn't one that A can make unilaterally, and it isn't one that B can foist onto A. Creating a trust relationship is sort of like creating a treaty between countries; you need signatures from both sides to make it legal. Now, we realize that in many cases one person—probably you—will be the domain administrator on both sides, but you will nevertheless have to establish credentials on both domains before you'll be able to create that domain.

Four Kinds of Trusts

In a Windows Server 2008 R2 world, there are four kinds of trusts that can be created manually: external, shortcut, forest, and realm. These trusts were also available in Windows Server 2003. Only external and shortcut trusts were available on Windows 2000 servers. You will probably work only with the external and, on rare occasions, forest trusts, but let's take a quick look at what they are:

External   External trusts are basically the kinds of trusts we've been mostly talking about when we talk about domain-to-domain trusts. Since they come directly from the NT trust technology, they're occasionally referred as *NT trusts*. If you want a domain in a forest to trust a domain *outside* the forest or, in Microsoft terms, an *external* domain, then you build an *external* trust. You'll use these for migration. For example, if you're migrating from a domain to a new empty Windows Server 2008–based AD domain, then you must first create an external trust between the two domains so that you can copy the user accounts and other things to the new domain.

Shortcut   Shortcut trusts help speed up authentication in large forests. Remember the earlier discussion concerning the Kerberos and high-school dating? It would be nice to cut out the extra jumps between you and the cute date. The shortcut trust is like that. For our example, Ecoast. Bigfirm.com could pass around Bigfirm.com and directly contact Consolidated.com with this. This isn't a real impressive example. Only a forest with several trees or great-great-grandchild domains would actually benefit from this feature.

Forest   Forest trusts are the neat new-to-2003 trust that lets you build one trust relationship between two forests. Once done, every domain in the first forest trusts every domain in the second forest.

Realm   Realm trusts allow trust relationships with Unix systems that use Kerberos for authentication. (What we call domains, Unix Kerberos users call *realms*.)

We'll mostly use external trusts, but we'll show you how to build a forest trust also.

Understanding Transitive Forest Trusts

Since we can't graft forests together, we can't add a forest to another one. The best we can do is create a trust. The external trust is adequate for sharing resources across one domain. The forest trust is best for multiple domains.

However, forest trusts don't play under an AD forest that contains any Windows 2000 Servers as domain controllers. You can build forest trusts in an Active Directory composed of all Windows Server 2003 or Windows Server 2008–based DCs.

Like the automatic transitive trust relationships, the forest trust provides a gateway for all domains in one forest to trust the domains in the other. Thus, suppose Bigfirm buys Apex, both of which have an existing forest. Bigfirm wants its forest to work well with Apex's, so it creates a single forest-to-forest root trust, and trust is universal.

This is good news, but there are a few reasons why this may not be all that Bigfirm and Apex wanted. Here's why:

◆ First, this is possible only if both Bigfirm.com and Apex.com are upgraded to Windows Server 2003 forest functional level. In other words, they must upgrade every domain controller from Windows 2000 Server to Windows Server 2003. Not *one* DC can be running Windows 2000.

◆ Second, two trusting forests do not exactly equal a single forest as far as some AD-aware software is concerned. (Read: Exchange Server. Although it isn't the only one, it is the most important one.) That's because there is another very important bit of "glue" binding forests together in addition to their transitive trusts: the global catalog. Exchange Server sees your enterprise as one big firm no matter how many domains it has because Exchange Server thinks "all domains sharing a global catalog equal one enterprise." So, here's the problem: two separate trusting forests *still have two separate global catalogs*.

◆ Third, and this is probably a smaller issue, forest-to-forest trusts are, believe it or not, not transitive *across forests*. By that we mean if forest 1 trusts forest 2, then as you've seen, all of forest 1's domains trust all of forest 2's domains, and vice versa. But now let's say that you set up a transitive trust between forest 2 and forest 3. Now all of forest 2's domains trust all of forest 3's domains (and vice versa). But what about forest 1 and forest 3—what relationship do they have? None, as it turns out. Forest-to-forest trusts do not "flow through." You'd have to build a whole separate trust between forest 1 and forest 3 in order to have every forest around trust every other one.

You'll see the nuts and bolts of setting up trusts in the next topic "Manually Creating Trusts."

Manually Creating Trusts

The primary tool for managing trusts is the Active Directory Domains and Trusts (ADDT) console. Although those "old-school leatherneck admins" think wizards are for those "latte-sipping pencil-neck admins," the ADDT's New Trust Wizard gets the job done when you consider the complexity of the `netdom` command.

You can find the trusts of a domain on the Trusts tab of the properties of a listed domain within the console, as shown in Figure 23.19. This figure illustrates a one-way outgoing external trust for the Apex.com domain. Even using the "trusts" nomenclature, the idea of what the tab is telling you is thoroughly confounding.

FIGURE 23.19
The outgoing trust

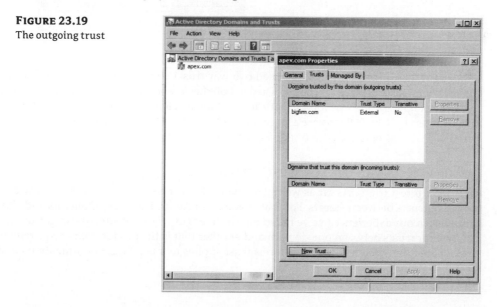

Referring to Figure 23.18, Apex.com is the domain with computers, printers, and files. The arrow is outgoing to the Bigfirm.com domain. On the Trusts tab, the top area, "Domains trusted by this domain (outgoing trusts)," lists the domains with the users and groups. In this case, users in Bigfirm.com can access files and printers in Apex.com. You can test this by creating a domain local group in the Apex.com domain's Active Directory Users and Computers snap-in. When you attempt to add members to the group, you can select users and groups from the Bigfirm.com domain. This domain local group can then be assigned permission to resources.

Figure 23.20 illustrates the incoming trust on Bigfirm.com. This is the same trust relationship discussed earlier and displayed on the Bigfirm.com domain controllers. Apex.com is in the bottom area, "Domains that trust this domain (incoming trusts)." Apex.com, the resource domain, trusts Bigfirm.com, which is the accounts domain.

FIGURE 23.20
The incoming trust

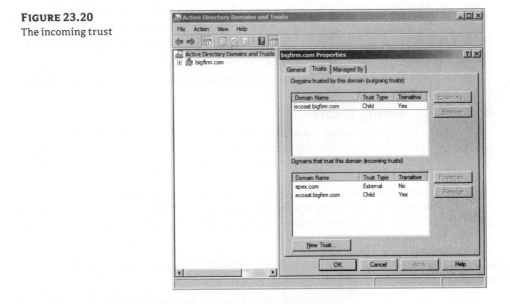

In Figure 23.20, the automatically created two-way trust between Bigfirm.com and Ecoast. Bigfirm.com is also displayed. Ecoast is listed in both fields, and thus it is two-way. On Ecoast, it will be set up the same way for the Bigfirm.com domain. Hence, automatic two-way transitive trust relations built by DCPromo are a lot easier to administer. There are no confusing the terms like *trusted* and *trusting* or *incoming* and *outgoing* with a two-way trust.

CREATING TRUSTS WITH THE NEW TRUST WIZARD

Let's cover forest trusts. As far as we can see, you can't get netdom to create the really cool transitive trusts between forests. For that, you'll need Active Directory Domains and Trusts. However, in our experience, we've relied on external trust. They're effective in getting the job done for trusts between one domain and another that is the predominant requirement in Active Directory environments. The forest trust applies to much larger organizations than the typical IT shop.

Creating trusts with the ADDT's New Trust Wizard is the same for each of the trusts, and they require the same configurations and information.

First, as always, check DNS with a few `NsLookup` commands to see that the folks in each forest, realm, or domain will be able to find domain controllers in the other forest. Although there are different ways of setting up resolving the names with in a different domain, we prefer setting up DNS stub zones. The stub zone can be configured as Active Directory integrated, so it will be automatically replicated to other domain controllers in the domain. It doesn't require modifications of the primary zone like a secondary zone would. Conditional forwarders accomplish the same thing.

Then, make sure that both of the forests are at Windows Server 2003 forest functional level or above.

Finally, make sure that you have the name and password of an account that is either in Enterprise Admins or in Domain Admins for the forest root domain—and you'll need one of those accounts from each forest.

Start Active Directory Domains and Trusts (Start ➤ Administrative Tools ➤ Active Directory Domains and Trusts), and right-click the icon representing the forest root domain (you can't create a forest trust from any other domain), choose Properties, and on the resulting page click the Trusts tab. Refer to Figure 23.19.

This figure shows how to create a forest trust between Bigfirm.com (which is, as you'll recall, a forest root domain) and Apex.com (which is the forest root of another forest). For the sake of this illustration, the trust in Figure 23.19 and Figure 23.20 was removed beforehand using the Remove button.

Click New Trust, and a Welcome to the New Trust Wizard screen appears; click Next, and you'll see something like Figure 23.21.

FIGURE 23.21
Who will
you trust?

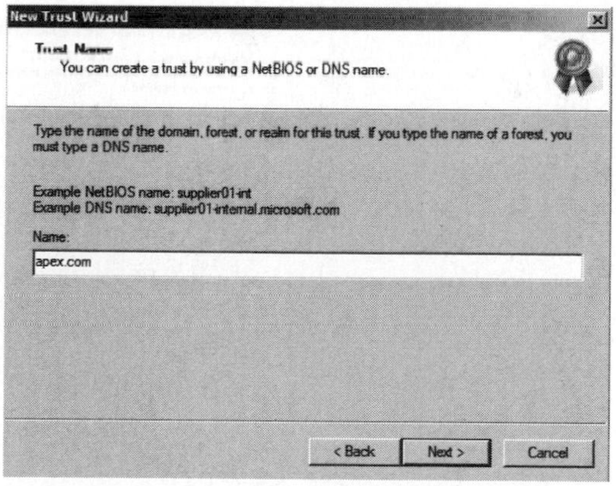

We've filled in **apex.com**. (This wizard is not case sensitive.) Click Next to see the *important* question, as shown in Figure 23.22.

Recall that an external trust is a simple domain-to-domain trust, and a forest trust is the transitive trust that you want. Choose Forest Trust, and click Next to see Figure 23.23.

As you've seen, at its heart a trust has two sides—the domain that trusts and the one that is trusted. This page lets you choose who trusts whom and whether trusts should just run bidirectionally. Choose Two-way, and click Next to see Figure 23.24.

FIGURE 23.22
What kind
of trust?

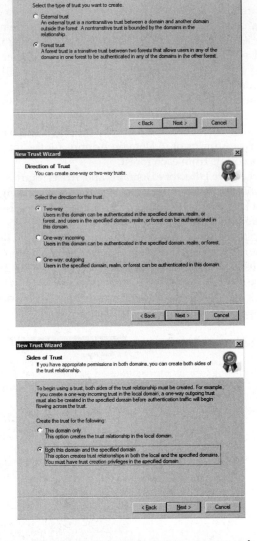

FIGURE 23.23
Which way should
the trust go?

FIGURE 23.24
Set up both sides
or just this one?

This is a real time-saver. As we said, one administrator can't create a trust for two domains; it takes admins from both sides. That used to mean that you'd first set up one side of the trust on one domain and then run over to a DC for the other domain and finish setting up the trust at the other domain. This, however, saves you the trouble. If you click "Both this domain and the specified domain," then the wizard will ask you for an administrator account and password on the other domain. Fill in the administrative account and password, click Next, and you'll see Figure 23.25.

FIGURE 23.25
The other guy's
credentials

FIGURE 23.25
The other guy's
credentials

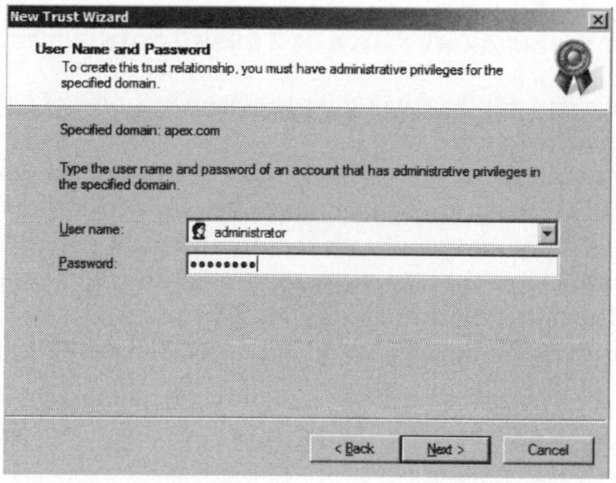

The next page will display the option for Forest-wide Authentication or Selective Authentication. In most cases, you create a forest trust because you want all the domains in one forest to trust all the domains in the other forest. If that's the case, then choose Forest-wide Authentication. If, on the other hand, you want to more finely tune the kind of authentication information that passes between the forests, then choose Selective Authentication. But if you do, you'll have a lot more work ahead of you! Then click Next, and the wizard will ask you the same question from the point of view of the other forest; select whatever you prefer, and click Next again. You'll get two more information panels confirming what you've selected; click Next to get past them. Then you'll be asked whether you want to confirm the link between forests. Then you'll end up at a final "This is what you did" page. Click Finish, and it's done—Apex and Bigfirm are working as one, sort of.

Figure 23.26 shows the results on the Trusts tab. Apex.com is the added in both fields. If you select to view the properties of a trust, you can run through the validation of the trust. This is useful in troubleshooting.

FIGURE 23.26
Trusts tab after
the wizard

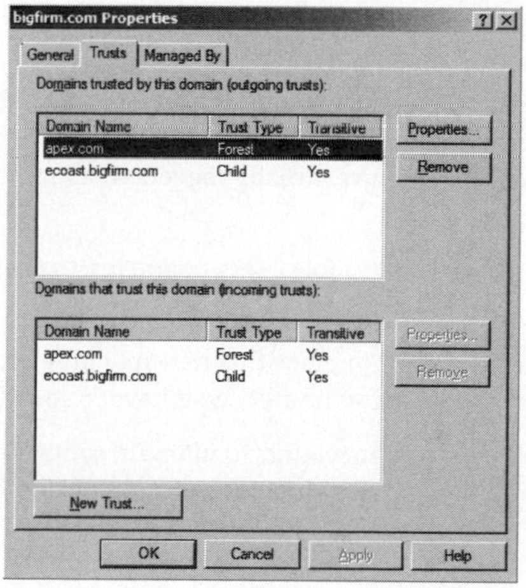

THE SWISS ARMY KNIFE OF TRUST TOOLS: NETDOM

As we've said, the true under-the-hood meaning of *trust relationship* extends beyond domain-to-domain trusts; it includes the connection between domain members and their DCs, meaning that even someone operating a one-domain enterprise deals with trusts. But there's a tendency for administrative tools to handle either domain-to-domain trusts or domain membership trusts; there's only one tool that we know of that envisages trusts in their entirety. It's called netdom. First introduced in the NT 4 days, netdom has become more powerful and useful with every version—and 2008's version is no exception. The sweet part of Windows Server 2008 R2 is that it is installed by default. No hunting for the support tools anymore!

Most of netdom's options affect domain membership trusts. We don't want to devote too much space to this, because we're mainly interested in discussing domain-to-domain trusts, but it's worth listing some of the netdom options.

netdom add adds a machine account to a domain. It doesn't join the machine to the domain; it only creates the machine account on the target domain, and, if the domain is an AD domain, you can even tell netdom what OU to put the machine account in. This is useful because a machine's local administrator can join that machine to a domain, *if* a domain administrator has already created a machine account for that machine on the domain. Here's what its syntax looks like:

```
netdom add machine /domain:domainname
/userd:destination-domain-admin-account
/passwordd:destination-domain-admin-password
/server:dcname /ou:destination-OU /DC
```

That looks like a mouthful; let's pick it apart to make it easier to understand. If you wanted to create a machine account in a domain, then you'd need to know the following:

◆ The name of the machine for which you wanted to create a domain account. That's what the *machine* parameter supplies.

◆ Next, you'd need to know what domain you were joining that machine to. That's what the /domain:*domainname* parameter supplies. If you don't specify this, then the machine account gets created in your current domain.

◆ That domain is only going to let you add a machine account if you're someone with the permissions to do that on the domain. That's what the /userd and /passwordd parameters supply. Of course, if you're already logged on as someone with those permissions, then you needn't resupply them.

◆ You might want to force this operation to occur on a particular DC. The /server option lets you do that.

◆ You might want to place this new machine account in a particular OU; the /ou option accomplishes that. Unfortunately, you have to specify the OU in LDAP terminology.

◆ Finally, machine accounts for domain controllers are a bit different from the rest of the machine accounts, so netdom includes the /DC option for that eventuality.

So, if you wanted to create a machine account named Matterhorn in a domain named Apex.com and place its account in an OU named Workstations, you'd type the following:

```
netdom add Matterhorn /domain:apex.com /ou:"ou=Workstations,dc=apex,dc=com"
```

Again, that does *not* join Matterhorn—there needn't even *be* a system named Matterhorn for this to work. But now it'd be possible for a local administrator at Matterhorn to join Apex.com, and she would not have to fill in a domain account/password to satisfy her workstation OS. But what if you wanted to both create the machine account *and* join the machine to the domain? For that, there's netdom join. It looks like the following:

```
netdom join machine /domain:domainname
/userd:destination-domain-admin-account
/passwordd:destination-domain-admin-password
/usero:local-machine-admin-account
/passwordo:/local-machine-admin-password
/ou:ou /reboot
```

Most of those options will seem pretty familiar. As before, you need to tell netdom what machine to join, what domain to join it to, and perhaps what OU in that domain to place the machine account in. Because this creates a machine account on the domain, you'll need to present domain-level administrative credentials. But now because you're also joining the machine to the domain, you'll need the *machine's* permission as well, so you'll need to show that you have an account that the machine recognizes as a local administrator account—that's what passwordo and usero do. (Think of the o at the end as "object," as in "We're joining this object to the domain." The same for userd and passwordd—they're the user account with administrative privileges on the *destination* domain.) Finally, /reboot tells the workstation or member server to reboot to make the changes take effect. Interestingly enough, you don't need to be anywhere near the target machine to do this—it'll work remotely without a problem! So, for example, suppose you wanted to move a system named Saturn into a domain named Planets.com. The administrator account on the Saturn machine is named satadmin with password *hi*, and Planets.com has a domain administrator named planadmin with password *so*. The command would look like this:

```
netdom join Saturn /domain:planets.com
/usero:satadmin /passwordo:hi
/userd:planadmin /passwordd:so
/reboot
```

We told you that netdom could help with migration by letting you move a machine from one domain to another—that's the netdom move command. It'll need *three* sets of account names and passwords, because to move a machine from domain A to domain B, you'll need to demonstrate administrator credentials on domain A, on domain B, and on the machine that you're moving. As before, you specify userd, passwordd, usero, and passwordo. But now you'll need to specify userf and passwordf—an account name and password on the *former* domain. By now, all the options should be familiar:

```
netdom move machine /domain:destination-domainname
/userd:destination-domain-admin-account
```

```
/passwordd:destination-domain-admin-password
/usero:local-machine-admin-account
/passwordo:/local-machine-admin-password
/userf:former-domain-admin-account
/passwordf:former-domainadmin-password
/ou:ou /reboot
```

So, suppose you wanted to move a machine named saturn.planets.com from a domain named Planets.com to one named Cars.org. Say that you have an administrative account on Saturn named satadmin, a domain admin account on Planets.com called planadmin, and a domain account on Cars.org called caradmin. Finally, let's suppose that each of those admin accounts has the password *hi*. The command would look like this:

```
netdom move saturn.planets.com /domain:cars.org
/usero:satadmin /passwordo:hi
/userf:planadmin /passwordf:hi
/userd:caradmin /passwordd:hi
/reboot
```

Before moving to netdom's domain-to-domain trust abilities, we'll mention that it can help out in other ways when maintaining domain member trusts:

◆ netdom reset resets a machine's account. Sometimes you'll sit down at a system and be unable to log onto the domain because the machine has lost its domain account, or so it says. Sometimes just resetting it does the job.

◆ netdom resetpwd resets a machine's domain password. You must be sitting at the machine for this to run. Sometimes if a machine has not connected to the domain for several weeks, then its account password expires; this can fix that.

◆ netdom remove removes a system from a domain.

◆ netdom renamecomputer renames a computer and its machine account. Be careful about doing this with certificate servers; they are installed to be name-dependent.

BUILDING DOMAIN TRUSTS WITH NETDOM

Now you'll learn how to build a trust with netdom. Recall that you'll work with two kinds of trusts: external (domain-to-domain nontransitive) and forest (forest-to-forest transitive) trusts. netdom can create external trusts. By now, it'll be easy to guess how netdom does it. You need to specify who will trust whom and present domain admin credentials for each domain.

Here's the syntax:

```
NETDOM TRUST trusting_domain_name /Domain:trusted_domain_name
  [/UserD:user] [/PasswordD:[password | *]]
  [/UserO:user] [/PasswordO:[password | *]]
```

Remember that in the most basic trusts, there is a *trusting* and a *trusted* domain. The trusting domain accepts authentications from the trusted domain. You can choose to make it two-way, but even if you do, `netdom` insists that you call one domain the trusting and one the trusted. (Of course, if you're building a two-way trust, then it doesn't matter which you make the trusted and which you make the trusting.) As before, you present credentials, but this time you use the /uo and /po parameters to specify the username and password for a domain admin from the trusting "resource" domain, and you use /ud and /pd to specify the username and password for a domain admin from the trusted "accounts" domain. The /add parameter says to create the trust, and the /twoway parameter says to build it in both directions. That's optional—if you *do* want a one-way trust, then don't include /twoway. /enablesidhistory makes a trust that can support migration tools that create SID histories. We discuss this in further detail in Chapter 24.

So, for example, to make Apex.com and Bigfirm.com trust each other, let's suppose that Apex.com has a domain admin named apexAdmin with password *@pex.c0m* and Bigfirm. com has a domain admin named bigfirmAdmin with password *B1gF1rm!* On the Bigfirm.com domain controller, the following command is used:

```
netdom trust apex.com /domain:bigfirm.com
/UserD:bigfirmAdmin /PasswordD:B1gF1rm!
/UserO:apexAdmin /PasswordO:@pex.c0m
/add /twoway /EnableSIDHistory
```

Trust relationships can fall apart for a variety of reasons, so if you create a trust, leave it for a few months, and then try to use it to migrate, you might find that it doesn't work. `netdom` can "refresh" a trust with the /reset option:

```
netdom trust apex.com /domain:bigfirm.com
/UserD:bigfirmAdmin /PasswordD:B1gF1rm!
/UserO:apexAdmin /PasswordO:@pex.c0m
/reset
```

It's the same as the command that creates the trust, but instead of ending with /add /twoway /enablesidhistory, you just use /reset. Or, instead of /reset, use /verify to just check that the trust is working; if not, then try /reset. We *strongly* recommend that you verify a trust just to make certain it's working. You can also verify the Apex.com trust like this:

```
netdom query /d:apex.com
/ud:apexAdmin /pd:@pex.c0m
/verify  trust
```

Then, once the trust isn't needed any more, you can break it with this syntax:

```
netdom trust apex.com /domain:bigfirm.com
/UserD:bigfirmAdmin /PasswordD:B1gF1rm!
/UserO:apexAdmin /PasswordO:@pex.c0m
/remove /twoway
```

The Bottom Line

Explain the fundamental concepts of Active Directory with clarity   The Active Directory environment gets back to nature with the forest and trees. The forest is the collection of domains built in relation to each other through DCPromo. The trees are domains within a hierarchal DNS namespace with "the same last name." The key to the relation between domains is the automatic and nonconfigurable two-way transitive trust relation.

Master it   When the first domain controller for the first domain is created, three partitions are created within the Active Directory database. What are these three partitions named, what is contained in them, and which are replicated to the other domain controllers of the forest?

Choose between using domains, multiple domains, or multiple forests with an Active Directory design   In planning an Active Directory design, you might decide you need multiple domains instead of using organizational units within a single domain. Replication limitations, legal requirements, and political forces are the top reasons for considering multiple domains.

Master it   What features of Windows Server 2008 eliminate two security-related reasons for multiple domains?

Add domains to an Active Directory environment   You have to use the domain controller promotion wizard (DCPromo) whenever you are going to build a new domain or replica domain controller in an Active Directory forest. In previous versions of Windows Server, the DNS structure needed to be in place prior to the installation. With Windows Server 2008 R2, everything is done for you.

Master it   Since DNS is now handled by Windows Server 2008 R2, it would be nice to know if it did it right. What four changes should you see if you add a new child domain?

Manage function levels, trusts, FSMO roles, and the global catalog   Several forest-related configurations were discussed, which would be managed by Enterprise Admins. The function levels for the forest and domains provide the availability of features of the latest Windows Server version. All domain controllers need to be upgraded to that level to benefit from these features. Although you can raise function levels, you can't lower them. The five FSMOs are specific roles assigned to domain controllers within the domains and forest. The PDC emulator, RID master, and infrastructure master are domain-related. The domain naming master and schema master are forest-related. Trusts are required to share resources between domains that are not part of the same forest. The exception is shortcut trusts, which reduce the trust path between two domains within the same forest.

Master It   The placement of FSMO roles is dictated by the domain to which it is assigned and the global catalog role. Which two roles had rules concerning placement in regard to the global catalog?

Chapter 24

Migrating, Merging, and Modifying Your Active Directory

Active Directory is a major component of an organization's network. Wherever Microsoft systems are deployed, odds are extremely high that Active Directory controls access to the computers, file and printer resources, email, databases, and applications.

Microsoft released Active Directory with Windows 2000. So, it has had almost a decade to become entrenched in organizations. Windows Server 2008 R2 is just the fourth major release of Active Directory. Organizations will upgrade to this version or a later one eventually.

As an essential part of business operations, the information technology and infrastructure becomes a discussion point when planning mergers, acquisitions, and spin-offs. Active Directory's design doesn't support domain grafting or pruning. In other words, you cannot add or take away an existing domain to a forest. Thus, separating or adding business operations will impact the Active Directory environment by manually migrating users, computers, and data while maintaining business continuity.

It's important to talk smartly about these operations to decision makers within management. In this chapter, you will learn to:

◆ Introduce new versions of Active Directory into a network

◆ Migrate domain accounts from one domain to another

◆ Restructure domains within a forest

Migration Strategies

We've been talking as if you were creating a new network where there was none before, but that's not likely these days. Instead, it's more likely that you already have an Active Directory domain and you want to move to a Server 2008–based Active Directory domain. Or you might have two ADs that you want to make into just one AD. Either way, that kind of work falls under the topic of migration.

Before we start talking about migration, however, we'll offer a bit of advice that quite frankly you would be crazy not to take. If you're migrating, then that means you probably already have a domain that currently works. You intend to convert this domain to a Server 2008–based AD domain that works. The scary part is in getting from the "before" to the "after." You'll really make people unhappy if you mess up partway, because a working domain is better than no domain at all…and messing up partway leaves you with a broken one. So, here's the advice: don't even think about starting your migration until you've tried the process on a test network. The availability of virtual technology makes the testing process quick and painless—almost a "no-brainer."

There are three basic philosophies of migrating to a Windows 2008 R2 domain:

In-place upgrades This would be conducted through the setup process of installing the Windows Server 2008 R2 operating system on top of an existing Windows domain controller.

Swing migration A Windows Server 2008 R2 member server is promoted as a replica domain controller of the existing domain. This is occasionally referred to as an Active Directory upgrade or domain migration.

Clean and pristine migration A "pure as the wind-driven snow" Windows Server 2008 R2 Active Directory is created. User accounts, groups, and computers are migrated into this new domain with the use of tools such as the Active Directory Migration Tool (ADMT). The latest released version is 3.1.

These approaches are explained in detail in the following sections.

Migrating with an In-Place Upgrade

In the in-place upgrade approach, you let Server 2008's Setup program convert your domain's Active Directory database to a Server 2008–based Active Directory. This process is straightforward, without a long laundry list of procedures. You run a couple preparatory procedures and then run the Setup program on the installation DVD on the domain controller.

When it is done, everything within the domain is pretty much the same. Users and groups are the same. Computers are the same. Everyone is happy because nothing has changed from their perspective. (People fear change, especially when it comes to accessing their email and documents.)

However, this is an all-or-nothing option. Upgrades of applications and operating systems tend to be nonevents. Vendors go through the ropes to ensure an upgrade is fail-safe just to avoid the costly support calls from customers. However, things can go wrong. If the upgrade of a domain controller bombs, the rollback would be very stressful and time-consuming.

UPGRADE PATHS

The available upgrade paths to Windows Server 2008 R2 are slim. Basically, it follows the basic guidelines: Windows Server 2003 or later, same processor such as x64 to x64, and the same or better edition. Windows Server 2008 R2 doesn't come for an x86 processor, so the in-place upgrade may not be an option for many organizations.

If an organization has a Windows 2000 Active Directory, an upgrade to Windows Server 2003 must be conducted first.

GETTING READY FOR THE UPGRADE

Before you do this, make absolutely sure you have your DNS infrastructure in place—perform checks of the service resource records using `NsLookup` and `DcDiag` that we covered earlier in this book, in Chapter 5.

And just to be certain that you have something of a fallback position, go to all domain controllers, synchronize them, and back them up. If the upgrade fails, perform a restore on the domain controller with its original system state data. (But let's hope it doesn't come to that.)

Some suggest taking a domain controller offline for safety like we did in the days of the NT 4 primary domain controller upgrade. However, the Windows Server 2008 upgrade process attempts to contact all domain controllers. So, taking one offline doesn't help. If it cannot contact the offline domain controller, it will balk at the operation.

HOW TO DO AN IN-PLACE UPGRADE FROM A 2003-BASED AD

The in-place upgrade involves these basic steps:

1. Prep the forest's schema to be compatible with Windows Server 2008 R2.

2. Prep the domain for Windows Server 2008 R2.

3. Run the Setup program to upgrade the domain controller.

Prepping the Forest/Schema and Domain

During an in-place upgrade, not all domain controllers must be Windows Server 2003. However, some FSMO roles are required to be located on this operating system. The domain naming master of the forest, which by default is the first domain controller in the forest, must be Windows Server 2003. The PDC emulators of each domain within the forest are required as well. These by default are the first domain controller in each domain.

In addition, all Windows 2000 domain controllers need to have Service Pack 4 applied. Also verify that the domain functional level is Windows 2000 native or better.

Even if you're going to upgrade only one domain in your 2003-based forest to Server 2008, you have to change your domain's schema before 2008 can install on the target domain controller. But, as you know, there isn't any such thing as a *domain* schema—all domains in a forest share the same schema. So, you have to change your entire forest's schema. You'll do that on the forest's schema operations master/FSMO. Pop the Windows Server 2008 R2 Setup CD into the computer's CD drive, open a command prompt, and navigate to the support\adprep directory on whatever drive holds the CD. So, for example, if your CD drive were drive D, you'd open a command prompt, type **D:**, and press Enter; then you'd type **cd \support\adprep** and press Enter. adprep.exe is compiled in 64-bit. If the schema master is running on a 32-bit server, use adprep32.exe.

Now run adprep by typing **adprep /forestprep** or **adprep32 /forestprep**, and press Enter. You'll see something like this:

```
D:\support\adprep>adprep32 /forestprep

ADPREP WARNING:

Before running adprep, all Windows 2000 Active Directory Domain Controllers
in the forest should be upgraded to Windows 2000 Service Pack 4
(SP4) or later.

[User Action]
If ALL your existing Windows 2000 Active Directory Domain Controllers
```

```
meet this requirement, type C and then press ENTER to continue. Otherwise, type
any other key and press ENTER to quit.
```

At this point, you might skip reading text and hit Enter. This abruptly ends the command. We recommend that you read the text. You are supposed to type **c** and then press Enter to see adprep in action. This will produce a blur of text and an innumerable number of periods.

This goes on for a while as AD imports and installs a bunch of schema changes. Finally, it says the following:

```
Adprep successfully updated the forest-wide information.
```

A rollback after changing the schema requires a restore of the system state data on the domain controller with the schema master role. The system state data will contain the latest backup of the Active Directory database. The schema master is the primary domain controller for schema replication, so restoring its Active Directory database will include the schema. This will be replicated to the other domain controllers.

Now you're ready to prep your domain. Go to the infrastructure operations master/FSMO, insert the CD, and get ready as before to run adprep. Type **adprep /domainprep /gpprep**, and it'll look like the following. domainprep prepares the domain for a Windows Server 2008 R2 domain controller. gprep modifies permissions on Group Policy objects for replication to Windows Server 2008 R2 domain controllers.

```
D:\support\adprep>adprep32 /domainprep /gpprep

Adprep successfully updated the domain-wide information.

Adprep successfully updated the Group Policy Object (GPO) information.
```

And for the fun of it, run adprep for read-only domain controllers. Given a production environment, you may not have a better opportunity to get this knocked out down the road. Type **adprep /rodcprep**.

To summarize, before you can upgrade a Windows 2003–based AD domain to a Server 2008-based AD domain, you must do the following:

1. Apply Service Pack 4 to all Windows 2000 domain controllers.

2. Upgrade the forest by running adprep /forestprep on the schema FSMO computer for your forest, even if that machine is not in the domain that you're going to upgrade.

3. Upgrade the domain structure by running adprep /domainprep /gpprep on the infrastructure FSMO for the domain that you are going to upgrade.

4. Optionally, run /rodcprep to prepare for read-only domain controllers.

Running Setup

Now you're ready to run Setup. Put the DVD in, double-click it in My Computer if it doesn't autostart, and select the Upgrade option. It will warn you about anything that will change in this upgrade. It will also check that you've forest-prepped and domain-prepped properly. From there, Setup runs hands-off, and there's nothing to do until it's done and you log onto your newly upgraded Server 2008 DC for the first time. At this point, you're upgraded!

In-Place Upgrades: Pros and Cons

To summarize, the things in favor of in-place upgrades are the following:

◆ They don't require new machines.

◆ Your users keep their old SIDs, and the domain keeps its old trust relationships, so any servers in other domains—resource domains containing perhaps file and print servers or email servers, for example—will still recognize those users without trouble.

◆ The users keep their old passwords.

◆ It's a simple, quick upgrade.

◆ If you're going from 2003-based ADs to 2008-based ADs, then the upgrade seems pretty trouble-free.

Although in-place upgrades have a lot going for them, we recommend that many people *not* do them. Here's why:

◆ The upgrade path is very limited. Windows Server 2008 R2 is 64-bit only. Many organizations deployed with 32-bit domain controllers when Windows Server 2003 came around, so it may not be an option.

◆ It's all or nothing. You upgrade *all* the accounts, and it's a one-way trip—there's no AD rollback wizard. (However, you can, as we've suggested, restore the system state data.) We prefer more gradual approaches.

◆ Any leftover junk remains in your Active Directory database.

Migrating with a Swing Migration

One gradual approach is the swing migration, also known as an *Active Directory migration*. This would involve adding a Windows Server 2008 R2 replica domain controller into an Active Directory domain. The environment would remain essentially the same, but the existing domain controllers can be upgraded or replaced at the convenience of the administrators. The drawback is the requirement for more hardware.

The all-or-nothing nature of the server upgrade is avoided because the replica domain controller doesn't threaten the integrity of the Active Directory database. The replica is just receiving a copy. This process still requires prepping the schema and domains, but these procedures are less intrusive than the upgrade.

For penny-pinching companies, purchasing a new server is consistently a showstopper. An alternative is performing the swing on a spare server or loaner and then redeploying the original hardware with Windows Server 2008 R2. This provides an opportunity to install Windows Server 2008 R2 on the existing domain controller after a successful swing migration.

A domain controller redeployment does involve some complications that require some planning. The source domain controller is probably an important part of the environment. It may have FSMO roles and the global catalog assigned to it. It may have other services such as DNS, DHCP, file shares, and printers that users depend on regularly. There may be scripts and group policies that point to this domain controller. Homework needs to be done to find out what would happen when this server is removed from the network. Resolutions to these gaps must be determined. Possibly, the new Windows Server 2008 R2 can assume these roles and services.

The swing migration involves these basic steps:

1. Prep the forest's schema to be compatible with Windows Server 2008 R2.

2. Prep the domain for Windows Server 2008 R2.

3. Prep the source domain controller for possible decommission or change of configurations.

4. Prep the member server and run DCPromo.

5. Perform post-migration procedures considering FSMO placement, IP address changes, or other changes.

6. Redeploy the source domain controller as necessary.

PREPPING THE FOREST/SCHEMA AND DOMAIN

Like with the in-place upgrade, the existing forest and target domain need to be prepped for Windows Server 2008 R2's Active Directory changes. ForestPrep, DomainPrep, and GPprep are required to be run as listed in the "Migrating with an In-Place Upgrade" procedures.

Rollback procedures at this point of the game are the same as for the in-place upgrade. Restore the system state data on the schema master domain controller.

BUILDING A WINDOWS SERVER 2008 R2 MEMBER SERVER

The target domain controller will start as a Windows Server 2008 R2 member server in the original domain. In preparation, the Active Directory Domain Services role and DNS role are installed prior to the DCPromo run.

VERIFYING DNS

Since the new domain controller will support DNS, it should be added as a name server to the applicable forward and reverse zones. Once the member server is promoted as a domain controller, the DNS zones will be replicated.

To ensure proper name resolution of the domain controllers, the DNS resolution should be tested. Perform checks of the service resource records using NsLookup and DcDiag that we covered earlier in this book, in Chapter 5.

PREPPING THE SOURCE DOMAIN CONTROLLER

Plans for what will be done with the source domain controller should be decided prior to the operation. If the server is to remain in the domain as a domain controller, little needs to be done. If it will be redeployed, you must consider how to replace the network's reliance on this server.

Data for the source server should be collected to apply similar settings to the target member server after the domain controller promotion:

◆ Server name.

◆ IP addresses (IPv4 and IPv6).

◆ Assigned Active Directory site.

- Assigned OU.

- Applied GPOs and RSOP output. You can type **gpresult /scope computer >
  GPOResult.txt** to push the results to a text file.

- Assigned FSMO roles. These would be transferred if the server will be decommissioned.

- Global catalog role.

- Additional services such as DHCP, File and Print Shares, and Internet Authentication
  Services for VPN connections.

Finally, perform system state data backup for all domain controllers and file system backups
for essential services to be migrated outside Active Directory Domain Services.

PROMOTING THE MEMBER SERVER

The Active Directory Domain Services Installation Wizard, affectionately referred to as DCPromo,
does the meat of the work. You'd select the option "Add a domain controller to an existing domain"
for the deployment configuration. Also, you should enable the options for the DNS and global catalog roles as required.

After the bulge has traveled through the network cable and the restart is performed, the DNS
should be configured on the target domain controller. Although the Active Directory integrated
DNS zones have been replicated to the domain controller, the DNS service may not be listing them.

1. On the source server, enumerate the DNS zones and application partitions:

```
dnscmd /enumdirectorypartitions
Enumerated directory partition list:

        Directory partition count - 2

   DomainDnsZones.bigfirm.com               Enlisted Auto Domain
   ForestDnsZones.bigfirm.com               Enlisted Auto Forest

   Command completed successfully.
```

dnscmd /enumzones

```
Enumerated zone list:
        Zone count = 6
```

Zone name	Type	Storage	Properties
.	Cache	AD-Domain	
_msdcs.bigfirm.com	Primary	AD-Forest	Secure
1.168.192.in-addr.arpa	Primary	AD-Forest	Update Rev
Bigfirm.com	Primary	AD-Domain	Secure
TrustAnchors	Primary	AD-Forest	

2. On the target server, enumerate the DNS application partitions and zones using the same previous command. Compare the results between the two servers. If they are not listed, the `dnscmd /enlistdirectorypartitions` command will force the new DNS server to start sharing the partitions. The zones should be listed since the domain controller is listed as a name server for the zones.

```
dnscmd /EnlistDirectoryPartition <FQDN of partition>
```

Perform the following steps if you plan to replace the source domain controller's DNS service with the new one. This will ensure a complete copy of DNS configurations are transferred to the new server.

1. On the source server, stop the DNS service.

2. Export the registry settings for the DNS service. This can be used with `regedit` or with the following commands. Notice the export file is saved to the DNS service's directory for this example.

```
reg export HKEY_LOCAL_MACHINE\System\CurrentControlSet
    \Services\DNS\Parameters
    C:\Windows\System32\DNS\Dns-Service-hive.REG
reg export "HKEY_LOCAL_MACHINE\SOFTWARE\Microsoft\Windows NT
    \CurrentVersion\DNS Server"
    C:\Windows\System32\DNS\Dns-Software-hive.REG
```

3. Copy the contents of C:\Windows\System32\DNS to a temporary location on the target server.

4. Start the DNS service on the original domain controller.

5. Stop the DNS service on the target domain controller.

6. Apply the `.reg` files exported from the original domain controller.

7. Copy the files to the C:\Windows\System32\DNS folder.

8. Start the DNS service.

9. Verify the zones are listed in the DNS Management snap-in.

10. Push DNS replication between the servers to ensure the latest DNS entries are listed. Kicking off replication in Active Directory Sites and Services will take care of Active Directory integrated zones. Secondary zones could be transferred from the master.

POST-MIGRATION PROCEDURES

You should verify the domain services. You can perform tool-based tests with the Event Viewer, `DcDiag`, and `NetDiag` to see if there are any initial problems. You should perform user acceptance tests as well, such as attempting to log on and accessing network resources with the new domain controller as the available authentication service.

Given the plans for the migration process, you should perform the following:

◆ FSMO role transfers and GC assignment.

◆ IP address reassignment.

- Network name reassignment. The domain controller can be renamed using the System applet (`sysdm.cpl`) in Control Panel or the `netdom renamecomputer` command.

- For DNS, the reassignment of the standard primary zones may be required.

Rollback is not complex. If the promotion process fails, running `DCPromo` again on the target domain controller should remove any record of the computer from the Active Directory database. If not, manual deletion of its computer object in Active Directory Sites and Services should resolve this.

REPURPOSING HARDWARE

The swing migration provides the opportunity to redeploy an existing domain controller as a Windows Server 2008 R2 domain controller, although it may not have the correct upgrade path available. For example, you may have a domain controller capable of running both 64- or 32-bit versions of Windows Server. Remember, Windows Server 2008 R2 comes in 64-bit only, so upgrading the original server wouldn't be possible.

This procedure requires an available virtual machine or hardware that can support Windows Server 2008 R2. This spare machine provides an intermediate phase between the two Active Directory states. Follow these general steps:

1. Prep the forest/schema and domain.

2. Build a Windows Server 2008 R2 member server on the spare machine.

3. Verify DNS is supporting Active Directory adequately.

4. Prep the source server.

5. Promote the spare member server.

6. Similar to the post-migration procedures, you will want to ensure everything is stable within the network and that users can access resources. Run `DCPromo` to uninstall Active Directory from the original domain controller. After that, it will be listed as a member server in the domain.

7. Build a Windows Server 2008 R2 member server on the original hardware. You can use the same name and IP address of the original server as long as you delete the computer account in Active Directory.

8. Promote the member server as a domain controller.

9. Perform post-migration procedures including reviewing the FSMO placement. The spare domain controller may have FSMO roles assigned it through the decommissioning of the source domain controller.

10. Once the domain and the domain controller services are validated, the spare can be decommissioned with `DCPromo`.

SWING MIGRATION: PROS AND CONS

To summarize, these are the benefits of swing migrations:

◆ They are gradual in implementation. Once the first Windows Server 2008 R2 domain controller is introduced, the rest of the domain controllers can be upgraded or replaced as necessary.

◆ Your users keep their old SIDs and the domain keeps its old trust relationships, so any servers in other domains—resource domains containing perhaps file and print servers or email servers, for example—will still recognize those users without trouble.

◆ The users keep their old passwords.

◆ The swing migration offers the opportunity to redeploy Windows Server 2008 R2 on the original server.

There are few disadvantages of this method. These are the most common pain points:

◆ More preparation and planning are required to ensure a smooth delivery.

◆ Any leftover junk remains in your Active Directory database.

Migrating with a Clean and Pristine Migration

The third approach is characterized as *clean and pristine* (C&P). In this approach, you leave your existing domains (2000-based AD or 2003-based AD domains) alone and create a new, empty AD domain. Then you use a program called a *migration tool* to copy user and machine accounts from the old domain (or domains) into the new AD domain.

The advantage of this method is that it is gradual. The migration can span a period of time where testing can be conducted and issues can be resolved. During this period of time, users will still need access to their data. Access can be maintained by reassigning permissions or relying on the capability of SID history.

C&P Is Gradual

In specific cases, we prefer the C&P approach. For one thing, it's gradual. With an in-place upgrade, you walk your domain through a one-way door. If you find later that Server 2008–based ADs just aren't the thing for you, then too bad; you're stuck. But if you have a new domain and you copy some subset of your users over to that domain, then you just tell those users to log in to this new domain. If they start using the new domain and you find after a week or two that the AD is just not the tool for you, then you can always just tell the users to go back to their old domain accounts.

Although the swing migration approach is gradual as well, the process still leaves the junk that may have contributed to the poor performance and issues that instigated the migration in the first place. Over time, unknowledgeable administrators can configure Active Directory in some manner that confound the wise chaps who've read this book. These changes will still be there to work through after the domain is migrated to a later version.

The C&P approach also provides an intermediate phase that is not available with the other two. During this phase, you have the opportunity to test the process, proving users will be able to access their resources and uncovering some common issues that may arise with later production runs of the migration. This reduces the headaches and heart attacks that could arise upon crossing the threshold of the one-way door.

INTRAFOREST MIGRATIONS

Keep in mind that these same processes are applicable to intraforest migrations too. "Intra-what?" you might ask. This merely means within a forest. In Chapter 23, you learned the forest is a group of domains built in relation to each other.

Users, computers, and groups may need to be transferred to another domain within the forest. You migrate these objects from one domain to another domain "in the forest" using these procedures. The primary difference is that objects, like users and groups, must be moved rather than copied. The source user account is deleted after the target account is created. The ADMT is used to migrate the accounts back to the source domain in a rollback. New computer accounts are created in the new domain, but the old computer account is disabled for rollback purposes.

There are two combinations of objects that need to be migrated together. This is referred to as *closed sets*.

Users and global groups   Global groups allow only users and global groups from the same domain as members. When the user changes domains, it can't be a member of their original group. When a global group is moved, the members from the original domain are dropped as well. These need to be migrated together to maintain access within the limits of global group membership rules.

Resource computers and domain local groups   Resources cannot assign permissions to domain local groups from other domains. If the computer is migrated without the assigned domain local groups, the computer will not be able to "see" the group's SID on the user's security token to provide it access. As an alternative, you can opt to change the scope of the domain local group to universal, but this will impact the global catalog size.

HANDLING PERMISSIONS WITH THE NEW DOMAIN

Suppose you decide to go that C&P route. Since there will be an intermediate phase, you can expect the users of the organization will be members of old domains or the new one. This will require users in the new domain to be able to access files and other resources in an old one. Straddling the two domains, the organization will be heavily dependent on the trusts between the domain controllers until all servers that hold the resources are on the same side of the users.

How will the users in the new domain maintain the same access to resources as they did in the old domain? Business continuity is big-ticket item for management; they need to ensure their people will be able to get to their data. A seamless migration will minimize any access outages.

There are two approaches to maintain access to the resources: re-ACLing and SID histories. ACL stands for *access control list*, a techie term for the security tab of a resource like a shared folder. The SID is the security identifier, which is the unique number assigned to accounts to identify it within the permission structure. If you don't blink after opening the security tab of a file, you may see the SID listed on the ACL before the computer resolves the SID to a friendly display name.

🌐 Real World Scenario

THE RANDOM HORDE AND THEIR JUNK

A group of venture capitalists acquired two IT private firms. The management of the newly formed corporation wanted to merge the two firms' Active Directory forests into one to provide a unified message system based on Exchange and reduce the administrative overhead.

The network environment of one firm seemed to be held together with duct tape and superglue. Unexplained system downtime was common, and performance slowed down after a few days of operations between reboots.

You might think that an IT firm would be able to apply its expertise to their environment. They had the know-how to deliver a top-of-the-line example of their services. However, did they have the time and money to do so? No.

As one employee explained, the environment was the result of a random horde. To address issues in an aging and piecemeal environment, part-time administrators and IT professionals provided stop-gap measurements. These in turn became the long-term solutions. Similar solutions existed in Active Directory. The number of user accounts tripled the number of actual employees. The number of computer accounts surpassed the number of actual computers as well. The undocumented VPN solution that relied on the original domain controller could not be reconfigured. (They lost the admin password.) Thus, an upgrade or swing migration would potentially collapse the remote users' tunnel into the network. A C&P approach was a must.

Re-ACLing the Server

One approach is the obvious (and somewhat laborious) way: just walk over to all those old servers and add Joe's new account to the permissions lists on those servers. This is called *re-ACLing* because the other name for a list of permissions on a network service is the access control list. It can be a real pain, but some migration tools will do that for you automatically.

Outside of the total excitement this process offers, especially when you may have to do this for 100+ shares for 100+ groups or users, the potential of error is high. The possibility of unintentionally removing access for one group, adding access to the wrong group, or forgetting to add another required group will ensure this to be a fun-filled adventure for all involved!

Using SID Histories

You know that every user has a SID. That's been true since NT 3.1. But under Windows 2000 native and Windows Server 2003 domain functional levels, Active Directory lets users keep more than one SID. As migration tools create the new AD user accounts, those accounts of course get new SIDs. But the migration tools can tack the user's old SIDs onto the new user account as well, exploiting a feature called *SID history*. Then, when a user tries to access some resource that he had access to under his old account, his workstation tries to log him in to that resource using his new Active Directory account.

As with all domain logons, AD builds a *token* for the user that contains both his user SID and the SIDs of any global and universal groups to which he belongs. Here's the trick to SID histories:

AD says, "He's a member of a group with *this* SID" and sends along his old SID from the old domain! Even though it's a user account's SID, the AD domain controller passes the SID along as if it were a global group SID, and apparently this is acceptable. The resource, reviewing the token, says, "Hmmm…do I know any of these guys? Well, there's this user SID…nope, I don't know that guy…but wait, look, he's a member of the 'Joe from the old domain' group. I have an ACL for that 'group,' so I guess he's in." Thus, even though Joe is logged in as a person from the new group with a new SID, he's dragging the old SID around, and it gets him access to his old stuff.

Using this method is preferred over the re-ACLing method because the resources' permissions can remain unchanged. The key is ensuring that the SID history is recorded during the migration and the trusts do not filter them when the user is "crossing the trust" to access the resource.

WHAT YOU NEED TO CREATE SID HISTORIES

Several notes about SID histories are important:

◆ You need a migration tool that knows how to create SID histories. Microsoft's free Active Directory Migration Tool, which we'll cover a bit later in this chapter, can do that. Other migration tools are available, but you have to pay for them. Quest Software, for example, offers a suite of industry-approved migration tools.

◆ Migration tools create SID histories as they copy user accounts from older domains to your new 2000 native/2003 functional level domain. (Remember, Windows Server 2008 R2 can exist in these function levels.) Before a migration tool can work, you must create a trust relationship between the old and new domains. But no matter which migration tool you have, your migration tool cannot create SID histories unless you have created that trust relationship with netdom or with ADDT's New Trust Wizard. Refer to discussion on this topic in Chapter 23, "Creating Larger Active Directory Environments: Beyond One Domain."

◆ You can create SID histories only on domains with a functional level of Windows 2000 native or better. So, when you create that new clean-and-pristine AD domain, then make sure that it's already shifted into Windows Server 2008 R2 functional level—after all, you're building a fresh new domain, you may as well get the most out of it—before creating the trust relationship and running the migration tool.

You can keep SID histories for quite a while; systems running Windows 2000 Service Pack 3 or Windows Server 2003 can store up to 120 old SIDs. But SID histories are really just temporary measures, because you really only need your old SIDs as long as your old domains are around. That probably won't be for long. Once you've moved all your servers and workstations out of the old domain, the old SID is of no value. So, it'd be convenient to be able to trim those old SID histories off your user accounts. You can do that with a short VBScript that Microsoft describes in Knowledge Base article 295758 (http://support.microsoft.com/kb/295758).

Using Microsoft's Free Migration Tool: ADMT

If you're thinking about a clean and pristine migration, then you need a migration tool…and if you've priced migration tools, then you might be reconsidering a C&P. But you needn't, because Microsoft offers a migration tool called the Active Directory Migration Tool. Originally written for Microsoft by NetIQ, ADMT v3.1 maintains the ease of use of the first version and adds some nice features as well.

CLEAN AND PRISTINE MIGRATION: PROS AND CONS

Here are C&P's advantages:

◆ C&P lets you do gradual upgrades.

◆ C&P *copies* user accounts; it doesn't *move* them. The old accounts are still there if something goes wrong.

◆ C&P lets you create your DCs from clean installs, avoiding the extra complexity and potential bugs of an in-place upgrade.

◆ C&P lets you consolidate domains, collapsing a morass of many domains into just one, or just a few.

Although we've said that C&P has the advantage of reversibility, thus helping you manage your risk, it's not without costs:

◆ You need more machines than you would if you were just upgrading. You'll need machines to act as domain controllers in the new domain.

◆ Most migration tools cannot copy passwords. ADMT provides a separate service to install on the source domain for this. Otherwise, the users will then have to create new passwords the first time they log in to the new AD domain. This isn't a showstopper, but for a large remote workforce, this would cause heartache.

◆ You have to buy a migration tool. There *is* ADMT, but it's really intended for small-scale migrations of 1,000 users at best. These tools aren't cheap, starting somewhere in the neighborhood of $10 per user. That's *per user*, not per administrator, so those pictures of Alexander Hamilton can start adding up.

◆ You cannot create an Active Directory domain with the same NetBIOS name or FQDN as the original domain, because that would require you to be able to create two domains with the same name (since you don't decommission the old domains when you do a clean and pristine migration).

◆ It's more work. You have to worry about when to move any given set of users and groups, you may have to re-ACL or translate local profiles, and so on.

VERSION INCOMPATIBILITY

At the time of this writing, ADMT 3.1 was the latest version for this tool. However, it is not compatible with Windows Server 2008 R2. What possibly could be the difference between Windows Server 2008 R2 and Windows Server 2008 concerning ADMT is beyond us. Our guess is that the OS build number doesn't match up with what was coded in ADMT 3.1 as compatible operating systems, and that's all. So, the following examples for ADMT migration use Windows Server 2008.

An Example Migration Setup

To provide a basic run-through of this utility, we'll use this example: Bigfirm has purchased the OtherDomain company. OtherDomain is a Windows Server 2003 Active Directory domain. Bigfirm has built a clean-and-pristine Windows Server 2008 domain Bigfirm.com for consolidating its domains into one. The administration department needs to be migrated from the OtherDomain's Windows Server 2003 domain. The administration department shares a workstation (they don't get a lot of work done), and their user folders are located on the domain controller named Od1. During the migration, the department members will need to access their home folders and log on to their workstation to perform their work until these are migrated to the new domain too. In this example, we'll cover the following:

- How to migrate user accounts and groups across two forests.

- How SID histories allow the migrated user to access resources on the old domain whose ACLs have not been changed

- How ADMT can re-ACL the workstation in the old resource domain. This will also reassign the local profiles of the users to their new accounts.

- How ADMT can migrate member servers from the old domain to the new AD domain.

To make this work, we'll set up three systems—two in OtherDomain.local and one in Bigfirm.com. The two in OtherDomain.local are as follows:

- A DC for OtherDomain.local named Od1. On Od1, we create the following:

  - A shared folder named Users with Everyone assigned Full Control permissions. The Active Directory Users and Computers snap-in will configure the NTFS permissions for the specific user accounts.

  - An organizational unit named Administration.

  - Domain user accounts for those dependable Administration people.

  - A home folder mapped to the Z drive with the UNC path of \\OD1\users\%username%.

  - A global group named Administration Group and its members.

  - A shared folder named Administration with the Administration Group assigned Full Control permissions.

- A workstation for OtherDomain.local named Odxp1. On Odxp1, we logged into each user account. To identify each account profile, we performed the following:

  - We changed the desktop background from the "Teletubbies meadow scene" to another image. This will prove that the profile was translated to the new user account.

  - We created a text file in each home folder to test permissions.

The Active Directory domain contains one machine: a DC for Bigfirm.com, our old friend Bf1. Bigfirm.com.

The following are the goals:

◆ Copy the administration accounts to Bigfirm.com without interrupting their ability to access the shares on Od1 while it is still a domain controller of the OtherDomain.local domain.

◆ Maintain their access to their profiles on Odxp1 during the migration.

◆ Eventually migrate Odxp1 and other servers to Bigfirm.com so that we can shut down the OtherDomain.local domain altogether. Decommissioning the domain would also include migrating their home folders as well, but this will not be discussed here.

Before we go any further, check that you won't have any name resolution problems—either point all the systems to the same DNS servers or ensure that each system's DNS servers talk to one another. Our preferred method is the latter. Modifying systems' DNS configurations can be done automatically with DHCP scopes and VBScripts for systems with statically assigned IP addresses. However, this is prone to error and lag-time issues. DNS stub zones ensure the DNS servers are forwarding the name requests to the appropriate servers in the other domain. Refer to Chapter 5 concerning stub zones.

Establishing the Trust

Next, establish the trust between the two domains. The quickest method for this example is using the Active Directory Domains and Trusts console (`domain.msc`). Use the New Trust Wizard for the following:

◆ Specify the type of trust. An external trust is simple and effective for this procedure.

◆ Specify a two-way trust. Accounts from each domain will need to access the other's resources.

◆ Create the trusts on the other domain. This will require domain admin credentials on that domain.

◆ Validate the trust to make certain things are working fine.

We like to stop and test things at this point—is the trust working, and are the permissions correct on Od1? Since users and global groups from any domain can be members of domain local groups and member server local groups, we attempt to add a user from the opposite domain to a built-in group on the domain controller. This is a required step down the road. So, we search and add the Bigfirm\Administrator to the built-in Administrators group of OtherDomain in Active Directory Users and Computers.

But adding users to groups is not what we *really* want. We want the migrated accounts to be able to access resources in the opposite domain. This is where SID history comes into play. As stated earlier, the SID history is treated as another group on the security token that will be passed to the resource domain for access to the migrated accounts' resources. If you weren't paying attention to the New Trust Wizard and clicked every Next and OK button like a mind-numb automaton, then you may have missed the window shown in Figure 24.1.

What was that? SID filtering is enabled. SID history can be exploited by an evil hacker in an elevated privilege attack. He could construct a security token with a SID of a domain administrator within the trusting resource domain. Since the SID is recognized as a domain administrator, his account would have the same level of access. SID filtering strips any SIDs that don't originate from the trusted user domain. Basically, our users' security token wouldn't buy a gumball in the source domain with SID filtering enabled because the SID history value would be stripped off. So, following the useful hyperlink "Securing external trusts" in the window, we learn we can use the `netdom` command to disable and enable SID filtering for migrations such as these.

FIGURE 24.1
SID filtering
warning

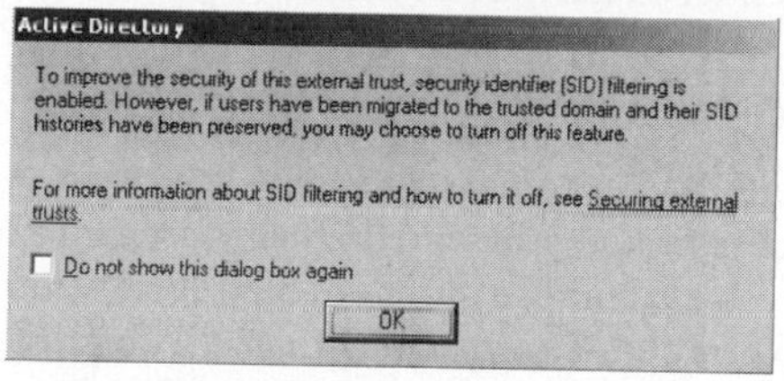

The `netdom` command comes installed with Windows Server 2008, but earlier versions had it available in the Support Tools. Microsoft released a later version of Support Tools after Windows Server 2003 Service Pack 2, so be sure to search its site for the latest version.

The following commands are run to disable SID filtering. The `/quarantine:no` parameter does the trick. You should be able to deduce how SID filtering would be enabled.

```
Rem performed on bf1.Bigfirm.com
Netdom trust otherdomain /domain:bigfirm /quarantine:No
/usero:administrator /passwordo:P@ssw0rd

Rem performed on the od1.OtherDomain.local:
Netdom trust bigfirm /domain:otherdomain /quarantine:No
/usero:administrator /passwordo:P@ssw0rd
```

Getting Both Sides ADMT-Friendly

ADMT can be an absolutely frustrating nightmare of a program because of its needs. It's a program that takes information that is fairly private and internal to a domain—user accounts and passwords—and reveals them to a completely different domain. Before ADMT can do that, you'll have to open up a number of locked doors. The following is what you have to do.

PUTTING A DOMAIN ADMIN IN EACH OTHER'S ADMINISTRATORS GROUPS

The ADMT utility needs an account that is both a member of the Domain Admins group in the target domain, Bigfirm.com, and a member of local Administrator groups of servers and workstations in source domain, OtherDomain.local. This will allow the ADMT utility to perform changes to permissions, user rights, and other nifty stuff that all powerful Administrators have the privileges to do. In this example, we created an account with the imaginative name of ADMT in the Bigfirm.com domain and assigned it to the Domain Admins group. Using the trust relation between the two domains, it was also assigned to the built-in Administrators group in OtherDomain.local and the local Administrators group on Odxp1.

On the source domain, OtherDomain.local, a similar requirement is needed for the Password Encryption Service (PES). This is an additional service that will read the password of the migrating account, encrypt it, and then store it with the new account's properties. It needs to be a member of the Domain Admins group in the source domain, OtherDomain.local, and a member of the built-in Administrators group in the target domain, Bigfirm.com. We created an account with an equally imaginative name, PES, in OtherDomain.local. Over at Bigfirm.com, we opened up Active Directory Users and Computers and drilled down to the `Builtin` folder to find the Administrators group. Then we made the PES account a member of that group.

TURNING ON AUDITING

ADMT has some specific auditing needs, presumably so that it can monitor how it's doing. The source domain—the one the users are being copied from, OtherDomain.local—needs both success and failure audit enabled for user and group management.

On the target and source machines (Bf1.bigfirm.com and Od1.OtherDomain.local), we enable auditing by modifying a group policy called Default Domain Controller Policies. In a standard Windows Server 2003 installation, you can use Active Directory Users and Computers to do this. Right-click the Domain Controllers OU, and choose Properties and then the Group Policy tab; double-click Default Domain Controllers Policy, and the Group Policy editor appears. With Windows Server 2008 R2, the Group Policy Management Console is installed automatically. After opening this console, you drill down to the Group Policy Objects container. Then right-click the Default Domain Controllers Policy, and select Edit.

To get to the policy you're looking for, open Computer Configuration, then Windows Settings, then Security Settings, and then Local Policies; finally inside Local Policies you see Audit Policy. Inside Audit Policy, double-click Audit Account Management, and make sure that Define These Policy Settings is selected, as is Success and Failure. Then click Close…but don't close the GP editor; your work is not nearly done yet.

ENABLING CRYPTOGRAPHIC SETTINGS ON THE TARGET DOMAIN

To migrate computers with previous versions of Windows to a target domain with domain controllers running Windows Server 2008, another GPO setting is required on the target domain. Within the Security options of the Domain Controller GPO, enable "Allow cryptography algorithms compatible with Windows NT 4.0."

Further south in Computer Configuration, go to Administrative Templates\System\Netlogon. Right-click "Allow cryptography algorithms compatible with Windows NT 4.0," click Edit, click Enabled, and then click OK.

INSTALLING ADMT AND PES

ADMT is available as a download from Microsoft. Installing the utility is straightforward for a C&P installation since you will not be importing databases from previous versions. It does ask whether the database will be on SQL Express or a standard installation of SQL. In most cases, SQL Express will be the preferred option.

Creating a Password Key on the Target

Now, you want your users' passwords to move over with their accounts, and ADMT can do that with the help of the PES. Before it will migrate passwords, ADMT requires that you create a password encryption file on Bf1 and then copy that over to Od1, and Od1 will use that to be able to send passwords over the wire—but encrypted.

To do this, you have to run ADMT from the command line. The following is an example of the command syntax:

```
admt key /option:create /sourcedomain:otherdomain
/keyfile:c:\temp\password.pes /keypassword:P@ssw0rd
```

This says to prepare a key that OtherDomain.local can use to transfer passwords to Bigfirm.com. (Bigfirm is not explicitly mentioned because you're working on a Bigfirm.com DC.) The C:\temp\password.pes file just says where to put the file. If your server has a floppy drive, then A:\ works fine too. It doesn't matter where you put it—just understand that you'll have to transport that file to the OtherDomain.local DC, Od1, somehow. When it runs properly, ADMT will return a message looking something like this:

```
The password export server encryption key for domain 'otherdomain' was
successfully created and
saved to 'c:\temp\password.pes'
```

You're done on Bf1.Bigfirm.com for the moment. It's time to move to the Od1.

Moving Over the PES File

Once logged in at Od1, you need to get that PES file from Bf1 to a local drive; we usually just create a share and copy it across the network. You can alternatively put it on a floppy, a CD-ROM, or whatever you want—but it has to get over to Od1 one way or another.

Installing the Password Migration DLL on the Source DC

The Password Encryption Service was once included with earlier versions of ADMT. The 3.1 release is available as a separate download.

The PES is installed with an MSI file called PWMIG.MSI; double-click it to start the ADMT Password Migration DLL Installation Wizard, perhaps the world record-holder for wizard name length. The key ingredients required in the installation are the password file and the service account that was created earlier. After the installation, you should be prompted to reboot. Remember the service's autostart configuration is set to Manual. This restart of the source domain controller will have you scratching your head on why the ADMT utility isn't working if you don't verify that the service is running.

A LITTLE HOUSEWORK ON THE WORKSTATION

If computers are to be migrated, we need to cover some additional steps. The ADMT installs an agent service on a computer to perform security modifications and to trigger a domain membership change. The utility will perform a few checks prior to the install to ensure things are flying correctly. One is a test of the File and Print Sharing. With XP, Vista, and Windows 7, the firewall can cause these tests to bomb.

- ◆ In firewall.cpl, on the Advanced tab, configure the ICMP settings to "Allow incoming echo requests." This is for your own benefit.

- ◆ On the Exception tab, select File and Print Sharing to make it an allowed service.

In addition, we recommend the following:

- ◆ Add the ADMT account as a member of the local Administrators, as mentioned earlier.

- ◆ Reset the local Administrator account to a known password. If the domain membership change fails, this account may be the only way into the workstation to fix it.

Starting Up ADMT and Migrating

When migrating users and computers from one domain to another, the basic sequence of events is as follows:

1. Set up the trusts, registry entries, and so on.

2. Migrate services accounts. For brevity, we're not going to detail this here. A service account is migrated to the new domain, and servers are modified on the source domain's servers to use this new account.

3. Migrate the global groups from the old domain to the new domain. The new global groups get SID histories from the old ones, so anyone in the new BIGFIRM\ Administration group will have access to anything that people in the OtherDomain. local\Administration group had access to. This means that as you migrate users from OtherDomain.local to Bigfirm.com, the users can be automatically placed in the Administration group in Bigfirm.com, and they will have immediate access to all their old stuff.

4. Migrate the users. Once you have the global groups migrated, you can migrate the users at whatever pace works for you. Users migrated to the new domain will be able to access file shares, shared printers, and other resources from the old domain, because the migrated user accounts have SID histories from the old domain.

5. Migrate the workstations and servers to Bigfirm.com. Change the domain membership from OtherDomain.local to Bigfirm.com.

6. Translate security objects. User rights, file and share permissions, and local group membership are a few objects that can be re-ACLed by the ADMT. To ensure access to the resource, new account and group SIDs need to be applied to servers and workstations. Depending on how the migration is conducted, this type of operation can happen before server migration. In our example, the workstation's local profiles need to be mapped to the new accounts. During a long migration, the user and his/her workstation may not be migrated simultaneously. So, profiles should be translated prior to a computer's domain membership change.

7. Repeat migration processes to fill in gaps. Membership of groups may change, user accounts may need to be enabled or disabled, and additional security objects may need translation. All of these require planned runs of the ADMT utility.

8. Migrate domain local groups.

9. Once all the member servers are moved over to Bigfirm.com and you've checked that all the permissions have been correctly changed from OtherDomain.local references

to Bigfirm.com references, you can decommission OtherDomain.local—break the trust relationship, shut off the OtherDomain.local DCs, and trim the SID histories from the migrated user accounts.

It's time to migrate the global groups and users, so let's do it. Move over to Bf1.Bigfirm.com, and start up ADMT (Start ➢ Administrative Tools ➢ Active Directory Migration Tool). It's a kind of sparse-looking UI, as shown in Figure 24.2, but here is a list of a few of its available functions:

- ◆ Migrate groups
- ◆ Migrate service accounts
- ◆ Migrate users
- ◆ Translate local user profiles
- ◆ Migrate workstations and member servers

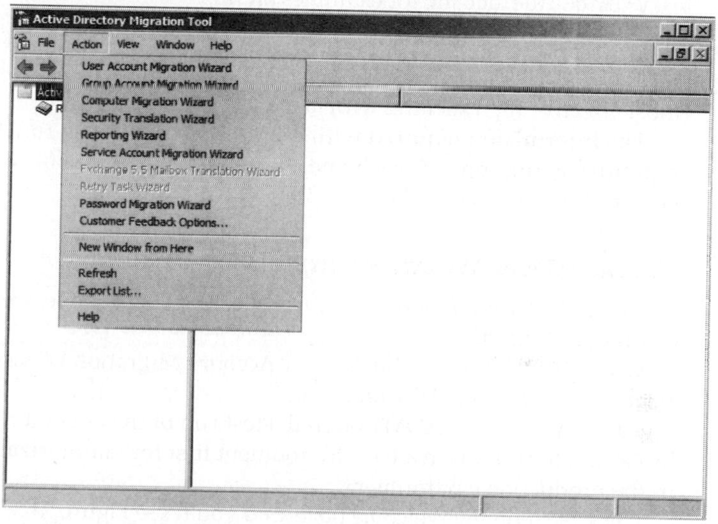

FIGURE 24.2

The Spartan ADMT console

ADMT does a *lot* of things, more than we can cover in a short time. We'll just cover the basics here. We *strongly* recommend that you read the Help file that comes with it, because ADMT is a powerful and useful tool that can migrate users, groups, machines, and even Exchange setups! In addition, the V31MigGuide.doc file that is available for download from Microsoft provides the same information in a Word document.

GUI, COMMAND LINE, OR VBSCRIPT

The ADMT utility provides three interfaces for performing the migrations. Each has advantages:

GUI   Based on the Microsoft Management Console technology, the ADMT snap-in offers wizards to walk you through each function. This is useful if you are not familiar with the options and required parameters to migrate a specific object. However, it is tedious to click through the wizard for a large quantity of objects.

Command line Batch files can be created using the command-line ADMT tool. This is useful for migrating larger numbers of accounts. Each command is limited to delivering the accounts to one organizational unit, so it cannot be all-encompassing. The following is the listing of functions available with it. We'll cover some examples in the following sections.

```
admt
The syntax of this command is:

ADMT [ USER | GROUP | COMPUTER | SECURITY | SERVICE |
        REPORT | KEY | PASSWORD | CONFIG | TASK ]
```

VBScript Scripting offers logic to control the operations of the ADMT operations. It also provides the functionality of reading input text files and performing individual operations on each entry. So, handling larger numbers with different requirements could be bundled into a batch job more readily. It does require expertise on writing scripts. Refer to the V31MigGuide.doc file for examples on this.

We highly recommend performing these operations in a test environment to get a feel for the utility and to develop a game plan on a specific migration. A mix of different methods may be most effective than sticking with just one.

The information required with each method and each function is similar, so it can look repetitive going through each one. Here, we will show some examples of the operations in GUI and command-line format.

USER AND GROUP MIGRATION WITH THE ADMT SNAP-IN

Group and user migration are very similar. In this example, we will walk through the User Migration Wizard.

On the ADMT menu, choose User Account Migration Wizard, and click Next to see the first panel, the all-familiar Welcome page.

Earlier versions of ADMT offered a test run of the operations. Version 3.1 isn't as timid. So, be certain to run this in a test environment first for familiarization and then on pilot accounts in the production environment.

Click Next on the Welcome page, and you'll see Figure 24.3.

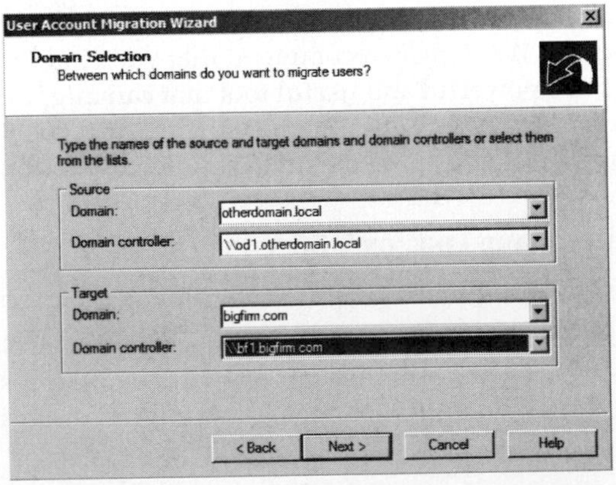

FIGURE 24.3
Choosing source
and destination
domains

This page is straightforward; you pick the domain that you're moving from and the one that you're moving to. But it's actually quite useful as well, because it serves as a test of connectivity. If Od1 wasn't up, your only options on both "from" and "to" would be Bigfirm.com...which wouldn't be a very interesting migration. Once you choose the domains, click Next, and you'll notice a pause as the DCs connect, as shown in Figure 24.4. The option "Read objects from an include file" requires a file that lists users or groups that would be imported into the wizard. In this case, "Select users from domain" is selected.

FIGURE 24.4
User Selection
Option page

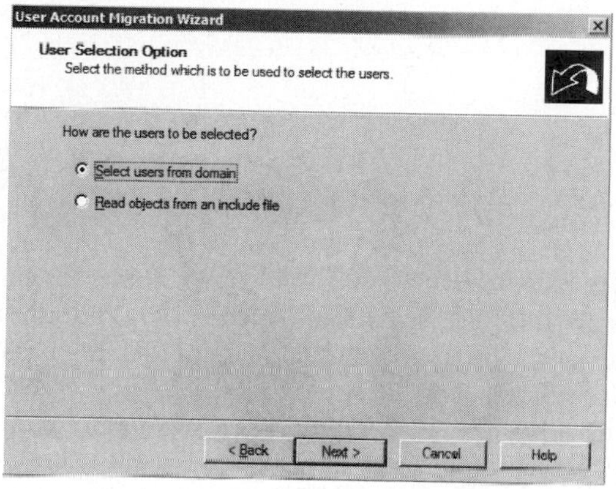

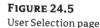

This option displays the User Selection page, as shown in Figure 24.5, which allows you to select which object, or in this case, which users, to migrate. The Add button will provide the typical search dialog box you'd see in Active Directory Users and Computers. For this example, we clicked Add and chose DPaise, although we could have chosen any number of user or groups given the wizard.

FIGURE 24.5
User Selection page

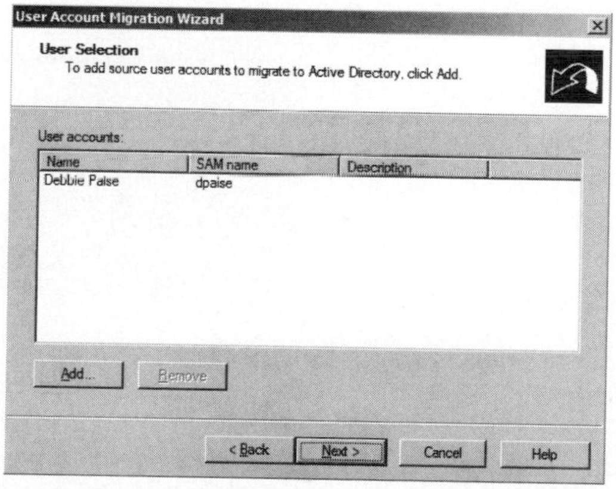

Click Next, and you're led to Figure 24.6, which allows you to choose OU in the target domain. Like all good AD-aware tools, ADMT lets you choose what OU to place the migrated group into. But don't worry that you have to master that cumbersome LDAP-ese—you can click the Browse button, and ADMT then lets you navigate though the AD structure.

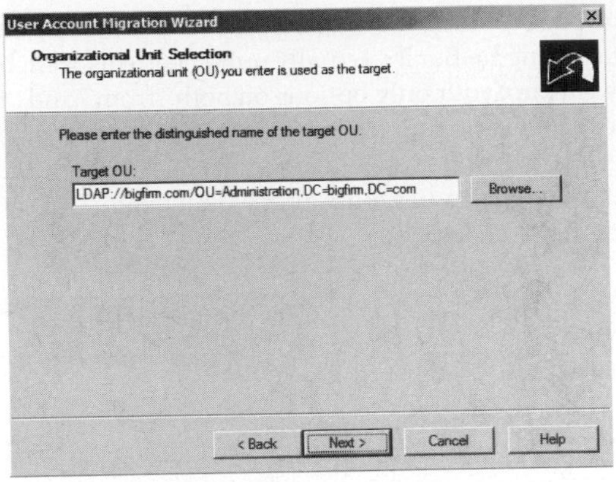

FIGURE 24.6
Organizational
Unit Selection page

Click Next to see Figure 24.7, which displays the password migration options. Since passwords are unique to user accounts, password options will be seen only in the User Account Migration Wizard. Basically, you can migrate the passwords or have ADMT come up with new ones for your users. The former needs the PES server. The latter needs a location to store the text file with all these new passwords. As you can imagine, distributing this file to your users should not be done as an email attachment to the All Users distribution group. So, you will have an additional challenge to get the passwords to the users after the migration.

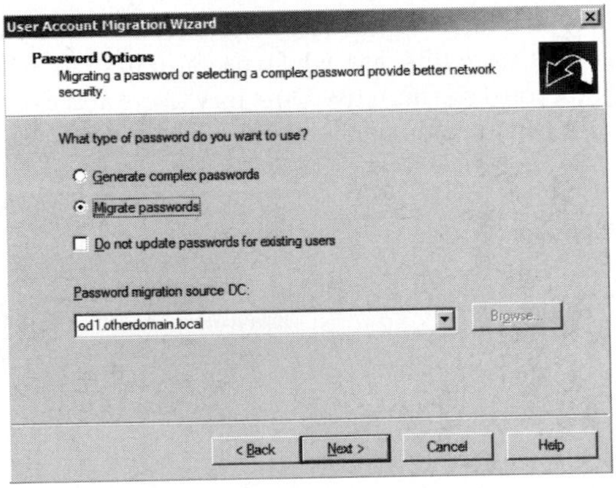

FIGURE 24.7
Password
Options page

The next page is entitled Account Transition Option, as displayed in Figure 24.8. This determines how to handle the target and source accounts after migration. Given the scenario, the accounts may need to be disabled for a period of time. The ADMT can handle both sides. Keep an eye out for the "Migrate user SIDs to target domain" check box. In Mexico, they would say, "Está muy importante." This creates the SID history on the user or group. This is ADMT's way of saying "Create a SID history item in Bigfirm.com for the DPaise user account." Clicking Next on this page is something of a useful diagnostic—if something isn't in place to allow the SID history mechanism to work, ADMT emits an error message. Or it issues the warning such as creating the OtherDomain$$ helper group and enabling auditing if you forgot to do so.

FIGURE 24.8
Account Transition
Option page

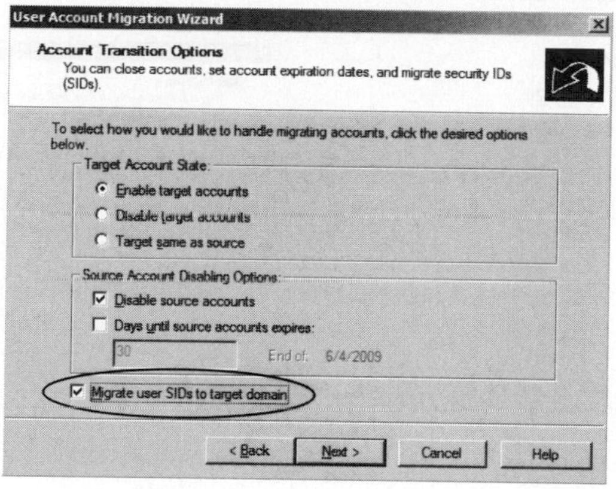

Whenever you use a SID history, the ADMT checks with the old domain, OtherDomain.local in this case, to check whether creating the helper group is acceptable. This group has something to do with how ADMT ensures that the SID histories will work right, but the wizard checks anyway to ensure that it's OK to create the group. Click Yes, and you'll see a login screen, shown in Figure 24.9, as if you haven't already presented your credentials frequently enough.

FIGURE 24.9
SID history
credentials

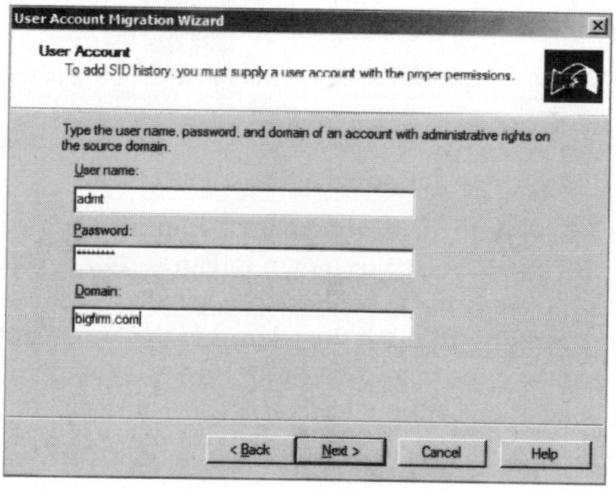

Clicking Next takes you to Figure 24.10. Typically, the preferred option for the first migration is "Fix users' group memberships." This will update the SIDs in the groups of which it was a member. The other options can be used later in remigrating the account to assist in stripping off the old SID history. "Update user rights" will replace the SIDs with the new one. "Translate roaming profiles" will reassign permissions to the new SID.

Specific properties can be excluded from the migration (see Figure 24.11). Say Bigfirm doesn't want the department or company fields of a user account migrated; these can be singled out and excluded with this page.

FIGURE 24.10
User Options page

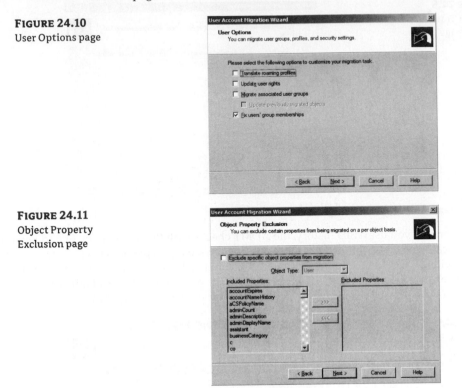

FIGURE 24.11
Object Property
Exclusion page

You're migrating a group named Administration, but what if there already *is* a group named Administration? The page shown in Figure 24.12 answers the question—skip the migration, zap the existing Administration group, or add a prefix to the name.

After walking through the wizard to the Finish button, the migration kicks off. It will display the statistics of the migration process, as shown in Figure 24.13. If errors pop up, view the log with the available button. You can also visit the logs in the c:\windows\admt folder. The log files are named with a date/time stamp.

MIGRATING WITH THE COMMAND LINE

As mentioned earlier, the command-line utility ADMT.exe offers batch operations, which avoids the tedious button clicking required with the console's wizards. The first example migrates the Administration global group:

```
rem global group migration
admt group /N "administration group" /sd:"otherdomain.local"
 /td:"bigfirm.com" /to:"administration" /mss:yes /fgm:yes
 /ugr:yes /mms:no /co:Merge+REMOVEUSERRIGHTS+REMOVEMEMBERS
```

FIGURE 24.12
Conflict
management

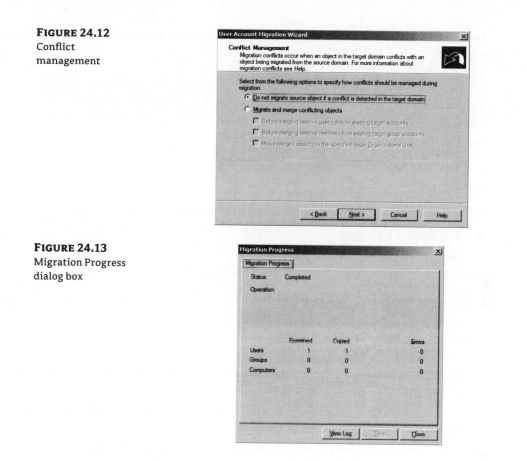

FIGURE 24.13
Migration Progress
dialog box

Although this example doesn't exhaust all the options for this command, each option is represented with the wizards:

◆ /N: The SAM Account name of the group. Additional group names could be listed as well.

◆ /sd: Source domain.

◆ /td: Target domain.

◆ /to: Target organizational unit.

◆ /mss: Migrate SIDs. This is equivalent to the check box named "Migrate user SIDs to target domain."

◆ /fgm: Fix group membership.

◆ /ugr: Update group rights.

◆ /mms: Migrate members. If yes, all user accounts as members would also be migrated.

◆ /co: Conflict options. In this case, the group will be merged with one of the same name, user rights will be removed from that group and any existing members removed.

The following command migrates the rest of the user accounts in the Administration organizational unit:

```
rem user account migration
admt user /N "bdavis" "llong" "croscoe" "nlanders" /sd:otherdomain.local
/td:bigfirm.local /to:"administration" /mss:yes /co:ignore /po:copy
/ps:od1.otherdomain.local /dot:disablesource+enabletarget /uur:yes /fgm:yes
```

The additional parameters are user-specific:

- /po: Password option

- /ps: PES server

- /dot: Transition options, which manage the state of the accounts after migration

- /uur: Update user rights

Testing the Migrated Group's Access to Resources

Because the migrated Administration group in Bigfirm.com has a SID matching the one of the Administration group in OtherDomain.local and *that* group has access to \\od1\Administration, then anyone in the new Administration group should be able to get to \\od1\Administration. Let's try it:

1. In the Bigfirm.com domain, log on as the Administrator, and attempt to access the \\od1\Administration share. This should produce an "access denied" message because the account doesn't have permissions to the share.

2. Assign the Administrator account to the newly migrated Administration group in Bigfirm.com.

3. Log off and log back on as the Administrator. Note that you will need to do this to rebuild the security token.

4. Attempt to connect to the \\od1\Administration share again.

Lo and behold, the Administration share opens! The SID history works.

Translating Local Profiles

Assuming the user accounts were successfully migrated, the users will be able to access resources within the OtherDomain.local domain. However, they still have to work on the workstation located in that domain. If they log onto the Odxp1 workstation now, they will have a new profile created for each of them. They will whine and gripe that they can't find their photographs of loved ones, or, worse yet, their Internet favorites are gone!

To prevent this headache, the Security Transition Wizard provides reassignment of the SIDs on existing profiles on all Windows platforms *except Vista*. (Isn't that swell?)

For XP machines, you could consider using an alternative method that was available in the Windows Server resource kit. The moveuser utility can assign one profile to another account. You may consider using this if the translation of local profiles bombs.

```
MOVEUSER [DOMAIN/]user1 [DOMAIN/]user2 [/c:computer] [/k] [/y]
Key:
user1 A local existing user profile.
```

user2 The user account that will inherit the user1 profile. In this case, we would use the newly migrated account.

/c:computer The computer on which to make the changes. The format is the UNC form "\\computername"

/k Keep user account *user1* (only applies to local users)

/y Overwrite an existing profile for *user2*.

To use MOVEUSER, you must be logged in with admin rights to create and modify user accounts on both the source and target machine.

```
MOVEUSER otherdomain\bdavis bigfirm\bdavis /c:\\odxp1
```

However, this isn't available for Vista either. Microsoft has provided WMI namespace Win32_UserProfile, which includes the moveuser capability. This can be downloaded and installed on Vista computers. See http://support.microsoft.com/kb/930955. With the use of VBScript, this can automate the process.

The Security Translation Wizard is used for several types of procedures. The translation of local profiles is just one. It can also reassign permissions for user rights, files and shares, printers, local groups, and registry settings. The following section will familiarize you with this function.

TRANSLATING PROFILES WITH THE ADMT SNAP-IN

You can start the Security Translation Wizard from the Action drop-down menu (shown earlier in Figure 24.2). It asks for many of the same things that the User and Group Migration wizards require:

- Source domain and domain controller.

- Target domain and domain controller.

- Object selection, in this case computers. These are chosen through the typical search dialog box. In our example, Odxp1 is the desired computer that the local profiles will be reassigned to for the migrated user.

Then it gets into security specifics (see Figure 24.14). This lists the type of security objects to translate. The ADMT's Help details when to translate each of these. In this example, just the "User profiles" check box is selected.

FIGURE 24.14
Translate
Objects page

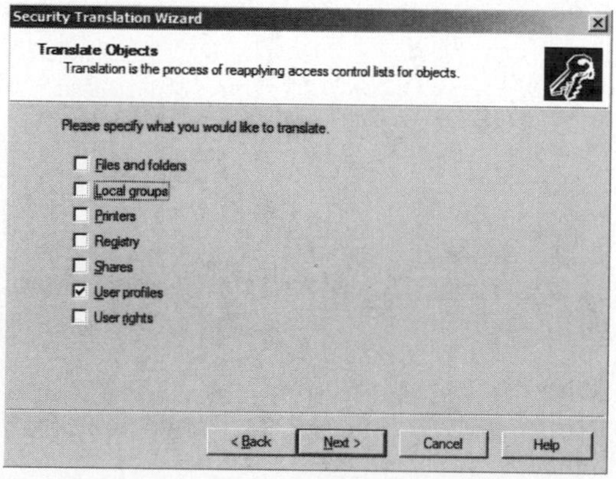

On the next page, shown Figure 24.15, the three options Replace, Add, and Remove treat the old SID as described in the window. The ADMT's help file specifies which option is required for each type of security object. In this case, the local profiles need to have the security replaced. The Add option with local profiles has a tendency to break software application packages deployed with Group Policy objects.

FIGURE 24.15
Security Translation Options page

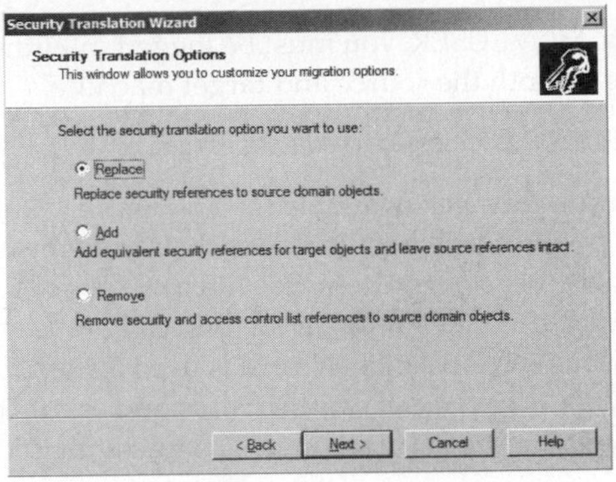

The old SID will be replaced with the user account's new SID, so when Bigfirm\BDavis logs on the workstation, it identifies the original profile with the new account.

After the wizard is complete, a different window displays, as shown in Figure 24.16. The Active Directory Migration Tool Agent Dialog window (say *that* ten times fast) runs the actual operation on the workstation. You must launch the operation with the desired radio button: "Run pre-check" or "Run pre-check and agent operation." (If you use the ADMT command-line utility, the operation starts automatically.) The pre-check, as mentioned, will test the File and Print Services, but more specifically it checks whether the ADMT account can access the administrative shares like \\odxp1\ admin$. The agent operation will install the agent on Odxp1 and then perform the translation.

FIGURE 24.16
Active Directory
Migration Tool
Agent Dialog
window

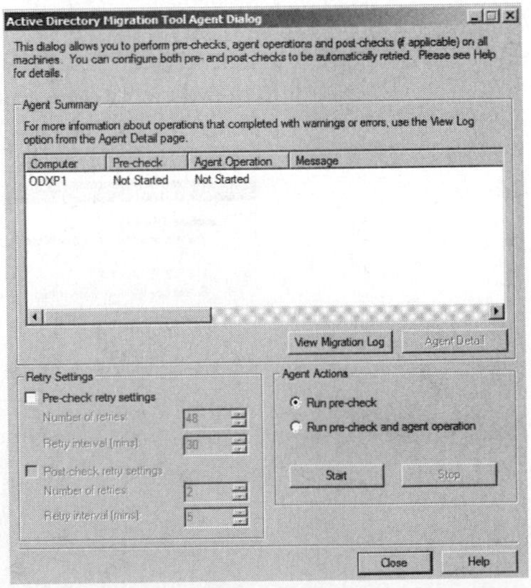

The Agent Summary field displays the progress. For further information, you can view the migration log and agent detail. The agent detail provides another window detailing the agent's installation and run events.

The users need to be logged off the workstation while this operation occurs. A locked workstation will also lock access to the profile. This causes the agent to perform an add operation, but it still could produce an error or unexpected reactions. From our experience, some users may not understand the difference between logged off and locked. We recommend asking users to restart their workstations when knocking off from work. Then run the operation in off-hours.

After the agent operation is completed, the user can log on with the new user account. Their old desktop should be presented, and all the other profile specific settings are available. In this case, their mapped drives to their home folder should be available. Their access to the home folder will verify whether the SID history is working as well.

In additional runs of the Security Translation Wizard, permissions on the home folder can be re-ACLed.

Migrating Computer Accounts

The process of migrating computer accounts looks similar to the Security Translation Wizard and the Active Directory Migration Tool Agent (see Figure 24.17)

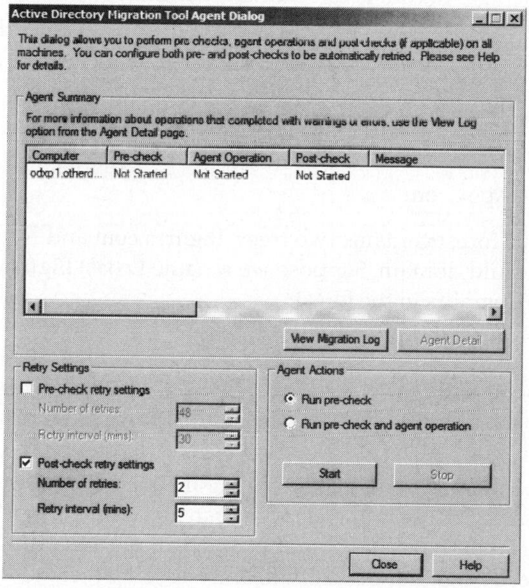

FIGURE 24.17
Active Directory
Migration Tool
Agent Dialog window for computer
migrations

The Agent Summary field includes a Post-check column. The operation performs the domain membership change, which will require a reboot. The verification of change is performed in the post-check. The reboot makes the post-check retry settings important. This sets the number of retries and the interval between each attempt. With a little patience, the operation completes.

Rollback Considerations

The greatest advantage to the C&P migration is its gradual nature. This also lends itself to gradual rollback plans. Phases of the migration will uncover wrinkles and hiccups. You want these to emerge early in the pilots. If issues or obstacles arise, you can avoid performing a showstopping "no-go" rollback. Issues can be addressed individually and with proper planning, "workarounds" and intermediate states can be expected.

The migration process involves copies of accounts and groups. Thus, source accounts and groups are still in place and can be reenabled and used as necessary. Only a few security objects require rollback procedures such as local user profiles. Tools such as `moveuser` can assist in rolling the changes back to regain access.

So, for each migration phase, plan and test the rollback to the state prior to the specific change within the phase.

Renaming a Domain

So, you say you want to rename your domain from Ecoast.Bigfirm.com to Acme.com? Well, we have just one question for you, pardner…*are you sure?*

Server 2003 made it possible to rename domains, so you could indeed rename an AD named Ecoast.Bigfirm.com to one named Acme.com. But there's more to it than just renaming, because renames also let you *rearrange* a forest. For example, suppose we have a forest containing three domains:

◆ Bigfirm.com

◆ Ecoast.Bigfirm.com

◆ Apex.com

This forest contains two trees, Bigfirm.com and Apex.com. One of the trees—Bigfirm.com—has a child domain. Suppose we rename Ecoast.Bigfirm.com to Acme.com. Then we have these three domains in the forest:

◆ Bigfirm.com

◆ Acme.com

◆ Apex.com

See the difference? Still three domains, but now we have three trees as well and no child domains. So, renaming is more than just cosmetic—it's a forest rearranger. Renaming cannot, unfortunately, merge domains; for example, renaming Ecoast.Bigfirm.com to Apex.com will not result in all of Ecoast.Bigfirm.com being melded into the existing Apex.com. The outcome of a rename operation must always leave as many domains in the forest as there once were. And you can't use renaming to change which domain is the forest root, although you can rename the forest root domain.

A domain rename rates a 10 on the pucker factor. A *pucker* is an anatomical phenomenon occurring during high levels of stress and risk. Other similar events with a 10 pucker factor include the following:

◆ Attempting for the third time to land a fighter jet on an aircraft carrier at night in the middle of the Indian Ocean

◆ Vacationing at a beach resort in South Florida because "it's paid for" despite the region being under a hurricane warning for a Category 5 storm

Obviously, there are times when there are no other options except enduring such risk, and there are times when you don't have to endure. The domain rename is the latter.

The reasons for this operation and alternatives must be considered at length. As you saw earlier, the domain rename doesn't buy much. It just renames or reorders. Administration will remain the same.

For the user, the change will be minimal. Pardon the pun, but when it comes to Active Directory, they can't see the forest from the trees. At most, the user would sign on with a different NetBIOS name. If that is important, you can change the UPN suffix and instruct them to log on with the user principal name. In addition, an intraforest migration could provide the same effect without the all-or-nothing consequences.

If there is a decision maker with a wild hair to go through with this, we highly recommend that they are made completely aware of the requirements, operations, and potential risks.

Understanding the Requirements

The following is the list of requirements. Most are doable; however, there is one significant showstopper:

◆ Only an Exchange Server 2003 Service Pack 1 organization is supported by the Windows Server 2008 domain rename. Exchange Server 2003, Exchange Server 2003 SP2, Exchange Server 2007, or Exchange Server 2007 SP1 are not supported. Exchange 2000 and 5.5 are out too. This should knock out 99 percent of the Active Directory implementations in the world.

◆ The Certificate Authority role (either Windows Server 2003 or Windows Server 2008) is not installed on the domain controllers of the renamed domain.

◆ All domain controllers must be Windows Server 2008 or Windows Server 2003.

◆ The forest function level is Windows Server 2008 or Windows Server 2003.

◆ Enterprise Administration credentials are required.

◆ A Windows Server 2008 or 2003 member server is required as a control station.

◆ A stand-alone Distributed File Server (DFS) server must be available.

Affecting Business Operations

This is not an exhaustive list of what needs to be done for a domain rename. It's the big-ticket items that will impact the network and business operations that the decision maker should know:

◆ Domain-based Distributed File System (DDFS) needs to be migrated to stand-alone DFS. After the name change, namespaces for these DDFS will be broken.

◆ Folder redirection and roaming user profiles addressing the DDFS will need to be relocated before the operation.

- Group Policy objects will need to be rebuilt, if the GPO is linked across domains and one of the domains is the renamed one. The GPO assignments will break down because the Group Policy object cannot be found.

- In your Exchange 2003 Service Pack 1 organization, the Exchange Domain Rename Fix-up Tool (Microsoft marketing didn't get a chance to name this one, folks) must be run on all Exchange 2003 Service Pack 1 servers. This will be followed by two restarts.

- Smart cards may have to be reissued. If a domain user is not assigned an explicit UPN such as bdavis@bigfirm.com, then user's UPN will have the original domain name like bdavis@ecoast.bigfirm.com. The name change to Acme.com will invalidate the certificate and authentication path.

- Significant modifications must be performed on the certificate authorities within the renamed domain.

- All local member computers require two reboots. This must be a standard software system shutdown, not a single-finger salute on the power button.

- All remote computers need to be unjoined from the domain and rejoined to the newly renamed domain via VPN connections. You'll feel the love from help desk after they hear about this one.

- All domain controllers in the renamed domain must run through a rename procedure to modify the primary DNS suffix.

Understanding the Business Risks

The loss of business productivity is a significant risk with this operation. The procedure is all-or-nothing. The rollback will involve lengthy procedures including restoring every domain controller's system state data. Here is another short list of the potential risks:

- Workstations fail to switch domain names, resulting in logon issues.

- Users' profiles are not "found," separating them from their expected work environment.

- Remote users are required to bring their laptops into the office to rejoin the domain since it failed via VPN.

- Exchange Server may suffer downtime with loss of email access.

- Domain controllers that fail in the domain rename process must be immediately removed from the network.

It all sounds good, doesn't it? Well, get ready for the bad news…it's a fairly lengthy process.

Performing the Domain Rename

The following hits the high-level steps of the operation. Domain renaming is sufficiently complex that we can't even cover it in detail here without adding at least another 60 pages to the book; Microsoft has about 100 pages of documentation on it online, and trust us, there's not a lot of fluff there. So, just take this as an overview of what you'll have to do when renaming a domain, and please get the Microsoft papers and read them—the object of the following sections is to give you a feel what a domain rename will entail.

PSYCHIATRIC RECOMMENDATION

If you are still with us on this topic, we expect you are a glutton for punishment or suffer from severe insomnia. We recommend seeking psychiatric counseling. If you are reading this because you want to perform a domain rename, you should schedule the psychiatric appointment now. If you are forced by your employer to perform this operation, the visit to the "shrink" should be scheduled upon completion of the operation.

PREPARING FOR A DOMAIN RENAME

The preparation phase ensures the requirements are in place:

1. Configure a DNS zone for the new domain name so that there's a dynamic zone ready to receive new SRV records for the new domain name. In this case, create a DNS zone named Acme.com and make it dynamic on the Ecoast.Bigfirm.com domain controllers. We opt to create a separate application partition for Acme.com so domain controllers outside Ecoast can control the zone. Be sure not to name the partition the same as the domain name. The name of the partition will conflict with the planned domain name during the rename process.

2. Verify that it's set to a forest functional level of Windows Server 2003 or better. Open Active Directory Domains and Trusts, and right-click the Active Directory Domains and Trusts icon; then choose Properties and ensure that the forest functional level is Windows Server 2003 instead of Windows 2000. If it's not at a 2003 level, then refer to Chapter 23 to see how to raise the functional level.

3. Create shortcut trusts. Then build a shortcut trust from the domain that you're going to rename to its future parent, if it's going to move in the forest. However, in our example, it is not allowed in the Active Directory Domains and Trusts snap-in. The automatic trust is already in place; thus, it will kick back with an error.

4. Relocate DDFS structures to a stand-alone DFS server. A DDFS uses the domain name in the address such as \\ecoast.bigfirm.com\DFS. To ensure users can still get to their data, the stand-alone DFS server will provide a temporary solution.

5. Redirection folders using the DDFS need to be reassigned to the stand-alone DFS server. Through Group Policy objects, users' My Documents can be redirected to another location. If it references the DDFS address, this needs to be changed.

6. Assign roaming profiles using the DDFS to the stand-alone DFS server too.

FOLDER MIGRATIONS

We can't stress enough that steps 4, 5, and 6 significantly contribute to the high pucker factor. Moving or reassigning user data tremendously impacts the business operations if not done flawlessly. Most IT shops treat this as a separate project in itself. This would require planning, testing, pilot phases, and the production rollout. Taking it as a simple step of just one project is not recommended.

WHY DO WE NEED A SHORTCUT TRUST?

The idea is that as the rename is happening, there's a brief time when the old automatically built trust will be broken and the new one won't yet be in place. So, create a two-way shortcut trust between the domain that's being renamed and its future parent because the renamed domain will have to communicate with the parent *during* the rename process. For example, suppose you were renaming Bld2.Se.Acme.com to just Bld2.com. The old parent domain was se.acme.com, and now the future parent domain will be whatever is the root domain. So, you'd create a shortcut trust to that root domain. But what about Ecoast.Bigfirm.com? As you're moving from a child domain to a tree of its own, does its parent change? No, not in this case, because Ecoast.Bigfirm.com's parent is Bigfirm.com...which happens to be the forest root. Both Ecoast.Bigfirm.com and Acme.com end up with the same trust relationship.

Now, if you're not 100 percent sure whether you need to create a trust, go ahead and build one—it doesn't hurt. Use Active Directory Domains and Trusts to create the trust as you saw earlier in our discussion of forest trusts in Chapter 23. The wizard is smart enough to keep you from creating unnecessary trusts.

7. Configure workstations and member servers to automatically change the primary DNS suffix. This suffix is assigned to the computer's hostname and is used to dynamically register the computer within the DNS structure. It also is appended to hostnames when searching DNS if an FQDN is not used. By default, Windows operating systems are set do this. So, you must verify that the computers are still set to do this or modify it. This can be set with a Group Policy object.

8. Prep the certificate authorities (CAs). First, CAs must be migrated off domain controllers within the renamed domain. Second, certificates that identify the CA and certificate revocation list (CRL) need to be renewed if they are about to expire. If a member computer recognizes these are out-of-date, they will attempt to find the new ones from the CA. It will attempt to find it with the listed FQDN, which will be unavailable through the domain rename process. This measure of renewing the CA certificate and CRL mitigates this occurrence. In the post-operation phase, steps are made to resolve the inevitable recurrence of certificate and CRL expirations.

DOING THE RENAME

After you've finished the full network configuration changes to prepare for the operation, you can get down to the nitty-gritty of kicking off the process:

1. Install the tools on the control station, which can be either a Windows Server 2008 or a 2003 member server. Although there isn't a requirement on which domain it should be a member, we opt for one in the forest root. The domain naming master is located in that domain. The tools for Windows Server 2008 R2 are part of the Remote Server Administration Tools Pack. This is another feature you can add just as you would add a role like Active Directory Domain Services. It is loaded in the c:\windows\system32 folder.

THE DYNAMIC DNS UPDATE BOW WAVE

Modifying the DNS suffix on workstations and member servers might seem innocuous. If the default setting is sufficient for the operation, then what could go wrong? The problem arises when all the computers see that they have a new DNS suffix to register under. They all are going to attempt it at once! This can overload network bandwidth, stifle DNS performance, and result in loss of name resolutions within the network. Following this, Active Directory replication will be affected by the changes in the Active Directory integrated DNS zones. So, you have some considerations on how to mitigate this bulge in the network cable:

◆ How many computers can be configured at a time? GPOs which trigger the change could be limited to computers in an organizational unit or to a group of computers. The change can be done in phases.

◆ When can you modify the primary DNS suffix? The GPO settings could set the DNS suffix before the domain change or after.

◆ How will computers manage name resolution with the change? If the primary DNS suffix is changed, the computers will encounter name resolution issues. The DNS suffix search order can be populated with the old domain name and the new one. Obviously, we would have to decide which would go first. In one of our environments the DNS suffix search configurations in GPOs didn't work as advertised; thus, you need to test and verify.

---

2. Freeze the forest. Although this generates images from the *Chronicles of Narnia*, you need to ensure no other Active Directory–related activity is occurring during the procedure. As if renaming a domain is not intensive enough for an IT shop, we have to make sure procedures such as creating domains, adding trusts, creating application directories, or other similar enterprise admin-level operations are *not* happening. The random utility is going to throw all domain controllers into a "read-only" type mode until the process is complete. This will seriously impact other forest actions.

3. Back up the domain controllers—all of them.

4. Log on to the control station as an enterprise administrator. Open a command line, and change the directory to the system directory, c:\windows\system32, and type **rendom /list**. You'll get a response "The operation completed successfully." rendom created a file called domainlist.xml in the working directory. Just in case, save it to an alternate location before perusing it. Open domainlist.xml with Notepad. The following is the result of the example forest of Bigfirm.com, Ecoast.Bigfirm.com, and Apex.com domains. We've added comments in italics:

```
<?xml version ="1.0"?>
<Forest>
    <Domain>
        <!-- PartitionType:Application -->
        <Guid>fea67a5d-b376-4d31-bfcd-bf348cd78b24</Guid>
        <DNSname>DomainDnsZones.apex.com</DNSname>
        <NetBiosName></NetBiosName>
```

```
            <DcName></DcName>
        </Domain>
        <Domain>
            <Guid>a5078b58-02c2-4a9e-8fd7-5198665bb138</Guid>
            <DNSname>apex.com</DNSname>
            <NetBiosName>APEX</NetBiosName>
            <DcName></DcName>
        </Domain>
        <Domain>
    <!-- This is the custom application partition
for the newly created Acme.com DNS zone-->
            <!-- PartitionType:Application -->
            <Guid>c73b27d7-2a9b-4d85-aa63-0fd219e7a4c0</Guid>
            <DNSname>acme.com.DNSzone</DNSname>
            <NetBiosName></NetBiosName>
            <DcName></DcName>
        </Domain>
        <Domain>
<!-- This is the default application partition for the Ecoast DNS zone. It
will be modified with the new Acme.com name. -->
            <!-- PartitionType:Application -->
            <Guid>414ced6f-4c43-4776-9826-9282da14b4e9</Guid>
            <DNSname>DomainDnsZones.ecoast.bigfirm.com</DNSname>
            <NetBiosName></NetBiosName>
            <DcName></DcName>
        </Domain>
        <Domain>
<!-- This is the domain partition for the Ecoast domain. It will be modified
with the new Acme.com domain. -->
            <Guid>11c4eed6-a4b2-49c9-b1e5-e123c07f2598</Guid>
            <DNSname>ecoast.bigfirm.com</DNSname>
            <NetBiosName>ECOAST</NetBiosName>
            <DcName></DcName>
        </Domain>
        <Domain>
            <!-- PartitionType:Application -->
            <Guid>fc64dd09-9b1d-4485-b2d6-7ed0423f3e64</Guid>
            <DNSname>DomainDnsZones.bigfirm.com</DNSname>
            <NetBiosName></NetBiosName>
            <DcName></DcName>
        </Domain>
        <Domain>
            <!-- PartitionType:Application -->
            <Guid>0c396cb8-a744-4065-ab89-3073d6bb915a</Guid>
            <DNSname>ForestDnsZones.bigfirm.com</DNSname>
            <NetBiosName></NetBiosName>
            <DcName></DcName>
```

```
    </Domain>
    <Domain>
        <!-- ForestRoot -->
        <Guid>49dc40f3-4902-47eb-bb42-7cb50ac1ec44</Guid>
        <DNSname>bigfirm.com</DNSname>
        <NetBiosName>BIGFIRM</NetBiosName>
        <DcName></DcName>
    </Domain>
</Forest>
```

In case you've never seen an XML file before, it's a way of storing data in what is intended to be a self-describing way. (Get used to it. If you haven't noticed this in the book already, Microsoft has shifted to this format for almost all output and input files.) The things in the angle brackets are called *tags*—<Domain>, <DNSname>, <NetBiosName>. Notice that every tag has a partner tag with a / in the front of its name, like </Domain>, </DNSname>, and </NetBiosName>. Think of these <tag> and </tag> pairs as being sort of like left and right parentheses that also describe the data between them. For example:

```
<NetBiosName>ECOAST</NetBiosName>
```

This means "This particular object has a NetBiosName of ECOAST." Armed with this information, you can see a few things. First, the whole file describes a forest, as you can see from the fact that the very first line is <Forest> and the last is </Forest>. Within that are several <Domain> and </Domain> sets. Each domain contains a GUID, a DNSname, a NetBiosName, and a DcName—we'll need to use the DNSname and NetBiosName sections. Notice that the first Domain entry is an application partition named DomainDNSzones.apex.com, which holds the Apex.com Active Directory integrated DNS zone. The next entry is for the Apex.com domain and its NetBiosName is Apex.

5. Believe it or not, the way that you tell **random** to rename the domain is to directly edit this file—so change Ecoast.Bigfirm.com to Acme.com and "ECOAST" to "ACME," and save the file. In our example, the change is pretty straightforward. If the change is related to changing the parent-child DNS suffix, the DNSzone application partitions would have to be modified too. In this case, the DomainDNSzones.ecoast.bigfirm.com application partition is renamed to DomainDNSzones.acme.com.

6. Next, check your work by typing **random /showforest** to make sure that you didn't mess up the XML file. The output will look something like this:

```
c:\Windows\System32>random /showforest
acme.com [FlatName:ACME]
        DomainDnsZones.acme.com [PartitionType:Application]
acme.com.DNSzone [PartitionType:Application]
apex.com [FlatName:APEX]
        DomainDnsZones.apex.com [PartitionType:Application]
bigfirm.com [ForestRoot Domain, FlatName:BIGFIRM]
        DomainDnsZones.bigfirm.com [PartitionType:Application]
        ForestDnsZones.bigfirm.com [PartitionType:Application]
```

```
The operation completed successfully.
```

That looks correct—Ecoast.Bigfirm.com is gone, and Acme.com is visible. Note the "FlatName" represents the NetBios name. Since "spelling counts" in computers, this is a great opportunity to double-check it.

7. Now run **rendom /upload**. This will take the edited `domainlist.xml` file and create the domain rename instructions to deploy to the domain controllers.

8. In the working directory, the **rendom /upload** command also generated a `dclist.xml` file. This lists the domain controllers within the forest. Examine that file to ensure every domain controller in the ecoast.bigfirm.com has the `<State>Initial</State>` attribute and the domain controller with the domain naming master role has the initial state. (We also recommend investigating why any domain controller doesn't have that state.) The following is an example of the file:

```xml
<?xml version ="1.0"?>
<DcList>
    <Hash>oHuq2Mzlp7sxnd1vJ9B4N2jEbHI=</Hash>
    <Signature>ViDbL849veWjknGm5mLE3LeSJsE=</Signature>
    <DC>
        <Name>ap1.apex.com</Name>
        <State>Initial</State>
        <Password></Password>
        <LastError>0</LastError>
        <LastErrorMsg></LastErrorMsg>
        <FatalErrorMsg></FatalErrorMsg>
        <Retry></Retry>
    </DC>
    <DC>
        <Name>ec1.ecoast.bigfirm.com</Name>
        <State>Initial</State>
        <Password></Password>
        <LastError>0</LastError>
        <LastErrorMsg></LastErrorMsg>
        <FatalErrorMsg></FatalErrorMsg>
        <Retry></Retry>
    </DC>
    <DC>
        <Name>bf1.bigfirm.com</Name>
        <State>Initial</State>
        <Password></Password>
        <LastError>0</LastError>
        <LastErrorMsg></LastErrorMsg>
        <FatalErrorMsg></FatalErrorMsg>
        <Retry></Retry>
    </DC>
</DcList>
```

9. Now, the uploaded domain rename instructions need to be promulgated to all domain controllers in the forest. You could allow the Active Directory replication to handle this on its own. This would give you some time to grab another piece of cold pizza that the IT manager brought in for the Saturday night "party." However, in larger environments that span several sites, this could take much longer than he's willing to wait. So, the repadmin tool could speed up the process by triggering replication to occur. The following would trigger the domain controllers to synchronize with the domain naming master:

```
repadmin /syncall /d /e /P /q bf1.bigfirm.com
```

10. The DNS service locator records need to be verified for the new domain name. A check of its DNS zone using the DNS Management console can help with this. The Acme.com DNS zone should be populated with the service locator folders so a check of the zone in the DNS Management console should validate that they were registered by the domain controller of Ecoast.Bigfirm.com Also, DCDiag can perform the operation:

```
Dcdiag /test:DNS /DnsRecordRegistration /s:ec1.ecoast.bigfirm.com
```

11. Then run rendom /prepare, which reads the dclist.xml file and uses it to find DCs and get them ready for the domain rename. In large organizations, you may need to run this command multiple times until all domain controllers are prepared. The dclist.xml file will be modified after each run. It's recommended that you save a copy of the file prior to each run. You'll see output something like this:

```
c:\Windows\System32>rendom /prepare
Waiting for DCs to reply.
Waiting for DCs to reply.
bf1.bigfirm.com was prepared successfully
ap1.apex.com was prepared successfully
ec1.ecoast.bigfirm.com was prepared successfully
3 servers contacted, 0 servers returned Errors

The operation completed successfully.
```

12. Now you're ready for the big step—rendom /execute. Like the prepare step, the dclist. xml file will be modified with the new state of the domain controllers. The Done or Error are completed states. When a domain controller is done, an automatic reboot will occur. If a domain controller is listed as Prepare, you will have to run this command again. Our output looks like this:

```
c:\Windows\System32>rendom /execute
Waiting for DCs to reply.
Waiting for DCs to reply.
The script was executed successfully on bf1.bigfirm.com
The script was executed successfully on ap1.apex.com
The script was executed successfully on ec1.ecoast.bigfirm.com
3 servers contacted, 0 servers returned Errors

The operation completed successfully.
```

ERROR STATE

Domain controllers that reach the error state will have to be removed from the forest. This will require running DCPromo to remove the service from that server.

---

13. Run the Exchange Domain Rename Fix-up Tool. Remember that this is for those Exchange Server 2003 Service Pack 1 servers.

14. Unfreeze the forest. With the equivalent privileges of Aslan the Lion within the Bigfirm. com forest, we run `rendom /end`, which will release the domain controllers from the "read-only" type state.

15. Reestablish and verify external trusts.

16. Run the GPOFixup tool to change the references of the old domain name in the GPOs.

17. Perform some certificate authority operations that will make your head spin. For starters, create a CNAME for the certificate authorities in the old domain's DNS zone that points to its new host record. This will remain until the old CRLs and CAs certificates expire. The publishing of new CRLs and CA certificates are also required, but the list goes on.

18. A boatload of little configuration changes too tedious for us to mention. To peruse the array of miscellaneous tasks, you can visit `http://technet.microsoft.com/en-us/library/cc816896.aspx`.

19. Back up the domain controllers.

20. Reboot all member servers and workstations in the renamed domain *twice*. You need both reboots to confirm the membership and change the domain suffix. If the workstations are remote, they must be unjoined from the domain and rejoined through a VPN connection. (We can't stop laughing when we read this step. It's sort of a maniacal laugh.)

21. Run the `rendom /clean` command. This must be done after all the previous steps are completed, including fixing up the CAs and restarting the entire lot of domain computers.

22. Rename the domain controllers of the new domain. The primary DNS suffix doesn't change automatically on domain controllers like the member computers. So, you have to do it by hand—go to each DC and change its DNS suffix from the old domain name to the new one. Now, this procedure is a little bit different from Windows Server 2003. Right-click Computer on the Start menu and choose Properties; then in the System window, under the "Computer name, domain and workgroup settings" section, click the Change Settings hyperlink. This will open the System applet in Control Panel that you may be familiar with from Windows Server 2003. On the Computer Name tab, click the Change button, and then click the More button. There, you can change the DNS suffix to Acme.com.

It's dusk on Sunday. You're bleary-eyed and smell funny. The domain rename is over, and the IT manager has given you kudos for an extremely stressful and challenging network change. It's time for a brewsky. In our example, the process involved only a few domain controllers and a member server, so it is hardly reflective of an enterprise environment where this procedure may apply. Remember for you to earn that brewsky, you will have to research, plan, and run through this in a virtual environment several times. Don't rely only on this description.

The Bottom Line

Introduce new versions of Active Directory into a network   The release of a new version of Windows Server means you need to upgrade existing domain controllers. There are two basic methods to add a new version of Active Directory into an organization: upgrading a domain controller or upgrading the domain by adding a new domain controller.

> **Master it**   Both operations require the Active Directory database to be modified using the `adprep.exe` utility. What three options need to be run? What option can also be run?

Migrate domains accounts from one domain to another   The requirement, to move users and groups from an existing domain to a clean and pristine domain, often happens when companies merge or spin off. In addition, this can be required when a forest restructuring is justified. Microsoft offers the ADMT utility to perform domain migrations.

> **Master it**   After a user account is migrated to the new domain, what gives the user access to resources within the original domain?

Restructure domains within a forest   The options to changing the domain structure are limited. One option is performed by migrating the domain accounts with the ADMT utility. The other alternative is renaming a domain. The former is gradual and complicated. The latter is an all-or-nothing complex operation offering a great deal of risk.

> **Master it**   The domain rename operation is limited by the version of Exchange Server deployed in the environment. What version is supported by Microsoft for a domain rename?

Chapter 25

Installing, Using, and Administering Remote Desktop Services

Using Remote Desktop Services (RDS)—formerly known as Terminal Services—and an RD Session Host server makes it possible to install and manage applications, or desktops, in one location but be controlled by end users in another location.

Applications that run on the RD Session Host server are called RDS RemoteApp applications. From the end-user perspective, these applications look and feel as though they are running on their local system. The user's keystrokes and mouse movements are sent to the server. Images are sent back to the user's system. Even thin clients can easily run sophisticated applications with ease, though RDS RemoteApps are most commonly run on regular desktop systems.

The old Remote Desktop Services came in two flavors: TS for Administrators and TS in application mode. TS for Administrators is now known as Remote Desktop for Administration, and TS in application mode is known as Remote Desktop Services with an RD Session Host server. Remote Desktop for Administration was covered in Chapter 14, and this chapter covers Remote Desktop Services with an RD Session Host server. Topics include adding the RDS role, configuring an RD session host server, adding RDS RemoteApp applications, and connecting to RDS sessions.

In this chapter, you will learn to:

◆ Limit the maximum number of connections

◆ Add an application to an RD Session Host server

◆ Add a RemoteApp for Web Access

◆ Add a RemoteApp to the Start menu

Who Needs Remote Desktop Services?

Remote Desktop Services can be used to enable end users to run a Windows-based program on a remote server from their desktop computer. The server hosting the application is called a Remote Desktop Session Host (RD Session Host) server. It's also possible for the end users to access a full desktop session on the RD Session Host server.

As an administrator, you can do the following:

◆ Deploy and manage applications on a few RDS servers instead of on hundreds or thousands of client computers.

◆ Provide applications to end users whom you cannot easily support because they're in another office—or another country.

- ◆ Reduce the impact of client hardware failures by keeping all applications on a central server. If a client's computer dies, plug in a new one, and they're back to work.

- ◆ Avoid misconfigured computers.

- ◆ Get out of the hardware rat race that constantly requires more updates to support the latest and greatest software.

- ◆ Use computers in environments that are not compatible with desktop computers.

- ◆ Simplify help-desk and training support.

If any of these tasks are important to you, then you should seriously consider using Remote Desktop Services with a Session Host server.

Centralized Deployment of Applications

One great benefit to Remote Desktop Services is how it simplifies application deployment. Instead of deploying an application to all the clients using Group Policy or Microsoft System Center Configuration Manager (SCCM), you can install it once on the RD Session Host server.

As an example, your business may have a line-of-business application that 100 users need to access. Instead of installing the application on all 100 desktop computers, an RD Session Host server could be used. The application could be installed once on the server, and each user could then access the application remotely.

Even better, when the application needs to be upgraded or patched, you need to do it only once—on the RDS server.

Supporting Remote Users

Remote Desktop Services can be used for remote access or branch-office access. Some applications have difficulty performing over low-speed connections or need special ports opened on the firewall. Instead of running the application over the low-speed connection, the application can be hosted on the RDS server within a well-connected network.

Clients can still connect via a VPN or low-speed dial-up connection. However, since the application is running on the RD Session Host server in a well-connected network, its performance isn't impacted by the slower connections.

More and more people are telecommuting at least a couple of days a week. Many U.S. government agencies have a legal requirement to support telecommuters, and many telecommuters often don't even have offices or desks. Rather than trying to maintain desktop computers for all the staff, many companies are giving users computers to take home and providing their applications via remote servers.

Supporting PC-Unfriendly Environments

The dream of "a PC on every desktop" will remain a dream, if for no other reason than in some environments the conditions are bad for the desktop PC or the desktop PC is bad for the conditions. In other words, it's not feasible to put a desktop PC anywhere.

Some environments are bad for PCs. PCs don't like dust, excessive heat, or vibration, and you won't like maintaining the PCs if you try to use them in an environment that has any of these characteristics. Of course, PCs can be built to work in extreme conditions such as temperatures as high as 120 degrees or even underwater. And for the companies and people who must have them in these extreme environments, engineers have engineered solutions—but at a cost. When cost is an issue and a thin client will work, Remote Desktop Services can be a good solution.

We've also seen terminals in health club cafes and coffeehouses set up so that only the monitor is visible, thus reducing the chances of someone dropping a strawberry-banana low-fat smoothie with a shot of wheatgrass juice down the vents. For that matter, if someone does drop the smoothie down the terminal's vents, then, because the applications are installed on and running from the RDS server, replacing the device to provide an identical environment is as simple as unplugging the sticky terminal and plugging in a new one. If you drop a smoothie down a computer's vents, then restoring an identical working environment is significantly more complicated.

What about PCs being bad for the conditions? Clean rooms where chips and boards are made are good candidates for Windows terminals. You can't have dust in a clean room, and the fans in a PC kick up dust. Additionally, becoming sanitized to enter a clean room is neither simple nor inexpensive; you don't want to put devices that need care and feeding from the IT staff in there. Another factor applies to many situations, not just clean rooms: anyplace where space is at a premium is a good candidate for a Windows terminal.

Clients can be running thin clients or just about any desktop operating system including Windows, Linux, and Macintosh (though security is optimized on Windows Vista or Windows 7).

This section isn't to sell you on the idea of Windows terminals but to point out that sometimes they're useful, even required—and you can't use them without an RDS server.

🌐 Real World Scenario

POWER STRUGGLES

Another aspect of the environment-unfriendly PC applies to the power a desktop PC uses. Several studies have been published on the cost savings of thin clients vs. desktop PCs. With the cost of power these days, the savings can be significant.

One study titled "Power to the People: Comparing Power Usage for PCs and Thin Clients in an Office Network Environment" by Stephen Greenberg, Christa Anderson, and Jennifer Mitchell-Jackson (www.thinclient.net/power/Power_Study.pdf) shows some of the possibilities. For example, a single thin client averaged about 10 watts a day while a desktop PC averaged 69 watts. This doesn't include the monitor, but both thin clients and PCs can use low-power LCD monitors instead of the power-hungry CRTs of the past.

The study estimated the cost of power at .10 per kWh and .20 per kWh, which is a good range of power costs within the United States. For 100 clients, this equated to savings of between $3,000 and $6,000 annually.

Saving on power costs isn't the only reason to use Windows terminals, but if you're tossing around the idea of replacing PCs with terminals, it's a compelling argument in favor of it.

Reducing Hardware Refreshes

Does it take a 2.5GHz Pentium with 3GB of RAM installed to check email, do accounting, and poke around on the Web a bit? Of course not, but, as of mid-2009, that's not an unusual hardware profile for a desktop computer. Not that these computers are too expensive in absolute terms;

we're wryly amused that every time we buy a new computer, we pay less for a system more powerful than the last one we bought.

Still, even though they're not too expensive in absolute terms, the new computers aren't always worth it because what you're doing doesn't demand all that much from your hardware. Ironically, unless your job is something demanding such as computer-assisted design, you're often more likely to need a powerful computer at home than at work because game hardware requirements are so high. It takes more computing power to play a few swift rounds of the most recent version of WarCraft than it does to write this chapter. (Fighting orcs is hard work!)

The trouble is, sometimes you do need those more powerful computers if you're planning to keep up with existing software technology. True—you don't need the world's fastest computer to do word processing. You may, however, need a computer faster than the one you have if you're going to keep up with the latest and greatest word processing package that everyone is using. If you want to be able to read all those charts and graphs, you can't always do it when the word processor you're using is six years old, even if it still suits your in-house needs. And you can't always run that new word processor if your computer is six years old.

However, if you're using Remote Desktop Services with an RD Session Host server, the client only displays applications running on the RDS server, rather than running them locally—you don't have to concern yourself with whether the applications will run on the client computer, just the server. If the application will run on the RD server and the client can get to the RD server, then the application will display on the client.

Simplifying the User Interface

Another potential benefit to Remote Desktop Services is it can simplify the user interface (UI). Using a computer isn't as easy for everyone as the marketing world would have you believe. Experienced users find it easy to customize their interface, but those who are less experienced find all sorts of pitfalls when it comes to using their computers: so many options that they get confused and too many ways to break something. Colorful icons with rounded corners do not a simple UI make.

If the people you're supporting need only a single application, then you can save yourself and them a lot of grief by providing a connection that runs this application in a remote desktop and nothing else. This is particularly true with Windows-based terminals, which are little more than a monitor, a box, a keyboard, and a mouse.

Or, if the users are already running a desktop operating system, you can use RemoteApp applications. RemoteApp applications deployed via RDS are as easy to use as any other applications on the end user's computer. RemoteApp applications can be launched from the Start menu, from a desktop icon (of an .rdp file), or from a web page.

Providing Help-Desk Support

Finally, Remote Desktop Services can make application support easier, not just in terms of installing new applications and applying fixes but in helping people learn to use those applications. Remote Control lets help-desk personnel or administrators connect to another person's remote session either to watch what they're doing or to interact with the session. (This isn't the security hole it may seem—permissions to do this can be controlled.)

When you have remote control of another user's session, you can either watch what they're doing and coach them (perhaps over the telephone) or actually interact with the session so that you can demonstrate a process. This beats standing over someone's shoulder saying, "Click the File button at the top left. No, File. The FILE button," or trying to figure out what they're doing when your only information comes from their description of the screen.

Deploying RDS RemoteApp

RemoteApp programs are applications that are running on the RD Session Host server but appear to the end user to be running on their desktop. This is often easier for an end user to conceptualize. They don't have to manage multiple desktops but instead can simply launch another application from their main desktop.

Windows Server 2008 introduced RemoteApp programs, and they've been improved in Windows Server 2008 R2. It does take a little bit of configuration to support RemoteApp programs. Once you've configured all the pieces, users can access RemoteApp applications using the following methods:

Through a web browser If RD Web Access is configured, users can access the web page and click a link to launch the application.

Using a Remote Desktop Protocol (.rdp) file Users can simply double-click a properly configured .rdp file to launch the RemoteApp application.

Through the Start menu or a program icon RemoteApp applications can be installed using traditional Windows Installer (.msi) packages (also called Microsoft Installer packages). Once installed, users can launch the applications just as any other installed application.

You'll learn how to install all the components and deploy RemoteApp applications for each of these methods in the section "Adding Remote Desktop Services" later in this chapter.

Understanding the Remote Desktop Services Processing Model

Thin-client networking or *server-based computing* (same thing, different emphasis) refers to any computing environment in which most application processing takes place on a server enabled for multiuser access, instead of a client. The terms refer to a network by definition, so that doesn't include stand-alone small computing devices such as personal digital assistants (PDAs) or handheld PCs, although you can add thin-client support to some of these devices.

What makes thin-client networking and computing "thin" is neither the size of the operating system nor the complexity of the apps run on the client, but how processing is distributed. In a thin-client network, most if not all processing takes place on the server. Instructions for creating video output travel from server to client, mouse clicks and keystrokes pass from the client to the server, and all video output is rendered on the client.

Son of Mainframe?

You may have heard thin-client networking described as "a return to the mainframe paradigm." (We have heard this less politely phrased as "You just reinvented the mainframe, stupid!") This comparison is partly apt and partly misleading. It's true that applications are stored and run on a central server, with only output shown at the client.

Netbooks and Thin Clients

Netbooks are exploding on the scene, and you may be wondering how they may fit in here. In case you've just gotten off a deserted island, a netbook is a small (7- to 10-inch screen) portable computer designed for communication on the Internet (hence the *net* in netbook). They have more resources than a thin client but significantly less than a full-blown desktop PC. Because of their size, they are highly mobile. They use less processing power, less RAM, and simpler graphics, which all contribute to using less power and to a longer battery life.

It's entirely possible to use netbooks as part of a Remote Desktop solution. The netbook could connect to the Remote Desktop server either directly over the Internet using RD Gateway or via a VPN. The applications or desktops can be executed on the Remote Desktop server so that the netbook's hardware resources aren't overly taxed.

However, the applications being run in the thin-client environment are different from those run in a mainframe environment; mainframes didn't support word processing or slide show packages, and the video demands on the graphical Windows client are necessarily greater than they were with a text-based green-screen terminal. Yet the degree of control that thin-client networking offers is mainframe-like, and we've heard one person happily describe thin-client networking and the command it gave him over his user base as "a return to the good old mainframe days."

Why the move from centralized computing to personal computers and back again? Business applications drove the development of PCs—the new applications simply couldn't work in a mainframe environment. Not all mainframes were scrapped, by any means, but the newer application designs were too hardware-intensive to work well in a shared computing environment. But those applications came back to a centralized model when it became clear that the mainframe model had some things to offer that a PC-based LAN did not:

◆ Grouping of computing resources to make sure none are wasted

◆ Centralized distribution and maintenance of applications

◆ Clients that don't have to be running the latest and greatest operating system with the latest and greatest hardware to support it

◆ Client machines that don't require power protection because they're not running any applications locally

All in all, reinventing the mainframe has its advantages. Just as PCs didn't replace mainframes, server-based computing isn't replacing PCs. However, it's nice to have the option to use server-based computing when it makes more sense than installing applications on the desktop.

Anatomy of a Thin-Client Session

A thin-client networking session has three parts:

◆ The *RDS server,* running a multiuser operating system

◆ The *display protocol,* which is a data link layer protocol that creates a virtual channel between server and client through which user input and graphical output can flow

◆ The *client,* which can be running any kind of operating system that supports the terminal client

These are explained in detail in the following sections.

THE RDS SERVER

Remote Desktop Services is one of the optional components you can choose to install on Windows Server 2008 R2. If you've added the Remote Desktop Services role, RDS begins listening at TCP port 3389 for incoming client connection requests as soon as the server boots up and loads the core operating system.

Understanding Sessions

When a client requests a connection to the server and the server accepts the request, the client's unique view of the RDS server is called its *session*. In addition to the remote sessions, a special client session for the console is created.

> #### DESKTOP PCS CAN'T RUN RDS
>
> Some have asked whether there's any way to make Windows XP, Windows Vista, or Windows 7 into a multiuser server (of sorts). Nope—no Microsoft desktop operating system includes full-fledged Remote Desktop Services, and there is no way to add it. Windows XP, Windows Vista, and Windows 7 all include the Remote Desktop feature that allows someone to connect to the computer via the RDP display protocol. However, only one connection is supported at a time. The Remote Desktop Services feature we discuss in this chapter is solely a server-class feature.

All sessions have unique session IDs that the server uses to distinguish the processes running within different RDS sessions on the same computer. In this context, processes are roughly equivalent to executable files. When a client connects to the RDS server, a session ID is created for the session.

Figure 25.1 shows the Remote Desktop Services Manager monitoring several sessions running on an RDS server.

FIGURE 25.1

Remote Desktop Services Manager

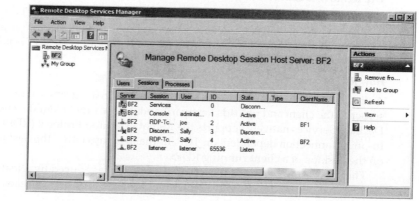

Every desktop session has several base processes running within it to support the user. Additional processes in the session will depend on the applications the user is running.

> ### EXECUTABLES, IMAGES, AND THREADS
>
> In Windows operating systems, an executable file is internally known as an *image*. This is because, technically speaking, an application isn't the piece getting processor cycles but instead is a collection of commands called *threads* that get processor time to do whatever they need to do. The threads have an environment called the *process* that tells them where to store and retrieve their data. The part of the process that does something is collectively called the *image* or *executable*. For the sake of consistency with the interface, we'll refer to programs running on the RDS server as *processes*.

The session keeps per-session processes from corrupting each other or viewing each other's data. However, although the sessions are allowed to ignore each other, they still have to coexist. All sessions use the same resources—processor time, memory, and operating system functions— so the operating system must divide the use of these resources among all the sessions. To do so, the RDS server identifies the processes initiated in each session not only by their process ID but by their session ID as well.

Each session has a high-priority thread reserved for keyboard and mouse input and display output, but ordinary applications run at the priority they'd have in a single-user environment. Because all session threads have the same priority, the scheduler processes user input in round-robin format, with each session's input thread having a certain amount of time to process data before control of the processor passes to another user thread. If the sessions are very active, they'll be much more competition for processor time.

The number of sessions an RDS server can support depends on how many sessions the hardware (generally memory but also processor time, network bandwidth, and disk access) can support and how many licenses are available. When a client logs out of her session, the virtual channels to that client machine close, and the resources allocated to that session are released.

THE REMOTE DESKTOP PROTOCOL

You can run all the sessions you like on the RDS server, but that won't do you any good unless you can view the session output from a remote computer and upload your input to the terminal server for processing. The mechanism that allows you to do both is the *display protocol*.

How RDP Works

A display protocol downloads instructions for rendering graphical images from the terminal server to the client and uploads keyboard and mouse input from the client to the server. Remote Desktop Services natively supports the Remote Desktop Protocol (RDP). RDP provides a point-to-point connection dependent on TCP/IP that displays either the desktop or a single application on the desktop of a client running RDP.

The processing demands placed on the client are reduced by a feature called *client-side caching* that allows the client to "remember" images that have already been downloaded during the session. With caching, only the changed parts of the screen are downloaded to the client during each refresh. For example, if the Microsoft Word icon has already been downloaded to the client, there's no need for it to be downloaded again as the image of the desktop is updated. The hard disk's cache stores data for a limited amount of time and then eventually discards data using the least recently used (LRU) algorithm. When the cache gets full, it discards the data that has been unused the longest in favor of new data.

AUTOMATIC REFRESH TIMING

The image on the screen is updated at very short intervals when the session is active. If the person logged in to the session stops sending mouse clicks and keystrokes to the server, then the RD server notes the inactivity and reduces the refresh rate until client activity picks up again.

Note that in addition to each client session, there's also a session for the server's use. All locally run services and executables run within the context of this server session.

RDP VERSION 6.0 AND VERSION 6.1

RDP has been around since NT 4.0 days (the first version was RDP 4.0) and has had a lot of upgrades. The current version available with Windows Server 2008 R2 is version 6.1.

Version 6.0 came out with Windows Vista. The biggest change was the ability to connect to individual applications using RemoteApp instead of launching a full desktop. It also provided support for monitor spanning or using multiple monitors in remote sessions.

Microsoft released version 6.1 in February 2008 and included it with Windows Server 2008. Mostly, this was used to provide support for advanced features to Windows XP SP3 clients. If you're running Windows XP SP3, you should check out the Knowledge Base article at http://support.microsoft.com/kb/952155.

Server and Client Requirements

The computing model for thin-client networking means that the horsepower is concentrated on the server end, not the client end. Because the server will be supporting dozens of people — maybe hundreds—this is not the time to skimp on power.

Server Hardware

The notion of using a bigger server so that you can skimp on client-side hardware isn't new. That's all a file server is: a computer running a big, fast hard disk so that you don't have to buy big, fast hard disks for everyone in the office. RDS servers are designed on a similar principle—if most of the processing takes place in a single location, you can concentrate the hardware resources needed to support that processing in a single location and worry less about power on the client end.

USE A POWERFUL RD SESSION HOST SERVER

Since an RD Session Host server will be serving applications or full desktops to clients, you'll need to purchase or build a powerful server. Processing power and RAM are the most important resources. Depending on the types and number sessions you're supporting, you may also want to consider boosting disk access and network bandwidth.

On the surface, calculating the needs seems straightforward. Just follow these steps:

1. Calculate the resources needed for the operating system.

2. Calculate the resources needed for a small number of sessions (such as five).

3. Multiply the resources needed for your sessions based on the total number of sessions you plan to support. If you planned to support 100 sessions and you measured five sessions, you'd multiply by 20 (20 * 5 = 100 sessions).

4. Add the total session resources needed for sessions to the resources needed for the operating system.

Although this seems like simple math, it never seems to work out that way. Synergy is often hard to predict. Synergy (where the whole is greater than the sum of its parts) often results in something unexpected. Additionally, if the deployment is successful and users are happy with what they can do, they may end up using it much more than you anticipated.

You don't need to tell this to the budget people, but it's best to add a buffer for the unknowns and to plan for expansion. Additionally, you should do some independent research starting with Microsoft's Remote Desktop Services home: www.microsoft.com/windowsserver2008/en/us/rds-product-home.aspx.

CORE HARDWARE RESOURCES

For the purposes of running an efficient RD Session Host server, the bare minimum required to run Server 2008 R2 won't cut it. Although there are no hard-and-fast specifications for an RDS server, some general guidelines for server sizing follow:

Processor Faster is better to a point. More important than a fast processor is one with enough cache so that it doesn't have to reach out to the (slower) system memory for code and data. Faced with a choice between more cache and more speed, go with more cache. Most RDS servers these days have multiple processors, and these processors have multiple cores. Although only multithreaded applications will actually use more than one processor at a time, if there are multiple processors, then threads needing execution can line up at both.

Memory RDS servers tend to be memory bound, not processor bound. Get high-speed, error-correcting memory; get plenty of it; and be prepared to add more as you add more users or applications to the RDS server. The amount of memory you'll need depends on the applications that people use, the number of concurrent sessions, and the memory demands of the files opened in those sessions—computer-aided design (CAD) programs will stress the system more than, say, Notepad. Thankfully, the 64-bit operating system goes well beyond the 4GB limit. Start your calculations with at least 8GB of RAM for the server, and start adding based on the of number of users and memory required by the applications they'll run on the server. Windows Server 2008 R2 will support up to 2TB of RAM.

Disk   Consider Serial Computer System Interface (SCSI) disks on an RDS server if at all possible. A SCSI disk controller can multitask among all the devices in the SCSI chain. Most people believe that SCSI performs much better both Serial Advanced Technology Attachment (SATA) and Enhanced Integrated Drive Electronics (EIDE) disks, though some people are starting to find that high-end SATA solutions perform better than low-end SCSI solutions. Disk performance is an important capability in any server, especially so in an RDS server. Additionally, consider a Redundant Array of Inexpensive Disks (RAID) solution to increase the performance and/or fault tolerance of the drives. For a high-end RDS server, a RAID 1+0 solution provides both performance gains and redundancy.

Network   On a busy RDS server, consider load-balancing high-speed network cards, which can assign multiple NICs to the same IP address and thus split the load of network traffic. Another alternative is a multihomed server with one NIC dedicated to RDS session traffic. As far as network *speed* goes, sending application output and client-side input back and forth requires little bandwidth, but client-print jobs sent to mapped printers can take quite a bit of bandwidth. Mapped drives may also increase the load by making it possible to copy files back and forth across the RDP connection.

USING THE PERFORMANCE MONITOR

The Performance Monitor (discussed in Chapter 17) can help you get an idea of how RDS sessions are stressing the server. Server load should scale closely with the number of people using the server; therefore, as long as you pick a representative group of about five people, you should be able to extrapolate your needs for larger groups. The key objects and counters for measuring general server stress introduced in that chapter will help you size your RDS servers. But a couple of Performance Monitor objects are worth examining to give you detailed information for your RDS server.

PERFORMANCE MONITOR OBJECTS STILL CALLED TERMINAL SERVICES

Although the name of Terminal Services has changed to Remote Desktop Services in Windows Server 2008 R2, it's still called Terminal Services in Performance Monitor. It might look like a typo, but the two objects are called Terminal Services and Terminal Services Session.

First, the Terminal Services object has counters representing the number of active sessions (sessions where the user has connected to the RD Session Host server and successfully logged on), inactive sessions (where the user is still logged onto the RDS server but has stopped using the session), and the total combined.

Besides simply monitoring activity, you could use this to alert you when the number of active session reaches a certain threshold. Say you wanted to know when a server hosts more than 100 sessions. You could do this with a data collector set.

Chapter 17 discussed data collector sets in more depth, but it's possible to set up a simple user-defined data collector set with an alert. This is done by creating the user-defined data collector set manually (not with a template), selecting Performance Counter Alert, and then setting the threshold for the active sessions. You can then set a task for the alert to notify you with a basic script or log the event to a file.

Although you can get some session-level information from the Remote Desktop Services Manager, a performance object called Terminal Services Session provides quite a bit more data. Use the Remote Desktop Services Manager to find the session you want to monitor—sessions are identified in Performance Monitor by their session numbers, not user login name—and then add counters to monitor that session. Each session object has processor and memory counters that should look familiar to anyone who's used Performance Monitor, but it also has session-specific counters such as the ones in Table 25.1. We haven't included all the counters here, just the ones to show you the kind of information that will be useful when you're calculating the load on the server and looking at the kind of performance the sessions are getting.

TABLE 25.1:   Key Terminal Services Session Performance Monitor Counters

COUNTER	DESCRIPTION	SEE ALSO
% Processor Time	Percentage of time that all of the threads in the session used the processor to execute instructions. On multiprocessor machines the maximum value of the counter is 100 percent times the number of processors.	
Total Bytes	Total number of bytes sent to and from this session, including all protocol overhead.	Input Bytes, Output Bytes
Total Compressed Bytes	Total number of bytes after compression. Total Compressed Bytes compared with Total Bytes is the compression ratio.	Total Compression Ratio
Total Protocol Cache Hit Ratio	Total hits in all protocol caches holding Windows objects likely to be reused. Hits in the cache represent objects that did not need to be re-sent, so a higher hit ratio implies more cache reuse and possibly a more responsive session.	Protocol Save Screen Bitmap Cache Hit Ratio, Protocol Glyph Cache Hit Ratio, Protocol Brush Cache Hit Ratio
Working Set	Current number of bytes in the Working Set of this session.	Virtual Bytes, Page Faults/Sec

WAIT ON THE LICENSE SERVER

When experimenting with Remote Desktop sessions to find out how many users you'll be able to support for each session, do not set up a license server; let the RDS server issue its temporary 120-day licenses for this purpose. Although this sounds counterintuitive, using the temporary licenses prevents you from unwittingly assigning per-device licenses to test equipment. See the "Licensing Mode" section for an explanation of how licensing and license allocation works.

Client Hardware

When connecting to an RD Session Host server via a native RDP client, you'll most often use a PC with a Windows operating system loaded, a Windows terminal, or a handheld PC using Windows CE.

NATIVE RDP CLIENT

In this context, a native RDP client means one available from Microsoft and thus implies Windows. Although Microsoft does not support other platforms (except for its OS X Macintosh client, available for download at www.microsoft.com/mac/products/remote-desktop/default.mspx), Hobsoft link sells a cross-platform (Windows, Mac, Linux, DOS) Java client at www.hobsoft.com/products/connect/jwt.jsp, and there is a free Linux RDP client available at www.rdesktop.org.

WINDOWS TERMINALS

In its narrowest definition, a *Windows terminal* is a network-dependent device running Windows CE that supports one or more display protocols such as RDP or Independent Computing Architecture (ICA), the display protocol used to connect to Presentation Server servers. Many Windows terminals also support some form of terminal emulation.

For this section, think of a Windows terminal as any terminal device designed to connect to a Windows RD Session Host server; it can run any operating system that has an RDP client. A Windows-based terminal (WBT) is such a device that's running a Windows operating system locally—CE or (more rarely) Windows XP/Vista for Embedded Systems—and follows the Microsoft system design requirements for WBTs.

The main thing defining a Windows terminal is its thin hardware profile: because the main job of most Windows terminals is to run a display protocol, they don't need much memory or processing power, and they don't use any storage. A Windows terminal includes a processor; some amount of memory, network, and video support; and input devices such as a keyboard (or equivalent) and mouse (or equivalent). The terminals don't generally have hard disks, CD-ROMs, or DVD players. The operating system is stored in local memory. Beyond those similarities, Windows terminals range physically from a "toaster" form factor to a pad to a small box that can attach to the back of a monitor—or even be part of the monitor itself. Some models of Windows terminals are wireless tablets, intended for people (such as doctors and nurses) who would ordinarily use clipboards and folders to store information.

Although most Windows terminals are entirely dependent on their RDS server, a small set of them can run applications locally. The devices still don't have hard disks; the applications are stored in ROM like the operating system. The types of applications available depend on the terminal's operating system, since locally stored applications must run locally instead of just being displayed. Generally speaking, however, it's more common for Windows terminals to depend on an RDS server for applications.

Windows terminals are most popular in environments where people are using a single application, where supporting PCs would be logistically difficult, or anywhere else that PCs aren't a good fit. However, PCs still outnumber Windows terminals as thin clients. Part of this is because many environments can't depend totally on server-based computing. Companies already have

PCs, and unless they're refreshing the desktop entirely, taking away a powerful PC to replace it with a less-powerful terminal doesn't really make sense.

PC Clients

At this point, people are using more than twice as many PCs as Windows terminals for RDS server client machines. This isn't surprising. First, unless they're starting fresh, people already have the PCs. Even though WBTs are a little less expensive than low-end PCs (not much, though), they're still an added cost. Second, not all applications work well in an RDS server environment. It's often best to run some applications from the RDS server and some locally. Unless you're buying new hardware and don't anticipate any need to run applications locally, you're likely to have to work with PCs for at least some of your terminal clients.

To work with Remote Desktop Services, the PCs must be running a Windows operating system, have the RDP display protocol installed, and have a live network connection using TCP/IP and a valid IP address.

Handheld PCs

We're surprised that handheld PCs (H/PCs) aren't more popular than they are, given how handy they are. They're a terrific substitute for a laptop—inexpensive, lightweight, and thrifty with their power so that you can actually use them during the entire flight instead of having to give up two hours after takeoff. (You can also use one on a plane without worrying that the person in front of you will suddenly recline their seat and crack your laptop's display.) Usually, they run Windows Mobile (previously known as Pocket PC). You can use wired, wireless LAN, or dial-up connections to connect to an RDS server.

What an H/PC looks like depends on who makes it. Some (mine among them) look like a laptop's baby brother. Others fold into a little portfolio shape or are a flat tablet. Some are small pocket-sized deals that are too small to really work on. Some—the ones we prefer—have keyboards; others have only pointers. What all this comes down to is that an H/PC isn't really in a position to replace a desktop PC. Instead, it's usually used in cooperation with a desktop machine with which it's partnered.

Adding Remote Desktop Services

You can add the Remote Desktop Services role to any Windows Server 2008 R2 server using Server Manager. Server Manager includes wizards that allow you to add many roles, and you've probably already used it by now.

When adding the RDS role, you'll be prompted to answer some questions. The following sections will give you the knowledge you need to answer these questions and successfully add the role. Some of the topics related to an RD Session Host server installation include the following:

◆ Additional role services

◆ Network Level Authentication

◆ Licensing mode

◆ Local Remote Desktop Users group membership

◆ Adding applications

After the role is installed, you'll need to take some steps to configure the server. This section will guide you through the decision-making process and the steps to add and configure the server.

REMOTE DESKTOP SERVICES NOT NEEDED FOR ADMINISTRATOR CONNECTIONS

Remote Desktop Services is not needed to connect to a server for administrator connections. Chapter 14 covered remotely connecting to a server using Remote Desktop Connection (RDC) or Remote Desktops. To use these tools, you don't need to install Remote Desktop Services. Instead, you only need to enable Remote Desktop connections on the server.

A significant difference between remotely connecting for administrator purposes and using an RD Session Host server is that licenses aren't needed for administrator connections. Any server can support as many as two remote administrator connections without a license. However, licenses are required for RD Session Host server connections on one-to-one basis. In other words, you'll need a license for every connection.

Required Role Services

Remote Desktop Services is a server role and includes several role services. All of the services aren't required for every installation. You'll need to evaluate what you're trying to accomplish to determine which services to add.

Remote Desktop Session Host   The RD Session Host service enables the server to host Windows-based programs or a full Windows desktop. This is a required service for the role.

Remote Desktop Virtualization Host   The RD Virtualization Host service is integrated with Hyper-V to allow users to connect to a virtual machine on a server hosting Hyper-V. It can be configured so that users will connect to their own unique virtual machine and allow users to run multiple operating systems simultaneously. This service requires the Hyper-V role service and is needed if you are using the Hyper-V role service.

Remote Desktop Licensing   The RD Licensing service manages the client access licenses (RDS CALs) that are needed to connect to an RD Session Host server. It's possible to run Remote Desktop Services without licenses for a limited grace period of 120 days. This allows you to deploy, configure, and test the server.

Remote Desktop Connection Broker   The RD Connection Broker service is used for session load balancing and session reconnection in an RD Session Host server farm. It's also required to support RDS RemoteApp applications that allow users to launch applications on the RD Session Host server via Internet Explorer.

If you are using multiple RD Session Host servers, the RD Connection Broker can redirect connections to the servers that are the least busy, which provides load balancing. Additionally, if a user is disconnected, the RD Connection Broker will ensure they are reconnected to the same server where their session is active.

Remote Desktop Gateway   The RD Gateway service is used to allow users to connect to RD Session Host servers and remote desktops over the Internet. This service requires additional role services including the Web Server (IIS), Network Policy and Access Services, RPC over HTTP Proxy, and the Remote Server Administration Tools.

Remote Desktop Gateway was covered in much greater depth in Chapter 14, including how to add the required services and enable it.

Remote Desktop Web Access The RD Web Access service allows users to access RemoteApp and Remote Desktop Connection through a web browser. If the clients are running Windows 7, they can access these through the Start menu on their system. This service requires additional supporting role services including Web Server (IIS) and Remote Server Administration Tools. IIS is short for Microsoft's Internet Information Services.

APPLICATION COMPATIBILITY

If you plan on using the RD Session Host server to host applications for end users, you should install it first before installing the applications. Applications that are installed before adding the RD Session Host role may not work correctly in a multiple user environment.

Although some applications will work in multiuser mode even if they've already been installed, many will not. If you've already installed applications that you want to use with RD Session Host server, you should consider uninstalling the application before adding the Remote Desktop Services role.

Easy Print

A neat new feature available since Windows Server 2008 is called Easy Print. Easy Print ensures that client printers are always installed in remote sessions without requiring printer drivers to be installed on the terminal server.

This might not seem like much, but in the past, you were required to install printer drivers on the terminal server for all the printers used by clients. If you have just 50 clients and they were using 10 different print devices, you'd then need to install printer drivers for all 10 print devices on the server even if they were already installed on the client's systems.

Now you may wondering what you need to do to support Easy Print. Almost nothing. The support is there automatically as long as Remote Desktop Services is installed on Server 2008 R2 (or Terminal Services is installed on Windows Server 2008).

Clients need to be running RDC 6.1 and the Microsoft .NET Framework 3.0 with SP1. RDC 6.1 is backward compatible to XP SP3 with a download, as mentioned earlier. Microsoft .NET Framework 3.0 with SP1 is available for download for XP clients from Microsoft's download site: www.microsoft.com/downloads. Search for *Microsoft .NET Framework 3.0 Service Pack 1*.

Single Sign-On

Single sign-on is when users are able to provide their credentials once and these credentials are used for the entire session. As long as these credentials have adequate permissions, the user isn't asked to provide their credentials again. Without single sign-on, users can be queried several times to provide the same username and password.

You can implement single-sign for clients that access the RDS server using Windows XP SP3, Windows Vista, and Windows 7 clients or from Windows Server 2008 or 2008 R2 servers.

Two settings are required in the RDP TCP/IP Connection properties. You'll see graphics of these later, but here are the two settings:

♦ Ensure that the Security layer is set to either Negotiate or SSL (TLS 1.0) on the General tab of the RDP TCP/IP Connection properties.

♦ Ensure that "Always prompt for password" is not selected in the "Log on" settings of the RDP TCP/IP Connection properties.

Network Level Authentication

Network Level Authentication (NLA) can be used in Remote Desktop sessions to provide better security. When adding the Remote Desktop Services role, you need to specify whether NLA is required. Your decision is based on the clients the RD Session Host server will support.

NLA ensures that the authentication is completed before a full Remote Desktop connection is established. Without NLA, there is a small window of opportunity for a malicious user or malicious software to attack, even if authentication is unsuccessful.

NLA is available by default in Windows Vista and Windows 7. It relies on the Credential Security Service Provider (CredSSP). If all the clients are running Windows Vista or Windows 7, then you should require Network Level Authentication on the RD Session Host server.

Windows XP doesn't natively support NLA. However, if you upgrade to SP3 and enable CredSSP, you can use NLA. You need to modify the registry to use CredSSP in Windows XP SP3. Check out these two Microsoft Knowledge Base articles for more information:

♦ KB article 951608, Description of the Credential Security Service Provider (CredSSP) in Windows XP Service Pack 3:
http://support.microsoft.com/kb/951608/

♦ KB article 951616, Description of the Remote Desktop Connection 6.1 client update for Terminal Services:
http://support.microsoft.com/kb/951616

If your clients are older than Windows XP SP3, they cannot use NLA, and NLA should not be required. The older clients will not be able to connect using NLA.

Licensing Mode

You'll be prompted to select the licensing mode when you add the Remote Desktop Services role. The licensing mode specifies what type of Remote Desktop Services Client Access Licenses (RDS CALs) you'll use. You have three choices:

Configure Later   You can postpone your decision and simply select Configure Later. You'll have a grace period of 120 days to configure licensing and select a licensing mode. It's common to choose this option early in the deployment cycle and then configure the RDS CALs once you've worked out the kinks in your RD environment.

Per Device   A per-device CAL is issued to a client computer or device. If the licensing mode is set to Per Device and a licensing server has been configured, the licensing server will issue the device a temporary license the first time the device connects. The second time the device connects, the licensing server will attempt to issue it a permanent license.

The licensing server will enforce per-device CALs. In other words, if a per-device CAL doesn't exist for the device and an RDS CAL isn't available to be issued, the connection will be blocked.

You should use per-device CALs if multiple users will use the same device to connect to an RD Session Host server.

Per User A per-user CAL allows a user to connect to an RD Session Host server from any number of devices. Interestingly, the license server doesn't track the per-user CALs. This can make things both easier and more difficult. It's easier to manage on a day-to-day basis because the RD Session host server won't stop users from connecting. However, administrators still have a responsibility to ensure that appropriate CALs have been purchased, which does take some extra administration.

It is possible to configure the maximum connections supported by the server to coincide with the number of purchased CALs. This is done on the Network Adapter page of the RDP-Tcp Properties in the Remote Desktop Session Hosts Configuration console. This isn't exact since users can legitimately connect to more than one session at a time unless you've limited users to only a single connection at a time.

You should use a per-user CAL if users will connect to an RD Session Host server from multiple devices.

A Remote Desktop Services Licensing server needs to be configured to install, issue, and track RDS CALs. Clients won't be able to connect to the RD Session Host server if RDS CALs haven't been purchased and added to the licensing server before the grace period.

Remote Desktop Users Group

Users need to be members of the local Remote Desktop Users group in order to connect to the RS Session Host server. You can add them when you add the role or add them later. The Administrators group is added to the Remote Desktop Users group by default.

Two Remote Desktop Users groups exist: one in the domain and a local group on the RD Session Host server. You need to add users and groups into the *local* group to grant access for them to connect.

It's not uncommon for an administrator to incorrectly add users to the domain Remote Desktop Users group thinking this will grant access to the RD Session Host server. After a little bit of head banging or hair pulling, the little word *local* is noticed. Once users are added to the local group, things work just as advertised.

Adding the Remote Desktop Services Role

You can use the following steps to install Remote Desktop Services. A word of warning, though: you really need to install this on a computer that isn't a domain controller. In our example environment, we're using one server as a DC (named BF1) and another server as the RDS server (named BF2) in a domain named bigfirm.com. If you try install RDS on a DC, you'll receive a couple of warnings and later realize some things just can't work. For example, you'll need to manipulate local groups, but local groups don't exist on a DC.

1. Log onto a member server.

2. If Server Manager doesn't launch automatically, launch it by selecting Start ➤ Administrative Tools ➤ Server Manager.

3. In Server Manager, select Roles, and click the Add Roles link.

4. If the Before You Begin page appears, review the information, and click Next.

5. Select the Remote Desktop Services role. Your display will look similar to Figure 25.2. Click Next.

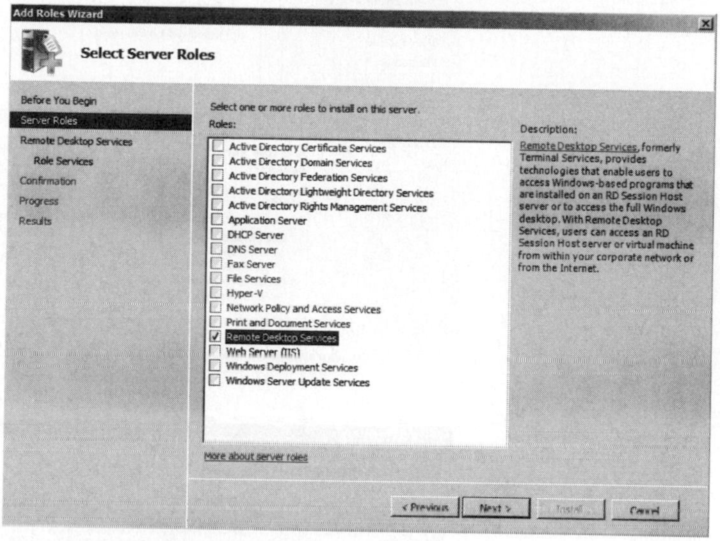

FIGURE 25.2
Adding the
Remote Desktop
Services role

6. Review the information on the Introduction to Remote Desktop Services page, and click Next.

7. On the Select Role Services page, select the check boxes for Remote Desktop Session Host, Remote Desktop Licensing, Remote Desktop Connection Broker, and Remote Desktop Web Access. When you select the check box for Remote Desktop Web Access, a dialog box will appear similar to Figure 25.3. Click the Add Required Role Services button, and click Next.

8. Review the information on the Applications for Compatibility page. Click Next.

9. Review the information on the Authentication Method page, and select Require Network Level Authentication if your clients are running at least Windows Vista or Windows XP SP3 with the registry modification to enable CredSSP. Select Do Not Require Network Level Authentication if the clients are older. Click Next.

10. On the Specify Licensing Mode page, select Configure Later, and click Next.

11. The User Groups page will appear and includes the Administrators group. You can add users or groups using this page, and they will automatically be added to the local Remote Desktop Users group. Click Next.

12. The Configure Client Experience page will appear, as shown in Figure 25.4. If clients are running Windows 7, you can use this page to enable additional functionality that mimics Windows 7. Select the check boxes for each to install the Desktop Experience feature on the server. It can be disabled later if desired. Click Next.

FIGURE 25.3
Adding required
role services

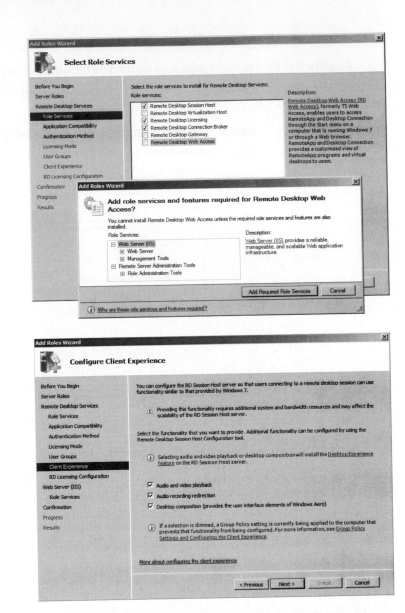

FIGURE 25.4
Configuring the
client experience

13. Review the information on the RD Licensing Configuration page. Leave the check box deselected so that discovery scope is not configured for the license server. Click Next.

14. The Web Server (IIS) installation will begin. As a reminder, this is required to support Remote Desktop Web Access. Review the information on the Web Server (IIS) page, and click Next.

15. The Role Services page will show with the required role services already selected. Review the selected services, and click Next.

16. Review the information on the Confirmation page. A warning stating you may need to reinstall existing applications is normal. It's just reiterating that applications installed before Remote Desktop Services is installed may not work in multiuser mode unless they are reinstalled. Click Install.

17. The installation will take several minutes to complete. When it completes, the Installation page will appear indicating a restart is pending. Click Close. When prompted to restart the server, click Yes. The installation will continue during the restart process. This may take several minutes to complete, so feel free to take a cappuccino break.

18. After the system reboots, log on using the same account, and the configuration wizard will resume. When the installation completes, review the information in the Installation Results page, and click Close.

It's normal to get informational messages related to the Remote Desktop Services Server License server since it has not been configured yet. Additionally, you'll see a warning indicating that RD Web Access requires additional configuration, which is covered later in this chapter.

Adding Applications

Although many applications will work automatically in multiuser mode (such as Paint, Calculator, and Notepad), other applications need to be installed. Previous versions of Remote Desktop Services (called Terminal Services) required extra steps to install the applications, but the process is much simpler with RDS.

After the role has been added, you can install any application using an .msi (Windows Installer) file or via the Control Panel's Add Remove Programs Wizard. If the application will install via one of these methods, that's all that's necessary.

However, if you have a legacy application that won't install via one of these methods, you'll need to use the Change User command. The three-step process is as follows:

1. Execute the Change User /install command from the command prompt. This puts the RDS server into installation mode.

2. Install the application.

3. Execute the Change User /execute command from the command prompt. This returns the RDS server to the normal mode of operation.

Connecting to an RDS Session

After adding the RDS role, clients that are members of the local Remote Desktop Users group can access desktop sessions on the RD Session Host server. During the installation, you had an opportunity to add users and groups to the Remote Desktop Users group, and you may have done so. Members of the administrators are automatically in the group and can't be removed.

Use the following steps to add a user or group into the local Remote Desktop Users group and verify the RDS server supports remote sessions:

1. Log onto the RD Session Host server.

2. If Server Manager doesn't launch automatically, launch it by selecting Start ➢ Administrative Tools ➢ Server Manager.

3. Browse to the Configuration\Local Users and Groups\Groups node.

4. Double-click the Remote Desktop Users group. Add a user or group from the domain that you'll use to test connectivity. In Bigfirm.com, two users (Joe and Sally) are added, as shown in Figure 25.5. Add any users on your system that you want to be able to access the RD Session Host server. Click OK.

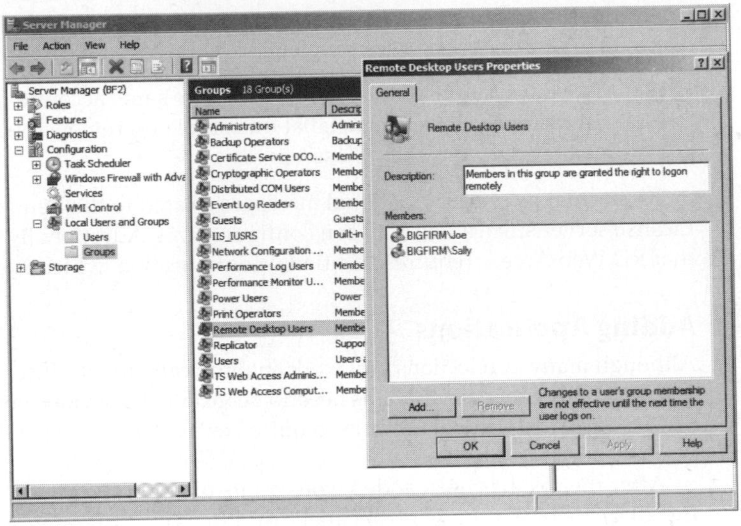

FIGURE 25.5
Adding users to the local Remote Desktop Users group

5. Click Start, type **MSTSC** in the Search box, and press Enter. This will launch the Remote Desktop Connection console. For a full description of all the options available in this tool, you can check out Chapter 14.

6. Click the Options button. Enter the name of the computer hosting RDS in the Computer box, and enter the username of a user in the local Remote Desktop Users group. Your display will look similar to Figure 25.6. Click Connect.

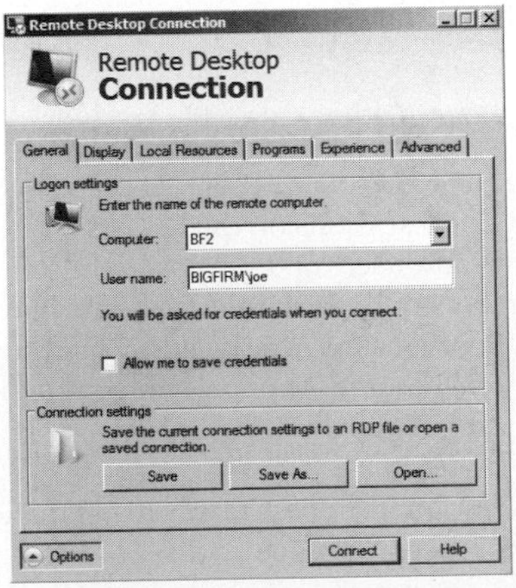

FIGURE 25.6
Connecting with Remote Desktop Connection

7. A Windows Security screen will appear, and you will be prompted to enter the password for the user. Enter the password, and click OK. Security will be negotiated, and after a moment, you will be connected to the desktop.

8. Depending on how MSTSC was configured, the connection may start as a window on the desktop or in full-screen mode. Figure 25.7 shows the connection. Notice it has a Windows 7 look and feel.

FIGURE 25.7
Connected to the RD Session Host server using Remote Desktop Connection

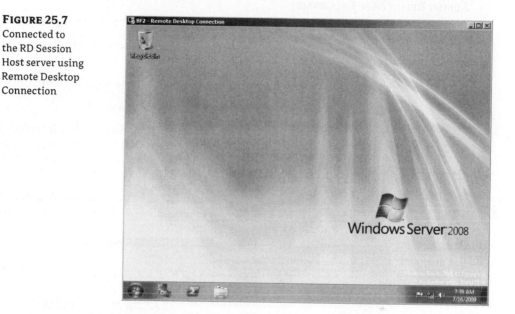

Although this verifies that you have successfully installed RDS and can connect to RDS sessions, the sessions are still plain desktops. You can install applications on the RD Session Host server and make them available to all users, or you can use RD RemoteApp applications to allow users to run the applications in Windows on their desktops.

Adding an RDS RemoteApp Application

Remote Desktop RemoteApp applications are a neat feature with RDS. Once added and configured, they will run in their own window on the end user's computer. Instead of a user launching a full desktop of another operating system, the RemoteApp application appears just like another application.

Another neat feature is that you can restrict access to the RemoteApp programs by identifying which users and groups can access the program. By default, all authenticated domain users will have access.

There are a lot of steps to get RemoteApp applications to work, but hang in there. None of the steps are that difficult by themselves. As an overview, the following steps need to be taken and are included in this section:

1. Add an RDS RemoteApp program to the RDS server.

2. Add the RDS server to the TS Web Access Computers group.

3. Configure your RD Session Host server to serve RD RemoteApp applications.

4. Identify your RDS server as an RD RemoteApp source.

You'll then be able to launch RD Remote Applications using Internet Explorer from any system in your network.

ADDING REMOTEAPP PROGRAMS

Use the following steps to add one or more programs to the RemoteApp program list:

1. Launch the RemoteApp Manager by selecting Start ≻ Administrative Tools ≻ Remote Desktop Services ≻ RemoteApp Manager.

2. The Actions pane on the right includes a link to Add RemoteApp Programs. Click this link.

3. Review the information on the Welcome page, and click Next.

4. The RemoteApp Wizard displays a list of programs that are currently installed on the server and can be added to the RemoteApp Programs list. Select the check box for Paint and any other programs you may want to add. You can also click Browse, and browse to other executable programs on your system that don't show in this list.

5. Click Properties. Select the User Assignment tab. Your display will look similar to Figure 25.8. Notice you can restrict access to programs to specific users and groups here.

FIGURE 25.8

Adding programs to the RemoteApp Programs list

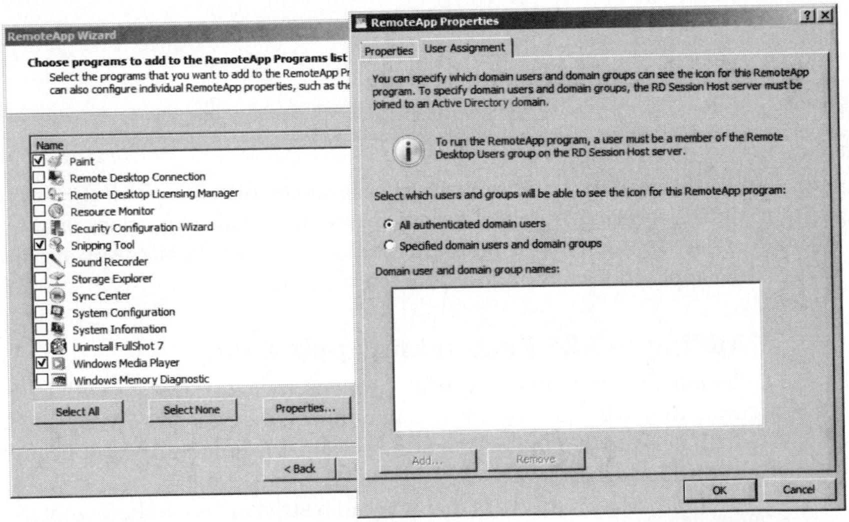

6. Click OK to dismiss the RemoteApp properties sheet. Click Next on the program selection list page.

7. Review your choices on the Review Settings page, and click Finish.

ADDING AN RDS SERVER TO THE TS WEB ACCESS COMPUTERS GROUP

These next steps will add your RDS server to the TS Web Access Computers group:

1. Launch Server Manager by selecting Start ➤ Administrative Tools ➤ Server Manager.

2. Browse to the Configuration\Local Users and Groups\Groups node.

3. Double-click the TS Web Access Computers group, and click Add.

4. In the Active Directory search page, click Object Types.

5. Select the check box next to Computers to include computers in the search. Click OK.

6. Type in the name of the computer hosting RDS, and click OK. Your display should look similar to Figure 25.9. Click OK.

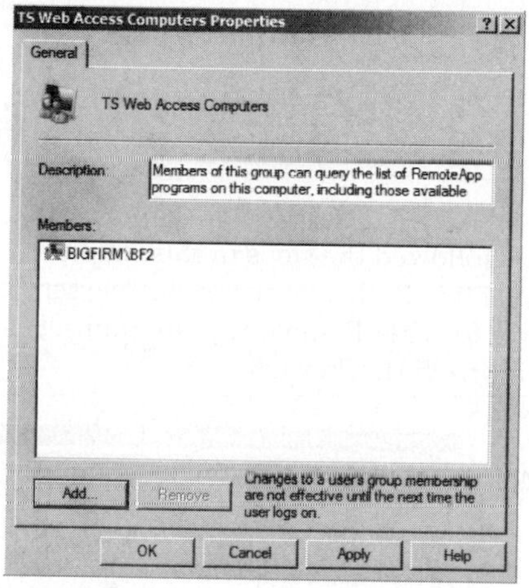

FIGURE 25.9
Adding the computer to the TS Web Access Computers group

CONFIGURING THE RDS SERVER TO SERVE RD REMOTEAPP APPLICATIONS

With the RDS server added to the TS Web Access Computers group, you can now configure the RD Session Host server to serve the RD RemoteApp applications via a web browser.

1. Launch the Remote Desktop Web Access Configuration console by selecting Start ➤ Administrative Tools ➤ Remote Desktop Services ➤ Remote Desktop Web Access Configuration. This will launch Internet Explorer with the address of the RD web server.

2. Unless you've added a certificate from a trusted authority, you will receive an error indicating there is a problem with the website's security certificate. This is normal. The certificate is self-signed, which is good enough for a test environment, but you'll want to install a certificate from a trusted certificate authority for a production server. Click "Continue to this website (not recommended)."

3. After a moment, the Remote Desktop Services Default Connection page will appear. Enter the domain and username for an administrator account and the associated password. Your display will look similar to Figure 25.10. Click the Sign In button.

FIGURE 25.10
Remote Desktop
Services Default
Connection page

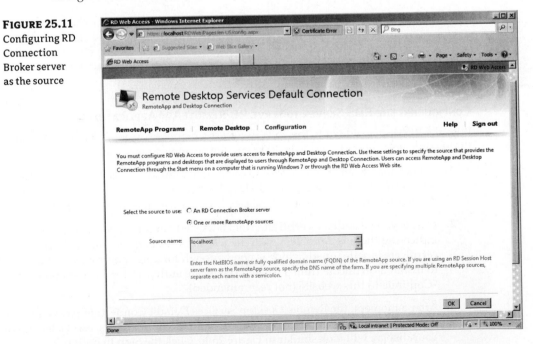

4. If you followed the steps in this chapter to install RDS, you included the Remote Desktop Connection Broker as one of the role services installed on the server. This will be the source for your RemoteApp programs. Select An RD Connection Broker Server, as shown in Figure 25.11. Click OK.

FIGURE 25.11
Configuring RD
Connection
Broker server
as the source

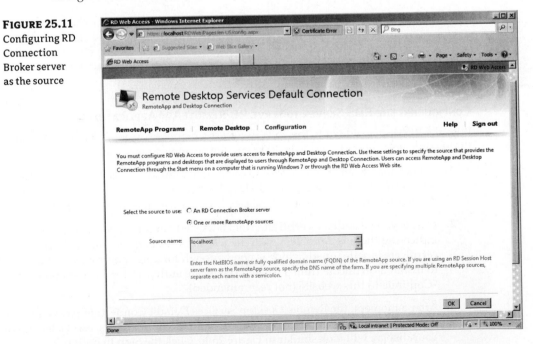

5. At this point, Remote Desktop Web Access is configured, and the Enterprise Remote Access web page will appear with the RemoteApp Programs selected. However, the list is empty.

Even though you added several RemoteApp programs previously, none of them appears because the server hasn't been identified as a RemoteApp source. It's time to do that now.

ADDING AN RDS SERVER AS A REMOTEAPP SOURCE

You'll now add your RDS server as a RemoteApp source:

1. Launch the Remote Desktop Connection Manager by selecting Start ➤ Administrative Tools ➤ Remote Desktop Services ➤ Remote Desktop Connection Manager.

2. Select RemoteApp Sources in the navigation tree pane on the left, and then click Add RemoteApp Source in the Actions pane on the right.

3. Enter the name of the server where you've installed RDS. Your display should look similar to Figure 25.12. Click Add.

FIGURE 25.12
Using Remote Desktop Connection Manager to add a RemoteApp source

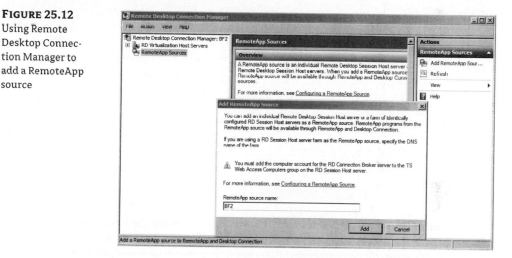

4. Your server will appear as one of the RemoteApp sources. Close the Remote Desktop Connection Manager.

LAUNCHING A REMOTEAPP FROM INTERNET EXPLORER

Launch a RemoteApp from Internet Explorer with the following steps. You can do this from your RDS server, or if desired, you can do it from another computer in your network.

1. Launch Internet Explorer.

2. Enter the following URL into the address bar: **https://localhost/rdweb**.

If you're accessing this from a remote host, enter the name of the server in place of *localhost*. For example, our server name is BF2, so we would enter it as **https://bf2/rdweb**.

3. Since the server is using a self-signed certificate, you'll see an error. Click the Continue to This Website (Not Recommended) link.

4. If prompted by the Internet Explorer Enhanced Security Configuration, click Add to indicate you trust this website. Click Add again, and click Close.

5. The RemoteApp and Desktop Connection page will appear.

6. Enter a username in the format of *domain\user name* and a password for an account that is in the local Remote Desktop Users group of the RDS server. We've created an account named Sally in the Bigfirm.com domain, so we have entered it as **bigfirm\Sally**, as shown in Figure 25.13.

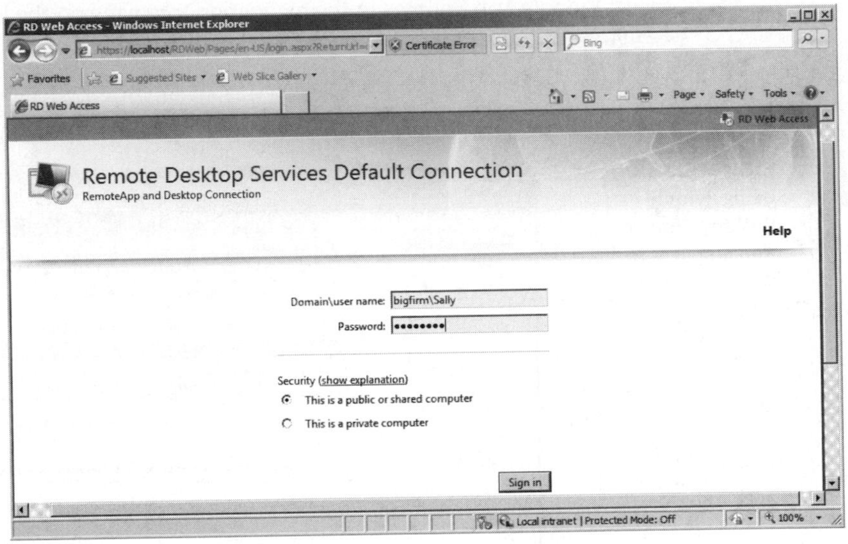

FIGURE 25.13
Logging into the Enterprise Remote Access website

Notice that you can also select whether you're accessing the RemoteApps from a public or private computer. The private setting allows a longer period of activity before logging you off. It's strongly recommended that users close the session as soon as they are finished to flush any remnant data from the session.

7. Enter the user's password, and click Sign In.

8. The RemoteApp programs that have been published to the server are listed, as shown in Figure 25.14.

9. Click the Paint application. A warning will appear providing a warning to the user that the RemoteApp program is starting. Click Connect.

10. Enter the credentials of the same account you used to access the website, and click OK. After a moment, the credentials will be validated, and the Paint program will start.

If you launch Paint from the Accessories menu, you'll see there is very little difference between the local Paint program and the RemoteApp Paint program. They function the same, but the border of the RemoteApp program may be a little different.

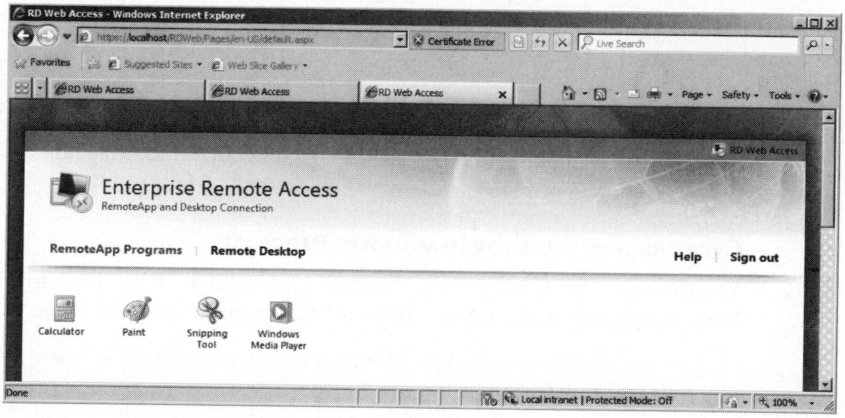

FIGURE 25.14

Accessing Remote-
App programs
using Internet
Explorer

11. Leave the Paint program open, and click another RemoteApp program on the web page. You'll receive the warning again, but after you click Connect, this program will launch without requiring you to enter credentials again.

12. Return to the Internet Explorer web page showing the Enterprise Remote Access menu. Click Remote Desktop.

13. On the Remote Desktop page, click Options. Your display will look similar to Figure 25.15.

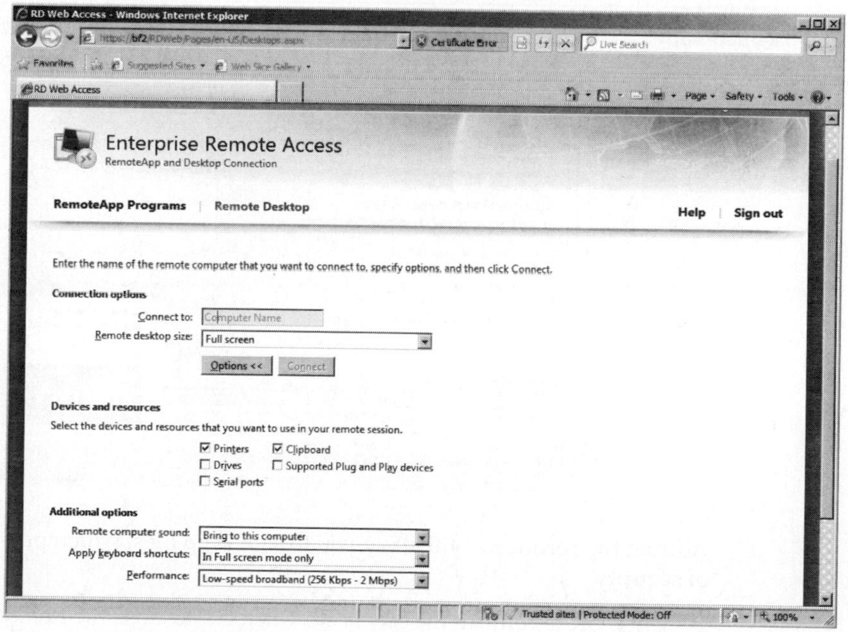

FIGURE 25.15

Accessing Remote
Desktop options
using Internet
Explorer

Notice that you can select many of the same options that are available in the Remote Desktop Connection tool from this page.

14. Enter the name of the RD Session Host server in the Connect To box, and click Connect.

15. A warning will appear as it did before. Review the information, and click Connect.

16. After a moment you will be connected to a full desktop session running on the server.

17. Log off the RemoteApp desktop session, and close all the RemoteApp applications.

CREATING .RDP FILES FOR REMOTEAPP PROGRAMS

You can use a Remote Desktop Protocol (.rdp) file to allow users to easily connect to an RD RemoteApp application. You can create the .rdp file with these steps:

1. Launch the RemoteApp Manager by selecting Start ➤ Administrative Tools ➤ Remote Desktop Services ➤ RemoteApp Manager.

At the bottom of the RemoteApp Manager, you should see one or more RemoteApp programs that were added in previous steps in this chapter. You will also see a warning icon in the Digital Signature Settings area. It indicates a digital certificate has not been configured.

2. Click Change next to Digital Signature Settings to add a digital certificate. Select the "Sign with a digital certificate" check box, and click the Change button. Your display will look similar to Figure 25.16.

FIGURE 25.16
Adding a certificate to RemoteApp Manager

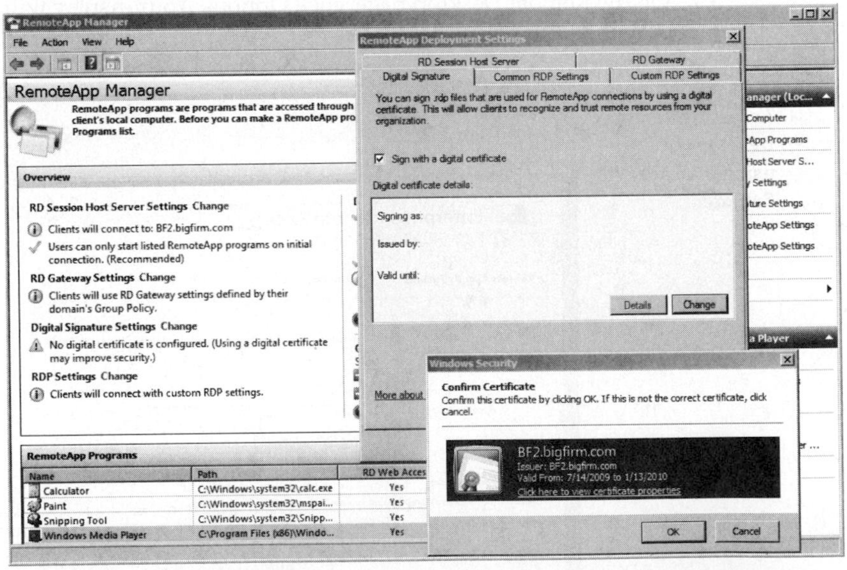

Adding the certificate will allow you to sign .rdp files, which provides clients an added layer of security.

3. Click OK to confirm the certificate. Click OK to close the RemoteApp Deployment Settings property page. You'll see that the warning icon on the Digital Signature Settings page will disappear.

4. Locate the Paint program in the RemoteApp Program list. Right-click it, and select Create .rdp File.

5. Review the information on the Welcome page, and click Next.

6. The Specify Package Settings page will appear, as shown in Figure 25.17. You can change any of these settings, but the defaults will work for most deployments. Click Next.

FIGURE 25.17
Specifying package settings for the .rdp file

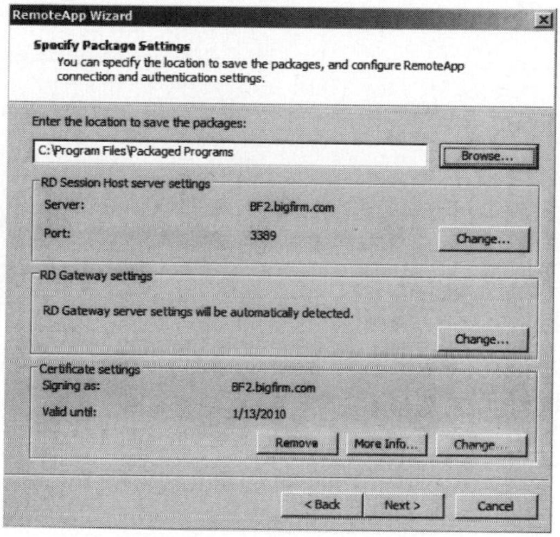

7. Click Finish on the Review Settings page.

8. Windows Explorer will open in the C:\Program Files\Packaged Programs folder. It will include the mspaint.rdp file.

This file can be copied to other computers or shared. Once it is available to other computers in the network, it can simply be double-clicked to start the application.

LAUNCH .RDP FILES REMOTELY

RDS doesn't seem to like it when you launch RemoteApp programs on the RemoteApp server. If you try to double-click the .rdp file on the RDS server, it may work, but often it just doesn't respond. It's best to test your .rdp files from another system within the network, even if that other system is a remote desktop launched from within your RDS server.

---

9. Copy the mspaint.rdp file to another computer in your network.

10. Double-click the .rdp file on the other computer. Even though the .rdp file is signed with a certificate from the RD Session Host server, the server's certificate isn't in the trusted root authority store, so you will receive an error similar to Figure 25.18.

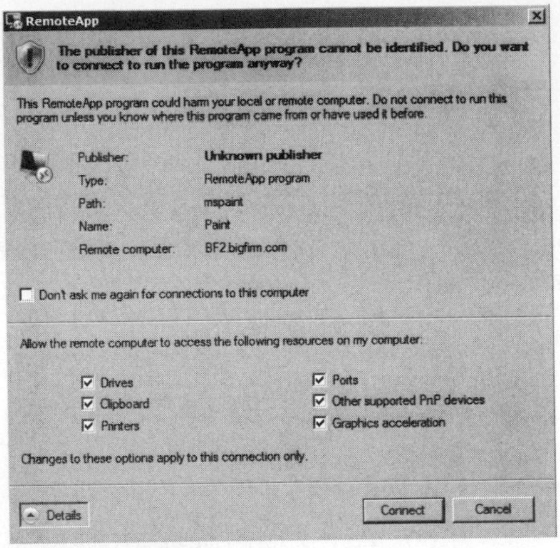

FIGURE 25.18
Unknown Remote-App publisher warning

If you click the Details page, you can view additional options showing what local resources will be available to the RemoteApp program. Click Connect.

11. Enter the credentials of an account that is in the local Remote Desktop Users group on the RDS server, and click OK. After a moment, the credentials will be verified, the connection will be established, and the program will launch and appear on your desktop.

At this point, you've seen how to launch a RemoteApp application using WebAccess and using an .rdp file. Once the program is launched, there isn't any difference in how it works between the two methods.

CREATING WINDOWS INSTALLER PACKAGES FOR REMOTEAPP PROGRAMS

Another way you can deploy RemoteApp applications is by creating a Windows Installer (.msi) file and deploying the application using the .msi file.

The big benefit of using Windows Installer files is that they can easily be deployed using Group Policy. Once the installer file has been created, you can create GPOs to assign or publish them to users and computers in your domain.

Applications installed with the Windows Installer files can be available via the Start menu and via icons placed on the desktop, depending on what you choose. Use the following steps to create a Windows Installer package for a RemoteApp application:

1. Launch the RemoteApp Manager by selecting Start ➤ Administrative Tools ➤ Remote Desktop Services ➤ RemoteApp Manager.

2. Locate the Paint program in the RemoteApp Programs list. The Paint program was added in previous steps within this chapter. Right-click Paint, and select Create Windows Installer Package.

3. Review the information on the Welcome screen, and click Next.

4. The Specify Package Settings page will appear. This page is the same page that you saw when you created an .rdp file. Click Next.

5. The Configure Distribution Package page will appear, as shown in Figure 25.19. Notice that you can add shortcut icons for the program on the desktop and on the Start menu. Additionally, you can have the RemoteApp take over the client extensions. For example, if the .bmp client extension was set to launch the local Paint program, you can change it to launch the RemoteApp Paint program instead. Select the "Start menu folder" check box only, and click Next.

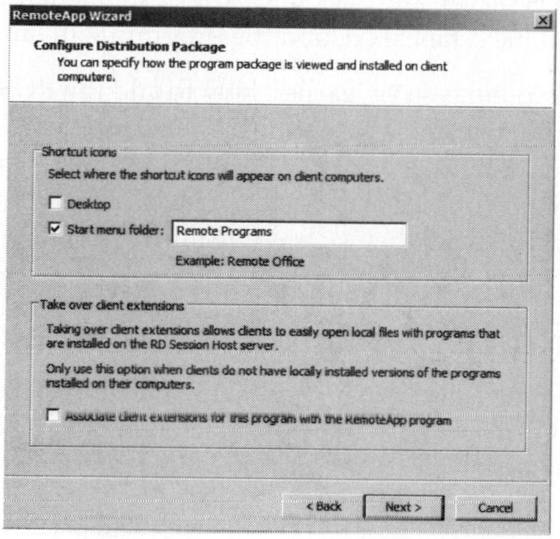

FIGURE 25.19
Configuring the distribution package

6. Review your settings, and click Finish.

7. Windows Explorer will open in the C:\Program Files\Packaged Programs folder. It will include the mspaint.msi file. Additionally, the mspaint.rdp file may be in the same directory from the previous set of steps.

You could deploy this Windows Installer file via Group Policy or by simply executing it on a computer.

This file can also be copied to other computers or shared. Once it is available to other computers in the network, it can simply be double-clicked to start the installation.

8. Copy the mspaint.msi file to another computer in your network.

9. Double-click the .msi file on the other computer. You will receive an error similar to Figure 25.20, but since you created the .msi file, you know it is safe. Click Run.

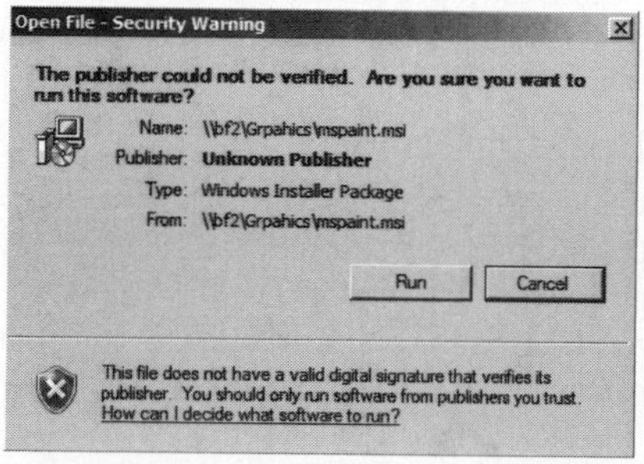

FIGURE 25.20
Windows Installer security warning

10. The Windows Installer file will run and create a shortcut on the start menu. Select Start ➢ Remote Programs ➢ Paint.

11. After a moment, the RemoteApp warning will appear because the certificate is not trusted. This is the same issue you saw with the .rdp file in the previous exercise. Click Connect.

12. Enter the credentials of an account that is in the local Remote Desktop Users group on the RDS server, and click OK. After a moment, the credentials will be verified, the connection will be established, and the program will launch and appear on your desktop.

At this point, you've learned how to add the RDS role, configure the RD Session Host server, and add RemoteApp applications. You've also learned how to deploy RemoteApp programs using Web Access, .rdp files, and Windows Installer files.

Although you've learned a lot so far, there's more. You'll also want to know how to manage these services after they've been installed.

Monitoring Remote Desktop Services

Once Remote Desktop Services is up and running, you'll need to monitor and manage it. Several RDS tools are available from the Start menu by selecting Start ➢ Administrative Tools ➢ Remote Desktop Services. The tools are as follows:

- Remote Desktop Services Manager
- Remote Desktop Session Host Configuration
- RemoteApp Manager
- Remote Desktop Web Access Configuration
- Remote Desktop Licensing Manager
- Remote Desktop Connection Manager
- Remote Desktops

Three menu items are available here without the Remote Desktop Services role installed. They are used to manage remote connections for administration and RDS. For example, Remote Desktops (covered in Chapter 14) is used to remotely administer clients and is included in a default installation. The other two items are Remote Desktop Services Manager and Remote Desktop Session Host Configuration.

The Remote Desktop Connection Manager, RemoteApp Manager, and Remote Desktop Web Access Configuration tools were covered earlier in this chapter.

Remote Desktop Services Manager

The Remote Desktop Services Manager is used to view information about users, sessions, and processes on a Remote Desktop Session Host server. You can also interact with sessions from this tool using Remote Control.

When you launch the Remote Desktop Services Manager from the computer hosting the RD Session Host server, the local server will automatically be added. However, if you manage more than one RD Session Host server, you can add all the servers to a single console. For large environments, you can even group the RD Session Host servers using the My Group node in the console.

USERS, SESSIONS, AND PROCESSES

When you're connected to an RD Session Host server, you'll have three tabs available. You can use these tabs to monitor and interact with activity on the server. Figure 25.21 shows the Remote Desktop Services Manager with the Processes tab selected.

FIGURE 25.21
Remote Desktop Services Processes tab

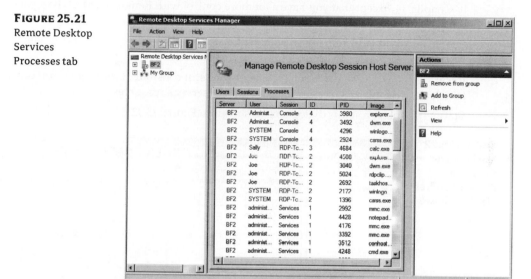

In the figure, we have clicked the User header to order the list based on the user spelling. Sally is using a RemoteApp application (`calc.exe`), and Joe has a full desktop running. Notice that only one process is running for Sally, while Joe's session requires several supporting processes.

The three tabs are as follows:

Users   This tab lists all the users who have sessions running on the server. It includes sessions that are active and disconnected.

Sessions   The Sessions tab shows all the sessions for the server. It includes the RDS supporting sessions: Console, Services, and Listener. If any users connect, it will show their sessions as *RDP-TCP#x* (where *x* is the number assigned to the session).

Processes   The Processes tab shows all the processes running on the server. You can right-click any process listed here and select End Process to kill it.

The Users and Sessions tabs give you many additional options to interact with sessions. If you right-click any of the sessions, you'll have the following choices:

Connect   Allows you to connect to a user's session. When you connect to this session, the user will be disconnected.

This feature will work only when you access it from a Remote Desktop Services client session. It is disabled if you try to access it from the console session.

Disconnect Disconnects a user from an active session. Be nice, though. Send the user a message, and give them some time to clean up and log off before simply disconnecting them.

Send Message Sends a message to a session. The message will appear as a dialog box. The title will include who sent the message and when it was sent.

Remote Control Allows you to connect and interact with a remote session. This can be used to provide assistance to a user by either showing the user how to perform an action or watching and talking them through it. It is very similar to Remote Assistance, covered in Chapter 14, except that you have a lot more control with Remote Control than you'd have with Remote Assistance.

This feature will work only when you access it from a Remote Desktop Services client session. It is disabled if you try to access it from the console session.

Reset Deletes a session. Disconnected sessions still consume resources, so you can use this to delete a disconnected session and free up the server's resources.

Status Displays a status dialog box, as shown in Figure 25.22.

FIGURE 25.22
Session status
from Remote
Desktop Services
Manager console

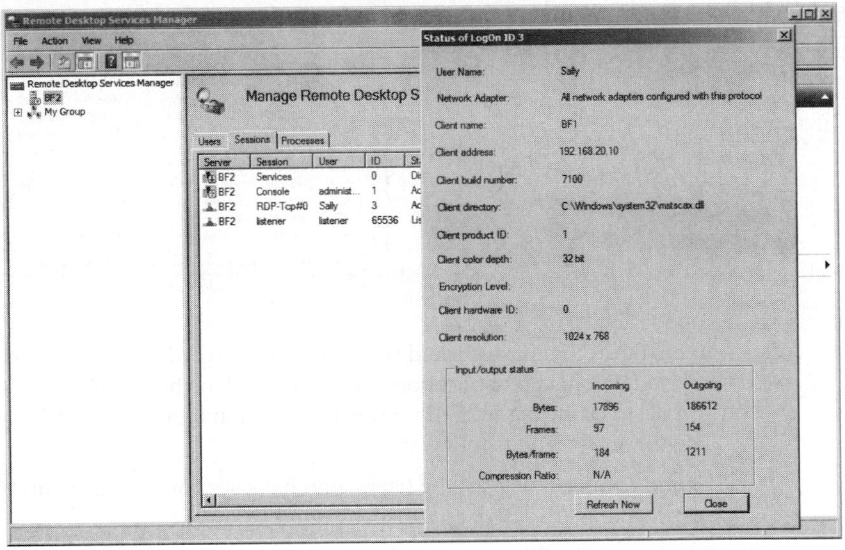

Figure 25.22 was launched by right-clicking the RDP-Tcp#0 session and selecting Status.

COMMAND-LINE TOOLS

In addition to the Remote Desktop Services Manager GUI, you can use several command-line tools to manage users, sessions, and processes in place of the Remote Desktop Services Manager, as shown in Table 25.2.

For more information about any of these tools, enter them from the command line with /? for help. Examples are given for each these with the assumption that a user with a username of Sally has an active session with a session ID of 1.

TABLE 25.2:   Remote Desktop Services Manager Command-Line Tools

COMMAND	ACTION
logoff	Logs a user off from a session and deletes the session on the RD Session Host server. The number would the session ID number and can be obtained with query session. logoff 1
msg	Sends a message to a user on an RD Session Host server. The message will appear as a pop-up. Msg Sally Message CTRL + Z Enter
query process, qprocess	Displays information about processes running on an RD Session Host server. No arguments are needed. query process
query session, qwinsta	Displays information about sessions running on an RD Session Host server. No arguments are needed. This can be used to identify the session ID, the username, and the session name of all sessions. query session
query users, quser	Displays information about user's sessions running on an RD Session Host server. This can be used to determine whether the session is active, how long it's been idle, and when the user logged on. If executed without arguments, it shows all information on all users. If executed with the name of an active user, it shows only that user's information. query user query user Sally
Tsdiscon	Disconnects an active session on an RD Session Host server. Tsdiscon 1
Tscon	Connects to a disconnected session on an RD Session Host server. Tscon 1
Tskill	Ends a process running in a session on an RD Session Host server. Processes can be identified with the query process command. Tskill mstsc

Remote Desktop Session Host Configuration

You can use the Remote Desktop Session Host Configuration console to configure many of the settings for your RD Session Host server. Settings in this console will affect all the users who connect to the server. Figure 25.23 shows the configuration console.

FIGURE 25.23
Remote Desktop
Session Host
Configuration
console

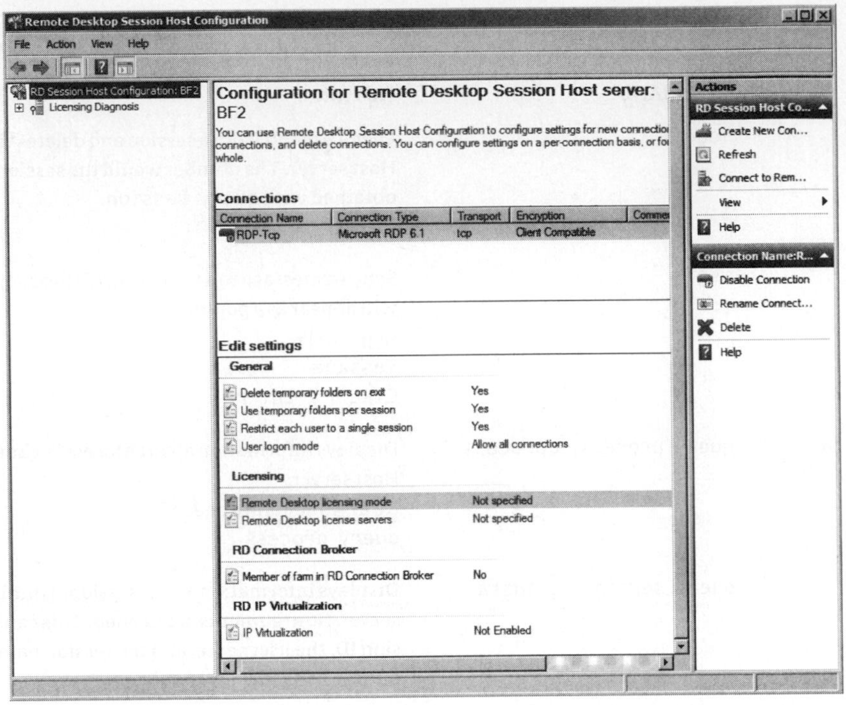

There are three major types of settings you can configure with the majority of the server configuration done through the RDP-Tcp Connection property page.

RDP-Tcp Connection settings You can use the RDP-Tcp Connection properties to configure all the connections to the RD Session Host server. This includes security settings, session settings, remote control settings, and more. The majority of the configuration for the RD Session Host server is done through these properties.

Edit Settings The Edit Settings section shows the current settings for four additional areas. If you double-click any of the areas, you can see the properties sheet with the four tabs that can be used to supplement the RDP-Tcp Connection settings.

Licensing Diagnoses If you are receiving errors related to RDS licensing, you can use the Licensing Diagnoses tool to help you identify the problem. Select this in the tree pane on the left.

RDP-TCP CONNECTION

You can view and modify the properties of RDP-Tcp Connection by either double-clicking it or right-clicking it and selecting Properties. The properties sheet includes eight tabs.

This connection is available even if the Remote Desktop Services Session Host role has not been installed. Before the role is added, this connection will allow two connections for administrator purposes. When the role is added, it is changed to allow unlimited connections.

You can add connections if your server includes multiple network adapters.

RDP-Tcp Properties General Tab

Figure 25.24 shows the General tab. You can add a comment here that may be useful if you have multiple NICs and multiple connections you're using on your RD Session Host server. However, the primary use of this page is to configure security.

FIGURE 25.24
RDP-Tcp Properties General tab

RDS supports both the RDP Security Layer and SSL (TLS 1.0). SSL (TLS 1.0) is more secure than RDP Security Layer. If the Security Layer is set to Negotiate (as shown in the figure), the RDS server will attempt to use SSL (TLS 1.0) first. If the client doesn't support it, it will use RDP Security Layer instead, which provides weaker security.

Earlier, single sign-on was mentioned, and this is one of the settings you need to verify to support single sign-on. It must be set to Negotiate or SSL (TLS 1.0). You'll also need to verify the "Always prompt for password" option is not selected on the Log On Settings tab.

Additionally, you'll need to use a certificate to use SSL (TLS 1.0). If you installed RDS using the exercises in this chapter, an autogenerated (self-signed) certificate was created and added.

SELF-SIGNED OR TRUSTED CERTIFICATE

Although you can create a self-signed certificate, Microsoft recommends you obtain a certificate from a trusted certificate authority (CA) for better security. This trusted CA can be a public one such as VeriSign or Thawte or an Active Directory Certificate Services server built internally. However, for small organizations where the server is used internally only, you can use a self-signed certificate without any problems.

You can select from one of four encryption levels. This can encrypt the data sent to and from the server to prevent sniffing attacks. The choices are as follows:

Low   Data sent from the server to the client is not encrypted. Data sent to the server from the client is encrypted using 56-bit encryption.

Client Compatible   Data is encrypted to and from the server using the maximum key strength supported by the client. This is the default setting.

High   Data is encrypted to and from the server using 128-bit encryption. Clients that don't support 128-bit encryption can't connect.

FIPS Compliant   Data is encrypted to and from the server using Federal Information Process Standard (FIPS) 140-1 validated encryption methods. FIPS is a series of documents published by the National Institute of Standards and Technology (NIST). When this is selected, clients that don't support FIPS 140-1 encryption can't connect.

RDP-Tcp Properties Log On Settings Tab

You can configure what credentials are used for sessions through the Log On Settings tab of the RDP-Tcp properties sheet. A user always has to provide their own credentials to determine whether they should be able to access the server, but you can use this page to alter the credentials used for the session.

Figure 25.25 shows the Log On Settings tab.

FIGURE 25.25

RDP-Tcp Properties dialog box's Log On Settings tab

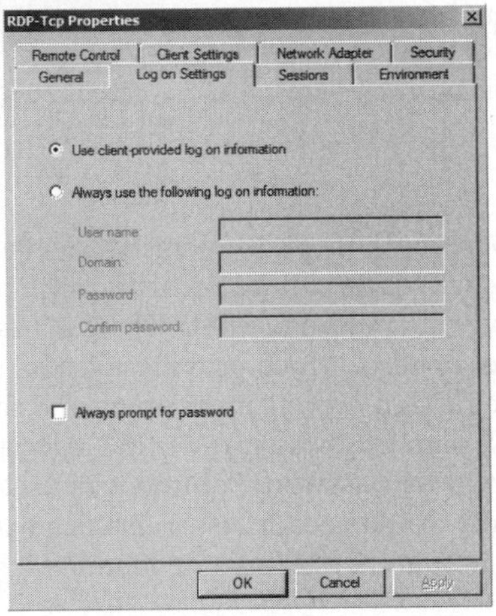

The default is to use the client-provided logon information. However, you could also create an account with specific permissions and privileges on the RD Session Host server. Then, when users connect and authenticate, the session will start with the credentials you provided. This can be useful if you're hosting an application with special rights and permissions.

The "Always prompt for password" setting has two possible uses. First, if you want to configure single-sign-on as discussed earlier, you would ensure that this box is deselected and the security layer (on the General tab) is set to either Negotiate or SSL (TLS 1.0). However, if your clients frequently access the RDS server from public places and you want to add another layer of security, you can select this box. It will force users to always provide a password even if they've configured their password to be saved. This prevents an attacker from launching an RDS session if a valid user leaves their system unlocked. The attacker will be prompted for a password. As long as the user didn't write down their password on a little yellow sticky attached to the monitor, the attack is thwarted.

RDP-Tcp Properties Sessions Tab

The Sessions tab can be used to override user settings for how to handle disconnected sessions, active session limits, and idle session limits. By default, these settings are configured on a per-user basis using Active Directory Users and Computers.

However, if you want all users who connect to the server to have the same settings, you can use this page to override the individual settings. This tab was covered in more depth in Chapter 14.

RDP-Tcp Properties Environment Tab

The Environment tab can be used to launch a specific application when a user connects. It's very common to use an RD Session Host server to host a line-of-business application. If you're specifically using RDS to host an in-house application, it makes a lot of sense to launch the app as soon as the user connects.

Figure 25.26 shows the Environment tab. The default setting is shown. You can override this for every user by either specifying that applications should not be launched or identifying a specific application to run when the user logs on.

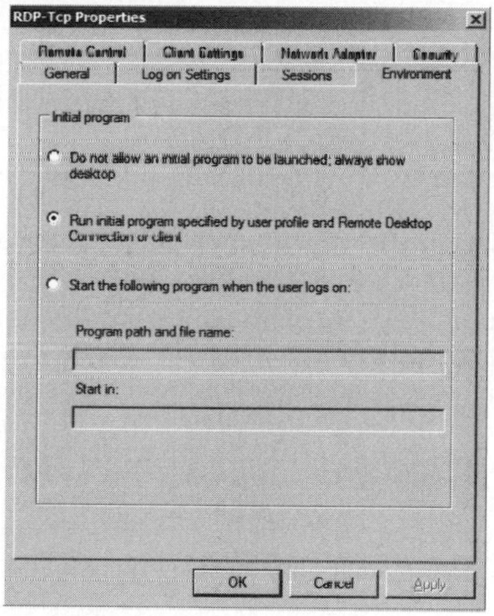

FIGURE 25.26

RDP Tcp Properties Environment tab

To specify a starting application, you simply provide the program path and filename of the application. Some applications require the starting path to be specified so that the application can access specific application data. If necessary, you can specify the path in the Start In text box.

RDP-Tcp Properties Remote Control Tab

Remote Control is a neat feature available with an RD Session Host server. As mentioned earlier, an administrator can use it to interact with a user's session to either show a user how to accomplish a task or talk a user through the task while observing the actions on the screen.

Figure 25.27 shows the Remote Control tab. The default setting is shown using the default user settings. You can also completely disable remote control or configure remote control with special settings that apply to all users connecting to the server.

FIGURE 25.27
RDP-Tcp
Properties Remote
Control tab

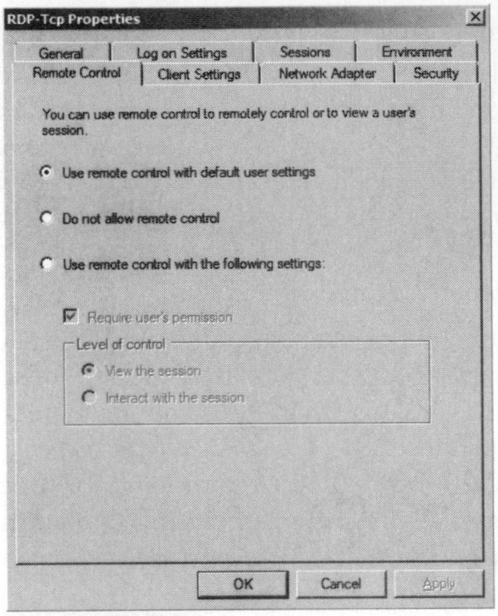

When configuring server settings for remote control, you can set it to require the user's permission or not. Additionally, you can configure the level of control to either view the session or interact with the session.

If your company is managing an RD Session Host server, there's nothing wrong with setting it to not require the user's permission in many instances. Although it makes sense to require the user's permission in a peer-to-peer Remote Assistance scenario, it's different when users are connecting to a corporate RDS server.

The user (an employee within the company) is asking for help, and the help-desk professional (another employee within the company) is there to provide assistance. Requiring the help-desk professional to request permission from the employee to connect is often just an extra step that isn't required. Of course, if employees may be accessing sensitive data that the help-desk professional shouldn't see, then requiring the user's permission to connect is appropriate.

If you do set it so that the user's permission is not required, you may want to provide some type of notification to the user that their sessions may be monitored. Many companies provide this notification in an acceptable use policy.

RDP-Tcp Properties Client Settings Tab

The Client Settings tab is useful if your users are experiencing performance issues. You can reduce some of the capabilities to provide better performance.

For example, you can reduce the color depth if users are connecting over a slow connection. The different settings are 15 bits, 16 bits, 24 bits, or 32 bits per pixel. For most users and most applications, the reduced color depth may not be noticeable, while the increased speed will be greatly appreciated.

Figure 25.28 shows the Client Settings tab. Notice that you can also disable redirection for several devices from this page.

Redirection allows users to access local resources in the remote session. For example, a user may want to be able to access files on their local C drive on their system. With the check box deselected (not selected to *disable* redirection), they can configure redirection.

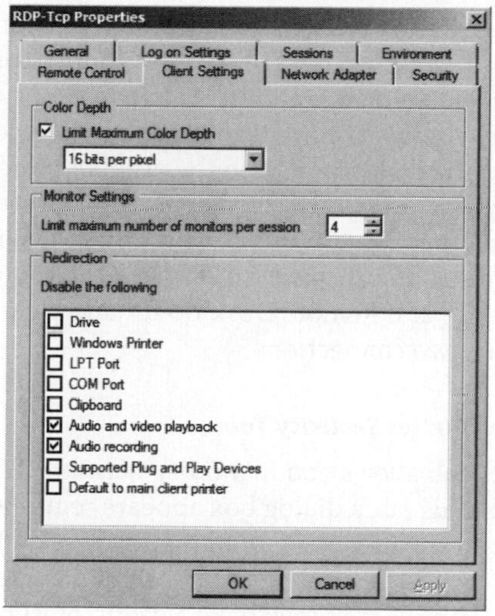

FIGURE 25.28
RDP-Tcp Properties
Client Settings tab

A key point is that this page is used to disable redirection on a global scale. If redirection is not disabled, users have the ability to select or deselect redirection for individual items on a per-connection basis. If you refer to Figure 25.18 earlier in this chapter, it shows that the user has several choices for redirection. Users have similar choices if they connect with Remote Desktop Connection.

RDP-Tcp Properties Network Adapter Tab

If your RD Session Host server is multihomed, you can configure which network adapters will be used for the RDP-Tcp connections.

Figure 25.29 shows the Network Adapter tab. In the figure, it's set to use all network adapters, but if you select the drop-down box, you'll see that you can select individual NICs.

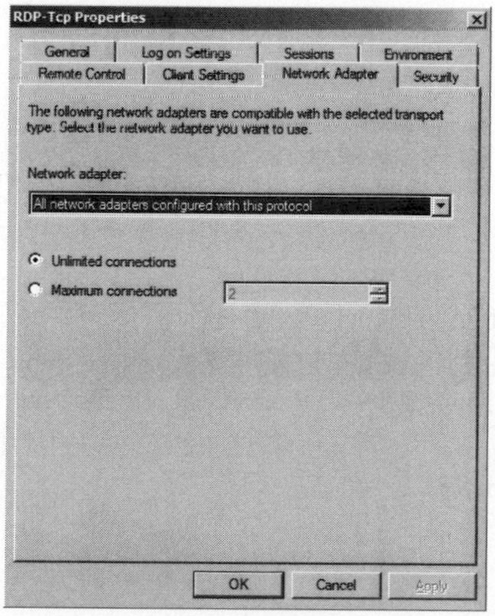

FIGURE 25.29
RDP-Tcp
Properties
Network
Adapter tab

When the server is configured as an RD Session Host server, it is set to "Unlimited connections." You can also use the "Maximum connections" setting to limit the number of connections the server will accept. If you find that an RDS server functions best below a certain number of connections, you could configure the maximum connections to this threshold.

You are still legally limited to the number of licenses you've purchased for the server. If you're using per-user CALs, the license server doesn't track the CALs, but you can configure the maximum connections on this page to coincide with the number of licenses you've purchased.

Before you configure a server as an RD Session Host server, the "Maximum connections" setting is set to 2. If Remote Desktop for administration is enabled, the server will support a maximum of two connections.

RDP-Tcp Properties Security Tab

The Security tab allows you to modify permissions granted to users (see Figure 25.30). As soon as you select this tab, a dialog box appears reminding you to use the local Remote Desktop Users group to control who can log onto the RD Session Host server.

In other words, you only need to use this tab to modify advanced permissions for a special group. For example, you may have a group of RD administrators that need to be able to do anything on your RD Session Host server. You could use a Windows Global group to organize the users, add them to the Security page, and allow Full Control permissions.

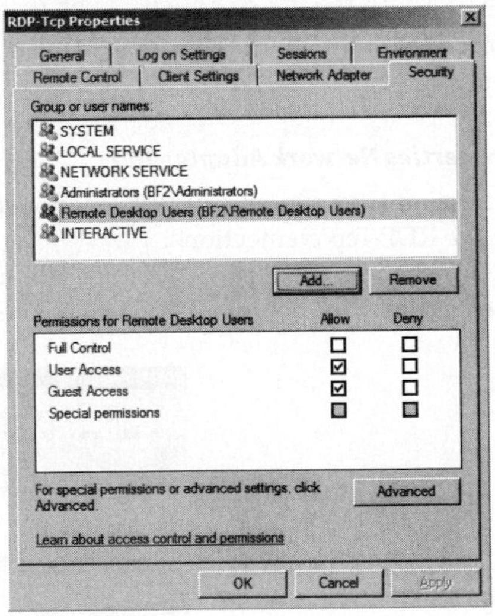

FIGURE 25.30
RDP-Tcp Properties
Security tab

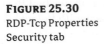

The Security tab includes four permissions:

Full Control   Full Control includes the following permissions: query information, set information, remote control, logon, logoff, message, connect, disconnect, and virtual channels.

User Access   User Access includes the following permissions: query information, logon, and connect.

Guest Access   Guest Access includes only the Logon permission.

Special permissions   Any of the following special permissions can be individually allowed or denied: query information, set information, remote control, logon, logoff, message, connect, disconnect, and virtual channels.

EDIT SETTINGS

The Edit Settings property page includes four tabs. You can access any of these settings by double-clicking any of the settings in the General, Licensing, RD Connection Broker, or RD IP Virtualization sections.

General Tab

Figure 25.31 shows the General tab. It's recommended to keep all the check boxes selected for the best performance of the server. Notice the last check box prevents users from opening more than one session—this refers to full desktop sessions, not RemoteApp applications. Users will be able to launch multiple RemoteApp applications with this selected.

FIGURE 25.31
Edit Settings
General tab

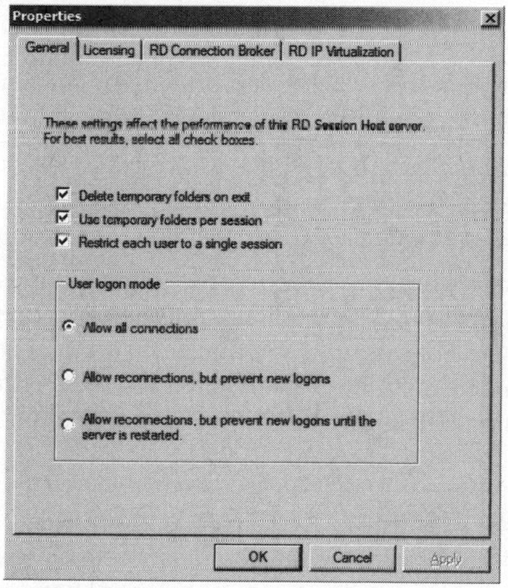

Licensing Tab

The Licensing tab allows you to choose between Per Device or Per User. As a reminder, it's recommended to postpone configuring a licensing server until your RD Session Host servers are up and running. Figure 25.32 shows this tab.

Before the 120-day grace period, you'll need to revisit this page and set the licensing mode. When you select either Per Device or Per User, you'll also need to specify the license server. In very large organizations, you can use multiple licensing servers. A single licensing server can manage licenses for multiple RDS Session Host servers.

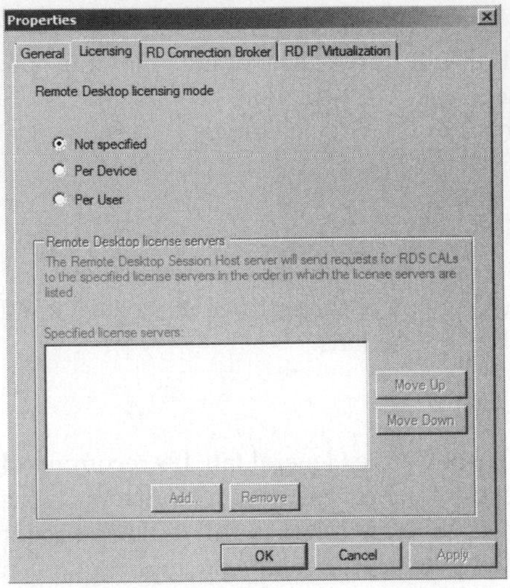

FIGURE 25.32
Edit Settings
Licensing tab

RD Connection Broker Tab

RD Connection Broker is needed only if you have more than one RD Session Host server. The RD Connection Broker provides two important features:

Load balancing If you have multiple RD Session Host servers, you can add the servers to a Connection Broker farm. When a user connects, the RD Connection Broker will determine which server has the lightest load and will redirect the connection to that server.

Reconnects users to the correct session If a user becomes disconnected from a session, the RD Connection Broker will ensure they are connected back to the same session on the original server. For example, say that Sally is connected to BF2 but the network has a problem and disconnects her. When she reconnects, the Connection Broker recognizes she has an active session on BF2 and will redirect her connection to that server.

RD IP Virtualization Tab

If an application requires each connection to have a separate IP address, you can use RD IP Virtualization. Normally, every session will have a single IP address. Although this works for the majority of applications, there are a few instances where separate IP addresses are required.

RD IP Virtualization also requires a DHCP server to be configured to provide virtual IP addresses.

LICENSING DIAGNOSIS

The last tool you have available in the Remote Desktop Session Host Configuration console is Licensing Diagnosis. When licensing issues crop up, they've been challenging to resolve in past versions of Windows and Terminal Services. This tool is a welcome addition.

Figure 25.33 shows some of the information provided from the Licensing Diagnosis console.

FIGURE 25.33
Licensing
Diagnosis tab

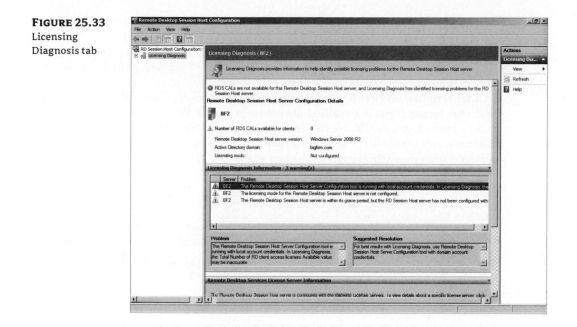

In the figure, licensing hasn't been configured yet, and RDS CALS have not been added. However, by reviewing the entries in the center panes, the issue is easy to identify. This tool becomes an easy reference to identify any licensing issues.

Remote Desktop Licensing Manager

Although you have a grace period when RDS will function normally, after the grace period ends, RDS will no longer accept connections if licensing is not configured. The grace period lasts for 120 days or until the first permanent RDS CAL is issued by a license server, whichever occurs first.

As mentioned previously, you can choose between per-user or per-device Remote Desktop Services Client Access Licenses (RDS CALs). The licensing server must first be activated before you can install the licenses.

After you've configured your RDS environment, you'll want to configure the license server. The RD Licensing Manager is used to install, issue, and track the availability of RDS CALs on a Remote Desktop license server. Licenses are purchased through a variety of different methods, depending on your company's relationship with Microsoft, such as the following:

◆ Enterprise Agreement

◆ Campus Agreement

◆ School Agreement

◆ Services Provider License Agreement

◆ Other Agreement

If you have one of these agreements with Microsoft, the best way to obtain licenses is through this agreement. It's also possible to purchase licenses through retail channels by purchasing a license pack. For detailed information on how to purchase licenses, check out this page: http://technet.microsoft.com/library/cc786167.aspx.

The license server can be on the same server as the RD Session Host server, or for larger implementations of Remote Desktop Services with multiple servers, a single license server will manage licenses for multiple RDS servers.

Older Terminal Services license servers used a discovery scope to allow TS servers to locate the license server. If you're installing the license server on Windows Server 2008 R2, this is not needed. Instead, you should use the Remote Desktop Session Host Configuration tool to specify a license server for the RD Session Host server to use. This is done on the Licensing tab of the RDP-Tcp Connections Properties dialog box where you identify the type of RDS CALs used for the server (per user or per device).

If you've performed the steps in this chapter to install and configure an RD Session Host server, you can configure the RD Licensing Manager by following these steps:

1. Launch the RD Licensing Manager by selecting Start ➢ Administrative Tools ➢ Remote Desktop Services ➢ Remote Desktop Licensing Manager.

2. Click the plus (+) to expand All Servers, and you'll see your server marked with a white X in a red circle.

3. Select your server. Right-click your server, and select Activate Server.

4. Review the information on the wizard's Welcome page, and click Next.

5. On the Connection Method page, accept the default of Automatic Connection (Recommended). Use this method if the RDS server has access to the Internet. If the server doesn't have access to the Internet, you can connect with another computer over the Internet or via a telephone. Click Next.

6. The Company Information page will appear. Enter your first name, last name, company, and country. This information is used if you need help from Microsoft. Click Next.

7. Enter the additional information requested on the Optional Company Information page. Click Next.

8. A dialog box will appear with a progress bar. The server is connecting to the Microsoft Clearinghouse and is being activated. When it completes, the completion page will appear.

9. Deselect the Start Install Licenses Wizard Now check box, and click Finish. At this point, the licensing server is activated, but there aren't any RDS CALs installed.

SET PER USER OR PER DEVICE

It may be necessary to return to the Remote Desktop Session Host Configuration console and set the Remote Desktop licensing mode. After launching the console, double-click the Remote Desktop licensing mode to access the property page. Select Per Device or Per User depending on what type of licenses you have purchased, and enter the name of the license server.

---

10. Right-click your server, and select Install Licenses. This will launch the wizard to install your licenses. There are multiple paths this can take, depending on what type of licenses you've purchased and where you've purchased them from.

The Bottom Line

Limit the maximum number of connections   You can limit the maximum number of connections for the server for performance reasons or to help ensure you remain compliant with the licensing agreement.

Master It   You want to limit the maximum number of connections to 100. How can you do this?

Add an application to an RD Session Host server   Once the RDS role is added and the RD Session Host server is configured, you can add applications to make them available to the server.

Master It   Your company has purchased an application that supports multiuser access. You want to install it on the RD Session Host server. What should you do?

Add a RemoteApp for Web Access   RemoteApp applications can be configured so that they are accessible to users via a web browser. Users simply need to access the correct page and select the application to launch it.

Master It   Assume you have already configured your environment to support RemoteApp applications. You now want to add a RemoteApp application. What should you do?

Add a RemoteApp to the Start menu   RemoteApp applications can be configured so that they are accessible to users from the Start menu of their system. Once configured, users simply select the item from their Start menu to launch it.

Master It   Assume you have already configured your environment to support RemoteApp applications. You now want to add a RemoteApp application so that it is accessible to users via the Start menu. What should you do?

Chapter 26

Connecting Mac OS X Clients

More and more organizations are integrating Apple Macintosh computers into their Active Directory networks each year. This is being facilitated both by Apple including better networking features and by Microsoft adding federation services that make it easier for diverse network clients to take advantage of Active Directory.

In this chapter, we cover ways to connect your Mac clients to your Windows Server 2008 R2 network and how to access various features such as file shares and printers from the Mac.

In this chapter, you'll learn to:

◆ Prepare Active Directory for Mac OS X clients

◆ Connect a Mac to the domain

◆ Connect to file shares and printers

◆ Use Remote Desktop from a Mac client

Preparing Active Directory for Mac OS X Clients

In the past, the process of connecting a Mac client to a Windows Server machine required additional software to let the Mac understand the Server Message Block (SMB) file protocols used by Windows. In Mac OS X, you have all the necessary pieces included with the operating system. This is because Apple has included a version of Samba with OS X. Samba lets Unix-like operating systems, such as Linux and OS X, talk the native SMB dialects that are used by Windows operating systems. So, the issue in connecting your Mac clients is more a matter of authentication than one of basic connectivity.

Even though Macs can speak SMB, Windows Server 2008 R2 expects a certain default level of security for SMB communication that OS X cannot provide natively, namely, SMB packet signing. Packet signing helps a Windows server and client communicate more securely by digitally signing every packet that is sent by SMB. This technique can relieve some of the risk of the packets being intercepted and manipulated in a so-called man-in-the-middle attack.

To let your Mac clients communicate effectively with Windows Server 2008 R2 Active Directory environments, you will need to disable the requirement for SMB packet signing. But in the interest of network security, you don't want to do away with packet signing altogether. Fortunately, the setting you want to make will enable SMB packet signing for clients that support it but not require it for clients (such as Macs) that don't.

To enable Mac clients running OS X to connect to your Active Directory domain, you must set the following Group Policy settings:

Microsoft network server: Digitally sign communications (always) Set this policy to Disable to turn off the requirement for SMB packet signing on client-to-server communications.

Microsoft network server: Digitally sign communications (if client agrees) Set this policy to Enable to allow Windows clients to still use SMB packet signing when communicating with Windows servers.

Network security: LAN Manager authentication level Set this policy to Send LM & NTLM; use NTLMv2 session security if negotiated. This policy will provide access to Mac clients while still permitting Windows clients to negotiate a higher security level.

You can set these policies in the local policies for domain controllers, which will enable access for Mac clients across the network. To set these policies, follow these steps:

1. Open Group Policy Management. You can do so in the following ways:

    ◆ Select Start ➢ Administrative Tools ➢ Group Policy Management.

    ◆ In Server Manager, expand Features, and then click Group Policy Management.

2. Open the Default Domain Policy.

In Server Manager, expand Group Policy Management, expand your forest, expand Domains, expand your domain, right-click Default Domain Policy, and click Edit. The location is shown in Figure 26.1. If you are prompted at this point, click OK.

FIGURE 26.1
Opening the Default Domain Policy in Server Manager

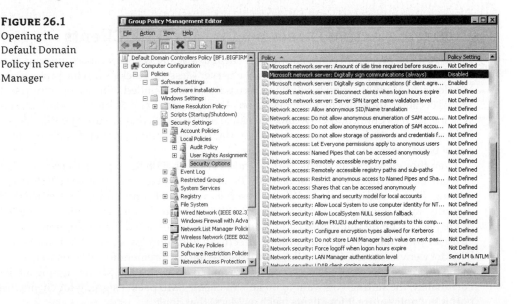

Through Group Policy Management in Administrative Tools, expand your forest, expand Domains, expand your domain, right-click Default Domain Policy, and then click Edit. The location should look similar to Figure 26.2. If you are prompted at this point, click OK.

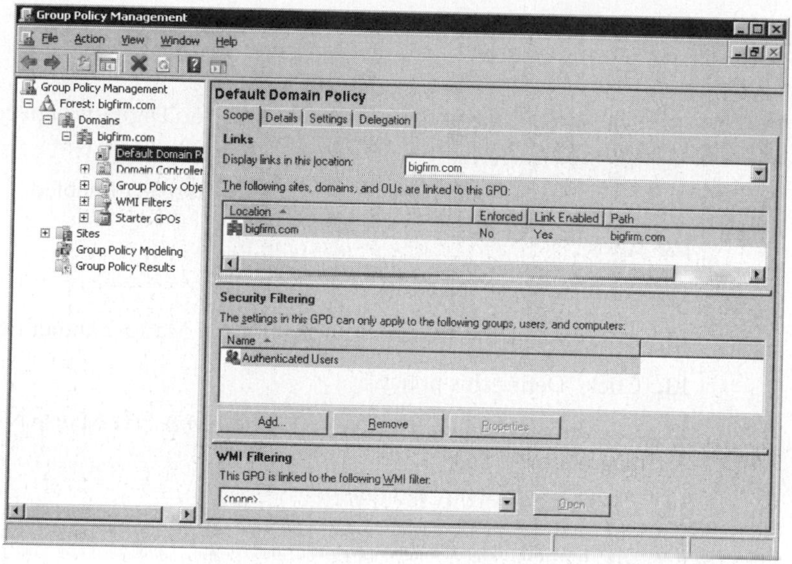

FIGURE 26.2
Using Group Policy
Management

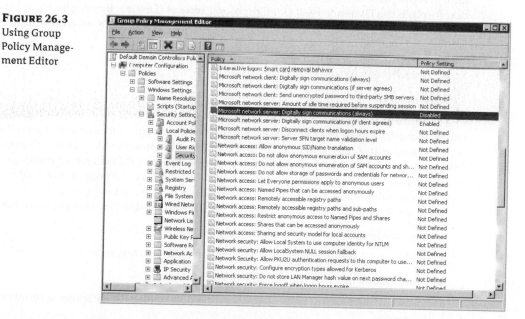

3. In the Group Policy Management Editor, go to Computer Configuration\Policies\
Windows Settings\Security Settings\Local Policies\Security Options, as shown in
Figure 26.3.

FIGURE 26.3
Using Group
Policy Manage-
ment Editor

4. Scroll down to "Microsoft network server."

5. Double-click the "Microsoft network server: Digitally sign communications (always)" policy.

6. Click "Define the policy setting," and then select Disabled.

7. Click OK.

8. Double-click the "Microsoft network server: Digitally sign communications (if client agrees)" policy.

9. Click "Define the policy setting," and then select Enabled.

10. Click OK.

11. Scroll down to "Network security."

12. Double-click the "Network security: LAN Manger authentication level" policy.

13. Click "Define this policy."

14. Use the drop-down list to select "Send LM & NTLM; use NTLMv2 session security if negotiated."

15. Click OK.

Connecting a Mac to the Domain

Before you can bind your Mac OS X client to Active Directory, you must complete some preparatory steps. Some of them may be completed already if the clients receive their IP configuration through the Dynamic Host Configuration Protocol (DHCP). Before you try to bind your Mac client to Active Directory, ensure the following items are configured on your Mac:

◆ IP address

◆ DNS server address

◆ Default gateway

The Domain Name System (DNS) server address is the critical part. In most organizations using Active Directory, the DNS servers will likely be domain controllers, or at least they will be integrated with Active Directory. This is important because the Mac client will perform a DNS query to find the Lightweight Directory Access Protocol (LDAP) server responsible for the domain name. An Active Directory integrated DNS server will respond with the IP address of a domain controller, which is what you want in order to join the domain.

These are some additional bits of information you will need to provide during the bind process:

◆ User credentials with permission to add a computer to the domain

◆ Your Mac's computer name as it will appear in Active Directory

◆ Fully qualified domain name (such as bigfirm.com)

◆ Distinguished path to the organization unit (OU) where the computer account should be created

◆ Administrator account credentials for your Mac

With this information in hand, or at least in mind, you are ready to join your Mac client to your Active Directory domain. Log on to your Mac OS X computer, and perform the following steps:

1. Open Directory Access.

2. Open a new Finder window.

3. Click Applications in the left pane.

4. Double-click Utilities.

5. Double-click Directory Access.

6. Click the closed lock in the lower-left corner, and then provide your administrator username and password. Click OK.

7. Click the Show Advanced Settings button.

8. Click the Services tab.

9. Double-click Active Directory.

10. In Active Directory Domain, type the fully qualified domain name, such as **bigfirm.com**.

11. In Computer ID, type the name for the Mac client computer; do not include dashes in the name.

12. Click Bind. When prompted, provide your Mac administrator name and password to permit the change. Click OK.

13. Provide the distinguished name for an account with permission to add the Mac client account to Active Directory, such as **administrator@bigfirm.com**.

14. Enter the password for the account.

15. Verify the distinguished path to the OU where this computer account will be created, as shown in Figure 26.4. Click OK.

FIGURE 26.4
Providing the
distinguished
path to the OU

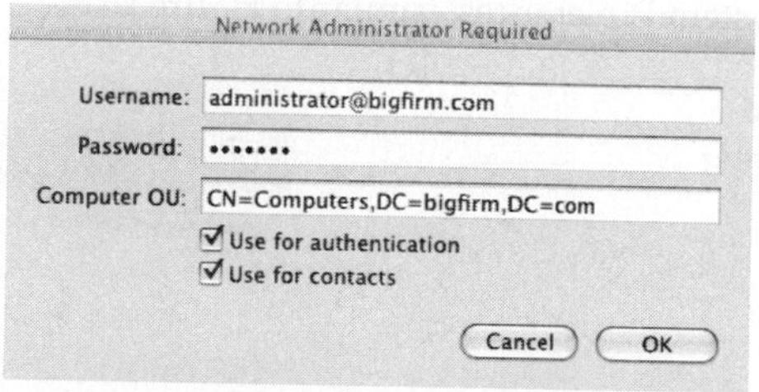

16. Click OK to save the Active Directory settings.

17. When prompted, enter your Mac administrator credentials, and click OK.

Connecting to File Shares

Once your Mac client is part of the Active Directory domain, connecting to shared folders is almost the same process as connecting to an OS X Server. The single exception is that you must specify that the Finder will use the SMB protocol to connect to the share. Use the format *smb:// servername/sharename* to define the path, similar to Figure 26.5.

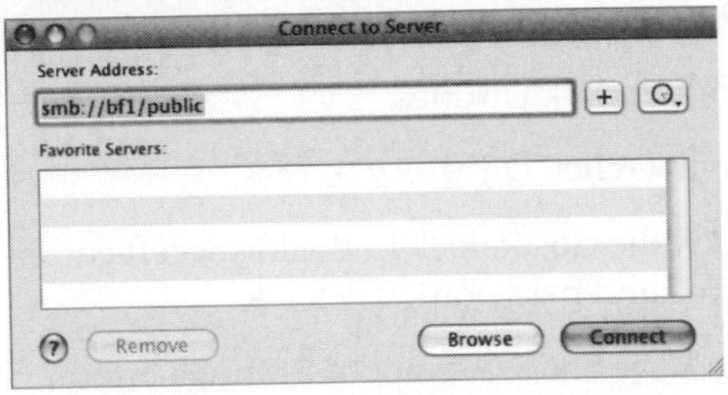

FIGURE 26.5
Defining the path to the Windows server

To connect your Mac client to a Windows Server 2008 R2 shared folder, use these steps:

1. In the Finder, click the Go menu, and then click Connect to Server.

2. Type the path to the shared folder using the format *smb://servername/sharename*.

3. Optionally, click the plus sign (+) to add this server to your list of favorite servers. If you do, you will be able to click the server name in the list; then click Connect.

4. Click Connect.

5. Provide your Active Directory user credentials, and click OK.

Connecting to Printers

Like connecting to shared folders, connecting to network printers that are published in Active Directory is a relatively straightforward task. Once the Mac client has joined the Active Directory domain, published printers will be displayed on the Default tab when adding a printer in Print & Fax in System Preferences, similar to Figure 26.6.

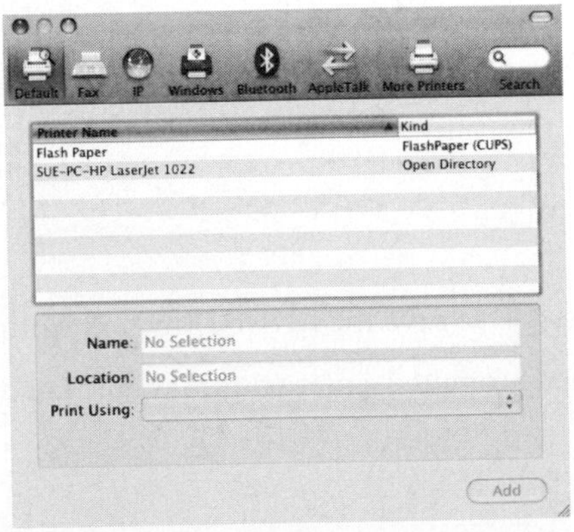

FIGURE 26.6
Adding a printer from Active Directory

To add a printer that is published in Active Directory, use these steps:

1. Open System Preferences.

2. Click Print & Fax.

3. Click the plus sign (+) to add a new printer.

4. On the Default tab, click the name of the printer you want to add.

5. Click Add.

To add printers in a Windows workgroup environment, the process is similar. You would still use the Print & Fax page of System Preferences to add the new printer, but instead of finding the Active Directory printers listed on the Default tab, you would use the Windows tab and browse for them.

Using Remote Desktop from a Mac Client

Now that you have added your OS X client to your Active Directory domain and you can access file shares and printers, how can you do your network administration? Fortunately, Microsoft has created a Remote Desktop client for OS X that lets you access your Windows Server 2008 R2 computers from your Mac. You can download the Remote Desktop Connection for Mac 2 (RDC) for OS X for free from either Microsoft's (www.microsoft.com/downloads) or Apple's (www.apple.com/downloads) download sections. Search the sites for *Remote Desktop Connection*.

To install the Remote Desktop Connection client, follow these steps:

1. Download the latest version of Remote Desktop Connection. The disk image package will automatically mount and start the setup. Click Continue.

2. Review the Read Me information, and then click Continue.

3. Review the license, and then click Continue. Click Agree if you accept the license.

4. Click Install to perform a standard installation, where the Remote Desktop Connection for Mac 2 icon will be placed in your Applications folder on your primary hard disk. You can change the install destination by clicking Change Install Location. Click Install. Figure 26.7 shows the Installation Type page.

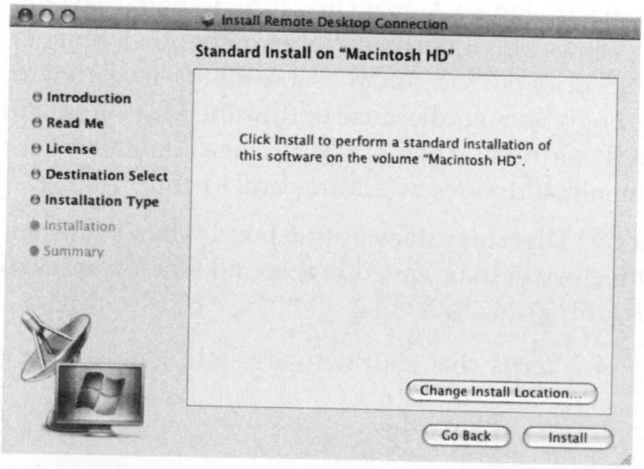

FIGURE 26.7
Selecting the location to install RDC

5. Provide your Mac administrator password to approve the installation, and then click OK.

6. When the installation process finishes, click Close to exit the installer.

Using the RDC is similar to using Remote Desktop in Windows, except that the interface has been changed somewhat to match the OS X style. The initial window contains only a space to enter the name of the computer to which you want to connect. To supply logon credentials and adjust any preferences, use the RDC menus at the top of the screen. Just like the Windows version of Remote Desktop, when you first connect to a remote computer, you will be prompted to provide your username, password, and domain name. RDC does save you some time by letting you store your Windows credentials in the Preferences screen and then save them in your Keychain.

⊕ Real World Scenario

ADMINISTERING WINDOWS SERVER 2008 R2 FROM A MAC

One of our clients expressed his frustration at having to keep a Windows client computer on his desk in addition to his new Mac running OS X 10.5. It seems that he performed his normal work entirely on the Mac but needed the Windows computer to handle occasional administration tasks in Active Directory.

Once he was introduced to the Remote Desktop Connection for Mac, he discovered that he could use RDC to perform his administration tasks without having to keep the Windows client on his desk. In the end, he had more space on his desk, and the Windows computer was passed on to another employee who needed it.

Troubleshooting

In this section, we offer some troubleshooting tips if you experience these issues while trying to bind your Mac client to Active Directory:

You have an issue with AD domains ending in .local   Many people have reported issues connecting to an Active Directory domain that ends with .local (such as is often used with Windows Small Business Server networks). Bonjour, Apple's implementation of Multicast DNS, does not see .local as a valid top-level domain and assumes that it should be resolved through Bonjour. Because of this, the Mac client will not query the DNS server to retrieve an IP address for any host in a .local domain. You can enable your Mac to look up .local domain addresses by adding *local* to your list of search domains, as shown in Figure 26.8.

Active Directory does not respond when binding   If you receive an error that the Active Directory domain failed to respond when you try to bind your Mac to the domain, there are a few things to check:

◆ Verify that your network settings specify a valid DNS server in the domain.

◆ Verify that SMB packet signing has been set correctly in Active Directory, as described in the "Preparing Active Directory for Mac OS X Clients" section in this chapter.

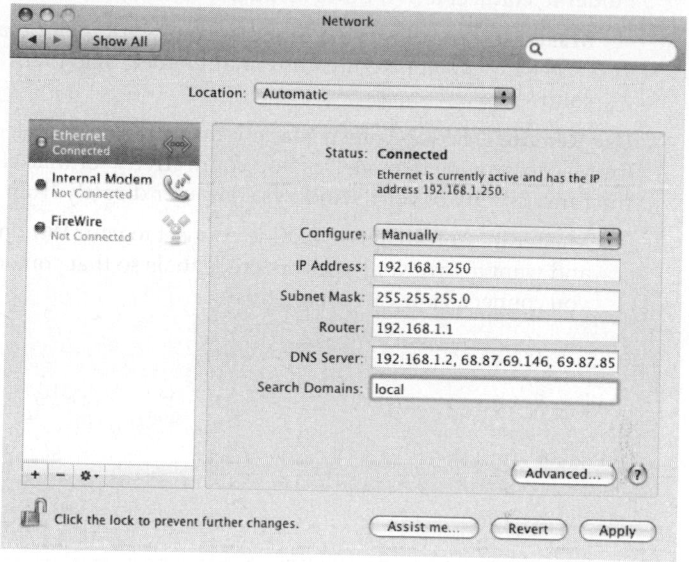

FIGURE 26.8
Adding *local*
to your search
domain order

Active Directory stops responding Various versions of OS X have had challenges connecting to Active Directory. Make sure you have the latest updates for the operating system. If your Mac client loses contact with Active Directory, try unbinding from the domain and then binding again.

The Bottom Line

Prepare Active Directory for Mac OS X clients Although Mac OS X can join Active Directory domains, you must take some preparatory steps to ensure they can communicate with Windows Server 2008 R2.

Master it You want your Active Directory users who have Mac clients to connect to your Windows Server 2008 R2 servers using a single Active Directory logon. What network security feature of Windows must you change to permit Mac clients to communicate with your Windows Server 2008 R2 domain?

Connect a Mac to the domain Mac OS X can connect to Active Directory and join domains. SMB protocol support is provided by a built-in version of Samba, letting OS X connect to Windows for file shares and printers.

Master it You want to add your Mac OS X client to your Active Directory domain. Which OS X utility should you use?

Connect to file shares and printers   OS X connects to Windows file shares and printers using the SMB support provided by Samba. Because support is integrated, you can use the Finder to connect to Windows resources directly rather than adding additional software.

Master it   You are trying to access a network folder that is shared on a Windows Server 2008 R2 computer from your domain-joined Mac client. How can you use the Finder to connect?

Use Remote Desktop from a Mac client   Microsoft created the Remote Desktop Connection for Mac to provide Remote Desktop connectivity for Mac clients. Using RDC, you can access the functionality of your Windows computer directly from your Mac clients.

Master it   You are using RDC to connect to your Windows Server 2008 R2 server computer and want to save your network credentials so that you don't have to enter them every time you connect. How can you do this?

Chapter 27

Patch Management

Patch management refers to the process by which software updates are installed on computers managed by your organization. In recent years, software updates have become a necessary evil in today's connected world. The rate of time at which you deploy updates can mean the difference between pulling a weekend-long install-fest rebuilding compromised computers or enjoying the weekend with a margarita by the pool.

Software updates seem like a never-ending cycle, and unless you enjoy walking around to every computer to install updates, you need tools to help you do the job. Beyond the tools, you also need a sound patch management process. You need to know whether each update is applicable to computers on your network, whether it is compatible with your existing applications, and how urgent it is to deploy this update.

This chapter covers some issues to consider when you are developing a patch management policy, including the different phases that you should go through when a new software update is released. After that, we analyze security updates and then take a detailed look at Windows Server Update Services (WSUS), which is a free Microsoft tool to help you keep your network computers up-to-date.

In this chapter, you will learn to:

◆ Use Windows Automatic Updating to check for new updates on a computer running Windows 7

◆ Use the Windows Update Stand-Alone Installer to silently install a security update

◆ Identify the four phases of patch management

The Four Phases of Patch Management

Installing updates on the computers on your organization's network is critical to protect the security of the network and to keep the organization's client computers performing optimally. How updates are rolled out on your network requires planning and testing to ensure a successful installation. Microsoft recommends a four-phase approach to patch management, as shown in Figure 27.1. Each of the four phases is discussed in the following sections. You can find more detailed information on the four phases on the Microsoft TechNet website at http://technet .microsoft.com/library/cc700845.aspx.

Phase 1: Assess

The Assess phase is when you look at your current patch management policies and procedures, collect information about the computers on your network, and determine the effectiveness of your current patch management infrastructure.

FIGURE 27.1
The four phases of
patch management

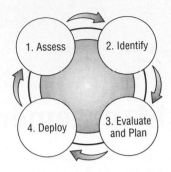

First, you should examine your current patch management policies and procedures. If they don't exist, create them! Once the policies and procedures have been finalized and approved, you should communicate these to all the users on your network. The communication should include a copy of each policy and procedure as well as expectations for the end user. For example, one expectation could be that users will not install any software on their computers that has not been approved by the IT department. By doing this, you decrease the number of applications that need to stay up-to-date.

Next, having a detailed inventory of all the computers connected to your network is important when an update is released. This will help you determine the overall impact that the update may have on your business. The inventory should list the hardware components on the computer, the version of operating system that the computer is running, and all installed applications and their version numbers. In large organizations, it is unrealistic to expect an inventory list can be 100 percent up-to-date all the time. In this case, you should consider splitting up the computers into logical groups. For example, all SQL Server database servers within your organization could be grouped together. When an SQL Server update is released, you can narrow down the number of computers that must be assessed by looking at only the computers in that SQL Server database servers group.

Finally, you should look at your current patch management infrastructure and determine whether it can accommodate the updates that you are planning on deploying. If you determine that the current infrastructure is inadequate, you should use this step in the phase to choose a new product that will suit your organization's needs. Later in this chapter, we will cover the different free patch management tools provided by Microsoft, designed for small to medium-sized organizations. Larger organizations should consider an enterprise-class patch management product, such as one from the Microsoft System Center family of products (www.microsoft.com/systemcenter).

Phase 2: Identify

The Identify phase of a patch management process is broken into three parts: being notified when an update is available, determining whether the update is applicable to computers on your network, and ranking the priority at which the update should be deployed.

Staying on top of when updates are released and then determining whether an update affects computers on your network can be a daunting task. The Identify phase should be used to research and subscribe to the notification method that best suits your needs. Microsoft offers several different methods by which you can be notified when security updates are available, such as email notifications, Really Simple Syndication (RSS) feed subscriptions, or Windows

Live alerts. You can sign up for these notification methods on the Microsoft TechNet website at www.microsoft.com/technet/security/bulletin/notify.mspx.

There are also several websites you can use to find out what is going on before an update is released for a particular vulnerability. This will keep you ahead of the game by letting you know at the same time as the bad guys find out that a vulnerability has been exposed.

Here are several websites we recommend:

Microsoft Security Response Center (MSRC) blog The Microsoft Security Response Center is in charge of issuing security updates for Microsoft. The site also issues advisories for issues that were not disclosed but that it's investigating. The MSRC blog is a good way to get current information. See http://blogs.technet.com/msrc.

The United States Computer Emergency Readiness Team (US-CERT) US-CERT consists of several public and private organizations that partner with the Department of Homeland Security to communicate security advisories for Microsoft and non-Microsoft products. See www.us-cert.gov.

SANS Internet Storm diary The SANS Internet Storm diary is made by handlers who volunteer their time to post security happenings as they occur. See http://isc.sans.org.

Full Disclosure mailing list The Full Disclosure mailing list was created for security researchers who choose not to follow responsible disclosure practices and publish vulnerability details to the Web before the manufacturer has a chance to develop an update for them. Whereas full disclosure is strongly discouraged, it still happens. This mailing list can be good to stay in step with what the bad guys are doing; however, not everything posted to this list is accurate. See http://archives.neohapsis.com/archives/fulldisclosure/.

University of Michigan Virus Busters The University of Michigan Virus Busters is a group of IT professionals from the University of Michigan. The site provides the information about malware in an administrator-friendly format. It also includes information on hoaxes that may be circulating on the Internet. See http://virusbusters.itcs.umich.edu/.

Symantec Security Response The Symantec Security Response website provides a knowledge base of information about malware and other potentially harmful software that may be installed on your computer. The site owners often post information about current threats sooner than other websites. See www.symantec.com/security_response/index.jsp.

Next, you should determine whether the update is applicable to computers on your network. This step of the Identify phase is dependent on your detailed inventory that was gathered in the first phase, Assess. Microsoft security updates are all accompanied by a security bulletin that includes a section titled "Affected and Non-Affected Software." This section lists all the operating systems supported by Microsoft and whether the security update applies to it. If you find that your computers are not affected by this update, you can move to the next one. However, if you find that your computers are affected, you must determine how quickly the update should be deployed on your computers.

Finally, once you've determined that an update applies to computers on your network, you should decide how quickly you need to deploy the update. The security bulletin can be a good place to start to decide the priority at which the update should be deployed. The following are some key sections in the bulletin:

Recommendation This is a general recommendation from Microsoft on how quickly the update should be deployed. However, this is just a recommendation and should serve only as a starting point to determine a patch's installation priority.

Known issues This section lists any known compatibility issues that this update may introduce. For example, if SQL Server is critical to your business and there is a known compatibility issue with a specific update and SQL Server, you may want to hold off on deploying the security update until the issue has been addressed.

Aggregate severity rating This rating can be Critical, Important, or Moderate. An update with a severity rating of Critical should be deployed faster than an update with a severity rating of Moderate.

Workarounds Any suggested workarounds are covered in this section. A workaround, such as disabling a service, setting an ActiveX kill bit, or changing firewall rules, can be used as a temporary fix until the security update can be deployed. However, a workaround does not replace the necessity for the security update because the binary is still vulnerable.

END-OF-LIFE PRODUCTS ARE NOT LISTED

Only affected products that are still supported by Microsoft are listed, even if a product may be affected. For example, Windows 2000 is no longer supported. If an update is released that affects Windows 2000, it will not show up on the list because it is no longer supported. You can find out which Microsoft products are no longer supported at www.microsoft.com/windows/lifecycle/default.mspx.

Phase 3: Evaluate and Plan

Once you have determined that an update is applicable to computers on your network, you must then submit a change request to deploy the update, prep the computers for the update, and determine how the update will be deployed.

A change request is dependent on organizational policies and procedures. Oftentimes, a change has to be approved by a committee and then scheduled with enough time to communicate any downtime to end users. All approved change requests should be performed within change management windows and should include a contingency plan in case something goes wrong with the deployment. Change management windows are often during nonpeak times when the impact on the business is the slightest.

Prepping the computers for the update includes looking for anything that may block the installation of the update during the deployment. Some of these blockers may include insufficient disk space, the computer not being powered on, or software restriction policies or other Group Policy objects that may block the installation.

Finally, determining how the update will be deployed means writing scripts, building tools, or using patch management software to deploy the update. Fortunately, most, if not all, Microsoft security updates have standardized on the same installer, so deploying these updates should be easier. Windows Server Update Services—discussed in detail later in this chapter—is a free product that will deploy Microsoft updates. Non-Microsoft updates can be packaged and deployed by using the System Center family of products (www.microsoft.com/systemcenter).

Phase 4: Deploy

The last phase is the Deploy phase. In this phase, the update is tested on a subset of computers, the specific details of the deployment are communicated to end users, and then the update is deployed to all affected computers on your network.

Testing the update on a subset of computers is important to identify any unknown compatibility issues or other last-minute changes that need to be addressed. When choosing the subset, you should pick computers that will not significantly impact your organization's business.

Next, the details of the deployment should be communicated. This includes the time at which the update will be installed (preferably within a change management window), the expected downtime required to perform the update, and a support channel in the event something goes wrong. For example, in your communication, you could include a number to the help desk or an email address through which end users can contact you with problems.

Finally, it's time to deploy! After the deployment is complete, assess whether it was successful and request sign-off from stakeholders in the process. Additionally, you should frequently revisit the patch management policies and procedures with stakeholders and management to ensure that no process changes are required.

Real World Scenario

WHERE WERE YOU WHEN BLASTER HIT?

For those of you who have been around for a few years, you probably remember the MSBlaster worm that rocked the IT industry. For those of you who don't, consider yourself lucky! The MSBlaster worm, released in August 2003, exploited a vulnerability in the remote procedure call (RPC) Distributed Component Object Model (DCOM) interface. Once your computer was infected, the worm would start scanning your network and look for other victims. The MSBlaster worm was especially nasty because it did not require any user interaction—having a computer connected to the Internet was enough.

It's always entertaining to hear what other people were doing "when Blaster hit." It seems like any system administrator on duty during that time remembers what they were doing. For one of the authors of this book, it started the weekend before: "I was a system administrator at the time, and we were still working out our patch management strategy. We had just purchased a new patch management product a few weeks before, so I thought it would try it with some free time. The product performed well, and I was able to get the majority of the client computers updated that were affected. However, the next few weeks were a nightmare. Not all departments had kept up on their security updates, so, once it was inside the network, it spread like wildfire. It got to the point where if you brought a new computer onto the network without the security update installed, you would be infected within minutes. It took several months to get everything back under control."

MSBlaster enforced the need for many organizations to take a careful look at their patch management strategy (if one existed) and figure out how they could avoid this in the future. In our opinion, Microsoft also learned a few things from this. It was not too long after MSBlaster that Microsoft released Automatic Updates, the Windows Firewall, and Windows Server Update Services. MSBlaster served as a wake-up call for many people but, in the end, helped the industry (and its consumers) as a whole.

Dissecting a Security Update

Starting with Windows Vista and Windows Server 2008, the way updates are distributed has changed. In the previous versions of Windows, a security update was installed by using update.exe. Now, security updates are packaged within an MSU file. The package contains the following files: a cabinet (CAB) file for the update, an XML file that describes the update, and a properties file that includes the strings used by the installer. The Windows Update Stand-Alone Installer process (wusa.exe) installs the security update.

The Windows Update Stand-Alone Installer accepts three command-line switches, as shown in Table 27.1.

TABLE 27.1:   Command-Line Switches Supported by wusa.exe

SWITCH	DESCRIPTION
/help, /h, or /?	Shows the command-line help for the Windows Update Stand-Alone Installer.
/norestart	Defers a reboot if required by the installation of the update.
/quiet	Quiet mode. Nothing is shown to the user while the update is installing.

You may have noticed that several switches are no longer supported by the Windows Update Stand-Alone Installer. For example, it is not possible to use the /X switch to extract the files any longer. However, you can still extract the files by using expand.exe or a file compression utility, such as 7-Zip (www.7-zip.org). Another switch that is no longer available is /integrate. This switch gave you the ability to integrate the updates into an offline installation so that the update is already installed when the computer is set up for the first time. One workaround is to add these updates to a Windows Image (WIM) file and deploy the image to new computers. You can find out more information about integrating updates and deploying WIM files by downloading the Windows Automated Installation Toolkit from the Microsoft Download Center (http://tinyurl.com/6368wo). You can find more information about the Windows Update Stand-Alone Installer at http://support.microsoft.com/kb/934307/.

Digging into Windows Server Update Services

WSUS is an update-management product designed to deploy updates to Windows client computers on your network. It includes rich reporting and status updates on all computers within your network.

Features of WSUS 3.0

Several new features have been added to WSUS 3.0. Some of them are listed here:

◆ More supported products. The full list is shown in Table 27.2.

◆ The ability to automatically download updates by product, update classification, or language.

◆ Email notification when new updates are ready or scheduled status reports on the overall compliance of your network.

♦ The ability to scan WSUS clients for needed updates before deploying them. This is handy to create reports when conducting the Identify phase of the patch management process.

♦ The ability to target updates to a group of computers. This can be used in conjunction with the Evaluate and Plan phase when you need to test the updates on a subset of computers.

♦ The ability to install the WSUS Administration Console on a computer other than the WSUS server.

TABLE 27.2: Supported Products for WSUS 3.0

Windows 2000 with Service Pack 4	Office XP, 2003, and 2007
Windows XP	Office Communications Server 2007
Windows Vista, Windows Vista Ultimate Extras, and Windows Vista Language Packs	Microsoft Internet Security and Acceleration (ISA) Server 2004, 2006, and firewall client for ISA Server
Windows Media Player	Internet Explorer 7 and 8
Windows 7	Internet Explorer 7 and 8
Windows Server 2003, 2008, and 2008 R2	Exchange Server 2000, 2003, and 2007
Microsoft Expression Media v1	System Center Configuration Manager 2007 and Systems Management Server 2003
Windows Essentials Business Server 2008 and Windows Small Business Server 2003	Virtual Server 2005 and Virtual PC 2007
Compute Cluster	Microsoft Data Protection Manager 2006
CAPICOM SDK Components	System Center Virtual Machine Manager 2007
Visual Studio 2005 and 2008	Microsoft Forefront
Windows Defender	Network Monitor 3
Windows Live	SQL Server 2005
	Microsoft Silverlight

Software Requirements for WSUS Servers and Clients

Before installing WSUS in your environment, you must ensure that both the WSUS server(s) and clients meet the minimum software requirements.

The WSUS servers must have at least the following installed:

♦ Windows Server 2003 with Service Pack 1, Windows Server 2008, or Windows Server 2008 R2.

♦ Internet Information Services (IIS).

- ◆ Windows Installer 3.1 or newer.

- ◆ .NET Framework 2.0 or newer.

- ◆ If you are using a separate database server, you must have a computer installed that is running SQL Server 2005 with Service Pack 2 or newer.

To run the WSUS Administration Console, you must have the following installed:

- ◆ Windows XP with Service Pack 2, Windows Vista, Windows Server 2003, Windows Server 2008, Windows Server 2008 R2, or Windows 7

- ◆ Microsoft Management Console 3.0

- ◆ Microsoft Report Viewer Redistributable 2005

WSUS clients must be running one of the following operating systems:

- ◆ Windows 7

- ◆ Windows Server 2008 R2

- ◆ Windows Server 2008

- ◆ Windows Server 2003

- ◆ Windows Vista

- ◆ Windows XP

- ◆ Windows 2000 with Service Pack 4

WSUS can use either the Windows Internal Database or SQL Server to host the WSUS update information. The one you should choose depends on the size of your WSUS installation. For larger installations, using SQL Server 2008 is recommended.

REMOTE CONNECTIONS NOT SUPPORTED WITH THE WINDOWS INTERNAL DATABASE

The Windows Internal Database does not support remote connections, so you will not be able to install the WSUS Administration Console on another computer if you are using the Windows Internal Database.

Deployment Scenarios

WSUS 3.0 can be broken down into three main deployments: small businesses, medium businesses, and business with limited connectivity to either the Internet or within your enterprise network (your *intranet*). For large businesses, you should consider a product from the System Center family (www.microsoft.com/systemcenter).

A small business normally comprises one WSUS server that synchronizes directly with Microsoft Update. All WSUS clients are geographically close, and all are behind the same firewall, as shown in Figure 27.2.

FIGURE 27.2
Small-business
WSUS deployment

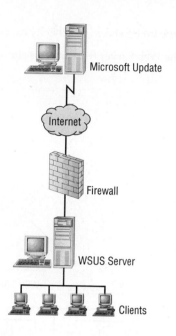

A medium-size business may be comprised of more than one WSUS server serving clients that are geographically close. One WSUS server may synchronize with the other (shown in Figure 27.3), or they may get their updates separately from Microsoft Update (shown in Figure 27.4). An advantage of having only one server synchronizing with Microsoft Update
is that the other WSUS server is not exposed to the Internet.

In a limited-connectivity deployment scenario, all computers that are connected to your enterprise network are isolated from the Internet. In this case, you could set up an external WSUS server, export the update metadata from this server, and manually import it into the internal WSUS server, as shown in Figure 27.5.

Configuring Prerequisites for WSUS 3.0

There are two prerequisites that need to be configured before you can install WSUS on a computer running Windows Server 2008. The first one is to install IIS, including the components needed for WSUS, as described in a moment. The other prerequisite is to install the Report Viewer 2008 SP1 Redistributable on the computer that will be running the WSUS Administration Console. In this chapter, we will show you how to run the WSUS Administrator Console on the WSUS server itself.

First, install IIS:

1. Log on to the computer as a member of the local Administrators group.

2. Select Start ➢ Administrative Tools ➢ Server Manager.

3. In the Roles Summary section, click Add Roles.

4. On the Before You Begin page, click Next.

   5. Select the Web Server (IIS) check box, click Add Required Features, and then click Next.

   6. Read the Web Server (IIS) page, as shown in Figure 27.6, and then click Next.

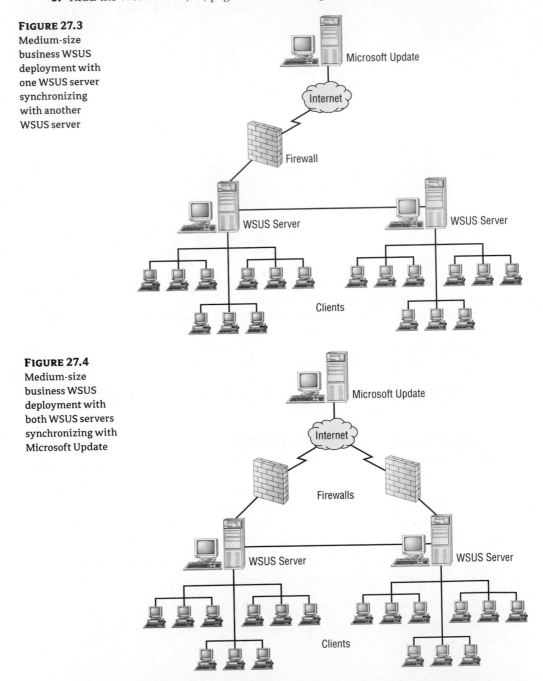

FIGURE 27.3
Medium-size business WSUS deployment with one WSUS server synchronizing with another WSUS server

FIGURE 27.4
Medium-size business WSUS deployment with both WSUS servers synchronizing with Microsoft Update

FIGURE 27.5
Limited-
connectivity
deployment

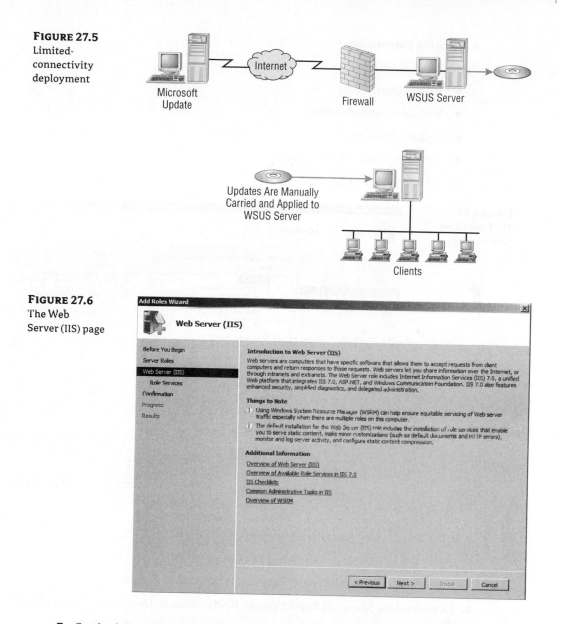

FIGURE 27.5
Limited-
connectivity
deployment

FIGURE 27.6
The Web
Server (IIS) page

7. On the Select Role Services page, ensure that only the following check boxes are selected, and then click Next, as shown in Figure 27.7:

◆ Static Content

◆ Default Document

◆ ASP.NET

- ◆ .NET Extensibility

- ◆ ISAPI Extensions

- ◆ ISAPI Filters

- ◆ Windows Authentication

- ◆ Request Filtering

- ◆ Dynamic Content Compression

- ◆ IIS 6 Metabase Compatibility

FIGURE 27.7
The Select Role
Services page

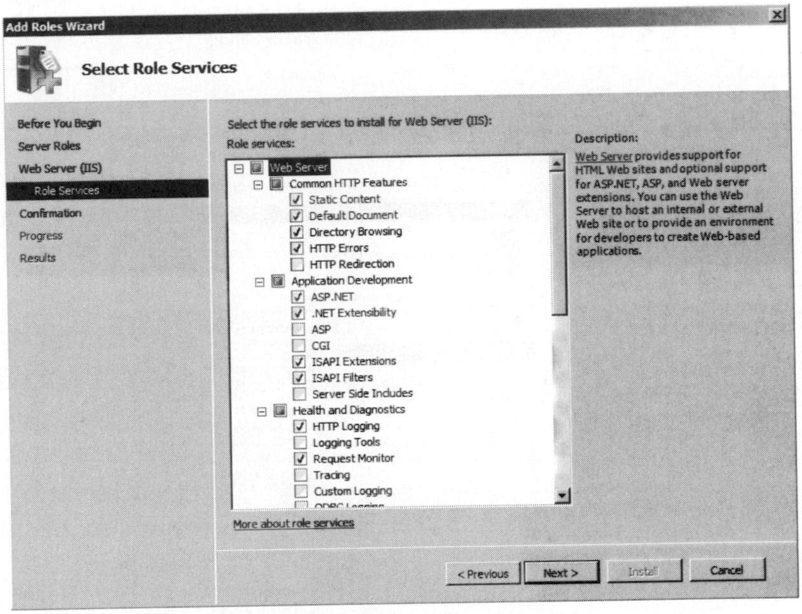

8. Click Install. This may take a few minutes to complete.

9. When the installation is complete, click Close.

Finally, you can install the Report Viewer 2008 SP1 Redistributable:

1. Download the Microsoft Report Viewer Redistributable from `http://tinyurl.com/16oex2`.

2. Double-click `ReportViewer.exe`, and then click Next to start the installation.

3. Select the "I have read and accept the license terms" check box, and then click Install.

4. When the installation is complete, click Finish.

Installing and Configuring WSUS 3.0

WSUS 3.0 is packaged as a stand-alone installer available from the Microsoft Download Center. In this section, you will learn how to download WSUS 3.0 and install and configure it on a Windows Server 2008 computer. After that, you will configure a Group Policy object that points to WSUS clients to the new WSUS server.

Follow these steps to install and configure WSUS 3.0 on Windows Server 2008 using the Windows Internal Database (Note: This is included as a role in Windows Server 2008 R2):

1. Download WSUS 3.0 with SP2 from the Microsoft Download Center, and double-click the executable to start the installation.

2. On the Welcome to the Windows Server Update Services 3.0 SP2 Setup Wizard page, click Next.

3. On the WSUS Installation Mode Selection page, select the "Full server installation including Administration Console" option, and then click Next, as shown in Figure 27.8.

FIGURE 27.8

The WSUS Installation Mode Selection page

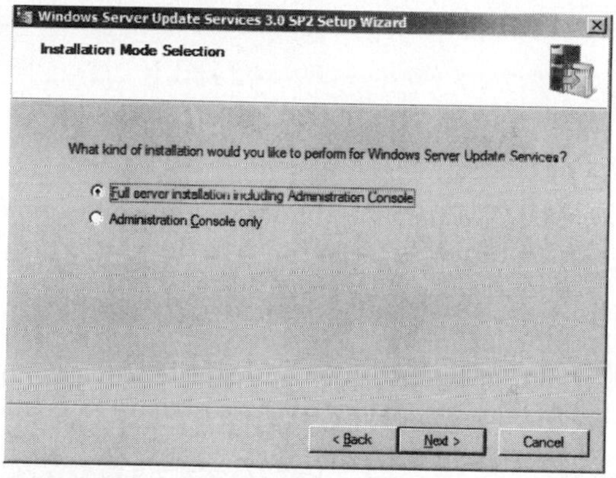

4. On the License Agreement page, select the "I accept the terms of the License agreement" option, and then click Next, as shown in Figure 27.9.

FIGURE 27.9

The License Agreement page

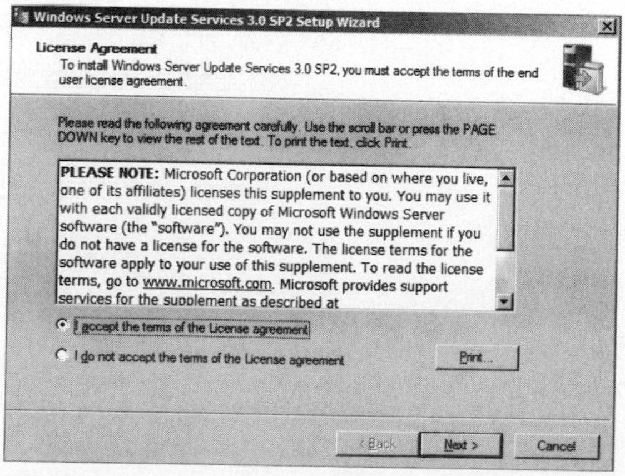

5. On the Select Update Source page, click the Stores Update Locally check box, and then click Browse to choose a directory in which to store the updates. In this chapter, we will use C:\WSUS, as shown in Figure 27.10.

FIGURE 27.10
The Select Update
Source page

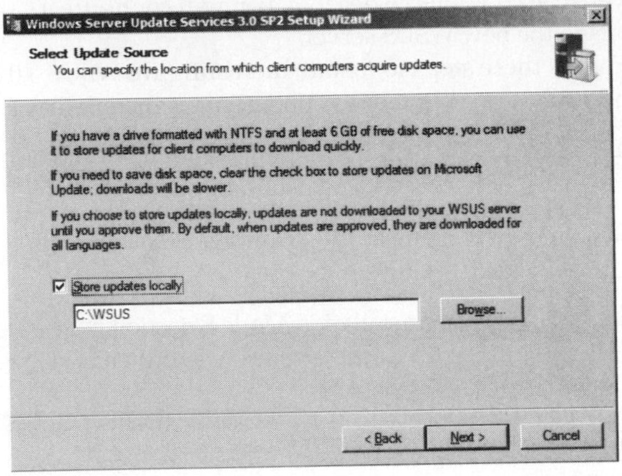

6. Choose the database installation:

   A. On the Database Options page, if you want to use the Windows Internal Database for WSUS, select the "Install Windows Internal Database on this computer" option. This option is what we will use in this chapter and is shown in Figure 27.11.

   B. If you have a SQL Server on your network that you would like to use, select the "Use an existing database server on a remote computer" option, and then enter the machine name and database instance name in the following format: *Machinename\Instancename.*

FIGURE 27.11
The Database
Options page

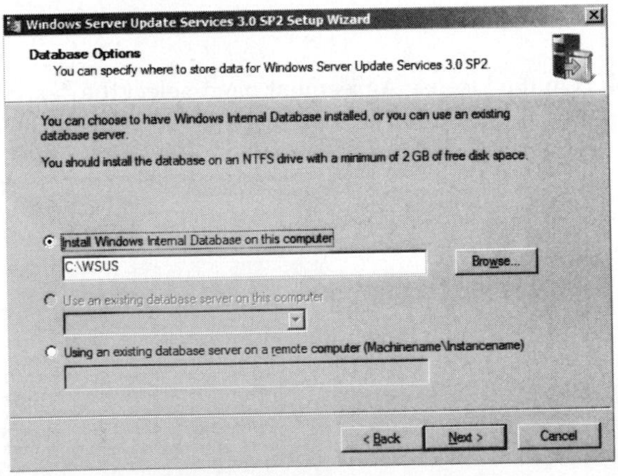

7. Click Next.

8. On the Web Site Selection page, choose whether you want to use the existing default IIS website or to create a new website. In this chapter, you will use the existing default website, as shown in Figure 27.12. Click Next.

FIGURE 27.12
The Web Site
Selection page

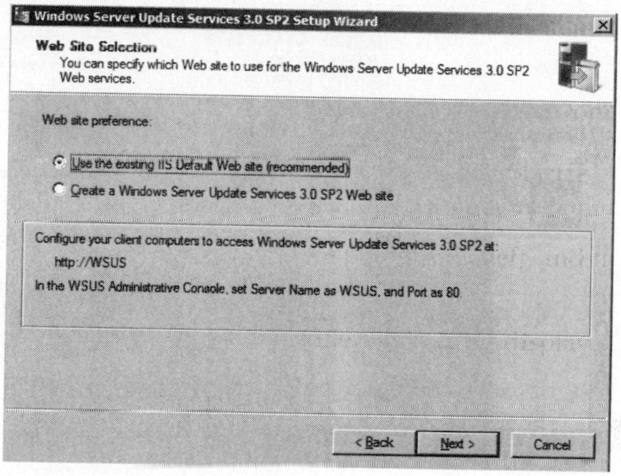

9. Click Next to start the installation. This may take a few minutes to complete.

10. When the installation has finished, click Finish.

The WSUS Configuration Wizard automatically starts. Follow these steps:

1. On the Before you Begin page, click Next.

2. On the Join the Microsoft Update Improvement Program page, select the "Yes, I would like to join the Microsoft Update Improvement Program" check box, and then click Next.

3. Choose the WSUS upstream server:

   A. In this chapter, you will synchronize the WSUS server directly with Microsoft Update by selecting the Synchronize with Microsoft Update option on the Choose Upstream Server page, as shown in Figure 27.13.

   B. If you already have a WSUS server on your network that you want to synchronize with, select the "Synchronize from another Windows Server Update Services server" option, type the WSUS computer name in the "Server name" box, choose to use SSL when synchronizing update information, and decide whether this server is a replica of the upstream server.

4. Click Next.

5. On the Specify Proxy Server page, if you are using a proxy server, enter the appropriate credentials, and then click Next.

6. On the Connect to Upstream Server page, click Start Connecting. This will download the type of updates that are available, products that can be updated, and available languages. This may take several minutes to complete.

FIGURE 27.13
Choosing the
upstream server

FIGURE 27.13
Choosing the
upstream server

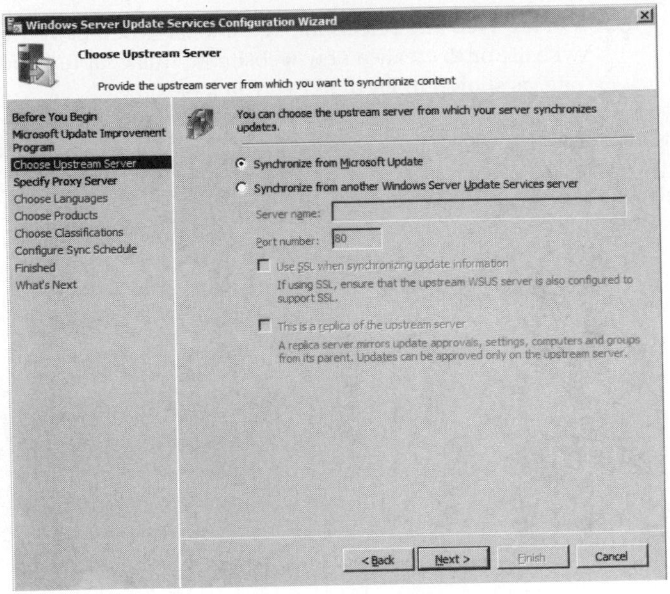

7. When it has finished, click Next.

8. Choose the languages for which this server will download updates, and then click Next. For this chapter, select English only, as shown in Figure 27.14.

FIGURE 27.14
Choosing
languages

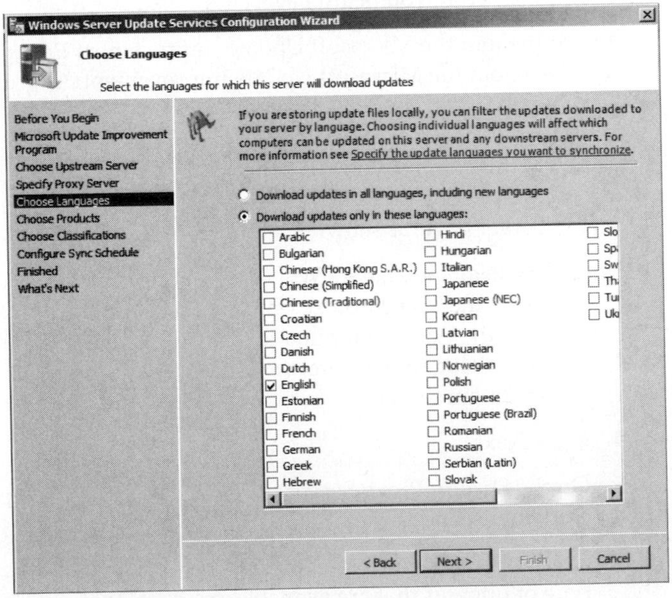

9. Choose the products that you want to update. By default, WSUS chooses all Windows and Microsoft Office updates. For the purposes of this chapter, use the defaults. Click Next.

10. Choose the classification of updates. By default, WSUS chooses only critical updates, definition updates, and security updates, which is what you will use in this chapter. Click Next.

11. On the Set Sync Schedule page, choose the "Synchronize manually" option, and then click Next, as shown in Figure 27.15. If you would rather choose automatic synchronization, you can do it from this step in the configuration wizard.

FIGURE 27.15
Choosing the sync schedule

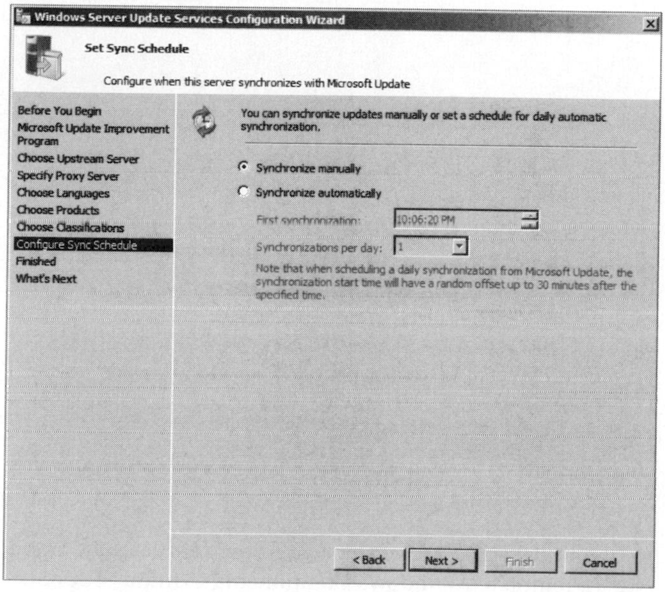

12. On the Finished page, click Finish to launch the WSUS Administration Console and begin initial synchronization, as shown in Figure 27.16.

You can also do an unattended installation of WSUS. This can come in handy if you need to install WSUS in many computers at once or if your organization requires unattended installation scripts for all applications in the event of a server failure. You can find more information about doing an unattended installation of WSUS on Microsoft TechNet at http://technet. microsoft.com/library/cc708476.aspx.

Pointing Your Clients to the WSUS Server

Client computers use the Windows automatic updating client to receive WSUS updates and can be configured by using a Group Policy object. A GPO drastically reduces the administrative overhead because one GPO can be deployed to all computers in an Active Directory installation at once. Configuring Windows automatic updating through a GPO is done by using the Group Policy Object Editor.

FIGURE 27.16
Finishing the
WSUS Configura-
tion Wizard

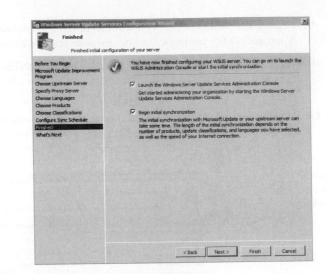

OPERATING SYSTEM SUPPORT FOR WSUS UPDATES

You must be running one of the following operating systems to receive WSUS updates: Windows 7, Windows Server 2008 R2, Windows Vista, Windows Server 2008, Windows Server 2003, Windows XP Professional with Service Pack 2, Windows 2000 Professional with Service Pack 4, or Windows 2000 Server with Service Pack 4.

To configure Windows automatic updating settings, follow these steps:

1. In the Group Policy Object Editor, navigate to Computer Configuration\Administrative Templates\Windows Components\Windows Update.

2. Double-click Configure Automatic Updates, and then select the Enabled option.

   A. For the "Configure automatic updating" box, select the appropriate setting. The choices are "Notify for download and notify for install," "Auto download and notify for install," "Auto download and schedule the install," and "Allow local admin to choose setting."

   B. If you choose "Auto download and schedule the install," you must enter the day and time for which the updates are scheduled, as shown in Figure 27.17.

3. Point the WSUS clients to the WSUS server by specifying the intranet Microsoft Update service location.

   A. Select the Enabled option.

B. In the "Set the intranet update service for detecting updates" and "Set the intranet statistics server" boxes, type the name of the WSUS server, as shown in Figure 27.18.

C. Click OK.

FIGURE 27.17
Configuring Automatic Updates

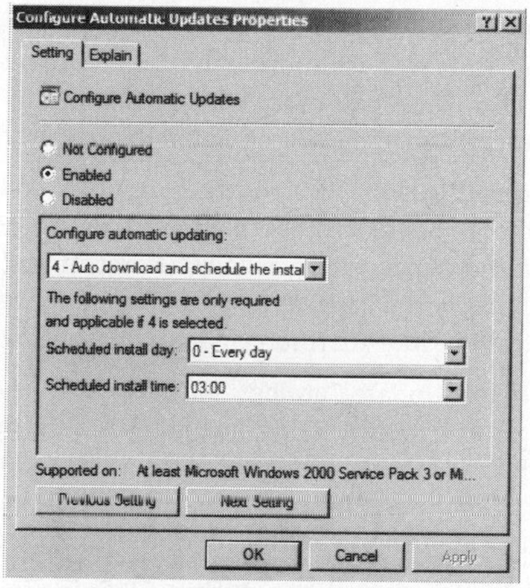

FIGURE 27.18
Configuring WSUS server

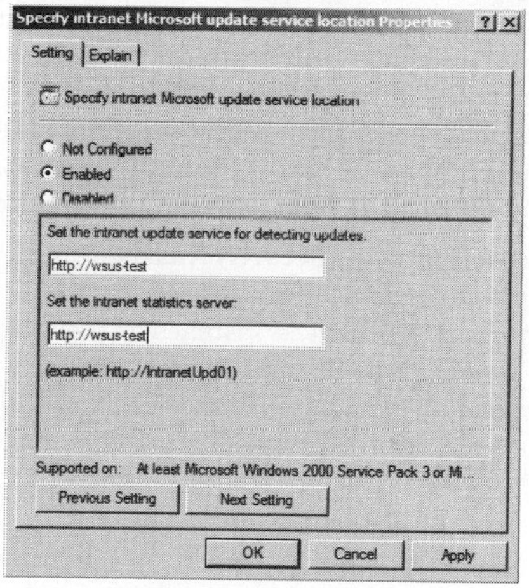

4. If required, configure the other options within this Group Policy setting. For more information, see the topic "Configure Clients Using Group Policy" on Microsoft TechNet at http://technet.microsoft.com/library/cc708574.aspx.

5. If you would rather configure the WSUS clients by using the registry, all the registry settings are located in HKEY_LOCAL_MACHINE\Software\Policies\Microsoft\Windows\ WindowsUpdate. You must do this for each WSUS client individually.

ADDITIONAL PATCH MANAGEMENT TOOLS PROVIDED BY MICROSOFT

Although we're focusing on WSUS in this section, Microsoft has several other tools that can assist you in deploying updates to your organization:

Microsoft Download Center   All updates are posted to the Microsoft Download Center. You can download these and use the updates to manually install them on computers, incorporate them into custom scripts, or package them for use by a patch management system. The Microsoft Download Center is available at http://download.microsoft.com.

Microsoft Update   Microsoft Update is an enhancement to Windows Update that offers you updates to products other than Windows, including Microsoft Office. Starting with Windows Vista and Windows Server 2008, Microsoft Update has been integrated into the operating system as a Control Panel item. For operating system versions prior to Windows Vista and Windows Server 2008, the Microsoft Update site is available at http://update.microsoft.com.

Microsoft Update Catalog   All files available on Microsoft Update are available in the Microsoft Update Catalog, including drivers, updates, security, and other updates to Microsoft products. One nifty thing about the Microsoft Update Catalog is the ability to add multiple files to your shopping basket and download them all at once. You can find the Microsoft Update Catalog at http://catalog.update.microsoft.com.

Windows Automatic Updating   This is a feature in Windows that allows you to schedule updates so they can be automatically installed when you are not using the computer. You can choose to automatically download and install updates, download updates and prompt you for installation, check for updates and notify you when new updates are available for download and installation, or never check for updates. In operating systems prior to Windows Vista and Windows Server 2008, this feature was known as Automatic Updates. You can configure Windows Automatic Updating and Automatic Updates through the Control Panel.

Microsoft Baseline Security Analyzer (MBSA)   You can use this tool to scan local and remote computers for missing security updates or a configuration that is not secure. For example, if SQL Server is installed on the computer being scanned, MBSA will check that the SA password is not blank. If it is, it will notify you. The MBSA is only for reporting and will not fix anything that it finds. You can find out more information about MBSA on Microsoft TechNet at http://technet.microsoft.com/security/cc184924.aspx.

The Bottom Line

Use Windows Automatic Updating to check for new updates on a computer running Windows 7   Windows Automatic Updating is a Control Panel item used to check the Microsoft Update site to see whether any updates are available for your computer.

Master It   On a Windows 7 computer, use Windows Automatic Updating to see whether any new updates are available for your computer.

Use the Windows Update Stand-Alone Installer to silently install a security update The Windows Update Stand-Alone Installer is used to install security updates on all Windows operating systems since Windows Vista and Windows Server 2008.

Master It Install a security update in quiet mode and defer a required reboot by using the Windows Update Stand-Alone Installer.

Identify the four phases of patch management According to Microsoft, there are four phases in planning a patch management strategy.

Master It Which of the following is not one of the four phases of patch management?

1. Identify

2. Troubleshoot

3. Evaluate and Plan

4. Assess

5. Deploy

Chapter 28

File Shares Made Even Better: Windows SharePoint Services 3.0

Information—everything from a multinational company's finances down to the middle name of your mother's aunt's cousin—has become the focus of the century. For better or worse, modern technology makes it possible to store almost every detail about almost any topic. Between regulations and sound business tracking, it is safe to say that virtually all of the information pursuant to a company's decisions will end up being kept for many years. Becoming well informed is no longer the challenge; the new dilemma is where the heck to *store* all of this information!

Data organized into files can reside in a number of repositories. For the past several generations, the solution has been to store individual files in a flat file system, such as the Microsoft NT File System (NTFS) or the File Allocation Table (FAT) file system. But imagine your office cluttered from floor to ceiling with hundreds of file cabinets and all of your business intelligence data stored in the form of paper documents filed away in those cabinets, probably typed up with an old manual typewriter. Forget the time it takes to produce each document—think of the time involved in finding and retrieving all of the details you need to make one simple decision! File systems, like file cabinets, still have a limited purpose but cannot support the immediate gratification—pardon us, immediate *response*—most business users seek when making decisions. Now imagine all of that data stored efficiently in searchable electronic tables with additional qualifying details about each document stored along with the document content itself. Breathing easier? Welcome to Windows SharePoint Services.

In this chapter, you will learn to:

- ◆ Understand the features and requirements of Windows SharePoint Services 3.0
- ◆ Consider Windows SharePoint Services 3.0 installation issues and processes
- ◆ Understand SharePoint site and document library provisioning
- ◆ Understand document management and access in Windows SharePoint Services 3.0
- ◆ Understand advanced Windows SharePoint Services 3.0 administration

Overview of Windows SharePoint Services 3.0

Windows SharePoint Services 3.0 (WSSv3 for short or WSS for even shorter) was included in Windows Server 2003 R2 as an installable server application, much like IIS 6 or the DNS Service. The original Windows Server 2003 sans SP/SP1 product did not have WSS embedded, but the installation programs could be easily downloaded from Microsoft. In Windows Server 2003 R2, it was embedded. Therefore, in the early betas of Windows Server 2008, all the way up to Beta 3, there was hope that SharePoint would continue to be included in the OS. Alas, there must have been some parting of the ways between the SharePoint team and the Windows Server team because unexpectedly Windows SharePoint Services 3.0 was dropped from the Windows Server 2008 OS just prior to release. However, SharePoint presents such a superior mechanism to file shares for storing and accessing shared data that it just had to be included in any intelligent narrative on Windows Server 2008, which is why we've included this chapter.

WSSv3 offers free document management services that can be downloaded from Microsoft and installed on Windows Server 2008 or 2008 R2. And although WSSv3 is so much more than simply a document management utility (see Table 28.1), for the purpose of this chapter we will examine the features of WSS that make it a uniquely qualified candidate to replace traditional file shares for individual file/document storage.

TABLE 28.1: WSS 3.0 Features

FEATURE	DESCRIPTION
Lists and libraries	Organizes and manages files, nonfiles, and their metadata
Web parts	Exposes lists, libraries, and other programmable content
Master pages	Provides central editing of web-wide branding and style
Galleries	Manages content templates for redistribution
Central Administration	Provides one-stop administration of the WSS environment
Office 2007 integration	Enforces consistency and supports user collaboration
Security	Protects data, trims the UI per user, provides auditing
Indexing	Provides content crawls that are schedulable
Information rights management (IRM)	Provides controls for document access offline

WSSv3 is optimized for Windows Server 2003, so running WSSv3 on a Windows Server 2008 operating system brings its own set of challenges. Windows Server 2008 includes IIS 7.0 and Windows Server 2008 R2 includes IIS 7.5, the latest version of IIS. But WSSv3 was written for IIS 6. As such, the new architecture in IIS 7.0 and 7.5 (hereafter referred to together as simply IIS 7) affects SharePoint services to a certain degree. Details about IIS 7 appear elsewhere in this book, but as a reminder, these are some of the ways in which IIS 7 differ from IIS 6:

◆ IIS 7 includes new processing modes, such as *integrated application pool mode*, which integrates IIS and ASP.NET pipelines for seamless processing, and *classic application pool mode*, which mimics IIS 6 worker process isolation mode.

◆ IIS 7 includes Windows Communication Foundation (WCF) listeners to support web applications that use protocols other than HTTP or HTTPS.

◆ The new Windows Process Activation Service (WAS) is the listener adapter for HTTP.sys.

♦ IIS 7 offers both native modules and managed modules to support both static and managed code content.

♦ The IIS 6 `metabase.xml` configuration file has been replaced by several XML files that work together to provide the distributed configuration for IIS 7 (`applicationhost.config`, `machine.config`, root `web.config`, site-unique `web.config`).

♦ A new CLI application, `appcmd.exe`, grants flexible, scriptable administration of IIS 7, while the new WinRM-based remote management allows access from anywhere through commonly exposed TCP ports.

How Does WSS Work?

One of the major differences between file shares and WSSv3 is the storage facility behind each technology. File shares organize multiple files in a hierarchically organized nonrelational file system. But Windows SharePoint Services stores each file as a large object in a Microsoft SQL Server table. In fact, where file shares use file attributes to provide metadata about a document, WSS stores the metadata separately from the actual document content in the SharePoint content SQL database. But it is not as simple as a one-to-one relationship between the document and the table row. In fact, the metadata about a given document is distributed and stored in many tables within the SharePoint content database in SQL Server. Reconstructing a single document requires querying multiple tables. In this respect, a file share's method of storing attributes attached to the document content would appear simpler, but in fact it restricts manipulation and hinders flexibility.

Another vast chasm between file shares and SharePoint is the method of delivery. Microsoft file shares are accessed via SMB protocol requests either through NetBIOS over TCP/IP or supported directly by TCP/IP over TCP port 445 (Windows 2000 OS and newer). But SharePoint documents are accessed by contacting a web application running on IIS via a web browser application or Office suite productivity application such as Word or Excel. The web-based delivery of files stored in SharePoint opens up a bevy of web application customizations that can improve user experience, data security, and network efficiency.

In fact, Windows Server 2008 R2's IIS 7.5 introduces new and improved web application features that can be employed to improve a user's SharePoint experience. Cool features such as tracing, compression, remote management, compartmentalized modules, URL filtering, IPv6 address restriction, and application pool warm-up lend well to optimizing and maintaining a SharePoint website. For more details about directly managing IIS 7, check out Microsoft's IIS website at www.iis.net. Also, be aware that Microsoft discourages direct configuration of SharePoint sites through IIS Manager or direct management of SharePoint databases through the SQL Server Management console. Like the old saying goes, "If you break it, you bought it!" Don't expect a warm reception from Microsoft Product Support in the event your customizations in IIS 7 or SQL Server have disabled your SharePoint sites!

Prerequisites

Windows SharePoint Services owes its functionality and slick good looks to a variety of supporting Microsoft products. There are several software prerequisites that must be involved to support a SharePoint environment. First, you need Microsoft SQL Server, without which there would be no repository in which to store either SharePoint application's configuration information or the actual user content. Second, Microsoft IIS provides HTTP/HTTPS listening and web page delivery, among other things. Also, WSSv3 uses several components of the .NET Framework v3+ to offer IRM, collaborative communication, and automation workflows (more on those later). Without the Windows Communication Foundation and Workflow Foundation provided by the .NET Framework, WSSv3 would simply be a storage library and nothing more. Also, a current XML parser is needed because most SharePoint pages, both system provided and user created, are of the `.aspx` format.

The SQL Server version installed to support WSS can be SQL Server 2000, SQL Server 2005, or SQL Server 2008 (though WSSv3 was written for SQL Server 2005). In fact, WSS is so dependent on SQL Server that if the SQL Server application is not already installed at the moment of WSS installation, the WSS install program will install a free edition of SQL Server called SQL Server Embedded Edition (also known as the Windows Internal Database). Similarly, WSS depends on Windows Server 2008 R2's Web Server role. Be aware that Windows Server 2008 R2 does not install the Web Server role by default, so you will need to add the Web Server role to the OS prior to beginning to install WSS.

Also, consider the front-end client application that users will engage to interface with the WSS web pages. Microsoft recognizes two separate tiers of web browser applications. The first tier consists of browsers capable of delivering all administration and end-user consumption functionalities. It's no surprise this top tier boasts only Microsoft Internet Explorer (versions 6 and newer). The second-tier browsers offer a user interface for retrieving and submitting documents/files but little administration functionality. This second tier includes non-Microsoft web browsers such as Safari, Mozilla, and Netscape.

WEB BROWSER ADD-ONS

Some of the second-tier web browsers offer add-ons that mimic Internet Explorer to add administration functionality for SharePoint sites, but installing the add-on does not make the non-Microsoft browser application a top-tier client. It just adds functionality.

Now, if you're sold on the benefits of storing documents and business data files in the SharePoint content database for stability, recoverability, and programmability, then read on for WSS installation and management strategies!

Installing WSSv3

Before you can launch WSSv3 installation files on the server, you must first install the necessary software prerequisites. And although it doesn't really matter in what order you install the required applications so long as they are all properly installed and configured prior to beginning the WSSv3 installation, things will go easier if you install IIS first and then the .NET Framework. And there is no substitute for a well-thought-out installation planning document. Such a blueprint could include the names of servers onto which WSS is being installed, as well as direct IP addresses to each. Also, be sure to include any scaling plans or service account information (see Table 28.2) for each application. These decisions are best made prior to beginning the actual install process.

TABLE 28.2:   WSS Service Accounts

ACCOUNT	PURPOSE	DEFAULT ASSIGNMENT
Application Pool Identity	IIS application pool worker threads	Network Service
WSS Database Content Access	Content database access	Network Service
WSS Search Content Access	Content crawling to build index	Network Service
WSS Search Service Account	Searching	Local Service

🌐 Real World Scenario

REPLACING BIGFIRM FILE SHARES WITH WSSV3

Let's say you want to replace some departmental shared folders on the file server with SharePoint document libraries at a company called Bigfirm. You have decided to implement departmental WSS sites for each of the following Bigfirm departments: accounting, human resources, sales, and services. Each site will host document libraries containing files regarding the specific department and utilized primarily by only that department's employees. But before you jump into installing WSSv3, you must sit down and plan your SharePoint Service Account assignments.

As for the WSS installation files, they can be easily downloaded from the www.microsoft.com/downloads website; just search the site for *WSS*, and you'll get links to different platforms (32- or 64-bit), different builds (slipstreamed with service packs), and even different languages of the product. The self-extracting executable is named simply SharePoint.exe and *must* contain the streamed SP2 to install onto Windows Server 2008 R2. The WSS installation program itself requires only a few installation decisions, but the SharePoint Products and Technologies Wizard that follows will configure far more details about the SQL Server database location, IIS application pools, and service account configuration. But enough talk, let's install!

Loading IIS 7.5

Windows Server 2008 R2 uses the concept that installs functionality by setting the OS to act as certain *roles* that was introduced in Windows Server 2008. Assigning a role installs the corresponding services and antecedents. For example, to install IIS, you must engage the Web Server role in the OS. Since this book focuses on the Windows Server 2008 R2 OS product and all that is included with it, we shall deliberately begin with enabling IIS 7.5 and leave the SQL Server prerequisite to the WSS installation program's free SQL Server 2005 Embedded Edition product.

A SharePoint Service Account Soapbox

At the risk of sounding preachy, we would be remiss if we didn't warn you about the importance of proper service account designation. Trust us when we tell you that many of our consulting clients have found the demon of their SharePoint woes to be a single inadequate service account assignment. Determine your service accounts with care, because there are limitations to using the accounts assigned by default.

To begin with, the Network Service account of an Active Directory Service (ADS) member server is only recognized during authentication within trusted domains of an ADS forest. Unless you can convince your ADS administrators to construct domain- or forest-level external trusts just for the privileged use of your SharePoint servers, you will find it difficult to stretch your SharePoint farm across ADS forests should your company employ a distributed ADS model. In addition, the Local Service account of the WSS Search Service is limited to resources on the local machine only, which can wreak havoc on search results if the query server is a different machine from the Indexing server in a SharePoint farm.

The practice of using ADS domain user accounts as SharePoint service accounts has its own challenges, especially concerning the user rights and permissions required for each service's account. Luckily, Microsoft TechNet has a great article available at `http://technet.microsoft.com/library/cc288210.aspx` that outlines the security requirements, advantages, and disadvantages of various service account strategies. Check it out before you decide under which security context each of your SharePoint services should run. If your SharePoint enterprise is already up and running, don't worry; you can always change a service account assignment using Central Administration.

For our scenario at Bigfirm, we will use the default service account assignments. We can also assume that the WSSv3 installation files have already been downloaded from Microsoft. Before we can actually install WSSv3, however, we must take care of the small matter of loading the prerequisite software.

A Word About SQL Server Embedded Edition

WSS basic installation will install the freely licensed edition of SQL Server 2005 called Embedded Edition. This is not SQL Server 2005 Express Edition, although the two products share the same acronym of SSEE, and the SQL Instance property is inaccurately valued as Express Edition should you query for it. Embedded Edition is often referred to as the Windows Internal Database (WID) and does not suffer as many limitations as Express Edition, but it also ships with no management utilities. If using an alternative SQL Server product's `sqlcmd.exe` from the CLI to manage your Embedded Edition databases is inconvenient, you can force-feed an instance of Embedded Edition into SQL Server 2005 Management Studio (Full or Express) by using the instance name of `\\.\pipe\mssql$microsoft##ssee\sql\query` in the SSMS connection dialog box (of course, this is not supported by Microsoft). For more information about SQL Server 2005, see the www.microsoft.com/sql website.

To engage the Web Server role using the GUI, launch Server Manager from the Administrative Tools program group, and look to the Roles node in the left tree pane. Click the Add Roles hyperlink in Server Manager's Roles node (Figure 28.1) to launch the Add Role Wizard. Alternatively, you could use the command line to install IIS 7.5 onto Windows Server 2008 R2 ServerManagerCMD.exe or pkgmgr.exe. Either way, the IIS 6.0 Management Compatibility role service is required. This is not a role service that is part of the default Web Server role installation, so be sure to deliberately select it.

FIGURE 28.1
Server Manager open to the Roles node

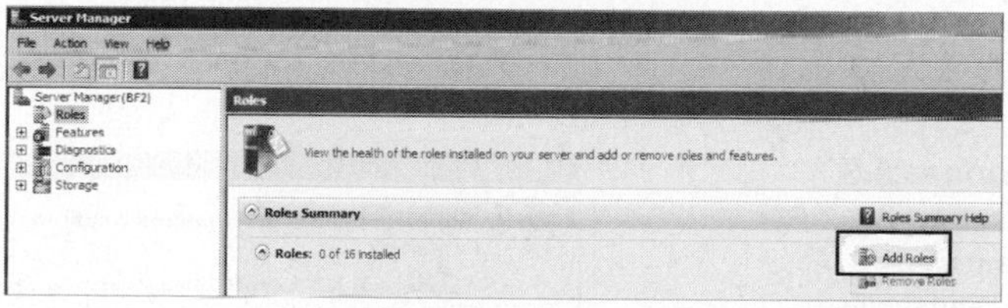

To install IIS 7.5 via the Server Manager (GUI) Add Role Wizard, follow these steps:

1. Select Web Server (IIS) in the Select Server Roles menu, select IIS 6.0 Management Compatibility, and then click Next.

2. In the resulting pop-up, click Add Required Features to also employ the services on which IIS 7.5 depends, and then click Next.

3. On the Web Server (IIS) page, simply click Next.

4. In the Available Role Services selection list, just accept the defaults, and click Next to continue.

5. The Confirm page merely reminds you of your choices thus far, so click Install and wait through the progress to reach the Installation Results page before clicking Close.

Alternatively, to fully install IIS 7.5 from CLI via ServerManagerCMD.exe, simply enter the following:

```
ServerManagerCMD.exe -install Web-Server -allsubfeatures
```

Remember that you can add setting configurations to each feature during installation via ServerManagerCMD.exe by adding the -setting switch. Lastly, to fully install IIS 7 via the Package Manager CLI, enter the following:

```
pkgmgr /iu:
```

and then type in each IIS service role by name delimited with semicolons.

Loading the .NET Framework

The .NET Framework 3 feature set is bundled with Windows Server 2008 R2 but is not part of the default OS install. To add the .NET features to the OS, simply use Server Manager to add features and add the .NET Framework v3 Features (see Figures 28.2 and 28.3).

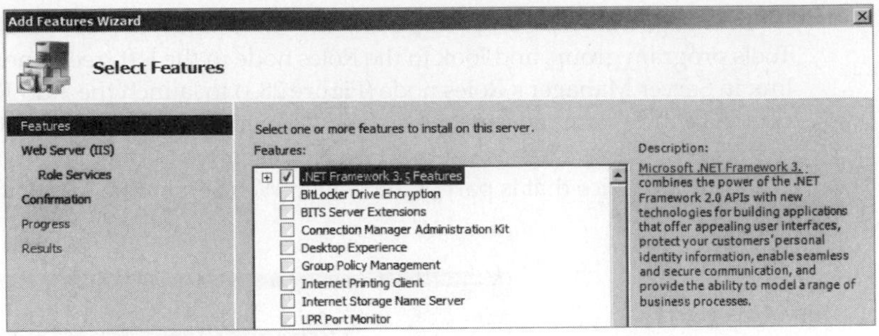

FIGURE 28.2
Installing the .NET
Framework

FIGURE 28.2
Installing the .NET
Framework

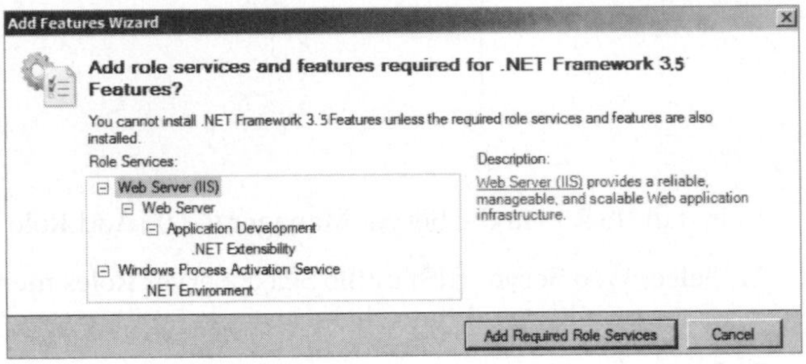

FIGURE 28.3
Installing the .NET
Framework
Dependencies

Loading WSS 3.0

Getting WSS installed onto Windows Server 2008 R2 once the prerequisite software is resident and configured requires an SP2 slipstreamed version of the SharePoint installation files. Windows Server 2008 R2 is compatible only with WSSv3 SP2, and any attempt to install a prior version of SharePoint will abort in a Program Compatibility Assistant error. WSSv3 with SP2 can be downloaded from Microsoft Downloads or if you already have an existing pre-SP2 version of the WSSv3 installation files you can SP2 slipstream them manually. Luckily, creating an SP2 slipstreamed version of the SharePoint installation files isn't too difficult. Essentially, once you have a copy of the extracted pre-SP2 installation files in a file system directory, you can extract the contents of an SP2 download into an updates child directory using the following syntax:

```
{package name}.exe /extract:{path}\updates
```

The final window of the SharePoint installation program contains fine print about launching the SharePoint Products and Technologies Configuration Wizard (see Figure 28.4). This tool must be used to configure SharePoint prior to creating structure and publishing content. If you didn't have the time to immediately follow up this installation with the configuration wizard, you could deselect the check box and launch the wizard later from its icon in the Administrative Tools program group. But sooner rather than later you'll have to run the configuration wizard. If you don't run the wizard you'll have no SharePoint Central Administration site to begin setting up your WSS structure that will eventually publish content.

Keep in mind that Windows Server 2008 R2 Server Core, though it now supports the .NET Framework, still does not support a GUI install program. The WSSv3 installation package, `SharePoint.exe`, can be extracted via the syntax stated previously in this section, and a quiet installation of WSSv3 can be accomplished by modifying the sample `custom.xml` file to reflect your configuration choices. *Voila*! No GUI necessary.

PERFORMING AN INSTALLATION PROCEDURE OF WSS 3.0

Generating slipstreamed installation files for Microsoft products, including WSSv3, falls a bit outside the scope of this chapter. For details about how to create an SP2 slipstreamed version of the WSSv3 installation files, check out the Microsoft TechNet article cc261890 at http://technet .microsoft.com/library/cc261890.aspx.

To install WSSv3 SP2 on Windows Server 2008 R2, run the slipstreamed SharePoint.exe installation file, wait for files to extract, and begin the install procedure:

1. Read and accept the EULA, and click Continue.

2. Choose between Basic and Advanced.

   Basic

   This is a single-server install with all the necessary SharePoint services being installed onto the one server using the default configuration, including the free SSEE Windows Internal Database. The server farm cannot be expanded in the future to include additional SharePoint servers.

   Advanced

   The Advanced install offers a choice of Web FrontEndOnly server (WFE) or Stand-Alone server installation. WFE installs only the SharePoint services required to support HTTP requests, indexing, and querying. This choice will not, however, install SQL Server, so make sure you already have a SQL Server instance loaded on the server. Stand-Alone is like a basic single server where everything gets installed onto a single box, but you cannot add more SharePoint servers to the farm later (and it's the default!).

3. If you chose Advanced, on the Data Location tab specify the file system destination for the index catalog.

4. If you chose Advanced, on the Feedback tab choose whether to participate in Microsoft's Customer Experience Improvement Program.

5. Click Install Now to begin file transfer and installation.

Pretty short and simple, huh? Ah, but where were the choices for service account assignments? We aren't done yet!

FIGURE 28.4
Final screen
of WSS install
program

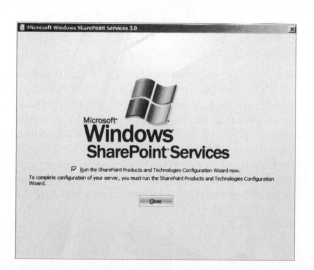

Configuring Products and Technologies

You can launch the SharePoint Products and Technologies Configuration Wizard from the final screen of the WSS installation program or from a shortcut icon in the Administrative Tools program group. There is also a third method of launching the SharePoint Products and Technologies Configuration Wizard (albeit reverse psychology): attempt to launch the SharePoint Central Administration shortcut found in Administrative Tools immediately following installation but before the configuration wizard has been completed. Windows Server 2008 R2 will open the dialog box in Figure 28.5 from which the configuration wizard can be launched.

FIGURE 28.5
Error launching SharePoint Products and Technologies Configuration Wizard

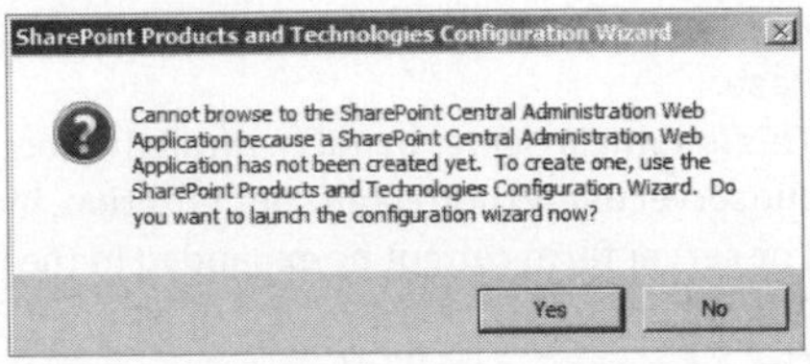

Upon launching the configuration wizard, WSSv3 Setup completes by automatically accomplishing the following (with no user input):

1. Initializing configuration

2. Creating the WSS configuration database in SQL Server

3. Installing help collections

4. Securing SharePoint resources

5. Registering SharePoint services

6. Registering SharePoint features

7. Provisioning the Central Administration web application

8. Creating sample data

9. Installing application content files

10. Finalizing configuration

Soon into the configuration wizard, prior to commencing configuration tasks, a message box will announce that there are three services to be started/restarted: IIS, SharePoint Administration Service, and SharePoint Timer Service. In the Windows Server 2008 Services administrative tool, these services are named World Wide Web Publishing Service, Windows SharePoint Services Administration, and Windows SharePoint Services Timer, respectively. Do not attempt to configure these services directly in the OS prior to running the SharePoint configuration wizard, or the wizard may produce an error because of unexpected failure during service starts. If the WWW Publishing Service has been customized because IIS has been installed and utilized prior to WSS installation, just verify that the service is properly configured to restart without issue, and realize that the SharePoint configuration process is going to briefly take existing websites away from users.

SHAREPOINT PRODUCTS AND TECHNOLOGIES CONFIGURATION WIZARD ON THE CLI

There is a CLI version of the SharePoint Products and Technologies Configuration Wizard found in the bin directory of the "12 hive" (%ProgramFiles%\Microsoft Shared\web server extensions\12). The executable file psconfig.exe can be used to accomplish many of the same tasks the GUI wizard performs and offers the opportunity to customize each task with optional parameters. Microsoft TechNet offers a reference article for this utility at http://technet.microsoft.com/ library/cc288944 .aspx that outlines each command. For errors experienced during the GUI wizard, an alternative option via psconfig.exe may successfully install WSS (such as creating a new configuration database when WSS has previously been installed and uninstalled, but the first configuration database was never cleaned out of SQL Server). This utility is also imperative for Windows Server 2008 R2 Server Core installations because of the absence of GUI support in that OS.

Upon completion of the SharePoint Product and Technologies Configuration Wizard, the default Internet browser is launched from the OS and immediately delivered to the newly minted SharePoint Central Administration website. Remember that Internet Explorer Enhanced Security Configuration (IE ESC) is engaged by default on the Windows Server 2008 R2 OS, so you may need to add the site to the Trusted Sites list or disable IE ESC via Server Manager and then launch Central Administration from the Administrative Tools program group. Now that you have WSS installed and fully configured, let's look around Central Administration!

Introducing Central Administration

The Central Administration site in SharePoint is a one-stop shop for managing the logical structure of WSS. The site is a SharePoint website and therefore can be managed like any user-focused site by adding web parts, lists, and libraries. But before you go hog-wild customizing Central Administration, know this: if you inadvertently incapacitate the site, you will be unable to maintain your SharePoint environment! Furthermore, future patches and service pack installations may fail to install or may undo your customizations or, worse, break Central Administration. We realize it is a painful stretch of the imagination to think that a Microsoft patch or service pack could actually do more damage than good (because surely that has never happened before!), but realize that customizing Central Administration is done at your own risk.

Not just anyone can access the Central Administration website. Only the accounts listed in Table 28.3 have access to Central Administration by default. Notice that the Farm Administrators and HelpGroup group objects are security principals within SharePoint (called *SharePoint group objects*), not Windows group accounts from the local OS or an Active Directory domain. This is important because SharePoint groups are managed strictly within SharePoint. Of course, you can always add additional users to the permission set for Central Administration if you are going to be delegating server, web application, or site collection–level administration tasks (we'll talk more about security and advanced administration later in this chapter).

TABLE 28.3:   Central Administration Default Permission Set

USER/GROUP	PERMISSION	DEFAULT MEMBERS
Account that performed WSS install	Full Control	n/a
Farm Administrators SharePoint Group	Full Control	Account that performed WSS install; Windows Server 2008 OS BuiltIn Administrators local group
HelpGroup SharePoint Group	Limited Access	Account that performed WSS install; Windows Server 2008 OS Network Service system account

The Home page of Central Administration (Figure 28.6) has a helpful web part called *Administrator Tasks* that exposes the actual Administrator Tasks list object within the Central Administration site collection root site. This list outlines Microsoft-recommended follow-up tasks that should be performed to complete the setup of your new WSS environment. The difference between this task list and the mandatory SharePoint Products and Technologies Configuration Wizard is that these task list settings are conducted after initial SharePoint services have been configured and are totally optional. You need to complete only the administrator tasks for settings you actually plan to employ. For example, if you are not going to allow WSS to receive email in the form of email-enabled lists and libraries, then there is no reason to configure incoming email settings. However, if you do click one of the administrator tasks to complete an optional configuration, the task title hyperlink will deliver you straight to the configuration web page pursuant to the referenced setting, and upon completion of configuring said setting, the administrator task will be automatically marked complete and removed from the web part view on the Home page. Pretty nifty, yes?

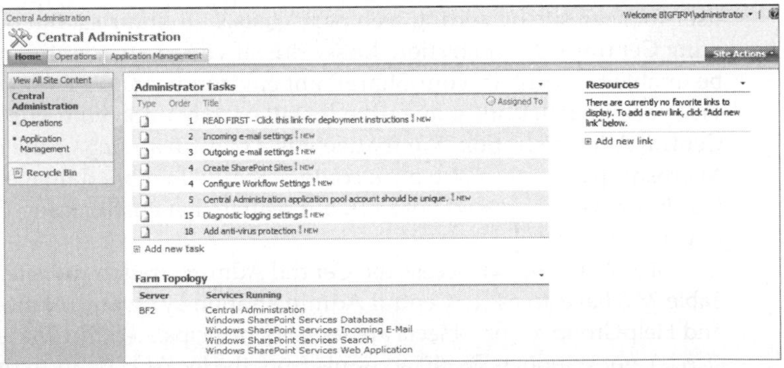

FIGURE 28.6
SharePoint Central Administration's Home page

The Operations page of Central Administration (Figure 28.7) offers links to management pages that configure server-level settings such as SharePoint farm settings, global defaults, security and auditing, backup, and database parameters for the SharePoint SQL Server databases. In fact, since WSS installs SQL Server Embedded Edition by proxy (for which there is no GUI administration utility) and because Microsoft Best Practices has frowned upon directly managing a SharePoint database via SQL Server tools, the Operations page of Central Administration is the preferred utility for managing SharePoint databases.

FIGURE 28.7
SharePoint Central Administration's Operations page

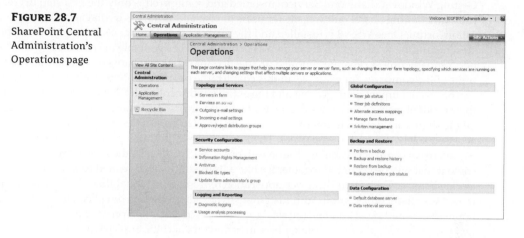

The Application Management page of Central Administration (Figure 28.8) provides access to management pages that configure web application–level settings such as Web Application Definition (sites hosted in IIS), Site Collection Definition (SharePoint logical components of a web application), Web Application Security, Workflow settings, and External Service Connections. Remember that the creation and maintenance of all IIS objects related to SharePoint should take place here on the Application Management page of Central Administration, not in the IIS Manager console. Although each web application listed here represents a tangible website over in IIS, the SharePoint-specific configuration parameters about each SharePoint-managed website will not be available in the IIS Manager console.

FIGURE 28.8
SharePoint Central Administration's Application Management page

Got a feel for navigating Central Administration? Great, let's get started creating the sites and document libraries that will eventually provide users with an alternative place to store files and collaborate!

SharePoint Website Provisioning

Getting Windows SharePoint Services installed and configured is only the first step in creating a fully functioning SharePoint website for users to visit and utilize as a collaboration and communication forum. Once WSSv3 is installed and the services are running, it's time to plan and build the structure of the WSS sites, an art known as *provisioning*. The general rule of thumb is one "portal" per company unless separate "portals" are needed for external visitors or autonomous business units of the company. For example, in this chapter, the purpose of WSS is to take the place of file servers, so document management and the entire sundry configuration of document libraries and their resident websites becomes the focus of our endeavors. Assuming current Bigfirm departmental file shares are limited to internal use only, it stands to reason that the WSS environment will be accessed solely by internal employees. Therefore, a single "Intranet portal" site will be sufficient.

Before we begin, a vocabulary lesson is in order. Microsoft calls the logical areas of SharePoint content that will be packaged together for like administration and related functionality *SharePoint web applications*. Each SharePoint web application represents an actual IIS website created and maintained via SharePoint Central Administration. In fact, these used to be called *virtual servers* in IIS, but market branding of another, unrelated Microsoft virtualization product precludes the continued use of the *virtual servers* moniker here in SharePoint and IIS. Suffice it to say that SharePoint's use of the term *web applications* corresponds to web applications within IIS 7.5 that represent the programmable settings of a particular website. Additionally, the Microsoft term for the hierarchically arranged virtual directory structures within an IIS WSS-managed website is *SharePoint site collection*. Each site collection is an administrative and object collection boundary and can be said to represent a company *portal*. Unless certain WSS sites require different site collection–level configuration settings or object galleries, there are few reasons to create separate site collections in WSS.

Before you can decide how many web applications and site collections to create, you must classify all the data that will be stored in SharePoint. Designing a good taxonomy for WSS blends the best possible administrative ease with intuitive navigation. There are many taxonomy designs, but two of the most popular strategies out of the four supported by WSS are organization based (such as department sites) and function based (the purpose of the files such as to inform vs. to instruct). The taxonomy design will influence the number of site collections necessary and whether multiple site collections will reside in a single web application or multiple web applications. Of course, determining structure layout depends on knowing the configuration parameters that are set at the web application as opposed to those configured at the site collection level (and no, they don't overlap). But we'll discuss advanced administration later.

⊕ Real World Scenario

CREATING BIGFIRM'S LOGICAL SHAREPOINT DESIGN

For the purpose of this chapter, remember that the company Bigfirm has decided to implement departmental WSS sites for each of its four departments: accounting, human resources, sales, and services. Each site will host document libraries restricted primarily to only that department's employees, although there may be some interdepartmental readers here and there.

To keep things simple, Bigfirm is planning only a single site collection for today (although growth could require a potential second site collection in the future). Therefore, since site collections do not traverse web applications, you can deduce that a single web application is in store as well, dictating a single content database in SQL Server. Bigfirm's logical SharePoint design is shown here.

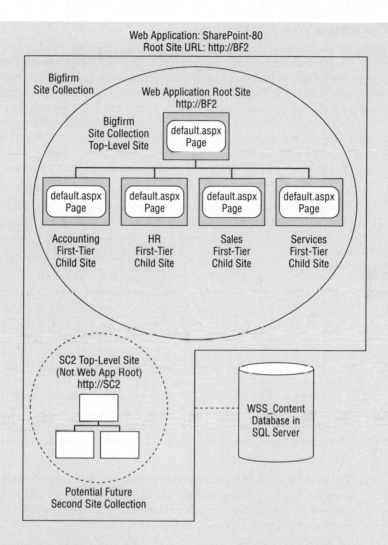

Notice in the figure that the web application root site happens to be the Bigfirm site collection top-level site (because the Bigfirm site collection top-level site will be the first site created in the first site collection generated in the web application). However, if a second site collection gets generated in the future, that site collection's top-level site will not be honored with the role of web application root site. Furthermore, the second site collection's top-level site cannot have the same URL as our Bigfirm site collection's top-level site.

Since a WSSv3 installation automatically generates a SharePoint-80 web application with a single sample site collection in it comprised of only a top-level site entitled Team Site, most of our work for generating this planned environment for Bigfirm is already done! All we need to create are the first-tier children sites for each of Bigfirm's departments.

Creating a Web Application

Lucky for us, the installation and configuration of WSSv3 automatically creates two web applications: SharePoint Central Administration (take one guess as to the site collection residing in here) and SharePoint-80, containing a single site collection created in it that has only a top-level root site based on the WSS Team Site template. Using SharePoint Central Administration (not the IIS Manager console), you can generate new web applications if necessary by visiting the Application Management page. Remember to exercise caution and create additional web applications only if absolutely necessary; excessive web applications overpopulate IIS and are difficult to manage. Though our scenario for Bigfirm does not require additional web applications, we just thought you would like to know that the process of creating web applications goes like this:

1. Launch Central Administration, and navigate to the SharePoint Web Application Management section of the Application Management page. Click Create or Extend Web Application, and then click "Create a new web application" to begin (see Figure 28.9).

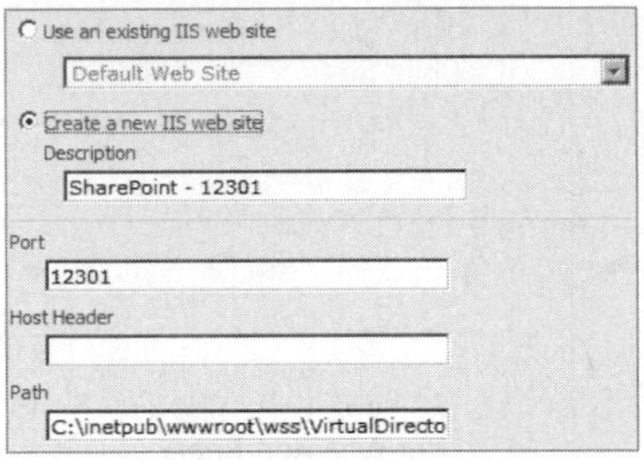

FIGURE 28.9
Creating a web application: IIS website

2. Choose between using an existing IIS website or create a new one. Creating a new site will generate a new website in IIS. Using an existing requires that the existing website have SharePoint extensions (translation: it was originally created with SharePoint, but SharePoint management was disabled for maintenance or troubleshooting reasons and now is being reinstated).

3. Fill in the site description, and differentiate the WSS site from other already existing IIS sites by assigning it a custom port and/or a custom host header. Notice that when creating a new web application, SharePoint automatically assigns a description and random port number. Simply edit these.

4. Specify the path to the site's virtual directory storage on the file system.

5. Choose an authentication provider for *all* sites in this web application (see Figure 28.10): NTLM for older or unknown clients, Kerberos for Windows 2000, and new operating system clients in trusted Active Directory domains.

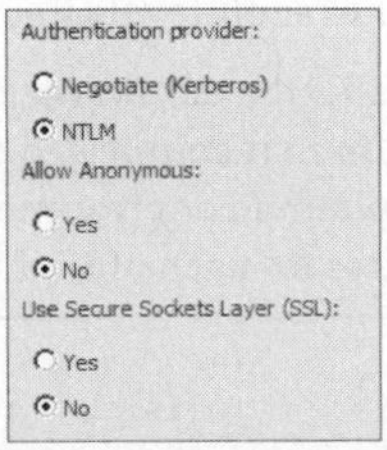

FIGURE 28.10
Creating a web application: security

6. Select whether *all* sites in this web application will honor anonymous access.

7. Select whether *all* sites in this web application will require SSL protection.

8. Specify a load-balanced URL (see Figure 28.11) if the site will be created on multiple SharePoint servers that are grouped together, and provide a single identity to the network (for example, to handle more client traffic efficiently, you might have set up multiple SharePoint web front-end servers and use Microsoft Network Load Balancing to "cluster" them together as a single entity on the network).

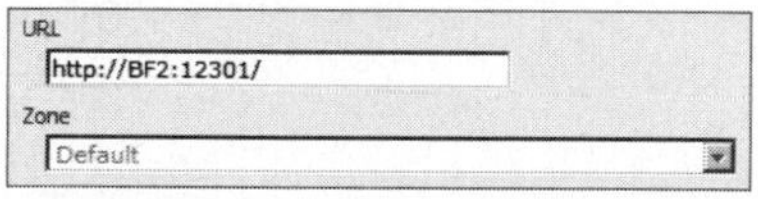

FIGURE 28.11
Creating a web
application: load-
balanced URL

9. Mandate whether the web application (translation: IIS website) will use an existing IIS application pool to manage its worker threads across the CPU or create a new, isolated application pool on the fly (see Figure 28.12). Using an existing application pool may put the WSS websites in danger if any other websites using that same application pool abnormally end on the CPU without releasing the resource.

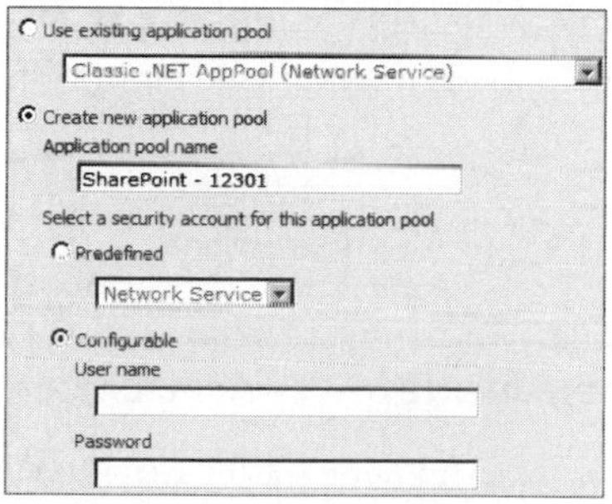

FIGURE 28.12
Creating a web
application: appli-
cation pool

10. Assign a unique credential by which the application pool will identify itself (as mentioned earlier in Table 28.2, the default credential is the Windows Server 2008 Network Service system account).

11. Choose whether to restart IIS services automatically upon completion of web application creation (see Figure 28.13). New websites in IIS 7.5 do not start automatically upon creation but are, by default, set to start automatically when the IIS 7.5 services start. So manually or automatically, you will need to restart IIS.

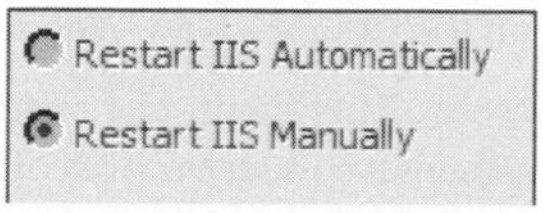

FIGURE 28.13
Creating a web
application:
reset IIS

12. Define SQL Server settings for the new web application including which instance of SQL Server in your SQL environment the web application will store its content database on, what the name of that content database will be, and the credential WSS should identify itself with when requesting entry into SQL Server (see Figure 28.14). If the SQL Server administrator has informed you that a SQL Server–resident SQL login has been created for WSS, enter it under "SQL authentication." Otherwise, choose Windows Authentication to access SQL as the Windows SharePoint Services Content Access service account.

FIGURE 28.14
Creating a web application: database name and authentication

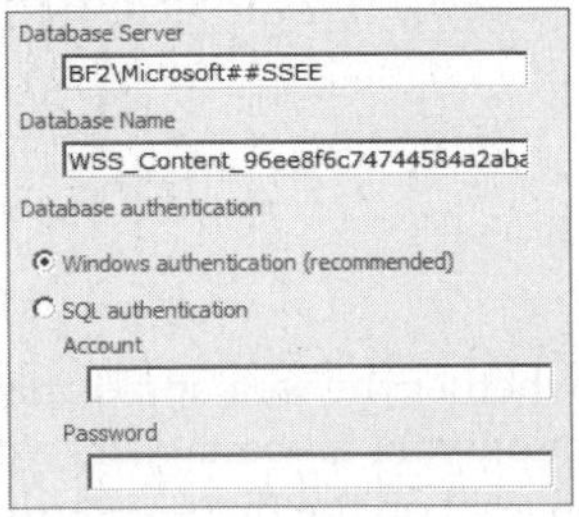

13. In a large environment containing multiple WSS servers, you may choose to point the new web application to an alternate search server so that user requests for search that are delivered via sites in this web application will actually get redirected to another SharePoint Search server (see Figure 28.15).

FIGURE 28.15
Creating a web application: search

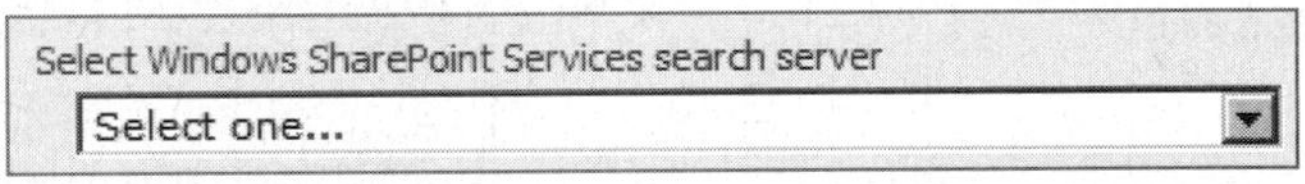

WHEN CREATING NEW WEB APPLICATIONS...

Be sure to open the inbound traffic pattern for your new web application's TCP/IP port number in the Windows Firewall and Advanced Security service of the OS. By default, Windows Server 2008 R2 ships pretty well locked down, so be sure the inbound traffic allowances in the activated domain profile found in Advanced Security's Overview section reflect your SharePoint ports.

Also, remember that each web application gets its own content database by default. The first content database created for the automatically generated SharePoint-80 web application is named simply WSS_Content by default. All subsequent web application creations will, by default, uniquely generate one content database each named WSS_Content_GUID by default (with the GUID being a unique identifier). The need to store site data in a separate SQL Server database may be a specific reason to create multiple web applications. If, however, you want to store multiple web applications in a single WSS_Content database, use Central Administration's Extend Existing Web Application choice rather than the Create a New Web Application link.

One of our recent consulting clients had overlooked web application design when they installed WSSv3 and instead simply created several site collections into the default SharePoint-80 web application. Over time, their WSS_Content database became unmanageable, and they called for our help. Luckily, an Extend Existing Web Application operation from Central Administration successfully spread the web application across multiple content databases. Don't make the same mistake—plan ahead!

Creating a Site Collection

Site collections are logical groupings of multiple websites that require like administration. These logical groupings are serviced by web applications in a many-to-one relationship. A single web application may service one or many site collections. A single site collection can be associated with only one web application at a time. Reassociating site collections from one web application to another requires complex migration tools, so consider relationships carefully before creating a new site collection.

Recall that the WSSv3 installation process automatically generated a web application containing a single site collection called simply Team Site. For the purpose of this chapter, we will rename and expand that site collection to include our departmental sites. But if, while planning your data taxonomy, you determine multiple site collections are necessary, here are the steps to creating a new site collection:

1. Launch Central Administration, and navigate to the SharePoint Site Management section of the Application Management page (see Figure 28.16). Click Create Site Collection to begin.

FIGURE 28.16

Creating a site collection: web application

Web Application: **http://bf2/**   ▾

2. Choose the web application into which the new site collection will be created by clicking the Change Web Application drop-down link and highlighting the web application of choice from the resulting page.

3. Specify a title and description that will appear on the Home page of the new site collection's root site when readers visit the site via a web browser (see Figure 28.17).

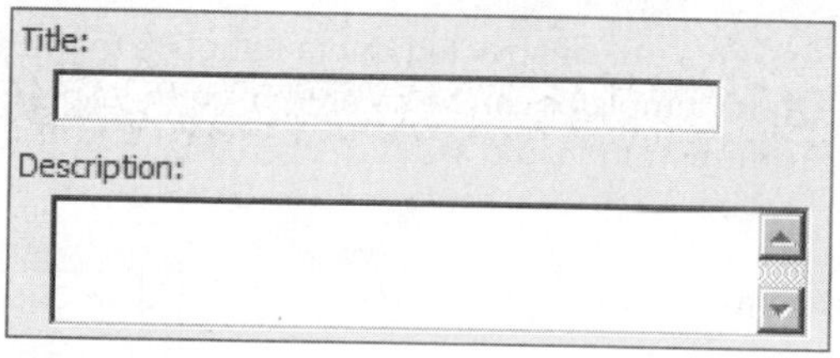

FIGURE 28.17

Creating a site collection: title and description

Title:

Description:

4. Specify a URL for the new site collection by choosing an IIS managed path from the drop-down list and entering the site collection root site's resolvable name (requires DNS resolution), as shown in Figure 28.18.

FIGURE 28.18

Creating a site collection: website address

URL:

http://bf2/sites/ ▾

5. Choose from the 10 system-supplied site templates in WSSv3 (see Figure 28.19). Each template builds a preconfigured set of pages, lists, and libraries, so choose the template that is closest to what you need, and customize the site once it exists. As you highlight each choice, the caption under the graphic will describe the highlighted template so you can make an informed decision.

Choose site templates *carefully*. Once a site has been generated, its template assignment cannot be changed without dropping and re-creating the site itself (or the entire site collection if you find you must drop the root site). This is because the site template is responsible for more than just initial creation. It also continues to supply some page content on attached pages (formerly called *ghosted pages*) each time the page is browsed by a visitor.

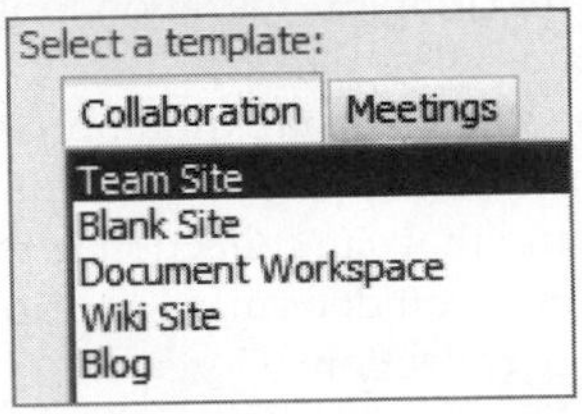

FIGURE 28.19

Creating a site collection: template

Select a template:

Collaboration	Meetings

Team Site
Blank Site
Document Workspace
Wiki Site
Blog

6. Enter only one single value into the Site Collection Administrator fields (see Figure 28.20). The Primary Site Collection Administrator field should be the party most held accountable for management of the SharePoint environment. The Secondary Site Collection Administrator field is optional and can also include one entered value. To grant multiple folks the Primary Site Collection Administrator role, consider bundling them into a Windows group and adding that group as a member of the site collection administrator field.

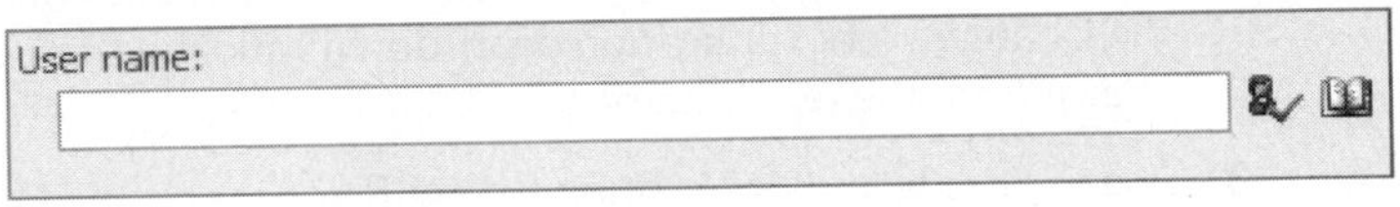

FIGURE 28.20

Creating a site collection: Site Collection Administrators

User name:

7. Assign a preconstructed quota template to the new site collection, as shown in Figure 28.21. Quota templates can be created from the Application Management page of Central Administration and will be covered later in this chapter.

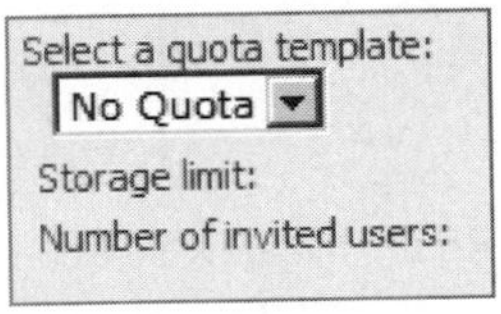

FIGURE 28.21

Creating a quota template

Select a quota template:

No Quota ▼

Storage limit:

Number of invited users:

Adding Sites to a Site Collection

Creating new site collections for different entities would not be practical if they all needed the same security structure, Recycle Bin administrator, and Features (more on *Feature* features later in this chapter). If different groups need separate areas to store their SharePoint content in but have the same administration and security requirements, consider creating children sites in an existing site collection rather than creating separate site collections for each group (see

Figure 28.22). But before we can discuss the process of creating new sites into a site collection, it would behoove you to learn a little navigation first.

FIGURE 28.22
Typical site
diagram

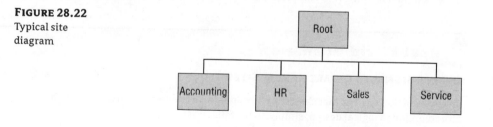

When managing a WSSv3 site, one of the base concepts you must understand is that WSSv3 uses security trimming to simplify the graphical user interface. In other words, if you are logged into the site as someone who does not have permission to a link's destination, then you won't see the link at all. So, creating subsites (children) underneath an existing parent site requires elevated privileges, or the necessary tool links for creating site collection structure won't even appear for you.

To create new sites into a site collection, start at the site that will play parent to the new child subsite you want to create. Once your browser application is nestled on any of the pages within the parent site, either click the Site Actions drop-down and choose Create to begin or alternatively click View All Site Content at the top of the Quick Launch Bar on the left and click the Create link in the resultant page's toolbar to begin (both methods deliver you to the same page). See Figure 28.23.

FIGURE 28.23
Creating site links

All Site Content
Create

Site Actions
Create
Add a new library, list, or web page to
this website.

Once you arrive at the Create Site page, choose the Sites and Workspaces template link under the Web Pages category, and begin filling out the required information on the resultant Create Site web page:

1. Give the website a descriptive title and optional description to further assist users in deciding on the proper use of the site.

2. Complete the URL alias for the new site, noting the default path choice of /sites. Alternative paths can be added via Central Administration.

3. Choose from the 10 system-supplied site templates in WSSv3. Remember to choose carefully; template choice cannot be easily changed after creation.

4. Specify whether the new child site should inherit the parent site's permissions structure or configure permissions of its own.

5. Specify whether links to the new site will appear in the Quick Launch Bar and Top Link Bar of the parent site.

6. Specify whether the child site will inherit the parent site's Top Link Bar.

7. Click the OK button to complete site creation.

🌐 Real World Scenario

CREATE BIGFIRM'S DEPARTMENTAL SITES

To generate the four first-tier child sites for our Bigfirm chapter scenario company according to the aforementioned logical design, simply do the following:

1. Navigate to the root site of the Bigfirm site collection by launching a web browser application and visiting http://BF2.

2. Log into the Team Site as a user with the authority to create subsites, and then choose Create Site from the Site Actions menu.

3. Name the first child site **Accounting** with a description of **Departmental site for the Accounting department**, and fill in **http://BF2/sites/accounting** as the URL.

4. Use the default site template of Team Site, the default security behavior of Inherit...from parent, and the default navigation tools. Simply click the OK button to finish.

Imagine that we have repeated these site creation steps three more times to produce the remaining departmental sites named accordingly HR, Sales, and Service. Now the users at Bigfirm are ready to begin using the new SharePoint environment for file storage. To visit their department's site, users need only type the URL for their site into their web browser application (such as **http://BF2/sites/accounting** for the accounting department's users).

In the next section, we will examine some of the document management features of WSSv3 that make it more useful than traditional shared folder file storage. So, read on for more information about how to convince your users to save their documents in SharePoint!

Creating SharePoint Document Libraries

Once a SharePoint structure has been erected according to data taxonomy plans, it is important to create appropriate storage libraries for the multitude of data files users will eventually store in SharePoint. WSSv3 ships with several list and library templates for storing collaborative information, but the library this chapter will focus on is the Document Library template. We don't want to imply that many of the features discussed are not also available in other library templates; some are. But for the purpose of replacing traditional shared folders with SharePoint libraries, the Document Library template fits our scenario's business need quite nicely. Very little custom programming is necessary to provide a functional document library that meets many business and data requirements.

Different site templates that can be called upon to create a new WSS site (as performed in the previous section of this chapter) will automatically produce different collections of site objects including libraries (see Table 28.4). Before creating a new document library, consult your taxonomy plan to determine whether a separate library is really necessary or whether using the default created library that came as part of the site template will suffice.

TABLE 28.4: Site Template Document Library Creation

LIBRARY NAME	PURPOSE	SITE TEMPLATES THAT INCLUDE SAID LIBRARY
Shared Documents	Store documents	Team Site, Document Workspace
Document Library	Store documents	Basic Meeting Workspace, Decision Meeting Workspace
Wiki Pages	Store web pages	Wiki
N/A	None	Blank Site, Blog Site, Blank Meeting Workspace, Social Meeting Workspace, MultiPage Meeting Workspace

Creating a Document Library

To begin creating a new document library, first navigate to the site in question, and then use the Create link found either under the Site Actions menu or on the View All Site Content page:

1. On the Create page, choose the appropriate object template.

2. Enter a descriptive title and description for the new library. Notice the lack of opportunity to enter a URL. WSS will generate the URL from the title, so keep it short and URL friendly. You can always return to the library's settings after it is created to change the spelling of the Title property.

3. Choose whether a link for the new library will appear in the Quick Launch Bar for the site. The default is Yes.

4. Choose whether version information will be maintained about all items stored in the library. The default is No.

5. Choose the default document template for all new files created in the library by clicking the New link on the document library toolbar. Though the default selection will be Microsoft Office Word 97–2003, if you are sure all your clients are running Office 2007, then you can change the default document template to the Microsoft Office Word choice instead (which indicates the new file format of Office 2007 and beyond).

6. Click the OK button to complete library creation.

Document libraries automatically inherit the security structure of the site into which they are created. To alter the permission set for a document library, inheritance must first be disabled, and then unique permissions for the library can be created. There are no options on the creation page that allow you to define permissions during creation. This chapter will discuss security more in a bit. If you will be creating several document libraries that will all need the same construct of custom permissions, consider creating a site to build them in that has the custom security settings already defined at the site level. And don't think a Document Library template will help you. Unfortunately, library templates do not carry security settings, so simply generating a template from an existing document library that already has the custom permissions defined will not generate the same security structure later.

Real World Scenario

CREATE BIGFIRM'S DEPARTMENTAL DOCUMENT LIBRARIES

For the sake of our scenario at Bigfirm, you should create a new document library at each of the four departmental sites that will hold department documents that will be accessed only by the resident department's employees. For example, the Accounting site will have a document library full of documents that are restricted to only accounting department employees. The new document library will be named after each department using the nomenclature "*{department}* Departmental Docs." To begin, follow these steps:

1. Navigate to http://BF2/sites/accounting, and then choose Create from the Site Actions menu.

2. Choose the Document Library object template, and name the new library Accounting Departmental Docs. Then add a description such as **Library for documents to be submitted and read only by Accounting Department personnel**.

3. Choose Default Appearance on the Quick Launch Bar, turn off default versioning, and keep the default choice of Word 97–2003 for the default document template. Click OK to create.

4. Repeat these steps with the appropriate titles and descriptions at the HR site, then the Sales site, and then the Services site.

Notice that library creation does not offer a separate fill-in text box to provide a URL for the new object. Instead, WSS uses the Title string to generate the URL. To create a resolution-friendly URL (that is, no spaces, short abbreviations), simply fill in the Title field with the intended URL for the library. We know, it's ugly, but once the new library exists, you can then go into its document library settings and correct the Title field to a more aesthetically pleasing string (the URL, however, will remain unchanged).

Populating a Document Library

Creating a document library is only the beginning. The library is not very useful until it contains important information that users need. Allowable document formats are dictated by WSSv3's list of blocked file types found in Central Administration (more on advanced administration later in this chapter). Populating a document library includes creating new documents in it either straight from the browser or by launching a local application and/or uploading existing files from a file system. The two processes are quite different, so let's look at each separately.

CREATING NEW DOCUMENTS

Users may choose to create new documents in a document library rather than uploading existing files. There are two methods of initiating creation, but both essentially launch a client-side application to provide the creativity interface. First, a user may visit the document library itself via a web browser and click the New link on the toolbar or use the associated drop-down to select New Document. At this point, the OS on the user's client PC gets involved to determine what application is associated with the file type of the document library's default document template. Remember step 5 in the previously outlined document library creation process? Selecting the appropriate default document template is important because it determines the client application that will be used to create new items into the library. Of course, the default document template can changed at any time by visiting the Advanced Settings area of the library's document library settings. The second method a user may employ to create a new document in the library is simply launching a client-side application directly, generating a new document, and pointing to the WSS document library during the Save As procedure.

Keep in mind that despite how the generating client-side application gets launched, the true art of populating the WSS document library resides in how the user *saves* the new document. A user may initially launch the client-side application from the browser via the New link on the document library with the best of intentions. But if the inexperienced user selects an alternative location from the client application's Save menu, they could inadvertently end up saving the document to a traditional file system folder instead of into the SharePoint library. Users must be trained to select the appropriate document library from the generating application's Save menu when initially saving a new document.

So, if the document library's toolbar displays only the New Document option under the New drop-down menu, how can you provide additional alternative document templates for a user to create from scratch via the library? Can you say *content types*? Site content types are SharePoint objects that allow you to define a default document template, associated workflows, custom metadata, and other custom properties ahead of time and then engage the content type later from a document library for the purpose of creating new items. Creating new content types is fairly simple and will be covered a bit later in this chapter.

UPLOADING DOCUMENTS

Instead of creating new documents in a document library, users may need to create an item from an already existing file on a file system. Uploading documents into a SharePoint document library is as simple as clicking the Upload link on the document library's toolbar. Notice that users are limited to uploading a single document at a time and that the GUI has automatically selected the option to overwrite existing files of the same name (see Figure 28.24). This can be dangerous for users who may not realize that a file of similar name but different text content already exists in the document library. Again, users must be trained to validate their upload choice prior to performing the upload so they don't inadvertently overwrite valuable documents.

FIGURE 28.24
WSS upload
document GUI

In the event that you need to upload multiple documents on a large scale into WSSv3, consider purchasing a migration management utility from a third-party software vendor. To search for Microsoft-certified partner software manufacturers, visit the http://office.microsoft.com/sharepointtechnology website.

An important concept to understand is that once a document is stored in a WSS document library, it is resident in the WSS content database of SQL Server. In the event you uploaded the document instead of creating it anew, the original document file will still reside in the original file system location. And although that file is still a viable document, users should be discouraged, nay *prohibited*, from interacting with it or risk confusion and inconsistency. You see, nothing in WSS is going to keep the original file synchronized with the SharePoint instance of that document stored in SQL Server! Consider altering the original file system's security settings to prevent continued use of the original file once it has been uploaded to SharePoint.

Another thing to keep in mind while populating WSS document libraries is that SharePoint technologies are optimized to provide single-instance storage. In principal, single-instance storage means storing a given document only once into only one document library. Additional sites or pages that need quick reference to the document then need only be configured with a hyperlink straight to the document's URL in its resident library. This can be accomplished using the *HyperLink to a Document* content type. Uploading or creating the same document more than once into more than one library defeats the purpose of SharePoint. That being said, however, you may have a viable need to store the same file twice such as in the case of differing permission sets for extranet WSS sites vs. intranet WSS sites. Although a link from the extranet WSS server to the URL of the intranet library would be preferable and may be possible in theory, firewall or other IP network restrictions may make such a link impractical. In this case, storing the same document in two libraries may be advantageous. Just remember that each instance of the file increases the size of your WSS content database!

Managing SharePoint Documents

Now we are to the part of this chapter where WSS document libraries begin to outshine their antiquated shared folder predecessors. Simply creating and populating document libraries is really no more exciting than creating and populating shared folder storage. OK, maybe it's a little more exciting because of the fancy web interface! But now we will take a look at the advantages WSS offers over traditional file systems for organizing, managing, and securing documents.

Document Metadata

Metadata is nothing more than a fancy term for information maintained about valuable data. Metadata is usually presented in the form of properties or attributes that are given specific values and, when combined, uniquely identify a given piece of data. In the case of WSS, document metadata can include anything from the name of the document file to the date and time it was last modified and by whom. File systems such as Windows NTFS also maintain metadata about their files that can be accessed by going to the properties of the folder or file. However, these attributes are not maintained while uploading the document into SharePoint. So, if you need to take the last modification timestamp with you as you upload a document into SharePoint, consider purchasing a third-party migration solution.

WSS presents document metadata by producing a column in the document library for each metadata property. Table 28.5 outlines the default properties that ship with the system-supplied Document Library template. However, you are not limited to these properties. To add custom metadata to a document library for the purpose of maintaining custom information about the documents stored within, simply add custom columns to the library!

TABLE 28.5:   Default Document Library Columns

COLUMN	PURPOSE	DISPLAYED IN DEFAULT ALL ITEMS VIEW
Type (icon linked to document)	Graphic display of file format	Yes
Name (linked to document with Edit menu)	File name with associated application edit menu	Yes

TABLE 28.5:   Default Document Library Columns   *(CONTINUED)*

COLUMN	PURPOSE	DISPLAYED IN DEFAULT ALL ITEMS VIEW
Modified	Last modification date/time	Yes
Modified By	User who last modified item	Yes
Check In Comment	Comments by last check-in	No
Checked Out To	User holding current checkout	No
Content Type	Content type associated with item	No
Copy Source	Source of file	No
Created	Creation date/time	No
Created By	User who initially created item	No
Edit (link to edit item)	Links to Edit Item page	No
File Size	File size in KB	No
ID	GUID number of item	No
Name (for use in forms)	Filename in XML acceptable format	No
Name (linked to document)	Filename with associated application	No
Title	Item title separate from filename	No
Version	Version number of item	No

In fact, if you will need the same column of custom metadata maintained on multiple libraries, consider creating a site column at the site level. Site columns are independent column definitions that can be employed on multiple lists and libraries. Design the column once, and use it repeatedly to save administrative steps! Even better, if a change needs to be made to the column's definition, you need only modify the site column and choose to allow WSS to distribute the new change to all columns on all libraries that were built using that site column. How easy is that? You'll learn more about site columns later in the chapter.

CREATING LIBRARY-CENTRIC COLUMNS

To create a column in a document library, first you must choose whether to create a library-centric column that will exist only in the library into which it is created or a site column that will be created at the site level and then added to a library in need of it. For the purpose of this chapter's scenario, let's assume we need both kinds of columns in our environment. First we will look at the steps required for creating a library-centric column:

1. Navigate to the document library requiring a new column.

2. Click the Settings drop-down arrow, and choose either Create Column from the menu or enter Document Library Settings from the menu; then click the Create Column link found in the "Columns management" section.

3. Name the column descriptively, but make it programmable-friendly. Remember that the column name will appear on the library page as well as in other management windows such a view creation.

4. Choose an appropriate data type for the new column. The remainder of the creation choices for the new column will change in context depending on the type chosen. Keep in mind that currency and date and time data types will display pursuant to the language WSS has been installed with.

5. Provide additional configuration per data type choice. Pay close attention to the Yes/No setting entitled "Require that this column contains information." If you create a required column, Office 2007 applications will prompt for required values before allowing users to save items. Also, uploaded documents may remain checked out to a user until they fill in the required columns' values. Be careful.

6. Click the OK button to complete column creation.

CREATING SITE COLUMNS

Columns that will be needed on multiple libraries can be created once and administered from one spot, the Site Column Gallery found at the site level. Site Column Gallery columns are available to all libraries within that same site as well as libraries in any and all sites below that site (all the way down the site hierarchy). In a multilayered site collection, choose carefully which site's gallery you build the new site column in: the higher the site in which you build the new site column, the more potential children sites whose libraries can make use of the new site column. Some WSS administrators choose to build all site columns at the root site of the site collection to make them available across the whole site collection. To create a new site column, follow these steps:

1. Navigate to the site hosting the Site Column Gallery that will house the new site column.

2. From the Site Actions menu, click on Site Settings.

3. Under the Galleries section, click the "Site columns" link.

4. Notice the bold group names that help to organize the list of existing site columns. Choose which group you will create your new site column under or plan to generate a new group name on the fly during column creation.

5. Click the Create link in the toolbar of the gallery.

6. Notice that the creation options of a site column are the same as the options of a library-centric column with the addition of the gallery group under which the new site column will appear.

7. Name the column descriptively yet friendly for programming (e.g., no special characters or embedded spaces). Remember that the column name will appear on the library page as well as in other management windows such as view creation.

8. Choose an appropriate data type for the new column. The remainder of the creation choices for the new column will change in context depending on the type chosen. Keep in

mind that currency and date and time data types will display pursuant to the language WSS has been installed with.

9. Provide additional configuration per data type choice. Again, beware of the "Require that this column contains information" setting.

10. Provide your choice of existing gallery groups, or create a new gallery group under which this new site column will appear within the gallery.

11. Click the OK button to complete column creation.

Now that the new site column exists, adding it to a library is very easy. Navigate to the Document Library Settings page of the desired library, scroll down to the "Columns management" section, and click the "Add from existing site columns" link. Then simply choose the desired site column from the list by clicking the right-arrow Add button to move the column name from the "Available site columns" box to the "Columns to add" box, specify whether to add the new site column to the default view, and click OK. *Voila!* Of course, your next understandable inquiry is whether a single site column can be pushed en masse to multiple libraries simultaneously. Alas, WSS administration interfaces are not that sophisticated; they require adding the site column from each individual library's point of view. But the good news is, once the site column has been added to the library, it can then be customized for that particular library.

⊕ Real World Scenario

ADDING CUSTOM COLUMNS TO BIGFIRM'S DEPARTMENTAL DOCUMENT LIBRARIES

Let's assume that the Bigfirm accounting department uses a custom column on its departmental document library that provides a link to the standards information by which each document was created. The following illustration displays a possible creation configuration for the new Standards Information column. Though this new column works well for the accounting department, none of the other departments need such a column on their libraries, so we should create the Standards Information column as a library-centric column on the Accounting Department Docs library.

Column name:

Standards Information

The type of information in this column is:

- ○ Single line of text
- ○ Multiple lines of text
- ○ Choice (menu to choose from)
- ○ Number (1, 1.0, 100)
- ○ Currency ($, ¥, €)
- ○ Date and Time
- ○ Lookup (information already on this site)
- ○ Yes/No (check box)
- ○ Person or Group
- ⦿ Hyperlink or Picture
- ○ Calculated (calculation based on other columns)

Description:

Provide link to the governing standards documentation for this item

Require that this column contains information:
- ○ Yes ⦿ No

Format URL as:
Hyperlink ▾

☑ Add to default view

To illustrate site columns, imagine that Bigfirm requires a column on all document libraries that dictates the federal regulations governing each document. The column will be entitled Regulatory and will provide choices of HIPAA, SOX, or OTHER for the designation value. The following illustration displays the settings that might be appropriate for such a site column created in the Site Column Gallery of the Bigfirm site collection root site.

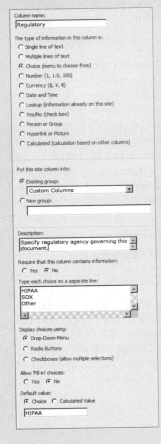

The following illustration shows the accounting department's library with a new document recently uploaded entitled "Accounts Payable Procedures."

Accounting Departmental Docs

Departmental data for the exclusive use of the Accounting Department.

New ▾ | Upload ▾ | Actions ▾ | Settings ▾   View: **All Documents** ▾

Type	Name	Modified	Modified By	Standards Information	Regulatory
📄	Accounts Payable Procedures ! NEW	10/2/2008 2:56 PM	BIGFIRM\administrator	http://www.sox.org	SOX

Notice the two rightmost columns in the library!

Choosing between library-centric and site columns requires knowing the broadness of the metadata and its association with various documents or content types. Since there is no easy way to convert a library-centric column into a site column (or vice versa), building the column correctly initially will save duplicate administration down the road. Microsoft encourages using the system-supplied site columns when possible and creating new site columns only when absolutely necessary. However, Microsoft does not advocate modifying any of the system-supplied site columns found in the Site Column Gallery at the site collection root site (even though they are editable) because future fixes or service packs may inadvertently overwrite your customizations. So if you like a system supplied site column but wish you could just change one little thing about it, rather than modifying the system supplied site column create a custom site column of your own that is almost identical but with your desired alterations.

When it comes to modifying an existing column, both library-centric columns and site columns behave similarly. First, you may only modify the column's type selection to those other limited types that are compliant with the existing structure. For example, our choice-type site column created a moment ago can be modified only into a text, number, currency, or date and time column type. This makes perfect sense because you would not want to invalidate all existing values stored in the column by inadvertently changing the column type to an incompatible data type restriction! In fact, the only real difference when editing a site column vs. a library-centric column is the additional site column option stating whether all lists using the site column should be updated with the newly changed settings (it is a simply a Yes/No choice, an all-or-nothing proposition).

Ordering and Indexing Columns

To put the finishing touches on column construction, you can specify what order the columns appear in when users are creating or editing the properties of an item. Furthermore, you can ask SharePoint to build indexes on popularly queried columns to improve search performance. Note, however, that choosing column order only affects the order in which editable metadata appears on the Edit Item page. The view chosen on the library page itself will determine the order the columns appear from left to right. And beware of building too many indexes because they can overpopulate your SQL databases! Column indexes only benefit those users who tend to search for items from the library by querying for that column's values.

To change the column order on the Edit Items page or to build an index on a particular column, navigate to the Document Library Settings page of the library, and click the Column Ordering or Indexed Columns link. Figure 28.25 shows the respective edit pages.

Figure 28.25
Column ordering and indexing configuration

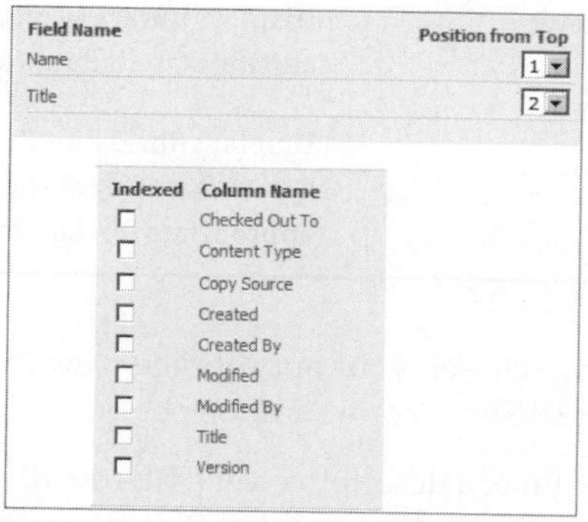

Field Name	Position from Top
Name	1
Title	2

Indexed	Column Name
☐	Checked Out To
☐	Content Type
☐	Copy Source
☐	Created
☐	Created By
☐	Modified
☐	Modified By
☐	Title
☐	Version

COLUMN EXPOSURE: VIEWS

Once the item metadata has been stipulated for a document library by defining its columns, you may need to limit viewership of certain pieces of metadata for specific scenarios. WSSv3 makes it simple to change the metadata displayed about document library items by offering different views of the library. The two views built by default are the All Documents view and the Explorer view. The All Documents view displays all items by the file type, filename, and creation/modification information in a vertical list style. The Explorer view, on the other hand, displays the library like the GUI called Computer, with folder icons and item icons in small icon format (see Figure 28.26).

FIGURE 28.26
Explorer view of a populated document library

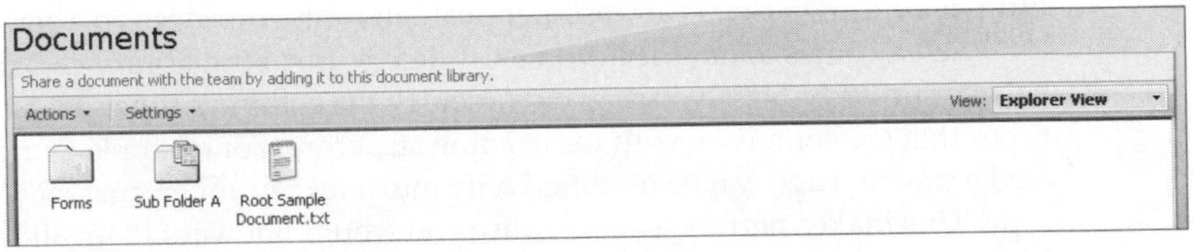

To create a new view, navigate to the document library's Document Library Settings page, scroll to the Views section, and click the Create View link. Or, a less wandering method is to navigate to the library and use the view choice drop-down menu to click Create View. Either way, you are delivered to the Create View administration web page and offered four possible view formats to build, as outlined in Table 28.6. Alternatively, you are offered the choice to begin your new view build from an existing view object and the existing views of the library are available as hyperlinks to choose from (except Explorer view).

TABLE 28.6:   System-Supplied View Formats

NAME OF FORMAT	PURPOSE
Standard view	Displays library on web page as itemized vertical listing
Calendar view	Displays data as daily, weekly, or monthly calendar (less appropriate for document libraries than for event or tasks lists)
Datasheet view	Displays library in an editable spreadsheet format convenient for bulk editing of metadata values
Gantt view	Displays library in standard format vertical list of items plus a timeline Gantt chart across the top for relating items in durations and phases (less appropriate for document libraries than for event or tasks lists)

Once you have chosen your appropriate view format, complete the creation of your new view by making the following configuration choices:

1. *Name*: Enter a descriptive yet URL friendly name because, much like document library creation, view creation does not stipulate a separate URL. You can always rename the view later and may notice that when modifying a view, the name and URL are separate text boxes.

2. *Default*: Decide whether the new view will become the "default" view of the library that all users will initially see when visiting the library URL without specifying a view page choice. This is an on or off setting via check box.

3. *Audience*: Stipulate whether the new view will be available to all readers of the library or only the view creator as a personal view.

4. *Columns*: Specify which metadata columns will be included in the new view and what order they will appear in from left to right (USEnglish language interface).

5. *Sort*: Select up to a maximum of two columns by which to sort the view items.

6. *Filter*: Display a subset of items according to filter criteria, and improve performance by establishing an indexed column as the first filter criteria. The filter criteria can employ parameters to substitute the threshold values.

7. *Group By*: Select up to a maximum of two columns by which to group and then subgroup the view's items.

8. *Totals*: Indicate which metadata columns of a numerical data type should display totals.

9. *Style*: Choose a view style of Basic Table (horizontal divider lines are added under each item), Document Details (each document is a thumbnail section exposing metadata in a graphic text box), Newsletter/Newsletter-NoLines (same as basic table but with edit icons for quickly editing document metadata), Shaded (every other item in vertical listing is shaded like greenbar paper), Preview Pane (document items are listed vertically by filename only on the left, and a permanent contextual details grid of metadata values is centered in the library to display only the currently hovered-over item's details), or Default (the style associated with the system-supplied view format chosen earlier).

10. *Folders*: Dictate whether the view exposes folders or simply displays all items at once.

11. *Item Limit*: Set a display limit for the maximum number of items either in batches with Previous and Next links or hard limited to the number of items setting and no more.

12. *Mobile*: Dictate whether the new view is available to mobile devices and if the new mobile view is, in fact, the default mobile view all mobile users will see who visit the library URL without specifying a view page.

FIGURING OUT VIEW FILTER SYNTAX

It never fails, the minute you start to program a new platform, it turns out that the application uses a completely different set of system functions in its code! Thought you were writing in C# .NET? Not for SharePoint view filters. More of a VB .NET or Visual Basic Script hound? Those function names won't work here in the browser GUI during SharePoint view creation. So, what functions are you allowed to use when creating filtered views of a list or library?

You can get a list of supported SharePoint system functions from the help files of a MOSS 2007 server or the Access help files of any Office 2007 installation or by browsing the help catalog of SharePoint Designer 2007. But the most up-to-date and easily accessible source of valid functions is available on the Office product site at http://office.microsoft.com/en-us/sharepointserver/CH101760291033.aspx.

Remember that all WSSv3 user interfaces are security trimmed, so a user's permissions will determine whether the Create View and Modify View links appear in the view choice drop-down menu. Also, users who do not have any permission to an item will not see the item no matter which view they employ on the library. This can result in empty views for a user if the view they choose has a filter that results in only exposing those items to which the user has no permissions. This can be quite confusing for your users! Be sure to train users on proper view selection. Microsoft endorses using views generously in document library management for good reason, so use them to create intuitive interfaces of your lists and libraries and make it easier for your users to find the item they need.

Document Library Settings

Effectively managing document items within a document library involves managing the overall library. The General Settings section of a library's Document Library Settings page gives you plenty of opportunity to manage library-wide configuration options such as whether to allow subfolders or whether the library should show up in search results. The "Title, description and navigation" link will change exactly those three settings (navigation means whether a link to the library should appear in the Quick Launch Bar), while Table 28.7 outlines the Advanced Settings options available. Configuring any of these options will affect all documents stored in the library, so be sure before setting them.

TABLE 28.7: Document Library Advanced Settings

SETTING	PURPOSE	VALUES
Content Types	Allows management of content type objects associated with the library	Yes/No (No is the default)
Document Template	Sets the URL of the template document by which all new documents will be created directly into the library	URL to a Template File (by default the template is specified during library creation)
Browser-enabled Documents	Allows library items to be displayed as web pages in the event the visitor does not have necessary client-side application	Open In Client App/Display as a Web Page (the default is Open In Client App)
Custom Send To Destination	Sets the name/URL for one custom target to appear in the Send To context menus on library items	Destination Name/URL (none is the default)
Folders	Allows subfolders to be created	Yes/No (the default is Yes)
Search	Allows library to appear in appropriate search results	Yes/No (the default is Yes)

The Browser-enabled Documents Advanced Setting requires that you point your SharePoint server to the HTML Viewer server in your environment. HTML Viewer configuration is performed via the HTML Viewer link under the External Services Connectors section of the Application Management page in SharePoint Central Administration. A word to the wise, however: at the time of this writing, the HTML Viewer product available from Microsoft is for WSSv2.0 only and does not work on WSS 3.0 because of security limitations. Unfortunately, Microsoft does not currently plan to offer a WSSv3/Office 2007–compatible HTML Viewer because of a lack of market popularity of the predecessor version.

Content Types

The first option under Advanced Settings is whether to allow content type management on a document library. As mentioned earlier, content types are objects independent of any library that define default document template, metadata, workflow, and other properties for any future library item that gets created based on that content type. Independent content type objects are stored in the site-level Site Content Types Gallery. Much like the Site Column Gallery, the Site Content Type Gallery items are available to all lists and libraries within that same site as well as all sites below it in the hierarchy. So again, create new content types into a site high in the site collection hierarchy to make them available to many different lists and libraries.

If you change the Content Type management setting to Yes on a document library, it will add a new section to the Document Library Settings page called appropriately Content Types (see Figure 28.27). This new section allows you to associate additional content types with the library, as well as configure which content types to make visible on the library's New drop-down menu and specify which content type will be the default initiated when a user simply clicks the New button of the library toolbar.

FIGURE 28.27
Document
Library Settings:
Content Types

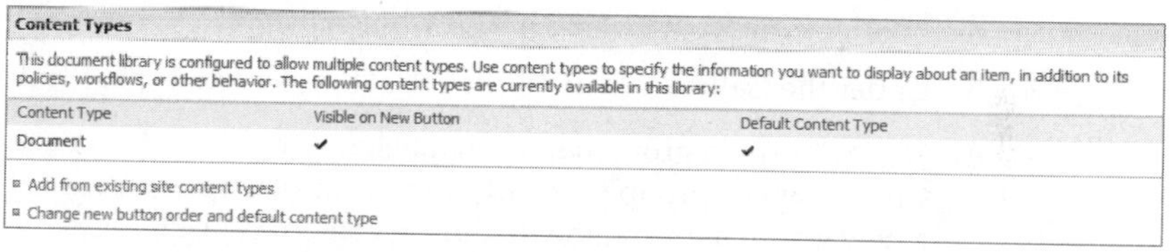

Content Types			
This document library is configured to allow multiple content types. Use content types to specify the information you want to display about an item, in addition to its policies, workflows, or other behavior. The following content types are currently available in this library:			
Content Type	Visible on New Button		Default Content Type
Document	✔		✔
▫ Add from existing site content types			
▫ Change new button order and default content type			

🌐 Real World Scenario

BIGFIRM CONTENT TYPES

Before you create a new content type, you must envision a scenario in which multiple content types being stored into a single library would be appropriate. Imagine at Bigfirm that the sales department employees are allowed to submit their own travel expense reports and receipts to a document library on the Sales WSS site. If all employees were required to fill in a very simple text document with information about their trip, providing a blank form would be convenient. Also, some users prefer to submit picture files of their receipts, while others simply provide a URL to the web folder in which the sales department secretary has compiled their receipts. In this scenario, we need an Expense Report document library that can support the creation of new completed text forms, new pictures, and new web links. Let's get started!

Assume we have already created the Expense Report document library on the Sales site using the system-supplied Document Library template with the default settings. Additionally, we have already turned on content type management in the Advanced Settings of our new library. Before we can add new content types to the library, we must decide whether one of the system-supplied content types will do or if we need to create a new site content type object. In our scenario, the system-supplied Picture content type will satisfy users who want to upload their receipts as picture files. And the system-supplied Link To a Document content type will suffice for users who want to provide links to their receipt files stored in a web folder. But none of the system-supplied content types uses a custom text form that Bigfirm wants to provide when users create new expense reports directly within the library, so we'll need to create that one.

The Site Content Type Gallery is found at the site level by navigating to the Site Settings page of the desired site. Much like site columns, the site content types are listed in the gallery organized by group headings to make finding them easier. Also like with site columns, Microsoft best practices encourage using one of the system-supplied content types when possible and creating new objects only if absolutely necessary. Microsoft also discourages modifying any of the system-supplied content type objects to avoid losing customizations during overwrites by future patches or service packs. So, the same rules this chapter mentioned earlier for site columns apply to site content types as well.

The creation of a new site content type occurs in two stages: object generation and object configuration. To begin object generation, follow these steps:

1. Navigate to the site with the Site Content Types Gallery that will house the new site content type.

2. From the Site Actions menu, enter Site Settings.

3. Under the Galleries section, click the "Site content types" link.

4. Notice the bold group names that help organize the list of existing site content types. Choose which group you will create your new site content type under, or plan to generate a new group name on the fly during content type creation.

5. Click the Create link in the toolbar of the gallery.

6. Provide a name and description for the new content type. This information will appear on the drop-down menu for users to verify their template choice when creating new items into a library, so be descriptive!

7. User-defined content types cannot just be manufactured out of thin air; they must be based on an existing content type object. If this is the first user-defined content type, it must be based on one of the system-supplied content types. Subsequent user-defined content types can be based on either a system-supplied content type or an already existing user-defined content type. Choose an appropriate existing content type from an appropriate group heading on which to base the new content type object.

8. Provide your choice of existing gallery groups, or create a new gallery group under which this new content type will appear within the gallery.

9. Click the OK button to complete column creation.

Real World Scenario

BIGFIRM EXPENSE FORMS

Figure 28.27 displays possible settings for creating the new Expense Form content type in our Bigfirm sales scenario. Clicking OK to the New Site Content Type page immediately begins the second stage of the content type creation, which is object configuration. On the Settings page of the new content type object, we can now begin adding custom metadata by adding site columns from the Site Column Gallery, or we can associate custom workflows with the content type or provide Advanced Settings such as whether the content type object will be read-only and protected from modification (the content type object itself, not new library items created using it). In fact, our Expense Form content type for Bigfirm requires us to set the document template to an existing text form that will open with blank values each time a user submits a new expense report, as shown here.

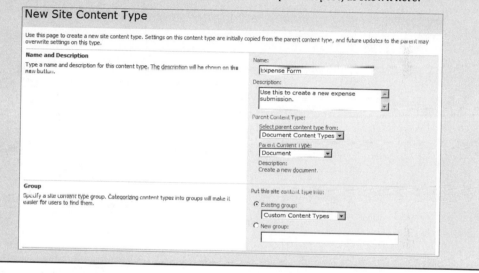

VERSIONING SETTINGS

One of the biggest reasons to convert from traditional shared folder file storage to Windows SharePoint Services is the new version control feature in WSSv3. Being able to maintain previous history of what the document used to look like is monumental as a recovery tool, not to mention sometimes important for regulatory compliance. SharePoint maintains version history on all documents stored in a document library that has had versioning enabled at the library level. That's right; version history is a library-level decision, not document by document. So, be careful, because the more volatile documents you save into a version-enabled library, the bigger your SharePoint content database is getting in SQL Server!

To enable versioning for a library, navigate to the library's Document Library Settings, and click the Versioning Settings found in the General Setting section (Figure 28.28). The first option you may notice is the Content Approval setting; you may be wondering what content approval has to do with version control. Well, in a volatile library, it would be worth putting each new change in front of an impartial judge to determine whether the changed document is warranted before taking up another version history slot. The Content Approval setting shown here is a holdover from WSSv2.0 and is simply an on or off decision. This is not an approval workflow; any user who has been granted the Approve Items permission on the library can single-handedly approve or reject each new or changed item. Engaging content approval will add a column to the default view called Approval Status to expose whether each published major version document is pending, approved, or rejected. Rejected items can only be seen by users who have been granted Approve Items permission on the library.

FIGURE 28.28
Document Library Versioning Settings

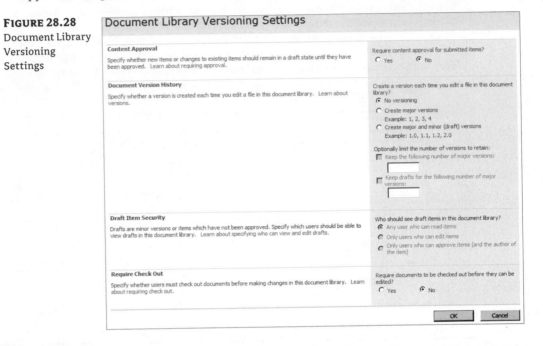

The next setting, Version History, is where the real magic begins. You can choose to invoke only major version control or major and minor version control. Major Versioning creates a new major version represented by sequential whole numbers for each change to an item. Consider that item changes include not only changes to the content inside a document but any change to the document item's metadata as well! In this case, very inconsequential changes to a piece of metadata may be excessively advertised as a major change even though they are actually quite simple changes. Alternatively, major and minor versioning can be set to flag simple metadata changes and work-in-progress content changes as minor revisions represented by fractional numbers and save major version whole numbers for significant revisions.

Introducing minor version control exposes an additional versioning setting called Draft Item Security. Using this configuration property of the document library, you can limit which groups of visitors will be able to see the minor versions of all documents. There are three choices: all readers, only those with Edit Items permission, or only those with the Approve Items permission. The last choice, approvers only, will not become available to select unless you also invoke content approval. Limiting minor version viewing can be advantageous if the documents will cause unnecessary concern among library visitors during work-in-progress stages.

When you invoke major and minor version control on an already populated document library, all existing items receive an initial major version number of 1.0. From then on, changes made to the items will be deemed either major or minor by the content editor at save/check-in time. However, if you invoke major and minor version control on an empty library, newly uploaded items will receive a minor revision number of 0.1, and newly created items will be deemed either major or minor by the content editor at save/check-in time. Once a minor or "draft" version of a document is ready to be converted to a major version number and exposed to all readers of the library, anyone with the Edit Items permission to the library can hover over the item to produce a drop-down context menu and click Publish a Major Version.

To view an item's version history, simply hover over the item to produce an item context menu, and choose Version History (see Figure 28.29). Both major and minor versions will be listed along with comments made by the publishing or editing user. Notice on the toolbar you can choose to delete all *minor* versions in one fell swoop or all versions. You can also hover over any previous version of a document and choose to either restore or view. Restore does what it sounds like; it restores the previous version to the current version status without deleting all versions in between. View, however, is misleading. Clicking the View choice only displays the metadata property values of the item, not the document content. To read a previous version of a document, click the document version date and timestamp to produce the actual document in the associated client-side application.

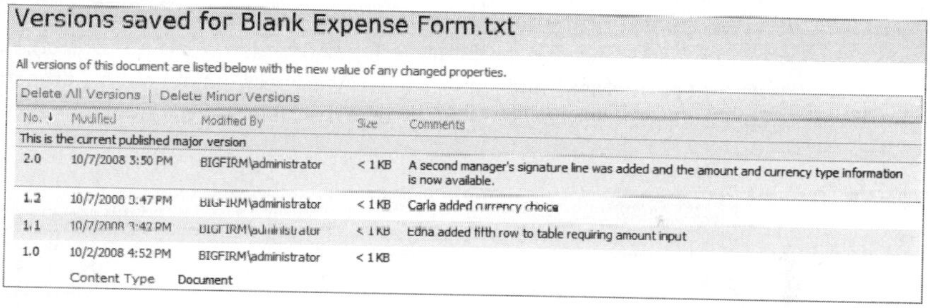

FIGURE 28.29
Single-item
version history

Versions saved for Blank Expense Form.txt				
All versions of this document are listed below with the new value of any changed properties.				
Delete All Versions	Delete Minor Versions				
No. ↓	Modified	Modified By	Size	Comments
This is the current published major version				
2.0	10/7/2008 3:50 PM	BIGFIRM\administrator	< 1 KB	A second manager's signature line was added and the amount and currency type information is now available.
1.2	10/7/2008 3:47 PM	BIGFIRM\administrator	< 1 KB	Carla added currency choice
1.1	10/7/2008 3:42 PM	BIGFIRM\administrator	< 1 KB	Edna added fifth row to table requiring amount input
1.0	10/2/2008 4:52 PM	BIGFIRM\administrator	< 1 KB	
	Content Type	Document		

CHECKING IN AND OUT

The final setting on the Versioning Settings page is Force Check Out. Another holdover from WSSv2.0 checkout is the ability to lock a document for editing prior to launching the associated client-side application and opening the document for writing purposes. However, back in WSSv2 the checkout operation was invoked solely at the user's discretion, an honor system of sorts, and if user B forgot to check out a document before editing it while user A was already editing the document, save conflicts could occur. New to WSSv3, the checkout process can be mandated at the library level to force users to check items out before editing them. Since items may be locked by only one checkout at a time, the potential for save conflicts is virtually eliminated.

Checking a document out of a library can be a manual operation of hovering over the document to produce a drop-down context menu and clicking Check Out. Or, depending on the Name column type, the item drop-down menu may offer an option called "Check and Edit with *[associated client side application name here]*." Third, the Office 2003 and Office 2007 applications offer the ability to check out a document that was initially opened from SharePoint without a lock, placing a checkout lock on the fly in case a reader suddenly decides to edit the document.

Sometimes a user may check a document out of a library and forget to check it back in. To alleviate a checkout that has outlived its purpose, users who have been granted the Override Check Out permission to the library or document item can hover over the checked-out document to produce a context drop-down menu and click Discard Check Out. This option will check the document back into the library without the offending editor's revisions that have yet to be saved. Also, the document library settings offers a "Manage checked out files" link under the Permissions and Management section that will list all document items that do not have any checked-in versions. This may include documents that were uploaded to the document library missing critical required metadata and have remained checked out to the contributing user since upload. The checkout manager can then select specific document items from the list and click the Take Ownership of Selection link so they can modify the item or its metadata as necessary and check it into the library.

🌐 Real World Scenario

PUTTING IT ALL TOGETHER

Now let's see what happens if we invoke all the versioning settings at once: Content Approval, Major and Minor Versioning, Draft Item Security, and Force Check Out. Imagine that in our Bigfirm scenario the human resources department has a document library called Benefits on its site with three documents that were already in the library when versioning was invoked (so the items are currently all major version 1.0). Also, users who visit the library include Administrator (Full Control), Heather Human (Contributor with Edit permission), and Randy Reeder (View permissions only). At the start, Randy can see the three major documents called Benefits, Direct Deposit, and Retirement, as shown here.

The Direct Deposit document was originally published as major version 1.0 at 4:15 p.m. At 4:30 p.m., imagine Heather checks out the Direct Deposit document and edits it but saves and checks her revisions back into the library as a minor (draft) version of number 1.1 pending further approval by Administrator. This means at 4:31 p.m., though Randy still sees a Direct Deposit item when he visits the library, when he reads it, he discovers that it is the 4:15 p.m. version prior to Heather's edits. Randy cannot read any of Heather's edits until the document gets published as a major version. Why? Because we have set Draft Item Security limited to "Only users who can approve items (and the author of the item)." This means both Heather (the author) and Administrator (an approver) can see Heather's edits, but not Randy.

At 4:45 p.m. Heather decides to publish her revisions as a major version. So, she hovers over the Direct Deposit item in the Benefits document library to produce the item context drop-down menu. Then she selects Publish a Major Version and revises her check-in comments from earlier to indicate the document is now a major version. Even though Heather did not check the document out first, she was able to publish it as a major version because content approval will still block the final version from Randy's view until it is approved by Administrator.

At this point, Administrator must use his Approve Items permission to approve the published major version of the document, as shown here. Imagine Administrator approves the newly published major version 2.0 of the Direct Deposit document and adds some comments indicating his acceptance of Heather's revisions. Upon approval, Randy can now see the 4:45 p.m. version of Direct Deposit including Heather's edits.

Using a real-world scenario, you have now walked through version control, one of WSSv3's selling points for document management. Keep in mind that the more version control you invoke, the more data that is being stored by SharePoint. So, be sure to use the maximum settings for both your major and minor versioning to cap the amount of historical versions you are saving about the documents in a particular library. Also, remember that all version settings, including the maximum settings, are configured at the library level and cannot be altered folder by folder or document item by document item.

Workflows

Probably one of the biggest selling points of WSSv3 is its integration with the Windows Workflow Foundation provided by the .NET Framework. The Workflow Foundation (WF) supports automated programmatic processing according to a user-defined configuration. WSSv3 relies on the WF to run workflow definitions created by library or content type administrators. Defining workflows is an intricate process and one that should be restricted to administrative SharePoint users who understand logic flow and parallel vs. the serial execution of steps. The beauty of WSSv3 and WF is any process you can dream up, you can write as a workflow…from the simple to the complex.

As you can well imagine, the topic of workflows could constitute its own book. In the context of this chapter, we will limit our discussion to the procedure of creating only one workflow on a single document library. Keep in mind that, as detailed as this discussion becomes, it is constrained within the scenario and does not elaborate on every possible faction of workflow planning, creation, and maintenance. Suffice it to say if anyone were to ask, "Can a workflow be used to…," you can feel confident stopping them right there and offering the industry-standard answer of "Yes." Programmatically, there are few limits to what a workflow can be configured to accomplish!

WSSv3 ships with only one system-supplied workflow feature, the Three State Workflow. The Three-state template can be used to build simple item-tracking workflows via the Internet Explorer browser application. Alternatively, custom workflows can be defined via client-side applications such as SharePoint Designer 2007 or Visual Studio. Or additional workflow features can be purchased and added to WSS, providing additional workflow templates in the browser.

CREATING A SIMPLE THREE-STATE WORKFLOW

To begin creating a new workflow for a library, navigate to the library's Document Library Settings, and click the Workflow Settings link found in the Permissions and Management section. If this is the first workflow ever designed for the library, the Workflow Settings link will automatically call up the Add a Workflow admin page (AddWrkfl.aspx). However, if even just one workflow already exists and is associated with the library, the Workflow Settings link will call a page listing all the existing workflows and links to their status reports (wrksetng.aspx). This workflow settings page will also include an "Add a workflow" link, offering the opportunity to create additional workflows on the library. Arriving at the creation page by either method (Figure 28.30), you may then configure the new workflow as follows.

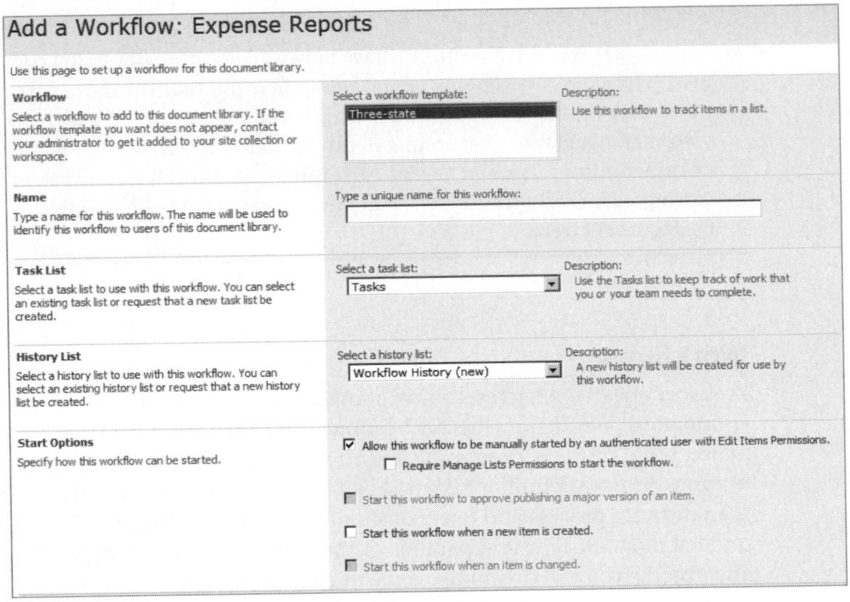

FIGURE 28.30
Creating a workflow: phase I

1. *Workflow*: Select the workflow template. (Three-state is the only template offered by default.)

2. *Name*: Give the workflow object a unique, descriptive name.

3. *Task list*: Specify an existing or build a new Tasks list from the Tasks List template that will organize the task items created during workflow processing. Workflows use task lists to store required user action information and notify assignees via email.

4. *History list*: Specify an existing or build a new History template list that will organize the history items created automatically during workflow processing. Workflows use history lists to store incremental processing information about run instances that are helpful during troubleshooting and auditing.

5. *Start options*: Select which actions will initialize the workflow. The choices depend on the workflow template. For example, the Three-state workflow template offers manual start and/or start when a new item is created. Other templates may include options to start the

workflow when a minor version item is published as a major version in a library requiring approval so as to automatically approve publishing a major version of an item. Yet other templates may offer an option to start the workflow when an item is changed. Start options are inclusive check boxes, so multiple options can be engaged at once.

6. *Phase II: customization*: Clicking Next after specifying start options will call a Customize page offering configuration settings pursuant to the workflow template chosen in step 1. Each workflow template requires different parameters. The Three-state template in our scenario bases its actions on known values in a specific metadata column of the library (see Figure 28.31), so the remaining instructions are specific to Three-state workflows only.

FIGURE 28.31

Customizing a Three-state workflow

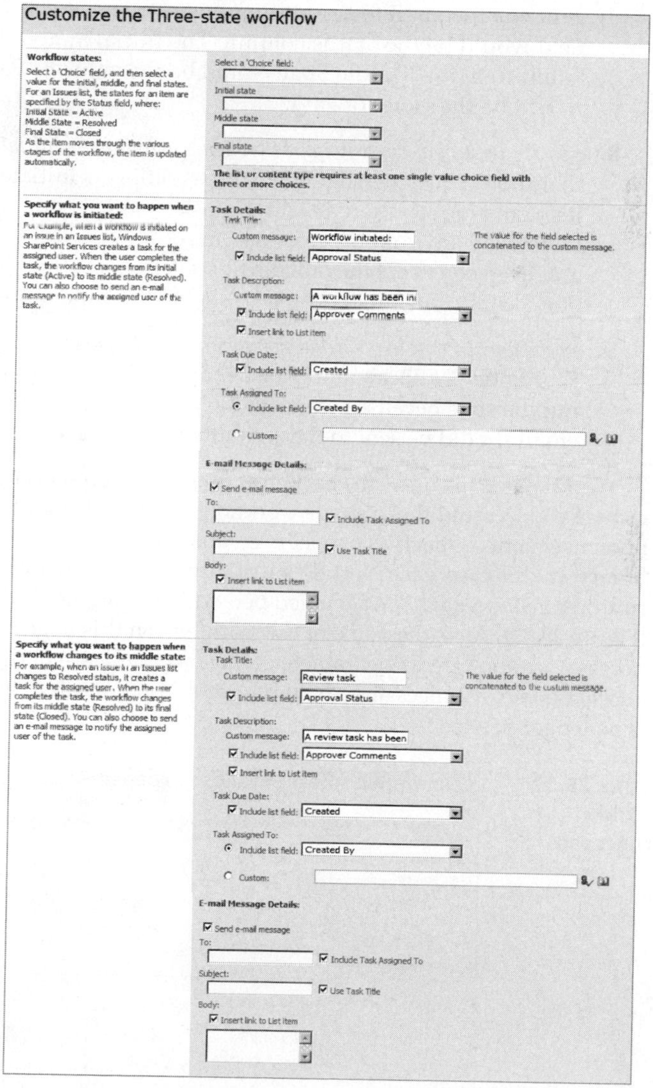

7. *Workflow states*: There are three states to a Three-state workflow: Initial (workflow start), Middle (second stage), and Final (workflow end). One single-value column of the column type Choice from the library must be designated as the workflow's Choice Field. For example, assume the Expense Reports document library in our scenario has a choice column titled Status that users can fill in with one of three prewritten values: Submitted, PendingPymt, or Paid. Now assume that when a user changes the Status value on an expense report item to the value Submitted, our Three-state workflow must generate an email to the employee's supervisor notifying them that reimbursement has been requested. Furthermore, when a supervisor changes the Status value on an expense report item to the value PendingPymt, our Three-state workflow must generate an email to accounting requesting a check. In this case, the workflow's Choice field would be the Status column. The Initial State setting would be the value of Submitted, the Middle State would be the value of PendingPymt, and the Final State would be the value of Paid.

8. *Specify what you want to happen when a workflow is initiated*: Provide details about the task that should be generated when the workflow is initiated either manually or upon new item creation. You can dictate the task message body, add a link to the library item of interest by any column value as a description, specify a due date and assignee to the task, and even construct the outgoing email message that will be sent to the task assignee. In our scenario, an email should be sent to the supervisor of the requestor.

9. *Specify what you want to happen when a workflow changes to its middle state*: Similar to step 8, provide details about the task that should be generated when the workflow enters its middle state because a value in the Choice field has been changed. In our scenario, an email should be sent to the accountant to request a check.

Workflows will run in the background on the WSS server to accomplish their configured tasks. Keep in mind that a single workflow that has start options set to automatically start upon user actions (such as new item creation or item changes) may initialize multiple times per library. In this case, each workflow instance is a separate program, and the number of currently running instances will be divulged per workflow on the Workflow Settings page of the library (Figure 28.32). Also, the name of the workflow on this page is a hyperlink to edit the workflow if necessary, although new parameter values will only affect future initializations of the workflow and not those instances already in progress. You may also remove a workflow from a library if it is no longer needed.

FIGURE 28.32
Workflow
Settings page

Change Workflow Settings: Expense Reports

Use this page to view or change the workflow settings for this document library. You can also add or remove workflows. Changes to existing workflows will not be applied to workflows already in progress.

Workflows

Workflow Name (click to change settings)	Workflows in Progress
Request Check	1

▫ Add a workflow
▪ Remove a workflow

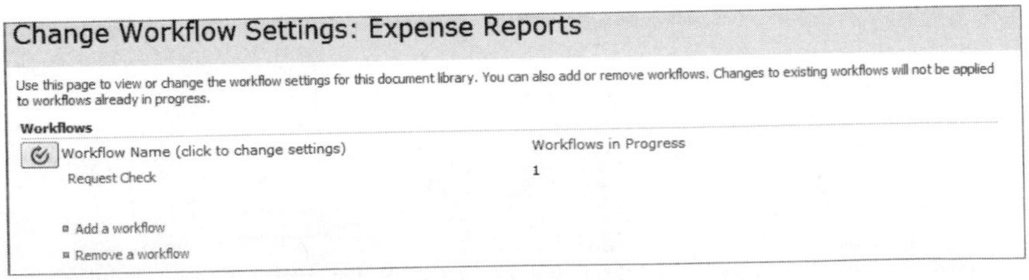

🌐 Real World Scenario

THREE-STATE WORKFLOW IN MOTION

Imagine that the Expense Reports document library we built earlier in this chapter for the Bigfirm sales department needs a Three-state workflow to track expense report status (submitted, approved pending payment, and paid). The Three-state workflow we create will automatically generate a new column on the Expense Reports library, and the workflow status of In Progress will appear as the column value while the workflow instance runs on each new item into the library. Additionally, a visit to the Tasks list identified during workflow creation will offer proof that a new task is assigned upon each new item creation in the library according to the initial state actions we defined during workflow creation.

The moment the task assignee changes the task status to Completed, the sales supervisor acknowledges the expense request, then our Three-state workflow enters its middle state, and finally a new task is added to the associated task list informing accounting of the need for a check. The Status column on our Expense Reports library is automatically altered from a value of Submitted to a value of PendingPymt for the new report. As soon as an accountant issues the check and changes the status of their task to Completed, the Status column on our Expense Reports library is automatically altered from a value of PendingPymt to a value of Paid for the new report, and the Request Check workflow column changes from In Progress to Completed.

You can review a history of each workflow instance's actions by clicking the value In Progress or Completed link in the workflow's Status column. Tasks that were created will be listed along with task details such as the assignee and due date. Also, the workflow event history will outline the time each step of the workflow occurred along with a helpful description that can aid in troubleshooting and auditing, as shown here. Any errors encountered along the way during workflow processing will be reported in the Status column in the library as well as in the individual document's Workflows link in the item context drop-down menu. These links will also call the Workflow Status page shown here, but with errors listed on the specific step in the history section that caused the failure. Unfortunately, the error descriptions are rarely if ever revealing, so additional monitoring tools such as Windows Server 2008 Event Viewer may be required to decipher the problem.

Workflow Status: Request Check

Workflow Information

Initiator: BIGFIRM\administrator	Document:	Jamie Expenses
Started: 10/8/2008 1:43 PM	Status:	Completed
Last run: 10/8/2008 1:50 PM		

Tasks

The following tasks have been assigned to the participants in this workflow. Click a task to edit it. You can also view these tasks in the list Tasks.

Assigned To	Title	Due Date	Status	Outcome
Randy Reeder	Expenses Submitted Jamie Expenses.txt ! NEW	10/8/2008	Completed	The task has been completed.
	Request Check Jamie Expenses.txt ! NEW	10/8/2008	Completed	The task has been completed.

Workflow History

The following events have occurred in this workflow.

Date Occurred	Event Type	User ID	Description	Outcome
10/8/2008 1:43 PM	Workflow Initiated	BIGFIRM\administrator	Three-state workflow started on http://bf2/sales/Expense Reports/Jamie Expenses.txt.	
10/8/2008 1:47 PM	Task Completed	BIGFIRM\administrator	Three-state workflow state change on http://bf2/sales/Expense Reports/Jamie Expenses.txt. Expense Reports.Status is now PendingPymt.	The task has been completed.
10/8/2008 1:50 PM	Task Completed	BIGFIRM\administrator	Three-state workflow state change on http://bf2/sales/Expense Reports/Jamie Expenses.txt. Expense Reports.Status is now Paid.	The task has been completed.
10/8/2008 1:50 PM	Workflow Completed	BIGFIRM\administrator	Three-state workflow completed on http://bf2/sales/Expense Reports/Jamie Expenses.txt.	

You can enable/disable user-defined workflows at the web application level by navigating Central Administration to the Application Management page and clicking the "Workflow settings" link under the Workflow Management section. You can also restrict task notifications to internal vs. external users.

BE CAREFUL WITH WEB APP SETTINGS

These settings are web application wide. They apply to every site in every site collection throughout the entire web application!

Accessing SharePoint Documents

Populating WSS document libraries and even managing document versions and workflows are all fine and good, but the documents themselves are useless unless users can easily navigate to them and their content is relevant. Designing an efficient access strategy for SharePoint documents involves the following:

- Enforcing security to protect sensitive data

- Creating useful navigation links to libraries and to individual items

- Keeping SharePoint indexes up-to-date to provide accurate search results

- Notifying users of library or item changes via alerts and RSS feeds

- Protecting offline copies via information rights management

Keep in mind, of course, as you construct user-friendly access solutions, that the principle of single-instance storage should be forefront in your design. In WSS, the direction of data access should consist of bringing users to the data, not the other way around as in traditional file system storage and email attachments. The whole point is to store a document only once and bring all readers, editors, and administrators to that one instance of the data so everyone can keep up with versions, metadata, and content in one place! Uploading the same document to multiple libraries defeats this purpose because WSS will manage each instance of the document in each separate library as a separate object, with different library settings affecting each and different workflows processing against each and, by the way, no automatic synchronization. Try to build efficient navigation and search solutions that allow users in one site to see links to items in document libraries on another site. Encourage users to access the single instance of each document via those links rather than uploading the document from the file system a second time to their own site's document library.

Enforcing Security

Perhaps the most significant responsibility of any site or library administrator is enforcing security. Effective security is neither too tight, thus stifling creativity and productivity, nor too loose, allowing inappropriate access. And although this may be a fine design tightrope to walk, the granularity of WSSv3's security model will help you balance without falling. Permissions can be defined right by individual right or in compilations of related rights known as permission levels (PLs for short). These permissions can then be assigned to individual users or groups of users called *SharePoint groups* to simplify administration. Those assignments can then be granted to any level of WSS objects from an entire site all the way down to an individual item within a list. Sound like a lot to manage? It is, so let's get started.

The Concept of Inheritance

Before we begin dissecting permissions, groups, and securable objects, we'll take a moment to point out the default behavior of SharePoint's security model. Industry-wide, the term *inheritance* represents the act of propagating certain settings from one level of architecture to another. In Microsoft vocabulary, the word *inheritance* is used more specifically to describe a downward flow of parent-level settings into the child levels (and their children and those children's children, and so on). Whereas the word *propagate* in Microsoft vernacular is more apt to describe child object data being forced upward to the parent object (and their parent and that parent's parent, and so on, up to the root).

In SharePoint, any permission-level compilations and security group configurations that are defined at the root site of a site collection are, by default, inherited down the architecture to all sites throughout the site collection as well as to all lists and libraries within each site. The individual items within each list or library then also inherit their permission structure from the list or library in which they reside. Inheritance is on by default all the way down a site collection B-tree because the default security setting when creating a new site is "Use same permissions as parent site" (refer to step 4 in the "Add Sites to a Site Collection" procedure explained earlier in this chapter). If an administrator creating a new site in the site collection were to instead choose the "Use unique permissions" radio button for the Permissions parameter during site creation, they would then be breaking inheritance for that new site and its future children. We will discuss more about disabling inheritance on children sites and site objects in the next section.

Permissions and Permission Levels

Perhaps now is a good time to point out that Microsoft changed some of the security vocabulary in WSSv3. Back in the predecessor version, WSSv2, the access authority an administrator could give to a user was called a *right*. New to WSSv3, these authority settings have been renamed what they truly are, *permissions*. However, in the next few paragraphs we'll use the terms *right* or *privilege* to indicate a permission object's given authority as opposed to the permission entity itself.

To view the permissions and permission levels of an entire site collection using inheritance throughout, you must navigate to the root site of the collection. From any page in the root site, administrators can access the Site Actions menu to visit the Site Settings for the root site (Figure 28.33). In the Users and Permissions section, there are three links for managing SharePoint security:

People and groups Manages SharePoint group objects (`people.aspx`)

Site collection administrators Specifies users receiving full control over all websites in the collection (this link appears on the root site of the site collection only)

Advanced permissions Manages SharePoint group/user to permission-level mappings (`user.aspx`).

FIGURE 28.33

Site Settings: Users
and Permissions

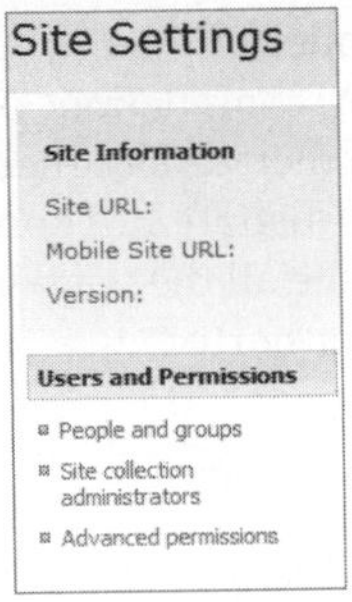

Permissions and permission levels can be most easily accessed from the "Advanced permissions" link in Site Settings. Once on the target page, the Settings menu on the toolbar offers a Permissions Levels link. The resultant Permission Levels page (`role.aspx`) can be used to add custom permission levels or change the privileges compiled for each permission level (Figure 28.34). You can even delete existing permission levels (except for Full Control and Limited Access) if you don't plan to ever assign their prescribed compilation of rights.

FIGURE 28.34

System-supplied
permission levels

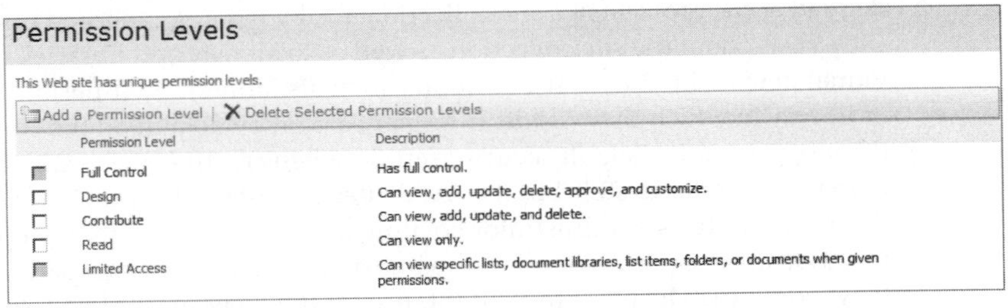

To add a new custom permission level, click the Add a Permission Level link in the toolbar, enter a revealing name and description, and then grant specific privileges to be included in the new level. Although individual permissions are well described, deciding which permissions are related can be challenging. However, the WSS GUI makes it easy by automatically selecting any necessary dependencies when you select a particular permission. For example, selecting the Manage Lists permission to add it to your new permission level will also automatically select the View Items permission it depends on. Need it even easier? Open one of the existing permission levels that is close to what you desire by clicking its name link, and then use the Copy Permission Level button to create a new permission level identical to the existing level. Now all you have to do is name the new level descriptively and alter a few of the permission choices to tailor it to your needs. How cool is that?

Microsoft discourages modifying the system-supplied permission levels because there is no guarantee that future patches, fixes, or service packs will not reset the permissions compilations of these levels back to factory default, thus obliterating all your customizations. Best practice is to create new custom permission levels bearing your special compilations instead.

PEOPLE AND GROUPS

Once you have permission-level compilations defined, it's time to begin deciding who will be assigned them. The "who" in that statement are referred to in our industry as security *principals*.

Again, Microsoft has rearranged the vocabulary in WSSv3 to reflect security principals as new terminology: people objects or SharePoint group objects (back in WSSv2 these objects were called *users*, *groups*, and *cross-site groups*). Keep in mind that SharePoint group objects do not necessarily map one-to-one to a Windows or Active Directory group object. Although such a mapping is possible to define, it is not an automatic assignment. SharePoint group objects exist within SharePoint and are created and managed independently of Windows security principal objects in the underlying OS or Active Directory domain.

To view a list of all SharePoint group security principals that are defined for the site collection, navigate to the Site Actions menu of the root site, and use the People and Groups link in the Users and Permissions section. The resulting page (`people.aspx`) will open focused on the first SharePoint group listed for the site and display the membership information for each SharePoint group, both autogenerated and user-defined (as in Figure 28.35, note that the default Members group has no one in it by default). The SharePoint groups generated automatically during site creation depend on the site template employed. For example, the Team Site template used to generate the initial automatically created site collection during WSSv3 installation will produce three system-generated SharePoint groups:

{Site Name} Members   Granted the Contribute PL and containing no members

{Site Name} Visitors   Granted the Read PL and containing no members

{Site Name} Owners   Granted the Full Control PL and containing as its only default member the user account who created the site

FIGURE 28.35
People and Groups

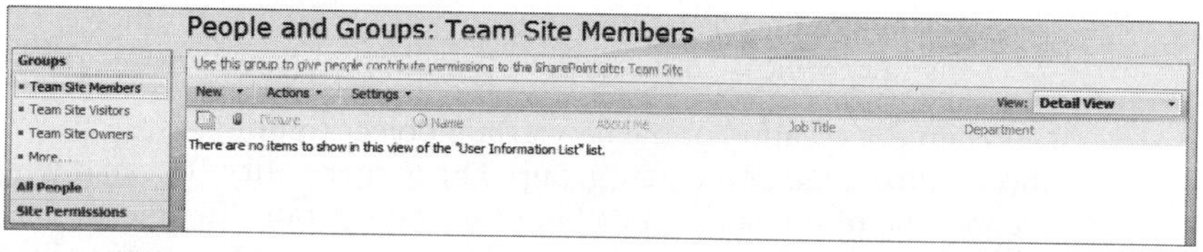

Additionally, the All People link in the Permissions navigation links on the left of all security pages will display an alphabetical listing of all SharePoint People objects regardless of which SharePoint group they are a member of. This listing assists in quickly contacting (the Email or Call/Message option in Actions menu) or eliminating (the Delete User from Site Collection option in the Actions menu) certain people objects.

Creating and Deleting SharePoint Groups

The SharePoint groups autogenerated during site creation may not be sufficient for your custom security structure design. Creating new SharePoint group objects should be carefully planned and strategically invoked to minimize repetitive administration yet provide adequate protection for the data. To create a new SharePoint group that will recognize only specific users as its members, follow these steps:

1. Navigate to the People and Groups link from Site Settings at the site level.

2. Regardless of which group object the page opens to, use the New drop-down menu from the toolbar, and click the New Group link.

3. Configure the new group as follows:

   A. *Name and About Me Description*: Give the new group object a concise name and description. Notice the description text box is entitled About Me (because it is the same description text box used to create a new people object) and that it offers rich-text editing that may include hyperlinks, pictures, and HTML editing.

   B. *Owner*: Specify the owner of the group object. By default, this field will populate with the user logged in and creating the new group. Whoever is deemed as Owner will have full control over the group and can manage membership and delete the group entirely. This is a single-value field; however, either an individual user or a group security principal from the Windows OS or ADS domain can be the single value.

   C. *Group Settings*: Dictate whether only group members or everyone with view security authority can view the membership list of the group. Dictate whether only the group owner or all group members can edit the membership list of the group.

   D. *Membership Requests*: Specify whether you will allow users to send an email request to join or leave the group. If requests are allowed, then set whether the system will autoaccept requests (thus only providing an email trail of requests for audit purposes). Also, specify the email address all new requests will be sent to.

   E. *Give Group Permission to this Site*: Assign the appropriate permission level(s) to the new group. You can choose not to select any of the options and leave the group unauthorized at the site level so that you can later grant them authority at a lower-level object such as a specific list or library.

When the creation of the new group object completes, the GUI returns to the People and Groups page of the new group. The owner entity chosen during group creation will become the initial single member of the new group. To determine the group ID number of a SharePoint group, notice the MembershipGroupID=x query at the end of the URL while visiting the People and Groups page of that particular group. The x will be the ID number of the group.

To delete an existing SharePoint Group, follow these steps:

1. Make absolutely certain it is not actively providing data security on any sites, lists, libraries, folders, or list items.

2. Once you are certain you really need to eliminate the group, navigate to the People and Groups link of Site Settings at the site level, and select the group to be deleted.

3. Click the Group Settings link under the Settings drop-down menu on the toolbar.

4. Click the Delete button found at the bottom of the page (near the OK and Cancel buttons) to delete the group object.

Bear in mind that you do not need to remove all users or remove the group's permission assignment first, so there is little safety net beyond the screen message asking for confirmation of the deletion. Be careful!

Real World Scenario

BIGFIRM CUSTOM GROUP

Suppose that Bigfirm needs a SharePoint group that will represent Heather Human and Randy Reeder as the two people responsible for populating a new document library on the Services site called Suggestions. However, we are not interested in using the autogenerated Members SharePoint group object because its membership list includes users other than Heather and Randy who should not have contribute permission to the Suggestions library. Following the process previous outlined, we can create a custom SharePoint group populated only with Heather and Randy as members. This new custom group, let's call it Suggestions Contributors, could then be assigned the necessary permission level to the Suggestions library.

Modifying Existing Groups

During the life span of a SharePoint group object, management and maintenance will need to be performed. To modify the configuration parameters, membership list, or permissions assignments of an existing SharePoint group, navigate to the People and Groups link of Site Settings at the site level, and select the group to be modified from the Groups Quick Launch menu. Then perform any of the following operations:

To add new members Click the Add Users from the New drop-down menu on the toolbar, or simply click the New toolbar link. Both operations deliver the Add Users page (adinv. aspx). This page offers a People Picker text box in the Add Users section wherein multiple values can be listed separated by semicolons and then verified with the Check User icon, or the Browse icon can be used to invoke a People Search dialog box for choosing members. Additionally, the Give Permission section allows you to choose the SharePoint group that the new users will be made members of (and it doesn't have to be the group you initially intended to modify in step 2 earlier) or allows you to assign permission levels directly to the users, not making them members of a SharePoint group at all!

To remove existing members Select the check box of the desired member, and then click the Remove Users from Group link under the Actions drop-down menu on the toolbar. To select all members' check boxes, select the column header Select All check box. You may want to use the one of the contact links under the Actions menu first to alert the desired users of their pending removal (Email or Call/Message).

To modify group settings Modify any of the settings configured during site creation by clicking the Group Settings link under the Settings drop-down menu on the toolbar.

To view the permissions assigned to the group Click the View Group Permissions link under the Settings drop-down menu on the toolbar.

To change the permissions assigned to the group Click the Site Permissions link in the Groups Quick Launch menu, and select the check box of the group to be modified. Then click the Edit User Permissions link under the Actions drop-down menu on the toolbar.

To restrict the list of SharePoint Groups appearing in the Groups Quick Launch Bar while visiting the group's pages Click the Edit Group Quick Launch link under the Settings drop-down menu on the toolbar.

To edit the member metadata displayed on the page Click the List Settings link under the Settings drop-down menu on the toolbar.

> **BEWARE OF ALTERING SYSTEM-SUPPLIED SHAREPOINT GROUPS**
>
> Much like system-supplied permission levels, Microsoft cautions against modifying the system-supplied SharePoint groups because of the risk of future patches, fixes, or service packs may reset the groups back to the factory defaults.

Group Membership Strategies

When it comes to planning SharePoint group membership, there seems to be two schools of thought in the industry. First, segregated IT departments may benefit from adding only individual user accounts from the network directory service into SharePoint groups and then nesting multiple SharePoint groups into other SharePoint groups as members to organize permission to SharePoint data. In this model, the security of SharePoint data is managed strictly within SharePoint and is not affected by group structures existing in the network directory service.

Second, in smaller integrated IT departments where the same person manages SharePoint and the directory service, it may be less effort to create the necessary group structure in the directory for providing non-SharePoint benefits such as email distribution lists for Exchange or NTFS permission security principals for shared folders and printers. Then those directory groups that already exist can be leveraged by making the directory group object a member of a SharePoint group in SharePoint for the purpose of granting permission to SharePoint data. In this model, the security of SharePoint data depends on the correct management of directory group object memberships. This strategy is most successful in environments where directory group resource requirements match the needs for SharePoint resources.

Whether defining SharePoint groups by adding individual user accounts as members or by adding directory group objects as members, the method employed to populate the group membership is the same (see the earlier section "Modifying Existing Groups"). However, even though the SharePoint group pages will display the name of the directory group object when a group is made a member, rest assured that SharePoint is enumerating the group object at each action on a SharePoint site. Audit reports and document metadata such as Created By will always display the individual username who committed the action.

DISABLING INHERITANCE

Inheritance can be disabled or reenabled at any security level throughout the hierarchy. When inheritance was previously enforced and gets disabled, the previously inherited users/groups and their permissions to the object will be automatically added to the object as new unique security entities (see Figure 28.36). From there, the administrator can begin removing previously inherited access that should no longer be on the object or add new assignments that are unique to the object.

The inheritance of PL objects is handled separately by SharePoint from the inheritance of SharePoint group objects. Disabling inheritance on one does not affect inheritance on the other. The advantage is collections of power-granting permissions can be managed centrally from the root of the site collection, while the art of personnel grouping can be delegated to managers who are more in tune with which users need which level of access to SharePoint resources. The disadvantage is that if both permission mixes and user gatherings need to be delegated, then increased administration and documentation is required.

FIGURE 28.36
Changes in library permissions because of disabling inheritance

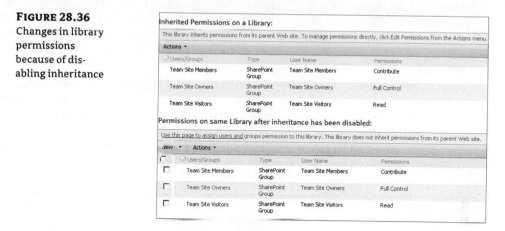

The act of disabling inheritance is performed at the object level on which inherited security structure is no longer desired. This can be on a subsite, a page, a list or library, a folder, or an individual item within a list or library.

Creating Useful Navigation

Knowing you have a million dollars is not nearly as useful and being able to put your hands on it. Similarly, knowing that a document has been uploaded into some document library in SharePoint but not being able to find the item is futile. Once documents have been uploaded into SharePoint, it may become necessary in a multisite environment to begin creating intuitive navigation hyperlinks to the libraries and their items. Otherwise, users may lose interest and perhaps even give up on using SharePoint to store their files. Luckily, SharePoint navigation tools make designing links to frequently accessed documents quite easy on SharePoint site pages:

Links list   This is a custom list built using the Links list system-supplied template and populated with URLs to SharePoint libraries, lists, folders, or individual items. These lists can also be populated with URLs to resources outside the immediate SharePoint enterprise (such as the external Internet or other companies' SharePoint destinations). To create a new Links list, visit the Create choice of the Site Actions menu, and choose the Links template from the Tracking menu.

Quick Launch Bar   The Quick Launch Bar can be customized to include additional links to both other SharePoint resources and external Internet destinations. Additionally, the tree view can be invoked to expose the site's entire hierarchy of objects as hyperlinks (the tree view is context specific). To modify the Quick Launch Bar, visit Site Settings, and click either Quick Launch or *Tree View* in the Look and Feel menu.

Global Navigation tabs   The Global Navigation tabs can be reordered, renamed, and added to so as to provide more hierarchical navigation across the entire site collection. To modify the Global Navigation tabs, visit Site Settings and click "Top link bar" in the Look and Feel menu.

Link to a Document content type   This is a system-supplied content type that allows library items to be created that do not actually contain a document but rather provide a hyperlink straight to an existing document in a different folder or library. Using links, it is possible to advertise a document in a related library without uploading a second instance of the document into SharePoint (thus violating single-instance storage). The best part is that the link to another document will be treated like any other item in its resident library according to security and workflows! To associate the Link to a Document content type with a library, merely modify the library's settings as discussed earlier in this chapter.

Send To destinations   Each document library can be configured to support custom Send To destinations that allow a user to publish their item to an alternate library, thus creating a second instance of the document. Although this method violates single-instance storage, it places the document close to users who need it and makes it easier for said users to navigate to the document. To add a custom Send To destination, visit the library's settings, and click Advanced Settings in the General Settings menu.

THE THREE-CLICK RULE

There is an old web design adage called the *three-click rule* that discourages web designers from placing commonly desired content more than three hyperlinks away from the interface a user commonly works in. And back during the infancy of the Web when many users were just learning to traverse hyperlinks, this rule may have been helpful. But most of today's web users are hyperlink savvy and can navigate a breadcrumb trail or navigation link thread to find a desired document library or item in SharePoint. So, keeping link navigation to three or fewer hyperlinks is no longer necessary and, in fact, may not be a practical design for your SharePoint site.

Be sure to record your navigation modifications so they can be easily duplicated in the event other WSS administrators undo them. Also, documentation helps plan additional navigational tool implementation without reinventing the wheel. For instance, if a Links list already exists on another page of the WSS site that includes all the hyperlinks you need, it would be easier to expose that list on your page than to re-create it entirely from scratch!

Updating Search Indexes

Windows SharePoint Services offers indexing and search capabilities to assist those users who choose to hunt for documents rather than navigate to them. But don't get too excited, because WSS has very limited search capabilities. For one thing, WSS search will seek the desired search string only within the scope of the site from which the search is initiated. If you already know where the item is, would you really need search? If you require alternative search scopes, custom content sources, incremental content crawls, and/or a custom manner in which your users can perform their search, consider implementing Microsoft Search Server 2008 or MOSS 2007. The WSS search index must be updated as new content is added or existing content is edited in a way that would change its focus. By default, the index is scheduled to crawl the entire content of all site collections every five minutes.

You can alter the frequency at which WSS crawls its content to update the search index by modifying the configuration of the Windows SharePoint Services Search service. First, identify which server in your WSS farm is running this all-important service for you (if you have a scaled farm). Then, visit Central Administration, and click the Services on Server link in the Topology and Services menu of the Operations page. Be sure to focus the resulting Configure Windows SharePoint Services Search Service Settings page on the server you noted earlier. In the list of services running on the given machine, click the hyperlink that is the name of the Windows SharePoint Services Search service, and scroll down to the Indexing Schedule section at the bottom of the page (see Figure 28.37).

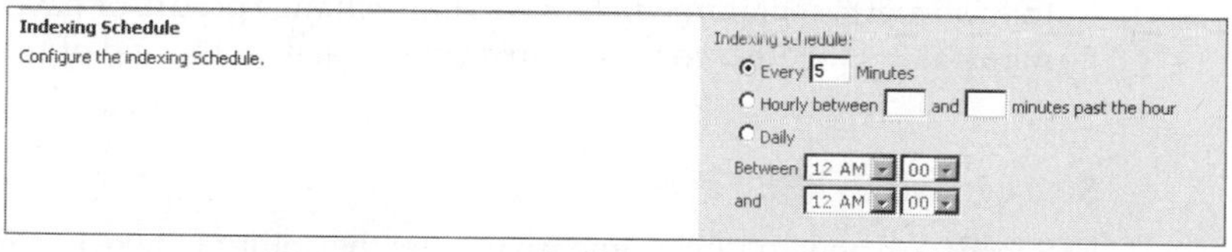

FIGURE 28.37
Indexing Schedule settings for Windows SharePoint Services search

You should set the index crawls to a schedule that least impacts user activity or performance on the server while providing the necessary frequency of updates to produce accurate search results. If the WSS content data tends to be static, set the crawls to occur nightly or during off-peak hours. If the data is volatile, more frequent crawls may be necessary, but beware if you set the crawls too frequently on a large WSS implementation; they will not finish within the time allotted, and the index will be broken. No index means no search results!

Using Alerts and RSS

Modern computers have yet to become artificially intelligent enough for users who wish for a system intuitive enough to anticipate their needs. But while you wait, wouldn't it be nice for SharePoint to tell you what it has for you rather than you having to take the initiative to go find it? Guess what, SharePoint does. Alerts and RSS feeds allow you to sign up for notifications from the WSS server when new content is added or existing content has been modified. And although alerts have been around since the previous version, WSSv3 has expanded alert functionality to allow delegation. RSS feeds eliminate the opportunity for users of consequence to claim that they never received the information of interest.

SIGNING UP FOR ALERTS

Alerts notify recipients via email. To sign yourself or some other unsuspecting party up for an alert, simply visit the list or library you want to be notified about, choose Alert Me from the Actions menu, and then specify the following settings:

Name   The alert must be uniquely named on the library.

Send Alerts To   Though this multivalue field automatically fills in with the name of the user currently connected to the library, you can remove your name and replace it with someone else or add many alert recipients. The ability to construct an alert bound for someone else is new to WSSv3.

Change Type   Select whether to receive an alert only when new items are added, only when existing items are modified, only when existing items are deleted, or all of the above. Unfortunately, each choice is mutually exclusive, so it's an all-or-only-one decision. If the library happens to be a discussion board, there is also a choice for only when the web discussion updates.

Send Alerts for These Changes   Once the change type has been selected, you can narrow the alert down to only when someone else changes a document (you will not receive alerts for your own work), only when someone else changes a document created by you, only when someone else changes a document that was last modified by you, or all of the above. Like Change Type, each choice is mutually exclusive.

When to Send Alerts   If you chose a wide breadth of alerts (all changes of all types), you may want to tone down the volume of email messages arriving in your inbox. You can choose to have alerts sent immediately when the change occurs or have the SharePoint server bundle many alerts together to be sent in a single email at the end of the day or only one day a week.

SUBSCRIBING TO RSS FEEDS

RSS feeds are new to WSSv3 and give users the ability to take advantage of RSS readers such as those found in IE 7 and Outlook 2007. RSS subscriptions differ from alerts because library changes are exposed immediately and automatically. Better still, the information in the RSS item contains an excerpt from the changed document, not just a link to the document as is sent in an email alert. Users can make a better informed decision whether to visit the library or not.

By default document libraries are enabled for RSS as shown in the RSS Settings under the Communications menu of the document library settings. But RSS feeds are not limited to document libraries; picture and form libraries can also be configured for RSS. But wait, there's more! Announcement and calendar lists, blogs, surveys, and discussion boards can also be set up with RSS feeds. To RSS-enable one of these repositories, first verify that the resident site is in a site collection whose web application has been configured to support RSS in Central Administration. Second, visit the repository's settings, and click the RSS Settings under the Communication menu. Once you are looking at the Modify List RSS Settings: {list name} item, fill out the configuration of the feed, but be careful not to include too many columns or set the item limit too high (see Figure 28.38). Many mobile devices now have RSS readers, but the screen is much smaller! To subscribe as a client, enter the URL of the SharePoint list into your RSS reader application.

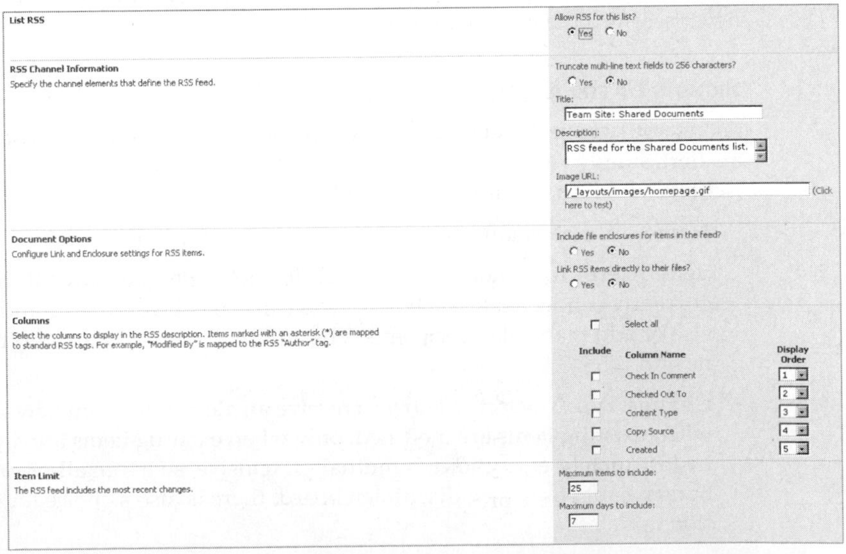

FIGURE 28.38
RSS feed settings on the Shared Documents library

Managing Information Rights

Despite Microsoft's best intentions, occasionally documents from SharePoint need to be printed or taken offline. After all, not every possible use of a document can be carried out on a computer using an Internet browser. If you've been to a physician lately, you have undoubtedly noticed the labels and bar codes plastered across every page of that dubious chart, which seems to hold your entire life history. How does that bar code get on the page? Similarly, what if you need to protect a document by forbidding printing or setting encryption once the document is down-loaded from SharePoint? If your documents are stored in WSSv3, you can configure information rights management on your SharePoint server to control what happens to a document that is opened from a document library.

IRM configuration begins not in WSS but rather in the Windows network. A Rights Management Services platform must be configured with the laws of the land regarding document encryption, feasibility (printing, editing, and saving offline), and labeling (bar codes, labels, water-marks, and so on). Once a RMS platform is online, the RMS client included in the Windows Server 2008 OS will connect to the RMS server advertised in Active Directory or configured directly in the RMS client application's properties. Setting up and configuring a Rights Management Services platform falls outside the scope of this chapter. For more information on RMS in Windows Server 2008, see the TechNet article at http://technet.microsoft.com/en-us/library/cc771234.aspx.

To configure WSS to engage RMS, use the Information Rights Management link under the Security Configuration menu on the Operations page of Central Administration. There are three possible settings for IRM:

Do not use IRM on this server   IRM is disabled.

Use the default RMS server specified in Active Directory   This directs WSS to employ the Rights Management Services server advertised in ADS and is only an appropriate choice if your WSS server is a member server in an Active Directory domain.

Use this RMS server   This allows you to specify the FQDN of an RMS server in your environment other than the RMS server advertised in ADS (if your WSS server is a member server in an Active Directory domain) or an independent RMS server (if your WSS server is a stand-alone server in a workgroup).

Once you have IRM enabled on WSS, configuration is merely a matter of choosing which libraries or lists you want to engage IRM. Visit the Information Rights Management link under the Permissions and Management menu of the library's Settings page. Choose which RMS poli-cies you want to have employed against that library, and all documents within all folders will begin adhering to the chosen IRM rules. But be careful, because this is a library-wide setting. If one out of the 20 documents you have stored in the library should not be restricted by the IRM policy assigned to the library, then you've got a problem because it will be held accountable to the same laws as the other 19 documents. You should plan with pen and paper before assigning IRM to a library.

Advanced WSS Administration

At this point in the chapter, it is probably apparent that WSSv3 is an intense topic to discuss in a single chapter. The SharePoint product line has virtually become a platform in its own right with third-party programs written specifically for it and entire document management solutions designed around it in large enterprises. But you're in the home stretch, so hang in there! We'll cover a few advanced administration topics to illustrate SharePoint's flexibility and extensibility.

Don't Double Dip!

If your environment has already engaged RMS outside SharePoint and documents are being created in Windows RMS–compliant editors (such as Word 2007) and saved to a file system (to be uploaded to SharePoint later), then the documents are already protected on the file system before you upload them into SharePoint. Uploading protected documents renders the documents unsearchable in WSS, and even those users who have SharePoint permissions to the item in the library will not see the item in their related search results.

If this becomes an issue, consider asking users to create new documents directly into the SharePoint library without protection and allowing WSS IRM to protect the documents on the fly when other users download them from the library. Then the items in the library will be searchable. Of course, check with your security engineers first. Storing the document in an unprotected format while it resides in SharePoint may not meet your company's security standards or regulatory compliance requirements.

If you must upload already protected documents into SharePoint because of security standards yet want to be able to search those items, you will need to employ a more robust third-party search tool than the WSSv3 search service.

Authentication Providers

The default authentication provider used to identify users in WSS is Windows. It stands to reason that a Windows user account authenticating into a Windows Vista client OS and launching Internet Explorer without secondary logon would expect to enter SharePoint as itself. If the SharePoint URLs have been added to the Intranet security zone of IE, then the Windows user account should be passed through to the IIS services that by default are configured to use Windows integrated authentication. Therefore, the user will not be prompted to provide their account for the second time that day upon entering the WSS web page. But if the SharePoint URLs have not yet been added to the Intranet security zone of IE or if the security zone's settings have been altered, it is possible that the user will be prompted to provide their Windows logon information upon requesting a WSS web page.

But what can we do for non-Windows users who need access to SharePoint? Perish the thought, but you may actually need to support users of non-Windows clients such as Mac or Linux. Or you may have a public-facing WSS environment and do not want to create a Windows user object for every conceivable human on the planet who has Internet access. You could open your WSS server up to anonymous access both in IIS and in WSS by enabling anonymous access both in the IIS Manager console (on the site) and in Central Administration (on the WSS web application), but this may be too generous. Instead, consider using one of the other authentication providers included with WSSv3: forms or web single sign-on (note: Selecting authentication providers is a web application–level decision):

1. On Central Administration's Application Management page, click the Authentication Providers link in the Application Security menu.

2. In the upper right of the toolbar, choose the web application for which you want to change providers.

3. Click the zone name link to change the authentication provider for a zone.

During initial creation of a web application, only the default zone is generated. Thereafter, you can extend an existing web application to set up load-balanced URLs to add URLs by which different groups of users will access the SharePoint site. For example, internal employees may type **http://servername** while extranet users type **http://partnerinfo.publicdomain**, yet both are delivered to the same content. Each load-balanced URL must be assigned a zone: Internet, Intranet, Custom, or External. These zone names will show up in the list of zones on the Authentication Providers page in Central Administration. Therefore, it's possible to use a different authentication provider for internal employees than for extranet users. For more information on load balancing, see http://technet.microsoft.com/en-us/library/cc287954.aspx.

The Edit Authentication page is authentication type–specific. If you choose the Windows authentication type, you will see an IIS Authentication Settings section requiring you to specify Kerberos vs. NTLM and offering "Basic clear text" as an option. If instead you choose the forms or web single sign-on authentication types, no IIS Authentication Settings section is displayed. Instead, Membership Provider Name and Role Manager Name sections are displayed. The Membership Provider Name setting must match exactly the information manually added to the `web.config` file of the IIS website supporting SharePoint. Programming the authentication data source for forms or web single sign-on providers falls outside the scope of this chapter.

Managing Features

Adding functionality to your WSS environment is not as labor intensive as you might think. Many sets of programming code have already been written to bring different useful tidbits to your sites. These easily pluggable, freely redistributable components of code are called *Features*. Yes, Features with a capital *F* as the first letter. Maybe the WSS product designers just couldn't come up with a more distinguishable, less confusing moniker, but you may sleep better if you agree that at least the title reflects the actual purpose of the object: to add features to your WSS sites.

Features are managed within WSS in a hierarchical fashion. Features available at the farm level can be employed web application by web application. Features available on a certain web application can then be enabled site collection by site collection. Features enabled at the site collection level can be employed or disabled site by site within that site collection. You can acquire Features from various third parties or from the Microsoft WSS product pages on the Internet. Depending on whom you purchase your Feature from, it may self-install. But if not, you can install a new Feature using the following `stsadm.exe` syntax:

```
Stsadm -o installfeature -filename {path&file} -name {new directory for Feature}
```

Both the -filename and -name parameters must contain paths that are relative to the \12\ TEMPLATE\FEATURES path of the WSS program directory. By default, this would be %SYSTEMDRIVE%:\

`Program Files\Common Files\Microsoft Shared\web server extensions`. There is also an optional `-force` parameter that will overwrite an existing Feature of the same name to install updates.

Once a new Feature has been installed, you enable it at the farm level using the "Manage farm features" link under the Global Configuration menu on the Operations page of Central Administration. You can then use the "Manage Web application features" link under the SharePoint Web Application Management menu on the Application Management page of Central Administration to employ the feature on a specific web application. Then selectively enable or disable the new Feature using the "Site collection features" link under the Site Collection Administration menu of Site Settings or using the "Site features" link under the Site Administration menu of Site Settings. If you have disabled a Feature at all four levels (site, site collection, web application, and farm) because you no longer need the feature, consider uninstalling the Feature from WSS so it cannot be exploited. To uninstall a Feature, use the `uninstallfeature` operation of `stsadm`, which requires the same `-filename` and `-name` parameters as the `installfeature` operation with an additional required parameter called `-id` that demands the GUID of the feature to be removed.

Limiting Content

In an effort to control and properly maintain your WSS environment, you may find it necessary to limit the amount and type of data that users are allowed to input. WSSv3 ships with several filename extensions blocked so that users cannot upload files of these types into libraries or attach them to list items that allow attachments. WSSv3 also allows creation of site quota limits to put the brakes on uncontrollable growth of the content databases in SQL Server. Using these configuration settings wisely can help you avoid future headaches and potential attacks. And speaking of attacks, you should also employ a worthy antivirus solution on your WSS servers.

VIEWING BLOCKED FILE TYPES

To see the list file types blocked from being uploaded into WSS by default, visit the Operations page of Central Administration. Under the Security Configuration menu, the "Blocked file types" link produces a list of those file types prohibited globally throughout your WSS implementation (see Figure 28.39). Notice that the list is web application–specific via the drop-down on the right side of the toolbar. This allows you to prohibit a specific file type in one web application (thus all sites in said web application) without impacting other web applications. To remove a prohibited file type or to add additional forbidden file types, merely edit the text box.

THE GHOST IN THE MACHINE...

If you read the fine print on the Blocked File Types page above the text box shown in Figure 28.39, the last sentence notes that in order to allow a previously blocked file type, you must remove it from both the global and web application lists. This is a holdover from the previous version of SharePoint and no longer applies because WSSv3 no longer has a global blocked file types list. Oops, we guess someone in technical editing missed the *obsolete* wording when they proofread the web page! In WSSv3, you need only remove the blocked file type in the web application list of interest to begin allowing files of said type to be uploaded into SharePoint sites residing in that web application.

FIGURE 28.39
Blocked file
types from the
Operations page

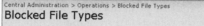

Central Administration > Operations > Blocked File Types

Blocked File Types

Use this page to prevent specific file types from being saved or retrieved from any site on this server. If a user tries to save or retrieve a blocked file type, he or she will see an error, and will not be able to save or retrieve the file. NOTE: To allow a file type that is currently blocked, you must delete it from both the global and Web application lists.

Web Application: **http://spserver/** ▾

Type each file extension on a separate line.

```
ade
adp
app
asa
ashx
asmx
asp
bas
bat
cdx
cer
chm
class
cmd
com
config
cpl
crt
csh
der
```

Filenames that include braces (for example, filename.{doc}) are blocked automatically.

OK   Cancel

ESTABLISHING QUOTA LIMITS

Setting quota limits on a WSS site restricts the amount of data users can build into sites whether that information is a web part, list, library, individual item, or additional web pages. Quota limits are set at the site collection level, and if several site collections will use the same storage limits, it's worth creating a quota template ahead of time in Central Administration and then calling that template in the configuration settings of a given site collection. To define quota templates, follow these steps:

1. Visit the Application Management page of Central Administration.

2. Click the Quota Templates link under the SharePoint Site Management menu.

3. In the resultant page's Template Name section, specify a name for the new template. The name must be unique throughout the hosting web application.

4. If the new template is similar to an existing template, you may choose the existing template in the "Template to start from" field and simply modify its name and limit values. This does not create a dependency. The existing template you chose to emulate while creating your new template can be modified or deleted without affecting your template.

5. In the Storage Limit Values section, dictate a maximum size limit and/or warning threshold in megabytes that will be invoked if an administrator chooses to use this quota template.

To set quotas on a specific site collection, click the "Site collection quotas and locks" link from the SharePoint Site Management menu on the Application Management page of Central Administration. Be sure to focus the resultant page on the site collection you want to influence, and then configure the Site Quota Information section by either employing an existing quota template or setting limits unique to the site collection. Notice that you can also lock the site collection from this page to prohibit access entirely (so as not to publish a proactively created site collection until a future date) or isolate the site collection during maintenance by rendering it read-only or read/update/delete-only, which doesn't allow new inserts ("Adding content prevented").

THWARTING VIRUSES

Perhaps one of the worst threats to shared documents is virus infection. As multiple users open a SharePoint document library item in their own client application, the potential for infection from a virus increases. WSSv3 does not include antivirus software, but if you have installed a compliant antivirus application onto your SharePoint server, you can control how and when WSS content will be scanned. Always check with your antivirus software manufacturer to verify their application is SharePoint aware before assuming it is protecting your WSS content successfully. And be sure to install your new antivirus application onto all web front-end servers in your WSS farm, or you could be missing the opportunity to scan certain documents. Microsoft offers a SharePoint-aware security program called Microsoft Forefront Security for SharePoint, which can be downloaded from http://technet.microsoft.com/en-us/bb738112.aspx; it includes not only antivirus but also filtering tools for inappropriate content.

Once you have installed an appropriate antivirus software, visit the Antivirus link under the Security Configuration menu on the Operations page of Central Administration (see Figure 28.40). From this page you can set a timeout value for antivirus scans, limit the parallelism of the scanning threads, specify when scanning will take place (upload vs. download), and dictate whether infected documents will be quarantined and/or cleaned.

FIGURE 28.40
Antivirus settings

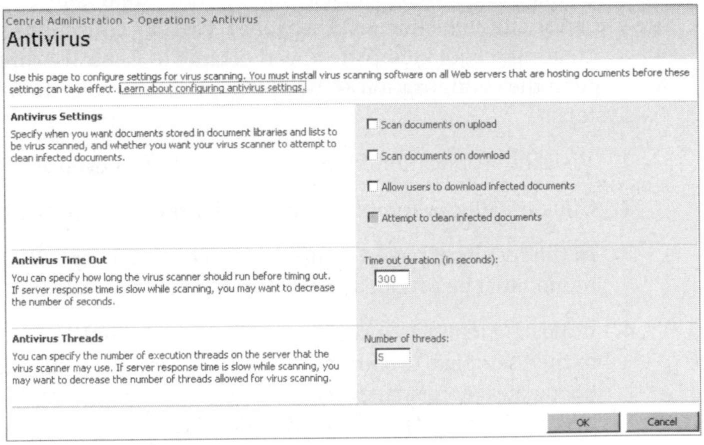

Integrating Client Software

One last quick thing worth mentioning about WSSv3, which amazingly has little to do with the server, is the degree of client application integration SharePoint offers your users. This chapter has, so far, unveiled the sophisticated features of SharePoint that make it a much more appealing storage facility for critical business data than traditional file system folders on network file servers. But all of these features don't necessarily have to make it more difficult for users to interact with that business data. Here is a peek at how painless it can be!

Internet Explorer Integration

From the information in the first section of this chapter, it is easy to see that SharePoint is a web-based service platform. Its dependency on IIS gives this fact away. So, it is no surprise that most of the SharePoint content can be quickly accessed via a web browser application. In fact, some SharePoint content, such a graphical web parts and SharePoint-centric lists, is available only via a browser unless other front-end applications are purchased or written to expose them. But this chapter focuses on replacing traditional file shares with SharePoint, so files stored in SharePoint libraries are the priority here.

Opening documents and files from SharePoint libraries via a web browser application, by default, launches a native application associated with the file's extension type, such as Microsoft Word for DOC files or Acrobat Reader for PDF files. However, if you support SharePoint users who access computers that fall outside your political control, then you may not be able to guarantee that their client OS will have a native application installed that can handle your SharePoint library items. You may need to employ a third-party solution to convert documents into HTML pages so they can be rendered by the web browser application.

WSSv3 Central Administration appears to offer a Document Conversion setting that taps a SharePoint server in the farm to convert documents to HTML for those libraries that have been configured to deliver their items as web pages. But don't get too excited; the HTML document conversion in WSSv3 never seemed to be a priority for Microsoft because of minimal interest from the market. It is heavily flawed with little improvement expected in this version of SharePoint.

Office 2007 Application Integration

Windows SharePoint Services was essentially written to be a back-end server to Microsoft's wildly popular productivity application suite, Office 2007. In fact, most of the WSSv3 product web pages can be found within the Microsoft Office product websites on the Internet. SharePoint integration with Office depends on the correct options being selected during Office installation. There is an option called Support for Windows SharePoint Services that must be selected during Office installation to reap the relationship rewards of WSS and Office.

Outlook 2007

Outlook is by far the most versatile of the Office suite applications when it comes to SharePoint integration. WSSv3 allows you to bidirectionally and persistently synchronize certain lists with Outlook 2007 by choosing Connect to Outlook from the Actions menu of the list (see Figure 28.41). The following list template types can be connected to Outlook 2007:

- Contacts List
- Calendar (Events) List
- Tasks List
- Discussion Board (List)
- Document Library

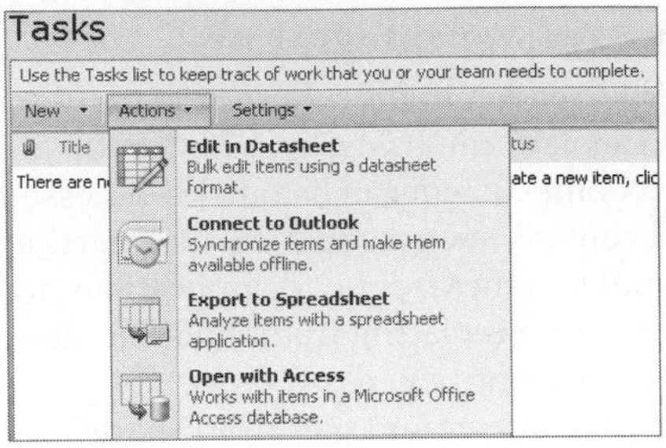

FIGURE 28.41
Actions menu of
Task list type

The first four list types seem pretty obvious companions to the personal organizer features of Outlook 2007. Contact, Calendar appointment, and To-Do entries are commonplace in Outlook. In fact, Outlook can even be employed as an RSS reader or community message board client, so it's easy to accept SharePoint Discussion Board lists can be synchronized with Outlook. But document libraries?

Outlook 2007 now offers a document preview feature that allows the user to open (in a read-only format) any file for which a native application is associated. This is helpful for email attachments but is also invaluable for linking WSS document libraries to Outlook. Keep in mind the preview tool is a read-only utility; Outlook is not a fully fledged document-editing software (at least not yet!). But still, Outlook fanatics who prefer to launch most of their productivity from this email client application's interface will delight in being able to add and alter SharePoint list items and preview SharePoint documents without leaving Outlook.

EXCEL 2007

SharePoint lists and libraries also offer the Export to Spreadsheet option in their Actions menu. This produces a one-way, one-time export of the list or library row values (but not library files themselves) to an Excel spreadsheet. Beware, this is not the same degree of integration that Excel enjoyed with the previous version of SharePoint. The menu choice is called Export; if items are added to the spreadsheet, once inside Excel those items will not also reside in SharePoint. Worse, the next refresh of the Excel spreadsheet from its SharePoint data source will overwrite the Excel content with only the SharePoint items, thereby eliminating any items added only in the spreadsheet. There is no bidirectional synchronization; this functionality is only one-way from SharePoint and must be refreshed in Excel manually. Also, keep in mind that only the metadata about a document or file will be written into the Excel spreadsheet when a SharePoint library is exported to spreadsheet. The actual file or document itself does not become embedded into the Excel spreadsheet.

ACCESS 2007

SharePoint lists (but not libraries) can now be turned into Access 2007 databases by choosing Open in Access in their Actions menu. This allows SharePoint lists to be configured, edited, and populated using the Access application instead of a web browser or SharePoint Designer 2007. Access replaces Excel as the application for editing SharePoint lists outside SharePoint. However, remember this option is available only for lists and not libraries, so it won't help you with maintaining your SharePoint alternative to file shares.

SharePoint Designer 2007

Although SharePoint Designer 2007 is not bundled with any of the Office editions, it warrants mention in this chapter because it is the only SharePoint-compliant web page editing application on the market at the time of this writing. Born of its predecessor FrontPage 2003, SharePoint Designer 2007 can be used to manipulate and customize libraries to include custom metadata and file formats. SharePoint Designer 2007 is very robust website editing software that requires expertise and experience to operate, the details of which already fill numerous other technical books. And the best news is that it can be downloaded for free (at least at the time of this writing).

The Bottom Line

Understand the features and requirements of Windows SharePoint Services 3.0   WSSv3 offers great versatility and control to document management but also has several prerequisite software and mandatory hardware requirements. The web services are heavily influenced by the web hosting prerequisite software, and storage considerations in the repository can affect content delivery. But overall, the benefits outweigh the extra management required to manage documents in SharePoint instead of file systems.

> **Master It**   WSSv3 is dependent upon which three Microsoft applications?

Consider Windows SharePoint Services 3.0 installation issues and processes   Though a free service, WSSv3 is by no means small. From service accounts to farm topology, several objectives must be planned and documented prior to beginning the installation process. And not just SharePoint, but the IIS 7.5 installation and SQL Server configuration must also be carefully planned.

> **Master It**   You are planning a multiserver SharePoint farm using servers that reside in separate trusting domains throughout your ADS forest. Under what security context will you configure your WSSv3 service accounts?

Understand SharePoint site and document library provisioning   Planning SharePoint logical design encompasses data taxonomy classifications, administrative models, and document management requirements. There is no one correct design for SharePoint; that's what makes it so versatile! Templates for sites and for site objects such as lists and libraries make it easy to enforce consistency, while system-supplied templates can be customized and then saved as custom templates to enhance the look and feel of a WSSv3 environment.

> **Master It**   You have three different groups of SharePoint users who all want exclusive authority over their own content. What are two alternative logical SharePoint designs you could build to accommodate them?

Understand document management and access in Windows SharePoint Services 3.0   WSSv3 has distinct advantages over file systems for managing document versions, approval processes, editing conflicts, metadata, archiving, and more. Single-instance storage guidelines prevent multiple unsynchronized copies of the same file without preventing necessary user access. The challenge is in setting up the initial environment.

Master It You need to create a selective workflow within a document library that houses multiple items. You want the workflow to kick off in response to only one specific item type being created. How would you implement this?

Understand advanced Windows SharePoint Services 3.0 administration In addition to managing individual document libraries and sites, overall administration of the entire SharePoint environment must be dutifully performed in order to provide users with a comfortable, usable document management platform. And though advanced administration usually entails settings that are planned and set early on and rarely changed, they have no less impact on user experience than day-to-day maintenance.

Master It Because of limited storage space on your SQL Server, you need to make sure that SharePoint users do not overpopulate their sites with content. You want to invoke a standard limit to site size that can be overridden on a site-by-site basis when justified. How would you design a solution?

Chapter 29

Server Virtualization with Hyper-V

If there is anything that the IT industry has shown us, it must be that technologies go in and out of fashion but seem to be resurrected when their time comes again. Server virtualization is one of these topics. Mainframes did it 30 years ago, and now virtualization is becoming big in the Windows world. With Windows Server 2008, Microsoft has introduced its own native server virtualization software, called Hyper-V. In Windows Server 2008 R2, Microsoft has upgraded Hyper-V with new possibilities and higher performance. The two versions are mostly compatible, and where relevant we will note the differences.

Virtualization is a huge subject. Typically, server virtualization is a game of big iron: many large multiprocessor servers, loads of memory, storage area networks, Fibre Channel networks, clustering technologies, management software, and so on. In one chapter of a general-purpose book on Windows Server 2008 R2, such as this one, it is impossible to cover all of that. In this chapter, you can expect an introduction on Hyper-V, sufficient to get you to first base and enabling you to build your own small environment using only native Windows software. We address topics such as what server virtualization is and what it's used for, how to install and use Hyper-V, the constituent components of Hyper-V and how they work together, how Hyper-V works with Windows Server Core, and how to manage Hyper-V installations, including Live Migration.

In this chapter, you will learn to:

♦ Determine whether a server can run Hyper-V

♦ Determine when it makes sense to virtualize a server

♦ Decide which technology to use to quickly move a virtual machine between hosts

♦ Advise on a backup strategy

What Is Server Virtualization?

The term *virtualization* is used for a lot of different things nowadays. It is used in association with applications, storage, network, servers, screen presentation, and so on. In this chapter, *virtualization* means the ability to run a full operating system on a software platform in such a way that the OS thinks it is running on a "real" computer. This type of virtualization is called *hardware virtualization* or *server virtualization*. So, why would you want to have that?

Chances are that you are a system administrator, responsible for a number of servers in your organization. If you have been in the business a while, you will have noticed the trend that server power tends to grow faster than the resource hunger of applications.

Nowadays, you buy a low-end server with at least 4GB and probably 8GB or more. Moreover, you buy a 64-bit capable machine. Most such servers are just idling away with 5 percent CPU usage, have multiple gigabytes of free memory, and have I/O bandwidth to spare. Clearly, this is a waste of resources. This is where virtualization helps you out.

With virtualization, you can consolidate many servers on the same hardware. Not only will these servers make more effective use of the hardware, but because you have fewer physical servers, you will use less power and rack space. Even better, with the right software, you can move virtual servers between physical servers easily, giving you a flexible configuration.

To illustrate the principle, Figure 29.1 shows one physical server running Windows Server 2008 with Hyper-V virtualization software and a number of virtual machines (VMs). The machine running Hyper-V is known as the *host*.

FIGURE 29.1

Hyper-V on Windows Server 2008 R2 running multiple VMs

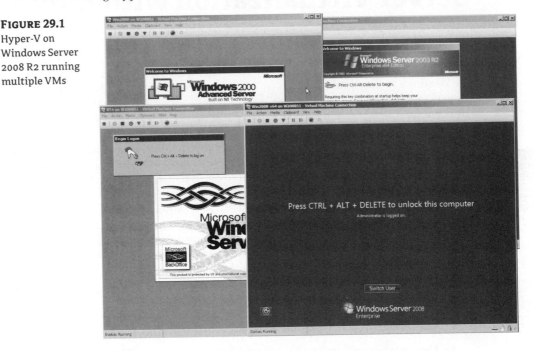

How does this work, generally speaking? Clearly, you cannot have two operating systems accessing the same hardware at the same time. One has to be in charge (that would be the host), and the other (the VM) will need to access that hardware through emulation or some other means. In principle, the same goes for the execution of CPU instructions and even memory access. Some virtualization systems can really emulate a different CPU than their own, but as you can imagine, VMs in such a system have nowhere near native performance. They need to translate each CPU instruction of the emulated system into ones that they can understand themselves. Such systems can still be useful, though, because they can solve problems that cannot be done in any other way. For instance, such systems might emulate an Intel PC on a Macintosh running a PowerPC CPU or the other way around. Another example is CCS64, which you can use to run a trusty old Commodore 64 on your Windows desktop—and quite a bit faster than the original if you want!

Modern dedicated virtualization systems like Hyper-V go out of their way to use system resources as efficiently as possible. They use real memory, and the CPU directly executes the code of the VM—with some exceptions that we will discuss later. The same argument holds for high-performance devices such as network, disk, or video interfaces. Emulation where existing hardware behavior needs to be simulated will cost you performance. Sometimes this is unavoidable, but

Hyper-V takes a different route. It uses its own driver architecture for each type of device to reduce such overhead as much as possible. This design tightly integrates with the computer architecture. From the VM you will see and use the same CPU that the host uses, so cross-CPU emulation is impossible. But that was not the point anyway. The point was to run a VM as fast as possible.

What Use Is Server Virtualization?

Now that you have some idea of what virtualization is about, let's discuss what to use it for. Some important applications are testing, consolidation of servers, and disaster recovery. These all benefit from the high degree of flexibility that virtualization offers.

The technology really got started as a test method. Administrators and consultants in need of hardware for a quick test were only too happy to use an existing machine with virtualization software to run a couple of VMs. Similarly, virtualization is great for giving technology demos. Because of the low-performance requirements for demos, you can run multiple VMs on a powerful laptop and show people how it actually works.

Testing still is a mainstay of virtualization. Larger organizations usually have multiple testing environments for various purposes. With virtualization, you can quickly add and remove VMs as required. Some organizations use a "network in a box": multiple VMs that taken together are a functionally representative copy of (part of) the production network. Whenever a new application comes along or a new infrastructure component needs to be integrated, a "network in a box" is deployed for the project to use.

A lot of administrators have a couple of VMs for their own private use so that they can quickly test and research changes before actually applying them in a production network. For instance, as an Active Directory specialist, you might run four or five DCs plus a Vista workstation in VMs on a normal 4GB desktop that is running Windows Server 2008 with Hyper-V. You might use this to research the fine points of Active Directory replication or the effects of a Group Policy change on the Vista client.

Testing is one thing, but the largest deployments of server virtualization are no doubt in datacenters where lots of servers are consolidated. A virtualized server offers the following advantages:

Conserves resources and saves costs   One host running multiple VMs saves a lot of rack space, electrical power, and cooling capacity. It would not be unreasonable to consolidate 10 or 20 lowly utilized physical machines to one host machine.

Shares hardware   A host offers the same "virtual" hardware to each VM. In other words, all VMs share common hardware. This makes them predictable and makes the maintenance of drivers easy. Deploying VMs is much easier than doing the same for physical machines, mainly because drivers are no longer a factor.

Increases flexibility   The same feature of identical virtual hardware makes for a high degree of flexibility. You can move VMs between hosts for load distribution or maintenance.

Joins legacy operating systems   A lot of organizations will be running a mix of operating systems—not only Windows 2008 but likely also older systems running Windows 2003 or even Windows 2000. Chances are that those older systems don't require much in the way of computing power on modern hardware. This makes them ideal candidates for consolidation. One host will have enough power for many of these *legacy* systems. Legacy consolidation will also benefit from the uniform virtual hardware.

In large environments with large storage area network (SAN) deployments, mirrored datacenters, and similar infrastructure, server virtualization is an asset for disaster recovery. Not only is server consolidation a benefit here, but all virtual machines have the same type of virtual hardware. You will have *no* driver or HAL issues when restarting a virtual machine on a new host, assuming of course that the new VM has the same configuration as the old one.

Each technology has its downside, and virtualization is no exception. Some may impact you more than others, but here are a few:

Increases complexity Virtualization adds a layer of complexity to the existing environment. You now need to know whether a given server is a VM or a physical server, or perhaps a host for VMs. Let's take the example of a SQL Server administrator. Before, he would be responsible for all the SQL Server: software, hardware, and configuration. If SQL Server is virtualized, he needs to depend on the administrators of the host server to keep his VM running. Any impact on the host will also impact the SQL Server VM.

Strains infrastructure A full-blown VM environment will need additional infrastructure: a SAN is mandatory in large environments, as is dedicated management software and a dedicated high-speed IP network.

Can cause large-scale failure If you are not specifically designing for service availability, a host is a single point of failure. If it goes down unexpectedly, for instance because the CPU overheats and shuts down, it will take all running VMs down with it.

Requires special maintenance If you have a library of offline VMs, you will need to do some form of maintenance on those as well, such as applying patches.

Creates unique security issues There are some nonobvious security considerations related to virtualization. For instance, in a SAN-based environment, you will have two additional groups of administrators who can access data in a VM: the administrators responsible for the host machines and the SAN administrators. A SQL Server administrator responsible for a VM may not be aware that those other administrators can in principle access his data at will, assuming the desire and knowledge to do so.

Requires a learning curve When you deploy a new technology, you need to learn it. While you are learning it, you will make mistakes. Some of those will impact your production environment. That's nothing new, but it's still a factor to consider.

Clearly, it's a balancing act. For most organizations (but not all), the advantages will outweigh the downsides. The main point to take away here is that server virtualization has arrived and is here to stay. If your organization has not deployed it yet, chances are that you will soon.

What Do You Need to Get Started with Hyper-V?

Not surprisingly, there are hardware and software requirements for running Hyper-V. In addition, there are some intricate licensing questions involved, which we'll discuss later in this chapter.

HARDWARE REQUIREMENTS

The base requirements for running Hyper-V are quite simple. You need an x64-based CPU, hardware-assisted virtualization, and hardware Data Execution Prevention (DEP). Most, but not all, computers meeting these minimum requirements will run Hyper-V. A common problem is that although these features are offered by the system, they are not enabled in the BIOS. Make sure these features are turned on. If you need to change the DEP or virtualization settings, be aware that a cold boot is required: the computer must be turned completely off. A reset or software reboot is not sufficient. Note that server hardware from 2008 or earlier may need a BIOS upgrade as well.

Both Intel and AMD support DEP on the hardware level with modern processors, but they call it differently. Intel has the XD bit (eXecute Disable), and AMD has the NX bit (No eXecute). Look for that in the BIOS. The situation is a bit different for the virtualization extensions. Intel and AMD both created their own extensions around the same time in 2006. They roughly do the same thing but are incompatible. However, all major server virtualization products including Hyper-V support both the Intel and AMD extensions. One point to be aware of is that some BIOS systems for AMD CPUs refer to AMD-V as "SVM" or "secure virtualization." Also, because of incompatibilities, some early systems featuring AMD-V cannot actually run Hyper-V or can do so only with a specific BIOS version.

If you want to be really sure that the servers you will buy will run Hyper-V, you should check directly with your vendor. They are responsible for testing that Hyper-V actually runs on their hardware. Most large vendors also participate in the "Certified for Windows Server 2008" program, which requires them to test their hardware using Microsoft-standard procedures. After the server passes the test, the vendor can submit the configuration to Microsoft for inclusion on the public catalog. However, not all vendors submit all of their hardware. That's why you should ask them directly. The Microsoft catalog is at http://windowsservercatalog.com. You can specifically search for *Hyper-V compatible systems*.

Let's talk about the specifics now that you know generally what features to look for. There are two things to keep in mind when selecting hardware for virtualization: VMs like a lot of memory, and disk I/O bandwidth is critical. For a low-end testing system dedicated to virtualization, you should probably select something with at least 8GB of memory and a single or dual CPU motherboard with quad-core CPUs.

Get as many disk spindles as you can reasonably afford. Four independent medium-capacity disks will be faster than two large-capacity disks when using multiple VMs. If you have the money for it, invest in high-RPM disks. SATA disks are OK for testing and nondemanding applications. For best performance, SCSI or SAS are better, generally speaking. Avoid a RAID-5 configuration because it is slow on write operations. RAID 0 and RAID 1 combinations are fine for low-end systems. For high-end applications, consider RAID 10. Finally, think about the networking. The general recommendation is to have at least two NICs, one to manage the host and another for the VMs to access the network. If you expect high network throughput or iSCSI connections that require dedicated NICs, you will need even more.

SOFTWARE REQUIREMENTS

Now that you have your hardware sorted, we'll discuss the software side. The first thing to note is that a 64-bit version is required. Of course, this is the only option with Windows 2008 R2, but Windows 2008 also has 32-bit editions. Table 29.1 summarizes the options.

TABLE 29.1:   Windows 2008 Editions and Hyper-V

WINDOWS 2008 EDITION	HAS HYPER-V ROLE
Windows Server 2008 (R2) Standard edition x64	Yes
Windows Server 2008 (R2) Enterprise edition x64	Yes
Windows Server 2008 (R2) Datacenter edition x64	Yes
Microsoft Hyper-V Server 2008 (R2)	Yes
Windows Server 2008, any x86 edition	No
Windows Web Server 2008 (R2)	No
Windows Server 2008 (R2) for Itanium	No

Note the specific edition named Hyper-V Server. This is basically a 64-bit version of Server Core with Hyper-V enabled by default. We will discuss it briefly later in this chapter. Its main benefit over the regular Server Core editions is that it's available as a free download. The remaining editions differ in their failover clustering capabilities and licensing models. Briefly, Standard comes with one license for a Windows-based VM and has no clustering option. Enterprise has four VM licenses and allows clustering. Datacenter is licensed per physical CPU and allows unlimited VMs with clustering.

> **WINDOWS SERVER 2008 VERSIONS WITHOUT HYPER-V**
>
> As you can see from Table 29.1, not all editions of Windows 2008 R2 can run Hyper-V. Although that is clear enough, the situation was confused with its predecessor Windows 2008. It has Standard edition, Enterprise edition, and Datacenter editions with Hyper-V, and once again without Hyper-V at a minimal price difference. The reason for that was never really clear, but it is probably related to market regulation efforts. If you are buying Windows 2008, make sure you get the one with Hyper-V.

From the table it's clear that Hyper-V is a server component. Microsoft will not release a version of Hyper-V for a client OS such as Windows 7, Vista, or XP. Also, Windows 2008 is the first server version to support Hyper-V. It will not be implemented for earlier releases of the Windows operating system. If you want to run server virtualization on any of these other platforms, you need to look at other products in the market. Finally, if you're running Itanium servers (IA64), you should know that when Hyper-V was released, it did not run on IA64, and it probably never will.

The Hyper-V Feature Set

We'll now cover the functionality that Hyper-V offers in Windows Server 2008 R2. Since the first version in Windows Server 2008 SP1 (remember, there never was a SP0), there have been some quiet changes in certain limits, such as the number of supported processor cores or number of virtual machines. Those limits may well change again, so check the Microsoft site for the current feature set. For now, see Table 29.2.

TABLE 29.2: Windows 2008 R2 Hyper-V Feature List

FEATURE	WINDOWS HYPER-V SERVER, STANDARD EDITION	ENTERPRISE EDITION, DATACENTER EDITION
x86 VM	Yes	Yes
x64 VM	Yes	Yes
IA64 VM	No	No
Maximum number of VMs	384	384
Maximum host memory	32GB	1TB
Maximum host processors	64 cores	64 cores
Maximum VM memory	32GB	64GB
Hot-add VM memory	No	No
Maximum VM processors	4 per VM	4 per VM
Hot-add VM processor	No	No
IDE adapters	2	2
Maximum IDE devices	4	4
SCSI adapters	4	4
Maximum SCSI devices	255	255
Hot-add hard disk	Yes	Yes
Virtual networks	Unlimited	Unlimited
Maximum number of VM network cards	8	8
Hot-add virtual NIC	No	No
Failover clustering support	No*	Yes
Live Migration	No**	Yes

* Hyper-V Server R2 does support clustering and Live Migration.
** Live Migration is not included with Windows 2008. It's new with R2.

There is not much difference between the editions until you really start to scale up in memory or require high availability using the various clustering options. Most of these limits are hard limits, in the sense that they cannot be exceeded. The exception is the maximum number of VMs per host. This is a soft limit, determined by the Microsoft testing labs. Perhaps the most stringent limit here is the maximum number of virtual processors, which translates to the number of physical CPU cores actually used. Currently, you cannot have a VM with more than four virtual CPUs, which means that your maximum CPU power is limited. On the other hand, if you have an application that really uses all your CPUs to the maximum, then it's probably not a great candidate for virtualization anyway. One notable missing feature is USB support, which would be great for lab situations. Microsoft's point of view is that Hyper-V is a server role where USB is not required, so there is little chance of ever having this feature added. Another feature set that is likely to change is the type of devices that support the ability for adding or removal from a running VM. Currently, this works only with virtual hard disks. It would certainly be nice to be able to do the same thing for memory, NICs, and CPU. Microsoft is planning this for future releases.

The final two items in the list are failover clustering support and Live Migration. Briefly, *failover clustering* is the ability to move a running application (such as a virtual machine!) from one server to another, either on-demand or after a detected hardware or failure. Shared storage between the servers is required, using Fibre Channel or iSCSI connections. Live Migration builds on failover clustering to move VMs between hosts with subsecond downtime. The point of this feature is that online users of the VM won't even know that the move occurred. With Live Migration, you can build a very flexible virtualization farm. We will walk you through how to set up Live Migration in the "Moving VMs: Quick Migration and Live Migration" section.

Installing the Host with a Virtual Machine

This book aims to be a practical resource for you. Although some theory is essential to fully understand Hyper-V, we can leave that for later. In this walk-through, you will learn how to install Hyper-V on Windows Server 2008, how to get a VM going, and how to connect to its console. Along the way, you will pick up practical details dealing with Hyper-V.

To get started, you need the following:

◆ You need Hyper-V capable hardware. Remember, VMs like memory and lots of disk I/O. One NIC is required; two would be nice.

◆ You need a version of Windows 2008 or 2008 R2 that supports Hyper-V. If you are using Windows 2008, make sure to install SP2 or newer first.

◆ An ISO file with your Windows OS of choice will come in handy but is not strictly required.

◆ You need IP addresses to use for the host and the VM.

WHY YOU SHOULD AVOID WINDOWS SERVER 2008 SP1

The first version of Windows Server 2008 has the Hyper-V role but in a beta version. Don't use it! Although there have been interim updates to get the Hyper-V version up to 1.0, your best option is to simply install SP2 for Windows Server 2008, which includes many additional fixes. Of course, Windows Server 2008 R2 has no such problems since it includes the production version of Hyper-V 2.0.

Installing and Configuring Hyper-V

Since you have gotten this far in the book, you know how to install a server, join it to a domain, and so on. We will skip the details for the base installation. Table 29.3 shows the suggested configuration for a test setup. Feel free to vary the instructions as you see fit. This walk-through uses Windows 2008 R2, but there is hardly any difference if you use Windows 2008.

TABLE 29.3:   Hyper-V Host System

SETTING	CONFIGURATION
Internal memory	8GB; 4GB is the practical minimum.
Hard disks	2×200GB or more. One disk is acceptable for a test system, but expect low performance.
Partitions	Disk 1: System on C. Disk 2: Reserved for Hyper-V on E.
Network	2×1Gbit highly recommended. One NIC acceptable for test.
Operating system	Hyper-V enabled editions of Windows 2008 R2 or Windows 2008 SP2.
Installation type	Full GUI to follow the examples; Server Core is discussed later.
Hostname	bf5 to follow the examples; anything you like is fine.
IP configuration	Address: 192.168.1.54/24. Gateway: 192.168.1.1. DNS: 192.168.1.51.
Active Directory	Domain-joined recommended for production. Workgroup is workable for testing, although remote management is not possible because it requires Active Directory.

Just about the only thing you need to decide before you install the Hyper-V role is which NIC to use for managing the Hyper-V host. The idea is to have at least two NICs in the host, although you can do with one if you really must. Expect no performance miracles in that case. With two NICs available, dedicate one to managing the host and the second for VM network traffic. To make this obvious, one trick is the rename the network connections, as shown in Figure 29.2.

Let's start with the installation of the Hyper-V role:

1. Install the server using the parameters in Table 29.3 for the version, server name, IP configuration, and so on. Make sure to have dedicated disks or partitions for Hyper-V data.

2. Join the computer to the domain if you want to follow some of the later examples. The domain bigfirm.com is used throughout this book.

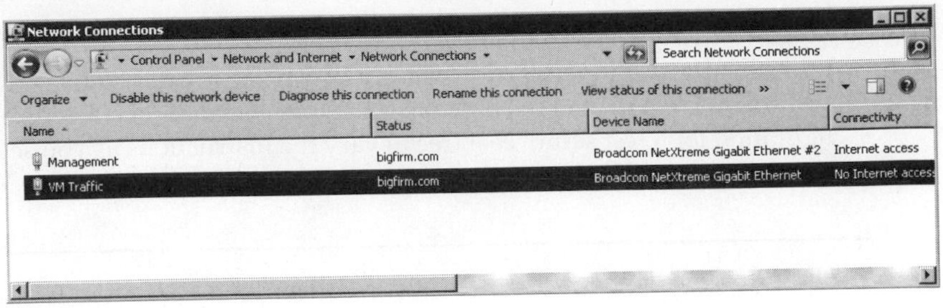

FIGURE 29.2
Renaming the network connections to reflect their role in the Hyper-V host

After you install the Hyper-V host server, you are ready to install the Hyper-V role. You might want to do this using a console session and avoid Remote Desktop. During the installation, the network connection will be broken once or twice because of upgraded network components.

3. Log on to the console on the host. At this time, do not use an RDP session, but use the physical console.

4. Open Server Manager, as shown in Figure 29.3. Click Add Roles, and select the Hyper-V role. As you can see, this is a clean server without any additional roles. This is the best practice for a Hyper-V host. Any other functionality should go to the VMs. In fact, the licensing structure for VMs stipulates that you do not use the host for anything but Hyper-V. We discuss the details later.

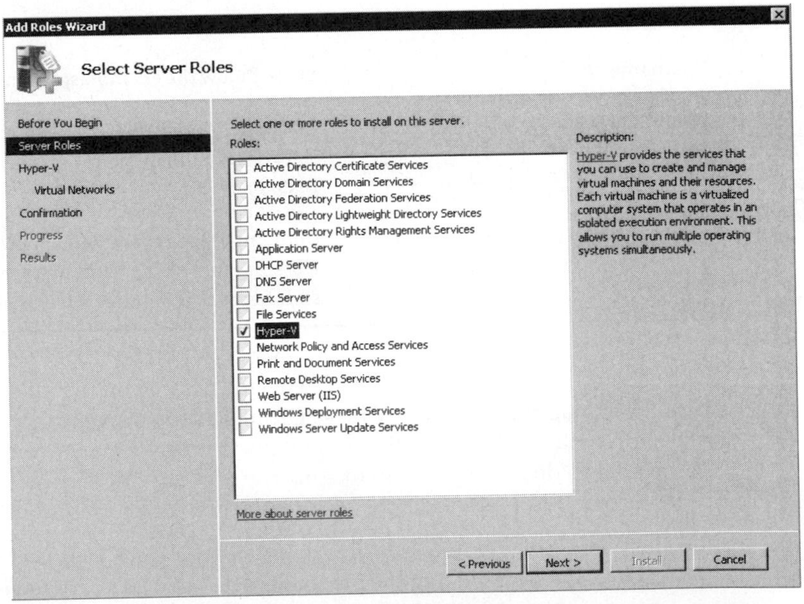

FIGURE 29.3
Adding the Hyper-V role using Server Manager

5. Click Next to start the Hyper-V role wizard, and read the introduction to Hyper-V if you like.

6. Click Next for the NIC selection screen, as shown in Figure 29.4. This requires you to select a NIC for a virtual network. You will find the details later in this chapter, but briefly, a virtual network is a Hyper-V software network switch. For each NIC that you select here, one such switch will be created. If you have two NICs or more, you should leave one blank. An unselected NIC will not have a switch associated with it and can be used to manage the host. If you have only one NIC, select it. If you don't select any NIC, your VMs have no easy way to communicate with the outside world, although you could correct this later. Because we remembered to give sensible names to the network connections, it's now easy to select the one we will use for VM network traffic.

FIGURE 29.4
Select one NIC to
use for VM traffic.
The unselected NIC
is used to manage
the Hyper-V host.

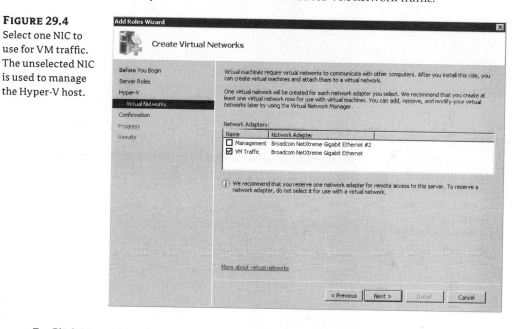

7. Click Next. A confirmation screen appears telling you that a reboot might be required. In fact, count on it.

8. Click Install. This should not take longer than a minute. After it's done, it tells you again that a reboot is needed, as shown in Figure 29.5.

9. Click Close. A dialog box offers to reboot the machine for you. Click Yes to accept its offer. The machine will reboot.

10. When it comes back, log on using an Administrator account. After the desktop initializes, the configuration process will resume. Give it some time to do its job and finalize the installation (Figure 29.6).

Let's take a look at what you've got now. Start the Hyper-V Manager from Administrative Tools. We have a console to administer the Hyper-V host setting with the usual layout, as shown in Figure 29.7. The left pane holds the Hyper-V host service you want to manage. Shown is the current server bf5, but you can have more than one server listed. Later, when we discuss a Server Core setup, you will add that server here.

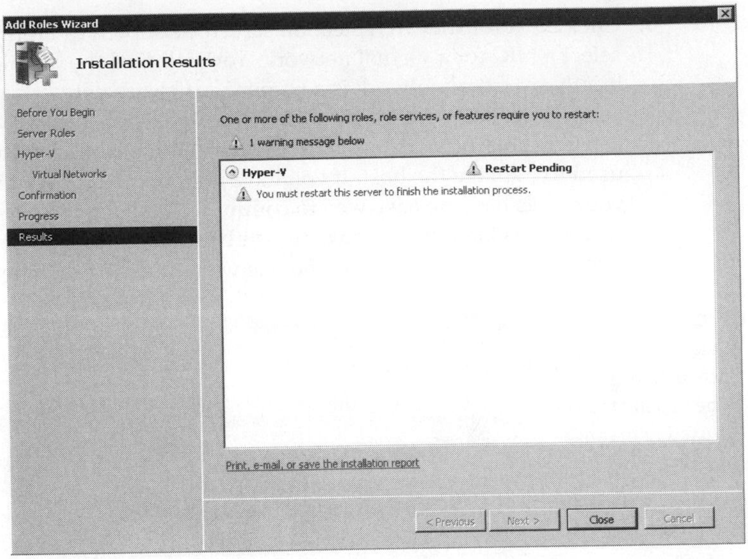

FIGURE 29.5
The final step of
the wizard tells
you that all is fine
and that a reboot
is required.

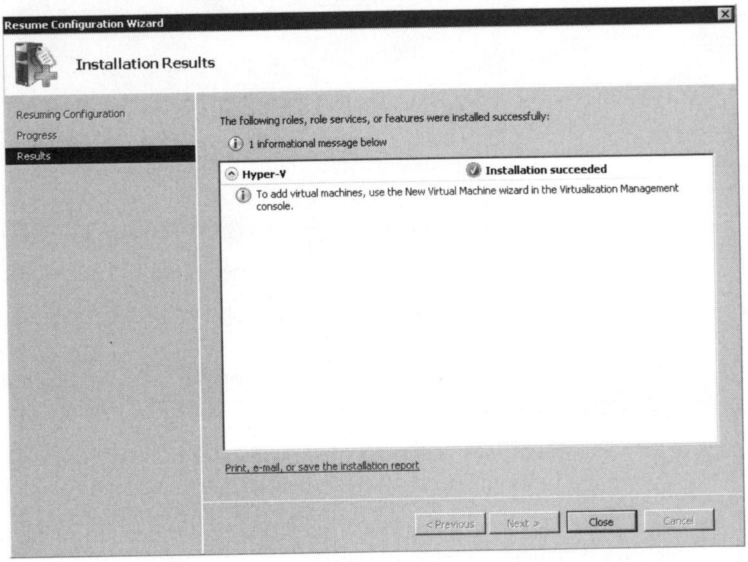

FIGURE 29.6
After the reboot
and logging on,
the Hyper-V instal-
lation wizard
finalizes the instal-
lation. After this,
Hyper-V is ready
for use.

The middle pane has three regions:

Virtual Machines   The list of VMs on this host with some relevant parameters such as its
current state (running, off, saved, and so on).

Snapshots   Briefly, these are point-in-time disk images, including memory and CPU states.
You create a snapshot of a server if you want to be able to roll back to such an image. We will
discuss this extensively later in the chapter.

Details   This contains extra information on the currently selected VM—if any.

FIGURE 29.7
The Hyper-V management console

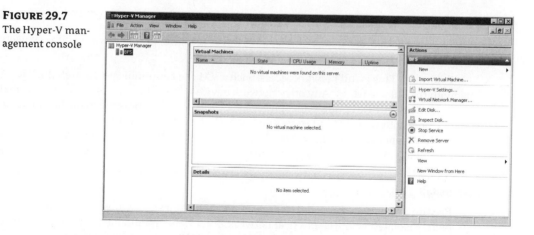

The rightmost Actions pane is the most interesting for now. It allows you to manage various aspects of the Hyper-V setup. Some are pretty obvious, such as stopping or starting the Hyper-V Virtual Machine Management Service or removing the current server from the console. Others such as the Network Manager, Edit Disk, and Inspect Disk are not so obvious if you are new to the virtualization game. Before we go on with configuring Hyper-V, we'll take a step back and discuss virtual disks and virtual networks.

VIRTUAL DISKS: THE SHORT VERSION

When you create a virtual machine, you assign virtual devices for network, video, and so on. Your VM also needs a virtual disk, of course. The question is, what disk? The physical disks are in use by the host! The solution is simple and obvious. because we are virtualizing and emulating already, use a file instead and present that to the VM as a disk. So, a virtual disk is nothing more than a very large file.

In fact, you can have multiple flavors. For test purposes, use a dynamically expanding disk. A virtual disk in this format will allocate the physical disk space it needs, and no more. For instance, you might allocate 127GB for a Windows 2008 Server VM, which only uses less than 10GB after a basic install. Every time the VM needs more disk space, the file is expanded. The expanding virtual disk makes best use of the available disk room on the host. But as you can imagine, there is a performance cost involved when an expansion is needed, and you run the risk of fragmentation. Also, a clear disadvantage is that you may run out of disk space on the host when dynamic virtual disk expands beyond available room. When that happens, all VMs are frozen by Hyper-V, and the event log turns red.

To get rid of overhead, you can also choose to use a fixed disk size. The full size of the virtual disk will be allocated when the disk is created. This is the recommended format for most production loads. The third flavor is a pass-through disk, where you assign a physical disk for dedicated use by a VM. This is possible when this disk is not used by the host. Pass-through disks are useful to connect a VM directly to a SAN or to an iSCSI target. Generally speaking, you will only use a pass-through disk in clustering scenarios and similar. If you don't need them, stick with normal virtual disks and let the host mount disks on the SAN or iSCSI target.

In fact, there is one more flavor: you can have a virtual floppy disk. Interestingly, you do not have the option to connect a VM to a physical floppy drive—not that you are likely to have one.

VIRTUAL NETWORKS: THE SHORT VERSION

Early on in the server virtualization game, it was recognized that it would be very useful to have multiple types of network connections for VMs:

External This is full network access. Such a VM can communicate through the NIC of the host with the outside world. Any other network device will see the VM as if it were a normal computer. The only exception is the (physical) network switch connected to the host. This switch sees one host with two MAC addresses and two IP addresses. Be aware that some secure network environments may not allow this. The symptom would be that your VM can talk to your host but not to any other machine on the network even though you have specified external access.

Internal This is access between the host and VM only. This is suitable for most test installations.

Private VMs are connected to each other but cannot see the host. Effectively, they are completely isolated from the physical network. Again, this is suitable for testing. For instance, when you test the DHCP features of Windows 2008, you would not want to try this on the physical network. In some companies, that could get you fired! When in doubt, a private network is the safest option.

Later, this concept was expanded from virtual NICs to virtual switches with the same type of behavior. You will not be surprised to learn that Hyper-V implements them. Virtual switches are 100 percent software but are not visible outside of a host and its VMs since they are implemented in software. They deliver high-speed connections between VMs. On a virtual switch, you "plug in" virtualized NICs of VMs. A useful feature of virtual switches is that you can change their scopes. You might start a switch as internal and connect it to a physical NIC later.

Using virtual switches, you can generate quite complicated networks inside the host. Clearly, this is most useful in test situations; in production scenarios, all VMs should be able to talk to the physical network. Using three virtual switches, you could, for instance, build a classic DMZ setup: one switch for the outside interface connected to a physical NIC, one switch for the DMZ hosts, and one switch for the internal LAN.

CONFIGURING THE HYPER-V HOST

With those asides out of the way, we can return to configuring the Hyper-V service in the right Actions pane of the Hyper-V management console. The New Wizard and the Import Virtual Machine Wizard deal with creating VMs and virtual disks, so we'll leave that for the next section.

The Hyper-V Settings dialog box shown in Figure 29.8 allows you to set some parameters for Hyper-V. Not many, actually. Hyper-V was really designed to run out of the box with minimal tuning.

Each parameter shows its current setting. The two most important parameters are the default paths for virtual hard disks and for virtual machine configurations. In this example, they have been changed to point to a folder on E, a nonsystem partition and preferably a dedicated drive. In the Hyper-V philosophy, the files for virtual disks are separate from virtual machine settings. Make sure you set them to something sensible and different from each other. By default they end up somewhere in your local profile. Microsoft should probably have made these mandatory inputs during the Hyper-V setup.

The remaining settings are all related to the way you use Hyper-V and access the VMs:

Keyboard Specify how Windows special keys should behave in the VM console.

Mouse Release Key   Specify what keyboard combination should be used to release input focus from a VM console.

User Credentials   Specify what user ID should be used to access a VM console. By default, this is the currently logged on user. If you deselect this option, you will be required to supply a user ID and password when connecting to a VM console. These credentials can be cached, if you choose to do so.

Delete Saved Credentials   If you have ever saved credentials, this dialog box has a button that will clear them.

Reset Check Boxes   At various points in the Hyper-V console you can select boxes indicating that you never want to see a particular dialog box again. This option brings them all back.

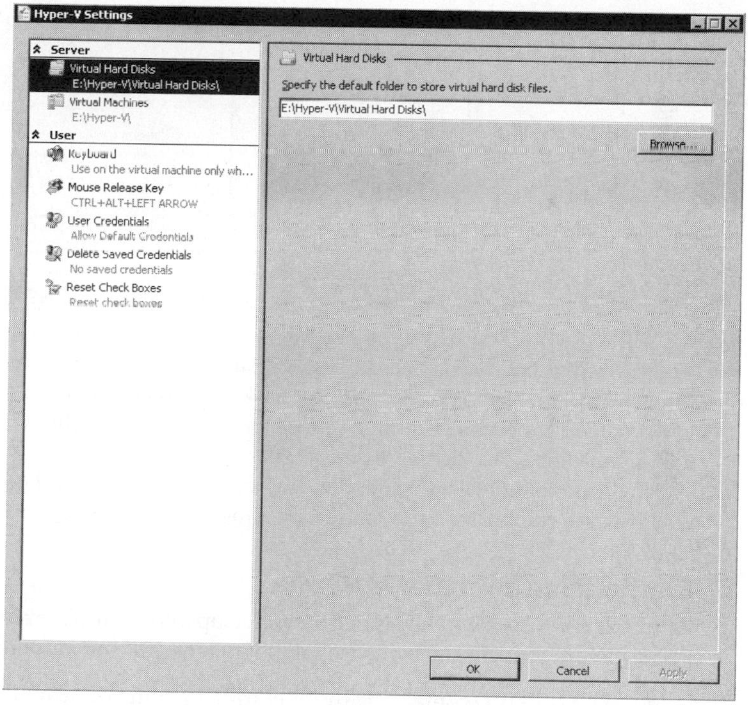

FIGURE 29.8
The Hyper-V Settings dialog box. Set the default folders for virtual hard disks and VMs before you do anything else.

Continuing the overview of the Actions pane, we have three more wizards to discuss briefly. Virtual Network Manager is the central management point for virtual switches (or *networks*, as Hyper-V prefers to call them). Using this wizard, you view, create, and edit networks. Networks of type External can be assigned to physical NICs. In this example, we used the Hyper-V setup wizard to assign one NIC to the VMs, as shown in Figure 29.9. Be default, the corresponding virtual switch is set to External. Also, the host can access this switch, meaning that traffic between the VMs and their host can use this internal virtual switch.

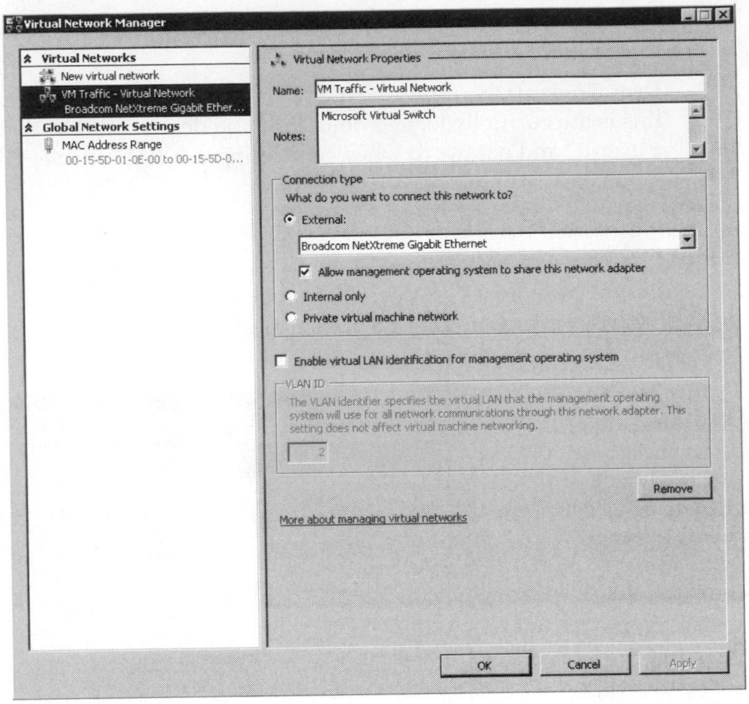

FIGURE 29.9

The virtual network manager after setup. The virtual switch called VM Traffic is currently the only one available for VMs.

Surprisingly perhaps, the Edit Disk Wizard cannot be used to create virtual disk. That activity is reserved for the New Wizard. The Edit Disk Wizard does allow you to change a disk from dynamic to fixed, to expand its size, and to remove blank space from the virtual disk file. The Inspect Disk dialog box inspects a virtual disk for consistency.

Now that you have an understanding of how to install and configure the Hyper-V service, we'll turn to the heart of the matter: creating and managing virtual machines.

Configuring a Virtual Machine

At this point, you have the Hyper-V service up and running and are ready to start configuring a VM. Before you get started, check that you have all that you need:

◆ A CD or DVD containing the operating system you want to install. A good alternative would be to use an ISO image of this CD/DVD, because an ISO image works much faster and is more convenient. In this example, we'll use an ISO file for Windows Server 2008 R2. The server bf5 has been set up with a share hosting the ISO files: \\bf5\ISO.

◆ A name for the new server.

◆ An idea on which network (External, Internal, or Private) you want to use the VM, and an IP address to go with it.

◆ How much memory to use. Make sure you are not too conservative with this. If the VM needs to start swapping its memory, it puts a heavy load on the disk I/O capacity of the host—capacity that would be better used to accommodate more VMs. For a base install or Windows Server 2008 R2, use 1GB.

◆ The virtual disk type to use: dynamic for testing or fixed for production purposes.

Conceptually, it takes two steps to create a VM from scratch. First you configure the virtual hardware of the VM, and then you boot the VM and start installing the operating system. The New Wizard takes care of configuring the VM.

1. Open the Hyper-V management console, and select New ➢ New Virtual Machine. Figure 29.10 shows the first screen of the wizard, telling you briefly what a VM is for. Use the check box to skip this screen in the future. At this point, you could even use Finish to create a VM with the default settings, but that's not a good idea. Generally, no two VMs are the same.

FIGURE 29.10
The start of the VM creation wizard. Select the check box to never see this first screen again.

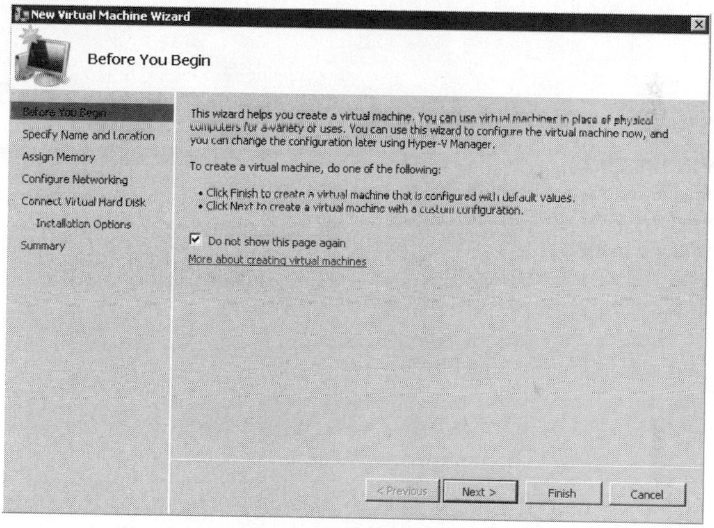

2. Enter the name for the VM, as shown in Figure 29.11. Note that this is the friendly name used in the management console, not the actual hostname. Of course, it would make sense to make those names (almost) the same. To follow the example, set the name to bf10. By default, this name will also be used for its first virtual disk. To be clear, bf10 is not the hostname of the VM, although it makes good sense to keep the VM name and its hostname the same. If you want the configuration of the VM in a nondefault place, select the check box and the path you want. Remember, you should have set the default while configuring the host.

3. Click Next. The Assign Memory page asks you to specify the amount of memory for the VM. Specify 1024MB, as shown in Figure 29.12, as a minimum for a Windows Server 2008 R2 VM. Make sure to use enough memory. If the OS is too low on memory, it will start swapping it to disk and slowing down other VMs using the same disk. This is a general point to keep in mind: disk I/O is a precious resource on a virtualization host. Use it wisely.

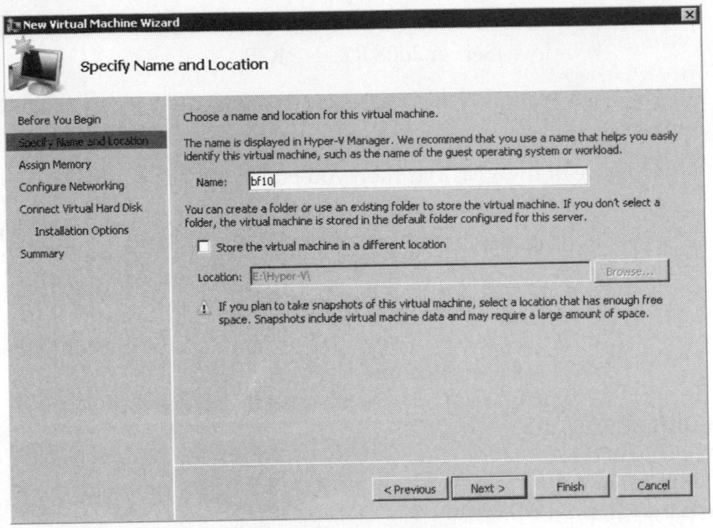

FIGURE 29.11
Give the new
VM its name.

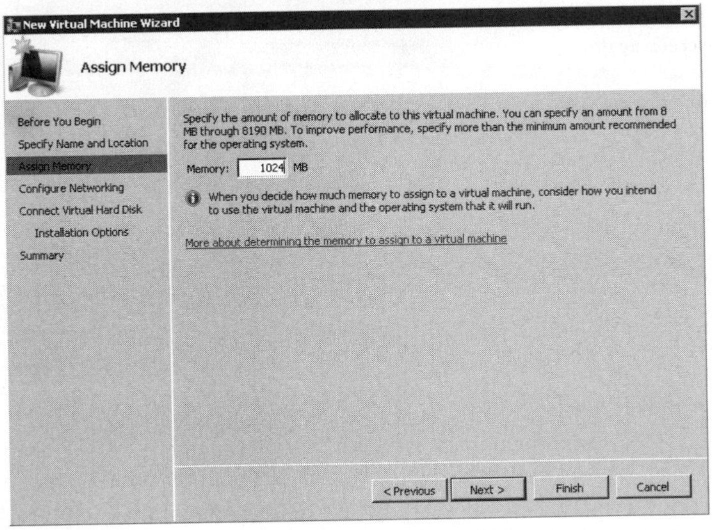

FIGURE 29.12
Specify enough
memory for the OS
you will install.

4. Click Next. The Configure Networking page shown in Figure 29.13 is used to specify the virtual switch to use. The default is Not Connected, which is a safe but not very useful option. Select the VM Traffic virtual switch to connect to. Remember, this switch is external and allows the VM to talk to the outside world directly.

5. Click Next for the Connect Virtual Hard Disk page shown in Figure 29.14. Here you will create a new virtual disk or assign an existing one. The defaults are good for a test setup: a new virtual disk in the default location, 127GB in size. Although the dialog box does not show it, this disk will be dynamic. If you want a fixed size disk, you must build one before you create the VM or attach it afterward. The wizard proposes a default name for the virtual disk. Accept it if you like it.

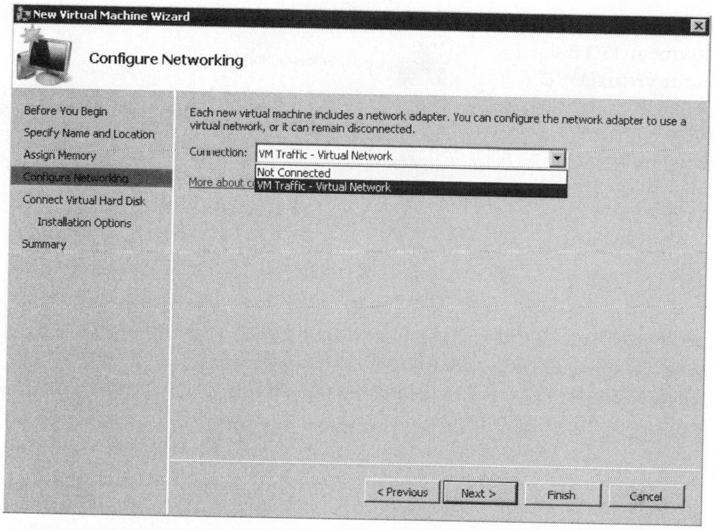

FIGURE 29.13
Connect the VM to the outside world using an externally connected virtual switch.

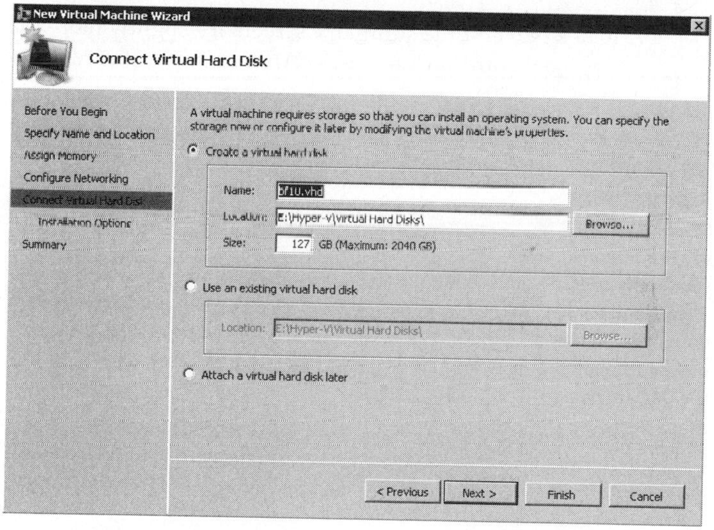

FIGURE 29.14
The new virtual disk is dynamic, which means that its real-world size is roughly as large as the data it contains, much less than 127GB usually.

6. Click Next for the final options. This page basically allows you to set the initial installation media: a physical or virtual (ISO) CD/DVD, a virtual floppy disk, or something from the network. In this example, you install using an ISO file. Use the radio button "Install an operating system from a boot CD/DVD-ROM" to get started. Here you see one of the great conveniences of the VM world: you can use ISO files directly, as shown in Figure 29.15. Browse to the spot where you have stored the ISO for Windows 2008 R2. Of course, if you only have the physical DVD, you can use that as well.

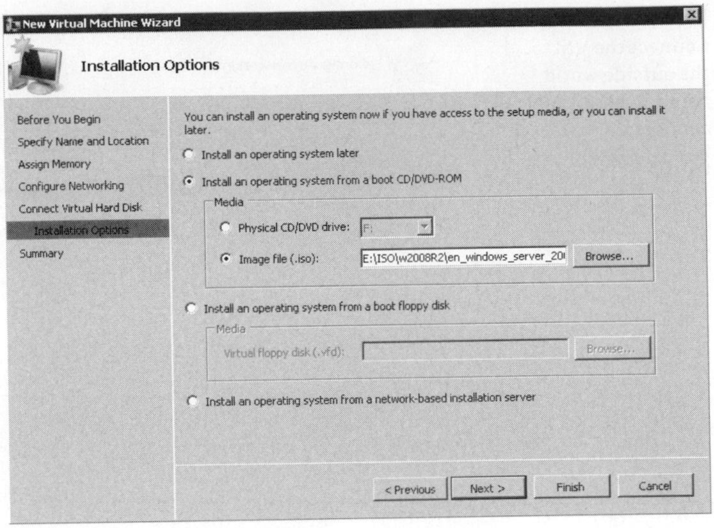

FIGURE 29.15
Mount an ISO file in the virtual DVD player of the VM. When starting the VM, it will boot from it.

7. Click Next for the summary screen. It's slightly more than just a summary. Click Finish to let the wizard start working. After a couple of seconds, you will have a new VM.

In the Hyper-V Manager, you will now have your first VM. Select this VM, and the Actions pane is extended to display specific options for the VM (named bf10), as shown in Figure 29.16.

FIGURE 29.16
Select a VM to see the actions that apply to it. This menu varies, depending on the power state of the VM among other things.

Click the Settings menu to take a look at the VM configuration, as shown in Figure 29.17. This is one dialog box you will see a lot in the future. There is no point in covering all items here exhaustively, but we'll talk about the most important ones. The left pane has two sections, Hardware and Management.

FIGURE 29.17

Managing all VM parameters from the Settings dialog box

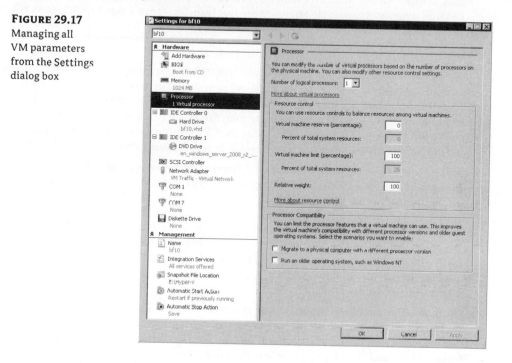

The Hardware section manages all virtual hardware. The topmost entry is for the Add Hardware Wizard, although the choices are limited. You can add a SCSI controller that you can use in turn to add virtual SCSI drives. You can have up to four SCSI controllers, with 255 devices each; that should be enough. One thing to note here: you cannot boot from a virtual SCSI disk. It must be an IDE disk. However, because of the way Hyper-V implements the virtual IDE and SCSI adapters, there is no performance penalty for using IDE.

The second entry is BIOS. Contrary to some other virtualization software, there is no direct access to the BIOS screen from the VM console. If you boot the VM from the console, there is no function key to get you to a BIOS menu. Here you see again the idea that the hypervisor should run mostly out of the box with little tuning. The BIOS entry in the VM settings allows you to select the order of boot devices: disk, CD/DVD, floppy, or network. And for some reason, you can also tell the VM to turn Num Lock on or off on boot.

The Memory entry specifies the amount of memory available to the VM, as you have seen before. The Processor entry is more interesting. You can specify the number of logical processors configured for this particular VM. On boot, the VM will see that number of processors. Of course, they are not by default reserved to that particular VM. The hypervisor is the sole owner of the processors and decides which VM gets how much time. The host itself is under the control of the hypervisor in this aspect. To say this another way, you can have many more virtual CPUs in total than the number of real CPU cores.

DO NOT GIVE A WINDOWS 2003 VM MORE THAN TWO CPUS

Although Hyper-V allows you to assign up to four logical CPUs to a VM, this is not always a good idea. It turns out that Windows 2003 may react badly when presented with three or four virtual CPUs on Hyper-V. Anyway, the Microsoft product team for Hyper-V supports Windows 2003 with one or two CPUs only.

Using the "Resource control" settings, you specify what percentage of the selected processors should be reserved for this VM. The grayed-out boxes tell you how much this is in terms of the full host capacity. This is a lower limit that is always available. The upper limit is set by the virtual machine limit. The VM will never use more than this particular percentage. That feature is very useful to limit misbehaving applications that use CPU resources for no good reason.

At the bottom are two check boxes to tweak processor functionality:

Migrate to a physical computer with a different processor version   This is used in a situation where you have clustered machines with slightly different physical CPUs. Before, such a configuration would block features such as Live Migration and Quick Migration where you move online VMs between hosts. Select the box to improve your chances. Tests show that compatibility between CPUs of the same family is quite good, but beyond that it doesn't really help. You will certainly not be able to do online moves between AMD and Intel systems. The feature works by disabling certain CPU instructions whose functionality varies between processors, such as SSE3, SSE4, 3dNow!, and others. The price you pay is potential lower performance, depending on your workload.

Run an older operation system, such as Windows NT   This is required to run OSs that were built before the year 2000, roughly speaking. It alters the behavior of some processor instructions, notably CPUID. In the Windows 2008 version of Hyper-V, this check box was obscurely called "Limit processor functionality." Not something you would think of using in case of trouble.

The next items on the list are the two IDE controllers. You cannot delete them. The first IDE controller is used for the virtual hard disk that you configured. As usual, you can have two IDE devices per controller. The second IDE controller has the CD/DVD drive. Using this setting you can change the configuration while the VM is running. Why is that useful? Well, you can mount other ISO files or connect to a physical CD/DVD drive if you want. There also is a default SCSI controller if you're running Windows 2008 R2, but it has no devices connected.

Next are the network adapter, the COM ports, and the floppy drive. Most notable about the network adapter is that you can change its binding while the VM is running. This is equivalent to pulling the cable from a physical NIC and connecting it to another switch. One use for it is to install the operating system, patch it on Windows Update, and then connect it to an internal switch for testing. The COM ports are not quite what they seem. The do *not* connect to any physical COM port your server may have. Instead, they can connect only to a named pipe, which in turn must have a process behind it to talk to. Similarly for the floppy drive, it does not connect to a physical drive, but only to a file image. A virtual floppy is created using the New Wizard; then select Floppy Disk.

Continuing the discussion of the left pane, we come to the Management section. Normally you don't need to change any settings here, since the defaults are sensible. You can change the name of the VM here, configure the Integration Services components, specify the snapshot file location (discussed later when we fully discuss virtual disks), and decide what should happen when the host starts up or shuts down. Of these settings, the Integration Services setting deserves extra discussion.

You can only configure the Integration Services setting from the host. You have five options to choose from. All of them are enabled by default, and again, the defaults should be good for most situations:

Operating System Shutdown   This allows the host to signal to the VM that it should start the regular shutdown procedure right now, as opposed to just turning off. This is a neat trick, because this allows you to shut down the host, which in turn will cleanly shut down all the VMs for you. Clearly, this works only when this option is enabled and for VMs that actually have Integration Services installed.

Time Synchronization   As you probably know, this option is critical in an Active Directory domain, because Kerberos authentication relies on accurate timekeeping. If the host is a member of the same Active Directory forest as its VMs, you can make the host responsible for timekeeping of the VMs; this is the default. If the time of the host is not managed in any way, you must deselect this setting to allow the VM to manage its own time source.

Data Exchange   With this option, it's possible for the host and VM to exchange data through selected registry keys.

Heartbeat   This is used by the host to keep track of the state of the VM. When heartbeats stop coming, the host signals that the VM is in trouble.

Backup (volume snapshot)   This important setting enables Volume Shadow Copy Services (VSS) integration for the VM. In other words, a backup application on the host can signal the VM that it is going to be part of a backup and should make sure all its applications are ready for it.

🌐 Real World Scenario

WHY ACCURATE TIMEKEEPING IS IMPORTANT

Accurate timekeeping is not just important for Kerberos. Many applications depend on good time administration to work reliably and may act strangely if time is reset into the past. If you are lucky, the application just completely stops working when its internal administration is corrupted. Jumps into the future are usually fine. After all, that is not really different from turning a server off and turning it on a year from now. The trouble starts when you set the time back to the present after a jump into the future.

To illustrate what might go wrong, consider a real-world example of a VM running an Active Directory domain controller (DC). It is running on a host that is not joined to a domain. Instead, it takes its time from a network component, a centrally located switch. During maintenance, the switch gets a new firmware update and accidentally sets the time a year ahead. The host picks this up and also sets its time a year ahead. Then the virtual DC does the same. At that point, it stops replicating with its peers because Kerberos authentication is broken.

Another problem is that the internal Active Directory administration for deleted objects goes badly wrong if the time jumps ahead too far. Some objects will be permanently deleted; others will not. The result is a badly corrupted forest. The list goes on and on, if you start thinking about it.

Bottom line: in a production environment, make really sure to have a correct time synchronization configuration, especially for VMs.

We are not done discussing the Actions pane in Figure 29.16 yet. With a VM selected, you have these additional options:

Connect   Used to start the virtual console.

Settings   To configure the VM, as discussed.

Start   To boot the VM. Depending on the state of the VM, you will have more options here such as Shutdown and others.

Snapshot   To create a point-in-time image of the VM.

Export   To save the entire VM, including configuration and virtual hardware.

Rename   To give the VM another name.

Delete   To remove the VM configuration, but not its virtual hard disks.

Actually, the exact items in the Actions pane vary with the power state of the VM. The previous assumes that the VM is still turned off. When a VM is running, you have additional items to turn the VM off, reset, shut down, and so on.

Installing a Virtual Machine

With the VM configured, the hard part is done. The next step is to install the operating system in the VM. When you are used to dealing with physical servers, the details of installing in a VM are a bit different.

The first question is how to connect to the console of the VM. After all, you want to see what is going on. To do that, open Hyper-V Manager, select the VM (bf10) you want to connect to, and click Connect in the lower-right corner. A virtual console opens, as shown in Figure 29.18. Another way to do this is to double-click the thumbnail at the bottom.

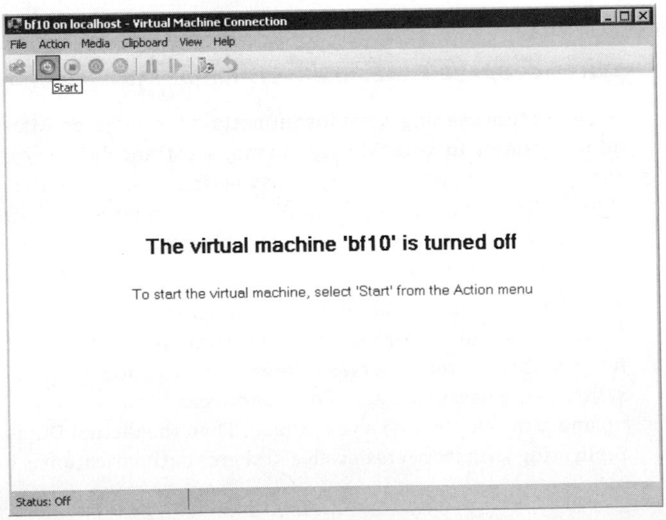

FIGURE 29.18
Connecting to a
VM shows you
its console

The virtual console has a menu bar and a button bar. Most of the functions have duplicates in the Hyper-V management console that you are already familiar with. The black screen telling you that the VM named bf10 is turned off is your virtual screen. When you boot the VM, this will show you the familiar messages of Windows progressing from boot to full GUI. Before you go ahead and boot the VM, there is something you need to be aware of. It's clear how the screen works, but what about the keyboard and mouse?

The console can "capture" the keyboard and mouse. You do so by clicking the virtual screen. When captured, all input from keyboard and mouse are sent to the VM. Initially, you cannot release control from the VM by just moving the mouse. You press the key sequence Ctrl+Alt+left arrow for release. In a fully running VM with Integration Services installed, the experience is much better: you can move the mouse out of the virtual screen onto the desktop, and when that happens, the host has control of the keyboard and mouse again. There is one special case: the Ctrl+Alt+Del sequence is special. Even when the VM has control, the host will process it. To send the Ctrl+Alt+Del sequence to a VM, you can either press Ctrl+Alt+End or use the console menu Action (Ctrl+Alt+Delete).

THE VIRTUAL CONSOLE UNDER THE HOOD

The Hyper-V virtual console uses the Remote Desktop Protocol (RDP) to talk to the VM, the same protocol that is used for Remote Desktop Services. The difference is that it does not use the default RDP port but instead uses TCP port 2179. When you start the virtual console from the Hyper-V Manager, it starts a client application called vmconnect.exe, located in %programfiles%\hyper-v. This application is similar to the Remote Desktop Client but additionally allows you to select the VM you want to connect to. The Virtual Machine Management Service is the listening service. When you connect to it using vmconnect.exe, it tells the client which VMs are available and makes sure the RDP traffic goes to the correct VM. In other words, this service acts as an RDP multiplexer.

Using the RDP protocol and client code means that VMConnect shares a number of keyboard shortcuts with RDP and introduces some of its own. Table 29.4 lists the most relevant ones.

TABLE 29.4:   Hyper-V Virtual Console Keyboard Shortcuts

HYPER-V KEY	WINDOWS KEY	EXPLANATION
Ctrl+Alt+End	Ctrl+Alt+Del	The well-known three-finger salute to display the logon screen or security dialog box
Alt+Page Up	Alt+Tab	Switches to next program
Alt+Page Down	Shift+Alt+Tab	Switches to previous program
Ctrl+Alt+left arrow		Releases keyboard and mouse focus from the VM
Ctrl+Alt+Pause		Toggles full-screen mode

If you open the Media menu on the virtual console and select DVD drive, you will see that the ISO file for Windows Server 2008 R2 is mounted—assuming you are following the example to the letter. With the DVD ready for booting, you are ready to go. You can find Start under the Action menu, but the quickest way is to just push the green power-on button. The console will display a few messages and quickly show the familiar boot screen of Windows Server 2008 R2. Click the virtual console to let it capture the keyboard and mouse. Don't forget: to release the mouse, you need to press Ctrl+Alt+left arrow.

Install the operating system in the usual way using a full installation—not Server Core. We will get to a Server Core installation later in this chapter.

🌐 Real World Scenario

INSTALLING OLDER OR UNSUPPORTED OPERATING SYSTEMS

Hyper-V was developed to run only current and common operating systems. The programmers at Microsoft do not test with older operating systems such as Windows NT 4, Windows 98, OS/2 Warp, Linux distributions, and so on. This does not mean that such operating systems will not work as a VM on Hyper-V, but it does mean that they will not have Integration Services. They will have to rely on the legacy (emulated) devices, which will be much slower than enlightened VMs.

We tested some old operating systems, just to see what would happen. Windows NT 4 is known to run on Hyper-V, while Windows 98 does not boot. DOS 6.22 runs fine, even with network access. We took one old OS from a different vendor: OS/2 Warp from IBM. It did not install.

After the installation and final reboot, you end up with a fully running Windows Server 2008 R2 VM. If you have DHCP on the LAN connected to its virtual switch, it will be fully network enabled as well.

However, the work is not quite done. Unless your VM runs the same OS and service pack as the host system, its Integration Services will not match that of the Hyper-V host. In fact, any OS older than Windows 2008 will not have Integration Services at all. In both cases, you need to install the latest version. This is easily done using the built-in ISO file with the Integration Services software. The details may vary a bit, depending on the OS version and/or previously installed versions of Integration Services.

1. Log on to the VM using an Administrator account.

2. Select Console ➢ Action ➢ Insert Integration Services Setup Disk.

3. After a short while, the Autoplay dialog box should offer to run Setup, as shown in Figure 29.19. If this does not happen, perhaps because Autoplay is disabled, you can run Setup directly from the virtual DVD drive in the VM.

4. Run Setup. After this, you know the drill. One or more reboots may be required.

If you look through the VM using the virtual console, there is little that shows that it's a VM. From its own point of view, it's just another server. One place where it shows its virtual nature is in the Device Manager. This is actually a good place to check that all is well with your VM. Table 29.5 lists the names for the virtual drivers of Hyper-V. If you *don't* see these, something went wrong. You might be missing a reboot, installed the wrong version of the Integration Services, or something like that.

FIGURE 29.19
Autoplay dialog
box for setting
up Integration
Services

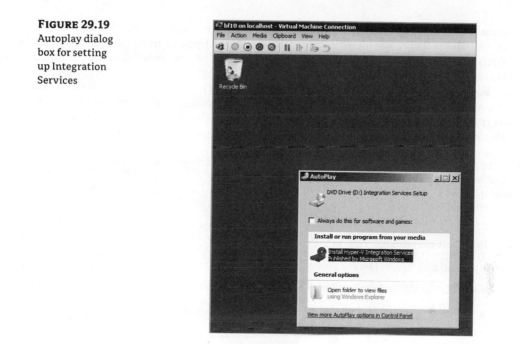

TABLE 29.5:   Hyper-V Devices in the VM

TYPE OF DEVICE	NAME
DVD/CD-ROM	Msft Virtual CD/ROM ATA Device
IDE/SATA disk	Virtual HD ATA Device
SCSI controller	Storvsc miniport
SCSI disk	Msft Virtual Disk SCSI Disk Device
Display adapter	Microsoft Virtual Machine Bus Video Device
Mouse	HID-compliant mouse
Network adapter (enlightened)	Microsoft Virtual Machine Bus Network Adapter
Network adapter (legacy)	Intel 21140 Based PCI Fast Ethernet Adapter or DEC PCI Fast Ethernet DECchip 21140
System devices	Many, such as the Integration Component drivers, the Virtual Machine Bus, and various filter drivers

A final word on the power states of a VM: you can boot, shut down, hibernate, suspend, and reset a physical machine. But a VM has an additional power state: it can be in a "saved state." This feature is very nice to have in a test environment. It is similar to a hibernated state but initiated from the host. This means that it always works, no matter what OS is installed in the VM. The "save state" action can be found in the usual place in the Hyper-V management console or the VM virtual console. Start the VM again, and the saved stated will be reloaded to resume exactly where you left off.

For some tests, it's useful to freeze the VM in place. This is different from a saved state because no data is saved to disk. A freeze (or *pause*, as Hyper-V calls it) just stops the VM in its tracks, instantaneously. This is again a feature that is hard to find on a physical machine. Figure 29.20 shows the power state buttons on the Hyper-V console.

FIGURE 29.20
Virtual machine power state buttons on the console

From left to right, you can do the following:

◆ Send a Ctrl+Alt+Del sequence to the VM.

◆ Start the VM after a shutdown or saved state.

◆ Turn off the VM directly. Windows will ask you whether you are sure you want this. It is the equivalent of pulling the plug.

◆ Shut down the VM. This works only with properly installed Integration Services. The Hyper-V host will work with the VM to initiate a normal shutdown sequence. Quite useful! There's no need to log on to the console anymore.

◆ Save the current state of the VM. For test, this is probably the one we use most.

◆ Pause (or freeze) the VM. Hit the button again to resume.

◆ Reset the VM, similar to a hardware reset on a physical host.

◆ Snapshot the VM: save all current state and configuration, and bookmark it. The VM continues running, but you can revert to the saved snapshot later. This is very useful, but it's potentially dangerous, as you will see later

◆ Revert to a saved snapshot.

Understanding Hyper-V Architecture

By this time, you should have a feeling for the basic functionality of Hyper-V. You have learned what server virtualization is used for and how to set up a basic server running Hyper-V with some VMs. However, to understand what's going on and to be able to troubleshoot problems, you need a deeper understanding of how Hyper-V was designed. In this section, you will learn more about the software architecture of Hyper-V.

CPU capabilities play an essential role in the implementation of server virtualization. The Intel/AMD model for Pentium-class processors has four privilege levels, known as *rings*. Ring 0 has the highest privilege. The Windows kernel and device drivers use this level. Processes in ring 0 are able to access any hardware in the system. Ring 1 and ring 2 are not normally used in current versions of Windows. Ring 3 is the lowest level. It runs normal "user" programs. In practice, this (should) mean any code that does not require kernel privileges. The trick here is that the CPU forbids any code running in a higher ring to write data or code belonging to a lower ring. In other words, it's a hardware security feature.

Let's take a look at the various ways that server virtualization is implemented in general. The oldest methods have a hybrid architecture that is similar to the diagram shown in Figure 29.21. The label Hybrid means that it is a merger of a normal kernel and a kernel that is aware of virtualization. The (now free) Microsoft Virtual Server product line is an example of such a hybrid architecture.

FIGURE 29.21
Overview of a hybrid virtualization platform, where the host and the virtualization layer are on the same level

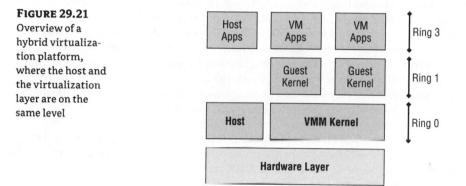

The host kernel is split in two pieces. The normal kernel runs side by side with code that takes care of all virtualization aspects related to hardware: the Virtual Machine Manager (VMM) kernel. The VMM kernel takes care of all interactions of the VMs with the host. The VMM runs in ring 0 and has full access to all hardware. The VMs have their own kernel. This kernel should believe that it's running in ring 0, but as you can see from the diagram, it is really running in ring 1. The VMM kernel is taking care of this translation. The principle is known as *ring compression*. To make this work, both the host and the VM kernels need adjustments, and the VMM needs to translate certain VM requests to the host.

Contrast this with a hypervisor architecture. A *hypervisor* is a software layer between the hardware and the operating systems running on the host. This is known as the *bare-metal* approach: virtualization at the lowest possible level. The main purpose of the hypervisor is to create isolated execution environments (partitions) for all operating systems. In line with that function, it is responsible for arbitrating access to the hardware. Figure 29.22 illustrates the point.

FIGURE 29.22
With a hypervisor, the host operates on the same level as the VMs: atop a hypervisor layer.

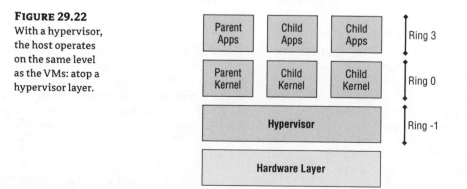

Let's take a look at the ring structure. You will note the addition of ring -1. This is not a mandatory feature of a hypervisor, but most modern hypervisors use it. This ring is the main feature of the CPU virtualization additions discussed earlier: Intel VT and AMD-V. It's a new access level of even higher priority than ring 0. It allows all kernels to really run on ring 0 without the tweaking that is required in a hybrid model. This makes for a cleaner architecture, implying fewer bugs in code and ideally better performance.

The diagram uses Microsoft's terminology for the technology. It illustrates that all VMs are created equal but that one is more equal than the others: the *parent* partition that is responsible for the management and high-level arbitration of all VMs. It is the default owner of all hardware resources and controls the startup and shutdown of the *child* partitions.

The Hyper-V hypervisor is *microkernelized*. As the term suggests, this means it was written to be as lean and mean as possible. It contains no drivers, no GUI code, but just enough intelligence to do its main job: manage memory and regulate access to the hardware. Other (non-Microsoft) hypervisors may take a different approach. In the monolithic approach, the hypervisor contains drivers and takes more responsibility for inter-VM communication. One advantage of a monolithic hypervisor is that it theoretically can deliver a higher maximum performance because of its tighter integration with drivers to access the hardware. On the other hand, if this hypervisor has no drivers for your specific hardware, you are out of luck. For mature products, this should not be a real problem, though. In the microkernel hypervisor, the drivers actually reside in the parent partition, which in the case of Hyper-V must be a Windows 2008 (R2) server. The parent partition has the drivers, so if your hardware has drivers for Windows 2008, it can work with Hyper-V.

Let's step away from the generalities and take a look at the specifics of Hyper-V. Microsoft designed it with the following goals in mind:

◆ The hypervisor should be as lean and mean as possible.

◆ It should be manageable using open APIs.

◆ Reliability and performance should be maximized.

◆ It should be a built-in feature of the Windows Server.

What they came up with is an implementation roughly along the lines of Figure 29.23. You will probably need to look at this a couple of times before it starts to make sense. We know we did the first time.

The bottom of the diagram shows the by-now-familiar layers of the hardware and the hypervisor. On top of the hypervisor run four VMs in this particular example. From left to right we have the parent partition and three types of child partitions. Let's start with the parent partition.

The Hyper-V Parent Partition

The parent really has two parts. The lower block runs in ring 0, or kernel mode. It contains four blocks, three of which are new in this discussion: the VMbus, the independent hardware vendor (IHV) drivers, and the virtualization service provider (VSP). The upper block corresponds to ring 3 code, or user mode. Shown here are only the components that are relevant to Hyper-V. The parent partition must run Windows Server 2008 or newer in order to support the hypervisor. Depending on your needs, this can be a full GUI version or the Server Core edition.

FIGURE 29.23
Hyper-V architecture: the hypervisor, the virtual machines, and their relations

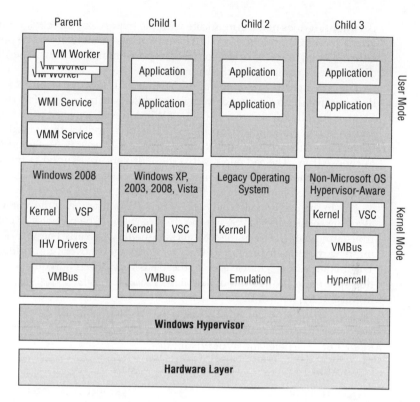

> **INSTALLATION AND BOOT PROCESS OF THE HYPERVISOR**
>
> You may wonder about this chicken and egg problem: the hypervisor needs a Windows 2008 parent to manage it, but the parent needs the hypervisor before it can do anything. What happens is this. You first install the Windows Server 2008 edition with Hyper-V, such as Standard, Enterprise, or Datacenter. At this point, there is no hypervisor. When you enable the Hyper-V role, Windows will install all required software components such as the VMbus and the VSP, but not the hypervisor.
>
> Instead, Windows installs the device driver Hvboot.sys, which will load the actual hypervisor on next boot. This can either be the %Systemroot%\System32\Hvax64.exe hypervisor for AMD processors or %Systemroot%\System32\Hvix64.exe for Intel. These files are both less than 1MB on the initial version of Windows 2008, illustrating their microkernel nature. Once loaded, the hypervisor uses the virtualization extensions of the CPU to insert itself as a ring -1 process, taking over control of the hardware. It proceeds to load the Windows 2008 kernel of the parent partition, prepared with the VMbus and VSP.

Coming back to the ring 0 part of the parent partition, you see the VMbus component at the lowest level. As the name suggests, the VMbus is used for data communication. It is 100 percent virtual, meaning that it has no hardware components. It is a point-to-point connection between partitions. It does not communicate with the hypervisor directly and uses shared memory and Inter Process Communication (IPC) mechanisms to share data. The point to note here is that data is shared and not copied for obvious performance reasons. The VMbus is an important differentiator compared to the hybrid model.

The IHV drivers live on top of the VMbus, but only in the parent partition. This illustrates that you install no external drivers in the child partitions. The IHV drivers are the usual drivers that are supplied with every version of Windows: disk drives, SCSI bus, RAID, network, video, and so on. A characteristic for this virtualization model is that you depend on exactly the same drivers as you would for nonvirtualized Windows servers. The good news is that you have a lot to choose from. The bad news is that those drivers are as good as the vendor chooses to make them, since they are not written or verified by Microsoft. Make sure you use drivers that are digitally signed and supported by your vendor.

Key to the performance of Hyper-V is the combination of the VSP in the parent and the virtualization service client (VSC) in the child partition. The parent VSP component is responsible for translating data between the VMbus and the IHV drivers. The VSP is actually a combination of multiple modules for each hardware type: storage, networking, video, input devices, and so on. This makes sense, because each of these has very different requirements regarding the transaction speed and the amount of data to be processed. Table 29.6 shows an overview of the most important hypervisor files.

TABLE 29.6: Relevant Hypervisor Files

FUNCTION	PATH TO FILE
Hypervisor boot driver	`%systemroot%\system32\drivers\hvboot.sys`
Hypervisor (for AMD)	`%systemroot%\system32\hvax64.exe`
Hypervisor (for Intel)	`%systemroot%\system32\hvix64.exe`
Virtual Machine Management service	`%systemroot%\system32\vmms.exe`
VM worker process	`%systemroot%\system32\vmwp.exe`

These VSP modules are paired with corresponding VSC modules. For example, the storage module of the VSC will communicate with the storage module in the VSP. Where the VSC communicates only with the VSP in the parent partition, the VSP communicates with all VSC components. It's possible for non-Microsoft developers to design and build their own modules since the relevant APIs are open to all.

We have covered the kernel mode part of the parent partition and progress to the user mode components. The Virtual Machine Management service (VMM service) is responsible for managing all child partitions. Whenever a child partition is started, the VMM service starts a new virtual machine worker process (VMW process) for this child. This process doesn't really do any work, except for monitoring, starting up, shutting down, and so on.

WHAT PROCESS "RUNS" THE VM?

Contrary to similar worker processes in the hybrid model, the VMW process does not really "run" the child partition. It just controls it. You cannot tell from the CPU usage of the VMW process if the child is doing anything, with the exception of data transfer by legacy (nonenlightened) devices.

In fact, all child partitions may be running up to 100 percent CPU without anything showing up in the parent partition directly. To find out what the child is doing, you either need to connect to the child directly using normal server management tools, use Performance Monitor counters from the parent, or access the WMI provider in the parent partition.

The final component in the parent partition is the WMI provider. Years ago Microsoft has decided that WMI would be the preferred way to manage and monitor system resources, and Hyper-V is no exception. The WMI provider is publicly documented on MSDN and provides the following functionality:

◆ Status reporting on mouse and keyboard

◆ Access to the VM BIOS

◆ Managing and reading the configuration of networking, serial devices, storage, guest partitions, and so on

◆ Reading current CPU properties

◆ Managing power state

From this feature set you can see that the WMI provider has all the functionality required to manage the Hyper-V environment. In fact, most management systems for Hyper-V are expected to use WMI. Unfortunately, the WMI interface is a little too involved to use directly for most daily management activities, although we will discuss some examples later in this chapter. Only people with extensive WMI programming experience will be able to work productively with this.

THE TWO HYPER-V APIS

Hyper-V actually has two built-in APIs. Besides WMI, it has the Hypervisor interface. The Hypervisor API is a low-level interface capable of configuring the hypervisor, managing partition states, handling interpartition communication (VMbus), handling the scheduler, and so on. The Hypervisor interface is really meant for those writing their own VSP/VSC modules and other system-level coding. As an administrator, you will certainly never touch the Hypervisor interface API directly.

To complete the parent overview, you should have an idea of the services running in the Hyper-V parent partition. There are three of them:

◆ Hyper-V Virtual Machine Management. This is for managing virtual machines from the parent partition.

◆ Hyper-V Image Management Service. This is dedicated to managing disk snapshots.

◆ Hyper-V Networking Management Service.

All three services are set to start on boot.

Hyper-V Child Partitions

Now you have most of the picture. Just the child partition architecture is left to discuss, and we have actually already covered some elements of that. The first child partition in Figure 29.23 runs an operating system that is aware of the hypervisor. Microsoft calls such an OS *enlightened*, while others may call it *paravirtualized*. As such, it has a VMbus interface and a Virtualization Service Client. The question is, how does the child partition become enlightened? In the parent, you installed the Hyper-V role, but clearly you need to do something else in a child partition to supply the required software components. The Hyper-V software for VMs is Integration Services. Its version must match the Hyper-V server version.

ENLIGHTENMENT COMES IN TWO FLAVORS

Enlightenment exists in two variants, a general and a more specific one. Generally speaking, an operating system that works with the VMbus interface is enlightened. That includes older systems such as Windows XP and Windows 2003 that need the Integration Services to be enlightened. The specific variant applies to the kernel: if the kernel natively knows about the hypervisor, the operating system is said to have an *enlightened kernel*. This would include Windows 2008 and Vista SP1 and newer versions. The advantage of an enlightened kernel is that it can further optimize access to the VMbus. For instance, Windows 2008 can bypass some internal software layers for network and disk access when it realizes the data is intended for a virtual device.

Only Windows 2008 and newer have a version of Integration Services built in, although you will probably need to upgrade that version to match the current Hyper-V version. For other operating systems, you will need to install them explicitly. One of the ways to do this is to insert an ISO file with Integration Services into the VM. This ISO file comes with Hyper-V.

Integration Services is actually a set of modules installed in %systemroot%\ Virtualization\<version> in the child partition. There is one <version> folder for each update of Integration Services. Taking a deeper look at its functionality, you can see that it is really split into two parts. On one hand, there are drivers for storage, video, and network. Another driver directly integrates with the kernel to optimize its performance running as a VM. On the other hand, there is a multipurpose service (vmicsvc.exe) executable that is started four times with different arguments to provide the following functionality:

Shutdown service On request of the parent partition, this service will shut down the VM in an orderly manner.

Heartbeat service The parent needs a way to tell whether the child is still alive. If the parent can no longer hear the heartbeats, it is safe to assume the child has a severe problem.

Time Synchronization service A child partition has no direct access to the hardware clock. This service offers an alternative. Don't use this feature in an Active Directory domain environment, because that has its own time synchronization infrastructure.

Data Exchange service   This service is the only way for user (ring 3) processes in the parent and child services to communicate outside of the regular devices. It works through certain registry keys.

Shadow Copy Requestor service   This service will work with a backup service on the parent to provide consistent backups for both the parent and the child partitions, using VSS technology.

It's worth noting that Integration Services cannot be configured from the child partition. The only (proper) way to do it is through the parent partition, either using the Hyper-V management console or using the WMI interface.

Continuing the discussion of child partitions, let's look at the second child partition in the diagram. It's labeled as a "legacy operating system." What this really means is that the operating system is not enlightened. This may be because Integration Services are not installed or are not available. For instance, you can have Windows 2003 installed both as a legacy system and as enlightened. For older systems such as Windows 2000 or Windows NT 4, Microsoft will not write Integration Services, although in principle a third party could do so. Lack of Integration Services does not mean that the VM will not install or run, but it does imply that it will never reach a high level of performance. On the other hand, many legacy operating systems should perform just fine on modern hardware, even if virtualized. The diagram shows that a legacy system has no VMbus or VSC provider.

The third and final type of child partition runs a non-Microsoft operating system using a custom hypervisor adapter, such as the Hypercall adapter of SUSE Linux. These are kernel-level drivers that provide access to the VMbus infrastructure. On top of that you see the usual VMbus component, which in turn is used by enlightened drivers from the VSC provider, again written specifically for that operating system. You may expect near-native performance from such an enlightened system. At the time Hyper-V came on the market, the only such operating system was SUSE Linux with a Xen-enabled kernel.

Security Design in Hyper-V

Now that you have a good overview of the Hyper-V architecture, we should say a few words about security. After all, you can now run multiple computers on the same hardware, separated only by a thin layer of hardware and software. If one of the partitions gets compromised, what could it do to the others? It could attack the hypervisor and, if it succeeds in compromising it somehow, attack the other partitions. In other words, the hypervisor is the key to the whole thing. Hyper-V was designed with such security issues in mind. We'll cover what was done to make an attack as hard as possible, but keep in mind that no sane person could ever guarantee 100 percent that an attack from one VM to the other through the hypervisor is impossible. It is software, and any piece of software has bugs.

As discussed, the Hyper-V hypervisor was designed to have a small footprint. That by itself is good for security: the less code and complexity, the better. Also, the Hypercall APIs that are needed to talk to the hypervisor are open to public scrutiny. Therefore, Microsoft had to make the assumption that all possible Hypercall functions are accessible to attackers and took measures to protect against invalid arguments, bad usage, and so on.

A basic premise of the Hyper-V security model is that the parent must be trusted, both by the hypervisor and by the child partitions. After all, all system resources are controlled by the parent. For instance, if an attacker controls the parent partition, he or she can stop and start VMs at will, inspect their disks, and so on. Given that premise, the Hyper-V architecture has to defend against two avenues of attack against the parent: external and internal.

An external attack against the parent is nothing more than a normal hacking attack: guess a password, try to compromise a running service, intercept management traffic, and so on. To minimize the attack surface, we recommend you use a Windows 2008 Server Core or the dedicated Hyper-V Server edition for the parent and use only the strict minimum of services required. Don't fall into the temptation of using it for a file server, domain controller, or anything else. If it's not related to Hyper-V functionality, it needs to go into a VM.

An internal attack would have to come from a compromised child partition, using Hyper-V resources such as the VMbus, VSC, or Hypercall API to try to attack services in the parent partition. Also, an attack from one VM to another VM on the same host would constitute an internal attack. To illustrate the principle, take a look at Figure 29.24.

FIGURE 29.24
The dashed lines are security boundaries in a Hyper-V machine.

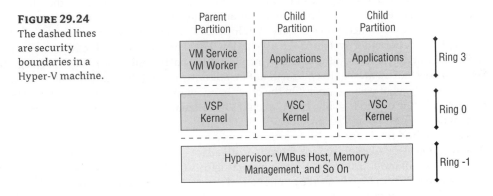

Each dashed line represents a security boundary, either as a ring transition in the CPU or the software separation between partitions. To defend against an internal attack, the Hyper-V architecture has implemented the following measures:

◆ The hypervisor uses unique resource pools for each partition. In other words, no VM-specific data is shared with other VMs. Such data cannot be used for a direct attack. Along the same line, no memory is shared between VMs. Each VM has its own memory space.

◆ There is no direct communication from one child to another. All communication either goes through the parent or goes through a really external medium such as the network.

◆ Each child has its own VMbus instance to the parent. So, even if one VMbus instance is compromised, this has no direct influence on other child partitions.

◆ Each child has its own controlling process in the parent, a VM worker process, as noted earlier.

◆ DMA attacks between VMs are not possible because a child partition can never own a physical device.

There's more. Architecture is one thing; actual coding is quite another. The programmers of the hypervisor have taken steps to make an attack as difficult as possible and to try to detect an attack if it happens. Some of these include the following:

◆ The hypervisor uses Address Space Layout Randomization (ASLR) whenever possible. This is a technique where different pieces of code are always loaded at different addresses.

This makes buffer overrun attacks very hard, since those depend on a predictable starting point for executable code.

♦ Hardware Data Execution Prevention is mandatory, meaning that only in-memory code that is marked as executable can actually be run. This protects against stack overflow attacks. In addition, memory pages containing code are marked as read-only. Any attempt to modify such data should generate a blue screen.

♦ Stack Guard cookies are known pieces of data on the stack that the hypervisor uses with certain internal functions. If these cookies are modified, the system will know there has been a stack overflow or an illegal but successful modification of the stack. A blue screen will probably be the next event.

♦ Last but not least, the hypervisor file is digitally signed. Any attempt to modify it offline will stop it from loading.

All of these countermeasures against internal attacks are no guarantee that an attack cannot succeed. But they do indicate that Microsoft has taken security very seriously.

Using Virtual Disks

In your day-to-day working with Hyper-V, the virtual disks of your VMs play an important role. To use them effectively, you need a good understanding of the various types of disks and their performance characteristics. We will also discuss VM snapshots and disk maintenance.

Virtual Disks and Their Controllers

A *virtual disk* is a file with a specific format. Its normal extension is .vhd, and it's common to all Microsoft virtualization products. Even more important, its structure is published and freely usable by anyone. The specification is low level from a disk point of view, meaning that it does not assume any type of filesystem in the VM. The VM may run Windows with NTFS, FAT32, or FAT or run Linux with EX2, ReiserFS, or whatever will be developed in the future. The open specification of VHD files means that it can be used for virtualization products from other companies and that anyone can write tools to handle them.

Windows accesses disks through controllers, and a VM running on Hyper-V is no different. The two usual types are present: IDE and SCSI. In a physical machine, SCSI systems generally perform better on a server. Not only are SCSI disks faster than IDE disks (very generally speaking!), but the SCSI interface was designed to handle multiple I/O requests at the same time. Interestingly, from a Hyper-V VM perspective, there is no performance difference. In an enlightened VM, both IDE and SCSI data transfers are quickly translated to VMbus requests that in turn depend on the storage system of the host. In fact, the .vhd file has no knowledge of its controller. This means that the same .vhd file can be used with an IDE and SCSI controller.

Still, there is one important difference between virtual SCSI and IDE controllers: you cannot boot a VM from a SCSI controller. The reason behind this is the magic that Hyper-V needs to perform to make the enlightened controllers work. If you have read the section "Understanding Hyper-V Architecture," you will know that the VMbus drivers are not the first ones to load in the boot process. If the VMbus is required for booting, we would have a deadlock situation. Hyper-V solves this by making the IDE controller automorphing, meaning that it behaves as a legacy IDE controller when this is necessary. As soon as an enlightened driver starts talking to it, the controller will use the VMbus instead of using emulation. The virtual SCSI controller has no such auto-morphing capability, explaining why it cannot be used to boot a VM. In practice, it should not be a problem because the virtual IDE performance is equal to that of virtual SCSI.

VHD DISKS AS FIRST-CLASS CITIZENS

Previously, virtual disks based on VHD were just files that needed to be run by a virtualization engine. Both Windows Server 2008 R2 and its little brother Windows 7 offer native support for VHD files. Not only can you mount them as you can with physical disks, but you can also boot from them.

Virtual Disk Types and When to Use Them

Hyper-V has three types of virtual disk systems to offer to a VM, as you can see when you start the wizard for a new virtual hard disk (shown in Figure 29.25). All these virtual disks are implemented as normal files on an NTFS volume.

FIGURE 29.25
The New Virtual
Hard Disk Wizard

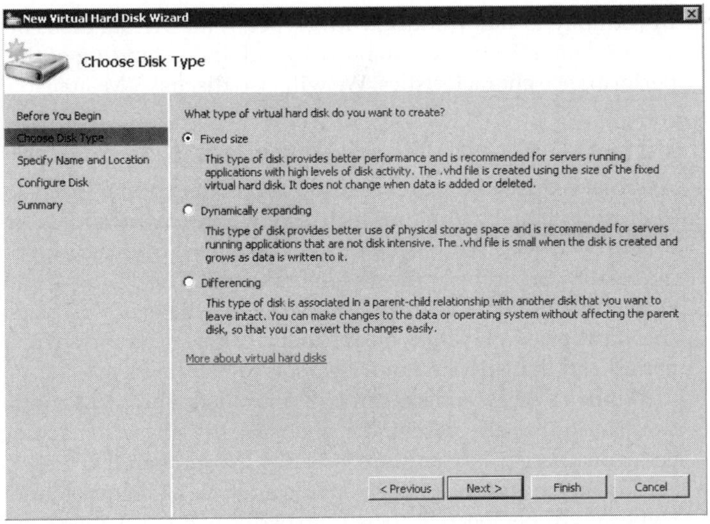

Dynamically expanding disk   You create such a disk with a virtual size. For instance, you create the disk with a size of 127GB. The VM using this disk will indeed see 127GB. However, on the host, the file will allocate only as much space as it really needs. This is very useful for test situations, but it's not as fast as a fixed-size disk. Another disadvantage is that the host may run out of disk space unexpectedly because of growing virtual disks. You will definitely want to avoid this in production situations. Finally, each time the host needs to allocate new disk space to expand the disk, you will take a (brief) performance hit. Although a dynamically expanding disk is the default selected by the wizard, it is really only suitable for testing.

Fixed size disk   When you create such a disk, a file is created with the full size that you specify. During creation, the file is filled with binary zeros. This may take quite some time, depending on the size you specified. A fixed size disk should be your default for production systems.

Differencing disk   This is an interesting feature where you have a parent-child relation between two virtual disks. The parent disk is a static, read-only reference. The differencing disk (child) stores all changes with respect to the parent. The point of this feature is to save disk space on the host and be able to create a new VM really quickly. However, if the VM using the differencing disk is writing a lot of new data, the advantage of saving disk space will disappear quickly. Clearly, this feature is suitable only for test purposes.

A VM can use any type of virtual disk. However, it is also possible to use a physical disk on the host. This is known as a *pass-through disk*. To dedicate a physical disk to a VM, it must appear as a physical disk to the Windows host machine. This may be a local disk, a disk on a SAN, an iSCSI disk, and so on. It cannot be a partition. It really must be a full disk, as visible in Disk Manager. Also, to be able to use the disk in a VM, it must be offline in the host to stop the host from using it. You can set a disk offline or online in Disk Manager or using the command-line tool `diskpart`.

A pass-through disk is the fastest possible configuration, in theory. In practice, the performance difference with a fixed disk will be very small. In some cases, a pass-through disk has another advantage: it may be larger than 2TB, which is the limit for a virtual disk. You can decide for yourself if it is wise to use such a large volume, considering the time it would take to back up or restore such a volume or to run the command-line tool `chkdsk` on it to verify the filesystem integrity.

A pass-through disk has some disadvantages. You cannot copy it to another machine as you would with a virtual disk, although you can convert a physical disk to a virtual disk when creating a virtual disk. A pass-through disk cannot be part of a differencing set, and you cannot snapshot a VM that has such a disk.

In short, your default type of drive for production purposes should be a fixed-size virtual disk. Use pass-through disks for the scenarios that require them, such as some clustering configurations. Use dynamically expanding and differencing disks only for testing.

Adding a Disk to an Existing VM

When you create a VM using the New Virtual Machine Wizard, you have the option to add the boot disk. To add more disks, you can either prepare a disk using the New Disk Wizard directly from the Hyper-V console or, more conveniently, start this wizard from the VM settings. In this example, we use the hot-add feature of Hyper-V V2; this won't work on Windows 2008 Hyper-V. We will add a disk to the SCSI controller. Remember, the .vhd virtual disk format is interchangeable for IDE and SCSI because it is the same for both. We could have added it to an IDE controller except for the little fact that IDE does not support hot-add!

1. Select the VM, and open its Settings menu. Select the SCSI controller on the left, and then select Hard Drive on the right, as shown in Figure 29.26. The Add button will activate.

2. The next step is to select an unused SCSI channel. Channel 0 is reserved for the controller, so picking channel 1 for the first disk makes sense. You now have the option to select an existing virtual hard disk using the Browse button or to create a new one using New. This enters the familiar New Disk Wizard. In the screenshot of Figure 29.27, we have created a new 127GB fixed-size disk (the default!) and used a name that relates it to its VM.

FIGURE 29.26
Adding a new
virtual disk to the
SCSI controller

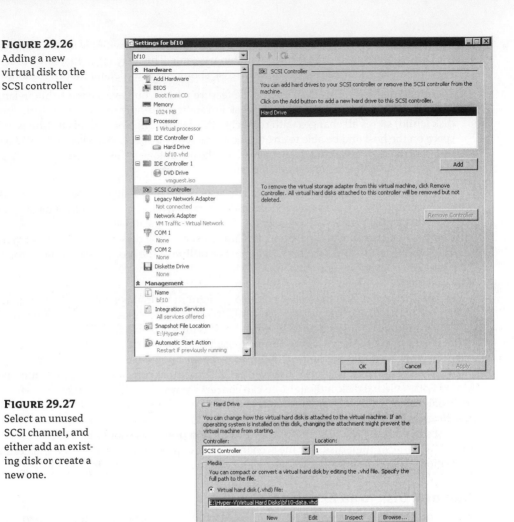

FIGURE 29.27
Select an unused
SCSI channel, and
either add an exist-
ing disk or create a
new one.

3. Click OK to finalize your changes. Now, let's see if the hot-add worked. Log on the
VM with an Administrator account, and start Server Manager. Open Storage and Disk
Management. You will see the newly added disk, ready to be initialized and formatted,
as shown in Figure 29.28. Interestingly, you can even remove an online disk on operating
systems that support it, such as Windows Server 2008 R2.

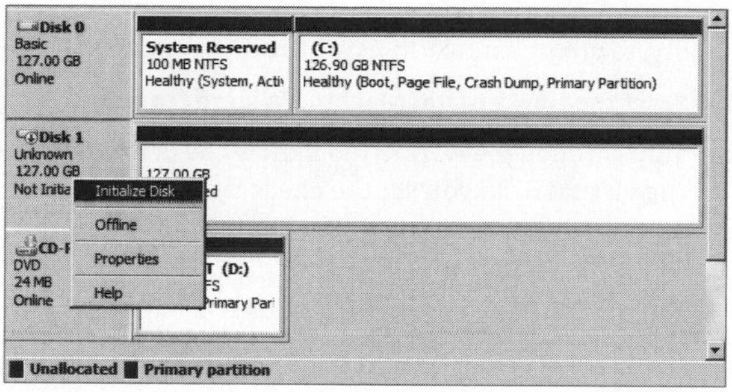

FIGURE 29.28
The newly added
disk is visible in the
VM and just needs
to be initialized
and formatted.

USING DIFFERENCING DISKS WITH A BASE IMAGE

Let's take a closer look at the use for differencing disks. We often have the need to quickly try
something in a lab. For instance, say we want to examine the effects of raising the Active Directory
domain and forest levels. How would we quickly build a one-shot lab to try this? The trick is to
use a base installation of Windows Server 2008 and make differencing disks from that VM. From
each differencing disk, you can create a new VM. This is similar to working with an image, so you
must take care to apply sysprep to the new VMs. These are the basic steps that you would take in
preparation:

1. Prepare a VM with a dynamically expanding virtual hard disk. Take note of the full path of the
   corresponding .vhd file.

2. Install Windows Server 2008 R2 as usual, including Integration Services. Apply service packs
   and patches as required. Do not join it to a domain, make it a domain controller, or install any
   service or application.

3. Install tools that you might need in each VM, such as resource kits, the Sysinternals tooling,
   and so on.

4. Run sysprep:%systemroot%\system32\sysprep /generalize /oobe /shutdown.

5. Find to the .vhd file, and mark it as read-only.

You would have the same preparation even if you planned to copy the virtual disk afterward to
deploy a new VM. In this case, for each new VM you want to create, you need to create a differencing
disk to use it for a new VM. To create the differencing disk, follow these steps:

1. Start the New Hard Disk Wizard from the Hyper-V console.

2. Click Next to skip the welcome screen.

3. Select Differencing Disk.

4. Click Next, and enter a name for the virtual disk such as vm2-diff.vhd. Specify the full path
   to the disk as well, or accept the default.

5. Click Next, and browse to the parent virtual disk that you have marked as read-only when you
   prepared it.

6. Click Next and Finish to create the differencing disk.

Finally, to create a new VM using the differencing disk, follow these steps:

1. Start the New Virtual Machine Wizard from the Hyper-V console.

2. Step through the wizard (you know the drill), and when you get to the step where you specify the virtual disk, you set the check box for an existing virtual disk. Browse to the virtual disk you created, vm2-diff.vhd in this example.

3. Boot the VM, and the sysprep procedure will do its work to create a new instance of Windows.

Those are all the steps—it's quicker than copying the full virtual disk of the parent and uses less disk space.

There are two things you can do to speed things up a bit. The first and rather obvious suggestion is to create the differencing disks on a different physical disk for better performance. The second is to use NTFS compression on the differencing disks. Experience teaches us that differencing disks compress very well. A CPU decompressing such a file will outperform an uncompressed file in terms of MB per second, as long as the CPU is not too busy. Again, this is for testing purposes only, as you know by now.

Finally, a note of warning. If you change the parent disk at any time, you will completely invalidate all its children. Setting the parent disk to read-only prevents such accidents.

🌐 Real World Scenario

VMs Mysteriously Running Slow

Bigfirm has deployed a number of Hyper-V servers as a test environment. Each server has 16GB of internal memory and 2TB in usable disk space. The Hyper-V hosts are run by the IS department. Other departments use and manage the VMs.

One day, complaints start coming in that certain VMs are slow to respond, although there is no obvious load on the VMs. The IS department takes the complaints and investigates. None of the VMs shows any sign of trouble. The CPU usage is normal, all applications are running, the OS is not swapping, and there is no memory pressure. In short, there is no obvious cause. One pattern emerges: most "slow" VMs share the same host.

The IS department starts running performance counters on the host, including the CPU and Logical Disk objects. After an hour of measuring, it is noted that some counters are consistently high: the counter "disk seconds/read" averages in at 30 milliseconds, and the counter "disk seconds/write" is mostly over 50 milliseconds. The "average disk queue length" counter of the disk hosting the VMs often peaks at more than 20. Compared to other hosts, these are really high values. Clearly, the host has trouble delivering the required disk I/O.

An inspection of the host shows that the VM disk is a RAID 5 configuration, which is good at reads but slow at writes. The combined disk I/O of all VMs has pushed the host capacity over the limit. The problem is solved by rearranging the disks in a RAID 10 configuration and adding more disks to increase the maximum I/O throughput.

This case illustrates the added complexity of managing a virtualized server environment. The combined VMs may put the host in trouble.

Disk Maintenance

The most essential parts of a VM are its disks. Not only do they contain the data, but they determine in large part the performance of the VM. In this section, you will learn how to maintain virtual disks.

We'll discuss disk fragmentation first. You are familiar with NTFS fragmentation, where a file may get chopped into many pieces for several reasons. For large files there may not be sufficient continuous space on disk to create an unfragmented file. More commonly, a file may get updated many times and write to a different section of the disk each time. If you think about it, you see that VMs using virtual disks may suffer doubly from fragmentation! Not only does it have fragmentation in its own file systems, but its virtual disk may also fragment. There are some measures you can take to reduce the effects of fragmentation.

First, it is good to realize that a very large file having a few fragments does not impact performance significantly. If you have a 127GB fixed size virtual disk in a 100 pieces, each piece is still larger than 1GB on the average. Reading one such chunk from disk will take multiple seconds, while skipping to another section on disk takes no more than a few milliseconds. You won't notice the few additional milliseconds loading that data. So, fragmentation on this level is nothing to worry about.

Second, dynamic and differencing disks are different. They increase their size on demand and may get fragmented quickly. The most reliable way to get a dynamic disk back in shape is to defragment it. But how do you defragment a single file? The built-in tools can defragment only a complete volume. One way to do it is to use the command-line tool contig.exe, which you can download from www.microsoft.com/sysinternals. Assuming you have downloaded and unzipped contig.exe, you could do it like this (as illustrated in Figure 29.29):

1. Copy contig.exe to a convenient spot, such as E:\downloads\sysinternals.

2. Stop the VM whose disk you want to defragment, either by shutting down or saving its state.

3. Open a command prompt or PowerShell window, and change the working directory to E:\Hyper-V\Virtual Hard Disks.

4. To analyze the virtual disk named bf10.vhd, type **E:\downloads\sysinternals\contig .exe -a bf10.vhd**.

5. If the file is significantly fragmented, fix it by typing **E:\downloads\sysinternals\ contig.exe bf10.vhd**.

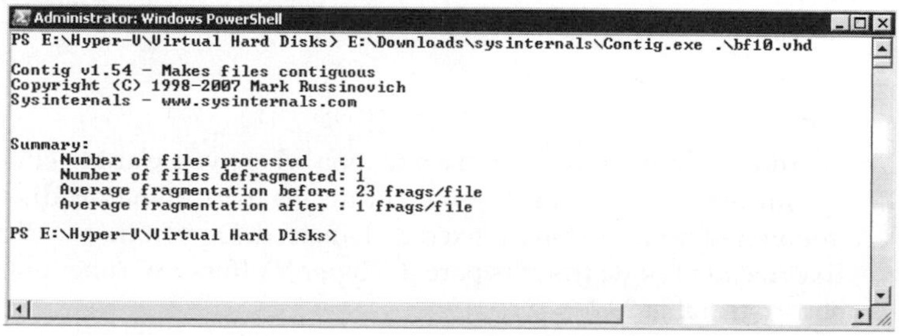

FIGURE 29.29
Defragmenting files using the Sysinternals tool contig.exe

There is another fragmentation-like effect that only affects dynamic and differencing disks. If you create a lot of data and then remove it, you will leave a lot of empty space on the disk. In other words, the virtual disk is larger than it needs to be. Hyper-V can remove this empty space with an operation called *compaction*. To do that, it mounts the virtual disk in the parent partition. If the file system on the virtual disk is NTFS, the parent can inspect its data structures to figure out where the empty space is. It uses this information to reduce the size of the file representing the virtual disk. If you have any other file system, such as FAT32 or EXT2, you must use some means to fill the empty space with zero bytes first. The compaction procedure recognizes such zero bytes and can adjust the VHD file to remove them. Tools to fill empty space with zeros are not included with Hyper-V, so compaction is effectively limited to NTFS file systems. If you do try to compact a FAT32 disk, it will start the process but will probably not do much because it will not find many zero byte sequences to compact.

To compact a virtual disk, the corresponding VM cannot be running. You must shut it down or save its state. Once that's done, it goes like this:

1. From the Actions pane in the Hyper-V management console, start the Edit Disk Wizard.

2. Locate the virtual disk you want to compact, such as the familiar bf10.vhd.

3. In the Choose Action dialog box, select the default action Compact.

4. Click Finish. The actual process may take a while.

Interestingly, you can open Disk Manager and see that the virtual disk is mounted while the compaction process works. In Figure 29.30, disk 2 is the virtual disk being compacted. Note that it has no drive letter assigned to it and is mounted read-only. Clearly, it shows the virtual size and not the real size of the disk. Note that there is a potential issue with mounting the virtual disk like this. If the host is running something like an antivirus or indexing program, it might find this disk and start analyzing it as well.

FIGURE 29.30
Disk Manager while the compaction operation is running. The VM disk of 127GB is actually mounted in the host!

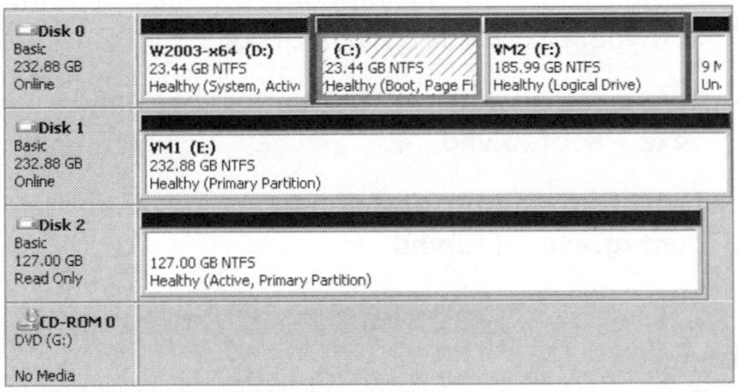

You might find yourself in a situation where you want to change the type of disk you are working with. For instance, you may decide that a dynamic disk was not a great choice and that you would prefer to have a fixed disk instead. Or, you have a differencing disk that you would like to disentangle from its parent. Hyper-V offers a number of disk conversion options, as shown in Table 29.7.

TABLE 29.7:   Disk Operations

TYPE OF DISK	POSSIBLE OPERATIONS
Dynamically expanding disk	Create a new fixed size disk, compact, expand.
Fixed-size disk	Create a new dynamic disk, expand.
Differencing disk	Merge with parent disk, compact, or reconnect to a parent disk that was moved to a different path.

These options are all accessed from the Edit Disk Wizard. If you do a lot of testing using differencing disks, you will at some point want to create stand-alone disks, because a much-used differencing disk will be larger than its parent—exactly the point you wanted to avoid. We'll show an example. Say you have a differencing disk called bf11-differencing.vhd, and you want to create a new independent virtual disk. Again, for such a procedure, the VM must be turned off.

1. From the Actions pane on the Hyper-V management console, start the Edit Disk Wizard.

2. Locate the disk you want to merge, which is bf11-differencing.vhd in this example. The wizard will determine that it's a differencing disk and present you with the relevant options only.

3. From the Choose Action dialog box, select the Merge option.

4. A subdialog box appears giving you two basic options. Do you want to merge the differencing disk into its parent, or do you want a new dynamic of fixed differencing disk? Be really careful when merging a disk into its parent because any other child disks will be invalidated. For testing, you will want to create a new dynamic disk. Choose a suitable name, such as bf11-dynamic.vhd, as shown in Figure 29.31.

5. Click Next and Finish to start the actual procedure.

6. To use the new disk, edit the virtual machine properties, and replace the current differencing disk.

From the discussion you may have seen that virtual disks come in various types. The .vhd extension does not tell the whole story. If you look at the Actions pane of the Hyper-V management console, you see one additional menu related to disks: Inspect Disk. This is a simple dialog box that does nothing more than to open a virtual disk and tell what type it is with some additional information. It has one useful feature for differencing disks: if the parent disk is missing, it will tell you. It will give you the option to reconnect it to its parent, which you do by browsing to it.

Time Travel with Snapshots

As you have seen, a lot of features of Hyper-V help you with testing. Dynamic disks save you valuable disk space, and differencing disks allow you to quickly deploy new VMs. But wouldn't it be nice if you could prepare a VM for testing and save it easily so that you can revert to it when things go wrong? This is what snapshots offer you—and more besides.

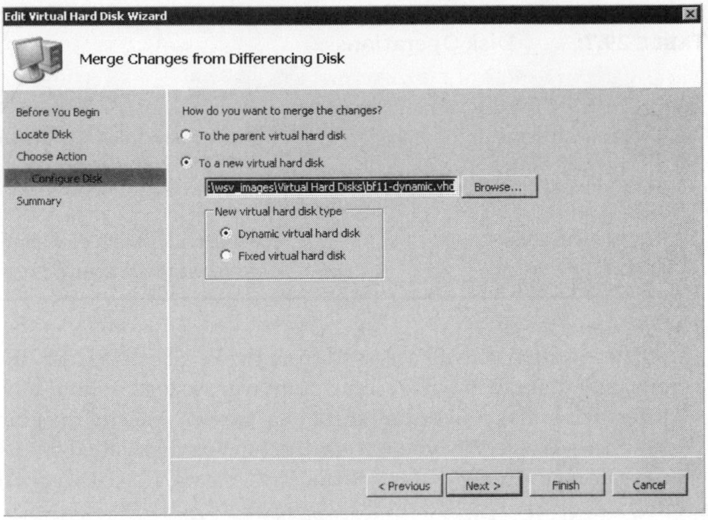

FIGURE 29.31

Merging a difference disk and its parent to a new (dynamic) virtual hard disk

A *snapshot* is best understood as a point-in-time copy of a VM. The copy includes virtual disks, memory, processor state, and configuration of the VM. The VM may be turned off, may be running, or may be in a saved state—it doesn't matter. Of course, not all the VM is really copied. Hyper-V is efficient about it. When you snapshot a VM, Hyper-V does the following:

1. The VM is paused.

2. For each virtual disk connected to the VM, a new differencing disk is created.

3. The virtual disks are decoupled from the VM and are replaced by the corresponding differencing disks.

4. The files containing the configuration of the VM are copied.

5. The VM is resumed. Usually, at this point, you have less than a second of downtime.

6. While the VM is running, its memory is written to disk. If the VM writes to memory, the write action is intercepted, and the original memory is quickly written to disk. Then the write action is allowed to succeed. In this way, all the memory at the time of the snapshot is preserved, while allowing the VM to keep running.

7. When the memory dump is completed, the snapshot is done.

If you look at this carefully, you can conclude some interesting things. First, it allows a true undo. Not only are the disk contents preserved, but the memory and even the configuration are too. You could change memory and add disks and networks and still be able to revert to the original situation. Second, there is no reason why you could not repeat this process. You can have a chain or even multiple chains of snapshots. A limitation of this process is that it works only with virtual disks. If your VM uses pass-through disks, you cannot snapshot it. Finally, taking a snapshot is quick. Anyone using the VM would not notice much downtime, perhaps a second or so.

Taking a snapshot can be done in various ways, similar to changing power states. To do it from the Hyper-V management console, select the VM, and take the snapshot from the Actions pane. Figure 29.32 illustrates what this looks like.

FIGURE 29.32
A VM with multiple snapshot trees. The base snapshot is "After install" and has two subtrees called *domain join* and *sysprepped*.

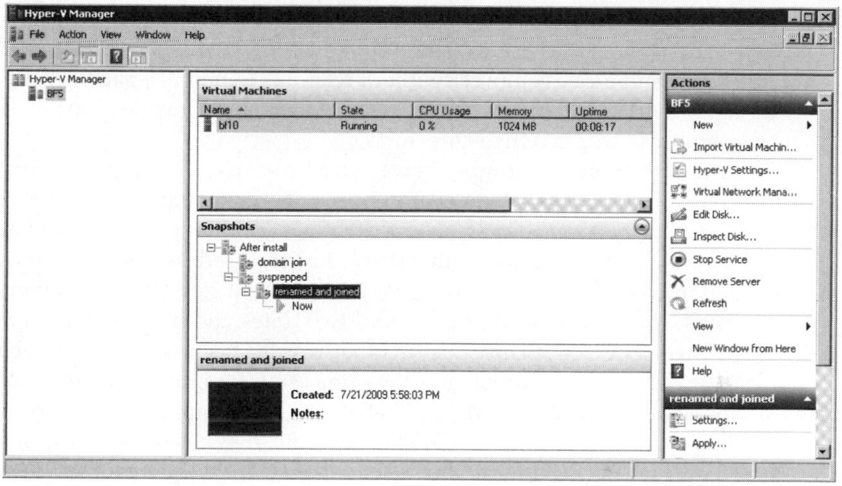

This example already has a number of snapshots. The current snapshot is highlighted. Its icon is different from the others. The default name is the current time and date, but renaming it immediately makes more sense.

It's not hard to move around between snapshots. However, if you want to preserve the current state, you need to take a new snapshot first. If you don't, the latest preserved state is that of its latest snapshot. So, to go to a different snapshot while the current one is running, you do the following:

1. Select the snapshot you want to move to. You can select any one you like, even the ones in the middle of a chain.

2. Use the Apply action from the snapshot menu.

3. You get a dialog box with three choices: Take Snapshot and Apply (the default), Apply, and Cancel.

4. Make your choice, and after a couple of seconds, the selected snapshot starts running.

In the same way, you can also delete any snapshot you want. From the management console, this seems simple, but under the hood there is more going on. The key to snapshots is the use of differencing disks. So, what happens if you remove a snapshot in the middle of a chain? In that case, the differencing disks of the removed snapshot are preserved, keeping the disk chain intact. Just the configuration files are removed. When VM is shut down, the host will merge the orphaned differencing disks into their parents. The Hyper-V management console will show a status of "Merging... (34%)." There are more scenarios to consider here, but the key point is that Hyper-V is aware of them and will do the right thing.

One particular example is when you remove a VM that has snapshots. The dialog box will tell you that it will not remove the associated virtual disks. That's only partially true. When you do delete the VM, it will take longer than you might expect. A dialog box stays on-screen telling you that it is "Destroying… (12 percent)" and counting. It is not removing the disks; it is merging the active snapshot with its parents, leaving you with just one .vhd file. That's probably the right thing to do, because it leaves you with just one .vhd representing all the data of the VM you just deleted.

As a testing feature, snapshots are just great. You can mess up your environment all you want, and you have your get-out-of-jail-free ticket ready to bail you out. Always? No, not always. There are some situations where applying an earlier snapshot can get you into serious trouble. For a stand-alone computer without relations to others, snapshots are perfectly safe. For any situation where computers share some configuration, you need to be careful. The most well-known example of this is Active Directory.

In fact, there is a number of ways where snapshots can get you into trouble with Active Directory. The most obvious example is where you have a snapshot of a member server taken 40 days ago. As you know, a server that is a member of a domain changes its password every 30 days. Since 40 days ago, that server has changed its password in Active Directory at least once and maybe twice already. In its local database, it stores two passwords, the current and the previous. If it has changed its password two times, the snapshotted server no longer has a matching password in Active Directory. In other words, it is no longer a member of the domain and needs to be rejoined. This problem is the same as with regular backups. However, there is a more subtle and dangerous problem that affects only domain controllers.

For domain controllers (DCs) to replicate, they need some administration that tells them what information they already have received from their partners and what they are still missing. This administration depends on the update sequence numbers (USNs) that each DC generates with each modification of its database. Any change has a unique USN associated with it. The point is, when you restore a snapshot of a DC, you also restore the USN configuration of that time. The problem is that the other DCs do not know this has happened! When they look at the DC that had a snapshot restored, they see that they already have processed the current USN of that DC. So, the replication partners of that DC see no need to replicate any data. Effectively, that DC will not replicate until its USN is finally higher than its partners have administered. All data that the affected DC generates in that period will never leave the DC.

This complicated but very serious problem is known as *USN rollback* and is documented in Knowledge Base article 875495. Luckily, if the DC detects that this is going on, it will immediately stop all Active Directory activity and log the problem in the Directory Services event log. The point of this illustration is to make you aware that using snapshots can lead to unexpected problems, even in systems you think you know well. The best thing to avoid such problems is to snapshot computers as a group after shutting them down and to restore them as a group. You may wonder why such problems do not occur when you do a regular backup of a DC and restore it. The reason is that the Windows restore operations are aware of the Active Directory replication administration and reset it. When a restored domain controller comes online, it signals to its partners that it should be treated as if it has never replicated before.

SNAPSHOTS AND DISK IMAGING ARE VERY SIMILAR

If you look at how snapshots work, you'll realize that it's technically similar to disk imaging. The difference is, most modern disk-imaging software (not all!) is aware of this problem and takes measures to prevent it. In most cases, this requires the use of software agents.

SANs that are capable of making disk snapshots face a similar problem. Make sure that you install the required agent software on all computers whose disks may be snapshotted.

To finish up this section on Hyper-V snapshots, the two key summary points are probably these:

- Snapshots are a great testing feature that can make your life a lot easier.

- Snapshots should not be used in production networks.

Using Virtual Networks

Once you have set up the virtual networks on your Hyper-V hosts, you won't have to think about them much. In fact, once you have set the defaults during the setup of the Hyper-V role, chances are that you won't touch them again. Still, they offer some interesting possibilities and have some limitations that you should be aware of. In this section, we'll discuss everything you need to know about virtual networks for your daily job.

In addition to virtual network interface cards (NICs), Hyper-V supports virtual switches. You really should think of them like that, because they do have some of the characteristics of physical switches. The Hyper-V architecture is such that a virtual NIC must be connected to a virtual switch. You cannot connect a virtual NIC directly to a physical one. Clearly, the Hyper-V virtual switches play an essential role. In fact, there are three types of virtual switches: external, internal, and private. You might take a look at the diagram in Figure 29.33 while reading the following explanation. The diagram shows the Hyper-V parent partition (the host) and two virtual machines. Connections to the virtual switch of type external are solid lines, to internal are dashed, and to private are dotted.

FIGURE 29.33
Three types of
virtual switches:
external, internal,
and private

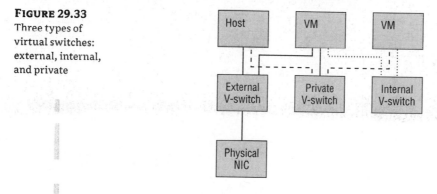

An *external* switch is one that is connected to a physical NIC on the host. This allows the VM to communicate directly with the outside world. Any other computers on the network will see two different machines, since the VM and its host each has different MAC and IP addresses. From the physical switch connecting the host, the situation looks different: one (physical) NIC with multiple MAC addresses and IP addresses for each VM. Although most switches allow this configuration by default, on some corporate networks this would not be allowed by policy. Note that there is a one-to-one relation between external switches and physical NICs. External switches cannot share NICs, and you cannot have more than one switch per NIC. If you require load balancing or redundancy on the NIC level, you will need software and drivers from the NIC manufacturer.

The *internal* switch is interesting. It allows communication between all VMs with the host but not directly to the outside world. For each internal virtual switch that you create, Hyper-V creates an additional Local Area Connection directly connected to the new switch. There is no DHCP on that particular NIC (unless you put it there), so everything on that switch will get an APIPA address. So yes, there is network connectivity, but to use it, you need to configure the IP settings yourself. Another way of generating an internal switch would be to configure a loop-back network adapter on the host and create an external switch connected to it. In fact, this is how Virtual Server and Virtual PC work. The existence of the internal switch is to make your life easier in this aspect.

The *private* switch is now easy to understand. There is no host NIC or Local Area Connection associated with it. Only VMs can connect to it, which is a great feature for testing. There is no way a fully internally connected VM can reach the host or the external network directly.

Understanding Virtual Switches

There are two parts to configuring virtual networking: virtual NICs and virtual switches. The switches are managed using the Virtual Network Manager, which you open from the Actions pane in the Hyper-V management console, as shown in Figure 29.34. In the screenshot, the virtual switch VM Traffic – Virtual Network is selected. This switch was created when we installed the Hyper-V role and told the wizard which NICs to use for VM traffic. Look back to Figure 29.4 to see this again.

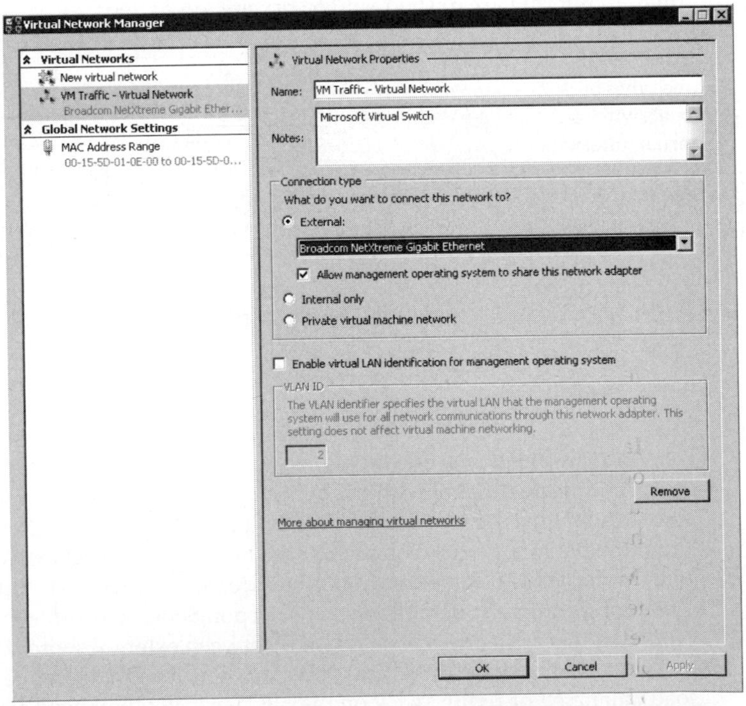

FIGURE 29.34
The Virtual Network Manager dialog box. Open this from the Actions pane of the Hyper-V management console.

A virtual switch has a number of properties: a name, some notes if you like, a network scope (external, internal, or private), and an optional VLAN tag. This switch is external and connected to physical NIC Broadcom NetXtreme Gigabit Ethernet. The LAN connection in the host for this NIC is called VM Traffic; unfortunately, that does not show here. Note the important check box "Allow management operating system to share this network adapter." With this check box, a new virtual NIC is created in the host, allowing network traffic from the host to the internal VM world.

The result of this configuration can be slightly confusing if you look at the networking configuration of the host. Figure 29.35 shows host bf5, which has the Hyper-V role enabled.

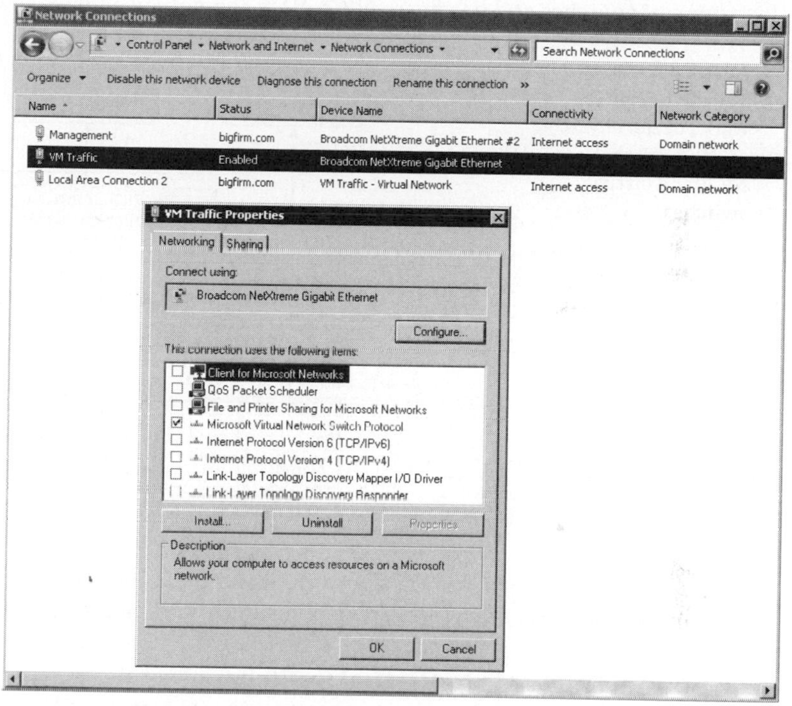

FIGURE 29.35

Hyper-V host with one NIC dedicated to VM traffic. The virtual NIC Local Area Network 2 shows up because of the enabled check box "Allow management operating system to share this network adapter."

We have three NICs here, one more than we started with when we built the machine. Let's look at them all:

Management   This NIC is physical and dedicated to the host. Remote management of VMs goes through this NIC. This is a best-practice configuration: have at least two physical NICs, leave one for dedicated host and management traffic, and use the other one(s) for VM traffic. The NIC is connected to the device Broadcom NetXtreme Gigabit Ethernet.

VM Traffic   This is also a physical NIC but with a much different configuration. Look at the binding properties for this NIC. All protocols are deselected, except for Microsoft Virtual Network Switch Protocol. So, it has no IP stack, cannot act as a server, and is effectively invisible. Give the command `ipconfig /all`, and the NIC does not show up. The NIC is connected to Broadcom NetXtreme Gigabit Ethernet, illustrating that this is a link to the outside world for the VMs.

Local Area Network 2 This is a virtual NIC. Its configuration is the same as the Management NIC, except that it connects to the virtual switch VM Traffic – Virtual Network. All protocols are bound, except the Virtual Network Switch Protocol. This NIC is created when you select the check box "Allow management operating system to share this network adapter." And yes, it will go away when you deselect it. Using this NIC, the host is connected to the outside network through the virtual switch.

Figure 29.36 sums it all up. The physical NICs talk to the outside world and are connected to the parent partition directly or to a virtual switch. The host (parent partition) can use both virtual switches and hardware NICs. VMs can only use virtual switches.

FIGURE 29.36
The virtual network puzzle: physical NICs, virtual NICs, and virtual switches

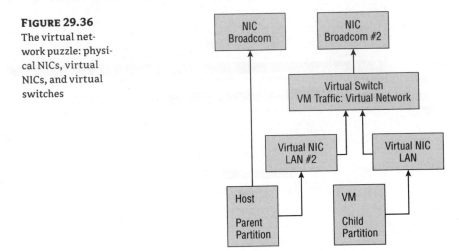

These virtual switches are a powerful concept. Using them, you can create an internal network as complex as you like. Great for testing and exploring new technology!

Connecting VMs to Virtual Switches

Virtual network connections are managed from the VM settings dialog box. This VM has only one NIC. For each NIC, you can select any virtual switch you like, as shown in Figure 29.37. The interesting setting is where you choose which network (virtual switch, really) to use for the selected NIC. You can change this while the VM is running. From the VM point of view, this is like pulling the cable from one switch and plugging it into another.

The option to use a static MAC address should not be necessary. Hyper-V manages its own pool of MAC addresses. Unless you encounter a MAC conflict, you should probably leave this setting at Dynamic.

Then there is the option "Enable spoofing of MAC addresses." That sounds like a bad thing, doesn't it? Well, it was the only behavior available in Hyper-V 1.0. One compromised VM could start flooding the switch or impersonate another VM. Hyper-V 2.0 is by default more secure. The virtual switch learns which MAC corresponds to which VM and does not allow it to change its MAC address anymore. Usually this is not a problem, except for those situations where you really do need multiple MAC addresses. Can't think of one? Consider network load balancing or failover clustering.

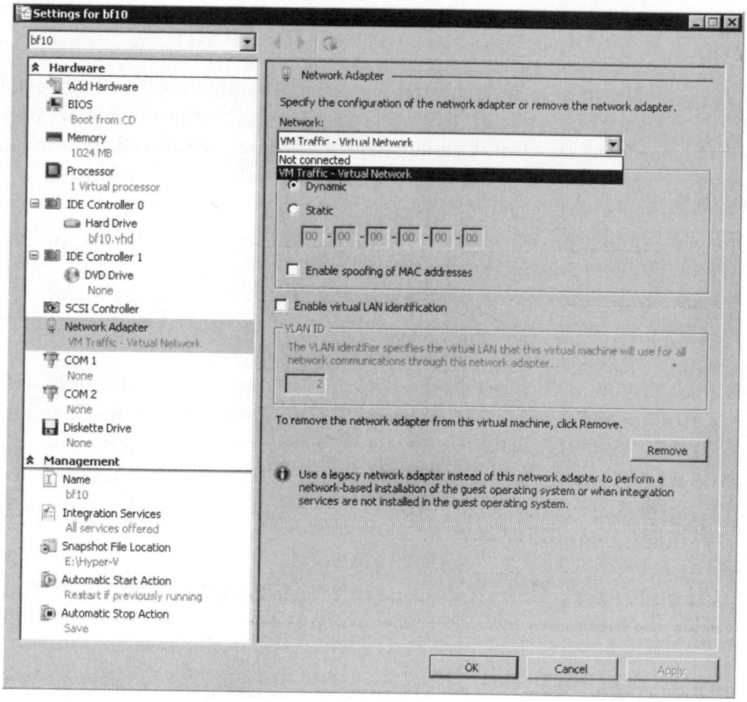

FIGURE 29.37
Configuring VM
network settings.
The important
choice is which
virtual switch to
use: none (the "Not
connected" option)
or VM Traffic –
Virtual Network.

When you configured the switch, you saw the option to configure a VLAN tag. A similar option is present in the dialog box for a virtual NIC. A VLAN is a virtual LAN on the network level. The term has been in general use since the late-90s and is unrelated to Hyper-V virtualization.

Briefly, a virtual LAN (VLAN) can be regarded as a broadcast domain. It operates on the OSI network layer 2. The exact protocol definition is known as 802.1Q. Each network packet belonging to a VLAN has an identifier. This is just a number between 0 and 4095, with both 0 and 4095 reserved for other uses. Let's assume a VLAN with an identifier of 10. A NIC configured with the VLAN ID of 10 will pick up network packets with the same ID and will ignore all other IDs. The point of VLANs is that switches and routers enabled for 802.1Q can present VLANs to different switch ports in the network. In other words, where a normal IP subnet is limited to a set of ports on a physical switch, a subnet defined in a VLAN can be present on any switch port—if so configured, of course.

Getting back to the VLAN functionality in Hyper-V: both virtual switches and virtual NICs can detect and use VLAN IDs. Both can accept and reject network packets based on VLAN ID, which means that the VM does not have to do it itself. The use of VLAN enables Hyper-V to participate in more advanced network designs. One limitation in the current implementation is that a virtual switch can have just one VLAN ID, although that should not matter too much in practice. The default setting is to accept all VLAN IDs.

NETWORK TRACING ON HYPER-V SWITCHES

What all these virtual switches have in common is that they do not behave like network hubs, but like true switches. This includes the capability to transport packets from port to port without offering them to all connected NICs. Usually this means nothing to you, but there is one situation where you will notice it. A VM will see only its own MAC address on the virtual switch port. This means that there is no way to analyze the network with a NIC in promiscuous mode. The port will simply see no traffic that is not directly targeted at its VM. To see all traffic, you would need to be able to assign one port as a monitor, duplicating all traffic in the switch. This feature is not present in versions 1.0 and 2.0 of Hyper-V, although it is being considered for later versions.

If you look at the status of a NIC in Figure 29.38, you may note one unusual feature. It has a link speed of 10Gbit per second! That's clearly not realistic in most cases. There is a subtle point here. What speed do you assign to a software NIC connected to a software switch? It really doesn't matter. Hyper-V will move the data as fast as it can. The Hyper-V development team arbitrarily chose to label the link speed as 10Gbit per second, and perhaps you may even reach that rate under some circumstances.

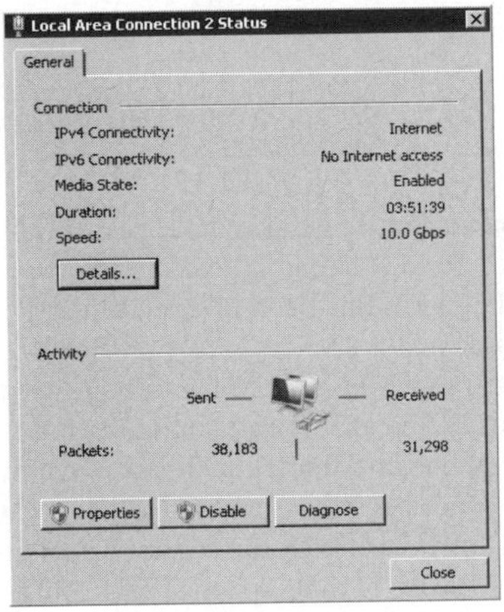

FIGURE 29.38
A virtual NIC is
connected to its
switch using a link
speed of 10Gbit
per second.

NIC TEAMING: BE CAREFUL

Using NIC teaming, you can logically combine two or more physical NICs and present them to the OS as a single NIC. The idea is to supply redundancy or load balancing. Many NIC vendors supply teaming drivers for this purpose. The problem is, most teaming solutions (anno 2009) don't work in combination with Hyper-V, with the exception of specifically designed drivers.

So, before you deploy teaming on your Hyper-V hosts, make really sure that your teaming solution supports Hyper-V.

Managing Virtual Machines

In the previous sections of this chapter, you learned the main points of Hyper-V: how to install it, its software architecture, and the ins and outs of virtual disk and networks. There is a lot more to say about server virtualization that would deserve a book on its own. In this remaining sections, we will discuss some of these aspects, some just for awareness, and others more in depth.

Licensing Hyper-V Hosts and Their VMs

As with all commercial software, you need a license to run Hyper-V legally. Generally, licensing aspects are an uninteresting bit of overhead when you buy and deploy software. But with virtualization, there is something important going on. Since 2006, Microsoft has had a specific licensing scheme for server virtualization. Before we get into that, you should realize that such licensing may change over time. To get the current state of affairs, please visit www.microsoft.com/licensing. To have the exact details explained to you, you should call Microsoft. It has people trained in the science of Microsoft licensing; rumor has it that such training takes years.

Anyway, the point is this. If you buy a Windows server license enabled for virtualization, you obtain the right to run one or more VMs with a Windows Server operating system on it using that same license. In other words, you do not have to buy an additional license for the VM—under certain conditions. This right is valid for Windows 2003 R2 licenses and later versions of Windows Server. Table 29.8 lists the main points.

TABLE 29.8:   Virtual Machine Licensing

SERVER VERSION	EXTRA LICENSE RIGHTS
Hyper-V Server	None
Standard edition	One VM
Enterprise edition	Four VMs
Datacenter edition	Unlimited VMs, licensed per *physical* processor

Here is how it works. A license for a higher edition always gives you permission to run a lower edition. Buy Enterprise edition, and you are allowed to run Standard edition as well. Assume you want to run 10 new VMs with Standard edition. The host server has two physical processors. Again, note that licensing depends on these physical processors (motherboard sockets) of the host, not on the number of processor cores or on any hyperthreading features. Your options for these 10 VMs are as follows:

◆ Buy 10 licenses for Standard edition.

◆ Buy two licenses for Enterprise edition, giving you the right for $2 \times 4 = 8$ VMs and two additional licenses for Standard edition. This gives you exactly what you need, but no more.

◆ Buy three licenses for Enterprise edition for $3 \times 4 = 12$ licenses. Yes, two too many, but that is room to expand.

◆ Buy two licenses for Datacenter Edition, one for each processor on the host. In this case, you have unlimited expansion room with your licenses.

The cost effectiveness depends on your future growth plans and on the prices for each edition. As you can see, you may have some unexpected options to license your VMs. Note that the license you buy does not require you to install that particular operating system edition as a host or VM. A typical scenario might be to buy a high-end four-processor quad-core server with 128GB of internal memory, where you will run 50 or maybe even 100 lightly used servers, most of them probably running Standard edition. You will certainly buy four Datacenter licenses for the host, but you do not have to install Datacenter just to run Hyper-V. A Standard or Enterprise edition with Hyper-V is good enough.

What's really interesting about this licensing mechanism is that it does not talk about a specific virtualization technology. The license does not specify what edition of Windows to install on the host, as noted, but it in fact allows you to install anything you like as a virtualization host. This includes Microsoft's own products such as Virtual Server R2 but also any server virtualization products by the competition.

What operating system are you licensed for, exactly? There are not only editions to think about but also versions. The host will be Windows 2008 or newer if you run Hyper-V, but what about the operating system in the VMs? Unfortunately, the answer is that it depends on your licensing scheme. Some have downgrade options allowing you to install Windows 2003; others do not. Contact Microsoft or talk to your reseller to find out.

You may be planning to virtualize existing physical machines in your environment. Clearly, you have already paid for those licenses. There is no need to purchase extra licenses from this special virtualization licensing scheme.

One point about the spirit of the license. If you buy one Enterprise edition, you are allowed to run four VMs, but including the host with Hyper-V, you are really running five instances of Windows. The stipulation is that the host should not do anything except be a virtualization platform. You should not make the host a domain controller, run DHCP, and so on. If you plan on doing so, it costs one license, which would leave you with only three licenses for VMs.

Moving VMs Around: Export and Import

One important benefit of server virtualization technology is that the VM no longer strongly depends on the physical server. With a physical server, you would at the very least need to move physical disk around, which works only if the hardware is similar enough. With dissimilar hardware, you would probably have to reinstall the whole machine. Because all Hyper-V hosts offer almost identical hardware to their VMs (with the possible exception of the CPU) and most VMs will use virtual disks, VMs are much easier to move around. With additional tools, it becomes easier still, but moving a VM with Hyper-V is not hard. All you need for this section is a regular high-speed network because of the amount of data you are moving. A SAN is not required.

A VM has three parameters: configuration, current state, and data. When moving a VM to another Hyper-V host, you need to make sure that all of these come along. There is no easy way to do this by hand, though in a pinch you could just take the virtual disks and re-create the VM from there. The Hyper-V console has the Export Wizard, which appears only when the VM is not running. This wizard collects all relevant data, including snapshots, and copies it to a target folder. On the Hyper-V host where you want to run the VM, you run the Import Wizard, and that is all there is to it—well, almost.

The first point to be aware of is that an export operation simply copies all the VM: configuration, state, and data. The import operation is different. You have two choices to make:

♦ Do you keep the old virtual machine ID (default) or generate a new one?

♦ Do you use the export files directly to run the VM or copy them first? If you do not copy the files, you can import only once.

VIRTUAL MACHINE IDS

As most experienced Windows administrators know, many objects in the Windows world have multiple names. A well-known example is an Active Directory object. Its "true" name is a *globally unique identifier* (GUID), but we prefer to use human-readable names such as *display name* or *common name*. It's the same with VMs. Their true name is a GUID, which cannot change. Then there is the display name, which can be anything you like. Other objects in the VM world also have GUIDs, such as virtual switches and NICs.

An interesting property of VMs is that their IDs need to be unique, but the display names may be identical. This typically happens when you import a VM on the same host that you used for export. As long as you use a different ID on import, this will work fine.

A second, more subtle point is that of the virtual network configuration. How does the VM know which virtual switches to use on the new host? Internally, each virtual switch is known by its GUID, allowing you to give the switch any name you like without interfering with its relations to virtual NICs. But if you create a virtual switch on another host, it will have a different GUID. Hyper-V has one little trick to get around this. On import, it looks for virtual switches with exactly the same display name (including character case) as the ones included in the export files. If it finds them, the virtual NICs are connected. If not, the imported VM will have disconnected NICs.

Let's walk through an example where you export and import a VM. Any VM will do, but in this case we will use bf10. Ideally you should have a second Hyper-V host for import, but the example works with one host.

Assume you have a second host name, bf6. Create a shared folder with a descriptive name like Imported Virtual Machines. The required share permissions are a bit tricky. The export process runs as SYSTEM, not as you. So, the share should have permissions for the host computer account to write data. Use either the computer account (bf5) or the Everyone security principal to give write access. Then, start the Export process on the source host, bf5:

1. On the Hyper-V management console, select the VM you will export, which is bf10 in this example.

2. If the VM is still running, shut it down. A saved state may work but requires compatibility on the CPU level between hosts. For the attentive reader, yes, enabling the ability to migrate to a computer with a different processor version will definitely help to migrate saved states. You would set this on the virtual CPU properties.

3. Select Export, and enter a destination path for your export. It could be a local drive, USB drive, or a remote network location. This time, we will export directly to another Hyper-V host: `\\bf6\Imported Virtual Machines`. If the path does not exist, the wizard will create it. Whatever path you specify here, the wizard will create a subdirectory with the name of the VM.

After the export procedure is finished, you will import the VM. You can to this from the Hyper-V management console on bf5 by adding bf6 as an additional managed machine, but for the example you will log on to bf6:

1. Log on to bf6.

2. If you want the virtual NICs to connect automatically on import, make sure there are virtual switches with exactly the same names. If you have followed the examples, you need to create Management and VM Traffic.

3. Start the Hyper-V management console.

4. From the Actions pane in the Hyper-V management console, select Import Virtual Machine, as shown in Figure 29.39. Specify the location of the VM using the full path: `D:\Imported Virtual Machines\bf10`. The default settings in the dialog box deserve some attention. Keeping the same unique ID (see the "Import/Exports in Hyper-V 1.0" sidebar) makes sense. But if you plan to use this export again, you should select "Duplicate all files so the same virtual machine can be imported again."

FIGURE 29.39
Importing an exported VM

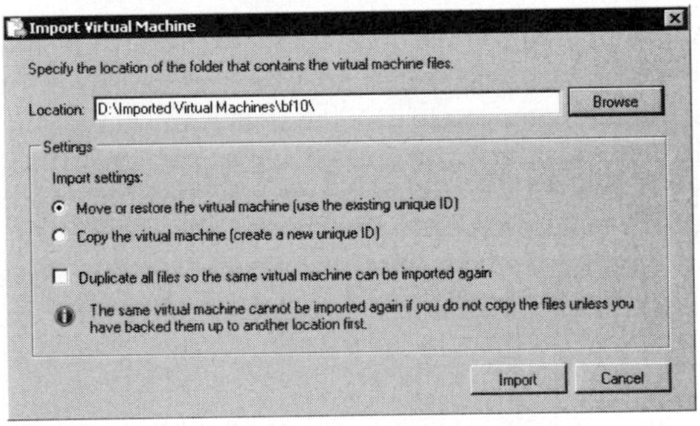

5. Click Import to start the process. It will take just a few seconds and come back with a status update. If there was a problem, you need to search the event log. A common issue is that no matching virtual switch was found, leaving the NICs unconnected.

6. Select the newly imported VM. You will see that the snapshots came along. Check the VM properties, and note the paths to the virtual disks. Verify the connection state of the NICs.

Now that you have imported this VM, you might be tempted to turn it on. But remember, you have now effectively cloned the old VM. You'd have two identical machines on the network if you were to turn them both on! Good idea? You be the judge.

IMPORT/EXPORTS IN HYPER-V 1.0

The first version of Hyper-V in Windows Server 2008 has different behavior on export and import operations. In fact, to call it broken would not be far from the truth.

In Hyper-V 1.0, if you imported a VM, it would always use the import location directly. The GUI offers no option to copy the import files first. So, unless you thought to copy them yourselves, you could import the exported VM only once. More than a few people have been caught out with this, because this behavior is totally nonobvious—unless you know exactly how it works.

A second point is that Hyper-V 1.0 does not deal elegantly with snapshots. On export you would get all the intermediate files as well. In 2.0, the whole snapshot tree is merged on export, leaving you with one .vhd file.

Just when you think you have the whole concept nailed, there comes one more point to consider. While reading about snapshots, you learned about the risks of rolling back images or restoring image-like backups. Exported VMs are no different. If you export a VM and start it again, the exported VM becomes an image-like backup. If you import the VM on another host, two bad things might happen: you have two almost identical computers running (same name, same IP address, same roles, and so on), and at the same time you did the trick of going back in time for the VM. As noted in the snapshot discussion, this exposes you to issues such as USN rollback and related fun. The safe thing to do is never to use a VM again after you export it. The export mechanism is used to store a VM offline. It is not a replacement for backup.

You may be interested to know how Hyper-V actually keeps track of VM configuration. The actual VM configuration is the easy part. When you create a VM, you tell it where to put the top-level folder containing the VM configuration. Figure 29.40 shows the configuration on Hyper-V host bf5 at E:\Hyper-V.

FIGURE 29.40
The file structure in the default Hyper-V folder

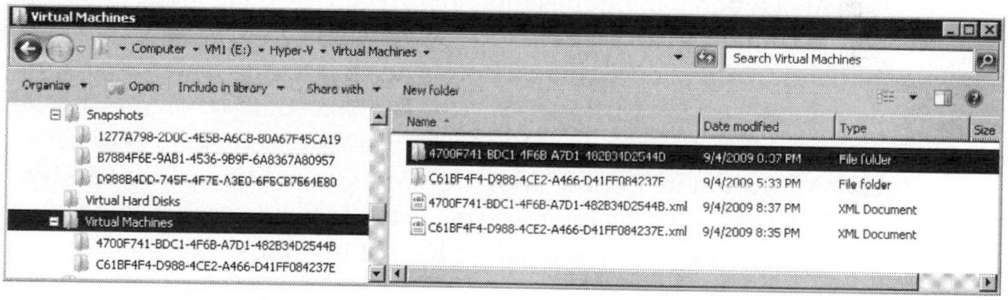

The screenshot shows three folders: Snapshots, Virtual Hard Disks, and Virtual Machines. There are two virtual machines registered here. Each has one folder named after its GUID, which is the real name of the virtual machine. For instance, the folder name C61BF4F4-D988... corresponds to bf10. This folder contains the current memory state if you save its state. Each VM also has an XML document, again named after the GUID of the VM. This document is fully readable, although you probably should not edit it by hand. If you look though it, you will find the entire configuration of the VM. As an illustration, the XML file has all virtual switches the VM is connected to listed by the GUID of the virtual switch, not by the friendly names.

The Snapshot folder has GUID folders, containing state information of each snapshot: the current configuration of the processes and virtual hardware in a .vsv file, and all of virtual memory in a .bin file. The difference files of the snapshots are saved as .avhd files in the Virtual Hard Disks folder.

As you know, the VM configuration may be all over the place. When creating a VM or virtual disk, you can put it basically any place you like. So, how does Hyper-V know where to find everything? It uses *symbolic links*, which are very small files that refer to other files in a way that is transparent to applications. In this case, all relevant symbolic links are in the central configuration location for Hyper-V: %systemdrive%\ProgramData\Microsoft\Windows\Hyper-V. The folder ProgramData is hidden; it's visible only if you tell Explorer to not hide hidden and system files. Starting with Windows 2008 R2, you can actually view symbolic links as such from Explorer. In Figure 29.41, you can see from the small curved arrows in the icons that these are symbolic links, not ordinary files. Also, the file size of 0 bytes gives it away. In earlier versions of Windows, you would need to revert to the command prompt to tell the difference between symbolic links and normal files.

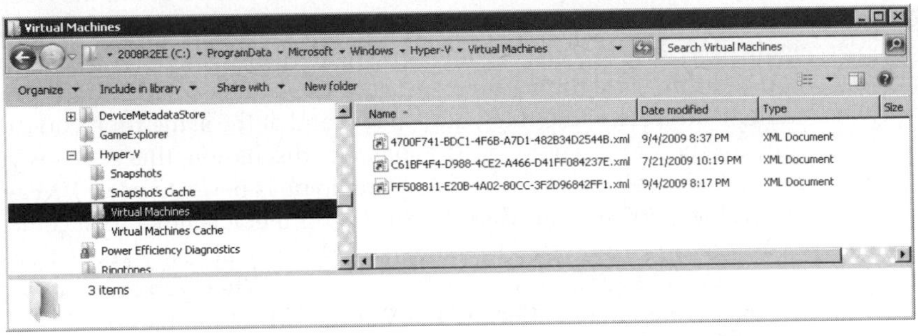

FIGURE 29.41
The starting point for Hyper-V configuration files. All files here are symbolic links, pointing to the physical location of the XML files that define virtual machines.

This Hyper-V folder has four subdirectories: Snapshots, Snapshots Cache, Virtual Machines, and Virtual Machines Cache. The screenshot shows the Virtual Machine folder containing three symbolic links to XML files. This is one more than Figure 29.41 actually shows. The third VM definition is not in E:\Hyper-V*, but it turns out to be on C:\ClusterStorage*, which is used for Live Migration. The Cache folders are also used to support Live Migration. Read more about Live Migration in section "Moving VMs: Quick Migration and Live Migration."

Knowing how this reference mechanism works can be quite useful for repairing the Hyper-V configuration after some disaster. Keep it in mind!

Backing Up and Restoring Virtual Machines

From a systems management point of view, you should treat VMs as if they were physical machines, with some exceptions. When it comes to backup and restore, there are some special issues to consider. If you look at a Hyper-V host machine running a number of VMs, you may wonder whether you can back up all of that in one go. In the ideal world, you could do the following:

◆ Back up all VMs, and do so incrementally.

◆ Make all VMs aware of the backup so that they can do the right thing on restore. This is particularly important for Active Directory and Exchange.

◆ Restore VMs individually.

In principle you could do it this way. The reality is different, however. We'll review briefly how a modern Windows backup works.

Since the days of Windows 2003, we have had Volume Shadowcopy Services (VSS). This component does two things for the backup process. First, it can freeze a disk volume, take a snapshot, and unfreeze the disk again. The snapshot stays on the volume. It works using a differencing algorithm and takes little space. Second, the VSS service interacts with applications during the backup to allow them to clean up and prepare, such as flush buffers, stabilize data structures, and so on. You can see how this benefits complex applications. VSS allows them to be backed up quickly and with data structures intact. Such applications would be Active Directory, SQL Server, Exchange Server, and of course...Hyper-V.

So, to make VSS work in a virtual environment, you need a VSS provider for Hyper-V and a component in the VM that integrates with this provider. How else would the applications in the VM be aware that there is a backup going on? In other words, it's a two-stage rocket: the VSS process in the host needs to trigger the VSS process in the VM during backup, using the Hyper-V VSS provider as the communication channel. In the VM itself, it's the Integration Services that takes care of the integration. This is an important point to note: without working Integration Services, you cannot have a real backup from the host. Yes, using VSS you can back up the .vhd files that make up the VM, but the VM will not be aware of the backup. It would be nothing better than a live image backup with all its limitations.

Let's recap. You have two options to back up operating systems and applications in a VM:

♦ Run a backup from the host, using a backup tool that is VSS aware. The Integration Services in the VM are required.

♦ Treat the VM as a physical machine, and run backups software from the virtualized OS.

There is a lot going for the second option. It will fit right it with your existing backup system, it won't break anything, and you know how to do it. This way, the host can be a black box that can be replaced at will. Be aware that a backup initiated from a VM generates a lot of disk I/O. If you have 10 VMs on one host all doing their backup at the same time, you generate 10 times the load on the host. It takes pretty good hardware to keep up with that!

On the other hand, backing up all those VMs in one shot is attractive as well, so let's take a look at that. The built-in tool for the job is Windows Server Backup. There is one problem you need to take care of before you start. By default, Hyper-V is not registered with VSS. If you made a backup now, the VSS service in the VMs would not be used. The following steps show you how to install WSB and to register the Hyper-V VSS provider. For more details, please read Knowledge Base article 958662.

1. Start Server Manager, select Features, then select Add Features. Find Windows Server Backup Features, select all subfeatures, and install it.

2. Start the registry editor, `regedit.exe`. Browse to HKLM\SOFTWARE\Microsoft\Windows NT\ CurrentVersion.

3. Create a new key called WindowsServerBackup.

4. Below this key, create a new key called Application Support.

5. Below this key, create a new key called {66841CD4-6DED-4F4B-8F17-FD23F8DDC3DE}. Yes, we're serious. This is the GUID corresponding to the Hyper-V VSS writer. Don't forget the curly brackets.

6. Below this key, create a new REG_SZ value called `Application Identifier`.

7. Set this value to `Hyper-V`, as shown in Figure 29.42.

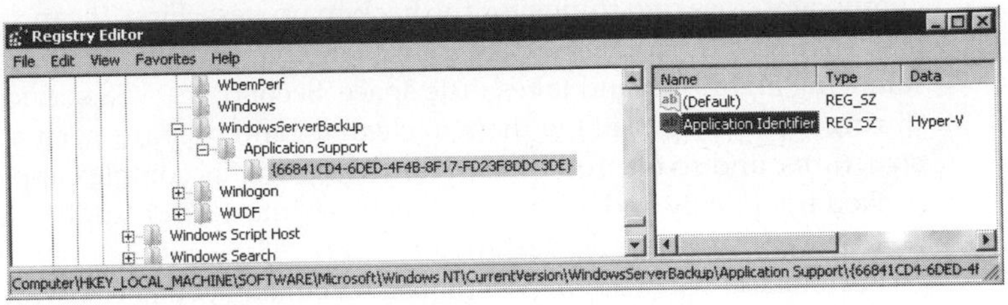

FIGURE 29.42
Required registry setting to register the Hyper-V VSS writer with Windows Server Backup

If you are going to do this more than once, you will probably want to export this key into a .reg file. There is no need to reboot. Windows Server Backup looks for VSS registrations every time it starts.

To get all VMs and their configuration, you must back up all volumes where you have the VMs, as well as the system volume that stores the Hyper-V configuration. In most cases, the best thing is to back up all volumes except the one that will hold the backup files. For this example, you'll to do a one-time backup to a local USB drive:

1. From the Administrative Tools, start Windows Server Backup. In the Actions pane, select "Backup once."

2. On the first screen, just click Next for Different Options.

3. Select Custom, and click Next.

4. Add Items, and select the system partition (C, most likely) and all partitions containing VMs.

5. Click Next to select the destination drive. This can be a local drive or a remote share. Figure 29.43 shows the summary screen.

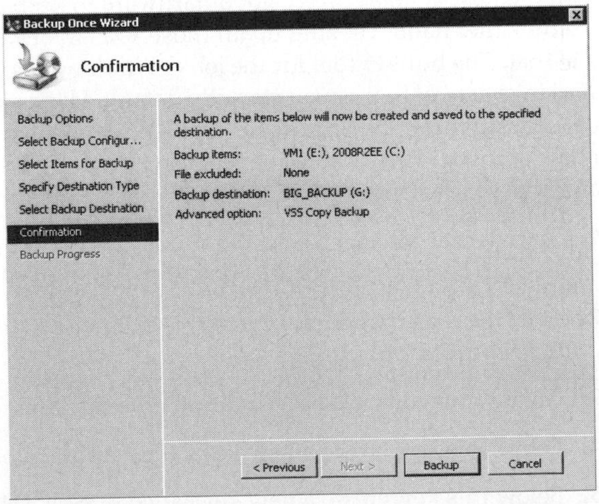

FIGURE 29.43
Windows Server Backup, about to start the Hyper-V backup

6. Click the Backup button to start the process.

Although this is clear enough, the restore process is not nearly as nice. WSB offers no way to restore individual VMs. Either you can restore all the Hyper-V configuration and data or you need to hand-pick the VHD files you want recovered. Still, the full restore is good enough in a disaster recovery situation where the whole host is lost and you need to recover the VM setup. If that is your main purpose, you are all set!

HYPER-V BACKUP IN THE REAL WORLD

The limitations of Windows Server Backup make it unsuitable for larger companies. Its worst problem is not being able to restore individual VMs. Not only does this force you to jump through hoops for VM recovery, but it means you need to know on which host the VM was running at the time. So, what to do?

You probably have third-party backup software already. Many vendors have promised support for Hyper-V host-based backup, so with a bit of luck, you have a solution already in-house. The only supported solution from Microsoft is to use Data Protection Manager 2007 SP1, or any newer edition.

It may have occurred to you to use the Export feature as a backup. Still, an exported VM is not equivalent to a normal backup because there is no VSS integration. When you import a VM, it does not know it has been "restored." The downsides of using exports are that you do them one by one and that importing them requires you to delete the current VM first (if it still exists). If you know what you are doing, an export/import will do in a pinch. Otherwise, it's not a backup solution.

Server Core and the Hyper-V Server

If there is one scenario where the Server Core edition really shines, it's virtualization. What would you like in a virtualization host? Minimal memory footprint, as few services as possible, locked down by default, small attack surface, reduced patch frequency—Server Core has it. There is just one little disadvantage: you must manage it remotely because there is no MMC on Server Core and no out-of-the-box command-line interface to Hyper-V. In larger environments, this is no problem, since remote management should be the default option anyway. In this section, we show you how to install Server Core with Hyper-V and how to manage it remotely. This example is suitable for both Windows 2008 and Windows 2008 R2. In reality, the R2 version of Server Core is easier to manage because it includes a menu-oriented command named sconfig to manage many configuration settings. Similarly, the Hyper-V Server has the command hvconfig to do the same thing.

The system requirements for Hyper-V on Server Core are basically the same as for a full installation of Windows Server 2008, with one strong recommendation: join the host to a domain. Remote management is just so much easier when the server is a member of an Active Directory forest. To recap, Table 29.9 is the suggested minimal configuration.

TABLE 29.9: Hyper-V on Server Core

SETTING	CONFIGURATION
Internal memory	8GB; 4GB is the practical minimum
Hard disks	2×200GB or more
Partitions	Disk 1: System on C Disk 2: Reserved for Hyper-V on E
Network	2×1Gbit highly recommended.
Operating system	Windows 2008 SP2 or later with Hyper-V, 64-bit edition
Installation type	Server Core
Hostname	bf6 to follow the examples
IP configuration	Address: 192.168.1.55/24 Gateway: 192.168.1.1 DNS: 192.168.1.51
Active Directory	Domain-joined strongly recommended

Next, you will install Server Core, configure the network and firewall, name the server, join it to a domain, and install the Hyper-V role. Since Server Core is covered extensively elsewhere in this book, we will not show you the full installation. Please refer to Chapter 3, "The New Server: Introduction to Server Core," to remind yourself how it was done and to familiarize yourself with the command-line tools you might need.

In this example, the Server Core installation will work closely with the first Hyper-V host you installed (bf5). The IP configuration is compatible. Make sure they are connected to the same network using a hub or switch. Now perform the following steps:

1. Install Windows Server 2008 with Hyper-V, using the Server Core installation option. Install to the point where you log on for the first time using Administrator with a blank password, and set it to something meaningful. The next step is to set the IP configuration.

2. Examine the LAN interfaces. Take note of the IDX (index) number of the interface that you need to use. Enter the following at the command prompt:

   ```
   netsh interface ipv4 show interfaces
   ```

3. Set the IP number, mask, and interface using the IDX number from the previous step:

   ```
   netsh interface ipv4 set address name="<IDX>" source=static↵
   address=192.168.1.55 mask=255.255.255.0 gateway=192.168.1.1
   ```

4. Add a DNS server using the IP address of the DC bf1.bigfirm.com:

   ```
   netsh interface ipv4 add dnsserver name="<IDX>" address=192.168.1.51 index=1
   ```

With the IP configuration done, next up is giving the server a proper name and joining it to the domain bigfirm.com:

1. Rename the server to bf6:

```
netdom renamecomputer localhost /NewName:bf6
```

2. As the netdom command told you, a reboot is required:

```
shutdown /r /t 0
```

3. Let the machine restart, and log on again using the password you set in step 1.

4. To double-check, verify that you can resolve the domain. The following command should succeed and give you the IP address of at least one domain controller of the domain bigfirm.com:

```
nslookup bigfirm.com
```

5. Join the server to the domain. You use the Administrator of the domain and need its password. The asterisk causes netdom to prompt you for the password:

```
netdom join localhost /domain:bigfirm.com /userD:Administrator /passwordD:*
```

6. Again, a reboot is required:

```
shutdown /r /t 0
```

To use the server in a domain with Hyper-V, you need to make it more manageable than its current locked-down state. Enable Remote Desktop, allow remote management through MMCs on other computers, and allow remote computers to access file shares:

1. Log on using a Domain Admin account such as BIGFIRM\Administrator.

2. Enable Remote Desktop:

```
cscript \windows\system32\scregedit.wsf /ar 0
```

3. Optionally, you might want to allow older systems than Windows 2008 to use RDP:

```
cscript \windows\system32\scregedit.wsf /cs 0
```

4. Enable the use of remote management tools:

```
netsh advfirewall set currentprofile settings remotemanagement enable
```

5. Allow remote computers to access shared folders on this server:

```
netsh advfirewall firewall set rule group="File and Printer Sharing" new enable=Yes
```

The final step is to install Hyper-V:

1. Log on to bf6 using Domain Admin credentials.

2. Install the Hyper-V role:

   ```
   ocsetup Microsoft-Hyper-V
   ```

3. Click Yes in the dialog box to restart. The server may reboot again automatically.

At this point, bf6 is a fully prepared Hyper-V host. As noted, it's not easy to manage Hyper-V from the command line without additional tools. WMI scripts are your only option using native instrumentation. Normally, you will use another server with a Hyper-V management console to control your Server Core hosts. As an illustration, follow these steps:

1. Log on to bf5, and start the Hyper-V management console.

2. Right-click Hyper-V Manager, and add bf6 as an additional server.

> **USE GROUP POLICY TO CONFIGURE SERVER CORE**
>
> Take advantage of the power of Group Policy to configure Server Core (or Hyper-V Server) as much as possible. After the computer has joined the domain, you can use a firewall policy, use startup scripts, and so on.

Moving VMs: Quick Migration and Live Migration

It's impossible to have a full discussion of server virtualization without mentioning Quick Migration and Live Migration. These are related but different technologies to move virtual machines between hosts using shared storage and shared high-speed networks. Live Migration is the newer technology. Its key feature is that the unavailability of the VM during the actual move is very short. Subsecond times are not unusual. This time is short enough to keep TCP/IP sessions alive. In other words, anyone using that VM will at most notice a subsecond delay, but everything keeps working.

The ability to move VMs quickly between hosts opens up some interesting scenarios. Let's say you have at least three of four Hyper-V hosts deployed, and you are running all your VMs on shared storage with Live Migration enabled.

Easier host management   Any time you need to do something on a host that requires downtime, you can move all VMs away without downtime for those VMs. Think hardware maintenance like adding memory, patching, and so on.

On-demand resource allocation   You may have VMs that are running "hot" and are using a lot of CPU or disk I/O resources. With Live Migration, you can move this VM to a lightly loaded host or, alternatively, get other VMs out of the way instead.

Enabling green IT   With Live Migration, you have the potential to shut down lowly used hosts, although in the real world you would need additional tooling to pull this off. The idea is that you move VMs away from lightly used hosts, putting them all on a few hosts that are well utilized—say, up to 60 percent average CPU time or whatever you prefer. The hosts without VMs can be shut down until they are needed again, with corresponding power savings.

All the major server virtualization vendors offer similar features but may use different names. However, shared storage implies SANs, iSCSI, and other storage technologies that we can't fully discuss here. Still, we'll cover the basic principles and show you a brief walk-through assuming that you are able to set up the basic storage infrastructure yourself. If you have never worked with remote storage before, we will have some hints to help you along.

Live Migration relies on failover clustering, known as *server clustering* in Windows 2003 and 2000. *Failover clustering* is the ability to transfer running applications between hosts, including all their data and current state. This transfer (also known as *failover event*) can be initiated by the user, but usually a number of conditions are set that should trigger the failover. Dependencies of the application are good examples of such a condition: disks, networks, certain services that should be running, and so on. If any of these goes missing, failover clustering will trigger a failover. An application needs to know that it's running on a cluster and take action when requested. Well-known examples are SQL Server, Exchange Server, File and Print Services, and so on. You can see where the shared storage comes in: a data disk for an application running on one node needs to go to another node if the application fails over.

Each server taking part in a clustering setup is a node. Since Windows 2008, the maximum number of nodes has been pushed to 16, an increase from 8 in Windows 2003. The main point of failover clustering is to provide high availability: if one host goes down, either planned or unexpectedly, the clustering services ensure that the application is restarted on another node.

An important limitation of Quick Migration in Hyper-V version 1 is that each VM requires its own logical unit (LUN). A LUN is a unit of storage on a SAN that is presented as a single disk to Windows. This leads quickly to drive letter exhaustion and other administrative complications. One of the major changes in Windows 2008 R2 is the introduction of a cluster shared volume (CSV). This is a way to store multiple files on a single LUN, simultaneously shared among two or more hosts. There is a locking mechanism that determines which node actually owns which file. CSV was written with Live Migration in mind, although it also works with Quick Migration. Its main function is to make life easier by simplifying the setup and configuration of a Hyper-V cluster and its VMs.

With failover clustering applied to Hyper-V virtual machines, you actually have two different failover technologies. First, Quick Migration works by saving the state of the VM, transferring control of its disk to another node, and restarting it on that node. This process is predictable and reliable but not so fast that it passes unnoticed. Time is lost during saving and restoring the VM state, which may take up to perhaps a minute for VMs with a lot of memory. Still, this is not a problem during a maintenance window where you need to work on the cluster node(s).

The second technology is Live Migration, called that because it is fast enough to move a VM to another node without loss of service. It works roughly like this; the key difference with Quick Migration is the way the VM memory is transferred:

1. The migration is initiated. The VM configuration is transferred to the destination host, which builds a skeleton VM.

2. The memory store of the VM is locked, and a difference file is started. All memory changes are written to this file.

3. The memory store of the VM is transferred to the destination node using the shared network. Clearly, this network should be as fast as possible. The destination node starts loading this memory into the skeleton VM.

4. The first difference file is locked, and a second one is started. The first difference file is transferred to the destination node. This process repeats until the difference files become small.

5. Up to now, the VM keeps running, but at this point, the VM is frozen, and the final difference file is transferred as well.

6. Control of the VHD files of the VM is transferred to the destination node. This happens quickly.

7. The VM configuration is removed from the original node and registered on the destination node.

8. The VM starts running on the destination.

HOW TO CHOOSE BETWEEN LIVE MIGRATION AND QUICK MIGRATION

Why would you ever want to use Quick Migration when you can have Live Migration? Well, one reason is that you might be running Hyper-V on Windows 2008, which works only with Quick Migration.

Another reason is that Live Migration could sometimes fail. If you look at how it works, you can see its theoretical weak spot: it needs to transfer memory faster to the destination host than the VM is changing it. If you have an application that writes a lot of data to memory very quickly and keeps doing this, it could make Live Migration impossible. Clearly, a fast network is required to make Live Migration reliable. Your legacy 10Mb Ethernet is not going to cut it.

But this does show the advantage of Quick Migration: it is deterministic because it saves and restores the VM state between migrations. So, if Live Migration ever fails, try it with Quick Migration.

After all this explaining, let's get on with the walk-through. Take a look at Figure 29.44 for the basic setup. To make this work, you need to get hold of some servers and shared storage:

◆ Two similar servers. The CPU and motherboard need to be as closely matched as possible. The Failover Clustering Wizard will tell you if you have a problem. The servers need two NICs.

◆ Installation media for a cluster-enabled version of Windows 2008 R2, meaning Enterprise edition or Datacenter.

◆ An exported VM ready for import will be very convenient. Alternatively, you will build a VM from scratch.

◆ Shared network, at least 1Gbit.

◆ Shared storage, either iSCSI or Fibre Channel. Standard two-node shared SCSI no longer works for clustering since Windows 2008. The simplest setup uses iSCSI, and this is what we will use as an example. There are many ways to get hold of an iSCSI storage device. Lots of NAS devices support it nowadays, there is Windows Storage Server, and if you have a TechNet or MSDN subscription, you can even download a software iSCSI target to install on Windows Server.

FIGURE 29.44
Moving VMs between hosts using Live Migration requires a high-speed network and shared storage.

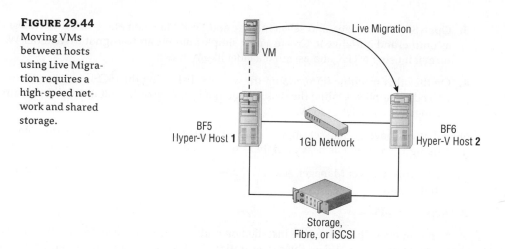

In preparation, configure the following. Yes, we are assuming that you know how to set up and configure your iSCSI storage here or that you can have somebody do it for you. Apologies if this turns out to be a problem!

1. Install two Hyper-V servers, named bf5 and bf6. A setup as described before for server bf5 will do fine. Use one NIC for management traffic and another for the VMs. The key point is to *make sure to use the same name for the virtual networks on both nodes*. Also, deselect the check box on the virtual network called "Allow management operating system to share this network adapter," because you don't want the cluster to become confused about which NIC to use.

2. Use static IP configuration for bf5 and bf6. In our example, we use 172.16.1.5/24 and 172.16.1.6/24. Find an unused IP address to be used as cluster IP address, such as 172.16.1.9.

3. Join both machines to an Active Directory domain, such as bigfirm.com, as used in this book.

4. Set up a LUN on your iSCSI device for the shared cluster information (a witness disk). This one needs to have a size of at least 1GB.

5. Set up another LUN for the VM that we will use for Live Migration; 50GB should be a comfortable size.

6. Both LUNS should be configured to be used by the two Hyper-V machines simultaneously.

The next step is to create the witness disk and to assign it a drive letter. W seems like a good choice, though any unused drive letter will do. All machines in the cluster must use the same drive letter for the witness disk, though. We will deal with the shared VM disk later. Note that the order in which you do this does matter. Another order may "confuse" the Create Cluster Wizard when it looks for disks and networks to use.

1. Start out with bf5, and log on using a Domain Admin account.

2. Using the iSCSI Initiator console, add the LUN intended as the witness disk. Make sure to add it to the list of favorite targets, ensuring the drive stays mounted after a reboot.

3. Open Server Manager, and select Storage and Disk Management. Mark the witness disk as online, and initialize it. Create a new simple volume, and assign it drive letter W. Then, format it using NTFS, and assign it a label like Witness.

4. On the other machine (bf6), mount the witness disk using the iSCSI initiator. The same procedure applies. Online the disk, but do not initialize or format it; we did that already. Change the drive letter to W.

Now that you have storage set up, you can install the failover clustering features. No, it's not a role, although something as heavyweight as failover clustering should deserve to be one.

1. On bf5, open Server Manager, select Features, and add the Failover Clustering role. A reboot is not required.

2. Repeat for bf6.

With the Failover Clustering role installed on both nodes, you can configure the failover cluster itself. Step 1 is to validate the configuration; step 2 is to create the cluster. These are the most critical steps. If any of the following fails, you should go back and troubleshoot.

1. On bf5, open Failover Cluster Manager from the Administrative Tools. In the right pane, select Validate a Configuration.

2. The Validate a Configuration Wizard starts. Close the opening screen, and add bf5 and bf6 to the list of servers to be tested on the next screen.

3. Next up is the choice for which tests to run. Just run them all.

4. For some reason, you need to confirm this step in the next stage.

5. Start the actual validation. This could take several minutes.

6. The wizard will present you with the results that look something like Figure 29.45. Examine any warnings, and fix all errors before proceeding. The warnings shown in the figure are because we have only one NIC for cluster communication, which is a single point of failure. No problem for a test, of course.

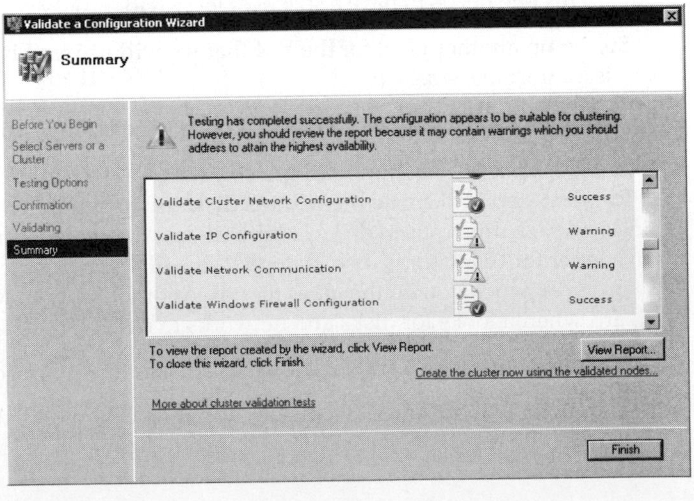

FIGURE 29.45
The results of the cluster validation should look like this. If all is well, you are in a good position to go ahead and configure Live Migration for these nodes.

7. Go back to Failover Cluster Manager, and select Create a Cluster.

8. The Create Cluster Wizard starts. Click away the opening screen, and add bf5 and bf6 as nodes to be added to the cluster.

9. The next screen is for the access point of the cluster. Enter a network name for the cluster, such hv1. The name must be unique in the Active Directory forest. Additionally, specify an IP address for this cluster name such as 172.16.1.9 in our setup.

10. Again, you need to confirm that you're sure you really want this.

11. Create the cluster. The wizard will look for the witness disk itself and configure it to be used accordingly.

12. If all is well, you end up with Figure 29.46. Note the warning that says that the second disk that it found is not considered as a witness. This is exactly what we need, because this disk will be used to hold the VMs.

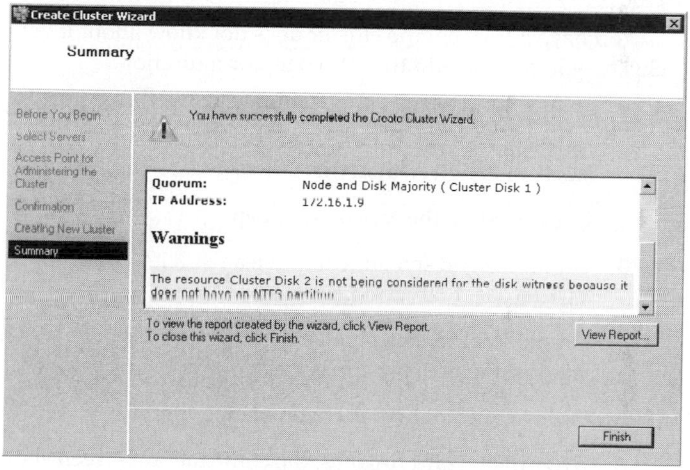

FIGURE 29.46
Finalizing the cre-
ation of the Hyper-
V cluster

So, we have a cluster, but there is no Hyper-V in sight yet. That is changing now. The next step is to enable CSV and to add the prepared VM disk.

1. On bf5, open Failover Cluster Manager. Select the cluster configuration (hv1.bigfirm.com), right-click, and Enable Shared Cluster Volumes. You will need to approve a notice.

2. From Server Manager, open the Disk Manager. Mark the disk intended for VMs as online, and initialize it. Create a new simple volume, and assign it drive letter V. Then, format it using NTFS, and assign it a label like VMDISK1.

3. Back to the Failover Cluster Manager, right-click Storage, and select Add a Disk. From the dialog box, pick the disk you just created (should be only one).

4. On Failover Cluster Manager, right-click Cluster Shared Volumes, select Add Storage, and add the new disk.

To check that all is well, you should look for a newly created folder named C:\ClusterStorage\ Volume1 on both nodes. At this point, you have a shared volume that you can use for virtual machines. You are almost there now. The whole system is ready for use. The next step is to create a virtual machine that you can use for testing. Create or import a new VM named bf11 (or whatever you prefer) on Hyper-V host bf5, and make sure that you do the following:

1. Place the virtual hard disks on the shared cluster storage at C:\ClusterStorage\Volume1.

2. Start the VM, and install the Integration Services, if required.

3. For networking, pick the network that you have created for use by VMs. Remember, this network should have the same name on both machines.

4. Give it an IP address that is reachable from the hosts, such as 172.16.1.50. Test this before you continue.

5. After you finalize the configuration, shut down the VM. Note: saving state is not sufficient, a shutdown is needed.

You have a VM, but the cluster does not know about it yet. To bring it under control of the cluster, you need to add the VM to its configuration.

1. On bf5, open Failover Cluster Manager. Select the cluster configuration (hv1.bigfirm.com), right-click Services and Applications, and select Configure a Service or Application. This starts the High Availability Wizard.

2. Click Next on the welcome screen.

3. On the second screen, you'll see a list with applications suitable for high availability. Pick Virtual Machine, and proceed.

4. On the final screen, choose the VM you want to make highly available. Pick the machine you just created, probably bf11.

5. Once again, confirm that you want to do this.

6. After the wizard finishes, the confirmation screen should show all green like Figure 29.47.

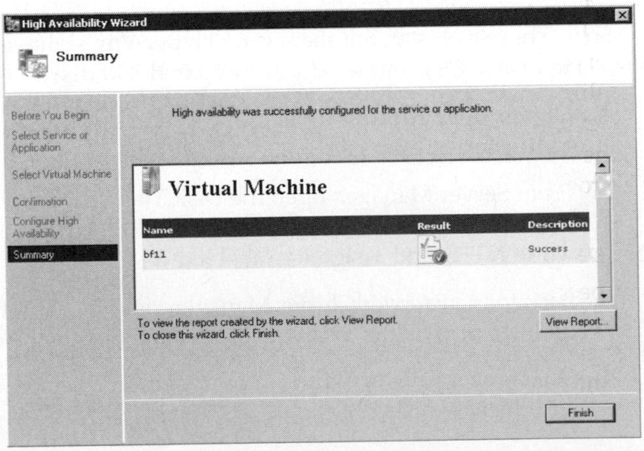

FIGURE 29.47
You just made virtual machine BF11 highly available.

7. Finally, verify that the VM is ready to be used with Live Migration. In Failover Cluster Manager, open Services and Applications again, and select your VM. In the Summary pane, select the properties of virtual machine bf11. It has a tab called "Network for live migration." Make sure that at least one cluster network is selected. Note: you may have to refresh the GUI or to start the VM first to actually see this tab. We have seen some inconsistencies here.

The configuration is done: the VM is ready for Live Migration and Quick Migration as well. To set up the test, a nice trick is to connect a remote desktop to the VM and play with Explorer or do a ping /t 172.16.1.50 from a remote machine to keep checking availability during the Live Migration. To initiate Live Migration, follow these steps:

1. Open Failover Cluster Manager, expand Services and Applications, and select bf11 (the VM that is enabled for Live Migration).

2. Right-click the VM, and select "Live Migrate virtual machine to another node." A list will expand showing all available nodes; pick one, and keep watching the ping window. After about 10 seconds, the VM will have moved to the other node while you have missed at most one ping—if all went well, of course.

3. Similarly, you can test quick migration and see that this is not as quick. Most of our tests kept the migration time under 10 seconds, which is short enough to keep a remote desktop session alive. During the migration, this desktop is frozen because the VM is being saved and restored.

That about sums it up. Configuring Live Migration is not a one-step process, but once you get the hang of it, it is easy enough. Having seen how it works, there are some final points you need to know.

First, there is backup and restore. In the section "Backing Up and Restoring Virtual Machines," we discussed how to back up a VM using Windows Server Backup and its VSS integration. However, in Hyper-V versions 1 (Windows 2008) and 2 (Windows 2008 R2), there is no VSS integration for clustered disks. So, you are back to making backups from inside the virtualized OS or need to use an external backup application that is cluster aware.

Second, you have some choices about which OS to use. As noted, both Enterprise edition and Datacenter editions are enabled for clustering and Live Migration. It does not matter if you install the full operating system or the Server Core edition. However, you have an additional choice: the Windows 2008 R2 Hyper-V Server is a valid cluster node. This is not a bad choice as a virtualization platform. It has a minimal footprint in terms of memory, disk space, and features. It can even be run from an USB device. The downside is that you only have the command line and the built-in menu system hvconfig. Still, for a large virtualization cluster, this should not be a problem.

Malware Protection and Patching

Most people are convinced by now that having some type of malware protection on servers is a good idea. The question is more, to what extent do you need protection? Do you need continuous scanning, or can you get away with daily or weekly scans? As long as you are in position to counter new threats, you are probably OK.

There is a possible complication with virtualization that may have occurred to you. Not only do you have the host to consider, but disk I/O is a precious resource on a virtualization platform. If you have a host with 10 VMs, all of them performing continuous malware scanning, the I/O system of the host gets 10 times more load because of scanning than a single server would have. In practice, this is not often a limiting factor. Modern antimalware software, certainly the server-class kind, knows how to be careful with I/O bandwidth. So, for VMs, the advice is clear: install malware scanners in all of them. Treat a VM the same way as a physical server.

But what about the Hyper-V host? If it runs no services except Hyper-V, what is the need for malware scanning? Especially on Server Core, there is little to attack for malware. Although that's true, that's not quite the point. Any operating system connected to a network is potentially vulnerable to attacks. Even a flaw in the TCP/IP stack could lead to a compromise of the system. So if you want full protection, you need to scan the host as well. Consider that by far the most disk activity will be performed by the VMs and you see that the performance impact of a malware scanner on the host will be low. Clearly, you will need to exclude the virtual disks and the Hyper-V processes from scanning. To be precise, exclude the default VM Configuration folder, the VHD folder, the Snapshot folder, VMMS.exe, and VMWP.exe.

Although malware scanning is a direct form of protection, keeping up-to-date with patches is indirect but just as important. There's no need to tell you that you should patch the VMs and the host. Patching the host may require a reboot, taking all the VMs offline. That requires planning and may cause problems if you cannot shut down VMs reliably. That's why Integration Services are so important. One of its functions is to initiate the save-state procedure in the VM when the host asks for it. The default action configured on each VM is that is saves state when the host shuts down. Clearly, the fewer patches the host needs, the less server interruption you will have. That is one of the reasons that Server Core makes a good virtualization platform—it needs fewer patches than a full server.

Scripting Hyper-V

One of the focus points of this book is to show you how to manage your network from the command line. The bad news is that there is no direct command-line interface to Hyper-V. There are no built-in tools to query the configuration of the host, start or stop VMs, and so on. The good news is that there is an extensive WMI interface to Hyper-V. This same interface is used by the Hyper-V management console. Theoretically speaking, you should be able to write a script to do anything the Hyper-V console can do. In practice, this is not easy. The WMI model of Hyper-V is quite complex, to put it mildly.

However, there are some simple and useful illustrations that show the basics of working with WMI to manage Hyper-V. All of the examples use VBScript, which is guaranteed to be present on any Windows Server, including Server Core. The scripts shown are stripped of all nonessentials so as to not distract from the main points. Production-quality scripts should include error checking, use explicitly declared variables, and so on.

Unfortunately, if you are not familiar with scripting or WMI, these scripts will make little sense to you. However, you will still be able to run a script using the following steps:

1. Find a folder to run these scripts, such as C:\scripts.

2. Open Notepad, type the script literally, and save it in C:\scripts with a descriptive name such as list-vm.vbs. Note that the .vbs extension is required.

3. Open a command prompt, and change the directory to C:\scripts.

4. Type **cscript list-vm.vbs**.

A typical example of working with WMI is to ask a Hyper-V host which VMs it has. The following script asks the local host (.) for its VMs. The WMI root namespace for Hyper-V is \root\virtualization, and the object class you need is Msvm_ComputerSystem. From this class, you can query the registered virtual machines.

```
strHost = "."
Set objWMIService = GetObject("winmgmts:\\" & strHost & "\root\virtualization")
Set vmCollection = objWMIService.ExecQuery("SELECT * FROM Msvm_ComputerSystem",,48)

For Each vm In vmCollection
    Wscript.Echo vm.Elementname & ", " & vm.Description & ", " & vm.EnabledState
Next
```

The output of this script is useful but shows some of the complications that are typical of the WMI interface to Hyper-V:

```
C:\tools>cscript list-vms.vbs
Microsoft (R) Windows Script Host Version 5.7
Copyright (C) Microsoft Corporation. All rights reserved.

bf5, Microsoft Hosting Computer System, 2
bf11, Microsoft Virtual Machine, 3
bf10, Microsoft Virtual Machine, 32769
```

In addition to the VMs (bf10, bf11), it also shows the parent partition (bf5). This is not so strange considering that the parent partition is just a special type of VM, but the result is probably not what you expected. The Description field can be used to distinguish between them. The EnabledState field is a number indicating the current power state. Not very intuitive, is it? Table 29.10 shows what the numbers mean. Interpreting the table, bf5 is running (of course, it is the host!), bf11 is shut down, and bf10 is powered off with a saved state.

TABLE 29.10: WMI Power State Codes

POWER STATE	MEANING
0	Unknown
2	Running
3	Powered off
4	Shutting down
10	Resetting
32768	Paused

TABLE 29.10:   WMI Power State Codes   *(CONTINUED)*

POWER STATE	MEANING
32769	Saved (state)
32770	Starting up
32771	Snapshot in progress
32772	Migrating
32773	Saving State
32774	Stopping
32775	Deleted
32776	Pausing
32777	Resuming
<anything else>	Unknown/undocumented

Using this knowledge, you can take it one step further. These codes are used in other places, for instance to change the current power state of a VM. In the previous script, you see the object called vm, representing a virtual machine. This object has a method named RequestStateChange(), which accepts the desired power state as an argument. The method has a variety of return codes. The most important one is 4096, indicating that the start procedure was initiated successfully. The method is asynchronous, meaning that it directly returns control and does not wait until it knows that the action has fully succeeded. It just tells you it has started the action. The final complication here is that you do not want to start the host itself. The easiest way to check which VM is the host is to check the Description field of the VM object. The following script tries to start all VMs on the Hyper-V host it's run on.

```
strHost = "."
Set objWMIService = GetObject("winmgmts:\\" & strHost & "\root\virtualization")
Set vmCollection = objWMIService.ExecQuery("SELECT * FROM Msvm_ComputerSystem",,48)

For each vm In vmCollection

if vm.EnabledState <> 2 and vm.Description <> "Microsoft Hosting Computer System"
Then
        StatusCode= vm.RequestStateChange(2)

        if StatusCode = 4096 Then
            Wscript.Echo "Start signal sent to " & vm.ElementName
```

```
        Else

Wscript.Echo "An error occurred while starting " & vm.ElementName & ": " &
StatusCode
        End If
    End If
Next
```

The script uses code 2 from the table to check whether it is not running and start the VM. Change it to 32769, and the VM will save its state instead. Of course, you would check first that current state is 2 (running). These are the simplest kinds of examples of what you can do with the Hyper-V WMI interface.

Another class type worth knowing about is Msvm_ImageManagementService, which represents virtual hard disks. The following example does something very interesting: it mounts a .vhd file as a disk in the parent partition. To do that, it uses the first object returned by Msvm_ImageManagementService. This object always belongs to the parent. Using the Mount() method, the VHD file is made visible to Windows, although it will be offline at first if you use Windows Server 2008 Enterprise edition or Datacenter edition. The following script mounts the virtual disk belonging to bf10, specified by the variable strVHD:

```
strVHD = "E:\wsv_images\Virtual Hard Disks\bf10.vhd"
strHost = "."

Set objWMIService = GetObject("winmgmts:\\" & strHost & "\root\virtualization")
Set objVHDService = objWMIService.ExecQuery("SELECT * FROM Msvm_
ImageManagementService").ItemIndex(0)
objVHDService.Mount(strVHD)
```

To examine how this works, try the following:

1. Turn off or save-state the VM bf10. You cannot mount a .vhd file if it is in use by a running VM.

2. Open a command prompt, and start the Disk Manager by typing **diskmgmt.msc**.

3. Start Notepad, type the script, and save it as c:\scripts\mount-vhd.vbs on the Hyper-V host bf10.

4. From the command prompt, type **cscript c:\scripts\mount-vhd.vbs**.

5. Check the Disk Manager, and notice a new disk appears. The disk may be offline, as indicated by a red arrow pointing downward. On Windows 2008 Standard edition, it will be online.

6. Right-click the new disk, and select Online.

7. A drive letter is automatically assigned. At this point, you can open the drive in Explorer and change anything you like. From Windows' point of view, the .vhd file is now a local drive.

To reverse this, taking the drive offline is not enough. You need to unmount it. One way to do it is to use almost exactly the same script, but to replace the Mount() method by Unmount(). If you want to automate the online/offline procedure of the disk, investigate the command diskpart.

To finish up this section, we will cover another command-line trick, just to show you that there is more in life than WMI. Likely, you will have more than one Hyper-V host in your Active Directory forest. Is there an easy way to find them? Not surprisingly, there is such a way, and it's related to the computer account of the Hyper-V host.

As you know, each domain-joined computer has its own account in Active Directory. Any object in Active Directory is allowed to have child objects, although not all types are allowed. One of the child objects any computer account allowed to have is a Connection object. You may be familiar with Print Queue objects, allowing you to find printers just by querying the global catalog. Services such as Hyper-V can implement their own specific type of service connection point (SCP). This is a child object of any domain-joined Hyper-V host. Its name is always Microsoft Hyper-V.

Armed with this knowledge, you can find all Hyper-V hosts in your forest. If you want to script this, you will need the ADSI interface, not WMI. Both scripting technologies are covered on http://technet.microsoft.com, but there is another and simpler way to do it. Because the information is stored in Active Directory, you can use any LDAP query tool to read it. On a computer with the RSAT tooling or a Directory Services role installed, you will have the command-line tool dsquery. You will search for objects named Microsoft Hyper-V, of type serviceConnectionPoint. You ask specifically for the attribute serviceBindingInformation. From a command prompt, run the following:

```
dsquery * forestroot -filter↵
"&(cn=Microsoft Hyper-V)(objectCategory=serviceConnectionPoint)" -attr
serviceBindingInformation
```

The output will be similar to the following. It's a bit cryptic, but it's perfectly usable. The query returned two Hyper-V hosts in the forest, bf5 and bf6. serviceBindingInformation is a multivalued attribute, and its first member is always the name of the host. The second member is interesting as well; it tells you which TCP port to use for a remote connection using VMConnect.

```
serviceBindingInformation

bf5.bigfirm.com;
RDP listener port=2179;
msxml://C:\ProgramData\<…>\InitialStore.xml;

bf6.bigfirm.com;
RDP listener port=2179;
msxml://C:\ProgramData\<…>\InitialStore.xml;
```

The Bottom Line

Determine whether a server can run Hyper-V   You are buying new servers whose main role will be to run Hyper-V. However, you are concerned that the new servers may not be capable of running Hyper-V because they do not meet the minimum requirements.

> **Master It**   What are the CPU requirements to run Hyper-V? What brands may be considered, and are there other factors to be considered?

Determine when it makes sense to virtualize a server   Your company is standardizing on Hyper-V virtual machines for all production servers. The strategy is to virtualize all servers, unless there is a good reason not to do so. One of the critical business applications (CalcIT) is a multithreaded modeling application that is very CPU intensive and may take days to run even on a big 16-core server.

> **Master It**   Decide whether CalcIT is a good candidate for virtualization. If it is, explain why. If it is not, you need good arguments to convince your management to deviate from the standard.

Decide which technology to use to quickly move a virtual machine between hosts   You are designing a Hyper-V testing lab. One of the requirements is that the hardware is used effectively for a varying collection of virtual machines. The idea is to maximize the use of available hardware and do so with the least overhead the next time the VM collection changes. Also, the process must be as reliable as possible.

> **Master It**   What technology would you use, and how would your choice meet the requirements?

Advise on a backup strategy   As an IT consultant you are hired by a company to have a look at their Hyper-V configuration. They are especially proud of their backup system, describing it as simple and effective. Using a script, they save the state of all VMs one by one, and during the suspended period, they copy the VHD file to a backup location.

> **Master It**   Give the customer your opinion of their backup methods. If it is fine, compliment them on their choice, and leave a (self-)satisfied customer. If there is a problem, explain it to them, and propose an alternative. What do you recommend?

Chapter 30

Advanced User Account Management and User Support

You learned about the basics of user and group management in Chapter 7. We're going to take user management to the next level in this chapter. You'll be utilizing some of the skills that you have developed while reading this book, such as managing file shares, Distributed File System (DFS) namespaces, and Group Policy objects (GPOs). Using these technologies, you can develop a flexible, fault-tolerant, and mobile working environment, something that Microsoft refers to as *dynamic IT*.

We'll cover how you can deploy solutions where a user's data and settings follow them around on the network using home directories and roaming profiles. You'll see how you can force a user to work in a locked-down environment using mandatory profiles. You'll then learn how you can use GPOs to change things up a little. You can control a user's personal profile using Group Policy settings. You can allow a user to have different roaming profiles for different locations or for Remote Desktop Services. Many organizations have chosen to not adopt roaming profiles because of the complications of mixing operating systems or even software configurations on different PCs. Active Directory allows you to still have a mobile working environment by using redirected folders. This technology allows you to take the folders on a PC and move them to the server, invisibly to the user.

Redirected folders have existed for some time now but were always a little limited. Windows Server 2008 and Windows Vista allowed you to redirect more important folders to file servers so that users' personal working environments are available wherever they log in—all without the complications of roaming profiles.

You will also look at logon scripts and how you can run a set of commands whenever a user logs in or even when a user logs out, thanks to logoff scripts. You'll want to learn about the best ways to connect users to the resources that you have invested time in preparing. We'll give you real-world solutions that utilize these solutions for many of the scenarios that you will face when working with advanced user management.

In this chapter, you'll learn to:

◆ Deploy home directories to multiple users

◆ Set up mandatory roaming profiles

◆ Create logon scripts to automate administration

Experiencing the Flexible Desktop

The ideal scenario for a user's working environment is that the desktop, the laptop computer, or even the Remote Desktop server is nothing more than an appliance.

WHAT IS REMOTE DESKTOP SERVICES?

Users of Windows Server 2008 may be confused by this talk of Remote Desktop Services. Microsoft expanded (to include virtual desktop infrastructure) and rebranded *Terminal Services* as *Remote Desktop Services* in Windows Server 2008. Whenever we refer to Remote Desktop Services or Remote Desktop Servers, Windows Server 2008 users should think of Terminal Services or terminal servers.

Consider the help-desk engineer who gets a call from a user having problems with their Office installation. For some reason, Word won't work correctly. The legacy deployment of a desktop network would require that the engineer sit at that desktop until the problem was resolved. The desktop has a large collection of software installed. The user has all of their business data on a "data partition." The user's settings, including their mail archive, mail contacts, and web browser favorites, are all local on the PC. There is no alternative but to fix that Office installation, no matter how long it takes.

What's the most likely component in a PC to fail? It's probably the device with the moving parts. That's right; it's the hard disk. What happens when the hard disk fails? You guessed it. IT is to blame for the user losing business data. Even worse, you've lost the most "important" information that the user had—their web browser favorites and their mail contacts. We've been there, and it isn't a pretty situation. Sure, Windows Vista and Windows 7 have a backup tool, but do you really want to manage backups for hundreds or tens of thousands of desktops and laptops?

What would happen in these scenarios if the user's PC was nothing more than an appliance? You could build the PC using something like Windows Deployment Services, Microsoft Deployment Toolkit, or another paid-for cloning solution like System Center Configuration Manager (SCCM/ConfigMgr) 2007 R2 or Ghost. That allows you to deploy an image of a configured operating system in minutes. Software deployment can be automated using solutions such as Group Policy, ConfigMgr 2007 R2, or something like Microsoft's application virtualization solution, App-V. That configures the PC to a previously known and managed standard in a few more minutes. Patches are quickly deployed using Windows Software Update Services (WSUS) or ConfigMgr 2007 R2. Group Policy configures the environment. Now the PC is secured. This is all great because now the PC is back to a healthy state and Office is working correctly for the user. This entire process probably took no more than 30 minutes. That's probably much less time than the help-desk engineer would have taken to resolve the issue.

But what of the data the user had on the PC? Either you've formatted the disk by rebuilding the PC or their data was lost during the hard disk failure. Don't worry; the data was on a server all along. If they had a laptop, you made it available locally using a synchronized cache. The user will still have access to all their data when they log into their newly built PC.

Using the practices we'll cover in this chapter, you will see how to do the following:

◆ Simplify backups

◆ Make data more available

◆ Allow the user to be mobile from one PC to another or to a Remote Desktop server while maintaining access to data in a consistent manner

◆ Reduce time for troubleshooting

◆ Have happier users

◆ Create secure working environments where there is a shared computing solution

◆ Preconfigure the working environment to apply security policies or to even make the environment easier to use

---

🌐 Real World Scenario

WHEN TO REBUILD THE PC

Here is a simple rule of thumb when you deploy this approach. If a problem is unique to the PC (that is, not a network or shared services issue) and it looks like it will take more than 30 minutes to resolve, then rebuild the machine. It ends up being a time-saver for IT, the user, and the business. It also gives the user a long-term stable solution. You may even find that educated users will be able to rebuild the PC for themselves in this scenario if you allow them.

Of course, this assumes you have used the techniques that are contained in this chapter to keep user data off the PC and on the servers. You'll also need something like System Center Configuration Manager or similar to automatically deploy applications that are not contained within your standard images.

Configuring Home Directories

What is a home directory? A *home directory* is a shared folder or a folder within a network share that is dedicated to a user. Each user has their own home directory on a file server. The concept is that you want users to store data on servers so that the data is easy to back up, audit, and archive. Some organizations will use company policy and Group Policy to prevent users from using the drives on their PCs so that they are forced to use their home directories for their personal data. Organizations use home directories in two basic ways. The most common is that the directory's permissions are set up so that the home directory is private; in other words, the user is the only person with access to the contents. Local administrators and local systems on the server will also probably need access for administration, backup/recovery, and archive operations. An alternative you might see in some deployments is that there is no privacy on the home directory. It's treated as the user's personal share for sharing data with others on the network when the normal team, departmental, or company shares aren't appropriate.

This is where some people will argue that there is a lot of cheap disk on every PC and that server storage is relatively expensive. Isn't it more economic to keep data on the PC and distribute it via email? We'd argue that you're looking at the short-term costs. Email is not a great way to share files. It's a great way to ensure that differing versions of the same file are all being viewed as the current version of that file by different people in the same team or department. If you're using a mailbox-style server such as Exchange or Lotus Notes, then the file is being stored on the mail server, possibly many times over if the mail server doesn't support single-instance storage. But most important, an organization must be able to ensure that its business data is being backed up or even archived to a secure store and retained for several years. These are legal requirements for many organizations, either public or private, across the world. How are you going to back up your PCs? How are you going to archive files without user intervention? You'll find that it's a lot cheaper, easier to use, and much more reliable to centralize your data storage and perform one backup and manage one automated archive.

The other argument against home directories that one often hears comes from the HR/personnel or accountancy departments. They don't want IT to be able to see their data, so they want to keep it on the PC. We're sorry to burst your bubble, but if someone is a motivated administrator, then they can get into your data no matter where it is. There was once an HR department that decided to store sensitive data on a USB-attached hard drive that they'd store in a safe. Can you imagine storing critical company payroll data on a non-fault-tolerant device with moving parts that are likely to fail? The best solution is to have independently monitored auditing of file server data access with clearly documented and communicated policies and actions that follow up any contravention of those policies.

We'll now cover how you can configure home directories for the users in your business.

Setting Up the Lab

In this example, you'll be working with two servers. BF1 is a Windows Server 2008 R2 domain controller for the BigFirm organization. BF2 is a Windows Server 2008 R2 file server. The network will also have a desktop called Win7 that is running...well, Windows 7. We strongly recommend that you do any work in a test lab and have everything documented before approaching your production system.

You're going to see how to use DFS namespaces whenever using file shares within this chapter. There are two reasons that you'll do this:

◆ *You can abstract the physical location of the file shares*: Users and applications map to a logical name rather than to a physical server. This means that you can move the file shares from one server to another without having to change user configurations, logon scripts, or application configurations. This is very convenient when a server becomes obsolete or during a server failure when you need to recover data to an alternate location. You can quickly adjust the namespace without having to make many changes that you would otherwise have to make elsewhere.

◆ *You can take advantage of DFS replication (DFS-R) while maintaining the same drive mappings in user configurations, logon scripts, and application settings*: This means that you can replicate user data to another server in another site. If a disaster destroys your production server or even the site, then the data is available in an alternate location using the same drive mappings. You can also introduce more creative backup strategies. For example, you can use Volume Shadow Copy Service (VSS) for short-term operational backups in the production site and use the DR site for long-term backups that might otherwise interfere with network performance in the production site.

You should have already learned about how to set up a namespace and how to configure DFS-R. You are going to be using a namespace called \\bigfirm.com\BigFirmShares. You'll see later how you will add folders to this namespace that redirect to the shares that will contain the user's personal data.

Creating the Home Directories

You need to create a directory for each user and ensure that it is appropriately secured. You must ask the following questions when you are doing this:

◆ *Who must be able to access each user's home directory?* The norm is to allow only the user, administrators and System to access to the folder. Some organizations choose to treat the home directory as a personal folder that the user can use to share data with everyone else. We'll demonstrate the more usual private approach in this section.

◆ *How will you name the folders?* Some people use something predictable. They name the folder after the user who owns the home directory. For example, the user Joe Bloggs has a username of JBloggs. His home directory will be called JBloggs. This makes it easier to perform automated tasks such as connecting the user to the share.

◆ *How will you share the folder?* Some choose to share each and every home directory. That's a lot of work. Others prefer to create one generic share and create a folder underneath for each user. This suits the DFS approach discussed earlier because there's only one DFS link to alter if you need to restore or move the home directory share to a new location. The shared folder will be made available via a DFS namespace.

Let's start creating some home directories. We'll reuse the lab network used in Chapter 7. You have a number of users in the \bigfirm.com\BigFirm\Users organizational unit (OU), as shown in Figure 30.1. You'll be configuring a working environment for these users throughout this chapter.

FIGURE 30.1
The Joe Bloggs
test user

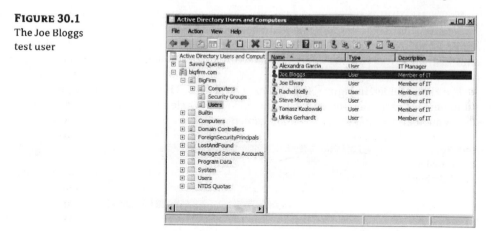

You'll be creating a shared folder called Home on BF2. Some administrators like to create all of their shares in a single folder on the file server. This serves a couple of purposes:

◆ It keeps things tidy, and the administrators can find all of their shares in one location.

◆ It makes automation tasks such as backup or directory replication much easier because there is only one folder to select.

Create a folder called Shares on the C drive, as shown on the next page in Figure 30.2.

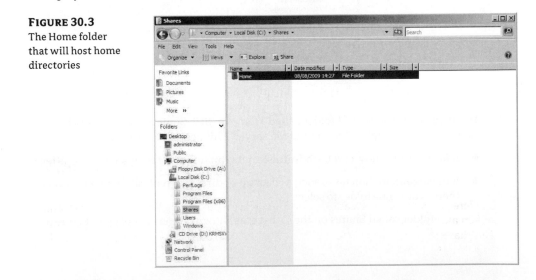

FIGURE 30.2
The Shares
folder on BF2

Disable folder permission inheritance, and set the folder permissions as follows:

GROUP	PERMISSION
BF2\Administrators	Full
System	Full

You're doing this because any folders you create in C:\Shares will inherit these permissions by default. This makes the new shared folders secure by default. It will be up to you and other administrators to assign access to the correct users or security groups. It will also prevent non-administrators from creating folders in here without permission. Now create a folder in C:\Shares called Home.

The Home folder, in Figure 30.3, will now be shared. This will mean that you can create subfolders for each user and only have to manage a single share. The aim of this is to simplify deployment and to make security management as easy as possible.

FIGURE 30.3
The Home folder
that will host home
directories

You are now going to use the Share and Storage Management administrative tool for this. The tool shown in Figure 30.4 will appear when you start it from Administrative Tools.

FIGURE 30.4
Share and Storage
Management

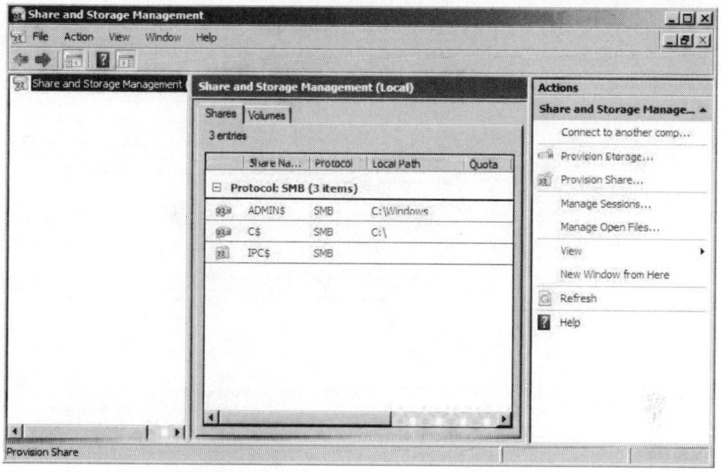

You click Provision Share to start the wizard shown in Figure 30.5.

FIGURE 30.5
Shared folder
location

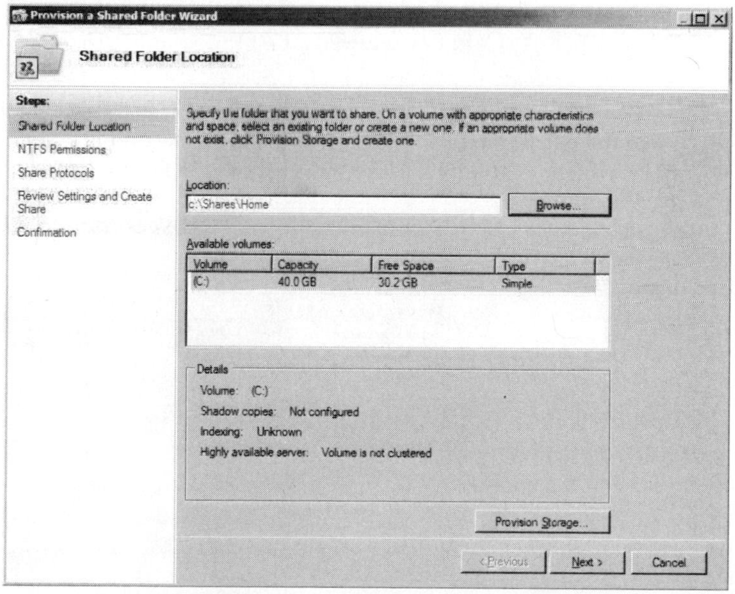

Here you specify the location of the folder that you want to share. Click Next, and the next screen allows you to set the NTFS permissions. You've already done this, so you can skip ahead. The share protocol for the Windows network will be SMB. The share name will be Home$.

The screen shown in Figure 30.6 allows you to document the share. It makes sense to describe the shared folder for when someone else needs to diagnose/fix an issue and you're not around to help. Enter a description for the share.

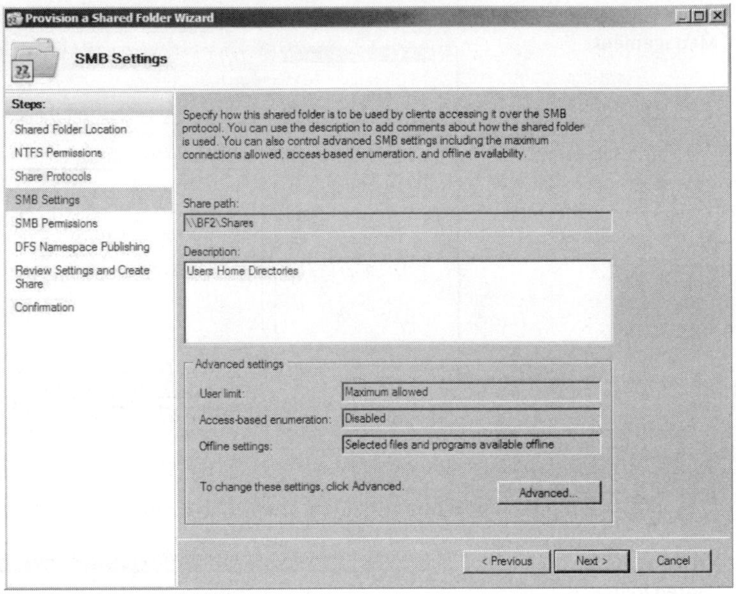

FIGURE 30.6
Home directory share description

It is best practice to lock down permissions on a shared folder in two ways. The first is to lock down the permissions on the NTFS folder. The second is to lock down permissions on the SMB share, which you will do in the screen shown in Figure 30.7.

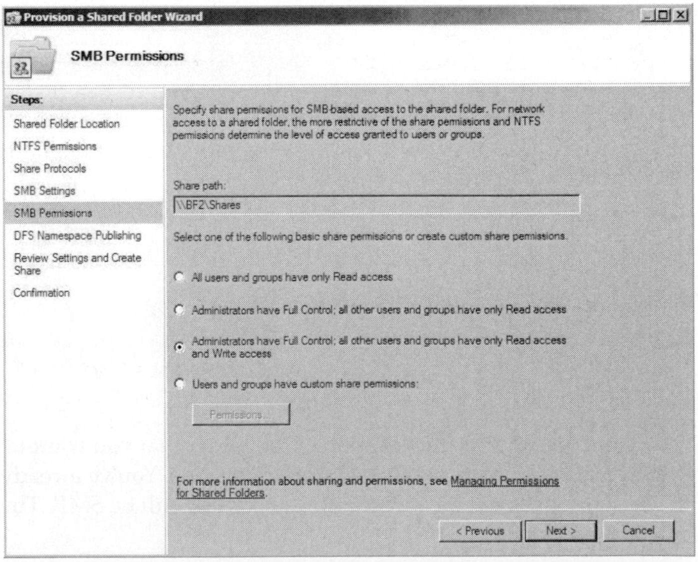

FIGURE 30.7
Setting the SMB permissions

The combined effects of the folder and share permissions are as follows:

- Users will be able to pass through the Home share to folders beneath it. However, they cannot create anything here. This is thanks to the NTFS permissions in the folder.

- The user will be able to modify the contents of anything within Home$ *as long as they have permission*. This is required so that the user can create and modify files and folders within their home directory. As it stands, users can't do anything much on the Home$ share, but that will change when you create their personal home directories.

The share is now ready to be made available via the DFS namespace. The Provision a Shared Folder Wizard allows you to do this, which is very convenient. You can see this in Figure 30.8. Alternatively, you can do this in the DFS administration tool.

FIGURE 30.8
Adding the home directory share to the DFS namespace

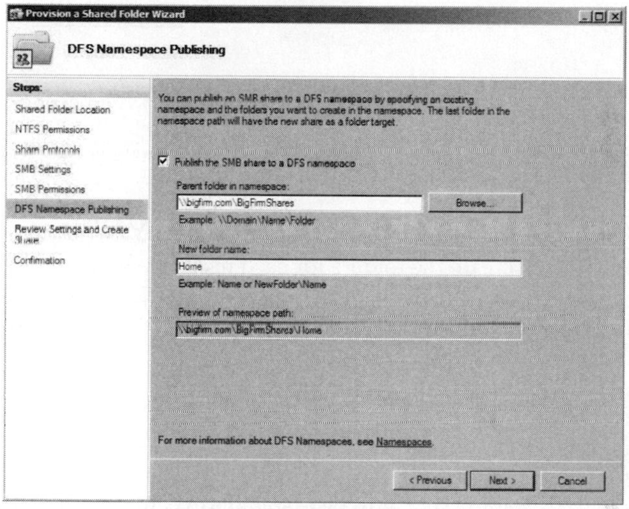

You are setting up the folder within the BigFirmShares namespace with a new folder name of Home. This folder will be available on the network as \\bigfirm.com\BigFirmShares\Home.

Once the wizard is complete, you should verify that the share was created and that it is accessible. As shown in Figure 30.9, you can do this by browsing to the UNC path of the share within the DFS namespace. Check it with administrator and nonadministrator accounts to be sure that the permissions are correct.

You could use DFS to set up folder replication if you had a duplicate server in a disaster recovery (DR) site. If you do this and the DR plan is invoked, users can log in to PCs or Remote Desktop servers in the DR site, and they'll still use the same UNC paths to browse to or connect to their home directories. No user objects or scripts need to be modified.

Thanks to the abstraction provided by DFS namespace, you can easily move the Home folder to another server. All it requires is a quick change of the mapping for the folder within the namespace. No user objects or scripts would need to be modified to reflect the move.

Administrators have used both of these approaches in the past and kept user disruption to a minimum. Administrators using the traditional file shares without DFS will find that there is some effort required to introduce DFS. However, the gains are worth the effort once the migrations are complete.

FIGURE 30.9
Checking the
new share

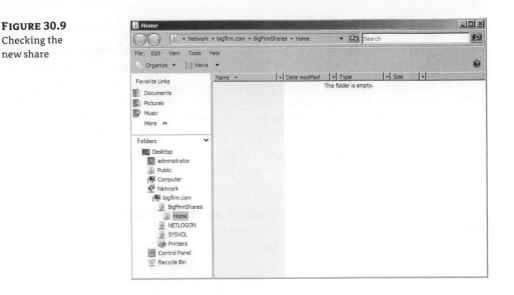

Creating Home Directories: The Easy Way

It's time to create the folders for each user. You're really going to like how easy this can be.

Log into your domain controller and launch your preferred Active Directory administrative tool, either Active Directory Users and Computers (ADUC) or Active Directory Administrative Center (ADAC). For this example, log into BF1, launch ADUC, and navigate to where the users are in \BigFirm\Users.

Select all the users, right-click, and chose Properties. This opens the dialog box shown in Figure 30.10. This will allow you to configure all of these users with a home directory at the same time. You can see that we have configured the home directory to be mapped as Z:\ when the users log in. They will be mapped to \\bigfirm.com\BigFirmShares\Home\%Username%. The %Username% is where the magic is.

FIGURE 30.10
Setting home
directories for
many users

This automatically completes the path using the username of the account in question. For example, when you check the Home Folder setting in the JBloggs user object, you can see it has been mapped to `\\bigfirm.com\BigFirmShares\Home\JBloggs`. You can see this in Figure 30.11, where we have opened the properties of the JBloggs user account.

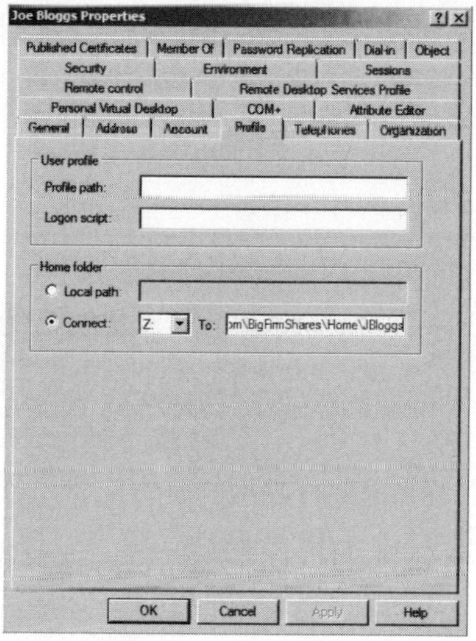

FIGURE 30.11

Checking the user object home directory setting

Here's the cool bit: Windows creates the folder and sets the correct permissions for you on your file server. This is visible on the file server, as shown in Figure 30.12.

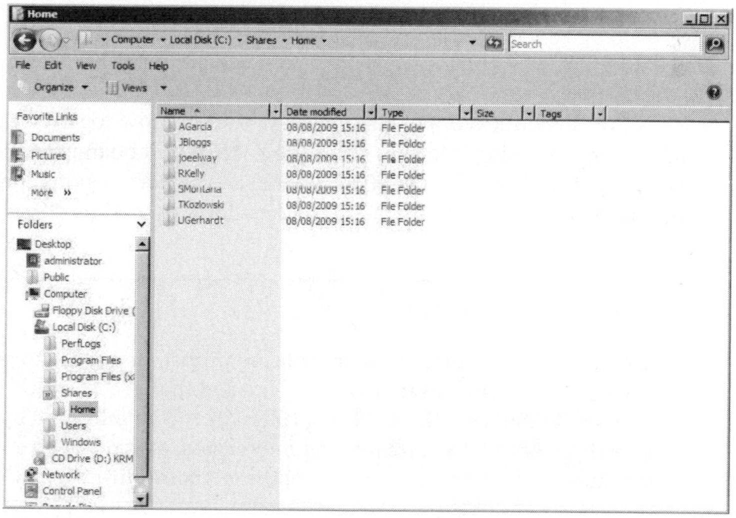

FIGURE 30.12

The automatically created home directories

You can see in Figure 30.13 that the home directory for each user has inherited the permissions on the Home folder. Each user has been granted Full Control permissions over their own folder:

GROUP	PERMISSION
BF2\Administrators	Full
System	Full
BigFirm\<User>	Full

FIGURE 30.13
The home directory's automatically created permissions

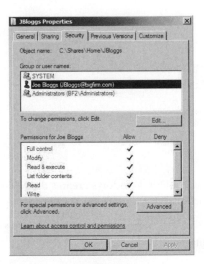

All of the work is done! It's that easy. You can now log on using one of those users. In our lab, JBloggs will log into Win7, and the Z drive will be mapped to JBloggs' own home directory. We've shown this in Figure 30.14. Thanks to the permissions that are on each folder, the user in question cannot access a home directory that is owned by somebody else.

SHARING HOME DIRECTORIES

We previously mentioned that some organizations choose to give users other than the owner access to the home directories. You can add that access quite easily by adding Authenticated Users to C:\Shares\Home. This permission will be inherited by every home directory. You can give them Read & Execute for read-only access, or you can give them Change rights so that they can modify the contents of another person's home directory.

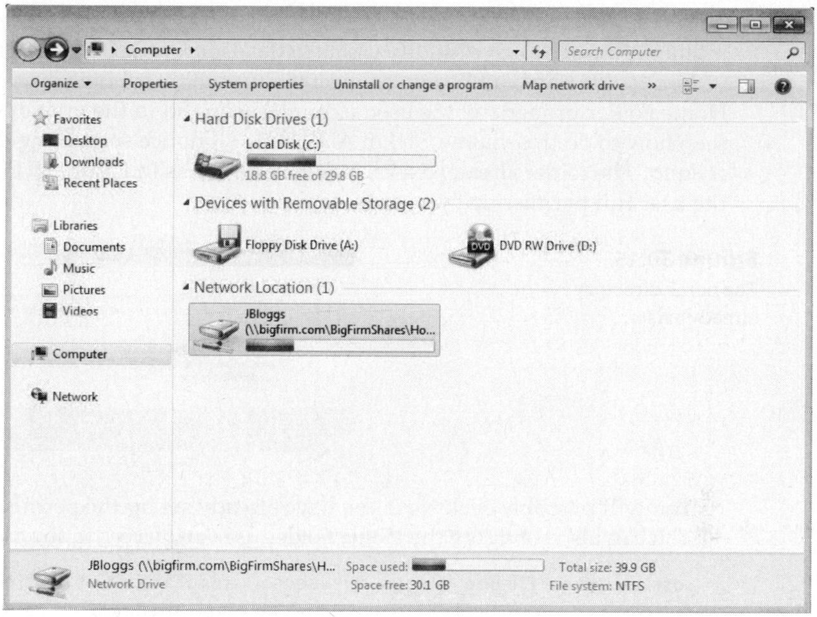

FIGURE 30.14
The user sees the home directory on their PC.

Unfortunately, this method cannot be re created using a command-line tool. You'll have to do a few more steps to set up home directories from the command prompt.

Creating Home Directories: The Hard Way

This process requires that you set up each folder and set the permissions on it one by one. You're now asking why you might want to do it this way, right? As you've just seen, there is no command-line way to set up home directories the easy way. You need an alternative. You also may not like the default permissions that are assigned to the home directory when they are set up the easy way. This approach gives you complete control over the process.

You are assuming that you've already set up your user accounts. Check out Chapter 7 if you need to learn how to do this. There we have documented ways to create user objects using ADUC, ADAC, the command prompt, and even PowerShell.

You have created a directory for each user in C:\Shares\Home. Each user's home directory is named after the user, as in the previous method. The permissions can be set as you require them, but the most common approach treats the home directory as a user's private store:

GROUP	PERMISSION
BF2\Administrators	Full
System	Full
BigFirm\<User>	Full

As we mentioned earlier, you can customize this to whatever you need; for example, you might only want to give Modify rights to the user for their home directory.

You have a choice of how to connect the user to their home directory. You can configure the Home Folder property of the user account as you did in the previous method. You've already seen how to do this via the GUI in ADUC. You'll notice something different happens this time around. The folder already exists, so you're asked, as in Figure 30.15, whether you should grant the user full permission over the folder.

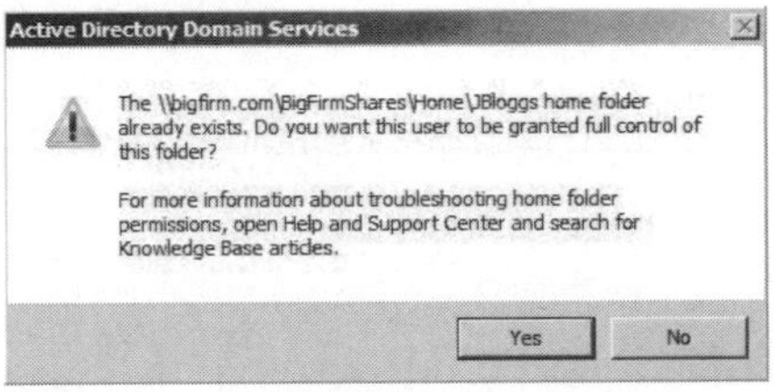

FIGURE 30.15
The home directory
already exists.

You will probably click No if you have already set up the permissions to what you require. You can also configure the Home Folder user property via the command prompt:

```
dsmod user "CN=Boe Bloggs,OU=Users,OU=BigFirm,DC=bigfirm,DC=com" -hmdir
\\bigfirm.com\bigfirmshares\Home\JBloggs -hmdrv Z
```

The syntax for this command is as follows:

```
dsmod user <Distinguished Name of User> -hmdir <Path to the user's home
directory>
-hmdrv <letter to use to map the drive>
```

The command-line approach does not attempt to configure the permissions of the home directory.

Windows Server 2008 R2 also allows you to configure this setting using the Active Directory module for PowerShell. Here's how you can set a home drive for the JBloggs user by setting Z to map to \\bigfirm.com\bigfirmshares\Home\JBloggs. You'll be using the Set-ADUser cmdlet:

```
PS C:\Users\Administrator> set-aduser jbloggs -homedrive Z -homedirectory
 "\\bigfirm.com\bigfirmshares\Home\JBloggs"
```

This PowerShell alternative will also not set the home directory permissions.

Some organizations choose to not configure the user object's Home Folder attribute. Their opinion is that it is easier to map the drive using a logon script. A logon script runs every time a user logs in and runs a set of commands. You'll look at them later. If the drive moves to another server, then it's easy to change a single logon script command instead of changing hundreds or even thousands of users. The counter opinion on this is that you have made your solution for home directories very dynamic by using a DFS namespace to abstract the physical location of the share. You can move the share, and all users will retain their mappings once you modify the single folder mapping in the DFS namespace. In addition to this, there are some environment variables in Vista and Windows 7 for the user's home directory that are available when you set up the Home Folder user attribute. These may be used by your scripts or by applications:

HOMEDRIVE Represents the letter used to map the home directory, for example, Z:.

HOMEPATH   Represents the path within the HOMEDRIVE where the home directory is contained, for example, \. The total path is %HOMEDRIVE%%HOMEPATH% or Z:\.

HOMESHARE   This is the UNC path to the user's home directory, for example, \\bigfirm.com\BigFirmShares\Home\JBloggs.

You can now test the user, and you will find that the home directory is mapped as required.

Home Directory vs. Local Storage

You have given your users a centralized storage mechanism. You should consider communicating to your users that data should be stored on this drive and not on the local drive of the PC. You can use Group Policy to enforce this policy. The following are keys to success:

◆   Communicate that home directories are backed up and that PCs are not. There is no service-level agreement for data stored on PCs.

◆   Enable the Volume Shadow Copy Service on your file servers, and educate users how to use the Previous Versions Client to recover their own files.

◆   Data on the PC is not secure. Educate the users about the need for data security.

◆   Use auditing where required to reassure users about sensitive files. Maybe even take a look at using Active Directory Rights Management Services to allow users to control at the file level who can see or edit a file.

You will look at some automated mechanisms a little later that will further encourage users to keep data on the server instead of on the PC.

This section has discussed how to allow a user to make their personal data available to them no matter what server or PC they log into. We'll now cover roaming profiles and discuss how they can do the same thing with their working environment.

Creating Roaming Profiles

A *profile* is a folder that contains all the settings pertaining to a user's working environment. By default, the profile is stored in the C:\Users directory in Windows Vista, Windows 7, Windows Server 2008, and Windows Server 2008 R2. Windows 2000, XP, and Server 2003 stored them in C:\Documents and Settings, and Windows NT stored them in the \Windows\Profiles folder. A *roaming profile* is stored on the network instead of the local drive of the machine where the user logs in. However, it is cached locally by default. The advantage of a roaming profile is that a user can log in to any machine in the domain and have a consistent working environment. However, you have to watch out for the profile containing information that is specific to a computer, application, or operating system that won't apply to all machines that the user might log into.

A profile has two types of content:

◆   Files and folders

◆   ntuser.dat

A user's Windows and application settings are usually stored in HKEY_CURRENT_USER in the registry. This needs to be available to the user every time they log in. It is stored in a file called NTUSER.DAT.

Other types of content are stored as files in specially named folders in the profile. For example:

My Documents   This is the default location where programs such as Microsoft Office look to store documents.

My Music   This is where music players look to store and load music by default.

Favorites   Internet Explorer keeps your Favorites link files here.

AppData   Windows and other programs will store files and settings here that are configuration oriented but shouldn't be visible by default in order to simplify things for the user.

Desktop   The user's desktop contents are stored here.

Profiles are stored in C:\Users by default in the newer versions of Windows, that is, Windows Vista, Windows 7, Windows Server 2008, and Windows Server 2008 R2. Windows 2000, Windows XP, and Windows Server 2003 stored them in C:\Documents and Settings. (Windows NT stored them in C:\Windows\Profiles.)

A new profile needs to be created for a user when they log into the machine for the first time. Out of the box, Windows generates one by copying the default profile. A new profile is created and is named after the user. You'll see a new folder in C:\Users that is named after the user, for example, C:\Users\JBloggs. That will be secured so that only System, Administrators, and the user have access to it. When the user logs in, the settings from the profile are loaded into the user's working session. When they log out, the changes are saved. Depending on the version of Windows you're using, you will see a message telling you that settings are either being loaded or saved when you log in or out.

At this point, you may have noticed that the profile is a local resource by default. This means that the data and configuration that you have on one PC will be different on another PC. Imagine how ticked off your users will be if their browser favorites or their email contacts are missing when they log into a different machine. This problem will occur in different scenarios:

◆   Users log into a farm of Remote Desktop servers or virtual desktops. They never know which server they will be on, so their user configuration is different on every server.

◆   You have a hot-desk office where users sit down at different PCs every day. Their profile will be different on each machine.

◆   A user's PC fails or is replaced. They will lose their entire personal configuration. Think of the business data that might be permanently lost because PCs are not normally backed up.

You can see how all this conflicts with your desire for the appliance PC and dynamic IT. Users will rebel against IT as soon as they know that there is a risk of them losing their data or having an inconsistent working environment.

And old solution to this problem is the roaming profile. The concept is that the user's profile is stored on a file share that is similar in structure to the one you've set up for home directories. The profile is downloaded from the file server whenever a user logs in. It is cached in C:\Users (or in the other locations mentioned earlier for legacy operating system clients) on the computer that the user is logged into. The contents of the profile that have changed are saved back to the file server when the user logs out. That can sound like a lot of files moving around the network. Potentially, it can be. However, Windows will download or upload only those files that need to be. For example, when a user is logging into a PC with a roaming profile, only the files that are not already downloaded will be transferred. When the user logs out, only the files that have been changed will be uploaded.

Let's take a look at two ways to create roaming profiles. One is very quick and easy to set up. The second takes things a little further by increasing security, but it does require a little more work.

Creating a Roaming Profiles Share: The Easy Way

We'll now go through the process of configuring roaming profiles for the users in BigFirm. With this approach, you'll set up the profile settings in the user objects. Unlike the easy approach for setting up home directories, a folder will not be created for you once you set up the roaming profile attribute. Instead, the user's roaming profile will be set up automatically when the user logs in.

You'll start by using an approach often recommended by Microsoft that allows for the easy deployment of profiles. You'll create a file share on BF2, the file server.

Create a folder called Profiles in C:\Shares, as shown in Figure 30.16.

FIGURE 30.16
The roaming
Profiles folder on
the file server

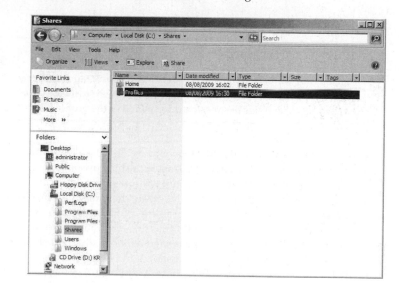

Disable inheritance of permissions on the folder, and configure the permissions as shown here (and shown in Figure 30.17):

GROUP	PERMISSION	WHERE
Creator Owner	Full Control	Subfolders and files
BF2\Administrators	Full	This folder, subfolders, and files
System	Full	This folder, subfolders, and files
Authenticated Users	List Folder/Read Data;	
	Create Folders/Append Data; Read Attributes	This folder, subfolders, and files

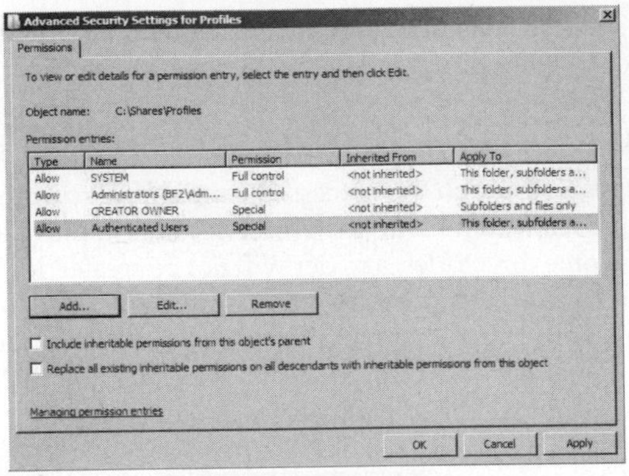

FIGURE 30.17
The advanced
permissions of the
Profiles folder

WHY READ ATTRIBUTES?

Notice that we've added that last permission for Read Attributes. It isn't documented in any Microsoft documentation that we have read. However, a user's profile will fail to completely save to the file server if this permission is not added to the profile folder.

These permissions will allow a user to create a folder within the share where their roaming profile will be stored. There is a downside to this approach. A user could create a folder within this share and then store data within it without approval. This is required because, with this approach, the user's rights are used to create their roaming profile. The user, unbeknownst to them, will be setting up their own roaming profile folder on the file server when they log in.

You're now going to share the Profiles folder and add it to the DFS namespace.

Launch the Share and Storage Management console, and click Provision Share to launch the Provision and Shared Folder wizard shown in Figure 30.18. Then set the location as C:\Shares\ Profiles; that's the location of the folder that you are going to use to store roaming profiles.

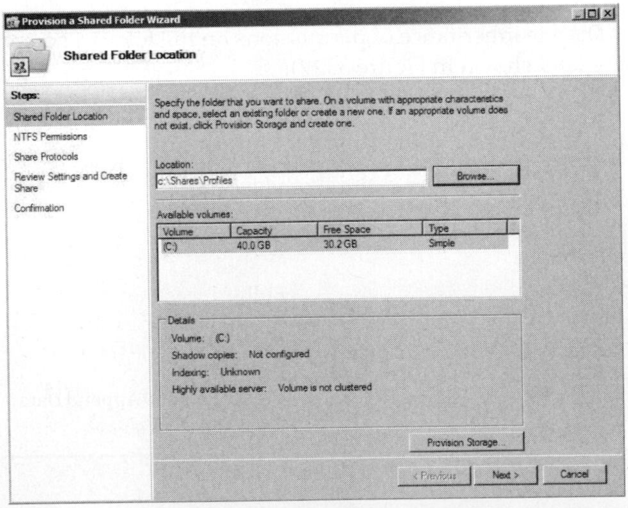

FIGURE 30.18
Profiles shared
folder location

The NTFS Permissions screen is next. You've already set the permissions, so you can skip this and proceed to the Share Protocols screen.

Share the Profiles folder as a hidden share called Profiles$, as shown in Figure 30.19. The next screen allows you to set a description. In this example, enter **Users roaming profiles share** for the description of this share.

FIGURE 30.19
Profiles share
protocols

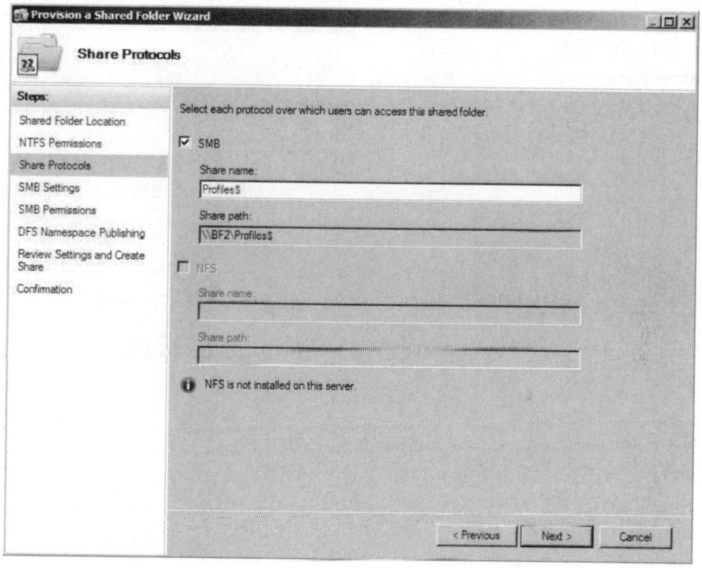

In Figure 30.20, you can see that the permissions are set to give Administrators Full Control. Authenticated users will have modify permissions, that is, read and write access.

FIGURE 30.20
Setting the
profile's share
permissions

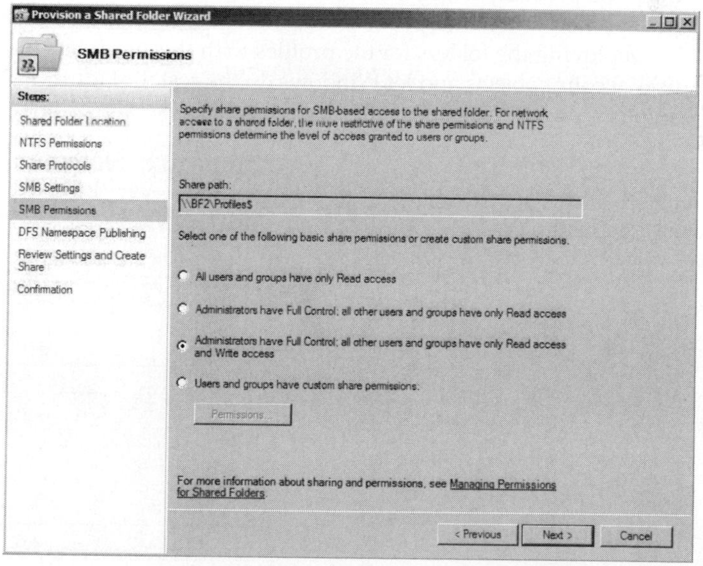

You'll be using the DFS namespace again to make the profile share available to the network. You can see this happening in Figure 30.21. This means that you can replicate the folder or move it when you need to without having to make any huge adjustments when the system is in production.

FIGURE 30.21
Adding Profiles$ to the DFS namespace

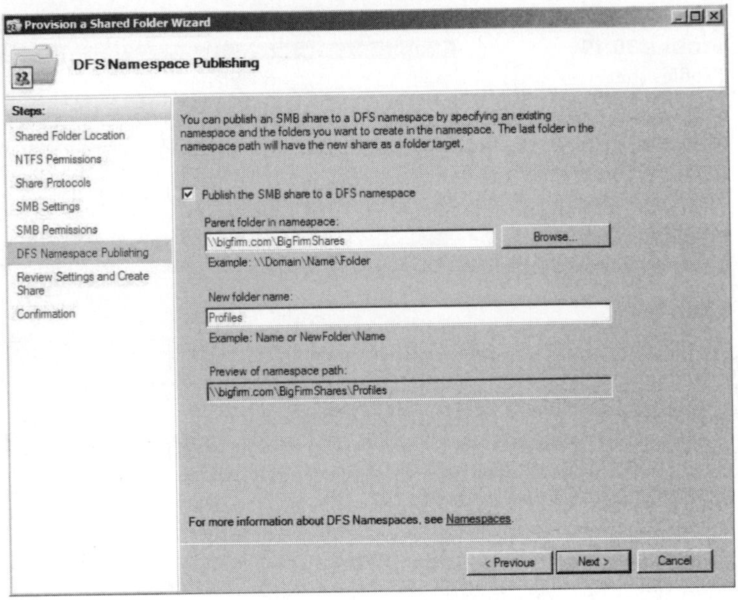

When you've completed the wizard, you should verify that you can browse to \\bigfirm. com\BigFirmShares\Profiles. If you can, then you're ready to move onto the next step. If not, then you probably have an issue with permissions on the share, or you need to wait for or force the updated DFS namespace settings to replicate between domain controllers.

Deploying the folders for the profiles with this approach is easy. You simply configure the user account objects and let Windows do the rest. In Figure 30.22, you've selected all the user accounts at once and opened their properties to set the profile property.

FIGURE 30.22
Configuring many users with a roaming profile

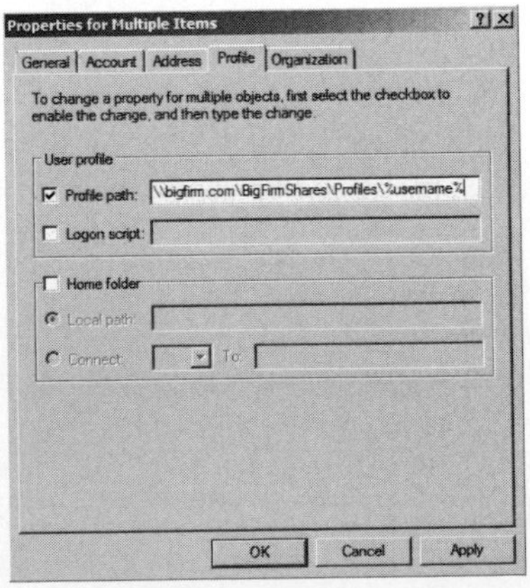

Alternatively, you can do this by editing a single user object, as you can see in Figure 30.23.

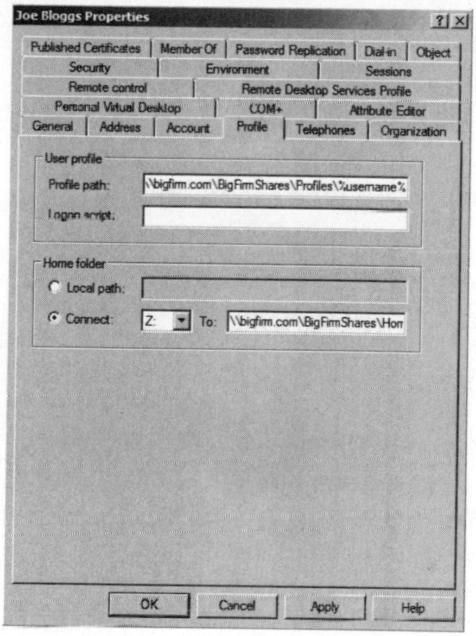

FIGURE 30.23
Configuring a
single user with
a roaming profile

When you do this, no folder is created. Remember that the folder will be created on behalf of the user when they log in. So, don't be surprised to find no new folders in the Profiles folder yet. You'll have to test it first.

You can also set a user's roaming profile at the command prompt by using the dsmod user command:

```
dsmod user "CN=Joe Bloggs,OU=Users,OU=BigFirm,DC=bigfirm,DC=com" -profile
\\bigfirm.com\bigfirmshares\Profiles\JBloggs
```

The syntax is as follows:

```
dsmod user <distinguished name of the user object> -profile <path to the profile>
```

Administrators of Windows Server 2008 R2 can also use PowerShell to configure the roaming profile attribute of a user object:

```
PS C:\Users\Administrator> set-aduser jbloggs -profilepath "\\bigfirm.com\
bigfirmshares\Profiles\JBloggs"
```

You're now ready to test this, which is a very necessary step before allowing your users to log in. You're going to notice a few things here.

A profile is created on the workstation (or Remote Desktop server) when the user logs in for the first time. You can see this in Figure 30.24.

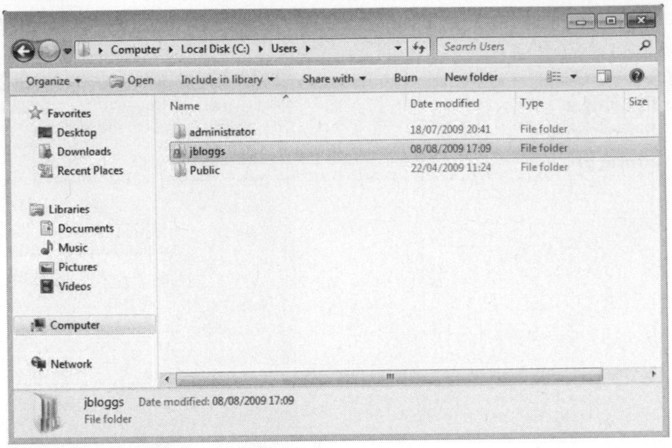

FIGURE 30.24
The cached profile
on the PC

A new and empty folder is created on the profile share for the user, as shown in Figure 30.25. Note the name has a **.V2** extension. This signifies that the profile is a *version 2* profile and was created by either Windows Vista, Windows 7, Windows Server 2008, or Windows Server 2008 R2. This is done because these newer operating systems cannot load profiles from legacy operating systems. Profiles without the **.V2** extension are created by legacy operating systems such as Windows XP, Windows Server 2003, or Windows 2000. *Do not make the mistake of specifying* .V2 *in the profile path*. It's an easy trap to fall into. For example, specifying a profile as \\bigfirm.com\ BigFirmShares\Profiles\JBloggs.V2 will cause the profile to not load. Windows will automatically add that extension to the folder name as required.

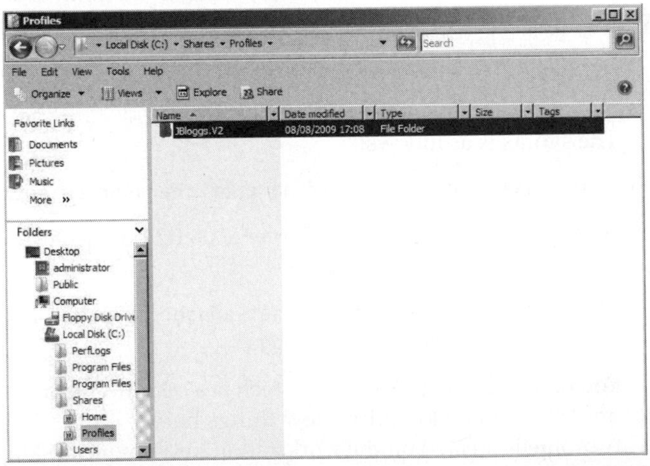

FIGURE 30.25
The roaming pro-
file in the roaming
profile's share

Log your user out, and the user's profile is uploaded from the workstation to the file share. It is now possible for this user to roam from workstation to workstation and maintain the same working environment. However, they cannot share a roaming profile between legacy operating systems and the current generation of Windows, that is, Server 2008, Server 2008 R2, Vista, and Windows 7. You'll look at a solution for that later in this chapter.

> ### CHECKING FOR ERRORS
>
> Be sure to log in and out a few times as the user. Check for errors in the notification area and in the Application log in Event Viewer. Any errors are typically related to misspellings or permissions issues.

Hold on a second! How do you know if there's anything in that profile folder? You've probably just re-created this scenario and noticed that administrators don't have any access to the profile. That's actually the way this is meant to work. The user has created their own folder, and as Creator Owner they have full and *sole* access to it. That's a bit of a pain because it makes things like backup/recovery and helping the user a little impossible!

It's messy to go grant administrators to user profiles. Ideally, there would be a way to grant access as required. You can do this with a Group Policy setting that you can apply to the computers creating the profiles. However, this solution must be applied before the profiles are created. It has no retrospective effect.

Log into the domain controller, BF1, and launch the Group Policy Management Console from Administrative Tools. Create and link a new Group Policy object, as shown in Figure 30.26, to the Computers OU where Win7, the workstation, resides.

FIGURE 30.26
The new Group Policy object

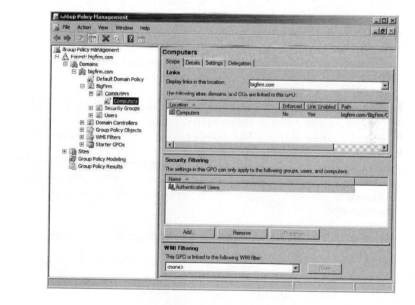

The policy that you will be enabling applies to the computer that the user will be logging into, not the user and not the file server where the profile is created. That's why the policy is linked to Computers and not Servers where the file server resides.

The policy that you are enabling is "Add the Administrators security group to roaming users profiles," which can be found in Computer Configuration\Policies\Administrative Templates\System\User Profiles. You can see it in Figure 30.27. Set it to Enabled, and this policy will grant Administrators Full Control to any newly created profile.

FIGURE 30.27
Configuring
the Group
Policy Object

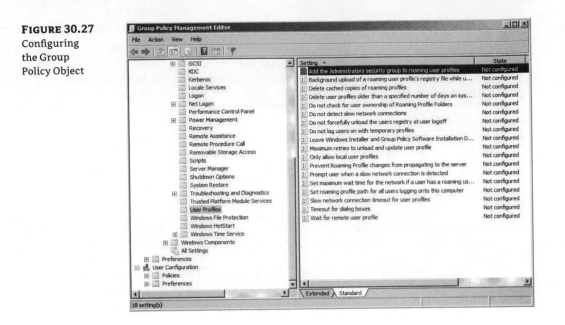

Remember that policies don't apply straightaway. In a production scenario, you will probably have to wait for the length of the refresh period. In a test or lab scenario, you can run the following command to force a computer to apply a computer configuration from inherited GPOs:

```
gpupdate /target:computer /force
```

Figure 30.28 shows that when you test this, you will see that Administrators will have Full Control over the profile. This will make user management and troubleshooting a lot easier for administrative staff and allow services that run as an administrator user to access the contents.

FIGURE 30.28
Administrators
have access to
roaming profile
folders.

You've managed to deploy roaming profiles just by creating a shared folder and configuring the user accounts. That was pretty simple. However, we did mention that the security of the Profiles folder isn't as tight as you might like thanks to the permissions required for this "self-service" technique. A sneaky user could start creating folders in the Profiles$ share and storing data there. You might want to look at an alternative way to deploy user profiles.

Creating a Roaming Profiles Share: The Hard Way

You can adopt this solution if you want 100 percent control over the contents of the folder containing the roaming profiles. You manually create every folder and set the permissions.

Create the Profiles folder in the same location as the previous sections. Disable inheritance, but do not copy the inherited permissions. Now assign these permissions to the folder:

GROUP	PERMISSION
BF2\Administrators	Full
System	Full
Authenticated Users	Read & Execute

Make sure that Authenticated Users does not have any special permission that allows the group to create folders in the Profiles folder. Set up the Profiles$ share as shown here:

GROUP	PERMISSION
BF2\Administrators	Full
BigFirm\Authenticated Users	Full

Don't worry about Authenticated Users having full permission on the share; they'll be restricted by the folder permissions to read everything. The user will be later granted additional permissions to their own profile folder. You can now link the Profiles$ share using a folder in the DFS namespace.

This is the extra step that requires much more work. You must manually create and set the permissions of a folder that will contain a user profile. A profile folder will not be automatically created when the user logs in because of the restrictive permissions set on the Profiles folder. For example, the user Joe Bloggs will require the folder C:\Shares\Profiles\JBloggs.V2. That folder must have permissions set on it as follows:

GROUP	PERMISSION
BF2\Administrators	Full
System	Full
BigFirm\JBloggs	Modify

You'll note that you must disable permissions inheritance to get the previous permissions set. You can now configure the user accounts with their profile path. The total solution is this:

◆ The user can navigate through the Profiles$ share with read-only permissions.

◆ The user has Change permissions only on their profile, which is enough for complete functionality.

◆ The user cannot create folders or files in the Profiles$ share through any means without administrative rights.

When you test this, you'll find that nothing appears in the user's roaming profile folder on the file server until they log out. Make sure you do two things when you are testing:

1. Log in and out as a single user several times to make sure the profile loads and saves correctly. Be sure to make some changes when you are logged in.

2. Make sure that the non-administrator user cannot read other people's profiles and cannot create folders in the Profiles$ share outside of their own profile.

⊕ Real World Scenario

HANDY TROUBLESHOOTING TIPS

As you are experimenting, you will find that you'll have little niggling things that annoy you.

First, remember that Windows Server 2008, Windows Server 2008 R2, Windows Vista, and Windows 7 require that the name of the roaming profile folder for the user on the file server must have a .V2 extension. For example, the folder for JBloggs on the file server will be called JBloggs.V2. Legacy operating system users such as those using Windows XP must not have that .V2 extension on their personal file server roaming profile folder.

You can delete locally cached roaming profiles (for example, on your Vista or Windows 7 machine) by right-clicking My Computer in the Start menu and selecting Properties. That launches System from Control Panel (that's a handy shortcut). Then click Advanced System Settings. Click Settings in the User Profiles section of the Advanced tab. That dialog box will display the profiles that are cached on the PC. You can select one and delete it if required.

You shouldn't try to delete the profile of a logged-in user. But sometimes (OK...usually), even if you log that user out and log in as an administrator, you still can't delete that cached profile because there's still an open or locked file or folder. You usually have to resort to rebooting the PC.

If the PC gets a bit messy, it can be hard to find the user's cached profile folder in C:\Users. It's possible to have several versions of the profile whenever there's a corruption or access issue with the user probably using the latest one. You can identify which folder the user is using by using regedit.exe, the registry editing tool. Browse to \HKEY_LOCAL_MACHINE\SOFTWARE\Microsoft\Windows NT\CurrentVersion\ProfileList. Here you'll see the security identifiers (SIDs) of the users. If this is a test machine, it won't be hard to identify which one to look at. Go into the key that is named after the SID of the relevant user. The ProfileImagePath value will contain the path to this user's locally cached profile.

While you test, take a look at the folders on the file server and the PC that you're testing. It's a good learning experience. You'll see that Windows caches the profile on the PC. That's handy for PC users, especially laptop users, whenever the file server is not available when the user logs in. Imagine if a laptop user goes home and can't download their profile. If there's no cache, then they get a temporary profile that doesn't contain their files and their settings. Thanks to the cache, they still have their files and settings.

It's worth doing some fun things in your test lab to re-create real-world scenarios. Change permissions on the Profiles folder so the user has no permissions. Rename the profile on the file server without changing the user object. You'll find that Windows will load a locally cached copy or will generate a temporary profile from the default user profile. Now you can try some troubleshooting.

You've now seen how to create roaming profiles in two different ways. This allows users to take their customized working environment around the network wherever they work. But what if your organization needs to lock down the user's working environment to maximize security and simplify the user interface? That brings us to mandatory profiles, a variation on the roaming profile.

Configuring Mandatory Profiles

Ask a veteran administrator what the cause of many problems is in a desktop environment, and you'll be sure to find that user configuration is not far from the top of the list. You may want a solution that provides users with a clean user configuration every time they log in.

The solution that we're talking about is a mandatory profile. This works by pre-creating a profile for users, configuring it as a mandatory profile, and making it available to all the required users as their roaming profile. No matter what changes the user makes, they will not be saved. Every time the user logs in, their profile will be reset to what the administrator had defined.

Other benefits include the following:

♦ You can provide the user with a preconfigured and consistent working experience.

♦ You can always ensure that the user has the required shortcuts for applications available.

♦ You will reduce the administrative workload and complexity associated with roaming profiles.

These are typical scenarios where you find mandatory profiles:

♦ Remote Desktop Services server farms

♦ Environments where there may be significant staff churn and where training time is minimal, for example, call centers

You'll now learn how to create a mandatory profile.

LEGACY OSS

Remember that you will need to have different mandatory profiles for legacy operating systems (2003, XP, and 2000) than for current operating systems (2008, 2008 R2, Vista, and Windows 7).

You'll now learn how to set up a roaming mandatory profile for the users on Windows 7. We say "roaming" because it's going to be available on the network no matter where the users log in. You're going to use a sample non-administrative user called JElway that is an Active Directory user account. Once you've logged into the Win7 PC with that user, you'll configure the environment exactly the way you want it to be for all users. You can set up a quick test by changing the way the Start menu is presented and by adding some shortcuts onto the desktop. You can log out to save the profile, and now you can convert this local profile into a roaming mandatory profile.

Now this is where the craziness with mandatory profiles begins. There is what we will call a "feature change" with Windows 7/Server 2008 R2, where part of this next step is not possible. There is no issue with Windows Vista/Server 2008. We'll show you how it works in Windows Vista and then jump back and show you how it works with Windows 7.

Mandatory Profiles on Windows Vista

Imagine that the workstation you set up the user profile on is running Windows Vista. You have logged in as an administrator on the workstation. From there open the system properties and then open Control Panel ➢ System ➢ Advanced System Properties, as shown in Figure 30.29.

FIGURE 30.29
System properties
on the Vista lab PC

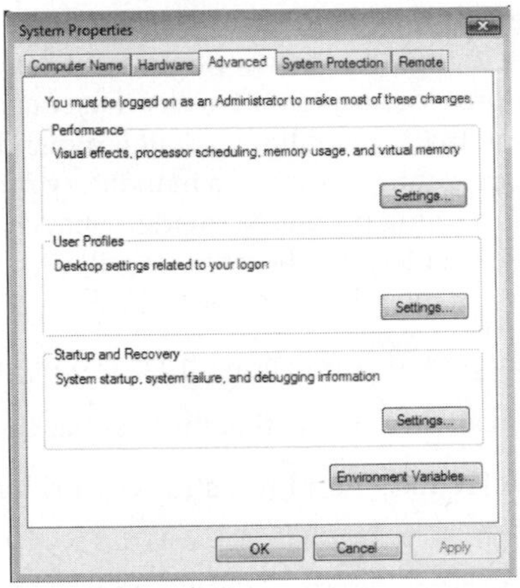

Click Settings under User Profiles to manage the profiles that are stored locally on the workstation. Of course, this may be a server if you're preparing a mandatory profile for Remote Desktop Services.

As shown in Figure 30.30, select the local profile that you used to create your mandatory profile. You want to copy this profile to the file server, BF2, so click Copy To. The Copy To dialog box opens, as shown in Figure 30.31.

The Copy To dialog box allows you to do the following:

◆ Select where to copy the profile to, for example, \\bigfirm.com\BigFirmShares\Profiles\ Mandatory.V2. Note the .V2 is being used because you're using profiles on the newer versions of Windows.

◆ Specify which user or security group will have permission to use the profile. We've selected Authenticated Users in the example, but you might need to use another group for more granular control. Failing to do this will cause users not to be able to log on with this profile. It changes registry permissions in the NTUSER.DAT file in the profile.

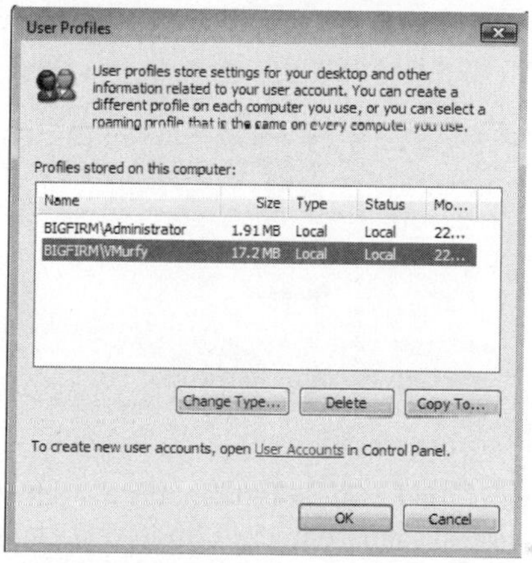

FIGURE 30.30
User profiles on
the Vista lab PC

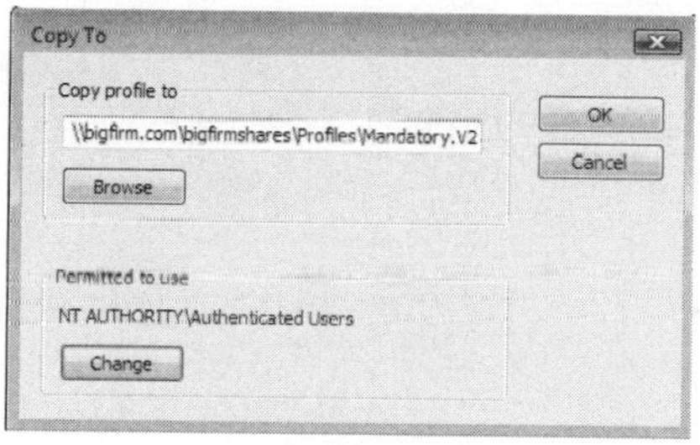

FIGURE 30.31
Copying the user
profile from the
Vista lab PC

Clicking OK will copy the profile to the file server. You need to set permissions for the folder appropriately now. This will require logging onto the file server. We'll show Windows 7 administrators how to re-create that button click. You should now jump ahead to the section titled "Completing Mandatory Profiles" if you are worried about Windows Vista only. The next section deals with creating a mandatory profile for Windows 7.

MANDATORY PROFILES ON WINDOWS 7

The previous Windows Vista profile copy will not work in Windows 7. It appears Microsoft disabled (accidentally or deliberately) the ability to copy a user profile on Windows 7 by graying out the Copy To button.

Therefore, you're going to have to manually re-create the process that the Copy To button has been doing since the days of Windows NT. Let's go back in time and log out as the sample user that you used to configure the profile.

As shown in Figure 30.32, open Windows Explorer, and browse to C:\Users. Here you can see the cached profiles on the PC. The one you're interested is C:\Users\JElway. You are going to copy this folder to the Profiles share on the file server, that is, \\bigfirm.com\BigFirmShares\Profiles\.

FIGURE 30.32
The profiles on the
Windows 7 lab PC

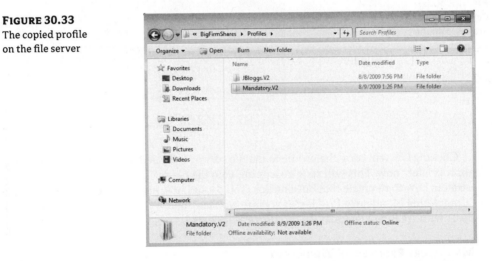

Once it has copied, you should rename it. Make sure that it has a **.V2** extension for users on newer operating systems, namely, Windows Vista, Windows 7, Windows Server 2008, and Windows Server 2008 R2. We've renamed the profile folder to Mandatory.V2, as shown in Figure 30.33.

FIGURE 30.33
The copied profile
on the file server

Figure 30.34 shows you the two folders that you need to delete from the roaming profile:

◆ AppData\Local

◆ AppData\LocalLow

Part of the profile is a file called NTUSER.DAT. It contains the HKEY_CURRENT_USER hive from the Windows registry. It has internal (not NTFS or file system) permissions. They protect the contents of the registry file so that only the assigned user (Joe Elway in this case) and administrators have access. You need to change that so users of the new mandatory roaming profile will have access to the contained HKEY_CURRENT_USER registry hive.

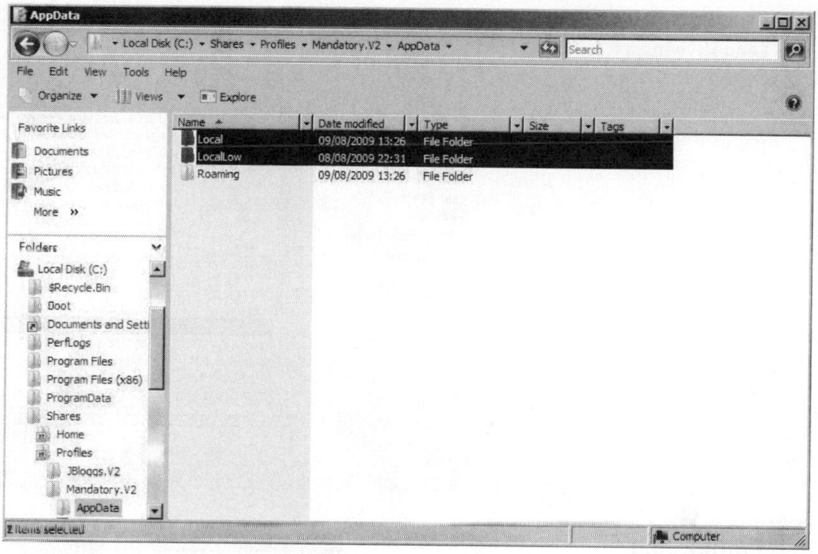

FIGURE 30.34
Deleting folders from the roaming profile

What you're going to do now is open up the NTUSER.DAT file in regedit.exe, the registry editor, and change the permissions of the HKEY_CURRENT_USER hive in that file.

Launch regedit.exe on the file server, and browse to HKEY_USERS, as shown in Figure 30.35.

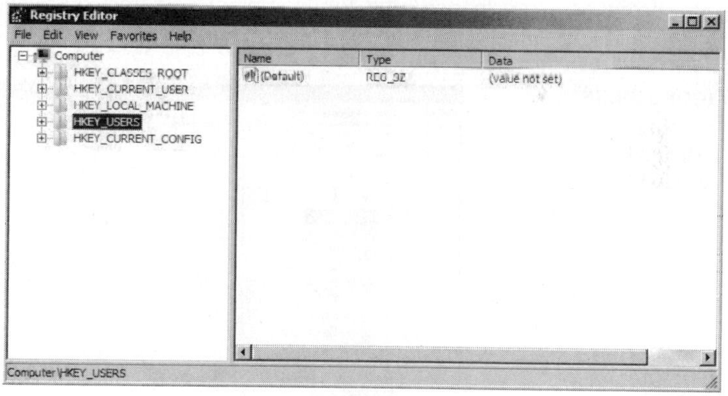

FIGURE 30.35
Opening the registry editor

Select File ➢ Load Hive. That opens the dialog box shown in Figure 30.36. Browse to where the NTUSER.DAT file is contained on the file server. In our case, that is C:\Shares\Profiles\ Mandatory.V2\NTUSER.DAT. Open that file.

You'll need to give the loaded hive a new name; you can't have a second HKEY_CURRENT_USER. Don't worry, this is only a temporary label that will be used while you're editing the opened NTUSER.DAT file. For the sake of simplicity, we've named the hive after the profile, that is, Mandatory.V2, in Figure 30.37.

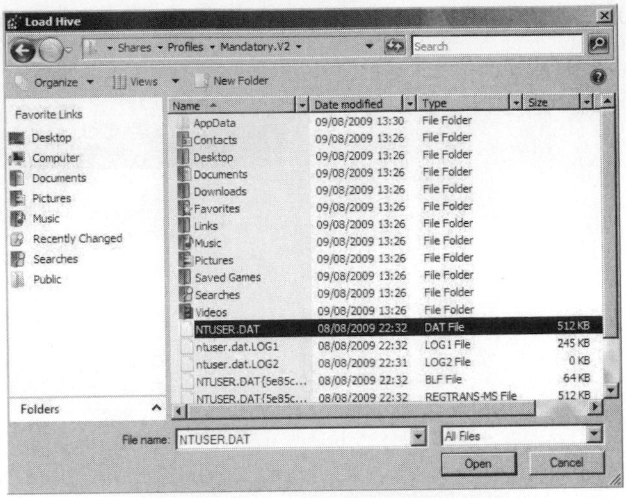

FIGURE 30.36
Load Hive in
regedit.exe

FIGURE 30.37
Naming the loaded
registry hive

Browse to your loaded hive, for example, Mandatory.V2 as shown in Figure 30.38, and right-click it. Select Permissions from the pop-up menu.

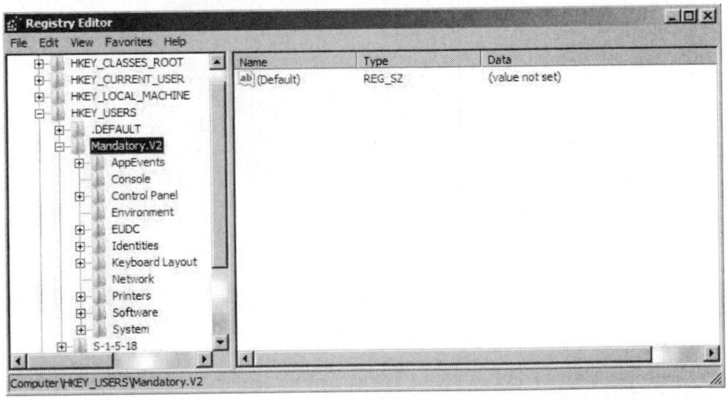

FIGURE 30.38
Browsing to
the loaded
registry hive

What you see in Figure 30.39 is the permissions for HKEY_CURRENT_USER as contained within the NTUSER.DAT file in the new roaming profile. Do two things to the permissions:

◆ Remove the entry for the user that was used to create the profile, that is, JElway.

◆ Add an entry for a security group that will require access to the roaming mandatory profile. In this case, it is Authenticated Users from the domain. Grant this group Full Control over the hive.

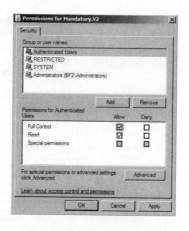

FIGURE 30.39
Permissions for the loaded registry hive

Close the permissions dialog box, and then select File ➢ Unload Hive in regedit.exe. You'll be asked whether you want to unload the key and its subkeys. Say Yes to that, and your modified NTUSER.DAT is saved. You cannot use this roaming profile until you unload the hive.

At this point, the Windows 7 administrators have caught up with the Windows Vista administrators. That was *a lot* of work that you had to do instead of clicking a single button. Both Windows Vista and Windows 7 administrators will continue the mandatory profile process in the next section.

COMPLETING THE MANDATORY PROFILES

At this point, all you have done is create a roaming profile that could be used by anyone. You haven't made it a *mandatory* roaming profile. The conversion is quite easy. Navigate into the roaming profile you created, and rename NTUSER.DAT to NTUSER.MAN, as shown in Figure 30.40. The extension is what tells Windows that no changes should be saved to this profile; that is, it is a mandatory roaming profile.

You need to correctly secure the mandatory roaming profile folder on the file server. Disable the inheritance of permissions from the parent folder, and set the mandatory profile's permissions as follows:

GROUP	PERMISSION
BF2\Administrators	Full
System	Full
BigFirm\Authenticated Users	Read & Execute

You've granted access to the Authenticated Users security group. You should choose a group that matches the group to which you granted access to the NTUSER.DAT registry hive.

Setting the folder permissions does two things for you. It provides Authenticated Users (or whatever security group you choose to use) with access to the mandatory roaming profile but prevents members from changing it.

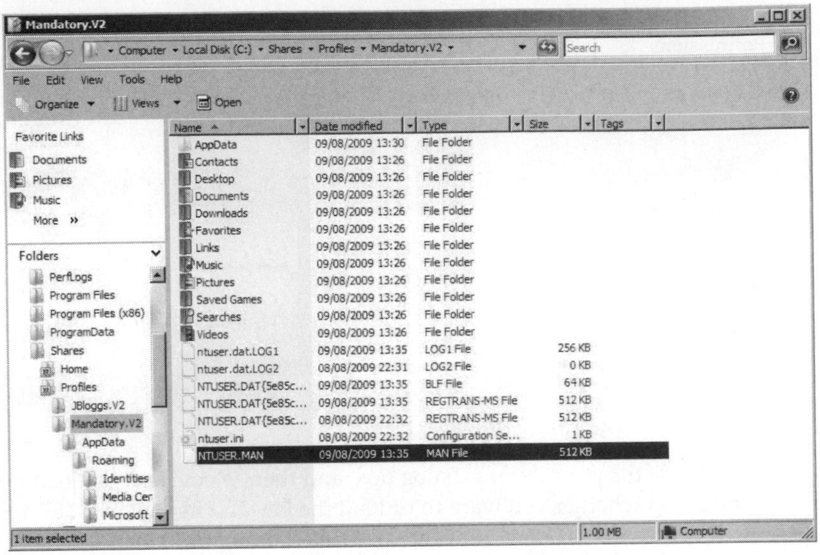

FIGURE 30.40
Rename
NTUSER.DAT
to NTUSER.MAN

Now you need to test the mandatory roaming profile. Simply navigate to a test user, and change the profile entry to \\bigfirm.com\BigFirmShares\Profiles\Mandatory.

WHERE'S THE ".V2"?

Notice that you did not add the .V2 extension. Consider it to be silent; the newer versions of Windows will add it as required as discussed earlier.

Log in as the test user, and verify that the customizations to the mandatory roaming profile are loaded. Make some changes; then undo the customizations, and make a few of your own. Log out and log in again. You should find that the loaded profile is reset to what was set up in the original mandatory roaming profile; no changes were saved. If that's what is happening, then you have a correctly functioning mandatory roaming profile.

You've configured JBloggs with \\bigfirm.com\BigFirmShares\Profiles\Mandatory.V2 as the path to his profile.

Joe Bloggs will now attempt to download the mandatory profile every time he logs in. If you log in now as JBloggs on a workstation, you will find that the entire profile is identical to that of JElway. You can still make changes. However, when you log out, those changes are not saved. You can log in again and get the same mandatory profile that you had before, without any of the previously made and unsaved changes.

Configuring Super Mandatory Profiles

There are some scenarios where you are using mandatory profiles but you cannot afford to allow anyone to be logged in if the mandatory profile cannot be downloaded for some reason, such as because a network issue or a file server problem. When could this be a realistic option?

We're probably talking about something like a kiosk or a publicly accessibly computer where it's better to have no service rather than a service that isn't tightly controlled.

So, it appears that you need to find a solution for this scenario. Luckily, you have one in the form of *super mandatory profiles*. Implementing this solution isn't all that different from mandatory profiles.

Setting up a super mandatory profile is just an extension of setting up a mandatory profile. Follow the previously described steps for configuring a mandatory profile, and follow it up with the following:

1. Rename the folder profile on the file server so it has a .MAN.V2 extension; for example, rename Mandatory.V2 to Mandatory.MAN.V2.

2. Configure the user's profile to include the .MAN extension. Ignore the .V2 component; for example, set the profile to \\bigfirm.com\BigFirmShares\Profiles\Mandatory.MAN.

That's it! You've just set up a super mandatory profile for the user. The profile will act like a normal mandatory profile, not allowing any changes to be saved to the file server. However, unlike a normal mandatory profile, this user will not be able to log in if the super mandatory profile cannot be downloaded.

There's an easy mistake that you can re-create to test this "no logon" functionality. Rename the NTUSER.MAN file in the super mandatory profile to NTUSER.DAT. Now try to log on as JBloggs. You'll be informed that the profile could not be downloaded and that the user cannot logon. Don't forget to rename the file back to NTUSER.MAN when you're finished!

Configuring a Default Network Profile

A *default profile* is used to build a user's profile if they don't already have one. Consider a user who has no roaming profile configuration and is logging into Windows Vista or Windows Server 2008. Their new profile is created by copying the contents of C:\Users\Default to the user's new profile folder in C:\Users\<username>.

There is a way for administrators to provide users with a customized default profile on the network. Domain member computers will automatically look for a default network profile. If one exists, then this is used instead of the default profile that is stored locally on the computer. You would use a default network profile when you want to provide a preconfigured working environment for users. This sounds like a mandatory profile, doesn't it? The difference is that the default network profile simply is copied to become the user's own profile. The user is free to save changes to their own profile.

The process for creating a default network profile is very similar to the one you used for creating a mandatory profile:

1. Create a template user.

2. Log in as that user on a sample computer. Remember that Windows Vista and Windows Server 2008 profiles are incompatible with legacy operating systems. Be sure to log into the correct operating system for your users.

3. Configure the template user's profile, and log out.

4. Log into the computer as an administrator, and copy the template user's profile to \\<Active Directory Domain Name>\Netlogon\Default User.V2. In the chapter's example, this would be \\bigfirm.com\Netlogon\Default User.V2.

Notice the **.V2** extension. This signifies version 2 profiles for Windows Vista and Windows Server 2008. You should use a folder called Default User to share a default network profile for legacy operating system support. Make sure that Authenticated Users is permitted to use this new profile when you copy it. Check out the process that you used to copy and permission Windows 7 profiles earlier in this chapter.

This default network profile will now be copied to every new user on the network.

The flaw with this solution is in that last sentence. This default network profile defines the user configuration for a user. This includes things such as regional settings. Consider an organization where there are branch offices in foreign countries. Those users will probably need different regional settings to match their keyboard, and so on. It'll be a bit of a pain to change these settings for the user when they first log in. You also need to be careful about keeping location-specific settings in the profile. You don't want to save drive mappings for a file server in New York and have someone logging in at the San Francisco office 3,000 miles away to find that they have a file server that's appearing to be very slow.

You cannot have a "per-location" default network profile. The profile can be stored only in a specific folder. And this folder is copied to all domain controllers via SYSVOL replication.

Default network profiles are fine for simple networks where everyone shares the same basic configuration. You should think long and hard about deploying default network profiles in more complex networks where users require different basic configurations such as regional settings. Yes, the user can change those settings when they first log in, but that might prove to generate lots of help-desk tickets. You might want to look at an automated configuration. You could use a GPO to define regional settings once a user has logged in, but this locks a user down. A common experience is that not everyone shares the same configuration in an office in this environment. Instead of default network profiles, consider a scripting or Group Policy solution that will make those localized configurations when a user logs in for the first time. This allows those few users who are not the norm to alter their own configuration and retain those settings.

Managing Roaming Profiles

Roaming profiles require considerable thought if you have different operating systems, users roaming between branches with limited network links, and Remote Desktop Services. You can do some advanced management of profiles by using Group Policy, as you saw earlier when you granted rights to automatically generated profiles to Administrators.

Let's look at a few examples where you might have issues. If you have a farm of Remote Desktop servers, then a user could log into any one of them. If you have 1,000 users logging into 10 servers, you could end up with 10,000 cached roaming profiles. That's a lot of disk space being wasted.

Speaking of disk space, you might want to consider how big a roaming profile can get. For example, users could upload their entire MP3 collection into My Music. It might be an innocent action where they think they're only consuming local storage. But these are roaming profiles; 1,000 users all doing something like this soon adds up to terabytes of storage being consumed on the organization's file servers with nonbusiness data. Should the organization be paying for this?

The solution is to use machine and user Group Policy objects to control how roaming profiles behave in these and other circumstances.

Machine Settings

You'll now look at how you can control roaming profiles on a per-machine basis using Group Policy. Every user logging onto a machine inheriting the Group Policy settings that you configure will be subject to these settings.

CLEANING UP THOSE PROFILES

If you look, you'll find that a locally cached copy of the mandatory profile is created and *kept* on the workstation on the Remote Desktop server. When you think about it, it probably makes no sense to keep a copy of it in environments where you are using a mandatory profile.

Even if you're not using mandatory profiles, you might want some way to clean up older profiles when a computer reboots. Group Policy gives you some tools to do this (see Table 30.1).

TABLE 30.1:   Cached User Profiles GPO

PATH	ENTRY	DESCRIPTION
Computer Configuration\Policies\Administrative Templates\System\User Profiles	Delete cached copies of roaming profiles	Locally cached copies of a roaming profile will be deleted when the user logs out.
Computer Configuration\Policies\Administrative Templates\System\User Profiles	Delete user profiles older than a specified number of days on system restart	Profiles older than a specified number of days will automatically be deleted when a computer restarts.

MULTIPLE SITES AND ROAMING PROFILES

What do you do with a user who has a roaming profile and that user travels between branch offices across the world? By default, the computer that the user is logging into will measure the network speed between itself and the location where the profile is stored. If the link is considered too slow, then the profile will not be downloaded. Instead, the user will be offered a temporary local profile. However, remember that this won't work with super mandatory profiles. You can control how this measurement process works using GPO (see Table 30.2).

TABLE 30.2:   Slow Networks and User Profiles GPO

PATH	ENTRY	DESCRIPTION
Computer Configuration\Policies\Administrative Templates\System\User Profiles	Do not detect slow network connections	You can prevent a computer from detecting whether a profile download will take too long. Be very careful with this because a user logon could take a *very* long time and flood a branch-office WAN link.

TABLE 30.2: Slow Networks and User Profiles GPO *(CONTINUED)*

PATH	ENTRY	DESCRIPTION
Computer Configuration\Policies\Administrative Templates\System\User Profiles	Prompt user when a slow network connection is detected	If a slow network connection is detected, the user can be prompted. This allows the user to choose to download their roaming profile despite the network issue. Again, be very careful with this.
Computer Configuration\Policies\Administrative Templates\System\User Profiles	Slow network connection for user profiles	This allows you to define what "slow" means when measuring the link to the file server hosting the user's profile. This is done using kilobits per second and latency measured in milliseconds.
Computer Configuration\Policies\Administrative Templates\System\User Profiles	Wait for remote user profile	This directs the system to wait as long as it takes for a roaming profile to download. It is ignored if "Do not detect slow network connections" is enabled.

This gives you a pretty crude mechanism for giving users a roaming profile when the users travel to other locations. You have some other ways to make the environment flexible to business needs.

If your users have a predictable travel pattern, then you might be able to take advantage of DFS replication (DFS-R). Now you're seeing why we like to use DFS for hosting home directories and user profiles. You can choose to replicate selected folders to servers in other branch offices. You'll find that this could get difficult to manage, so you will want to manage things very carefully.

An alternative is to allow users to have different roaming profiles in each site. This would mean that their roaming profile wouldn't actually roam between sites, only between computers within a site. You can configure this using the following GPO settings:

Path   The path is Computer Configuration\Policies\Administrative Templates\System\User Profiles.

Entry   The entry is "Set roaming profile path for all users logging onto this computer."

Description   You can specify a path for roaming profiles for any users logging into the computer. Use the %username% variable to have different profiles for users. This takes precedence over the profile specified in the user object.

REMOTE DESKTOP SERVICES

There are several complications to consider when dealing with Remote Desktop Services and roaming profiles:

◆ It is a bad idea to mix a user's desktop roaming profile with the profile that will be used on a Remote Desktop server/virtual desktop because registry settings and shortcuts from the different systems will be mixed together.

◆ You may employ the concept of "application silos" in a Remote Desktop server farm; in other words, Server1 and Server2 might have BizzApp installed, but Server3 might not. You don't want shortcuts for BizzApp to appear when a user is logged into Server3 with a roaming profile.

◆ A common use for Remote Desktop servers is to share applications from a central site with users in branch offices. You do not want branch-office roaming profiles to load across the WAN, but you do want some sort of roaming profile solution.

You can apply this Group Policy object to disable roaming profiles on the machine:

Path The path is Computer Configuration\Policies\Administrative Templates\System\User Profiles.

Entry The entry is Only Allow Local User Profiles.

Description Disable the usage of roaming profiles on this computer.

This is a rather crude solution. It turns off the ability to download a roaming profile and returns you to a scenario where the user does not have a consistent working environment.

Alternatively, you might configure users with specific roaming profiles for farms of machines. For example, when a user logs into a Remote Desktop server farm, they will use a dedicated profile from a Remote Desktop server roaming profile share. When they log into their PC, they will use a dedicated profile from a PC roaming profile share. When they log into a virtual desktop, they will use a dedicated profile from a virtual desktop roaming profile share. Table 30.3 shows the settings required to do this.

TABLE 30.3: Remote Desktop Services Profile GPO

PATH	ENTRY	DESCRIPTION
Computer Configuration\ Policies\Administrative Templates\Windows Components\Remote Desktop Services\Remote Desktop Session Host\Profiles	Set path for TS roaming user profile	You can specify the path of a profile for a user account when logging in via Remote Desktop Services. This takes precedence over all other profile settings. You can use %username% to allow multiple profiles or simply use one folder for all users.
Computer Configuration\ Policies\Administrative Templates\Windows Components\Remote Desktop Services\Remote Desktop Session Host\Profiles	Use mandatory profiles on the Remote Desktop Server	When enabled, this turns the profile specified in the previous GPO setting into a mandatory profile.

The second settings in Table 30.3 allows you to tell the computer to treat any roaming profile as a mandatory profile, that is, to never save any changes made by the user. This is an alternative to the previously described method for creating a mandatory roaming profile.

For Windows Server 2008, you'll find these GPO settings in Computer Configuration\Policies\Administrative Templates\Windows Components\Terminal Services\Terminal Server\Profiles.

SPECIFYING A REMOTE DESKTOP SERVICES PROFILE

There is an option in the user account to specify a Remote Desktop Services profile. That's a rather simple solution that implies that there will only ever be one possible profile for that user that is suitable for all Remote Desktop servers. This might be suitable for smaller organizations with one or maybe two Remote Desktop servers. We recommend that you think long-term and adopt the GPO approach to manage Remote Desktop Services roaming profiles.

You will need to clean up cached profiles (covered earlier in the chapter) if using roaming profiles on your Remote Desktop servers. They can quickly eat up a lot of space on your system drive if left unmanaged.

ADDITIONAL ROAMING PROFILE GPO SETTINGS

You've seen only about half of the GPO settings you can use to configure roaming profiles. Table 30.4 shows the rest.

TABLE 30.4:   Miscellaneous GPO Settings for Roaming Profiles

PATH	ENTRY	DESCRIPTION
Computer Configuration\Policies\Administrative Templates\System\User Profiles	Background upload of a roaming user profile's registry file while user is logged on	You can configure a schedule to regularly upload the NTUSER.DAT file to the file server in the background while the user is logged in.
Computer Configuration\Policies\Administrative Templates\System\User Profiles	Do not check for user ownership of Roaming Profile Folders	By default Windows checks for user ownership of the profile before downloading it. This policy can reverse this practice.
Computer Configuration\Policies\Administrative Templates\System\User Profiles	Do not forcefully unload the users registry at user logoff	When a user logs off, their applications should close and release their open file handles on the registry. Faulty applications may not do so. Windows will then force the registry to close. There may be scenarios when this is undesirable.
Computer Configuration\Policies\Administrative Templates\System\User Profiles	Do not log on users with temporary profiles	This has the same effect as the super mandatory profile. When the user's assigned profile cannot be loaded, then the user will be immediately automatically logged out after their login attempt.

TABLE 30.4:   Miscellaneous GPO Settings for Roaming Profiles *(CONTINUED)*

PATH	ENTRY	DESCRIPTION
Computer Configuration\ Policies\Administrative Templates\System\User Profiles	Leave Windows Installer and Group Policy Software Installation Data	It is possible to install applications for a user via Group Policy. This stores data in the user's profile. Deleting the profile causes this data to be deleted and thus causes applications to be installed again. This policy prevents nonrequired repeat installations.
Computer Configuration\ Policies\Administrative Templates\System\User Profiles	Maximum retries to unload and update user profile	This allows an administrator to specify how many times Windows will try to save the NTUSER.DAT file to the file share. You might need to increase this if faulty applications are slow to update it at logoff. By default Windows tries it a maximum of 60 times over 60 seconds.
Computer Configuration\ Policies\Administrative Templates\System\User Profiles	Prevent Roaming Profile changes from propagating to the server	Any changes made to the user's profile on this machine are not saved to their roaming profile.
Computer Configuration\ Policies\Administrative Templates\System\User Profiles	Set maximum time for the network if a user has a roaming user profile or remote home directory	Windows will wait up to 30 seconds if the file server with those shares is unavailable. You can override that setting. You might use this on wireless networks when you notice roaming profiles are not downloaded and home directories are not connected, and the only issue is timing.
Computer Configuration\ Policies\Administrative Templates\System\User Profiles	Timeout for dialog boxes	Windows will pop up a dialog box when it needs human interaction to make a decision. The default is 30 seconds. You can change this from between 0 and 600 seconds.

These are all settings for a machine; that is, they will affect all users who log into the machine that the policy is applied to. You can also apply policies to user objects to control roaming profiles.

User Settings

You can use some settings to manage roaming profiles on a per-user basis. You might want to control the contents of the roaming profile or even control the size of the roaming profile itself with the settings shown in Table 30.5.

TABLE 30.5:   Roaming Profile Contents GPO Settings

PATH	ENTRY	DESCRIPTION
User Configuration\Policies\ Administrative Templates\ System\User Profiles	Exclude directories in roaming profile	You might find some folders that you do not want to make available on all computers. You can specify them here. The Appdata\ Local and Appdata\LocalLow folders and their contents are not replicated to a file server by default.
User Configuration\Policies\ Administrative Templates\ System\User Profiles	Limit Profile Size	You can determine a quota for roaming profiles. Operating systems prior to Windows Vista simply refused to allow a user to log out if the quote was exceeded. Vista allows the user to log out without saving the profile to the file server. Users can be notified of an issue and reminded using a set message at set times.

Be careful of the Limit Profile Size policy. Remember that folders like My Documents and Desktop are contained within there. You'll need to find a way to move them to another location—you'll be looking at that soon.

Redirecting Folders

Roaming profiles have been pretty common practice in the Windows world. They work, but they are far from perfect.

We've already mentioned that you cannot have a single roaming profile that works on both current operating systems (2008, Vista, and later) and legacy operating systems (2003, XP, and 2000). The current operating systems use different versions of roaming profiles that are signified by the .V2 extension. If you have mixed operating systems and roaming profiles, then it's possible that your users may have two profiles with different configurations to support the two versions.

There are complications with files being loaded, unloaded, and corruptions. Things can get very complicated. That brings us to *folder redirection*.

Folder redirection allows you to move special folders within the user profile to another, more suitable location. For example, instead of storing these folders in a roaming profile, you could store them in the user's home directory. Windows 2000, 2003, and XP allowed you to redirect a limited number of folders. However, Windows Vista and Server 2008 and later allow you to redirect:

- ◆ AppData (Roaming)
- ◆ Desktop
- ◆ Start Menu
- ◆ Documents
- ◆ Pictures

- Music

- Videos

- Favorites

- Contacts

- Downloads

- Links

- Searches

- Saved Games

ORIGIN OF FOLDER REDIRECTION

Folder redirection was introduced as part of IntelliMirror in Windows 2000. The concept of IntelliMirror was to provide the user with a mobile working environment that followed the user wherever the user moved. The brand name seems to have slipped by the wayside over the years, unfortunately.

When you look at that list, it appears to be everything that is important within a profile. If you can store these folders in some special folder, why would you even want to have roaming profiles?

That's a very good question. In fact, many organizations don't bother deploying roaming profiles anymore. You've seen that deploying a roaming profile in addition to a home directory doubles the amount of administration that you must do. By storing them in the user's home directory, you could halve the amount of file share administration on the network. That simplifies deployment, backup/recovery, security, auditing, archiving, and disaster recovery planning/implementations. There are many complications with roaming profiles such as their mobility between machines with different software configurations and between machines with different operating systems.

So, what exactly does folder redirection do? Quite simply, you configure each of these listed special folders to point to an alternate location outside of the profile. This location would be a file share unique to the user. Such a folder probably already exists—you've probably created home directories for each of your users so you can configure folder redirection to map there instead of to the profile. For example, My Documents normally exists as Documents in the profile. Using folder redirection, it could exist as Documents in the home directory. This accomplishes a number of things:

- You can redirect all the required folders to the home directory so that a user can have a consistent working environment on current and legacy operating systems; that is, the data exists outside the restrictions of profile versions.

- By redirecting folders that contain user data, you can reliably apply profile size quotas without impacting business data contained in folders such as My Documents.

- You can probably eliminate the need for profiles altogether by redirecting all the folders that are important to the organization. Roaming profiles can be a source of trouble and are considered an obsolete technology by some administrators.

Before you move on, we should quickly address a question that might be popping up at this point. What use is something like My Documents if it is redirected to a file server and you're a user who travels around with a laptop? By default, redirected folders are replicated to the local computer using Offline Files. Offline Files creates a secure cache of the files on the computer. When connected to the network, the computer will synchronize the Offline Files cache with the shares on the file server(s).

Basic Folder Redirection

You're probably itching to see how to do this right about now. We won't delay any longer. Folder redirection is controlled using Group Policy settings that are applied to users. Say all your users reside in \bigfirm.com\BigFirm\Users. You've created and linked a policy called Users to this OU.

Edit the policy object that will be applied to the user accounts for whom you want to redirect folders. Create and link a policy to the Users OU, as shown in Figure 30.41.

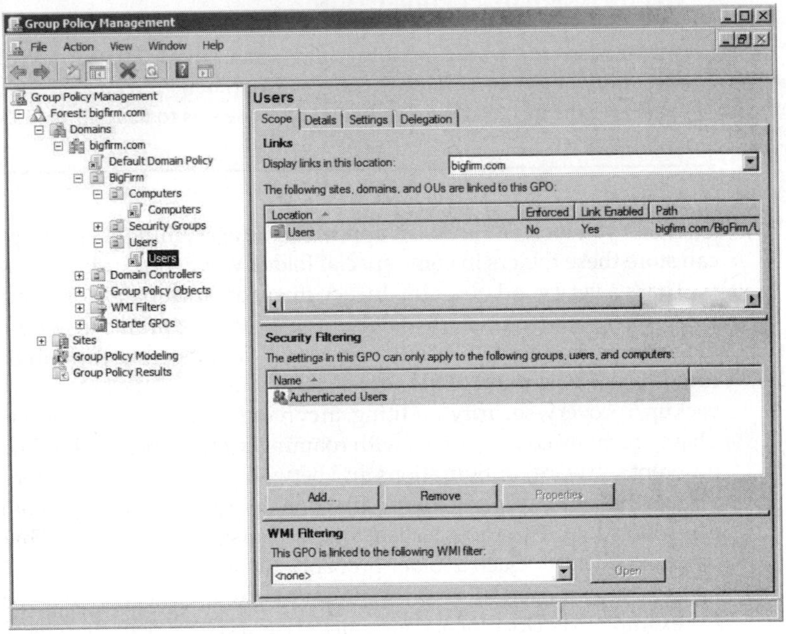

FIGURE 30.41
A new GPO object for user folder redirection

Navigate into User Configuration\Policies\Windows Settings\Folder Redirection. It is here that you can see all the folders that you can redirect on a current Windows operating system computer, as shown in Figure 30.42.

You are going to start out by redirecting Documents to the user's home directory. Right-click Documents, and select Properties.

This opens a dialog box, shown in Figure 30.43, where you can configure the redirection of the folder. You have three choices here:

Not configured This disables folder redirection.

Basic redirection   This allows you to configure all users to redirect to a common location. For example, all users have their home directory in a common file share, so redirect all folders to \\bigfirm.com\BigFirmShares\Home. It's a "one-size-fits-all" policy that usually is the appropriate choice.

Advanced – Specify locations for various user groups   This allows you to specify unique paths for different groups. You'll go with this one when your OU layout doesn't match up with your desired folder redirection design.

FIGURE 30.42
The folder redirection policies

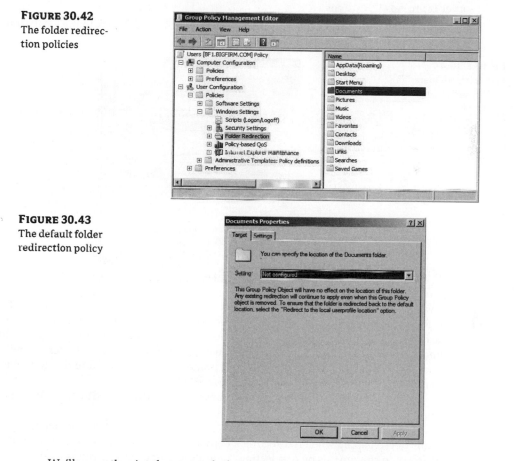

FIGURE 30.43
The default folder redirection policy

We'll cover the simple approach that you are most likely to apply, that is, basic redirection. Select Basic, as shown in Figure 30.44.

Target Folder Redirection offers you a number of choices depending on which folder you are redirecting:

Redirect to the user's home directory   This very simple solution will redirect the folder to the user's home directory. It does not create a subfolder for the redirected folder. Instead, it just dumps contents to the root of their home directory. Things will get impossible for users if you redirect many folders.

Create a folder for each user under the root path This will create a folder named after the redirected folder within the path you specify; for example, Documents will be created in \\bigfirm.com\BigFirmShares\Home\JBloggs if you specify \\bigfirm.com\BigFirmShares\Home. Do you see how it intelligently adds the username? This will solve the previous confusion problem we mentioned.

Redirect to the following location This is a simple redirection where all users will share a common folder. This might be suitable if redirecting a Start menu for a Remote Desktop server farm.

Redirect to the local user profile location This forces the folder back to the local profile.

FIGURE 30.44

Redirecting folders to the user's home directory

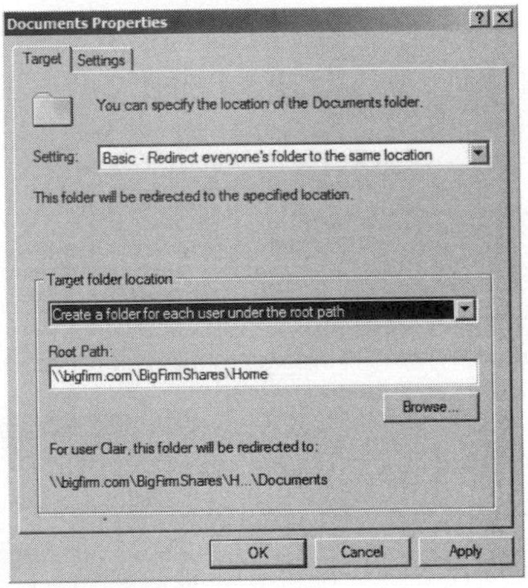

As shown in Figure 30.44, select to redirect Documents to a subfolder within the user home directory. Remember that you set up the home directories in a DFS namespace. You can move the physical storage location of the folders, and you won't have to change this policy. You just need to update the link in the DFS namespace. You can do this with further folders knowing that the user will see a distinct folder within their home directory for each redirected folder—nice and simple and fewer help-desk tickets!

Clicking the Settings tab shows you how Windows will handle the redirection. We'll go through the settings in Figure 30.45 in a moment.

By default, the user will get exclusive rights to any folders created during folder redirection. Note that this doesn't apply when redirecting Documents to the home directory itself (and not a subfolder). You can change this by deselecting "Grant the user exclusive rights to Documents." You will probably want to do this so that you can perform administrative tasks with Documents to assist the user or if you use administrator accounts for services such as archiving or backup/recovery. We've done this in Figure 30.46.

You can move all contents of Documents in the profile when the redirection policy applies. This is on by default and is probably what you will want to do. However, you do have the option to turn this behavior off.

By default, your redirection policies will not apply to legacy operating systems even if they support redirection for this folder. Some redirections (depending on legacy operating system support) can be configured for legacy operating systems by selecting the "Also apply redirection policy to ..." check box. Note that this will be grayed out when those legacy operating systems cannot support this function; in other words, legacy operating systems are capable of redirecting only a few key folders. You'll want to enable legacy redirection where possible to allow the sharing of profile data between version 2 and legacy user profiles.

FIGURE 30.45
Default Documents folder redirection settings

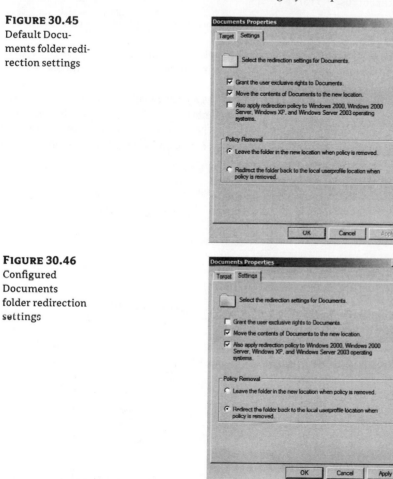

You can change what will happen when the policy you are now configuring no longer applies to a user. The default is that the redirected folder and contents are left where they are when redirection is disabled. You can redirect the folder and its contents back to the profile in this situation.

Figure 30.46 shows disabling exclusive access to the folder, moving the contents, and turning on legacy support. The folder will also be redirected back to the profile when the policy no longer applies.

You'll now want to test this. Log into your test workstation using a user account that is inheriting the new policy. Use JBloggs to log into Win7; JBloggs is configured to not use a roaming or mandatory profile. In a lab, you won't want to wait for policies to refresh, so you'll want to run the following on your test workstation:

```
gpupdate /target:user /force
```

You have used the /force flag here because of how some GPO settings can take two refreshes to apply.

You will be told that you need to log out to apply new policy settings. This is a sign that your folder redirection is working—it applies only during logon. Log back in, and check out where Documents is now located.

Log in as JBloggs, and open the properties of the Documents library. Windows Vista administrators should check the properties of the My Documents folder. The location of My Documents shows you that the folder has been redirected to the user's home directory. You can see in Figure 30.47 that in this example it has been moved to a folder called Documents in the user's home directory on the file server.

FIGURE 30.47
Checking the redirected folder properties

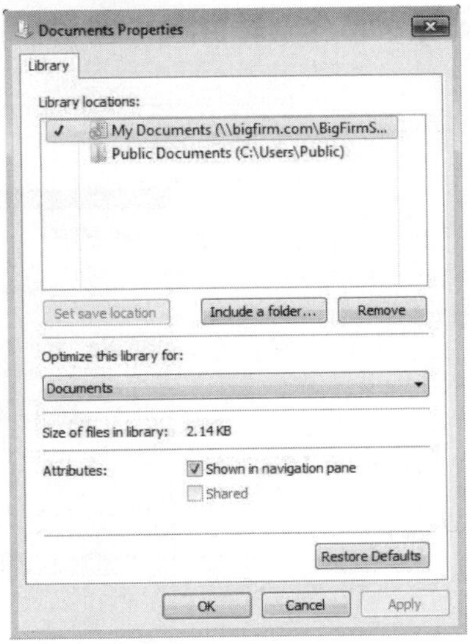

Opening Windows Explorer and browsing to JBloggs' home directory shows that a special folder called Documents has been created for the user. You can see this in Figure 30.48.

Interestingly, browsing into Documents shows you that the following folders are automatically redirected as subfolders of Documents, as shown in Figure 30.49. That's a time-saver!

◆ My Music

◆ My Pictures

◆ My Videos

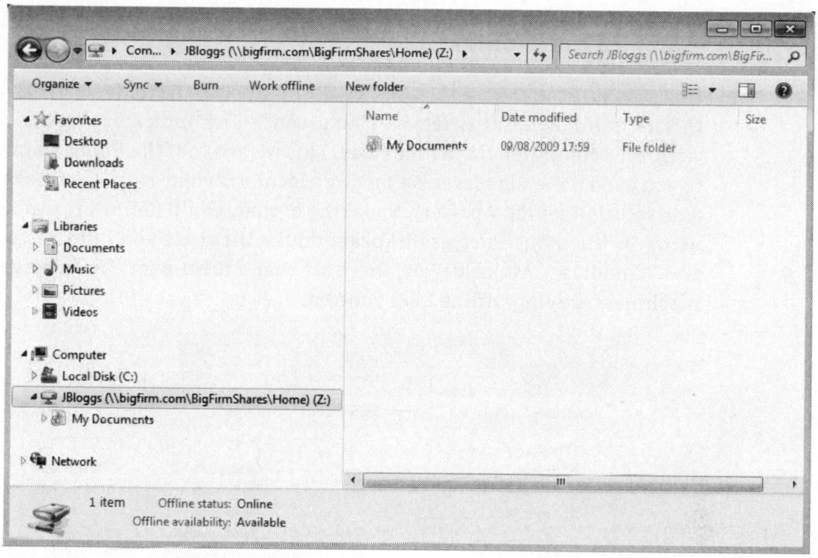

FIGURE 30.48
The redirected folder in the home directory

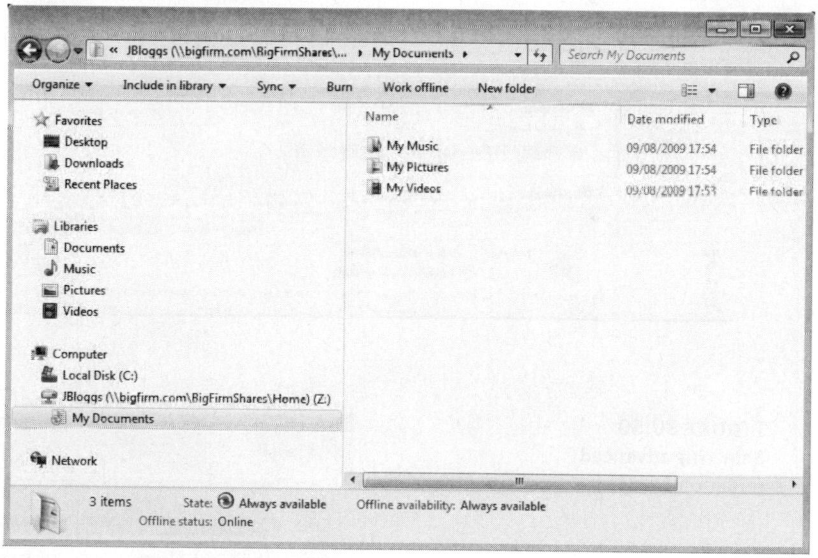

FIGURE 30.49
The contents of the redirected Documents

This is because the default Group Policy setting for these folders is that they should follow My Documents to wherever it is redirected to.

Figure 30.50 shows an example of where we have redirected almost all the possible folders to the user's home directory. There's actually enough of the user's data here where you can consider completely abandoning the concept of profiles!

FOLDER SYNCHRONIZATION

Have you noticed the little green circular symbol on the folder icon for My Documents? You can see this in the following illustration. That green "swirl" indicates that this folder is being synchronized with your computer via Offline Files. This means that the folder and its contents will be available to you even if the file server isn't using a locally cached copy. This makes folder redirection a workable solution for laptop users. Speaking of that, you'll definitely want to look at laptop security if using Offline Files, such as BitLocker on the Ultimate and Enterprise editions of Windows Vista and Windows 7. Alternatively, there are many third-party alternatives to protect those roaming machines carrying Offline Files content.

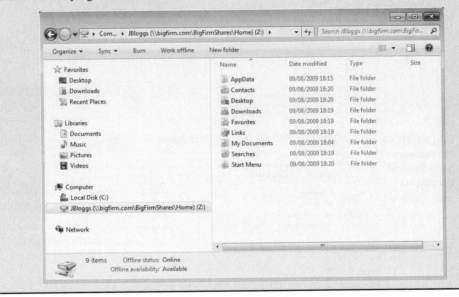

FIGURE 30.50
Selecting advanced folder redirection

This example of basic folder redirection will suit organizations where the OU design is similar to how you want to handle folder redirection. You'll now move on to doing some more advanced folder redirection.

Advanced Folder Redirection

Basic folder redirection configures everyone who received the policy to redirect their folders in a similar way. This is probably fine in most situations, but there are times when you might want to apply a single policy where users redirect to different locations depending on their group membership rather than just OU location. Here are a few examples:

- You apply different security policies to home directory shares to different groups in the organization. This means that user A might have her profile in a different share than user B.

- You control DFS replication of home directories on a per-share basis.

- You have been forced to deploy multiple servers for home directory file shares.

You can use advanced folder redirection to apply your policy to security groups. Each security group will receive a different configuration for the folder redirection policy. This will become a little clearer when you look at it in action.

Open the GPO and properties of the folder that you want to redirect. In the previous example of folder redirection, you selected basic folder redirection. This time, as you can see in Figure 30.51, you are going with "Advanced – Specify locations for various user groups." You can click Add to specify a user group and a location for the folder redirection.

The dialog box shown in Figure 30.51 allows you to do the following:

- Select a security group to apply this policy to.

- Define how the folder will be redirected. This has an identical set of options as Target Folder Location in basic folder redirection.

- Specify the path where the redirected folder will reside.

FIGURE 30.51
Setting up
advanced folder
redirection under
a root path

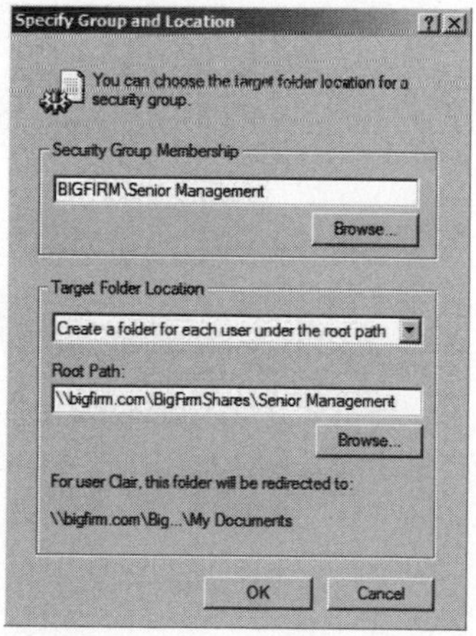

You can see in Figure 30.52 that you can configure folder redirection of a single folder for security groups differently using a single GPO.

FIGURE 30.52
Advanced folder redirection to the user's home directory

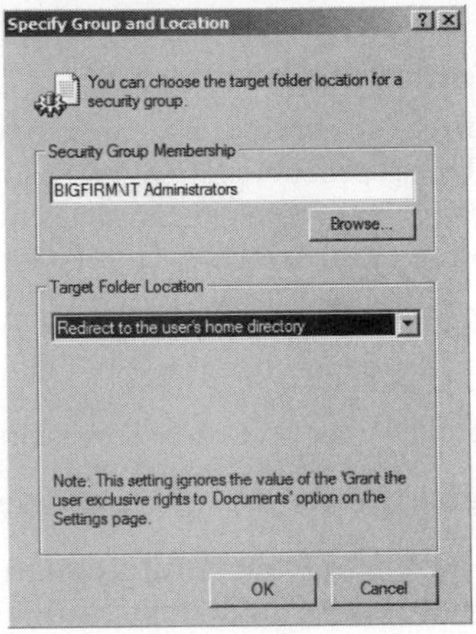

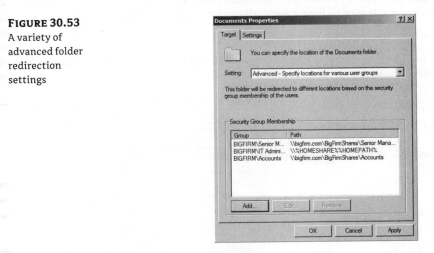

In Figure 30.53, you have configured three different security groups to redirect Documents using various methods within a single Group Policy object. This demonstrates how flexible folder redirection can be and how it can adjust to the needs of the organization.

FIGURE 30.53
A variety of advanced folder redirection settings

Managing Folder Redirection

You use Group Policy to configure folder redirection (see Table 30.6). You can use other Group Policy settings to manage how folder redirection is processed.

TABLE 30.6:   Folder Redirection Management GPO

PATH	ENTRY	DESCRIPTION
Computer Configuration\Policies\Administrative Templates\System\Folder Redirection	Use localized subfolder names when redirecting Start and My Documents	The special folders in a profile will normally be localized; for example, what you see in an American English version of Windows will be different from a German version. By default, folder redirection does not maintain these names. Enabling this policy will allow localized names on a per-system basis.
Computer Configuration\Policies\Administrative Templates\System\Group Policy	Folder Redirection policy processing	You can force folder redirection to work over slow links (off by default). You can also configure a folder redirection policy to process even if the policy has not changed.
User Configuration\Policies\Administrative Templates\System\Folder Redirection	Do not automatically make redirected folders available offline	Redirected folders automatically are synchronized using Offline Files. You can disable this behavior.
User Configuration\Policies\Administrative Templates\System\Folder Redirection	Use localized subfolder names when redirecting Start and My Documents	The special folders in a profile will normally be localized; for example, what you see in an American English version of Windows will be different from a German version. By default, folder redirection does not maintain these names. Enabling this policy will allow localized names on a per-user basis.

Managing the Desktop Using Group Policy

Mandatory profiles allow administrators to provide a consistent working experience for users when they log in. No changes can be saved. However, what if you do not want to allow users to make any changes at all? Mandatory profiles can't be considered a security solution because they don't stop users from doing what they want. Consider the following:

- ◆ A Remote Desktop server where you want to restrict users to a locked-down experience where they can only start certain programs

- ◆ A kiosk where only one program can be run and there is no other interaction with the system

- ◆ A PC in a security- or regulatory-conscious organization where administrators need to tie down what a user can do

All of these types of problem require a solution where the user cannot make changes. Clearly, mandatory profiles aren't the complete solution.

Windows provides the ability to lock down the desktop using registry edits. A wide variety of options are available to administrators such as restricting what is on the Start menu, disabling browsing on the C drive, and restricting access to Control Panel. You probably don't want to deploy your security solution using registry edits because of the excessive work involved. Luckily, a number of built-in Group Policy settings are included in the administrative templates in Windows Server 2008 and Windows Server 2008 R2. You can use these to configure Group Policy for those users and/or computers that you need to secure. You'll take a look at a *few* of those now that you can use to tie down your computers or Remote Desktop server desktops. There are *many* more settings available to use, but these are ones that you might find more important to start working with.

Using the settings in Computer Configuration\Policies\Administrative Templates\Network \Offline Files, you can manage offline files on a per-system basis; that is, the settings you apply here will affect all users who log onto the targeted computers (see Table 30.7).

TABLE 30.7: Computer Configuration: Offline Files

ITEM	DESCRIPTION
At logoff, delete local copy of user's offline files	Use this option if you decide that you need to remove all offline files from a computer when the user logs off.
Encrypt the offline files cache	Data on a computer is vulnerable to attack if not encrypted. Enabling this setting forces the offline files cache to be secured by encryption. Users cannot turn this off.
Prohibit "Make Available Offline" for these files and folders	You can specify certain folders that must not be made available offline. There may be certain information that you cannot risk being on laptop computers because of the risk of theft in order to obtain access to that information.
Synchronize all offline files before logging on	All marked files and folders are synchronized before a user is logged on. This guarantees that changes made by a user while traveling with their laptop are copied to the file server.
Synchronize all offline files before logging off	This guarantees that the user will have the latest copy of all files when they take their laptop away from the office.
Prohibit user configuration of Offline Files	Users are often the cause of faults on computers. You can configure offline files using a GPO and prevent users from tampering with that configuration.

Computer Configuration\Policies\Administrative Templates\Windows Components\ Internet Explorer contains a nested set of GPO settings for controlling how a user can manage Internet Explorer on a computer (see Table 30.8).

TABLE 30.8:   Computer Configuration: Internet Explorer

ITEM	DESCRIPTION
Disable automatic install of Internet Explorer components	By default, users are prompted to download components when a web page requires them. You can prevent this behavior using this policy.
Make proxy settings per machine (rather than per user)	You can configure proxy settings for the machine and force those settings on all logged-in users.
Security Zones: Do not allow users to add/delete sites	A zone in Internet Explorer changes the permissions for the sites in that zone and how IE will behave. Adding or deleting sites to or from a zone changes how IE will handle those sites. Enabling this setting forces a per-system configuration on all users to prevent them from editing zone memberships.
Internet Control Panel\Disable the connections page	This prevents users from being able to alter the way IE connects to the Internet, for example, proxy settings.

A number of settings for controlling applications are built into Windows. You might need to preconfigure these applications, lock down their configuration, or prevent access to them. Some applications such as Microsoft Office allow you to add templates to do this. Windows Messenger (see Table 30.9) is an example of a built-in one, and it can be managed on a per-system basis using the settings in Computer Configuration\Policies\Administrative Templates\Windows Components\Windows Messenger.

TABLE 30.9:   Computer Configuration: Windows Messenger

ITEM	DESCRIPTION
Do not allow Windows Messenger to be run	This prevents Windows or users from starting Windows Messenger.
Do not automatically start Windows Messenger initially	This turns off the default setting to start Windows Messenger when a user logs in. However, this setting can be overridden if a user chooses to do so.

That's just a small sample of the munitions that are available in an administrator's arsenal to lock down a user's desktop experience on a per-system basis. Let's look at what you can do on a per-user basis.

One of the things that you will probably need to do is preconfigure Internet Explorer. You can do this on a per-user basis using the settings contained within User Configuration\Policies \Windows Settings\Internet Explorer Maintenance (see Table 30.10). This is an *interesting* collection of Group Policy settings. Some of the settings work by importing the IE settings from the computer that the administrator is working on. As the administrator, you will need to configure IE on your computer in order to import those settings into your GPO. You'll also find that some of these policies apply only when a user logs in and not during a normal refresh.

TABLE 30.10:   User Configuration: Internet Explorer Maintenance

ITEM	DESCRIPTION
Connection\Connection Settings	This allows you to import the connection settings of IE from your computer including dial-up and the proxy configuration.
Connection\ Proxy Settings	This allows you to type in the proxy configuration for IE and other Windows applications.
URLs\Favorites and Links	You can prepopulate the favorites of IE with important sites, for example, the IT help desk, business applications, SharePoint, or the corporate Intranet.
Security\Security Zones and Content Rating	You can import the security zone configurations and memberships from your workstation to force a configuration on targeted users.

Control Panel is one of those things where a user can really get into trouble. You can remove a user's ability to access the components of Control Panel or even their ability to open it (see Table 30.11). This is controlled in User Configuration\Policies\Administrative Templates\Control Panel.

TABLE 30.11:   User Configuration: Control Panel

ITEM	DESCRIPTION
Hide specified Control Panel items	You can list specific modules from Control Panel that should be made unavailable to a user.
Show only specified Control Panel items	It might be easier to reveal only certain items in Control Panel than to list almost all of them. This setting will allow a user to be able to access only the modules that are listed.
Prohibit access to Control Panel	You can prevent a user from being able to see or use Control Panel.
Personalization\Force specific screensaver	This forces a specific screen saver to be selected by the user.
Personalization \Screen Saver timeout	This configures a timer for the screen saver; in other words, it will be activated after x seconds of inactivity.
Personalization \Enable screen Saver	This enables the screen saver. It requires the previous two entries to be configured.
Personalization \Password protect the screen saver	This forces the user to enter their password to unlock the screen saver.

Note that in Windows Server 2008 the screen saver policies are slightly different:

◆ Display\Screen Saver executable name

◆ Display\Screen Saver timeout

◆ Display\Screen Saver

◆ Display\Password protect the screen saver

🌐 Real World Scenario

TAKE CARE WHEN IMPLEMENTING SCREEN SAVER SECURITY

Be careful with forcing policies such as a screen saver configuration. Best practice in terms of security is that the screen saver should be active for everyone and require a password to unlock it. A common experience is that the people who most require this security are the ones who will hate it the most. Directors and sales staff hate things like screen savers with password locking. You should find the balance between IT security and sustained employment it's good to get guidance on something like this from the business after presenting a considered briefing on best-practice security before going gung-ho and applying policies by yourself.

Windows Explorer is locked down to some extent in most GPO deployments. You can configure Windows Explorer in User Configuration\Policies\Administrative Templates\Windows Components\Windows Explorer (see Table 30.12).

TABLE 30.12:   User Configuration: Windows Explorer Configuration

ITEM	DESCRIPTION
Do not track shell shortcuts during roaming	This disables a computer from trying to track back to the original remote target of a shortcut if a local target cannot be found.
Remove CD burning features	Windows Explorer includes the ability to create CDs. You can disable this ability using this setting.
Hide these specified drives in My Computer	You can hide a combination of the local drives or all drives on a computer in Windows Explorer. This does not restrict access to resources on those drives, for example, programs. This can be bypassed using tools other than Windows Explorer.
Prevent access to drives from my computer	You can prevent access to a combination of the local drives or all drives on a computer using Windows Explorer. This does not restrict access to resources on those drives; you can still launch programs installed there via the normal shortcuts. This can be bypassed using tools other than Windows Explorer.

As you can see, many options are available for per-user configuration. You will likely use a mixture of per-user and per-system configurations. For example, an OU containing Windows kiosks can be efficiently locked down using Computer Configuration policies. An open office plan featuring "hot-desking" will probably rely more on the use of User Configuration policies. The reason is that a per-system policy will not suit the wide variety of users who may use a single computer. It would be better to configure the users rather than the computers.

What method you use to test and develop your lockdown policy will determine the success of your deployment and how easy it will be to manage. You've seen just a very small sample of the available settings. There are many more included with Windows Server 2008 and Windows Server 2008 R2. More still can be added via templates for applications, for example, for Microsoft Office. You can also implement custom templates by editing them yourself or by using third-party utilities.

Our advice is that you build a lab environment that is as identical to your production network as you can afford. This can be a virtual network; this would give you an opportunity to deploy Hyper-V! Building your policies should be a very gradual and deliberate process. Add one policy setting at a time. Only then can you test to see what the true effect of the policy is. If you implement many policies at once, how can you truly know which one is causing a problem? You should test to see when the policy applies, for example, every logon, after a second logon, or during a normal policy refresh. We recommend logging in several times because you have seen complex scenarios where a policy implementation can be inconsistent. You can use the Group Policy Management Console to document your policies once they are complete and to export them for implementation in your production network.

Managing Users with Logon Scripts

So far in this chapter you have seen how to set up network resources for a user such as a profile, a home directory, and redirected folders. Other resources are available on the network such as file shares, DFS namespaces, and printers. How do you connect a user to those? There are methods for doing this via a GPO that are quite powerful. The more traditional solution is to use a script that runs every time a user logs in. This is known as a *logon script*. There are some advantages to this approach over Group Policy.

◆ A script can feature a decision-making process that is flexible regarding user or computer configuration and the location.

◆ An administrator can use one of many scripting solutions, such as command-prompt executables (also known as a *batch*), VBScript, PowerShell, or even third-party solutions.

◆ A script can do things that GPOs cannot, such as move files, create folders, or run commands to configure third-party applications.

Earlier in this chapter we deployed a DFS namespace called \\bigfirm.com\BigFirmShares, shown in Figure 30.54. We have since added a number of file shares to allow users to work with each other on a team or departmental basis. Say you want to automatically map this namespace for all users as the Y drive on their computers. This means all users will see all file shares using a single drive letter.

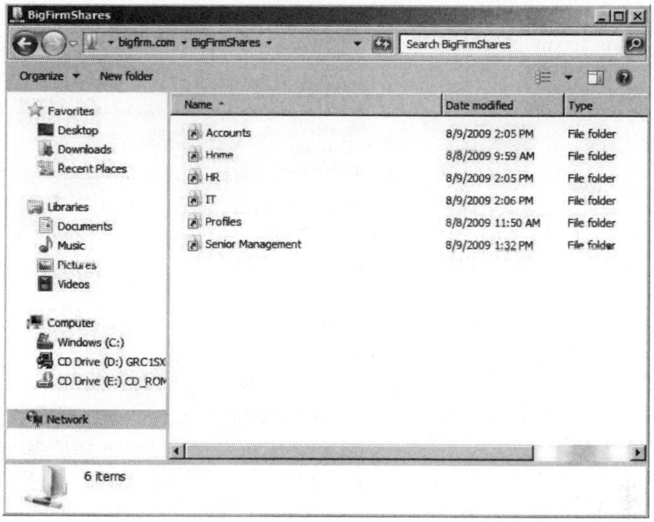

FIGURE 30.54
BigFirm's
populated DFS
namespace

Say you've also deployed an antivirus application that you will run a command for every time that a user logs in. The command is MyAVApp -configure. The script that you want everyone to run when they log in is as follows:

```
net use Y: \\bigfirm.com\BigFirmShares /persistent:no
MyAVApp -configure
```

Can you see that this command uses the /persistent:no parameter? That means the drive mapping will not be saved when the user logs out. This is handy when you want to be able to reuse this drive letter for this user when they run other logon scripts, such as when they visit another branch office that has its own file shares.

Launch Notepad, type in the previous commands, and save this as Logon.bat on your workstation. That's the logon script, and you want it to run every time a user logs in. That will cause the contained commands to run every time the user logs in. You could use Visual Basic Scripting (VBS) or PowerShell instead. You need to make this logon script available to all users in the domain in all locations where they can log in. Fortunately, there is a share on every domain controller that is part of SYSVOL and hence is replicated for you. This share is called NETLOGON and can be found in \\bigfirm.com\SYSVOL\bigfirm.com\scripts as well as \\bigfirm.com\Netlogon. You can also find it on every domain controller in \\<servername>\NETLOGON, such as \\bf1\NETLOGON. Copy all your logon scripts into here, as shown in Figure 30.55.

You would want to think about the name of your logon script if you have a large domain and will have many logon scripts. A naming standard that describes the role of the script and who it will be associated with will simplify keeping track of the script.

You need to decide how this logon script will be linked to your users. There are several ways you can do this.

The simplest solution is to define the logon script on a per-user basis, which you can see in Figure 30.56. The "Logon script" field in the user object allows you to specify a script that is contained within the NETLOGON share on your domain controllers. The logon script *must* be contained in NETLOGON.

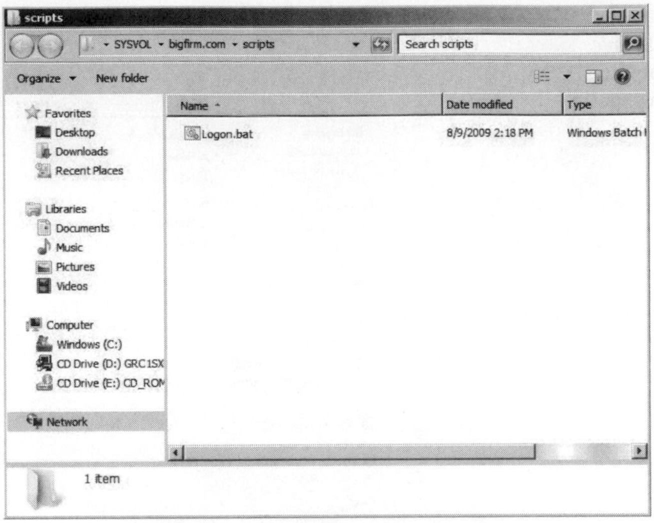

FIGURE 30.55
The logon script
in SYSVOL

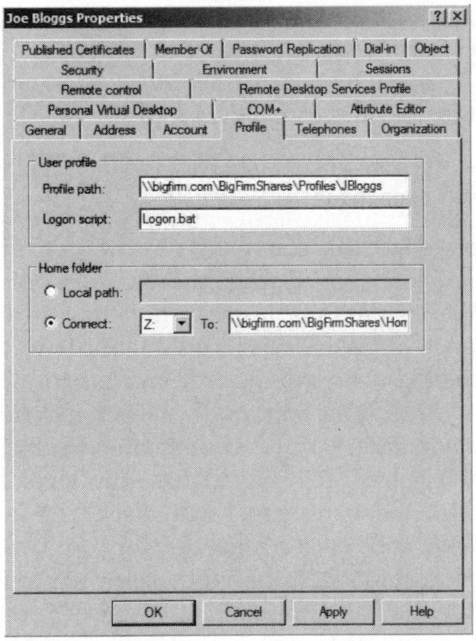

FIGURE 30.56
Configuring the
user object "Logon
script" attribute

This method is fine if there are only a few users or if the user has a unique script. However, you will want a different mechanism if there are many users to configure.

A much better way to configure users with a logon script is to use a GPO. Think about this for a moment:

◆ A single GPO can apply to many users.

◆ A GPO can be linked to an OU; that is, a logon script can be linked to a unit of the logical structure of the organization.

◆ A GPO can be linked to an Active Directory site; that is, a logon script can be linked to a unit of the physical structure of the organization. For example, maybe certain things should be done when anyone logs into specific local networks in a site.

◆ You can use loopback policy processing to associate a different logon script with a user when they log on to certain computers.

Create and link a GPO, and open it for editing, as you can see in Figure 30.57. Navigate to \User Configuration\Policies\Windows Settings\Scripts (Logon/Logoff).

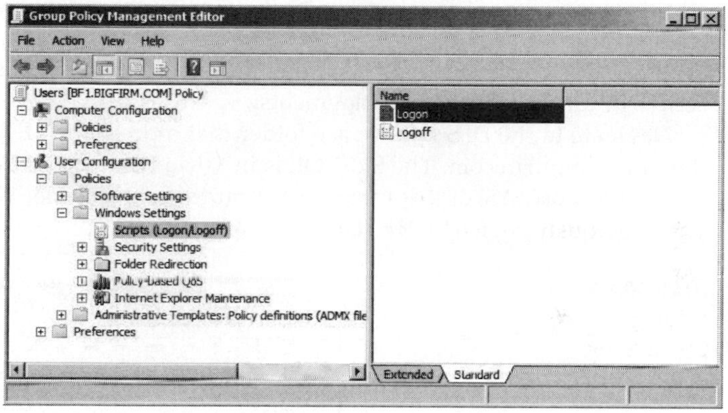

FIGURE 30.57
The Logon/Logoff Scripts option in Group Policy

You cannot argue that this isn't a more powerful approach. Some organizations have chosen to use the per-user configuration. Their reasoning was that each user had a unique logon script. Any reasoning for this approach can be eliminated by utilizing OUs, security groups, and decision making in your logon script. You'll now use it to deploy a script using a GPO. Double-click Logon in the GPO to edit the logon script settings.

This opens the dialog box, depicted in Figure 30.58, where you can add a logon script. You can do this by clicking Add.

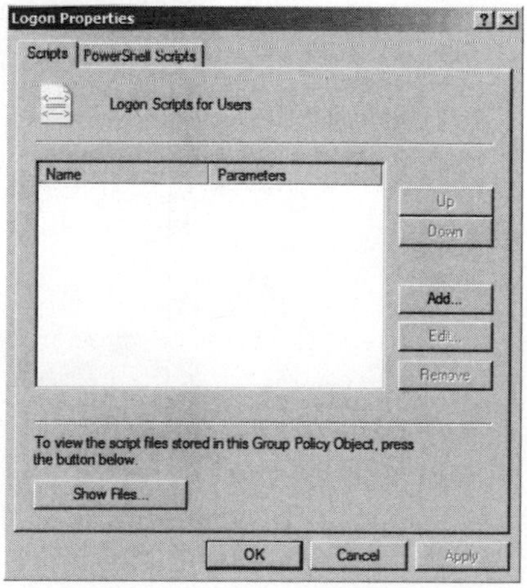

FIGURE 30.58
Logon Properties dialog box for a logon script GPO

This opens the dialog box in Figure 30.59, which allows you to do the following:

1. Select a specific logon script.

2. Feed parameters to the logon script that will change its behavior. This is an example of how you can use decision making in your scripts to reduce the number of scripts you need to implement.

Click Browse to open a wizard in order to select an existing logon script. The default location that it chooses is a folder (\User\Scripts\Logon) within SYSVOL where the GPO that you are editing is contained. This is a nasty location to find when you aren't editing the GPO. That's why we didn't recommend it as a place to keep your logon script! However, the entirety of SYSVOL is available to everyone as a share, so you might consider using this default location for your logon scripts in very complex AD deployments.

Navigate to the DFS namespace folder that represents NETLOGON in your domain. Our domain is bigfirm.com. The SYSVOL is in \\bigfirm.com\SYSVOL. The NETLOGON share is in \\bigfirm.com\SYSVOL\bigfirm.com\scripts. In this folder you will find the logon script that you previously copied to NETLOGON.

FIGURE 30.59
Specifying
the logon script
in SYSVOL

The logon script is now displayed in the Add a Script dialog box. Click OK in the Logon Properties dialog box shown in Figure 30.60, and you have finished deploying your logon script via a GPO. You should test this now before configuring users.

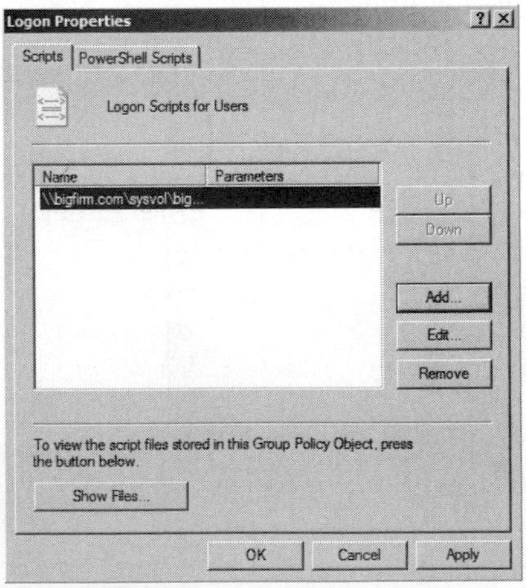

FIGURE 30.60
The configured
logon script
Group Policy

As shown in Figure 30.61, log in as one of the test users who inherits the Group Policy object, and you can see that the logon script has run and mapped the Y drive to your DFS namespace.

FIGURE 30.61
The results of running the login script policy

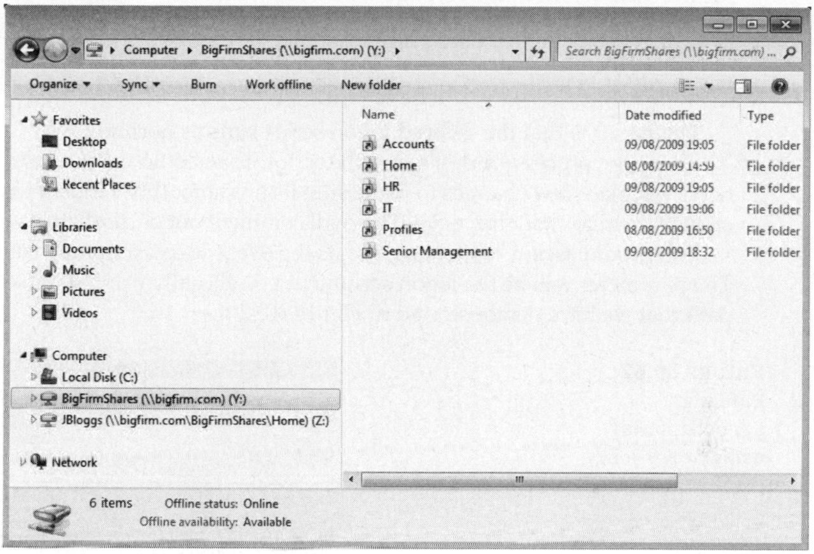

User Access Control and Logon Scripts

There is a chance when you've been testing logon scripts that the script just fails to run for some unknown reason. This section explains a common cause of issues with logon scripts on the current generation of Microsoft Windows.

User Access Control (UAC) was added in Windows Vista and Windows Server 2008 to reduce the risk of attack on the computer. You can read about it in great detail at http://tinyurl.com/24cfcr. The idea of UAC is that processes should always run with the least required privilege. This is done by using *tokens*. A token describes the user, the user's group memberships, and the user's privileges.

With UAC you will run most programs or processes with limited privileges as defined by a limited token. It is only when the process requires your full privileges that the process will run with your elevated token. As an administrator, you will have seen this take place every time you've launched an administrative tool or attempted to make any system changes. You are prompted to confirm that you want to run that task to run with elevated rights. That's the process looking to gain access to your elevated token. UAC prevents processes with lower privileges from sharing information with processes running with higher privileges.

When a user logs into Windows Vista, Windows 7, Windows Server 2008, or Windows Server 2008 R2, the login process runs using both the user's limited and elevated tokens. Downloading and applying Group Policy requires your elevated token. This includes running your logon script as defined by Group Policy. Loading your desktop is done using your limited token.

A nonadministrative user's limited and elevated tokens are almost identical. When a nonadministrative user logs into their GPO, the defined logon scripts will run normally. However, an administrator's limited token is very different from their elevated token. This difference can cause problems with the logon script when it runs.

You can work around this issue using a solution described by Microsoft on `http://tinyurl` `.com/yenok6`. This uses an alternate logon script called `launchapp.wsf`. You can copy the code for the script from that web page. This script works by doing the following:

◆ It runs using the user's limited token.

◆ It takes the desired logon script as a parameter and schedules that desired script to run.

The result is that the desired logon script runs as normal.

Here's the process for deploying the script. You should copy it from Microsoft's website. You will need to make a few changes to make sure it runs smoothly. Find all instances of `wscript.echo`, and change them to `'wscript.echo`. This will comment out or disable those lines.

You should assign `launchapp.wsf` as the user's logon script instead of the normal logon script. The parameter will be the logon script that you actually wanted to use. Remember to use the UNC path that we have demonstrated in Figure 30.62.

FIGURE 30.62
Running
Launchapp.wsf
using Group Policy

The end result of this solution is that your logon script will be executed, and it will operate normally, even for administrators.

Multiple Logon Scripts

You can associate multiple logon scripts with a user if you use Group Policy assignment. Each of these scripts will run for the user.

Figure 30.63 shows where you have added multiple logon scripts using a single GPO. You can change the ordering of the logon scripts using the Up and Down buttons. The script that is listed on top is the first to be executed.

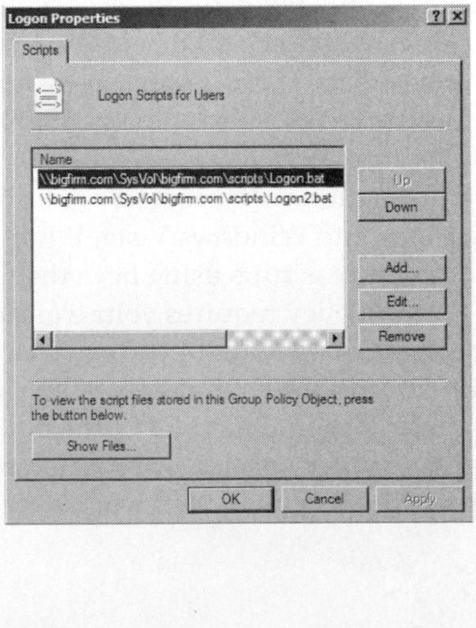

FIGURE 30.63
Configuring many
logon scripts using
Group Policy

You may have a situation where you have multiple logon scripts assigned by multiple Group Policy objects. Figure 30.64 shows an example in the Group Policy results.

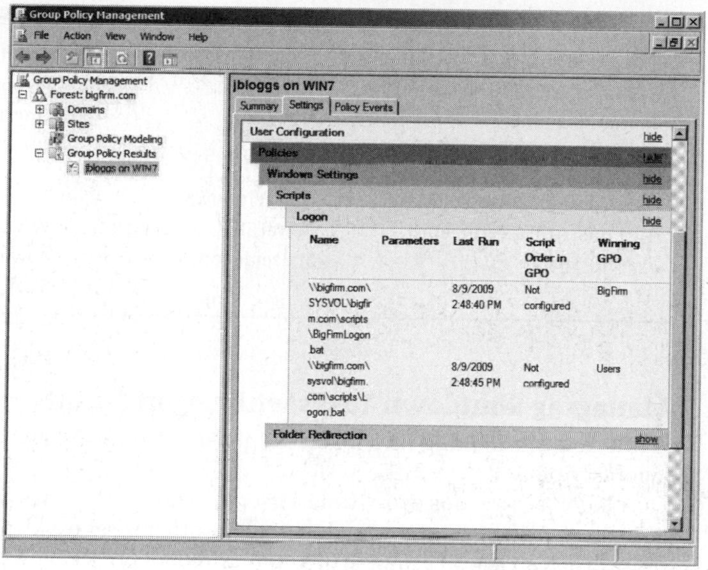

FIGURE 30.64
Group Policy
results showing
multiple logon
scripts

FIGURE 30.64
Group Policy
results showing
multiple logon
scripts

This is an example where a logon script performs tasks that are common for all users underneath the bigfirm.com domain. Another logon script performs tasks for the Users OU. The members of the Users OU will run both logon scripts. Normal policy execution order (site, domain, OU, child OU) is maintained. In this example, the logon script for bigfirm.com runs before the Users logon script.

Managing Logon Scripts with Group Policy

You can use a number of Group Policy settings to manage how logon scripts are processed (see Table 30.13). You can do this on a per-system or per-user basis.

TABLE 30.13: Logon Script GPO

PATH	ENTRY	DESCRIPTION
Computer Configuration\Policies\Administrative Templates\System\Scripts	Maximum wait time for Group Policy scripts	This defines the number of settings that Group Policy processing will allow a script to run before terminating the process. The default is 600 seconds.
Computer Configuration\Policies\Administrative Templates\System\Scripts	Run logon scripts synchronously	Enabling this setting forces Windows Explorer to wait until all logon scripts have run before allowing the user to do anything.

TABLE 30.13:   Logon Script GPO   *(CONTINUED)*

PATH	ENTRY	DESCRIPTION
User Configuration\Policies\ Administrative Templates\ System\Scripts	Run logon scripts visible	The default is that users cannot see the logon script running. Enabling this setting allows users to see the commands running in a window.
User Configuration\Policies\ Administrative Templates\ System\Scripts	Run Windows PowerShell scripts first at user logon, logoff	This runs only on Windows 7 and Windows Server 2008 R2. By default, PowerShell scripts run before non-PowerShell scripts. You can reverse this policy.

Managing Shutdown Tasks with Logoff Scripts

While you were setting up a logon script using Group Policy, you will have seen an option for logoff scripts.

A logoff script runs every time a user logs off. This allows administrators to define some tasks that can be run every time a user logs off. It is set up identically to how you set up a logon script. You can see an example of a configured logoff script in Figure 30.65.

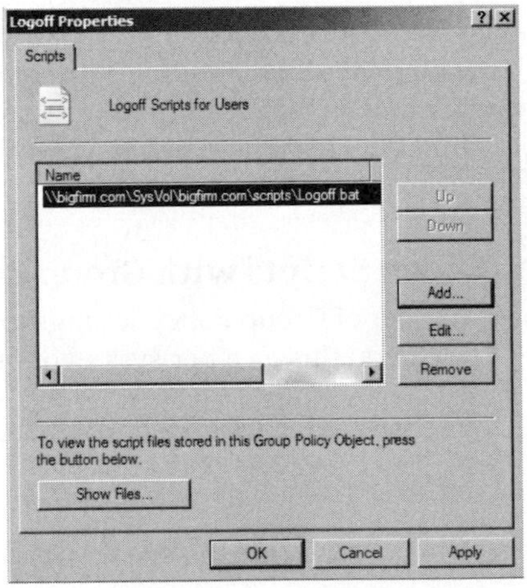

FIGURE 30.65
A configured
logoff script in
Group Policy

Note that a logoff script will not run if a user just turns off their PC without going through a clean shutdown. It also doesn't run if a user puts their machine into hibernation or disconnects a Remote Desktop Services session.

The Bottom Line

Deploy home directories to multiple users   Home directories allow a user to have a personal store of information stored on a file server. This makes their data available to them no matter where they log in on the network.

Master It   You've been tasked with deploying home directories to many users in the OU that you manage. You want to do this as quickly as possible. Your backup application uses an administrator user account, so you need to ensure that it has access to the users' home directories on the file server. How will you set this up?

Set up mandatory roaming profiles   Mandatory roaming profiles can be used to provide users with a preconfigured working environment and to prevent them from saving changes to it.

Master It   Your manager has asked you to set up a mandatory roaming profile for users of Windows 7. You're also asked to see whether there is a way to prevent users from logging in if the mandatory roaming profile cannot be loaded.

Create logon scripts to automate administration   Administrators can use logon scripts to run a series of commands to preconfigure the working environment for a user when they log in. Administrators can use scripting languages such as command-prompt commands, VBScript, or PowerShell.

Master It   You are designing an Active Directory for a large multisite organization. You need to be able to set up logon scripts for different scenarios:

- There are global commands that must be run for everyone.

- Anyone in the Accounts OU must have access to certain resources.

- Anyone, including visitors, logging in at the Dublin Active Directory site must connect to a local shared drive.

You are asked what the running order will be for any user who will run all of the logon scripts.

Appendix: The Bottom Line

Chapter 2: Installing and Upgrading to Windows Server 2008 R2

Upgrade your old servers   Microsoft has provided several upgrade options for Windows Server 2008 and Windows Server 2008 R2.

Master It   You have a Windows 2000 file server. What will your upgrade path be to Windows Server 2008 R2?

Solution   Windows 2000 was not available as an x64 build. Windows Server 2008 R2 is available only as an x64 build. You will have to prepare a new machine with Windows Server 2008 R2. You will then migrate the services and data from the Windows 2000 machine to the Windows Server 2008 R2 machine.

If you are building machines now with Windows Server 2003 or Windows Server 2008, then you should try to use an x64 build to allow future in-place upgrades where appropriate.

Configure your server   Windows Server 2008 allows you to use Server Manager and servermanagercmd.exe to add or remove roles, role services, and features.

Master It   You have started to deploy Windows Server 2008 R2. You are planning on automating as much of the build process as possible. What tool will you use to add or remove roles, role services, and features?

Solution   servermanagercmd.exe was the right tool to use on Windows Server 2008. It is still available on Windows Server 2008 R2. However, Microsoft is deprecating it and suggests that you use PowerShell instead on Windows Server 2008 R2 to future proof your efforts. Import-Module will add the following PowerShell cmdlets. Get-WindowsFeature will list the install status of every role, role service, and feature. Add-WindowsFeature will allow you to install a component, and Remove-WindowsFeature will allow you to uninstall a component. You can write PowerShell scripts to automate your configuration changes.

Build a small server farm   Installing Windows Server normally requires that you sit in front of the machine and answer a number of questions. This is time-consuming and distracts administrators from other engineering or project tasks that they could be working on. A number of alternative techniques can be employed.

Master It   You have been instructed to build four new servers with Windows Server 2008 R2. This will be the first time your organization will deploy Windows Server 2008. Your department is short-staffed because a number of your colleagues are on vacation. You want to do this job quickly and efficiently. How will you do it?

Solution   If you had more time, you could look into preparing a server with Windows Deployment Services (WDS). However, you need to work quickly. You can download and install the latest Windows Automated Installation Kit (WAIK) from Microsoft's website. You use Windows System Image Manager (WSIM) to prepare an unattended answer file called autounattend.xml, copy that file onto a USB stick, insert the Windows Server 2008 DVD into each server, and boot the server from the DVD. Insert the USB stick in the server, and the Windows Installer will load the answer file from the USB stick and automate the installation of Windows. Your next step on the server is to change the Administrator password and log in.

Chapter 3: The New Server: Introduction to Server Core

Explain the purposes for Server Core   The Windows Server 2008 R2 Server Core operating system is a trimmed-down version of its full installation. The removed code reduces the profile for security threats to leverage and also reduces performance demands. The primary administration interface is the command prompt. It can perform several but not all of the roles available with the full installation.

> **Master It**   The Windows Server 2008 R2 Server Core version differs from the original release in Windows Server 2008. What are those key differences, and how does that impact the roles the server can perform?

> **Solution**   The original version of Server Core lacked the .NET Framework. The latter release includes a tailored version of the .NET Framework. With this inclusion, Server Core can act as an Internet Information Services server for ASP.NET websites. In addition, it can support other ASP.NET-based services such as Active Directory Certificate Services. PowerShell, which is built on the .NET Framework, is also available.

Install and configure Server Core   The installation of Server Core is the same as installing a full installation of Windows Server 2008 R2. The full installation provides a list of initial configuration tasks such as joining the domain, initiating automatic updates, and installing features. Each of these operations has a command associated with them.

> **Master It**   Server Core has a specific script to perform several common tasks that edit the registry. What is this script's name? What parameter can provide a list of additional commands to perform much of the common configuration tasks?

> **Solution**   The scregedit.wsf script located in c:\windows\system32 performs several configurations such as enabling automatic updates and enabling Remote Desktop. The /cli parameter lists the additional commands for performing the initial configuration tasks.

Set up Server Core for a branch-office deployment   The branch-office deployment was one possible purpose of the Server Core implementation. The infrastructure roles of Active Directory Domain Services, DNS server, DHCP, and File Services and Print and Document Services would be installed and configured on a server, which would provide these basic services to the users within a small office environment. The configurations of these services could be performed remotely.

> **Master It**   To configure Active Directory Domain Services and DNS, the Active Directory Domain Services Installation Wizard (DCPromo) is run from the command line. What is needed to enter the parameters for the command?

Solution   DCPromo requires an answer file to install on Server Core. Since much of the graphic capabilities are removed from the installation, the utility cannot be run interactively. The command to use the answer file is dcpromo /unattend:answerFile.txt.

Remotely manage the operating system   Server Core can be remotely managed by three options. Remote Desktop administration is available, but only the command prompt and provided GUIs with Server Core can be used. The MMC console snap-ins can connect to the server's services to manage with the standard Windows tools. Finally, a new service, Windows Remote Shell, provides single-command connections to the server.

Master It   The Windows Remote Shell offers a quickconfig option. What are the security concerns that system administrators should be aware of when using this option? What can be done to address these concerns?

Solution   The Windows Remote Shell in the quickconfig option sets up the service to listen for requests on TCP port 5985 using the HTTP protocol. This means the command and results will be transmitted unencrypted. In addition, the server is unauthenticated, which could result in configuring the wrong server. One way to resolve this is to set up IPsec between the servers and clients. Another way is to configure the service to use the HTTPS protocol with TCP port 5986, which would encrypt the transmissions and authenticate the server.

Chapter 4: Windows Server 2008 IPv4: What Has Changed?

Understand the next-generation TCP stack   The next-generation TCP stack includes technologies to optimize how data is sent across a network connection.

Master It   Can you name the technologies included in the next-generation TCP stack and what they do?

Solution

♦ Autoscaling allows Windows to be more efficient in sending and receiving data. The TCP receive window is scalable and allows more data to be sent in a frame at once.

♦ Compound TCP allows a computer to send larger amounts of data to a computer with a large TCP receive window across latent connections, in other words, slow turnaround times.

♦ SMB 2.0 allows file sharing to take advantage of these technologies by sending more data and fewer frames.

Troubleshoot the improvements in the next-generation TCP stack   You may encounter issues when you deploy the newer versions of Windows, such as Server 2008, Server 2008 R2, Vista, and Windows 7, on an older network or when roaming users are in airports or hotels.

Master It   What are the commands for configuring the TCP receive window when you encounter network appliance compatibility issues?

Solution   Check to see what the current configuration is:

```
netsh interface tcp show global
```

Reduce the amount of optimization slightly by using the restricted setting:

```
netsh interface tcp set global autotuning=restricted
```

If that still doesn't work, then you can highly restrict the amount of scaling being done:

```
netsh interface tcp set global autotuning=highlyrestricted
```

You may need to completely disable the TCP receive window:

```
netsh interface tcp set global autotuning=disabled
```

This is the command to reset the TCP receive window to its default:

```
netsh interface tcp set global autotuninglevel=normal
```

Control bandwidth usage Windows Vista, Windows 7, Windows Server 2008, and Windows Server 2008 R2 all include functionality that allows you to fully utilize any bandwidth that you have.

Master It Users in a branch office are complaining that access to network services that are hosted in your headquarters office are unbearably slow on a frequent basis. Network engineers report that the link between headquarters and the branch-office network has been fully utilized since you upgraded from Windows XP and Windows Server 2003. You need to resolve the issue.

Solution You work with the business to identify critical applications that must receive priority over all others on the network. You then work with the network engineers to implement policy-based QoS. Using Group Policy, you define the application ports and destinations that must receive priority. The network devices are configured by the network engineers to implement actions based on the Differentiated Services Code Point (DSCP). The result will be that business-critical applications will be prioritized over other network traffic.

Chapter 5: DNS and Naming in Server 2008 and Active Directory

Explain the fundamental components and processes of DNS DNS relies on integrated servers that manage a hierarchal naming structure. On the Internet, this structure starts with root servers and then top-level domain servers, which delegate subdomains to other DNS servers. Within a DNS server, the database of records is known as a *zone*, and it can be replicated between other DNS servers to provide distributed query resolution for a given namespace.

Master It Several common DNS records were discussed in this chapter. The SRV and MX records both have a parameter named priority. If there were two SRV records for the same service with a priority parameter of 10 and 20, which SRV record would be selected first?

Solution The priority parameter can have a value from 0 to 65535 on SRV records. However, the lowest number has the highest priority. Therefore, the record with the priority parameter of 10 would be selected first.

Configure DNS to support an Active Directory environment Active Directory requires a DNS namespace to be available to support the assigned name of the domain. Windows Server 2008 R2 provides an automatic capability to create the required DNS structure through the domain controller promotion process. The DNS zones can be stored in the Active Directory database, which provides multimaster replication of the DNS records. With the use of SRV records and DDNS update, the domain controllers can register their services in DNS for clients to access them.

Master It The DNS service on DCs can create Active Directory integrated zones. In which locations within the Active Directory database can the zones be placed? What scope do these locations provide?

Solution There are four locations that can be chosen when creating a new zone:

- ◆ Domain partition accessible by all domain controllers in the domain including Windows 2000 domain controllers.

- ◆ Domain DNS application partition accessible by all domain controllers in the domain.

- ◆ Forest DNS application partition accessible by all domain controllers in the forest.

- ◆ A custom DNS application partition that can be accessed by all domain controllers in the forest. They must enlist in the replication of the partition before supporting it.

Manage and troubleshoot DNS resolution for both internal and external names Internal and external name resolution relies on the connectivity between DNS servers. Forwarding and root hints are the primary methods to provide DNS servers to send queries between them. Several tools are available to assist troubleshooting and monitoring DNS configurations and performance, including nslookup, DNSCmd, DCDiag, and DNSLint.

Master It The SRV record registration for domain controllers is performed by the netlogon service. It is a very complex and demanding task to attempt to perform this manually. What tests can be performed to verify whether SRV records are correctly registered within a domain?

Solution The DCDiag utility and the DNSLint utility provide tests to verify whether SRV records are available within the specified domain. dcdiag /registerindns validates that the domain controller can perform updates to the domain zone using DDNS updates.

Chapter 6: Creating the Simple Ad: The One-Domain, One-Location AD

Create a single-domain forest Any Windows Server 2008 R2 server can be promoted to a domain controller to create a single-domain forest. A DC hosts an instance of Active Directory Domain Services.

Master It You want to promote a server to a DC and create a single-domain forest. What should you do?

Solution Run DCPromo, and follow the wizard to create a new forest.

Add a second DC to the domain   A single DC represents a potential single point of failure. If it goes down, the domain goes down. Often administrators will add a second DC to the domain.

Master It   You want to add a second DC to your domain. What should you do?

Solution   Run DCPromo on a Windows Server 2008 R2 server, and follow the wizard to add a second DC to an existing domain.

Decide whether to add a global catalog   A global catalog server hosts a copy of the global catalog. Any domain controller can become a GC, but only the first domain controller is a GC by default.

Master It   You are promoting a second server to a domain controller in your single-domain forest. Should you make it a GC?

Solution   Yes. In a single-domain forest, all domain controllers should also be global catalog servers. This provides redundancy in the domain without any additional overhead.

Create accounts   Any domain needs to host user and computer accounts representing users and computers that will access the domain. There are several ways to create user and computer accounts.

Master It   What are two methods that can be used to create a user account? One is a GUI, and the other is a command-line tool.

Solution   Active Directory Users and Computers and the DSAdd command-line tool.

Create fine-grained password policies   Windows Server 2008 introduced the ability to create multiple password policies within a domain by using fine-grained password policies. You can use a fine-grained password policy to assign a different password policy to a user or group within the domain.

Master It   You want to create a fine-grained password policy for a group of administrators in your network. What should you create, and what tool should you use?

Solution   Create a password settings object using the ADSI Edit tool. You can also apply the PSO object to users or groups using Active Directory Users and Computers.

Chapter 7: Creating and Managing User Accounts

Manage local users and groups   Local users and groups are stored on a computer and cannot be used to log in to or access resources on other computers.

Master It   You have 25 PCs with 25 users on a workgroup network, in other words, a network with no Active Directory or Windows domain. You are installing two file servers. You want to provide authorized-only access to shared resources on the file servers. How will you do this?

Solution   You will need to create a user account for each of the 25 users. However, because there is no domain, you will need to create the user account on the users' PCs and on each of the two servers. The username and password will have to be identical on their PCs and each of the two servers. You can speed the process up by using a scripted option, such as using the net user command in a script.

Manage users and groups in Active Directory   Users and groups can be stored in Active Directory. That means administrators can create a single copy of each user and group that is stored in a replicated database and can be used by member computers across the entire Active Directory forest. You can use Active Directory Users and Computers and the command prompt to manage users and groups on Windows Server 2008 and Windows Server 2008 R2. Windows Server 2008 R2 adds a new task-oriented console called the Active Directory Administrative Center and an Active Directory module for PowerShell.

Master It   List the different types of Active Directory group types and scopes. Why would you use each of them?

Solution   There are two Active Directory group types:

- The *distribution group* type is used to collectively communicate with the group members via a single mail address that is associated with the group.

- The primary purpose of the *security group* type is to manage assigned permissions for a collection of members.

The members of an Active Directory group may be users or other group objects. There are three group scopes:

- A *domain local group* can be used only within the domain that it was created in. It can contain user/computer accounts, global groups, and universal groups from any domain in the forest and domain local groups from the same domain.

- The default scope when you create a group in Active Directory is the *global group*. A global group can be used by computers within the domain that it is a member of and by members of other domains in the Active Directory forest. It can contain user/computer accounts from the domain that the global group is created in.

- The *universal group* is the third and final group scope. A universal group is stored on domain controllers that are configured as global catalogs. The universal group is replicated to domains across the entire forest. That allows a universal group to not only be able to be used by all computers in the forest but also to contain members from any domain within the forest. Universal groups can contain user/computer accounts, global groups, and other universal groups from any domain in the forest.

Manage users and computers in Windows Server 2008 R2   Windows Server 2008 R2 adds two new ways to manage users and computers in an Active Directory. Once Active Directory Web Services is installed on one domain controller in the domain, you can manage its users and computers using either PowerShell or the new Active Directory Administrative Center (ADAC). ADAC makes it quicker and easier for administrators to perform day-to-day operations such as resetting passwords, unlocking user accounts, and finding objects in the forest that they want to manage. The Active Directory module for Windows PowerShell offers a new command-line interface and way to script Active Directory management tasks. You can use this to automate repetitive tasks using scripts or to perform complex and large operations that would consume too much time using an administrative console.

Master It   You are managing the Windows Server 2008 R2 Active Directory forest for an international corporation. The directors have announced that a new call center with 5,000 employees is to be opened soon. The human resources department will be able to produce a file from its database with the names of the new employees thanks to some in-house developers. You want to create the user objects as quickly as possible with minimum human effort. How will you do this?

Solution   You can work with the in-house developers so that the new employee export from the human resources application will be a CSV file. The header row will describe the entries in the following rows. Each of the following rows will contain the values that you would use in the PowerShell New-ADuser cmdlet. For example:

```
Name,SamAccountName,GivenName,Surname,DisplayName,Path,UserPrincipalName,
AccountPassword
Rachel Kelly,RKelly,Rachel,Kelly,Rachel Kelly,"OU=Users,OU=BigFirm,DC=bigfirm,
DC=com",RKelly@bigfirm.com,NewPassw0rd
Ulrika Gerhardt,UGerhardt,Ulrika,Gerhardt,Ulrika Gerhardt,"OU=Users,OU=BigFirm
,DC=bigfirm,DC=com",UGerhardt@bigfirm.com,
NewPassw0rd
Tomasz Kozlowski, TKozlowski,Tomasz,Kozlowski,Tomaz Kozlowski,"OU=Users,OU=Big
Firm,DC=bigfirm,DC=com",TKozlowski@bigfirm.com,
NewPassw0rd
```

You will then run a PowerShell command that reads each line of the CSV file and runs the New-ADuser cmdlet using the values in each row to create the new user objects, for example:

```
PS C:\Users\Administrator> Import-CSV c:\users.csv | foreach {New-ADUser -Name
$_.Name -SamAccountName $_.SamAccountName -GivenName $_.GivenName -Surname $_.
Surname -DisplayName $_.DisplayName -Path $_.Path -UserPrincipalName $_.
UserPrincipalName -AccountPassword (ConvertTo-SecureString -AsPlainText $_.
AccountPassword -Force) -Enabled $true -ChangePasswordAtLogon 1}
```

This command will rapidly read the file and create each of the 5,000 user objects in the organizational unit(s) of your choice. Instead of spending days creating objects using a console, you will spend one minute typing this command.

Delegate group management   Part of the power of Active Directory is the ability to delegate administrative rights. You can grant permissions to users or groups to manage any organizational unit or object in the domain. You can limit those rights so people only have permissions to do what they need to do for their role in the organization.

Master It   You are a domain administrator in a large organization. Your network contains several file servers. File shares are secured using domain-based security groups. You have delegated rights to help-desk staff to manage these groups. The organization is relying on the help desk to know who should have read, read/write, and no access to the file shares. Mistakes are being made and changes are taking too long, causing employees to be unable to access critical information. You've considered a paper-based procedure where the business owners of the file shares document who should have access. This has proven to be unpopular because it slows down the business. You have been asked to implement a solution that ensures the business is not delayed and where only authorized people have access to sensitive information.

Solution

1. Create a Read Only and Read and Write domain-based security group for each file share.

2. Grant each of these groups the appropriate permissions on the shares.

3. Create an additional Owners domain-based security group for each file share.

4. Add the business owners of the information in the shares to each Owners group.

5. Edit the properties of the Read Only and Read and Write groups.

6. Add the appropriate Owners groups as a manager of the Read Only and Read and Write groups on the Managed By tab.

The result of this solution is that anyone who is a member of the Management Owners group for the Management share will be able to manage the membership of the Management Read Only and the Management Read and Write groups. The business owners know who should have access to their file shares. The help desk cannot know this. The business owners are now empowered to make the appropriate changes in the group memberships. IT is no longer involved in the process. This reduces the communication process and allows employees of the organization to access information without delay.

Deal with users leaving the organization It is important to understand that Windows tracks users, groups, and computers by their security identifier and not by their visible friendly name. When you delete and re-create an object, the new object is actually a different object and does not keep the old object's rights and permissions.

Master It The personnel department has informed you that an employee, BKavanagh, is leaving the organization immediately under bad circumstances. The security officer informs you that there is a security risk. You have been asked to deal with this risk without any delay. What do you do? Two hours later you are told that the personnel department gave you the wrong name. The correct name was BCavanagh. BKavanagh has called the help desk to say that she cannot do any work. What do you do to rectify the situation?

Solution When you originally disable BKavanagh, you should have disabled the user account. This prevents the account from being usable. When you get the call that this was the wrong user account, you can simply reenable the account, and BKavanagh can start working again.

If you have a Windows Server 2008 R2 Active Directory and you deleted the BKavanagh account, then you should reanimate it from the Active Directory Recycle Bin.

If you deleted the user account and don't have a Windows Server 2008 Active Directory, then you will have to re-create it and add the user to all the groups that she was in before. This is a time-consuming process.

You should disable the BCavanagh account to comply with the security officer and the personnel department. You can delete the account after a predetermined time has passed and the user has not returned to the organization.

Chapter 8: Group Policy: AD's Gauntlet

Understand local policies and Group Policy objects   Every Windows computer from Windows 2000 Professional and up has a local Group Policy. Windows Vista has many local group policies, which can accommodate for various situations where the computer might be located. There are Group Policy objects stored in Active Directory too, which allow for central administration of computers and users who are associated with the domain.

Master It   Which of the following is not a local Group Policy?

◆ Local Computer Policy

◆ Administrator

◆ Non-Administrator

◆ All Users

Solution   All Users is not a local Group Policy.

Create GPOs   Group Policy Objects can, and should be, created within your Active Directory domain. These additional GPOs will allow you to control settings, software, and security on the different users and computers that you have within the domain. GPOs are typically linked to OUs but can be linked to the domain node and to AD sites as well. GPOs are created within AD by using the Group Policy Management console.

Master It   Create a new GPO and link it to the HRUsers OU.

Solution

1. Create the HRUsers OU under the domain.

2. Within the GPMC, right-click the HRUsers OU, and select the option to create and link a GPO.

3. Give the new GPO a name of HRUserSecurity.

Troubleshoot group policies   There are times when a GPO setting or Group Policy itself fails to apply. There can be many reasons for this, because there are many tools to help you investigate the issue. There are some tools, such as the `rsop.msc` tool, which are presented in a resulting window, and other tools, such as `gpresult`, which is a command-line tool. Regardless of your tool that you use, troubleshooting Group Policy is sometimes required.

Master It   Which tool would you use to ensure that all settings in all GPOs linked to Active Directory have applied, even if there have not been any changes to a GPO or a setting in a GPO?

Solution   `gpupdate /force`

Chapter 9: Active Directory Delegation

Delegate control using organizational units   Delegation is a powerful feature in Active Directory that allows domain administrators to "delegate" tasks to junior administrators. The idea is that the delegation granted is narrow in scope, providing only limited capabilities within Active Directory and the objects contained within.

Master It   Establish delegation on the HRUsers organizational unit such that the HRHelpDesk can reset the passwords for all users in the HRUsers OU.

Solution

1. Create the HRHelpDesk security group under the Users container.

2. Create the HRUsers OU under the domain.

3. Run the Delegation of Control Wizard by right-clicking the HRUsers OU.

4. Grant permissions to the HRHelpDesk group.

5. Grant the Reset Password permission.

6. Complete the delegation.

Use advanced delegation to manually set individual permissions   There are thousands of individual permissions for any given AD object. Advanced delegation provides the ability to set any of these permissions to give a user or security group access to the object for the specified permission. The Delegation of Control Wizard is a useful tool to grant common tasks, but when the wizard does not provide the level of detail required, you must grant delegation manually.

Master It   *Delegation* is another term for which of the following?

◆ Replicating AD database

◆ Read-only domain controller

◆ Setting permissions on AD objects

◆ Using Group Policy to set security

Solution   Setting permissions on AD objects

Find out which delegations have been set   It is unfortunate, but the Delegation of Control Wizard is a tool that can only grant permissions, not report on what has been set. To find out what delegations have been set, you have to resort to using other tools.

Master It   Name a tool that you can use to view what delegations have been set.

Solution   dsacls is a command-line utility that comes with Windows Server 2008 for viewing detailed delegation settings.

Chapter 10: Files, Folders, and Shares

Install the File Services role on a server The File Services role includes services designed to optimize serving files from the server. A significant addition is the File Server Resource Manager, which can be used to manage quotas, to add file screens, and to produce comprehensive reports.

Master It How do you add FSRM to the server?

Solution Install the File Services role, and include the File Server Resource Manager role service.

Combine share and NTFS permissions When a folder is shared from an NTFS drive, it includes both share permissions and NTFS permissions. It's important to understand how these permissions interact so that users can be granted appropriate permission.

Master It Maria is in the G_HR and G_HRManagers groups. A folder named Policies is shared as Policies on a server with the following permissions:

NTFS: G_HR Read, G_HR_Managers Full Control

Share: G_HR Read, G_HR Change

What is Maria's permission when accessing the share? What is her permission when accessing the folder directly on the server?

Solution Maria's permission when accessing the share is Change. You can determine the result of combined NTFS and share permissions can be accomplished in three steps:

- *Determine cumulative NTFS permissions*: She has Read and Full Control, so her cumulative NTFS permission is Full Control.

- *Determine cumulative share permissions*: She has Read and Change, so her cumulative share permission is Change.

- *Determine which of the two provides the least access (or is the most restrictive)*: Change is more restrictive than Full Control.

If the folder is accessed directly, share permissions do not apply. So, she would have Full Control permission.

Implement BitLocker Drive Encryption BitLocker Drive Encryption allows you to encrypt an entire drive. If someone obtains the drive that shouldn't have access to the data, the encryption will prevent them from accessing the data.

Master It What are the hardware requirements for BitLocker Drive Encryption, and what needs to be done to the operating system to use BitLocker?

Solution BitLocker requires Trusted Platform Module 1.2, which is a hardware component and is typically included in the motherboard on systems that have it. It is possible to use BitLocker without TPM using either a password or a smart card and a pin. BitLocker needs to be added as a feature using Server Manager before it can be implemented.

Chapter 11: Creating and Managing Shared Folders

Add a File Services role to your server   Before you can create and use DFS, NFS, share files and folders, or any other file-related function across the domain in Server 2008, you will need to install the File Services role.

Master It   Go into the server master, and add the server role File Services.

Solution

1. Select Start ➢ Administrative Tools ➢ Server Manager.

2. In Server Manager's Action drop-down list, click Add Roles.

3. In the Add Roles Wizard, click File Services, and then click Install.

4. After the wizard completes, go back into the Server Manager, expand Roles, and you should see File Services installed.

If done correctly, your server will show that the File Services role is installed.

Add a shared folder using NFS   Once the File Services role has been added, you can then share folders, such as a folder called APPS.

Master It   Create a shared folder called APPS on your Server 2008 server; when done, the wizard should show a successful share.

Solution   Once you set up the permissions on your share, click Next to see the final screen of the Share a Folder Wizard, which lists the results and gives you the option to run the wizard again.

1. Select Start ➢ Administrative Tools ➢ Computer Management ➢ Shares ➢ New ➢ Share.

2. Follow the wizard, and browse to the folder you want to share. Click Next, and then set the kind of permissions you want for the shared folder. Click Finish.

Add a DFS root   If your organization ends up with a lot of file servers created over time, you may have users who do not know where all the files are located. You can streamline these operations by creating a DFS root and consolidate the existing file servers into common namespaces.

Master It   Create a new namespace called MYFIRSTNS on your Windows Server 2008 server; when done, the wizard should show a new namespace called MYFIRSTNS.

Solution   In the upper-right side of the DFS Management screen, click New Namespace. You will then see the Namespace Server Wizard. Follow the steps through to completion:

1. Select Start ➢ Administrative Tools ➢ DFS Management.

2. In DFS Management, click the Action drop-down, and select New Replication Group.

3. In New Replication Group Wizard, select the group type. Enter the name of the replication group (MYFIRSTNS), add any descriptions, and click Next.

4. Add the servers, and then click Next.

5. Select the topology, and then click Next.

6. Add the hub members, and click Next.

7. Select the replication group schedule, and click Next.

8. Set whether it is a primary member, and click Next.

9. Now add the folders to replicate, and click Next.

10. Review the settings, and click Finish.

Chapter 12: SYSVOL: Old and New

Understand the File Replication Service   In the old world of SYSVOL (everything up until Windows Server 2008 R2), the duties of replicating the shared SYSVOL folder were handled by the File Replication Service. Any domain that has a domain functional level of Windows 2008, or later, can be migrated to DFSR.

Master It   You have decided to adjust the replication schedule for FRS in your network. You are interested in setting the replication to occur continuously. Which replication setting would you choose?

Solution   The replication schedule can be configured to take place four, two, one, or zero times per hour. Setting it for four times per hour is tantamount to continuous replication.

Migrate to Distribute File System Replication   If you desire the benefits of remote differential compression displayed in DFSR, you can migrate your domain replication method from FRS to DFSR. This migration will occur in a series of four standard states: start, prepared, redirected, and eliminated.

Master It   Use the Active Directory Domains and Trusts tool to move your domain to the Windows Server 2008 functional level.

Solution   First, each domain controller must be running Windows Server 2008 or Windows Server 2008 R2. To raise the domain functional level to Windows Server 2008, perform the following steps:

1. Open Active Directory Domains and Trusts.

2. Right-click the domain, and click Raise Domain Functional Level.

3. In the domain functional level box, select Windows Server 2008.

4. Click Raise.

5. In the warning message box, click OK.

6. In the confirmation box, click OK.

Discover the current migration state of a domain controller using the dfsrmig **command-line utility**   The process of migrating from the start state to the eliminated state is handled only by using the dfsrmig command-line utility. This utility is used to set the global state and to get the global migration state. This utility is used to move the process of migration forward and backward through its stages.

Master It   Use dfsrmig to discover the current migration state of a domain controller.

Solution   Open a command prompt, and type **dfsrmig /getmigrationstate**.

Chapter 13: Sharing Printers on Windows Server 2008 R2 Networks

Add the Print and Document Services role   Windows Server 2008 R2 servers can be configured to perform as print servers. One of the first steps you must take is to add the Print and Document Services role. There are different steps needed if you're adding the role to a full installation of Windows Server 2008 R2 vs. a Server Core installation.

Master It   What tool would you use to add the Print and Document Services role on a full installation of Windows Server 2008 R2? What tool would you use to add the Print and Document Services role on a Server Core installation of Windows Server 2008 R2?

Solution   Use Server Manager to add the Print and Document Services role on a full installation of Windows Server 2008 R2. Use the Ocsetup command-line utility to add the Print and Document Services role on a full installation of Windows Server 2008 R2. The actual command is as follows:

```
Ocsetup Printing-ServerCore-Role
```

Manage printers using the Print Management console   After adding the Print and Documents Services role to the server, you can use the Print Management console to manage other print servers, printers, and print drivers.

Master It   Your company has purchased a new print device, and you want it to be hosted on a server that is configured as a print server. How would you add the printer to the print server?

Solution   You can add printers through the Print Management console. Right-click the printer's node within the desired server, and select Add Printer to start the Add Printer Wizard.

Manage print server properties   The spool folder can sometimes take a significant amount of space on the C drive, resulting in space problems and contention issues with the operating system. Because of these issues, the spool folder is often moved to another physical drive.

Master It   You want to move the spool folder to another location. How can you do this?

Solution   Launch the PMC, and browse to the server. Right-click the server, and select Properties. Change the location of the spool folder on the Advanced tab. Any spooled documents will be lost, so you should ensure users aren't currently printing to any printers hosted by the server.

Manage printer properties Printers can be added to Active Directory so that they can be easily located by searching Active Directory. Printers must be shared first, but they aren't published to Active Directory by default when they are shared.

Master It You want users to be able to easily locate a shared printer. What can you do to ensure the shared printer can be located by searching Active Directory?

Solution Launch the PMC, and browse to the printer. Right-click the printer, and select List in Directory, or access the Sharing tab of the printer's properties, and select List in Directory.

Chapter 14: Remote Server Administration

Configure Windows Server 2008 servers for remote administration Servers must be configured to allow remote administration before administrators can connect remotely.

Master It Configure a server to allow remote connections by clients running RDC version 6.0 or greater.

Solution Click Start, right-click Computer, and select Properties. Click Remote Settings. Select "Allow connections only from computers running Remote Desktop with Network Level Authentication (more secure)." Click OK.

Remotely connect to Windows Server 2008 servers using Remote Desktop Connection You can remotely connect to servers to do almost any administrative work. Servers are often located in a secure server room that is kept cool to protect the electronics. They can be in a different room, a different building, or even a separate geographical location, but they can still be remotely administered using either RDC or Remote Desktops.

Master It Connect to a server using RDC. Ensure your local drives are accessible when connected to the remote server.

Solution Launch RDC by selecting Start ➢ Accessories ➢ Remote Desktop Connection. Alternatively, you could enter **mstsc** from the command line or Run line. Enter the name of the remote server in the Computer text box. Click Options. Select the Local Resources tab. Click More, and select Drives.

Remotely connect to Windows Server 2008 servers using a Remote Desktop Protocol file If you regularly connect to a remote server using RDC, you can configure an RDP file that can be preconfigured based on your needs for this server. This RDP file will store all the settings you configure for this connection.

Master It Create an RDP file that you can use to connect with a server named Server1. Configure the file to automatically launch Server Manager when connected.

Solution Launch RDC by selecting Start ➢ Accessories ➢ Remote Desktop Connection. Click Options, and select the Programs tab. Select the Start the Following Program on Connection check box, and enter **ServerManager.msc** in the text box. Click the General tab, and enter **Server1** in the Computer text box. Click Save As, and save the file.

Configure a server for Remote Assistance   When your environment includes remote locations where junior administrators may occasionally need assistance, you can use Remote Assistance to access their session and demonstrate procedures.

Master It   Configure a server for Remote Assistance.

Solution   Launch Server Manager by selecting Start ➢ Administrative Tools ➢ Server Manager. Select Features, and add the Remote Assistance feature. Once the wizard has completed, ensure Remote Assistance is enabled: click Start, right-click Computer, select Properties, and select Remote Settings. Verify the Remote Assistance check box is selected.

Install the Remote Server Administration Tools   The Remote Assistance Server Administration Tools (RSAT) include the snap-ins and command-line tools needed to manage Server 2003 and Server 2008 servers from Windows Vista and Windows 7.

Master It   Obtain and install RSAT on a Windows Vista or Windows 7 system.

Solution   Obtain RSAT by going to Microsoft's download site at www.Microsoft.com/downloads and typing in **RSAT**. Install RSAT by double-clicking the downloaded file and following the wizard. Enable the tools by adding the Remote Server Administration Tools feature via Control Panel ➢ Programs ➢ Turn Windows Features On or Off.

Chapter 15: Connecting Windows Clients to the Server

Verify your network configuration   DHCP provides centralized IP address configurations, and all Windows clients understand DHCP without any additional installations required.

Master It   You need to verify that a client machine has received the correct IP address configuration via DHCP for the network you are working on. Which of the following commands would return these results?

- `ipconfig /all`
- `ipconfig /refresh`
- `msconfig /show`
- `msconfig`

Solution   The `ipconfig /all` command returns Local Area Connection configuration information including the following:

- IP address
- DNS IP addresses
- DHCP server IP address
- Domain name suffix

Join a client computer to a domain   Joining an Active Directory domain is key for workstations, because this provides centralized management from the Domain Admins within the domain. Group Policy is centralized, security can be established, and even software can be controlled centrally.

Master It Is the following statement true or false? "When joining a computer to an Active Directory domain, the only way this can occur is if the user joining the computer to the domain is a Domain Admin."

Solution False. Domain users can also add computers to the domain, but they can only do so up to 10 times. Users can also be delegated the right to add computers to the domain.

Change user passwords By default Windows AD provides a 42-day maximum password age limit. This limit is preceded by a 14-day reminder that you need to change your password. The 42-day maximum is designed to maintain a certain level of security for the enterprise, not allowing passwords to become stale.

Master It A user has become paranoid and wants to change his user account password right away. He does not know how to do this and calls the help desk. The computer he is using is running the Windows 7 operating system. What do you tell him?

Solution Tell the user to open the Start menu, click the Windows and Security button, and then click "Change a password." He will need to input his old password and his new password and then click the arrow button.

Connect to network resources Here's a typical scenario: a user wants to connect to a printer on the domain that does double-sided printing and also stapling. But the user does not know where the company keeps these printers. The user calls the help desk.

Master It Which of the following is the most efficient way for the user to find printers matching this description?

A. Tell the user to walk around the office complex and check each printer to see whether it has these features.

B. Tell the user to use the net view command to check for shared printers on a per-computer basis.

C. Tell the user to start the Add Printer Wizard and then select the Search Active Directory option.

Solution C. The user should search Active Directory using the Add Printer Wizard. Using this wizard, the user can specify specific printer feature criteria and see all the printers that are published to Active Directory that have the feature set the user needs.

Chapter 16: Working the Web with IIS 7.0 and 7.5

Understand IIS 7 architecture and capabilities IIS 7 redefined the structure of Microsoft's web server by compartmentalizing functionality and vertically managing behavior in a hierarchy. The new features of IIS 7.5 enhance application pools and include native modules for application protocols such as FTP that were absent from the previous revision. A dependency for many other services, IIS has become an integral part of the OS.

Master It Which of the following does *not* require IIS?

- Remote Server Administration Tools

- AD Rights Management Services

- Windows SharePoint Services 3.0

- Windows Management Service

- Federation Service

Solution Windows Management Service supports IIS remote administration but does not rely on IIS.

Plan for and install IIS 7.5 Relatively lean by default, IIS 7.5 must be carefully and painstakingly planned so as not to install more modular functionality than you need. More than a resource concern, leaving unnecessary role services off the server is also a method of securing your websites. As always with Microsoft, there are multiple ways to install IIS 7.5, from interactive GUI to CLI utility scripting to Windows PowerShell.

Master It You are planning a Windows Server 2008 R2 web server and need to make sure the requisite features are already installed in the OS. What three role services should you verify are installed?

Solution

- Windows Process Activation Service (WAS)

- Process Model

- Configuration APIs

Manage IIS 7's modularity and delegated administration IIS 7.5 modules are only one piece of evidence of the product's compartmentalization. Web applications and individual configuration settings per site can be independently managed as well. A hierarchical ladder of global, web, application, and page settings allow granular administration by multiple engineers.

Master It What is feature delegation?

Solution Feature delegation is the art of allowing site administrators to configure a specific IIS feature at their own sites rather than accepting the feature behavior dictated by the global settings on the server. Delegation is enabled by unlocking specific sections of the web.config files on one or more sites.

Create and secure websites in IIS 7 Designing and generating new websites in IIS 7.5 can be accomplished via the GUI or CLI, allowing you to automate routine site creation. Permission structure can be copied from one site to another or managed from the upper layers of the settings hierarchy to simplify permission granting. IIS 7.5 eases site generation by packaging your website.

Master It You need to create a new website that has all the characteristics of the Default Web Site but must also support ASP.NET pages. You do not want to add ASP.NET support to the Default Web Site for fear of adding vulnerability to existing web content. How would you implement this?

Solution   Create a new website, and add the ASP.NET module to the new site. Use a custom TCP/IP port number or host header to differentiate the new site from existing sites. Consider configuring a unique application pool identity for the site to isolate ASP.NET activity during troubleshooting.

Manage IIS 7 with advanced administration techniques   Day-to-day site maintenance and content posting may be the bulk of your IIS 7.5 administration. But additional higher-level management is what assures consistent and uninterrupted service of your web pages. Important configuring tasks including recovering from disasters, monitoring performance, setting access or code security, and defining encryption can be accomplished either locally or remotely.

Master It   Because of limited storage space, you are revising your disaster recovery plan. You are considering delaying backups of the IIS `applicationhost.config` file to monthly. However, you are concerned that minor global configuration changes made throughout the month may get lost if a failure occurs before the monthly backup. How would you recover a mid-month edit?

Solution   IIS 7 maintains a configuration history of `applicationhost.config` according to the default schedule found in the `iis_schema.xml` file. These can be restored with the `appcmd.exe` restore backup command. By default, the automatically generated historical versions of `applicationhost.config` are stored in the history subdirectory under `%systemdrive%\inetpub`.

Chapter 17: Watching Your System

View administrative events on your system   The Event Viewer includes many logs showing events on your system. It includes a built-in custom view that can be used to view all administrative events from multiple logs.

Master It   Access the Administrative Events custom view log.

Solution   Select Start ➤ Administrative Tools ➤ Event Viewer. Select Administrative Events within the Custom Views folder.

Attach a task to an event   You can create a response to any event by attaching a task. The response can be a notification with a dialog box, an email, or the execution of a program.

Master It   Create a task to display a dialog box if the Print Spooler service stops.

Solution   Launch the Services applet, and stop the Print Spooler service. Launch the Event Viewer, and select the System log. Right-click the event that was logged when the Print Spooler service was stopped, and select Attach Task to This Event. Follow the wizard, and select Display a Message as the action.

View the System Performance data collector set report   Data collector sets can be used to measure and monitor the performance of a server. The Performance Monitor includes built-in data collector sets that can be run on demand, and you can also create your own user-defined data collector set.

Master It   Run the System Performance data collector set, and view the resulting report.

Solution   Select Start ➤ Administrative Tools ➤ Performance Monitor. Browse to the Data Collector Sets ➤ System folder. Right-click the System Performance data collector set, and select Start. When it completes, right-click the data collector set, and select Latest Report.

Chapter 18: Windows Server 2008 R2 and Active Directory Backup and Maintenance

Use Windows Server Backup to back up and restore a Windows Server 2008 R2 computer Windows Server Backup is installed as a feature in Windows Server 2008 R2 and can be used to create various types of backups to protect your server computer. Full server backups contain the operating system, critical volumes, and all data on the server, while critical volume backups protect all volumes the operating system depends on but not necessarily the additional data stored on the server.

Master It   Your server contains two hard disks; the first contains the operating system, and the second contains user data. How can you use Windows Server Backup to protect the operating system and the user data?

Solution   Perform a full server backup, which will by default back up both volumes.

Defragment AD DS offline   In Windows Server 2008, you had to restart a domain controller in DSRM to perform an offline defragmentation and integrity check of the AD DS database. Windows Server 2008 R2 gives you the ability to perform these tasks without having to restart the computer and enter DSRM. Instead, you can stop AD DS and then use Ntdsutil.exe from an elevated command prompt to perform the offline defragmentation and integrity check.

Master it   You want to defragment your AD DS database but do not want to shut down the server and restart it in DSRM. How do you do that?

Solution   Stop AD DS, and then use Ntdsutil.exe from an elevated command prompt to defragment the Ntds.dit database.

Install the Active Directory Recycle Bin   In previous versions of Windows Server, recovering deleted objects in Active Directory required recovering from a backup. Windows Server 2008 R2 introduces the Active Directory Recycle Bin, which enables you to recover objects from Active Directory as if you were restoring a file that had been sent to the Windows Recycle Bin.

Master it   You want to provide additional protection against accidental deletion of objects in Active Directory. How can you provide an extra 180 days of recovery for deleted objects?

Solution   Use Windows PowerShell to install the Active Directory Recycle Bin.

Create and recover a system state backup for Active Directory   Because domain controllers contain all the database information for Active Directory, recovering a failed domain controller server is critically important. When using Windows Server Backup or the command-line utility Wbadmin.exe, perform backups containing the system state at a minimum to preserve Active Directory.

Master it You want to protect your Active Directory data from the possibility of complete hardware failure of the server computer. Which type of backups will provide this protection?

Solution Use a system state backup at a minimum. Critical volume and full server backups also include all the information necessary to recover Active Directory.

Chapter 19: Advanced IP: Routing with Windows

Document the life of an IP packet routed through your network Understanding how the routing components work inside your hosts and routers will allow you to predict where network traffic will travel throughout your network. With this understanding comes the ability to troubleshoot network issues that appear perplexing.

Master It In the Carthage/Rome network from Figure 19.1, use your understanding of the route taken by an IP packet from host A to host G to determine which addresses you should ping in order to discover routing issues that are preventing packets from traveling between A and G.

Solution When using the ping tool to track traffic from one host to another, it is important to realize that you are tracking return traffic. If a route is broken, it may well be in the return journey. Having said that, when debugging router issues from system A to system G, you should ping, in order, the following IP addresses:

A—199.34.57.10—to ensure that IP is configured on host A

D—199.34.57.40—to ensure that the router is on the network

E—156.40.10.60—to ensure that the router is routing traffic

G—156.40.10.50—to ensure that host G is receiving, and responding to, traffic

Explain the class-based and classless views of IP routing When discussing routing with networking professionals, it is important to understand the old class-based terminology to allow for conversations and documentation that may still linger on these terms. Understanding how classless IP routing works is key to avoiding inefficiencies brought on by too strict an adherence to class boundaries in network addressing.

Master It The address 172.24.255.255 lies inside class B, whose default netmask is 255.255.0.0. It also lies in the 172.16/20 RFC 1918 private network range, whose default netmask is 255.255.240.0. Given this information, is the address 172.24.255.255 a host address or a subnet broadcast address?

Solution The information given is insufficient to determine whether the address 172.24.255.255 is a host address or a subnet broadcast address. The default netmask is not relevant; only the netmask that is actually in use is relevant. If this is a network built by a network designer who was not thinking about supernetting or CIDR, this address may very well be treated as a subnet broadcast address. It is more likely, given that RFC 1918 talks about supernetting this address range, that this is a simple host address.

Use NAT devices to route TCP traffic Until we all switch to using IPv6, we will need to use NAT devices to route TCP traffic from our many networked hosts to the outside world, while using only a few of the increasingly rare public IP addresses. Understanding how NAT devices change the source and destination addresses of IP packets will allow you to read network packet traces and interpret which systems are intended as recipients of data.

Master It   A user complains that when he tries to connect to an FTP site, the connection initially succeeds, but the first time that a file listing is attempted, his connection is severed, and the server states that it cannot connect to 192.168.0.10.

What are likely causes of this problem, and how could this be addressed?

Solution   FTP, like SIP and several other protocols, often includes the IP address of the host in its communication.

Whenever an RFC 1918 address such as 192.168.*.* is seen as part of an error, your first thought should be that there may be a problem with a NAT router between the two hosts. With the FTP protocol, there are a number of possible causes and fixes:

◆   The FTP ALG in the NAT should be changing the IP address and port in the control channel—the usual cause for it not doing so is that the FTP server is running on a port other than the default port, 21. If possible, moving the server back to port 21 will allow the ALG to work correctly.

◆   If the FTP server is on port 21, it is possible that encryption is being used on the control channel, using FTP over SSL or FTP over GSSAPI. In this case, the ALG cannot see or modify the traffic.

◆   Many FTP clients allow the user to select "passive mode" communications for data transfers, in which case it is the server's IP address that needs to pass through the NAT, and this may allow for data to travel between client and server.

◆   If this is not possible, the use of an FTP proxy service may prove necessary to ensure that data connections can flow correctly.

Chapter 20: Getting From the Office to the Road: VPNs

Add the Network Policy and Access Services role   The first step to create a VPN server is to add the Network Policy and Access Services role. Once the role is added, you can take additional steps to configure the VPN server.

Master It   You need to add the Network Policy and Access Services role to create a VPN server. How can you accomplish this?

Solution   Launch Server Manager, select Add Roles, select the Network Policy and Access Services role, and add the Routing and Remote Access Services.

Configure a VPN server   You have added the Network Policy and Access Services role and now want to configure your VPN server to accept connections from clients.

Master It   What should you do to configure your VPN server?

Solution   Launch Routing and Remote Access by selecting Start ➢ Administrative Tools ➢ Routing and Remote Access. Right-click the server, and select Configure and Enable Routing and Remote Access. Use the wizard to complete the configuration.

Create a remote access policy to allow VPN connections   Even after the VPN role has been added and the Routing and Remote Access service has been configured, the VPN server will not accept any connections until the default remote access policies are modified or new ones are created.

Master It   You want to allow users that have domain accounts to be able to access the VPN server remotely. What should you do to create a remote access policy?

Solution   Launch Routing and Remote Access. Right-click Remote Access and Logging, and select Launch NPS. Right-click Network Policies, and select Create New. Follow the wizard to create the policy using a condition that users must be a member of the Domain Users group.

Use IPSec to encrypt traffic   IPSec can be used to encrypt normal IP traffic between two computers to protect it against sniffing attacks. Policies can be created with Group Policy or via a local policy.

Master It   You want to ensure that traffic between two DNS servers is encrypted. What should you do?

Solution   Create two IPSec policies (one on each DNS server) to encrypt all traffic.

Chapter 21: Adding More Locations: Sites in Active Directory

Create a site   Site objects are added to Active Directory to represent well-connected physical locations that will host domain controllers. Once a decision has been made to place a DC in a physical location, you need to add a site.

Master It   Create a site to represent a new business location in Virginia Beach.

Solution   Launch Active Directory Sites and Services. Right-click Sites, and select New Site. Name the site **VB**, select an existing site link, and click OK.

Add subnets to sites   Active Directory uses clients' subnets to determine which site they are in. For this to work, subnet objects need to be created and associated with sites.

Master It   Create a subnet object to represent the 10.15.0.0/16 subnet that exists in the Virginia Beach location. Associate the subnet object with the VB site.

Solution   Launch Active Directory Sites and Services. Right-click Subnets, and select New Subnet. Enter **10.15.0.0/16** as the prefix, and select the VB site. Click OK.

Configure a site link to replicate only during certain times   It's often desirable to restrict when replication occurs between sites. If the defaults are used, replication will occur every 180 minutes. If the WAN link is heavily used during certain periods, you can configure the schedule so that it replicates only during certain times.

Master It   Configure the Default-First-Site-Name site (or another site) to replicate only between midnight and 5 a.m.

Solution   Launch Active Directory Sites and Services. Right-click the DefaultIPSiteLink site link, and select Properties. Click the Change Schedule button. Click Replication Not Available to change the schedule so that replication isn't scheduled. Use your mouse to highlight the hours 5 a.m. to midnight for all seven days of the week. Click Replication Available, and click OK.

Configure Group Policy for the next nearest site   If a domain controller can't be reached in a client's site, the client will look for any domain controller without regard to how close it is. This can negatively impact logons for enterprises with several locations connected with different speed WAN links. You can configure Windows Vista (and newer) clients to locate and log on to a DC in the next nearest site if a DC can't be located in their site. This can be done using Group Policy or the Registry Editor.

Master It   Which of the following Group Policy settings can be manipulated to enable the next nearest site setting?

1. Computer Configuration ➤ Policies ➤ Administrative Templates ➤ System ➤ Logon ➤ DC Locator DNS Records

2. Computer Configuration ➤ Policies ➤ Administrative Templates ➤ System ➤ Net Logon ➤ DC Locator DNS Records

3. User Configuration ➤ Policies ➤ Administrative Templates ➤ System ➤ Logon ➤ DC Locator DNS Records

4. User Configuration ➤ Policies ➤ Administrative Templates ➤ System ➤ Net Logon ➤ DC Locator DNS Records

Solution

- ◆ Computer Configuration ➤ Policies ➤ Administrative Templates ➤ System ➤ Net Logon ➤ DC Locator DNS Records. The setting applies to computers, not users. Additionally, it affects how the `netlogon` service (not the logon process) locates domain controllers.

Chapter 22: The Third DC: Understanding Read-Only Domain Controllers

Prepare a forest and a domain for RODCs   RODCs are new to Windows Server 2008 and can't be added until the forest and domain are prepared. The preparation will modify the schema and permissions.

Master It   Identify the command that needs to be executed to prepare the forest to support RODCs.

Solution   The adprep command needs to be executed from the command line. The following command will prepare the forest: `adprep /forestprep`.

Prepare the domain   In addition to preparing the forest, you must also prepare the domain before RODCs can be added.

Master It   Identify the two commands that need to be executed to prepare the domain to support RODCs.

Solution The `adprep` command needs to be executed from the command line. The following two commands should be executed after `adprep /forestprep`:

◆ `adprep /domainprep`

◆ `adprep /rodcprep`

If a forest is created with all Windows Server 2008 servers as domain controllers, it's not necessary to execute `adprep /forestprep` and `adprep /domainprep`, **but** `adprep /rodcprep` still must be executed.

Allow passwords on any RODC The RODC can cache passwords for users based on how it's configured. When a user's password is cached on the RODC, the authentication process doesn't have to traverse the WAN link and is quicker. However, a cached password is susceptible to an attack, so privileged accounts should not be cached on the server.

Master It What should you modify to allow users to have their passwords cached on any RODC in the domain?

◆ The Allowed RODC Password Replication group

◆ The Denied RODC Password Replication group

◆ The password replication policy

Solution You should modify the Allowed RODC Password Replication group. Members of this group can have their passwords replicated or cached on any RODC in the domain.

Allow passwords on a single RODC It's possible to configure the environment so members of a group can have their passwords replicated and cached to any RODC in the domain. It's also possible to configure the environment so that the passwords will be replicated or cached only to a single RODC.

Master It What should you modify to allow users to have their passwords cached on a specific RODC in the domain?

◆ The Allowed RODC Password Replication group

◆ The Denied RODC Password Replication group

◆ The password replication policy

Solution You should modify the password replication policy. Each RODC has a Password Replication Policy tab that can be modified to allow users to have their passwords cached or replicated onto that RODC.

Chapter 23: Creating Larger Active Directory Environments: Beyond One Domain

Explain the fundamental concepts of Active Directory with clarity The Active Directory environment gets back to nature with the forest and trees. The forest is the collection of domains built in relation to each other through DCPromo. The trees are domains within a hierarchal DNS namespace with "the same last name." The key to the relation between domains is the automatic and nonconfigurable two-way transitive trust relation.

Master it   When the first domain controller for the first domain is created, three partitions are created within the Active Directory database. What are these three partitions named, what is contained in them, and which are replicated to the other domain controllers of the forest?

Solution   The three partitions are the domain partition, the schema partition, and the configuration partition. The domain partition contains objects pertaining to the domain such as computer and user accounts and is replicated to domain controllers of the domain. The schema partition defines the objects of Active Directory and which data values are assigned to each object. The configuration partition holds data concerning Active Directory replication and other forest-related configurations. The schema and configuration partitions are replicated throughout the forest.

Choose between using domains, multiple domains, or multiple forests with an Active Directory design   In planning an Active Directory design, you might decide you need multiple domains instead of using organizational units within a single domain. Replication limitations, legal requirements, and political forces are the top reasons for considering multiple domains.

Master it   What features of Windows Server 2008 eliminate two security-related reasons for multiple domains?

Solution   The two security-related reasons for multiple domains were password policies and poor security at branch offices. The feature of fine-tuned password policies that can be applied to users through the use of GPOs relieved the need for creating separate domains for differing password policies. The read-only domain controller with password caching reduces the risk of a stolen domain controller getting into the hands of an evil hacker and retrieving passwords from the Active Directory database or replicating corrupt changes to the rest of domain controllers.

Add domains to an Active Directory environment   You have to use the domain controller promotion wizard (DCPromo) whenever you are going to build a new domain or replica domain controller in an Active Directory forest. In previous versions of Windows Server, the DNS structure needed to be in place prior to the installation. With Windows Server 2008 R2, everything is done for you.

Master it   Since DNS is now handled by Windows Server 2008 R2, it would be nice to know if it did it right. What four changes should you see if you add a new child domain?

Solution   You should see these changes:

◆   In the IP configurations, the domain controller is listed as the DNS server using loopback addresses for IPv4 and IPv6.

◆   The DNS zone for the new child domain is supported on the domain controller as an Active Directory integrated zone.

◆   The parent domain controller is listed as the forwarder for the DNS service.

◆   The child domain's DNS domain name is delegated to the new domain controller in the parent DNS zone.

Manage function levels, trusts, FSMO roles, and the global catalog   Several forest-related configurations were discussed, which would be managed by Enterprise Admins. The function levels for the forest and domains provide the availability of features of the latest Windows Server version. All domain controllers need to be upgraded to that level to benefit from these features. Although you can raise function levels, you can't lower them. The five FSMOs are specific roles assigned to domain controllers within the domains and forest. The PDC emulator, RID master, and infrastructure master are domain-related. The domain naming master and schema master are forest-related. Trusts are required to share resources between domains that are not part of the same forest. The exception is shortcut trusts, which reduce the trust path between two domains within the same forest.

Master It   The placement of FSMO roles is dictated by the domain to which it is assigned and the global catalog role. Which two roles had rules concerning placement in regard to the global catalog?

Solution   The domain naming master, which is located in the forest root domain, had to be placed on a domain controller with the global catalog role. The infrastructure master role, which is located in each domain, could not be located on a domain controller with the global catalog role. However, in a single-domain Active Directory environment, this didn't apply.

Chapter 24: Migrating, Merging, and Modifying Your Active Directory

Introduce new versions of Active Directory into a network   The release of a new version of Windows Server means you need to upgrade existing domain controllers. There are two basic methods to add a new version of Active Directory into an organization: upgrading a domain controller or upgrading the domain by adding a new domain controller.

Master it   Both operations require the Active Directory database to be modified using the adprep.exe utility. What three options need to be run? What option can also be run?

Solution   /forestprep modifies the schema of the Active Directory forest to support Windows Server 2008 R2's Active Directory.

/domainprep prepares the domain for a Windows Server 2008 R2 domain controller.

/gpprep modifies permissions on Group Policy objects for replication to Windows Server 2008 R2 domain controllers.

/rodcprep prepares the forest for deploying the read-only domain controllers. This is optional and can be run at another point.

Migrate domains accounts from one domain to another   The requirement, to move users and groups from an existing domain to a clean and pristine domain, often happens when companies merge or spin off. In addition, this can be required when a forest restructuring is justified. Microsoft offers the ADMT utility to perform domain migrations.

Master it   After a user account is migrated to the new domain, what gives the user access to resources within the original domain?

Solution   Resources in the original domain have permissions assigned, allowing access to listed security principles such as user accounts. The permissions, also named ACEs, list the user's SID. After a user account is migrated, its SID changes. However, the original SID is saved as SID history. When the user authenticates in the other domain, the SID history will identify with the permission on the resource.

SID filtering, which is enabled by default on domain trusts, will prevent this action from happening. You must manually disable this security feature.

Restructure domains within a forest The options for changing the domain structure are limited. One option is performed by migrating the domain accounts with the ADMT utility. The other alternative is renaming a domain. The former is gradual and complicated. The latter is an all-or-nothing complex operation offering a great deal of risk.

Master it The domain rename operation is limited by the version of Exchange Server deployed in the environment. What version is supported by Microsoft for a domain rename?

Solution The only supported version is Exchange Server 2003 Service Pack 1. If the forest has any other versions from 5.5 to 2007 Service Pack 1, this operation is not available for the company.

Chapter 25: Installing, Using, and Administering Remote Desktop Services

Limit the maximum number of connections You can limit the maximum number of connections for the server for performance reasons or to help ensure you remain compliant with the licensing agreement.

Master It You want to limit the maximum number of connections to 100. How can you do this?

Solution Launch the Remote Desktop Session Host Configuration tool. Double-click RDP-Tcp to access the properties sheet. Select the Network Adapter tab. Set "Maximum connections" to 100.

Add an application to an RD Session Host server Once the RDS role is added and the RD Session Host server is configured, you can add applications to make them available to the server.

Master It Your company has purchased an application that supports multiuser access. You want to install it on the RD Session Host server. What should you do?

Solution Install the application using the `.msi` (Windows Installer) file or using the Control Panel Add/Remove Programs Wizard.

If the application can be installed via one of these methods, it is not necessary to use the `Change User` command that was required in older versions of Terminal Services. If it can't be installed using the `.msi` file or Add/Remove Programs, you must use the `Change User /install` command before installation and the `Change User /execute` command after the installation.

Add a RemoteApp for Web Access RemoteApp applications can be configured so that they are accessible to users via a web browser. Users simply need to access the correct page and select the application to launch it.

Master It Assume you have already configured your environment to support RemoteApp applications. You now want to add a RemoteApp application. What should you do?

Solution Launch the RemoteApp Manager, and select the Add RemoteApp Program link in the Actions menu. Follow the wizard to add the program.

Add a RemoteApp to the Start menu RemoteApp applications can be configured so that they are accessible to users from the Start menu of their system. Once configured, users simply select the item from their Start menu to launch it.

Master It Assume you have already configured your environment to support RemoteApp applications. You now want to add a RemoteApp application so that it is accessible to users via the Start menu. What should you do?

Solution Launch the RemoteApp Manager, and select the Add RemoteApp Program link in the Actions menu. Follow the wizard to add the program. Right-click the RemoteApp program, and select Create Windows Installer package. Use the package to install the application on the user's system.

Chapter 26: Connecting Mac OS X Clients

Prepare Active Directory for Mac OS X clients Although Mac OS X can join Active Directory domains, you must take some preparatory steps to ensure they can communicate with Windows Server 2008 R2.

Master it You want your Active Directory users who have Mac clients to connect to your Windows Server 2008 R2 servers using a single Active Directory logon. What network security feature of Windows must you change to permit Mac clients to communicate with your Windows Server 2008 R2 domain?

Solution You must change the local policy for domain controllers to not always require SMB packet signing.

Connect a Mac to the domain Mac OS X can connect to Active Directory and join domains. SMB protocol support is provided by a built-in version of Samba, letting OS X connect to Windows for file shares and printers.

Master it You want to add your Mac OS X client to your Active Directory domain. Which OS X utility should you use?

Solution Use Directory Access in your Utilities folder to configure and connect to Active Directory and create a computer account in the domain.

Connect to file shares and printers OS X connects to Windows file shares and printers using the SMB support provided by Samba. Because support is integrated, you can use the Finder to connect to Windows resources directly rather than adding additional software.

Master it You are trying to access a network folder that is shared on a Windows Server 2008 R2 computer from your domain-joined Mac client. How can you use the Finder to connect?

Solution In the Finder, click the Go menu, and select Connect to Server; then type the path using the format **smb://servername/sharename**.

Use Remote Desktop from a Mac client   Microsoft created the Remote Desktop Connection for Mac to provide Remote Desktop connectivity for Mac clients. Using RDC, you can access the functionality of your Windows computer directly from your Mac clients.

> **Master it**   You are using RDC to connect to your Windows Server 2008 R2 server computer and want to save your network credentials so that you don't have to enter them every time you connect. How can you do this?

> **Solution**   Enter your Active Directory credentials in Preferences under the RDC menu, and select the option to save the credentials in your Keychain.

Chapter 27: Patch Management

Use Windows Automatic Updating to check for new updates on a computer running Windows 7   Windows Automatic Updating is a Control Panel item used to check the Microsoft Update site to see whether any updates are available for your computer.

> **Master It**   On a Windows 7 computer, use Windows automatic updating to see whether any new updates are available for your computer.

> **Solution**

> 1.   Click Start, and then click Control Panel.

> 2.   Click System and Security, and then click Windows Update.

> 3.   Click "Check for updates."

> If updates are available for your computer, you will be prompted to install them.

Use the Windows Update Stand-Alone Installer to silently install a security update   The Windows Update Stand-Alone Installer is used to install security updates on all Windows operating systems since Windows Vista and Windows Server 2008.

> **Master It**   Install a security update in quiet mode and defer a required reboot by using the Windows Update Stand-Alone Installer.

> **Solution**   Run *executable* `/quiet /norestart` at an elevated command prompt where *executable* is the file name of the security update.

Identify the four phases of patch management   According to Microsoft, there are four phases in planning a patch management strategy.

> **Master It**   Which of the following is not one of the four phases of patch management?

> 1.   Identify

> 2.   Troubleshoot

> 3.   Evaluate and Plan

> 4.   Assess

> 5.   Deploy

Solution Troubleshoot is not one of the four phases of patch management. The four phases in order are as follows:

1. Identify

2. Evaluate and Plan

3. Assess

4. Deploy

Following a standardized, documented process helps bring order to the chaos of patch management.

Chapter 28: File Shares Made Even Better: Windows SharePoint Services 3.0

Understand the features and requirements of Windows SharePoint Services 3.0 WSSv3 offers great versatility and control to document management but also has several prerequisite software and mandatory hardware requirements. The web services are heavily influenced by the web hosting prerequisite software, and storage considerations in the repository can affect content delivery. But overall, the benefits outweigh the extra management required to manage documents in SharePoint instead of file systems.

Master It WSSv3 is dependent upon which three Microsoft applications?

Solution .NET Framework 3.0+, Internet Information Services v6.0+, and Microsoft SQL Server 2005+

Consider Windows SharePoint Services 3.0 installation issues and processes Though a free service, WSSv3 is by no means small. From service accounts to farm topology, several objectives must be planned and documented prior to beginning the installation process. And not just SharePoint, but the IIS 7.5 installation and SQL Server configuration must also be carefully planned.

Master It You are planning a multiserver SharePoint farm using servers that reside in separate trusting domains throughout your ADS forest. Under what security context will you configure your WSSv3 service accounts?

Solution Choose either the Network Service account or a specially created ADS domain user account to facilitate communication between hosts. Since all the servers reside in trusting domains within a single ADS forest, the network service account would work and simplifies authentication by using each server's computer account in ADS. Alternatively, creating a special domain user account increases security and administrative reach. Avoid configuring WSSv3 services with any "local" account because doing so will restrict the SharePoint services to resources only on the local server, defeating the multiserver farm topology design.

Understand SharePoint site and document library provisioning Planning SharePoint logical design encompasses data taxonomy classifications, administrative models, and document management requirements. There is no one correct design for SharePoint; that's what makes it so versatile! Templates for sites and for site objects such as lists and libraries make it easy to enforce consistency, while system-supplied templates can be customized and then saved as custom templates to enhance the look and feel of a WSSv3 environment.

Master It   You have three different groups of SharePoint users who all want exclusive authority over their own content. What are two alternative logical SharePoint designs you could build to accommodate them?

Solution   You could build each group their own exclusive site collection, providing complete autonomy not only over their content but over their quota limits and site collection maintenance as well. Or, you could build separate sites for each group within a single site collection and disallow security inheritance to uniquely configure content permissions on each site.

Understand document management and access in Windows SharePoint Services 3.0
WSSv3 has distinct advantages over file systems for managing document versions, approval processes, editing conflicts, metadata, archiving, and more. Single-instance storage guidelines prevent multiple unsynchronized copies of the same file without preventing necessary user access. The challenge is in setting up the initial environment.

Master It   You need to create a selective workflow within a document library that houses multiple items. You want the workflow to kick off in response to only one specific item type being created. How would you implement this?

Solution   Create a custom content type in the Site Content Type Gallery that has the workflow attached to it (instead of creating the workflow on the library itself that would affect all items throughout the library). Then add the new custom content type to the library via its Library Settings.

Understand advanced Windows SharePoint Services 3.0 administration   In addition to managing individual document libraries and sites, overall administration of the entire SharePoint environment must be dutifully performed in order to provide users with a comfortable, usable document management platform. And though advanced administration usually entails settings that are planned and set early on and rarely changed, they have no less impact on user experience than day-to-day maintenance.

Master It   Because of limited storage space on your SQL Server, you need to make sure that SharePoint users do not overpopulate their sites with content. You want to invoke a standard limit to site size that can be overridden on a site-by-site basis when justified. How would you design a solution?

Solution   Create a quota template in Central Administration that specifies the standard warning and limit sizes. Then invoke the new quota template on the user site collection using Central Administration. All sites in the site collection will now be held to the limits of the new quota template but can be adjusted at the Site Settings of an individual site by one of the administrators.

Chapter 29: Server Virtualization with Hyper-V

Determine whether a server can run Hyper-V   You are buying new servers whose main role will be to run Hyper-V. However, you are concerned that the new servers may not be capable of running Hyper-V because they do not meet the minimum requirements.

Master It What are the CPU requirements to run Hyper-V? What brands may be considered, and are there other factors to be considered?

Solution Both Intel and AMD have processors with features to support Hyper-V. The first deciding factor is that the CPU must be 64 bits. For Intel, select a processor with at least the features VT and XD. For AMD, select AMD-V and NX. Note that the BIOS of your server must expose these features, or you can't enable them.

Bonus points if you noted that Itanium processors with VT and XD bits should be able to run Hyper-V but cannot since Microsoft did not write a version for Itanium.

Determine when it makes sense to virtualize a server Your company is standardizing on Hyper-V virtual machines for all production servers. The strategy is to virtualize all servers, unless there is a good reason not to do so. One of the critical business applications (CalcIT) is a multithreaded modeling application that is very CPU intensive and may take days to run even on a big 16-core server.

Master It Decide whether CalcIT is a good candidate for virtualization. If it is, explain why. If it is not, you need good arguments to convince your management to deviate from the standard.

Solution Hyper-V VMs can use no more than four virtual CPUs, which limits the total CPU power a VM can use even on big servers. In addition, server virtualization is best suited to lowly utilized VMs sharing a host. CalcIT is a multithreaded application, meaning that it can effectively use many cores and CPUs. As a VM, it cannot use more than four cores at the same time. Runtime may increase by a factor of four after virtualization. So, it is definitely not a good candidate. Virtualization would hurt the business in this case.

Decide which technology to use to quickly move a virtual machine between hosts You are designing a Hyper-V testing lab. One of the requirements is that the hardware is used effectively for a varying collection of virtual machines. The idea is to maximize the use of available hardware and do so with the least overhead the next time the VM collection changes. Also, the process must be as reliable as possible.

Master It What technology would you use, and how would your choice meet the requirements?

Solution You have quite a number of possible solutions for this:

- Move the VHD files between machines, and re-create the VM from scratch.

- Export the VM, and import it again on a different machine.

- Back up all VMs, and restore on a different machine.

- Deploy a clustered configuration, and use Quick Migration or Live Migration.

However, all solutions except Quick Migration and Live Migration will involve a lot of slow, manual, error-prone steps.

You define a solution where an iSCSI SAN is used for central storage. For a test lab, iSCSI is a good solution to keep costs down. For a new lab, you can specify to use Windows 2008 R2 which supports Live Migration.

Advise on a backup strategy As an IT consultant you are hired by a company to have a look at their Hyper-V configuration. They are especially proud of their backup system, describing it as simple and effective. Using a script, they save the state of all VMs one by one, and during the suspended period, they copy the VHD file to a backup location.

Master It Give the customer your opinion of their backup methods. If it is fine, compliment them on their choice, and leave a (self-)satisfied customer. If there is a problem, explain it to them, and propose an alternative. What do you recommend?

Solution Of course, copying VHDs around is no substitute for a backup. In fact, it is potentially crippling to their network! This method is functionally the same as using a disk image for a backup. The worst problem is with distributed systems such as Active Directory and Exchange Server, which need to know that they have been restored in order to reconfigure themselves. Just restoring a VHD leaves no hint to the VM OS and applications that they were restored.

You explain to your customer firmly that they are on a road to disaster and need to start using a real backup solution right now. One way is to use a Hyper-V aware backup solution to back up the host. Alternatively, back up from the VM, and store the backup in a remote location.

Chapter 30: Advanced User Account Management and User Support

Deploy home directories to multiple users Home directories allow a user to have a personal store of information stored on a file server. This makes their data available to them no matter where they log in on the network.

Master It You've been tasked with deploying home directories to many users in the OU that you manage. You want to do this as quickly as possible. Your backup application uses an administrator user account, so you need to ensure that it has access to the users' home directories on the file server. How will you set this up?

Solution

1. Create a file share on the file server to contain your home directories, and set the permissions appropriately.

2. Configure a Group Policy object for your OU. Enable "Add the Administrators security group to roaming users profiles," which can be found in Computer Configuration\Policies\Administrative Templates\System\User Profiles.

3. Navigate to the OU in Active Directory Users and Computers. Select all of the user objects in the OU, right-click, and select Properties. Enter the path of the home directory file share, and add \%username to the end.

Your home directories will be automatically created and administrators on the file server will have access to them.

Set up mandatory roaming profiles Mandatory roaming profiles can be used to provide users with a preconfigured working environment and to prevent them from saving changes to it.

Master It Your manager has asked you to set up a mandatory roaming profile for users of Windows 7. You're also asked to see whether there is a way to prevent users from logging in if the mandatory roaming profile cannot be loaded.

Solution You need to configure a super mandatory roaming profile:

1. Log in as a sample user on a PC. Configure the working environment as required.

2. Log back into the PC as an administrator, and copy the sample user's profile onto the network. You need to ensure that the required Active Directory security group has Full Control over the registry hive in the profile using `regedit.exe`.

3. Rename `NTUSER.DAT` in the profile to `NTUSER.MAN`. This will cause the profile to become a mandatory profile.

4. Rename the profile to something like `Mandatory.V2` knowing that the `.V2` is required for Windows 7 users.

5. To make this roaming mandatory profile into a super mandatory profile, you can rename the profile folder to `Mandatory.MAN.V2`.

Create logon scripts to automate administration Administrators can use logon scripts to run a series of commands to preconfigure the working environment for a user when they log in. Administrators can use scripting languages such a command-prompt commands, VBScript, or PowerShell.

Master It You are designing an Active Directory for a large multisite organization. You need to be able to set up logon scripts for different scenarios:

- There are global commands that must be run for everyone.

- Anyone in the Accounts OU must have access to certain resources.

- Anyone, including visitors, logging in at the Dublin Active Directory site must connect to a local shared drive.

You are asked what the running order will be for any user who will run all of the logon scripts.

Solution Write the three logon scripts, and save them into SYSVOL. Create three Group Policy objects. Link the first GPO to the domain, and edit it to run the logon script for everyone. Link the second GPO to the Accounts OU, and edit it to run the logon script for the Accounts OU. Link the third GPO to the Dublin Active Directory site, and edit it to run the Dublin logon script.

The running order for GPOs is site, domain, OU, child OU. The running order of the logon scripts for a user inheriting all of the policies will be as follows:

- Dublin

- Domain

- Accounts

Index

Note to the Reader: Throughout this index **boldfaced** page numbers indicate primary discussions of a topic. *Italicized* page numbers indicate illustrations.

A

A (Host) records, 192, **195–196**, 206
ABO (AdminBaseObject), 690
access. *See* security
Access Client IPv4 and IPv6 Addresses policy, 865–866
access control entries (ACEs), **426–427**, 442
access control lists (ACLs), **426–427**
   C&P migration, **1033–1034**
   Group Policy, **377–378**, *377–378*
Access databases, **1212–1213**
Access permission, 1110
accidental deletion protection, 252
Account is disabled option
   domain user accounts, 300
   local user accounts, **282**
Account is sensitive and cannot be delegated option, 300
Account lockout duration setting, 400
Account lockout threshold setting, 400
Account Policies category, 388, 391
Account tab
   domain user accounts, **298–301**, *298*
   locked out accounts, **332**, *332*
Account Transition Option, 1046, *1047*
accounting configuration in VPNs, **884–886**, *885*
Accounting providers setting, 888
accounts
   domain. *See* domain accounts
   user. *See* users and user accounts
ACEs (access control entries), **426–427**, 442
ACK states, 834–835
ACLing, **1033–1034**
ACLs (access control lists), **426–427**
   C&P migration, **1033–1034**
   Group Policy, **377–378**, *377–378*
Action page
   events, 760, *761*
   inbound firewall rules, 137–138, *139*
actions, IPSec, **896**, 899, **901–902**, *901–902*
Actions tab
   task events, 762
   user-defined data collector sets, 789–790, *790*
Activate Windows task, 46
activation, 26, 46, **121–122**, 156

Active Directory, **227**
   accounts, **257–259**, *257–259*, 939
   backups. *See* backups
   connectivity issues, **974**
   database integrity, **805–807**
   defragmenting, **804–805**
   delegating control, **261–262**, *261–262*, **419**
      best practices, **425**
      manually setting permissions, **424–428**, *426–428*
      vs. NT domains, **419–421**
      using OUs, **421–424**, *422–424*
      reporting on, **428–429**, *429*
   design guidelines, **978–980**
   DFS, 498
   and DNS, **209–215**, *214–215*, **234–235**, *235*
   domains. *See* domains; multiple domains
   empty roots, **976–977**
   file lookup, 510
   fine-grained password policies, **3–4**, *4*, **271–276**, *274–276*
   and FRS, 520
   and GPOs, 360
   groups
      creating, **259–261**, *260*, **324–330**, *324–328*
      working with, **321–324**, *323*
   introduction, **227–230**
   Mac OS X clients, **1117–1120**
   migration strategies. *See* migration
   network resources connections, 659
   new features and changes, **2–5**, *4–5*
   OUs. *See* organizational units (OUs)
   political considerations, **973–974**
   PowerShell. *See* PowerShell
   printers, **663–665**, *663*
   Recycle Bin, 4, *4*, **84**, 239, 265–266, **811–812**, *812*
   replication, **225**, **228**, **974**
   restores, **811–815**, *812*, *814*
   schemas, **228**, **996**, 1002
   searching, **662–663**, *662*, **672–673**, *672*
      network drives, **447**
      printer deployment, **562–565**, *562–565*
      shares, 439, *440*
   second domain controllers, **245–250**, *246–249*
   for shares, **435**, **439**, *440*
   single-domain forests. *See* single-domain forests

sites. *See* sites
snapshots, **807–809**, *807–808*
stopping and restarting, **803–804**
upgrading, **82–87**
verifying, **527–528**
Active Directory Administrative Center (ADAC),
84, 333
home directories, 1304
navigating, **336–343**, *336–343*
as new feature, **4–5**, *5*
overview, **333–336**, *334–336*
Active Directory Certificate Services, 858, 878
Active Directory Client Certificate
authentication, 738
Active Directory Diagnostics data collector set,
783–784
Active Directory Domain Services (AD DS), **228**,
803–804
Active Directory Domains and Trusts
(ADDT), 1038
domain functional levels, 528
forest functional levels, 266–268, 947, *947*,
989–990, *989*
FSMO roles, 1002, *1002*
trusts, 1009, 1013–1015, *1014*
Active Directory Integrated (ADI)
DNS, **264–265**, *265*, 917, **964**
zones, **189–192**, *189–190*, 246
Active Directory Migration Tool (ADMT), 978,
1035–1036
auditing, **1040**
command-line, **1048–1050**
computer accounts, **1053–1054**, *1053*
Domain Admins groups for, **1039–1040**
domains renaming. *See* domains
group and user migration, **1044–1048**,
1044–1048
installing, **1040–1041**
interfaces, **1043–1044**
local profiles, **1050–1053**, *1051–1052*
PES, **1040–1041**
resource access in, **1050**
rollback plans, **1054**
setup example, **1037–1038**
starting up, **1042–1043**, *1043*
trusts, **1038–1039**, *1039*
Active Directory Migration Tool Agent Dialog
window, 1052–1053, *1052–1053*
Active Directory Object Type page, 261
Active Directory Recovery Mode (ADRM),
803–804

Active Directory Search tool
printer deployment, **562–565**, *562–565*
shares, 439, *440*
Active Directory Service (ADS) member
servers, 1154
Active Directory Services Interface (ADSI)
OUs, 255–256
passwords, 274, *274*
site replication, 912
Active Directory Sites and Services, 913, *913*
Default-First-Site-Name, 915
printer location, 551
RODCs, 951
site links, 922
site replication, 925, *925*
Active Directory Users and Computers (ADUC)
accounts, **257–258**, *257–258*
for auditing, 1040
decommissioning domain controllers, 264
delegation of control, 261
DNs, 291
domains, 976
functional levels, 266, 945, 986–987
joining, 648
time, 269, *270*
user accounts, 285–289, *286–287*, *289*,
296, 307
event log subscriptions, 775
FSMO roles, 1002
groups, 260
home directories, 1304
locked-out accounts, 331–332
OUs, **251–252**, *251–252*, 422–423, 426–427, *426*
passwords, 330–331
PSOs, 276, *276*
RID FSMOs, 1000, *1000*
RODCs, 951, 955, 957, 959
shares, 439
trusts, 1014
Active Directory Web Services (ADWS), 84, 343
Active Server Pages (ASP), 686, **688**
AD. *See* Active Directory
ADAC (Active Directory Administrative Center),
84, 333
home directories, 1304
navigating, **336–343**, *336–343*
as new feature, **4–5**, *5*
overview, **333–336**, *334–336*
Add a new printer using an existing port
option, 548
Add a Script dialog box, 568, *568*, 1356, *1356*

Add a TCP/IP or Web Services Printer by IP address or hostname option, 548
Add a Wireless Device To The Network Wizard, 666
Add-ADGroupMember cmdlet, 352–353
Add dialog box for groups, 423
Add EAP dialog box, 874
Add features task, 46
Add Features Wizard
    GPMC, 406, *407*
    .NET Framework, 1155, *1156*
    Remote Server Administration Tools, 131, *131*
    Server Backup, 795
    Server Manager, 76–77, *76–77*
    SMTP, 727–728
Add FTP Site Publishing dialog box, 733–734, *733–734*
Add Group dialog box, 391
Add Hardware Wizard
    local area connections, 635, 637
    virtual machines, 1235
Add Network Location Wizard, 667, 669, *670*, 678, *678*
Add Network Place Wizard, 672, 678–679, *679*
Add or Remove Snap-ins dialog box
    LGPOs, 363–364
    security templates, 390
Add Printer Driver Wizard, 152, *152*
Add Printer window, 561–562, *561*
Add Printer Wizard, 664–665, *664–665*, 674–675, *674–675*
Add Remove Programs Wizard, 1087
Add/Remove Servers page, 557
Add/Remove Snap-in window, 131, 995
Add Role Service dialog box, 703, *703*
Add Role Wizard
    domains, 981–982
    IIS, 1155
    Server Manager, 127, 182, 697
Add roles task, 46
Add Roles Wizard, 59–63, *60–63*
    Hyper-V, 1224–1225, *1224–1226*
    NFS, 512
    Print and Document Services role, **544–545**, *545*
    RDS, 1085–1086, *1085–1086*
    Remote Desktop Gateway, 612
    RRAS, 838–841, *838–841*, 859, *859*
    WSUS, 1135–1138, *1137–1138*
add scope command, 145
add server command, 144
Add Server window, 131, *132*
Add Standalone Snap-in dialog box, 995

Add Virtual Directory dialog box, 712–713, *712*
Add Web Site dialog box, 714, *714*
Add-WindowsFeature cmdlet, 70–71, 699
Additional Domain Controller Options page
    RODCs, 953, *953*, 960
    second domain controllers, 249, *249*
Additional Drivers window, 554, *554*
Address Assignment Range page, 844, *844*
Address Resolution Protocol (ARP), **820–821**, *820*
Address Space Layout Randomization (ASLR), 1250
Address tab, 297, *298*
addresses
    IP. *See* IP addresses
    MAC, 819–820, 1263, 1266
ADDT (Active Directory Domains and Trusts) 1038
    domain functional levels, 528
    forest functional levels, 947, *947*, 989–990, *989*
    FSMO roles, 1002, *1002*
    trusts, 1009, 1013–1015, *1014*
AddWrkfl.aspx page, 1190
ADI (Active Directory Integrated)
    DNS, **264–265**, *265*, 917, **964**
    zones, **189–192**, *189–190*, 246
Admin logs, 758
ADMIN$ share, 449
AdminBaseObject (ABO), 690
administration
    delegating, **723–724**
    Group Policy, **410–412**, *411*
    separating, **285–286**
administrative (ADM) templates
    IE restrictions, **396–397**
    legacy, **394**, *395*
    new, **395–396**, *396*
    software restrictions, **397–398**, *398*
    time servers, **399**
Administrative Events Properties page, 748, *748*
Administrative Events view, 748
administrative shares, 449
administrative tools
    IIS, 688
    RRAS policies, 862, *862*
administrative workstations, 89
Administrator Tasks list, 1160
administrators
    accounts, **280–281**
    LGPOs, **362–363**, *363*
    passwords, 32, *32*, **117**, *117*
    roles, **83**
    trust involvement, **1011**

Administrators have full access; other users have no read and write option, 476
Administrators have full access; other users have read-only access option, 476
adminpak.msi package, 131
ADML files, **395–396**, *396*
ADMT. *See* Active Directory Migration Tool (ADMT)
ADMX files, **395–396**, *396*
adprep tool
    forest upgrades, 87
    in-place upgrades, **1025–1026**
    Recycle Bin preparation, 811
    RODCs, 944–945, **947–951**
    swing migration, 1028
ADPREP Warning dialog box, 949
ADRM (Active Directory Recovery Mode), 803–804
ADS (Active Directory Service) member servers, 1154
ADSI (Active Directory Services Interface)
    OUs, 255–256
    passwords, 274, *274*
    site replication, 912
adsiedit tool, 809
ADUC. *See* Active Directory Users and Computers (ADUC)
Advanced Features view, 296
advanced folder redirection, **1345–1346**, *1345–1346*
Advanced Password Replication Policy page, 957
Advanced permissions link for WSS documents, 1195
Advanced Subscription Settings dialog box, 770–771, *771, 776, 777*
Advanced tab
    ADMT, 1041
    local area connections, 637, 640, 642
    My Network Places icon, 661
    network resources connections, 671, 673
    permissions, 488
    printers, **581**, *581*
        available hours, **582–583**
        priorities, **583**
        searches, 564–565, *565*
        separator pages, **584–587**, *585*
        servers, **572–573**, *572*
        spooling, **583–584**
Advanced WSS installations, 1157
ADWS (Active Directory Web Services), 84, 343
AES encryption algorithm, 300–301
aggregate severity rating, 1130
aging caches, 523
AH (Authentication Header) protocol, 895

alerts for WSS documents, **1203–1204**
ALGs (Application Layer Gateways), **837**
Alias (CNAME) records, **196**
all 0s addresses, 826
all 1s addresses, 826
all-all-0s addresses, 827
all-all-1s addresses, 827
All Documents view, 1180
All Drivers printer filter, 589
All files and programs that users open from the share are automatically available offline option, 468
All Printers filter, 589
All users have read-only access option, 475
Allow Clients to Connect without Negotiating an Authentication Method option, 883
Allow connections from computers running any version of Remote Desktop (less secure) option, 57
Allow connections only from computers running Remote Desktop with Network Level Authentication (more secure) option, 57
Allow permissions
    assigning, **442**
    description, **480**
    precedence, **443**
    printers, 579
    RRAS, 867
Allow processing across a slow network connection option, 372
Allowed EAP Types setting, 866
allowed lists for RODCs, 941, **957**, *958*
Allowed RODC Password Replication group, **941–944**, *944*, 957
Always prompt for password setting, 1106
Analytic logs, 758
AND operations, 829
Anderson, Christa, 1069
anonymous website accounts, 722, 738
answer files
    creating, **92–106**, *93, 95–99*
    unattended scripts, 68
    using, **107–108**
antivirus settings, **1210**, *1210*
appcmd.exe command
    backups, 741
    FTP, 734
    server-level control, 709–711
    site-level control, 706
    website creation, 718
    WSS, 1151
AppData folder, 1310

Append Data permission, 483
Application and Services Logs option, 752
Application Layer Gateways (ALGs), **837**
Application log, 452, 752, **757–758**
Application Management page
 authentication, 1207
 Central Administration, 1161, *1161*, 1164,
  1167–1168
 quota limits, **1209**
 WSS features, 1208
Application Pool Defaults dialog box, 716, *716*,
 722, *722*
application silos, 1333
applicationhost.config file
 administration delegation, 724
 backups, 741–742
 feature delegation, 694
 FTP, **731–733**
 global settings, 708
 IIS, 701, 705–707
 NTFS permissions, 709
 sections, **710**
 websites, 718–719
 WSS, 1151
applications
 partitions, **210**, 1029–1030
 pools, 722, *722*, 1165, *1165*
 RDS, **1068**, **1087**
 web, **686**, 708, **1164–1166**, *1164–1166*
Applications for Compatibility page, 1085
Apply Policy Before the Data Collector Starts
 option, 790
Archive the log when full, do not overwrite events
 option, 764
archives, websites, 721
ARP (Address Resolution Protocol), **820–821**, *820*
ARP tables, 820, *820*
ASLR (Address Space Layout
 Randomization), 1250
ASP (Active Server Pages), 686–687
 IIS integration, **688**
 role service, 705
 services, 702
ASP.NET Impersonate authentication, 738
.aspx format, 1152
Assess phase in patch management,
 1127–1128
Assign Memory page, 1231, *1232*
assigning permissions, **442**, **485–491**, *486–491*
atomic permissions, **481–483**
attached pages in site collections, 1168

Attribute Editor tab
 distinguished names, 291, *291*
 domain user accounts, 303, *304*, 309
attributes
 permissions, 483, 1312
 RODCs, 939–942
auditing
 Active Directory, **84**
 ADMT, **1040**
 infrastructure, 20
 printers, **579–580**, *580*
 web sites, **737–740**, *738*
Auditing tab, **579–580**, *580*
auditSystem configuration pass, 94
auditUser configuration pass, 94
Authenticated Users group, 378
authentication
 Active Directory, 85
 domains, 300, **971–972**
 fine-grained password policies, 3
 and FRS, 520
 FTP, 734, *734*
 IPSec, **896–897**
 RRAS, 866, 874, 887–888
 SMTP, **729**
 synchronization for, 269
 VPN, **882–885**, *883*, *885*
 web sites, **738**
 WSS, **1206–1207**
Authentication Header (AH) protocol, 895
Authentication Method page, 903,
 903, 1085
Authentication Type setting, 866
authoritative restores, **814–815**
authorization, FTP, 734, *734*
Autoconfiguration Enabled setting, 631
Automatic Classification tab, 459
automatic operations
 DNS configuration, **210–211**
 FSRM classification, 459
 server updates, **124–126**, *125*
 synchronization of Offline
  Files, 466
 updating and feedback, 46
Automatic Updates service, 124–125
Autoplay dialog box, 1240, *1241*
autoscaling
 transaction time, **167–173**, *168–170*
 troubleshooting, **171–172**
available printer hours, **582–583**
.avhd files, 1274

B

Back up Group Policy Object dialog box, 408
background operations
    GPO refresh, 370, 372
    printing, 583
    zone loading, **215**
backup domain controllers (BDCs), 186
Backup (volume snapshot) option, 1237
backups, **793–795**
    Active Directory, **809–810**, **813**
    and event log subscriptions, 767
    files and folders, **801–802**, *802*
    full servers, **795–798**, *796–798*
    GPOs, **408–409**, *409*
    Server Core, **157–162**
    virtual machines, 1237, **1274–1277**, *1276*
    web site data, **741–742**
    Windows Backup, **2–3**
Bandwidth Allocation Protocol (BAP), 871
bandwidth for replication
    Active Directory, **975**
    DFS, **507**
bare-metal approach, 1243
baseboard management controllers (BMCs), 735
baselines for data collector sets, 785, 788
Basic authentication, 738
Basic Encryption, 872
basic folder redirection, **1338–1343**, *1338–1343*
Basic WSS installations, 1157
batch timeouts for event log subscriptions, 771
batches for event log subscriptions, 771
BDCs (backup domain controllers), 186
best-effort protocols, 822
Best Practices Analyzer, 49
.bin files, 1274
binary AND operations, 829
BIND DNS servers, 183
bindings
    IIS, 708
    site, unique, 722
BIOS for virtual machines, 1235
BitLocker Drive Encryption technology, **461**
    enabling, **463–464**, *463–465*
    hardware requirements, **461–462**
    recovery keys, **462–463**
BitLocker To Go, 461, **465**
blobs, 646
block transmissions security level, **894**
Blocked File Types page, 1208, *1209*
blocking GPO inheritance, **380–381**

BMCs (baseboard management controllers), 735
boot process for hypervisors, **1245**
BranchCache, 176
    for Network Files, 433
    working with, **466–467**
bridgehead servers, 912–913, **927**, *928*
bridges for sites, 912
broadcast addresses, **827**
broadcast-based protocols, 821
Browse for Printer page, 674, *674*
Browse for Shared Folders dialog box, 504, *504*
Browser-enabled Documents Advanced
    Setting, 1183
By Log and By Source filtering options, 754

C

C$ share, 449
C&P (clean and pristine) migration, **1032–1036**
CA certificates, **881**, 884
cached credentials
    RODCs, 940–941
    sites, **917–918**, *918*
caches
    client-side, 1074
    FRS, 523
    on networks, 176
    Offline Files, 467, *467*
caching-only servers, 186
Caching tab, 467, *467*
cacls.exe utility, 149–150
Calendar view for WSS, 1180
cards, monitoring, **850–851**, *850*
CAs (certificate authorities), 1058
case sensitivity
    PowerShell, 255
    XML tags, 750
catalog files, 95–96, *95–96*
CCS64 emulator, 1216
CDs/DVDs for answer files, 107
Central Administration, **1159–1161**, *1160–1161*
    authentication, 1207
    blocked files, 1208
    document conversion, 1211
    documents search indexes, 1202
    features, 1208
    quota limits, **1209**
    site collections, 1167–1169
    virus protection, 1210, *1210*
    web applications, 1164, 1166
    website provisioning, 1162

centralized application deployment, **1068**
certificate authorities (CAs), 1058
certificate revocation lists (CRLs), 1058
Certificate Store page, 881
certificates
    domain user accounts, 304, *305*
    IPSec, 896
    RemoteApp applications, 1096, *1096*
    self-signed, 1105
    Server Core, **133–135**, *134*
    VPNs, **878–882**, *879*
certutil command, 133, *134*, 137
CGI (Common Gateway Interface), 686
Challenge Handshake Authentication Protocol
    (CHAP), 883
Change Password dialog box, 657–658, *657–658*
Change permission, 441, 478, 577
Change Permissions permission, 483
Change Type setting, 1203
changes in Windows Server 2008, **17–18**
    64-bit support, **21**
    installation requirements, **19–21**
    media, **18–19**
CHAP (Challenge Handshake Authentication
    Protocol), 883
checking in and out library documents, **1187–1188**
checksums in FRS, 522–523
child domains, 982–983, *982–983*
child partitions, **1248–1249**
chkdsk tool, 1253
Choose a connection option page, 876
Choose a Deployment Configuration page
    DCPromo, 242
    RODCs, 952, *952*, 961
    second domain controllers, 248
Choose Action dialog box, 1259
Choose Languages page, 1142, *1142*
Choose Upstream Server page, 1141, *1142*
CIDR (Classless InterDomain Routing) format,
    822, 825
    private addresses, **830**
    subnets, 919
cl command, **766**
classes of IP addresses, **825–826**
classic application pool mode, 689, 1150
Classless InterDomain Routing (CIDR) format,
    822, 825
    private addresses, **830**
    subnets, 919
clean and pristine (C&P) migration,
    1032–1036

clean installations, **23–33**, *24–33*
cleaning up profiles, **1331**
clearing logs, **766**
CLI. *See* command line
Client Compatible encryption, 1106
client connections to servers, **627–628**
    client-side software requirements, **628–629**
    domain and local accounts, **629–630**
    domain user password changes, **653–659**,
        655–659
    joining domains, **642**
        Windows 7, **643–649**, *643–645*, *649*
        Windows 2000, **652–653**
        Windows Vista, **649–651**, *649–651*
        Windows XP, **651–652**, *651–652*
    local area connections
        verifying, **630–632**, *631*
        Windows 7, **634–637**, *634–636*
        Windows 2000, **642**
        Windows Vista, **637–640**, *637–639*
        Windows XP, **640–642**, *640–641*
    network resources, **659–660**
        Windows 2000, **679–680**
        Windows Vista, **660–671**, *661–665*,
          667–671
        Windows XP, **671–679**, *672–679*
    testing with ping, **632–634**, *633–634*
Client for Microsoft Networks, 630
Client (Respond Only) policy, 899
Client Settings tab, **1108–1109**, *1109*
client-side caching, 1074
client-side extension (CSE) DLLs, 360
client-side sockets, 834
clients
    closest sites, **929–931**, *929*, *931*
    DNS, **203**
        configuring, **206–208**, *206–207*
        dynamic updates, **208–209**, *209*
        hostname resolution, **203–206**, *204*
    KMS server, **156–157**
    Mac OS X. *See* Mac OS X clients
    NFS, 511
    printer deployment, **561**
        Active Directory search, **562–565**, *562–565*
        GPOs, **565–568**, *566–568*
        manual process, **561–562**, *561*
        viewing, **568–569**
    RDS, **1079–1080**, **1108–1109**, *1109*
    server connections. *See* client connections
        to servers
    thin-client sessions, **1072–1075**, *1073*

VPN
authentication, 882–884, 883
configuration and connections, 875–877, 875–877
WSS software, 1210–1213, 1212
WSUS, 1143–1145, 1144–1145
closed sets in intraforest migrations, 1033
CLOSED states, 835
closest sites for clients, 929–931, 929, 931
closing command prompt, 116–117
cluster shared volumes (CSVs), 1281, 1285
clustering virtual machines, 1281
cmdkey command, 130
cmdlets, 5, 69
CN (component name), 289
CNAME (Alias) records, 196
code access security, 739–740
Cogswell, Bryce, 480
collections, provisioning, 1167–1170, 1167–1169
collector computers for events, 766, 766, 772–773
collector-initiated subscriptions
configuring, 767–768, 768
creating, 773–777, 774–777
collector sets, 783
reports, 789–791, 789–790
system, 783–785, 784–785
user-defined, 785–788, 787, 789
Colors tab, 114, 115
columns in WSS documents, 1176–1182, 1177–1180
COM ports for virtual machines, 1236
COM+ tab, 303, 304
combining permissions, 445–446
comma-separated value (CSV) files, 346, 349
command line
ADMT, 1044, 1048–1050
domain user accounts, 309–311
full server backups, 798, 798
full server restores, 801
groups, 317, 328–330
IIS installation, 698–699
IIS module management, 706
local user accounts, 284
printer additions, 663, 663, 674
Remote Desktop Services Manager, 1102–1103
server configuration, 57
website creation, 717–718
WSS configuration, 1159
Command-Line Reference A-Z, 118
command prompt, closing, 116–117

commands
finding, 118
remote, 132–133, 132
syntax, 118–119
Commodore 64 emulator, 1216
Common Gateway Interface (CGI), 686
Common Queries tab, 479
common shares, 449
compaction of virtual disks, 1258, 1258
Company Information page, 1114
compatibility
ADMT, 1036
operating systems, 232–233, 234
RDS applications, 1082
SMB 2.0, 459–460
upgrade installations, 42–43, 42–43
WSS, 1156
complex passwords, 381–382
complexity from server virtualization, 1218
compmgmt.msc snap-in, 10
compmgmtlaucher.exe utility, 48
component name (CN), 289
components in answer file, 96–100, 97–98
Compound TCP, 169
compression
FRS, 519
RDC, 524
site replication, 911–912
computer accounts migration, 1053–1054, 1053
computer certificates, 880–881
Computer Configuration node, 359, 371, 371
Computer Configuration settings, 368, 383–386
Computer Management console, 117
local user accounts, 280, 280, 283, 283
permissions, 477
shares, 474–476, 474–476
Computer Name Changes dialog box, 652, 652
Computer Name/Domain Changes dialog box, 650–651, 650
Computer Name tab, 54–56, 54
DNS, 207–208
domains, 263, 263, 650–651, 650
Computer window, 671, 671
computers
joining to domains. See joining domains
names, 46, 53–56, 54
domains, 263, 263
providing, 124
remote desktop, 615
renaming, 268
shared folders, 475
refresh intervals, 371

concurrent users licensing, 438, **474**
conditional forwarders, **184–185**, *185–186*
conditions
　　RRAS policies, **862–865**
　　task events, 763
conficker virus, **221**
Configuration page for RRAS, 859, *860*
Configuration Authentication Methods page, 883, *883*
configuration partitions, 970
configuration passes in installation, **92–94**
Configuration section in Server Manager, 80
Configure Authentication Methods page, 874, *874*
Configure Automatic Updates option, 1144
Configure Client Experience page, 1085, *1086*
Configure Constraints page, 874
Configure Distribution Package page, 1099, *1099*
Configure Local File Logging page, 885, *885*
Configure Native Modules dialog box, 704, *704, 707, 707*
Configure Networking page, 1232, *1233*
Configure networking task, 46
Configure Settings page, 874
Configure Storage Usage Monitoring page, 433, *434*
Configure Windows Firewall task, 47, *47*
Configure Windows SharePoint Services Search Service Settings page, 1202–1203
Confirm Installation Selections page, 878
Conflict Management page, 1048, *1049*
conflicts
　　ADMT, 1048, *1049*
　　credentials, **448**
　　FRS, **519**
　　permissions, **491**
　　roles, 61
　　schemas, **997–998**
Connect to Server screen, 1122, *1122*
Connect to Upstream Server page, 1141
Connect Virtual Hard Disk page, 1232, *1233*
Connection Method page, 1114
Connection Properties category, 865–866
connections
　　Active Directory, **974**
　　DFS replication, 507–508
　　IIS Manager, 711–714, *711*
　　Mac OS X client
　　　　to domains, **1120–1121**, *1121*
　　　　file shares, **1122**, *1122*
　　　　printers, **1122–1123**, *1123*
　　networks, **50**, *50*
　　printers, **558**

RDS sessions, **1087–1089**, *1088–1089*
RRAS, 865–866, **881–882**
to shares, **446–449**, *446–447*
TCP, 818
virtual switches to virtual machines, **1266–1268**, *1267–1268*
web sites, **737–740**, *738*
Windows clients to servers. *See* client connections to servers
Connections setting
　　DFS replication, 507–508
　　IIS Manager, 711–714, *711*
Connections to Microsoft Routing and Remote Access Service Policy, 862
Connections to Other Access Servers policy, 862
Connectivity Test Succeeded dialog box, 774
consistent desktop and Start menu, 398
consolidated enterprise resources, **509**
constraints in RRAS policies, 863, **869–870**, *869*
contacts, 326
Content Approval page, 1185, *1186*
content in WSS
　　limiting, **1208–1210**, *1209–1210*
　　type, 1173, **1183–1184**, *1183*, **1201–1202**
contig.exe tool, 1257, *1257*
continuous replication, 520
Control access through NPS Network Policy option, 867
control delegation. *See* Active Directory
Control Panel
　　BitLocker Drive Encryption, 463–464
　　Group Policy for, **1350**
　　IIS, 696
controllers
　　domain. *See* domain controllers (DCs)
　　virtual machines, 1235–1236, **1251–1253**, *1254*
copy-and-paste operations for SYSVOL, 518
Copy To dialog box, 1322–1323, *1323*
copying
　　Event Viewer views, **751–752**, *752*
　　mandatory profiles, 1322–1323, *1323*
costs
　　power, 1069
　　server virtualization, 1217
　　sites, 914, **923–924**, *924*, **929–931**, *929, 931*
counters, performance, 781, 787, *787*
CPU tab, 782
Create a Basic Task Wizard, 760, *761*
Create a folder for each user under the root path option, 1340
Create a new port and add a new printer option, 548

Create a Shared a Folder Wizard, 475–476, *475–476*
Create Cluster Wizard, 1285, *1285*
Create Files permission, 483
Create Folders permission, 483
Create page for document libraries, 1171
create partition primary command, 147
Create Site page, 1169
Create the Data Collector Set page, 786
CreatePartitions component in answer files, 100
Credential Security Service Provider
     (CredSSP), 1083
credentials. *See also* passwords; usernames
     cached, **917–918**, *918*, 940–941
     conflicts, **448**
     domains, 644–645, *645*, 651–652, 982, *982*
     RODCs, 952, *953*, 959, 961, *962*
CredSSP (Credential Security Service
     Provider), 1083
Critical events, 747
critical volumes backup, 810
CRLs (certificate revocation lists), 1058
cross-site groups, 1197
cryptography algorithms
     ADMT, **1040**
     single-domain forests, 233
cscript command, 122
CSE (client-side extension) DLLs, 360
CSV (comma-separated value) files, 346, 349
CSVs (cluster shared volumes), 1281, 1285
cumulative GPOs, **361**
cumulative permissions, **442–443**, *443*, **577**
current state in virtual machines, 1270
custom filters for printers, 546, **588–590**, *589–590*
Custom IPSec policy setting, 888
Custom View Properties page, 749, *749*
custom views in Event Viewer, **748**
     copying, **751–752**, *752*
     creating, **752–753**, *753*
     exporting and importing, **755–756**, *756*
     filtering, **753–755**, *754*
     properties, **748–749**, *748–749*
Customize Start Menu dialog box, 661, *661*

D

D$ share, 449
DAC (discretionary access control) model, 442
DACLs (discretionary access control lists), 442
data collector sets, **783**
     reports, **789–791**, *789–790*
     system, **783–785**, *784–785*
     user-defined, **785–788**, *787*, *789*

Data Exchange option, 1237
Data Exchange service, 1249
Data Execution Prevention (DEP), 1218–1219
Data Location tab, 1157
Data Manager tab, 789–790, *789*
data parameter for virtual machines, 1270
Database Mounting Tool, 84
Database Options page, 1140, *1140*
databases
     Access, **1212–1213**
     Active Directory, **805–807**
     security templates, **392–393**
     WSUS, 1140, *1140*
Datasheet view in WSS, 1180
Day and Time Restrictions screen, 865, *865*
DC (domain component) in domain user
     accounts, 289
DcDiag command
     domain renaming, 1063
     events, 747
     swing migration, 1030
     working with, **223–224**
dclist.xml file, 1062
DCPromo, 227
     DNS service, 210
     domain controllers
          decommissioning, 264, **993**
          second, 245, **248–250**, *248–249*
          site, 914
     domains, 969–970, 980–984, *981*
     FRS, **521–522**
     new features, 5
     parameters, 244
     RODCs, **954–955**, 960–963, *962–963*
     Server Core, 142
     single-domain forests
          creating, 231–241, *232*
          process, **242–244**, *242–243*, *245*
     swing migration, 1029, 1031
     trusts, 1014
DCs. *See* domain controllers (DCs)
DDFS (Domain Distributed File System), 1055, 1057
DDNS (Dynamic DNS) update protocol, 182,
     208–209, *209*
Debug Logging tab, 219, *220*
debug logs, 219, *220*, 758, 892
decimal dot notation, 193
decommissioning domain controllers, **263–264**, **993**
Default Domain Controller Policies policy, 1040
Default gateway setting, 631–632
default.htm web page, 685

defaults
    address selection, 195
    domain policies, 229
    IPSec policies, **899**
    local groups, 312, *312*
    permissions, **513**
    profiles, **1329–1330**
    separator pages, 585
    site links, 920
    sites, 914
defining
    permissions, **477–480**, *478–479*
    sites, **915–916**, *915*
defragmenting Active Directory, **804–805**
delegation
    Active Directory. *See* Active Directory
    DNS, 181
    domain user accounts, 306
    GPOs, 368, *368*, 377
    Group Policy administration,
      410–412, *411*
    IIS features, **694–695**
    OUs, **251**
    permissions, 572, **579**
    RODC administration, **943–944**
    subdomains, **211**, **225**
    website administration, **723–724**
Delegation of Control Wizard, 261–262, *261–262*,
    423–424, *423–424*, 429
Delegation of RODC Installation and
    Administration page, 954, *954*, 960
Delegation tab, 368, *368*, 377
Delete option for GPOs, 409
Delete permission, 483
Delete Saved Credentials option, 1229
Delete Subfolders and Files permission, 483
Deleted Objects container, 811
deleting
    credentials, 1229
    GPOs, 409
    mapped drives, 669
    objects, **310–311**
    printers, **548**
    roles, **72–75**, *72–73*
    SharePoint group members, 1199
    SharePoint groups, 1198
delivering
    event log subscriptions, **770–771**, *771*
    file reports, 456
    web pages, **685**
Delivery tab, 456

demilitarized zones (DMZs)
    hosts, 837
    IIS, 695
    VPNs, 853
demoting DCs, 5
denied lists, 941
Denied RODC Password Replication group,
    941–943, *943*, 957.
deny by default, 836
Deny permissions
    assigning, **442**
    description, **480**
    managing, **492**, *492*
    precedence, **443**
    printers, 579
    RRAS, 866–868
DEP (Data Execution Prevention), 1218–1219
dependencies
    FRS, **520**
    roles, 61
Deploy GPO screen, 566
Deploy phase in patch management, 1131
Deploy with Group Policy screen, 565, *566*
deployed printers, 547
deployment
    applications, **1068**
    patch management, **1131**
    printers, **561**
      Active Directory search, **562–565**,
        562–565
      GPOs, **565–568**, *566–568*
      manual process, **561–562**, *561*
      viewing, **568–569**
    RemoteApp applications, **1071**
    second domain controllers, **246**, *247*
    single-domain forests, 233
    websites, **720–721**
    WSUS scenarios, **1134–1135**, *1135*
Description tab, 901
descriptions
    content types, 1184
    IPSec policies, 901
    SharePoint groups, 1198
    site collections, 1167, 1169
desktop
    consistent, 398
    flexible, **1295–1297**
    Group Policy for, **1347–1352**
    RDC. *See* Remote Desktop
"Destination host unreachable"
    message, 633

Details settings
    GPOs, 367, *367*
    Group Policy, 415–416
    Hyper-V, 1226
    .rdp files for, 1098
detecting network printers, **548–551**, *549–551*
device drivers. *See* drivers
Device Manager
    local area connections, 635, 637, 642
    opening, 630
    virtual machines, 1240
Devices and Printers applet, 663
DFS. *See* Distributed File System (DFS)
DFS Management screen, 499–500, *500*, 504, *505*
DFSR. *See* Distributed File System
    Replication (DFSR)
dfsrmig utility, 525–527
    getglobalstate, **529**, *529*, 532, *532*, 534, *534*
    getmigrationstate, 529–530, *530*, 532–535,
        533, *535*
    setglobalstate, 528, *529*, 532, *532*, 534, *534*
DHCP. *See* Dynamic Host Configuration
    Protocol (DHCP)
DHCP Enabled setting, 631
DHCP Management Console, 145
DHCP Server Tools feature, 131
DHTML (Dynamic HTML), 684
Diagnostic Report Wizard, 531, *531*
Diagnostics section in Server manager, 80
Dial-in tab
    local user accounts, **296**, *296*
    RRAS policies, 867, *868*
differencing disks, 1253, **1255–1257**
Differentiated Services Code Point (DSCP)
    value, 173
Digest authentication, 695, 738
digital certificates. *See* certificates
Digital Signature Settings page, 1096
Digitally sign communications (always) policy, 1118
Digitally sign communications (if client agrees)
    policy, 1118
digitally signing packets, 460–461
dir command, 133
DirectAccess connectivity, 177
directed state, migrating to, **532–533**, *532–533*
direction of trusts, **1010**, *1010*
directories. *See* folders; home directories
Directory Integrated zones, **189–192**, *189–190*
Directory Services Restore Mode (DSRM), **241**,
    241, 804
Directory Services Restore Mode Administrator
    Password page, 243, 963

Directory tab for user-defined data collector sets, 786
dirquota.exe tool, 452
Disable-ADAccount cmdlet, 351
disabling
    IIS, 389–390
    replication groups, **507–508**
    spooling, 584
    users, 311, **351–355**
    WSS permissions inheritance,
        1200–1201, *1201*
disaster recovery in single-domain forests, 231
Discard Check Out option, 1188
disconnected sessions, 293
discretionary access control (DAC) model, 442
discretionary access control lists (DACLs), 442
Disk Management Console, 146
Disk Manager, 1253, 1258, *1258*, 1285, 1291
Disk subcomponent in answer files, 100
DiskPart command, 146–147
disks
    for answer files, 100, 107
    RDS servers, **1077**
    requirements, 19–20
    virtual. *See* virtual disks
dism command, 10, 127–128, 198
display protocols for thin-client sessions,
    1074–1075
display requirements, 20
displayed columns in Event Viewer, **756**, *757*
distinguished names (DNs)
    domain user accounts, 289
    LDAP, **252–253**, 948
    Mac connections, 1121
    obtaining, 291, *291*
    viewing, 933
    working with, 932
Distributed Cache mode, 467
distributed configuration model, **688**
Distributed File System (DFS), 432, **496**, *497*, 524
    consolidated enterprise resources, **509**
    FRS requirements and dependencies, **520**
    life-cycle management, **510**
    replications. *See* Distributed File System
        Replication (DFSR)
    roots, 496–497
        creating, **499–503**, *500–503*
        links to, **503–504**, *504*
    security requirements, 509
    sharing replicated folders, **508–509**
    stand-alone vs. domain-based, **498–499**
    terminology, **496–497**

Distributed File System Replication (DFSR), 432, **496**, 517
    configuring, **504–506**
    managing, **507–510**
    migrating to, **525**
    migration states, **525**
        eliminated, **534–536**, *534–536*
        prepared, **527–531**, *528–531*
        redirected, **532–533**, *532–533*
        stable, **525–526**
        transition, **526**, *526*
    overview, **506**, **524–525**
Distributed Scan Server service, 544
distribution groups, 260, **322**
djoin.exe utility, **645–649**, *649*
DLLs
    CSE, 360
    unregistering, 996
DMZs (demilitarized zones)
    hosts, 837
    IIS, 695
    VPNs, 853
DNs. *See* distinguished names (DNs)
DNS. *See* Domain Name System (DNS)
DNS Management Console, **219–221**, *220*
DNS Suffix setting, 631
DNS tab
    clients, 207, *207*
    DHCP, 209, *209*
    local area connections, 637, 640, 642
dnscmd command, 143
    diagnostic commands, **220**
    directory partitions, 190–191
    forwarders, 199
    global query block lists, 213–214
    GlobalNames feature, 214
    records, 202
    swing migration, 1029–1030
    zones, 200–201
DNSLint tool, **225**
DNSSec zones, **215**
Do not apply during periodic background processing option, 372
Do not overwrite events (Clear logs manually) option, 764
Do not require Kerberos preauthentication option, 301
Do not use IRM on this server option, 1205
Document Library Settings page, 1177, 1180, **1182–1183**
    Content Type, **1183–1184**, *1183*
    versioning, **1185–1188**, *1186–1187*

Document Library template, 1170
documents
    printer permissions, 577
    WSS. *See* Windows SharePoint Services 3.0 (WSSv3)
dollar signs ($) for separator pages, 586–587
domain accounts
    client connections to servers, **629–630**
    creating, **284–289**, *286–289*
    local computer groups, **643**
    multiple. *See* multiple domains
    password changing, **653–659**, *655–659*
    properties, **296–311**, *297–299*, *301–309*
Domain Admins group, 420, **1039–1040**
domain-based DFS, **498–499**
domain-based groups
    nested, 327
    policies, 365, **393**
domain component (DC) in domain user accounts, 289
domain controllers (DCs), 5
    bridgehead servers, **927**, *928*
    decommissioning, **263–264**, **993**
    and DNS servers, **917**
    global catalog servers, 918, *918*
    multiple, **977**
    prestaging, **521–522**
    read-only. *See* read-only domain controllers (RODCs)
    refresh intervals, 371
    in remote locations, **916–919**, *918–919*
    renaming, **268**
    replicating, 1262
    RODCs, 2
    second domains
        adding, **245–250**, *246–249*
        preparing for, **981**, *981*
    security, 968
    Server Core, **142–143**
    sites, 910, 913–914
    swing migration, **1028–1029**
Domain Distributed File System (DDFS), 1055, 1057
domain.msc console, 1038
Domain Name System (DNS), **179**, 181
    and Active Directory, **209–215**, *214–215*, **234–235**, *235*
    ADI, **264–265**, *265*, 917, **964**
    background zone loading, **215**
    clients, **203**
        configuring, **206–208**, *206–207*
        dynamic updates, **208–209**, *209*
        hostname resolution, **203–206**, *204*

components, **179**
configuring, **210–211**
DCDiag for, **223–224**
DNS Management Console and DNSCmd for, **219–221**, *220*
DNSLint for, **225**
external domains, **216–217**
external namespaces, **218–219**, *218*
forwarders, 984, *985*
fundamental concepts, **180–182**, *180–181*
global query block lists, **213–214**
GlobalNames feature, **214–215**, *214–215*
infrastructure
    Active Directory design, **979**
    and FRS, 520
    in-place upgrades, 1024
Internet-based resolution, **216–219**, *218*
new features, **212**
nslookup for, **221–223**
record types, **196–198**, *197*
on RODCs, **963–964**, *963*
second domain controllers, **246–247**, *247*
Server Core, **142–143**, **198–203**
servers, **179**, **182–183**
    and DCs, **917**
    integrating, **183–186**, *183–186*
    local area connections, 631–632
    Mac connections, 1120
swing migration, **1028**
troubleshooting, **219–225**, *220*
zones. *See* zones
domain naming FSMOs, **991–992**, **999**
Domain Rename tool, 235
domainlist.xml file, 1059, 1062
domains, 419, **967**
    accounts. *See* domain accounts
    Active Directory, 228
    ADI DNS troubleshooting, **264–265**, *265*
    controllers. *See* domain controllers (DCs)
    functional levels
        overview, **236–238**
        raising, **265–268**, *266–267*, **528**, *528*
        RODC, **944–946**, *946*
        working with, **986–988**, *987*
    in-place upgrades, **1025–1026**
    joining. *See* joining domains
    local groups, 260, 322
        adding members to, 318
        intraforest migrations, 1033
    Mac connections to, **1120–1121**, *1121*
    misspelled, **985**

multimaster replication, **968–970**
multiple. *See* multiple domains
names, **979**
renaming, **1054–1055**
    business operations, **1055–1056**
    business risks, **1056**
    difficulties, **235**
    preparation phase, **1057–1058**
    process, **1059–1065**
    requirements, **1055**
    steps, **1056**
restartable services, **84**
security, **968–969**
SMTP servers, **728–729**
swing migration, 1028
time management, **269–271**, *270*
DOS, 174
dotted quads, 818
Download and install updates task, 46
downloading server updates, **126**
drivers
    adding, 571
    client connections to servers, 628
    printers. *See* printers
    stores, **554–555**, *554*
    upgrade installations, 36, 39
Drivers tab, 571
drives
    clean installation options, 29–30, *29*
    mapping
        to drive letters, **447**, *447*
        to hidden shares, 495, *495*
        just-in-time, 406
        to shared folders, **666–669**, *667–669*, **675–678**,
            676–677
dsa.msc file, 385
dsacls command, 429
dsadd command
    accounts, **258–259**, *259*
    dsadd group, 328–329
    dsadd user, 288–289
    OUs, **253–254**
dsamain.exe tool, 84, **808–809**
DSCP (Differentiated Services Code Point)
    value, 173
dsmod group command, 329
dsmod user command
    domain accounts, 309
    home directories, 1308
    passwords, 331
    roaming profile shares, 1315

DSMove tool, 269
dsquery command, 1292
    dsquery server, 948
    dsquery user, 309, 311
DSRM (Directory Services Restore Mode), **241**, *241*, 804
dsrm command, 330
    Active Directory backups, 813–814
    domain user accounts, 311
DVD-ROM
    for installation, 23
    requirements, 19–20
DVDBURN tool, 89
Dynamic bandwidth control using BAP or BACP option, 891
dynamic disks, **1252**, 1257
Dynamic DNS (DDNS) update protocol, 182, **208–209**, *209*
Dynamic Host Configuration Protocol (DHCP)
    client connections to servers, 629
    local area connections, 631
    managing, **131–132**, *132*
    Network Access Protection for, **177**
    Server Core, **143–146**
    servers
        DDNS process, 209
        RRAS, 888–889
Dynamic HTML (DHTML), 684
dynamic IT, 1295
dynamic updates for DNS clients, **208–209**, *209*
dynamic web pages, **685–687**

E

E-mail Message tab, **451–452**, *452*
EAP (Extensible Authentication Protocol), 866, 882, 884
EAP-MS-CHAP-v2 authentication, **884**
Easy Print feature, **1082**
echo command, 149
Edit Anonymous Authentication Credentials dialog box, 723, *723*
Edit Authentication page, 1207
Edit Disk Wizard, 1230, 1259
Edit Items page, 1179
Edit Schedule dialog box, 507
Edit Settings properties
    RD Connection Broker tab, **1112**
    Remote Desktop Session Host Configuration console, **1111–1112**, *1111–1112*
editing Registry, **120**

effective permissions, **493–494**, *493*
EIDE (Enhanced Integrated Drive Electronics) disks, 1077
el command, 763–764
elements in XML, 705
eliminated state, migrating to, 525, **534–536**, *536*
Email Notifications tab, 458
emails
    as event response, 760
    File Server Resource Manager, 458
    SMTP, **729–730**, *730*
empty roots in Active Directory, **976–977**
Enable-ADAccount cmdlet, 351
Enable-ADOptionalFeature cmdlet, 812
Enable advanced printing features option, 584
Enable automatic updating and feedback task, 46
Enable broadcast name resolution option, 889
Enable Remote Desktop task, 46
enabling
    Offline Files, **467–468**, *467*
    Remote Desktop, 46, **57**, *58*, **128–129**
    user accounts, **351**
encrypt transmissions security level, **894–895**
Encrypted Authentication (CHAP) option, 883
encrypted RPC, 519
encryption
    BitLocker Drive Encryption, **461–465**, *462–465*
    domain accounts, 300–301
    IPSec, **894–896**, 901
    RDS, **1105–1106**
    RRAS, **872**, 874
end user license agreement (EULA)
    clean installations, 28, *28*
    upgrade installations, 40, *41*
    WAIK, 89, *90*
    WSS, 1157
ending processes, 782
Enforce password history option, 399, 654
Enhanced Integrated Drive Electronics (EIDE) disks, 1077
Enhanced Unix support in NFS, 510
enlightened kernels, 1248
enlightened OS, 1248
Enterprise Admins group, **973**
Enterprise Remote Access screen, 1093, 1095, *1095*
Environment tab
    local user accounts, **292**, *292*
    RDP-Tcp Properties, **1107**, *1107*
environments issues, RDS for, **1068–1069**
epl command, **765–766**
Error events, 747

error indication in TCP, 833
error status for roles, 78, *78*
escape characters for separator pages, 585 586
ESENT (extensible storage engine), 805
Esentutl.exe program, 806
ESTABLISHED state, 834
EULA. *See* end user license agreement (EULA)
Evaluate and Plan phase in patch
    management, **1130**
event IDs, 755
Event Log category, 388, 391
Event Log Readers group, 768, 770, 776, *776*
Event Log tab, **452**, *453*
Event Viewer, **745–747**, *746*
    displayed columns, **756**, *757*
    event levels, **747**
    Group Policy, **416**
    logs, **757–760**, *758*, *760*
    new features, **12**
    roles, 79, *79*
    with Server Core, **763–766**
    tasks attached to events, **760–763**, *761–762*
    views, **748**
        copying, **751–752**, *752*
        creating, **752–753**, *753*
        exporting and importing, **755–756**, *756*
        filtering, **753–755**, *754*
        properties, **748–749**, *748–749*
Event Viewer logs, 219
events
    forwarding, **777–780**, *778*
    logs. *See* logs
    roles, 79, *79*
Everyone group, 478
Excel spreadsheets, **1212**
Exceptions tab, 513–514, 1041
Exclusions tab, 802
executables, 1074
eXecute Disable (XD) bit, 1219
Execute File permission, 482
Explorer for shared folders, **473**, *473*
Explorer view for WSS, 1180
Export Custom View File dialog box, 756, *756*
Export Wizard, 1270
exporting
    Event Viewer views, **755–756**, *756*
    logs, **765–766**
    printers, 573
    virtual machines, **1270–1274**, *1272–1274*
extended attributes, 483
extending schemas, 229

Extensible Authentication Protocol (EAP), 866,
    882, 884
Extensible Markup Language. *See* XML (Extensible
    Markup Language)
extensible storage engine (ESENT), 805
Extensions tab, 879, *879*
external DNS domains, **216–217**
external namespaces, **218–219**, *218*
external switches, 1263–1264, *1263*
external trusts, **1012**
external virtual networks, **1228**

F

fail closed devices, 836
failover clustering
    server virtualization, 1222
    virtual machines, 1281, 1284–1287, *1285*
Failover Clustering Manager, 1284–1287
failover events, 1281
FastCGI, 14
FAT (File Allocation Table) file system, 1149
fault-tolerant replication path, 520
Favorites folder, 1310
features
    adding, **75–78**, *75–77*, **127–128**
    defined, 58
    IIS, 690, **694–695**
    printers, 564, *564*, 673, *673*
    removing, **75–78**, *75–77*
    Server Core, **141–142**
    troubleshooting, **78–80**, *78–80*
    WSS
        managing, **1207–1208**
        overview, **1149–1151**
Features tab
    network resources connections, 673
    printer searches, 564, *564*
    printers, 673, *673*
feeds, RSS, **1204**, *1204*
File Allocation Table (FAT) file system, 1149
File Replication Service (FRS), 13, **517**
    benefits, **519–520**
    DFS replication, 506
    file and folder replication, **522–523**
    file system junctions, **518–519**
    overview, **519**
    prestaging domain controllers, **521–522**
    requirements and dependencies, **520**
    scheduling replication, **523**
    with SYSVOL, **521**

File Screen Audit tab, 458
File Screen Policy page, 437
File Server Resource Manager (FSRM), 61, *61*,
  64–68, **449**
  description, 432
  file screen policies, **454–455**, *455–456*
  opening, 434
  options, **458–459**
  quota policies, **450–454**, *450–454*
  reports, **456–458**, *457*
File Server screen, 512
file servers, **146**
  description, 432
  folders, **148–151**, *150*
  primary partitions, **146–148**
File Services role, 59–60, *61*
  adding, **433–434**, *434–435*
  components, **432–433**
  overview, **431–432**, *432*
File System category, 388, 391
file system junctions, **518–519**
File to Import page, 880
File Transfer Protocol (FTP) server
  integration into web pages, **730–735**, *731,*
    733–734
  new features, **15**
files
  backups, **801–802**, *802*
  blocked types in WSS, **1208**, *1209*
  FRS replication, **522–523**
  offline. *See* Offline Files
  permissions. *See* permissions
  reading, **119**
  restores, **802–803**
  screening policies, **454–455**, *455–456*
  sharing, **13–14**
    access, **118**
    Mac OS X clients, **1122**, *1122*
    SMB, **174–176**, *175*
  single-domain forests, **239–240**, *240*
Filter Action tab, 903
Filter Actions dialog box, 901
Filter Current Custom View, 754, *754*
Filtering Platform API, 167
filters
  Event Viewer views, 749, *749*, **753–755**, *754*
  GPOs, 361, 366–367
  Group Policy, **377–380**, *377–380*
  IP, **871**
  IPSec, **895–896**, **899–901**, *900*, 903
  packets, **904–907**, *906–907*

  printers, 546, **588–590**, *589–590*
  Resource Monitor results, 782
  SIDs, 1038, *1039*
  WSS document columns, 1181
FIN states, 834–835
Final (workflow end) state, 1192
Find Printers dialog box
  adding printers, 563–565, *563–565*, 663, *663*
  filters, 665, *665*, 673, *673–674*
Find Shared Folders window, 667, *667*, 675, *676*
Find Users, Contacts, and Groups dialog box,
  672–673, *672*
Find Users, Groups, and Contacts dialog box,
  662–663
fine-grained password policies
  creating, **271–276**, *274–276*
  as new feature, **3–4**, *4*
  objective, **82**
FIPS Compliant encryption, 1106
firewall.cpl file, 1041
firewalls
  configuring, 47, *47*, **129–130**, *129*
  DMZs, 853
  IPSec, 895
  KMS server, 156
  NAPT as, **837**
  printers, 552
  Server Core rules, **137–141**, *138–141*
  shares, 439
  stealth, **847**
  upgrade installations, 37
fixed size disks, 1227, 1253
flexibility, server virtualization for, 1217
flexible desktop, **1295–1297**
flexible single master of operations (FSMOs), 991
  domain naming, **991–992**, *999*
  global catalogs, **992–993**, *994*
  importance, **992**
  infrastructure masters, **1000–1001**
  multimaster vs. single-master replication, **991**
  PDC emulators, **1001–1002**
  RID pool, **999–1000**, *1000*
  role transfers, **1002–1005**, *1002*
  roles, **994–999**, *995–997*
  time synchronization, **1005–1008**
flow control in TCP, 833
Folder Action page, 790
folders
  backups, **801–802**, *802*
  file servers, **148–151**, *150*
  FRS replication, **522–523**

network, **669–671**, *670–671*
permissions. *See* permissions
redirection
    advanced, **1345–1346**, *1345–1346*
    basic, **1338–1343**, *1338–1343*
    benefits, **385–386**, *387*
    managing, **1346–1347**
    overview, **1336–1338**
restores, **802–803**
shared. *See* shares and sharing
synchronized, **1344**, *1344*
Force Check Out option, 1187–1188
forcing
    complex passwords, **381–382**
    intersite replication, **928–929**
FOREACH cmdlet, 348
Forest-wide Authentication option, 1017
forests, **970–971**
    Active Directory, **230**
    functional levels
        overview, **238–239**, *238*
        raising, **265–268**, *266–267*
        RODC, 944, **946–947**, *947*
        working with, **989–990**, *989*
    in-place upgrades, **1025–1026**
    multiple-domain, 248
    rearranging, 1054
    RODC, 948
    root, 971
    single-domain. *See* single-domain forests
    transitive trusts, **1012–1013**
    trees in, **972–973**
forgotten passwords, **330–331**, *331*
forms, printer, 547, **556**, **569**, *569*
Forms authentication, 738
Forms tab, **569**, *569*
forward lookups, 193
Forwarded Events log, 757
forwarders
    adding, 199, 210
    conditional, **184–185**
    DNS, 984, *985*
    external namespaces, 218
Forwarders tab, 184–185, *185*
forwarding events, **777–780**, *778*
forwarding servers, 182
FPSE2002 (FrontPage Server Extensions), 690
FQDNs (fully qualified domain names), 774
    DNS, 180, 193, 207–208
    root domain names, 234
    SMTP, 728

fragmentation
    Active Directory, **804–805**
    disk, 1257
framed protocols, 866
freezing virtual machines, 1242
FrontPage Server Extensions (FPSE2002), 690
FRS. *See* File Replication Service (FRS)
FSMOs. *See* flexible single master of
    operations (FSMOs)
FSRM. *See* File Server Resource Manager (FSRM)
FT cmdlet, 353–354
FTP (File Transfer Protocol)
    integration into web pages, **730–735**,
        731, 733–734
    new features, **15**
Full Control permission, 441, 478, 484
    limiting, 425
    RDS, 1110
Full Disclosure mailing list, 1129
full installation vs. Server Core, 27
Full name field, 282
full servers
    backups, **795–798**, *796–798*
    restores, **798–801**
fully qualified domain names (FQDNs)
    DNS, 180, 193, 207–208
    root domain names, 234
    SMTP, 728
functional levels
    domains
        overview, **236–238**
        raising, **265–268**, *266–267*, **528**, *528*
        RODC, **944–946**, *946*
        working with, **986–988**, *987*
    forests
        overview, **238–239**, *238*
        raising, **265–268**, *266–267*
        RODC, 944, **946–947**, *947*
        working with, **989–990**, *989*

G

Gantt view for WSS documents, 1180
Gateway/Interface Name column, 824
gateway-to-gateway VPNs, **854**, *855*
gateways
    local area connections, 631–632
    VPN, **854**, *855*, **866**
GCs. *See* global catalogs (GCs)
GDI (Graphics Device Interface), **544**
general health reports, 531

General tab
  domain user accounts, **297**, *297*
  Edit Settings properties, 1111, *1111*
  Group Policy, 416
  groups, 325–326, *326*
  IPSec policies, 902
  IPSec rules, 905–906
  local area connections, 641, *642*
  printers, **574**, *574*
  RDP-Tcp Properties, **1105–1106**, *1105*
  RRAS, **886**, *887*
  task events, 762
Generalize configuration pass, 94
Generate Storage Reports dialog box, 457
Get-ADGroupMember cmdlet, 353, 355
Get-ADuser cmdlet, 349–353, 355
Get-ExecutionPolicy cmdlet, 71, 256
get-items cmdlet, 134
Get-WindowsFeature cmdlet, 69–70, 699
getglobalstate command, **529**, *529*, 532, *532*, 534, *534*
getmigrationstate command, 529–530, *530*, 532–535, *533*, *535*
GetObject command, 255
Getting Started page, 800
ghosted pages, 1168
GID (group identifier) field, 510
global catalogs (GCs)
  Active Directory, **230**
  and cached credentials, **917–918**, *918*
  forest functional levels, 990
  FSMOs, **992–993**, *994*
  replication, **998–999**
  RODCs, 950
  second domain controllers, **247**
  sharing, 974
  sites, 916–917
  universal group membership caching, **918–919**, *918–919*
global groups
  creating, 260, *260*
  intraforest migrations, 1033
  scope, 322
Global Navigation tabs, 1201
global query block lists, **213–214**
Global Search tool, **334–336**, *334–336*
global settings for websites, **708–710**
globally unique identifiers (GUIDs), 1271, 1273–1274
GPC (Group Policy container), 415
gpedit.msc (Group Policy tool), 362
GPMC. *See* Group Policy Management Console (GPMC)

GPME. *See* Group Policy Management Editor (GPME)
GPOFixup tool, 1064
GPOs. *See* Group Policy and GPOs
gpotool.exe tool, 412, **415**
GPP (Group Policy preferences) settings, 12, **401–406**, *402*, *405*
gpresult command, 412
  swing migration, 1029
  working with, **414–415**
GPTs (Group Policy templates), 360, 415
gpupdate command, 382
  client updates, 930
  folder redirection, 1342
  printers, 567–568
  roaming profile shares, 1318
grafting
  domains, 973
  namespaces, 518
Grant access permissions, 866, 868
Graphics Device Interface (GDI), **544**
Greenberg, Stephen, 1069
group identifier (GID) field, 510
Group Policy and GPOs, 359
  account lockout, **400**
  Active Directory, **229**
  administration, **410–412**, *411*
  application, **374–376**, *375–376*
  backing up and restoring, **408–409**, *409*
  closest sites, **930**, *931*
  complex passwords, **381–382**
  concepts, **359–361**
  creating, **365–369**, *365–368*
  cumulative, **361**
  desktop, **1347–1352**
  Event Viewer, **416**
  filtering, **377–380**, *377–380*
  folder redirection, **385–386**, *387*, 1338–1339, *1338–1339*, 1343, 1345–1347, *1346*
  GPMC. *See* Group Policy Management Console (GPMC)
  GPP settings, **401–406**, *402*, *405*
  Hyper-V Server Core, 1280
  inheritance, **361**, **380–381**
  IPSec, 897
  item-level targeting, **405–406**, *405*
  local, **362–364**, *362–364*
  logon scripts, **1355–1360**, *1356–1359*
  new features, **12**
  for OUs, **250–251**
  passwords, **399–400**

policies, **371–374**, *371–374*
printer access, 579–580
printer deployment, **565–568**, *566–568*
refresh, **361**, **370–372**
removing, **370**
replication, **369–370**
roaming profiles, 1317–1318, *1317–1318*,
    1333–1336
scripts, **383–385**, *384–385*
security, **386–394**, *387, 391*
settings, **382–383**
slow links, **373–374**, *374*
source computer-initiated subscriptions,
    769, *769*
starter, **407–408**, *408*
summary, **416–417**
templates. *See* templates
time changes, 270
troubleshooting, **412–416**, *413–414*
Group Policy container (GPC), 415
Group Policy folder, 362
Group Policy Inheritance tab, 375, *376*
Group Policy Management Console (GPMC), 359
    auditing, 1040
    closest sites, 930
    desktop, 1352
    GPOs
        backing up and restoring, **408–409**, *409*
        creating, **365–369**, *365–368*
        starter, **407–408**, *408*
    Group Policy modeling, **414**
    Group Policy results, **412–414**, *413–414*
    IPSec, 897
    Mac OS X clients, 1118, *1119*
    new features, **406–407**
    printers, 567, *567*, 580, *581*
    roaming profile shares, 1317, *1317*
Group Policy Management Editor (GPME), 359,
    362, *362*
    GPO editing, 368–369, *368*
    logon scripts, 1355
    Mac OS X clients, 1118–1119, *1118–1119*
    nodes, 383, *383*
    printer access, 580–581, *581*
Group Policy Object Editor
    LGPOs, 363–364
    WSUS, 1143–1144
Group Policy objects. *See* Group Policy and GPOs
Group Policy preferences (GPP) settings, 12,
    401–406, *402, 405*
Group Policy Results Wizard, 413–414, *413*

Group Policy tab, 1040
Group Policy templates (GPTs), 360, 415
Group Policy tool (gpedit.msc), 362
groups, **312**
    Active Directory
        creating, **259–261**, *260*, **324–330**, *324–328*
        working with, **321–324**, *323*
    ADAC, **342–343**, *342–343*
    adding, 487
    ADUC, **422–423**, *422*
    Group Policy. *See* Group Policy and GPOs
    local. *See* local groups
    membership
        domain user accounts, **305**, *305*
        security templates, **389**
        viewing, 934
    migrating, 1033, **1044–1048**, *1044–1048*
    names, 312, **325**
    nesting, 322–323, *323*
    permissions, 490
    Remote Desktop Users, **1084**
    removing, **356**
    replication, 524
    RODCs, 944, 951
    SharePoint, 1195, **1197–1200**
Groups condition in RRAS policies, **865**
Guest Access permission, 1111
Guest account, **280**
GUIDs (globally unique identifiers), 1271, 1273–1274

H
H-node, 207
handheld PCs (H/PCs), 1080
handshake protocol, 818, 833
hard quota limits, 451
hardware
    BitLocker Drive Encryption, **461–462**
    RDS clients, **1079–1080**
    RDS servers, **1075–1077**
    refreshes, **1069–1070**
    server virtualization, **1218–1219**
    sharing, 1217
    swing migration, **1031**
    virtual machines, 1215, 1235
Hardware Data Execution Prevention, 1251
hashes, 460
Hashing Message Authentication Code
    (HMAC), 460
HCAP (Host Credential Authorization Protocol),
    857, 865

headers, IP, 819
Health Registration Authority (HRA), 857
Heartbeat service
Hyper-V, 1248
virtual machines, 1237
help-desk support, **1070–1071**
hidden shares, **494–496**, *495*
hierarchical DNS naming structure, **180**, *180*
High Availability Wizard, 1286, *1286*
histories, SID, 987, **1034–1035**, 1047
History tab, 763
HMAC (Hashing Message Authentication
Code), 460
Hold mismatched documents option, 584
home directories
creating, **1299–1304**, *1299–1304*
easy way, **1304–1307**, *1304–1307*
hard way, **1307–1309**, *1308*
vs. local storage, **1309**
overview, **1297–1298**
sharing, 1306
Home folder setting, 291
Home pages
Central Administration, 1160, *1160*
site collections, 1167
HOMEDRIVE variable, 1308
HOMEPATH variable, 1309
HOMESHARE variable, 1309
Host Credential Authorization Protocol (HCAP),
857, 865
Host name setting for websites, 715
Host (A) records, 192, **195–196**, 206
Hosted Cache mode, 467
hostname command, 124
hostname resolution. *See* Domain Name
System (DNS)
hosts
DMZ, 837
Hyper-V, **1228–1230**, *1229–1230*
multiple websites, **719–724**, *722–723*
unusable addresses, **826**
virtual machines, 1216, 1280
HOSTS file, 180, 203, *204*
How do you want to connect? page, 876
HRA (Health Registration Authority), 857
.htm extension, 684
HTML (HyperText Markup Language), 684
HTTP (HyperText Transfer Protocol), 686, 772
HTTPS
event log subscriptions, 772
SSTP, 856

Hvboot.sys device drivers, 1245
hvconfig command, 1277
hybrid virtualization, 1243, *1243*
Hyper-V
architecture, **1242–1244**, *1243, 1245*
child partitions, **1248–1249**
feature set, **1220–1222**
hosts
configuring, **1228–1230**, *1229–1230*
licensing, **1269–1270**
installing, **1223–1227**, *1224–1227*
overview, **7–8**
parent partitions, **1244–1248**, *1245*
scripting, **1288–1292**
security design, **1249–1251**, *1250*
Server Core, **1277–1280**
server virtualization. *See* server virtualization
virtual disks, **1227**
virtual machine installation, **1238–1242**, *1238,
1241–1242*
virtual networks, **1228**
Hyper-V Settings dialog box, 1228–1229, *1229*
HyperLink to a Document content type, 1174
HyperText Markup Language (HTML), 684
HyperText Transfer Protocol (HTTP), 686, 772
hypervisors, **1243–1246**, *1243*

I

ICT. *See* Initial Configuration Tasks (ICT) utility
IDE controllers, 1235–1236, 1251–1252
Identify phase in patch management, **1128–1130**
idle sessions, 294
Idle time-out setting, 890
Idle Timeout constraint, 870
IDs
event, 755
GUIDs, 1271, 1273–1274
session, 1073
SIDs. *See* security identifiers (SIDs)
UIDs, 510
virtual machines, 1271
VLAN, 1267
Idx column for netsh, 824
IE (Internet Explorer)
Group Policy for, **1349–1350**
launching RemoteApp applications from,
1093–1096, *1094–1095*
restricting, **396–397**
WSS integration, **1211**
IE ESC (Internet Explorer Enhanced Security
Configuration), 1159

ifm command, 959

Ignore user account dial-in properties option, 868

IHV (independent hardware vendor) drivers, 1244, 1246

IIS. *See* Internet Information Services (IIS)

IIS 6 Metabase Compatibility services, 726–727

IIS Manager, 688
  native module registering, **704–706**, *704*
  SMTP, 726–727, *726*
  website setup, **711–716**, *711–712*

IIS Manager Permissions page, 738, *738*

IKEv2 (Internet Key Exchange version 2), **856**, **889–890**, *889*

Image Management Service, 1248

images
  differencing disks, **1255–1256**
  executable files, 1074
  install, **94–95**, *95*

IMAGEX command, 101

implicit denies, **442–443**, *443*

IMPORT-CSV cmdlet, 348

Import-Module cmdlet, 699

Import Virtual Machine dialog box, 1272, *1272*

Import Virtual Machine Wizard, 1228

Import Wizard, 1271

importing
  Event Viewer views, **755–756**, *756*
  security templates, **394**
  virtual machines, **1270–1274**, *1272–1274*

in-place upgrades, **1024–1027**

inbound firewall rules, **137–141**, *138–141*

indentation in HTML files, 684

independent hardware vendor (IHV) drivers, 1244, 1246

indexed sequential access manager (ISAM) database engine, 805

indexes for WSS documents, **1179**, *1179*, **1202–1203**, *1203*

Information events, 747

Information Rights Management (IRM), **1205**

infrastructure
  auditing, 20
  roles, **948**

infrastructure masters, **1000–1001**

inheritance
  GPOs, **361**, **380–381**
  permissions, **485**, **489**
  roles and features, 58
  WSS documents, **1195**, **1200–1201**, *1201*

Initial Configuration Tasks (ICT) utility, 33, *33*
  domains, 981
  Server Core, 121, *121*
  server customization, 127
  tasks, **46–47**, *47*
  web servers, 696, *696*

Initial (workflow start) state, 1192

input device requirements, 20

install images, **94–95**, *95*

Install now button, 25, *25*

install.wim file, 94–95

Install Windows window
  clean installations, 24–31, *24–31*
  upgrade installations, 38–43, *39–44*

Installation Results page, 698

Installation Type page, 1123, *1123*

InstallFeature.xml file, 77

installing
  ADMT, **1040–1041**
  DNS role, 198–199
  Hyper-V, **1223–1227**, *1224–1227*
  IIS, **695**
    command line, **698–699**
    renovation, **701–707**, *702–704*, *707*
    Server Core, **700–701**, *701*
    Web Server role, **695–698**, *696–697*
  NAT, **838–846**, *838–844*
  Print and Document Services role, **544–546**, *545*
  printer drivers, **554–555**, *554*
  printers, **551–553**, *552*
  RODCs, **950–955**, *951–954*, **958–963**, *960–963*
  Server Core, **113–115**, *114–115*
  virtual machines, **1238–1242**, *1238*, *1241–1242*
  Windows Automated Installation Kit, **89–92**, *90–92*
  Windows Server 2008, **17**
    64-bit support, **21–22**
    Active Directory upgrades, **82–87**
    changes from Windows Server 2003, **17–18**
    media, **18–19**
    operating system. *See* operating systems
    requirements, **19–20**
    sample server network, **108**
    server configuration. *See* Server Manager
    unattended, **88–108**, *90–93*, *95–99*, *104*
  Windows Server Backup, **795**
  WSS, **1152–1153**
  WSUS, **1139–1143**, *1139–1143*

integrated application pool mode, 689, 1150

integration
    DNS servers, **183–186**, *183–186*
    FTP onto web pages, **730–735**, *731, 733–734*
    SMTP into web pages, **724–725**
        e-mail feature, **729–730**, *730*
        server features, **726–728**, *727*
        server setup, **728–729**
        starting, **725–726**, *726*
    WSS client software, **1210–1213**, *1212*
Integration Services, 1255
    Hyper-V, 1248
    virtual machines, 1275
integrity
    Active Directory database, **805–807**
    FRS replication, 520
IntelliMirror concept, 1337
Inter Process Communication (IPC)
    mechanisms, 1246
Inter-Site Topology Generator (ISTG), 926
interactive mode in nslookup, 222
interim domain functional levels, 988
internal switches, 1263–1264, *1263*
internal virtual networks, 1228
Internet-based DNS resolution, **216–219**, *218*
Internet Domain Survey, 683
Internet Explorer (IE)
    Group Policy for, **1349–1350**
    launching RemoteApp applications from,
        1093–1096, *1094–1095*
    restricting, **396–397**
    WSS integration, **1211**
Internet Explorer Enhanced Security Configuration
    (IE ESC), 1159
Internet Information Services (IIS), **683**
    7.0 vs. 7.5, **686–689**
    advanced administration, **735**
    application pools, 1165, *1165*
    backing up and restoring data, **741–742**
    disabling, 389–390
    feature delegation, **694–695**
    FTP integration into pages, **730–735**, *731,
        733–734*
    global settings, **708–710**
    installing, **695**
        command line, **698–699**
        renovation, **701–707**, *702–704, 707*
        Server Core, **700–701**, *701*
        Web Server role, **695–698**, *696–697*
    loading, **1153–1155**, *1155*
    modules, **689–694**
        CLI management, 706
        native, **704–706**, *704*

new features, **14–15**, *15*
SMTP integration into web pages, **724–730**, *724,
    726–727, 730*
virtual servers, 1162
web applications, 1164–1165, *1164–1165*
Web Management Service, **735–740**, *736, 738*
websites
    creating, **683–686**, *685*, **711–718**, *711–712, 714,
        716–717*
    multiple sites hosting, **719–724**, *722–723*
    provisioning, **707–708**
    settings, **718–719**
    setup, **711–716**, *711–712*
Windows System Resource Manager tool,
    740–741
and WSS, 1150–1151, **1153–1155**, *1155*
Internet Information Services (IIS) Manager, 688
    native module registering, **704–706**, *704*
    SMTP, 726–727, *726*
    website setup, **711–716**, *711–712*
Internet Key Exchange version 2 (IKEv2), **856,
    889–890**, *889*
Internet Printing Protocol (IPP), 544
Internet Protocol. *See* IP (Internet Protocol)
Internet Protocol Version 4 (TCP/IPv4) Properties
    page, 636, *636, 639, 639*
intersite replication
    bridgehead servers, **927**, *928*
    configuring, **924–926**, *925–926*
    forcing, **928–929**
intersite routing, 990
Intra-site Automatic Tunneling Addressing Protocol
    (ISATAP), 213
intraforest migrations, **1033**
Intranet portal sites, 1162
Introduction to File Services page, 433
IP (Internet Protocol), 165
    filters, **871**, 900, *900*
    headers, 819
    IPv4. *See* IPv4
    IPv6. *See* IPv6
    layers, 819–820
    packets, **817–818**
        no routing required case, **819–822**,
            820–821
        routing required case, **822–825**,
            823, 825
    properties, 210
    RRAS policies, **871–872**
    site links, **921**
    as unreliable protocol, 818
IP Address Assignment page, 860

IP addresses, 818
    classes, **825–826**
    DHCP, 143
    domain controllers, 232, *232*
    domains, 981, *981*
    IPSec policies, 901
    local area connections, 631, 633
    printers, 541, 552, *552*, 556, 560
    private, **233**, **827–833**, *829*
    RRAS, 860, *861*, 872, **888–889**, *888*
    second domain controllers, 245
    unroutable, **827**
    unusable host addresses, **826**
    virtual networks, 1263
    VPN clients, 876
IP Filter Properties dialog box, 900, *900*
IP-HTTPS protocol, 177
IP Security. *See* IPSec (IP Security)
IPC (Inter Process Communication)
    mechanisms, 1246
IPC$ share, 449
ipconfig command, 52–53
    domains, 984
    ipconfig /all, 122, 207, *631*
    ipconfig /displaydns, 205–206
    ipconfig /flushdns, 205
    local area connections, 631–632
    working with, **848–849**
IPP (Internet Printing Protocol), 544
IPSec (IP Security), **893–894**
    authentication, **896–897**
    filters, **895–896**, **904–907**, *906–907*
    L2TP with, 855
    policies, **897–899**, *898*
        custom, **899–904**, *900–903*
        default, **899**
    security levels, **894–895**
    tunneling, 908
IPSec Policy Wizard, 902
ipsecmon command, 904
IPv4, **165**
    Address Resolution Protocol, **820–821**, *820*
    autoscaling, **167–173**, *168–170*
    file and printer sharing, **174–176**, *175*
    history, **165–167**, *166*
    local area connections, 632
    policy-based QoS, **173–174**
    properties, 51–52, *51–52*
    RRAS, **888–889**, *888*
    subnets, 919
IPv4 Address setting, 632

IPv4 tab, **888–889**, *888*
IPv6, 8
    Neighbor Discovery, **821–822**, *821*
    RRAS, **889**
    subnets, 919
    tunnel commands, **846**
IPv6 tab, **889**
IRM (Information Rights Management), **1205**
ISAM (indexed sequential access manager) database
    engine, 805
ISATAP (Intra-site Automatic Tunneling
    Addressing Protocol), 213
ISO files, 89, 1233, *1234*
ISO Recorder tool, 89
isolating print drivers, **13–14**, **592**, *592*
ISTG (Intersite Topology Generator), 912, 926
item-level targeting in Group Policy, **405–406**, *405*
iteration in DNS, 182

J

jams, paper, **590**
Java, 686
jobs, print, **559**, **587–588**, *587–588*
Join a Domain or Workgroup Wizard, 645
Join the Microsoft Update Improvement Program
    page, 1141
joining domains, **642**
    netdom command, **56**, *56*, **269**
    offline, 85
    process, **262–263**, *263*
    Windows 7, **643–649**, *643–645*, *649*
    Windows 2000, **652–653**
    Windows Vista, **649–651**, *649–651*
    Windows XP, **651–652**, *651–652*
Jones, Alun, 15
junction points, **518–519**

K

KCC (Knowledge Consistency Checker), 520, 926
Keep printed documents option, 584
Kerberos authentication, 943
    domains, 300, **971–972**
    and FRS, 520
    IPSec, 896
    synchronization for, 269
kernels
    enlightened, 1248
    Hyper-V, **1242–1244**, *1243*, *1245*
Key Management Service (KMS), 122, **155–157**

Keyboard or input method setting, 25
keyboards
    Hyper-V, 1228
    installation settings, 24–25
KMS (Key Management Service), 122, **155–157**
Knowledge Consistency Checker (KCC), 520, 926
known issues in patch management, 1130
krbtgt account, 943

L

L2TP (Layer 2 Tunneling Protocol), 855
LAN Manager authentication level policy, 1118, 1120
languages in installation, 24, *24*, 36
large-scale failures from server virtualization, 1218
last writer wins rule, 519
latency
    event delivery, 770–771
    local area connections, 632
    network, **168–173**, *168–170*
launchapp.wsf script, 1358, *1358*
launching RemoteApp applications, **1093–1096**, *1094–1095*
Layer 2 Tunneling Protocol (L2TP), 855
Layfield, Rhonda, 91
LDAP. *See* Lightweight Directory Access Protocol (LDAP)
LDAP Data Interchange Format (LDIF) tool, 273
Ldp.exe tool, 809, **812–813**
learning curve in server virtualization, 1218
legacy administrative templates, **394**, *395*
legacy logon scripts, 385
legacy operating systems
    mandatory profiles, 1321
    server virtualization for, 1217
legal considerations for multiple domains, **975**
levels
    event, **747**
    functional. *See* functional levels
    Hyper-V privileges, **1242–1244**, *1243*, *1245*
    IPSec security, **894–895**
LGPOs (local GPOs), **362–364**, *362–364*
libraries, WSS, **1170–1174**, *1173*, **1182–1189**, *1183*, *1185–1189*
library-centric columns, **1174–1180**, *1177–1180*
License Agreement page, 1139, *1139*
licenses
    in answer file components, 102–103
    clean installations, 26–28, *28*
    concurrent users, 438, **474**
    Hyper-V hosts, **1269–1270**

Key Management Service for, **155–157**
RD Licensing Manager, **1113–1115**
RDS Host Configuration console, **1112–1113**, *1113*
RDS modes, **1083–1084**
RDS sessions, 1078
upgrade installations, 36, 40, *41*
WAIK, 89, *90*
WSS, 1157
WSUS, 1139, *1139*
Licensing Diagnosis tool, **1112–1113**, *1113*
Licensing tab
    Edit Settings properties, 1111, *1112*
    RDP-Tcp Connections Properties, 1114
life-cycle management in DFS, **510**
Lightweight Directory Access Protocol (LDAP)
    Active Directory names, 421
    distinguished names, **252–253**
    Mac connections, 1120
    printers, 560
    sites, 916
Lightweight Directory Access Protocol (LDAP) directory database, 807
Line Printer Daemon (LPD) service, 544
Line Printer Remote (LPR) service, 544
Link control protocol (LCP) extensions option, 891
Linked Group Policy Objects tab, 376
links
    DFS, 496, **503–504**, *504*
    GPOs, 360
    sites. *See* sites
    symbolic, 1274
Links list for WSS documents, 1201
list disk command, 147
List Folder permission, 482–483
List Folder Contents permission, 441, **484–485**
list partition command, 147–148
listeners for Server Core, **135–137**
LISTENING state, 834
listing logs, **763–764**
lists of group memberships, 934
Live Migration, 1222, **1280–1283**, *1283–1284*, 1287
LMHOSTS file, 203, *204*, 206
load balancing
    RD Connection Broker, 1112
    web applications, 1165, *1165*
Load Hive dialog box, 1325, *1326*

loading
  background zones, **215**
  IIS, **1153–1155**, *1155*
  .NET Framework, 1155, *1156*
  WSS, **1156–1157**, *1157*
Local Area Connection Properties dialog box,
  50–51, *51*, 636–642, *636*, *639*, *641*
Local Area Connection Status window, 635–638,
  635, *638*, 640, *640–641*
local area connections
  verifying, **630–632**, *631*
  Windows 7, **634–637**, *634–636*
  Windows 2000, **642**
  Windows Vista, **637–640**, *637–639*
  Windows XP, **640–642**, *640–641*
Local Area Network NICs, 1265–1266, *1265*
local computer groups, **643**
local disks, backups to, 795
local domain accounts, **629–630**
.local domains, 1124–1125, *1125*
local GPOs (LGPOs), **362–364**, *362–364*
local groups, **312**, *312–313*
  creating, **312–317**, *313–316*
  intraforest migrations, 1033
  members
    adding, **317–320**, *317–319*
    removing, **320–321**, *320–321*
  policies, 376
  Remote Desktop Users, 1084
  security templates, **389**
local policies
  vs. domain-based, 897
  migrating, **1050–1053**, *1051–1052*
  security settings, 390
Local Policies category, 388, 391
Local Security Policy snap-in, 897
local storage vs. home directories, **1309**
local user accounts
  creating, **280–284**, *280*, *282–283*
  properties, **289–296**, *290–296*
  security, 968
localhost address, 827
Location for Database, Log Files, and SYSVOL page
  second domain controllers, 249
  single-domain forests, 243
Location property, 551
locations
  groups, 327, *327*
  printers, **551**
Locations dialog box, 327, *327*
locked-out users, **331–332**, *332–333*

lockout
  accounts, 272
  Group Policy, **400**
Log additional Routing and Remote Access
  information (used for debugging) option, 892
Log On Settings tab, **1106**, *1106*
Logging tab, **891–892**, *891*
logical units (LUNs), 1281, 1283
logoff command, 1103
logoff scripts
  Group Policy settings, 383
  shutdown tasks, **1360**, *1360*
Logon Hours tab, 298, *299*
Logon Properties dialog box, 1355–1356, *1355–1356*
logon scripts, **1352–1357**
  GPOs, **1355–1360**, *1356–1359*
  Group Policy, 383–384, *384*, **406**
  home directories, 1308
  local user accounts, 290
  multiple, **1358–1359**, *1358–1359*
Logon Workstations dialog box, 299, *299*
logons
  with clean installations, 32–33, *32*
  domain password changes, **655–657**, *655*, *657*
  hours settings, 298, *299*
  names, 258, 288
  Remote desktop Services, **1106**, *1106*
  RODCs, 939, 963–964, *963*
logs, **757**
  Application and Services, **758**
  clearing, **766**
  configuration information, **764**
  DNS, **219**
  exporting, **765–766**
  Group Policy, 416
  listing, **763–764**
  properties, **758–760**, *758*, *760*
  queries, **765**
  quotas, **452**, *453*
  RRAS, **891–892**, *891*
  subscriptions, **766**, *766*
    advanced options, **770–772**, *771*
    collector-initiated, **773–777**, *774–777*
    configuring, **772**
    event selection, **770**
    protocols, **772**
    types, **766–770**, *768–769*
  VPN, 884–885
  XML-based, 755
loopback addresses, 632, 827

Loopback processing mode: when you want a particular machine option, 372–373, *373*
LPD (Line Printer Daemon) service, 544
LPR (Line Printer Remote) service, 544
LUNs (logical units), 1281, 1283

M

MAC (Media Access Control) addresses, 819–820, 1263, 1266
Mac OS X clients, **1117**
    Active Directory, **1117–1120**
    connections
        domains, **1120–1121**, *1121*
        file shares, **1122**, *1122*
        printers, **1122–1123**, *1123*
        remote desktop from, **1123–1124**
        troubleshooting, **1124–1125**, *1124*
machine.config file, 1151
machines
    roaming profiles settings, **1331–1335**
    virtual. *See* virtual machines (VMs)
mail exchanger (MX) records, **196**
mainframe paradigm, **1071–1072**
maintenance of virtual disks, **1257–1259**, *1257–1258*, *1260*
major versions of document libraries, 1186–1187
MAK (Multiple Activation Key), 156
Malicious Software Removal Tool (MSRT), 221
malware protection, 1129, **1287–1288**
man-in-the-middle hackers, 176
Manage Documents permission, 572, 577
Manage Filter Actions tab, 905–906
Manage Printers permission, 571
Manage Server permission, 572
Manage this printer permission, 577
Managed By tab, 328–329, *328*
managed IIS modules, 694
management NICs, 1265
Management Properties dialog box, 326–328, *326–328*
management tools, new features, **10–12**
Managing Multiple Remote Access Servers page, 860
mandatory profiles, 295, **1321–1322**
    completing, **1327–1328**, *1328*
    super, **1328–1329**
    Windows 7, **1323–1327**, *1324–1327*
    Windows Vista, **1322–1323**, *1322–1323*
manually setting permissions, **424–428**, *426–428*

Map Network Drive dialog box, 447, *447*, 667–668, *668*, 676
mapping drives
    to drive letters, **447**, *447*
    to hidden shares, 495, *495*
    just-in-time, 406
    to shared folders, **666–669**, *667–669*, **675–678**, *676–677*
mapsvc.exe tool, 514
masks, 195, 631–632, 828–829, *829*
Maximum Folders setting, 790
Maximum password age setting, 400, 654
Maximum Root Path Size setting, 790
MBSA (Microsoft Baseline Security Analyzer), 1146
MD5 checksums, 522–523
media
    RODC installation, **958–959**
    Windows Server 2008 installation, **18–19**
Media Access Control (MAC) addresses, 819–820, 1263, 1266
Media Streaming option, 662
Member Of tab
    domain user accounts, **305**, *305*
    event log subscriptions, 776, *776*
    groups, 319, *319*, 327, *327*
    local user accounts, 290, *290*
member servers, 263
members
    Active Directory groups, 326–327, *326–327*
    domain user accounts, **305**, *305*
    event log subscriptions, 776, *776*
    local groups
        adding, **317–320**, *317–319*
        removing, **320–321**, *320–321*
    replication groups, 524
    security templates, **389**
    SharePoint groups, **1199–1200**
    viewing, 934
Members tab, 326, *326*
Membership tab, 531
memory
    64-bit systems, **6**
    RDS servers, **1076**
    requirements, 19–20
    virtual machines, 1231, 1235
memory sticks for answer files, 107
Merge mode for GPOs, 373
messages as event response, 760
Met column for netsh, 824
metabase.xml file, 726–728, 1151

metadata
  answer files, 102
  printer drivers, 543
  WSS documents, **1174–1182**, *1177–1180*
metrics in routing, 825
microkernelized hypervisors, 1244
Microsoft Baseline Security Analyzer (MBSA), 1146
Microsoft Download Center, 1146
Microsoft Encrypted Authentication
  (MS-CHAP), 883
Microsoft Encrypted Authentication version 2
  (MS-CHAP-v2), 883
Microsoft Forefront Security for SharePoint
  program, 1210
Microsoft Management Console (MMC), **130–132**,
  131–132
Microsoft Point to Point Encryption (MPPE), 872
Microsoft Search Service 2007, 1202
Microsoft Security Response Center (MSRC)
  blog, 1129
Microsoft Update, 1146
Microsoft Update Catalog, 1146
Microsoft Virtual Server product line, 1243
Middle (second stage) state, 1192
Migrate to a physical computer with a different
  processor version option, 1236
migration, **1023–1024**
  Active Directory, **1023–1024**
    ADMT. *See* Active Directory Migration
      Tool (ADMT)
    clean and pristine, **1032–1036**
    in-place upgrades, **1024–1027**
    intraforest, **1033**
    swing, **1027–1032**
  to DFSR, **525**
  printers, **573**, *574*
  states, **525**
    directed, **532–533**, *532–533*
    eliminated, **534–536**, *534–536*
    prepared, **527–531**, *528–531*
    stable, **525–526**
    transition, **526**, *526*
  virtual machines, 1222, **1280–1287**, *1283–1286*
Migration Progress dialog box, 1048, *1049*
Minimize Bandwidth option, 770–771
Minimize Latency option, 770–771
Minimum Free Disk setting, 790
Minimum password age setting, 400, 654
Minimum password length setting, 400, 654
minor versions of document libraries, 1186–1187
misspelled domains, **985**

Mitchell-Jackson, Jennifer, 1069
MMC (Microsoft Management Console), **130–132**,
  131–132
modes
  IIS, **688–689**
  RDS, **1083–1084**
Modify dialog box, 813
Modify permission, 441, 484
ModifyPartitions component in answer files, 100
modules, IIS, **689–694**
  CLI management, 706
  native, **704–706**, *704*
molecular permissions, **484–485**
monitoring
  DNS, 219, *220*
  Event Viewer. *See* Event Viewer
  Network Monitor, **850–851**, *850*
  Performance Monitor. *See*
    Performance Monitor
  Reliability Monitor, **783**
  Remote Desktop Services Manager. *See* Remote
    Desktop Services Manager
  report space, 458
  Resource Monitor, **781–783**, *782*
  storage, 450
Monitoring tab, 219, *220*
MOSS 2007 searches, 1202
most restrictive permissions, 445
Mount method, 1291
mounting Active Directory snapshots, **808–809**, *808*
Mouse Release Key option, 1229
Move Server screen, 920, *921*
moveuser utility, **1050–1051**
moving
  accounts into OUs, **422**
  spool folder, 573
  virtual machines, **1270–1274**, *1272–1274*,
    1280–1287, *1283–1286*
MPPE (Microsoft Point to Point Encryption), 872
MS-CHAP (Microsoft Encrypted
  Authentication), 883
MS-CHAP-v2 (Microsoft Encrypted Authentication
  version 2), 883
MSBlaster worm, **1131**
msdeploy.exe, 720–721
msDS-AuthenticatedToAccountList
  attribute, 942
msDS-NeverRevealGroup attribute, 941–942
msDS-Reveal-OnDemandGroup attribute, 941
msDS-RevealedList attribute, 942
msDS settings, 272–275

msg command, 1103
.msi (Windows Installer) files, **1098–1100**, *1099*
MSRC (Microsoft Security Response Center)
  blog, 1129
MSRT (Malicious Software Removal Tool), 221
Msvm_ImageManagementService class, 1291
multicast addresses, 821
multilink connections, 871, 891
multimaster replication, **968–970**, **991**
Multiple Activation Key (MAK), 156
multiple domains, **967**
    domain functional levels, **986–988**, *987*
    editing, **308**, *308–309*
    forest functional levels, **989–990**, *989*
    forests, 230, 248, **970–971**
    FSMOs. *See* flexible single master of
      operations (FSMOs)
    multimaster replication, **968–970**, **991**
    names, **980**
    need for, **975–976**
    second domains
        creating, **982–985**, *982–985*
        preparation, **981**, *981*
    security, **968–969**
    trees, **971–972**, *972*
    trees and forests together, **972–973**
    trust relationships. *See* trusts
multiple logon scripts, **1358–1359**, *1358–1359*
multiple permissions, **491**
multiple sites with roaming profiles, **1331–1332**
multiple users and groups, 487
multiple websites, **719–724**, *722–723*
MX (mail exchanger) records, **196**
My Documents folder, 1310
My Music folder, 1310
My Network Places
    network resources connections, 671–672, *672*
    shared folders, 678–679, *679*
My Network Places icon, 661

N

Name and Address Translation Services page, 842
Name and Domain screen, 505, *505*
Name server (NS) records, **198**
name servers. *See* Domain Name System (DNS)
Name Servers tab, 187, *188*
named pipes, 449
names
    alerts, 1203
    computers, 46, **124**, **268**

    content types, 1184
    default site links, 920
    distinguished. *See* distinguished names (DNs)
    domains, **979**
    groups, 312, **325**
    home directories, 1299
    inbound firewall rules, 138, *140*
    loaded registry hives, 1325, *1326*
    local user accounts, **281–282**
    logon, 258
    logon scripts, 1353
    Mac connections, 1121
    multiple domains, **980**
    objects, **310–311**
    printers, 582–583
    replication groups, 505
    resolving. *See* Domain Name
      System (DNS)
    root domains, **234–235**, *234*
    servers, **53–55**, *54–55*
    SharePoint groups, 1198
    shares, 473
    sites, 715, **915**
    trees, **979**
    virtual machines, 1231
Namespace Server Wizard, 500, *500*
Namespace Type screen, 501, *501*
namespaces
    DFS, **496**, **500–503**, *500–502*
    DNS, 180, **186–194**
    external, **218–219**, *218*
    grafting, 518
naming contexts, 933
NAP (Network Access Protection), 856
    for DHCP, **177**
    as new feature, **9**
NAPT (network address/port
    translator), **836–837**
NAT (Network Address Translation)
    installing, **838–846**, *838–844*
    L2TP, 855
native domain functional levels, 987
native IIS modules, 694, **704–706**, *704*
native RDP clients, 1079
navigating
    ADAC, **336–343**, *336–343*
    WSS documents, **1201–1202**
nbtstat command, 204
NCSA Mosaic browser, 835–836
Neighbor Discovery (ND), **821–822**, *821*
neighbors, displaying, **849–850**

nested groups
  considerations, 322 323, *323*
  domain-based, 327
nested XML tags, 750
.NET framework, 113, 1155, *1156*
net localgroup command, 316–321
net share command
  Active Directory verification, 527
  domain controllers, 530
  folders, 150
  migration verification, 533
  SYSVOL, 535, *535*
net start command, 125
net start netlogon command, 265
net start spooler command, 592
net stop command, 125
net stop netlogon command, 265
net stop spooler command, 592
net use command
  logon scripts, 1353
  mapped drives, 118, 668, 677–678, *677*
  shares, 447–448
  on WANs, **448–449**
net user command
  Administrator password, 117
  delegation, 421–422
  domain user accounts, 311
  local user accounts, 284, 296
net view command, 204
  file shares, 118
  mapped drives, 669, *669*, 676–678, *677*
NetBIOS
  configurations, 206–208, 213–214
  naming system, 182, 203, *204*
netbooks, **1072**
NetDiag, 1030
netdom add command, **1018–1019**
netdom computername command, 268
netdom join command, 56, 124, 269, **1019**
netdom move command, **1019–1020**
NetDom Remove command, 269
netdom renamecomputer command, 55, 124, 1031
NetDom Reset command, 269
NetDom ResetPwd command, 269
netdom trust command, **1020–1021**, 1039, 1279
netlogon service
  cached credentials, 918
  DDNS requests, 211
  RODCs, 963–964
  SYSVOL folder, 521
NETLOGON share, 449, 519, 1353, 1356

netmasks, 195, 828–829, *829*
netsh command, 514, *515*
netsh advfirewall firewall command
  firewall configuration, 129
  firewall enabling, 156
  inbound rules, 137, 139
  print services, 557
  remote management, 1279
  shares, 439
netsh dhcp command, 144–146
netsh firewall command, 556
netsh interface ip command, 51–52
netsh interface ipv4 add dnsserver command, 1278
netsh interface ipv4 add route command, 124, 143, 832
netsh interface ipv4 delete route command, 143, 832
netsh interface ipv4 set address command, 123, 1278
netsh interface ipv4 set interface command, 124, 851
netsh interface ipv4 show interface command, 1278
netsh interface ipv4 show neighbors command, 820, *820*
netsh interface ipv4 show routes command, 822, *823*
netsh interface ipv6 add v6v4tunnel command, 846
netsh interface ipv6 delete command, 143
netsh interface ipv6 show neighbors command, 821, 850
netsh interface ipv6 show routes command, 822, *823*
netsh interface portproxy command, 845–846
netsh interface tcp command, 172
Network Access Protection (NAP), 856
  for DHCP, **177**
  as new feature, **9**
network access services (NAS) servers. *See* virtual private networks (VPNs)
Network Adapter page, 1084, **1109–1110**, *1109*
network address/port translator (NAPT), **836–837**
Network Address Translation (NAT)
  installing, **838–846**, *838–844*
  L2TP, 855
Network and Sharing Center
  local area connections, 634–635, *634*, 637, *637*
  network resources connections, 660–661
  printers, 549
  VPN clients, 877, 882
Network applet
  network resources connections, 662, *662*
  printers, **664–666**, *664–665*
  shared folders, 667
network cards. *See* network interface cards (NICs)
Network Connection Details window, 635, *635*, 638, *638*, 641, *641*

Network Credentials page
    RODCs, 952, *953*, 959, 961, *962*
    second domain controllers, 248, *248*
Network Diagnostics applet, 637
Network Discovery
    network resources connections, 659
    Server Core, 556
    wireless devices, 666
Network File System (NFS), 433, 436, **510–514**, *511*, *515*
network folders
    creating, **669–671**, *670–671*
    printers, 664
network interface cards (NICs)
    client connections to servers, 628
    configuring, 50
    Hyper-V, 1225, *1225*
    RDS servers, **1077**
    virtual networks, 1263, **1265–1268**, *1265–1266*, *1268*
    VPNs, 853, 859–860, *860*, 875
Network Level Authentication (NLA), 597, **1083**
Network Load Balancing, 1165, *1165*
Network Location Awareness (NLA), 373
Network Monitor, **850–851**, *850*
Network Outage Time setting, 890
Network Policy and Access Services page, 858
Network Policy Server (NPS), **856**, *857*
Network Printer Installation Wizard, 152 153, *153*, 547–548, *547*
network printers
    adding, **663–666**, *663–665*, **673–675**, *673–675*
    detecting, **548–551**, *549–551*
    setting up, 152–153, *153*, 547–548, *547*
network resources connections, **659–660**
    Windows 2000, **679–680**
    Windows Vista, **660–671**, *661–665*, *667–671*
    Windows XP, **671–679**, *672–679*
Network Time Protocol (NTP), 270
network tunneling, **845**
Networking Management Service, 1248
networks
    access policies. *See* Routing and Remote Access Service (RRAS)
    configuring, 46
    connections, **50**, *50*
    default profiles, **1329–1330**
    location shortcuts, **678–679**, *678–679*
    new features and changes, **8–9**
    properties, **50–53**, *50–52*
    settings, **122–124**

    virtual, **1263–1268**, *1263–1268*
    wide area networks, 176
New-ADGroup cmdlet, 351
New-ADuser cmdlet, 344–346, 348
New Disk Wizard, 1253
New Filter Actions Properties dialog box, 901, *901*
New GPO dialog box, 366, 408, *408*
New Group dialog box, 312, *313*
New Hard Disk Wizard, 1255
New Inbound Rule Wizard, 137–141, *138–140*
New Local User Properties dialog box, 402, *402*
New Namespace Wizard, 500–502, *500–502*
New Network Policy dialog box, 872–874, *873–874*, 883, *883*
New Object - Group dialog box, 324, *324*, 422–423, *422*, 951, *952*
New Object - Site dialog box, 915, *915*, 951, *951*
New Object - Site Link dialog box, 922, *922*
New Object - Subset dialog box, 919, *920*
New Object - User Wizard, 287, *287*
New Printer Filter Wizard, 589–590, *589–590*
new printer setup, **582–583**
New Replication Group Wizard, 505, *505*
New Rule Properties page, 907
New Security Method dialog box, 901, *902*
New Site Content Type page, 1184, *1184*
New SMTP Domain Wizard, 729
New Trust Wizard, **1014–1017**, *1015–1017*, 1038
New User dialog box, 281–283, *282*
New Virtual Hard Disk Wizard, 1252, *1252*
New Virtual Machine Wizard, 1231–1234, *1231–1234*, 1253, 1256
New Wizard, 1228, 1230, 1236
New WMI Filter dialog box, 380
New Zone Wizard
    ADI zones, 189–192, *189–190*
    DNS updates, 208, *209*
    reverse lookup zones, 193
    standard primary zones, 187
NFS (Network File System), 433, 436, **510–514**, *511*, *515*
NICs. *See* network interface cards (NICs)
NIST time server, 271
NLA (Network Level Authentication), 597, **1083**
NLA (Network Location Awareness), 373
nltest.exe command, 747
No eXecute (NX) bit, 1219
No files or programs from the share are available offline option, 468
Non-Administrators LGPOs, **362–363**, *363*
Normal mode for event log subscriptions, 770–771

Notepad for text files, **119**
Notification Limits tab, 458
notification process for site replication, 911
NPS (Network Policy Server), **856**, *857*
NPS console, **884–885**
NS (Name server) records, **198**
nslookup command
    external name resolution, 224
    GlobalNames feature, 214
    overview, **221–223**
    reverse lookup, 193
    trusts, 1015
NT 4 operating system, 969
NT domains, **419–421**
NT File System (NTFS), 30, 1149
NTBackup Utility, 157, 794
ntds.dit file, 517
    defragmenting, **804–805**
    integrity checking, 805–806
    RODCs, 959
    security boundaries, 968
NTDS Settings properties sheet,
    918–919, *918–919*
NTDS Site Settings sheet, 926
ntdsutil command, 143
    Active Directory snapshots, 807
    authoritative restores, 815
    database file integrity, 805–807
    defragmentation, 804–805
    DSRM passwords, 241
    FSMOs, 1003–1004
    moving files, 240
    RODCs, 959
NTFS (NT File System), 30, 1149
NTFS permissions, 435, **441**
    applicationhost.config, 709
    security templates, 389, 392
NTFS Permissions screen, 435, 1313
NTFSDOS utility, 480
NTP (Network Time Protocol), 270
ntpquery.exe tool, 1007
ntuser.dat file
    mandatory profiles, 1323–1329,
        1325, 1328
    roaming profiles, 1309
NX (No eXecute) bit, 1219

O

Object Property Exclusion page, 1048, *1048*
Object tab, **306**, *307*
Object Types dialog box, groups, 313, *314*

objects
    access auditing, 581, *581*
    Active Directory, **228**
    GPOs. *See* Group Policy and GPOs
    information on, **306**, *307*
    Performance Monitor, 781
    renaming or deleting, **310–311**
oclist command, 127, 556, 701, *701*
ocsetup command, 10
    Hyper-V Server Core, 1280
    IIS installation, 700–701, 703
    print services, 556
    roles, 127–128, 696
OEM (original equipment manufacturer)
    clean installation licenses, 26
    client connections to servers drivers, 628
off-site disk backups, 797
Office 2007, **1211–1213**, *1212*
offline Active Directory defragmenting, **804–805**
Offline Files, **465**
    BranchCache, **466–467**
    enabling, **467–468**, *467*
    Group Policy for, **1348**
    operation, **465–466**
offlineServicing configuration pass, 94
on-demand resource allocation, 1280
100% Threshold Properties page, 454, *454*
Only the files and programs that users specify are
    available offline option, 468
oobeSystem configuration pass, 94
Open Database dialog box, 392
Open Packaging Conventions (OPC), 543
Open Saved Log dialog box, 759–760, *760*
Open XML Markup Compatibility
    specifications, 543
Operating System Compatibility page
    DCPromo, 242, *242*
    RODCs, 952, 959, 961
    second domain controllers, 248
    single-domain forests, **232–233**, *234*
Operating System Shutdown option, 1237
operating systems, **22–23**
    clean installations, **23–33**, *24–33*
    Initial Configuration Tasks utility, **46–47**, *47*
    new features and changes, **5–8**
    upgrade installations, **33–46**, *35, 38–45*
Operational logs, 416, 758
operations masters, 968
    FSMOs. *See* flexible single master of
        operations (FSMOs)
    RID, 1000, *1000*
    transferring, 264

Operations page
    blocked files, 1208
    Central Administration, 1160, *1161*
    virus protection, 1210, *1210*
    WSS, 1202, 1208
Optimized for performance option, 468
optimizing event log subscriptions, **770–771**, *771*
Optional Company Information page, 1114
Optional Component Setup, 696, 700–701, 703
order
    RRAS policies, **863–865**
    WSS document columns, **1179**, *1179*
Organization tab, **302–303**, *303*
Organizational Unit Selection page, 1045, *1046*
organizational units (OUs), **250**, 420
    Active Directory, **229**
    ADUC, **251–252**, *251–252*
    creating, **250–251**, 422
    delegation, **251**, **421–424**, *422–424*
    domain user accounts, 286–289, *287*
    dsadd for, **253–254**
    GPOs for, **250–251**, 360
    groups, 323
    moving accounts into, **422**
    need for, **978–979**
    password reset control, **423–424**, *423–424*
    PowerShell for, **255–257**
    Windows Scripting Host for, **254–255**
original equipment manufacturer (OEM)
    clean installation licenses, 26
    client connections to servers
        drivers, 628
oscdimg command, 107
OUs. *See* organizational units (OUs)
outbound logs in FRS, 522
Outlook 2007, **1211–1212**, *1212*
output to text files, 764
Override Check Out permission, 1188
Overview tab
    Resource Monitor, 781–782, *782*
    RRAS policies, 866, *868*
Overwrite events as needed (oldest events first)
    option, 764
owners
    permissions, **494**
    SharePoint groups, 1198

P

Package Manager, 696, 698–700
packages, 382

packets
    digitally signing, 460–461
    IP, **817–818**
        filtering, **871**, **904–907**, *906–907*
        no routing required case, **819–822**, *820–821*
        routing required case, **822–825**, *823*, *825*
pages, website. *See* websites
PAP (Password Authentication Protocol), 882–883
paper jams, **590**
parallel ports for printers, 547
parameters with PowerShell, 933
paravirtualized OS, 1248
parent partitions in Hyper-V, **1244–1248**, *1245*
partitions
    ADI zones, 190–191
    applications, **210**
    configuration, 970
    domain, 303, 969–970
    Hyper-V
        child, **1248–1249**
        parent, **1244–1248**, *1245*
    primary, **146–148**
    schemas, 970
    Server Core, **114–115**, *114*
    swing migration, 1029–1030
pass-through disks, 1227, 1253
passphrases
    benefits, **283**
    domain users, 654
    local users, 282
Password Authentication Protocol (PAP), 882–883
Password Encryption Service (PES), **1039–1041**
Password Migration DLL Installation Wizard, 1041
Password must meet complexity requirements
    setting, 654
Password never expires option
    domain users, 300
    local users, 282
Password Options page, 1046, *1046*
Password Replication tab, 306, *306*
Password Replication Policy tab, 940–942, *941*,
    955–957, *956*
Password Settings Object (PSO), **272–276**, *273–276*
passwords
    administrator, 32, *32*, **117**, *117*
    ADMT, **1039–1041**, 1046, *1046*
    BitLocker Drive Encryption, 462
    certificates, 880
    changing, **653–659**, *655–659*
    clean installations, 31–32, *32*
    complex, **381–382**

domain accounts, 288, **300**, 306, *306*
DSRM accounts, **241**, *241*
event log subscriptions, 775–776
fine-grained
    creating, **271–276**, *274–276*
    as new feature, **3–4**, *4*
    objective, **82**
forgotten, **330–331**, *331*
Group Policy, **399–400**
IPSec policies, 899
joining domains, 644–645, *645*, 651–652
locked-out accounts, 332, *332*
Mac connections, 1121
PAP, 882
PDC emulators FSMOs, 1001–1002
RDS, 1106
RemoteApp applications, 1094
replication policy, **940–942**, *941*
reset control delegation, **423–424**, *423–424*
RODCs, 939–940, **954–957**, *956*, 961, 963
setting, **345–346**
user accounts, 257–258, *258*, 282
VPN clients, 877, *877*
Passwords must meet complexity requirements
    option, 400
PAT (port/address translator), 836
patch management, **1127**, *1128*
    Assess phase, **1127–1128**
    Deploy phase, **1131**
    Evaluate and Plan phase, **1130**
    Identify phase, **1128–1130**
    security updates, **1132**
    tools, **1146**
    WSUS. *See* Windows Server Update
        Services (WSUS)
paths for profiles, 290
pausing virtual machines, 1242
PC-unfriendly environments, RDS for, **1068–1069**
pcl.sep separator page, 585
PDC tab, 269, *270*
PDCs (primary domain controllers)
    domain time, 269, *270*
    elimination of, 968
    emulators, **1001–1002**
    purpose, 186
PDF (Portable Document Format) documents, 543
PEAP (Protected EAP), 884
People and Groups page, 1198
People and groups permissions, **1195–1200**, *1196*
people.aspx page, 1197
People Search dialog box, 1199

per-device RDS licensing, **1083–1084**, 1111, 1114
per-user RDS licensing, **1084**, 1111, 1114
Perflogs folder, 790
Perform machine health check only option, 882
performance
    BitLocker Drive Encryption, 461
    NFS, 510
Performance Counter Properties dialog box, 787, *787*
Performance Monitor, **780–781**
    data collector sets, **783**
        reports, **789–791**, *789–790*
        system, **783–785**, *784–785*
        user-defined, **785–788**, *787*, *789*
    RDS servers, **1077–1078**
Permission Levels page, 1196, *1196*
permissions, **440**
    Allow and Deny, **442–443**, **480**, **492**, *492*
    applicationhost.config, 709
    assigning, **442**, **485–491**, *486–491*
    atomic, **481–483**
    C&P migration, **1033**
    Central Administration, 1160
    combining, **445–446**
    conflicting, **491**
    creating, **477–480**, *478–479*
    cumulative, **442–443**, *443*
    defaults, **513**
    delegation, 262, *262*, 572, **579**
    description, **480**
    effective, **493–494**, *493*
    file servers, **149–150**
    home directories, 1300–1302, *1302*, 1305–1307
    inherited, **485**, **489**
    managing, **492**, *492*
    mandatory profiles, 1326–1327, *1327*
    manually setting, **424–428**, *426–428*
    modifying, **444–445**, *444–445*
    molecular, **484–485**
    multiple, **491**
    NTFS, 435, **441**
    ownership, **494**
    precedence, **443**
    printers, **571–572**, **576–579**, *576*, *578*
    RDS, **1110–1111**
    roaming profile shares, 1311–1314, *1312–1313*,
        1319–1320
    RODC, 944
    RRAS policies, 863, **866–868**, *868*
    security templates, **389–390**, 392
    shares, **440–446**, *443–445*
    types, **480–482**, *481*

web sites, **738–739**, *738*
WSS documents, **1195–1196**, *1196*
    disabling, **1200–1201**, *1201*
    people and groups, **1196–1200**, *1196*
Permissions page, 262, *262*, 444–445, *444–445*
permit transmissions security level, **895**
Personal Virtual Desktop tab, 303, *303*
PES (Password Encryption Service), **1039–1041**
PHP, 686
physical site locations, 911, 914
ping command, 53
    local area connections, **632–634**, *633–634*
    remote computers, **847–848**
pizza boxes, 112
PKI (Public Key Infrastructure) certificates, 896
PMC. *See* Print Management console (PMC)
Point-to-Point Protocol (PPP), 866, **890–891**, *890*
Point-to-Point Tunneling Protocol (PPTP), 855
pointer (PTR) records, **196**
policies
    Active Directory, 229
    file screen, **454–455**, *455–456*
    fine-grained password, **3–4**, *4*, **82**, **271–276**, *274–276*
    group. *See* Group Policy and GPOs
    IPSec, **897–899**, *898*
        custom, **899–904**, *900–903*
        default, **899**
    quotas, **450–454**, *450–454*
    RODCs, 956–957, *956*
    RRAS. *See* Routing and Remote Access
        Service (RRAS)
policy-based QoS, **173–174**
Policy Events tab, 414
Policy Usage tab, 956–957, *956*
political considerations with Active Directory, **973–974**
pools
    application, 722, *722*, 1165, *1165*
    printers, **575–576**
populating document libraries, **1172–1174**, *1173*
port/address translator (PAT), 836
Port setting, 715
Portable Document Format (PDF) documents, 543
portal sites, 1162
portproxy tunneling, **845–846**
ports
    printers
        adding, 152, *152*, **560**
        creating, 548
        description, 547

server settings, **570**, *570*
settings, **570**, *570*, **575–576**, *575*
viewing and editing, **555–556**, *555*
RRAS, **893**, *893*
sockets, **834–835**
TCP, 513–514, 818, 833
UDP, 513–514
virtual machines, 1236
web applications, 1166
websites, 715
Ports tab, **570**, *570*, **575–576**, *575*
pound signs (#) for separator pages, 586
power costs, 1069
"Power to the People: Comparing Power Usage
    for PCs and Thin Clients in an Office Network
    Environment", 1069
PowerShell
    Active Directory, **84**, **343–344**
        disabling accounts, **351–355**
        enabling accounts, **351**
        passwords, **345–346**
        Recycle Bin, 812
        removing groups, **356**
        unlocking accounts, **349–351**
        users, **344–346**
    certificates, 134
    cmdlets, 699
    as new feature, **4–5**, *5*
    OUs, **255–257**
    Server Manager, 50
    sites, **931–934**
    unattended scripts, 69–71
PPP (Point-to-Point Protocol), 866, **890–891**, *890*
PPP tab, **890–891**, *890*
PPTP (Point-to-Point Tunneling Protocol), 855
preferred bridgehead servers, 913, **927**, *928*
Prefix column for netsh, 824
prepared states, migrating to, 525, **527–531**, *528–531*
preshared key option, 896
prestaging
    domain controllers, **521–522**
    RODC accounts, **959–963**, *960–963*
primary domain controllers (PDCs)
    domain time, 269, *270*
    elimination of, 968
    emulators, **1001–1002**
    purpose, 186
primary partitions, **146–148**
primary read-only zones, 964
principals, security, 1196–1197

Print and Document Services role, 151, **544–546**, *545*, **556–560**
print devices, 539
Print Management console (PMC)
    components, **546–547**, *546*
    new features, **13–14**
    print jobs, 587–588, *587*
    printers
        adding, **547–548**, *547*
        deleting, **548**
        deploying, 562, *562*
        detecting, **548–551**, *549–551*
        setup, 151–153, *151–152*
    settings and resources, **553–556**, *553–555*
Print permission, 571, 577
Print Server service, 544
PRINT$ share, 449
Print spooled documents first option, 584
Printer Driver page, 549
Printer Found page, 550
Printer Name and Sharing Settings page, 550, *550*
printers, **539**
    adding, **547–548**, *547*
    advanced settings, **581**, *581*
    available hours, **582–583**
    background printing, 583
    connections, **558**, **1122–1123**, *1123*
    deleting, **548**
    deploying, **561**
        Active Directory search, **562–565**, *562–565*
        GPOs, **565–568**, *566–568*
        manual process, **561–562**, *561*
        viewing, **568–569**
    drivers
        adding and updating, 152, *152*, 547, **571**
        GDI, **544**
        installing, **554–555**, *554*
        isolating, **13–14**, **592**, *592*
        managing, **553**, *553*
        scripts, **559**
        types, **541–542**
        views, **553**, *554*
        XPS, **542–543**
        XPSDrv, **543**
    filters, 546, **588–590**, *589–590*
    forms, 547, **556**, **569–570**, *569*
    General settings, **574**, *574*
    GPP, 406
    installing, **551–553**, *552*
    locations, **551**
    Mac OS X clients, **1122–1123**, *1123*

migrating, **573**, *574*
network
    adding, **663–666**, *663 665*, **673–675**, *673–675*
    detecting, **548–551**, *549–551*
    setting up, 152–153, *153*, 547–548, *547*
permissions, **571–572**, **576–579**, *576*, *578*
pooling, **575–576**
ports. *See* ports
Print and Document Services role, **544–546**, *545*, **556–560**
print jobs, **587–588**, *587–588*
Print Management console overview, **546–547**, *546*
priorities, **583**
publishing, **560**
queues, 539, **560**, **587–588**, *587–588*
security, **571–572**, *571*, **576–581**, *576*, *578*, *580–581*
separator pages, 576, **584–587**, *585*
servers
    adding, 546, *546*
    migrating, **573**, *574*
    properties, **569–573**, *569–572*
    Server Core, **151–155**, *151–153*
service overview, **539–540**, *540*
settings and resources, **553–556**, *553–555*
sharing, **13–14**, **174–176**, *175*, 575
spoolers, **540–541**, 583–584
troubleshooting, **590–592**, *592*
Printers and Faxes applet, **674–675**, *674–675*
Printers Not Ready filter, 589
Printers with Jobs filter, 589
printui command, **557**
priorities for printers, **583**
private IP addresses, **827–828**
    CIDR, **830**
    IP, **233**
    subnets and supernets, **828–830**, *829*
    TCP routing, **830**, **832–833**
private switches, 1264
private virtual networks, 1228
privileges
    Hyper-V, **1242–1244**, *1243*, *1245*
    permissions. *See* permissions
prncnfg.vbs script, 153, **558–559**
prndrvr.vbs script, 153–154, **559**
prnjobs.vbs script, 153, **559**
prnmngr.vbs script, 153, **558**
prnport.vbs script, **560**
prnqctl.vbs script, **560**

Process even if the Group Policy objects have not changed option, 372
processes
    description, 1074
    ending, 782
    Remote Desktop Services Manager, **1101–1102**, *1101–1102*
Processes tab, 1101
processing modes, **688–689**
% Processor Time counter, 1078
processors
    RDS servers, **1076**
    requirements, 19–20
    Resource Monitor, 782
    virtualization, 1216, 1222, 1235–1236
product keys
    in answer files, 102
    clean installations, 25–26, *26*
    Server Core installations, **121–122**
Profile page
    domain users, 301, *301*
    inbound firewall rules, 138, *140*
    local users, **290–292**, *291*
profiles
    default, **1329–1330**
    mandatory. *See* mandatory profiles
    roaming. *See* roaming profiles
program icons, 1071
program startup as event response, 760 761
progress bar engineering, 96
promotions
    DCs, 5
    in swing migration, **1029–1030**
propagation dampening, 911
propagation reports, 531
Protect container from accidental deletion feature, 252
Protected EAP (PEAP), 884
protocol analyzers, 894
Protocols and Ports page, 137, *138*
Provide Computer Name and Domain task, 46
Provision a Shared Folder Wizard, 435
    home directories, 1301–1302, *1301–1302*
    roaming profile shares, 1312–1314, *1312–1314*
provisioning
    machines in joining domains, 647
    site collections, **1167–1170**, *1167–1169*
    web applications, **1164–1166**, *1164–1166*
    websites, **707–708**, **1162–1163**, *1163*
pruning domains, 973
psconfig.exe utility, 1159

pscript.sep separator page, 585
PTR (pointer) records, **196**
Public Folder Sharing option, 662
Public Key Infrastructure (PKI) certificates, 896
Public Key Policies category, 388
Publish column for netsh, 824
Published Certificates tab, 304, *305*
publishing
    printers, **560**
    shares, **439**, *440*
pubprn.vbs script, **560**
pucker factor, 1054, 1057
PushPrinterConnection.exe utility, 567–568
PWMIG.MSI file, 1041

Q

qe command, **765**
qprocess command, 1103
Quality of Service (QoS), **173–174**
query process command, 1103
query session command, 1103
query users command, 1103
querying logs, **765**
question marks (?) in command syntax, **118–119**
queues, print, 539, **560**, **587–588**, *587–588*
Quick Launch Bar, 1201
Quick Migration, **1280–1282**, 1287
Quota Policy page, 436
Quota Properties page, 454
Quota Templates screen, 450, *450*
quotas
    applying, 436
    creating, **453–454**
    policies, **450–454**, *450–454*
    templates, **450–453**, *450–453*
    WSS, **1209–1210**
quser command, 1103
qwinsta command, 1103

R

RADIUS (Remote Authentication Dial-in User Service) servers
    client properties, **866**
    clients vs. VPN clients, **867**, *867*
    NPS, 856
    RRAS, 888
RAID (Redundant Array of Inexpensive Disks), 1077
Raise Domain Functional Level page, 266

Raise Forest Functional Level page, 267, *267*
raising functional levels, **265–268**, *266–267*, *528*
RAM
    64-bit systems, **6**
    RDS servers, **1076**
    requirements, 19–20
    virtual machines, 1231, 1235
RD Connection Broker tab, **1112**
RD IP Virtualization tab, 1112
RD Licensing Configuration page, 1086
RDC (Remote Desktop Connection), 1081
    description, 292
    Mac OS X clients, **1123–1124**, *1123*
    RDS sessions, 1088–1089, *1088–1089*
RDC (Remote Differential Compression), 524
RDP. *See* Remote Desktop Protocol (RDP)
RDP Security Layer, 1105
RDP-Tcp Properties dialog box, **1104**
    Client Settings tab, **1108–1109**, *1109*
    Environment tab, **1107**, *1107*
    General tab, **1105–1106**, *1105*
    Licensing tab, 1114
    Log on Settings tab, **1106**, *1106*
    Network Adapter tab, **1109–1110**, *1109*
    Remote Control tab, **1107–1108**, *1108*
    Security tab, **1110–1111**, *1110*
    Sessions tab, **1107**
RDS. *See* Remote Desktop Services (RDS)
re-ACLing in C&P migration, **1033–1034**
Read and Execute permission, 441, 484
Read Attributes permission, 483, 1312
Read Data permission, 482–483
Read Extended Attributes permission, 483
Read-Host cmdlet, 345–346, 349
read-only DNS, **964**
read-only domain controllers (RODCs), 646
    adprep tool, **947–951**
    allowed lists, **957**, *958*
    changes on, **938**
    contents, **939–944**, *939, 941, 943–944*
    DNS on, **963–964**, *963*
    domain functional levels, **944–946**, *946*
    installing, **950–955**, *951–954*, **958–963**, *960–963*
    introduction, **937–938**, *938*
    as new feature, 2
    overview, **83**
    properties, **955–957**, *956*
    remote locations, 916
    requirements, **944–949**, *946–947*
    and server applications, **950**
Read permission, 441, 478–479, **484**, 577

Read Permissions permission, 483
reading text files, **119**
realm trusts, 1012
rebooting
    command for, **120**
    for printer problems, 591
rebuilding PCs, 1296–1297
recommendations for patches, 1129
Reconnects users to the correct session setting, 1112
records, DNS
    managing, **202–203**
    types, **196–198**, *197*
recovery. *See* restores
recovery keys in BitLocker Drive Encryption,
    462–463
recursion, DNS, **180–181**, *181*, 183
Recycle Bin, Active Directory, 4, *4*
    benefits, 239
    description, **84**
    functional levels for, 265–266
    object recovery from, **811–812**, *812*
redircmp tool, 257
Redirect to the following location option, 1340
Redirect to the local user profile location
    option, 1340
Redirect to the user's home directory option, 1339
redirected state, migrating to, 525, **532–533**, *532–533*
redirection of folders
    advanced, **1345–1346**, *1345–1346*
    basic, **1338–1343**, *1338–1343*
    benefits, **385–386**, *387*
    managing, **1346–1347**
    overview, **1336–1338**
reduced functionality mode (RFM), 121
Redundant Array of Inexpensive Disks (RAID), 1077
refreshes
    GPOs, **361**, **370–372**
    hardware, **1069–1070**
    RDS, 1075
regional settings, 24
Register Native Module dialog box, 704, *704*
RegisterInDNS test, 224
registering native IIS modules, **704–706**, *704*
Registry
    access restrictions, 398
    closest sites, **930–931**
    editing, **120**
    GPP, 406
    permissions, **390**
    security templates, 388, 391
    virtual machine backups, 1275–1276, *1276*

Registry category, 388, 391
Registry Editor
    automatic server updates, 125, *125*
    closest sites, 931, *932*
    mandatory profiles, 1325, *1325*
relative identifier (RID) pool FSMOs, **999–1000**, *1000*
Reliability Monitor, **783**
reliable protocols, 818
Remote Access Clients node, **892–893**, *892–893*
remote access policies, 861
remote access services (RAS) servers. *See* virtual
    private networks (VPNs)
remote administration
    enabling, 57, *58*
    Server Core, **130–141**, *131–132, 134, 138–140*
remote applications, 12
Remote Authentication Dial-in User Service
    (RADIUS) servers
    client properties, **866**
    clients vs. VPN clients, **867**, *867*
    NPS, 856
    RRAS, 888
remote computers
    pinging, **847–848**
    shares on, **437–439**, **474–476**, *474–476*
Remote Control tab
    local users, **294–295**, *294*
    RDP-Tcp Properties, **1107–1108**, *1108*
Remote Desktop
    enabling, 46, 57, *58*, **128–129**
    from Mac OS X clients, **1123–1124**
    Server Core, **130**
Remote Desktop Connection (RDC), 1081
    description, 292
    Mac OS X clients, **1123–1124**, *1123*
    RDS sessions, 1088–1089, *1088–1089*
Remote Desktop Connection Broker, 1081,
    1092, *1092*
Remote Desktop Connection Manager,
    1093, *1093*
Remote Desktop Gateway, 1081–1082
Remote Desktop Licensing Manager, **1113–1115**
Remote Desktop Licensing service, 1081
Remote Desktop page, 1095
Remote Desktop Protocol (RDP), 57
    Hyper-V virtual console, 1239
    operation, **1074–1075**
    .rdp files
        creating, **1096–1098**, *1096–1098*
        RemoteApp access through, 1071
    versions, **1074–1075**

Remote Desktop Services (RDS), **1067**, 1296
    adding, **1080–1081**
    applications, **1068**, **1087**
    client requirements, **1079–1080**
    Easy Print feature, **1082**
    licensing modes, **1083–1084**
    monitoring. *See* Remote Desktop
        Services Manager
    need for, **1067–1071**
    Network Level Authentication, **1083**
    as new feature, **11–12**
    processing model, **1071–1075**, *1073*
    Remote Desktop Users group, **1084**
    RemoteApp applications. *See*
        RemoteApp applications
    required, 1081
    roaming profiles, **1332–1334**
    role, **1084–1087**, *1085–1086*
    server requirements, **1075–1078**
    session connections, **1087–1089**, *1088–1089*
    single sign-on, **1082–1083**
    thin-client sessions, **1072–1074**, *1073*
Remote Desktop Services Default Connection page,
    1091, *1092*
Remote Desktop Services Licensing server, 1084
Remote Desktop Services Manager, 1073, *1073*,
    1100–1101
    command line, **1102–1103**
    local user accounts, 292
    Remote Desktop Licensing Manager, **1113–1115**
    Remote Desktop Session Host Configuration
        console
        Edit Settings properties, **1111–1112**,
            1111–1112
        Licensing Diagnosis, **1112–1113**, *1113*
        RDP-Tcp Connection properties, **1103–1111**,
            1104–1110
    users, sessions, and processes, **1101–1102**,
        1101–1102
Remote Desktop Services Profile tab, **295**, *295*
Remote Desktop Services Server License
    server, 1087
Remote Desktop Session Host Configuration
    console
    Edit Settings properties, **1111–1112**, *1111–1112*
    Licensing Diagnosis, **1112–1113**, *1113*
    RDP-Tcp Connection properties, **1103–1111**,
        1104–1110
Remote Desktop Session Host servers, 1067, **1076**
Remote Desktop Session Host service, 1081
Remote Desktop Users group, **1084**, 1088, *1088*

Remote Desktop Virtualization Host, 1081
Remote Desktop Web Access, 1082
Remote Differential Compression (RDC), 524
remote locations, DCs in, **916–919**, *918–919*
remote management, **80–81**, *81*
Remote Procedure Call (RPC), **11**
    and FRS, 520
    IP site links, 921
Remote Server Administrative Tools (RSAT), 342
remote services for websites, 721
remote users, RDS for, **1068**
RemoteApp and Desktop Connection page,
    1094, *1094*
RemoteApp applications, **1070–1071**
    adding, **1089–1090**, *1090*
    deploying, **1071**
    launching, **1093–1096**, *1094–1095*
    .rdp files for, **1096–1098**, *1096–1098*
    RDS servers for, **1091–1093**, *1091–1093*
    Windows Installer files for, **1098–1100**, *1099*
RemoteApp Manager, 1090, 1096, *1096*
RemoteApp Wizard, 1090, *1090*
removable disks for backups, 795
Removable Storage Manager feature, 77
Remove-ADGroup cmdlet, 356
Remove-ADGroupMember cmdlet, 354–355
Remove-ADuser cmdlet, 351
Remove Features Wizard, 77, *77*
Remove Roles Wizard, 72–73, *72–73*
Remove-WindowsFeature cmdlet, 74–75
RemoveFeature.xml file, 78
RemoveFileServer.xml file, 74
removing
    features, **77–78**, *77*
    GPOs, **370**
    groups, **356**
    members from local groups, **320–321**, *320–321*
    roles, **72–75**, *72–73*
    site links, 922, *923*
renaming
    computers, 124, **268**
    default site links, 920
    domains. *See* domains
    objects, **310–311**
    sites, **915**
rendom command, 1059, 1061–1064
renovating IIS construction, **701–707**, *702–704, 707*
repadmin tool, 527, 534, 815, 928, 1063
reparse points, 518
repeated password prompts, 656
Replace mode in GPOs, 373

Replica Set command, 522
replicas in DFS, 497
Replicate every property, 914, 923
replicated folders, sharing, **508–509**
Replicated Folders tab, 509
replication
    Active Directory, **225**, **228**, **974**
    bandwidth issues, **975**
    DFS, **496**
        configuring, **504–506**
        overview, **506**
    DFSR. *See* Distributed File System
        Replication (DFSR)
    domain controllers, 1262
    FRS. *See* File Replication Service (FRS)
    global catalogs, **998–999**
    GPOs, **369–370**
    intersite
        bridgehead servers, **927**, *928*
        configuring, **924–926**, *925–926*
        forcing, **928–929**
    multimaster, **968–970**, **991**
    password policy, **940–942**, *941*
    sites, **910–912**, *911*
    SYSVOL, **13**
replsingleobj switch, 928
replsingleobject switch, 928
Report tab, **453–454**, *454*
Report Locations tab, 458
reports
    data collector sets, **789–791**, *789–790*
    FSRM, **456–458**, *457*
    propagation, 531
    quotas, **453–454**, *454*
Request Handling tab, 878
"Request timed out" message, 633
RequestStateChange method, 1290
Reset account lockout counter after setting, 400
Reset Check Boxes option, 1229
Reset Password dialog box, 330–332, *331,
    333*, 428
resolving external namespaces, **218–219**, *218*
resource access in migration, **1050**
resource computers in intraforest
    migrations, 1033
Resource Monitor, **781–783**, *782*
Resource Policy setting, 790
resources for virtual machines
    allocating, 1280
    savings in, 1217
restartable Active Directory domain services, **84**

restarting
    Active Directory, **803–804**
    spooler service, **592**
Restore-ADobject cmdlet, 5
restores
    Active Directory, **811–815**, *812, 814*
    authoritative, **814–815**
    domain user accounts, **311**
    files and folders, **802–803**
    full server, **798–801**
    GPOs, **408–409**, *409*
    virtual machines, **1274–1277**, *1276*
    web site data, **741–742**
Restricted Groups category, 388, 391
Resultant Set of Policy (RSOP) Tool, **412**
reverse engineering Server Core, **119**
reverse lookup zones, 190, **193–194**, *194*
Review Settings page, 1090
RFC 1918 subnetting, 830
RFM (reduced functionality mode), 121
RID (relative identifier) pool FSMOs, **999–1000**, *1000*
rights. *See* permissions
Rights Management Services platform, 1205
ring compression, 1243
rings in Hyper-V, **1242–1244**, *1243, 1245*
roaming profiles
    creating, **1309–1311**
    GPOs, **1333–1336**
    machine settings, **1331–1335**
    managing, **1330**
    multiple sites, **1331–1332**
    Remote Desktop Services, **1332–1334**
    shares
        easy creation method, **1311–1319**, *1311–1318*
        hard creation method, **1319–1321**
        troubleshooting, **1320**
    user settings, **1335–1336**
RODCs. *See* read-only domain controllers (RODCs)
role.aspx page, 1196
Role Services page, 1086
roles
    administrators, **83**
    FSMO, **994–999**, *995–997*
    Hyper-V, 1224, *1224*
    IIS, **690–694**, 1153, 1155, *1155*
    RDS, **58–72**, *59–64*, **127–128**
    removing, **72–75**, *72–73*
    Server Core, **141–142**
    Server Manager, 49
    troubleshooting, **78–80**, *78–80*
Roles Summary section, 59, *59*, 64, *64*

rollback plans in ADMT, **1054**
root applications, 708
root domain names, **234–235**, *234*
root hints, 183–184, *183–184*, 218–219
root servers, 181
roots
    DFS, 496–497
        creating, **499–503**, *500–503*
        links to, **503–504**, *504*
    empty, **976–977**
    forests, 971
round-robin technique, 195
route add command, 832, 845
route del command, 832
route print command, 822, *823*
routers, **845**
routing, **817**
    Application Layer Gateways, **837**
    classes, **825–826**
    displaying, **849–850**
    IP packets. *See* IP (Internet Protocol)
    NAT installation, **838–846**, *838–844*
    network address/port translator, **836–837**
    sockets and ports, **833–835**
    testing and troubleshooting, **846–851**
    Winsock, **835–836**
Routing and Remote Access Server Setup Wizard, 842, *842–844*
Routing and Remote Access Service (RRAS), 856
    accounting configuration, **884–886**, *885*
    adding, **858**
    authentication, 866, 874, **882–884**, *883*
    capabilities, **857–858**
    certificates, **878–882**, *879*
    configuring, **858–861**, *859–861*
    NAT installations, **838–844**, *838–844*
    policies, **861–863**, *862*
        configuring, **870–872**, *870–871*
        constraints, **869–870**, *869*
        creating, **872–875**, *873–874*
        order, **863–865**
        permissions, 863, **866–868**, *868*
        properties, **865–866**, *865*
    ports, **893**, *893*
    Remote Access Clients node, **892–893**, *892–893*
    server properties, **886–892**, *887–891*
    VPN clients, **875–877**, *875–877*
routing tables, **824–825**, *825*, **831–832**
RPC (Remote Procedure Call), **11**
    and FRS, 520
    IP site links, 921

RRAS. *See* Routing and Remote Access Service (RRAS)
RSAT (Remote Server Administrative Tools), 342
RSOP (Resultant Set of Policy) Tool, **412**, *413*
RSS subscriptions, **1204**, *1204*
Rule type screen, 137, *138*
rules
    firewalls, **137–141**, *138–141*
    IPSec, **896**, 899, **902–907**, *903*, *906–907*
Run an older operation system, such as Windows NT option, 1236
runtime status of event subscriptions, **777–778**, *778*
Russinovich, Mark, 480

S
SAM (security account management) database, 968
SANS Internet Storm diary, 1129
SATA (Serial Advanced Technology Attachment), 1077
Save unattend file dialog box, 244
Saved Logs folder, 759
saving
    library documents, 1173
    log files, **759**
    web pages, **684–685**
sc (server config) command, 143–144, 437, 439
scaling
    transaction time, **167–173**, *168–170*
    troubleshooting, **171–172**
SCCM (System Center Configuration Manager), 1068
Schedule property, 923
Schedule tab, 788, *789*
schedules
    backups, 796–798, *797–798*
    data collector sets, 786, 788, *789*
    DFS replication, **507**
    FRS replication, 520, **523**
    reports, 457, *457*
    site links, 923
    site replication, 914, 926, *926*
    SYSVOL, 524
    WSS documents indexes, 1203, *1203*
schema masters, **948**, **994–999**, *995–997*
schema redefines, 990
schemas
    Active Directory, **228**, **996**, 1002
    changing, **996–998**, *997*
    conflicts, **997–998**
    forests, 990

in-place upgrades, **1025–1026**
partitions, 970
swing migration, 1028
sconfig tool, 57, 1277
Scope tab, 366, *366*, 378
SCPs (service connection points), 1292
screen saver security, **1351**
scregedit.wsf script, 120, 124, 128–129
Scripting Center, 254
Scriptomatic tool, 380
scripts
    event response, 761
    Group Policy settings, **383–385**, *384–385*
    home directories, 1308
    Hyper-V, **1288–1292**
    logon. *See* logon scripts
    Server Core printer, **557–560**
    unattended, **68–72**
    WMI, 380
SCSI (Serial Computer System Interface) disks and controllers
    RDS servers, 1077
    virtual machines, 1235–1236, 1251–1253, *1254*
Search Active Directory dialog box
    folders, 667
    printers, 675
search indexes, **1202–1203**, *1203*
Search the network for printers option, 548–549
Searcher.Findall command, 933
searches
    Active Directory, **662–663**, *662*, **672–673**, *672*
        network drives, **447**
        printer deployment, **562–565**, *562–565*
        shares, 439, *440*
    ADAC, **334–336**, *334–336*
    WSS documents, **1202–1203**, *1203*
secedit.exe tool, 389, 393
second domain controllers, **245**
    computer configuration, **245–246**, *246*
    DCPromo, **248–250**, *248–249*
    deployment configuration, **246**, *247*
    DNS, **246–247**, *247*
    global catalog, **247**
second stage (Middle) state, 1192
secondary zones, **187–189**, *188*
secpol.msc file, 897
Secure Hashing Algorithm-256, 460
Secure Server (Require Security) policy, 899
Secure Socket Tunneling Protocol (SSTP), **9**, **855–856**, 872

Secure Sockets Layer (SSL)
   IIS, 689, 716
   RDS, 1105
   RRAS policies, 872, 888
   in SSTP, 856
   web sites, 740
Secured password (EAP-MS-CHAP-v2) option, 884
security
   authentication. *See* authentication
   BitLocker Drive Encryption, **461–465**, *462–465*
   C&P migration, **1033**
   DFS, 509
   domains, **968–969**
   Group Policy, **386–394**, *387, 391*
   groups, 260, **322**
   Hyper-V, **1249–1251**, *1250*
   IPSec. *See* IPSec (IP Security)
   mandatory profiles, 1327–1328
   OUs, **426–427**, *427*
   permissions. *See* permissions
   printers, **571–572**, *571*, **576–581**, *576, 578,*
      580–581
   RDS, 1089, 1105
   RRAS, 881, **886–888**, *887*
   screen savers, **1351**
   server virtualization, 1218
   SMB 2.0, **460–461**
   trusts, **1011**
   updates, **1132**
   VPN clients, 875, *876*
   VPN servers, 879
   web sites, **737–740**, *738*
   WSS
      authentication providers, **1206–1207**
      documents, **1194–1195**
      inheritance, **1195**
      permissions, **1195–1201**, *1196, 1201*
security account management (SAM) database, 968
Security Association data size limit setting, 890
Security Association expiration time setting, 890
Security Configuration and Analysis tool, 390
Security Filtering settings, 366
security identifiers (SIDs)
   filtering, 1038, *1039*
   histories, 987
      ADMT, 1047
      C&P migration, **1034–1035**
   objects, 310
   overview, **999–1000**
   permissions, 442
   security principals, 321

security.inf file, 391
Security log, 757–758
security principals, 321
Security Settings dialog box, 377, *377*
Security tab, 426, *426*
   certificates, 879
   domain users, **306–307**, *307*
   permissions, 481, *481*, 486–487, *487–488*
   printers, **571–572**, *571*, **576–581**, *576*
   RDP-Tcp Properties, **1110–1111**, *1110*
   RRAS, 881, **886–888**, *887*
   VPN clients, 875, *876*
   web sites, 739
Security Transition Wizard, 1050–1053, *1051–1052*
Security Translation Options page, 1052, *1052*
Select a Domain page
   RODCs, 953, 962
   second domain controllers, 249
Select a Site page
   RODCs, 960
   second domain controllers, 249
Select Accounting Options page, 885
Select Backup Configuration page, 802, *802*
Select Backup Date page, 800
Select Features page, 795
Select GPO dialog box, 366
Select Group page, 873, *873*
Select Group Policy Object dialog box, 363–364
Select Network Policy Name and Connection Type
   screen, 872, *873*
Select Recovery Type page
   file and folder restores, 803
   full server restores, 800
Select Role Services page
   certification, 878
   File Services role, 433, *434*
   printers, 545, *545*
   RDS, 1085, *1086*
   WSUS, 1138, *1138*
Select Server Roles screen, 697
   DFS, 496, *497*
   printers, 544, *545*
   RDS, 1085, *1085*
   RRAS, 858
Select the driver to be installed screen, 30, *30*
Select Update Source page, 1140, *1140*
Select Users dialog box, *314–316*, 316
Select Users, Computers, or Groups dialog box,
   313, *313*
Select Users or Groups dialog box, 479, *479*, 486–487
Selective Authentication option, 1017

self-signed certificates, 1105
Semantic database analysis command, **806–807**
Send Alerts for These Changes setting, 1203–1204
Send Alerts To setting, 1203
Send To destinations options, 1202
separator pages, 576, **584–587**, *585*
sequencing in TCP, 833
Serial Advanced Technology Attachment
  (SATA), 1077
Serial Computer System Interface (SCSI) disks and
  controllers
    RDS servers, 1077
    virtual machines, 1235–1236, 1251–1253, *1254*
Serial Line Interface Protocol (SLIP), 866
serial ports for printers, 547
server-based computing, 1071
server config (sc) command, 437, 439
Server Core, **111**
  backups, **157–162**
  computer information for, **121–124**
  DHCP service, **143–146**
  domain controllers and DNS, **142–143**
  events on, **763–766**
  file server setup, **146–151**, *150*
  vs. full installation, 27
  guidelines, **116–120**, *116–117*
  Hyper-V server, **1277–1280**
  IIS installation, **700–701**, *701*
  installing, **113–115**, *114–115*
  licenses, **155–157**
  overview, **6**, **111–113**
  Print and Document Services role, **556–560**
  print servers, **151–155**, *151–153*
  printer scripts, **557–560**
  remote administration, **130–141**, *131–132, 134,*
    138–140
  RODC installation on, **954–955**
  roles and features, **141–142**
  server customization, **127–130**, *129*
  server updates, **124–127**, *125*
Server Manager, **47–48**, *48*
  Active Directory, 804, 813
  backups, 795–796, 813, 1275
  BitLocker Drive Encryption, 463
  changes to, **49–50**
  Event Viewer view, 748
  features
    installing and removing, **75–78**, *75–77*
    troubleshooting, **78–80**, *78–80*
  file and folder restores, 803
  file screen templates, 455, *455*

File Services role, 433–434, *435*
Hyper-V roles, 1224
IIS, **696–698**
joining domains, **56**, *56*
local user accounts, 280
network properties, **50–53**, *50–52*
as new feature, **10–11**, *10*
permissions, 444
quotas, 453
RDS requirements, **1075–1078**
remote administration, **57**, *58*
remote management, **80–81**, *81*
roles, 1155, *1155*
  adding, **58–72**, *59–64*
  removing, **72–75**, *72–73*
  troubleshooting, **78–80**, *78–80*
server names, **53–55**, *54–55*
shares, **437–439**
upgrade installations, 45–46, *45*
Server Manager console, 127
Server Message Block (SMB) protocol, **459–461**
  file and printer sharing, **174–176**, *175*
  Mac OS X client file shares, 1122
  new features, **13**
  permissions, 436, *437*, 1302, *1302*
  user limits, 438
Server (Request Security) policy, 899
server-side sockets, 834
server virtualization, **1215**, 1254, 1284–1285
  benefits, **1217–1218**
  hardware requirements, **1218–1219**
  Hyper-V
    architecture, **1242–1244**, *1243, 1245*
    child partitions, **1248–1249**
    feature sets, **1220–1222**
    host configuration, **1228–1230**, *1229–1230*
    installing, **1223–1227**, *1224–1227*
    parent partitions, **1244–1248**, *1245*
    security design, **1249–1251**, *1250*
  IIS, 1162
  overview, **1215–1217**, *1216*
  SMTP, **728–729**
  software requirements, **1219–1220**
  virtual disks. *See* virtual disks
  virtual machines. *See* virtual machines (VMs)
  virtual networks, **1263–1268**, *1263–1268*
servermanagercmd.exe tool, 10, 48
  features, 76–77
  IIS installation, 698–700, 703, *704*
  roles, 59, 64–68, 72–73
  SMTP installation, 728

servers
    authentication certificates, **878–880**, *879*
    bridgehead, 912–913, **927**, *928*
    client connections. *See* client connections
        to servers
    clustering, 1281
    configuration. *See* Server Manager
    customization, **127–130**, *129*
    DHCP
        DDNS process, 209
        RRAS, 888–889
    DNS, **179, 182–183**
        and DCs, **917**
        integrating, **183–186**, *183–186*
        local area connections, 631–632
        Mac connections, 1120
    names, **53–55**, *54–55*
    NFS, 511
    placement in sites, **920**, *921*
    printers
        adding, 546, *546*
        migrating, **573**, *574*
        properties, **569–573**, *569–572*
        Server Core, **151–155**, *151–153*
    RODCs, **950**
    updating, **124–127**, *125*
    virtualization. *See* server virtualization
serverweroptin.exe command, 126
service accounts, 326
    Active Directory, 85
    WSS, **1154**
service connection points (SCPs), 1292
service location (SRV) records, 182, **196**, *197*
    Active Directory, 211
    KMS servers, 156
    viewing, 264–265, *265*
Service Type setting, 866
services
    IIS, **686–694**
    roles, 60
    RRAS policies, 866
    Web Server role, **702–703**, *702–703*
Services applet, 592
Services for Network File System console, 510, *511*
Services Logs folder, **758**
Session Timeout constraint, 870
sessions
    RDS, **1087–1089**, *1088–1089*
    Remote Desktop Services Manager, **1101–1102**,
        1101–1102
    thin-client, **1072–1075**

Sessions tab
    local user accounts, **293–294**, *293*
    RDP-Tcp Properties, **1107**
    Remote Desktop Services Manager, 1101
Set-Adaccountpassword cmdlet, 349
Set-ADuser cmdlet, 350 351, 1308
Set Domain Functional Level page, 242
Set-ExecutionPolicy cmdlet, 71, 256
Set Forest Functional Level page, 242
Set Report Options page, 433
Set Sync Schedule page, 1143, *1143*
Set time zone task, 46
setglobalstate command, 528, *529*, 532, *532*, 534, *534*
SetInfo command, 255–256
Settings dialog box for virtual machines, 1235, *1235*
Settings tab
    folder redirection, 1340, *1341*
    Group Policy, 367, *367*, 414
    task events, 763
Setup log, 715, 757
Setup program, 38, *38*
    in-place upgrades, **1026–1027**
    new features, **9–10**
SetupUILanguage component, 99
severity ratings in patch management, 1130
Shadow Copy Requestor service, 1249
Share and Publish Replicated Folder Wizard, 509
Share and Storage Management node, 434, *435*
Share and Storage Management tool
    DFS roots, 503, *503*
    home directories, 1301, *1301*
    quotas, 453
    roaming profiles, 1312
    shares and permissions, 444, 467
Share Permissions tab, 477–478, *478*
Share Protocols screen, 435, 1313
Shared Folder Location page, 435, *436*
Shared Folders tab, 675
SharePoint. *See* Windows SharePoint
    Services 3.0 (WSSv3)
SharePoint Administration service, 1158
SharePoint Designer 2007, **1213**
SharePoint Products and Technologies
    Configuration Wizard, 1156, 1158–1160, *1158*
SharePoint Timer service, 1158
shares and sharing
    accessing, **118**
    common, **449**
    connecting to, **446–449**, *446–447*
    creating, **435–439**, **471–476**, *472–476*
    credentials conflicts, **448**

DFS. *See* Distributed File System (DFS)
global catalogs, 974
hidden, **494–496**, *495*
home directories, **1299–1303**, *1300–1304*, 1306
Mac files, **1122**, *1122*
Network File System, **510–514**, *511, 515*
printers. *See* printers
publishing, **439**, *440*
roaming profiles
    easy creation method, **1311–1319**, *1311–1318*
    hard creation method, **1319–1321**
    troubleshooting, **1320**
shared folders, **150–151**, *150*
    creating, **471–476**, *472–476*
    mapping drives, **447**, *447*, **666–669**, *667–669*,
      675–678, *676–677*
    permissions. *See* permissions
    replicated, **508–509**
SMB 2.0, **174–176**, *175*
on WANs, **448–449**
Sharing tab
    folders, 473, *473*
    printer deployment, 562
    printer drivers, 554, *554*
    printers, 575
Shiva Password Authentication Protocol
    (SPAP), 883
shortcut trusts, **1012**, **1057–1058**
shortcuts for network location, **678–679**, *678–679*
show scope command, 145
shutdown, **120**
    GPOs, 383
    Hyper-V service, 1248
    logoff scripts, **1360**, *1360*
shutdown command, 120
SIDs. *See* security identifiers (SIDs)
sign transmissions security level, **895**
signatures in IPSec, **896**
Simple Mail Transfer Protocol (SMTP)
    integrating into web pages, **724–725**
      e-mail feature, **729–730**, *730*
      server features, **726–728**, *727*
      server setup, **728–729**
      starting, **725–726**, *726*
    site links, **921–922**
Simple Network Management Protocol
    (SNMP), 556
Simple Network Time Protocol (SNTP) servers,
    1007–1008
Simple Object Access Protocol (SOAP), 133
single-command queries, 222

single-domain forests, **230**
    Active Directory and DNS, **234–235**, *235*
    benefits, **231**
    creating, **231**
    DCPromo process, **242–244**, *242–243, 245*
    deployment configuration, 233
    domain functional levels, **236–238**
    DSRM, **241**, *241*
    file location and SYSVOL, **239–240**, *240*
    forest functional levels, **238–239**, *238*
    operating system compatibility, **232–233**, *234*
    root domain names, **234–235**, *234*
    server configuration for, **232**, *232*
single-master replication vs. multimaster, **991**
single sign-on
    Active Directory, 228
    RDS, **1082–1083**
Site Bindings dialog box, 740
Site Collection Administrator fields, 1168, *1168*
Site collection administrators permissions, 1195
Site Column Gallery, 1176
Site Content Type Gallery, 1183–1184
site level, IIS module configuration at,
    706–707, *707*
sites, **909**
    Active Directory, **229**
    cached credentials, **917–918**, *918*
    closest, **929–931**, *929, 931*
    collections, **1167–1170**, *1167–1169*
    concepts, **909–910**
    DCs in remote locations, **916–919**, *918–919*
    defining, **915–916**, *915*
    GPOs, 360
    links, *921–924*
      adding, **920–921**, *921*
      cost calculations, **923–924**, *924*
      creating, **922**, *922–923*
      IP, **921**
      properties, **923**
      SMTP, **921–922**
    operation, **913–914**, *913*
    PowerShell cmdlets, **931–934**
    providing information on, 913
    renaming, **915**
    replication, **910–912**, *911*
      compression, **911–912**
      configuring, **924–929**, *925–926, 928*
    RODCs, 951
    server placement in, **920**, *921*
    subnets, 912, 914, **919–920**, *920*
    terminology, **911–912**

64-bit technology
 requirements, **6**
 support, **21–22**
size of log files, 759
sl command, **764**
sliding windows, 833
SLIP (Serial Line Interface Protocol), 866
slmgr.vbs script, 26, 121
slow links, Group Policy over, **373–374**, *374*
Smart card is required for interactive logon
 option, **300**
smart cards
 BitLocker Drive Encryption, 462
 description, **884**
 domain user accounts, **300**
SMB. *See* Server Message Block (SMB) protocol
SMB permissions screen, 436, *437*, 1302, *1302*
SMB Settings page, 436, 438
SMTP. *See* Simple Mail Transfer Protocol (SMTP)
SMTP Server Tools feature, 727
snapshots
 Active Directory, **807–809**, *807–808*
 Hyper-V, 1226
 virtual disks, **1259–1263**, *1261*
 websites, 721
Snapshots settings, 1226
sniffers, 883, 894
SNMP (Simple Network Management Protocol), 556
SNTP (Simple Network Time Protocol) servers,
 1007–1008
SOA (Start of Authority) records, **197–198**, 964
SOAP (Simple Object Access Protocol), 133
sockets in routing, **833–835**
soft quota limits, 451
Software compression option, 891
software requirements
 client connections to servers, **628–629**
 server virtualization, **1219–1220**
 WSUS, **1133–1134**
software restrictions, 388, **397–398**, *398*
Software Restrictions Policies category, 388
solicited node multicast addresses, 821
source computer-initiated subscriptions,
 768–770, *769*
source computers
 events, 766, *766*, 772
 swing migration, **1028–1029**
SPAP (Shiva Password Authentication Protocol), 883
special permissions, 1111
Special Permissions permission, **485**, 572
Specialize configuration pass, 94

Specify a Printer page, 674, *674*
Specify Access Permission page, 874
Specify Conditions page, 873–874, *873*
Specify Licensing Mode page, 1085
Specify Package Settings page, 1097–1098, *1097*
Specify Proxy Server page, 1141
Specify Recovery Options page, 803
Specify the Computer Name page, 959, *960*
splash screens in WAIK, 89, *90*
split-brain DNS, 198, **216–217**
spoolers
 moving, 573
 print, **540–541**, **583–584**
 restarting, **592**
SQL Server
 web applications, 1166, *1166*
 for WSS, 1152
SQL Server Embedded Edition, 1152, *1154*
SRV (service location) records, 182, **196**, *197*
 Active Directory, 211
 KMS servers, 156
 viewing, 264–265, *265*
SSL. *See* Secure Sockets Layer (SSL)
SSL certificate binding setting, 888
SSL certificate field, 716
SSTP (Secure Socket Tunneling Protocol),
 9, **855–856**, 872
stable migration states, **525–526**
Stack Guard cookies, 1251
staged RODC installations, **958–963**, *960–963*
stand-alone DFS, **498–499**
standard primary zones, **186–187**, *187*, 200
standard secondary zones, **187–189**, *188*, 200
Standard view for WSS documents, 1180
Start a Program page, 761
start command for printer additions, 674
Start menu
 consistent, 398
 My Network Places icon, 661
 RemoteApp access through, 1071
Start of Authority (SOA) records, **197–198**, 964
start state, 525
startcd.exe utility, 89
starter GPOs, **407–408**, *408*
startup scripts for Group Policy settings, 383
states
 migrating. *See* migration
 system, 793, **799–801**
 workflow, **1192**
static IP addresses, 232, *232*, 245
stealth firewalls, **847**

Stop Condition tab, 786, *787*
stopping Active Directory, **803–804**
storage
    monitoring, 450
    reports, 456–458, *457*
    Server Manager, 80
Storage and Disk Management, 1254, 1284
Storage Reports Management node, 456–457, *457*
Storage Reports tab, 458
Store password using reversible encryption option,
    300, 400
stores, drivers, **554–555**, *554*
Strong Encryption option, 872
Strongest Encryption option, 872
stsadm.exe utility, 1207–1208
stub zones, **192**, *192*, 1015
subdomains
    delegating, **211**, **225**
    DNS, 180
Subject Name tab, 879
Subnet mask setting, 631–632
subnets, **828–830**, *829*
    Active Directory, 229
    local area connections, 631–632
    sites, 912, 914, **919–920**, *920*
subscriptions
    event logs. *See* logs
    RSS, **1204**, *1204*
suffixes, UPN, 288
Summary page
    DCPromo, 243–244, *243*
    Group Policy, 414
    second domain controllers, 249
    task events, 762
super mandatory profiles, **1328–1329**
superbar, 48
supernets, **828–830**, *829*
Support tab, 640
swing migrations, **1027–1032**
switches in virtual networks, **1263–1268**, *1263–1268*
Symantec Security Response website, 1129
symbolic links, 1274
SYN states, 834–835
synchronization
    domains, **269–271**, *270*
    folders, **1344**, *1344*
    FSMOs, **1005–1008**
    Hyper-V, 1248
    Offline Files, 466
    time, **269–271**, *270*
    virtual machines, 1237

sysdm.cpl applet, 1031
sysprint.sep separator page, 585
sysprtj.sep separator page, 585
System and Security Center, 463–464, *464*
System applet, 643, *643*, 649, *649*
System Center Configuration Manager
    (SCCM), 1068
System Default (Shared) option, 592
System Diagnostics data collector
    set, 783–785
System log, 747, 757
system monitoring, **745**
    event forwarding, **777–780**, *778*
    event logs. *See* logs
    Event Viewer. *See* Event Viewer
    Performance Monitor. *See*
        Performance Monitor
System Performance data collector
    set, 783–784
System Properties dialog box
    computer names, 54–56, *54*
    domains, 263, *263*, 644, *644*, 650–651,
        650–651
    product keys, 27
System Services category, 388, 391
system settings for Group Policy, 383
system state
    backup and recovery, 793
    full server restores, **799–801**
SYSVOL_DFSR folder, 530, *530*, 533, 535–536
SYSVOL share, 449, **517**
    FRS. *See* File Replication Service (FRS)
    replication changes, **13**
    schedules, 524
    single-domain forests, **239–240**, *240*

T

tables
    ARP, 820, *820*
    routing, **824–825**, *825*, **831–832**
tags
    HTML, 684
    XML, 750, 1061
Take Ownership permission, 483, 578
targets
    ADMT domains, **1040**
    DFS, 497
Task Manager, **116**
Task Scheduler, 762, *762*
Taskpad views, 425

tasks
  delegating, 261, *261*
  events, **760–763**, *761–762*
  shutdown, **1360**, *1360*
Tasks to Delegate page, 261, *261*
tattooing issue, 370
TCP. *See* Transmission Control Protocol (TCP)
TCP/IP protocol, 165
  local area connections, 630
  printer ports, 152, *152*
  printers, 664, 666
  web applications, 1166
TCP receive window, 169
teaming, NIC, 1268
Telephones tab, 301, *302*
templates
  administrative
    IE restrictions, **396–397**
    legacy, **394**, *395*
    new, **395–396**, *396*
    software restrictions, **397–398**, *398*
    time servers, **399**
  default profiles, 1329–1330
  Document Library, 1170
  file screen, 455, *455*
  Group Policy, 360, 415
    database, **392–393**
    domain-based group policies, **393**
    importing, **394**
    leveraging, **388–389**
    settings, **389–390**
    working with, **390–392**, *391*
  quotas, **450–453**, *450–453*
  site collections, 1167–1168, *1168*
Terminal Services, 1296
  local users, 293
  RDS servers, 1077–1078
  replacement for, **11–12**, 1296
testing
  client connections to servers, **632–634**, *633–634*
  event log subscription connectivity, 774, *774*
  network connectivity, 53
  routing, **846–851**
  Server Core, **141**
  virtualization, **1217**
text files
  output to, 764
  reading, **119**
thin-client networking
  description, **1071–1072**
  sessions, **1072–1075**

This account supports AES 128 bit encryption
    option, 300–301
This account supports AES 256 bit encryption
    option, 301
threads, 1074
three-click rule, 1202
Three State Workflow, **1189–1194**, *1190–1193*
three-way handshakes, 833
throttling, 173
tickets in Kerberos
  ticket-granting ticket accounts, 943
  trust relationships, 972
Time and currency format setting, 25
Time and Date control panel, 122
time servers, **399**
time synchronization
  domains, **269–271**, *270*
  FSMOs, **1005–1008**
  Hyper-V, 1248
  virtual machines, 1237
time zones, 46, **122**, 1006
titles for site collections, 1167, 1169
TLS (Transport Layer Security), 884
tokens
  C&P migration, **1034–1035**
  SID, 1034
  UAC, 1357
Tolly Group, 171
tombstone lifetime, 926
tombstoned objects, 811
Total Bytes counter, 1078
Total Compressed Bytes counter, 1078
Total Protocol Cache Hit Ratio counter, 1078
TPI (two-person integrity), 425
TPM (Trusted Platform Module), **461–462**
trace logs, 892
traceroute command, **848**, *849*
transactions
  autoscaling, **167–173**, *168–170*
  logs, 240
transferring FSMO roles, **1002–1005**, *1002*
transition states, **526**, *526*
transitive trusts, 990, **1011–1013**
Translate Objects page, 1051, *1051*
translating profiles, **1050–1053**, *1051–1052*
Transmission Control Protocol (TCP)
  autoscaling for, **167–173**, *168–170*
  description, 818
  DHCP and NAP, **177**
  history, **165–167**, *166*
  new features and changes, **8–9**

ports, 513–514
routing, **830**, **832–833**
Transport Layer Security (TLS), 884
Traverse Folder permission, 482
tree view in ADAC, 337, *337*
trees, 970
Active Directory, **230**
in forests, **972–973**
multiple domains, 980
names, **979**
trusts, **971–972**, *972*
Triggers tab, 762
troubleshooting
ADI DNS, **264–265**, *265*
autoscaling, **171–172**
DNS, **219–225**, *220*
event forwarding, **777–780**, *778*
Group Policy, **412–416**, *413–414*
IIS tools, 688
Mac OS X clients, **1124–1125**, *1124*
printers, **590–592**, *592*
roaming profile shares, **1320**
roles and features, **78–80**, *78–80*
routing, **846–851**
trust anchors, 215
trust levels for web sites, **739–740**
trusted certificates, 1105
trusted domains, 1010, *1010*, 1020–1021
Trusted Platform Module (TPM), **461–462**
trusted root enterprise certificate authorities, 133
trusting domains, 1010, *1010*, 1020–1021
trusts, 420, 968, **1009**
ADDT, **1038–1039**, *1039*
administrator involvement, **1011**
creating, **1013–1020**, *1013–1017*
direction, **1010**, *1010*
forests, 990, **1012–1013**
netdom for, **1018–1021**
overview, **1009**
security, **1011**
shortcut, **1057–1058**
transitive, 990, **1011–1013**
trees, **971–972**, *972*
types, **1012**
Trusts tab, 1013–1014, *1013–1014*, 1017, *1017*
TS for Administrators, 1067
TS Web Access Computers group, **1091**, *1091*
Tscon command, 1103
Tsdiscon command, 1103
Tskill command, 1103
Tunnel Type setting, 866

tunneling
IP, **845–846**
IPSec, 908
ISATAP, 213
PPTP, 855
SSTP, **9**, **855–856**, 872
VPN, **855–856**, 866
Turn off background refresh of Group Policy
option, 372
two-factor authentication, 300
two-person integrity (TPI), 425
Type 3 - User Mode drivers, 541–542
Type column for netsh, 824

U

UAC (User Access Control), 1357
UDP (User Datagram Protocol), 513–514, 818
UIDs (Unix user identifiers), 510
UILanguage property, 99
Ultrasound tool, 527, 530, 533
unattended DCPromo, 250
unattended installations, **88**
answer files
creating, **92–106**, *93*, *95–99*
using, **107–108**
RODCs, **954–955**
scripts, **68–72**
WAIK, **89–92**, *90–92*
Unattended Windows Setup Reference, 96
unbound sockets, 833
unconnected sockets, 833
Unencrypted Authentication (PAP, SPAP)
option, **883**
unfriendly environments, RDS for, **1068–1069**
unique site bindings, 722
unique websites, **722**, *722*
United States Computer Emergency Readiness
Team (US-CERT), 1129
universal groups, 260
membership caching, **918–919**, *918–919*
overview, **322**
Universal Plug and Play (UPnP), 628
University of Michigan Virus Busters, 1129
Unix support by NFS, 510
Unknown Remote-App publisher warning, *1098*
Unlock-ADAccount cmdlet, 349
unlocking user accounts, **349–351**
Unmount method, 1292
unregistering DLLs, 996
unreliable protocols, 818

unroutable addresses
  broadcast, **827**
  private, **827–833**, *829*
unusable host addresses, **826**
update sequence numbers (USNs), 1262
updates
  DNS, **208–209**, *209*
  printer drivers, 571
  search indexes for WSS documents,
    1202–1203, *1203*
  security, **1132**
  servers, **124–127**, *125*
upgrades
  Active Directory, **82–87**
  in-place, **1024–1027**
  library documents, **1173–1174**, *1173*
  operating systems in, **33–46**, *35, 38–45*
UPN suffixes, 288
UPnP (Universal Plug and Play), 628
UPNs (user principal names)
  domain user accounts, 288
  properties, 995, *996*
US-CERT (United States Computer Emergency
  Readiness Team), 1129
USB memory sticks for answer files, 107
USB thumb drives for installation, 23
Use custom share and folder permissions
  option, 476
Use Kerberos DES encryption types for this account
  option, 300
Use the default RMS server specified in Active
  Directory option, 1205
Use this RMS server option, 1205
User Access Control (UAC), 1357
User Account Migration Wizard, **1044–1048**,
  1044–1049
user accounts. *See* users and user accounts
User Assignment tab, 1090, *1090*
User cannot change password option
  domain users, 300
  local users, 282
User Configuration node, 359, 371, *371*
User Credentials option, 1229
User Datagram Protocol (UDP), 513–514, 818
user-defined data collector sets, **785–788**, *787, 789*
User Groups page, 1085
User Limit area for shares, 474
User Limits tab, 438, *438*
User must change password at next logon option
  domain uses, 300
  local users, **282**

User Options page, 1048, *1048*
user principal names (UPNs)
  domain users, 288
  properties, 995, *996*
User Selection page, 1045, *1045*
User Selection Option page, 1045, *1045*
user-specific LGPOs, **363–364**, *364*
UserData subcomponent, 102
Userenv.log file, 416
%username% system variable, 149
usernames
  domain users, 288
  event log subscriptions, 775–776
  joining domains, 644–645,
    645, 651–652
  local users, **281–282**
  RemoteApp applications, 1094
  RODCs, 961
  VPN clients, 877, *877*
users and user accounts, 257
  ADAC, **333–343**, *334–343*
  adding, 487
  ADUC, **257–258**, *257–258*
  anonymous, 722, 738
  creating, **344–346**
  disabling, 311, **351–355**
  domain
    creating, **284–289**, *286–289*
    properties, **296–311**, *297–299, 301–309*
  dsAdd, **258–259**, *259*
  enabling, **351**
  event log subscriptions, **770**, *775, 775*
  groups. *See* groups
  intraforest migrations, 1033
  local, **279**
    creating, **280–284**, *280, 282–283*
    properties, **289–296**, *290–296*
    security, 968
  locked-out, 272, **331–332**, *332–333*, **400**
  logon scripts. *See* logon scripts
  migrating, **1044–1048**, *1044–1049*
  moving into OUs, **422**
  passwords, **330–331**, *331*
  refresh intervals, 371
  Remote Desktop Services Manager, **1101–1102**,
    1101–1102
  rights. *See* permissions
  roaming profile settings, **1335–1336**
  unlocking, **349–351**
  WSS security, 1197
users.csv file, 346, 348

Users pages
LPGOs, 364
Remote Desktop Services Manager, 1101
Users or Groups page, 261
USN journal, 522–523
USNs (update sequence numbers), 1262

V

V31MigGuide.doc file, 1043–1044
Validate a Configuration Wizard, 1284, *1284*
VBS (Visual Basic Scripting), 1353
VBScript
ADMT, 1044
Hyper-V, 1288
VDI (virtual desktop infrastructure), 286
Verbose event level, 747
verifying
Active Directory, **527–528**
local area connections, **630–632**, *631*
Version History setting, 1186–1187,
1186–1187
versions
ADMT, 1036
document libraries, **1185–1188**,
1186–1187
View option, *409*
View Server permission, 572
views
deployed printers, **568–569**
Event Viewer, **748**
copying, **751–752**, *752*
creating, **752–753**, *753*
exporting and importing, **755–756**, *756*
filtering, **753–755**, *754*
properties, **748–749**, *748–749*
GPOs, 409, *409*
printer drivers, **553**, *554*
WSS documents, **1180–1182**, *1180*
Virtual Clone Drive tool, 89
virtual desktop infrastructure (VDI), 286
virtual directories, 708
virtual disks
adding, **1253–1256**, *1254–1255*
controllers, **1251–1253**, *1254*
maintenance, **1257–1259**,
1257–1258, *1260*
overview, **1227**
snapshots, **1259–1263**, *1261*
types, **1252–1253**, *1252*
virtual LANs (VLANs), 1267

Virtual Machine Manager (VMM)
child partitions, 1246
kernel, 1243
overview, **7–8**
virtual machine worker processes (VMW
processes), 1246–1247
virtual machines (VMs), 1216, *1216*, **1269**
backing up and restoring, **1274–1277**, *1276*
configuring, **1230–1238**, *1231–1235*, 1270
Hyper-V hosts licensing, **1269–1270**
Hyper-V scripting, **1288–1292**
installing, **1238–1242**, *1238*, *1241–1242*
malware protection, **1287–1288**
moving, **1270–1274**, *1272–1274*, **1280–1287**,
1283–1286
Server Core, **1277–1280**
virtual switch connections to, **1266–1268**,
1267–1268
Virtual Machines settings, 1226
Virtual Network Manager, 1229, *1230*, 1264, *1264*
virtual networks, **1263–1268**, *1263–1268*
virtual private networks (VPNs), 845–846, **853**
accounting configuration, **884–886**, *885*
clients
authentication, **882–884**, *883*
configuration and connections, **875–877**,
875–877
gateway-to-gateway, **854**, *855*
names for, **854**
overview, **853–854**, *854*
RRAS. *See* Routing and Remote Access
Service (RRAS)
security. *See* IPSec (IP Security)
tunneling protocols, **855–856**, 866
virtual servers. *See* server virtualization
virtual switches, **1263–1268**, *1263–1268*
virtualization service clients (VSCs), 1246
virtualization service providers (VSPs), 1244
viruses
conficker, **221**
WSS protection, **1210**, *1210*
Visual Basic Scripting (VBS), 1353
VLANs (virtual LANs), 1267
VM settings dialog box, 1266
VMbus, 1246, 1251
vmconnect.exe application, 1239
vmicsvc.exe, 1248
VMM (Virtual Machine Manager)
child partitions, 1246
kernel, 1243
overview, **7–8**

VMMS.exe tool, 1288
VMs. *See* virtual machines (VMs)
VMW processes (virtual machine worker processes), 1246–1247
VMWP.exe tool, 1288
Volume Shadow Copy Service (VSS)
    Active Directory snapshots, 807
    enabling, 1237
    file and folder backups, 802
    virtual machines, 1275–1276, *1276*
volumes in clean installations, 30
VPN Connection page, 860, *860*
VPN Reconnect feature, 856
VPNs. *See* virtual private networks (VPNs)
VSCs (virtualization service clients), 1246
VSPs (virtualization service providers), 1244
VSS (Volume Shadow Copy Service)
    Active Directory snapshots, 807
    enabling, 1237
    file and folder backups, 802
    virtual machines, 1275–1276, *1276*
VSS Settings tab, 802
.vsv files, 1274

W

W32tm (Windows Time Service), 270–271, 1007
WADNs (wide area data networks), 176
WAIK (Windows Automated Installation Kit), **88**
    installing, **89–92**, *90–93*
    WIM files, 101
WANs
    in Active Directory design, 978
    net use on, **448–449**
Warning events, 747
WAS (Windows Process Activation Service), 698, 1150
wbadmin utility
    Active Directory backups, 810, 813
    Active Directory restores, 814
    file and folder restores, 803
    full server backups, **798**, *798*
    full server restores, 801
    working with, **158–162**
WBTs (Windows-based terminals), 1079
WCF (Windows Communication Foundation) services, 689, 698, 1150
weak receives, 851
weak sends, 851

web applications, 708
    creating, **1164–1166**, *1164–1166*
    overview, **686**
web-based services, **14–15**, *15*
web browsers, RemoteApp access through, 1071
web.config file, 1151
    default sites, 718–719
    feature delegation, 694–695, 739
    IIS modules, 706–707
    site-specific settings, 688, 708, 720
Web Deployment Tool, 720–721
Web FrontEndOnly servers (WFEs), 1157
Web Management Service (WMSVC), **735–740**, *736, 738*
web pages
    FTP integration into, **730–735**, *731, 733–734*
    SMTP integration into, **724–725**
        e-mail feature, **729–730**, *730*
        server features, **726–728**, *727*
        server setup, **728–729**
        starting, **725–726**, *726*
Web Proxy Automatic Discovery Protocol (WPAD), 213
Web Server (IIS) page, 698, 1155
Web Server role
    adding, **695–698**, *696–697*
    IIS. *See* Internet Information Services (IIS)
    new features, **14–15**, *15*
    services, **702–703**, *702–703*
Web Site Selection page, 1141, *1141*
websites, **683**
    anonymous accounts, 722, 738
    backing up and restoring data, **741–742**
    creating, **683–686**, *685*, **711–718**, *711–712, 714, 716–717*
    delegating administration, **723–724**
    global settings, **708–710**
    multiple, **719–724**, *722–723*
    provisioning, **707–708**, **1162–1163**, *1163*
        site collections, **1167–1170**, *1167–1169*
        web applications, **1164–1166**, *1164–1166*
    site settings, **718–719**
    unique, **722**, *722*
    Web Management Service, **735–740**, *736, 738*
    WSRM tool, **740–741**
Wecutil (Windows Event Collector) service, 772–773, **778–780**
well-connected sites, 911
wevtutil (Windows Event utility), **763–766**
WFEs (Web FrontEndOnly servers), 1157
When a Specific Event Is Logged page, 760

When to Send Alerts setting, 1204
Where do you want to install Windows? screen,
    29–30, *29*
WID (Windows Internal Database), 1134, 1154
wide area data networks (WADNs), 176
wide area file networks, 176
WIM (Windows Image) files, 94, 1132
%windir% environment variable, 892
Windows 7
    joining domains, **643–649**, *643–645, 649*
    local area connections, **634–637**, *634–636*
    mandatory profiles, **1323–1327**, *1324–1327*
Windows 2000
    domain functional levels, **986**
    domain password changes, **656–659**, *657–658*
    global catalog replication, **998–999**
    joining domains, **652–653**
    local area connections, **642**
    network resources connections, **679–680**
Windows 2003 global catalog replication, **999**
Windows authentication, 738
Windows Automated Installation Kit (WAIK), **88**
    installing, **89–92**, *90–93*
    WIM files, 101
Windows Automated Installation Toolkit, 1132
Windows Automatic Updating feature, 1146
Windows Backup Server
    new features, **2–3**
    working with, **157–162**
Windows-based terminals (WBTs), 1079
Windows Communication Foundation (WCF)
    services, 689, 698, 1150
Windows Event Collector (Wecutil) service, 772–773,
    778–780
Windows Event utility (wevtutil), **763–766**
Windows Event Viewer. *See* Event Viewer
Windows Explorer Configuration, **1351**
Windows Firewall
    configuring, 47, *47*
    printers, 552
    upgrade installations, 37
Windows Groups page, 873, *873*
Windows Image (WIM) files, 94, 1132
Windows Installer (.msi) files, **1098–1100**, *1099*
Windows Internal Database (WID), 1134, 1154
Windows logs, **757–760**, *758, 760*
Windows Management Instrumentation command
    (WMIC), **620–621**
Windows Messenger, **1349**
Windows NTFS permissions dialog box, 392

Windows Process Activation Service (WAS),
    698, 1150
Windows Remote Management (WinRM) service,
    11, **772–773**
Windows Remote Shell, **132–133**, *132*
Windows Scripting Host (WSH) program, **254–255**
Windows Search Service, 433
Windows Security dialog box
    password changes, 656, *656*, 658, *658*
    RDS, 1089
Windows Server 2000 functional levels, 945–946
Windows Server 2003
    domain functional levels, 945, **988**
    forest functional levels, 946, **990**
Windows Server 2003 File Services, 433
Windows Server 2008
    domain functional levels, 945, **988**
    forest functional levels, 945–946, 990
    servers as routers, 857
    servers for swing migration, 1028
Windows Server Backup (WSB), **793–794**, 1276–1277
    Active Directory backups, 813
    file and folder backups, 801–802
    file and folder restores, 803
    full server backups, 796
    full server restores, 798–801
    installing, **795**
    limitations, **794**
Windows Server Migration Tools feature, 76, *76*
Windows Server Update Services (WSUS), **15**,
    1132–1146
    clients with, **1143–1145**, *1144–1145*
    deployment scenarios, **1134–1135**, *1135*
    features, **1132–1133**
    installing and configuring, **1139–1143**,
        1139–1143
    prerequisites, **1135–1138**, *1136–1138*
    software requirements, **1133–1134**
Windows SharePoint Services 3.0 (WSSv3), 1149
    authentication providers, **1206–1207**
    Central Administration. *See* Central
        Administration
    client software integration, **1210–1213**, *1212*
    content
        limiting, **1208–1210**, *1209–1210*
        types, 1173, **1183–1184**, *1183*, **1201–1202**
    documents
        accessing, **1194**
        alerts, **1203–1204**
        information rights, **1205**

libraries, **1170–1174**, *1173*, **1182–1189**, *1183,*
1185–1189
metadata, **1174–1182**, *1177–1180*
navigating, **1201–1202**
RSS feeds, **1204**, *1204*
search indexes, **1202–1203**, *1203*
security, **1194–1201**, *1196–1197, 1201*
workflows, **1189–1194**, *1190–1193*
features
managing, **1207–1208**
overview, **1149–1151**
group objects, 1159
groups, 1195
IIS 7.5 for, 1150–1151, **1153–1155**, *1155*
installing, **1152–1153**
loading, 1155
.NET Framework for, 1155, *1156*
operation, **1151**
Products and Technologies configuration,
1158–1159
requirements, **1151–1152**
service account designations, **1154**
viruses, **1210**, *1210*
website provisioning, **1162–1163**, *1163*
site collections, **1167–1170**, *1167–1169*
web applications, **1164–1166**, *1164–1166*
Windows SharePoint Services Administration
tool, 1158
Windows SharePoint Services Timer tool, 1158
Windows System Image Manager (WSIM), 88,
92–94, *93*
Windows System Resource Manager (WSRM) tool,
735, 737–738, **740–741**
Windows terminals device, **1079–1080**
Windows Time Service (W32tm), 270–271, 1007
Windows Update Stand-Alone Installer, 1132
Windows Vista
domain password changes, **655–656**, *655–656*
joining domains, **649–651**, *649–651*
local area connections, **637–640**, *637–639*
mandatory profiles, **1322–1323**, *1322–1323*
network resource connections, **660–671**,
661–665, 667–671
wireless devices, 666
Windows XP
domain password changes, **656–659**, *657–658*
joining domains, **651–652**, *651–652*
local area connections, **640–642**, *640–641*
network resource connections, **671–679**,
672–679
windowsPE configuration pass, 94

winrm command
shares, 437
winrm create command, 137
winrm quickconfig command, 133
WinRM (Windows Remote Management) service,
11, **772–773**
WinRS as new feature, **11**
winrs client, **141**
WINS tab, 206, *206*
Winsock, **835–836**
winver.exe utility, 38
wireless devices, **666**
WMI
Group Policy, 367, 374, **378–380**, *379–380*
Hyper-V scripting, **1288–1292**
providers, 1247
WMI Query Language (WQL) filters, **378–380**,
379–380
WMIC (Windows Management Instrumentation
command), **620–621**
WMSVC (Web Management Service), **735–740**,
736, 738
workarounds in patch management, 1130
workflow end (Final) state, 1192
Workflow Foundation (WF), 1189
Workflow Settings page, 1192, *1192*
workflow start (Initial) state, 1192
workflows for WSS documents, **1189–1194**,
1190–1193
workgroups
Active Directory, **227–228**
client connections to servers, 629
Working Set counter, 1078
workstations, administrative, 89
World Wide Web Publishing Service, 1158
WPAD (Web Proxy Automatic Discovery
Protocol), 213
writable DCs, 938
Write permission, 441, **484**
Write Attributes permission, 483
Write Data permission, 483
Write Extended Attributes permission, 483
Write-Host cmdlet, 932–934
wrksetng.aspx page, 1190
WSB. *See* Windows Server Backup (WSB)
WSH (Windows Scripting Host) program, **254–255**
WSIM (Windows System Image Manager), 88,
92–94, *93*
WSRM (Windows System Resource Manager) tool,
735, 737–738, **740–741**

WSSv3. *See* Windows SharePoint Services 3.0 (WSSv3)

WSUS. *See* Windows Server Update Services (WSUS)

WSUS Configuration Wizard, 1141

WUA_SearchDownloadInstall.vbs script, 126

wuauclt command, 126

wusa.exe process, 1132

X

XD (eXecute Disable) bit, 1219

XML (Extensible Markup Language), 543
  domain renaming process, **1059–1065**
  Event Viewer views, 749
  for IIS, 705
  logs, 755
  overview, **750–751**
  static web pages, 684
  tags, 750, 1061

XML Paper Specification (XPS), **542–543**

XML tab, 749

XPath, **750–751**

XPS (XML Paper Specification), **542–543**

XPSDrv printer driver, **543–544**

XPSPort printer port, 547

Z

Zone Transfers tab, 187, *188*

zones
  adding, **200–202**
  background loading, **215**
  description, **186**
  new domains, 984, *984*
  record management in, **202–203**
  reverse lookup, **193–194**, *194*
  standard primary, **186–187**, *187*
  standard secondary, **187–189**, *188*
  stub, **192**, *192*, 1015
  swing migration, 1029–1031
  WSS, 1207